The New Century

Classical Handbook

—The New Century—
Classical Handbook

EDITED BY CATHERINE B. AVERY

EDITORIAL CONSULTANT,
JOTHAM JOHNSON,

HEAD OF THE DEPARTMENT OF CLASSICS,
NEW YORK UNIVERSITY, AND CHAIRMAN
OF THE DEPARTMENT OF CLASSICS,
WASHINGTON SQUARE COLLEGE.

Appleton-Century-Crofts, Inc • New York

Preface

Western culture arose in ancient Greece. There a restless, active, imaginative people considered the universe and evolved a wonderful variety of ideas and conclusions about it and themselves. Their Roman conquerors admired and preserved much of the brilliant civilization of the Greeks. To it they made contributions of their own. The combined eras of the two peoples is known as the Classical Age: a name that recognizes the standard of excellence then set up for succeeding ages.

The purpose of this book is to provide convenient and detailed information on the Classical Age in a form that is readily accessible to the general reader and to the student. Included are the figures of myth and legend, gods and heroes, persons and places, fact and fancy. There are biographies of dramatists, poets, sculptors, painters and potters; philosophers, generals, statesmen, and politicians; lost ladies and scoundrels. Résumés supply the reader with a working knowledge of the *Iliad, Odyssey, Argonautica,* etc., and acquaint him with the great dramas of Aeschylus, Sophocles, and Euripides. Places of mythological, historical, and archaeological interest are listed, with notice of recent archaeological finds. There are articles on rivers, mountains, shrines, ancient works of art; sibyls and seers; magic herbs, descriptive words; ruins and monuments.

The aim of these articles is to present the material as it appeared to the ancients, rather than to apply modern interpretations. For example, many of the traditions and legends set down by Herodotus and Plutarch about actual people are included. The emphasis is on the stories the ancients told each other, and believed in varying degrees, about people and places of history as well as about figures of mythology. The theory is that the way they themselves saw life and the universe is the most potent factor in the enduring quality of their influence. There is less emphasis on early scientific thought, the area in which, perhaps, the achievements of modern man are most markedly separated from ancient origins. Generally speaking, the period of time covered runs from the mist-shrouded days of prehistory in Greece to the last of the Julian emperors of Rome (68 A.D.). However, the final limit has been flexible in order to include later Roman figures and events that had some special association with the preceding period.

To aid the reader, each figure, whether mythological or historical, appears as a separate entry, rather than in cross-references under the heading of a story in which he took part. When, as sometimes happens, the same name is shared by a mythological figure, a historical figure, and a place, the entry for the mythological figure is given first, for the historical figure next, and for any other subject of the same name last. Dates distinguish historical from mythological figures. Greek names are subject to various spellings in the Latin alphabet. No single rule or group of rules answers every problem that arises in this connection. For this reason, a number of cross-references are included to cover variant spellings. Since, in general, the Romans took over Greek myths and legends with very little change, the Greek names are given.

Sixty-four of the line cuts in the volume were drawn expressly for this work from the originals, from photographs, or from previously published drawings. The figures in the drawings, arbitrarily removed from the shapes and decorations that completed and confined them, are intended rather as illustrations of Greek stories and ideas than as examples of Greek art. The originals are among the most precious examples of that art.

The Editorial Consultant, Professor Jotham Johnson, assisted by Professors Abraham Holtz and Philip Mayerson of New York University, has read the manuscript for historical accuracy, verified and, where necessary, corrected or supplied spellings and pronunciations. Those articles to which their initials are appended have been composed or substantially revised by Professors Johnson, Holtz, and Mayerson.

The editor wishes to thank Miss Margaret Thompson, Curator of Greek Coins, and Miss Joan Fagerlie, Curator of Roman and Byzantine Coins, both of The American Numismatic Society, for their friendly suggestions and help in choosing the coins to be illustrated, and to thank also The American Numismatic Society for the photographs of Greek and Roman coins. Grateful acknowledgment is also made here to the *American Journal of Archaeology* for the plan of Nestor's Palace on page 950; to The Metropolitan Museum of Art; the Museum of Fine Arts, Boston; the Antikensammlungen and the Glyptothek, Munich; the Staatliche Museen, Berlin; the British Museum; the Louvre; the German Archaeological Institute, Athens; the Museo delle Terme, Rome; the Royal Greek Embassy Press and Information Office; the Italian State Tourist Office; and the Spanish National Tourist Office for photographs which they have supplied. Finally, the editor is profoundly grateful for the many courtesies extended by the Connecticut College Library at New London, Connecticut, and the New York Public Library.

The NEW CENTURY CLASSICAL HANDBOOK is offered as a reference tool to those whose studies or work requires a knowledge and understanding of the Classical Age. For the general reader, it is hoped that it will be a source of interest, information and pleasure to all who have the curiosity and the desire to be informed concerning the basis of our western civilization.

THE EDITOR

New York
1962

List of Photographs

Following page 1008

Gold stater of Croesus, 561–546 B.C. Obverse: Foreparts of lion and bull facing.
Reverse: Two incuse squares.   *The American Numismatic Society*

Silver stater, Aegina, early 6th century B.C. Obverse: Sea turtle. Reverse: Incuse.
The American Numismatic Society

Silver stater, Corinth, early 6th century B.C. Obverse: Pegasus. Reverse: Incuse,
swastika.   *The American Numismatic Society*

Silver stater, Poseidonia, second half of 6th century B.C. Obverse: Poseidon. Reverse:
Incuse.   *The American Numismatic Society*

Silver stater, Croton, second half of 6th century B.C. Obverse: Tripod. Reverse: Incuse.
The American Numismatic Society

Silver stater, Sybaris, second half of 6th century B.C. Obverse: Bull with head reverted.
Reverse: Incuse.   *The American Numismatic Society*

Silver tetradrachm, Syracuse, c530–510 B.C. Obverse: Quadriga. Reverse: Incuse
square with archaic head.   *The American Numismatic Society*

Silver tetradrachm, Athens, late 6th century B.C. Obverse: Head of Athena. Reverse:
Owl.   *The American Numismatic Society*

Silver tetradrachm, Gela, early 5th century B.C. Obverse: Quadriga crowned by Nike.
Reverse: Forepart of man-headed bull.   *The American Numismatic Society*

Silver tetradrachm, Syracuse, c485–479 B.C. Obverse: Quadriga crowned by Nike.
Reverse: Female head surrounded by dolphins. *The American Numismatic Society*

Silver tetradrachm, Athens, 5th century B.C. Obverse: Head of Athena. Reverse: Owl.
The American Numismatic Society

Silver tetradrachm, Aenus, c450 B.C. Obverse: Head of Hermes. Reverse: Goat.
The American Numismatic Society

Silver tetradrachm, Mende, c450–423 B.C. Obverse: Dionysus on an ass. Reverse:
Vinestock with grapes.   *The American Numismatic Society*

Silver tetradrachm, Naxos (Sicily), second half of 5th century B.C. Obverse: Head of
Dionysus. Reverse: Silenus with cantharus.   *The American Numismatic Society*

Silver decadrachm, Syracuse, late 5th or early 4th century B.C. Obverse: Quadriga
crowned by Nike. Reverse: Head surrounded by dolphins.
The American Numismatic Society

Silver stater, Tarentum, c420–380 B.C. Obverse: Galloping horseman. Reverse: Taras
on a dolphin.   *The American Numismatic Society*

Silver tetradrachm of Alexander the Great, c336–334 B.C. Obverse: Head of Heracles.
Reverse: Zeus holding an eagle.   *The American Numismatic Society*

Silver stater, Cnossus, 4th century B.C. Obverse: Head of Demeter or Persephone.
Reverse: Labyrinth in the form of a swastika. *The American Numismatic Society*

Silver tetradrachm of Demetrius Poliorcetes, 292–291 B.C. Obverse: Diademed and
horned head of Demetrius. Reverse: Poseidon. *The American Numismatic Society*

The New Century

Classical Handbook

A

Abacus (ab′a-kus). In architecture, the slab or plinth which forms the upper member of the capital of a column or pillar, and upon which rests, in classic styles, the lower surface of the architrave. In the Greek Doric it is thick and square, without sculptured decoration; in the Ionic order it is thinner, and ornamented with moldings on the sides; in the Corinthian also it is ornamented, and has concave sides and truncated corners.

Abae (ā′bē). [Also: **Abai**.] In ancient geography, a city in Phocis, Greece, noted for its temple and oracle of Apollo. Looted and largely destroyed during one of the Persian invasions of Greece, it was later partly rebuilt under the Roman emperor Hadrian. Ruins of parts of the town still exist.

Abantes (a-ban′tēz). According to Homer (*Iliad*), a warlike tribe of Euboea, who allied themselves with the Greeks in the Trojan War. They were fierce fighters, and it was their custom to shave the hair from the fore parts of their heads to prevent their enemies from grasping the forelock in close combat. Theseus emulated their practice. The Abantes are also named in legend as a people of Epirus among whom the Colchians, frustrated in their attempt to capture Jason and Medea, settled rather than return to Colchis and face the wrath of Aeëtes.

Abarbarea (a-bär-ba′rē-a). In Homeric legend (*Iliad*), a fountain-nymph. She was the mother, by Bucolion, of twin sons, Aesepus and Pedasus, who were slain by Euryalus in the Trojan War.

Abaris (ab′a-ris). [Called **the Hyperborean**.] Mythical Greek sage, assigned by Pindar to the 6th century B.C., by Eusebius to the 7th. According to these writers and to Herodotus, Apollo gave him a magic arrow on which he traveled and which he gave to Pythagoras in exchange for instruction in the latter's philosophy. He was believed to have worked miraculous cures, and was widely invoked by the ancient Greeks in oracles and charms.

Abas (ā′bas). Named by Homer (*Iliad*), as a son of the dream-interpreter and diviner Eurydamas. He was slain by Diomedes in the Trojan War.

Abas. According to legend, a son of Celeus, king of Eleusis, and Metanira. Demeter, searching for Persephone, was hospitably received by Metanira and given barley-water to quench her thirst. Abas, unaware of her identity, mocked her for drinking greedily and was changed into a lizard by Demeter.

Abas. The legendary grandson of Danaus. He was a king of Argolis and possessed a shield with such marvelous powers that the mere sight of it put his enemies to flight. He mar-

fat, fāte, fär, fãre, errant; net, mē, hėr ardent; pin, pīne; not, nōte, möve, nôr, actor; up, lūte, pull; oi, oil; ou, out; ᴛʜ, then; ḍ as d or j, ṣ as s or sh, ṭ as t or ch, ẓ as z or zh.

I

ried Aglaia and had twin sons, Acrisius and Proetus.

Abas. A legendary companion of Diomedes. He accompanied Diomedes on his voyage to Italy after the Trojan War. Aphrodite continued to persecute Diomedes because he had wounded her during the war. She sent storms at sea and war on land to harass him. Abas and others were transformed into birds by Aphrodite because a companion, Acmon, defied her to prevent Diomedes' company from reaching sanctuary in Italy.

Abdera (ab-dir′a). A maritime city in Thrace on Cape Balastra, opposite the island of Thasus in NE Greece. According to legend, it was founded by Heracles, who had gone there to fetch the man-eating mares of Diomedes of Thrace, in memory of Heracles' servant Abderus who was slain by the mares while Heracles sought Diomedes. The city is now known to have been colonized (c650 B.C.) by people from Clazomenae. Destroyed some time before 550 B.C. by Thrace, it was resettled (c540 B.C.) by refugees from the Persian occupation of Teos, and became during the next 200 years one of the most prosperous of Greek cities. Thereafter it declined in importance, and the ancient city is now entirely in ruins. A small agricultural community still occupies part of the original site. The air of the region was thought in ancient times to cause people to become dull, and from this came a folk belief among the ancient Greeks that all Abderites were stupid. This conviction persisted despite the fact that a number of famous men, including Protagoras and Democritus, either were born in or were residents of Abdera.

Abderus (ab-dir′us). According to some accounts, a son of Hermes. While tending the man-eating mares of Diomedes for Heracles, he was torn to pieces by them. Heracles founded the city of Abdera beside his tomb and established games in his honor.

Abia (ab′i-a). In Greek tradition, a nurse of a descendant of Heracles, who raised a temple of Heracles in Ira in Messenia. To honor her, the name of the town was changed to Abia.

Abradatas (ab-ra-dā′tas). King of Susa, fl. 6th century B.C. He was at first an enemy, then an ally, of the Persians under Cyrus the Great. The story of the love of Abradatas and his wife Panthea (the earliest example

of sentimental romance) is given by Xenophon (*Cyropaedia*). The story ends with the death of Abradatas in battle and the suicide of Panthea and her eunuchs.

Abrocomes and Atheia (a-brok′ō-mēz; a-thē′a). [Called **Ephesian Stories;** also, **Abrocomas and Anthia, Habrocomas and Anthia.**] Romance in five books by a Hellenistic writer named Xenophon of Ephesus, in which he describes a handsome young Greek couple of the period, their marriage and the complicated series of adventures by which they were separated and finally reunited. The later writers Chariton and Heliodorus are believed to have used this work as a pattern for some of their writing.

Absyrtus (ab-sér′tus). See **Apsyrtus.**

Abydos (a-bī′dos) or **Abydus** (-dus). In ancient geography, a town in Mysia, Asia Minor, on the Hellespont. It was colonized by Ionians from Miletus. It was from Abydos that Leander swam across the Hellespont each night to visit his beloved Hero at Sestos. From Abydos Xerxes caused a double bridge to be constructed across the Hellespont by which his army could march into Europe to attack Greece. However, when it was completed a great storm arose and dashed the whole work to pieces. Xerxes was so angry when he learned of the destruction of the bridge that he gave orders for the Hellespont to receive 300 lashes, and that fetters should be hurled into it. Some say he ordered the waters of the Hellespont branded with a hot iron, and commanded those who carried out the task of lashing the water to say the following as they did so: "Thou bitter water, thy lord lays on thee this punishment because thou hast wronged him without a cause, having suffered no evil at his hands." When the waters had thus been punished, those who had been in charge of constructing the bridge had their heads cut off, new engineers were appointed and the work was recommenced. This time the bridge was made of boats—triremes and penteconters (50-oared ships). The keels of the boats ran parallel to the current of the Hellespont to ease the strain on the cables which fastened them together. The ships were also made fast with heavy anchors. In the middle of the strait a gap was left between the ships so that light vessels could pass through them into or out of the Euxine Sea. Sawn planks from tree trunks were laid on the cables and fastened to them, brushwood and earth were packed down on top of the planks to form a roadway, and on each side of the bridge a fence was raised high enough so that the animals passing across could not see the water and become frightened. When Xerxes learned in Sardis that the bridge was ready he set out with his vast army and arrived for the crossing. Now he took a golden goblet and poured a libation into the Hellespont as he prayed for success in his conquest of Greece. Then he cast the golden goblet, a golden bowl, and a sword into the waters. Perhaps this was to make amends for having scourged the waters, or perhaps this was an offering to the sun. Having carried out these rites his vast host successfully crossed over from Abydos into Europe. The people of Abydos did not accompany him into Greece; they were left behind to guard the bridge. However, when Xerxes returned, after the disaster of Salamis (480 B.C.), he found his bridge of boats had been scattered by storms, and this time he crossed back to Asia in his ships which had sailed back from Greece.

Abyla (ab'i-la). [Also: **Abyla Columna, Abyla Mons.**] A promontory in Africa, the modern Jebel Musa at Ceuta, opposite the ancient Calpe (the modern Gibraltar). One of the pillars supposed to have been set up by Heracles, either to narrow the opening between the ocean and the inner sea and keep ocean monsters out, or as a headland which he made by cutting a passage from the ocean into the inner sea, hitherto separated by a continuous range of mountains between the European and African continents.

Acacallis (a-ka-kal'is). According to legend, a daughter of Minos and Pasiphaë. She was beloved by Apollo. Her father learned that she was about to bear the god's son and banished her to Libya where she bore Amphithemis, who was also known as Garamas.

Academus (ak-a-dē'mus). A legendary Arcadian who had moved to Athens. When the Dioscuri came to Attica in search of their sister Helen who had been kidnaped by Theseus, Academus is said to have revealed to them her hiding place in Aphidna. As a reward for his services on this occasion the

Spartans ever after treated him with great honor and courtesy. After his death, when the Spartans warred on Athens they spared his estate on the Cephissus River. The estate of Academus with its pleasant garden came to be used as a meeting place for philosophers and became known as the Academia or Academy.

Academy. [Greek, **Akademeia, Akademia.**] Name applied to what was originally a public pleasure-ground on the Cephissus River about one mile NW of ancient Athens, on land said to have belonged to Academus, an Arcadian who is supposed to have revealed the place where Theseus had hidden Helen. It was surrounded with a wall built by Hipparchus and was further adorned by Cimon, the son of Miltiades who bequeathed it to the citizens of Athens. It was the resort of Plato who taught in its groves for nearly 50 years.

Acamas (ak'a-mas). In Homeric legend (*Iliad*), one of Antenor's sons. He accompanied Aeneas at the siege of the Greek fortifications and slew Promachus to avenge the death of his brother Archelochus at the hands of Telamonian Ajax. Acamas was slain by Meriones, Idomeneus' comrade.

Acamas. According to legend, a son of Theseus and Phaedra. He went on a mission to Troy with Diomedes to demand the return of Helen. While there he met Laodice, King Priam's daughter, and fell in love with her. She bore him a son, Munitus. Later he was one of the Greeks who entered Troy in the Wooden Horse and on the fall of the city regained his son. In the meantime he had left behind a Thracian princess, Phyllis, when we went to fight at Troy. Grieving at his long absence she was changed into an almond tree. When Acamas returned and embraced the tree, it burst into flower.

Acamas. Named by Homer (*Iliad*), as a son of Eussorus. He was a captain of the Thracians, allies of Troy, and was slain by Telamonian Ajax.

Acanthus (a-kan'thus). In ancient geography, a town situated on the base of the peninsula of Acte in Chalcidice. It was colonized by Andros and allied to Athens. The Spartan general Brasidas moved to attack it in 424 B.C. The Acanthians allowed him to enter their city alone, to present reasons why they

actor; up, lūte, púll; oi, oil; ou, out; ᴛʜ, then; ḍ as d or j, ş as s or sh, ṭ as t or ch, ẓ as z or zh.

should surrender to him. It was time to harvest the grapes and they did not want to lose the vintage. Thus, "not being a bad speaker for a Lacedaemonian," the arguments of Brasidas persuaded them to revolt against Athens and to submit to Sparta.

Acarnan (a-kär′nan). In classical legend, a son of Alcmaeon and Callirrhoë, daughter of the river-god Achelous. When he was a child, his mother prayed to Zeus that he might grow to manhood in a single day, along with his brother Amphoterus, so that they could avenge the murder of their father who had been slain by the sons of Phegeus, a king who had once purified him. Zeus answered her prayer. Acarnan and his brother grew up at once and went to Nemea where they found the sons of Phegeus and killed them. Before a full day had passed, they found and killed Phegeus also. After these murders the brothers fled to Epirus and founded Acarnania, named after Acarnan.

Acarnania (ak-ar-nā′ni-a). In ancient geography, a division of Greece, bounded by the Ambracian Gulf on the N, by Amphilochia on the NE, by Aetolia on the E (partly separated by the Achelous River), and by the Ionian Sea on the W. Its ancient inhabitants were the Leleges and Curetes. They were considered rude mountaineers by the people of the Greek city-states, but were nevertheless regarded as Hellenes and as such were allowed to participate in the Panhellenic games.

Acastus (a-kas′tus). An Argonaut, the son of Pelias. According to legend, he joined Jason in the expedition for the Golden Fleece in spite of his father's objections. When the expedition returned to Iolcus and Pelias was killed by the wiles of Medea, Acastus became king of Iolcus. He purified Peleus of an accidental murder. Later he challenged Peleus to a hunting contest because his wife Cretheïs falsely accused Peleus of making advances to her. Peleus won the contest with the aid of a sword forged by Daedalus. While Peleus slept Acastus stole the sword and hid it but it was returned to Peleus by Chiron the centaur. Later Peleus returned to Iolcus, captured the city, and killed Acastus and his wife.

Acca Larentia (ak′a la-ren′shi-a) **or Acca**

Laurentia (lô-ren′shi-a). Variously identified in Roman legend: 1) as the wife of Faustulus and nurse of Romulus and Remus, her nickname Lupa (she-wolf, or courtesan) being perhaps the source of the story that they were raised by a wolf; 2) as a beautiful woman won in gambling by Hercules, wife of an Etruscan whose wealth she bequeathed to the Romans, honored by their festival called Larentalia.

Accius (ak′shi-us), **Lucius**. [Also: **Attius**.] Roman tragic poet and prose writer, born c170 B.C.; died c86 B.C. He was noted for his adaptations of the Greek cycles, especially the Trojan War, and also dealt with Roman subjects such as the expulsion of the Tarquins. He was greatly esteemed as a tragic poet under the Republic. Of his works only the titles and a few fragments survive.

Acerbas (a-sėr′bas) or **Akerbas** (-kėr′-). [Also: **Sicharbas**.] In classical legend, uncle and husband of Elissa, a wealthy and powerful Tyrian noble, high priest of the Tyrian god Melkarth. In Vergil's *Aeneid* Acerbas was Sychaeus, husband of Dido (Elissa), murdered for his riches by her brother Pygmalion. Dido was able, however, when she fled from Tyre and founded Carthage, to take the treasure with her.

Acesius (a-ses′i-us). An epithet of Apollo, meaning "Healer."

Acessamenus (a-ses-a-mē′nus). According to Homer (*Iliad*), a king in Thrace and the father of Periboea.

Acestes (a-ses′tēz). [Also: **Aegestes**.] According to legend, a son of the Sicilian river-god Crimisus and Egesta (Segesta), a Trojan woman. After the Trojan War in which he took part, he settled near Mount Eryx in Sicily. He is said to have founded the cities of Segesta (named for his mother), Entella (named for his wife), Eryx, and Asca. He entertained Aeneas and his companions when they stopped in his kingdom on their flight from Troy. Again, when Aeneas had left Carthage, he entertained the Trojans. He took part in the archery contest in the funeral games honoring Anchises, but since the target, a dove, had already been shot to the ground by a contestant, he loosed an arrow into the air with such great speed and power that it took fire as it sped through the heavens. Aeneas regarded this as a favorable omen and gave Acestes first prize. While the funeral games were in progress, the Trojan women, in despair at their continual wandering, set fire to Aeneas' ships in the hope the loss of the ships would compel them to settle down with Acestes, their countryman. Acestes gave his consent and welcome to those who wanted to stay and make their homes in his kingdom. Aeneas and those of his comrades who still had a thirst for glory continued their journey until they should reach their destined home in Latium.

Acetes (a-sē′tēz). A legendary Lydian pilot. He alone recognized a youth who had been captured by the crew of his ship as a god, and protected him from the crew's violence. When the sailors threatened to throw Acetes overboard, the youth entreated the sailors to take him to Naxos. The sailors, pretending to accede to this request, sailed in a different direction. When the youth (really Dionysus) realized what had happened, he used his divine powers. The ship stood still in the sea. Ivy suddenly grew up the masts of the ship and entwined itself about the oars. The youth, crowned with grapes and holding a thyrsus, revealed himself as the god Dionysus. Suddenly lions, tigers, and other wild beasts appeared on the deck around him. The sailors, either maddened by the god or in fear of punishment for their ill treatment of him, leaped into the sea and were changed into dolphins. Acetes sailed on to Naxos with the god and became one of his followers. Later he was bound and imprisoned by Pentheus, who was trying to wipe out the worship of Dionysus in his realm, but the chains fell from his limbs and the doors of his prison opened of themselves to free him.

Achaea (a-kē′a). [Also: **Achaia**; called **Achaea Phthiotis**.] In ancient geography, a small region in S Thessaly, containing Phthia. It was probably the original home of the Achaean people, and it retained its name as late as the time of Herodotus. According to tradition, this was the home of Deucalion who with his wife survived the great flood sent by the gods to destroy wicked mankind. The land was ruled by Xuthus, son of Hellen and grandson of Deucalion. Xuthus left it to help the Athenians in a war. Later, Achaeus, son of Xuthus, returned and won back his father's realm for himself and named it Achaea.

Achaea. [Also: **Achaia**; original name, **Aegialus** or **Aegialea**, meaning "the Coast."] In ancient geography, a mountainous district in the Peloponnesus bordering on the Gulf of Corinth, N of Elis and Arcadia. According to tradition, Achaeans from Argos and Lacedaemon under the leadership of Tisamenus, son of Orestes, invaded this land when they were driven from Argos and Lacedaemon by the Dorians. Driving out the Ionians who inhabited it, they took the land for themselves and named it Achaea.

Achaean League (a-kē′an). A religious confederation in Achaea, at the time of Herodotus consisting of 12 cities: Pellene, Aegira, Aegae, Bura, Helice, Aegium, Rhypes, Patrae, Pharae, Olenus, Dyme, and Tritaea. Somewhat later, Rhypes and Aegae fell into decay, and their places in the confederacy were taken by Leontium and Cerynia.

Achaean League. A political confederation of Achaean and other Greek cities extending over the period of 281–146 B.C. After the death of Lysimachus in 280 B.C., the Achaean cities Dyme, Patrae, Tritaea, and Pharae formed a confederation to resist the Macedonian domination, and were afterward joined by the other Achaean cities, except Olenus and Helice. In 251 B.C. the confederation acquired new strength by the accession of Sicyon, under the leadership of Aratus. In 245 Aratus was elected *strategus* (general) of the league, which under his guidance rapidly rose to national importance. In a short time it embraced Athens, Aegina, Salamis, and the whole of the Peloponnesus with the exception of Sparta, Tegea, Orchomenus, Mantinea, and Elis. It was destroyed by the Romans in 146 B.C., and with it fell the last stronghold of freedom in Greece. The Achaean League is remarkable as one of the most perfect types of federal government which has been handed down from antiquity. The confederation was inseparable, every city having equal rights with the others; in foreign affairs the federal government was supreme. Common affairs were regulated at general meetings held twice a year by the citizens of all the towns.

Achaeans (a-kē′anz). [Also: **Achaei**, **Achaians**, **Achivi**.] One of the four principal peoples of ancient Greece (the Aeolians, Dorians, and Ionians were the other three). The Achaeans were one of the invading tribes which settled in the Peloponnesus. According to tradition, Xuthus, son of Hellen, came from his realm in Thessaly to help the Athenians in a war and was given Creusa, daughter of King Erechtheus, as a reward. After the death of Erechtheus, Xuthus was appointed to choose his successor. He named Cecrops, son of Erechtheus, but the other sons of Erechtheus did not approve this choice and Xuthus was compelled to flee. He went to Aegialus, a land in the north of the Peloponnesus between Elis and Sicyon. Achaeus, a son of Xuthus and Creusa, left Aegialus and won back his father's land in Thessaly, but he left behind two sons who married two daughters of Danaus and settled in Lacedaemon and Argos. The descendants of these two sons of Achaeus, dwellers in Lacedaemon and Argos, were at first the only Greeks in the Peloponnesus to be known as Achaeans. (The Achaeans of Argos were also known as Danaans.) The descendants of Achaeus in Thessaly in the region about Phthia were also called Achaeans. Ion, son of Apollo and Creusa but thought by Xuthus to be his son, remained in Aegialus, married Helice, daughter of King Selinus, and succeeded his father-in-law as king of the Aegialians whom he now named Ionians after himself. Generations later the Heraclidae (Dorians) returned to the Peloponnesus and drove the Achaeans out of Argos and Lacedaemon. These Achaeans sought asylum with the Ionians of Aegialus, but the Ionians resisted them by force. Tisamenus, son of Orestes, was the leader of the Achaeans. He was killed, but his followers defeated the Ionians. The Ionians fled to Helice and later left the region under a truce. The Achaeans divided up their land, which they renamed Achaea, and settled in their cities which now became known as the 12 Achaean cities. These cities were Dyme, Olenus, Pharae, Tritaea, Rhypes, Aegium, Cerynia, Bura, Helice, Aegae, Aegira, and Pellene. The Achaeans furnished the largest contingent in the Greek force that Agamemnon led against Troy to recover Helen of Sparta. In the Persian War the Achaeans of Achaea played no heroic part as they scorned to be

led by Dorians (Spartans), and to the extent that they did not help their fellow Greeks they helped the Persians. The name *Achaean* is applied generally to all Greeks in Homeric poetry, and to some extent by poets in later times. The Achaeans formed the ethnic basis of the Achaean League which lasted until 146 B.C. when the Romans finally subjugated the Greeks.

Achaemenes (a-kē′me-nēz). [Old Persian, **Hakhāmaniš**, meaning "the Friendly."] Probably the leader (fl. c7th century B.C.) under whom the Persians first settled in the country subsequently called Persia, and the eponymous founder (possibly mythical) of the ancient Persian royal family of the Achaemenidae. He was, initially, ruler of Anshan, in SW Persia. His name was later used as a family name, beginning (550 B.C.) with Cyrus.

Achaemenes. A son of Darius, and the brother of Xerxes I. He accompanied Xerxes as one of the commanders of the fleet in the Persian War. He advised Xerxes to keep his fleet together for the attack on Salamis, in opposition to the advice of Demaratus, the Spartan. The latter had advised Xerxes to send a part of his fleet directly against Sparta and so pin down the Spartans while the land army of Xerxes was subjugating Greece. Achaemenes was killed at Papremis by Inarus the Libyan.

Achaemenidae (ak-ē-men′i-dē). [Also: **Achaemenides, Achemenides, Achemenids.**] Ancient royal family of Persia, founded c600 B.C. Its leading members were Achaemenes, Cyrus the Great, Cambyses (Gaumata, the Magian usurper), Darius Hystaspes, Xerxes I, Artaxerxes I, Xerxes II, Sogdianus, Darius Ochus, Artaxerxes Mnemon, Ochus, Arses, and Darius Codomannus.

Achaeus (a-kē′us). Legendary son of Xuthus and Creusa. He fled with his father from Athens to Aegialus in the Peloponnesus. Two of the sons of Achaeus married two daughters of Danaus, settled in Argos and Lacedaemon and their descendants became known as Achaeans. They later invaded Aegialus, took over the region and named it Achaea. Achaeus left Aegialus and went to Thessaly where he won back his father's lands, and named the region Achaea and the people Achaeans for himself. Thus there were two groups in Greece known as Achaeans, those in Achaea in the Peloponnesus, and those in Thessaly in the region of Phthia. The name *Achaean* was also sometimes applied as a collective name for all the Greeks.

Achaeus or **Achaios** (a̯-kā′os). Greek poet of Eretria in Euboea; fl. c484–448 B.C. He was the author of from 24 to 44 plays, only fragments of which remain and of which the titles of only 19 are now known. He contended with Sophocles and Euripides in the great Hellenic dramatic contests of his day, and won the prize once.

Acharnae (a̯-kär′nē). Deme in Attica where the ivy plant was said to have first appeared. Here Dionysus Kissos (*Ivy*) and Dionysus Melpomenus (*Singer*) were invoked. Apollo Agyieus and Heracles were also worshiped here.

Acharnians (a̯-kär′ni-a̯nz), **The**. Comedy of Aristophanes, first brought out under the name of Callistratus, at the Lenaea, or rural Dionysia at Athens in 425 B.C. It was awarded first prize. It was an attempt to support the aristocratic peace-party against the intrigues and intimidations of the democratic war-party represented by the chorus of Acharnians. In form it is an extravagant farce rather than a comedy.

Achates (a̯-kā′tēz). In Roman legend, a Trojan, the faithful friend and companion of Aeneas. He accompanied Aeneas on the flight from Troy and was his inseparable companion in all his adventures.

Acheloïdes (ak-e̯-lō′i-dēz). A name for the legendary Sirens, daughters of Achelous.

Achelous (ak-e̯-lō′us). The river-god of the Achelous River in NW Greece which formed part of the boundary between Aetolia and Acarnania. He was the oldest of the 3000 sons of Oceanus and Tethys, and as such was worshiped throughout Greece and in the colonies. His name in religious rites became synonymous for any stream, and sacrifices to Achelous were always prescribed along with the prophecies given out by the oracle of Dodona. He had the power to assume three forms: that of a man with a bull's head, that of a speckled serpent, and that of a bull. Achelous was one of many who courted Deianira, supposed daughter of Oeneus of Calydon. When Heracles also came wooing her, all her other suitors left the field to him and Achelous. Achelous claimed her on the ground that he was a deity. Heracles boasted that he could give her Zeus for a father-in-law. To this Achelous retorted that if it were so, which he doubted, then Alcmene, Heracles' mother, was an adulteress. Heracles, enraged at this slur on his mother's honor, proposed that he and Achelous wrestle for the hand of Deianira, the winner to become her husband. Achelous wrestled first in his form as a bull-headed man, and Heracles succeeded in throwing Achelous. The river-god, finding himself pinned by the mighty Heracles, transformed himself into a serpent. But Heracles laughed, told him he had strangled serpents in his cradle, and grasped Achelous firmly in his fists. Achelous now assumed the shape of a bull. Heracles seized him by the horns and hurled him to the ground, thus defeating him in all his forms. One of Achelous' horns was broken off in his fall and, according to some, naiads took it and filled it with fruits. It became the Cornucopia (Horn of Plenty), and was always miraculously filled. To cover the spot where the horn had been Achelous ever after wore a wreath of river reeds. Achelous was said to have been the father of Pirene, who was transformed into a fountain. He was also said by some to have been the father, by the muse Terpsichore, of the Sirens. He fell in love with Perimele, daughter of Hippodamas, and ravished her. Her father hurled her into the sea but Achelous caught her and held her up. He prayed that she might be given a resting place or that she herself would be changed into such a place. She was transformed into an island, one of the Echinades islands which lie at the mouth of the Achelous River. Achelous purified Alcmaeon for the murder of his mother and gave his daughter Callirrhoë to Alcmaeon for a wife.

Achelous. [Modern names, **Akheloos, Aspropotamos.**] River in NW Greece which rises in Epirus, in the Pindus Mountains, forms part of the boundary between what was ancient Aetolia and Acarnania, and flows into the Ionian Sea.

Achemenides (ak-e̯-men′i-dēz). A legendary Greek who fought at Troy and sailed for home with Odysseus after the fall of the city. He accompanied Odysseus when he visited the cave of Polyphemus in Sicily but was left behind when Odysseus and his remaining companions escaped from the giant. When Aeneas later stopped at the island Achemenides came running out of hiding and warned him that there were many giants there, as huge and cruel as Polyphemus. He advised Aeneas to flee and begged him to take him with them, even though as a Greek he was their former enemy. Aeneas pitied him and carried him off in his ship.

Achemenides or **Achemenids** (ak-ẹ-men′idz). See **Achaemenidae.**

Acheron (ak′ẹ-ron). In ancient geography, the name of several small rivers in Greece, of which the chief (the modern Gurla) was in Thesprotia in Epirus. It flowed through Lake Acherusia, received the waters of the Cocytus (the modern Vuvos), and emptied into the Ionian Sea.

Acheron. In Greek mythology, one of the five rivers surrounding Hades, the river of woe. The souls of the dead had to bathe in it or cross it. Later it became synonymous with the lower world in general.

Acherusia Palus (ak-ẹ-rö′si-ạ pā′lus). [Eng. trans., "Acherusian Bog."] In ancient geography, the name of several small lakes supposed to be connected with the lower world. The most important were the lake through which the Acheron flowed, and one about 11 miles W of Naples, the modern Fusaro Lake. Like Acheron, the name came to be applied, in ancient literary usage, to the lower world itself.

Achilleis (ak-i-lē′is). [Also: **Achilleid.**] Name given to the part of the *Iliad* comprised by Books I, VIII, and XI–XXII, regarded by some critics as constituting a poem of which the theme is the "wrath of Achilles," and which is distinct from, and older than, the rest of the *Iliad.* The name *Achilleis* was first applied to these books by Grote.

Achilles (ạ-kil′ēz). In Greek legend, a son of Peleus (for this reason he was also called Pelides) and the sea-goddess Thetis. He was the grandson of Aeacus (for this reason he was also known as Aeacides), and thus a descendant of Zeus. He was the youngest of seven sons born to Peleus and Thetis. His mother, wishing to immortalize her sons, one by one placed his older brothers in the flames to destroy their mortal parts and sent

the immortal remains to Olympus. When Achilles was born she anointed him with ambrosia by day and placed him in the fire at night to burn away his mortal parts. Peleus interrupted her as she was performing this ritual and cried out in terror. She dropped her infant and fled back to the sea in anger. Some say Achilles' entire body had been made invulnerable by the ministrations of his mother, except for one anklebone which had been scorched but not burned. Peleus replaced the ankle-bone with one taken from the giant Damysus.

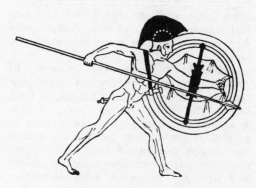

ACHILLES
Red-figured Greek crater, Berlin Painter,
c480 B.C. *British Museum*

Others say Thetis rendered her son invulnerable by dipping him in the Styx. The ankle by which she held him in the water was his only vulnerable spot. When Thetis disappeared into the sea, Peleus entrusted his infant son to the care of Chiron, the centaur. The kindly centaur reared him on Mount Pelion, feeding him on the entrails of bears and lions to give him courage and, some say, on honey and the marrow of fawns to give him swiftness of foot. He learned to ride, hunt, play on the lyre, and to master the arts of healing. He was taught how to sing by the muse Calliope. He was so swift of foot and had such courage that at the age of six he overtook and subdued wild animals and dragged them back to Chiron's cave. Although Thetis had left the house of Peleus she did not lose interest in her son, of whom it had been predicted that he would be greater than his father. (It was because of this prophecy that Zeus gave up his pursuit of Thetis and married her to Peleus.) She was a sea-goddess and had the gift of prophecy. When the Greeks massed to sail to Troy to recover Helen, Thetis knew that if Achilles accompanied them he would gain glory and die young. She sent him to the court of Lycomedes on the island of Scyrus to save him from this fate. There he was dressed as a girl and lived among the women, and there he fathered Neoptolemus on Deidamia, the daughter of Lycomedes.

The Greeks were informed by a seer that they could not overcome the Trojans without the aid of Achilles. Odysseus, Nestor, and Ajax (as some say), the cousin and friend of Achilles, therefore went to Scyrus to fetch him. Some say Odysseus brought jewels, girdles, and other things of interest to ladies. Lycomedes welcomed these envoys but disclaimed all knowledge of Achilles. Odysseus, ever ready with a scheme, asked permission to make gifts to the ladies of the court. He displayed his rich gifts, among which were included a shield and a spear. As the ladies hovered over the treasures, a loud trumpet blast was heard. One of the maidens instantly seized the shield and spear, and prepared to rush into battle. Others say Odysseus came to Scyrus disguised as a merchant and that among his wares he included a few weapons. Achilles revealed himself by lovingly handling the weapons. In either case, Achilles revealed himself to the triumphant Odysseus and promised to lead his Myrmidons against Troy. But others say these are just tales to exalt the ingenuity of Odysseus. According to their accounts, Achilles readily agreed to march against Troy when Nestor and Odysseus came to his father's court in Phthia. Peleus armed him with an ashen spear and golden armor, and gave him immortal horses, and sent him off with Phoenix, his trusted friend and tutor. Patroclus, his beloved friend, and his Myrmidon warriors also accompanied him.

Achilles was the handsomest, the swiftest, the strongest, and the bravest of the Greeks who went to Troy. The mere sight of him struck terror into the hearts of his enemies. Accompanied by Patroclus, Phoenix, and the Myrmidons, he sailed from Aulis with the other Greeks. Under the impression that it

was the Troad, they attacked the coasts of Asia Minor. Achilles and Patroclus attacked Mysia. Telephus, king of Mysia, bravely drove the Greeks back but in pursuing them he tripped over a vine and was wounded by Achilles' spear. After the Greeks left Asia Minor, their fleet was scattered by a storm and they returned separately to their homelands. Achilles went back to Scyrus and married Deidamia. At the second gathering at Aulis, the Greeks were wind-bound. Calchas the seer said that only the sacrifice of Iphigenia, Agamemnon's daughter, would appease Artemis and secure favorable winds. In order to secure the presence of Iphigenia, Agamemnon told his wife Clytemnestra that Iphigenia was to be married to Achilles. Achilles was furious when he learned that his name had been used to bring Iphigenia to Aulis so that she could be sacrificed. He offered to defend her, but Iphigenia readily consented to be sacrificed and, the rites having been performed, favorable winds sprang up and the Greeks put to sea again. They sailed to the island of Tenedos near the Troad. Achilles had been warned by his mother that if he killed a son of Apollo, he would die by Apollo's hand, and he took Mnemon, a servant, with him to remind him not to attack the sons of Apollo. When the Greeks neared Tenedos, King Tenes, said to be a son of Apollo, refused them permission to land and hurled huge stones at their ships. Achilles impulsively leaped into the sea, swam ashore, and killed Tenes. Too late he remembered his mother's warning and then killed Mnemon for failing to remind him of it. But some say Achilles killed Tenes because of a quarrel that arose over Tenes' sister Hemithea. An embassy which the Greeks sent to Troy from Tenedos to demand the restoration of Helen was unsuccessful. They now sailed past the headland of Sigeum and beached their ships before Troy. There was a prophecy that the first to land at Troy would be the first to die. For this reason Achilles did not leap ashore immediately; some say he was the second and some say the last to land. When he did reach shore, he was attacked by Cycnus, a son of Poseidon who had been rendered invulnerable to sword, spear, and arrow. Cycnus had killed many Greeks before he confronted Achilles.

Achilles hurled his spear at him only to see it bounce harmlessly aside. His sword also being ineffective, Achilles battered Cycnus about the head with his shield until he fell, whereupon Achilles strangled him with the straps of his own helmet. But some say Achilles killed Cycnus on Tenedos by crushing his head with a stone. It is said that after landing at Troy, he found Troilus, said by some to be a son of Apollo. He was in the sanctuary of Thymbraean Apollo, which was in neutral territory, when Achilles came upon him and killed him. He captured Lycaon, son of Priam, and sold him as a slave. But Lycaon was ransomed and returned to Troy where, 12 days later, he again fell into the hands of Achilles, who killed him. He made a raid on the cattle of Aeneas. Until this time Aeneas had been neutral in the struggle, but because of this raid, in which he barely escaped capture, Aeneas went over to the side of the Trojans. In raids which Achilles made in Asia Minor and the Troad, he seized and sacked 11 inland cities and 12 seacoast towns, among them: Lesbos, Phocaea, Colophon, Smyrna, Clazomenae, Cyme, Aegialus, Tenos, Adramyttium, Side, Endium, Linnaeum, Colone, Hypoplacian Thebes, Lyrnessus, Antandrus, and others. To Agamemnon, as commander of the expedition, he handed over the lion's share of the booty from these conquests. For himself, he kept Briseis, wife of Mynes of Lyrnessus whom he had slain and whose kingdom he had destroyed. Briseis was the cause of the famous quarrel between Achilles and Agamemnon. The latter, on being forced to relinquish his captive Chryseis to placate Apollo, demanded Briseis from Achilles in her place. As Agamemnon was the commander Achilles had no choice but to obey and yield Briseis whom he had come to love dearly. But to punish Agamemnon and the Greeks, Achilles withdrew from the fighting, taking Patroclus and his Myrmidons with him. He persuaded his mother to ask Zeus to make the Greeks suffer at the hands of the Trojans, to atone for the arrogance of Agamemnon and the injuries inflicted by him. Agamemnon soon regretted his rash action in arousing the ire of Achilles. As the Greeks were battered by the Trojans, he sent an embassy to Achilles to try to persuade him to

return to the war. The ambassadors offered to restore Briseis, to give Achilles any one of several rich cities, and also one of the daughters of Agamemnon for his wife. Achilles rejected their offers, saying that all Agamemnon's proffered gifts he could acquire, but the soul of a man is never won by pillage or capture. Agamemnon, Achilles said, could not soothe his injured spirit with bribes. He

ACHILLES BINDING THE WOUNDS OF PATROCLUS
Red-figured Greek cup, Sosias Painter, 5th century B.C. *Berlin*

threatened to take his ships and his men and go home; he remembered his mother's prophecy that if he fought at Troy he would gain everlasting fame but would die young. On the other hand if he returned to his homeland he would enjoy a long life, but one without glory. The disasters which overtook the Greeks when they no longer had the irresistible aid of Achilles, the death of Patroclus, and Achilles' return to the battle, are described in the *Iliad*. After Achilles had avenged the death of Patroclus by slaying Hector, whose body he shamefully mistreated until it was ransomed by Priam, he buried Patroclus and remained in his tent, mourning his loss with his dear friend and cousin, Telamonian Ajax. Ajax heard the clamor of battle as it increased to a roar and roused Achilles. They sped to the battle and found that Penthesilea the Amazon had come

fat, fāte, fär, fãre, errant; net, mē, hér ardent; pin, pīne; not, nōte, möve, nôr,

to the aid of the Trojans, boasting that she would kill Achilles. Fighting with glorious valor, she had driven the Greeks back to their ships. Achilles sought her out and, mocking her for her daring, he slew her. He removed the helmet from his fallen foe and saw her young face, lovely as a sunrise even in death. Instantly he fell in love with her beauty and was pierced with wild regret for her death. Thersites, the ugliest man of the Greek expedition, sneered at him for his tears over his dead enemy. Achilles flew at him in a rage and killed him. Odysseus took Achilles to the island of Lesbos where, after he had sacrificed to Apollo, Artemis, and Leto, he was purified for the murder. Memnon, the son of Eos, next came to aid the Trojans. He and Achilles met in combat. Each boasted of his immortal forbears; each swore to kill the other. But Memnon's fate, clad in black, came to his side, and after a glorious struggle, Achilles slew him. Hector, dying before the Scaean gate, had prophesied that Achilles would die at the hands of a god and a hero. Other omens, oracles, and prophecies made it plain that Achilles would not survive the war. Apollo meant to avenge the deaths of Troilus and Tenes. Poseidon resolved to avenge the death of his son Cycnus. Achilles' hour had now come. Paris directed an arrow at him as he fought before the Scaean gate and pierced his ankle, his only vulnerable spot. Some say Apollo guided the arrow of Paris, and some say the god shot it himself, disguised as Paris. Achilles drew the arrow out of his foot and flung it from him; it was instantly sped back to Apollo. Achilles wrathfully demanded to know who shot him. Glaring and warlike to the last moment, he grasped his spear, hurled it, and slew one more Trojan before he expired. Telamonian Ajax lifted his body and protected it, though besieged on all sides by the Trojans. All day the battle raged for possession of Achilles' body, but Ajax stood firm, and succeeded in carrying it back to the ships. Then Zeus sent a great storm to end the fight. However, others say Achilles died in quite another way. They say he saw Polyxena, daughter of Priam, as she stood on the walls of Troy casting down rings and bracelets to make up the ransom for Hector's body, and that Achilles fell in love

with her. He secretly entered into negotiations with Priam, who promised to give him Polyxena if he would persuade the Greeks to raise the siege of Troy. When Achilles went alone and unarmed to the sanctuary of Thymbraean Apollo to confirm the negotiations, he was treacherously slain by Deïphobus. Or, as some say, Paris shot him from ambush when Achilles went to the sanctuary to ratify the treaty of marriage with Polyxena. On the death of Achilles, Thetis rose with a great cry from the sea. Accompanied by her Nereids, she came to mourn her son. The Muses also grieved. Thetis commanded the Greeks, grievously wounded by his loss, to hold funeral games in his honor, and to award his armor, which Hephaestus had made for him at her request, to the bravest of the Greeks. His ashes along with those of his beloved friends Patroclus and Antilochus were placed in a golden urn fashioned by Hephaestus, and buried on the headland of Sigeum. Thetis took his spirit to Leuce, an island off the mouths of the Ister which was given to Achilles by Poseidon. There, according to some accounts, he married Helen and lived happily. Travelers who sailed near the island said they could hear the voices of Achilles and his friends across the water as they recited the verses of Homer which extolled their own exploits, accompanying themselves on the lyre as they sang. But some say Achilles married Medea and went to live in the Isles of the Blest. Homer, however, says he went to Tartarus, and when Odysseus visited the Underworld on his way home from Troy, he saw Achilles striding unhappily about the Fields of Asphodel, bitterly lamenting his fate, and declaring that he would far rather be a live slave than a dead hero. The women of Elis honored Achilles with funeral rites at the opening of the Olympic Festival, and the Thessalians sacrificed to him annually. He was honored and worshiped at many places, the most revered of his shrines being his tomb on the Hellespont.

Achilles Tatius (tā′shus). Greek astronomer who flourished in the late 2nd century (or during the 3rd century) A.D. He was one of the many commentators on the astronomical work, in verse, *Phenomena* (or *Phainomena*) written by Aratus of Soli. His commentary, entitled *On the Sphere,* is preserved in a fragmentary condition.

Achilles Tatius. Greek rhetorician and novelist who flourished probably in the 4th century A.D. at Alexandria in Egypt. He was the author of the Greek romance, in eight books, on the adventures of Clitophon of Tyre and Leucippe of Byzantium. This tale of two lovers who suffer many adventures before at last they meet continued to be popular until the fall of Byzantium in the 15th century. It is well constructed, and in the telling of it the author exhibits his wide reading by his descriptions of places, works of art, and natural phenomena.

Achilleum (ak-i-lē′um). In ancient geography, a place on the promontory of Sigeum, in NW Asia Minor, in the Troad, containing, according to tradition, the tomb of Achilles.

Acidalia (a-si-dā′li-a). Epithet of Aphrodite, from a fountain named Acidalius near Orchomenus, in which the goddess was said to bathe with the Graces.

Acis (ā′sis). In classical legend, a beautiful Sicilian youth, the son of Faunus and the sea-nymph Symaethis. He was beloved by Galatea and was slain by the Cyclops Polyhemus, his unsuccessful rival. Galatea transformed the blood of his crushed body into a river which bore his name.

Acmon (ak′mon). A legendary Greek follower of Diomedes. When Diomedes at last returned to his own home after the Trojan War, he was driven out by his wife and her lover. With a number of his followers, among them Acmon, he set out for Italy. But because he had once wounded Aphrodite in the Trojan War she continued to harass him, sending storms to scatter his ships at sea and besetting him with war on land. The followers of Diomedes became discouraged by so many misfortunes. Acmon sought to hearten them. Their condition could not be any worse, he said; they should therefore defy the goddess who persecuted them and press on to Italy. For his defiance Aphrodite transformed him and a number of the followers of Diomedes into birds.

Acontius (a-kon′shi-us, -shus). Principal character in the tale of Acontius and Cydippe, told by Aristaenetus and by Ovid. "Acontius gathered an orange in the garden of Venus, and having written on the rind the words, 'By

Artemis, I will marry Acontius,' threw it in Cydippe's way. She took it in her hand, read out the inscription, and threw it from her. But Artemis heard the vow, and brought about the marriage." William Morris took the legend for the subject of one of his poems in *The Earthly Paradise.*

Acrae (ak′rē). In ancient geography, a city of SE Sicily, situated about 20 miles inland and W of Syracuse. It was founded (664 B.C.) by colonists from Syracuse. Quarries near the ancient city are filled with tombs dating from various periods. The ancient city was built on a hill above the modern town of Palazzolo Acreide.

Acraea (ak-rē′a). An epithet of Aphrodite in her aspect as a goddess of the heavens and the winds, meaning "Of the Height."

Acragas (ak′ra-gas). [Latin, **Agrigentum;** modern names, **Agrigento, Girgenti.**] In ancient geography, a city of Sicily, situated on a high hill near the shore on the SW coast of the island. It was founded c582 B.C. by colonists from the Dorian city of Gela. Shortly after its founding it was compelled to defend itself, perhaps under the tyrant Phalaris, from attacks by the Carthaginians (c560–550 B.C.). By the beginning of the 5th century B.C. it was a flourishing and prosperous city, called by Pindar "the fairest of mortal cities." It outstripped Gela and became second only to Syracuse among the Greek cities of Sicily. Under the tyrant Theron (died c472 B.C.) the city was greatly enlarged: its walls were extended to include both eastern and western summits, a water supply was provided, and the foundations were laid for a magnificent row of temples along the south wall between the rivers Acragas and Hypsas. Following the defeat of the Carthaginians at Himera (480 B.C.) the city flourished. In 472 B.C. the tyrants were overthrown and a democracy was established. A high degree of prosperity and even luxury was attained and the temples begun by Theron were completed. In 406 B.C. the Carthaginians besieged the city, which had refused immunity in return for neutrality in the struggle that Carthage now undertook to reduce and conquer Greek Sicily. After a siege of eight months, in which they were deserted by their allies and mercenaries, most of the inhabitants abandoned their city. Under cover of darkness they marched out, leaving those either unable or unwilling to go to be butchered by the Carthaginians under the command of Himilco, who sacked the city. It remained a Punic city until c340 B.C., when it was rewon and recolonized by Timoleon, the general sent by Corinth to rescue her colony of Syracuse. During the Punic Wars the city was sacked by the Romans (261 B.C.) and by the Carthaginians (255), and finally fell to Rome (210 B.C.). Many remains of the magnificent temples constructed in the 5th century B.C. are to be found on the site, including temples of Zeus, Heracles, Concordia, and Hera, as well as remains of the 4th century B.C. temples of Demeter, Castor and Pollux, and Hephaestus. The poet and philosopher Empedocles was a native of Acragas.

COIN OF ACRAGAS
Silver decadrachm issued by Acragas shortly after 413 B.C. Obverse, chariot of Helius, engraved by Myron; reverse, eagles with hare, engraved by Polycrates. *British Museum*

Acrisius (a̱-kris′i-us). In classical legend, a son of Abas and Aglaia, and the great-grandson of Danaus. He was the twin of Proetus with whom he struggled in his mother's womb and with whom he was destined to struggle all his life. Their father, king of Argos, left his kingdom to his twin sons with instructions that they should rule alternately. But Acrisius refused to give up the throne when it was Proetus' turn to rule, and drove him out of the kingdom. Proetus fled to Iobates in Lycia. He later returned with reinforcements supplied him by Iobates and waged war on Acrisius. The battle was indecisive and the brothers decided to divide the kingdom between them: Acrisius took Argos and Proetus became ruler of Tiryns. Acrisius' wife Aganippe, or as some say, Eurydice, bore him a daughter, Danaë. Acrisius, who wanted a son, consulted an oracle and was told that he would have no sons and that he would meet his death at the hands of Danaë's son. To prevent the fulfillment of the oracle, Acrisius confined Danaë in a prison with bronze doors. Zeus, however, came to Danaë in a shower of gold and she bore him a son, Perseus. Acrisius, on learning of this, doubted the paternity of his grandson; nevertheless, he wanted to destroy him. Reluctant to kill his own daughter and her son, he locked them in a chest and set them adrift on the sea. The chest was washed ashore on Seriphus, and Danaë and Perseus were saved. Perseus grew to manhood and carried out his mission to secure the head of Medusa. Acrisius learned of his exploits and, mindful of the oracle, fled from Argos to Larissa. Perseus, unaware that his grandfather was there, also went to Larissa to take part in funeral games. In the discus-throwing contest his discus was carried out of its course by the wind or by fate. It struck and killed Acrisius who was standing as a spectator, unaware of the fact that his grandson was one of the contestants. Thus the oracle concerning the death of Acrisius was fulfilled. He was buried in the temple of Athena on the acropolis of Larissa.

Acroceraunia (ak″rō̱-sē̱-rô′ni-a̱). [Also: **Akrokeraunia**; modern Greek, **Glossa**; Italian, **Linguetta**.] In ancient geography, a promontory projecting from what was then the NW part of Epirus (and is now SW Albania) into the

actǫr; up, lūte, pu̇ll; oi, oil; ou, out; ŦH, then; ḏ as d or j, ṣ as s or sh, ṭ as t or ch, ẓ as z or zh.

Ionian Sea. The name has sometimes been incorrectly extended to the whole range of the Ceraunian Mountains.

Acrocorinthus (ak"rō-kō-rin'thus). [Also: **Akrokorinthos, Acro-Corinth.**] Hill, about 1885 feet high in Greece, under the N slope of which lies the city of Corinth. According to legend, Poseidon and Helius struggled for control of the land about Corinth. Briareus awarded the hill to Helius. He in his turn gave it to Aphrodite. On the slopes of the hill were many temples and altars, and on the summit a temple of Aphrodite. The spring behind the temple was given to the city by the river-god Asopus to reward Sisyphus for informing him that it was Zeus who had carried off his daughter Aegina. Some say this spring and the Pirene spring are the same, that the water flows underground from one to the other. The hill, celebrated for its extensive view, is now covered with ruins. There are scanty remains of the ancient fortifications and of the celebrated temple of Aphrodite and other religious structures.

Acropolis (a-krop'ō-lis). A general name for the citadel of an ancient Greek city. The name is especially appropriated to that of Athens, whose Acropolis is a precipitous rock that rises about 260 feet above the city, extends 1000 feet from E to W, and is 400 feet in its greatest width. It forms a natural citadel, and in earliest times was the site of ancient Athens itself, strongly fortified and containing the palace of the king. It was a center of worship from most ancient times. Here were the palaces of Cecrops and Erechtheus, and here Athena vied with Poseidon for control of the city.

The well of Clepsydra, below the northwest corner of the Acropolis and reached in ancient times by a covered stairway, supplied the citadel with water. Nearby was the cave where Apollo is said to have ravished Creusa, daughter of Erechtheus, and fathered Ion, ancestor of the Ionians. Traces of settlements of the Neolithic Age have been found on the slopes of the Acropolis. The first palace on its upper surface was erected between 1900 and 1600 B.C. Traces of structures of the age of Cecrops (traditional date, 1581 B.C.), Erechtheus, and other early kings include a palace, parts of Pelasgian walls, and the platform where the temple of Nike

stands. Traces of a temple from the period 1100–750 B.C. also survive. Down to about the 7th century B.C. the Acropolis was a fortified citadel. After that time it came to be considered as a sacred area and private dwellings were removed from it, leaving a few temples and a simple propylaeum. The foundations of an ancient temple of Athena, lying between and partly under the sites where the *Erechtheum* and the *Parthenon* now stand, were recognized and studied by Dörpfeld in 1885. The Doric, peripteral temple, which measured 70 by 137 feet, went through three phases. The earliest part of it was raised on the foundations of a prehistoric Mycenaean palace about the time of Solon (c638–c559 B.C.), and was entirely dedicated to Athena Polias. Toward the end of the 6th century B.C. the Pisistratidae, seeking to equal the beautiful temple erected by their rivals the Alcmaeonidae at Delphi, transformed the naos of the temple and, 520–510 B.C., added 12 columns on the flanks, six columns on the façades, and painted marble pediments. The temple was destroyed by the Persians, 480 B.C., and was partly restored. In 454 B.C. the treasury of the Confederacy of Delos was brought from Delos and placed in the restored temple. On completion of the Parthenon the treasury was removed thither. After the completion of the Erechtheum (407 B.C.), the restored section of the ancient temple of Athena Polias fell into disuse. It was destroyed by fire in 406 B.C. and its foundations were covered over by a terrace. In the 6th century B.C. there was a temple on the present site of the Parthenon, and many smaller temples and treasuries as well on the Acropolis. In this century Pisistratus and Clisthenes made additions to the temples. All of these were completely destroyed when the Persians attacked, took the citadel and burned it, 480 B.C. After the successes of the Greeks at Salamis (480) and Plataea (479 B.C.), the Athenians returned to the city which they had abandoned when the Persians swept down on it. Themistocles, the successful commander at Salamis and the most influential man in Athens, immediately set about rebuilding the walls of the city and those on the north side of the Acropolis as well, using drums of the columns of the ancient temple of Athena and other marble fragments created by the Persian destruction as building materials. These fragments, set into the wall in a kind of pattern and plainly visible to all, were a constant reminder to the Athenians of the Persian vandalism. Cimon continued the work of Themistocles. He built walls on the east and south slopes and increased the top area by filling it in with the rubble that was strewn about the Acropolis. By the time of Pericles (c495–429 B.C.), the Acropolis had been shored up by walls and its area increased but its surface was a mass of ruins. Cleared of ancient structures of varying periods, it presented a site for a planned development of new buildings. Pericles seized this opportunity to create here a great religious center and artistic memorial to the victory of the Greeks over the Persians. Ictinus, Callicrates, and Phidias were given the responsibility and authority to carry out his plan. The buildings and remains from this period (last half of the 5th century B.C.) make of the Acropolis a world-famous monument of the Classical period. The traveler Pausanias describes the Acropolis as it was in the 2nd century A.D. His description, the only complete contemporary account of any age, provides a full description of buildings, statues, and altars that have since disappeared, and also makes possible the identification of many objects that have remained.

In the Pelasgic period (1600–1100 B.C.) the Acropolis could be approached by a stairway cut into rock at the northeast corner. This led to the palace of the ancient kings. The natural entrance was on the west, through the *Enneapylon*, the nine gates that were added to the Acropolis perhaps in the 10th century B.C. By the time of Pausanias the main entrance was by a great gate, the *Propylaea* on the west. This vast, never-completed structure was designed by Mnesicles. His design, majestic and symmetrical, had to be altered when priests of Athena Nike and Brauronian Artemis refused to allow their ancient precincts to be invaded to make room for the south side of the proposed Propylaea. Work on the structure was begun in 438 B.C., but was halted 431 B.C. by the outbreak of the Peloponnesian Wars. The design was modified in succeeding centuries and additions were made to it. Among the last of these was that by Caligula in 40 A.D. The present approach to the Propylaea is by the *Beulé Gate,* so-called because it was uncovered by the French archaeologist Ernest Beulé in 1853. A western extension of the Propylaea, it was added perhaps in the 2nd century A.D., and was covered by the Turks when they used the Acropolis as a fortress. The Propylaea were transformed into an archbishop's palace (12th century), and were later used for administrative offices; about the middle of the 17th century the Turks who had occupied the Acropolis since 1394 stored gunpowder in it. This was ignited by a thunderbolt and exploded. Thus, part of the structure was destroyed (1640). It is now being restored. In ancient times a winding path was followed by the sacred processions to the Acropolis in the Panathenaic festival. This was replaced by a marble ramp that led to the Propylaea. On the south or right side of the Propylaea is the little temple of Athena Nike, goddess of Victory, built on a bastion that juts out to the west, on a site that was from ancient times a precinct of Athena. The ancient cult image was of wood, and depicted the goddess without wings, holding in one hand a pomegranate, symbol of peace and fertility, and in the other her war helmet. This edifice came to be known as the temple of *Nike Apteros* (Wingless Victory) perhaps from the ancient statue. Here, some say, Victory was presented as wingless so that she could never fly from Athens. The exquisite relief sculptures of the Victories, including the charming *Victory Loosing Her Sandal,* from the balustrade of the temple, are now in the museum on the Acropolis. On the site of the temple of Athena Nike, so legend says, Aegeus stood to look over the sea, watching for the ship whose sails would tell him the fate of Theseus. From here, when he saw the black sails of death, he hurled himself to the rocks below. The temple of Athena Nike, built 440 B.C., was pulled down by the Turks in 1687, and its material was used by them to build a rampart against the Venetians. It was carefully reconstructed from its original pieces in 1835, later found to be near a state of collapse, and in 1936–41 was rebuilt again, when remains of an older temple were found.

To the left of the Propylaea was what Pausanias referred to as a building with pictures, the *Pinacotheca*. Among the pictures he mentions in it were representations of Diomedes taking the Palladium from Troy, Odysseus fetching Philoctetes at Lemnos, Orestes killing Aegisthus, Pylades killing the sons of Nauplius who had come to the aid of Aegisthus, and Polyxena about to be sacrificed on the tomb of Achilles. There were many more pictures, but all of these and the foregoing have been lost. Inside the Propylaea, at the entrance to the Acropolis, was a figure of *Hermes of the Gateway*. Near it was a small stone on which Silenus was supposed to have sat and rested when he came in the train of Dionysus to Athens.

To the south center of the Acropolis is the Parthenon, a temple that for strength and simplicity, perfect proportions and harmonious relation to its site, has never been equalled. This was Athena's great temple, named from her epithet Athena Parthenos. Pericles engaged Ictinus as architect and gave Phidias general charge of its construction and ornamentation. Periods in history when such a fortunate combination of geniuses lived at the same time have been rare. Work on the temple, which faces the east, was commenced in 447 and completed in 438 B.C. On its pediments were great sculptured scenes, skillfully designed to fit the awkward and constricted area of a thin elongated triangle with perfect grace. The scene at the birth of Athena was on the east pediment; the west pediment showed the contest of Athena and Poseidon. The building was richly decorated inside and out. Great artists worked on it; rich gifts were made to it in succeeding times, among them the golden shields presented by Alexander the Great after the battle of the Granicus, 334 B.C. In later times, when Christianity spread over the Mediterranean world and the Emperor Theodosius II destroyed many of the great monuments, the Parthenon was dedicated as a Christian church (630 A.D.). Later it was turned into a mosque and equipped with minarets by the Turks, who had occupied the Acropolis since 1394, and it was used by them as an arsenal in a war with the Venetians. During the siege a shot from the Hill of the Muses pierced the roof, ignited the gunpowder

stored there, and blew the magnificent building apart (1687). This was the worst disaster that had ever befallen it. Afterward its monumental sculptures, statues, altars, and columns lay in broken heaps on the ground. In succeeding years some of the marble was carried away and used for building material. Early in the 19th century Lord Elgin, ambassador of Great Britain in Constantinople, received permission from the Sultan to gather up what he wished of the fallen and neglected marbles and to carry them off to England, where they were placed in the British Museum, 1816. Across from the Parthenon, to the north, rises the Erechtheum, built after 421 B.C., on the site of one of the oldest sanctuaries of the Acropolis. Here, according to tradition, Athena and Poseidon vied for control of Athens. Poseidon struck the rock with his trident, and a fountain of sea water gushed forth. Athena gave the olive tree as her gift to the city. It was voted the more useful to man and she was awarded the city and became its chief goddess. The Erechtheum housed the ancient shrines of the rivals. The cella in the east of the building was that of Athena. In it was the ancient olive-wood image of the goddess, said to have fallen from heaven in the time of Cecrops. It was burned when the Persians destroyed the Acropolis, or, as some say, was saved by being taken aboard a Greek ship just before the battle of Salamis (480 B.C.). Behind the cella of Athena, to the west, was the cella of Poseidon-Erechtheus. Thus the two rival immortals, Athena and Poseidon, were united in one temple. In Poseidon's cella was enclosed the fountain of sea water, sometimes called the "Sea of Erechtheus," brought forth by Poseidon's trident, as well as the marks of his trident. It was said that when the south wind blew the cistern gave forth the sound of waves. There were also altars to Hephaestus, a god closely associated with Athena in the arts of civilization, and to Butes, an ancient priest of Athena and ancestor of the priestly family, the Butadae. Behind the cella of Poseidon was the *Pandroseum,* the sanctuary of Pandrosos, daughter of Cecrops and first priestess of Athena. In the enclosure was the sacred olive tree Athena planted as a gift to Athens. The tree was burned during the Persian Wars, but

fat, fāte, fär, fãre, errạnt; net, mē, hẽr ardẹnt; pin, pīne; not, nōte, möve, nôr,

according to tradition it immediately put forth a new shoot. The famous *Porch of the Maidens* formed a south wing of the Erechtheum, and a north porch was a place of sacrifices to Zeus. The Erechtheum was converted into a church, probably in the 7th century A.D., and in the time of the Turkish occupation it housed the harem of the Turkish commander on the Acropolis. Many altars and statues were on the Acropolis, among them the statue of *Athena Lemnia* by Phidias, said by Pausanias to be his finest work. There were also numberless statues representing scenes from mythology, images of the gods, and of such mortals as Pericles, Xanthippus, and Anacreon of Teos, the poet. On the south slope of the Acropolis was the sanctuary of Asclepius, begun c420 B.C., an important healing center until its close in the 5th century A.D. To the east of the sanctuary of Asclepius are the remains of a theater of Dionysus built in the 4th century B.C. on the site of the ancient theater in which the plays of Aeschylus, Sophocles, and Euripides had been performed. At the southeast corner on the lower slopes was the *Odeum*, constructed about the same time as the Parthenon.

In 86 B.C. Sulla besieged Athens and destroyed many buildings on the south slope of the Acropolis. In Roman times additions were made to the Propylaea and buildings were added on the Acropolis. A circular shrine dedicated to the goddess Roma and to the Emperor Augustus was erected 14 B.C. Hadrian made rich gifts and repaired buildings. Herodes Atticus, wealthy Athenian and generous donor of buildings, built the theater named for him on the south slope, in memory of his wife Regilla, c160 A.D. From the reign of Theodosius II (401–450 A.D.), the Acropolis ceased to be a center of worship. He caused the monuments to be mutilated or destroyed in a ruthless campaign of Christianization. As noted earlier, the Acropolis was occupied by the Turks for about 400 years. In 1833, following the liberation of the Greeks, the royal ensign of their first king, Otto I, was hoisted on the Acropolis. Almost immediately work was begun on the restoration of the monuments, among the most precious in the western world. Excavations have revealed succes-

sively earlier stages of development, before the time of Pericles. The site, crowned by the Parthenon, the Erechtheum whose more delicate outlines, façade, and famous Porch of the Maidens are in good state of preservation, and the temple of Athena Nike, is a center of artistic and cultural pilgrimage. Large marble fragments and the drums of columns of these and other structures remain where they fell, in the hope that means will be found to reassemble and raise them.

Acta Diurna (ak′ta dī-ėr′na). [Eng. trans., "Daily Events."] Roman official daily chronicle which contained regulations by the magistrates, transactions and decrees of the Senate, accounts of accidents and family news communicated to the editors in addition to official reports of events in the imperial family, and of state and city affairs. The *Acta* were publicly exhibited on a whitened board (*album*), which anyone might read and copy, and there were men who made a business of multiplying and transmitting such news to the provinces. After a time the originals were placed among the state archives for the benefit of those who wished to consult them. The publication of such news was made official by Julius Caesar; it ceased, apparently, on the transfer of the capital to Constantinople.

ACTAEON BEING TORN TO PIECES BY HIS HOUNDS
Red-figured Greek crater, Pan Painter, 475–450 B.C. *Museum of Fine Arts, Boston*

Actaeon (ak-tē′on). In mythology, a son of Aristaeus and Autonoë, daughter of Cadmus. He lived in Orchomenus. Weary one day from hunting, he sought rest in a grove which, unknown to him, was sacred to Artemis. As he wandered through the grove he inadvertently came on the spring where Artemis and her nymphs were bathing. To punish him because, through no fault of his, he had seen the goddess in her bath, Artemis splashed water in his face and transformed him into a stag. In his new form Actaeon fled. His own hounds, which some say were the Telchines that had fled from Rhodes, picked up the scent of the stag and gave chase. Overtaking him at last, they tore their former master to pieces.

Actaeus (ak-tē′us). According to some accounts, the first king of what later became Attica. In his reign the land was called Actaea. His daughter Aglauros (or Agraulos) married Cecrops who, on the death of Actaeus, succeeded him to the throne.

Actis (ak′tis). In mythology, one of the six sons of Rhode and Helius. Banished from Rhodes for killing his brother, he went to Egypt and founded the city of Heliopolis. There, inspired by Helius, he taught the Egyptians astrology. The Colossus of Rhodes was built in his honor.

Actium (ak′shi-um, -ti-um) In ancient geography, a promontory on the NW coast of Acarnania, in Greece. The ancient *peribolos* or sacred enclosure, rectangular in plan and built in *opus reticulatum,* the seat of the famous Actian games of Augustus, still remains. Modern excavations have laid bare extensive ruins of several successive temples, one of the latest of which is that dedicated by Augustus after the victory of 31 B.C. A famous naval battle was fought (Sept. 2, 31 B.C.) near Actium by Octavian (the future Augustus) against Mark Antony and Cleopatra. It was decided by the flight of Cleopatra, Mark Antony's land forces thereupon surrendering to Octavian. The victory secured for Octavian supreme rule over the Roman dominion.

Actor (ak′tor). In classical legend, a brother of Augeas, king of Elis, and reputedly the father by Molione of Eurytus and Cteatus. His descendants are called the Moliones, after their mother.

Actor. In legend, a son of Myrmidon and Pasidice. He was king of Phthia and received Peleus when the latter fled to his court after the murder of Phocus. Actor's adopted son Eurytion purified Peleus for the murder. Actor gave his daughter Polymela to Peleus in marriage and one-third of his kingdom as her dowry.

Actoridae (ak-tôr′i-dē), or **Actoriones** (-tôr-i-ō′nēz). Descendants of Actor. See **Moliones.**

Acusilaus (a-kū-si-lā′us). Called **Acusilaus of Argos,** although he was born in Boeotia, probably mid-6th century B.C. He was a Greek commentator and chronicler, who paraphrased the *Theogony* of Hesiod in prose. It was said that his father found the *Theogony* inscribed on bronze tablets buried in his garden, and that it was from these that Acusilaus rewrote the work in prose. He was regarded by some as one of the seven wise men.

Ada (ā′da). Sister and wife of Idrieus, ruler of Halicarnassus. When her husband died she succeeded him as ruler, but was driven out by her brother Pixodarus. Alexander the Great, having defeated the Persians at the Granicus River (334 B.C.), marched through Asia Minor, overthrowing the tyrannies established by the Persians in the Greek cities there. Ada sought his protection. He adopted her as his mother, and when he had taken Halicarnassus by force he restored Ada and made her ruler of the satrapy of Caria.

Adamas (ad′a-mas). Named by Homer (*Iliad*) as a son of the Trojan ally Asius. In his chariot he accompanied his father at the attack on the Greek fortifications. His attempt to kill Antilochus, Nestor's son, was foiled by Poseidon, who caused his spear to break off in the shield of Antilochus. As the unarmed Adamas retreated, Meriones followed and killed him.

Addaeus (a-dē′us). Greek epigrammatist of Macedonia, active c320 B.C.

Addua (ad′ö-a). [Modern name, **Adda.**] River in N Italy, which rises in the Rhaetian Alps, traverses Lacus Larius (Lake Como), and joins the Po River about eight miles W of Cremona.

Adige (ä′dē-jä). See **Athesis.**

Admete (ad-mē′tē). According to legend, a daughter of Eurystheus. Because she ardently desired to possess the golden girdle of

Ares that belonged to the Amazon queen, Hippolyte, Heracles was commanded to fetch it as one of his 12 labors.

Admetus (ad-mē′tus). A legendary king of Pherae in Thessaly. He was a son of Pheres. He joined in the Calydonian Hunt and was also a member of the expedition of the Argonauts. When he returned from that expedition, Apollo was sent to labor for him for one year as a punishment for killing the Cyclopes. Apollo served him well and was his good friend. He helped Admetus to yoke a lion and a boar to a chariot, a condition which Pelias set for the suitors of his daughter, Alcestis, and thus Admetus won Alcestis for his bride. Admetus forgot to sacrifice to Artemis on the wedding day and in anger the goddess punished him. Apollo interceded and won her forgiveness, and also won a promise from Artemis that when Death came for Admetus he could win a reprieve on condition that some one else could be found to take his place. Too soon, Hermes came to take Admetus to the Underworld. Apollo made the Fates drunk so that they did not immediately snip the thread of his life. This gave Admetus time to search for a substitute. He asked his father and mother but, though very aged, they loved life and neither would give it up for Admetus. Only Alcestis, his devoted wife, was willing to cut short her life that Admetus might prolong his: she went with Hermes to the Underworld in his place. Admetus, grieving at her loss, let her go.

Adonia (a-dō′ni-a). A festival held in midsummer in honor of Adonis. In the celebration of the festival small images of the dead Adonis were carried in procession and exposed to the public view, while the women who accompanied them beat their breasts and mourned, and imitated the burial rites. After this, the women rejoiced as at the resurrection of Adonis. As part of the festival pots of earth were sown with plants that grew quickly. These were tended carefully for eight days and then allowed to wither and die and were thrown into the sea with the images of the dead Adonis. They represented the rapid coming to youthful beauty of Adonis and his death in the bloom of youth.

Adonis (a-don′is, a-dō′nis). In mythology, a son of Myrrha and Cinyras, her own father.

Cinyras had not realized that the young girl with whom he was consorting was his own daughter. When he learned the truth, he was horrified and sought to kill her. She fled and was transformed into a myrrh tree. When it was time for her child to be born the birth goddess Lucina split the trunk of the tree and Adonis tumbled out. He was cared for by nymphs and grew to be a young man of surpassing beauty. According to another account, Aphrodite, repenting that she had caused Myrrha to fall in love with her father, saved the infant Adonis when he was born from the trunk of the tree and hid him in a chest which she gave to Persephone to guard, with admonitions not to look inside the chest. Persephone disobeyed her command and was so struck by the beauty of the child in the chest that she brought him up herself, and refused to give him up when Aphrodite demanded him. The muse Calliope, who was called on to judge the dispute between Aphrodite and Persephone, decided that Adonis, now a handsome youth and the lover of both, should spend a third of the year with Aphrodite, a third with Persephone, and should have a third for himself. But Aphrodite, with the aid of the magic girdle of love, persuaded him to spend most of his time with her thus violating the terms of the decision. She bore him a son Golgos and a daughter Beroë. Although she cautioned Adonis to avoid ferocious beasts when he followed his favorite pastime of hunting, he could not resist the thrill of the chase. His hunting dogs raised a wild boar from its lair and Adonis eagerly gave chase. He shot at the boar but his arrow only wounded and maddened the animal. It turned savagely on Adonis and tore him to pieces. A blood-red flower sprang from the drops of his blood that fell to the earth, the anemone, which flourishes briefly. Its handsome blossom grows swiftly to beauty and as rapidly dies, even as Adonis died in the full bloom of youth. Some say it was Ares in the shape of a boar who destroyed him, because he was jealous of Aphrodite's love for him. Aphrodite was heartbroken at the death of her youthful lover. She appealed to Zeus and persuaded him to allow Adonis to spend the summer months of the year with her. The rest of the time his shade lingers in the Un-

actor; up, lūte, pull; oi, oil; ou, out; ᵮн, then; d̦ as d or j, ș as s or sh, ț as t or ch, z̧ as z or zh.

derworld. Adonis has been considered by some scholars to have been originally an oriental deity of nature, typifying the withering of nature in winter and its revival in summer. By way of Asia Minor his cult came first to Greece, then passed to Egypt, and thence finally was brought to Rome. The yearly festival of Adonis in the spring was a special favorite with women. In the Old Testament reference is made to the weeping of the women over Tammuz, the Babylonian equivalent of Adonis (Ezek. viii. 14), a name which may be a form of the Semitic *'adon,* "lord."

Adramyttium (ad-ra̯-mit′i-um) or **Adramyti** (-i). [Modern name, **Edremit**.] In ancient geography, a town in the Troad near the head of the Gulf of Adramyttium (Gulf of Edremit) NE of the island of Lesbos. It was one of the towns seized and sacked by Achilles during the Trojan War, according to legend.

Adramyttium, Gulf of. [Modern name, **Gulf of Edremit**.] In ancient geography, an arm of the Aegean Sea on the coast of Mysia. It separates the mainland from the island of Mytilene. Length, about 50 miles; width, about 15 miles.

Adraste (a̯-dras′tē). In Homeric legend (*Odyssey*), an attendant of Helen in the court of Menelaus.

Adrastea (ad-ras-tē′a̯) or **Adrastia** (ad-ras-tī′a̯). A Cretan nymph, daughter of Melisseus, to whom Rhea entrusted the infant Zeus to be reared in the Dictaean grotto. According to some accounts, Zeus rewarded her by giving her the horn of the goat Amalthea, which thereafter was filled with whatever food or drink its possessor desired, and became known as the "Cornucopia" or "Horn of Plenty."

Adrastea. "Inescapable"; an epithet of Nemesis, goddess of divine vengeance.

Adrastus (a̯-dras′tus). [Also: **Adrastos**.] A mythical grandson of Bias. He was a king of Argos. His two daughters Aegia and Deïpyle had so many powerful suitors that Adrastus hesitated to choose among them for fear the disappointed suitors would become his enemies. He consulted the oracle at Delphi and was told to yoke a boar and a lion that fought in his palace. Shortly thereafter Tydeus, son of Oeneus of Calydon,

and Polynices, son of Oedipus of Thebes, came to Argos. When these two exiles began to quarrel in his palace Adrastus remembered the oracle, for the emblem of Calydon is a boar, and the emblem of Thebes is a lion. (Some say Tydeus was clad in a boar's hide and Polynices in a lion's skin.) He pacified their quarrel and gave his daughter Aegia to Polynices and his daughter Deïpyle to Tydeus. Polynices had been refused the throne of Thebes when it was his turn to rule, by his brother Eteocles. Tydeus had been banished from Calydon for a murder. Adrastus promised to restore them both to their lands. He called his chieftains together for a march against Thebes to restore Polynices. The Seven against Thebes who assembled were Adrastus, Capaneus, Hippomedon, Parthenopaeus, Amphiaraus, Polynices, and Tydeus. Amphiaraus, brother-in-law of Adrastus, was unwilling to go. He was a seer and foresaw disaster. But some years previously he had quarreled with Adrastus and driven him to Sicyon. Their quarrel was later resolved and Amphiaraus married Eriphyle, the sister of Adrastus, who made them both promise that in any future dispute they would abide by her decision. In this case, bribed by Polynices, she decided that Amphiaraus should be one of the expedition. Amphiaraus yielded to her decision though he knew it would cause his death. In the war against Thebes, the Seven met with disaster, as Amphiaraus had foreseen. Every one of the champions was killed except Adrastus who escaped on the winged horse Arion, which had been given to him by Heracles. Some years later the sons of the Seven against Thebes, known as the Epigoni, again attacked Thebes to avenge their fathers. Aegialeus, the son of Adrastus, was among the Epigoni and was killed in the attack. When Adrastus learned of his death he died of grief. But some say Adrastus accompanied the Epigoni to Thebes and died of grief over his son's death at Megara, on his way home from the successful attack. He was worshiped as a hero at Athens, Sicyon, and Megara.

Adrastus of Aphrodisias. Greek philosopher; fl. at Aphrodisias, in Caria, about the beginning of the 2nd century B C. He wrote commentaries on Aristotle (*Ethics, Logic, Phys-*

ics), on Theophrastus (*Ethics*), and on Plato's *Timaeus*. His commentary on the *Timaeus* dealt with mathematical and astronomical questions. He also wrote a treatise on the order of the Aristotelian writings.

Adrestus (a̤-dres′tus). In Homeric legend (*Iliad*), a son of the seer Merops of Percote. He and his brother Amphius went to the aid of Troy, in spite of their father's prophecy that if they did so they would never return to their homeland. He was slain by Diomedes.

Adrestus. In Homeric legend (*Iliad*), a Trojan ally. He was captured by Menelaus when his horses, fleeing in terror, overturned his chariot. He begged Menelaus to spare his life, promising him a rich ransom. Menelaus agreed to do so, but Agamemnon then came upon the scene and reminded Menelaus that he had not been so kindly treated by the Trojans, and slew Adrestus himself.

Adria (ā′dri-a̤). In ancient geography, the sea now called the Adriatic, and also (about the 1st century A.D.) that part of the Mediterranean which lies between Crete and Sicily.

Adriatic Sea (ā-dri-at′ik, ad-ri-at′ik). [Italian **Mare Adriatico;** Latin, **Adria, Mare Adriaticum.**] That part of the Mediterranean Sea which lies between Italy on the W and NW, and Yugoslavia and Albania on the E, and is connected with the Ionian Sea by the Strait of Otranto. Its chief arms are the Gulfs of Manfredonia, Venice, Trieste, and Quarnero (Velik Kvarner), and its largest tributaries are the rivers Po and Adige. Length, about 500 miles; area, about 51,000 square miles; average depth, about 795 feet; greatest known depth, 4590 feet.

Adymnus (a̤-dim′nus). Name which the Cretans gave to the son Eos bore to Cephalus. Others called him Phaëthon. Aphrodite stole him while he was still a child and made him watchman of her most sacred shrines.

Adytum (ad′i-tum). In ancient worship, a sacred place which the worshipers might not enter, or which might be entered only by those who had performed certain rites, or only by males or by females, or only on certain appointed days, etc. Also, a secret sanctuary or shrine open only to the priests, or whence oracles were delivered, hence in general the most sacred or reserved part of any place of worship. In Greece an adytum was usually an inner recess or chamber in a temple as in that of Hera at Aegium; but it might be an entire temple as that of Poseidon at Mantinea, or a grove, inclosure, or cavern, as the sacred inclosure of Zeus on the Lycaean mount in Arcadia. The most famous adytum of Greece was the sanctuary of the Pythic oracle at Delphi.

Aea (ē′a̤). In ancient geography, a city on the Phasis' River in Colchis, where King Aeëtes lived and to which Jason and the Argonauts journeyed on the quest for the Golden Fleece. Some say it was named for a huntress who was transformed into an island of this name to save her from the pursuit of the river-god Phasis. Aea seems to mean "Land, the Mainland," and may be the same word as *Asia*. *Aeëtes* is "Man of the land, Lands-man." This whole tale is full of allegory: *Argo* "Swift," *Jason* "Healer," *Medea* "Wise girl," etc.

Aeaea (ē-ē′a̤). A name applied to two homes of the enchantress Circe. One was an alder-fringed island at the head of the Adriatic Sea near the mouth of the Po River. It is described as gloomy and heavily wooded, but on the other hand was sometimes called the Island of the Dawn. The other was identified with a promontory or small rocky island (in ancient times an island, now connected to the mainland) off the west coast of Italy near Terracina. Jason and Medea went to Aeaea to be purified by Circe of the slaying of Apsyrtus on their way to Iolcus from Colchis. Odysseus also visited Circe in her island home of Aeaea and remained with her a year. The name Aeaea was sometimes applied to the enchantress herself.

Aeacides (ē-as′i-dēz). A term meaning "Descendant of Aeacus." It was applied especially to Peleus, Telamon, and Achilles.

Aeacus (ē′a̤-kus). A mythological son of Zeus and Aegina, the daughter of the river-god Asopus. He was born on the island of Oenone, or Oenopia, whither Zeus had taken Aegina when he carried her from her father's land. Aeacus became king of the island and renamed it Aegina in his mother's honor. By his wife Endeïs, the daughter of Sciron, Aeacus was the father of Peleus and Telamon. By the sea-nymph Psamathe he was the father of Phocus. Phocus was his father's favorite and caused such jealousy on the part of his brothers that, with the encouragement of their mother, they murdered him. Telamon and Peleus fled but Telamon sent word to his father from Salamis that he was innocent, and asked permission to plead his case. Aeacus refused to let him land on the island. Telamon was forced to plead his case from a mole which he secretly constructed in the harbor. But Aeacus was unmoved by his plea and refused to permit Telamon to return. Some say that Aegina was an unpopulated island, and that Zeus transformed ants into men who became subjects of Aeacus, and that this was the origin of the famous Myrmidons. But others tell a different story: Hera, when she learned that Aeacus was the child of Zeus by one of her rivals, and that an island had been named for this rival, was infuriated as usual. She vowed to punish the inhabitants of the island. In pursuit of this vow she sent a plague of serpents to infest the rivers and springs of the land. She caused the hot south wind to blow across the island for four months, thus parching the fields and ruining the crops. The springs and fountains were poisoned by the serpents; men and beasts died of drinking the waters. In the towns men sickened and died. The people prayed for relief to Zeus, but the animals prepared for the altars collapsed and died before they could be sacrificed. Men became desperate under the dire pestilence, and a wave of crime and impiety broke out. Soon nearly all the inhabitants were dead. Aeacus continually prayed to Zeus for relief. One day his prayer was answered by a shattering thunderclap. He prayed that if he were really the son of Zeus, his father would either repopulate his land or let him die. Pointing to a nearby oak tree that had grown from the acorn of a sacred Dodonian oak, Aeacus asked Zeus to send him as many men as there were in the army of ants busily carrying grain up the trunk of the tree. When Aeacus made this request the oak trembled and the leaves rustled although there was no wind. In the night Aeacus dreamed that a shower of ants fell to the ground from the oak tree and were transformed into men. Next morning his son Telamon called to him that an army of men, all of the same age and size, had ar-

rived. Aeacus recognized them from his dream as ants that had been transformed by Zeus into men in answer to his prayer. He called them Myrmidons, "ants," and they were ever after marked by the thrifty, energetic qualities of the ants from which they had sprung. At the same time, the plague of serpents was lifted, the south wind stopped blowing, and a heavy rain fell on the parched land. Aeacus divided his lands among his new people and gave thanks to Zeus.

According to some accounts, Apollo and Poseidon enlisted the aid of Aeacus when they built the wall of Troy, for they knew that unless a mortal assisted in the building of the wall it would be impregnable and the inhabitants within it could defy the gods. After they had finished building the wall, three serpents slithered up and tried to scale it. Two fell back and died. The third, making his attack on the part of the wall built by Aeacus, was successful. Apollo prophesied that the wall would be breached and the city destroyed by the descendants of Aeacus; as indeed it was, by Telamon and later by Ajax.

Aeacus was renowned as a pious and wise man and as the powerful ruler of a strong country. He was often appealed to in disputes, as when Sciron and Nisus quarreled over Megara. Aeacus was asked to decide; his judgment was that Nisus should be king but that Sciron should command the army. He was considered so powerful that many Spartans and Athenians wished to fight in his army. When the Athenians caused the death of Androgeus, son of Minos of Crete, Minos waged war on Athens and sought Aeacus as his ally. But Aeacus announced that he was closely allied to Athens and offered the Athenians his aid instead. He had made it nearly impossible for any power to attack his island by surrounding it with a sunken wall of rocks, and though Minos threatened, he did not dare attack. In the war that followed, all Greece was afflicted by a drought; or as some say, by earthquakes and famine. The oracle at Delphi, appealed to by the Greeks, advised them to ask Aeacus to pray to Zeus for relief. Aeacus heeded their request. He ascended Mount Panhellenius, the highest peak of the island. As he stretched out his hands to Zeus a loud

fat, fāte, fär, fãre, errạnt; net, mē, hėr ardẹnt; pin, pīne; not, nōte, möve, nôr,

thunderclap was heard, a cloud settled on the mountain top, rain began to fall, and the drought was broken. The earthquakes ceased in all of Greece except Attica, which had to make amends to Minos in another manner. In gratitude, Aeacus built a sanctuary to Zeus on the mountain, which could be seen from the shores of the mainland. Ever after, a cloud hovering over the peak of Mount Panhellenius was a sign of rain. But some say the drought that afflicted Greece and which Aeacus caused to be broken with his prayers to Zeus had come because Pelops, in a war against Stymphalus, king of Arcadia, treacherously slew Stymphalus during a truce in which he pretended friendship, and scattered his mangled limbs.

Aeacus, greatly honored during his lifetime, was equally honored after death. Zeus made him one of the three judges in Tartarus. It is said that he makes decisions concerning the souls that come from Europe; and also that he is the keeper of the keys of Tartarus.

Aeanes (ē′a̲-nēz). In mythology, named as a son of Amphidamas and elsewhere named Clitonymus, who was killed by Patroclus in a childish quarrel over a game of jackstones. It was because of this murder that Patroclus fled to Phthia, where he became the beloved friend of Achilles.

Aeantis (ē-an′tis). An epithet of Athena, meaning "Ajacian." Telamonian Ajax dedicated an image of Athena Aeantis on the citadel at Megara when, as some say, he succeeded Alcathous as king of Megara.

Aechmagoras (ēk-mag′ō̲-ra̲s). In Greek legend, a son of Heracles and Phialo. When he was born, his grandfather thrust him and his mother out on the mountainside to die. The child's crying was heard by a jay. The bird flew off to Heracles and, mimicking the infant's cries, led Heracles to the spot where Aechmagoras and his mother were dying of hunger. Heracles saved them. The spring near which he found them was named Cissa after the jay that had warned Heracles of their plight.

Aechmis (ēk′mis). King of Arcadia. He and his countrymen openly fought for Aristodemus, king of Messenia, in the First Messenian War between Messenia and Sparta.

Aedile (ē′dīl). In ancient Rome, a magistrate whose duty was originally the superintendence of public buildings and lands, out of which grew a large number of functions of administration and police. Among other duties, that of promoting the public games was incumbent on the aediles, and cost them large sums of money. Later, under the Empire, their functions were distributed among special officials, and their importance dwindled.

Aëdon (ā-ē′do̤n). In legend, a daughter of Pandareus of Ephesus. According to Homer she was the wife of Zethus, king of Thebes, and the mother of Itylus. Inspired by envy of Niobe, the wife of Amphion, who had seven sons and seven daughters, she formed the design of killing Niobe's eldest son, but by mistake destroyed her own son Itylus. To relieve her grief she was changed by Zeus into a nightingale, and her song became one long lament for her lost son. According to another account which closely follows the story of Procne in some respects, Aëdon was the wife of Polytechnus. She and her husband so gloried in their happiness that she boasted they were a happier couple than Zeus and Hera. To punish her arrogance Hera sent Eris to cause strife between them, and Eris caused Aëdon to arrange a contest between herself and her husband: that whoever completed specified tasks first should be presented with a slave by the other. Aëdon won the contest. Polytechnus angrily went to Pandareus in Ephesus and carried off Chelidon, the sister of Aëdon, under the pretext that he was taking her on a visit to her sister, and on the journey he ravished her. He bound her to secrecy and gave her, disguised, as a slave to Aëdon. Aëdon learned that this was her sister and conspired with her to punish Polytechnus. Together the sisters slew Itylus, the son of Aëdon and Polytechnus, dismembered his body, cooked it, and gave it to his father to eat. When he had eaten, the nature of his meal was revealed to Polytechnus. He sought to kill the sisters, but as he pursued them, the gods transformed them into birds. Aëdon became a nightingale, Chelidon a swallow, and Polytechnus a pelican.

Aedui (ed′ū-ī). [Also: **Haedui, Hedui.**] Celtic people in C Gaul, W of the Sequani between what are now the Saône and the Loire rivers. Their capital was Bibracte (the Roman Augustodunum, modern Autun). They were allies of the Romans, but joined in the revolt of 52 B.C.

Aeëtes (ē-ē'tēz). In classical myth, a son of Helius and Persa, and the brother of Circe, Pasiphaë, and Perses. He was king of Aea in Colchis at the far end of the Euxine Sea. By the nymph Asterodia he was the father of Chalciope. His second wife was Idyia, who bore him Medea and a son Apsyrtus. Phrixus, son of Athamas, landed on his shores when he fled from Orchomenus on the ram with the Golden Fleece. Aeëtes welcomed him hospitably, despite the reputation of the Colchians for hostility to strangers, and gave him his daughter Chalciope for a wife. The ram, according to its own instructions, was sacrificed to Zeus. Its fleece was hung in a grove sacred to Ares in Colchis and was guarded by a dragon that never slept. Phrixus died after fathering several sons and his ghost was said to haunt Pelias, king of Iolcus, demandng that the fleece be restored to Hellas. For this reason, and also to get rid of him, Pelias sent Jason to Colchis to fetch the Golden Fleece. When Aeëtes learned the reason for Jason's arrival on his shores, he was enraged. Only the laws of hospitality prevented him from slaying Jason at once. He thought also that his grandsons, whom Jason had rescued at sea and brought with him to Colchis, were plotting to seize his throne with Jason's help. He schemed to bring about the death of Jason without actually being involved in it himself. He said he would give Jason the fleece if he could do what Aeëtes himself had done: yoke two fire-breathing bulls, plow a field, and sow in it the dragon's teeth which had been given to Aeëtes by Athena. With Medea's help Jason successfuly performed this feat. Then, being warned by Medea of her father's intention to betray him, Jason fled, taking Medea with him. Aeëtes pursued the Argonauts with a great fleet but he was delayed, according to some accounts because he stopped to gather up the pieces of Apsyrtus' body which Medea had cut up and flung into the sea. Others say Apsyrtus did not go with the Argonauts but pursued them and was betrayed and slain by Jason. Aeëtes never did overtake the fleeing Argonauts and all his attempts to secure the return of Medea

ended in failure. However, some years later when his throne was seized by his brother Perses, Medea returned to Colchis, killed Perses, and restored her father to his throne.

Aegae (ē'jē). In ancient geography, a town on the Crathis River, under the Crathis Mountains, situated on the south shore of the Gulf of Corinth, in Achaea. According to Homer it was one of Poseidon's cities. He had an underwater palace nearby, in the stables of which he kept his white horses with bronze hoofs and golden manes, and his golden chariot in which he rode to still storms at sea. The town later was abandoned and fell into ruin.

Aegae. In ancient geography, the fortified capital of Macedonia, situated in the foothills of mountains about 50 miles to the W and N of the Thermaic Gulf. Philip II who had moved his capital from Aegae to Pella, c356 B.C., was murdered at Aegae, 336 B.C. According to an ancient oracle the kingdom of Macedonia would approach its dissolution if any of its kings was buried anywhere but in the ancient capital. The oracle was confirmed when Alexander the Great died in Asia and his empire was divided by his generals. Througout antiquity Aegae remained one of the most important cities of Macedonia. In Roman times the name was changed to Edessa, which it bears today.

Aegaeon (ē-jē'on). See **Briareus.**

Aegaeus (ē-jē'us). The god of the river of the same name in the land of the Phaeacians. He was the father of the nymph Melite, who became the mother, by Heracles, of Hyllus. This Hyllus is not to be confused with that Hyllus who was the son of Heracles and Deianira.

Aegaleos (ē-gā'lē-os), **Mount.** In ancient geography, a mountain in W Attica, W of Athens. It ended in a promontory (Amphiale), opposite the island of Salamis, from which Xerxes is said to have witnessed (480 B.C.) the defeat of his forces by the Greeks in the Battle of Salamis. Elevation, about 1534 feet.

Aegates (ē-gā'tēz) or **Aegadian** (ē-gā'di-an) **Isles.** [Modern name, **Egadi Islands.**] Group of small islands W of Sicily. The Romans defeated the Carthaginians in a naval battle near the islands in 241 B.C.

Aegean Sea (ē-jē'an). [Latin, **Mare Aegaeum.**]

fat, fāte, fär, fāre, errant; net, mē, hėr ardent; pin, pīne; not, nōte, möve, nôr,

Name given to that part of the Mediterranean Sea which lies between Greece on the W and N, and Turkey on the E. It communicates with the Sea of Marmara (Propontis) and thence with the Black Sea (Pontus, Pontus Euxinus) by the strait of of the Dardanelles (Hellespont). It contains many islands, of which the best known are Aegina, Euboea, the Cyclades, the Sporades, Samos, Chios, Lesbos, Samothrace, and Thasus. According to Greek legend, it received its name from the Athenian king Aegeus who threw himself into the sea believing that his son Theseus had been killed. The term *Aegean* has been used to designate the Bronze Age civilization of the Greek mainland, islands, and the mainland of Asia Minor, Thrace, and Macedonia. Length, about 400 miles; greatest width, over 200 miles; area, about 69,000 square miles; average depth, 1910 feet.

Aegesta (ē-jes′ta). See **Egesta**.

Aegestes (ē-jes′tēz). See **Acestes**.

Aegeus (ē′jē-us, -jŏs). In mythology, a son of Pandion the Younger, king of Athens, and Pylia. His brothers were Pallas, Nisus, and Lycus. But some say Aegeus was an adopted son of Pandion and therefore was not a true descendant of Erechtheus. Pandion had been driven from Athens but after his death his sons marched against Athens, drove out their enemies and divided Attica into four parts. Aegeus, being the oldest, became king of Athens. Pallas claimed that Aegeus was not a true son of Pandion. He and his 50 sons were ever plotting to unseat Aegeus as king, and another brother, Lycus, became so threatening that Aegeus exiled him. Aegeus married twice, but neither of his wives bore him a child. He visited the oracle at Delphi to inquire what he should do to procure an heir. The oracle answered that he should not untie the neck of the bulging wine-skin until he came to the highest point of Athens or he would die of grief. Aegeus did not understand the meaning of this pronouncement. On his return from Delphi he stopped in Corinth. There he saw Medea, the sorceress Jason had brought back from Colchis, and promised her that if she ever needed help he would provide it for her. In return Medea promised to get him an heir by her magic. Aegeus visited his friend Pittheus in

Troezen and told him of the oracle's warning. Pittheus, affected from afar by Medea's magic, entertained him lavishly, pressed wine on him, and when he was drunk sent his daughter Aethra in to lie with him. The next day Aegeus told Aethra if she should bear a son, she was to raise him in secret in Troezen, and when he grew up she was to send him to Athens if he could recover a sword and sandals that Aegeus now hid under a huge rock. Aegeus departed for Athens to celebrate the Athenian Festival. Some say that at these games Androgeus, son of Minos of Crete, won all the contests and that the Athenians were furious with jealousy. To get rid of Androgeus, Aegeus sent him to capture the Marathonian Bull, a fierce animal brought from Crete by Heracles. Androgeus was killed in his attempt to subdue the bull. But others say he was killed when he was ambushed by jealous Athenians, or that Aegeus ordered him ambushed and slain because he feared that Androgeus might persuade Minos to help the sons of Pallas who were plotting to seize the throne from Aegeus. Minos, king of Crete, waged war on Athens to avenge his son's death. He could not defeat the Athenians and prayed the gods to punish them. The gods sent famine and pestilence against Athens, and lifted these scourges only when the Athenians agreed to give Minos any amends he might demand. He demanded a tribute of seven youths and seven maidens to be sent to Crete every nine years to be devoured by the Minotaur.

In the meantime, Medea had fled from Corinth to Athens and reminded Aegeus of his promise to help her. He not only gave her asylum; he married her. She bore him a son, and Aegeus, not knowing that Aethra had already borne his son Theseus, thought this child, Medeus, was the heir that Medea had promised him. But Theseus, now grown to young manhood, took up the tokens Aegeus had hidden under the rock and, after many adventures, arrived in Athens. Medea, through her arts, instantly realized this was Aegeus' first-born and warned Aegeus that the young stranger was a threat to his kingdom. She induced Aegeus to hand him a cup of poisoned wine. But just as Theseus raised it to his lips, Aegeus noted the hilt of the young man's sword, recognized it as his own, and realized that this was his son whom he had never seen. He dashed the cup from his hand and welcomed his son with delight. Medea was obliged to flee from Athens for her plots, but Aegeus provided an escort for her and her son. Shortly after, the time for sending tribute to Minos arrived. In spite of the pleas of Aegeus, Theseus resolved to go as part of the tribute. He promised to return, however, and told his father that on the return journey he would substitute, for the black sail the ship customarily carried, a white sail to show that he had vanquished the Minotaur.

Theseus, however, forgot to change the sail on the return journey. Aegeus mounted to the top of the Acropolis, to a point where the little temple of Athena Nike later stood. Each day he scanned the horizon for a sail. When at last he saw the black sail from afar, he read in it a message of his son's death and hurled himself from the Acropolis, to his death in the vale below. The Latin writers say Aegeus hurled himself into the sea which henceforth bore his name. Theseus, returning safely, buried him and erected a shrine in his honor.

Aegia (ē-jī′a) or **Argia** (är-jī′a). According to legend, a daughter of Adrastus, king of Argos. She and her sister had so many suitors Adrastus feared to give them in marriage to any of the young men lest he make enemies of the disappointed suitors. Upon consulting the oracle he was told to yoke his daughters in marriage to the boar and the lion that fought in his palace. He gave Aegia to Polynices of Thebes, who bore the device of a lion on his shield. She was the mother of Thersander.

Aegiae (ē′ji-ē). A town in Laconia, called *Augiae* by Homer. A temple of Poseidon with an image of the god was near a lake called "Poseidon's Lake." The people of Aegiae dared not fish in the waters of this lake because whoever fished in it was transformed into a fish called the fisher, a species that caught its prey with long feelers.

Aegialeus (ē-jī′a-lūs). In Greek legend, a son of Adrastus and Demonassa. He was the only one of the Epigoni to be killed at the second expedition against Thebes, to avenge the original Seven against Thebes, all

of whom were killed except Adrastus. According to a prophecy, Thebes would fall when all of the original Seven were dead. Adrastus, on learning of his son's death, died of grief and Thebes fell, thus fulfilling the prophecy.

Aegialia (ē″ji-a-lī′a) or **Aegiale** (ē-ji′a-lē). Named by Homer (*Iliad*) as the daughter of Adrestus, king of Sicyon. While her husband Diomedes was away fighting in Troy she was persuaded by Nauplius, whose son had been put to death as a traitor by the Greeks, to believe that Diomedes had taken a Trojan concubine. She then took Cometes, son of Sthenelus, as her lover and when Diomedes returned from Troy she and her lover forced him to flee.

Aegialus (ē-jī′a-lus) or **Aegialea** (ē″ji-a-lē′a). Original name of the ancient district of Achaea, in the Peloponnesus. According to tradition, the land was named Aegialus after Aegialeus, the son of the river-god Inachus and the nymph Melia.

Aegicores (ē-ji-kô′rēz). According to tradition, one of the four sons of Ion. One of the four ancient tribes of Athens was named for him. His brothers were Argades, Geleon, and Hoples.

Aegimius (ē-jim′i-us). According to tradition, a son of Dorus. He was a king of the Dorians. In a boundary dispute with Coronus, king of the Lapiths, Aegimius sought the aid of Heracles. In the war which followed, the Lapiths were defeated and their king was slain. Aegimius kept one-third of his kingdom, which he had promised to Heracles in return for his aid, in trust for the descendants of Heracles and later adopted Hyllus, the son of Heracles and Deianira.

Aegina (ē-jī′na). In mythology, a daughter of the river-god Asopus and Metope. She was carried off by Zeus to Oenone, or Oenopia, an island in the Saronic Gulf which was subsequently renamed Aegina in her honor by Aeacus, the son she bore to Zeus.

Aegina. An island in SE Greece, in the Saronic Gulf, or the Gulf of Aegina. According to legend it was to this island, once known as Oenone or Oenopia, that Zeus brought Aegina, the daughter of the river-god Asopus. The island was renamed Aegina by Aeacus, the son of Aegina and Zeus, who became king of the island. Hera was infuriated when

fat, fāte, fär, fãre, errant; net, mē, hèr ardent; pin, pīne; not, nōte, möve, nôr,

she learned that the island had been named in honor of one of her rivals. She sent a plague which poisoned the waters, and a hot south wind to parch the fields and pastures; the land was infested by serpents; animals collapsed and died; hopeless men relapsed into licentious behavior. At the end of four months Aeacus appealed to Zeus: if indeed Zeus was his father he should either lift the plague or let Aeacus die with his people. Zeus answered his prayer and the plague was ended, but Aegina had been nearly depopulated. Once again Zeus heeded the prayers of Aeacus: hordes of ants climbing the trunk of a sacred oak tree were transformed into men who became known as Myrmidons.

ATHENA
From the west pediment of the so-called Temple of Aphaea at Aegina, c510 B.C. *Munich*

Historically, Aegina was conquered and colonized in very ancient times by the Dorians, and it was an important Greek commercial state and center of art in the 6th and 5th centuries B.C. In 459 B.C. it was defeated for the first time by Athens, and some three decades later (431 B.C.) relegated to a position of comparative insignificance when the Athenians carried out a mass deportation of its population. The principal ancient remains are a late archaic (early 5th century B.C.) Doric temple of Aphaea, where the Aeginetan Marbles now in Munich were found, and scanty remains of a temple of Apollo. Aeginetan coins, bearing the image of a tortoise, were widely circulated in the Greek world and many Greek states adopted the Aeginetan standards of weights and measures.

Aegina, Gulf of. [Also: **Saronic Gulf**; Latin, **Saronicus Sinus**.] Arm of the Aegean Sea, lying SW of Attica and NE of Argolis, Greece. It contains the islands of Salamis and Aegina. Length, about 50 miles.

Aeginaea (ē-ji-nē′a̤). An epithet of Artemis, meaning "Goat-goddess." There was a sanctuary of Artemis Aeginaea at Taenarus.

Aeginetan Marbles (ej-i-nē′tan). Pediment sculptures and acroteria from the temple of Aphaea on the Greek island of Aegina, found in 1811 and now in the Glyptothek, Munich. Study of them is complicated by the fact that three sets of pediment sculptures survive, suggesting that perhaps one of the original sets was damaged and replaced. They were restored by the sculptor Thorwaldsen, who sawed off the broken stumps of limbs the more neatly to attach his restorations, with the result that when 20th-century excavators found additional fragments it proved impossible to refer them to their original positions. All three pediments show scenes of combat between Greeks and Trojans. They date from c510 B.C. and the period of 490–480 B.C. (JJ)

Aegiochus (ē-jī′ō-kus). Epithet of Zeus, meaning "Aegis-bearing," from his goatskin aegis. Some say Zeus had this name in honor of the goat that suckled him in his infancy.

Aegipan (ē′ji-pan). In Greek mythology, a name sometimes used for the goatish god Pan. In some forms of the myth he is identified with Pan. He is variously called the son of Zeus and Aega, Pan's wife, and also the father of Pan. On one occasion together with Hermes he restored to Zeus the sinews taken from him by the giant Typhon.

Aegira (ē-jī′ra). Town on the coast of Achaea, named by Homer as Hyperesia. It was given the name Aegira (from *aigos*, goat) for the following reason: During a war with Sicyon the inhabitants of the town, knowing they were about to be invaded and that they were vastly outnumbered, gathered all the goats of the area together and tied torches on their horns. In the depths of the night they lighted the torches. The Sicyonians, seeing great numbers of blazing torches, thought that allies had come to help their enemy and withdrew. Henceforth the inhabitants called their town Aegira in honor of the goats, and where the handsomest goat, the leader, had crouched they raised a sanctuary of Artemis Agrotera (*Huntress*) in gratitude to the goddess for having inspired the trick that caused the Sicyonians to withdraw. In Aegira there was an oracle of Hera. Here the priestess drank bull's blood which was deadly poison to all other mortals but which was supposed to inspire the priestess of Hera with the gift of prophecy.

Aegis (ē′jis). The wondrous and terrifying breastplate of Zeus and Athena, sometimes loaned to Apollo. In the center of the breastplate was the head of the Gorgon Medusa, and in Homeric legend it is often spoken of as being encircled with flames.

Aegisthus (ē-jis′thus). In Greek legend, the son of Thyestes and Pelopia, his own daughter. As an infant he was exposed by his mother to die but was rescued by shepherds and brought up by Atreus, whom Pelopia had married, as his own son. When very young, he was ordered by Atreus to kill Thyestes as he slept, unaware that the latter was his true father. Thyestes escaped the blow and, recognizing the sword which Aegisthus had aimed at him as the one he had lost the night he ravished Pelopia, he asked Aegisthus where he had gotten it. When Aegisthus told him his mother had given it to him, Thyestes realized that this was indeed his son. He sent Aegisthus to fetch his mother, and when she came and learned that she was the mother of Aegisthus by her own father, she plunged the sword into her breast in horror. Thyestes next commanded Aegisthus to kill Atreus, king of Mycenae. Thyestes then became king and ruled until he was forced into exile by Atreus' son Agamemnon. Aegisthus fled from Mycenae at the same time but returned while Agamemnon and Menelaus were away at the Trojan War. To get revenge on the house of Atreus, because Atreus had served Aegisthus' brothers to Thyestes in a ghastly banquet and because Agamemnon had become king of Mycenae, he became Clytemnestra's paramour and plotted with her to kill her husband Agamemnon. When the latter returned from Troy he was welcomed by both Aegisthus and Clytemnestra, according to their plot. They prepared a banquet for him, and as he emerged from his bath, ready to enjoy the feast, he was struck down. According to some accounts it was Aegisthus who split his skull with a two-headed ax. According to other accounts Clytemnestra stabbed her husband. In the *Odyssey* Zeus complained of the wickedness of men citing Aegisthus' wickedness in wooing Clytemnestra and killing Agamemnon, in spite of the fact that he had been especially warned by Hermes not to do so. Clytemnestra and Aegisthus ruled in Mycenae for seven years after the death of Agamemnon. Clytemnestra was the real ruler while Aegisthus, on the whole a cowardly sort, lived in fear that her son Orestes would return to Mycenae, from which he had been sent before his father's death, and slay him. In the eighth year after the murder of Agamemnon Orestes did return and killed both Aegisthus and Clytemnestra, thus fulfilling the command of the oracle of Delphi and avenging his father's murder.

Aegium (ē′ji-um). [Modern name, **Aiyion.**] In ancient geography, a harbor town of Achaea, on the Gulf of Corinth. Men of Aegium went to the Trojan War under the command of Agamemnon. In later times the Achaean League met there, and the city was enlarged by absorbing the survivors of the earthquake and flood that destroyed the town of Helice.

Aegle (ēg′lē). In mythology, one of the Hesperides who guarded the Golden Apples. At the approach of the Argonauts she first became dust and earth, and then transformed herself into a willow tree. But when she learned the Argonauts were not hostile, she told them that Heracles the day before had slain the dragon that guarded the Golden Apples, and then told them where they could find a spring to quench their thirst after carrying the *Argo* for 12 days across the Libyan desert. See **Hesperides.**

Aegle. A naiad, sometimes said to have been the mother of the Charites (Graces) by Helius.

Aegle. In mythology, a daughter of Helius and the Oceanid Clymene. With her sisters she was one of the Heliades who was changed into a poplar tree that wept tears of amber because of grief over the death of their brother Phaëthon, who died driving the fiery chariot of Helius across the heavens to prove his divine parentage.

Aegleis (ĕg-lē'is). A daughter of Hyacinthus the Spartan. See **Hyacinthides.**

Aegospotami (ē"gos-pot'a̤-mī). [Also: **Aegospotamos.**] In ancient geography, a small river and a town in that part of ancient Thrace known as the Chersonesus Thracica (geographically identical with what is now called the Gallipoli Peninsula of Turkey in Europe). The area of the river's mouth is noted as the scene of the decisive naval victory of the Spartans under Lysander over the Athenians, in 405 B.C., which led to the close of the Peloponnesian War. The Athenians maintained that they were not honorably beaten in battle but had been betrayed by their commanders who they claimed had been bribed by Lysander. This was all in fulfillment of two oracles, they said. The oracles were:

"And then on the Athenians will be laid grievous troubles
By Zeus the high-thundered, whose might is the greatest,
On the war-ships battle and fighting,
As they are destroyed by treacherous tricks, through the baseness of the captains."

And this oracle from the writings, so it was said, of Musaeus:

"For on the Athenians comes a wild rain
Through the baseness of their leaders, but some consolation will there be
For the defeat; they shall not escape the notice of the city, but shall pay the penalty."

Nevertheless, the Athenian fleet was de-stroyed and but for the alert action of Conon, the commander in chief, against whom incidentally there was no accustation of having accepted a bribe, Athens herself would have been threatened. He knew that it was customary to remove the sails when the ships went into battle. He therefore, having escaped, swooped down on the Spartan ships and carried off their sails, so that they could not pursue him nor sail immediately against Athens.

Aegusa (ē-jö'sa̤) or **Aethusa** (ē-thö'sa̤). [Modern name, **Favignana.**]. Largest island of the Aegates, W of Sicily.

Aegyptus (ē-jip'tus). In classical myth, a son of Belus, king in Egypt, and Anchinoë, and the twin of Danaus. He became ruler of Arabia and conquered the land which, according to some accounts, he later named Egypt after himself. By various women he was the father of 50 sons, whom he wished to marry to the 50 daughters of his brother Danaus. Danaus refused his consent to the marriages and fled. Aegyptus sent his sons in pursuit of the Danaids with orders not to return without them. In Argos, whither Danaus and his daughters had fled, they ultimately compelled Danaus to give them his daughters, but all save one of the sons of Aegyptus were murdered on the wedding night. Aegyptus followed his sons to Argos, but when he learned of their murders he fled. He died and was buried in the Peloponnesus.

Aegyptus. The name which Homer used to indicate the Nile River.

Aegyptus. Latin name of **Egypt.**

Aelius Paetus (ē'li-us pē'tus), **Sextus.** Roman jurist; fl. 2nd century B.C. He was consul in 198 B.C., censor in 193. Author of the *Tripartita* (or *Jus Aelianum*) containing a recension of the Twelve Tables (450 B.C.) with commentary.

Aella (ā-el'a̤). In Greek legend, an Amazon. Her name, which means "Whirlwind," was given to her because she was so swift. She fought Heracles personally in his war against the Amazons and was slain by him.

Aello (ā-el'ō). In Greek mythology, one of the Harpies.

Aemilian Way (ē-mil'i-an). See **Via Aemilia.**

Aenaria (ē-nâr'i-a̤). An ancient name of **Ischia.** See **Pithecusa.**

Aeneades (ē-nē'a̤-dēz). A name meaning

"Descendant of Aeneas." It was applied especially to Ascanius and to the members of the Julian family of Rome, and was also applied to the Romans collectively.

Aeneas (ē-nē′as). In classical myth, the son of Anchises and the goddess Aphrodite. Some say he was brought up for the first years of his life by the nymphs of Mount Ida in the Troad. Others say Alcathous, his sister's husband, reared him. Anchises, king of the Dardanians, was crippled by a thunderbolt from Zeus because he boasted of having lain with a goddess. Unable to rule his kingdom, he was succeeded by Aeneas. Some say Aeneas accompanied Paris when the latter went on his voyage to Sparta and abducted Helen. He did not immediately offer his aid when Troy was attacked by the Greeks to recover her. Some say he was on cool terms with his relative, King Priam of Troy, either because Priam did not accord him the honor Aeneas thought fitting, or because Priam feared fulfillment of the prophecy that Aeneas would rule the Trojans. However, in the ninth year of the war against Troy, when Achilles was raiding the surrounding country and sacking the cities in it, he made a raid on the cattle of Aeneas during which Aeneas barely escaped with his life. Thenceforth Aeneas allied himself and his Dardanians with the Trojans, and fought with great valor and skill. He was honored by the Trojans for his piety and his spirit. The gods protected him in battle because he was destined to found a new home for the Trojan race in Italy. In the course of the war, Diomedes flung a huge boulder at Aeneas and felled him, but Aphrodite swooped down to rescue her son. When she too was wounded by Diomedes, Apollo rescued Aeneas and bore him off to Pergamus where Leto healed him. He then returned to the battle and slew many of the enemy. At the attack on the Greek fortifications protecting their ships Aeneas was in the vanguard. Later, as the Trojans were being driven back in the struggle for the body of Patroclus, Apollo appeared to him in the guise of a herald and encouraged him to inspire the Trojans to new efforts. Again, encouraged by Apollo, he was the first to go out to meet Achilles, although his courage failed him at first as he remembered how

Achilles had driven him from Mount Ida and Lyrnessus when he sacked that town. But Apollo filled him with bravery and he pressed forward against Achilles. His spear, however, could not pierce Achilles' magic armor, and Aeneas found himself in deadly peril. To save him, Poseidon sent a mist to dim Achilles' eyes, then he spirited Aeneas away. Poseidon, who in all other respects favored the Greeks against the Trojans, saved Aeneas to preserve the line of Dardanus, from whom he had sprung, and because he pitied Aeneas, who was fighting another man's war. He promised Aeneas that no other Achaean would take his life and that he would live to fulfil his destiny. Aeneas rescued the body of the Lycian Glaucus when he was slain by Telamonian Ajax, and then was himself wounded by Ajax in the struggle for possession of Achilles' body. He withdrew into the city to nurse his wound. Later, Aeneas scorned the proposal of Polydamas to withdraw to the city and there to fight from the safety of its towers. He preferred, he said, death in the open, fighting bravely, to death like a trapped animal. As leader of the Trojans, Hector being dead, again and again Aeneas returned to the attack, aided by the gods. He slew many Greeks in engagements in which Penthesilea, Memnon, and Eurypylus, each of whom had come to help the Trojans, were killed. When Neoptolemus came to the aid of the Greeks, Thetis, out of respect for Aphrodite, prevented him from coming face to face with Aeneas. When Athena aided the Argives and they drove the Trojans back, Aphrodite snatched Aeneas away in a mist. But the bitter struggle was hopeless, and at last Zeus, though grieving, abandoned Troy to its long delayed fate. Various accounts are given of the fate of Aeneas in the sack of Troy. Some say he was captured by Neoptolemus, carried off to Greece as the most valuable of the spoils of the war and ultimately ransomed by the Dardanians. Others say he was spared by the Greeks because he had favored the return of Helen to Menelaus, and that he reigned, as did his descendants, in the Troad. Still others say he defended Troy bravely until the last then, seeing that the cause was hopeless, retired with the aid of Aphrodite to Mount Ida, taking his father, his son, the sacred images of Troy and a few followers with him. Later he went to Pellene (Pallene) in Thrace and died there, or in Orchomenus. The Romans say that after he retired to Mount Ida with his father, son, wife, and the sacred images (for they say Diomedes stole only a copy of the Palladium from the citadel of Troy), he fled from the Troad at the command of the gods and set out to found a new home for the Trojans in Italy. Having fulfilled his destiny, he fell in battle and was taken to heaven. His adventures in pursuing his destiny are described in Vergil's *Aeneid* (q.v.). In Homer, Aeneas is the greatest of the Trojans after Hector, a favorite of the gods, and a brave, reasonable, and pious man, whose piety and courage are leavened with a few human and endearing weaknesses. In the *Aeneid* the character of Aeneas suffers a great change; from a man of admirable but believably human traits, he becomes a symbol of the divinity which the Romans considered fitting in the founder of their nation. In the *Aeneid*, "pious Aeneas" is often insufferably conscious of his divine mission.

Aeneas Silvius (sil′vi-us). In Roman mythology, a king of Alba Longa. He was supposedly a direct descendant of Aeneas.

Aeneas Tacticus (tak′ti-kus). [**The Tactician.**] An Arcadian contemporary of Xenophon who flourished about 360 B.C. He had seen service in the Aegean and in Asia Minor and wrote on military tactics. In the fragment that has come down to us he explains how to conduct defensive warfare and how to resist a seige (*Commentarius poliorceticus*). This book, containing valuable historical information, was very probably composed in 357–356 B.C. The hydraulic telegraph which he invented was described by Polybius. Aeneas also explained a system of cryptography.

Aeneid (ē-nē′id). An epic poem in 12 books, by Vergil. It had been completed, but not corrected, at the time of Vergil's death in 19 B.C. The purpose of this national epic was to emphasize the divine origin of the Romans—as descendants of Venus through Aeneas—by portraying the historical background of the nation, and to glorify Augustus, who had suggested the theme to Vergil. In many passages the *Aeneid* obviously derives from the *Iliad*, but it holds its own as a classic through the beauty and grace of its language and the ingenuity of its literary devices in weaving actual history, legend, and mythology into a unified story. The plot of the *Aeneid* revolves around the continuing struggle of Aeneas, bitterly opposed by Juno, to reach his destined home in Italy after the Trojan War. According to Vergil, Juno's hatred was inspired by the insulting Judgment of Paris and her fear that Aeneas would raise up a nation that would destroy her beloved Carthage.

Book I: Juno harries Aeneas and his followers without mercy. In the seventh year of their wanderings a disastrous storm which she caused Aeolus to unleash, but which Neptune calmed, has driven Aeneas ashore near Carthage. Venus, mother of Aeneas, receives from Jove a renewal of his promise that Aeneas will found a great race in Italy. She appears to Aeneas in disguise and tells him to seek out Dido in whose kingdom he has landed. She then sends her son Cupid to take the place of Ascanius, son of Aeneas, so that he can practice his art on the unfortunate Dido, cause her to fall in love with Aeneas, and assure his safety as long as he remains in her realm. At a great feast Dido asks Aeneas to tell his story from the beginning.

Book II: Aeneas describes the end of the Trojan War. The Greeks had left a huge Wooden Horse on the beach before Troy, and Laocoön, a priest, suspected it and advised the Trojans not to accept it as a Greek offering. Just then Sinon, a captive, was brought forward. He said he was a Greek who had been persecuted by Ulysses, and that the Greeks had sailed for home and had left the Wooden Horse to propitiate Pallas Athena. When twin serpents glided out of the sea, seized Laocoön and his two sons in their mighty coils, and disappeared with them to the shrine of Pallas Athena, it was interpreted as a sign that the gods were angry at Laocoön for doubting the Wooden Horse. The Trojans immediately hauled it inside their walls. But Sinon was a spy sent by Ulysses. During the night he freed the Greeks hiding in the Horse. They opened the gates and the other Greeks swarmed into the city. Aeneas,

actọr; up, lūte, pu̇ll; oi, oil; ou, out; ᴛʜ, then; ḍ as d or j, ṣ as s or sh, ṭ as t or ch, ẓ as z or zh.

warned in a dream by Hector, awoke to find the city in turmoil. He fought his way through the flames to Priam's palace and saw Pyrrhus, the son of Achilles, kill Priam on his own altar. He found Helen hiding in the palace and would have killed her, but Venus appeared and stayed his hand. She urged him to leave Troy. As he fled, bearing his aged father on his back and holding Ascanius by the hand, his wife Creusa who was following got lost in the commotion. Her ghost later appeared to Aeneas and said that the gods did not intend for her to go with him. Heartbroken, he went to an appointed meeting place and found a number of people who had made up their minds to go into exile with him.

Book III: Aeneas built a fleet and sailed to Thrace, but he was warned by the ghost of a son of Priam not to settle there. At Delos, his next stop, the oracle told him to go to the land of his fathers. They sailed to Crete, but there the images of the gods of Troy told him in a dream that the oracle had meant Hesperia (Italy), where Dardanus, founder of the Trojan race, was born. Winds drove them to the Strophades, where they fought the Harpies and were warned by Celaeno that they would endure a famine that would compel them to devour their tables. On this gloomy note they proceeded along the coast of Greece to Buthrotum, where they found Andromache, Hector's wife, and Helenus, Hector's friend. They had settled on the Chaonian plains and had built a miniature Troy. Helenus prophesied that Aeneas would recognize his ultimate home as the spot where he found a white sow and 30 piglets, but that he would have troubles and wars beforehand. He warned Aeneas of places to avoid on his journey, urged him to be zealous in paying homage to Juno, and instructed him to consult the Cumaean sibyl in Italy. Through storm and hardship they made their way slowly around Italy and the coast of Sicily to Drepanum, where Anchises died. It was after this that the great storm inspired by Juno had driven them to Dido's kingdom.

Book IV: In the days following his arrival Dido, impelled by Venus and Cupid, falls desperately in love with Aeneas. Her sister Anna encourages her to stop mourning for Sychaeus, her murdered husband, and advises her that an alliance with Aeneas will strengthen her against her enemies. Juno and Venus, for different reasons, engineer a plot to throw Aeneas and Dido alone together and during the next winter their life is an open scandal. The story is spread throughout the land by Rumor who delights in tale-bearing. Jove sends Mercury to remind Aeneas that it is not so that he can dally with Dido that he has been saved from Troy. If he cares nothing for his own destiny, he should think of Ascanius, get on with his voyage and stop building a city to please a woman. Mercury finds Aeneas and delivers the message. Dido, made sensitive by her love, soon realizes that Aeneas is planning secretly to leave. She accuses him and he replies that he is compelled by the gods. When she sees that her love and her generosity cannot persuade him to stay, she tricks her sister into building a great funeral pyre. As Aeneas, warned again by Mercury, makes ready to sail, Dido places his armor on the funeral pyre. She calls for eternal enmity between her people and those of Aeneas to the last generation, then flings herself on his sword and dies in her sister's arms. Thus Vergil accounts for the hostility between Rome and Carthage in the Punic Wars.

Book V: The smoke from Dido's funeral pyre is the last sight Aeneas sees as he sails away. High winds then buffet his fleet and compel him to set a course for Sicily. There he is welcomed by the Trojan Acestes, who has established a kingdom near Mount Eryx. Aeneas holds funeral games in honor of Anchises, and as the boat race, foot race, boxing match, archery contests and cavalry maneuvers take place, Juno sends Iris to stir up the Trojan women. Iris, in the guise of a Trojan matron, reminds them of the ills they have endured and predicts worse to follow. She inspires them to set fire to the ships so that they can cease their endless voyaging. On discovering the fire, Aeneas prays to Jove and immediately a torrential rain smothers the flames. Aeneas is advised to leave with King Acestes those Trojans who are weary of wandering; he should repair the ships and proceed to Italy with those who still thirst for glory. Anchises' ghost instructs

fat, fāte, fär, fãre, errạnt; net, mē, hėr ardẹnt; pin, pīne; not, nōte, mȯve, nôr,

him to follow this advice and adds that Aeneas must visit Anchises in the Underworld to learn more of the future. In the heavens, Neptune promises Venus that he will give Aeneas calm seas to Cumae, asking in return that one life, in exchange for the safety of many, be given to him.

Book VI: At Cumae Aeneas visits the Sibyl and learns that he will successfully found a kingdom in Latium after bloody wars caused by marriage to a foreign bride. The Sibyl tells him he must find a Golden Bough—destined as a gift for Proserpina—if he wishes to visit Anchises in the Underworld. Led by a pair of doves, he discovers the Golden Bough in the woods and plucks it. He and the Sibyl then enter the Underworld through a cave at Avernus. In Hades he meets the fabulous monsters of mythology and sees the Tree of Dreams, images of War, pale Disease, and Sleep, brother of Death. Among those compelled to haunt the banks of the River of Death for a hundred years because they have not been properly buried, Aeneas recognizes Palinurus, his steersman, who had been lost at sea on the way to Cumae. His was the one life Neptune took in return for giving Aeneas calm seas. Charon ferries Aeneas and the Sibyl across the river, where they see Cerberus and the ghosts of infants and those who have been unjustly condemned. They see Minos, now a judge in the Underworld, and the unhappy souls who had died for love. Here is Dido, who refuses to answer to Aeneas' call and turns her back on him. Passing the entrance to Tartarus they see the courts of Rhadamanthys, a judge who metes out justice to those who had escaped punishment for their misdeeds in the upper world. This is the final home of the wicked and here are those who have offended the gods. In the Fields of the Blest Aeneas finds the shade of Anchises. His father foretells the future in definite detail, giving Aeneas the names of the rulers of Italy who will follow him, and describing the vast and peaceful empire that will belong to his descendants. When he has told him of the coming wars in Latium, he sends him away.

Book VII: The Trojans next sail to the mouth of the Tiber River and land in Latium. A meal is prepared and the hungry Trojans eat the flat cakes of meal on which their food was served, thus fulfilling Celaeno's prophecy that they would devour their tables. Aeneas sends messengers to the king, Latinus, who receives them kindly and informs them that his only daughter, Lavinia, is sought in marriage by Turnus, king of the Rutuli, but signs from Heaven warning Latinus to give his daughter to a stranger have held up this alliance. Latinus thinks that Aeneas must be that stranger. Juno, watching from Heaven, is enraged that Aeneas is about to achieve success in spite of her. She sends Alecto, a Fury, to delay the fulfillment of his destiny. Alecto first stirs up Amata, wife of King Latinus and a strong backer of Turnus, so that she foments a rebellion among the Latin women against Aeneas. Then Alecto taunts Turnus for tamely giving up Lavinia to Aeneas until, in a frenzy, he issues a call to arms. Finally Alecto causes Ascanius to kill a stag, unaware that it is a famous pet of the countryside. The aroused country folk seize clubs and stones to attack Ascanius and the war begins. Latinus, unable to restore order, blames Turnus, predicts an evil outcome, and gives up control of his government. The whole country is inflamed; men and their leaders flock from all Latium to join Turnus and drive the Trojans out.

Book VIII: Tiberinus, the god of the Tiber, now appears to Aeneas. He tells him he will find the white sow and 30 piglets, site of his future city, in an oak grove on the river bank and advises Aeneas to seek the aid of King Evander. Aeneas finds the sow, sacrifices her to Juno, and sets out for Evander, who had known Anchises and had promised to help Aeneas. Meanwhile, Venus reminds her husband Vulcan that he had once made arms for Achilles and asks him to make some for Aeneas. He agrees. Evander sends Aeneas to Tarchon, leader of the Etruscans. They are already clamoring for war against Turnus because he has refused to give them Mezentius, a tyrannical ruler whom they had driven out of their land and who had fled to Turnus. They will make enthusiastic allies, especially since a seer has told them they must await a foreign commander. In addition, Evander sends his only son Pallas to fight at Aeneas' side. That night Venus comes down from Heaven and presents

Aeneas with the magic armor made by Vulcan.

Book IX: While Aeneas is away, Juno sends Iris to inform Turnus that this is an opportune time to attack and destroy the garrison that Aeneas has left behind in charge of Ascanius. Since the Trojans refuse to come out and fight on the plains when Turnus challenges them, he attacks their ships. These had been constructed of wood sacred to Cybele, and rather than see them destroyed by fire, she instantly transforms them into sea-goddesses, who swim away before the astounded gaze of Turnus. During the night, Nisus and Euryalus seek a way out of the besieged camp to go and warn Aeneas. They kill many of the sleeping enemy before they are discovered and slain. At daybreak, Turnus attacks again. Savage fighting ensues. Turnus gets inside the walls and kills many Trojans before the tide turns against him. He retreats and plunges into the river, whose waters buoy him up and return him to his friends.

Book X: Aeneas reaches Tarchon, makes a treaty with him, and sets off with a large number of Etruscan leaders and their men for his garrison. Cymodoce, one of his ships that had been changed into a sea-nymph, swims alongside his ship during the night, tells him what is happening at the encampment, then, to speed him back to his men, she gives his ship a mighty push and disappears. At daybreak Aeneas and his allies beach their ships at the garrison. Relentless fighting takes place. Evander's young son Pallas fights like a demon and kills many, but is finally slain by Turnus, who strips off the youth's armor and golden sword belt. Aeneas fights savagely to avenge the death of Pallas and to break the siege. Turnus is lured away from the danger by Juno, and Mezentius takes his place. He leads a counterattack against the Trojans. He meets Aeneas head on, is wounded, and is joined by his son Lausus, who saves his father's life at the cost of his own, for Aeneas kills Lausus. In pity for the brave youth, Aeneas does not strip him of his armor, but sends the fully armed body back to Mezentius. Mezentius is in a frenzy when he learns of his son's death. Death itself does not frighten him now that Lausus is dead. He calls for Aeneas,

and after a furious struggle lies helpless, pinned beneath his fallen horse. He asks no mercy, offers his throat to Aeneas' sword and is killed.

Book XI: A truce is observed for the burial of the fallen. Aeneas declares he has no quarrel with the Latin people. He says his quarrel is with Turnus and challenges Turnus to meet him in single combat. Latinus calls a council, but his willingness to cede land to Aeneas and to make peace is scorned by Turnus, who calls for a renewal of the war. Camilla, a Volscian maiden skilled in cavalry warfare, is ordered to engage the Trojans on the plain while Turnus waits for Aeneas in a pass in the hills. In the battle on the plains Camilla is felled by a spear. Dying, she sends word to Turnus to come and defend the city. He leaves his ambush just before Aeneas arrives in the pass where he might have been cut off and destroyed. Instead, Aeneas and his men march safely forward and consolidate their position on the plain.

Book XII: Turnus still refuses to yield to Latinus' desire for peace. He agrees to fight Aeneas in single combat. Terms for the duel are arranged but Juno interferes and the truce is broken. Aeneas is treacherously wounded as he makes ready to fight Turnus. Fighting again breaks out. Juno sends Juturna, a deity and the sister of Turnus, to spirit him away from the fighting. In the meantime Aeneas, having been healed by Venus, decides to attack the city. He sets fire to the walls, and Amata, blaming herself for the war and despairing because she thinks Turnus is dead, hangs herself. Turnus sees the flames of the burning city, recognizes his sister and tells her to stop interfering. He wants to fight Aeneas and rushes to find him. Aeneas hurries to meet him. The soldiers lay down their arms as at last Turnus and Aeneas meet face to face. Jove watches the conflict from on high. He commands Juno to stop harrying Aeneas for he must fulfill his destiny. She agrees to desert Turnus on condition that the Trojan name and language be lost and that the race, name, and language of the Latins will prevail in Italy. In the battle between Aeneas and Turnus Aeneas gains the upper hand. Turnus, who knows he has been abandoned by the gods, is forced to his knees. Aeneas would have spared his life, but he catches sight of the sword belt Turnus had taken from young Pallas. This reminder of the loss of Pallas and all that he and his companions had suffered causes Aeneas to harden his heart. He plunges his sword into Turnus' breast. The death of Turnus ends the war with the Latins, and at last Aeneas can proceed with the founding of the Roman race and nation.

Aenesidemus (ē-nes-i-dē′mus). Greek Skeptic philosopher, born at Cnossus on the island of Crete, and active in the 1st century B.C. He was notable for his teaching at Alexandria in Egypt, and was the author of *Pyrrhonian Principles* and other works.

Aenius (ē′ni-us). Named by Homer (*Iliad*) as a Paeonian ally of the Trojans in the Trojan War. He was slain by Achilles when the latter was savagely avenging the death of Patroclus.

Aeolia (ē-ō′li-a). The island home of Aeolus, the ruler of the winds. It was supposed to be one of the Lipari Islands which in ancient times were known as the Aeolian Islands.

Aeoliae Insulae (ē-ō′li-ē in′sū-lē). [Modern name, **Lipari Islands**.] Group of volcanic islands in the Tyrrhenian Sea, N of Sicily. The chief islands are Lipara, Strongyle, Didyme, Thermessa or Vulcania, and the small islands of Ericussa, Phoenicussa, and Euonymus or Hicesia. According to Greek legend, this was the island kingdom of Aeolus, keeper of the winds, and his wife Enarete. Lipara was said to be a floating island surrounded by a bronze wall. Its cliffs, rising sheer from the sea, confined the winds. When Aeolus, their master, wished to free one of the winds he pierced the side of the cliff and let it out; when he wished to stop the wind he stopped up the hole in the side of the cliff. According to tradition, in a war with the Etruscans the Liparaeans sent envoys to Delphi for advice. The priestess told them to engage the Etruscans with the smallest possible number of ships. The Liparaeans sent five ships against them. The Etruscans, not to be outdone in bravery, sent five ships to meet them. These were captured by the Liparaeans, as were succeeding groups of five Etruscan ships, and the Liparaeans were victorious. Accordingly, they dedicated as many statues to the god at Delphi as the number of Etruscan ships they had captured.

Aeolians (ē-ō′li-anz). [Also: **Aeoles, Aeoli**.] One of the four great divisions of the ancient Greeks (the Achaeans, Dorians, and Ionians were the other three).

Aeolides (ē-ō′li-dēz). Name applied to a son or descendant of Aeolus; it was applied particularly to Athamas, Idmon the Argonaut, Melampus, Minyas, and Phrixus.

Aeolis (ē′o-lis). [Also: **Aeolia**.] In ancient geography, originally the W coast of Asia Minor between the river Hermus and Lectum, settled by Aeolians. Later it extended along Troas (the Aegean coastal territory in the vicinity of the ancient city of Troy).

Aeolus (ē′ō-lus, ē-ō′lus). In mythology, a son of Hellen and the nymph Orseïs, and a grandson of Deucalion and Pyrrha. He was the brother of Dorus and Xuthus, and succeeded his father as king of Magnesia in Thessaly. By Thea, a daughter of Chiron whom he seduced, he was the father of Arne and grandfather of the twins Aeolus and Boeotus; the former became keeper of the winds. He bequeathed part of his kingdom to his grandson Boeotus who became the ancestor of the Boeotians. By his wife Enarete, Aeolus had seven sons: Athamas, Cretheus, Deion, Magnes, Perieres, Salmoneus, and Sisyphus, and five daughters: Alcyone, Calyce, Canace, Pisidice, and Perimedes.

Aeolus. In mythology, a son of Poseidon and Arne, daughter of Aeolus, king of Magnesia in Thessaly. He and his twin brother, Boeotus, were exposed to die on Mount Pelion at the order of their mother's foster father. They were saved by a shepherd and handed over to Theano, the childless wife of Metapontus, king of Icaria. She presented them to her husband as her own children. Metapontus was delighted with them, thinking they were his own sons. Even when his wife later bore twins of her own, he preferred Aeolus and Boeotus. Grown, the twins frustrated a plot arranged by Theano in which they were to be killed by their foster brothers. Instead Aeolus and Boeotus killed Theano's sons with the aid of their father, Poseidon. They then fled. Poseidon came to them and revealed that he was their father and told them to free their mother, who had been imprisoned since their birth

actor; up, lūte, pull; oi, oil; ou, out; ŦH, then; ḍ as d or j, ş as s or sh, ṭ as t or ch, ẓ as z or zh.

by her foster father. They freed Arne, who married Metapontus, Theano having killed herself, but after a time Metapontus put her aside in favor of a new wife. Aeolus and Boeotus took their mother's part and killed the new wife, after which they fled. Aeolus and some companions sailed to the Tyrrhenian Sea and there they established a kingdom on an island, usually thought to be one of the Aeoliae Insulae (Lipari Islands). He was on friendly terms with the gods and was entrusted with the task of guarding and controlling the winds. These were locked behind the sheer cliffs of the island. When he wanted to release any of the winds, he pierced the side of the cliff with his spear and the wind streamed through the opening. To shut off the wind he simply stopped the hole. Aeolus and his wife, whom some call Enarete, had six sons and six daughters. They all lived in great happiness and prosperity on their island until Aeolus discovered that his six sons and daughters had formed incestuous unions, unaware that such marriages were frowned upon by the gods. He broke up these combinations by requesting some of his sons to emigrate. Odysseus visited Aeolus on his wanderings at the end of the Trojan War, and was royally entertained. Aeolus gave him a skin in which all the winds were confined to help him on his journey home. The ship was in sight of Ithaca when his comrades, while Odysseus slept, thinking that the skin Aeolus had given him contained a rich treasure, opened it to take their share. All the winds flew out and raised a great storm. Odysseus was blown to sea again. He revisited Aeolus and told him what had happened. But Aeolus would not help him again, on the ground that a man who had such bad luck must be hated by the gods, and therefore there was nothing he could do to help such a man. (In the *Aeneid,* at Juno's behest, Aeolus sent winds to raise a storm at sea in an attempt to destroy Aeneas and his ships but the plan was thwarted by Neptune.) Aeolus fulfilled his duties as guardian of the winds so capably that Zeus did not permit him to die, but placed him on a throne in the Cave of the Winds where he continues to perform his duties faithfully.

Aepea (ē-pē′a). City on the Gulf of Messenia,

in Messenia. It was one of the seven gift cities offered by Agamemnon to Achilles if he would give up his quarrel with Agamemnon and return to the battle in the Trojan War. Its name was later changed to Corone (q.v.).

Aepy (ē′pi). In ancient geography, a town in Nestor's realm in Elis. According to Herodotus, it was one of six cities founded by the Minyans who had come to Laconia from the island of Lemnos but who fled to this region and settled, to escape the threats of the Laconians. Men of Aepy accompanied Nestor to the Trojan War. The town, which was also called Aepium, Epium, or Epeum, was ultimately taken over by the Eleans and demolished. Among its ruins are remains of a theater and several temples.

Aepytus (ē′pi-tus). In mythology, a son of Elatus. He reared Evadne, daughter of the nymph Pitana and Poseidon. Although she tried to hide it from him, Aepytus knew that Evadne was about to bear a child. He consulted the oracle at Delphi and was reassured that the child, Iamus, was destined to become a famous seer.

Aepytus. According to legend, a son of Merope and Cresphontes, and the grandson of Heracles. Cresphontes, king of Messenia, and two of his sons were murdered in a rebellion. His mother sent Aepytus away to Arcadia for safe-keeping. Polyphontes seized the throne and married Merope, unaware that her third son was still alive. When Aepytus grew up he returned to Messenia. His mother mistook him for the murderer of Aepytus and would have killed him but he revealed his real identity to her and together they murdered Polyphontes. Aepytus then took the throne. The tomb of Aepytus was said to be in Arcadia.

Aepytus. A king of Arcadia and a descendant of Stymphalus. It is said that he entered the sanctuary of Poseidon at Mount Alesium near Mantinea, forbidden to mortals, and that he was struck blind for his presumption and shortly afterward died. Aepytus was the father of Cypselus who succeeded him as king of Arcadia.

Aequi (ē′kwī). Warlike tribe of Latium, neighbors of the Volscians and Latins. They joined Turnus in his war against Aeneas. In historic times they were often allied with the

fat, fāte, fär, fãre, errạnt; net, mē, hėr ardẹnt; pin, pīne; not, nōte, mŏve, nôr,

Volscians and at war with the Romans. They were subdued at the end of the Second Samnite war in 304 B.C.

Aero (ē′rō). Another name for Merope, daughter of Oenopion, king of Chios. See **Merope**.

Aërope (a̧-er′ō̧-pē). In Greek legend, the daughter of Catreus, king of Crete. Because her father had been told by an oracle that he would be killed by one of his own children, he sold Aërope and her sister Clymene as slaves to Nauplius. Aërope became the mother of Agamemnon, Menelaus and Anaxibia; according to some accounts Plisthenes was their father. According to other accounts, Atreus whom she married, was their father; in any case they were brought up as his own children. Aërope fell in love with Thyestes, Atreus' brother, and on learning of her unfaithfulness Atreus cast her into the sea.

Aërope. In Greek mythology, a daughter of Cepheus, king of Tegea. Heracles sought the aid of Cepheus in his war to punish the sons of Hippocoön. To protect the city against attack while Cepheus was assisting him, Heracles gave Aërope a lock of the hair of the Gorgon Medusa which Athena had given to him, telling her if the city was attacked she should exhibit the lock of hair three times from the city walls and this would cause any enemy to flee.

Aesacus (ē′sa̧-kus). In classical myth, one of the 50 sons of Priam, king of Troy. His mother was Arisbe, the daughter of Merops the seer. After the birth of Aesacus Priam gave Arisbe to Hyrtacus for a wife, and Priam married Hecuba. From his grandfather Aesacus learned the art of prophecy. Hecuba, about to bear Paris, dreamed that she produced flames and fiery serpents, and awoke in terror under the impression that Troy was in flames. Aesacus interpreted the dream to mean that the child she was about to bear would bring ruin to the city and must be destroyed. The day Paris was actually born Aesacus again prophesied, saying that the son born to the royal house of Troy that day must be done away with. But Priam and Hecuba did not apply the prophecy to their own child, but to another princeling of Troy who was also born that day. Aesacus withdrew to the country where he fell desperately in love with Asterope, or Hesperie,

a daughter of the river-god Cebren. She did not return his love immediately and fled from his ardent embraces. As he pursued her she stepped on a serpent, was bitten by it, and died. Aesacus, in a torment of remorse and grief, sought to kill himself by leaping into the sea but Thetis transformed him into a bird, and he continues to dive savagely into the sea in an attempt to destroy himself.

Aeschines (es′ki-nēz). Athenian philosopher who was active in the first half of the 4th century B.C. He became a disciple of Socrates and, like his master, tried to live without money, his few needs being supplied by gifts from his friends and pupils. After the death of Socrates he went to the court of Dionysius of Syracuse. Later he returned to Athens and supported himself by composing dialogues admired for their faithful descriptions of Socrates.

Aeschines. ["The Orator."] Athenian orator. He was born in 389 B.C., and died on the island of Samos in 314 B.C. He was a cultivated man of good family, but war had destroyed his family's fortunes and he was compelled to work. He was for a time an actor and then, through his association with Athenian statesmen, secured a post as a clerk in the public service. He yoked the legal training he received in the public service with his talents as an actor and became a public speaker and a political figure. He was one of ten commissioners sent to make peace with Philip of Macedon (346 B.C.). Demosthenes, also one of the commissioners, alone refused to accept the peace terms which he rightly considered dangerous to Athens and accused Aeschines of treason (345 B.C.). He defended himself of the charge in a brilliant speech and was acquitted. Subsequently he was again compelled to defend himself when Demosthenes, who had become his enemy, charged that he had accepted bribes from Philip of Macedon. In the end, his enmity for Demosthenes brought his downfall. He made a speech, *Against Ctesiphon* (330 B.C.) but really aimed at Demosthenes, charging that Ctesiphon had acted illegally in proposing a golden crown for Demosthenes. Demosthenes counterattacked strongly and brought suit against him in a speech, *On the Crown*. Aeschines lost the case, was compelled to pay

actǫr; up, lūte, pu̇ll; oi, oil; ou, out; ŦH, then; d̦ as d or j, ş as s or sh, ț as t or ch, ẓ as z or zh.

a fine, and went into voluntary . exile at Rhodes. From there he went to Samos, where he subsequently died. Three of his orations, *Against Timarchus* (an ally of Demosthenes who had joined him in the attack on Aeschines in 345 B.C.), *On the False Embassy* (a reply to an oration of the same name which Demosthenes made against him, 342 B.C.), and *Against Ctesiphon,* survive. The force and grace of the orations of Aeschines caused him to be ranked next after Demosthenes among the orators of his period.

Aeschines the Orator. Greek statue from Herculaneum, in the National Museum at Naples, of high rank among works of its class. The orator stands quietly, his arm wrapped in his mantle; the expression is preoccupied but full of dignity.

Aeschylus (es′ki-lus). Athenian tragic dramatist. He was born at Eleusis, 525 B.C., the son of Euphorion, a member of the old nobility. In 490 B.C. he took part with his countrymen at the Battle of Marathon, in which his brother lost his life. To judge by his own epitaph which he wrote, this was the greatest moment of Aeschylus' life. The epitaph simply gives his name and lineage and adds the brief and proud comment, "His might the sacred grove of Marathon has witnessed, and the deep-tressed Mede has known." There is no mention of his life work as a tragic poet. Again with the Athenians, he retired to Salamis (480 B.C.) and took part in the great sea battle in which the Greeks defeated the Persians. Some say he fought also at Plataea and in Thrace. He made at least two visits to Sicily. On his first visit he wrote a play, *Women of Aetna,* honoring the town of Aetna that had only recently been founded (476–475 B.C.) on the slopes of that mountain. The play has been lost. About 456 B.C. he again went to Sicily. He died in that year, at Gela; some say an eagle flying overhead dropped a tortoise on his skull and killed him. The Gelans erected a splendid monument in his honor. Later, on the motion of Lycurgus the orator, the Athenians set a bronze statue of him in the theater. Euphorion, the son of Aeschylus, was also known as a tragic poet, as were several others of his descendants.

Aeschylus began to write in his youth, appearing as a rival of Pratinas and Choerilus.

Some date his first presentation in the year 499 B.C. He entered the annual Athenian competition of tragic drama more than 20 times, and won first prize 13 times. He won first prize in 484 B.C., and from that time forward was recognized as the leading figure in Attic drama. In 468 B.C. Sophocles took the first prize but the following year Aeschylus again won. He has been called the father of Greek drama and the first tragedian. To the choral lyric in honor of Dionysus which had existed up to his time and which consisted only of a chorus and leader, he added a second actor and thereby supplied the action and reaction between characters which is the essence of drama. He also designed costumes for his players, introduced stage settings and stage machinery, drilled his choruses in their songs and dances, invented dance figures, and took part in his own dramas, as was the custom. However valuable his innovations were, they were additions to an existing structure. But the addition of the second actor completely changed the shape of that structure and produced drama where before there had been only choral lyrics. The technique is of tremendous significance, but it is his approach to life of lofty, universal and compelling interest, all expressed in language of surpassing beauty, that has kept his work alive for nearly 2500 years. After his death a special law was passed governing the presentation of his works; by a decree of the people a chorus was granted for every performance; and he was awarded the prize as if he had been still living. By the time of Plato (428–348 B.C.) his work was numbered among the classics and has remained so since.

Aeschylus wrote approximately 90 plays. The titles of 82 are known; seven survive in their entirety, and others are known from papyrus fragments and quotations in later writings. Critics date *The Suppliant Maidens* as the earliest of the extant plays, because of its simple, archaic structure and because of the importance of the chorus. This concerns the 50 daughters of Danaus who fled from Egypt to escape marriage with their cousins, the sons of Aegyptus. They seek asylum with Pelasgus, king of Argos. Pelasgus, knowing it would bring war with the sons of Aegyptus, will not take the re-

fat, fāte, fär, fãre, errạnt; net, mē, hér ardẹnt; pin, pīne; not, nōte, möve, nôr,

sponsibility of sheltering them without consulting his people. The Argives vote to accept the suppliants and to defy the herald sent to demand their return. The maidens offer prayers of gratitude to Zeus and ask blessings on the people of Argos. However, they also vow to remain virgins, and lay the basis for future woes by thus offending Aphrodite. *The Suppliant Maidens* was followed by two other plays, now lost. They were: *The Maker of the Bride Bed,* in which Danaus, having been defeated by the sons of Aegyptus and compelled to deliver his daughters to them, orders his daughters to murder their husbands on the wedding night; and *Danaides,* about the one daughter Hypermnestra who defied her father's order and spared her husband. She was tried for defying him, defended by Aphrodite and acquitted. The earliest play of known date is *The Persians* (472 B.C.). It takes place in the Persian capital and is concerned with the defeat of the forces of Xerxes at Salamis. This is the first account by a great poet of a great historical event in which the poet himself had taken part. It memorializes the epic achievement of the Greeks in throwing back the vast host of the Persians, and it illustrates the thesis that the gods punish impiety. In 467 B.C. Aeschylus won the prize with his trilogy on Thebes. The first play was *Laius,* the second was *Oedipus,* the third—the only surviving one of the three—is *Seven Against Thebes.* It concerns the siege of Thebes, in which the two sons of Oedipus, fighting on opposite sides, kill each other and carry out the curse laid on them by their father, and it brings to an end the horrors of the house of Laius which began when Laius defied the gods. Some time after this came the Promethean trilogy, of which only the *Prometheus Bound* is extant. The other two were *Prometheus Unbound,* which obviously follows, and *Prometheus the Fire-Bearer,* which some name as the first of the trilogy and some as the last. In *Prometheus Bound* Prometheus appears as the unconquerable spirit, and as the champion of man as opposed to the tyranny of the new lord of the universe, Zeus. The scene of the drama lies in the furthest reaches of mythological time; all the actors (there were only two but one actor could take more than

one part) and the chorus are immortals. In the drama Aeschylus set himself a formidable obstacle by keeping his protagonist completely immobilized and on the stage throughout. What action there is lies with the second actor who comes to plead with Prometheus to be expedient (Oceanus) or to threaten him for defying Zeus (Hermes), and in the chorus which comes to offer sympathy, fears his intransigeance, but elects to share his fate. The chorus of *Prometheus Bound* "is perhaps in character and dramatic fitness the most beautiful and satisfying known to us on the Greek stage." (Gilbert Murray.) Aeschylus won his last victory (458 B.C.) with the great Orestean trilogy, his own highest achievement and perhaps the greatest achievement of all Greek drama. The trilogy includes *Agamemnon,* on his murder, when he returns from Troy, by his wife Clytemnestra who had been grievously sinned against and in her turn sins grievously. Among other things, *Agamemnon* is marked by stunning psychological insight in the counterpoint provided by the characters of Agamemnon and Clytemnestra. Second in the trilogy is the *Choëphoroe,* named for the chorus, which recounts the terrible dilemma of Orestes, son of Agamemnon, called on by Apollo to avenge his father by killing his mother, and thus outraging one of the most sacred laws of the Greeks and bringing on him the terrible persecution of the Furies. The trilogy ends with the *Eumenides,* which brings a halt to the endless involvement of the house of Atreus in blood guilt, and substitutes courts of law for vengeance. In the trilogy Aeschylus offers the view that it is not capricious fate that causes disaster, but the deeds of men. In the *Orestea* every human act, stretching back to the time of Thyestes and Atreus, produces a new act of horror until at last, in the *Eumenides,* reconciliation between the blind avenging Furies and a rule of law is achieved through the divine will (Athena). This view—that previous acts and conditions and not irresistible fate bring suffering—appears often enough in the work of Aeschylus to be taken as a part of his basic approach to life. The trilogy taken as a whole also presents a clear example of one of the essential principles of Greek art, a principle which appears to a lesser degree in each of its individual parts; this is: to loosen the tension at the close. The "pity and terror" of the first two plays are maintained almost to the very last line. The *Eumenides* drifts to a relaxed and artistic close. By modern standards it collapses; for the Greeks a release from the high pitch of horror in the first two plays was considered a desirable necessity.

From his work it appears that Aeschylus was an enthusiastic theoretical democrat, using the last word as it would have been applied in his time. The principles of law and justice which appear in such grandeur in his plays express his own search for a law and a morality in the universe. That he conceived of a law of sublime wisdom and reason is apparent in his religious piety, which seems to question the idea of "gods" but to accept the idea of "god." His plays were based on cycles of myths, or woven of unrelated myths and legends. The gods appear in them with the greatest ease and frequency, but seldom in the role of "deus ex machina" to help the playwright out of a predicament that could be solved only by the help of the gods. Though they appear often, the role the gods play is subordinate to the suffering and epic struggle of man. Aeschylus seemed to see life as an exhilarating and terrible struggle against superior forces; a struggle that inevitably arises when a mighty will is aroused to action by intellect, emotion, or passion. The struggle, a noble one, causes suffering, whence comes wisdom.

Aesculapius (es-kū-lā′pi-us). See **Asclepius**.

Aeson (ē′son). In Greek legend, a son of Tyro and Cretheus, founder and king of Iolcus. He was the half-brother of Pelias and Neleus, Tyro's twin sons by Poseidon. After the death of Cretheus Pelias seized the throne of Iolcus and kept Aeson, the rightful heir, a prisoner. Aeson had a son by his wife who is variously known as Perimede, Amphinome, Alcimede, and Polymede. The child, who was first named Diomedes but is known as Jason, was brought up by Chiron the centaur on Mount Pelion. Aeson was still a virtual prisoner of Pelias when Jason arrived in Iolcus and claimed the throne. After Jason had departed on the quest for the Golden Fleece, Pelias believed that he would not return. He threatened to kill Aeson but allowed him to commit suicide by drinking bull's blood, which only the immortals could imbibe and survive. But some say Aeson did not commit suicide, that he still lived, an aged and broken man, when Jason returned from Colchis; and that Medea restored his youth with her magic arts learned from Hecate.

Aesonis (ē-sō′nis). A city of Magnesia, named for Aeson, the father of Jason. It was the home of Pelias.

Aesop (ē′sop). [Also: **Esop**.] According to tradition, a Greek fabulist of the 6th century B.C., represented as a dwarf and originally a slave. Samos and other places claimed the honor of being his birthplace. After obtaining his freedom, he visited Lydia and Greece. Of the so-called fables of Aesop there have been several editions, but they are all considered to be spurious. Indeed, Aesop was probably not an actual historical personage. Several of the fables which he is popularly supposed to have written have been traced to sources which considerably antedate his own alleged period of life; some, in fact, may be found in Egyptian materials dating from approximately the 14th century B.C. He was represented in later art as deformed, "perhaps to indicate his nearer approach to the lower animals and his peculiar sympathy for their habits."

Aesepus (ē-sē′pus). In Homeric legend (*Iliad*), a son of Abarbarea, a fountain nymph, and Bucolion, and the twin of Pedasus. The brothers were slain by Euryalus in the Trojan War.

Aesepus. A river of Mysia, passed by the Argonauts on their way to Colchis. Homer names it as one of the rivers of the Troad which was diverted from its course by Poseidon and Apollo and directed against the wall built by the Greeks to protect their ships during the Trojan War. After the war was over, Poseidon and Apollo with the help of Zeus sent the rivers against the wall and washed it into the sea. See **Rhesus**, river.

Aesernia (ē-ser′ni-a). [Modern name, **Isernia**.] Town of SE Italy, situated on a tributary of the Volturnus River. It became a Roman colony in 265 B.C., and was conquered by Sulla in the Roman civil war (80 B.C.).

Aesyetes (ē-si-ē′tēz). Named by Homer (*Iliad*), as the father of Antenor. His grave-mound outside the walls of Troy was used as a lookout post by Polites, a Trojan sentinel and a son of Priam.

Aethalia (ē-thal'i-a̱). [Modern name, **Elba.**] An island off the coast of northern Italy where the Argonauts stopped briefly on their roundabout journey home from Colchis.

Aethalides (ē-thal'i-dēz). In Greek legend, a son of Hermes by Eupolemeia, daughter of Myrmidon. He was born near the Amphrysus River in Thessaly. He joined Jason in the quest for the Golden Fleece, and served as herald of the Argonauts. Aethalides was given two remarkable gifts by his father: the ability to live either in the Underworld or on earth, and an infallible memory. Since he could remember everything, even in the Underworld, his soul remembered, even after death, that it had migrated from Aethalides to Euphorbus, to one Hermotimus, and then to the philosopher and mathematician Pythagoras.

Aether (ē'thėr). In Greek mythology, the son of Chaos and Darkness, and the brother of Night, Day, and Erebus; in the Orphic hymns, the soul of the world and source of life; later, the expanse of heaven or abode of the gods.

Aetheria (ē-ther'i-a̱). In mythology, a daughter of Helius and the Oceanid Clymene. With her sisters she was one of the Heliades, and like them she was changed into a poplar tree that wept tears of amber because of her grief over the death of her brother Phaëthon, who died driving the chariot of Helius across the heavens to prove his divine parentage.

Aethiopis (ē-thī'ō-pis). [Also: **Lay of Aethiopia.**] Greek epic poem of the Trojan cycle (by Arctinus of Miletus, the oldest [c776 B.C.] certainly known epic poet), so named from one of its heroes, Memnon the Aethiopian. It was a continuation of the *Iliad,* reaching "from the death of Hector to that of Achilles, and telling of the arrival of the Amazons and the Aethiopians to aid Troy."

Aëthlius (a̱-eth'li-us). According to some accounts, a son of Hermes and the father, by Calyce, of Endymion. Others say he was a son of Zeus and Protogenia, the daughter of Deucalion. He was the first to rule in the land later known as Elis.

Aethra (ēth'ra̱). In Greek legend, a daughter of Pittheus, king of Troezen. She was the mother, by Aegeus, of Theseus. She cared for Helen when the latter was abducted as a child by Theseus, returned with her when she was rescued by the Dioscuri, and later went with her as a captive when Helen was carried off to Troy by Paris. In Troy she reared her great-grandson Munitus, and fled with him to the Greek camp when Troy fell. Her grandson, Acamas, recognized her and demanded of Agamemnon that he be allowed to take her home to Greece. Agamemnon agreed, but stipulated that in return Acamas should forego any other spoils of war.

Aethra. In mythology, one of the Oceanids, a daughter of Oceanus and Tethys. She was the mother, by Atlas, of many daughters and one son, Hyas. Seven of the sisters died of grief over the death of their brother and were translated to the heavens where they became known as the Hyades, the rain stars.

Aethyia (ē-thwī'a̱). An epithet of Athena, meaning "Gannet" or "Diver-bird." Pandion of Athens was buried on the Rock of Athena Aethyia at Megara.

Aethylla (ē-thil'a̱). According to some accounts, a sister of King Priam of Troy. Some say that she was captured at Troy and carried off by Protesilaus who, according to this account, was not the first man killed at Troy, but on the contrary, survived the war. Aethylla and other Trojan women captives set fire to the ships in which they were carried from Troy when the fleet put in at a harbor. Some say the spot where the women burned the ships was at Pellene, in the Thracian Chersonese (Macedonia), and that Protesilaus founded the city of Scione on this site since he could proceed no farther without his ships. But others say it was the followers of Protesilaus, driven hither by storms on the way home from Troy, who founded the city. And still others say the ships were burned by the Trojan women in Italy, and that Protesilaus had nothing to do with their capture.

Aëtion (a̱-ē'shi-on). Greek painter, mid-4th century B.C., probably a contemporary of Apelles. He is noted for his painting *The Marriage of Alexander and Roxana.*

Aetna (et'nä). A nymph of Sicily. Some say she was a daughter of Uranus and Gaea; others say Briareus was her father. In a dispute between Hephaestus and Demeter for control of Sicily, Aetna, according to some accounts, was the arbitrator. By Zeus or by Hephaestus she was the mother of the Palici. The volcanic mountain in Sicily was named for her. Some say that Hephaestus had one of his forges under this mountain, and that it was in this forge that the Cyclopes made the thunderbolts for Zeus. The mountain also figures in the stories of Enceladus the Giant, who was buried under it after he had been charred by the lightning of Zeus. They say that when Enceladus turns over to ease his aching sides, all Sicily quakes and rumbles. Typhon, the hideous monster who warred against Zeus and was defeated by him, is also buried under Mount Aetna. On the slope of the mountain, Hiero, tyrant of Syracuse, founded a city which he named Aetna (c476 B.C.).

Aetolia (e-tō′li-a). [Also: **Aitolia**.] In ancient geography, a district of Greece, bounded by Epirus and Thessaly on the N, Doris on the NE, Locris on the E and SE, the Corinthian Gulf on the S, and Acarnania on the W. According to tradition, it was the land of the Curetes but was invaded from the Peloponnesus by Aetolus, a son of Endymion, and renamed for him.

Aetolian League (ē-tō′li-an). Confederation of Greek cities whose organization was copied from that of the Achaean League. It waged war against Macedon in 323 B.C., against the Gauls in 279 B.C., and against the Achaean League in 220 B.C. In the period 211–192 B.C. it was allied with Rome. It was dissolved in 167 B.C.

Aetolus (ē′tō-lus). In mythology, one of the sons of Endymion. He competed with his brothers for the throne of Elis, his father's kingdom, but lost. In the course of funeral games for Azan, son of Arcas, the first ever held in Greece according to some accounts, he accidentally killed Apis, the son of Phoroneus. He was banished and crossed the Gulf of Corinth to the land of the Curetes. There he killed his hosts, Dorus, Laodocus, and Polypoetes, the sons of Apollo and Phthia, and made himself ruler. He named the land Aetolia after himself. He married Pronoë, a daughter of Phorbas, who bore him two sons. Two cities he founded in Aetolia were named Pleuron and Calydon after these two sons.

Afranius (a-frā′ni-us), **Lucius**. Roman comic poet, active c100 B.C. He was an imitator of the Greek Menander. Extant fragments of his work, 40 titles of which survive, indicate that he dealt, like Menander, chiefly with middle-class life.

Afranius, Lucius. Roman general, died in Africa, 46 B.C. He was an adherent of Pompey who assisted him to become consul (60), he was defeated by Caesar at Ilerda, Spain, in 49 B.C. Despite a promise not to serve thereafter against Caesar, he joined Pompey's forces and was present at the defeats of Pompey at Pharsalus (48 B.C.) and Thapsus (46 B.C.). He was captured in the last-named battle and taken to Caesar, whose soldiers thereupon put him to death.

Africa (af′ri-ka). In ancient geography, the designation for either the entire continent, or for that portion of the northern coastal area along the Mediterranean comprising the Roman province of Africa, approximately coterminous with modern Tunisia. To the Greeks the continent was known as Libya. (JJ)

African War. Name sometimes applied to the war between Julius Caesar and the followers of Pompey who had collected in the Roman province of Africa after the defeat at Pharsalus in Greece, in 48 B.C., and were overthrown at Thapsus in 46 B.C.

Agacles (ag′a-klēz). Named by Homer (*Iliad*) as a king of the Myrmidons in Budeum. He was the father of Epigeus, a follower of Achilles.

Agamede (ag-a-mē′dē). In mythology, a daughter of Augeas, king in Elis and the owner of the famous stables. According to Homer she knew all the herbs that grew on the earth, and was skilled in the arts of using them for healing. Her husband, Mulius, was slain by Nestor when Augeas warred with Neleus, Nestor's father.

Agamedes (ag-a-mē′dēz). In mythology, a son of Erginus the Argonaut. He was the brother of Trophonius. The brothers were born in their father's old age, after he had taken the advice of an oracle and married a young wife. They were famous builders. With his brother Agamedes built the temple of Apollo at Delphi and the brothers were guardian spirits of its threshold until they were replaced by Neoptolemus. They also built a treasury for King Hyrieus of Boeotia.

fat, fāte, fär, fãre, errant; net, mē, hèr ardent; pin, pīne; not, nōte, möve, nôr,

In it they so placed a stone that it could be removed from the outside and thus they were able to rob the treasury at will. According to some accounts, Hyrieus arranged a trap and caught Agamedes stealing in this manner. Trophonius cut off his brother's head in order to save himself. The gods were angry with Trophonius and swallowed him up in the earth in a grove at Lebadia. The oracle of Trophonius at Lebadia thereafter became famous, and suppliants there, before entering the pit where the oracle gave answers, ate of a ram that had been sacrificed to the shade of Agamedes. According to other accounts, as a reward for building the temple of Apollo at Delphi the god granted them seven days of pleasure, at the end of that time they received their reward: they went peacefully to sleep and died.

Agamemnon (ag-a-mem′non). In Greek mythology, the son of Atreus and Aërope and the brother of Menelaus and Anaxibia. Following the murder of their father by Aegisthus, Agamemnon and Menelaus remained at the court of Oeneus, a king in Aetolia, until they were restored to their own kingdom by Tyndareus, king of Sparta. Agamemnon became king of Mycenae and, making war on Tantalus, king of Pisa, slew him and his infant, and compelled his widow to marry him. She was Clytemnestra, a daughter of Tyndareus, and she bore Agamenmnon Orestes, Electra (sometimes known as Laodice), Iphigenia (sometimes known as Iphianassa), and Chrysothemis. When Paris abducted Helen, Menelaus reminded the Grecian princes who had been her suitors of their oath to assist whomever she married in case any ill came to him as a result of the marriage. A great expedition was organized to go to Troy and recapture Helen. Agamemnon, brave but vain and eager for glory, yearned to be made leader of the expedition, although he pretended with a great show of humility that he did not seek the honor. As he had planned, however, he was chosen captain of the Greek armies which gathered to go to Troy. The Greek fleet, assembled at Aulis, was prevented from sailing by violent storms or, according to another account, by a calm. Calchas the seer said that the storms were caused by the anger of Artemis, because Agamemnon had killed a stag, one

of her creatures. Only the sacrifice of Agamemnon's daughter would appease the goddess and quiet the storms. Urged on by Menelaus, Agamemnon sent a message to Clytemnestra, telling her to send their daughter Iphigenia to Aulis to be married to Achilles. This scheme had been hatched by Odysseus to make sure that Clytemnestra would send Iphigenia. Agamemnon regretted his decision to sacrifice his own child and would have changed his order, in spite of his overwhelming desire to be the leader of the glorious expedition, but he was persuaded that events had moved too fast: the armies knew of Calchas' interpretations and demanded the sacrifice so that they could proceed. Menelaus taunted him with seeking power and glory but being unwilling to take the responsibilities that went with them if personal sacrifice was involved. When Iphigenia arrived, unexpectedly accompanied by Clytemnestra, the sacrifice was performed, despite the latter's pleas and Agamemnon's own misgivings. The fleet then sailed.

For nearly ten years the Greeks raided the allies of Troy and the cities of the Troad. In the tenth year they attacked the city itself, but were beset by a plague of arrows sent by Apollo. Calchas informed Agamemnon that Apollo was angry because Agamemnon had taken Chryseis, daughter of a priest of Apollo, as a captive and refused to return her to her father who had offered a rich ransom for her. Agamemnon agreed to give her up, but demanded Briseis, a captive who had been awarded to Achilles, in her place. This aroused the famous wrath of Achilles and caused that hero to withdraw from the war, and so it was that Agamemnon's arrogance and hasty temper brought great losses and near disaster to the Greeks. Brave, rash, and vain, Agamemnon wanted the glory of leadership but did not know how to exercise it. He therefore constantly sought advice from Nestor who encouraged him to remain and fight when, discouraged, he would have given up and sailed for home. Also he continually turned to Odysseus who was ever ready with some scheme to save the situation. In the last year of the war Agamemnon volunteered to fight Hector in single combat but was eliminated by the drawing of lots. As the battle went against the

actǫr; up, lūte, pŭll; oi, oil; ou, out; ᴛʜ, then; ḍ as d or j, ş as s or sh, ţ as t or ch, ẓ as z or zh.

Greeks he regretted his arrogance toward Achilles and tried to lure him back into the struggle with the offer of rich rewards. Achilles refused, and Agamemnon threw himself into the fighting until he was compelled by a wound to withdraw. After the death of Patroclus he admitted his fault to Achilles, saying he was spurred on by Ate, the goddess of mischief, and returned Briseis, untouched, to her former master. When Achilles later was killed, Agamemnon, possibly jealous of Telamonian Ajax' glorious fame, voted to award the armor of Achilles to Odysseus, whereupon Ajax, divinely inspired with madness by Athena, committed suicide. It was only the persuasive intervention of Odysseus that prevented him from denying honorable burial to Ajax. It was Odysseus again who persuaded him to order Astyanax, young son of Hector, to be hurled from the towers of Troy when that city had fallen, lest at a later date he gather the Trojans and again make war on the Greeks. Agamemnon took Cassandra, daughter of Priam and Hecuba, as his captive from Troy and began preparations to return to Greece. Once again weather prevented the sailing and Calchas informed him that the spirit of Achilles demanded the sacrifice of Polyxena, youngest daughter of Priam and Hecuba, on his funeral pyre. He ordered the sacrifice and commanded that her body be returned to her mother for burial. However, when he went to Hecuba to learn why she had not claimed the body, she appealed to him at least to permit her to avenge herself on Polymnestor, a former ally of Troy who had murdered the young son of Priam and Hecuba left in his care for safe-keeping. He agreed to let her take whatever vengeance a captive woman could, but would give her no assistance. The Greeks then sailed for home. Agamemnon was one of the few Greek leaders who arrived home directly. When he landed, Clytemnestra, who had learned of his approach by an elaborate system of beacon fires, welcomed him so extravagantly that he was uneasy but yielded to her efforts to treat him almost as a god. She invited him and his captive Cassandra, who seemed to be in a frenzy and was raving of bloody baths, into the palace for purification rites. As he stepped out of the cere-

monial bath, Clytemnestra wrapped him in a robe that immobilized him and, according to Aeschylus, stabbed him three times, and then killed Cassandra. According to Homer, it was Aegisthus, her paramour, who actually killed Agamemnon. After the murders, with wild elation, Clytemnestra told the stunned subjects of Agamemnon that she had taken vengeance on her husband for the sacrifice of her daughter and for bringing back Cassandra as a rival wife.

Agamemnon. A tragedy by Aeschylus, the first in the Orestean triology with which Aeschylus won first prize in 458 B.C. The trilogy treats the curse on the House of Atreus, how it operated and how it was lifted. The tragedy *Agamemnon* deals with the murder of Agamemnon, who has returned victorious from Troy after an absence of ten years. The tragedy, marked by the psychological insight with which Aeschylus draws the character of Clytemnestra, the dramatic intensity of the Cassandra scene, and the powerful scene in which Clytemnestra stands triumphant over her husband's corpse, is considered by many to be Aeschylus' masterpiece.

The scene is the place before Agamemnon's palace at Argos. From the palace roof a watchman prays the gods to bring his vigil to an end. He has been stationed there for a year by Clytemnestra—in whose woman's breast, he says, beats a man's heart—to watch for the signal that will announce the fall of Troy. A beacon flashes and he shouts for joy, then immediately curbs his tongue as he thinks of the tales the house could tell its master of his wife. A chorus of Argive Elders enters. The Elders sing of the years, the ships, and the men lost since Agamemnon and Menelaus set out for Troy to recover Helen. With foreboding they recall the omens that seemed to promise victory for the Greeks, but a victory clouded with evil. Uneasily they remember the seer's prophecy that Iphigenia, daughter of Agamemnon and Clytemnestra, must be sacrificed, and their fear that it would arouse a resentment that could be appeased only with blood. They state that Agamemnon chose the responsibility for sacrificing his innocent daughter in order to lead a war to regain a false wife. The burden of the choice was his. Through

fat, fāte, fär, fāre, errạnt; net, mē, hėr ardẹnt; pin, pīne; not, nōte, mȯve, nôr,

their song runs a thread of fear, caused by their knowledge of what Clytemnestra has done and the guilt that Agamemnon bears for the sacrifice of his daughter. Zeus, they say, has decreed that men must learn through suffering, and that Justice will not be denied. At the close of their ode they ask Clytemnestra, who has been lighting altar fires, what news has caused her to order sacrificial fires throughout Argos. She tells them Troy has fallen and explains the system of beacon fires she has caused to be set up to carry the message across the seas to her. She hopes the Greeks, in their joy at success, will risk no impiety to the gods of Troy lest the gods in their turn take revenge on the victorious Greeks. The Elders sing a paean of thanksgiving to Zeus for the victory which has brought retribution to Paris and which has proved again that there is no protection for the guilty. But many in Greece, they say, will grieve for the losses they have sustained in the war for a false wife, and resentment will rise against Agamemnon. A herald of Agamemnon enters. He bids the Argives prepare to welcome their king who has crushed Troy, overthrown its altars, and wiped out the race of the Trojans. He weeps for joy to be home again. Farewell to the woes they have suffered, he says, there is no profit in remembering the losses and hardships they endured in the war. Clytemnestra approaches. She plans how she may best honor Agamemnon, speaks extravagantly of her joy at his homecoming, and claims she has been a faithful watchdog over his interests in his absence. The herald applauds her speech but, as she withdraws, the Elders hint that her speech does not square with her actions. The herald tells of the hardships of the war and of the storms that scattered the Greek fleet on the voyage home. When he leaves the Elders sing a long ode on the beauty of Helen and of the evil it brought Troy, not for itself but because the gods were angered when Paris violated the laws of hospitality and the Trojans upheld him. Some hold that ease and security bring a curse on the children of those who possess them. The Elders say it was not beauty or wealth that brought Troy's downfall, but an evil deed. A past impiety or an old crime breeds a young curse, they say, which in the appointed time results in doom. This choral ode prepares the way for Agamemnon, who now enters in a chariot, followed by his captive Cassandra and a great company of Argives. The Elders welcome him, congratulate him on his victory, and suggest that time will tell who has been loyal and who faithless in his absence. He acknowledges their greeting, and arrogantly points out that it was he and the gods who meted out justice to Troy. Clytemnestra greets him. She speaks in the most extravagant language of her love for him, her loneliness in his absence, the agonizing rumors of his death; his presence now is as the return of the sun. She commands her maids to spread a purple carpet for Agamemnon, the conqueror of Troy. He rebukes her, reminding her that the purple is for gods, not for mortals. Clytemnestra insists. She plays on his vanity as a great conquerer, suggests that fear should not prevent him from setting foot on the purple, and finally says that a victor can also afford to yield in order to please his wife. He has his sandals removed by a slave and, uttering the hope that no god's jealousy will be aroused (by an act he knows to be impious), sets his feet on the carpet. He tells his servant to lead Cassandra into the palace and withdraws. The Elders, alone with Cassandra, are filled with a nameless fear. Clytemnestra comes from the palace to fetch Cassandra for the rites which warriors undergo to cleanse themselves of the blood of those they have slain, but the captive, who has been silent throughout, remains motionless and speechless. Clytemnestra impatiently withdraws.

The Elders pity Cassandra who begins a chant of woe and calls on Apollo, saying he has destroyed her again. Wildly she cries that the palace is cursed, that she sees bloodstained hands smiting their kin, and a strangling noose. When she refers to Thyestes and the horrible banquet at which he was caused to eat of his children's flesh, the Elders recognize her allusion. Now, she cries, a worse crime is plotted. It was a treacherous welcome, the bath is prepared, the snare is set. The Elders do not understand but they are chilled with terror. She predicts her own death. So that the chorus will believe her prophecies, she tells them that Apollo gave her the gift of prophecy in return for her promised love but that she refused to fulfill her promise and the god, though he respected her refusal of his suit, doomed her to be a true prophet who would never be believed. Apollo did not ravish her, but what the god left untouched, Agamemnon took for his own. When she again describes her own death and that of Agamemnon, the curse of Apollo operates and the Elders refuse to believe her. However, it does not matter, she says, as events will soon prove her tale is true. She warns that a son will avenge his father's blood, prays that her death will be swift, and enters the palace. Presently Agamemnon's cry for help is heard from within the palace. The Elders are confused. While they debate what should be done, the doors of the palace are flung open to reveal Clytemnestra standing over the corpses of Agamemnon and Cassandra. She exults as she describes to the horrified Elders how she entrapped Agamemnon in a netlike robe as he stepped from the ritual bath and then stabbed him three times. She makes no apologies and no appeals in justification of her deed. No one cried out, she reminds the Elders, when Agamemnon sacrificed Iphigenia, but that deed has now been atoned for by this murder. The chorus and Clytemnestra chant alternately. The Elders lament: he who slays today will die tomorrow, and the wage for woe is woe. Clytemnestra replies that her deed has ended the curse on the House of Atreus. Aegisthus enters. He describes the horrible crime Atreus, father of Agamemnon, wrought against Thyestes, his own father, and of the curse Thyestes laid on the sons of Atreus—Agamemnon and Menelaus. Agamemnon has suffered from the curse, and Aegisthus rejoices. The leader of the chorus heaps scorn on Aegisthus as a coward who did not join the war, an adulterer who seduced Agamemnon's wife, and a plotter who hid behind a woman. They predict the return of Orestes to slay both plotters. In answer to his claim that he is now their ruler, the Elders prepare to attack Aegisthus. Clytemnestra intervenes. Enough blood has been shed; it was necessary to kill Agamemnon but she hopes this will be the end. Aegisthus threatens the Argives. They mock him for

appearing to be brave only when Clytemnestra is there to protect him. She persuades him to withdraw, saying together they will rule and that all will turn out well.

Aganippe (ag-a-nip′ē). According to some myths, the wife of Acrisius and the mother of Danaë. Others name Eurydice as the mother of Danaë.

Aganippe. In ancient geography, a fountain near Mount Helicon, in Boeotia, Greece, sacred to the Muses. It was believed to inspire those who drank of it, and it gave the name "Aganippides" to the Muses.

Aganus (ag′a-nus). Named by some mythographers as a son of Helen and Paris. He died in Troy in infancy when a house collapsed on him.

Agapenor (ag-a-pē′nor). In Greek mythology, a son of Ancaeus, the Arcadian Argonaut. He became king of Arcadia, as successor to Echemus. He was the leader of the Arcadians who accompanied the Greeks to Troy to secure the return of Helen. On the way home after the Trojan War, his ships were scattered by storms. Agapenor and his Arcadians landed in Cyprus, and founded the city of Paphos and built the sanctuary of Aphrodite at Palaepaphos (*Old Paphos*).

Agariste (ag-a-ris′tē). Daughter of Clisthenes of Sicyon (fl. 580 B.C.). Her father invited such of the young princes and heroes of Greece as desired to do so to come to his court and sue for the hand of Agariste. Many came from the wealthiest and noblest families. In Sicyon they stayed a year, and were there put through various tests so that Clisthenes could determine the one best fitted to become his son-in-law. After a year in which the suitors endured such athletic contests as foot racing and wrestling, and such social affairs as banquets where their deportment and prowess as trenchermen were observed, the field was narrowed to the Athenians Hippoclides, son of Tisander, and Megacles, son of Alcmaeon. In the end, Hippoclides frittered away his chances by making a spectacle of himself through excessive dancing at a banquet. Agariste was given to Megacles. One of her sons was Clisthenes the Athenian who divided the Athenians into ten tribes. Her granddaughter, another Agariste, married the Athenian nobleman Xanthippus. When

fat, fāte, fär, fãre, errant; net, mē, hėr ardent; pin, pīne; not, nōte, möve, nôr,

she was expecting a child, she dreamed she had given birth to a lion. Soon afterwards she bore Xanthippus a son, Pericles.

Agasias (a̱-gā′shi-as). Name of two Greek sculptors of the Ephesian school who lived sometime during the 1st century B.C.: 1) Son of Dositheus. His name is inscribed on the base of the *Borghese Gladiator* in the Louvre in Paris. 2) Son of Menophilus. A military statue done by him is in the Athens national museum.

Agastrophus (a̱-gas′tro̱-fus). Named by Homer (*Iliad*) as a son of Paeon. He was a noted spearman. Diomedes killed him, and was himself wounded by an arrow from the bow of Paris as he stooped to strip Agastrophus of his armor.

Agatharchides of Cnidus (ag-a̱-thär′ki-dēz; nī′dus). [Also: **Agatharcus, Agatharchus.**] Greek geographer and historian, born at Cnidus and active during the first half of the 2nd century B.C. at Alexandria. His *On the Erythraean Sea*, which has been preserved through Photius, contains valuable geographic and ethnographic information on Arabia and Ethiopia. He also wrote a geography and history of Asia in ten books, and a geography and history of Europe in 49 books.

Agatharchus (ag-a̱-thär′kus). Athenian painter; born on the island of Samos in the Aegean Sea; fl. c460–417 B.C. He is said by Vitruvius to have painted a scene for a tragedy by Aeschylus, and thus is sometimes credited with having been the inventor of scene-painting for the theater.

Agathocles or **Agathokles** (a̱-gath′o̱-klēz). Sicilian despot, tyrant of Syracuse (317–289 B.C.), born at Thermae, Sicily, 361 B.C.; died 289 B.C. He seized power with an army of exiles and Campanian hirelings and shortly became involved in war with Carthage, traditional enemy of the Sicilian Greeks. He made his way through the Carthaginian forces around Syracuse and crossed the Mediterranean to attack Carthage in 310 B.C., but returned to find Syracuse rumbling with incipient revolt. He thereupon made peace with the Carthaginians and put down his opposition, but died before he could renew the attack on Carthage.

Agathon (ag′a̱-thon). Named by Homer (*Iliad*) as one of the 50 sons of Priam, king of Troy. He was slain in the Trojan War some time after the death of Hector.

Agathon. Athenian tragic poet. He was born c450 B.C. and died c400 B.C., probably in Macedonia whither he had gone with his friend Euripides. He was also a friend of Plato, and was noted for his culture and beauty. The banquet he gave to celebrate his first dramatic victory (416 B C.) at the Lenaea is the scene of Plato's *Symposium*. He is considered to have been the first Athenian dramatist to devise an original plot, having abandoned the myths as source material for his works, and to sever the link between plot and choral odes.

Agathyrsi (a̱-ga̱-thir′si). A tribe dwelling near the Maris River on the border of Scythia. According to tradition, they were descendants of Heracles through their eponymous ancestor Agathyrsus, the son of Heracles and the Fish-maiden of Scythia. According to Herodotus, they were luxurious in their tastes and fond of wearing gold. Men and women lived together promiscuously to the end that all children would be brothers and thus cherish no hatred or envy toward one another. In other respects they were similar to the Thracians. When Darius attacked the Scythians, the latter called on the Agathyrsi for aid. The Agathyrsi refused to give it on the grounds that the Scythians had provoked the attack. If Darius attacked them they would resist, but they would not go to the aid of the Scythians. The Scythians developed a policy for resisting Darius and punishing those who had refused them aid at the same time. They kept a day's march in front of the Persians and led them through the lands of those who had refused them aid; thus those countries were invaded twice. But the Agathyrsi, having observed this maneuver of the Scythians, rushed to their borders and forbade the Scyths to enter their land. Their evident intention to resist passage by the Scyths, as well as by the Persians, caused the Scythians to deflect their course and the land of the Agathyrsi was spared invasion.

Agathyrsus (ag-a̱-thir′sus). According to legend, a son of Heracles and a fabulous serpent-tailed maiden of Scythia. His brothers were Scythes and Gelonus. Because he failed in a task which Heracles instructed his mother to set him, she sent him out of the land.

Agave (a-gā′vē.) In Greek mythology, a daughter of Cadmus and Harmonia. She was the wife of Echion, one of the "Sown Men" of Thebes, and was the mother of Pentheus. When Dionysus made his appearance in Thebes, Pentheus denied the divinity of the god and sought to suppress his worship. Agave, who had been driven mad by Dionysus because she too denied his godhead, joined her sisters and other Theban women who were participating in the revels of Dionysus on Mount Cithaeron. There Pentheus, also inspired with madness by Dionysus as a punishment for his doubts, went to spy on the women. They seized him and, frenzied with wine and religious ecstasy, tore him to pieces. Agave herself, under the impression that she was subduing a lion, wrenched his head from his mangled body and bore it impaled on her thyrsus to the palace at Thebes. When she was restored to her senses, she was horrified and lamented the death of her son. Dionysus appeared to her and told her this was her punishment for her unbelief and sentenced her to exile from Thebes. She went to Illyria, as did her mother and father, and there married the king. When she later learned that her father had become commander of a force of Encheleans in Illyria, she murdered her new husband and turned his kingdom over to her father .

Ageladas (aj-e-lā′das). [Also: **Hageladas, Hagelaidas.**] Greek sculptor, a native of Argos; fl. c520–c460 B.C. He was noted for his statues of gods and athletes in bronze, of which no originals now exist, and is thought to have been the instructor of Myron, Phidias, and Polyclitus.

Agelaus (aj-e-lā′us). In Greek mythology, the chief herdsman of Priam, to whom Paris was given as an infant with instructions to kill him. Not having the heart to slay the babe, Agelaus left him on the mountain to die. A few days later Paris was found alive and well, having been suckled by a she-bear, and Agelaus, convinced that Paris had been saved by divine intervention, took him and brought him up with his own son.

Agelaus. In Homeric legend (*Iliad*), a Trojan, the son of Phradmon. He was slain when Diomedes hurled his javelin into his back as he fled in his chariot, after Zeus had sent an omen favorable to the Greeks which inspired them to renew their struggle against the Trojans.

Agelaus. In Homeric legend (*Odyssey*), a son of Damastor. He was a suitor of Penelope and advised Telemachus that it was not right to delay the choice of a husband for Penelope any longer. It had been proper to wait some time after the end of the Trojan War for the return of Odysseus, but he had now been gone twenty years, and Agelaus considered that a more than sufficient interval of waiting.

Agelaus. According to some accounts, a son of Heracles and Omphale, queen of Lydia. Some say he was the ancestor of the Lydian king, Croesus.

Agenor (a-jē′nôr, -nor). In mythology, a son of Poseidon and Libya, and the twin of Belus. He was a descendant of Io and Zeus, and was a king of Phoenicia. He left Egypt and went to Canaan (afterward Phoenicia). His wife Telephassa bore him Cadmus, Cilix, Phineus, Phoenix, Thasus, and Europa. When Europa was carried off by Zeus in the the form of a bull, Agenor commanded his sons to find her, threatening them with exile if they were unsuccessful. His sons departed on their mission but, being unsuccessful, never returned. They became the ancestors of peoples in Greece and Asia.

Agenor. A Trojan, named by Homer (*Iliad*) as the "great-hearted" son of Antenor and Theano, and as one of the bravest of the Trojans. He led a group at the siege of the Greek fortifications, and later, when Achilles chased the Trojans to the walls and would have followed them and taken the city, Agenor did not flee before him. Inspired by Apollo, he concluded that even Achilles was a mortal whose flesh could be wounded with a spear, and he stood firm to fight Achilles. The magic armor of Achilles protected him from Agenor's spear thrust, however, and lest Achilles harm him, Apollo veiled Agenor in a thick cloud and spirited him away. But Agenor's courage in facing Achilles had given the Trojans time to get inside the walls of the city and close the gates after them.

Agesander (aj-e-san′dèr) or **Agesandros** (-dros). Greek sculptor, a native of Rhodes, active

42–21 B.C. With Athenodorus and Polydorus of Rhodes he carved the famous sculptured group known as the *Laocoön*. This depicts the episode narrated by Aeneas in the second book of Vergil's *Aeneid,* when, following the priest Laocoön's bidding the Trojans to trust not the Wooden Horse ("I fear the Greeks even bearing gifts"), two great serpents emerge from the sea and attack Laocoön and his two sons. A copy of this sculpture (or possibly the original), is in the Vatican Museum, Rome. Fragments of sculpture recently found in a cave of Sperlonga, Italy, were at first assigned to a second Laocoön group, but some scholars prefer another interpretation. (JJ)

Agesilaus (a̲-jes-i-lā′us) or **Agesilaos** (-os). King of Sparta (c399–c360 B.C.), born c444 B.C.; died in Libya, c360 B.C. He was a younger son of Archidamus II, of the Eurypontid line of Spartan rulers, by his second wife Eupolia. Because his older half-brother Agis was the heir, Agesilaus was not trained for kingship, but shared in the regular training of Spartan youths. Archidamus had been fined by the Spartans when he married Eupolia, because she was a small woman and would bear, they said, "not kings but kinglets." To the extent that Agesilaus was of modest stature and lame, their prophecy was carried out. He did not let his lameness interfere with his activities; rather, he was the bolder in spirit to compensate for it. When Agis died (398 B.C.) Lysander, a Spartan general and intimate of Agesilaus, promoted Agesilaus for the throne on the grounds that Leotychidas, who passed as the son of Agis, was actually the son of Alcibiades who was rumored to have had a liaison with the wife of Agis when he deserted Athens for Sparta. However, an oracle stood in the way of the accession of Agesilaus; "Bethink thee now, O Sparta, though thou art very glorious, lest from thee, sound of foot, there spring a maimed royalty . . ." Diviners said the oracle forbade Sparta to take a lame king. Lysander countered by saying the "maimed royalty" of the oracle referred to the illegitimacy of Leotychidas, who was not a true descendant of Heracles. His view prevailed and Agesilaus became king (c399 B.C.). He won the respect of the ephors by his seeming deference, and won the love of the people by

the simplicity of his personal life. Having done so, he had the essence rather than the appearance of power. He showed himself honorable in dealing with his enemies and supported his friends unreservedly, even when their actions were unjust or harmful to the state. His loyalty to his friends, in fact, sometimes led to disaster. When word came that the Persians were gathering their forces, Lysander persuaded Agesilaus to march against them and to help the friends he had established in power in Asia Minor. Agesilaus, who dreamed of conquering Persia, went to Aulis to assemble his forces, following in the path of Agamemnon, "king of men." At Aulis he was advised in a vision to sacrifice to Artemis as Agamemnon had done before sailing to Troy. Agesilaus promised a sacrifice that would be pleasing to the goddess but would not imitate the cruelty of Agamemnon's sacrifice of his daughter. He ordered a hind to be garlanded and offered up by his own priests. The Thebans, enraged that a foreign priest should sacrifice on their soil without their permission, disrupted the ceremony and carried off the thighs of the victim. Agesilaus was troubled by this unfavorable circumstance, and never forgave the Thebans. He went to Ephesus where he found that Lysander, who had been in the region before and had many friends, was the center of attention and was regarded as the real commander of the expedition. Up to this time, relations between Agesilaus and Lysander had been very close. Now Agesilaus found his own ambitions hindered by the respect in which Lysander was held, and feared that if he did succeed in Asia Lysander would win all the credit. He resolved to nullify Lysander's influence. He refused his advice. Then he denied those who were recommended by Lysander and came to him for help, and aided those known to be unfriendly to Lysander. Instead of giving Lysander a military post of command, he appointed him as his official meat-carver. Lysander, appreciating the situation, asked for and received permission to depart to a region where he could be of real service to his country. Agesilaus marched through Phrygia and conquered many cities. In the spring of 395 B.C. he defeated the Persians on the plain before Sardis. He followed his victory by ravaging Phrygia, the satrapy of Pharnabazus. Pharnabazus came to parley with him. With dignity, he remonstrated with Agesilaus, saying he had been the faithful ally of Sparta in her wars against Athens and now he was rewarded by having his satrapy devastated. Was this justice, he asked, or gratitude? Agesilaus answered that since he was at war with Persia, all satraps must be regarded as his enemies, and invited Pharnabazus to desert the Persian king and join him as an ally. Pharnabazus replied that while he held a post under the Persian king he would support him, and wage war against Sparta with all his power. Agesilaus admired his loyalty. He promised to leave the satrapy and to respect it in the future. Before his interview with Pharnabazus he had received word from Sparta putting him in command of the fleet which was to be assembled. This was the first time the posts of general and admiral had been united in one person. He unwisely entrusted the the command of the fleet to his brother-in-law Pisander, a man of no experience, in order to please his sister. This appointment is an extreme example of the extent to which Agesilaus was at the mercy of his affections with disastrous results for Sparta. He restored order in Asia Minor and planned to pursue and capture the Persian king Artaxerxes II at Susa, in order to bring to an end the continual interference of Persia in Greek affairs, supporting now one now another of them in their internecine wars. Before he could embark on the project, he was called home to subdue the Corinthian League of Greek states that had formed an alliance against Sparta. He marched overland by the route Xerxes had taken when he invaded Greece (480 B.C.), asking permission of the tribes along the way to pass through their territory. Most gave it. One tribe, however, demanded 100 talents of silver and as many women as the price for passage through their land. Agesilaus, retorting that they must come and get it, fought and defeated them. The king of Macedonia said he must deliberate before giving permission to the Spartans to cross his land. "Let him deliberate then," said Agesilaus, "but we will march on." The Macedonian prudently refrained from interfering. The Spartans ravaged Thessaly in their passage because of ancient enmity with the Thessalians. On his homeward journey Agesilaus learned of a battle near Corinth in which some Spartans and many of their enemies had fallen. "Alas for Hellas," he groaned, "which has by her own hands destroyed so many brave men. Had they lived, they could have conquered in battle all the barbarians in the world." On orders from Sparta he invaded Boeotia. At Chaeronea there was an eclipse of the sun. The unfavorable omen was followed by news that Pisander had been thoroughly defeated off Cnidus by a fleet under the command of Conon, the Athenian admiral, and Pharnabazus (394 B.C.). All his work in Asia Minor was now undone, and the Spartan fleet was destroyed. He concealed the news from his army and marched quickly to Coronea where he met the allies—Thebes, Athens, Corinth, and Argos—arrayed against him. He was badly wounded in the battle (394 B.C.) but was awarded the victory when the Thebans asked for a burial truce. The victory was fruitless, as he dared not stay in the area but withdrew to Sparta, where he was warmly welcomed. In 391 B.C. he captured Lechaeum, one of the ports of Corinth, and the following year marched again to the Isthmus and took over the presidency of the Isthmian Games, then being celebrated. The Corinthians nullified his presidency by holding the games all over again as soon as he left. He supported the King's Peace (386 B.C.), handed down by Artaxerxes II, under which the Greek cities of Asia Minor were abandoned to Persia and the Greek states were declared autonomous. However, he violated its terms by sanctioning the seizure of the Theban citadel (382 B.C.) by Phoebidas and the government friendly to Sparta that he set up in Thebes. When the Thebans expelled the Spartans (379 B.C.) he waged war on them, leading expeditions against Thebes in 378 and 377 B.C. The expeditions accomplished nothing and Agesilaus was badly wounded. The wars against Thebes were provoked by Agesilaus more from his hatred of the city than for strategic reasons, and were an open violation of the peace. Even Xenophon, a great admirer of Agesilaus and Spartan institutions, was critical of these violations. He attributed the

fat, fāte, fär, fãre, errant; net, mē, hér ardent; pin, pīne; not, nōte, möve, nôr,

ultimate downfall of Sparta to retribution by the gods for her harsh and unjust actions toward other states. Agesilaus was rebuked by one of his generals, when he was wounded, who said to him, "Indeed, this is a fine tuition-fee which thou art getting from the Thebans, for teaching them how to fight when they did not wish to do it and did not even know how." The expeditions also caused discontent among the Spartan allies. In 371 B.C. an attempt was made to end the crippling warfare by the Peace of Callias. Agesilaus demanded of Epaminondas, the Theban envoy, that the Boeotian cities be permitted, as independent cities, to sign the peace treaty separately. Epaminondas retorted that it would be permitted if Agesilaus acknowledged the independence of the Laconian cities. Agesilaus had no intention of so doing, and Thebes was not a party to the treaty. In the same year the Thebans, under Epaminondas, defeated the Spartans at Leuctra. The following year they invaded the Peloponnesus and pushed into Laconia itself, the first time in 600 years that its borders had been violated. Agesilaus kept the Thebans out of the city of Sparta and withstood a series of attacks, culminating in a campaign by four armies against the unwalled city (369 B.C.) The Spartans, safe within their borders for centuries, were in despair when war touched their land. They longed for peace and began to plot against Agesilaus for preventing it. He seized the plotters and put them to death without trial. He again defended the city (362 B.C.) against a Theban army, and a few days later marched at the head of a force to take part in the battle of Mantinea in which Epaminondas was slain. Afterward, Agesilaus refused to take part in the general peace settlement. His countrymen, worn out by war, no longer honored and respected him; they considered his obstinacy dangerous to his country and his friends. Now in his eighties, he put himself at the head of a band of mercenaries and set out (361 B.C.) for Egypt. He agreed to help the Egyptian Tachos in return for money that he needed to carry on Sparta's wars. The Egyptians knew of Agesilaus by reputation. When they saw the simply clad, lame old man, they mocked him, and he did not receive supreme command

of their expedition as he had expected. A revolt broke out against Tachos. Agesilaus joined the conspirators against him and helped them to gain control in Egypt. They begged him to remain, but he was anxious to return to Sparta. Loaded with honors, gifts, and 230 talents for the war at home, he set sail. On the return voyage he died (c360 B.C.) at a place called the Harbor of Menelaus, on the coast of Libya. His body was enclosed in melted wax and taken to Sparta for burial. He had been a dominating figure in Sparta for over 40 years. He had witnessed his country's triumph over Athens in the Peloponnesian War, and was its king during the period of its greatest power. A story goes that a visitor marveled that Sparta, with its many enemies, had no walls. Agesilaus is said to have pointed to the citizens in arms and replied, "These are the walls of Lacedaemon." He was still king when Sparta lost the rich land of Messenia and was compelled to defend its very citadel against invaders. Wrong-headed but indomitable, he made a final contribution to his country by serving as a mercenary to replenish its empty treasury.

Agger of Servius Tullius (ag'ẽr; sẽr'vi-us tul'i-us). Name given to a stretch of the so-called Servian Wall of Rome, extending from the Colline Gate across the low ground to the Esquiline Gate, adjoining the existing Arch of Gallienus, at the foot of the Esquiline. In the middle of the Agger there was a third gate, the Porta Viminalis. The Agger consisted of a great mound of earth, in front of which there was a ditch 30 feet deep and 100 feet wide. The mound had a massive retaining wall in front, rising 30 feet above the top of the ditch, and a lighter wall at the back.

Agias (ā'ji-as). Greek cyclic poet of Troezen, in the Peloponnesus, fl. c740 B.C.; author of the *Nostoi* (Homeward Voyages) of the Achaean heroes after the siege and fall of Troy.

Agidae (ā'ji-dē) or **Agids** (ā'jidz). Descendants of Agis, the son of Eurysthenes, the senior of the two royal houses of Sparta.

Agis I (ā'jis). Traditionally, king of Sparta (c1032 B.C.). He was the reputed founder of the royal line known as the Agiadae, or Agidae.

actor; up, lūte, pull; oi, oil; ou, out; ᴛʜ, then; ḍ as d or j, ş as s or sh, ṭ as t or ch, ẓ as z or zh.

Agis II. King of Sparta (c427–399 B.C.). He was the son of Archidamus II, of the Eurypontid line of Spartan kings. In 418 B.C. he defeated Athens and her allies in a great battle at Mantinea and restored the prestige to Sparta which it had lost by the surrender at Sphacteria (425 B.C.). In 413 he led an expedition that took and fortified Decelea, from which point the Spartans commanded all Attica. In 405 B.C. he moved his forces up to the walls of Athens, but finding them impregnable he withdrew. The Athenians, defeated at Aegospotami (405), asked for peace and the long Peloponnesian Wars came to an end (404 B.C.). Agis had been one of the two kings of Sparta for almost the entire duration of the wars. During the reign of Agis, Alcibiades, the Athenian general, repudiated at home, came to Sparta. Because of Alcibiades' notorious liaison with Timaea, wife of Agis, her son was not recognized by Agis as his heir on the grounds that he was actually the son of Alcibiades. However, in his last illness Agis was prevailed upon to declare this son, Leotychidas, as his legitimate heir. His earlier refusal to recognize him made it possible for Agesilaus, halfbrother of Agis, to succeed him as king in place of Leotychidas.

Agis III. King of Sparta (338–331 B.C.). He was allied with Persia against Macedon. In an attempt to throw off Macedonian control, while Alexander the Great was in Asia, he was defeated by Antipater, Alexander's regent, at Megalopolis (331 B. C.), where he lost his life in battle.

Agis IV. King of Sparta (244–240 B.C.); son of Eudamidas II of the Eurypontid line of Spartan rulers. He proposed to recruit additions to the ranks of the Spartans from among the Perioeci, and advocated a redistribution of the landed property. In these measures of reform he was opposed by his colleague Leonidas II, of the royal line known as the Agidae, and after some transient successes he was captured and sentenced to death by the Spartan ephors.

Aglaia (ā-glā′i-a). The youngest of the Charites (Graces). Some say she was the wife of Hephaestus. See **Charites.**

Aglaia. In classical legend, the mother, by Abas, of Acrisius and Proetus.

Aglauros (ā-glô′ros). Name used interchangeably with Agraulos, to indicate either the wife or the daughter of Cecrops. See **Agraulos.**

Aglaus (ā-glā′us). In mythology, a son of Thyestes and a naiad. With his brothers Callileon and Orchomenus he was dragged from the altar of Zeus where they had taken refuge, and dismembered by Atreus. The extremities of the three children were kept to one side; the rest of their bodies were cut up, boiled in a cauldron and served to their father at a feast given him by Atreus. This was to punish Thyestes for his adultery with the wife of Atreus. After Thyestes had eaten, the extremities of the children were brought in to prove to Thyestes that he had eaten the flesh of his own sons.

Agora (ag′o-ra). The Greek term meaning "market-place," analogous to the forums of Roman cities. Essentially, it is a considerable open space within the walls; the political, social, and commercial focus of the community where farmers bring their produce for retail sale, businessmen meet their clients and associates, and popular assemblies may be convoked. It is often bordered by stoas (colonnades, porticoes), public offices, and a temple or two. One who speaks of "the Agora," without specifying which city's agora he means, presumably refers to that of Athens, most famous for its association with the city's intellectual and artistic, as well as political and economic, leadership of classical Greece. The Athenian Agora is a broad area extending from the northwest slopes of the Acropolis to the terrace on which the Temple of Hephaestus stands, revealed by extensive excavations conducted by an American mission from 1931 to the present. (JJ)

Agoracritus (ag-ō-rak′ri-tus) or **Agorakritos** (-tos). Greek sculptor, born on the island of Paros in the Aegean Sea, and active in the 5th century B.C. He was a favorite pupil of Phidias and a rival of Alcamenes. He is now remembered chiefly for his work on the *Nemesis at Rhamnus,* fragments of which are in the British Museum and Athens Museum. But some say this statue was by Phidias himself. The bronze image of *Athena Itonia* in the temple at Boeotia was made by Agoracritus.

Agoraea (ag-o-rē′a). An epithet of Athena, meaning "Of the Market-place."

fat, fāte, fär, fâre, errant; net, mē, hėr ardent; pin, pīne; not, nōte, mȯve, nôr,

Agoraeus (ag-o̜-rē'us). Epithet, meaning "Of the Market-place." It was applied especially to Zeus and to Hermes. There were sanctuaries of Zeus Agoraeus (among others) at Sparta, Olympia, and Thebes.

Agrae (ā'grē). Suburb of ancient Athens extending E from opposite the temple of Olympian Zeus over the hills of the S bank of the Ilissus. In it lies the Panathenaic Stadium. In this area, southeast of the Acropolis on the Ilissus River, the Lesser Mysteries, established by Demeter in honor of Heracles, were celebrated.

Agraeus (ag-rē'us). An epithet of Apollo, meaning "Hunter."

Agraulos (a̜-grô'lus). In Greek mythology, the wife of Cecrops, the first king of Attica, and the mother of Agraulos the Younger, Herse, and Pandrosos. Athena entrusted her with a casket to guard, with orders not to look inside it. One day, overcome by curiosity, Agraulos and her daughters opened the casket and beheld in it the infant Erichthonius whose body ended in a serpent's tail. Agraulos and her daughters were so terrified they leaped to their deaths from the Acropolis. But some say Agraulos leaped from the Acropolis during an attack on Athens in response to an oracle which said the city would be saved by such a sacrifice. There was a sanctuary of Agraulos on the Acropolis, where young Athenian warriors took an oath "to regard wheat, barley, the vine, and the olive as the natural boundaries of Attica" and to defend those boundaries with their lives.

Agraulos the Younger. In Greek mythology, a daughter of Cecrops, king of Athens, and Agraulos. She demanded much gold from Hermes in return for furthering his cause with her sister Herse. Having offended Athena, Agraulos was made to fall in love with Hermes, and in an attempt to bar him from seeing Herse she was turned to stone. Some say Agraulos was a daughter of Alcippe by Ares. See **Herse.** (AH)

Agreus (a̜-grē'us). A name, meaning "Wild," which was given by the myrtle-nymphs to Aristaeus when they were rearing him.

Agricola (a̜-grik'ō-la̜), **Cnaeus Julius.** Roman soldier and politician; born at Forum Julii (now Frejus, France), 40 A.D.; died at Rome, 93 A.D. He was the father-in-law of Taci-

tus. Quaestor in Asia (63) under Salvius Titianus; made commander (70) of the XXth Legion in Britain by Vespasian; governor of Aquitania (74–76); elected consul (77) and assigned to southern Britain, where in seven campaigns (78–84) he extended Roman law to the northern boundary of Perth and Argyll. He may have been poisoned by agents of the emperor. Tacitus' *Agricola,* an account of his life and accomplishments, is generally considered to be an outstanding example of good classical biography.

Agrigentum (ag-ri-jen'tum). See **Acragas.**

Agrionia (ag-ri-ō'ni-a̜). An annual feast, held at Orchomenus, in which the sacrifice of Hippasus by his mother Leucippe and her sisters was ritually reënacted. The feast was to atone for the murder.

Agriope (ag-rī'ō̜-pē). A name sometimes given to Eurydice, wife of Orpheus.

Agrippa (a̜-grip'a̜), **Marcus Vipsanius.** Roman soldier and politician, born at Rome, 63 B.C.; died in Campania, 12 B.C. He rose from a humble birth to become son-in-law, friend, and counselor to Augustus. He put down the Aquitanian revolt (38 B.C.) in Gaul, was elected consul (37) and defeated (36) Sextus Pompeius Magnus (often called Pompey the Younger) at Mylae and Naulochus. He became aedile in 33, and defeated (31) Antony's fleet at Actium. Recalled from the governorship of Syria to become (23) Augustus' chief counselor, he shared the tribuneship with Augustus (18 B.C. *et seq.*). Agrippa was married to a daughter of Octavia the niece of Augustus but when Julia, the daughter of Augustus, was widowed, Augustus persuaded Agrippa to divorce his wife, the mother of his children, and marry Julia who was young enough to be his daughter and whose reputation for immoral living was to become the scandal of Rome. Julia bore three sons, Gaius, Lucius, and Agrippa Postumus, to Agrippa, and two daughters, Julia and Agrippina the Elder. Many of the military successes of the reign of Augustus were due to the capacity of Agrippa. He is also known for his geographical writings.

Agrippa Postumus (pos'tū-mus). Posthumous son of Marcus Vipsanius Agrippa by Julia, the daughter of Augustus. He was born 12 B.C. and died 14 A.D. He was adopted by Augustus in 4 B.C. Accused of plotting against Augustus, he was exiled. On the accession of Tiberius, he was murdered, possibly by the order of Livia, widow of Augustus, who was determined that none of the heirs of Augustus' body should be left living as a possible threat to her own son Tiberius.

Agrippina (ag-ri-pī′na), **Julia.** [Called **Agrippina the Younger.**] Daughter of Germanicus and Vipsania Agrippina. She was born at Oppidum Ubiorum (later named, for her, Colonia Agrippina, now Cologne), c15 A.D. She was killed near Baiae (now Baia), on the Bay of Naples, 59 A.D. She married Domitius Ahenobarbus and by him was the mother of the future emperor Nero. She later married Crispus Passienus and in 49 A.D. her uncle, the emperor Claudius, whom she poisoned (54) after excluding his son Britannicus from the throne in favor of Nero. She was influential during the early part of Nero's reign, but was eventually murdered at his orders after she threatened to support the claims of Britannicus.

Agrippina, Vipsania. [Called **Agrippina the Elder.**] Roman matron, born c13 B.C.; died at Pandataria, 33 A.D. She was known for the loftiness of her character. She was the youngest daughter of Marcus Vipsanius Agrippa and Julia, daughter of Augustus, and the wife of Germanicus and mother of Caligula. She accompanied her husband on his military campaigns and was with him at Antioch when he was poisoned (19 A.D.). She returned to Rome and publicly denounced the governor of Syria, Calpurnius Piso, as the poisoner. By implication, her accusation involved the emperor Tiberius himself. Her accusation, the popularity with which her husband had been regarded, and the popular feeling which his death aroused, promoted the jealous hatred of Tiberius and Sejanus. She was banished to the lonely island of Pandataria (Ventotene) off the Campanian coast, where she was flogged so savagely that she lost an eye. Her sons, the elder of them at least, were ordered starved to death. Agrippina, some say, starved herself to death, although Tiberius ordered her jaws pried apart for forcible feeding. But others say Tiberius himself ordered her to die by starvation.

Agrius (ā′gri-us). In Greek mythology, one of the Giants, a son of Gaea and the blood of Uranus, who waged war on the gods. In the battle the Fates crushed his head with a brass pestle and Heracles dispatched him.

Agrius. In Greek mythology, a centaur who, aroused by the aroma of the wine of Dionysus, attacked Heracles when he was visiting Pholus on his way to capture the Erymanthian Boar. Heracles drove him off.

Agrius. In Greek mythology, one of the three sons Circe bore to Odysseus when he visited her on her island. The other two were Latinus and Telegonus.

Agrius. In Greek legend, an Aetolian, the father of Thersites. The latter was noted as the person with the foulest tongue and ugliest appearance of all the Greeks at Troy.

Agrotera (ag-rŏ′te-ra). An epithet of Artemis, meaning "the Huntress." Alcathous, son of Pelops, raised a sanctuary of Artemis Agrotera at Megara in gratitude to the goddess for her help in killing the Cithaeronian Lion. Apollo Agraeus (*Hunter*) shared the sanctuary with her. There was a temple of Artemis Agrotera across the Ilissus, the river of Athens, in a district called Agrae. The image in the temple carried a bow, for they say that Artemis first hunted here when she came from Delos. Five hundred goats were annually sacrificed to Artemis Agrotera on the anniversary of the battle of Marathon. This was done because, before the battle, the Athenians had vowed to sacrifice to Artemis as many goats as would equal the number of Persians they slew. But they killed so many of their enemy that they did not have goats enough to fulfill the vow. Instead they resolved to sacrifice 500 goats every year.

Agyieus (a-gwī′ūs). An epithet of Apollo. As Apollo Agyieus he was "God of Streets," who kept out the bad and let in the good. Before each house was his symbol, a plain pillar with a conical top, or sometimes a pillar with a head or face painted on the top. This symbol was honored with offerings of wreaths and ribbons.

Agyieus. Named by some as a Hyperborean priest who established the worship of Apollo at Delphi.

Ahala (a-hā′la), **Cnaeus Servilius Structus.** Roman patrician, master of the horse in 439 B.C. (according to the common chronology), and slayer of the popular leader Spurius Maelius.

fat, fāte, fär, fãre, errant; net, mē, hèr ardent; pin, pīne; not, nōte, mõve, nôr,

Ahasuerus (a̧-has-ū-ē′rus). In the Old Testament, a Persian shah, mentioned as the father of Darius the Mede (Dan. ix. 1). He has been variously identified as Astyages and Cyaxares.

Ahasuerus. In the Old Testament, a great ruler of Persia, and husband of Esther, probably identical with Xerxes I. He is mentioned in Ezra, iv. 6., and throughout the Book of Esther.

Ahenobarbus (a̧-hē-no̧-bär′bus, a̧-hen-o̧-), **Cnaeus Domitius.** Roman official, fl. 104–92 B.C. He was the father of Lucius Domitius Ahenobarbus. A tribune (104 BC.), pontifex maximus (103), consul (96), and censor (92), he framed the law, later repealed by Sulla, that priests of certain classes should be selected by the lay citizenry rather than by each other.

Ahenobarbus, Lucius Domitius. Roman official and political opportunist, fl. 54–48 B.C.; son of Cnaeus Domitius Ahenobarbus. He was a consul in 54 B.C. and Caesar's successor as governor of Gaul in 49 B.C. He opposed both Caesar and Pompey, but later attached himself to Pompey and was slain after the defeat at Pharsalus.

Aidoneus (ā-i-dō′nūs, -nȩ̄-us). In Greek legend, a king in Thesprotia. Some say it was his wife whom Pirithous and Theseus tried to steal, and not Persephone the wife of Hades. Perhaps confusion was caused because Aidoneus is a poetic term meaning Hades. In any event, those who hold to this story say that Aidoneus captured the would-be abductors, hurled Pirithous to the dogs, and cast Theseus into a dungeon from which he was subsequently rescued by Heracles.

Aidos (ī′dos). In Greek mythology, the personification of Conscience, or the shame that is caused by conscience. Her altar was on the Acropolis at Athens, near the temple of Athena, whose nurse she was said to have been. Aidos was thought to be a deity that ranged the earth, and did not live among the immortal gods in Olympus. At the theater of Dionysus a seat was reserved for the priestess of Aidos.

Aigai (ī′gī). [Modern name, **Nimrud-Kalessi.**] In ancient geography, a town in Aeolia, Asia Minor. On its site are the ruins of various ancient structures.

Aigion (e′yôn). [Also: **Aiyion, Aegion.**] See **Aegium.**

Aissa (a̧-is′a̧). One of the names, meaning "Fleet," under which Achilles is said to have been known when, in order to avoid serving with the Greek forces at Troy, he lived at the court of Lycomedes in Scyrus disguised as a girl.

Aius Locutius (ā′i-us lo̧-kū′shus). In Roman legend, a voice that was heard in the dead of night (c390 B.C.). Marcus Caedicius, a Roman citizen, was walking along the Via Nova on his way home when he heard a great voice. He turned but could see no one. Again he heard the voice, which said in loud, clear tones, "Harken, Marcus Caedicius; early in the morning go and tell the magistrates that within a little time they must expect the Gauls." The next day Marcus Caedicius went to the magistrates as he was bid, but the tribunes mocked him and paid no attention to the warning. Not long afterward (390 B.C.) the Gauls came and sacked Rome. When they were at last driven out, the warning voice was remembered and Camillus, the victorious Roman dictator, raised a temple and an altar to Aius Locutius (the *Voice,* or the *Announcing Voice*), on the exact spot where Marcus Caedicius stood when he heard it.

Ajax (ā′jaks), **Telamonian** or **Great.** In Greek legend, a son of Telamon of Salamis and Periboea. Before he was born, Heracles visited his parents in Salamis. Observing that Periboea was about to produce a child, he prayed to Zeus that she would bear a son whose skin was as tough as a lion's and whose courage would match it. Zeus sent an eagle to show that his prayer was heard. When Ajax was born, Heracles covered him with his own lion's skin, and made him invulnerable except in the neck and armpit that had not been covered by the skin. Ajax became king of Megara, and was a suitor of Helen. Like her other suitors, he took an oath to defend the man she chose as her husband if that man should ever suffer ill on account of his marriage. To carry out his oath, he joined Achilles, his beloved cousin, and the other Greek captains who sailed to Troy to recover Helen when she was carried off by Paris. Next to Achilles he was the handsomest and the bravest of the Greeks. He also stood head and shoulders above them in stature. In the tenth year of the Trojan War he accepted Hector's challenge to the Greeks to engage in single combat. They fought all day and when the contest ended with neither gaining the advantage the heroes exchanged gifts, each praising the other's prowess.

AJAX CARRYING THE BODY OF ACHILLES
Black-figured Greek crater, signed by Cleitias and Ergotimus, c570 B.C. *Archaeological Museum, Florence*

Hector gave Ajax his sword and Ajax gave Hector his gleaming belt. In the war Ajax fought side by side with his half-brother Teucer who was a skilled bowman. Teucer dodged out from the shelter of Ajax' shield to shoot his deadly arrows. Among his many deeds in the Trojan War he acted as one of the envoys who went to Scyrus to fetch Achilles to the war; later he was one of the ambassadors who went to Achilles' tent to try to persuade him to return to the war after his quarrel with Agamemnon; with Menelaus he rescued Odysseus when the latter was cut off and surrounded by the Trojans; with the Lesser Ajax he held off the enemy from the Greek ships; he defended the body of Patroclus and fought off the Trojans until it could be rescued by his comrades. When Penthesilea the Amazon came to the aid of the Trojans after the death of Hector, she furiously drove the Greeks back. Ajax, mourning with Achilles over the death of Patroclus, heard the clamor

and roused Achilles. They immediately joined the fray. Penthesilea sprang at them like a leopard. She hurled her lance at Ajax but it glanced off harmlessly, as fate had decreed that no enemy's blade would taste his blood. He drove the Trojans back and left Achilles to deal with Penthesilea. Together, Ajax and Achilles seemed irresistible, but Ajax' courage and skill were his undoing. As he left his home his father admonished him to go forth and win, but to win with the gods on his side. Ajax boasted that any fool could win with the help of the gods; he would gain honor and glory by himself. He refused to acknowledge Agamemnon as his commander on the grounds that he had come to Troy of his own free will, in fulfillment of his oath, and was not subject to anyone. In battle he rejected the aid of Athena and advised her to go and help those who needed it, for the line would not break where he was in command. The gods did not forget. After the death of Achilles, his mother Thetis commanded that her son's arms be given to the mightiest of the Argives. Only Odysseus and Ajax dared claim them, although it was Ajax who had borne the body of dead Achilles back to his comrades through the very ranks of the enemy. Ajax suggested that Idomeneus, Nestor, and Agamemnon should choose which of them had earned the arms. Nestor grieved; for he said that whoever was not selected would be lost to the Greeks. He suggested that they let the captive Trojans decide who had done them the most harm—Ajax or Odysseus. Ajax was insulted. He accused Odysseus of cowardice, reminding him that he had tried to escape coming to Troy in the first place. He scornfully pointed out that Odysseus had his ships in the center of the line where they would be protected, whereas Ajax had his own ships guarding the flank of the line. He challenged Odysseus to a duel to decide who should have the arms. Odysseus replied that strength was not wisdom, and that his wisdom had meant more to the Greeks than the strength of Ajax. The Trojan captives agreed with Odysseus that his cunning had harmed them more than Ajax' valor, and the armor was awarded to Odysseus. Ajax was infuriated, feeling that the armor was rightly his. Moreover, Odysseus was his ancient enemy and he scorned him as an intriguer who fought with words, not with weapons. Crazed with jealousy, he resolved to kill the Greeks who had been responsible for the award. Athena maddened him, so that through one long night he slaughtered innocent cattle under the impression that they were his Greek enemies. He seized a ram and hung it up in his tent and tortured it, thinking that it was Odysseus. Then in the midst of his frenzy Athena restored his sanity. He was appalled and humiliated to learn that he, the bravest of the Greeks, had so disgraced himself by the slaughter of animals. Too late he recognized that he was being punished for his pride. Bidding goodby to his captive wife Tecmessa, who loved him dearly, and to their young son Eurysaces, he went off alone to wash himself clean in the salt sea and to pray to the gods. Finally he fixed his sword, which Hector had given him, in the foreign sands of Troy and hurled himself upon its point. From his blood was said to have sprung up a purple flower bearing on its leaves the letters *ai,* which were the first letters of his name in Greek, and also an exclamation of woe: *alas!* According to some accounts, Menelaus tried to prevent his heartbroken brother Teucer from giving honorable burial to his corpse, and Agamemnon agreed with him, but they were persuaded by Odysseus, who now acknowledged the great contributions and courage of his old enemy, and who even offered to help Teucer with the funeral rites. But others say Agamemnon grieved over the loss of Ajax, and that Odysseus did too, saying that he would never have taken the arms of Achilles if he had known how much they meant to Ajax. It is also said that Ajax' body was not burned as was the custom for warriors who fell in battle, but that he was buried on the headland of Cape Rhoeteum. The arms of Achilles were later given to Neoptolemus, Achilles' son. On the way home from Troy they were lost in the sea during a great storm. Thetis found them and, as recompense to Great Ajax in death, she caused them to be washed ashore on his tomb. Ajax was worshiped as a hero by the Athenians. Each year young men sailed from Athens to Salamis to sacrifice to him.

Ajax the Lesser, or **Oilean Ajax.** In Greek legend, a son of Oileus and Eriopis. He was a captain of Locrians who went with the Greeks to Troy, and although he was small and wore only a linen corselet, he surpassed all the Greeks in skill as a lancer. Also, next to Achilles he was the fleetest runner of the Greeks. As did others, he accepted Hector's challenge to single combat but was eliminated by the drawing of lots. Poseidon, in the guise of Calchas, came to encourage the Greeks after Hector had driven them back to their ships, and put divine strength into the two Ajaxes to stand firm. Ajax, a runner himself, could tell by the legs and ankles that it was not Calchas and realized it was a god who aided them. He fought savagely and, being so swift, slew more Trojans in that fight than any of the other Greeks. He cut off the head of Imbrius and hurled it into the Trojan camp, and when the Trojans at length breached the fortifications he and Telamonian Ajax held them off from the ships. After the fall of Troy the Greeks sacked the city. Ajax found Cassandra in the temple of Athena and dragged her away from the sacred image as his concubine. However, Agamemnon wanted Cassandra. To get her, Odysseus spread the tale that Ajax had committed sacrilege in Athena's shrine. This aroused the wrath of all the Greeks and Cassandra was taken away from him. On the way home from Troy Ajax' ship was wrecked on the Gyraean rocks. Ajax saved himself by climbing onto the rocks but, according to some accounts, was slain by a thunderbolt hurled by Athena to punish him for violating her shrine, in spite of the fact that he had expiated this crime. According to other accounts, it was Poseidon who sundered the rocks with his trident and drowned him. Thus did the gods easily change sides to bring disaster to those they had formerly aided. The spirit of Ajax went to the island of Leuce where it consorted with the spirits of Achilles and Helen. Thetis rescued his body and buried it on the island of Myconus, and for many years thereafter his countrymen annually launched a ship with black sails and burnt it in his honor.

Ajax. Probably the earliest extant tragedy by Sophocles. It treats the death of Ajax, and the respect and compassion felt by

actǫr; up, lūte, pŭll; oi, oil; ou, out; ŦH, then; d̦ as d or j, ş as s or sh, ț as t or ch, z̧ as z or zh.

Odysseus for the brave man who had been his bitter rival.

The scene is before the tent of Ajax in the Greek camp near Troy. Athena addresses Odysseus, who is seen furtively approaching the tent. She asks him why he is at the tent of Ajax, which guards the flank of the camp. He answers that in the night someone slaughtered the cattle and sheep the Greeks had taken as booty; Ajax is suspected of the butchery. It was indeed Ajax, the goddess informs him. He did it to punish the Greeks for awarding the arms of Achilles to Odysseus rather than to him. He intended to kill his fellow Greeks but the goddess inspired Ajax with madness. He slew cattle, roped many of them, and drove them to his tent as prisoners. Odysseus shall see for himself. She calls Ajax. Still under the spell of madness, he comes from his tent and greets Athena but does not see Odysseus whom the goddess has hidden from him. He has killed Agamemnon and Menelaus, he says, for taking away his prize and he has that crafty fox Odysseus trussed up in his tent. He will torture his ancient enemy and then kill him. So saying, he returns to his tent. Athena gloats over the power of the gods to punish those who in their pride of strength blaspheme them, as she has punished Ajax. Odysseus pities his old enemy for the awful fate which has him in its grip. They withdraw. A chorus of sailors, companions of Ajax, enter. They link their fate with that of Ajax. Odysseus has been spreading tales about Ajax, they say. If his tale is true it was the work of a man inspired with madness by some angry god. They appeal to Ajax to come out, to protect and command them. Tecmessa, Ajax' captive wife, comes out. Mighty Ajax has been brought low, she tells the sailors; in a fit of madness he killed cattle under the impression that they were his Greek enemies. But now Ajax has been restored to his senses and his state is even more grievous, for he knows what he has done. She describes his wild rage when the madness was on him, and his terrible anguish when his sanity was restored and he beheld his handiwork. In his present despair she fears he will do some dreadful thing. The sailors hear Ajax groaning and suggest it may calm him to look upon the faces of

his friends. Tecmessa opens the tent door and Ajax, sitting among the slaughtered beasts, is revealed. He asks the sailors, his only friends, to put him out of his misery. He torments himself by picturing the scorn Odysseus and the Greeks will heap upon him—Ajax—the fearless fighter who has slaughtered innocent beasts. This is the end of Ajax, he cries. Well is he named *Aias,* which means "Alas!" He recalls the honor of his family and his own valor in battle. It was Athena's work that he was maddened as he was about to avenge himself on Odysseus and the Atridae for denying him the arms of Achilles, and that he slaughtered dumb beasts instead. And what is now left for him, hated alike by the gods, his fellow-Greeks, and the Trojans? He cannot go home to his father in disgrace. He will have honor in life or he will seek it in death. Tecmessa pleads with him to think what will happen to her if he dies. She loves him. Can he forget that and desert her and their son? He rejects her pleas, then in an address to the sailors he seems to change his mind. Nothing is impossible, he says. The most sacred oath is fallible, a will of iron may bend. He is loath to leave a widow and child among his enemies. He will go to the sea and wash himself clean. Discipline is necessary; henceforth he will obey his commanders, and he will remember that though he now hates his enemy, the time may come when he will have need of him. He asks Tecmessa to pray to the gods for him. Telling his sailors that when next they see him he will be safe, he withdraws.

Presently a messenger enters with the news that Ajax' brother Teucer has returned and has given orders that Ajax must not leave his tent. If he does so, Calchas the seer had warned Teucer that he would never see Ajax again. Calchas said the gods were angry with Ajax for blasphemous boasting, as when he had told his father that any fool could win with the gods beside him but he intended to win glory and honor on his own account. Again, when Athena came to help him in battle he told her to go help others, that he had no need of her assistance: Athena resolved to punish him. But if he could live through this day, he might be saved from the anger of the gods. This is

fat, fāte, fär, fãre, errant; net, mē, hėr ardent; pin, pīne; not, nōte, möve, nôr,

the reason for Teucer's order. But Ajax has already gone. All scatter in alarm to look for him.

In a new scene Ajax appears on the sands. He plants his sword firmly in the earth by the hilt, with the point up. This is Hector's sword, he says, and he will die by it here on enemy soil. He prays to Zeus that Teucer will find his body, that death will come swiftly, and that the Furies will hound the Atridae for causing his death. He bids farewell to the bright day, to his dear and sacred land of Salamis, even to the soil of Troy, then hurls himself on his sword and dies. The sailors and Tecmessa come on the scene. All lament the loss of their leader and protector when Tecmessa finds his body. Teucer rushes in. He is heartbroken at the death of his beloved brother. He says he failed Ajax in his hour of need, and fears the reproaches of his father when he returns without him. He pulls out the sword on which Ajax is impaled, recognizes it as the one Hector had given to him after their duel, and notes sadly that Hector had slain Ajax from beyond the grave. As he prepares to bury Ajax, Menelaus approaches and forbids the burial on the grounds that Ajax was a traitor who would have killed them if it had not been for Athena. Therefore he must suffer the most horrible punishment—denial of the sacred rites of burial. They could not control Ajax while he lived but in his death they can put him in subjection. Teucer hotly defends Ajax. He and Menelaus exchange insults and the latter withdraws. Tecmessa approaches with her son Eurysaces. The sailors grieve. Ajax could protect them; now that he is gone, who knows what will happen to them? Agamemnon strides in and assails Teucer, and also forbids the burial. Teucer cannot believe that the man for whom Ajax fought so valiantly would forget so quickly. As Agamemnon and Teucer wrangle, Odysseus enters. The sailors appeal to him to resolve the quarrel. Odysseus is Agamemnon's most trusted adviser. He advises the latter not to anger the gods by denying this brave man, once his own enemy, the sacred rite of burial; not to let obstinacy betray him into an act of impiety. He is thinking not only of Ajax, he says, but of himself; for one day he will require these

same rites. Agamemnon does not understand, but yields to Odysseus' advice and departs. Teucer, astonished that it should be Odysseus who would champion Ajax, thanks him warmly but politely declines the assistance Odysseus now offers in performing the rites, as he thinks it would be displeasing to Ajax even in death. Odysseus accepts this decision, and Teucer calls on the dead man's son Eurysaces to help prepare the rites for his father.

Alabanda (al-a-ban′da). Ancient city of Caria, Asia Minor, on the site of the modern Arap Hissar. It is said to have been founded by Alabandus, who was later regarded by the inhabitants as a deity. (JJ)

Alabastrum (al-a-bas′trum) or **Alabastron** (-tron). In ancient Greece, a small elongated vase for unguents or perfumes, rounded at the bottom and provided with a broad rim about a small orifice. Vases of this class were originally so called because made of alabaster; but the name was applied also to vessels of similar form and use in other materials, as metal, glass (sometimes richly ornamented in color), or pottery.

Alalcomenae (al-al-kọ-mē′nẹ). In ancient geography, a village of Boeotia, named, some say, for the aboriginal Alalcomeneus who brought up Athena; others say it was named for Alalcomenia, a daughter of the aboriginal Boeotian king Ogygus. Nearby was a stream named Triton near which the inhabitants claimed Athena was born. The temple of Athena in the village housed an ivory image of the goddess. When the Roman Sulla was raging through Greece in the 1st century B.C., he is said to have stolen the ivory image.

Alalcomenean (al-al-kọ-mē′nẹ-an) **Athena.** An epithet of Athena, with reference to the story that she was brought up in the home of Alalcomeneus in Boeotia, and was thereafter considered to be the guardian of Boeotia.

Alalcomeneus (al-al-kọ-mē′nūs). According to legendary accounts, the first man. He appeared near Lake Copaïs in Boeotia. He was the founder of Alalcomenae in Boeotia, and was said to have brought up Athena in his house. He built a temple to Athena in Alalcomenae.

Alastor (a-las′tọr). In Greek mythology, an

epithet of Zeus as the avenger; also applied to any avenging deity or demon.

Alba Fucentia (al′ba̤ fu-sen′shi-a̤) or **Alba Fucens** (fu′senz). [Modern name, **Alba Fucense, Albe.**] Village near Avezzano, in C Italy, in the province of Aquila. It contains an ancient amphitheater of the usual Roman elliptical plan, 114 by 305 feet, estimated to have seated 20,000 people. The arena measures 68 by 159 feet. The site also preserves extensive polygonal limestone fortification walls of c300 B.C., and in recent years excavations have revealed a forum of unusual archaeological interest.

Alba Longa (al′ba̤ long′ga̤). In ancient geography, a town in Latium, Italy, about 15 miles SE of Rome, the ancient center of the Latin League. Its foundation is traditionally ascribed to Ascanius, son of Aeneas, and its destruction (665 B.C.) to Tullus Hostilius.

Alban Hills (al′ba̤n). [Italian, **Monti Laziali, Monti Albani.**] Mountain group SE of Rome, near Albano Laziale. Its highest point is Monte Cavo.

Albanus, Lacus (al-bā′nus lā′kus). [Italian, **Lago (di) Albano, Lago di Castello.**] Small lake in C Italy, noted for its picturesque scenery and occupying the crater of an extinct volcano. At the beginning of the 4th cenuty B.C. the Romans were besieging the Etruscan city of Veii. According to the tale, in the course of the ten-year siege the waters of the Alban Lake, confined within their rocky walls, were observed to rise gently in an extremely dry summer. The waters rose steadily, overflowed the crater's rim and rushed down to flood the surrounding fields. News of this prodigy reached the enemy in Veii. An Etruscan soothsayer there laughed with glee when he heard of it. A Roman soldier who had become friendly with the soothsayer during the long siege lured him to the Roman camp, where he was imprisoned and compelled to interpret the prodigy concerning the waters of Albanus Lacus. He said there was an ancient oracle that Veii could never be captured until the waters of the Alban Lake overflowed and then were reconfined so that they did not mingle with the waters of the sea. The Roman Senate distrusted the enemy soothsayer, and sent to Delphi to inquire into the matter. The priestess told the Roman envoys that the Romans had neglected certain ceremonies in connection with the Latin feasts. She added that the waters must be confined; they must under no condition be allowed to flow to the sea. If the Romans could not force them back, they were instructed to dig ditches and canals to absorb the waters and thus prevent them from flowing to the sea. On receiving the instructions from Delphi the Roman priests offered sacrifices; the Romans set to work and dug canals and ditches to drain off the water. Shortly thereafter, under Camillus in 396 B.C., the Romans captured Veii. Another explanation for the construction of the canals and the channel bored through rock (still in existence) lies in the utilization of the water for purposes of irrigation.

Albinus (al-bī′nus), **Spurius Postumius.** Roman consul (334 and 321 B.C.); fl. late 4th century B.C. He was a commander at the defeat of the Romans by the Samnites at the Caudine Forks.

Albunea (al-bu′nē-a̤) or **Albuna** (al-bū′na̤). In Roman mythology, a fountain nymph who had the gift of prophecy. She was said to have inhabited a fountain near the grove of Faunus.

Alcaeus (al-sē′us). A legendary son of Perseus and Andromeda. He was the father of Amphitryon and Anaxo by Astydamia, daughter of Pelops; or by Laonome, or by Hipponome, daughter of Menoeceus. His grandson Heracles was called Alcaeus before he was given the more famous heroic name.

Alcaeus. In Greek mythology, a son of Androgeus, and a grandson of Minos, king of Crete. He was bequeathed the island of Paros by Rhadamanthys, his great-uncle. Heracles, on his way to fetch the girdle of the Amazon queen, stopped at Paros for water. Two of his crew were killed by the inhabitants. In retaliation he waged war on the Parians. At length they sued for peace and offered him any two men he might choose to atone for the two sailors they had killed. Heracles chose Alcaeus and his brother. They went aboard his ship and accompanied him to the land of the Amazons.

Alcaeus (al-sē′us) or **Alkaios** (-kī′os). Greek poet who flourished in Mytilene in Lesbos, c611–580 B.C. He fought against Athens for possession of Sigeum but was defeated and lost his shield to the enemy. Next, because he joined with the aristocrats of his native city in their struggle against the tyrants, he was banished, and spent many years traveling about as a soldier of fortune. Ultimately he was pardoned and invited to return to Mytilene. The lyrics of Alcaeus, in Aeolic dialect, are thought to be the prototype of Sappho's who was a contemporary of his. The existence of fragments of complimentary verses exchanged between the two poets has led some to believe that they were romantically attached to each other. Fragments of the hymns, political songs, drinking songs, and love songs, which made up ten books in the Library at Alexandria, survive. He was the probable inventor of the Alcaic verse, a metrical form much used by later classical poets.

Alcaids (al-kā′idz). A name meaning "Descendants of Alcaeus." It was applied especially to the children of Megara and Heracles as supposed descendants of Alcaeus.

Alcamenes or **Alkamenes** (al-kam′e̞-nēz). Greek sculptor, born at Lemnos or Athens and active c450–c400 B.C. According to Pausanias he was the most skillful pupil of Phidias and, like him, worked in gold, ivory, and bronze as well as in marble. He probably assisted Phidias in the decoration of the Parthenon. He is known to have done *Aphrodite of the Gardens* (a copy of which is now at Athens), which is considered a masterpiece of his period, and bronze cult statues of Athena and Hephaestus in the temple of Hephaestus overlooking the Athenian Agora. The famous caryatids of the Maiden Porch of the Erechtheum on the Athenian Acropolis have also been attributed to him, on stylistic grounds.

Alcandre (al-kan′drē). In Homeric legend (*Odyssey*), the wife of Polybus, king of Egyptian Thebes. She entertained Menelaus and Helen when they stopped there on their way home from Troy, and gave Helen rich gifts.

Alcathous (al-kath′o̞-us). In Greek mythology, a son of Pelops and Hippodamia. He won Euauchme, daughter of King Megareus, according to some accounts, by killing a lion that had slain Megareus' son. He succeeded Megareus as king of Megara and with the help of Apollo rebuilt the walls of the city. In the course of constructing the walls Apollo leaned his lyre against one of the stones and ever afterward that stone sounded a musical note when it was struck with a pebble.

Alcathous. In the *Iliad,* a Trojan chieftain who was married to Aeneas' sister, Hippodamia. He led a group at the siege of the Greek fortifications and was slain by Idomeneus.

Alcathous. In Greek legend, one of the last Trojans slain by Achilles. Achilles had been wounded and his life, but not his fighting spirit, was draining away when he flung his spear at Alcathous and killed him.

Alcathous. In Greek legend, one of the suitors of Hippodamia, daughter of Oenomaus. He was killed by Oenomaus after being overtaken in the race which Oenomaus required of all the suitors of Hippodamia. Some say that he was buried near the racetrack at Olympia and that it was his ghost that ever after frightened the horses of charioteers, making them rear and overturn the chariots, unless the spirit was propitiated with appropriate sacrifices.

Alcestis (al-ses′tis). A legendary daughter of Pelias, king of Iolcus. According to some accounts, she refused to take part with her sisters in the spurious rites Medea proposed to prolong her father's life, but which resulted in his death. These accounts say that Jason then gave her as wife to Admetus, king of Pherae. Others say that Admetus won her by yoking a boar and a lion to a chariot and successfully driving them. In any event, she was the wife of Admetus, who had been promised by Artemis that when Death came for him, he would be spared if he could find a substitute to go in his place. When the time came all too soon, no one was willing to go in place of Admetus except his devoted wife Alcestis. She gave her life that Admetus might be spared. But she did not remain long in the Underworld. On learning of her sacrifice Admetus' friend Heracles went to the Underworld, wrestled with Death to secure her release, and restored her to Admetus. The story of Alcestis' nobility and unselfishness, contrasted with Admetus' willingness to give up what he most loved in order to live a little longer, is told by Euripides in his drama *Alcestis* (q.v.).

Alcestis. A tragi-comedy by Euripides, produced in 438 B.C. It deals with Alcestis, wife

actŏr; up, lūte, pŭll; oi, oil; ou, out; ₮н, then; ḍ as d or j, ş as s or sh, ţ as t or ch, ẕ as z or zh.

of King Admetus of Pherae, who consented to die in her husband's place.

The scene is at Pherae, outside the palace of King Admetus. Apollo, carrying a golden bow, comes from the palace. Angered because a thunderbolt had felled his son Asclepius, Apollo killed the Cyclopes who forged the thunderbolt. To punish him, Zeus commanded Apollo to serve Admetus as a herdsman. Admetus was kind and just. To reward him, Apollo secured a promise from the Fates that on the day Admetus was meant to die, he could escape his fate if another would consent to take his place. When that day came none could be found; not even his aged father and mother, who were almost at the end of their lives, would make this sacrifice. At last Alcestis, the loyal wife of Admetus, volunteered in order to save her husband. Now the day for her departure for the realm of death is here. Apollo must leave in order to escape pollution. Death enters with a drawn sword in his hand. He berates Apollo for cheating him of his true prey. Apollo jests with him, and attempts to dissuade him from taking Alcestis, but in vain. Death enters the palace to find his quarry and Apollo departs. A chorus of elders enters, mourning for Alcestis, and unsure whether she is dead or still alive. One of the handmaidens of Alcestis tells them that her mistress is already in her death robes. She has prepared herself for death, prayed for the welfare of her children, and said farewell to her marriage bed. All in the palace weep for her. The agony of Admetus will be worse than if he had died as fated. The chorus prays for a reprieve, for a rescuer who will save Alcestis.

A funeral procession comes from the palace. Admetus supports his fainting wife. Their children are with them. Alcestis calls out that death is near. She reminds Admetus, who begs her not to leave him, of the gift of life she gives him with her death, a gift not even his own parents would proffer. She begs him not to set another woman over her children. Admetus promises. He wishes he might charm the gods as Orpheus did; then he would recover Alcestis from Hades. He swears that when he dies, he will be put in the same tomb with her. Alcestis grows faint and dies. All mourn. Admetus swears

to honor her above all, since she alone would die for him. Her body is carried back into the palace, with Admetus and his children in attendance. The elders sing an ode in praise of Alcestis.

Heracles, clad in a lion's skin, enters and addresses the elders. He is on his way to fetch the mares of Diomedes as one of his labors for Eurystheus. While he talks, Admetus, dressed in mourning, comes from the palace. He welcomes Heracles, but does not speak of his loss. He says merely that he must bury a corpse and answers Heracles' questions evasively, so that the latter does not know who has died. Heracles does not wish to intrude and prepares to leave, but Admetus insists that he remain and assures him that his visit will not be marred by the sound of lamentation, for he will put Heracles in a secluded part of the palace. Some attendants lead Heracles off to his quarters. The chorus cannot understand why Admetus has hidden from Heracles the news of Alcestis' death. Admetus tells them that if Heracles knew of his misfortune, he would never enter the palace. Rather than violate the laws of hospitality, Admetus has not exhibited his private grief and will not let it affect Heracles, although he knows some will criticize him for this. He enters the palace and returns, leading the funeral procession for Alcestis. Among the mourners is Pheres, father of Admetus. He greets the body of Alcestis. Admetus berates him. If Pheres had been a proper father, he would have died in Admetus' place and Alcestis would be alive. Each accuses the other of cowardice, the one on the ground that, though he is old, he would not die for his son; the other because he let his wife die for him. Admetus sends his father away, saying he is no true father, and leads the procession to the funeral pyre.

A servant in mourning hurries out of the palace and complains about the strange guest who has come. This guest does not honor the grief of the king. Instead he puts flowers on his head and is making merry with wine. Heracles reels out and chides them all for their gloomy faces. He would like to see a little gaiety. He urges them to take a drink and to cheer up. As he talks the servant realizes that Heracles does not know who it

---

fat, fāte, fär, fâre, errạnt; net, mē, hėr ardẹnt; pin, pīne; not, nōte, mŏve, nôr,

was that has died, and at last he tells him. Heracles is smitten with remorse for his levity. He resolves to rescue Alcestis from Hades. He will go down there, wrestle with Death and restore Alcestis to her husband. He departs.

Admetus returns from the funeral pyre, mourning the loss of Alcestis. The chorus tries to encourage him, but it is useless. He now knows it would have been better to have died himself than to permit the sacrifice Alcestis has made and so bring shame on himself as well as grief. He covers his head and weeps. Now Heracles returns, leading a veiled woman. He blames Admetus for not telling him Alcestis was dead, but to show he forgives him he offers Admetus the veiled woman whom he says he won in a wrestling match. He asks Admetus to take her into his house and care for her. Admetus protests that he will take no woman into his house. He will always honor Alcestis and keep his promise to her. He begs Heracles to take away this woman, whose form is so like that of Alcestis. The chorus says he must take a gift offered by the gods. Heracles tells him that he cannot mourn forever; it is true that he has lost a good wife but time will heal his wound. He persists and at last Admetus, protesting that he loves only Alcestis and always will, agrees to take the woman's hand and lead her into the palace. He puts out his hand but turns his head away. Heracles places the hand of the veiled woman in the hand of Admetus and snatches off the veil. Saying that Admetus will not deny that Heracles is a grateful guest, he commands Admetus to look at the woman and see if she is not like Alcestis. Admetus does so, and is startled, but is finally persuaded that this is his dear Alcestis, restored to him by Heracles. He welcomes her with rapture.

Alcibiades (al-si-bĭ′a-dēz). Athenian general and politician, born c450 B.C. at Athens; killed at Melissa, Phrygia, 404 B.C. His father was Clinias, who claimed descent from Eurysaces, the son of Telamonian Ajax. On his mother's side he was a member of the wealthy Alcmaeonid family. His father, who had fought bravely at Artemisium (480 B.C.), was killed (447) fighting the Boeotians and Alcibiades was brought up as a ward of Pericles, one of his kinsmen. From child-

hood he loved rivalry and sought preëminence. A story is told that once as a youth he was wrestling, and to prevent his opponent from gaining a fall, he bit him. His opponent accused him of biting "as women do." "Not as women do," Alcibiades retorted, "but as lions do." He pursued his studies successfully but was not a docile scholar. He refused to play the flute on the ground that it made men look ridiculous when they puffed and blew out their cheeks. He justified his refusal to play it by citing the goddess Athena, who threw the flute away in disgust when she saw how it distorted her face, and the god Apollo, who flayed the flute-player Marsyas. He consented to play the lyre, which a gentleman could play with dignity, while at the same time he could converse or sing in company with it. As he grew up he drew many prominent and able men to him with his brilliant youthful beauty, and in the fashion of the time had many who sought his company. To them he displayed unparalleled insolence, which had the effect apparently of binding them even more securely to him. Once, it is said, Anytus, one of his most ardent admirers, invited him to a banquet. Alcibiades did not attend. He spent the evening drinking with his companions; then going to the house of Anytus and, observing the gold and silver cups on the banquet table, he sent in a servant to sweep up half of them and carried them away. Anytus refused to be insulted. On the contrary, he remarked that Alcibiades had shown great kindness in taking only half of his cups. On another occasion because of a wager he struck Hipponicus, the father of Callias, with his fist. The unwarranted assault aroused great indignation in the city. The next day Alcibiades went to the house of Hipponicus, took off his cloak, and invited Hipponicus to beat him. Hipponicus forgave him, refused to scourge him and later gave him his daughter Hipparete in marriage. Hipparete was a discreet and affectionate wife and bore his children. However, Alcibiades continued to carry on scandalous and public affairs with various courtesans. Hipparete left him and finally sued for divorce. When she appeared in court, Alcibiades strode in, seized her and carried her off through the agora to his home. She lived with him until her death, which occurred not long afterward. He had a famous stable of horses and once entered seven racing chariots in the games at Olympia—the only man ever to enter so many—and won first, second, and fourth (or third) prizes. Such an extravagant display made a great stir in Athens and in the other cities as well, and Nicias cited it as an instance of the arrogance of Alcibiades. Alcibiades justified his extravagance on the ground that it glorified Athens. The people were delighted with his retort. Along with his arrogance and lawlessness, he had such brilliance and excellent native qualities that he won the devoted friendship of Socrates, the only man he respected and loved. Socrates feared that Alcibiades would be ruined by those who pandered to him and had no hesitation in pointing out to him the many areas in which he fell short of excellence, and bent his efforts—unsuccessfully as it turned out—to developing his great native talents. When Alcibiades served in the campaign against Potidaea (432–431 B.C.), Socrates shared his tent and was his companion in arms. In a fierce action Alcibiades fought bravely and was wounded. Socrates with conspicuous bravery defended his fallen comrade and saved him together with his armor. At a later time Alcibiades returned the service. When Socrates was participating in the general retreat at Delium (424 B.C.), Alcibiades came by on horseback and protected him from the encompassing enemy.

Because of his birth, wealth, and courage in battle, his many friends and followers, and his personal magnetism, it was natural that he should enter public service. Fundamentally aristocratic in his views, having stated that democracy is "acknowledged folly," he yet used the tools of democracy to further his ambitions which were without limit. His initial appearance in public life was the occasion on which he made the first of his many large contributions to the state. He soon became a leading figure and, as leader of the radical party, he was the rival of Nicias. Hyperbolus, a "base fellow" according to Thucydides, thought to take advantage of this rivalry for his own ends. He engineered a vote of ostracism with the idea that either Alcibiades or Nicias would be ostracized.

When Alcibiades became aware of it, he joined forces with Nicias and the result, astonishing to all, was that Hyperbolus himself was ostracized. However, the unity with Nicias was short-lived. Alcibiades schemed to break the peace with Sparta negotiated by Nicias (421 B.C.). He plotted with the Argives. He attacked Nicias in the assembly, accused him of treachery and raised a great outcry against him. When Spartan envoys came to negotiate, he secretly met with them, it is said, and persuaded them to say that they did not have full powers to negotiate, as in fact they had. When they then stated in the assembly that their powers were limited, Alcibiades accused them of lying. Nicias was confounded by their change and the negotiations collapsed. Alcibiades was then appointed general (420 B.C.), and urged the Athenians to extend their dominion on land, as was required by the oath young warriors took "to regard wheat, barley, the wine, and the olive as the natural boundaries of Attica." He brought the Argives, Mantineans, and Eleans into alliance with Athens and persuaded Argos and Patrae to build walls to the sea. But after the Spartan victory at Mantinea (418 B.C.) he was not reelected as general and Nicias took his place. Conservative and respectable men feared him for his influence and were indignant at his personal life, for all his public acts were accompanied, as Plutarch says, "with great luxuriousness, with wanton drunkeness and lewdness, with effeminacy in dress—he would trail long purple robes through the agora—and with prodigal expenditures." He carried a golden shield the device of which was an Eros armed with a thunderbolt. But the people, though they feared his insolence, admired his military skill, were charmed by his discourse and looked indulgently on his excesses, excusing them as the high spirits of youth. According to Aristophanes, the public "yearns for him, and hates him too, but wants him back." (*Frogs.*)

When the Egestaeans of Sicily sent envoys to Athens (416 B.C.) and asked for aid against Selinus, Alcibiades was foremost in urging the Athenians to answer their appeal. By his eloquence, which even the comic poets acknowledged, he inspired the Athenians with the wildest hopes and dreams of conquest.

fat, fāte, fär, fāre, errant; net, mē, hèr ardent; pin, pīne; not, nōte, möve, nôr,

Some say his interest was to win glory for himself, and that Sicily was to be but the stepping stone for the conquest of Carthage and Libya. Nicias and some others, among them Socrates, opposed the expedition and on good grounds. But Alcibiades fanned the enthusiasm of the young men with extravagant hopes and set their elders to dreaming of past glories. The exercise grounds were crowded with men who daily drew maps of Sicily, Carthage, and Libya in the sand. Those who considered such an expedition to be folly found it prudent to say nothing of their doubts. An expedition was voted and a great armament was prepared. Alcibiades, Nicias (against his will), and Lamachus were named generals with full powers. Two unfavorable omens marred the carnival-like atmosphere in which the fleet made ready to sail. It was discovered that many of the Hermae—square stone figures surmounted by a head of the god Hermes which stood at the entrances to temples and before private houses—had been mutilated. This act of impiety greatly aroused and disturbed the Athenians and large rewards were offered for information concerning its authors, and of any other acts of impiety to the gods. Alcibiades was implicated in a charge of having taken part in a drunken mockery of the rites of Eleusinian Demeter. The two impieties were thought to be connected and his enemies claimed that they were part of a plot by which he planned to overthrow the democracy. He demanded a trial before he set out on the expedition for he understood how perilous it was to be starting off with such suspicions hanging over him, and he wanted at once either to be cleared of the charges, or to be executed for impiety. His enemies feared he would be acquitted by the people. They claimed that some of the allies in the expedition might withdraw if Alcibiades was not the commander; therefore he should sail and stand trial on his return. He could not persuade them otherwise. The day for the departure fell on the festival of Adonia, in which small images of the dead Adonis were carried in procession and were given burial rites. This was thought to be unfavorable as foretelling that the splendid armament would fade in its glory as had the youthful beauty of Adonis. Neverthless, in

the summer of 415 B.C. the splendid fleet sailed.

Hardly had the expedition arrived in Sicily when a galley came from Athens bearing news of Alcibiades' recall. He went aboard willingly, but when the galley put in at Thurii he went ashore and escaped. When news of his escape reached Athens, he was tried *in absentia* on a charge of impiety. His property was confiscated, priestesses were ordered to curse his name, and he was condemned to death. When he heard the sentence in the Peloponnesus whither he had gone, he exclaimed, "I'll show them that I'm alive!" He went to Sparta, where he asked for immunity and offered his aid. The Spartans were instantly charmed by him. All were amazed to see the luxury-loving Athenian adopt the rigid Spartan ways, even to sharing the simple diet of black pudding with the soldiers. He urged the Spartans to send help to Syracuse against the faltering Athenians under Nicias. He also persuaded them to renew the war against Athens at home and lastly, and most devastating for the Athenians, he advised them to fortify Decelea. This was a mountain fortress of Attica, about 14 miles from Athens, which commanded the Attic plain and the routes to Euboea and Boeotia. The Spartans adopted his advice and effectively removed from Athenian control all the farmland that had supplied Athens with food. Although the Spartans used the advice of Alcibiades to their advantage, he ultimately lost their good will. Their leaders became jealous of him. While King Agis was away, Alcibiades seduced his wife Timaea, and the child she subsequently bore was presumed to be his. He went to Ionia on a successful mission to stir up revolt against Athens. While there, he learned that the Spartans had sent orders demanding his death. He went (412 B.C.) to the Persian satrap Tissaphernes whom he advised to be less generous in his aid to Sparta. Rather, he suggested, Tissaphernes should encourage Athens and Sparta to exhaust themselves and then they would be easy prey for the Persian king. Athens was in straitened circumstances and desired the return of Alcibiades. In 412–411 B.C. he sent secret messages to the Athenian forces at Samos, hinting at aid from Tissaphernes

actor; up, lūte, pull; oi, oil; ou, out; ᴛʜ, then; ḍ as d or j, ṣ as s or sh, ṭ as t or ch, ẓ as z or zh.

for Athens if the democracy was overthrown. However, he did not return to Athens when the Four Hundred seized control there in June, 411 B.C. He went to Samos and took command of a fleet. By his advice he prevented the Athenians at Samos from sailing to the Piraeus to overthrow the Four Hundred, for they would have left the Hellespont and Ionia defenseless before the Spartan fleet operating in nearby waters. When the Four Hundred were overthrown in Athens (Sept., 411 B.C.), he was invited to return. He wanted some military successes to take back with him. He defeated the Spartans at Abydos and then went to Tissaphernes, who had been his great friend. Tissaphernes, however, now feared Athens and cast him into prison. Within a month he escaped and joined the Athenians at Cardia in the Thracian Chersonese and led them to victory over the Spartan commander Mindarus at Cyzicus (410 B.C.). In the following year he routed both the Persian satrap Pharnabazus and the Spartan Hippocrates, plundered the satrapy of Pharnabazus, and captured Selymbria on the Hellespont. In 408 B.C. he took Byzantium and was now ready to return to Athens. He sailed back from Samos with a fleet decked with the trophies of his victories and was wildly acclaimed when he landed. His property was restored, he was crowned with a gold crown, and he was elected general with sole powers by land and by sea. In his prosperity he determined to celebrate the rites at Eleusis and clear away any lingering shadow as to his piety. Since the Spartans had occupied Decelea the procession had been carried to Eleusis from Athens by sea. He resolved to take it across the ancient sacred way and to protect it with his soldiers, and carried out his resolve. He became so popular that the people sought to make him their tyrant. There were others who feared him, however, and encouraged him to sail and pursue the Spartans. He assaulted Andros but failed to take the city (Oct., 408 B.C.). Plutarch says he was ruined by his own reputation for success, for when he failed it was thought he did so deliberately, and now his enemies renewed their attacks on him. But the truth was that the Athenians had voted him full power but no money, and he had to occupy himself sailing

about to collect funds. While he was doing this he left the fleet at Notium in charge of Antiochus, with strict orders not to engage the Spartans. Antiochus disobeyed and was lost with the ships that went to his aid in an engagement with the Spartans at Ephesus (407 B.C.). When Alcibiades learned of it he set out against the Spartan commander Lysander but the latter refused to fight. This was held to be treachery on the part of Alcibiades. The fickle Athenians again turned against him. He fled to Thrace with some mercenaries and occupied a stronghold near Pactye. Before the battle of Aegospotami (405 B.C.) he saw the peril in which the Athenian fleet had placed itself vis-à-vis the Spartans, and rode down to the Athenian camp to warn the generals. They invited him to go away and were utterly defeated in the ensuing battle with Lysander. After the defeat of Athens, Alcibiades retired to Bithynia, then proceeded to the satrap Pharnabazus, a good friend of Sparta, and offered his services to the Persian king Artaxerxes. The Spartans sent orders to have him slain. It is said that when he was visiting the courtesan Timandra, he dreamed that he was lying in her arms and that she was robing him in women's clothing and painting his face. According to one account, when he was in his house with her, the minions of Pharnabazus set fire to his house. He rushed out unscathed to quell his attackers. But they dared not meet him hand to hand and slew him with javelins and arrows. Some say Timandra recovered his body, dressed it in her own sumptuous robes, and gave it as brilliant a burial as was possible.

Alcidamas (al-sid′a-mas). Greek rhetorician, born at Elaea, Asia Minor, who flourished in the 4th century B.C. He was a pupil of Gorgias. Alcidamas was the only one of the Sophists to propose the actual abolition of slavery as a practical matter. He was instructor in eloquence at Athens and last of the purely sophistical school of rhetoricians. Two extant declamations, one on composing written speeches and the other—the authenticity of which is questioned—an indictment of Palamedes by Odysseus, are ascribed to to him.

Alcides (al-sī′dēz). An epithet applied to Heracles as a descendant of Alcaeus, father of Amphitryon, who was Heracles' supposed father.

Alcidice (al-sid'i-sē). In legend, the wife of Salmoneus. She died when her daughter Tyro was born.

Alcimede (al-sim'e-dē). According to some accounts, the mother of Jason. She was a daughter of Clymene, granddaughter of Minyas, and for this reason the Argonauts were often called "Minyans." She tried to persuade Jason not to go to Colchis.

Alcimedes (al-si-mē'dēz). In Greek legend, one of the seven sons of Jason and Medea. The others were Medeus, who was sometimes called the son of Aegeus, Mermerus, Pheres, Tisander, Thessalus, and Argus. According to Euripides, when Jason deserted Medea for Glauce, a princess of Corinth, Medea sent two of her children with a poisoned robe to Glauce which burned her to ashes when she donned it and gave off such flames that the palace was set on fire and Creon, her father, was consumed in the flames. Then, according to the story, she murdered her two children. Others, however, claim that the Corinthians bribed Euripides to write that Medea destroyed her children. These claim that the Corinthians seized all Medea's children except Medeus from the altar of Hera's temple where they had gone for sanctuary, and stoned them to death to avenge the deaths of Glauce and King Creon by their mother's magic arts. The children's bodies were buried in the temple on instructions from the oracle at Delphi, and their souls became immortal. Ever after, the Corinthians expiated the crime of killing the children, including the seven daughters of Jason and Medea, by sending seven boys and seven girls, with shaven heads and clad in black garments, to spend a year in the temple where the murder of the children had taken place.

Alcimedon (al-sim'e-don). A legendary Arcadian hero whose daughter Phialo was ravished by Heracles. When she bore a son Alcimedon banished them from his mountain cave, bound and gagged Phialo, and left her and her baby on the mountain to die. Her child's cries were heard by a jay which, mimicking the infant's cries, flew off to Heracles. Thus he was led to the spot where Phialo and her child were lying and he rescued them.

Alcimedon. In Homeric legend (*Iliad*), a son of Laerces. He was a captain of the Myrmidons under Patroclus. He took charge of the immortal horses Balius and Xanthus when Patroclus fell and Automedon, Patroclus' charioteer, remained to fight on foot.

Alcinous (al-sin'ō-us). In Homeric legend (*Odyssey*), a king of the Phaeacians. He was the husband of Arete and the father of Nausicaä. Odysseus managed to get ashore on the island kingdom of Alcinous after the raft on which he had sailed from Calypso's island broke up in a storm. Encountering Nausicaä on the shore, Odysseus prevailed upon her to conduct him to her father's court. Alcinous, encouraged by his wife, welcomed him as a stranger and promised to provide a ship to take him home. In the course of a feast Odysseus was called on to tell his name and history, and many of the adventures which he had experienced since leaving Troy are told for the first time during his stay with the Phaeacians. When Alcinous learned who he was, he wanted to keep Odysseus as a son-in-law, but refused to hold him against his will. He gave him many gifts and sent him in one of the Phaeacians' ships to Ithaca. In later legend it is said that Jason and Medea landed on the island of the Phaeacians in their flight from Colchis. Here the Colchians overtook them and claimed Medea. But Alcinous, advised by his wife, refused to surrender Medea if she was married to Jason. A marriage was hurriedly arranged and some of the disappointed Colchians, fearing to return to Colchis without Medea, settled among the Phaeacians.

Alciphron (al'si-fron). Greek writer; fl. 2nd century A.D. In particular, he was the writer of imaginary letters which, though models of Attic style, purported to be the work of contemporary lower-class Athenians. The approximately 124 letters extant constitute a valuable description of social conditions and manners of the period; those supposedly written by famous hetaerae reflect the work of New Comedy writers, especially Menander.

Alcippe (al-sip'pē). In Greek legend, a daughter of Ares and Aglauros (or Agraulos), the daugther of Cecrops and Agraulos. Halirrhothius, a son of Poseidon, tried to violate

actor; up, lūte, pull; oi, oil; ou, out; ŦH, then; ḍ as d or j, ş as s or sh, ṭ as t or ch, ẓ as z or zh.

her and was killed by Ares. For this murder Ares was brought to trial at a place that came to be known as the Areopagus, meaning "Hill of Ares," and was acquitted by the Olympian gods sitting in judgment on him. This is said to have been the first murder trial.

Alcippe. In Greek mythology, the wife of Evenus and the mother of Marpessa who was won by Idas in a contest with Apollo.

Alcippe. Sometimes named as the legendary wife of Metion, son of Erechtheus, and the mother of Daedalus.

Alcippe. In Homeric legend (*Odyssey*), an attendant of Helen at the court of Menelaus in Sparta.

Alcis (al'sis). According to some accounts, a daughter of Antipoenus of Thebes, a descendant of the Sparti. When Heracles decided to resist Erginus, king of the Minyans who was attacking Thebes, an oracle foretold victory if a descendant of the Sparti voluntarily died for Thebes. Alcis and her sister Androclea gladly killed themselves for the good of their country, and were afterward worshiped as heroines in the temple of Artemis in Thebes.

Alcithoë (al-sith'ō̆-ē̆). In Greek legend, one of the three daughters of Minyas, king of Orchomenus. Her sisters were Arsippe and Leucippe. Dionysus invited them to participate in his revels. They denied the divinity of the god, and even after he had transformed himself successively into a lion, a bull, and a panther to demonstrate his powers, they continued to mock him and refused to join the revels. To punish them Dionysus inspired them with madness. In their frenzy the sisters seized Hippasus, son of Leucippe, tore him to pieces and devoured him. But some say they remained at home occupied with their weaving during the revels, and that their looms turned green and their thread was changed into twining ivy. In the end they were transformed by Dionysus into bats.

Alcmaeon (alk-mē'on). In Greek legend, a son of Amphiaraus the seer and Eriphyle. Ten years after the disastrous expedition of the Seven against Thebes, in which Amphiaraus disappeared into the earth, the Epigoni (sons of the original Seven) proposed to make war on Thebes and avenge their fathers.

They learned from an oracle that the expedition would be successful if Alcmaeon commanded it. According to some accounts, before Amphiaraus had departed on the first expedition, he had left orders commanding his sons to kill their mother Eriphyle and to march on Thebes when they grew up. Because he had not yet punished his mother, Alcmaeon was reluctant to lead the new expedition. Others say he thought it was unwise and disputed with his brother Amphilochus about the matter, and that they agreed to submit the question to their mother for a decision. She, bribed by Polynices' son Thersander, advised them to make war on Thebes. The expedition was successful, but Alcmaeon overheard Thersander boasting that he had brought about the success by bribing Eriphyle, as his father had bribed her before the first expedition. Alcmaeon was furious when he learned of this second bribe that might have caused his death as the first bribe had caused his father's. He consulted the oracle at Delphi and interpreted the answer to mean that he should kill his mother. This he did with the help, some say, of Amphilochus. As she was dying Eriphyle uttered a curse, praying that no land should offer shelter to her murderers. Alcmaeon, pursued by the Furies, first fled to his grandfather Oicles in Arcadia then went to Phegeus, king of Psophis. He took with him the necklace and robe with which his mother had been bribed. Phegeus purified him and gave to him in marriage his daughter Arsinoë. Alcmaeon gave the fatal necklace and robe to his new wife. But Eriphyle's curse was operating and he was hounded by the Furies. The land of Psophis became barren. An oracle advised him to go to the river-god Achelous. Achelous purified him and gave him his daughter Callirrhoë in marriage. Alcmaeon colonized the land that had been deposited as silt by the Achelous river; this land, not having been formed at the time of his mother's curse, was free to receive him and here he lived peacefully for some years. Callirrhoë bore him two sons, Acarnan and Amphoterus. Some time later Callirrhoë coveted the ill-omened necklace and robe of Eriphyle and commanded Alcmaeon to fetch them for her. He went to Phegeus and told him an oracle had instructed him to take the

fat, fāte, fär, fãre, errant; net, mē, hèr ardent; pin, pīne; not, nōte, möve, nôr,

necklace and robe to Delphi and he would be cured of his madness. Phegeus, with Arsinoë's consent, gave him the robe and necklace but on learning that Alcmaeon had taken another wife for whom he sought the robe and necklace, Phegeus commanded his sons to kill Alcmaeon and take the robe and necklace to Delphi where they could bring no further disasters. The sons of Phegeus carried out their father's orders. Alcmaeon was killed. The robe and necklace were taken to Delphi where, according to Pausanias, they remained until the 4th century B.C. when they were stolen. According to Euripides, when Alcmaeon and the Epigoni took Thebes, Alcmaeon took Manto, a daughter of the seer Tiresias, and became the father of a son Amphilochus and a daughter Tisiphone by her. He later sent Manto to Delphi as part of the booty from Thebes and gave his two children to be brought up by Creon, king of Corinth. Tisiphone grew to be so beautiful that Creon's wife, jealous of her beauty, sold her as a slave. The purchaser, unaware of her identity, was Alcmaeon.

Alcmaeon of Croton (krō'ton). Greek physician and philosopher, born at Croton, Italy, and active c500 B.C. He was a younger contemporary of Pythagoras and perhaps his disciple. He was the most famous of the Greek physicians preceding Hippocrates, and has been called "the father of Greek medicine." His book is lost and only a few fragments of his writings have remained, but it is known that he was one of the first to perform dissection, by means of which he discovered the optic nerve, distinguished in the cadaver empty veins and veins carrying blood, and knew the trachea. He gave explanations of sleep, of the origin of sperm, of sense impressions, and made physiological experiments. He was the first to recognize that the brain is the central organ of intellectual activity, and held that health and disease are respectively an equilibrium and a rupture of equilibrium of the organism.

Alcmaeonidae (alk-mē-on'i-dē). Noble family of Athens, a branch of the family of the Nelidae which, according to tradition, came from Pylus in Messenia to Athens about 1100 B.C. Among the more notable members of the family are Alcmaeon, an Athenian general in the Cirrhaean war; Megacles, a son of Alcmaeon and a rival of Pisistratus; Clisthenes the legislator and son of Megacles; Pericles, the celebrated Athenian statesman, great-grandson of Megacles; and the scarcely less-famous Alcibiades, cousin of Pericles. The family was banished for sacrilege about 596 B.C. on account of the action of the Alcmaeonid archon Megacles, who in 632 B.C. put to death the participants in the insurrection of Cylon while they clung for protection to the altars. They returned through an alliance with Lycurgus, carried on with varying fortunes a struggle with Pisistratus and the Pisistratidae, and were finally restored in 510 B.C.

Alcman or **Alkman** (alk'man) or **Alcmaeon** (alk-mē'on). Greek poet, founder of the Doric school; fl. in the middle of the 7th century B.C. Because of some references in one of his works to Lydia it was thought that he had been born in Lydia, had been captured in war, and taken as a slave to Sparta where his poetry caused the Spartans to free him and give him citizenship. This is legend; he was a Spartan from birth. His poetry, in a non-literary dialect, expresses his personal emotions and enthusiasm in clear and simple meters. For these reasons and for the personal feeling and simplicity of expression, he is often considered the inventor of love poetry. He wrote, especially for choral performance, hymns, paeans, processionals, and *parthenia* (maidens' songs). In 1855 there was discovered on an Egyptian papyrus a parthenion which is one of the earliest poems to show a definite tendency toward intentional rhyme.

Alcmaon (alk'mā-on). In Homeric legend (*Iliad*), a Greek, the son of Thestor. He was slain by Sarpedon, in revenge for having wounded Glaucus, the dear comrade of Sarpedon. With his death Sarpedon surmounted the Greek rampart, thus opening the way for many Trojans to follow him.

Alcmene (alk-mē'nē). In Greek mythology, a daughter of Electryon and the mother of Heracles. Her father promised her to Amphitryon but she would not allow the marriage to be consummated until the deaths of her eight brothers had been avenged. While Amphitryon was away fighting the Taphians for this purpose, Zeus visited

Alcmene. He had decided to make her the mother of a mighty hero, and because he knew she was chaste he came to her disguised as her husband. Alcmene was the last mortal woman Zeus embraced. He told her that her brothers had been avenged and spent with her one night, which he caused to be prolonged to three times the usual length. Amphitryon returned the next day but Alcmene, having entertained Zeus in the belief that he was her husband, did not welcome the returned warrior with great enthusiasm. In due time she bore twin sons, Heracles and Iphicles. Heracles, who she learned from the seer Tiresias was the child of Zeus, she abandoned out of fear of Hera, but he was restored to her by Athena. Iphicles was the child of Amphitryon. Alcmene outlived her famous son and was the protectress of his children. She accompanied them to Athens, the only Greek city willing to defy Eurystheus' order to banish them, and when he made war on Athens and was defeated, Alcmene ordered his death. After the death of Amphitryon Alcmene married Rhadamanthys, who had fled from Crete to Greece, and lived with him at Ocalea. She died at a great age and a tomb at Haliartus was said to be the tomb of Alcmene and Rhadamanthys. But some say she died in Thebes, where she was worshiped as a goddess. These claim that when Alcmene died Zeus sent Hermes to steal her body from the coffin. Hermes substituted a stone for the body of Alcmene and carried her off to the Elysian Fields and it was there that she married Rhadamanthys. The Heraclidae, carrying the coffin in the funeral procession, were astonished at its great weight. After some discussion they set the coffin down, opened it, and found the stone Hermes had put inside. This they set up in a sacred grove at Thebes where there was later a shrine of Alcmene. But still others say she died in Megara where there was also a shrine of Alcmene.

Alcon (al'kon). In Greek legend, a skilled archer who accompanied Heracles on his mission to obtain the cattle of Geryon. He could shoot through rings on the helmets of soldiers standing in file, and could split arrows that were impaled on spear points. He was the father of Phalerus the Argonaut and once killed with an arrow, without harming the boy, a serpent that that had coiled around his son's body.

Alcon. Known as a Trojan warrior, the son of Megacles. In the struggle for possession of Achilles' body, Alcon wounded Odysseus but was in turn slain by Odysseus.

Alcyone (al-sī'ọ̄-nē). In Greek mythology, a daughter of Aeolus and the wife of Ceyx. After her husband's death she was changed into a kingfisher (*alcyon*); it was said that her father causes the winds to cease for seven days at the beginning of the winter solstice and seven days after it, so that the seas will be calm while the kingfishers nest. See **Ceyx.**

Alcyone. In Greek mythology, a daughter of Pleione and Atlas; one of the Pleiades. By Poseidon she was the mother of Hyrieus (sometimes also called Anthas). With her sisters, her image was placed among the stars. See **Pleiades.**

Alcyone. A sister of King Eurystheus. In the legend, Homadus, a centaur, attacked her and attempted to ravish her. Heracles, hearing her cries, ran up, killed him, and won great praise for protecting the sister of his enemy.

Alcyone. In Homeric legend *(Iliad),* a name sometimes given to Cleopatra, wife of Meleager, because her mother Marpessa had cried like an alcyon (kingfisher) when she was carried off by Apollo.

Alcyoneus (al-sī'ọ̄-nus). In Greek mythology, one of the Giants, a son of Gaea and the blood of Uranus, who waged war on the gods. Heracles pierced him with his arrow and threw him to the ground but as it was his native soil Phlegra, he sprang up renewed. On the urgent advice of Athena Heracles then carried him into Boeotia which was not his native soil, and killed him with a club.

Alcyoneus. In Greek legend, a giant herdsman who twice stole the cattle of Helius. He won control of the Isthmus of Corinth and when Heracles sought to cross with the cattle he was driving back from Geryon's land, Alcyoneus flung a huge stone to prevent him from crossing. Heracles batted the stone back at Alcyoneus with his club; it struck and killed him.

Alea (ā′lē-a). Epithet of Athena. The ancient sanctuary of Athena Alea in Tegea was said to have been founded by Aleus, great-grandson of Zeus and Callisto. An oracle predicted that a child of Auge, daughter of Aleus, would slay his uncles. Aleus determined, therefore, that she should bear no children and made her a priestess in the temple of Athena Alea. But Heracles, visiting Aleus, seized Auge near the fountain of the sacred precinct and ravished her. The land was smitten by a blight and was relieved only when the profanation of Athena Alea's temple was revealed and Auge was removed from it. Among the objects dedicated in the ancient temple were: a sacred couch of Athena, the tusks and hide of the Calydonian boar, the bronze manger taken from the camp of Mardonius after the Battle of Plataea (479 B.C.), and the fetters the Spartans had brought to bind the Tegeans. However, having defeated the Spartans in battle, the Tegeans used these to bind the Spartans. The sanctuary of Athena Alea at Tegea was respected by all in the Peloponnesus as a place of refuge for suppliants. To it Leotychides, the Spartan victor at Mycale (479) fled in 476 B.C., having been accused of bribery in his war against Thessaly. Nearly a century later (395 B.C.), the Spartan king Pausanias also sought refuge here, having been accused of cowardice in a war in Boeotia. The ancient sanctuary was destroyed by fire (c394 B.C.) and was replaced by a magnificent temple, of which Scopas was the architect and sculptor. The priest in the temple had to be a boy who had not yet reached puberty. The ancient image of Athena Alea (and some say, the tusks of the Calydonian boar also) was carried off by the Emperor Augustus (63 B.C.–14 A.D.) and set up in the Forum at Rome. Other images of Athena Alea were on the road from Amyclae to Therapne in Laconia, and at Alea in Arcadia.

Alea. In ancient geography, a city on the E border of Arcadia, near Argolis. According to tradition the city was founded by Aleus, grandson of Arcas and great-grandson of Zeus. The city was noted for its great sanctuaries of Ephesian Artemis and Athena Alea. A festival of Dionysus, the Scieria, was celebrated every other year here, at which time the women were flogged as the Spartan boys were flogged before the image of Artemis Orthia. Alea was abandoned shortly after 371 B.C. when its inhabitants went to live in the new city of Megalopolis.

Alebion (a-lē′bi-on). [Also: **Albion.**] According to mythology, a son of Poseidon. He and his brother Dercynus attempted to steal some of the cattle which Heracles had taken from Geryon as Heracles was driving them through Liguria. Heracles fought them off until his supply of ammunition was exhausted. He then prayed to Zeus, who sent a shower of stones onto the plain. Heracles picked up the stones, flung them at Alebion and Dercynus and killed them. The spot where the shower of stones fell became known as the "Stony Plain." It is near Marseilles.

Alecto (a-lek′tō). In mythology, one of the three Erinyes, or Eumenides, born of the blood of Uranus which fell on Gaea when Cronus mutilated him. Alecto was called the "unresting." Juno called on Alecto, as a maker of grief who revels in war, violence, and quarrels, to rouse the Latins against Aeneas when he had come peacefully to the kingdom of Latinus.

Alesia (a-lē′zha). A city founded, according to legend, by Heracles on his journey into Iberia to seize the cattle of Geryon. The name commemorated the wanderings of his companions and himself. The city remained free until Caesar took it by storm, 52 B.C., from Vercingetorix. The site is occupied by the modern village of Alise on the Côte d'Or in France.

Alesium (a-lē′zhi-um), **Mount.** Mountain in Arcadia, on the road between Mantinea and Tegea. Its name, which means "wandering," was given to it because here Rhea wandered when she was looking for a place to bear Zeus. On the mountain was a grove sacred to Demeter. At the foot of the mountain was a sanctuary of Poseidon Hippius, the original of which was said to have been built by Agamedes and Trophonius. It was forbidden to mortals to enter the sanctuary and across its entrance the builders stretched no barrier but a thread of wool. Inside the sanctuary, according to ancient legend, was a fountain of sea water. Aepytus, king of Arcadia, disregarded the prohibition against entering the sanctuary, cut the woolen

actor; up, lūte, pull; oi, oil; ou, out; ᴛʜ, then; ḍ as d or j, ṣ as s or sh, ṭ as t or ch, ẓ as z or zh.

thread and went in. As he did so a wave of sea water swept into his face and blinded him. Centuries later when the ancient sanctuary was in ruins, the Roman Emperor Hadrian commanded that a new sanctuary be built over the ruins of the old one. Workmen detailed to complete the task were forbidden either to look into the old sanctuary or to move any of the ruins.

Aletes (a̲-lē′tēz). In Greek legend, a son of Clytemnestra and her paramour Aegisthus. After Clytemnestra and Aegisthus were slain by Orestes, Aletes became ruler of Mycenae. Orestes, after great suffering and wandering, at length was purified of his crime. He returned to Mycenae, slew Aletes and regained his inheritance as ruler of Mycenae.

Aletes. In Greek legend, a son of Hippotes, and a descendant of Heracles. After the Heraclidae invaded the Peloponnesus, he learned that he could win the city of Corinth only if he was given a clod of earth. Later when he asked a Corinthian peasant for bread he was given a lump of earth instead. Outside the city walls he met the daughters of the king of Corinth. On his promise to marry the youngest daughter, he persuaded her to open the gates of the city so that he could conquer it. Thus 30 years after the invasion of the Peloponnesus by the Heraclidae, he took possession of Corinth. When he was waging war against Athens he was informed by an oracle that he would take the city if its king remained unharmed. Codrus, king of Athens at the time, also learned of the oracle and some say that he killed himself, or took measures that led to his death, in order to fulfill the oracle and and save his country.

Alethia (al-ē-thī′a̲). In Greek mythology, the personification of Truth. She was supposedly a daughter of Zeus. Her Roman counterpart was called Veritas.

Aleus (ā′lē̲-us). In Greek legend, king of Tegea and the father of Amphidamas, Auge, Cepheus, and Lycurgus. The oracle at Delphi informed him that his wife's brothers would be slain by his daughter's son. To prevent the fulfillment of the prophecy Aleus made his daughter Auge a priestess of Athena and therefore dedicated to chastity. His attempts to prevent her from bearing sons

were unsuccessful, as Heracles violated her and she bore him Telephus.

Alexander (al-eg-zan′dẻr). Another name for Paris, son of Priam and Hecuba, brother of Hector, and abductor of Helen.

Alexander. [Called **Alexander Lyncestes.**] Fl. 4th century B.C. A native of Lyncestis in Macedonia (whence his surname "Lyncestes"), he was implicated with his brothers in the murder of Philip II of Macedon in 336 B.C. Because he was the first to do homage to Alexander the Great the latter pardoned him and raised him to a high position in the army, but afterward put him to death for treasonable correspondence with Darius III.

Alexander I (of *Epirus*). King of Epirus; died c330 B.C. He was the son of Neoptolemus and the brother of Olympias, mother of Alexander the Great. His youth was spent at the court of Philip II of Macedon who made him king of Epirus. Philip II gave him his daughter in marriage to strengthen his ties with Epirus and her king, whose sister Olympias he had recently cast aside. At the celebration of the marriage of Alexander and Philip's daughter, Philip was murdered. Alexander's aid against the barbarians of Italy was sought by Tarentum in 334 B.C. His arms met with such success in southern Italy that Rome thought it expedient to make an alliance with him. Subsequently, Tarentum came to fear the conqueror who had come to her aid, renounced her alliance with Alexander, and during a battle that ensued at Pandosia Alexander was stabbed in the back and killed.

Alexander II (of *Epirus*). King of Epirus, son of Pyrrhus and Lanassa, the daughter of Agathocles, tyrant of Syracuse. He succeeded his father in 272 B.C. He was dispossessed of Epirus and Macedonia by Demetrius, whose father, Antigonus Gonatas, had been deprived of Macedonia by Alexander. Epirus was recovered subsequently chiefly with the aid of the Acarnanians.

Alexander I (of *Macedon*). King of Macedon (c500–c454 B.C.). He was a son of Amyntas I, whom he succeeded. In the Persian Wars he was allied to Persia, both by ties of marriage and by force, for his father had given earth and water to Darius in token of his submission to the Great King. In the spring of 479 B.C. Mardonius sent him as an envoy to Athens because he was aware of Alexander's friendship for Athens. Alexander was authorized to tell the Athenians that Mardonius would forgive the wrong they had done to the Persians, restore their territory, and rebuild their temples if Athens would join an alliance with him. Alexander added his own words, as a known friend of Athens, to persuade them to make an alliance. For, he said, they could never overcome the power and might of the Persian Empire. To him the Athenians replied, "So long as the sun keeps his present course, we will never join alliance with Xerxes. Nay, we shall oppose him unceasingly." According to Herodotus, when the Greeks were encamped at Plataea, waiting favorable omens to engage Mardonius, a man rode up on horseback to their camp at night, and asked to speak to the generals, but would not give his name. He told the generals that out of friendship for Athens, and at great peril to himself, he had come to inform them that the Persians had been unable to obtain favorable omens for many days and had decided to attack without them on the next day. He also told them that Mardonius' supplies were running low. Then he asked them to do something for his freedom if they were successful. Finally, he announced to them that he was Alexander of Macedon, turned his horse and rode back to the Persian camp and took up the station assigned to him.

Alexander II (of *Macedon*). King of Macedon (369–368 B.C.). He was a son of Amyntas II, whom he succeeded. He was murdered by his mother's paramour, Ptolemy Alorus (368 B.C.).

Alexander III (of *Macedon*). See **Alexander the Great.**

Alexander Balas (bā'las). Usurper of the Syrian throne. He was born at Smyrna and occupied the Syrian throne from 150–145 B.C. Of humble origin, he was the self-alleged son of Antiochus Epiphanes. He was the protegé of a coalition including Ptolemy Philometor of Egypt which seized the throne from the Seleucid king Demetrius Soter. He was murdered in 145 B.C. by an Arabian ruler to whose domain he had fled.

Alexander Cornelius (kôr-nē'li-us, -nēl'yus). [Called **Alexander Polyhistor**.] Greek writer, fl. 1st century B.C. He was a native of

either Ephesus or Cotiaeum in Lesser Phrygia. He wrote a geographical-historical account in 42 books of nearly all the countries of the ancient world, and many other works of which only the titles and fragments have been preserved.

Alexander the Great. [Also: **Alexander III** (of *Macedon.*)] Macedonian ruler and conqueror of the civilized world, born at Pella, Macedonia, 356 B.C.; died at Babylon, June 13, 323 B.C. Alexander claimed descent from Heracles and from Aeacus, the ancestor of his favorite hero, Achilles. He was the son of Philip II of Macedon and the Epirote princess Olympias, whom Philip met in Samothrace when he was initiated into the mysteries there. Some say he inherited his military ability from his father, a rough mountain king of genius, while from his mother came his mysticism and impetuousness. Before he was born there were potent omens of his future greatness: his mother dreamed a thunderbolt fell on her body from which great flames sprang, spread all about, and were then extinguished; his father dreamed he sealed up his wife's body with a seal bearing the impression of a lion, a portent that she would bear a son as courageous as a lion. On the day of his birth the great temple of Artemis at Ephesus burned—some said this was because the goddess was absent assisting at his birth—and seers mourned over the ruined temple, foretelling that the day brought forth the ruin of Asia. Philip, victorious at Potidaea, on the same day received news that his horse had won at the Olympic Games, that Parmenio, his general, had conquered the Illyrians, and that his wife had borne him a son. Born amid so many successes, Alexander was considered destined for spectacular success himself.

Among his earliest teachers was Leonidas, a kinsman of his mother who trained him for conquest. A story is told that once when the lad was preparing to sacrifice, he filled both hands with incense to pour on the altar fire. Leonidas rebuked him, advising Alexander to be more sparing of his offerings until he had conquered the lands that produced them. Later (332 B.C.), when Alexander had taken Tyre, he remembered his old tutor. He sent him 500 talents of frankincense and 100 talents of myrrh, accompanying his gift with a message that Leonidas would no longer need to be stingy in his offerings to the gods. It is said that as a boy Alexander was unhappy when he learned of any new success won by his father for the more Philip won, the less there would be for him to conquer. Philip had a handsome horse in his stables, so high-spirited none could ride him and Philip ordered the horse destroyed. Alexander begged to be allowed to try his skill, and Philip reluctantly gave his permission. Alexander had observed that the horse was terrified by its own shadow. He turned its eyes into the sun, stroked and talked to it, succeeded in mounting, and was the first, and from thereafter the only one, to ride Bucephalus. On this occasion Philip is said to have told him proudly that he must find a kingdom for himself, "For Macedonia is too small for thee." Bucephalus was the mount preferred above all others by Alexander when he went into battle. Once when the horse was captured, he threatened to put to the sword all the inhabitants of the town where Bucephalus had been taken unless his horse was restored. Bucephalus was returned and Alexander then showed great moderation to the city. When at last Bucephalus died of old age after the crossing of the Hydaspes River in India, Alexander grieved as for a dear companion and built a city on the banks of the river which he named Bucephalia in his honor.

Philip was a great admirer of the Greeks whom he had subdued, and of Greek culture, and wished to be identified with them. In 343 B.C. he sent for Aristotle to come as a tutor to Alexander. Alexander studied literature and languages with him, and learned something of medicine, but did not subscribe to the philosophy subsequently evolved by Aristotle, and in later years his affection for the philosopher cooled. He was a great reader. His favorite book was the *Iliad* which he kept under his pillow at night along with his dagger. When he had embarked on his conquests he came into possession of a magnificent jeweled casket. In it he placed his copy of the *Iliad*, the only article that he felt worthy of the precious box. Ambassadors from Greece and the East coming and going at Philip's court gave him an

education in political and diplomatic affairs. At the age of 16, Philip left him in charge of Macedonia while he was absent. Alexander subdued the hill tribes on the northern border of the kingdom and founded the city of Alexandropolis in his father's absence. In 338 B.C. he accompanied his father in the expedition against the Greek allies and led the charge against the Sacred Band in their defeat at Chaeronea. This was the first time the Sacred Band had suffered defeat. Philip was proud of his son's bravery but intrigues in his court caused a breach between father and son. Olympias, no longer secure in the affections of Philip, sought his downfall. When Philip took another wife (the Macedonian rulers practised polygamy) Olympias encouraged Alexander to take her side against his father. In 336 B.C. Philip was murdered, perhaps at the instigation of Olympias and possibly with the knowledge of Alexander. His infant son by his new wife Cleopatra was murdered as was Alexander's cousin Amyntas, thus removing rival claimants to the throne. Supported by the army, Alexander disposed of other rivals for the throne. He became king of Macedonia and leader of the Greeks in war against the predatory Persian Empire that had never ceased to intrigue with one after another of the Greek states to bring ruin to all Greece. Alexander spent two years restoring order in his father's turbulent kingdom, first pacifying the tribes in his rear. With the death of Philip, the Greek cities he had defeated burst into rebellion. Believing Alexander to be in Macedonia, they rose up to throw off his rule. By a forced march, so rapid as to be unbelievable, he arrived at rebellious Thebes. He offered to spare Thebes the violence of attack if the city would submit. The Thebans refused. Alexander stormed the city and razed it to the ground. By his order the temples and the house of Pindar the poet were left standing. Six thousand Thebans were massacred in the city before Alexander put an end to the slaughter, and 30,000 were sold into slavery. The furious destruction of Thebes must be ascribed largely to his Phocian and Boeotian allies, who thus brought low the proud city that had lorded it over them for many years. Alexander later regretted the destruction of

fat, fāte, fär, fāre, errant; net, mē, hėr ardent; pin, pīne; not, nōte, mŏve, nôr,

Thebes, and attributed whatever misfortunes later befell him to the anger of Dionysus for having ruined his city. Now, however, he was truly master of the Greece he admired so ardently. He forgave the Athenians for going into mourning and omitting the celebration of the mysteries on the fall of Thebes; he never wavered in his admiration and respect for their city, and continued to treat the Athenians with courtesy and to enrich them with gifts. Before he made his forced march from Macedonia to Thebes, Alexander had marched through Greece and had been named general of the league of Hellas to lead the invasion of Persia. In Corinth, where he had been elected general, he had his famous encounter with the Cynic philosopher Diogenes, in which the latter requested the young king and general to "stand from between me and the sun." Alexander expressed admiration for Diogenes, and said if he were not Alexander he would choose to be Diogenes. He had also gone to Delphi and sought an oracular response on a day when it was forbidden to give them. He seized the priestess to compel her, and her remark, "My son, you are invincible," was oracle enough for him.

With order restored in Macedonia and Greece submissive, he set out (334 B.C.) to reduce Persia. His highly professional army which was devoted to him consisted of 30,000 heavy- and light-armed infantry and 5000 cavalry, with a superior siege train, commissary, and intelligence service. Crossing the Hellespont, he stopped at Troy to visit the ancient battleground, sacrificed to Athena, and honored the heroes who had fallen in the Trojan War. He ran naked, as was the custom, around the tomb of Achilles to honor his favorite hero. From Troy he marched to the Granicus River where the Persian forces were encamped and and there he defeated them (334 B.C.). Of the great spoils taken, he kept little for himself, sent some to the Athenians, and the rest to his mother. Following his victory at the Granicus many of the cities of Asia Minor, including Sardis, surrendered to him, and the object of the league, the liberation of the Greek cities of Asia Minor from Persia, was accomplished. The tyrannies favorable to Persia were overthrown and democracies

were established. Halicarnassus and Miletus resisted him and were taken by force. In Caria he restored the princess Ada to the throne and adopted her as his mother. According to Plutarch, while Alexander was deliberating what to do next, a fountain in Lycia overflowed and washed up on its banks a copper plate on which was written, in ancient characters, a prophecy that the time would come when the Greeks would destroy the Persian Empire. Taking this as a sign, he marched by the sea through Cilicia and Phoenicia along the coast of Pamphylia where, some say, divine power held back the waves so that his army could make its way on the beach (others say his soldiers waded in water up to their armpits), to Phaselis, where he stopped and danced about a statue of Theodectes he found in the market-place to honor this philosopher he had once known. He subdued the Pisidians, conquered the Phrygians, and turned inland to Gordium where he was shown the famous knot on the yoke of the chariot of Gordius. Concerning the knot, an oracle had decreed that whoever untied it would rule the world. Some say Alexander looked at it and impatiently cut it through with his sword. Others say he unloosed it by withdrawing the pin in the yoke about which it was tied. He reduced Paphlagonia and Cappadocia, and now Darius III led his Persian forces against him. At Tarsus, Alexander became very ill. None of his physicians dared prescribe for him lest he die and they be accused. Alexander's friend Philip, an Acarnanian, anxious for his health, concocted a potion to cure him. Philip did not know that Alexander had received a letter which accused him of plotting against the young king's life. He took the medicinal draft to Alexander and handed it to him. Alexander drank it, then handed the letter of accusation to Philip, having already indicated his perfect trust in his friend by drinking the medicine. Whether it was by reason of Philip's medicine or of nature, Alexander was soon well again and advanced to meet Darius who had mocked his delay as cowardice. The armies met in the mountainous defiles near the town of Issus. In such cramped quarters the large armaments of the Persians could not act effectively; the terrain was of

actor; up, lūte, pull; oi, oil; ou, out; ŦH, then; ḏ as d or j, ş as s or sh, ṭ as t or ch, ẕ as z or zh.

great advantage to Alexander. In the thick of the battle Alexander was wounded, some say by Darius himself, but his forces surged on and the Persians were overwhelmed. Darius saw that the battle was lost. He abandoned his war chariot and fled on horseback, leaving his mother, his wife and his children behind in his camp. When Alexander learned of their presence among his captives he sent word that they need not grieve for Darius who still lived, nor fear him, as he intended to accord them the honor and service due their royal estate. Alexander kept his promise. Though Statira, wife of Darius, was counted the most beautiful princess living, he did not seek her out but had all the women of Darius' household maintained according to their customary standard. From his victory at Issus (333 B.C.), he took great spoils, the largest share of which he gave to his Thessalian horsemen because they had fought most gallantly. After Issus he resolved to render the Persian fleet harmless by winning control of the ports on the coast. He conquered Phoenicia, except for Tyre. Without a fleet, it seemed an impossible task to conquer Tyre, a city on an island. Alexander accomplished it by building a mole from the mainland to the island and after a siege of seven months the city fell (332 B.C.). He scattered its inhabitants, selling vast numbers of them into slavery. He took Gaza after a siege, and went on to Egypt (332 B.C.), where he was welcomed as a deliverer of the Egyptians from Persian tyranny. In Egypt he founded the city of Alexandria on the mainland opposite the island of Pharos, a site chosen, it is said, because of a dream in which Homer appeared to him and named Pharos. Alexandria was the first of 70 communities founded by him which became powerful forces for the Hellenization of the non-Greek world. While the city was being erected he made the difficult and dangerous journey across the desert to the oracle of Ammon in Libya, though seers advised him not to go. On the way the gods protected him, it was said, by sending rain so that his band would not perish of thirst, and by sending ravens to lead him when he was lost in the desert. The priest of Ammon addressed him as the son of Zeus and predicted that he would

conquer the world. His circle encouraged him to believe he was the son of a god and it appeared that he was frequently willing to do so.

With the eastern coasts of the Mediterranean now in his possession he turned inland (331 B.C.). Darius had earlier sent word to him asking that he be allowed to ransom his family, and offering to partition his empire with him, ceding to Alexander all the lands west of the Euphrates. Parmenio, a general in his army who had served under Philip, said if he were Alexander, he would accept the offer of Darius. Alexander replied, "So would I, if I were Parmenio." But being Alexander, he wrote Darius a letter worthy of a conqueror, informing him that if Darius would come and surrender himself, he would be treated with every courtesy. Otherwise, Alexander was prepared to go and fetch him. Darius could not accept such terms and prepared to march against him. When the Macedonians arrived before the camp of Darius at Gaugamela (for the battle sometimes called the Battle of Arbela, 331 B.C.), the fires from the Persian camp at night gave stunning evidence of the vast forces Darius had arrayed against them. Alexander's generals advised that the attack be made at night when darkness would conceal the dangers of the battle. Alexander answered that he would not "steal a victory," went to bed, and slept so soundly he had to be awakened when it was time to muster his army. Dressed in spectacularly rich armor and mounted on Bucephalus, he charged the enemy at the head of his cavalry, the phalanx of foot soldiers following. The Persians were overwhelmed. Again Darius left his chariot and fled on horseback. Alexander would have pursued, but Parmenio sent a message calling for help in his sector. Alexander went to his aid, but from that time on he suspected Parmenio, now an old man, if not of treachery, at least of incompetence. After the victory at Issus Alexander was proclaimed king of all Asia. Of the rich spoils taken he sent some to Greece, some to the Greek cities of Italy, and with the rest he rewarded his friends and followers. He now proceeded into the heart of the Persian empire, first putting to the sword the many prisoners who were an encumbrance. At Susa he found fabulous treasure. Going on to Persepolis, the royal city, he found untold riches and sat upon the Great King's throne. Some say that at a banquet in the Persian king's palace his generals and their mistresses were present. Thais, the Athenian mistress of his general Ptolemy, when the company was flushed with wine, proposed that the palace be burned in revenge for the burning of Athens by Xerxes (480 B.C.). Alexander gave his permission, and the diners with heads garlanded paraded through the palace putting it to the torch. But soon Alexander regretted the wanton destruction and ordered the fire quenched. From Persepolis, having subdued Persia, Alexander set out after Darius. He pursued him through Media, where he left Parmenio to guard the treasures taken at the Median capital Ecbatana. With a small band, by a series of tireless marches, he chased Darius past the Caspian Gates and overtook him near Thara south of the Caspian Sea. The Persian nobles accompanying Darius, chief of whom was his cousin Bessus, stabbed him when he refused to continue the flight and deserted him. When Alexander arrived, Darius had just died (330 B.C.). In pity, some say, Alexander threw his own cloak over the body of the Great King, and later sent it with great pomp to the dead king's mother for burial with his ancestors.

From here he took his army through Parthia, south to Seistan in Drangiana (modern Iran), swung north and passed through Arachosia and Bactria to Maracanda (Samarkand) in Sogdiana, fighting and conquering all the way. The wealth he won and distributed to his friends began to have its effect on them. Some of them soon acquired a taste for luxury and extravagant living. He feared they would become soft and vulnerable. "Have you not yet learned," he asked, "that the end and perfection of our victories is to avoid the vices and weaknesses of those we conquer?" For himself, he kept in good physical condition by violent sports and hunting. He ate with moderation and, contrary to legend, he rarely drank but did enjoy sitting long over the wine in conversation with his friends. His mother wrote to scold him for enriching his companions for, as she said, if they became the equal of kings in

wealth, they might attack his own kingship. He showed the letters to his dear friend Hephaestion and then ensured the latter's silence on these matters by placing his seal ring against Hephaestion's lips. He continued to send his mother rich presents from his spoils, but did not let her advice interfere with his plans. When he went through Parthia, he adopted Persian dress, and it seemed to his men that he wished to be honored as a god. More and more he adopted barbarian (Persian) customs, but at the same time he attempted to introduce Greek ways. He had 30,000 Persian boys chosen to be educated in the Greek tongue and the Macedonian military discipline. He married Roxana, a Bactrian princess, some say to make a stronger bond between the Macedonians and the Persians. The changes in his personal life and habits made his Macedonians uneasy. Of his dearest friends, Hephaestion followed Alexander in adopting barbarian ways, and was used as his emissary in dealing with them. Craterus kept to the Macedonian customs. Alexander was said to have had affection for Hephaestion, whom he called "Alexander's friend," and to have respected Craterus, whom he named "the king's friend." Wealth and luxury brought enmity and envy in its train. Philotas, son of Parmenio, became arrogant in his display of riches. His father advised him to be "less great," for he knew Alexander had received complaints of him. Philotas took no heed, and boasted that it was he and his father who had won the great victories for which Alexander claimed the credit. His boasts were repeated to Alexander who at first disregarded them. But when an abortive plot to kill Alexander was wrongly ascribed to Philotas, Alexander had him tortured and put to death. Afterward, he sent men to kill his father Parmenio who had faithfully served Philip as well as himself. Now many of his friends began to fear him. The Macedonians resented what they considered to be Persian domination over him. Clitus, one of his companions, during a long evening in Maracanda (Samarkand) in which much wine was drunk, accused Alexander of preferring the Persians who bowed the knee to him to the company of free-born men who dared to speak their minds. Clitus had saved his life in battle at the Granicus and reminded Alexander of it. Friends of both at the gathering tried to quiet Clitus. Alexander himself tried to change the subject. But the resentment he had stored up drove Clitus on. When he was hustled out of the room by guards, he returned through another entrance and shouted a verse from Euripides' *Andromache*: "In Greece, alas! how ill things ordered are." The lines that follow in the play (which Clitus did not speak) contained the insult:

"When trophies rise for victories in war,
Men count the praise not theirs who did
    the deed,
But to the one commander give the meed;
Who, sharing with ten thousand more the
    fight,
For one man's service takes the general
    right."

Infuriated, Alexander seized a spear and ran Clitus through. Instantly he came to his senses, drew the spear from the body of his friend, and would have killed himself but for the intervention of his guards. He mourned for days, but his grief was at last eased by the self-made philosopher Anaxarchus, who told him, "Zeus is represented to have Justice and Law on either hand, to signify that all the actions of a conqueror are lawful and just." Alexander was able to convince himself with this, that his acts as ruler were just, thus doing irreparable damage to the qualities of moderation and justice he had formerly possessed. He became convinced that Callisthenes, a philosopher in his train who had been brought up in Aristotle's household, was in a plot against him. He seized Callisthenes, and with no grounds at all cast him into prison. There he died (327 B.C.) or as some say, was killed by Alexander's order.

His march of conquest now carried him from Maracanda north to Tashkent, across the Jaxartes River. He then turned south again, went through Bactria and on to the Indus River, which he crossed, and entered India (326 B.C.). He marched to the Hydaspes River where he defeated King Porus. Porus, badly wounded, fell into his hands. When Alexander asked Porus how he expected to be treated, he replied, "Like a king," and he was treated so. Proceeding from the Hydaspes, the Macedonians rebelled at the proposal to cross the Ganges, and he was compelled to turn back. He returned by way of the Indus valley and at the mouth of the Indus sent his admiral Nearchus on a voyage to the mouth of the Euphrates. Part of his own overland journey was made through deserts with great privation, and his forces were enormously reduced by lack of supplies. On the way he was harassed by hostile tribes and impeded by the necessity of subduing their cities. At one city of the Malli he performed an exploit of personal valor and recklessness that was typical of him. He climbed the wall of the town with a few companions in his impatience to take the place, and leaped in among the hostile forces. He was badly wounded before his army could gain entrance to the city and rescue him. At Carmania he came upon abundance again and spent days feasting and resting his army. Nearchus had met him at Gedrosia and gave such reports of his voyage that Alexander resolved to make one himself, but various parts of his empire were in revolt. Olympias had seized Epirus and Cleopatra had taken control in Macedonia. Returning through Persepolis, he married Statira, a daughter of Darius III, at Susa, as well as a second Persian wife, and gave the noblest of the Persian ladies to his friends. These marriages were intended to cement the ties between the Persians and Macedonians. Great feasts and celebrations attended the weddings. His friends grieved, however, to see him become Persianized. In 324 B.C. an open rebellion broke out in his army when he discharged some of his Macedonian veterans. In the end he quelled it by the force of his personality and his threat to take a Persian guard. Then he forgave the dissidents, rewarded the veterans too old for combat and sent them home. When Hephaestion died of a fever at Ecbatana (324 B.C.), he ordered the manes and tails of all his horses and mules cropped in mourning, destroyed the fortifications of neighboring cities, crucified the physician who attended Hephaestion, and forbade the playing of music until at last word came from the oracle of Ammon in Libya instructing him to make sacrifices to Hephaestion and to worship him as a hero. He fell upon the Cossaeans and put the whole tribe to the sword, some say as a sacrifice to Hephaestion. Proposing to go to Babylon, he was told by Nearchus that Chaldean diviners ordered him not to go there. He ignored the warnings, but as he proceeded unfavorable omens occurred in rapid succession: a tame ass kicked the finest lion he had and killed it; a man appeared, clad in the king's clothes, and seated himself on the king's throne, saying he was sent by Serapis. Alexander had him put to death, but the incident depressed him. Embassies from all over the world came to Babylon to honor him as the acknowledged conqueror. He planned and prepared a voyage to explore a route from Babylonia around Arabia to Egypt. All was in readiness, and on the approach of the departure, Alexander and one of his favorites drank deep to celebrate the departure for two days and nights. On the third day he was afflicted with a fever which he at first disregarded, but it persisted and with the elapse of ten more days he had succumbed and lost his speech. The Macedonians were led through his tent to say farewell to their king and commander. The next day (June 13, 323 B.C.), not yet 33 years of age, weakened by his old wounds and disease, he died at Babylon. Napoleon called him the greatest general in history. Alexander strongly believed in the fusion of races; all his wives were eastern princesses. His life altered the course of history, for he created a new world-society based on a common Greek culture. He became after his death a legendary figure to medieval Europe and to the Orient of all periods.

Alexandra (al-eg-zan′drạ). Another name for **Cassandra.**

Alexandretta (al″ig-zan-dret′a). [Modern name, **Iskenderun** or **Iskanderun.**] A seaport on the Gulf of Alexandretta (Issus, Iskenderun) near Antioch, in the NE extremity of the Mediterranean Sea. The town was founded by Alexander the Great in 333 B.C.

Alexandria (al-eg-zan′dri-ạ). Name given to a number of cities, newly founded, reorganized by, or in the name of Alexander the Great during his campaigns in Egypt and Asia (334–323 B.C.). Those of special historical interest are listed below.

Alexandria. [Arabic, **Al-Iskandariyah, Iskan-**

deriyeh.] Seaport in NE Africa, in Egypt, founded (332 B.C.) by Alexander the Great, from whom the city took its name. It is situated at the NW extremity of the Nile delta on the strip of land which lies between the Mediterranean Sea and Lake Mareotis, about 133 miles NW of Cairo. The modern city occupies what was anciently the island of Pharos, together with the isthmus now connecting it with the mainland where the ancient city stood. According to Plutarch, Alexander chose the site of the ancient city because of a dream in which Homer appeared to him and mentioned Pharos. Surveying the location, Alexander remarked that Homer was a good architect. The lines of the city, which were laid out with flour, were devoured by flocks of many kinds of birds that swooped down. Alexander feared that the erasure of the lines by the birds was an unfavorable omen. However, seers convinced him that it meant not only that his city would be great but that it would become the nurse and feeder of many nations because there were so many kinds of birds in the flocks that fed on the flour. Ancient Alexandria was the capital of Egypt during the Ptolemaic period and became an important seat of Greek culture and learning. In 30 B.C. it was annexed by Rome and long ranked as the second city of the Roman empire.

Alexandria Arachosiae (ar-ạ-kō′si-ē). In ancient geography, a city of Arachosia, C Asia, founded by Alexander the Great, 329 B.C. The ancient site is now occupied by the city of Kandahar, SE Afghanistan.

Alexandria Arian or **Arion** (ãr′i-ạn, a-rī′ọn). In ancient geography, a city of Aria, in C Asia, so named by Alexander the Great (330 B.C.) who made it the capital of his province of Aria. The site of the ancient city is now occupied by Herat in NW Afghanistan.

Alexandria Eschata (es-kā′ta). In ancient geography, a city on the Jaxartes River where it crossed the borders of Sogdiana in C Asia. The city was founded by Alexander the Great, c328 B.C., and was named Eschata (*Furthest*) to indicate that it marked the northeastern limit of his empire. The site of the ancient city is now occupied by Leninabad (formerly Khodjend) in the Tadzhik Soviet Socialist Republic, U.S.S.R.

Alexandrine War (al-eg-zan′drin, -drēn). The name given to the episode of 48–47 B.C. when Julius Caesar, infatuated with Cleopatra and wishing to have her recognized as queen of Egypt, established himself with a small garrison in the royal quarter of Alexandria and found himself besieged by furious mobs aided by the royal troops of Ptolemy XIII, Cleopatra's elder brother. Mithridates of Pontus, a free-lance adventurer, raised a force of irregulars and broke the siege; Ptolemy XIII was defeated and killed; the crown was assumed by Cleopatra, then about 23, and her younger brother, then a child of ten or 11, who became Ptolemy XIV. A short historical account, *On the Alexandrine War,* of uncertain authorship, is extant. (JJ)

Alexiares (a-lek″si-ār′ēz). According to Greek legend, one of the sons born to Heracles after he had been apotheosized and had married Hebe.

Alexicacus (a-lek″si-kā′kus). An epithet of Apollo, which means "Averter of Evil." It is said that the epithet was given him in recognition of the fact that by an oracle of Delphi he stayed the plague that afflicted the Athenians in the Peloponnesian War in 430 B.C. Apollo Alexicacus was much invoked and greatly honored.

Alexis (a-lek′sis). Greek dramatist at Athens; born at Thurii, Magna Graecia, Italy; fl. 4th and 3rd centuries B.C. He was a master of the Middle Comedy. A prolific writer, he was the author of about 245 plays, including one on the emancipation of women, fragments of which are extant.

Alilat (ā′li′lat) or **Alitta** (a-lit′a). An Arabian goddess, later identified with Aphrodite, who came to be worshiped by the Persians. The Assyrians called her Mylitta. The name may mean "the Goddess."

Alkaios (al-kī′os). See **Alcaeus.**

Alkamenes (al-kam′e-nēz). See **Alcamenes.**

Alkmene (alk-mē′nē). See **Alcmene.**

Allia (al′i-a). [Also: **Alia;** modern name, **Aga.**] In ancient geography, a small river in Latium, Italy, joining the Tiber about ten miles N of Rome. On its banks in c390 B.C., the Gauls under Brennus defeated the Romans. The battle was followed by the capture and sack of Rome.

Allobroges (a-lob′rō-jēz) or **Allobrogi** (-jī). In ancient history, a Celtic people of SE Gaul, dwelling between the Rhodanus (Rhone) and the Isara (Isère) rivers, northward to Lacus Lemmanus (Lake Geneva). They occupied also a tract on the W bank of the Rhodanus. The chief town of the tribe was Vienna, now Vienne. They were made subject to Rome in 121 B.C. by Cnaeus Domitius Ahenobarbus and Quintus Fabius Maximus.

Aloeus (al-ō′ūs). Named by Homer as the father of the giants, Otus and Ephialtes. Other accounts say they were the sons of Poseidon and Iphimedia, or Canace, and that Aloeus married their mother and brought up her sons by Poseidon as his own. See **Aloidae.**

Aloidae (al-ọ-ī′dē). Ephialtes and Otus, the sons of Poseidon and Iphimedia or Canace. In Greek mythology they were called the Aloidae, "sons of Aloeus," because he was their mother's husband and their foster father. The handsome children grew at an astonishing rate each year, and by the time they were nine years old they felt equal to waging war on the gods. They seized Ares in Thrace, bound him and imprisoned him in a bronze vessel. After 13 months Ares was freed by the cunning of Hermes. They then piled Mount Pelion on Mount Ossa and attacked Olympus itself. Poseidon persuaded them to cease their attack on Olympus in return for the promise of Zeus not to punish them for their arrogance. This armistice was easier to arrange because of a prophecy that no other men or gods could kill the Aloidae. They next decided to carry off two goddesses. Otus chose to abduct Hera and Ephialtes desired Artemis. They first sought Artemis, but that goddess, on the advice of Apollo, fled over the sea to Naxos. Like all the sons of Poseidon, the Aloidae could skim over the sea and they followed her. She disappeared in a wood on the island and a white hind appeared in her place. The brothers separated to pursue it and approached it from opposite sides of the wood. Unaware that his brother was on the other side of the hind, each hurled his spear at the same time and, as the hind vanished, the spear of each went unerringly into the heart of the other. Thus the prophecy that no other men or gods could kill them was fulfilled, and Artemis had her revenge

Acropolis at Athens, from the west.

Left: Temple of Nike, Acropolis, Athens.

Erechtheum.

Temple of
Apollo Epicurius,
Bassae.

Left: Temple of Apollo,
Delphi.

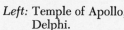

Above: Temple of Poseidon,
Sunium.

Left: Temple of Hera,
Olympia.

Italian State Tourist Office

Temple of Poseidon and Basilica,
Paestum.

Italian State Tourist Office

Temple of Apollo,
Pompeii.

Amphitheater,
Pompeii.

Italian State Tourist Office

Olympeium,
Athens.

Mary E. Dolbeare

Roman Forum and Arch of Septimius Severus.

Flavian Amphitheater (Colosseum),
seen through the Arch of Titus, Rome.

Roman theater,
Mérida.

on them for daring to desire a goddess by causing the devoted brothers to kill each other. The Aloidae were the first mortals to worship the Muses; they were also paid the honors due to heroes by the people of Naxos. Their bodies were carried back to Boeotia for burial but their souls descended to Tartarus and were tied to posts with ropes of writhing serpents.

Alope (al'ọ-pē). A legendary daughter of Cercyon, king in Arcadia. She was violated by Poseidon and bore a son, Hippothous who, though twice exposed to die, was saved. She was imprisoned by her father who did not believe Poseidon was the father of her child, and died and was buried near the road between Eleusis and Megara. Poseidon transformed her body into a spring of the same name.

Alope. In ancient geography, a city of S Thessaly, near the Sinus Maliacus (Gulf of Lamia). It was named, some say, for Alope, the daughter of Cercyon.

Alopecus (al-ō'pē-kus). According to tradition, a Spartan prince who is said by some to have found the wooden image of Artemis that Orestes brought back from Tauris. It had been lost a long time, and when Alopecus and Astrabacus came upon it in a thicket where it was held upright by willow osiers twining around it, they went mad at the sight of the image.

Alphaea (al-fē'a). An epithet of Artemis at Letrini in Elis. According to legend, the river-god Alpheus fell in love with her. When he realized he could not win her by persuasion he resolved on a violent course of action. With the intention of seizing her he went to the revels the goddess was holding at Letrini with her nymphs. Artemis suspected his intentions and daubed her face and the faces of her nymphs with white clay, whence the epithet, Alphaea. The river-god could not distinguish the goddess among the mud-daubed nymyhs and went away disappointed. From this the custom thereafter arose that at the celebration for the goddess in Letrini the celebrants daubed their faces with white clay.

Alpheaea (al-fē-ē'a). See **Alphaea.**

Alphesiboea (al''fē-si-bē'a). An I n d i a n nymph. When Dionysus traveled in India he met her and fell passionately in love with

her but she rejected his advances. Dionysus, transforming himself into a tiger, some say, compelled her to ride across the Sollax River on his back, and from this incident the river was renamed the Tigris.

Alphesiboea. In legend, the mother, by Phoenix, son of Agenor, of Adonis. But the general account is that Adonis was the son of Cinyras by his own daughter Myrrha.

Alphesiboea. A variant name of Arsinoë, daughter of Phegeus who married Alcmaeon.

Alphesiboea. In Greek legend, a daughter of Bias and the wife of Pelias, but the name of the wife of Pelias is usually given as Anaxibia.

Alpheus (al-fē'us, al'fē-us). River-god of the Alpheus River in Elis. On one occasion Arethusa, one of the chaste companions of Artemis, was bathing in his waters, and was terrified to feel an embracing movement about her. She leaped to the bank and fled. Alpheus pursued her and she called on Artemis for help. Artemis took her away to Ortygia near Syracuse, rent the earth and transformed Arethusa into a fountain that flowed from the chasm. Alpheus dived under the sea and made his way to Ortygia, and there mingled his waters with those of the fountain of Arethusa. It was said that a flower thrown into the Alpheus River in Greece would ultimately turn up in the fountain of Arethusa at Ortygia, having followed the route under the sea that was taken by Alpheus. On another occasion Alpheus went to Letrini where Artemis was holding revels with her companions with the intention of seizing the goddess. But Artemis suspected him and disguised herself and her maidens with white clay. Alpheus was unable to distinguish the goddess and was compelled to retire, as the maidens laughed at his disappointment. See **Alphaea.**

Alpheus River. [Also (for parts of its course): **Rouphia, Rufia, Ruphia;** Greek **Alpheios.**] River in Greece, in the Peloponnesus, flowing generally NW from S Greece into the Ionian Sea. The plain of Olympia touches its N bank, and its name is mentioned repeatedly in the legend and history of Greece. In more modern times, it occurs in English literature as the original of Coleridge's river Alph, mentioned in *Kubla Khan.* In Greek mythology, it was the river diverted by Heracles in order to clean the Augean stables. It flows at one point under the ground, and was for this reason believed by the ancient Greeks actually to flow under the sea to Sicily.

Alps (alps). [Latin, **Alpes**.] The most extensive mountain system in Europe, comprising a part of what is now SE France, most of Switzerland, a part of N Italy, a part of S Germany, and parts of Austria and Yugoslavia, and consisting of a number of ranges separated by deep valleys. The system was divided in ancient times into: 1) the Maritime Alps (Alpes Maritimae), including the Ligurian Alps, highest peak, Punta Argentera (10,184 feet) in NW Italy; 2) the Cottian Alps (Alpes Cottiae or Cottianus), highest peak, Monte Viso (Mons Vesulus) (12,605 feet) SW of Turin, NW Italy, near the French border; 3) the Graian Alps (Alpes Graiae), which include the Little St. Bernard Pass (7177 feet) over which Hannibal is thought to have marched into Italy in 218 B.C., highest peaks, Gran Paradiso (13,324 feet) in NW Italy, and the Barre des Écrins (13,462 feet) in SE France; 4) the Pennine Alps (Alpes Penninae), the highest portion of the system, which includes the Great St. Bernard Pass (Mons Penninus) (8111 feet) between Switzerland and N Italy and the summits Mont Blanc (15,781 feet) in SE France on the Italian border, Monte Rosa (15,217 feet) on the border between Switzerland and Italy, and Mont Cervin or the Matterhorn (14,780 feet) on the border between Switzerland and Italy; 5) Rhaetian Alps (Alpes Raeticae), including Saint Gotthard Pass (6935 feet) and Finsteraarhorn (14,026 feet) in SC Switzerland, and Piz Bernina (13,295 feet) in the extreme SE corner of Switzerland; 6) the Noric Alps (Alpes Noricae), with Eisenhut (8006 feet) and Gross Glockner (12,461 feet) in the Tirol, S Austria; 7) the Carnic Alps (Alpes Carnicae), with the summit Kellerwand (9217 feet) on the border between Austria and Italy; 8) the Venetian Alps (Alpes Venetae), also called the Dolomites, with the summit Marmolada (10,965 feet) in NE Italy; and 9) the Julian Alps (Alpes Juliae) in NW Yugoslavia with the summit Triglav (9394 feet). Outlying ranges in Hungary and Yugoslavia are respectively: Karawanken (Caravanca Mons) and the Dinaric Alps (Alpes Dinaricae).

The length of the range from the Pass of Giovi (N of Genoa) to Semmering Pass (SW of Wiener Neustadt, Austria) is over 600 miles, and its width is from 90 to 180 miles. The average height of the system is about 7700 feet.

Altes (al′tēz). In Homeric legend (*Iliad*), a king of the warlike Leleges. He was the father of Laothoë who became Priam's concubine.

Althaea (al-thē′a). In Greek legend, a daughter of Thestius. She was said to be the wife of Oeneus, king of Calydon in Aetolia, and the mother of Meleager, Tydeus, and Deianira. According to some accounts, Meleager was her son by Ares and Deianira was her daughter by Dionysus. Shortly after Meleager's birth the Fates prophesied that he would live only as long as a brand at that time burning in the fire was unconsumed. She seized the brand, quenched it and hid it away, thus saving his life. When, following the hunt for the Calydonian Boar, Meleager killed her brothers, Althaea recovered the partly burned brand and hurled it into the flames, thus causing Meleager's death. In despair at the violation of her maternal feelings she then hanged herself.

Althaemenes (al-thē′mē-nēz). In Greek mythology, a son of Catreus, king of Crete. His sisters were Aërope who married Atreus and became the mother of Agamemnon and Menelaus, Clymene who married Nauplius and bore Palamedes and Oeax, and Apemosyne. On learning from an oracle that Catreus would perish by the hand of one of his own children, Althaemenes and Apemosyne left Crete so that they should not be the instrument to fulfill the oracle. They went to Rhodes and settled at Camirus. Althaemenes raised an altar to Zeus on a nearby mountain-top. He surrounded the altar with a ring of bronze bulls which roared whenever danger threatened Rhodes. His sister Apemosyne was ravished by Hermes and Althaemenes, mocking her story that Hermes had attacked her, killed her. Years later Catreus came to Rhodes in search of his son. He landed at night, was mistaken for a pirate, and killed by a spear flung by Althaemenes. When Althaemenes learned that he had killed his father and that the oracle had been fulfilled in spite of his self-imposed

fat, fāte, fär, fãre, errant; net, mē, hér ardent; pin, pīne; not, nōte, möve, nôr,

exile, he prayed to be swallowed up by the earth. The earth parted and he disappeared. He was honored as a hero in Rhodes.

Altilia (äl-tē′lya). See **Saepinum**.

Altis (al′tis). The sacred precinct of Zeus at Olympia. About the sacred grove rose the installations connected with the Olympic Games, including the temples of Zeus and Hera, treasuries, administrative buildings, and the stadium.

Alyattes (al-i-at′ēz). Son of Sadyattes, whom he succeeded as king of Lydia c617 B.C. and reigned until 560 B.C. He waged war on the Medes under Cyaxares, drove the Cimmerians out of Asia, and extended the conquests of the Lydian kings on the coast of Asia Minor by conquering Smyrna, a colony of Colophon, and attacking Clazomenae. He attempted to extend his empire by taking Miletus. Twice he defeated the Milesians in battle but did not take the strongly walled city which commanded the sea. Since siege under these circumstances was hopeless, each year he marched through the country surrounding the walled city and burned the standing crops but spared the houses of the farmers, as he wanted them to return and plant more crops for him to plunder. The sixth year that he did this flames from the burning grain were carried by a high wind to the temple of Athena Assesia and burned it to the ground. The army of Alyattes withdrew to Sardis and there, in a short while, Alyattes fell sick. As his illness could not be cured he sent messengers to Delphi for information but his messengers were told that no answer would be given him until he rebuilt the temple of Athena at Assesus. Alyattes now sought a truce that would give him time to rebuild the temple. But Thrasybulus, tyrant of Miletus, had been informed of the oracle by his friend Periander of Corinth and prepared a trick by which he hoped to bring the war to an end. He ordered all the meager supply of grain to be brought to the market-place, commanded the Milesians to dress in their finery and gather there, and to be ready at a signal to fall to feasting and revelry. When the herald of Alyattes arrived he found the Milesians feasting and making merry as if they had not a care in the world. On his return he reported the prosperity of the city to Alyattes who was astonished, for he had hoped to starve the city into submission by burning the crops. The news brought by the herald convinced Alyattes that it was fruitless to prosecute a war against a city that seemed to thrive on it. He made an alliance of friendship with Miletus and brought the war to an end. He then built two temples of Athena at Assesus to replace the one he had burned and shortly afterward recovered from his illness. Alyattes was the father of Croesus who succeeded him as king. The tomb of Alyattes north of Sardis, his capital, was an outstanding monument of antiquity.

Amalthea (am-al-thē′a). In Greek mythology, a goat-nymph who provided milk for the infant Zeus when he was reared by nymphs in a cave in Crete. According to some accounts, Zeus borrowed one of her horns and gave it to the nymphs. This horn, the "Cornucopia," had the property of being filled with whatever food or drink its possessor required. In gratitude to Amalthea, Zeus set her image among the stars as the constellation Capricorn.

Amalthea. In Roman legend, the Sibyl who sold the Sibylline books to Tarquin.

Amanus (a-mā′nus). [Modern name, **Alma Dagh** (or **Dağ**).] In ancient geography, a mountain group, a branch of the Taurus range on the borders of Cilicia and Syria.

Amaranth (am′a-ranth). A flower (the word means "unfading" or "everlasting"), often planted on graves and therefore poetically associated with death. (JJ)

Amarynceus (a-mar′in-kus). In Homeric legend (*Iliad*), a king in Messene who shared the rule of Elis with Augeas. He was slain by Nestor in a war that the Eleans waged on the Pylians and was buried at Buprasium. Nestor won all the contests except the chariot race in the funeral games held in honor of Amarynceus. Diores, son of Amarynceus, led a company against Troy in the Trojan War.

Amarynthia (a-mar-in′thi-a) or **Amarysia** (-is′i-a). Epithet of Artemis. It comes from the town of Amarynthus in Euboea, which was named for a hunter of Artemis by that name. Artemis Amarynthia was also worshiped in Attica.

Amasis II (a-mā′sis). [Also: Amosis, Aahmes, Ahmes.] Egyptian king, the fifth of the XXVIth dynasty, fl. c569–525 B.C. According to Herodotus, Amasis was sent by Apries, king of Egypt, to quell a rebellion of the soldiers after they had been defeated by the Cyrenaeans. As Amasis was exhorting the soldiers one came up behind him and placed a helmet on his head, saying he thereby crowned him king. The soldiers acclaimed him and instead of quashing the revolt in the army, Amasis marched at the head of it to seize power from Apries. Apries sent a man of high rank to go and bring Amasis back with him. The envoy soon saw what Amasis planned and hastened back to tell Apries. But the latter was so enraged with his envoy for returning without Amasis that he cut off his ears and nose. This barbarous act to a man of high rank caused the Egyptians, who up to now had supported Apries, to go over to the side of Amasis to whom they now offered their aid. Apries, at the head of a force of mercenaries, marched against Amasis and was defeated. Amasis took Apries captive and returned with him to Saïs, where he took over the palace of Apries. He treated Apries kindly until criticism of his kindness to an enemy caused him to turn Apries over to his former subjects, who strangled him. Amasis now became king. At first he was somewhat despised by his subjects because he had been a mere private citizen before seizing the throne but he won their respect by diplomacy rather than force. He caused a golden vessel in which he had habitually washed his feet to be melted down. From this he made a golden image of one of the gods and set it up in the city. The Egyptains immediately began to worship it. Amasis called his people together and revealed that the image had been made of a vessel formerly used for bathing the king's feet yet now it was given unquestioning worship. He compared himself to the vessel. Once he had been a private person and nobody paid much attention to him; now he was king and he ordered them to honor and obey him. His lesson was not lost on his subjects. Herodotus says of Amasis that from dawn to noon he carried on the public business with great earnestness. But from noon on he joked, feasted, and drank wine, enjoying himself as much as he might. Criticized for his light-hearted manner after carrying on affairs of state all morning, Amasis replied with an analogy. Bow-

men, he said, string and bend their bows when they want to shoot; when shooting is over, they unstring the bows for if the bow was kept always tautly strung it would break and in time of need would fail the bowman. For the same reason, he divided his own time between business and pleasure. It is said that before Amasis became king he was in the habit of stealing when he needed funds to carry on his pleasures. When discovered on various occasions if he denied that he was a thief he was brought before the nearest oracle. Sometimes the oracle would say he was guilty, sometimes it would declare he was not a thief. When he became king, he neglected the temples of the oracles that had pronounced him innocent of his thefts because he judged them to be utterly unreliable and worthless. But those that had rightly judged him guilty he honored with great reverence.

Amasis had treaties of alliance and friendship with Polycrates of Samos and with Croesus, king of Lydia. He extended his kingdom by conquering Cyprus and he exerted great influence in Cyrene. Egypt was immensely prosperous during his reign. He erected many monuments and made gifts to the temples. He built a gateway to the temple of Isis at Saïs, added a number of colossal statues and sphinxes and a recumbent colossus. At Memphis also he gave a recumbent colossus to the temple and built a temple of Isis. Remains of his monuments still exist. He welcomed Greeks to his kingdom (Solon was one of his visitors), established them in the port city of Naucratis and allowed them to set up temples and altars to their gods. He contributed the very large sum of 1000 talents to the rebuilding of the temple of Delphi that had burned in 548 B.C.; and also gave rich gifts to the temple of Athena in Cyrene, the home of his wife Ladice, daughter of King Battus; to the temple of Athena at Lindus in Rhodes, because the daughters of Danaus stopped there on their flight from Egypt; and to the temple of Hera at Samos, because he was a bond friend of Polycrates, tyrant of Samos. Later Amasis dissolved the bond of friendship with Polycrates because, according to Herodotus, Polycates enjoyed too good fortune. Amasis said he knew that such uninterrupted good

fat, fāte, fär, fãre, errạnt; net, mē, hė́r ardẹnt; pin, pīne; not, nōte, möve, nôr, fortune would surely bring down the envy and wrath of the gods on Polycrates. He therefore no longer wished to be his bond friend so that he would not be obliged to grieve on his account when the inevitable doom overtook him. This is the story Herodotus gives for the dissolution of the alliance between Amasis and Polycrates. Others, however, say that the alliance may have been weakened when Amasis learned that Polycrates was intriguing with the Persians against Egypt when Cambyses, son of Cyrus, proposed a campaign against Egypt. It was supposedly because of anger against Amasis that Cambyses resolved to make war on Egypt, but by the time Cambyses reached Egypt with his army Amasis had died and been succeeded by his son Psammenitus (Psammetichus III), 525 B.C. When he came to Saïs Cambyses ordered that the body of Amasis should be brought from its tomb. His tomb was in the sacred precinct of Isis at Saïs near the tomb of the king he had deposed. Cambyses commanded his soldiers to stab Amasis' body and pull out the hair, but since the body had been embalmed it did not fall apart under this treatment and Cambyses ordered it to be burned, an act of the most frightful impiety to the Egyptians. But some say that Amasis, having been warned by an oracle of what would happen to him after his death, had given orders for his body to be entombed in a secret place in the sanctuary and another body substituted in his tomb so that Cambyses did not, after all, defile his body. However, Herodotus, who tells this story, does not believe it and thinks the Egyptians made it up to preserve the dignity of their king.

Amasis. Attic potter of the 6th century B.C. Eight vessels signed "Amasis made me" are extant. They date from c555–525 B.C. The decorator of his vessels worked in the black-figure style and is called the Amasis Painter. Among his extant works an amphora (Paris) shows Dionysus holding a cantharus. Two maenads, an arm of each about the other's neck, approach to offer him small animals. An amphora (Metropolitan Museum, New York), c550 B.C., attributed to the Amasis Painter, shows warriors departing for battle.

Amata (a-mā′ta). In Roman legend, the wife of King Latinus and the mother of Lavinia.

She promised Lavinia in marriage to Turnus, leader of the Rutuli. When Latinus, in obedience to the command of an oracle, gave Lavinia to Aeneas, Juno sent the Fury Alecto to inspire Amata with madness. Under this spell, Amata stirred up the Latin women to rebellion which led to war between the forces of Aeneas and those of Turnus. After two disastrous defeats by Aeneas, Amata begged Turnus not to meet Aeneas in single combat as Aeneas proposed. He agreed. Aeneas and his forces made another violent attack on the city and set it afire. Amata, fearing that Turnus had died in the attack, blamed herself for the war and destruction and hanged herself.

Amathus (am′a-thus). In ancient geography, a city of Phoenician origin on the S coast of Cyprus near the site of the modern Limassol. It contained a sanctuary of Aphrodite. According to some accounts, when Theseus fled from Crete, having killed the Minotaur, his ship, bearing him and Ariadne, daughter of King Minos, was caught in a great storm. As they neared Cyprus Ariadne, who was suffering from seasickness, asked to be put ashore at Amathus. Theseus reboarded his ship which was caught up in a gale and driven to sea again, and he never returned for Ariadne. The women of Amathus were very kind to Ariadne and took good care of her as she was soon to bear Theseus' child. These accounts say she died giving birth to the child and that the people of Amathus gave her a splendid funeral. They say Ariadne's tomb is in Amathus in a grove sacred to her, and on Cyprus an annual festival of Ariadne was celebrated in which a youth groaned and writhed in imitation of a woman in labor. Because Amathus refused to join the other Cyprians in the revolt against Persia (c499 B.C.), Onesilus who had seized the throne of Cyprian Salamis laid siege to Amathus. While he was so occupied a Persian force landed and gave battle to Onesilus. The Cyprians were defeated and Onesilus was slain. Because he had besieged their city the people of Amathus cut off his head and set it up over their gates. The skull was eventually reduced to bone by the passage of time, and a swarm of bees settled in it and filled it with a honeycomb. The Amathusians observed the prodigy and con-

actor; up, lūte, pull; oi, oil; ou, out; ᴛʜ, then; d̪ as d or j, s̪ as s or sh, t̪ as t or ch, z̪ as z or zh.

sulted the oracle. The advice they received was to take down the head, bury it, and sacrifice to Onesilus as to a hero and their affairs would prosper. This they did, and they continued to sacrifice to Onesilus annually.

AMAZONOMACHIA
Sarcophagus. *Louvre*

Amazonomachia (am″a-zon-ō-mak′i-a). In Greek antiquity, a battle of Amazons. There were several of these mythical battles: 1) the invasion of Lycia by the Amazons; 2) the invasion of Phrygia by the Amazons; 3) the battle with Heracles, his ninth labor, in which Hippolyte, queen of the Amazons, was slain; 4) the battle with Theseus to liberate Antiope; 5) the battle at the close of the Trojan War when the Amazons came to the assistance of Priam; 6) the Amazons' invasion of the island of Leuce at the mouth of the Ister. Since it furnished many interesting arrangements of men, women, and horses in action, the Amazonomachia was a favorite subject with Greek artists. One of the finest representations is a series of bas-reliefs in the British Museum which was found in the ruins of the Mausoleum at Halicarnassus.

Amazons (am′a-zonz). In Greek legend, a race of warrior women supposed to have dwelt near the Thermodon River on the coast of the Euxine Sea, and in the Caucasus Mountains. They are represented as forming a state from which men were excluded. They were governed by a queen. Girl children had their right breasts cut off (the name Amazon has been said by some to mean "breastless") so as not to interfere with the bow arm. Male children were slain in in-

fancy. The Amazons devoted themselves to war and hunting. Bellerophon fought them. Heracles, as one of his labors for Eurystheus, went to their country to fetch the girdle of the Amazon queen Hippolyte. By a misunderstanding inspired by Hera he made war on the Amazons, who had been inclined to be friendly, killed many and took some prisoners. According to Herodotus the Amazons who were being shipped back to Greece rose up and massacred the Greek crews. Unfamiliar with the ways of ships, they then were carried by the winds to the shores of Lake Maeotis. Here they went ashore, fell among the Scythians and seized their horses. After some time, these Amazons mingled with the Scythians and formed a new race. The new race, ancestors of the Sauromatae according to Herodotus, moved to lands north of the Tanais River and settled there. The women continued to hunt and make war and it was one of their laws that no girl should marry until she had killed a man in battle.

AMAZON
Red-figured Greek amphora, c440–430 B.C.
Metropolitan Museum of Art

fat, fāte, fär, fāre, errant; net, mē, hėr ardent; pin, pīne; not, nōte, mŏve, nôr,

During the reign of Theseus, the Amazons remaining about the Thermodon River marched to Athens and attacked it. Some say this was done because Theseus had accompanied Heracles on his raid and had carried off the Amazon Antiope, who became the mother of his son Hippolytus. The Amazons were defeated by the Athenians and were driven off. In the Trojan War the Amazons under their queen Penthesilea came to the aid of the Trojans. They were defeated by the Greeks and Penthesilea was slain by Achilles. Plutarch reports of the Amazons that they annually met with the Albanians on the banks of the Thermodon River for two months, after which they withdrew again to their own country and lived without the company of men. The wars between the Amazons and Greeks were a favorite subject with Greek painters and sculptors. Many friezes of temples, vase paintings, and metopes were devoted to this subject.

Amber Islands (am'bėr). [Also: **Electrides.**] In ancient geography, a name given by the Greeks in later times to the islands in the North Sea off what is now Denmark, Germany, and the Netherlands. See also **Glessariae.**

Ambiorix (am-bī'ọ̄-riks). Gallic chief; fl. 1st century B.C., leader of the Eburones. He is famous for his campaigns against the Romans (54–53 B.C.) in which he twice defeated them in what is now Belgium but fled across the Rhine at the approach of Julius Caesar.

Ambracia (am-brā'shi-ạ). [Modern name, **Arta.**] In ancient geography, a city in NW Greece situated on the Arachthus River, N of the Ambracian Gulf. It was founded as a colony by the Cypselids of Corinth in the 7th century B.C., but following the death of Periander of Corinth (585 B.C.) Ambracia detached itself from the mother city and set up a democracy. In the Peloponnesian War the city appealed to Sparta for aid against Athens and her allies, the Amphilochians and Acarnanians. The Peloponnesians sent a force but in 426 B.C. betrayed the Ambracians by a secret agreement with the Athenian general Demosthenes, under which the Peloponnesians stole away without the knowledge of the Ambracian allies and left them to the mercy of Demosthenes. Demosthenes and the Amphilochians inflicted a stunning

defeat on the Ambracians at Idomene. Of such magnitude was the disaster, according to Thucydides, that he did not record the number of the dead "because the amount stated seems so out of proportion to the size of the city as to be incredible." Following the defeat the Ambracians made a 100-year treaty with the Amphilochians and Acarnanians and withdrew from the war. Philip II of Macedon placed a garrison in the city after defeating the Greeks at Chaeronea (338 B.C.). This garrison was expelled after his death (336). Under Pyrrhus, the city became the capital of Epirus, 294 B.C.

Ambracian Gulf (am-brā'shi-ạn). [Also: **Gulf of Arta.**] Inlet of the Ionian Sea in W Greece. Length, about 25 miles, greatest breadth, about ten miles.

Ambrosia (am-brō'ẓiạ). Literally, "immortality." A celestial substance, commonly represented as the food of the gods, sometimes as their drink, and also as a richly perfumed unguent. When eaten by mortals it conferred immortality on them. It was also supposed to preserve against decay and corruption. In the *Iliad* the bodies of Hector, Patroclus, and Sarpedon were preserved and made whole by applications of ambrosia by the gods.

Ameipsias (ạ-mēp'si-ạs). A Greek poet of the Old Comedy who was contemporary with Aristophanes and flourished toward the end of the 5th century B.C. His *Connus*, in which Socrates was the hero, won first prize over Aristophanes' first version of *Clouds* in 423 B.C. In 414 B.C. he again won with his *Revellers* over Aristophanes who presented his *Birds*. Only fragments of his work survive.

Amestratus (ạ-mes-trā'tus). [Modern name, **Mistretta.**] Town on the island of Sicily, situated near the N coast between Messana and Panormus.

Amestris (ạ-mes'tris). Daughter of Otanes, according to Herodotus, but daughter of Onophas, according to Ctesias, and the favorite wife of Xerxes, to whom she bore at least five children. Her crimes and cruelties are related by Ctesias at some length, and are mentioned by Herodotus. She is believed by some to be the Vashti of the Book of Esther.

Amisodarus (ạ-mi-sō'dạ-rus). Named by

Homer (*Iliad*) as a king of Caria who reared the Chimaera. His sons Atymnius and Maris were comrades of Sarpedon in the Trojan War. They were slain, the one by Antilochus, the other by Thrasymedes, sons of Nestor.

Ammon (am'on). The Greek and Roman conception of the Egyptian sun-god, Amon (Amon-Re), Amen (Amen-Ra). The Greeks called him Zeus-Ammon to identify him with Zeus. The Romans called him Jupiter-Ammon. According to the Greeks, when Typhon attacked the gods Zeus transformed himself into a ram and fled to Egypt. Later when Heracles was in Libya in quest of the Apples of the Hesperides, he visited the oracle of Ammon and demanded to see Zeus. The god did not wish to show himself but when Heracles persisted, Zeus killed a ram, flayed it, and cut off its head. The god then held the ram's head before him, covered himself with the rams fleece and in this guise he presented himself to Heracles. It is for this reason, according to Herodotus, that the Egyptians show their images of Zeus-Ammon with the face and horns of a ram, and it is for this reason that rams are held sacred by the Thebans of Egypt and are not sacrificed except on the one day of the year when the festival of Zeus-Ammon is celebrated. On this day they kill one ram and flay it. They cover the image of Zeus with the fleece and then present to the fleece-covered statue of Zeus an image of Heracles, after which they mourn the ram and bury it in a sacred spot. The oracle of Zeus-Ammon in Libya (situated at what is now the Oasis of Siwa in NW Egypt) was greatly venerated and was consulted by seekers from all over the ancient world. Laomedon, king of Troy, sent to the oracle of Ammon to learn how he could rid his land of the plague and sea monster that Apollo and Poseidon had sent against his land because he did not pay them as he had promised for their help in building the walls of Troy. The oracle told him to sacrifice his daughter Hesione to the monster. Cepheus, father of Andromeda, consulted the oracle to learn how he could be delivered from a monster that was ravaging his land and received similar advice. Croesus, king of Lydia, consulted the oracle of Ammon among others, when he was considering a war against Cyrus and the Persians. This oracle was founded, according to some accounts, in obedience to the command of a black dove that flew from the temple of Egyptian Thebes to this place, and ordered the inhabitants to establish an oracle of Zeus. Remains of the ancient temple of Zeus-Ammon on the site are still to be seen. The Spartans, who consulted the oracle of Ammon more frequently than the other Greeks, had their own sanctuary and oracle of Ammon in Sparta.

Ammonia (a-mō'ni-a). Epithet of Hera as the wife of Zeus-Ammon; these names were given to them by the Libyans. The Eleans poured libations and sang hymns to Hera Ammonia at Olympia once a month.

Amopaon (a-mō'pa-on). In Homeric legend (*Iliad*), a Trojan warrior, the son of Polyaemon. He was slain by Teucer, who used the shield of his brother Ajax as a bastion from behind which he shot his arrow and killed Amopaon.

Amor (ā'môr). The Roman counterpart of the Greek god of love, Eros.

Amorgos (ä-môr-gôs'). Island in the Aegean Sea, one of the Cyclades, about 16 miles SE of Naxos. It was the birthplace of the Greek poet Simonides. Area, about 50 square miles.

Ampelius (am-pē'li-us), **Lucius.** Roman author who was active probably sometime after 100 A.D. He is best known for a concise history, *Liber Memorialis*, which contains also a number of geographical and mythological entries. Although much of the material is not trustworthy, it includes the only known classical reference to the sculptures at Pergamum.

Ampelos (am'pe-los). A beautiful satyr who fell and was killed when plucking grapes from a vine that grew up an elm tree. He was a favorite of Dionysus, who placed him among the stars. A genus of singing birds that haunt vines, among them the Carolina waxwing, was named for him.

Amphiale (am-fī'a-lē). Promontory on Mount Aegaleos opposite the island of Salamis. From this spot Xerxes is said to have witnessed the Persian defeat at the Battle of Salamis (480 B.C.).

Amphianax (am-fī'a-naks). Another name for Iobates, king of Lycia, who received Proetus

fat, fāte, fär, fāre, errant; net, mē, hėr ardent; pin, pīne; not, nōte, möve, nôr,

and gave him his daughter Antia (Stheneboea) in marriage.

Amphiaraus (am″fi-a-rā′us). In Greek legend, an Argive seer and hero; he was the son of Oicles and was married to Eriphyle, sister of Adrastus, king of Argos. He took part in the Calydonian Hunt and accompanied Jason as an Argonaut on the voyage to Colchis to secure the Golden Fleece. When Adrastus proposed to march against Thebes to restore his son-in-law Polynices to the throne, he asked Amphiaraus to accompany him on the expedition as one of the leaders. Amphiaraus, who foresaw that all except Adrastus would perish, was reluctant to go and tried to discourage the others. His wife Eriphyle, however, had once settled a quarrel between him and Adrastus and had extracted a promise from each that they would abide by her decision in any future difference of opinion. Polynices now bribed her to compel Amphiaraus to march with Adrastus. She reminded him of his promise and he consented to go, but he left orders with his sons Alcmaeon and Amphilochus to kill their mother and march against Thebes when they grew up. Amphiaraus saw an omen of disaster in the death of the child Opheltes at Nemea who was killed by a serpent while his nurse showed the Argives where they could get water. At the assault on Thebes all the champions were killed except Adrastus. Amphiaraus fled in his chariot. Before Periclymenus who was pursuing him could cast his spear into his back, Zeus cleft the earth with his thunderbolt and Amphiaraus, his chariot, and his charioteer vanished into the chasm. The spot where he disappeared into the earth was shown not far from Thebes on the road to Potniae. Zeus made Amphiaraus, the one upright man in a lawless company, immortal. He was deified and worshiped as a divine, oracular hero at various places. He had a temple at Oropus in Attica and a famous oracle of Amphiaraus there was noted for the interpretation of dreams. Some say Amphiaraus, by means of an oracle, proposed to the Thebans that they make a choice: either to take him as their prophet or as their helper in war. The Thebans decided to take him as their helper in war. For this reason it was unlawful for the Thebans to consult him as an oracle; it was therefore forbidden to them to sleep in his temple and receive his prophecies in dreams.

Amphiareum (am″fi-ar′e̯-um). Sanctuary and oracle of Amphiaraus, near Oropus, in Boeotia, Greece. In Greek legend, Amphiaraus was one of the Seven who marched against Thebes, and was here swallowed up by the earth at the will of Zeus, to save him in his flight. The sanctuary occupies a narrow area on the bank of a torrent; it includes a temple and altar, a large portico, a long range of bases for votive statues, and a theater. All the existing ruins are of Hellenistic date. The oracle enjoyed great renown, and the deified seer had a high reputation for healing sickness. Excavations were made (1884 *et seq.*) here by the Archaelogical Society of Athens.

Amphictyon (am-fik′ti-o̯n). According to some accounts, a son of Deucalion and Pyrrha, but others say he sprang from the soil. He rose against Cranaus, king of Attica, and seized the throne. He entertained Dionysus and is said to have been the first man to mix water with wine, a wise precaution for preventing disputes at the meetings of the Amphictyonic Council. After a reign of 12 years Amphictyon in his turn was driven from the throne by Erichthonius, the earthborn son of the spilled seed of Hephaestus.

Amphictyony (am-fik′ti-o̯-ni) or **Amphictyonic League** (am-fik-ti-on′ik). In Greek history, a league of peoples inhabiting neighboring territories or drawn together by a community of origin or interests, for mutual protection and the guardianship in common of a central sanctuary and its rites. There were several such confederations, but the name is specially appropriated to the most famous of them, that of Delphi. This was composed of 12 tribes, and its deputies met twice each year, alternately at Delphi and at Thermopylae. Its origin dates back to the beginnings of Greek history. It exercised paramount authority over the famous oracular sanctuary of the Pythian Apollo and over the surrounding region, and conducted the Pythian games; and it constituted, though in an imperfect way, a national congress of the many comparatively small and often opposed states into which Greece was divided. The 12 members

actor; up, lūte, pull; oi, oil; ou, out; ᴛʜ, then; ḍ as d or j, ş as s or sh, ṭ as t or ch, ẓ as z or zh.

of the Delphic Amphictyonic League were the Thessalians, the Boeotians, the Dorians, the Ionians, the Perrhabeans, the Magnetes, the Locrians, the Oeteans, the Phtyiots, the Malians, the Phocians, and the Dolopians.

Amphidamas (am-fid′a-mas). In Greek legend, a son of Aleus. He and his brother Cepheus left their home in Tegea in Arcadia and joined the Argonauts on the quest for the Golden Fleece. When the Argonauts approached the island of Ares they were afraid to land because of the birds of Ares that dropped iron feathers and attacked with bronze bills and claws. Amphidamas suggested that the Argonauts should cover their heads with their shields and clash their weapons together to frighten the birds away. This ruse was successful and the Argonauts landed on the island of Ares as they had been advised to do by Phineus.

Amphidamas. Named by Homer (*Iliad*) as a king of Cythera to whom Autolycus gave a tusk-covered helmet. He gave it to Molus, father of Meriones, as a guest-gift and the latter carried it with him to the Trojan War.

Amphilochia (am-fi-lō′ki-a). In ancient geography, a region on the eastern shore of the Ambracian Gulf, inhabited by a tribe from Epirus.

Amphilochus (am-fil′ō-kus). In Greek legend, a son of Amphiaraus and Eriphyle, and the brother of Alcmaeon. Like his father, he was a seer. Some say he accompanied the Epigoni on their expedition against Thebes and that he helped Alcmaeon kill Eriphyle when they learned that she, by being bribed, had caused the death of their father by urging him to go as one of the original Seven Against Thebes. He accompanied the Greeks to Troy and after the war he traveled overland with Calchas and Podalirius to Colophon where they met the seer Mopsus, and where Calchas died. Amphilochus did not return to Argos immediately but remained in Cilicia where he founded the city of Mallus with Mopsus. After some time he departed for Argos, leaving Mopsus as ruler of Mallus but later he returned from Argos and sought to resume his former role as joint ruler of Mallus. He and Mopsus quarreled bitterly when Mopsus refused to share the powers. They attempted to resolve their quarrel in a duel, in the course of which

they killed each other. After their bodies had been consumed to ashes on funeral pyres, the ghosts of Amphilochus and Mopsus became intimate friends. An oracle was established in their names which came to be regarded as most infallible. Questions were written on wax tablets and the answers were revealed in dreams.

Amphimachus (am-fim′a-kus). In the *Iliad*, a grandson of Cteatus. He was a chief of the Epeans in the Trojan War and was slain by Hector.

Amphimarus (am-fim′a-rus). A son of Poseidon. According to some accounts he was the father of the poet Linus by the muse Urania.

Amphinome (am-fin′ō-me). In Greek legend, a daughter of Pelias, king of Iolcus. Deceived by Medea, she and her sister Evadne cut their sleeping father into small pieces and boiled these in a cauldron. They did this under the impression that Pelias would be rejuvenated, as Medea had promised would be the case if they followed her instructions. Pelias, however, was not restored to life. When Jason regained control of Iolcus he overlooked Amphinome's crime, which was committed in innocence, and found a husband for her. But some say that Amphinome, in horror, committed suicide.

Amphinomus (am-fin′ō-mus). In Homeric legend (*Odyssey*), a son of Nisus of Dulichium. Of all the suitors of Penelope he was the most pleasing to her, and according to some accounts, was the father by Penelope of Pan. In general, he was kinder and more sympathetic than Penelope's other suitors. He protested against the plan of Antinous to ambush and kill Telemachus as he returned from Sparta. Because he was a good man, Odysseus, when he returned to Ithaca disguised as a beggar, advised Amphinomus to leave Ithaca. He warned him that death awaited the wooers. But Amphinomus did not follow this advice. He remained and was slain by Telemachus during the slaughter of the suitors.

Amphion (am-fī′on, am′fi-on). In Greek mythology, a son of Antiope and Zeus and twin brother of Zethus. The twins were exposed on Mount Cithaeron to die when they were born but were found and raised by a herdsman. As young men they slew Dirce, who had mistreated their mother, by causing her

fat, fāte, fär, fãre, errant; net, mē, hér ardent; pin, pīne; not, nōte, möve, nôr,

to be dragged to death by a bull. They made themselves masters of Thebes and built part of the city. Amphion, a gifted musician, played so beautifully on the lyre which Hermes had given him, while the walls were being constructed, that the stones slid into place by themselves. He married Niobe and became the father of seven sons and seven daughters. When his children were slain by Artemis and Apollo because of Niobe's boasting, Amphion, in grief, killed himself. According to other accounts Amphion was killed by Apollo and was punished in the Underworld for attacking the priests of Delphi in revenge for the slaying of his children by Apollo.

Amphion. In Greek legend, a son of Hyperasius. He and his brother Asterius left their home in Achaea and joined the Argonauts in the quest for the Golden Fleece.

Amphipolis (am-fip′ọ̄-lis). In ancient geography, a city in Macedonia, on the Strymon River, about three miles from the Aegean Sea. Originally a Thracian town, it was colonized by Athens c436 B.C., and was captured (424 B.C.) by Sparta. Near it the Spartans under Brasidas defeated (422 B.C.) the Athenians under Cleon. It later became a Macedonian and then a Roman possession.

Amphiprostylus (am-fi-prọ̄-stī′lus). A Greek or Roman rectangular temple with a portico at both front and rear, but no columns on the flanks.

Amphis (am′fis). A Greek poet and writer of Middle Comedy. He was one of the earliest to write a play with the emancipation of women as the subject.

Amphissa (am-fis′a). In Greek legend, a daughter of King Echetus of Epirus. She was ravished by Aechmodicus and bore a child. To punish her, her father blinded her. He promised to restore her sight when she had ground barley corns that were made of iron into real flour. Amphissa was also sometimes known as Metope.

Amphissa. According to some accounts, a granddaughter of Aeolus. She was the offspring of Macareus and Canache, the son and daughter respectively, of King Aeolus, and she was loved by Apollo.

Amphissa. Town in Phocis, C Greece, N of the Gulf of Corinth, situated at the foot of the W slope of Mount Parnassus. In an-

cient times it was a Locrian city whose people claimed to be Aetolians, as they were ashamed to be thought of as Ozolian Locrians. According to tradition, it was named for Amphissa, beloved by Apollo. She was a daughter of Macareus and a descendant of Aeolus. On the citadel of the ancient city was a temple of Athena, in which was a bronze image said to have been brought from Troy. The Amphissians celebrated mysteries in honor of the Boy Kings, but no one could say who the Boy Kings were. Some said they were the Dioscuri, others that they were the Curetes, and still others claimed they were of the Cabiri. The Amphissians went to the aid of Delphi in the Sacred War of 356 B.C., but arrived too late and were repulsed by the Phocian general Philomelus. In 340 B.C., Amphissa was accused by Aeschines of Athens of cultivating the sacred plain of Crissa. The Amphictyonic League marched against Amphissa, imposed a fine on the city, but being unable to collect it, invited Philip of Macedon to come to the aid of the League. Philip captured and destroyed Amphissa. The rivalry and jealousy of the Greek city-states led some of them to invite Philip in; once in, they could not get him out. Athens and Thebes, however, alarmed at his rapid progress into Greece banded together to oppose him. They were completely defeated at the battle of Chaeronea (338 B.C.).

Amphissus (am-fis′us). In Greek mythology, a son of the nymph Dryope and Apollo. He was brought up by his foster father Andraemon, and was said to have founded the city of Oeta, where he built a temple to Apollo.

Amphithemis (am-fith′e-mis). In Greek mythology, a son of Apollo by Acacallis, daughter of King Minos of Crete. He was born in Libya whither his mother had been banished by Minos. Amphithemis is also known as Garamas.

Amphitrite (am-fi-trī′tē). In early mythology, the personification of the sea; the goddess who sends the waves and governs the inhabitants of the sea. In later mythology she is a Nereid, the daughter of Nereus and Doris. Some say Poseidon saw her dancing on the island of Naxos and carried her off to be his wife. Others say she fled to Atlas from his advances. He sent Delphinus as an ambassador to plead his cause, and this he did so successfully that Amphitrite consented to marry Poseidon. She bore him Triton, Rhode, and Benthesicyme. She was jealous of her many rivals for Poseidon's affections. She punished Scylla, a daughter of Phorcys whom Poseidon loved, by changing her into a hideous monster with six heads and twelve feet. Amphitrite is represented with a net about her hair and with crab claws on the top of her head. As queen of the sea she rides over the waves in a chariot made of shells and drawn by Tritons or dolphins, or sometimes she simply rides on the backs of the creatures of her domain. The Romans identified Amphitrite with their Salacia.

Amphitryon (am-fit′ri-on). In Greek legend, a descendant of Perseus. When Electryon, king of Mycenae, warred against the Taphians and the Teleboans because they had made a raid on his cattle and killed his eight sons, he left Amphitryon to rule in his place, and promised him his daughter Alcmene if he ruled well. Amphitryon learned that the Eleans had Electryon's cattle and bought them back. On learning that he was expected to pay for his own cattle Electryon was furious, and charged Amphitryon with incompetence. In the course of the dispute, Amphitryon hurled a club at one of the cattle and accidentally struck and killed Electryon. He was then banished from Mycenae and went with Alcmene to Thebes. However, she would not allow the marriage to be consummated until the murder of her eight brothers by the Taphians was avenged. Amphitryon was permitted by Creon, king of Thebes, to raise an army for that purpose on condition that he catch a ravaging fox, the Teumessian vixen, which by a decree of fate could not be caught. Amphitryon borrowed Laelaps, a dog which fate had decreed should catch whatever animal it might pursue, and went after the fox. Under these conditions the gods resolved the problem posed by these two animals by turning them both into stone. Amphitryon now attacked the Taphians but could not overcome them so long as the chief Pterelaus, who was rendered immortal by one golden hair, continued to live. Comaetho, daughter of Pterelaus, cut off this hair for love of Am-

phitryon, and Pterelaus perished. Amphitryon was successful, but he killed Comaetho for her betrayal of her father. While Amphitryon was away at the war Zeus, disguised as her husband, embraced Alcmene, telling her the deaths of her brothers had been avenged. When Amphitryon returned, he learned from a seer that Alcmene had been loved by a god. Later twin sons, Heracles and Iphicles, were born a day apart, to Alcmene. According to some accounts, Amphitryon put two harmless serpents into the children's cradle while they were yet babes in order to find out which child was his. Heracles seized the serpents in his bare hands and strangled them gleefully. Iphicles screamed, and Amphitryon knew this was his son. But others say it was Hera who sent the serpents in order to destroy Heracles. In the war between Thebes and Erginus, leader of the Minyans, Amphitryon was killed and was buried in Thebes.

Amphius (am′fi-us). In Homeric legend (*Iliad*), a Trojan ally. He was the son of Merops, a seer who exceeded all others in divining. Merops tried to persuade his two sons not to march to war in Troy as he knew they would never return if they did. But he could not preserve them from their fate and Amphius accompanied his brother Adrestus to Troy where both were slain.

Amphora (am′fō-ra). A tall, slender vessel, having two handles or ears, a narrow neck, and generally a sharp-pointed base for insertion into a stand or into the ground: used by the Greeks and Romans for transporting and storing wine, oil, honey, grain, etc. They were commonly made of hard-baked, unglazed clay, but Homer mentions amphorae of gold. Amphorae with painted decoration, having lids and provided with bases enabling them to stand independently, served commonly as ornaments among the Greeks and were given as prizes in racing and athletic contests. The Panathenaic amphorae were large vases of this class, bearing designs relating to the worship of Athena. Filled with oil from the sacred olives, they were given at Athens as prizes to the victors in the Panathenaic games.

Amphoterus (am-fō′te-rus). In Greek mythology, a son of Alcmaeon and Callirrhoë, and a brother of Acarnan. Their mother

AMPHORA
Athlete carrying a tripod, c540 B.C. *Metropolitan Museum of Art*

prayed that her infant sons might grow to manhood overnight and avenge the murder of their father by the sons of Phegeus. Her prayer was answered. Amphoterus and Acarnan met Phegeus and his family as they were going to Delphi, slew them, and took the robe and necklace of Harmonia, which Phegeus had intended to dedicate to Apollo, and carried them to Delphi.

Ampsanctus, Lacus (amp-sank′tus, lā′kus) or **Amsanctus Lacus** (am-sank′tus). [Modern: **Amsancti.**] Small lake in a valley of the same name in Samnium (modern province of Avellino), SW Italy, E of Naples, noted for its sulfurous vapors and cave.

Ampycides (am-pi′si-dēz). A name, meaning "Son of Ampycus," applied to Mopsus, a seer who accompanied the Argonauts.

Amulius (a̱-mū′li-us). In Roman legend, a son of Proca and a younger brother of Numitor, ruler of Alba Longa. Amulius revolted against Numitor, drove him out, killed his sons, and seized the throne. To make sure that there would be no legitimate heirs of Numitor, Amulius made his niece Rhea, Numitor's daughter, a vestal virgin, which

automatically compelled her to chastity. However, Mars is said to have visited and embraced Rhea, and she bore him twin sons, Romulus and Remus. Amulius seized and bound her, and cast her into prison. He ordered the infants committed to the Tiber River. The twins were saved. When they reached manhood, Remus, some say, was seized by brigands and handed over to Amulius, who recognized him as one of the infants he had ordered to be destroyed so many years before. Romulus gathered his followers, stormed the house of Amulius, and freed his brother. He killed Amulius and restored Numitor to the throne.

Amyclae (a̱-mī′klē). In ancient geography, a town on the Eurotas River in Laconia, Greece, about three miles S of Sparta. According to tradition, it was founded by Amyclas, a son of Lacedaemon, and it was the legendary seat of Tyndareus. The town was sacred to Apollo, and contained the most famous precinct of the god in Laconia. In it was a magnificent throne, made by the Magnesian sculptor Bathycles. The reliefs on the throne depicted a large number of figures of mythology as well as a band of dancers who represented the Magnesian assistants of Bathycles. The throne, as described by Pausanias, consisted of several seats, the center one of which was reserved for the image of the god. The Spartans used gold sent by Croesus to adorn the image and each year the women wove a tunic for it. The tomb of Hyacinthus, son of Amyclas, was under the throne. There was a sanctuary of Cassandra at Amyclae as well as what was supposed to be a tomb of Agamemnon. The Amyclaeans worshiped Dionysus as "Psilax," the Doric word for "wings," because wine uplifts men and lightens their spirits. Amyclae was laid waste by the Dorians and never recovered. According to a legend, the inhabitants of Amyclae had been so often alarmed by false reports of the hostile approach of the Spartans that all mention of the subject was forbidden; hence when they did come no one dared announce the fact and the town was captured. "Amyclaean silence" thus became a proverb.

Amyclas (a̱-mī′klas). According to Spartan legend, a son of Lacedaemon and Sparte (or Sparta), the daughter of Eurotas. He

built a town in Laconia and named it Amyclae for himself. Amyclas was the father
of Hyacinthus.

Amyclas. In Greek mythology, a son of Niobe
and Amphion. According to some accounts,
when Apollo slew the other sons of Niobe
he was spared because he offered up a propitiatory prayer to Leto.

Amycus (am′i-kus). In Greek legend, a son
of Poseidon and the nymph Melia. He succeeded his brother as king of the Bebryces.
He was very proud of his skill as a boxer
and challenged all travelers who came his
way to box with him. If they refused, he
hurled them into the sea; if they accepted,
he killed them in the match. When the
Argonauts landed on his shores he refused
to give them water and supplies unless they
would send their best man to box with him.
Polydeuces accepted his challenge and according to one tale, although he was older
and smaller than Amycus, he defeated and
killed him. The Argonauts then sacrificed
20 red bulls to appease Poseidon for the
slaying of his son.

Amymone (a-mi-mō′nē). In Greek mythology,
one of the 50 daughters of Danaus. Danaus
instructed his daughters to appease Poseidon
who had dried up the streams of Argolis in
anger. Amymone, while searching for water,
disturbed a satyr who attempted to ravish
her. She called for help. Poseidon appeared
and hurled his trident at the satyr, but the
satyr avoided the blow and fled. The trident
was implanted in the rock. Poseidon fell
in love with Amymone and embraced her.
When he learned that she was searching for
water, he caused a spring to gush from the
rock where the three prongs of his trident
had struck it. This spring, known as the
fountain of Amymone, became the source
of the Lerna River and never dries up, even
in midsummer when the other streams of
Argolis are dry. The Hydra of Lerna, child
of Echidna, was born under a plane tree near
this fountain of Amymone. Amymone bore
Nauplius, the famous navigator, by Poseidon.

Amyntas I (a-min′tas). King of Macedonia;
died c498 B.C. He was a son of Alcetas and
fifth in descent from Perdiccas, the founder
of the dynasty. He presented earth and
water as a token of his submission to the
Persian commander Megabazus, whom

Darius, on returning to Persia, had left at
the head of 80,000 men in Europe.

Amyntas II. King of Macedonia (394–370
B.C.); nephew of Perdiccas II. He obtained
the crown of Macedonia proper in 394 B.C.
by the murder of Pausanias, son of the
usurper Aëropus. He was forced to flee
from his kingdom (385 B.C.) when Argaeus,
the son of Pausanias and supported by the
Illyrians, invaded it. He left the southern
districts of Macedonia and the cities on the
Thermaic Gulf to the Chalcidian League, a
federation of some of the cities of Chalcidice
under the leadership of Olynthus. When he
was restored to his throne by the Thessalians
with whom he had taken refuge, Olynthus
refused to give up the cities he had handed
over. Amyntas asked the aid of Sparta.
The Spartans answered his appeal, defeated
the Olynthians, broke up the Chalcidian
League, and restored his coastal cities to
Amyntas. Amyntas died in 370 B.C. and was
succeeded by his son Alexander II, the oldest
brother of Philip II.

Amyntas III. King of Macedonia (360–359
B.C.); died 336 B.C. He was the grandson
of Amyntas II. He was an infant at the
death of his father in 360 B.C., and was excluded (359) from the throne by the regent,
his uncle Philip of Macedon, at whose court
he was brought up and whose daughter he
married. He was executed by Alexander the
Great for a conspiracy against the king's life
(336 B.C.).

Amyntor (am′in-tôr). In Greek mythology, a
king of Ormenium, at the foot of Mount
Pelion. Heracles sought his daughter, Astydamia, and when Amyntor refused to give
her to him on the ground that Heracles already had a wife, Heracles attacked his city,
killed Amyntor, and carried off Astydamia.
She, according to some accounts, bore him
Tlepolemus. But others say her son was
Ctesippus.

Amyntor. In Homeric legend (*Iliad*), a son
of Ormenus. He was the father of Phoenix,
tutor of Achilles, by his wife Cleobule.
Cleobule asked Phoenix to seduce the mistress of Amyntor. When Amyntor learned
that Phoenix had done so, he cursed him,
praying that Phoenix should never have a
son of his own. Amyntor was the owner of
a famous tusk-covered helmet, the Casque

fat, fāte, fär, fãre, errạnt; net, mē, hėr ardẹnt; pin, pīne; not, nōte, mŏve, nôr,

of Amyntor. It was stolen from him by Autolycus, from whose hands it eventually passed and came to those of Meriones, the squire of Idomeneus of Crete. Meriones loaned the helmet to Odysseus when he went with Diomedes to spy on the Trojan camp.

Amythaon (a-mi-thā′on). In Greek legend a son of Cretheus of Thessaly and Tyro. He was a brother of Aeson and strongly supported Jason in his claim to the throne of Iolcus. Amythaon lived in Pylus where he was noted for his wisdom, and by his wife Idomene, the daughter of his brother Pheres, he was the father of Bias and of the seer Melampus.

Anabasis (a-nab′a-sis). Account by the Greek soldier-historian Xenophon, in seven books (original number uncertain) of the campaign of the Persian prince Cyrus the Younger against his brother Artaxerxes II, and of the retreat of the 10,000 Greek mercenaries after Cyrus′ death in the battle of Cunaxa near Babylon. The events cover the years 401–399 B.C. After the death of Cyrus the Greeks were faced with the problem of withdrawing from a hostile country. Although the title strictly applies only to the inland march, the major portion of the work is devoted to the famous retreat. Xenophon, at first present merely as a guest and observer, assumed command after most of the Greek commanders had fallen victim to Persian treachery. He does not hesitate to emphasize his own good judgment and ability in conducting the Greek force to the Black Sea at Trapezus, from which point the Greeks finally returned to Byzantium. (AH)

Anabasis of Alexander. Important historical work by Arrian, in seven books, all of which, with the exception of a few pages, has survived. It begins with the accession of Alexander the Great, and describes his campaigns and victories.

Anacharsis (an-a-kär′sis). Scythian prince, brother of Saulius, king of Thrace, active c600 B.C., and a contemporary of Solon. He traveled widely and visited Athens, where he obtained a great reputation for wisdom. By some he was reckoned among the legendary seven great sages of ancient times. On his way back to Thrace he stopped at Cyzicus. There he found the inhabitants celebrating a festival to Cybele, the Great Mother. He was so impressed by the magnificence of the festival that he vowed to create a similar festival if he returned safely to his homeland. On his arrival in Thrace he went to a sequestered place and performed the rites. Some Scythians, who observed him in the course of the ritual, informed his brother, King Saulius, of what they had seen and Saulius went to see for himself. Such was the hatred of the Scythians for foreign customs and rituals that when he beheld Anacharsis carrying out the rites for Cybele, Saulis shot Anacharsis with an arrow and killed him.

Anacreon (a-nak′rē-on). Greek lyric poet; born at Teos, in Asia Minor, c570 B.C.; died there, c478 B.C. His work concerns itself chiefly with love and wine. He was widely imitated in the Alexandrian period, and later, in a form of verse called, from him, Anacreontics. He is supposed to have been driven from Teos by the invasion (545 B.C.) of Cyrus the Great, to have fought briefly in the resisting army, and to have been tutor to Polycrates of Samos, at whose court he became a favorite. He was called to Athens on Polycrates′ death by Hipparchus, the patron of Simonides and other literary figures; he probably returned to Teos after Hipparchus was assassinated (514 B.C.). Valerius Maximus′ account, probably mythical, of his death by choking on a grape seed, gives the key to his reputation as a celebrator of the gay and leisurely life, though various writers attest to his sobriety. Although only fragments of his work are now extant, imitations, from the pseudocollection by Stephens (1554) to Thomas Moore (1800), demonstrate the popularity of his short, facile lyrics.

Anadyomene (an″a-dī-om′e-nē). An epithet of Aphrodite, in allusion to her origin from the sea.

Anaitis (a-nī′tis). [Also: **Anait, ′Anat;** Egyptian, **Anta.**] Syrian goddess whose worship was introduced into Egypt in the 15th century B.C. She was a war goddess, and is usually depicted with helmet, shield, and battle-ax. The Greeks identified her with Athena.

Ananius (a-nā′ni-us). A satirical writer of classical times.

Anaphe (ä-nä′fē). [Modern name, **Anafi** or **Anaphi.**] An island, seven miles long, in the SE Cyclades. Its name means "revealing"

actor; up, lūte, pu̇ll; oi, oil; ou, out; ŦH, then; ḏ as d or j, ṣ as s or sh, ṭ as t or ch, ẕ as z or zh.

and was given to it for the following reasons: When the Argonauts were returning from Colchis with the Golden Fleece they were overtaken by a great storm and were lost in pitch darkness. Jason called on Apollo to save them and at once there was a flash of light from the silver bow of Apollo. The flash of light revealed the island; Ancaeus, helmsman of the *Argo,* was able to beach the ship there. The Argonauts landed and gave thanks to the god and named the island for the flash of revealing light which saved them.

Anaurus (a̱-nou′rus) **River.** In ancient geography, a small river of Thessaly. According to legend, Jason, on his way to Iolcus, was stopped on the bank of the river by a crone who asked him to carry her across. He courteously agreed to do so and won the good will of the goddess, Hera, who had thus disguised herself to test him. On the way across the river Jason lost one of his sandals in the mud and did not bother to replace it before he appeared at the court of Pelias in Iolcus. Pelias had been warned concerning a man wearing one sandal; it was for this reason that he sent Jason off to Colchis to fetch the Golden Fleece.

Anax (a′naks). In Greek mythology, a giant son of Uranus and Gaea who was ruler of the land later known as Caria. His son, also a giant, named Asterius, succeeded him as ruler of the land.

Anaxagoras (an-aks-ag′ō-ra̱s). Greek philosopher, born at Clazomenae, in Ionia, c500 B.C.; died at Lampsacus in Mysia, c428 B.C. He was born of a noble family but gave up his inheritance to devote himself to science, and went to Athens. He was the first philosopher to settle permanently at Athens (c464–c434 B.C.), thus establishing Athens as a home of philosophy. There he became the teacher of Pericles, Thucydides, Euripides, and perhaps of Socrates. His theory of the universe, based on astronomical observation (which among other things led him to the correct explanation of eclipses) and the teachings of Anaximander, brought a charge of impiety against him because it denied the gods which were recognized by the state. Pericles, his good friend, defended him against the charge which was largely an expression of political hostility to Pericles himself, and he was acquitted. However, he felt compelled to emigrate and went to Lampsacus where he died soon after. Anaxagoras introduced a dualistic explanation of the universe as deriving from a chaotic and inextricable mass in which infinitely small particles (or "seeds"), existing in larger or smaller numbers and of varying taste, color, and size, constitute the distinction between different kinds of matter; on these the controlling function of mind (*nous*) is exercised to bring order via motion. The first half of this concept (which is fundamental to the atomic theory) and his description of the sun as a mass of molten metal, of heavenly bodies as rocks torn from earth, and of men and animals as being born from moist clay, to which they ultimately returned, were abhorrent to the pantheism of his time; the second half, through Aristotle and Averroës, became an absorbing topic of medieval speculation. His doctrine was expressed in a work in the Ionic dialect, *On Nature,* fragments of which survive.

Anaxandrides (an-aks-an′dri-dēz). Co-king of Sparta, with Ariston, in the time when Croesus was king of Lydia. According to tradition, during his reign Anaxandrides consulted the oracle at Delphi to learn how the Spartans might achieve success in their wars against Tegea, for of all the peoples the Spartans fought, only the Tegeans were invariably successful against them. The priestess at Delphi told the messengers of Anaxandrides that if Sparta wished to be successful against the Tegeans the bones of Orestes must be recovered from their Tegean grave. Once this was accomplished, through the cleverness of the Spartan Lichas, Sparta had the advantage in future engagements with the Tegeans.

Anaxandrides. Greek poet of Middle Comedy; fl. first half of the 4th century B.C. He went to Athens from Rhodes (or perhaps from Colophon) and won his first victory there in 376 B.C. Titles of 42 of his works as well as some fragments, survive.

Anaxarchus (an-aks-är′kus). Greek philosopher of Abdera, who was active c350 B.C. He was a disciple of Democritus. He attended Alexander in his Asiatic campaigns, and is said to have consoled the king after the murder of Clitus by maintaining that a king can do no wrong. Plutarch called him a self-made philosopher and deplored the means by which he consoled Alexander and encouraged him to depart from the principles of morality and justice he had once admired and practised. According to Plutarch, Anaxarchus had not been highly regarded as a philosopher before he attached himself to Alexander. He tells that once Anaxarchus and Callisthenes, a philosopher who was brought up in Aristotle's household, were discussing whether the climate of Greece or of Persia was the milder. Anaxarchus maintained that Persia was warmer. Callisthenes affected surprise, and pointed out that whereas in Greece Anaxarchus wore but one threadbare cloak, here in Persia in Alexanders' train he was covered with three thick warm coats. Either Persia was colder or the fortunes of Anaxarchus had changed considerably.

Anaxarete (an″ak-sar′ē̠-tē). In Greek mythology, a Grecian princess who was beloved by Iphis, a man of humble birth. He sent messages of love to her and adorned the doorposts of her house with garlands and wreaths of flowers. Anaxarete mocked him and scorned his love. In despair, Iphis resolved to place one final testimonial of his love on the doors of her house. He fixed a noose to the lintel and hanged himself. His funeral procession passed by Anaxarete's house, and as she watched it without compassion, the gods turned her to stone. The stone statue was placed in a temple in Salamis as a warning to hard-hearted maidens who mocked their lovers.

Anaxibia (an-ak-si′bi-ạ). In Greek legend, a daughter of Atreus and Aërope, and the sister of Agamemnon and Menelaus.

Anaxibia. In Greek legend, the wife of Nestor and mother of his sons. Her name is sometimes given as Eurydice.

Anaxilaus (ạ-nak-si-lā′us) or **Anaxilas** (-nak′si-lạs). Tyrant of Rhegium (494–476 B.C.); died 476 B.C. He won control of Zancle, which thereafter was known as Messana (Messina), and thus controlled both sides of the straits between Sicily and Italy.

Anaxilaus. Pythagorean philosopher and physician of the 1st century B.C. He was banished as a magician from Italy by Augustus in 28 B.C.

Anaximander (ạ-nak-si-man′dẽr). Greek philosopher (the second of the Ionian or Milesian school) and mathematician; born at Miletus, 610 B.C.; died c547 B.C. He was a friend and pupil of Thales. He taught that the principle of all things is a substance of indeterminate quality and limitless quantity, "immortal and imperishable," out of which all things arise and to which all return; eternal motion creates opposites, conflict between which brings about order and destroys it, in a continuing cycle. This substance, according to some accounts, he regarded as having a nature intermediate between that of water and air. He was probably the author of the first philosophical treatise in Greek prose. He is said to have discovered obliquity of the ecliptic, to have introduced the sundial and gnomon to Greece, and to have made the first map of the earth. His teachings had, after his death, some considerable influence on the theories of Anaxagoras.

Anaximenes of Lampsacus (an-ak-sim′ē̠-nēz; lamp′sạ-kus). Greek rhetorician and historian; born at Lampsacus in Mysia, c380 B.C., died c320 B C. He was a companion of Alexander the Great on his Persian campaigns. Author of histories of Greece, and biographies of Philip of Macedon and of Alexander, the latter in epic form, he is also the probable author of a treatise on rhetoric, *Rhetorica ad Alexandrum*, the only existing work on the subject prior to Aristotle (and formerly attributed to him).

Anaximenes of Miletus (mī-lē′tus, mi-). Greek philosopher; born at Miletus, in Asia Minor; fl. c546 B.C. He was the third of the Ionian or Milesian school, a contemporary and friend of Thales and Anaximander, usually reckoned a disciple of the latter. He regarded air as the principle of all things, various kinds of matter being created by its expansion with heat and contraction with cold.

Anaxo (ạ-nak′sō). In Greek mythology, a daughter of Alcaeus, son of Perseus. She was the sister of Amphitryon and married Electryon, her uncle, and became the mother of Alcmene. Alcmene married Amphitryon and Anaxo became her brother's mother-in-law.

Ancaeus (an-sē′us). In Greek legend, a son of Poseidon. He left his palace in Tegea and joined the Argonauts on the voyage in quest of the Golden Fleece. From his father

actor; up, lūte, pull; oi, oil; ou, out; ŦH, then; ḍ as d or j, ṣ as s or sh, ṭ as t or ch, ẕ as z or zh.

he had great skill in navigation, and after the death of Tiphys in the land of the Mariandyni Ancaeus became the helmsman of the *Argo*. He guided the ship to the Phasis River in Colchis and acted as steersman on the voyage of return from Colchis. After the many perils of the voyage Ancaeus returned safely to his home in Tegea. He had been told by a seer that he would not survive to taste wine from recently planted grape vines. On his return the vines had flourished, grapes had been harvested, and wine pressed. Ancaeus, about to set a cup of the wine to his lips, reminded the seer of his old prophecy and accused him of being a false prophet. The seer replied that "there is many a slip between the cup and the lip." At that instant a tumult arose over a wild boar that had been discovered in the vineyard. Ancaeus set down the cup, the wine untasted, and rushed off to slay the boar but the animal charged him and gored him to death.

Ancaeus. According to some accounts, a son or grandson of Lycurgus. Others say he was a son of Aleus and the brother of Amphidamas and Cepheus. He left his home in Arcadia and joined the Argonauts in the quest for the Golden Fleece. He wore a bearskin and carried a two-edged battle-ax because his grandfather had hidden his armor in an effort to prevent him from joining Jason. Next to Heracles, he was the strongest of the Argonauts and rowed on the same bench with Heracles. He was killed by the boar in the Calydonian Hunt.

Anchesmius (an-kes'mi-us). Epithet of Zeus, from his image on the low hill near Athens called Mount Anchesmus.

Anchiale (an-ki'a-lē). A nymph. According to some accounts, she produced the Dactyls in the Dictaean cave as she grasped the land of Oaxus.

Anchinoë (an-kin'ọ-ē). In Greek mythology, a daughter of the river-god Nilus. She was the wife of Belus, a king in Egypt, and bore him the twin sons Aegyptus and Danaus.

Anchises (an-kī'sēz, ang-). In mythology, a son of Capys and Themiste, and a descendant of Dardanus and Ilus, founders of the Trojan race. While he was tending his flocks Aphrodite came to him, disguised as the daughter of a Phrygian king. The goddess, who became the mother of Aeneas by An-

chises, later revealed her true identity to him, and made him vow that he would never reveal it. However, Anchises, having overindulged in wine, boasted that he had lain with a goddess. For this he was struck by a shaft of lightning and crippled in his limbs. After the fall of Troy he expressed his determination to remain and end his days in the city. He said he was old and useless and did not wish to flee with his son Aeneas. He was persuaded to go by a sign—a curl of flame settled on his young grandson's hair but didn't burn it—and a falling star confirmed the favorable omen. Carrying the gods of Troy, he rode out of the city on Aeneas' shoulders. When the oracle of Delos told the Trojans to seek out their mother country, Anchises took this to mean Crete, but a dream informed Aeneas that the oracle meant Italy, whither they then journeyed. Anchises died, according to Vergil, in Drepanum in Sicily, after having been a bulwark of advice and counsel to Aeneas. Even after his death he continued to aid his son. When the Trojan women, despairing that their journeying never ceased, burnt the ships in Italy, Anchises' shade appeared to Aeneas and advised him to leave those who were weary of wandering where they were, and to proceed to carry out his destiny with those who still had a love of glory. He also told Aeneas that he must visit him in Hades to find out what the future held. In accordance with these instructions, Aeneas entered the Underworld near Cumae. Anchises welcomed him and pointed out the souls in the Underworld that were waiting to be reborn and to win honor in Rome. He also gave Aeneas a very wide look at the future history of the empire he was destined to found.

Anchisia (an-kī'si-a), **Mount.** Mountain in Arcadia. Some say that Anchises, father of Aeneas, died here on the way to Italy after leaving Troy, and that this mountain, where he was buried, was named for him.

Ancile (an-sī'lē). The sacred shield of Mars, said to have fallen from heaven in the reign of Numa, and declared by the seers to be the palladium of Rome so long as it should be kept in the city. With 11 other ancilia, made in imitation of the original, it was given into the care of the Salii, or priests of Mars, who carried it annually in solemn procession through Rome during the festival of Mars in the beginning of March.

Ancius (an'shi-us, -shus). According to legend, one of the centaurs who, aroused by the aroma of the wine of Dionysus, attacked Heracles when he was visiting Pholus on his way to capture the Erymanthian Boar. Heracles drove him off.

Ancus Marcius (ang'kus mär'shi-us, -shus). According to Roman legend, the fourth king of Rome, who succeeded Tullus Hostilius and was said to have reigned from 640–616 B.C. He was a grandson of Numa Pompilius. If we are to believe the legends, it was in his reign that the Janiculum was added to Rome and fortified; the first bridge was built across the Tiber (this was the Pons Sublicius, "Pile Bridge," so-named because it was made of wooden piles, that was destroyed by the Romans while Horatius held the Etruscans at bay); a prison, the Carcer, was built; Rome's boundaries were extended and its seaport, Ostia, was founded. Ancus conquered the Latin village of Politorium and moved its people to Rome where he settled them on the Aventine Hill. He also defeated the Latins in one of the many wars the Romans had with their neighbors.

Andania (an-dā'ni-a). Ancient city in C Messenia, founded, according to tradition, by Polycaon, the Lelegian who conquered the country. Polycaon and his wife Messene had their palace here, and to this place the mysteries of Demeter were first brought into the country. Generations later, when Cresphontes secured control of the country by guile, in the return of the Heraclidae, the king's palace was at Stenyclarus. Andania was the center of the revolt against the Spartans which was inspired by Aristomenes and led to the Second Messenian war. The Messenians moved from Andania to Mount Eira to continue their defense, and after their sufferings and defeat in the war never wanted to return to Andania. When the Messenians returned to their country, nearly three hundred years later, Epaminondas, the Theban, helped them to build a new city near Ithome, which was named Messene.

Andocides (an-dos'i-dēz). Attic potter, active at the end of the 6th century B.C. Seven vessels signed by him as potter are extant. Four of these were decorated by the same painter, who for this reason and because his own name is not known, is known as the Andocides Painter. Twenty-six other works

HERACLES FEASTING
Red-figured Greek amphora, Andocides Painter, c510 B.C. On the other side of the amphora the same scene is presented in black-figure. *Munich*

actọr; up, lūte, pùll; oi, oil; ou, out; ᵺH, then; ḍ as d or j, ş as s or sh, ṭ as t or ch, ẓ as z or zh.

have been attributed to the Andocides Painter. He was one of the first and most important of the vase painters to use the red-figure technique. He also used the black-figure style to decorate the craters and cups he painted. An amphora (Munich) has on one side Heracles feasting, attended by Athena, Hermes and a cupbearer, in the black-figure style. On the other side Heracles feasting, attended by Athena, appears in the red-figure style (c510 B.C.). Works signed by Andocides as potter and decorated by the Andocides Painter include: an amphora (Louvre) with a man playing the cithara, and a combat; an amphora (Louvre) with women bathing; a kylix (Palermo) with archers and a trumpeter; and an amphora (Berlin) with Heracles and Apollo struggling for the Delphic tripod. Other works include an amphora (Boston) c520 B.C., with Heracles driving a bull, and an amphora (Louvre) with Heracles dragging Cerberus from Hades.

Andocides. Athenian orator and politician, born c440 B.C. at Athens; died c390 B.C. He was a member of a distinguished aristocratic family. In 415 B.C. he was accused of mutilating the statues of Hermes. The defacing of the sacred images before the start of the Athenian expedition to Sicily caused a near panic in Athens. Three hundred people were denounced for the act of impiety, which was probably committed in a spirit of skepticism and youthful exuberance (see **Alcibiades**). To save himself and others who might be innocent, Andocides agreed to give information about his aristocratic accomplices under a promise of amnesty. In spite of the promise he was deprived of some of his civic rights. He went to Cyprus and became a trader, in which occupation he made many shrewd deals for the benefit of Athens to show his patriotism. Twice he sought to have his status restored, and at last in 403 B.C., he was readmitted to Athens under a general amnesty which followed the establishment of the democracy. On his return he was active in public life, successfully defending himself against charges of impiety based on the old scandal of 415 B.C. In 391 B.C. he was sent as an ambassador to negotiate peace with Sparta. One of his orations, still extant, was made in behalf of the treaty

he brought back on this occasion. The treaty was rejected and he went into exile. Of two other orations which are preserved, *About Returning Home* pleaded for the restoration of his status as an Athenian, and was made in 410 B.C. In another he defended himself again against the old charges of impiety which were resurrected in 399 B.C.

Andraemon (an-drē′mon). In Homeric legend (*Iliad*), the husband of Gorge and son-in-law of Oeneus, king of Calydon. Diomedes made Andraemon king of Calydon in Aetolia after Oeneus, whom Diomedes had protected from his nephews, became too old to rule. He was the father of Thoas, a captain of Aetolians in the Trojan War.

Andraemon. According to mythology, he married the nymph Dryope after she had been ravished by Apollo and had borne a son to the god. Andraemon came upon his wife as she was being turned into a lotus tree because she had plucked the lotus blossoms, and heard her last instructions for the upbringing of her infant son just before the bark which was enclosing her whole body grew up over her face.

Androclea (an-drō-klē′a). In Greek legend, a daughter of Antipoenus of Thebes, a descendant of the Sparti. See **Alcis**.

Androcrates (an-drok′ra-tēz). According to legend, a mythical hero who founded Plataea in Greece. On the eve of the Battle of Plataea (479 B.C.), the Greeks drew up their battle array against the Persians in or near the sacred precinct of Androcrates.

Androgeus (an-droj′ē-us). In Greek legend, a son of Minos, king of Crete, and Pasiphaë. On a visit to Athens he defeated all competitors in the Panathenean games. According to some accounts, King Aegeus, to get rid of him, then sent him on a mission to kill the Marathonian Bull, which Heracles had brought back from Crete as one of his labors. It was now roaming the plains of Marathon, destroying men and cattle. Androgeus found the bull, but was killed by it. Others say that King Aegeus, fearing Androgeus would support a rebellion against him, had Androgeus ambushed and though he fought valiantly he was killed. In revenge for his son's death, Minos waged war on the Athenians, and compelled them to send a tribute of seven maidens and seven youths to Crete every nine years. These youths and maidens were given to the Minotaur.

Andromache (an-drom'a-kē). In Greek legend, a daughter of Eëtion, king of Thebes in Cilicia. She was the wife of Hector and the mother of Astyanax. In the tenth year of the Trojan War when the city was besieged by the Greeks, she tried to persuade Hector not to engage in the battle on the plain. Since her father and her seven brothers had been killed by Achilles when he took Thebes, and her mother, though ransomed, had died, she told Hector that he was father, mother, and brother to her as well as husband. She warned him that his courage would be his undoing as the Greeks would certainly make him their prime target. She asked him to take pity on her and on their infant son and to remain within the walls of the city. With great compassion and nobility of spirit Hector refused her request to keep apart from the battle. Weeping, Andromache returned to the palace as Hector put on his war helmet and set out for the battlefield. She never again saw him alive. When his body was ransomed and returned to Troy she clasped dead Hector's head in her arms and mourned, grieving bitterly that he had not been able to give her any word in farewell. With Hector dead she foresaw doom for herself, her son, and for Troy. Penthesilea the Amazon came to the aid of Troy and boasted that she would kill Achilles. Andromache doubted her good sense in speaking so recklessly of the man who had killed Hector. After the fall of Troy, Astyanax was taken from Andromache's arms and hurled to his death from the towers of the city. Andromache was taken as the captive and concubine of Neoptolemus. He took her to Thessaly and she bore him sons: Molossus, Pergamus, and Pielus. For ten years Neoptolemus treated her with kindness. At the end of that time he married Hermione, the daughter of Helen and Menelaus, but he did not abandon Andromache and her children. However Hermione, who remained childless, jealously persecuted Andromache and with the help of her father would have slain her and her sons during Neoptolemus' absence. Peleus arrived in time to save Andromache and her

children. Neoptolemus, who was slain at Delphi, bequeathed Andromache to Helenus. She married him and accompanied him to Epirus where he built a miniature Troy at Buthrotum. There Aeneas, on his way to Italy, found her as she was performing rites for Hector. She had never stopped mourning for him and told Aeneas that the women who died at Troy were fortunate; they had been spared the life of slavery and humiliation which had been her fate. Following the death of Helenus Andromache returned to Asia with her son Pergamus.

Andromache. A drama by Euripides, concerning the misfortunes of Andromache and the son she bore to Neoptolemus (son of Achilles), whose captive she became after the fall of Troy, and of the sorrows of Peleus, father of Achilles.

The scene is at the temple of Thetis beside the palace of Neoptolemus in Phthia. Andromache, alone on the altar steps, weeps for her past life as the wife of Hector and bemoans her present evil state. Neoptolemus has married Hermione, daughter of Helen and Menelaus. Now he is away at Delphi to inquire why his wife bears him no children. Hermione has taken advantage of his absence to persecute Andromache because she is jealous of the son Andromache has born to Neoptolemus. Andromache instructs a captive Trojan handmaid loyal to her to go to Peleus and ask his help. A chorus of Phthian maidens sympathizes with the woes of Andromache but as they fear Hermione's wrath they are unwilling to help her. Hermione enters and accuses Andromache of putting a spell on her that prevents her from bearing children. She threatens Andromache with death. Her proud spirit has been brought low, she says, and now there is no one to protect her. Only a barbarian, Hermione adds, would consent to live with the man who had slain her husband. Andromache replies that as a slave she can do nothing else. Moreover, Hermione need not fear that her slave sons will ever be allowed to rule. She has put no spell on Hermione; it is her own proud and arrogant nature, that does not match that of Neoptolemus, that causes her barrenness. If Hermione did not set her father above her husband she would win her husband's love. Hermione again taunts Andromache with Trojan barbarianism. She tries to force Andromache to leave the altar, for she dares not contrive her death on the sacred steps. When she fails, she threatens Andromache. Andromache spiritedly tells her that the Trojans were not responsible for the death of Achilles; Helen caused it. The chorus sings of the Judgment of Paris who, in awarding the prize to Aphrodite and winning Helen as a reward, incurred the hatred of Hera and Athena for Troy. Menelaus now enters with Molossus, son of Andromache and Neoptolemus. He threatens to kill Molossus unless Andromache leaves the altar. Andromache first scorns him and then tries to reason with him. If he kills her Hermione will not escape pollution. If he kills Molossus he will have to face the anger of Neoptolemus. Murder will not draw Neoptolemus and Hermione together, and no one will want Hermione if Neoptolemus abandons her. Andromache is the more fearful because it was also a woman's quarrel that brought disaster to Troy. Menelaus speaks arrogantly of his royal state. He insists that he will champion his daughter: either Andromache or Molossus must die to satisfy Hermione. Andromache argues that she has been the concubine of Neoptolemus against her will. She recalls her wretched history. All she has left is this one child, and he has now become a new source of suffering and danger. To save him, she agrees to leave the altar. The chorus chides Menelaus for his cruelty. Unmoved, he orders Andromache bound and then announces that he will let Hermione decide what to do about Molossus. To the outcry against this gross treachery Menelaus is indifferent. Andromache again tries to reason with him. Death is not grievous for her, for her death came when Hector was slain. However, she will never fawn on Menelaus. If he is great in Sparta, she was great in Troy. As she has been brought low, so he will be too. But Menelaus ignores her and takes her away.

The chorus grieves for the evils of a divided house that lead to a divided state. They predict that Andromache will be avenged. Menelaus now returns, dragging Andromache and Molossus. Peleus follows. He commands Menelaus to cease his lawless plots and orders the bonds removed from

Andromache. Menelaus countermands his order. Peleus accuses him of cowardice in binding a woman and defying an old man. Andromache is the captive of Neoptolemus, not of Menelaus. The Spartan women are loose, he says, and the men careless. Helen was a wanton, but it was the fault of Menelaus. He had warned his grandson Neoptolemus not to link himself with a wanton's daughter. He remembers that Menelaus caused Agamemnon, "poor fool," to sacrifice his daughter for Menelaus' worthless wife, and that Menelaus, who said he would kill Helen when Troy was taken instead saw her bosom and forgave her everything. Peleus removes the bonds that have been put on Molossus and scornfully asks Menelaus if he thought he was binding a lion that he put such heavy fetters on a child. Menelaus, finding his plans set at naught, leaves to return to Sparta. Andromache and Molossus depart with Peleus.

A nurse comes from the palace and tells the chorus Hermione is trying to commit suicide. As she speaks Hermione rushes in. She fears the wrath of Neoptolemus when he learns how she has persecuted Andromache, feels abandoned by her father, and longs to die. While the nurse tries to calm her Orestes approaches. He inquires solicitously about his dear kinswoman Hermione. She falls at his feet as a suppliant. In justification of her cruel conduct, she says her jealousy of Andromache was incited by women's talk. She begs Orestes to take her away from Phthia. Orestes reminds her that Menelaus had betrothed her to him. Menelaus betrayed his promise and gave her to Neoptolemus in order to win him from Scyrus to help the Greeks take Troy. Now Orestes will take his revenge on Neoptolemus and make Hermione his wife. He departs with her to carry out his plans.

The chorus mourns the evils that have come to Greece. On the arrival of Peleus they tell him that Orestes is planning the death of Neoptolemus. Peleus sends a messenger to warn him, but almost immediately a second messenger enters and announces that Orestes has stabbed Neoptolemus at Delphi. The second messenger is followed by bearers with the corpse of Neoptolemus. Peleus mourns; he lost his son Achilles at Troy; now

fat, fāte, fär, fāre, errạnt; net, mē, hėr ardẹnt; pĭn, pīne; not, nōte, mŏve, nôr, his grandson is dead. He is an old man, alone in his empty halls. As he grieves Thetis, mother of Achilles, appears to him. She instructs him to bury Neoptolemus under the threshold of the temple of Apollo at Delphi; to send Andromache and Molossus to Helenus in Molossia for from Molossus will spring a line of kings, descendants of Peleus and Thetis. Finally, she assures Peleus that he will dwell with her in the palace of Nereus under the sea and that he will again see Achilles. After burying Neoptolemus, Peleus must go to the Rock of Sepias where he first met her. There she will come for him. Peleus departs to carry out her wishes.

Andromeda (an-drom′e̅-dạ). In Greek legend, the daughter of Cepheus, king of Joppa in Ethiopia, and Cassiopea. She was betrothed to Phineus, the brother of Cepheus according to some accounts. Her mother boasted that she and her daughter were more beautiful than the Nereids of the sea. This boast angered Poseidon. He sent a savage sea monster to devastate the land as a punishment for the foolish arrogance of Cassiopea. Cepheus, on appealing to the oracle of Ammon, was told that only the sacrifice of Andromeda to the monster would appease Poseidon and cause him to relieve the country of the depredations of the beast he had sent. Cepheus had no choice; he chained Andromeda, naked except for her jewels, to a rocky cliff at the edge of the sea. Phineus felt unable to take any steps to save her. Perseus, returning with the head of Medusa, flew over the shores of Ethiopia and saw the beautiful maiden chained to a rock. Instantly he fell in love with her and flew down to learn the reason for her unhappy state. He learned the story from Cepheus and promised to slay the monster if Cepheus would reward him with Andromeda's hand in marriage. Cepheus willingly promised. When the monster emerged from the sea Perseus cut off its head with one stroke and freed his bride. The marks made by her chains on the rocks were visible for generations afterwards. At the wedding festivities for Perseus and Andromeda, Phineus and a company of his followers burst in and asserted that he was betrothed to Andromeda and she could not marry Perseus. Andromeda insisted that her father's promise be fulfilled. Cepheus weakened, now that all danger was past. Phineus attacked Perseus, but he exhibited the head of Medusa and turned them all to stone. Andromeda departed for Greece with Perseus. She bore him six sons and a daughter, and during their life together she enjoyed the knowledge, unusual for the wife of a Greek hero, that her lord was constant in his affection for her. After she died Athena placed her image among the stars.

Andromeda. A northern constellation surrounded by Pegasus, Cassiopea, Perseus, Pisces, Aries, and others, and supposed to represent the figure of a woman chained. The constellation contains three stars of the second magnitude, of which the brightest is Alpheratz.

Andron (an′dron) or **Andrus** (an′drus). In Greek mythology, a son of Anius, priest of Apollo and king of Delos, and the brother of Elaïs, Spermo, and Oeno. He was given the gift of augury by Apollo. According to some accounts, Rhadamanthys bequeathed to him the island of which he became king and which was named Andros in his honor. Agamemnon sought to capture his sisters because of their miraculous powers of turning whatever they wished into wine, grain, and oil. Two of the sisters fled to Andron on his island, but he, fearing the power of Agamemnon, surrendered them. Some say that as the fetters were about to be placed on the maidens to convey them to Agamemnon, they were transformed into doves and flew away.

Andronicus (an-drō-nī′kus, an-dron′i-kus), **Livius.** See **Livius Andronicus.**

Andronicus of Cyrrhus (sir′us). [Called **Cyrrhestes.**] Greek astronomer, born at Cyrrhus; fl. 1st century B.C. He was the builder, at Athens, of the "tower of the winds," still standing; it is an octagonal tower decorated with sculptured figures of the winds, and was surmounted by a bronze Triton which turned with the wind. It was perhaps the first weather-vane in history.

Andronicus of Rhodes (rōdz). Greek philosopher, fl. in the middle of the 1st century B.C. He was head of the Peripatetic school at Rome, and was the author of commentaries on, and paraphrases of, Aristotle, and editor of the works of Aristotle and Theophrastus.

Androphagi (an-drō-fā'jī, an-drof'a̱-jī). According to Herodotus, a cannibal tribe dwelling on the upper Borysthenes (Dnieper) River. They were nomads who lived without justice or law and, unlike other tribes bordering Scythia, they were man-eaters. In dress they were like the Scyths but their language was peculiarly their own. They refused to give aid to the Scythians when the latter were attacked by Darius. To punish them, the Scythians, according to their plan of never coming in contact with the Persian forces, led the Persians into the land of the Androphagi and caused great disturbance among them with two successive invasions—that of the Scyths followed by the Persians in pursuit.

Androphonos (an-drof'ō-nos). An epithet of Aphrodite meaning "Man-slayer."

Andros (an'dros). Northernmost island of the Cyclades, E Greece, situated in the Aegean Sea, about six miles SE of Euboea. According to legend, the island was named for Andron, the son of Anius, priest of Apollo and king of Delos. Andron, who had the gift of prophecy, became king of the island and named it for himself. In the Persian War the people of Andros joined forces with Xerxes for the invasion of Greece. After the defeat of the Persians at Salamis the Greeks pursued their fleet as far as Andros. There they stopped and held a council to decide if they should sail to the Hellespont and destroy the bridges, the exit route of the Persian army. Having decided against this plan, they besieged Andros because the islanders refused to pay a tribute required of them by Themistocles. The Andrians said their gods were Poverty and Helplessness, and they did not have the money to pay, siege or no siege. Under the circumstances, the Greeks lifted the siege and sailed away. The island was anciently a possession successively of Athens, Macedon, Pergamum, and Rome. It is a mountainous island, about 25 miles long and ten miles wide in its greatest width.

Androtion (an-drō'shi-on). Athenian orator, fl. c350 B.C., a contemporary of Demosthenes and pupil of Isocrates. He was a chronicler of Attica, whose work was probably contained in ten books, only fragments of which survive. He is known chiefly as a subject of attack by Demosthenes in one of his early orations.

Anemone (a̱-nem'ō̱-nē). The blood-red flower that sprang up from the drops of blood spilled by Adonis when he was gored and slain by a boar while hunting. The flower blooms quickly and as quickly perishes, just as Adonis perished, in the full bloom of youth. The traditional derivation from Greek *anemos*, "wind," which has provided the popular name Windflower, is not accepted by modern philologists, who prefer to derive it from the Semitic *na 'aman*, "the handsome," an epithet of Adonis. (JJ)

Anemotis (a̱-nem'ō̱-tis). Epithet of Athena, meaning "Of the Winds." In the temple of Athena Anemotis in Messenia an image of Athena Anemotis was dedicated. This was in gratitude to the goddess, for when the land was being damaged by violent and unseasonable winds prayers to the goddess caused them to cease.

Anesidora (a̱-nes-i-dôr'a̱). Epithet of Demeter; altars to Demeter Anesidora (*Sender-up of Gifts*) were raised in various places throughout Greece.

Angerona (an-je̱-rō'na̱) or **Angeronia** (-ni-a̱). In Roman mythology, a goddess whose attributes and powers are not definitely known. She was, perhaps, the goddess connected with anguish and secret grief. Her statue stood in the *Sacellum Volupiae*, and she was represented with her finger upon her bound and sealed lips.

Angitia (an-ji'shi-a̱, -sha̱). After Medea's plot to poison Theseus was exposed, she was forced to flee. According to some accounts, she went to Italy and, having taught the inhabitants the art of snake-charming, was afterward worshiped by them as a goddess under the name Angitia. The name is more likely that of a diety of the Marsi in C Italy, whose native name was Anagtia. She seems to have been a goddess of healing.

Anicetus (a-ni-sē'tus). In Greek legend, one of the children born to Heracles after he had been apotheosized and married Hebe.

Anigrus (a̱-nī'grus). River in Elis, in Greece, which gave off a very unpleasant odor and in whose waters no fish lived. It is said that Chiron, when accidentally wounded by an arrow of Heracles, bathed his wound in its waters. The water of the river stank horribly ever after because of the Hydra's blood on the arrow. But others say the extremely disagreeable odor of the river was caused by Melampus, who cast into its waters the means by which he had purified the daughters of Proetus. In a cave nearby, persons suffering from certain diseases could go to pray to the nymphs of the river. They promised certain sacrifices, wiped the affected parts of their bodies, then swam in the river. The disease was left in the water and the sufferer emerged from it cleansed and healthy. Another cave nearby is said to have been sacred to the daughters of Atlas and was the site where Dardanus was born to Electra. In the *Iliad*, the Anigrus is called the Minyeius River.

Anio (än'yō). [Modern name, **Aniene,** and also, in its lower course, **Teverone.**] River in C Italy that flows into the Tiber just above Rome. It is the source of a famous waterfall, about 330 feet high, at a point just below Tivoli. It has been since ancient times a source of water for the city of Rome. Camillus, as general and dictator of the Romans, defeated the Gauls at the Anio, c366 B.C., when they marched against Rome a second time.

Anius (an'i-us). In classical mythology, a son of Apollo. He and his mother Rhoeo were put into a chest and cast onto the sea. The chest floated to Delos, where Anius later became king as well as a priest of Apollo. His son Andron was taught augury by Apollo and became king of Andros. Anius and his wife Dorippe also had three daughters: Elaïs, Oeno, and Spermo. They were given the power by Dionysus, to whom their father had dedicated them, of turning whatever they wished into oil, wine, and grain. Because of their gifts Anius was able to supply the Greek fleet, anchored at Aulis, with provisions. He invited the Greeks to remain with him on Delos for nine years, since he knew of the oracle that Troy would not fall until the tenth year but they refused his offer and instead carried off his three daughters (see **Elaïs**). Anius, as an old friend of Anchises, welcomed Aeneas and the Trojan exiles when they stopped in Delos after the Trojan War to consult the oracle in the temple of Apollo.

Anna (an'a). In Roman legend, Dido's sister. She advised Dido to stop mourning for her dead husband and to yield to her love for Aeneas. She went to Italy after Dido's death and was hospitably received by Aeneas. Lavinia, wife of Aeneas, became jealous and Dido warned Anna in a dream of her jealousy. Anna drowned herself in the river Numicius, and was later worshiped as the river-nymph Anna Perenna.

Ansedonia (an-sā-dō'nya). Promontory on the coast of Etruria, in Italy, south of the lagoon of Orbetello, on which in 273 B.C. was established the Latin colony of Cosa (q.v.), recently identified and in part excavated by an American mission. (JJ)

Antaea (an-tē'a). Epithet signifying the goddesses to whom men may pray. It was applied to Rhea, Demeter, and Cybele.

Antaeus (an-tē'us). In Greek mythology, a Libyan giant and wrestler, son of Poseidon, god of the sea, and Gaea, the earth. He was invincible so long as he remained in contact with his mother. He compelled strangers in his country to wrestle with him, and built a house to Poseidon of their skulls. Heracles discovered the source of his strength, and, lifting him into the air, crushed him.

Antagoras (an-tag'ō-ras). In Greek legend, a shepherd on the island of Cos. When Heracles was on his way home after having punished Laomedon of Troy, Hera caused him to be shipwrecked by storms. His vessel landed on Cos and there he met Antagoras and asked him for a ram. Antagoras offered to give him the ram as a prize if Heracles could defeat him in a wrestling match. Antagoras and Heracles wrestled, but they were interfered with by assistants on both sides. The countrymen of Antagoras rushed in to help him, while shipmates came to the aid of Heracles. But Heracles and his men were outnumbered. Heracles fled to the home of a countrywoman of Cos, who disguised him in woman's clothes and helped him escape.

Antalcidas (an-tal'si-das). Spartan diplomat, politician, and warrior; fl. in the first half of the 4th century B.C. He was sent (c393 B.C.) to undermine Athenian relations with the Persian satrap in Asia Minor. He proceeded (388 B.C.) to the Persian court, where aid against Athens was finally obtained, and shortly thereafter he defeated the Athenian

actor; up, lūte, pull; oi, oil; ou, out; ŦH, then; d̦ as d or j, ș as s or sh, ț as t or ch, z̦ as z or zh.

fleet near the Hellespont. He prevented the grain ships from reaching Athens and was thus able to compel Athens to accept the "Peace of Antalcidas" (or "King's Peace") in 386 B.C., which provided that all of Asia Minor as well as Cyprus and Clazomenae would be abandoned to Persia, while all remaining Greek city-states would be independent except for Imbrus, Lemnos, and Scyrus, which remained Athenian.

Antalya (än-täl-yä′) **Gulf of.** [Former name, **Gulf of Adalia**; ancient name, **Pamphylian Gulf**; Latin, **Pamphylicus Sinus**.] Arm of the Mediterranean Sea, on the S coast of Turkey, on which the city of Antalya, founded by Attalus II of Pergamum, is located. Length, about 100 miles; width, about 40 miles.

Antandrus (an-tan′drus). In ancient geography, a city in the Troad, in Asia Minor. It was one of the cities attacked, taken, and sacked as an ally of Troy by Achilles in the Trojan War. In the time of Cambyses II it fell to Persia. Subsequently it belonged to Mytilene, and in the Peloponnesian Wars it was a battleground for the forces of Lesbos, Athens, and Sparta, falling now to one now to another. It was especially desirable because of its location near the Hellespont.

Antefix (an′tē-fiks). In classical architecture, an upright ornament, generally of marble or terra-cotta, placed at the eaves of a tiled roof, at the end of the last tile of each ridge of tiling, to conceal the joining of the tiles. Antefixes were also often placed at the junction of the tiles along the ridge of a roof, forming a cresting. In some Roman examples the antefixes were so disposed and combined with water channels as to serve as gargoyles.

Antenor (an-tē′nor). In Greek legend, a Trojan, husband of the priestess Theano. As one of Priam's counselors he advised the Trojans, after the duel between Hector and Ajax in the tenth year of the war, to return Helen and all her possessions to Menelaus. His advice was disregarded. In the closing days of the war he was sent to negotiate peace with Agamemnon but instead, according to some accounts, because of his hatred of Deïphobus, son of Priam, he plotted with Agamemnon to help Odysseus enter the city secretly and steal the Palladium, the sacred image of Athena which protected the city as long as it remained within the walls. When Troy was taken by the device of the Wooden Horse, Menelaus hung a leopard's skin over the door of Antenor's house as a sign that it should not be plundered in the sack of the city. Antenor, Theano, and his remaining sons, slipped through the Greek lines and crossed over to Thrace. At length he sailed up the Illyrian Gulf and founded a city at the head of the Adriatic which was called "New Troy." Its inhabitants were afterward known as Venetians. Antenor is also said to have founded Padua, shortly before the arrival of Aeneas in Latium.

Antenor. Athenian sculptor of the 6th century B.C. He executed the first bronze statues of Harmodius and Aristogiton which the Athenians set up in the Agora and which were carried off to Susa by Xerxes I. After his conquest of Persia, Alexander the Great is said to have sent the statues back to Athens. A statue-base found on the Athenian Acropolis bears the signature of Antenor, and to this has been joined a marble *Kore*, also found on the Acropolis and plausibly ascribed to him.

Antenorid (an-tē′no-rid). A name applied to any of the sons of Antenor.

Anteros (an′tèr-os). In Greek mythology, a son of Aphrodite and Ares, and brother of Eros. He was sometimes represented as the avenger of unrequited affection and sometimes as the symbol of mutual love and tenderness.

Antevorta (an-te-vôr′ta). [Also: **Porrima** (pôr′i-ma) or **Prorsa** (prôr′sa).] In Roman mythology, with Postvorta, described as sisters or companions of Carmenta. Antevorta knew the future, Postvorta knew the past. Originally, they were perhaps two attributes of Carmenta, but later they came to be regarded as separate from, and companions of, Carmenta. They had two altars at Rome. Pregnant women invoked them to avert the dangers of childbirth.

Anthas (an′thas). In Greek mythology, a son of Poseidon and Alcyone. He founded the cities of Anthaea and Hyperea which were afterwards united into Troezen. He is also said to have sailed to Caria where he founded the city of Halicarnassus.

Anthea (an-thē′a). Epithet of Hera, meaning "Flowery." The women of the Pelopon-

fat, fāte, fär, fāre, errant; net, mē, hér ardent; pin, pīne; not, nōte, möve, nôr,

nesus annually celebrated a flower festival in honor of Hera Anthea. Before the temple of Hera Anthea at Argos was the common grave of women who had come from the Aegean islands to help Dionysus in a war. Because they had come from the islands the women were called Haliae (*Women of the Sea*).

Anthedon (an'thĕ-don). In ancient geography, a harbor town of Boeotia. Some say it was named for a nymph. Others say it was named for Anthas, son of Poseidon and Alcyone, who was despot here. There was a sanctuary and grove of the Cabiri at Anthedon, and a temple of Demeter and Core. Glaucus, the fisherman who ate grass and was transformed into a sea god, was said to have come from Anthedon. Some say the Aloidae who killed each other were buried here.

Antheia (an-thē'a). City in Messenia, near the Gulf of Messenia. It was one of the seven gift cities offered by Agamemnon to Achilles if he would give up his quarrel with Agamemnon and return to the battle in the Trojan War. Its name was later changed to Thuria and in the time of Augustus it was given to the Spartans because the inhabitants of the city lent aid to Antony.

Antheis (an-thē'is). A daughter of Hyacinthus the Spartan. See **Hyacinthides.**

Anthela (an-thē'la). In ancient geography, a place near the pass of Thermopylae, in Greece. It was the original seat of the Amphictyonic Council which was composed of representatives of the "dwellers around" the shrine of Demeter at Anthela. The meetings of the Council were held there, and later at Delphi also.

Anthemion (an-thē'mi-on). In art and archaeology, a characteristic palmette or honeysuckle ornament, varying in detail but constant in type, of frequent occurrence both in single examples and in series, in vase-painting, in architectural sculpture, in jewelry and dress fabrics, and in all other decorative work of Greek origin from very early times, and later in ornament derived from the Greek. This ornament in its original shape was borrowed by Greek artists from the Orient, and was probably first adopted by the Ionians. It was much used upon antefixes, both sculptured and terra-cotta, and in the composition

of acroteria, particularly those of the tall and slender Greek funeral slabs.

Anthemion frieze or molding. A molding or frieze ornamented with a series of anthemia, usually in graceful alternation of two forms. Sometimes the effect is diversified by the introduction of flowers or tendrils more literally expressed, and occasionally birds are represented perching on the tendrils, as in examples at Athens and Argos. The most elegant examples of anthemion molding are those beneath the capitals of the north porch columns, and forming one of the friezes, of the Erechtheum at Athens.

Anthesteria (an-thes-tē'ri-a). In ancient Greece, the third in order of the Attic feasts in honor of Dionysus. It was held in the spring on the 11th, 12th, and 13th days of the spring month Anthesterion (the beginning of March). The people wore garlands of the brilliant anemones which deck the Attic plain at that season, and certain mystic ceremonies and sacrifices were performed by priestesses in the guise of bacchantes. The festival was a time of merrymaking, and also a time for sacrifices to the forces of the Underworld and for the laying of ghosts. The first day of the festival was called Pithoigia, from *pithos* a large pottery jar for the storing of wine and wheat that was set into the ground. These pithoi were also used from time to time as burial jars, and as such, the Pithoigia may also have represented a day in which the ghosts of the grave-jars were banished. On Pithoigia the jars of wine made the previous season were tapped, a libation was poured to Dionysus and the celebrants of the festival at Athens also partook of the wine. Among the Boeotians the first day of the festival was called the Day of the Good Spirit. The broaching and drinking of the new wine set off a day of revel and feasting. The second day was called Choes (*Cups*). The merrymaking continued on this day. A drinking contest was held in which the winner deposited his victory wreath at the temple of Dionysus in the Marshes. The only day in the year that this temple was opened was on Choes. On this day also, the wife of the chief Archon was ritually married to Dionysus. According to some accounts, the people believed that the spirits of the dead rose up on Choes, and to protect themselves from the shades they chewed buckthorn all day and covered their doors with pitch. The latter had the quality of repelling evil by its own purity. On Choes each man drank by himself. Some say this custom arose because Orestes, after the murder of his mother, arrived in Attica at the time of Choes. Since it would have violated religious custom to drink with a man polluted by his mother's blood, the order was given for each man to drink separately, so that none should be polluted, and the custom continued. The third day was Chytroi (*Pots*). The word *chytroi* was also applied to natural holes, or "pots," in the ground, that were sometimes used as burying places. Chytroi was marked by a dramatic contest and the revel continued. In addition, sacrifices were made to Hermes of the Underworld. Dishes of seeds and beans were prepared, but no one tasted them, as they were offerings to the dead in the Underworld. The Anthesteria ("The festival of flowers") was thus a festival of the spring, of the opening of the new wine and rejoicing at the flowering of the earth. It was also a festival of purification after the evils of winter when the ghosts of the dead were appeased.

Anthesterion (an-thes-tē′ri-on). The eighth month of the Attic year, containing 29 days and corresponding to the last part of February and the beginning of March.

Antheus (an′thē-us). In Greek legend, a son of the Trojan Antenor. He was accidentally killed by Paris.

Anthium (an′thi-um). A place on the road from Eleusis to Megara where Demeter, disguised as an old woman, sat and rested in her search for her daughter Persephone. Here, at this place whose name means "Flowery Well," the daughters of Celeus found her and took her to their father's house.

Anthology, The. Collection of several thousand short Greek poems by many authors, written for the most in the elegiac meter. In it every period of Greek literature is represented, from the Persian war to the decadence of Byzantium. The first *Anthology* was compiled by Meleager of Gadara in the 1st century B.C., and to this additions were made by Philippus of Thessalonica about 40 A.D. In the collection by Agathias of Myrina (6th century) the poems are (for the first time) arranged by subjects. The so-called Palatine Anthology, a version compiled probably in the 10th century by Constantinus Cephalas, is the oldest one still extant.

Anthus (an′thus). In mythology, a son of Antonous and Hippodamia. He was killed by his father's horses and was changed into a bird that imitates the sound of horses and flies in front of them.

Antia (an-tī′a). In Greek legend, the daughter of Iobates, king of Lycia, and the wife of Proetus, king of Tiryns in Argos. Bellerophon, a guest in her husband's house with whom she fell in love, honorably spurned her advances. As a woman scorned she accused him falsely to her husband of making the very advances he had repelled, and urged that he be put to death. She is also known as Stheneboea.

Antianeira (an′′ti-a-nī′ra). In Greek mythology, a daughter of Menetes. She was the mother by Hermes of the Argonauts Erytus and Echion.

Anticlea (an-ti-klē′a). A daughter of Autolycus. She was the wife of Laertes the Argive but was seduced by Sisyphus and some say Sisyphus was the father of her son Odysseus, although Laertes passed as his father. Odysseus, who had not known of her death, met her shade when he visited the Underworld to consult the seer Tiresias on his way home from Troy. Although she assured him that Penelope was faithful to him she discreetly refrained from telling him of the number of suitors who were besieging Penelope. She told Odysseus that his father had retired to the country and was grieving for him, and that she had died, not from illness or a shaft from the gods, but because of her longing for his return from Troy.

Anticlus (an′ti-klus). In Greek legend, one of the Greeks who entered Troy in the Wooden Horse. Helen, inspired by Aphrodite to see if the Wooden Horse was a trap, imitated the voices of the Greeks' wives and called to the Greek heroes by name. When Anticlus heard what he thought was his wife's voice, he tried to answer but Odysseus choked him so that he could not give them away, and Anticlus perished in one of the hollow legs of the horse.

Anticyra (an-tis′i-ra). In ancient geography,

a city in Locris, Greece, situated near Naupactus.

Anticyra. In ancient geography, a city in
Phocis, Greece, situated on the Corinthian
Gulf. It was noted for the medicinal plant
hellebore (the ancient remedy for madness)
obtained in its neighborhood.

Anticyra. In ancient geography, a city in
Thessaly, Greece, situated on the Sperchius.
Like Anticyra in Phocis, it was noted for
hellebore, the ancient remedy for madness.

Anticythera (an-ti-si-thir′a). Small island in
the Sea of Crete, NW of Crete. The *Ephebe
of Anticythera* and other antiquities that had
been lying at the bottom of the sea as a result of ancient shipwrecks were found near
here by divers from Syme.

Antigone (an-tig′ọ-nē). In Greek legend, a
daughter of Oedipus by his mother Jocasta.
She was the sister of Eteocles, Polynices, and
Ismene. According to some accounts, she
faithfully accompanied Oedipus as he fled
through Greece pursued by the Furies because he had killed his father and sired children by his own mother. They came at last
to Colonus in Attica where Oedipus died
and there, with the aid of Theseus, Antigone
buried him. She returned to Thebes where
her brother Eteocles was now on the throne.
By agreement with Polynices, Eteocles was
to rule for a year and then yield to Polynices
for a year. However, at the end of his
term Eteocles refused to give up the throne.
Polynices enlisted the aid of Adrastus, king
of Argos. The latter, accompanied by the
Argive chieftains who made up the Seven
against Thebes, marched with Polynices
against Thebes and waged an ill-fated war
to restore Polynices to the throne. In the
battle Eteocles and Polynices met in single
combat and slew each other. Creon, uncle
of Antigone, now became king. He ordered
funeral honors for Eteocles, the valiant defender of the city, but gave orders that the
body of Polynices should be cast outside the
walls to become the prey of scavenger birds
because he had treacherously attacked his
own city. Antigone, moved by the claims
of blood loyalty, resolved to bury Polynices
in defiance of Creon. She attempted to enlist her sister's aid in the project but Ismene
dared not risk rousing Creon's anger. Antigone succeeded in giving Polynices the mini-

mum rites of burial by sprinkling dust over
his body. Some say that she heaped a burial
mound over his body or burned it on a pyre.
When Creon learned that his order had been
defied he demanded death for the person
who had disobeyed him, and was not deterred even when he learned that the culprit
was his own niece. He ordered her to be
buried alive. Some say Antigone was entombed alive in a cave, or in the family tomb,
and hanged herself, and that Haemon, the
son of Creon, to whom she was betrothed,
slew himself on her tomb. Others say that
Creon handed Antigone over to Haemon with
orders to destroy her. Haemon pretended
to carry out his father's order but he secretly
married Antigone and sent her away to live
among his shepherds. She bore him a son.
Years later the son returned to Thebes to
take part in funeral games. Creon recognized him as a son of Antigone by the birth-
mark which all the descendants of the Sparti
bore on their bodies. He charged Haemon
with having disobeyed his orders, and in
spite of the pleas of Heracles for clemency,
ordered punishment for Antigone and Haemon. Haemon, to forestall Creon's vengeance, killed Antigone and then slew himself.

Antigone. A tragedy by Sophocles, of uncertain date. It treats a part of the Theban
saga and describes how Antigone, daughter of
Oedipus, defied her uncle, Creon, who assumed the throne after the death of her
brothers Eteocles and Polynices. Her defiance, in the name of a divine law and of
loyalty to her own blood, is pitted against the
man-made law of Creon.

The scene is before the royal palace of
Thebes, in the early morning of the day following the deaths of Eteocles and Polynices
and the defeat of the Seven Argive chieftains
who marched against Thebes. Antigone calls
her sister Ismene from the palace and informs her of Creon's order: that Eteocles, the
defender of the city, is to be honorably
buried, but that Polynices shall be denied
burial and left as prey for the birds; moreover, whoever disobeys the order is doomed
to death. She asks Ismene to help her to
bury their brother in defiance of the order.
Ismene reminds her of the fate of their father,
self-blinded when his obstinate search revealed his own sins; of their mother's suicide

actọr; up, lūte, pꞟll; oi, oil; ou, out; ᴛн, then; ḍ as d or j, ŝ as s or sh, ṭ as t or ch, ẓ as z or zh.

by hanging; and of the mutual doom their brothers wrought on each other. Now they will both perish more miserably than the rest if they disobey Creon. Ismene says that she, a weak woman, will bow before the superior strength of Creon. Antigone tells her to do as she likes, but for her part she intends to obey the divine law and bury the dead brother she loves. Ismene cannot persuade her that such defiance is impractical and inexpedient. The sisters retire into the palace. A chorus of Theban elders enters and sings of the army which Polynices led against Thebes. Zeus drove the attackers back and the two brothers killed each other. Creon enters. He says he has called the elders together to assure them he will guard Thebes' greatness. He makes known his order forbidding the burial of Polynices, whom he accuses of having sought to destroy the city and his own kin. This is his justification for denying him the burial sanctioned by the gods. A guard comes to Creon. He makes sure that he will not be blamed for the news he brings, then tells Creon that someone has buried Polynices in defiance of the order. The guard does not know who did it, and all the guards are ready to give their oath that they did not sprinkle dust on the body, nor had they seen anyone else do it. They decided that Creon should be informed and the lot fell on him to carry the message. He is most unhappy about it for no man likes to be the bearer of bad news. The leader of the chorus suggests that this burial may be the work of the gods. This angers Creon, who says the gods do not honor the wicked. He remembers that from the first there have been some in Thebes who disapproved his order, and decides that someone has been bribed to bury Polynices. He orders the guard to find the culprit on pain of death, and withdraws to the palace. The guard, relieved that he has not suffered for bringing bad news, departs. The chorus sings of the wonders man has accomplished, and of the skill that brings him now to evil, now to good. The guard reënters, leading Antigone. Creon approaches and learns that Antigone is the one who has defied him. The guard is regretful concerning Antigone, but the ill he brings to his friends is much less important to him than his own safety. Antig-

one freely admits that she disobeyed Creon's order in full knowledge of it and of the consequences. She says she fulfilled a law of Zeus in breaking a law of Creon. Her life is so full of sorrow and evil, she says, that if she must die for it death will be a gain. Creon accuses her of adding insolence to her crime. If he does not now punish her as he said he would punish the culprit, she will have gained a victory over him. Antigone asks him not to delay. She claims glory for having buried her brother and says the others would agree with her if they dared speak. Creon insists on his view that Eteocles, being good, deserved honorable burial, but that Polynices, having evilly attacked his own city, must be punished even in death. Antigone holds to her view that she loves her brothers equally and has done right in obeying the divine law and burying Polynices. Creon declares that no woman is going to rule him; she must die.

Ismene is now brought forward. She wishes to share Antigone's fate but Antigone scorns her. Since she had no part in the deed, and did not wish to, Antigone does not want her company now; Ismene chose to live, now she must live. Ismene reminds Creon that his son Haemon is betrothed to Antigone, but he retorts that there are other women his son can marry. He orders the servants to take the sisters away. The chorus sings of the evils that have ever attended the house of Labdacus, and now when it seemed that peace would come, the gods, foolish speech, and frenzied emotions have brought more trouble. The gods can cause men to make evil seem good. Haemon enters. He assures his father that no marriage is worth more to him than his father's good opinion. Creon is gratified, and repeats his intention to kill whoever disobeyed his command, rather than to break his word to the city even though the culprit happens to be one of his own kin. For a ruler, he says, must be obeyed; disobedience ruins cities and makes homes desolate; the cause of order must be served; and above all a woman must not be allowed to get the better of the king. Haemon modestly says it is not for him to question his father, but he feels it is right to point out that many disapprove of his order to slay Antigone. They even say her

fat, fāte, fär, fãre, errạnt; net, mē, hėr ardẹnt; pin, pīne; not, nōte, möve, nôr,

deed in burying her brother was glorious. He declares that no treasure is so precious as his father's welfare, but suggests that perhaps in this instance his father's word is not the only word that is right; no man should think that he alone is wise; all must learn to bend sometimes, even as the tree gives way before the wintry wind. He tries to persuade his father to change his mind. The leader of the chorus, representing the Thebans, adds his agreement with Haemon. Creon refuses to be guided by one so young as Haemon and he also denies the Thebans a voice in this matter. If he is to rule he is going to rule by his own judgment. The words between Creon and Haemon become hotter as Haemon accuses him of injustice and adds that the death of Antigone will bring another death. Haemon flees before his father's threat to have Antigone killed before his eyes. Creon tells the chorus he will entomb Antigone alive. She is brought out. When she laments that she is looking her last on the sunlight the chorus reminds her that she has chosen her own course; they suggest that she is paying for her father's sins. As the servants lead her away Antigone's proud defiance wavers and she cries out to know what law of heaven she has broken that she must now die. The blind seer Tiresias now approaches Creon. All the omens say, he tells him, that it is a mistake not to bury Polynices. He should admit his error and change his order; there is .no profit in slaying the slain anew. He gives this counsel to Creon because he is interested in Creon's welfare. Creon is angered. He threatens Tiresias and accuses him of having accepted a bribe. Tiresias is unable to convince him of his high purpose. He predicts the death of Haemon, because Creon has hidden one who belongs in the sunlight, and put in the sun one who should be hidden in the shade. He leaves, prophesying a wave of hatred against Creon. Creon is shaken by these warnings. He decides to take the advice of the leader of the chorus and release Antigone; he will free her himself for he had caused her to be entombed. He hurries off, and the chorus appeals to the gods to bring peace to Thebes.

A messenger enters. Creon, he says, who once had everything has now lost all; his son Haemon is dead. Eurydice, wife of Creon, comes from the palace. The messenger tells her that Creon, having changed his mind, found the body of Polynices and buried it, then went to the vault where Antigone was entombed to free her. He found that Antigone had hanged herself. Haemon, who was embracing her dead body, thrust himself through with his sword when his father called to him. Without saying a word, Eurydice reënters the palace, followed by the messenger who is disturbed by her silence. Now Creon returns, carrying the shrouded body of Haemon. He mourns his son and blames his own stubbon folly. It was the gods, he cries, who made him so cruel. The messenger, running from the palace, tells Creon that Eurydice has stabbed herself. Creon mourns. At last he knows that these deaths can be laid at his door. He wishes to die. As he is led into the palace the chorus sings that wisdom is the supreme happiness, and that the sins of the proud are punished with great blows. Perhaps with time wisdom is achieved.

Antigonidae (an-ti-gon'i-dē). The descendants of Antigonus I of Macedonia (died 301 B.C.), one of the generals of Alexander the Great. The principal members of the family were Demetrius I (Poliorcetes), king of Macedonia (died 283 B.C.), son of Antigonus I; Antigonus II (Gonatas), king of Macedonia (died 239), son of Demetrius I; Demetrius of Cyrene (died 250), son of Demetrius I; Demetrius II, king of Macedonia (died 229), son of Antigonus II; Antigonus III (Doson), king of Macedonia (died 221), son of Demetrius of Cyrene; Philip V, king of Macedonia (died 179 B.C.), son of Demetrius II; and Perseus, king of Macedonia, conquered by the Romans in 168 B.C.

Antigonus I (an-tig'ō-nus) (of *Macedonia*). [Surnamed **Cyclops** or **Monophthalmos**, meaning the "One-Eyed."] King of Macedonia (306–301 B.C.), born c382 B.C.; killed at the battle of Ipsus, 301 B.C. He was one of the generals of Alexander the Great. After the latter's death he received the provinces of Greater Phrygia, Lycia, and Pamphylia. He carried on war against Perdiccas and Eumenes, made extensive conquests in Asia, assumed the title of king in 306 B.C., and was overthrown at Ipsus in Phrygia by a coalition of his enemies.

Antigonus II (of *Macedonia*). [Called **Antigonus Gonatus.**] King of Macedonia (283–239 B.C.), son of Demetrius Poliorcetes, born c320 B.C.; died 239 B.C. He assumed the title in 283, after the death of his father, but did not actually reign until 276. He suppressed the Celtic invasion and was temporarily driven from his land by Pyrrhus in 273 B.C.

Antigonus III (of *Macedonia*). [Called **Antigonus Doson.**] King of Macedonia (229–221 B.C.), nephew of Antigonus II and a great-grandson of Antigonus I, Alexander's general. He died 221 B.C. He was appointed guardian of Philip, son of Demetrius II, and on the death of Demetrius (229 B.C.) he married his widow and ascended the throne. He successfully supported Aratus and the Achaean League against Cleomenes, king of Sparta, and the Aetolians, and defeated the former at Sellasia in 222 B.C. He is said to have been dubbed "Doson" because "he was always about to give, and never did."

Antigonus of Carystus (ka̲-ris'tus) or **Antigonus Carystius** (-ti-us). Greek writer and bronze worker of the middle of the 3rd century B.C., who worked chiefly at Pergamum although he was a native of Carystus, Euboea. He was the author of biographical works on the philosophers and of a natural-history work entitled *Collection of Wonderful Tales*, portions of which are still extant. He helped fashion the statues which celebrated Attalus' Gallic victory .

Antilochus (an-til'ō̲-kus). In Greek legend, a son of Nestor, who had been exposed by his mother to die on Mount Ida but was nursed by a bitch until found and saved. He had been left at home as too young to accompany his father when the latter sailed off to the Trojan War. A few years later he followed the Greeks to Troy and appealed to Achilles to soften his father's wrath because he had defied him and joined the fighting. He became a great friend of Achilles. Though he was one of the youngest Greeks at Troy the handsome lad was a brave fighter. He slew many Trojans and on occasion was protected by Poseidon from the spears of the enemy. Because of his friendship with Achilles and his fleetness of foot he was sent to tell Achil-les of the death of Patroclus. At Troy one of Nestor's horses was pierced by an arrow. The other horse became frenzied. As Antilochus hurried to his father's assistance, Memnon the Ethiopian killed him. Achilles avenged the death of his friend Antilochus as he did that of Patroclus. The three friends were buried in the same mound, and were seen by Odysseus walking together over the asphodel meadows of the lower world.

Antimachides (an-ti-mā'ki-dēz). Sixth century B.C. Greek architect associated with Antistates, Callaeschrus, and Porinus in preparing the original plans for the Olympieum, the colossal temple of Zeus Olympius at Athens projected by the Pisistratids. (JJ)

Antimachus (an-tim'a̲-kus). In Homeric legend (*Iliad*), a Trojan chieftain who advised the Trojans not to return Helen to Menelaus. His sons were slain by Agamemnon.

Antimachus. [Called **the Colophonian.**] Greek epic and elegiac poet of Clarus, a part of the dominion of Colophon, who flourished c410 B.C. His chief work was the *Thebais*, a voluminous epic poem on the first expedition against Thebes. His elegy on Lyde, his wife (or mistress), which tells of famous lovers separated by death, was much admired in antiquity. He also published a critical edition of Homer. The Alexandrians admired him as a learned poet and for this reason placed him next after Homer among the epic poets, but as a critic remarked, "next" does not necessarily mean "near." His style, preserved only in fragments, became rigid and artificial in his attempts to attain dignity of language and to avoid common or popular expressions.

Antinous (an-tin'ō̲-us). In the *Odyssey*, the most arrogant of the suitors of Penelope during Odysseus' long absence. He complained to her son Telemachus that Penelope would not make up her mind which of her suitors to choose and he accused her of guile in weaving a web, supposedly a shroud for her father-in-law, which she unraveled each night. Antinous assured Telemachus that the wooers would camp on him until she chose a husband. He was enraged when he learned that Telemachus had gotten a ship and set out for Pylus for news of his father, and resolved to ambush and kill Telemachus on his way home. He was most abusive when

Odysseus returned to his own house disguised as a beggar, and he was the first one Odysseus killed.

Antiochus (an-tī′ọ-kus). A legendary son of Heracles and Meda, daughter of a Dryopian king. Antiochus was said to have founded the Attic deme which bore his name.

Antiochus. Athenian sea captain; died 407 B.C. He chanced to be in the assembly at Athens when contributions were being made to the state. Alcibiades, passing by, heard the applause and inquired the reason for it. When he was told, he entered the assembly and offered a large contribution himself. In the applause that followed he forgot that he was carrying a quail in his cloak. The bird escaped, and all took part in the scramble to retrieve it. Antiochus caught it and restored it to Alcibiades. Henceforth he became a great favorite with Alcibiades and served loyally under him. In 407 B.C. when Alcibiades, general in command on land and sea, sailed to collect money for his operations, he left the main body of the fleet at Notium under the command of Antiochus with strict orders not to engage the Spartan fleet under Lysander at Ephesus. Antiochus disobeyed his orders, sailed out and taunted the Spartans. Lysander sailed out against him and destroyed his ship and the Athenian ships that had come to his aid. Fifteen ships were lost in all.

Antiochus I (of *Commagene*). King of Commagene, a petty principality between the Euphrates and Mount Taurus, whose capital was Samosata, at one time a part of the Syrian kingdom of the Seleucidae. He concluded (64 B.C.) a peace with Pompey, and later (49) supported him in the civil war with Caesar. He died c30 B.C.

Antiochus II (of *Commagene*). King of Commagene; fl. late 1st century B.C. He was the successor to Mithridates I. He was summoned to Rome and executed (29 B.C.) for having caused the murder of an ambassador sent to Rome by his brother.

Antiochus III (of *Commagene*). King of Commagene; fl. early 1st century A.D.; died 17 A.D. He was probably the father of Antiochus IV of Commagene. Very little is known about either his accomplishments or dates of rule.

Antiochus IV (of *Commagene*). [Called An-tiochus IV Epiphanes.] King of Commagene; fl. middle of 1st century A.D. He was probably a son of Antiochus III of Commagene. He was a friend of Caligula, who restored (38 A.D.) to him the kingdom of Commagene, which had been made a Roman province at the death of his father in 17. Subsequently, however, he was deposed by Caligula, but was restored (41) on the accession of Claudius. He was finally deprived (72 A.D.) of his kingdom by Vespasian who incorporated it in Syria.

Antiochus I (of *Syria*). [Called **Antiochus I Soter**.] King of Syria (280–261 B.C.), born 324 B.C.; killed c261 B.C. He was a son of Seleucus I Nicator. It is said that when he fell sick from love of Stratonice, the young wife of his father, Seleucus, on the advice of the physician Erasistratus, allowed Stratonice to marry his son, and invested him with the government of Upper Asia giving him the title of king. On the death of his father Antiochus succeeded to all his dominions, but relinquished his claims to Macedonia on the marriage of Antigonus II of Macedonia to Phila, the daughter of Seleucus and Stratonice. He was the greatest founder of cities after Alexander the Great.

Antiochus II (of *Syria*). [Called **Antiochus II Theos**.] King of Syria; killed 247 B.C. He was the second son of Antiochus I, whom he succeeded in 261 B.C. He became involved in a ruinous war with Ptolemy Philadelphus, king of Egypt, during which Syria was further weakened by the revolt of the provinces of Parthia and Bactria, Arsaces establishing the Parthian empire in c250 B.C., and Theodotus the independent kingdom of Bactria about the same time. Peace was concluded with Egypt in 250 B.C. Antiochus was obliged to reject his wife Laodice and to marry Berenice, the daughter of Ptolemy. On the death of Ptolemy (247 B.C.), he recalled Laodice (who, it is thought, caused Ptolemy's murder) and also Berenice and her son. The connection between Syria and Egypt is referred to in Daniel, xi. 6.

Antiochus III (of *Syria*). [Called **Antiochus the Great**.] King of Syria (223–187 B.C.), the most famous of the Seleucidae. He was born c241 B.C.; died 187 B.C. He was the second son of Seleucus II and grandson of Antiochus II, and succeeded his brother

Seleucus Ceraunus at the age of 15. His epithet "the Great" was earned by the magnitude of his enterprises rather than by what he accomplished. He subdued (220 B.C.) his rebellious brothers Molo and Alexander, satraps of Media and Persia, and was forced (after having undertaken an aggressive war against Ptolemy Philopator) by the battle of Raphia, near Gaza, to relinquish (217 B.C.) his claims to Coele-Syria and Palestine. He defeated and killed (214) Achaeus, the rebellious governor of Asia Minor; attempted (212–205 B.C.) to regain the former provinces Parthia and Bactria; and was compelled to recognize (205) the independence of Parthia. The victory of Paneas (198) gave him back the Egyptian provinces of Coele-Syria and Palestine. He made peace, however, with Ptolemy Epiphanes to whom he betrothed his daughter Cleopatra, promising Coele-Syria and Palestine as a dowry. He conquered (196 B.C.) the Thracian Chersonese from Macedonia; received (195) Hannibal at his court; carried on (192–189) a war with the Romans who demanded the restoration of the Egyptian provinces and the Thracian Chersonese; was defeated at Thermopylae in 191, and at Magnesia in 190; and sustained naval losses at Chios (191) and at Myonnesus (190 B.C.). He purchased peace by consenting to the surrender of all his European possessions, and his Asiatic possessions as far as the Taurus, and the surrender of Hannibal, who escaped, and by giving up his elephants and ships of war. Antiochus was killed by his subjects in an attempt to plunder the rich temple of Elymaïs in order to pay the Romans, an event which, like his defeat by the Romans, is supposed by some to be referred to in Daniel, xi. 18, 19.

Antiochus IV (of *Syria*). [Called **Antiochus IV Epiphanes**.] King of Syria (175–c163 B.C.); third son of Antiochus III; died 163 B.C. He reconquered Armenia, which had been lost by his father, and made war on Egypt in the period 171–168 B.C., recovering Coele-Syria and Palestine. His policy of destroying the Jewish religion, in pursuance of which he took Jerusalem by storm in 170 B.C. (when he desecrated the temple) and again in 168, led to the successful revolt under Mattathias, the father of the Maccabees (167 B.C.).

Antiochus V (of *Syria*). [Called **Antiochus V Eupator**.] King of Syria (163–162 B.C.); son of Antiochus IV, whom he succeeded at the age of nine years, under the guardianship of Lysias. He was born c173 B.C.; died 162 B.C. He concluded a peace with the Jews who had revolted under his father, and was defeated and killed by Demetrius Soter (the son of Seleucus Philopator) who laid claim to the throne.

Antiochus VII (of *Syria*). [Called **Antiochus VII Sidetes**.] King of Syria (c139–c129 B.C.); born c159 B.C.; died c129 B.C. He was the second son of Demetrius Soter. He carried on war with the Jews, taking Jerusalem in 133 B.C., after which he concluded peace with them on favorable terms. He was killed in a war with the Parthians.

Antiochus VIII (of *Syria*). [Called **Antiochus VIII Grypus**, meaning "the Hook-nosed."] King of Syria (125–96 B.C.); died 96 B.C. He was the second son of Demetrius Nicator.

Antiochus XIII (of *Syria*). [Called **Antiochus XIII Asiaticus**.] King of Syria, the last of the Seleucidae. He took refuge in Rome during the mastery of Tigranes in Syria in the period 83–69 B.C. Given (69) possession of the kingdom by Lucullus, he was deprived (64 B.C.) of it by Pompey.

Antiochus of Ascalon (as′ka̤-lon). Greek eclectic philosopher, born in Palestine; early in the 1st century B C. He was the founder of the so-called Fifth Academy. He sought to reconcile the philosophies of the Stoic Mnesarchus and the Skeptic Philo, each of whom had been his teacher.

Antiochus of Syracuse (sir′a̤-kūs). Greek historian; fl. in the 5th century B.C. His *History of Syracuse* provided a record to 424 B.C. and was used as a source by Thucydides. He also wrote an account of the Greek colonization of Italy which is referred to by Strabo and Dionysius of Halicarnassus.

Antiope (an-tī′ō̤-pē). In Greek mythology, the daughter of Nycteus of Thebes. She was seduced by Zeus in the form of a satyr and fled from her father's wrath to the king of Sicyon. Her father secured a promise from his brother Lycus to help him capture and punish Antiope and she was brought back from Sicyon by force, her father having died. The twin sons she bore to Zeus, Amphion and Zethus, were left on Mount Cithaeron to die, but were saved by a herdsman. Antiope was cruelly treated by Lycus and his wife Dirce. She fled to the hut where her sons, now grown up, were living. Dirce pursued and told the twins to put the runaway to death by tying her by the hair to the horns of a wild bull. As they were about to do so the herdsman informed them that Antiope was their mother. Thereupon they seized Dirce and put her to death in the manner she had suggested for Antiope. According to other accounts, Antiope was the daughter of the river-god Asopus and was married to Lycus who divorced her to marry Dirce. In both accounts she was persecuted by Dirce and avenged by her Zeus-fathered sons.

Antiope. In Greek mythology, an Amazon queen, sister of Hippolyte. She became Theseus' captive and bore a son, Hippolytus, to him. In the war which the Amazons and Scythians waged against Athens she fought loyally at Theseus' side against her own countrywomen. According to some accounts she was killed in the battle. Others say Theseus killed her when she tried to prevent his marriage to Phaedra.

Antiparos (an-tip′a̱-ros). See **Oliarus.**

Antipater (an-tip′a̱-tẽr). Macedonian general and diplomat, born c398 B.C.; died 319 B.C. He was one of the ablest and most trusted of the ministers of Philip II of Macedon. Philip sent him (346 B.C.) to Athens as an ambassador to receive the oaths by which the Athenians accepted the peace imposed by Philip after the fall of Olynthus. He also acted in the peace negotiations after the defeat of the Athenians and Thebans at Chaeronea (338 B.C.). After the death of Philip, Antipater served Alexander the Great as regent of Macedonia while the king was in Asia. As regent he suppressed a Spartan revolt under Agis III through a victory at Megalopolis (330 B.C.). Olympias, mother of Alexander, constantly sent letters of accusation against Antipater to her son. In his turn he constantly complained to Alexander of her intrigues. On Alexander's death (323 B.C.) the partition of the empire left Macedonia under Antipater's control as joint ruler with Craterus; he defeated a Greek attempt (322 B.C.) to throw off Macedonian rule in the Lamian war. As conditions for peace with Athens following this war, he ordered modifications in the democratic constitution, placed a Macedonian garrison in Munychia at the Piraeus, and demanded the surrender of Demosthenes and Hyperides, the orators who agitated for revolt against Macedonia. Demosthenes fled to Calauria and committed suicide. Hyperides fled to the temple of Aeacus in Aegina. He was captured, taken to Antipater, and put to death. Antipater is said by some authors to have died of illness and by others to have been killed in battle.

Antiphanes (an-tif′a̱-nēz.) Greek comic poet, outstanding writer of the so-called Middle Comedy. He was born c388 B.C., and died c311 B.C. He is believed not to have been a native Athenian, but to have migrated there from Larissa in Thessaly. He was a most prolific author. Titles of about 120 of his plays are known, and more than 300 fragments of text survive. He won first prize 13 times with his comedies.

Antiphas (an′ti-fa̱s). In mythology, one of the twin sons of the priest Laocoön. He and his brother Thymbraeus were crushed to death by a serpent which Apollo sent from the sea to punish Laocoön for defaming his temple. But the Trojans thought the serpent was sent as a punishment because Laocoön doubted the divinity of the Wooden Horse the Greeks left before the walls of Troy.

Antiphates (an-tif′a̱-tēz). In mythology, a son of Melampus the seer. He was the father of Oicles who was the companion of Heracles and was killed when he went to Troy with him.

Antiphates. In Homeric legend (*Odyssey*), a chieftain of the Laestrygones, man-eating giants of Italy. His followers destroyed all but Odysseus' own ship when his fleet anchored in their harbor. Odysseus anchored his ship outside the harbor and escaped when the cannibals attacked the other ships and devoured the crews.

Antiphates. In Homeric legend (*Iliad*), a Trojan warrior who was slain by Leonteus in the battle at the Greek ships in the Trojan War.

Antiphellos (an-ti-fel′os). In ancient geography, a town on the SW coast of Lycia, Asia Minor. Its site contains a Lycian necropolis of rock-cut tombs, which are architecturally important because the façades are in exact reproduction of a framed construction of square wooden beams, with doors and windows of paneled work, and ceilings of round poles laid closely together. These tombs evidently represent ancient dwellings, and the imitation is carried out in some of the interiors. There is also an ancient theater, the *cavea* of which is well preserved, with 26 tiers of seats.

Antiphilus (an-tif′i-lus). Greek painter of the second half of the 4th century B.C. His work included portraits of Philip of Macedonia, Alexander the Great, and others.

Antiphon (an′ti-fon). Athenian orator and politician, the oldest of the "ten Attic orators." He was born at Rhamnus, Attica, c480 B.C. He taught political eloquence in his own school of rhetoric and also prepared speeches which he sold to others to deliver. He trained his aristocratic friends for legal practice in the democracy with exercises in speech-craft. His method was to take an imaginary case and prepare two speeches for the prosecution and two speeches for the defense. Three of these so-called tetralogies are extant. In addition, there are three extant speeches which were delivered in actual murder cases. These, though written by Antiphon, were delivered by others. As a member of the aristocratic party, he was brought to trial (411 B.C.) for his share in establishing government by the Four Hundred. This revolution was the death-blow to the democracy. He had spent all his life preparing for this revolution to restore the aristocrats and an oligarchy, and the speech he made in defense of his actions (the only instance of his delivering publicly one of his own speeches) was considered by Thucydides to be the greatest speech in the world. In spite of it he was condemned to death and executed (411 B.C.)

Antiphus (an′ti-fus). In Homeric legend (*Iliad*), a son of Talaemenes and the nymph of the lake of Gygaea. He and his brother Mesthles captained the Maeonians who came from Mount Tmolus as allies of Troy. Homer says their mother was "the lake of Gygaea."

Antiphus. Named by Homer (*Iliad*) as one of Priam's 50 sons. His mother was Hecuba. In the early days of the war he and his half-brother Isus were captured by Achilles but were released for ransom. He joined the battle against the Greeks and, in an attempt to kill Telamonian Ajax, killed Leucus, a valiant companion of Odysseus, and was later slain himself by Agamemnon.

Antiphus. In Greek legend, a Greek chieftain who fought at Troy. Eurypylus, a descendant of Heracles, tried to kill him but he fled as it was his fate to die in Sicily. He sailed from Troy with Odysseus and was one of the Greeks devoured by Polyphemus when Odysseus and his companions were trapped in Polyhemus' cave in Sicily.

Antipoenus (an-ti-pē′nus). In Greek legend, a Theban descendant of the Sparti. When Heracles decided to resist Erginus, king of the Minyans who was attacking Thebes, an oracle foretold victory if a descendant of the Sparti voluntarily died for Thebes. Antipoenus was unwilling to give up his life for his city but his daughters, Alcis and Androclea, gladly did so.

Antissa (an-tis′a). Cave on the island of Lesbos where, according to tradition, the head of Orpheus was laid to rest but where it continued to prophesy. At last Apollo, fearful for the reputation of his own oracles at Delphi, Gryneum, and Clarus, ordered the head of Orpheus to cease prophesying, and it fell silent.

Antistates (an-tis′ta̱-tēz). Greek architect, 6th century B C., associated with Callaeschrus, Antimachides, and Porinus in preparing the original plans for the Olympieum, the colossal Doric dipteral temple of Zeus Olympius at Athens, construction of which was begun about 530 B.C. by the Pisistratids. Work on the temple was abandoned on the expulsion of Hippias, c510, resumed in 174 B.C. under the direction of the Roman architect Cossutius, and completed in the reign of the emperor Hadrian. (JJ)

Antisthenes (an-tis′the-nēz). Athenian philosopher, born at Athens, c455 B.C.; died there c360 B.C. His mother was a Thracian. He was a pupil of Gorgias in his youth. In later life he became a follower and intimate friend of Socrates. He founded a school in Athens which admitted those who were not full citizens of Athens. His followers were known as *Cynici* and the school he founded was the Cynic School. The doctrine he taught was that Virtue is only good, that it can be taught, that the essence of virtue is self-control, and that pleasure is an evil if sought for its own sake. He regarded riches, fame, ease, and enjoyment as worthless. Two works on the contest for the arms of Achilles survive but the attribution of them to Antisthenes is disputed. He is said to have written dialogues, interpretations of Homer, and fictitious orations but save for some fragments, none of these has survived.

Antium (an'shum, -shi-um). [Modern name, **Anzio**.] Town in C Italy, situated on the Tyrrhenian Sea, about 32 miles S of Rome, at one time part of the nearby community of Nettuno: a seaside resort already known to the Romans. In ancient times a Volscian stronghold, it was incorporated into Rome in 338 B.C. It was the birthplace of Nero and of Caligula who later patronized the town. The statue known as the Apollo Belvedere was discovered here in 1485.

Antoninus Liberalis (an-tō-nī'nus lib-e-rā'lis). Greek grammarian of the middle of the 2nd century A.D. He was the author of a collection of mythical metamorphoses based on Hellenistic sources.

Antonius (an-tō'ni-us), **Marcus.** Roman politician and orator, born 143 B.C.; killed at Rome, 87 B.C. He was consul (99), and censor (97 B.C.), and was put to death by the Marian party.

Antony (an'tō-ni), **Mark.** [Also: **Marc Antony;** Latin, **Marcus Antonius.**] Roman triumvir and general, born c82 B.C.; died at Alexandria, in August, 30 B.C. He was the grandson of Marcus Antonius the orator. He served in Palestine and Egypt; was quaestor in 52 and tribune in 49 B.C. He became a prominent adherent of Caesar, and when he was expelled from Rome he fled to Caesar, who thereupon commenced the civil war. He commanded the left wing at the battle of Pharsalus, was master of the horse in 47 and became consul in 44 B.C. He engaged in intrigues after Caesar's death, and was denounced by Cicero. After having fled from Rome, he formed with Octavian (the future Augustus) and Lepidus the Second Triumvirate in 43. He defeated Brutus and Cassius at Philippi in 42 B.C., summoned Cleopatra to Asia and later followed her to Alexandria, and renewed the triumvirate in 40 and 37 B.C. From c40 B.C. he lived chiefly at Alexandria with Cleopatra, abandoning his wife Octavia, the sister of Octavian. He conducted an unsuccessful expedition against Parthia in 36. He was defeated by Octavian at Actium in 31 B.C., returned to Egypt and committed suicide before Octavian's entry into Alexandria.

Anubis (a-nū'bis). In Egyptian mythology, the son of Osiris often identified by the Greeks with Hermes. He is represented with a jackal's head and was the ruler of graves and supervisor of the burial of the dead.

Anyte (ä'ni-tē). Greek epic poetess of Tegea in Arcadia of whom little is known except from mention of her by other writers. She was active c290 B.C. and was once called "the feminine Homer." Twenty Doric epigrams are preserved in the *Anthology*.

Anytus (a'ni-tus). Athenian politician; fl. end of the 5th century B.C. He was an ardent admirer of Alcibiades who treated him with the utmost insolence. He was a democrat and fled to Thebes when the government of Athens was in the control of the Thirty Tyrants (404 B.C.). With Thrasybulus and other exiles from Athens he seized the fortress of Phyle in Attica and took part in the overthrow of the Tyrants, 403 B.C. Anytus was among those who brought the charge of impiety against Socrates that resulted in the death of the aged philosopher. Part of the charge against Socrates was that he corrupted the young men by his teachings. Some say this was a particular reference to the influence of Socrates on Alcibiades, who had been a pupil and friend of the philosopher and had insulted Anytus, and who had brought disaster to Athens by his military advice to Sparta.

Aonia (ā-ō'ni-a). In ancient geography, a district in Boeotia, Greece. The name is often used as synonymous with Boeotia.

Aornis (ā-ôr'nis). In Greek mythology, one of the five tributaries of the river Styx in the Underworld. The others were Acheron, Phlegethon, Cocytus, and Lethe.

Aornum (ā-ôr'num). A place in Thesprotia where there was said to be a passage to Hades. Some say Orpheus used this entrance when he descended to Hades in search of Eurydice.

Aornus (ā-ôr'nus). [Also: **Aornos.**] In ancient geography, a rock stronghold situated between the Indus and Swat rivers, taken (c327 B.C.) by Alexander the Great from native defenders.

Apamea (ap-a-mē′a). [Also: **Apamea Cibotus.**] In ancient geography, a city in Phrygia, Asia Minor, near the modern Dinar, Turkey.

Apamea. [Also: **Apamea ad Orontem.**] In ancient geography, a city in Syria, situated on the Orontes River about 50 miles SE of Antioch; the medieval Famieh, and the modern Qal'at el Mudiq, originally called Pharnake.

Apaturia (ap-a-tū′ri-a). An epithet of Athena, meaning, in this sense, "Deceitful." Aethra, before she became the mother of Theseus, in obedience to a dream sent to her by Athena, waded across from Troezen to the island of Sphaeria to offer libations to Sphaerus, the charioteer of Pelops who was buried there. On the island Poseidon overpowered her and violated her. (For this reason, Theseus sometimes claimed he was the son of Poseidon.) Aethra changed the name of the island to Hiera (*Sacred Isle*), and raised a temple to Athena Apaturia. Henceforth it was decreed that Troezonian maidens must dedicate their girdles to Athena Apaturia before their wedding day.

Apaturia. In Greek antiquity, the solemn annual meeting of the *phratries* (family brotherhoods) for the purpose of registering the children of the preceding year whose birth entitled them to citizenship. It took place in the month Pyanepsion (falling variously in October or November), and lasted three days. The registration took place on the third day.

Apelles (a-pel′ēz). Greek painter, born in Ionia, and active in the 4th cenutry B.C. He is considered one of the great ancient artists. He is said to have been a pupil first of an otherwise unknown Ephorus of Ephesus, later of Pamphilus of Sicyon, and his style is described as a blend of Ionian and Dorian elements. He was celebrated particularly for his portraits, including one of Alexander the Great with the thunderbolts of Zeus, for the temple of Artemis at Ephesus, and those of such other Macedonian notables as Archelaus, Clitus, and Antigonus. He also painted a procession of the high priest of Artemis, Artemis and her nymphs, and the *Aphrodite Anadyomene* (Aphrodite wringing out her hair as she rises from the sea) painted for

the temple of Asclepius at Cos. This last was probably his most noted work. It was taken to Rome by Augustus and set up in the temple of Caesar.

Apemius (a-pē′mi-us). Epithet of Zeus, meaning "Averter of Ills." There was an altar of Zeus Apemius on Mount Parnes near Athens.

Apemosyne (a-pe-moz′i-nē). In Greek mythology, a daughter of Catreus, king of Crete. She left Crete with her brother, Althaemenes, to avoid fulfilling an oracle which said Catreus would die at the hands of one of his own children. She and Althaemenes went to Rhodes and settled in Camirus. Hermes fell in love with her but she fled from his advances. One evening he cornered her, and when she tried to flee she fell on wet hides that he had placed across her path. He caught her and ravished her. Althaemenes did not believe her story that she had tried to escape. He killed her for what he thought were her immoral ways.

Apennines (ap′e-nīnz). [Latin, **Appenninus.**] Central mountain system of Italy. It forms the backbone of the peninsula and extends from the Ligurian Alps in the neighborhood of Savona SE to the extremity of the peninsula. The highest point is Monte Corno (9585 feet), in the Gran Sasso d'Italia. Length, about 800 miles; average elevation, about 4000 feet.

Apesantius (a-pe-sān′shi-us, -shus). Epithet of Zeus, from Mount Apesas near Nemea in Argolis where some say Perseus first sacrificed to Zeus of Apesas.

Aphaea (a-fē′a). Name under which Britomartis was worshiped on the island of Aegina, because she "vanished" when pursued by King Minos of Crete. The well-preserved Doric temple on Aegina, first thought to have been dedicated to Athena, is now known to have been the temple of Aphaea. At the site were found the much-admired late archaic pediment sculptures, the Aeginetan Marbles now in Munich. (JJ)

Aphareus (af′ar-yūs). In Greek mythology, the son of Gorgophone and Perieres, and the grandson of Perseus. He married his half-sister Arene, and by her was the father of Lynceus. He acted as foster father to Idas, Arene's son by Poseidon. According to tradition, Aphareus founded the city of Arene,

fat, fāte, fär, fãre, errant; net, mē, hėr ardent; pin, pīne; not, nōte, möve, nôr,

named for his wife, and with his brother Leucippus succeeded to the throne of Messenia on the death of Perieres. When Neleus was driven out of Iolcus by Pelias, Aphareus received him kindly and gave him Pylus. Lycus, son of Pandion, also came to Aphareus and, some say, revealed the rites of Demeter to the Messenians.

Aphesius (a-fē′shi-us, -shus). Epithet of Zeus, meaning "Releaser." At a time when all Greece was afflicted by a prolonged drought the oracle advised the Greeks to ask Aeacus to pray to Zeus for them. Aeacus went to the top of a mountain on the island of Aegina and sacirficed to Zeus Panhellenius (*God of all the Greeks*). In answer to the prayers of Aeacus Zeus sent a torrent of rain and released the land from the drought, hence the epithet "Releaser." Near the Molurian rock in Argolis, where Sciron was in the habit of tossing passers-by into the sea, the Greeks raised a temple of Zeus Aphesius.

Apheta (af′ē-ta) or **Aphetae** (-tē). A name meaning "Starting place," attached to several places. 1) It was the name of a street in Argos because it was from here that suitors for the hands of the Danaids were to start their race. The race was arranged by Danaus to marry off his daughters after they had all, at his request, slain their husbands, the sons of Aegyptus, on the wedding night. The winner of the race, in which there were few contestants, was to have first choice of a bride, the others were to choose brides in the order in which they finished the race. 2) Apheta was also the name of a place in Sparta which was said to have been the starting point of a race in which Odysseus won Penelope as a bride. 3) The name was also given to a place in Magnesia from which the *Argo* sailed on the expedition for the Golden Fleece.

Aphidas (a-fī′das). In Greek mythology, a son of Arcas and either Meganira, the nymph Chrysopelia, or the dryad Erato. He became the ruler of Tegea in Arcadia, and was the father of Aleus, who founded the famous temple of Athena Alea in Tegea, and of Antia who married Proetus.

Aphidna (a-fid′na). In ancient geography, a city of Attica. According to legend, here Theseus hid Helen after abducting her from Sparta. He left her here (she was ten years old at the time) because he feared the Athenians disapproved of his deed.

Aphidnus (a-fid′nus). In mythology, a friend of Theseus who with Theseus' mother Aethra took care of Helen when Theseus abducted her. When Helen was rescued by her brothers, Castor and Polydeuces, Aphidnus adopted them as his sons. In Roman legend, a friend of Aeneas, killed by Turnus.

Aphneius (af′nē-ūs). Epithet of Ares. Some say that Ares embraced Aërope, daughter of Cepheus, king of Tegea, and that she died in giving birth to her child. The child clung to its mother even though she was dead, and through the will of Ares sucked great quantities of milk from her breasts and lived. For this reason the name Aphneius (*Abundant*) was given to Ares. There was a sanctuary of Ares Aphneius on Mount Cresius near Tegea in Arcadia where all this took place.

Aphrodisias (af-rō-diz′i-as). In ancient geography, a town in Caria, Asia Minor, situated on the Maeander River (modern, Menderes) in what is now SW Turkey. The site contains the remains of an ancient hippodrome which coincide on one side with the city walls. Both ends are semicircular. The length is 919 feet, the breadth 270; the arena is 747 by 98 feet. There are 26 tiers of seats, divided into sections by flights of steps and bordered above by an arcaded gallery. There is also a comparatively well preserved Roman temple of Venus. It is Ionic, octastyle, pseudodipteral, with 15 columns on the flanks, in plan 60 by 119 feet. The peristyle columns are 35¾ feet high.

Aphrodite (af-rō-dī′tē). One of the 12 Olympian deities, goddess of love and beauty who ruled the hearts of gods and men and symbolized the irresistible generative powers of nature operating on land, in the sea, and in the air. Only Artemis, Athena, and Hestia among the goddesses were successful in denying the power of the great goddess of love. All others, including Zeus himself, were under her sway. Conscious of her power to give beauty and love, Aphrodite punishes those who fail to honor her or who attempt to deny her, and willingly aids those who honor and seek her.

Some say that Aphrodite was the daughter of Zeus and the Titaness Dione. But others say that when Cronus emasculated his father

Uranus with a sickle and flung his dismembered parts into the sea, foam gathered about them; and from this sea foam Aphrodite rose and was borne to land on a sea-shell, whence her epithets Aphrogeneia (*Foam-born*), and Anadyomene (*Risen from the Sea*). She first stepped ashore on the island of Cythera, and then went to Paphos on Cyprus. Paphos was the most ancient seat of her worship, and every spring the priestess of her temple renewed herself by bathing in the sea. From these two islands, Aphrodite has the names Cytherea and Cypris. Wherever she treads, according to the ancient Greeks, flowers spring up, and doves and sparrows murmur in the air about her. She possesses a magic girdle which imparts surpassing grace and charm to whomever wears it and compels all who behold it to fall in love with the wearer. Some say Eros and Himeros (*God of Longing*), her constant companions, along with the Horae and the Charites, were born with her.

She was given in marriage by Zeus to the lame god Hephaestus, to whom she was notoriously unfaithful, especially with the magnificent war god Ares. To Ares she bore Phobus (*Fear*), Deimos (*Terror*), and Harmonia, who married Cadmus, and some say Eros and Anteros (*Unrequited Love*) were also her children by Ares. Helius, who saw everything in his circuit across the heavens reported to Hephaestus that Aphrodite was entertaining Ares in his absence. Hephaestus laid a trap for them. He pretended that he was going to Lemnos but secretly spied on them. He found Aphrodite and Ares together and cast a great bronze net he had forged over them, from which they could not escape. He then called the gods to witness their disgrace and his own dishonor. He demanded that the gifts he had given Zeus on his marriage to Aphrodite be returned as a condition for releasing the lovers from the net. Zeus was disgusted by the public spectacle Hephaestus had made of his private affairs and refused to return the marriage gifts. Poseidon, who was in love with Aphrodite, guaranteed that Ares would pay the equivalent of the marriage gifts to Hephaestus in return for his freedom from the net, and if Ares failed to do so Poseidon promised that he himself would pay He-

phaestus and take Aphrodite as his wife. Ares was freed, but never did pay, as he claimed that since Zeus had refused he could do the same. Aphrodite renewed herself by bathing in the sea. Afterward she rewarded Poseidon for his good offices and bore him two sons, Rhodus and Herophilus. Hermes, who had expressed his admiration for her as she struggled in Hephaestus' bronze net, received her favors. She bore him Hermaphroditus, who had the features of both sexes. But Eos, who seduced her lover Ares, she punished. She caused Eos to have a fatal weakness for young and beautiful mortal boys. In the end, Hephaestus took Aphrodite back as his wife on her own terms, as he was madly in love with her. In later myth she is the wife of Ares. She subsequently bore the fertility god Priapus to Dionysus.

APHRODITE RIDING ON A GOOSE
Attic cup, white ground, Pistoxenus Painter, 500–475 B.C. *British Museum*

By her power to rule the hearts of gods as well as men, Aphrodite many times caused Zeus to fall in love with mortal maidens. To make her understand what it was like to love a mortal, Zeus caused her to fall in love with

Anchises, son of Capys. She went to the herdsman's hut of Anchises, on the "cloud-kissing" peaks of Mount Ida near Troy, and appeared to him when he came in from tending his flocks. Anchises was stunned by her loveliness, and instantly took her for a goddess. But she told him she was a mortal, the daughter of the Phrygian King Otreus, and that she had been brought to Mount Ida by Hermes to become Anchises' wife. Anchises was enchanted and at once embraced her. Afterward he fell into a deep sleep. As he slept Aphrodite donned her immortal robes, and then woke him, and revealed to him that he had embraced a goddess. Anchises was terrified, for he knew what terrible punishments were visited on mortals who embraced gods. However, Aphrodite reassured him. She said she would bear him a son who would be named Aeneas, "the Terrible," because of the terrible pain she suffered in loving a mortal. This son would be brought up by the nymphs of Mount Ida for five years. At the end of that time he would return to Anchises, who must say that he was the son of a mountain nymph. Aphrodite promised Anchises a long and prosperous life on condition that he never mention that he had lain with a goddess. Anchises readily agreed but later, either bemused by wine or for some other reason, he revealed that he had embraced Aphrodite. Instantly Zeus struck him with the lightning, and though he was saved through the intervention of Aphrodite his strong straight body was permanently crippled. Some say that before this happened, Aphrodite bore him not only Aeneas but another son Lyrus who died childless.

For all her grace and charm, Aphrodite is an exacting goddess. Smyrna, daughter of Cinyras, scorned her power or, as some say, Smyrna incurred her wrath because her mother boasted that Smyrna was more beautiful than Aphrodite. Aphrodite caused her to fall in love with her own father, to meet him in darkness so that he didn't know what maiden he was embracing, and to conceive a son by him. When Cinyras learned that the maiden who visited him was his own daughter he was horrified, and sought to kill her. Smyrna fled, and Aphrodite transformed her into a myrrh tree. From the

trunk of the tree Smyrna's son Adonis was born. Aphrodite rescued him and gave him to Persephone to rear. Persephone fell in love with him as he grew to be a handsome youth, and refused to give him up to Aphrodite. The muse Calliope was called on to judge the case. She divided the year into three parts—Adonis was to spend one third of it with Persephone, one third with Aphrodite, and the last third by himself. In the end, Aphrodite persuaded him, by means of her magic girdle, to give her the third he was supposed to have by himself. Some say that Aphrodite grieves so during the time Adonis spends with Persephone that she withdraws her generative powers, and vegetation withers, and this is the winter. At her joy over his return she causes the earth to flower in the spring. Some say, however, that Aphrodite was so enraged by Calliope's decision that it was she who caused the Thracian maenads to go mad and tear Calliope's son Orpheus to pieces. The muse Clio, who mocked her love for Adonis, she caused to fall in love with Pierus and to bear him a son who some say was Hyacinthus. Again, Aphrodite inflicted a most terrible punishment on Hippolytus, son of Theseus, because he scorned her powers and denied her due honor. She caused his stepmother Phaedra to fall in love with him and brought about the catastrophe which cost the lives of Phaedra and Hippolytus. Aphrodite aided Melanion (or as some name him, Hippomenes) to win Atalanta by giving him three golden apples. But some say the pair forgot her help in their happiness and were transformed into beasts as a punishment. It was Aphrodite who caused the men of Lemnos to prefer their captive women to their own wives, because the Lemnian women denied her power. This led to the slaughter of all the males of Lemnos by the women to avenge the insults the men had directed toward them.

But for Theseus, who took Aphrodite as his guide on the advice of the Delphic oracle when he set out on his mission to Crete, she caused Ariadne to fall in love with him and to make possible his escape from the labyrinth of the Minotaur and from Crete. And at the request of Hera and Athena, she furnished a love charm to insure that Medea's passion for Jason would endure and that she would help him in his trial at Colchis and to secure the Golden Fleece. This love charm consisted of a wryneck (a fish-eating bird) stretched to a fire-wheel, and was considered by the Greeks to be a potent love charm. To Paris who awarded her the Apple of Discord (prize of beauty thrown among the wedding guests at the marriage of Peleus and Thetis) she promised the most beautiful woman in the world. She helped him to win Helen, although she was the wife of Menelaus, and carry her off to Troy. This interference by Aphrodite led to the Trojan War, disastrous for Troy. In the course of the war Aphrodite aided the Trojans, saved Paris when he was about to be slain by Menelaus in a duel, and rescued her son Aeneas when he was wounded by Diomedes. Diomedes also wounded the goddess, who fled to Olympus to be cured by her mother Dione. Hera and Athena scorned her when she arrived in Olympus, but Zeus smiled, and advised her to "busy herself with the gladsome duties' of wedlock" and leave war to the gods and goddesses who were suited to it. Dione comforted her, healed the wound, and promised that Diomedes would be punished for his temerity in attacking an immortal. At the sack of Troy some say it was Aphrodite who interposed and prevented Aeneas from killing Helen, and some say that it was she who caused love to surge anew in the heart of Menelaus when he saw Helen again, so that instead of killing her, as he had said he would do, he forgave her and lovingly carried her off to his tent.

When the Argonauts sailed by the island of the Sirens on their way home from Colchis, Orpheus played so sweetly that their music was unheard except by Butes who leaped into the sea, maddened by the strains of the Sirens. Aphrodite rescued him and bore him to Lilybaeum in Sicily where she bore him a son, Eryx.

The myrtle, rose, apple, and poppy were sacred to Aphrodite, as were the dove, sparrow, swan, swallow, hare, goat, and ram. Incense and flowers were offered to her in sacrifice. The principal seats of her worship were at Amathus, Idalion, and Paphos on the island of Cyprus, in the latter of which was the most ancient temple of Aphrodite in the Greek world; on the island of Cythera; at Cnidus, where her temple held the famous statue of her by Praxiteles; at Mount Ida in the Troad; Cos; Abydos; Athens; Thespiae; Megara; Sparta; Sicyon; and Corinth; and at Eryx in Sicily.

Many epithets signified her varied aspects. She was Aphrodite Acraea (*Of the Height*), Doritis (*Bountiful*), and Epistrophia (*She who turns men to love*). Having sprung from the sea, she was regarded as a goddess of the sea who protected sailors and navigation and was named Euploia (*Fair Voyage*), Limenia (*Of the Harbor*), and Pontia (*Of the Deep Sea*); when Zeus and Typhon struggled and all the gods were forced to flee, Aphrodite escaped by transforming herself into a fish, a symbol of the fertility of the sea. She was a goddess who gave victory and was worshiped in Sparta as Area (*Warlike*), possibly because of her connection with Ares. Hypermnestra, daughter of Danaus, dedicated an image to Aphrodite Bringer of Victory, after she was acquitted by the Argives for defying her father and refusing to murder her husband. When Theseus, some time after his safe return from Crete, federated the demes of Attica he instituted the worship of Federal Aphrodite and Persuasion, another aspect of the goddess. Most of all she was the goddess of love. As goddess of the physical love that unites men and women there was a sanctuary of Aphrodite Migonitis (*Uniter*) opposite the island of Cranaë, raised by Paris to commemorate his first embrace of Helen. In Memphis in Egypt, whither some say Paris and Helen were blown by storms on the way to Troy, there was a temple of Aphrodite the Stranger, said to have been dedicated by Helen herself. Theseus raised a sanctuary of Aphrodite Nymphaea (*Bridal*) when he abducted the youthful Helen and made her his wife. She was Aphrodite Melaenis (*Black*), some say because men invoke her at night for love-making, but others say it was because of her role as a goddess of the Underworld, in which role she was also called Scotia (*Dark One*), Androphonos (*Man-slayer*), and Epitymbria (*Of the Tombs*). As a goddess of marriage and family life she was Aphrodite Pandemos (*Common to All*). This aspect was perverted in the time of Solon, so that Aphrodite Pandemos came to be a goddess of prostitution, with temple prostitutes. As a goddess of the spiritual love of mankind she was worshiped widely as Aphrodite Urania (*Heavenly*), and had many temples. In this aspect she was also goddess of the heavens and the winds and many of her temples were on elevated headlands, as at Eryx in Sicily. As a goddess of the heavens she was also Pasiphaë (*Shining on all*) and Asteria (*Starry*). At Thebes the ancient temple originally contained three wooden images made from the figureheads of the ships that brought Cadmus to Greece, that were dedicated by Harmonia. The images represented Aphrodite Urania (*Heavenly*) of the pure love of mankind, Aphrodite Pandemos (*Common*), to represent the goddess of the family and community life for all the people, and Aphrodite Apostrophia (*Rejecter*), the goddess who helps men to reject unlawful passion and sinful acts. Tyndareus dedicated an image of Aphrodite Morpho (*Shapely*), representing the goddess veiled and with fetters on her ankles. Some say this represented the bonds of faithfulness and modesty in marriage. Under the special circumstances surrounding the daughters of Tyndareus, however, it could have been an ironic reminder to the goddess.

Some say that Aphrodite was originally the Assyrian goddess Ishtar, and that her worship was brought to Paphos in Cyprus by the Phoenicians of Ascalon, who called her Astarte, and from whose ancient temple the Paphians copied their temple. And they say that the Phoenician traders who came to Cythera taught worship of her to the Cytheraeans. Among the Syrians, a goddess similar to her was called Derceto. The Babylonians worshiped Mylitta and the Arabians Alilat, who were equivalent to Aphrodite in some respects. Whatever the origin of her worship, the Greeks evolved the worship of Aphrodite, in all its aspects, into a purely Greek conception. The Romans who claimed Aphrodite as their ancestress through her son Aeneas, worshiped her as Venus. Aphrodite was one of the favorite subjects in art. Of her representations in classical art the most famous are the replica of her statue of Cnidus by Praxiteles, the original statutes of Melos in the Louvre, of Capua at

Naples, the Medicean at Florence, and the Capitoline at Rome.

Aphrogeneia (af-rō-je-nī′a̧). An epithet of Aphrodite, meaning "Foam-born" and referring to the circumstances of her birth from the foam that gathered around the dismembered parts of Uranus which were flung into the sea by Cronus.

Apis (ā′pis). In Greek legend, a son of Phoroneus. He was accidentally killed by the chariot of Aetolus, son of Endymion, at the funeral games for Azan, son of Arcas. Because of this Salmoneus banished Aetolus from Elis.

Apis. In Greek legend, a son of Apollo. He went from Naupactus to Argos, where he drove all the serpents out of the land, for which reason Argos was sometimes called "Apian" land.

Apis. In Egyptian mythology, the sacred bull of Memphis, worshiped by the ancient Egyptians. He was believed to be the incarnation of Osiris, and was the sacred emblem of that god. Sometimes he is portrayed as a man with a bull's head. The Greeks sometimes identified Apis with Epaphus, the son of Io and Zeus, born on the banks of the Nile after the long wanderings of Io. According to Herodotus, Apis is the calf of a cow that becomes barren after his birth. Apis, in the form of a bull, is black, with a square white spot on his forehead, the figure of an eagle on his back, and a beetle on his tongue. The hairs in his tail are double. Apis in the form of a bull appeared from time to time in Egypt, and when he did so it was a time of great rejoicing.

Apocolocyntosis (a̧-po″ko-lō-sin′tō-sis). Mock-serious title (it may be translated as "Pumpkinification") of a ruthless satirical sketch of the reception, by the Olympian Gods, of the emperor Claudius, i.e., his deification; composed in Latin in a medley of prose and verse, shortly after Claudius' death (54 A.D.) and attributed to L. Annaeus Seneca the Younger, statesman, orator, philosopher, essayist, dramatist, and court wit. (JJ)

Apollino (ä-pōl-lē′nō). Statue in the collection of the Uffizi, Florence. It is an antique copy from a Greek original, probably of the 4th century B.C., representing a delicately built type of the youthful Apollo, standing easily and gracefully.

actor; up, lūte, pu̇ll; oi, oil; ou, out; ᴛʜ, then; ḏ as d or j, ş as s or sh, ṭ as t or ch, ẕ as z or zh.

Apollo (a-pol′ō). "Lord of the Silver Bow," one of the great Olympian gods. He was the god of music, poetry, and the dance, and in classical times came to be regarded also as god of the plastic arts and of science and philosophy, the god of the intellect and the enemy of barbarism. He was the protector of flocks and herds, the patron of the founding of towns and colonies who helped build the walls of Troy and Megara, and to whose oracle all went before setting out to found colonies. He was the god of healing, Alexicacus (*Averter of Evil*), who was called on to dispel plagues and heal sickness; and he was the god of prophecy. Above all, he was the god of light: of the physical light that dispels darkness, of the light of spring and summer that puts the winter to flight, and of the spiritual and moral light that dispels the darkness of ignorance from men's minds and evil from their hearts. The worship of Apollo was one of the most potent of the forces that brought Greek civilization to full flower.

When Leto was about to bear her children by Zeus she fled throughout the world. No place would receive her, for jealous Hera had decreed that Leto could not bear her children in any place where the sun shone. At last she came to the tiny floating island of Delos. Delos gladly received Leto, but feared that her future son, "the Archer-king," would scorn the modest island and would thrust it under the sea. Leto swore an oath that her son would build his first temple there, and would honor it above all other places, whereupon Delos welcomed her warmly. Some say Leto first bore Artemis on the neighboring island of Ortygia, and that when she was born Artemis helped her mother across to Delos where her twin was to be born. Even here Hera's jealousy afflicted her for she kept Ilithyia, the goddess who helps women in childbirth, on Mount Olympus by guile. Leto's labor lasted nine days and nights. Then the goddesses—Dione, Rhea, Themis, Amphitrite—who were all present, sent Iris to Olympus to fetch Ilithyia. That goddess, informed of the circumstances, hurried to Delos at once. Leto knelt on the ground, clasped a palm tree in the shadow of Mount Cynthus, and gave birth to Apollo. The goddesses washed him and clothed him. Themis fed him on nectar and ambrosia. He was born on the seventh of the month, and ever after the number seven was sacred to him, and sacrifices were made to him on the seventh of every month. The palm tree beneath which he was born was one of the sights of antiquity from the time of Homer to the time of Pliny. Other places in the Greek world claimed to be his birthplace, as the grove of Ortygia in Ephesus, Tegyra in Boeotia, and Zoster in Attica, but Delos in generally honored as the birthplace of Apollo, and it was there that his universal sovereignty began. After his birth the island was covered with golden flowers in its joy, and as a reward for its kindness to Leto it was anchored in the sea and ceased to float about. Four days after he was born Apollo sundered the golden bands of his swaddling clothes, leaped up, and proclaimed that he would in future announce the will of Zeus to men. Some say at this time he called for bow and arrows, which Hephaestus at once gave him, and declared them and the lyre sacred to him. And some say that when he was four years old he built an altar at Delos entirely composed of the horns of goats shot by his sister Artemis. In search of a place to found his oracle he left Olympus, where clad in royal raiment he had given a concert to the delighted gods, and passed through Pieria to Euboea. He then crossed the Euripus and went by Teumessus and the site where the city of Thebes would one day stand, passed Onchestus, crossed the Cephissus River on the border of Phocis, and so arrived at Haliartus. There he thought to found his oracle, but the fountain nymph, Telphusa, advised him not to found an oracle in her domain because she did not want to share the honors with him, and suggested that he go on to Crisa (Delphi). There he slew with his arrows the dragon that guarded the spring. Some say this dragon had, at Hera's orders, pursued Leto across the world before her children were born, and it was for this reason that Apollo killed it. Others say the dragon was slain because it tried to prevent Apollo from approaching the chasm of an ancient oracle. In any event, the world was rid of a murderous pest and the place where the creature's body was left to rot was named Pythos, "the place of the rotting," and Apollo acquired the epithet Pythian. But some say the dragon was named Python, and this was the reason for Apollo's epithet, and the reason why his priestesses at Delphi were called Pythonesses. He laid the foundations for his temple, for which Trophonius and Agamedes paved the floor with marble and scores of laborers raised the structure, and founded his oracle. But some say there was formerly an oracle of Gaea there, and then one of Themis, and that it was from the latter that Apollo took the oracle. And some say Apollo was compelled to go to Tempe to do penance and to be purified for the slaughter of the dragon, which they say was Hera's earthborn child or was the guardian of an ancient oracle. The killing of the dragon and the purification of Apollo were memorialized every eighth year (for he was in Tempe seven years atoning for the murder) in a festival at Delphi, and the Pythian Games held at this time were instituted to propitiate the dead dragon. Because he had endured penance and purification himself, Apollo could purify others, and in this function the worship of Apollo encouraged the substitution of law and penance for blood vengeance. After slaying the dragon Apollo remembered that Telphusa had advised him to come to this spot but had not warned him of the serpent. To punish her, he sealed up her fountain in Haliartus with a huge stone. On the spot he erected an altar, and thereafter Apollo was worshiped and Telphusa was forgotten. Having built his temple near Crisa (at Delphi) Apollo pondered how he should choose priests to serve in it. He gazed far out to sea and beheld a Cretan vessel on its way to Alphaean Pylus. Instantly he changed himself into a dolphin, swam out to the vessel and leaped aboard. The Cretan crew tried to hurl the dolphin into the sea, but he shook the ship so that they were afraid and dared not even man the tiller. Under Apollo's unseen guidance the ship sailed around the Peloponnesus to the Gulf of Crisa (an inlet in the Gulf of Corinth) where a strong wind blew it ashore. Apollo went to his shrine and lit an altar fire, as all the people acclaimed him. He returned to the Cretan ship and invited the crew to stow their tackle and come ashore for food and rest. The captain replied that he did not know what land they were in,

that his vessel had been brought there by a a god, and that he wished to go home. Apollo revealed himself as a god and announced that they would never return to Crete, but would become his priests and be the most honored among men. He instructed them to build an altar there by the sea and to worship him as the Delphian god, because he had first appeared to them as a dolphin. As Delphian Apollo, or Apollo Delphinius, he was the patron of sailors and ports, and at Athens was worshiped as the patron of the founding of colonies. Jason sacrificed a yoke of oxen to Apollo Embasius (*Apollo of Embarkations*), before setting out on his journey to Colchis. And as a god of sailors and sailing he was worshiped as Apollo Ecbasion (*Apollo of Disembarkations*), who assures successful landings. Diomedes raised a temple of Apollo Epibaterius (*Seafaring*), in gratitude for his having weathered the storms that scattered the Greeks at sea on their way home from Troy.

Apollo, "Lord of the Silver Bow," received his bow and arrows from Hephaestus, who forged them for him, and used them to punish the wicked and arrogant. He slew Tityus, the monstrous son of Zeus and Elara, because he attacked Leto as she was going to Delphi. Again, for the greater honor of his mother, he and his sister Artemis killed the children of arrogant Niobe who had boasted that she was at least equal to Leto who had only two children. It was Apollo who sent the plague of arrows on the Greeks encamped before Troy, because Agamemnon haughtily denied the plea of Apollo's priest Chryse to accept ransom for his daughter Chryseis. In the battle with the Giants, Apollo shot Ephialtes in the left eye, and Heracles dispatched him by shooting him in the right eye. Apollo was a helpful god, as when he appeared to the Argonauts, caught in a black and raging storm on their way home from Colchis, and by a flash of light revealed an island where they could find haven. The Argonauts built an altar to Radiant Apollo, and named the island Anaphe (*Revealed,* or *Unexpected*). As Apollo Parnopius (*Locust-god*) he lifted a plague of locusts that infested Attica. He was also Acesius (*Healer*), Patroüs (*Paternal*), Archegetes (*Founder*), Prostaterius (*Protecting*), and Boëdromius

(*Rescuer*). In the Trojan War he rescued Hector many times, and abandoned him to death only at the command of Fate.

Under the leadership of Hera, Apollo took part in the conspiracy of the gods to bind Zeus. Zeus was freed by the intervention of Thetis. To punish Apollo, Zeus ordered him to work with Poseidon to build the walls of Troy for Laomedon. (But some say the gods labored on the walls to prove the wickedness of Laomedon; and some say Apollo served as the herdsman of Laomedon.) When the walls were completed Laomedon not only refused to pay as he had promised, but threatened to cut off the ears of the gods and sell them as slaves. Apollo sent a pestilence to afflict Troy, and Poseidon sent a sea monster. Both afflictions were removed when Heracles came and killed the monster. In the Trojan War Apollo aided the city whose walls he had helped to build. When the gods who actively participated in the conflict fell to quarreling and attacking each other, Apollo refused to quarrel with Poseidon although the latter taunted him for aiding the descendants of the man who had tricked them over the building of the walls. In this case it was beneath his dignity to fight. On another occasion he showed his willingness to take vigorous action to protect his property. Heracles came to the shrine at Delphi to inquire how he could cure himself of a sickness. The priestess refused to give him an answer. Enraged, Heracles seized the tripod and said he would found his own oracle. Apollo sprang to the defense of his priestess and wrestled with Heracles. Zeus parted them with a thunderbolt and compelled them to make friends, and the two went off together and founded the town of Gythium.

Apollo had many loves. He was the father of Linus by the muse Calliope, according to some accounts. Some say he was the father of the Corybantes by the muse Thalia. By Phthia he was the father of Dorus, Laodocus, and Polypoetes who were killed by Aetolus, who took their land and named it Aetolia after himself. Aria bore him Miletus who afterward fled from Crete to Caria and founded the city of Miletus. His son Amphissus by the nymph Dryope founded the city of Oeta and raised a temple of Apollo

there. Anius, king of Delos and Apollo's priest there, was his son by Rhoeo. Some say that Hector and Troilus, reputed sons of Priam, were Apollo's children. By Creusa he was the father of Ion, founder of the Ionian race. Again, it is said that Apollo was the father of Tenes, king of Tenedos. When the Greeks landed on Tenedos on their way to Troy Achilles killed Tenes. It had been foretold that if Achilles killed a son of Apollo he would die by Apollo's hand. According to some accounts, when Achilles fell at the Scaean Gate of Troy the arrow that killed him, though shot by Paris, was guided by Apollo and was wafted back to Apollo when Achilles pulled it from his ankle. Others say Achilles was killed in the sanctuary of Thymbraean Apollo in the Troad. On one occasion Apollo saw the huntress Cyrene struggling with a boar, fell in love with her, and asked Chiron the centaur if he should woo Cyrene. Chiron said Apollo would take Cyrene to a luxuriant land and that she would bear him a son. Apollo carried her off to Libya, where she bore him Aristaeus and Idmon the seer. Another of his loves was Coronis. She was unfaithful to him while she was carrying his child and the news was brought to the god by a white raven he had set to guard her. Apollo turned the raven's feathers black for bringing him the news (which he already knew by divination) instead of pecking out the eyes of Coronis' lover. He went to Coronis and caused her death. But as she was lying on the pyre he regretted his harsh act; he commanded Hermes to snatch the unborn child from her womb, and sent it to Chiron to be reared. This son was Asclepius who inherited his father's skill in healing and was so successful in his art that he raised men from the dead. Some say Zeus feared he would teach his skill to others; others say Hades complained to Zeus that owing to the ministrations of Asclepius the population of his realm was decreasing, and Zeus struck Asclepius dead with his thunderbolt. In anger at the loss of his son, Apollo killed the Cyclopes who had forged the thunderbolt of Zeus. Zeus would have banished him to Tartarus, but yielded to the pleas of Leto to spare her son and sentenced Apollo to serve Admetus, king of Pherae, for a year. While in his service as a herdsman Apollo caused all his flocks to bear twins. He also helped Admetus to win Alcestis for a bride by yoking a boar and a lion to a chariot for a race, one of the conditions her successful suitor must fulfill. Admetus forgot to honor Artemis properly at his marriage ceremonies, and in anger Artemis declared he must die. Apollo went to the Fates, who control the span of life, got them drunk, and exacted a promise from them that they would spare Admetus' life, but only on condition that someone who loved him would consent to die in his place. When he had completed his term of penance by serving Admetus, Apollo never again defied Zeus, but learned to control himself and became a force for moderation in all things.

Apollo did not enjoy unvarying success in his love affairs. Idas, the only mortal who dared to struggle with him, vied with him for the affections of Marpessa. Marpessa, given the choice by Zeus, chose Idas, for she feared that as she aged she might lose the love of the god and would have a better chance of happiness with Idas, who would grow old and lose his beauty even as she would. Apollo pursued the nymph Daphne, daughter of the river-god Peneus in Thessaly. Leucippus was his rival in this case, and disguised himself as a girl that he might be in the company of the chaste nymph. Apollo learned of his ruse by divination and revealed the disguise when he advised the nymphs to bathe naked. He now sought Daphne but she fled, and when she was about to be overtaken prayed to her father to so transform her beauty that Apollo would cease his pursuit. Her prayer was answered: as Apollo was about to clasp her to him she was changed into a laurel tree. Even transformed, Apollo still loved her and made the laurel (or bay) his sacred tree and gave it never-fading leaves. Wreaths of laurel crowned the victors at the Pythian Games, and leaves of laurel were chewed by the priestesses of Apollo to inspire them with prophetic powers. Another of Apollo's loves was Hyacinthus. Thamyris the musician and Zephyrus (West Wind) were Apollo's rivals. Thamyris was deprived by the Muses of his sight and of his gift for song because he had boasted of his art. Zephyrus, a jealous rival, came one day when Apollo was teaching

Hyacinthus how to throw the quoit, seized the quoit in a gust of wind and hurled it back with such force that it struck Hyacinthus on the head and killed him. Others say that Hyacinthus was killed when the quoit ricocheted from the ground and struck him on the forehead.

APOLLO
Red-figured Greek psykter, Pan Painter, c490
B.C. *Munich*

Apollo was the god of prophecy and divination, an attribute which some say he had received as a gift from Zeus, and others say he learned from Pan. In his role as seer he passed on to men the will of Zeus, but men did not always interpret his prophecies correctly; for that reason he was called Loxias (*Crooked,* or *Ambiguous*). Some hold this epithet to mean Interpreter. Many famous seers claimed to have received their powers from Apollo. He taught the art of divination to Melampus, Helenus, Epimenides, and the Cumaean Sibyl; and Idmon, the Argive Argonaut, and Mopsus, son of Manto, inherited the gift as Apollo's sons. He could give the gift to others. When he fell in love with Cassandra he gave her the gift of prophecy in return for the promise of her favors. She refused to honor her promise, however, and since the god would not take back what he had given he turned her gift into a curse by decreeing that, although she would make true prophecies, no one would believe her.

Apollo was the god of flocks and herds. One day some of his cattle were missing from their pasture in Pieria. By his powers of divination, or as some say, by watching the flight of a long-winged bird, he knew that Hermes, a new-born infant, had stolen the cattle. He went to the cave on Cyllene where Hermes was lying in his cradle and accused him of the theft. Hermes protested his innocence of a crime that would be, he claimed, impossible for one of his tender age. Nevertheless, Apollo took him off to appear before Zeus, and Hermes was compelled to admit the theft and led Apollo to where he had set them to graze. Arrived at the spot, Hermes played on the lyre which he had just invented, and so charmed Apollo that he agreed to give up the cattle to Hermes in exchange for the lyre. Hermes gave it to him, and immediately invented a shepherd's pipe, made of reeds, on which he played so artfully while the cattle grazed that Apollo demanded the new instrument also, and offered Hermes the golden wand he used when herding cattle in exchange for it. Hermes agreed to give him the pipe if Apollo would throw in the art of divining as well as the wand. As protector of flocks, Apollo was Lycius (*Wolf-god*) who destroys the wolves that prey on flocks.

As the god of music, poetry, and the dance, he influenced the Muses to leave their frenzies on Mount Helicon and join him in stately dances, and so earned the epithet Musagetes (*Leader of the Muses*). As god of music he brooked no rivals. Marsyas challenged him to a musical contest, contending that his instrument, the flute, was superior to Apollo's lyre, and was defeated in the contest of which the Muses were the judges. To punish him for his presumption Apollo flayed him and hung up his skin on a pine tree. On another occasion, he took part in a contest with Pan. Midas, the Phrygian king, and Tmolus, the mountain god, acted as judges. Tmolus awarded the prize to Apollo, but Midas stubbornly clung to his opinion that Pan was the better player. Apollo caused asses' ears to grow from Midas' head, as being worthy ears for one who was such a donkey as to prefer the music of Pan to that of Apollo.

Apollo had many epithets. He was Phoebus (*Bright,* or *Pure god*), and the "Far-darter." In his role as a god of agriculture he was "Ruler of the Seasons," and was accompanied by the Horae. As "Rearer of Boys" he fostered young men and was patron of their athletic training grounds, and to him they sacrificed the first clippings of their hair. He was Apollo Smintheus (*Mouse-god*), an epithet which may have applied to his role as god of healing, for mice were associated with disease and its cure, and white mice were kept in Apollo's temples to protect against plague and against plagues of mice. He was Apollo Agyieus (*God of Streets*), who let in the good and kept out evil, and whose symbol, a pillar with a pointed top, stood before the doorways of houses and was honored with offerings of wreaths and ribbons. He was also Agraeus (*Hunter*), Platanistius (*God of the Plane-tree Grove*), Theoxenius (*Strangers' God*), Spodius (*God of Ashes—of victims*), and Moeragetes (*Guide of the Fates*). The Spartans worshiped him as Apollo Carneus and held a splendid festival for him in August, the Carnea. In addition to the epithets celebrating a particular role or incident concerning him, he had numerous epithets which associated him with places, as Apollo Actius (*of Actium*), Apollo Acritas (*of Acritas*), Apollo Ismenius (*of Ismenium*).

Some among the ancients considered Apollo to be a god of the Hyperboreans, who were all priests of Apollo and who lived in a land of perpetual light and happiness far to the North. The center of their cult was at Delos, and to it the Hyperboreans sent offerings wrapped in wheaten straw. Although most anciently he was a Dorian or a non-Greek deity, his worship became pan-hellenic. In later times he came to be identified with and worshiped as the Sun. Among the Greek colonists of Asia Minor the golden cicada was his emblem as the Sun-god. But earlier Apollo and the Sun-god, Helius, had been regarded as two separate deities. His most sacred oracles were at Delphi, the most influential oracle of the ancient world, and at Tempe. Other oracles were at the Lyceum and on the Acropolis at Argos; at Ismenium in Boeotia, where oracles were derived from the inspection of entrails by priests; at Clarus

fat, fāte, fär, fāre, errạnt; net, mē, hẻr ardẹnt; pin, pīne; not, nōte, mŏve, nôr,

near Colophon, where the priests drank the waters of a secret well and gave the oracles in verse; at Telmessus in Asia Minor, where the oracles were revealed in dreams; and in many other places.

The attributes of Apollo were the bow, the lyre, and the tripod. Sacred to him were the laurel, commemorating Daphne, and the palm tree, under which he had been born. The wolf, swan, hawk, raven, snake, mouse, and grasshopper, were also sacred to him. His festivals were the *Delphinia*, held at Athens in April to celebrate the end of winter storms and the opening of the seas to navigation; the *Thargelia*, held in the spring as a fertility rite; in midsummer the Athenians offered him sacrifices of hecatombs, so that the hot sun would not destroy their crops. At this time the Spartans held the *Hyacinthia*. In the autumn when the crops were harvested first fruits were offered to Apollo at the *Pyanepsia*. In addition there were the *Carnea, Daphnephoria, Delia, Stepteria, Apollonia*, and *Pythia*.

By the Romans, who derived all their ideas of Apollo from the Greeks, he was worshiped primarily as a god of healing. They raised a temple to him in 430 B.C., in obedience to an oracular command and in order to arrest a plague A second temple was erected in 350 B.C. Augustus greatly furthered the worship of Apollo. He dedicated a portion of the spoils of his victory at Actium to him, reconstructed and beautified the temple of Apollo Actius, and instituted the Actian Games. He also built a new temple at Rome.

Apollo was one of the favorite subjects in ancient art, and was represented in the full majesty of youthful manhood, usually unclothed or only lightly draped, and usually characterized by the bow and arrows, the lyre, the oracular tripod, the serpent, or the dolphin.

Apollo Belvedere (bel-ve̱-dir′; Italian, ä-pôl′lō bel-vä-dä′rä). Most famous extant statue of Apollo, a marble figure carved during the early Roman empire, now in the collection of the Belvedere, Vatican, Rome, discovered (1485) at Antium (now Anzio, Italy). It was copied from a Greek original in bronze. Just over life size, it depicts a vigorous, youthful god wearing a chlamys around the neck and over the extended left arm. The left hand, one of the parts restored by Montorsoli, a pupil of Michelangelo, holds part of an object variously though to have been an aegis, a bow from which he has shot an arrow, or another weapon. The original may have been a commemorative figure erected at Delphi to celebrate the expulsion of the Gauls (279 B.C.) from the temple of Apollo.

Apollodorus (a-pol-o̱-dō′rus). Athenian grammarian and historian, who flourished in the second century B.C. He wrote on grammar, mythology, geography, and history. Of his work which has survived, the *Bibliotheca* (Library) is an important source of mythological material, covering the gods and the Age of the Heroes. It is thought to be an abridgement of a larger work.

Apollodorus. [Surnamed **Sciagraphus**, meaning "Shadow Painter" or "Shadower."] Greek painter, contemporary of Zeuxis and Parrhasius. He was born at Athens and flourished in the late 5th century B.C. He seems to have been the first important painter to abandon the old schematic arrangements for shading by gradation of color and foreshortening observed from nature.

Apollodorus of Carystus (ka̱-ris′tus). Greek comic poet of the new Attic comedy. He was born at Carystus, in Euboea, and flourished at Athens 300–260 B.C. He was the author of 47 plays, and was five times a prizewinner. He supplied Terence with models for his *Hecyra* and *Phormio*.

Apollonia (ap-o̱-lō′ni-a̱). [Modern name, **Marsa Susa**.] In ancient geography, the port of Cyrene, a Greek city in N Africa, in what is now E Libya.

Apollonia. In ancient geography, a city in Illyria, in what is now W Yugoslavia.

Apollonia. [Modern name, **Arsuf**.] In ancient geography, a town in Palestine, situated on the Mediterranean between Joppa (modern Jaffa) and Caesarea.

Apollonia. [Modern name, **Sozopol**.] In ancient geography, a city in Thrace, situated on the Euxine Sea. It is now only a small village in Bulgaria.

Apollonius (ap-o̱-lō′ni-us). [Called **the Sophist**.] Alexandrian grammarian who flourished in the late 1st century A.D. He was the author of a Homeric lexicon (still extant in an abridged form) based on Aristarchus and Apion.

actọr; up, lūte, pull; oi, oil; ou, out; ᴛʜ, then; ḍ as d or j, ş as s or sh, ṭ as t or ch, ʐ as z or zh.

Apollonius Dyscolus (dis'kō-lus). Greek scholar, born at Alexandria, active 2nd century A.D. He was educated in Alexandria and, after having served as a teacher in Rome under Antoninus Pius, returned to Alexandria and became a member of the Museum. As the first critical student of Greek syntax his great contribution was to reduce grammar to a system. His only extant works are *On Syntax* and three treatises on adverbs, pronouns, and conjunctions.

Apollonius Molon (mō'lon). Greek rhetorician at Rhodes, born at Alabanda, Caria; fl. 1st century B.C. He was the instructor of Cicero and Caesar. He advocated "Atticizing," or moderating, the florid Asiatic style.

Apollonius of Perga (pėr'ga). [Also: **Apollonius Pergaeus.**] Greek geometrician, born at Perga, Asia Minor; fl. 247–205 B.C. He was educated at Alexandria and was the author of a treatise on *Conic Sections* in eight books, of which four are extant in Greek and three others in Arabic. His work includes the theories of Euclid and others, as well as new deductions.

Apollonius Rhodius (rō'di-us). [Also: **Apollonius of Rhodes.**] Greek epic poet who flourished at Alexandria and Rhodes in the 3rd century B.C. He was a pupil of Callimachus in Alexandria but did not follow the brilliant epigrammatic style of his teacher. He wrote the *Argonautica*, a long poem in four books, in the epic style. This work, which celebrates the adventures of Jason and the Argonauts in the quest for the Golden Fleece, was not enthusiastically received at Alexandria. Apollonius blamed Callimachus for its poor reception, and left Alexandria in disgust. He went to Rhodes. There he wrote a second version of his poem which was acclaimed by the Rhodians. He became a citizen of Rhodes, hence his surname. His *Argonautica*, in simple epic style, was much admired by the Romans and was imitated by Vergil, whose Dido and Aeneas are somewhat stately copies of Jason and Medea, as well as by Varro, Marianus, and others. Apollonius was also a librarian of the famous Alexandrian Library.

Apollonius of Tralles (tral'ēz). Greek sculptor, born at Tralles, in Caria, who was active probably in the 1st century B C. With his brother Tauriscus he carved the so-called *Farnese Bull,* representing the death of Dirce.

Apollonius of Tyana (tī'a-na). [Also: **Apollonius Tyanaeus.**] Greek Neo-Pythagorean philosopher, reputed magician and wonderworker. He was born at Tyana, Asia Minor, and was active in the 1st century A.D. He was educated and lived in the temple of Asclepius at Aegae until he was 20 years old. He then gave away his property and devoted himself to travel and learning. He studied in Greek schools at Tarsus, traveled in Babylonia, Persia, and India, where he absorbed Eastern mysticism, and set up a school at Ephesus. His biography by Philostratus is largely fabulous and untrustworthy. Hierocles of Nicomedia, an anti-Christian writer, compared the miracles of Apollonius with those of Jesus. He was considered divine by some for his supposed miracles, and his bust was placed by Alexander Severus in his *lararium* with those of Abraham, Orpheus, and Christ. Eighty-five letters attributed to him survive.

Apollo Sauroktonos (a-pol'ō sô-rok'tō-nos). [Also: **Sauroctonus;** Eng. trans., "the Lizard-slayer."] Name of two copies, one in bronze (Vatican, Rome) and one in marble (Paris), of a lost bronze statue by the Greek sculptor Praxiteles. The god leans against a tree and is apparently about to strike with an arrow, possibly as a method of divination, the lizard which climbs up the trunk. The relaxed, curving figure is typical of Praxiteles' choice of youthful subjects and his graceful, humanizing treatment of the gods.

Apology of Socrates (sok'ra-tēz). The unconciliatory speech delivered by the Athenian philosopher Socrates in his own defense at his trial in 399 B.C. on capital charges of introducing strange gods and of corrupting the youth of Athens, following which the jury found him guilty and sentenced him to death. A version by Plato and an inferior one attributed to Xenophon are extant. (JJ)

Apomyius (ap-ō-mī'i-us). An epithet of Zeus, in Elis, meaning "Averter of Flies." The Eleans sacrificed to Zeus Apomyius because the flies brought pestilence, and no sooner was the sacrifice offered than the flies disappeared. It was said that during the Olympic festival the flies voluntarily disappeared across the Alpheus River, and after the festival was over they swarmed back.

---

fat, fāte, fär, fāre, errant; net, mē, hėr ardent; pin, pīne; not, nōte, mȯve, nôr,

Apostrophia (a̯-pos-trō-fī′a̯, -trō′fẹ-a̯). An epithet of Aphrodite in her aspect of goddess of love, meaning "Rejecter." In this aspect the goddess helps men to reject unlawful passion and sinful acts.

Appian (ap′i-a̯n). [Latin, **Appianus;** Greek **Appianos.**] Greek historian, born in Alexandria; flourished about the middle of the 2nd century A.D. In early life he went to Rome and pursued a career in the legal field. Later he was sent to Egypt as procurator by the emperor Antoninus Pius. He was the author (in Greek) of an ambitious work in 24 books on the development of the Roman empire from earliest times to the time of Trajan. Eleven books survive. Chiefly a compilation from earlier writers and marred by errors in chronology and by omissions, nevertheless the work has a special value for the use Appian made of authorities whose writings have since been lost, and for the history of the Civil Wars.

Appian Way. [Latin, **Via Appia.**] Most famous of the ancient Roman highways. It ran from Rome to Brundisium (now called Brindisi), and is probably the first great Roman road which was formally undertaken as a public work. It was begun in 312 B.C. by Appius Claudius Caecus, the censor, who carried it as far as Capua. The next stage of the work extended it to Beneventum (Benevento), and it probably did not reach Brundisium until 244 B.C., when a Roman colony was inaugurated there. At present the Appian Way, for a long distance after it leaves Rome, forms one of the most notable memorials of antiquity in or near Rome, bordered as it is by tombs and the ruins of monumental buildings. Long stretches of the pavement remain perfect, and show that the width of the roadway proper was only 15 feet. Length, about 350 miles.

Apple of Discord. A golden apple, inscribed "To the Fairest," thrown into an assembly of the gods (at the marriage of Thetis and Peleus) by Eris, goddess of Discord, who had not been invited to the feast. Aphrodite, Hera, and Athena claimed it, and its award to Aphrodite by Paris of Troy, selected by Zeus as judge, so inflamed the jealousy of Hera and her hatred toward all the Trojan race that she did not cease her machinations till Troy was destroyed.

Apples of the Hesperides (hes-per′i-dēz). According to mythology, Mother Earth gave Hera, as a wedding gift when she married Zeus, a tree which bore golden apples. Hera planted the tree in her own orchard. Some say the orchard was located in the land of the Hyperboreans, some say it lay on the slopes of Mount Atlas in Mauretania, others say it was in a region beyond the western ocean, or on two islands near Ethiopia. Atlas was the gardener in the orchard, and the tree was guarded by his daughters, the Hesperides, and by Ladon, a never-sleeping dragon. As his eleventh labor for Eurystheus, Heracles fetched the Golden Apples. He took them to Eurystheus, but as the apples were sacred Eurystheus returned them to Heracles who then gave them to Athena. She restored them to the orchard of the Hesperides.

Apries (ap′ri-ēz). [Called in the Bible, **Hophra.**] Egyptian ruler, fourth Pharaoh of the Saite XXVIth dynasty; reigned 589–570 B.C. as successor to his father, Psamtik II. Rivalry with Babylon's Nebuchadnezzar led him to attack Tyre and Sidon, as well as to attempt the relief of Jerusalem which was besieged by the Babylonians. He failed (586 B.C.) to save Jerusalem or to overthrow Babylonian rule in Syria despite a series of military and naval victories, and was finally himself overthrown and killed by his former ally, Amasis II.

Apsyrtus (ap-sėr′tus) or **Absyrtus** (ab-). In Greek legend, a son of Aeëtes, king of Colchis, and, according to some accounts, of the Caucasian nymph Asterodia. Others say his mother was Idyia. He commanded a fleet of ships in pursuit of his sister Medea who had fled with Jason after the latter stole the Golden Fleece. According to some accounts, Medea tricked him into meeting her in an isolated spot to arrange for her own return to Colchis and he was slain by Jason who was hiding nearby. His leaderless men then gave up the pursuit of the Argonauts. Others say that he fled with Medea and Jason from Colchis and that Medea, to delay the pursuit of her father Aeëtes, killed him and cast the pieces of his body into the sea. Aeëtes, stopping to recover them to give his son proper burial, was left behind.

actọr; up, lūte, pull; oi, oil; ou, out; ᴛʜ, then; ḍ as d or j, ş as s or sh, ṭ as t or ch, ẓ as z or zh.

Apuleius (ap-ū-lē′us), **Lucius.** [Also: **Lucius Appuleius.**] Roman rhetorician and Platonic sophist, born in Numidia (or, according to some authorities, at what is now Bône, Algeria), c123 A.D., and active chiefly at Carthage. He was notable as a clever and versatile writer with an encyclopedic range of interests. In completion of his education he went to Athens to study the philosophy of Plato. He then traveled widely in Greece and was everywhere initiated into the mysteries. He spent some time in Rome as an advocate then returned to Africa and settled in Carthage. He is probably now best known for his *Metamorphoses,* or *The Golden Ass,* the sole Latin novel that survives entire. The extraordinary adventures (including metamorphosis into the shape of an ass) attributed by Apuleius to the hero of this fictional work were later freely adapted and used by Fielding, Smollett, Boccaccio, and Cervantes. Among the episodes woven into the story of the man who was metamorphosed into an ass is the tale of *Cupid and Psyche.* As an ass, the hero of the romance had ample opportunity to observe the absurdities of human kind and commented freely and satirically on them, thus preserving a picture of his age. Apuleius is also of some considerable importance, although less well known, for his scientific writings. His most important work in this field (particularly for the historian of medicine) was his book on magic (*De magia* or *Apologia*) which dealt with various matters not unrelated to those which were the concern of the first alchemists, and thus historically linked to what was later to emerge as modern science. In this work Apuleius also defended himself on the charge that he had bewitched a rich woman, much older than he, into marrying him. All the other scientific writings of Apuleius, including a translation of an early text on arithmetic, have now been lost except for *De mundo (On the World),* and some scholars have questioned the authenticity of this.

Apulia (a-pū′li-a). In ancient geography, a region of S Italy, lying S of the Frentani and E of Samnium. It was conquered by Rome in the 4th century B.C. Later it included the Messapian Peninsula. The ancient inhabitants were the Dauni, Peucetii, and Salentini or Messapians. Throughout the centuries, Apulia was a place of entrance for Greek and Oriental influences. The region saw bitter fighting in the Punic Wars.

AQUARIUS
Pictured according to ancient descriptions.

Aquarius (a-kwā′ri-us). The eleventh sign of the zodiac—the Water-bearer—which the sun enters about the 21st of January. Also, a zodiacal constellation, supposed to represent a man standing with his left hand extended upward, and with his right pouring out of a vase a stream of water which flows into the mouth of Piscis Australis (*the Southern Fish*).

Aqueus (ā′kwē-us). Epithet applied to Zeus at Dodona, meaning "Watery" or "Flowing." At Dodona a spring welled from the roots of the sacred oracular oak. The murmuring of the water of the spring was heard as the voice of the god and the sounds were interpreted to pilgrims by the ancient priestess as oracles of the god.

Aquila (ak′wi-la). A northern constellation situated in the Milky Way nearly south of Lyra, and containing the bright star Altair. It has for its outline the figure of a flying eagle carrying in its talons the boy Antinous, the favorite of the emperor Hadrian. It is also called **Aquila et Antinous.**

fat, fāte, fär, fãre, errant; net, mē, hėr ardent; pin, pīne; not, nōte, möve, nôr,

Aquileia (ä-kwa̧-lā′ya̧). Town in NE Italy, situated at the head of the Adriatic Sea, near what is now Trieste. Founded by the Romans in 181 B.C., it became one of the chief market cities of the Empire, the strategic key to Italy on the NE. It was destroyed by Attila in 452 A.D., but rebuilt.

Aquilius (a̧-kwil′i-us). Latin writer; fl. 2nd century B.C. He is mentioned as a writer of comedies. Two fragments are attributed to him.

Aquilo (ak′wi-lō̧). The Roman name for Boreas, the north wind.

Ara (ā′ra̧). An ancient southern constellation—the Altar. It is situated south of Scorpio.

Arabia Deserta (a̧-rā′bi-a̧ dȩ-zėr′ta̧). [Eng. trans., "desert," or "uninhabited," Arabia.] In ancient geography, the N and C portions of Arabia.

Arabia Felix (fē′liks). [Eng. trans., "flourishing," or "happy," Arabia.] In ancient geography, the comparatively fertile region in the SE and S parts of Arabia, contrasted with the uninhabited and barren N and C portions.

Arabia Petraea (pȩ-trē′a̧). [Eng. trans., "stony" Arabia.] In ancient geography, the NW part of Arabia.

Arabicus (a̧-rab′i-kus), **Sinus.** Latin name of the **Red Sea.**

Arachne (a̧-rak′nē). In Greek legend, a maiden of Colophon in Lydia. She was so skilled in spinning and weaving that her reputation spread throughout Lydia. Admirers of her work suggested that she must have been taught by Athena. Arachne scorned the suggestion and boasted that she could compete with Athena. The goddess, jealous of Arachne's fame in an art that was considered peculiarly her own, learned of her boast and appeared to her disguised as an old woman. She advised Arachne that it was unwise to vie with the gods, that it was enough to excel all mortals. Arachne repeated her boast and demanded that Athena come to her in person and meet her challenge. Athena then revealed herself and agreed to a contest which was begun at once. Athena's work portrayed the Olympian gods in all their majesty. Arachne wove into her work scenes of the more scandalous love affairs of the gods, but so delicately and beautifully that no flaw could be found in

her work. It was evident that the goddess had not surpassed the maiden, and in a frenzy of jealousy Athena destroyed her rival's work, then touched the girl on her forehead and made her conscious of her presumption and impiety. Arachne hanged herself from a rafter, and as she was hanging there Athena condemned her to hang on a thread and spin eternally by transforming her into a spider.

Arachosia (ar-a̧-kō′zha̧, -zhi-a̧). In ancient geography, a region in ancient Persia corresponding to part of modern Afghanistan.

Arachthus (a̧-rak′thus). River in NW Greece, in Epirus, which flows into the Ambracian Gulf about eight miles below Ambracia.

Araethyrea (a-rē-thē′rē-a̧). In ancient geography, the former name of Phlius. It was named for the daughter of the aboriginal king, Aras. Phlias changed the name to Phlius. The place was known as Araethyrea in the time of Homer, who listed it as one of the places that sent men to the Trojan War under the command of Agamemnon.

Araros (ar′a̧-ros). Athenian comic poet of the early 4th century B.C. He was the son of Aristophanes and brought out his father's *Plutus* in 388 B.C. He appeared as an original poet c375 B.C.

Aras (a′ras). According to legend, an earthborn man who in the time of Prometheus became the first king of the land later known as Phliasia.

Aratus of Sicyon (a̧-rā′tus; sish′i-on, sis′i-). Greek general, born at Sicyon, near Corinth, Greece, 271; died 213 B.C. He was the leader of the second Achaean League. He liberated (251 B.C.) Sicyon from the usurper Nicocles and set up a democracy; elected (245 B.C.) strategus (military leader) of the Achaean League, he took the citadel of Corinth in 243 B.C., and brought Athens and Argos into the League. Defeated in a succession of campaigns by the Spartans under Cleomenes III, he formed an alliance with Antigonus III of Macedonia (Antigonus Doson), who defeated Cleomenes at the battle of Sellasia near the city of Sparta in 222 B.C., but thus brought the League under Macedonian domination. He carried on an unsuccessful defensive war (221–219 B.C.) against the Aetolians.

Aratus of Soli (sō′li). Greek didactic poet at

the court of Antigonus II of Macedonia (Antigonus Gonatas) and Antiochus I of Syria; born at Soli, in Cilicia, c315 B.C.; died in Macedonia, 240 B.C. He was the author of *Phenomena* (or *Phaenomena* or *Phainomena*), a work in 1154 verses on astronomy, later very popular with Roman writers. It contained a section on weather signs (*Prognostica* or *Diosemeia*) used by Cicero, Vergil, and others, and an invocation to Zeus quoted by Saint Paul in his address to the Athenians on the Areopagus (Mars' Hill). Acts, xvii. 28.

Arbela (är-bē′la̩). [Also: **Arbaïlu**: modern name, **Erbil**.] In ancient geography, a town in Assyria. It was an early seat of the worship of Ishtar, and a place of considerable importance. Sixty miles from here at Gaugamela, a Macedonian force said to have numbered 47,000 under Alexander the Great defeated a much larger Persian army (some estimates have run as high as one million) under Darius III, in 331 B.C. This battle, often called the Battle of Arbela, led to the final overthrow of the Persian empire.

Arcadia (är-kā′di-a̩). In ancient geography, a region in Greece, in the heart of the Peloponnesus, bounded by Achaea on the N, by Argolis on the E, by Laconia and Messenia on the S, and by Elis on the W. All but isolated by mountains and intersected by them, it was proverbial for its rural simplicity. It was the favorite haunt of the pastoral god Pan, who was born on Mount Maenalus within its borders and whose worship was especially strong throughout the region: caves, springs, blasted trees, mountains, etc., were sacred to him. The Arcadians also claimed that Athena was born in their country. They said that near Aliphera in western Arcadia is a stream called Tritonis and that near here Athena was born from the head of Zeus. For this reason they set up an altar of Zeus Lecheates (*In Childbed*) at Aliphera. The mountains and forests of Arcadia were a favorite hunting ground of Artemis, and Arcadia was one of the strongest centers of her worship. The mountains and woods also abounded in nymphs. The Arcadians are aboriginal to their region (they say they have lived in their land since before the birth of the moon), and they were never driven out, as were the inhabitants of the other states of

the Peloponnesus. According to their own account, the first man in Arcadia was Pelasgus, a son of earth, who was the first king and who named the land Pelasgia after himself. When Arcas, son of Zeus and Callisto and a descendant of Pelasgus on his mother's side, ascended the throne he changed the name of the land to Arcadia, after himself, and this was the name by which it was known ever afterward. When the sons of Heracles under Hyllus attempted to return to the Peloponnesus, Echemus, king of Arcadia, accepted the challenge of Hyllus to decide the control of the Peloponnesus by single combat. Echemus killed Hyllus and the Heraclidae withdrew as they had agreed to do if Hyllus lost in the duel. In the second Dorian invasion by the sons of Aristomachus, the Arcadian king Cypselus gave his daughter to Cresphontes, son of Aristomachus, in marriage, and so made an ally of Cresphontes. For this reason the Arcadians were not disturbed nor dislodged from their country by the Dorian invasion. The Arcadians played an active role in the Trojan War, to which they journeyed in ships loaned them by Agamemnon as they had no fleet of of their own. In the wars between Messenia and Sparta the Arcadians allied themselves with the Messenians. Aechmis, king of Arcadia, and his countrymen fought openly on the side of Aristodemus, king of Messenia, in the First Messenian War. In the Second Messenian War the Arcadians were again allied with Messenia, and when they learned that their own leader Aristocrates had accepted bribes from the Lacedaemonians to betray their allies the Arcadians stoned him to death. Arcadians took part in the Persian War, especially at Thermopylae (480 B.C.) and Plataea (479 B.C.). Under compulsion, they joined with the Spartans to fight against Athens in the Peloponnesian Wars (431–404 B.C.). As Spartan allies, they were defeated at Leuctra (371 B.C.) by the Theban Epaminondas, and as their alliance with Sparta was an unwilling one, after this defeat the Arcadians broke away from their Spartan alliance. The cities of Arcadia, Tegea, Mantinea, and others, formed a confederation c370–360 B.C.

Arcas (är′ka̩s). In Greek mythology, a son of the nymph Callisto and Zeus. His mother was transformed into a bear through the jealousy of Hera, and Arcas was brought up by Maia in Arcadia. When, as a youth, he was hunting wild beasts in the forest, he came face to face with his mother in her guise as a bear. She recognized him and approached him, but he did not know her and would have killed her as the wild animal he thought she was. Zeus lifted her to the heavens in a whirlwind and set her among the stars as the constellation of the Great Bear. A common account also has Arcas translated to the heavens as the Little Bear. Arcas succeeded his uncle, Nyctimus, son of Lycaon, on the throne of the land that was then known as Pelasgia. He changed its name to Arcadia after himself, and is said to be the ancestor of the Arcadians. Some say that Arcas was taught how to cultivate crops by Triptolemus, and that he in turn taught the arts of agriculture to the Arcadians and also taught them how to bake bread and the crafts of spinning and weaving. Some say Arcas had two sons—Elatus and Aphidas—and that their mother was either Meganira or the nymph Chrysopelia. Others say the dryad Erato bore him three sons—Azan, Aphidas, and Elatus. Azan became ruler of Azania in Arcadia; Aphidas became ruler of Tegea; Elatus inherited the region of Mount Cyllene. Arcas was buried on Mount Maenalus in Arcadia, but his bones were removed and placed near an altar of Hera at Mantinea in obedience to the following command of an oracle:

"Maenalia is storm-swept, where lies
Arcas, from whom all Arcadians are named,
In a place where meet three, four, even five roads;
Thither I bid you go, and with kind heart
Take up Arcas and bring him back to your lovely city.
There make Arcas a precinct and sacrifices."

The place of his grave was called the Altars of the Sun. The image of Arcas was translated to the heavens, where it was known as Arcturus. Located behind the Great Bear, Arcturus is the guardian or watcher of the Great Bear, his mother.

Arce (är'sē). In Greek mythology, a daughter of Thaumas, and the sister of Iris and the Harpies. Because she aided the Titans in their war against Zeus, he took away the wings of Arce, after the Titans had been defeated and banished, and gave them to Thetis as a wedding present when she married Peleus. Some say Thetis gave the wings to her son Achilles, and this accounted for his fleetness. After Zeus had taken away her wings he banished Arce to Tartarus.

Arcesilaus (är-ses-i-lā'us). According to some accounts, a son of Odysseus and Penelope.

Arcesilaus or **Arcesilas.** Name of several kings of Cyrene, of the Battiadae dynasty. Arcesilaus I (590–574 B.C.) was the son of Battus, founder of the Greek city of Cyrene and of the dynasty. In the reign of Arcesilaus II (c560–c550 B.C.), grandson of Arcesilaus I, the city of Barca was founded by dissidents from Cyrene. A black-figure cup of Cyrene shows Arcesilaus II overseeing the weighing out and packing of silphion, a medicinal plant. The sale of the plant, which was widely exported, was the monopoly of the king and brought him great wealth. See **Battiadae.**

Arcesilaus or **Arcesilas** (är-ses'i-las). Greek Skeptic philosopher, born at Pitane, in Aeolis, c315 B.C.; died c241 B.C. He was the founder of the so-called Second Academy, an opponent of Stoicism and exponent of the Socratic method. Holding that both senses and reason are untrustworthy, he based his system of ethics on assumption of probability.

Arcesius (är-ses'i-us). In mythology, a son of Zeus and Euryodia, according to some accounts. Others say he was the son of Cephalus and Procris, and still others say he was the son of Cephalus and a she-bear. He was the father, by Chalcomedusa, of Laertes, and the grandfather of Odysseus.

Archegetes (är-kē'je-tēz). An epithet of Apollo, meaning "Founder." An altar of Apollo Archegetes was set up at Naxos, in Sicily, whither winds had blown the first Greek colonists who sailed to that island. It became the custom for envoys thereafter arriving from Greece to offer sacrifices on this altar as soon as they arrived in Sicily.

Archelaus (är-ke-lā'us). In Greek legend, a son of Temenus and a descendant of Heracles. When he arrived at the kingdom of Cisseus in Macedonia after fleeing from his brothers in Argos, he was promised the throne and the hand of Cisseus' daughter if he overcame the enemies of Cisseus. Archelaus was successful but instead of fulfilling his promise Cisseus plotted to kill him. However, a slave warned him of the pit of hot coals Cisseus had concealed in his path, and Archelaus hurled Cisseus into it and fled. Archelaus is the traditional founder of the Macedonian royal house.

Archelaus. Greek sculptor of the 1st century A.D. A bas-relief, the *Apotheosis of Homer*, carved by him, is in the British Museum.

Archelaus (of *Athens*). [Surnamed **Physicus**, meaning "the Physicist."] Greek philosopher of the Ionian (or Milesian) school, active c450 B.C. He was a pupil of Anaxagoras, and was said to have been an instructor of Socrates and Euripides. He regarded heat and cold (derived by condensation and rarefaction of "primitive matter" or "original substance," which he took to be air), mixed with mind, as the basic principles of generation.

Archelaus (of *Cappadocia*). Cappadocian general under Mithridates VI; fl. in the 1st century B.C. He served in Mithridates' wars against Rome. Sent to Greece (87 B.C.) with a large force, he made Athens his headquarters, occupied Piraeus, and stirred up revolt against Rome in the other Greek states. Sulla came from Rome to command the war against Mithridates, and defeated Archelaus at Chaeronea (86) and at Orchomenus (85 B.C.). Mithridates came to distrust Archelaus who then deserted to the Romans (81 B.C.).

Archelaus (of *Cappadocia*). King of Cappadocia, c34 B.C.–17 A.D.; a grandson of Archelaus (of Egypt). He owed his elevation to Mark Antony, who was captivated by the charms of Archelaus' mother, Glaphyra. He sided with Antony in the war with Octavian (Augustus), but was permitted after the defeat of Antony to retain his kingdom, to which was subsequently added part of Cilicia and Lesser Armenia. He was finally summoned to Rome by Tiberius, where he was held prisoner until his death. Cappadocia became, after his death, a Roman province.

Archelaus (of *Egypt*). King of Egypt in 56 B.C.; a son of the general Archelaus (of Cappadocia). He became high priest at Comana in 63 B.C., and secured the hand of Berenice, queen of Egypt, by representing himself to be the son of Mithridates VI Eupator. He

was defeated and slain by the Romans after a reign of six months.

Archelaus (of *Macedonia*). King of Macedonia (c413–399 B.C.); son of Perdiccas II. He was a patron of Hellenic art and literature, and attracted to his court Zeuxis, Euripides, and Agathon, and invited Socrates who declined.

Archelochus (är-kel′ō-kus). In Homeric legend (*Iliad*), a Trojan, the son of Antenor and Theano. He accompanied Aeneas at the siege of the Greek fortifications. Telamonian Ajax killed him.

Archemorus (är-kem′ō-rus). A name given to Opheltes, son of Lycurgus of Nemea. It means "Beginner of Doom." Opheltes' nurse left him unguarded for a short time while she directed the Seven against Thebes, who were passing through Nemea, to a spring. When she returned a serpent had killed Opheltes. This was regarded as an evil omen, and for this reason the new name was given to him.

Archeptolemus (är-kep-tol′ē-mus). In Homeric legend (*Iliad*), a Trojan, the son of Iphitus. He replaced Hector's fallen charioteer. Teucer, attempting to kill Hector, aimed an arrow at him but Apollo deflected it and Archeptolemus was killed instead.

Archestratus (är-kes′tra̤-tus). Greek writer of Gela, in Sicily, who was a contemporary of Aristotle and flourished about the end of the 4th century B.C. He wrote a humorous poem about food and the cooking of it. Fragments which survive show him to have been a witty and talented writer.

Archias (är′ki-a̤s). According to Greek tradition, a descendant of Heracles. He lived in Corinth. Some say he went with a companion to visit the oracle at Delphi. The priestess asked him to choose between wealth and health. Archias chose wealth, and his companion, Myscellus, chose health. In later times Archias went to Sicily and founded Syracuse (734 B.C.), which became noted for its wealth. Myscellus went with a colony to Croton, which became noted for its physicians.

Archidamus I (är-ki-dā′mus). King of Sparta, of the Eurypontid house of Spartan kings, who reigned after the close of the Second Messenian War (7th century B.C.).

Archidamus II. King of Sparta, of the Eury-

fat, fāte, fär, fãre, erra̤nt; net, mē, hėr ardᶒnt; pin, pīne; not, nōte, möve, nôr, pontid house of Spartan kings, who reigned c476–c427 B.C. He was the son of Zeuxidamus, who did not reign, and the grandson of Leotychides, the hero of Mycale (479 B.C.). He was a friend of Pericles. Early in his reign (c471 B.C.) he defeated the Arcadian League at Dipaea. In 432 B.C. when the allies of Sparta asked her to declare war on Athens for having broken the Thirty Years Peace by aiding Corcyra against Corinth, by the seizure of Potidaea, and more immediately, by assisting the Plataeans against Thebes, Archidamus prudently counseled moderation. He advised the Spartans to delay, on the ground that Sparta was not financially prepared for war and lacked a fleet. He was over-ruled. In the ensuing war he fought so bravely and well that the early years of the Peloponnesian War (431–421 B.C.) are called the Archidamean War. In the spring of 431 B.C. he led a large part of the Peloponnesian forces in an invasion of Attica, first however, sending an envoy from the Isthmus to make one last attempt to settle the disputes between Athens and the Peloponnesians. His envoy was not received. Archidamus besieged the fortress of Oenoë on Mount Cithaeron but could not take it. He marched to the plain of Eleusis and devastated it, crossed the plain of the Cephissus and encamped under Mount Parnes, from where he could see the Acropolis of Athens. Before this threat the populace poured for refuge into the city. The following year he invaded Attica again and ravaged the area south of the city. But the Athenians had a worse enemy inside their walls. Plague broke out. Among those who succumbed to it was Pericles. In 429 B.C. Archidamus led his forces against Plataea. The Plataeans appealed to him to refrain from violating their territory in the name of the heroes who had fallen there in the Persian War, among whom were many Spartans whose memories were annually honored by the Plataeans. Archidamus replied that he would so refrain if the Plataeans detached themselves from Athens and remained neutral. This the Plataeans were unwilling to do, and were besieged. In 428 B.C. Archidamus and the allies invaded Attica for the third time, destroyed the standing crops and, having used up the supplies they brought with them, retired.

Archidamus III. King of Sparta, of the Eurypontid line of Spartan kings. He reigned from 360/359 to 338 B.C. He was the son of Agesilaus II, whom he succeeded. After the defeat of the Spartans at Leuctra (371 B.C.) he was made commander of a Spartan force sent to the relief of the survivors of that battle. He defeated the Arcadians, Messenians, and Argives in 368 B.C. in a fight called "the Tearless Battle," because although great loss was suffered by the Arcadians and their allies, not one Spartan lost his life. In 364 B.C. he occupied the fortress of Cromnon, between Megalopolis and Messenia. The garrison he placed there was besieged by the Arcadians and their allies, and when he sought to relieve it he was driven off with losses. He fought bravely to defend Sparta from the attacks of Epaminondas and the Thebans in 362. In 356 B.C. he supported the Phocians in their Sacred War to seize Delphi. In 343 B.C. he answered an appeal from Taras (Tarentum) in Italy for aid against the Italian tribes. Leading a band of mercenaries he sailed to Italy, waged inconclusive war there for some years and was killed (338 B.C.) at Manduria.

Archilochus (är-kil′ō̄-kus). Greek lyric poet, born at Paros, in the Cyclades, and active c700–650 B.C. A sensitive and highly intelligent man, he was embittered by poverty, and turned his talents to satire and invective. He took part in the colonization of Thasus but was compelled to leave there, some say because he dropped his shield and ran from a battle, others because he made so many enemies with his lampoons. He returned to Paros and became engaged to the daughter of a fellow townsman. But the father of his betrothed broke off the engagement and, later tradition says, Archilochus wrote such biting lampoons that both father and daughter hanged themselves. Thereafter, Archilochus wandered about as a soldier of fortune and freebooter, and reports have it that he was killed in a battle against Naxos. Fragments of his powerful and incisive work remain. Archilochus is regarded as a great innovator in meter, language, and the subjects of poetry. He used iambics in satires praised by Horace and Hadrian, among others. He was the author also of hymns (one of which was sung in the Olympics), elegies, and lampoons. He used the trochee in his serious works, and was the first to alternate long and short verses in the form called epode. Counted among the greatest of the poets by the ancients, the legend is that when the man who killed him appeared at Delphi the priestess refused to admit him, on the ground that he had slain one of the Muses.

Archimedes (är-ki-mē′dēz). Greek mathematician, engineer, and physicist, now usually considered to have been in each of these fields the outstanding figure of the ancient world. He was born at Syracuse, Sicily, c287 B.C., and was killed there, 212 B.C. He was the discoverer of principles and the author of treatises basic to the subsequent study of geometry and calculus, particularly on the dimensions of the circle, sphere, cylinder, and parabola; in physics, developer of the displacement theory known as Archimedes' principle, and supposedly also of that of the lever (of which, according to tradition, he said, "Give me a place to stand, and I will move the world"); in mechanics he was the inventor of the Archimedean screw and various machines of war. The son of an astronomer, he was a student at Alexandria where he probably met Conon of Samos. He spent much of his life at the court of Hiero II of Syracuse (who is said to have been his relative). Given the problem of determining the proportions of gold and silver in Hiero's crown, he is supposed to have cried "Eureka!" ("I have found it"), as, stepping into his bath, he discovered the relationship between weight and displacement of water, the principle now applied to determining the displacement of ships and specific gravity. His engines of war, which struck terror among the Romans and held them off for three years in their siege of Syracuse (214–212 B.C.), were considered unimportant by him. According to one tradition, he devised a huge burning-glass and set fire to the Roman ships as they sailed up to the wall of the city. Some say he was killed at the fall of Syracuse while drawing geometrical figures in the sand, though the Roman commander had ordered him spared for his great learning. The Roman was deeply grieved, ordered that an honorable burial be given him, and made provision for his survivors. His tomb, which was found, nearly covered with brambles,

by Cicero in 75 B.C., was marked by a cylinder circumscribing a sphere with the ratio 3/2, in accordance with his expressed wish. For in his own opinion his discovery of the relation between the surface and volume of a sphere and the cylinder that circumscribed it was his most important achievement.

Archipelago (är-ki-pel′a-gō). [Also: **Greek Archipelago**; Turkish, **Jezairi-Bahri-Sefid.**] In ancient geography, a name for the various islands in the Aegean Sea, or for the sea itself.

Arch of Augustus. [Also: **Porta Romana.**] Roman triumphal arch at Ariminum (Rimini), Italy, built in 27 B.C., in honor of the restoration of the Flaminian Way. It is of white travertine, 45.9 feet high and 28.8 thick, with a single arch 29.5 feet high and 26.9 wide. A Corinthian fluted column on each side of the archway supports an entablature, above which there is a low pediment.

Arch of Constantine. Triumphal arch in Rome, SW of the Flavian Amphitheater ("Colosseum"), built by Constantine the Great to commemorate his victory over Maxentius at the battle of the Milvian Bridge in 312 A.D., and preserved with only superficial damage from weathering, abrasion, and vandalism. It has three passageways, a large central arch flanked by smaller arches. It is richly decorated with columns, architectural moldings, statues, and relief sculptures. The most important of the reliefs were removed from public monuments of the Flavian and Antonine periods to embellish Constantine's work. In the attic is Constantine's dedicatory inscription. In the 10th century the arch was incorporated into a castle, eventually coming into the possession of the Frangipani family, by which circumstance it escaped the despoiling to which most ancient monuments of Rome were subjected. (JJ)

Arch of Drusus. Roman arch (wrongly named) built by Caracalla (188–217 A.D.) to carry an aqueduct for the supply of his thermae over the Appian Way near the gate of San Sebastiano. It is built of travertine, faced with white marble, and decorated with composite columns, and originally had on each side an entablature and a pediment.

Arch of Hadrian. Triumphal gateway at Athens, probably built by Hadrian, between the old city and his new quarter. It is 59

fat, fāte, fär, fāre, errant; net, mē, hėr ardent; pin, pīne; not, nōte, möve, nôr,

feet high, with a single arch 20 feet high. Above the arch there is an attic with three large openings, originally closed. Above the central opening there is a pediment. The arch was decorated on each side with Corinthian columns.

Arch of Janus Quadrifrons. Roman arch at the NE extremity of the Forum Boarium. It is a four-way arch of marble, largely built of older architectural fragments. The interior is covered with a simple groined vault. The four fronts bear 48 niches for statues. The construction is that of the late 3rd or early 4th century A.D. and is probably to be referred to the time of Constantine.

Arch of Septimius Severus. Roman arch in the Forum, erected in 203 A.D. in honor of Severus and his sons Geta and Caracalla in commemoration of victories over the Parthians. It is of Pentelic marble, with a central arch and two side arches, flanked by four Corinthian columns on each face. There are sculptured panels over the side arches and a frieze above all with reliefs of Roman triumphs. The attic bears inscriptions, originally of bronze letters inlaid in the marble; scrap dealers have pried out the metal, but the matrices remain and can be clearly read, except for the name of Geta which was chiselled away at Caracalla's order.

Arch of Titus. Roman arch in the Forum, built in commemoration of the taking of Jerusalem. It has a single archway, the opening flanked on each face by four composite columns. The spandrels bear Victories in relief, and on the high attic is the dedicatory inscription. The vault is richly coffered and sculptured, and the interior faces of the piers display reliefs of Titus in triumph, with the plunder of the temple at Jerusalem, in which the seven-branched candlesticks are conspicuous.

Arch of Trajan. Arch over the Appian Way at Benevento, Italy, dedicated in 114 A.D., and one of the finest of ancient arches. It is of white marble, 48 feet high and 30½ wide, with a single arch measuring 27 by 16½ feet. On each face there are four engaged Corinthian columns, with an entablature, above which is a paneled attic. The arch is profusely sculptured with reliefs illustrating Trajan's life and his Dacian triumphs. There are Victories in the spandrels and dedi-

catory inscriptions on the central panels of the attic.

Arch of Trajan. Arch erected at Ancona, Italy, in 115 A.D. It is of white marble, and stands at the end of the breakwater built by Trajan, and is perhaps the best-proportioned of all Roman triumphal arches. It has a single opening 46 by 29½ feet, two engaged Corinthian columns on the face of each pier, and a high attic above the entablature.

Archon (är′kon). A chief magistrate of some states in ancient Greece, and particularly Athens. After the abolition of the title of king in Attica there was chosen a single archon, who exercised for life essentially royal prerogatives. The term of office was afterward reduced to ten years, and in 683 B.C. it was made annual, and the duties of the archonship were distributed among nine persons. The first was the *archon eponymos* (name-giving archon), whose functions were executive and judicial, and who gave his name to the civil year; the second was the *archon basileus* (archon king), whose duties were chiefly religious and ceremonial; the third was the *archon polemarchos* (archon generalissimo), who was, first in fact and then nominally, commander of the military power and whose main duties were judicial; and the remaining six were the *thesmothetae,* or administrators of justice, whose most important duty it was to pass carefully in review, each year, the whole body of laws of the state in order to make sure that no errors or contradictions had crept in, that repealed laws had been duly cancelled, and that repetition was avoided. It rested with the thesmothetae, also, to see that all the laws that were in vigor were strictly enforced, and to bring to trial any public official who had failed in his trust. They also had charge of all cases not specifically within the jurisdiction of the other archons. At the end of their year of office all the archons, unless they were found guilty of malfeasance, by virtue of their office entered the council of the Areopagus.

Archytas of Tarentum (är-kī′tas; ta-ren′tum). Greek Pythagorean philosopher, mathematician, statesman, and general; fl. c400–350 B.C. He was a friend of Plato. Believed by some to have furnished certain ideas used by Plato and Aristotle, he is known to have been the first to set up a system of analytical geometry and to distinguish harmonic progression. He was a notable contributor to the theory of proportion and the study of acoustics and music. Finally, he was the inventor of a method of doubling the cube, supposedly also of the pulley, and even, according to one account, of a flying machine.

Arctinus (ärk-tī'nus). Greek poet of Miletus, to whom three lost poems of the Epic Cycle are attributed; fl. c776 B.C.; said to have been a pupil of Homer. Author of *Aethiopis*, an epic poem which continued the narrative of the Trojan War from the point where it is dropped by the *Iliad*. From that point it described the arrival of the Amazon Penthesilea, and recorded her glorious exploits in battle, her death in combat at the hands of Achilles, the death of Memnon, the death of Achilles, and the rivalry between Ajax and Odysseus for the arms of Achilles that resulted in the suicide of Ajax. Another epic poem attributed to Arctinus, the *Iliu Persis* or Sack of Troy, told of the stratagem of the Wooden Horse, the taking and sack of Troy, and the departure of the Greeks. A third epic, the *Titanomachia* or War of the Titans, was also attributed to Arctinus. The works are known from quotations in later writers, inscriptions, and a late epitome.

Arcton (ärk'ton). In ancient geography, a mountain ("Bear Mountain") near Cyzicus on the Pontus. Here the Argonauts, after the tragic accident of slaying Cyzicus, king of the land, sacrificed to Rhea and prayed to her to calm the storms that beset them on their way to Colchis.

Ardea (är'de̦-a̦). In ancient geography, a town in Latium, Italy, about 24 miles S of Rome. It was the chief town of the Rutulians, and later a Roman colony. In Republican times it served as a State prison. While Camillus, Roman tribune and dictator, was in voluntary exile here, the Gauls attacked, took, and sacked Rome (389 B.C.). Camillus, it is said, gathered a force of Ardeans and destroyed a part of the army of the Gauls that had encamped outside Ardea. From this victory he went on to free Rome. Ardea has the best example of early Italic fortifications of mounded earth, the agger, and interesting masonry fortifications in the volcanic stone known as tufa. Excavations have brought to light decorative architectural terra-cottas from several Italic temples of the 4th–2nd centuries B.C., and Swedish explorations have cleared the tufa foundations of a large temple and an early basilica. (JJ)

Ardys (är'dis). Son of Gyges, king of Lydia. Assurbanipal, king of Assyria (668–626 B.C.), relates in his annals that Gyges rebelled against him, but that his son Ardys, as a result of the invasion of Lydia by the Cimmerians, submitted to him and invoked his help.

Area (a̦-rē'a̦). [Also: **Areia**.] An epithet applied to Aphrodite by the Spartans, meaning "Warlike," or "Devoted to Ares." Artemis and Athena also were given this epithet. Orestes is said to have dedicated an altar of Athena Area on the Hill of Ares (*Areopagus*) after he had been acquitted in his trial on the charge of murdering his mother. Nearby, unhewn stones were located, on which the defendants and prosecutors in a trial stood. One of the stones was the stone of Outrage; the other was the stone of Ruthlessness (see **Areopagus**). The sanctuary of Athena Area at Plataea was built by the Plataeans with their share of the spoils from the victory at Marathon (480 B.C.). The image in the temple at Plataea was by Phidias, and on the walls was a painting by Polygnotus showing Odysseus and the slain suitors.

Areïthoüs (a̦-rē-ith'ō̦-us). In Homeric legend (*Iliad*), the father of Menesthius of Arne. He was called Corynetes (*The Mace-man* or *Club-man*) because he used an iron mace rather than a lance or spear in battle. He was trapped by Lycurgus, son of Aleus of Tegea, in a narrow place where he could not swing his mace and was slain by Lycurgus, who then took his armor. According to Pausanias, the tomb of Areïthoüs was near Mantinea in Arcadia.

Areius (a̦-rā'us). Stoic or Pythagorean philosopher of Alexandria; fl. c30 B.C. He was the friend and preceptor of Octavian, the future Augustus, and is said to have overcome the latter's hesitation to put to death Caesarion the son of Cleopatra, reputedly by Julius Caesar, by the following parody of Homer's famous praise of monarchy: "'Tis no good thing, a multitude of Caesars."

Arene (a̦-rē'nē). In Greek mythology, the

half-sister and wife of Aphareus, and mother by him of Lynceus. By Poseidon she was the mother of Idas.

Arene. City of Messenia, founded, according to tradition, by Aphareus and named for his wife and half-sister, the daughter of Oebalus and Gorgophone. The city played a part in the war between the Epeans and Pylians, in which Nestor as a youth won his spurs. Men of Arene followed Nestor to the Trojan War.

Areopagus (ar-ē-op′ạ-gus). [Eng. trans, "Hill of Ares."] Low rocky hill at Athens, Greece, continuing westward the line of the Acropolis, from which it is separated by a depression of ground. On the S side near the top there is a flight of 15 rock-cut steps, and portions of the summit are hewn smooth to form platforms, doubtless for altars. Upon this hill sat the famous court of the same name. Two unhewn stones were nearby. On one of them, the Stone of Outrage, the accuser stood during the trial; on the other, the Stone of Ruthlessness, stood the accused. This court, originally a Council of Elders, exercised supreme authority in all matters in ancient times. Under the developed Athenian constitution it lost many of its ancient powers but retained jurisdiction in cases of homicide (including wounding with intent, and arson) and in religious concerns, and exercised a general censorship. In ancient times murder and manslaughter had been avenged by the family of the slain person either by slaying the slayer or by accepting a payment in compensation. As the worship of the dead souls and of the gods of the Underworld developed, the principle arose that a murderer had offended them and must be purified of his offense in order to satisfy the avenging Erinyes or Furies. Furthermore, until purification had been achieved the wrath of the Erinyes fell not only on the murderer, but on the community of which he was a part as well. Hence purification was a matter concerning the state and one on which the community was compelled to act. It became the function of the Areopagus to adjudicate these matters. According to mythology, the very first trial for murder that took place was that of Ares for the murder of Halirrhothius, a son of Poseidon. Ares claimed he had resorted to murder to save his daughter Alcippe

from being violated by Halirrhothius and was acquitted. Some say the hill and the Council was named Areopagus in commemoration of this trial, and some say the name comes from Athena's epithet "Areia," for in the second trial Orestes was acquitted of the murder of his mother when Athena cast the deciding vote in his favor. The trials of myth and legend reinforced a developing principle: the substitution of justice and law for the blind vengeance symbolized by the Erinyes or Furies. In historic times the Areopagus was constituted of all archons who, after their year of office, had successfully proved themselves guiltless of malfeasance, in accordance with the provisions of law.

Ares (ār′ēz). One of the 12 Olympian gods. He was the hated and feared god of war who engaged in bloody strife for love of combat itself. He flung himself impetuously into battle, accompanied by his sister Eris *(Strife)*, and other deities of relentless battle. Of all their gods, for whom the Greeks showed on the one hand reverence and on the other interested affection and curiosity, Ares alone won no sympathetic attention. As a symbol of an evil that exists, and the sorrow and suffering it causes, Ares was acknowledged but not loved.

Ares was the son of Zeus and Hera, both of whom disliked him, and Zeus often hinted that it was from his mother that Ares got his quarrelsome temper. The only one of the gods who appreciated Ares was Hades, for by his activities the population of Hades' realm was greatly increased. The various myths attached to Ares indicate that the Greeks were pleased to think their war god sometimes got a taste of his own medicine, and that he was by no means invulnerable. The Aloidae, giant sons of Iphimedia and Poseidon, captured Ares before they made war on the gods and shut him up in a bronze vessel. There he languished for 13 months before he was released through the intervention of Hermes. In the war of Heracles against Pylus, Athena aided Heracles, while Ares—along with Hera, Poseidon, and Hades—aided the Pylians. With Athena's aid Heracles wounded Ares twice and compelled him to withdraw. In the fight between Heracles and Cycnus, son of Ares,

Ares sided with his son and was again wounded by Heracles. In this instance Athena led him away to Olympus to be healed.

Homer tells that Aphrodite, married to the lame god Hephaestus, fell in love with the straight and handsome Ares, and entertained him frequently in her husband's absence. Hephaestus, informed by Helius of his wife's unfaithfulness, laid a trap for the lovers. He made a brazen net of mesh so fine as to be invisible and as strong as it was fine. This he draped on the bed where Ares and Aphrodite were accustomed to disport themselves. He told Aphrodite that he was going on a journey to his favorite haunt, the island of Lemnos. As soon as he had gone Ares came joyfully to his house and embraced Aphrodite. The net fell on the lovers and bound them fast. Hephaestus, again informed by Helius, returned and published their disgrace by calling the gods to witness how Aphrodite had dishonored him. He vowed he would not release the lovers until Zeus repaid him the rich marriage gifts he had made when he was given Aphrodite's hand. Ares promised to repay him, and Poseidon offered his guarantee that if Ares failed to keep his promise he would assume the debt. Aphrodite and Ares were freed. Ares went off to Thrace, his favorite dwelling place because of its warlike people and savage country. Aphrodite went to the isle of Cyprus and was purified by the nymphs. This, however, was not the end of the affair. Eos seduced Ares, and Aphrodite, out of jealousy, punished Eos. And when Aphrodite fell in love with Adonis, Ares, some say, disguised himself as a wild boar, one of his sacred animals, and killed Adonis. To Ares, Aphrodite bore Harmonia, later the wife of Cadmus, and Eros, Anteros, Deimos, and Phobos. He had many other children, among them: Oxylus, whose mother was Protogonia, daughter of Calydon; Demonice bore him Evenus, Molus, Pylus, and Thestius; some say he was the father of Althaea's son Meleager; Ascalaphus and Ialmenus, the Argonauts, were his sons; Cyrene bore him Diomedes of Thrace, master of the man-eating mares; Pyrene bore him that Cycnus who fought with Heracles on the Echedorus River in Macedonia and was only saved by

the intervention of Zeus; Pelopia bore him another Cycnus, who also fought with Heracles at Pagasae and was slain; Phlegyas, who became a king in Boeotian Orchomenus, was his son; Tereus of Thrace, the seducer of Philomela, claimed Ares as his father; and some say he was the father of Atalanta's son Parthenopaeus. Among his daughters were the Amazon Penthesilea, and Alcippe, for whose sake Ares slew Halirrhothius. For this killing he was tried, the first ever to stand trial for murder, on the Hill of Ares, afterwards known as the Areopagus and sacred to him. He was acquitted on the ground that he was protecting his daughter's honor. Ares gave arms and swift horses to Oenomaus who, some say, was his son. He gave the belt to the Amazon Hippolyte, which led to her death when Heracles came to fetch it as one of his labors for Eurystheus. Some say the dragon that guarded the spring at Thebes, slain by Cadmus, was a son of Ares. To atone for its murder Cadmus was compelled to serve Ares for a great year, that is, for eight years. The descendants of Cadmus also felt the wrath of Ares on account of the slaying of the dragon. In the war of the Seven against Thebes Menoeceus, son of Creon, voluntarily sacrificed himself to Ares on the advice of an oracle, to appease him and to give victory to Thebes. Another dragon guarded the Golden Fleece that hung in a grove sacred to Ares in Colchis. Colchian was one of his epithets, from his temple in Colchis.

Wherever conflict broke out, there Ares delighted to be. Some say it was Ares, with his sister Eris, who caused the wars between the Lapiths and the centaurs, because Pirithous, king of the Lapiths, had not invited them to his marriage to Hippodamia. In the Trojan War Ares helped the Trojans at the request of Aphrodite, and by so doing he roused his mother's (Hera's) anger against himself. But whereas he was a strong and violent fighter, he was not skilled in strategy. Athena twice worsted him in battle. She inspired Diomedes with immortal courage and encouraged him to attack Ares himself. She seized the spear Ares had hurled at Diomedes and deflected it, but the lance Diomedes threw, guided by her hand, found its target. Wounded, Ares withdrew to

Olympus to be healed, and complained to Zeus about Athena. Zeus sternly advised him not to come whining to Olympus, and addressed him as the most hateful to him of all the gods of Olympus, because all his joy was in strife and battle. Zeus also mentioned the untamed temper of Ares' mother, and observed that it might be by her will that Ares had been wounded. However, since Ares was his own son, Zeus commanded that he be healed. If he had not happened to be his son, Zeus assured him that he would long ago have banished him to Tartarus. Later in the war Ares came face to face with Athena and accused her of encouraging Diomedes to attack him and of guiding his lance. He rushed at her, vowing vengeance. As he lunged with his spear she took up a huge boulder, flung it at him and flattened him. Ares' bright hair lay in the dust. Athena stood over him and laughed at his boasts and his foolish belief that his strength could overcome her skill.

Ares was worshiped by the Spartans, and had sanctuaries under the name Enyalius in several places, but unlike the other Olympians, he had no cities, with the exception of Thebes, where he was especially worshiped. The Spartans called him "Theritas," and the oldest sanctuary of Ares in Laconia was that of Ares Theritas on the road from Therapne to Amyclae. In the sanctuary was an image said to have been brought back from Colchis by the Dioscuri. According to Pausanias, the name Theritas came from a Colchian nurse of Ares, called Thero. But, Pausanias adds, his opinion is that the name comes from a word meaning "wild beast," because it is necessary to cast aside all the qualities of gentleness and humanity when one engages in battle. The Spartans sacrificed dogs to Ares under his title of Enyalius. Near Tegea on Mount Cresius is a sanctuary of Ares Aphneius. The story is that Ares embraced Aërope, a daughter of Cepheus, and that she died in giving birth to a child. However, the child clung to its mother, even though she was dead, and through the will of Ares sucked great quantities of milk from her breasts. For this reason Ares was named Aphneius (*Abundant*). At Tegea also, he was worshiped as Gynaecothoenas, because when the women of Tegea armed themselves

and drove out the Spartans who had attacked them under Charillus, the women offered sacrifice to Ares for their victory on their own account. They gave the men no share in the meat of the victims, and named Ares Gynaecothoenas (*He who entertains women*).

The attributes of Ares are the spear and the blazing torch. Sacred to him were the vulture, the dog, and the boar. Priests of Ares marched in front of the armies and hurled the blazing torches at the enemy as a signal for battle to begin. In art Ares is represented as a muscular, handsome man, sometimes bearded and wearing armor, sometimes clean-shaven and wearing only the helmet. He is often shown also in company with Aphrodite and their son Eros. In the decipherment of the bronze-age tablets in the Linear B script appears the name *Enyalios,* which later appears as an epithet or alternate name of Ares, indicating that Ares had been equated with a Mycenaean divinity.

Arete (a-rē′tē). In mythology, wife of Alcinous, king of the Phaeacians. She exerted great influence over her husband and, according to her daughter Nausicaä, it was important to make a good impression on her. So Nausicaä advised Odysseus when he was swept ashore on the island of the Phaeacians. Arete received him kindly and Alcinous therefore welcomed him. It was Arete, according to a late mythographer, who persuaded Alcinous not to surrender Medea to the Colchians. Arete reminded Alcinous of the horrible things irate fathers had done to their daughters, and prevailed on him to refuse to surrender Medea if she were married to Jason. Arete supervised the arrangements for the wedding and frustrated the Colchians in their attempt to fetch Medea back to her father.

Arete. Daughter of Dionysius the Elder, of Syracuse (c430–367 B.C.), and Aristomache. She was the wife of her uncle, Dion, but when he was banished (366 B.C.) by her half-brother, Dionysius the Younger, she was compelled to marry one of her half-brother's friends. When Dionysius was besieged in the citadel of Syracuse by the forces of Dion who had returned to lead a revolt, Arete was kept with him as a captive. Dionysius escaped from the citadel and his forces there later were compelled to surrender. Arete came out with them and was received by her weeping husband Dion, who took her back as his wife. After the death of Dion, Arete, sailing with her mother to the Peloponnesus, was seized by Hicetas, tyrant of Leontini, and drowned.

Arete. In Greek mythology, the personification of courage, or the manly virtues.

Arethusa (ar-ē̱-thū′sạ). In mythology, a nymph of Elis, or Achaea, and a companion and follower of Artemis. Her remarkable beauty was only a nuisance to her as she preferred the pleasures of the chase. One time when she sought refreshment after a hot day of hunting she came to the bank of a cool stream, slipped off her robes, and splashed in the waters. As she was bathing she heard a curious murmuring in the river and, frightened, leaped out onto the bank. The river-god Alpheus, in whose waters she had bathed, fell in love with her and sought to embrace her. In terror she ran naked over fields and mountains, though he cried out to her with loving words. At last she knew her strength was failing and that the river-god would overtake her. She called on Artemis to save her. The goddess responded at once. She wrapped Arethusa in a mist and swept her off to Ortygia, an island in the harbor of Syracuse in Sicily. There the goddess split open the ground and Arethusa, transformed into a fountain, gushed forth from the chasm. Alpheus plunged into the ground of Elis and, passing under the sea, came at last to Ortygia and mingled his waters with those of the fountain of Arethusa. It was said that a flower dropped into the Alpheus in Greece ultimately floated to the surface of the waters of the fountain of Arethusa in Sicily, having traveled under the sea along the path taken by Alpheus when he pursued Arethusa. Various springs in ancient Greece also bore the name Arethusa.

Aretus (ạ-rē′tus). Named by Homer (*Iliad*) as one of Priam's 50 sons. He was slain by Achilles' charioteer, Automedon, as he struggled for possession of Achilles' immortal horses after the death of Patroclus, who had been loaned the horses by Achilles.

Areus (ạ-rē′us). [Also: **Areius**.] In Greek legend, a son of Bias and Pero. With his brothers, Leodocus and Talaus, he accompanied Jason in the *Argo* on the quest for the Golden Fleece.

Areus. [Also: **Areius**.] An epithet of Zeus, meaning "Warlike." Pelops sacrificed to Zeus Areus before his race with Oenomaus. The kings of Epirus also sacrificed to Zeus Areus.

Argades (är′gạ-dēz). According to tradition, one of the four sons of Ion. One of the four ancient tribes of Athens was named for him. His brothers were Aegicores, Geleon, and Hoples.

Arganthonius (är-gan-thō′ni-us). In ancient geography, a mountain ridge in Bithynia, Asia Minor, near the Propontis.

Argeiphontes (är-jī-fon′tēz) or **Argiphontes**. An epithet of Hermes, meaning "Slayer of Argus." It was given to him because, at the command of Zeus, he first lulled hundred-eyed Argus who was guarding Io (transformed into a heifer) to sleep with his stories and his wand, and then killed him.

Arges (är′jēz). In Greek mythology, one of the Cyclopes, a son of Gaea and Uranus. His brothers were Brontes and Steropes. See **Cyclopes**.

Argia (är-jī′ạ). In mythology, a daughter of Oceanus and Tethys. Some say she was the sister and wife of the river-god Inachus and the mother of Io.

Argia. According to some accounts, the mother of that Argus who, with the aid of Athena, built the *Argo* for Jason. Her husband was Polybus.

Argia. In Greek legend, the wife of Aristodemus, one of the Heraclidae, and the mother of Eurysthenes and Procles.

Argia. See Aegia, daughter of Adrastus.

Argillus (är-ji′lus). In ancient geography, a colony of Andros in Macedonia. It revolted from Athens c424 B.C.

Arginusae (ạr-ji-nū′sē). In ancient geography, a group of small islands off the coast of Asia Minor, SE of Lesbos. Near here the Athenian fleet under Conon defeated (406 B.C.) the Spartans under Callicratidas.

Argiope (är-jī′ō-pē). In mythology, the wife of Agenor and the mother by him of Cadmus, Cilix, Phineus, Phoenix, Thasus, and one daughter, Europa. Argiope is also known as Telephassa.

Argiope. A daughter of Teuthras, king of

Mysia. According to some accounts of the myth, Teuthras gave her to Telephus, son of Heracles and Auge, when he came to Mysia searching for news of his parents.

Argiope. A nymph, sometimes said to be the mother of Cercyon the Arcadian.

Argive Heraeum. A famous sanctuary of Hera, patron goddess of Argos, situated on a spur of Mount Euboea between Argos and Mycenae. It contains on three terraces the remains of a 6th-century Doric temple which was burned in 423 B.C., the late 5th-century Doric temple which replaced it, and a number of stoas or colonnades excavated in 1892-95 by the American School of Classical Studies at Athens under the direction of Charles Waldstein. The temple was notable for its cult statue in gold and ivory by Polyclitus. In legend, it was at this shrine that the Greek chieftains swore allegiance to Agamemnon before leaving for Troy, and Herodotus tells Solon's story of Cleobis and Bito, sons of a priestess of Hera, who, when the team assigned to draw their mother to the shrine failed to arrive, yoked themselves to the car and drew her to the Heraeum. After which, having sacrificed and feasted, they lay down, never to awake. (JJ)

Argives (är′jīvz). Name often used for the Greeks of Argolis. As a result of the important part they played under their king Agamemnon in the Trojan War, their name is extended by Homer in the *Iliad* to all the Greeks. See **Argolis.**

Argo (är′gō). The name of the famous fifty-oared ship in which the Argonauts sailed with Jason to Colchis to fetch the Golden Fleece. It was built by Argus, son of Arestor, and supposedly named after him. Its prow contained a beam, supplied by Athena, from a sacred talking oak of Dodona, which occasionally gave advice to the Argonauts on their journey. According to ancient writers the *Argo* was the first ship that ever sailed the sea.

Argo. An ancient southern constellation, the largest in the heavens. It contains Canopus, after Sirius the brightest of the fixed stars.

Argolis (är′gō-lis). In ancient geography, a division of the Peloponnesus, Greece, surrounded by Sicyonia, Corinthia, the Aegean (with the Saronic and Argolic gulfs), La-

conia, and Arcadia, and containing the plain of Argos. According to one tradition, Inachus was the first king of the land. He named the river for himself and sacrificed to Hera. Others says Phoroneus, son of Inachus, was the first king. Hera and Poseidon struggled for control of Argolis and the river-gods Inachus, Cephissus, and Asterion were named to settle their dispute. They awarded Argolis to Hera. It became a land much loved by her and contained one of her holiest sanctuaries, the Heraeum. But Poseidon was enraged by the decision of the river-gods, and dried up all the rivers of Argolis. Later, out of love for Amymone, daughter of Danaus, he brought forth the fountain of Lerna, source of the river Lerna whose waters never cease to flow. Phoroneus collected his followers, the Pelasgians, and founded a city in Argolis which he named Phoronicum for himself. The Argives denied that Prometheus gave man the gift of fire, although they claimed his tomb was in their country. They said Phoroneus was the discoverer of fire, and they had an eternal fire that they called "the fire of Phoroneus." The Argives made offerings to him as to a hero. The name of the city founded by him was later changed to Argos by Argus, his descendant. Gelanor was king of the land when Danaus, fleeing thither from Egypt with his 50 daughters, arrived in Argolis and claimed the throne. Gelanor, who had no idea of yielding it to him, retired on the pretext of considering his demand. During the night a wolf fell on his cattle and destroyed his prize bull. This was considered to be an omen, and the following day Gelanor gave up his throne to Danaus. The latter established his own dynasty over Argolis, raised a temple to Lycian Apollo in gratitude for the omen and dedicated an image therein. His tomb is in Argolis. The kingdom was ruled by his descendants. Acrisius and Proetus, his great-grandsons, divided it. Acrisius kept the region around the city of Argos. Proetus took over the Heraeum, the cities of Midea and Tiryns, and the region of the coast. Acrisius tried to destroy his own grandson Perseus, because of an oracle that he would die at Perseus' hands. When he learned that Perseus was returning from his adventures with the Gorgon Medusa, whose head, the

Argives claimed, was buried in Argolis, Acrisius fled. The oracle was fulfilled, however, for Perseus followed him to Larisa and accidentally killed him. After this Perseus did not wish to return to his kingdom, and he exchanged Argos for the kingdom of Tiryns, ruled by his cousin Megapenthes. On his way to take up the throne Perseus founded the city of Mycenae. The region of Argos was divided into three parts for the daughters of Proetus were afflicted with madness, and Melampus, who offered to cure them, demanded that the kingdom be divided between himself, his brother Bias, and the king. In time Atreus, son of Pelops, became ruler of the Argolid city of Mycenae. He extended his power and in the time of his son Agamemnon, all of Argolis, as well as most of the rest of the Peloponnesus and the islands, was under the domination of Mycenae. In fact, Agamemnon's influence extended throughout Greece. When Paris abducted Helen and carried her off to Troy Agamemnon recruited forces from all over and led them against the Trojans to recover his brother's wife. The names Danaans (descendants of Danaus) and Argives (descendants of Argus) are those Homer habitually used in the *Iliad* to describe the Greeks; he never used the word "Greek." Some of the Argives returning from Troy were shipwrecked at Caphareus on the coast of Euboea. Those who escaped drowning were afflicted by cold and hunger. They prayed to their gods to save them and withdrew to a cave on the shore. Inside the cave they found an image of Dionysus. They also found there a herd of wild she-goats that had taken refuge from the storm. They killed and ate them and clothed themselves in goatskins. When they returned to Argos they took the image with them and dedicated it in the temple of Dionysus, near the house of the Argive king Adrastus who led the Seven against Thebes. Agamemnon was murdered on his return from Troy and was succeeded, after an interval in which Clytemnestra and Aegisthus held sway, by his son Orestes. In the reign of Tisamenus, son of Orestes, the Heraclidae (Dorians) invaded Argolis, basing their claim to the land on an earlier conquest by Heracles who, they said, had left it in trust for his descendants. Tisa-

menus and his sons were driven out and fled to Achaea. The Nelidae, descendants of Bias and Pero, fled to Athens, where two tribes, the Paeonidae and the Alcmaeonidae, were named for them. The sons of the Heraclid Temenus seized the land.

Argolis was rich in mythological associations. Here was an altar of Zeus, God of Rain, over which the allies of Polynices, in the war of the Seven against Thebes, swore they would take Thebes or die in the attempt. There was also an image of Zeus Mechaneus (*Contriver*) to which, some say, the Greeks made the same vow with regard to the taking of Troy. In the temple of Tyche (*Fortune*) in Argolis, Palamedes dedicated the dice he invented, and which helped the Greeks while away the time in their ten-year war against Troy. Among the many sanctuaries was a temple of Leto, said to have been raised by Meliboea and Amyclas, the children of Niobe who escaped the arrows of Apollo and Artemis by praying to Leto. The temple contained a statue of Leto carved by Praxiteles. In a temple of the Dioscuri stood the wooden images of the Dioscuri, their wives Hilaira and Phoebe and their sons, reputedly carved by Scyllis and Dipoenus, pupils, some say, of Daedalus. The Argives claimed Helen raised a temple of Ilithyia here, for they say when the Dioscuri had rescued her from Theseus she gave birth to a child, the daughter of Theseus. She gave the child to her sister Clytemnestra. This daughter, according to the poets, was Iphigenia.

The legend of Danaus probably explains an early influx of an eastern people who mingled with the Pelasgian inhabitants of Argolis. After the invasion of the area by the Dorians the city of Argos, thanks to its position and its access to the sea, became the chief city of the area. Other important cites of Argolis where Tiryns, Mycenae, Midea, and Nauplia.

Argonautica (är-gō-nô′ti-ka). Title of a lost poem on the adventures of the Argonauts, in the Epic Cycle, attributed by one source to Epimenides. (JJ)

Argonautica. An epic poem, extant in four books, by Apollonius Rhodius. It describes the adventures of Jason and the Argonauts on their expedition to obtain the Golden

fat, fāte, fär, fāre, errant; net, mē, hėr ardent; pin, pīne; not, nōte, mȯve, nôr,

Fleece, some time before the Trojan War.

Book I: Jason, the son of Aeson, arrives before Pelias, King of Iolcus, shod in one sandal only. Pelias, having seized the throne from Aeson, had been warned by an oracle to beware of a man wearing one sandal. He therefore sends Jason on a perilous mission: to fetch the Golden Fleece from King Aeëtes in Colchis, and return it to Hellas. Argus, aided by Athena, builds a ship, the *Argo*, and heroes and demigods from all over Greece gather to accompany Jason. Among them are: Orpheus; Polyphemus, who had fought the centaurs; Mopsus, who had learned the augury of birds from Apollo; Oileus, the father of the Locrian Ajax; Menoetius, the father of Patroclus; Canthus; Telamon, father of Ajax; Peleus, father of Achilles; Tiphys, the helmsman of the *Argo;* Heracles, who interrupts his labors for Eurystheus; Idmon, a seer, the son of Apollo; Polydeuces and Castor; Taenarus, Erginus, and Ancaeus, sons of Poseidon; Meleager, from Calydon; Zetes and Calais, sons of Boreas; Acastus, Pelias' own son; Argus; and many others. Atalanta wishes to join but Jason, chosen leader when Heracles refused the task, fears her presence would cause strife.

The *Argo* sails from Magnesia and goes to Lemnos where the Lemnian women, angered because their husbands preferred captive maidens to their lawful wives, had recently slain all the males of the island. Hypsipyle, their queen, is persuaded by her old nurse to let the Argonauts land; she invites them to remain and share her kingdom. They linger a year after which, chided by Heracles for abandoning their mission, they put to sea again. They sail by Samothrace, cross the Euxine Sea, pass through the Hellespont and land at the island of the Doliones, where they are welcomed and entertained by King Cyzicus. The night after the *Argo* leaves the Doliones it is blown back again by unfavorable winds, and in the darkness the Doliones mistake the Argonauts for raiders; a fight ensues, and Jason kills Cyzicus. Daylight reveals the bitter mistake. The Argonauts make sacrifices of mourning to Rhea and leave for Mysia. On the way Heracles, rowing alone because his companions are weary, breaks his oar. He goes into the

forests of Mysia to find a tree from which he can fashion a new oar and Hylas, his squire, goes to look for water. Hylas is captured by a nymph of a spring, and while Heracles and Polyphemus search for him the Argonauts sail. A fierce quarrel breaks out among them over the abandonment of Heracles and Polyphemus but is quieted when Glaucus, a sea god, rises and tells them Heracles must finish his labors for Eurystheus, Polyphemus will found a city, and Hylas has become the husband of a nymph. The Argonauts then proceed to Bebrycia.

Book II: Amycus, king of the Bebryces, arrogantly challenges all travelers to box with him. Polydeuces accepts the challenge for the Argonauts and kills him. The Argonauts then fight the Bebryces and defeat them. Passing through the Bosporus, they land on the coast opposite Bithynia, where they find Phineus, who had been endowed with the gift of prophecy by Apollo. Zeus had blinded Phineus and sent Harpies to befoul his food so that he was always at the point of starvation because Zeus was enraged that a mortal should have the gift of complete prophecy. Phineus had eagerly awaited the arrival of the Argonauts for he knew they could help him. At his request, Calais and Zetes pursue the Harpies but are prevented from killing them by Iris, messenger of Zeus, who promises that they will not hound Phineus again. Phineus gives some advice and makes certain predictions to the Argonauts, although he does not tell them complete prophecies for fear of Zeus, and they leave him. When they come to the Clashing Rocks (Symplegades) they take the advice of Phineus and send a dove to test the passage through the rocks. The rocks part for the dove and the *Argo* follows swiftly, aided by Athena. After passing the isle of Thyrias they push on to the land of the Mariandyni, where they are especially welcome because they had defeated the Bebryces, enemies of the Mariandyni. Idmon the seer is killed by a wild boar while they are with the Mariandyni, and Tiphys, helmsman of the *Argo*, also dies here. Ancaeus, a son of Poseidon who has great knowledge of the sea, takes his place. After passing Sinope, being driven by winds away from the land of the Amazons and passing the bleak home of the Chalybes, an iron feather from a bird of Ares falls and wounds Oileus. This informs them they are near Aretias, Ares' isle, where Phineus had told them to land and find help from the sea. Since it is impossible to kill Ares' birds they frighten them away by creating a fearful din with their shields, and then they land. Here they find the four sons of Phrixus and Chalciope who had been shipwrecked on their way from Colchis to Hellas. These sons, grandsons of King Aeëtes, are the help from the sea promised by Phineus. They are taken aboard and the voyage continues, passing the rock to which Prometheus is chained and from which they hear his screams as the eagle tears at his liver. At last they arrive at the Phasis, river of Colchis, and see the towers of Aeëtes' city.

Book III: Hera and Athena, watching the progress of the Argonauts from the heavens, ask Aphrodite to send her son Eros to smite Medea, Aeëtes' daughter, with love for Jason so that she, a powerful sorceress, will help the Argonauts. Hera is angry with Pelias because he does not properly honor her and she favors Jason because, when she was disguised as an old crone, he had helped her across the raging floods of the Anaurus River. Aphrodite bribes Eros with a golden ball that had once been the plaything of Zeus, and when Jason appears before Medea and her sister Chalciope, Eros sends an arrow that transfixes Medea and instantly she falls wildly in love. The eldest son of Phrixus accompanies Jason to the palace and explains his errand. Aeëtes is enraged; only the laws of hospitality prevent him from despatching the Argonauts at once, along with the sons of Phrixus whom he accuses of plotting to gain his throne. Jason reassures him and offers to fight the enemies of Aeëtes in return for the Golden Fleece. Aeëtes craftily replies that he will give Jason the Fleece if he succeeds in a trial of courage: to yoke two fire-breathing bronze bulls, plow a field with them, sow dragon's teeth, and then slay the armed men who will spring up from the teeth. Aeëtes says he asks Jason to do only what he himself has done, but secretly he is sure Jason will perish. Jason accepts the challenge. Chalciope, mother of Phrixus' sons, urges Medea

to help Jason so that he will protect her sons, and Medea, consumed by love for Jason, agrees to betray her father. That night she meets Jason at the shrine of Hecate and gives him a charm which, when steeped in water and sprinkled on his body and his weapons, will render him invulnerable for a day. She tells him to throw a boulder among the armed men who will spring up from the dragon's teeth and they will slaughter each other. Jason performs all the rites Medea ordains and next day, protected by the charm, he successfully yokes the bulls and fulfills the remainder of the task Aeëtes had set for him.

Book IV: Aeëtes, enraged at Medea's treachery, plots to kill Jason. Medea, frantic with love and guilt, flees to Jason. She warns him to leave, begs him to take her with him and promises to help him secure the Golden Fleece. In return he promises to make her his wife. Together they approach the dragon that guards the Fleece. Medea lulls it to sleep with a magic song; Jason seizes the Fleece; they return to the ship and cast off at once. Aeëtes and his son Apsyrtus pursue them. Apsyrtus takes a short cut and traps the Argonauts when they stop to sacrifice to Hecate. Rather than give up the Golden Fleece, Jason proposes to surrender Medea to her brother. She reproaches him bitterly for breaking his oath to marry her and advances a plan to get rid of Apsyrtus. She carries it out by inducing Apsyrtus to come to her alone, tells him she had been carried off by force and that she wishes to return to Aeëtes. Jason, hiding nearby, leaps out and kills him and buries his body. The Colchians are then prevented from further pursuit by heavy storms sent by Hera. But Zeus is angry at the murder of Apsyrtus, and vows many woes to the Argonauts. They learn this from the *Argo* itself. It had been made from sacred Dodonian oak, and now speaks to them, telling them they must go to Circe to be cleansed of this murder. It is thus that they go to Aeaea and are purified by Circe, the sister of Aeëtes.

When they leave Aeaea, Hera sends Iris to smooth the seas for the *Argo*. They pass the island of the Sirens and are saved from succumbing to their lures by the songs of Orpheus. Thetis and the Nereids propel the *Argo* through Charybdis and past Scylla, and carry it in the air over the treacherous Rolling Rocks (Planctae). At length they come to Drepane (Corcyra), the land of Alcinous, king of the Phaeacians. Here the Colchians catch up with them again and demand Medea but Arete, wife of Alcinous, persuades him to make this decision: if Medea is a virgin he will return her to her father, otherwise he will not separate her from her man. Arete thereupon urges Jason to marry Medea and this is done. The Golden Fleece serves as a marriage couch and Orpheus sings the marriage song. The Colchians admit defeat, and rather than face the wrath of Aeëtes they settle among the Phaeacians. After leaving the Phaeacians the *Argo* is blown onto the shoals of Syrtis. On the advice of some nymphs the Argonauts carry their ship on their shoulders across reefs and sand to the Tritonian Lake. Here they see the Hesperides, mourning because only the day before Heracles slew the dragon who guarded the golden apples. Here also Canthus is killed by a shepherd whose sheep he is trying to steal, and Mopsus the seer dies as the result of stepping on a poisonous serpent. Triton then appears to the Argonauts and guides them out of the lake to the sea. They stop at Crete where Medea brings about the death of bronze Talos, the guardian of Crete who walks around its shores three times a day; they sail by Aegina and at last return safely, carrying the Golden Fleece, to Pagasae, the port where the *Argo* was built.

Argonautica. The title of a Latin epic poem in eight books, by the Roman poet Valerius Flaccus (1st century A.D.), recounting the legendary adventures of the Argonauts. (JJ)

Argonauts (är′gō̤-nôts). The Greek heroes and demigods who sailed with Jason on the *Argo* to fetch the Golden Fleece from Colchis. Various writers have drawn up varying lists of Argonauts, until finally the roster, which originally may have included only Minyans from Iolcus, Orchomenus, and Pylus, came to include representatives from all over Greece. Thus, every part of Greece shared in the expedition (which may have had an historical basis in an early trade venture), and therefore shared the glory and any future advantages which might derive from it. Following is the list of Argonauts given by Apollonius Rhodius in his *Argonautica:*

Acastus, son of King Pelias of Iolcus
Admetus, prince of Pherae, son of Pheres
Aethalides, son of Hermes
Amphidamas, son of Aleus, from Arcadia
Amphion, son of Hyperasius, from Pellene
Ancaeus, son of Lycurgus, from Arcadia
Ancaeus, a steersman, son of Poseidon, from Tegea
Areus, a son of Bias
Argus, builder of the *Argo*
Asterion, son of Cometes
Asterius, brother of Amphion
Augeas, son of Helius, from Elis
Butes, son of Teleon, from Athens
Canthus, son of Canethus, from Euboea
Calais, winged son of Boreas and Orithyia
Castor, one of the Dioscuri, from Sparta
Cepheus, son of Aleus, from Arcadia
Clytius, son of Eurytus, from Oechalia
Coronus, son of Caeneus, a Lapith from Thessaly
Echion, herald of the Argonauts, son of Hermes
Erginus, son of Poseidon, from Orchomenus
Eribotes, son of Teleon, from Athens
Erytus, brother of Echion, from Alope
Euphemus, son of Poseidon, from Taenarus
Eurydamas, son of Ctimenus, a Dolopian
Eurytion, son of Irus
Heracles, son of Zeus, from Tiryns
Hylas, squire of Heracles
Idas, son of Aphareus, from Arene
Idmon, a seer, son of Apollo, from Argos
Iphiclus, son of Thestius, from Aetolia
Iphiclus, son of Phylacus, from Phylace
Iphitus, brother of Clytius
Iphitus, son of Naubolus, from Phocis
Jason, son of Aeson, captain of the expedition
Laocoön, uncle of Meleager
Leodocus, brother of Areus
Lynceus, brother of Idas
Meleager, son of Oeneus, from Calydon
Menoetius, son of Actor
Mopsus, son of Ampycus, a Lapith
Nauplius, son of Clytonaeus, from Argos
Oileus, father of Ajax the Lesser, from Locris
Orpheus, the musician and poet, from Thrace

Palaemonius, lame son of Hephaestus, from Aetolia

Peleus, father of Achilles, from Phthia

Periclymenus, son of Nestor, from Pylus

Phalerus, archer from Athens

Phlias, from Araethyrea

Polydeuces, one of the Dioscuri, from Sparta

Polyphemus, son of Elatus, from Arcadia

Taenarus, son of Poseidon

Talaus, brother of Areus

Telamon, father of Great Ajax, from Salamis

Tiphys, the steersman, son of Hagnias, from Boeotia

Zetes, winged brother of Calais

Others listed as members of the Argonauts by other writers include:

Actor, son of Deion, from Phocis

Amphiaraus, the seer, from Argos

Ascalaphus, son of Ares, from Orchomenus

Atalanta, the virgin huntress, from Calydon

Caeneus, the Lapith, father of Coronus

Euryalus, son of Mecisteus, one of the Epigoni

Iphitus, from Mycenae

Laertes, son of Acrisius, from Argos

Melampus, son of Poseidon, from Pylos

Peneleus, son of Hippalcimus, from Boeotia

Phanus, son of Dionysus, from Crete

Poeas, father of Philoctetes, from Thessaly

Staphylus, brother of Phanus.

Argoön (är′gō-on). A harbor on the island of Aethalia (Elba) into which, as legend would have it, the Argonauts put on their roundabout way home from Colchis. They gave it this name in honor of their ship, the *Argo*. The site is now occupied by Portoferraio, the chief city in the island of Elba.

Argos (är′gos, -gŏs). Town in S Greece, in the district anciently called Argolis, in the Peloponnesus. It is situated about nine miles NW of Nauplia and the coast. According to legend, an ancient city was founded here by Phoroneus, son of Inachus, and his Pelasgian followers. He named it Phoronicum and sacrificed to Hera. Argus, a descendant of Phoroneus, changed the name of the city to Argos. It is regarded as the oldest city in Greece, and was one of the cities most beloved by Hera, who, the Argives claimed, was born in Argos. The region of Argolis fell under the domination of Danaus who fled hither from Egypt with his 50 daughters. He established his dynasty in Argolis and erected a temple to Lycian Apollo. His descendants Acrisius and Proetus partitioned the kingdom. Acrisius became ruler of the region around Argos. In a later generation Perseus, grandson of Acrisius, exchanged the kingdom of Argos for Tiryns. Argos was the home of Adrastus, father-in-law of Tydeus and Polynices and the leader of the expedition of the Seven against Thebes. By the time of the Trojan War Argos was under the influence of the ruler of Mycenae, of the dynasty of Pelops, and at the request of Agamemnon, its king, sent many Argives against Troy. They won great distinction under their leader Diomedes. The word "Argives" was habitually used by Homer in the *Iliad* to designate the Greeks. The great kingdom over which Agamemnon had ruled was diminished in the reign of his grandson, Tisamenus, by the Dorian invasion, the so-called return of the Heraclidae, for the Dorians based their claim to Argos on ancient conquests by Heracles, who left it in trust for his descendants. The Heraclid Temenus became ruler of Argos, but such was the Argive love of liberty, according to some, that the king had but little power.

As a Dorian city Argos, thanks to its position in the plain (the name means "plain"), and its access to the sea, became the dominant city in this area of the Peloponnesus. Under the rule of King Pheidon, in the early 7th century B.C., Argos was the equal of any of the city-states of Greece. Pheidon coined the first Greek money in Aegina. Argos was a center of trade and in this period controlled Mycenae and Tiryns, destroyed Asine, and defeated the Spartans at Hysiae (669 B.C.). Pheidon captured Olympia from Elis and returned the management of the Olympic Games to Pisa. With the rise of Sparta the power of Argos declined, and she was unable to assist Pisa when Elis attacked and won back control of Olympia. In the 6th and early 5th centuries the power of Argos was reduced by Cleomenes I, king of Sparta, who defeated her at Sepeia (c494 B.C.) in her own territory. Six thousand Argives perished when Cleomenes set fire to the sacred grove in which they had taken refuge.

The city itself would have fallen at this time if it had not been for the bravery of the poetess Telesilla. From that time forward, though remaining independent, a dangerous enemy or a valued friend, Argos was a second-rate power. Enmity toward Sparta caused the Argives to refuse to submit to Spartan leadership when Greece was threatened by the Persians and the city-state played no part in the Persian War. However, she could not prevent her former subject-cities of Mycenae and Tiryns from sending men to help the Greeks at Thermopylae and Plataea. After the Persians had been driven out of Greece, Argos attacked and destroyed Mycenae and Tiryns. Some say the attack was out of jealousy for the renown they had won in the Persian War. Others say it was because they had sheltered slaves escaped from Argos. Following the Persian Wars, Argos recovered some of her former power. A democratic constitution was adopted and an alliance with Athens against Sparta was concluded. With her allies, Athens, Corinth, and Mantinea, Argos was defeated by the Spartans at the first battle of Mantinea (418 B.C.). Argive hatred of the Spartans persisted and Argos took part on the side of Thebes in the defeat of Sparta at the second Battle of Mantinea (362 B.C.). In 229 Argos joined the Achaean League against Macedonia. The League was defeated (146 B.C.) by the Romans. Argos fell under Roman domination and enjoyed a new prosperity.

The citadel of Argos was on a rocky hill to the west, called Larissa. Cut into the flank of the hill are the remains of an ancient theater that seated 20,000 spectators. The upper tiers of seats of the cavea are rock-hewn; below these are tiers of masonry. Twenty tiers in all survive, the lowest consisting of thrones of honor. There are remains of a Roman stage and of several modifications of the Greek stage structure. An underground passage ran from behind the proscenium to the middle of the orchestra. Up the hill from the theater was a temple of Aphrodite. Near the summit was an ancient temple of Hera Acraea (*Of the Height*). North of the city, near the summit of the hill called Aspis, was a sanctuary of Pythian Apollo and Athena. In the sanctuary was an oracle. Oracular responses were given in the following manner: each month a lamb was sacrificed in the night; a woman forbidden to cohabit with a man drank the blood of the lamb and then prophesied. In this sanctuary Diomedes is said to have dedicated an image of Athena Oxyderces (*Bright-eyed*) in gratitude to the goddess for clearing the mists from his eyes when he was wounded in the Trojan War. Near the citadel were buried the heads of the sons of Aegyptus, who were killed by their brides on their wedding night. Their bodies were buried at nearby Lerna. Argos was noted for its school of sculpture, in which Ageladas (late 6th century B.C.) and Polyclitus (5th century B.C.) were outstanding examples.

Argus (är′gus). In Greek mythology, a son of Niobe and Zeus. He reigned in the Peloponnesus and named it Argos after himself. His great grandson, the son of Agenor, who bore the same name and was called Argus Panoptes (*All-seeing*), had a hundred eyes placed all over his body. No matter how many of his eyes were resting, two were always awake. He killed a bull that was ravaging Arcadia and wore its hide. He came upon the monster Echidna while she was sleeping and killed her. It was Argus Panoptes to whom Hera had given the task of guarding Io, after the latter had been transformed into a heifer by Zeus to protect himself from the jealousy of Hera. Argus guarded Io night and day. At length Zeus sent Hermes to rescue her. Hermes beguiled Argus with many stories and songs, accompanying himself on the syrinx, until at last every one of Argus' hundred eyes fell asleep. Hermes touched them with his magic sleep-inducing wand, lest they open suddenly, and then cut off Argus' head. Hera placed the hundred eyes of Argus in the tail of the bird sacred to her, the peacock, where they make a brilliant display and perpetuate the memory of Argus.

Argus. In Greek legend, a son of Phrixus and Chalciope, and the grandson of Aeëtes, king of Colchis. He tried to persuade Aeëtes to give Jason the Golden Fleece. See **Phrontis.**

Argus. He built the *Argo* for Jason, according to tradition, and sailed in her on the quest for the Golden Fleece. His parentage and nationality are variously given.

Argus. Son of Jason and Medea. See **Alcimedes.**

Argus. In the *Odyssey*, Odysseus' hound. He recognized Odysseus when he returned to his home after an absence of twenty years, wagged his tail once, and died.

Argyra (är′ji-ra̱). A nymph of a spring of the same name in Achaea. She loved the beautiful youth Selemnus, but her love for him died when his beauty faded. See **Selemnus.**

Argyrotoxus (är″gi-rō-tok′sus). An epithet of Apollo, meaning "Lord of the Silver Bow." It was given to him because of the silver bow and arrows made for him by Hephaestus with which he punished the wicked and arrogant.

Aria (ä′ri-a̱, a̱-rī′a̱). A nymph. She was loved by Apollo and bore him a son Miletus who, according to tradition, founded the city of that name in Caria.

Ariadne (ar-i-ad′nē). In Greek mythology, a daughter of Minos, king of Crete, and Pasiphaë. She was the sister of Acacallis, Androgeus, Catreus, Glaucus, and Phaedra. When Theseus came to Crete as one of the 14 Athenian youths and maidens who were sent as tribute to Crete every nine years to be thrown to the Minotaur, Ariadne fell in love with him. She offered to help him overcome the Minotaur and to find his way out of the Labyrinth if he would promise to take her back to Athens and marry her. Theseus agreed. Ariadne gave him a ball of golden thread which she had obtained from Daedalus, the builder of the Labyrinth in which the Minotaur was housed. According to some accounts, she held the end of the thread, but others says Theseus instructed to fasten the end of it to the door post of the Labyrinth. As he penetrated the Labyrinth Theseus unwound the ball of thread. Instructed by Ariadne, he seized the Minotaur by the hair and, as some say, killed him with a sword given to him by Ariadne, and sacrificed him to Poseidon. He then found his way out of the Labyrinth by rewinding the golden thread until he came again to the entrance. Ariadne who was awaiting him led the Athenians to the ships which had been made ready, and all escaped. On the island of Naxos, where they stopped, Ariadne fell asleep. When she awoke Theseus and the Athenians had sailed away.

Some say that Dionysus appeared to Theseus in a dream and warned him to leave Ariadne, and this was what caused him to forget his promise. In any case, while Ariadne wept alone and demanded vengeance on Theseus, Dionysus came to her. He fell in love with her and married her immediately. Later he set the golden marriage crown, made by Hephaestus, among the stars. Zeus made Ariadne immortal. She bore Dionysus many children, including Oenopion, Thoas, Staphylus, Latromis, Euanthes, and Tauropolus. But some say Dionysus did not marry Ariadne. On the contrary, he asked Artemis to slay her because she had profaned his shrine with Theseus. And others say that Ariadne was put ashore at her own request and that the fleet of Theseus was blown away in a violent storm, and when Theseus returned he found Ariadne had died. Ariadne was given divine honors. Festivals were held for her at Naxos, in which women first wailed to commemorate her abandonment by Theseus, and then reveled to celebrate her marriage to Dionysus. In the palace at Crete there was an elaborate mosaic floor, said to have been laid out by Daedalus, which was made for Ariadne to dance upon.

Ariadne's Crown. See **Corona Borealis.**

Ariana (ar-i-ā′na̱, ar-i-an′a̱). In ancient geography, a region in Asia, of vague boundaries, extending from Media on the W to the Indus River on the E, and from Hyrcania and Bactriana on the N to the Persian Gulf and Arabian Sea on the S.

Aricia (a̱-rish′a̱). [Modern, **Ariccia.**] An ancient Latin town, situated in the Alban Hills, 16 miles SE of Rome. There was a grove sacred to Diana (Artemis) to which Artemis brought Hippolytus after he had been restored to life by Asclepius. The grove surrounded a lake and was itself set off by steep cliffs. In the grove was an ancient oak tree, the branches of which were sacred. If a runaway slave, fled to the grove for sanctuary, chanced to break off one of the branches of the oak then the priest of the temple of Diana was compelled to fight him, and if he was killed in the fight the slave became priest. All the priests were drawn from runaway slaves, and each priest obtained his position by killing his predecessor. In later times the temple of Diana Nemo-

fat, fāte, fär, fãre, errant; net, mē, hėr ardent; pin, pīne; not, nōte, mŏve, nôr,

rensis was one of the most famous and wealthy in Italy. The Romans also said that there was a nymph Aricia, the mother of a Virbius said to be the son of Hippolytus.

ARIES
Pictured according to ancient descriptions.

Aries (ā′ri-ēz). The first sign of the zodiac— the Ram—which the sun enters at the vernal equinox, March 21, and leaves April 20. Also, a zodiacal constellation. Owing to the precession of the equinoxes, the sign Aries has moved completely out of the constellation of the same name, and is now in the constellation Pisces.

Arimaspians (ar-i-mas′pi-anz). In classical mythology, a one-eyed people of Scythia. They were at war with the Griffins whose gold they sought.

Ariminum (ä-rim′i-num). [Modern name, **Rimini**.] In ancient geography, a town of N Italy, situated on the Adriatic Sea. It was an Umbrian, then a Gallic settlement, and became a Roman colony in 268 B.C. It was the starting point of Julius Caesar in the civil war of 49 B.C. As the terminus of the Via Flaminia which, coming from Rome, here reached the Adriatic Sea, and of the Via Aemilia, it was of great military importance, and long dominated communications between Rome and upper Italy. Among the Roman antiquities are an amphitheater, triumphal arch, and the marble bridge of Augustus across the Marecchia River. The bridge is one of the most perfect of ancient bridges.

Arimnestus (ar-im-nēs′tus). Plataean general who commanded the Plataeans at the battles of Marathon (490 B.C.) and Plataea (479 B.C.). According to tradition, before the battle of Plataea the Greeks were in some doubt as to whether they should withdraw their forces to Attica, in obedience to an oracle of Delphi that seemed to command it. Arimnestus was visited by Zeus in a dream. The god told him the Greeks had misinterpreted the oracle, for the precinct of Eleusinian Demeter where the oracle told them to fight was at Plataea, not at Eleusis as the Greeks thought. When Arimnestus awoke he called the elders to him and told them of the dream. They searched for a sanctuary of Eleusinian Demeter, and at last found a very ancient one nearby, near Hysiae, at the foot of Mount Cithaeron. This site they found well adapted for battle, and thanks to the dream of Arimnestus, some say, the Greeks remained and defeated the Persians at Plataea.

Ariobarzanes (ar″i-ọ-bär-zā′nēz). Soldier and satrap of the Persian empire who, after the battle of Gaugamela (331 B.C.), secured the pass through the so-called Persian Gates. Alexander the Great was able to force the pass and continue to the east only by stratagem.

Ariobarzanes I (of *Cappadocia*). [Also: **Ariobarzanes I Philoromaeus**.] King of Cappadocia; fl. about the beginning of the 1st century B.C. He was several times expelled by Mithridates VI of Pontus and restored by the Romans.

Ariobarzanes II (of *Cappadocia*). [Also: **Ariobarzanes II Philopator**.] King of Cappadocia, son of Ariobarzanes I, whom he succeeded c63 B.C.

Ariobarzanes III (of *Cappadocia*). [Also: **Ariobarzanes III Eusebes, Ariobarzanes III Philoromaeus**.] King of Cappadocia; died 42 B.C. He was a son of Ariobarzanes II, whom he succeeded c51 B.C. He aided Pompey against Julius Caesar in the civil war but was pardoned by Caesar. He was put to death by Cassius.

Ariobarzanes I (of *Pontus*). Satrap of Pontus; fl. 5th century B.C. He was the father of Mithridates I of Pontus.

Ariobarzanes II (of *Pontus*). King of Pontus (363–337 B.C.); son and successor of Mithridates I of Pontus. He revolted (362 B.C.) against Artaxerxes II of Persia, and founded the independent kingdom of Pontus.

Ariobarzanes III (of *Pontus*). King of Pontus

(266–c240 B.C.); son of Mithridates III of Pontus.

Arion (a̯-rī′on). A reputed son of Poseidon and the nymph Oneaea, but more likely the son of Cycleus, of Methymna in Lesbos. He was a skilled musician from Lesbos (fl. 628–625 B.C.). He journeyed from Corinth to Taenarus in Sicily and there won such great riches for his playing on the lyre that it is said the sailors on the ship bearing him home decided to kill him and steal his treasure. He asked to be allowed to sing one song before death, and sang so beautifully that dolphins gathered around the ship to listen. On finishing his song he leaped into the sea. A dolphin bore him up on its back and speedily took him to Corinth, arriving there before the ship. When the sailors were questioned about Arion when they came to Corinth, they said he was still in Sicily. On being confronted with him in person they acknowledged their guilt and were put to death. Apollo is said to have placed an image of Arion and his lyre among the stars. According to legend, Arion invented the dithyramb, a choral song in honor of Dionysus, and taught it to Corinthian choruses.

Arion. In Greek legend, a fabulous horse. It was said to be the offspring of Poseidon by Demeter (or, in other accounts, Gaea or a Harpy) who to escape him had metamorphosed herself into a mare. It was successively owned by Copreus, Oncus, Heracles, and Adrastus. It possessed marvelous powers of speech, and its right feet were those of a man.

Ariovistus (ar″i-ō-vis′tus). Germanic leader, active from c71–58 B.C. He was a chief of the Suevi, who crossed the Rhenus (Rhine) and invaded Gaul c71 B.C. to aid the Sequani, conquering the Aedui in 61 B.C. He was made an ally of Rome by Julius Caesar, but on an appeal by the Gauls Caesar engaged him in battle at Vesontio (now Besançon, France) and finally defeated him near what is now Mulhouse, France, in 58 B.C.

Arisbe (a̯-ris′bē). In Greek legend, a daughter of Merops, the seer. She was the first wife of Priam, king of Troy, and bore him a son, Aesacus. After the birth of Aesacus Priam gave Arisbe to Hyrtacus as his wife, and she was the mother by him of Asius and

Nisus. She lived outside Troy on the slopes of Mount Ida. Helenus, a son of Priam and Hecuba, left Troy after the death of Paris and went to the town in the Troad named for Arisbe.

Arisbe. According to some accounts, the daughter of Teucer and the wife of Dardanus. She came from Crete and, some say, she gave her name to the town of Arisbe in the Troad. Others say the town was named for the first wife of Priam, and some say the name of the wife of Dardanus was Batia.

Aristaeum (ar-is-tē′um). In ancient geography, a city near Mount Haemus, in Thrace. It was said to have been founded by Aristaeus during his travels about the earth, and after founding this last city he disappeared.

Aristaeus (ar-is-tē′us). In Greek mythology, a son of Apollo and Cyrene. He was born in Cyrene, whither his mother had been brought by Apollo, and was reared by nymphs who taught him how to make cheese, to build beehives, and to raise the cultivated olive. From Libya he went to Boeotia, where Apollo took him to Chiron's cave in order that he might be instructed in the Mysteries. The Muses taught him the arts of healing and of prophecy and when he had grown to manhood they married him to Autonoë, by whom he became the father of Actaeon and Macris, the nymph who cared for the infant Dionysus. Instructed by the Delphic oracle to visit Ceos, he immediately sailed to that island and found it suffering from a plague. This plague was caused by the Dog Star because the murderers of that Icarius who was the first to make wine were hiding among the Ceans and had not been punished. Aristaeus lifted the plague by raising altars to Zeus, on which he offered sacrifices, and by finding and slaying the murderers of Icarius. Ever after this Zeus caused the cooling summer winds to blow on Greece and the islands for forty days following the rising of the Dog Star. The islanders annually offered sacrifices to appease the Dog Star, and gave divine honors to Aristaeus in gratitude for relief from the plague. From Ceos Aristaeus went to Arcadia. In the valley of the Peneus River near Tempe he came on Eurydice, wife of Orpheus. He attempted to ravish her and she fled. In so doing she stepped on a ser-

fat, fāte, fär, fāre, errant; net, mē, hėr ardent; pin, pīne; not, nōte, mŏve, nôr,

pent and died of its bite. Shortly afterward, all of Aristaeus' bees died. He appealed to the naiads of the Peneus River and they advised him to consult the sea-god Proteus. He caught Proteus as he slept on the island of Pharos; seized the god and held him fast through all the changes he underwent in an effort to escape from Aristaeus' clasp. At last Proteus resumed his own form and told Aristaeus his bees had died because he had caused the death of Eurydice. Aristaeus now appealed to his mother. She told him to raise altars to the dryads, companions of Eurydice, and to offer sacrifices of bulls and heifers, and to leave the animals' carcasses at the altars. After nine days Aristaeus returned; a swarm of bees rose from the decaying carcasses. He captured the swarm and put it into a hive. Later Aristaeus sailed to Sardinia and taught all he had learned from the nymphs and Muses to the inhabitants there, as he had done wherever he went. He also visited Sicily and Thrace and taught the arts of agriculture there. He founded the city of Aristaeum in Thrace and finally disappeared. As the deity who presides over hunting and herds and the domestic arts of beekeeping, wine-making, and olive-growing, he was worshiped in Thessaly, Boeotia, and various other parts of Greece, as well as in the islands, in Cyrene, Thrace, Sicily, and Sardinia.

Aristagoras (ar-is-tag'ō-ras). Tyrant of Miletus (fl. c500 B.C.). He was the nephew and son-in-law of Histiaeus, former tyrant of Miletus who was, under the guise of friendship, kept a virtual prisoner at the court of Darius at Susa. Aristagoras thought to enrich himself by restoring some exiled leaders to Naxos, and secured the aid of the Persian satrap for this venture by proposing to him the conquest of the Cyclades and Euboea, with the capture of Naxos as the first step in this program. He assured the Persian that such a conquest would be easy and on gaining the consent of Darius for his expedition, he set out at its head to carry through his purpose. But the expedition was a complete failure. On the way Aristagoras quarreled with the Persian admiral who was sent to help him, and as a result of the quarrel the admiral warned the Naxians of the coming attack. Thus forewarned, they made preparations and were able to withstand Aristagoras and his forces. After four months of an expensive and useless siege he was compelled to retire. Rather than winning the island and the plaudits of the Persians he had wasted their money, and incurred the distrust of the Persian satrap and the enmity of the Persian admiral. To recoup his fortunes he resolved to foment a revolt of the Ionian cities which were already seething with unrest under the tyrants the Persians had placed over them. At this point, according to Herodotus, a messenger came to him from his uncle Histiaeus in Susa. The only message he bore was a request that the courier's head be shaved. Aristagoras did so, and on the messenger's scalp was pricked a command from Histiaeus to raise revolt in Ionia. This fitted in with the plans of Aristagoras to save himself from the wrath of the Persians because of the failure of the Naxian venture. He stirred the Ionians to revolt, and to make them the more eager to throw off the Persian yoke he called on the cities to throw off their tyrants, and he himself stepped down as tyrant of Miletus. He journeyed to Sparta to ask the help of Cleomenes. He showed Cleomenes a map of the world engraved on bronze, the first map Cleomenes had ever seen, and pointed out to him the rich Persian empire it would be so easy for him to conquer. But when Cleomenes asked him how long a journey it was from Ionia to Susa and heard that it was three months, he told Aristagoras to quit Sparta before sunset. Aristagoras did not give up. He returned as a suppliant to Cleomenes' house and attempted to bribe him. As Herodotus tells the story, Cleomenes listened as Aristagoras raised the bribe from ten to 50 talents. At that point the nine-year-old daughter of Cleomenes appealed to her father to send the stranger away before he was corrupted, and so Aristagoras lost again. He went next to Athens and Eretria, where he was more successful and won some support. But Aristagoras had neither the courage nor the ability to weld the Ionians into a united fighting force. The Persians gathered their forces and began to win systematically. In the face of their successes Aristagoras gathered his leaders together and discussed with them whether it would be

actor; up, lūte, pull; oi, oil; ou, out; ŦH, then; ḍ as d or j, ş as s or sh, ṭ as t or ch, ẓ as z or zh.

wise to flee to Sardinia and establish a colony there, or to carry on his operations in Thrace. In the end he went to Thrace and was killed while besieging a city there (497 B.C.).

Aristarchus of Samos (ar-is-tär′kus; sā′mos). [Also: **Aristarchos.**] Greek astronomer and mathematician of the Alexandrian school; fl. c280–264 B.C. According to Archimedes, he was the first to maintain the heliocentric theory of the universe and the rotation of the earth on its axis. In order to reconcile the apparent immobility of the fixed stars with the revolution of the earth around the sun, he assumed that the sphere of the fixed stars was incomparably greater than that containing the earth's orbit. That is, the universe conceived by him was incomparably greater than that conceived by his predecessors. In his only extant treatise, *On the Sizes and Distances of the Sun and Moon,* he gave a scientific method to make these measurements. His results were grossly inaccurate, but the method was sound. This treatise is also of great mathematical interest because it contains the calculation of ratios which are in fact trigonometrical ratios. The discovery of an improved sun dial (a concave hemispherical surface with a gnomon in the center) was ascribed to him. He also wrote on vision, light, and colors.

Aristarchus of Samothrace (sam′ō-thrās). [Also: **Aristarchos;** called **Coryphaeus of Grammarians.**] Greek grammarian and critic; fl. at Alexandria, c217–c145 B.C.; died on Cyprus. He was a leading Homeric scholar of antiquity, now considered to have been one of the greatest philologists of the ancient world. A student of the school of Aristophanes of Byzantium, and the successor (c153 B.C.) of Apollonius as librarian at Alexandria, he was the founder of a school of philology known as Aristarcheans. A prolific commentator on and editor of Hesiod, Pindar, Aeschylus, Sophocles, and other Greeks, his version of the Homeric language and the arrangement into 24 books of the *Iliad* and *Odyssey* is a basis of many modern texts.

Aristarchus of Tegea (tē′jē-a). Greek tragic poet of Tegea; contemporary of Euripides (c480–406 B.C.). He is said to have written 70 tragedies, of which the titles of two survive.

Ariste (ar-is′tē). An epithet of Artemis, meaning "Best." Wooden images of Artemis Ariste stood on the road to the Academy near Athens.

Aristeas (a-ris′tē-as). [Sometimes called the **Wandering Jew.**] Greek poet, assigned to various periods, from the 6th century B.C. to the time of Homer. The accounts of his life are legendary; he is represented as a magician who rose after death, and whose soul could occupy or abandon his body at will. It is said that he dropped dead one day in a fuller's shop in Proconnesus. The fuller shut up his shop and went to gather the relatives of Aristeas. On their way to the shop to recover his body, they were met by a man who assured them that the poet was not dead, that he had just met him on the road to Cyzicus and spoken with him. The fuller was equally positive that Aristeas had died in his shop and the party proceeded there. When they arrived Aristeas had vanished. Seven years later he reappeared in Proconnesus and it was then, inspired by Apollo, that he was reputed to have written the epic poem *Arimaspea,* in three books, which described the one-eyed Arimaspi and contained revelations about the Hyperboreans and the gold-guarding Griffins. The information on these subjects, he claimed, was revealed to him while he was in a trance. After this Aristeas disappeared a second time. He turned up at Metapontum in Sicily and commanded the inhabitants to set up an altar to Apollo because, he said, Apollo had visited Metapontum alone of all the Italian cities, and he, Aristeas, had accompanied the god, in the form of a crow. Therefore, the Metapontines should set up a statue of Aristeas of Proconnesus near the altar of Apollo. Having said this, Aristeas vanished. The Metapontines, on the advice of the oracle of Delphi, carried out his instructions.

Aristeas or **Aristaeos.** [Surnamed **the Elder.**] Greek mathematician; fl. about the end of the 4th century B.C. He collaborated with Euclid in the composition of the "treasury of analysis," a geometrical method for advanced students. He wrote on the "comparison of the five figures" (i.e., the five regular solids) and proved that "the same circle circumscribes both the pentagon of the dodecahedron and the triangle of the icosahedron when both solids are inscribed in the same sphere." He also wrote five books of solid loci connected with the conics (that is, a treatise on conics regarded as loci). This treatise is now usually considered by historians of science to be more important and more original than the one written later by Euclid on the same subject, although its object and point of view were different. Aristeas called the conics, respectively, sections of right-angled, acute-angled, and obtuse-angled cones, and he discussed the three-line and four-line locus.

Aristias (a̱-ris'ti-a̱s). Greek tragic poet; son of Pratinas and a younger contemporary of Aeschylus (525–456 B.C.).

Aristides (ar-is-tī'dēz). [Also: **Aristeides**; surnamed **the Just.**] Athenian statesman and general, born c530 B.C.; died probably at Athens, c468 B.C. He was the son of Lysimachus, a man of modest circumstances of the tribe of Antiochus in Athens. As a great admirer of Lycurgus the Spartan lawgiver and, after the expulsion of the Pisistratidae from Athens, a particular friend of Clisthenes, grandson of the tryant of Sicyon, he had a leaning toward aristocracy. A conservative and an advocate of Athens as a land power, he was continually opposed by Themistocles. Some say they had been rivals from boyhood. He came to oppose Themistocles almost as a matter of principle for, he said, the good of Athens. He was aware that he made this a practice. Once he successfully opposed Themistocles in a matter that was really advantageous to the public, and remarked, "The affairs of the Athenians will never prosper unless they throw Themistocles and myself in the Barathron (a deep pit into which condemned persons were hurled)." He was appointed public treasurer and found that the public funds had been mishandled, especially by Themistocles. The latter raised a hue and cry against him and, some say, would have had him condemned but the court (the Areopagus) was so aroused that they not only caused the charge to be dropped but got Aristides reëlected chief treasurer. Aristides now pretended he had been too strict and closed his eyes, apparently, to those who pilfered the public money. Those who profited thereby praised him and urged that he be reëlected. He now came

before the people and said that when, as an honest man, he did right and looked out for their interests, he was abused and condemned, but when he let robbers steal the public monies he was praised. He added, "I am more ashamed of the present honor than I was of the former disgrace, and it is with indignation and concern that I see you esteem it more meritorious to oblige bad men than to take proper care of the public revenue."

Aristides was one of the ten generals sent by the Athenians to repel the Persians at Marathon (490 B.C.), and there fought with valor. The practice, some say, was to rotate the command among the ten generals, so that each commanded a day in turn. Some say that realizing the ability of Miltiades, when his day came to command Aristides voluntarily yielded it to Miltiades, and by his example caused the other generals to do the same.

He was chosen archon eponymus in 489 B.C. The people admired him most for his justice, and gave him the name "the Just." This name made him first loved, and then envied. Because he was so much in demand as a mediator, Themistocles accused him of usurping judicial power and sought to have him ostracized. (Ostracism was a means of removing from the city, for a stated time, any man who seemed to be becoming too powerful or who appeared capable of causing disorder in the state; it was not a punishment for crimes. According to the system, 6000 votes must be cast or the total voting was void. Of the 6000, the man whose name was written on the greatest number of *ostraka*—a tile or broken piece of pottery—was banished for ten years.) When the day for voting arrived, Aristides was in the marketplace where the votes were cast and counted. An illiterate citizen, unaware who he was, approached him and asked him to write the name Aristides on his *ostrakon*. He was asked whether Aristides had ever injured him in any way. "No," said the citizen, "I don't even know him, but I'm tired of hearing everyone call him 'the Just'." Aristides made no reply, but took the shell and wrote his own name on it as requested. He received the most votes and was banished (483 B.C.). A number of *ostraka* inscribed with Aristides' name, ballots used in this voting, have been found in the Agora excavations.

Themistocles also wished him banished because Aristides did not agree with his policy of building up the Athenian fleet. When he was leaving Athens he prayed that the people of his state would never see the day when they would be forced to remember him. When Xerxes marched into Greece (480 B.C.) all who had been banished by ostracism were recalled. Aristides did all he could to encourage resistance to the Persians, contrary to the fears of some who thought that since he had been ill-treated by the Athenians he might go over to the Persians. After the burning of Athens the Greek forces withdrew to Salamis. There Themistocles wished them to make a fight with their fleet, as the advantage in the narrow strait would lie with the Greek ships, as against the Persian ships. But the Spartans wished to withdraw to the isthmus and make a stand there. While they debated the Persians surrounded Salamis. Aristides, at great peril, sailed through the Persian fleet to Salamis and called Themistocles from the council. He urged that they forget their personal quarrel in the face of the common danger and told him there was now no question of withdrawing to the isthmus, as the Greeks were surrounded. In the battle that followed, he took a force to the island of Psyttalia and wiped out the Persian garrison there. After the Greek success at Salamis (480 B.C.) he opposed sailing to the Hellespont to cut off the Persian retreat. On the contrary, he was eager to carry the war against the enemy vigorously to the end that the Persians would the sooner be driven out of Greece, rather than to destroy their means of exit and force them to ravage Greece. Xerxes left at once to return to Persia. Mardonius was left in command of a vast land force of Persians and their allies. He sought to separate the Athenians from their allies by bribes. The Spartans heard of this and sent urgent envoys to Athens, offering in their turn what amounted to bribes if the Athenians would stay in the war and help them to resist the Persians. Aristides was grieved that the Spartans would think the Athenians capable of such deeds.

To their envoys he said, "The people of Athens would not, for all the gold either above or under the ground, barter the liberties of Greece." As for the envoys of Mardonius, he pointed to the sun and said, "As long as this luminary shines, so long will the Athenians carry on war with the Persians, for their country which has been laid waste and for their temples which have been profaned and burned."

At the battle of Plataea (479 B.C.), he commanded 8000 Athenian foot soldiers. In drawing up the battle line both the Tegeans and the Athenians claimed the honor of the left wing and hot words were uttered by both in defense of their claims. Aristides addressed Pausanias, the Spartan general in command, "The post neither gives valor nor takes it away, and whatever post you assign us, we will endeavor to do honor to it, and take care to reflect no disgrace upon our former achievements. For we are come hither not to quarrel with our allies, but to fight with our enemies." His words restored calm and Pausanias awarded the left wing to the Athenians. After Plataea, he was a commander at Byzantium (c479 B.C.) and succeeded Pausanias as admiral after the Ionian revolt. After the Persian war he won the friendship and support of the Greek allies of Athens through his mildness and fair treatment. He was sent to assess the tax that the members must pay to support the Delian League, and won the gratitude of all by the fairness of his assessments. He drew up the articles of alliance between the Greek states, and confirmed them for Athens with an oath. But he yielded to expediency later on the occasion of transferring the treasure of the League from Delos to Athens, though this was contrary to the treaties. In agreeing to the change he said, "It is not just, but it is expedient."

To the end of his days he enjoyed honor and though he wielded vast power, especially in financial matters, he spent his life in relative poverty. The circumstances and whereabouts of his death are obscure. A monument was erected to him at the public expense at Phalerum. Athens continued to honor him by giving dowries for his two daughters and a sum of money, a pension, and land to his son. He was noted for his

fat, fāte, fär, fãre, errant; net, mē, hėr ardent; pin, pīne; not, nōte, möve, nôr,

moderation, his steady service to the state, and for his justice. He was neither elated with honors nor unduly cast down by failures. He refused to seek support by granting favors, and he treated his enemies with justice. Once, it is said, he prosecuted a man and the judges, influenced because it was Aristides who prosecuted, were about to pass sentence without giving the accused a hearing. Aristides sprang up and insisted that he be heard before sentence was passed. Another time he was the mediator between two citizens. One of them sought to influence him by saying the other had done many injuries to Aristides. He replied, "Don't speak of that, but tell me what injury he has done you, for it is your cause that I am judging, not my own." The following verses are from *The Seven Against Thebes*, the tragedy by Aeschylus:

"To be and not to seem, is this man's choice;
Reaping the fruits that in a rich mind grow,
Whence sage advice and noble actions flow."

When they were recited upon the stage everyone in the audience looked at Aristides as being the man whose reputation for justice and service best exemplified the sentiments of the verses. According to Plutarch, "Plato, among all that were accounted great and illustrious men in Athens, judges none but Aristides worthy of real esteem."

Aristides of Miletus. [Also: **Aristeides.**] Greek writer; fl. c150–100 B.C. He was the author of the *Milesiaca* or *Milesian Tales*, so-named because of their setting, considered to have been the first Greek prose romance. Translated into the Latin, these stories were especially admired by the Romans.

Aristides of Thebes. [Also: **Aristeides.**] Greek painter; fl. 4th century B.C. He did battle scenes, hunting scenes, and other works, prized by Alexander and others for their expression of the mind and passions of man. His most famous painting represented a conquered city. In it a mother, dying, thrusts back the infant who seeks her breast, to prevent the child from sucking blood.

Aristides, Publius Aelius. [Also: **Aristeides;** surnamed **Theodorus.**] Greek rhetorician; born in Mysia, Asia Minor, c120 A.D.; died at Smyrna, c180 A.D. He was the author of treatises on speech, declamations, sacred discourses and others, used as models of Attic style. He traveled widely in Asia, Egypt, Greece, and Italy. Felled by a sickness that lasted 13 years, he continued his studies, and fashioned his rhetoric on that of Demosthenes and Plato. He was greatly admired in his lifetime, and so impressed Marcus Aurelius with his account of the destruction (178) of Smyrna by earthquake that the emperor was persuaded to rebuild the city. In addition to two treatises, 55 of his ceremonial speeches are extant. They are powerful and concise exhibitions of profound thinking, and treat of historical subjects, deities, and cities. In a series of six orations, called the Sacred Orations, he described the hints given to him while he was in a trance, by Asclepius on how to cure his long illness. He also composed eulogies on Athens, Rome, and Smyrna.

Aristides, Quintilianus. [Also: **Aristeides.**] Greek author; fl. between 3rd and 4th centuries A.D. He was the author of a treatise on music (printed in a collection in 1652), in three books. The first book treated harmony, rhythm, and meter. The second described the elevating influence of music. The third, based on Pythagorean principles, compared harmonic intervals and the harmony of the universe. The work is considered by some as the most important ancient book on the subject of music.

Aristippus (ar-is-tip′us). Greek philosopher; born at Cyrene, Africa; fl. c435–386 B.C. He was a pupil of Socrates and the founder, or the grandfather of the founder, of the Cyrenaic school, also known as the Hedonistic system. Starting with the Socratic principles of virtue and happiness, he based his ethics on the pursuit of pleasure, tempered with prudence in order to avoid pain. Little is known of his life, and it is uncertain how much of his theory actually originated with him, and how much was developed by his followers.

Aristobulus (a-ris-tō-bū′lus, ar″is-tō-). Greek historian from Cassandrea; fl. 4th century B.C. He was a companion of Alexander the Great on the Asiatic expedition. His account of Alexander's campaigns was later used by Plutarch, Arrian, and others.

Aristocrates (ar-is-tok′ra̲-tēz). According to Greek tradition, a son of Aechmis, king of Arcadia. On the border of Orchomenus, near Mantinea in Arcadia, was a temple of Artemis Hymnia, the priestess of which was a virgin. Aristocrates violated the priestess, and when his deed was discovered he was stoned to death. After this, the priestess of the temple had to be an old woman, rather than a young virgin. The grandson of Aristocrates, Aristocrates the second, was also stoned to death because the Arcadians discovered that he had accepted bribes from the Lacedaemonians to betray Messenia, the ally of Arcadia.

Aristodemus (a̲-ris-tō̲-dē′mus). According to tradition, a son of Aristomachus, and the brother of Cresphontes and Temenus. He was a descendant of Hyllus, son of Heracles. He was the father and founder of the two royal Spartan houses. The wife of Aristodemus was Argeia, a descendant of Polynices, son of Oedipus. Shortly after she bore Aristodemus twin sons he died. The Lacedaemonians wished to make the elder of the twins king in his father's place, but didn't know which was the elder. Their mother claimed she didn't know which of them was the first-born herself, although, according to Herodotus, she knew perfectly well but hoped that both might become kings. The Lacedaemonians sent to the oracle to inquire what they should do. The priestess instructed them to make both boys kings, but to show greater honor to the elder. This left the Spartans about where they were before, still ignorant of which was the elder. At length it was suggested to them that they set a watch on Argeia, to observe whether she habitually bathed, fed, and tended one of her sons first, or whether she varied, sometimes taking the one and sometimes the other first. The Spartans acted on this suggestion, and observed that she did in fact always tend to the same one first. Since this child was the one more honored by his mother the Spartans concluded he was the first-born and gave him the most honor also. The twins were Eurysthenes, the elder, and Procles, and from them sprang the two royal houses of Sparta. They ruled as co-kings, and there was always great enmity between them. According to the Spartans themselves, Aristodemus led them into the land, later known as Lacedaemonia, after he had drawn it in the lots by which he and his brothers divided up the Peloponnesus. Some say, however, that he was shot by Apollo because he failed to visit the oracle at Delphi, or that he was murdered by the sons of Pylades and Electra, and that in the division of the Peloponnesus a representative drew his lot on behalf of his sons. Still others say he was killed by a stroke of lightning at Naupactus just as he was about to sail with the Dorians for the invasion of the Peloponnesus. In any case, his sons inherited his share, which was Sparta.

Aristodemus. Messenian king, 8th century B.C. (c731–724 B.C.), and traditional hero of the First Messenian war with Sparta which, according to tradition, lasted 20 years and ended 724 B.C. An oracle told the Messenians they would be successful if a father willingly sacrificed his virgin daughter. Aristodemus offered his daughter, but she was betrothed, and her young prospective husband, wild with grief at the thought of losing her, first claimed Aristodemus no longer had authority to offer her up for Messenia. Since she was to be his wife he alone could make such a decision. His claim being denied he then declared that she was not a virgin but was about to become a mother. Aristodemus was enraged at this accusation; he killed his daughter and opened her body to prove that she was not pregnant. His impious rage offended the gods, and her death did not satisfy the oracles. Grief-stricken in his turn, Aristodemus was haunted by evil dreams, despaired of defeating the Spartans, and at length committed suicide on his daughter's tomb.

Aristomachus (ar-is-tom′a̲-kus). In Greek legend, the father of Hippomedon of Argos who was one of the Seven against Thebes.

Aristomenes (ar-is-tom′ē̲-nēz). Messenian national hero of the Second War against Sparta, which took place in the first half of the 7th century B.C. He was the son of Nicomedes, or, as some say, of a god who assumed the shape of a serpent when he embraced Aristomenes' mother. In the years following the end of the First Messenian War against Sparta, Aristomenes urged the defeated Messenians to revolt, with such success that they

fat, fāte, fär, fâre, errant; net, mē, hėr ardent; pin, pīne; not, nōte, mȯve, nôr, gathered a force and waged war on Sparta. Aristomenes, noted for his daring, went secretly at night to the temple of Athena of the Bronze House, in Sparta, and fixed thereon a shield. This shield, a goad to the Spartans, was inscribed that it was a gift to the goddess from Aristomenes, and was a shield he had taken from the Spartans. In the battle which the Spartans waged against the Messenians Aristomenes fought like a whirlwind and threw the Spartans into such confusion that they broke and fled. Before the battle Aristomenes was warned by a seer not to pass a certain pear tree where the Dioscuri, protectors of Sparta, were sitting. In his ardor to pursue the Spartans he forgot the seer's warning and lost his shield for disobeying the seer. While he looked for it the Spartans escaped. Later he recovered his shield and took it to Lebadia, where he dedicated it at the shrine of Trophonius. When he returned to Messenia he was received with the wildest acclaim. He made a successful cattle raid on Laconia, and though wounded drove the stolen cattle back to Messenia, but when he made an attack on Sparta at night he was deterred by the appearance of Helen and the Dioscuri. In the continuing war, he was taken prisoner in a sanctuary but escaped during the night. The Arcadians were allies of the Messenians, but Aristocrates, their leader, accepted a bribe to betray the Messenians. In the midst of a battle Aristocrates, without letting his people know he had been bribed, ordered his men to retreat. He led them through the thick of the battling Messenian forces, throwing them into utter confusion, so that the Spartans cut them to pieces. Aristomenes collected the survivors and took them to Mount Eira. There they withstood siege for 11 years, plundering the countryside to maintain themselves. In a sharp engagement with the Spartans Aristomenes was struck on the head by a stone, and while stunned was set upon by the enemy and taken prisoner with about 50 of his followers. The Spartans resolved to kill them all by hurling them into a jagged chasm that had no outlet, but when Aristomenes was hurled forth an eagle swooped down and rescued him, and deposited him unharmed in the bottom of the pit. As he could not escape he prepared himself for death, but soon observed a fox scavenging on the dead bodies of his comrades who had been cast into the pit. Aristomenes realized that there must be some entrance to the pit by which the fox had come in. He seized the animal and followed it to a hole just large enough for the fox, but he enlarged it, escaped, and returned to Mount Eira and resumed his command of the Messenians. He attacked and slew a force of Corinthians on their way to the aid of Sparta, and the Spartans asked for a truce. During the truce Aristomenes was careless and was seized by some Cretan archers in Spartan employ. They were elated with his capture and sent messengers to tell the Spartans, while they took their captive to a farmhouse for safe-keeping. But there he was freed by a maiden of the house, in accordance with a dream she had had. He gave her to his son for a wife. An oracle now foretold the destruction of Messenia. According to the oracle, when a he-goat drank of the waters of the Neda, Messenia would fall. The seer who related this oracle to Aristomenes, in secret, said that a wild fig tree which grew on the banks of the Neda was now leaning over the bank to such an extent that its branches were in the water. The Messenians used the same word for the fig tree as for he-goat and Aristomenes realized that the end was at hand, but did not tell the Messenians. He took certain secret things and buried them in a secret place at Ithome, calling on Zeus as he did so to honor the pledge, for an oracle had said that if these things were preserved the Messenians would recover their country. After this he exhorted his followers to defend themselves on the acropolis at Mount Eira. But their citadel was betrayed by an adulterous woman. In a violent storm the Spartans attacked with ladders, and the Messenians could not hold out much longer. The seer who knew of the oracles told Aristomenes to lead out as many Messenians as he could, and to save them and himself, while a few brave Messenians held up the Spartans to cover their retreat. Aristomenes followed his advice and took his Messenians to Arcadia. There he and his followers were cordially received, for the Arcadians had never learned that their king betrayed the Messenians for

actor; up, lūte, pŭll; oi, oil; ou, out; ŦH, then; ḏ as d or j, ş as s or sh, ţ as t or ch, ẕ as z or zh.

money. Now he prepared to betray them again, but was discovered and stoned to death by the Arcadians themselves. Aristomenes went to Rhodes on his way to Persia, but died while at Rhodes, and was honored by a splendid tomb built for him by the Rhodians.

Ariston (a-ris'ton). A descendant of Procles, son of Aristodemus, and hence of the junior branch of the royal house of Sparta. He was co-king of Sparta with Anaxandrides, in the time of Croesus. Ariston had been twice married but neither of his wives bore him any children. He now fell in love with the very beautiful wife of his most intimate friend. This woman had once been as ugly as she was now beautiful. Her parents commanded her nurse to take her every day to the temple of Helen at Therapne and beg the goddess to take away the child's ugliness. One day as the nurse was leaving the temple a woman came to her and asked to see the child. At first the nurse refused as she had been ordered to do by the child's parents, but at last yielded. The stranger looked at the little girl and prophesied that one day she would be the most beautiful woman in Sparta. From that day, the child's appearance began to change. She grew up to be a beautiful woman and married Agetus, the friend of Ariston. Ariston resolved to win her from her husband. He proposed to his friend that each give as a gift to the other whatever his friend most desired of all his possessions. Agetus agreed. He made his request and received what he had asked for. Ariston now asked for the wife of Agetus. Agetus was thunderstruck, but as he had given his oath he was compelled to give up his wife. Ariston now put aside his second wife and took the wife of Agetus. After a time she bore a son, Demaratus. See **Demaratus.**

Ariston or **Aristo** (-tō). Greek Stoic philosopher; born on the island of Chios in the Aegean Sea; died c250 B.C. He was a disciple of Zeno and later, according to Diogenes Laertius, of the Platonist Polemo. Of the various branches of philosophy he recognized only ethics as a legitimate study.

Aristophanes (ar-is-tof'a-nēz). Athenian writer of Greek comedies; born between c450 and 446 B.C.; died c385 B.C. Out of the buf-foonery of Greek comic plays Aristophanes created an artistic comedy. A conservative and a passionate believer in the good old days of Marathon, he attacked with triumphant vigor "progressive" education (Socrates), new ideas in philosophy (the Sophists), melodrama, rhetorical claptrap, and bizarre musical innovations in contemporary tragedy (Euripides), and above all demagoguery and corruption in politics (Cleon and Hyperbolus). His criticism of the tragedies of Aeschylus and Euripides in *The Frogs* is the earliest piece of literary criticism in existence. His comedies are characterized by a wealth of imagination, a freshness of wit, a pungency of satire, and bursts of pure lyric poetry that can be found in no other comedies except perhaps those of Shakespeare. He took the role of public critic seriously, and his political satire was so effective that he was awarded by the Athenian state a crown of wild olive for the good advice he had given the city. Because his work often dealt with satire of current events some of it is obscure to a later age; at the same time, passages of rollicking humor, brilliant wit, and eloquent poetry are timeless. According to Gilbert Murray (*The Literature of Ancient Greece*), "His most characteristic quality, perhaps, is his combination of the wildest and broadest farce on the one hand, with the most exquisite lyric beauty on the other." Of his many comedies these 11 survive: *The Acharnians* (425 B.C.), *The Knights* (424), *The Clouds* (423), *The Wasps* (422), *The Peace* (421), *The Birds* (414), *Lysistrata* (411), *The Thesmophoriazusae* (411), *The Frogs* (405), *The Ecclesiazusae* (391), and *The Plutus* (388 B.C.). Of these plays, *The Acharnians, The Birds,* and *Lysistrata,* as well as the lost *Babylonians,* were produced under the name of Callistratus, and *The Wasps* and *The Frogs* under the name of Philonides. The titles of at least 20 lost plays are recorded, and hundreds of fragments survive as quotations in later writers.

Aristophanes of Byzantium. Greek grammarian, critic, and lexicographer; born c257 B.C.; died c180. He is now considered to have been perhaps the greatest philologist of the ancient world. He went to Alexandria in his youth and succeeded Eratosthenes as librarian of the Alexandria museum (c194 B.C.). A pupil of Zenodotus and Callimachus, he was one of the Alexandrian scholars from whom our traditional explanation of Homer is derived, and was an instructor of Aristarchus of Samothrace, who succeeded him as the leading Homeric scholar of the day. Besides Homer, he edited Hesiod, Alcaeus, Anacreon, Pindar, Plato, and the Greek dramatists, wrote commentaries on Aristophanes (the playwright) and on Callimachus' literary history *(Pinakes),* compiled word lists, and introduced diacritical marks in an effort to systematize the pronunciation and accentuation of Greek. The invention of punctuation is sometimes ascribed to Aristophanes, but systematization is perhaps a more exact description of his contribution.

Aristotle (ar'is-tot-l). [Sometimes called **the Stagirite.**] Greek philosopher, one of the greatest thinkers of antiquity, and a continuing influence on philosophic speculation; born at Stagira (whence the name above), on the NW Aegean coast, 384 B.C.; died at Chalcis, in Euboea, 322 B.C. He was the son of Nicomachus, the personal physician of Amyntas II of Macedonia, and probably spent part of his childhood at the Macedonian court. When he was 17 he went to Athens and attended the Academy of Plato where he remained until Plato's death. He then went to Assus as the guest (348–347 B.C.) of Hermias, the ruler of Atarneus and Assus, and married Hermias' niece, Pythias. After the death of Hermias in 345 B.C., he went to Mytilene, and there carried on zoological studies. In 343–342 B.C. Philip of Macedonia invited him to Pella to act as the tutor of his son, Alexander. In 335 B.C., after Philip's death, he returned to Athens and founded outside the city a school which took its name (the Peripatetic School) from a covered court, or *peripatos,* in the garden of the school. The school had a communal life and an extensive library, and was a center of research in every field of contemporary knowledge. When Alexander died there was an outbreak of feeling against the Macedonians, and Aristotle was charged with impiety. He left Athens and went to Chalcis, and there died in 322 B.C. of a digestive disease.

Written Works. His works were of three kinds: 1) early writings published by himself, mostly in the form of Platonic dialogues, and Platonic in spirit, which survive only in fragments, e.g. the *Protrepticus;* 2) later didactic works in which he moved away from Platonism towards his more mature views, and which also survive only in fragments, e.g. the *Theodectea;* and 3) the works of his maturity, many of which still survive. The body of surviving works accredited to him does contain some which are spurious, but for the most part the works are genuine. The extant writings may be conveniently divided into the classes used by the ancient editors: 1) the *Organon,* or group of writings on logic, which includes the *Prior* and *Posterior Analytics;* 2) the works on natural science which include the *Physics, On the Soul,* and the *History of Animals;* 3) miscellaneous writings, which include the *Problems;* 4) the work on primary philosophy, called the *Metaphysics;* 5) the works on moral philosophy, which include the *Nicomachean Ethics* and the *Politics;* and 6) the works on art, the *Rhetoric* and the *Poetics.* To these must be added one historical work, the *Constitution of Athens,* written on papyrus and discovered in Egypt in the latter part of the 19th century.

Influence as Philosopher. Aristotle has been the philosopher *par excellence* of the western world, and his influence is still significant. He was primarily a philosopher of moderation and common sense. In metaphysics he believed in both matter and mind, in both the natural and the supernatural. In ethics he believed in both physical wellbeing and spiritual contemplation. In political theory he advocated constitutional government and rule by the middle class. Aristotle's philosophy is an inspired common sense governed by a critical insight into the meaning of human experience.

Aristotle and the History of Science. Aristotle was one of the founders of the inductive method. He was the first to conceive the idea of organized research, and himself contributed considerably to the organization of science by his systematic survey and classification of the knowledge of his time. He took pains to make as clear as possible the fundamental principles of each science in particular, and of science in general. He may be called the founder of logic, and his systematization of it in the *Organon* was so masterful that it still dominates much of the teaching of today. He prepared the systematization of geometry by his investigations of its more fundamental and philosophical aspect, in particular by his introduction of new or better definitions and his discussion of the concepts of continuity and infinity. He completed the system of homocentric spheres of Eudoxus and Callippus, using a total of 55 spheres to account for all the celestial motions. He offered proofs of the sphericity of the earth, and attempted to estimate its size. To the four elements he added a fifth (the quintessence) called *aether,* the natural movement of which was circular. The celestial bodies are made of aether and are perfect and incorruptible (this theory stood until 1610). If the mechanical writings be genuine, Aristotle had done much profound thinking on the subject, but whether he was fundamentally right or fundamentally wrong depends entirely upon one's interpretation of his thought. He is said to have discovered the law of the lever, and that sound is transmitted by vibrations of the air. He made the first systematic study (and wrote the first textbook) of meteorology, as well as the first treatise on chemistry.

Contributions to the Natural Sciences. Aristotle carried on immense botanical, zoological, and anatomical investigations. He clearly recognized the fundamental problems of biology: sex, heredity, nutrition, growth, adaptation. He outlined both a theory of evolution *(scala naturae)* and of scientific classification of animals. He proposed theories of generation and heredity. He may be called the founder of comparative anatomy (e.g., comparative study of the womb). Many of his anatomical descriptions are admirable (e.g., reproduction of selachians, especially placental development of the dogfish, embryonic development of the chick, stomach of ruminants, and others). Some of Aristotle's errors, however, retarded scientific progress because of the uncritical acceptance of his investigations. Thus his denial of the sexuality of plants (he assimilated their reproduction to nutrition and growth) was the main cause of the enormous

delay in its discovery (Camerarius, 1694). In spite of earlier Hippocratic views, he considered the heart as the seat of intelligence, the function of the brain being then simply to cool the heart by the secretion of phlegm and to prevent its overheating. He realized that the arterial system duplicates the venous system, but failed to understand the real difference between arteries and veins; he believed that arteries contain air as well as blood. Here again Aristotle's views were the main cause of the extraordinary tardiness of the discovery of the circulation of the blood (Harvey, 1628).

Other Contributions and Summary. He attempted an inductive study of politics, and wrote a history and critical account of Greek constitutional law. One of the modern definitions of psychology as "the positive science of the behavior of living things" is a return to the standpoint of Aristotle. His theory of dreams was far more rational than that of Democritus (he tried to explain them by the persistence of sense impressions, having observed the exaggerated excitement caused by slight stimuli if they interrupt a dream). Aristotle's influence, for good or evil, in every department of knowledge, was so tremendous that a good history of Aristotelianism would include a large part of the history of science and thought down to the 18th century. The prodigious activity of Aristotle marks the climax of the golden age of Greece. The very existence of his works proves not simply that he had an encyclopedic mind of the highest order, but also that a large amount of scientific research had already been accomplished by his time. Unlike Plato's successor, Speusippus, Aristotle was not essentially a mathematician. He had a deep mathematical knowledge, but that knowledge was happily balanced by a very extensive acquaintance with every branch of natural history.

Aristoteles (ar-is-tot′ē̆-lēz) or **Aristotle.** The original name of Battus, son of Polymnestus of Thera and Phronima. See **Battus.**

Aristoxenus (ar-is-tok′sē̆-nus). Greek music theorist and philosopher of the Peripatetic School; student of Aristotle; born at Tarentum, Italy; fl. 4th century B.C. Now usually considered to have been the greatest music theoretician of ancient times, he was the founder of the school of musicians known as Aristoxeneans; his *Elements of Harmony* (of which three books are partly preserved) is of value to music historians. Author also of *Elements of Rhythm* (which exists in fragments), and of more than 430 lost works.

Arius (a̱-rī′us). [Also: **Areius**.] In Greek legend, a despot of Teuthrania. During his rule Pergamus, son of Andromache and Neoptolemus, came into his land with his mother. Pergamus killed Arius, took his city, and named it Pergamum after himself.

Arminius (är-min′i-us). [Latinized name of **Armin**; German, **Hermann**.] German chieftain of the Cherusci (near modern Hanover); born c17 B.C.; assassinated 21 A.D. He was immortalized as the liberator of the Germans from Roman rule. He entered the Roman military service in 1 A.D. and became a Roman citizen of the equestrian order, but on his return to Germany he found his people oppressed by Roman rule and secretly organized a revolt of the Cherusci. He surprised Quintilius Varus, the Roman governor, in the Teutoburgian Forest in 9 A.D. and destroyed him and three complete legions of Roman troops. The news of this disaster caused a near panic at Rome. The massacre of the three legions by Arminius forced the withdrawal of the Roman frontier from the Elbe to the Rhine. This was the worst disaster suffered by Roman arms during the rule of Augustus, and he never ceased to mourn it. Germanicus Caesar defeated him in 16 A.D., and captured his wife, but he still maintained the independence of the right bank of the Rhine. The victory of Germanicus had been so costly that he was recalled and the frontier on the Elbe was abandoned. Arminius overthrew Maroboduus, head of the Marcomanni, but was killed in a feud among rival chiefs.

Arnaeus (är′nē-us). In Homeric legend (*Odyssey*), the real name of Irus, the beggar who had the monopoly of begging in the halls of Odysseus' palace. He was given the nickname Irus, a distortion of Iris, because he was used by the suitors of Penelope as an errand boy.

Arne (är′nē). In Greek mythology, a daughter of Thea (daughter of Chiron the centaur), and Aeolus, king of Magnesia in Thessaly. Her mother was transformed into a mare by Poseidon before Arne was born, and Arne's first appearance into the world was as a foal which bore the name Melanippe. She was then transformed into an infant girl by Poseidon, and was given by Aeolus, who renamed her Arne, to Desmontes to bring up. When she grew up she was seduced by Poseidon. Desmontes, on discovering that she was about to bear a child, blinded and imprisoned her. She bore twin sons, Aeolus, who became guardian of the winds, and Boeotus, ancestor of the Boeotians. Desmontes ordered the twins exposed on Mount Pelion but they were saved by shepherds. They were given to Theano, the childless wife of Metapontus, king of Icaria, who presented them to her husband as her own children. Metapontus was delighted with them, thinking they were his own children. Later Theano bore twins of her own but Metapontus still preferred Aeolus and Boeotus. Theano now wanted to be rid of them. She advised her sons to attack them on a hunting expedition and kill them. But her scheme miscarried. Poseidon came to the aid of his sons and they killed Theano's children. Aeolus and Boeotus, on being informed by Poseidon that he was their father, were then ordered to kill Desmontes and to free their mother who was still languishing in prison. They did as commanded and were reunited with Arne whose sight was restored by Poseidon. When Metapontus learned the truth he married Arne and adopted her sons. Later he tired of her and put her aside to take a new wife. Aeolus and Boeotus took their mother's part and slew the new queen. They then fled. Arne and Boeotus went to Thessaly, to the home of her father Aeolus. He gave Boeotus part of his kingdom, which Boeotus renamed Arne in honor of his mother.

Arne. In Greek mythology, a princess of the island of Siphnus. Minos, desiring to win her friendship for his war against the Athenians, bribed her with gifts of gold and secured her aid. To punish her greed she was changed into a magpie, ever attracted by the glitter of bright things.

Arno Valley (är′nō). [Italian, **Val d'Arno**.] The fruitful valley of the upper Arno River, in N central Italy. See **Arnus**.

Arnus (är′nus). [Modern, **Arno**.] River in Tuscany, N central Italy, which rises in the

Apennines, flows S, W, NW, and then W, and empties into the Mediterranean about six miles SW of Pisae. Pisae (Pisa) and Florentia (Florence) are situated on it.

Arpi (är′pī), or **Argyripa** (är-ji′ri-pa). Named in the *Aeneid,* as a town built by Diomedes in Garganus in Apulia, after he had fled from his native Calydon on his return from the Trojan War. The town, lying near the Adriatic coast, is the site of modern Foggia.

Arpinum (är-pī′num). [Modern name, **Arpino.**] In ancient geography, a town of C Italy, situated near the Liris River, SE of Rome. The ancient town was first Volscian, then belonged to the Samnites, was taken by the Romans in the Second Samnite War, and was made a Roman ally with voting rights in 188 B.C. It was the birthplace of Marius and Cicero.

Arpoxaïs (ar-pok′sa-is). According to tradition, the second son of Targitaus, the first inhabitant of Scythia. He was the founder of the Scythian tribes known as the Catiari and the Traspians. See **Colaxaïs.**

Arrephoria (är-e-fôr′i-a). In ancient Athens, a festival celebrated by maidens. Four young girls of noble birth were selected. These maidens were called Arrephoroi and lived for a time in the temple of Athena Polias on the Acropolis, where two of them were engaged in weaving the peplus that was annually presented to Athena. At the time of the festival the girls were clothed in white garments and performed the following ceremony at night. The priestess of Athena put laden baskets on their heads which the maidens carried by an underground passage to a sanctuary nearby. Neither the priestess who put the burdens in the baskets nor the maidens who carried them knew what they were. After the girls delivered what was in their baskets they received something in its place and returned to the priestess. Some say this festival commemorated the acts of the daughters of Cecrops, to whom Athena gave a chest with orders to guard it but not to look inside. They disobeyed her command and discovered within the chest the infant Erichthonius, half-man and half-serpent. The sight of him drove them mad and they hurled themselves from the Acropolis. Only Pandrosos, of the sisters, did not disobey the command

of the goddess. She became the first priestess of Athena and had a sanctuary on the Acropolis.

Arretium (a-rē′shum, -shi-um). [Modern name, **Arezzo.**] In ancient geography, a city in C Italy in Tuscany, situated in the Clanis valley, near the junction of the Arnus and Clanis rivers, about 38 miles SE of Florentia. An ancient Etruscan city, it was colonized by the Romans and became the terminus of the Via Flaminia. Arretium refused to take part in an Italian coalition against Rome (285–282 B.C.) and was besieged by the whole force of the confederacy, including paid hordes of Gallic Semones. Lucius Caecilius Metellus went to the relief of the city, but was defeated and slain, with seven military tribunes and 13,000 men, the rest of the army being made prisoners. The city contains many remains from the Etruscan and Roman periods. In the 1st century B.C. potters of Arretium perfected the production of a fine tableware known as *terra sigillata,* decorated in relief in imitation of embossed metal ware, with an excellent red glaze, which came to enjoy wide vogue in the Mediterranean and was widely imitated in western Europe. It appears in museums and excavation reports as Arretine Ware.

Arrhidaeus (a-ri-dē′us). Macedonian soldier; half brother of Alexander the Great; killed 317 B.C. He was one of the military leaders who disputed the empire after Alexander's death in 323 B.C., being elected by the soldiers under his command in Babylonia. He was put to death by order of Olympias, mother of Alexander.

Arria (ar′i-a). Roman woman whose husband, Caecina Paetus, was condemned to death for conspiracy against the emperor Claudius. As her husband hesitated to destroy himself, she stabbed herself (42 A.D.) and handed him the dagger with the words *"Paete, non dolet"* ("Paetus, it does not hurt").

Arrian (ar′i-an). Greek meteorologist; fl. first half of the 2nd century B.C. He wrote a book on meteorology and a short monograph on comets, but his work was largely absorbed in later writings and only three fragments of it now are extant.

Arrian. [Latin, **Flavius Arrianus.**] Greek historian and philosopher; born at Nocomedia, Bithynia; fl. 2nd century A.D. Because of his culture and ability he was made a citizen of Rome and of Athens, and held high offices in the state. Hadrian appointed him governor of Cappadocia (c131), and he served as consul (c146) under Antoninus Pius. He spent his last years in his native town as a priest of Demeter. He was a friend and follower of Epictetus, whose lectures he published and on whose philosophy he wrote a manual. The latter became so popular, because of its tersely expressed moral precepts, that much later it was used as a textbook. He was the author also of valuable historical works in the style of Xenophon, notably his *Anabasis* of Alexander, based on first-hand accounts by Aristobulus and others, the *Indica* on Nearchus' expedition to India, the *Periplus of the Euxine* (Black Sea), and the *Cynegeticus*, on hunting.

Arsinoë (är-sin'ō̇-ē). In Greek mythology, a daughter of Phegeus, king of Psophis. Phegeus gave her in marriage to Alcmaeon who had fled to his court to be purified. Alcmaeon gave her the necklace and peplus of Harmonia, which he had brought with him and which caused disaster to whomever possessed them. Alcmaeon, pursued by the Erinyes for the murder of his mother, went to the river-god Achelous for purification. On his return to Psophis he asked Arsinoë to surrender the necklace and peplus to him. This she willingly did, unaware that during his absence he had married the daughter of Achelous and wished to give the necklace and peplus to her. When Phegeus learned the truth he had Alcmaeon killed. Arsinoë would not listen to the truth about Alcmaeon and prayed that her father and brothers would die before the next new moon to punish them for having widowed her. Her father locked her in a chest and gave her to the king of Nemea for a slave. But her prayer was answered, her father and brothers were dead within a month.

Arsinoë. In Greek legend, the nurse of Orestes. According to some accounts, after the murder of Agamemnon, Aegisthus plotted to kill Orestes. Arsinoë, who knew of the plot, nobly substituted her own son in Orestes' bed, and he was slain. She secretly carried Orestes off to Strophius, king of Phocis and uncle of Orestes, for safety.

Arsinoë. In Greek mythology, a daughter of Leucippus and Philodice, and a sister of Hilaira and Phoebe, who became the wives of the Dioscuri. By Apollo, she became the mother of Eriopis, and some say she also bore him Asclepius, but the general account is that Coronis was the mother of Asclepius. Arsinoë was given a hero's honors in Sparta, where she also had a sanctuary.

Arsinoë I. The daughter of Lysimachus of Thrace, and first wife of Ptolemy II; fl. in Egypt, c280 B.C. Suspected of plotting against her husband's life, she was for a time banished.

Arsinoë II. Daughter of Ptolemy I of Egypt, wife of Lysimachus and, afterward, of Ptolemy II. She was born c316 B.C.; died 270.

Arsinoë III. Fl. c220 B.C. The wife of Ptolemy IV Philopator, by whose order she was put to death.

Arsinoë IV. Killed at Miletus, 41 B.C. Queen of Egypt in 47 B.C., put to death by Mark Antony at the instigation of her sister Cleopatra.

Arsinoë. In ancient geography, a city on the E coast of Cyprus near ancient Salamis. It was built by Ptolemy II of Egypt. The name of the city now on the same site is Famagusta.

Arsinous (är-sin'ō̇-us). In Homeric legend *(Iliad),* a man of Tenedos, the father of Hecamede, the prize of war given to Nestor for his maid-servant by Achilles.

Arsippe (är'si-pē). In Greek mythology, a daughter of Minyas and the sister of Alcithoë and Leucippe. The sisters were driven mad for denying the divinity of Dionysus. See **Minyades.**

Artabanus (är-ta̲-bā'nus). Brother of Darius the Great (king of Persia, 521–c485 B.C.). When Xerxes, son of Darius, decides to wage war on the Greeks Artabanus reminds him that he advised his father not to make war on the Scythians. Darius ignored his advice and so lost many good men before making a safe retreat from Scythia. The Greeks, he says, are much more valiant than the Scythians, and are bold fighters on sea and land. He advises Xerxes of the dangers that so nearly befell Darius in crossing the Hellespont, and warns him of the worse dangers an invasion of Greece would present. But at least, he urges Xerxes to withdraw from the council that is discussing war against the Greeks and think well what course he should follow before he makes up his mind to go to war, as his other chiefs advise; or to refrain from war, as Artabanus advises. He reminds Xerxes that the gods knock down the tallest trees in the forest with the lightning, for the gods love to cut down all things and men that stand above their fellows, and thus a great host (the Persians) can, by the will of the gods, be destroyed by a small force (the Greeks). Artabanus chides Mardonius, a counselor who strongly advises war, for belittling the Greeks and stirring up Xerxes' will to war. He suggests that if war is determined on Xerxes should remain in Persia. He proposes that he and Mardonius put up their sons as pledges, that Mardonius march at the head of as large an army as he feels is necessary to defeat the Greeks. If Mardonius is successful, Artabanus and his sons must perish, but if he is not successful Mardonius and his sons must be slain. This advice from Artabanus infuriates Xerxes. He commands Artabanus to remain at home with the women and decides in favor of war. Later Xerxes thinks it over and decides that Artabanus has given good advice. He makes up his mind to abandon the war. In the night he dreams a man appears to him and tells him not to abandon his plans for war. He pays no attention to the dream, and next day calls his chiefs together and acknowledges that Artabanus is right, and he will not make war. The Persians are delighted. That night Xerxes has the same dream; the figure that appears to him threatens that unless he makes war he will be brought low. Xerxes sends for Artabanus and tells him the dream. If, as he thinks, the dream was sent by the gods it will be sent to Artabanus too, if only Artabanus clothes himself in Xerxes' raiment and sleeps in his bed. Artabanus tries to soothe him, saying man is likely to dream of what is uppermost in his mind, and the war against the Greeks had occupied them above all else for many days. However, if the dream was really sent by the gods it will come to him too. Although, he tells Xerxes, the dream will not be so simple-minded as to be fooled by the disguise of Xerxes clothes. Yet he agrees to put them on. He sits on the

throne, dons Xerxes' garments, and lies down on Xerxes' bed to sleep, thinking that thus he will prove Xerxes is mistaken. But the same dream comes to him, and threatens him for advising Xerxes not to make war. Artabanus springs up and hurries to Xerxes. He agrees that the dream has come from the gods, who desire the war against the Greeks, and he now gives it his support. Xerxes makes preparations for the war. After four years a host is assembled at the Hellespont. Artabanus now expresses his fears about two things: land and sea. For the army is too great to live off the land and the fleet is too vast to find harbor in case of storms. Xerxes upbraids him for his fears. If a man were to consider every possible hazard before he acted he would never act at all. He tells Artabanus Persia would never have grown so great if his predecessors had been so afraid of taking a chance as Artabanus. Xerxes, taking the three sons of Artabanus with him as captains, leaves his sceptre and his empire in Artabanus' hands and sends him back to Susa as he leaves for the invasion of Greece. Subsequent events proved that Artabanus was correct in all his fears, that the gods could indeed cut down the mighty forces of Persia.

Artabazus (är-tạ-bā′zus). Persian general of the Parthians and Chorasmians in the campaigns of 480 and 479 B.C. His forces took no part in the battle of Plataea (479 B.C.), and after the defeat of Mardonius there he retreated to Asia.

Artabazus. Persian general under Artaxerxes II; fl. c362–328 B.C. He was satrap of Phrygia and rebelled (c356 B.C.) against Artaxerxes III, aided by the Athenian general Chares. He was pardoned (c349) for his uprising through the intercession of Mentor, fought at Gaugamela (331 B.C.) under Darius, and was made satrap of Bactria by Alexander the Great.

Artachaees (är-tak-ā′ēz). Persian engineer; died c481 B.C. He was one of the engineers in charge of the construction of a canal across the Athos peninsula, near Acanthus in N Greece, to allow the passage of Xerxes' fleet in 480 B.C. Xerxes wanted the canal to spare his fleet the dangerous winds that had buffeted his father's ships when they rounded the peninsula in 490 B.C.

Artacia (är-tā'shi-a̲, -sha̲). In the *Odyssey*, a spring in the land of the Laestrygonians where the companions of Odysseus met the daughter of King Antiphates.

Artaphernes (är-ta̲-fėr'nēz). Persian general; fl. c500 B.C. He was a brother of Darius the Great (of Persia), by whom he was appointed satrap of Sardis. He interfered ineffectually in behalf of Hippias, the expelled tyrant of Athens, and took part in suppressing the revolt (499–498 B.C.) of the Ionians against Persian rule.

Artaphernes. Persian general; son of the foregoing Persian general of the same name. He commanded, with Datis, the Persian army which invaded (490 B.C.) Greece and was defeated at Marathon, and led the Lydians in the expedition of Xerxes I against Greece ten years later which ended in the defeat of the Persians.

Artaxerxes I. (är-ta̲-zẻrk'sēz). [Surnamed **Longimanus**, meaning "the Long-handed"; name in the Old Testament, **Artachshast**.] King of Persia (464–425 B.C.). He was a younger son of Xerxes I. Aided by the vizier who had murdered his father, he ascended the throne (464 B.C.). When, some time later, he discovered this vizier was his father's murderer and the author of other crimes, Artaxerxes killed him and his sons in a hand-to-hand struggle in the palace. According to ancient writers he was handsome, brave, of a mild disposition, and greatly influenced by his mother and his wife. Early in his reign he was forced to put down the rebellion of one of his satraps. Following this the Libyan Inarus raised a rebellion in Egypt and called in the Athenians to help him. After a long struggle (460–454 B.C.) in which the Athenians sailed up the Nile and took possession of most of Memphis (459), Egypt was subdued. The forces of Artaxerxes were defeated (449 B.C.) on sea and land in a double action at Salamis in Cyprus by the Athenians. That same year peace was concluded with the Athenians under which the Persians agreed not to invade the Aegean, while the Athenians abandoned their interest in Cyprus and pledged to honor the coasts of the Persian Empire. This peace, known as the Peace of Callias, ended the great struggles with Persia for over a hundred years.

Artaxerxes is presumed to have instigated the mission of Ezra and Nehemiah (his cupbearer) to Jerusalem, thus furthering Judaism. He won the epithet "Longimanus" because of the excessive length of his right hand.

Artaxerxes II. [Surnamed **Mnemon**.] King of Persia (404–358 B.C.). He was the son of Darius II and Parysatis, and succeeded his father on the throne of Persia (404 B.C.). His mother, who had great influence over him, preferred to see her younger son, her favorite Cyrus, as king, and plotted unsuccessfully to secure the throne for him. Cyrus, with a band of Greek mercenaries that included Xenophon and a body of Asiatic troops, took the field and prepared to seize the throne from Artaxerxes. He marched across Asia Minor, along the Euphrates, and into Babylonia. At the village of Cunaxa, outside Bablyon, Artaxerxes came out to oppose him. Cyrus was killed (401 B.C.), his Asiatic troops fled, and Artaxerxes retained his throne. He willingly gave the Greek mercenaries permission to depart, after which they made the famous march to the sea celebrated in Xenophon's *Anabasis*. At the beginning of the 4th century B.C. a Peloponnesian force under the Spartan king Agesilaus II invaded the coasts of Asia Minor and temporarily freed the Greek cities there (396). The Spartan triumphs were shortlived, as Agesilaus was called home to fight the Greek enemies of Sparta. In 388 B.C. the Spartan Antalcidas journeyed to Susa to make peace with Artaxerxes. By the terms of the peace, concluded in 386 B.C. and called the "King's Peace," the cities of Asia Minor and Cyprus fell to Persia, and the other Greek cities were declared autonomous, except Lemnos, Imbrus, and Scyrus which continued to belong to Athens. Having concluded peace with Sparta Artaxerxes was compelled to turn his attention to the series of rebellions within his empire. Satraps in the provinces from the Hellespont to the Nile rose up against him; Egypt freed herself from Persian domination. In his last years Artaxerxes had given himself up to the pleasures of the harem, had put his three eldest sons to death as a result of the intrigues of their brother Ochus, but by the time of his death (358 B.C.), thanks largely to the jealousy and intrigues of the various revolting satraps against each other, the king's authority over the empire had been restored.

Artaxerxes III. [Surnamed **Ochus.**] King of Persia (358–338 B.C.). He was the son of Artaxerxes II, and cleared his path to the throne by inducing his father to put to death the three older brothers who stood in his way. He succeeded to the throne on the death of Artaxerxes (358 B.C.). On his accession he put to death most of his relatives who might have contested his right to rule. He energetically and harshly asserted his power over his satraps, compelled them to disband their mercenary armies, and succeeded (343 B.C.) in conquering Egypt which he thereupon treated with great cruelty. He was poisoned (338 B.C.), along with his older sons, by his favorite, the eunuch Bagoas, who had come to have great power.

Artemidorus Daldianus (är″tē-mi-dō′rus daldi-ā′nus). Greek soothsayer of Daldis, in Lydia; fl. c170 A.D.; author of a four-book treatise on the interpretation of dreams, valuable to modern scholars as a source of information on ancient rites and superstitions. He also wrote treatises on auspices (divination based upon the observation of birds) and on chirognomy (palmistry), but these have been lost.

Artemidorus of Ephesus (ef′ẹ-sus). Greek geographer; fl. c104–100 B.C. He was at one time the Ephesian ambassador to Rome. He is better known, however, as the author of an 11-volume geographical work, now lost, largely based on earlier writers and in turn used by Strabo and others. It purported to deal with the whole "inhabited world," and attached much importance to physical geography and distances between places cited.

Artemis (är′tẹ-mis). One of the 12 Olympian gods, the daughter of Zeus and Leto, and the twin sister of Apollo. As with Apollo, the worship of Artemis was supposed to have come from the Hyperboreans, for which reason she was known as Hyperborean Artemis. Armed like Apollo with a silver bow, she was a mighty hunter, a "Rainer of Arrows," who sent them to punish the wicked and impious, and who could also heal and reward. Sudden death occurring in women

was attributed to the arrows of Artemis. She did not share with Apollo the gift of prophecy, nor had she any connection with the arts. She was the virgin huntress, devoted to the chase, the goddess of streets and the founding of towns, the protectress of all young animals, and the goddess of flocks. As Apollo was a god of light, sometimes identified with the sun, so Artemis was also a goddess of light and was identified with the moon, particularly with Selene and Hecate.

ARTEMIS
Red-figured Greek crater, Pan Painter, 475–450 B.C. *Museum of Fine Arts, Boston*

Leto was compelled to wander through the earth searching for a place to bear her children, because jealous Hera had decreed that no place where the sun shone could receive her rival. At last she came to the tiny island of Ortygia. There she bore Artemis, and because she was born without pain Artemis became the goddess invoked by women in childbirth, and was sometimes known as Ilithyia, the birth-goddess. As soon as she was born Artemis helped her mother across the narrow strait to the neighboring and slightly larger floating island of Delos, which offered to receive Leto in spite of Hera's threats. On Delos Artemis acted as midwife and helped her mother to bear Apollo, her twin. But some say Artemis was born on Delos itself, and some say she was born in the Ortygian grove at Ephesus. While she was yet a child, her father Zeus took her on his knee and asked what gifts she desired of him. At once, Artemis asked for the gift of eternal virginity. This was granted her, and she became one of the three goddesses whose heart could not be moved by the power of Aphrodite (the others were Athena and Hestia). She also asked for bow and arrows like her brother's, for 60 ocean nymphs to be her companions, and 20 river nymphs from Crete to look after her hunting gear and her hounds. Besides, she wanted all the mountains of the world and just one city, for she expected to spend most of her time hunting on the mountains. Zeus promised her all she asked and more, and made her goddess of roads and harbors. Artemis went off to the realm of Oceanus and to Crete, where she chose her companions. Then she went to visit the Cyclopes, at the invitation of Hephaestus. Brontes, who had been told to make whatever she asked, took her on his knee, but she did not care for his fondling, and tore a handful of hair out of his chest to express her annoyance. At the time of her visit the Cyclopes were at work on a silver trough for Poseidon. Artemis imperiously told them to interrupt the work and make her a silver bow and a quiver of arrows, and promised to give them the first thing she shot with them as a reward. The Cyclopes did as she bid. Armed with her bow, Artemis went to Arcadia. There she met Pan, who gave her hounds for the chase. Next she captured alive two pairs of golden-horned, bronze-hoofed stags and harnessed them to a golden chariot. In this she set off for Thrace to try out her weapons. Her first two arrows struck trees; her third slew a wild beast; and her fourth was used to punish a city of unjust men.

Artemis jealously guarded the honor of her mother and her brother. She helped Apollo kill Tityus when he attacked Leto as she was on her way to Delphi. She killed the daughters of Niobe who had boasted of her many sons and daughters, taunted Leto because she had only two children, and recommended to the Thebans that they worship her instead of Leto. Some say that she slew Coronis the Lapith with her arrows when Apollo complained to her that Coronis had been unfaithful to him. But others say she helped Coronis when she was bearing Apollo's son Asclepius. Artemis sent heavy punishments on those who failed to give her due honor. Oeneus of Calydon forgot her when he was sacrificing first fruits to the gods. Helius informed Artemis of this oversight, and she sent a monstrous boar to ravage Calydon, the realm of Oeneus. Meleager, the son of Oeneus, called together a group of heroes and the boar was at length slain, but Meleager quarreled with his uncles and finally killed them and brought about his own death. Artemis turned all but two of his wildly grieving sisters into guinea-hens. Admetus also offended her by neglecting her at his marriage rites. When he went to the marriage chamber he found it filled with writhing serpents. Apollo, who was serving as bondman of Admetus at the time, told him how to appease Artemis. Atreus, son of Pelops, promised to sacrifice the best of his flocks to Artemis. Hermes, who wanted to punish the Pelopidae because Pelops had murdered his son Myrtilus, schemed with Pan, and put a lamb with golden fleece and a horn of gold into the flocks that Pelops had left to his sons Atreus and Thyestes. Atreus claimed the lamb with golden fleece, and did indeed kill it and offer the flesh to Artemis but he took the skin, stuffed it, and hid it in a chest. But some say it was Artemis herself who put the lamb with golden fleece among the flocks of Atreus, to test him. By withholding the golden fleece from the sacrifice he incurred her wrath, and she punished his family, especially his son Agamemnon. Broteas, son of Tantalus, was a great hunter. He failed to honor Artemis and, some say, she drove him mad; he cast himself on a pyre and so perished. On the other hand, she rewarded those who honored her. Hippolytus, son of Theseus, worshiped Artemis above all, and even denied the power of Aphrodite. Aphrodite caused his death, not because he honored Artemis, but because he denied her, the goddess of love. Artemis begged Asclepius to restore Hippolytus. He did so with a magic herb, and Artemis wrapped him in a cloud and carried him off to Italy. There in her sacred grove of Aricia she changed his name to Virbius and gave him the nymph Egeria for a wife.

Artemis, the chaste goddess, resisted all would-be lovers. Otus, one of the Aloidae, sought to embrace her. With his brother Ephialtes he pursued her to the island of Naxos. As the brothers were about to discover her, Artemis transformed herself into a hind. The brothers separated to attack from opposite sides. With the hind between them, each hurled his spear, but Artemis disappeared, and the spears so forcefully hurled sped on; each brother was pierced by the other's spear. Some say that Orion, returning from the East with his sight restored after Oenopion had blinded him, met Artemis as he sought Oenopion for revenge. She persuaded him, as a mighty hunter, to give up the idea of revenge and go hunting with her. Apollo, fearing that Orion might melt the heart of his virgin sister, caused a great scorpion to attack him. Orion fought the monster with his arrows and his sword, but could not kill him. He fled into the sea to escape the scorpion and swam off toward Delos. Apollo now approached Artemis. He pointed to the speck on the sea made by Orion's head as he swam rapidly away and challenged her to hit it with one of her arrows. Artemis took aim, shot at the speck, and killed Orion. When she learned that she had killed Orion she begged Asclepius to restore him to life, but Asclepius was killed by the thunderbolt of Zeus before he could do so. Artemis then set Orion's image among the stars, with the image of the scorpion ever in pursuit. But some say Artemis herself sent the scorpion against Orion, either because he had attempted to violate her, or pursued one of her maidens who had come from the Hyperboreans, or because he challenged her to a match at quoits, and that Orion died of the scorpion's bite. Unfortunate Actaeon, who accidentally happened to pass a fountain where the goddess and her companions were refreshing themselves, stopped to watch the goddess in her bath. When he was discovered Artemis transformed him into a stag and he was pursued and torn to pieces by his own hounds. Artemis escaped the amorous advances of the river-god Alpheus at Letrini in Elis by daubing her own face and the faces of her companions with white clay. For this she was given the epithet Alphaea *(Whitish)*. When Alpheus came in search of her he could not tell which was the goddess and was forced to withdraw disappointed. And Artemis punished those of her companions who forgot their vows of chastity. When she noticed that Callisto, loved by Zeus, was about to have a child, she transformed her into a bear and set her companions to hunt her, but Zeus saved Callisto by translating her to the heavens. Others say it was not Artemis who transformed Callisto into a bear, but Zeus, to save her from Hera, and that Artemis and her maidens were tricked by Hera into pursuing the bear.

Artemis loved all animals, but the hind was her favorite. She transformed the Pleiad Taÿgete into a hind to help her escape the embraces of Zeus. Afterward, Taÿgete dedicated a hind with golden horns and bronze hoofs to Artemis in gratitude. Inscribed on the hind was the legend, "Taÿgete dedicated me to Artemis." But others say this hind, called the Cerynian hind because it roamed the Cerynian Hill, was one of five hinds with bronze hoofs and horns of gold that Artemis had seen as a child. She captured four of them and harnessed them to her chariot, but the fifth escaped. Heracles was ordered by Eurystheus to catch the Cerynian hind as one of his labors. Because it was sacred to Artemis he was reluctant to harm it. He pursued it for a year, and at last transfixed the forelegs of the creature with one arrow and captured it alive. Artemis reproached him for having harmed her sacred hind, but forgave him when he explained the necessity under which he was operating, and allowed him to carry it off to Eurystheus at Mycenae.

Some say that Artemis visited her anger at Atreus on his son Agamemnon because Atreus failed to sacrifice the golden-fleeced

lamb to her as he had promised. Others say
that she punished Agamemnon because he
killed a hare that was about to bear young,
or because he killed a stag and boasted that
"Artemis herself could not have done better."
As the Greek fleet was gathered at Aulis in
preparation for the voyage to Troy, it was
windbound. Calchas the seer said Artemis
was angry, and would not send favorable
winds until Agamemnon had sacrificed his
daughter Iphigenia to her. Agamemnon secured the presence of Iphigenia at Aulis by
a trick, and made ready to sacrifice her. As
she bared her throat to receive the knife,
Artemis spirited her away and left a hind in
her place. She took Iphigenia to her temple
in Tauris and made her a priestess there,
while the goddess went off and, like Apollo,
helped the Trojans in the war. In the temple
of Artemis at Tauris was an ancient wooden
image of the goddess that had fallen from
heaven. Strangers who were forced by
storms to land on the coast were sacrificed
to the Taurian Artemis, who was also called
Artemis Tauropolus, Artemis Dictynna,
Hecate, and Trivia. Certain preparatory
rites were performed on the victim. He
was then clubbed to death and his head
severed from his body. The head was nailed
to a cross and the decapitated body was cast
into the sea from the cliff on which the
temple of Taurian Artemis stood. If the
victim was of noble blood he was killed with
a sword by the priestess herself, and his
corpse was burned in a sacred flame that
rose from Tartarus. While Iphigenia was
serving as priestess, Orestes, her brother,
came, in obedience to an oracle, to fetch the
image and take it back to Greece. Like other
strangers, he was about to be sacrificed, but
Iphigenia recognized him and with her help
he escaped, taking her with him, and returned to Brauron, near Athens, with the
image. Some say the goddess made
Iphigenia immortal, and that she was sometimes known by the name Iphigenia herself.
A temple of Artemis was raised at Brauron,
and Iphigenia was its first priestess. At the
temple, in obedience to instructions from
Athena, the rites included pricking the throat
of a man with a knife just enough to draw
blood, in commemoration of the narrow escape of Orestes at Tauris. Brauronian Ar-

temis was worshiped at Athens and Sparta,
and stags and goats were sacrificed to her.
An oracle said the altar of the Taurian image
of Artemis should be stained with blood, as
was the marble altar at Tauris, and at first
human sacrifices were offered to her. In the
time of Spartan Lycurgus this practice was
changed. Young boys were scourged in the
temple while the priestess held the image of
the goddess. If the scourgers did not lay on
heavily enough the image grew so heavy
the priestess could scarcely hold it. When
the scourgers laid on with more vigor the
image became light. An image of Brauronian Artemis, made by Phidias, was in her
sanctuary on the Acropolis at Athens. Some
say the ancient wooden image of Taurian
Artemis was at Brauron, and that it was
taken by Xerxes in the Persian War and given
to the Syrians, who still claimed it was in
their possession in the 2nd century A.D., but
the Lydians and the Cappadocians each also
claimed that they had the image. And others
say Orestes took it to the sacred grove of
Artemis at Aricia, in Italy, and that the Romans later returned it to Sparta. But the
Spartans, who claimed they had the true
image, said the Taurian image was lost.
After centuries it was found in a thicket of
willows at Limnaeum in Laconia by two
noble Spartans who subsequently went mad.
Because the image was held upright by
willow fronds that twined around it, Artemis
has the epithet Orthia *(Upright)* and Lygodesma *(Willow-bound)*. This image at Limnaeum, the Spartans say, is the true image.
   When Zeus asked Artemis what gifts she
would like from him she asked for as many
names as her brother Apollo. In addition to
the epithets already mentioned, she was
Agrotera *(Huntress)*, Coryphaea *(Of the
Peak)*, Limnaea and Limnatis *(Of the Lake)*,
Daphnaea *(Of the Laurel)*, Lyceia or Lycea
(Wolfish), Aeginaea *(Goat-goddess)*, Caryatis *(Of the Walnut-tree)*, Cedreatis *(Of the
Cedar)* from an image of the goddess set in
a cedar tree, and Eurippa *(Horse-finder)*
from a sanctuary raised by Odysseus in Arcadia where he found his mares for which
he had been searching throughout Greece.
She was Hiereia *(Priestess)*, Pyronia *(Fire-
goddess)*, Peitho *(Persuasion)*, Selasphorus
and Phosphorus *(Light-bearer)*, Ariste

actọr; up, lūte, pụll; oi, oil; ou, out; ŦH, then; ḍ as d or j, ş as s or sh, ṭ as t or ch, ẓ as z or zh.

(*Best*), Calliste (*Fairest*), and Paedotrophus (*Nurse of Children*). Artemis Savior was worshiped in many places. In Megara there was an ancient sanctuary of Artemis Savior erected by grateful Megarians because the goddess helped them to defeat a force of Persians during the Persian War. The Persians lost their way in the hills at night. Thinking the enemy was nearby they shot off a volley of arrows. The arrows struck rocks, which Artemis caused to groan. Under the impression that they were killing Greeks, the Persians fired all their arrows, and the next day when the Megarians attacked them had no ammunition with which to defend themselves and were slain. Theseus raised a temple of Artemis Savior at Troezen in gratitude for her help in overcoming the Minotaur; and the people of Boeae in Laconia worshiped Artemis Savior because she helped them to find a site for their city. At Condylea, in Arcadia, she was worshiped as Condyleatis and as the Strangled Lady because some children playing near the sanctuary found a rope and tied it around the neck of the image, and said the goddess was being strangled. The Calydonians worshiped her as Laphria. At Patrae an annual feast was held, called Laphria. A circle of green logs was set up around the altar. A procession marched to the temple. The maiden priestess rode in a car drawn by a deer at the end of the procession. The next day, great numbers of live wild beasts were hurled on the fire that was lighted within the circle of green logs. Some say Artemis got the epithet Laphria from a Calydonian man named Laphrius. Others say the name was given her because her wrath weighed more lightly (*elaphroteron*) on the Calydonians and Oeneus as time passed. In Arcadia she was also Hemerasia (*She who Soothes*) because at her sanctuary Melampus cured the daughters of Proetus of their madness. At Pyrrhicus in Laconia she was worshiped as Astrateia because she stayed the advance of the Amazons there.

The worship of Artemis was universal in Greece, Delos, Crete, Sicily, and southern Italy, and was especially strong in Arcadia, where she had many temples and sanctuaries, and throughout the Peloponnesus. In Thrace, Artemis was Tauropolus, to whom human sacrifices were made, and who drove men mad. Later, the Thracians sacrificed dogs to her. In Greek Asia she was widely worshiped. At Ephesus, where the Amazons were said to have introduced her worship, she was a fertility goddess. In the magnificent temple of Artemis there, was an image of Artemis Polymastus (*Many-breasted*), which had many breasts and bore a mural crown on the head. The symbol of Artemis Polymastus at Ephesus was a bee. Chaste Artemis, the huntress who roamed the mountains and streams and in whose care were all animals, led her nymphs in the groves and received sacrifices on woodland altars. She was known as Arcadian Artemis. Artemis of Ephesus, known as Ephesian Artemis, was an Asiatic deity adopted and adapted by the Greeks who settled in Asia Minor. The laurel and the fir tree were sacred to Artemis, as were the hind, the bear, the dog and the boar. Her attributes were the bow and quiver, torch, javelin, and crescent. In art she is represented as a young woman of noble and severe beauty, tall and majestic, and generally bearing bow and quiver as the huntress or mountain goddess, and often accompanied by a hind or a dog. She was identified by the Romans with their Diana, an original Italian divinity.

Artemisia (är-tẹ-miz'i-ạ, -mish'i-ạ). A daughter of Lygdamis, who succeeded to the throne of Halicarnassus on the death of her husband, and ruled over the Dorian cities of Halicarnassus, Cos, Nisyrus, and Calydna. As a vassal of Persia she furnished five triremes to Xerxes I in the Second Persian War. Her ships, says Herodotus, were the most famous of the fleet after those of the Sidonians. She acted as a counselor to Xerxes and stood high in his favor. She advised Xerxes not to risk a sea fight with the Greeks after he had taken Athens, because she considered the Greeks superior at sea and besides, he had accomplished what he set out to do—made himself master of Athens. In her opinion the Greeks who had gathered on Salamis would not be able to hold out against him, cut off as they were from supplies, and she did not think it likely that they would do battle on behalf of Athens. Thus a sea fight was unnecessary in her view. She expressed the fear that if he undertook such a battle and was unsuccessful at sea great harm would come to his land forces. In addition, she had no very high opinion of some of the allies on whom he would be forced to rely in a sea fight. Xerxes was delighted that Artemisia, who had fought bravely at Euboea, dared to differ from his other captains in her advice which, however, he did not take. The fleet was ordered to Salamis and the army began to march towards the Peloponnesus. The Athenians were so indignant that a woman dared appear in arms against them that they offered a reward of 10,000 drachmas to whoever could capture her. The reward was never claimed. At the Battle of Salamis (480 B.C.) the Persian fleet was in confusion. Artemisia's ship was pursued by an Athenian trireme. In the press of ships which choked the escape route Atemisia rammed a Calydnian ship, one of the Persian allies, and sank it without a trace. This act of destroying one of her allies brought her luck from two sides. The Athenian ship, seeing her sink the Calydnian, thought she was a Greek ship or a Persian deserter and gave up pursuit, thus saving her life. Xerxes, watching the battle, saw her sink a ship and thought it was a Greek ship, as his advisers assured him it was. He is said to have remarked, "My men have behaved like women and my women like men." Since there were no survivors of the Calydnian ship there was no one to expose her. After the Persian defeat at Salamis Xerxes again asked advice of Artemisia: whether to return to Persia and leave Mardonius behind with a land army, as Mardonius wished. She advised Xerxes to go home, so that the Persians would still have their master. What happened to Mardonius was unimportant, she thought. If he were successful it would redound to the credit of Xerxes; if he failed it would be the loss only of a slave. This time Xerxes took her advice and, entrusting certain of his children to Artemisia, he departed for Persia.

Artemisia (of *Caria*). Queen of Caria, in Asia Minor, 352–c350 B.C.; fl. middle of 4th century B.C. In memory of her husband Mausolus, she built at Halicarnassus a tomb, the Mausoleum, which was regarded by the ancients as one of the seven wonders of the world. To give further proof of her affection she is said to have mixed her husband's ashes with a precious liquid and to have drunk the potion so prepared.

Artemisium (är-tẹ-mish'i-um). A promontory in N Euboea, Greece, crowned by a temple of Artemis. Here where the sea runs in a narrow channel between the island of Sciathus and the mainland of Magnesia, the Greeks sent a fleet to engage the Persian fleet while their army was being engaged at the pass of Thermopylae. Alarmed over the fate of their country, now being invaded by the Persians, the people of Delphi consulted the oracle and were told to pray to the winds, for the winds would do Greece great service. When the Persian fleet assembled near Artemisium it was scattered by a great storm that lasted four days. The Athenians said Boreas sent the winds to help them, and raised a temple to Boreas on the Ilissus River. The Persians claimed that they brought the storm to an end by sacrificing to Thetis, for it was near where their fleet was anchored, Cape Sepias, that Peleus had seized Thetis, and the area was sacred to her. The Persians regrouped at Aphetae. The Greeks would have withdrawn, being greatly outnumbered, but some say Themistocles was bribed by the Euboeans to remain at Artemisium and risk a battle. The Persians thought to surround the small Greek fleet, and sent a fleet of 200 ships around Euboea to bottle up the Greeks in the strait. The Greeks, commanded by Eurybiades, were warned of the Persian plan by an Ionian who deserted from the Persians, and they resolved to sail against the Persian ships at Artemisium. The Persians thought they were mad when they saw the few Greek ships coming against them, and expected they would easily overcome them. The Greeks executed a maneuver: at a signal they brought the sterns of their ships together, the prows facing outward in a circle toward the enemy. At a second signal they attacked. They captured or sank 30 Persian ships. The battle was still raging when night fell. The Persians retired to Aphetae, the Greeks to Artemisium. During the night a crashing storm buffeted the Persian fleet at Aphetae and completely destroyed the 200 ships that were on their way around Euboea. After two more days of sea fights the Greek fleet withdrew, having inflicted heavy damage on the Persians but without reaching a decisive result. The battle at Artemisium took place at the same time as the nearby land battle at Thermopylae (480 B.C.). The two battles represented a desperate attempt to keep out the Persian invaders; neither of the battles succeeded in this aim.

In 1928, in the Straits of Artemisium, Greek sponge-divers located an ancient wreck containing fragments of classical sculpture, and further diving recovered the now famous Zeus of Artemisium, a bronze statue of the middle of the 5th century B.C. showing the god hurling his thunderbolt, and a Hellenistic group of a horse and diminutive jockey.

Artemisius (är-te-miz'i-us), **Mount.** Mountain on the border of Arcadia and Argolis, near Mantinea. Here the Inachus River rises. On the mountain was a temple and image of Artemis, for whom the mountain was named.

Aruns (ar'unz). In Roman legend, the Trojan ally who slew Camilla, the ally of Turnus. Camilla had been dedicated to Diana by her father, and on her death the goddess sent Opis to kill Aruns and avenge Camilla, and rescue her body.

Arval Brothers (är'val). In ancient Rome, a priesthood of 12 members, including the emperor, who offered public sacrifices for the fertility of the fields.

Aryballus (ar-i-bal'us). A form of Greek vase. Probably in ancient times this name was applied to a large vase with a small neck, used for carrying water to the bath. In later archaeological nomenclature, it generally denotes a small vase shaped like a ball, with a short neck and a small orifice surrounded by a broad flat rim, used like the alabastrum in anointing the body with oil.

Ascalabus (as-kal'a-bus). In mythology, a son of Misme of Eleusis. When Demeter, searching for her lost daughter Persephone, came to the house of Misme she was received kindly and given water to drink. In her thirst, Demeter drank it hastily and Ascalabus mocked her for her greed. To punish him, Demeter sprinkled some of the water on Ascalabus and transformed him into a lizard. A similar story is related of Abas, the son of Celeus.

Ascalaphus (as-kal'a-fus). In mythology, a son of Acheron, the river-god, and Orphne, a nymph of the groves of Avernus. He was a gardener in the Underworld and saw Persephone eat seeds from a pomegranate when she was abducted by Hades. On learning that Persephone could leave the Underworld provided she had eaten no food there, he informed Hades that she had eaten the pomegranate seeds. For this reason Persephone was compelled to divide her time between earth and the Underworld. Demeter changed Ascalaphus into an owl, or put him under a great stone, as a punishment for his tale-bearing.

Ascalaphus. In Greek legend, a son of Ares and Astyoche. He and his brother, Ialmenus, accompanied Jason in the *Argo* on the expedition for the Golden Fleece. The brothers were suitors of Helen, daughter of Leda and Zeus, and took the oath with the other suitors, to come to the aid of the man who became her husband should any ill befall him as a result of his marriage. When Helen was carried off to Troy by Paris, Ascalaphus joined with others from Boeotian Orchomenus who served under Agamemnon in the Trojan War. Ascalaphus served as a sentry. In the fighting before Troy he was killed by Deïphobus.

Ascalon (as'ka-lon). [Also: **Ashkelon, Askelon, Eshkalon**; Assyrian, **Isqualuna**; modern name, **Migdal Ashkalon**.] In ancient geography, one of the five chief cities of Philistia, situated on the Mediterranean about 39 miles SW of Jerusalem. According to Herodotus, it was the site of the most ancient of all the temples of Aphrodite, even antedating that at Cyprus which was built in imitation of it. The temple was pillaged by Scythians when, having overrun Media, they were on their way to Egypt. As a punishment for their desecration of the temple Aphrodite caused these Scythians and many of their descendants to suffer from the "female sickness," that is, they were afflicted with a tendency to impotency. The temple to which Herodotus referred was later identified as the temple of Derceto, a Syrian goddess whose form was half-maiden and half-fish, and whose sacred lake was nearby. Ascalon is mentioned in Phoenician and Assyrian inscriptions; the names of four of its kings (Sidka, Sarludari,

Rukibti, and Mitenti) appear in the annals of Sennacherib (705–681 B.C.) and Esarhaddon (680–668 B.C.). Herod I, whose birthplace it was, adorned the city with many edifices.

Ascania (as-kā′ni-ạ), **Lake.** [Modern Turkish, İsnik or Iznik.] In ancient geography, a lake in Bithynia, Asia Minor, draining finally into the Sea of Marmara. Nicaea was situated at its E extremity. Length, about 11 miles.

Ascanius (as-kā-ni-us). In Roman legend, the son of Aeneas and Creusa. He accompanied his father on the flight from Troy. When the Tro:ans were shipwrecked on the shores of Carthage Cupid, sent by Venus, assumed the form of Ascanius to cause Dido to fall in love with Aeneas. Jupiter, to reassure Venus who was complaining of the ills which beset Aeneas, foretold a 30-year reign for Ascanius in Italy, and that his dynasty would rule for 300 years, until a priestess should bear twin sons by Mars who would found the Roman nation. In Latium Ascanius shot a tame stag and inflamed the Latins against the Trojans; this was one of the causes of the war between the Latins and the Tro:ans, in the course of which Ascanius used his bow against men for the first time. But he was prevented from taking an active part by Apollo, who restrained him in order to preserve him for his destiny. Ascanius moved the kingdom founded by Aeneas from Lavinium and made Alba Longa, on the slopes of the Alban Mount, his stronghold. Here, as Jupiter had foretold, his descendants ruled after his death. Latin writers also call him Iulus.

Asclepiadae (as-klē̱-pī′ạ-dē). Primarily, a word meaning the sons or descendants of Asclepius. It came to apply to a priestly family that gathered and preserved medical information, traditions, and practices over the course of many years. The material so gathered and preserved was handed down secretly from father to son. Hippocrates belonged to this family.

Asclepiades of Bithynia (as-klē̱-pī′ạ-dēz; bi-thin′i-ạ). Greek physician; fl. c100 B.C. He is notable as the first eminent one of his country to practice at Rome. He opposed the theories of Hippocrates, asserting that disease springs from a disordered movement of the corpuscles and that a cure is achieved by soothing remedies, such as diet, moderate

exercise, bathing, wine, and (for the insane) music. He achieved considerable success in Rome by his methods. Portions of his written works are preserved.

Asclepiades of Samos (sā′mos). Greek lyric poet and writer of epigrams. He was a native of Samos, a younger contemporary of Theocritus, and was active in the early 3rd century B.C. He is the earliest, and considered by some the most important, of his school. According to some scholars his graceful love poems gave the name Asclepiadean to that type of verse. Some 40 epigrams of his are found in the Greek *Anthology*.

Asclepius (as-klē′pi-us). In Greek mythology, a son of Coronis and Apollo. Apollo caused Coronis' death, before Asclepius was born, because he found she had been unfaithful to him. As her body lay on the funeral pyre he was overcome with remorse and resolved at least to save his son. He sent Hermes to snatch the unborn child from his mother's womb. Hermes took the infant to Chiron the centaur, who brought him up and taught him the arts of healing and hunting. Asclepius was much more interested in the medical arts than in sport, and soon outstripped his master. Aided also by instruction from Apollo, he became a skilled surgeon and highly successful in prescribing drugs. Some say Athena gave him two phials of the blood of Medusa when her head was cut off by Perseus. The blood that was drawn from the left side was used to restore the dead to life; that from the right side he used to destroy life. But others say Athena divided the blood drawn from Medusa between herself and Asclepius. She used her share for destructive ends; Asclepius used his share for healing. Asclepius was the father of Podalirius and Machaon, the physicians who accompanied the Greeks to Troy, and of Hygea. Asclepius is said to have used the blood of Medusa, or an herb known only to him, to restore Lycurgus, Capaneus, Tyndareus, Glaucus, Orion, and Hippolytus to life. Hades complained to Zeus, some say, that Asclepius was taking away his subjects by restoring them to life, and Zeus killed him with his thunderbolt. Others say Asclepius accepted a bribe in defiance of divine law, and restored the dead to life, and was slain by the thunderbolt of Zeus. Apollo, infuri-

actor; up, lūte, púll; oi, oil; ou, out; ŦH, then; ḍ as d or j, ṣ as s or sh, ṭ as t or ch, ẓ as z or zh.

ated at the slaying of his son, killed the Cyclopes, because they had forged the thunderbolt of Zeus. To punish him, Zeus ordered him to serve Admetus of Pherae for a year without pay. Some say Asclepius was later restored to life himself, thus fulfilling a prophecy that he would fulfill his destiny twice. His image was set among the stars. Asclepius was worshiped throughout Greece as a hero and god of healing for centuries. One of his most famous shrines was at Epidaurus. In his temple there several serpents were kept, for serpents, annually renewing themselves by shedding their skins, were connected in some mysterious way with the art of healing. Asclepius was always shown with a serpent, usually carrying a staff about which a serpent was coiled. The cock was commonly sacrificed to him. Patients who went to the healing shrine at Epidaurus slept in the temple, presided over by an image of Sleep or Dreams, and their cures were related to them in dreams. A great festival in honor of Asclepius was held every five years at Epidaurus. There were temples and shrines to Asclepius throughout Greece. At Pergamum, founded by a colony from Epidaurus, there was another famous shrine; as there was also at Tricca in Thessaly, whose inhabitants claimed that their town was the birthplace of the healing god. After 293 B.C. Asclepius was worshiped in Rome, under the name Aesculapius. He had been brought to Rome in the form of a serpent; his shrine was on the Tiber island.

Asconius Pedianus (as-kō'ni-us pē-di-ā'nus), **Quintus.** Roman historian and grammarian, born probably at Patavium (Padua), 9 B.C.; died 76 A.D. He was notable for his commentaries on Cicero's speeches.

Asculum Apulum (as'kū-lum ap'ū-lum). [Modern name, **Ascoli Satriano.**] In ancient geography, a town of SW Italy, in the region of Apulia, on the slopes of the Apennines. The town was founded by the Romans. It was the scene of the costly victory (279 B.C.) of Pyrrhus over the Romans.

Asculum Picenum (pī-sē'num). [Modern name, **Ascoli Piceno.**] A town in the Abruzzi on the Adriatic slope of the Apennines, capital of the Picentes, which fought against Rome in the Social War and was destroyed by Pompey, but rapidly regained importance

under the empire. It has many antiquities: fortification walls, a gate, the *Porta Romana,* remains of an aqueduct, a Roman bridge over the river Truentus (modern Tronto), still in use, a second Roman bridge whose arch fell recently, a well-preserved Roman temple of the 1st century A.D., now the church of S. Gregorio, and Romanesque churches and houses of exceptional interest. Ancient cemeteries in the vicinity have yielded evidence of early commerce via the Adriatic with central Europe and S Italy, the Aegean, and the Balkans. (JJ)

Ascus (as'kus). In mythology, a giant who helped Lycurgus to put Dionysus in chains on the border of Thrace, or, as some say, cast him into a river. Zeus or Hermes came to the rescue of Dionysus. They slew Ascus and took his hide for a wineskin. Some say that the city of Damascus in Syria got its name from this incident.

Asea (a-sē'a). Town in Arcadia, in the central Peloponnesus, with a fortified acropolis commanding the Asean Plain, celebrated for its springs which flow to the Alpheus, and capital of the short-lived Asean League. (JJ)

Asia (ā'zha). To the ancient Greeks, Asia meant the lands bordering the eastern end of the Mediterranean Sea. The name also embraced the few parts of Africa known to them, and it was only after the Nile began to be considered as a dividing river that the countries W of it were separated from Asia, while Egypt was still included in it. Moreover, the knowledge of the ancients with regard to Asia did not reach far beyond the boundaries of the Perso-Macedonian empire. The parts S of the Himalaya range were called India, those to the N Scythia. The west was termed Upper and Lower Asia, the Tigris being the dividing line between both.

Asia Minor (mī'nor). Peninsula of W Asia which lies between the Euxine Sea and the Propontis on the N, the Aegean Sea on the W, and the Mediterranean Sea on the S; the E boundary is vague. The chief divisions in ancient times were Mysia, Lydia, Caria, Lycia, Pamphylia, Pisidia, Phrygia, Bithynia, Paphlagonia, Galatia, Lycaonia, Cilicia, Cappadocia, and Pontus. The surface is in the main a plateau, traversed by the Taurus and other ranges. The chief rivers are the Sangarius, Halys, Maeander, Sarus, and Hermus.

It was the seat of Troy, Lydia, and other ancient powers, and of the Ionian Greek civilization; its possession has been disputed by Persia, Macedonia, Syria, Rome, the Byzantine empire, Parthia, the Saracens, the Seljuks, and the modern Turks. According to Herodotus, there were 15 races or nations in Asia Minor: in the S part the Cilicians, Pamphylians, Lycians, and Caunians; W of the great central plateau, close to the coast, the Carians, Lydians, Mysians, and Greeks; on the shores of the Euxine, Thracians, Mariandynians, Paphlagonians, and Cappadocians; in the interior, the Phrygians, Chalybes, and Matieni.

Asinara (as-i-nä′ra), **Gulf of.** Arm of the Mediterranean, off the NW coast of Sardinia. See also **Insula Herculis.**

Asinarus (as-i-nä′rus). [Italian names, **Falconare, Fiume di Noto.**] In ancient geography, a small river near Syracuse, Sicily. To this stream came the Athenians under Nicias, after their total defeat at Syracuse, 413 B.C. Tormented by thirst, they rushed into the river. The Syracusans, with their Peloponnesian allies, manned the steep bank on the opposite side of the river and shot them down ruthlessly as they plunged into the water to drink. Nicias surrendered here to stop the slaughter of his men. To celebrate the anniversary of their great victory, the Syracusans established Asinarian Games, named for the river where the total destruction of the enemy took place.

Asine (a′si-nē). In ancient geography, a city of Argolis, on the Gulf of Argolis. The people were Dryopes, who originally came from Mount Parnassus. They were captured by Heracles and taken as slaves to Delphi, but the oracle commanded that they be taken to the Peloponnesus. The people of Asine claimed they were not taken as slaves to Delphi but abandoned their town when Heracles assaulted it, and appealed to Eurystheus, who gave them Asine near Hermion in Argolis out of enmity to Heracles. These Dryopes of Asine were the only Dryopians who were proud to be called Dryopes. Men of Asine went to the Trojan War under the command of Diomedes and his friend Sthenelus. Asine was destroyed by Argos in the 7th century B.C. Excavations have re-

vealed substantial remains of a settlement of the bronze age.

Asine. City of the Peloponnesus, on the western shore of the Gulf of Messenia. It was given to people who had been driven out of Argos by the Spartans, after the First Messenian War, and the Argives occupied it ever after. At the end of the Second Messenian War, which resulted in the conquest of Messenia, Asine alone was left separate in the division of the land.

Asius (ā′si-us). In Homeric legend (*Iliad*), the son of Hyrtacus. He came from Arisbe on the banks of the Selleis river in the Troad as an ally of the Trojans. Polydamas advised the Trojans not to attack the Greek moat and wall in their chariots, lest the horses stumble into the moat, upset the chariots, and make the warriors an easy prey for the Greeks. Asius refused to take his advice. He drove at the Greeks in the way which the Greeks used to return in their war-cars, but once inside the walls he was unable to maneuver. He descended from his chariot, and in an attempt to kill Idomeneus was himself slain by that hero. His horses were captured by Antilochus, son of Nestor.

Asius. In Homeric legend (*Iliad*), a son of Dymas, and the brother of Hecuba. When Patroclus had driven the Trojans back to the gates of Troy, Hector paused to decide whether to fight on or withdraw inside the walls. Apollo assumed the form of Asius, Hector's uncle, and urged him to turn on Patroclus and perhaps Apollo would give him victory. Asius was slain by Ajax.

Asklepios (as-klē′pi-os). See **Asclepius.**

Asopus (a-sō′pus). The god of the Sicyonian river of the same name. By his wife Metope, the daughter of Ladon, he was the father of two sons, Pelasgus and Ismenus, and 12 (or as some say, 20) daughters—Corcyra, Salamis, Aegina, Pirene, Cleone, Thebe, Tanagra, Thespeia, Asopis, Sinope, Ornia, and Chalcis. His beautiful daughters were harassed by the attentions of various gods who carried them off and ravished them. Sinope was carried off by Apollo, according to some accounts, and bore him a son, but later shrewdly frustrated the attentions of Zeus. Corcyra and Salamis were abducted by Poseidon. Thebe disappeared with Zeus.

When Aegina too disappeared Asopus lost patience with the gods and determined to recover her. He learned that Sisyphus of Corinth had information concerning her whereabouts, but Sisyphus never gave away anything for nothing. It was necessary for Asopus to bribe him by giving Corinth the never-failing Pirene Fountain, to tell what he knew. Sisyphus then divulged that Zeus had carried off Aegina. Asopus pursued Zeus and overtook him in a forest. Zeus, who was carrying no thunderbolts at the time, fled and changed himself into a huge stone to escape the wrath of Asopus. When Asopus had passed by Zeus resumed his shape, returned to Olympus, and from there hurled thunderbolts at Asopus. He wounded Asopus and lamed him. It is for this reason that the Asopus River flows sluggishly, and the thunderbolts hurled by Zeus at Asopus are said to account for the lumps of burned coal that are sometimes found in the river bed.

Asopus. A town in Laconia, on the eastern promontory of the Peloponnesus on the Gulf of Laconia. It was noted for a sanctuary of Asclepius, who was here given the epithet Philolaus, "Loved by the people." Athena here was named Cyparissia, "Cypress goddess."

Asopus. [Modern name, **Oropo.**] In ancient geography, a small river in Boeotia, Greece, flowing into the Euripus in N Attica.

Asopus. [Modern name, **Hagios Georgios.**] In ancient geography, a small river in Sicyonia, Greece, rising in Phliasia and flowing through Sicyonia to empty into the Corinthian Gulf about four miles NE of Sicyon. According to tradition, the water of the Asopus came under the sea from the Maeander River in Caria.

Aspasia (as-pā'zha). Greek courtesan, born at Miletus, in Ionia; fl. c440 B.C. She was renowned for her wisdom, beauty, and wit. She was for many years the mistress of Pericles, who was so attracted to her that he left his wife and would have married her except for his own law of 451 B.C., which forbade Athenians to take foreign wives. Her brilliance made her house a center of Athenian literary and philosophical life. According to some accounts, she advised Pericles on public policy and helped him write his speeches. Accused of impiety, she was saved from death by Pericles' eloquence; her son, by Pericles, was legitimized under his father's name by a special Athenian decree after the death of Pericles' two sons by his first wife.

Aspendos (as-pen'dos). [Also: **Aspendus.**] In ancient geography, a city in Pamphylia, Asia Minor, on the Eurymedon. It contains a Roman theater which is one of the best-preserved of all ancient structures of the kind. The cavea is quite intact. There is also a Roman aqueduct which crosses the valley by a long range of arches.

Asphalius (as-fal'i-us). Epithet of Poseidon, as a god who grants safety to harbors and to navigation in general. Poseidon was worshiped under this name in several towns of Greece.

Asphodel Fields (as'fō-del.) Named by Homer as the meadow of the dead, where the shades of heroes wandered disconsolately. In Greek mythology the asphodel was the peculiar plant of the dead, its pale blossoms covering the meadows of Hades; perhaps because in Greek lands it is a very common weed, plentiful in barren and desert places and about tombs.

Assaracus (a-sar'a-kus). In Homeric legend (*Iliad*), a son of Tros and Callirrhoë, and a descendant of Dardanus and Ilus, the founders of the Trojan race. He was a king in Phrygia, and the brother of Ganymede, Ilus the Younger, and Cleopatra. Through his son Capys he was the ancestor of Aeneas.

Assus (as'us). [Also: **Assos**; modern Turkish, **Behram** or **Behramköy.**] In ancient geography, a city situated on the Gulf of Adramyttium, Mysia. The site, in what is now W Turkey, was thoroughly explored and excavated (1881–82) by the Archaeological Institute of America, with the important result of illustrating the architectural and topographical development of a minor Greek city with a completeness comparable to the body of information supplied by Pompeii concerning Roman towns under somewhat similar conditions. The remains studied include very extensive fortifications of successive periods, and temples ranging from the archaic Doric to foundations of the Christian era, a theater, baths, porticoes, a gymnasium, private dwellings in great variety, a remarkable and highly adorned street of tombs, and a Greek bridge.

Assyria (a-sir'i-a). [Greek, **Syria;** ancient name, **Assur, Asur,** or **Ashur;** Persian, **Athura.**] Ancient Asiatic state which at the period of its greatest power covered a territory of about 75,000 square miles, bounded by Armenia on the N, the Lower Zab River on the S, the Zagros Mountains on the E, and the Euphrates River on the W. The name was derived from that of the national deity, Assur, and was first applied to the city situated about 50 miles S of the modern Mosul. The city of Assur is not mentioned in the Old Testament, but it survived Nineveh, being still in existence in the time of Cyrus of Persia (Cyrus the Great), the conqueror of Babylon. The name Assur, besides being given to the city (and thence to the country), was also an element in the names of many Assyrian rulers. The Persians called the city Athura. The Greeks included under the name Assyria, or its shortened form Syria, the entire territory between Babylonia and the Mediterranean, sometimes applying it even to Babylonia. The N and E portions of the country were mountainous but the greater part was flat, being an extension of the Babylonian plain. Its principal rivers were the Tigris, the Upper and Lower Zab, the Kurnib, the Khoser, and the W Khabur. It was a fertile country, and abounded in all sorts of animals, among others the stag, roebuck, wild bull, and lion. The hunting of the lion was the favorite sport of the Assyrian kings. According to Genesis (x. 8–12, 22) the Assyrians were descendants of Shem and emigrants from Babylon. Their Semitic-Babylonian origin is fully attested by their sculptures and inscriptions. Their language is, apart from a few dialectical and orthographical variations, identical with Babylonian, and closely akin to Hebrew. Assyria derived its civilization from Babylonia. Its religion was the same as that of the mother-country, with the exception of the national god Assur, who was placed by them at the head of the pantheon. Assyrian architecture was a slavish copy of that of Babylonia. Although stone abounded in Assyria, bricks continued to be used in imitation of the practice in Babylonia, where no stone existed. The Babylonian emigrants who founded

Assyria have been dated by some scholars as leaving Babylonia c2000 B.C., although some recent archaeological research indicates the probability of a settlement at an even earlier date. In the 15th century B.C., Assyria was involved in a war with Babylonia. War continued between the two countries for a long time with varying success. Finally, however, Assyria became supreme and Babylonia the vassal state. The chief maker of Assyria's glory was Tiglath-pileser I (c1120–1100 B.C.), who conquered the city of Babylon, other cities of Babylonia, and penetrated as far as the Mediterranean. His more important successors were Assurdan II (930–911 B.C.), Assurnazirpal (884–860 B.C.), Shalmaneser III (860–824 B.C.), who came in contact with Damascus and Israel, Tiglath-pileser III (Phul in the Old Testament), 745–727 B.C., whose power extended to the confines of Egypt and who put the crown of Babylon on his head, Sargon (722–705 B.C.), the conqueror of Samaria, who defeated the Egyptians of Raphia, Sennacherib (705–681 B.C.), and Esarhaddon (680–668 B.C.). These last two kings mark the height of Assyrian power, and Esarhaddon was enabled by his conquests to add to his name the title king of Upper and Lower Egypt and Ethiopia. Under Assurbanipal (the Sardanapalus of Greek writers), 668–626 B.C., the decline of the empire began. In some respects this reign was most prosperous and brilliant; it was the golden age of art and literature. Under this reign too, Susa was conquered and destroyed. But signs of the approaching disintegration were seen in the constant uprisings of the oppressed nations. The downward course was rapid. Once, c625 B.C., Assyria succeeded in repelling an attack of the Medes and Persians, but later, Cyaxares in union with Nabopolassar of Babylon repeated the attack (606 B.C.), Nineveh fell, and Assyrian power entirely disappeared.

Astacus (as'ta-kus). [Modern Turkish name, **Izmit.**] In ancient geography, a Greek colony in Bithynia, Asia Minor, near Nicomedia.

Asta Pompeia (as'ta pom-pē'a). An ancient name of **Asti,** city in the Piedmont region of N Italy.

Astarte (as-tär'te). [Also: **Ashtoreth.**] Semitic

actor; up, lūte, pull; oi, oil; ou, out; ᴛʜ, then; d̯ as d or j, s̯ as s or sh, t̯ as t or ch, z̯ as z or zh.

goddess of fecundity and love, among the Phoenicians equivalent to the Ishtar of the Assyro-Babylonians; often considered to be an equivalent of the Greek Aphrodite. She is the female counterpart of Baal, with whom she held the first place in the Phoenician pantheon. Baal was identified with the sun, and Astarte with the moon, and she is often represented under the symbol of the crescent. The chief seat of her worship was at Sidon. The pomegranate and the dove were sacred to her. The favorite places of her worship were sacred groves, and she herself was often adored under the symbol of a tree, the *asherah* (translated "grove") often denounced in the Old Testament. Her cult in later times was combined with orgiastic celebration.

Asteria (a-stē′ri-a). In Greek mythology, a daughter of the Titans, Coeus and Phoebe, and the mother, by Perses, of Hecate. Pursued by Zeus, she assumed the form of a quail and leaped into the sea to escape him. She was then transformed into an island, Ortygia, which floated in the sea. Later, when her sister, Leto, sought refuge to bear her children, the tiny island received her gladly; four pillars rose from the sea floor to anchor it, and the modest island, thereafter called Delos, became famed as the birthplace of Leto's children, Apollo and Artemis.

Asteria. An epithet of Aphrodite in her aspect as a goddess of the heavens, meaning "Starry."

Asterion (as-tē′ri-on), or **Asterius** (-us). According to tradition, a son of Cometes. He sailed with Jason on the *Argo*.

Asterion. In ancient geography, a river of Argolis, Greece. When Hera and Poseidon contended for control of Argos the river-god Asterion was one of the judges of the dispute. He awarded the land to Hera. In a rage at the decision, Poseidon dried up his waters. The stream Asterion flowed past the Argive shrine of Hera, called the Heraeum. Some say one of the nymphs who cared for Hera in her childhood was the nymph of this river named Asterion.

Asterius (as-tē′ri-us). In Greek mythology, the king of Crete when Europa was brought there by Zeus. After Zeus left Europa, with the three sons she had borne him, Asterius married her, and since this marriage was childless he adopted her three sons and made them his heirs. Asterius or Asterion was also the name given to the Minotaur, the monster that Pasiphaë bore as a result of her unnatural union with the Cretan Bull.

Asterius. In mythology, a giant, the son of Anax. He succeeded his father as ruler of the land later known as Caria. Miletus, fleeing from King Minos of Crete, came to his land and killed Asterius. His body, later disinterred from its grave on a neighboring island, was found to be over ten cubits long.

Asterius. In Greek legend, a son of Hyperasius. With his brother Amphion he was one of the Argonauts who accompanied Jason on the quest for the Golden Fleece.

Asterodia (as-tėr-ō-dī′a). A Caucasian nymph. She was the mother, by Aeëtes, king of Colchis, of Apsyrtus.

Asteropaeus (as-tėr-ō-pē′us). In Homeric legend (*Iliad*), a Trojan ally. He was a Lycian from Paeonia, a son of Pelegon, and a descendant of the river-god of the Axius River. He accompanied Sarpedon at the siege of the Greek moat and walls. He was later slain by Achilles on the banks of the Scamander River and Achilles bore off his remarkable armor.

Asterope (as-ter′ō-pē). Another name for Sterope, one of the Pleiades.

Astrabacus (as-trā′ba-kus). According to tradition, a Spartan prince who with Alopecus found the wooden image of Artemis that Orestes brought back from Tauris.

Astraea or **Astrea** (as-trē′a). In classical mythology, the goddess of justice.

Astraeus (as-trē′us). In Greek mythology, a son of the Titan Crius and Eurybia, and the brother of the Titans Pallas and Perses. He was the father of the winds and the stars by Eos, the goddess of Dawn.

Astrateia (as-tra-tī′a). An epithet of Artemis, meaning "Stayer." There was a sanctuary of Artemis Astrateia at Pyrrhicus, in Laconia, because the advance of the Amazons was stayed there.

Astronomica (as-trō-nom′i-ka). A Latin hexameter poem on astrology, of which five books survive, by the Roman poet Marcus Manilius, a contemporary of Augustus and Tiberius. (JJ)

Astyages (as-tī′a-jēz). Son of Cyaxares, king of the Medes. According to Herodotus, who is the source of the following information, he married a daughter of Alyattes, king of Lydia, and thus was the brother-in-law of Croesus, who later became king of Lydia. Astyages succeeded his father as king of the Medes and reigned in the period 584–c549 B.C. He had a daughter Mandane, of whom he dreamed that such a flood of water flowed from her that it covered all Asia. The interpretation which the Magi put on this dream terrified him. As a consequence, he married his daughter to a Persian nobleman, Cambyses, who was of the royal race of the Persians and their hereditary monarch, but since at that time the Persians were subject to the Medes he was looked on as inferior as a husband to a Mede of a lower class. After Mandane was married to Cambyses and had gone to his home in Persia, Astyages dreamed again. This time it seemed that from his daughter's womb grew a tree which overshadowed all of Asia. The Magi interpreted this to mean that Mandane's offspring would become king if he lived long enough. Astyages sent to Persia and ordered Mandane brought back to his court. He gave orders that the child she was about to bear should be destroyed as soon as it was born. Soon afterward Cyrus was born. He was given into the hands of Harpagus, a trusted aid of Astyages, to be destroyed. As it happened the orders of Astyages were not carried out— the shepherd to whom Harpagus gave the task brought up the child as his own son— but Astyages and Harpagus were unaware of this. Years later a boy was brought before Astyages on the complaint of a Median noble, who accused the lad of playing the king and insulting the son of the nobleman. Astyages was struck by the appearance of the boy, and soon learned that it was his own grandson, whom he thought had been slain. He sent the child, Cyrus, to his mother in Persia, having been assured that his dream was fulfilled because Cyrus had acted as king among his playmates. But Harpagus he punished for his disobedience by slaying his son, cutting the body in pieces, and serving it to Harpagus at a banquet. At the end of the banquet he asked Harpagus how he had enjoyed it. When Harpagus answered that he had enjoyed it very much, Astyages order his servants to bring in the hands, feet,

and head of Harpagus' son, that the father might know on what flesh he had feasted. (This story appears in various myths, as in the story of Atreus and Thyestes.) Harpagus maintained his composure, saying that whatever pleased the king pleased him, but thenceforth he determined on revenge. He enlisted the interest of some powerful Median nobles who chafed under the harsh rule of Astyages. When Cyrus grew to manhood Harpagus sent messages to him, urging him to lead the Persians in a revolt against Astyages, and assuring him of the coöperation of the Median nobles and himself. The Persians had long been anxious to throw off the Median yoke, thus when Cyrus proposed that they revolt they accepted him as their leader with enthusiasm. Astyages got wind of the plot and summoned Cyrus into his presence. When Cyrus came it was at the head of an army. Astyages, forgetting the cruelty he had earlier inflicted on Harpagus, sent out an army against Cyrus that was commanded by Harpagus and, according to plan, this army was quickly put to flight. When Astyages learned of the defeat of his army he sent for the Magi who had advised him to send Cyrus to his parents in Persia, because the dream had been fulfilled, and impaled them. Then at the head of a hastily gathered force he marched out against Cyrus and was utterly defeated by him in battle (c549 B.C.). Astyages had ruled for 35 years when he was defeated by Cyrus and his people passed under the dominion of Persia. Astyages spent the remainder of his days in the court of Cyrus, where he was courteously treated. Later he encountered Harpagus, who taunted him with having lost his kingdom and bragged that he had engineered the revolt. Astyages answered him that if it was true he was powerful enough to stir up the revolt then he was a fool not to have led it himself and made himself sovereign; and moreover, he had done an evil service to his own countrymen, the Medes, by helping to set a Persian over them.

Astyanax (as-tī′a̱-naks). In Greek legend, the son of Hector and Andromache. At the fall of Troy Odysseus advised Agamemnon to kill Astyanax lest, when he was grown up, he assemble the Trojans and make war on the Greeks. In consequence of this advice and a prophecy by Calchas, Astyanax was taken from his mother's arms and hurled from the towers of Troy. Astyanax was also known as Scamandrius.

Astydamas (as-tī′da̱-mas). Name of two Greek tragic poets, father and son, of the 4th century B.C. Fragments are all that remain of their works.

Astydamia (as″ti-da̱-mī′a̱). In Greek legend, a daughter of Amyntor of Ormenius. It is extremely difficult to disentangle the various mothers of the many children of Heracles, but according to some accounts her father refused to give her to Heracles, on the ground that he already had a wife; Heracles then slew Amyntor and abducted Astydamia, and she bore him a son, either Tlepolemus or Ctesippus. Other accounts however, say that Astyoche was the mother of Tlepolemus.

Astydamia. According to some accounts, a daughter of Pelops and Hippodamia, and the mother of Amphitryon.

Astyoche, Astyocheia (as-tī′ō̱-kē, as″tī-ō̱-kī′a̱). In Greek mythology, a daughter of Phyleus, king of Ephyra on the Selleis River. When her father's city was attacked by Heracles she was carried off as a captive and became the mother, by Heracles, of Tlepolemus.

Astypalaea (as″ti-pa̱-lē′a̱). [Also: **Astropalia;** Italian, **Stampalia.**] Greek island in the Aegean Sea, about 77 miles NW of Rhodes; one of the Dodecanese Islands. Length, about 13 miles.

Atabyrian (a-ta̱-bī′ri-an). Epithet of Zeus, from his sanctuary on Mount Atabyrium (or Atabyrum or Atabyris), the highest peak on the island of Rhodes. The sanctuary was founded at Althaemenes, son of Catreus, who had voluntarily gone into exile at Rhodes from his native Crete so that he would not be the one to fulfill an oracle predicting that Catreus would meet death at the hands of one of his children. From the sanctuary, which was still highly esteemed in the 1st century B.C., the homesick Althaemenes could see his native Crete in the distance. Atabyrian Zeus was worshiped in the form of a bull, and bronze images of bulls on the mountain were said to bellow when any evil threatened.

Atalanta (at-a̱-lan′ta̱) or **Atalante** (-tē). In Greek legend, the supposed daughter of Iasius of Arcadia, but some say Zeus was her father. Iasius had hoped for a son. In his disappointment over the birth of a daughter he exposed the child on a mountain to die. Artemis became her protector and sent a she-bear to nurse the infant until she was found by a band of hunters. They rescued her and brought her up. Once later, when Atalanta was fainting from thirst she called on Artemis for help, and struck the earth with the point of her spear. Artemis caused a stream of water to gush forth. Atalanta was warned by the oracle at Delphi against marriage, but the oracle added that she would marry and that she would not enjoy her marriage. She therefore shunned the society of men and devoted herself to hunting, as did the virgin goddess Artemis. She became a skilled and fearless hunter, and once killed two centaurs who pursued her in the forest. According to some accounts, she accompanied the Argonauts in the quest for the Golden Fleece, but others say that Jason refused her request to be admitted as a member of his company on the ground that the presence of one woman among so many men would cause trouble. When she heard of the great company that Meleager of Calydon was assembling to hunt the Calydonian Boar she eagerly went to join the group. Meleager saw her lovely face, fell in love with her charm, which was boyish and feminine at the same time, and welcomed her as a member of the hunt. But the great heroes who had come at Meleager's call objected strongly to the presence of a woman in their midst, and some threatened to withdraw. Meleager announced that they must accept Atalanta or he would abandon the project of the hunt entirely. They reluctantly agreed to accept her. When the boar was raised from its lair many of the noble hunters sprang to attack it, but none succeeded in wounding it. On the contrary, the boar killed some of the hunters and drove others to cover. Atalanta was the first to draw blood by striking it in the head with one of her arrows. Ancaeus, who scoffed at Atalanta because she hadn't killed the boar, boasted that he would show her how to hunt, but as he went to the attack the boar charged him and disembowelled him with its tusks. Meleager administered the final blow to the boar after it had

been wounded by Atalanta. He awarded
the boar's hide and tusks to her because she
had drawn first blood. To honor a woman in
this way was a humiliation in the eyes of
some of the hunters. Meleager's uncles
protested the award. They said either Meleager, who had killed the boar, should have
the hide, or it should be awarded to one of
them, as those most to be honored among
those present. Their anger in this matter led
to their own and Meleager's deaths. Some
say that Atalanta bore a son to Meleager in
secret and that she exposed the child, Parthenopaeus, on a mountain to die, and afterward pretended that she was a virgin. After
her success in the Calydonian Hunt Atalanta
returned to her father's house and was delightedly received. He wished her to marry,
as he hoped for grandsons. Atalanta, mindful of the warning of the oracle, agreed to
marry, but set up certain conditions which
her future husband must first meet. Relying
on her swiftness of foot, she said any suitor
for her hand must run against her in a race.
If he won she would marry him; if he lost
she would kill him. In spite of the harsh
conditions there were many suitors, and
many lost the race and their lives. Hippomenes came to watch the contest. He was
astonished that any man would be so foolish
as to take such a risk, thought no woman
alive was worth it. But when he saw Atalanta's beauty he changed his mind. He fell
in love with her and decided to race for her
hand himself. When he made known his
intentions Atalanta looked at him and her
heart softened. She did not want him to die,
and hoped he would win. Before the race
began Hippomenes appealed to Aphrodite
for help, because, he said, it was Aphrodite
who had caused him to fall in love with Atalanta and take such a mad risk. Aphrodite
answered his prayer by giving him three
golden apples and instructions for the use
he should make of them. As the race started
the runners were even for a time but soon
Atalanta fleetly drew ahead. Hippomenes
cast one of the golden apples in front of her.
On seeing it Atalanta hesitated, then bent
and picked it up. This gave Hippomenes
a chance to draw ahead. When she again
overtook him and widened the space between them he used a second apple, and

toward the end of the course it was necessary
for him to use the third. With their help he
was able to beat Atalanta and win her for
his bride. As Atalanta had already fallen in
love with him before the race everyone was
delighted. But in their happiness they forgot to show their gratitude to Aphrodite.
That goddess, in anger because they had so
quickly forgotten her and also to punish
Atalanta for denying the power of love for
so long, caused them to profane the temple of
Cybele with their love-making. Cybele
avenged the outrage to her shrine by transforming them into lions and yoking them to
her car. Sometimes Atalanta is called the
daughter of Schoeneus of Boeotia, and her
husband is variously named as Melanion; and
some think the Atalanta of Arcadia and the
Atalanta of Boeotia were two different maidens who had almost identical histories.

Atalanti (at-a̯-lan′ti; Greek, ä-tä-län′dē), **Channel** (or **Gulf**) **of.** [Also: **Channel** (or **Gulf**)
of Atalante (or **Talanti**).] The NW portion of
the sea passage which separates Euboea from
the mainland of Greece.

Atargatis (a̯-tär′ga̯-tis). Syrian goddess, worshiped in Carchemish, corresponding approximately to Astarte and the Assyro-Babylonian
Ishtar. At Ascalon she was worshiped by the
Philistines under the name of Derceto in the
form of a woman terminating in a fish. She
also had a temple at Ephesus, and her numerous retinue of priestesses, which the Greeks
found there, is supposed by some to have
given rise to the legend of the Amazons.

Ate (ā′tē.) A daughter of Zeus (according to
Homer) or of Eris (according to Hesiod).
She was the goddess of mischief, who en-
snared the feet of mortals and caused them
to act rashly and unreasonably. It was Ate
who so blinded Zeus to his own interests
on the day when he was awaiting the birth of
his hero son Heracles, that he promised Hera
that the first son born that day would be lord
over all those who dwelt around him. Hera
then delayed the birth of Heracles until after
Eurystheus, grandson of Perseus, was born,
in consequence of which Heracles had to
serve Eurystheus. For causing this mischief
Zesus clutched Ate by the hair and flung her
out of heaven. Agamemnon blamed his
rash act in taking Briseis from Achilles on
Ate, naming her the goddess who strikes

actọr; up, lūte, pŭll; oi, oil; ou, out; ŦH, then; d̦ as d or j, ş as s or sh, ț as t or ch, z̧ as z or zh.

men with blindness and makes them stumble and fall.

Atella (a-tel′a). In ancient geography, a town in Campania, Italy, about ten miles N of Naples.

Aternus (a-tėr′nus). [Modern name, **Aterno**.] Upper course of the river Pescara, in C Italy.

Athamas (ath′a-mas). In Greek mythology, a son of Aeolus and Enarete, and the brother of Sisyphus and Salmoneus. He was a king of Orchomenus in Boeotia. At Hera's command he married Nephele, a cloud in the shape of a woman, and by her had two sons, Phrixus and Leucon, and one daughter, Helle. Tiring of his phantom wife, he abandoned Nephele in favor of Ino, the daughter of Cadmus, and had two sons by her, Melicertes and Learchus. Ino, to get rid of his heirs by Nephele, duped him into believing that a famine which was devastating the land could be lifted by the sacrifice of Phrixus. As Athamas prepared to carry out the sacrifice a winged ram with golden fleece, sent by Hermes, arrived at the altar and carried Phrixus and his sister Helle away on its back. Nephele complained to Hera because she had been replaced by Ino. The goddess resolved to punish Athamas, both because of his treatment of Nephele and because Ino had sheltered Dionysus, the son of Zeus and Semele. Hera laid a divine frenzy on Athamas, in which he killed his son Learchus and would have killed Ino too but with the aid of Dionysus she escaped, carrying Melicertes in her arms. Athamas' remaining son Leucon died. Since he was banished from Boeotia for his crimes, Athamas consulted the oracle at Delphi to learn where he should go. He was told that he should settle where wild beasts provided his dinner. He wandered into Thessaly and there came upon wolves mauling sheep that they had just killed. The wolves fled at the approach of Athamas and his companions. The slain sheep provided Athamas and his friends with a hearty meal and, in accordance with the instructions of the oracle, he founded a city, Alos, on the site. In Thessaly he married again and raised a new family.

Athena (a-thē′na) or **Athene** (-nē). [Also: **Pallas Athena**.] One of the 12 Olympians. Although she was worshiped throughout Greece, her cult was especially strong in Attica, where she was a national divinity, and where her worship was gloriously memorialized in the Parthenon, the Temple of the Maiden Goddess on the Acropolis at Athens. The worship of Athena is essentially an expression of developing ethical and social principles. She is a goddess of war who fights in righteous causes. Like Zeus, she wields the thunderbolt and the lightning. She personifies the clear upper air as well as mental clearness and acuteness, embodying the spirit of truth and divine wisdom; she wears the aegis, symbolizing the dark storm-cloud, and is armed with the resistless spear (the shaft of lightning). She participates with skill and wisdom in wars to defend the state, but does not fight, like Ares, with uncontrolled ferocity for sheer love of strife. Her activities in war restore order, and thus she is a goddess of peace. She upholds law and order, encourages the arts by which the state is strengthened, and has invented so many aids to mankind that she is called the *Contriver*. Athena is also the goddess who taught and encourages the household arts of spinning, weaving, and cooking. She is the protectress of the young, the patroness of agriculture, of construction of all kinds, of healing, and of music. She is especially devoted to the interests of mankind for, some say, when Prometheus fashioned men of clay and water it was Athena who breathed life into them.

Some say Athena was born beside the lake Tritonis in Libya, and that Poseidon was her father. By the temple of Hephaestus at Athens was a blue-eyed statue of Athena, signalizing her relationship to Poseidon with blue eyes like his. But she quarreled with Poseidon and appealed to Zeus, who then adopted her as his daughter. Others say she was reared by the river-god Triton, and that his daughter Pallas was her dear companion. They often played at war games together, and one day Athena accidentally struck and killed her. In memory of her grief, Athena placed the name of her playmate before her own, and was henceforth known as Pallas Athena. She made a wooden image of Pallas, wrapped it in her aegis, and set it up and honored it. This image, the Palladium, afterwards dropped, or was hurled, from heaven. It fell into the Troad

fat, fāte, fär, fãre, errạnt; net, mē, hėr ardẹnt; pin, pīne; not, nōte, mȯve, nôr,

and was found by Ilus, who made a temple in which he set it up, and it became the sacred image that protected Ilium (Troy) as long as it remained in the citadel. Others say the winged giant Pallas was the father of Athena, and that he attempted to violate her and she killed him. She flayed him, they say, and used his skin for her aegis, and attached his wings to her own feet. The generally accepted account is that Zeus fell in love with the Titaness Metis, called by some his first wife, and embraced her. An oracle of Gaea predicted that Metis would bear a girl child, and if she should have another child it would be a son who would destroy Zeus, as he had destroyed his father Cronus. On learning of this oracle Zeus swallowed Metis. Some months later as he walked beside Lake Tritonis in Libya he was smitten with a violent headache and roared with pain. Hermes recognized the cause of his anguish and called Hephaestus, or as some say, Prometheus, who took up an axe and smote Zeus on the forehead. Out of his cloven skull Athena leaped, fully armed. She became the favorite of her father Zeus, and sat at his right hand, giving him counsel. Oaths taken in her name, along with those of Zeus and Apollo, were most sacred. Some say her epithet *Tritogeneia* means "Triton-born," and was given to her because she was born near Lake Tritonis. Because of the connection with Triton in the varying accounts of her birth, any place that had a lake or a river named Triton claimed to be her birthplace. The oldest seat of her worship in Greece was on the Triton River that flows into Lake Copaïs, in Boeotia, for it was here that the river-god was said to have reared her. But some say she came to Greece from Libya by way of Crete, and that Alalcomeneus, the first man, brought her up near Lake Copaïs, for which reason she had the epithet *Alalcomeneis*.

As a goddess of war Athena was called Area (*Warlike*). She took part in the war between the gods and the giants, but first she prudently sought out Heracles, for an oracle had foretold that the gods could not defeat the giants without his help. She found him and helped him to find the magic herb that would make him invulnerable, then conveyed him to the battle, where she advised him how to kill Alcyoneus. Because she drove a chariot—which she invented—in the struggle with the giants, she was given the name Hippia (*Horse-goddess*). She pursued Enceladus and flattened him with a rock so that he became the island of Sicily, and some say the Pallas whose skin she used for her aegis was a giant she killed in this war. Athena contended with Hera and Aphrodite for the prize of beauty, thrown among the wedding guests at the marriage of Peleus and Thetis by Eris. She promised Paris, who was given the task of awarding the prize, victory in all his battles, but when he gave the prize to Aphrodite she became an implacable enemy of Paris and the Trojans. In the Trojan War her services were always on the side of the Greeks. She so inspired Diomedes with valor that he wounded Aphrodite and then, with Athena riding beside him in his chariot and guiding his spear, he wounded Ares. When Diomedes was wounded by Pandarus Athena cleared the mist from his eyes and filled him with new courage. In gratitude for her help, Diomedes dedicated a sanctuary to Athena Oxyderces (*Bright-eyed*) at Corinth when he returned from the Trojan War. She was a protector of Achilles. When Hector stood alone before the walls of Troy Athena assumed the guise of his brother, Deïphobus, and stood beside him and tricked him into remaining to face Achilles and death. It was Athena, some say, who inspired the stratagem of the Wooden Horse and helped Epeus to build it. On the side of the Horse was an inscription that dedicated it to Athena. After the capture and sack of Troy, Locrian Ajax (Ajax the Lesser) seized Cassandra as she clung to the image of Athena in the sanctuary whither she had fled for refuge. In tearing Cassandra from the sanctuary he bore off the image which she clasped with her. This brought the wrath of Athena on Ajax, and on the Greeks because they did not punish him. She caused the death of Ajax in a storm at sea on his way home, and for 1000 years afterward the Locrians were compelled to propitiate Athena by supplying two Locrian maidens to serve in her sanctuary at Troy. Odysseus was one of her favorites. He raised several sanctuaries to Athena Celeuthea (*Lady of the Road*), along the road in Laconia on which he had raced for the hand of Penelope. Athena caused Telamonian Ajax to go mad to save Odysseus from his wrath when the armor of Achilles was awarded to Odysseus instead of to him. Though she could not prevent Poseidon from harrying Odysseus on his voyage home from Troy, she took the opportunity, when Poseidon was absent, to appeal to Zeus to let Odysseus, already delayed ten years on his journey, return home. She helped Odysseus regain his own shores and instructed and aided him so that, with his son Telemachus, he slew the suitors who had been reveling in his halls at his expense and won back his wife and his kingdom. Agamemnon, who had made proper sacrifices to Athena before leaving Troy, had a speedy voyage home. Menelaus, angry at the gods for allowing the war to last so long, refused to sacrifice to the goddess, and was punished by being driven about the seas for seven years before he was permitted to return to Sparta.

ATHENA WITH HERACLES
Red-figured Greek cup, Duris, c480 B.C.
Munich

In the reign of King Cecrops, Athena and Poseidon contended for control of Athens. Poseidon struck the rock of the Acropolis with his trident and a fountain of sea water gushed forth, and whenever the south wind blows the sound of waves can be heard in this fountain. Athena's gift to Athens was an olive tree, as Cecrops testified. (Both the well and the olive tree were later enclosed in the Erechtheum. When this temple was burned during the Persian War (480 B.C.) the olive tree was destroyed, but instantly a new shoot sprang forth from the burned trunk, and the tree was shown to the traveler Pausanias in the 2nd century A.D.) The gods, called on to decide which gift was of more benefit to the people of Athens, voted in favor of the olive tree and Athena. In a rage, Poseidon flooded the plain. Athena's town of Athenae was engulfed by the flood, whereupon she took Athens as her city and gave it her own name. On another occasion she contended with Poseidon for Troezen. By a decree of Zeus they were directed to share it, and the Troezenians raised a temple of Athena Sthenias (*Strong*) on their citadel.

Athena was one of three goddesses (the others were Artemis and Hestia), who did not yield to the power of love exerted by Aphrodite; she remained a virgin. Hephaestus, tricked by Poseidon into thinking she would welcome his advances, once tried to make love to her when she entered his forge. She repulsed him, and his spilled seed fell to the ground and fertilized Earth. When the child Erichthonius was born of this accidental union Earth refused to have anything to do with him. Athena took the child, half-man and half-serpent, put him in a chest and gave the chest to the daughters of Cecrops—Aglauros, Herse, and Pandrosos—with the admonition to take good care of it but not to look inside. Curiosity compelled the maidens, with their mother, to open the chest. When they saw the strange creature inside they were seized with fear, and leaped to their deaths, some say, from the Acropolis. A white crow brought the news to Athena as she was carrying a huge rock to fortify the Acropolis. She dropped the rock, which stayed where it fell and became Mount Lycabettus, and punished the crow for bringing her the distressing news by changing its feathers to black and forbidding crows to perch on the Acropolis in future. She took Erichthonius up into her aegis and reared

fat, fāte, fär, fāre, errant; net, mē, hėr ardent; pin, pīne; not, nōte, möve, nôr,

him in the Erechtheum, the oldest temple on the Acropolis, and thereafter sacred serpents were kept in the temple in his honor. Erichthonius became king of Athens and instituted the Panathenaea in her honor. In another case, Athena rescued the heart of Zagreus, who had been torn to pieces by the Titans, enclosed it in a clay figure, and breathed life into it, making Zagreus immortal.

Athena Promachus (*Champion*) was the protector and defender of heroes and freely gave them her aid. Cadmus, desiring to sacrifice the cow that had led him into Boeotia to Athena, killed the dragon that guarded the sacred spring whither he had gone to fetch water for the sacrifice. Athena appeared to him and thanked him for the sacrifice. She told him to sow half the dragon's teeth and gave him the city of Thebes. She gave the other half of the dragon's teeth to Aeëtes of Colchis. She advised Danaus to build a ship and flee with his daughters from Egypt. He set up an image of Athena at Lindus, in Rhodes, in acknowledgment of her help. Afterward, on the order of Zeus, Athena and Hermes purified the daughters of Danaus for the murder of their husbands, and Danaus raised a sanctuary of Athena Saitis (*Sais*, the name of the Egyptian goddess identified with Athena) on the hilltop at Lerna where, some say, the heads of the murdered men were buried. Athena helped Perseus when he went to fetch the head of Medusa. She gave him a bright shield to use as a mirror when he cut off Medusa's head, and guided his hand as he did so. After he had put Medusa's head to good use Perseus gave it to Athena and she placed it in her aegis, or as some say, in the middle of her shield. Some say the Gorgon Medusa was transformed from a beautiful maiden into a hideous monster because she had vied with Athena in beauty. Others say she was transformed for committing impious acts with Poseidon in a sanctuary of Athena. Athena gave Cepheus of Tegea a lock of Medusa's hair to protect his city, and to Asclepius she gave some of Medusa's blood. Some say the blood that came from the left side of Medusa was used to bring death, and that from the right side was used for healing; and some say all the blood of Medusa that was given to Asclepius

was used by him for healing and restoring life. She gave Erichthonius two drops of Medusa's blood, one to bring death and the other to cure, contained in vials, and fastened them with golden bands to his body. Bellerophon owed much to her, for she bridled Pegasus, for which reason she was called Chalinitis (*Bridler*) and gave the winged horse to him. Brave Tydeus, father of Diomedes, was especially loved by Athena. When he was wounded in the fighting of the Seven against Thebes, she hurried off to Zeus and fetched an herb that would make him immortal. She arrived with the magical herb just in time to see Tydeus gulp the brains of Melanippus from his dismembered head. This sight so disgusted her that she refrained from healing his wound and making him immortal, as she had intended to do, and let him die. Heracles was another of her favorites, and by one of her devices he was restored to his mother when he had been abandoned as an infant. She gave him a robe when the gods were arming him with gifts, gave him bronze castanets with which to frighten the Stymphalian birds, advised him how to attack the Lernaean Hydra, helped him fetch the Apples of the Hesperides (which were later returned to her as it was unlawful for mortals to keep them), and guided him to the Underworld to fetch Cerberus. Heracles raised a sanctuary of Athena Axiopoenus (*Just Requital*) in Laconia after he had avenged the death of Oeonus by slaying Hippocoön and his sons. In all his labors and trials Athena stood as his friend; twice she took his part in battles against the gods, and when he was immortalized she led him to the gods of Olympus. She was a friend to Jason and helped Argus build the *Argo* for the expedition for the Golden Fleece, and inserted in the keel a beam of oracular oak from the sacred grove at Dodona which gave Jason good advice on his journey.

As a patroness of law and order, Athena compelled the Erinyes to allow Orestes to come to trial before the Areopagus for the murder of his mother, and when the vote was even she cast her vote in favor of Orestes. This strengthened the Areopagus and substituted law and mercy for vengeance. In gratitude, Orestes dedicated an altar to

Athena Area (*Warlike*). The Erinyes were much exercised at what they considered a perversion of their ancient privileges. They threatened to lay a blight on Athens if the verdict was not reversed but Athena persuaded them, with promises of gifts and honor from the Athenians for all time, to dwell peacefully in a grotto on the Acropolis. In return for honors and sacrifices from the Athenians the Erinyes promised favorable winds for Athena's ships, fertility for her land, and prosperous marriages for her people. The Erinyes, henceforth known as The Kindly Ones, were then led in a torchlight procession to their new home on the Acropolis, which became an oracular shrine and a place of sanctuary.

Athena is credited with having invented many things. She constructed the double flute of stag's bones, but when she played on it Hera and Aphrodite laughed, although she drew from it delightful music. One day she went to a quiet pool, and watching herself in its surface, she played on her flute. When she saw how distorted her face was, with her cheeks puffed out, she cast the flute from her and laid a curse on whoever should pick it up. It was found by Marsyas and caused his death. Some say she also invented the trumpet, and Hegeleos, son of Tyrsenus, raised a sanctuary of Athena Salpinx (*Trumpet*) in Argos. But others say it was Tyrsenus, son of Heracles and a Lydian woman, who invented the trumpet, and that Hegeleos taught the Dorians how to play it. Among her other inventions were earthenware pots, the plow, the ox-yoke, bridle, chariot, ship, and the science of numbers. She also made dice from knucklebones and used them for divination.

On the whole, Athena was not a vindictive goddess. She did transform Arachne, who had the arrogance to challenge her to a weaving contest, into a spider. But when Tiresias, the son of her dear companion Chariclo, happened to see her as she bathed in the Hippocrene Spring on Mount Helicon, he was blinded at the will of the gods for having seen what was unlawful. But some say Athena laid her hand over his eyes and blinded him. When Chariclo reproached her Athena could not restore his sight, because he had seen what was unlawful, but

she gave him the gifts of prophecy and divination, and a long life.

Athena had many epithets. As Athena Polias (*Of the City*), she had temples on the Acropolis at Athens, at Troezen, in Arcadia, and at Erythrae in Asia Minor. As Poliatas (*Keeper of the City*) she had a sanctuary at Tegea into which the priest entered but once a year, and as Poliuchus (*City-protecting*) she had a citadel in Sparta. The citadels at Athens, Argos, Sparta, Epidaurus, Troezen, Pheneus, and Troy and Smyrna, among others were all sacred to her, and illuminate her important role as a guardian and strengthener of cities. As patroness of the useful and decorative arts she was Ergane (*Worker*), a name first given to her by the Athenians. There was a sanctuary of Athena Ergane on the citadel at Sparta, and an altar at Olympia in Elis. The descendants of Phidias, known as Burnishers or Cleansers because they had the hereditary task of cleaning and polishing the great statue of Olympian Zeus, sacrificed to Athena Ergane before they began their work. The cock, a bird supposedly very ready to fight, was sacred to Athena Ergane. At Elis there was also an altar to Athena Leitis (*Goddess of Booty*), and the Eleans worshiped her as *Mother* in gratitude for the repopulation of Elis after the destruction of the population by Heracles. A temple of Athena Narcaea, raised by Narcaeus, son of Dionysus and Physcoa, also stood in Elis, as well as a temple of Athena Cydonia. This last was said to have been founded by Clymenus, a descendant of the Cretan Dactyl Heracles, who came from Cydonia in Crete. Pelops sacrificed to Cydonian Athena before he began his race with Oenomaus for the hand of Hippodamia. As Paeonia (*Healer*) Athena had an image at Athens and an altar at Oropus, and as *Health* she had an image on the Acropolis at Athens. Amphitryon dedicated an image of Athena Zosteria (*Girder*) at Thebes because here he put on his armor when he went to fight against Chalcedon and the Euboeans; Castor and Polydeuces raised a temple of Athena Asia in Laconia, near Gythium, when they returned from Colchis, in honor of the Colchian shrine of Athena Asia. The temple of Athena Anemotis (*Of the Winds*) was founded in Messenia after prayers to the goddess had caused violent and unseasonable winds that were damaging the country to cease. The sanctuary of Athena Alea in Tegea was founded by Aleus, great-grandson of Zeus and Callisto, and was respected throughout the Peloponnesus as an inviolable place of sanctuary. The sanctuary of Athena Itonia in Boeotia was named, some say, for Itonius, son of Amphictyon. The bronze image in it was made by Agoracritus, a pupil of Phidias. In the sanctuary the Boeotians gathered annually for their general assembly. One story concerning the sanctuary is that Iodama, a priestess, entered the sacred precinct at night and Athena appeared to her. When Iodama saw the head of Medusa in Athena's aegis she was turned to stone. Ever after, fire was put on the altar of Iodama each day, with the thrice repeated chant that Iodama lives and is asking for fire. But some say Athena was a daughter of Itonius, and that Iodoma was her sister. There was another sanctuary of Athena Itonia between Larisa and Pherae. The Spartans dedicated a bronze image of Athena on the citadel at Sparta; the bronze sanctuary in which it was housed, and for which reason the image was called Athena of the Bronze House, was begun by Tyndareus and was finished early in the 6th century B.C. by the Spartan Gitiadas. At other places there were images and sanctuaries of Athena Promachorma (*Protector of the Anchorage*), Pronaea (*Of the Fore-temple*), Pronoia (*Forethought*), Xenia (*Hospitable*), Larisaea (*Of Larisa*), Ophthalmitis (*Of the Eye*), Cissaea (*Ivy-goddess*), Cyparissia (*Cypress-goddess*), Coryphasia (*Of Coryphasium*), Aeantis (*Ajacian*), Aethyia (*Gannet*), Agoraea (*Of the Market-place*), Apaturia (*Deceitful*), and Hippolaitis (*Of Hippola*). As Athena Nike (*Victory*) she had a special temple on the Acropolis at Athens, and was sometimes depicted holding a figure of Victory in her outstretched hand. To the Athenians she was especially Parthenos (*Virgin* or *Maiden*), and for her they built the Parthenon. Inside the temple the gold and ivory image of Athena Parthenos, by Phidias, was set up (438–7 B.C.). The face, hands, and feet were of ivory; precious stones formed the pupils of the eyes. The robe was of gold. The gold, which weighed 40 talents, could be removed from the image, and because of this Phidias was acquitted of a charge that he had stolen some of it, for when it was weighed it was found that the 40 talents were all accounted for. In the image the goddess wears her aegis. On her left side is her shield, on the outside of which is depicted in relief the battle of the Amazons and the Athenians. Into this scene Phidias put a portrait of himself, a bald-headed old man lifting a stone, and a portrait of Pericles, the face of which is somewhat obscured by his arm raised to hurl his spear. Because of these two portraits on an image of the goddess Phidias was convicted of impiety. On the inside of the shield the Battle of the Giants was shown. In her extended right hand Athena held an image of Victory wearing a golden crown. In her left hand, beside the shield, was her spear. Under the shield was a golden serpent, and on her helmet was the Sphinx. The war between the Centaurs and the Lapiths was depicted on her sandals, and the pedestal showed the birth of Pandora. Also on the Acropolis was the great bronze Athena Promachus (*Champion*) by Phidias, made from the spoils taken by the Athenians at the Battle of Marathon, and a third image, dedicated by the Lemnians and thought by some to be the most beautiful, called Lemnian Athena. All of these works have perished; descriptions from ancient writers and some copies of the Athena Parthenos are all that remain.

The chief festival of Athena was the great Panathenaea, at which time a peplus embroidered by the Athenian women was presented to the goddess, games and contests were held, and the festival was terminated by a great procession to the Acropolis. Other festivals of Athena were held at various times of the year to mark the progress of the crops. The sea-eagle, cock, serpent, and olive tree were sacred to her, but above all she was identified with the owl, symbol of wisdom. The coins of Athens bore the head of Athena on one side, and her sacred owl on the other. As a goddess of war she is represented in art with a helmet, shield, and spear; as a goddess of peace and the useful arts she is sometimes represented without her helmet and holding a distaff. The Romans identified their Minerva with Athena.

Athenae (a-thē′nē). Town near Eleusis, Greece. According to mythology, it was Athena's town, and when Poseidon lost in his contest with her for control of Athens, he flooded the plain in his rage and Athenae was engulfed. Athena then took Athens for her city and gave it her own name.

Athenaeum (ath-e-nē′um). A famous school or university at Rome, founded by the emperor Hadrian. It was named for Athens, and was situated on the Capitoline Hill.

Athenaeus (ath-e-nē′us). Greek mechanician; fl. possibly about the end of the 2nd century B.C. He wrote a book on siege engines which contains historical information on these engines.

Athenaeus. Greek grammarian, rhetorician, and philosopher, born at Naucratis in Egypt. He was active c200 A.D. He wrote *The Learned Banquet (Deipnosophistae)* in 15 books, ten of which survive. The work purports to describe the conversation of a number of learned men, including Galen the physician and Ulpian the jurist, at a banquet given by a rich and cultivated Roman. The conversation covers the subject of cookery and banqueting in encyclopedic detail, providing a sourcebook of information on the customs, vessels, foods, wine-vessels, and entertainment in antiquity. It also includes comments on the weaknesses of philosophers, on subjects connected with social life, manners, customs, trade, art, and science. The work provides abundant evidence of the immense reading the author had done in many ancient authorities, and by quoting from many of the prose-writers and poets, especially from the masters of Middle and New Comedy, he has preserved fragments of many ancient writers' works otherwise lost. The work also contains what is believed to be the first account in history of a rain of fishes.

Athenagoras (ath-e-nag′ō-ras). Syracusan demagogue; fl. end of the 5th century B.C. He was an opponent of Hermocrates, whom he accused of trying to frighten the Syracusans when the latter warned that the Athenians were on their way and urged the Syracusans to prepare to resist them.

Athena Nike (a-thē′na nī′kē), **Temple of.** Small Ionic amphiprostyle tetrastyle marble temple, dedicated to Athena as goddess of Victory.

Pausanias called it the Temple of Nike Apteros or *Wingless Victory;* inscriptions indicate that the official designation was as Athena Nike. It was erected c427–424 B.C., on the site of an earlier temple, to designs by Callicrates, one of the architects of the Parthenon, and stands at the SW extremity of the Acropolis at Athens on a bastion projecting before the S wing of the Propylaea. Measuring 18 by 27 feet on the stylobate, it has a continuous frieze sculptured in high relief, with an assembly of gods on the E and battle scenes elsewhere. Four slabs of the frieze, among the Elgin Marbles in the British Museum, have been replaced with casts in the reconstructed temple. The small pediments also had sculptures. Along the north, east, and south faces of the bastion was a parapet, the Nike Parapet, sculptured with *Nikai* or Victories in relief, including the famous *Victory Loosing her Sandal,* among the most precious of all Greek sculptures.

The temple was pulled down by the Turks in 1686 to furnish the material for a rampart in front of the Propylaea. In 1834, when this rampart in turn was taken down, the stones of the temple were recovered, and in due course it was rebuilt, but with minor inaccuracies so that in 1936–1940 it was again dismantled and rebuilt. The temple, begun c427 B.C., had been commissioned c449 B.C.; during the interim Callicrates had used the plans in constructing the very similar temple on the Ilissus, which was seen and drawn by Stuart and Revett and was still standing in 1778 but subsequently vanished, torn down presumably for its materials. (JJ)

Athena Parthenos (pär′the-nos). Ivory and gold statue by Phidias, once in the Parthenon. It was one of the most admired works of antiquity. Only copies of the work survive, the most important of which, for its careful reproduction of details, is the Roman copy belonging to the collection of the National Museum at Athens. According to the writer Pausanias (2nd century A.D.), the face, hands, and feet of the image were of ivory; precious stones formed the pupils of the eyes. The robe was of gold. In the image the goddess wore her aegis. On her left side was her shield, on the outside of which was depicted in relief the battle of the

Amazons and the Athenians. On the inside of the shield appeared the Battle of the Giants. In her extended right hand the goddess held an image of Victory wearing a golden crown. In her left hand, besides the shield, was her spear. Under the shield was a golden serpent, representing Erichthonius, and on her helmet was the Sphinx. Her sandals were decorated with a scene showing the war between the Centaurs and the Lapiths, and the pedestal showed the birth of Pandora.

Athenion (a̯-thē′ni-on). Leader in the second slave insurrection in Sicily, 103–99 B.C. He is said to have been the commander of bandits in Cilicia, where he was captured and sold as a slave into Sicily. He was chosen leader of the insurgents in the western part of the island, made an unsuccessful attack on Lilybaeum, joined Tryphon (Salvius), king of the rebels, by whom he was for a time thrown into prison, fought under Tryphon in the battle with Lucius Licinius Lucullus, and on the death of Tryphon became king. He was slain in battle by the hand of Marcus Aquillius who put down the revolt.

Athenodorus (a̯-thē-no̯-dō′rus). Greek sculptor, born at Rhodes; fl. 1st century B.C. He collaborated, according to Pliny the Elder, with Agesander (believed by some to have been his father) and Polydorus on the group of the *Laocoön*.

Athenodorus Cananites (kā-na̯-nī′tēz). Stoic philosopher and tutor of Augustus, born at Tarsus, Asia Minor; fl. 1st century B.C. His influence over his one-time pupil is alleged to have been great even in later years; he was a friend also of Strabo and Cicero.

Athenodorus Cordylion (kôr-dil′i-o̯n). Stoic philosopher and librarian at Pergamum; fl. early 1st century B C. He lived at Rome during most of his later life.

Athens (ath′enz). [Greek, **Athenai, Athinai;** Latin, **Athenae.**] Capital of Greece, situated about five miles from its seaport Piraeus (on the Saronic Gulf) in E central Greece and Euboea, at the SW end of the Attic peninsula. The city lies at 350 feet above sea level on the Attic plain. Surrounding it are the mountains Aegaleos, Parnes, Pentelikon, and Hymettus on the W and E, which sometimes assume at dusk a delicate lavender color and give to the city its epithet "violet-crowned." Within the city limits stands the steep, rocky hill of Lycabettus. The Acropolis, around which the ancient city grew up, rises in the center of the city; it is the site of the earliest settlement and a place of many historical remains. In ancient times, on it were the royal palace and the dwellings of the Eupatrids. To the W is the Areopagus, or Hill of Ares, the site of the most ancient court of Athens, and the place where Saint Paul preached; farther W are the Hill of the Muses, the Pnyx, and the Hill of the Nymphs. In the 5th century B.C. long walls joined the city to its port. The city was founded, according to the old account, by an Egyptian colony led by Cecrops. It became the chief place in Attica, with Athena as its especial divinity, and was ruled by kings, among whom Erechtheus, Theseus, and Codrus are legendary and famous. Gradually the city spread to the lower slopes around the Acropolis and to the banks of the Illisus River. Thither the Eupatrids (nobles) moved and established the ancient aristocratic city described by Thucydides. Besides the Eupatrid enclave, other groups of dwellings to the north and northwest of the Acropolis formed the quarters occupied by artisans and tradesmen, such as the section known as the Ceramicus, alongside the ancient agora which, in the 7th and 6th centuries B.C. became the civic heart of the city. According to tradition, it was Theseus who united the twelve independent communities of Attica into a federal union governed by delegates to Athens. He renamed the Athenian Games the Panathenaea and invited all Attica to share in them, and he united the suburbs mentioned above to the city proper. Furthermore, he invited his fellow Greeks to become Athenian citizens, and many came to Athens. He is said to have divided the population thus enlarged into three classes: the Eupatrids, or nobles; the Georges, or farmers, and the Demiurges, or artisans. Lastly, he gave Athens a constitution, some say, and resigned his throne to further the democracy. After 1132 B.C., the legendary date of the death of Codrus, Athens was ruled by the Eupatrids, and had archons as magistrates, who were successively perpetual, decennial, and (after 683 B.C.) annual. Scholars have ques-

actor; up, lūte, pull; oi, oil; ou, out; ᴛʜ, then; d̯ as d or j, ş as s or sh, ţ as t or ch, z̯ as z or zh.

tioned the historical value of much of this legendary material. The laws of Draco were enacted in 621 B.C., and those of Solon in 594. Pisistratus became tyrant in 560 B.C. and his sons were expelled in 510. The reforms of Clisthenes (508 B.C.) made Athens (for its day) a pure democracy; popular assemblies of all its citizens (but not all, or even most, of its adult inhabitants were citizens) made the laws. The glorious period began with the Persian wars, in which Athens took a leading part, as at Marathon (490 B.C.) and Salamis (480). The city was temporarily held by the Persians (480 B.C.) who burned it and destroyed the buildings on the Acropolis. Athens became the head of the Delian League in c477 B.C., and for a short period had an extensive empire and was the first power in Greece. The Athenians in the "Age of Pericles" (c461–429 B.C.) at the onset of the Peloponnesian Wars are described by Thucydides. He puts the following speech into the mouth of the Corinthian envoy who addresses the Spartan assembly considering whether to declare war on Athens:

"You have never considered, O Lacedaemonians, what manner of men are these Athenians with whom you will have to fight, and how utterly unlike yourselves. They are revolutionary, equally quick in the conception and in the execution of every new plan; while you are conservative—careful only to keep what you have, originating nothing, and not acting even when action is most necessary. They are bold beyond their strength; they run risks which prudence would condemn; and in the midst of misfortune they are full of hope. Whereas it is your nature, though strong, to act feebly; when your plans are most prudent, to distrust them; and when calamities come upon you, to think that you will never be delivered from them. They are impetuous and you are dilatory; they are always abroad, and you are always at home. For they hope to gain something by leaving their homes; but you are afraid that any new enterprise may imperil what you have already. When conquerors, they pursue their victory to the utmost; when defeated, they fall back the least. Their bodies they devote to the country as

though they belonged to other men; their true self is their mind, which is not truly their own when employed in her service. When they do not carry out an intention which they have formed, they seem to have sustained a personal bereavement; when an enterprise succeeds they have gained a mere installment of what is to come; but if they fail, they at once conceive new hopes and so fill up the void. With them alone to hope is to have, for they lose not a moment in the execution of an idea. This is the lifelong task, full of danger and toil, which they are always imposing upon themselves. None enjoy their good things less, because they are always seeking for more. To do their duty is their only holiday, and they deem the quiet of inaction to be as disagreeable as the most tiresome business. If a man should say of them, in a word, that they were born neither to have peace themselves nor to allow peace to other men, he would simply speak the truth."

In the short period from the victory over the Persians at Marathon (490 B C.) and Salamis (480), to the defeat of Athens by Sparta (404 B.C.), the tremendous Athenian vitality described by Thucydides produced some of the world's greatest poetry, architecture, and sculpture. At the same time, Athenian commercial and maritime activity predominated in the Mediterranean. The Peloponnesian War (431–404 B.C.) resulted in the displacement of Athens by Sparta in the hegemony of Greece. Athens was defeated by Sparta in 404 B.C. and an aristocratic faction was put in power, but moderate democracy was restored a year later by Thrasybulus. Athens under the influence of Demosthenes resisted Macedonia, but was overthrown at the battle of Chaeronea (338 B C.), and was generally after this under Macedonian influence. It was subjugated by Rome in 146 B.C., and pillaged by Sulla in 86 B.C.

The ancient architectural masterpieces are mostly on the Acropolis (q.v.), the chief ancient landmark. Other important structures are: the theater of Dionysus on the S slope of the Acropolis, where all the famous Greek dramas were produced. It was orginally of wood, and was not completed in stone until the end of the 5th century B.C. The existing remains of the orchestra and stage structures are modifications of Roman date. East, and somewhat south of the Acropolis, are the remains of a temple of Olympian Zeus. According to legend, the first temple on the site was raised by Deucalion, in gratitude for his deliverance from the great flood. About 515 B.C. Pisistratus planned to raise a great temple on the site but the plan was not realized. In the 2nd century B.C., Antiochus IV, king of Syria, revived the plan of building a temple here, but work on it was suspended when he died. It was not until the Roman emperor Hadrian's time that the temple was completed (132 A.D.). Several columns with elaborate Corinthian capitals still stand. Also noteworthy are the Gate of the Oil Market, or New Agora, a gate built with gifts from Julius Caesar and Augustus; the Agora, to the north of the Acropolis and adjoining the quarter known as Ceramicus. This was the center of Athenian public life and after the Acropolis the heart of the city. Nearly in the center of the Agora was the altar of the Twelve Gods, from which distances from Athens were measured. Among other structures, there were temples of Apollo and of Ares, and an Odeum that held 1000 spectators. Many roads led to the Agora, which was not only the center of Athens but of all Attica. Here were such official buildings as the Bouleterium (Senate), the Tholos, and the Metroun. Here the votes for ostracism were cast. Here were colonnaded galleries for shops and meeting places, the Painted Portico, and various stoas. Public figures, artists, philosophers, and ordinary citizens gathered in the Agora. Religious activity was concentrated about its temples and altars, and through it wound the sacred Panathenaic procession on its way to the Acropolis. Excavations of the site have been carried on at intervals from the 19th century. Since 1931 the American School of Classical Studies has undertaken systematic excavations and restoration on a vast scale. Aided by large grants from John D. Rockefeller Junior and by Marshall Plan funds, and by a law authorizing the demolition of the structures which covered the ancient Agora, the site has been cleared and the excavations of the Agora have shed light on the entire history of Athens, from Neolithic times forward. On a

slight rise which gives a splendid panoramic view of the Agora stands the well-preserved temple of Hephaestus commonly known as the Theseum. The "Long Walls," traces of which have now almost entirely disappeared, were two massive fortification walls extending from the ramparts of the city to those of the Piraeus, at a distance apart, except near their diverging extremities, of about 550 feet. Built between 461 and 456 B.C., they made the port and the metropolis practically one huge fortress, and assured Athenian supplies by sea while rendering possible Athenian naval triumphs at times when the Spartans held their land without the walls. They were destroyed in 404 B.C. when Athens fell before Sparta but were restored in 393 B.C. by Conon. The Long Walls followed the crests of the group of hills SW of the Acropolis. The arena of the Panathenaic stadium, a stadium still practically complete except for its sheathing of marble, measures 109 by 850 feet, and is bordered on its long sides and its semicircular E end by the slopes which supported the spectators' seats (about 60 tiers). There were at intervals 29 flights of steps to give access to the seats. The original stadium was begun about 330 B.C.; its stone tiers were covered with Pentelic marble through the generosity of Herodus Atticus c143 A.D. In 1895 money was given to restore the stadium in preparation for the Olympic Games of 1896; thus today it gleams with marble not even yet weathered to match other monuments.

Athesis (ath'e-sis). [Modern name, **Adige.**] River in N Italy, rising in the Rhaetian Alps and flowing S through the Alps to the plain of the Padus (Po). It sends arms to the Padus, and flows into the Adriatic N of the mouths of the Padus. On it are Tridentum (Trent) and Verona.

Athlete, The. Greek statue, held to be a copy of the famous Doryphorus (spear-bearer), the canon or type of Polyclitus, found at Pompeii, and added to the collection of the Museo Nazionale, Naples. The undraped figure is well proportioned and holds a simple, naturalistic pose.

Athos (ath'os). [Also: **Acte, Akte.**] Easternmost peninsula of Chalcidice in Macedonia, NE Greece. It projects into the Aegean Sea and is connected with the mainland by a narrow isthmus. Length, about 30 miles. As part of his preparations for his invasion of Greece, Xerxes, the Persian king, caused a canal to be cut through the isthmus. The purpose of this canal, which was about a mile and a half long, was to save the Persian fleet from rounding the stormy headland of Mount Athos where a large part of the fleet of Mardonius, son-in-law of Darius, had been destroyed (492 B.C.) by storms. Once past this headland, the promontory would protect the fleet from the tempestuous north-east winds. In addition, the canal would allow the ships to keep contact with the army of Xerxes as it proceeded along the coast. The dry ditch which marks the course of Xerxes' canal can still be followed.

Atilius (a-til′i-us), **Marcus.** Latin writer; fl. 2nd century B.C. Little is known of him except that he is mentioned as an early writer of comedies. Three fragments are attributed to him.

Atlantides (at-lan′ti-dēz). See **Hesperides; Pleiades.**

Atlantis (at-lan′tis). Legendary island in the Atlantic Ocean, NW of Africa, referred to by Plato and other ancient writers, which with its inhabitants (who had achieved, according to most accounts, a high degree of civilization) was said to have disappeared in a convulsion of nature. The belief in the possibility of such a place has continued to exist even into modern times, and many writers (including Francis Bacon in his work *The New Atlantis*) have taken the name as an equivalent for a utopian state. A modern scholar has ingeniously suggested that the legend might have arisen from a prehistoric inundation of the bronze-age palace on the island known as Gla (an Albanian name; the ancient name is not recorded, unless indeed it was Atlantis) in the Copaic Lake in Boeotia, which was subject to periodic flooding.

Atlas (at′las). In Greek mythology, a Titan, the son of Iapetus and the nymph Clymene. His brothers were Prometheus, Epimetheus, and Menoetius, and he was the father of the Pleiades (by Pleione), of the Hyades (by Aethra), of the Hesperides (by Hesperis), and according to Homer, the father of Calypso. He lived in the western lands, beyond the stream of Ocean, in the land of the Hyperboreans, or some say in Mauretania, and was the proud gardener of the orchard where grew the tree with the golden apples which had been a wedding present to Hera. According to Hesiod he was condemned by Zeus for his part in the battle of the Titans, in which he was the leader, to stand at the western extremity of the earth near the habitation of the Hesperides, upholding the heavens with his shoulders and hands. His station was later said to be in the Atlas Mountains in Africa. Heracles, seeking the golden apples as one of his labors for Eurystheus, sought the aid of Atlas, but he hesitated to help him for he remembered a prophecy that one day a son of Zeus would rob him of the golden fruit. He told Heracles he feared Ladon, the hundred-headed serpent that guarded the apples. Heracles immediately shot Ladon with one of his arrows, and then offered to hold up the heavens if Atlas would pluck the apples for him. Atlas was so glad to get rid of his burden that he agreed, and while Heracles assumed the heavens he fetched the apples. He offered to take them to Eurystheus himself, but Heracles had no intention of holding up the heavens indefinitely, and cunningly agreed to this plan, if Atlas would just take back the heavens for a moment so that he could pad his shoulders, which were getting sore from the unaccustomed weight. Atlas amiably resumed the burden, and was then amazed and distressed as Heracles walked off, leaving him holding the heavens as before. Another story concerning Atlas is that Perseus, returning from slaying Medusa, visited him and asked for refreshments. Atlas remembered the prophecy about a son of Zeus and treated him inhospitably. Perseus punished him by showing him the head of Medusa and turned him to stone, and it is this huge bulk of stone which is now called the Atlas Mountains in Africa.

Atossa (a-tos′a). Queen of Persia in the 6th century B.C. She was a daughter of Cyrus the Great and Cassandane, and the full sister of Cambyses. The latter fell in love with her and since it was not the custom for Persians to marry their own sisters he asked the Persian judges if there was any law which permitted the king to marry his sister. The judges said there was no such law but, on

the other hand, there was a law which permitted the king of Persia to do whatever
he chose. In this way the judges allowed
Cambyses to do what he planned to do and
at the same time to save their own skins.
Cambyses married Atossa. She did not accompany him on his expedition to Egypt,
for by that time he had fallen in love with
another of his sisters and took her with him
to Egypt. On the death of Cambyses Atossa
became the wife of his successor, the False
Smerdis, as it was the custom for the successor to inherit wives as well as throne.
When the False Smerdis was exposed and
slain by a group of conspirators who set
Darius on the throne in his place, Atossa
married Darius. She bore him four sons,
the eldest of whom was Xerxes. Such was
her power and influence over Darius that,
although he had older sons by a woman he
had married before he became king, Atossa
was able to persuade him to appoint her son
Xerxes as his heir. She survived Darius and
lived to see her son Xerxes I return from
Greece defeated.

Atrax (ā′traks). In Greek mythology, a son
of the river-god Peneus and Bura. The town
of Atrax in Hestiaeotis, N Greece, was named
for him. He was the father of Hippodamia,
who married Pirithous, and of the maiden
Caenis, who was transformed into a man by
Poseidon.

Atreus (ā′trē-us, -trös). In Greek legend, a
son of Pelops and Hippodamia, and the
brother of Thyestes, with whom he was fated
ever to struggle. After the death of his half-
brother, Chrysippus, in which he may have
had a hand, he fled from Elis to Mycenae
where he succeeded Eurystheus as king and
wielded the sceptre, made by Hephaestus
and given to him by Pelops. He first married Cleola, who died after giving birth to
a son, Plisthenes. He then married Aërope
and by her was the father of Agamemnon,
Menelaus, and Anaxibia. He had a horned
lamb with golden fleece which he claimed
authorized whoever possessed it to be king.
It had been sent to him by Hermes who
wanted to avenge the death of Myrtilus by
Pelops. Hermes was sure that Atreus would
not, as he had vowed to do, sacrifice the
golden lamb along with the finest of his
flocks, to Artemis. He did kill the lamb but

had it stuffed and mounted and decreed that
whoever possessed it was endowed with royal
power. Thyestes, in a plot with Aërope who
had fallen in love with him, stole the lamb
and was acknowledged as king. Atreus then
proposed that if he could cause the sun to
reverse its path through the heavens—to go
from West to East—Thyestes should acknowledge him as the rightful king. With the help
of Zeus and Eris the sun did just this. Atreus
became king again and Thyestes went into
exile. This by no means ended the struggle
between the brothers. Thyestes arranged
the murder of Plisthenes and then, on being
lured back to Mycenae, was served his own
sons in a ghastly banquet of welcome given
him by Atreus. After Thyestes had eaten,
Atreus revealed that it was the flesh of his
own children he had enjoyed. Thyestes laid
a curse upon the House of Atreus and again
went into exile. An oracle told Atreus to
bring back Thyestes in order to end a famine
that then wasted Mycenae. He sought him
in Sicyon, where he met Pelopia and, unaware of her true parentage and that she was
soon to bear a child, he married her, having
cast Aërope into the sea because of her unfaithfulness with Thyestes. Pelopia bore
Aegisthus, whom she exposed, but he was
rescued and brought up by Atreus as his
own son. In fact this was the child of
Thyestes and his own daughter, Pelopia,
although she did not know that it was her
father who had ravished her when she was
sacrificing to Athene one night. After some
years Atreus brought Thyestes back to Mycenae, threw him in prison, and commanded
Aegisthus, still a child, to kill him. Aegisthus
tried to obey but was foiled by Thyestes,
and by means of the sword which his mother
had given him Thyestes identified him as
his own son. Together they then killed
Atreus.

Atropos (at′rō-pos). In Greek mythology, that
one of the three Fates who severs the thread
of human life.

Atta (at′a), **Titus Quinctius.** Latin poet; fl.
early in the 1st century B.C. Fragments of
his work survive.

Attalus (at′a-lus). [Also: **Attalos.**] Macedonian
general; died c336 B.C. He was a general
under Philip II of Macedon. Philip cast
aside his wife Olympias to marry Cleopatra,

actor; up, lūte, pull; oi, oil; ou, out; ŦH, then; ḍ as d or j, ş as s or sh, ṯ as t or ch, ẕ as z or zh.

daughter or niece of Attalus. At the wedding feast, Attalus urged those present to pray for a legitimate heir, thus impugning the virtue of Olympias, who had borne Alexander to Philip. Alexander, who was present, flung a wine-cup into the face of Attalus. Attalus was sent to Asia with other generals to prepare for Philip's planned attack on the Persian Empire. When Philip was murdered, he supported the claims of Cleopatra's infant son to the throne, thus incurring again Alexander's hatred. At the latter's order he was murdered in Asia (c336 B.C.).

Attalus I. [Also: **Attalos**; surnamed **Soter**.] King of Pergamum (241–197 B.C.); born 269 B.C.; died 197 B.C. He carried on war with the Galatians, with Syria, and with Macedonia, and was allied with Rome against Macedonia in the latter part of his reign. Votive groups were set up by him on the Acropolis at Athens in honor of his victory over the Gauls. These groups of figures of about half life-size, depicted a battle of the gods and giants, combat between Athenians and Amazons, the victory of Marathon, and destruction of the Gauls by Attalus. Four figures from these groups were acquired by the National Museum at Naples: a fallen giant, a dead Amazon, a fallen Persian, and a dying bearded Gaul. Attalus was an outstanding patron of literature, philosophy, and the arts. He presented Delphi with a colonnade (stoa) for the shelter of pilgrims. His successors, Eumenes II and Attalus II, presented similar stoas to Athens.

Attalus II. [Also: **Attalos**; surnamed **Philadelphus**.] King of Pergamum (c159–138 B.C.); born 220 B.C.; died 138 B.C. He was a son of Attalus I and successor to his brother Eumenes II. He was an ally of Rome. Like all the Attalids he was interested in letters and the arts. He presented Athens with a stoa which bears his name. Restoration of the Stoa of Attalus in the Agora was completed in 1956 by the American School of Classical Studies.

Attalus III. [Also: **Attalos**; surnamed **Philometor**.] King of Pergamum (138–133 B.C.); born 171 B.C.; died 133 B.C. He was a nephew of Attalus II. By his will he left his kingdom to the Romans. He is of some interest to historians of science for his studies in botany and, more narrowly, in agriculture

(a treatise by him in this field was used by Pliny). However, his interests in these fields seem to have had a very practical motive not unrelated to the political hazards of his day: his chief interest was in poisonous plants, and he prepared and experimented with a number of poisons.

Atthis (at'this). In mythology, a daughter of Cranaus, king of Cecropia. Some say that she died before marriage, and in her honor her father renamed his kingdom Attica; others say that she was the mother of Erichthonius.

Attic (at'ik). One of the dialects of ancient Greek, spoken in Athens and the surrounding district (Attica). Three periods can be distinguished in the history of the Attic dialect: 1) Ancient Attic, till the end of the 5th century B.C.; 2) Middle Attic, from the end of 5th century B.C. to the middle of the 4th century B.C.; and 3) New Attic, from the middle of the 4th century B.C. to the death of Alexander the Great. Attic was considered the most highly cultivated of the Hellenic dialects.

Attica (at'i-ka). In ancient geography, a division of C Greece, bounded by Boeotia (partly separated by Cithaeron) on the NW, the Gulf of Euripus (separating it from Euboea) on the NE, the Aegean Sea on the E, the Saronic Gulf on the SW, and Megaris on the W. It contained several mountains (Cithaeron, Parnes, Pentelicus, and Hymettus) and the plain of Attica, watered by the Cephissus and Ilissus rivers. Its chief city was Athens, with whose history it is in general identified.

Atticus (at'i-kus), **Titus Pomponius**. Roman scholar and bibliophile, born at Rome, 109 B.C.; died 32 B.C. He is best known for a collection of letters from Cicero, his intimate friend, which he edited and published. A man of great political discretion, he was also simultaneously the friend of Pompey and Caesar, both of whom Cicero opposed. His surname derives from a 20-year residence at Athens during the Roman civil war.

Attis (at'is). See **Atys**.

Attius (at'i-us), **Lucius**. See **Accius, Lucius**.

Attius (at'i-us) or **Attus** (at'us), **Navius**. Augur under Tarquinius Priscus. According to legend, Tarquinius Priscus, in a war against the Sabines, wished to make some changes in the army as organized by Romulus. However, the Senate would not consent to the changes without consulting the auguries. Tarquinius was impatient and scornful of the ability of the sacred birds to pass on such a matter. To prove, as he thought, that augury in this case was a waste of time, he mockingly requested the augur Attius to tell him if what he was thinking would come to pass. Attius took the auspices and replied that what Tarquinius was thinking would surely come to pass. Tarquinius laughed in triumph and announced he was thinking that the augur would sunder a whetstone with a razor. Addressing Attius, he handed him these objects. "Take them," he commanded, "and accomplish what your birds declare is possible!" Attius took them and immediately cut the whetstone in two with the razor. A statue of Attius, with his head covered, was afterward raised on the spot where he performed this feat.

Atymnius (a-tim'ni-us). In Homeric legend (*Iliad*), a son of Amisodarus of Caria, and the brother of Maris. He accompanied Sarpedon as an ally of Troy in the Trojan War. He was slain by Antilochus.

Atys (ā'tis) or **Attis** (at'is). Mythical personage in the worship of the Phrygian goddess Cybele. Some say he was the son of the Lydian supreme god Manes. Others say Nana, daughter of the river-god Sangarius, ate the fruit of an almond tree and as a result bore Atys. He was a beautiful Phrygian youth beloved of Cybele. The goddess wished to make him a guardian of her temple to keep him for herself. She exacted a promise from him to remain faithful to her, and he swore to do so, saying, "If I lie, may the love for which I break faith be my last love." But Atys forgot his pledge. He fell in love with and embraced the nymph Sagaritis. Wild with rage and grief, Cybele hacked down the tree in which the nymph lived and so killed her. Atys was driven mad. He fled to the top of Mount Dindymus and there mutilated himself and dragged his head in the dust. He died at a pine tree, which received his spirit while from his blood sprang violets. A tomb was raised to him on Mount Dindymus, in the sanctuary of Cybele, and henceforward the priests of Cybele emasculated themselves and tossed their hair in feigned madness in commemoration of Atys. A festival of orgiastic character, lasting three days, was celebrated in his honor in the spring. A pine tree covered with violets was carried to the shrine of Cybele as a symbol of the departed Atys. Then, amidst tumultuous music and the wildest exhibition of grief, the mourners sought for Atys on the mountains. On the third day he was found, and the rejoicing which followed was as extravagant as the mourning which preceded. (A similar ceremony was observed by women and girls to commemorate the death and rebirth of Dionysus.) The myth may be considered as the counterpart of the Greek legend of Aphrodite and Adonis, which itself is reminiscent of the Semitic legend of Tammuz and Ishtar.

Auge (ô'jē). In Greek mythology, a daughter of Aleus, king of Tegea, and Naera. Her father made her a priestess of Athena in an attempt to circumvent a prophecy that her son would kill her mother's brothers. Heracles, who was being entertained by Aleus, violated her nevertheless. When it became apparent that she was about to bear a child, Aleus, who mocked her plea that Heracles had ravished her, gave his daughter to Nauplius with instructions to drown her. Nauplius departed for the coast with her. On the way Auge felt that the time to give birth to her child had come. She went into a thicket on Mount Parthenius and gave birth to Telephus, whom she left to die on the mountain, but he was rescued. Auge and Nauplius proceeded on their journey and Nauplius, who had no intention of killing Auge, sold her to some traders who took her to Mysia and sold her to King Teuthras. According to some accounts Teuthras married her, and many years later Telephus came to Mysia on the advice of the oracle and was reunited with his mother. Other accounts say that Auge was adopted as a daughter by Teuthras, and that when Telephus arrived, gave him his adopted daughter as a wife in return for Telephus' aid in a war. But on the wedding night the miraculous appearance of a serpent caused their true relationship to be revealed.

Augeas (ô'jē-as, ô-jē'as) or **Augeias** (ô-jē'as). In Greek mythology, a son of Helius (or of Phorbas). He was a king of the Epeans in

Elis, and one of the Argonauts. Augeas was the owner of a herd of 3000 oxen, including 12 white bulls sacred to the sun. His cattle, by a gift of the gods, were extremely fertile and never sickened and died of disease. They were kept in a stable that had not been cleaned in 30 years. As one of his labors for Eurystheus, Heracles undertook to clean the stables in one day, and Augeas agreed to pay him one-tenth of his herds if he fulfilled the task in the time stipulated. Phyleus, son of Augeas, was called as a witness to the bargain. Heracles carried out his contract by diverting the rivers Alpheus and Peneus and washing them through the stables. Augeas refused to honor his agreement, on the ground that Heracles had been commanded to carry out this task by Eurystheus and furthermore, he had been assisted by the river-gods. He banished Phyleus, who upheld Heracles. Heracles ultimately had his revenge; he gathered a force and attacked and killed Augeas and his other sons, and made Phyleus ruler of the kingdom.

Augiae (ô-jī′ē). Homer's name for the Laconian town of Aegiae.

ROMAN AUGUR WITH STAFF AND CHICKEN
Roman relief, 2 B.C. The *lituus* (curved staff) was used for marking off the heavens. *Florence*

Augur (ô′gẽr). Among the ancient Romans, a functionary whose duty it was to observe and to interpret, according to traditional rules, the auspices or reputed natural signs concerning future events. It was the function of the augur to announce the approval or disapproval of the gods with respect to proposed activities, rather than to make specific predictions. These auspices were studied, with a fixed ceremonial, in the following classes of phenomena: 1) signs from the heavens, including thunder and lightning, and other meteorological manifestations; 2) signs from the direction of flight or the various cries of birds; 3) signs from the manner of eating of domestic hens kept for this purpose; 4) signs from the movements and attitudes of animals; 5) evil omens from various fortuitous incidents, such as the fall of an object, the gnawing of a mouse, the creaking of a chair, etc., occurring during the augural ceremonies, or when these were about to begin. The official or public augurs, who constituted a college probably founded by Numa, were originally three in number. By the time of the Tarquins they had been increased to six. (For an interesting legend concerning augury during the time of Tarquinius Priscus, see **Attius, Navius**.) After 300 B.C., the number of augurs was raised to nine, of whom five had to be plebeians. Sulla made the number 15; Julius Caesar, 16, not including his own official membership in his character of perpetual chief priest and dictator; and toward the close of the empire the number was still further increased. The augurs wore the sacerdotal praetexta, or toga with a broad purple border, and their distinctive emblem was the curved rod called the *lituus*, with which they marked out the limits of the templum or boundary within which the omens with which they had to do were to be observed. Before any public business or ceremony was undertaken, the augurs decided whether the auspices were propitious, or whether unfavorable omens demanded interruption or delay; they conducted the inauguration or exauguration of priests, establishment of temples and places such as new settlements, and fixed the times of movable festivals. Augural advice was not always followed, and Roman history relates numerous occasions on which the rejection of such advice was followed by disaster.

Augusta (ô-gus′tạ). In ancient Rome, a title conferred as a supreme honor upon women of the imperial house. It was first borne by Livia, then by Antonia, grandmother of Caligula, and first as consort of the emperor by Agrippina, wife of Claudius. Later it was bestowed, with the consent of the emperor, upon others beside the consort of the reigning Caesar.

Augusta Praetoria (ô-gus′tạ prē-tôr′i-ạ). [Modern name, **Aosta.**] Town in NW Italy at the foot of the Alps, situated on the Duria Major River. It was the ancient capital of the Gallic tribe of the Salassi, and became a Roman colony under Augustus. Roman walls, towers, gates, arches, and theaters are preserved.

Augustodunum (ô-gus-tọ-dū′num). [Modern name, **Autun.**] Large town in Gaul, founded by Augustus in 12 B.C., supplanting the earlier Bibracte, with important Roman remains including fortifications and two town gates. (JJ)

Augustus (ô-gus′tus). [Original name, **Caius Octavius;** called later **Caius Julius Caesar Octavianus.**] The first Roman emperor. He was the son of a wealthy knight, Caius Octavius, and Atia, the niece of Julius Caesar. He was born just before sunrise, on Sept. 23, 63 B.C.; died August 19, 14 A.D. Some say he was born in the Palatine district in Rome, and the room in which he was said to have been born became a shrine after his death. But the people of Velitrae, the home of his father and his ancestors, insisted that Octavius was born there in a small room on his father's estate. Later, it was forbidden to enter this room before ceremonies of purification had been performed. Numerous legends have been preserved concerning his birth and predictions of his future greatness. In ancient times part of the wall of Velitrae had been struck by lightning. Seers foretold that a native of the city would become ruler of the world. On the night that Octavius was born, a seer, on learning the hour of his birth, prophesied that the ruler of the world had been born. Later, Octavius consulted the priests of Dionysus in Thrace concerning his son's future. When the priests poured wine for the sacrifice over the altar, a pillar

of flame rose from it. This same sign had appeared when Alexander the Great sacrificed at the same altar. That night Caius Octavius dreamed that his son appeared, armed like Jupiter with the thunderbolt, crowned, and riding in a chariot decked with laurel branches. Other dreams and omens confirmed that he would wield supreme power. At the ceremonies in honor of his coming of age, the gown of a senator that Caesar permitted him to wear, split apart and fell about his feet. This was interpreted as a sign that the Senate itself would one day be brought to his feet.

Before he was legally entitled to them, he was given many honors. At the age of 18 he followed Caesar to Munda in Spain to help him against the sons of Pompey. At Munda, Caesar noticed a palm tree and ordered his men not to cut it down as the palm was a symbol of victory. The tree suddenly put out a new shoot that grew so fast it overshadowed the original stock. Doves nested in it. Some say that this omen confirmed Caesar in his intention to name Octavius as his heir. In the following year Octavius was in Apollonia, in Illyria. While he was there news of Caesar's death reached him (44 B.C.). He returned to Rome at once. Having learned that Caesar had adopted him and made him his heir, he took the name Caius Julius Caesar Octavianus, and was henceforth known as Octavian. He took command of the army and assumed the reins of government.

In Rome he was at first scorned by Mark Antony, who ridiculed his pretensions; Brutus and Cassius, the chief conspirators against Caesar, thought him beneath their notice and retired to their estates. But Octavian maneuvered shrewdly. He gained the influence of Cicero, the Senate, and the people against Mark Antony. After defeating Mark Antony at Mutina (43 B.C.), he became reconciled with him, and in the same year formed the Second Triumvirate with him and Marcus Lepidus. The three members divided the western provinces between them. Brutus and Cassius held the eastern provinces in the name of the Republic. The triumvirs consolidated their power by proscribing a large number of citizens and confiscating their estates as well as the territories of many cities, which they handed over to their soldiers. Those citizens of republican complexion who escaped the proscription went to Brutus and Cassius in the east. In 42 B.C. Octavian and Mark Antony pursued them. It is said that on his way to Philippi, Octavius met a Thessalian who assured him that he had met the ghost of Julius Caesar on the road and that the ghost foretold the victory of Octavian over the forces of Brutus and Cassius. In his first encounter with the enemy at Philippi, he was unsuccessful, and was forced to flee to the camp of Mark Antony. It was said that he escaped death only by the intervention of a friend's dream. The dream caused him to leave his tent, which was afterwards surrounded by an enemy party that cut the tent to ribbons under the impression that Octavian was in it. In the second engagement at Philippi he defeated Brutus and Cassius (42 B.C.). Both the conspirators committed suicide. Some say that Octavian cut off the head of Brutus and sent it to Rome to be flung at the feet of Caesar's divine image as proof that he had avenged Caesar's death. After the success at Philippi, Octavian and Mark Antony, whose friendship had never been strong, quarreled. Lucius, brother of Antony, raised a revolt at Perusia. Octavian proceeded to the city and laid siege to it. It is said that one day as he was sacrificing before the walls, a party of the enemy raided his camp and carried off the sacrificial vessels as well as the carcasses of the victims. Soothsayers foretold that the dangers threatened by the omens, which had been unpropitious on the victims, would now fall on those who had carried them off. Octavian forced the city to capitulate. Some say that after its fall he chose 300 prisoners from the upper ranks of citizens and offered them as human sacrifices on the Ides of March to the god Julius (Caesar). In 40 B.C. Octavian and Mark Antony were again reconciled. Antony married Octavia, the sister of Octavian, and departed to rule the eastern half of the empire. Lepidus was given 20 legions and command of one province in Africa. Sextus Pompey, son of Pompey the Great, had control of Sicily and was constantly threatening to cut off the grain supply on which Rome depended. Octavian waged war on him

(43–35 B.C.). Two stories are told of propitious omens in connection with the battle against Sextus. One, that when he was walking near the shore before a naval battle off Sicily, a fish leaped out of the water and fell at his feet. The other, that he met a peasant driving a donkey and asked him his name. The peasant answered that his name was Eutychus (*Prosperous*) and his donkey's name was Nicon (*Victory*). In spite of these favorable omens, the war dragged on; Antony at first refused to send assistance. Octavian lost two fleets in violent storms, but raged that he would win this war "whatever Neptune may do." Antony finally did send some help and the war ended in victory for Octavian. He was greatly aided by the services of his good friend and admiral, Marcus Vipsanius Agrippa, to whom he gave his daughter Julia in marriage, despite the fact that Agrippa was already married and that Julia was very much younger and already becoming well known for her vices. Sextus Pompey fled to Asia and perished there soon afterwards. Lepidus, whose ideas of his own importance had become highly exaggerated, demanded the leading place in the government and was expelled from the triumvirate for his presumption, and went into permanent exile (36 B.C.). For the next five years Octavian and Antony shared power, but whereas Antony accomplished little in the East except for promoting his liaison with Cleopatra, Octavian consolidated his power in the West. When Antony cast aside Octavia, the sister of Octavian, and when it was discovered that in his will he had made his children by Cleopatra his heirs, Octavian had a proper reason for declaring war on him and eliminating the only serious rival who opposed him. He met Antony at Actium in Epirus, and defeated him decisively (31 B.C.). After the battle he was compelled to go to Brundisium and put down a mutiny, which he did with dispatch. He then pursued Antony to Alexandria, besieged the city, and forced Antony to sue for peace. As a condition of the peace he compelled Antony to promise to commit suicide, and saw that he had carried out the promise by inspecting the corpse. He was so anxious to have Cleopatra in the triumphal procession that would follow this victory that, some say, he tried to have her restored by sending a snake charmer to suck out the poison of the asp that she had allowed to bite her. This was a failure, and with some magnanimity Octavian permitted Antony and Cleopatra to be buried in the same tomb. But he dragged Antony's son by Fulvia from the image of the god Julius whither he had fled for sanctuary and had him slain. He also sought out and had killed Caesarion, Cleopatra's son by Caesar. But the children of Antony and Cleopatra he brought up with as much care as if they had been members of his own family. In memory of his victory at Actium he founded the city of Nicopolis (*City of Victory*) near the scene of the battle, and instituted public games to be held every five years there.

With the defeat of Antony, Octavian became sole ruler of the Roman dominion, and remained sole ruler for the next 44 years. In 28 B.C. he was made *princeps senatus* (First senator). On Jan. 17 of the following year he received the title of Augustus, by which title he is best known in history. Augustus preserved the republican forms, but united in his own person the consular, tribunician, proconsular, and other powers. His generals carried on various wars in Spain, Africa, Germany and elsewhere, but the Roman advance in the last-named country received a definite setback through the defeat of Varus by Arminius in 9 A.D. The loss of Varus and three legions with all their officers and men was a blow from which Augustus never completely recovered. It was said that when he heard the news, he went into a state of depression, and let his hair and his beard grow, and that he was often observed to beat his head on a door while he shouted, "Quintilius Varus, give me back my legions!" The anniversary of the loss was observed as a day of mourning. Yet Augustus preferred to avoid war if he could. During his reign the gates of the Temple of Janus on the Quirinal, which were open during times of war, were closed three times, signifying that the country was at peace. From the founding of Rome up to his time, they had been closed only twice before. Augustus was a strict disciplinarian over the army, did not encourage the creation of new citizens lest he dilute Roman blood,

built libraries, and beautified the city. He boasted that he had found Rome a city "of sun-dried brick and left it clothed in marble." Among the structures for which he was responsible were the Forum, a temple of Apollo on the Palatine, and a temple of Jupiter the Thunderer on the Capitoline. He also urged such Romans as could afford it to raise new temples and public monuments and to restore such of the existing ones as stood in need of it. He revived ancient religious rites and customs; restored the calendar, which had been allowed to lapse, and named one month (formerly Sextilis) for himself; he tidied up the civil and administrative forms that had fallen into disorder during the years of civil war; he provided the most elaborate public spectacles ever to be presented to the Roman public; and he encouraged the growth of an indigenous Roman literature, which under him reached its greatest point. Above all, he consolidated the empire and brought peace to it. He was in fact, supreme ruler and emperor. Twice he thought of restoring the republican constitution, but was persuaded that the time was not ripe to do so. He rejected divine honors as well as the title "Father of his Country."

Augustus married first, Claudia, stepdaughter of Antony, for reasons of state, but divorced her when he quarreled with her mother. His second wife was Scribonia, who bore him a daughter, his only child, Julia. Julia caused him great sorrow, for though he attempted to raise the moral tone of Roman life, the activities of Julia his daughter and Julia his granddaughter were a public scandal. When he learned what all Rome knew, he had them both banished and refused all pleas to forgive them, or to lessen the severity of their punishment. He adopted his grandsons, the children of Julia and Agrippa, Caius, Lucius, and Agrippa Postumus. Caius and Lucius died in young manhood. Agrippa Postumus was accused of plotting against him, was banished, and died under mysterious circumstances. The third wife of Augustus was Livia Drusilla, whom he took from her husband Tiberius Nero, though she was pregnant at the time. He adopted her son Tiberius and, having lost the heirs of his body, made him his heir. There is no doubt that Livia Drusilla was a strong character and that she exerted great influence on Augustus. Some say that her constant aim in the exercise of her influence was to strengthen the office of emperor and to see to it that her son Tiberius eventually filled it. Whether, as is sometimes hinted, she hastened the end of Augustus by the judicious use of poison, can probably never be proved. Omens foretold his death: lightning struck his name on one of his statutes, for example. On Aug. 19, 14 A.D., after a very brief illness, he died in the same room at Nola where his father had died. His body was burned and the ashes placed in the mausoleum on the Tiber that he had built for himself and his family. By a decree of the Senate, Augustus was named one of the gods to be worshiped by the Romans. He had prepared an official biography, the *Res Gestae Divi Augusti* or *Index Rerum Gestarum,* containing lists of his public honors, of his public benefactions from his private purse, and of the military successes of the Romans during his principate, and a statement of his attitude toward and position in the Roman state. In accordance with his wishes this was engraved on two bronze tablets and placed on his mausoleum. Copies, in Latin and in an official translation, have been found at Ancyra (Ankara) in Galatia, and at Apollonia and Antioch in Pisidia, the most nearly complete of which, inscribed on the walls of the temple of Rome and Augustus at Ancyra, is known as the *Monumentum Ancyranum,* a term consequently sometimes used synonymously for the official title.

Aulis (ô′lis). In ancient geography, a town on the E coast of Boeotia, Greece, said by some to have been named for a daughter of Ogygus. Twice the Greek fleet assembled here for the expeditions against Troy. The second time the fleet was held windbound through the will of Artemis. In accordance with instructions from a seer, Agamemnon made ready to sacrifice his daughter, Iphigenia, to appease Artemis and secure favorable winds. One tradition has it that Iphigenia was actually sacrificed. According to another account, as the sacrificial knife was at her throat, Artemis substituted in her place a hind, and took Iphigenia away to Tauris. In the temple of Artemis at Aulis

were two white marble images of the goddess, one carrying a torch and the other showing the goddess in the act of shooting an arrow. Also in the temple was preserved the plane tree in which the eight nestlings and their mother were swallowed by a mottled serpent, just before the Greeks sailed to Troy, thus indicating that the war would last ten years. The traveler Pausanias, writing in the 2nd century A.D., says he saw the plane tree in the temple, and that he was also shown the bronze threshold of Agamemnon's tent at Aulis.

Aura (ô′ra). In Greek mythology, a daughter of Lelas and Periboea. She was a huntress and a companion of Artemis. Dionysus pursued her but she rejected his advances. Dionysus appealed to Aphrodite to cause Aura to return his love. She then yielded to him and bore him twins. But afterward she was stricken with madness, killed one of her children, and cast herself into the Sangarius river. Zeus transformed her into a spring.

Auriga (ô-rī′ga). A northern constellation, the Charioteer or Wagoner, containing the first-magnitude star Capella. It is supposed to represent a charioteer kneeling in his vehicle. He is often represented with a kid on his left shoulder.

Aurora (ȧ-rō′ra). [Greek, **Eos.**] In Roman mythology, the goddess of the dawn. The poets represented her as rising out of the ocean in a chariot, her rosy fingers dropping gentle dew.

Aurunci (ô-run′sī). A dialectal form of the name of an Italic people, the Ausones (q. v.), who formerly occupied the Vescian Plain and the valley of the river Liris, on the border between Latium and Campania. (JJ)

Ausona (ô-sō′na). One of three *oppida,* Ausona, Vescia, and Minturnae, of an Italic people known as the Ausones or Aurunci, who formerly occupied the Vescian Plain and the valley of the river Liris on the border between Latium and Campania. The site has not been identified. (JJ)

Ausones (ô′sō-nēz). An Italic people, known also as the Aurunci, who formerly occupied the Vescian Plain and the valley of the river Liris, on the border between Latium and Campania. Their three principal villages, or *oppida,* were Ausona, Vescia, and Minturnae,

fat, fāte, fär, fāre, errant; net, mē, her ardent; pin, pīne; · not, nōte, möve, nôr,

which according to Livy were captured by the Romans in 314 B.C., after which the independent history of the Ausones ceases; but at Minturnae (q.v.) a colony of Roman citizens was established in 295 B.C. and it thereafter became an important Roman industrial and commercial city. The shrine of a local nature-goddess, the Dea Marica, now explained as the Goddess of the Marshes, on the right bank of the Liris near its mouth, survived into Imperial times. The sites of Ausona and Vescia are lost; echoes of the Ausones survive in the nomenclature of the region, the Montes Aurunci to the west, the Via Ausonia, the Ager Vescinus or Vescian Plain, the Montes Vescini, the Latin colony of Suessa (now Sessa) Aurunca, the usually dry streambed known as the Ausente, a Roman bridge known locally as the Ponte Ronaco (= Aurunco), a hamlet called Rongolisi (= Auruncolisium), the Roman family name Ausonius, and so on. Among Greek and Latin writers Ausonia, the land of the Ausones, became a poetic or romantic name for Italy. (JJ)

Ausonia (ô-sō′ni-a̯). A term for the region, on the border between Latium and Campania, formerly occupied by the Italic people known as the Ausones (q.v.) or Aurunci, occasionally used by Greek and Latin poets as a name for Italy. (JJ)

Autolycus (ô-tol′i-kus). In Greek mythology, a son of Hermes and Chione, and the twin half-brother of Philammon, whose father was Apollo. He was a famous thief and possessed the power, given him by his father, of making himself and the things that he stole invisible or of giving them new forms. He stole the cattle of Sisyphus but Sisyphus found them, and seduced Anticlea, the daughter of Autolycus. Autolycus was the grandfather of Odysseus and gave him his name, which means the "angry one." He gave Odysseus rich gifts when the latter visited him as a child, and it was during this visit that he received the scar from a gash of a boar, by which Odysseus was recognized when he returned to Ithaca ten years after the end of the Trojan War. Autolycus was the thief who stole the cattle of Eurytus of Oechalia and, after changing their color, sold them to Heracles.

Autolycus. Greek mathematician and astronomer, born at Pitane in Aeolis; fl. late 4th century B.C. He was the author of two treatises still extant: one a work on the motion of points on a sphere (the oldest Greek mathematical work preserved as a whole) and the other a study of the apparent rising and setting of fixed stars. Autolycus was the first to try to explain certain difficulties involved in the theory of homocentric spheres in astronomy, notably the fact that the apparent differences in the relative sizes of the sun and moon, and in the brightness of the planets, suggest variations in their distances from the earth.

Automedon (ô-tom′e̯-don). In Homeric legend (*Iliad*), a son of Diores. He was Achilles' charioteer, the driver of the immortal horses Balius and Xanthus. After the death of Patroclus, who had borrowed the horses from Achilles, the horses wept and refused to leave the battlefield. Automedon could not persuade them to move but he stayed with them and finally, after Zeus had assured them that they would never fall into Hector's hands, Automedon drove them back to Achilles.

Autonoë (ô-ton′ō-ē). In Greek mythology, a daughter of Cadmus and Harmonia, and a sister of Agave. She married Aristaeus at the order of the Muses and bore him a son Actaeon, who was torn to pieces by his own hounds. When Dionysus arrived in Thebes, his divinity and his worship were denied by Pentheus, king of Thebes and son of Agave. To punish him, Dionysus drove Agave and her sisters and other Theban celebrants mad. Under this spell the Theban women mistook Pentheus, who was caught spying on them from a treetop, for a wild beast. They shook the tree until he fell from it and, under the impression that he was a young lion, Autonoë helped Agave tear him limb from limb. Autonoë, like Agave, had been punished by the god for originally doubting his divinity, and with her sister was forced to go into exile.

Auxo (ôk′sō). In Athens only two Charites (Graces) were recognized. Auxo (*Increase*) was one of them. In Greek mythology, Auxo is also recognized as one of the goddesses of the seasons. See **Charites.**

Aventine Hill (av′en-tīn). [Latin, **Mons Aventinus;** Italian, **Monte Aventino.**] Name of

---

actor; up, lūte, pull; oi, oil; ou, out; ᵺ, then; d̦ as d or j, s̩ as s or sh, t̩ as t or ch, z̩ as z or zh.

the southernmost of the seven hills of ancient Rome, rising on the left bank of the Tiber, S of the Palatine. Below it to the N lay the Circus Maximus, and to the E the Baths of Caracalla. According to some accounts, the hill was named for Aventinus, a king of the ancient city of Alba Longa, who was buried on it.

Avernus, Lacus (a-vėr′nus, lā′kus). [Modern: **Lake Averno**; Italian, **Lago d'Averno**.] Small lake near Puteoli in Campania, Italy, about nine miles W of Neapolis, anciently believed to be the entrance to the infernal regions.

Axine (ak′sin). An early name for the Euxine (Black) Sea, meaning "Unfriendly."

Axiopoenus (ak″si-ọ-pē′nus). Epithet of Athena, meaning "Just Requital." Heracles raised a sanctuary of Athena Axiopoenus in Laconia, after he had avenged the killing of Oeonus, who had accidentally killed one of their dogs, by killing Hippocoön and his sons.

Axius (ak′si-us). [Modern name, **Vardar.**] In ancient geography, a river of Paeonia, about 200 miles long. It flows south and empties into the Myrtoan Sea (Thermaic Gulf).

Azan (ā′zan). In mythology, a son of Arcas and the dryad Erato. He became ruler of the district of Azania, named for himself, in Arcadia. Some say the first funeral games ever celebrated in Greece were held in his honor.

Azani (a-zā′nī). [Also: **Azanion, Aizani.**] In ancient geography, a city in Phrygia, Asia Minor.

—B—

Baalbek (bäl′bek). See **Heliopolis.**

Babrius (bā′bri-us). [Also: **Babrias, Gabrias.**] Greek writer and fabulist, who flourished possibly in the 1st century A.D. or later, in Syria. He is chiefly known for having put into choliambic verse the fables attributed to Aesop.

Babylon (bab′i-lon). [Possibly the Biblical **Babel**; ancient Persian, **Babirus.**] In ancient geography, a city in Mesopotamia, the capital of Babylonia, situated on both sides of the Euphrates River, above the modern city of Hilla, S central Iraq, about 50 miles S of Baghdad. The etymology of the name is, as ascertained by many passages in the cuneiform inscriptions, Bab-Ili (meaning "Gate of God"), from *bab* ("gate") and *ilu* ("god"). Babylon was one of the oldest cities of Mesopotamia, and was the undisputed capital of Babylonia at the time of the Elamite conquest, in the third millennium B.C. As capital of the country it shared in all its vicissitudes, and was the principal target of the Assyrian invasions. It was first conquered (c1270 B.C.) by the Assyrian king Tukulti-Adar, then (c1110 B.C.) by Tiglath-pileser I. Of Shalmaneser II (860–824 B.C.) and his son and grandson it is recorded that they victoriously entered Babylon and sacrificed there to the gods. It was customary with the Assyrian kings, in order to be recognized as fully legitimate kings, to go to Babylon and there perform the mysterious ceremony termed by them "seizing the hands of Bel." Sennacherib sacked it (690 B.C.), and completely razed it to the ground. His son and successor Esarhaddon undertook, 11 years later, the restoration of the city. But it was under Nabopolassar (625–604 B.C.), the founder of the new Babylonian empire, and especially under his successor Nebuchadnezzar (605–562 B.C.) that it became "Babylon the Great." The ruins, now covering both banks of the Euphrates, are those of the Babylon of these kings and their successors, and convey some idea of its former magnitude and splendor. Nebuchadnezzar, who took more pride in the buildings constructed under his auspices than in his victorious campaigns, concentrated all his care upon the adorning and beautifying of his residence. To this end he completed the fortification of the city begun by his father Nabopolassar. The city itself was adorned with numerous

fat, fāte, fär, fãre, errạnt; net, mē, hėr ardẹnt; pin, pīne; not, nōte, mȯve, nôr,

temples, chief among them Esagila ("the high-towering house"), temple of the city and of the national god Merodach (Babylonian, Marduk) with his spouse Zirpanit. In its neighborhood was the royal palace, the site of which was identified with the ruins of Al-Kasr. Sloping toward the river were the Hanging Gardens, one of the seven wonders of the ancient world, the location of which is in the N mound of ruins, Babil. The temple described by Herodotus is that of Nebo in Borsippa, not far from Babylon, which Herodotus included under Babylon, and which also in the cuneiform inscriptions is called "Babylon the second." This temple, which in the mound of Birs Nimrud represents the most imposing ruin of Babylonia, is termed in the inscriptions Ezida ("the eternal house"), an ancient sanctuary of Nebo (Assyrian, Nabu), and was restored with great splendor by Nebuchadnezzar. It represents in its construction a sort of pyramid built in seven stages, whence it is sometimes called "temple of the seven spheres of heaven and earth," and it has been assumed that the narrative of the Tower of Babel in Genesis xi. may have been connected with this temple. Concerning Babylon proper, Herodotus mentions that it had wide streets lined with houses of three and four stories. In the conquest (538 B.C.) of Cyrus of Persia, the city of Babylon was spared. Darius the Great razed its walls and towers. Xerxes (486–465 B.C.) despoiled the temples of their golden statues and treasures. Alexander the Great wished to restore the city but was prevented by his early death. The decay of Babylon was hastened by the foundation (300 B.C.) in its neighborhood of Seleucia, which was built from the ruins of Babylon. The last who calls himself in an inscription "king of Babylon, restorer of Esagila and Ezida," was Antiochus the Great (223–187 B.C.). In the time of Pliny (23–79 A.D.) Babylon was a deserted and dismal place.

Babylonia (bab-i-lō′ni-a̱, -lōn′ya̱). In ancient geography, a region and country of SW Asia. Its extent and boundaries are matters of divergence of opinion, some scholars considering it to have been coextensive with the whole, but others with the S part only, of Mesopotamia. Before the rise of Babylon to power,

S Mesopotamia was known as Chaldea and as Sumer. A line running from the Euphrates near Hit to a little below Samarra on the Tigris has been suggested as an approximate boundary between Sumer to the south and Akkad to the north. Some, however, apply the name Sumer to the whole region; some also identify it with the Biblical Shinar (also spelled Shanhar, Shenar), which others differentiate from Sumer and apply only to N Mesopotamia.

Culture. The N part of the area between the Tigris and the Euphrates is an upland; the S part is an alluvial plain resulting from deposits of silt by the two rivers. This alluvial land advances into the Persian Gulf at the rate of about 115 feet a year. From this it is known that Eridu, anciently a seaport and now 130 miles inland, existed 6000 years ago. It is widely believed that man first attained civilization in this alluvial plain. The ruins of many cities and towns have been discovered, with artifacts of Stone Age and Bronze Age cultures. There is evidence that from an early age this was a region where many peoples met. The Sumerians drained swamps, built canals, practiced flood control, developed agriculture and trade, and developed skills in metal-working, pottery, and textiles. They had an advanced understanding of astronomy and also practiced astrology, and acquired such a reputation for magic that their other name, Chaldeans, was for ages a synonym for magicians. Their religion was polytheistic; different Semitic and non-Semitic deities were popular in different periods, and each city had its particular god or goddess. At Nippur, Bel was especially worshiped, but within the precincts of his temple there were shrines to 24 other deities. One of the great Sumerian achievements was the cuneiform alphabet, perhaps the first ever to take form. Systems of weights, measures, and accounting were also invented in Sumer and later highly developed in Babylon.

History. The Sumerians, a non-Semitic people, were conquered by the Akkadians, generally supposed to have been Semites, under Sargon I; the Akkad dynasty may be dated c2400–2200 B.C. At this time the city of Babylon began to dominate the entire region from the mountains E of the Tigris to the Arabian or Syrian Desert and from the

Persian Gulf to the borders of what is now Armenia. Thus the ancient Babylonian empire occupied approximately the area now comprised in the kingdom of Iraq. From about 2200 B.C. it was ruled for some centuries by the Guti, a highland people; about 1850 B.C. it was conquered by the Amorites, who were probably Semites. The capture of Mari, chief city of the Amorites, by the Sumerian Hammurabi is now generally dated about 1700 B.C. Under Hammurabi the village of Babylon became a great city, and the laws were written down in the famous Hammurabian Code. Babylonia, however, was far from through with invasions, being conquered thereafter by Horites and Hittites and, about 1270 B.C., by the Assyrians. For centuries Assyria had been a vassal state of Babylonia, but now for more than 600 years the Assyrians were supreme. Under Nebuchadnezzar (605–562 B.C.) Babylonia enjoyed its greatest power and Babylon its peak of wealth and glory; but in 538 B.C. Cyrus of Persia put an end to Babylonian power. After the Persians, Babylonia was ruled by Alexander the Great, by the Seleucids, the Parthians, the Arabs, and the Turks. Throughout the later centuries the ancient system of drainage and irrigation was neglected, and the land became almost a wilderness, while ancient cities and towns were leveled by war or abandoned by their inhabitants.

Bacchae (bak′ē) or **Bacchantes** (ba̧-kan′tēz). [Also: **Maenads**.] In ancient Greece and Italy, female worshipers of the god of wine, generally called by the Greeks Dionysus, and by the Romans Bacchus.

Bacchae, The. A drama by Euripides, produced after his death, in 405 B.C. It is concerned with the strange and awful punishment which Dionysus inflicted on Pentheus and the daughters of Cadmus for denying his divinity. The scene is before the royal palace at Thebes. Dionysus enters and proclaims that he is the son of Zeus and Semele, daughter of Cadmus. He describes his travels through Lydia, Phrygia, Persia, and all of Asia, during which he established his worship. He is now in Thebes to teach his mother's sisters and Pheneus, ruler of Thebes, that he is indeed a god. Because of their doubts, he has already driven the women

mad; they are raging on the hills. A chorus of Asian women enters and sings in praise of Dionysus.

Tiresias and Cadmus come in. Only they of all Thebes are going to the mountain to take part in the rites for Dionysus. They only are wise; the rest are fools to question the gods. Pentheus joins them. He says he has heard of the women's revels, and that he has ordered them captured and imprisoned. He sneers at the claims of Dionysus and vows to cut off his head. He mocks Cadmus and Tiresias, clad in fawnskins and bearing the thyrsi of Dionysus, and blames Tiresias for introducing the pestilential rites into Thebes. Tiresias answers by declaring that Dionysus, giver of wine, and Demeter, giver of grain, are the two greatest gods. He advises Pentheus to welcome the god. Cadmus also admonishes him, and suggests that he wear the ivy crown of Dionysus. Pentheus disregards their warnings. He orders his attendants to find and bind Dionysus. Tiresias and Cadmus depart, predicting woe for Pentheus, as the chorus sings of the folly of the obstinate and then praises Dionysus, who demands faith from all.

Pentheus returns, followed by attendants who have brought Dionysus with them. They say that he, disguised as a mortal, came with them willingly. Furthermore, the captives have been freed: the chains miraculously dropped from their limbs. After questioning his captive and finding his answers evasive, Pentheus orders him chained and imprisoned. The chorus sings to Dirce, the sacred fountain of Thebes, foretelling the time when the city will accept Dionysus, and praying the god to free them of their chains. They hear the voice of Dionysus. An earthquake follows, in which the monument of Semele is wreathed in flames. Dionysus approaches and comforts the chorus. Pentheus also comes out, looking for his captive. A herdman now enters and describes the wild revels of the women on the mountain. He speaks of a miraculous fountain of wine that gushed from the earth when the thyrsus struck the ground. He earnestly advises Pentheus to welcome the wonder-working god. But Pentheus refuses to be convinced. Instead he proposes to take up arms against the women. He disregards the repeated

fat, fāte, fär, fãre, erra̧nt; net, mē, hėr ardȩnt; pin, pīne; not, nōte, mȯve, nôr, warnings of Dionysus not to provoke a god, but agrees to his suggestion to go and observe the revels. Dionysus says he must go disguised as a woman, otherwise the maenads will kill him. Pentheus goes off to effect his disguise. The god now informs the chorus of his intended revenge on Pentheus: he will make him mad, cause him to go through the streets garbed as a woman after all his terrible threats, and bring about his death at the hands of his own mother. Thus all Thebes will know that Dionysus is the son of Zeus. The chorus sings of the doom that awaits those who in their folly exalt their own unbelief.

Pentheus reappears in his woman's robes. Dionysus ridicules him by fixing his hair and adjusting his robe, but as Pentheus is now completely mad, he submits and departs. The chorus calls on Justice to avenge his impiety, and to punish him because he fears neither the gods nor the laws.

Presently a messenger enters and announces the death of Pentheus. He had climbed to the top of a tree to spy on the women. Informed of his presence by Dionysus, the women threw stones and their thyrsi at him and finally, in a frenzy, uprooted the tree and brought him down. Agave, his mother, attacked him. He tried to tell her he was her son, but she paid no heed. Under the impression he was a lion, she tore him limb from limb. She then impaled his head on her thyrsus and was even now returning to the city in triumph, bearing it aloft.

Agave enters. She calls Cadmus and Pentheus to share her triumph, to see the head of a young lion she has caught with her bare hands. Cadmus follows her, bearing the fragments of Pentheus' body. He regards his daughter with anguish and speaks of the just but ruthless stroke by which Dionysus has ruined them. Gradually he brings his daughter to a realization of what she has done and tells her that this is a punishment for denying the divinity of Dionysus. Aware of the horror she has committed under a spell of madness, Agave laments for her dead son. Dionysus, now revealed as a god, enters. He declares that Agave and her sisters were involved in the punishment of Pentheus because of their unbelief. They shall be exiled permanently. Even Cadmus and his wife are

sentenced to exile and ultimately they will be transformed into serpents. Dionysus is deaf to Agave's plea that his punishment is too extreme and too similar to human vengeance. They must go into exile. The play closes, as many of Euripides' plays close, with words to the effect that the ways of the gods are too mysterious for mortals to understand.

Bacchanalia (bak-a-nā′li-a, -nāl′ya). Festival in honor of Bacchus (Dionysus). Introduced into Rome from the Greek communities in S Italy, the Bacchanalia (the name is a Latin equivalent of the Greek *Dionysia*) originally consisted of secret rites practiced by women only (the Bacchae or Bacchantes) on three days of the year. Later the rites were opened to men and were celebrated five days each month; they became drunken orgies, at which it was supposed that crimes were plotted and conspiracies were hatched, and the Roman Senate by decree in 186 B.C. prohibited them throughout Italy, under penalty of severe punishments.

Bacchiadae (ba-kī′a-dē). Ruling family of Corinth. They were descendants of Heracles, and took their name from Bacchis, said to have been king of Corinth in the period 926–891 B.C. As members of the ruling class they intermarried, lived luxuriously, and displayed the utmost arrogance toward the people. They were deposed by Cypselus, 657 B.C., and many of them fled to other parts of Greece and to Italy.

Bacchiglione (bäk-kē-lyō′nä) **River.** See **Meduacus Minor.**

Bacchus (bak′us). In classical mythology, a name of Dionysus, the son of Zeus and Semele. He was the god of wine, personifying both its good and its bad qualities. Bacchus was the current name of the god among the Romans. The orgiastic worship of Bacchus was especially characteristic of Boeotia, where his festivals were celebrated on the slopes of Mount Cithaeron, and extended to those of the neighboring Parnassus. In Attica the rural and somewhat savage cult of Bacchus underwent a metamorphosis, and reached its highest expression in the choragic literary contests, in which originated both tragedy and comedy, and for which were written most of the masterpieces of Greek literature. Bacchus was held to have taught the cultivation of the grape and the preparation of wine. It is thought that while the worship of Dionysus originated in Phrygia, the name *Bacchus* is Lydian in origin.

Bacchylides (ba̱-kil′i-dēz). Greek lyric poet (fl. 5th century B.C.), born on the island of Ceos, in the Aegean Sea. He was a nephew and pupil of Simonides, and a contemporary and rival of Pindar. He lived for a time at the court of Hiero I of Syracuse. He wrote, as did Pindar, odes or hymns for athletic victors, as well as paeans, processionals, and other works. Among his extant works is a poem on the meeting of Theseus and Minos in Crete and a poem in praise of peace. Horace is said to have been influenced by the work of Bacchylides.

Bacis (bā′sis) or **Bakis** (-kis). In Greek legend, a name given to several seers or prophets, the most celebrated of whom was the Boeotian Bacis, whose oracles were delivered at Heleon in Boeotia. Specimens of these (spurious) oracles, in hexameter verse, have been preserved. According to Herodotus, Bacis had warned the Euboeans of the Persian invasion in the following oracle:

> "When o'er the main shall be thrown a
> byblus yoke by a stranger,
> Be thou ware, and drive from Euboea the
> goats' loud-bleating."

But the Euboeans made light of the oracle and took no precautions, to their great loss. Bacis also foretold the eventual and total defeat of the Persians in the following pronouncements:

> "When they shall bridge with their ships
> to the sacred strand of Artemis . . .
> Mad hope swelling their hearts at the
> downfall of beautiful Athens—
> Then shall godlike Right extinguish
> haughty Presumption."

This oracle referred to the victory of the Greeks at Salamis. The following was to the victory over Mardonius at Plataea:

> "By Thermodon's stream, and the grass-clad banks of Asopus,
> See where gather the Grecians, and hark
> to the foreigners' war-shout—
> There in death shall lie, ere fate or
> Lachesis doomed him,
> Many a bow-bearing Mede, when the day
> of calamity cometh."

Bactra (bak′tra̱). [Also known anciently as **Zariaspa**; modern, **Balkh**.] In ancient geography, a city in SW Asia, supposed by most authorities to have been the capital of the ancient country of Bactria. It was the center of Zoroastrianism, and Zoroaster is said to have died there. Bactra, which its natives called "Mother of Cities," anciently rivaled Ecbatana, Nineveh, and Babylon. It was conquered by Cyrus the Great and by Alexander the Great.

Bactria (bak′tri-a̱). In ancient geography, a country in C Asia, N of the Paropanisus Mountains (now Hindu Kush) on the upper Oxus River (now the Amu Darya), nearly corresponding to the modern district of Balkh in Afghanistan. The ancient capital was Zariaspa, Baktry, or Bactra (now Balkh). Bactria was the cradle of the Persian religion which Zoroaster reformed c600 B.C. At a very early period it was the center of a powerful kingdom which was conquered first by the Medes, then (as part of the domain of the Medes) by the Persians, and finally by Alexander the Great, who took a Bactrian princess, Roxana, as one of his wives. It was a part of the kingdom of the Seleucidae (a dynasty of rulers in Asia that stemmed from one of Alexander's generals), and from 256 B.C. for about 100 years an independent Greco-Bactrian kingdom which extended to the Kábul and Indus rivers. Bactria belonged thereafter to the Sassanidae until c640 A.D., and has since been under Moslem rule. Bactria played in ancient times an important cultural role, acting as an intermediary between the civilizations of the Greek world, India, and China.

Baetica (bē′ti-ka̱). In ancient geography, the southernmost division of Hispania (Spain). It was also known as *Hispania Ulterior*.

Bagoas (ba̱-gō′as). Favorite eunuch of Alexander the Great; fl. second half of the 4th century B.C.

Bagoas. Egyptian eunuch, originally in the service of Artaxerxes III of Persia. For a short time he virtually usurped the sovereignty of the empire. He put to death Artaxerxes (338 B.C.) and his son Arses (336 B.C.), but was himself compelled to drink poison (336 B.C.), which he had intended for Arses' successor, Darius III.

Baiae (bā′yē). [Modern name, **Baia**.] Seaport

in SW Italy, in the Campania, near Cape Misenum on the Gulf of Puteoli, W of Neapolis. It was a great seaport and the leading Roman watering-place, especially in the times of Horace, Nero, and Hadrian. It was famous for its luxury, and contained the villas of many celebrated Romans. Among the antiquities of Baiae are: 1) A Temple of Diana, so-called, in reality part of a Roman bath. It is octagonal without, circular within, with a pointed dome 97 feet in diameter. The walls have four ornamental niches. The structure is in *opus incertum* cased in masonry of brick and stone. 2) A Temple of Mercury, so-called, in reality part of a Roman bath, three subdivisions of which survive. The chief of these is the *frigidarium*, or cold bath, a circular domed structure 144 feet in diameter, with a circular opening at the apex, as in the Pantheon at Rome. The two others are rectangular and vaulted, the vault of one having excellent ornament in relief. 3) A Temple of Venus, so-called, in fact part of a Roman bath, an octagonal buttressed structure of *opus incertum* cased in brick, and *opus reticulatum*, circular within, 94 feet in diameter, and domed. It has eight windows above, four doors below, and had lateral chambers containing stairs.

Balbus (bal'bus), **Lucius Cornelius.** [Called **Lucius Cornelius Balbus Major.**] Roman politician, born in Gades (now Cádiz, Spain); fl. in the 1st century B.C. He was surnamed "Major" to distinguish him from his nephew Lucius Cornelius Balbus. He served in Spain in the war against Sertorius, and was made a Roman citizen in 72 B.C. His right to the citizenship was successfully defended (c55 B.C.) by Cicero. He sided with Caesar against Pompey, having been entrusted with the management of the former's affairs at Rome. On the death of Caesar he attached himself to Octavian, under whom he obtained the consulship in 40 B.C.

Balbus, Lucius Cornelius. [Called **Lucius Cornelius Balbus Minor.**] Roman politician, surnamed "Minor" to distinguish him from his uncle Lucius Cornelius Balbus. He was quaestor (44–43 B.C.) to the propraetor Asinius Pollio in Spain, where he acquired a large fortune through oppression of the native population. He subsequently became proconsul of Africa, and enjoyed a triumph (19

B.C.) in consequence of a victory over the Garamantes.

Balius (bā'li-us). In Homeric legend *(Iliad)*, one of a pair of immortal horses belonging to Achilles. See **Xanthus.**

Balkh (balch). See **Bactra.**

Baltia (bal'shi-a̤). In ancient geography, an unidentified island off the coast of Scythia, mentioned by Pliny and other writers. The name of the Baltic Sea is derived from it.

Bantia (ban'shi-a̤). In ancient geography, a town in S Italy, SE of Venusia and NE of the modern Potenza. The inhabitants spoke Oscan as evidenced by the *Tabula Bantina,* found in 1793 and now in the Naples Museum.

Baphyra (bä'fi-ra̤). According to Greek mythology, when the maenads who had torn Orpheus limb from limb attempted to wash away the blood that stained their hands in the waters of the Helicon River, the river, rather than be of any assistance to the murderers, plunged underground. In this way it avoided being an accessory in any way to the murderesses. The river emerged from the ground several miles away and took the name Baphyra.

Barathron (bar'a̤-thron). Steep ravine on the W slope of the Hill of the Nymphs, at Athens, Greece, outside of the ancient walls, rendered more precipitous by ancient use of it as a quarry. In antiquity this was the "pit" into which the bodies of criminals were thrown after execution, or in some cases while still living.

Barca (bär'ka̤). In ancient geography, a city in Cyrenaica, N Africa, situated near the coast: one of the cities of the Pentapolis.

Bardiya (bär'di-ya̤). A son of Cyrus the Great and the brother of Cambyses. He was known to the Greeks variousy as **Mardos, Smerdis, Maruphius, Merphis, Tanaoxares** or **Tanyo-oxarces.** See **Smerdis.**

Basento (bä-sen'tō). See **Casuentus.**

Basilis (bas'i-lis). In ancient geography, a town in Arcadia, founded by that Cypselus who gave his daughter in marriage to Cresphontes. It was the site of a sanctuary of Eleusinian Demeter.

Bassae (bas'ē). Place in Arcadia, Greece, near Phigalia. It is noted for its ruined temple of Apollo Epicurius, built in the second half of the 5th century B.C., probably by Ictinus, the architect of the Parthenon. According to Pausanias, the temple was raised to Apollo Epicurius (*Reliever*) in gratitude to the god for lifting a plague that afflicted the Phigalians during the Peloponnesian War, c420 B.C. Armor found near the temple indicates that Apollo Epicurius may originally have been a war god and shows that the site of his temple on the height (over 3700 feet) was used as a place of refuge for the Phigalians in their wars with Sparta. Set back in the solitude of the mountains of Arcadia, the existence of the temple was forgotten for centuries. It was discovered by a French archaeologist in 1765. According to one account, he overheard an Arcadian shepherd telling a friend that he had left his sheep "up by the pillars." The Frenchman inquired about the "pillars," investigated, and found the temple, one of the best preserved in Greece. It is a Doric peripteros of six by 15 columns, in plan 41 by 125 feet, the cella with pronaos and opisthodomos of two colums *in antis*. In the interior of the cella six piers project from each side wall, their faces formed by Ionic three-quarter columns. A portion toward the back of the cella has no piers, and has a door in the side wall facing the east; it is probable that this was the cella proper, and that the main part of the cella was merely a monumental court, open to the sky—a unique arrangement. The famous frieze, about two feet high (often called the Phigalian Marbles; since 1814 in the British Museum), surrounded the interior of the cella, above the architrave; it is in high relief, and represents combats of Greeks with Amazons and of Lapithae with Centaurs.

Bastarnae (bas-tär′nē) or **Basternae** (-tèr′-). Germanic tribe. They appear in history in the 2nd century B.C., as auxiliaries of Perseus against the Romans in the Third Macedonian War in the region about the Euxine Sea N of the Ister, whither they had come from their original seat, apparently on the upper Vistula. During the succeeding centuries they were in frequent conflict with the Romans, but disappear in the 3rd century A.D. They appear to have been among the first Germanic people to leave their old homes in the north, and were the forerunners, accordingly, of the southward movement that afterward became general.

Batavi (ba̱-tā′vī). Germanic tribe, a branch of the Chatti. The Batavi inhabited the Insula Batavorum (between the Rhine, Waal, and Meuse rivers) in Roman times, were subjugated, probably by Drusus, and became the allies of the Romans (c15 A.D.) serving in the Roman armies, especially as cavalry. Later they took part in the rising (69–70 A.D.) under their own countryman, Civilis. They were ultimately merged in the Salic Franks.

Bathos (bā′thos). A place near Trapezus in Arcadia. The legend states that here the giants made a last stand in the battle against the gods. Pausanias reported that the ground still burned and smoldered and that occasionally a giant's bones were turned up by plowmen.

Baths of Caracalla (kar-a̱-kal′a̱). Baths in ancient Rome, begun by the emperor Lucius Septimius Severus in 206 A.D. The thermae proper occupied a space of 750 feet by 380 feet, in a large square enclosure of about 33 acres, bordered by porticoes and connected foundations. The remains include walls, arches, and vaults, which are among the most imposing ruins of ancient Rome, and portions of the figured mosaic pavements.

Baths of Diocletian (dī-ọ̄-klē′sha̱n). Baths in ancient Rome, begun by the emperor Diocletian in the late 3rd century A.D. They were not opened, however, until 306 A.D., the year after the abdication of Diocletian.

Baths of Titus (tī′tus). Baths in ancient Rome, constructed in the 1st century A.D. by the emperor Titus, situated NE of the Flavian Amphitheater ("Colosseum").

Bathycles (bath′i-klēz). Greek sculptor, born at Magnesia (now Manisa, in Turkey), and active probably about the middle of the 6th century B.C. He was commissioned by the Spartans to construct a throne for the colossal image of Amyclaean Apollo in Laconia. On the throne he and his Magnesian assistants carved reliefs representing mythological scenes—Zeus carrying off Taÿgete, Heracles battling Cycnus, the battle of the Centaurs at Pholus, Theseus leading the Cretan Bull, Perseus beheading Medusa, and many more well-known figures of mythology. Under the throne was the tomb of Hyacinthus.

Bathyllus of Alexandria (ba̱-thil′us). Freedman of Maecenas; fl. c20 B.C. He was noted as a comic dancer in the *pantomimi,* a popular dramatic form of the Hellenistic period.

Batia (ba̲-tī′a̲). A nymph who, according to some accounts, bore Hippocoön to Oebalus. The other sons of Oebalus were Icarius and Tyndareus.

Batia. In Greek legend, a daughter of Teucer. When Dardanus came to his shores, Teucer gave Batia to him in marriage, and she bore him Erichthonius, whom Homer described as the richest of men and the owner of 3000 magnificent horses.

Baton (bā′ton). In Greek legend, the charioteer of Amphiaraus, and member of the same family, the Melampodidae. He accompanied Amphiaraus in the war of the Seven against Thebes, and was swallowed up in the earth with him when Zeus made a chasm in the earth to save Amphiaraus from the spears of his enemies.

Batrachomyomachia (bat″ra̲-kō̲-mī″ō̲-mā′ki-a̲). [English, **The Battle of the Frogs and Mice.**] Ancient Greek mock epic in hexameters, of which 316 lines are extant. Although its authorship is, at best, a matter of conjecture, it was formerly attributed to Homer, and by some critics to Pigres of Halicarnassus, brother of Artemisia, queen of Caria. The poem is a parody of the heroic epics, which describes a fierce battle between frogs and mice, in which finally, the gods intervene and send a large force of crabs to aid the frogs, hard-pressed by the mice.

Batrachus (bat′ra̲-kus) or **Batrachos** (-kos). Greek sculptor and architect at Rome in the time of Augustus.

Battiadae (ba̲-tī′a̲-dē). Dynasty of Greek rulers in Cyrene in N Africa, which reigned from the 7th to the 5th century B.C. They have been classified as follows: Battus I (630–590 B.C.), founder of the city; Arcesilaus I (590–574 B.C., his son); Battus II (the Happy, his son, 574–c560 B.C.); Arcesilaus II (the Ill-tempered, his son, c560–c550 B.C.); Battus III (the Lame, his son, c550–c530 B.C.); Arcesilaus III (his son, c530–c510 B.C.); Pheretima, regent c515–c514 B.C.; Battus IV (the Fair, son of Arcesilaus III, c510–c470 B.C.); Arcesilaus IV (his son) ascended the throne c470 B.C., gained a Pythian victory in 462, and lived until c450 B.C. With his death the dynasty ended and a popular government was established.

Battus (bat′us). In Greek mythology, a peasant who saw the child Hermes steal Apollo's cattle. He promised Hermes that he would not reveal that he was the thief. To test him, Hermes appeared to Battus in disguise and offered him a bribe if he would reveal the name of the thief. Battus succumbed to the bribe and, as he had broken his promise, Hermes turned him to stone.

Battus. According to Greek tradition, a son of Polymnestus of Thera and Phronima. His name was originally Aristotle or Aristoteles; he was given the name *Battus,* the Libyan word for "king," either by the oracle of Delphi or because he became king. He was born with an imperfection which hindered his speech and when he was grown, journeyed to Delphi to consult the oracle about his stammering. The priestess, addressing him as Battus, commanded him to found a colony in Libya. He returned to Thera. Later, finding the people of the island afflicted by sufferings, he sent envoys to the oracle at Delphi. They returned with the reminder from the oracle that he must found a colony at Cyrene in Libya. He sent out two ships, the crews of which settled on an island near the coast of Libya, but their settlement did not prosper. A third visit to the oracle at last convinced Battus that he must go himself and settle in Libya proper if he wished to relieve the sufferings of the people of Thera. With his followers he sailed to Libya and, through the deceit of his Libyan guides who saw to it that his party passed through the best parts of Libya at night, settled in one of the least appealing parts of the country. On his journey through the Cyrenaean desert he was cured of his stammer. It is said that he was faced by a fierce lion there, and was so terrified that he cried out in a loud, clear voice, and ever after spoke without any impediment. His colony survived, and under his descendants won large portions of the richest and pleasantest areas of the land. See **Battiadae.**

Baubo (bô′bō). According to some accounts, an aged nurse in the house of Celeus at Eleusis. When Demeter, disguised as an old woman, came to the house of Celeus in her search for her daughter Persephone, she pretended she had escaped from pirates and was seeking refuge. She seemed so sad that

Baubo sought to cheer her up. She gave her a cup of mint-flavored barley-water, and then she groaned as if she were in labor. Suddenly Baubo brought Demeter's own son from under her skirt. Because she had given the goddess a cup of mint-flavored barley-water, it became the custom at the Eleusinian Mysteries to give the worshipers this mixture to drink. In a fragment of an Orphic hymn a vulgar gesture which caused Demeter to smile, despite her grief, and accept the drink, is attributed to a servant, Iambus. Baubo came to have a place in the nocturnal mysteries of Eleusis. These details are probably inventions of a later date to provide a basis for certain aspects of the worship of Demeter at Eleusis.

Baucis (bô'sis) and **Philemon** (fi-lē'mon, fī-). Zeus, disguised as a mortal, once visited the earth with Hermes, according to a Greek myth. They went to many homes, seeking refreshment and rest, but wherever they knocked, they were turned away. At last they came to a humble cottage in Phrygia. It was inhabited by an old couple, Baucis and Philemon, who had spent their lives together in this dwelling. They welcomed the strangers who knocked at their door, warmly invited them in, and set about to make them comfortable. Baucis stirred up the fire and prepared vegetables while her husband set out the meat. Whatever of comforts they had in their home they offered to the strangers who had come. When the meal was ready, Baucis and Philemon happily served their unknown guests. They set a jug of their local wine on the table. As the meal progressed and the wine was passed around, Baucis and Philemon observed that no matter how much wine was drunk, the jug remained filled. In the presence of this obvious miracle they were frightened. Zeus now revealed that he was a god and that his companion was Hermes. He told Baucis and Philemon that they were the only ones in the area who had shown kindness to strangers. Because of their surly attitude Zeus resolved to punish those who had been unfriendly to the disguised gods, but he wished to spare Baucis and Philemon. He told them to climb the nearby mountain for safety. They did as the god commanded. When they reached the top of the mountain they looked back and saw that the land below was covered with marshy water. Only their poor hovel was spared. It was miraculously transformed into a golden-roofed, marble temple. As they watched, pitying those who had lost their homes, Zeus spoke to them. He promised to give them whatever boon they desired. After thinking it over, they told Zeus they would like to serve as priests in his temple for the rest of their lives. When it came time to die, they asked that they might be allowed to die in the same instant, that neither would have to bear the grief of losing the other. Zeus granted their wish. For the remainder of their lives the good and pious couple looked after the temple. One day, in their extreme old age, as they stood on the temple steps talking of their life, each noted that the other was gradually becoming covered with leafy foliage. Bark grew up around their bodies. Before their faces were enclosed, they bade each other goodby and both were transformed into trees at once. Standing side by side, the two trees were later honored with floral wreaths as befitted those whom the gods loved and who had loved the gods.

Baucis. Greek poetess of Tenos, a friend of Erinna and a disciple of Sappho. An epitaph upon her by Erinna is extant.

Bavius (bā'vi-us). Roman poetaster; died in Cappadocia, 35 B.C. He was an enemy of Vergil and Horace. His name is always associated with that of Maevius, who shared his vindictive feelings toward those greater poets and his lack of poetical ability.

Bebryces (beb-rī'sēz). A people of Bithynia, dwelling on the Euxine Sea. According to legend, Heracles defeated them under their king, Mygdon, and gave the land to the Mariandyni, who founded a city and named it Heraclea in his honor. The Bebryces won the land back under their new king, Amycus, a son of Poseidon, but lost it again when Amycus was slain by Polydeuces, whom he had challenged to a boxing match. After the death of Amycus, the Argonauts won his land and restored it to the Mariandyni.

Bedriacum (bē-drī'a̯-kum). [Also: **Bebriacum**.] In ancient geography, a village in N Italy, E of Cremona. The exact location is undetermined. Here the forces of Vitellius, under Cecina and Valens, defeated (April, 69 A.D.)

the forces of Otho; later in the same year, the forces of Vespasian, under Antonius, defeated those of Vitellius.

Behistun (bā-his-tön'). [Also: **Bisitun, Bisutun**; ancient name, **Baghistan**.] In ancient geography, a place in C Asia, about 23 miles E of what is now the city of Kermanshah, Iran. It is the site of a monument of Darius the Great, called the "Rosetta Stone of Asia," consisting of bas-reliefs and trilingual inscriptions 500 feet up the face of a sheer cliff, 1700 feet high. The bas-reliefs include a sculpture showing Darius with his foot on the prostrate form of the False Smerdis (Gaumata). In front of Darius are nine of the rebel chiefs, their hands bound behind them and a rope around their necks. Over all is a winged figure of the god Ahura Mazda. The inscriptions are in three kinds of cuneiform writing (Old Persian, Elamite, and Accadian), and tell how he killed the False Smerdis after the death of Cambyses, won victory over the rebels, and "with the aid of his good horse and his good groom, got himself the kingdom of the Persians." The inscriptions, deciphered (c1846) by Sir Henry Rawlinson, provided the first key to the ancient Assyrian writings.

Belgae (bel'jē). In ancient history, a people in northern Gaul, mainly of Celtic origin, occupying the area that now comprises Belgium, Luxembourg, NE France, the S part of the Netherlands, and part of W Germany. They were conquered in 57 B.C. by Julius Caesar.

Bellerophon (be-ler'ō̧-fon). In Greek legend, a son of Glaucus and the grandson of Sisyphus. His name was originally Hipponous but was changed to Bellerophon after he killed Bellerus, a countryman. Following this death and the accidental killing of his brother, he left Corinth and went to Proetus, king of Tiryns. There Antia (Stheneboea in some accounts), the wife of Proetus, fell in love with him but he rejected her advances. Enraged, she told Proetus that Bellerophon had made love to her against her will and asked Proetus to kill him. Proetus was unwilling to take such drastic action against a guest. Instead he sent Bellerophon to Iobates, king of Lycia, who was Antia's father. With him he sent a letter, asking Iobates to kill the bearer for the insult to

Antia. But Iobates also hesitated to act himself. He imposed a task on Bellerophon that he felt sure would bring about his death: to slay the Chimaera, a monster that shot flames from its lion's head, had the body of a goat and a slashing serpent's tail. Bellerophon was advised by a seer to catch the winged horse Pegasus to assist him in this task. Aided by Athena, who gave him a golden

BELLEROPHON MOUNTED ON PEGASUS
Proto-Corinthian lecythus, 675–640 B.C.
Museum of Fine Arts, Boston

bridle, he found Pegasus drinking at a spring, slipped the bridle over his head and tamed Pegasus. He leaped on Pegasus' back and sped off to find the Chimaera. According to some accounts, he first attacked it with arrows as he soared above it, then when it was weakened and gasping he poured molten lead into its mouth and dispatched it. Iobates was amazed at Bellerophon's success in this venture and sent him off to fight the Solymi and the Amazons. The special advantage of flying over his enemies and attacking from above again gave him success. Iobates then sent Lycian warriors to lie in wait for Bellerophon and kill him, but he defeated them with the aid of a flood sent by Poseidon. This convinced Iobates that he was dealing with the offspring of a god and he gave up further attempts to have him killed. Instead he made him the heir of his kingdom and gave him his daughter Philonoë in marriage. Three children were born of this marriage: Isander, Hippolochus, and

Laodamia. But Bellerophon's successes went to his head. He felt he was the equal of the gods and decided to fly up to Olympus on Pegasus. Such arrogance offended the gods. As he rose through the air on Pegasus' back, Zeus sent a gadfly to sting Pegasus; the winged horse reared, and Bellerophon fell to earth and was lamed and blinded by the fall. Pegasus continued to Olympus. From that time on Bellerophon was hounded by the gods and became a miserable, solitary wanderer until he died.

Bellerus (bel'er-us). A man of Corinth who was killed by Hipponous, the son of Glaucus. Because of his death Hipponous was known as "Bellerophontes," "killer of Bellerus," and widely known in mythology as "*Bellerophon*." (q.v.).

Bellona (be-lō'na). In Roman mythology, the goddess of war, regarded sometimes as the wife and sometimes as the sister of Mars. She was, probably, originally a Sabine divinity, and her worship appears to have been introduced at Rome by a Sabine family, the Claudii. She is represented as armed with shield and lance.

Belus (bē'lus) or **Belos** (-los). In Greek mythology, a son of Poseidon and Libya, and the twin of Agenor. He was a descendant of Io and Zeus. He became king of Chemmis (later Panopolis) on the Nile River, and was the father of the twins Aegyptus and Danaus, and of Cepheus.

Belus. According to some accounts, the father of Dido, and conqueror of Cyprus.

Benacus, Lacus (be-nā'kus, lā'kus). [Modern name, **Lake Garda**; Italian, **Lago di Garda**.] Large lake in N Italy, in Transpadane Gaul. The Mincius River carries its waters into the Padus. The lake is noted for storms.

Beneventum (ben-e-ven'tum). [Modern name, **Benevento**.] In ancient geography, a city in S Italy, about 35 miles NE of Neapolis. It was an ancient Samnite town that became a Roman colony, with its name changed from Mal(e)ventum, in 268 B.C., after the victory of the Romans over Pyrrhus which took place there. The town was pillaged by Hannibal after his victory at Cannae in 216 B.C. Among the many Roman monuments that remain are the Arch of Trajan, built in 114 A.D. and some Roman bridges.

Benthesicyme (ben-the-sis'i-me). In Greek mythology, the daughter of Poseidon and Amphitrite. She brought up her half-brother, Eumolpus, son of Poseidon and Chione, and gave him one of her daughters in marriage. When she learned that he had fallen in love with another of her daughters, she banished him to Thrace.

Berecyntia (ber-e-sin'ti-a). Another name for Cybele, a Phrygian goddess identified with Rhea. Her worship was common in Phrygia, in the Berecynthian forest or on Mount Berecynthus.

Berenice (ber-e-nī'sē). Daughter of Ptolemy II (Philadelphus) of Egypt and wife of Antiochus II (Theos), king of Syria. She was murdered in 246 B.C.

Berenice. Sister of Cleopatra, slain by the Romans in 55 B.C.

Berenice I. Wife of Ptolemy I (Soter) of Egypt and the mother of Ptolemy II (Philadelphus); fl. 4th and 3rd centuries B.C.

Berenice II (of *Cyrene*). Egyptian princess; wife of Ptolemy III (Euergetes); fl. 3rd century B.C. She is said to have dedicated her hair in the temple of Arsinoë at Zephyrium for the safe return of her husband from an expedition to Syria. The astronomer Conon of Samos reported that her hair had been transformed into the constellation called *Coma Berenices*.

Beroë (ber'ō-ē). In Greek legend, the nurse of Semele. Hera assumed her form in order to persuade Semele to ask Zeus, who was at that time in love with Semele, to appear to her in all his splendor. Hera knew that no mortal could live who had seen Zeus in his Olympian array, and took the form of Beroë to wheedle Semele into making this demand of Zeus.

Beroë. Named by some as a daughter of Adonis and Aphrodite. In Roman legend, Beroë was a Trojan woman married to one of the companions of Aeneas on his flight to Italy. Iris assumed her form when she persuaded the Trojan women to set fire to the ships while Aeneas and his followers were celebrating funeral games for Anchises on the coast of Sicily.

Beroea (be-rē'a). In ancient geography, a town on the Haliacmon River, in Macedonia. It was taken and held briefly by Pyrrhus, king of Epirus, in 286 B.C. After that it remained a Macedonian town until the arrival of the Romans, 168 B.C., who came to fight Perseus, and to whom the town of Beroea was one of the first Macedonian towns to submit. Pompey spent the winter of 49–48 B.C. encamped here.

Berosus (be-rō′sus) or **Berossus** (-ros′us). Babylonian historian who flourished in the early 3rd century B.C. He was a priest of Bel in Babylon. He was the author of a history of Babylonia (in Greek) in three books, founded on the chronicles of the priests of Bel. Fragments which have been preserved by later writers, including Josephus and Eusebius, show it to have been a valuable source for the ancient history of the region.

Bessus (bes′us). Persian soldier and satrap of Bactria, fl. 331–330 B.C. He commanded the left wing of the Persian army at the battle of Gaugamela (Arbela), 331 B.C., and when the Persians were overwhelmed there by Alexander the Great, he fled with Darius III, king of Persia. In the flight of Darius and his noble companions through Media and past the Caspian Gates, Bessus and the rest refused to halt when Darius wanted to stand and make another fight against Alexander. With the consent of the other nobles, Bessus plotted against Darius to make himself king of the Persians in his place. Darius became virtually a prisoner of his companions. When Alexander, hotly pursuing Darius now that he had subdued the lands behind him drew near, Bessus stabbed Darius (330 B.C.), and fled to Bactra where he assumed the title "Great King" of the Persians under the name Artaxerxes. In 328 B.C., having secured his rear, Alexander pursued Bessus, whose cavalry now deserted him, across the Oxus River into Sogdiana. The people there had no desire to endure warfare for the benefit of Bessus, and sent word to Alexander offering to surrender him. He was brought to Alexander's camp and placed naked and in chains, by Alexander's order, by the side of the road as the army marched by. When Alexander came up to him and asked why he had murdered Darius, he replied that he had done it to win Alexander's favor. This did not please Alexander, for having made himself by conquest the successor of Darius, he held that Darius was under his protection. He ordered Bessus to be scourged. He was then sent to Bactra, tried for the murder of Darius, and found guilty. He was sentenced to have his ears and nose cut off and was afterward crucified.

Bia (bī′a). In Greek mythology, a daughter of Pallas and Styx and an attendant of Zeus. According to some accounts, she was one of those directed by Hephaestus to bind Prometheus to the rock in the Caucasus as a punishment for stealing fire from the gods for man. Her name means "Force."

Biadice (bi-a-dī′sē). In Greek legend, the wife of Cretheus. According to some accounts, she fell in love with her nephew Phrixus, son of Athamas, and wooed him passionately. He honorably spurned her advances. She thereupon made false accusations against him, and this is sometimes given as a reason why Phrixus was chosen to be sacrificed when Boeotia suffered from a famine and was told by messengers from the oracle at Delphi that only a human sacrifice would lift the famine. The messengers from the oracle were later found to have been bribed to give this false message.

Biancavilla (byäng-kä-vēl′lä). See **Inessa**.

Bias (bī′as). According to Greek legend, a son of Amythaon and Idomene, and the brother of the seer Melampus. He was promised his cousin Pero for wife if he could deliver the oxen of Phylacus (or Iphiclus) of Thessaly to her father Neleus, king of Pylus. With the help of Melampus he secured the cattle and married Pero. After the death of Pero he married Iphianassa, daughter of Proetus, king of Argos. See **Melampus**.

Bias. One of the "Seven Sages" of Greece, noted for his apothegms. He was born at Priene in Ionia, and was active in the second half of the 6th century B.C. When Harpagus, general of Cyrus the Great, was subduing the Ionian cities of Asia Minor (c540 B.C.), Bias addressed the Ionian Greeks gathered at the festival of the Panionium. He advised them to join in one body and set sail for Sardinia, where they should found a single Pan-Ionian city and make themselves master of what the Greeks at that time thought was the largest island in the world. The Ionians did not take his advice.

Biblis (bib′lis). See **Byblis**.

Bibracte (bi-brak′tē). In ancient geography, a hill-town in C Gaul, the capital of the

Aedui, about eight miles W of Autun, France, with which it was formerly identified. Near it Caesar defeated the Helvetii in 58 B.C.

Bibulus (bib'ū-lus), **Marcus Calpurnius.** Roman politician. He was Julius Caesar's colleague as aedile and praetor. In 59 B.C. he was consul with Julius Caesar, after having been elected through the efforts of the aristocratic party. After an ineffectual attempt to oppose Caesar's agrarian law, he shut himself up in his own house, whence he issued edicts against Caesar's measures. Pompey appointed him commander of the fleet in the Ionian Sea in 49 B.C. to prevent Caesar from crossing over into Greece. His vigilance was, however, eluded by the latter in January of the following year, and Bibulus died in the same year (48 B.C.) near Corcyra (now Corfu).

Bion (bī'on). Greek bucolic poet, born at Phlossa, near Smyrna, Asia Minor. He was active c2nd–1st century B.C.; died in Sicily. In addition to some minor poems, his chief extant poem is the *Epitaphios Adonidos* (Lament for Adonis), noted for its imagery and graceful style. He is said to have been the teacher of Moschus.

Birds, The. Comedy of Aristophanes, exhibited in 414 B.C. and awarded second prize. It has been called Aristophanes' masterpiece. In a delightful manner it pokes fun at the current Athenian mood of hope for a wondrous change in the fortunes of Athens as the result of the departure of an expedition to capture Syracuse in Sicily. Two Athenians, Pithetaerus ("Persuader") and Euelpides ("Hopeful"), having realized, from Sophocles and other poets, that Tereus was a king of Athens before he was transformed into a hoopoe and made king of the Birds, decide to find Tereus and form a Bird-republic. Pithetaerus is fired with ambition and energy in this cause. He finds Tereus, reveals his design to the angry Birds and persuades them to cooperate. He has wings made for the new citizens, writes a constitution, erects buildings, and prepares defenses. Multitudes apply for citizenship in the Bird-republic. He arbitrarily admits some, such as a poet, and rejects those, seers and scientists, whom he considers unnecessary in the new state. The new land interferes with the communications between gods and men; the gods' supply of incense is cut off. Iris, messenger of the gods, is arrested for trespassing on the territory of the Birds. Prometheus deserts the gods and, hiding under an umbrella so that the gods on high cannot see him, arrives among the Birds. The gods send Poseidon, a sage, Heracles, a dullard, and Triballus, an absolute fool, to come to terms with Pithetaerus and the Bird-republic. Pithetaerus dominates the proceedings; Zeus awards the rule of the world to the Birds, gives Pithetaerus his own daughter in marriage, and Cloudcuckooland, the Bird-republic, is safely and unalterably established.

Bithynia (bi-thin'i-a). In ancient geography, a division of Asia Minor, lying between the Propontis (Sea of Marmara), Bosporus, and Euxine (Black Sea) on the N, Mysia on the W, Phrygia and Galatia on the S, and Paphlagonia on the E. Its inhabitants were of Thracian origin. Nicomedes I became (c278 B.C.) its first independent king; and Nicomedes III bequeathed (74 B.C.) the kingdom to Rome. It was governed by Pliny the Younger. The chief cities were Chalcedon, Heraclea, Prusa, Nicaea, and Nicomedia.

Bithynians (bi-thin'i-anz). A Thracian tribe, dwelling near the Strymon River and while they dwelt there, called Strymonians. According to their own account, as set down by Herodotus, they were driven out of their land by the Mysians and Teucrians and crossed the Thracian Bosporus into Asia. They settled west of the Halys River and took the name of Bithynians. Their dress in war consisted of fox skins for their heads, coats of many colors for their bodies, and buskins of fawn skins for their feet and legs. Their weapons were javelins and dirks. Croesus, in expanding his domain, brought them under his control and they later formed part of the Persian Empire.

Biton and Cleobis (bī'ton; klē'ō-bis). In Greek legend, the sons of Cydippe, priestess of Hera at Argos. During a festival, the priestess had to ride to the temple in a chariot, and, as the oxen were not at hand, Biton and Cleobis dragged the chariot 45 stadia to the temple. There they fell asleep; in answer to a prayer of their mother to Hera to reward this act of filial piety with the

fat, fāte, fär, fāre, errant; net, mē, hėr ardent; pin, pīne; not, nōte, mõve, nôr, greatest boon possible for mortals, they were given painless and swift death in their sleep. Herodotus makes Solon relate this story to Croesus.

Black Sea. See Euxine Sea.

Blue Grotto. Cavern on the shore of the island of Capreae.

Boae (bō'ē) or **Bavo** (bā'vō). [Modern, **Čiovo**; also: **Bua**.] Island off the Dalmatian coast, just W of Spalatum (now Split). It was a place of banishment under the Roman emperors.

Boeae (bē'ē). A city in Laconia, near the end of the southeastern promontory of the Peloponnesus. According to tradition, it was founded by Boeüs, a descendant of Heracles. He collected the inhabitants of three cities (Etis, Side, and Aphrodisias), who had been expelled from their cities, and set out to found a new city. The oracle of Artemis told them the goddess would show them where to go. When they came to the inner shore of the promontory, they saw a hare. They followed it until it dived under a myrtle tree. Taking this as a sign from Artemis, they built their city on the spot where the hare disappeared, and ever after worshiped the myrtle tree.

Boëdromion (bō-ē-drō'mi-on). The third month of the Attic year, corresponding to the latter part of September and the early part of October. During this month the festival called Boëdromia was celebrated, in commemoration of the succor given by Theseus against the Amazons.

Boëdromius (bō″ē-drō'mi-us). An epithet of Apollo, meaning "Rescuer."

Boeotarch (bē-ō'tärk). One of the chief magistrates of the Boeotian confederacy. Two were chosen by Thebes, and one by each of the other members of the league. They held office for one year.

Boeotia (bē-ō'sha). In ancient times, a district in C Greece, bounded by Locris Opuntia on the N, Attica and the strait of Euripus on the E, Attica, Megaris, and the Gulf of Corinth on the S, and Phocis on the W. Its surface was generally level, forming a basin in which was Lake Copaïs, now drained. Through this region Cadmus was said to have driven a cow, as instructed to do by the oracle at Delphi, following it until it sank to the ground to rest. On that

spot he built the city of Thebes. The area was named Boeotia to commemorate the journey of the cow through it, according to some accounts; others say it was named for Boeotus, who was a son either of Poseidon or of Itonus and Melanippe; but still others say it was named for Mount Boeon in Epirus, the land from which the Boeotians came. The cities of Boeotia were loosely united into the Boeotian League, of which Thebes was the leading and dominant city. Plataea refused to join the League. This caused a war with Athens to whom the Plataeans turned for aid, in which the Boeotians were defeated (509 B.C.). Plataea maintained close ties with Athens thereafter. The Athenians took many Boeotians prisoners in the war and kept them in iron fetters until they were ransomed. Afterward the Athenians hung the fetters in their citadel, and with a tenth of the ransom they constructed a bronze chariot with four horses which they dedicated to Athena on the Acropolis with the following verses:

> When Chalcis and Boeotia dared her might,
> Athens subdued their pride in valorous fight;
> Gave bonds for insults; and, the ransom paid,
> From the full tenths these steeds for Pallas made.

When Xerxes invaded Greece (480 B.C.), the Boeotians, except those of Plataea and Thespiae, sent him earth and water as tokens of submission and agreed to march with him as allies against their fellow countrymen. The Greeks who had taken up arms to resist the Persians, swore an oath against those Greeks who "delivered themselves to the Persians without necessity." In the battle of Plataea (479 B.C.), the Boeotians fought valiantly on the Persian side against the Athenians, but were defeated. The history of Boeotia after the Persian War is largely the history of Thebes, which took the commanding place among the Boeotian cities. According to ancient Greek tradition, the inhabitants of Boeotia were all extremely stupid (but this, like most other Greek traditions, has come down to us through Athenian sources, and the Athenians had little love for the people or cities of Boeotia, for obvious reasons); but some say that the worship of Dionysus and the art of writing were introduced into Greece through Boeotia, for they were brought there by Cadmus.

Boeotian League or **Confederacy** (bē-ō'shan). League of independent cities in Boeotia, supposed to have been at various times from 11 to 14 in number, with Thebes at the head (although Theban leadership was always resented, to some extent, by certain of the member cities). Its common sanctuaries were the temple of the Itonian Athene near Coronea, where the Panboeotia were celebrated, and the temple of Poseidon in Onchestus. Its chief magistrates were called *boeotarchs*, and were elected annually, two for Thebes and one for each of the other cities. It was finally dissolved, in 171 B.C. or in 146 B.C.

Boeotus (bē-ō'tus). In Greek legend, a son of Arne and Poseidon, and the twin brother of that Aeolus who became guardian of the winds. They were exposed to die as infants but were saved and brought up by Theano and Metapontus. Theano had passed them off to her husband as her own children. When she had sons of her own, she plotted to have them kill Boeotus and Aeolus but they were killed instead. They slew Desmontes, who had imprisoned and blinded their mother, then they freed their mother, and caused Theano to kill herself. Metapontus married Arne but later cast her aside, whereupon the twins killed the new queen. Boeotus fled to his grandfather Aeolus, and got from him the part of his kingdom which he renamed Arne, the home of the Boeotians.

Boëthus (bō-ē'thus). Greek sculptor of the Alexandrian school, born at Chalcedon (or Carthage, according to Pausanias); fl. in the 2nd century B.C. He was famous in antiquity for genre work of a high character. Pliny mentions a bronze figure of a boy strangling a goose, of which there is a replica in the Louvre. The boy extracting a thorn, found in replica in many museums, is supposed to represent Boëthus' statue of the same subject.

Boges (bō'jēz). Persian governor of Eion, a fortress at the mouth of the Strymon River. He was besieged by the Athenians under the command of Cimon (476–475 B.C.). Cimon offered him terms to withdraw and return

to Persia, but Boges refused, rather than appear as a coward who would surrender his trust to save his own life. Instead he held out. When all supplies were exhausted, he caused a huge funeral pyre to be erected, slew his wife, children, and all those attached to his household, and threw their bodies on the blazing pyre. Then he collected all the treasures of gold and silver in the fortress and hurled them into the Strymon River, beyond the reach of the Athenians. When all this was accomplished, he flung himself onto the funeral pyre. Though Eion was taken by Cimon, the Persians long honored Boges for his bravery.

Boii (bō'i-ī). Ancient Celtic people who entered Italy from Gaul c400 B.C. and settled between the Padus and the Apennines. They were overcome by the Romans in 282 B.C., but continued to struggle against them. After 191 B.C. they were not heard of again in Italy. It is thought that they migrated to what is now Bohemia, to which they gave their name. They disappeared from there also, c50 B.C. Another group of Boii joined the Helvetii in their invasion of Gaul in 58 B.C.; to them Caesar assigned land in the territory of the Aedui.

Bola (bō'la). A town of the Aequi in Latium. It was a nameless site at the time when Aeneas visited his father in the Underworld. Anchises pointed out to him the shade of the man waiting to be born who would found the city.

Bomilcar (bō-mil'kar). Carthaginian general; fl. at the end of the 4th century B.C. He commanded (310 B.C.) the Carthaginians against Agathocles, the tyrant of Syracuse. Possibly impressed by the example of Agathocles, he conspired in 308 B.C. to make himself tyrant of Carthage with the aid of 500 citizens and a number of mercenaries, but was captured and crucified.

Bona Dea (bō'na dē'a). In Roman mythology, the goddess of fecundity, worshiped only by women. She was the female counterpart of Faunus (in various accounts, she is called his sister, wife, or daughter) and bore, in this relationship, the name Fauna. However, she was so exclusively a woman's goddess that the name used by women (Bona Dea) has come to be her usual name.

Bonus Eventus (bō'nus ē-ven'tus). In Roman

mythology, a god of agriculture who later came to be regarded as a god of good luck.

Boötes (bō-ō′tēz). A northern constellation containing the bright star Arcturus, and situated behind Ursa Major. It is supposed to represent a man holding a crook and driving the Bear (Ursa Major).

Boreadae (bō-rē′a-dē). In Greek mythology, a name for the descendants of Boreas. It was applied especially to Calais and Zetes, his twin sons by Orithyia, the daughter of Erechtheus, king of Athens. These youths sailed with Jason in the *Argo* on the expedition for the Golden Fleece. In the course of the voyage the Argonauts landed in Thrace, and found Phineus, a blind seer, who had been married to Cleopatra, the sister of the Boreadae. Phineus promised to help the Argonauts if they would free him from the visits of the loathsome Harpies who polluted his food and kept him constantly on the verge of starvation. Calais and Zetes, who had grown wings as they attained manhood, pursued the Harpies and caught them. They would have killed them but Iris came as a messenger from the gods and warned them not to kill "the hounds of Zeus." In return, Iris promised the Boreadae that the Harpies would cease to harass Phineus. Grateful for being freed from the pestilent Harpies, Phineus gave the Argonauts much useful advice about their course to Colchis. Earlier in the voyage, when the Argonauts had landed in Mysia, Hylas, the squire of Heracles, had disappeared. Heracles searched frantically for him and delayed his return to the *Argo*. Some of the Argonauts wished to await the return of Heracles, but the Boreadae supported Jason's decision to proceed without him. It was in revenge for this that, long after the voyage of the *Argo,* Heracles killed them on the island of Tenos as they were returning from Pelias' funeral games. He buried them there and set up two columns, one of which moved at the breath of the North Wind.

Boreas (bō′rē-as). In Greek mythology, the North Wind, the son of Astraeus and Eos, or of Aeolus, and the brother of Hesperus, Zephyrus, and Notus. He fell in love with Orithyia, daughter of Erechtheus, king of Athens, and wished to marry her. Her father delayed the marriage, and Boreas abandoned his hitherto patient wooing, swooped down to the banks of the Ilissus River where Orithyia was playing, and carried her off in a gust of wind to his home in Thrace. Their children were Cleopatra, Chione, and the winged twins, Calais and Zetes. Enamored of the mares of Erichthonius, Boreas changed himself into a black stallion and produced 12 swift fillies by them that could run over standing grain without bending it and over the waves of the sea. A violent and stormy character, he was often appealed to by the gods to torment mortals, or even demigods, who were under the displeasure of the gods, as, for example, Hera appealed to him to shipwreck Heracles on Cos. Because he had carried off Orithyia from the

BOREAS CARRYING OFF ORITHYIA
Red-figured Greek amphora. *Munich*

banks of the Ilissus River at Athens and married her, the Athenians came to regard Boreas as kin to them. During the Persian War, when the Persian fleet lay at anchor off Chalcis in Euboea, an oracle came to the Athenians, instructing them to seek help from their son-in-law. They offered sacrifice to Boreas and Orithyia and prayed for their aid. A violent storm arose and battered the Persian fleet. Four hundred Persian ships and uncounted men and treasure were engulfed in the raging storm. In gratitude to their son-in-law Boreas, the Athenians erected a sanctuary to him on the bank of the Ilissus River. Boreas was identified by the Romans with their Aquilo.

Borghese Gladiator (bôr-gā′zā). [Also: **Borghese Warrior, Fighting Gladiator.**] Ancient Greek statue by Agasias of Ephesus, representing a warrior or an athlete. It is in the collection of the Louvre, Paris, having formerly been in the collection of the Villa Borghese, Rome. It dates from late 2nd to early 1st century B.C. The vigorous figure, undraped, is in at attitude of rapid advance, the left arm, encircled by the shield-strap, raised above the head, and the right (restored) extended downward and backward in the line of the body, grasping the sword.

Borghese Mars. Antique statue of Mars in the collection of the Louvre, at Paris.

Bosporus (bos′pō-rus). [Also: **Bosphorus;** Turkish, **Karadeniz Boğazi;** ancient name, **Bosporus Thracius, Thracian Bosporus.**] Strait which connects the Euxine (Black) Sea and Propontis (Sea of Marmara) and separates Europe from Asia. On it are Byzantium (now Istanbul) and Chrysopolis (now Usküdar). The name means "Oxford": so named from the legend that Io, transformed into a heifer, swam across it. Length, about 20 miles; greatest width, about 2½ miles; narrowest, about 800 yards.

Bouphonia (bö-fō′ni-a) or **Buphonia** (bū-fō′ni-a). In ancient Attica, a ceremony which was part of the festival of *Dipoliea* (*Dipolia*) in honor of Zeus Polieus (*Protector of the City*), celebrated on the 14th day of Scirophorion (about the end of June). According to the ritual, wheat and barley, or cakes made of them, were placed on the altar of Zeus Polieus on the Acropolis at Athens. An ax and a knife, sharpened with water provided by maidens, were given to butchers. An ox was led before the altar and was permitted to eat the cakes, whereupon the ox was slain by the butchers, one of whom felled it with the ax and the other slit its throat. The butchers then fled. The ox was skinned, its flesh roasted, and all partook of the feast. Then the skin of the ox was stuffed with straw and the stuffed animal was set up and yoked to a plow. This action was followed by a trial to find out who had murdered the ox, of all animals one most valuable to man. All concerned in the ceremony were involved in the trial. The maidens who brought the water for whetting the ax and the knife accused the butchers; the butchers accused the knife and the ax. The knife and the ax were found guilty and were hurled into the sea. Under the procedure, a feast was provided for celebrants, but lest they be polluted for the murder of the ox, the ax and knife were found guilty, suffered just punishment, and the ghost of the ox was placated.

Bovianum (bō-vi-ā′num). In ancient geography, a city in Samnium, Italy.

Branchidae (brang′ki-dē). The site of a famous temple of Apollo and an oracle, situated in the territory of Miletus in Ionia near the port of Panormus. The oracle was frequently consulted by both the Ionians and Aeolians. Croesus, who made many rich offerings to the temple, sent to test the accuracy of this oracle when he was considering whether to attack the Persians. Evidently he was not satisfied with its accuracy, for he ultimately posed the question whether he should attack Persia to the oracle at Delphi, with disastrous results. A story is told that the people of Cyme, in Aetolia, captured a Lydian whom the Persians demanded that they surrender. The Cymaeans feared to give up one who had come to them as a suppliant, and consulted the oracle to know what they should do. The oracle told them to surrender the suppliant. However, the leader of the Cymaeans on hearing of this advice thought the oracular response must have been misunderstood, and went with a delegation to consult the oracle again. The same response was given, whereupon this Cymaean leader, who had really been prepared to hear it, went about the temple and robbed all the nests that he found therein of their nestlings. A voice issued from the sanctuary and asked how he dared have the impiety to tear suppliants from the temple. The Cymaean replied that if the oracle was so desirous of protecting his own suppliants, why did he advise the Cymaeans to give up their suppliant? The voice repeated the command to surrender the Lydian to the Persians, and added that for their impiety the Cymaeans might the sooner perish, and furthermore, should not consult the oracle again. Hecataeus, the historian and wise counselor, when he failed to dissuade the Milesians from their intention of revolting against the Persians, advised them at least to take the precaution of taking the treasures of the temple of Apollo at Branchidae, including a huge shield in gold which Croesus had dedicated there, and use them to build a fleet with which they could secure control of the sea. If the Milesians did not take the treasures, he said, the Persians would. His advice was ignored and the event turned out as he had foretold. When the Persians came to put down the revolt of the Milesians, the hereditary priests of the temple (who were also called Branchidae) surrendered the treasure to them (c494 B.C.). The Persians carried it off and burned the temple. Many of the men of Miletus were slain. Some of the women and children were sent up to Susa as slaves. Later Xerxes sent the Milesians who were considered responsible for the betrayal of the temple to Sogdiana, in C Asia, to save them from the vengeance of the Greeks. At Sogdiana these Greeks founded a small settlement in which they preserved their Greek customs, religion, and speech. When, over 150 years later (c327 B.C.), Alexander the Great came to their settlement in his march into Asia, the Branchidae of Sogdiana, so it is said, rushed to welcome him as a Greek and to give him their loyalty. Some say that Alexander could think of them only as the Greeks who had betrayed their trust concerning the temple of Apollo and had taken the side of the Persians against the Greeks. He submitted the case of the Branchidae to the men of Miletus in his army. These could not agree on a judgment against the descendants of the priests who had betrayed the temple.

Alexander himself decided their fate, so some say. The settlement was seized and every one of its inhabitants was massacred to avenge the dastardly crime of their ancestors. Magnificent ruins of the Ionic temple of Apollo of Branchidae, near Miletus, and of the ancient port, remain.

Branchus (brang′kus). In Greek legend, the son of Apollo and a woman of Miletus. During his birth his mother had a vision that the sun was passing through her body. The priests interpreted this as a favorable omen. Apollo loved his son and gave him the gift of prophecy. Branchus founded an oracle at Didyma, near Miletus, which was highly regarded, especially by the Ionians and the Aeolians. The descendants of Branchus became priests of the oracle and were said to have built the temple of Apollo at the place that became known as Branchidae.

Brasiae (bras′i-ē). Name by which the Laconian town of Prasiae was sometimes known.

Brasidas (bras′i-das). Spartan general; killed at Amphipolis, Macedonia, 422 B.C. He was the son of Tellis, and was noted for his incomparable bravery, eloquence, simple honesty, justice, moderation, and for his frank and winning manner. In 431 B.C., at the outbreak of the Peloponnesian War, the Athenians sent 100 ships around the Peloponnesus and attacked Methone on the coast of Messenia. Brasidas commanded a defense force in the area. When he learned of the attack, he rushed to the relief of Methone with a hundred heavy infantry. The Athenians, attacking the wall of the city, were completely surprised when he appeared from behind them. He and his men made their way through the enemy with small loss and entered the city. By his daring raid he saved Methone and was publicly thanked by Sparta for his exploit, the first to win such an honor in the war. In the Spartan attack (425 B.C.) on Pylus in Messenia, which had been taken and fortified by the Athenians, Brasidas distinguished himself by his bravery. It was difficult and hazardous to bring the Spartan ships in against the defenders. Brasidas, observing the reluctance to risk their vessels, shouted to the Spartan captains that "they must never allow the enemy to fortify himself in their country for the sake of saving timber, but must wreck their vessels and force a landing." He ordered his own steersman to run his ship aground. In the landing he received many wounds, fainted, and lost his shield in the water. It was afterward found by the Athenians and set up in the victory trophy they erected. The following year he hurried from the northeast of the Peloponnesus to relieve Megara, which was under Athenian attack, and the Athenians withdrew. Next (424 B.C.) he marched through Thessaly to Acanthus, on the Chalcidian peninsula, and by his eloquence and personality persuaded Acanthus to detach herself from the Athenian Confederacy. The burden of his plea to the Acanthians, who admitted him alone to present his case, was that the Spartans "were taking up arms to protect the liberties of Hellas against Athens." Stagira and Argilus in the same area followed Acanthus, and enabled Brasidas to capture Amphipolis, one of the most important cities of the Athenian empire. In the following year, with the aid of traitors, he captured Torone, on the Sithonian peninsula of Chalcidice, and completed his highly successful campaign against the Athenian cities in the region. His successes were not viewed with unmixed admiration by the Spartans themselves; rather, they aroused jealousy of the brilliant commander. Scione, on the Pallene peninsula of Chalcidice, revolted against Athens, put herself in his hands (423 B.C.), put a golden crown on his head as the liberator of Hellas, and wreathed him with garlands of victory. Such adulation, and his acceptance of it, made the Spartans uneasy and spurred his own ambitions. A one-year truce between Athens and Sparta had meanwhile been concluded. Nevertheless, when Mende, a neighbor of Scione, also revolted, Brasidas accepted the offer of an alliance with Sparta and continued his activities in the area. At the expiration of the truce (422 B.C.) the Athenians sent a fleet against Scione. Brasidas was unable to arrive in time to save it and withdrew to Amphipolis. Hither the Athenians under Cleon followed, but decided not to engage him and began to withdraw. Brasidas rushed out after them. Cleon was slain in the battle. Brasidas received a mortal wound. He was carried into the city and expired. The people of Am-

phipolis gave him the honors of a hero. They removed all the monuments of the actual founder of their city, the Athenian Hagnon, and named Brasidas their founder. Sacrifices were offered to him, and games were celebrated annually in his honor. He was the outstanding general of the first ten years of the Peloponnesian War.

Brauron (brô′ron). In ancient geography, a village on the east coast of Attica. It was to this place, some say, that Orestes and Iphigenia returned from Tauris, bearing the ancient wooden image of Taurian Artemis with them. The image was brought to this place on the instructions of Athena, and in obedience to her commands the temple of Artemis Tauropolus was raised to house the image. As part of the ritual in honor of Artemis Tauropolus, the throat of a man kneeling before the altar was pricked by a sword just enough to draw blood. This was in memory of the narrow escape Orestes had in Tauris, and was also a substitute for the human sacrifices that had been offered to Taurian Artemis. Iphigenia was the first priestess in the temple of Artemis at Brauron, and some say Artemis made her immortal and she became Hecate. Excavations carried out by the Greek Archaeological Society (1958) have revealed remains of an early 5th century B.C. Doric temple of Artemis at Brauron, on the site where, according to Euripides' *Iphigenia in Tauris,* Orestes and Iphigenia were commanded to raise the temple of Artemis. Votive offerings, statuettes, and inscriptions found in the nearby marshes confirm the ritual described above. The Athenians celebrated the festival called the *Brauronia* in honor of Artemis at Brauron. Once when the Athenian women were celebrating this festival, some Pelasgians, who had driven the Minyans from the isle of Lemnos, swooped down on the women at Brauron and carried them away to Lemnos with them as their wives. Later, the sons of these women, born on Lemnos, showed such pride and strength that the Pelasgians killed them all, and their mothers with them. The modern village of Vravron is near the site of ancient Brauron.

Brauronia (brô-rō′ni-a). In Greek antiquity, a festival held at the shrine of Artemis at Brauron, in Attica, at regular intervals of several years. At this festival, little Attic girls performed a bear-imitation ceremony.

Brennus (bren'us). Roman name for a leader of the Gauls who marched on Rome early in the 4th century B.C., and sacked it. Brennus first marched his forces into Italy and laid siege to the Etruscan city of Clusium. The Romans sent ambassadors to treat with him, to see if they could persuade him to withdraw. When asked what his purpose was, Brennus is said to have replied that his purpose was the same as that of the Romans: to take land from people who had so much they could not till it and give it to his own people who needed it. As the Romans made war to satisfy their needs, so did the Gauls, said Brennus. The Roman ambassadors, seeing they could accomplish nothing, withdrew into Clusium. In a subsequent engagement the Gauls attacked Clusium and one of the Roman ambassadors took part on the side of Clusium. He was recognized by the Gauls, who demanded his surrender. For it was against all the rules of war, they said, for an ambassador to take part in a battle. The Romans refused to surrender their envoy. At once the Gauls marched on Rome. They did no damage to the country they passed through, for, they said, their quarrel was with Rome because of the violation of the laws concerning ambassadors. When they arrived at Rome they found the gates of the city open and unguarded, and the city almost abandoned, so terrified were the Romans at news of their coming. A small force under Marcus Manlius had withdrawn to the citadel on the Capitoline Hill, and a few priests and magistrates sat quietly in the Forum, having refused to abandon their city. The Gauls suspected a trap, but as they proceeded into the city, they found there was no resistance. They came upon the speechless, unarmed men in the Forum, who neither looked up nor moved at their approach. One of the barbarians approached a seated Roman and gently stroked his long beard. The Roman took up his staff and brought it down heavily on the barbarian's head. The Gaul at once drew his sword and killed him. Following this, the Gauls, who had up to this point done no damage, killed the rest of the men in the Forum, plundered the city, and put all those they found in it to the sword. But they could not take the Capitol, which was defended by Marcus Manlius. Brennus kept part of his forces in Rome, having burned most of the city, to keep up the siege of the Capitol. After seven months, those on the Capitol were weakened by lack of supplies, and the Gauls in the ruined city were weakened by disease. Brennus agreed to withdraw his forces in return for 1000 pounds of gold. The defenders in the Capitol brought the gold to him to be weighed. As Brennus was weighing it, the Romans saw that he was tipping the scales and cheating them. When they protested, he laughed, took off his sword and belt, and flung them on the scales. They asked what this meant and he mocked them, saying, "Vae victis!" (that is, "Woe to the vanquished," conveying approximately the same meaning as, in modern times, "to the victor belong the spoils"). However, Brennus was not to be victor after all. While the weighing of the gold was proceeding, Camillus entered with a force he had gathered, took up the gold and gave it to an attendant, and gave the scales back to Brennus, to whom he said that Rome was accustomed to delivering herself with iron, not with gold. Brennus withdrew to a camp outside the city. The next day Camillus fell upon him and routed his forces with great slaughter.

Brennus. A leader of the Gauls. Attracted by the weakness of the Greeks and the wealth of their sanctuaries, he led an attack against them, 279 B.C. His army, or part of it, eluded the Greeks and swam across the Spercheus River, using their shields as rafts. They plundered the country around Thermopylae but were defeated by the Greeks, with the aid of ships from Athens, at Thermopylae. The Gauls would now have retired in discouragement, but Brennus rallied them. He sent part of his forces into Aetolia to draw off the Aetolians, and they sacked and murderously ravaged the town of Callium. As Brennus had expected, the Aetolians rushed back from Themopylae to protect their cities. Some Greeks at Thermopylae who, according to Pausanias, were not so much traitors as they were anxious to get rid of the Gauls, led Brennus and a large part of his force around the pass at

Thermopylae, even as the armies of Xerxes had been led around it 200 years earlier. From there Brennus began his march to Delphi to plunder the rich sanctuary there. But again, they say, the god Apollo came to protect his own, as he had done in the time of the Persian War. When the Gauls drew near, the ground shook with earthquakes; thunder and lightning assaulted the Gauls, rock slides fell on them, and lastly, during the night snow fell. The Greeks attacked them at sunrise, surprising them from the rear. Brennus was wounded. The same night Pan came to aid the Greeks by spreading panic among the barbarians. They thought they heard the sound of horses galloping, and rushed to arms and fell on each other, under the delusion they were fighting off enemies. The Greeks, beholding this, attacked them relentlessly and drove them off. Brennus, seeing that all was lost, com-

Briareus to free Zeus. The gods called him *Briareus* but men called him *Aegaeon*.

Brimo (brī'mō). A Greek goddess variously identified with Hecate, Persephone, or Demeter.

Brindisi (brĕn'dē-zē). See **Brundisium**.

Brisea (brī-sē'a̤). A town in Laconia. See **Bryseae**.

Briseis (brī-sē'is). In Homeric legend (*Iliad*), a daughter of Briseus and the wife of Mynes, king of Lyrnessus. On a raid on Lyrnessus, Achilles killed her husband and took her captive. She was awarded to him as part of the spoils from the raid and he loved her dearly. Agamemnon took her from Achilles when his own captive, Chryseis, was restored to her father at Apollo's demand. After the death of Patroclus, Agamemnon restored Briseis to Achilles, untouched, and she wept over dead Patroclus, who had always been so good and gentle to her.

BRISEIS TAKEN BY AGAMEMNON
Red-figured Greek skyphos, early 5th century B.C. *Louvre*

mitted suicide. According to legend, he brought his life to a close by drinking undiluted wine.

Briareus (brī-ār'e̤-us). In Greek mythology, the son of Uranus and Gaea and the brother of Gyges and Cottus. He was a sea giant who had one hundred arms. When Hera, Poseidon, and Athena confined Zeus in chains as he slept, Thetis, a sea-goddess, called on

Briseus (brī'sūs). In Homeric legend (*Iliad*), the father of Briseis. According to a later account, he hanged himself in despair when his daughter was taken captive by Achilles.

Britannicus (bri-tan'i-kus). [Original name, **Claudius Tiberius Germanicus**.] Roman noble, born c41 A.D.; died at Rome, 55 A.D. He was the son of the emperor Claudius and Messalina, and was heir apparent to the throne until the intrigues of his stepmother, Agrippina, and her paramour, the freedman Pallas, secured from Claudius the precedence for Nero, Agrippina's son by a former marriage. He is thought to have been poisoned at a banquet by Nero, whose mother had sought to work upon the fears of her rebellious son by threatening to bring the claims of Britannicus before the soldiery. The name *Britannicus* was given to him by the Senate because of the conquest of Britain about the time of his birth.

Britomartis (brit-ō-mar'tis). A Cretan divinity of hunters and fishermen. The name probably means "Sweet Maiden." According to some accounts, she was a daughter of Leto. Minos pursued her and she fled from him and hid in the marshes. Later he pursued her over mountains and hills and to save herself, she flung herself into the sea. She was caught in fishermen's nets, which she is said to have invented, and saved. Artemis immortalized her and in Crete, where there are many temples to her, she was called Dictynna. In Greece she was identified with Artemis.

Brize (brī'zē). The gadfly sent by Hera to goad Io and chase her all over the eastern end of the Mediterranean.

Brizo (brī'zō). A goddess worshiped by women and known for prophecy through dreams. She was also a protectress of sailors. Her seat was the island of Delos.

Brome (brō'mē). In Greek mythology, one of the nymphs who helped care for the infant Dionysus in a cave on Mount Nysa. With other nymphs who performed this service, she was rewarded by Zeus by having her image placed among the stars as one of the Hyades.

Bromius (brō'mi-us). An epithet of Dionysus, meaning "Thunder," and given to him from the thunder that pealed at his birth.

Brontes (bron'tēz). In mythology, one of the Cyclopes, a son of Gaea and Uranus. His brothers were Arges and Steropes. See **Cyclopes.**

Bronze Age. One of the Ages of Man described by Hesiod. It was the third of the five ages, each of which was worse than the last. In the Bronze Age men ate flesh. They armed themselves with weapons and delighted in warfare. Death carried them all off.

Broteas (brot'ē-as). In Greek mythology, a son of Tantalus and the brother of Pelops. He had a son Tantalus, named for his father (Thyestes is also named as the father of this Tantalus). He carved an image of the Mother of the gods in the living rock of Mount Sipylus, high above the plain, which is still visible. He refused to honor Artemis, boasting that even fire could not hurt him. In punishment for his arrogance, he was divinely inspired with madness, and cast himself into a fire and burned to death. But some say that Broteas was a son of Zeus and was blinded by Zeus for his wickedness. Others say that he was so ugly that in discouragement he killed himself.

Brundisium (brun-dizh-'i-um). [Modern: **Brindisi.**] City in Apulia, in SE Italy, situated on a land tongue between two bays of the Adriatic Sea. The ancient town, occupied by the Romans c266 B.C., became a Roman colony (246) and a naval station (244 B.C.). It assumed great strategic importance as the terminus of the Appian Way and port of embarkation for Greece and the Levant.

Bruttii (brut'i-ī). [Also: **Bruttium, Bruthius; Bruttiorum Ager.**] In ancient geography, the southernmost division of Italy, corresponding to the modern provinces of Reggio di Calabria, Cosenza, and Catanzaro, and approximately coextensive with the modern region of Calabria.

Brutus (brö'tus), **Decimus Junius.** [Surnamed **Gallaecus** or **Callaicus.**] Roman consul and military leader; fl. 138 B.C. The surname Gallaecus (Callaicus) derived from his conquest of the Gallaeci (Callaïei), a people of NW Spain. He also repulsed the forays of the Lusitanians into the Roman colonies in Spain. He was consul in 138 B.C. He is remembered not only as a soldier, but also as a patron of poets, especially of Accius.

Brutus, Decimus Junius. [Surnamed **Albinus.**] Roman general; executed 43 B.C. He was one of the assassins of Julius Caesar. He was put to death by order of Mark Antony, with whom he disputed the province of Cisalpine Gaul. At the time of his death, Brutus was consul-designate. He is not to be confused with Marcus Junius Brutus, Caesar's chief assassin.

Brutus, Lucius Junius. Roman consul in 509 B.C., known as "The Founder of the Roman Republic." According to legend, he feigned idiocy (whence the name *Brutus* "stupid"; probably an erroneous etymology) to avoid exciting the fear and enmity of his uncle Tarquin the Proud (Tarquinius Superbus), who had put to death the father and the elder brother of Brutus to possess himself of their wealth. Tarquin, alarmed at the prodigy of a serpent appearing in the royal palace, sent his sons Titus and Aruns to consult the oracle at Delphi. They took with them for amusement Brutus, who propitiated the priestess with a hollow staff filled with gold. When the oracle in response to an inquiry of Titus and Aruns as to who should succeed to the throne, replied, "He who first kisses his mother," Brutus stumbled to the ground and kissed mother earth. When Tarquin seized and violated Lucretia, wife of Tarquinius Collatinus (whose father was a cousin of Tarquin the Proud), she called her husband and her father to her house. Brutus was one of several prominent Romans who accompanied Tarquinius Collatinus. Lucretia told them all that had happened, begged them to punish her ravisher, and then, in spite of their pleas, she took up a dagger and plunged it into her breast. Brutus, casting aside forever his pretense of idiocy, took up the blood-stained dagger, held it before them all, and swore by Lucretia's blood, once so pure, that he would "pursue Tarquin the Proud, his wicked wife and their children, with fire and sword: nor will I ever suffer any of that family, or any other whatsoever, to reign at Rome." He called the gods to witness his oath, then gave the dagger to the other men present and asked them to swear the same oath. With the aid of Publius Valerius, Brutus drove Tarquin out. The people immediately wanted to choose a new leader, but with the memory of the tyranny of Tarquin before them, they decided to divide the rule between two consuls. Brutus and Tarquinius Collatinus, as the man most implacably the enemy of Tarquin, were chosen consuls (509 B.C.), and established the Roman Republic.

On the understanding that he would give up his attempts to regain the throne and reëstablish the kingship, envoys of Tarquin were allowed to reënter Rome to collect his personal treasure and belongings. While in the city, they plotted with two of the leading families of Rome to kill the consuls and restore Tarquin. Two young sons of Brutus were involved in the conspiracy. When the plotters were discovered, brought before the consuls and accused, they made no defense, since the proof against them was incontrovertible. They stood in silence. In the stillness Brutus addressed his sons, "You, Titus, and you, Tiberius, why don't you defend yourselves of this charge?" As they made no answer, Brutus turned to the lictors and delivered his sons into their hands. The lictors flogged them, then stretched them on the ground and cut their heads off. The others present averted their eyes before the scene, the humiliation of Brutus, but he sternly watched to see that justice was done for the crime against Rome. Some said his face showed neither grief nor pity, but others said that to the dignity of his expression was added a look of fatherly anguish. When his sons were dead, he left the Forum. Immediately afterward, Publius Valerius and Tarquinius Collatinus began to dispute as to what should be done with the other conspirators, some of whom were related to Collatinus. Valerius called for Brutus. He returned to the Forum and informed them that, he having pronounced judgment on his own sons, it was up to the people to pronounce judgment on the other traitors. The matter was put to a vote, and the conspirators were condemned to death and at once beheaded. But Tarquin had not given up his determination to regain power at Rome. He sought aid from the Etruscans and marched with a great force against Rome. Brutus and his new colleague as consul, Publius Valerius, led the Roman troops against them. Aruns, the son of Tarquin, met Brutus on the field. They charged headlong at each other and killed each other.

Brutus, Marcus Junius. [Adoptive name, **Quintus Caepio Brutus.**] Roman politician and general, born c85 B.C.; died near Philippi, Macedonia, 42 B.C. Of a prominent Roman family, on his father's side he claimed descent from Lucius Junius Brutus who expelled the Tarquins from Rome. His mother was Servilia, a sister of Cato the Younger. She was a descendant of Servilius Ahala, who slew Spurius Maelius (439 B.C.) for plotting to usurp power in Rome. Thus, on both sides of his family, Brutus had a heritage of hatred of tyrants. He was well educated, and was particularly devoted to the philosophy of Plato. In the disturbances that shook Rome before Caesar won control, he was noted for his conspicuous devotion to the ideals of the republic and for the fact that he was impervious to bribery and flattery. Pompey was responsible for the death of his father, and though on this account he would not even speak to Pompey, when the struggle for power between Pompey and Caesar erupted, Brutus unhesitatingly chose to ally himself with Pompey who had legality on his side. He voluntarily joined Pompey in Macedonia before the battle of Pharsalus. It is said that when Caesar learned that Brutus was in the enemy camp, he gave particular orders to his men not to harm him in the fighting; if possible, he was to be taken prisoner, but if he refused to give up, Caesar ordered his men to leave him. Some say Caesar did this out of regard for Brutus' mother Servilia, who was the woman most loved by Caesar. And some say that Brutus was Caesar's son by Servilia. At all events, Brutus was not harmed in the battle of Pharsalus (48 B.C.), which ended in the defeat of Pompey. Brutus then wrote to Caesar, who forgave him and made him one of his companions. Caesar appointed him governor of Cisalpine Gaul (46 B.C.), where he won the devotion of the province by his wise rule and by his refusal to enrich himself by plundering it. In 44 B.C. Caesar made him first praetor (*praetor urbanus*), and it appeared that there was no limit to his future in Rome. But there were many in Rome who hated and feared Caesar on personal or public grounds. For there was no doubt that under him the ancient liberties of the republic had vanished. Cassius, married to Brutus' sister Junia, was continually warning of the dangerous power Caesar held. Others who felt the same turned to Brutus because of his incorruptible spirit and because his name and heritage made him a natural choice to pull down tyranny. Urged on by Cassius and others, Brutus at last agreed to a plan to kill Caesar

for the good of the republic. Some of the most prominent men in Rome joined the conspiracy, and it was decided that the deed would be committed at a meeting of the Senate which Caesar was expected to attend on the Ides of March (March 15, 44 B.C.). On that day the conspirators met at the Portico of Pompey. For various reasons, among them the omens of disaster that came to his wife Calpurnia, Caesar delayed his coming to the meeting, and the conspirators felt alarm that the plot might have been exposed. At last, however, Caesar arrived. As the conspirators gathered about him, Cassius turned his eyes to the statue of Pompey as if to invoke his spirit. Casca was first to strike at Caesar with his dagger. He hit him a glancing blow. Others approached and he fended them off, but when he saw Brutus threatening him, Caesar murmured "Et tu, Brute?" (*You, too, Brutus?*), covered his head with his robe, and ceased to defend himself. The thrust of Brutus went home. It was said that of the 23 wounds that struck Caesar on that day it was the second one, that inflicted by Brutus, that caused his death. When Caesar was dead, the senators fled. The conspirators had wanted to kill Antony also, but Brutus forbade it as they had agreed not to kill anyone else. Following the assassination, Brutus made a speech on the Capitol, exhorting the Romans to take back their liberties. There was no immediate outcry against the conspirators. On the contrary, Brutus was taken to the Forum with an escort of honor, but when Cinna, one of the conspirators, began to revile Caesar, the crowd murmured against him. The next day the Senate met and voted not only to give amnesty to the conspirators but also to honor them. Brutus was entertained by Lepidus. The following day the Senate met again and distributed the provinces, awarding Crete to Brutus. Mark Antony, who had fled in disguise after the murder of Caesar, returned and proposed that Caesar be given a public funeral. Cassius opposed him, but Brutus gave permission for it and also for a public reading of Caesar's will. When the will, bequeathing largesse to the citizens, was read, the crowd was moved by sympathy and affection for Caesar. Antony, aware of the tide of opinion that was rising, inflamed the crowd, praising Caesar, and holding up the blood-stained robe in which he died. His speech precipitated a riot, and Brutus and the other conspirators withdrew from the city.

Brutus went to Greece, where he was honored and welcomed, and from there to Asia, where he began to gather money and men to fight against Octavian (heir of Caesar) and Antony, who had temporarily given up the struggle between themselves for control in order to unite against Brutus. At Sardis, Brutus met Cassius, who had also by this time collected a large force. Before he left Asia, Brutus was sitting alone in his tent, late at night, meditating on the forces that he was about to set in motion. He thought he heard someone enter his tent, and looking up saw a phantom of monstrous shape. "Who of gods or men are you?" he asked, "and what is your errand with me?" "I am your evil genius, Brutus," the phantom answered, "and you will see me at Philippi." Turning back to his work, Brutus said, "I shall see you." There were other evil omens: when the armies of Brutus and Cassius embarked on their ships, two eagles perched on the leading standards and went with them, but flew off the day before the battle; at the sacrifices performed before battle was joined at Philippi, there were so many unfavorable omens that even the skeptic Cassius became alarmed. In a discussion before the battle Brutus and Cassius agreed that in case of failure they would commit suicide. In the first battle of Philippi (42 B.C.), Brutus was victorious over Octavian, who barely escaped with his life, but the forces of Cassius were overwhelmed by Antony. Cassius did not know that Brutus had been successful and he committed suicide. Twenty days later the forces of Brutus again met those of Octavian. The night before, the monstrous shape that had come to Brutus in Asia appeared in his tent again, but departed without saying a word. Next day the battle began in the afternoon. The army of Brutus was surrounded. He escaped with some friends and hid in a cave. He asked his companions to hold his sword, that he might fall upon it, but they refused. He then grasped the hilt of his naked sword

with both hands and fell upon it (42 B.C.). According to Plutarch, when Antony found the body of Brutus, he wrapped it in one of his own costly robes for burial and sent the ashes of Brutus to his mother Servilia. But others say the head of Brutus was cut off and sent to Rome, where it was flung at the feet of a statue of Caesar.

Bryaxis (brī-ak′sis). Greek sculptor; fl. 4th century B.C. He is best known as one of the four sculptors (the others being Scopas, Leochares, and Timotheus) who created the Mausoleum, the tomb of Mausolus, satrap of Caria, at Halicarnassus, which was completed c333 B.C. The relief panel of the Amazon frieze from the northern face is attributed to Bryaxis. It is believed that Bryaxis was the sculptor of an *Apollo* which stood in the grove of Daphne near Antioch, and other notable ancient works have been attributed to him. A tripod having a base with sculptured figures of horsemen, recovered at Athens in 1891, is shown by its signature to have been his work.

Brygos (brī′gos). Attic potter, active at the beginning of the 5th century B.C. Five vessels signed by him as potter were decorated by the same painter, who became known as the Brygos Painter (because his true name is unknown) and was one of the foremost painters of his time. He has been recognized as the painter of over 170 vessels, chiefly cups. The inside of a cup (Munich) c490 B.C., has a maenad painted in black outline on a white ground. On the outside, in red-figure style, Dionysus appears with a troop of maenads and satyrs. A cup in the Louvre shows an *Iliupersis* (Sack of Troy), and one in the British Museum shows satyrs attacking Iris and Hera. On a cantharus (Boston), Zeus pursues Ganymede; on another (New York), two satyrs relax to music.

Bryseae (brī-sē′ē). A town in Laconia, whose inhabitants sailed under Menelaus to the Trojan War. In the temple of Dionysus here, only women were permitted to see the sacred image, and the rites they performed in its presence were secret.

Bryson of Heraclea (brī′son; her-a-klē′a). Greek mathematician, a member of the Pythagorean school; fl. 5th century B.C. He went a step further than his contemporary Antiphon toward the squaring of the circle by considering not simply inscribed polygons of an increasing number of sides, but also circumscribed polygons. He believed, erroneously, that the area of the circle was the arithmetical mean between the areas of inscribed and circumscribed polygons.

Bubares (bū′ba̤-rēz). Persian engineer who helped direct the construction of a canal across the Athos peninsula, near Acanthus, in Greece, to allow the passage of Xerxes' fleet in his invasion of Greece, 480 B.C.

Bubona (bū-bō′na̤). In Roman mythology, a female divinity, protectress of cows and oxen. The Romans placed small images of Bubona, and the companion goddess Epona, protectress of horses, in niches in stables, or painted pictures of the divinities over the mangers.

Bucephalus (bū-sef′a̤-lus). Favorite horse of Alexander the Great which, after accompanying its master through his principal campaigns, died (326 B.C.) at the age of 30. Alexander buried the horse with great pomp on the banks of the ·Hydaspes River (now the Jhelum) in India, and built at the site the city of Bucephalia, traces of which exist across the river from the modern town of Jhelum in Pakistan.

Bucolion (bū-kol′i-on). In Homeric legend (*Iliad*), the eldest son of Laomedon. He was the father of twin sons, Aesepus and Pedasus, by the nymph Abarbarea.

Bunaea (bū-nē′a̤). Epithet of Hera, from the temple raised to her on the Acrocorinthus at Corinth by Bunus, son of Hermes.

Bunus (bū′nus). In Greek legend, the son of Hermes and Alcidamea. He ruled Ephyraea for Aeëtes when the latter migrated to Colchis.

Buphagus (bū-fā′gus). In Greek legend, a son of Iapetus and Thornax. He was an Arcadian of Pheneus, who received Iphicles, the brother of Heracles, when he was wounded in the fighting between Heracles and Augeas. Buphagus cared for him until he died. Afterward, Buphagus was slain by Artemis because of his presumption in pursuing her.

Buphagus. Epithet, meaning "Ox-eater." It was given to Heracles following a contest with Lepreus, part of which consisted in devouring a whole ox.

Buphagus. In ancient geography, a river in Arcadia. It was said to have been named for Buphagus, the son of Iapetus and Thornax, who was slain by Artemis because he attempted to violate her on Mount Pholoë.

Bura (bū′rä). A city in Achaea, near the southern shore of the Gulf of Corinth. An oracle of Heracles there gave answers as the result of the throw of four dice. It was destroyed by an earthquake in 373 B.C. It joined (275 B.C.) the Achaean League.

Buraicus (bū-rā′i-kus). Epithet of Heracles, derived from the town of Bura in Achaea. Nearby Heracles had an oracle in a cave. Those who consulted the oracle took four dice from a pile and cast them on a table. The message was then gleaned from certain markings on the dice, which were interpreted in accordance with a painting hanging on the wall of the cave.

Burrus or **Burrhus** (bur′us), **Sextus Afranius.** Roman officer; died 62 A.D. He was appointed sole praetorian prefect by Claudius in 51 A.D., and was, together with Seneca, entrusted with the education of Nero. By his influence with the praetorian guards he secured the undisputed succession of his pupil in 54. He is thought to have been put to death by poison, probably for having offended Nero.

Busiris (bū-sī′ris). According to Greek legend, a king of Egypt, who was the son of Poseidon and, as some say, Lysianassa, daughter of Epaphus. During his reign Egypt was afflicted with a famine that lasted nine years. Phrasius a learned seer of Cyprus, visited the land and told the Egyptians the famine would cease if they sacrificed one stranger each year on the altar of Zeus. Busiris adopted his advice and began by sacrificing Phrasius himself. When Heracles came to the land, after he had secured the apples of the Hesperides for Eurystheus, Busiris seized him and dragged him off to the altar to be sacrificed. At the altar Heracles burst his bonds and slew Busiris, his son Amphidamas, and all his followers, an event commemorated in several Greek vase-paintings.

Butes (bū′tēz). In Greek legend, a son of Poseidon or Pandion, and the twin of Erechtheus, king of Athens. He was the brother of Procne and Philomela. After Pandion died

actor; up, lūte, pull; oi, oil; ou, out; ŦH, then; ḏ as d or j, ş as s or sh, ţ as t or ch, ẕ as z or zh.

of grief over the fate of his daughters, Butes succeeded him as priest of Athena and Poseidon. He married his brother's daughter, Chthonia. He is the legendary ancestor of the family of hereditary priests of Poseidon in the Erechtheum.

Butes. According to the legend, a son of Teleon, who joined Jason and the Argonauts on the expedition for the Golden Fleece. On the way home from Colchis the Argonauts passed the island of the Sirens and were prevented from succumbing to their enchanting songs by the even sweeter singing of Orpheus. Only Butes yielded to their spell. He leaped overboard and would have perished at the Sirens' hands, but Aphrodite snatched him up and placed him on the Lilybean height, a promontory in Sicily, where he dwelt thereafter, and by Aphrodite became the father of Eryx.

Butes. In Greek legend, a son of Boreas. He was driven into exile from Thrace because he plotted against his brother, Lycurgus, and was discovered. With some companions he seized the island of Strongyle (Naxos) in the Cyclades. He pillaged passing ships and raided the mainland for women, since there were no women on Strongyle. In Thessaly he found the women celebrating the festival of Dionysus and seized Coronis, a Lapith princess, and ravished her. She appealed to Dionysus to avenge her and the god afflicted Butes with madness. In a spell he plunged into a well and was drowned.

Buthoë (bū′thō-ē). A city in Illyria, on Lake Lychnitis. It was built by Cadmus who, having resigned his Theban throne, had migrated to Illyria. Illyrius, the son of Cadmus in his old age, became its king.

Buthrotum (bū-thrō′tum). [Modern name, **Butrinto, Vutrinto.**] In ancient geography, a seaport in Epirus, now in Albania. It is said to have been founded by Helenus, son of Priam.

Buxentum (buk-sen′tum). [Modern name, **Policastro.**] Town of Greek origin in Lucania, situated on an arm of the Tyrrhenian Sea about 60 miles SE of Salernum. It was colonized by the Romans after the Second Punic War.

Byblis (bib′lis). According to legend, a daughof Miletus, and the twin sister of Caunus, with whom she fell in love. When she con-

fessed her love, he fled in horror to Lycia. In despair Byblis searched for him through many lands, until she fell of exhaustion. As she lay weeping, the Lelegian nymphs changed her and her tears into a fountain that never fails, and over the spot there grew an ilex tree.

Byblus (bib′lus). [Also: **Byblos;** modern name, **Jubeil,** also spelled **Djebeil, Jebail, Jebeil, Jubayl;** in the Bible, **Gebal.**] In ancient geography, a city in Phoenicia, situated on a hill close to the Mediterranean Sea, about 18 miles N of what is now Beirut. It was one of the earliest of the Phoenician settlements, and second in importance only to Tyre and Sidon. Its inhabitants, the Gebalites, are mentioned as skillful in hewing stones (1 Kings, v. 18) and in shipbuilding (Ezek. xxvii. 9). The word "Bible" comes (through Greek *biblion*, book) from the ancient name of the city, which exported papyrus. The city was most celebrated as the oldest seat of the cult of Adonis, to whom the city was sacred, and after whom the river it stood on was named. Gebal is mentioned as a kingdom paying tribute to Assyria in the annals of Tiglath-pileser II and Esarhaddon. It was taken by Alexander the Great. Excavations carried on there have unearthed numerous tombs and sarcophagi and the substructions of a large temple, perhaps that of Adonis.

Byrsa (bėr′sä). See under ancient **Carthage.**

Byzantium (bi-zan′shi-um, -ti-). [Greek, **Byzantion.**] In ancient geography, a Greek city built on the E part of the site of Constantinople (modern Istanbul), into which it was formally merged by the emperor Constantine I in 330 A.D. It was noted for the beauty of its location, for its strategic position controlling the entrance to the Euxine (Black) Sea, and for its control of the all-important grain trade between the Euxine region and Greece. It is said to have been founded by colonists from Megara under Byzas, for whom it was named, in 667 B.C. The Megarians had first founded Chalcedon, on the opposite shore of the Bosporus. When they returned to the oracle of Delphi, they were chided by the priestess for their blindness in overlooking the more advantageous spot to which they returned and where they founded Byzantium. In the reign of Darius the Great the city was destroyed. Pausanias, the Spartan victor at Plataea (479 B.C.), seized and recolonized it, 477, but was driven out by the Athenians, 476 B.C. The city became a member of the Athenian Confederacy, from which it revolted in 440 and 411 B.C. Alcibiades conquered it in 408 B.C. by means of a blockade and the treachery of the Athenian party inside the city. Lysander the Spartan took it in 403 B.C. and set a Spartan governor to rule it. The Athenians regained control in 390, and at last recognized it as independent in 354 B.C. In 340 B.C. it was besieged by Philip of Macedon and relieved by Phocion. During the reign of Alexander the Great it fell under Macedonian dominion, but with the disinte-

gration of the Macedonian empire after Alexander's death it became a free city. It was allied to Rome, at first as a free city, then as a subject city, and was at length besieged by Severus (196 A.D.), who took it, destroyed its walls, and put the population to the sword. Constantine recognized the advantages of its location, rebuilt it, and transferred the government there, 330 A.D., and it became the capital of the long-lived Byzantine Empire.

Byzas (bī′zas). In Greek legend, a son of Poseidon and Ceroëssa, daughter of Zeus and Io. Some say he was the founder of Byzantium. Others say that a Byzas led a colony of Megarians to the Black Sea and founded Byzantium, c667 B.C.

C

Caanthus (kā-an′thus). In Greek mythology, a son of Oceanus. He was sent to look for his sister Melia, who had disappeared. He found that she had been carried off by Apollo, and when he was unable to rescue her, he threw fire into the sacred grove of Apollo. For his impiety Apollo slew him. According to Pausanias, the tomb of Caanthus was near the Ismenus River, at Thebes, on the spot where he was killed.

Cabirea (ka-bī′rē-a). Epithet of Demeter. The Thebans said that on the site occupied by the grove of Cabirean Demeter outside Thebes, there was once a city occupied by the Cabiri. Demeter taught them her rites and entrusted a sacred object into their keeping. The Cabiri were driven from their homes in the war that the Epigoni waged against Thebes, but later returned and revived the rites. Only the priests were permitted to perform the rites. If private persons made the attempt, they were swiftly punished by the anger of the gods, as were also those who profaned the sacred places. During the Persian War some soldiers from the army of Mardonius entered the sanctuary of Demeter Cabirea in Boeotia. According to the account, they were struck with madness and hurled themselves into the sea.

Cabiri (ka-bī′rī). [Also: **Cabeiri, Kabeiri**.] In Greek mythology, certain beneficent deities of whom little is known. They were worshiped in parts of Greece and in the islands of Imbrus, Lemnos, and Samothrace. They are possibly of Phrygian origin. Their rites were secret. The mysteries of the Cabiri of Samothrace were regarded as inferior only to the Eleusinian. Later they became associated with the Dioscuri and gave protection against mishaps, especially by sea.

Caca (kā′ka). In Roman mythology, an ancient goddess of the hearth. Her place was later taken by Vesta. Caca was supposed to have been the sister of Cacus who stole the cattle Hercules had seized from Geryon. This occurred while Hercules rested in Italy on his return with the cattle to Greece. Caca is said to have reported the theft to Hercules.

Cacus (kā′kus). In Roman mythology, a giant, a fire-breathing, man-eating, half-human son of Vulcan, living near the spot on which Rome was built. He stole from Hercules some of the cattle of Geryon, dragging them backward into his cave under the Aventine, so that their footprints would not show the direction in which they had gone; but Hercules found them by their lowing. He ripped off the top of the mountain in a cave of which

actor; up, lūte, pᵾll; oi, oil; ou, out; ᴛʜ, then; ḏ as d or j, ş as s or sh, ṭ as t or ch, ẓ as z or zh.

Cacus had hidden the cattle, hurled in stones and arrows, and, when these failed to hurt Cacus, jumped in and slew the monster, thus ridding the land of a pestilence and winning the gratitude of the inhabitants.

Cadmea (kad-mē′a). In ancient times, the citadel or acropolis of Thebes in Boeotia, Greece, named from its mythical founder, the hero Cadmus. The remains of the ancient fortifications include a stretch of ruined Cyclopean wall on the north side, and fragments of more recent walls on the southeastern slope.

Cadmeans (kad-mē′anz). Graeco-Phoenicians (their name merely signifying "the Easterns") who in pre-Trojan times were said to have occupied the country which was afterward called Boeotia. Their name may have been derived from the legendary figure of Cadmus, whose name means "man of the East."

Cadmus (kad-mus). In Greek mythology, a son of Agenor of Phoenicia and Telephassa, and the brother of Cilix, Phoenix, and Europa. When Europa was carried off by Zeus, who had taken the form of a bull on this occasion, Agenor commanded his sons to find her, and threatened them with exile if they failed to do so. Cadmus, accompanied by his mother, sailed to Rhodes. He dedicated a bronze tripod in the sanctuary of Athena at Lindus, in Rhodes. This tripod was inscribed with Phoenician letters, and thus it was that Cadmus brought the alphabet into the Greek world. He also founded a temple of Poseidon in Rhodes, in fulfillment of a vow made during a storm at sea. He touched at the island of Thera and founded a colony there. Still in search of Europa, he journeyed to Thrace. Telephassa died there and Cadmus buried her. He next proceeded to Delphi to make inquiries of the oracle as to how he could find his sister. The priestess told him to give up his search. She instructed him to follow a cow, and where it should lie down, there he must build a city. Cadmus traveled through Phocis. He detached a heifer which had white marks in the shape of a full moon on its flanks from the herd of King Pelagon, and drove it through Boeotia. At last the cow lay down on the site of the city which later came to be known as Thebes. Cadmus wanted to sacrifice the cow to Athena at once. He sent his followers to a nearby spring for

water. This was a spring of Ares, and was guarded by a fierce dragon that killed the companions of Cadmus. Cadmus slew the dragon and, on the advice of Athena, sowed part of its teeth. Instantly armed men sprang up from the soil; these were the Sparti, "sown" men. Cadmus flung stones into the midst of the Sparti and they, thinking they were being assaulted by some of their own number, fell to fighting among themselves and all except five were slain. The five survivors were Echion, Udaeus, Chthonius, Hyperenor, and Pelorus. They agreed to help Cadmus build his city, and became the ancestors of five of the leading families of Thebes. But Ares was angry with Cadmus for killing his dragon, and as a punishment compelled Cadmus to serve him for a Great Year, that is to say, for eight years, for such was the term of a "Great" or "Eternal" year. At the end of his term of service Athena made him king of Thebes, which at that time was known as Cadmea, and its inhabitants as Cadmeans. Zeus gave him Harmonia, the daughter of Aphrodite and Ares, for a wife, and all the gods attended the wedding. This was the first wedding of mortals which the gods honored with their presence.

Cadmus built the upper city of Thebes and reigned peacefully, but his descendants suffered grievously for his fault in killing the dragon of Ares. Harmonia bore Cadmus four daughters: Autonoë, Semele, Ino, and Agave, and one son, Polydorus. After some time, Cadmus gave up the throne in favor of his grandson, Pentheus, the son of Agave. In this time Dionysus came to Thebes. Pentheus doubted the divinity of the god and ordered the Thebans not to take part in the revels. Dionysus punished him by driving him mad and by causing his mother, who had also at first refused to believe that Dionysus was a god, to tear Pentheus to pieces while she was under a spell of divinely inspired madness. After this Cadmus and Harmonia fled, grief-stricken, from Thebes. They went to the land of the Encheleans, who were at war with their neighbors, the Illyrians. The Encheleans were informed by an oracle that they would defeat the Illyrians if Cadmus was their leader. They therefore made him their leader and defeated the Illyrians. Thus Cadmus became king of the

Illyrians, and when a son was born to him in his old age, he named him Illyrius. In the end, Cadmus and Harmonia were turned into spotted serpents by Zeus, and finally went to the Elysian Fields.

Cadmus of Miletus (mī-lē′tus). Greek historian, called Cadmus of Miletus from his chief work, but by birth a Phoenician. He flourished probably in the middle of the 6th century B.C. He is generally considered to be the earliest of the Greek chroniclers and the first to write historic prose, a prose it should be noted, that was still marked by the poetic character of the earlier epics. According to tradition, he wrote his chronicle, a history of Miletus and the colonization of Ionia, immediately after he had invented letters. He also speculated on the cause of the periodic floods of the Nile.

Caduceus (ka̱-dū′se̱-us). The rod or wand borne by Hermes, or Mercury, as an ensign of authority, quality, and office. It was originally merely the Greek herald's staff, a plain rod entwined with fillets of wool. Later the fillets were changed to serpents; and in the conventional representations familiar at the present day the caduceus is often winged. The caduceus is a symbol of peace and prosperity and in modern times figures as a symbol of commerce, Hermes being the god of commerce. It is also used as an emblem by physicians in this country. The rod represents power; the serpents represent wisdom; and the two wings, diligence and activity.

Caecilius (se̱-sil′i-us, -sil′yus). [Surnamed **Calactinus** and, erroneously, **Callantianus;** original name, **Archagathus.**] Hellenistic historian, critic, and teacher, of Calacte in Sicily (whence his surname); active in the 1st century A.D. He was naturalized at Rome, where he took the name of his patron, one of the Metelli. He enjoyed high repute at Rome in the time of Cicero and Augustus, but his works are lost, with the exception of a few fragments.

Caecilius Statius (stā′shi-us, -shus). [Also: **Statius Caecilius.**] Roman comic poet, who died 168 B.C. He was by birth a member of the Celtic tribe of the Insubrians, and was brought as a prisoner to Rome c200 B.C. His comedies, of which only fragments survive, were adaptations of Attic originals.

Caeculus (se̱′kū-lus). In Roman legend, the

son of Vulcan and a young woman of a family of shepherds. As the young woman was sitting near the hearth, a spark, which was Vulcan, flew into her lap, and from this union Caeculus was born. His mother abandoned him, but he was found and brought up by shepherds. As a young man he became a wandering robber; later, with a band of companions, he is said to have founded the town of Praeneste. He asked Vulcan for a sign to prove to his doubting followers that he was truly of divine birth. Vulcan instantly answered his request by surrounding them with a ring of flames. Satisfied with this proof, Caeculus then requested Vulcan to cause the flames to subside so that his companions, their doubts now at rest, would not be injured. Vulcan again complied.

Caecus (se̱′kus). See **Claudius, Appius.**

Caelian Hill (se̱′li-a̱n). [Latin, **Caelius Mons.**] Southeastern hill of the group of Seven Hills of ancient Rome, adjoining the Palatine, and between the Aventine and the Esquiline. The Lateran lies on its widely extending eastern slope. According to legend, the Caelian Hill was added to the growing city of Rome by Tullus Hostilius, third king of Rome (672–640 B.C.). He won dominion over Alba Longa, destroyed that city, and moved its inhabitants to Rome, where he settled them on the Caelian Hill.

Caelius (se̱′li-us). [Full name, **Marcus Caelius Rufus.**] Roman politician, born at Puteoli, Italy, May 2, 82 B.C.; died 48 B.C. He was a friend and correspondent of Cicero. It is said that his education was supervised by Crassus and Cicero, and he was an especially close friend of the latter during the great orator's public career. He was also for a time intimate with Catiline, but according to Cicero was not involved in the latter's conspiracy, and in fact he exposed the part played by C. Antonius in that intrigue. In 56 B.C. his mistress Clodia, the sister of Publius Clodius and the *Lesbia* of the poems of Catullus, charged him with an attempt on her life, but he was acquitted with the aid of Cicero, whose oration in his defense, *Pro Caelio,* is one of the latter's most famous efforts. A tribune in 52 B.C. and an aedile in 50, Caelius supported Julius Caesar against Pompey in 49 B.C. Caesar appointed him *praetor peregrinus* (that is, judge of legal actions between persons at least one of whom was not a Roman citizen). But whether from a resentful feeling that this reward was insufficient to his services, or from impatience with what he considered the slow pace of Caesar's measures to cancel debts (of which Caelius had many), Caelius joined in a foredoomed conspiracy against Caesar's rising power. In 48 B.C. he was killed by soldiers whom he was attempting to win over to his rebellious plans.

Caelius Mons (monz). Latin name of the **Caelian Hill.**

Caelus (sē'lus). In Roman mythology, a god of the sky. He was later identified with Uranus.

Caeneus (sē'nūs). In Greek legend, a Lapith, originally the girl Caenis, daughter of Elatus, who was violated by Poseidon. He promised to grant any wish she might make and fulfilled her request to be changed into a man. She became a warrior who was invulnerable to the sword or spear and was renamed Caeneus and later had a son, Coronus. Caeneus was so powerful the Lapiths made him their king. He took part in the quest for the Golden Fleece and in the Calydonian Hunt. In the battle with the centaurs which broke out at the marriage of Pirithous and Hippodamia, the centaurs tried in vain to slay Caeneus, who was killing centaurs unmercifully. At length they entombed him beneath huge tree trunks. His soul flew out in the form of a bird, and when the Lapiths sought his body to bury it, it was found transformed back to its original form as a girl.

Caenis (sē'nis). In Greek legend, the daughter of Elatus. She was violated by Poseidon who, in accordance with his promise to grant her any wish, transformed her into a man. See **Caeneus.**

Caepio (sē'pi-ō), **Quintus Servilius.** Roman consul in 106 B.C. As proconsul in Gaul (105 B.C.), he was defeated with Mallius by the Cimbri.

Caere (sē'rē). [Earlier name, **Agylla.**] In ancient geography, a city in Etruria, Italy, situated about 25 miles NW of Rome. It was supposed to have been founded by a warlike tribe from Lydia. In the *Aeneid*, it is spoken of as one of the towns that was oppressed by Mezentius, and for this reason Aeneas was advised to seek its aid by Evan-

der, in his war against the Rutulians. According to some accounts, when the Gauls took Rome (389 B.C.), the vestal virgins fled with the sacred fire and their sacred vessels to Caere, and there performed the rites. From this event, some say, the rites came to be known as *ceremonies*, after Caere. The site of Caere is occupied by the modern village of Cerveteri (i.e., Caere Vetere, "Old Caere," to distinguish it from the new town, Cere Nuovo), noted for Etruscan ruins.

Caesar (sē'zạr). In ancient Rome, a patrician family of the Julian gens, of which the origin was fancifully traced to a legendary Julius, son of Aeneas, and hence claimed descent from the goddess Venus. The first Caesar actually to be noted in the annals was Sextus Julius, who was a praetor in 208 B.C. Lucius Julius Caesar, consul in 90 B.C., had an important part in shaping Roman institutions by securing the enactment of the law granting Roman citizenship to such of the Italian allies as had not fought against Rome in the Social War or who had laid down their arms at once. Lucius Julius Caesar was killed in 87 B.C., during the civil war, and with him his brother Caius Julius Caesar Strabo Vopiscus, whom Cicero numbered among the Roman orators. A son of Lucius Julius Caesar, bearing the same name, served in Gaul under that other Caius Julius Caesar (c100–44 B.C.) who made the family name one of the most noted in history. This younger Lucius Julius Caesar accompanied his great relative in the campaign which secured for the latter mastery of the Roman world, and after his assassination, joined the avenging forces of Mark Antony, whose mother, Julia, was a sister of Lucius. He quarrelled with Antony, however, and was saved from proscription only by Julia's intervention.

Caesar (sē-zạr), **Caius Julius.** Roman general, statesman, orator, and writer, born July 12, 100 B.C. (according to Theodor Mommsen, 102 B.C.); killed at Rome, March 15, 44 B.C. It is said that Caesar had a charger, each of whose hoofs was cloven into five parts, resembling toes. Soothsayers foretold that the master of the horse would one day rule the world. Caesar reared it carefully, was the first and only man ever to ride it, and eventually raised a statue of it before the Temple of Venus. Early in his career

Caesar made an enemy of the dictator Sulla, who stripped him of his office as a priest of Jupiter and forced him to go into hiding. Sulla ceased to hound him at the plea of influential members of the aristocratic party, but when he did so, he warned them never to forget that the man they pleaded for would one day cause the ruin of their party. Caesar served in Mytilene in 80 B.C., and was awarded a crown of oak-leaves for saving a soldier's life there. While on the way to Rhodes (76 B.C.) he was captured by pirates and held for ransom. He sent his staff to procure it and swore to the pirates that as soon as he was free, he would capture and crucify them. On the arrival of the ransom he sailed off, raised a fleet, and pursued, captured, and crucified the pirates as he had sworn to do. In 68 B.C. he was appointed quaestor and went to Spain. There, at Gades (now Cadiz), he saw a statue of Alexander the Great in the Temple of Hercules, and is said to have sighed because at an age when Alexander had already conquered the world, he had accomplished nothing. He returned to Rome and was made curule aedile (65 B.C.) and began his program of winning the commons to his side with public spectacles, wild beast hunts, gladiatorial combats, and plays. By bribery he succeeded in getting himself elected pontifex maximus (63 B.C.). The following year he became praetor, and the year after that, propraetor in Spain. Successful in Spain, he returned to Rome, was elected consul, and formed the "First Triumvirate" with Pompey and Crassus in 60 B.C. By this maneuver he associated himself with the popularity and influence of Pompey and won access to the wealth of Crassus. He was named proconsul in Gaul and Illyricum in 58 B.C.; defeated the Helvetii and Ariovistus in 58, and the Belgae in 57; invaded Britain in 55 and 54; was the first Roman to build a military bridge across the Rhenus (Rhine), crossed it in 55 and 53 B.C., inflicting heavy losses on the Germans; and defeated Vercingetorix in 52 B.C.

His extraordinary military successes did not allay the fears of those who suspected him of plotting against the aristocratic party and the Republic. The consul in Rome proposed that since the Gallic War was over, Caesar should be recalled, his armies disbanded, and a new commander appointed to take his place. It was further proposed that he should not be allowed to stand for the consulship unless he was present in Rome, for this was the law. In the meantime, Caesar had won many to his side, with bribes, gifts, public spectacles, triumphs and their accompanying holidays. He now crossed into Cisalpine Gaul and came to Ravenna. The choice before him was to return to Rome as a private citizen and stand trial for all manner of alleged crimes and irregularities before a hostile court, or to march on Rome at the head of his loyal army and embroil it in civil war. He advanced to the river Rubicon, the boundary between Gaul and Italy. It is said that when he was considering whether to cross the Rubicon and bring on civil war, an apparition of great size and beauty was observed sitting on the bank of the river and playing a pipe. Shepherds gathered to listen and were joined by some soldiers from Caesar's army. When the soldiers neared, the apparition seized a trumpet from one of them, ran to the river, stopped there, blew a blast on the trumpet, and then crossed over. Caesar cried out this was a sign from the gods that they should cross over too. "The die is cast," he said, led his army across (49 B.C.) and began the civil war. In this he was eminently successful. Pompey, for the defense of the Republic, led an army opposed to him. Caesar defeated him (48 B.C.) at Pharsalus in Greece, and pursued him to Alexandria in Egypt. There he found that Ptolemy had murdered him. In his turn, Caesar murdered Ptolemy and gave the rule of Egypt to Cleopatra and her younger brother. (Cleopatra lived with Caesar at Rome, 46–44 B.C., and bore him a son, Caesarion.) He went next to the Near East and defeated Pharnaces at Zela in 47 B.C. In the triumph for Zela at Rome, one of the chariots carried the inscription, "Veni, vidi, vici." (I came, I saw, I conquered.) He defeated the followers of Pompey at Thapsus in 46 B.C. and at Munda in 45 B.C. He reformed the calendar in 46 B.C., brought the Senate up to strength, beautified the city, set about codifying the laws, and proposed many great public works, as the draining of the Pontine Marshes and Lake Fucinus.

Caesar first married Cornelia, daughter of

the consul Cinna. She bore him a daughter, Julia. His second wife was Pompeia, a granddaughter of Sulla. He divorced her because she was implicated in an impiety with Publius Clodius, who, disguised as a woman, invaded the feast of the Bona Dea, a sacred festival from which men were excluded. The charge was never proved, nor was an accusation against her of infidelity with Publius Clodius. Caesar divorced her, he said, because "Caesar's wife must be above suspicion." His third wife was Calpurnia, daughter of the consul Lucius Piso.

Caesar was a persuasive and cogent orator, and a lucid writer. The *Commentaries* (or Memoirs), the only one of his literary works extant, contain the history of the first seven years of the Gallic War in seven books, and three books of the Civil War. As a brilliant military leader he was idolized by his soldiers. He had played brilliantly on the caprices of the people and won their entire support. The crown was offered to him on several occasions, the last of these being Feb. 15, 44 B.C., when he refused it as he had done before. However, as his power increased, he made powerful enemies, some of whom feared for the Republic and others who had personal reasons for enmity. He also lost some of the support of the people with his infringement of their ancient liberties. A plot was hatched to assassinate him. According to tradition, many omens, signs, and auguries foretold his death. Veterans who had been sent to colonize in Capua unearthed the tomb of Capys, the legendary founder of the city. With it was a bronze tablet bearing an inscription in Greek warning that if any disturbed the bones of Capys "a man of Trojan stock will be murdered by his kinsmen, and later avenged at a great cost to Rome." (Caesar claimed descent from Venus and Aeneas, hence his "Trojan stock.") An augur warned him that he would not be safe until the Ides of March had passed. The night before he was assassinated his wife Calpurnia dreamed that a temple-like gable, voted in his honor, had collapsed, and that he lay stabbed in her arms. Some say that before he went to the Senate on his last day, he was handed a note describing the plot, but he saved it to read later. Victims sacrificed before he went to the Senate were unfavor-

able. He saw the augur who had made the prediction about the Ides of March and taunted him, saying, "The Ides of March have come." The augur answered, "Yes, they have come, but they have not gone." He entered the Senate and was immediately surrounded by a ring of daggers. About 60 men were in the plot. The first dagger thrust wounded him, but he parried it. When he saw Marcus Brutus, who had defected from Pompey and become one of Caesar's lieutenants, preparing to make the second thrust, he sorrowfully murmured, "You, too, Brutus?" before he received the wound. Then he drew the top of his robe over his face and ceased to defend himself. Some say that of the 23 wounds he received, only the second was mortal. At news of his death great lamentation rose throughout the city. The conspirators dared not seize control. The blood-stained robe in which Caesar died was placed on an ivory funeral couch and set in a gilded shrine. At his funeral, a dispute arose as to whether his body should be cremated at the Temple of Capitoline Jupiter or in Pompey's Assembly Hall. According to one account, suddenly two divine beings appeared, armed with spear and sword, and set fire to the couch on which his body rested. The crowd of mourners added branches to the flames; those in the funeral procession who were wearing the robes he himself had worn at his triumphs, tore them to pieces and flung them on the flames. Women tossed on their jewelry, the soldiers contributed their weapons. As soon as the funeral was over, the crowd snatched brands from the pyre and ran to burn the houses of Brutus and Cassius, the two chief conspirators, but were prevented from doing so. Later a column of Numidian marble was raised in the Forum. Inscribed on it were the words, "To the Father of his Country." It became the custom to offer sacrifices at the foot of this column, to make vows there, and to settle disputes by taking oaths in Caesar's name. He was deified immediately by the Senate. At the games given by Augustus in honor of Caesar the god, a comet appeared, and shone thereafter for seven days in a row. This was said to be Caesar's soul, taken up to heaven, and in his honor a star was placed above the forehead of his divine image. The hall where he was murdered was closed. The Ides of March were henceforth known as "The Day of Parricide." The name *Caesar* was assumed by all male members of the Julian dynasty, and after them by the successive emperors, as inseparable from the imperial dignity. It thus became the source of the German *Kaiser* and the Russian *Tsar* or *Czar*. After the death of Hadrian the title *Caesar* was specifically assigned to those who were designated by the emperors as their successors and associated with them in the government.

Caesar, Drusus. See **Drusus Caesar.**

Caesarea (sē-za̱-rē′a̱). A name given to various cities of the Roman empire in honor of an emperor.

Caesarea Philippi (fi-lip′ī, fil′i-pī). See **Paneas.**

Caesarion (sē-zãr′i-on). Egyptian ruler, son of Cleopatra and (probably) Julius Caesar; born 47 B.C.; died 30 B.C. He was executed by order of Octavian. As Ptolemy XV he was, with his mother, a nominal ruler of Egypt from c44 B.C. to the time of his death.

Caieta (kā-yē′ta̱). [Also: **Portus Caieta;** modern name, **Gaeta.**] In ancient geography, a town and port of Latium, situated on a promontory between Rome and Naples. According to legend, after he had visited his father in Hades and learned from him what his future and the future of his race would be, Aeneas coasted along the shores of Italy and put in at this place. Here his old nurse, Caieta, died and was buried, piously mourned by Aeneas. The town that grew up on this spot was named for her. Historically, Caieta was a Greek colony that ultimately became a Roman town.

Caieta, Gulf of. [Modern name, **Gulf of Gaeta.**] Indentation of the Mediterranean Sea N of Neapolis, Italy.

Caius Caesar (kā′us, kī′us; sē-za̱r). See **Caligula.**

Caius Cestius (ses′ti-us), **Pyramid of.** Massive sepulchral monument of brick and stone, at Rome, about 114 feet high, encrusted with marble. Each side of the base measures 90 feet. The small burial chamber is painted with white arabesques. The pyramid is of the time of Augustus.

Calabria (ka̱-lā′bri-a̱). See **Bruttii.**

Calactinus (kal-ak-tī′nus). See **Caecilius.**

Calais (kal′a̱-is). An Argonaut, the winged

son of Boreas and Orithyia, and the twin of Zetes. See **Boreadae.**

Calamis (kal′a̱-mis). Greek artist, predecessor of Phidias, who was active at Athens, 480–450 B.C. He was a master of the older style of sculpture, and worked in marble, gold, ivory, and bronze. His works ranged from reliefs on small silver vessels to heroic statues in bronze. Among his works was a group of bronze boys with their hands outstretched, that was dedicated at Olympia. A heroic statue of Apollo at Apollonia in Pontus was carried off to Rome by Lucullus and set up in the Capitol. He was unrivalled for his horses, and produced figures of horsemen and four-horse chariots. The work of Calamis retained some of the archaic stiffness, but also showed an interest in and developing capacity for natural expression.

Calanus (kal′a̱-nus). [Also: **Kalanos.**] Indian philosopher; fl. 4th century B.C. He accompanied Alexander the Great from India. Becoming ill, he threw himself upon a funeral pyre in the presence of Alexander and his Macedonian officers three months before Alexander's death (323 B.C.), which he had predicted. His name is also given as **Sphines.**

Calauria (ka̱-lôr′i-a̱). [Modern name, **Poros.**] In ancient geography, a small island off Troezen on the E coast of the Peloponnesus. According to legend, it was given to Poseidon by Apollo in exchange for the former's share of the oracle at Delphi. A religious association of maritime towns—Athens, Aegina, Epidaurus, Troezen, Hermione, Nauplia, Prasiae, and Orchomenus in Boeotia—joined together to promote the worship of Poseidon on the island; they built a stone temple (7th century B.C.) for their god, and sailors of the member towns propitiated him there with sacrifices. The sanctuary was served by a maiden priestess, who retired in favor of a younger one when she reached marriageable age. Demosthenes, the Greek orator, was exiled to this island after the unsuccessful uprising which he promoted against the Macedonians. He was later recalled but banished a second time. He returned to Calauria and committed suicide by taking poison in the temple of Poseidon (322 B.C.). His tomb is at Calauria, where he was especially honored.

Calchas (kal′kas). In Greek legend, a son of Thestor, a scion of Idmon, the seer who accompanied the Argonauts. He learned the art of divination from his father and became, according to Homer, the wisest of seers, "who knew all that has been, now is, or shall be in the future." His prophecies and interpretations of omens encouraged the Greeks to fight through the ten years of the Trojan War. He said Troy could not be taken without the help of Achilles; the Greeks accordingly sent for Achilles. When the Greeks first assembled at Aulis to sail against Troy, a crimson-backed serpent wound its way up a nearby plane tree, swallowed eight young sparrows in their nest and devoured their mother. The serpent, still coiled about the tree, then turned to stone. Calchas interpreted this to mean that the Greeks would fight nine years, in the tenth year would take Troy. In the second gathering at Aulis, after years of raiding the coasts of the Troad because they did not know the course to follow to Troy, the Greeks were held windbound. Calchas advised Agamemnon that only the sacrifice of his daughter, Iphigenia, to Artemis would bring favorable winds. Iphigenia was sacrificed and the storm winds ceased. Calchas then confirmed that the course which had been given them by a Mysian was correct and the Greeks sailed once more. While they were encamped before Troy, they were harassed by a rain of arrows sent by Apollo. Calchas offered to tell the reason for this plague on condition that Achilles would protect him from Agamemnon's anger. Achilles agreed and Calchas explained that Apollo was sending the arrows to punish Agamemnon for refusing to accept the ransom offered by a priest of Apollo for his daughter, Chryseis, Agamemnon's captive. Agamemnon was indeed angry and accused Calchas of always prophesying evil for him. However, he restored Chryseis to her father and the rain of arrows ceased. Other predictions that Calchas made and that the Greeks acted on were: 1) that Troy, after the death of Achilles, could not be taken without the aid of Achilles' son, Neoptolemus; 2) that the bows and arrows of Heracles, at that time in the possession of Philoctetes, who had been abandoned by the Greeks in Lemnos, were necessary for the taking of Troy; 3) that only Helenus, a son of Priam, could tell them what protected Troy and therefore he should be captured; and 4) that Troy could not be taken by direct siege but must be captured by stratagem. This last led to the ruse of the Wooden Horse, and some say Calchas was one of those who entered the city in it. After the taking of Troy he told the Greeks to spare Aeneas because it was his destiny to found a new nation in Italy. He prophesied that Astyanax, young son of Hector, would grow up and raise an army which he would lead against the Greeks if he were spared. Astyanax was slain. He said that Polyxena, daughter of Priam, must be sacrificed on Achilles' tomb; otherwise Achilles' shade, wrathful that he had not been duly honored, would raise great storms and prevent the Greeks from returning home. When the Greeks left Troy, he was forewarned by his prophetic powers of the disasters that would overtake them at sea. He therefore went by land to Colophon. It had been prophesied that Calchas would die when he met a seer wiser than himself. In Colophon or Clarus, he met Mopsus, a son of Apollo and Manto. Calchas challenged him to give the number of figs growing on a tree nearby. Mopsus answered that there were 10,000 figs, plus one bushel, plus one fig left over. When the tree was stripped and the figs counted, Mopsus was found to be correct. He then challenged Calchas to say how many pigs a sow that was about to farrow would produce. Calchas looked at the sow and said there would be eight male piglets, born within nine days. Mopsus disagreed. There would be three piglets, he said, only one a male, and they would be born the next day at noon. Again Mopsus proved correct and Calchas, having met a seer wiser than himself, died of a broken heart and was buried at Notium. But some say he committed suicide on account of the injury done his pride.

Caletor (ka-lē′tôr). In Homeric legend (*Iliad*), a Trojan, the son of Clytius. He was a cousin of Hector, a descendant of Dardanus, Ilus, and Tros. He was slain by Telamonian Ajax as he attempted to set fire to the Greek ships in the Trojan War.

Caligula (ka-lig′ū-la). [Original name, **Caius**

Julius Caesar Germanicus.] The third emperor of Rome (37–41 A.D.); born at Antium, Italy, Aug. 31, 12 A.D.; killed at Rome, Jan. 24, 41 A.D. He was the youngest son of Germanicus and Agrippina the Elder. As a child he was a great pet with his father's troops and wore a miniature uniform of the private soldier, even including the half-boot (*caliga*), whence the name Caligula, "Little Boot," given him by the soldiers. His popularity with the troops was such that when they rioted on hearing of the death of Augustus, the threat to remove Caligula to safety calmed them. He accompanied his father on his expedition to the East (18 A.D.), and after the death of Germanicus (19 A.D.), lived at Rome with his mother until she was banished (29 A.D.) by Tiberius, after which he lived with his grandmother Livia. At the age of 19 he went to Capreae at the request of Tiberius. There he behaved with such obsequiousness that he escaped the fate of his relatives, most of whom had been murdered by Tiberius. He refused to be tricked into making any complaint against the emperor, either in behalf of his relatives or on any other grounds, and in general behaved so slavishly that it was said of him, "Never was there a better slave, or a worse master." It is said that his unnatural obsession with brutality and his addiction to scandalous living manifested themselves early. Tiberius is said to have remarked of him, "I am nursing a viper in Rome's bosom. I am rearing a Phaëthon who will mishandle the fiery chariot of the sun and burn up the world." He succeeded Tiberius (37 A.D.), whose death he had caused or accelerated. Some say he caused Tiberius to be poisoned, and that before the emperor died, an attempt was made to remove the imperial ring from his finger. Tiberius would not let it go and he was smothered with a pillow. When Caligula became emperor, he was warmly regarded by the Romans, who had adored his father Germanicus. The Senate gave him absolute power and ignored Tiberius' will, by which his other grandson, Tiberius Gemellus, was named coheir. The Romans were so pleased at the accession of Caligula that, so it is said, 160,000 victims were sacrificed in thanksgiving. Among his first acts was to give the funeral oration in honor of Tiberius, shedding copious tears as he did so, and to give him a splendid funeral. He then recovered the bones of his mother and his brother Nero and returned them to Rome with great solemnity in proof of his devotion. He awarded honors in memory of his father and gave his grandmother Antonia —whose death he afterward hastened by his indifference and cruelty—all the honors once awarded to Livia, and, at first, he demanded that his sisters, Agrippina, Drusilla, and Livilla, be honored in Rome as himself. He recalled political exiles, dismissed long-standing criminal charges, published the imperial budget, restored the authority of the magistrates, carried out the bequests in Tiberius' will, and performed many other acts which won him great popularity. So great was the initial enthusiasm for him that the festival of Parilia, which commemorated the birth of Rome, was changed to the day when he became emperor, as if Rome had been born again. Among his public works was the completion of the Temple of Augustus and Pompey's Theater, begun by Tiberius, the commencement of an aqueduct to bring water to Rome, the rebuilding of the walls and temples of Syracuse, and the completion of the Temple of Didymaean Apollo at Ephesus. He ardently wished to cut a canal through the Isthmus of Corinth, but the project was abandoned. He was consul four times, in 37, 39, 40, and 41 A.D.

The moderation with which his reign began did not last long. Suetonius says he had suffered from epilepsy as a child, and that this caused mental as well as physical illness and perhaps accounts for his cruelty and his profligacy. He soon gave up the pretense that he was the ruler of a republic. Not only did he wish to be regarded as emperor; he wished to be treated as a god. He sent for the most famous statues of the Greek gods, including that of Zeus at Olympia, had their heads removed and his own head put in their places. He established a shrine to himself with priests, costly sacrifices, and a life-sized golden image. His reign was marked by wholesale killings of extreme brutality and by personal licentiousness little short of madness. On every occasion he showed his contempt for the people, and is said once to have exclaimed in a fit of vexation, "Would that the

Roman people had only one head!" with the clear implication that this would considerably simplify their beheading. He was not content merely with the extermination of his enemies, real or imagined, but wanted them slain in the most cruel and lingering fashion. "Make him feel that he is dying," was a frequent order with him. He built a marble stable and an ivory manger for his horse Incitatus, and had the stable furnished with luxurious appointments for the occasions when guests had been invited in the name of Incitatus. Some say he planned to make the horse a consul. He made a fruitless expedition into Gaul in 40 A.D., and advanced to the English Channel where he ordered his men to pick up sea shells as spoils of the sea for Rome. On his return he demanded a triumph, but it was postponed. His extravagance, licentiousness, and savageries had the expected results. Plots against his life were discovered. There were omens that his life was drawing to a close. One was that when his men were preparing to move the statue of Olympian Zeus from the temple at Olympia, the statue burst into a roar of laughter and frightened the workmen away. An oracle warned him to "beware of Cassius." Thinking the governor of Asia was meant, he ordered the murder of Cassius Longinus. On Jan. 24, 41 A.D., as he left the Palatine Games to go for luncheon, he was set upon by Cassius Chaerea, tribune of a praetorian cohort, and murdered in the passageway that led from the theater he had just left. Cassius, so some say, asked him the password, and when he replied, "Jupiter," Cassius shouted "So be it!" and plunged his dagger into Caligula's throat. Caligula had married Junia Claudilla, daughter of a senator. She died in childbirth. He is said to have had incestuous relations with his sisters, one of whom, Drusilla, he treated publicly as his wife. Many other women had suffered his attentions. Some say he loved best Caesonia, who was wildly extravagant and notoriously promiscuous. She seemed to love him too, and he threatened to torture her to find out why she loved him. After Caesonia had borne him a daughter, Julia Drusilla, Caligula married her. Both Caesonia and Julia Drusilla were murdered following his own murder.

Calippus (ka-lip′us). See **Callippus**.

Callaeschrus (ka-lēs′krus). Sixth century B.C. Greek architect, associated with Antistates, Antimachides, and Porinus in preparing the original plans for the Olympieum, the colossal temple of Zeus Olympius at Athens projected by the Pisistratids. (JJ)

Callantianus (ka-lan-shi-ā′nus). See **Caecilius**.

Callias (kal′i-as). Athenian statesman, 5th century B.C. He is known to have fought in the battle of Marathon (490 B.C.). A member of one of the oldest Attic families, he was in his time the wealthiest citizen of Athens. It seems certain that he undertook an embassy to Artaxerxes I of Persia in 449 B.C. and secured that monarch's promise to refrain from attacks upon the Delian League and from sending Persian war vessels into Greek waters, in return for Athenian acceptance of Persian hegemony in Asia Minor. Many authorities, however, doubt that there ever was a "Treaty of Callias" in the form of a written agreement of this sort, and the story that upon his return to Athens he was accused of treason and fined 50 talents is also open to doubt. The agreement, however formal or informal, was beneficial to the cities of the Delian League, for it freed them from Persian interference for several decades. The "Treaty of Callias" is sometimes referred to as the "Peace of Callias," by confusion with a pact proposed many years later and in very different circumstances by another Callias, the grandson of the Callias here referred to.

Callias. Athenian soldier (died 370 B.C.) and leading citizen; grandson of Callias (5th century B.C.). A wealthy man, he was ridiculed in some of the plays of Aristophanes for his profligacy and ostentation. In 392 B.C., he commanded the Athenian hoplites in the victory over Sparta at Corinth. His name is associated with the so-called Peace of Callias, which was a proposal put forward by him at a conference in Sparta (371 B.C.). This, however, was disrupted by a quarrel between Sparta and Thebes. Callias was a friend of Xenophon and of Plato.

Callias, Peace of. Peace concluded at Sparta in 371 B.C., between Athens and Sparta, including their allies, from which, however, Thebes was excluded. It took its name from

Callias, one of the Athenian envoys, prominent in the conferences.

Callichorus (ka̲-lik′ō̲-rus). A river of Paphlagonia, the river of fair dances. It was so named because Dionysus, on his way back from India, held dances and revels in a cave nearby.

Callicrates (ka̲-lik′ra̲-tēz). Athenian architect and sculptor of the 5th century B.C. His great claim to fame is that he was the collaborator of Ictinus in designing the Parthenon on the Acropolis of Athens. He is also known to have designed the much-admired small marble temple of Athena Nike on the Acropolis near the Propylaea, which was completed c424 B.C.

Callicratidas (ka″li-krat′i-da̲s). Spartan admiral; killed in battle, 406 B.C. He was named navarch (admiral) in 406 B.C. to succeed Lysander, whose one-year term was up. Some say that out of enmity to him Lysander purposely sowed disaffection among the men of the fleet. At first Callicratidas was successful: the Spartan fleet took the fortified place of Delphinium on the island of Chios and the town of Methymna in Lesbos, and blockaded part of the Athenian fleet at Mytilene. Callicratidas left part of his fleet to maintain the blockade and sailed to Arginusae, a group of small islands south of Lesbos, to engage the remainder of the Athenian fleet. A great battle was fought at Arginusae (406 B.C.). Callicratidas was slain and the Athenians were victorious.

Callidice (ka-lid′i-sē). In Greek legend, a queen in Thesprotia. According to some accounts, Odysseus, after his return to Ithaca, sought to appease Poseidon by going to a land whose people had never heard of the sea and there making sacrifices to the god. He went to Thesprotia where he married Callidice and became king. She bore him a son Polypoetes. After the death of Callidice Odysseus gave the throne to Polypoetes and returned to Ithaca.

Callimachus (ka̲-lim′a̲-kus). Greek sculptor, active toward the end of the 5th century B.C. He is credited with having originated the Corinthian capital, and with having been first to use the running drill for imitating the deep folds of drapery in statues. He made a golden lamp for the image of Athena on the Acropolis, and over the lamp he placed a bronze palm to draw off the smoke. He claimed to be the first to drill holes through stones, some say, and for the excessive elaboration of his techniques was given the title "Enfeebler of his Art."

Callimachus. Greek grammarian, critic, and poet. He was born at Cyrene, in North Africa, probably in the early part of the 3rd century B.C., and died at Alexandria c240 B.C. He was one of the first five of the great librarians of the Library at Alexandria, an office he held until his death. One of his great services to literature was the arranging and cataloguing of the numerous writings that had been collected there. The result of this labor was the *Pinakes,* or *Tablets,* an annotated catalogue of books which can be regarded as a literary history. He is said to have produced some 800 works, few of which are extant, and was one of the most influential personalities in literature between the times of Plato and Cicero. Eratosthenes, Aristophanes of Byzantium, and Apollonius of Rhodes were among his pupils. Instead of attempting to write epics in the manner of Homer and Hesiod, he advocated and wrote short, polished poems, as artificial and perfect in their limited scope as the epics of Homer were simple, sweeping, and moving. The emphasis of Callimachus was on learning artistically expressed in poems that represented the tastes of his own age. Fragments of his work which survive bear abundant witness to his learning. The polished verses give small evidence of poetic genius. Apollonius of Rhodes was no slavish follower of his master, and quarreled with him. The influence of Callimachus was largely responsible, Apollonius thought, for the failure of his epic, *The Argonautica,* in Alexandria. He went to Rhodes where a second version was very favorably received. Later ages have found the work of his rival Apollonius more interesting in its simple, honest story-telling and moving imagery than the cold, pedantic writings of Callimachus. He was greatly admired and imitated by the Romans, Ovid and Catullus, among others, having used the poems of Callimachus as models on occasion.

Callinus (ka̲-lī′nus). Greek elegiac poet of Ephesus, who flourished early in the 7th century B.C. He is the oldest known writer (and sometimes considered the originator) of elegiacs. His poems were war-songs concerning the wars of the Cimmerians against Magnesia. There is extant one long fragment, attributed to Callinus, which is a patriotic exhortation to the young men of his age.

Calliope (ka-lī′ọ-pē). In Greek mythology, one of the nine daughters of Zeus and Mnemosyne. She is the chief of the Muses, the Muse of epic or heroic poetry, and her attributes are a scroll and stylus. Calliope was the mother of Orpheus by Oeagrus, a king in Thrace, and is sometimes said also to have been the mother of the poet Linus and of the Thracian Rhesus who went to the aid of Hector in the Trojan War. In a dispute between Aphrodite and Persephone over possession of Adonis, Calliope decided that Adonis' year should be divided into three parts: one third to be spent with Aphrodite, one third with Persephone, and one third by himself. See **Muses.**

Callipolis (ka-lip′ọ-lis). In Greek legend, a son of Alcathous, king of Megara. His older brother, Ischepolis, went to help Meleager capture the Calydonian boar, and was slain in the hunt. Callipolis, who was the first to hear the news, rushed to the Acropolis where Alcathous was preparing to sacrifice to Apollo, and knocked the logs from the sacrificial fire in token of mourning. Alcathous, unaware of the death of his son Ischepolis, thought Callipolis had committed an impiety. He struck him on the head with one of the green logs from the sacrificial fire and killed him.

Callipolis. [Modern name, **Gallipoli.**] Seaport on a rocky island in the Gulf of Tarentum, connected with the mainland by a bridge, founded by Dorian colonists from Tarentum. It submitted to Rome in 266 B.C., but supported the Carthaginians in 214; passed finally to the Romans in 213 B.C. It was known to the Romans as Anxa.

Callipolis. [Modern names, **Gelibolu, Gallipoli.**] Seaport in the Chersonesus Thracica, on the Hellespont.

Callippus or **Calippus** (ka-lip′us). Greek astronomer, born at Cyzicus, Asia Minor; fl. in the 4th century B.C. He instituted the "Callippic" cycle of 76 years, formed by quadrupling the Metonic cycle (19 years) and subtracting one day.

Callirrhoë (ka-lir′ọ-ē). In legend, a daughter of Scamander, the god of the great river of Troy. She was the wife of Tros and the mother of Cleopatra, Ilus the Younger, Assaracus and Ganymede. She was an ancestor of Aeneas.

Callirrhoë. In Greek legend, a daughter of the river-god Achelous. She married Alcmaeon, who had abandoned Arsinoë, daughter of King Phegeus, for her, and bore Alcmaeon two sons, Acarnan and Amphoterus. Later she asked Alcmaeon to secure the robe and peplus of Harmonia, which were in the possession of Arsinoë, for her. When he attempted to do so Phegeus learned that Alcmaeon was now married to Callirrhoë. Phegeus, angry at the insult to his daughter, ordered his sons to kill Alcmaeon. When Callirrhoë learned of his death, she prayed to the gods to cause her young sons to grow to manhood in a day's time so that they could avenge their father's death. The gods answered her prayer. Her sons came to manhood, found Phegeus and his sons and killed them.

Callirrhoë. According to legend, a maiden of Calydon who was loved by Coresus, a priest of Dionysus. She scorned his love and Coresus appealed to Dionysus. The god sent a plague of madness on the people, which the oracle said could be relieved only by the sacrifice of Callirrhoë. When preparations for sacrificing Callirrhoë were complete, Coresus, overcome by his love for her, killed himself in her place. When he was dead, Callirrhoë was stricken with remorse and killed herself, and presumably the plague was lifted.

Callirrhoë. Historic fountain at Athens, architecturally adorned and provided with conduits by Pisistratus; the use of its water was prescribed for ceremonial rites. From the earliest study of Athenian topography, this fountain has been identified with the copious spring flowing in the bed of the Ilissus, near the temple of Olympian Zeus. Wilhelm Dörpfeld, however, demonstrated the probability that this identification is incorrect, and that the fountain was in fact situated at the SW angle of the Areopagus, on the border of the Agora. Excavation has re-

fat, fāte, fär, fāre, errạnt; net, mē, hér ardẹnt; pin, pīne; not, nōte, möve, nôr,

vealed a water conduit of the Pisistratid epoch ending at the site indicated, which accords with literary testimony.

Calliste (ka-lis'tē). An epithet of Artemis, meaning "Fairest."

Calliste. The ancient name for the island of Thera, one of the Cyclades. It was said to have arisen from the sea when Euphemus the Argonaut cast into the sea a clod of earth that had been given to him as a gift by Triton. It became the home of the sons of Euphemus.

Callisthenes (ka-lis'thȩ̄-nēz). Greek philosopher and historian, born at Olynthus, Macedonia, c360 B.C.; died 327 B.C. He was a cousin and pupil of Aristotle, and was educated in the latter's household. He joined Alexander the Great in his campaigns in Asia, and sought to persuade Alexander to rebuild his native Olynthus (destroyed 348 B.C. by Philip II), as Philip had rebuilt and repopulated Stagira, Aristotle's city. Callisthenes would not abandon his austere and moralistic philosophy to curry favor with the young conqueror. He incurred his ill will by his criticism of Alexander's adoption of Oriental customs and by opposing the introduction of the practice of obeisance which was common in the presence of Oriental monarchs. Furthermore, he would not subscribe to the doctrine that "a king can do no wrong." Alexander became convinced, without any grounds, that Callisthenes was involved in a plot against him and had him executed in 327 B.C. This incident ended the friendship between Alexander and Aristotle. Callisthenes wrote a history of Alexander's campaigns in Asia up to the death of Darius III, fragments of which survive. In following years, other histories of Alexander appeared which falsely bore the name of Callisthenes and formed the basis of the popular romances written about the life of Alexander.

Callisto (ka-lis'tō). In Greek mythology, a daughter of Lycaon, a king of Arcadia who had been transformed into a wolf because of his wickedness. Zeus fell in love with Callisto and she bore him a son, Arcas. According to some accounts, Artemis was angry with Callisto, who had been one of her chaste companions, and transformed her into a bear. Others say it was Zeus who transformed her to save her from the wrath of

Hera. When Arcas reached young manhood, he was hunting wild beasts in the forest, and seeing a bear, would have killed it, unaware that she was his mother. Zeus rescued Callisto by carrying her off in a whirlwind and translating her to the heavens, where she became the constellation Ursa Major (the Great Bear). Hera was jealous of the honor that had come to Callisto of being placed in the skies, and persuaded Poseidon to forbid Callisto ever to bathe in the sea. For this reason the Great Bear never sinks below the horizon.

Callistratus (ka-lis'tra̧-tus). Athenian actor who was active toward the end of the 5th century B.C. A friend of Aristophanes, the latter produced several of his pieces under the name of Callistratus, who was consequently proclaimed as the author. Although it was well known that Aristophanes wrote the plays, Callistratus, as the named author, trained the choruses and received the payment from the state for producing the plays.

Callistratus. Greek grammarian; fl. about the middle of the 2nd century B.C. He was the author of commentaries on the major poets of Greece, which were held in considerable repute by the ancients, but which are now lost.

Callynteria (kal-in-ter'ī-a̧). One of the two principal days of a festival celebrated at Athens the 19th–25th of the month Thargelion (last of May and beginning of June). On this day the temple of Athena on the Acropolis was swept and garnished in preparation for the return of the sacred image and for the offering of the first fruits of the harvest to the goddess. The other of the two chief days was the Plynteria.

Calpe (kal'pē). A promontory on the southern coast of the Iberian peninsula, modern Gibraltar, opposite the ancient Abyla (the modern Jebel Musa at Ceuta). It is one of the pillars supposed to have been set by Heracles. See **Pillars of Heracles.**

Calpurnia (kal-pėr'ni-a̧). Daughter of Lucius Calpurnius Piso Caesoninus. She was the third and last wife of Julius Caesar. On the night before he was murdered, she dreamed that a temple-like gable dedicated in his honor fell from its place and was smashed, and that Caesar lay dying in her arms.

Calpurnius Siculus (kal-pėr′ni-us sik′ū-lus), **Titus.** Latin pastoral poet who lived about the time of Nero. Seven eclogues and two fragments of bucolic poems are attributed to him. The panegyric, *Laus Pisonis,* formerly attributed to Calpurnius Siculus, is of uncertain authorship. Four other eclogues formerly regarded as his are now referred to Nemesianus, a poet once thought to be identical with Calpurnius.

Calvus (kal′vus), **Caius Licinius Macer.** Roman poet and forensic orator; born 82 B.C.; died 47 B.C.

Calyce (kal′i-sē). In Greek mythology, a daughter of Aeolus, king of Magnesia in Thessaly, and Enarete. She was the mother of Endymion; according to some accounts, Zeus was the father of Endymion; others say Aëthlius was his father.

Calydon (kal′i-don). In mythology, a son of Aetolus and grandson of Endymion. The city of Calydon, in Aetolia, was named for him. He was the father of Epicaste and Protogonia.

Calydon. In ancient geography, a city of Aetolia, in C Greece, situated near the river Evenus. It is the legendary scene of the hunt of the Calydonian boar (q. v.).

Calydonian Boar. A huge, savage boar sent by Artemis to ravage the land of Calydon in Aetolia because Oeneus, the king, had forgotten to sacrifice first fruits to her when he made offerings to the other gods and goddesses. The boar was wounded by Atalanta and killed by Meleager in a great hunt in which many of the legendary heroes of Greece participated.

Calymna (ka-lim′na). [Also: **Kalymna**; modern name, **Kalimnos**.] Dodecanese island in the Aegean Sea SW of Asia Minor, between the islands of Lerus and Cos. According to tradition, some of the Greek heroes returning from the Trojan War were shipwrecked on its rocky coasts. Those who survived founded a settlement there. Sculptured tombs found there indicate that the island was settled from early times. Area, 49 square miles.

Calypso (ka-lip′sō). A nymph who was, according to some accounts, the daughter of Oceanus and Thetis; others say Nereus or Atlas was her father. She lived in a tree-shrouded cavern on the island of Ogygia.

Odysseus drifted to her shores after losing all his ships and men as he attempted to return to Ithaca after the Trojan War. Calypso welcomed him warmly and offered him eternal youth and immortality if he would remain with her. As he had no means of leaving the island, he remained with her seven years and, some say, she bore him Latinus as well as the twins Nausithous and Nausinous. At the end of seven years Athena appealed to the gods on Olympus to allow Odysseus to return to his home. Zeus, taking advantage of the absence of Poseidon who was the enemy of Odysseus, commanded Hermes to go to Calypso and instruct her to provide Odysseus with whatever was needed for his journey. She bowed to the god's command, helped Odysseus to build a raft, furnished stores for his needs on the voyage, and sent him on his way, although she assured him that if he knew the troubles still in store for him, he would prefer to stay with her, notwithstanding the charms of his wife Penelope.

Camares (ka-mä′rēz). See **Kamares.**

Camarina (kam-a-rī′na). In ancient geography, a city on the S coast of Sicily, about 45 miles SW of Syracuse. It was founded by colonists from Syracuse (599 B.C.), was wrested from Syracuse by Hippocrates, tyrant of Gela (491 B.C.), razed to the ground and its inhabitants moved to Syracuse by Gelon of Syracuse (484), rebuilt, and then (405 B.C.) abandoned by its inhabitants at the instance of Dionysus the Elder, tyrant of Syracuse, who betrayed it to Carthage.

Cambyses (I) (kam-bī′sēz). [Old Persian, **Ka(m)bujiya.**] Persian king whose historical character is doubtful. In the genealogy of Xerxes, as given by Herodotus, both he and his son Cyrus are omitted, and Diodorus, where he gives this name, seems to mean the father of Cyrus the Great. On the other hand, a Cambyses is mentioned whose sister was the ancestress in the fourth degree of one of the seven conspirators who put Darius on the throne. Possibly Cambyses I was one of the sons of Theispes (on the cuneiform monuments Chishpaish), and grandson of Achaemenes.

Cambyses II (or I). Persian ruler, c600 B.C.; the son and successor of Cyrus I, and the father of Cyrus II, called "Cyrus the Great." According to Herodotus he was merely a Persian nobleman. Astyages, king of the Medes, had a wondrous dream about his daughter Mandane which seemed to warn him that her son would dethrone him. He accordingly gave her not to a Median nobleman, but to Cambyses, a Persian nobleman of a conquered race. Their son, Cyrus the Great, did in fact dethrone Astyages. But Xenophon states that Cambyses was king of Persia, and his statement is confirmed by native records. In those chronologies which do not recognize the historically dubious Cambyses covered by the entry immediately preceding this one, he is shown as Cambyses I.

Cambyses III (or II). The son of Cyrus the Great and Cassandane. He succeeded Cyrus and reigned 529–521 B.C. According to some accounts, he suffered from the "sacred disease," epilepsy, and this accounted for his mad periods; others ascribed his eventual madness to the many impieties he committed. He conceived the idea of subjugating Egypt and prepared to march against that country (c525 B.C.), taking Ionian and Aeolian Greeks, vassals of his father, with him. Amasis was king of Egypt at the time. Having crossed the Arabian desert safely he mounted the attack. By this time Amasis had died; his successor was his son Psammenitus (Psammetichus). In the battle at Pelusium (525 B.C.) the Egyptians, after stubborn resistance, were forced to retreat. They retired to Memphis whither Cambyses pursued them, besieged the city, compelled its surrender, and incorporated Egypt in the Persian Empire. The Libyans bordering Egypt, the Cyreneans, and the Barcans surrendered to Cambyses without a struggle. He went to Saïs, ordered the body of Amasis to be brought to him, desecrated it, and finally ordered it burned. This was the most impious act he could commit, according to the laws of both the Persians and Egyptians, for the Persians looked upon fire as a god that they would not desecrate by burning bodies, whereas the Egyptians regarded fire as an animal which devours whatever it can. By his act of ordering the body of Amasis to be burned Cambyses set at nought the most deeply felt of the Egyptian

religious convictions. He planned a conquest of Carthage, but gave it up when his Phoenician allies, the backbone of his fleet, refused to attack Carthage. He then set out, without proper provisioning for his forces, to conquer Ethiopia. On the way he detached a large body of his troops and sent them to attack the Ammonians, and to burn the oracle of Zeus there. Before he had proceeded one-fifth of the distance to Ethiopia the supplies for his army were exhausted. Nevertheless Cambyses, madman that he was, persisted in going on. It was only when he learned his men had resorted to cannibalism that he gave up his plan for the conquest of Ethiopia and returned to Egypt, having lost great numbers of his men through starvation, according to Herodotus. The troops which he had sent against the Ammonians never reached their destination and never returned to Egypt. Some say they were buried in a sandstorm.

Returned to Memphis, Cambyses committed many outrages against the Egyptians as well as against members of his own entourage. According to Herodotus, he opened the ancient tombs, insulted the images in the temples, went into the most sacred enclosures and burned the statues, and in every way outraged the religious laws and feelings of the Egyptians, to no purpose. While he was in Agbatana, in Syria, heralds reported that Smerdis had seized his throne in Persia. His instant reaction was that Prexaspes, whom he had ordered to slay Smerdis, had betrayed him and had not slain his brother. Prexaspes convinced him that the Smerdis who had seized the throne was an imposter. Cambyses determined to proceed at once to Susa and expose the false Smerdis. In leaping to his horse he pierced his thigh. The wound did not heal, and when he realized he was in Agbatana in Syria he recalled an old oracle that foretold his death in Agbatana. When he first heard the oracle he assumed that it meant Agbatana in Persia. Now he realized that his end had come. He called his chiefs before him, told them he was dying, revealed that his brother Smerdis had been slain at his command, and urged them with the threat of unending curses, to regain the throne for the Persians. Shortly thereafter he died (521 B.C.), having reigned about seven and a half years, and leaving no son to succeed him.

Camenae (ka̯-mē′nē). In Italian mythology, four prophetic divinities, identified by Roman poets with the Muses.

Camilla (ka̯-mil′a̯). In Roman legend, a virgin warrior of the Volscian nation. She had been consecrated to Diana in her childhood owing to the following circumstances: Her father, Metabus, a tyrannous ruler, fled from Privernum, carrying his daughter with him. He was pursued and about to be overtaken when he came to a stream, the Amasenus River. He fastened the infant Camilla to his spear and, vowing to dedicate her to Diana if he was successful, hurled the spear carrying his daughter across the stream. He then jumped into the flood and swam across. Upon reaching safety with his child, he dedicated her to Diana as he had vowed. She grew up to be skilled in the arts of war, an expert horsewoman and, as she was devoted to Diana, an excellent archer. In the war that the Latins fought against Aeneas, she led a troop under the command of Turnus. When Aeneas besieged Latinus' capital, she commanded the cavalry and Turnus commanded the infantry. Fighting with one breast bared to give freedom to her bow arm, she was a merciless killer and slew many. But she fell at last to a spear hurled by Arruns. As she was dying, she sent word to Turnus to take her place in the defense of the city.

Camillus (ka̯-mil′us), **Marcus Furius**. [Called "The Second Founder of Rome."] Roman general and statesman; died 365 B.C. The traditional accounts of his career probably contain many embellishments to suit the purposes of various authors. In his early years he served with distinction in a war against the Aequi and Volscians (429 B.C.), in which he was wounded in the thigh by an enemy javelin, but he plucked it out and continued to fight. He was made censor and in this important post one of his acts was to compel bachelors to marry, for there were many widows in Rome as a result of the frequent wars. In 396 B.C. he was appointed tribune, and then dictator, to bring an end to the siege of Veii. The Romans had been besieging that Etruscan city for seven years, and were getting discouraged. He renewed

their flagging spirits, vowed games to the gods, and promised to consecrate the temple of Mater Matuta if he was victorious. After defeating the Faliscans, he went to Veii, mined the walls, and took the city which he allowed his troops to plunder. As he stood on the citadel of Veii, he wept and prayed that if the gods must send a misfortune to balance the good fortune of the Romans in taking the city, such misfortune would fall on him personally and not on the Roman people. Finishing his prayer, he turned, stumbled, and fell. His associates were alarmed, but Camillus was delighted. The trifling inconvenience to him, he said, was the misfortune that balanced the good fortune of Rome. He resolved to carry the image of Juno in Veii to Rome, and prayed to her, inviting her to take up her abode in Rome. According to legend, the image replied softly that she was ready and willing to go to Rome. For his capture of Veii (c396 B.C.) he was honored with a triumph, but incurred the displeasure of the Romans by riding into the city in a chariot drawn by white horses, which no commander had ever done before, as white horses were used only to draw images of Jupiter. The ungrateful citizens were also angered because he, with other leading citizens, thought it would be harmful to Rome if half her people were removed to Veii, as they wished to do in order to relieve the overpopulation of Rome, and he opposed it. In addition, they were irate because he had not carried out his vow to give one-tenth of the plunder of Veii to Apollo. It was decided to make a golden bowl and dedicate it at Delphi, and when it was found that there was not enough gold in Rome for the purpose, the ladies of the leading families contributed their golden ornaments. In a war with the Falisci, Camillus was again tribune and laid siege to Falerii. The Falerians felt so secure within their walls that life was carried on as usual. A schoolmaster of Falerian boys resolved to betray the city. He led his charges outside the walls and into the camp of Camillus, where he presented them as hostages to the Romans. Camillus was incensed at the treachery. "War," he said, "is indeed a grievous thing, and is waged with much injustice and violence; but even war has certain laws which good and brave men will respect . . . the great general will wage war relying on his own native valor, not on the baseness of other men." So saying, he gave the Falerian schoolboys rods and ordered them to flog their schoolmaster back into the city. The Falerians were so struck with his honor in this instance that they surrendered to him. Camillus exacted an indemnity from the Falerians and made an alliance with them. His soldiers were disappointed because they were not allowed to plunder the city, and brought a charge of fraud against him, saying he had taken booty for himself. When he found that he could not be acquitted of the charge, he chose to go into exile (389 B.C.). On reaching the gates of Rome, he prayed that if he had been driven out unjustly, the Romans would quickly repent of it and express to the world their need of him.

His prayer was swiftly answered. The Gauls, under Brennus, attacked and defeated the Romans at Allia (389 B.C.). They marched on the city, which had been almost abandoned by the terrified Romans, plundered and burned it, and put all who were taken captive to the sword. Only a handful, under Marcus Manlius, resisted them successfully on the Capitol. Camillus, living in exile at Ardea, rallied the young men there. Brennus had divided his forces and sent half of them to ravage the country, while the others remained in Rome. Part of the barbarians were encamped outside the walls of Ardea. In the night Camillus led out the Ardeans and killed them in their camp while they slept. News of his victory came to the Romans, who were forced to remember and long for him. They named him dictator, but he would not accept the office until he was properly appointed by the citizens of Rome on the Capitol. This posed a great difficulty, since the Capitol was surrounded by the forces of Brennus. Pontius Cominius volunteered to go through the enemy lines to the Capitol to secure the appointment, and he was successful. Camillus collected a great force and prepared to free Rome. In the meantime, the citizens on the Capitol were suffering from lack of provisions; the Gauls were suffering from the unaccustomed heat and from disease. Brennus agreed to withdraw on receipt of 1000

pounds of gold. As the gold was being weighed out, Camillus entered with his forces. He took the gold from the scales and gave it to an aide, saying to Brennus that Rome was accustomed to deliver herself with iron, not with gold. He was dictator, he announced, and agreements made with any other were invalid. After a skirmish Brennus withdrew and made camp outside the city. The next day Camillus and his Romans, now full of courage, attacked and routed the forces of Brennus with great slaughter. Camillus was honored with a triumph, made sacrifices to the gods, purified the city, restored the temples, and raised a temple of Aius Locutius. He set the Romans to rebuilding the city, but they were discouraged by the overwhelming task, and talked again of Veii. They wished to occupy that city and abandon the ruins of Rome. Their clamor was so great that Camillus brought up the subject for debate in the Senate. In the silence before the vote was taken on whether or not Rome should be abandoned, the voice of a centurion outside the chamber was heard. He commanded the standard bearer of his squad to halt, "for this is the best place to settle down and stay." The senators interpreted this as divine intervention and all voted to stay in Rome. Now the Romans fell to rebuilding their city with new courage and hope. They built feverishly and without plan, so that the city was honeycombed with narrow lanes, crooked passages, and winding streets; nevertheless, the city was raised again with a year, and Camillus was named "The Second Founder of Rome." Before the city was completely restored, the Aequians, Volscians, and Latins rose against Rome. Camillus was appointed dictator again and defeated them. When he was quite an aged man, the Volscians rose against Rome again, and Camillus was made tribune for the sixth time, although he at first refused the post because of his age and ill health. He defeated the Volscians and returned to the city with great booty. He took Tusculum and gave its people Roman citizenship. Word now came that the Gauls were on the move. Camillus was again appointed dictator, although he was nearly 80 years old, and defeated them at Anio. Shortly thereafter, plague struck Rome.

Many citizens succumbed to it, including Camillus, but he was, as Plutarch says, "full ripe for death, if any man ever was, considering his years and the completeness of his life." In the time of Camillus the selection of consuls was changed so that thereafter one of them was chosen from the plebeians. Camillus himself, though he was tribune six times, dictator five times, and celebrated four triumphs, never served as consul.

Camirus (ka̱-mī′rus). In Greek mythology, a son of Cercaphus and Cydippe, and a grandson of Helius. Some say the town of this name on the island of Rhodes was named for him. Others say the town was built by the Telchines and named for one of the daughters of Danaus who died there on the flight from Egypt to Argos. According to Homer, Tlepolemus, son of Heracles founded the town.

Campagna di Roma (käm-pä′nyä dē rō′mä). Large plain in C Italy, surrounding Rome, lying between the Mediterranean Sea and the Sabine and Alban mountains. It corresponds in great part to the ancient Latium. It is of volcanic formation, and has been for centuries noted for its malarial climate, though in antiquity it was covered with villas and towns and was brought to a high state of cultivation. It has been largely reclaimed.

Campania (kam-pā′ni-a̱). In ancient geography, a region in S Italy, lying between Latium on the NW, Samnium on the N and E, Lucania on the SE, and the Mediterranean Sea on the W. Its original inhabitants were probably of the Oscan or the Ausonian race; it was settled later by the Greeks, and submitted to Rome in 343 B.C. It contained the ancient cities of Cumae, Capua, Baiae, Puteoli, Herculaneum, and Pompeii. Ever since Roman times the region has contained numerous seaside resorts. Campania came to include Latium in early imperial times and the name was gradually restricted to Latium (see immediately preceding article).

Campaspe (kam-pas′pē). [Also: **Pancaste, Pacate**.] Favorite concubine of Alexander the Great. She is said to have been the model for the picture Venus Anadyomene of Apelles.

Campe (kam′pē). In Greek mythology, the aged jailer of Tartarus. She guarded the Hecatonchires and Cyclopes when Cronus cast them into Tartarus. Zeus slew her in order to get her keys and free the Cyclopes to help in his war against the Titans.

Campus Martius (kam′pus mär′shus). [Italian, **Campo Marzio** (käm′pō mär′tsyō); Eng. trans., "Field of Mars."] Historic area in ancient Rome, lying between the Pincian, Quirinal, and Capitoline hills and the Tiber River. Throughout the early history of Rome this plain remained free of buildings, and was used for popular assemblies and military exercises. During the reign of Augustus it had become encroached upon from the S by the building up of the Flaminian Meadows, and from the E by public and other buildings on the Via Cata, corresponding closely to the later Corso. Under Augustus, however, a great extent of the plain still remained free, and served for chariot races and horse races, ballplaying, and other athletic sports; it was surrounded by the finest monuments of the city, and presented an imposing spectacle. It is now occupied by one of the most important quarters of modern Rome, including the Pantheon and the parliament buildings.

Canace (kan′a̱-sē) or **Canache** (kan′a̱-kē). In Greek mythology, one of the six daughters of Aeolus and Enarete. She killed herself at the command of her father, after bearing a child to her brother Macareus.

Canachus (kan′a̱-kus). Greek sculptor (6th century B.C.), of Sicyon in Achaea. Little is known of his work except that, according to Pausanias, he executed two famous statues of Apollo, one in bronze for the city of

CANCER
Pictured according to ancient descriptions.

Miletus in Asia Minor, and one in cedar for Thebes. The former is represented on some of the coins of Miletus.

Canathus (kan′a̱-thus). A spring near Argos where, according to some accounts, Hera bathed regularly to renew her virginity.

Cancer (kan′sėr). A constellation and also a sign of the zodiac. It shows the limits of the sun's course northward in summer; hence, the sign of the summer solstice. It is represented in the form of a crab. According to the Greeks, Hera sent a huge crab to help the Hydra with many heads that Heracles was attempting to kill for Eurystheus. Heracles crushed the crab, and Hera rewarded it by translating it to the heavens, where it became the constellation Cancer.

Candaules (kan-dô′lēz) or **Myrsilus** (mėr-sī′lus). King of Lydia in the 8th or 7th century B.C. He was the last Heraclid king of that country. According to Herodotus, he compelled his aide and friend Gyges to spy on his beautiful wife. When she discovered that Gyges had watched her with Candaules' consent, she forced Gyges to murder Candaules, to marry her, and to succeed Candaules on the throne.

Candia (kan′di-a̱). See **Heracleum.**

Canens (kan′ēnz). In Roman mythology, reputed to have been a daughter of Janus. She was the wife of Picus, a king of Italy. When her husband disappeared while hunting boars (he was transformed into a woodpecker because he spurned the love of Circe), Canens sought him for six days and nights, then dissolved in tears and disappeared on the banks of the Tiber River at a spot which afterward bore her name.

Canidia (ka̱-nid′i-a̱). Neapolitan courtesan; fl. in the 2nd half of the 1st century B.C. She was loved by Horace. When she deserted him, he reviled her as a sorceress. Her real name is said by some authorities to have been Gratidia.

Caninefates (ka̱-nin-e̱-fā′tēz). [Also: **Canninefates.**] German tribe, first mentioned by Tacitus, on the North Sea, to the north of the Rhine delta, closely related to the Batavi, their neighbors on the south. The Caninefates were subjugated to the Romans by Tiberius, but took part in the rising of Civilis. With the Batavi they were originally a part of the Chatti. They were ultimately merged with the Salic Franks.

Canis Major (kā′nis mā′jor). The Great Dog, a constellation SE of Orion, and containing Sirius, the brightest star in the sky.

Canis Minor (mī′nor). The Little Dog, a small ancient constellation following Orion and S of Gemini. It contains the star Procyon, of the first magnitude.

Cannae (kan′ē). In ancient geography, a town in Apulia, Italy, situated S of the river Aufidus. Near here (and N of the river), Hannibal with a Carthaginian force of about 50,000 men virtually annihilated (216 B.C.) the Roman army of about 80,000–90,000 under Varro and Aemilius Paulus. It was one of the greatest military disasters ever suffered by the ancient Romans, and the site is still called locally the "Field of Blood" (Italian, *Campo di Sangue*). The Battle of Cannae remains even to this day of interest to military historians from the fact that it provides (with the earlier victory at Lake Trasimenus) clear evidence of Hannibal's military genius. Carthaginian fortunes were at their peak after Cannae, but lack of support from Carthage made it impossible for Hannibal to press his advantage and led finally to the defeat (201 B.C.) of Carthage by Rome in the Second Punic War.

Canopic Mouth of the Nile (ka̱-nō′pik). In ancient geography, a branch of the Nile River, NE Africa, the westernmost of the important mouths.

Canopus (ka̱-nō′pus). [Also: **Canobus.**] In ancient geography, a seaport of Egypt, about 15 miles NE of Alexandria, on the Canopic Mouth of the Nile. It had considerable trade and wealth.

Cantharus (kan′tha̱-rus). [Also: **Kantharos.**] In ancient Greece, a wide-mouthed cup or vase, with a foot, and two handles rising above the rim. It was used especially for drinking wine.

Canthus (kan′thus). In Greek legend, an Argonaut from Euboea. He was slain in Libya, on the return from Colchis, by a shepherd whose sheep he was trying to steal for his comrades.

Capaneus (kap′a̱-nūs). In mythology, the son of Hipponous and the father of Sthenelus. He was an Argive chieftain, and marched against Thebes as one of the Seven against Thebes. As he climbed the wall of Thebes, he was struck by a thunderbolt because he had boasted that not Zeus himself could stop him. When his body was returned to his homeland for funeral honors, his wife Evadne, who had been watching from a rocky height, leaped down on to his funeral pyre and was consumed by the flames.

Caphaurus (ka̤-fô′rus). A Libyan. According to legend, he was a son of Amphithemis and a Tritonian nymph, and the grandson of Apollo and Acacallis. He slew the Argonaut, Canthus, in Libya, to prevent him from stealing his sheep.

Caphyae (kaf′ĭ-ē). In ancient geography, a city in Arcadia. It was said to have been founded by fugitives from Aegeus of Athens. Cepheus, king of Arcadia at the time, received them kindly, and they founded this city whose name is a form of Cepheus in the Arcadian dialect. The people of Caphyae annually celebrated mysteries of Artemis on their mountain, Cnacalus, for which reason they called her Artemis Cnacalesia. The people of the town believed that Menelaus came here when he was collecting his army to go to Troy, and planted a plane tree beside a spring outside the walls of their city.

Capitoline Museum. One of the chief museums of antiquities of Rome. It was founded in 1471 by Pope Sixtus IV, who presented the papal collections to the Roman people, and designated the Capitol as the place where the art treasures of Rome should be preserved. The museum was greatly enriched by Popes Clement XII and Benedict XIV. The collections now occupy the palace on the left-hand side of the Piazza del Campidoglio, which was built in the 17th century from modified designs of Michelangelo. Among the most noted of the antiquities acquired by the Capitoline Museum are the colossal statue of *Mars* in armor, the *Dying Gaul*, the *Satyr* of Praxiteles, the *Centaurs* by Aristeas and Papias, and the *Capitoline Venus* (after Praxiteles).

Capitolium (kap-i-tō′li-um), **Capitol.** 1) At Rome, one of the traditional seven hills, Rome's inner citadel, with two summits, sometimes distinguished as *Arx et Capitolium*, the northern summit being the *arx* or citadel proper, the southern the *Capitolium*, dominating from the west the Forum Romanum. On the arx stood the temple of Juno Moneta, on the Capitolium the ancient

triple-cella temple to the Capitoline Triad of Jupiter Optimus Maximus, Juno, and Minerva, focus of Roman state worship. With its religious, political, and military associations, it was regarded as the historic center of Rome, symbol of Rome's greatness. It is also referred to as *Mons Capitolinus* or Capitoline Hill. In modern Rome, the name has been corrupted to *Campidoglio;* the Piazza del Campidoglio, designed by Michelangelo, approached from the west by a monumental stairway, occupies the saddle between the two peaks; it contains the Museo Capitolino or Capitoline Museum, the Palazzo del Senatore, the Palazzo dei Conservatori, the fine bronze equestrian statue of Marcus Aurelius, other sculptures, milestones, etc.; near the site of the temple of Juno Moneta stands the church of S. Maria in Aracoeli; on the summit of the arx is the dazzling Victor Emmanuel Monument; on the southern summit, partly built over by the Palazzo Caffarelli, are the tufa foundations of the temple of Jupiter, Juno, and Minerva. 2) The term *Capitolium* was also applied to the triplecella temple to the Capitoline Triad, Jupiter Optimus Maximus, Juno, and Minerva, alternatively known as the temple of Jupiter Capitolinus, said to have been dedicated in the first year of the republic, 509 B.C., rebuilt after fires in 83 B.C., 69 A.D., and 80 A.D., repeatedly repaired and embellished, and systemically vandalized from the 5th century on. Only a few courses of the tufa foundations remain. 3) Outside of Rome, at first in Roman colonies and eventually elsewhere, the term *capitolium* was applied to a temple with three cellas, or with tripartite division indicated by chapels or niches, dedicated to the Capitoline Triad in emulation of Rome; examples at Ostia, Cosa, Minturnae, Pompeii, and elsewhere. (JJ)

Cappadocia (kap-a̤-dō′sha̤). In ancient geography, a country in the E part of Asia Minor, lying W of the Euphrates, N of Cilicia, and E of Phrygia; in a wider sense, the territory in Asia Minor between the lower Halys and Euphrates rivers, and the Taurus mountains and Euxine Sea; an elevated tableland intersected by mountain chains. The inhabitants of this region were called *Cappadocians* by the Persians and *Syrians* by the Greeks of Herodotus' time. Before the rise of Persia the area was subject to the Medes.

It was invaded by Croesus and then came under the control of Persia under Cyrus. As warriors, the Cappadocians wore braided helmets, carried small shields, and fought with spears, javelins, and daggers. Under the Persians the area constituted two satrapies, afterward two independent kingdoms; they were Cappadocia on the Pontus, later called Pontus; and Cappadocia near the Taurus, called Great Cappadocia, the later Cappadocia in a narrower sense. In 17 A.D. Cappadocia became a Roman province. It had then only four cities, Mazaca, near Mount Argaeus, the residence of the Cappadocian kings, later called Eusebia, and by the Romans Caesarea, the episcopal see of Saint Basil (modern Kayseri); Tyana; Garsaura, later called Archelais; and Ariarathea. Of its other cities, Samosata (Samsat), Myssa, and Nazianzus, the birthplaces or seats of celebrated ecclesiastics, are noteworthy.

Cappotas (kạ-pō′tas). Epithet of Zeus. Orestes, driven mad and fleeing from the Furies, sat down on a rough stone near Gythium in Laconia, and there temporarily his madness left him. For this reason the stone was named Zeus Cappotas (*Reliever*).

Capreae (kap′rẹ-ē). [Modern name, **Capri**.] Island off the coast of Campania, S Italy, situated about 19 miles S of Neapolis. It was famous in antiquity for the beauty of its scenery and its caves, especially the Blue Grotto. It was used as a resort by Augustus, and the emperor Tiberius spent his last ten years on Capreae, communicating by letter with the Senate at Rome. Area, five square miles.

Capri (kä′prē). See **Capreae**.

CAPRICORN
Pictured according to ancient descriptions.

Capricorn (kap′ri-kôrn) or **Capricornus** (-kôr′-nus). The tenth sign of the zodiac—the Goat—which the sun enters about the 22nd of December, the winter solstice. Also, an ancient zodiacal constellation between Sagittarius and Aquarius, represented on ancient monuments by the figure of a goat, or a figure having the fore part like a goat and the hind part like a fish.

Capua (kap′ū-ạ). Ancient city in Campania, Italy, about 17 miles N of Neapolis, famous for its wealth and luxury. It was founded by the Etruscans (c600 B.C.), was taken (c440 B.C.) by the Samnites, and came (c343 B.C.) under Roman rule. It opened (216 B.C.) its gates to Hannibal, whose army wintered there (216–215 B.C.). In 211 B.C. it was retaken by the Romans, and severely punished. It afterward flourished until sacked (456 A.D.) by Genseric. It was destroyed (840) by the Saracens, and its inhabitants colonized modern Capua. Its site is occupied by the village of Santa Maria di Capua Vetere. It contains the ruins of a triumphal arch and of a Roman amphitheater which dates from the early empire. The amphitheater was an imposing monument, much resembling the Roman Colosseum, and nearly as large. The axes of the outer ellipse are 557 and 458 feet; of the arena, 250 and 150 feet.

Capys (kā′pis). In mythology, a son of Assaracus, and a descendant of Dardanus, Tros and Ilus, the founders of the Trojan race. He was the father, by Themiste, of Anchises, and the grandfather of Aeneas. Anchises pointed out his shade to Aeneas when the latter visited Anchises in the Underworld.

Capys. In legend, a Trojan who mistrusted the Wooden Horse when it was first seen outside the walls of Troy, and advised that it be cast into the sea. When the city fell he accompanied Aeneas on his flight from Troy, and eventually became the founder of the city of Capua.

Car (kär). In mythology, a son of Phoroneus and the nymph Cerdo. His brothers were Pelasgus, Iasus, and Agenor. Some say he founded the city of Megara in Greece, and that the acropolis of the city was called Caria for him. Another Car, mentioned by Herodotus, was the brother of Lydus and Mysus. Three peoples of Asia—the Carians,

Lydians, and Mysians—were named for these three brothers.

Carbo (kär′bō), **Cnaeus Papirius.** Roman plebeian leader, soldier, and consul; born c130 B.C.; died 82 B.C. A member of one of the most prominent of the plebeian families, Carbo vigorously supported Marius and fought in the Marian forces against Sulla. In 85 B.C. he became consul with Cinna and remained as sole consul after Cinna's murder. In 82 B.C. he checked Sulla near Clusium (modern Chiusi), but suffered disastrous defeat at the hands of Metellus Pius, one of Sulla's lieutenants, near Faventia (modern Faenza). Carbo fled abroad but was taken by Pompey on the island of Pantelleria near Sicily and was put to death.

Cardamyle (kär-dam′i-lē). A city of Laconia, on the Messenian Gulf. It had formerly belonged to Messenia. This was one of the "gift" cities which Agamemnon promised to Achilles if he would return to the battle and forget his quarrel with Agamemnon. Near here, according to some accounts, the Nereids came up from the sea to see Neoptolemus when he was on his way to Sparta to wed Hermione.

Cardea (kär′dȩ̄-a̧). In Roman mythology, a household goddess. She was loved by Janus. In return for her favors he made her protectress of door hinges and gave her the power to prevent evil spirits from passing through doorways. She was thus a protectress of family life, and was especially the protectress of young children at night, when it was supposed that they were the most vulnerable to evil spirits that might suck their blood.

Cardia (kär′di-a̧). In ancient geography, a city on the Thracian Chersonesus, founded by colonists from Miletus and Clazomenae.

Cardo and Decumanus (kär′dō, dek-ū̧-mā′nus). In Roman surveying, the *cardo* was a north-south line, crossing the *decumanus,* or west-east line, at right angles. The resulting + is the basis of all Roman land surveys and measurement, and becomes particularly important in city-planning and the laying-out of new settlements. The intersection of the streets corresponding to the principal cardo and principal decumanus was regarded as the center of the city, and minor *cardines* and *decumani* were marked out parallel to the principal ones, at regular intervals, to form a grid or checkerboard as large as required, extending where desired beyond the walls into the countryside. In practice, any north-south street may be called a cardo and any west-east street a decumanus. It is usually easy to distinguish the principal decumanus of a Roman city as at Ostia and Minturnae: it transects the city from gate to gate, forms the main through artery, and is bordered by important public buildings. Identification of the major cardo is not always so easy, unless the locations of north and south gates are known. It should be remarked that in the observation of the north-south line Roman surveyors were prone to err, the direction of the major cardo often varying considerably from true north. Lacking the compass, which had not been invented, the most reliable determination was the observation of the pole-star, Polaris, at night; perhaps observations made at night were not trusted by day.

The word cardo means "door-post," the timber extending above and below the door into lintel and threshold on which the door turned, and the north-south line represented by the cardo as surveyed was thought of as parallel to the cardo of the earth, the pole or axis, real or imaginary, on which the earth was believed to rotate in space. Surveys were carried out with the aid of a *groma* (Greek *gnomon*), a crude sort of transit which may be roughly described as consisting of two alidades fixed at right angles to each other. Roman surveyors' manuals, the *Agrimensores,* were illustrated with tantalizing diagrams of cardo-and-decumanus grids laid out with the groma, and in some manuscripts these diagrams have been preserved, but archaeology has still to confirm them by actual excavation. (JJ)

Caresus (kär-ē′sus). Named by Homer (*Iliad*), as one of the rivers in the Troad which Apollo and Poseidon diverted from its course to break down the Greek wall, after the war was over and the Greeks had sailed for home. See **Rhesus,** river.

Caria (kär′i-a̧). In ancient geography, a division of Asia Minor, lying between Lydia on the N, Phrygia and Lycia on the E, and the Aegean Sea on the S and W. The Maeander (modern Menderes), a noted river, flows through it. According to Herodotus, the Carians went to the mainland of Asia Minor from the islands, where they were formerly called Leleges and were subjects of King Minos of Crete. They were noted sailors and served brilliantly in the navies of Minos. They were the first to put crests on their helmets and devices on their shields, and they invented handles for shields, which were formerly worn suspended by straps around the necks of warriors. The Greeks borrowed these usages from the Carians. Herodotus says the Carians were driven from the islands by the Dorians and Ionians and settled on the mainland. The Ionians of the islands and of Asia Minor insisted that they were of pure stock, but in fact, says Herodotus, they were a mixture from the mainland of Greece. When they came among the Carians, they killed the men and forced marriage on the women; their descendants were thus inevitably of mixed race. The Carian women, compelled to marry the Ionians, vowed they would never sit at table with their husbands, or call them by name, because they had slain their fathers, sons, and husbands, and they handed this practice down to their daughters. But the Carians themselves, according to Herodotus, say they were aboriginal to the mainland and never bore any other name. They claimed they were named for Car, and showed a temple of Carian Zeus in which the Mysians and Lydians, brother races of the Carians as the descendants of Mysus and Lydus, had the right to worship along with the Carians, and no other people could worship in that temple. In the Trojan War the Carians were allies of Troy. In the time of recorded history, Caria became subject to Croesus and later to Cyrus, falling to the Persian forces without much of a fight. Under Darius Caria was part of the first of the 20 satrapies into which Darius divided his empire, and paid a tribute to him of 400 talents of silver annually. In the Ionian revolt against Persian domination the Carians fought valiantly but were subdued. They furnished 70 ships to the Persian navy in the Persian Wars. The chief cities of Caria were Miletus, Myus, Halicarnassus, and Priene. The area fell to Alexander the Great and was later incorporated by the Romans into the province of Asia (129 B.C.).

Carius (kär′i-us). Epithet of Zeus, from his temple at Mylassa in Caria. This temple was shared by the brother races—Carians, Lydians, and Mysians. Zeus Carius was also worshiped in Thessaly and Boeotia.

Carmania (kär-mā′ni-a̲). In ancient geography, a division of Ariana on the plateau of what is now Iran. It was a province of the Persian Empire, bounded on the N by Parthia, on the E by Drangiana and Gedrosia, on the S by what is now known as the Persian Gulf, and on the W by Persis and Media. Alexander the Great passed through it on his return from India (325 B.C.) and added it to his empire. Carmania occupied about the same area as the modern Iranian region of Kerman.

Carmanor (kär-mā′nôr). Legendary Cretan king who is said by some to have received Apollo and Artemis and to have purified them after they had slain the Python at Delphi. While he was at the house of Carmanor, Apollo fell in love with Acacallis, who later bore him a son. Carmanor was the father of Eubulus and Chrysothemis. The latter, a son, was said to have been a poet, and to have won the first victory at the Pythian Games with a hymn to Apollo.

Carme (kär′mē). In mythology, a daughter of Eubulus. She was the mother by Zeus of the Cretan goddess Britomartis.

Carmenta (kär-men′tä). In Roman mythology, one of the Camenae, fountain nymphs of Italy who could foretell the future and who were goddesses of healing as well. Her sister Roman divinities were Antevorta, Postvorta, and Egeria. Carmenta had a temple at the foot of the Capitoline Hill at Rome, and altars near the gate called after her. Some claim Carmenta was originally an Arcadian, named Nicostrate, who was given the name Carmenta because of her prophetic powers. This Carmenta was said to be the mother by Hermes of Evander, with whom she fled from Arcadia to Italy, where she gave her oracles, to Heracles among others. It is also said of her that she changed the 15 characters of the Greek alphabet, brought with her from Arcadia, to the Roman letters. Some say she was slain in very old age by her son, who then awarded her divine honors.

Carnea (kär-nē′a̲). Ancient Spartan festival

(observed also by some of the other Doric peoples), lasting nine days in the month of Karneios (a sacred month, approximating the modern August), held in honor of Apollo Carneus, in his aspect of god of flocks and fertility (Carneus probably being a more ancient fertility god assimilated to Apollo by the Dorians).

Carneades (kär-nē′a̯-dēz). Greek Skeptic philosopher and rhetorician; born at Cyrene, 213 B.C.; died 129 B.C. He was called the founder of the Third or New Academy. Holding a firm belief in the necessity for suspending judgment at all times, he advocated probability in its various degrees as the only truly practical basis for human action. Excavators have found in the Athenian Agora the base of a statue of him.

Carneus (kär-nē′us). Epithet of Apollo. Some say it was an epithet of the god in his role as protector of flocks and herds. Some say he was given this epithet because the Greeks in Troy cut down some cornel trees in a grove sacred to Apollo. The god was angry at the violation of his grove. To propitiate him, the Greeks made sacrifices and called him "Carneus" from the cornel trees.

Carnus (kär′nus). In Greek legend, an Acarnanian soothsayer. He came to the army that the sons of Aristomachus—Temenus, Cresphontes, and Aristodemus—had gathered at Naupactus for the invasion of the Peloponnesus. Carnus recited frenzied verses to them and they killed him, thinking he was a magician sent by the Peloponnesians to destroy them. In his anger at the death of his seer, Apollo caused the fleet the Heraclidae had assembled to be destroyed and the army was so afflicted by famine that it was disbanded. Temenus consulted the oracle and learned that these calamities resulted from the slaying of Carnus. He was told to banish the slayer for ten years and take the "Three-eyed One" for a guide. From this time forward the Dorians continued to offer sacrifices to Carnus to propitiate him. Some say Apollo's epithet, Carneus, under which he was especially worshiped by the Spartans, came from this incident.

Carnutes (kär-nū′tēz) or **Carnuti** (-tī) or **Carnutae** (-tē). Ancient tribe of central Gaul, living in the vicinity of what are now Orleans and Chartres, and involved (52–51 B.C.) in wars against Caesar. The Carnutes, who lived in an area distinguished for its forests, are considered the center of Druidic worship.

Carpathus (kär′pa̯-thus). [Greek, **Karpathos**; Italian, **Scarpanto**; Turkish, **Kerpe**.] Island in the Aegean Sea, about 30 miles SW of Rhodes: one of the Dodecanese group. According to some accounts, it was here that Aristaeus caught Proteus and compelled him to tell him why it was that all of his bees had died. Proteus told him it was because Aristaeus had caused the death of Eurydice, wife of Orpheus. In ancient times the island was under the rule of Rhodes. Area, about 108 square miles; length, about 32 miles.

Carpo (kär′pō). A goddess of summer fruits. She was worshiped at Athens as one of the Horae.

Carpophorus (kär-pof′o̯-rus). Epithet, meaning "Fruit-bringer." It was applied equally to Demeter and her daughter Persephone, called "The Maid."

Carrhae (kar′ē). [Also: **Charran**; modern name, **Haran**.] In ancient geography, a city of Mesopotamia, situated on the Bilichus River (Belikh), a small affluent of the Euphrates, about 23 miles SE of Urfa. It was the city named Haran in the Old Testament. Nearby was the scene of the defeat (53 B.C.) of Crassus by the Parthians, who killed him shortly thereafter while he was engaged in an interview with one of their satraps.

Carthage (kär′thāj). [Latin, **Carthago**; Phoenician, **Karthadasht**, meaning "New Town."] Ancient city and state in N Africa, situated on the Mediterranean, a few miles NE of modern Tunis, and not far from the ancient city of Utica. It was founded by Phoenicians about the middle of the 9th century B.C. (According to tradition, Dido founded the city, having bought as much land as could be circumscribed by a buffalo hide; this she cut in strips with which, laid end to end, she encircled a sizable piece of ground and on it built the citadel called Byrsa, from the Greek word "hide.") It was a great commercial and colonizing center as early as the 6th century B.C., and was one of the largest cities of antiquity. It had two harbors, a naval and a mercantile. Its first treaty with Rome was made in 509 B.C. It was defeated at Himera in Sicily in 480 B.C., but overthrew

Selinus and other Sicilian cities c400 B.C. It was the rival of Syracuse under Dionysius, Agathocles, and others. At the height of its power it had possessions in Sicily, Corsica, Sardinia, N Africa, and Spain. Its wars with Rome have the following dates: First Punic War, 264–241 B.C.; Second Punic War, 218–201 B.C.; Third Punic War, 149–146 B.C. It was recolonized as a Roman city by Caius Gracchus and successfully by Augustus c29 B.C., was taken by the Vandals in 439 A.D., and was retaken by Belisarius in 533. At present some cisterns, broken arches of an aqueduct, the Roman Catholic monastery of Saint Louis, and a museum mark the site of the former rival of Rome.

Carthaginian Wars (kär-tha-jin′i-an). See **Punic Wars.**

Carus (kär′us), **Titus Lucretius.** See **Lucretius.**

Carvilius (kär-vil′i-us), **Spurius.** Roman freedman, in the second half of the 3rd century B.C. He is noted as one of the first to open a public school at Rome (meaning here a school open to those members of the public who paid its fees rather than one supported by public funds). He is credited, by Plutarch and others, with having devised the letter G for the Roman alphabet. (The differentiation between C and G has also been attributed to Appius Claudius.) The need for this letter arose from the fact that C was employed ambiguously to denote both the sound of K (as in *kin*) and "hard G" (as in *gap*). Carvilius, by a slight modification of the sign for C, produced the G, and put it in the alphabetical place of the little-used Z (which was only restored, together with Y, in the time of Cicero, when they were placed at the end of the alphabet). But such spellings as Caius (abbreviated C.), Caia, and Cnaeus (abbreviated Cn.) persisted through the empire.

Carya (kar′i-a). In mythology, a Laconian maiden who was loved by Dionysus. When she died suddenly at Caryae, the god changed her into a walnut tree. Artemis brought the news of the death of Carya to the Laconians and they built a temple to her, Artemis Caryatis. It is from this temple that Caryatids, female statues that act as columns, get their name.

Caryae (kar′i-ē). A place in Laconia sacred to Artemis and the nymphs. Here Carya,

daughter of a Laconian king died, and the Laconians had the news of her death from Artemis. The Laconians built a temple of Artemis, the columns of which were made in imitation of the dancing girls who performed at the annual festivals of Artemis. There was an image of Artemis Caryatis in the open. The dance the Spartan maidens performed at their annual festival was originally taught them by the Dioscuri. The name Caryae means "walnut trees," and was associated with Carya, the beloved of Dionysus, who was transformed into a walnut tree.

Caryatid (kar-i-at′id). See **Caryatis.**

Caryatis (kar-i-at′is). An epithet of Artemis, meaning "Of the Walnut tree." Artemis received the name for bringing news of the death of Carya to the Laconians. They raised a temple of Artemis Caryatis in which female statues served as columns, hence the name "caryatid" by which such columns came to be known (especially those of the Erechtheum on the Acropolis in Athens).

Carystius (ka-ris′ti-us), **Diocles.** See **Diocles Carystius.**

Casca (kas′ka), **Publius Servilius.** Roman politician; died after 42 B.C. He was one of the conspirators against Caesar (44 B.C.), and was the first of them to strike Caesar with his dagger at the base of Pompey's statue in the Senate house.

Casilinum (kas-i-lī′num). An ancient name of **Capua.**

Casius (kā′si-us). [Also: **Bargylus.**] Ancient name of the mountainous region in Asia Minor S of Antioch. According to Greek mythology, here the monster Typhon overcame Zeus in his battle against the gods and cut the sinews of his hands and feet.

Caspiae Portae or **Pylae** (kas′pi-ē pôr′tē, pī′lē). [Also: **Albanian Gates; Caspian Gates;** Latin, **Albaniae Pylae; Caucasiae Portae.**] An old name of the defile of Derbent between the Caucasus and the Caspian Sea. It has long been a trade route.

Caspian Gates (kas′pi-an). See **Caspiae Portae.**

Caspium, Mare (kas′pi-um, mā′rē). [Also: **Mare Hyrcanium;** modern, **Caspian Sea.**] Salt inland sea N of Media and Hyrcania. Length, 760 miles; greatest width, about 270 miles; area 169,330 square miles; elevation at surface, 85 feet below sea level.

actor; up, lūte, pull; oi, oil; ou, out; ᴛʜ, then; ḍ as d or j, ṣ as s or sh, ṭ as t or ch, ẓ as z or zh.

Cassander (ka-san′dėr). King of Macedonia; born 358 B.C.; died 297 B.C. He was the eldest son of Antipater, who had been made regent of Macedonia while Alexander the Great was engaged on his Asiatic campaigns. Olympias, mother of Alexander, was constantly sending accusations against Antipater to her son. Cassander went to Babylonia to meet Alexander and defend his father. On the death of Antipater (319 B.C.), Cassander waged war on the successors of Alexander, especially on Polysperchon, who had been appointed regent of Macedonia by Antipater. Ptolemy Soter and Antigonus were in alliance with him, and most of the Greek states, including Athens, came under his dominion. He made an alliance with Eurydice, wife of Philip Arrhidaeus of Macedon, but Olympias soon had them slain. Cassander then marched against Olympias, compelled her to surrender at Pydna, and put her to death (316 B.C.). In 311 B.C. he was made regent for Alexander IV, the young son of Roxana and Alexander the Great. In the same or the following year, he had them both slain. After the battle of Ipsus (301 B.C.) and the death of Antigonus, he was recognized as king of Macedonia and ruler of Greece. He married Thessalonica, sister of Alexander the Great, restored Thebes, which had been destroyed by Alexander, changed the name of Therma to Thessalonica, and rebuilt Potidaea, which was thereafter known as Cassandrea.

Cassandra (ka-san′dra). In Greek legend, one of the 12 daughters of Priam, king of Troy. Her mother was Hecuba, and she was the twin of Helenus. According to some accounts, the children fell asleep in the temple while their parents were celebrating a festival of Apollo. Sacred serpents came and licked their ears as they slept, but on being discovered by Hecuba, who screamed in terror at the sight, the serpents glided away. However, because they had been ministered to by sacred serpents, from that time forth both children were endowed with the power of divination. Other accounts say that Apollo fell in love with Cassandra and promised to give her prophetic powers in return for her love. The god thereupon taught her the art of prophecy but Cassandra refused to carry out her end of the bargain. Apollo could not withdraw the gift he had given her, but in revenge he turned it into a curse by decreeing that although she would correctly foretell the future, no one would ever believe her. Her name has become synonymous for those prophets of doom whose warnings go unheeded until it is too late. The more accurately she predicted disaster, the more convinced her hearers were that she was mad. She predicted that if Paris carried out his intended voyage to Sparta he would bring ruin to Troy. Her father ignored her warnings and provided the fleet in which Paris subsequently abducted Helen. From the beginning of the Trojan War Cassandra incessantly prophesied that it would end in disaster. She was scorned and kept as a virtual prisoner so that the Trojans would not have to listen to her gloomy predictions. In appearance Cassandra, the fairest of Priam's daughters, was described as a rival of Aphrodite, and she had many suitors. Towards the end of the Trojan War, Priam promised her to Eurypylus, descendant of Heracles, in return for assistance in the defense of Troy, but he was killed. Cassandra protested violently against bringing into the city the Wooden Horse which had been left outside the walls of Troy by the Greeks. She said there were armed men in it and predicted that Troy would become dust, Priam and Polyxena would die, Hecuba would be metamorphosed into a dog, and she herself carried off into slavery. Priam rebuked her for her raving and the Horse was dragged into the city. The Trojans wreathed it with garlands and offered sacrifices. The sacrificial fires poured forth blood-red smoke and then fizzled out. The statues of the gods wept. Cassandra correctly interpreted these omens of disaster but no one heeded her. In desperation she tried to set the Horse afire, but was prevented from doing so by her countrymen. In the sack of Troy she sought refuge at the altar of Athena. There, according to some accounts, Ajax the Lesser seized her and violated her. Others say no such thing happened, and that this was a malicious lie spread by Odysseus, and indeed, Cassandra did not claim that Ajax had injured her. In the awarding of captives Cassandra was taken by Agamemnon as his concubine and, according to some, subsequently bore him twin sons. Before she left Troy, she promised to destroy her most bitter foes by her alliance with Agamemnon. In a spell of what seemed to be madness, she declared that Agamemnon had lost what he loved most—his wife and his children—and declared that the Greeks fought and died in foreign lands, while the

AJAX SEIZING CASSANDRA FROM THE
IMAGE OF ATHENA AT TROY
Red-figured Greek amphora, c450 B.C.
Metropolitan Museum of Art

Trojans had the glory of dying in defense of their homeland. She predicted the death of Agamemnon, the long wanderings of Odysseus, and her own death, and then left her mother to go off as a captive to Greece. On his arrival in Argos Agamemnon was royally acclaimed by Clytemnestra. Cassandra remained mute until the reunited pair entered the palace for the feast which Clytemnestra said she had prepared for her returning husband. Then Cassandra broke into frenzied speech. She cried out at the smell of blood that came from the palace; she expressed horror at the frightful deeds kinsmen were committing on kinsmen. In this she was saying that Clytemnestra was murdering Agamemnon, as was, in fact, the case. But the citizens who had come to the palace to welcome Agamemnon home listened compassionately, convinced that her sufferings had unhinged her mind, and made no effort to go

to Agamemnon's assistance. However, when she alluded to the ghastly feast which Thyestes, uncle of Agamemnon, had made on the flesh of his own sons, and recalled his curse, they were filled with foreboding and uneasy wonder that one from so far away should know the horrible history of the House of Atreus. Again she spoke of the death of Agamemnon and foretold that one (Orestes) would some day come to avenge him. Then, knowing her own death to be at hand, she appealed to the gods to make it swift and entered the palace. There Clytemnestra, who had just murdered Agamemnon, set upon Cassandra and killed her. In the mêlée which followed the murders, the sons of Cassandra and Agamemnon were slain. Cassandra was known sometimes as Alexandra. Her character, with its tragic element of impotent wisdom, has been variously introduced into later literature.

Cassandra (kä-sän′drä). [Also: **Kassandra, Pallene.**] Westernmost peninsula of Chalcidice, NE Greece.

Cassandra, Gulf of. See **Toronaicus, Sinus.**

Cassandrea (kas-an-drē′a̠). The name Cassander gave to Potidaea, a Macedonian city, when he rebuilt it after its destruction. See **Potidaea.**

Cassiopea (kas″i-ō̠-pē′a̠) or **Cassiepea** (kas″i-e̠-) or **Cassiope** (ka̠-sī′ō̠-pē). In Greek legend, the wife of Cepheus, king of Joppa in Ethiopia, and the mother of Andromeda. Her boasts that she and her daughter were more beautiful than the Nereids angered Poseidon and he sent a sea monster to devastate the land. To appease Poseidon, Andromeda was offered to the monster in accordance with an oracle. She was saved by Perseus, however, and became his bride. Cassiopea was unwilling to have Perseus for a son-in-law, as she preferred Phineus, brother of Cepheus, in that role. At the wedding of Perseus and Andromeda she supported the cause of Phineus when he burst in on the festivities and attempted to seize Andromeda. Perseus turned Phineus and his other enemies, including Cepheus and Cassiopea, into stone by exhibiting the head of Medusa. Poseidon set the image of Cassiopea among the stars, but in such a way as to humiliate her, for at certain times of the year she appears hanging in the heavens upside down.

Cassiopea or **Cassiepea.** A circumpolar constellation, supposed to represent the wife of Cepheus seated in a chair and holding up both arms. It contains 30 stars brighter than the sixth magnitude, and is always found opposite the Great Bear on the other side of the pole-star. In this constellation there appeared in 1572 a temporary star brighter than Venus at its brightest.

Cassius Dionysius (kash'us dī-ō-nish'us). Greek writer on botany and materia medica; fl. c88 B.C. His works include a translation from Punic to Greek of the Carthaginian Mago's great treatise on agriculture (to which he added many Greek examples), a work on roots, and a reported illustrated pharmacopoeia.

Cassius Longinus (lon-jī'nus), **Caius.** Roman general and politician, who died near Philippi, Macedonia, 42 B.C. He was distinguished in the Parthian war of the period 53–51 B.C. A participant in the battle of Pharsalus, he was subsequently pardoned by Caesar. Nevertheless, in 44 B.C. he was one of the leading conspirators against Caesar. A commander in Syria and Asia (44–42 B.C.), he was defeated by Antony at Philippi in 42 B.C. and killed himself.

Cassius Longinus, Quintus. Roman politician; died 45 B.C. Although he was accused of corruption during his tenure of the quaestorship in Spain in 54 B.C., he became a tribune, and with his colleague in that office, Mark Antony, in 49 B.C. vetoed a decision of the Senate to order Julius Caesar to relinquish command of his army. When the Senate nevertheless persisted in its purpose, Cassius and Antony joined Caesar, who thereupon crossed the Rubicon and began the campaign which made him master of Rome. In 47 B.C. Cassius was given a command in Spain, and presently was faced with a rebellion which he was unable to handle, so that Caesar had to come to his rescue.

Cassius Parmensis (pär-men'sis), **Caius.** Roman poet, born at Parma in Italy (whence his surname). He was one of the conspirators against Julius Caesar. He fled to Athens where, by order of Octavian, c30 B.C., he was executed.

Cassius Viscellinus (vis-e̱-lī'nus), **Spurius.** Roman reformer; died c485 B.C. There is little doubt that Spurius Cassius Viscellinus was a historic person, though so much legend has gathered about him as to give him an almost mythical character. He appears to have held the consulship several times, and is named as the negotiator in 493 B.C. of treaties between Rome and the cities of Latium. Trouble between the Roman patricians and the lower orders had long been festering because of the continual arrogation of public lands by the patricians. Cassius, while consul in 486 B.C., proposed a redistribution of lands, but the patricians accused him of courting popular support with the object of becoming king, and brought about his death in the following year.

Cassotis (kas'ō-tis). [Also: **Kassotis.**] Spring at Delphi on the slopes of the hill above the theater. According to some accounts, it was named for a nymph of Mount Parnassus. The waters of the spring were said to sink into the ground and flow into the shrine of the priestesses of Apollo who, on drinking of them, were then inspired to prophecy.

Castalia (kas-tā'li-a̱, -tāl'ya̱). A fountain at the eastern foot of the deep gorge that separates the rocks known as the Phaedriades, on the slopes of Mount Parnassus, Greece. The fountain was sacred to the Muses and to Apollo. Its waters were said to have the power of inspiring those who drank of them. Some say the fountain was named for a native woman, or for a man named Castalius. Others say it was named for Castalia, a daughter of the river-god Achelous. They say the spring was given to Castalia by the river-god Cephissus. On certain days the people of Lilaea threw cakes into the waters of the Cephissus River on the other side of Mount Parnassus. These cakes were said to reappear in the fountain of Castalia. The fountain was sealed off by earthquakes for centuries and its site was lost. Ensuing earthquakes opened it up and caused its waters to flow again. The basin, to the west on a slope above Castalia, where rites were performed before pilgrims approached the sanctuary of Apollo, may still be seen with streams from the fountain trickling into it.

Castalides (kas-tal'i-dēz). A name for the Muses, derived from the fountain of Castalia on the slopes of Mount Parnassus, Greece. sacred to them.

Castel Sant' Angelo (än'jä-lō). [Also: **Hadria-**

neum, **Moles Hadriani, Hadrian's Mole, Hadrian's Tomb.**] The name by which the mausoleum of the emperor Hadrian, together with the medieval and renaissance fortifications which enclose it, on the right bank of the Tiber in Rome, are now known. Begun by Hadrian in 136 A.D., the mausoleum was completed in 139 A.D. by his successor Antoninus Pius, and used as a place of burial for all the emperors and members of their families from Hadrian to Caracalla. It was originally about 165 feet high, in the form of a cylinder c220 feet in diameter on a base c280 feet square, faced with marble revetment which has now almost entirely vanished, and decorated with columns, statues, and a cupola on which stood a quadriga with the emperor. Soon after 400 A.D. the tomb was converted to a fortress. It was said that in 590 A.D. Pope Gregory the Great, returning from a procession to pray for deliverance from a plague then raging, saw in the skies above the fortress the figure of the Archangel Michael sheathing his sword, a sign that the plague would shortly cease. In commemoration of this Pope Boniface IV built, c610 A.D., on the summit of the tomb a chapel of Sanctus Angelus inter Nubes, from which the modern name is derived. After the return of the papal court from Avignon to Rome in 1377 the popes established their residence at the Vatican, to which the Castel Sant' Angelo was connected by a covered passage. The bronze statue of the Archangel Michael sheathing his sword, which now stands on the summit, dates from 1752. In addition to its original tomb chambers and the apartments, tribunals, storerooms, and dungeons associated with the papal occupancy, the Castel Sant' Angelo now contains a museum of engineering. (JJ)

Castor (kas'tor). The twin brother of Polydeuces (Pollux). See **Dioscuri.**

Castores (kas-tô'rēz). A Roman name for the Dioscuri, Castor and Polydeuces (Pollux).

Castrum Inui (kas'trum ī'nō-ī). "Fort of Inuus," a town in Latium near Antium and Ardea. It was a nameless site at the time when Aeneas visited his father in the Underworld. Anchises pointed out to him the shade of the man waiting to be born who would found the city.

Casuentus (kas-ū-en'tus). [Modern: **Basento** or **Basiento.**] River in S Italy which flows into the Gulf of Tarentum (now Taranto) near Metapontum about 27 miles SW of Tarentum.

Cataebates (kat-ē-bā'tēz). An epithet of Zeus, meaning "Descender," because he descends in the thunderbolt. The Greeks enclosed places that had been struck by lightning, as they considered such spots sacred.

Catamitus (kat-a-mī'tus). A Roman name for Ganymede, the pretty Trojan youth said to have been carried off to Olympus to be the gods' cup-bearer and Zeus' favorite, whence the disparaging term "catamite." (JJ)

Catana (kat'a-na) or **Catina** (kat'i-na). [Greek, **Katane**; modern, **Catania.**] City on the island of Sicily, situated on the Gulf of Catana on the E coast of the island. Founded by Greeks from Naxos in 729 B.C., the city lies in a very fertile plain at the foot of Mount Aetna, and because of its location and rich soil has often been contested. When the Athenians sent an expedition against Syracuse under the command of Alcibiades (415–413 B.C.), Catana was allied with Athens and served as a base for the Athenian fleet. In 404 B.C. Catana allied itself to the neighboring city of Leontini for protection against Dionysius the Elder, tyrant of Syracuse. However, the city fell into the hands of Dionysius by treachery. Traitors, bribed by Dionysius, opened the gates of the city to his forces (403 B.C.); he plundered the city, rounded up its inhabitants and sold them into slavery, and gave what remained of the city to his Italian allies, the Campanians. In the First Punic War (264–241 B.C.), Catana was one of the first Sicilian cities to be taken by the Romans (263 B.C.), and later, from the time of Augustus, it became one of the first cities of Sicily as an ally of Rome. Remains of a theater, odeum, and amphitheater of Roman times have been found at the site.

Catania (kä-tä'nyä). See **Catana.**

Catharsius (ka-thär'si-us). Epithet of Zeus, meaning "Purifier." There was an altar of Zeus Catharsius at Olympia.

Catiline (kat'i-līn). [Full name, **Lucius Sergius Catilina.**] Roman politician and conspirator, born c108 B.C.; killed at Faesulae (now Fiesole), Italy, 62 B.C. He was of an old but impoverished patrician family. As a partisan of Sulla he rendered himself infamous by his complicity in the horrors of the proscription, destroying with his own hand his brother-in-law, Q. Caecilius. He was praetor in 68 B.C. and governor of Africa in 67 B.C. After an abortive attempt, in conjunction with P. Autronius, to murder the consuls-elect for 65 B.C., with a view to seizing power, and after an unsuccessful candidacy in the consular elections of 64 B.C., he organized a widespread conspiracy against the republic, whose object is said to have been the cancellation of debts, the proscription of the wealthy, and the distribution among the conspirators of all offices of honor and emolument. It was defeated by the vigilance and eloquence of Cicero, who was then consul. The rebellion having broken out in Etruria on Oct. 27, Cicero pronounced in the Senate on Nov. 8, his first oration against Catiline, which caused the latter to leave the city. On Nov. 9 Cicero delivered in the Forum his second Catilinian oration in which he acquainted the people with the events in the Senate and the departure of Catiline from Rome. On Dec. 3 documentary evidence of the conspiracy was obtained from an embassy of Allobroges, which had been tampered with by the Catilinians, and in the evening Cicero delivered in the Forum his third oration, in which he acquainted the people with the events of the day and the seizure of the conspirators remaining at Rome. On Dec. 5 Cicero delivered in the Senate his fourth oration, which was followed by the execution in prison of some of the conspirators. Meanwhile Catiline had assumed command of the revolutionary force, which amounted to about two legions, but was overtaken by the army of the Senate as he was attempting to escape into Gaul, and was defeated and slain in the battle which ensued.

Catina (kat'i-na). A Latin name of **Catana** (q.v.).

Cato (kā'tō), **Marcus Porcius.** [Called **Cato the Elder** and **Cato the Censor;** surnamed **Priscus.**] Roman statesman, general, and writer, born at Tusculum, Italy, 234 B.C.; died 149 B.C. He was quaestor under Scipio in 204 B.C., served as consul in 195, served in Spain in 194 and against Antiochus in 191, was censor in 184, and was ambassador to Carthage in 157 or 153 B.C. He sought to restore the integrity of morals and the simplicity of manners prevalent in the early days of the Republic, his severity as a censor earning him the epithet "Censorius." The prosperity of Rome's old enemy Carthage led him to advocate a third Punic war. In his effort to initiate this war, for years he closed every speech in the Senate with the words, "Ceterum censeo Carthaginem esse delendam" ("Furthermore, I am of the opinion that Carthage ought to be destroyed."). He wrote voluminously; his *De Agri Cultura* survives, but of his historical *Origines,* in seven books, and his speeches, letters, and essays, only fragments have reached us.

Cato, Marcus Porcius. [Called **Cato the Younger;** surnamed **Uticensis,** meaning "Of Utica."] Roman patriot and Stoic philosopher; great-grandson of Marcus Porcius Cato (234–149 B.C.), born at Rome, 95 B.C.; committed suicide at Utica, North Africa, 46 B.C. He fought under Gellius Publicola against Spartacus in 72 B.C., served as military tribune in Macedonia in 67, and was quaestor in 65, tribune of the people in 62, and praetor in 54 B.C. He supported Cicero against the faction of Catiline, and sided with Pompey against Caesar on the outbreak of the civil war in 49 B.C. After the battle of Pharsalus he retired to Utica, where he put himself to death on receiving intelligence of the victory of Caesar at Thapsus. He had a reputation for scrupulous fairness and honor, and his death was considered noble and courageous.

Catreus (kā'trūs). In Greek legend, a son of Minos, king of Crete, and Pasiphaë. He was the father of three daughters, Aërope, who married Atreus and became the mother of Agamemnon and Menelaus, Clymene, who married Nauplius and became the mother of Palamedes and Oeax, and Apemosyne. He had one son, Althaemenes, whom he dearly loved. An oracle predicted that he would die at the hands of one of his own children. To avoid beng the instrument that would fulfill the oracle, Althaemenes and Apemosyne went into voluntary exile at Rhodes. Catreus, on discovering his daughter Aërope entertaining a lover, proposed to cast her into the sea. But as Catreus suspected both Aërope and Clymene of plotting against his life, he was instead persuaded to sell them as slaves to Nauplius on condition that they never return to Crete. Years later, Catreus went to Rhodes, seeking his beloved and pious son. He landed on Rhodes at night and in the darkness was mistaken for a pirate. Although he tried to explain who he was, the uproar drowned his voice. Althaemenes, rushing up and unaware of the stranger's identity, hurled a spear at him and killed him, thus fulfilling the oracle.

Catullus (ka̱-tul′us), **Caius Valerius.** Roman poet; born at Verona, Italy, c84 B.C.; died c54 B.C. Particularly effective in simple short lyric poems, he is ranked by many with Sappho and Shelley. Coming to Rome, he became acquainted with the most celebrated men of his day, including Julius Caesar (whom he attacked in his verses but to whom he later was reconciled), Cicero, Asinius Pollio, Cornelius Nepos, and Calvus. His love poems are addressed to Lesbia, whose real name, according to Apuleius, was Clodia, the beautiful and fascinating, as well as ambitious and unscrupulous, wife of Caecilius Metellus and sister of the demagogue Clodius, Cicero's enemy. The stormy love affair (which gave to some of the poems a bitterness not usually found in lyric verse) ended in unhappiness for Catullus. The extant poems number 116 (3 are considered spurious), and include lyrics, epigrams, elegies, and even a short epic ("epyllion") of 408 lines about the marriage of Peleus and Thetis. They fall into three groups: short lyrics, four longer poems (including two wedding hymns and the epic), and a group of epigrams and elegies. The themes of some of his most famous and charming poems are the death of Lesbia's pet sparrow, the "thousand kisses," the dinner invitation, the homecoming to Sirmio, the love of Acme and Septimius, the marriage of Torquatus, the death of a brother. The *Attis,* in galloping galliambics, is a metrical tour de force of extraordinary effectiveness. Catullus greatly influenced Horace in his *Odes,* Vergil in the *Aeneid,* Ovid and the other elegists, and the epigrammatist Martial.

Catulus (kat′ū-lus), **Caius Lutatius.** Roman general; fl. 3rd century B.C. He was chosen consul for the year 242 B.C. When he entered office, the First Punic War had been waged since 264 B.C. and the Senate, dis-

couraged by numerous losses, had abandoned the war at sea. He obtained command of a fleet built by wealthy patriots at Rome, and in 241 B.C. gained the decisive victory at the Aegadian Islands which resulted in a treaty of peace favorable to Rome.

Catulus, Quintus Lutatius. Roman general; born c152 B.C.; died 87 B.C.; father of Quintus Lutatius Catulus (died 60 B.C.). He was consul with Marius in 102 B.C., and was associated with him in the victory over the Cimbri at Vercellae in 101 B.C. He joined Sulla in the civil war and, having in consequence been proscribed by Marius, he is said to have committed suicide in 87 B.C.

Catulus, Quintus Lutatius. Roman politician; died 60 B.C.; son of Quintus Lutatius Catulus (c152–87 B.C.). Consul in 78 B.C. and censor in 65 B.C., he was a strong supporter of Cicero against the conspiracy of Catiline in 63 B.C.

Caucasus (kô′ka̱-sus) **Mountains.** Mountain system between the Black and Caspian seas. On a crag in these mountains, according to legend, Prometheus was chained at the command of Zeus, and eagles daily gnawed at his liver. Heracles at last freed Prometheus, with the consent of Zeus. The mountains extend SE and NW and are often taken as the conventional boundary between Europe and Asia. There are numerous passes, some of them reaching an elevation of 10,000–11,000 feet. The glaciers rival those of the Alps, but lakes are almost entirely lacking. The mountains have been extremely important historically as a barrier to migrations. Length of the system, about 800 miles; greatest width, about 120 miles.

Caucon (kô′kon). According to tradition, a son of Lycaon, but others say Poseidon was his father. He brought the mysteries of the Great Goddess (Demeter) from Eleusis to Messenia. The Messenians sacrificed to him, but the chief seat of his worship was at Lepreus in Elis, a city built by his son.

Caudine Forks (kô′din). [Latin, **Furculae Caudinae.**] Two passes in the mountains of ancient Samnium, Italy, leading to an enclosed valley between Capua and Beneventum. Here the Romans under the consuls Spurius Postumius Albinus and T. Veturius were forced (321 B.C.) to surrender to the Samnites under Pontius. The Romans were forced to swear to a treaty of peace, and to give 600 Roman *equites* (knights) as hostages, while the whole Roman army was sent under the yoke (thus symbolizing their collective submission). Infuriated by this last humiliation, which was one of the worst ever accepted by a Roman military force, the Roman Senate refused to approve the treaty, and delivered the consuls to the Samnites, who refused to accept them.

Caulonia (kô-lō'ni-ạ). In ancient geography, a city in Bruttii, S Italy, situated on a rocky elevation near the Mediterranean Sea. According to the *Aeneid*, Aeneas passed by Caulonia on his way to his destined homeland in Italy, and saw the temple of Juno there. The city was founded by Achaeans, perhaps from Croton or from Greece itself, in the 7th century B.C. It was captured by Dionysius the Elder, tyrant of Syracuse, in 389 B.C. He destroyed the city and gave its territory to the neighboring city of Locri. It was soon after restored, but was again taken by Pyrrhus, king of Epirus (c318–272 B.C.), and thereafter was almost abandoned. Excavations at the site have revealed remains dating from the 7th and 6th centuries B.C., and part of a temple of the 5th century B.C.

Caunians (kô'ni-ạnz). A people of Caunus in S Asia Minor south of Caria. Herodotus thought they were autochthonous but recorded that they themselves claimed to have come from Crete. Their language was similar to that of the Carians. According to Herodotus they decided they would no longer worship in the foreign temples that had been established for a long time among them, but would worship only their own ancient gods. The youths of the land armed themselves, and beating the air with their spears they marched to the frontiers, declaring that they were driving out the alien gods. The Caunians fell under the dominion of the Persians in the reign of Cyrus the Great.

Caunus (kô'nus). In legend, a son of Miletus of Caria and Cyaneë He was the brother of Byblis, who fell in love with him. He rebuffed her advances and fled to Lycia when he became aware that she could not overcome her guilty love for him.

Cavo (kä'vō), **Monte.** [Also: **Monte** (or **Mount**) **Albano.**] Highest summit of the Alban Hills, situated about 13 miles SE of

Rome. On it are the ruins of the temple of Jupiter Latiaris. Height, 3115 feet.

Caÿster (kạ-is'tẽr). The river-god of the Caÿster River in Lydia. Some say he was the son of Achilles and the Amazon queen Penthesilea, and the father, by Derceta (the Syrian Aphrodite) of Semiramis of Babylon.

Caÿster. [Also: **Caystrus** (kạ-is'trus).] In ancient geography, a river in Lydia, Asia Minor, which flows into the Aegean Sea about 35 miles S by SE of Smyrna (Izmir); now called the Bayindir or, sometimes, the Little Menderes. The ancient city of Ephesus was near its mouth.

Cebes (sē'bēz). Greek philosopher; fl. at Thebes, Boeotia, in the 5th century B.C. He was a friend and pupil of Socrates; in Plato's *Phaedo* he is one of the interlocutors. Three works were ascribed to him, probably erroneously, one of which, *Pinax*, is a philosophical explanation of a table symbolically representing the dangers and vicissitudes of life.

Cebriones (seb-rī'ọ-nēz). In Homeric legend (*Iliad*), a brother of Hector who became Hector's charioteer when the regular driver was slain by Teucer. He was the leader of a group who assaulted the Greek fortifications, and was later slain by Patroclus before the walls of Troy.

Cecropia (sē-krō'pi-ạ). An ancient name for Attica, from the ancient king Cecrops.

Cecrops (sē'krops). In Greek mythology, a son of Gaea. He was a man in his upper parts and a serpent in his lower parts. He is said to have been the first king of Attica and the land was sometimes called Cecropia in his honor. It was Cecrops who divided Attica into the 12 demes. He also built temples and established the worship of the gods, especially Athena and Zeus. He established the custom of monogamy and abolished human sacrifices. Some say he also gave the people their institutions of burial and writing. By his wife Agraulos (or Aglauros) he was the father of three daughters, Agraulos II (or Aglauros), Herse, and Pandrosos. During his reign Athena and Poseidon struggled for control of Athens. Poseidon struck the rock of the Acropolis with his trident and salt water gushed out and formed a deep well. This was his gift to the people. (Some say a horse came forth when he struck the rock.) But Athena gave the people the olive tree and Cecrops, who was to judge which gift was more valuable, according to some accounts, awarded the city to her. Others say the women, who outnumbered the men, voted to give Athena control of Athens. A second Cecrops was a son of Erechtheus, and was made king of Athens by his brother-in-law Xuthus, but his brothers quarreled over this decision and to save him Athena, disguised as a bird, carried him off under her wings to safety.

Cedalion (sē-dā′li-on). According to legend, one of the workers at the forge of Hephaestus on the island of Lemnos. He was seized by Orion, who had been blinded, and compelled to act as Orion's guide to farthest Ocean, where Orion's sight would be restored as the rays of Helius, rising from the sea, fell on his eyes.

Cedreatis (sed-rē-ā′tis). An epithet of Artemis, meaning "Of the Cedar Tree." It was given to her because of an image of the goddess set in a cedar tree.

Cefalù (chā-fä-lö′). See **Cephaloedium.**

Celaenae (se-lē′nē). In ancient geography, an important and large city of Phrygia, situated at the source of both the Marsyas and Maeander rivers. Traditionally, Apollo flayed Marsyas here after he had beaten the latter in a musical contest. The city was the site of a royal residence in the time of Xerxes. The modern town on the ancient site is Dinar, Turkey.

Celaeno (se-lē′nō). A daughter of Pleione and Atlas; one of the Pleiades. By Poseidon she was the mother of Lycus and Nycteus, or, as some say, the mother of Lycus by Prometheus. With her sisters, her image was placed among the stars. See **Pleiades.**

Celaeno. In the *Aeneid*, one of the "bird-bodied, girl-faced" Harpies. She told Aeneas, when he landed in the Strophades, that famine would force him and his men to eat their tables before he would be able to build his walled town in Italy. The prophecy was fulfilled when Aeneas and his men ate the thin cakes made of meal on which their food was served when they landed in Italy.

Celer (sē′lėr), **Quintus Caecilius Metellus.** See **Metellus Celer, Quintus Caecilius.**

Celeus (sē′le-us). In Greek legend, a king of Eleusis whose wife and daughters, unaware of her true identity, offered hospitality to the goddess Demeter when she was searching for Persephone. Later, the goddess revealed herself and, at her command, Celeus helped to build a temple in her honor at Eleusis. In return he was initiated into the sacred rites and mysteries of Demeter by the goddess herself. See **Demophoön** and **Triptolemus.**

Celeuthea (sel-ū-thē′a). Epithet of Athena, meaning "Lady of the Road." In gratitude to Athena for his success, Odysseus set up several sanctuaries of Athena Celeuthea along the road in Laconia on which he had raced for the hand of Penelope.

Cella (sel′a). The room or chamber which formed the nucleus of an ancient Greek or Roman temple and contained the image of the deity, as distinguished from the additional rooms, porticoes, etc., often combined with the cella to form the complete temple.

Celsus (sel′sus), **Aulus Cornelius.** Roman writer; fl. in the first half of the 1st century A.D. He was the author of a comprehensive encyclopedia treating of farming, medicine, military art, oratory, jurisprudence, and philosophy. The medical part, the only one extant, is a fundamental source for the history of Alexandrian medicine, surpassed only by the works of Hippocrates and Galen. Celsus' attitude was one of moderation between empiricism and methodism; theory and practice to him were equally indispensable.

Cena Trimalchionis (sē′na trī-mal″ki-ō′nis). The longest episode in Petronius Arbiter's novel (which is commonly known as the *Satyricon* and was composed probably before 61 A.D.), this passage (discovered c1650 at Trau, Dalmatia) describes the Feast or Dinner-Party given by Trimalchio, a wealthy freedman, to a number of his fellow-freedmen and a group of educated but dissolute scholars (accompanied by one full and one assistant professor). A plethora of rich, frequently fantastically disguised viands is accompanied by musical and acrobatic performances. The host recites miserable doggerel and shows off both his wealth and his ludicrous pretensions to learning. All this satirizes the conspicuous bad taste of the newly-rich—criticism for which Petronius,

---

actor; up, lūte, pull; oi, oil; ou, out; ᴛʜ, then; ḍ as d or j, ṣ as s or sh, ṭ as t or ch, ẓ as z or zh.

Nero's "Arbiter of Elegance," was particularly fitted. As host and guests grow more intoxicated, they swap riddles, anecdotes, stories of werewolves and witches, until the rising uproar finally alerts the fire brigade, and the feast ends. The *Cena* is remarkable not only because of its high literary merit as a thoroughly amusing piece of characterization, but also from the linguistic viewpoint. For the first time in Latin literature, educated and vulgar speech levels are clearly distinguished and reproduced. The spoken Latin of the lower classes (which had been banned from the literature of the classical period but had, of course, been vigorously alive all along) emerges from its underground existence to supply invaluable information on Roman slang, proverbs, everyday speech, and thereby on the eventual development of the Romance languages. See also, **Petronius Arbiter, Satyricon, Trimalchio.** (HS)

Cenaean (sē-nē′an). Epithet of Zeus, from his altar at Cenaeum, a headland of Euboea. See **Cenaeum.**

Cenaeum (sē-nē′um). A promontory on the northwestern tip of Euboea. It was here that Heracles prepared to sacrifice to Zeus and donned the shirt poisoned with the blood of Nessus which led to his death.

Cenchreae (seng′krē-ē). In ancient geography, the harbor of Corinth, named for Cenchrias, a child of Poseidon and Pirene. Nearby was a temple of Artemis, and in the town, a temple and stone image of Aphrodite. The region was sacred to Poseidon, and a mole running out into the sea was crowned by a bronze image of him. Opposite Cenchreae was a stream of warm salt water that flowed from a rock into the sea and was known as *Helen's Bath.* Near Cenchreae was the common grave of the Argives who conquered the Lacedaemonians at Hysiae in the 7th century B.C.

Cenchrias (seng-krī′as). In Greek mythology, a child of Pirene and Poseidon. He was unintentionally killed by Artemis and his mother's tears flowed unceasingly in her grief. She was changed into a fountain and the place where he died was named Cenchreae.

Cenomani (sen-ō-mā′nī). Celtic people, a part of the army of Bellovesus, which with his

sanction crossed (c400 B.C.) the Alps under a legendary leader, Etitovius, and settled north of the Padus about Brixia (Brescia) and Verona, according to the detailed account of Livy. They were a branch of the Aulerci. Their original seat in Gaul, where they were called Aulerci Cenomani, was on the Sarthe River near what is now Le Mans. The Aulerci were included among the tribes constituting the Armorici.

Censor (sen′sor). One of two superior magistrates of ancient Rome, who in the latter half of the 5th century B.C. succeeded to certain powers which had before been exercised by the consuls. Their functions included—1) the keeping of a register (census) of all Roman citizens, with the amount of their property, for the purposes of taxation, and for the classification of the citizens according to their possessions, from the rank of senator down; 2) the disciplinary control of manners and morals, in which their power was absolute, both in sumptuary matters and in the degradation of any citizen from his proper class for reasons affecting the moral or material welfare of the state, or in the imposition of fines at will upon those deemed by them to be offenders; 3) the practical administration of the public finances, including the control under the Senate of both direct and indirect taxation, the determining of the expenditures of the state other than fixed charges, the letting of public contracts, and the supreme direction of public works. The magistracy of the censors was interrupted at the time of the civil wars, and under Augustus and succeeding emperors was reëstablished at various times, but with greatly diminished powers.

Centaurs (sen′tôrz). In mythology, the descendants of Ixion and Nephele, a cloud-born woman. They dwelt in Thessaly and were conceived of as being half man and half horse. In general, they were wild and savage, more like beasts than men but some of them, notably Chiron, had close associations with men as friends and teachers. The centaurs were invited to the marriage of Pirithous, king of the Lapithae, and Hippodamia. There, inflamed by wine, they attacked the women, in particular, the bride. A fierce battle took place in which the Lapithae succeeded in driving off the centaurs. On another occasion the centaurs, again maddened by the fumes of wine, attacked Heracles as he visited Pholus, one of their number, in a cave near Mount Pholoë. Nephele sent a violent rain to help her descendants. The centaurs, being four-footed, had an advantage over Heracles in the slippery mud. Nevertheless, Heracles slew many of them and drove the rest away. In later times the centaurs were thought of as peaceful followers of Dionysus and Eros.

Centaurus (sen-tô′rus). In mythology, the son of Ixion and Nephele, a woman who was shaped from a cloud. By Magnesian mares he became the father of the centaurs. (See preceding article.)

Centaurus. An ancient southern constellation, situated between Argo and Scorpio, pictured to represent a centaur holding a Bacchic wand. Its brightest star is third brightest in the sky. Its second star is about as bright as Betelguese, and is reckoned the eleventh in the heavens in order of brightness. The two stars are situated near each other on the parallel of 60° S, a little E of the Southern Cross. Centaurus has, besides, two stars of the second magnitude and seven of the third. Alpha Centauri and Proxima Centauri, a faint star within the constellation, are thought to be the closest (4.3 light years) stars to our solar system.

Centimani (sen-ti-mā′nī). A Roman name for the hundred-handed monsters whom the Greeks called Hecatonchires: Briareus (also called Aegaeon), Cottus, and Gyges (or Gyes).

Centumcellae (sen″tum-sel′ē). Also: [**Portus Trajani**; modern name, **Civitavecchia** or **Civita Vecchia**.] In ancient geography, an Etruscan town in C Italy, situated on the Mediterranean Sea, NW of Rome. The port was constructed in the time of the emperor Trajan.

Centuripae (sen-tū′ri-pē). [Also: **Centorbi**; modern name, **Centuripe**.] In ancient geography, a very old Sicel city in Sicily, in the eastern half of the island near Mount Aetna. It was allied with Athens against Syracuse in the Peloponnesian Wars, and was later allied to Dionysius the Elder, tyrant of Syracuse, in his wars against the Carthaginians. It was an independent city up to the time of the First Punic War (264–241 B.C.). It

flourished under the Romans, and a number of antiquities of this period are preserved.

Century. [Latin, **Centuria**.] In Roman antiquity: 1) A division of the people (originally so called, probably, with reference to the approximate number of its members, though there was no fixed limit), instituted by Servius Tullius, formed with reference to taxation and to the election of magistrates and enactment of laws. All the citizens were divided into classes, according to their wealth, and each of the classes was divided into from ten to 40 senior and junior centuries, according to age, in all 193 or 194. Each century had one vote in the *comitia centuriata*, the wealthier classes voting first and generally controlling the others. 2) A subdivision of the legion, corresponding to a modern military company of infantry, and consisting nominally of 100 men.

Ceos (sē′os). [Also: **Keos, Kea, Tzia, Zea, Zia**.] Island of the Cyclades in the Aegean Sea about 13 miles SE of Attica. According to legend, the island suffered a terrible scorching drought which afflicted it because the murderers of Icarius had taken refuge there. On learning from the oracle at Delphi that he would find honor there, Aristaeus went to Ceos, offered sacrifices to Zeus, and by killing the murderers of Icarius appeased the Dog-Star (the faithful hound of Icarius which had been translated to the heavens), which was causing the drought. From that time on cooling winds, the Etesian winds, now annually strike the islands for 40 days. Ceos formerly contained four cities, and was the birthplace of the poets Simonides and Bacchylides. Area, about 65 square miles.

Cephallenia (sef-a-lē′ni-a). [Modern **Cephalonia**; also: **Kefallinia, Kephallenia**.] The largest of the Ionian Islands, W of Greece. Its surface is mountainous. Some say the island is the one called Same or Samos by Homer who, some think, meant this island as the center of the Kingdom of the Islands of which Odysseus was the ruler. There were four main cities there in ancient times: Cranii, Pale, Same, and Pronni. Remains of Cyclopean walls have been found at the sites of each of these cities. Tombs and graves of the Mycenaean period and the period of the Trojan War have revealed a rich store of vases and other objects that indicate a flourishing state of civilization from most ancient times. In later centuries, the 13th and 12th centuries B.C., rivals of Cephallenia—Mycenae, Thebes, Athens—waged war against her. According to legend, Amphitryon of Thebes, the foster father of Heracles, waged war on the Taphians and Teleboans, aided by Cephalus. Because of the assistance of the latter, Amphitryon awarded the island of his defeated enemies to Cephalus and its name was changed to Cephallenia in his honor. At the outbreak of the Peloponnesian War (431 B.C.), Cephallenia was allied to Corinth, but was forced to change its allegiance to Athens. It became subject to Rome in 189 B.C. Length of the island, 30 miles; area, about 300 square miles.

Cephaloedium (sef-a-lē′di-um). [M o d e r n name, **Cefalù**.] In ancient geography, a city on the N coast of the island of Sicily, situated at the foot of a headland over 1200 feet above sea level, from whence it derived its name (Greek, *kephale*, "head"). It was founded by the Sicels, one of the earliest tribes in the island and from whom the whole island ultimately took its name. The city was conquered by Dionysius the Elder, tyrant of Syracuse, c395 B.C., by the Romans in 254 B.C., and by the Saracens in 858 A.D. Among the ancient remains to be seen there are fortifications, a primitive sanctuary known as the "Temple of Diana," and a fine Norman church with superb Byzantine mosaics.

Cephalus (sef′a-lus). According to some accounts of the legend, a son of Hermes and Herse, daughter of Cecrops, king of Athens. Others say he was a son of Deion. He was married to Procris, daughter of Erechtheus, king of Athens, and loved her deeply. One day while he was hunting, Eos saw him and fell in love with him. She carried him off, offering her love. Cephalus rejected her advances, saying he had sworn undying fidelity to Procris. Eos, the dawn-goddess, scoffed at his pledge and mocked his belief that Procris was equally faithful. To prove her contention, she transformed him into a handsome youth with the name Pteleon, and sent him back to Procris. In this guise he approached his wife, who was grieving for her lost husband, and finally persuaded her with rich gifts and ardent protestations of love to weaken and yield to him. Immediately he revealed himself, denounced her for infidelity, and deserted her. Later he met a handsome youth, Pterelas, who was the owner of a hound, Laelaps, that could not fail to catch its quarry, and of a spear that could not fail to reach its target. He offered Pterelas a large sum for these two marvellous aids to hunting, but was told that Pterelas would only give them up for love. Cephalus then offered his love. At this Pterelas threw off his disguise and was revealed as Procris. The couple was reconciled and Cephalus enjoyed many successful hunts with his hound and spear, and recovered his devotion to Procris. But Procris, who had not forgotten his absence with Eos, was jealous and thought when she overheard him calling for a breeze to cool him that he was calling a lover. She followed him and hid in a thicket to watch him. Cephalus' keen eye detected a slight movement of the bushes in which she was hidden, and thinking it was caused by a wild beast, hurled his spear. It went straight to the mark and transfixed Procris. Afterward, Cephalus was banished from Athens for murder. He went to Thebes, and loaned his hound to Amphitryon, foster father of Heracles, to catch the Teumessian fox that was ravaging the countryside. Since the fox, by decree of the gods, could not be caught, and the hound must catch its quarry, both were turned to stone by Zeus. Cephalus also helped Amphitryon in his war against the Taphians and Teleboans. In return for his aid he was awarded the island which was named Cephallenia in his honor. But he never recovered from the death of Procris, and blamed himself for the disguise which he had assumed to test her, as well as for her death. He built a temple to Apollo on Cape Leucas and one day went there and, calling his wife's name, leaped into the sea.

Cepheus (sē′fūs, -fē-us). In Greek legend, a son of King Belus and Anchinoë, and brother of the twins Danaus and Aegyptus. He was king of Joppa in Ethiopia and was the father of Andromeda by his wife Cassiopea. He was turned to stone when Perseus exhibited the head of Medusa. Poseidon set the image of Cepheus among the stars. See **Andromeda**.

fat, fāte, fär, fãre, errant; net, mē, hèr ardent; pin, pīne; not, nōte, mŏve, nôr,

Cepheus. In Greek mythology, a son of Aleus, king of Tegea in Arcadia, and the brother of Amphidamas. He went to Calydon and joined Meleager in the hunt for the Calydonian Boar, although he had at first refused to take part when he learned that Atalanta was also a member because he did not like to hunt with women. He was also one of the Argonauts who joined Jason on the expedition to Colchis in quest of the Golden Fleece. He became king of Tegea and, reluctantly, joined with Heracles when the latter waged a war to punish the sons of Hippocoön. Cepheus and 17 of his 20 sons fell in the war.

Cepheus. One of the northern constellations, recognized in ancient times, between Cassiopea and Draco. It is figured to represent the Ethiopian king Cepheus wearing a tiara and having his arms somewhat extended. Its brightest stars are of the third magnitude. The Cepheid variables, a class of stars varying in brightness because of internal pulsation, are called after one of the stars in this constellation.

Cephisodotus (sef-i-sod′ō-tus). Name of two Greek sculptors, often confused with each other, of the 4th century B.C. One was a relative, possibly the father or a brother, of Praxiteles, and something is known of his work from a copy, at Munich, of a statue of Pluto, or Wealth, as an infant in the arms of Irene, or Peace. The other Cephisodotus was a son of Praxiteles; it is known that he made portrait sculptures, but no examples of his work survive.

Cephissus (sē-fis′us). [Also: **Cephisus, Kephisos.**] In ancient geography, a river in Attica, Greece, flowing through the plain of Eleusis into the Gulf of Eleusis.

Cephissus. [Also: **Cephisus, Kephisos.**] In ancient geography, a river in Attica, Greece, flowing through the plain of Athens into the Saronic Gulf.

Cephissus. [Also: **Cephisus, Kephisos.**] In ancient geography, a river in Phocis and Boeotia, Greece, flowing into Lake Copaïs. This was the sacred river of the shrine of Delphi. Beside it was the shrine of Themis, where Deucalion and Pyrrha went after the great flood to pray to the gods, and where they learned how to repopulate the world.

Cer (sēr) or **Ker** (kēr). In Greek mythology, a goddess of violent death, according to some accounts, a daughter of Nyx, and the sister of the Moerae. There were several goddesses representing different sorts of death, and together they were called Ceres. They were described as hateful and dreaded because they carry man off to the hopeless halls of Hades. But it was thought that the Ceres were not entirely free agents; Zeus and the other gods could control them, and sometimes even men could do so. In battle the Ceres were accompanied by Eris, and wandered about in blood-stained garments, quarrelling among themselves over the wounded and the dead. Epidemic diseases were sometimes associated with them, and they came in time to be regarded as goddesses who punish men for their crimes. For this reason they came to be identified with the Erinyes.

Cerambus (sē-ram′bus). In Greek mythology, a man of Pelion who was changed into a beetle by the nymphs and flew to Mount Parnassus to escape the flood which Zeus sent to destroy mankind for its wickedness. This was the same flood from which Deucalion and Pyrrha were spared because of their piety.

Ceramicus (ser-a-mī′kus). Large area on the NW side of ancient Athens, Greece, so named from the early gathering in it of potters, attracted by the presence of water and excellent clay. It was divided into parts, the Inner Ceramicus, within the walls, traversed by the Dromos Street from the Dipylon Gate, and including the Agora; and the Outer Ceramicus, continuing the first division outside of the walls. The Outer Ceramicus became a favorite place of burial for the Athenians, and here were interred those honored with a public funeral. The tombs were ranged beside and near the various roads which radiated from the Dipylon Gate. Little trace of them remains, except of the unique group upon and near the inception of the Sacred Way to Eleusis, a group which was preserved by being buried in 86 B.C. in the siege *agger* (earthwork) of Sulla, and contains historical and plastic memorials of very high value, among them the sculptured monument of Dexileus, who fell (393 B.C.) before Corinth, and tombs of Euphrosyne, Hegeso, Aristion, Demetria, and Pamphile.

Ceramus (ser'a-mus). In Greek mythology, a son of Dionysus and Ariadne. According to some accounts, the district called the Ceramicus at Athens was named for him.

Ceraunii Montes (sē-rô'ni-ī mon'tēz). [Also: **Ceraunian Mountains; Acroceraunia** or **Acroceraunian Mountains.**] In ancient geography, a chain of mountains in NW Epirus, terminating in the promontory Acroceraunia.

Ceraunian Mountains. In ancient geography, a range of mountains in the E part of the Caucasus system, exact position undetermined.

HERACLES DRAGGING CERBERUS FROM HADES
IN THE PRESENCE OF HERMES
Red-figured Attic plate, c520 B.C.
Museum of Fine Arts, Boston

Cerberus (sėr'bėr-us). In Greek mythology, the watchdog at the entrance to the Underworld, whose duty it was to devour the living who attempted to invade the infernal regions or the shades that attempted to escape from them. Orpheus, Aeneas, and Odysseus successfully passed Cerberus on visits to the Underworld. He was an offspring of Typhon and Echidna, and was usually represented as having three heads, a serpent's tail, and a mane of serpent's heads. As one of their burial customs, the Greeks buried with the corpse a honey cake with which the spirit was to quiet Cerberus so that it might pass the monster-dog on its way to Elysium; thence the expression "a sop to Cerberus." The last labor of Heracles was to bring Cerberus up from the Underworld. Hades permitted him to do this if he could take Cerberus without weapons. Heracles grasped him firmly around the neck, disregarding the stings of the serpent's tail with which Cerberus lashed him, and choked him until he yielded. As Cerberus faced the light of earth for the first time, either at Troezen or at Heraclea on the Euxine Sea, foam fell from his jaws onto the ground. From the foam sprang the poisonous plant aconite, which, it was claimed, flourished ever after around Heraclea.

Cercinitis Lacus (sėr-si-nī'tis lā'kus). [Also: **Cercinites, Kerkinitis, Limne Kerkinitis.**] In ancient geography, the lake or enlargement near the mouth of the river Strymon in Macedonia.

Cercopes (sėr-kō'pēz). A legendary race of men in Lydia. They are sometimes conceived of as mischievous gnomes, who attacked Heracles as he slept, when he was serving Queen Omphale, and stole his weapons. Awakened, Heracles was amused by their attempts. He gathered them up in his lion's skin and took them to Omphale. Others say that they were deceitful men who were changed into apes by Zeus, and that Heracles captured them and carried them, head down on a pole, to Omphale. The Pithecusae (Ape) islands of Ischia and Procida, off the coast of Naples, were named for them.

Cercops. Greek poet of Miletus, of the 6th century B.C. A poem on the war of Aegimius, king of the Dorians, against the Lapithae is assigned by some to him; by others it is attributed to Hesiod.

Cercyon (sėr'si-on). In Greek mythology, a son of Hephaestus or of Poseidon. He was a king in Arcadia and the father of Alope, whom he imprisoned because she bore a son to Poseidon. He ordered her son, Hippothous, exposed to die but the child was rescued. Cercyon was in the habit of challenging strangers in Eleusis to wrestle with him, whereupon he crushed them to death in his powerful arms. When Theseus passed through Eleusis, he met Cercyon on the road between Eleusis and Megara near Alope's grave, accepted his challenge to wrestle, and killed him by dashing him to the ground.

Cercysera (sėr-sī'se-ra). One of the names under which Achilles is said to have been known when he lived at the court of Lycomedes in Scyrus disguised as a girl.

Ceres (sir′ēz, sē′rēz). In ancient Italian mythology, the goddess of grain and harvest, later identified by the Romans with the Greek Demeter. Her cult was quite old; one of the *flamens* (15 priests, each assigned to one god and his cult observance) was the *flamen Cerealis.*

Cerveteri (cher-ve′tä-rē). See **Caere.**

Cerynean Hind (ser-i-nē′an). A fabled creature in Greek mythology, referred to in the legend of Heracles. With golden horns and hoofs of bronze, this creature, sacred to Artemis, was as fleet as the wind. Its capture was one of the 12 labors imposed upon Heracles. Some say he pursued it through Arcadia and finally transfixed its forefeet with one arrow as it stopped at the Ladon River to drink. He then carried it to Eurystheus. Others say that after a long pursuit, he drove it into a deep drift of snow in a northern region and thus captured it without injuring it.

Cerynia (ser-i-nī′a). In ancient geography, one of the 12 towns in Achaea occupied by the Achaeans after the Ionians had left the land. It was built on a high hill between the Cerynites River and Mount Cerynia, from which it took its name according to some accounts. The sanctuary of the Eumenides in Cerynia was said to have been founded by Orestes. Of this sanctuary it was said that whoever entered it, guilty of murder or impiety, at once became insane with fright.

Cerynitia (ser-i-nish′a). Forested region in Arcadia where Heracles found the golden-horned, bronze-hoofed Cerynean stag (or hind) which he pursued for a year before capturing it alive as his third labor for Eurystheus.

Ceryx (sē′riks). In Greek mythology, a son of Hermes and Herse. Some say he was the first herald of the Eleusinian Mysteries.

Cestrinus (ses-trī′nus). In Greek legend, said to have been a son of Andromache and Helenus, born in Epirus after the Trojan war and the death of Neoptolemus. After the death of his father he took land beyond the Thyamis (Calamas) River in Epirus and settled there.

Cestus (ses′tus). Aphrodite's magic girdle, which had the power of enhancing the beauty of any who wore it and of inspiring love in those who beheld the wearer of it. Hera borrowed the cestus from Aphrodite to charm Zeus, during the Trojan War, so that he would forget about helping the Trojans in his aroused love for her, and thus give her favored Greeks a chance to drive back the Trojans. The cestus played an important role in many of the myths.

Cethegus (sē-thē′gus), **Marcus Cornelius.** Roman general; died 196 B.C. He was curule aedile (213 B.C.), praetor (211), censor (209), and consul (204 B.C.). In the following year he commanded as proconsul in Cisalpine Gaul, where, with the aid of the praetor Quintilius Varus, he defeated the Carthaginian general Mago, brother of Hannibal.

Ceto (sē′tō). In Greek mythology, a daughter of Gaea and Pontus. By her brother Phorcys she was the mother of the Graeae, the gray-haired sisters who share one eye and one tooth between them, and of the Gorgons, winged sisters who dwelt in Libya. According to some accounts, Ceto and Phorcys were also the parents of Echidna, an immortal monster, half-maiden and half-serpent; the Hesperides, who dwelt in the garden called by their name; and of Ladon, a many-headed monster who guarded the Apples of the Hesperides.

Cetus (sē′tus). A southern constellation—the Whale—situated west of Orion. It was anciently pictured as some kind of marine animal, possibly a seal.

Ceyx (sē′iks). In Greek mythology, a son of Phosphorus, the Morning-Star. He was a king in Trachis who welcomed Heracles when he went into exile there with his wife Deianira for an accidental murder, but was not strong enough later to defy the order of Eurystheus to banish Heracles' children. Ceyx was celebrated for the tender love he bore his wife Alcyone. On a journey to Clarus to consult the oracle of Apollo, he was drowned at sea. His wife, who had pleaded to accompany him, was informed in a dream sent by Hera that her husband was dead. She went to the water's edge to weep and discovered her husband's body, which had been washed to his native shores. Alcyone grieved so over the loss of her husband that the gods in pity changed her and Ceyx into kingfishers (alcyones), whose affection for each other in the mating season is proverbial. The Halcyon Days, a period of 14 days when the sea is calm, are named for them. According to another version of this myth, Ceyx and Alcyone were so happy that they dared to compare themselves to Zeus and Hera. Their arrogance so annoyed the gods that Zeus sent a storm which wrecked the ship in which Ceyx was sailing to consult the oracle, and he was drowned. According to this version also, the gods in pity for Alcyone's grief changed the pair into kingfishers, or into a sea-mew (Ceyx) and a kingfisher (Alcyone).

Chabrias (kā′bri-as). Athenian general; fl. 388–357 B.C.; killed near Chios, 357 B.C. In 388 B.C. he was sent to the assistance of Evagoras, king of Cyprus, against the Persians. On the way he landed at the island of Aegina, which the Spartans were using as a base, and by an ambush defeated the Spartans in battle and seized and killed Gorgopas, the Spartan commander. In 378 B.C., in a campaign against Agesilaus, he acquired great celebrity by the adoption of a new maneuver, which consisted in receiving the enemy's attack on one knee with spears presented and shields resting on the ground. In 376 B.C. the island of Naxos revolted against the reconstituted Athenian Confederacy. Chabrias sailed against the island to put down the revolt. The Spartans sent a fleet to the relief of Naxos. Chabrias engaged their fleet and utterly defeated the Spartans. Eleven Spartan ships were allowed to escave while Chabrias, mindful of the fate of the Athenian victors at Arginusae (406 B.C.), stopped to rescue from the water his men whose ships had been wrecked. Thus the Spartan fleet was not completely destroyed, but the victory was impressive. Chabrias sailed about the Aegean and enrolled new members in the Athenian Confederacy. He acted as military adviser to the king of Egypt (c373 B.C.). The island of Ceos revolted from the Confederacy (364 B.C.), and was subdued by Chabrias in the same year. On the outbreak of the Social War (357 B.C.) he was placed in command of the Athenian fleet, which coöperated with the army under Chares. Chios revolted. He was sent to put

down the revolt and was killed at the siege of the island (357 B.C.).

Chaereas and Callirrhoë (kē′rē-as; ka-lir′ō-ē). Greek romance (c2nd century A.D.) by Chariton Aphrodisiensis, only a part of which is extant.

Chaeremon (ker-ē′mon). Greek tragic poet, a contemporary of Plato, and active at Athens early in the 4th century B.C. A few fragments of his work remain.

Chaeronea (ker-ō-nē′a). [Also: **Chaeroneia.**] In ancient geography, a town in W Boeotia, Greece. Some say it was once called Arne, after the daughter of Aeolus, who also gave her name to a city in Thessaly. Others say the city was named for Chaeron, a son of Apollo. The Chaeroneans claimed they found on their borders the scepter Hephaestus made for Zeus, who sent it by Hermes to Pelops, and that was ultimately held by Agamemnon. They worshiped it under the name "Spear." It was not kept in a public temple. Priests of the "Spear" took turns keeping it in their own houses for a year each. Sacrifices were offered to it daily. Offerings of meats and all kinds of cakes were placed on a table near it. Chaeronea was the birthplace of Plutarch and it was here that he spent most of his life and did his work. It was a dependency of Orchomenus. Here Philip of Macedon defeated (338 B.C.) the Thebans, Athenians, and their allies. The Thebans gathered the bodies of those of the Sacred Battalion who had fallen in the battle and buried them in a common tomb. Over it the famous marble *Lion of Chaeronea* was raised as a memorial. The monument was broken apart by a chieftain who thought to find treasure there and it was not until 1818 that the lion was found lying in a field. In the early part of the 20th century it was restored and remounted on its ancient base. Nearby the lion a small theater was cut into the rocks of the hill called Petrachus. This hill was, some say, the place where Rhea deceived Cronus by handing him a stone wrapped in swaddling clothes in place of her new-born son Zeus. Chaeronea was the place where Sulla (86 B.C.) with 30,000–40.000 men defeated the army of Mithridates VI (about 110,000) under Archelaus. In ancient times the Chaeroneans were noted for their skill in distilling

Above: Marble lion,
   Delos, 6th century B.C.

Left: Standing female figure with
   pomegranate, early 6th century B.C.

Below: Heracles, from the E pediment
   of the so-called Temple of Aphaea,
   Aegina, c 490 B.C.

Head of Athena,
from the E pediment
of the so-called Temple of
Aphaea, Aegina, c 490 B.C.

Museo delle Terme, Rome

Female flute-player, side panel from
the so-called Ludovisi Throne, c 460 B.C.

Museum of Fine Arts, Boston

Boy with lyre, detail from
a three-sided relief, 470–460 B.C.

British Museum

Equestrian group, W frieze of the
Parthenon, c 440 B.C.

Louvre

Head of Apollo
of Piombino, c 475 B.C.

Nike of Paeonius, Olympia,
after 421 B.C.

Hermes carrying the infant Dionysus,
Praxiteles, Olympia.

Detail, Head of Hermes. *YDAP*

Terra-cotta portrait head,
late Roman Republic.

unguents from the lily, rose, narcissus, and iris, that cured many human ills.

Chair of Forgetfulness. A seat in the Underworld to which whoever sat on it was irrevocably fastened. The stone of the chair grew up around the sitter's body. On a journey to the Underworld to abduct Persephone, Pirithous was tricked into sitting on this chair and remains there forever.

Chalcedon (kal′se-don, -don; kal-sē′don). [Modern Turkish name, **Kadiköy.**] In ancient geography, a town in Bithynia, situated on the Bosporus opposite Byzantium. It was founded (c685 B.C.) by Megarian colonists.

Chalcenterus (kal-sen′tėr-us). Surname of **Didymus.**

Chalcidice (kal-sid′i-sē). [Also: **Chalkidike, Khalkidhiki, Khalkidike, Khalkidiki.**] In ancient geography, the chief peninsula of Macedonia, terminating in the three smaller peninsulas of Pallene, Sithonia, and Acte, projecting into the Aegean Sea. It was settled (c7th century B.C.) by Euboeans. Its chief cities were Olynthus and Potidaea.

Chalciope (kal-sī′ō-pē). In Greek legend, a daughter of Aeëtes, king of Colchis, and the nymph Asterodia. She was the sister of Medea. Aeëtes gave her in marriage to Phrixus when he alighted in Colchis on the ram with the golden fleece. Her four sons by Phrixus (Argus, Cytissorus, Melas, and Phrontis) were shipwrecked while on their way from Colchis to Hellas after the death of their father, and were rescued on the island of Ares by Jason and the Argonauts, with whom they returned to Colchis. In gratitude to Jason for saving her sons, Chalciope persuaded Medea to help Jason to win the Golden Fleece.

Chalcis (kal′sis). In Greek legend, a daughter of the river-god Asopus and Metope. According to some accounts, she was the mother of the Curetes, who were the earliest inhabitants of Chalcis, and of the Corybantes. The town of Chalcis in Euboea is said to have been named for her.

Chalcis. [Also: **Chalkis, Egripo, Evripos, Negropont.**] City in C Greece, situated on the W coast of the island of Euboea on the Euripus strait about 34 miles N of Athens. It was the chief town in ancient Euboea, and sent out many colonial settlers. Cumae in

Italy and Naxos in Sicily were colonized by Chalcidians, and the colonies of Chalcis in Italy and Sicily exceeded in number those of any other state. Chalcis was subdued (506 B.C.) by Athens, and was an important trading and colonizing center. Isaeus the orator and Lycophron the poet were born in Chalcis, and Aristotle died here in 322 B.C.

Chalinitis (kal-i-nī′tis). Epithet of Athena, meaning "Bridler." She is credited with having invented the bridle, and assisted Bellerophon in his attack against the Chimaera by bridling the winged horse Pegasus and giving him to Bellerophon. There was a temple of Athena Chalinitis near the tomb of Medea's children in Corinth.

Chalybes (kal′i-bēz). A people of Pontus, near the Euxine Sea. They were noted as ironworkers, living entirely from the work of their forges. Jason and the Argonauts sailed by their land on their way to Colchis. The Chalybes were subdued by Croesus.

Chamyne (kam′i-nē). Epithet of Demeter. There was a sanctuary of Demeter Chamyne at Olympia. The priestess of Demeter Chamyne at Olympia had a marble altar from which she could watch the Games. Some say the name *Chamyne* was given to this sanctuary at Olympia because here the earth opened (*chainein*) for the chariot of Hades to emerge, and closed (*mysai*) to swallow up the chariot when Hades had seized Persephone. Others say the name comes from a man, Chamynus, who was put to death by a tyrant of Pisa, and whose property was used to build the sanctuary.

Chaon (kā′on). Named in the *Aeneid* as a brother of Helenus of Troy. Helenus accidentally killed him while hunting, and to commemorate his name Helenus named a part of his country, which he ruled in Epirus after the Trojan War, Chaonia.

Chaos (kā′os). In Greek mythology, the original formless state of the universe; or, the diety presiding over it. Perhaps no other myth exhibits quite so much confusion and variety as are found in the concepts of Chaos. The one thing common to all versions was the idea of infinite space in which matter existed without form and in complete darkness; to some of the ancient poets, this was Chaos, and alone existed, but others said that Earth and Eros were coeval with Chaos. In some cosmogonies, the first of all things was Chronos (Time), from whom proceeded Chaos and Aether (Light, or the upper air). But in another formulation, Chaos was the deity presiding over the formless mass with his wife Nyx (Night). Their son Erebus (Darkness) slew or dethroned Chaos and married his mother; from this union came Aether and Hemera (Day), who with the aid of their son Eros (Love) created Pontus (the Sea) and Gaea (the Earth). But in other accounts, Gaea proceeded directly from Chaos, and was the mother of Eros as well as of Tartarus (the Nether World).

Chares (kā′rēz, kär′ēz). Athenian general; died after 332 B.C. In 357 B.C. he captured Sestus in the Chersonesus, put the inhabitants to the sword, and regained the Chersonesus for Athens. In the same year he was sent to put down a revolt of the Athenian ally Chios with Chabrias as his co-general. Chabrias was killed in attempting to force a landing. Chares withdrew but later returned, sharing the command with two admirals. They refused to support his plan for attacking Chios. He attacked without them and was driven off with loss. He accused them of treachery; they were tried on a charge of bribery and Chares was vindicated. As sole commander, he now went to Asia Minor to subdue the revolting Athenian allies. In Asia he helped a rebellious satrap of the Persian king to a brilliant victory (355 B.C.) and was rewarded by the grateful satrap with the money he urgently needed to maintain his army. But the Persian king made strong representations against the Athenians for helping his satrap in a rebellion. Peace was made (354 B.C.) between Athens and her revolting allies, and Chares was recalled. He went next (349 B.C.), to help the Phocians against Philip II of Macedon, but accomplished little. In 340 B.C. he was sent to aid Byzantium to resist a siege by Philip. The Byzantines, mindful of his ruthlessness at Sestus, refused to receive him in their city. He was one of three Athenian commanders at the Battle of Chaeronea (338 B.C.) in which the Greeks were overwhelmed by Philip. After Alexander the Great conquered Thebes, he demanded the surrender of Chares, but the latter fled to the east and, some say, entered the service of the Persian king, Darius III.

Chares. Rhodian sculptor, born at Lindus, Rhodes; active c292–c280 B.C. He is noted as the creator of the Colossus of Rhodes. He was a pupil of Lysippus and is considered the founder of the Rhodian school. The Colossus of Rhodes was made to commemorate the successful defense of that place against Demetrius I (Demetrius Poliorcetes) in 305 and 304 B.C. It required 12 years for its completion, and was probably finished before 280 B.C. Representing the Rhodian sun-god, Helius, it was over 105 feet high, and was considered one of the seven wonders of the ancient world. Its cost is said to have been defrayed from the engines of war which Demetrius was obliged to abandon.

Chariclo (ka-rik′lō). A nymph who was dear to Athena and accompanied the goddess everywhere. She was the mother by Everes of Tiresias the seer. Athena blinded Tiresias, according to some accounts, because he had inadvertently surprised the goddess while she was bathing in the Hippocrene Spring with Chariclo. Chariclo reproached the goddess for blinding her son, at that time only seven years old. Athena could not restore the sight she had taken away, but in answer to Chariclo's plea gave Tiresias long life and the gift of understanding the prophetic birds, or the power of prophecy and divination.

Charidemus (ka-ri-dē′mus). Greek mercenary captain; executed 333 B.C. He served under the Athenian general Timotheus in an unsuccessful attempt to recapture the city of Amphipolis (364–362 B.C.). After being dismissed by Timotheus, he went over to the Thracian king Cotys, one of whose daughters he married, and opposed the Athenians. After the murder of Cotys, he became the chief minister of his son, Cersobleptes, and defeated an Athenian fleet that was sent to take over the Chersonesus (c359 B.C.). When the Chersonesus was at length retaken by the Athenians (357 B.C.), Charidemus was able so to twist the appearance of his activities that the Athenians not only again invited him to serve them but honored him as well. In following years he commanded Athenians against Philip II of Macedon, who had now won control over large parts of Thrace, but without great success. He was one of those whose surrender Alexander the Great demanded after his capture and destruction of Thebes. He escaped and fled to Darius III, king of Persia, whom he served as a mercenary. According to some accounts, he was put to death by the Persians (333 B.C.) for insubordination concerning the preparation Darius was making to meet Alexander the Great before the battle of Issus.

Charila (kar′i-lạ). According to Plutarch, a maiden of Delphi. Delphi was afflicted by a famine. The people went to the gates of the king's palace with their wives and children as suppliants. The king gave grain and oil to the noblest of the suppliants, as there was not enough to go around. Among the suppliants was a young orphan girl. When she appealed to the king, he struck her with his shoe and then hurled it in her face. Humiliated, the child went off into the woods and hanged herself. Afterward pestilence was added to the famine that afflicted Delphi. The Delphians consulted the oracle and learned that they must appease the shade of Charila, a maiden who died by her own hand. No one knew who Charila was at first, but after some time it was discovered that she was the child into whose face the king had flung his shoe and who subsequently hanged herself. A ceremony of appeasement was enacted in which the king distributed the grain to the people as before. An image of Charila was brought before him and was struck by the king's shoe. The leader of the Thyiades then took the image and hanged it in a cavern. Afterward, the image was cut down and buried where the child Charila was buried. This ceremony of appeasement was performed by the Delphians every nine years.

Charillus (kar-il′us) or **Charilaüs** (kar-i-lā′us). A Spartan king of the Eurypontid house. He was the son of Polydectes and the father of Nicander. In his time he devastated Argolis. Then the Spartans wished to conquer Arcadia and went to consult the oracle at Delphi on the matter. Persuaded by a deceptive oracle, they attacked Tegea. The reply that the priestess had given them was as follows:

"Cravest thou Arcady: Bold is thy craving.
  I shall not content it.
Yet I do not begrudge thee:
I will give thee Tegea to beat with the feet
  in dance,

And the fair plain thereof to measure off
  with line."

Feeling that he had the sanction of the oracle, Charillus attacked. While the men of Tegea fought valiantly, the women armed themselves and lay in ambush under a hill, called afterward Phylactris (*Sentry Hill*). In the midst of the battle the women rushed out and put the Lacedaemonians to flight. Charillus himself was taken prisoner, but was freed without ransom on his pledge never again to attack Tegea. The Spartans who were taken captive were bound in the fetters that they had brought with them to bind the Tegeans, and fulfilled the oracle of Delphi when they were forced to measure the plain of Tegea as they tilled it as slaves. The Tegeans later dedicated the fetters in the temple of Athena Alea.

Charis (kā′ris). According to Homer, one of the Graces and the wife of Hephaestus.

Charites (kar′i-tēz). The Greek name for the Graces, goddesses of the beauty, brightness, and joy in nature and humanity. Some say they are the daughters of Helius and Aegle, a naiad. Others say they are the daughters of Zeus and Eurynome. Their most familiar names are Aglaia (Brilliance), Euphrosyne (Joy), and Thalia (the Bloom of Life). The Charites are associated with the Muses, with whom they dwell on Mount Olympus, as the inspiration for music, poetry, the arts of painting and sculpture, beauty and knowledge. They are also associated particularly with Aphrodite, Eros, and Dionysus. Their shrine at Orchomenus in Boeotia, where they were worshiped with Aphrodite and Dionysus, was said to be the oldest there. In it were ancient stone images, said to have fallen from heaven. In Athens, where only two graces, Auxo (Increase) and Hegemone (Queen), were recognized, the Athenian youths, on first receiving their shields and spears, swore by these goddesses to be loyal to their country. The Charites were worshiped in Athens, Sparta (where also only two were recognized), Messene, and elsewhere in Greece.

Chariton of Aphrodisias (kar′i-ton; af-rō-diz′i-as). [Also **Chariton Aphrodisiensis**.] Greek novelist who flourished c2nd century A.D. He was the author, probably under an assumed name, of the well-constructed and naturally-expressed romance of *Chaereas and Callirrhoë* (q.v.).

Charmides (kär′mi-dēz). Dialogue of Plato, the narration by Socrates of a conversation on the subject of temperance (moderation or practical wisdom) between himself, Charmides (a beautiful youth renowned for his moderation), Critias, and Chaerephon, which took place at Athens at the Palaestra of Taureas near the porch of the King Archon immediately after the battle of Potidaea, from which Socrates had just returned. Charmides was an Athenian, son of Glaucon, cousin of Critias, and uncle of Plato.

CHARON RECEIVING A DEAD SOUL FROM HERMES
Attic lecythus, early 4th century B.C. *Munich*

Charon (kār′on). In Greek mythology, a son of Erebus. He is the ferryman who transports the souls of the dead (but only of those who have been properly buried) across the river Styx to the Underworld. His fee is an obolus or other coin, and this is placed for him in the mouth of the dead at the time of burial. Few have passed Charon in defiance of the rules concerning proper burial. Orpheus so charmed him that he was ferried over; Heracles terrified him into taking him across; and Aeneas bribed him with the Golden Bough. There were, however, several back entrances to the Underworld, and by using these Charon and his fee could be avoided.

Charon. Greek chronicler of Lampsacus, active in the middle of the 5th century B.C. He wrote about his own town, about Persian and Ethiopian history, voyages beyond the Pillars of Heracles, and incidents in the life of Themistocles.

Charon. Theban patriot; fl. in the first half of the 4th century B.C. At great risk to himself he made his house available as a hiding place for Pelopidas, a Theban exile, and five of his colleagues. These had secretly returned to the city with the intention, which they successfully carried out, of ridding Thebes of its pro-Spartan polemarchs and their Spartan garrison (378 B.C.).

Charondas (ka-ron′das). Sicilian lawgiver, born at Catana, Sicily; active c500 B.C. He legislated for the cities of Chalcidian origin in Sicily and Italy.

Charops (kā′rops). An epithet of Heracles, meaning "With bright eyes." The Boeotians raised an image of Heracles Charops on Mount Laphystium in Boeotia, because they said that here Heracles ascended from Hades, dragging the hound Cerberus with him.

Charybdis (ka-rib′dis). In Greek mythology, a monster, the daughter of Gaea and Poseidon. Because of her greed Zeus struck her with his thunderbolt and hurled her into the sea near Sicily. There, three times a day she gulps in the waters and spews them out again. Odysseus twice narrowly escaped death passing by Charybdis. In later times Charybdis was identified as a whirlpool in the Straits of Messina.

Chatti or **Catti** (kat′ī). German tribe, a branch of the Suevi, first mentioned by Strabo. They originally occupied the Taunus region N of the Moenus (Main) River, but were assigned by Drusus to the old territory of the Sugambri further northward, back from the Rhenus (Rhine), in the region about the middle Visurgis (Weser) River. They took part in the rising under Civilis, and were afterward, down into the 3rd century A.D., in frequent conflict with the Romans. They were one of the most powerful of the German inland tribes. Two minor tribes of the Chatti, the Batavi and the Canninefates, were ultimately merged with the Salic Franks. Those left behind in the old territory became finally the Hessians, a name which first appears early in the 8th century A.D.

Chauci (kô′sī). German tribe, first mentioned by Strabo, in the region along the Mare Germanicum (North Sea), on both sides of the Visurgis (Weser) River from the Amisia

(Ems) River to the Albis (Elbe) River. Pliny divides them into "greater" and "lesser." They were brought by Drusus and Tiberius into subjection to the Romans. In the 3rd century A.D. they became part of the confederation of the Franks, and thereafter gradually lost their tribal identity in history.

Chelidon (ke-lī´don) or **Chelidonis** (-dō´nis). In Greek mythology, a daughter of Pandareus of Ephesus, and the sister of Aëdon. She was violated by her brother-in-law Polytechnus as he was escorting her on the journey from her father's house to Aëdon. Polytechnus disguised her as a slave and gave her to Aëdon, his wife. Chelidon revealed herself to her sister and helped her to punish Polytechnus. She was transformed into a swallow by Artemis. See **Aëdon.**

Chelone (ke-lō´nē). In Greek legend, a maiden who refused to attend the wedding of Zeus and Hera. To punish her, Hermes cast her house into a river and transformed Chelone into a turtle, which carries its house on its back.

Chelydorea (kel´´i-dō´rē-a). In ancient geography, a mountain in Arcadia, on the boundary between Pheneus in Arcadia and Pellene in Achaea. The inhabitants were mostly Achaeans. The mountain, near Mount Cyllene, the birthplace of Hermes, was said by some to be the place where Hermes found the tortoise from which he constructed the first lyre. The name Chelydorea means "Mountain of the flayed tortoise."

Chemmis (kem´is). [Also: **Panopolis;** modern **Akhmin.**] An ancient city on the right bank of the Nile, in Upper Egypt, between Asyut and Thebes. It was the seat of the cult of Ammon Chem. Chem was identified with Pan and the city was called Panopolis by the Greeks and Romans. According to legend, Perseus stopped in the city as he returned from Libya after securing the head of Medusa. There was a precinct sacred to Perseus in the city, and an image of him in the temple. The people of Chemmis declared, in the time of Herodotus, that Perseus often appeared to them. They said also that frequently a huge sandal belonging to Perseus was found, and on those occasions all Egypt prospered. The people of Chemmis claimed that Perseus himself had ordered them to establish the festival in his honor which they celebrated annually in the Greek manner with games and other contests. This honoring of Perseus was all the more unusual in that the Egyptians were decidedly averse to adopting the customs of other nations, and were especially hostile to Greek customs. It was accounted for by their belief that Perseus was of Egyptian origin through his ancestor Danaus, who was said to have been native to Chemmis before he fled with his daughters to Argos.

Chersiphron (kėr´si-fron). Cretan architect, born at Cnossus, Crete, active c576 B.C. He is traditionally considered the designer of the first Artemisum (temple of Artemis) at Ephesus. He was associated with his son Metagenes, and with Theodorus. The Artemisium was more than 100 years in building, and was finished c456 B.C. It was later destroyed by fire, and rebuilt about the time of Alexander the Great by Dinocrates; this building, usually called the Temple of Diana of Ephesus, was one of the seven wonders of the ancient world.

Chersonesus (kėr-so-nē´sus). [Also: **Chersonese.**] Ancient Greek word for peninsula, specifically applied to the following: 1) Chersonesus Aurea, the modern Malay Peninsula. 2) Chersonesus Cimbrica, the modern peninsula of Jutland, Denmark. 3) Chersonesus Taurica or Scythica, the modern Crimea, U.S.S.R. 4) Chersonesus Thracica, the modern Gallipoli Peninsula, between the Hellespont and the Gulf of Saros.

Chersonesus. [Also: **Cherson, Chersonesus Heracleotica.**] Ancient city situated on the SW tip of the Crimean Peninsula, near what is now Sevastopol, founded by the Ionians at the beginning of the 5th century B.C. Because of its situation, it soon became an important trading city-state. Alliance with the kingdom of Cimmerian Bosporus was followed by subjection to the Roman Empire. It is archaeologically of interest, containing the remains of city walls and towers of the Byzantine era, foundations of some private dwellings, and foundations of basilicas, with mosaic floors and traces of frescoes. Many old Greek inscriptions were found here, and the necropolis contains numerous objects of the Greco-Roman and Byzantine periods. Some traces of a neolithic culture have been found here.

Cherusci (ke-rus'ĭ). German tribe, in the time of Caesar, dwelling about the middle Visurgis (Weser) River in territory extending as far E as the Albis (Elbe) River. They were subjugated to the Romans by Drusus Germanicus and Tiberius, but rose (9 A.D.) against Varus under the leadership of their own countryman, Arminius. In the time (c100 A.D.) of Tacitus they had sunk into comparative unimportance. They are thought to have become ultimately a constituent part of the Saxons.

Children of Heracles, The (Heraclidae). A drama by Euripides, produced about 430 B.C. It is concerned with the war which Athens undertook to protect the rights of suppliants, the noble sacrifice which the gods required as the price of victory, the gift of rejuvenation to an aged warrior, and the vengeance claimed by Alcmene, the mother of Heracles. The scene is a court in the temple of Zeus to which the children of Heracles, accompanied by their father's faithful friend, Iolaus, have come as suppliants. Eurystheus, their father's enemy, has ordered them banished from all the cities of Hellas. In despair they have sought sanctuary at Marathon, a dependency of Athens. Copreus, herald of Eurystheus, enters the court. He knocks down Iolaus and seizes the children to take them to his master. Iolaus, now a very aged man, calls for help. A chorus of old men of Marathon enters and hears the story of the persecutions with which Eurystheus has harried the children of Heracles. The chorus tells the herald that suppliants at an altar cannot be surrendered. Demophon, son of Theseus, now appears and hears the story. To his charge that Copreus, though dressed as a Greek, must be a barbarian, Copreus answers arrogantly, naming his land, his king, and his errand—to seize the children of Heracles. He threatens Athens with war if the Heraclidae are not surrendered. Iolaus appeals to the pride of Athens; if the city is really free, it will not bow to the demands of Eurystheus. He reminds Demophon of the kinship between the sons of Theseus and the sons of Heracles, and recalls that Heracles rescued Theseus from Hades. He pleads with Demophon not to disgrace Athens by surrendering them to Eurystheus. Demophon cites these very

remarks as reasons why he will refuse the demands of Eurystheus and sends Copreus back to his master, scorning his threats of war. In thanking Demophon, Iolaus says noble birth makes noble men, and adds that in all Hellas only Demophon has dared defy Eurystheus and protect the Heraclidae. The chorus states that Athens has always been a friend to the helpless, even if it means war, as it will in this case. Demophon departs to gather his forces.

As Iolaus and the Heraclidae wait at the altar, Demophon returns. All is in readiness. The forces of Eurystheus have appeared on the plain. But Demophon is troubled: an oracle has told him that Athens will be victorious in the war only if a highborn maiden is sacrificed. He would do almost anything for the children of Heracles, but he is not willing to sacrifice his daughter, nor is he willing to ask another to make a sacrifice which he will not make. His city is on the verge of civil war, one faction insisting on war to protect the rights of suppliants, and the other fearing disaster without the sacrifice and insisting on peace. Iolaus understands the position of Demophon but he finds this fresh disappointment too heavy to bear just when he thought they were safe. He volunteers to go as a captive to Eurystheus. But Demophon tells him that Eurystheus is not interested in the capture of an old man, he wants to annihilate the descendants of Heracles.

In the midst of this discussion Macaria, daughter of Heracles, comes from the temple. She learns of the oracle and immediately offers herself. It would be cowardly and unjust, she says, to seek the assistance of Athens, and then to expect Athens to risk defeat because one was unwilling to carry out the instructions of the oracle. To Iolaus' suggestion that lots be drawn, she has a proud answer: she will die of her own free will and choice and not as a plaything of chance. She bids goodby to Iolaus and her brothers and leaves to be sacrificed.

Presently a messenger from Hyllus, Heracles' oldest son, comes with good tidings. Alcmene, mother of Heracles, comes from the temple to hear the news. When Iolaus learns that Hyllus has arrived with an army, he announces that he will join the army.

The others think he is joking, but he persists and arms himself with weapons taken from the temple (as Heracles had done so many years before at Thebes). Alcmene and the chorus try to dissuade him, it is madness for a weak old man to think of going to war. Iolaus pays no attention, he arms himself, prays, listens to the chorus pray for success in the war to defend the right of sanctuary, and departs.

Soon a servant comes to tell Alcmene that the Athenians have won and Iolaus has fought gloriously. Hyllus had offered to settle the war by a duel but Eurystheus was afraid to meet him. Both armies were engaged. Iolaus jumped into a chariot and pursued Eurystheus, praying to the gods for one day of youthful prowess. In answer two stars lit on the yoke of his chariot and threw him into shadow. When the shadow lifted, Iolaus had become young again. He overtook Eurystheus, captured and bound him, and is even now bringing him into the city. Alcmene asks why Iolaus had not slain Eurystheus. Because, the servant replies, he wanted to bring Eurystheus to her. In her joy Alcmene frees the servant who has brought her the good news. Now Iolaus enters with Eurystheus. Alcmene is to have the privilege of deciding his fate. She tells him that in Athens he found free men and a free city who feared him not. To fight Athens was a different matter from fighting against an old woman and helpless children, and now he must die. The chorus objects to her sentence of death; no one who has been captured in war can be killed. But Eurystheus interrupts. He is not afraid. He acted only at the instigation of Hera. It was the goddess who caused him to torment Heracles and his children after him. Alcmene is implacable. She orders the death of Eurystheus and frees Athens of the blood-guilt by assuming it herself.

Chilon (kī′lon) or **Chilo** (kī′lō). Spartan sage; fl. in the first part of the 6th century B.C.; noted as one of the Seven Sages of Greece. He was ephor eponymus at Sparta in 556 B.C. and is said to have died of joy caused by the victory of his son in boxing at the Olympic Games.

Chimaera (kī-mē′ra̧, ki-). In Greek mythology, a fire-breathing monster of divine origin. It had the head of a lion, the body of a goat, and the tail of a serpent. It dwelt in Lycia and was slain by Bellerophon. Hesiod says it was the offspring of Echidna and Typhon and described it as having three heads: a lion's, a goat's and a serpent's. It was supposed by the ancients to represent a volcanic mountain of the same name in Lycia, the top of which was said to be the home of lions, the middle that of goats, and the foot that of serpents.

CHIMAERA
Proto-Corinthian lecythus, 675–640 B.C.
Museum of Fine Arts, Boston

Chione (kī′ō̧-nē). In Greek mythology, a daughter of Boreas and Orithyia, and the mother, by Poseidon, of Eumolpus. Fearing her father's anger, she cast her infant son into the sea. He was rescued by Poseidon and washed ashore on the coasts of Ethiopia.

Chione. In Greek mythology, a beautiful daughter of Daedalion. She won the love of Apollo and Hermes, who both visited her on the same night. By them she was the mother of twin sons; Apollo was the father of Philammon and Hermes was the father of Autolycus. Chione boasted that she was as beautiful as Artemis, and was slain by the goddess for her arrogance.

Chionides (kī-on′i-dēz). One of the earliest (early 5th century B.C.) writers and founders of Attic comedy.

Chios (kī′os). [Also: **Khios**; Italian, **Scio**; Turkish, **Saki-Adasi**, **Saki-Adassi**.] Greek island in the Aegean Sea, situated W of

Asia Minor. It is 30 miles long and has an area of 355 square miles. The surface is hilly and rocky. The island has been noted in ancient and modern times for wine and fruit. The inhabitants are mostly Greeks. According to legend, the island was named for a son of Poseidon, who seduced a nymph here. When the time came for her to bear her child, snow (*chion*) fell. Poseidon named his son Chios, and from him the island took its name. Oenopion and his sons sailed to Chios from Crete and settled there. Orion the mighty hunter was said to have fallen in love with his daughter and to have slain all the wild beasts of the island for her sake. But Oenopion refused to fulfill his promise and give Orion his daughter in marriage. Instead, he got him drunk and blinded him. It was from Chios that Orion set out for the East to recover his sight. In later times, Carians and Abantes from Euboea settled in the island. In the 6th century B.C. it came under Persian rule and revolted against Persian rule at the beginning of the 5th century B.C. In 494 B.C. the Chians, deserted by their Samian and Lesbian allies, fought with splendid valor against the Phoenician fleet that had come to the siege of Miletus, but were forced to withdraw, after inflicting great damage on the enemy ships and losing many of their own. After the Persian War Chios joined the Confederacy of Delos but revolted in 413 B.C. and was laid waste by the Athenians. Chios was noted in the ancient world as a center of art and literature, particularly for its school of epic poets.

Chios. [Also: **Kastro, Khios;** Italian, **Scio.**] Chief city of the island of Chios, E Greece, situated on the E coast. It is one of seven cities which claimed to be the birthplace of Homer.

Chiron or **Cheiron** (kī′ron). In Greek mythology, a wise and just centaur, the friend and teacher of many of the heroes of Greece, and renowned for his powers of healing and prophecy as well as for his skill in hunting and music. In his gentle and beneficent qualities he was the direct opposite of his wild and unruly brothers. Some say Cronus consorting with Philyra on a tiny island which afterward bore her name, was surprised by Rhea. He transformed himself into a stallion.

The child which Philyra subsequently bore was half-man and half-horse, the kindly centaur Chiron. Others say that Zeus was Chiron's father. But still others say that he was a descendant of Ixion, who fathered Centaurus on the cloud Nephele. Centaurus in his turn fathered the race of centaurs on mares and Chiron, the king of the centaurs, was one of these. Many instances are recorded of Chiron's kindness to and friendship for men. He saved Peleus when he was abandoned by Acastus and attacked by centaurs; he told Peleus how he could capture the sea-goddess Thetis by holding fast to her no matter what transformations she might assume to escape his embrace. Peleus, successful, was married to Thetis in Chiron's cave on Mount Pelion; Chiron gave him an

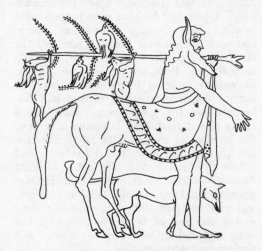

CHIRON
Black-figured Greek amphora.

ashen spear for a wedding gift, which was afterward used by Achilles at Troy. When Thetis deserted Peleus, he gave his infant son Achilles into Chiron's charge, and the centaur reared him. He taught Achilles to ride and hunt, and instructed him in the arts of healing. Later, he is said to have restored the sight of Phoenix, who became Achilles' tutor and second father. He reared and instructed Jason and, some say, his son by Medea, Medeus. Others he nurtured were Asclepius, who excelled his teacher in

fat, fāte, fär, fãre, errạnt; net, mē, hẽr ardẹnt; pin, pīne; not, nōte, möve, nôr, the art of healing, Castor and Polydeuces, and Actaeon. When the centaurs were driven away from Mount Pelion by the Lapiths, Chiron went to Malea and dwelt in a cave there. Hither his friend Heracles pursued the centaurs who had attacked him in Pholoë. By accident, one of Heracles' poisoned arrows pierced Chiron's leg. Heracles immediately withdrew it but nothing could heal the wound. Chiron suffered unbearably, and could not be released from his sufferings by death as he was immortal. Zeus, at the plea of Heracles, offered to release Prometheus from his chains on the rock if he could find someone to take his place in Tartarus. Chiron offered his immortality to Prometheus and went to Tartarus in his stead, and won release from his suffering at last. Zeus set his image among the stars.

Chiusi (kyö′sē). See **Clusium**.

Chlidanope (klī″da̱-nō′pē). A naiad. According to mythology, she was the wife of the Lapith Hypseus and the mother of Cyrene.

Chloë (klō′ē̱). An epithet of Demeter, meaning "Green." There was a sanctuary of Demeter Chloë near the entrance to the Acropolis at Athens, whose priestess had a reserved seat in the theater of Dionysus and received certain allowances of meat, wheat, honey, oil, and firewood. At Myconus two sows (one of them pregnant) were sacrificed annually to Demeter Chloë, and in the spring all men joyfully sacrificed to her because of their joy at the sight of the green earth and the promise of new crops.

Chloris (klôr′is). In Greek legend, the wife of Neleus and the mother of his children. According to some accounts, she was the daughter of Amphion and Niobe, and was spared by timely supplication, when the other daughters of Niobe were slain by Artemis for Niobe's insult to Leto. Her name, according to these accounts, was Meliboea but she turned so pale with fear when her sisters were falling before the bow of Artemis that she was given the name Chloris. Some say Chloris was the first victor at the games established in honor of Hera by Hippodamia, wife of Pelops.

Choëphoroe (kō̱-ef′ō̱-rē), **The**, or **The Libation-Bearers**. A tragedy by Aeschylus, so named because of the chorus bearing vessels with offerings to the tomb of Agamemnon (the name literally meaning "bearers of a drink-offering," or "libation-bearers"). It is the second of a trilogy, known as the *Orestea*, with which Aeschylus won first prize in 458 B.C., and deals with the vengeance Orestes took on his mother, at the command of Apollo, for the murder of his father.

The scene is at the grave of Agamemnon outside the walls of Argos. Orestes and Pylades, his friend, stand near the burial mound. Orestes calls on Hermes, who guides dead men's souls below the earth, to hear his prayer and win the sanction of Agamemnon for the deed of vengeance he is about to undertake. He sees Electra approaching the grave, prays to Zeus to grant him vengeance, and withdraws to eavesdrop on Electra. She and a chorus of female servants enter. The chorus sings that it has been sent by Clytemnestra, who was frightened by a dream, to offer libations to appease Mother Earth, but they regard it as blasphemous for one who murdered her husband to command these rites, and predict that Justice will crush the evil-doers. Electra asks the women what she can say as she offers these false libations. They advise her to pray for all who hate Aegisthus, her mother's lover, reminding her that her brother Orestes is one of these. They tell her to pray for one to come and shed blood for the blood that has been shed by Clytemnestra and Aegisthus. Electra addresses her father's spirit. She asks aid for herself and for the exiled Orestes, and she calls for vengeance. The chorus joins in the prayer for an avenger. Electra notes that the wine she has poured on the earth has been absorbed. She further notices locks of hair left as an offering on her father's grave, and in great excitement decides that it must be from Orestes' head, as no one else would make such a sacrifice. She is certain Orestes has returned when she discovers footprints shaped like her own. At this Orestes and Pylades emerge from their hiding place. Orestes tells her that the prayers she has uttered are now about to be answered. He reveals himself as her longed-for brother. She doubts him and he chides her with being able to recognize his hair and footprints but not his person. She is convinced and welcomes him rapturously. Orestes invokes Zeus to help the "eagle's brood" avenge their

actǫr; up, lūte, pu̇ll; oi, oil; ou, out; ꜰʜ, then; ḍ as d or j, ş as s or sh, ṭ as t or ch, ẓ as z or zh.

dead father. He has been commanded by Apollo on pain of dire punishment if he disobeys, to shed blood for blood. Even if he cannot trust such oracles, Orestes says he must obey, and in addition free the proud citizens who conquered Troy from the slavery imposed by a woman, or two women, for Aegisthus is a weak woman in his eyes. Electra, Orestes, and the chorus alternately invoke the spirit of Agamemnon. Electra grieves for her father, his miserable death, and her own state as a virtual slave of her mother. Orestes prays to avenge his dishonored house and reclaim his inheritance. The chorus demands retaliation. All seek by prayers to rouse the dead, that the wrongs suffered by Agamemnon and his children may be righted with the blood of Clytemnestra and Aegisthus. They end by naming the curse that lies on the house of Atreus and demanding to know when the suffering will end. The chorus bids Orestes plan his course. Orestes agrees it is time to act, yet he wonders why his mother at this late date, seven years after his father's murder, has sent an offering to the grave of Agamemnon. The chorus tells him her act was inspired by a dream. She dreamed that she bore a serpent, lulled it in her bosom, and that it sucked blood from her breast. The terror of the dream compelled her to order the libations. Orestes prays the dream will come true; he is the snake she dreamed of and the dream commands that he must be her murderer. They make their plans and depart. The chorus sings of man's rash heart and stubborn will, of woman's desperate love and hate. They cite Althaea who caused her own son's death, Scylla who killed her father, and the Lemnian massacre, as examples of woman's wild passion when she is scorned, disfranchised and dispossessed by men.

The scene changes to the front of the palace. Orestes knocks at the door and calls out to be admitted. Clytemnestra comes and welcomes him. He tells her (she has not recognized him) that he is from Phocis and bears the message that Orestes is dead. Clytemnestra mourns, or seems to, at the news that her son is dead. She invites Orestes into the palace. The chorus gird themselves to help Orestes in any way they can. Presently an old nurse comes weeping from the palace and tells them Orestes is dead, and that she is on her way to fetch Aegisthus, who will hug himself for joy at the news. The chorus, who know she nursed Orestes as a baby and hates Aegisthus, tells her to instruct Aegisthus to come without his armed guard to the palace. The chorus then prays to the gods for help in the deed of vengeance, and call on Orestes not to be softened by his mother's prayers but to redeem the house of Atreus from the curse. Aegisthus approaches, speaks of the news, and asks if it is true that Orestes is dead. The chorus advises him to go into the palace and ask the man who brought the news himself. He goes in. Almost at once Aegisthus is heard to shriek. A servant rushes out and says Aegisthus is dead. Clytemnestra comes out. The servant tells her the dead have come to life to kill the living. Clytemnestra understands; she killed by craft and by craft she is to die. She calls for a weapon; the whole bitter story is about to reach its end, she says. Orestes strides out and tells her she is to die as Aegisthus died. She exerts her authority as a parent and orders her son to put down his sword. Orestes refuses and she appeals to him to spare the mother who gave him life. Orestes is shaken by her appeal but Pylades firmly reminds him of Apollo's command. Orestes agrees that he must kill her and rejects every claim Clytemnestra makes as a parent. He will be pursued by his father's curse if he relents, and so he does not fear his mother's curse. He drives her into the house. The chorus exults that Justice has at last triumphed. The scene changes. Orestes is shown standing over the bodies of Aegisthus and Clytemnestra. He exhibits the blood-stained, netlike robe in which Clytemnestra had entangled Agamemnon and then killed him. He calls the gods to view it so that when he goes on trial for murdering his mother, they will understand that he had to do it; it was she who planned the horrible crime of Agamemnon's murder and had made the robe to trap him. But he says his victory over his mother tortures him, pollutes his life. The chorus reminds him that no man can pass through life untouched by pain. He is afraid he is going mad; before he does, he wants to proclaim that it was no sin to kill his mother who was marked with his father's blood, and that he had acted on the command of Apollo. He will now depart to Apollo's shrine for refuge, as he had been told to do. The chorus does not understand his doubts and misgivings. He has set Argos free, they say, and should not fear that ill will come. But Orestes sees the Furies who have come to hound him for killing his mother, and with a cry of despair he rushes away. The chorus recalls the ancient curse, and says it has now struck three times: first, Thyestes' children were murdered, then Agamemnon, and now Orestes is pursued by the Furies. When will the fury of the curse be spent? The fate of Orestes is the subject of the third play of the trilogy, **Eumenides** (q.v.).

Choerilus (kē′ri-lus). Athenian tragic poet who flourished in the 6th century B.C. He was a contemporary of Aeschylus and Pratinas, and was most popular as a writer of satyr-plays.

Choerilus of Samos (sā′mos). Greek epic poet, born in Samos c470 B.C. He lived at Athens for a time, later was a member of the entourage of the Spartan general Lysander, and afterward went to the court of Archelaus in Macedon, where he died. Because he thought that the subjects of mythology and legend had been exhausted, he turned to poems on historical subjects. Like his friend Herodotus, he took the Persian invasion as his subject. His epic, *Perseis* or *Persica,* was the first historical epic.

Choerilus the Younger. Greek epic poet of little ability, of Caria (4th century B.C.), who celebrated the achievements of Alexander the Great. Alexander is said to have offered to pay him a gold coin for every good line he wrote about him, but this same story has been told of others. This Choerilus may be the grandson of Choerilus of Samos.

Chronicle of Paros (pār′os, pā′ros). Greek historical inscription found on the island of Paros, and now preserved among the Arundel marbles in the Ashmolean Museum at Oxford. It extended originally from the mythical reign of Cecrops, king of Athens, taken as c1581 B.C., to the archonship of Diogenetus, 264 B.C.; but the end is now lost, and the surviving part extends only to c354 B.C. The chronicle embraces an outline of Greek history, with special attention to festivals, poetry, and music. Political and military events are less carefully recorded, many of importance being omitted entirely. A second, similar marble, of later date and covering a subsequent period (c365–c299 B.C.) is in a museum on Paros.

Chrysaor (krī-sā′ôr, kris′ạ-ôr). In Greek mythology, a warrior who sprang fully grown from the body of Medusa when Perseus cut off her head. Poseidon was his father. Chrysaor was the father by Callirrhoë, daughter of Oceanus, of the three-headed Geryon and dwelt in Erythea. According to later accounts, Chrysaor was a king in Iberia who had three stalwart sons, symbolized in the three-headed Geryon.

Chryse (krī′sē). See **Comana.**

Chryseis (krī-sē′is). In Homeric legend (*Iliad*), a daughter of Chryses, priest of Apollo on the island of Sminthus. Known also as Astynome, she was taken captive by Achilles in the Trojan War and was awarded to Agamemnon as his share of the spoils. Apollo sent a plague of arrows against the Greeks because Agamemnon refused to accept a rich ransom for her from her father, and to appease the god Agamemnon sent her back to Chryses by Odysseus, although she was perfectly willing to remain where she was, according to later accounts. The return of Chryseis to her father caused the famous quarrel between Agamemnon and Achilles, for to make up for her loss Agamemnon took Achilles' captive, Briseis.

Chryses (krī′sēz). In Homeric legend (*Iliad*), a priest of Apollo on the island of Sminthus, and father of **Chryseis** (q.v.).

Chrysippus (krī-sip′us, kri-). In Greek legend, a bastard son of Pelops and the nymph Astyoche, a Danaid. Laius, king of Thebes, fell in love with the boy and carried him off to Thebes. Hera sent the Sphinx, a monster that devoured those who could not answer the riddle she propounded, to punish Thebes because its king had abducted Chrysippus. Hippodamia, wife of Pelops, killed Chrysippus, either alone or with the aid of her sons Atreus and Thyestes, because she feared that Pelops might leave his kingdom to him rather than to her own sons.

Chrysippus. Greek Stoic philosopher; born at Soli, Cilicia, c280 B.C.; died at Athens, c207 B.C. He was a disciple of Cleanthes, whom he succeeded as head of the Academy. He was considered, next to Zeno, who founded the Stoic school and who died in the early 3rd century B.C., the most eminent of the Stoic philosophers. He is said to have died from an immoderate fit of laughter on seeing an ass eating some figs destined for his (Chrysippus') own supper. (In one account, the sight of the ass solemnly eating human food so delighted him that he cried, "Give him a bumper of wine," to the old woman who was attending him, and thereupon sank, exhausted by his merriment, into death.)

Chrysopolis (kri-sop'ō̦-lis). In ancient geography, a city on the Bosporus, opposite Byzantium. From ancient times it was important as a center of traffic from the Euxine Sea. In the last years of the Peloponnesian War Athens seized it and set up a toll-station there at which ships coming from the Euxine had to pay a percentage of the value of their cargoes.

Chrysostom (kris'o̦s-to̦m, kri-sos'to̦m) or **Chrysostomus** (kri-sos'tō̦-mus), **Dio.** See **Dio Chrysostomus.**

Chrysothemis (kri-soth'e̦-mis). According to Homer and Sophocles, a daughter of Agamemnon and Clytemnestra. In the *Iliad*, Agamemnon offered her or either of her two sisters to Achilles as part of a rich peace offering if Achilles would forget his quarrel with Agamemnon and take up his arms again to help the Greeks defeat the Trojans. When Agamemnon returned from Troy and was murdered by his wife and Aegisthus, Chrysothemis and her sister Electra remained in their mother's house. She shared Electra's hatred of Clytemnestra and Aegisthus, but felt that she was helpless to do anything about it and accepted her fate with resignation. She urged Electra to refrain from publicly accusing their mother and Aegisthus of being murderous adulterers and to make the best of her lot. She thought Electra's desire for vengeance for her father's death was mad and refused to help Electra kill Aegisthus on the ground that she was only a weak woman, who would rather be miserable and alive than heroic and dead.

Chrysothemis. According to some accounts, a son of Carmanor, the Cretan who purified Apollo for the murder of Pytho. According to tradition, Chrysothemis was the first winner of the musical contests held in what later became the Pythian Games at Delphi.

Chthonia (thō̦'ni-a̦). In Greek legend, one of the seven daughters of Erechtheus, king of Athens, and his wife Praxithea. She married her uncle, Butes.

Chthonia. Epithet of Demeter, meaning "Of the Lower World." Some say the sanctuary of Demeter Chthonia at Hermion was founded by Clymenus and Chthonia, the children of Phoroneus. But the Argives told a different story. They said that when Demeter came to Argos in her search for her daughter, some welcomed her, but Colontas did not receive her or pay her any mark of respect. His daughter, Chthonia, rebuked her father for his conduct, but he ignored her. Colontas was punished for his presumption but Chthonia was spared. Demeter took her to Hermion and there she founded the sanctuary of Demeter Chthonia. At the annual festival that had the same name, Chthonia, there was a great procession. First came the priests, next the civil officers, then the townspeople, followed by children dressed in white and wearing wreaths made of the iris. The iris, marked with the letters of mourning, commemorated Demeter's grief when she lost Persephone. When the procession arrived at the temple, four cows in succession were driven into the temple; there they were killed by four elderly women. But, according to Pausanias, the thing they worshiped most in the temple had never been seen by any man. Demeter Chthonia was also widely worshiped by the Spartans.

Chthonius (thō̦'ni-us). One of the Sparti who sprang from the earth when Cadmus sowed the dragon's teeth. His name means "Sprung from the earth." See **Sparti.**

Chthonius. Epithet of Zeus, meaning "Of the Lower World." Under this epithet the powers and functions of Zeus extended to the death of vegetation and its renewal from the lower world. Among other places, there were altars of Zeus Chthonius at Olympia and Corinth.

Cibalis (sib'a̦-lis). [Also: **Cibalae** (-lē).] In ancient geography, a town in Pannonia, near what is now Osijek in Yugoslavia. Here Constantine defeated Licinius (314 A.D.).

Cibyra (sib'i-ra̦). [Called **Cibyra Magna** (mag'na̦).] In ancient geography, a town in Phrygia, Asia Minor, near the site of the Turkish village of Korzum, about 65 miles NW of Antalya. It was surnamed "Magna" to distinguish it from a smaller town of the same name in Pamphylia. Its ruins comprise an odeum, 175 feet in diameter, with 13 tiers of seats visible above ground. The front wall is noteworthy, and is practically complete; it has five arched doorways between two square ones. There are also an ancient theater of some size and considerable interest, and a stadium, in part excavated from a hillside. There are 21 tiers of seats in marble, which remain in place around the curved end. There was a monumental entrance, consisting of three lofty arches.

Cicero (sis′e-rō), **Marcus Tullius.** [Formerly called **Tully.**] Roman orator, philosopher, and statesman; born at Arpinum, Italy, Jan. 3, 106 B.C.; assassinated near Formiae, Italy, Dec. 7, 43 B.C. He was the son of Marcus Tullius Cicero and Helvia. His father, a member of the equestrian order and a man of comfortable means, wished to give his sons a sound education, and to that end took young Marcus and his younger brother Quintus Tullius (102–43 B.C.) to Rome. There Cicero came into contact with some of the foremost intellects of the time: the poet Archias of Antioch who, according to Cicero, gave him a love for literature; the celebrated orators Lucius Licinius Crassus (140–91 B.C.) and Marcus Antonius (143–87 B.C., grandfather of the triumvir), who interested him in oratory and a legal career; the noted jurists Quintus Mucius Scaevola the Augur (c159–c88 B.C.) and Quintus Mucius Scaevola the Pontifex Maximus (died 82 B.C.); the philosophers Diodotus the Stoic, Phaedrus the Epicurean, and Philo of Larissa, who was head of the Academy; and the rhetorician Molo of Rhodes. In the course of a two-year journey (79–77 B.C.) which he took for his never robust health, he went to Athens where he attended the lectures of Antiochus of Ascalon, to Rhodes, where he heard Posidonius the Stoic, and once more studied with Molo. That master chided him for his florid style. Cicero took his comments to heart, pruned the excesses of which Molo complained, and thereafter assiduously cultivated the style that made his the classic pattern of oratory. Before returning to Rome

he visited Asia Minor, where he heard the lectures of the Greek rhetorician and historian, Dionysius of Halicarnassus, and those of Menippus of Gadara, the Cynic. Some time before 68 B.C. he met Pomponius Atticus who became his lifelong friend and confidant, and the recipient of many revealing letters.

Earlier, Cicero had fulfilled his military service in the Marsic War (89 B.C.), under Pompeius Strabo and Sulla. He had also delivered (81) his earliest extant oration, *Pro Quinctio* (For Quinctius). In 80 he had defended Sextus Roscius (*Pro Sextus Roscio*) on a trumped-up charge of murdering his father. To defend Roscius and oppose Chrysogonus (a favorite of Sulla) took courage on Cicero's part, as Sulla was dictator at the time. He won his case and shortly after (79) went on the journey for his health, not entirely, as it was sometimes said, to escape Sulla's possibly wrathful notice. When he returned to Rome (77) he married Terentia, a strong-willed woman who subsequently bore him his beloved daughter Tullia (c76–45 B.C.) and a son Marcus (born 65 B.C.). In 75 he went to Lilybaeum in Sicily as quaestor and won admiration there for honest and conscientious administration of his office —a rare experience for Sicilians under Roman officials. The following year he entered the Senate and energetically embarked on his legal career in Rome. In 70 he was asked to lead the prosecution of Verres, who as governor of Sicily had ravaged that province for three years. Hortensius, the most famous orator in Rome at the time, defended Verres. Cicero marshaled such testimony in the first action (*In Verrem*) against Verres that the latter decided to go into voluntary exile. The material prepared for the second action against Verres was not delivered, but was subsequently published in five parts by Cicero. He was curule aedile (69) and praetor (66). As praetor he favored (*De Lege Manilia,* For the Manilian Law), the proposal by the tribune Caius Manilius to give Pompey vast power as general in command of the Mithridatic War. His argument dealt less with the constitutional questions posed in awarding such great power to one man than with the virtues and qualities of Pompey, among which he named the good luck with which Pompey seemed to be blessed.

Devoted to the principles of the Republic and the maintenance of order, Cicero's natural sympathies were with the *optimates* (the aristocratic and conservative party). However, he was regarded with some hostility by them as a "new man," and had won influence with the *populares* (popular party) by his victory in the prosecution of Verres. Seeking the consulship, he wavered for a time between the two, but when, with the help of the optimates he defeated Catiline and became consul (63), his loyalty to the optimates never thereafter failed. As consul he was at the height of his power and influence. But in this turbulent period between civil wars the cause for which he lived, and ultimately died, was already almost lost. The great days of the Republic, which in any event existed only in an idealized version in his mind, were irretrievably lost. He delivered three speeches, *Contra Rullum* (Against Rullus) or *De Lege Agraria* (On the Agrarian Law), against a proposal by the tribune Servilius Rullus, who sought to win popularity by a distribution of land to the poor. The proposal lost, and Cicero lost favor with the populares. He defended the agéd Rabirius (*Pro Rabirio*), who was charged with having illegally put to death Saturninus in 100 B.C. This old charge was revived to warn those in authority against dealing summarily, as Rabirius had done, with suspected rebels. Rabirius was not acquitted, but after some complicated maneuvering went free, and Cicero shortly proceeded to ignore the warning presented by the charge against Rabirius. The most dramatic episode of his consulship was his discovery, energetic exposure, and suppression of the Catilinarian conspiracy. Catiline, a renegade aristocrat, plotted to overthrow the government, and kill the most prominent men of Rome, including Cicero. The night of Nov. 7, 63, was fixed for the murder of Cicero. He learned of the plot, as he had of other intrigues by Catiline, and took steps to protect himself. On Nov. 8 he rose in the Senate, in the presence of Catiline himself, and delivered the first of four orations *In Catilinam* (Against Catiline). He accused him, and urged him and his followers to

withdraw, that Rome might be relieved of the fear that had gripped it since Catiline first organized his band of rebels and rumors of his intentions had got abroad. Cicero noted that it was once considered virtuous for patriotic men to punish a traitorous citizen even more harshly than a foreign foe. However, he sought the withdrawal of Catiline with his followers lest the well-deserved execution of the latter leave embers which his supporters, if still in the city, might fan to a conflagration of revolt at a later time. Catiline fled to Etruria that same night. On Nov. 9 Cicero delivered the second oration to a tremendous gathering, in order to quiet the fears which the flight of Catiline to his camp outside Rome had aroused. On Dec. 2 it was learned from the Allobroges, with whom Catiline was conspiring to attack Rome, that Catiline meant to strike on Dec. 19. The third oration, in which these plans were exposed, was delivered, Dec. 3, to another huge crowd. Some of the conspirators, not including Catiline, were seized. The fourth oration, in which Cicero favored the death penalty for the conspirators, was delivered before the Senate on Dec. 5. Subsequently, they were put to death without trial, and early in the next year Catiline and his followers were destroyed in battle. Although he was given the title *pater patriae* for his services, on leaving the consulship Cicero was increasingly subject to attack. He prosecuted (61) Clodius Pulcher on a charge of impiety: that of invading the ceremony of the *Bona Dea* (a sacred festival from which men were excluded) disguised as a woman. Clodius was acquitted and became Cicero's mortal enemy. Amid rising disorder, Caesar and Pompey approached him and invited him to join a secret coalition to control Rome. After great hesitation, he refused (Dec., 60) and opposed them. In 58 Clodius, who was tribune, proposed a law that any Roman who had put citizens to death without trial should be outlawed. This was directly aimed at Cicero, for his part in the death of the Catilinarian conspirators. Having put himself at odds with Pompey and Caesar, they now left him to his fate at Clodius' hands, and he went into exile at Thessalonica. His property in Rome was seized and destroyed; the site of his house was consecrated to Liberty by Clodius. The next year he was recalled to Rome and was greatly honored. However, he was out of favor with the Triumvirate (formed 60 B.C., by Caesar, Pompey, and Crassus), and so played small part in political affairs. Instead, he occupied himself with his legal career and with literary pursuits. In 53 he was elected augur; in 51 he was made proconsul of Cilicia. Although he had not wanted a province, he carried out his office efficiently and honestly, put down a revolt in Cappadocia, and waged successful war on the tribes of Mount Amanus. By 50, when he returned to Rome, the differences between Caesar and Pompey made civil war inevitable. After great vacillation, for Cicero recognized the vigor and qualities of Caesar, he elected to join Pompey in Greece. Following the latter's defeat by Caesar at Pharsalus (48), Cicero, who had not taken part in the battle because of illness, abandoned Pompey and went to Brundisium, where he waited a year for Caesar's forgiveness. When it came he returned to Rome, was generously treated by Caesar but kept apart from public affairs. Private sorrows occupied him. He divorced Terentia (46), made a disastrous marriage with his young and wealthy ward, and lost his beloved daughter Tullia (45). In this period he consoled himself with literary work and the study of philosophy.

The murder of Caesar (March 15, 44 B.C.) brought him once more from retirement. His great aim was to restore order and to bring about a reconciliation between the rival factions. To this end he secured an amnesty for the conspirators. However, the intrigues of Caesar's partisans caused him to leave Rome. He was recalled, and began to express his intense hostility to Mark Antony in the first of the 14 *Philippicae* (Philippics). Cicero put his hopes in Octavian (Caesar's heir), who had always shown him the greatest respect, and while Octavian struggled to enter into his inheritance Cicero became the acting head of state, although he held no office. In his optimism, he thought he could influence Octavian to restore the Republic. He realized to what extent he had deluded himself when Octavian formed the Second Triumvirate (43) with Antony and Lepidus. Cicero, who had shown unrelenting hostility to the last two, prepared to fly. His ship was driven back by contrary winds, he was seized by agents of the triumvirs (but against the wishes of Octavian, it is said), and put to death near Formiae, Dec. 7, 43 B.C. His head and right hand were cut off and sent to Rome, where Antony caused them to be nailed to the rostra.

For all his great activity in public affairs, Cicero could not shape the time in which he lived. His monument rests in the contributions he made as the greatest enricher and stylist of the Latin language that Rome had ever produced. His contributions and example were consciously employed in the next 15 centuries to shape literary and linguistic expression. Aside from some early attempts at verse-writing and the translations from the Greek which he made from time to time throughout his life, his literary output may be divided into four groups. *The Orations,* of which 58 survive, in whole or in part: *Pro Quinctio* (81); *Pro Sextus Roscio* (80); *Pro Roscio Comoedo* (77); *Pro Tullio* (71?); *In Caecilium Divinatio, In Verrem* (The First Action against Verres, the Second Action against Verres, six speeches altogether) (70); *Pro Fonteio, Pro Caecina* (69); *Pro Lege Manilia, Pro Cluentio* (66); *Contra Rullum* (three speeches), *In Catilinam* (four speeches), *Pro Murena* (63); *Pro Sulla, Pro Archia* (62); *Pro Flacco* (59); *Post Reditum ad Quirites, Post Reditum in Senatu, De Doma Sua* (57); *De Haruspicum Responso, Pro Sestio, In Vatinium, Pro Caelio, De Provinciis Consularibus, Pro Balbo* (56); *In Pisonem* (55); *Pro Plancio, Pro Rabirio Postumo* (54); *Pro Milone* (52); *Pro Marcello, Pro Ligario* (46); *Pro Rege Deiotaro* (45); *Philippicae* I–XIV (44–43). In *Pro Fonteio* he defended Marcus Fonteius, former governor of Gaul, on charges similar to those on which he had secured the conviction of Verres the year before. *Pro Cluentio* was notable for the clever handling of a highly equivocal case in behalf of a client for whom Cicero had little use. The two speeches, *Post Reditum ad Quirites* and *Post Reditum in Senatu,* were addressed to the Roman people and Senate on his recall from exile. *De Doma Sua* was a plea for the restoration of his house, and *De Haruspicum Responso* was a disseration on an Etruscan soothsayer's interpretation of an earthquake, which Clodius had taken to mean disapproval of the restoration of Cicero's property. In *Pro Caelio* he defended Marcus Caelius Rufus who was charged, among other things, with an intention to poison Clodia, sister of Clodius Pulcher, and with having bought the poison with gold given to him by Clodia herself. In the speech Cicero defended the sowing of wild oats by the young man and castigated Clodia for her morals and manner of living. With the two speeches *De Provinciis Consularibus* and *Pro Balbo,* Cicero made his peace with Caesar and Pompey; in the first he dealt with the command in Gaul, and in the second he upheld the claim to citizenship of Pompey's protégé Lucius Cornelius Balbus. The published speech *Pro Milone* is not the same as that delivered in defense of Titus Annius Milo, accused of slaying Cicero's old enemy Clodius Pulcher. Milo was condemned and went into exile. *Pro Marcello, Pro Ligario,* and *Pro Rege Deiotaro* were addressed to Caesar in behalf of former supporters of Pompey.

Rhetoric: De Inventione (84); *De Oratore* (55); *Oratoriae Partitiones* (c54); *De Optimo Genere Oratorum* (52); *Brutus* or *De Claris Oratoribus* (46); *Orator* (46); and *Topica* (44), which last was an adaptation and exposition of a work by Aristotle. These works form a compendium of Circero's ideas and conclusions on the subject of oratory. They include observations on style, the arrangement of subject-matter, use of language, manner of delivery, the qualities the orator himself must have, and a form of history of oratory in Greece and Rome.

Philosophy. Through Cicero Greek philosophy passed to western Europe. He did not claim to be an original thinker. On the contrary, he said of his philosophical writings that they were just copies; that he supplied nothing but the words, of which he had plenty. "Supplying the words" may be taken quite literally, for Latin, lacking a philosophical tradition, also lacked the words with which to express philosophical concepts. Cicero provided them, as well as clear, simple expositions of the concepts themselves. In periods of political inactivity he turned to philosophy. *De Republica* (54), in six books, is a blueprint for the best constitution for Rome, and ends with the famous "Dream of Scipio." *De Legibus* (of which three books

survive) discusses the function of law and sets forth laws as he thinks they should be. *Hortensius* (45?) and *De Consolatione* (45) have been lost. The first concerned the orator Hortensius and is said to have caused St. Augustine to study philosophy. The second is Cicero's consolation to himself on the death of his daughter. *Paradoxa Stoicorum* (46?) deals with certain Stoic maxims. *Academica* (45) in two books, is an exposition of the Academic school, descended from Plato, which most nearly coincided with Cicero's own conclusions. *De Finibus Bonorum et Malorum* (45?) discusses Epicureanism and Stoicism in the first four books, and ends, in the fifth book, with statements of Academic ideas. *Tusculanarum Quaestionum* (45?), in five books, treats fear of death, pain, grief, other disturbances of the soul, and virtue, which last is declared to be sufficient for happiness; the whole is ornamented with many quotations from Greek and Roman writers and with many examples. In the three books of *De Natura Deorum* (45?) the Epicurean, Stoic, and Academic precepts are again set forth. *De Divinatione,* in two books, argues the validity of oracles; *De Fato* discusses whether man's fate and actions are predestined. *Cato Major* or *De Senectute* is an essay in which Cicero has Cato the Elder describing the advantages and comforts of old age to Laelius and the younger Scipio. The work was dedicated to Cicero's friend Atticus. *Laelius* or *De Amicitia* (44) is concerned with friendship. For his son Marcus, who stood in need of it, Cicero wrote *De Officiis* (44), in three books, on duties.

Letters. Cicero was a tireless letter writer. Thirty-seven books of his letters are extant, and represent only a part of the letters known to antiquity. From those that have been preserved, especially those to such intimates as Atticus, emerges a vivid picture of turbulent Rome, and a portrait in depth of the hopes and fears, weaknesses and strength, of its most articulate citizen.

Cicero, Quintus Tullius. Roman commander; born 102 B.C.; killed 43 B.C. He was a younger brother of Marcus Tullius Cicero. He distinguished himself in Gaul in 54 B.C. He was condemned to death by the same proscription issued against his brother. He was the author of letters and an epistle to his brother.

Cicones (sik'ọ-nēz) or **Ciconians** (si-kō'ni-ạnz). In Homer, a people of Thrace, dwelling on the shores of the Aegean near the Hebrus River. Orpheus settled among the Cicones, and it was the Ciconian women, either inspired with madness by Dionysus, or enraged because he scorned them, who set upon Orpheus, a priest of Apollo, and tore him limb from limb. According to some accounts, it was the practice thereafter for the Ciconian women to be tattooed as a warning against the murder of priests. Odysseus, on his way home after the Trojan War, landed on their shores and plundered their chief city of Ismarus. The Ciconians rallied their neighbors and made an attack on the forces of Odysseus who, in spite of his urgings for a speedy departure, lingered and enjoyed themselves over their wine. The Ciconians killed six men from each of Odysseus' ships before he was able to withdraw. A priest of the Ciconians, Maro, grateful that he and his family had been spared in the attack on the city, gave Odysseus several skins of a special wine which Odysseus later used to good advantage when he was confined by Polyphemus, the Cyclops. The Ciconians had been allies of Troy in the Trojan War, which was enough reason for Odysseus to plunder their city.

Cilicia (si-lish'ạ). In ancient geography, a province in SE Asia Minor, separated by the Taurus range from Lycaonia and Cappadocia on the N, and by the Amanus range from Syria on the E, and extending toward the sea. This describes the general area of Cilicia, but in fact the boundaries were subject to several shifts. According to some accounts the inhabitants were anciently called Hypachaeans. They took the name Cilicians from Cilix, a son of Agenor, who came into the land in search of his sister Europa and, abandoning his search, settled there. During the Syrian period many Greeks and Jews settled in Cilicia. It was repeatedly invaded by the Assyrian kings, but was one of the few areas west of the Halys River that did not fall to Croesus, king of Lydia. It was conquered by the Persians and constituted the fourth of the 20 satrapies into which Darius divided his empire. The Cilicians paid a tribute to Darius of 360 white horses and 500 talents of silver annually. In the Persian Wars they furnished 100 ships. Cilicia later fell under Macedonian, Syrian, and Roman dominion. The dreaded Cilician pirates were subdued (67 B.C.) by Pompey.

Cilician Gates (si-lish'ạn). [Also: **Beilan Pass, Syrian Gates**; Latin, **Pylae Ciliciae**.] Pass between the Taurus mountains and the NE angle of the Mediterranean, about 25 miles N of Tarsus, leading from Cilicia to Syria. The pass has been in use for almost 3000 years as a passageway through the Taurus.

Cilissa (sī-lis'ạ). According to some accounts, the name of Orestes' nurse. Some say that she placed her own son in Orestes' bed and allowed him to be murdered by Aegisthus, after the murder of Agamemnon, in order to protect Orestes. It was she who recognized him when he returned many years later to avenge his father's death, and told Aegisthus, falsely, that he could go unarmed to the palace and thus made it possible for Orestes to capture and kill Aegisthus.

Cilix (sil'iks). In Greek mythology, a son of Agenor of Canaan (afterward Phoenicia) and Telephassa. He was the brother of Cadmus, Phineus, Phoenix, Thasus, and Europa. When Europa was carried off by Zeus in the form of a bull, Agenor sent his sons to search for her. Cilix journeyed to Asia and there, wearying of his search, settled in the land of the Hypachaeans. The name of the country was changed to Cilicia in his honor.

Cilla (sil'ạ). According to legend, the daughter of Laomedon and the sister of Priam, king of Troy. Priam interpreted a prophecy that a mother and son of the royal house would cause the destruction of Troy to mean Cilla and her son, who was born the same day as Paris was born to Hecuba and Priam. Priam had Cilla and her child slain.

Cillus (sil'us). In Greek mythology, Pelops' charioteer. On the journey to Elis in Pelops' winged chariot, Cillus died on the island of Lesbos, some say, because the flight across the sea was so swift. He appeared to Pelops in a dream and asked to be given funeral honors. Pelops performed the rites and founded a sanctuary of Cillaean Apollo near his barrow on Lesbos. Some say the ghost of Cillus aided Pelops in his race for the hand of Hippodamia.

Cimbri (sim′brī). Ancient people of central Europe, of uncertain local habitation and ethnographical position. They probably pushed into the Roman provinces in 113 B.C., and in company with the Teutons and Gauls engaged with and defeated Roman armies in southern Gaul and elsewhere (the most notable defeat being that at Arausio of Caepio and Mallius in 105 B.C.) until 101 B.C., when they were defeated and virtually exterminated by Marius near Vercellae in the Padus Valley, N Italy. The peninsula now known as Jutland was named by ancient geographers the Chersonesus Cimbrica (peninsula of the Cimbri) after them.

Cimmeria (si-mir′i-a). Country of the legendary Cimmerians of ancient Greek tales, fabled to be a place of perpetual darkness. Odysseus sailed to the edge of the world to the mist-enshrouded land of the Cimmerians where he made his descent to Tartarus, as instructed to do by Circe, when he was trying to get home to Ithaca after the Trojan War. The Cimmerians of legend are not to be confused with the historical Cimmerians who lived near the Euxine Sea.

Cimmerian Bosporus (si-mir′i-an bos′pō-rus). [Also: **Bosporus Cimmerius**.] In ancient geography, the name of a kingdom in S Sarmatia and also of the strait (modern Kerch Strait) between the Euxine Sea and the Palus Maeotis (now Sea of Azov). The Crimean side was colonized (c600 B.C.) by a Greek expedition from Miletus which founded Panticapaeum (now Kerch) there. It flourished until absorbed in the dominions of Mithridates VI of Pontus, and for some centuries afterward experienced alternating periods of hardship and prosperity. Close relations were early established with Athens, which sent oil, jewelry, and works of industrial art in return for Crimean wheat. The chief city was Panticapaeum, the center of the highly important archaeological discoveries which have been yielded by this region as well as by the territory around it. The first systematic excavations were made in 1816. After 1832 explorations were regularly conducted by the Russian imperial government, and their results, rich in Greek industrial antiquities, were placed in the Hermitage Museum at St. Petersburg. The architectural remains are scanty, perhaps the chief of them being the fine revetment, in quarry-faced ashlar with margin-draft, of the so-called Tumulus of the Czar at Kerch. The sculpture found, too, is scanty in quantity, late in date, and poor in style. The great archaeological wealth of the region lies in its abundant burial tumuli and catacombs. It was the practice of the ancient inhabitants to bury with their dead a large part of their possessions; hence the remarkable harvest of jewelry, vases, implements, and even textile fabrics and a pair of woman's leather boots, found in these graves. Little or nothing discovered is older than the 4th century B.C.; the finest specimens of jewelry and pottery are Athenian, and include some of the most beautiful work known in their classes. Many of the vases are decorated in brilliant polychrome; others have gilded ornament, and others bear figures in relief. Some of the tomb chambers bear interesting mural paintings.

Cimmerians (si-mir′i-anz, ki-). [Older variant names: **Gimir, Kimmerians**.] Early inhabitants of the N shore of the Euxine Sea, between the Ister (Danube) and Tanais (Don) rivers. The Cimmerians were forced into Asia Minor by Scythian pressure during the 8th cenutry B.C. They plundered the cities of Asia Minor and entered Asia as far as Sardis. They came into conflict with the Assyrians and Phrygians, and after they were defeated by the Lydians in the 7th century B.C., disappeared from history. In the time of Herodotus there were still traces of the Cimmerians in Scythia. He mentions Cimmerian walls and speaks of a settlement the Cimmerians made in the peninsula where the city of Sinope was later situated. Herodotus also says that the strait which unites the Palus Maeotis and the Euxine Sea was called the Cimmerian Bosporus. In the Old Testament the Cimmerians are mentioned by the name of Gomer (Gen. x. 2).

Cimon (sī′mon). An Athenian noble, father of Miltiades who commanded the Athenians at Marathon. According to Herodotus, he won the four-horse chariot race at the Olympic Games and was banished by Pisistratus. At the next Olympiad he won again with the same team, but he had the victory declared in the name of Pisistratus because he had agreed with the latter that he would do so in exchange for being allowed to return to Athens. Later he won again with the same mares, and the sons of Pisistratus sent men to lie in wait for him and kill him. He was buried outside the city. According to Herodotus, only one other man had ever won the four-horse chariot race three times with the same horses.

Cimon. Son of Miltiades, who gained the victory at Marathon, and Hegesipyle, daughter of Olorus, prince of Thrace. It is said that he led a gay and irresponsible life as a young man, but when Aristides recognized his latent ability and encouraged him to enter public life, he gained popularity quickly with his generosity and his honesty, and added to it with his military victories. One of his first acts was to pay the 50 talents his father had been fined for having deceived the Athenians about the use he intended to make of the 70 ships they had granted him some time after his victory at Marathon. Payment of this sum was a heavy financial burden, but Cimon managed it. He served under Aristides in the Athenian fleet and later (477 B.C.) was made head of the Confederacy of Delos to carry on the war against Persia. He commanded a squadron sent out by the Athenians against Pausanias, the Spartan hero of Plataea, who at this time seemed ready to betray his country to the Persians. Cimon seized Sestos on the Hellespont and drove him out of Byzantium (476 B.C.). He captured Eion (476–5 B.C.), a fortress at the mouth of the Strymon River, from its Persian governor, Boges, and wrested all the cities of the seaboard of Thrace, except Doriscus, from the Persians. After the battle of Marathon, in which the image of Theseus was said to have aided the Athenians, the priestess of Delphi had ordered that the bones of Theseus be recovered from the island of Scyrus and brought to Athens. Scyrus was infested with Dolopian pirates, who continually preyed on Athenian commerce, and the Athenians were warned that the raids would continue so long as the bones of the Athenian hero remained in Scyrus. Cimon led an expedition against Scyrus (c474 B.C.), cleared the pirates from the island, and reduced the natives to slavery. But the inhabitants would not tell him where Theseus was buried. According to tradition, Cimon saw

an eagle tearing at the earth with its talons. He regarded this as a sign from heaven, went to the spot, and dug in the hole started by the eagle. A stone coffin was revealed, in which rested the bones of a very tall man and a bronze spear and sword. As the bones of Theseus, these were reverently carried back to Athens and reburied with a great public ceremony in the sanctuary of Theseus. The recovery of the bones of Theseus added greatly to the popularity of the already popular general. As a final blow at Persian power he led an expedition against the Persians in southern waters off Asia Minor, in which he delivered the Greek towns of Caria from Persian rule, brought the Lycian cities into the Confederacy of Delos, and overcame the Persian land and sea forces at the battle of the Eurymedon (468 B.C.). Plunder taken in the expedition was used to rebuild the walls of the Acropolis at Athens. About 463 B.C. he put down a revolt on the island of Thasus and forced the inhabitants to pull down their walls, surrender their ships, and pay tribute to Athens. After the death of Themistocles and Aristides, Cimon had become the dominant figure in Athens and was elected general of the Confederacy year after year. He was a noble and, conservative in his views, did not forward the democracy that was developing in Athens, although by his victories he helped to make it possible. With the rise of Pericles his influence was threatened. He was accused of having accepted a bribe from the Macedonians, but was acquitted. When he led a force to aid Sparta to put down a revolt of the helots, the Athenians were rebuffed by Sparta, who feared the rising power of Athens, and Cimon's policy of friendship with Sparta was repudiated by the Spartans themselves. In his absence from Athens, Pericles and Ephialtes, his political enemies, made many democratic and popular reforms. When Cimon returned, his Spartan policy discredited and Athens insulted, he was denounced as a lover of Sparta and was ostracized (461 B.C.). At the battle of Tanagra (457 B.C.), Cimon appeared at the Athenian camp and asked permission to fight for his country against Sparta, but permission was denied. Nevertheless, his supporters fought so stubbornly that although Athens was defeated, the Spartans were forced to withdraw. Cimon's action in this case prepared the way for his recall. Athens was exhausted by the long war with Sparta and wanted a truce; Cimon was recalled to bring it about (451 B.C.), after which he retired to a place outside Athens. Later he was recalled by Pericles to command an expedition against Persia. At the head of a large fleet he sailed to Cyprus to attack the Phoenician fleet gathered there to keep Cyprus under Persian control. He died at Citium in Cyprus (c450 B.C.) and was buried in Athens. The main points of Cimon's policy were to prosecute the war against Persia, which he did successfully, and to remain on friendly terms with Sparta, for with Athens as a great sea power and Sparta a great land power, a united Greece would be invulnerable. Because of Sparta's fear of the growing power of Athens, this part of Cimon's policy was a failure. One of the main effects of his dominance in Athens was the change in the voluntary nature of the Confederacy of Delos; it became an organization in which membership was compulsory. Carystus, Naxos, and Thasus were forced to pay tribute to it. This marked the emergence of Athens as an empire.

Cimon of Cleonae (klē̲-ō′nē̲). Greek painter, born at Cleonae, in Chalcidice, famous in antiquity. He is mentioned in two epigrams of Simonides.

Cincinnatus (sin-si-nā′tus, -nat′us), **Lucius Quinctius.** Roman hero, to whose life later writers have added embellishments, born c519 B.C.; fl. 1st half of the 5th century B.C. He was consul suffectus in 460 B.C. and distinguished himself as an opponent of the plebeians in the struggle between them and the patricians in the period 462–454 B.C. In 458 B.C. a Roman army under Lucius Minucius having been surrounded by the Aequi in a defile of Mount Algidus, he was named dictator by the Senate whose deputies, dispatched to inform him of his appointment, found him digging in the field on his farm beyond the Tiber. He gained a complete victory over the Aequi, and laid down the dictatorship after the lapse of only 16 days, then returning to his farm. In 439 B.C., at the age of 80, he was appointed dictator to oppose the traitor Spurius Melius, who was

defeated and slain. The details of his story vary; the story of the first dictatorship is probably legendary embellishment on a factual basis; that of the second dictatorship is probably wholly false.

Cineas (sin′ē̲-as). Thessalian politician in the service of Pyrrhus, king of Epirus; died probably in Sicily, c277 B.C.· He was ambassador to Rome after the battle of Heraclea in 280 B.C., in which Pyrrhus had defeated the Romans, but could not persuade the Senate to accept his terms.

Cinna (sin′a), **Caius Helvius.** Roman tribune and poet; a friend of Catullus. On the occasion of the funeral of Julius Caesar (44 B.C.), he was slain by the populace, who mistook him for Lucius Cornelius Cinna (fl. 44 B.C.).

Cinna, Lucius Cornelius. Roman general and statesman; slain in a mutiny at Brundisium, Italy, 84 B.C. He was celebrated as a leader of the popular party and an opponent of Sulla; father of Lucius Cornelius Cinna (fl. 44 B.C.). He was consul with Octavius in 87 B.C., with Marius in 86 B.C., and was also consul in the period 85–84 B.C. During his first consulship he took advantage of Sulla's absence from Rome to recall Marius and attempted to pass a voting bill in opposition to Sulla's partisans. Cinna was defeated in his attempt and was removed as consul. He raised a force and besieged the city. A massacre of Sulla's supporters took place after Marius' return. Cinna's daughter Cornelia was Julius Caesar's first wife.

Cinna, Lucius Cornelius. Roman politician; active 44 B.C. He was the son of Lucius Cornelius Cinna (d. 84 B.C.) and brother-in-law of Julius Caesar. He was praetor in 44 B.C. ·He sided with the conspirators against Caesar.

Cinyras (sin′ē̲-ras). A mythical king of Cyprus. He was a descendant of Pygmalion and Galatea and established the worship of Aphrodite on the island of Cyprus. It was he who built the famous temple to the goddess there, and it was said that he was the first to use songs in connection with the worship of Aphrodite. For this reason he was noted as one of the earliest musicians. He promised, as one of Helen's former suitors, to send Agamemnon 50 ships to help the Greeks carry on war against Troy. In fact, he sent only one ship and 49 clay models manned with dolls. But he did send a magnificent corselet to Agamemnon, which the latter wore at the siege of Troy. The wife of Cinyras boasted that her daughter Myrrha, or Smyrna as she was sometimes called, was more beautiful than Aphrodite herself. Aphrodite instantly took vengeance on her for her arrogant boast by causing Myrrha to fall in love with her own father. With the aid of a doting nurse Myrrha was brought to her father either in disguise or while he was befuddled by wine. When, after several such meetings, he discovered that his lover was his own daughter, he was filled with horror and tried to kill her. She fled from his sword and was transformed into a myrrh tree, from the trunk of which sprang her child, Adonis, the fruit of her incestuous union with her father. Cinyras was so revolted by the situation that he committed suicide.

Circaeum or **Circeium Promontorium** (sẽr-sẽ′um prõ″mon-tôr′i-um). [Also: Latin, **Circeius Mons**; modern, **Monte Circeo, Circeio** or **Circello**.] Promontory or isolated rock on the W coast of Italy, near ancient Tarracina. It was a frequented resort in ancient times. It has some antiquities of the Roman town Circeii, and abounds in grottoes.

Circe (sẽr′sẽ). In Greek mythology, an enchantress learned in the use of herbs, charms, and spells. She was the daughter of Helius and Persa, and the sister of Aeëtes and Pasiphaë. As it was the custom in Colchis, where she at first dwelt, to bury only women, and as the Colchians did not follow the Greek way of burning bodies on pyres, Circe had a cemetery outside Aea in Colchis where the bodies of men, wrapped in ox-hides, were suspended from willow trees. There as they swayed in the breezes, the birds ate them. Some say that Circe was the daughter of Hecate and Aeëtes, that she was the sister of Medea, and that both sisters excelled in the black arts, but that Circe used her skill for evil purposes, whereas Medea used hers for good. According to these accounts, Circe married a king of Scythia, but poisoned him after a time. She was so wicked and violent she was at last compelled to flee. Some say she went to Italy, and made her home on a promontory which bore her name, Circaeum. But others say she fled to the sea and established her home on an island ringed with alders. This island, which lies at the head of the Adriatic, near the mouth of the Padus, was known as Aeaea. Circe was noted for her cruel transformations. She fell in love with Picus, and when he spurned her advances, she transformed him into a woodpecker. Glaucus, the sea-god, appealed to her when his love was rejected by Scylla. Circe fell in love with him and suggested that he abandon his love for Scylla and transfer his affections to her. Glaucus refused, saying nothing could change his love for Scylla. Circe was enraged. She could not harm Glaucus, because he was immortal. Therefore she took her revenge on Scylla by transforming her into a hideous and dangerous sea-monster. But she had some loyalty for members of her family. When Jason and Medea visited her island on their way home from Colchis, she purified them of the murder of Apsyrtus by sprinkling the blood of a suckling pig over their hands. On his way home after the Trojan War Odysseus beached his ships on Circe's island. Though they were weary and thirsty, the Greeks hesitated to go ashore in a strange place after the disastrous experiences they had suffered in other unknown lands. By lot, 23 men under the leadership of Eurylochus were chosen to investigate the island. As they approached Circe's palace they were terrified by hordes of lions, wolves, bears, and other animals which came rushing to meet them. But the beasts licked their hands and fawned over them in a most unbeastly fashion. The envoys from Odysseus found Circe in her palace. She welcome them and invited them in. All entered save Eurylochus, who lurked outside to see what would happen. As he watched, he saw Circe give his companions a refreshing drink which they gulped greedily. She then lightly touched their heads and they were instantly turned into swine. Eurylochus fled back to the ship in terror and told all he had seen to Odysseus and begged him to sail with his remaining men at once. However, Odysseus determined to rescue his men. He set out alone for Circe's palace. On the way, Hermes met him and gave him a magic herb which would protect him from Circe's enchantments. He ate the herb, or some say, he merely sniffed

actor; up, lūte, pŭll; oi, oil; ou, out; ᴛʜ, then; ḍ as d or j, ş as s or sh, ṭ as t or ch, ẕ as z or zh.

it, and entered the palace. He too was graciously welcomed and given a potion to drink. But when she touched him to transform him, he drew his sword and threatened her. At this Circe fell at his feet and appealed for mercy. She retransformed his men from swine to men again and also at Odysseus' command, transformed the wolves, bears, lions, and other animals back to men. She invited Odysseus and his companions to remain with her and entertained them royally. The Greeks stayed with her a year or more and Circe bore three sons to Odysseus— Agrius, Latinus, and Telegonus. Before Odysseus left Circe to return to Ithaca, she told him that he must go to Tartarus and find Tiresias the seer, who would tell him what to expect in the future. She gave him full directions for the voyage to Tartarus and instructed him what to do when he got there: he must fill a trench with the blood of a young ram and a black ewe; when the shades came to drink of the warm blood, he must keep all except Tiresias away. Tiresias, after drinking the blood, would tell him all he wanted to know. She then sent a fair wind and Odysseus sailed away. But when he was in Tartarus, he met the shade of one of his companions who had been killed on Circe's island and had not been properly buried. So after he had consulted Tiresias, he sailed back to Circe's land to bury the dead sailor. This time she gave him useful advice about how to pass the Sirens in safety and warned him not to harm the cattle of Helius. Some say that Odysseus, having learned from an oracle that his son would kill him, sent Telemachus into exile. He went to Circe's land and married the enchantress.

Circeii (sẽr-sē'ī). In ancient geography, a town in Latium, Italy, situated on a former island now attached to the mainland by dune sand, about 57 miles SE of Rome. It belonged (340 B.C.) to the Latin League. Extensive fortifications of the 4th and 3rd centuries B.C. remain.

Circus Maximus (sẽr'kus mak'si-mus). Great Roman circus which occupied the hollow between the Palatine and Aventine hills at Rome. According to tradition, the site was already used for athletic exhibitions and provided with wooden seats under the legendary Tarquinius Priscus (c600 B.C.). Under Caesar and Augustus it was for the first time largely built of stone, and splendidly adorned. The present obelisks of the Piazza del Popolo and of the Lateran ornamented its *spina* (wall within the arena). It was rebuilt by Nero, and again by Domitian and Trajan, and in its final form is said to have accommodated, according to various estimates, from 140,000 to 385,000 spectators. Some of the vaulted substructures which upheld the seats survive, and there are considerable ruins about Santa Maria in Cosmedin of the *carceres*, or pens, from which the racers were started. The length of the arena was about 2200 ft.

Circus of Romulus (rom'ū-lus) or **Maxentius** (mak-sen'shus). Roman circus built at Rome in 311 A.D., outside the Porta Appia, considered to be the most perfect ancient circus surviving. It is 1580 feet long and 260 wide. The outer wall remains almost complete, and the central *spina* (the wall down the center of the arena), 892 feet long, can be traced throughout. At the west end, between two towers, are the chief entrance and 12 pens (*carceres*) for competing chariots; the east end is semicircular. In the middle of the N side can be distinguished the imperial box.

Cirrha (sir'a). In ancient geography, the seaport of Crisa (with which it is often confused) in Phocis, Greece. It was destroyed (c575 B.C.) in the First Sacred War, on account of sacrilege in interfering with pilgrims to Delphi.

Cissaea (si-sē'a). Epithet of Athena, meaning "Ivy-goddess." On the citadel at Epidaurus stood a wooden image of Athena Cissaea.

Cisseus (sis'ūs). In Greek legend, a king of Thrace, the father of Hecuba and Theano, Antenor's wife.

Cisseus. In Roman legend (*Aeneid*), a son of Melampus, the companion of Hercules, and a brother of Gyas. He fought with a club, as did Hercules. He was an ally of Turnus in the war against Aeneas and, in spite of his club, was killed by Aeneas.

Cithaeron (si-thē'ron). In Greek legend, the brother of Helicon. He was a fierce and savage man, who murdered his father and attempted to kill his brother, but as he hurled Helicon from a rocky height, both fell and were dashed to death. The gods changed them both into mountains. Mount Cithaeron in Boeotia is a wild and rugged mountain, where children were often exposed to die, as was Oedipus. It was also a home of the Furies, and ferocious beasts had their lairs there. Even so, many of the children who were exposed on Mount Cithaeron were saved because of the number of shepherds and herdsmen who watched their flocks on its slopes. Mount Cithaeron was sacred to Zeus and to Dionysus, and its name figures in many Greek myths and legends. According to another account, Cithaeron, a king of Plataea, was loved by the Fury Tisiphone, but he scorned her love and was bitten by one of the serpents of her snaky locks. He died on the mountain and it thereafter bore his name.

Cithaeronian (sith-ẽr-ō′ni-an). Epithet of Zeus, from Mount Cithaeron in Boeotia, which was sacred to Zeus.

Cithara (sith′a-ra). A musical instrument with strings and a sounding-board, from which are derived the lute and other instruments, including the cithern, zither, guitar, and others which bear names derived from *cithara* or *kithara*. (JJ)

Civilis (si-vī′lis), **Julius** (or **Claudius**). Batavian warrior; fl. 70 A.D. He was leader of the Batavian revolt against Rome in the period 69–70 A.D. The uprising, begun in Germany, spread to Gaul. Civilis was successful until defeated by Cerealis in 70.

Civitavecchia (chē″vē-tä-vek′kyä). See **Centumcellae.**

Clarius (klär′i-us). Epithet of Zeus, meaning "Of Lots." The spot in Tegea, in Arcadia, where most of the altars of the gods were set up was called the place of Zeus Clarius. Some say the name comes from the casting of lots by which the sons of Arcas divided his kingdom. Here the Tegeans annually celebated a festival of Zeus Clarius.

Clarus (klär′us). Seat of an ancient oracle of Apollo near Colophon in Asia Minor. Seers at the oracle drank water from a secret well and gave their pronouncements in verse.

Classis (klas′is). In ancient geography, the harbor of Ravenna. Built up by Augustus, it served in Roman times as a port and arsenal.

Claudia Quinta (klô′di-a kwin′ta). In Roman legend, a woman, probably the sister of Appius Claudius Pulcher. About 204 or 206

B.C., when the ship conveying the image of Cybele stuck fast in a shallow at the mouth of the Tiber and the soothsayers announced that only a chaste woman could move it, she cleared herself from an accusation of incontinency by stepping forward from among the matrons who went forth to receive the image, and towing the vessel to Rome. The story is one of numerous ancient legends in which the woman accused proves her chastity by coming victoriously through some such test, also often called the "act of truth."

Claudius I (klô′di-us). [Full name, **Tiberius Claudius Drusus Nero**; surnamed **Germanicus.**] Emperor of Rome in the period 41–54 A.D. He was born at Lugdunum in Gaul, Aug. 1, 10 B.C.; died 54 A.D. He was the grandson of Tiberius Claudius Nero and Livia Drusilla, who afterward became the third wife of Augustus, and son of Drusus Germanicus (sometimes called Drusus Senior) and Antonia, the daughter of Mark Antony. He was excluded from public affairs by Caligula, his predecessor, although the empty honor of consulship was bestowed on him in 37 by his nephew Caligula, on whose murder in 41 he was proclaimed emperor by the praetorian guards. Because Claudius was naturally of a mild and amiable disposition, his accession was signalized by acts of clemency and justice, which, however, under the influence of his third wife, Valeria Messalina, and his favorites, the freedmen Narcissus, Pallas, and others, were subsequently obscured by cruelty and bloodshed. He visited Britain in 43. In 49, after the execution of Messalina, who, during Claudius' absence at Ostia, had contracted a public marriage with Caius Silius, he married his niece Agrippina the younger. She persuaded him to set aside his own son Britannicus, and to adopt her son by a former marriage, Lucius Domitius, as his successor. When he repented of this step soon after, he is thought to have been poisoned by Agrippina, and Lucius Domitius ascended the throne under the name of Nero. The Claudian aqueduct at Rome was built during his reign and named for him. Claudius was noted for his writing, but none of his works is extant.

Claudius, Appius. [Surnamed **Sabinus Inregillensis** or **Regillensis.**] Original name, Attus or Attius Clausus. Roman consul.

Coming from Regillum in the Sabine country to Rome c504 B.C., with others of the Claudian family, of whom some were patricians and some plebeians, he seems to have gathered a number of families into a tribe which evidently was a force to be reckoned with, for he was admitted to the ranks of the patricians, at that time taking the name Appius Claudius, and was elected consul in 495 B.C. In that office he applied the laws concerning debts with a severity which caused the plebeians to take refuge on the sacred mount.

Claudius, Appius. [Surnamed **Crassus.**] Roman consul (471, 451 B.C.). In 451 B.C. he was a decemvir (one of ten magistrates) appointed to draw up a new code of laws. These decemvirs held virtually complete ruling powers during their time in office. In 450 B.C. the group was reconstituted, and Appius Claudius became its leading member, popular with patricians and plebeians alike, although his suggested legislation favoring plebeians roused considerable opposition. He remained in office until the group resigned in 449 B.C. Legend connects Claudius with Virginia, a young woman supposedly killed by her father, Virginius, to save her from being possessed by Appius Claudius, and advances this story as the cause for the public indignation that brought about the fall of the decemvirs. In fact, however, there may not be any connection at all.

Claudius, Appius. [Surnamed **Caecus,** meaning "the Blind."] Roman statesman, who died after 280 B.C. He was censor in the period 312–c308 B.C., and consul in 307 and 296 B.C. He advised the Romans not to make an alliance with King Pyrrhus of Epirus. He commenced the Appian Way and completed the Appian aqueduct, the first at Rome. He abolished the limitation of the full right of citizenship to landed proprietors.

Claudius, Appius. [Surnamed **Pulcher.**] Roman politician; brother of Clodius (Publius Clodius Pulcher); died in Euboea, c48 B.C. Before serving as governor in Sardinia he had been praetor in 57 B.C. He was consul in 54, proconsul in Cilicia from 53 to 51, and censor in 50 B.C. In 49 B.C. he was a follower of Pompey.

Claudius, Publius. [Surnamed **Pulcher.**] Roman consul of the 3rd century B.C.; son of

the consul Appius Claudius (surnamed Caecus). While consul in 249 B.C., he commanded the Roman fleet in the course of the First Punic War, and was disastrously defeated at Drepanum. It was believed that this disaster resulted from an impious act by Claudius. Just before the Roman and Carthaginian fleets clashed, the sacred chickens carried on the Roman ships are said to have refused to eat. This act was an alarming omen. Claudius said, "If they will not eat, let them drink," and ordered them thrown overboard. For this and certain other acts, he was accused of treason and heavily fined. It is thought that he died in 246 B.C. or earlier, probably a suicide.

Claudius Ptolemaeus (klô'di-us tol- e-mē'us). Second century A.D. Alexandrian astronomer and geographer, author of the 13-book *System of Mathematics* best known by its Arabic title, *Almagest*, the eight-book *Geography*, and other works surviving in whole or in part. (JJ)

Claudius Tiberius Germanicus (tī-bir'i-us jėr-man'i-kus). Original name of **Britannicus.**

Clazomenae (kla-zom'e-nē). In ancient geography, an Ionian city in Asia Minor, situtated about 20 miles SW of Smyrna (Izmir). It was colonized by Cleonaeans and Phliasians who had been driven out of their cities in the Peloponnesus by the Dorians. In its turn it sent colonists to Cardia in the Thracian Chersonese. Clazomenae was conquered by Alyattes, king of Lydia and father of Croesus, and later fell under the dominion of Persia.

Cleanthes (klē-an'thēz). Greek Stoic philosopher, born at Assos, Asia Minor, 331 B.C.; died at Athens, 232 B.C. He was a boxer who attended the lectures of Zeno at Athens, and earned his living at night as a water-carrier. After studying with Zeno for 19 years, he succeeded his master as head of the Stoic school. He is said to have committed suicide by starving himself to death.

Clearchus (klē-är'kus). Greek sculptor of Rhegium, who was active c540–500 B.C. He is said to have made the first image in bronze. According to Pausanias, it was an image of Zeus, made in several pieces, and fastened together with nails. This image was in Sparta. According to legend, Clearchus was a pupil of Daedalus.

Clearchus. Lacedaemonian general, born at

Sparta; executed by Artaxerxes II, 401 B.C. He fought at the battle of Cyzicus in 410 B.C. when the Spartan fleet was destroyed by Alcibiades. In 408 B.C. his tyrannous conduct as governor of Byzantium during the siege by the Athenians led to the surrender of the city by the inhabitants during his absence in Asia, whither he had gone to collect a force to raise the siege. In 406 he fought under Callicratidas at the naval battle of Arginusae, where the Spartans again were defeated, this time by Conon. After the Peloponnesian War he persuaded the *ephors* (magistrates) to send him as general to Thrace to protect the Greeks against the natives. Having proceeded thither in spite of an order for his recall which overtook him on the way, he was condemned to death. Defeated by a force sent against him, he fled to Cyrus the Younger, who was seeking to wrest the Persian throne from his brother Artaxerxes II. Clearchus offered him his services and raised a force of over 13,000 Greek mercenaries to fight in his cause. A young Athenian officer, Xenophon, later known for his writings, was one of the Greek volunteers in the force. Clearchus, alone of the Greeks, knew that the object of the expedition which now set out under command of Cyrus was Babylon, where Artaxerxes II maintained his forces. When it became apparent to the Greeks that they were on the way to Babylon, a three months' march from the sea, they rebelled. Clearchus, a strict disciplinarian, attempted to put down the rebellion by force, but was unsuccessful. He resorted to a trick. The forces by this time had marched from Celaenae in Phrygia to Tarsus. They were a long way from home. Clearchus called his soldiers together, and then stood before them and wept before he spoke. Then he told them that their rebellion had placed him in an extremely difficult position: either he must break his pledged word to Cyrus or desert the Greeks. What, he asked his men, did they propose to do? They must decide, since he would not command them and could not pay them. They decided to go on as soldiers of Cyrus. Arrived, after a long march, before Babylon, Clearchus refused to adopt the wise plan of battle outlined by Cyrus, but Cyrus did not insist. In the battle against the forces of Artaxerxes II the Greeks were

successful, but Cyrus, in his eagerness to slay his hated brother, was slain when he was on the point of victory; his forces fled in confusion. Thus the Greeks found themselves alone in the midst of enemies, and a long march from the sea. Artaxerxes was delighted to get rid of them and let them go. They were to be guided by the Persian satrap Tissaphernes, who marched with his forces ahead of them. On the way the suspicion and hostility between the two forces became so sharp that Clearchus sought a conference with Tissaphernes. Tissaphernes advised him to meet in his tent and to bring the leading Greek generals with him. Clearchus went to the Persian satrap's tent with his principal generals. They were all treacherously seized by Tissaphernes, bound in fetters, and sent to the court of Artaxerxes, where they were executed. The surviving Greeks chose new generals and accomplished the famous retreat known as the "Retreat of the Ten Thousand," the story of which is told in Xenophon's *Anabasis.*

Cleisthenes (klīs′thē̱-nēz).   See **Clisthenes.**

Cleitias (klī′ti-a̱s).   [Also: **Kleitias.**]   Attic vase-painter in the black-figure style, active in the second quarter of the 6th century B.C. The François vase (c570 B.C.), named for its finder and now in Florence, is an amphora signed by Cleitias as the painter and Ergotimus as the potter. There are more than 200 figures on the vase, many of which are identified by inscribed names. The scenes of the decoration include the *Calydonian Hunt, Funeral Games for Patroclus, Procession of the gods to the Marriage of Thetis and Peleus, Achilles Pursuing Troilus, Hephaestus Returning to Olympus, Ajax Carrying the Body of Achilles, Battle of the Pygmies and Cranes,* and various monsters. A stand in New York and various extant cups also bear the signatures of Cleitias and Ergotimus as painter and potter respectively.

Cleitus (klī′tus).   See **Clitus.**

Clementia (kle-ment′i-a̱).   In later Roman mythology, the personification of forbearance.

Cleobis (klē′o̱-bis).   See **Biton and Cleobis.**

Cleobulus (klē-o̱-bū′lus, klē-ob′ū-lus).   Tyrant of Lindus, born at Lindus, Rhodes, and flourished in the 6th century B.C. He was one of the Seven Sages of Greece. The reputed author of various riddles, he is credited with having formulated the first literary riddle. His daughter Cleobulina shares his reputed skill in riddles, being credited with inventing the riddle on the year: "A father has 12 children, each has 30 daughters, white on one side, black on the other; all are immortal, yet they die."

Cleodaeus (klē-ọ̄-dē′us). In Greek tradition, a son of Hyllus and the grandson of Heracles. Through his grandson Aristodemus he was the ancestor of the two royal houses of Sparta, and the ancestor of many illustrious Spartans.

Cleodice (klē-od′i-sē). A daughter of Lacedaemon and Taÿgete. See **Himerus.**

Cleombrotus (klē-om′brọ-tus). Regent of Sparta early in the 5th century B.C. He was the son of Anaxandridas, king of Sparta. Anaxandridas was married to his niece, whom he loved dearly, but as she bore him no children, the Spartan ephors and elders asked him to put her aside and take another wife that he might have an heir to the throne. Anaxandridas refused to give up the wife he loved. He agreed, however, to act on a suggestion of the ephors and elders, which was to take an additional wife, while he continued to love and honor his first wife as before. As a result of this advice he had two wives and lived with them in two separate houses; this was quite contrary to Spartan custom. The new wife bore him Cleomenes, who became his legitimate heir. Then the first wife produced, in rapid succession, Dorieus, Leonidas (the hero of Thermopylae), and Cleombrotus. Cleombrotus was regent of Sparta during the Persian War and commanded the forces that gathered at the Isthmus of Corinth after the death of Leonidas and built a wall across the Isthmus to keep the Persians out of the Peloponnesus. When the wall was built, Cleombrotus sacrificed victims to learn whether he should march against the Persians. As he was offering the sacrifices, the face of the sun was darkened in mid-sky. Cleombrotus interpreted this as a warning and marched his army back to Sparta, where shortly thereafter he died. The prodigy of the darkened sun was a partial eclipse which occurred October 2, 480 B.C.

Cleombrotus I. King of Sparta, 380–371 B.C.; killed at Leuctra, 371 B.C. He was co-king with Agesilaus, and was sent to Boeotia (378 B.C.) when the pro-Spartan rulers of Thebes were slain and the Spartan garrison expelled from the city as the result of a plot by the Theban patriot Pelopidas. Various maneuvers carried on by Cleombrotus in the vicinity were fruitless. He could not enter Boeotia because the mountain passes of Cithaeron were securely held by the Thebans. In 371 B.C. he led an army from Phocis against Thebes, to free the Boeotian cities from the Boeotian Confederacy which some had joined under compulsion. This march was a distinct violation of the Peace of Callias, concluded in the same year, by which all the signatories, Sparta among them, agreed to bring their armies home and remove their garrisons from foreign cities. Cleombrotus went first to the port of Creusis on the Gulf of Corinth, seized it and captured some Theban ships at anchor there. He then proceeded toward Thebes. The Thebans under Epaminondas marched out against him and barred his way at Leuctra. The Thebans took up position on the hills on one side of the Asopus River; the Spartans ranged themselves on the hills across the stream. When the opposing forces moved down the hills and engaged, the army of Cleombrotus was shattered by the impact of the Thebans, spearheaded by the Sacred Band. Cleombrotus was slain in the fighting and his army admitted defeat by asking for a truce to bury their dead (371 B.C.). This defeat marked the end of Spartan leadership in Greece that had been unquestioned since the end of the Peloponnesian Wars (404 B.C.).

Cleomedes (klē-ọ̄-mē′dēz). According to Pausanias, an athlete of Astypalea who killed his opponent in a boxing match at the Olympic Games. Being fined for foul play and denied the prize, he went mad. He went to a school in Astypalea and pulled down the roof on 60 children. The people of the town stoned him, and he fled to the sanctuary of Athena and hid in a chest there. The people followed him into the sanctuary and tried to pull up the lid of the chest. For a time it resisted them, and when they did succeed in opening the chest, they found no trace of Cleomedes. Being perplexed, the citizens consulted the oracle at Delphi and were told:

"Last of heroes is Cleomedes of Astypalea;
Honor him with sacrifices as being no
  longer a mortal."

Ever after, the people of Astypalea honored Cleomedes as a hero.

Cleomedes. Greek astronomer (c1st century B.C.). His birthplace and residence are unknown. He wrote a treatise on astronomy and cosmography, entitled *The Circular Motion of the Heavenly Bodies,* in which he maintains that the earth is spherical, that the number of the fixed stars is infinite, and that the moon's rotation on its axis is performed in the same time as its synodical revolution about the earth. His treatise contains also the first notice of the theory of atmospheric refraction.

Cleomenes I (klē-om'ē-nēz). King of Sparta from c519–487 B.C. He was the son of Anaxandridas, king of Sparta, and half-brother to Cleombrotus (q.v.), Dorieus, and Leonidas. He succeeded his father as king. Maeandrius, a man of Samos, fled to Sparta to seek aid against the Persians. He sought to bribe Cleomenes, but the latter refused to accept the bribe and advised the Spartan ephors to send Maeandrius away, lest he succeed in bribing someone else to give aid to Samos. Aristagoras also sought his aid when he was stirring up the Ionian revolt against the Persians. He painted a glowing picture of the ease with which Cleomenes could overcome the Persians and of the treasures he would gain thereby. Cleomenes, on learning that the Persian capital was a three-month march from the sea, refused to consider fighting the Persians and ordered Aristagoras to leave Sparta before sunset. Aristagoras persisted. He took an olive branch and went as a suppliant to Cleomenes' house. He offered him ten talents if he would bring Sparta to the aid of the Ionians. Cleomenes shook his head. Aristagoras raised the offer, and continued to raise it each time Cleomenes shook his head. At last Gorgo, the eight or nine year old daughter of Cleomenes who was present at this interview, interrupted and advised her father to send the stranger away before he was corrupted. Cleomenes thought her advice was good and sent Aristagoras away. At the

same time, he again proved his own honesty. In 510 B.C., as a consequence of repeated reminders from the oracle at Delphi to free the Athenians from the tyrannical Pisistratidae, Cleomenes led a force of Spartans against Athens and drove Hippias out of the city. He interfered in a struggle for control of Athens by ordering Clisthenes (one of two men who sought to rule the city) and his followers to leave Athens. He also sent 700 Athenian families into exile at the request of Isagoras and established the latter as ruler of Athens. But when he attempted to dissolve the Athenian council, the council resisted and, supported by the rest of the Athenians, compelled Cleomenes to withdraw. Thus was the oracle fulfilled, for when Cleomenes first went to the citadel of Athens and attempted to enter the temple, the priestess rose up and told him to withdraw. At the time Cleomenes ignored her command, but in the end he was forced to withdraw from the city. Cleomenes felt that the Athenians had insulted him and resolved to punish them. He gathered a large force and invaded Eleusis, where he cut down the sacred grove of the goddess. The Athenians marched to Eleusis to engage him, but as the two forces were about to go into battle, the Corinthian allies of Cleomenes withdrew. Demaratus, co-king of Sparta with Cleomenes, withdrew his forces also, and the other allies, seeing that the kings were not agreed, also withdrew. Cleomenes was compelled to retire. After this Cleomenes contrived the removal of Demaratus as co-king (491 B.C.), on the grounds that Demaratus was not the true son of Ariston, king of Sparta. Cleomenes achieved success in this matter by bribing the priestess at Delphi to say that Demaratus was not the true son of Ariston. After this Leotychides, son of Menares, became co-king with Cleomenes. When the Spartans learned of the bribe, Cleomenes was forced to flee, first to Thessaly, and then to Arcadia. There he stirred up the Arcadians against Sparta. The Spartans learned of his activities, and fearing that he might raise a war against them, invited him to return to Sparta and be king as before. On his return Cleomenes, who according to Herodotus had never been of very sound mind, was overcome by outright madness. This was caused, according to the Spartans, because of his habit of drinking wine unmixed with water. He struck every Spartan he met on the face with his scepter. The Spartans saw that he was mad and put him in prison, binding him in stocks. From a frightened helot he secured a knife and so gashed himself that he died of the wounds. The Greeks in general thought he had become mad for seducing the priestess of Delphi, but the Athenians considered that his horrible end was a punishment for destroying the sacred grove at Eleusis. The Argives had another account of his end. Once he had thought the oracle at Delphi told him he could take Argos. He led a force of Spartans to the Erasinus River to cross over to Argos. At the banks of the river he offered sacrifices but the victims were not favorable. He therefore embarked this forces on ships and went to Nauplia. The Argives marched to meet him and were defeated. Many of them sought refuge in the sacred grove of Argus. Cleomenes called for the leading Argive warriors by name, one at a time, pretending he had received their ransoms. When they came out of the grove, he treacherously killed them. His treachery being discovered, no more Argives came forth when he called their names. He now ordered his helots to set the grove afire, and some 6000 Argives who had taken refuge therein perished. When he learned that the grove was sacred to Argus, he felt that the oracle that told him he would take Argos had deceived him, and that now the oracle was fulfilled. The Argives said his end at his own hands was caused by his violation of the sacred grove and by his later blasphemy at the temple of Hera in Argos. As he had no son, only the one daughter Gorgo, Cleomenes was succeeded by his half-brother Leonidas, the older half-brother Dorieus having died.

Cleomenes III. King of Sparta, c225–c220 B.C., who died c219 B.C. He abolished the ephorate (a magistracy controlling the kings) in 225 B.C., waged war with the Achaean League and Macedonia in the period 225–222 B.C., and was defeated at Sellasia in 222 B.C.

Cleon (klē′on). Athenian demagogue, killed at Amphipolis, Macedonia, 422 B.C. He was the son of Cleaenetus, a tanner, and was one of a new class of leaders who came to the forefront in Athens during the Peloponnesian Wars. He was of the people as distinguished from the former leaders who had come from the aristocratic class, and won his place by his eloquence, shrewdness, daring, and ability. As unofficial leader of the Athenian Assembly, he was an opponent of Pericles whom he accused of maladministration. After the death of Pericles (429 B.C.) he became one of the foremost men in Athenian public life. He was an imperialist, whose policy it was to keep a tight rein on the Athenian allies and to maintain Athenian power by force. In furtherance of his policy he belonged to the war party that urged and supported continuation of the war against Sparta. In 428 B.C. Mytilene, a free ally of Athens, revolted. The revolt was put down after a siege in 427 B.C. Cleon used his influence in the Athenian Assembly to demand death for all the adult males of Mytilene and enslavement of the women and children. He argued that to be a strong state and rule an empire strong measures must be used to crush opposition. The sentence he urged was so voted, but a reaction immediately set in and the sentence was reconsidered and revoked the next day. In succeeding years Cleon opposed Nicias, one of the chief military leaders of Athens and the head of the aristocratic party, who advocated peace with Sparta and the conclusion of the Peloponnesian War. As leader of the democratic party he called himself "the people's watch-dog" and opposed those whom he suspected of undermining the democracy. Under his leadership the pay of jurors was increased, partly to help the citizens impoverished by the war, the tribute required of the allies was greatly increased, and the temple treasuries were depleted of some of their treasures "borrowed" to help defray the costs of the war. When the Spartans occupied Pylus in Messenia, they were attacked by the Athenians, driven to the island of Sphacteria lying off the shore of Pylus, and blockaded by an Athenian fleet. They asked for a truce and sent an embassy to Athens proposing peace terms that would allow the Athenians to keep the advantages they had won owing, as the

fat, fāte, fär, fãre, errant; net, mē, hėr ardent; pin, pīne; not, nōte, mȯve, nôr,

Spartans said, to Spartan "misfortunes." Cleon countered with such terms as he knew the Spartans could not accept. The Spartan embassy returned to Sphacteria and the garrison there submitted to siege (425 B.C.). As the weeks passed and the Spartan garrison continued to withstand the siege, Cleon suffered some loss of popularity because he had prevented peace. He expressed impatience with the delay in taking the island. He criticized the generals in Athens for not going to Pylus and taking charge of the siege themselves, and ended by saying that if he were commander, he would go and capture the Spartan garrison himself. Nicias, the commander, offered to give Cleon whatever forces he required and to send him there. As described by Thucydides, when Cleon saw that Nicias was in earnest, he tried to back out, saying that Nicias, not he, was the general. But Nicias formally gave him the command in the presence of the Assembly. Cleon tried again to withdraw, but the more he shrank from the undertaking, the more the people called on him to head the expedition. Finding himself boxed in by his own words, he asked for certain troops and promised either to take the Spartan garrison on Sphacteria alive or kill them on the spot, and within 20 days. These bold words evoked laughter from the Athenians, for it was well-known that Spartans were never taken alive. In Thucydides' words, "sensible men comforted themselves with the reflection that they must gain in either circumstance; either they would be rid of Cleon, which they rather hoped, or if disappointed in this expectation, would reduce the Lacedaemonians." As it turned out, the latter circumstance was fulfilled. Contrary to all expectations, Cleon brought about the surrender of the Spartan garrison within the promised 20 days, largely, to be sure, through the skill of his colleague, the Athenian general Demosthenes. Two hundred ninety-two Lacedaemonians were taken alive to Athens. Nothing that had happened in the war surprised the Greeks as much as this, for such was the reputation of the Spartans for fighting either to victory or death that it was impossible to believe that Cleon, a man of no military experience, had compelled them to surrender. The victory completely vindicated Cleon, reëstablished his popularity, and gave him immense advantage over his political rivals. In the spring of 422 B.C. Cleon sailed as commander of an expedition to recover Amphipolis in Macedonia, which had been taken by the Spartans in 424 B.C. He marched toward Amphipolis, but on observing the Spartan commander Brasidas sacrificing in the city, and noting what seemed to be large forces, he ordered his men to retreat without engaging in battle. Noting the retreat, Brasidas sallied out and fell on the Athenians. They were thrown into confusion by the onslaught and fled. Cleon joined them in panic-stricken flight, and was killed by the enemy as he fled. Cleon was satirized by Aristophanes in the *Acharnians,* the *Wasps,* and especially in the *Knights* (424 B.C.), in which Aristophanes himself was forced to play Cleon, as none of the players dared to take the role that showed the popular hero in an unfavorable light. However, Aristophanes' picture of Cleon was colored by the fact that the latter had hailed him before the courts because of an earlier comedy. Thucydides too, who gives an unfavorable portrayal of Cleon in his history of the Peloponnesian Wars, was undoubtedly prejudiced by the fact that Cleon had caused him to be exiled after the loss of Amphipolis (424 B.C.).

Cleonae (klē-ō′nē). In ancient geography, a city on the road between Corinth and Argos, in Greece. Some say it was named for Cleones, a son of Pelops, who founded the city. Others say it was named for Cleone, a daughter of the river-god Asopus. Here Heracles ambushed Eurytus and Cteatus as they were going from Elis to the Isthmian Games and killed them, and here they had their tomb. Men of Cleonae went to the Trojan War under the command of Agamemnon. In the city was a temple of Heracles. According to some accounts, he established it himself after he had killed Eurytus, son of Augeas, near there. Others say he would not have been so presumptuous as to set up a temple to himself as if he were a god; therefore, it must have been established after his death.

Cleone (klē-ō′nē). In Greek mythology, a daughter of the river-god Asopus. Some say the city of Cleonae in Argolis was named for her.

Cleopatra (klē-ō̇-pā′trạ, -pat′rạ). In Greek mythology, a daughter of Tros and Callirrhoë, daughter of the river-god Scamander. She was the sister of Assaracus, Ilus, and Ganymede.

Cleopatra. In Greek legend, a daughter of Boreas and Orithyia, and the sister of Calais and Zetes. She was the wife of Phineus by whom she had two sons. According to some accounts, after the death of Cleopatra, Phineus married Idaea, who falsely accused Cleopatra's sons. Phineus tortured them and cast them in prison. They were freed later, when Phineus learned from Calais and Zetes that the accusations were false. Other accounts say that Phineus cast aside Cleopatra in favor of Idaea, and blinded Cleopatra's sons; and that Calais and Zetes restored the sight of their nephews and gave the kingdom of Phineus to Cleopatra.

Cleopatra. In Greek legend, the daughter of Marpessa and Idas, and the wife of Meleager. According to one account, she persuaded Meleager to resume an active part in the fight, from which he had withdrawn in anger at his mother, to drive off the Curetes who were attacking the gates of Calydon. When Meleager later died as a result of his mother's wrath, Cleopatra killed herself. She was also known as Alcyone.

Cleopatra. Wife of Philip II of Macedon; died c335 B.C. She was the niece of Attalus, one of Philip's generals. Philip divorced his wife Olympias, the mother of Alexander, to marry her. After the murder of Philip (336 B.C.), Cleopatra's father was murdered, her infant was slain in her arms, and she was forced to hang herself. These murders were brought about by Olympias in revenge for being cast aside by Philip. They also removed a possible rival of Alexander for the throne and those who might contest his right to it.

Cleopatra. [In the chronology of Egyptian queens, **Cleopatra VII.**] Last Macedonian queen of Egypt, born at Alexandria, Egypt, 69 B.C.; died there, 30 B.C. She was the daughter of Ptolemy XII, called Ptolemy Auletes. In accordance with Egyptian tradition, she was wife of and joint ruler with her brother Ptolemy XIII from 51 to 49 B.C.,

when she was expelled by him. Her reinstatement in 48 B.C. by Caesar gave rise to war between Caesar and Ptolemy. The latter was defeated and killed, and his younger brother, Ptolemy XIV, was elevated to the throne in his stead and married to her. Cleopatra lived with Caesar at Rome from 46 to 44 B.C., and had by him a son, Ptolemy XV, usually known as Caesarion because of his father; the child was afterward put to death by Augustus. She returned to Egypt after the murder of Caesar, and in the civil war which ensued sided with the Triumvirate (Octavian, Antony, and Lepidus). Mark Antony having been appointed ruler of Asia and the East, she visited him at Tarsus in Cilicia in 41 B.C., making a voyage of extraordinary splendor and magnificence up the Cydnus. She gained by her charms a complete ascendancy over him. On her account he divorced his wife Octavia, the sister of Octavian, in 32 B.C. Octavian declared war against her in 31 B.C. The fleet of Antony and Cleopatra was defeated in the same year as the battle of Actium, which was decided by the flight of Cleopatra's ships, Antony being forced to follow. After the death of Antony, who killed himself on hearing a false report of her death (according to some, a report deliberately spread by her in an attempt to win Octavian's favor by causing his death), she poisoned herself to avoid being exhibited at Rome at the triumph of Octavian, but not until she had made an attempt to charm Octavian as she had Caesar and Antony. According to the popular belief, she applied to her bosom an asp that had been secretly conveyed to her in a basket of figs. Octavian was so anxious to have her in his triumphal procession that, some say, he sent a snake charmer to try to revive her by sucking out the poison. Cleopatra had three children by Antony. Besides extraordinary charms of person, she possessed an active and cultivated mind, and is said to have been able to converse in seven languages. Her reputed personality and the events of the latter part of her reign, as described by Plutarch, form the basis of Shakespeare's *Antony and Cleopatra*.

Cleophon (klē′ō̇-fon). Athenian demagogue; executed 404 B.C. He was a lyremaker, and was said to be of Thracian origin. He came

fat, fāte, fär, fãre, errạnt; net, mē, hėr ardẹnt; pin, pīne; not, nōte, mŏve, nôr,

to the forefront in the last years of the Peloponnesian War. He favored a strong imperialist policy, was a leader of the war party, and opposed the oligarchical party. As a popular leader he instituted the "two-obol" payment, which is thought to have been a kind of dole to those whose livelihoods had been destroyed by the long war with Sparta, and he provided employment for the impoverished Athenians by a program of public works, among them being the completion of the Erechtheum. After the Athenian victory over the Peloponnesian fleet at Cyzicus (410 B.C.), Sparta made peace offers to Athens which would have ended the war in a draw. Cleophon opposed the terms and they were rejected. Again, in 406 B.C., following the Athenian victory at Arginusae, Sparta proposed peace and again Cleophon used his considerable influence to oppose it. A year later the Spartans defeated the Athenians at Aegospotami and followed up their victory by blockading Athens. Athens was now compelled to seek peace. Cleophon, who had twice prevented the conclusion of an honorable peace, now prevented the acceptance of terms that were humiliating. However, the Athenians, blockaded and starving, had no longer any choice. In a wave of feeling against him, Cleophon was sentenced to death in 404 B.C. by the Athenian council and executed.

Cleophrades (klē-of′ra-dēz). Attic potter, active at the beginning of the 5th century B.C. The painter who decorated his work, in the red-figure style, is known as the Cleophrades Painter. Over 100 large vessels—craters and hydriai—attributed to the Cleophrades Painter are extant. Of these, there are nine Panathenaic amphorae (the ceremonial vessels awarded at the great festival), in the traditional black-figure style. Two calyx craters (New York and Tarquinia) show youths arming. An amphora (Munich) c500 B.C., shows Dionysus with maenads and satyrs on the body of the vessel, and scenes of the palestra on the neck. Of two more amphorae in Munich one shows the departure of a warrior and scenes of the palestra in red-figure, with a hunting scene on the rim of the vessel and a chariot race on the lid, in black-figure. The other amphora has a figure of Heracles on one side, prepared to do battle with the centaur on the other side. An amphora (New York) similarly decorated with a single figure on each side shows Apollo raising his bow on one side, against Heracles, who is carrying off the Delphic tripod on the other. A hydria (Naples) has an *Iliupersis* (Sack of Troy). The Cleophrades Painter, known by that name for lack of knowledge as to his real name for a long time, has been identified by his real name, Epictetus, but is not to be confused with the vase-painter Epictetus who lived a generation earlier.

Cleostratus (klē-os′tra-tus). Greek poet of Tenedos, active in the 6th century B.C. He observed the stars from Mount Ida, and was the first poet on record to use astronomy as a subject for his poems.

Cleothera (klē-ō-thē′ra). A daughter of Pandareus and Harmothoë. See **Merope.**

Clepsydra (klep′si-dra). Spring on the slope of Ithome in Messenia. The Messenians say that after the Curetes had stolen him to protect him from his father Cronus, Zeus was brought to Messenia and reared there by two nymphs, Ithome and Neda. The mountain in Messenia was named for Ithome and the river for Neda. The nymphs bathed Zeus in the spring of Clepsydra, and ever after water from this spring was daily carried to the sanctuary of Zeus at Ithome.

Clide (klī′dē). A nymph of the island of Naxos. According to some accounts, she helped care for the infant Dionysus when he was brought to the island of Naxos for safekeeping.

Clinias (klī′ni-as). Athenian commander; killed at the battle of Coronea, 447 B.C. He was the father of Alcibiades. In the Persian War he furnished a vessel and provided 200 men at his own expense. He served with distinction at the battle of Artemisium in 480 B.C.

Clinias. Pythagorean philosopher; fl. c400 B.C. He was a friend of Plato, and a native of Tarentum.

Clinis (klī′nis). According to legend, a Mesopotamian who lived near Babylon. He was beloved by Artemis and Apollo. He wanted to sacrifice asses to Apollo, as the Hyperboreans did, but Apollo forbade him to do so and commanded him to sacrifice only sheep, goats, and heifers. However, the sons of Clinis disobeyed the god's command and sacrificed asses. To punish them, Apollo caused the animals to go into a frenzy and attack the family of Clinis. The other gods took pity on them and transformed them into birds to save them from the maddened animals.

Clio (klī′ō). One of the nine daughters of Zeus and Mnemosyne. She is the muse who sings of glorious actions; specifically, the muse of History. She is usually represented with a scroll in her hand and a *scrinium* (case for manuscripts) by her side, and sometimes with the trumpet of fame in her hand. According to some accounts, as a punishment because Clio had mocked Aphrodite for her attachment to Adonis, Aphrodite caused her to fall in love with Pierus, to whom she bore Hyacinthus. See **Muses**.

Clisthenes (klĭs′thē̇-nēz) or **Cleisthenes** (klĭs′-). Tyrant of Sicyon, a city in the Peloponnesus, early in the 6th century B.C. (fl. 580 B.C.). He was leader of the Ionian part of the population, who turned upon the conquering Dorians and subjected and humiliated them. When he was at war with Argos, a Dorian city, he decreed an end to the contests of the rhapsodists at Sicyon because Argos and the Argives figured so prominently in the Homeric poems. He also sought to extinguish the worship of the Argive hero Adrastus in Sicyon. Clisthenes consulted the oracle at Delphi on this matter. The priestess said to him, "Adrastus is the Sicyonians' king, but you are only a robber." After this discouraging reply Clisthenes dared not use direct means to expel Adrastus, and sought to end his worship by establishing a shrine of Melanippus in Sicyon. Melanippus was a Theban hero and a great enemy of Adrastus, having slain his brother and his son-in-law Tydeus. Once Clisthenes had established the shrine of Melanippus he took away all the honors formerly bestowed on Adrastus and accorded them to Melanippus. He also renamed the Sicyonian tribes so that they would not have the same names as the Argive tribes. He had a daughter, Agariste, for whom he wished to find the best husband in Greece. At the Olympic Games, at which he won the chariot race, he had a proclamation made in which he invited all who considered themselves worthy to be his son-in-law to come and visit him for a year in Sicyon, at the end of which time he would choose one of them for his daughter. Many nobles from all over the Greek world accepted his invitation. They assembled from Italy, Aetolia, all over the Peloponnesus, Athens, Euboea, and Thessaly. Clisthenes prepared athletic grounds to test their prowess. In the year following their arrival the suitors were observed and tested as to their backgrounds, characters, accomplishments, and above all, their social accomplishments, and for this reason many hours were spent over the banquet table. During the year Clisthenes watched them closely, and found that the two who pleased him most were Hippoclides and Megacles, both of Athens; and of the two he preferred Hippoclides. When the time came for him to announce the successful suitor, he sacrificed 100 oxen and gave a great feast. The suitors entertained with speech and song. Hippoclides called to the flute players for a dance, whereupon he himself got up and began to dance. Clisthenes observed him with misgiving. Then Hippoclides called for a table, leaped upon it and continued to dance wildly. As Clisthenes watched with growing disgust, Hippoclides stood on his head on the table and made his feet do a jig in the air. Clisthenes lost all patience with him and called out, "You have danced your wife away." But Hippoclides was besotted with his own dancing and replied, "What does Hippoclides care?" From then on his reply became proverbial. Clisthenes now announced that the Alcmaeonid Megacles was his choice for a son-in-law. He gave rich presents and many compliments to the unsuccessful suitors and sent them back to their homes. Among the famous descendants of Clisthenes from this marriage were Clisthenes of Athens and Pericles. Clisthenes supported the Amphictyonic League in defending Delphi in the First Sacred War (590 B.C.). The men of Crisa (Cirrha), in whose territory the oracle of Apollo had been founded at Delphi, claimed control of it and levied toll on all visitors passing through their land to Delphi. The Delphian priests wished to be masters of their oracle and sought help from the Amphictyonic League, to which Clisthenes also gave his aid for the holy war in defense of the oracle. Crisa was taken after a struggle and destroyed. The land around the city was dedicated to the god, and the gulf formerly called Crisaean was henceforth known as the Gulf of Corinth. From this time the priests at Delphi became independent, and from this dates the period of the ascendancy of the Delphic oracle. The Pythian Games were splendidly reorganized, and Clisthenes won in the first chariot-race of the reorganized games. Valiant and able in war, Clisthenes was reputed a wise and humane ruler.

Clisthenes or **Cleisthenes.** Athenian politician of the 6th century B.C. He was the son of Megacles and the grandson of Clisthenes, tyrant of Sicyon, and was the most prominent of the Alcmaeonidae, the noble family important in Athenian politics at that period. Clisthenes and Isagoras struggled for control of Athens after the Pisistratid tyrants had been expelled with the aid of Cleomenes the Spartan (510 B.C.). Clisthenes won the advantage. He developed in a democratic spirit the constitution of Solon (adopted 594 B.C.) by substituting ten new for four old tribes, with a view to breaking up the influence of the landowning aristocracy, the new tribes being composed not of contiguous *demes* (local administrative communities), but of demes scattered through the area and interspersed with those of other tribes. The new tribes, which he named for native Athenian heroes, included new classes of free inhabitants and, with an enlarged council of 500, formed the basis of a popular government. Clisthenes, his followers, and 700 families who supported him were expelled in 507 B.C. by Isagoras, leader of the aristocratic party, aided by a Spartan army under Cleomenes, but he was recalled in the same year by the populace, which compelled the Spartans to withdraw and sent Isagoras into exile. On regaining his power he feared the Spartans, and sent envoys to King Darius in Susa to ask a treaty of alliance with the Persians. Darius agreed to an alliance provided the Athenians would give him earth and water as tokens of their submission to the Persians. The envoys agreed to this, but when they returned to Athens, they were

disgraced for their submission to Darius and the treaty of alliance was abandoned. According to tradition, Clisthenes established ostracism, the power of the sovereign popular assembly, the *ecclesia,* to decree, by means of a secret ballot, the banishment of any citizen who endangered the public liberty.

Clite (klī′tē). In Greek legend, the wife of Cyzicus, king of the Doliones. She had just married Cyzicus when the Argonauts came to his shores. He welcomed them warmly and they parted on friendly terms, but during the night they were driven back to his shores in a storm and by a tragic mistake they killed Cyzicus. Clite hanged herself in despair at the loss of her husband. The nymphs of the grove wept so for her that their tears created a fountain, to which her name was given.

Clitomachus (klī-tom′a-kus). [Original name, **Hasdrubal.**] Carthaginian philosopher; born c186 B.C.; died c110 B.C. He settled at Athens about 146 B.C., and succeeded (c127 B.C.) Carneades as leader of the New Academy.

Clitor (klī′tor). In ancient geography, a city in Arcadia, Greece. According to tradition, Clitor, the son of Azan and the grandson of Arcas, was a powerful king in Arcadia, who lived in Lycosura. He founded the city of Clitor and named it for himself. The city was on a level spot surrounded by low hills. It had several temples, of Demeter, Asclepius, Ilithyia, and the Dioscuri, among others, and, according to Ovid, a fountain called the Clitorium, the water from which was said to destroy the desire for wine. The river Clitor flowed nearby. It was supposed to contain dappled fish that sang like thrushes.

Clitumnus (klī-tum′nus). [Modern name, **Clitumno.**] River in Umbria, Italy, an affluent of the Tinia. It is celebrated (especially through the descriptions of the younger Pliny) for its sanctity and beauty. He mentions especially the existence of shrines to the river deity (Clitumnus) at its source.

Clitus (klī′tus). According to legend, a son of Mantius and the grandson of Melampus the seer. Eos fell in love with his beauty and carried him off.

Clitus. [Also: **Cleitus**; surnamed **Melas,** meaning "the Black."] Macedonian general, died at Maracanda (Samarkand), Sogdiana,

328 B.C. He was the friend and foster brother, so-called, of Alexander the Great, and accompanied him on the campaigns in Asia. At the battle of the Granicus River (334 B.C.) he saved Alexander's life. As Alexander increased his conquests and penetrated deeper into Asia, he adopted Oriental customs which were greatly resented by many of his Macedonian friends. At Maracanda Alexander summoned his friends, Clitus among them, to a feast. In former years Alexander had been most temperate in his habits, but on the march through Media and into the depths of Asia he and his men became accustomed to drinking the strong wine of the country as the only means of quenching their thirst; since the water in many places was not fit to drink. On this, as on other evenings, much wine flowed. The poets and musicians who accompanied the army sang the praises of Alexander, comparing him to the Dioscuri in whose honor the feast was given. Clitus, having drunk deep, suddenly leaped up and accused the singers of blasphemy. Inflamed by wine and deep resentment, he accused Alexander of preferring the conquered barbarians, who bowed the knee to him, to the company of free-born Greeks who dared speak their minds. Friends of both tried to quiet Clitus, but he insisted on pouring out his grievances and complaints against Alexander and went so far as to imply that Alexander unjustly took credit for victories his friends had won. Elders in the company removed Alexander's sword, but when Clitus reminded Alexander that he had saved his life and recited some verses of Euripides with an implied insult, Alexander seized a spear and ran it through his old friend's body. Although he instantly came to his senses and would have killed himself in his remorse for the death of his friend, the slaying of Clitus by Alexander in a drunken brawl marks the beginning of a definite change, for the worse, in Alexander's relation to his own Macedonians and in his ideas of kingship.

Cloaca Maxima (klō-ā′ka̱ mak′si-ma̱). Chief drain of ancient Rome, said to have been built by Tarquinius Superbus c600 B.C. Part of it is still in existence and much of it does not pre-date the 3rd century B.C. The outlet on the Tiber River is an arch about 12 feet high with three concentric tiers of massive voussoirs, fitted without cement.

Cloacina (klō-a̱-sī′na̱). See **Cluacina.**

Cloanthus (klō-an′thus). In Roman legend, a Trojan who accompanied Aeneas in his flight from Troy. His ship was driven apart from the others in a great storm off Sicily, and Aeneas thought that he had perished. But he was saved and, unaware that Aeneas still lived, he arrived at Dido's palace to seek help just as Aeneas was approaching it hidden in a cloud. In the funeral games in honor of Anchises in Sicily Cloanthus won the boat race. He was the legendary founder of the Roman family Cluentius.

Clodia (klō′di-a̱). Roman woman of patrician family; fl. 1st century B.C. The sister of Appius Claudius and of Publius Clodius (both surnamed Pulcher), she was reputedly of great beauty, intelligence, ambition, and extremely unconventional morals. Among her several lovers was Catullus, in whose poems she appears under the name of Lesbia. She was accused of murdering her husband Q. Caecilius Metellus Celer, and on her part she alleged that one of her lovers, M. Caelius Rufus, tried to murder her.

Clodius (klō′di-us), **Publius.** [Also: **Claudius;** surnamed **Pulcher.**] Roman adventurer and demagogue, born c93 B.C.; died Jan. 20, 52 B.C. He was the brother of Appius Claudius (also surnamed Pulcher) and of Clodia. He fought in the Third Mithridatic War, and when his services were not as well rewarded by Lucullus as he wished, he instigated a revolt, beginning the career of violence which made him notorious. In 62 B.C., disguising himself as a woman, he got admitted to the house of Julius Caesar during the observance of the Bona Dea ceremonies which were for women only. This caused a great scandal; one result was that Caesar divorced his wife Pompeia, who was said to have aided Clodius to gain entrance to the ceremonies. Another result was that Cicero prosecuted Clodius, who won acquittal by bribery and became Cicero's relentless enemy. Clodius, a member of a patrician family, arranged to be adopted by a plebeian so that he might qualify for the office of tribune, which offered the maximum opportunity for demagoguery. He was elected tribune in 58 B.C. and brought about the exile of Cicero and of Cato the Younger, causing Cicero's property, moreover, to be confiscated. Determined to dominate Rome, Clodius not only wooed public favor by demagogic means, but also organized gangs of strong-armed men to assault his enemies. Pompey and Milo organized a rival mob, and Rome was terrorized by the violent conflicts of these opposing forces until Clodius was killed by Milo's adherents. The disorders promoted by Clodius prepared the way for the civil war between Pompey and Caesar.

Cloelia (klē′li-a). In Roman legend, a maiden of Rome, delivered as a hostage to Lars Porsena c508 B.C. She escaped by swimming across the Tiber and returned to Rome. The Romans in all honor returned her into the hands of Porsena. He, however, in token of her courage, released her along with her fellow hostages.

Clotho (klō′thō). In Greek mythology, that one of the three Fates or Moerae who spins the thread of life.

Clouds, The. Comedy of Aristophanes, presented in 423 B.C. Strepsiades (Turncoat) sends his spendthrift son Phidippides to the phrontistery (thinking-shop) of Socrates, who appears as a sophist, to be reformed by training in rhetoric. Phidippides refuses to go; so Strepsiades goes himself and finds Socrates swinging in a basket observing the sun and ether. Socrates summons the Clouds, his new deities, and undertakes to make a sophist of Strepsiades and to free him from the religion of his fathers. Unfortunate results of his new knowledge show Strepsiades his error, and he abandons Socrates and sets the phrontistery on fire.

Cluacina (klu-a-sī′na). A Roman epiethet of Venus, with reference to her purifying powers. When Tatius and Romulus prepared to wage war on each other because of the rape of the Sabine women, they were prevented from fighting by the women themselves. Thereupon, the two opposing armies were purified with sacred myrtle branches, and on the spot where this occurred the temple of Venus Cluacina was raised.

Clusium (klō′zi-um). One of the chief cities of Etruria, located in Tuscany between Sena (Siena) and Volsinii (Orvieto). In the *Aeneid,* it is named as an ally of Aeneas in his war with the Latins. The town, originally one of the 12 confederated ancient Etruscan cities, is now named Chiusi, and has a museum of Etruscan antiquities. In the neighborhood are notable Etruscan tombs.

Clymene (klim′e-nē). In Greek mythology, a nymph, the mother of Phaëthon and the Heliades by Helius. She encouraged Phaëthon to seek his father and have all doubts of his parentage removed. This was because some had scoffed at Phaëthon's claim that he was the son of a god. After the death of Phaëthon, while driving the chariot of Helius, Clymene sought his remains throughout the world. She finally found his bones on the banks of the Eridanus River, where nymphs had buried them, and there too she watched his sisters turn into weeping poplar trees before her eyes.

Clymene. In Greek legend, a daughter of Catreus, king of Crete. Her sisters were Aërope, who became the mother of Agamemnon and Menelaus, and Apemosyne, and her brother was Althaemenes. Her father had been warned by an oracle that one of his children would kill him and, as he suspected Clymene of plotting against him, he was about to drown her. But Nauplius persuaded Catreus to sell him Clymene as a slave. Catreus did so with the stipulation that she be taken away from Crete and never allowed to return. Nauplius married her and took her to Nauplia, and she became the mother of his sons, Palamedes the inventor, and Oeax.

Clymene. In Homeric legend (*Iliad*), a handmaiden who accompanied Helen to Troy. She was given to Acamas when the Greeks defeated the Trojans.

Clymene. In Greek mythology, an ocean nymph. According to some accounts she was the mother of Prometheus by Iapetus.

Clymene. In Greek legend, a daughter of Minyas, king of Thessaly. She married Phylacus and bore him Iphiclus and Alcimede. Alcimede was the mother of Jason, according to some accounts, and her descent through Clymene from Minyas accounts for the name Minyans which was sometimes given to the Argonauts.

Clymenus (klī′me-nus). According to legend,

an Arcadian who fell in love with his own daughter Harpalyce, and ravished her. Later he gave her in marriage to Alastor, but did not give up his unnatural passion, and seized her again. Harpalyce bore a son. To punish Clymenus for his evil-doing, she slew her son, cut him up, cooked the pieces, and served them to her father, who was also the father of the child. Harpalyce was transformed into a bird and Clymenus hanged himself.

Clymenus. In Greek mythology, a king of Boeotian Orchomenus. He was accidentally injured by a stone flung in anger by a Theban charioteer at a festival of Poseidon in Onchestus. As he was dying, Clymenus charged his sons to avenge his death. Erginus, his eldest son, fulfilled his promise to his dying father by making war on Thebes and defeating the Thebans. He exacted heavy tribute from them for his father's death. Later, Heracles encountered the heralds who came to collect the tribute, cut off their ears and noses, and led the Thebans in a victorious war against Erginus.

Clytemnestra or **Clytaemnestra** (klī-tem-nes'tra, klit-em-). In Greek legend, a daughter of Tyndareus, king of Sparta, and Leda. She was the sister of Helen, Castor, and Polydeuces. Clytemnestra married Tantalus, son of Broteas, who was king of Pisa. Clytemnestra had just borne him a son when Agamemnon attacked Pisa, slew Tantalus and the infant at Clytemnestra's breast, and forced her to marry him. Her brothers would have avenged her but Agamemnon appealed to Tyndareus as a suppliant and was purified by him for the murder of Tantalus, and allowed to keep Clytemnestra as his wife. She bore him a son, Orestes, and three daughters: Electra (also known as Laodice), Iphigenia (also known as Iphianassa), and Chrysothemis. When the Greeks were massed at Aulis in preparation for the voyage to Troy to recapture Helen, unfavorable winds prevented them from sailing. Calchas the seer said Artemis had sent the winds because she was angry at Agamemnon for killing one of her sacred creatures. Only the sacrifice of Iphigenia to Artemis, Calchas advised, would appease the goddess and cause her to send favorable winds. Agamemnon sent for Iphigenia with the

message that she must come to Aulis to be married to Achilles. Clytemnestra, radiant with joy at this excellent match, accompanied Iphigenia to Aulis and there learned the truth. No pleas of hers could sway Agamemnon from his purpose of sacrificing Iphigenia, although he grieved to do so and had, in fact, tried to stop the messenger who went for her. But once she had arrived and the whole Greek army knew of the oracle he was persuaded by Odysseus that as commander of the 1000 ships assembled to sail to Troy he had a responsibility to do whatever was necessary for the conduct of the war. Thus Clytemnestra lost a second child to her warlike husband's ambition. Aegisthus, a cousin and an enemy of Agamemnon, had not joined the Greeks in the war against Troy. He now came to Argos. Although he had received special warnings from Zeus through his messenger Hermes not to encroach on Agamemnon's household, he now made elaborate plans to seduce Clytemnestra. He dispatched the bard whom Agamemnon had left behind to spy on Clytemnestra and went ahead with his plans. This was the easier to do because Nauplius, to avenge the death of his son Palamedes at the hands of the Greeks, had circulated rumors among the wives of the Greek heroes that their husbands had taken concubines in Troy whom they intended to bring home as wives. Clytemnestra readily believed such a tale of Agamemnon and, after some hesitation, yielded to the embraces of Aegisthus. For his success in becoming her lover Aegisthus offered rich gifts to the gods. To add to her many and painful grievances, Clytemnestra now learned that Agamemnon had taken Cassandra as his concubine. She and Aegisthus plotted to murder them both when they should come to Argos. She established an elaborate system of beacon fires which would inform her of the end of the Trojan War and of Agamemnon's progress towards Argos. A lookout watched from a tower for a year before the flash of fire signalling the approach of Agamemnon blazed over the sea. Aegisthus went to Nauplia to meet him. When he arrived in Mycenae, accompanied by Cassandra, Clytemnestra welcomed him extravagantly. She insisted that so glorious a victor must walk on a purple carpet into the palace. Agamemnon was reluctant to usurp a prerogative that was reserved for the gods but her appeals to his vanity induced him to follow her wishes. As he stepped onto the purple he piously hoped no jealous god would take offense. Clytemnestra led him into the palace for the ritual bath before the great feast which she said had been prepared for him. As he was stepping out of the bath she flung a netlike robe, without sleeves or a neck, over his head, and while he was helplessly trussed in it she, according to some accounts, killed him. Others say Aegisthus slew him and Clytemnestra cut off his head with a double-edged ax. She then, with the same weapon, slew Cassandra. A struggle between the supporters of Aegisthus and the followers of Agamemnon ensued, from which Aegisthus emerged victorious. Clytemnestra proclaimed the day as a monthly festival. Her claim was that the murder of Agamemnon was abundantly justified because he had killed Iphigenia and because of his insult in bringing Cassandra to Argos. For the next seven years she was the actual ruler of Argos, although ostensibly Aegisthus ruled. In fact he lived in terror of vengeance the whole time and did as Clytemnestra told him to do. She bore him three children, among them Erigone and a second Helen. But Clytemnestra's life was by no means serene. Her daughter Electra constantly charged her with being a murderess and an adulteress, and haunted her with the threat of vengeance. Orestes, who had been spirited away at the time of Agamemnon's murder, would surely return, Electra said, and avenge his father's death. In addition to the goading by Electra, Clytemnestra was troubled by dreams which seemed to indicate the furious return of Orestes. Eight years after the death of Agamemnon she received a false message that Orestes was dead. Her soul was divided; as a mother she must grieve at the death of her son, but as the murderer of his father she knew the greatest relief that now Orestes would not come seeking vengeance. The message had been planted by Orestes himself. He was in the neighborhood when Clytemnestra received it. He may, according to some accounts, actually have given it to her himself in disguise.

With the encouragement of Electra and the aid of his friend Pylades, he made himself known to his mother and, despite her pleas to be spared as the mother who had nursed him, he killed her and her lover Aegisthus. Whatever the estimate of Clytemnestra, whether as a strong and purposeful woman whose character was distorted by the wrongs she had suffered, or as a monster who was a disgrace to womankind, she was a fearless, intelligent, and arresting character. She arranged the plot to kill Agamemnon and did not flinch when it came to carrying it out. She ruled Argos with never an apology for the manner in which she obtained her power.

Clytië (klī'ti-ē or klish'i-ē) or **Clytia** (klish'i-ạ). In Greek mythology, a water-nymph so enamored of the sun-god Apollo that every day she watched his course across the sky. The gods took pity on her unrequited love and metamorphosed her into a heliotrope, a flower whose face follows the course of the sun. Hence, the heliotrope has come to symbolize unwavering love.

Clytië. Name sometimes given to one of the daughters of Pandareus. See **Merope**.

Clytius (klish'i-us). In Greek mythology, one of the giants, a son of Gaea and the blood of Uranus, who waged war on the gods. In the battle he was burned by the torches of Hecate and finished off by Heracles.

Clytius. Named by Homer *(Iliad)* as a son of Laomedon, and a descendant of Dardanus, Ilus, and Tros. He was the brother of Priam and the father of Caletor. He was slain by Heracles in the first sack of Troy, which only Priam of all the sons of Laomedon survived.

Clytius. In Greek legend, a son of Eurytus of Oechalia. He took part in the Calydonian Hunt and accompanied Jason on the quest for the Golden Fleece. He was killed when Heracles attacked his father's kingdom.

Cnaeus (or **Cneius**) **Pompeius Magnus** (nē'us pom-pē'us mag'nus). See **Pompey**.

Cnagia (nā'ji-ạ). Epithet of Artemis, from Cnageus, a Spartan who accompanied the Dioscuri in their war against Aphidna to recover Helen. He was taken prisoner and sold as a slave. As a slave he served in the temple of Artemis in Crete whither he had been transported. He escaped from Crete with the priestess of the temple, who carried the image of Artemis with her, and returned to Sparta.

Cnidia (nĭ′di-a̱). Epithet of Aphrodite, from Cnidus in Caria, where there was a celebrated statue of the goddess by Praxiteles.

Cnidus (nī′dus). Ancient city of Caria, Asia Minor, situated at the end of a narrow peninsula on the SW coast of what is now Turkey, between the islands of Rhodes and Cos. It was a Dorian city settled by the Lacedaemonians, and was a member of the Dorian Hexapolis of Asia Minor. Cnidus was a seat of worship of Aphrodite whom the Cnidians held in especially high honor. Their oldest sanctuary of the goddess was that of Aphrodite Doritis (*Bountiful*); others were the sanctuary of Aphrodite Acraea (*Of the Height*), and Aphrodite Euploia (*Fair Voyage*) or Cnidian Aphrodite. The famous statue of Aphrodite by Praxiteles was here. Some say Cnidus was founded by Triopas, for whom Triopium was named. The Cnidians dedicated an image of him at Delphi. They also dedicated images of Leto, and of Apollo and Artemis shooting Tityus, and of Dionysus. They had a treasury at Delphi, and their Lesche, or Club-room, at Delphi was decorated with paintings by the Thasian Polygnotus. One wall of the Lesche showed the taking of Troy and the Greeks sailing away, and contained figures of those who took part on both sides in the Trojan War. On another wall was depicted Odysseus visiting in Hades. At Triopium in Cnidus was a famous temple in which only the peoples of the Dorian cities of Lindus, Ialysus, Camirus (Dorian cities of Rhodes), Cos, and Cnidus had the right to worship. These were the cities of the Dorian Hexapolis, which had formerly included Halicarnassus. The Cnidians, to escape conquest when the Persians were subduing Ionia in the reign of Cyrus, attempted to make their land an island by cutting a channel across the neck of the promontory on which their city was located. As the work progressed, it was hampered by an unusual number of accidents, many workmen were injured about the eyes by splintering rocks. The Cnidians sent to Delphi to inquire of the oracle why the work of making their country into an island was being impeded. The oracular response was:

"Fence not the isthmus off, nor dig it through—
Zeus would have made an island, had he wished."

On hearing this, the Cnidians at once abandoned the project of making an island, and when the Persians advanced against them they gave up without a struggle. Following the Persian War Cnidus was a member of the Athenian Confederacy, from which it revolted, c412 B.C., during the Peloponnesian Wars. In 394 B.C. a naval battle off its shores saw Conon, the Athenian leader, defeat the Spartans under Pisander. Afterward, Cnidus joined Ephesus, Samos, and Iasus, with Rhodes, in a federation to protect themselves against the Persians and the Spartans. The Federation issued their own coinage on which appeared a figure of the young Heracles strangling the snakes, in a possible allusion to their hope of crushing tyrants. On the site of Cnidus, known at the present time as Cape Crio, are, among other ruins, those of an ancient theater. The *cavea* is 400 feet in diameter, with 36 tiers of seats divided by two precinctions, and survives almost perfect. There are considerable remains of the stage structure.

Cnossus or **Knossos** (nos′us). [Also: **Cnosus, Gnossus, Gnosus.**] In ancient geography, the capital of Crete, on the north coast and at the eastern end of the island. It was the site of a series of fabulous Minoan palaces. The site was discovered, 1886, by Heinrich Schliemann but he was unable to obtain the property at a price he considered fair, and abandoned his plan to excavate it. Sir Arthur Evans the English archaeologist visited the island in 1894, subsequently acquired the site of Cnossus, and began his excavations in 1900. His finds there were only equalled in importance by the earlier discoveries of Schliemann at Mycenae. The area of the palaces constructed at Cnossus was a low hill, in the valley of the Caeratus River. The discovery of wooden and bone utensils of the Neolithic Age showed that the site had been occupied since c3000 B.C. In succeeding ages two great palaces were erected at the site, the second of which was rebuilt after being partially destroyed. The first great palace was built about 2000 B.C. It was destroyed, by unknown means, c1700

B.C. Immediately a new and grander palace was erected on the ruins. The second palace was badly damaged, c1600 B.C., and was reconstructed, on a less extensive scale, in succeeding years. When, c1400 B.C., this palace too was destroyed, perhaps by an earthquake or by a sudden enemy raid, the site was thereafter only sparsely occupied. The second Minoan palace is the one associated with King Minos, Pasiphaë, the Minotaur, and the exploits of Theseus. The palaces were built on several levels connected by stairways and without any particular plan. Around a large central court groups of separate buildings were clustered. As more buildings were added, light and air were admitted to them by secondary courts and porticoes. With the passage of time, the buildings were connected by corridors to link them all into the complex that formed the palace. The builders were less concerned with the outside symmetry of the palace than with the comfort within it, and added chambers, courts, and porticoes with their connecting corridors as they were required, with the result that the corridors linking various parts

DOUBLE-AX
Red-figured Greek vase.

of the palace, the stairways by which different levels were approached, and the series of courts and porticoes, made it into a perfect maze. The double-ax, the word for which

was *labrys*, was a symbol of power, as well as a religious symbol and a mason's mark. It appeared in many places throughout the palace marked on walls and vessels, and double-axes were found in the chamber that came to be known as the "Room of the Double-Axes." The ending -*nth,* not of Greek origin, means "place of." Hence the palace was called *Labyrinth,* "place of the double-ax," but because of its mazelike arrangement the word "labyrinth" came to be thought of in succeeding years as a "maze." It may well be, therefore, that the story of Theseus and the Minotaur refers to the success Theseus enjoyed in the sport of bull-leaping in the central court around which the Labyrinth, "place of the double-ax," was built. Captives were commonly trained to take part in this sport, which consisted in baiting a huge bull. At the moment when the animal lowered its head and charged, the performer seized both its horns, turned a somersault over its head, and landed on the animal's back or on the ground behind it. Engravings on gems and other representations of the sport form a vivid basis for the story of Theseus. A small frescoed panel gives a complete picture of the sport. One of the paved courts of the palace is called the dancing-floor that was built for Ariadne by Daedalus.

Rather than attempt an ordered description of the conglomeration of courts, offices, magazines, baths, royal quarters, domestic quarters, treasure chambers, services areas, etc., it must suffice to mention some of the outstanding features of the palaces that sprawled on the hill at Cnossus. The outer walls were of stone or stone facing. The inner walls were of plaster and were decorated with richly colored frescoes. The frescoes have given valuable knowledge of the dress, life, and ceremonials of the times. They have also given names to some of the areas of the palace. A long corridor on the west is called the "Corridor of the Procession," from the fresco showing slim-waisted men, clad in loin cloths, bearing sacred vessels on their heads, and marching in a trim line across the wall. Another fresco shows an audience, including women, watching the sport of bull-leaping; and still another portrays elegant, black-haired ladies of the royal court. Wooden pillars, tapering from the top down and painted a rich terra-cotta color with blue bands at the top, rested on stone bases and supported the roofs and floors of the different levels. Water was brought from the hills by a "siphon" system and distributed through the palace by terra-cotta pipes and stone ducts. The supply was augmented by collecting rain-water from the roofs in shafts and causeways. Light and air were provided by light wells, covered shafts with openings cut into the walls below the roofs. Light and air were also provided by using the roof of one level as a portico for the next one. The great central court, lying N–S on the hill, was the center about which the rest of the palace was clustered.

for the royal visitors. The walls of the throne room were frescoed in strong colors with images of griffins and stylized vegetation. Opposite the throne is a sunken chamber, similar to others throughout the palace, that was probably used for purification rites. Its position so close to the throne indicates the close connection between the religious and temporal power of the king. To the east, the hill on which the palace stands drops away sharply. Here some of the underground rooms of the royal quarters have been preserved in their entirety, such as the Queen's Apartments, with blue-green dolphins leaping and playing on the frescoed walls. Four flights of the grand stairway that led down to the royal apartments have been preserved.

BULL-LEAPER
Fresco from the palace at Cnossus, before 1500 B.C. *Heraklion*

Just off it, on the west side, is a small chamber that has been named the throne room because in it, against the middle of one wall, a gypsum chair with rounded seat and high back was found. This is called the throne of Minos. On each side of it are stone benches

This is a most noble and serenely proportioned structure. Short flights, carefully designed for dignified ascent and set at right angles to each other, rise up the stair well. Pillars set on stone balustrades form an outer rail and add to the beauty of the structure.

fat, fāte, fär, fåre, errant; net, mē, hėr ardẹnt; pin, pīne; not, nōte, möve, nôr,

Ranged throughout the palace, on varying levels, are magazines under the protection of the double ax, where oil and grain were stored. Huge earthenware storage jars still stand as they were left thousands of years ago. Some of the magazines were used for the storage of treasure, judging by the bits of gold leaf that were found in them. Others were used for the sacred vessels belonging to the snake-goddess. Workshops containing fine painted pottery, unfinished stone vases, and material for producing other objects, were located in the north end of the east wing of the palace. Gathered about the palace were luxurious private villas that shared such features of the palace as light-wells, plumbing, porches, and lively frescoes. To the south of the palace, across a little stream, there are the remains of an inn that housed distant visitors to the palace. Cnossus was the center of a network of roads that radiated out over the eastern end of the island. The palace was unfortified, attesting to the unchallenged supremacy of Minoan sea power, as the richness of the palace, its comfort, and the highly developed techniques that built and furnished it attest to the brilliance of the Minoan civilization. Sir Arthur Evans, to whom the world is indebted for the evidences of this brilliant civilization, made a series of partial restorations of the palace. Following such clues as his excavations gave him he restored some of the frescoes, as that in the Corridor of the Procession (the original pieces of the fresco are in the Museum). Richly painted pillars were set up in certain places to restore porches and porticoes and more importantly, to replace the debris that was all that held up some of the upper floors. His restorations of porches, pillars, light-wells, and frescoes in several areas give a vivid impression of the style of architecture and decoration of the Minoan civilization, so different from those of the Classical Greek period.

Cocalus (kok′a-lus). In Greek legend, a king in Sicily. He welcomed Daedalus who fled to his kingdom when he escaped from Crete. The daughters of Cocalus were enchanted by the inventions of Daedalus and did not want to give him up when King Minos, from whom he had fled, came in search of him. When Minos demanded the surrender of Daedalus, the daughters of Cocalus, instructed by Daedalus, rigged a conduit over the bath in which Minos was resting, and poured boiling water, or as some say, hot pitch, on him and scalded him to death. Cocalus returned his body to his Cretan followers, with a tale that Minos had fallen into a cauldron of boiling water and so died.

Coccygius (kok-sī′ji-us). Epithet of Zeus. When Zeus first courted Hera she rejected his advances. He transformed himself into a cuckoo; Hera took up the bird and held it in her bosom. Zeus then assumed his own shape and ravished her. For this reason Zeus was given the name Coccygius (*Cuckoo*), and Mount Thornax, where the transformation took place, was renamed Mount Cuckoo. The famous statue of Hera by Polyclitus in the Heraeum at Argos showed the goddess holding a scepter on which a cuckoo perched.

Cocles (kō′klēz), **Publius Horatius.** Roman legendary hero, whose surname "Cocles" was a corruption of "Cyclops," and was given to him because he had lost one eye. Tarquinius Superbus (Tarquin the Proud), having been driven out of Rome, sought assistance from the Etruscan king, Lars Porsena of Clusium, and marched with a great force against Rome (c508 B.C.). In the battle outside the gates the Romans suffered heavy losses and withdrew inside the walls of Rome. As the Etruscans advanced toward the wooden Sublician bridge over the Tiber, Horatius with Titus Herminius and Spurius Lartius held the entire Etruscan force at bay until the bridge could be destroyed to prevent the Etruscans from attacking the gates. According to most accounts, Horatius alone held the bridgehead to the end. When it was destroyed, he jumped into the Tiber and swam to safety. As he swam, he was wounded in the thigh by an Etruscan spear and was henceforth lame. Publius Valerius (Publicola), who was consul at the time, passed a decree that every Roman should give him one day's provisions, that he be given as much land as he could encircle with a plough in one day, and that a bronze statue of him be erected in the temple of Vulcan. The statue was to be in the temple of Vulcan because that god, like Horatius, was lame.

Cocytus (kō-sī′tus). In Greek mythology, one of the five rivers surrounding Hades. Cocytus

actor; up, lūte, pull; oi, oil; ou, out; ŦH, then; ḍ as d or j, ş as s or sh, ţ as t or ch, ẓ as z or zh.

was the so-called Wailing River. The other four were: the Styx (Hateful), Acheron (Woeful), Pyriphlegethon (Fiery), and Lethe (Forgetful).

Codex (kō′deks). A form of book which made its first appearance in the 1st century B.C. or earlier, the ancestor of the modern book. It consisted of sheets of papyrus, vellum, or parchment folded once, arranged in quires, and assembled like the sheets of a modern newspaper. For economy (the text being written on both sides of the material), for convenience of storage and reference, and for durability, because it could be protected in a leather binding, the superiorities of the codex were substantial and it gradually superseded the older *volumen* or scroll. (JJ)

Codomannus (kō-dō-man′us), **Darius.** See **Darius III** (of *Persia*).

Codrus (kod′rus). Son of Melanthus, Messenian king who was driven from his land and became king of Athens. Codrus succeeded him and was the last king of Athens. He reigned (according to tradition) c1068 B.C. One legend is that Dorian invaders of Attica were assured by the Delphic oracle that success would come to that side whose king died. Codrus, having heard of this prophecy, disguised himself, and in unrecognizable, humble garb provoked a quarrel with some Dorian soldiers, taunting them until they killed him. This destroyed the premise by which the Dorians hoped to win, and Codrus thus saved his country by his own death. No one was considered worthy to succeed such a king. The archonship was established in Athens thenceforth, and Medon, son of Codrus, was appointed archon. But some say Codrus fell in battle. The sons of Codrus were the supposed founders of various Ionian cities, and thus connected Attica with Ionia. Among his sons was Neleus (or Nileus), named for the father of Nestor. He was said to have founded Miletus in Asia Minor. Other sons, and the cities they founded in Ionia, were Androclus (Ephesus), Damasichthon (Colophon), Andraemon (Lebedus), Damasus (Teos), Cyarethus (Myus), Cleopus (Erythrae), Promethus, and Naoclus.

Coes (kō′ēz). A Mytilenean general, contemporary with Darius the Great. He led the Mytileneans as allies of Darius when the latter bridged the Ister (Danube) and at-

tacked Scythia. Coes advised Darius not to destroy the bridge after the crossing of the army as he had proposed to do, but to leave a detachment to guard it so that it would provide a means of return. Darius was so pleased by his advice that he promised to give Coes any boon he asked. On the return of the Persians from Scythia Coes asked to be made king of Mytilene. Darius remembered his promise and granted his request. Coes was later stoned to death by the Mytileneans when Ionia revolted against Darius.

Coeus (sē′us). In Greek mythology, one of the Titans, children of Uranus and Gaea. He became the husband of Phoebe and father of Leto and Asteria. According to the Romans, he was the brother of Enceladus and Fama (Rumor), and the father of Latona.

Colaenis (kol-ē′nis). Epithet of Artemis, the name was derived from Colaenus, said to have been a king of Athens before Cecrops. Artemis Colaenis was worshiped in Myrrhinus, one of the small divisions of Attica.

Colaxaïs (kol-ak-sā′is). A son of Targitaus, who was said by the Scythians to be a son of Zeus and a daughter of the river-god Borysthenes, and the first inhabitant of Scythia. Colaxaïs was the youngest of the three sons of Targitaus. While they were in the land four golden objects, a plow, yoke, battle-ax, and drinking cup, fell from the sky. Lipoxaïs, the eldest of the three sons, ran to pick them up, but as he approached they blazed with fire and he was driven back. Next Arpoxaïs, the second son, approached and the same thing happened. But when Colaxaïs went near them the flames died out, he seized the golden objects and carried them away to his house. After this, the two older brothers acknowledged Colaxaïs as the king of the land, and from him sprang the tribe of Scyths called the Royal Scythians. The Royal Scythians kept the sacred golden objects and guarded them with the utmost care. At the annual festival, at which great sacrifices were offered in their honor, if the man guarding them fell asleep in the open air it was thought that he would not live the year out. Lipoxaïs was the founder of the Scythian tribe known as the Auchatae. The Catiari and Traspians sprang from Arpoxaïs.

Colchis (kol′kis). [Modern name, **Mingrelia.**]

In ancient geography, a country in Asia, lying between the Caucasus on the N, Iberia on the E, Armenia on the S, Pontus on the SW, and the Euxine (Black) Sea on the W. It was watered by the Phasis River (the modern Rion in Georgia, U.S.S.R.). Herodotus claimed that the Colchians were of Egyptian origin, descended from an Egyptian king, Sesostris (the exploits attributed to this king by Herodotus probably represent the combined efforts of Senusret I, Senusret III, and Ramses II), who journeyed into the land and left settlers there. He allied the Colchians to the Egyptians because of the similarity of their languages, because the two peoples, from ancient times, followed the practice of circumcision, and because the linen for which the Colchians were famous was woven in a manner used only by the Egyptians of all other peoples. At the time when Phrixus, riding a golden-fleeced ram, fled to Colchis from Orchomenus, the Black Sea was known as the Axine, or "Unfriendly" Sea. The land about it was inhabited by wild people who, nevertheless, received Phrixus kindly. The ram was sacrificed and its fleece hung in a sacred grove guarded by a fabulous monster. Nearby was a magnificent palace of Helius. Jason and the Argonauts journeyed to Colchis to recover the Golden Fleece. With the aid of Medea Jason was successful and escaped with the Fleece and Medea from Colchis. According to Herodotus, the abduction of Medea by Jason at her own request was one of the ancient causes of enmity between Europe and Asia that culminated in the Persian Wars. The Colchians, known to the Greeks as a barbarous and unfriendly people, did not bury or burn their male dead. Only women were buried. The men were wrapped in ox hides and exposed on trees to be eaten by the birds. Outside the city of Aea, Aeëtes' home in Colchis, Jason and his companions passed by such a cemetery, sacred to Circe, on their way to recover the Golden Fleece.

Colias (kō′li-as). Epithet of Aphrodite, from the promontory of that name in Attica where there was an image of Aphrodite Colias.

Coliseum (kol-i-sē′um). See **Flavian Amphitheater.**

Collatinus (kol-a-tī′nus), **Tarquinius.** Roman nobleman, fl. end of the 6th century B.C. His wife Lucretia was ravished by Tarquinius Sextus, son of the king Tarquinius Superbus. Collatinus, with others, vowed to punish the Tarquins whose harsh rule had made them very unpopular, and with Brutus and others he drove the Tarquins out of Rome. He was chosen (509 B.C.) with Brutus to be one of the two consuls who were to rule Rome in the place of the kings, and thus to transform it into a republic. Collatinus, though a nobleman and a relative of the Tarquins, was chosen because he would have the greatest reason for enmity to the Tarquins. However, when a plot by members of the Aquilii and Vitelii families to kill the consuls and restore Tarquin was exposed, Collatinus would have allowed the plotters, many of whom were related to him, to leave the city. In this he was opposed by Publicola and the conspirators were slain. Collatinus, who showed himself less hostile to the Tarquins than he was expected to be, resigned as consul and withdrew from the city.

Colline Gate (kol′in) or **Porta Collina** (pôr′ta kō-lī′na). Gate at the NE extremity of ancient Rome. Near here, in November, 82 B.C., Sulla defeated the Samnites under Pontius.

Colone (kō-lō′nē). In ancient geography, a small town in the Troad, in Asia Minor. It was seized and sacked by Achilles.

Colonna (kô-lôn′na), **Cape.** See **Sunium.**

Colonus (kō-lō′nus). [Also: **White Hill of Colonus; Kolonos Hippios.**] Site about one and a half miles NW of Athens, Greece, N of the Academy, on the banks of the Cephissus. It was the birthplace of Sophocles, and is immortalized by his description in the *Oedipus at Colonus.* It was a place sacred to the Furies in their later role of benign goddesses. Oedipus fled there with his daughter Antigone, and died there, comforted by the oracle. Upon the hill now stand the tombs of two noted archaeologists, the German Hellenist Karl Otfried Müller and the French Orientalist Charles Lenormant.

Colophon (kol′ō-fon). In ancient geography, one of the 12 Ionian cities of Asia Minor, situated near the coast, N of Ephesus. According to the Colophonians, the first Greeks who came there were colonists from Crete, who landed under their leader Rhacius and drove out the native Carians. Rhacius later married Manto, daughter of the seer Tiresias, and was, some say, the father of the seer Mopsus. Rhacius allowed the Thebans who came to Colophon with Manto to settle there, and his son Mopsus drove out the last. remaining Carians. After the Trojan War Calchas the seer went overland to Colophon, since he knew by his prophetic powers that heavy storms would assail the Greeks who sailed home from Troy. In Colophon he met Mopsus and, being defeated by him in a divining contest, died there and was buried at nearby Notium. In later years Ionians came to Colophon. They swore an oath of friendship with the Greeks already there and lived on equal terms with them. Some think that Gyges, the Lydian king, may have captured Colophon when he expanded his empire southward in the 7th century B.C., but he was forced to withdraw when the Cimmerians invaded his own country. The Colophonians took part in the Ionian revolt against Persia at the beginning of the 5th century B.C., and were subdued. Lysimachus, one of Alexander's bodyguards, completely destroyed the city (c302 B.C.), because its inhabitants fought against the Macedonians. At Clarus near Colophon was a famous oracle of Apollo.

Colossae (kō-los′ē). In ancient geography, a city in SW Phrygia, Asia Minor, situated on the Lycus. It was the seat of the early Christian church to which Paul wrote the *Epistle to the Colossians.*

Colosseum (kol-o-sē′um). See **Flavian Amphitheater.**

Colossus of Rhodes (kō-los′us rōdz). Large bronze statue of the sun god Helius, which anciently stood adjacent to the harbor of Rhodes on the Greek island of that name. Known in ancient and medieval times as one of the Seven Wonders of the World, it was designed by Chares of Lindus, and under his supervision erected between 292 and 280 B.C. It is reputed to have been 70 cubits high, or more than 100 feet, and is said to have been built from the abandoned bronze weapons and armor left by the soldiers of Demetrius I, king of Macedon, when they retired in defeat from their siege of Rhodes. The tradition that ships could sail between the colossal legs is erroneous. In 224 B.C. it was toppled by an earthquake. For many centuries great bronze fragments of the statue lay where they fell.

Colotes (kol-ō′tēz). Greek sculptor, a pupil of Phidias, who worked with him on the great statue of Olympian Zeus. He also made the table on which rested the victors' crowns at Olympia.

Column of Marcus Aurelius (mär′kus ô-rēl′-yus). [Also, **Antonine Column.**] A marble column erected in the Campus Martius at Rome between 175 and 193 A.D. to commemorate the victorious campaigns of Marcus Aurelius against the Dacians and Marcomanni in 172–175 A.D., similar to the Column of Trajan, having like the latter a shaft 100 Roman feet high on a high square pedestal, sculptured in spiral relief with scenes from the wars; the concept is of an artist's sketchbook in scroll form, unrolled to its full length and wound spirally around the shaft. The shaft is about 13 feet in diameter; within is a spiral staircase lighted by rectangular loopholes. On its Doric capital originally stood statues, long since vanished, of Marcus Aurelius and Faustina; the statue which now crowns it, of St. Paul, was placed there by Pope Sixtus V. It stands in what is now known as the Piazza Colonna. (JJ)

Column of Trajan (trā′jạn). Monument at Rome, dedicated in 114 A.D. in honor of the emperor. It is a Roman Doric column of marble, on a square basement, the total height, exclusive of the present statue of Saint Peter, being about 127½ feet. The base bears reliefs of warlike trophies and an inscription; the entire shaft is occupied by vigorous and lifelike reliefs ascending in a spiral, representing Trajan's campaigns. The reliefs contain about 2500 human figures, besides those of animals and inanimate objects.

Comaetho (kom-ē′thō). In Greek legend, a daughter of Pterelaus, king of the Taphians. Out of love for Amphitryon, who was attacking her father's kingdom, she cut off the lock of golden hair which rendered her father immortal and thus caused his death. Amphitryon ordered her killed for betraying her father, though he was victorious as a result of her treachery.

Comaetho. In Greek tradition, a priestess of Artemis in Patrae. She fell in love with Melanippus, but their love was opposed by both their parents. In defiance of their parents and religious custom, they profaned the sanctuary of Artemis by making love in it.

fat, fāte, fär, fãre, errạnt; net, mē, hėr ardẹnt; pin, pīne; not, nōte, möve, nôr,

Artemis sent a punishment on all the inhabitants of Patrae, the land became barren and strange sicknesses afflicted the people. Envoys were sent to appeal to the oracle at Delphi, to learn how the plagues could be lifted. The priestess told the envoys these evils came because of the impieties of Comaetho and Melanippus, and advised that in order to be free from them the Patraeans must sacrifice Comaetho and Melanippus to the goddess. Furthermore, each year they must crown a youth and a maiden with wreaths of ivy and grain and sacrifice them to Artemis Tridaria (*Threefold Assigner of Lots*). The practice of human sacrifice continued until Eurypylus arrived in the land, after the Trojan War, bearing a chest with the image of Dionysus. Thenceforth human beings were no longer sacrificed.

Comana (kō-mā′na). [Also: **Chryse**.] In ancient geography, a city in Cappadocia, Asia Minor, situated on the river Sarus. It was noted for its great temple to Ma, the Cappadocian mother goddess, with its elaborate festivals and great retinue of temple prostitutes and attendants, said to have numbered in the thousands.

Comana. In ancient geography, a city in Pontus, Asia Minor. It was perhaps a colony of the Cappadocian city of the same name and it was sacred to the same goddess, Ma.

Cometes (kom-ē′tēz). In Greek legend, a son of Diomedes' good friend Sthenelus. His father accompanied Diomedes to Troy and Cometes was left in charge of Diomedes' household. Thanks to the rumor Nauplius was spreading that the Greeks were taking concubines in Troy whom they would bring back as wives, Aegialia, wife of Diomedes, became the mistress of Cometes. When Diomedes returned from the Trojan War Cometes and Aegialia drove him out of his own country.

Cominius (kō-min′i-us), **Pontius.** Roman hero who volunteered to go through the enemy forces of the Gauls who had sacked and occupied Rome (389 B.C.), to the Capitol, which still held out under the command of Marcus Manlius. His mission was to secure an appointment as dictator for Camillus who would not accept the post until he was legally appointed by the citizens on the Capitol. Cominius took a number of pieces of cork and set out. When he came to the Tiber, he tied the cork about his body, leaped into the river, and propelled himself across. He made his way to the Capitoline Hill and up the lower slopes, using the bushes and shrubs to pull himself up. When he came to the steepest part of the hill, he called to the citizens on top. They hauled him up, gave him the appointment Camillus desired, and he returned the same way he had come.

Comitia (kō-mish′i-a). In Roman antiquity, assemblies of the people. They were of three kinds: 1) The most ancient assembly, that of the 30 curiae, or *comitia curiata*, in which the old patrician families found representation. Each curia had one vote, and the assembly acted on matters of state and affairs of family and religion. 2) The *comitia centuriata*, the assembly of the whole people by five fiscal classes, divided into centuries in the form of a military organization, according to the property census. There were 193 or 194 centuries, of which the first class had 98, so that the controlling vote lay with it. This assembly passed on laws and propositions with reference to which the Senate had the initiative, and had jurisdiction of capital offenses. 3) The *comitia tributa*, the assembly of the people by tribes or neighborhoods (a local division), 30—later 35—in number, without reference to rank. This assembly made nominations to the magistracy, had certain judicial powers extending to the imposition of fines and exile, and voted the laws called *plebiscita*. Under the empire the comitia were deprived of their judicial power, and of all influence upon foreign affairs, but retained a voice in the nomination or confirmation of certain magistrates.

Comitium (kō-mish′um, -mish′i-um). Paved area in ancient Rome, between the NE side of the Forum Romanum and the Curia, where the *comitia curiata*, or assembly of the patricians, met, and where the most important legal cases were tried. On the Comitium stood the original *rostra*, or official speakers' platform, and close to it was the *graecostasis*, the platform provided for foreign envoys.

Commagene (kom-a-jē′nē). [Called **Kummuh** in the Assyrian cuneiform inscriptions.] In ancient geography, a district in N Syria, between the Euphrates on the E and Cilicia on the W. At one time tributary of the Assyrian empire, it fell to Alexander, then to the Seleucids after his death, and was an independent kingdom from 65 B.C. to 17 A.D.

Comus (kō′mus).   In late Roman mythology, the god of mirth and drunken revelry, represented as a white-clad winged youth carrying a torch.

Concordia (kon-kôr′di-a).   In Roman mythology, the goddess of harmony and peace. There were several temples to her at Rome, the one on the Capitoline Hill dating from 367 B.C.   She is represented as a buxom matron with an olive branch in her right hand, the cornucopia in her left.

Condylea (kon-dil′ē-a).   A town in Arcadia, Greece.   Here there was a temple of Artemis Condyleatis.   According to Pausanias, one day some children, playing about the sanctuary, took a rope and put it about the neck of the image in the temple and said that the goddess had been strangled.   The people of the town, considering that the children had profaned the image, stoned them to death for impiety.   Afterward, the women of the town gave birth to dead babies, and when they consulted the Delphic oracle they were told this was a punishment for having unjustly killed the children.   The priestess ordered them to honor the children as heroes, and the stillbirths would cease.   From this incident the image of Artemis came to be known as "The Strangled Lady."

Condyleatis (kon-dil-ē-ā′tis).   An epithet of Artemis, from the place, Condylea (q.v.).

Confederacy of Delos (dē′los).   See **Delian League.**

Conius (kon′i-us).   Epithet of Zeus, meaning "Dusty."   There was a temple of Zeus Conius at Megara.

Conon (kō′non).   Athenian commander in the Peloponnesian War.   He succeeded to command of the Athenian fleet, 407 B.C., and shortly thereafter lost 30 of his 70 ships in an engagement with the Spartans at Mytilene. The Athenians melted down the gold and silver offerings that had been dedicated in the temples of the Acropolis and bought a new fleet with which (406 B.C.) he defeated the Spartans at Arginusae, south of Lesbos. Following the battle a fierce wind sprang up, and the Athenians did not rescue the crews of 25 of their own wrecked ships.   When news of the loss of these men reached Athens,

the city went into mourning, and a great hue and cry arose; the Athenian commanders were accused of negligence or worse, were tried, condemned to death, and six of them were executed.   Conon, however, was not included in the charges and no blame was attached to him.   In 405 B.C. the Athenian fleet under his command was disastrously defeated at Aegospotami by the Spartans. Conon prudently decided not to return to Athens on the heels of such a disaster.   He went to Salamis in Cyprus with part of the fleet and made plans and preparation to avenge the defeat.   He won the support of the king of Salamis and also at length received ships and money from the Persian court to wage war on the Spartans.   With such Persian aid he met an inferior Spartan fleet off Cnidus (394 B.C.), destroyed it and Spartan sea power, and avenged the disaster of Aegospotami.   He returned to Athens, rebuilt the Long Walls, and raised a temple to Cnidian Aphrodite at the Piraeus as a memorial of his victory.   In 392 B.C. Conon went as an envoy to parley with a Persian satrap friendly to Sparta.   The satrap treacherously imprisoned him.   He was released when the satrap was recalled and removed from power.   Conon went to Cyprus where he died soon afterward in the same year.

Conon.   Greek mathematician and astronomer, fl. 3rd century B.C.   A native or at least in early life a resident of Samos, and a friend of Archimedes, he traveled widely through the Greek world before settling at Alexandria. He was a student of solar eclipses and of the constellations, and in the history of mathematics is noted for his studies of conic intersections.

Consentes Dii (kon-sen′tēz dī′ī).   The Roman name for the gods of Olympus.

Constitution of Athens.   A monograph on the government of the Athenian state, by the 4th century B.C. philosopher Aristotle, lost for 1800 years and only recently recovered from the sands of Egypt.   Its reconstruction in almost complete form, a brilliant achievement of classical scholarship, was made possible by the contents of four papyrus rolls from Hermopolis in Egypt, identified at the British Museum in 1890.   These rolls had been used first for the accounts of the steward of an estate near Hermopolis; somewhat later, about 100 A.D., the *Constitution* had been written on their backs, and was buried with the owner in his grave. (JJ)

Consul. One of the two chief magistrates of the ancient Roman Republic annually chosen in the Campus Martius. In the first ages of Rome they were both elected from patrician or noble families, but about 367 B.C. the people obtained the privilege of electing one of the consuls from amongst themselves, and sometimes both were plebeians. The office of consul was retained under the empire, but was confined chiefly to judicial functions, the presidency of the Senate, and the charge of public games, and was ultimately stripped of all power, though remaining the highest distinction of a subject; it was often assumed by the emperors, and finally disappeared in the 6th century A.D.

Consus (kon′sus). In Roman mythology, a god, commonly called the god of good counsel, but having also certain very ancient agricultural and chthonian aspects. In his agricultural aspect of guardian of grain, the goddess Ops was his consort. His two festivals occurred in August and December. His underground altar in the Circus Maximus probably led the Romans to associate horses and horse racing with his festivals.

Copae (kō′pē). In ancient geography, a town on the shore of Lake Copaïs, in Boeotia, Greece. According to legend, Athamas settled on the plain before the town after he had killed his son in a fit of madness. Boeotians from Copae accompanied the Greeks to Troy. Among the temples of the ancient town were sanctuaries of Demeter, Dionysus, and Serapis.

Copaïs (kō-pā′is). In ancient geography, a lake in Boeotia, into which emptied the sacred river of Delphi, the Cephissus. Completely ringed by mountains, the Copaic Lake has no surface outlet, drainage in ancient times having been provided by natural tunnels ("katavothrae") in the limestone, whose choking was often followed by disastrous floods. Efforts to channel the waters and promote drainage began as early as the Bronze Age. From the lake bed rises a low rocky hill crowned with the massive defenses of a late Bronze Age palace, now known by the Albanian name of Gla or Goulas, the ancient name being unknown. Finally drained

at the end of the last century by a British engineering firm, Lake Copaïs has yielded to reclamation nearly 100 square miles of extremely fertile agricultural land. In antiquity, the lake was celebrated for its eels, pickled Copiac eels being a special delicacy. (JJ)

Copreus (kop′rös). In Greek legend, a herald, the son of Pelops and Hippodamia. He was purified of murder by Eurystheus and became his herald. It was Copreus who transmitted the orders of Eurystheus to Heracles and, according to some accounts, it was Copreus who threatened war, in the name of Eurystheus, against the Athenians for giving asylum to the children of Heracles. Copreus was at one time the owner of the marvelous horse Arion.

Cora (kō′rạ), **Core** (-rẹ), or **Kora, Kore.** A name meaning "Maiden," which was applied particularly to Persephone.

Cora. [Modern name, **Cori.**] Town in C Italy, situated about 30 miles SE of Rome. It was a town of the Volsci in Latium. Anchises predicted the founding of the town when Aeneas visited him in the Underworld, according to the *Aeneid.* It contains many Roman antiquities, such as columns, walls, and a temple of Hercules.

Corbulo (kôr′bū-lō), **Cnaeus Domitius.** Roman soldier and administrator, died 67 A.D. As legate under Claudius he governed Lower Germany, and caused a canal to be dug between the Rhenus (Rhine) and the Mosa (Meuse) which is still in service. Given command of Roman forces in the East, he waged successful campaigns against the Parthians and Armenians; but Nero, succeeding Claudius as emperor, seems to have suspected Corbulo of conspiracy, recalled him in 67 A.D., and compelled him to take his own life.

Corcyra (kôr′sī-rạ). In Greek mythology, a daughter of the river-god Asopus and Metope. Poseidon fell in love with her and carried her off to an island on the west coast of Greece which was subsequently named after her.

Corcyra. [Modern name, **Kerkyra, Corfu.**] The largest and most northern of the seven Ionian islands, separated from the coast of Epirus, Greece, by a broad channel. According to tradition, Poseidon fell in love with Corcyra, daughter of the river-god Asopus, and brought her to the island, which was then named for her. She bore Poseidon a son, Phaeax, who was the ancestor of the Phaeacians, according to some accounts. The island to which Corcyra was taken is a hilly land, heavily wooded with cypress trees, and was called "Black Corcyra" because of its somber woods. Some say the island was once visited by Demeter, and for this reason it was sometimes called Drepana, for Demeter's sickle. Others say it was called Drepana (Drepane or Drepanum) because Cronus threw the sickle with which he mutilated Uranus into the sea there and thus formed the island. The island was visited by Jason and Medea on their journey back from Colchis and it was here, in a cave of the nymph Macris, that they were married. Later, Odysseus was cast ashore here on his way home from the Trojan War and was graciously received by King Alcinous, a descendant of Corcyra and Poseidon. Hence, this island has been identified with **Scheria** and **Phaeacia** mentioned in the *Odyssey*.

The fertile soil and mild climate of Corcyra attracted settlers from an early time. Among the first to occupy it were the Eretrians. They were driven out when the island was colonized by Corinth, traditional date 734 B.C. The colony prospered and built up a strong fleet that dominated the surrounding waters. The Corcyraeans were said to take special pride in their fleet because they considered themselves to be descendants of the prime sailors of antiquity, the Phaeacians. As they increased in wealth and power, the Corcyraeans threw off their dependence on the mother city and defeated Corinth in a naval battle in the first half of the 7th century B.C. This was thought to be the first naval battle between two Greek powers. Subsequently, in their pride, the Corcyraeans denied Corinth the honors due a mother city and took every opportunity to show their contempt. Cypselus, tyrant of Corinth, brought them to heel and restored the sovereignty of Corinth over her colony. Corcyra incurred the wrath of Periander, son of Cypselus, by sheltering his son Lycophron. Lycophron refused all his father's pleas to return to Corinth while Periander was still there. At last Periander agreed that he himself would go to Corcyra and allow Lycophron to take his place as ruler of Corinth.

To keep Periander away, the Corcyraeans killed Lycophron, to whom they had hitherto granted asylum. Periander punished Corcyra by seizing 300 Corcyraean boys and sending them to Alyattes, king of Lydia, as eunuchs. On the way, the Corinthian ship carrying the boys touched at Samos, and the Samians, touched by the plight of the boys, and probably also to annoy the Corinthians, freed them and told them to seek sanctuary at the temple of Artemis in Samos. The Corinthians dared not violate the sanctuary, and attempted to force the boys out by cutting off their food supply. The Samians invented a festival in which Samian youths and maidens daily carried cakes of sesame and honey to the temple. The Corcyraean boys there in the sanctuary were allowed to snatch the cakes and so kept themselves alive. The festival continued to be observed long after the Corinthians, despairing of ever recapturing the boys, had given up and departed. When the Persians were invading Greece, 480 B.C., the assembled defenders sent to Corcyra, urging them to send help. The Corcyraeans readily promised to give assistance for, they said, if Greece fell, Corcyra would also fall. They manned 60 ships, but delayed putting them to sea. When at last their fleet did sail, it went only to the Peloponnesus and waited there to see how the war would go. For they fully expected the Persians to overwhelm the Greeks and wanted to be in a position to win Persian friendship when that result occurred. When the war was over, the successful Greeks reproached the Corcyraeans, who replied that they had indeed sent a fleet but that the Etesian winds had prevented it from rounding Cape Malea and joining the Greeks at Salamis.

Before the Persian War Corcyra had founded the colonies of Epidamnus and Apollonia in Epirus (7th century B.C.). Epidamnus was subsequently weakened by wars with her neighbors and by internal strife, and appealed to Corcyra for aid (436 B.C.). Corcyra rejected the plea. The Epidamnians next sought advice from the oracle at Delphi, and were told to put themselves under the protection of Corinth. The Epidamnians obeyed. Corinth sent an expedition to their relief. This infuriated the Corcyraeans. They commanded the Epidam-

nians to expel the Corinthian garrison, and
when they refused, sent a fleet, besieged the
city, and defeated the Corinthians at sea
(435 B.C.). This was one of the precipitating causes of the Peloponnesian Wars, for the
Corinthians drew Sparta to their side as
allies and the Corcyraeans appealed to, and
received the aid of Athens. In the long wars
that followed, Corcyra was weakened by internal strife and finally destroyed by revolution. In the next century the island was
taken by Sparta, and it ultimately fell to the
Romans.

Corcyraean (kôr-sī-rē′an) **Bull.** According to
Greek tradition, a great bull on the island of
Corcyra took up the custom of leaving the
cows in the pasture and going down to the
seashore, where he would stand and bellow
at the sea. When the herdsmen one day
followed him they saw the water in front of
him swarming with fish. They reported this
to the Corcyraeans, but when the fishermen
tried to net the fish they were unable to do
so. They sent an envoy ·to Delphi to inquire
about this circumstance. The oracle instructed them to sacrifice the bull to Poseidon. They did so, and immediately they
netted the fish. With a tithe of their catch
the Corcyraeans dedicated offerings at Olympia and Delphi. To Delphi they sent a
bronze image of a bull, and set it up beside
the Sacred Way to Apollo's temple. The
pedestal on which the image stood was seen
by Pausanias.

Cordaca (kôr-dā′ka). An epithet of Artemis
in Pisa. This epithet was given to the goddess because the followers of Pelops celebrated their victory over Oenomaus by dancing the *cordax*, a dance peculiar to the natives
of Mount Sipylus, from which Pelops had
come.

Coresus (kôr′ē-sus). In Greek legend, a priest
of Dionysus who loved Callirrhoë and killed
himself for her sake. See **Callirrhoë**, a
maiden of Calydon.

Corfinium (kôr-fin′i-um). In ancient geography, a town in C Italy, near the modern
Sulmona. It was the capital of the Paeligni,
and of the confederates in the Social War
(90–88 B.C.).

Corfu (kôr-fö′, kôr′fū). See **Corcyra**.

Cori (kō′rē). See **Cora**.

Corinna (kō-rin′a). Greek lyric poetess, born

at Tanagra in Boeotia, and active early in the
5th century B.C. She is sometimes called a
Theban from her long residence at Thebes,
whose local mythology formed the subject
of her work. She was a contemporary of
Pindar, from whom she is said to have won
the prize five times at the public games.
Although she wrote on mythological subjects
herself in the Boeotian dialect, she is said to
have advised Pindar not to overdo his use of
mythological allusion in his works, telling
him "to sow with the hand, not with the
whole sack." A few fragments of her poems
have been preserved.

Corinth (kôr′inth, kor′-). [Also: **Gortho**;
Greek, **Korinthos**; Latin, **Corinthia, Corinthus**;
ancient name: **Ephyra**.] City "in the corner
of Argos" in the Peloponnesus, situated near
the Isthmus and Gulf of Corinth. According
to tradition, it was founded c1350 B.C., some
say by Sisyphus. Poseidon and Helius contended for control of Corinthia, and Briareus
acted as arbitrator of their dispute. He
awarded the Isthmus and adjoining land to
Poseidon, and the height above the city (the
Acrocorinthus) to Helius. Thereafter, the
Isthmus was sacred to Poseidon, who had a
temple there in which were altars and images
of various sea-deities. The body of Melicertes, son of Ino and Athamas, was washed
ashore on the Isthmus and buried there, and
Isthmian Games were established in his
honor. The graves of Sisyphus and Neleus
were on the Isthmus, but their exact whereabouts was a well-kept secret. The region
was also the scene of some of the exploits of
Theseus. Theseus, Poseidon, and Corinthus
represent the original Ionian inhabitants of
Corinthia. Sisyphus, Jason, and Neleus represent the Aeolians who immigrated there.
Cenchreae was the east port and Lechaeum
was the west port of the Isthmus. A coin
of the time of the emperor Hadrian represents
the two harbors as two nymphs facing opposite ways with a rudder beween them. In
ancient times, ships were sometimes placed
on rollers and dragged across the Isthmus, to
save the long voyage around the Peloponnesus. Periander, tyrant of Corinth (c625–
585 B.C.), planned to breach the Isthmus
with a canal, but gave up the idea. Much
later, the emperor Nero began to cut a canal,
but he too abandoned the project. (The ex-

isting canal was completed in 1893.) In the Persian Wars, the Peloponnesians, under the leadership of Sparta, built a wall across the Isthmus as a fortification against the Persians. Some say the land about the Asopus River, in the NE corner of the Peloponnesus, was divided by Helius between his son Aeëtes to whom he gave Ephyraea (ancient name for Corinthia), and Aloeus to whom he gave Sicyonia. Aeëtes migrated to Colchis and left his kingdom in trust with Bunus, son of Hermes. After the death of Bunus the kingdom fell successively to the rule of Epopeus, then to his son Marathon, and then to his grandson Corinthus, for whom the name of the city was changed from Ephyra to Corinth. Corinthus died childless just at the time when Medea arrived from Colchis with Jason. She claimed the throne for Jason. Some say that when she was forced to flee from Cor-

CORINTHIAN JUG, 7TH CENTURY B.C.

inth, she gave her kingdom to Sisyphus. His descendants were ruling when the Dorians invaded the Peloponnesus in the 11th century B.C., defeated the Corinthians, and expelled them. The Dorian rulers were fol-

lowed by Bacchis (926–891 B.C.) and his descendants, the Bacchiadae, who were overthrown by Cypselus c657 B.C. The city of Corinth was well supplied with water. According to tradition, the river-god Asopus gave Sisyphus the never-failing Pirene spring in return for information about the whereabouts of one of his daughters, Aegina. It was at this spring that Athena bridled Pegasus for Bellerophon. In memory of the event, a temple of Athena Chalinitis (*Bridler*), was raised. The well of Glauce at Corinth was said to be the one in which Glauce, daughter of Creon, flung herself to get relief from the burning poison of the robe Medea had sent her. Nearby the well was the tomb of Medea's children. Some say they were stoned to death by the Corinthians in revenge for the death of Glauce. Afterward the Corinthians were punished until, at the command of the oracle, they offered annual sacrifices in honor of the dead children and set up a figure of Terror. As they were subject to Argos and Mycenae, the Corinthians had no leader in the Trojan War, but took part in it under the command of Agamemnon.

Corinth was noted in ancient times as a center of commerce, literature, and art, and as one of the wealthiest and most powerful of the ancient Greek cities. It sent colonies to Corcyra (Corfu) and Syracuse in 734 B.C., and founded Potidaea in Chalcidice and Apollonia on the coast of Epirus. During the rule of Periander (c625–585 B.C.) son of Cypselus, Corinth had reached a peak of cultural and commercial prosperity. The rise of Athens following the Persian Wars threatened the commercial supremacy of Corinth. A struggle over the Corinthian city of Potidaea, which was a tributary ally of Athens, was one of the precipitating causes of the Peloponnesian Wars, in which Corinth sided with Sparta against Athens. The alliance with Sparta disintegrated after the defeat of Athens in the Peloponnesian Wars, and Corinth engaged (395–387 B.C.) in the "Corinthian War" against Sparta. It was defeated by Sparta in 394 B.C. It later fell to the Macedonians and was held by them until 243 B.C., when it joined the Achaean League of which it was the capital. In 146 B.C. it was captured, sacked, and burned by the Romans, under Mummius; it was rebuilt by Julius Cae-

sar in 46 B.C. Pausanias visited the rebuilt
city in the 2nd century A.D. and has left descriptions of the monuments of the restored
city. He tells, for example, of an image of
Dionysus in the market-place that was supposed to have been made from the tree from
which Pentheus spied on the maenads as they
celebrated their revels, and from which he
was dragged to his death. He mentions a
temple of Palaemon (the name by which
Melicertes was known when he became a
god), and of Aphrodite Melaenis (*Black*).
Still to be seen are the ruins of an archaic
temple of Apollo, a Roman theater, an
odeum, the agora with basilicas, colonnades,
a hostelry, fountains, and other public buildings, the Fountain of Pirene, and much besides, excavated since the 1890's by the
American School of Classical Studies at
Athens.

Corinth, Gulf of. [Also: **Gulf of Lepanto;**
Latin, **Corinthiacus Sinus.**] Arm of the
Mediterranean Sea, with which it is connected by the Gulf of Patras. It separates
central Greece from the Peloponnesus.

Corinth, Isthmus of. Isthmus which connects
the Peloponnesus with central Greece. It is
now pierced by a canal. Width, 4–8 miles.

Corinthia (kō-rin'thi-a̯). [Also: **Corinth;** Greek,
Korinthos.] In ancient geography, a division
of Greece, lying between the Gulf of Corinth
on the N, Megaris on the NE, the Saronic
Gulf on the E, Argolis on the S, and Argolis
and Sicyonia on the W.

Corinthian Order (kō-rin'thi-an). In architecture, the most ornate of the classical orders,
and the most slender in its proportions. The
capital is shaped like a bell, adorned with
rows of acanthus leaves, and less commonly
with leaves of other plants. The usual form
of abacus (q.v.) is concave on each of its
sides, the projecting angles being supported
by graceful shoots of acanthus, forming volutes which spring from stalks originating
among the foliage covering the lower part of
the capital. These stalks also give rise to
lesser stalks and to spirals turned toward the
middle, and supporting an anthemion or other
ornament in the middle of each side of the
abacus. In the best Greek examples, the
shaft is fluted like the Ionic, and the base
called Attic is usual. The entablature also
resembles the Ionic. The Corinthian order

is of very early origin, though it did not come
into favor among the Greeks until comparatively late. The legend of the evolution of
the Corinthian capital by Callimachus, in the
5th century B.C., from a *calathus* (woman's

CORINTHIAN COLUMN

basket) placed on a maiden's tomb and
covered with a tile, about which the leaves
of a plant of acanthus had grown, is a fable.
Among notable Greek examples of the order
are the Tholos of Polyclitus at Epidaurus
(5th century B.C.), the choragic monument
of Lysicrates at Athens (c335 B.C.), and the
temple of the Olympian Zeus at Athens
(columns of which are a feature of the Athenian landscape), finished by the emperor
Hadrian. The rich character of the order
commended it to the Romans, who used it
freely, and modified it in accordance with
their taste.

Corinthus (kôr-in'thus). In Greek legend, a
son of Marathon or, as he claimed, a son of
Zeus. According to the Corinthians he was
the founder of the city of Corinth. Others
say he usurped the throne when Bunus, in
whose care Aeëtes had left the kingdom
when he migrated to Colchis, died. Some
say Corinthus died childless, and that on his
death Medea, as daughter of Aeëtes, claimed
the throne and made Jason the king.

Coriolanus (kō″ri-ō-lā′nus, kôr″i-, kor′i; kō″rī-ō-la′nus). [Surname of **Cnaeus** or **Caius Marcius**.] Roman legendary hero who was active in the first half of the 5th century B.C. He is represented as the champion of the patricians, and afterward as leading a Volscian army against Rome. He was the conquerer of the Volscian city of Corioli (whence his surname).

Corioli (kō-rī′ō-lī). In ancient geography, a city in Latium, Italy. Cnaeus Marcius conquered it c493 B.C., and took from it his name Coriolanus. Its exact site is unknown, but is probably not far from Ariccia.

Cornelia (kôr-nēl′ya). Roman matron of the 2nd century B.C. She was the daughter of the elder Scipio Africanus, wife of Tiberius Sempronius Gracchus, and mother of the Gracchi, the tribunes Tiberius and Caius Gracchus. She was celebrated for her accomplishments and virtues as a mother. After the death of her husband, she refused to marry again but devoted her life to her children. The story is told of her answering the boasts of another Roman matron about her jewels with the simple "These are my jewels," and pointing to her children.

Cornelian Laws (kôr-nēl′yan). [Latin, **Leges Corneliae**.] Body of laws introduced at Rome by the dictator L. Cornelius Sulla c80 B.C., with a view to restoring the aristocratic form of government, whose power had been weakened by the democratic legislation of the Gracchi and of Marius.

Cornopion (kôr-nō′pi-on). Epithet of Heracles. The people of Oeta in Euboea worshiped Heracles as Cornopion because he delivered them from a plague of locusts.

Cornucopia (kôr-nū-kō′pi-a). [Latin: **Cornu Copiae**.] See **Horn of Plenty**, which is the literal translation of the Latin phrase.

Cornutus (kôr-nū′tus), **Lucius Annaeus**. Roman Stoic philosopher, and commentator on Aristotle. He was born at Leptis Magna in Libya, c20 A.D., and died after 68 A.D. He was the friend and mentor of Persius, who dedicated his fifth satire to Cornutus.

Coroebus (kō-rē′bus). In Greek legend, a son of Mygdon, who allied himself with the Trojans in the hope of winning Cassandra, daughter of Priam, as his bride. He was killed by Diomedes in the sack of Troy.

Coroebus. In Greek legend, an Argive hero who killed the monster Poena, sent by Apollo to punish Argos for the deaths of Psamathe and her son Linus. After the slaying of the monster Argos was ravaged by a plague. Coroebus went to Delphi and confessed that he had killed Poena and asked that the plague be lifted. The priestess instructed him to carry a tripod from the shrine at Delphi. Where the tripod fell from his hands, he was to build a temple to Apollo. Coroebus did as he was bid. The tripod fell from his hands at Mount Gerania, and there he built the temple. The tomb of Coroebus, upon which was represented Coroebus slaying Poena, was at Megara.

Corona Australis (kō-rō′na ôs-trā′lis). An ancient southern constellation—the Southern Crown—about the knee of Sagittarius, represented by a garland.

Corona Borealis (kō-rō′na bō-rē-al′is, -ā′lis). [Also: **Ariadne's Crown** and **The Northern Crown**.] A northern constellation recognized by the ancients, between Hercules and Boötes, and represented as a garland with two streamers. According to mythology, it was the crown that Dionysus gave to Ariadne for a wedding present. When she died, he set it among the stars.

Corone (kō-rō′nē). Later name that was given to the ancient Messenian city of Aepea. Some say it was given this name because when the people were digging the foundations for the wall of the city they unearthed a bronze crow. Near this seacoast city, nestled under an overhanging mountain, the Messenians say Ino came ashore when she came from the sea transformed as the seagoddess Leucothea. The spring where the inhabitants got their drinking water rose in a hollow plane tree. See also, **Aepea**.

Coronea (kor-ō-nē′a). In ancient geography, a small town in Boeotia, Greece, situated W of Lake Copaïs. It was famous for two battles, in one of which (447 B.C.) the Boeotians defeated the Athenians, and in the other (394 B.C.) the Spartans under Agesilaus defeated the Thebans and other allied Greeks.

Coronis (kō-rō′nis). In Greek mythology, a daughter of Phlegyas, king of the Lapiths. She was beloved by Apollo, and during the absences of the god was guarded by his bird—a raven with pure white feathers.

fat, fāte, fär, fãre, errant; net, mē, hèr ardent; pin, pīne; not, nōte, mŏve, nôr,

During one of Apollo's absences Coronis fell in love with Ischys and was unfaithful to Apollo. The raven flew off to tell him, although, according to some accounts, the raven was warned by the crow, which had also once been white, not to be so anxious to be the bearer of bad news. On hearing the tale Apollo was enraged and turned the raven's snowy feathers black; some say because the raven had not driven off Ischys by pecking his eyes out; others say it was done because Apollo was so angry with the raven for bringing bad news. Either Apollo or his sister Artemis, to whom he had complained of Coronis' unfaithfulness, shot an arrow into the breast of Coronis. As she was dying Apollo repented of his anger, and in remorse tried to save her and his unborn child, but it was too late. He sorrowfully watched as her body was laid on the funeral pyre, then hastily called Hermes and asked him to snatch the unborn child free from its mother's womb. In this manner Asclepius, for so the child was named, was saved.

Coronis. A Lapith princess, according to some myths, or one of the nymphs of Naxos to whom Zeus entrusted the care of the infant Dionysus. Butes of Thrace, a son of Boreas, compelled her to marry him and she appealed to Dionysus. In answer to her pleas Dionysus drove Butes mad, and he cast himself into a well and drowned.

Coronis. According to some accounts, a daughter of Coroneus, king of Phocis. Poseidon pursued her and she appealed to Athena for help. Athena heard her prayers and transformed her into a white crow, so some say. Afterward, Coronis spied on the daughters of Cecrops, who disobeyed Athena's orders and looked inside the chest she had given them to guard. The chest contained the infant Erichthonius. Coronis flew off and told Athena of their disobedience. In anger at her talebearing, Athena forbade her to visit the Acropolis in future. But some say Athena turned Coronis' feathers black as a punishment.

Coronus (kō̱-rō'nus). In Greek legend, the son of Caeneus, the king of the Lapithae. He accompanied Jason on the quest for the Golden Fleece. Later he became king of the Lapiths and was killed by Heracles, who

aided the Dorians in a dispute with the Lapithae.

Corsica (kôr'si-ka̱). [Greek, **Cyrnos.**] Mountainous island in the Mediterranean Sea, N of the island of Sardinia. Phoenicians, Tyrrhenians, Etruscans, Greeks, Carthaginians, and Romans invaded the island, no one group ever completely suppressing the others. After the beginning of the First Punic War the Romans took the island from the Carthaginians. Remains of the ancient invaders have been found there. The Roman philosopher Seneca the Younger was banished (41 A.D.) to Corsica by the emperor Claudius, and had some very unkind things to say of the inhabitants, namely: that their first law consisted in avenging themselves, the second in living by rapine, the third in lying, and the fourth in denying the gods— but it must be remembered that Seneca's stay among the Corsicans was involuntary. Strabo speaks admiringly of their refusal to act the slave for Roman masters, who found them so intractable that they soon regretted the little they had spent in buying them.

Cortona (kôr-tō'nä). An ancient city of C Italy, in Tuscany, situated above the Mucellia River, about 50 miles SE of what is now Florence. It was one of the 12 great Etruscan cities. Important Etruscan and Roman antiquities, as well as ancient walls and a temple, remain.

Corvus (kôr'vus), **Valerius.** See **Valerius, Marcus.**

Corvus. An ancient southern constellation— the Raven or Crow—S of Virgo. A constellation anciently recognized, it presents a characteristic quadrilateral configuration of four stars of the second and third magnitude.

Corvus. The "Crow," a device for boarding an enemy warship, invented or perfected by the Romans and first used by them in the First Punic War (264–241 B.C.). It consisted of a hinged bridge or gangplank, which could be dropped on an enemy deck, fitted with a metal spike to embed in the planking and hold it in position while marines crossed to engage the enemy crew in the hand-to-hand combat at which Roman troops excelled. The Roman victory off Mylae, in 260 B.C., the first serious challenge to Carthaginian supremacy at sea, was credited to Duilius and his new corvus-equipped fleet. (JJ)

Corybantes (kor-i-ban'tēz). Priests of the Great Mother goddess in Phrygia, whose worship they celebrated by orgiastic dances. From the identification of Rhea with the Asiatic Great Mother, they are often equated with the Curetes, Rhea's satellite deities, since the priests were themselves representatives of these minor fertility gods. Some say the Corybantes were the children of Apollo and the Muse Thalia; others say they were the sons of Helius and Athena, or of Zeus and the Muse Calliope, or of Cronus. Still others say their mother was Rhea, and that she took them to the Holy Isle of Samothrace, and that the name of their father was revealed only to those who were initiated into the Samothracian mysteries.

Corycia (kō-rish'a̦). In Greek legend, a nymph beloved by Apollo, to whom she bore a son. The Corycian cave on Mount Parnassus was said to have been named for her.

Corynetes (kôr-i-nē'tēz). The nickname of Periphetes, meaning "Club-bearer," because he carried a bronze club. See **Periphetes.**

Coryphaea (kôr-i-fē'a̦). An epithet applied to the goddess who dwells on the top of the mountain. There was a sanctuary of Artemis Coryphaea (*Of the peak*) on Mount Coryphaeum near Epidaurus. The epithet was also used to designate the highest or supreme god, and was consequently sometimes given in the masculine form, Coryphaeus, as an epithet of Zeus.

Coryphasia (kôr-i-fā'sha̦). Epithet of Athena, from her temple at Coryphasium, the promontory on which Pylus in Messenia lies.

Coryphasium (kôr-i-fā'shi-um). Promontory in Messenia which became the site of Pylus, and which was afterward called Pylus.

Corythus (kôr'i-thus). A mythical king in Laconia whose herdsmen found Telephus, the son of Auge and Heracles, who had been born and abandoned on Mount Parthenius. The herdsmen took the infant to Corythus who reared him as his own son. At the same time, some of the shepherds of King Corythus found the infant Parthenopaeus, the child of Atalanta and Meleager, on the same mountain, and took him also to Corythus for shelter.

Corythus. The son of Paris and the nymph Oenone. Enraged that Paris had deserted her for Helen, Oenone sent Corythus to guide the avenging Greeks to Troy. There he was slain by his father because he too fell in love with Helen and aroused her interest.

Corythus. An ancient city of Etruria. Named, in the *Aeneid*, as the place in Italy where Dardanus was born and from which he emigrated to the Troad. The city was named for Corythus, a son of Zeus, and the father by Electra of Dardanus and his twin brother Iasion.

Cos (kōs) or **Kos.** One of the Dodecanese islands in the Aegean Sea, near the coast of Asia Minor. According to Homer, Hera raised a great storm and shipwrecked Heracles on this island. It is celebrated as the birthplace of the painter Apelles, Ptolemy Philadelphus, and the physician Hippocrates, and also for its sanctuary of Asclepius, a large and well-organized sanatorium and medical school established and directed by Hippocrates. Area, about 111 square miles.

Cosa (kos'a̦). A settlement on the coast of Etruria, founded as a Latin colony by Rome in 273 B.C. It stands on the hill of Ansedonia, between the Laguna di Orbetello and the Lago di Burano, some 85 miles northwest of Rome. Surface exploration combined with photographic reconnaissance from the air revealed the city walls, gates, street plan, forum, arx, Capitolium, and other buildings of the 3rd century B.C., and excavations directed for the American Academy in Rome by Frank E. Brown and Lawrence Richardson, beginning in 1948, have brought to light foundations of republican temples and public buildings, fragments of architectural decoration, and other finds. Air reconnaissance has also revealed the now silted port of Cosa, engineering measures taken in ancient times to prevent silting, and the secondary roads which linked colony and port with the Via Aurelia. The type of polygonal masonry represented by Cosa's massive limestone fortification walls was formerly assumed, on mistaken analogies with early walls in Greece, to belong to a relatively early period, the 6th century B.C. or earlier. This, plus its name, referred to a hypothetical Etruscan Cusi, and its loca-

tion led earlier generations of scholars to assume that Cosa's walls were in fact of Etruscan construction and date, and that excavation within them would reveal Etruscan
buildings and an Etruscan town plan. Professor Brown's demonstration that Cosa's
walls actually date from the 3rd century,
and that no construction earlier than 273
B.C. can be identified in the town, is a mile-
stone in the unraveling of Etruscan and
Italic chronology. The community which
grew up at the foot of Ansedonia, around
the port, appears to have been called Suc-
cosa, i.e., Sub-Cosa. (JJ)

Cosmetas (koz-mē′tas). Epithet of Zeus,
meaning "Orderer." Near the temple of
Zeus Cosmetas in Sparta was the tomb of
Tyndareus.

Cossaeans (ko-sē′anz). An ancient Elamitic
hill tribe which, when Sennacherib attacked
it in 702 B.C., was living in the NW mountains of Elam. It played an important part
in the history of Babylonia and in the course
of centuries was absorbed into the Babylonian population. In the time of Alexander
the Great the Cossaeans occupied the region
(Luristan, in modern Iran) lying about midway between the Caspian Sea and the Persian Gulf, and existed by preying on their
neighbors and travelers. Alexander conquered the tribe (c324 B.C.) and put many
to the sword, when he was on his return
journey from India. Some say he fell upon
the Cossaeans and killed them as an offering
to the shade of his friend Hephaestion who
had just died, for the oracle of Ammon in
Libya instructed him to make sacrifices to
Hephaestion and to worship him as a hero.
The Cossaeans are also known as Kassites.

Cossura (ko-sö′ra) or **Cossyra** (ko-sī′ra). [Mod-
ern names, **Pantalaria** or **Pantelleria**.] Island
in the Mediterranean Sea, off the W tip of
Sicily. The surface is rocky and volcanic.
It was early occupied by the Carthaginians,
but was taken by the Romans in 217 B.C.
It was highly favored as a place to which
members of the imperial family and other
prominent persons were banished in the time
of the Roman empire.

Cossutius (ko-sö′shus). Roman architect, engaged by the Seleucid emperor Antiochus
IV Epiphanes (175–164 B.C.) to prepare new
designs and resume construction, in the

Corinthian order, of the vast temple of Zeus
Olympius at Athens, which had been begun
as a Doric temple by the Pisistratids in the
6th century B.C. and abandoned on the exil-
ing of Hippias in 510 B.C. On Antiochus'
death construction was halted again and the
temple was completed only c132 A.D. during the reign of the Roman emperor Hadrian.
The employment of a Roman to design a
major Greek temple has been taken to indicate that Cossutius was an architect of
extraordinary ability, or that he was really
a Greek who had gained Roman citizenship
and name. (JJ)

Cottus (kot′us). In Greek mythology, one of
the Hecatonchires, the 100-handed giants
who were the children of Uranus and Gaea.
His brothers were Gyges and Briareus.

Cotyleus (kot′i-lūs). Epithet of Asclepius,
meaning "Of the Hip-joint." Heracles, engaged in a war with Hippocoön and his sons,
was wounded in the hip-joint and compelled
to retire. Asclepius healed his wound, and
to him Heracles gave the name "Cotyleus,"
and in gratitude raised a temple of Asclepius
Cotyleus near the Eurotas River in Laconia.

Cotys (kot′is) or **Cotytto** (ko-tit′ō). In ancient
Greek mythology, a Thracian goddess, resembling the Phrygian Cybele. Her festival,
the Cotyttia, was riotous and, later, licentious.

Cotys (kot′is). Any of several kings of Thrace,
but especially one who reigned between 382
and 358 B.C. One of his daughters married
the Athenian commander Iphicrates; another married the mercenary captain Charidemus. Cotys was an enemy of the Athenians and succeeded in wresting Sestos and
also all of the Thracian Chersonesus from
them. He was murdered in 358 B.C., and
his kingdom was divided between his three
sons.

Cranaë (kran′a-ē). [Modern name, **Mara-
thonisi**.] A small island in the Gulf of
Laconia, off the coast of Gythium. Here
Paris and Helen are said to have made their
first stop when they eloped from Sparta,
and here Helen first yielded in love to Paris.
A sanctuary of Aphrodite Migonitis (*Uniter*)
on the mainland opposite the island, commemorated the event, and the fulfillment of
Aphrodite's promise to Paris to give him
the most beautiful woman in the world in

return for his award to her of the Apple of Discord.

Cranaus (kran′ā-us). In Greek mythology, an earth-born man of what came to be known as Attica. He succeeded Cecrops on the throne. Cranaus had a daughter Atthis who died a maid. In her honor he named his land (formerly called Cecropia after Cecrops) Attica, after this daughter. It is said that it was during his reign that the flood of Deucalion took place in Thessaly. Amphictyon, said by some to be a son of Deucalion, and by others to be earth-born, rose against Cranaus and expelled him from Attica.

Crannon (kran′on) or **Cranon** (krā′non). [Also: **Ephyra.**] In ancient geography, a city in Thessaly, Greece, about ten miles SW of Larissa; its exact site is not known. Here, in 322 B.C., Antipater defeated the confederated Greeks.

Crantor (kran′tôr). Philosopher of the Old Academy (c335–c275 B.C.); born at Soli in Cilicia. He was the first commentator on Plato, and wrote a treatise, *On Grief,* from which Cicero borrowed extensively in his *Tusculan Disputations.*

Crassus (kras′us), **Lucius Licinius.** Roman orator and statesman; born 140 B.C.; died 91 B.C. He was consul in 95 B.C. and censor in 92 B.C. He is one of the chief speakers in Cicero's *De Oratore.*

Crassus, Marcus Licinius. [Surnamed **Dives,** meaning "the Rich."] Roman general and politician, born probably c112 B.C.; died 53 B.C. His father had been a censor and praetor, and he was reared modestly. His habits of life were temperate in the main. He married his brother's widow, entertained frugally, studied history and philosophy, and by cultivating the art of oratory made himself one of the most powerful public speakers in Rome. He was generous to strangers and educated his slaves for greater usefulness. But all his good qualities were obscured as he grew older by his great vice of avarice. He fattened on public calamities. It was said that when there was a fire in Rome, as often happened, he rushed to buy the burning property and then put out the fire with his own private fire brigade. The disorders of war and civil war afforded him opportunities to increase his wealth. Yet

the men he most despised were those whom he deemed guilty of avarice. Besides the great amount of real estate he owned in Rome he was the owner of silver mines, of valuable lands outside Rome, and of great numbers of slaves.

In the civil wars his father opposed Marius and finally committed suicide (87 B.C.) to avoid falling into his hands. The brother of Crassus also perished in the civil war. Crassus fled to Spain with some of his retinue to escape the proscriptions of Cinna, and hid in a cave for eight months. An acquaintance his father had made when he served as praetor in Spain sent food and other necessities and comforts of life to him during the whole period, but never allowed himself to see Crassus. When Crassus learned of the death of Cinna, he ventured out of the cave, gathered a band of followers, and marched about Spain. Some say he plundered Malaca (Malaga), but he denied it. He went to Africa and joined Metellus Pius, but failed to reach an accord with him and went over to Sulla, under whom he served in the campaigns of 83–82 B.C. During the proscriptions by which Sulla got rid of his enemies and seized their property Crassus enriched himself, profiting by the liberality of his chief and by the opportunities which the war offered for speculations in confiscated property. He became the richest man in Rome and used his colossal fortune to further his political ambitions. His great rival was Pompey, whom Sulla honored for his military victories. Since he could not equal Pompey in war, he turned to politics. He headed a moderate party between the aristocratic conservative party of Pompey and the radical party of Julius Caesar. Yet, says Plutarch, he was "neither a steadfast friend nor an implacable enemy, but readily abandoned both his favors and his resentments at the dictates of his interests." It is thought that he had some connection with the conspiracy of Catiline, and that for a time he secretly supported Publius Clodius, the enemy of Cicero. He won influence by the favors he granted and by the fear which the power of his wealth inspired. In 72 B.C. he was appointed by the Senate to put down the revolt of the gladiators under Spartacus, which two consuls had been

fat, fāte, fär, fāre, errạnt; net, mē, hèr ardẹnt; pin, pīne; not, nōte, möve, nôr, unable to quell and which spreading rapidly posed a great threat to Rome. In the course of fighting Spartacus one of his lieutenants disobeyed his orders, engaged Spartacus, was defeated, and fled with his men. Crassus chose 500 of those who had shown cowardice, divided them into 50 groups of ten men each, took one man from each group by lot and had him put to death as an example. He then pursued Spartacus to Rhegium and defeated a large part of his forces. In a succeeding engagement Spartacus was killed and the revolt was put down, but Pompey shared in the credit for the victory because he came upon those of the rebels who were fleeing from Crassus and killed them. Pompey was given a triumph, and Crassus had to be content with the knowledge that he had done his job well. This added to the jealousy he felt for Pompey and when, 70 B.C., he became consul with Pompey, he publicly disagreed with him on all matters. In 65 B.C. he was made censor but quarreled with his colleague and resigned. Caesar, who needed the military prestige of Pompey and the wealth of Crassus, succeeded in reconciling them and in winning their support. The three formed the First Triumvirate in 60 B.C., but when Caesar left for Gaul, the quarrels between Pompey and Crassus broke out anew. In 56 B.C. Caesar summoned them to Luca and again reconciled them, and urged them to run for the consulship again. There was some objection to this in Rome because they had accomplished so little when they earlier shared the consulship, but with liberal bribery, threats, and promises, as well as some juggling of the laws, they were elected (55 B.C.). In the division of spheres Crassus was awarded the province of Syria, Pompey got Spain, and Caesar was named proconsul of Gaul. Crassus was delighted. He meant to make war on the Parthians and win at last the military triumphs that would make him the equal of Pompey. Because there was no ground for a war against the Parthians his program was unpopular, and one of the tribunes of the people tried to prevent him from leaving Rome. The tribune was unsuccessful. Crassus sailed from Brundisium (54 B.C.) for the East. On the way he lost many vessels in a storm at sea. In the East he marched to the Euphrates River, crossed it, and took several cities in Mesopotamia. At Zenodotia 100 of his soldiers were slain. He captured the place, plundered and sacked it, and sold the inhabitants into slavery. He then went into winter quarters in Syria, plundered the temple at Jerusalem, and devoted himself to adding up the wealth he had taken. In the meantime the Parthians, thoroughly warned of his approach, made their preparations to resist him. A story is told that at a temple of Venus in Syria, Publius the son of Crassus stumbled and his father fell over him. He ignored the dire warning. His soldiers were terrified at the news they had of the Parthians, but Crassus was determined to proceed. His path was strewn with unfavorable omens. When he was crossing the Euphrates at Zeugma, a strange thunderstorm broke; the place where he intended to make camp was struck by two thunderbolts; the first Roman eagle set up turned around of its own accord and faced in the opposite direction; when rations were distributed to the men, lentils and salt, offerings customarily made to the dead, were offered them first. But most unfavorable of all was the combination in Crassus of military inexperience and unbridled ambition. He allowed himself to be duped by a barbarian chieftain pretending to be his friend into leaving the friendly valley of the Euphrates and striking out across the desert. The Parthians waited for him. When he was practically at a stand in the desert, his men weary from marching in sand and from thirst, the Parthians attacked. Publius, the son of Crassus, fought bravely. Crassus learned that he was in danger and rushed to his aid. But in the meantime Publius was wounded, and rather than submit to capture, he ordered his shield-bearer to kill him with his sword. When Crassus came up to aid him, he was met by the Parthians waving his son's head on the point of a spear. The battle was carried on furiously all day. Crassus suffered heavy losses. At night he retreated to Carrhae (modern Haran) in Mesopotamia, leaving his wounded behind to the mercy of the Parthians, who killed them all. After some days a message came to him in Carrhae, inviting him to a peace parley with the Parthians. He accepted the invitation and was treacherously slain. From the beginning to the end of the campaign, Crassus had displayed the utmost ignorance of military affairs and an obstinacy that resulted in disaster. Some 20,000 Romans are said to have lost their lives in the expedition that was undertaken to satisfy his ambition. According to Plutarch, the Parthians cut off his head and his hand, and carried the head to the pavilion of the Parthian king. The king was presiding over a banquet, at which a tragic actor was singing the lines of Euripides' tragedy, *The Bacchae*. As he came to the lines describing the frenzied Agave entering with the head of her own son, the head of Crassus was flung in and presented to the king.

Crataeis (kra̱-tē′is). Named by Homer *(Odyssey)*, as the mother of the sea-monster Scylla.

Crater (krā′tėr). An ancient southern constellation south of Leo and Virgo. It is supposed to represent a vase with two handles and a base.

Crater. [Also: **Krater.**] In ancient Greece, a large vessel or vase in which, as was Greek custom, water was mixed with wine according to accepted formulas, and from which it was dipped out and served to the guests in

CALYX CRATER
Theseus and the Marathonian Bull, 440–430
B.C. *Metropolitan Museum of Art*

the smaller pouring-vessels *(oinochoë)*. There are at least three types of craters. The bell crater is open and bell-like, with a foot, and a small handle placed very low on either side. The column crater, also footed, curves inward near the top to form a shoulder from which rises a neck of somewhat smaller diameter that ends in a rim; the handles rise as columns from the shoulder of the vessel to the rim. The volute crater, also footed, and like the column crater ending in a neck, has handles that rise from the shoulder and curl in a volute well above the rim. Many beautiful examples, richly decorated, are preserved.

Craterus (krat′ėr-us). Macedonian general, killed in Cappadocia, 321 B.C. He served Alexander the Great with distinction on the campaigns in Asia. He was one of Alexander's ablest and most trusted generals, and was often given the position of second in command as at Tyre (332 B.C.), Gaugamela (331 B.C.), and at the Hydaspes River (326 B.C.). Craterus built two cities—Bucephalia and Nicaea—on the banks of the Hydaspes while Alexander went on to the Indus River and into India. Craterus also prepared a fleet for transporting the army down the Hydaspes to the Indus and to the ocean when Alexander returned from India. From the mouth of the Indus Craterus marched inland on the homeward journey, to Arachosia to quell a revolt there and continued through Drangiana and Carmania, where he rejoined Alexander. In Asia Alexander increasingly adopted barbarian (Persian) customs to the dismay and resentment of his Macedonian veterans and friends. Craterus did not follow his commander in this, but maintained his Macedonian ways, and though he was highly respected by Alexander for his capacity, he did not enjoy the intimate affection with him that was shared by others. Nevertheless, on the occasion of a quarrel between Craterus and Hephaestion, Alexander rebuked them both, told them they were the two men he loved most in the world, but if such a quarrel ever arose again, he would kill them both, or, at least, the aggressor. In 324 B.C. Craterus was one of the leaders of the group of veterans Alexander sent home with rich rewards. Following the death of Alexander (323 B.C.) he became co-ruler

with Antipater of his empire. The Greek
states rebelled when they learned of Alexander's death. Craterus marched into Thessaly
and defeated them at Crannon (322 B.C.).
The next year he was killed in Cappadocia
(321 B.C.).

Crates (krā′tēz). Greek comic poet and actor
of the 5th century B.C. He is said to have
performed in the plays of Cratinus. He
wrote comedies in which he presented subjects of a general character rather than a
series of disparate antics and attacks on individuals, and is said to have been the first
to produce plays in which drunken men
appeared. Only fragments of his work
survive.

Crates. Greek Cynic philosopher; born in
Thebes; fl. c320 B.C. He was a disciple of
Diogenes.

Crates. Athenian, the pupil and successor of
Polemo in the Academy; fl. c270 B.C. The
friendship of Crates and Polemo was famous
in antiquity, and they were said to have been
buried in the same tomb.

Crates of Mallus. Greek grammarian, born
in Mallus in Cilicia; fl. c150 B.C. He was
the founder of the Pergamene school of
grammar. His chief work was a comprehensive critical and interpretive commentary on Homer. He went to Rome in 168–
167 B.C., and during a long stay there gave
lectures which aroused an interest in the
study of philology and literary criticism
among the Romans. Only fragments of his
work survive.

Cratinus (kra-tī′nus). Athenian comic poet,
born c484 B.C., died c419 B.C. He was a
bitter enemy of Pericles. His writing was
forceful but it is said he suffered from over-
fondness for wine. Aristophanes alluded to
him in the *Knights* as a fine man ruined by
drink. Nevertheless, Cratinus exhibited 21
plays and was victor nine times. His last
victory was won over Aristophanes with a
play in which he answered Aristophanes'
allusion to him in the *Knights* by writing a
satirical play against himself, in which his
wife of the play rescues him from the
clutches of Pytine (*Wine-jug*). He was
called by Mahaffy "the real originator—the
Aeschylus—of political comedy." The titles
and many fragments of his plays have survived.

Cratippus (kra-tip′us). Greek historian who
continued the history of Thucydides. Although he is given as a contemporary of
Thucydides in at least one source, it is felt
that he is a much later writer and the claim
of antiquity was made in order to secure
greater authority for his work. (AH)

Cratippus. Peripatetic philosopher of Mytilene; fl. c45 B.C. He was the friend and instructor of Cicero, who accounted him one of
the first philosophers of the Peripatetic
school. He accompanied Pompey in his
flight after the battle of Pharsalus, and endeavored to comfort and rouse him by engaging him in philosophical discourse. He
opened a school at Athens c48 B.C., which
was attended by many eminent Romans, including Brutus during his stay at Athens
after the murder of Caesar. He is thought
to have written a work on divination.

Cratus (krā′tus). In Greek mythology, a son
of Uranus and Gaea. He was the personification of strength or force, and in the
Prometheus Bound of Aeschylus, Cratus
goaded Hephaestus into binding Prometheus.
Some say Cratus was a son of the Titan
Pallas and Styx.

Cratylus (krat′i-lus). Greek philosopher, an
elder contemporary of Plato. He was a disciple of Heraclitus. Plato introduces him as
the principal speaker in one of his dialogues
(the *Cratylus*).

Cremera (krem′e-ra). In ancient geography,
a small river in Etruria which joins the Tiber
a few miles N of Rome. It is the traditional
scene of the defeat of the Fabii in c477 B.C.

Cremona (krē-mō′na; Italian, krä-mō′nä). City
in NW Italy on the Po River. It was founded
by the Gauls and became a Roman colony in
218 B.C. The old city, on the site of modern
Cremona, was destroyed in 69 A.D. in a
struggle between Vitellius and Vespasian.

Creon (krē′on). In Greek legend, a son of
Menoeceus of Thebes and a brother of
Jocasta, mother and wife of Oedipus. He
was ruler of Thebes after the death of Laius
but when Oedipus came to Thebes and freed
it of a plague by killing the Sphinx, Creon
gave him the throne and his sister, the widow
of Laius, in marriage, as he had promised he
would do for whoever rid Thebes of the
Sphinx. Plague again struck Thebes, some
years later, and ominous signs pointed to

Oedipus as the reason for it. He accused Creon of treachery and of spreading lies about him. But Creon was his loyal friend and when Oedipus left Thebes, having by this time learned the true reason for the plague, he left his children in Creon's care. Creon ruled until Eteocles was old enough to take the throne. In the war of the Seven against Thebes it was prophesied that Thebes would be victorious if a royal prince voluntarily sacrificed himself to Ares. Menoeceus, son of Creon, killed himself before the walls. In the fighting Eteocles was killed, Creon took command and drove the Argives back and Thebes was saved. He ordered a magnificent funeral for Eteocles, defender of the city, but forbade anyone, on pain of death, to bury Polynices, his other nephew who had inspired the attack on Thebes. Antigone, sister of Polynices, defied his order. She crept out of the city and buried her brother. When Creon learned of her defiance he ordered her to be buried alive. His son Haemon, to whom Antigone was betrothed, killed himself on her tomb. Theseus and the Athenians, some say, compelled Creon to yield the bodies of the other Argive dead and to restore them to their families for burial. To deny proper burial to the dead was the most wicked punishment that could be devised against an enemy, because the unburied had to wander for many years on the near side of the Styx before they could be ferried across to their final resting place in Hades. Creon ruled Thebes after the death of Eteocles until Laodamas, the son of Eteocles, grew up and assumed the throne.

Creon. In Greek legend, a king of Thebes. He was the father of Megara, whom he gave to Heracles in gratitude for his defeat of the Minyans under Erginus. According to some accounts he was slain in an uprising while Heracles was in the Underworld fetching Cerberus.

Creon. In Greek legend, a king of Corinth, father of Creusa, or Glauce, the intended wife of Jason. He perished when he tried to save his daughter, who was burning from the poisoned robe Medea had sent her. Creon attempted to pull the robe from his daughter and was destroyed with her.

Creontiades (krē-on-tī′a̱-dēz). According to some accounts, the second son of Megara

and Heracles. He was to have become king of Thebes but Heracles, in a fit of madness inspired by Hera, slew him and his other children by Megara.

Cresilas (kres′i-la̱s). Greek sculptor; born at Cydonia, Crete; active in the second half of the 5th century B.C. His career was made at Athens, where he was a contemporary of Phidias, and where he executed a portrait statue of Pericles. Copies exist of a figure of a wounded Amazon, which Cresilas carved at Ephesus in a competition with Phidias and Polyclitus.

Cresius (krē′shi-us). Epithet of Dionysus, meaning "Cretan." In the temple of Dionysus Cresius at Argos, some say, Ariadne was buried.

Cresphontes (kres-fon′tēz). According to legend, a son of Aristomachus, a descendant of Heracles, and brother of Temenus and Aristodemus. The brothers, as leaders of the Heraclidae (Dorians), conquered the Peloponnesus and decided to divide it between them by lot. Aristodemus having died, his share was to go to his twin sons, Eurysthenes and Procles. Lots were to be cast into an urn, and he whose lot came up first was to receive Argos, second Laconia, and third Messenia. The lot of Temenus came up first and he was assigned Argos. The sons of Aristodemus won dominion over Laconia. Cresphontes, who greatly desired the rich land of Messenia, won it by a trick. He put a clod of earth in the urn and poured water on it. As it was melted by the water, his lot came out last. After the lot-drawing, the Heraclidae set up three altars to Zeus Patrous (*Paternal*) and on the altar of each a sign appeared. On the altar of Cresphontes there was a fox. The seer interpreted this to mean that his people would be wily. In future wars between the Spartans and the Messenians, the Spartans based their claim to Messenia on an ancient right, saying Cresphontes had won it by trickery. Cresphontes was killed in a rebellion with two of his sons. A third son, Aepytus, was spared because he had been sent into Arcadia and later regained the throne.

Cressid (kres′id) or **Cressida** (kres′i-da̱). Mythical daughter of the Trojan priest Calchas, whose supposed infidelities have made her name a byword for female faithlessness. The name represents the accusative case of *Chryseis* (q.v.) The story of Cressid is believed to have originated with Benoît de Sainte-Maure, a 12th-century trouvère, who called his character Briseida (she was thus identified with Homer's Briseis). Guido delle Colonne later reproduced the story in a popular Latin work, the *Historia Trojana.* The story was later taken up by Boccaccio, Chaucer, and Shakespeare. A modern version may be found in Christopher Morley's *The Trojan Horse* (1937). Shakespeare's *Troilus and Cressida* is probably the best-known verision of the tale.

Creta (krē′ta̱) or **Crete** (-tē̠). In Greek mythology, a nymph who bore Pasiphaë, wife of Minos, to Helius. She was also known as Perseis. Some say she was a daughter of Asterius, and the wife of Minos.

Cretan Bull, The. In Greek mythology, a magnificent fierce bull, given to Minos, king of Crete, by Poseidon. Minos refused to sacrifice it to Poseidon, as he had promised to do, and as a punishment Poseidon caused Minos' wife to fall in love with the bull and to become by the bull the mother of the Minotaur. Heracles captured the bull as one of his labors for Eurystheus, and rode on its back as it swam from Crete to Greece. The bull was turned loose in Greece and roamed the countryside until it came to Marathon, where it terrified the populace. It then became known as the Marathonian Bull, and was responsible for the death of Androgeus, son of Minos. Theseus finally slew the bull.

Crete (krēt). [Also: **Candia**; Greek, **Kriti, Krete**; French, **Crète, Candie**; Italian and Latin, **Creta**; Old Turkish, **Kirid, Kirit**.] Island in the Mediterranean Sea, situated SE of Greece and SW of Asia Minor. It has an area of 3235 square miles, is 160 miles long, and 35 miles wide in its greatest width. Sharply rising mountain ridges separate the parts of the island from each other. The mountain slopes, once covered with cedar and cypress, are now largely bare. In the fertile plains and river valleys wheat, fruit, wool, olives, and wine are produced. According to legend, the inhabitants of Crete sprang from the soil. Their first king was Cres, for whom the island was named. Some say the Idaean Dactyls, who discovered the use of fire and metal-working, were born in Crete. The nine Curetes, either sprung from the earth or born of the Dactyls, originated in Crete, and the Titans, especially during the Golden Age of Cronus when men lived like gods, were associated with the island. In a cave on Mount Ida the Curetes protected the infant Zeus by clashing their shields to drown out his cries, while nymphs nourished him with milk and honey. To memorialize the contribution of the bees Zeus changed their color to copper that gleamed like gold in the sun, and made them impervious to changes in the weather, an important consideration in Crete. Athena was said by some to have been born from the head of Zeus at the source of the Triton River in Crete, where a temple was raised to her. The marriage of Zeus and Hera was also said by some to have taken place on the island. Cretans annually reënacted the ceremony at a temple that commemorated this event. Teucer, the ancestor of the Trojans, came from Crete, and Minos, Daedalus, Pasiphaë, the Minotaur, and many other figures of mythology and legend are associated with the island. Long before the Greeks on the mainland had developed their ideas of the great god Zeus, however, the Cretans had elaborated their own concepts of the gods. The chief figure in their worship was the Great Mother, who had power over life and death, who was the goddess of the forest and of wild beasts, and who occupied the central place in Cretan religion. Her attributes were the double ax, the *labrys,* a symbol of power, and the Horns of Consecration, which may have been connected with the bull, an animal that appears later in connection with the story of Europa. The Great Mother was a triple goddess, who ruled in heaven, on earth, and under the earth. The animals sacred to her came from each of her kingdoms—the dove from the air, the bull or lion from the earth, and the snakes from the underworld. Joined to the Great Mother was a male figure, a son-husband, he who was first named Zagreus by the Greeks and later developed by them into the great sky-god Zeus, whom the Cretans claimed was born on their island. They also claimed his tomb in the hill of Iuctas, the outline of which appears to be a giant lying on his back, pointing his great bearded profile at the sky. It was because the Cretans claimed to have the tomb of Zeus that the Greeks called them "liars," and gave them a bad reputation throughout the Greek world. Obviously, Zeus, being a god, could not have died and been placed in a tomb. Because Crete was subject to frequent earthquakes, there was a strong chthonic element to Cre-

SNAKE GODDESS
Faience statuette from the palace at Cnossus, 1600–1580 B.C. *Heraklion*

tan religion. The Cretans explained the earthquakes as the tossing of the earth on the great bull's horns, and propitiated him by offering him sacrifices of bulls.

The Cretans are thought to be of Libyan or Anatolian stock. Homer names them as Achaeans, Cydonians, Dorians, Pelasgians, and Eteocretans, the last of whom are believed to be the original non-Hellenic inhabitants. But Homer wrote long after the greatest ages of Cretan civilization had passed away. Cretan civilization existed before 3000 B.C., and was in a continuous state of development thereafter, reaching its height in the period 3000–1400 B.C. The German archaeologist Heinrich Schliemann believed that Crete was the legendary isle of Atlantis. He thought Crete might be the origin of the highly developed art he had found in Greece. He discovered the site of the palace of Cnossus in 1886, but was unable to carry out his plan for excavating it. It remained for Sir Arthur Evans the British archaeologist, who had visited the island in 1894, to acquire the site and, in 1900, to begin his excavations. Other excavations in various parts of the island have been carried on by the Italians, by the French School, the English School, by Americans, and by the Greeks. Sir Arthur Evans classified the distinctive periods into which Cretan civilization falls according to ceramic development, as follows:

Early Minoan I (E.M.I)		
		3400–2800 B.C.
" " II (E.M.II)		
		2800–2400 B.C.
" " III (E.M.III)		
		2400–2100 B.C.
Middle Minoan I (M.M.I)		
		2100–1900 B.C.
" " II (M.M.II)		
		1900–1700 B.C.
" " III (M.M.III)		
		1700–1580 B.C.
Late Minoan I (L.M.I)		
		1580–1450 B.C.
" " II (L.M.II)		
		1450–1375 B.C.
" " III (L.M.III)		
		1375–1100 B.C.

The relatively strict dates for each period are possible because of close synchronization with Egyptian history, for Cretan external relations were oriented toward Egypt from an early date. Habitations have been discovered beneath the palaces of Cnossus (q.v.) and Phaestus that date from the Neolithic Age, before 3000 B.C. Wooden

fat, fāte, fär, fâre, errant; net, mē, hėr ardent; pin, pīne; not, nōte, mōve, nôr, and bone utensils, and polished and incised pottery of this period have been found on these and other sites. In the period from 3000–2000 B.C. two great centers of civilization developed, that around the plain of Mesara, on the southern side of the island, and that at the eastern end of the island. In this period close commercial relations were held with the islands of the Cyclades, with Egypt, and with Asia Minor. This period saw the development of gray incised pottery, decorated with simple figures—zig-zags, herring-bones, groups of parallel lines, and rows of dots (E.M.I); pottery decorated with red and black on a natural clay ground (E.M.II); and pottery painted in white on a black glazed ground on which new patterns were introduced (E.M.III). Also in this period, great progress was made in metal-working and in the art of carving stone vases, employing the natural strata of the stone as decoration. In the Middle Minoan periods the polychrome style, called "Kamares ware" (because first examples of it were found by the English in a cave at Kamares, on the south slope of Mount Ida) was developed, with white, red, and yellow decorations on a black glazed ground. By the Middle Minoan periods I and II (2100–1700 B.C.), a brilliant civilization had evolved. The first palaces were built at Cnossus and Phaestus; the polychrome Kamares ware had become highly decorative with stylized figures, such as the octopus motif; and the refinement developed in the techniques of the potter's wheel led to the production of "egg-shell" vases, so named for their thinness with fluted bodies and rims of great delicacy. A system of hieroglyphic writing was in use; commercial relations in the Aegean were widened, continued with Egypt, and extended into Asia. At the end of this era of the fabulous development of a civilization far in advance of any that had developed on the Greek mainland at this time, some unknown catastrophe struck all the centers of Cretan civilization and destroyed them, about 1700 B.C. The interruption was temporary. Between 1700 and 1400 B.C. new and grander palaces were raised at Cnossus, Phaestus, and Mallia; comfortable private houses with oiled parchment for window panes were built around the palaces; new cities were founded; relations with Egypt and the Near East flourished; and Cretan colonies were sent out to the neighboring islands and to the Greek mainland. Cretan civilization and power was at its height. The age was characterized by the figure of King Minos, who had the largest and most powerful navy in existence and controlled the waters of the Mediterranean. Some say that the name "Minos" was a title similar to the Egyptian word "Pharaoh," and that it applied to at least two Cretan kings, and perhaps to a series of them. Palaces and houses were decorated inside and out with brilliantly colored frescoes that depicted naturalistic scenes, such as the human figure, sacrificial processions, and religious gatherings, thus recording much of the Cretan way of life. Sculptured stone vases, decorated pottery jars, some of great size, and golden cups worked in relief with consummate artistry, were in use in the palaces. Fragile vases and delicate figurines played a part in religious ceremonies or served for ornamentation. The king and others had exquisite seals cut in gems for sealing their documents. Seal engraving was developed to perfection in the Middle Minoan and following periods. Animals at rest and in action, birds in flight, human figures, were engraved with exquisite grace and fidelity on ivory, steatite, crystal, jasper, and other hard surfaces. From the miniature seal engravings of ceremonial scenes comes much of our knowledge of Minoan ritual. Relief decorations on cups and carving reached a peak of refinement. These are exemplified by the famous Vaphio cups (so-called because they were found at Vaphio, near Sparta, whither they had been carried from Crete), with their scenes of the bull hunt and of the bulls in pasture beautifully worked in repoussé, and by the extraordinary figure of the bull-leaper carved in ivory. Frescoes show large audiences, including women, watching the sport of bull-leaping, which differed from the bull-fight in that the performer must catch the horns of the bull as the animal charged, leap over its head, and land on his feet on its back. Many scenes and stories, as well as religious ceremonies, centered about the bull. Two styles of linear writing were in use in this period—the Linear Script A and Linear Script B—and indicated that the Cretans had an

---

actọr; up, lūte, pụll; oi, oil; ou, out; ₮ʜ, then; ḍ as d or j, ş as s or sh, ṭ as t or ch, ẓ as z or zh.

alphabet long before Cadmus introduced the Phoenician alphabet into Greece. The Linear Script B was deciphered, half a century after the first examples of it had been found, by the Englishman Michael Ventris, in 1952. In 1957 Prof. Cyrus H. Gordon of Brandeis University announced that an adaptation of Accadian was the language of the Linear Script A. In the houses and palaces of this era brilliant use of "light-wells" was made for ventilation and illumination; ingenious "siphon systems" brought water from the hills to the palaces, where it was then distributed by means of terra-cotta pipes and stone ducts. The household water supply was also augmented by rain water drained from the roofs. This period, so briefly described, was the era of Cretan supremacy, in commercial and maritime power, and in the refinement and brilliance of its civilization. About 1400 B.C. general catastrophe overcame the flourishing civilization and destroyed it, apparently at once. Some think it must have been a great natural disaster, as an earthquake, that put such a sudden end to the great palaces and Minoan cities. Others think it was perhaps a swooping raid by Achaeans from the mainland that utterly overthrew the Cretan civilization. The Athenian legend is that Theseus caused the overthrow of Cretan civilization, for when he fled with Ariadne, the Cretan fleet pursued him and in its absence the island was beset by enemies. Others say the island was exposed to raiders when King Minos sailed off in his fleet to recover Daedalus, who had escaped on waxen wings to the kingdom of Cocalus in Sicily. In the following centuries, 1400–1100 B.C., Crete was dominated by the Mycenaean culture. Its own became decadent, the palatial sites were not reoccupied to any great extent; the importance of Crete as a center of art, culture, and commerce declined completely. Homer mentions in the *Iliad* that Crete, "century-citied," sent soldiers against Troy under the leadership of Idomeneus and Meriones. In the *Odyssey* he describes the palace of Alcinous, with its gold and silver doors, and its decorations of blue enamel, and though some think the island home of Alcinous was Corcyra or Corfu, the description of the palace might equally well apply to the palaces of Crete. After the time of

the Trojan War the "hundred cities" of Crete warred so among themselves that they became an easy prey for the Dorians, who invaded their island, c1100 B.C., and put a period to the Minoan civilization. At the beginning of the era that culminated in the Classical period, c750 B.C., Cretan culture enjoyed a renascence. Cretan archaic art and skilled cratfsmanship, heirs of the master smith Daedalus, influenced developments on the Greek mainland. Independent cities coined their own money, and it was in this time that the famous Gortynian Code of Laws was promulgated—an extraordinary document that detailed all kinds of social and economic laws, and was engraved on the walls of a portico or arcade near Gortyna. Crete played no role in the Persian and Peloponnesian Wars. Its relations with the mainland were slight. By the height of the great Classical period its artistic developments had come to a halt. Its age of greatness was far in the past. In 66 B.C. the island fell, but not without difficulty, under the domination of the Romans.

Cretea (krē′tē̱-a̱). In ancient geography, a place on Mount Lycaeus, in Arcadia. The Arcadians said that here, in a place where no living creature casts a shadow, Zeus was born to Rhea. According to the Arcadians, this name Cretea was afterward taken to mean the island of Crete. But as far as they were concerned Zeus was born in Arcadia.

Cretheïs (krē′thē̱-is). In Greek mythology, the wife of Acastus, son of Pelias. Her name is also given as Astydamia (q.v.) and Hippolyta. She fell in love with Peleus, who had come to her husband's court to be purified for a murder, and when he rebuffed her advances she accused him to his wife Polymela of plotting to desert her and marry her (Cretheïs') daughter, Sterope. Polymela believed the lies of Cretheïs and hanged herself in despair. Cretheïs then made the same accusations against Peleus to Acastus and asked him to avenge the insult. Acastus was reluctant to kill a man he had purified and sought, unsuccessfully, to get rid of Peleus in another way. Some time later Peleus returned, attacked the kingdom, slew Acastus and Cretheïs, dismembered her body and drove his chariot through its scattered pieces into the city.

fat, fāte, fär, fāre, errant; net, mē, hėr ardent; pin, pīne; not, nōte, möve, nôr,

Cretheus (krē'thūs). In Greek legend, a son of Aeolus, king of Magnesia in Thessaly, and Enarete. He was the founder and king of Iolcus. He married his niece Tyro, daughter of Salmoneus, and adopted her twin sons Pelias and Neleus. By Tyro he was the father of Aeson, Pheres and Amythaon.

Cretheus. In the *Aeneid*, a Trojan companion of Aeneas on the flight from Troy to Italy. He was the darling of the Muses; his heart was given forever to song and the lyre. He was totally unequipped for war, and in the battle between the forces under Aeneas and those under Turnus in Italy he was slain by Turnus.

Creticus (krē'ti-kus), **Metellus.** See **Metellus, Quintus Caecilius** (d. c56 B.C.).

Creus (krē'us). See **Crius.**

Creusa (krē-ö'sa). In Greek mythology, a daughter of Erechtheus, king of Athens, and Praxithea. Apollo fell in love with her while she was still a very young girl and ravished her. Deserted by the god, whom she had called on for aid in vain, when her time came she bore Apollo a son in secret, and abandoned the child in the cave where he was born under the Acropolis. She was soon overcome by remorse and concern for her baby and returned to the cave to recover him but he had disappeared. Even the tapestried coverlet in which he was wrapped was gone, and there were no traces of blood to show that he had been devoured by animals. Creusa carried her sad and guilty secret alone. She later married Xuthus, the son of Hellen, who had fled to Athens from Thessaly and had helped Erechtheus in a war. The Athenians looked down on him as an alien, and thought it was just as well when some time had passed and no children were born to the couple. Xuthus longed for a son and went with Creusa to consult the oracle at Delphi. He was told that he should consider the first person he met on leaving the sanctuary as his son. Ion, a young and handsome priest of Apollo, was the first person he met and Xuthus joyously claimed him. Creusa, jealous because Xuthus had a son and she didn't know what had become of her child, and also incensed to think that Xuthus had a child by another woman, resolved to slay the youth. She offered him a cup of poisoned wine, but as he poured out part of

it as a libation to the gods a dove sent by Apollo flew down, drank of the wine, and instantly expired. Creusa's plot against him being exposed, Ion pursued her to the altar where she fled and would have killed her, but the priestess of Apollo appeared. She told Creusa and Ion how he had been brought by Hermes as an infant from a cave to Delphi. When she showed them the coverlet in which he had been wrapped Ion was overjoyed as he thought now he would be able to trace his mother. Creusa recognized the coverlet as one she had made herself and wrapped about her new-born child in the cave. She revealed to Ion that she was his mother and a reconciliation was effected. On instructions from the priestess Creusa did not tell Xuthus that Ion was her child. She allowed him to go on thinking that he was a gift to her husband from the oracle. Later she bore Xuthus two sons, Achaeus and Dorus.

Creusa. In the *Aeneid*, the daughter of Priam and Hecuba. She was the wife of Aeneas and the mother of Ascanius. During the flight through the burning city of Troy she was separated from Aeneas. He retraced his steps into the city but never saw her again. Her ghost appeared to him as he searched and told him to go without her, and to fulfill his destiny by establishing a race in another land.

Creusa. [Also: **Glauce.**] In Greek legend, daughter of Creon, king of Corinth. Jason the Argonaut, tiring of his wife Medea, fell in love with Creusa and planned to marry her. Medea sent Creusa as a wedding gown a magic robe which, when she put it on, burned her flesh and caused her to die in terrible convulsions.

Crimisus (kri-mī'sus). [Also: **Crimissus.**] In ancient geography, a river in W Sicily, probably near Segesta. Here Timoleon with 11,000 men defeated (339 B.C.) 70,000 Carthaginians. In the *Aeneid*, the river-god Crimisus is named as the father of Acestes by the Trojan woman Egesta or Segesta, for whom the town is named.

Criophorus (krī-of'ō-rus). An epithet of Hermes, meaning "Ram-bearer." It was given him by the people of Tanagra because he averted a pestilence by making a circuit of the city carrying a ram on his shoulders, one

actor; up, lūte, pull; oi, oil; ou, out; ᴛʜ, then; ḏ as d or j, ş as s or sh, ṭ as t or ch, ẕ as z or zh.

of the many instances in Greek lore of the apotropaic Magic Circle. Thereafter, at the feast of Hermes at Tanagra the handsomest youth marched around the walls carrying a ram on his shoulders in commemoration of this event. In his role as savior Hermes was also called Promachus (*Defender*). In many places Hermes was called Criophorus to signify his role as protector of flocks.

Crisa (krī′sạ). [Also: **Crissa**.] In ancient geography, a city in Phocis, Greece, situated SW of Delphi. It was styled "the divine" by Homer. It is often confused with its port, Cirrha.

Crispus (kris′pus), **Caius Sallustius**. See **Sallust.**

Critias (krish′i-ạs, krit′i-ạs). Athenian orator and politician, disciple of Socrates, and distinguished poet and orator. He was one of the Thirty Tyrants who governed Athens, opposed the revolution of 411 B.C., and proposed the recall of Alcibiades. He fell with the Tyrants in 403 B.C., perishing in the battle for the citadel of Piraeus. His reputation as a cruel, rapacious, and dissolute man may be unjust, as Plato seemed to admire him and introduced him in a dialogue which bears his name. He wrote on historical and political subjects, and was the author of several tragedies. Fragments of his political elegies survive.

Critius (krish′i-us, krit′-) and **Nesiotes** (nes-i-ō′tēz, nē-shi-). Greek sculptors of the 5th century B.C. Critius is thought to have been a pupil of Antenor, creator of the famous statues of Harmodius and Aristogiton, which were carried off from Athens by Xerxes and later recovered. Meanwhile Critius and Nesiotes executed new figures to replace those taken away by the Persians. Two sculptures at Naples have been identified as copies of these works, one of which, however, has been restored with a head of 4th century workmanship. Very little is known about Nesiotes, but Critius had a school of sculpture at Athens and among his works was a statue of Apollo with the lyre.

Crito (krī′tō). Athenian, a friend and follower of Socrates; fl. c400 B.C. He is a prominent character in the dialogue by Plato named for him.

Critolaus (krit-ō-lā′us). Achaean demagogue; died 146 B.C. He was the last *strategus* of the Achaean League, and was defeated by Quintus Caecilius Metellus at Scarphea near Thermopylae in 146 B.C.

Critolaus. Greek Peripatetic philosopher; fl. 2nd century B.C. He was sent to Rome in 156–155 B.C. as a member of the embassy of philosophers.

Crius (krī′us). In mythology, a Titan, the son of Gaea and Uranus. By Eurybia, the daughter of Pontus, he was the father of Astraeus, Pallas, and Perses.

Croceatas (krō″sē-ā′tạs). Epithet of Zeus, from his image at Croceae, a place in Laconia.

Crocus (krō′kus). According to some accounts, a youth who loved the beautiful youth Smilax. Smilax did not return his love, and the gods changed the unhappy Crocus into a saffron plant. Others say that Crocus was transformed into a saffron plant by Hermes, his friend, who had accidentally killed him while they were playing a game of quoits.

Croesus (krē′sus). King of Lydia in the 6th century B.C. He was the son of Alyattes, whom he succeeded in 560 B.C. He subjugated the Ionian, Aeolian, and other neighboring peoples, and at the close of his reign ruled over the region extending from the N and W coasts of Asia Minor to the Halys River (modern Kizil Irmak) on the E and the Taurus Mountains on the S. According to Herodotus, he was visited at the height of his power by Solon, to whom he exhibited his innumerable treasures. He asked Solon who, of all the men he had seen, he considered the most happy. Solon answered that Tellus of Athens was the happiest. Croesus, incensed because he had expected Solon to name him, a rich lord of many lands, asked why he had named Tellus. Solon replied that Tellus lived at a time when his country was flourishing, had fine sons whom he saw grow up and produce children of their own, and in the end perished gloriously fighting for his country. On being pressed to name the second happiest of mortals, Solon named Cleobis and Biton (q.v.). Croesus was still not satisfied; he thought surely Solon would have named him at the least as the second happiest of mortals, but he had to accept this dictum concerning happiness from Solon, "Account no man happy before his death." "It is the end that counts," said Solon, "for man is often given a gleam of happiness by the gods before being plunged into ruin." Almost immediately Croesus learned the truth of Solon's words. Of his two sons, one was a mute, the other, the apple of his eye, was accidentally slain in a hunting party. Croesus, deceived by a response of the oracle at Delphi to the effect that, if he marched against the Persians, he would overthrow a great empire, made war in 546 B.C. upon Cyrus, by whom he was defeated in the same year near Sardis and taken prisoner. He was, according to Herodotus, doomed to be burned alive, but as he was upon the

CROESUS ON HIS PYRE
Red-figured Attic amphora, Myson, 510–490 B.C. *Louvre*

pyre he recalled the words of Solon, and exclaimed "Solon! Solon! Solon!" Desired by Cyrus to state upon whom he was calling, he related the story of Solon, which moved Cyrus to countermand the order for his execution. He ordered his men to quench the fire which had already been lighted, but the flames were too hot and the men failed to check them. Thereupon Croesus, fettered to the pyre, called on Apollo to save him

and the day, which had been bright, suddenly darkened; a torrential rain fell and extinguished the flames. Cyrus was full of wonder at this and had Croesus brought to his side. As Croesus sat near him, watching the Persians plundering Sardis, he turned to Cyrus and asked if he might speak. Cyrus gave his permission. Croesus asked him what the Persians were doing. "Plundering your city," Cyrus replied, "and carrying off your riches." Croesus corrected him. It was not any longer his city nor his riches, he said; the Persians were plundering a city that now belonged to Cyrus and were carrying off riches that also now belonged to him. Cyrus was so impressed by the wisdom of this view that he kept Croesus henceforward in his train and bestowed upon him distinguished marks of favor. In return he often received valuable advice on military and other matters from Croesus. Later Croesus sent messengers and reproached the oracle at Delphi which had deceived him with a response that encouraged him to go to war against Cyrus. The oracle replied that though Apollo had tried to prevent the fall of Sardis in the lifetime of Croesus, not even a god could delay or deny the course of fate, and that Croesus had been punished, as he was fated to be, for the sins of his ancestors of five generations before. Moreover, said the oracle, Croesus had not taken the trouble to find out what the oracle meant. It had spoken truly in prophesying that a great empire would be destroyed. The empire of Croesus was destroyed and he had only himself to blame. On hearing this from the oracle Croesus humbly acknowledged the justice of it.

Crommyon (krom′i-on). In ancient geography, a place in the territory of Corinth, named, some say, for Cromus, a son of Poseidon. Here Phaea, the Crommyonian sow, was bred and was later slain by Theseus. Not far from here was an altar of Melicertes, for his body was brought ashore here by a dolphin. Sisyphus found the corpse, buried it on the Isthmus, and established the Isthmian Games in his honor.

Crommyonian (krom″i-ō′ni-an) **Sow**. In Greek legend, a savage sow that ravaged the countryside. It was killed by Theseus as he journeyed from Troezen to Athens. The sow was sometimes called Phaea after the woman who reared it. But some say this sow was really a fierce female bandit called a sow because of her greed and her notorious habits.

Cronia (krŏn'i-a̯). An ancient Greek festival in honor of Cronus (Kronos), held at Athens in midsummer, and resembling in its character of merriment the Roman Saturnalia.

Cronus (krō'nus) or **Cronos** (-nos). In Greek mythology, a Titan, the youngest son of Gaea and Uranus; he was the lord of the universe before the time of the Olympian gods. Gaea incited him to attack Uranus because he had imprisoned the Cyclopes, his sons, in Tartarus. She gave Cronus a sickle which had been forged by the Telchines. He used it to cut off his father's genitals and flung them and the sickle into the sea. Once Cronus and the Titans were victorious over Uranus they released their brothers from Tartarus and made Cronus the ruler. But Cronus again bound the Cyclopes and imprisoned them, along with the Hecatonchires, in Tartarus. The reïgn of Cronus was so peaceful and happy it was known as the Golden Age. Iron had not been beaten into swords and shields, thus there were no wars. There were no laws and no penalties, for men lived justly without them. The earth produced spontaneously, without any effort on man's part, and men ate what the earth of itself gave them. Cronus married his sister Rhea. She bore him Hestia, Demeter, Hera, Hades, and Poseidon. But as both Gaea and the dying Uranus had prophesied that he would be dethroned by one of his children he swallowed them as soon as they were born. When her sixth child was about to be born Rhea fled to Mount Lycaeus in Arcadia and there, where no shadow is cast, gave birth to Zeus. She gave her new-born son to Gaea for safekeeping and wrapped a stone in swaddling clothes which she presented to Cronus. He instantly swallowed it. Zeus was raised by nymphs in Crete. When he was grown he consulted Metis, a daughter of Oceanus, and learned from her how to compel Cronus to disgorge his sisters and brothers. He gave Cronus a potion which caused him to heave up first the stone which had been substituted for Zeus, and then his children. Zeus and his brothers and sisters then waged war on Cronus and the Titans, who were led by Atlas. The war lasted ten years. Then Gaea advised Zeus to free the Cyclopes and Hecatonchires from their prison in Tartarus and enlist their aid. He acted upon her advice and with their help was victorious. Cronus and the Titans were hurled into Tartarus, according to some accounts, and the Hecatonchires were set to guard them. Others say they were banished and fled to the west, where Cronus established another Golden Age in Italy and became known as Saturn. In Hades Cronus rules over Elysium. By the Oceanid Philyra, with whom he consorted in the form of a horse, Cronus was the father of Chiron the centaur. After the defeat of Cronus the universe over which he had ruled was divided among his three sons; Zeus won the sky, Hades the underworld, and Poseidon the sea. The earth remained common to all.

Cronus or **Cronius** (-ni-us), **Mount.** Low wooded hill N of the sacred precinct, the Altis, at Olympia.

Croton (krō'ton) or **Crotona** (krō-tō'na̯). [Modern name, **Crotone;** former name, **Cotrone.**] Town in S Italy, in Bruttii, situated on the Ionian Sea N of Catacium (Catanzaro). A Greek colony, one of the most important cities of Magna Graecia, it was noted for its devotion to athletics and as the seat of the Pythagorean school. There is a Greek temple of Hera Lacinia at the extremity of the nearby promontory on the Ionian Sea. This famous shrine has been greatly damaged by vandalism and earthquakes, but its platform of masonry and the results of excavations have supplied data for a partial restoration. It was of the 5th century B.C., Doric, hexastyle, with 14 columns on the flanks, and an interior range of four columns before the pronaos. The Crotonians destroyed the rival town of Sybaris in 510 B.C. but were defeated by the Locrians at the Sagras River in 480 B.C.; later the city submitted to Syracuse. It was occupied by the Romans in 277 B.C. Hannibal embarked here on his return to Africa in 203 B.C. The Romans founded a colony here in 194 B.C. A castle now stands on the site of the ancient acropolis.

Crotopus (krō-tō'pus). In Greek mythology, a king of Argos who was the father of Psamathe. Unbeknown to her father, Psamathe bore a son Linus to the god Apollo.

fat, fāte, fär, fãre, errant; net, mē, hėr ardent; pin, pīne; not, nōte, mŏve, nôr,

The child had been exposed to die but was found and brought up by shepherds. In his early youth he was torn to pieces by hounds belonging to Crotopus. When Crotopus became aware through her grief that Psamathe was Linus' mother, he slew her. Apollo sent a plague and a monster to punish the land for these deaths, which was not lifted until Crotopus left Argos.

Crotus (krō′tus). According to some accounts, a son of Pan by Eupheme, nurse of the Muses. He lived on Helicon, the mountain sacred to the Muses, and grew up as their beloved companion. He was a skilled archer and, at his own request, was placed among the stars as the constellation Sagittarius. But some say Crotus was a centaur.

Crow. The bird sacred to Apollo. Its feathers were originally snow white. According to one account, Apollo changed its feathers to black to punish the crow for bringing him the news that Coronis, the mother of Asclepius, was unfaithful to him. Apollo felt the crow would have done better to peck out the eyes of his rival. Others say it was Athena who changed the crow's feathers to deepest black, for bringing her the news that Agraulos and her daughters had leaped from the Acropolis to their deaths on discovering Erichthonius, the serpent child, in the casket Athena had given them to guard. Thenceforth crows were forbidden to visit the Acropolis.

Crown, Oration on the. [Latin, **De Corona.**] Oration of Demosthenes, delivered in 330 B.C. Ctesiphon had proposed that Demosthenes should be publicly presented with a golden crown as a reward for public services rendered after the battle of Chaeronea (338 B.C.), and for this was indicted by Aeschines as the proposer of an illegal act. In the oration Demosthenes defended his own acts and character, and attacked Aeschines who was defeated.

Crustumerium (krus-tū-mē′ri-um). In ancient geography, a city of the Sabines in Latium, Italy, situated a few miles NE of Rome. The town served as an arsenal supplying weapons to Turnus the Rutulian, when he was waging war against Aeneas.

Cteatus (tē′a-tus). In Homeric legend (*Iliad*), a son of Actor and Molione. See **Moliones.**

Ctesias (tē′zi-as). Greek historian and physician. He was born into the family of the Asclepiadae at Cnidus, Caria, in Asia Minor, and died after 398 B.C. As a member of the Asclepiadae he became physician to Artaxerxes Mnemon, king of Persia, in 416 B.C., and accompanied him on his expeditions, once, it is said, having cured him of a wound he suffered in battle. On his return to Cnidus, Ctesias wrote up the information he had collected on his Persian journeys. His history of Persia (*Persica*), in twenty-three books, was based on information he collected himself and from the royal archives. He also wrote *Indica,* a collection of observations he made on his journeys to India. The works of Ctesias were much used by ancient writers, but because of inaccuracies and "improvements" he made on stories such as those told by Herodotus, his work was more a source for romance than for history. Fragments of his works survive, and there is a meager abridgement of the *Persica* and *Indica* by Photius.

Ctesibius (tē-sib′i-us). Alexandrian physicist; born at Alexandria; fl. probably c250 B.C. He is noted for his mechanical inventions. He is said to have invented a clepsydra (water clock), a hydraulic organ, and other mechanical contrivances, and to have first applied the expansion force of air as a motive power.

Ctesiphon (tes′i-fon, tē′si-). Athenian of the 4th century B.C. Demosthenes defended him in his *Oration on the Crown.* (See **Crown, Oration on the.**) This speech of Demosthenes has sometimes been called the funeral oration on Greek freedom.

Ctesippus (te-sip′us). In mythology, a son of Heracles. His mother was either Deianira or Astydamia.

Ctesippus. Named in the *Odyssey* as one of Penelope's suitors. When Odysseus returned to Ithaca disguised as a beggar, Ctesippus hurled a cow's hoof at him and struck him. Later, when Odysseus revealed himself and fought to expel or kill the suitors who had taken over his halls, Philoetius, Odysseus' faithful herdsman, killed Ctesippus with his spear and avenged his master for the insult of the cow's hoof.

Ctesius (tē′si-us). Epithet of Zeus. Altars of Zeus Ctesius (*God of Gain*) were set up in some of the small parishes in Attica to honor him as the god who, by his will, gives or withholds benefits.

Cuba (kū′ba̱). In Roman mythology, a divinity who protected infants. See **Cunina.**

Cumae (kū′mē). In ancient geography, a city on the coast of Campania, Italy, about ten miles W of what is now Naples. It was founded (c1000 B.C.) by Greek colonists from Cyme in Euboea, was one of the chief Greek cities in Italy until the 5th century B.C., and became (338 B.C.) a Roman *municipium* (a town whose citizens enjoyed certain of the rights of Roman citizenship). Located near the haunted lake Avernus, it was the home of the Cumaean sibyl, the most famous of these prophetesses of antiquity. She gave her prophesies from a cave, in the hill of Cumae, which had 100 approaches from which 100 voices issued. Nearby were temples of Zeus and Apollo and a grove of Diana. Among the remnants of antiquity remaining at Cumae is a Roman amphitheater, imperfectly excavated, but displaying 21 tiers of seats. The axes of the great ellipse are 315 and 255 feet, of the arena 240 and 180 feet. The inhabitants of Cumae founded Neapolis (now Naples) and Puteoli (now Pozzuoli). The Vergilian Society of America maintains a summer school of classical studies in a villa located among the ruins.

Cumaean Sibyl. A seeress who wrote her prophecies on leaves and arranged them in order in the 100-mouthed cave where she gave her messages. If the wind disturbed the leaves, the seeress never bothered to put them in order again, with the result that as time passed it became impossible to unravel the prophecies. As instructed to do by Helenus, Aeneas visited the Sibyl when he landed in Cumae. Phoebus (Apollo) compelled her to give him information and she prohesied that Aeneas would come to power in Lavinium, but not without wars and struggle which would be caused, as was the Trojan War, by a foreign bride. The Sibyl then told Aeneas to find the Golden Bough, sacred to Proserpina, if he wished to go to the Underworld to see his father. She also told him to find and bury the body of a comrade. When he returned to her with the Golden Bough she conducted him to the Underworld, guided him through the different sections of it, and pointed out **various** great sinners

against the gods and the punishments which they were compelled to endure enternally. See also, **Sibyls.**

Cunaxa (kū-nak′sa̱). In ancient geography, a place in Babylonia near the Euphrates, probably about 75 miles NW of Babylon. Here, in 401 B.C., a battle took place between Artaxerxes II, king of Persia (with 400,000–1,000,000 men), and his brother Cyrus the Younger (with 100,000 Asiatics aided by 13,-000 Greeks). Cyrus was slain and his Asiatic forces fled; the Greek contingent, successful in the engagement, also succeeded in escaping eventually to the Euxine (Black) Sea, as Xenophon, one of their leaders, relates in his *Anabasis.*

Cunina (kū-nī′na̱). In Roman mythology, a good genius, one of three, who was worshiped as the guardian of babies sleeping in their cradles and to whom offerings of milk were made. The other two good genii associated with Cunina were Cuba and Rumina.

Cupavo (kū-pä′vō). In Roman legend (*Aeneid*), a son of that Cycnus who was changed into a swan as he grieved for Phaëthon. He was a Ligurian who came to the aid of Aeneas in his war against Turnus and Mezentius. He wore a swan's plume in his helmet in memory of his father.

Cupid (kū′pid). [Also: **Amor;** Greek **Eros.**] In ancient Roman mythology, the god of love, the son of Mercury and Venus. The parallel Greek Eros is similarly son of Hermes and Aphrodite. He is generally represented as a beautiful boy with wings, carrying a bow and a quiver of arrows, and is often spoken of as blind or blindfolded. The bow is used to shoot the arrows, which are invisible and which cause the one shot to fall irrevocably in love. Cupid originally was depicted as a young man, as he is in the story of Cupid and Psyche, but with time developed into the cherubic little scamp of later myth. The name is often given in art to figures of children, with or without wings, introduced, sometimes in considerable number, as a motif of decoration and with little or no mythological allusion.

Cupid and Psyche (sī′kē). Episode in the *Golden Ass* of Apuleius. The beauty of Psyche, the youngest of three daughters of a certain king, and the homage paid to it, arouse the wrath of Venus,

---

fat, fāte, fär, fãre, errȧnt; net, mē, hėr ardẹnt; pin, pīne; not, nōte, mȯve, nôr,

who commands Cupid to avenge her. In the attempt he falls in love with Psyche; she is borne to a lovely valley where every night Cupid, always invisible, visits her and commands her not to attempt to see him. Urged by her sisters and by her own curiosity, she violates this command, and is abandoned by the god. After toilsome wanderings in search of her lover, and many sufferings, she is endowed with immortality by Jupiter and united to Cupid forever. The tale, utilizing themes and motifs familiar in folk tales from all over the world, for example the taboo against looking at the supernatural husband and the search for the lost husband, is the clearest example of unadorned folk tale in classical literature. The story has served as a basis for many later accounts, such as the one by La Fontaine, and for paintings, one of the most familiar by Raphael.

Cupid and Psyche. Copy in marble, in the Capitoline Museum, Rome, of a Greek original of Hellenistic date, representing a boy and a girl embracing. Cupid is nude, Psyche draped from the hips down.

Cures (kū′rēz). In ancient geography, a city of the Sabines, about 24 miles NE of Rome. When Aeneas visited Anchises in the Underworld Anchises told him of Cures, a humble town from which a great law-giver would come. It was a legendary city of Numa Pompilius and Titus Tatius.

Curetes (kū-rē′tēz). In Greek mythology, attendants of Zeus, properly in Crete, who are often wrongly identified with the Corybantes, the Cabiri, and others. The Curetes were probably characters in a ceremony to Zeus the infant, and the myth explained their noisy dance. When Zeus was taken away and hidden from Cronus, who had swallowed his other children, the Curetes danced near him and, with the noise of spears and shields, drowned his infant cries so that his father might not hear them.

Curiatii (kū-ri-ā′shi-ī). In Roman legend, three brothers from Alba Longa, who fought against the three Horatii. They killed two of the Horatii, but the third slew the three Curiatii and then, when his sister Horatia grieved at the news because she was betrothed to one of the Curiatii, he slew her.

Curio (kū′ri-ō), **Caius Scribonius.** Roman general and politician; died 53 B.C. He fought

with Sulla against Mithridates II of Parthia, was tribune (90 B.C.), consul (76), proconsul in Macedonia (75–73), and became pontifex maximus, the chief priest of the state religion, in 57 B.C. He was the first Roman general to reach the Danube in Moesia, c73 B.C. He was an opponent of Julius Caesar.

Curio, Caius Scribonius. Son of Caius Scribonius Curio (d. 53 B.C.); a partisan of Caesar in the civil war. After struggling in Roman politics to prevent any action by the Senate against Caesar, he took the field as leader of military forces, taking Sicily and besieging a Pompeian force in Utica, in Africa, where he was killed, 49 B.C.

Curitis (kū-rī′tis) or **Quiritis** (kwī-rī′tis). In Roman mythology and religion, an epithet of Juno, meaning "Of the Spear." As wielder of the spear or lance, Juno was the chief of the goddesses.

Curium (kū′ri-um). Ancient city in Cyprus, W of the river Lycus, said to have been founded by the Argives. Its ruins contain a Phoenician temple, remarkable especially for its crypt of four rock-hewn chambers, about 23 feet in diameter, connected by doors and a gallery. The objects in gold and silver constituting the "Treasure of Curium" in the Metropolitan Museum, New York, were found in these chambers.

Curtius (kėr′shi-us, -shus), **Marcus.** Roman legendary hero of the 4th cenutry B.C. In 362 B.C., a chasm having been formed in the Forum by an earthquake, the soothsayers announced that it could be closed only by the sacrifice of Rome's greatest treasure. The people were at a loss to interpret the oracle when Marcus Curtius, a noble youth, stepped forward and, declaring that the state possessed no greater treasure than a brave citizen in arms, leaped, mounted on his steed and in full armor, into the chasm, which closed after him. The Forum stood where a marsh, the Lacus Curtius, formerly existed, and this is simply one of three legends intended to explain the name, the others being that Mettius Curtius, a Sabine, fell here before Romulus' pursuit, and that Caius Curtius was consul when lightning struck here to make the spot sacred.

Curtius Rufus (rö′fus), **Quintus.** Roman historian of the time of Claudius; fl. c50 A.D. He was the author of a history of Alexander the Great in ten books, of which books 3–10 are preserved. Curtius was probably the first Roman historian to deal with an entirely foreign subject.

Cyane (sī′a̯-nē). In mythology, a nymph of Syracuse who was a companion of Persephone. She tried to prevent Hades from carrying Persephone to the Underworld. Unsuccessful in this, she wept so that she was transformed into a fountain. Since she had lost the power of speech she could not tell Demeter, frantically searching for her daughter, what had happened to Persephone but she washed Persephone's girdle, which had dropped off as she was carried away, to Demeter's feet when the goddess came to the rim of Cyane's fountain searching for her daughter. On the spot where this occurred, the people of Syracuse annually celebrated a festival, said to have been established by Heracles, in the rites of which a bull was cast into the fountain as a sacrifice.

Cyane. In Greek legend, a daughter of Cyanippus of Syracuse. Unaware that she was his own daughter, her father violated her. The gods punished this act by sending a plague on the people. The people learned that the plague could be lifted only by the sacrifice of a guilty man. Cyane, who had recognized her father by a ring he wore, killed him and then herself, and the plague was lifted.

Cyaneë (sī-an′ẹ-ē). According to legend, a princess of Caria. She married Miletus and became the mother of the ill-fated twins Caunus and Byblis.

Cyanippus (sī-an-ip′pus). In mythology, a son of Pharax of Thessaly. He neglected his wife, Leucone, in order to indulge his passion for hunting. One day, as she secretly followed him, she was discovered by his dogs and torn to pieces by them. Cyanippus found her body and burned it. Then, in remorse, he killed himself.

Cyathus (sī′a̯-thus). According to some accounts, a Calydonian youth, cupbearer to Oeneus. When Heracles was visiting Oeneus Cyathus fumbled in serving him. Heracles, in annoyance, struck him with a careless blow, and although it seemed light to Heracles he was so forceful the blow killed Cyathus. A chapel in his honor was built beside the temple of Apollo.

Cyathus. [Also: **Kyathos.**] In ancient Greece, a form of vase or cup with a long handle, used especially for dipping, as for taking wine from the crater to pour into the oinochoë or directly into the cup. It was often made in the form of a ladle.

Cyaxares (sī-ak′sa̯-rēz). King of the Medes (625–584 B.C.). In the cuneiform inscriptions his name is Uvakshtra. He was the son and successor of Phraortes, and may be considered as the founder of Media's power and greatness. According to Herodotus, he was a capable and ambitious ruler. He organized his Asiatic forces into separate divisions of spearmen, archers, and cavalry. At the head of his forces and accompanied by his allies, he marched against Nineveh, where his father had been slain in an attempt to take the Assyrian capital. He had made a successful attack and settled down to besiege the city when Media was overrun by hordes of Scythian invaders. After some years the Scythians were driven out. According to Herodotus, Cyaxares and his chiefs invited a great number of the Scyths to a banquet, got them drunk, and slew them. In any case, having driven them out, he captured Nineveh (608 B.C.), in alliance with Nabopolassar, viceroy of Babylonia, and destroyed the Assyrian empire. Toward the W Cyaxares conquered Armenia, and thus extended his dominion as far as the river Halys in Asia Minor. Herodotus says that Cyaxares received some Scythian suppliants and treated them kindly. He came to respect them and gave the care of a number of Median boys into their hands with instructions to teach them to shoot with the bow. Every day the Scythians went hunting, and every day they brought back game. One day they returned empty handed. In a rage, Cyaxares insulted them. They were so deeply offended that they resolved to punish him. They took one of the Median boys under their care, slew him, and dressed his flesh as if it were game. They cooked it and served it to Cyaxares and his guests and then fled to Sardis, to the court of the Lydian king Alyattes. Cyaxares demanded that Alyattes surrender them. He refused, and this, according to Herodotus, was the reason for the war between the Lydians and the Medians. Fighting continued for five years during which fortune

fat, fāte, fär, fãre, errant; net, mē, hėr ardẹnt; pin, pīne; ṇot, nōte, mȯve, nôr, favored first one side then the other. In the sixth year another battle took place. As the struggle waxed hot, suddenly day was turned to night by an eclipse of the sun (May 28, 585 B.C.). The phenomenon had been foretold by Thales of Miletus, the first man who had learned enough about the stars in their courses to predict such an occurrence. However, the Lydians and the Medians were both so terrified by the portent that they immediately laid down their arms and agreed to a peace. According to the terms of it, the daughter of Alyattes married the son of Cyaxares. This son was Astyages, who became the grandfather of Cyrus the Great.

Cybele (sib′e-lē). [Also known as **Berecynthia, Cybebe, Dindymene,** and the **Great Idaean Mother.**] An oriental goddess of Phrygia and Lydia. She came to be identified by the Greeks with Rhea, the wife of Cronus and mother of the Olympian gods, and by the Romans with Ops, wife of Saturn. She was the "Great Mother of the Gods." Early seats of her worship were Mount Ida, Mount Sipylus, Cyzicus, and Sardis. As well as being the "Great Mother of the Gods" she was the great mother of Nature, a fertility goddess symbolizing the powers of reproduction and fruitfulness in man, plants, and animals. As the goddess who presided over the wild forests and fastnesses of mountains she was worshiped on the mountains, and was conceived as traversing them in a chariot draw by lions. As the goddess and giver of the rich treasures hidden in the earth she was worshiped in caves and grottoes. She came to be regarded as the mother of the arts of civilization and the special protectress of cities. Her priests, called Corybantes and Galli, were emasculated to commemorate the emasculation of Atys, the beloved of Cybele, and dressed like women to achieve unity with the goddess. Her festivals were celebrated with wild dances and orgiastic excesses amid the resounding music of drums and cymbals. From Asia Minor her worship spread through Thrace and thence to Greece, where it was known in Boeotia in the 6th century B.C. During the Second Punic War her cult was brought to Rome in 205–204 B.C. and established in a temple on the Palatine in obedience to a Sibylline prophecy that said that a foreign enemy could be expelled if the Great Idaean Mother was brought to Rome. The *Megalesia,* and later also the *Taurobolia* and *Criobolia,* were celebrated in Rome in her honor. The oak, pine, and lion were sacred to her. Among her other attributes were the drum, cymbals, flute, and horn. She is usually represented enthroned between lions, with a turreted crown on her head and a small drum or cymbal, the instrument used in her rites, in her hand.

Cychreus (sī′krös). In Greek mythology, a son of Poseidon and Salamis, daughter of the river-god Asopus. His daughter was Glauce, who became the wife of Telamon. Cychreus was made king of Salamis, the Serpent Isle, for slaying a destructive serpent that was ravaging the island. Some say he kept a young serpent that caused as much damage until it was expelled by Eurylochus, after which it went to Eleusis and became an attendant of Demeter. Others say it was Cychreus himself, called the "serpent" because of his cruelty, who was banished and went to Eleusis to become an attendant of Demeter. Cychreus was one of the guardian heroes of Salamis. There he was buried, facing the west, and sacrifices were offered at his tomb. In the famous naval battle between the Greeks and Persians in the bay of Salamis in 480 B.C., Cychreus was said to have appeared in serpent form among the Greek ships.

Cyclades (sik′la-dēz). [Also: **Kikladhes, Kyklades, Kykladon Nesoi.**] Group of islands belonging to Greece, situated in the Aegean Sea. The name, from the Greek word for "circle," derived from the belief that they formed a ring about Delos. Among the major islands are Andros, Tenos, Ceos, Syrus, Naxos, Melos, and Paros.

Cyclic Poets (sī′klik). The authors of Greek epic poems, composed between 800 B.C. and 550 B.C., relating to the Trojan War and the war against Thebes. Among these poems are *Cypria* (The Cyprian Lays), *Aethiopis* (The Lay of Ethiopia), *Iliu Persis* (The Sack of Troy), *Ilias Parva* (The Little Iliad), *Nostoi* (The Homeward Voyages), *Telegonia* (The Lay of Telegonus), all belonging to the Trojan cycle, and the *Thebais* and the *Epigoni,* belonging to the Theban cycle. A few fragments of these poems are extant.

Cyclopes (sī-klō′pēz) or **Cyclops** (sī′klops). In Greek mythology, three sons of Gaea and Uranus: Arges, Brontes, and Steropes. They were giants with but one eye, which was circular and in the middle of the forehead. They were great builders, said to have built the walls of Mycenae and other fortifications, and they were master smiths, said by some to have made Artemis' silver bow. Uranus hated his one-eyed sons and hid them away in Tartarus. They were freed temporarily by Cronus after he had overthrown Uranus, but then imprisoned again, along with their brothers the Hecatonchires. Zeus made war on his father Cronus for ten years. At the suggestion of Gaea, his grandmother, he freed the Cyclopes and enlisted their aid against Cronus. The Cyclopes gave Zeus the thunderbolt, forged a trident for Poseidon, and gave Hades a cap of darkness. With these weapons and with the help of the Hecatonchires, whom Zeus also freed, the Olympian gods defeated Cronus and divided up his universe. The Cyclopes dwelt in Thrace, Crete, and Lycia, and their descendants went to Sicily, or islands near Sicily, where Odysseus ran afoul of them on his way home from the Trojan War. Aeneas also landed on the island of the Cyclopes,

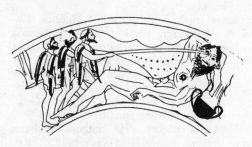

BLINDING OF THE CYCLOPS
Greek vase, late 6th century B.C. *Berlin*

on his way to Italy, but hurriedly departed on learning on what land he had come ashore. Some say the Cyclopes, or their descendants, worked in Hephaestus' forge. Apollo, to avenge the death of his son Asclepius, killed by Zeus' thunderbolt, slew the Cyclopes. Their ghosts dwell under

Aetna in Sicily, and cause it to rumble and roar, and sometimes to spout flames and red-hot boulders.

Cycnus (sik′nus). In Greek mythology, a son of Poseidon and Calyce. He was born in secret and exposed by his mother on the seashore. Swans that flew down to comfort him revealed his hiding place to some fishermen, who rescued him and cared for him. He became a king of Colonae in Phrygia and married Proclea, who bore him Tenes (but some say Tenes was the son of Apollo), and a daughter Hemithea. After the death of Proclea, Cycnus married Phylonome. She tried to seduce Tenes, and when he rejected her advances she falsely accused him to his father, and produced a witness that Tenes had tried to ravish her. Cycnus put his two children in a chest and cast them into the sea. The chest floated safely to an island which Tenes named Tenedos and of which he became ruler. Later Cycnus learned that Phylonome had lied. He buried her alive and sought Tenes to ask his forgiveness. Tenes angrily cut the cables of his ship when he put in at Tenedos, but later was reconciled to him, and Cycnus settled near his son on Tenedos. Cycnus was an ally of the Trojans in the Trojan War, and when the Greeks landed in the Troad he slew them in droves. Achilles rushed up to attack him, but as he was invulnerable neither spear nor sword could make any impression on his body. Achilles flung his spear at him in vain, although each time the spear struck Cycnus, and Achilles blunted his sword on Cycnus' invulnerable flesh. In a rage Achilles battered Cycnus' head with his shield and forced him back. As he retreated Cycnus stumbled over a stone and fell on his back. Achilles planted his knees on Cycnus' chest and strangled him with the straps of his own helmet, but when he went to strip the body of its armor he found the armor empty. Poseidon had transformed his son into a swan and in that form Cycnus flew off.

Cycnus. According to legend, a son of Ares and Pyrene. He challenged Heracles to a duel at the Echedorus River in Macedonia. Heracles had come hither on his way to learn the location of the Garden of the Hesperides. Ares came to aid his son in the fight, but Zeus hurled a thunderbolt between the combatants and stopped the fight. Some say, however, that before the intervention of Zeus Heracles had killed Cycnus, and that Ares then transformed his son into a swan.

Cycnus. In Greek legend, a son of Ares and Pelopia. Some say this Cycnus was in the habit of cutting off the heads of passing strangers. He used the skulls thus acquired to build a temple to his father Ares. Others say he challenged all comers to a chariot duel with him. Apollo, enraged because Cycnus stole the cattle that were being sent to Delphi for sacrifice, encouraged Heracles to accept the challenge. Heracles armed himself with the armor the gods had given him and made ready to meet Cycnus. Iolaus, Heracles' charioteer, was to fight on his side, and Ares would support Cycnus. Athena, the patroness of Heracles, warned him that though he might kill Cycnus, he must not attack Ares, a god. She then mounted the war-car with him, to protect him. Both Heracles and Cycnus were hurled from their chariots by the shock when they collided at full speed. They then took up the battle on foot. Athena protected Heracles from the sword Ares was aiming at him, and Heracles killed Cycnus. Ares rushed to attack him and, forgetting Athena's warning, he defended himself and wounded Ares in the thigh. Since it was not fitting for Heracles to attack a god, Zeus sent a thunderbolt between them and broke up the fight. Athena led Ares away to Olympus to be cured. Heracles and Iolaus stripped Cycnus of his armor. Some say this duel took place in Itonus, a city of Phthiotis. Others say it was at the Peneus River, or at Pagasae in Thessaly. And some say Cycnus was buried near the Anaurus River in Thessaly, and that Apollo caused the river to rise and wash away the gravestone.

Cycnus or **Cygnus** (sig'-). According to Ovid, a son of Apollo and Hyrie. He compelled his friend Phylius to tame wild birds and a lion for him. Phylius resented the demands of Cycnus that he prove his love. When Cycnus also demanded that Phylius give him a bull he had won as a prize at funeral games Phylius refused. Enraged at Phylius' refusal, Cycnus flung himself over a cliff and was transformed into a swan.

Cycnus. In legend, a king in Liguria and a devoted friend of Phaëthon. When Phaëthon was struck by the thunderbolt of Zeus because he could not control the horses of the chariot of the sun, Cycnus gave up his kingdom. Grief-stricken, he haunted the banks of the Eridanus River, into which Phaëthon had fallen, and lamented. Apollo took pity on him and transformed him into a swan and placed his image among the stars.

Cydippe (sī-dip'ē). In Greek legend, an Argive priestess of Hera, she was the mother of two sons, Biton and Cleobis. Herodotus says she wanted to go to the Argive Heraeum to take part in the festival of Hera. The oxen could not be brought home from the fields in time to take her there, and so her two devoted sons hitched themselves to the cart and drew their mother in it the five miles to the sanctuary. As a reward for their devotion, Hera agreed to grant whatever their mother wished for them. Cydippe asked for the best gift Hera could offer. Acclaimed by the people for their devotion to their mother, the two youths went to sleep in the temple and never awoke again. Their peaceful death was Hera's best gift.

Cydippe. See under **Acontius.**

Cydnus (sid'nus). In ancient geography, a river of Cilicia, Asia Minor, flowing into the Mediterranean Sea about 12 miles S of Tarsus.

Cydonia (sī-dō'ni-a). Epithet of Athena. Some say that Clymenus, a descendant of the Cretan Dactyl Heracles, came from Cydonia in Crete and founded a temple of Athena Cydonia in Elis. Pelops sacrificed to Athena Cydonia before he began his race with Oenomaus for the hand of Hippodamia.

Cydonia. [Modern name, **Canea.**] City and seaport on the N coast of Crete. It was founded by Samians (6th century B.C.), who had been exiled from Samos. They sought to return to Samos with the help of Spartans, but failing in their attack on the island, they sailed to Crete and founded Cydonia. They prospered in Cydonia, and built many temples, among them a famous temple of Dictynna (Britomartis).

Cygnus (sig'nus). An ancient northern constellation representing a bird called a swan by Ovid and others, and now always so considered.

Cyllene (si-lē′nē). In Greek mythology, a nymph who nursed Hermes in a cave on Mount Cyllene in Arcadia. Silenus and the Satyrs, who had undertaken to find Apollo's stolen cattle for him for a reward, were attracted to the cave by strange musical sounds. Cyllene told them of the marvellous infant she was guarding, who grew like a god and who had constructed a musical instrument from a tortoise shell and some hides. Silenus and the Satyrs (*The Trackers*), suspected this infant of the theft of Apollo's cattle, especially when they learned from Cyllene that he had used hides in the construction of the instrument. She hotly rebuked them for their suspicions, citing Zeus and Maia, the honest parents of her charge.

Cyllene, Mount. In ancient geography, a mountain in Arcadia, Greece, reputed to be the birthplace of Hermes. Elatus, son of Arcas, inherited the region about Mount Cyllene as his share of his father's kingdom and named it Cyllene after his son, Cyllen. The mountain was the highest in Arcadia, and was noted in classical times for the fact that the blackbirds indigenous to the mountain were white. Hermes had the name *Cyllenian* from his mountain birthplace, and a sanctuary of Cyllenian Hermes stood on it.

Cyllene. In ancient geography, the port of Elis, situated on the Ionian Sea, north of the promontory of Chelonatas (*Tortoise Shell*). Among its public buildings were sanctuaries of Asclepius and of Aphrodite.

Cylon (sī′lon). An Athenian noble of the 7th century B.C. He was married to the daughter of Theagenes, tyrant of Megara. With the advice and help of Theagenes Cylon plotted to make himself master of Athens. He was instructed by the oracle of Delphi to seize the Acropolis on "the greatest festival of Zeus." Accordingly, with the aid of a few Athenian nobles and some Megarian soldiers, Cylon seized the Acropolis (c632 B.C.) at the time of the Olympic festival, which, since he had been an Olympic victor himself, he considered "the greatest festival of Zeus." He and his alien supporters were trapped in the citadel by the Athenians. During a long siege Cylon escaped, but his followers, weakened by failing supplies, sought refuge in the temple of Athena, and finally agreed to surrender under a guarantee of safe conduct. Megacles the archon persuaded the Athenians to ignore their promise to spare the lives of the conspirators, and they were put to death. Cylon was later informed by the oracle that he had misinterpreted the oracle: that "the greatest festival of Zeus" referred to the *Diasia,* which took place in March and was celebrated outside the city. Because he interpreted the oracle falsely his attempt failed and Cylon and his descendants were banished forever from Athens. But Athens had put itself under a curse by breaking the pledge and insulting Athena, in whose temple the conspirators had taken sanctuary. The Alcmaeonids, of whom Megacles was a member, were tried for sacrilege, their property was confiscated, and they and their descendants were banished forever. The city was finally purged by Epimenides (596 B.C.) but the curse on the Alcmaeonids, who in the course of time returned to Athens, plagued Pericles, a descendant of Megacles, some 200 years after the murder of the followers of Cylon.

Cyme (sī′mē). Ancient Greek city in W **Asia** Minor, about 28 miles N of Smyrna (now Izmir), on a small coastal bay. It was founded in the early Greek colonization of Aeolis, and rose to prominence as the principal city of this region. In the 7th century B.C. Cyme was ruled by a king, but later it had oligarchic rule. It was involved in the intrigues between Athens and Sparta, and changed hands numerous times in the struggles between Greek and Persian empires. In 17 A.D. it was severely damaged by an earthquake. The site of Cyme is supposed to be at the small village of Namúrt Kjöi.

Cyme. In ancient geography, a city on the coast of Campania, settled by Greek colonists from Chalcis in Eretria, and Cyme in Euboea. This is said to have been the earliest (c1000 B.C.) Greek colony on the Italian peninsula. Euboeans from Cyme in Greece brought the alphabet with them to their colony in Italy, and thus introduced the fundamental tool for the creation of the great civilization that developed in Italy. They also brought their Greek religion, gods, and heroes. These were adopted by the Italians so universally and from such an early date that they came to be considered as native Italian divinities.

Among the colonists of Cyme were some Graeans from Euboea. In Italy all the colonists, from peoples who had hitherto been variously called Achaeans, Danaans, Argives, and other names according to locality, came to be named Graeci after these Graeans, and from them the word Greece, a name unknown to Homer, is derived. Cyme appears in Latin as Cumae, and was the seat of the famous prophetess of Apollo, the Cumaean sibyl. See also **Cumae.**

Cymodoce (sī-mod'ō̠-sē) or **Cymodocea** (sī-mod''ō̠-sē'a̠). Named in the *Aeneid* as a Nereid or sea-nymph. She was originally one of the ships of Aeneas, made from the sacred wood of Cybele's forest. Turnus, the Latin enemy of Aeneas, set the ships on fire while Aeneas was absent from his camp. To save them, Cybele transformed the ships into sea-nymphs. Cymodoce met Aeneas as he was returning in his ship and told him what had befallen his camp during his absence. She urged him to hurry back and relieve his besieged garrison. To speed him on his way she rose up from the water and gave his ship such a mighty push that it was propelled swiftly back to the Trojan camp.

Cynaegirus (sin-ē̠-jī'rus). Athenian soldier; brother of Aeschylus. He distinguished himself at the battle of Marathon in 490 B.C., in which, according to Herodotus, he pursued the Persians to the sea and, having seized one of their triremes to prevent its putting off, fell with his right hand severed. Later writers add that, having lost both his hands, he seized the vessel with his teeth.

Cynaetha (sin-ē̠'tha̠). In ancient geography, a city in N Arcadia, Greece. The Cynaetheans dedicated an image of Zeus, bearing a thunderbolt in each hand, at Olympia. At their winter festival of Dionysus, greased men seized a bull from the herd and carried it to the sanctuary of Dionysus for sacrifice. The Cynaetheans had a spring, called Alyssus (*Curer of Madness*), whose waters would cure one bitten by a mad dog.

Cynics (sin'iks). School of Greek philosophers of whom the earliest may be considered to be Antisthenes of Athens (b. c444 B.C.) who sought to develop the ethical teachings of Socrates, whose pupil he was. The chief doctrines of the Cynics were that virtue is

the only good, that the essence of virtue is self-control, and that pleasure is an evil if sought for its own sake. They were accordingly characterized by an ostentatious contempt of riches, art, science, and amusements. The most famous Cynic was Diogenes of Sinope, a pupil of Antisthenes, who carried the doctrines of the school to an extreme and ridiculous asceticism. Although this school is named after Diogenes who was called "kyon" (meaning *dog*), Antisthenes is considered by many as the founder.

Cynortes (sī-nôr'tēz). In Greek legend, a son of Amyclas, king of Sparta, and Diomede, and the brother of Hyacinthus. He is sometimes named as the father of Perieres.

Cynosarges (sī-no̠-sär'jēz). A gymnasium of very early foundation in ancient Athens, combined with a sanctuary of Heracles, and possessing a grove. The philosopher Antisthenes taught here. The Cynosarges lay somewhat high up on the S slope of Lycabettus; its site is now occupied by the Monastery of the Asomatôn and the British and American schools of archaeology.

Cynoscephalae (sin-o̠-sef'a̠-lē). Heights in Thessaly, Greece, between about 10 and 20 miles SE of Larissa. Here the Thebans under Pelopidas defeated (364 B.C.) Alexander of Pherae, and the Romans under Flamininus defeated (197 B.C.) Philip V of Macedon.

Cynosura (sī-no̠-shō'ra̠). A nymph of Mount Ida, who was one of the nurses of the infant Zeus. She was metamorphosed into the constellation Ursa Minor.

Cynosuria (sī-no̠-shō'ri-a̠). See **Cynuria.**

Cynthia (sin'thi-a̠). Epithet of Artemis, from Mount Cynthus on the island of Delos where she was born.

Cynthius (sin'thi-us). Epithet of Apollo, the sun god, as the moon goddess is called Cynthia.

Cynthus (sin'thus), **Mount.** An eminence, conspicuous from the sea (height, 370 feet) and commanding a fine view of the Cyclades, on the small Aegean island of Delos, where according to early legend Leto bore Zeus' twin children Apollo and Artemis. On the western slope of Mount Cynthus are the remains of a primitive rock sanctuary, the Grotto of Apollo, and on the summit was once a shrine of Zeus and Athena. From this Apollo received the epithet Cynthius, and Artemis, Cynthia. (JJ)

Cynuria (sī-nū′ri-a). [Also: **Cynosuria.**] In ancient geography, a district in Greece in the E part of the Peloponnesus, situated on the Gulf of Argolis.

Cynurus (sī-nū′rus). In Greek tradition, a son of Perseus. He went from Argos to the valley between Argolis and Laconia, and founded a colony there which he named Cynuria.

Cyparissia (sip-a-ris′i-a). Epithet of Athena, meaning the "Cypress-goddess." There were sanctuaries of Athena Cyparissia on the citadel of Asopus, in Laconia, and at Cyparissia in Messenia.

Cyparissia or **Cyparissiae** (sip-a-ris′i-ē). [Modern name, **Kyparissia** or **Kiparissia.**] In ancient geography, a city of Messenia, situated on the Ionian Sea. Men of the city accompanied Nestor against Troy. The city fell into ruin but was rebuilt by Epaminondas as the port for the new city of Messene, which he built after the battle of Leuctra (371 B.C.). Among the landmarks of the city was a spring that Dionysus caused to gush forth by striking the earth with his thyrsus. Nearby, remains of an ancient temple of Apollo have been found.

Cyparissus (sip-a-ris′us). According to Ovid, the son of Telephus. He was beloved by the gods. When he accidentally killed his favorite stag, he grieved so that the gods, in pity, transformed him into a cypress tree; thus his mourning for the stag became a symbol of mourning for others.

Cyphanta (sī-fan′ta). A city of Laconia, on the Myrtoan Sea. Here a fountain of clear cold water springs from the rock. It was said that Atalanta, hot and tired from hunting, came to this spot and, being thirsty, struck the rock with her spear; the fountain immediately gushed forth. Nearby was a cave sacred to Asclepius, containing a stone image.

Cypria (sip′ri-a). [Also: **Cyprian Lays.**] One of the poems of the Trojan cycle, anciently attributed to Homer, and later to Stasinus. It dealt with Paris' abduction of Helen, with the help of Aphrodite (Cypria), and their flight from Sparta.

Cypris (sī′pris). An epithet of Aphrodite, from the island of Cyprus, to which she is said to have gone after she rose from the foam near Cytherea. The epithet "Cyprian" is also applied to Aphrodite for the same reason.

Cyprus (sī′prus). [French, **Chypre;** German, **Cypern;** Greek, **Kypros;** Italian, **Cipro;** Turkish, **Kibris.**] One of the largest islands of the Mediterranean, situated in its E corner, about 40 miles S of Turkey and about 240 miles N of Egypt, with the mountain range of the Lebanon on the mainland to the E and that of Taurus to the N. Its name is supposed to be derived from its rich mines of copper (Greek, *kypros*). Cyprus has limestone mountains averaging about 2000 feet in elevation along its N coast, and a higher and more extensive range occupies the S and W parts of the island, culminating in Mount Olympus, or Troodos (6000 feet). Between these ranges lies a fertile plain. Cyprus was celebrated in antiquity as the birthplace and favorite abode of Aphrodite, and was famous for its beauty and wealth, but also for its licentiousness. It was early settled by Phoenicians, who were followed by Greeks. Its principal cities were Paphos (still known by that name) on the W coast (a center of the cult of Aphrodite), Salamis (near modern Famagusta) on the E, Kittim, or Citium (on the site of modern Larnaca) on the SE, and Amathus (near modern Limassol) on the S. In the center of the island were the Phoenician mining cities Tamassus and Idalium (modern Dali), with the celebrated grove of Aphrodite. For a time Cyprus was tributary to Assyria. Its name in the cuneiform inscriptions is Yatnan, and the Assyrian king Sargon relates that seven kings from this island (probably chiefs of the Phoenician colonies) brought him costly gifts and "kissed his feet," i.e., acknowledged his sovereignty. He in turn presented them with a marble stele containing a full-length sculptured portrait of himself, and an inscription commemorating his principal deeds. This monument was found in 1846, well preserved, near Larnaca (the ancient Kittim or Citium), and was acquired by the Royal Museum of Berlin. Cyprus was in succession subject to Persia, Macedon, and Egypt, and in 57 B.C. became a Roman province.

Cypselus (sip′se-lus). Tyrant of Corinth,

c655–625 B.C.. He was the son of Eëtion, a descendant of the Lapiths, and Labda, a member of the Bacchiadae of Corinth. Before he was born, the oracle of Delphi foretold to Eëtion that the son his wife was about to bear would be a rock on which the Bacchiadae, the ruling oligarchy of Corinth, would founder. This oracle coming to their ears, the Bacchiadae resolved to kill the son of Eëtion. They went to his house and asked to see the child. Labda, thinking there was no harm in it, brought the infant and laid it in the arms of the man nearest her. The plan was for whoever received the child to dash it **to** its death at once, the infant smiled at **the** man who received him and so moved **him** that he could not bear to murder it. Instead he passed the child on to the next man. So the child was passed from hand to hand and none of the ten men there had the heart to murder it. They left the house without accomplishing their purpose. Once outside, they began to dispute together, blaming each other for the failure to kill the child. Labda overheard them and thus learned the purpose of their visit. Lest they return, she hid her baby in a corn-bin. The men did return, but having searched the house in vain for the child, they again took their departure. Because the baby had been hidden in a corn-bin, *cypsele*, he was given the name Cypselus. When Cypselus grew up, he went to the oracle at Delphi and heard the following response:

"See there comes to my dwelling a man
  much favored of fortune,
Cypselus, son of Eëtion, and king of the
  glorious Corinth,
He and his children too, but not his children's children."

This encouraged him to attack the Bacchiadae and gain the throne of Corinth. Successful in this, he enjoyed a prosperous reign of 30 years and was succeeded by his son Periander, thus fulfilling the first part of the oracle.

Cypselus. According to legend, a son of Aepytus, who succeeded his father as king of Arcadia. During the reign of Cypselus, the sons of Aristomachus (Dorians) invaded the Peloponnesus. Cypselus gave his daughter in marriage to Cresphontes, one of the sons of Aristomachus, and so won him for an ally. For this reason Arcadians were not disturbed nor dislodged from their land by the Dorian invasion, as were the other states of the Peloponnesus.

Cyrenaica (sir-ē-nā′i-ka). [Also: **Pentapolis**.] In ancient geography, a country in N Africa, lying between the Mediterranean on the N, Marmarica on the E, the desert on the S, and the Syrtis Major (modern Gulf of Sidra) on the W. It corresponded closely to the modern territory of the same name, in NE Libya, and was noted for its fertility. It was settled (c631 B.C.) by Thereans, was subject to Egypt from 321 B.C., and formed (67 B.C.) with Crete a Roman province.

Cyrenaics (sī-rē-nā′iks). School of Greek hedonistic philosophers, founded by Aristippus of Cyrene, a disciple of Socrates. Epicureanism was influenced by this school.

Cyrene (sī-rē′nē). In Greek mythology, a daughter of Hypseus, king of the Lapiths, and Chlidanope, a naiad. She was an ardent huntress and the guardian of her father's flocks and herds near the Peneus River. Apollo watched her wrestle with a lion and fell in love with her. He carried her away to Libya, to the site on which the city of Cyrene was founded, and made her queen of a realm in which hunters and farmers prospered. She bore Aristaeus and Idmon the seer to Apollo. When they needed her advice her sons repaired to a spring where they knew she would be visiting her naiad relatives and consulted her. By Ares, Cyrene was the mother of Diomedes of Thrace, the owner of the man-eating mares.

Cyrene. [Also: **Cirene**.] In ancient geography, the principal city of Cyrenaica in Africa, situated about ten miles from the Mediterranean coast. It was founded (c631 B.C.) by Thereans under Battus. According to Herodotus, Aristoteles, the son of Phronima of Crete and Polymnestus of Thera, was afflicted by a stammer. He went to the oracle at Delphi to inquire about his speech, and was ordered by the priestess, who addressed him as Battus, or "king," to establish a colony in Libya. Henceforth called Battus, he returned to Thera, and shortly all sorts of evils descended on the island. The inhabitants, unaware of what the priestess had told Battus, sent to Delphi and now learned that if Battus would found a colony at

Cyrene in Libya, everything would go well with them. After a false start Battus and the Thereans arrived on the coast of Libya, but were soon persuaded to move by the natives. The Libyans promised them a better site for a colony and undertook to lead them to it. They craftily arranged the journey so that all the most delightful and suitable places were passed during the night. At last the Libyans brought Battus and his companions to a place where there was a spring called Apollo's Fountain. Here, on two hills overlooking a plain, Battus founded Cyrene. Battus ruled 40 years, and was followed by his son Arcesilaus (for generations, the names of the Cyrenaean kings were alternately Battus and Arcesilaus), who reigned for 16 years. In the reign of the second Battus, who followed Arcesilaus, Greeks from many areas began to flock to Cyrene and the colony prospered mightily. The Libyans found themselves pushed back and appealed to Apries, king of Egypt, for aid against the Cyrenaeans. Apries sent an army against them which was utterly defeated. This led to the downfall of Apries. He was succeeded by Amasis II, who made a treaty of friendship and alliance with the Cyrenaeans, and married Ladice, daughter of their king. He was so delighted by her that he honored Cyrene by sending a statue of Athena, overlaid with plates of gold, to the city. In a later generation, the ruler of Cyrene (an Arcesilaus) quarreled with his brothers and they withdrew to another site in Libya and founded Barca. When Cambyses II conquered Egypt, the Cyrenaeans offered to submit to him, and afterward paid tribute to Darius. Cyrene was the only Greek colony in Africa to become strong and wealthy. It was a center of Greek learning and culture. One of her sons, Eugammon the poet, wrote a continuation of the *Odyssey,* the *Telegony.* In this work Odysseus was connected with the line of Cyrenaean kings. The Cyrenaeans also claimed Aristaeus as their ancestor, for it was to this spot that Apollo brought Cyrene, for whom the city was named, and it was here that she bore Aristaeus to the god. The Cyrenaeans were celebrated in ancient times as physicians. This was perhaps owing to their connection with Apollo, but it is more likely

that it was on account of a medicinal herb that grew in their land, called silphion, which through its export brought wealth to the king. The modern town on the site of Cyrene contains many antiquities. It was the birthplace of Aristippus, Eratosthenes, and other famous men.

Cyrnos (sir′nos, kür′nos). Greek name of **Corsica.**

Cyropaedia (sī″rō̠-pē̠-dī′a̠), **The.** Work of Xenophon, in eight books, describing the education of Cyrus, the founder of the Persian Empire, his great deeds, and his dying advice to his sons and ministers. The work is a highly idealized biography.

Cyrrhestes (sī-res′tēz), **Andronicus.** See **Andronicus of Cyrrhus.**

Cyrrhestica (sī-res′ti-ka̠) or **Cyrrhus** (sir′us). In ancient geography, a region in N Syria, W of the Euphrates and S of Commagene.

Cyrus (sī′rus). [Called **Cyrus the Great;** name in the Old Testament, **Koresh;** in the cuneiform inscriptions, **Kurush, Kurshu;** Old Persian, **Kurush.**] The founder of the Persian Empire, who died 529 B.C. All accounts of his birth and early youth are heavily encrusted by legends, among which is the following account given by Herodotus. Before Cyrus was born, his grandfather Astyages, the king of the Medes, dreamed that the child his daughter Mandane was about to bear to her husband, the Persian Cambyses, would be a king if he did not die too soon. Astyages, fearing his grandson would usurp his throne, gave orders for the child to be destroyed as soon as it was born. The man to whom he gave the orders, one Harpagus, did not wish to commit the murder himself. When Cyrus was born, Harpagus gave him into the hands of a herdsman, Mitradates. He instructed Mitradates to expose the child on the mountains, and when he was sure it was dead to send word to him. Mitradates took the infant to his house. There he found that his wife, who was awaiting the birth of her first child, had produced a still-born son. She begged Mitradates not to expose the healthy child given into their hands, and they decided to dress their own dead child in the robes worn by Cyrus and to lay him in a thicket in the mountains and to keep Cyrus as their own son. After a few days Mitradates sent for Harpagus and led him to the dead child. Harpagus duly reported to Astyages that the child was dead, and the cowherd's son was given a magnificent funeral, which pleased its parents. Cyrus, brought up with loving care by Mitradates and his wife, grew into a handsome, intelligent, manly child. When he was ten years old, he was chosen to be their king by a group of his playmates. One of the boys objected bitterly to being ordered about by the son of a cowherd, refused to do as he was bid, and was whipped by Cyrus for his insubordination. The boy complained to his father, who in turn complained to Astyages. Astyages sent for the cowherd and his son. In his own defense the boy said the others had voluntarily chosen him as king, and therefore bound themselves to obey his orders. When this one boy refused, he invited the punishment he received. Astyages was much struck by this speech, but more than that, a suspicion grew in his mind that this was his grandson, whom he had ordered destroyed. He sent Cyrus out of the room and questioned Mitradates until, by his threats, he forced the truth from him. Astyages now bethought him of his old dream and of the interpretation the Magi had put on it. He summoned them to learn what he should do, now that his grandson was found to be alive. The Magi listened to the whole story and concluded that the oracle had been fulfilled in a very harmless way; that as his comrades had chosen him as their king, Cyrus had already been king and his grandfather need have no further worry on that account. The omens, the Magi assured Astyages, were sometimes fulfilled in most inconsequential ways. Herodotus adds, in connection with the birth of Cyrus, that the report that he was suckled by a bitch was circulated by his parents when they recovered him after the events related above, because Cyrus talked continually of the goodness of Cyno, his foster mother. Cyno means "bitch." However, much information of some historical repute concerning his lineage has been obtained from the inscriptions, among them a cylinder belonging to Cyrus himself, discovered in the ruins of Babylon and Sepharvaim (Sippar), combined with the accounts of the Greek historians (Herodotus, Xenophon, and Ctesi-

phon). On his cylinder he calls himself the son of Cambyses, grandson of Cyrus and great-grandson of Shishpish (Theispes), who were all "Kings of Anshan." Anshan is evidently identical with Anzan, the plain of Susa, and stands for Elam, which was conquered by Theispes, the son of Achaemenes, founder of the dynasty. But the Magi had been right in their original interpretation of the dream of Astyages. In 549 B.C., Cyrus, after conquering Ecbatana or Agbatana (modern Hamadan), encouraged by Harpagus, who had spared his life, led a revolt of the Persians against their Median rulers. He completely defeated the army Astyages sent against him, and made himself master of the Medes and the Persians. He then directed his arms against the Lydian kingdom of Croesus (q.v.), who made an offensive and defensive alliance with Nabonidus, king of Babylonia, and the reigning pharaoh of Egypt. Croesus consulted the oracle at Delphi several times as he prepared for war against Cyrus, and received what he considered to be most reassuring answers, although in the event it developed that they were equivocal. He asked the oracle if he should attack Persia. The priestess replied that if he attacked the Persians he would destroy a great empire. He further asked if his kingdom would long endure. The priestess replied:

"Wait till the time shall come when a mule
   is monarch of Media;
Then, thou delicate Lydian, away to the
   pebbles of Hermus;
Haste, oh! haste thee away, nor blush to
   behave like a coward."

This was most reassuring to Croesus, for he doubted that a mule would ever be king of the Medes. In the war that he now waged against the Persians Cyrus disastrously defeated him (546 B.C.), captured him, and plundered his capital, Sardis. But Croesus had no complaint against the oracle when the matter was explained to him, for Cyrus, the son of a Median mother and a Persian father, was the mule to which the oracle referred. Cyrus kept Croesus, miraculously saved from the pyre on which Cyrus had meant to burn him, at his side in his court. He treated him with the utmost courtesy and consideration, and often, according to

Herodotus, turned to him for advice or accepted suggestions he volunteered. After the conquest of Lydia by Cyrus, the Ionian and Aeolian Greeks sent envoys to Cyrus and asked him to accept them on the same terms they had enjoyed when they were subject to Croesus. Cyrus listened carefully to their plea, then replied with a parable. Once a piper walking by the sea chanced to see fish swimming in the waters. He took out his pipes and played sweetly to them, hoping they would come out on land in response to his music, but the fish ignored him. Then he took a net, cast it in the sea, netted the fish, and brought them to land. Hereupon the fish began to leap and dance. Then the piper told the fishes they could cease their dancing, as they had not chosen to dance when he piped to them. And so it was with the Ionians and Aeolians: when Cyrus urged them to revolt, before his war with Croesus, they had ignored him, probably on the assumption that Cyrus would never overcome Croesus. Now that he was successful they offered him their allegiance on the old terms, but as his position was now different, he was a conqueror, so would his treatment of the Ionians and Aeolians be different. As it turned out, he was a very mild ruler over them. In the years following the conquest of Lydia, Cyrus consolidated his power in the conquered countries. In 538 B.C. he marched with a great army into Babylonia. Sepharvaim (Sippar) was captured without fighting, Nabonidus, who defended it, fled, and two days afterward Babylon itself, which was held by Nabonidus' son Belshazzar, fell into the hands of the conqueror, likewise "without battle and fight," as he records. According to Eusebius, Nabonidus after the fall of Babylon fortified himself in Borsippa; the city was besieged by Cyrus, and after it had capitulated he treated it and Nabonidus himself with mercy, allowing the latter to make his residence in Carmania (modern Kerman). It is certain that he showed great generosity and consideration to the conquered capital Babylon, sparing its inhabitants and their religious feelings; he even represented himself as having been called by Merodach (Marduk), the god of the city, to avenge his neglect at the hands of the preceding kings. Cyrus' attitude toward the Jewish exiles in Babylonia is well known from the Old Testament (Ezra, i.). He permitted them to return to their own country (thus ending the Babylonian Exile), to rebuild Jerusalem, and to restore the temple, and even returned to them the vessels of the temple which had been carried away by Nebuchadnezzar. According to Herodotus, because of his firm, just, and kindly qualities, he was known to the Persians as "father." His death, like his birth, is shrouded in legend. The most common view is that he fell in battle with the Massagetae, on the river Jaxartes (modern Syr Darya); in this connection, see **Tomyris**. The tomb of Cyrus was at Pasargadae, a city founded by him near the site where he had defeated his grandfather Astyages, king of the Medes. The tomb was inscribed,

"O man, whosoever thou art, and from whencesoever thou comest (for I know thou wilt come), I am Cyrus, the founder of the Persian Empire; do not grudge me this little earth which covers my body."

His plea was ignored; the officers Alexander the Great left at Pasargadae, 330 B.C., allowed the tomb to be plundered. When Alexander returned and learned that the tomb had been opened and plundered, he put the guardians of the tomb to torture but could not learn who had committed the sacrilege and outrage.

Cyrus the Younger. Persian satrap; killed at Cunaxa in Babylonia, 401 B.C. He was the son of Darius II, king of Persia, and Parysatis. He was sent to Sardis by his father, to be satrap with dominion over Cappadocia, Phrygia, and Lydia, and proved himself an able administrator. There he met the Spartan admiral Lysander, who won his confidence by his personal incorruptibility and his refusal to accept gifts from Cyrus. His contact with Lysander's Spartans gave him great respect for the fighting qualities of the Greeks. He promised money to Lysander to prosecute the war against the Athenians, and left Lysander, whom he trusted more than the Persian nobles, in charge of his satrapy when he was called back to the Persian court to attend his dying father. On the death of Darius his mother intrigued unsuccessfully to secure the throne

fat, fāte, fär, fãre, errạnt; net, mē, hėr ardẹnt; pin, pīne; not, nōte, mŏve, nôr,

for him in place of the legitimate heir,
Artaxerxes II. Cyrus resolved to win the
throne and began to collect a force of Greek
mercenaries for the purpose. As finally
gathered, the army of Cyrus included about
100,000 Asiatic troops and 13,000 Greeks,
among whom was the Athenian Xenophon.
Without telling the troops their precise destination, Cyrus led forth his army from
Sardis in the spring of 401 B.C. The path
wound across Asia Minor, through Lycaonia,
the Cilician Gates, the Pass of Beilan, and
along the Euphrates River to Babylonia. At
the village of Cunaxa outside Babylon, Artaxerxes marched out against him. The two
hosts engaged. The forces of Cyrus were
immediately successful, and Cyrus was already receiving congratulations when he suddenly spied his hated brother. With a few
followers he urged his horse forward intent
on killing Artaxerxes with his own hand, and
did wound him slightly. But the bodyguard
surrounding Artaxerxes wounded him in the
eye; he fell from his horse and was instantly
slain. As soon as news of his death reached
his Asiatic troops, they fled in terror; the
victory so quickly won was more quickly
turned into a rout. Only the Greek mercenaries stood fast. They did not surrender
to Artaxerxes but were allowed to depart
and made the famous return described in
Xenophon's *Anabasis* (q.v.).

Cythera (si-thir′ạ). [Also: **Cerigo, Cerigotto;**
Greek, **Kithira, Kythera, Kytherion.**] One of
the Ionian Islands in S Greece, situated between 8 and 10 miles S of Laconia. It was
near this island that Aphrodite was said to
have arisen from the foam of the sea, whence
her epithet "Cytherea." But some say the
worship of Aphrodite was brought to the
island by the Phoenicians. The sanctuary
of Aphrodite Urania (*Heavenly*) on the
island is the oldest of all the sanctuaries of
Aphrodite among the Greeks. A wooden
image of the goddess, armed, stood in it. In
ancient times the island was known as the
"Purple Island" because the shellfish of the
region yielded such a fine dye. The island,
once an Argive possession, came into the
hands of the Spartans, but was wrested from
them by the Athenians, 424 B.C., and became a base from which Athens attacked
Sparta. This fulfilled the warning made

generations earlier by the sage Chilon, that
Sparta would gain if Cythera were sunk to
the bottom of the sea, for he saw it, by its
location, as a dagger pointed at the heart of
Sparta. Area of the island, about 110
square miles.

Cytherea (sith-ẹ-rē′ạ) or **Cythera** (si-thir′ạ). In
classical mythology, epithets of Aphrodite,
from the island of Cythera, or from a place
of the same name which once existed in
Crete.

Cytissorus (sī″ti-sôr′us). In Greek legend, a
son of Phrixus and Chalciope, and a grandson of Aeëtes, king of Colchis. See **Phrontis.**

Cyzicus (siz′i-kus). A legendary king of the
Doliones in the country of Cyzicus. Jason
and the Argonauts landed there on their
way to Colchis on the expedition for the
Golden Fleece and were hospitably received.
When the Argonauts sailed away they were
driven back by unfavorable winds and,
landing again on the shores of Cyzicus in
darkness, were mistaken for enemies. The
Argonauts were unaware that the land to
which they had been driven was Cyzicus
and in the struggle which followed Jason
killed Cyzicus, the king who had entertained
him.

Cyzicus. [Also: **Cyzicum.**] In ancient geography, the peninsula projecting from Mysia,
Asia Minor, into the Propontis (Sea of Marmara); also, the Greek town on its isthmus,
named, according to legend, for Cyzicus,
king of the Doliones. Jason and the Argonauts stopped there on their way to Colchis
in the quest for the Golden Fleece. Among
its ruins are a Roman amphitheater, a temple
of Hadrian, and an ancient theater. The
Roman amphitheater dates from the 2nd
century A.D. The ruins still rise to a height
of 65 feet, built of rubble faced with rusti-
cated masonry in granite. There are 32
arched entrances in the lower story. The
longer axis of the ellipse is 325 feet. The
temple of Hadrian, dedicated in 167 A.D.,
was greatly admired in antiquity. It was
a Corinthian *peripteros* (building surrounded
by a row of columns) of six by 15 columns,
of white marble. The cella, or main chamber, was small, without *pronaos* (vestibule)
or *opisthodomos* (rear chamber); there were
four interior rows of columns in front and
two behind. The temple measured 112 by

301 feet; the cella 70 by 140 feet. The columns were seven feet in base-diameter and 70 feet high (the highest of any classical temple). The pediments and the cella were richly adorned. The ancient theater, apparently contemporaneous with the amphitheater, was in part built up of rough masonry and faced with marble. The diameter is 328 feet.

—D———

Dacia (dā′sha). In ancient geography, a province of the Roman Empire, lying between the Carpathian Mountains on the N, the Tissus or Tisia (Tisza) on the W, the Ister (Danube) on the S, and the Tyras or Danastris (Dniester) on the E. It corresponded approximately to modern Rumania, including Transylvania. The inhabitants were the Getae or Daci. It was invaded by Alexander the Great in 335 B.C., by Lysimachus c292 B.C., and its people defeated the generals of Domitian in 86–90 A.D. It was conquered by Trajan in 101 and succeeding years, and made a Roman province. It was abandoned by the Romans in the reign of Aurelian (270–275), but not before the Romans, during some 200 years of occupation, had left their imprint on the region by establishing the language that has developed into modern Rumanian.

Dactyls (dak′tilz) or **Dactyli** (dak′ti-lī) or **Daktyloi** (-loi). In Greek and Roman mythology, supernatural and magical beings living on Mount Ida in Phrygia, the discoverers of iron and copper and of the art of working them. They were transferred, in the legends, to Mount Ida in Crete, where they were said to have been born of the nymph Anchiale, as she grasped the earth with both hands, in a cave on Mount Dicte. According to this version, and a similar one in which they were born as Rhea grasped the earth in giving birth to Zeus, there were ten Dactyls, five male and five female. The males were fabulous ironworkers in Crete. The females were experts in the art of making magic spells and dwelt in Samothrace. In Crete, the Dactyls were sometimes identified with the Curetes, Corybantes, and other mountain-dwelling semi-divine beings. Their number, originally three, was increased, in various accounts, to ten, and even to 100.

Daedala (dē′da-la). A Boeotian festival of the Sacred Marriage, established by Hera to commemorate a reconciliation after one of her quarrels with Zeus. In a fit of jealousy she had left him and gone into hiding in Euboea. Zeus could not persuade her to return to him. He went, some say, to Cithaeron, the despot of Plataea, who was reputed to be very clever, and asked advice. Cithaeron advised Zeus to make a wooden image, dress it up, and transport it on a bullock wagon, in the meantime stating that he was celebrating his marriage with Plataea, the daughter of the river-god Asopus. Zeus followed his advice. Hera learned of the proposed marriage and returned at once, swooping down on the supposed bride as she was carried in procession. When she realized it was a wooden image she was so relieved that she became reconciled with Zeus, and founded this festival, which was named Daedala because that was the name given to wooden images. The Little Daedala was celebrated every six years by Plataeans only. The Plataeans went to an oak grove, spread out cooked meat, and observed the crows that came to take up the meat. They marked the tree which the first crow to take up the meat perched on, cut down that tree and made their wooden image from it. The Great Daedala was celebrated every 59 years. To that festival 14 Boeotian towns sent images. The 14 images were carried in procession to the Asopus River, thence to the top of Mount Cithaeron. There a cow was sacrificed to Hera and a bull to Zeus on a wooden altar. The victims were burned, with other victims contributed by the celebrants of the festival, after they had been anointed with incense and wine, and the altar was burned with them.

Daedalion (dē̱-dā′li-on). In legend, a son of Phosphorus, the morning star. He was the brother of Ceyx and the father of a beautiful daughter, Chione, who was loved by Apollo and Hermes. Daedalion was a fierce and valiant warrior, but when his daughter was slain by Artemis for her boastfulness he became frenzied with grief. He fled to Mount Parnassus and leaped from its summit. Apollo took pity on him and transformed him as he fell into a hawk, a bird like Daedalion in its ruthless and ferocious character.

Daedalus (ded′a̱-lus, dē′da̱-lus). A legendary Athenian; son of Metion and grandson of Erechtheus. He was a marvelous smith, having been taught by Athena, and was regarded as the personification of all handicrafts and of art, and as such was worshiped by artists' guilds in various places, especially in Attica, and was a central figure in various myths. He was said to have made various improvements in the fine arts, including architecture, and to have invented many mechanical appliances, as the ax, the awl, and the bevel. For the murder of his nephew Talus, of whose inventive skill he was jealous, he was banished or escaped to Crete, where he constructed, to contain the monster Minotaur, the famous Labyrinth, in which he and his son Icarus were confined for a time. In one legend the reason given for his imprisonment is that he built a cow disguise for Pasiphaë in order that the bull sent by Poseidon might mount her. Escaping, he and Icarus fled over the sea on wings of wax which they had made. Icarus, ignoring his father's warnings, soared too near the sun; his wings melted, and he fell into the sea (which has since been called, after him, the Icarian Sea). Daedalus circled over the waves where he fell, recovered his son's body and took it to a nearby island, now called Icaria. A partridge perched nearby and watched gleefully as he buried Icarus there. It was his sister, Polycaste, who had been transformed into a bird when she hanged herself in grief at the death of her son Talus, and who was now avenged by the sight of Daedalus, the murderer of Talus, burying his own son. In some accounts Perdix ("part-

ridge") is given as the name of Polycaste's son. In his flight from Minos, Daedalus went to Cumae and there built a golden-roofed temple. On the doors of the temple he depicted the story of Androgeus, of the Athenians and the tribute which they paid because of his death, of Pasiphaë, the Minotaur, Theseus, and Ariadne, but he had not the heart to engrave the story of his son's death. From Cumae he went to Sicily and settled in the realm of King Cocalus. Minos, in the meanwhile, had set out in pursuit of him. As a scheme to trap Daedalus, Minos announced that he would give a rich reward to whoever could run a thread through a spiraled triton shell. Cocalus, to whom Minos had given the shell, passed it on to Daedalus. Daedalus attached a thread to an ant. He then bored a hole at the apex of the shell and confined the ant in the mouth of the shell. The scent of honey smeared on the bored hole lured the ant into traversing the coiling chambers of the shell, drawing the thread with it, until it reached the honey at the other end. When Cocalus returned the shell, with the thread running through it, to Minos and demanded his reward, Minos knew that he had found Daedalus. He demanded his surrender. Cocalus, however, refused to give him up. Still seeking the return of Daedalus, Minos died in Sicily, either in a struggle for his recapture or by being scalded to death as he lay in his bath. Daedalus ultimately joined Iolaus, the nephew of Heracles, in the colonization of Sardinia, and ended his days in that island. Many archaic wooden images were, in ancient times, believed to be the work of Daedalus (and figures of the type are still called Daedalian).

Daira (dā̱-ī′ra̱). A daughter of Oceanus. Some say she was the mother by Hermes of Eleusis, for whom the town was named. Others say she was a sister of Styx. She was a goddess connected with the Eleusinian mysteries and, some say, this name which means "the Knowing," is simply another name for Demeter, Persephone, Aphrodite, or Hera, or all of those goddesses.

Daemon or **Demon** (dē′mon). In Greek mythology, a term which had two significances: 1) a supernatural agent or intelligence, lower in rank than a god; a spirit holding a middle place between gods and men, as the Corybantes, Curetes, Dactyls, Satyrs, and Sileni; 2) a ministering spirit, sometimes regarded as including the souls of deceased persons, which was generally considered by the Greeks to be a protective spirit.

Daldianus (dal-di-ā′nus), **Artemidorus.** See **Artemidorus Daldianus.**

Damarchus (da-mär′kus). An Arcadian of Parrhasia. According to legend, he was transformed into a wolf at the sacrifice of Lycaean Zeus. He kept this shape for nine years, at the end of which time, because he had eaten no men, he was restored to his shape as a man. Afterward he took part in the Olympic Games and won in the boxing match. His statue was set up at Olympia. Pausanias, who tells the story of his transformation into a wolf, doubts that the story is true. If it were, he says, it would surely have been inscribed on the pedestal of his image at Olympia.

Damastes (da-mas′tēz). The real name of Procrustes, the "Stretcher," whom Theseus killed on his way from Troezen to Athens. But some say his name was Polypemon, and that he was the father of Sinis, the "Pine-bender," who was also slain by Theseus. See **Procrustes.**

Damia (dam′i-a). Spirit of fertility, worshiped in Epidaurus and Aegina. A famine struck Epidaurus and to learn how they might find relief, the Epidaurians consulted the oracle at Delphi. The priestess told them to set up images of Damia and Auxesia (Increase). To the question whether the images should be of stone or bronze, the priestess replied that they should be made of olive wood. Having no olive trees of their own, the Epidaurians sent to Athens for permission to cut trees there. The Athenians gave permission on condition that the Epidaurians make annual offerings to Athena Polias (*Of the City*) and Erechtheus. The Epidaurians agreed; the images were made, and the Epidaurians made the annual offerings. Afterward the Aeginetans, subjects of Epidaurus, revolted, attacked Epidaurus and seized the images, which they took to Aegina and set up there. The Epidaurians now ceased their offerings to Athena and Erechtheus. The Athenians demanded offerings from the Aeginetans on the ground that they had the images. The Aeginetans refused, and also refused to give up the images to Athens. Enraged, the Athenians sailed against Aegina, made their way to the temple, and tried to seize the images. They could not move them. They bound them with ropes and tried to haul them from the temple. Instantly a great thunderclap was heard; all the crew of the Athenian ship were struck with madness and fell upon each other with such savagery that all save one were killed. He alone returned to Athens. This is the Athenian story. But the Aeginetans say that as the Athenians made to haul off the images, the statues fell to their knees, in which position they remained ever after. Meantime the Argives, forewarned by the Aeginetans, came and cut off the retreat of the Athenians. Both agree that only one Athenian escaped. He, when he returned, was set upon by the wives of those who had been killed. As each one asked where her husband was, she jabbed the unfortunate man with the pin of her brooch. In this manner the one who had escaped from Aegina was killed by the widows of his fellows. The Athenians were so shocked by this deed of the women that henceforth the Athenian women were compelled to adopt a style of dress which required no brooches.

Damocles (dam′ō-klēz). Syracusan, fl. in the first half of the 4th century B.C., a courtier of Dionysius the Elder. Cicero relates that Damocles, having extolled the good fortune of Dionysius, was invited by the tyrant to taste this royal felicity, and that, in the midst of a splendid banquet and all the luxury of the court, on looking up he beheld above his head a sword suspended by a single horsehair.

Damon (dā′mon). Greek musician; fl. latter part of the 5th century B.C. He was noted as a master of the theory of music and for his richly endowed intellect. He was one of the most distinguished teachers of Pericles, and because of his supposed influence upon the latter, he was ostracized.

Damon and Pythias (dā′mon; pith′i-as). Pythagorean philosophers of Syracuse; fl. in the first half of the 4th century B.C. They were celebrated for their friendship. Pythias (or Phintias) plotted against the life of Dionysius I of Syracuse, and was condemned to die. As Pythias wished to arrange his affairs,

Damon offered to place himself in the tyrant's hands as his substitute, and to die in his stead should he not return on the appointed day. At the last moment Pythias came back, and Dionysius was so struck by the fideilty of the friends that he pardoned the offender and begged to be admitted into their fellowship.

Damophon (dam′ọ-fon). Greek sculptor, born at Messene, Greece; fl. 2nd century B.C. He was one of the masters of Hellenistic art, and his work combines the decorative richness of his period with something of the monumental simplicity of the Phidian epoch. For a sanctuary of Demeter at Lycosura, in Arcadia, he designed a group of cult statues, of Demeter and Persephone, seated, flanked by standing figures of Artemis and the Titan Anytus, from which three heads and other fragments were recovered during excavations at the site. From the quality of the carving, scholars have speculated that the actual carving was done by apprentices from the master's clay models. Damophon is also credited with a statue of the Mother of the Gods for the agora of Messene, an acrolithic Ilithyia for Aegium, an Artemis, and many others. He worked also in gold and ivory, and it was he who restored the cracked ivory of Phidias' chryselephantine Zeus at Olympia. (JJ)

Damysus (dam′i-sus). In Greek legend, a giant. Some say that when Peleus interrupted Thetis as she was burning away the mortal parts of Achilles to make him immortal, all had been made immortal except one ankle-bone. Thetis departed in a rage at the interruption. Peleus took the ankle-bone from Damysus, whose skeleton had been disinterred, and replaced the charred ankle-bone of Achilles. This was his only mortal part and thus his only vulnerable spot.

Danaë (dan′ạ-ē). In Greek mythology, a daughter of Acrisius, king of Argos, and Aganippe. Some say that Proetus, the twin brother of Acrisius, with whom he fought in the womb, seduced Danaë. He was discovered by Acrisius and this brought on a furious quarrel, in which the brothers took up arms against each other, and Proetus was compelled to flee. Later Acrisius, who wanted a son, consulted the oracle. He was told that he would have no sons and that the son of his daughter would cause his

death. To prevent the fulfillment of the oracle, Acrisius imprisoned Danaë in a bronze underground chamber so that she should have no traffic with men. His precautions were in vain. Zeus visited Danaë in a shower of gold and embraced her. She subsequently bore him a son, Perseus. Acrisius refused to believe that the child was the son of Zeus and longed for his death. But he dared not risk the wrath of the gods and the avenging Furies by killing his own grandson. He shut Danaë and her child in a chest and cast it into the sea. The chest floated safely to the shores of the island of Seriphus. Dictys, a fisherman, found the chest, opened it, and took Danaë and her son to his house. There

DANAE AND THE SHOWER OF GOLD
Red-figured Greek vase from Caere in Etruria, early 5th century B.C.

he and his wife sheltered them and there they remained as Perseus grew up. Polydectes, king of the island and brother of Dictys, fell in love with Danaë, but as Perseus, now grown to manhood, stood in his way, he got rid of Perseus, as he thought, by sending him to fetch the head of the Gorgon Medusa. During Perseus' absence Polydectes so harassed Danaë that she, with Dictys, went into hiding to escape him. When Perseus returned and learned that his mother and Dictys had fled to a temple for refuge from Polydectes he went to the palace, exhibited the head of Medusa, and turned Polydectes and his unfriendly court to stone.

Danai (dan'ā-ī). [Also: **Danaoi, Danaans.**] In ancient Greek history, the Argives; used by Homer to denote the Greeks generally.

Danaidae (da̱-nā'i-dē). In Greek mythology, descendants of Zeus and Io, the 50 daughters whom Danaus sired on various women. Their mothers were naiads, hamadryads, princesses, and other mortals. Their uncle, Aegyptus, wished them to marry his 50 sons, but Danaus, fearing a plot and on consideration of an oracular pronouncement, fled with his daughters to the Peloponnesus. With them the Danaidae took the rites of Demeter, called by the Greeks the Thesmophoria, and taught these rites to the Pelasgians (Argives). Later, however, when the inhabitants of the Peloponnesus were harried by the Dorians, the observance of the rites ceased, except in Arcadia. The Danaidae also helped the Argives to find springs, and one of them, Amymone, secured a never-failing fountain from Poseidon which is the source of the Lerna River. Danaus made himself king of Argos, and presently the sons of Aegyptus came from over the sea in pursuit of his daughters. After a siege of the city Danaus yielded to their demands to make his daughters their wives, but in secret he gave each of his daughters a sharp pin and ordered them to kill their husbands on the wedding night. All except Hypermnestra obeyed their father. She, divinely inspired, spared her husband Lynceus. The Danaidae buried their husbands' heads at Lerna and their bodies below the walls of Argos. At the command of Zeus, Athena and Hermes purified the Danaidae of the murder of their husbands. Even so, they were punished in the Underworld for their crimes. They were ordered by the judges in Tartarus forever to fetch water in jars that leaked like sieves. After their purification, Danaus sought husbands for his daughters, and awarded them to various men who took part in a foot race, the winner to have first choice, the runner-up second choice, and so on. The descendants from these marriages were known as Danaans, or Danai, a name given in honor of Danaus and sometimes applied to all Argives, and used by Homer to apply to all the Greeks who fought at Troy. According to some accounts the Danaidae, sisters of Hypermnestra, were slain by her husband Lynceus to avenge the deaths of his brothers.

Danaus (dan'ā-us). In Greek mythology, a son of Belus, king of Egypt, and Anchinoë. He was the twin of Aegyptus. Danaus, who became ruler of Libya, was the father of 50 daughters by various nymphs and mortal women. After the death of Belus, Danaus and his brother quarreled about the inheritance. Aegyptus suggested that the 50 daughters of Danaus marry his 50 sons, and thus consolidate the family power. But Danaus, warned by an oracle that he would die at the hands of a son-in-law, fled with his daughters from Libya. With the aid of Athena he built a ship; according to some, it was the first ship ever built, but others say it was the first 50-oared ship. He put to sea with his daughters and sailed to Rhodes, where he raised a temple to Athena and dedicated an image to the goddess. Some say three of his daughters—Lindus, Camirus, and Ialysus—died in Rhodes and gave their names to three cities there. Danaus next sailed to the Peloponnesus. Landing near Argos he informed the Argives, or the Pelasgians as they were also called, that he had been chosen by the gods to be their king. The Argives, who already had a king, were not disposed to accept this dictum but decided to sleep on the question. During the night a wolf attacked the herds of the Argives and killed the best bull. The Argives took this as an omen warning them to accept Danaus willingly or risk violence. Their king, Gelanor, or as some name him, Pelasgus, stepped aside and Danaus became king. In gratitude for the omen Danaus built the temple of Lycian Apollo in Argos, for he thought the wolf was Apollo in disguise. Danaus became a powerful ruler. He built the Acropolis of Argos and later taught the inhabitants how to dig wells, for Poseidon, enraged that Inachus had awarded the land to Hera instead of to himself, had dried up all the springs. Aegyptus now sent his 50 sons in pursuit of the daughters of Danaus, and ordered them not to return without their brides. Danaus remained adamant in his refusal to let his daughters wed their cousins. The sons of Aegyptus besieged Argos, and since there were no fountains in the citadel, Danaus was compelled to capitulate. He agreed to the marriages of his daughters, but in secret he furnished each of them with a lethal rapier and ordered them to kill their bridegrooms on the wedding night. All of his daughters except Hypermnestra obeyed his command. The daughters of Danaus buried the heads of their husbands at Lerna. Now Danaus decided to choose other husbands for his daughters. He arranged a race for the suitors of his daughters and announced that the winner would have first choice of a wife, the runner-up second choice, and so on until all his remaining daughters had husbands. This race was run on a street in Argos and was afterward celebrated by the Argives in a contest commemorating it. There were not enough contestants in the first race, as many men were reluctant to wed known murderesses, but ultimately all the daughters were wed. Their descendants were known as Danaans, or Danai, after their ancestor Danaus. Danaus met his end at the hands of the one bridegroom who had been spared among the sons of Aegyptus. He was Lynceus, who after murdering his father-in-law, took the throne.

Daphnaea (daf-ne′a). An epithet of Artemis, meaning "Of the Laurel." The laurel was sacred to her.

Daphne (daf′ne). In Greek mythology, a nymph, the daughter of the river-god Peneus, or, in other accounts, of Ladon, an Arcadian. She delighted to spend her days in the forest hunting, as did the virgin goddess Artemis, and rejected all suitors for her hand. Her father pleaded with her to take a husband and give him grandsons, but Daphne became so tearful at the prospect of marriage that Peneus did not insist. But Daphne was so beautiful that many fell in love with her. Apollo, wounded by one of the arrows of Eros because the god of love wished to punish him for mocking his skill with the bow and arrow, saw Daphne and fell in love with her. Leucippus, son of Oenomaus, also loved her. Leucippus, seeing that he could make no progress with Daphne, disguised himself as a maiden and joined Daphne and the nymphs in their hunting expeditions in order to be near the object of his adoration. Apollo, jealous of Leucippus' proximity to Daphne, suggested that the nymphs bathe naked in the mountain stream, and thus Leucippus' disguise was betrayed, whereupon the nymphs tore him to pieces. Apollo then pursued Daphne when she was separated from her companions. She fled from him in terror, some say because Eros had shot her with the arrow that drives away love. The more Apollo called to her of his love, the faster she flew from him. Nearly at the end of her strength in her flight, she approached the Peneus River and called out to her father to save her from the embraces of Apollo. Her prayer was answered. As Apollo was about to clasp her in his arms, she was transformed into a laurel tree. He embraced the tree, still quivering from the chase, and declared that its leaves would always be green and that he would always bind them around his head in memory of his love for Daphne. From then on the laurel wreath replaced the oak wreath as the prize to the victors in Apollo's festival of the Pythian Games, and laurel became the symbol of victory.

Daphne. In Greek legend, a daughter of Tiresias, the seer of Thebes. When the Thebans fled before the Epigoni Daphne remained in the city and was captured. The Epigoni sent her to Delphi as part of the fruit of their victory and dedicated her to the service of Apollo. She became famous for composing many of the oracular responses, and some say Homer borrowed some of his verses from her.

Daphne. In ancient geography, a famous grove and sanctuary of Apollo, situated about five miles SW of Antioch, in ancient Syria. It was established by Seleucus Nicator.

Daphnephoria (daf″ne-fo′ri-a). A festival in honor of Apollo, a kind of May-pole ceremony, observed in Thebes. It occurred once in eight years, but was probably annual at first. A boy, richly dressed and with his long hair let down, headed the procession. He was followed by his nearest relative carrying the decorated pole, and by a band of singing girls bearing olive branches.

Daphnis (daf′nis). In mythology, a son of Hermes and a Sicilian nymph. He was exposed by his mother in a laurel grove, but was found and brought up by shepherds. Pan taught him to sing and play the flute, the Muses endowed him with a love of poetry, and he was the companion of Apollo and Artemis. He was a shepherd who tended his flocks in Sicily. A nymph, Nomia, fell in love with him, and made him swear to be faithful to her. One of her rivals, Chimaera, made him drunk and then seduced him. When Nomia heard of it she blinded him. Daphnis, who is said to have invented pastoral or bucolic poetry, mourned the loss of his sight in song and Hermes took pity on him and transformed him into stone and caused a spring, named Daphnis, to flow from the earth near his home in Sicily. Annual sacrifices were offered there in memory of Daphnis.

Daphnis and Chloë (klō'ē). Greek pastoral romance attributed to Longus (3rd century A.D.?), a Greek sophist. It recounts the loves and pastoral life of Daphnis, foster son of Lamon, a goatherd, and Chloë, foster daughter of Dryas, a shepherd. The principals were each found as infants, and the circumstances surrounding the sites where they were found indicated divine birth. After various vicissitudes, they are united and their at least noble birth is acknowledged.

Dardanelles (där-da-nelz'). See **Hellespont**.

Dardani (där'da-nī). Ancient Illyrian people of the southern highland of Moesia. The Dardani became subject to the Macedonians under the Antigoni, and later to the Romans. Their chief city was Dardanus, after which the strait of the Dardanelles was named.

Dardani. Inhabitants of Dardania, mentioned in the *Iliad*.

Dardania (där-dā'ni-a). [Also: **Dardanice**.] In ancient geography, a territory in Mysia, with uncertain boundaries. It is mentioned, indefinitely, in the *Iliad*.

Dardanus (där'da-nus). In Greek mythology, a son of Zeus and the Pleiad Electra, and the ancestor of the Trojans. He migrated from Arcadia to Phrygia and built a city near the foot of Mount Ida, which he named Dardania. He brought with him to the Troad the sacred images of the gods which had formed part of his wife's dowry, and instituted their worship into the region. According to an oracle, his city would remain safe as long as the images remained in it. The city which Dardanus founded later became part of Ilium, or Troy. The children of Dardanus were Erichthonius, Ilus, Deimas, Idaeus, and one daughter, Idaea.

Dardanus. [Also: **Dardanum**.] In ancient

geography, a city in Mysia, Asia Minor, situated on the Hellespont, about nine miles SW of Abydos.

Dares (dâr'ēz). In the *Aeneid*, one of the companions of Aeneas on the flight from Troy. He was a famous boxer who used to spar with Paris. In the games honoring Anchises in Sicily, Aeneas had to stop his match with the much older Entellus, because Dares was being battered to pieces by Entellus. Dares was later slain by Turnus in the war with the Latins.

Dares Phrygius (dâr'ēz frij'i-us, dā'rēz). Priest of Hephaestus in Troy mentioned in the *Iliad*. *De Excidio Troiae*, a Latin poem on the fall of Troy, composed about the 5th century A.D., of little merit, was alleged to be a translation of an original poem by Dares Phrygius. (JJ)

Darius I (of *Persia*) (da-rī'us). [Called **Darius the Great**: also known as **Darius Hystaspes**.] King of Persia, born c558 B.C.; died 486 B.C. He was a son of Hystaspes; his brothers were Artaphernes, Artabanus, and Artanes; and he was fifth in the descent from Achaemenes. He succeeded (521 B.C.) Cambyses on the Persian throne, after defeating the magian Gaumata, who claimed to be Bardiya (the Greek Smerdis), brother of Cambyses and son of Cyrus. According to Herodotus, he won the throne in the following manner: While Cambyses was on his campaign in Egypt, the Median magus Patizeithes, whom he had left in charge of his household, plotted with his brother Bardiya to seize the throne of Persia. He set up Bardiya, pretending that he was Smerdis, the brother of Cambyses and son of Cyrus, and had him proclaimed king. He felt safe in doing this as he knew the real Smerdis had been secretly slain at Cambyses' order. Cambyses died before he could return to Susa and expose the False Smerdis. There were several Persian nobles who suspected, and finally proved to their own satisfaction, that the reigning Smerdis was not the son of Cyrus but an imposter. Six of these nobles took Darius into their confidence, proposing to overthrow the False Smerdis, who was a Mede, and regain the throne for a Persian. Darius had also suspected that this Smerdis was an impostor and now urged instant action. He threatened the other six nobles—Otanes, Gobryas,

Intaphernes, Megabyzus, Aspathines, and Hydarnes—that he would reveal their plot to Smerdis himself unless they acted at once. He would do so to protect himself, before the knowledge that he had been discovered reached the ears of Smerdis and caused him to take action against them. Darius convinced them, and they set off to the palace, planning to enter and slay the False Smerdis. On the way news reached them that Smerdis had been disclosed as an impostor by Prexaspes, the man who at Cambyses' order had secretly slain the real Smerdis. The conspirators now hesitated, and considered whether they should not delay a bit while the capital was in such a ferment. Darius again insisted on immediate action. As they discussed the matter, two pairs of vultures, pursued by seven pairs of hawks, flew by. The hawks overtook the vultures and tore them to pieces. At this omen the seven agreed to proceed at once. When they came to the palace the guards let them enter the courtyard without question. Eunuchs inside tried to stop them from entering the palace, but they were slain and the conspirators pushed on to the apartments of the king. The two magi heard the clamor and rose to defend themselves. One was instantly slain. The other rushed to an inner room. Darius and Gobryas followed. In the darkness Gobryas seized the magus but Darius, unable to see, hesitated. Gobryas asked why he hesitated and, hearing that Darius feared to strike lest he wound Gobryas, told him to strike anyway, even if both were killed by his blow. Darius obeyed and fortunately killed only the magus. After the slaying of the two magi, the seven nobles rushed from the palace, shouting what they had done and killing every magus they could lay their hands on.

Some days later they met to decide what they should do. After some discussion of the various merits of a monarchy, oligarchy, and democracy, they decided to restore the monarchy and choose one of their own number as king. They agreed to ride out of the city together the next morning, and that he whose horse was first to neigh after sunrise should become king. Darius was determined that the choice fall to him. He took his groom into his confidence, and was assured by him that if the choice depended on the neighing of the horse, Darius could cease to worry, as with the help of a mare he would cause Darius' stallion to neigh first. The next day the nobles, all except Otanes who favored a democracy and did not wish to become king, rode out as planned. As they rode along, they came to the spot where the groom had tethered a mare the night before. Darius' stallion leaped forward and neighed. At the same time there was a flash of lightning followed by a clap of thunder. The five other nobles leaped from their horses, knelt before Darius, and acknowledged him as their king. Thus he became ruler of all that was then known as Asia except the part occupied by the Arabians. In his own record of his reign, as set forth in the inscriptions of Behistun in three languages (Old Persian, Elamite, and Accadian), Darius caused the following to be inscribed: "Darius, son of Hystaspes, by aid of his good horse and his good groom Oebares, got himself the kingdom of the Persians." Darius, who was already married to a daughter of Gobryas, now married Atossa, daughter of Cyrus, who had been the wife of her brother Cambyses and then of the False Smerdis; she had great influence with him. He also married Phaedima, daughter of Otanes, who had proved that Smerdis was an impostor; Artystone, said to have been his favorite, another daughter of Cyrus; and Parmys, a granddaughter of Cyrus; and Phratagune, the daughter of his brother Artanes. Among the sons produced by these wives were: Artabazanes and Ariabignes, by the daughter of Otanes; Xerxes (his heir), Achaemenes, Hystaspes, and Masistes, by Atossa; Arsames and Gobryas, by Artystone; Ariomardus, by Parmys; Abrocomes and Hyperanthes (both of whom fell at Thermopylae, 480 B.C.), by Phratagune.

After gaining the throne, Darius turned his attention to putting down the revolts which broke out all over Persia following the unmasking of the impostor Smerdis. This was followed by two uprisings in Babylonia, led by Nidintu-Bel and Arachus, who made claim to be Nebuchadnezzar, son of Nabonidus. He marched to Babylon and besieged the city. But the Babylonians had taken thorough measures to prepare for a siege, and jeered at the Persians, saying their city would not fall until mules foaled. More than a year and a half passed, and still the city held out. In the twentieth month from the beginning of the siege a mule belonging to Zopyrus (son of that Megabazus who had helped to overthrow the False Smerdis), gave birth to a foal. With a stratagem worked out by Zopyrus, Darius now won entrance into the city and took it a second time. He destroyed the walls of the city and crucified 3000 of the leading citizens. He honored Zopyrus by making him governor of the city for life, free from tribute. The other countries under Persian dominion revolted in turn, but at last were brought to submission. He besieged and took Samos and gave it to Syloson to repay him for an act of generosity Syloson had shown toward him when he was a mere member of Cambyses' bodyguard with no prospects of ever becoming king. After restoring order in the empire, Darius turned his attention to reorganization and reforms of the administration. He divided the whole land into 20 satrapies, each ruled by a governor, introduced regular taxation and uniformity of coinage, constructed roads, and founded a kind of postal system by placing stations and relays with saddled horses at regular intervals on the road between Susa and Sardis. To the capitals Susa in Elam, Ecbatana in Media, and Babylon, he added Persepolis in Persia proper, which was destroyed by Alexander the Great, but the imposing ruins of which have survived. On account of his attention to trade, taxes, and industry he was called "the Huckster." He sent an expedition to explore the Indus River, and to sail to its mouth; he dug a canal from the Nile to Suez, and compelled North Africa to pay him tribute. He also explored the shores of Sicily and Italy (Magna Graecia); Herodotus relates that this was a spying trip in preparation for war on Greece, and that the idea for it was proposed by Atossa to honor her promise to Democedes, a physician of Crotona, to secure his return to his homeland.

Throughout his empire he encouraged and promoted the native religions and priests. For this reason the oracles of Asia Minor supported the side of the Persians, and in Egypt he was regarded as a great benefactor. He is referred to in the Old Testament in connection with the building of the temple of Zerubbabel. In the second year of his reign he allowed the resumption of the building, and in the sixth it was completed (Ezra, vi. 15). In 512 B.C., over the protests of his brother Artabanus, who felt the rewards of the undertaking were not worth its difficulties, he prepared an expedition against Scythia with the idea of securing the northern boundaries of his empire. At the head of a great host he marched to the Thracian Bosporus, leaving inscribed pillars along the way to commemorate his passage. He caused the Bosporus to be bridged and passed over it into Europe. On the advice of Ceos of Lesbos he did not destroy the bridge, as he had intended to do, but left it to secure his return or possible retreat. Histiaeus, tyrant of Miletus, was left in charge of the Ionians who guarded the bridge, and fulfilled his charge well. Both Ceos and Histiaeus were richly rewarded by Darius, who never lost his gratitude to them. Now that they were in Europe, the Scythians refused to meet the hosts of Darius in open battle. Instead they kept always one day's march ahead of Darius, destroying the lands through which they passed and leading the Persians deep into Europe, to the lower steppes of Russia. Darius was exasperated with this manner of fighting and did not know which way to turn. According to the account given in Herodotus, he sent messengers to the Scythian chiefs, and asked them if they were afraid to stand and fight why they did not surrender. The Scythians sent back a bird, a mouse, a frog, and five arrows, but the Persians did not immediately understand the meaning of these tokens. After Darius had received these gifts, a part of the Scythian force was drawn up in battle array against the Persians as if to engage in battle. Suddenly a hare ran in front of their ranks. The Scyths broke their formation and went in loud pursuit of the hare. Darius, observing their action, asked what they were doing. When he was told the Scythians were pursuing a hare, he decided that these strange people were making sport of him, that they neither feared him nor would fight him. The interpretation now put on the tokens sent by the Scythians was that unless the Persians became birds and could fly off into the sky, or mice and burrowed in the ground, or frogs and sought refuge in the marshes, they would never escape the Scythians but would die of their arrows. Darius decided to withdraw. He returned to the bridge and, leaving a part of his force in Europe to subdue Thrace, crossed safely back into Asia. Now Histiaeus, who had maintained the bridge in safety against the Scyths, was brought to Susa to become the king's counselor and friend, but he longed to return to Miletus where he had been tyrant. He sent secret messages to his nephew and son-in-law Aristagoras, and urged him to stir up the Ionian cities to revolt, assuring Aristagoras that Darius would send him, Histiaeus, to put down the revolt, and thus get him away from Susa. Aristagoras busied himself in this pursuit, and soon all Ionia was in open rebellion. The Athenians and Eretrians went to the aid of the Ionians, seized Sardis and burned it. When Darius heard of this, he shot an arrow into the air and prayed that he might be allowed to avenge the burning of Sardis. He commanded his servant to remind him each day to "Remember the Athenians." The revolt of the Ionians was put down, city by city. Histiaeus, whom Darius never suspected, fled when he realized that Artaphernes knew of his part in the revolt. He was ultimately captured and beheaded by a group of Persians, who killed him because they feared if he were returned to Darius, the king would forgive and restore him. And in fact, Darius was angry when he knew what they had done. He dressed the head of Histiaeus, which had been sent to him, and buried it with all the honor befitting one who had been a benefactor to himself and to Persia, because he had saved the bridge by which the Persians withdrew from Scythia. On many occasions Darius showed great magnanimity to his fallen enemies. After the revolts in Ionia had been quelled, he sent his son-in-law, Mardonius, to rehabilitate Ionia, and the latter deposed the tyrants and restored the governments to the people. Darius sent heralds to Greece demanding earth and water

from the different states as tokens of submission. Many sent him the required tokens, but the Athenians threw the heralds who came to them into a pit, and the Spartans hurled their heralds into a well and told them to fetch their own earth and water. Reminded every day by his servant to "Remember the Athenians," constantly urged by the exiled sons of Pisistratus, who had fled to him, to seize Attica, and now inflamed by the outrage to his heralds, he sent Mardonius into Greece (492 B.C.) but the latter was unsuccessful and was relieved of his command. In his place Datis and Artaphernes, guided by the Athenian Hippias, went with a host to Marathon. There the Persians suffered a great defeat in one of the decisive battles of history (490 B.C.) at Marathon, and withdrew. Darius was now more avid than ever to conquer the Athenians. He set about preparing a great expedition against Greece, and at the same time, an expedition to put down a revolt that had broken out in Egypt. Before he could put his forces in motion he died (486 B.C.). His reign had lasted 36 years. On his death he was succeeded by Xerxes, his son by Atossa. The tomb of Darius is hewn in the rock at a place called Naksh-i-Rustam, near Persepolis, and is adorned with sculptures and inscriptions complementing those of Behistun.

Darius II (of *Persia*). [Original name, **Ochus**; Greek surname, **Nothus**, meaning "Bastard."] Persian king from c423 to 405 B.C.; son of Artaxerxes I. Through his son Cyrus the Younger, and Tissaphernes and Artabazus, satraps in Asia Minor, he pushed the plan to conquer the Athenian power, allying himself with Sparta, about 412 B.C., in the Peloponnesian Wars.

Darius III (of *Persia*). [Surnamed **Codomannus**.] Last king of Persia, died 330 B.C. He reigned 336–330 B.C., when he was dethroned by Alexander the Great. Fearing that Alexander might cross into Asia, he offered money to the Greeks to wage war against him. This maneuver failed. Alexander came to Asia and Darius met him at Issus. In the battle of Issus (333 B.C.) Alexander directed his attack at the spot where Darius, standing in his war chariot and surrounded by a guard of Persian nobles, was located. Alexander broke through; Darius wheeled his chariot

actor; up, lūte, pull; oi, oil; ou, out; ŦH, then; ḍ as d or j, ş as s or sh, ṭ as t or ch, ẓ as z or zh.

and fled. Although his cavalry was successful on the other side of the river, when they heard the king was fleeing their line broke, they wavered and then fled. Darius abandoned his wife Statira and his mother in the camp at Issus, and when he had outdistanced his pursuers he abandoned his chariot, his armor, and his royal cloak, and continued his flight on horseback. Alexander gave up his pursuit of Darius at nightfall, returned to the Persian camp, and dined in the Great King's tent. He heard the wailing of women nearby and on inquiry learned that it proceeded from the abandoned family of Darius. Alexander sent word to them that Darius still lived, and that he would accord his royal captives all the respect due to royalty. Darius wrote Alexander from beyond the Euphrates, calling him an aggressor, asking that the royal captives be restored and proposing that a treaty of friendship and alliance be concluded between them (333 B.C.). Among other things, Alexander wrote the following in reply. "Your ancestors invaded Macedonia and the rest of Greece, and without provocation inflicted wrongs upon us. I was appointed leader of the Greeks, and crossed over into Asia for the purpose of avenging those wrongs; for you were the first aggressors. . . . I have overcome in battle, first your generals and satraps, and now yourself and your host, and possess your land, through the grace of the gods. . . . I am lord of all Asia, and therefore do thou come to me. . . . You have only to come to me to ask and receive your mother and wife and children, and whatever else you may desire. And for the future, whenever you send, send to me as to the Great King of Asia, and do not write as to an equal, but tell me what your need is, as to one who is lord of all that is yours. Otherwise I will deal with you as an offender. But if you dispute the kingdom, then wait and fight for it again, and do not flee; for I will march against you wherever you may be." Darius could not bring himself to submit to this arrogant, but perhaps justified, demand, and prepared to oppose Alexander. The forces met at Gaugamela (331 B.C.) for the battle often called the Battle of Arbela, from a town 60 miles away. Before the battle a eunuch from the train of Statira escaped from Alexander's camp and came to inform Darius that his wife had died in childbirth. Darius is said to have sighed that perhaps her death ended dishonor for her and for him at Alexander's hands, but the eunuch assured him that Alexander had never abused any of the women from Darius' household. On the contrary, he had treated them with great honor for, added the eunuch, "Alexander is as gentle after victory as he is terrible in the field." Convinced of the noble and honorable treatment Alexander had shown his wife, Darius, according to Plutarch, prayed to his gods that he might be allowed to restore the fortunes of Persia, but if fate decreed that Persia must be conquered, he prayed that Alexander would be the conqueror. In the battle of Gaugamela the forces of Alexander completely overwhelmed the superior numbers in Darius' army. Once again Darius fled before the onslaught. Again he abandoned his war car, and again on horseback, he galloped to the mountains of Media. Accompanied by a group of Persian nobles, he went deep into Asia past the Caspian Gates. Alexander consolidated his gains before pursuing him; then, true to his letter, took up the pursuit. Darius fell under the domination of his nobles, especially his cousin Bessus, and as Alexander, by a series of unbelievably swift rides with a small band, began to overtake him, Bessus urged Darius to mount again and flee. Darius refused; Bessus and the other Persians stabbed him (330 B.C.) at a place near Thara, south of the Caspian Sea, and deserted him. Plutarch says the dying king expressed his trust in Alexander and signified it by saying to his friend or servant, "I give him my right hand." But when Alexander arrived, the king had just died. In pity, he is said to have thrown his own cloak over the corpse, which he sent, with great pomp, to the dead king's mother for burial.

Darius the Mede (mēd). In the Bible, king of Chaldea or Babylonia after the overthrow and death of Belshazzar; 6th century B.C. He is said to have been a son of Ahasuerus (see Daniel, v. 31; vi. 28; ix. 1; xi. 1; and other passages). Some historians identify him with Cyaxares, son of Astyages, and uncle to Cyrus the Great.

Dascylus (das′ki-lus). In Greek legend, a son of Lycus, king of the Mariandyni. His father sent him to accompany the Argonauts on their voyage to Colchis, as his presence would assure friendship in the lands they must pass through. Lycus did this out of gratitude to the Argonauts for defeating his ancient enemies, the Bebryces.

Datis (dā′tis). Median general, who with Artaphernes, commanded the army that Darius I sent to punish the Eretrians and the Athenians for their interference in the Ionian revolt (c499 B.C.), and the burning of Sardis. On the way to Greece the Persian fleet stopped at Naxos and burned the temples and houses of the town, which had been abandoned by the Naxians in terror. The Delians, informed of the approach of Datis, fled to Tenos. Datis anchored at Rhenia, a tiny island lying near Delos, and sent a message to the Delians, asking why they had fled, and assuring them that he would not harm the country that gave birth to the two gods (Apollo and Artemis). He offered a valuable sacrifice on the altar at Delos and sailed away to Eretria. There he besieged the city for six days, at the end of which time it was betrayed, according to Herodotus, by two citizens, and fell to the Persians, who plundered and burned the temples and the town to avenge the burning of Sardis, and carried off the inhabitants as captives. The Persians then proceeded toward Athens. They drew up their forces on the plain of Marathon and suffered overwhelming defeat (490 B.C.) at the hands of the Athenians and Plataeans. Datis sailed back to Persia. On the way, when he reached Rhenia, he was visited by a vision in a dream. The next day he caused a search to be made throughout the ships. When a golden image of Apollo was found abroad a Phoenician vessel in his fleet, he sailed to Delos and placed it in the temple there.

Daulis (dô′lis). In ancient geography, a city in Phocis, Greece, situated about 12 miles E of Delphi. Some say the city was named for a nymph, a daughter of the river-god Cephissus. The Daulians were renowned in ancient times for their size and strength. It was in Daulis, they say, that Procne and her sister Philomela served up the flesh of his son to Tereus. All three were transformed into birds by the gods. Philomela was changed into a swallow and Procne into a nightingale. Because of their never-ending fear of Tereus, who became a hawk, swallows do not lay eggs or hatch their young, nor even nest in Daulis, and the nightingales no longer sing there. There was a sanctuary of Athena at Daulis that contained a wooden image of the goddess, said to have been brought to Daulis from Athens by Procne.

Daunia (dâ′ni-a). In ancient geography, a kingdom in Apulia, in Italy. The Daunians were hostile to Aeneas and the Trojans when they landed in Italy. Their king, Daunus, had given his daughter in marriage to Diomedes, who came into the land after the Trojan War.

Daunus (dâ′nus). Named in the *Aeneid* as a king of Daunia in Apulia. He was the father of Turnus by the nymph Venilia. When Diomedes came into his land after the Trojan War, Daunus gave him his daughter Euippe in marriage.

Dea Dia (dē′a dī′a). One of the most primitive deities of Italian mythology. Nothing is known of the rites associated with her cult until after the reorganization of religious ceremonies by Augustus; from these later ceremonies much may be inferred concerning the earlier rites. The worship of this goddess was entrusted to the Arval Brothers, from which it is thought that she may be in fact Acca Larentia, the mother of the original 12 Arval Brothers. There was a grove dedicated to her at Rome, and a temple in it, where professional priests assisted the 12 members of the brotherhood, which after Augustus always included the emperor, in rites which included the sacrifice of animals, prayer to wine jars, the wearing of wheat-ears as crowns, and ceremonial banquets. It is quite clear, especially as the chief ceremonies in her honor occurred in December and in May, that this was a goddess of the fields and the harvest; moreover, since Dea Dia is not a proper name but a descriptive term, it is certain that she was one of the very ancient deities whose names it was considered impious and dangerous to pronounce.

Deae Matres (dē′ē mā′trēz). [Also: **Deae Matronae.**] Fertility deities worshiped in ancient times in Belgic Gaul, and among the Teutons. Altars and inscriptions to these or similar deities have been found in those areas. Representations on altars and other monuments depict the Deae Matres as three seated women with baskets or bowls of fruit.

De Amicitia (dē am-i-sish'i-a̯). [Eng. trans., "On Friendship;" also called **Laelius.**] Treatise by Cicero, in the form of a conversation between Laelius and his sons-in-law, C. Fannius and Q. Mucius Scaevola, devoted to the praise of friendship.

Decebalus (dē-seb'a̯-lus). Title of honor among the Dacians, meaning "chief" or "king," and borne by several of their kings; especially by a king, d. c106 A.D., who was at war with the Romans in the reigns of Domitian and Trajan. He committed suicide after his defeat by Trajan, and Dacia became a Roman province.

Decelea (des-e̯-lē'a̯). In ancient geography, a city and mountain citadel in Attica, Greece, situated about 14 miles from Athens and commanding the Attic plain and the routes to Euboea and Boeotia. On the advice of Alcibiades, Athenian general who fled to Sparta to escape trial for impiety, the Spartans under King Agis seized and fortified Decelea in the course of the Peloponnesian War, 413 B.C. This was a crushing blow for Athens. Hitherto the Spartans made raids into Attica and then withdrew, so that it was still possible for Athens to be supplied from the surrounding farms and from Euboea. With the continued occupation of Decelea the Spartans effectively cut off the farmlands as a source of supply, for they continually patrolled the area from the fortress, and cut off supplies from Euboea. This compelled Athens to import supplies by sea and caused great hardship. The Spartans held Decelea until the end of the Peloponnesian War, 404 B.C.

Decelean War (des-e̯-lē'an). Name frequently given to the third or final stage of the Peloponnesian War, on account of the occupation of Decelea by the Spartans (Lacedaemonians).

Decemvirate (dē-sem'vi-rāt). In Roman history, the commission of ten, presided over by Appius Claudius, sent c450 B.C. to Greece to study Greek law and codify the Roman law. It was renewed the next year, and drew up the Twelve Tables. During its existence it superseded provisionally the regular machinery of government. On account of its tyranny it was overthrown by a popular insurrection after Appius Claudius had attempted to make a slave of Virginia, daughter of Virginius, who became tribune after the decemvirs were deposed.

Decii (dē'shi-ī). Several illustrious Romans of consular rank of the Decian gens, especially the father, son, and grandson Decius Mus: the father killed in the battle of Vesuvius, 340 B.C., the son killed in the battle of Sentinum, 295 B.C., the grandson killed in the battle of Ausculum Apulum, 279 B.C.

Decimus Junius Juvenalis (des'i-mus jön'yus jö-ve̯-nā'lis). Full Latin name of the Roman satirist Juvenal.

De Corona (dē kō-rō'na̯). See **Crown, Oration on the.**

Decumanus (dek-ū-mā'nus). See **Cardo and Decumanus.**

De Finibus (dē fin'i-bus). [Full title, **De Finibus Bonorum et Malorum,** meaning "Of the Boundaries of Good and Evil."] Treatise in five books by Cicero, in the form of a dialogue, consisting in a presentation of the doctrines of the Greek schools concerning good and evil. It was written in 45 B.C.

Deianira (dē-ya̯-nī'ra̯). In Greek mythology, a supposed daughter of Oeneus, king of Calydon, and Althaea, but actually Dionysus was her father. After the death of her brother, Meleager, Artemis changed his grieving sisters into guinea hens, but Dionysus persuaded the goddess to let Deianira and Gorge keep their human forms. Heracles, on a journey to the Underworld to fetch Cerberus, promised Meleager that he would marry Deianira on his return to earth. After some years he went to Calydon and fought Achelous, the river-god and an unwelcome suitor of Deianira, and won her hand. She bore him Hyllus, Hodites, Glenus, possibly Ctesippus, and his only daughter, Macaria. On a journey from Calydon to Trachis, Deianira and Heracles came to the Evenus River. Here Nessus, a centaur, offered to ferry Deianira across on his back. He did so and attempted to ravish her. Heracles shot him with one of his poisoned arrows. Before he died Nessus secretly told Deianira to preserve his blood, that it would be a powerful love charm by which she would hold Heracles if his interest ever strayed to another woman. Deianira gathered up the blood and kept it. When Heracles left to wage war on Eurytus of Oechalia he told Deianira that he would return at the end of fifteen months and pass the rest of his days peacefully or, at the end of that time, he would be dead. He was successful in his war against Eurytus, and sent Iole, daughter of Eurytus, back to Deianira as his captive and his concubine. Deianira, although she had nothing but sympathy for the young and beautiful captive, decided that the time had come to make use of the love charm Nessus had given her. She rubbed it on a robe which Heracles had sent his herald Lichas to fetch so that he could wear it as he sacrificed to Zeus at Cenaeum, and gave the robe to Lichas. After the herald had left, she noticed that a bit of wool with which she had anointed the robe had fallen to the ground and had caused the ground to smoulder. In fear she tried to recall Lichas but it was too late. Heracles received the robe, put it on, and soon his body was burning with the poison of the Hydra with which Heracles had coated the arrow that killed Nessus. When Deianira learned that Nessus had merely sought revenge by telling her of the love charm, and of the effect it had on Heracles, she hanged herself. Thus the poisoned robe killed Heracles long after Nessus had died, in accordance with a prophecy that no living man could kill him, but that he would fall at the hands of a dead enemy. Deianira was the innocent tool of that dead enemy, Nessus.

Deicoön (dē-ik′ọ-on). In Greek legend, the third son of Megara and Heracles. He was intended to be the ruler of Oechalia but Heracles killed him when he was afflicted with madness.

Deidamia (dē″i-da-mī′a̱). In Greek legend, a daughter of Lycomedes, king of Scyrus. When Achilles, disguised as a girl, was hidden at her father's court in an attempt to prevent him from going to Troy, he seduced Deidamia and she became the mother of his son Neoptolemus. The attempt to hold Achilles was unsuccessful and Deidamia sorrowfully watched him depart for Troy. According to some accounts, he returned during the first years of the war, which were occupied by raids on the coasts of the Troad, and married Deidamia. Some years later, after the death of Achilles, Odysseus and

Diomedes came to Scyrus to fetch Neoptolemus to the war. Deidamia, mindful of how Achilles had perished, tried to persuade Neoptolemus to remain safe at home, but was unsuccessful. When the war was over, Neoptolemus went to Greece. He gave Deidamia to Helenus as his wife to reward him for his good advice.

Deileon (dē-il′ẹ-on). In Greek legend, a son of Deimachus of Tricca. He lived with his brothers, Autolycus and Phlogius, near the Halys River on the Assyrian shore, whither they had wandered away from Heracles. The Argonauts encountered them there on their way to Colchis.

Deimos (dī′mos). Fear, or Terror, personified in the *Iliad,* and later regarded as a son of Ares.

Deinocrates (dī-nok′ra̱-tēz). See **Dinocrates.**

Deïoces (dē′yọ-sēz). According to some accounts, the founder (reigned c700–647 B.C.) of the Median dynasty who led the Medes in revolt against Assyria and freed them. According to Herodotus, Deïoces achieved his ambition of supreme power over his fellow-countrymen by the use of intelligence and psychology. In his own village he became so noted for his just dealings that his fellow townsmen made him mediator in their disputes. At this time the Medes lived in scattered villages and lacked the discipline of law. The reputation of Deïoces for justice spread and it became the practice for disputants in other villages to come to him to settle their affairs. As he was increasingly sought out to pronounce judgments, he suddenly gave notice that he would no longer occupy himself with securing justice for others because, by spending his whole day in regulating other men's affairs, he was neglecting his own. When he withdrew from his acknowledged position as judge, robbery and lawlessness broke out and so harried the Medes that they met together and decided to invite Deïoces to become their king and restore order. He agreed to do so on condition that he be given a personal bodyguard and that the Medes build him a palace suitable to his new rank. Moreover, he demanded that they build him a new capital city. This was the city of Ecbatana. Surrounding the city on a hill was a series of seven encircling walls. According to Herodotus, the walls were coated, beginning with the outer one, in white, black, scarlet, blue, and orange colors, and the two innermost walls were coated respectively with silver and gold. Inside this fastness Deïoces had his palace and treasury. He retreated into it and thenceforth became a power remote from the eyes of the people, for, says Herodotus, if those who had been brought up with him and considered themselves his equals saw him often, they would become jealous of the power he had acquired, though he was no better than they, and might conspire against him. Therefore he decreed that no one could come into his presence. Petitions from his subjects were communicated to him by messengers. When he had secured his bodyguard, his palace fortress, and his city, Deïoces continued to dispense justice as before, but whereas in former times he had been freely sought out as an arbiter, now his judgments were imposed from above, and a complex spy system kept him informed of the affairs of his kingdom. Some say that Deïoces was in fact probably a local chieftain named' Dayukku whose grandson Cyaxares founded the Median empire in 625 B.C. and whose name was included in the list of Median kings as a matter of policy.

Deïon (dē′i-on). In Greek mythology, a son of Aeolus, king of Magnesia in Thessaly, and Enarete. He became king of Phocis. He married Diomede, daughter of Xuthus, and became the father of four sons: Aenetus, Actor the Argonaut, Phylacus, and Cephalus, and one daughter: Asterodia.

Deïope (dē-ī′ō-pē). According to some accounts, the daughter of Triptolemus and the mother of Eumolpus by Musaeus. But others say she was the mother of Triptolemus.

Deïotarus (dē-yot′a-rus). Tetrarch and king of Galatia, and an ally of the Romans; died 40 B.C. He was defended before Caesar by Cicero in 45 B.C. on a charge of plotting to assassinate Caesar. `Throughout the Roman struggle for power he kept his throne, siding successively with Pompey, Caesar, Brutus, and the triumvirate of Octavian, Antony, and Lepidus.

Deïphobe (dē-if′ō-bē). In the *Aeneid,* a daughter of the prophetic sea-deity Glaucus. She became a sibyl at Cumae in Italy.

Deïphobus (dē-if′ō-bus). In Greek legend, a son of Priam and Hecuba, and one of the great heroes of the Trojan War. He led a group at the siege of the Greek fortifications and slew many. He himself was wounded by Meriones. As Hector was fleeing around the walls of Troy before Achilles, Athena assumed the shape of Deïphobus and encouraged Hector to make a stand against Achilles. But when Hector hurled his spear in vain at Achilles, and turned to his supposed brother for another one, Deïphobus had disappeared, and Hector knew that the gods had forsaken him. After the death of Paris, Helen was given to Deïphobus because of his deeds in the war. He married her by force. When the Wooden Horse had been dragged inside the walls of Troy Deïphobus accompanied Helen, who walked around it and imitated the voices of the wives of the Greeks in an attempt to find out whether there were actually Greeks hiding inside the horse. Menelaus and Odysseus prevented the Greeks inside from answering Helen's calls and convinced the Trojans that the Horse was indeed a divine gift. In the sack of Troy Deïphobus was slain, and his body terribly mutilated, either by Menelaus or Odysseus. According to the *Aeneid,* Aeneas met his shade in the Underworld and learned that he had been betrayed by Helen, who revealed his hiding place to Menelaus and Odysseus. Other accounts say that it was Helen herself who killed him, by stabbing him.

Deïphobus. In Greek legend, a son of Hippolytus. He was a king of Amyclae, who purified Heracles for the murder of Iphitus, son of Eurytus.

Deiphontes (dē-i-fon′tēz). In Greek legend, the husband of Hyrnetho, daughter of Temenus. Temenus favored him and planned to pass his kingdom on to him rather than to his own sons. The sons of Temenus killed their father to prevent him from carrying out his plan, but Deiphontes inherited the kingdom anyway. He also won Epidaurus without a struggle, and the Argives took possession of it. The sons of Temenus sought to hurt Deiphontes. They knew he was most vulnerable through his love for their sister and decided to take her away from him. They went to Epidaurus and sent a herald to ask their sister for an interview with them. When she acceded to their request, they denounced her husband, urged her to come with them to Argos, and promised her a much better husband. Hyrnetho defied them; she defended her husband as a good man and labeled her brothers as murderers for the death of their father. The brothers realized they could not make her accompany them willingly. They seized her and carried her off in their chariot. Deiphontes learned that she had been seized and pursued, aided by the Epidaurians. He overtook the sons of Temenus and shot one of them, but dared not aim at the other because he was holding Hyrnetho before him as a shield. As the chase continued, Hyrnetho was slain by her brother and flung from the chariot. Deiphontes and his sons took up her body and buried it in a place that came to be known as the Hyrnethium. They built a hero-shrine for her and declared that all the pieces that break off from olive trees were sacred to Hyrnetho, and henceforth any such pieces were placed in her shrine.

Deipnosophists (dīp-nos'ŏ-fists). "The Banquet Philosophers." Set of imaginary dialogues by Athenaeus of Naucratis, in which 29 dinner guests spend several days recounting tales and anecdotes. In this way the author manages to present many stories and quotations from Greek literature. Among the imaginary guests are included some of the most eminent literary figures of the empire, for example Masurius Sabinus, Ulpian, and Galen. Athenaeus wrote in the third century A.D.

Deïpyle (dē-ip'i-lē). In Greek legend, a daughter of Adrastus, king of Argos. Her sister was Aegia or Argia. The sisters were wooed by many suitors and Adrastus was perplexed as to whom he should give his daughters. Following the instructions of an oracle, to yoke the boar and lion that fought in his palace to a two-wheeled chariot, Adrastus gave Deïpyle to Tydeus of Calydon, whose emblem was a boar. Aegia was wed to Polynices of Thebes, whose emblem was a lion. Deïpyle became the mother of Diomedes.

Deïpylus (dē-ip'i-lus). In Greek legend, a son of Ilione and Polymnestor, king of Thrace, and a grandson of Priam. According to some accounts, he was mistakenly killed by his father, who had intended to kill his mother's young brother Polydorus.

Dejaneira (dej-a-nī'ra). See **Deianira**.

Delia (dē'li-a). Epithet of Artemis, from the island of Delos, her birthplace. Similarly Apollo, the sun god, was called Delius.

Delian League (dē'li-an). [Also: **Confederacy of Delos**.] A Hellenic league, formed probably c477 B.C., with its political center at Athens and its treasury at Delos (removed later to Athens). The term is sometimes applied also to a similar league of 378–338 B.C. The great danger of conquest by the Persians compelled the Ionian Greek states, jealous of their independence, but mostly located on islands and individually indefensible against Persian power, to find some means of collaboration. Beginning in 489 B.C. such maritime states as Aegina, Megara, Naxos, Thasus, Lesbos, Chios, Samos, and others accepted the plan of a league with a treasury and a council on the island of Delos, the assessments for the treasury to be set by Athens, and the council to be under Athenian presidency. The League accomplished its purpose of nullifying the Persian peril, but when, after the death of Xerxes, Naxos and Thasus attempted to withdraw from it, their secession was prevented by Athens. By diplomacy and by their greater power, the Athenians were able to hold the confederacy together and to increase its adherents, which eventually numbered well over 200 states. In 457 B.C. Sparta was deterred from a threatened attack, and Thebes was subdued. But in 454 B.C., when under the pretext of new danger from the Persian quarter, the treasury was removed to Athens, the League became in fact an Athenian empire, which lasted for a troubled half century but came to an end with the close of the Peloponnesian War, disastrously for Athens, in 404 B.C. Subsequent restoration of Athenian sea power led in 378 B.C. to the formation of a new league, Athenian-dominated, but its course was also a troubled one, and in 338 B.C. it was extinguished by the power of Macedon. The story of the Delian League is the story of the fatal unwillingness of the small Greek states to coalesce into a nation, and of the inability of Athens to enforce unity. It was the high point of the hope for such an eventuation, and its failure made inevitable first the Macedonian hegemony and eventually the conquest by Rome.

Delium (dē′li-um). In ancient geography, a place in Boeotia, Greece, situated on the coast about 24 miles N of Athens. Here during the Peloponnesian War the Boeotians defeated (424 B.C.) the Athenians. Socrates took part in the battle. During the retreat as he made his way with others through the enemy, Alcibiades came along on horseback and protected him from the attacks of the enemy and saved his life.

Delius (dē′li-us). Epithet of Apollo, from his birthplace in Delos.

Delos (dē′los). [Also: **Mikra Dilos**; ancient names, **Asteria, Ortygia**.] Smallest island of the Cyclades, Greece, situated in the narrow passage between the islands of Myconus and Rhenia. Area, two square miles. Here, according to some accounts, Asteria, daughter of the Titans Coeus and Phoebe, leaped into the sea to escape the embraces of Zeus and was transformed into a quail. A city was named Asteria for her, but afterward renamed Delos. Delos was also known, in her memory, as Ortygia, "quail." Leto, about to bear her children by Zeus, was pursued all over the world by a serpent sent to harass her by jealous Hera. As the time for her confinement neared, no place on earth would receive her out of fear of the anger of Hera. At last she came to Delos, at that time a floating island, and there she was welcomed and kindly received. Some say her children, Artemis and Apollo, were both born on the tiny island, but others say Artemis was born on neighboring Rhenia, and as soon as she was born, helped her mother across to Delos. The birth of Apollo took place in the shadow of the Hill of Cynthus, where the stream of the Inopus issues from the hill. The palm tree there, that Leto clasped when she bore Apollo, was one of the sights of antiquity from the time of Homer to that of Pliny. In its joy at being the birthplace of the god, the island covered itself with golden blossoms. Some say four pillars rose from the sea after the birth of the twin gods and moored the island, so that henceforth it ceased to float. Others say Apollo himself anchored the island, to reward it for receiving his mother. From

earliest times, Delos was connected with the Hyperboreans. When Apollo and Artemis were born, some say, two Hyperborean maidens, Arge and Opis, came to Delos to help the birth goddess deliver the children of Leto. The Hyperborean damsels died on Delos and were entombed behind the temple of Artemis. Ever after they were honored by the Delian women from whom the rest of the islanders learned to honor them also. Later two more Hyperborean maidens, Hyperoche and Laodice, came to Delos, accompanied by several men. They brought offerings wrapped in wheaten straw. These maidens also died on Delos and were entombed. In their honor the maidens of Delos cut off a lock of their hair before their wedding day and laid it upon the graves of the Hyperborean damsels. The youths also made offerings of their hair on their tombs. When the Hyperboreans saw that their envoys did not return, they ceased to send them to Delos. Instead they sent their offerings to Scythia, from where they were conveyed in relays to Delos.

Delos became the seat of a great sanctuary in honor of Apollo, one of the most famous religious foundations of antiquity. From the time of Solon, Athens sent an annual embassy to the Delian festival, in which the "tunic-trailing Ionians" honored Apollo with boxing, dancing, and song. When Pisistratus regained control of Athens for the third time, he purified Delos, on the advice of an oracle, by having all the bodies that were buried within sight of the temple dug up and reburied in another part of the island. Only the tomb of the two Hyperborean maidens who came to assist at the birth of Apollo and Artemis were left untouched. This spot was sacred and was not disturbed. In the Persian War, Datis assembled the Persian fleet off Delos. The Delians fled from their island and refused to return, even though Datis assured them that he would do no harm to the land that was the birthplace of two gods. On the contrary, he landed and made an offering of 300 talents' weight of frankincense on the altar at Delos and then sailed away. After he left, Delos was shaken by an earthquake. This was the first time such a thing had occurred and was taken as a warning of evils to come to Greece, and as a fulfillment of the oracle that had predicted:

"Delos self will I shake, which never yet has been shaken."

But Datis himself so much respected the sacred place that on his way back to Asia, after Marathon, he stopped at Delos and left a golden image of Apollo that had been stolen by some of his Phoenician allies and hidden on their ship. He asked the Delians to return it to the temple from which it had been stolen. Twenty years later, in obedience to an oracle, the Delians did so.

After the Persian War, Delos was the center of the Delian League (q.v.), formed (c477 B.C.) to resist Persian aggression. In 454 B.C. the sacred treasure of Delos, contributed by the members of the League, was removed to the Athenian Acropolis. In 426 B.C., Delos was purified again; all the dead who had been buried on the island were removed. Thenceforth no one was permitted to be born on the island, and no corpses could be buried there. The seriously ill were removed to some other place so as not to desecrate the island by dying there. Expectant mothers were taken off well before their time came so that no mortal children should first see the light of day in the island where Apollo was born. Games in honor of Apollo were restored, and a few years later all the inhabitants of the island were removed and it became purely a sacred place. The island was an Athenian dependency down to the Macedonian period, when it became semi-independent, and in the 2nd century B.C. it again became subject to Athens. The city of Delos was made a free port by the Romans and developed into a great commercial mart. It was raided in 88 B.C. by the forces of Mithridates VI and soon fell to the status of an almost uninhabited place. Now it is uninhabited. The sanctuary of Apollo was excavated by the French School at Athens, beginning in 1873. The work ranks as one of the chief achievements of its kind. The buildings disclosed lie for the most part within the enclosure or temenos of Apollo, which is of trapeziform shape, and about 650 feet to a side. Mosaic floors, bathing rooms, large underground drainage wells, and the floor plans of many buildings have been uncovered. In addi-

tion to the interesting finds of architecture and sculpture, epigraphical discoveries of the highest importance have been made, bearing upon history and particularly upon the ceremonial and administration of the sanctuary.

Delos, Confederacy of. See **Delian League.**

Delphi (del'fi). [Also: **Delphoi.**] In ancient geography, a town in Phocis, Greece; the seat of the world-renowned oracle of Pythian Apollo, the most famous oracle of antiquity. It lies at an altitude of about 2000 feet, on the slopes of Mount Parnassus, whose peak rises to a height of more than 8000 feet to the NE. Towering 800 feet immediately above the sanctuary, on the N and E, are two great bare gray rocks, the Phaedriades or "shining ones." The Phaedriades are separated by a deep gorge at whose eastern foot is the sacred spring of Castalia. To the S, the ground falls away swiftly to the ravine cut by the Plistus River as it flows into the Gulf of Corinth at the ancient port of Cirrha (Itea), six miles away. The area is subject to earthquakes and the menace of rock slides. Fissures opened up in the ground, and closed again by tremors, exhaled vapors said to inspire the priestesses who inhaled them to prophecy. In its location alone, Delphi is majestic and dramatic, the "wild and rocky glen" described by the poets.

From remote ages this was the seat of an oracle. Because it was subject to violent earthquakes, the earliest oracle belonged to the chthonian gods, those who hold sway under the earth. The most ancient oracle belonged to Gaea (Earth). Some say Poseidon, "the earth-shaker," shared the oracle with her. Through her prophetess Daphnis, a nymph of Mount Parnassus, Gaea gave her oracles. Poseidon uttered his through priests called Pyrcones. Gaea set the serpent Pytho to guard the chasm whence the prophetic vapors emanated. Her priestesses were called Pythia. Some say Gaea gave her share of the oracle to Themis, but Pytho continued to guard it. This was the situation until Apollo arrived, a relative newcomer to an ancient oracle. Some say he took the form of a dolphin (hence his epithet *Delphian Apollo*), and swam with a Cretan ship to the port of Cirrha. Arrived there, he resumed his divine form and commanded the Cretans to become his priests. When they protested that no one would come to worship at such a remote spot, he promised that so many would bring offerings that the sacrificial axes would never be idle. Having reassured them, he went to the chasm and slew the dragon that guarded the oracle. Some say the place was first named Pytho, "the place of the rotting," because he left the bones of the dragon to rot there, and that it was later named Delphi because Apollo had come to the nearby shores in the shape of a dolphin. But some say it was named Delphi in honor of Delphus, a son or a descendant of Apollo. Apollo received Poseidon's share in the oracle in exchange for a place near Troezen, in the Peloponnesus, and became sole master at Delphi. Having killed Pytho, Apollo was compelled to seek purification, and was away doing penance for eight years. The penance and purification of Apollo were commemorated in a sacred drama that was enacted at Delphi, at first, every eight years. The epithet *Pythian* was given to Apollo because he slew the dragon; his priestesses were called Pythia, or sometimes, Pythonesses. Others say, and the two legends existed side by side, that Apollo came from the land of the Hyperboreans at the back of the north wind, and seized the oracle. These say that his first prophet, the only man who ever served in this capacity, was Olen, a Hyperborean. But most say that Phemenoë was his first prophetess, and that she pronounced her oracles in hexameter verse. At first the priestess was available for consultation only once a year, on Apollo's birthday. In later times she prophesied once a month, or every day, if the omens were favorable. Those who sought advice from the oracle came as suppliants, wearing laurel wreaths and fillets of wool; they purified themselves, sacrificed a victim, and inquired whether it was worth their while to ask a question. If the response to this query was favorable, they approached the priestess in her shrine. Three priestesses served in turn. The priestess was purified, drank the waters of the spring of Cassotis, chewed laurel leaves, and seated herself on a tripod over the chasm from which the vapors issued and which stimulated prophetic

utterance. Only a priest was present when the priestess gave her responses. His function was to interpret the utterances, which were often obscure or, at the least, capable of two interpretations. Heracles, seeking information from the oracle, was denied by the priestess because of his impurity. Enraged, Heracles attempted to seize the sacred tripod and threatened to set up his own oracle. Apollo came to protect his shrine and the two struggled until Zeus parted them by a

HERACLES SEIZING THE DELPHIC TRIPOD OF
APOLLO
Black-figured Greek hydria.

thunderbolt and forced them to compose their differences. The priestess gave Heracles a response, and the sanctuary remained firmly in Apollo's hands. Some say that the myth of the fight between Heracles and Apollo symbolizes the Dorian invasion of Greece (c1100 B.C.). Most of the Dorians went on into the Peloponnesus, but some remained in Doris and continued to have great influence over the sanctuary. After the Dorian invasion the influence and power of the sanctuary flourished, and in the succeeding period of more than a thousand years, was felt from the shores of Asia to Rome. Other gods came to share the sacred spot with Apollo. Athena Pronoea (*Forethought*) had her place. Her sanctuary was on a slope below the temple of Apollo. (The temples in her precinct fell into ruin and the spot became known as the *Marmaria,* roughly, "the marble quarry," from the many fragments there.) Dionysus, an oracular god who prophesied during the winter, when Apollo was off with the Hyperboreans, was consulted. He was considered a god who died and was reborn annually, and his tomb at Delphi was the scene of rites held by women. Delphi also possessed the "omphalos" (*navel*), a stone that represented the exact center of the world. The myth was that Zeus sent out two eagles in opposite directions to make a circuit of the universe. They met at Delphi, and established it as the center. Another stone, or possibly it was the same one, was also called "omphalos," and was the stone given by Rhea to Cronus in place of her new-born son Zeus. A sacred city grew up around the oracle and these cult objects. According to tradition the first temple erected on the site was a hut of branches of laurel, a tree sacred to Apollo. This was replaced by a temple made by the bees, of beeswax and feathers, and sent to Delphi by the Hyperboreans. The third temple was of wood, covered with bronze plates and was made, some say, by Hephaestus. Of these three temples no trace has ever been found. The fourth temple was of stone. Trophonius and Agamedes, according to tradition, were the builders.

Delphi was at first under the control of Crissa, in Phocis, whose territory included the port of Cirrha. Pilgrims, making their way to the sanctuary, were subject to all sorts of dues and exactions by the Crissaeans. The priests of Delphi complained to the Amphictyonic Council, a group of representatives from 12 Greek cities (mostly Thessalian and Dorian), that had its seat at Anthela. The members were pledged to aid each other. The Amphictyons acted against Crissa. Solon of Athens and Clisthenes, tyrant of Sicyon, lent their assistance in the Sacred War (c600–c590 B.C.). Crissa was destroyed, its territory was dedicated to Apollo and henceforth the tilling of the Crissaean plain was forbidden, and Delphi became autonomous. The management of the sanctuary was left in the hands of the Am-

phictyonic Council. The Pythian Games, descended from the old religious drama representing the purification of Apollo (the *Stepteria*), and with the addition of musical and athletic contests, also came under the supervision of the Council. Thereafter, from 586 B.C., the Games were held every four years. The end of the Sacred War marked the beginning of a period of great prosperity for Delphi. The treasuries of Corinth and Sicyon were dedicated. Cypselus, tyrant of Corinth (c655–625 B.C.), was said to have dedicated the former, and Clisthenes the latter. These treasuries, the earliest of many, were small temple-like structures erected and dedicated by individual city-states. In them sacred, and often precious, vessels for religious ceremonies were kept. Rich offerings were made to them, and they also served as meeting places for pilgrims and officials from the cities that had dedicated them. The Lydian kings, Gyges (c685–653 B.C.), and Croesus (6th century king who reigned from 560–546 B.C.), made rich gifts to the sanctuary in gratitude for favorable oracles. Amasis II (fl. c569–525 B.C.), of Egypt was also a contributor. In 548 B.C. the temple built by Trophonius and Agamedes was destroyed by fire. The Alcmaeonidae, aristocrats who had been exiled from Athens, raised a great sum to rebuild it. Croesus and Amasis II again made large contributions for this cause. Spintharus of Corinth was the architect. At their own expense, it was said, the Alcmaeonidae had the temple faced with Parian marble instead of the limestone that was called for by the plan. The treasury of the Siphnians, one of the richest of them all, was dedicated c524 B.C. (Large fragments of its pediments and friezes, depicting the Greeks and the Trojans in combat, War of the Giants, the Judgment of Paris, and the exploits of Heracles, are preserved in the museum at Delphi.) The Cnidians raised their *Lesche,* a kind of club house, in the first half of the 5th century B.C. Its walls were decorated with paintings by the Thasian artist Polygnotus.

Croesus, who had made such rich gifts to Delphi in return for favorable responses, was later one of the most ill-fated victims of its obscure pronouncements. Having made every provision to secure the most reliable oracle, he sent to Delphi to ask if he should wage war on Cyrus. He learned that if he crossed the Halys River and marched against the Persians, he would destroy a great empire. Greatly encouraged, he attacked Cyrus and destroyed a great empire—his own. When he reproached the priestess, he was told that he had misinterpreted the oracle, which had been duly fulfilled. Croesus humbly acknowledged his error, so it is said. Not all the answers, however, were equivocal. In a later time the question was put: who was the wisest man in the world? The priestess replied with the flat statement that there was no man in the world wiser than Socrates.

When the Persians invaded Europe in 490 B.C., Delphi feared to be destroyed if it resisted, and "medized," that is, it was favorable to the Persians. But the priests were able to gloss over this period of weakness, and the Athenians dedicated the treasury of Athens at Delphi with the spoils taken from the Persians at Marathon. The walls of their treasury were covered with inscriptions, many of which record the gratitude of freed slaves. Among the inscriptions is also a hymn to Apollo bearing the only recorded musical notations ever found in Greece. (The rebuilt treasury of Athens can still be seen at Delphi. The fitting together of its scattered and broken walls was greatly facilitated by matching the inscriptions.) Ten years after Marathon the Persians returned. When Xerxes had taken the pass at Thermopylae, he sent an army into Phocis to plunder the sanctuary of Delphi, of whose treasures, according to Herodotus, he knew more than those in his own palace; he had heard so much about them. The Delphians were stricken with terror and asked the oracle if they should bury the treasures or remove them to another place. The god replied, through his priestess, that he was well able without their help to protect his own. On receiving the response the Delphians concentrated on saving themselves and their goods. They retired, some across the Gulf of Corinth and some to the heights of Parnassus. Only 60 men and a prophet remained in the sanctuary. When the Persians approached, the prophet saw the sacred

armor divinely removed from the shrine. The Persians advanced to the shrine of Athena Pronoea. Suddenly there was a crack of thunder. Two immense crags split off from Mount Parnassus and rolled down on the Persians, crushing a great number of them, while from the temple of Athena were heard a war-cry and a shout of victory. The Persians, terrified by the portents, fled in confusion. The Delphians, seeing how the god protected his own, fell on the Persians and slaughtered them wholesale. Those who escaped were pursued into Boeotia by two gigantic armed warriors, heroes who had sacred precincts at Delphi. Herodotus, who tells this tale, saw the huge stones that had crushed the Persians in the precinct of Athena Pronoea. Before this miraculous event, the Athenians had sent envoys to consult the oracle as to their defense against the Persians. The priestess replied:

"Wretches, why sit ye here? Fly, fly to
 the ends of creation,
Quitting your homes, and the crags which
 your city crowns with her circlet.
All—all ruined and lost. Since fire, and
 impetuous Ares,
Speeding along in a Syrian chariot, hastes
 to destroy her."

The envoys refused to return to Athens with such a gloomy reply. They returned to the shrine as suppliants and vowed to die in the sanctuary rather than leave without some more encouraging word. It would be the greatest impiety if any died in the shrine. The priestess grudgingly and obscurely uttered the following:

"Safe shall the wooden wall continue for
 thee and thy children."

Themistocles interpreted the "wooden wall" to mean the fleet, worked to build it up, and went on to defeat the Persians at Salamis. The temporizing of Delphi was forgotten when the Persians were driven out. Rich offerings of trophies, statues, and tripods were made for the victories of Salamis, Plataea, and Mycale. The offering for Plataea was a golden tripod set upon a pillar of three bronze intertwined serpents. On its base were inscribed the names of the Greek peoples who dedicated it.

Following the Persian War, Delphi became embroiled in the disputes between the various city-states, and lost some of its credit, because it seemed to take sides and because the charge of bribery leveled against it was never satisfactorily cleared. In the Second Sacred War (c448 B.C.), Pericles returned control of Delphi to the Phocians, but it regained its autonomy by the Peace of Nicias (421 B.C.), according to the terms of which the common temples of Greece were to be free to all. As a great sanctuary, it continued to receive gifts and offerings from the rival city-states and from foreign rulers as well. In 373 B.C. the temple was destroyed by an earthquake. Funds were raised by international subscription, and construction of a new temple was begun which was finished c330 B.C. Before its completion, a Third Sacred War broke out (357–346 B.C.) when the Phocians cultivated the sacred plain of Crissa and were punished by the Amphictyonic Council. Philomelus, the Phocian general, pillaged the rich treasures of the sanctuary to build a fortress. Philip of Macedon intervened, crushed the Phocians and imposed a heavy fine on them. Peace was short-lived. The city of Amphissa committed impiety against Delphi (339 B.C.), and brought on the Fourth Sacred War. Philip of Macedon, who had taken the place of the Phocians in the Amphictyonic League, interfered to "restore order." The Athenians and Thebans, fearing his growing power in Greece, resisted him, and he overwhelmingly defeated them at Chaeronea, 338 B.C. In 279 B.C., the Gauls, under Brennus, attacked Delphi and were driven off, so it was said, by the direct intervention of the god, who sent earthquakes, snow, and bitter cold to repulse them. After 189 B.C., Delphi came under the dominion of the Romans. In 91 B.C. the temple was burned by Thracians. In 86 B.C. Sulla pillaged the sanctuary. The story is that the priests, to deter Sulla from his purpose, set a harpist to playing in a concealed place and warned Sulla that the god was playing to forbid him to violate his temple. Sulla turned their remark by saying that the god was playing to show that he welcomed a friend, and proceeded to carry off what he wished. Later, the Emperor Nero carried off over 500 statues from the sacred city, but 3000 or so were still left there. Even so, Delphi re-

tained great wealth. But it had lost its place as the center of the universe, and enjoyed only a short revival as a religious center under Hadrian. In the reigns of Constantine and Theodosius many of its treasures were stolen to adorn other capitals, including the golden tripod of Plataea, which Constantine set up in the city named for him. Theodosius II, a Christian emperor, delivered the final blow to Delphi when he silenced the oracle, destroyed (390 A.D.) the temple, and systematically mutilated the statues and images.

The influence of Delphi was felt throughout the Mediterranean world for a period of centuries. It received pilgrims and envoys from all quarters, and became a great clearing house for receiving and spreading information. No colonizing force set out from Greece before consulting the oracle. Political decisions were based on its responses. It was the arbiter in education, art, and literature, as well as in religion. It was an enlightening and elevating force, emphasizing as it did on many occasions, a rule of law rather than of vengeance, moral purity rather than purifying rites. With the Pythian Games it brought the Greeks together, in athletics, musical contests, and literary competitions, and stressed the tendencies that unified the Greeks rather than those which divided them. In addition, as the recipient of rich gifts from city-states, generals, heroes, kings, victors in athletic contests, grateful individuals, and even beautiful women, Delphi was the art center of Greece. Images and statues by the finest sculptors over the course of centuries adorned the sanctuary and its environs. Among them was the famous bronze *Charioteer* on view in the museum at Delphi today. The site was occupied by a great temple of Apollo, to which pilgrims ascended by a winding sacred way that was lined with treasuries and votive offerings. All around the temple were other shrines and buildings, as well as uncounted hundreds of statues. In the flanks of the hill that rises sharply behind Apollo's temple was a theater, near the fountain of Cassotis whose waters flowed underground into the shrine and were drunk by the priestesses. Above the theater was a stadium where certain of the contests were held. The stadium, remains of which can still be seen, replaced an earlier one on the plain around Crissa. The sacred monuments and temples were carried off or destroyed, early in the Christian era. Earthquakes and landslides covered the site. A village, Castri, grew up over the buried remains. In 1892, the entire village having been removed to a new site, French excavators began work there. In succeeding years, many remains of the ancient site have been uncovered, including the temple of Apollo, the theater, bases of votive offerings and sites of treasuries, so that today it is possible not only to admire the imposing majesty of the physical scene, but to recreate, with the help of some imagination, the profusion and richness of the site as it existed in an earlier time.

Delphinia (del-fin'i-ä). A festival of Apollo Delphinius (the Dolphin or protector of navigation), of expiatory character, celebrated at Athens and Aegina, and generally among Ionian colonies along the Mediterranean coasts. At Athens it was held at the end of March, toward the close of the period of winter storms at sea, and included a procession in which seven boys and seven maidens bore olive branches, bound with fillets of white wool, to the Delphinian temple near the temple of the Olympian Zeus.

Delphinius (del-fin'i-us). An epithet of Apollo, meaning "Dolphin." It was attached to the god because as a god of sailors and seaports he often took the form of a dolphin. It was also in the form of a dolphin that he sought his first priests on a Cretan ship, according to some accounts. There was a sanctuary of Apollo Delphinius near the temple of Olympian Zeus at Athens. According to one legend, when the temple was completed except for the roof, Theseus arrived in the city, unknown. Wearing a long tunic, and with his hair neatly braided, he approached the temple of Apollo Delphinius. Laborers working on the roof of the temple observed him and mocked him. They asked what a marriageable virgin was doing walking about by herself. In sudden anger, Theseus unyoked oxen from a nearby cart and hurled them over the top of the temple.

Delphinus (del-fi'nus). In Greek mythology, an agent of Poseidon who followed Amphitrite to the Atlas Mountains, whither she had fled to escape the attentions of Poseidon. He pleaded Poseidon's cause so successfully that Amphitrite yielded and agreed to marry Poseidon. As a reward for his services, Poseidon placed Delphinus among the stars, where he was known in ancient times as the constellation Dolphin.

Delphinus. An ancient constellation, representing a dolphin. It is situated east of Aquila.

Delphus (del'fus). According to some accounts, a son of Poseidon and Melantho, daughter of Deucalion. Others say he was a son of Celaeno and Apollo. Some say Delphi, Apollo's shrine, was named for him.

Delphyne (del-fi'nē). In Greek mythology, a monstrous earth-born serpent who guarded the oracle at Delphi and, according to some accounts, gave the site his name. Apollo slew Delphyne at Delphi, and made the oracle his own from that time forth. The serpent is also known as *Python*.

Delphyne. In Greek mythology, a fabulous creature, half maiden and half beast, that guarded Zeus when Typhon imprisoned him in a cave in Cilicia. The sinews of Zeus' hands and feet had been severed by Typhon and given to Delphyne to guard. Hermes and Pan went to the cave and stole the sinews and restored them to the body of Zeus, after which Zeus escaped and returned to Olympus.

Demades (dem'a-dēz). Athenian orator, born c350 B.C.; died 319 B.C. By his eloquence and complete lack of scruples he rose to a position of prominence in Athens. He was a member of the peace party and opposed Demosthenes, who urged war on Philip of Macedon. Demosthenes' policy prevailed. At the battle of Chaeronea (338 B.C.) Philip inflicted a disastrous defeat on the Greeks. Demades was one of 2000 captives taken. According to one story Philip celebrated his victory by drinking much wine, and after a drunken carousal went to the place where the prisoners were under guard. He mocked them and sneered at the great Demosthenes, who had fled. Demades rebuked him, saying, "O King, fortune has given you the role of Agamemnon, and you play the part of Thersites." Philip was immediately sobered by the rebuke, freed Demades, and sent him as one of the envoys to make peace with Athens, the terms of which were re-markably lenient in comparison with his treatment of Thebes at the same time. After the death of Philip (336 B.C.) Thebes revolted against his successor, Alexander the Great. Athens prepared to help Thebes, but Alexander swooped down from the north, completely defeated Thebes, and destroyed the city. Alexander demanded the surrender of the leaders of the war party at Athens, including Demosthenes. Demades, who had proposed that an embassy from Athens be sent to congratulate Alexander on his victory at Thebes, was sent as a peacemaker from Athens, and persuaded Alexander to let Athens deal with the offenders. From this time on Demades supported Phocion (q.v.), the Athenian general who played a large part in guiding Athens away from her rash desire to wage war on Macedonia. Along with Phocion, and even Demosthenes, he persuaded the Athenians not to help the Spartan king Agis in a war against Macedonia (331 B.C.), and he continued to support the peace policy of Phocion in the 12 years between the fall of Thebes (335 B.C.) and the death of Alexander (323 B.C.). At the same time that he supported the Macedonian party, he accepted bribes from their opponents, was discovered, and was several times fined. Nevertheless, he maintained his position. When news of Alexander's death reached Athens, men could scarcely believe it. Demades declared, "If he were indeed dead, the whole world would have been filled with the stench of his corpse." Nevertheless, he was indeed dead. Athens rose again in rebellion, spurred on by Demosthenes, and was defeated at Crannon, 322 B.C., by the Macedonians under Antipater. Again Demades acted as a peace envoy, but this time the terms were not so lenient, for Antipater did not share the admiration and respect for Athenian culture held by Philip and Alexander. From this time Demades conducted affairs at Athens so as to please Antipater, and excused his servile conduct on the ground that he was "in command of a shipwrecked state." According to Plutarch, his life and administration were so outrageous that Antipater said of him, when he was an old man, that he was like a victim when the sacrifice was over:

nothing left but tongue and guts. Antipater also said he had two friends at Athens: Phocion, whom he could not persuade to take anything, and Demades, to whom he could never give enough. After the death of Antipater (319 B.C.) Demades went to Cassander, his son, to plead for relief from the payment Athens had agreed to make after the battle of Crannon. Cassander had found a letter written by Demades to Perdiccas, which was a betrayal of Antipater. He had Demades slain for his ingratitude and his treachery (319 B.C.).

Demaratus (dem-a-rā′tus). A son of Ariston and co-king of Sparta with Cleomenes; fl. c510–480 B.C., and shared the throne with Cleomenes from 510–491 B.C. He shared with Cleomenes the command of the army sent in 510 B.C. to assist the Athenians in expelling Hippias. In 506 B.C. when Cleomenes sought to restore Hippias, Demaratus withdrew at the moment when battle was to be joined. Demaratus later brought charges against Cleomenes for a war he was waging against the Aeginetans, and when he returned from the war, Cleomenes sought to drive Demaratus from his office as king and adopted the following means to do so: He claimed that Demaratus was not the true son of Ariston because when he was born to the third wife of Ariston, the latter, on reckoning the time he had been married, exclaimed an oath that this could not be his son. Ariston later became convinced that Demaratus was truly the son he had prayed for and forgot all about the matter. But Cleomenes revived the early incident. The oracle at Delphi was consulted. To make sure that a favorable answer was given, Cleomenes sent bribes to the oracle, which thereupon declared Demaratus was not the son of Ariston and therefore not rightfully a king of Sparta. Demaratus, on losing the throne (491 B.C.), sacrificed an ox to Zeus and questioned his mother. He begged her to tell him the truth. If he were not the son of Ariston but the offspring of a groom, as some claimed, he would forgive her as such an eventuality might come to anyone, but he wanted to know the truth of his origin. His mother told him that an apparition had come to her in the appearance of Ariston, embraced her, and placed garlands on her head. The same night Ariston came, again as she thought, and asked where the garlands had come from. To her reply that he himself had placed them there, he made strong denials. The conclusion, on consultation of the priests, was that he who placed the garlands on her head and embraced her was the spirit of a hero whose shrine was nearby. His mother ended her story by telling Demaratus that he was either the son of that hero or of Ariston; which, she did not know. Demaratus now fled from Sparta, pursued by the Spartans, and sought asylum with King Darius in Susa. The bribery of the oracle was later disclosed and the priestess was removed, and when Cleomenes' part became known, he was forced to flee. Demaratus, meanwhile, was received as a guest in King Darius' court, and afterward became the bond-friend of his son and successor Xerxes. He accompanied Xerxes when the latter invaded Greece. After the Persians had crossed into Europe, Xerxes called Demaratus and asked him whether he thought the Greeks would resist the onslaught of his mighty army. Demaratus replied that even if all the other Greeks submitted, the Spartans would not submit to the slavery Xerxes proposed to subject them to; and if there were only 1000 Spartans, they would resist, no matter what the size of the Persian host. Xerxes scoffed at what he considered a ridiculous estimate of the bravery of the Spartans. Demaratus insisted. He said the Spartans, as free men who submitted voluntarily to the discipline of law, were the bravest men in the world, for the law forbade them to flee in battle, but commanded them to stand firm and conquer or die. Xerxes laughed. Just before the battle of Thermopylae, when Xerxes was opposed by 1000 Greeks, Spartans and Thespians, he again questioned Demaratus, and received the reply that if he could subdue the Spartans at Thermopylae and those in Lacedaemonia, he would have all Greece at his feet. After the battle of Thermopylae Xerxes was compelled to admit that Demaratus had not lied about the bravery of the Spartans. He asked his advice how to conquer those still in Lacedaemonia. Demaratus advised him to attack them directly by sea. Xerxes ignored his advice, saying at the same time that he knew Demaratus meant it for his good but in this instance he was mistaken. But some say that Demaratus had sent a message warning the Spartans of what the Persians intended before they ever left Susa.

Demeter (dḗ-mē'tẻr). One of the great Olympian deities; the golden-haired giver of the fruits and flowers of the earth, protectress of social order and of marriage, she was "Mother Earth," "the Good Goddess," and the great benefactress of mankind. The gentle goddess of the fertility of the earth and of man was called "the greatest help and cause of joy to the undying gods and mortal men." In the Greek theogony she is one of the most important and revered of the gods, and her mysteries are among the holiest of the Greek rites.

Demeter was the second child of Cronus and Rhea, and like the first, Hestia, was swallowed by Cronus as soon as she was born. Zeus, with the aid of Metis, caused Cronus to disgorge her, along with his sisters and brothers. In her youth, some say, Demeter, during the wedding festivities of Cadmus and Harmonia, lay with Iasion, son of Electra and Zeus, in a thrice-plowed field and bore Plutus (*Wealth*) to him. Some say the thrice-plowed field where Iasion loved Demeter was a fertile district in Crete. And some say Zeus slew Iasion with a thunderbolt because he embraced the goddess. But others say Iasion was slain by his brother Dardanus. By her brother Zeus, Demeter was the mother of Iacchus and Core (*The Maid*), who is widely known as Persephone, and some say that it was she who bore Dionysus to Zeus. The rape of Persephone by Hades is the heart of the legend and worship of Demeter, symbolizing as it does the death and rebirth, or disappearance and reappearance, of the nourishing produce of the earth.

According to the myth, Hades saw Persephone and desired her. (Some say it was Aphrodite, wishing to extend her sway over Tartarus as well as over Earth and Sea, who caused her son Eròs to shoot his arrows into the heart of Hades and awaken love for Persephone in him.) With the connivance of Zeus, who did not like to thwart his brother, Hades planned to seize Persephone. One day as she was gathering flowers with her maidens, Persephone wandered away from them, enticed by a strange and beautiful flower, which some say was a kind of narcissus. As she bent to pluck the flower the earth parted; a great chariot drawn by black horses thundered forth, swept down on Persephone, and the black-clad charioteer swept her into his car. She cried out for help but her companions neither heard her nor saw the stranger who carried her off, for the chariot flew over the meadow and disappeared in a chasm that opened in the earth. The Sicilians say that the abduction took place near Enna, in Sicily. Others claim it was at Colonus in Attica, or at Hermion in Argolis, or at Pisa, Lerna, Pheneüs, Nysa, or Crete, but the priests of Demeter say it was at Eleusis. Demeter was heartbroken when she learned of the disappearance of her daughter. For nine days she searched frantically for her, carrying blazing torches through the night and stopping neither to eat nor to bathe. Of all those she questioned, gods and men, none would tell her the truth. On the ninth day she met Hecate, who said she had heard Persephone's cries, but when she rushed up to assist her, she had disappeared without a trace. Together, Demeter and Hecate went in search of Helius and questioned him on whether in his passage through the skies he had seen anything. Helius told Demeter that Hades had carried off Persephone with the consent of Zeus, and he advised Demeter not to grieve, for the ruler of Tartarus was not an unworthy son-in-law. But some say that Demeter, as she wandered about looking for Persephone, learned from the people of Hermion that it was Hades who had carried off her child, and the chasm through which he disappeared into the earth in their land was the same one by which Heracles dragged Cerberus to the upper air from Tartarus. And some say that the nymph Cyane, in Sicily, saw Hades as he prepared to steal Persephone, and that she attempted, without success, to stop him. Afterward, in grief, Cyane was transformed into a fountain, so that when Demeter came her way, she was unable to tell the goddess what had happened, but on the waters of her fountain she caused Persephone's girdle, dropped when she was caught up into Hades'

chariot, to float. Demeter saw the girdle and knew that Persephone had passed that way. In any event, when Demeter learned that it was by the consent of the gods that Hades had abducted Persephone, she left Olympus and wandered all over the face of the earth to search for her. As she roamed through Arcadia, Poseidon saw her and pursued her. Demeter, weary and grief-stricken, wished to elude Poseidon and his amorous intentions. She transformed herself into a mare and grazed with the mares of Oncus. But Poseidon would not be denied. He changed himself into a stallion and ravished her. From this union was born the marvelous horse, Arion, and a girl child whose name it was unlawful to utter, but some say this child's name was Despoena. Demeter was so infuriated by the outrage of Poseidon that the people of the region gave her the name Erinnys (*Fury*), but afterward her rage subsided, and she cleansed herself by bathing in the Ladon River, whence her epithet Lusia (*Bather*). In her temple at Thelpusa, in Arcadia, were two images, one for each of these names. The images had face, hands, and feet of marble, but the body was of wood. Also in Arcadia, Demeter went to the city of Pheneüs and was received kindly by the inhabitants. To reward them she gave them every kind of pulse except the bean, which was considered to be impure by the Pheneatians. Wherever she was treated kindly in her wanderings, Demeter rewarded the people, as she gave the fig tree to Phytalus, who welcomed her when she stopped beside the Cephissus River on the Isthmus. The Argives say that when she came to Argos, Pelasgus received her, and that one Chrysanthis, knowing of the rape of Persephone, told it to her. Disguised as a humble old woman she came to Eleusis. Some say it was in the reign of King Pandion of Athens that she came to Eleusis; others say it was when Erechtheus, son of Pandion, was king that wheat was first sown by Triptolemus, and that the mysteries of Demeter were first celebrated by Eumolpus. On the road from Megara to Eleusis she sat down on a rock, called *Laughless* because of her sorrow when she rested on it. Nearby was a well where the inhabitants came to draw water; some name this well Anthium

(*Flowery*) and some name it Callichorum (*Well of Fair Dances*). While the goddess rested here the four daughters of Celeus came to fetch water. They saw the sàd old woman and spoke kindly to her, and asked her what fortune had brought her to their land. Demeter told them she had escaped from pirates who had carried her away from her home in Crete and intended to sell her as a slave, and that she had made her way alone to this place seeking refuge. She asked the maidens if they knew a house where she might be welcome as a nurse or helper. The daughters of Celeus said there were many who would be glad to welcome her, but that they would like best to have her come to their father's house, and asked her to wait while they went and consulted with their mother. They soon returned and invited Demeter to go home with them. When she entered the doorway of Celeus' house, a heavenly radiance glowed about her. Metanira, wife of Celeus, was awed by the sight, and asked her to be seated, but Demeter would take only the lowliest stool, denying herself all comforts in her grief. The family of Celeus welcomed her warmly, but she seemed so sad that Iambe, the lame daughter of Celeus, made bawdy jokes and caused her to smile, and Baubo, nurse of the new-born son of the house, Demophoön, gave her barley water flavored with mint, and to make her laugh, Baubo groaned as if in labor, and suddenly produced Demeter's own son Iacchus from beneath her skirt. The child leaped into his mother's arms and kissed her. Because of the kindly efforts of these two to cheer Demeter in her grief, it became the custom to make broad jests at Demeter's feast of the Thesmophoria, and the cup of mint-flavored barley water was the cup offered to worshipers at the great mysteries of Eleusis. As Demeter drank, Abas, an older son of Celeus, mocked her because she drank so thirstily. Some say she threw the liquid in his face, in her anger, and transformed him into a spotted lizard, and some say that it was by a look alone that he was transformed into an animal that needs very little water and slithered away before his stricken mother's eyes. Demeter became the nurse of Demophoön, and because of the kindness of his

parents, she decided to make the child immortal. Under her care he flourished like a god. By day she fed him ambrosia, and each night she plunged him into the fire to burn away his mortal parts. One night as she was engaged in this ritual, she was surprised by his mother, who cried out in fear and broke the spell. Some say Demeter dropped the child, revealed herself in all the glory of her godhead, and told Metanira and her astonished household who she was. Now, she said, she could not make Demophoön immortal, but because he had been nursed by a goddess, great honor would come to him. Others say that when she dropped the child, he was consumed in the fire, and to make up for the loss of this son, Demeter

DEMETER, TRIPTOLEMUS, AND PERSEPHONE
Votive relief to the Eleusinian deities, c440
B.C. *National Museum, Athens*

promised to make his brother Triptolemus immortal. Some say she chose to confer immortality on Triptolemus because he had recognized her as a goddess, and had told her that some days before his brothers— Eumolpus and Eubuleus—had seen the earth open, and into it a chariot bearing a black-clad figure clasping a maiden had disappeared. This had happened as they were tending their father's swine and cattle in the fields, and Eumolpus had made a song about the event. It is because of this that the priests of Demeter say the rape of Persephone took place at Eleusis. Demeter commanded Celeus to raise a temple to her at Eleusis, and instructed him and Eumolpus, as well as Triptolemus, in her mysteries. (Later, when Heracles came to Eleusis, she established the Lesser Mysteries in his honor.) Then she sat in her temple and mourned her lost daughter. At her command the earth became barren; men plowed, but as fast as the plants sprang from the soil they withered. Some say this continued for a year, and then Zeus sent Iris to persuade her to return to Olympus, and to restore fertility to the earth, for he did not wish mankind to die, nor to lose the rich sacrifices and gifts men made to the gods of Olympus. But Demeter ignored his messenger because he had turned his head while Hades seized Persephone; and when the gods themselves, bearing gifts, came and tried to persuade her she still refused to return to Olympus, and declared the earth must remain barren until Persephone was restored to her. At last Zeus sent Hermes to Hades with an order to him to restore Persephone to her mother; and from Hades Hermes went to Demeter to inform her that Persephone would be returned on condition that she had not eaten anything while she was in Tartarus. When Hades received his message, he had no choice but to let Persephone go, but he spoke regretfully to her, and reminded her that it was no small thing to be his wife and a queen in Tartarus. Hermes came to fetch her; as she set out Ascalaphus, a gardener in Tartarus, said that he had seen her eat some seeds of a pomegranate, and therefore, as she had eaten of the food of the dead, she must return to the world of the dead. Demeter was overjoyed when Persephone returned to her at Eleusis, but was immediately downcast when she learned of the pomegranate seeds, and hurled a great stone on Ascalaphus for his tale-bearing. She refused to restore fruitfulness to the earth if Persephone was compelled to return to the Underworld. In the end a compromise was worked out by Rhea; Persephone, having eaten some of the food of the dead in the form of the pomegranate seeds (some say she ate seven), must spend one third of the year in the kingdom of the dead; the rest of the time she could spend with her mother. On this basis, with Hecate watching to see that the agreement was faithfully carried out, the matter was settled, and Demeter returned to her home among the gods. But before she left Eleusis she gave Triptolemus the gift of wheat and a wooden plow, and taught him the arts of sowing and threshing on the Rharian Plain in a place that came to be known as the "Threshing Floor," and which annually ever after was plowed in commemoration of this event. Then, in a car drawn by winged dragons, she sent him all over the earth to teach men how to cultivate crops. The time that Persephone spends with her mother represents the time of the sowing, growing, and harvesting of crops; the time when she must reign as a queen in the kingdom of the dead is the period of barren and blasted fields. The great Eleusinian Mysteries, among the holiest rites celebrated by the Greeks, were established at Eleusis by Demeter herself. When Athens conquered Eleusis, the Athenians won the right to share in them, and Eleusinia were also established in the other Greek states, but those at Eleusis were always the most sacred. The mysteries are thought to have been a reënactment of the suffering and grief of Demeter over the loss of her daughter, and of her joy when Persephone was restored. By extension, the mysteries and their symbolism were an expression of the idea of the immortality of the soul. But the rites of the mysteries were a well-kept secret; only the initiated knew them and they never betrayed the secret.

Demeter is a kind and gentle goddess, the giver of good to man. She takes no part in war and strife, and seldom is aroused to wrath. Erysichthon, however, did feel her just anger. He cut down a tree, the home of a nymph, in her sacred grove. Demeter appeared to him, disguised as her own priestess, and remonstrated with him when she heard the cries of the nymph, but Erysichthon defied her and proceeded to cut down her sacred trees. To punish him, Demeter sent insatiable hunger to destroy him.

Eleusis and Athens were the most ancient seats of the worship of Demeter, but she was worshiped throughout Greece; and Sicily, noted for its fertility, was said to be one of her favorite haunts. Among her many names, Demeter was called Black Demeter, for the time, during the loss of Persephone, when she clothed herself in black and went into seclusion in a cave in Phigalia in Arcadia. The Phigalians say that after Poseidon, in the form of a stallion, ravished Demeter, disguised as a mare, she clothed herself in black and hid in this cave. The Phigalians later set up an image in the cave; it was a figure of a woman seated on a rock, but instead of a woman's head it had a horse's head, out of which grew serpents and other beasts. In one of her hands the image held a dolphin, in the other, a dove. This was the image called "Mare-headed Demeter." She was known as "Cabirea" because she instructed the Cabiri of Thebes in her rites and entrusted a sacred thing into their keeping. Because of her connection with the kingdom of the dead through the annual loss of Persephone she was called Chthonia (*Of the Lower World*), and a festival of the same name was held annually in her honor. She was widely known as Eleusinian Demeter and had many sanctuaries in this name. As Thesmophorus (*Law-giver*), she was worshiped at the great festival of the Thesmophoria, and had many sanctuaries. She was also called Lernaea (*Of Lerna*) because, some say, Hades disappeared into the earth with Persephone at Lerna; Carpophorus (*Fruit-bearer*); Malophorus (*Sheep-bearer* or *Apple-bearer*); Mycalessia (*Of Mycalessus*), after the city in Boeotia where her sanctuary was said to be opened each morning and closed each night by Heracles the Dactyl; Mysia, from Mysius, an Argive who entertained her; Panachaea (*All Achaea*) from her sanctuary in Aegium, in Achaea; Pelasgis, because Pelasgus founded a sanctuary for her in Argos; Stiria or Stiritis (*Of Stiris*) from her sanctuary at that place in Phocis; Thermasia (*Warmth*); Thesmia (*Law-goddess*); Chloë (*Green*); and Anesidora (*Sender-up of Gifts*).

The festivals of Demeter, celebrated in conjunction with rites for her daughter Persephone, were the Great Eleusinian Mysteries and the Thesmophoria. Fruit, honey, the cow and the sow were offered to her. Her attributes were the poppy, a flower that grows with the wheat and is also a symbol of sleep and death, and stalks of wheat. In art she was sometimes also depicted with a basket of fruit and a piglet, or with a torch or a serpent. The Romans of the end of the Republic and of the empire assimilated to the Greek conception of Demeter the primitive Italic chthonian divinity Ceres.

Demeter of Cnidus (nī′dus). Greek statue (4th century B.C.) of the school of Scopas, now in the British Museum at London. The goddess is represented, fully draped and seated, as mourning for her daughter, and conveys a feeling of profound grief.

Demetrius I (dē-mē′tri-us). [Surnamed **Poliorcetes**, meaning "Taker of Cities" or "Besieger."] King of Macedonia (294–288 B.C.); born 336 B.C.; died at Apamea, in ancient Syria, 283 B.C. He was a son of Antigonus I, who was called Antigonus Cyclops. He liberated Athens and Megara in 307 B.C., defeated Ptolemy I in 306, unsuccessfully besieged Rhodes (305–304), and was defeated at Ipsus in 301 B.C. He was chosen king by the army in 294 B.C., gained control (293–289 B.C.) of Greece, and invaded Asia, which Antigonus had held, with an inferior force in 287 B.C. He surrendered to Seleucus I in 285 B.C. and drank himself to death.

Demetrius II. King of Macedonia; born c276 B.C.; died 229 B.C. He was a son of Antigonus II Gonatus, whom he succeeded c239 B.C. During his reign the Macedonians fought to preserve their territory; the Demetrian War, so called, was fought against the Aetolian League and the Achaeans, but Demetrius was defeated in the north. Philip V of Macedon was his son by his second wife Phthia (or Chryseis).

Demetrius I (of *Syria*). [Surnamed **Soter**, meaning "Savior."] King of Syria from 162 B.C.; born 187 B.C.; killed 150 B.C. He was a grandson of Antiochus the Great. After living as a captive in Rome while his uncle, Antiochus IV, and his cousin, Antiochus V, sat on the throne, he escaped (162 B.C.), killed his cousin, and became king himself. He suppressed the revolt of Timarchus in Babylon and put down the Maccabee uprising in Palestine. But Alexander Balas, a pretender, claimed the throne, and, with the help of the Maccabees, Egyptians, and others, overthrew Demetrius.

Demetrius II (of *Syria*). [Surnamed **Nicator**.] King of Syria (145–141 and 129–126 B.C.); son of Demetrius I. He was born c161 B.C.; died near Tyre, 126 B.C. He overthrew Alexander Balas, the usurper, with the aid of Ptolemy VI (Ptolemy Philometor), obtaining both the throne and Ptolemy's daughter, Cleopatra Thea, wife of Alexander Balas. He defeated the attempt (145–142 B.C.) to place Antiochus VI, son of Alexander Balas, on the throne. In 141 B.C. he was captured by the Parthians and remained their prisoner for about ten years, his brother Antiochus VII occupying the throne in his absence and marrying Cleopatra, Demetrius' wife. Demetrius regained the throne in 129 B.C. but was soon after killed in a civil war. He was succeeded by his sons Seleucus V and Antiochus VIII.

Demetrius III (of *Syria*). [Surnamed **Euergetes** and **Philometor**.] King of Syria 94–88 B.C.; son of Antiochus VIII Grypus. He struggled for the throne with his cousin Antiochus X and his brother Philip; he was defeated, captured, and held prisoner until his death by the Parthians.

Demetrius Phalereus (fa̲-lē′rös, fa̲-lir′ē̲-us). Athenian statesman and orator; born at Phalerum, in Attica, 345 B.C.; died in Upper Egypt, 283 B.C. He entered public life c325 B.C. as a supporter of Phocion, and in 317 B.C. was placed by Phocion's successor, Cassander, at the head of the administration of Athens. Expelled from Athens in 307 B.C. by Demetrius I of Macedonia (Demetrius Poliorcetes), he retired to the court of Ptolemy Lagus at Alexandria, where he devoted himself wholly to literary pursuits. He was exiled by Ptolemy's successor to Upper Egypt, where he is said to have died of the bite of a snake.

Demiphon (dem′i-fon). According to legend, a king whose land was smitten by a pestilence. He was commanded by an oracle to sacrifice one noble maiden each year and the pestilence would be lifted. Annually thereafter one noble maiden's name was drawn by lot and she was sacrificed. At last one Mastusius, whose daughter was sacrificed, learned that the names of Demiphon's own daughters were never placed among the lots to be drawn. He invited Demiphon and his daughters to a banquet and had the daughters murdered. He then served Demiphon with a cup containing their blood. When Demiphon discovered the horrible deed, he caused Mastusius and the cup to be hurled into the sea.

Democedes (dem-ọ̄-sē′dēz). A native of Croton, in Magna Graecia in Italy (now Crotone in Calabria), who flourished in the second half of the 6th century B.C. He was the most skilled physician of his day. He left his home in Croton to escape his father's harshness and went to Aegina. There he soon became the most skilled physician of the area. In a few years his reputation was so great that Polycrates of Samos heard of him and hired him away from Aegina. He went to Samos and became a friend of Polycrates. When Polycrates went to Oroetes, governor of Sardis, Democedes accompanied him, although he had tried to persuade Polycrates not to go. Polycrates was treacherously and horribly slain by Oroetes and his followers, among them Democedes, were enslaved. Darius, king of Persia, having injured his foot, suffered grievously, for the Egyptian physicians who treated him were clumsy and only aggravated the injury. One who had heard of Democedes recommended him to the king. Darius sent for him. He was found among the slaves of Oroetes, who had only recently been slain at the command of Darius, and was brought into the presence of the king, clothed in rags and still shackled in fetters. Darius asked him if he understood medicine. Democedes answered that he did not, for he feared if Darius found him to be a skillful practitioner he would never be allowed to depart for his home, which it was his ardent wish to do. Darius suspected him of deceit and ordered him to be scourged, whereupon Democedes confessed that he had some slight knowledge of medicine and agreed to treat the king's injured ankle. In a few days he had reduced the swelling and cured the injury so that Darius, who had feared to lose the use of his foot altogether, was completely restored. He presented Democedes with two sets of fetters wrought of pure gold. Democedes reproached him with doubling his sufferings because he had restored him to health. Darius was pleased with the remark and made him a present of much gold. From that time Democedes was treated royally by Darius and wanted for nothing except the one thing his heart most desired: liberty to return to his native land. Atossa, the wife of Darius, now approached him to cure an abscess on her breast. He promised to cure it if she would give him her oath that once it was healed she would grant whatever he requested of her, assuring her he would make no dishonorable demands. She agreed and after a few days he cured the abscess. His request was that she should secure his return to his homeland. Atossa did not directly ask Darius for the release of Democedes. Instead she inspired him with the idea of conquest and suggested that she would like to have some Greek serving women and advised him to consider the conquest of Greece. She proposed to Darius that he send Democedes, as the man who knew the most about Greece, to act as a guide for spies. Darius acted on her suggestion. He told Democedes he wished him to go with 15 Persians, and spy out the land for him. He suggested to Democedes that he take all his riches with him as gifts to his parents, and even offered to fit out a merchant ship and load it with gifts for the relatives of Democedes. Herodotus, who tells this story, feels sure that Darius had no ulterior motive in making these generous offerings, but Democedes feared that if he accepted and removed his treasure from Persia, Darius might suspect that he did not mean to return. Therefore he gratefully declined the king's offer to take his treasures with him. He departed in a ship with the Persian spies. They sailed along the shores of Greece, noting all that they saw, and went to Tarentum in Magna Graecia. There the ruler, out of friendship for Democedes, took the rudder off the ship and detained the Persians as spies. Democedes escaped to Croton. The Persians, released from Tarentum, pursued him but the people of Croton refused to give him up, and the Persians

sailed away. According to Herodotus, who gives this story as one of the opening chapters of the impending Persian Wars, these were the first Persians to come from Asia into Greek lands, and their purpose was to spy out the land for the purpose of invasion.

Demochares (dẹ-mok'ạ-rēz). Athenian orator; fl. 322–280 B.C. He was a nephew of Demosthenes. He came forward in 322 B.C. as an orator of the anti-Macedonian party, and after the restoration of democracy by Demetrius I of Macedonia (Demetrius Poliorcetes) in 307 B.C. became the leader of the popular party. He was several times expelled by the anti-democratic party, returning the last time in 287 or 286. He was sent as ambassador to Lysimachus c282, and disappears from view in 280 B.C.

Democoön (dẹ-mok'ọ-on). In Homeric legend (*Iliad*), a bastard son of Priam, king of Troy. In the Trojan war he was slain by Odysseus to avenge the slaying of Odysseus' "valiant companion," Leucus.

Democritus (dẹ-mok'ri-tus). [Called **the Abderite**, and **the Laughing Philosopher**.] Greek philosopher, born at Abdera, in Thrace, c460B.C.; died c370 B.C. He inherited an ample fortune, which enabled him to visit the chief countries of Asia and Africa in pursuit of knowledge, and through his studies and his travels became, according to some, the most learned of the Greeks before Aristotle. He adopted and expanded the atomistic theory of Leucippus, applying it even to the soul, which he considered to be compounded of smooth atoms, with the qualities of fire, that are constantly in motion and permeate the entire body. The soul he considered to be a manifestation of the real existence of the body and perishes with the body. He left a number of works, written in a lively manner, on ethics, physics, astronomy, mathematics, art, and literature, fragments only of which are extant. He is said to have been of a cheerful disposition, which prompted him to laugh at the follies of men (hence the epithet "the Laughing Philosopher"). According to tradition he put out his eyes in order to be less disturbed by outward things in his philosophical speculations. He distinguished between the things belonging to a substance by convention (heat, hardness) and in reality (atoms). His mechanistic philosophy extended to the gods, mortal to Democritus, though composed of finer atomic stuff than man was. His ethical system was based on pleasure, tempered by self-control, as an end, and he believed man could secure happiness by doing good for its own sake, not through fear or the promise of a reward.

Demodocus (dē-mod′ō-kus.) In the *Odyssey*, a blind minstrel of Alcinous, king of the Phaeacians. It was said of him that the gods took away his sight but gave him in its place the great gift of song. During the stay of Odysseus at the court of Alcinous he delighted the guests by recounting the feats of the Greeks at Troy, but as he sang of the quarrel between Odysseus and Achilles, Odysseus, whose true identity was unknown to Alcinous, wept. At the request of Odysseus Demodocus sang of the Wooden Horse, and ended with singing of the amours of Aphrodite and Ares.

Demodocus. Greek epigrammatist of Lerus, active c537 B.C. Writer of witty maxims.

Demonassa (dē-mon-as′a). In Greek tradition, a daughter of Amphiaraus and Eriphyle, and the wife of Thersander. She was the mother of Tisamenus.

Demonice (dē-mon′i-sē). In Greek mythology, a daughter of Agenor and Epicaste, descendants of Endymion. By Ares she was the mother of Evenus, Molus, Pylus, and Thestius.

Demophon (dē′mō-fon). In Greek mythology, a son of Theseus. Some say his mother was Phaedra; others say his mother was the Amazon Antiope. He and his brother Acamas accompanied the Greeks to Troy. According to some accounts, Demophon was one of the envoys who went with Diomedes to the court of Priam at the beginning of the war to seek a peaceful restoration of Helen. The mission failed, but in the course of it Laodice, daughter of Priam, fell in love with Demophon and later bore him a son, Munitus. (Others say the father of Munitus was Acamas.) In the fierce fighting before Troy in the last year of the war Demophon fought valiantly. When Troy fell, he was reunited with his grandmother, Aethra, who had been carried to Troy with Helen. He demanded his grandmother as his part in the spoils of war, and with her and his son

set out for Greece. On the way he stopped in King Sithon's kingdom in Thrace. Phyllis, daughter of the king, fell in love with him and he promised to marry her. Before he did so however, he returned to Athens and regained the throne from Menestheus. When he did not return to Thrace on the appointed day, Phyllis hanged herself and was transformed into an almond tree. Demophon, returning too late, embraced the tree and instantly buds and leaves were put forth from it. (For another version of this story, see **Phyllis.**) In Athens again, Diomedes was blown ashore on the coasts of Attica by storms. He did not recognize the land and began ravaging the countryside. Demophon set out to repel the invading host, unaware of their identity. He took the Palladium of Troy from them, and killed an Athenian in the process, for which he was later tried in Athens on a charge of murder. Some say it was Demophon who helped the sons of Heracles in their struggles against Eurystheus, and who gave them land in Attica. And some say that when Orestes, pursued by the Furies, arrived in Attica Demophon received him kindly, but extended by one day the festival that was then in progress, fearing that Orestes in his guilt had polluted the first day of holy rites. In the paintings at Delphi Demophon was shown with Helen and Aethra, planning the rescue of his grandmother Aethra.

Demophoön (dē-mof′ō-on). In Greek mythology, a son of Celeus of Eleusis and Metanira. He was nursed by Demeter when she sought refuge in Celeus' house in her search for Persephone. The goddess fed him on nectar and ambrosia and each night she placed him in fiery embers to burn away his mortal parts and give him eternal youth. Metanira, unaware of the goddess' true identity, observed this ritual one night and screamed in alarm. Demeter dropped Demophoön and the spell which would have freed him from old age and death was broken.

Demosthenes (dē-mos′the-nēz). Athenian general in the Peloponnesian War. He died at Syracuse, 413 B.C. He led an expedition (426 B.C.) against the Aetolians which ended in failure. He did not dare return to Athens with the news that he had lost 120 Athenian

actor; up, lūte, pull; oi, oil; ou, out; ŦH, then; d̪ as d or j, ṣ as s or sh, ṭ as t or ch, ẓ as z or zh.

hoplites to the Aetolian javelins. Instead he went to Naupactus, where he drove off an attack by the Spartans, and followed this up by defeating the Ambracians, Spartan allies. In 425 B.C., sailing to the relief of the people of Corcyra, Demosthenes put in at Pylus, on the western coast of the Peloponnesus, and fortified it, in defiance of the jeers of his fellow commanders who thought it a forsaken, useless spot. He remained at Pylus with five of his ships when the rest of the fleet sailed on. The Spartans hurried to Pylus to destroy a fortress that the enemy had raised on their own soil. For a time they blockaded the Athenians under Demosthenes at Pylus. Then they occupied the island of Sphacteria in the mouth of the bay, but the Athenians destroyed the ships by which the Spartans had landed and in turn blockaded them on the island. The siege went on longer than was expected and the Athenians at home became impatient. They sent Cleon, who had boasted that he would take the Spartans alive or kill them on the spot, with enlarged forces to end the siege. He arrived at Pylus and with Demosthenes, who had worked out a plan of attack, as his co-commander, did succeed in bringing about the surrender of the Spartans on Sphacteria. Cleon claimed the credit for this great victory, glorious not for the importance of the place but because of the unheard-of exploit of taking Spartans alive. Such was their reputation that they were expected to fight to the death in any encounter, and "come home either with their shields or on them." Demosthenes had made the disposition by which the surrender of the Spartans was accomplished. Later he commanded under Nicias in the unsuccessful expedition against Syracuse in 413 B.C. Having been captured in the retreat, he was put to death by order of the Syracusan assembly.

Demosthenes. Greatest of Greek orators. He was born at Paeania, in Attica, 384 B.C., and died on the island of Calauria, in the Saronic Gulf, 322 B.C. When he was seven years old, his father died and the guardians entrusted with his property made off with it. When Demosthenes, a weakly child reared by his mother, grew up, he brought an action against the guardians and, though they were prominent and attempted to frighten him, he won the case. Although most of his fa-

ther's property had been lost, with the damages he won he fitted out a trireme and presented it to the Athenian fleet. He is said to have been the pupil of the orator Isaeus, and entered public life as a speaker in the popular assembly in 355 B.C. In that same year he delivered his speech *Against Leptines,* in which he favored the continuance of public grants of immunity from taxation which were awarded from time to time to those who had rendered outstanding service to the state. In 351 B.C. he delivered the first of a splendid series of orations directed against the encroachment of Philip II of Macedon, three of which are specifically denominated *Philippics.* In 346 B.C. he served as a member of the embassy which concluded with Philip the so-called peace of Philocrates. In the ten-member peace commission Demosthenes alone was not satisfied with the peace because of certain ambiguous clauses, and in the end refused the rich presents Philip offered the negotiators as was the custom, refused to be associated with them in the peace, and when he reached Athens proposed that the crown usually awarded to ambassadors be withheld from them all, including himself. As Philip immediately after broke this treaty, Demosthenes came forward as the leader of the patriotic party, in opposition to the Macedonian party which was headed by Aeschines. In the years immediately following, the ambassadors who had arranged the peace were violently attacked and some left Athens. Demosthenes came out against Aeschines in a speech *On the Embassy* (344 B.C.), but failed to convict him. In 340 B.C. he caused a fleet to be sent to the relief of Byzantium, which was besieged by Philip. On the outbreak of the Amphictyonic War, he persuaded the Athenians to form an alliance with Thebes against Philip, who defeated the allies at Chaeronea in 338 B.C., and usurped the hegemony of Greece. The Macedonian party in Athens attacked Demosthenes, who called unceasingly for the overthrow of Philip, but the people were loyal to Demosthenes, his accusers failed to convict him, and he was chosen to pronounce the funeral oration for the fallen of Chaeronea. Athens was powerless to free herself from the alliance Philip had imposed on her. Following the murder of Philip

fat, fāte, fär, fãre, errant; net, mē, hėr ardent; pin, pīne; not, nōte, möve, nôr,

(336 B.C.), Demosthenes was one of the leaders of the unsuccessful rising against Macedon. Alexander the Great razed Thebes to the ground and demanded that the leaders who had encouraged the Theban revolt, among them Demosthenes, be handed over to him. But on the representation of a trusted mediator, they were spared. In 324 B.C. Harpalus, treasurer of Alexander, fled with considerable treasure and some forces, his peculations and extravagance having been discovered, and came to Greece. The Athenians would not receive him as long as he was accompanied by an armed force. But when he came alone to Athens they received him and took from him, Demosthenes being the authority in charge, 700 talents which they placed in the Parthenon until such time as the stolen money could be returned to Alexander. This was a matter of honor with the Athenians. Before the money could be restored Harpalus escaped. The money that had been deposited in the Parthenon was counted and was found to amount to only about half the sum originally deposited. The Macedonian party raised a great hue and cry against Demosthenes, claiming he had taken it as a bribe. The amount he received, if any, could not be proved, but the case went against him and he was fined such a large sum he could not pay it and went into exile on the island of Calauria, off Troezen. On the outbreak of a fresh rising at the death of Alexander in 323 B.C. he was recalled by the patriotic party, and on the capture of Athens by Antipater and Craterus in 322 B.C. fled to Calauria again, where he took poison in the temple of Poseidon to avoid capture. His tomb was at Calauria, where he was especially honored. The chief of the orations of Demosthenes are three *Philippics* (351, 344, 341 B.C.), three *Olynthiacs* (349, 349, 348 B.C.), *On the Peace* (346 B.C.), *On the Embassy* (344 B.C.), *On the Affairs of the Chersonese* (341 B.C.), *On the Crown* (330 B.C.). This last-named speech, the most famous of Demosthenes' orations, was in answer to Aeschines, who prosecuted Ctesiphon for moving that a crown be given to Demosthenes for his services to the state. Demosthenes was the great opponent of the Macedonian conquest of Greece, holding that Athens, traditionally and actually, was the heart of any Greek nation, and that it was necessary that the spark be rekindled that had died during the Peloponnesian War. Many legendary stories are told of how he obtained his oratorical power: a stammerer, he taught himself to speak slowly by putting pebbles in his mouth; he went to the seashore and declaimed to the waves so that the noise of an audience would not disturb him; he would run uphill while orating in order to strengthen his weak voice; he shut himself in a cave and copied Thucydides' history eight times in order to attain to a fine style. He seems actually to have had a speech defect; his style in oratory was not complex, but simple and pithy and effective.

De Natura Deorum (dē nạ-tū′rạ dē-ō′rum). [Eng. trans., "On the Nature of the Gods."] Dialogues by Cicero, in three books, treating of the existence, nature, and providence of the gods.

Dendera (den′dẻr-ạ). See **Tentyra.**

Dendrites (den-drī′tēz). An epithet of Dionysus, meaning "Tree-youth."

Dentatus (den-tā′tus), **Manius Curius.** Roman tribune, consul, praetor, and censor; fl. in the first part of the 3rd century B.C. He is celebrated as a model of the early Roman virtues of simplicity, frugality, and patriotism. He defeated Pyrrhus in 275 B.C., and the Samnites (290) and the Lucanians (274 B.C.).

De Officiis (dē ō-fish′i-is). [Eng. trans., "Of Duties."] Treatise in three books, by Cicero, on moral obligations, written c44 B.C.

De Oratore (dē or-ạ-tō′rē.) [Eng. trans., "Of the Orator."] Rhetorical work by Cicero, in three books, written (55 B.C.) in the form of a dialogue, the principal characters being L. Crassus and M. Antoninus. Its style and varied contents make it one of Cicero's most polished works.

Derceto (dẻr′sẹ-tō). [Also: **Derketo.**] Principal Philistine female deity, worshiped especially in Ashkelon (Ascalon). She was represented in the form of a woman terminating in a fish, and is considered the female counterpart of Dagon. She was a nature goddess, the principle of generation and fertility, and corresponds in her attributes and the mode of her worship to Ashtoreth (Astarte) of the Canaanites and Syrians (the Assyro-Babylonian Ishtar), and to Atargatis of the Hittites;

and is sometimes thought of as an eastern counterpart of the Greek Aphrodite. She was the mother of Semiramis, who, though human, was the counterpart of the goddess.

Dercyllus (dẽr-sil'is). See **Dinias and Dercyllis.**

De Republica (dē rẽ-pub'li-ka). [Eng. trans., "Of the Republic."] Philosophical political treatise in six books, by Cicero, in the form of a dialogue between Africanus the Younger (in whose gardens the scene is laid), C. Laelius, and others. The theme is the best form of government and the duty of the citizen. It was published in 51 B.C. About one-third of it has survived.

De Rerum Natura (dē rē'rum na-tū'ra). [Eng. trans., "Of the Nature of Things."] Didactic poem by T. Lucretius Carus, in six books. Completed shortly before his death about 55 B.C., the poem is one of the monuments of Roman literature, an exposition of things as they are in the world as viewed by an Epicurean. Lucretius discusses superstition, the nature of matter and of the universe, atoms, the mind, mortality, the senses, dreams, sex, the earth, man and society, and the phenomena of nature in the sky and on earth.

De Senectute (dē sen-ek-tū'tē). [Eng. trans., "On Old Age;" also, **Cato Major.**] Short treatise by Cicero, in the form of a conversation, devoted to the praise (in the person of Cato the Censor) of old age. It was written in 45 or 44 B.C.

Desmontes (des-mon'tēz). In Greek legend, the foster father of Arne, whom he blinded and imprisoned when he learned she was about to bear a child. He exposed her twin sons, Aeolus and Boeotus, to die, but they were saved. When they grew up, they rescued their mother and slew Desmontes.

Despoena (des-pē'na). The name, meaning "the Mistress," given by the Arcadians to the daughter of Demeter and Poseidon. This goddess may be identified with Persephone, who is usually described as the daughter of Zeus and Demeter. Pausanias indicates his unwillingness to identify "the Mistress," but mentions Persephone as "the Maid." *Despoena* appears also as an epithet of Aphrodite and Demeter. The Arcadians worshiped Despoena more than any other gods. In their sanctuary of the Mistress near Acacesium, there were altars to Demeter and Despoena, and an image of them. The images,

along with the throne and pedestal for them, were carved from one block of stone. The Arcadians had dug this huge stone from the earth in obedience to a command given in a dream. Next to Demeter stood Artemis clad in a deer skin and accompanied by a hunting dog. Next to Despoena stood Anytus, a Titan who was thought to have reared her. The Arcadians made offerings of all kinds of cultivated fruits except the pomegranate. In the sacred grove behind the sanctuary an oak and olive tree grew from the same root. Also in the precinct there was an altar of Poseidon Hippius, the father of Despoena.

Deucalion (dū-kā'li-on). In Greek mythology, a son of Prometheus and king of Phthia. Because of the wickedness of mankind Zeus determined to send a flood to destroy the evil race of man. Deucalion, who because of his piety was intended to found a new race, was warned by Prometheus of the impending destruction. He and his wife Pyrrha, the daughter of Epimetheus, took refuge in a huge chest. Rather than set the earth afire with his thunderbolts, and risk destroying the heavens as well, Zeus enlisted the aid of Poseidon in his plan to destroy mankind. For nine days the rains fell, the winds blew, and the sea washed over the earth, inundating villages and farms and drowning all the inhabitants. At the end of that time the waters began to recede and the chest in which Deucalion and Pyrrha had ridden out the flood came to rest on Mount Parnassus. Now the water subsided, the winds ceased, and the earth was restored to its normal appearance, but as far as he could tell Deucalion and his wife were the only living creatures left in the land. Near the banks of the Cephissus River they found a temple still standing and entered it. Deucalion thanked the gods for saving him from the flood and prayed to Themis that the earth would be repeopled. Themis heard their prayers and instructed them, through an oracle, to leave the temple, veil their heads, loosen the girdles of their garments, and throw the bones of their mother behind them. Deucalion interpreted this to mean that their mother was the earth and that stones were her bones. They veiled their heads, loosened their garments, and picked up stones which they cast over their shoulders behind them. After a short time the stones were transformed: those which Deucalion had cast became men; those thrown by Pyrrha became women. Soon the land was repopulated, and animals, birds, and insects sprang up from the muddy earth which presently recovered its customary verdure. Thus a new and, it was to be hoped, better race of man populated the earth. Deucalion was the father of Orestheus, Amphictyon, and Hellen.

Deucalion. In Greek legend a king of Crete and father of Idomeneus. He was a son of King Minos.

Dexamenus (dek-sä′me̯-nus). In Greek mythology, a centaur, king of Olenus in Achaea. His twin daughters married the Moliones, twin sons of Actor and Molione. The centaur Eurytion wished to marry his youngest daughter, whose name, according to some accounts, was Mnesimache. Dexamenus did not approve of the marriage but dared not refuse his consent. On the wedding day Heracles arrived and slew Eurytion and his brothers.

Dexileus (dek-sil′e̯-us), **Monument of.** Monument on the Street of Tombs at Athens. It is a beautiful stele bearing in relief a youthful horseman who has ridden down an enemy. Dexileus fell before Corinth in 394 or 393 B.C.

Dia (dī′a̯). In Greek legend, a daughter of Eioneus. She was the wife of the Lapith, Ixion, and the mother of Pirithous. According to some accounts Ixion was his father. According to others, Zeus was the father of Pirithous.

Dia. An island in the Aegean Sea, one of the Cyclades. It was one of the homes of Dionysus, and was also the island on which Theseus abandoned Ariadne on his return from Crete after escaping the Minotaur. Here Dionysus found Ariadne and married her. This island is better known by its name Naxos.

Diablintes (dī-a̯-blin′tēz) or **Diablindi** (-blin′-dī). Tribe of NW Gaul, allies of the Veneti against Caesar in 56 B.C. The Diablintes are thought to have lived near what is now Le Mans. They were one of four tribes forming a group known as the Aulerci. The other three members of this group were the Cenomani, the Eburovici, and the Brannovici.

Diadochi (dī″ad′o̯-kī). The Macedonian generals of Alexander the Great who, after his death in 323 B.C., divided his empire. Literally, the name means "Successors." The several empires that were established were the Seleucid in Syria and Asia Minor, the Ptolemid in Egypt, the Attalid in Pergamum, and the Antigonid in Macedonia.

Diadumenos (dī-a̯-dū′me̯-nos). Athlete binding his brow with a fillet, by the 5th century Greek sculptor Polyclitus, known from a Hellenistic copy found at Delos, now in Athens, and a head in Dresden. (JJ)

Diagoras (dī-ag′o̯-ras). [Surnamed **the Atheist.**] Greek philosopher, born on the island of Melos; fl. last half of the 5th century B.C. He was accused by the Athenians of impiety because of his attacks on the Eleusinian mysteries.

Diana (dī-an′a̯). Ancient Italian divinity, goddess of the moon, protectress of the female sex, later identified with the Greek Artemis. Like Artemis she was goddess of the hunt and the woods, protectress of chastity, and patroness of childbirth. She was called Luna, as goddess of the moon; Hecate, as an infernal deity, invoked in magic rites; and Diana, as goddess of the chase. Her famous shrine in the grove at Aricia was the scene of the custom investigated by Sir J. G. Frazer in the *Golden Bough.* Her companion, Virbius or Hippolytus, was worshiped there with her. Her priest, who came to his office by killing his predecessor in single combat, likewise might be killed by one in similar straits (specifically, a runaway slave).

Diana of Versailles (vėr-sālz′, ver-sī′). [Also: **Diana the Huntress.**] Greek statue in the Louvre, Paris, commonly regarded as a companion piece to the *Apollo Belvedere,* though inferior in execution. The goddess is advancing, clad in the short Dorian tunic and himation girded at her waist; she looks toward the right, as with raised arm she takes an arrow from her quiver.

Diasia (dī-ā′si-a̯). In ancient Attica, a festival in honor of Zeus Meilichius (*Gracious*), celebrated annually in the latter half of the month Anthesterion (about the 14th of March). According to Thucydides, this was the greatest festival of Zeus celebrated by the Athenians. The ceremonies of the festival took place outside the city, and the entire population made sacrifices. In early times the sacrifice demanded was a holocaust of pigs, in which the victims were entirely consecrated to the god. In later times the victims were sometimes animals, but cakes made in the shape of animals came to be acceptable sacrifices. The sacrifices were not used as a feast shared by the god and the celebrants of the festival; they were for the god alone. The Diasia was celebrated in an atmosphere of gloom. Zeus Meilichius was a god of purification and, at the same time, an avenging god who must be placated. For in order to purify, the spilled blood that made purification necessary must be avenged. It seems likely that the familiar Zeus assumed the function of a chthonian divinity who is represented by a serpent. Part of the ceremony of purification involved the "fleece of Zeus." When the victim had been sacrificed he who sought purification put his left foot on the fleece, for the skins of victims were thought to have marvelous purifying properties. With the celebration of the Diasia, pollution of the city was removed, the city was cleansed and joy prevailed.

Dibutades (dī-bū′ta-dēz). Greek sculptor of Sicyon, the reputed inventor of relief sculpture.

Dicaearchus (dī-sē-är′kus). Greek geographer, historian, and philosopher of the Peripatetic school. He was born in Sicily but spent most of his life in Greece; fl. c320 B.C. He was a disciple of Aristotle. His *Life of Hellas*, in three books, describes the geography and political condition of Greece, details public and private life, and gives an account of Greek theater, games, and religions. Fragments of this work survive.

Dicaeopolis (dī-sē-op′ō-lis). See **Segesta**.

Dice (dī′sē) or **Dike** (dī′kē). In Greek mythology, one of the Horae, the personification of justice; daughter of Zeus and Themis (*Law*), and sister of Irene (*Peace*) and Eunomia (*Order*).

Dicte (dik′tē). A cave in the mountains of Lassithion, in E Crete. It was one of many caves where, according to legend, Zeus was born. In the Minoan and Archaic eras it was used as a cult site. It has two chambers; one held an altar and was a place for making sacrifices; the other, approached by a stairway, was a place where votive offerings were deposited.

Dictynna (dik-tin′a). A Cretan goddess, identified with Britomartis. She was the protectress of hunters and seafarers. In Sparta she was identified with Artemis; the Aeginetans worshiped her as Aphaea; but the Samians, who built her a temple at Cydonia, in Crete, worshiped her as Dictynna.

Dictys (dik′tis). In Greek mythology, a kind fisherman on the island of Seriphus who discovered the chest in which Danaë and Perseus had been cast on the sea. He rescued them and took them to his house where he and his wife cared for them for many years. His brother Polydectes was king of the island and wished to marry Danaë. She and Dictys fled from him and hid while Perseus was off on his expedition for the head of Medusa. When he returned, Perseus sought and found his mother and Dictys, turned Polydectes to stone, and made Dictys king of the island.

Dictys Cretensis (dik′tis krē-ten′sis). A native of Cnossus, Crete, depicted as a companion of Idomeneus, leader of the Cretans at Troy, asserted to be the author of a diary of the Trojan War, the *Ephemeris Belli Troiani*, claimed to have been discovered during the reign of Nero. The work is fictitious, one of the earliest recorded examples of the literary hoax, and was actually composed in the 2nd or 3rd century A.D. A 4th century A.D. Latin prose translation by one L. Septimius survives. This narrative, with the *De Excidio Troiae* of Dares Phrygius, was one of the chief sources from which the heroic legends of Greece passed into the literature of the Middle Ages. (JJ)

Dido (dī′dō). A daughter of Belus, king of Tyre. In Roman legend, her husband Sychaeus was secretly murdered for his wealth by her brother, Pygmalion, king of Tyre. The ghost of Sychaeus appeared to Dido, told her of the murder, and warned her to flee. She fled to North Africa with some companions. There she was allowed by the natives to purchase as much land as could be encompassed by a bull's hide. By cutting the hide into narrow strips a fabulous amount of land was encompassed. On it Dido built the citadel Byrsa (so-named from the Greek for "hide") around which the city of Carthage grew. When Aeneas was driven to her shores, Venus sent Cupid, in

the guise of Aeneas' son Ascanius, to cause
Dido to fall in love with Aeneas, so that she
would protect and succor him. Dido had,
up until this time, remained faithful to the
memory of Sychaeus, and had rejected many
suitors, including Iarbas, lord of a neighboring country. As a result of the interference
of Venus she now fell passionately and generously in love with Aeneas. She showered
him with gifts and showed him the utmost
generosity and understanding. After about
a year had passed, she suddenly heard that
Aeneas was planning to leave Carthage in
secret. She reproached him, reminding him
of what she had done for him and his
friends, and also pointing out to him that she
had lost her honor, had not even the consolation of having been faithful to the memory
of Sychaeus, and had made many powerful
enemies for love of Aeneas. Aeneas acknowledged that everything she said was true and
declared that if the decision were left to him,
he would certainly prefer to remain with her.
But, he said, he was compelled by the gods
to leave for his destined home in Italy. Dido
was in an agony of despair. When she
offered sacrifices, the water on her altars
turned black, wine changed to blood, and
voices spoke to her from her husband's statue.
She resolved to kill herself, and arranged a
great funeral pyre under the pretext that she
intended to burn relics and an effigy of
Aeneas on it. She duped her sister into helping her with the pyre by telling her a
Massylian sorceress had told her this would
cure her of the love for Aeneas which was
consuming her. When all was in readiness,
she saw Aeneas' ships putting to sea. Dido
sent her attendants to fetch her sister. While
they were gone, she uttered a curse against
the Trojans, and prayed that their people
and hers would be eternal enemies. She then
hurled herself on the sword she had once
given to Aeneas and fell dying in the arms
of her sister, who had just rushed in. Juno
sent Iris from heaven to cut a lock of Dido's
hair representing her life and to relieve Dido
of her agony, and then conduct her to the
Underworld. When Aeneas later visited
Anchises in the Underworld, he saw the
shade of Dido in the region reserved for those
who had died of unhappy love, but when he
called out to her, she turned her back on

him. Dido was also the epithet of the
Phoenician goddess of the moon (Astarte),
who was worshiped as the protecting deity
of the citadel of Carthage. This name was
taken by Elissa of Tyre, who fled from
Phoenicia and founded Carthage, and who
killed herself rather than submit to marriage
with Iarbas. The story of Elissa was the
basis on which Vergil constructed his story
of Dido, outlined above, in the *Aeneid.*

Didymaea (did-i-mē'ä). A festival in honor of
Zeus and Apollo held at Didyma near Miletus
in Asia Minor.

Didymaeum (did-i-mē'um). A temple or
shrine sacred to Zeus and Apollo at Didyma
or Branchidae near Miletus. There was a
sacred way leading to it which had been built
for an earlier temple on the site, and which
was bordered by a series of archaic seated
figures. The later building probably dates
from about 334 B.C. It was dipteral, with
the cella open to the sky.

Didyme (did'i-mē). Ancient name for one of
the Lipari islands, now called **Salina.**

Didymi (did'i-mī). The Greek name of the
sign of the Zodiac whose Latin name is
Gemini, the Twins. (JJ)

Didymus (did'i-mus). [Surnamed **Chalcenterus,** meaning "bowels of brass," because
he was such a tireless worker.] Greek
scholar of the Augustan Age, born in Alexandria in 63 B.C. He spent most of his life
in Rome. He was a prodigious worker and
profound student. Of his many works (4000
according to an estimate by Seneca), the
most important was a commentary on Aristarchus' edition of Homer. He also wrote on
Hesiod, the poets, and the orators, and is
responsible for the most valuable part of the
information in the lexicons and commentaries
of the Byzantines.

Dieneces (dī-ē-nē'sēz). A Spartan in the company of Leonidas at the defence of the pass
of Thermopylae (480 B.C.). According to
Herodotus, he was warned by a Trachinian
that the number of barbarians attacking was
so vast that when they shot their arrows the
face of the sun was darkened. Fearless,
Dieneces replied that this was good news, for
if the barbarians darkened the sun then the
Greeks would be able to fight in the shade.

Dinaric Alps (di-nar'ik alps). [Latin, **Alpae
Dinaricae.**] Mountain ranges in Illyria (now

Yugoslavia), which are a continuation of the main Alpine system. They run parallel to the Adriatic Sea coast.

Dindymene (din-di-mē′nē). [Also: the **Dindymenian Mother.**] Cybele, the Phrygian mother-goddess: so-called from Mount Dindymus in Galatia.

Dindymus (din′di-mus). [Also: **Dindymum.**] A mountain in Phrygia, sacred to Cybele. It was near the realm of Cyzicus, king of the Doliones. When Jason and the Argonauts were driven back to the shores of Cyzicus by storms and, in the darkness, were attacked in the belief that they were pirates, Jason killed Cyzicus, unaware that he was the king from whose hospitable shores he had recently departed. Daylight revealed the tragic mistake but, after proper funeral rites, the Argonauts were prevented from continuing their journey by a howling tempest. Mopsus, the seer, heard a bird singing that only sacrifices to Rhea (Cybele) on Mount Dindymus would calm the storm. The Argonauts went to the mountain and performed propitiatory sacrifices and engaged in dances, as commanded, in which they clashed their shields to drown out the sounds of mourning for Cyzicus. Rhea acknowledged their homage by sending favorable omens: trees suddenly bore fruit, beasts became tame, and a spring gushed forth. The tempest was stilled and the Argonauts could proceed on their journey.

Dine (dī′nē). In ancient geography, a place in Argolis, on the seacoast, where a fountain of fresh water rises out of the sea. The name means "whirlpool." The Argives used to cast bridled horses into this fountain of fresh water as offerings to Poseidon.

Dinias and Dercyllis (din′i-as; dėr-sil′is). Chief characters of a lost Greek novel, usually entitled *The Incredible Things beyond Thule.* Their love story furnishes the plot. According to Photius, who gives an abstract of it, it was written soon after the death of Alexander the Great; others, however, believed it had been written by Antonius Diogenes, who was thought to have lived in Syria c100 A.D.

Dino (dī′nō). One of the Graeae, a daughter of Phorcys and Ceto. See **Graeae.**

Dinocrates or **Deinocrates** (dī-nok′ra-tēz). Ablest of the architects of Alexander the Great; fl. 4th century B.C. He planned the new city of Alexandria, and rebuilt the Artemisium of Ephesus after its destruction by fire. He had a plan, never executed, of making a huge statue of a seated figure of Mount Athos (the mountain, personified, was to have a city in one hand and a basin to catch the rivers in the other).

Dio Chrysostomus (dī′ō kri-sos′tō-mus). [Also: **Chrysostom.**] Greek rhetorician and philosopher; born at Prusa, in Bithynia, c50 A.D. He died at Rome c117 A.D. He traveled widely, partly as a result of banishment due to political difficulties, and partly in obedience to the commands of the oracle at Delphi. He went to Egypt, Rome, the northern reaches of the Roman Empire, and finally, on the accession of his friend Cocceius Nerva, returned to Rome where he ended his days. He was a student of philosophy and an orator. His epithet Chrysostomus, "golden mouth," was a tribute to his powers as a speaker. The style and content of his speeches, 80 of which survive, were greatly admired by the Romans, and he was honored by Nerva and Trajan.

Diocles (dī′ō-klēz). Syracusan popular leader; fl. 5th century B.C. He was the reputed chief author of a code of laws named for him.

Diocles Carystius (ka-ris′ti-us). Greek physician, born at Carystus in Euboea; fl. 4th century B.C.

Diodorus (dī′′ō-dō′rus). [Surnamed **Siculus,** meaning "of Sicily."] Greek historian, born in Agyrium in Sicily, and active in the time of Caesar and Augustus. He traveled widely in Europe and Asia, and after 30 years of travel and study, and using the works of ancient writers that were available to him in Rome, he wrote a Universal History in 40 books. This was a history of the known world from the earliest times to his own era. The first six books covered the ancient history, religion, and mythology of the Egyptians, Asians of Western Asia, North Africans, and Greeks. In them he drew generously and uncritically from ancient authorities to describe the people, geography, and legends of the regions he studied. Although he apparently accepted the general beliefs of his time as to the gods, their powers, and their stories, wherever possible (and sometimes when it was impossible), he attempted to give a rationalistic explanation to the stories of mythology which he could, by straining, link with natural phenomena. Books VII through XVII covered the period from the Trojan War to the death of Alexander the Great. The last 23 books brought his history to Caesar's wars in Gaul. Of the 40 books, books I–V and XI–XX survive intact, and there are fragments, some quite large, of the others. Despite many imperfections, errors, and a prosaic and dull approach, particularly with regard to the mythology, his work is valuable as an important source (to some extent for the authorities he quotes), for the history of the ancient world, particularly for the ancient history of Sicily.

Diogenes (dī-oj′ē-nēz). Greek Cynic philosopher, famous for his eccentricities. He was born at Sinope in Asia Minor, c400 B.C., and died at Corinth, c325 B.C. He emigrated to Athens in his youth, where, according to one tradition, he became the pupil of Antisthenes, and lived, according to Seneca, in a tub. While on a voyage from Athens to Aegina, he was captured by pirates who exposed him for sale on the slave market in Crete. When asked what business he understood, he replied, "How to command men," and requested to be sold to some one in need of a master. He was purchased by Xeniades, a wealthy citizen of Corinth, who restored him to liberty, and in whose house he passed his old age. At Corinth he was, according to tradition, visited by Alexander the Great. Alexander inquired whether he could oblige him in any way. "Yes," replied Diogenes, "stand from between me and the sun." Diogenes taught and believed in an extreme of asceticism as a means of attaining truth and good. As a result he was looked down upon and in turn rejected his contemporaries. The story, true or not, of his search with a lighted lamp in broad daylight (as he said, "for an honest man"), vividly illustrates this.

Diogenes of Apollonia (ap-o-lō′ni-a). Greek natural philosopher, born at Apollonia, Crete; fl. in the 5th century B.C. According to tradition, he was a pupil of Anaximenes.

Diomedes (dī-ō-mē′dēz). In Greek legend, the "high-souled" son of Tydeus and Deïpyle. He was a king in Argos and was one of the Epigoni—the sons of the Seven against Thebes—who successfully attacked Thebes and avenged their fathers. In fulfillment of the oath he had taken as an ardent suitor of

Helen—to protect whomever she should choose as a husband—he rallied to Menelaus when Helen was carried off by Paris. In the war which followed he was one of Agamemnon's most loyal supporters. He went with Sthenelus and Euryalus to Troy as the commander of a great fleet of 80 ships carrying warriors from Argos, Tiryns, Hermione, Asine, Troezen, Eionae, Epidaurus, Aegina, and Mases. He was the darling of Athena, and next to Achilles was the mightiest of the Greek heroes. To his own reckless courage the goddess added unparalleled strength, marvelous skill at arms, and unfailing valor. He was fearless and at times held off the Trojans single-handed. When he was wounded by Pandarus, Athena saved his life and restored him. Later she guided the spear with which he killed Pandarus. He felled Aeneas with a huge stone and would have killed him, but Aphrodite came and saved her son. Undaunted by the interference of a goddess, Diomedes pursued her, wounded her, and drove her from the field. Athena now encouraged him to attack Ares. He caught the spear which Ares hurled at him and in his turn turned on Ares, wounded him and forced the god of war to quit the field. In addition to attacking the gods, he killed many Trojans. In the savage fighting he came face to face with Glaucus, the companion of the Lycian king Sarpedon. As they squared off to fight, each boasted of his ancestry and prowess, and thus it was that they discovered that their grandfathers had been friends. They put down their weapons and swore an oath of friendship. To bind the oath, they exchanged arms. In this Diomedes got by far the better bargain. He gave Glaucus his bronze armor. Glaucus graciously, but foolishly, handed over his own armor of pure gold. Several times when the war went against the Greeks, Agamemnon proposed that they give up the struggle and go home. This was a purely psychological gambit. Agamemnon knew he could count on the fearless Diomedes to regard such a suggestion as a personal insult and to rally the Greeks to fight harder than ever. Diomedes was one of those who accepted Hector's challenge to a duel, but he was eliminated in the drawing of the lots. He rescued Nestor from Hector's attack and was prevented from pursuing

Hector only by the thunderbolt of Zeus. He accused Agamemnon of cowardice when the latter, believing the gods favored the Trojans, wanted to leave Troy, and volunteered to go with Odysseus as a spy on the Trojan camp. On this expedition they captured and killed Dolon, a Trojan spy, raided the Trojan camp and slew Rhesus, a king of Thrace and an ally of Troy, captured his marvelous horses, and returned safely to the Greek camp. This patrol with Odysseus was one of many. He and Odysseus went to Lemnos to fetch Philoctetes, the owner of the arrows of Heracles, when it was learned that Troy could not be taken without them. Accompanied by Phoenix, they next went to Scyrus and successfully persuaded Neoptolemus, son of Achilles, to join the Greeks at Troy. The

DIOMEDES CARRYING OFF THE PALLADIUM
FROM TROY
From a coin of Argos, 4th century B.C.
Museum of Fine Arts, Boston

last mission was to steal from the citadel of Troy the Palladium, which guarded Troy as long as it remained in the city. In rags and tatters they made their way to the walls of the city. Diomedes, according to some ac-

counts, climbed on Odysseus' shoulders but refused to pull Odysseus up after him. He scaled the wall and entered the city alone, found and stole the Palladium, and rejoined Odysseus at the wall. As they were returning, Diomedes, who was carrying the Palladium ahead of Odysseus, caught a glint of moonlight reflected from Odysseus' naked sword. He whirled around in time to see Odysseus with his sword raised ready to strike him. Odysseus had planned to murder Diomedes so that he could return alone and reap the glory of having stolen the Palladium. Diomedes now laid about Odysseus' flanks and sides with the flat of his sword. Odysseus had no choice but to run before him, howling miserably from the whacks of Diomedes' sword, and in this undignified manner he was driven back into the Greek camp. From this incident arises the expression "Diomedes' compulsion"—to do something because necessity leaves no choice. Some say Diomedes, cousin of Thersites, was the only one who mourned him when he was slain by Achilles for mocking the latter as he grieved over the death of Penthesilea. Diomedes in a rage seized Penthesilea's body by the foot, dragged it to the river, and hurled it in. Her body was rescued and restored to the Trojans for burial. He was one of those who entered Troy in the Wooden Horse, and after the sack of the city, was according to some accounts, one of the few who had a prosperous voyage home to Greece. Others say Aphrodite caused him to be shipwrecked on the coasts of Lycia, and that he was saved from being sacrificed by the king only through the good offices of the king's daughter, who helped him to escape. Arrived in Argos he found that his wife, Aegiale, had been unfaithful to him, largely owing to false reports spread by Nauplius. She and her lover drove him out of his kingdom. He went to Corinth, and then to Calydon and restored his grandfather, Oeneus, to his throne. Ultimately he sailed to Italy and settled in Daunia. He married Euippe, daughter of King Daunus and founded many cities, among them Brundisium. The Latins asked his help in their war against Aeneas, who had also come to Italy. Diomedes cited the suffering the Greeks had endured during and after the Trojan War, and said he had

fat, fāte, fär, fãre, errạnt; net, mē, hėr ardẹnt; pin, pīne; not, nōte, mȯve, nôr,

had enough of fighting Trojans. As he refused to lend his aid to the Latins, he advised them, out of his own experience, to make peace with Aeneas and his Trojan followers. According to some accounts, Diomedes was murdered by King Daunus, who had become jealous of the wealth and power he had acquired in Italy, and he was secretly buried on the Diomedan Islands. Others say he was divinely spirited away, and that his followers were transformed into gentle birds which nest on these islands. The golden armor that he got from Glaucus was preserved by the priests of Athena in Apulia, and he was worshiped as a god in southern Italy and in the region around Venice.

Diomedes. In Greek mythology, a son of Cyrene and Ares. He was a king in Thrace and the owner of fierce mares which he fed on the flesh of human beings. Heracles captured and tamed the mares, as one of his labors for Eurystheus, by feeding them the flesh of their master. He then harnessed them to a chariot, although they had never been broken to the bridle, and drove them over the mountains to Eurystheus. He consecrated them to Hera and set them free. They were ultimately torn to pieces by wild beasts on Mount Olympus.

Dion (dī'on). Syracusan philosopher and statesman; born at Syracuse, c408 B.C.; assassinated there, 354 B.C. His sister Aristomache was one of two wives whom Dionysius the Elder, tyrant of Syracuse, married at the same time. Ultimately, Dion married Arete, the daughter of Dionysius and Aristomache. From his connection with Dionysius and because of his own wisdom and capacity, he gained an influential role in Syracusan affairs, and was one of very few who dared speak freely to Dionysius. Dionysius the Younger succeeded his father, and Dion became one of his counselors. Dion, a gifted and ardent disciple of Plato, earnestly wished Dionysius the Younger to put into practice some of Plato's theories of government. The young tyrant had had no education, because his father feared that if he mingled with intelligent and capable men, he might seek to overthrow him and seize the tyranny. Dion now encouraged him to seek the company of philosophers; he pointed out the magnificence in which the young ruler lived and advised him to furnish "the royal palace of his soul" as richly as he had furnished the palace of his body. He tried to instill in him the idea that with a just government his people would obey him out of respect and admiration rather than give him the sullen obedience they now rendered through fear. Dionysius was all enthusiasm for learning, and Plato was sent for. He arrived in Syracuse in 367 B.C. and was warmly welcomed, and a wave of enthusiasm for philosophy and letters swept Syracuse. It did not last long. Dion's influence was resented and feared by those who profited from the tyranny. They set all manner of criticisms of Dion afloat and declared that his aim was to depose Dionysius, seize power himself, and secure the succession for his sister's children. Dionysius, a weak and profligate man, believed the enemies of Dion, and when a letter Dion had written to the Carthaginians fell into his hands his suspicions against Dion seemed to be confirmed. By a trick he led Dion to the shore, accused him of treachery, commanded him to board a small boat waiting there, and ordered the crew to set Dion ashore in Italy. However, the Syracusans were so aroused by the departure of Dion that Dionysius was frightened and denied he had exiled him. He loaded two ships with the goods and treasure of Dion and sent them to him. After a time, Plato left Syracuse also, with a promise from Dionysius that he would recall Dion. Dion went to Athens and joined Plato. He visited cities throughout Greece and was widely welcomed, the Spartans even going so far as to make him a citizen. Dionysius made no attempt to recall him. On the contrary, he discontinued sending him the revenues from his estates and forced Dion's wife to marry one of his friends. News came to Dion from Syracuse that the people were so discontented that they would overthrow Dionysius if Dion returned. He decided to do so. He collected a small force of Greek mercenaries on the island of Zacynthus, made a splendid sacrifice to Apollo, gave a feast, and was ready to depart. On the eve of departure there was an eclipse of the moon which frightened his soldiers, but seers said it betokened the eclipse of Dionysius. Another omen, swarms of bees that settled on the prows of the ships, was not publicly interpreted for the soothsayers feared it ·meant Dion's efforts would first prosper and then fail. Yet there were other definitely favorable signs: an eagle seized a spear, flew up with it, and then dropped it into the sea; sea water became sweet and drinkable for a whole day. The forces of Dion landed at Minoa in Sicily and marched toward Syracuse. Dionysius was away from the city, and letters warning him of the approach of Dion with an army failed to reach him. Dion, whose forces were increased by volunteers along the way, entered Syracuse without a struggle (357 B.C.), and was welcomed with joy. A week later, Dionysius sailed into the harbor, and though envoys were treating with Dion, he treacherously attacked the city. Dion rallied the defenders and won a victory, but not before Dionysius had gained the citadel where he took refuge. Dion was master of the city, but his aloof manner and determination to teach the Syracusans how to govern themselves under his direction offended them. The fickle people now appointed Heraclides as admiral of the fleet, but when Dion rebuked them for infringing the supreme power they had already give him, they withdrew the appointment. Dion himself then appointed Heraclides admiral, though his friends warned that Heraclides was not a friend to him. Philistus, a Syracusan exile, returned with a fleet to help Dionysius, who was under siege in the citadel, but Philistus was defeated and slain. Dionysius escaped through Heraclides' fleet and the people rose up in anger against Heraclides, but he diverted them by criticizing Dion, claiming that Dion's mercenaries got the best rewards and rousing the people against the foreign soldiers. He also suggested a land reform and proposed that the Syracusans choose new generals. The foolish Syracusans swung over to his side and turned against Dion. All sorts of unfavorable omens occurred the day the new generals were to be chosen, but they were ignored. Twenty-five new generals were selected, among them Heraclides, and a threatening crowd sought to drive Dion and his mercenaries out of the city. The Greek mercenaries would have attacked the crowd but Dion would not turn against his own city. Instead, his loyal mercenaries repelled the hostile Syracusans with scowls and conducted

him safely to Leontini, where they and he were welcomed (356 B.C.). In a short time, Dionysius sent forces to Syracuse that took the city with great slaughter. Envoys were hurriedly sent to Dion in Leontini, begging him to come and save the city. Dion, according to Plutarch, made a moving speech to his mercenaries, telling them he meant to return to Syracuse himself, but would understand if they did not wish to accompany him. "If, however, in your displeasure at the Syracusans, you shall leave them to their fate, at least for your former bravery and zeal in my behalf may you obtain a worthy reward from the gods, and may you think of Dion as one who abandoned neither you when you were wronged, nor, afterwards, his fellow citizens when they were in distress." The mercenaries leaped to their feet and shouted for him to lead them back. When the enemy captain learned that Dion was coming to the relief of the city, he sacked it and put it to the torch. Dion found it in flames. With his mercenaries he overcame the forces of Dionysius, who again took refuge in the citadel, and put out the fires in the city. The son of Dionysius in the citadel was compelled to surrender, and was permitted to sail away. Dion was reunited with his wife and his sister, who had been held in the fortress ever since he returned from Greece. All the Syracusans, with wildest rejoicing, went down to the harbor to witness the departure of the son of Dionysius. Dion was now at the height of his power and prestige. He rewarded his friends, allies, and mercenaries, but continued to live simply and modestly himself. His friend Plato wrote that the eyes of the world were on him. But Dion did not propose to restore a democracy; he favored a limited monarchy. However, he was, in fact, a new tyrant of Syracuse. He brought in Corinthians to advise him and by so doing aroused resentment among the Syracusans. Once again Heraclides stirred up discontent and plotted against him. This time Dion, who had always forgiven him though he was a known enemy, permitted his friends, who had been urging it for a long time, to go to the house of Heraclides and slay him. Dion gave him a splendid funeral and followed his body to the grave, but the murder of Heraclides oppressed him;

he knew it was a stain on his honor. After this, a heavier blow fell. His dear friend, the Athenian Callippus, who had come to Syracuse with him, plotted to seize control. Dion's friends warned him, but he no longer wanted to struggle for the people of Syracuse or himself. He was ready to die, he said, if it had become necessary for him to live on his guard not only against his enemies, but even against his friends. Omens of death had already come to him. As he was sitting in his house, he saw a woman of great height, dressed like and resembling one of the Furies, and sweeping his courtyard with a broom; a few days later, his son threw himself from the roof in a fit of anger and was killed. Nevertheless, his friends, and especially his wife Arete and his sister Aristomache, tried to protect him. Callippus was charged with a plot but swore a most sacred oath that he was innocent. He then committed the greatest impiety of all. As Dion was sitting among friends, during the festival of the Coreia, in honor of the goddess in whose name Callippus had sworn his oath, Callippus attacked him and killed him (354 B.C.).

Dione (dī-ō′nē). In early Greek mythology, the consort of Zeus; his feminine counterpart as sky-deity, supplanted by Hera. In later mythological genealogy, she is a female Titan, daughter of Oceanus and Tethys. In the *Iliad*, she is named as the mother of Aphrodite, who comforted Aphrodite when the latter was attacked and wounded by Diomedes in the Trojan War. Dione foretold the death of Diomedes for waging war against immortals.

Dionysia (dī-ō-nish′a). Ancient Greek festivals in honor of Dionysus, a fertility god. Those held at Athens were the chief ones, and are usually considered to have been four in number: the Lesser or Rural Dionysia, the Lenaea, the Anthesteria, and the Greater or City Dionysia. The Anthesteria appears to be an older festival which was overlaid by a festival of Dionysus centered about the Lenaeum, or sanctuary of Dionysus in the marshes, whose shrine was opened on only one day in the year. The date of this festival was the 11th–13th of Anthesterion (about March 2–4). The Lesser Dionysia were wine-feasts of very early origin, a solstice celebration held throughout the Attic demes

between the 9th and 11th of Poseideon (about Dec. 19–22), accompanied by drinking, boisterous processions, and dramatic performances, of which those at the Piraeus had the chief reputation. The Greater Dionysia were celebrated at Athens, probably the 9th–13th of Elaphebolion (about March 28–April 2), a spring equinox observance. This, the best known of the festivals of Dionysus, was the occasion on which the Greek tragedies were presented at Athens. See **Dionysus.**

Dionysius (dī-ō-nish′i-us, -nish′us). [Surnamed **the Elder.**] Tyrant of Syracuse, born c430 B.C.; died at Syracuse, 367 B.C. He was of obscure birth and had served as a clerk in a government office. In the siege of Acragas (406 B.C.), he fought bravely with the Syracusans who went to the relief of the city, was wounded, and left for dead on the field. His experience convinced him that the democratic government of Syracuse was so weak that a strong man could easily take control. He resolved to be that strong man. In an assembly he rose and denounced the generals of Syracuse who had failed to relieve Acragas. His views coincided with those of the populace. The generals were removed and a new board of generals, of which he was a member, was named. He soon discredited his fellow generals on the new board; they were deposed and he was made sole general (405 B.C.). He caused a rumor to be spread that an attempt had been made on his life, demanded and was permitted a personal bodyguard. Through the fear of the Syracusans of Carthage they had allowed Dionysius to make himself tyrant of Syracuse, although he kept the outward forms of democracy.

He led a force to the relief of Gela, besieged by the Carthaginians, but through what was probably treachery on his part, an attack on the Carthaginian camp ended in failure. Rather than attempt to raise the siege he decided to remove the people of Gela; they abandoned their city at night. At Camarina he made the same decision, although Camarina had not even been attacked. His Italian allies withdrew in disgust. Some Syracusan horsemen thought he was a traitor, rode to his house, plundered it, and attacked his wife. Dionysius hurried to Syracuse, entered the city at night by burning the gate, and overcame his opponents. It seems that his activities in the case of Gela and Camarina were deliberate—he did not want the annihilation of Carthage in Sicily, for as long as Carthage presented a danger there was justification of his dictatorial power. In 404 B.C. he made a treaty with Himilco, the Carthaginian general, by which each side was to keep, in general, what it held at the time, but the significant clause of the treaty, from the standpoint of Dionysius, was that Carthage guaranteed his power in Syracuse.

He now set to work to fortify Syracuse, a city on an island. But his rule was not popular or secure. In a war against Herbessus the army mutinied. Dionysius withdrew to his fortified island and suffered siege by his own people (403 B.C.), who were assisted by forces from Rhegium and Messina. He called a council of his followers in the fortress. Some advised him to flee, others to stay; one Heloris remarked that "Sovereign power is a fair winding-sheet." Dionysius, as he did so often, resorted to stratagem. He asked the besiegers to let him depart from Syracuse with his possessions. They agreed, and so implicitly trusted him that they sent away some of their forces and relaxed the siege. Meantime, Dionysius sent a secret call for assistance to the Campanian mercenaries of Carthage. They came, in accordance with the treaty of Himilco guaranteeing his power. When they arrived they competely routed the rebels and Dionysius reestablished his control. He sold the inhabitants of the Greek cities of Naxos and Catana as slaves, gave Catana to Campanian mercenaries, and razed Naxos. Next he won back Leontini, which had been made independent by his treaty with Himilco. This left Sicily divided between Greek cities under control of Dionysius, and Carthaginian cities, except for Messina which remained independent. He expanded the fortifications of Syracuse, reorganized his army, introduced the catapult as an engine of siege warfare, and strengthened his fleet by building ships with five banks of oars. Having made such preparations, he was ready to move against the Carthaginians in Sicily. Gela, Camarina, Acragas, and Eryx gave him their allegiance. He besieged (398 B.C.) the Carthaginian city

of Motya, a fortified island city, and after a tremendous effort and despite heroic resistance, he reduced and took it. This was the first Phoenician town taken by the Greeks.

Himilco was sent from Carthage to protect the Punic cities. He took Eryx by treason and recaptured Motya. Dionysius did not oppose him. He withdrew to Syracuse and sent a fleet, under command of his brother Leptines, to attack the Carthaginian fleet at Catana (396 B.C.). He observed the defeat of the fleet from the shore and again retreated to Syracuse, although his men were eager to stand and fight. The Carthaginians sailed into the harbor, their army disembarked and encamped in the marsh nearby, and laid siege to Syracuse. During the 11-month siege, discontent in the city was great. Outside, the army of Himilco was attacked by pestilence and greatly weakened. Dionysius chose the moment to counterattack. He ordered his fleet against the Carthaginian ships and himself led a land force out of the city. His attack was a great success; the Carthaginian fleet was burned, the land forces of Dionysius were victorious. The Carthaginians were routed, but Dionysius, on receipt of 300 talents, treacherously allowed Himilco to escape with 40 triremes. Himilco's mercenaries, deserted by their commander, were enslaved or slaughtered. Again, Dionysius was unwilling, for the sake of his own power, to allow the annihilation of Carthage in Sicily.

Following the victory, he extended his power in Sicily. In 392 B.C. the Carthaginians, under the command of Mago, returned, and were again defeated. They sued for peace. By the terms of the peace Syracuse became the acknowledged master of all the Greek communities of Sicily. The city of Tauromenium, once unsuccessfully besieged by Dionysius, was awarded to him, and he now began to expand his power on the mainland of Italy. Rhegium was a personal as well as a political enemy, for when he asked for a maiden of Rhegium for a wife he was told that the only maiden of Rhegium he could have was the hangman's daughter; Rhegium had sent assistance to the rebels who besieged Dionysius in his own city; and Rhegium controlled the strait between Sicily and Italy. He defeated the Italians at Elleporus (388

fat, fāte, fär, fãre, errạnt; net, mē, hér ardẹnt; pin, pīne; not, nōte, mŏve, nôr,

B.C.), and instead of killing his captives or selling them as slaves or even demanding ransom, he let them all go free. Thus he won the gratitude and friendship of all the Italian towns from which they came, and also isolated Rhegium, which he now (386 B.C.) besieged and captured. He scourged the defeated commander through his army and then drowned him, with all his relatives. With the capture of Rhegium he controlled both sides of the strait (he had earlier restored Messina), and in 379 B.C. he captured Croton. Continuing his expansion, he founded commercial settlements along the Adriatic coast up to what is now Venice. The Carthaginians returned in 379 B.C., Dionysius was defeated and forced to accept a humiliating peace. In 368 B.C. he again marched against the Punic cities, but failed to take Lilybaeum and died before peace could be concluded.

The tyranny of Dionysius lasted 38 years. It was maintained by force against all attempts to depose him and restore the Republic. He was harsh and cruel to his political enemies, but on the whole did not indulge in vengeance and murder for personal reasons. He had great capacity and energy, and above all, his ability to protect Syracuse from its enemies abroad continually kept his enemies at home off balance. Vast sums were needed to carry on his wars. He raised them by levying heavy taxes and by plundering the temples of their treasures. He even planned a raid on the holiest of Greek sanctuaries, Delphi, but was unable to put his plan into execution. He sent aid to Sparta several times, and was in turn aided by the Spartans.

Dionysius' first wife, abused by the Syracusans who had attempted to seize his power, killed herself in shame at her dishonor. He then married, so it is said, two wives at the same time, to whom he was equally devoted. One was a Locrian and bore his eldest son, Dionysius the Younger. The other was Aristomache, sister of Dion, one of his most trusted advisers. Dionysius accused the mother of his Locrian wife of drugging Aristomache so that she would not bear children and had her killed. Aristomache later had children, one of whom, Arete, was given in marriage to her brother Dion. Busy as

he was in securing his own power, protecting Syracuse from Carthage and enlarging its sphere of influence, Dionysius found time to encourage letters. In 388 B.C. Dion invited Plato to Syracuse and became one of his most ardent disciples. He was anxious to have Dionysius hear the philosopher, in the hope that the tyrant might be imbued with some of his theories of a government based on law and justice. He took Dionysius to hear Plato lecture. That day the philosopher discoursed on the nature of tyrants. He branded them as timid men, who ruled with iron hands out of fear. He might have been speaking of Dionysius personally, for the tyrant was frighteningly aware of the hatred he had roused against himself among his own people. He was so afraid of assassination he would not allow a barber to cut his hair, but had it singed with live coals. No one was permitted to come before him who had not first taken off his clothes in an antechamber and put on robes supplied by the tyrant in which it would be impossible to conceal a weapon. On one occasion, his brother Leptines was describing some plans to him. To clarify his explanation he seized a spear and drew the plans in the sand. Dionysius had the man from whom the spear was borrowed slain for having brought a weapon into his presence. Once he dreamed a certain man had attempted to kill him. The next day he had the man put to death for his dream convinced him that this man would make an attempt on his life. He dared not trust his own children, and had his eldest son and heir, Dionysius the Younger, brought up in relative ignorance and isolation from public affairs, lest if he associated with intelligent men he try to overthrow his father. Nevertheless, to hear Plato discourse on the timidity of tyrants enraged him, and shortly thereafter Plato left Syracuse. Dionysius gave orders to the captain of the ship on which he sailed to kill Plato if it was possible to do so quietly; if not, to sell him into slavery, for, said Dionysius, Plato claimed a just man was blessed, and since he himself was just he would be happy even in slavery. The incident did not disturb Dion's relationship with Dionysius, and the latter continued to encourage letters and to work as a dramatic poet himself. He had several times sent his tragedies to compete in the Dionysia at Athens, and had won third and second prizes. In a later time, his son Dionysius the Younger met Philip of Macedon at a banquet in Corinth. Philip mockingly asked him when his father had found time to write the tragedies and poems he left behind. Dionysius the Younger answered, "When thou and I and all those whom men call happy are busy at the bowl." But Dionysius was not satisfied with second and third prizes. In 367 B.C., after his failure to take Lilybaeum from the Carthaginians, he learned that his tragedy, *Ransom of Hector,* had won first prize at the Lenaea in Athens. The news more than consoled him for his military failure. In his delight he celebrated mightily. He drank too much wine and was taken with a fever. The soporific drink he was given to calm him put him to sleep forever. Under the tyranny of Dionysius Syracuse became the leading state in Europe; his own power and influence are said to have exceeded those of any other Greek before Alexander the Great. Nevertheless, the "adamantine bonds" with which he boasted he had secured his power were loosened within a generation.

Dionysius. [Surnamed **the Younger.**] Tyrant of Syracuse, born c395 B.C.; died, probably at Corinth, after 343 B.C. He was the eldest son of Dionysius the Elder and his Locrian wife, Doris. His father deliberately denied him an education through the fear that if Dionysius mingled with intelligent and capable men he would attempt to seize the tyranny. Instead, Dionysius the Younger was kept in virtual isolation from public affairs, and occupied himself by making little wooden wagons, chairs, and tables, and in revelry with his friends. On the death of his father (367 B.C.), Dionysius the Younger became tyrant of Syracuse with no preparation for governing, but with a highly developed taste for debauchery and extravagant living. Dion, the adviser and brother-in-law of his father, now became adviser to the son. Dion was an ardent follower of the philosopher Plato. He hoped that with an education in philosophy Dionysius the Younger would become a wise and just ruler, that the tyranny might be converted into a benevolent monarchy under a constitution along the lines proposed by Plato in the *Republic.* Dion was not an advocate of democracy; rather he hoped for a state that would prosper under a philosopher-king. He urged on the young tyrant the pursuit of knowledge and prevailed on him to send for Plato. The philosopher was reluctant to come, for his experiences in Syracuse under Dionysius the Elder had been unfortunate, but he admitted that he must not refuse the chance to put his theories to the test and sailed to Syracuse. Dionysius welcomed him warmly, and flung himself into the task of becoming a philosopher. To prepare him to become a philosopher-king, Plato insisted on a solid foundation of scientific study and set Dionysius to studying geometry. Soon the whole court of Syracuse was feverishly engaged in drawing diagrams on the sand, which served as a blackboard. But the mastery of geometry was slow and difficult. Dionysius soon tired of it; he was weak, impressionable, and easily swayed by those about him. Those who resented and feared the influence of Dion and Plato now brought their influence to bear. They flattered Dionysius, pandered to his extravagant tastes, and at last openly accused Dion of plotting against him. A letter Dion had written to the Carthaginians concerning negotiations between them and Syracuse was intercepted. Dionysius seized on it as evidence of treachery, and sent Dion away from Syracuse (366 B.C.). Frightened by the anger this roused in the Syracusans and by the threat of revolt, he sent Dion's treasure after him, declared he had not exiled him, and sent him the revenues from his estates at regular intervals. Dion went to Greece, where he traveled widely. Dionysius kept Plato in Syracuse, and became passionately attached to him, and jealously demanded to be the most loved and admired of his disciples. However, his mental equipment was inadequate, his will to discipline himself with work flickered, and his appetite for pleasure never faltered. Plato realized that Dionysius would never become the instrument to bring the ideal state into being. Having secured a promise from Dionysius that he would recall Dion, he returned to Athens. Dionysius made no attempt to recall Dion. Instead, when he learned how popular his former adviser was with the Greeks in the homeland he became fearful of him, lest he return and seize power

fat, fāte, fär, fāre, errạnt; net, mē, hėr ardẹnt; pin, pīne; not, nōte, mȯve, nôr,

in Syracuse. He stopped sending the revenues of his estates to him and compelled his wife, his own half-sister, to marry one of his friends. He sent for Plato again, promising that he would show mercy to Dion if Plato returned, otherwise he would not. Whether it was from friendship for Dion or a lingering hope that he might influence Dionysius, Plato returned to Syracuse (361 B.C.). When he arrived, Dionysius, under the pretext of giving him an honor guard, kept him under virtual arrest for a time, then allowed him to return to Athens.

Syracuse was in a state of great unrest under the harsh, extravagant, and unpredictable rule of Dionysius. Dion returned with an army of Peloponnesian mercenaries and led a revolt against him. Dionysius was out of Syracuse when Dion arrived, and the city was taken without a struggle. A week later Dionysius sailed into the harbor with a fleet and attacked. He was defeated, but not before he had won the citadel of Syracuse, which was a fortified island guarding the city. Here he took refuge with many soliders, much material, and with the wife and sister of Dion as his captives. When he found he could not raise the siege, he left command of the citadel to his son and escaped through the Syracusan fleet. He went to his mother's home (356 B.C.), in Locri, ruled it with an iron hand, and indulged his taste for profligacy. The hatred of the Locrians was so intense that when Dionysius at last left their city, abandoning his wife and children to the care of a small garrison, the Locrians seized them, outraged them in the streets, and slew them. They chopped up the bones of their victims, as ghosts could not rise from pulverized bones to haunt them, and served their flesh to the people of Locri, compelling all to taste of it on pain of being put under a terrible curse. The ashes of their bones were cast into the sea, along with any remains of their diced flesh. This occurred when Dionysius, after ten years of exile, returned to Syracuse (346 B.C.) and reëstablished himself as tyrant. Shortly after his return Hicetas, tyrant of Leontini, who had made a treacherous agreement with the Carthaginians, besieged him in Syracuse. The city was in despair. Carthaginian ships were in the harbor, the forces of Hicetas were in the city, and Dionysius had shut himself up in the island citadel. Corinth, the mother city of Syracuse, sent a force under Timoleon to relieve Syracuse. Dionysius sent him a message offering to surrender to him. Timoleon sent a small force into the city in secret and took him off the citadel and passed him in safety through the encircling enemies. All the material Dionysius had stored in the citadel and 2000 soldiers fell to Timoleon. Dionysius sailed off to Corinth (343 B.C.) with his personal treasure. There he lived aimlessly, occasionally mingling with the great. On one occasion he was asked what was the cause of the quarrel between him and Plato. He answered that the worst evil of a tyranny was that no one spoke the truth to a tyrant, and this cost him the good will of Plato. When he had exhausted his treasure, he passed the rest of his life as a mendicant priest of Cybele.

Dionysius of Halicarnassus (hal″i-kär-nas′us). Greek rhetorician and historian, born at Halicarnassus in Caria, and died at Rome in 8 B.C. He went to Rome in the time of Cicero and there became a profound student of the Roman language and literature, particularly the historical literature of the Romans. He wrote a history of Rome (*Archaeologia*) from its mythological beginnings to the time of the Punic Wars, parts of which are extant. In this work, as the Scottish classicist Richard Jebb has pointed out, Dionysius "aimed at writing an *Introduction* to Polybius. He maintains, on fanciful grounds, that the Romans, who deserve to rule the world, are not 'barbarians,' but are of Greek descent." Although the work was intended to glorify the Romans to their Greek subjects, it was soundly based on ancient authorities and provides a valuable source of early Roman history. He was a teacher of rhetoric and wrote on that subject, including *On the Arrangement of Words*. He also wrote critical works on the Greek classics, some of which were cast in the form of letters to prominent Romans. Since his main interest was in style, all his criticisms of Plato, Isocrates, Isaeus, and others, are based on style as the criterion. As a rhetorician his influence was important in the development of prose style.

Dionysius Thrax (thraks). ["The Thracian."] Greek grammarian, born at Alexandria, in

Egypt, and active c100 B.C. He studied at Alexandria, taught there and at Rhodes and Rome, and wrote *The Art of Grammar*, the first written study of that subject in Greek. This work, which has come down to us, probably with later alterations and additions, is not exhaustive, but Dionysius' approach and method greatly influenced later grammarians. He is known also to have written commentaries on the works of ancient writers.

Dionysus (dī-ọ-nī′sus). God of the vine, and youngest of the Olympian gods. He was the son of Zeus and Semele, and the only god to have a mortal for a parent. Zeus fell in love with Semele, a daughter of Cadmus, and the sister of Ino, Agave, and Autonoë. He visited her in mortal guise, although he assured her that he was the god Zeus. A few months before it was time for her child to be born, Semele, inspired thereto by jealous Hera who had taken the guise of Semele's nurse for the purpose, pleaded with Zeus to appear to her in the same majesty he showed to Hera, and thus prove to her that her lover was really a god. Zeus tried to persuade her to ask any other boon, but Semele insisted this was the only boon she craved. Since he had sworn by the Styx, the most sacred of oaths, that he would grant whatever she asked, Zeus appeared to her in blazing majesty, armed with the awful thunderbolts. Mortal Semele

ZEUS DRAWING DIONYSUS FROM HIS THIGH
IN THE PRESENCE OF HERMES
Red-figured Attic lecythus, c450 B.C.
Museum of Fine Arts, Boston

could not stand the divine fire and was burned to ashes, but Zeus snatched her unborn child from her womb and sewed it up in his thigh. When the child reached maturity, he was born from the thigh of Zeus. Because he had been taken from his mother and also from Zeus, Dionysus was sometimes called the child of "the double door," or given the epithet "Twice-born." But some say this epithet came from another circumstance. They say he was born with a horn growing from his head, around which serpents twined, and that Hera commanded the Titans to seize him. This they did, although he transformed himself into various shapes to escape, and tore him to pieces. His grandmother Rhea gathered up the fragments of his body, which the Titans had boiled in a cauldron, and restored him to life. (A similar story is told of Zagreus, with whom Dionysus is identified.) Others say, to save his son from Hera, who always sought to destroy her rival's child, Zeus gave him to the nymphs Philia, Coronis, and Clide, to rear on the isle of Naxos. Still others say Zeus gave him to Hermes, with orders to convey him to Ino and her husband Athamas in Thebes. Ino disguised him as a girl and reared him in secret. But Hera unmasked the secret and drove Ino and Athamas mad. Zeus saved Ino for her kindess to Dionysus by transforming her into the sea-goddess Leucothea. To protect Dionysus from the wrath of Hera, Zeus now transformed him into a kid and Hermes transported him to the nymphs of Nysa, who cared for him. Some say these nymphs were afterward placed among the stars as the Hyades, to reward them, and that these stars rise in the rainy season that makes the vine grow. Nysa has never been definitely located: Asia, Ethiopia, Libya, Egypt, and Mount Helicon in Greece, as well as other places where the vine is cultivated, have all been named as the site which held the cave of Nysa where Dionysus was nurtured. The name Dionysus has been fancifully interpreted as a combination of Zeus (Dio) and Nysa. Silenus became the tutor of the young god, taught him the secrets of nature, and helped him to discover wine, a two-sided gift to man, for it could be the source of freedom and joyousness, or of weakness and brutality. The attributes of wine were also embodied in

fat, fāte, fär, fãre, errant; net, mē, hėr ardent; pin, pīne; not, nōte, mŏve, nôr,

the god, who could be merry and gentle or ruthless and powerful. He traveled about the earth teaching men the mysteries of his worship and how to cultivate the vine. Those who welcomed him received the gift of the vine; those who resisted him were visited with terrible punishments. According to tradition, Oeneus of Calydon was the first mortal to whom he gave the vine, Icarius of Attica was the first mortal to discover wine, and Amphictyon, who entertained Dionysus, was the first whom he taught to mix wine with water. In the vineyards, masks of Dionysus were hung, which turned in the wind and were supposed to make fruitful whatever vines they looked upon. Dionysus grew to be a beautiful girlish-appearing young man, but Hera recognized him and drove him mad. He began to wander about the world, accompanied by Silenus, satyrs, nymphs, other woodland deities, and a band of female followers called maenads. In his mad wanderings he went to Egypt, where he was warmly welcomed and taught the cultivation of the vine. With the help of the Amazons he waged a successful war. Next he went on toward India. He crossed the Euphrates River on a bridge of ivy and vines. When he came to another broad river, Zeus sent a tiger to carry him across, for which reason the river came to be called "Tigris." In India, where he taught the arts of cultivation, many became his willing worshipers; even lions and panthers submitted to him and willingly drew his triumphal chariot. On his way back from India he passed through Phrygia, where he was purified by Rhea of the murders he had committed during his madness, and where he learned the rites of initiation into her mysteries. She, some say, gave him the costume for his ceremonies: a fawn skin or panther skin draped about his body, a band of ivy or vine leaves for his head, and a reed, the narthex, tipped with a pine cone and wreathed with ivy for his staff. This reed-turned-staff was the thyrsus. Dionysus adopted it rather than a wooden staff so that his followers, flushed with wine, would not hurt each other when they beat about with it. In Phrygia he lost Silenus for a short time. Silenus was brought before Midas, the king, and entertained him so

delightfully with his stories that it was with regret that Midas restored him to Dionysus. In return for his courtesies to Silenus, Dionysus offered to grant Midas whatever he wished. Unhappily his greed got the better of him, and Midas wished for the golden touch. Dionysus was disappointed but granted the wish from which he ultimately freed him. From Phrygia he went to Thrace. Lycurgus, king of the Edonians on the Strymon River, did not welcome the wild new religion. He chased Dionysus with an ox-goad and captured his followers. Dionysus fled to the sea and was given asylum by the Nereid Thetis. Rhea freed the maenads and the gods (Rhea or Zeus) drove Lycurgus mad, so that he killed his own son Dryas, under the impression he was pruning a vine. Thrace was afflicted by a plague, which was lifted only when Lycurgus, guilty of the murder of his own kin, was torn to pieces by wild horses. Some say that when he was in Thrace, Dionysus found that Orpheus refused to honor him, and preached other mysteries, and to punish him Dionysus inspired the maenads to attack Orpheus and tear him to pieces. His dismembered head was flung into the Hebrus River and floated, still singing, to the island of Lesbos. Afterward it was laid to rest in a cave sacred to Dionysus. But others say this was not the case at all, that Dionysus did not cause the death of Orpheus, for it was the latter who invented the mysteries of Dionysus. Still others say, concerning these mysteries, that they were brought from Egypt to Greece by Melampus, who also introduced the ceremonies and phallic procession with which the god was honored, and these identify Dionysus with Egyptian Osiris. At the end of three years, or in the third year after his departure, Dionysus returned to Greece at the head of a great triumphal procession, in which Indian elephants were a feature. He freed the cities of Boeotia, and founded Eleutherae, the "city of freedom." When he came to his birthplace, Thebes, Pentheus, the king, who was the son of Agave and therefore a cousin of Dionysus, looked with misgiving on the revels of the followers of this new leader who claimed to be a god. The Theban women immediately accepted him and flocked to his

actǫr; up, lūte, pull; oi, oil; ou, out; ᴛʜ, then; ḍ as d or j, ṣ as s or sh, ṭ as t or ch, ẓ as z or zh.

revels on the mountain, but Pentheus denied his divinity and ordered him and his followers seized. This Pentheus did in spite of the warnings of Cadmus and the seer Tiresias, who warned him not to resist the gods. The walls of the prison where Pentheus had jailed the companions of Dionysus fell down of their own accord. Dionysus willingly appeared before Pentheus and endeavored by persuasion to secure his acceptance of the new god, but Pentheus would not be persuaded and ordered him bound; the fetters instantly fell from his limbs. Even these signs did not convince Pentheus; he arrogantly refused to recognize the divinity of the new god. Agave, his mother, had likewise refused to believe that Semele's lover was a god. Dionysus caused her and the women of Thebes to revel frenetically on Mount Cithaeron in celebration of his rites. He now caused Pentheus, who had refused every chance offered him to accept and worship the new god, to go mad. In his madness he went to the mountain to spy on the women at their revels, was discovered by them, and was torn to pieces by his own mother, who in her frenzy thought she had captured a young lion. From Thebes Dionysus went to Argos. There all the women except the daughters of King Proetus joined in his worship. To punish those who refused, Dionysus drove them mad, and they fled wildly over the mountains. They were ultimately cured of their madness by the seer Melampus. Wishing to go to Naxos, he hired a ship at Icaria and set off. The ship was manned by Tyrrhenian pirates, and they, observing the beauty of their young passenger and his rich robes, resolved to kidnap him and sell him for ransom. They changed the course of their ship and set out for Asia. When Dionysus accused them, they scorned him. Only one member of the crew, the steersman, recognized him as a god and warned his fellows, but they mocked him and ordered him to steer for Asia. Suddenly the ship stood still as if on rock; ivy grew up the mast, vine leaves covered the sails, wine streamed over the deck, and their passenger himself was transformed into a lion; or, as some say, lions and panthers were suddenly seen crouching at his feet. The pirates were maddened with fright and leaped into the sea, where they were transformed into dolphins. Only the steersman who had recognized his godhead was spared, and at his request steered the ship to Naxos. Theseus had stopped on Naxos with Ariadne on his way from Crete to Athens. There Dionysus, according to some accounts, fell in love with Ariadne. He appeared to Theseus in a dream and ordered him to leave Ariadne and depart for Athens. While Ariadne slept, Theseus obeyed his command. Dionysus woke her with a kiss and bore her away to Drius in Thessaly. She bore him Oenopion, Thoas, Staphylus, Latromis, Euanthes, and Tauropolus. But others say Theseus, for reasons unknown, abandoned Ariadne on Naxos, and that Dionysus came upon her weeping, fell in love with her, and married her. He loved her devotedly, and when she died he placed the gem-studded crown, made by Hephaestus, which he had given her as a wedding gift, among the stars as the *Corona Borealis,* or *Ariadne's Crown.* Dionysus was also said to have had a short-lived affair with Aphrodite, who bore him Priapus, and to have loved Carya, daughter of a king in Laconia, but she died suddenly and he transformed her into a walnut tree. At last, when he was universally recognized and worshiped as a god, Dionysus ascended to Olympus and took his place among the gods. As there were to be only Twelve Olympians, Hestia withdrew and gave her place to him. Once he had taken his place among the gods, he desired to fetch his mother from Hades. According to some accounts, he did not know the way, and asked a wayfarer to show him the path. The wayfarer agreed to do so in return for a reward. He led him to the Alcyonian Lake at Lerna, which was one of the entrances to Hades. Dionysus plunged into its bottomless depths and found his mother in the Underworld. He defied the lord of the Underworld to rescue her, or, as some say, he bribed Persephone with a gift of myrtle to free her, and returned with her to the upper air. When he returned, the wayfarer to whom he had promised a reward had died, but Dionysus honored his promise by placing the agreed sum on the dead man's grave. But some say he returned from Hades at a place near the bay of Troezen. The descent of Dionysus to Hades was annually celebrated with nocturnal rites on the bank of the Alcyonian Lake. A lamb was thrown into it as an offering to the guardian of Hades; trumpets were sounded with startling suddenness to summon Dionysus from the depths of the lake. When Dionysus took his mother to Olympus, he changed her name to Thyone so that the spirits who had been left behind in Hades would not know of her resurrection. The gods received her as the mother of a god and made her immortal.

Dionysus was the god of the vine, fertility, and of joyous life. He was the god of hospitality who brings joy to the feast and frees men from care. He was a god of peace, who brings men law and civilization. He was associated with Apollo and the Muses as a god of poets and musicians. He was honored with a special series of festivals, the *Oschophoria, Lesser Dionysia, Lenaea, Anthesteria,* and the *Greater Dionysia.* This last, celebrated in Athens in the spring (March–April), when the vine begins to sprout, and lasting for five days, was most splendid of all. During the celebration all the ordinary business of life stopped, prisoners were freed to take part, and no one was imprisoned during its course. The festival was marked by the Thymelic contest (the Thymele was the altar of Dionysus that stood in the center of the orchestra in the Greek theaters). These were performances of the works of poets given in open air theaters. Even to observe them was an act of worship. The works the poets and musicians wrote for the Greater Dionysia were the foundation, and ultimately, the whole magnificent structure of Greek drama. The dithyramb, the form used by the poets, was invented by Arion of Corinth in honor of Dionysus. In honor of Dionysus musicians were freed from paying taxes, and from the 4th century B.C. for 800 years thereafter, members of the guild of the Artists of Dionysus were freed from military service. Dionysus was the god of joy and freedom, of vegetation, of peace, and the arts of civilization, who was everywhere worshiped with merry revels. He was also a god of the earth. The death of the vine and vegetation with the coming of winter was associated with the flight or the death of the god. The renewal of the vine in the spring was associated with his rebirth. Every third year

festivals, celebrated by women and girls only, were held in his honor. Some say the festivals were held every third year because Dionysus was away on his travels this length of time before he returned to Greece. Others say the interval marks the period which Dionysus, as a son of Zeus and Persephone, spends in the Underworld, at the end of which he is reborn. The tomb from which he was resurrected was at Delphi. During the festival the rites symbolized frantic grief over the death of the god and wild joy over his resurrection. The women who performed them were the maenads (also called bacchants and Thyiades). The maenads celebrated his worship with wild dances, clashing cymbals, drums, and piping flutes. They did not worship him in temples, but rather held their revels in the umblemished fastnesses of mountain and forest, coursing through the wilderness with heads crowned with ivy and swinging torches to light their revels. They tore the flesh of sacrificial victims apart with their hands and ate it raw to commemorate the dismemberment of Dionysus by the Titans. The wildest orgies took place in Thrace and Asiatic Greece, in which latter area the worship of Dionysus came to be associated with that of Cybele (Rhea), Atys, and Sabazius. In Greece itself, the revelers retired to Mount Parnassus near Delphi, and to Mount Cithaeron and Taÿgetus for their orgies, as well as to various other places in Boeotia, Argos and Laconia. Some say there was another Dionysus, a son of Zeus and Persephone, who was called Zagreus and Sabazius. As Sabazius he was very wise, and was the first to yoke oxen, for which reason he was sometimes represented wearing a horn. Celebrations for Sabazius, particularly in Thrace, were held at night to cloak the disgraceful conduct attending them. Dionysus was also identified with Iacchus, the brother or lover of Demeter, and was worshiped at the Eleusinian Mysteries with Demeter and Persephone.

Dionysus had many epithets. Among them were Lenaeus, because he taught men how to crush grapes in vats—*lenoi;* Mitrephorus (*Mitre-bearer,*) because he wore a band around his head to prevent, according to some accounts, the headache which sometimes followed over-indulgence in wine;

Bromius, from the thunder which accompanied his birth; Pyrigenes, because he was born amid fire; Thriambus, because he was the first to celebrate a triumph on his return from India; and Lyaeus (*the Loosener*) because of the relaxing effect of wine. The vine, ivy, rose, laurel, and asphodel were sacred to him, as well as the lion, panther, lynx, tiger, dolphin, ox, and goat. In art he appeared sometimes as a mature, bearded man, but the more usual representation was as a slim youth of almost effeminate beauty, clad in the skin of a wild animal, and with his flowing locks crowned with a wreath of ivy or vine leaves. His attributes are the thyrsus and cup, or grapes, and often he is represented surrounded by satyrs, nymphs, maenads, Muses, or other members of his retinue.

Perhaps more than the other gods, except Demeter, Dionysus represented an enlightened symbolism on the part of the Greeks. The wine he gave to man was a power for good or ill, depending on the use to which it was put. His worship embraced wild and savage elements, as well as the most highly developed arts. The death and renewal of vegetation, symbolized by the death and resurrection of the god, was an intimation of immortality.

Diores (dī-ō′rēz). In Homeric legend (*Iliad*), a son of Amarynceus of Messene. He accompanied the Greeks to the Trojan War as a captain of the Epeans, and was slain by a Thracian ally of the Trojans.

Dioscuri (dī-os-kū′ri). In mythology, Castor and Polydeuces (Latin, Pollux), the twin sons of Leda, and the brothers of Helen and Clytemnestra. According to some accounts, Tyndareus of Sparta was the father of Leda's sons, and as such they were called *Tyndaridae*. Others say Tyndareus was the father of Polydeuces only, and Zeus was the father of Castor. Some maintain that Zeus was the father of both (*Dios-Kouroi*, i.e. "Sons of Zeus"), but the generally accepted account is that Castor and his sister Clytemnestra were the children of Tyndareus, and Polydeuces and Helen were the offspring of Zeus. In any event, they were such noble, manly youths that they were named Dioscuri, "striplings of Zeus," and became Spartan heroes. Castor was renowned as a tamer

of horses, and won prizes at the Olympic Games. Some say he taught Heracles the arts of fencing, cavalry tactics, and strategy. Polydeuces was noted for his skill in boxing, and also won prizes at the Olympic Games, as well as at the funeral games for Pelias. The brothers were among the Argonauts who accompanied Jason to Colchis to recover the Golden Fleece. In the course of the journey Polydeuces overcame Amycus, king of the Bebryces, in a boxing match, and killed him. The Dioscuri also took part in the Calydonian Hunt. Among their other deeds, they helped Peleus devastate Iolcus and kill Cretheïs, the wife of Acastus who had falsely accused Peleus. When their sister Helen was carried off at an early age by Theseus and Pirithous, they went to Athens to rescue her. They conquered Athens, and, as Theseus was at this time in Hades with Pirithous, they set Menestheus on the throne of Athens, found Helen in Aphidnae where Theseus had hidden her with his mother, and carried her and the mother of Theseus back to Sparta. When, much later, Helen stood on the walls of Troy and pointed out to King Priam various Greek heroes who were besieging the city to recover her, she looked in vain for her valorous brothers, unaware that they had died and been deified since she had been carried off from Sparta by Paris. The Dioscuri were invited to attend the marriage of the twins, Idas and Lynceus, to the daughters of Leucippus, Phoebe and Hilaira. At the wedding they seized the prospective brides and carried them off and had children by them. Phoebe bore Mnesilus to Polydeuces; Hilaira bore Anogon to Castor. At some later date the Dioscuri and Idas and Lynceus were reconciled, and united their forces to make a cattle raid in Arcadia. When it came time to divide the spoils, Idas, who had been chosen by lot to fix on a method of division, cut one of the cows into four parts and decreed that whoever ate his part first should have half the stolen cattle, and that he who finished his part next should get the other half. Idas thereupon gobbled down his quarter and immediately set to work to help Lynceus finish his. Thus having disposed of their two quarters the quickest, Idas and Lynceus claimed all the cattle and drove them off to Messenia. Castor and Polydeuces later followed them into Messenia, and while Idas and Lynceus were away sacrificing they seized the cattle, took other booty, and waited in a hollow tree to waylay Idas and Lynceus on their return. But Lynceus, who had such sharp eyes he could see through the bole of a tree, warned Idas, and as they came toward the place of ambush Idas hurled his spear and killed Castor. Polydeuces attacked him, and though felled by a stone Idas cast at him, he succeeded in killing Lynceus. At this point Zeus intervened to save his son, and killed Idas with a thunderbolt. (But some say this fight between the two sets of twins broke out when the Dioscuri carried off the brides of Idas and Lynceus.) Polydeuces was heartbroken over the loss of his brother, and after he had set up a trophy to commemorate his victory over Lynceus, he prayed that he might die too. But as the son of Zeus, he was immortal. He asked to share his immortality with his brother. Zeus agreed. Thereafter Castor lived in the upper air one day, while Polydeuces was under the earth, and the next day they changed places, and so they alternated. Or, as some say, Polydeuces spent every other day with the gods in Olympus, the intervening day being spent with his brother in Hades. But according to the Spartans, Polydeuces, the immortal twin, was the Morning Star and Castor was the Evening Star; as one set, the other rose. And some say that Zeus set the images of the Dioscuri in the heavens as the Twins to honor their devotion to each other. According to a story told by Pausanias, the house where the Dioscuri lived still stood in Sparta long after their disappearance from the earth. Once the Dioscuri, pretending to be strangers, appeared there one night and asked to be allowed to sleep in their old room. The owner, although welcoming them, regretfully refused their request for that room, as it was occupied by his daughter. The next morning the girl and everything in the room had disappeared. All that remained were images of the Dioscuri and some sprigs of an herb. The Dioscuri were regarded as the saviors of shipwrecked sailors: sailors in danger, seeing the sign of their presence in a flame at the masthead, prayed to them, vowed the sacrifice of a white lamb, and the danger

passed. They were renowned for their bravery and skill in arms, and were the patron gods of warlike youth, by whom they were honored as the composers of certain warlike dances and songs. They were also the protecting gods of the rites of hospitality. Their attribute is an egg-shaped cap crowned with a star. They were honored in Athens as gods, and at Sparta they were worshiped with Heracles and other heroes. The Spartans carried a symbol of the Dioscuri, consisting of two parallel beams connected by crosspieces, when they went into battle. The Dioscuri were said to have hated the Messenians, because two Messenian youths, Gonippus and Panormus, impersonated them in the Second Messenian War. The Dioscuri sat in a wild pear tree during a battle, and when Aristomenes, a Messenian hero, was driving the Spartans back, the Dioscuri seized his shield. While he looked for his shield, the Spartans escaped. Again, with their sister Helen, they drove Aristomenes back when he attempted to make a night attack on Sparta. Their enmity to the Messenians lasted until the founding of the new city of Messene (369 B.C.), when the Messenians sacrificed to them and won their forgiveness. At the Battle of Aegospotami (405 B.C.), the Dioscuri were said to have hovered over the Spartan fleet and to have helped them to the decisive victory they won over the Athenians there which brought the Peloponnesian Wars to a close. After this victory the Spartans dedicated two golden stars at the shrine of Delphi to commemorate their divine companions in the battle. Shortly before the Battle of Leuctra (371 B.C.), the golden stars fell from their place at Delphi and disappeared. The Spartans met disastrous defeat at the hands of the Thebans in this battle, from which Sparta never recovered. The worship of the Dioscuri passed to Italy in early times, and they were especially honored in Rome and Tusculum. The original temple of Castor in Rome, in which the Senate sometimes sat, was erected in the Forum in their honor in 484 B.C., in gratitude for their assistance at the battle of Lake Regillus that had taken place 12 years earlier. An annual review of the Roman knights was held in their honor on the 15th of July. Greeks and Romans also worshiped them as gods of the sea; before the invention of the compass, the twin stars Castor and Pollux were important aids to navigation.

Diphilus (dif'i-lus). One of the chief Athenian poets of the New Comedy, and a contemporary of Menander. He was born at Sinope, in Asia Minor, and was active c300 B.C. Of the 100 plays he is said to have written, titles of 60 and fragments of 50 survive. His subjects were drawn from every day life—an extant fragment of his work is concerned with the sign, the way the smoke rises from the hearth, by which he can tell whether he will get a good dinner when he is invited to dine out—and from mythology. He was greatly admired in antiquity; Plautus and Terence borrowed extensively from him.

Dipoenus and **Scyllis** (dī-pē'nus; sil'is). Greek sculptors of the archaic period (fl. c580 B.C.). They worked together and their names are always coupled. They executed sculptures in wood and ivory and also, it is thought, in marble. Some say they were sons or pupils of Daedalus, and that Scyllis invented the art of carving in marble. Little is really known about them, although Pliny the Elder mentions that they worked at Sicyon, and it is thought that the noted school of sculpture at that city owed its rise to them.

Dipolia (dī-pol'i-a) or **Diipolia** (dī-ip-ō-li'a). An ancient Athenian festival celebrated annually, with the sacrifice of an ox, about the end of June, on the Acropolis, in honor of Zeus Polieus—that is, Protector of the City. Also called Bouphonia (q.v.).

Dipylon Gate (dip'i-lon). Chief gateway of ancient Athens, traversing the walls on the NW side. As its name indicates, it was in fact a double gate, consisting of a strongly fortified rectangular court between an outer and an inner portal. Each portal also was double, having two doors, each 11⅓ feet wide, separated by a central pier. The foundations of this gate, alone among those of ancient Athens, survive in great part, and from it toward the SW extends a beautiful stretch of the original wall of Themistocles, built under Peloponnesian menace after the Greek victories over the Persians in 480 and 479 B.C. This wall, in its contrasted construction of admirably fitted blocks and rough stones, confirms literary witness to

the haste of work spurred on by emergency. The Dipylon is identical with the Sacred Gate, and among the roads diverging from it is the Sacred Way to Eleusis. It was long held that an opening in the wall immediately SW of the Dipylon was the Sacred Gate, but Dörpfeld found that this was a passage for the stream which he identified as the Eridanus.

Dirce (dėr'sē). In Greek mythology, the wife of Lycus, put to death by Amphion and Zethus, sons of Antiope, in revenge for her ill treatment of their mother. She was bound to the horns of a bull and dragged to death. (Her execution is represented in the famous sculpture group *The Farnese Bull*.) Her body was thrown into a well on Mount Cithaeron thereafter known as the fountain of Dirce.

Dis (dis). In Roman mythology, a name of Pluto, and hence of the lower world.

Discobolus (dis-kob'ō-lus). Statue of a discus thrower by Myron, Greek sculptor of the 5th century B.C., known from literary descriptions and from copies in Rome (the Lancalotti head, the torso in the Museo Nazionale, the Vatican restoration) and in the British Museum. The body is bent forward and turned toward the right as the heavy discus is swung back, wonderful art being shown in the choice and expression of the moment of repose when, the backward motion completed, the powerful cast forward is on the point of execution.

Discordia (dis-kôr'di-a). Latin name of **Eris**.

Dithyrambus (dith-i-ram'bus). An epithet of Dionysus, meaning "the Child of the Double Door," from the fact that he was born twice. From this epithet cames the dithyramb, a form of Greek lyric composition, originally a choral song in honor of Dionysus, afterward of other gods, heroes, etc. First given artistic form by Arion (c625 B.C.) and rendered by cyclic choruses, it was perfected, about a century later, by Lasus of Hermione, and at about the same time tragedy was developed from it in Attica. Its simpler and more majestic form, as composed by Lasus, Simonides, Bacchylides, and Pindar, assumed in the latter part of the 5th century a complexity of rhythmical and musical form and of verbal expression which degenerated in the 4th century into a mimetic performance rendered by a single artist. From these different stages in its history the word *dithyramb* has been used in later ages both for a nobly enthusiastic and elevated and for a wild or inflated composition.

Dittany (dit′a-ni). A plant which grew, among other places, on Mount Dicte in Crete, whence its name. In the *Aeneid,* it is named as an herb, prepared by Venus and given to the physician Iapis, without his knowledge, to heal the wound which Aeneas had received in the war with Turnus in Latium. It was often referred to as a sacred herb.

Dium or **Deium** (dī′um). Place in Macedonia near the Hebrus River. According to the legend, Orpheus withdrew to this spot after his final parting from Eurydice and played and sang for birds, beasts, and trees only, refusing to have anything more to do with women. Here he was set upon, according to some accounts, by maenads who were sent by Dionysus to punish him for denying his cult; according to others, it was the women of the Cicones who attacked him for keeping apart from the society of women. In any case, the women tore him limb from limb and cast his severed head into the Hebrus River. Afterward the women were transformed into oak trees.

Dives (dī′vēz), **Crassus.** See **Crassus, Marcus Licinius.**

Divitiacus (div-i-tī′a-kus). Aeduan noble, brother of Dumnorix. He was an ally of Rome and a warm personal friend of Caesar. He was the guest of Cicero during a political visit to Rome. He rendered services to Caesar against Ariovistus and against the Belgae. Through his intercession Dumnorix' treason in 58 B.C. was pardoned by Caesar.

Dodecanese (dō-dek-a-nēz′, nēs′). [Greek, **Dodekanesos,** meaning "Twelve Islands."] Group of Greek islands in the SE part of the Aegean Sea near the SW coast of Turkey. There are 12 main islands: Astypalea, Chalce, Calymna, Carpathus, Casus, Cos, Lerus, Nisyrus, Patmos, Rhodes, Syme, and Telus. In addition, there are many small ones.

Dodona (dō-dō′na). An ancient town in Epirus, probably situated on or near Mount Tomarus, SW of modern Ioannina. It was the seat of the oldest Greek oracle, dedicated to Zeus Naios in an oak grove hung with vessels of brass, by which the god's voice was

thought to be made audible. The priestess of the oracle instructed the ancient Pelasgi, according to Herodotus, to adopt the names of the gods that were brought to Greece by the Egyptians, for these names had not, as many thought, originated with the Greeks. Some say that two of the sacred women of the temple of Zeus in Egyptian Thebes were carried off by Phoenicians. One of them was sold in Libya, where she founded the oracle of Ammon. The other was sold in Greece and founded the first oracle in Greece, this one of Dodona. But the priestesses at Dodona said that two black doves flew away from Egyptian Thebes. One went to Libya. The other flew to Dodona, alighted on an oak tree there, and began to speak in a human voice. She said that on that spot there should henceforth be an oracle of Zeus. The people of Dodona, feeling they had received instructions from heaven, immediately set to work to build the shrine. The oaks of the grove were sacred, and had the power of speech and prophecy, as in the oaken beam that Athena put in the keel of the *Argo.* Sometimes the prophecies were made known by the rustling of the leaves of the sacred trees. This oracle, with those of Delphi and Zeus Ammon in Libya, enjoyed the highest repute throughout the ancient world.

Dodonian (dō-dō′ni-an). Epithet of Zeus from the famous sanctuary, grove and oracle of Zeus at Dodona in Epirus.

Dolabella (dol-a-bel′a), **Publius Cornelius.** Roman patrician; born c70 B.C.; died at Laodicea in Asia Minor, 43 B.C. He is noted chiefly as the son-in-law of Cicero. Ruined by his profligate habits, he sought to restore his fortunes by joining the standard of Caesar in the civil war. He commanded Caesar's fleet in the Adriatic in 49 B.C., and in 48 B.C. participated in the battle of Pharsalus. He obtained the consulship after the death of Caesar in 44 B.C. At first he acted in support of the Senate, but was subsequently influenced by bribery to join the party of Antony. He received from Antony Syria as his proconsular province, but was defeated at Laodicea by Cassius. He was, at his own request, killed by one of his soldiers in order not to fall into the hands of the enemy.

Dolabra (dō-lā′bra). In Roman antiquity, a cutting implement of various shapes, used, according to shape and purpose, as a hatchet, an ax, a knife, a chisel, a mattock, or a pickax. Dolabrae of an ornate form were employed by the priests in slaughtering their sacrificial victims.

Dolius (dō'li-us). In the *Odyssey,* a faithful slave given to Penelope by her father when she married Odysseus. He cared for Laertes in the country during the absence of Odysseus, welcomed Odysseus when he returned after 20 years, and helped him to defeat the relatives of Penelope's suitors after Odysseus himself had slain the suitors.

Dolius. An epithet of Hermes, meaning "Crafty."

Dolon (dō'lon). In Homeric legend *(Iliad),* a Trojan, the son of Eumedes. On condition that he be given the immortal horses of Achilles once they were captured, he volunteered to go as a spy to the Greek camp in the tenth year of the Trojan War. Clad in a wolf's skin, he set out on his mission, but was captured by Diomedes and Odysseus, who had set out to spy on the Trojan camp. He betrayed the positions of the Trojans and their allies, and advised Diomedes and Odysseus that Rhesus, leader of the Thracian allies, was encamped at some distance from the main body of the Trojans. As soon as they had learned what they wanted from Dolon, the two Greeks, ignoring his pleas, killed him and proceeded to the Trojan camp.

Dolonea (dō-lon-ē'a). The *"Adventures of Dolon,"* a name given by grammarians to the tenth book of the *Iliad.* (JJ)

Domitian (dō-mish'an). [Full Latin name, **Titus Flavius Domitianus Augustus.**] Roman emperor (81–96); born at Rome, Oct. 25, 51 A.D.; died there, Sept. 18, 96 A.D. He was the second son of Vespasian and Flavia Domitilla, and the brother of Titus, whom he succeeded. He undertook a campaign against the Chatti in 83, in the course of which he began the construction of a boundary wall between the Danube and the Rhine. This wall was guarded by soldiers settled upon public lands (*agri decumates*) along its course. He carried on (86–90) unsuccessful wars against the Dacians under Decebalus, finally purchasing peace by the promise of a yearly tribute. He recalled Agricola, whose victories (78–84) in Britain aroused his

jealousy. Though the beginning of his reign had been marked by sincere attempts to govern well, to enforce the laws, to build temples, and to supervise the government closely, the last years of his reign were sullied by cruelty and tyranny, induced by fear of revolt and assassination. He was murdered by the freedman Stephanus, at the instance of the empress and several officers of the court, who were in fear of their lives.

Domitius Ulpianus (dō-mish'us ul-pi-ā'nus). See **Ulpian.**

Dorian Hexapolis (dō'ri-an hek-sap'ō-lis). See **Hexapolis, Dorian.**

Dorians (dō'ri-anz). One of the traditional branches of the ancient Greek people. According to the tradition, they were descendants of Dorus, the youngest son of Hellen and Orseïs. They were probably of Illyrian stock and, fighting on foot instead of on horseback and carrying iron weapons, they pushed into Epirus and Aetolia and destroyed the civilizations they found there. The Dorian invasion of Greece, as a point of departure for subsequent legend and history, was equalled in importance only by the Trojan War. Some went into the region between Mount Oeta and the Corinthian Gulf, a part of which afterward came to be known as Doris, but played only a minor role in Greek history. Others took to the sea and established settlements in Crete and the Greek islands, bringing strife and warfare in their train. Important Dorian settlements were founded in Asia Minor, Cos, and Rhodes. The greatest number moved across the Corinthian Gulf, perhaps from Naupactus, as the legend states, and conquered the Peloponnesus (c1100 B.C.). Everywhere they went the names of their three tribes—the Hylleis, Pamphyli, and Dymanes—persisted. In the Peloponnesus the Dorians conquered Corinthia and Argos. The destruction of the strongholds of Mycenae and Tiryns is thought to have taken place at this time. The largest number settled in the valley of the Eurotas River in Laconia. And it was in this area that the impact of their race made its most consistent impression in the development of what came to be thought of as the Dorian character, for they subdued the inhabitants, making them their subjects, yet maintained the purity of their own race. In connection

fat, fāte, fär, fāre, errant; net, mē, hèr ardent; pin, pīne; not, nōte, mōve, nôr, with their conquest of the Peloponnesus the Dorians called their invasion a "return." They linked themselves to Heracles and claimed that they were regaining an inheritance in the Peloponnesus that he had won for them. The Dorian tribe called the Hylleis claimed that their name was derived from Hyllus, the son of Heracles. The Dorian invasion marks the end of the Mycenaean civilization and begins the so-called Dark Ages of Greece, a period of some 300 years during which extensive changes occurred in many aspects of Greek life.

Doric Order (dor'ik). In architecture, the oldest and strongest of the three Greek orders, in its external forms the simplest of all, but in its most perfect examples, especially as exhibited in the monuments of the age of Pericles at Athens, combining with solidity and force the most subtle and delicate re-

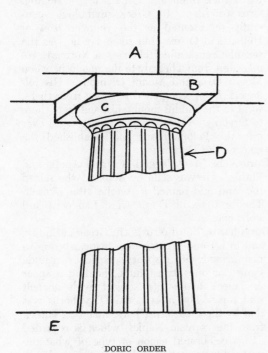

DORIC ORDER
A) architrave; B) abacus; C) echinus;
D) shaft; E) stylobate

finement of outlines and proportions that architecture has known. A characteristic of the Grecian Doric column is the absence of

a base; the channelings are usually 20 in number, and in section approximate to a semi-ellipse; the capital has generally no astragal (an ornamental molding), but only one or more fillets or annulets, which separate the channelings from the echinus (convex projecting molding of eccentric curve, supporting the abacus). The profile of the capital in the best examples is a carefully studied eccentric curve, neither flat enough to be hard in effect, nor full enough to be weak. The echinus prior to the time of perfection spread out far beyond the shaft; the later Greeks made it a frustum of a cone. In good Greek examples, as a rule, no horizontal lines are found in a Doric building, floor- and cornice-lines, etc., being curved slightly upward, the profiles of the column-shafts are slightly convex, and all columns are slightly inclined toward the center of the building. All these particularities have relation to the optical effects so subtle that their influence is felt rather than seen.

Dorieus (dôr'i-us). Son of Anaxandridas, king of Sparta, and the first of his two wives to whom he was married concurrently. According to Herodotus, the reason for this unusual marital state was that the first wife of Anaxandridas bore him no children. The Spartans urged him to take a second wife, since he would not give up the first one, and maintain the two in separate houses and with nearly equal honors. The second wife bore Anaxandridas a son, Cleomenes, who became the heir to the throne. Some time thereafter, the first wife, who up to this time had seemed to be incapable of bearing children, also produced a son, whom she named Dorieus. In rapid succession she also bore Leonidas, later to become the hero of Thermopylae, and Cleombrotus. Dorieus was the most promising of the sons and, since Cleomenes seemed to be mentally unbalanced at times, Dorieus fully expected to succeeed his father as king. However, when Anaxandridas died, the Spartans followed the law and made Cleomenes, the first-born son, the king. Dorieus could not bear to be subject to Cleomenes, and in anger sailed away with a company of Spartans to found a colony. In his disappointment, he failed to consult the oracle at Delphi, and to observe the customs before setting out to found a colony. He went to Libya and established a city there, but after three years was driven out. He returned to Sparta to consider what he should do, and was told by a seer to go to Heraclea in Sicily, for as a descendant of Heracles, he was entitled to the land. The claims of the Heraclidae to this region rested on the following grounds: When Heracles was driving the cattle of Geryon back to Argos, a bull escaped at Rhegium and swam across to Sicily. Heracles swam across after him. He landed in the kingdom of Eryx, in whose herds the bull had found a welcome. Eryx challenged Heracles to a series of contests, staking his kingdom against the bull. In the contests Heracles slew Eryx and won his kingdom, but left it to the inhabitants to enjoy until one of his descendants could come to claim it. Now Dorieus decided to be that descendant who recovered the land formerly won by Heracles. This time he went to the oracle at Delphi before he set out, and was assured by the priestess that he would gain the land as he intended. Dorieus returned to Libya, gathered up his followers, and proceeded to Sicily. On the way, according to some accounts, he stopped to help the people of Croton in a war against the Sybarites, and dedicated a temple to Athena in Sybaris after he had helped to take the city. The Crotoniats disclaimed this story entirely; they said Dorieus only came to their aid when victims foreshadowed defeat of the Sybarites, at which point he deserted them and came over to the side of the Crotoniats. From Sybaris he proceeded to Heraclea Minoa, in Sicily, helped the Selinuntians to overthrow their tyrant, and made himself tyrant of Selinus. After a while the inhabitants revolted against him, and though he fled to the altar of Zeus, they seized him and put him to death. Ironically, if Dorieus had been patient he would have become king of Sparta, for Cleomenes reigned only a short time and died without male issue. Leonidas, brother of Dorieus and half-brother of Cleomenes, became king in his place.

Doris (dō′ris, dôr′is). In classical mythology, the daughter of Oceanus and Tethys. She married Nereus, and their 50 daughters were called the Nereids. The name Doris is sometimes given to the sea by the poets, as by Vergil.

Doris. In ancient geography, a territory in C Greece, surrounded by Phocis, Locris, Aetolia, and Malis; a valley between Oeta and Parnassus. It was occupied by the Dorians, perhaps c1100 B.C. Although they moved on through Greece, conquered the Peloponnesus, made forays into Crete and the Aegean islands, founded many cities in Greece and Asia Minor, the small area of Doris was ever after considered as the motherland of the Dorians. This was its most important role in Greek history.

Doris. In ancient geography, a part of the coast of Caria, Asia Minor.

Doritis (dō-rī′tis). An epithet of Aphrodite meaning "Bountiful."

Dorium (dō-rī′um). In ancient geography, a town in Nestor's realm, in N Messenia. Here, some say, Thamyris engaged in a contest with the Muses. He lost in the contest and was struck blind and lost his art of singing.

Dorus (dō′rus). In Greek mythology, generally represented as the youngest son of Hellen and Orseïs (but some say he was the son of Creusa and Hellen's son Xuthus). He migrated from Thessaly to the region between Mount Ossa and Mount Olympus. His followers, being compelled to move from there, went to the Pindus mountains, and from there to Dryopis. From Dryopis they crossed over into the Peloponnesus and established the race of the Dorians.

Dorus. In Greek legend, a son of Apollo and Phthia. He was slain by Aetolus, who seized the land and named it Aetolia after himself. The brothers of Dorus were Laodocus and Polypoetes.

Doryphorus (dō-rif′ō-rus). In Greek antiquity, and in art and archaeology, a spear-bearer, a man armed with a spear; specifically, a nude figure, or one almost nude, holding a spear or lance: a favorite subject with ancient sculptors. The most noted Doryphorus was that by the great artist Polyclitus, best known from the copy in Naples, which is regarded as his celebrated canon or type of what the perfectly proportioned human figure should be.

Drabescus (dra̤-bes′kus). [Modern name, **Drama**.] In ancient geography, town in N Greece, situated between the Strymon and Nestus rivers, about 78 miles NE of Thessalonica.

Draco (drā′kō) or **Dracon** (drā′kon). Athenian legislator; fl. in the last half of the 7th century B.C. According to tradition, he was appointed (c621 B.C.) to reform existing laws and to formulate the first written code of laws for Athens. Among his reforms was the establishment of 51 Ephetae (judges), chosen from the Eupatrids (nobles), to try cases of bloodshed that did not come before the Areopagus. The court of the Ephetae sat in various places, depending on the nature of the offense, as at Delphi, in the temple of Apollo, or at Phalerum, the old port of Athens. Those who had committed the crime of manslaughter abroad were not permitted to set foot on Attic soil until they were cleared of the charge. Since they had to make their defense standing in a boat drawn up near the shore, the court went to Munychia, the hill above the Piraeus, to hear their cases. (Telamon, charged with the murder of his brother Phocus, was not permitted to land at Aegina, his father's home, to defend himself; he secretly built a mole and shouted his defense from the end of it that reached out into the sea.) According to Draco's code, one who was unable to pay a debt could be claimed as a slave by his creditor. On the completion of the code, there having been no written code previously, the people were so overjoyed that they smothered Draco accidentally under a deluge of cloaks. On account of the number of offenses to which it affixed the penalty of death, his code was said to have been written in blood. His code was superseded for the most part by that of Solon (594 B.C.).

Draco. A northern constellation—the Dragon. As pictured since ancient times, the figure is that of a serpent with several small coils. It appears at a very ancient date to have had wings in the space now occupied by the Little Bear.

Drama. *Greek Tragedy.* Greek tragedy (goat-song) came into being in the 6th century B.C. as part of the festival of Dionysus, god of wine. The circular threshing-floor, where the harvested grain was brought for threshing, provided a suitable stage, or so we assume from the form long preserved by the *orchestra* (dancing-place). At one side could be erected a tent (in Greek, *skene*, whence our word *scene*), where performers might rest, or change their costumes to appear in a new role. Presently someone added wooden bleachers, and the open-air *theatron* or theater (watching-place) was born. The temporary scene, replaced by a permanent structure in stone and wood, was the forerunner of the permanent scene-buildings of the Hellenistic theater and those of the still more elaborate Roman stage. After an accident, we are told, the wooden stands were given up, and the orchestra was moved to the foot of a hill, where spectators might stand or sit on the sloping ground, and where eventually stone seats were cut or set. As early as the 7th century B.C. we hear of the performance of dithyrambs, odes sung and danced by a chorus in honor of Dionysus, and c600 B.C. of Arion who fixed their form, gave them definite subjects, and trained Corinthian choruses to perform them. Introduced to Athens by one Lasus, the dithyramb quickly became popular, and by 508 B.C. the Athenians had established a competition in dithyramb at the Dionysus festivals; the old legends of the epic cycles provided hundreds of themes, and the list of winners includes Simonides, Pindar, and Bacchylides, but after 470 B.C. it was eclipsed by the towering popularity of the competition in tragedy, and ceased to attract leading poets. In the meantime, a critical date in the development of the drama at Athens had been 534 B.C., when an actor-producer of dithyrambs named Thespis (whence *thespian*) detached the chorus leader from the chorus, creating a character (*hypocrites,* meaning "answerer") and making possible monologue (e.g., a herald or messenger responds to questioning of the chorus by describing events which have occurred off-stage) and dialogue between character and chorus, as well as the purely choral odes. This is regarded as the birth of tragedy. The prize, we are told, was a goat, which the company might appropriately sacrifice to Dionysus and then eat.

After Thespis we hear next of Choerilus, Phrynichus, and Pratinas. Of Choerilus, we learn that he wrote 160 plays. Of Phrynichus, Herodotus tells us that when his *Capture of Miletus* was presented, the guilt-stricken Athenians, who had refused to support the Ionian city of Miletus in its disastrous revolt against Darius, fined him 1000

actor; up, lūte, pull; oi, oil; ou, out; ᴛʜ, then; d̩ as d or j, s̩ as s or sh, t̩ as t or ch, z̩ as z or zh.

drachmas and forbade further performance of the play; forty years after its beginnings, tragedy could prove a diet too strong for its audience. Phrynichus is said to have been the first to introduce female characters; female parts, however, were always taken by men or boys. By this time each playwright competing in the contest in tragedy was required to submit a tetralogy, consisting of a trilogy—three tragedies which might deal with the changing fortunes of an individual or a family (e.g., *Prometheus Bound, Prometheus Released, Prometheus Fire-Bringer*), or might be unrelated—and a fourth play known as a satyr-play. From the scripts submitted, officials selected three tetralogies for production. Apparently the prize was awarded for the best tetralogy, though some references seem to designate single plays as winners. Of the 33 tragedies which have chanced to survive, not all won first place; second- and third-place plays are also represented. The plots regularly center around a hero or heroine who because of some defect ("tragic flaw"), not necessarily his own, is involved in conflict and crisis. In the hands of a master playwright it became a medium of social criticism. The chorus is usually a group of citizens or bystanders, elders, old women, captives, sea-nymphs, spokesmen, insofar as the poet has chosen to employ them in this capacity, for the force of public opinion; but they may be principals in the plot, as in Aeschylus' *Suppliants*, in which the 50 daughters of Danaus seeking refuge form the chorus. Retaining at first from the dithyrambic competition the traditional chorus of 50, the number was presently reduced to 12, then increased to 15. The titles of tragedy are most often taken from the principal figure (*Agamemnon, Orestes, Electra, Oedipus, Medea*) or from the chorus (*Suppliants, Women of Trachis, Bacchae*).

Our knowledge of Attic tragedy is based largely on the three dramatists from whose pens survive complete plays: Aeschylus, Sophocles, and Euripides. That this represents a consensus of ancient approval cannot be denied, because popularity determined the demand for manuscript copies, which in turn increased the chances of survival of any given play. We must remember that not all the extant plays received the prize on their initial performance, the judges frequently awarding the prize to plays now known only by their titles or fragments. Aeschylus (525–456 B.C.) makes his appearance early in the 5th century. He fought at Marathon, probably also at Salamis, and won his first victory in 484 B.C. An innovator, he added a second actor, making it possible to portray two characters in conflict, whose implications were underscored by the comments of the chorus. Of his 90 or so plays, seven have survived. The earliest, the oldest surviving European drama, is *Suppliants*, mentioned above. *Agamemnon*, relating the victorious return from Troy of Agamemnon and his prompt murder by his embittered wife Clytemnestra, is usually regarded as Aeschylus' greatest play and by some as the greatest Greek play. No tetralogy has survived intact; the only complete Attic trilogy is Aeschylus' *Orestea*, consisting of *Agamemnon, Choëphoroe*, and *Eumenides*, which with its now lost satyr-play, *Proteus*, was presented in 458 B.C. and won the prize. Altogether, we are told, he won first prize 13 times.

After Aeschylus the next great tragic poet is Sophocles (c496–406 B.C.), like Aeschylus a profound thinker, a superb poët, and an innovator. Sophocles added a third actor, multiplying the possibilities of dramatic exchange, and we are told that it was he who increased the tragic chorus from 12 dancers to 15. Of his 125 or more plays, seven survive, and substantial fragments of others. In his first victory, 468 B.C., he defeated Aeschylus. Those who have sought a tragedy surpassing Aeschylus' *Agamemnon* have professed to find it in Sophocles' *Oedipus the King*, a play which in its initial performance took only second place, but many critics find *Antigone* also strangely moving. Contemporaries and rivals of Aeschylus and Sophocles were Aristias, the son of Pratinas, and Polyphrasmon or Polyphradmon, the son of Phrynichus, who in 467 B.C. competed, unsuccessfully, against Aeschylus' Theban tetralogy; Aristarchus of Tegea; and Ion of Chios. Later in the century we hear of Aeschylus' nephew Philocles, one of whose plays defeated (*sic*) Sophocles' *Oedipus the King*; Sophocles' son Iophon; Meletus, Sthenelus, Agathon, etc. Aeschylus' son Euphorion is said to have presented unproduced plays of his father, and with one of them in 431 B.C. to have won over both Sophocles and Euripides.

Euripides (c485–c406 B.C.), third of the three great tragic poets, made his first appearance in 455, but won his first victory only in 441 B.C. Of Greek dramatists, he was the least respectful of the Olympian gods, the most insistent in his demand for social reform, and the most modern in his appeal. His fellow Athenians regarded him as too advanced for their tastes, and he was repeatedly lampooned. In a long active career he was awarded the prize only five times, but among succeeding generations he was Greece's most popular tragic poet, the one whose plays were most frequently revived and the one most translated and adapted by the Romans. Of his 90-odd plays, the manuscript tradition has preserved 19 (or 18), of which those most frequently read today are *Alcestis, Medea, Hippolytus,* and *Bacchae.* Although in its own day it placed third, *Medea* has been staged for modern audiences with brilliant success. Of the obscure satyr-plays a single complete example, Euripides' *Cyclops,* has survived, but papyri from the trash-heaps of Egypt have yielded about 400 lines of Sophocles' *Ichneutae* and extended passages from Aeschylus' *Dictyulci* and *Isthmiastae.* For the traditional satyr-play of one of his tetralogies Euripides substituted *Alcestis,* a tragedy with a rare happy ending.

After Euripides we have the names of Neophron, Critias, Theodectes, Moschion, Polyidus, Chaeremon, Carcinus, Xenocles, two or even three poets named Astydamas, and many others, no play by any of whom did antiquity regard highly enough to preserve for posterity, unless *Rhesus* (which goes under Euripides' name) is in fact, as some scholars think, a 4th century composition. For fuller biographies and appraisals of Aeschylus, Sophocles, and Euripides, see their separate articles, and for synopses of surviving Attic tragedies see under their titles. *Roman Tragedy.* The Romans, considering themselves obliged to cultivate a theater more intellectual than the boisterous and rowdy native mime, found in their search for innovations of plot and characterization that the Greek dramatists had virtually exhausted the old legends. Much Roman drama was there-fore derivative—versions, adaptations, or even direct translations of familiar Greek plays. We are told that at Rome drama began in 240 B.C., when a manumitted Greek slave from Tarentum, Livius Andronicus (c284–c204 B.C.) presented both a Greek tragedy and a comedy in translation. We have the titles of eight tragedies and three comedies from his pen. His contemporary Cnaeus Naevius (c270–c201 B.C.) is credited with 34 comedies and seven tragedies adapted from Greek models, including an *Andromacha* and an *Iphigenia,* and two *fabulae praetextae,* historical dramas on Roman themes, a form of which he is regarded as the inventor. Quintus Ennius (239–169 B.C.) adapted from the Greek, especially from Euripides, at least 20 tragedies, and several unsuccessful comedies, and also composed two fabulae praetextae. Marcus Pacuvius (220–c130 B.C.), a nephew of Ennius, presented ten or more tragedies, one of which was a praetexta. Lucius Accius (c170–c85 B.C.), the most popular Roman tragic poet, admired and quoted by Cicero, imitated by Vergil, and frequently revived, adapted at least 45 Greek dramas, depending heavily on Euripides and Sophocles. We have also the titles, and a few fragments, of *Decius* and *Brutus,* two praetextae by Accius. After him the tragic theater in Rome consisted principally of revivals of earlier plays, but we hear of the success of a *Thyestes* by Varius, the editor of Vergil's *Aeneid,* and of a *Medea* by Ovid. Of this substantial corpus only fragments survive. In the 1st century A.D. the distinguished critic, orator, philosopher, essayist, and court wit, Lucius Annaeus Seneca, composed nine tragedies on Greek models; these are extant. Scholars have questioned whether they could ever have been successfully produced on the stage, though most are agreed that they are good armchair reading, and they profoundly influenced Elizabethan drama. *Octavia,* a praetexta, the only surviving example of a play of this form, has long had Seneca's name attached to it, but it is now held to be written by an imitator, later and less able, of Seneca's style. Repeated efforts to establish the native praetexta as an enduring attraction had failed, and thereafter in Rome the tragic stage is silent. *Greek Comedy.* The origins of Greek comedy, like those of tragedy, are obscure; the word seems to mean "revel-song," and most scholars agree that it probably originated in spontaneous and no doubt often ribald merry-making at rural agricultural festivals. Ancient sources allude to little farces or mimes enacted at Sparta, Tarentum, Megara, and Thebes, perhaps also at Sicyon. In due course someone gave these form, the unity implied by a central idea and a plot. According to the Parian Marble, the first performance of comedy, in Attica at least, took place at the village of Icaria, and the author-producer was one Susarion of Megara; the date would be somewhat before 560 B.C., but some scholars question the veracity of the statement. About 500 B.C. Epicharmus and Phormis founded a much-admired school of comedy at Syracuse in Sicily. Mention of a comic prize awarded to Chionides of Athens in 486 B.C. indicates that by that time a contest in comedy comparable to the tragic competition, and like it dedicated to Dionysus, had been established at Athens. Ancient critics divided comedy into two styles, Old Comedy, represented by the political satire of Aristophanes, and New Comedy, represented by the comedy of manners of Menander. Between Chionides and Aristophanes we hear of Magnes, Cratinus, Crates, Pherecrates, Teleclides, Hermippus, Eupolis, and Phrynichus. Of all their works antiquity selected none for preservation; we have only titles and occasional fragments; but ancient critics ranked Cratinus and Eupolis, at least, as Aristophanes' equals, and Aristophanes often had to settle for second prize, or third. Aristophanes won only four first prizes, Teleclides eight, Eupolis seven.

Old Comedy, as is clear from the surviving plays of Aristophanes (c450–c385 B.C.) and what is known of those of his rivals, was extremely adult political or social farce; e.g., Aristophanes' *Wasps*, a satire on the Athenian jury system, which presents Philocleon ("Loves-Cleon"), an indefatigable juryman, and his son Bdelycleon ("Hates-Cleon"), who in an effort to cure Philocleon of his addiction locks him up and prevents the chorus (of wasps: his fellow-jurymen) from rescuing him, but consents to his tapering off by holding court at home. Philocleon, trying the dog for stealing a Sicilian cheese, inad-

vertently votes to acquit, and when he realizes what he has done he collapses. The *Frogs* presents an uproarious debate in Hades, umpired by Dionysus, between Aeschylus and Euripides, who venomously attack each other's verse; the debate (*agon*) is a regular feature of Aristophanic comedy. In the *Acharnians*, Diceopolis, weary of war, negotiates a private peace with Sparta, purveyors of war-scarce delicacies flock to his market, and he ends up in the arms of two admiring flute-girls. In the *Lysistrata*, the women of Athens and Sparta, weary of war, withhold their favors from husbands and lovers, which soon brings a frantic embassy from Sparta to negotiate a truce. Of his 40 (or 44) plays 11 survive: *Acharnians* (first prize, 425 B.C.), *Knights* (first prize, 424 B.C.), *Clouds* (third prize, 423 B.C.; the text we have is a later revision), *Wasps* (second prize, 422 B.C.), *Peace* (second prize, 421 B.C.), *Birds* (second prize 414 B.C.), *Lysistrata* and *Thesmophoriazusae* (411 B.C.), *Frogs* (first prize, 405 B.C.), *Plutus* (408 B.C.; the surviving play is a revision presented in 388 B.C.), and *Ecclesiazusae* (391 B.C.). For comic effect Aristophanes employs situation, surprise, parody, ambiguity, and puns. He lodges charges of cowardice, effeminacy, thievery, and assorted rascalities against named Athenians who were presumably present in the audience; he repeatedly pillories the demagogue Cleon, and in the *Clouds* presents so grotesque a caricature of Socrates that at his trial, 24 years later, Socrates is still deploring it. The chorus, 24 in number, enthusiastically abet the principal character or violently oppose him; it plays an essential role in the unfolding of the plot, and at least once in each play turns to the audience and gives it a thorough scolding (the *parabasis*) for its faults and failings. Aristophanes' choral odes prove him a lyric poet of surpassing talent. His plays are sometimes described as "raw" or "pornographic"; it is true that he light-heartedly introduced a number of regrettable human weaknesses, but there is nothing in Aristophanes which, judged against the background of his times, would have seemed in bad taste to an audience of adult male Athenian citizens.

After Aristophanes comes a transitional period, for which critics of much later date devised the term Middle Comedy. Of the playwrights associated with Middle Comedy, and the 800 plays they are said to have presented, not enough survives to make possible a neat characterization of the style; but we are given to understand that in Middle Comedy personal abuse was gradually dropped and the chorus, perhaps because of its expense, much reduced in importance. When we find these changes in effect in Aristophanes' two latest surviving plays, *Plutus* and *Ecclesiazusae,* we conclude that these are in fact early examples of Middle Comedy. In *Plutus,* a humble citizen named Chremylus, honest and consequently poor, is advised by Apollo's oracle to take home with him the first person he meets. This turns out to be Plutus, god of wealth, who is blind. Chremylus conducts him to the sanctuary of Asclepius, where he is healed, to the lasting benefit of Chremylus and his friends and the confusion of rascals everywhere. Among younger contemporaries of Aristophanes who composed both Old and Middle Comedy we have the names of Plato, sometimes called Plato Comicus to distinguish him from Plato the philosopher, and Eubulus. Of other Middle Comedy writers, ancient critics singled out for special admiration Anaxandrides, Antiphanes, Diodorus of Sinope, Alexis, Xenarchus, Timocles, Sotades, and three sons of Aristophanes: Ararus, Nicostratus, and Philetaerus.

New Comedy developed out of Middle Comedy; by c320 B.C. the process of transition was complete. No New Comedy play has come down to us in the manuscript tradition. Until 1905 our knowledge of this style depended on a multitude of fragments, quoted by ancient grammarians to illustrate some point of grammar, diction, or meter, and the ubiquitous "cooking fragments," referring to the preparation of food, some hundreds of titles of lost plays, the comments of critics and literary historians, and translations and adaptations by Roman comic poets, who borrowed freely from New Comedy. New Comedy was a comedy of manners, its themes taken from daily life, involving misunderstandings, lovers' quarrels and reconciliations, lost children and recognition, coincidence, mistaken identity, and seduction, and a fairly constant cast of characters: the skinflint

father, the sex-directed son, the madam, the call girl, the ingenue, the impudent slave, and the parasite or scrounger. The ingenue is often a foundling, an exposed child sold into slavery and used as slaves are used, identified in the last act as freeborn, a citizen, and thereby eligible for matrimony with the undependable but repentant young man; in New Comedy it seems to trouble no one that the ingenue may at the same time be a prostitute. The emphasis is away from broad social problems and centered on the individual and his struggle to achieve happiness. New Comedy is a direct ancestor of modern drawing-room comedy. By this time, if not earlier, the permanent stage background had become fixed, three doorways, which may represent the entrances to three private houses; the stage itself represents a street, leading, by lateral exits (the *parodoi*) to market-place, harbor, or suburbs, as required by the plot. This arrangement was perpetuated in the still more elaborate façades of the Roman scene. To the extent that it puts a limitation on entrances and exits, it affects the poet's development of the plot.

Ancient critics agreed that the greatest of New Comedy playwrights was Menander (342–291 B.C.), who wrote more than 100 plays. He won only eight prizes; like Euripides, he was more appreciated after his death. In 1905 there was found in Egypt a papyrus containing important sections of Menander, comprising at least one-half of his *Arbitration,* about one-third of his *She Who Was Shorn* and his *Women of Samos,* and one scene from the *Hero.* Then in 1959 the Swiss scholar Victor Martin published a new papyrus discovery, sensational in that it contains the complete text of Menander's *Dyscolus* (Grouch), certainly not one of his greatest efforts—by current standards it is astonishingly dull—but containing a promise of more to come. Roman playwrights, among them Naevius, Plautus, Caecilius Statius, Terence, Luscius Lanuvinus, Turpilius, and Afranius, borrowed ideas, characters, scenes, plots, or entire plays from Menander. Of his rivals, the most successful, ranked as his peers by their contemporaries, were Philemon (c361–262 B.C.; 97 plays, known from 64 titles, over 200 fragments, and three adaptations by Plautus) and Diphilus (341?–289 B.C.;

about 100 plays, three prizes, and adaptations by Plautus and Terence). One Posidippus, we are told, won four prizes. Apollodorus of Carystus, who wrote 47 plays and won five victories, is represented by two adaptations by Terence, *Hecyra* and *Phormio*. Philemon's son Philemon is said to have won six prizes. A play by Demophilus was the original of Plautus' *Asinaria*. The records list many more.

Roman Comedy. Roman comedy, like Roman tragedy, was largely derivative. Finding in the New Comedy of the Greeks plots, themes, situations, and characters readily appreciated by Roman audiences, Roman playwrights for the most part set themselves to adapt Greek plays for Roman audiences, the adaptations in some instances approaching direct translations. Thus we are told of a beginning of a Roman theater in 240 B.C. when Livius Andronicus (c284–c204 B.C.), an emancipated Greek slave from Tarentum, presented Latin translations of a Greek tragedy and a Greek comedy, in Greek meters, setting a precedent for his successors who attempted both comedy (*fabula palliata*) and tragedy: Cnaeus Naevius (c270–c201 B.C.), credited with seven tragedies, 34 comedies mainly adapted from Greek New Comedy, and the creation of the Roman historical drama, known as the *fabula praetexta*; and Quintus Ennius (239–169 B.C.), author of 20 or more tragedies and of an undetermined number of comedies. Titus Maccius Plautus (c251–184 B.C.) confined his efforts to comedy; of his joke-packed comedies 21 have survived, and titles of others, among them unabashed adaptations from Menander, Philemon, Diphilus, and Demophilus; he was the most popular Roman comic poet, and his plays were repeatedly revived. Of Caecilius Statius, another manumitted slave, Roman comic poet next most admired after Plautus, we have titles and fragments, but no complete plays. Greek titles betray the source of most of his theater, and his *Plocium* was a close paraphrase of Menander's *Plokion*. Of Publius Terentius Afer (Terence), c195–159 B.C., still another manumitted slave, six plays survive, four adapted from Menander, two from Apollodorus of Carystus. Apparently these were all he ever presented, all very sophisticated and polished, too much so for his audience, it appears, for he never achieved popularity, even if the preservation of his plays indicates a measure of grudging respect. Terence was criticized for *contaminatio*, which seems to refer to his acknowledged practice of combining scenes from two or more Greek plays. Luscius Lanuvinus borrowed two plays from Menander, Sextus Turpilius six. Other Roman comic poets who adapted Greek New Comedy are hardly more than names: Quintus Trabea, Marcus Atilius, Aquilius, Licinius Imbrex. We hear also of a native Roman comedy, native insofar as it professed to abjure Greek models, the *fabula togata* or *tabernaria*, represented only by titles and fragments, whose principal poets were Titinius, Quinctius Atta, and L. Afranius. Thereafter the popular taste demanded less exacting fare, and farce and mime took over the Roman stage. (JJ)

Drama (drä′ma̱). See **Drabescus.**

Drances (dran′sēz). In the *Aeneid,* an aged and garrulous Latin, an enemy of Turnus. Following the death of Mezentius during the war between Aeneas and Turnus, Drances attempted to arrange a peace between Latinus and Aeneas so that the Latins could help to build the new Troy. He was unsuccessful in this attempt. He goaded and taunted Turnus and dared him to engage in single combat with Aeneas so that the rest of the Latins might be spared the horrors of further warfare.

Drangiana (dran-ji-ā′na̱). [Also: **Drangiane;** modern name, **Seistan.**] In ancient geography, a region in C Asia, bounded on the N by Areia, on the E by Arachosia, on the S by Gedrosia, and on the W by Carmania. It was a province of the ancient Persian empire, and was conquered by Alexander the Great, who brought it into his empire. The area lies in what is now SW Afghanistan and E Iran.

Drepana (drep′an-a̱). The island of the Phaeacians, later known as Corcyra (Corfu). The name Drepana means sickle and was given to this island either because it was formed from the sickle which Cronus threw into the sea after mutilating Uranus, or because Demeter, whose symbol is the sickle, once lived on the island. Still another explanation is that the outline of the island, as seen on a map, suggests the shape of a sickle.

Drepanum (drep'a-num). [Modern name, **Trapani.**] A cape and town on the west coast of Sicily. It was near the cape that Cronus threw the mutilated genitals of Uranus, along with the sickle that performed the emasculation, into the sea, according to some accounts. The discarded sickle gave the cape its name. Aeneas stopped at Drepanum on his way to seek his destined home in Italy after the Trojan War. Here Anchises, the father of Aeneas, died. In the First Punic War the city was one of the strongholds of the Carthaginians, was fortified by Hamilcar Barca, and was close to the scene of the great Carthaginian naval victory (249 B.C.) by Adherbal over the Roman fleet under Publius Claudius. It fell to the Romans only after a protracted siege in 241 B.C.

Drusilla (drö-sil'a). Daughter of Germanicus and Agrippina, and sister and mistress of Caligula.

Drusilla. Daughter of Caligula and Caesonia. She was murdered following the murder of Caligula.

Drusilla Livia. See **Livia Drusilla.**

Drusus (drö'sus), **Marcus Livius.** Roman politician, who died probably 109 B.C. He was tribune of the plebs conjointly with Caius Gracchus in 122 B.C., his election having been procured by the Senate, whose members were alarmed at the democratic innovations of the latter. In collusion with the Senate he opposed his veto to the bills brought forward by his colleague, and introduced instead bills of similar import, but making more extravagant concessions, which were passed by the Senate. He was consul in 112 B.C., and while governor of Macedonia, which he obtained as his province, defeated the Thracians and reached the Danube.

Drusus, Marcus Livius. Roman politician; son of Marcus Livius Drusus (d. 109 B.C.). Marcus Livius the son was assassinated at Rome in 91 B.C. He became tribune of the plebs (91 B.C.), whose favor he won by largesses of grain, and by the introduction of a bill providing for a new division of the public lands. This bill, together with another which restored to the Senate the places on the juries of which it had been deprived by Caius Gracchus, was passed by the comitia, but declared null and void by the Senate. He was assassinated as he was about to bring forward a proposal to bestow Roman citizenship on the Italians (that is to say, on the people of Italy as a whole and not simply those who lived in the city of Rome). His death gave the signal for the outbreak of the Social War.

Drusus, Nero Claudius. [Called **Drusus Senior;** surnamed **Germanicus.**] Roman general, born 38 B.C.; died in Germany, 9 B.C. He was the son of Livia Drusilla by Tiberius Claudius Nero, and was born shortly after the marriage of his mother with the emperor Augustus. With his older brother Tiberius, who later became emperor, he was adopted by Augustus, and at an early age married Antonia, the daughter of Mark Antony. He subdued a revolt in Gaul in 13 B.C., and, starting in 12 B.C. from the left bank of the Rhine, undertook four campaigns in Germany proper with his brother Tiberius. In the course of these campaigns, whence his name Germanicus, he led the Roman armies to the Weser and the Elbe. He died on the way back, in consequence of a fall from his horse.

Drusus Caesar. [Called **Drusus Junior.**] Son of Tiberius and Vipsania, born c13 B.C.; poisoned 23 A.D. He quelled a mutiny of the legions in Pannonia in 14 A.D., was consul in 15 A.D., was appointed governor of Illyricum in 17, was consul in 21, and in 22 was invested with the *tribunicia potestas,* whereby he was declared heir apparent to the throne. He is said to have lived an extremely dissolute life and so angered his father thereby, that when Drusus died, Tiberius curtailed the period of official mourning. Moreover, the tale is told that when an embassy from Troy arrived to offer condolences to Tiberius a month or two after the death of Drusus, Tiberius ironically offered condolences to the embassy on the loss of their eminent citizen, Hector. Later, Tiberius learned that Drusus had not died from his excesses, but that his wife Livilla had brought about his death by poison, in alliance with Sejanus, the commander of the Praetorian Guard, favorite of Tiberius, and Livilla's lover. When he learned this,

Tiberius energetically sought to investigate the crime and eventually ordered the death of Sejanus.

Dryad (drī′ad). A deity or nymph of the woods, or a nymph supposed to live in trees or preside over woods. See **Hamadryad**.

Dryas (drī′as). In Greek mythology, a son of Lycurgus of Thrace. Lycurgus, driven mad for his indignities to Dionysus, killed Dryas under the impression that he was pruning a tree. Thrace became barren because of this crime and could become fruitful again only if Lycurgus was punished. He was torn to pieces by wild horses.

Dryope (drī′ō-pē). In mythology, sometimes named as a nymph and sometimes as the sister of Iole, daughter of Eurytus. As she played with the hamadryads, Apollo appeared among them disguised as a turtle. Dryope picked up the turtle, which immediately changed into a snake and frightened the hamadryads away. Apollo then assumed his own form and ravished Dryope, who bore him a son, Amphissus. One day as she was carrying her infant son, she stopped to pick blossoms from a lotus tree for her child. Blood dropped from the blossoms and ran down the tree trunk, for Dryope had unfortunately chosen to pick flowers from a tree that was the home of the nymph Lotis. In terror Dryope tried to flee but her feet were rooted to the ground, her body became wooden, and as her husband, Andraemon, and her father came to look for her, bark grew up over her breast and neck. She had time only to plead with Andraemon to take care of her child before her face was forever enclosed in bark. In place of the nymph there stood a slender poplar tree.

Dryope. In Greek mythology, a nymph of the fountain, Pegae, in Mysia, who fell in love with Hylas, squire of Heracles, as he stopped to draw water, and pulled him into the spring to dwell with the nymphs.

Dryopes (drī′ō-pēz) or **Dryopians** (drī-ō′pē-anz). An ancient people of Greece. According to legendary accounts, Dryops was a son of Apollo and Dia, the daughter of Lycaon. Fearing her father's anger, Dia hid her infant son in a hollow oak tree, whence his name is derived. Dryops became the founder of the Dryopians, and settled with his people near Mount Parnassus. During the reign of Dryops' son Thiodamas, Heracles passed through the land on his way to Trachis. He saw Thiodamas plowing with a yoke of oxen and demanded one of them. Thiodamas refused his demand. Heracles killed him and carried off his son who, some say, was Hylas. Afterward Heracles conquered the Dryopians and carried off their leading citizens and dedicated them as slaves at Delphi. The priestess of Delphi ordered them to be taken to the Peloponnesus, where they sought asylum with Eurystheus, the enemy of Heracles. With other Dryopians, they built the Argive towns of Hermione, Asine, and Eion. Those Dryopians who did not go to the Peloponnesus fled to Euboea and Cyprus and ultimately lost their language, customs, and identity as a separate tribe. The Argives drove the Dryopians out of Argos and they went to Messenia. On the Messenian coast they occupied Messenian Asine. The Dryopians who settled there (some say the town was given to them by the Spartans after the Second Messenian War) were the only Dryopians who were proud to keep their name. They built a shrine to Dryops and celebrated mysteries in his honor every other year.

Duilius (dū-il′i-us), **Caius.** Roman general; fl. in the 3rd century B.C. He was consul in 260 B.C., when he defeated the Carthaginians near Mylae (modern Milazzo), on the N coast of Sicily. This was the first naval success gained by Rome. Duilius, a land officer placed in charge of the fleet by necessity, decided to fight the naval engagement as a land battle, and won by using his new device, the *corvus* (q.v.).

Dulichium (dū-lik′i-um). In ancient geography, an island in the Ionian Sea, near Ithaca. According to legend, it was a part of the island kingdom of Odysseus, and the home of some of the suitors of Penelope.

Dumnorix (dum′nō-riks). A chief of the Aedui; killed in Gaul, 54 B.C. He was a brother of Divitiacus, friend of Caesar. Pardoned once by Caesar for permitting hostile forces through his territory, he led his cavalry from the Roman camp as Caesar prepared the British invasion, and was captured and killed.

Dura (dū′ra). The Latin form of a Semitic word *dûr* "wall," which appears as the name of several fortified communities in western Asia, e.g. *dûr sharrukin* was Sargon's palace at Khorsabad. See **Europus (Dura).** (JJ)

Dura-Europus. See **Europus (Dura).**

Duris (dū′ris). Attic potter and painter in the red-figure style, active c500–470 B.C., fond of scenes from everyday life. Thirty vessels with his signature as painter are extant, and over 200 more have been attributed to him. Among his extant works is a kylix (Louvre) with Eos carrying off the body of her son Memnon, and a psykter (British Museum) with Satyrs. The inside of a cup (Munich) c480 B.C., shows Heracles resting as Athena pours wine into his cup. Scenes showing Peleus carrying off Thetis as her sisters run to their father for aid decorate the outside of the cup. This vessel was signed by Hieron as the potter. Another cup (Munich) shows a banqueter and a flute player on the inside, and Heracles striking his teacher Linus on the outside.

Duris. Greek historian. He was a native of Samos and was active in the first half of the 3rd century B.C. He wrote the *Samian Chronicle,* on the history of Samos, and a history of Greece and Macedonia, from 370 to about 281 B.C. in 23 books. Fragments of his works which survive show them to have been rather random collections of material on the regions with which he occupied himself.

Dying Alexander (al-eg-zan′dẽr). Name given to a sculptured head, held to be a Greek original of Hellenistic date, very remarkable for the intensity of its expression of pain, and of admirable execution.

Dying Gaul (gôl), **The.** [Formerly called **The Dying Gladiator.**] Ancient statue of the Pergamene school, in the Capitoline Museum, Rome. The warrior, nude, sits on the ground with bowed head, supporting himself with his right arm. The statue is considered especially fine in the mastery of anatomy displayed, and in its characterization of the racial type. It is thought possibly to have been commissioned by Attalus as a monument to his victories over the Gauls.

Dymas (dī′mas). Named in the *Iliad* as a king in Phrygia who dwelt near the San-

garius River. Homer calls him the father of Hecuba and Asius, and the grandfather of Hector.

Dymas. In the *Aeneid,* a Trojan who came to Aeneas' side fighting the Greeks on the night Troy fell. He had disguised himself in armor taken from a dead Greek in order to circulate freely among the Greeks and slay them. His Trojan comrades, thinking he was a Greek, slew him.

Dyme (dī′mē). In ancient geography, a city of Achaea in the Peloponnesus, situated on the Gulf of Calydon (Gulf of Patras). It was founded by the Epeans. It was the westernmost of the 12 Ionian cities of Achaea.

Dysaules (dī-sô′lēz). According to some accounts, a man of Eleusis who was the father of Triptolemus. But others say he was Celeus, and that he took the name Dysaules (*Unfortunate*) when he lost two of his sons. According to this account, Demeter came to his house in Eleusis in disguise when she was searching for Persephone. Abas, a son of the house, mocked her because, being thirsty, she drank greedily, and Demeter transformed him into a lizard. Then Demeter sought to make a second son of Celeus, Demophoön, immortal by burning away his mortal parts in the fire. The child's mother interrupted her and cried out in alarm, Demeter dropped the child, and he perished. It was then that Celeus took the name Dysaules. However, Demeter promised to make amends for the loss of his two sons by making a third one, Triptolemus, immortal and a great benefactor of mankind.

Dyscolus (dis′kō-lus), **Apollonius.** See **Apollonius Dyscolus.**

Dysponteus (dis-pon′tūs). In Greek legend, a son of Oenomaus. According to some accounts, he founded the town of Dyspontium (q.v.), on the Alpheus River in Elis.

Dyspontium (dis-pon′ti-um). Town near the Alpheus River, in Elis. According to some accounts, it was founded by Dysponteus, a son of Oenomaus. It was a vassal community of Elis, and was destroyed in the 6th century B.C. when it joined Pisa in a revolt against Elis.

—E—

Eagle. A bird sacred to Zeus. He appeared in the form of an eagle when he abducted Ganymede, according to some accounts, and frequently he sent the eagle as an omen.

Eburum (eb'ū-rum). [Modern name, **Eboli.**] Town in Campania, S Italy, situated near the Silarus River, about 45 miles SE of Naples. The ruins of ancient Paestum, including beautiful Greek temples, are nearby.

Ecbatana (ek-bat'a-na). In ancient geography, the capital of Media. According to the Greeks it was built by order of Deïoces in the first half of the 7th century B.C. The ancient city, on a hill, was surrounded by seven encircling walls which were coated, beginning with the outer one, in white, black, scarlet, blue, and orange colors, with the two innermost walls coated respectively with silver and gold. Ecbatana was taken from the Median king Astyages by Cyrus the Great (550 B.C.), and became the summer palace of the Persian and Parthian kings. Alexander the Great captured it in 330 B.C. When Alexander returned from India he stopped at Ecbatana for several months and held great feasts and celebrations. Here, 324 B.C., his friend Hephaestion died. Modern Hamadan, in W Iran, occupies the ancient site of Ecbatana, and is, according to tradition, the site of the tombs of Biblical Mordecai and Esther.

Ecclesia (ē-klē'zi-a). A Greek word meaning a "calling-forth," or convocation, and thus an assembly of, e.g., the voting populace, the people, as distinct from the *boule* or council of elders. Aristophanes' play *Ecclesiazusae* is "Women in the Assembly." A building designed as a meeting-place for the *ecclesia* might be called an *ecclesiasterion*, as at Priene. In Christian contexts *ecclesia* denoted an assembly of Christians, a congregation, and then came to refer to the building in which an *ecclesia* or congregation met to worship, a church, and as such survives, as in It. *chiesa,* Fr. *église,* Sp. *iglesia,* etc., and in such English derivatives as "ecclesiastic(al)." As the title of a book of the Old Testament, *Ecclesiastes,* means "Preacher." (JJ)

Ecclesiazusae (ē-kle″zi-a-zö'sē). Comedy of Aristophanes, exhibited in 392 B.C. In it the women of Athens meet in the Ecclesia or Assembly (whence the name, which means "Women in the Assembly"), and decide to take control of the state, with community of goods and husbands. The comedy ridicules alike rights for women and socialistic theories. The longest word in the Greek language, a compound of 169 letters, and 77 syllables, is found in the play.

Echecles (ē'kē-klēz). In Homeric legend *(Iliad)*, a son of Actor and a prince of the Myrmidons. He married Polymela, daughter of Phylas, who had born Eudorus to Hermes, and brought up Eudorus as his own son.

Echemus (ē'kē-mus). In Greek legend, a king in Arcadia. He was a descendant of Aleus. When Hyllus, son of Heracles, made his second invasion of the Peloponnesus, he proposed that control of the land be decided by single combat, in order to avoid bloodshed. Hyllus offered to fight any champion the Arcadians or other Peloponnesians named. He promised that if he was defeated the Heraclidae would withdraw for a long period of years, but if he won, the Heraclidae would assume power in the Peloponnesus. Echemus volunteered to accept the challenge of Hyllus, and on the boundary between Megara and Corinth the duel was fought. Echemus defeated and slew Hyllus, and the Heraclidae withdrew as they had promised. Echemus married Timandra, daughter of Tyndareus. His tomb was at Tegea, in Arcadia.

Echetus (ē'kē-tus). A mythical king of Epirus who put out his daughter's eyes with bronze spikes and set her to grinding grains of bronze in a dungeon, with the cruel promise that he would restore her sight when she had ground the bronze into corn. Arete recalled

fat, fāte, fär, fãre, errant; net, mē, hėr ardent; pin, pīne; not, nōte, mŏve, nôr,

her sufferings in order to persuade Alcinous, king of the Phaeacians, not to surrender Medea to the Colchians, who had pursued her and now demanded her return to Colchis.

Echidna (ē-kid′na̱). In Greek mythology, a monster, half beautiful maiden and half serpent. She was the daughter of Ceto and Phorcys (or of Chrysaor and Callirrhoë), and by Typhon was the mother of: two-headed Orthus, the hound of Geryon; Cerberus, the brazen-throated hound of Hades; the Hydra of Lerna; the fabulous Chimaera. By her own son Orthus she was the mother of the Theban Sphinx that was slain by Oedipus, and of the Nemean Lion, slain by Heracles. In addition, according to some accounts, she was the mother of Ladon, the vultures that gnawed Prometheus' vitals, and the sea monster Scylla. Echidna was slain while asleep by the many-eyed Argus.

Echinades (ē-kin′a̱-dēz). In ancient geography, a group of islands W of Acarnania in Greece, formed in and near the mouth of the Achelous River and now reunited, in part, to the mainland. According to Greek mythology, the islands were once naiads. These five naiads forgot to sacrifice to Artemis when they sacrificed to all the other rural deities at a festival. In her anger Artemis flooded the area where they were dancing, split it up into five parts and washed it into the sea where the land and the naiads became the islands known as the Echinades. Another one of the Echinades had formerly been the daughter of Hippodamas. She was loved by the river-god Achelous and transformed into an island when her father hurled her into the sea.

Echion (ē-kī′on). In Greek legend, a son of Hermes and Antianeira. With his brother, Erytus, he joined Jason on the voyage of the *Argo*. As herald of the Argonauts it was he who went ashore on Lemnos and convinced Hypsipyle, the queen, that the Argonauts were not hostile and persuaded her to let them land. They remained in Lemnos over a year.

Echion. In Greek mythology, one of the crop of armed men who sprang up when Cadmus sowed the dragon's teeth. He was one of the five who survived when the armed men warred among themselves, and later married Agave, daughter of Cadmus, and founded one of the five great families of Thebes. Pentheus was his son.

Echion. In Greek legend, one of the Greeks who entered Troy in the Wooden Horse. According to some accounts, when the Greeks silently descended the ladder from the belly of the horse, Echion fell and broke his neck.

Echo (ek′ō). In mythology, a talkative wood nymph who at last lost the power to originate any conversation. This came about because Hera, suspicious of the many amorous adventures of her husband Zeus, was too often delayed in discovering him in his affairs by listening to the chatter of Echo. To punish Echo for protecting Zeus in this manner Hera took away her power of speech, leaving her only the ability to repeat the last words spoken to her. By Pan, Echo was the mother of Iynx. Later she fell in love with Narcissus and, being scorned by him, wasted away until nothing was left of her but her voice.

Ecnomus (ek′nō-mus). Hill near the modern town of Licata, on the S coast of Sicily. Here the Carthaginians defeated (311 B.C.) the Syracusan tyrant Agathocles. Near here the Roman fleet defeated (256 B.C.) the Carthaginians.

Edile (ē′dīl). See **Aedile.**

Eëtion (ē-ē′ti-on). In Homeric legend (*Iliad*), a king of Thebes in Cilicia and ruler of the Cilicians. He was the father of Hector's wife Andromache. Achilles attacked his land in the years before the siege of Troy, killed Eëtion and seven of his sons, and sacked his city, but he gave Eëtion honorable burial, in full armor. Nymphs planted a grove about his grave.

Eëtion. In Homeric legend (*Iliad*), an Imbrian who ransomed Priam's son, Lycaon, from Euneus (who had bought him from Achilles), and sent him to Arisbe, from whence Lycaon returned home to the war and to his death.

Egeria (ē-jir′i-a̱). [Also: **Aegeria.**] In Roman mythology, one of the Camenae, or nymphs of springs, as well as a birth goddess and a prophetess. She had a fountain in the grove of Diana at Aricia. According to the Romans, she was the wife of Numa, and instructed him with regard to the forms of worship he was to introduce. Because of her role as instructress of a king, the name

actǫr; up, lūte, pu̇ll; oi, oil; ou, out; ᴛн, then; ḏ as d or j, ṣ as s or sh, ṭ as t or ch, ẓ as z or zh.

Egeria is sometimes applied to any woman adviser of statesmen, or others. On the death of Numa, Egeria went to Aricia and so disturbed the worship there by her lamentations that she was transformed into a fountain. Other accounts say that she married Hippolytus, son of Theseus, who was restored to life by Asclepius and carried to Italy by Artemis.

Egesta (ē-jes′ta) or **Aegesta**, or **Segesta** (sē-). In the *Aeneid*, a Trojan woman who was sold as a slave to Sicilian merchants by Laomedon, king of Troy. Aphrodite rescued her and she became the mother of Acestes, or Aegestes, by the river-god Crimisus in Sicily. The city of Segesta, founded by her son, was named for her. Some say Egesta later returned to Troy and bore Anchises to Capys.

Egypt (ē-jipt). [Biblical name, **Mizraim;** Latin, **Aegyptus;** Arabic **Misr.**] Country in NE Africa, famous for the great antiquity and former splendor of its civilization. It is bounded by the Mediterranean Sea on the N, and extends S, including the delta and the valley of the Nile River, to the second cataract of the Nile and the border of the Sudan. On the E it is bounded by Israel, the Gulf of Aqaba, and the Red Sea, and on the W by Libya. It includes the Sinai Peninsula, between the gulfs of Suez and Aqaba. The usual geographical divisions are the Nile valley region from Cairo south, called Upper Egypt, and the delta region, called Lower Egypt. To the ancient Greeks Egypt consisted of the delta and the land lying along the Nile, and was for this reason called, "The Gift of the River." According to them, the regions to the west and the interior of Africa were Libya (of indefinite boundaries), and those to the east and south were Aethiopia. Trade between Egypt and Crete began at least as early as the 16th century B.C. and probably from much earlier times. The Egyptians called the Cretans *Keftiu,* and evidence of commerce between the Keftiu kings and the Egyptian rulers exists from the XVIIIth Dynasty.

A history of ancient Egypt for Greek consumption was compiled in the 3rd century B.C. by the priest Manetho, who listed the kings in 31 dynasties. The dynasties are grouped thus by Breasted: the Old King-

dom (c3400–c2475 B.C.), Dynasties I–VI; the Middle Kingdom (c2445–1580 B.C.), Dynasties IX–XVII; the New Kingdom or Empire (1580–1090 B.C.), Dynasties XVIII–XX. The First Dynasty was founded by Menes c3400 B.C. During the early dynasties Memphis was the leading city, and in the time of the IVth Dynasty occurred the building of the Pyramids (c2900–2800 B.C.). The construction of Lake Moeris and the labyrinth are assigned to the XIIth Dynasty. Thebes now became the center, and later the invasion of the Hyksos occurred (in the XVth Dynasty). After a period of confusion and obscurity Egypt was united under the great Theban XVIIIth Dynasty, and under this and the XIXth Dynasty reached its highest point in extent and in the grandeur of its monuments. Among the great sovereigns were Thutmose III, Seti I, and Rameses II. The "Pharaoh" of the Exodus has frequently been identified with Merneptal or Meneptah of the XIXth Dynasty, and the date stated approximately at c1300 B.C., but he is now dated at 1225–1215 B.C. With the next dynasty began the decline of the country's power. There were some revivals of power, and in the 7th and 6th centuries Greek settlements began, but in 525 B.C. Egypt was conquered by Cambyses, and this Persian dynasty ranks as the XXVIIth. From 406 B.C. native rulers again held power, but in 340 B.C. a short-lived Persian dynasty (the XXXIst and the last of Manetho) began; this was overthrown in 332 B.C. by Alexander the Great. After his death Egypt was ruled by his general Ptolemy and Ptolemy's successors down to the death of the famous Cleopatra (Cleopatra VII or VI) in 30 B.C., when Augustus seized it as the private province of the emperor.

Eidothea (ī-dō′thē-a). See **Idothea.**

Eidyia (ī-dī′ya). See **Idyia.**

Eileithyia (ī-lī-thī′ya). Goddess who attended women in childbirth. See **Ilithyia.**

Eioneus (ē-yō′nē-us). In Greek mythology, the father of Dia. Ixion promised Eioneus rich gifts in return for Dia but instead of handing them over he laid a trap for Eioneus. He constructed in front of his palace a hidden pit, into which Eioneus fell and was burned to death by the charcoal fire in it.

Eioneus. Named by Homer as the father of

the Thracian king, Rhesus. Others give the river-god Strymon as the father of Rhesus.

Eirene (ī-rē′nē). See **Irene**, goddess of peace.

Elaïs (ē′lā̇-is). In Greek mythology, one of the three daughters of Anius, king of Delos, and his wife Dorippe. By a gift of Dionysus, to whom her father had dedicated her and her sisters, she could turn whatever she touched into oil if she first invoked Dionysus. Her sisters were Oeno and Spermo, and by gifts of the same god they could turn whatever they wished into wine and grain respectively. Agamemnon ordered them brought to Troy to provision the Greek fleet, and when their father refused to let them go, Odysseus, who had been sent to fetch them, bound them and carried them off. They escaped, but as Agamemnon threatened war, they surrendered. They appealed to Dionysus for aid and were transformed into doves by the god, for which reason doves were especially protected on Delos.

Elam (ē′lam). [Also: **Susiana**; ancient Greek, **Elymaïs**.] Ancient country and empire E of the lower Tigris, S of Media, and N of the Persian Gulf. It is a region of fertile and picturesque mountains, valleys, and ravines, the only flat tract being on the shores of the Persian Gulf; and was in very high antiquity the seat of a mighty empire of which Susa was the capital. The oldest historical information about Elam is that it subjugated Babylonia in the period c2300–2076 B.C. The Elamite dynasty is identical with the Median of Berosus, which ruled over Babylonia, c2300–2076 B.C. Among these Elamite kings is also very probably to be counted Chedorlaomer (Kudur–Lagamaru) of Gen. xiv. The next historical notice is that Elam was subdued by Nebuchadnezzar I, king of Babylonia, c1130 B.C. From the 8th century B.C. on, Elam was connected with the rivalry between Assyria and Babylonia, supporting the latter against the former. Elam was defeated by Sargon in 721 and 710 B.C., and by Sennacherib in several campaigns, especially in a decisive battle on the Tigris c691 B.C. In 645 B.C. Assurbanipal destroyed Susa. Soon after this catastrophe Elam is met with under the dominion of Theispes. In union with Media and Persia it helped to bring about the fall of Assyria

and Babylonia. It shared thenceforth the fate of the other Assyrian provinces, and had no history of its own. The ancient Elamites were not Semites. This is ascertained by the names of their kings, which are alien to all of the Semitic dialects, and by their representations on the monuments, which exhibit a type widely different from the Semitic. The enumeration of Elam among the sons of Shem in Gen. x. 22 may perhaps be accounted for by the fact that the Elamite valley was early settled by the Semites, who predominated over the non-Semitic element of the population, and also by the fact that the Elamites had for more than two centuries the upper hand in Semitic Babylonia. The name Elymaïs was used either as an equivalent of Elam or for a part of it.

Elaphebolion (el″ȧ-fē̇-bō′li-on). The ninth month of the Attic year, corresponding to the latter part of March to the middle of April, approximately. A feast of Artemis Elaphebolos in Phocis was held in this month.

Elaphios (ē-laf′i-os). Epithet of Artemis. Some say it refers to Artemis as a huntress of deer. Others say the epithet was given to her because Elaphios was the name of an Elean woman who was reared by the goddess.

Elara (ē′lā̇-rȧ). According to some accounts, the mother of Tityus by Zeus, but Gaea nursed him and gave him second birth.

Elatus (ē′lȧ-tus). In Greek mythology, a son of Arcas and either Meganira, the nymph Chrysopelia, or the dryad Erato. He inherited the region around Mount Cyllene in Arcadia as his share of his fathers′ kingdom, and named it Cyllene for his son. Some say he married Laodice, daughter of Cinyras, and that she bore him Stymphalus and Pereus. Others say he was also the father of that Ischys who was slain by the gods for causing Coronis to be unfaithful to Apollo; and of Aepytus and Cyllen. Elatus went to Phocis to assist the Phocians in a war, and remained to found the city of Elateia there.

Elea (ē′lē̇-ȧ). See **Velia**.

Eleatics (el-ē̇-at′iks). School of Greek philosophy founded by Xenophanes of Colophon (c570–480 B.C.), who resided in Elea, or Velia, in Magna Graecia. The most distinguished philosophers of this school were Parmenides and Zeno. The main Eleatic doctrines are developments of the conception that the One, or Absolute, alone is real.

Electra (ē-lek'trạ). In Greek legend, a daughter of Agamemnon and Clytemnestra, and the sister of Orestes, Iphigenia, and Chrysothemis. When Agamemnon returned victorious from Troy he was brutally murdered by Clytemnestra and her lover Aegisthus. Electra secretly gave the young Orestes into the charge of an aged tutor and commanded him to take the boy to Strophius in Phocis, where he would be safe from the evil designs of Aegisthus. Electra remained in Mycenae, kept in a state of virtual slavery by Clytemnestra and Aegisthus. However, her spirit was far from broken and she continually and publicly condemned her mother as an adulteress and a murderess. Electra had been betrothed to her cousin Castor, and after he died and was deified the leading princes of Greece sought her hand. But Aegisthus feared that she might bear a son who would avenge the murder of Agamemnon, and so rejected all her suitors. He wanted to have Electra slain but Clytemnestra heeded the prohibitions of the gods against the slaying of one's own kin and forbade him to do so. As she saw it was impossible to convince Electra that the murder of Agamemnon was justified, because of his sacrifice of Iphigenia at Aulis, she kept her in a state of misery, and according to some accounts, finally allowed Aegisthus to marry her to a peasant. But he, out of respect for his high-born bride, and out of fear of her brother, never consummated the marriage. Electra's one hope for release from her miserable state and for vengeance for her father's murder lay in the return of Orestes. She sent him frequent urgent reminders of his obligation and maintained her defiance of Clytemnestra and her scorn for Aegisthus by vociferously praying for the return of Orestes and with open expressions of her hope for vengeance. In the eighth year after the murder of Agamemnon Orestes secretly returned to Mycenae with Pylades, a son of Strophius and the faithful friend of Orestes. While his presence in Mycenae was still unknown to Clytemnestra he made himself known to Electra and was joyously reunited with her. Rapidly they made their plans. Orestes was troubled by doubts concerning

the deed he was planning, but Electra spurred him on: a son must avenge his father or risk the displeasure of the gods. She had been beside herself for years with grief over her father's hateful death, humiliation over her own state, and a burning desire for vengeance on Clytemnestra and Aegisthus. When Orestes wavered she stiffened his resolution. By pretending he was a messenger with news of Orestes' death he secured entry into the palace and killed his mother and Aegisthus. Electra ultimately married Pylades, after he had returned from Tauris with Orestes, and bore him two sons, Medon and Strophius. She died and was buried at Mycenae. See also *The Choëphoroe*, by Aeschylus, *Electra*, by Sophocles, and *Orestes*, by Euripides.

Electra. In Greek mythology, a daughter of Pleione and Atlas; one of the Pleiades. She was the mother of Dardanus by Zeus. With her sisters her image was placed among the stars but she withdrew from the group, according to some accounts, so that she would not have to witness the fall of Troy, a city inhabited by descendants of her son. See **Pleiades.**

Electra. In Greek mythology, an ocean-nymph. She was wedded to Thaumas and bore him Iris of the "fast-flying feet," and the Harpies—Aello and Ocypete.

Electra. A drama by Sophocles. Agamemnon, commander of the Greeks assembled to sail to Troy to recapture Helen, sacrificed his daughter, Iphigenia, in order to propitiate Artemis and obtain favorable winds for his fleet. When, ten years later, he returned victorious from Troy, his wife Clytemnestra, with the aid of her lover Aegisthus, murdered him, and she and Aegisthus became the rulers of his kingdom. Agamemnon's daughters, Electra and Chrysothemis, remained in the palace as virtual prisoners, but his young son Orestes had been sent away by Electra in the care of a trusted tutor. Grown to manhood, Orestes, at the command of Apollo, returned to avenge his father's death. The play relates the manner of his doing so.

Orestes, Pylades, his close friend, and the now-aged tutor enter. The tutor points out the house of Agamemnon, now the house of Aegisthus, at Mycenae, overlooking the plain and city of Argos, and tells him that now is the time to act. Orestes bids him enter the house and inform Clytemnestra that he is dead, killed in a chariot race. Meanwhile he goes with Pylades to make offerings to his father's grave. Electra then appears and bewails her unhappy fate. She longs for Orestes to return and avenge her father, whose skull was split with an ax by Aegisthus, and laments that she is now the only one who mourns him. A chorus of women of Mycenae try to comfort her. They tell her that since tears cannot lighten her sorrow she should hope for the return of Orestes and put her trust in god. But Electra is beside herself. She is outraged that Aegisthus is in her father's place, and implacable in her desire to punish her mother and her lover. Her sister Chrysothemis joins her and tries to persuade her to give up her defiance and her mad desire for vengeance. She feels that, being weak, helpless women, they must adjust themselves to their situation. Electra absolutely refuses to play any such part. Then Chrysothemis tells her that Clytemnestra is frightened; she dreamed that Agamemnon returned, took the sceptre from Aegisthus and planted it so firmly in the ground that it blossomed into a tree whose shade covered all Mycenae. Encouraged, Electra sends Chrysothemis to put a lock of her own hair on Agamemnon's grave, in place of the libations Clytemnestra had ordered to ward off the evil omen of the dream. Next there follows a bitter conversation between Clytemnestra and Electra, in which Clytemnestra justifies the murder of Agamemnon because he had sacrificed Iphigenia, and Electra defends the sacrifice, and adds that Clytemnestra's real reason for the murder was that she was Aegisthus' paramour. Clytemnestra then prays to Apollo to avert the evil foreshadowed in her dream. The tutor now enters and tells the two women that Orestes is dead. Clytemnestra is torn between maternal anguish at the loss of a child and great relief that he can no longer return and punish her for his father's death. Electra is in despair. As Clytemnestra departs Chrysothemis returns. In great excitement she says that Orestes has come home: she has found a lock of hair at their father's grave that can only be his. Desolately Electra tells her that Orestes is dead. But she is resolved on vengeance and asks Chrysothemis to help her,

since now there is no one else to do it. Chrysothemis points out that they are only weak women and, adding that she would rather be alive in misery than a dead heroine, refuses. When she has gone Orestes and Pylades come before Electra as messengers. They give her an urn which they say contains the ashes of Orestes, but on seeing her grief and learning that she is Electra, Orestes reveals himself to her. She rejoices. The tutor comes and warns Orestes to act at once: Clytemnestra is alone. Orestes and Pylades go inside. Presently Electra exults as she hears Clytemnestra scream. Now Aegisthus approaches and asks after the messengers who have brought news of Orestes. Informed that they are in the house and that he will see proof that they bring a message of death, he orders the doors to be flung open. A covered corpse, flanked by Orestes and Pylades, is revealed. Aegisthus, at the suggestion of Orestes, whom he has not recognized, draws back the sheet from the face of the corpse and looks on the face of Clytemnestra. Almost at once he realizes that the messenger is Orestes and knows why he has come. Orestes commands him to go to the place where Agamemnon was murdered, for it is there he intends to kill him. They go into the house. The play ends with the chorus saying that now at last the House of Atreus is free from suffering.

Electrides (ē-lek′tri-dēz). In Greek legend, the Amber Islands (where the trees weep amber), situated at the mouth of the fabulous river Eridanus (later identified with the Po River in Italy). See also **Amber Islands**.

Electryon (ē-lek′tri-on). In Greek mythology, the son of Perseus and Andromeda, and the grandfather of Heracles. He was a king of Mycenae. He left Amphitryon to rule in his place while he waged war against the Taphians, who had slain eight of his sons during a raid in which they stole his cattle, and promised his daughter Alcmene to Amphitryon if he ruled well during his absence. When he returned he found that Amphitryon had ransomed the cattle and expected him to pay the ransom. He refused. Amphitryon angrily hurled a club at one of the cattle, but it struck Electryon instead and killed him.

Eleia (ē-lī′a). See **Elis**.

Elements of Euclid (ū′klid). Most popular

mathematical work of all time, the earliest extant Greek treatise on mathematics, and the oldest scientific textbook still in actual use. It is a book on geometry, both plane and solid, and the theory of numbers, a compendium of mathematical knowledge of the time, arranged in logical order. It was composed by Euclid c300 B.C., was frequently copied in manuscript, and was first printed in 1482. Since that time over a thousand editions have appeared.

Eleusinian (el-ū-sin′i-an). Epithet of Demeter, from the Mysteries which she established at Eleusis. There were sanctuaries of Eleusinian Demeter in various parts of Greece. Among them was one at Pheneüs in Arcadia; in Laconia; and on the borders of Thelpusa in Arcadia. In this last there were stone images of Demeter and the Maid, as well as one of Dionysus. There were also sanctuaries of Eleusinian Demeter at Basilis in Arcadia near the Alpheus River, and at Plataea in Boeotia.

Eleusinian Mysteries. The famous Athenian mysteries and festival of Eleusis, developed from a local agrarian cult into a ritual of personal edification. The gods connected with the mysteries were Demeter, the Greek equivalent of the Roman Ceres, her daughter, Persephone (the Roman Proserpina), and the local Attic divinity Iacchus as the special protectors of agriculture and of all fruitfulness, and as the guardians of Athens. They were held at Eleusis, in Attica, about 14 miles W of Athens, and were the chief cause of its fame. At first initiation into the mysteries was limited to residents of Attica; later it was extended to all Greek citizens, and still later, Romans were admitted to the privileges of membership. Barbarians (which initially of course, included the Romans), murderers, and all who were guilty of serious crimes were barred. A candidate for initiation was proposed by an Athenian citizen who already belonged. The candidates were called *mystae* before full initiation, and *epoptae*, or seers of the highest rite, after. The mysteries were divided into two parts, the Lesser, held in Antestherion, corresponding more or less to February, and the Greater, in Boedromion, equivalent to part of the end of September and the beginning of October. The mysteries were regarded by the ancients themselves as having moral and ethical values in that they

promised, or seemed to promise, happiness after death as a reward for goodness. The chief rites are unknown. Hadrian and Marcus Aurelius did not think it beneath them to accept initiation. Valentinian, the Christian emperor, allowed the Eleusinian mysteries after he had abolished all others, but Theodosius did away with them at the end of the 4th century.

Eleusinium (el-ū-sin′i-um). Sanctuary at Athens, near the western foot of the Acropolis. In accordance with a law of Solon, the Council of 500 met there the day after the celebration of the Mysteries at Eleusis.

Eleusis (ē-lö′sis). A little town about 14 miles W of Athens, in Attica, situated near the bay and opposite the island of Salamis. It was said by some to have been founded by a hero of this name who was a son of Hermes, or of Ogyges. The Cephissus River, a more turbulent stream than the one of the same name in Athens, flowed through the plain of Eleusis into the Gulf of Eleusis. Near this stream is Erineus, where Hades, some say, descended into the lower world with Persephone, and it was nearby that Theseus killed Procrustes. In her desperate search for her daughter Persephone, Demeter, disguised as a humble old woman, came to Eleusis. The daughters of Celeus met her at a place called Anthium (*Flowery Well*) and offered her hospitality in their father's house. As a reward for their kind treatment the goddess, who revealed her identity to Celeus, commanded the people of Eleusis to build a temple for her. When it was completed she occupied it for a time, mourning for her lost daughter. While she mourned the earth was barren and, lest the people perish, the gods arranged for the return of Persephone so that Demeter would restore the fertility of the earth. After this Demeter chose a prince of Eleusis to be her priest, and taught him, Celeus, and others, the arts of agriculture and her sacred rites. At Eleusis is a well called Callichorum (*Well of Fair Dances*), where the women of Eleusis first danced and sang in honor of Demeter. Nearby is the Plain of Rharium, the first land to be sown to wheat and to bear crops. At the annual sacrifices here barley cakes were offered. Here too was the threshing-floor and an altar of Triptolemus who, some say, was the first to whom Demeter taught the arts of agriculture. Eumolpus was a priest of Demeter and the founder of her mysteries. In the time of Erechtheus the Athenians, under his command, and the Eleusinians, aided by Eumolpus, waged war. Eumolpus and his son were killed and the Eleusinians were defeated. Eleusis retained the right to have independent control of the mysteries of Demeter, but in everything else was subordinated to Athens.

Eleusis (*Advent*) was one of the oldest of the parishes of Attica, the seat of a very ancient cult of Demeter, and of the famous Eleusinian mysteries. It was annexed to Athens in the 7th century B.C., but kept control of the mysteries, in the celebration of which the Athenians, as well as Greeks from all other states, annually came for initiation into and celebration of the rites. The observation of the mysteries of Demeter and Kore (Persephone) continued down to the end of the 4th century A.D. Politically, Eleusis played no role in the development of Greece, but its religious significance was of paramount importance. The most important monuments lay within the sacred enclosure at Eleusis, which consisted of a spacious terrace on the E slope of an acropolis, surrounded by a massive wall and towers. The earliest sanctuary antedated the 7th century B.C., and was reconstructed and enlarged in the 6th century B.C. by the Pisistratidae. In succeeding years it was further enlarged as the importance of the mysteries increased. During the Persian Wars it was burned, but was restored by Cimon and Pericles. Entrance to the sanctuary of the Great Goddesses (Demeter and Kore) was forbidden, on pain of death, to the uninitiated. Those who had been initiated, like the traveler Pausanias, never described the buildings within the wall, only ruins of which now remain. Before the sacred enclosure was a large paved court, constructed in Roman times, and nearby an ancient spring where pilgrims purified themselves. Also in the area was a large altar and a ditch where victims, sacrifices to the gods of the Underworld, were burned. A sacred way led to the sanctuary. On the right of the sacred way a grotto cut into the flank of the hill was the precinct of Pluto and represented the entrance to the Underworld by which

Hades (Pluto) carried off Persephone. The sacred precinct was entered through two propylaea (of Roman construction) in succession, and its chief building was the Telesterion, where the rites of initiation took place, rites surrounded by a secrecy that was never entirely violated. The remains of the Telesterion date from the 6th century B.C., with additions made in the time of the Roman emperors, and replace much earlier buildings. The Telesterion was a huge, nearly square, roofed hall, on the four sides of which rows of seats, some of which were cut into the rock, were constructed for the *mystae* (initiated), who sat on them and observed the rites of initiation as they took place. The seats accommodated about 3000 spectators. The unique architecture of the Telesterion and its successive transformations, as well as remains of the entire precinct, were revealed by the excavations of the Archaeological Society of Athens and others, carried out at intervals since 1882.

Eleusis, Bas-relief of. Ancient Greek work of high artistic importance in the National Museum, Athens. It represents Demeter, Kore, and Triptolemus, and is most delicate in execution and expression. It dates from the early 5th century B.C.

Eleutherae (ē-lö′thėr-ē). When Dionysus returned from Asia he freed the cities of Boeotia and founded Eleutherae, the "City of Freedom." The city, originally in Boeotia, later allied itself to Athens, out of hatred of the Thebans. In a cave near Eleutherae Antiope left her twin sons, Amphion and Zethus, as soon as they were born. They were found by shepherds, who washed them in a cold spring beside the cave and took them to their huts to rear them.

Eleutherius (el-ū-thir′i-us). Epithet of Zeus, meaning "Liberator," or "God of Freedom." There was an image of Zeus Eleutherius at Athens. Near the common tomb of the Greeks who fell at the battle of Plataea (479 B.C.), an altar of Zeus Eleutherius was set up. For may years it was the custom to hold games every four years called the Eleutheria. The competitors ran, in armor, before the altar, and were awarded prizes.

Elgin Marbles (el′gin). Collection of Greek sculptures comprising the bulk of the surviving plastic decoration of the Parthenon, and a caryatid and column from the Erechtheum, and recognized as containing the finest existing productions of Greek sculpture. The marbles, now in the British Museum, were brought from Athens between 1801 and 1803 by Thomas Bruce, the 7th Earl of Elgin. The Parthenon sculptures were executed under the direction of Phidias, c440 B.C. The collection includes remains of the pediment statues in the round, a great part of the frieze, in low relief, about 525 ft. long, which surrounded the exterior of the cella, and 15 of the metopes of the exterior frieze, carved in very high relief with episodes of the contest between the Centaurs and the Lapiths. Among the chief of the pediment figures are the reclining figure of Theseus, Iris with wind-blown drapery, and the group of one reclining and two seated female figures popularly called the "Three Fates."

Elicius (ē-li'shus). A Roman epithet of Jupiter, as the god who sends the lightning, or as the giver of celestial signs and omens.

Elis (ē'lis). [Also: **Eleia**.] In ancient geography, a country in the W part of the Peloponnesus, Greece, lying between Achaea on the N, Arcadia on the E, Messenia on the S, and the Ionian Sea on the W. It comprised three parts: Elis proper or Hollow Elis, Pisatis, and Triphylia. Olympia, the site of the Olympic Games and the temple of Olympian Zeus, is in Elis; Elis, Pisa (later known as Olympia), Pylus, Lepreum, Letrini, and Hyrmine were some of the cities of Elis. According to tradition, the people of Elis came into the Peloponnesus from Calydon and Aetolia. Their first king was Aëthlius, the father of Endymion. Endymion later decided to award the throne to that one of his sons who won in a running race. Epeus was the victor and became king. He was succeeded by Aetolus, who was forced to flee, and the throne fell to Eleus, a son of Poseidon and the daughter of Endymion. Eleus called his people Eleans after himself. This Eleus was, according to some accounts, the father of Augeas (those who say Helius was the father of Augeas do so simply to glorify him), who hired Heracles to cleanse his stables and then refused to pay him as he had promised. Heracles made war on him, unsuccessful because Augeas was supported by the sons of

Actor, the Actoridae—Cteatus and Eurytus—and by Amarynceus. Later Heracles fell on the sons of Actor at Cleonae, during a truce for the Isthmian Games, and murdered them. Their mother, Molione, learned who their murderer was and demanded satisfaction from the Argives, among whom Heracles was living, at Tiryns. The Argives refused satisfaction. Molione sought to have the Argives banned thereafter from the Isthmian Games, but failing in this, she put a curse on any Eleans who should take part in the Games, and it was for this reason that the Eleans henceforth refused to compete in the Isthmian Games. Heracles, with an army of Argives, Thebans, and Arcadians, again attacked Elis. He destroyed Pylus but abandoned his expedition against Pisa because of an oracle. As master of Elis, he gave the land to Phyleus, son of Augeas, who had tried to persuade Augeas to pay Heracles as promised. Phyleus put the affairs of the country in order and departed to Dulichium. After the death of Augeas the kingdom fell to his son Agasthenes, and to the sons of the Actoridae. The Eleans sent 40 ships to accompany the Greek forces in the war against Troy. When the Heraclidae (Cresphontes, Temenus, and their nephews, Procles and Eurysthenes) decided to return to the Peloponnesus, on the ground that it belonged to them because Heracles had conquered it, they were told by an oracle to choose "one with three eyes" as their leader. They met Oxylus driving a one-eyed mule, and decided he was the leader indicated by the oracle. They promised him Elis in return for his services as leader of their expedition, thus Oxylus, an Aetolian, became ruler of Elis. In later times, Elis was afflicted by strife. The king, Iphitus, a contemporary of the Spartan law-giver Lycurgus, asked the oracle at Delphi how peace could be restored. The priestess told him to revive the Olympic Games, which had been abandoned for a time because of the war. She told him also to crown the victors, hitherto uncrowned, with wreaths of wild olive that had been cut from a tree shrouded in spider webs. Iphitus found such a tree in the sacred precinct at Olympia, and raised a wall around it. He revived the Olympic Games, some say in 793 B.C., and some say the time was 408 years after the fall of Troy (776 B.C.), and also persuaded the Eleans to worship Heracles, as the oracle had commanded, though hitherto he was always considered their worst enemy. The people of Elis were said to be the only Greeks to worship Hades, because when Heracles led his expedition against Pylus in Elis, Athena aided him, but Hades aided the Eleans, and even suffered a wound from Heracles for their sake. The Eleans raised a sanctuary to Hades, which was opened only once a year. They also worshiped Dionysus with the greatest reverence, and claimed that he attended their festival, Thyia. At the time of this festival three empty pots were brought into the temple by priests and set down empty in the presence of all who wished to see. The building was then sealed, in the presence of the onlookers. Next day, still with witnesses, the seals were broken, the pots were examined, and were found to be filled with wine. No mules can be bred within the borders of Elis. The Eleans claimed this is because of a curse of Oenomaus, who was a lover of fine horses.

Historically, the Eleans played their part in the Persian Wars. Later they reluctantly joined with Sparta (420 B.C.) in the invasion of Attica, but soon abandoned the alliance with their ancient enemy, which enmity had survived since Pisans of Elis aided the Messenians in their war with Sparta, and drove the Spartans (401–399 B.C.) out of the sacred precinct at Olympia. In 398 B.C. they submitted to Sparta and were compelled to allow the Spartans to take part in the Olympic Games, from which they had banned them. For a time they were unwilling allies of Philip II of Macedon, but after the death of Alexander they fought on the side of the Peloponnesians against Antipater and the Macedonians and were` defeated with their allies.

Elissa (ē-lis′a). [Also: **Elisa**.] In Phoenician legend, a princess of the royal house of Tyre, daughter of King Matgen (or Belus), grandson of Eth-Baal. She was married to her uncle Sicharbaal or Sicharbas (in Greek, Acerbas; in Latin, Sychaeus). Her brother Pygmalion having murdered Sicharbas, she sought safety in flight. With her sister Anna and a band of Tyrian colonists she set out for Africa, a term then applied to a section of the Mediterranean coast in what is now Tunisia. The local dynast contemptuously offering to sell the pilgrims as much land as could be enclosed within a bull's hide, Elissa had it cut following the margin in a cord some miles in length, with which she purchased enough land for her citadel, naming it Carthage, in Greek Byrsa. Unable to counter the insistence of the native king Iarbas that she marry him, she had a funeral pyre built and committed suicide by stabbing herself on it.

As appropriated by Vergil, the saga of Elissa becomes a key episode of the *Aeneid*. Carthage is newly founded, the scene of intense building activity; its governor is Elissa, who here appears as Dido, an epithet of the Phoenician Astarte as moon-goddess, still mourning Sychaeus; to Aeneas' storm-tossed companions she graciously grants haven. Dido and Aeneas, buffeted by fortune, form a romantic attachment, interrupted by the god's insistence that Aeneas continue his destined journey to Italy. When Aeneas dutifully sails away, Dido, dishonored and heartbroken, kills herself on her pyre, leaving a legacy of hatred between Carthage and Rome. (JJ)

Elpenor (el-pē′nôr). In the *Odyssey*, one of the companions of Odysseus on his return voyage from Troy. With others, he was changed into a swine by Circe and then, at Odysseus' command, changed back into a man by her. But in a drunken stupor he fell asleep on the roof of Circe's palace, and when it was time to leave he rolled off and was killed. Odysseus saw his shade when he visited the Underworld, and promised to do funeral honors for him so that he could cross the Styx, and to build a sepulchral mound for him and place his oar on it.

Elymus (el′i-mus). According to legend, a bastard son of Anchises. He fled from Troy to Italy with Acestes and helped the latter establish the city of Segesta in Sicily. He was reunited with Aeneas in Sicily, who arrived some time later, and the half-brothers celebrated funeral games in honor of Anchises together.

Elysian Fields (ē-lizh′an). Name given to a region near the ancient town of Baiae (modern Baia), Italy, which is particularly fertile and delightful, and is, therefore, supposed to

actor; up, lūte, pull; oi, oil; ou, out; ᴛʜ, then;   d̡ as d or j, ş as s or sh, t̡ as t or ch, z̧ as z or zh.

resemble the Elysium or Elysian Fields of Greek mythology.

Elysium (ē-liz′i-um, -lizh′um). [Also: **Elysian Fields.**] Abode of the souls of the good and of heroes exempt from death, in ancient classical mythology. It is described, particularly by later poets, as a place of exceeding bliss, and contrasted with Tartarus, an afterworld of torment. Some have thought it to be in the center of the earth, some in the Islands of the Blest, and some in the sun or mid-air. In the *Odyssey* it is a plain at the end of the earth "where life is easiest to man. No snow is there, nor yet great storm nor any rain."

Emathia (ē-mā′thi-a). An ancient name for Macedonia, or a region in Macedonia. The name was also sometimes applied to Thessaly and Pharsalia.

Emathion (ē-mā′thi-on). In Greek mythology, a son of Tithonus and Eos, goddess of the dawn. He seized the throne of his brother, Memnon, king of Aethiopia. Later Heracles, passing through his country in search of the golden apples of the Hesperides, killed Emathion and restored the throne to Memnon.

Empedocles (em-ped′ō-klēz). Greek poet, philosopher, and statesman, born in Acragas in Sicily, c493 B.C. He died probably in the Peloponnesus, c433 B.C. Although born of a rich and noble family, he was an ardent champion of liberty, and resisted the tyrants Theron and Thrasydaeus. On the expulsion of the latter he helped to set up a democratic constitution. Under it he exerted great influence through his vast learning, his powerful oratory, and his wealth. In later life it is thought he left Sicily, perhaps because of political disturbances, and went to the Peloponnesus, where he died. He followed Pythagoras and Parmenides in his teachings, but he was a real poet, and expressed his doctrine in poetic form. His system was based on the belief that there are four original elements—Fire, Earth, Water, and Air— and that these elements do not change in themselves but are mixed and moved by the action upon them of such non-physical forces as Love and Strife. The earth and all life on it originated from the endless mixing and moving of these elements. He also expressed in poetry his belief that the sinner who stained his hands with innocent blood, or was

false to his oath, must wander through untold eons, never attaining the peace of the dead, received and cast out by Air, Sea, Earth, and Sun, and endlessly being transformed from one mortal shape to another. He professed magic powers, prophecy, and a miraculous power of healing. In support of such professions he is said to have stopped the etesian winds, drained a vast swamp, and restored a dead woman to life. He also prophesied the hour when the gods would summon him and, according to some accounts, he disappeared without trace and was believed to have passed away without dying. Others said he threw himself into the crater of Aetna in order that, from his sudden disappearance, the people might believe he correctly prophesied his own passing and was a god. It is claimed by these latter that they knew he hurled himself into the crater because one of his brass boots was cast up by the volcano. The general tradition is that he died in the Peloponnesus. His influence on Greek and Arabian thought was great; books in his name appeared in both languages. Fragments of his hexameter poem, *On Nature*, survive. It was very highly regarded in antiquity for its content and its style. Some verses of his poem, *Purifications,* also survive.

Empusae (em-pū′sē). In Greek mythology, cannibal monsters with the legs of asses and hoofs of brass. Sometimes called the children of Hecate, at her direction they were sent to frighten travelers, disguised as bitches, cows, or even as beautiful maidens. The Lamiae were reckoned among the Empusae, who were believed eventually to devour their human lovers.

Enalus (ē′na̲-lus). According to legend, a young man who leaped into the sea because his sweetheart, Phineis, was chosen by lot to be hurled into the sea as a sacrifice to Amphritrite when colonists were first setting out for Lesbos. He was saved by a dolphin, who bore Enalus on his back to shore. The dolphin's mate rescued Phineis.

Enarete (en-ä′re̲-tē). In Greek mythology, the wife of Aeolus, king of the winds, and the mother of his six sons and six daughters.

Enceladus (en-sel′a̲-dus). In Greek mythology, one of the Giants, a son of Gaea and the blood of Uranus, who waged war on the gods. In the battle he was crushed flat by a huge stone flung at him by Athena as he fled. He now lies crushed under Aetna in Sicily. When he stirs the mountain shakes, and when he breathes it erupts.

ATHENA SLAYING ENCELADUS
Black-figured Attic amphora, late 6th century B.C. *Rouen*

Encheleans (en-ke-lē′anz). A people of Illyria. According to legend, Cadmus emigrated to their country after the death of Pentheus, his son-in-law, and was chosen by the Encheleans as their king. His tomb is in their land. Some of the Colchians who pursued Jason later settled among the Encheleans, rather than face the wrath of Aeëtes by returning to Colchis without Medea.

Endeïs (en-dē′is). In Greek mythology, the second wife of Aeacus, king of Aegina. She was the mother of Telamon and Peleus and encouraged them to murder their half-brother Phocus.

Endoeus (en-dē′us). Ionian sculptor, active in the latter part of the 6th century B.C. Some say he was a pupil of Daedalus and fled with him to Crete. Among his works, in the archaic style, was a statue of seated Athena on the Acropolis, and an ancient image of Athena at Tegea. He also made images for temples in Ionia, including an image of Artemis at Ephesus.

Endymion (en-dim′i-on). According to some accounts, he was a son of Zeus and the nymph Calyce; but some say he was a son of Aëthlius. He seized the throne of the region that was later known as Elis and made himself king. By his wife, whose name is variously given as Cromia, Asterodia, and Hyparippe, he was the father of three sons— Paeon, Epeus, and Aetolus—and a daughter, Eurycyda (or Eurydice). To choose a successor for his throne, he had his sons engage in a running race at Olympia. Epeus won, became king, and named the people of the land Epeans. Selene, the moon-goddess, came upon Endymion lying asleep in a cave, and fell in love with his beauty. She visited him nightly and bore him 50 daughters. Some say she asked Zeus to give him perpetual youth and eternal sleep. Others say that Endymion was a hunter on Mount Latmos in Caria, and that it was in a cave there that Selene found him, and that it was he himself who asked Zeus for immortality, eternal slumber, and undying youth. In all versions of his myth he is described as a youth of great beauty who kept his youth and his beauty in never-waking slumber. The Eleans (the name by which the Epeans came to be known) claimed that the tomb of Endymion was at Olympia in Elis, but others say he lies in eternal sleep in a cave on Mount Latmos in Caria, near Miletus.

Endymion, Sleeping. Classical statue in Parian marble, found in Hadrian's villa at Tivoli, Italy, and acquired by the National Museum at Stockholm, Sweden.

Engyum (en′ji-um) or **Enguium** (eng′gwi-um). In ancient geography, a city of Sicily, supposed to have been situated in the mountains N of Enna on a site near the modern town of Gangi. It possessed a celebrated temple of the Great Mother of the Gods.

Eniopeus (ē-nī′ō-pūs). Named in the *Iliad* as one of Hector's charioteers. He was slain by Diomedes.

Enipeus (ē-nī′pē-us). A river of Thessaly which flows into the Peneus (also sometimes called the Alpheus) River. According to mythology, Tyro, the daughter of Salmoneus, fell in love with the river-god Enipeus and wooed him daily, but he scorned her. Poseidon took the form of Enipeus when he wooed Tyro and became the father, by her, of Pelias and Neleus. Later Tyro cast the children adrift on the waters of the Enipeus when she learned that she had been tricked by Poseidon, according to some accounts. Others say she exposed them on a mountain.

Enna (en′a) or **Henna** (hen′a). [Former name, **Castro Giovanni**.] City of Sicily, situated in a mountainous region in the center of the island. In ancient times, Enna was the seat of the cult of the goddess Demeter, whose temple was here; Enna, more specifically the nearby Lake of Pergusa, was supposed to be the location at which the rape of Persephone, Demeter's daughter, occurred. The city was called the navel of Sicily, because of its position in the center of the island. It belonged to the Carthaginians, and fell into the hands of the Romans in the First Punic War. It was a headquarters of the slaves in the First Servile War, resisting the Roman armies for two years.

Ennius (en′i-us), **Quintus.** Roman epic poet, born at Rudiae, in Bruttii, 239 B.C. He died probably at Rome, 169 B.C. He was one of the founders of Latin literature and was admired by the ancients as the father of Latin poetry. He served in the Roman army in Sardinia (204 B.C.), in the Second Punic War, and there met Marcus Porcius Cato (Cato the Censor), who brought him to Rome, where he taught Greek and translated Greek plays. He became friendly with the Scipios and with Fulvius Nobilior, whom he accompanied to the Aetolian War in 189 B.C. and whose son secured Roman citizenship for Ennius in 184 B.C. He was the author of *Annales* (in 18 books, only fragments of which survive), an epic poem on the history of Rome from the fall of Troy down to his own time. With this poem he produced the first national epic of the Romans and also introduced the Greek hexameter as a literary form. This greatly influenced later Latin poets. He also wrote tragedies, modeled on those of Euripides, some comedies, and miscellaneous poems in various meters.

Ennomus (en′o-mus). Named by Homer (*Iliad*) as a seer or augur of Mysia, who fought as an ally of the Trojans and was slain by Achilles.

Ennosigaeus (en-o-sig′e-us). Epithet of Poseidon, meaning "Earth-shaker," as one who causes the earth to quake and tremble when he strikes it with his trident, thus causing chasms, valleys, springs, and river-beds. This epithet was particularly applied in regions which were subject to earthquakes. In one early attempt at cosmology, the continental land masses of the earth were held to be islands floating in the sea, and thus subject to disturbance at Poseidon's whim. There was a sanctuary of Poseidon Ennosigaeus near Therapne in Sparta, and an image of him in the harbor town of Gythium in Laconia.

Enope (e′no-pe). A town on the border between Laconia and Messenia. It was one of the "gift" cities that Agamemnon offered to Achilles if the latter would forget his quarrel with Agamemnon and return to the fight in the Trojan War. The town was later called Gerenia.

Entellus (en-tel′us). In the *Aeneid,* a noted Sicilian boxer who had been instructed by Eryx and who inherited the boxing gloves Eryx wore in the bout in which Heracles defeated him. In the funeral games for Anchises in Sicily Acestes persuaded him, against his will, to accept the challenge of Dares, a much younger man. In the match which followed he battered young Dares so murderously that Aeneas stopped the match and awarded Entellus the prize. With one great blow of his fist he smashed in the head of the bullock which he received as a prize and offered it to Eryx, and then announced that his boxing days were over.

Enyalius (e-ni-a′li-us). An epithet of Ares, "Slayer of Heroes." Appearance of this name in lists of divinities deciphered in the bronze-age Linear B tablets suggests that Enyalius was an early Greek or even pre-Greek god worshiped in Mycenaean times and later identified with Ares, a view supported by references in classical writers to temples of Enyalius in Salamis and the Megarid. (JJ)

Enyeus (e-ni′yūs). In Homeric legend (*Iliad*), a king of Scyrus whose fortress was captured by Patroclus in the years of the Trojan War before the siege of Troy began.

Enyo (e-ni′o). In Greek mythology, a goddess of war, sacker of cities, and companion of Ares. The Romans identified her with Bellona, destroyer of cities.

Enyo. One of the Graeae, a daughter of Ceto and Phorcys. See **Graeae.**

Eoiae (e-oi′e). Poem, attributed to Hesiod, celebrating Boeotian and Thessalian heroines who wedded gods. It formed a fourth book of the *Catalogue of Women,* an epic history of Dorian and Aeolian women. The name is sometimes used as being synonymous with the *Catalogue of Women*.

Eos (ē′ọs). The "rosy-fingered" goddess of the dawn. Clad in a saffron-colored mantle she drives her golden chariot, drawn by two white horses, from the east to Olympus each day to announce to men and gods the coming of her brother Helius. She is the herald of the day. Eos is a daughter of the Titans Hyperion and Thia, and by Astraeus she is the mother of the winds and the stars, especially the morning star. It is said that Eos once seduced Ares, the lover of Aphrodite, and so enraged the latter that she caused Eos to yearn for the fresh and youthful beauty of mortals. This accounts for her many mortal lovers. When Orion, blinded, came to the east Eos fell in love with him and caused her brother Helius to restore his sight by touching his lids with his rays. Eos then carried him off to Delos with her. She bore a son, Phaëthon, to Cephalus, whom she had caused to doubt his wife Procris. Some say it was Eos who carried off Ganymede, and that Zeus took him from her to be his cup-bearer. In return she asked Zeus

EOS AND TITHONUS
Red-figured Attic kylix, c480 B.C. *Museum of Fine Arts, Boston*

to grant eternal life to Tithonous, another Trojan whom she had carried off. Zeus granted her plea and she bore Memnon and

Emathion to Tithonous. In the Trojan War Memnon went to the aid of the Trojans. On the day he was fated to die Eos came reluctantly from the east. When death, at the hands of Achilles, overtook him that day, the children of Eos slipped down from heaven and rescued his body and carried it off. Eos threatened to withdraw her light from the earth. If Zeus loved Thetis and her son Achilles better than Eos and her son Memnon, let Thetis provide light to the world, she said. For some time darkness covered the earth, but the Horae came to Eos and led her to Zeus. At his command she resumed her daily course, but thenceforth she wept tears of dew each morning, in memory of Memnon.

Epaminondas (ē″pam-i-non′dạs). Theban general and statesman, born c418 B.C.; died at Mantinea, Arcadia, Greece, 362 B.C. He was of a noble but impoverished family. Modest and not personally ambitious, he determined to lighten his poverty by the study of Pythagorean philosophy, to which he had been introduced by Lysis, an exile from Tarentum. He was as interested in music as he was in physical prowess, and became an accomplished player on the lyre and the flute. Further to lighten his poverty, he denied himself the luxury of taking a wife. He was the good friend of Pelopidas, a man of wealth, and so high were his principles that he alone of the friends of Pelopidas refused to accept any financial help from him. Pelopidas, since he could not share his wealth with Epaminondas, decided to share the poverty of his friend—to some extent. Both were animated by ardent patriotism, both were noted for their integrity. They were colleagues in government and in command. At the battle of Mantinea (385 B.C.), Thebes was an ally of Sparta. Pelopidas fell, pierced by seven wounds. Epaminondas rescued him from the enemy and saved his life. The Theban alliance with Sparta was an unequal one. In 382 B.C. the Spartans seized the citadel of Thebes and set a Spartan governor, with a garrison of 1500 Spartan hoplites, over the Thebans. Pelopidas fled to Athens rather than live under Spartan rule. Epaminondas remained in Thebes, hoping for the day when Spartan control would be thrown off. By a daring coup, Pelopidas secretly returned to Thebes with six companions and killed the Spartan rulers. Epaminondas, in the turmoil that then broke out in the city, came to his aid with an armed band, and urged the Thebans to expel the Spartan garrison that had taken refuge in the citadel. But force was unnecessary, for the Spartans decided to withdraw under a truce. Thebes was thus freed of the Spartan yoke (378 B.C.) and a democratic constitution was proclaimed. An elite corps, called the Sacred Band, was created. It consisted of 300 young men of noble Theban families; 150 pairs of devoted friends determined to fight to victory or die together. The Sacred Band, maintained at the expense of the city, was the spearhead and rallying point of every attack. Epaminondas used it to revolutionize military tactics. In the years following the expulsion of the Spartans, Thebes repelled several Spartan attacks, and brought most of the Boeotian cities under her control. At a general peace conference between the various warring Greek states and their allies (371 B.C.), Agesilaus, the Spartan general, demanded that Epaminondas, the Theban envoy, allow every Boeotian city to sign the treaty separately. Epaminondas replied that he would if the Spartans would allow each of their vassal states to sign separately also. He knew that Sparta would not yield such control to her vassal states, and the result was that Thebes was not a party to the peace treaty. In the same year the Spartans, in violation of their treaty with their allies, decided to march against Thebes and free the Boeotian cities from Theban domination. At Leuctra they were met by Epaminondas and his army. The Thebans and their allies were appalled at the numbers and reputation of the forces marshaled against them and wished to withdraw. Epaminondas insisted that here was the place to make a stand, and his view prevailed. In accordance with a dream of Pelopidas, a roan colt was sacrificed to the daughters of the Theban Scedasus, Epaminondas permitted the Thespian allies, who had joined the Thebans against their will, to depart, and the next day, using the Sacred Band as a flying wedge, the Thebans defeated the Spartans at Leuctra (July, 371 B.C.). Cleombrotus, the Spartan king, was slain in the battle, 1000 Spartans fell, and 47 Thebans or their allies lost their

lives. The Spartans admitted defeat by asking for a truce and were permitted to withdraw. By defeating them at Leuctra, Epaminondas destroyed the Spartan superiority in Greece that they had obtained 30 years before in the Peloponnesian War. The destruction of Spartan influence in Greek affairs was the most important and lasting of the accomplishments of Epaminondas. The Thespians, fearing the anger of Epaminondas because they had left him on the eve of Leuctra, withdrew to one of their strongholds, that at Ceressus, which had never been captured in its history. However, there was an oracle of Delphi saying Ceressus would fall when "the Dorians have lost their glorious youth." Epaminondas marched to Ceressus and took it. He then (370 B.C.) carried the war to the Peloponnesus in support of the Arcadians against Sparta. He restored the Mantineans of Arcadia to their city and persuaded the Arcadians to join in building a great new city, Megalopolis, which would serve as a bastion against Sparta. He marched to the very borders of Sparta and ravaged southern Laconia. This created despair in Sparta, which, for generations, had not known war so near its own lands. Next he went to Messenia, for he was advised in a dream, some say, to restore the Messenians to their homeland from which they had been driven by the Spartans. Sparta now knew the humiliation of losing some of her territory. Messenia was detached from her control. Using the ancient citadel of Ithome as one wall, Epaminondas ordered the boundaries of the new city of Messene to be marked out to the piping of flutes. To the city he recalled the Messenian exiles. While he was in Messenia his one-year term as *boeotarch* (commander) expired. Although it was against the law, he retained his command, and when he returned to Thebes he was brought to trial for ignoring the law. The jury that heard the case did not even record their votes. Duly elected boeotarch again, Epaminondas again defeated the Spartans in the Peloponnesus. He marched into Sicyon (369 B.C.) and took many captives, including many Boeotians of cities now under Theban control who had fled into Sicyon. It was the practice for the Thebans to allow prisoners of war to be ransomed, but for any Boeotians captured in any engagement to be killed as traitors. As an example of his dislike for unnecessary harshness, in this case Epaminondas gave all the Boeotian captives a new nationality so that their lives might be spared. In 368 B.C. Pelopidas, who had gone to visit Alexander of Pherae after a campaign in Thessaly, was treacherously thrown into prison by Alexander. Epaminondas, no longer boeotarch, marched in the ranks of an army sent to rescue him. The Thebans were surprised by the army of Alexander in Thessaly and were thrown into confusion. The two legal boeotarchs voluntarily resigned their posts and handed over the command to Epaminondas. He skillfully extricated the Thebans from a dangerous position, and the following year secured the release of Pelopidas without striking a blow.

On the advice of Epaminondas, the Thebans created a navy, of which he became the first admiral. Events in the Peloponnesus then caused him to lead an army into that region for a fourth time, to bring the disaffected cities there under Theban control again. He attacked the enemy—Spartans, Athenians, Mantineans, and others who had united against Thebes—at Mantinea (362 B.C.) and overwhelmed them. As he pursued the fleeing enemy he was mortally wounded by a spear thrust. Dying, he sent for the two men whom he wanted to appoint to succeed him in command. On learning that they had been slain he advised that peace be made with the enemy. By his death, a crushing victory was transformed into a stalemate, for when he pulled the spear from his body and died there was no one to take his place. Epaminondas was a brilliant military innovator, whose tactics were successfully imitated by Alexander the Great. He was noted for his patriotism, his learning and his eloquence (which was seldom employed, but then to great effect), and for the nobility and purity of his character. Notably successful as a general, he was unable, as a statesman, to secure the dominant place in Greek affairs which he had won for Thebes, and after his death Theban influence declined.

Epaphroditus (ē-paf-rō-dī′tus). Freedman of Nero, and his secretary. He assisted Nero in his attempt at suicide. He was also secretary of Domitian by whom he was killed (95 A.D.). The philosopher Epictetus was the freedman of Epaphroditus.

Epaphus (ep′a̲-fus). In Greek mythology, a son of Zeus and Io. As foretold to Io by Prometheus when she visited him on his crag in the Caucasus, Zeus touched Io and she bore him Epaphus on the Nile, after she had completed many years of wandering. The Curetes, at the request of Hera, made off with Epaphus. When Zeus learned of their theft he slew them. Io searched for her son, found him in Syria, and returned with him to Egypt. According to some accounts, Epaphus married Memphis, a daughter of the Nile, and founded a city which he named Memphis in her honor. He became king of Egypt, and was the ancestor of the Danaids and of Heracles, as was also foretold by Prometheus. Epaphus was considered by some to be the divine bull Apis. His daughter Libya became the mother of the twins Agenor and Belus by Poseidon.

Epeans (ep-ē′a̲nz). Descendants of Epeus, one of the sons of Endymion. He won the throne by defeating his brothers in a running race, and named the people after himself. The Epeans dwelt in the land that was later known as Elis. Some say that Pelops took Olympia (formerly called Pisa) from the Epeans during the reign of Epeus. When Nestor was a youth he won his spurs in battle in a war between the Epeans and the Pylians, in which he drove off great numbers of Epean cattle, killed many, and completely routed the Epeans. In the Trojan War, Epeans from Epea in Elis were under the command of Nestor.

Epeiros (ancient, ē-pī′ros; modern, ē′pē-rôs). See **Epirus.**

Epeus (ep-ē′us). In legend, a son of Panopeus. Although he had the reputation of being a coward, and was, as a punishment to his father for breaking his oath, he accompanied the Greeks to the Trojan War. At the funeral games for Patroclus he won the boxing match, and again, at the funeral games for Achilles, he contended with Acamas, son of Theseus, in the boxing match. The match was stopped, as the contestants were evenly matched. Epeus, with the aid of Athena, built the Wooden Horse which led to the fall

actor; up, lūte, pu̇ll; oi, oil; ou, out; ᴛн, then; d̲ as d or j, s̲ as s or sh, t̲ as t or ch, z̲ as z or zh.

of Troy, and entered the city in it, although trembling with fear.

Epeus. According to legend, a son of Endymion. In a race arranged by his father against his brothers, he won and was awarded the throne of his land in the Peloponnesus. He named the people after himself, Epeans. He married Anaxiroë and had one daughter, Hyrmina, but no sons. During his reign, Pelops won the land of Pisa and neighboring Olympia after the death of Oenomaus, and separated it from the land of Epeus. The Eleans, the name by which the Epeans were later called, said that Pelops was the first in the Peloponnesus to erect a temple of Hermes. He did this to appease the god for the death of Myrtilus. Epeus was succeeded by his brother Aetolus, who was forced to flee from his country because he accidentally killed Apis at the funeral games for Azan. The kingdom fell to Eleus, son of Poseidon and the daughter of Endymion, who changed the name of the people to Eleans.

Ephebos (e-fē′bos) or **Ephebus** (-bus). In Greek antiquity, particularly at Athens, a young man, the son of a citizen, between the ages of 18 and 20. At Athens, upon attaining the age of 18 each youth was subjected to an examination as to his physical development and his legal claims to citizenship. During the next two years (later reduced to one year) his education, moral, physical and military, was taken in charge by the state, and conducted under the most rigid discipline, in conformity with a fixed course designed to prepare him to understand and to perform the duties of citizenship. Upon being admitted to take the sacred oath, at which time he was formally presented with a spear and a shield, he received some of the citizen's privileges, and he became a full citizen after completing with honor his two years as an ephebos. Hence, in works on Greek art, etc., the name is applied to any youth, particularly if bearing arms, or otherwise shown to be of free estate.

Ephesian Artemis. An ancient Asiatic divinity whose worship was adopted by the Ionian Greeks. She was a personification of the fruitfulness of nature, and was quite distinct from the Greek goddess, though assimilated

to her by the Ephesians from some resemblance of attributes. She was represented wearing a mural crown and with many breasts, and with the lower part of her body cased, like a mummy, in a sheath bearing mystical figures. Also called "Diana of the Ephesians."

DIANA OF THE EPHESIANS
National Museum, Naples

Ephesian Stories. See **Abrocomes and Atheia.**

Ephesus (ef′e̯-sus). In ancient geography, one of the 12 Ionian cities in Asia Minor, in Lydia, situated on the Caÿster River near its mouth, S of Smyrna. According to legend, it was founded by Ephesus, a son of the river-god Caÿster, and by Coresus. The first inhabitants were Leleges and Lydians,

and Amazons dwelt nearby. Later, Androclus, a son of Codrus, the legendary king of
Athens, drove out the natives and settled
there with Ionian colonists. They identified
the nature-goddess who was worshiped there
from very ancient times with their Artemis,
and allowed the natives who dwelt near the
ancient temple to remain, and exchanged
oaths of friendship with them. Androclus
died in battle and was buried at Ephesus.
Through its trade and its importance as a
port, the city flourished mightily. In later
times the tyrant of Ephesus married a daughter of Alyattes, king of Lydia and father of
Croesus, and the city became part of the
kingdom of Croesus when he succeeded his
father. Subsequently the city fell to the
Persians, but continued to thrive. Alexander
the Great established (334 B.C.) a democratic constitution there. While he was in
the city the artist Apelles painted a portrait
of him, holding the lightning in his hands,
that was set up in the temple of Artemis.
In 133 B.C. Ephesus was taken by the Romans but still remained great and powerful.
Through ancient times Ephesus, the city of
Artemis, was celebrated for its temple of
Artemis, and as a great commercial city
whose wealth was proverbial. It was sacked
by the Goths (262 A.D.), the temple was
destroyed, the harbor silted up and destroyed the importance of the city as a port,
and small villages and ruins covered the site.
Among its ruins are a theater, an odeum, a
stadium, and the temple of Artemis. The
great theater is mentioned in Acts, xix. 23.
It is Greek in plan, with Roman modifications. The *cavea* (auditorium), 495 feet in
diameter, has two precinctions (landings between tiers of seats), with 11 *cunei* (blocks
of seats) in the two lower ranges, and 22
in the highest, which is skirted by a colonnaded gallery. The orchestra is 110 feet in
diameter, and the proscenium 22 feet wide.
The odeum (a type of small theater) is
ascribed to the 2nd century A.D. In plan
it is a half-circle 153 feet in diameter. There
is one precinction, with five cunei below and
ten above it, and a rich Corinthian gallery
around the top. The orchestra is 30 feet
in diameter; the stage has five doors and
Corinthian columns. The stadium, ascribed
to the time of Augustus, is 850 feet long

and about 200 feet wide. The N side and
semicircular E end are supported on vaulted
substructions, the S side on the rock of the
hillside. A double colonnade was carried
along its entire length, and communicated
with the upper gallery of the stadium by a
series of stairways. The temple of Artemis
(Diana of the Ephesians) was a famous and
ancient sanctuary celebrated as one of the
Seven Wonders of the Ancient World. It
was burned in the 4th century B.C. and rebuilt. The temple was Ionic, dipteral,
octastyle, with 21 columns on the flanks,
and measured 164 by 342 feet. The base-
diameter of the columns was 6 feet, their
height 55 feet. The base-drums of 36 columns of the front and rear were beautifully
sculptured with figures in relief. Croesus
dedicated the golden heifers at the temple,
and gave most of the columns, on the bases
of which fragments of the words "Dedicated
by Croesus," can be seen. The cella had
interior ranges of columns, Ionic in the lower
tier, Corinthian above. Xenophon, author
of the *Anabasis,* deposited ransom money received for captives taken during the retreat
of the 10,000 in the temple at Ephesus. The
money was subsequently restored to him, and
he used it to build (c370 B.C.) a small replica
of the temple of Artemis at Ephesus at
Scillus, in Elis, and for an annual festival
of the goddess.

Ephialtes (ef-i-al'tēz). In Greek mythology,
a son of Poseidon. He was the brother of
Otus. See **Aloidae.** Ephialtes was also the
name of the nightmare demon of ancient
Greece.

Ephialtes. In Greek mythology, one of the
Giants, a son of Gaea and the blood of
Uranus, who waged war on the gods. In
the battle Apollo pierced him with an arrow
through one eye, and Heracles sent an arrow
through the other eye and killed him.

Ephialtes. A Greek of Malis who betrayed
the Spartans and other Greeks under the
command of Leonidas at the pass of Thermopylae (480 B.C.). In the hope of reward,
he went to Xerxes, whose forces had three
times been thrown back by the Greeks,
and offered to lead the Persians by a path
over the mountains so that they could attack from the rear the Greeks defending the
pass. Xerxes accepted his offer; Ephialtes

led them over the mountain, and the Greeks, fighting with enormous valor, were wiped out. Ephialtes afterward fled and a price was put on his head by the Greeks. Some time later he returned from his exile to Anticyra, and there was slain, his slayer being greatly honored by the Spartans.

Ephialtes. Athenian statesman and general; died 461 B.C. He was the friend and partisan of Pericles, and was the principal author of a law which abridged the power of the Areopagus and changed the government of Athens into a pure democracy (i.e., for citizens). Ephialtes opposed Cimon, the leader of the oligarchic and aristocratic party. With Pericles he brought charges against Cimon of having accepted bribes from the king of Macedon, but the charges were not pressed and Cimon was acquitted. Again, Ephialtes opposed Cimon's policy of aiding Sparta to put down a revolt of the Helots (462 B.C.). It was while he was off at the head of an expedition to aid Sparta in this affair that Ephialtes and Pericles put through the reforms that made Athens a democracy. When Cimon returned he was banished, and shortly afterward Ephialtes was mysteriously murdered. He was, according to Aristotle, assassinated by Aristodicus of Tanagra, at the instance of the oligarchs.

Ephor (ef'ôr). In ancient Greece, one of a body of magistrates common to many ancient Dorian constitutions, the most celebrated being that of the Spartans, among whom the board of *ephors* consisted of five members, elected yearly by the people. Their authority ultimately became superior to that of the kings, and virtually supreme before the office was abolished, c227 B.C., by Cleomenes III, who is said to have executed the incumbents. The term means "overseer" or "inspector," and in this meaning is widely used in Roman, Byzantine, and modern Greece.

Ephorus (ef'ọ-rus). Greek historian, born at Cyme, in Aeolis, and active in the first half of the 4th century B.C. He wrote a universal history, in 30 books, covering the period from the Dorian migrations to 340 B.C. Book 30 was added by his son. In his work he rejected the history of the earliest times as being mythical. He was a collector and critic of earlier authorities, whom he used

freely, and made an attempt to correct them by comparing and checking them against each other. His work, which includes ethnography, geography, and mythology, was greatly and justly admired and used. Fragments of his work have been preserved, and large parts of it appear in the extant parts of the *Universal History* of Diodorus Siculus.

Ephyra (ef'i-rạ). Ancient name of Corinth, in the Peloponnesus, named, according to some, for Ephyra, daughter of Oceanus. Some say that Helius divided the land around the Asopus River. That which was later called Sicyonia he gave to Aloeus. That known as Ephyraea he gave to his son Aeëtes. When Aeëtes migrated to Colchis he left his share in the care of Bunus, a son of Hermes and Alcidamea. After Bunus, Epopeus, the son of Aloeus, added Ephyraea to his kingdom. Marathon succeeded his father Epopeus, and he in turn was succeeded by his son Corinthus. Corinthus, for whom the city was renamed, according to the Corinthians, died childless, and it was then, some say, that Medea, daughter of Aeëtes, claimed the kingdom for Jason. Some say that when Medea was compelled to flee from Corinth she handed the kingdom over to Sisyphus. Others say Sisyphus founded the city, c1350 B.C., and that its first inhabitants were a race sprung from mushrooms. See **Corinth.**

Ephyraea (ef-i-rē'ạ). Ancient name for Corinthia.

Epibaterius (ep″i-bạ-tē'ri-us). An epithet of Apollo, meaning "Seafaring." Diomedes raised a temple to Apollo Epibaterius in gratitude for his safe return after storms had battered the Greek ships on their way home from Troy.

Epicaste (ep-i-kas'tẹ). Name used in Homer for **Jocasta.**

Epic Cycle. Cycle of legends and songs about events relating to the Trojan War, produced as a chronological narrative by later compilers from material by various epic poets of the Ionian school, between 776 B.C. and 550 B.C.

Epicharmus (ep-i-kär'mus). Greek comic poet born in Sicily or on the island of Cos, c540 B.C. At an early age he was carried to Megara, in Sicily, and thence, when Megara was sacked by Gelon, to Syracuse. He died at Syracuse at an advanced age (90 or 97). He was the leading writer of comedy in the Dorian dialect. His works were farces, employing no chorus, and were greatly admired by Plato, who is said to have learned the art of writing dialogue from them. He made free use of puns in his works, and took for his subjects the gods and heroes, whom he treated in a light-hearted manner, and incidents of everyday life. He was also the author of such philosophical sayings as "Character is destiny to man." Thirty-five titles of his comedies are extant, but only scanty fragments remain.

Epictetus (ep-ik-tē'tus). Attic potter and painter, active at the end of the 6th century B.C. His signature appears as potter on at least one vessel, and as painter on thirty vessels. He was one of the greatest masters of his time. About 80 of his works—mostly cups and plates—are extant. He worked in the red-figure style mainly, although in his early work he sometimes used the black-figure technique. A plate (British Museum) shows an archer, possibly an Amazon. Another shows a satyr holding a wineskin.

Epictetus. [Also: **Epictetus of Hierapolis.**] Greek Stoic philosopher, active about 100 A.D. He was a crippled Phrygian slave, born in Hierapolis in Phrygia, and went to Rome as a slave in the house of Epaphroditus (the freedman and favorite of Nero). He was a pupil of Musonius Rufus and, having been emancipated by his master, lectured on philosophy in Rome until c94 A.D., when he removed to Nicopolis in Epirus, in consequence of an edict of Domitian banishing the philosophers from Rome. At Nicopolis he became a friend of Trajan, formed a school, and made many disciples. Although he left no written works, his essential doctrines are preserved in a manual compiled by his pupil Arrian. He taught that the sum of wisdom is to desire nothing but freedom and contentment, and to bear and forbear; that all unavoidable evil in the world is only apparent and external; and that our happiness depends upon our own will, which even Zeus cannot break.

Epicurus (ep-i-kū'rus). Greek philosopher, the founder of the Epicurean school of philosophy. He was born on the island of Samos, 342 or 341 B.C., and died at Athens 271 or

270 B.C. He was the son of Neocles, an Athenian *cleruch* (colonist) settled on Samos, and belonged to the Attic *deme* of Gargettus (whence he is sometimes called the Gargettian). He revealed an early aptitude for philosophy, which he studied as a youth at Athens and subsequently taught as a young man at Mytilene and Lampsacus. In 306 B.C. he returned to Athens, where he established a school in a garden outside the city walls. There, in an atmosphere of quiet withdrawal, he devoted the rest of his life to teaching. We owe most of our information about him to a biography by Diogenes Laertius. Of the approximately 300 rolls which he is said to have written, only fragments remain. Fortunately, however, his biographer gives us the texts of three of his rather lengthy epistles, a transcript of his will, and some 40 propositions known as "Principal Doctrines," all of which contain the substance of his views on "physics" and ethics. As Epicurus developed his system of hedonism, he was influenced by Plato's views on pleasure as well as by the Cyrenaic doctrine of Aristippus. Pleasure, according to Epicurus, meant freedom from pain and peace in body and mind. With the ethical principle of pleasure as the highest good, Epicurus blended the physics of Democritus and the other atomists of the 5th century B.C. This materialistic physics asserted such principles as "nothing can come from nothing," and "all that exists is atoms and void." As such it could be supported by empirical evidence, and was easily made to integrate on rational grounds with a hedonistic ethic. Adhering to an enlightened view of pleasure, Epicurus primarily desired that his system should free mankind from religious superstition and fear of death. He argued that the view of the universe as consisting only of atoms and void would rid man of his besetting anxieties and hence would enable him to achieve that best of pleasures, inner calm and security. He advocated the principle of moderation, and urged men to seek the pleasures of friendship, of simple living, even to the extent of recommending withdrawal from active life. Only by these and like means, Epicurus insisted, could real freedom and its attendant peace be attained. So carefully articulated was his philosophy that

actọr; up, lūte, pụll; oi, oil; ou, out; ᴛʜ, then; ḏ as d or j, ş as s or sh, ṭ as t or ch, ẕ as z or zh.

it endured without significant change for centuries after his death.

Epidaurum (ep-i-dô′rum). In ancient geography, a maritime town in Illyricum. It was destroyed sometime after the reign of Justinian, and was replaced by Ragusa, now Dubrovnik, Yugoslavia. It was a Roman colony.

Epidaurus (ep-i-dô′rus). Ancient town on the E coast of the Peloponnesus, in the district called Argolis. It was named, according to the Eleans, for a son of Pelops. But others say the Epidaurus for whom the town was named was a son of Argus and a descendant of Zeus, and some say he was a son of Apollo. According to legend, the last king before the arrival of the Dorians was Pityreus, a descendant of Ion, son of Creusa and Apollo, though Xuthus was his acknowledged father. When Deiphontes, son-in-law of Temenus, marched into the land Pityreus handed it over to him without a struggle and went off to Athens. The land was especially sacred to Asclepius, for the Epidaurians said that when Phlegyas, the Lapith king, came to the Peloponnesus to spy out the land and learn whether its people were warlike, he brought his daughter Coronis with him, unaware that she was about to bear Apollo's child. When her child, Asclepius, was born, she exposed him on a mountain, formerly called Myrtium but subsequently named Nipple. A she-goat pastured on the mountain slopes nursed him, and the watch-dog of the flock stood guard over him. The shepherd of the flock remarked that one she-goat and the watch-dog were missing. He looked about for them and found them behind a bush, guarding an infant. As he approached to take up the infant, lightning flashed from the child's body. The shepherd concluded that it was a divine child and so left it to divine protection. (For another version of the birth of Asclepius, see **Asclepius.**) From the beginning Asclepius was a god, and his fame as a healer spread throughout the land. The most famous of his sanctuaries had their origin in Epidaurus. Throughout the flourishing period of Greek history Epidaurus was an independent state, possessing a small territory, bounded on the W by Argeia, on the N by Corinthia, on the S by Troezenia, and on the E by the Saronic Gulf. It was the most celebrated seat of the ancient cult of Asclepius. The sanctuary occupied a valley among hills, at some distance from the city. The sacred grove was enclosed and contained a temple of Asclepius, in which lived tame sacred serpents, the architecturally important *tholos* (round building) of Polyclitus, extensive porticoes which served as hospitals to the sick who came to seek the aid of the god and his priests, and many votive offerings. As at Delos, no birth or death could take place in the sacred enclosure, and all offerings must be consumed within it. In the temple was an ivory and gold image of the god, representing him seated, holding a staff in one hand, and the other hand held above the head of a serpent. A dog stretched out at the side of the image. Originally, suppliants at the temple slept in the open air, but in the time of the Romans shelters were built for them. On slabs about the precinct were inscribed the names of the people who had been cured by Asclepius and the diseases from which he had freed them. Pausanias tells of a very old slab on which it was recorded that Hippolytus dedicated 20 horses to the god, because Asclepius had raised him from the dead. Outside of the sacred enclosure were the stadium, a gymnasium, propylaea, and other buildings, the arrangements for the collection and distribution of water being especially noteworthy. The theater at Epidaurus built probably by Polyclitus the Younger, was, and still is, unrivaled in its acoustical perfection. Extensive excavations conducted by the Archaeological Society of Athens (1881, *et seq.*) have greatly added to our knowledge of the sanctuary of Epidaurus.

Epidaurus Limera (lī-mē′ra). In ancient geography, a town on the E coast of Laconia, Greece, about 22 miles NW of Cape Malea. According to tradition, some Epidaurians who were on their way to Cos, touched here and were warned by dreams to remain here. A snake they were bringing from Epidaurus escaped from their ship and disappeared into the ground near the shore. This event confirmed the dreams which instructed the Epidaurians to remain. On the spot where the snake disappeared into the ground they built altars of Asclepius and planted olive trees around them, and founded a city.

Epigeus (e-pī′jūs). In Homeric legend (*Iliad*), a son of Agacles, king of Budeum. He murdered a kinsman and fled to Peleus for sanctuary. He later followed Achilles, son of Peleus, to Troy as one of the Myrmidons. He was slain by Hector in the struggle for Sarpedon's body.

Epigoni (ē-pig′ō̞-nī). The name given to the sons of the Seven against Thebes; it means "the After-born." Ten years after the disastrous rout of the Seven against Thebes by the Thebans the Epigoni proposed to march against Thebes to avenge their fathers. An oracle foretold that they would be successful if Alcmaeon commanded the expedition. Alcmaeon was persuaded to do so and the expedition set out. The chieftains who made up the Epigoni were: Alcmaeon and Amphilochus, sons of Amphiaraus; Aegialeus, son of Adrastus; Diomedes, son of Tydeus; Promachus, son of Parthenopaeus; Sthenelus, son of Capaneus; Thersander, son of Polynices; and Euryalus, son of Mecisteus. The Thebans, under the command of Laodamas, son of Eteocles, met the Epigoni on the plain outside the walls of Thebes. Aegialeus was killed by Laodamas, but he in his turn was slain by Alcmaeon. The Thebans retired within the walls and were advised by Tiresias the seer to send a herald to negotiate with the Epigoni and to flee the city, for, said Tiresias, Thebes would fall when Adrastus, the only survivor of the original seven, died. And Adrastus would die of grief when he learned of the death of his son Aegialeus. The Thebans followed Tiresias' advice and fled to the north and founded Hestiaea in Thessaly. But some say they went to Illyria where the descendants of Cadmus ruled. The Argives entered Thebes, pulled down the walls, and took much booty, some of which they sent to Apollo at Delphi in fulfillment of a vow to give him the best fruits of their victory. Thersander and his heirs became the rulers of Thebes. The successful war of the Epigoni took place before the expedition of the Argonauts and before the Trojan War. It has been placed by some in the 14th century B.C.

Epigoni. Greek epic poem of the Theban cycle, by Antimachus of Clarus, relating to the renewal of the war between Argos and Thebes by the *epigoni* (descendants) of its heroes.

Epimelius (ep-i-mē′li-us). An epithet of Hermes, meaning "Keeper of Flocks."

Epimenides (ep-i-men′i-dēz). Cretan poet, religous teacher, and wonder worker who was active in the 7th and 6th centuries B.C. He was the Rip Van Winkle of Greek legend, for he was said to have gone into a cave to rest while looking for a lost sheep, to have fallen asleep, and to have awakened 20, 57, or 100 years later, unaware of the duration of his sleep. He came home to find his younger brother now an old man. He became a well-known sage and was called (596 B.C.) to Athens to determine the reason and cure for a plague. The oracle at Delphi told him that the plague was due to the murder of the supporters of Cylon, an Athenian noble who attempted to seize power, who had been killed (c632 B.C.) by Megacles despite a promise of safe-conduct. Epimenides performed the proper rites and freed the city of its impurity. He asked as his only reward that Athens and Cnossus, his home, should make treaties of friendship. Tradition assigned to him a number of mystical writings.

Epimetheus (ep-i-mē′thūs, -thē̞-us). In Greek mythology, a son of Iapetus, and the brother of Prometheus, Atlas, and Menoetius. Some say Epimetheus, whose name means "Afterthought," was given the task of creating animals to populate the world after it had been formed. He carelessly gave the best gifts to the animals—fur to keep them warm, feathers to soar into the air, cunning, and courage. When it came to man all the protections had been used up, and he sought the aid of Prometheus to find some means by which men could protect themselves. Prometheus made man to stand erect and stole fire from heaven and gave it to man. To counterbalance the gift of fire, Zeus commanded Hephaestus to make a maiden, Pandora. She was endowed with gifts by all the gods and taken by Hermes to Epimetheus as a gift. Epimetheus forgot until it was too late Prometheus' warning never to accept a gift from Zeus. He married Pandora. Up to this time there had been only men in the world, and they lived without evils or hardship. Pandora, in her character and in the dowry she brought with her, inflicted endless trouble and grief on men. Epimetheus and Pandora were the parents of Deucalion's wife Pyrrha.

Epinaos (ep-i-nā′os). An open vestibule behind the cella of some temples, corresponding to the pronaos in front.

Epione (ē-pī′ō-nē). According to some accounts, the wife of Asclepius. Her image was among those included in the sacred precinct of Asclepius at Epidaurus.

Epirus or **Epeiros** (ē-pī′rus). In ancient geography, that part of N Greece lying between Illyria on the N, Macedonia and Thessaly on the E, Aetolia, Acarnania, and the Ambracian Gulf on the S, and the Ionian Sea on the W (to the Acroceraunian promontory). In earlier times the name was given to the entire W coast S to the Corinthian Gulf. The kingdom of Epirus was at its height under Pyrrhus (295–272 B.C.). It was ravaged by Aemilius Paulus in 167 B.C., and was a part of the Roman Empire from 146 B.C. to 1204 A.D. The N part is now in Albania, the remainder in Greece.

Epistrophia (ep″i-strō-fī′a). An epithet of Aphrodite in her aspect as goddess of love, meaning "She Who Turns Men to Love."

Epistrophus (e-pis′trō-fus). In Homeric legend (*Iliad*), a son of King Evenus and a brother of Mynes. He was slain along with his brother when Achilles raided his land, Lyrnessus, during the Trojan War.

Epitymbia (ep-i-tim-bī′a). An epithet of Aphrodite in her aspect as goddess of death-in-life, meaning "Of the Tombs."

Epium (ē′pi-um). See **Aepy.**

Epona (ep′ō-na). In Roman mythology, a female divinity, protectress of horses. See **Bubona.**

Epopeus (ē-pō′pūs, -pē-us). In Greek legend, a son of Aloeus, and a grandson of Helius, but some say Poseidon was his father. Iphimedia was his mother and he was a brother of the Aloidae. Or, as some say, Canace was his mother. He was a king in Sicyon, having inherited the land about the Asopus River from his father. The adjoining land of Ephyra (Corinth) belonged to Aeëtes, and when Aeëtes departed for Colchis he left his realm in the care of Bunus. After the death of Bunus, Epopeus conquered Ephyra and added it to this kingdom. He was married to Antiope, daughter of Nycteus of Thebes. Some say Antiope fled to him when she was with child; others say Epopeus carried her off. In any event, his connection with Nycteus led to a war with Thebes, in which Nycteus was wounded. Epopeus was also wounded, but his forces won the battle. In gratitude for his success he raised a temple to Athena. When it was complete he prayed to the goddess to give him some sign that the temple was pleasing to her. The goddess caused olive oil to flow before the temple to express her satisfaction. Epopeus also raised sanctuaries of Apollo and Artemis and altars of Pan and Helius in Sicyon. He neglected his wound and died of it, and was buried before the altar in the temple of Athena.

Epyllion (ē-pil′i-on). A narrative poem in epic style, a "little epic," a literary form developed at Alexandria, or under Alexandrian influence, whose motif is usually a romantic episode from the life of a legendary hero or heroine. Epyllia by Theocritus, Bion, Moschus, Callimachus, Euphorion, Cicero, Catullus, Vergil, Ovid, and others survive, in whole or fragments. Catullus' "Wedding of Peleus and Thetis," in 408 polished Latin hexameters, well represents the form. (JJ)

Equuleus (e-kwö′lē-us). An ancient northern constellation, supposed to represent a horse's head. It lies west of the head of Pegasus.

Erasistratus (er-a-sis′tra-tus). Greek physician and anatomist; born probably on the island of Chios; fl. c300 B.C. He lived first at the court of the king of Syria, then went to Alexandria, where he founded a school of anatomy. He studied the convolutions of the brain, investigated the bile, spleen, liver, and the anatomy of the heart, named the trachea, and invented a catheter. In his investigation of the nerves he distinguished sensory and motor nerves. He also made studies of the arteries and veins, and believed that the elixir or substance vital to life was circulated by the arteries. According to his conclusions, the escape of this vital substance caused bleeding, and any impediment in its flow caused disease.

Erato (er′a-tō). One of the nine daughters of Zeus and Mnemosyne. She is the muse of lyric and amorous poetry. In art she is often represented with the lyre. See **Muses.**

Erato. In Greek mythology, an Arcadian dryad who, according to some accounts, was the wife of Arcas and the mother of his sons. She was also a prophetess of Pan, and gave his oracles.

Eratosthenes (er-a̱-tos'the̱-nēz). Alexandrian astronomer, geometer, geographer, grammarian, and philosopher, born at Cyrene, in Africa, c275 B.C.; died c194 B.C. He has been called "the founder of astronomical geography and of scientific chronology." He studied at Athens, and his reputation for learning became such that he was invited by Ptolemy III to become the chief librarian (the third to hold the position) of the great Library at Alexandria (247 B.C.). He wrote on a wide variety of subjects, as *On Ancient Comedy,* in which he described among other things the mechanics of production; he also composed a short epic on the death of Hesiod and the punishment of his murderers, and a celebrated elegy, the *Erigone,* which was probably part of his epic poem, *Hermes.* His greatest work was the *Geographica,* in three books, of which the first was on physical geography, the second was on mathematical geography and embraced a system for calculating latitude and longitude which he devised himself, and the third was on map-making. This work has been lost except for fragments preserved in the writings of later writers. His greatest accomplishment in mathematical geography was his measurement of the circumference of the earth. He also calculated the degree of inclination of the great circle of the earth and the magnitude and distance of the sun and the moon. He wrote on chronology and worked out a system into which he fitted such events as the dates of Heracles (1261–1209 B.C.), the voyage of the Argonauts (1225 B.C.), the Expedition of the Seven against Thebes (1213 B.C.), the Fall of Troy (1183 B.C.), the Return of the Heraclidae (c1100 B.C.), and the time of Lycurgus at Sparta (885 B.C.).

Ercta (ėrk'ta̱) or **Ercte** (ėrk'tē). [Modern name, **Monte Pellegrino.**] Isolated mountain peak just N of Panormus (Palermo), in Sicily, overlooking the city and harbor. It was occupied by Hamilcar in the First Punic War. Elevation, about 1900 feet.

Erebus (er'e̱-bus). [Also: **Erebos.**] In Greek mythology, the son of Chaos and some say, of Darkness, but others say Erebus was Darkness. He was the brother of Nyx (Night) and, according to some accounts, of Aether (Air) and Hemera (Day), but others say

Aether and Hemera were his children. By his sister Nyx he was the father of the Fates and such personified evils as Doom, Death, Slumber, Dreams, Misery, Deceit, Eld (*the Destroyer*), and Strife. In general, Erebus signified the unknown darkness.

Erebus. [Also: **Erebos.**] In Greek mythology, a place or region, and a state or condition. As the first, it is that part or section of the Underworld through which the souls of the dead must pass in order to reach Hades. As the second, it is "darkness" itself, and, in particular, the darkness of the west.

Erechtheum (e̱-rek'the̱-um). The popular name of a white marble temple of Athena, of the Ionic order, on the Acropolis of Athens, dating from the last quarter of the 5th century B.C. and one of the most remarkable creations of Greek architecture. In plan it is unique; whereas at this period Greek temples were almost invariably peristyle (surrounded by colonnades) or amphiprostyle (columned porches on front and rear), the Erechtheum has a conventional hexastyle porch on the E, but at the W, where the still more ancient sanctuary of Cecrops resisted encroachment, there are no steps and no free-standing columns, the order of the E front being suggested by four attached Ionic half-columns between antae, rising above a high basement. At the W end of the N flank is a deep porch, four columns in front and one behind each corner column, leading to the magnificent North Doorway which gave access to the W chambers. At the W end of the S flank is a porch ("Porch of the Maidens") in which six architectural statues of fully-draped young women ("Caryatids") take the place of columns, carrying the entablature on their heads. Around the cella block and north porch was a continuous frieze of separately-carved white marble figures attached by pins to a background of dark gray limestone. If the plan is awkward, or at least unorthodox, the decorative elements, capitals, bases, antae, cornice moldings, door and window frames, and ceilings, are widely admired; the North Porch, in particular, has been described as the finest expression of the Ionic order, while visitors are inevitably drawn to the graceful Caryatid Porch.

The interior has been repeatedly gutted,

but enough foundations remain to indicate that inside were four rooms on at least two levels. In addition to the cult of Athena Polias (*Protectress of the City*), which we may locate in the E chamber, we learn that Poseidon and Hephaestus were worshiped there, and Pausanias also reports altars of Erechtheus, legendary founder of Athens, the name of whose chapel was eventually extended to the whole building, and his nephew Boutes, while beside the N porch was an altar of Zeus Hypatos. A fenced opening in the floor of the N porch permitted a view of markings in the native rock, said to have been made by Poseidon's trident in his contest with Athena for possession of Attica. To the west was the Pandroseum, in which stood the sacred olive tree.

The name of the architect of the Erechtheum is not recorded, but it has been observed that the complex design would give ample scope for the versatility displayed by Mnesicles, architect of the Propylaea. Construction was begun about 420 B.C., suspended in consequence of the Sicilian disaster of 413, resumed in 409, and completed probably in 405 B.C. It suffered from interior fires in the 4th century B.C. and at least twice in Roman times. In the Byzantine period it became a Christian church and during the Turkish domination it became the residence of the Pasha. Protracted researches by a commission of architectural historians of the American School of Classical Studies at Athens have resolved many of the problems of reconstruction and detail. (JJ)

Erechtheus (ē-rek′thūs, -thē̱-us). A son of Pandion, the twin of Butes, and the brother of Procne and Philomela. He was a legendary king of Athens and a protegé of Athena, who gave him her shrine for a dwelling. By his wife Praxithea he had four sons: Cecrops, Metion, Orneus, and Pandorus, and seven daughters: Chthonia, Creusa, Orithyia, Otionia, Pandora, Procris, and Protogonia. During a war between the Athenians and the Eleusinians an oracle informed him that if he sacrificed his youngest daughter he would secure victory. She, Otionia, willingly gave her life for Athens. Protogonia and Pandora killed themselves also, as they had vowed that they would kill themselves if one of them died by violence. In the same

war, Erechtheus slew Eumolpus, leader of the Eleusinians, who was his own great-grandson. Poseidon, father of Eumolpus, took immediate revenge, either by destroying Erechtheus with his trident, or by invoking Zeus, who felled Erechtheus with a thunderbolt.

Eretria (e-rē′tri-ạ). In ancient geography, a city on the island of Euboea, Greece, about 29 miles N of Athens. It was a rival of Chalcis, was destroyed (490 B.C.) by the Persians, and was afterward rebuilt. An ancient theater has been excavated on its site by the American School at Athens. The *cavea* (auditorium) is supported on an artificial embankment. It was divided by radial stairways into 11 *cunei* (blocks of seats), and is 266 feet in diameter. The orchestra, 81½ feet in diameter, presents a highly important feature, here first recognized, in an underground passage leading from its center to the interior of the stage structure.

Ereuthalion (er-ū-thā′li-on). In Homeric legend (*Iliad*), an Arcadian who fought as the champion of the Arcadians, wielding the iron mace of Areïthoüs, in a single combat to decide a struggle between the Arcadians and Pylians. Nestor, who was his opponent in the duel, killed him. Nestor recalled his conquest of Ereuthalion in his youth as he regretted his age in the siege of Troy.

Ergane (ėr′gạ-nē). Epithet of Athena, meaning "Worker." As patroness of the useful and decorative arts the Athenians were the first to give her this name. The cock was sacred to Athena Ergane, and sanctuaries of Athena Ergane were erected in many places.

Erginus (er-jī′nus). According to some mythographers, a son of Clymenus, king of the Minyans in Orchomenus. Others say he was a son of Poseidon. In the course of the games for Poseidon at Onchestus, Clymenus was killed by a Theban. Erginus, who succeeded his father as king, forthwith attacked and conquered Thebes, and imposed a tribute of 100 head of cattle yearly for 20 years. Heracles met the heralds who were on their way to collect the cattle, and cut off their ears and noses, which he threaded on cords and hung around their necks. He then bound their hands behind their backs and sent them back to Erginus. Erginus again attacked the Thebans in retaliation for this outrage, but this time Heracles aided the Thebans. He routed Erginus, scattered his army, and forced the people of Orchomenus to pay double the tribute which Erginus had been exacting from the Thebans. Some say Erginus was killed in this battle. Others say he survived the defeat and later joined the Argonauts on their journey to Colchis. In his old age he followed the advice of an oracle and married a young wife who bore him the famous builders, Agamedes and Trophonius.

Erginus. A river of Thrace. Nearby is the rock of Sarpedon to which Boreas carried Orithyia when he carried her off from the banks of the Ilissus River.

Eriboea (er-i-bē'a). In Greek mythology, a wife of Aloeus and the stepmother of Ephialtes and Otus. Her stepsons imprisoned Ares in a bronze vessel and hid him in her house. Hermes tricked her into releasing him.

Erichthonius (er-ik-thō'ni-us). In Greek mythology, a son sprung from the seed of Hephaestus which fell on Gaea. Gaea abandoned him and Athena took the infant, who was half human and half serpent, put him in a chest, and gave him to the daughters of Cecrops, king of Athens, to guard. She gave them strict instructions not to open the chest. Ultimately, of course, their curiosity got the better of them. They opened the chest and when they saw the child with a serpent's tail for legs they were maddened with fear and leaped to their deaths from the Acropolis. A white crow brought Athena the news of the death of Agraulos and her two daughters. Athena was so saddened by the news she changed the crow's color from white to black and henceforth banished crows from the Acropolis. She put Erichthonius in her aegis and reared him herself. Some say she gave him the power to restore the dead to life by presenting him with two drops of the blood of the Gorgon Medusa. When he later became king of Athens he established the worship of Athena there. He invented the four-horse chariot and later was identified with the constellation Auriga on this account. The royal family of Athens claimed descent from Erichthonius, as well as from Erechtheus, with whom he is sometimes confused.

Erichthonius. In Homeric legend *(Iliad)*, a son of Dardanus. He succeeded to his father's kingdom in what later, from Erichthonius' son Tros, came to be known as the Troad.

Eridanus (ē-rid'a-nus). A large mythical river in northern Europe, later identified with the Rhone, or, usually, with the Po. According to legend, it had its source in the Elysian Fields of the Underworld. Its waters still steam from receiving blazing Phaëthon, a youth who fell into them when he failed successfully to drive the chariot of Helius across the sky and was felled by a thunderbolt of Zeus to save the world from burning up. Along its banks the Heliades, sisters of Phaëthon, were turned into poplar trees as they grieved for their fallen brother.

Eridanus. [Also: **Fluvius**, the River.] The ancient southern constellation of the River. It is situated south of Taurus, and contains the star Achernar, or Acanar, of the first magnitude.

Erigone (ē-rig'ō-nē). In Greek mythology, the daughter of Icarius of Athens. When her father was slain by peasants, made drunk by wine he had given them, his dog led her to his grave. Stricken with grief, she prepared to hang herself from the pine tree under which the peasants had buried him. She prayed that all Athenian daughters would suffer a death similar to hers until Icarius was avenged. When Athenian maidens began to be found swinging from trees, an oracle explained that this came about in answer to Erigone's prayer. The Athenians found the peasants who had murdered Icarius and killed them, extinguishing the curse.

Erigone. In Greek legend, a daughter of Clytemnestra and Aegisthus. According to some accounts, it was she who brought Orestes to trial for the murder of her mother and father, before the Areopagus. When Orestes was acquitted she hanged herself.

Erinna (ē-rin'a). Greek poetess, born at Rhodes or Telos probably in the middle of the 4th century B.C. She died at the age of 19. Fragments of the poem by which she is best known, *The Spindle*, survive, of the original 300 hexameters. The poem was written in memory of her friend Baucis, described girlhood experiences shared with her, and lamented her death. Of her other writings only a few epigrams are extant.

Erinyes (e-rin'i-ēz). Female divinities, avengers of iniquity, who live in Erebus and are older than Zeus and the Olympians. According to Hesiod, they are daughters of Gaea (Earth), sprung from the blood of Uranus when he was mutilated by his son Cronus. According to others, they are the children of Night and Darkness. The Erinyes are monstrous hags; coiling serpents stream from their dogs' heads, wings sprout from their black bodies, and in their hands they carry bronze scourges to attack their victims. They hunt down offenders, make them mad, and punish them in Tartarus. In later times the number of the Erinyes was limited to three: Alecto (*Unresting*), Megaera (*Jealous*), and Tisi-

ERINYS
Red-figured Greek vase, 4th century B.C.
Ruvo

phone (*Avenger*). The Erinyes are not vindictive; their punishments are impartial and impersonal; crimes, or other offenses, must be avenged to satisfy the souls of the dead whose representatives they are and who have called on them for vengeance. Orestes, who slew his mother, is hounded by the Erinyes, even though his act was fully in consonance with what he was required to do: he had killed his mother to avenge his father. But the Erinyes, called on by Clytemnestra's soul, demanded payment for his crime. Athena, goddess of law and order as well as

of wisdom, came to the defense of Orestes. She persuaded the Erinyes to let him stand trial before the Areopagus. In the trial the vote of the judges was evenly divided, whereupon Athena cast her vote in favor of Orestes and broke the tie. The Erinyes bitterly protested the trial and the verdict. If now, they said, a confessed murderer was to go free they would lose all authority as avenging deities. They threatened to put a blight on Athens if the verdict was not reversed. Athena cajoled them. She promised that the Athenians would honor them with offerings of first fruits and sacrifices. She invited them to take up their residence in a grotto on the Acropolis and receive their honors from the Athenians. In return for these honors the Erinyes were to promise prosperity for the land, ships, and marriages of the Athenians. The Erinyes accepted Athena's proposal, agreed to the promises she exacted from them, and were led away by torchlight procession to their new home in the grotto on the Acropolis, which henceforth became a shrine and a sanctuary. After this they were honored by the Athenians as the "Solemn Ones," their rites were performed in silence, and acquitted murderers sacrificed black victims to them. Other places in Greece had altars of the Solemn Ones. At Phyla, in Attica, sheep were sacrificed to them, and libations of honey were poured. Here flowers were worn at their processions instead of the myrtle wreaths that symbolize the Underworld. The Erinyes are also called the Eumenides. Some say this name, meaning "the Kind Ones," was given to them by Orestes, and some say the name was given to them because it was considered dangerous to mention them by the name Erinyes. And some say only three of the Erinyes agreed to Athena's proposal to cease hounding Orestes and make their home in the grotto on the Acropolis. They say that the other Erinyes, whose number varies, continued to pursue Orestes, and it was not until he had gone to Tauris and fetched the image of Artemis there that he was freed from their scourging. The Roman name for the Erinyes was Furiae or Dirae.

Erinys (e-rin′is, e-rī′nis). An epithet of Demeter. Tthe Thelpusians of Arcadia said that when Demeter was searching for Persephone she came to their land. Poseidon pursued her and she transformed herself into a mare to escape him. Poseidon then transformed himself into a stallion and ravished her as she grazed among the herds of Oncus. Demeter was so enraged that the Thelpusians gave her the name Erinys (*Fury*) and set up an image of Demeter Erinys in her temple.

Eriopis (er-i-ō′pis). Named by Homer as the wife of Oileus and the mother of Ajax the Less.

Eriphyle (er-i-fī′lē). In Greek legend, the wife of the seer Amphiaraus and the sister of Adrastus, king of Argos. She was the mother of Alcmaeon and Amphilochus. In a quarrel between Amphiaraus and Adrastus she intervened to prevent them from injuring each other, and made them each promise to abide by her decision in any future dispute which might arise between them. When Adrastus proposed to march on Thebes to restore his son-in-law, Polynices, to the throne, he asked the help of Amphiaraus in the expedition. Amphiaraus refused, because he knew all would perish except Adrastus. Polynices learned of the agreement between Adrastus and Amphiaraus to allow Eriphyle to settle any disputes between them. He gave Eriphyle the necklace of Harmonia which he had brought with him from Thebes and begged her to compel Amphiaraus to accompany the expedition. Eriphyle accepted the bribe, although Amphiaraus had forbidden her to accept any presents from Polynices, and persuaded her husband to accompany Adrastus to Thebes. As Amphiaraus had foreseen, the expedition ended in disaster; only Adrastus survived it. Ten years later the Epigoni, as the sons of the original Seven against Thebes were called, proposed to march against Thebes to avenge their fathers, and sought Alcmaeon as their leader. Alcmaeon was reluctant to go. He argued the matter with his brother Amphilochus and they agreed to let their mother decide it. Once again Eriphyle was bribed, this time by Thersander, son of Polynices, who gave her the robe of Harmonia, which had been given to Harmonia as a wedding gift by Athena. She advised Alcmaeon to lead the new expedition. The Epigoni were successful and captured Thebes. On his return Alcmaeon learned that Eriphyle's acceptance of the bribe of the necklace had caused his father's death, and that her acceptance of the robe might have caused his own. He consulted the oracle of Delphi and then killed Eriphyle, some say with the help of Amphilochus. As she was dying, Eriphyle uttered a curse: she called on all the lands of Greece and Asia to deny a home to her murderers.

Eris (ē′ris, er′is). [Latin: **Discordia.**] According to some accounts, a daughter of Zeus and Hera, and the twin of Ares. Others say she was a daughter of Nyx. She is the goddess of discord who stirs up strife by spreading rumors and by inciting men to jealousy. The most famous example of how Eris roused jealousy concerns the Apple of Discord. In revenge for not having been invited to the nuptials of Peleus and Thetis, she threw among the guests a golden apple bearing the inscription "To the Fairest." A dispute arose among Aphrodite, Hera, and Athena concerning the apple, whereupon Zeus ordered Hermes to take the goddesses to Mount Gargarus, to the shepherd Paris, who should decide the dispute. He awarded the apple to Aphrodite, who in return assisted him in carrying off the beautiful Helen from Sparta, thus giving rise to the Trojan War.

Eros (ē′ros, er′os). In Greek mythology, the god of love. Some say he was born from a silver egg laid by Nyx, that he set the world in motion, and was the first of the gods. According to Hesiod he is the offspring of Chaos, coeval with Earth and Tartarus, and the companion of Aphrodite; in later myths he is the youngest of the gods, son of Aphrodite and Ares, Hermes, or Zeus, represented as a beautiful winged boy, armed by Zeus with bow and arrows, or flaming torch. In the older view he was regarded as one of the creative powers of nature, the principle of union among the diverse elements of the world, more especially as the power of sensuous love, and also of devoted friendship. In the later legend he is characterized as a beautiful, wild, mischievous, irresponsible, and irresistible boy, who shoots his arrows of desire at random, without regard for former commitments or future welfare of those whose hearts he wantonly sets on fire. Although he was never given a place among the 12 Olympians, the gods had not the smallest compunction about employing him to further their own ends. For example, he was bribed by Aphrodite, at the request of Hera and Athena, to cause Medea to fall so madly in love with Jason that she betrayed her father and her country for his sake. Nor were the gods themselves immune to his arrows. He was worshiped at Thespiae in Boeotia, where a festival, the *Erotidia* or *Erotia,* was celebrated every five years in his honor. His brother is Anteros, the god of mutual love or the avenging god who punishes those who do not return love. The Romans identified Eros with Cupid or Amor, and the later Greeks adopted the Roman concept of a plural Eros.

Erulus (er'ū-lus). Named in the *Aeneid* as a son of Feronia, a goddess who presided over woods and orchards. He was a king in Italy. Because of gifts from his mother of three sets of equipment and three lives, Evander, a Trojan who had come to Italy before the Trojan War, had to kill him three times. Evander succeeded in doing this, all in the same day.

Erycina (er-i-sī'na). Epithet of 'Aphrodite or Venus. It comes from Mount Eryx in Sicily where her cult was established, according to various sources, by a legendary king named Eryx, by Aeneas, or by the Phoenicians. It was as Aphrodite Erycina that her worship was introduced to Rome c220 B.C.

Erymanthian Boar (er-i-man'thi-an). In Greek legend, a savage boar that roamed the slopes of Mount Erymanthus and ravaged the countryside. One of Heracles' labors for Eurystheus was to bring it alive to Mycenae. He drove it into a snow drift, captured it and carried it back to Mycenae slung across his shoulders. The scene, when Eurystheus, in terror of Heracles arriving with the still struggling boar, takes refuge in a large *pithos* or storage jar, whose lid he raises cautiously to follow the course of events, amused Greek artists and appears frequently in vase-painting and sculptured metopes.

Erymanthus (er-i-man'thus). [Also: **Olonos.**] Mountain peak on the border of Arcadia and Achaea, Greece. It was named after a son of Apollo who was blinded by Aphrodite because he saw the goddess bathing. It was the haunt of the Erymanthian Boar. The mountain was sacred to Artemis.

Erysichthon (er-i-sik'thon). In Greek mythology, a Thessalonian who cut down the trees in a grove sacred to Demeter. According to some accounts, when his servants refused to obey his order to cut down the tallest tree, he seized the ax and cut the tree himself. Some say the blood of the hamadryad who inhabited the tree flowed out and that her voice warned Erysichthon that Demeter would surely punish him. Others say that Demeter herself, in the guise of the priest of the grove, appeared and told him not to cut down the trees. In both cases he persisted in spite of warnings. Demeter punished him by sending Famine to embrace him, and from that time forward he could never eat enough to satisfy his hunger. He sold everything he had to buy food. Ultimately, he sold his daughter, Mestra. She, like some of the sea-gods, had the power of changing her shape at will, and as fast as she was sold she changed her form and returned to her father. She was then sold again, in this way providing an unending means of obtaining money for his insatiable hunger. But Famine grew ever more ravenous and at last Erysichthon turned upon his own body and devoured himself.

Erythea (er-i-thē'a). A legendary island far to the west beyond the Mediterranean Sea. It was the home of Geryon and his famous cattle. Heracles slew Geryon and took the cattle back to Hellas as one of his labors for Eurystheus. The island was also known as one where Helius kept one of his herds.

Erytheïs (er-i-thē'is) or **Erytheia** (-thī'a). In Greek mythology, one of the Hesperides who guarded the Golden Apples. At the approach of the Argonauts she transformed herself into an elm tree on the banks of the Tritonian Lake. See **Hesperides.**

Erythrae (er'i-thrē). In ancient geography, an Ionian city in Asia Minor, situated opposite the island of Chios. According to legend, it was founded by Erythrus, son of Rhadamanthys of Crete, and named for him. Lycians and Carians joined the Cretan settlers, and soon their city was further enlarged by the arrival of some Pamphylians who had wandered there with Calchas the seer after the fall of Troy. Some time later Cleopus, son of Codrus, the legendary king of Athens, attacked the city with a band of

Euboean and Boeotian colonists and secured control of it. There was a famous sanctuary of Heracles at Erythrae. According to some accounts, an image of Heracles, riding on a wooden raft, floated to a cape midway between Erythrae and Chios. The men of both places were most anxious to obtain the image, and strove mightily to pull it ashore but to no avail; they couldn't move it. A blind fisherman, one Phormio, had a vision that if the women of Erythrae would cut off their hair and make a rope of it the raft bearing the image could be pulled ashore. The women of Erythrae refused to cut off their hair, but the Thracian women who were in the city, both free and slave, volunteered to give their hair. The rope was made and the raft was then easily drawn ashore. A sanctuary of Heracles was raised in which the image was set, but only Thracian women were admitted to it. The rope of hair was also put in the sanctuary, and, it is said, that Phormio recovered his sight. Erythrae was called "The Crimson City" because of the purple dye obtained there by Tyrian traders.

Erythraean Sea (er-i-thrē′an). [Latin, **Mare Erythraeum**, also **Mare Rubrum**, meaning "Red Sea."] In ancient geography, a name given to the Arabian Sea, or to the Indian Ocean including the Red Sea and Persian Gulf.

Eryx (e′riks). According to mythology, a son of Butes, the Argonaut, and Aphrodite, and thus half-brother of Aeneas. He was in the habit of challenging strangers to box with him. If he won, his reward was to slay his opponent. Upon challenging Heracles he was defeated and killed, and buried on the mountain which henceforth bore his name.

Eryx. A mountain on the NW coast of Sicily. Butes, the Argonaut, was rescued by Aphrodite when he had leaped into the sea in answer to the Sirens' song, and was carried to this mountain by her. The mountain was named for the son of Butes and Aphrodite. Acestes, the Trojan, settled near this mountain, and it was on its slopes that Aeneas founded a shrine to Idalian Venus (Aphrodite) when he visited Acestes the second time, and divided his followers, leaving those who were tired of wandering to settle down with Acestes at the foot of Mount Eryx.

Eryx. [Modern name, **Erice**; formerly, **Monte San Ciuliano.**] Town on the island of Sicily, situated on a mountain 2465 feet high, overlooking the Tyrrhenian Sea. It was colonized by Phoenicians, later occupied by Greeks, captured (278 B.C.) by Pyrrhus, and was the base of the Carthaginian army under Hamilcar Barca in the First Punic War. The central seat of the cult of the goddess Venus (Greek, Aphrodite), it had a temple of which the ruins may still be seen. Fortification walls, some having Phoenician inscriptions, are also preserved.

Esquiline Hill (es′kwi-līn, -lin). [Latin, **Mons Esquilinus.**] Central hill of the three which form the E side of the group of Seven Hills of ancient Rome. It lies between the Viminal on the N and the Caelian on the S, and E of the Palatine. It is divided from E to W by a depression. On the part to the N, called the Mons Cespius, stands the Church of Santa Maria Maggiore; on that to the S, the Mons Oppius, rise the Church of San Pietro in Vincoli and the Baths of Titus. Here, too, were the houses of Horace, Vergil, and Propertius. Between the Esquiline and the Palatine stands the Flavian Amphitheater ("Colosseum").

Eteocles (ē-tē′ō-klēz). In Greek legend, a son of Oedipus and Jocasta. When Oedipus learned that he had killed his own father and produced children by his own mother he blinded himself in despair. According to some accounts, his sons Eteocles and Polynices shut him away to hide the shame of their family; others say they banished him. Still others say his sons gave him a slave's portion of a sacrificial victim. For one of these reasons Oedipus laid a curse on his sons: that they should divide their inheritance by the sword. After Oedipus left Thebes Eteocles and Polynices agreed to rule the kingdom by turns. Eteocles, being the elder, was first to rule. When his term was ended he refused to give up the throne, on the grounds of Polynices' violent character, and banished him. Polynices fled to Argos and enlisted the aid of Adrastus to lead an expedition against Thebes to recover the throne. This was the famous, ill-fated expedition of the Seven against Thebes. Eteocles mustered his forces within the city to meet the attack. He assigned one Theban chieftain to each of the seven gates of Thebes which were being attacked by the seven leaders of the enemy forces. When only three of the attacking Argives remained, the others having been killed, Eteocles and Polynices met in single combat to decide which should have the throne. They fought furiously and in the end slew each other, thus carrying out the curse which Oedipus had laid on his sons. The attackers then fled and Thebes was safe. Creon, uncle of Eteocles, succeeded to the throne. He commanded that Eteocles, as the valiant defender of the city, be given full funeral honors. But as for Polynices, who had treacherously attacked his home city, Creon commanded that his body be flung outside the walls to become the prey of scavenger birds.

Eteoclus (ē-tē'ō̱-klus). In Greek legend, an Argive, the son of Iphis. According to some accounts, he was one of the Seven against Thebes and perished in the attack on the city.

Ethiopia (ē-thi-ō'pi-a̱). [Also: **Aethiopia, Axumite Kingdom.**] In ancient geography, a country S of Egypt, corresponding to the kingdom of Meroe, from the neighborhood of Khartoum N to Egypt. In a more extended sense it comprised Nubia, the N part of modern Ethiopia, Sennar, and Kordofan. It was closely connected with Egypt. Conquered by Egyptian kings of the XIIth Dynasty, lost in the period of the Hyksos, and reconquered under the XVIIIth Dynasty, it remained with Egypt until after the XXth Dynasty. An Ethiopian founded the XXVth Egyptian Dynasty. The Greeks visited the country in the middle 7th century B.C. and gradually extended their relations with the inhabitants. In the 1st century A.D. a powerful Ethiopian state, with Axum as its capital, arose and remained powerful until far into the Byzantine era.

Etna (et'na̱). [Italian, **Monte Etna,** (Sicilian) **Mongibello.**] Chief mountain in Sicily, and the highest volcano in Europe, situated in the E part of the island. Elevation, about 10,758 feet. See **Aetna.**

Etruria (ē-trö'ri-a̱). In ancient geography, a division of Italy which extended along the Mediterranean, and was separated from Umbria, the Sabine territory, and Latium by the Tiber, and from Liguria by the Apennines. It nearly corresponds to modern Tuscany. It contained a confederation of 12 cities. The Etruscans developed as a great naval power, influential in N and C Italy, and had possessions on the Po and in Campania. Etruscan kings ruled at an early time at Rome (probably until c500 B.C.). The Etruscans were defeated by Syracuse in a naval battle in 474 B.C., and suffered from the invasion of the Gauls c400 B.C. Veii was lost to Rome in 396 B.C. Defeat by Rome at the Vadimonian Lake in 283 B.C. was followed by the fall of Tarquinii and the other Etrurian cities. In the *Aeneid,* Etruria is named as a land whose people were in rebellion against the cruelty of Mezentius, a former ruler. He was given asylum by Turnus and the Etrurians were up in arms and massed for war to recover Mezentius, but a seer had told them they must wait for a foreign commander. For this reason they welcomed Aeneas when he appealed to them for aid in his war against Turnus, and joined with him.

Etrurians (ē-trö'ri-anz). See **Etruscans.**

Etruscans (ē-trus'ka̱nz). [Also: **Etrurians.**] The people of ancient Etruria, a region in Italy corresponding to what is now Tuscany and part of Umbria. Exactly who or what these people were has never been satisfactorily determined. Their inscriptions have never been completely deciphered; only the proper names emerge with certainty; and their language still defies sure classification. It was entirely different from the language of their predecessors in the region. That it is not Indo-European is the consensus to date; the alphabet resembles the Greek and Phoenician. Several theories as to the origin of the Etruscans have been advanced: 1) the Greek historian Dionysius of Halicarnassus thought that they were the original inhabitants of Italy; 2) Herodotus said that during a famine in Lydia the current king divided his people into two groups, one group to remain in Lydia, the other to emigrate under the leadership of his son Tyrrhenus. The emigrants went first to Smyrna to build ships, and from there to the land of the Umbrians, where they settled, built towns, and called themselves Tyrrhenians; 3) Livy proposed that they came from invading Alpine peoples, probably the Rhaetians. The most recent specialists in Etruscan ethnology and archeology corroborate Herodotus, insofar as it is now believed that the Etruscans entered Italy in the 9th century B.C. from the sea, were probably from Asia Minor, subdued the Umbrians, and built a number of fortified towns which were eventually unified into a powerful state. That they came from the north is now a discredited theory, because archaeologists are satisfied that they entered Italy from the sea and that the northernmost of their settlements were the latest to be founded. Flinders Petrie believed in their Asiatic origin because their weights were unlike those in use throughout the Mediterranean region, but seemed related to those of India.

A new era of culture began with them, the most advanced in Italy before Roman arms overwhelmed it. The Etruscans were skilled ironworkers and bronze-workers, active traders, and their products were sought and bought not only by the Greeks, but even trickled into the area of what is now Germany, France, and Spain through the trade routes and passes. The Etruscans imported as assiduously as they exported, and many an "Etruscan" objet d'art has since been proved to be an imported piece of Greek workmanship. The greatest similarity between Etruscan and Greek art, however, lies in the fact that both arts derived from the same Eastern sources. The Etruscan peculiarity of style, reflecting both Asiatic and Egyptian influence, distinguishes their early productions; later Greek influence predominates and finally supersedes their own. The Etruscans are especially noted for their characteristic polygonal town walls (sometimes called Cyclopean) and their cupolaed sepulchers (also called tower-tombs). The sepulcher paintings depict a high level of life: banquets, dancers, musicians, races, wrestling matches, hunting scenes. Silver and gold objects and carved gems were found in the tombs, where the findings also reveal that these people were advanced in dentistry (artificial teeth, gold crowns, etc., bear testimony to this). They are much noted also for their black *bochero* pottery and terra-cotta vases and figurines. Of their twelve cities Tarquinii (modern Tarquinia) is noted for its tombs and tomb paintings. Caere (modern Cervetri) is noted for its necropolis; Veii (modern Veio) for its sculptures. Vetulonia is famous as one of the oldest Etruscan settlements. Clusium (modern Chiusi) was the stronghold of the king Lars Porsena, and is noted for its tombs. Cosa, Volteria, Perugia were among the other cities. By the 6th century B.C. the Etruscans had crossed the Apennines and founded Felsina (now Bologna). By the 5th century B.C. their expansion, power, and civilization was at its height. The Greeks repeatedly tried to curb Etruscan expansion and power, but it was the Romans who finally first halted them in the 5th century B.C. They became weakened by Gallic invasions, and after the Romans captured Veii (396 B.C.) the rest of the cities succumbed. Etruscan culture made its mark on Roman culture during the first two centuries of the Roman hold, throughout Latium especially. But as the Roman powers strengthened, Etruscan civilization weakened, and by the 1st century B.C. had disappeared.

Euaechme (ū-ēk′mē). In Greek legend, a daughter of Megareus, king of Megara. Alcathous won her for his wife by slaying a lion. She was the mother of Periboea.

Euboea (ū-bē′a̤). [Modern Greek, **Evvoia**; Italian, **Negroponte**; Turkish, **Egripo**; sometimes in English, **Negropont**.] Largest island belonging to Greece, in the Aegean Sea. It lies E of Phocis, Boeotia, and Attica, from which it is separated by the strait of Euripus. It is traversed by mountains, Delphi reaching the height of 5725 feet. The chief towns in ancient times were Chalcis and Eretria. It was subdued by Athens after the Persian wars. Length, about 98 miles; greatest width, about 30 miles.

Euboea. In ancient geography, a Greek city of Sicily, situated on the coast N of Syracuse. The city was abandoned after most of its inhabitants were moved to Syracuse by the tyrant Gelon (485 B.C.), and its exact location is now uncertain.

Eubuleus (ū-bū′lē-us). In Greek mythology, a son of Trochilus, priest of Argos who fled to Eleusis. He was the brother of Triptolemus and, some say, of Eumolpus, a shepherd. Some say Eubuleus was an oracular swineherd (his name means "good counsel"). He was feeding his animals in the fields one day when suddenly the earth parted and engulfed one of his swine. Almost at once a chariot drawn by black horses appeared, and before it too disappeared into the chasm, Eubuleus saw in the chariot a girl tightly clasped in the arms of a stranger. Eubuleus told Triptolemus of this sight, and he in turn gave the information to Demeter when she came searching for her lost daughter Persephone. In commemoration of the service of Eubuleus to Demeter live swine were hurled into a chasm in his honor at the festival of the Thesmophoria at Eleusis.

Eubulides (ū-bū′li-dēz). Greek philosopher of the Megarian school. He was born in Miletus and was active in the 4th century B.C. He wrote a satire against Aristotle and is said to have taught Demosthenes oratory and the art of disputation.

Eubulus (ū-bū′lus). Athenian statesman; fl. middle of the 4th century B.C. He was in charge of the Theoric Fund from 354 to perhaps 346 B.C. This fund consisted originally of surplus revenues of the state that were devoted to religious purposes, such as paying for the seats of the poor at the dramatic festivals. By the time of Eubulus the manager of the Theoric Fund was in effect the financial minister of Athens. Eubulus filled the office extremely ably. At a time when Athens was weak and the power of Macedon was growing Eubulus favored a policy of peace with Philip II of Macedon. Nevertheless, he sent a force to rescue the Phocians when Philip defeated them (351 B.C.) and prepared to march through the Pass of Thermopylae. Philip withdrew. Eubulus was an opponent of Demosthenes, who continually urged the Athenians to destroy Philip before his power became too great. After the fall of Olynthus (348 B.C.) which the Athenians had not arrived in time to save, Eubulus was compelled by the pressure of public opinion to send envoys to the cities of the Peloponnesus for the purpose of organizing united resistance to Philip. In this case Eubulus acted against his own policy, which continued to be one of peace with Philip, the effort to organize resistance failed, and he bluntly told the Athenians they must accept Philip's terms for peace (346 B.C.). A peace was made, but because of the inflammatory speeches of Demosthenes against the envoys who had agreed to it Eubulus lost some of his influence.

Eubulus. Greek Middle Comedy poet of the early 4th century B.C. He wrote mythological burlesques or parodies of tragedies. Fragments of the 100 or more pieces attributed to him survive.

Euchenor (ū-kē′nôr). In Homeric legend *(Iliad)*, a Corinthian, the son of the seer, Polyidus. On learning from his father that he would die worn out by affliction if he stayed home, or be overcome by the Trojans if he went to war, he chose to join the Greeks in the war against Troy. His father's prophecy was fulfilled: he was slain by Paris.

Euchidas (ū′ki-das). According to Plutarch, a Plataean runner. After the battle of Plataea (479 B.C.), the oracle at Delphi commanded that all the fires of Greece, which had been polluted by the barbarians (Persians), must be extinguished, and new fires kindled from the sacred fire at Delphi. The Plataeans extinguished their fires and sent Euchidas to Delphi to fetch new fire. He ran to Delphi, purified himself, put a laurel crown on his head, took fire from the sacred altar and returned with it to Plataea on the same day. Arrived at Plataea, having covered a journey of 1000 furlongs (125 miles) in one day, he saluted his companions, delivered the fire, and fell dead. The Plataeans buried him in the temple of Artemis Eucleia.

Euclid (ū′klid). Greek mathematician and physicist, active at Alexandria, c323–285 B.C. His systematization of the mathematical knowledge of his time remains to this day a basis for the teaching of elementary geometry. Despite the tremendous importance of this contribution, very little is definitely known about the man himself. He was probably trained in the Academy at Athens after the time of Plato, but several decades before the time of Archimedes. An Alexandrian scholar of the period has written that he was unassuming and of a notably mild temper, although by no means servile (according to one account, when he was asked by the reigning Egyptian king if there was not some easier way than his to learn geometry, he replied: "There is no royal road to geometry"). The type of man suggested by this fragmentary information is surely no humble slave, but a true scientist, and this conjecture is supported by the fact that much of the material in the 13 books of *The Elements* was probably original with him, and that the work as a whole is a synthesis of the highest order in the elaboration of which there is clear evidence of considerable genius. The formulation of the postulates (and more particularly, of the fifth postulate) was due to Euclid alone (and the many attempts since to prove the fifth postulate is an indirect tribute, surely, to his wisdom). In addition to this, Euclid discovered the earliest theorems of the theory of numbers (leaving aside some undatable Pythagorean knowledge) and fundamental principles of geometrical optics (including laws of reflection and propagation of light in straight lines).

Euclid's best-known work is, of course, *The Elements,* in 13 books (of which the first six are the ones chiefly used in introductory geometry). The translation of this, with commentary, by Thomas L. Heath (3 vols., 1908) is generally considered by historians of science to be not only the best one now existing in English, but one of the best ever to be made in any language. Among Euclid's other works are *The Pseudaria* (which are now lost, but are known to have been exercises in elementary geometry), *The Data* (also exercises, but in its modern form showing some deviation from that with which Euclid's contemporaries were familiar), *The Porisms* (three books which are now, and very unfortunately, no longer extant, but are known to have dealt with higher geometry), *The Phaenomena* (a treatise on astronomy or, more precisely, on spherical geometry), *The Optics* (although attribution of this to Euclid has been disputed by some authorities), and probably also various writings on musical theory.

Euclid of Megara (meg′a-ra). Greek philosopher, born probably in Megara, in the middle of the 5th century B.C. He was a friend and disciple of Socrates and the founder of the Megarian school. He tried unsuccessfully to combine Eleatic monism with Socrates' ethical teaching.

Eudemus of Rhodes (ū-dē′mus; rōdz). Greek philosopher of the 4th century B.C. He was a friend and student of Aristotle. He wrote on astronomy and mathematics, but only fragments of his works have come down to us. He edited the *Metaphysics* of Aristotle and his *Physics,* and is believed to have edited *Eudemian Ethics,* which is intended to be a summary of Aristotle's lectures on ethics rather than an original work. Eudemus interprets his master's doctrines theologically, making reason a divine element in man's nature. Some of his lost works, quoted by later writers, are histories of arithmetic, geometry, and astronomy, and treatises on logic and rhetoric.

Eudorus (ū-dôr′us). In Homeric legend *(Iliad),* a son of Polymela and Hermes, and a foster son of Echecles who later married Polymela. He was a commander of the Myrmidons and accompanied Patroclus when Achilles gave Patroclus permission to join the battle against the Trojans.

Eudoxus of Cnidus (ū-dok′sus; nī′dus). Greek astronomer, geometer, and physician. He was born c409 B.C. and died c356 B.C. He is said to have been the first to introduce the use of the celestial globe into Greece, to have improved the approximation of the length of the year, and to have adduced the fact that the altitude of the stars changes with the latitude as a proof of the sphericity of the earth.

Eudoxus of Cyzicus (siz′i-kus). Greek navigator, born at Cyzicus, in Asia Minor, and active in the late 2nd century B.C. He was in the service of Ptolemy Euergetes II of Egypt, for whom, after 146 B.C., he made two voyages to explore the Arabian Sea. He later went to Cádiz, after leaving the Egyptian king, to lead an expedition to circumnavigate Africa. According to Strabo, he traveled southward along the west African coast, after which all trace of him is lost.

Euemerus (ū-ē′mėr-us, ū-em′er-us). See **Euhemerus.**

Eugaeon (ū-jē′on). An Ionian chronicler from the island of Samos, active in the latter part of the 6th century B.C.

Eugammon (ū′ga-mon). Greek cyclic poet of Cyrene, who was active c566 B.C. He was the author of the *Telegonia,* which tells how Telegonus, son of Circe and Odysseus, sailed off in search of his father, unwittingly killed him, and married Penelope. He took Penelope and Telemachus to Circe's island, where they were made immortal by the enchantress. In Eugammon's work Telemachus marries Circe and Telegonus marries Penelope.

Euganean Hills (ū-gā′nē-an). [Italian, **Colli**

actǫr; up, lūte, pull; oi, oil; ou, out; ŦH, then; ḍ as d or j, ṣ as s or sh, ṭ as t or ch, ẓ as z or zh.

Euganei.] Chain of volcanic hills in NE Italy, SW of Padua. Highest point, 1800 feet.

Euhemerus (ū-hē′mėr-us, ū-hem′ẽr-us). [Also: **Euemerus, Evemerus.**] Greek mythographer of the second half of the 4th century B.C. He wrote a travel novel, the *Sacred History*, in which he gave a rationalistic explanation of current mythology. Euhemerus claimed that mythology was simply human history distorted, that the gods were originally men whose exploits had been twisted and magnified with time, and that the events of mythology could be explained as historical occurrences. He found a tomb in Crete bearing the inscription "Zeus, son of Cronos," which seemed to him to support his theory that the gods were only mortals who had come to be worshiped for their deeds by their superstitious or, in some cases, grateful, fellow mortals. Euhemerism, as this approach to mythology is still called, still finds its occasional supporters. At the time Euhemerus propounded his theory he was simply extending the current skeptical-scientific approach to matters which until that time had been accepted without question.

Euippe (ū-ip′ē). According to legend, a daughter of Daunus, king of Daunia in Italy. She married Diomedes, who came to her father's kingdom after the Trojan War.

Euippe. A name given to the mare into which Thea, daughter of Chiron the centaur, was transformed by Poseidon, in order to escape her father's wrath when she was about to bear a child by Aeolus. See **Thea.**

Eumaeus (ū-mē′us). In the *Odyssey*, the faithful swineherd of Odysseus. When Odysseus appeared to him, disguised as a beggar, he welcomed him and told him of his longing for the return of his gentle master. In the battle against the suitors of Penelope, Eumaeus aided Odysseus, who had by that time revealed his true identity.

Eumedes (ū-mē′dēz). In Homeric legend (*Iliad*), a Trojan herald and a man of great wealth. He had one son Dolon, and five daughters. Dolon was slain in the Trojan War.

Eumedes. A Trojan follower of Aeneas. Named in the *Aeneid* as the son of Dolon, famed in the *Iliad* as a Trojan spy who was captured and slain by Diomedes and Odysseus. Eumedes was slain by Turnus in the war with the Latins.

Eumelus (ū-mē′lus). In Homeric legend (*Iliad*), a son of Admetus and Alcestis and the grandson of Pheres. He was a leader of Thessalians in the Trojan War, and the possessor of remarkable horses. In the chariot race celebrating the funeral games for Patroclus Athena, who wanted Diomedes to win, shattered the yoke of Eumelus' chariot, causing it to veer sharply and hurling Eumelus to the ground. Diomedes won.

Eumelus. In the *Aeneid*, a Trojan who accompanied Aeneas on the flight from Troy. It was he who brought the news to Aeneas that the women had set the ships afire while the men were celebrating funeral games for Anchises in Sicily.

Eumelus. Greek epic poet of Corinth, who lived probably about the middle of the 8th century B.C. He was a member of the noble family of the Bacchiadae and is reputed to have been the author of a chronicle of Corinth, a *Europia* (about Dionysus), and works on Medea, the war of the Titans, and Hades, but all his works have been lost. He is sometimes spoken of as "the Corinthian Homer."

Eumenes (ū′mẹ-nēz). Secretary to Philip of Macedon and to Alexander the Great and one of the successors of Alexander the Great. He was born at Cardia, Thrace, c361 B.C.; and was put to death in Gabiene, Elymaïs (Elam), 316 B.C. He controlled Cappadocia, Pontus, and Paphlagonia and in the struggle for power among the Diadochi, or successors, he sided with Perdiccas against Antipater, Antigonus I, Ptolemy I, and Craterus. He defeated Craterus in 321 B.C., was defeated by Antigonus, and was betrayed by his soldiers to Antigonus. He kept the diary, the *Royal Journal*, of Alexander the Great which he perhaps published after Alexander's death.

Eumenes II. King of Pergamum 197–c159 B.C.; died c159 B.C. He was the eldest son of Attalus I, whom he succeeded. He cultivated the friendship of the Romans, whom he assisted in the war against Antiochus the Great. He was present in person at the decisive battle of Magnesia (189 B.C.), and, on the restoration of peace, was rewarded by the addition of the Thracian Chersonese, Mysia, Lydia, and Phrygia to his kingdom.

He was a patron of learning, and founded at Pergamum one of the famous libraries of antiquity.

Eumenides (ū-men′i-dēz). Euphemistic name, meaning "the gracious (or kindly) ones," for the Erinyes in Greek mythology.

Eumenides, The. A drama by Aeschylus, the third in his Orestean trilogy which won first prize in 458 B.C. In it the end of the curse on the House of Atreus and the establishment by Athena of a new order of justice founded on law rather than vengeance is treated.

The first scene is before the temple of Apollo at Delphi. Curtains conceal the shrine. The priestess invokes the gods and enters the shrine. She shrieks with terror and immediately reappears. She describes the loathsome Furies and the blood-stained suppliant she has found within and, horrified at this pollution of the shrine, withdraws. The curtains of the shrine are parted and reveal Orestes sitting by the altar and the black-robed Furies asleep on the floor. But now the shining figure of Apollo, flanked by Hermes, is also seen in the shrine. Apollo assures Orestes that he is his constant guardian. Although the Furies will continue to pursue him, he tells Orestes to take advantage of their present slumber to fly to the temple of Athena in Athens. There he must ask the goddess for a trial. He himself, who first commanded Orestes to slay his mother, will be his defender and will secure his deliverance from the avenging Furies. Orestes departs, under the protection of Hermes. The ghost of Clytemnestra now comes and accuses the Furies, to whom she had so often made libations, of allowing Orestes to escape. She exhorts them to awaken and pursue him, to hunt him to death for his crime in killing her, his mother, and so win honor for her in the Underworld. As the Furies rouse themselves the ghost of Clytemnestra vanishes. They see that Orestes has escaped and accuse Apollo, whom they call a younger god, of riding roughshod over the privileges of the older gods in order to save a matricide. The young gods have polluted the old justice. Orestes has sinned and must be hunted to death for it. Apollo enters and orders the Furies out of his shrine. They remind him that it is their duty and their high office to hound matricides. He asks why they didn't

hound Clytemnestra for the murder of Agamemnon. That was different, they answer, Clytemnestra was not the blood kin of Agamemnon. Apollo scorns this argument as an insult to the divine marriage of Hera and Zeus, as well as to the power of Aphrodite. He accuses them of injustice in persecuting Orestes and showing leniency to his mother. Athena must judge the case, he says. The Furies answer that they will never let Orestes go, and never give up their duty and privilege of hounding the guilty.

In a new scene, a year later, Orestes enters the temple of Athena in Athens and kneels before the image of the goddess. The Furies, having tracked him down, follow him in. Nothing can save him, they say. Whoever has broken the law of reverence due to parent, god, or guest must pay the inexorable penalty. Orestes says he has long since been purified, with drops of blood and pure water poured over his hands by many friends. He calls to Athena, wherever she may be, to come in divine authority and save his soul. The Furies repeat that neither Apollo nor Athena can save him. They never trouble the man whose hands are clean, they say, but they relentlessly claim the price in blood from one who has stained his hands with blood. This was the right they had held since the time of their birth. They have no concern with immortals, but any mortal who sins will inevitably suffer at their hands. This is the divine law. Athena enters and asks why they have come. The chorus tells her they are the Furies, and that no murderer can ever find rest from their pursuit. Orestes says he has killed his mother at the command of Apollo, to avenge his father. He will leave it to the goddess to judge whether what he did was right. Athena decrees that such a serious case must be decided by the wisest citizens, and goes to the city to fetch them. The Furies are enraged that the old law and justice are being overthrown by the new gods. Henceforth, they avow, the fear which keeps men from murder will disappear if sinners are allowed to appeal to a court. The judges assemble. Athena establishes the court, admonishes the judges to reverence their oath to give justice, and opens the trial. The Furies testify first. They establish that Orestes, on the advice of Apollo, killed his mother with a sword. Clytemnestra was not punished by them for the murder of Agamemnon because he was not of her own blood —that is the law. Orestes cannot refute their evidence and calls on Apollo to defend him. The god testifies that he acted on the authority of Zeus, the supreme authority, in giving Orestes the oracle which commanded him to kill his mother; that a warrior king's death by a woman's treachery does not compare with the death of an adulterous, murdering wife; that a mother is not a true parent in the same sense as a father because she only nourishes a seed, and he points to Athena herself as proof that a mother is not necessary. In the end he promises that Orestes, whom he has sent as a suppliant to Athena, will become a faithful ally of Athens. (Apollo's weak arguments are thus further undermined by an out-and-out bribe. The Furies have at least traditional law on their side. But their idea of vengeance on the sinner coupled with the gods' injunction that a father's blood must be avenged has put Orestes into a horrible dilemma from which there seems to be no escape.) Athena proclaims that the court she has established here on the Areopagus shall henceforth constitute a judicial council to try every case of homicide that occurs in Athens. She exhorts the judges not to taint pure laws with expediency, and commands them to establish a bulwark of law to strengthen the state. She announces that in case of a tie in the vote of the 12 judges she will vote for Orestes who has been purged of his guilt through suffering. The Furies threaten dire consequences on Athens if they lose the case, but when the votes are counted it is found that they are even. Athena breaks the tie as she had said she would and Orestes is acquitted. He expresses his deep gratitude to Athena, promises eternal loyalty and friendship to Athens, and joyously departs. The Furies rage: the new gods have robbed the old of their due; they will cast a blight on Athens. Athena says the trial was fair, the even vote represents no dishonor or defeat for the Furies. She persuades them to make their home in Athens, which she prophesies will become glorious and add glory to them with the honor the people will accord them. The Furies relent and now promise great blessings on Athens. They are led to a cave on the Acropolis by a great procession which has gathered to escort them to their new home. Henceforth they will be known as the dread and kindly powers who love and guard Athens. (The fear that keeps men from wrong-doing has not been destroyed by this change in the Furies, but a judicial procedure has been substituted for the personal vengeance which had brought generations of the House of Atreus to their doom.)

Eumolpus (ū-mol′pus). A priestly bard, reputed founder of the Eleusinian mysteries. According to the tale, he was the son of Chione, granddaughter of King Erechtheus of Athens, and Poseidon. In fear of her father's anger if he discovered she was the mother of a son, Chione cast her infant into the sea, but he was watched over by Poseidon and washed ashore in Libya. There he was brought up by Benthesicyme, a daughter of Poseidon and Amphitrite. She gave him one of her daughters in marriage when he grew up, but when he fell in love with another of her daughters she banished him to Thrace. There he plotted against the king, Tegyrius, and, having been discovered, was compelled to flee to Eleusis. In Eleusis he became the first priest of the rites of Demeter and Dionysus, and initiated Heracles into the Mysteries of Demeter and Persephone. Being highly skilled on the lyre and flute—he won the flute contest at the funeral games for Pelias —he taught the musical arts to Heracles also. He is said to have written hymns and to have discovered the art of cultivating trees and vines. The upright life he led in Eleusis caused King Tegyrius to forgive him for his earlier conspiracy, and he made Eumolpus the heir to his throne. When war broke out between Eleusis and Athens, Eumolpus, who had by now inherited the throne of Thrace, led a band of Thracians agains Athens and claimed the throne for himself as Poseidon's son. In the war the Athenians, under Ion, won and the Eleusinians, by the treaty of peace which was then concluded, became subject to Athens in all respects except that they retained control of the sacred Mysteries of Eleusis. Eumolpus was slain in battle by his great-grandfather Erechtheus, and was succeeded as priest of Demeter by his son. To avenge the slaying of Eumolpus,

Poseidon hurled his trident at Erechtheus and killed him, or, as some say, he appealed to Zeus to slay him with his thunderbolt. The family of the Eumolpidae were hereditary priests of Demeter at Eleusis.

Eumolpus. In Greek mythology, a flute-player of Colonae. He swore that Tenes, son of King Cycnus, had made improper advances to Phylonome, wife of Cycnus and stepmother of Tenes. The evidence he presented was a lie, and when later Cycnus learned that he had sworn falsely he ordered Eumolpus to be killed. Because of Eumolpus, no flute-player was ever allowed to set foot in the sacred precincts of the temple on the island of Tenedos.

Euneus (ū-nē′us). In Greek legend, a son of Jason and Hypsipyle. He lived in Lemnos, where his brother Thoas was king. He and Thoas rescued their mother, who had been sold into slavery by the Lemnian women, from Lycurgus of Nemea. When Lycaon, Priam's son, was captured by Achilles, Euneus bought him for a silver bowl. Later, Euneus supplied the Greeks at Troy with wine from Lemnos.

Eunomia (ū-nō′mi-a̯). One of the Horae, goddesses of the seasons and of nature. She was Order.

Eunomus (ū′nō̯-mus) or **Ennomus** (en′ō̯-). In Greek legend, a youth in the household of Oeneus, father of Deianira. Heracles cuffed him for carelessness when he was pouring water over the hero's hands before a feast. The blow was heavier than Heracles intended and killed the lad. In remorse, Heracles took Deianira and went into exile at Trachis.

Eupatridae (ū-pat′ri-dē) The landowning aristocracy in ancient Athens (Attica), as distinguished from the Georgi, or peasants, and the Demiurgi, or artisans. On the abolition of royalty they found themselves in exclusive possession of political rights. Their privilege was gradually curtailed, notably by Solon (594 B.C.) and Clisthenes (509 B.C.), until in the time of Pericles Athens was transformed into a pure democracy.

Euphemus (ū-fē′mus). In Greek legend, a son of Poseidon and Europa (daughter of Tityus). From his father he had the gift of being able to skim across the sea so swiftly his feet were hardly dampened. He was a member of the Calydonian Hunt and

went from Taenarus to join Jason on the expedition of the *Argo* to Colchis. He released the dove which prepared the way for the *Argo* through the Symplegades (Clashing Rocks). When the Argonauts were driven to the Tritonian Lake in Libya, Euphemus persuaded Triton to help them back to the sea. Triton gave him a clod of earth as a guest-gift, and because of this the descendants of Euphemus gained sovereignty over Libya. Euphemus, either in obedience to a dream or on the advice of Medea, cast it into the sea and the island of Calliste (Thera), afterward the home of his son, rose from it. Battus, who was born there, later founded Cyrene in Libya.

Euphorbus (ū-fôr′bus). In Greek legend, a Trojan, the son of Panthous. According to some accounts it was he who killed Protesilaus, the first Greek to leap ashore at Troy. It was he, too, who was the first to wound Patroclus when he attacked the walls of Troy and was stunned by a blow from Apollo. Immediately afterward Hector delivered the death blow to Patroclus, and in the struggle for possession of his body Euphorbus was slain by Menelaus and stripped of his armor. Menelaus dedicated the shield of the brave Euphorbus in the temple of Hera, near Mycenae. Pythagoras, who expounded the theory of metempsychosis, professed to be animated by the soul of Euphorbus, who in his turn was animated by the soul of the Argonautic herald and son of Hermes, Aethalides.

Euphorion (ū-fō′ri-on). According to some accounts, a son of Helen and Achilles, born after Achilles became a shade on the Islands of the Blest. He fled from Zeus, who loved him, and was slain by a thunderbolt.

Euphorion. Greek poet who lived in the middle of the 5th century B.C. He was the son of the tragedian Aeschylus. After his father's death, according to Suidas, he exhibited some of his unproduced works and won four prizes. Tragedies from his own hand were also produced with some success, so much so that he is said to have defeated Sophocles and Euripides in 431 B.C.

Euphorion. Greek poet and writer. He was born c276 B.C., at Chalcis in Euboea, and died in Syria, where he was librarian at the court of Antiochus the Great, c200 B.C. He wrote epics, elegies, and epigrams on many subjects, including mythology and history, and, with Callimachus and Philetas, was one of the chief exponents of the Greek elegy in the Alexandrian manner. This literary style, of great beauty and learning, greatly influenced later Roman poets. Only scanty fragments of his work survive.

Euphranor (ū-frā′nôr). Greek painter and sculptor in bronze and marble. He was born near Corinth, Greece, and was active in the middle of the 4th century B.C. His treatises on symmetry and color were much used by Pliny in the compilation of the 35th book of his *Natural History*. Lucian ranks his sculpture with that of Phidias, Alcamenes, and Myron, and his painting with that of Apelles, Parrhasius, and Aëtion. One of his most celebrated statutes was of Paris, the lover of Helen.

Euphrates (ū-frā′tēz). [Arabic, **Al Furat;** Armenian, **Yeprad;** Assyrian, **Purattu;** Hebrew, **Perath;** Turkish, **Frat;** Old Persian, **Ufrates.**] Great Mesopotamian river which has its origin in the Armenian mountains in NE Turkey. It is formed from the East Euphrates (Murad-Su), which rises NE of Erzurum, and a branch rising NW of Lake Van. The united river then makes a wide circuit W, breaks through the mountain chain of the Taurus, enters the terrace region at Birecik, and turns in a meandering course toward the Tigris. In the neighborhood of Baghdad these two rivers approach one another, and there the Babylonian canal system begins. In its lower course, below the site of Babylon, the Euphrates has changed its bed, shifting more and more westward. According to notices in classical authors, confirmed by the inscriptions, it came in ancient times nearer Sippara (Sepharvaim, modern Abu-Habba) and Erech (modern Warka) than now; and it did not empty into the sea, united with the Tigris, through the Shatt el-Arab, as at present. As late as the time of Sennacherib (705–681 B.C.) and his successors, the twin rivers flowed separately into the Persian Gulf, which extended then at least as far as the ancient city of Eridu, known to have been a seaport. Babylon has been rightly termed "the gift of Euphrates and Tigris." The soil is formed from the alluvial deposits of these rivers, and this formation still continues. During the winter months the Euphrates has but little water in its bed; but in the spring, and especially toward the summer solstice, it swells by the melting of the snow of the mountains, which often causes disastrous floods.

Euphronius (ū-frō′ni-us). Celebrated Athenian potter and vase-painter in the red-figure style, active at the end of the 6th and the beginning of the 5th centuries B.C. Five vessels signed by him as the painter and twelve signed by him as the potter are extant. A calyx crater (Louvre) signed by him as the painter shows Heracles wrestling Antaeus. The inside of a kylix (Munich), c510 B.C., is decorated with a figure of a youthful horseman. Inscribed near the figure of the young rider is the name Leagrus. Heracles slaying the triple-bodied Geryon is shown on one side of the outside of the cup, and the cattle of Geryon on the other. An inscription reads, "Chachrylion made, Euphronius painted." Another red-figured vessel by Euphronius (British Museum) shows Eurystheus taking refuge in his brazen vessel as Heracles attempts to deliver the Erymanthian boar to him. The exploits of Heracles and Theseus were favorite subjects in the paintings of Euphronius, and on the whole he favored the larger vessels—craters and amphorae—for his heroic subjects. It may be that Euphronius gave up painting for potting, for the vessels signed by him as potter are of somewhat later date than those signed by him as painter. The paintings on these vessels have been assigned to Onesimus, the Panaetius Painter, and the Pistoxenus Painter. Fifty-nine cups have been attributed to Onesimus, some of which were thrown by Euphronius. Of the 41 vessels attributed to the Panaetius Painter, six were signed by Euphronius as potter. They include a kylix (Louvre) with a scene showing Theseus and Amphitrite under the sea, whither Theseus had gone to recover King Minos' ring. Eighteen works have been attributed to the Pistoxenus Painter, most of whose work comes somewhat after the time of Euphronius. One of the loveliest of these, in technique and feeling, is a white-ground cup interior (British Museum) showing Aphrodite riding a goose.

Another of his masterpieces is a cup (Athens) showing the death of Orpheus.

Euphrosyne (ū-fros′i-nē). One of the Charites (Graces). See **Charites**.

Euploia (ū-ploi′a̱). An epithet of Aphrodite in her aspect as a goddess of the sea, meaning "Fair Voyage," or "Giver of Prosperous Voyages."

Eupolemia (ū″po̱-lē̱-mī′a̱). According to some accounts, a daughter of Myrmidon of Phthia, and the mother, by Hermes, of the Argonaut Aethalides.

Eupolis (ū′po̱-lis). Greek comic poet, born at Athens c445 B.C. He and his great contemporary and rival, Aristophanes, were among the first to give artistic form to the Old Comedy. They shaped the hitherto isolated farcical fragments into a plot and toned down or abolished the phallic element in Old Comedy. Their influence caused Comedy to develop rapidly. Eupolis is said to have presented his first piece at the age of 17, and to have won seven victories in his lifetime. He wrote political comedy, as did Aristophanes, in which he attacked, with graceful satire, the leaders of his day. According to some accounts, he drowned (411 B.C.) in the Hellespont in the course of a battle, and his death was said to have led to a ruling that professional poets would henceforth be exempt from military service. The titles and fragments of 15 of his pieces remain.

Eupompus (ū-pom′pus). Greek painter, born at Sicyon, Greece, and active in the 4th century B.C. He was the founder of the so-called Sicyonian school of painting. The work of Eupompus and his successor Pamphilus was to introduce the characteristics of Doric sculpture into painting.

Euripides (ū-rip′i-dēz). Athenian dramatic poet; with Aeschylus and Sophocles one of the great triad of Greek tragic writers. According to one tradition he was born on the Greek island of Salamis, whence his parents had fled from Athens on the invasion of Xerxes, on the very day of the great battle and victory of Salamis, 480 B.C. Others say he was born in a village of Attica, perhaps as early as 484 B.C. He died in Macedonia, 406 B.C. He was the son of Mnesarchus, of a middle-class, land-holding family. The comic poets claimed that Cleito, his mother, was a greengrocer, and that moreover her greens were bad. This was a goad they invented to plague Euripides, who appears to have had an exceptionally close relation with his mother, for she was actually of a noble family. Because his parents had received an oracle that he would win crowns of victory he was given careful gymnastic training as a youth, and did indeed win athletic victories at Athens and Eleusis. As a young man he served in the army in the frontier forts. He also held a position in the ceremonies of worship of Delphian Apollo. He was a disciple of Anaxagoras, the natural philosopher who was a friend of Pericles and was later banished from Athens for impiety, and studied rhetoric under Prodicus and Protagoras, the foremost Sophists of his day. He enjoyed a lifelong friendship with Socrates, of whom it was said that he never went to the theater except to see a play of Euripides. The influence of his sophistic training, which consisted of a search for "wisdom" (*sophia*, wisdom), and a rationalistic approach to religion, politics, and society, accounts to some extent for the highly intellectual quality characteristic of his work. The comic poets, for whom he was a ceaselessly interesting target, claimed that he divorced his first wife because of her sluttishness and took a second who was no better. The fact seems to be that he married once only, lived harmoniously with his wife, and had three sons by her. In his working adult life he avoided society and political life, withdrew to his estate on Salamis, and there, in a cave looking out over the sea, produced his dramas. About 408 B.C., harried at home as a traitor because he opposed the war party, and as dangerous because he questioned the traditional religious beliefs, and even suspected of immorality because of the speeches he put into the mouths of the characters in his plays, he left Athens and went into voluntary exile. He went first to Magnesia, near Ephesus in Asia Minor, where he had once served in an official post. Then, by invitation, he went to the court of King Archelaus of Macedonia. There he moved in the congenial company of Agathon the tragedian, Timotheus the musician, Zeuxis the painter, and perhaps Thucydides the historian. After 18 months he died (406

actȯr; up, lūte, pùll; oi, oil; ou, out; ᴛʜ, then; ḏ as d or j, ş as s or sh, ṭ as t or ch, ẓ as z or zh.

B.C.) at the Macedonian court (according to doubtful tradition being torn to pieces by a pack of hounds set upon him by two rival poets, Arrhidaeus and Crateuas), and was buried with great pomp by Archelaus, who refused a request of the Athenians for his remains.

The number of works produced by Euripides is variously given as 75, 78, and 92. Of these, 18 are extant in relatively complete form; a 19th, *Rhesus,* is sometimes attributed to him, and fragments of about 60 others are extant. In his lifetime he was awarded the first prize in dramatic contests four times. After his death his son produced *Iphigenia in Aulis* (405 B.C.), and it was awarded first prize. In 455 B.C. he presented his first tetralogy, fragments of which remain. It included *Peliades,* about the daughters of Pelias who slew their father, duped by Medea into thinking that by their action they would restore his lost youth. In 442 or 441 B.C. he won his first victory with a play now unknown. The other early works, of unknown date, were *Cyclops,* the only complete satyr-play to have survived, and *Rhesus.* The latter is generally considered to be spurious, but may have been an early play by Euripides that was worked over by later writers. It treats an incident from the *Iliad,* in which Rhesus, a Thracian chieftain, is murdered by Odysseus and Diomedes. Besides *Cyclops,* his extant works are: *Alcestis* (438 B.C.), *Medea* (431 B.C.), *Hippolytus* (428 B.C.), *Andromache, Hecuba* (425 B.C.), *The Suppliant Women* (c420 B.C.), *The Children of Heracles* (430 B.C.?), *The Madness of Heracles* (c416 B.C.), *Ion* (between 413 and 408 B.C.), *The Trojan Women* (c415 B.C.), *Electra* (c413 B.C.), *Iphigenia in Tauris, Helen* (c412 B.C.), *The Phoenician Maidens* (c409 B.C.), *Orestes* (408 B.C.), *Iphigenia in Aulis* (produced 405 B.C.), and *The Bacchae* (also produced after his death, 405 B.C.). (See separate entries under these titles.) All the works are based on myths or the heroes of legend, as was required of the dramas presented at the religious festivals. In his subject matter, therefore, Euripides was limited, but in his treatment of it he struck out in all directions. He departed from tradition by applying a realistic attitude to material hitherto sanctified by tradition. He adhered to the form but did violence to the content in a manner that jolted his audience. *Alcestis* took the place of the usual satyr-play in a tetralogy which included the lost plays the *Cressae* (Cretan Women), *Alcmaeon in Psophis,* and *Telephus.* It treats the legend of Admetus, who can avoid death only if he finds someone who is willing to die in his place. An appeal to his aged parents, already near death, is unavailing. Only his devoted wife Alcestis is willing to make the sacrifice. As a satyr-play *Alcestis* has its moments of humor, as in the antics of the drunken Heracles, but Euripides threw it out of perspective for the Athenians by pointing out the utter selfishness and egotism of Admetus in allowing his wife to die for him. *Medea* has been called one of the greatest masterpieces of Greek tragedy. It portrays the awful revenge Medea takes on Jason when, after she had saved him from the death her father had plotted and betrayed her home and her country for his sake, he announces that he is going to abandon her to marry the daughter of the king of Corinth. Medea's revenge is to bring death to his intended wife and her father, and to slay her own and Jason's children. The tragedy has been variously characterized as an example of the lengths to which love betrayed will drive a woman, and as an example of the havoc that is wrought in a so-called civilized society by a passion that is immune to civilizing influences. At the same time, Jason, traditionally regarded as a great hero, appears as a pompous, calculating, despicable hypocrite. *Hippolytus,* which won first prize, tells of Phaedra's love for her husband's son Hippolytus, and the death and disaster it brought in its train. It advances the thesis that single-minded devotion to one principle can be ruinous, as was Hippolytus' devotion to the chaste goddess Artemis and his denial of the power of Aphrodite. The date of the *Andromache* is unknown, but it is thought to have been produced about the beginning of the Peloponnesian War, as a political play aimed at the Spartans. In it Andromache, princess of Troy and widow of Hector, appears as the concubine of Neoptolemus, son of Achilles, the slayer of her husband. Hermione, daughter of Helen and Menelaus and the wife of

Battle of Greeks and Amazons, from the S frieze of the Mausoleum at Halicarnassus, Timotheus, c 325 B.C.

Head of a young goddess, Chios, c 300 B.C.

Bronze statuette, Beroea, c 400 B.C.

Aphrodite, terra-cotta statuette, end of 2nd century B.C.

Staatliche Museen, Berlin

Corinthian wine-jug, 625–600 B.C.

British Museum

Corinthian crater, end of the 7th century B.C. Heracles feasting with Eurytus.

Louvre

British Museum

Chalcidian crater, 550–530 B.C. Two youths preparing to go riding.

Attic black-figured dinos, beginning of the 6th century B.C. Death of Medusa.

Louvre

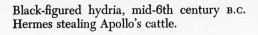

Black-figured hydria, mid-6th century B.C. Hermes stealing Apollo's cattle.

Louvre

British Museum

Attic black-figured amphora, c 510 B.C. Heracles delivering the Erymanthian boar to Eurystheus.

Louvre

Red-figured crater, signed by Euphronius, end of 6th century B.C. Combat of Heracles and Antaeus.

Neoptolemus, seeks to destroy Andromache and her son by Neoptolemus, on the ground that Andromache has bewitched her and caused her to be childless. The Spartans, Hermione and Menelaus, speak scornfully of the Trojans as barbarians, but by their own words convict themselves of barbarity. *Hecuba* describes the transformation of the noble queen of Troy into a maddened beast through suffering. *The Children of Heracles,* a patriotic drama, is about a war that Athens, as a humane and enlightened city, undertook to protect the rights of suppliants. In another patriotic drama, *The Suppliant Women,* Athens again appears as the champion of the oppressed. Here the suppliants are the mothers of those who fell in the Expedition of the Seven against Thebes. The Thebans defied all the laws of warfare and religion by refusing permission to the Argives to recover the bodies of their dead for burial. The Argive women appealed to the Athenians who, at the cost of war to themselves, recovered the bodies of the fallen, gave them honorable burial, and upheld the sanctity of the law. The play was looked upon as a plea for peace with Sparta and for alliance with Argos. In *The Madness of Heracles,* Athens, personified by Theseus, again is shown in an idealized light: Theseus refuses to deny his aid and sympathy to Heracles after the latter has, in a fit of madness sent by the gods, slain his wife and children. Instead, Theseus persuades him not to commit suicide, encourages him to shoulder the burden the gods have laid on him, and offers him a home in Athens, refuge of the oppressed. About 415 B.C., when the Athenians, with high hopes, had sent out an expedition to take Syracuse, Euripides produced the *Trojan Women,* probably one of the most powerful anti-war plays ever written. It portrays the capture of Troy, one of the proudest moments of Greek legendary history, in such a manner as to make it crystal-clear that though the conquered are miserable, the conquerers, brutalized by war, are despicable. It speaks volumes for the enlightened state of the Athenians that such a play could have been produced at all at such a time. *Iphigenia in Tauris* is a romantic exercise that tells of Iphigenia, serving as a priestess of Artemis at Tauris. Pre-

paring for the sacrifice to the goddess of two Greeks who have been captured, she discovers that one of them is her brother Orestes. In joyous reunion they plan to flee Tauris with the ancient image of the goddess Orestes has come to fetch. With the help of Athena they escape and return to Greece. In *Helen,* Euripides adopts the story of Stesichorus that it was not Helen at all who was carried off to Troy by Paris, but a phantom Helen, sent by the gods. *Electra* treats the same material as was used by Aeschylus in his *The Choëphoroe* and by Sophocles in his *Electra,* but the emphasis of Euripides is entirely different. His Electra is a twisted character who has no natural outlet for her passions and has channeled them all into hatred of her mother, a hatred that she justifies on the ground that her murdered father must be avenged, and that she persuades her brother Orestes to share. *The Phoenician Women,* named for the chorus, centers on the moment in the Oedipus legend when his sons Polynices and Eteocles, through lust for power, kill each other. *Orestes* was the last play Euripides produced in Athens. The melodramatic sequence of events involving Electra, Orestes, Menelaus, Helen, and Hermione, defies capsule description. Two of the three plays which Euripides wrote in Macedon survive. *Iphigenia in Aulis* is about the trick by which Iphigenia is brought to Aulis to be sacrificed and bring favorable winds for the Greeks waiting to sail to Troy, and the specious reasoning by which Agamemnon is persuaded that he has no choice but to sacrifice his daughter, who is, however, spirited away by the gods at the last moment. The last play, *The Bacchae,* shows Pentheus, king of Thebes, denying the godhead of Dionysus, a new god for whom there is no tradition. For his obstinacy and doubt Dionysus causes him to be slain by his mother.

Euripides speaks to each age according to its condition. The manner of his speech, his poetry, is eternal. In his own time he was the most celebrated of the Greek poets. Yet he was not loved as Sophocles had been. The Athenians admired his poetry but rebelled when he goaded them with new concepts. With his rationalistic approach to traditional religion he seemed blasphemous, as in *Ion,* in which the god of light and justice is depicted as a ravisher who abandons not only his victim but, seemingly, his own son, and is too craven to appear in his own defense when the son and mother are reunited. Nothing about the play inspired reverence for the god. Hecuba prays to whatever force there is in the universe, having been abandoned by her gods. Heracles, in *The Madness of Heracles,* openly doubts the old tales of the gods. Euripides' close friend, Protagoras, once read his book on theology in Euripides' house. The first sentence of the book was, "In regard to the gods I cannot know that they exist, nor yet that they do not exist, for many things hinder such knowledge—the obscurity of the matter, and the shortness of human life." Euripides might have said the same, for his attitude was not one of blasphemy, or denial of the gods, nor was it a supine acceptance of traditional beliefs. It was rather, as a good sophist, one of seeking for a principle that would embrace humanity and divinity on somewhat more equal terms than appeared in the popular religion. Almost without exception his plays end with a comment to the effect that the ways of the gods are mysterious. It is not certain that such comment was irony. On the other hand, his last play, *The Bacchae,* shows Pentheus perishing for his denial of a new god that he could not understand, and seems to say that there is not necessarily a rationalistic explanation for all the forces that are loose in the universe; that sometimes man must accept without understanding. A characteristic of his own humanity was his championship of the weak and silent. Any number of instances can be cited where it is a shepherd, servant, slave, or messenger who makes the reasonable and just comment, and shows himself to be far superior in qualities of the soul and spirit to the men who are in positions of power over him. This was taken as an extreme of democracy by his contemporaries, and aroused their distrust. He showed kings and leaders far too often in rags, as Telephus in the lost play of that name, and Menelaus in *Helen,* as if to indicate the unworthiness and destined end of those who were customarily in positions of leadership. The other large class of weak and silent defended

by Euripides was the women. His contemporaries considered him a woman-hater. Aristophanes' comedy, *Thesmophoriazusae,* is largely devoted to the schemes of the women in their annual festival to be revenged on Euripides for portraying them so unpleasantly in his plays. Modern critics consider that he often took up the cudgels on behalf of women; that he understood their problems and was sympathetic to them. Medea, driven to barbarism through passion and pride, yet points up the condition of virtual slavery in which women of Athens lived at that time, and can cry out about the suffering, incomparably greater than that endured in battle, that a woman experiences in bearing a child. Phaedra, consumed by a love she neither sought nor wanted, is more sympathetic than Hippolytus with his unrealistic purity. The virgin martyrs—Iphigenia, Macaria (*Children of Heracles*), Polyxena (*Hecuba*), are idealized maidens who could sublimate themselves and their lives in a higher cause. The results of the irresistible power of sex were taken for granted in the myths and legends. Euripides investigated the power itself, as in Medea and Phaedra, women in the grip of passion who escaped their frustration by plunging into disaster. A lost play, *Aeolus,* dealt with the sons and daughters of Aeolus who innocently married each other and were condemned. Another lost play, *Chrysippus,* had for its subject the abnormal relation between men and boys which, though accepted in fact, had not hitherto been considered as a fit subject for drama with the emphasis on sex rather than on the nobility of the relationship. Euripides would not ignore the heartlessness of the state vis-à-vis the individual. In *Iphigenia in Aulis,* Agamemnon as a father recoils at the idea of sacrificing his daughter, but as a commander of men on the business of the state, he orders her death; in *Hecuba,* as a man he would spare the Trojan queen further sufferings, but as a leader responsible for the safe return of the Greeks he adds to it by ordering the sacrifice of Polyxena on Achilles' tomb.

Two technical devices were much employed by Euripides. One was the Prologue, which served the double purpose of explaining the events that led up to the moment when the drama opened and provided a quiet base from which the intensity of the drama rose. The second device was the *Deus ex machina*. The technique here was to have a god or goddess appear at the end of the play to explain, reconcile, command, or prophesy. To a modern audience the appearance of the divinity seems awkwardly contrived and a great letdown. To the ancients such a letdown was desirable as a release from the tension of the drama, and as evidence of completion.

Euripides was the product and mirror of his age. His contemporaries were not quite ready to accept the clear portrait of their doubts, problems, and nascent individualism that he presented to them. He served as a model for dramatists for the next six centuries. Aristotle called him "the most tragic of poets," but complained that his plays were not well-made. Critics are virtually unanimous in acknowledging his intellectualism, his interest in dissecting and propounding an idea rather than in producing an architecturally perfect drama. His comment has timeless validity. His lines were often quoted, his language endlessly imitated, his lyricism never equalled.

Eurippa (ū-rip′a̯). An epithet of Artemis, meaning "delighting in horses." Odysseus lost his mares and searched for them throughout Greece. He found them at a place in Arcadia, and there raised a sanctuary of Artemis Eurippa.

Euripus (ū-rī′pus) or **Euripos** (-pos.). Narrowest portion of the channel between the island of Euboea and the mainland of Greece. It was near here, at Aulis, that Agamemnon's fleet en route to Troy was stormbound and Iphigenia was sacrificed. The strait is remarkable for the force of its current and its frequent changes of direction in response to the tides. Its width at the narrowest part (opposite Chalcis) is about 120 feet.

Europa (ū-rō′pa̯) or **Europe** (-pē). In Greek mythology, the daughter of Agenor, king of Tyre, and Telephassa. She was the sister of Cadmus, Phoenix, Cilix, Thasus, and Phineus. Zeus fell in love with her and sent Hermes to lure her to the seashore. Hermes did as he was bid, and one day as she was playing with her maidens on the shore near Tyre, Zeus transformed himself into a white bull with golden horns and approached her. Europa was charmed by the creature's beauty, and, as he appeared gentle, decked his horns with wreaths of flowers. When the bull knelt before her she climbed on his back. Instantly Zeus plunged into the sea and carried the maiden on his back to Crete. There Europa bore three sons to Zeus: Minos, Rhadamanthys, and Sarpedon. When Zeus left Europa she married Asterius, the king of Crete, and since he had no children, he adopted Europa's three sons and made them his heirs. But some say that it was Greeks from Crete who raided the Phoenician shores and carried off the king's daughter, and that this was one of the causes of the ancient enmity between Greece and Asia, which culminated in the Persian Wars.

EUROPA ON THE BULL
Black-figured Greek amphora, 6th century
B.C. *Museum of Fine Arts, Boston*

Europa or **Europe.** Epithet of Demeter. Some say Demeter was the nurse of Trophonius, and there was a sanctuary of Demeter Europa (*Broad-faced*) in the grove of Trophonius at Lebadia.

Europus (ū-rō′pus). Name of a city in Macedonia, in honor of which several cities founded by the Seleucids in Asia were named. (JJ)

Europus (Dura), often called **Dura-Europus**. A town founded c300 B.C., probably by Seleucus I, on the right bank of the middle Euphrates, as a military colony. It became an agricultural market and district administrative center of local importance, prospered, and was heavily fortified, to be held in turn by the Parthians and the Romans, and taken by siege and destroyed by the Sassanian king Sapor c256 A.D. Identified in 1921, it was excavated by the Belgian scholar Franz Cumont in 1922–23 and by a Yale University expedition, 1928–1937. The remarkable fortifications belong probably to the second century B.C. The planning is in regular rectangular blocks, entire blocks being devoted to temples, market, or private houses. The Temple of the Palmyrene Gods, built into a corner of the fortification walls, preserved mural paintings of extraordinary interest. In the dryness of the soil, wood, leather, wool, felt, paper, cordage, and other substances usually considered perishable are preserved, and Dura-Europus has yielded important and unique documents on parchment, vellum, and papyrus, including contracts and legal codes in Greek and the military records of the 3rd century A.D. Roman garrison, in Latin. Dura-Europus has also yielded hundreds of inscriptions in Greek, Latin, and dialects of Semitic, of which a gratifyingly large number contain exact dates; a horoscope scratched on a house wall, with other evidence, made possible the reconstruction of the *enneadecateris* or nineteen-year lunisolar calendar cycle adopted by the Seleucids and widely employed in Asia. The nomenclature of the parchments, papyri, and inscriptions indicates a mixed population descended from the Macedonian and Greek troops of the garrison and the native community. Dura-Europus has also provided a very early Christian chapel, with wall paintings illustrating scenes from the New Testament, an unprecedented synagogue with wall paintings from the Old Testament, a shrine of the soldiers' god Mithras, and many other places of cult. The reconstruction of the events of the final siege by Sapor, not recorded in the literary sources, is a master-

work of archaeological exploration and deduction. (JJ)

Eurotas (ū-rō′tas). In mythology, son of Myles and grandson of Lelex. He ascended the throne of Laconia after the great flood, and drained the marshes caused by the flood by constructing a trench to the sea. He named the river so formed after himself. Some say he had no son of his own and left his kingdom to Lacedaemon, the son of Taÿgete and Zeus, and gave him his daughter Sparta for wife. And some say that in a war with the Athenians he was warned to wait until the full of the moon to commence the battle. He ignored the warning and suffered a disastrous defeat. In humiliation at this defeat he leaped into the river in Laconia, and according to some, this was why the river came to be known by his name.

Eurotas. [Modern name, **Iri, Iris**] In ancient geography, a river in Laconia, Greece, flowing into the Mediterranean about 25 miles SE of Sparta.

Eurus (ū′rus). The east wind.

Euryale (ū-rī′a-lē). A Gorgon, one of the daughters of Ceto and Phorcys. See **Gorgons**.

Euryalus (ū-rī′a-lus). In Greek legend, a son of Mecisteus of Argos. He was one of the Epigoni who successfully attacked Thebes, and he accompanied Jason on the expedition of the Argonauts. As a leader of Argives he accompanied Diomedes to Troy, where he slew many Trojans. Although a skilled boxer, he was defeated by Epeus in the boxing match during the funeral games for Patroclus.

Euryalus. In the *Aeneid*, a son of Opheltes. He fought at Troy and accompanied Aeneas in the flight to Italy. Euryalus was the beloved young friend of Nisus. In the war with the Rutulians in Italy, Aeneas left his camp to go for aid. The garrison was attacked and besieged. Euryalus and Nisus volunteered to try to get through the enemy lines in order to warn Aeneas. During the night the two friends slipped out of the camp. As they went through the ranks of the sleeping enemy they took the opportunity to kill many of them. Euryalus seized the plumed helmet of one of his victims and put it on his own head. This brought disaster, for the light from a watch fire flickered on the shining helmet and aroused a dozing sentry who gave the alarm. Nisus and Euryalus were separated in the ensuing mêlée, and Euryalus was slain. His head was cut off and impaled on a spear, and the Rutulians triumphantly paraded it before the walls of the beleaguered Trojan camp the next day.

Eurybates (ū-rī′ba̱-tēz). In the *Odyssey*, a companion of Odysseus who accompanied him to Troy. When Odysseus returned to Ithaca after the Trojan War and his ten years' wanderings, he went to his own palace disguised as a beggar and talked to his wife Penelope. She did not know him, as he had planned, but wanting to assure her that Odysseus still lived, he proved he had seen Odysseus by speaking of Eurybates, who had gone with him to Troy.

Eurybia (ū-rib′i-a̱). In Greek mythology, a daughter of Pontus and Gaea. By the Titan Crius she was the mother of Astraeus, Pallas, and Perses.

Eurybiades (ū-ri-bī′a̱-dēz). Leader of the Spartan naval contingent during the Persian War; fl. 5th century B.C. Although the Athenians furnished the most ships in the war against the Persian invaders, the Spartans and the other Greek forces refused to serve under an Athenian commander. Eurybiades was appointed commander of the united fleet of the allied Greek states, with the consent of the Athenians. Aided by furious storms, he defeated the Persians in the naval battle of Artemisium, off the N end of Euboea, 480 B.C. The Persian army swept on down through Thessaly and occupied Attica. The Greek allies of Athens wished to withdraw to the Isthmus of Corinth and there make their defense against the oncoming Persians. Themistocles persuaded Eurybiades not to withdraw to the Isthmus, but to meet the Persians in the narrow waters between the island of Salamis and the mainland, where the Greek ships would have the advantage of maneuver over the heavier Persian ships. Eurybiades was obliged to accept the strategy of Themistocles when he learned that the Greek fleet in the waters of Salamis had been blockaded by the Persians. The victory the Greeks under Eurybiades won at Salamis (480 B.C.) was decisive.

Euryclea (ū-ri-klē′a̱) or **Euryclia** (-klī′a̱). According to Homer (*Odyssey*), a daughter of Ops. She was the nurse and attendant of Telemachus, son of Odysseus, and helped him secretly to prepare for his voyage to Pylus in quest of news of his father. She promised not to tell his mother until he was well on his way. When Odysseus returned to Ithaca, disguised as a beggar, Euryclea, who had also been his nurse, thought the beggar bore a strong resemblance to Odysseus. She was ordered by Penelope to wash the beggar's feet, and as she did so she recognized an old scar on his leg and knew that the beggar was in fact Odysseus. At his hissed command—and especially in view of the fact that his hands were clasping her throat—she did not reveal his identity. Later, when he had destroyed the suitors, she told him which of his serving women and men had been loyal to him during his long absence.

Eurydamas (ū-rid′a̱-mas). In Greek legend, an Argonaut, who went from Ctimene, near the Xynian Lake, to join Jason on the expedition for the Golden Fleece.

Eurydamas. In Homeric legend (*Iliad*), an aged Trojan dream-interpreter and diviner. His sons Abas and Polyidus were slain by Diomedes.

Eurydice (ū-rid′i-sē). In Greek legend, a daughter of Adrastus. She was the wife of Ilus and the mother of Laomedon.

Eurydice. In Greek mythology, the beloved wife of Orpheus. Aristaeus attacked her and as she fled from him she stepped on a snake, was bitten by it, and died. The bees of Aristaeus died as a punishment to him. Orpheus, overwhelmed with grief at the loss of Eurydice, descended to Tartarus in an effort to bring her back. This was granted on a condition that Orpheus lead the way, and not look back at her until they reached daylight. They had almost reached safety when in his anxiety Orpheus looked back and Eurydice's shade was snatched away forever. Some say he was ultimately reunited with her in Tartarus and that they could be seen strolling hand in hand in the Elysian Fields. See **Orpheus.**

Eurydice. Named by some as the wife of Acrisius and the mother of Danaë. She was the sister of Hyacinthus. But others say Danaë's mother was Aganippe. Another Eurydice, the daughter of Pelops and Hippodamia, is named by some as the mother of Alcmene and the grandmother of Heracles.

---

actọr; up, lūte, pu̇ll; oi, oil; ou, out; ŦH, then; ḏ as d or j, ş as s or sh, ţ as t or ch, ẓ as z or zh.

Eurydice. Wife of Amyntas II, king of Macedonia; fl. 4th century B.C. She was the mother of Alexander, Perdiccas, and Philip II of Macedon. She supported one of the Macedonian nobles, Ptolemy of Alorus, who rebelled against her son Alexander who had succeeded his father as king. Ptolemy murdered Alexander and married Eurydice.

Eurydice. Macedonian princess; daughter of Perdiccas III of Macedonia, and cousin of Alexander the Great.

Euryganeia (ū-ri-gā′ni-ạ, ū″ri-gạ-nī′ạ). According to some accounts of the legend, a daughter of King Hyperphas. Some say that Jocasta did not bear children to Oedipus. They say his sons Polynices and Eteocles were the children of Euryganeia. A painting by Onasias at Plataea depicted Euryganeia grieving because her sons fought each other.

Eurylochus (ū-ril′ọ-kus.) In the *Odyssey*, one of the companions of Odysseus on the voyage home from Troy. He led the group who went to Circe's palace but, suspecting a trick, he did not enter it with the others. As a result of his prudence he was able to return to Odysseus and inform him that his men had been turned into swine by Circe. Later in the voyage when Odysseus and his companions were stranded on the island of the Sun (Trinacria), Eurylochus persuaded the men, during an absence of Odysseus, to disobey his commands and to kill and eat the cattle of the Sun—which they had been expressly warned not to do by Circe and Odysseus. Eurylochus' argument for disregarding the warnings was that they might as well die as a result of the anger of a god as from starvation. They ate the cattle and they were later all destroyed, except Odysseus, in a great storm.

Eurylochus. Spartan commander in the Peloponnesian War; he besieged Naupactus, 426 B.C., and was driven off by the Athenian general Demosthenes. He was slain the same year in a battle near the Gulf of Ambracia.

Eurymachus (ū-rim′ạ-kus). In the *Odyssey*, a son of Polybus and a suitor of Penelope during the absence of Odysseus. He told Telemachus to command his mother to return to her father's house and choose among the suitors, otherwise they would stay and eat up his substance. He pretended to Penelope that he would protect Telemachus, while actually secretly planning to kill him. Eurymachus mocked Odysseus when he returned to Ithaca disguised as a beggar, but when after the death of Antinous, Odysseus revealed himself, Eurymachus blamed the ill-treatment of Telemachus and Odysseus (in his disguise as a beggar) on Antinous, and begged Odysseus to spare the other suitors. Odysseus killed him.

Eurymede (ū-rim′ẹ-dẹ) or **Eurymeda** (-dạ). According to some accounts, the wife of Glaucus and the mother of Bellerophon.

Eurymedon (ū-rim′ẹ-don). A name for Perseus, meaning "Wide-ruling," given to him by his mother.

Eurymedon. Athenian general in the Peloponnesian War; killed near Syracuse, 413 B.C. As commander of an Athenian fleet, he was at Corcyra, 427 B.C., during the revolution in which the democrats there overthrew the oligarchs. He took no steps to prevent the excesses on that occasion and the oligarchs were massacred, except for about 200 who escaped to the fortress of Istone. Two years later he commanded a fleet that helped the Corcyraean democrats besiege the fortress of Istone. The besieged oligarchs at last surrendered, on condition that the Athenians be allowed to decide their fate. This condition being granted, the oligarchs marched out from the fortress, whereupon the Corcyraeans brutally murdered them in the courtyard where they were assembled. Eurymedon made no effort to save them. In 413 B.C. he sailed to Sicily as co-commander of a force to rescue the expeditionary force sent out under Nicias to take Syracuse. He was slain in the fighting at Syracuse (413 B.C.), in which the Athenians were annihilated.

Eurymedon. [Modern Turkish name, **Köprü,** formerly also **Capri-Su.**] In ancient geography, a river in Pisidia and Pamphylia, Asia Minor, flowing from the Taurus Mountains generally S into the Mediterranean about 25 miles E of what is now Antalya, Turkey. Near its mouth, in 466 or 465 B.C., the Greeks under the Athenian general Cimon defeated the Persian fleet and army.

Eurynome (ū-rin′ọ-mē). In Greek mythology, a daughter of Oceanus or of Chaos. She and Ophion, whom she created from the wind, were the first rulers on Olympus according to some accounts, but she yielded her power to Rhea (Ophion yielded his to Cronus), and fell into the sea. She was the mother by Zeus of the three Graces, or Charites. Homer names Eurynome one of the ocean nymphs who helped Thetis to save Hephaestus when Hera hurled him out of heaven.

Eurypontidae (ū-ri-pon'ti-dē). Descendants of Eurypon, grandson of Procles, the junior of the two royal houses of Sparta.

Eurypylus (ū-rip'i-lus.) In Greek legend, a son of Telephus and Astyoche, and the nephew of Priam. His mother, bribed with a golden vine, sent him to Troy near the end of the war in command of a group of Mysians. He fought valiantly, slaying, according to some accounts, the Greek surgeon Machaon, and being at last slain himself by Neoptolemus, son of Achilles.

Eurypylus. In Greek legend, a son of Euaemon, and a leader of the Thessalians at Troy. As a former suitor of Helen he fought valiantly at Troy, and was one of several to accept Hector's challenge to single combat, but was eliminated in the drawing of lots. He went to the aid of Telamonian Ajax when the latter, stunned and wounded, was compelled to withdraw from the fighting. In defending Ajax he slew Apisaon, and was himself wounded by Paris as he bent to strip Apisaon of his armor. Patroclus tended his wound, and was convinced by Eurypylus that he should join the Greeks and fight against the Trojans even if Achilles still refused to aid his beleaguered countrymen. After the war Eurypylus received a chest as his part of the spoils of victory. Some say Aeneas abandoned the chest when he fled from Troy; others say Cassandra left it to be a curse to whatever Greek found it. Inside it was an image of Dionysus, made by Hephaestus and given to Dardanus by Zeus. When Eurypylus opened the chest he was driven mad by the image. In an interval of sanity he went to Delphi to inquire concerning his malady. The priestess told him to find a people making a strange sacrifice and to settle there. Eventually he came to Aroë, later a part of Patrae, where he found the people sacrificing a youth and a maiden to Artemis, to propitiate the goddess for the crime of Comaetho and Melanippus, who had polluted her shrine. Eurypylus understood that this was the strange sacrifice indicated by the priestess. The people of the town recognized him as a leader an oracle had said would come to them and made him their king. Henceforward Eurypylus recovered his sanity and the people of Patrae ceased to make human sacrifices. The tomb of Eurypylus is in Patrae, and ever after the people of the city sacrificed to him as a hero at the festival of Dionysus, and the city flourished.

Eurysaces (ū-ris'a-kēz). In Greek legend, a son of Telamonian Ajax and the captive princess Tecmessa. His name means "Broad" or "Thick Shield." When Ajax was about to kill himself he directed that his armor be buried with him, all except his shield, for which Eurysaces was named and which was of seven thicknesses of bull's hide, which he left to his son.

Eurysthenes (ū-ris'thē-nēz). In Spartan legend, a son of Aristodemus. He was the twin of Procles. Their father died in their infancy and the Lacedaemonians wished to make one of the sons their king, but did not know which one was the older. On the advice of the oracle at Delphi, both Eurysthenes and Procles were made kings, to reign together, and for this reason, it is said, Sparta henceforth had two kings. By watching their mother as she tended to her twin sons the Spartans decided that Eurysthenes was the first-born and accorded him more honor than Procles, thus his line was the senior line of the two Spartan royal houses. But some say that Aristodemus had died before the Heraclidae (descendants of Heracles) had successfully invaded the Peloponnesus to win back the land their ancestor Heracles had left in trust for them. The brothers of Aristodemus—Temenus and Cresphontes—took his sons, Eurysthenes and Procles with them when they made their successful invasion. After their conquest of the Peloponnesus they decided to divide it between them by lot. The sons of Aristodemus drew Laconia as their share. After the lot-drawing, the Heraclidae set up three altars to Zeus Patrous (*Paternal*) and on the altar of each a sign appeared. On the altar of Procles and Eurysthenes there was a serpent. The seer interpreted this to mean that their people would be terrible in attack. Eurysthenes was succeeded by his son Agis, and from him was sprung the royal family of the Agids, or Agidae. His descendant, Cleomenes III, who reigned c235–219 B.C., was the last king of Sparta.

Eurystheus (ū-ris'thē-us). In Greek mythology, a son of Nicippe and Sthenelus, king of Mycenae, and a descendant of Perseus. Thanks to Hera's activities in delaying the birth of Heracles and causing Eurystheus to be born two months ahead of time, he profited by Zeus' vow that the first child born to the house of Perseus would become ruler of Argos and the descendants of Perseus. Zeus could not withdraw his vow, and Eurystheus became king, but Hera agreed that after Heracles had performed whatever labors Eurystheus should demand of him, he would become immortal. It was thus that Eurystheus became the master of Heracles. When Heracles had carried out twelve great labors he returned to Mycenae, but Eurystheus, who was absolutely terrified of him, banished him from Argos, claiming he was a threat to the throne. When Heracles had been taken to live among the gods, Eurystheus banished his children from all Hellas, lest they grow up and seize his throne. Only Athens dared defy Eurystheus and offer protection to the Heraclidae. In the war which followed Eurystheus was captured by Hyllus, Heracles' son, and killed. According to some accounts, Hyllus cut off his head and Alcmene, mother of Heracles, gouged out his eyes. Others say the Athenians would have spared Eurystheus, but yielded to Alcmene's demand for his death.

Eurytion (ū-rit'i-on). In Greek mythology, a centaur who fought with Heracles on Mount Pholus and fled when Heracles overcame the centaurs there. Heracles later killed him for attacking the daughter of King Dexamenus at her marriage feast. Another centaur, also named Eurytion, was killed by Theseus and Pirithous because he attacked Hippodamia, the bride of Pirithous, at the wedding feast. This second centaur is sometimes called Eurytus.

Eurytion. According to the *Aeneid,* a brother of Pandarus, the famous Trojan archer. He was one of the companions of Aeneas on the flight from Troy. In the funeral games honoring Anchises in Italy, he took part in the archery contest. When the cord which held the target, a dove, to a pole was severed by a previous contestant, Eurytion transfixed the dove as it fluttered away.

Eurytion. In Greek legend, an adopted son of Actor, king of Phthia. He purified Peleus for the murder of his half-brother Phocus. He took part in the Calydonian Boar Hunt and was accidentally slain by the spear of Peleus.

Eurytion. In Greek mythology, a son of Ares. He was the giant herdsman who guarded the cattle of Geryon, and he was slain by Heracles, who felled him with his club, when Heracles went to fetch the cattle as one of his labors for Eurystheus.

Eurytus (ū'ri-tus). In Greek legend, the son of Melaneus of Thessaly. He was a king of Oechalia, and a famous archer who had been taught by Apollo, and who in his turn had taught Heracles. He promised his daughter, Iole, to whoever could defeat him in an archery contest. Heracles easily won the contest, but Eurytus, fearing a recurrence of Heracles' madness, refused to give him his daughter and banished him from his palace. Heracles thereupon raised an army and marched against him. He slew Eurytus and some of his sons, and took Iole captive. Eurytus' bow finally fell into the hands of Odysseus, who used it to kill Penelope's suitors. In another account, Eurytus challenged Apollo to an archery contest and the god, angered by his presumption, caused his early death.

Eurytus. In Greek legend, a son of Augeas, king of the Epeans. Heracles attacked Eurytus near Cleonae, as he was going to attend a festival, and killed him in revenge on Augeas, who had not honored his agreement to pay Heracles for cleaning the Augean stables.

Eurytus. A son of Actor and Molione. See **Moliones.**

Eurytus. In Greek mythology, one of the Giants, a son of Gaea and the blood of Uranus, who waged war on the gods. In the battle he was knocked down by the thyrsus of Dionysus and killed by Heracles.

Euterpe (ū-tèr'pē). One of the nine daughters of Zeus and Mnemosyne. She is the muse of music, a divinity of joy and pleasure, the patroness of flute-players. She invented the double flute, and favored rather the wild and

simple melodies of primitive peoples than
the more finished art of music, and was associated more with Dionysus than with
Apollo. She is usually represented as a
maiden crowned with flowers, having a flute
in her hand, or with various musical instruments about her. According to some accounts she was the mother of the Thracian
Rhesus by the river-god of the Strymon River.
See **Muses.**

Euthydemus (ū-thi-dē′mus). Dialogue of
Plato, the narration by Socrates of a conversation which took place at the Lyceum between himself, the sophists Euthydemus and
Dionysodorus, Crito, Clinias, and Ctesippus.
Its theme is virtue and instruction in virtue,
and it is a satire upon the Sophists and the
older philosophies.

DANCING SATYR
Red-figured Greek amphora, Euthymides,
c510 B.C. *Munich*

Euthymides (ū-thim′i-dēz). Celebrated Attic
vase-painter, active at the end of the 6th and
the beginning of the 5th centuries B.C. Six
vases with his signature as painter are extant.
An amphora (Munich) c510 B.C., in the red-
figure style, shows three dancing satyrs on one
side, and is notable for the successful foreshortening of the partly turned bodies of the
satyrs. On this side Euthymides, a contemporary, and perhaps a friendly rival, of
Euphronius, inscribed a remark to the effect
that Euphronius could never have painted
anything like it. On the other side he painted
Hector putting on his armor in the presence
of Priam and Hecuba. On this side the inscription reads "Euthymides, son of Polios,
painted." Another red-figured amphora
(Munich) shows Theseus carrying off Corone.
Other figures are identified by inscribed
names as Helen, Pirithous, and Heres.

Euxine (ūk′sīn) **Sea.** The Black Sea, in Latin,
Pontus Euxinus. Inland sea between SE
Europe and W Asia, bordered on the N and
E by Scythia, on the S by Cappadocia,
Paphlagonia, and Bithynia, and on the W by
Thrace, communicating with the Mediterranean by the Bosporus, the Propontis (Sea
of Marmora), and the Hellespont (Dardanelles). The word means "hospitable,
friendly to strangers." It had also been called
the Axine ("unfriendly"), presumably in reference to the hostile tribes living on its shores,
or to its frequent savage storms; but this may
have resulted from the operation of folk
etymology on a non-Greek term. A late
writer says that it was Heracles who changed
the name, from Axine to Euxine, because he
was hospitably received by the tribes who
dwelt there. According to legend, the voyage of the Argonauts (13th century B.C.?)
was the first Greek exploration of the Euxine.
Scholars, seeking for the Trojan War a more
cogent issue than the abduction of Helen,
have suggested that the war was fought to
end Troy's control and taxation of commercial
traffic between the Euxine and the Aegean
via the Hellespont. Between 800 and 600
B.C. Ionian Greeks explored the entire coastline and established numerous colonies. In
the 6th and 4th centuries B.C. the Crimea,
under Scythian domination, produced surplus wheat which was shipped in substantial
quantities to the Aegean, particularly to
Athens. In Roman times it was still regarded
as frontier country; as a punishment only
slightly preferable to death, Ovid was ordered
to exile at Tomis, modern Constanza. The
establishment at Constantinople of the east-

ern capital of the Roman empire intensified commerce throughout the lands bordering the Euxine, accelerating the advance of civilization and urbanization. Length, about 740 miles; greatest width, about 390 miles; estimated area, 168,500 square miles. (JJ)

Evadne (ē-vad′nē). In Greek legend, the wife of Capaneus, an Argive chieftain who was one of the Seven against Thebes and perished there. When his body was recovered from Thebes by Theseus and the Athenians it was placed on a funeral pyre for funeral honors. Evadne leaped into the flames, as she preferred death with one she loved to life by herself.

Evadne. In Greek mythology, a daughter of Poseidon and the nymph Pitana. She was reared by Aepytus, son of Elatus. Apollo loved her and she bore him a son, Iamus.

Evadne. In Greek legend, a daughter of Pelias, king of Iolcus. Under Medea's direction, she and her sister cut up their sleeping father and boiled the pieces in a cauldron, under the impression that this would make him young again as Medea had promised. But Medea had promised falsely, and Pelias was dead. When Jason took control of Iolcus he overlooked Evadne's crime of patricide, which was committed in innocence, and found a husband for her in the son of the king of the Phocians.

Evagoras (ē-vag′ō-ras). King of Salamis, in Cyprus (c435–374 B.C.). He claimed descent from Teucer, the half-brother of Telamonian Ajax who came to Cyprus and founded Salamis after the Trojan War. The descendants of Teucer ruled Salamis for centuries and then lost the throne to the Phoenicians. Evagoras won it back by his own courage and enterprise. He was said to be a wise and moderate ruler, who encouraged and revived Greek culture in his kingdom. After the defeat of the Athenians at Aegospotami (405 B.C.), Conon, one of the Athenian admirals who escaped, found hospitality and protection at his court, and he took part in the battle of Cnidus (394 B.C.) in which the Spartans were defeated by a Phoenician and Persian fleet under the command of Conon. Because of his friendship for Athens he was made a citizen and his statue was erected in Athens beside that of Conon. He had been a tributary of the Great King of Persia,

but as his own power grew in Cyprus, and was extended to the coast of Asia Minor the Persians waged war on him as on a rebellious subject (c389 B.C.). For the next ten years he resisted the Persians. After a serious defeat at sea he withdrew to Salamis and endured siege, which he resisted so stubbornly that the Persians offered to raise it if he would pay tribute to Persia, "as a slave to his master." Evagoras refused the terms but finally agreed to pay tribute, only, however, as one king to another, and the siege was raised. The Athenians had at first helped him by sending ten ships, but with the signing of the King's Peace (386 B.C.), by which Cyprus was acknowledged as a Persian tributary, the Athenians ceased to support him, and he had carried on his war alone. He was slain (374 B.C.) by the eunuch of a man who had been forced to flee for plotting against him. The story is that the eunuch, left in charge of the beautiful daughter of the exile, told both Evagoras and his son of the loveliness of the girl and arranged appointments for each of them separately. Neither the father nor the son knew of the other's appointment. Each arrived at the stated times and each was slain by the eunuch, who thus avenged his master.

Evander (ē-van′dėr). According to legend, a son of Hermes (Mercury) and the prophetic nymph Carmenta. His people were Arcadians, descended from Pallas, and migrated with him from Greece to Italy before the Trojan War. Destiny guided him to the spot where he built the town of Pallanteum, named for his ancestor, which gave its name to the Palatine Hill, when the glorious city of Rome afterward occupied the site of Evander's humble town. Evander had met Anchises, before he left Troy, and had received a quiver of Lycian arrows and other gifts from him. Thus, he welcomed Anchises' son when Aeneas arrived in Italy. In the *Aeneid*, Evander advised Aeneas to seek the help of the Etruscans in his war against Turnus. He told Aeneas that the Etruscans, already enraged against Turnus, were massed and ready for war but had been told by a seer to await a foreign commander. As he sent his only son Pallas to fight at Aeneas' side, Evander prayed to live if Pallas was destined to return safely; otherwise he asked the gods to let him die. In the war Pallas was killed. Evander, though grief-stricken, was proud that he had died gloriously and in the service of a noble commander. He asked the death of Turnus as vengeance. Evander is said to have introduced the worship of Pan (Faunus) into Italy, and Pan may be identical with Faunus. Some scholars believe that he is a native Italian deity to whom the Italians attached Greek attributes in order to have a link with the admired Greek world.

Evemerus (ē-vē′mėr-us, ē-vem′ėr-us). See **Euhemerus.**

Evenus (ē-vē′nus). In Greek mythology, a son of Ares, and father, by Alcippe, of Marpessa. He wanted his daughter to remain a virgin and therefore challenged all her suitors to a chariot race with him, with the understanding that the first one to defeat him would win Marpessa. Whoever raced and lost had his head cut off and nailed to the walls of Evenus' palace. When Idas defeated him, with the help of winged horses provided by his father Poseidon, Evenus killed his horses and flung himself into the river which from that time on bore his name.

Evenus. [Modern name, **Fidaris, Fidhari.**]

In ancient geography, a river in Aetolia, Greece, flowing into the Gulf of Patras (or Calydon) about seven miles SE of what is now Missolonghi.

Everes (ēv′ėr-ēz, ē-vē′rēz). In mythology, the father of the seer Tiresias by the nymph Chariclo.

Evius (ē′vi-us). An epithet of Dionysus, derived from the bacchantes' cry, "Evoë."

Evripos (ev′rē-pôs). See **Euripus** and **Chalcis.**

Exekias (ek-sē′ki-as). [Also: **Execias.**] Attic potter and painter in the black-figure style, active c550–525 B.C. He painted amphorae, craters, cups, and other vessels. Among his extant works are an amphora in the Vatican, showing Achilles and Ajax playing checkers, signed by him as both potter and painter; an amphora (Berlin), signed by him, showing the Dioscuri at home with Leda and Tyndareus; and a signed eye cup (Munich). The outside of the cup has two large eyes flanked by warriors near the handles; the inside shows Dionysus floating in a vine-swathed boat. The date of this cup, which is inscribed "Exekias made," is c540 B.C.

Expedition of the Seven against Thebes. See **Seven against Thebes, Expedition of the.**

F

Fabia gens (fā′bi-a). In ancient Rome, a patrician clan or house, possibly of Sabine origin, which traced its descent from Hercules and the Arcadian Evander. Its family names under the republic were Ambustus, Buteo, Dorso, Labeo, Licinus, Maximus, Pictor, and Vibulanus.

Fabius Maximus (fā′bi-us mak′si-mus), **Quintus.** [Surnamed **Rullianus.**] Roman general; died c290 B.C. While he was master of the horse he defeated the Samnites (325 B.C.). In spite of the victory he was degraded because in waging the battle he had disobeyed orders, and he was compelled to leave Rome for a time. He afterward became consul a number of times, the first time in 322 B.C. He was named dictator (315) and suffered defeat at the hands of the Samnites. In 310 he defeated the Etruscans.

As consul in 295 B.C. he distinguished himself in the third war against the Samnites, over whom and their allies he gained the decisive victory of Sentinum (295 B.C.).

Fabius Maximus, Quintus. [Surnamed **Cunctator,** meaning "the Delayer."] Roman general; died 203 B.C. He traced his descent from Hercules and a nymph, the parents of Fabius, founder of the Fabian family. Besides the well-known epithet, Cunctator, he was also surnamed *Verrucosus,* from a wart growing on his lip, and Ovicula (*Lambkin*), because he was so gentle as a child. Because he was deliberate and cautious as a youth some thought he was rather stupid. He trained himself for war, recognizing the menace of Carthage, and for oratory so that he could persuade the Romans to follow him in their own interest. He became consul for the first time in 233 B.C., when by a victory over the Ligurians he obtained the honor of a triumph. In 230 B.C. he was censor, and in 228 he held the office of consul for the second time. In 218 B.C. he was at the head of the legation sent by the Roman Senate to Carthage to demand reparation for the attack on Saguntum. According to the story, he held up a fold of his toga and asked the Carthaginians whether they chose peace or war. The Carthaginians indicated that it was a matter of indifference to them. Fabius then dropped his toga and said, "Then take war." In the same year Hannibal came into Italy and was victorious at the Trebia. Reports of ominous portents added to the fears of the Romans: shields sweated blood, grain cut at Antium was found to have blood on it, fiery stones fell from the heavens. Fabius, in opposition to the consul Caius Flaminius, advised the Romans to let Hannibal exhaust himself, far from his base and with no allies in Italy. Flaminius was undaunted by the portents, ordered the tribunes to call out the armies, and was disastrously defeated at Lake Trasimenus (217 B.C.). News of the defeat threw Rome into a turmoil, and Fabius was chosen dictator a second time by the people. He surrounded the office with all the pomp and ceremony of which it was capable in order to impress the Romans with his power and make them submissive. He called on the people to honor and propitiate the gods, whose anger, he said, at the neglect and scorn of religious rites had caused the defeat; he consulted the Sibylline Books, and vowed sacrifices and festivals to the gods. All this was intended to encourage a belief in the Romans that the gods would bring them victory. But he, according to Plutarch, "put all his hopes of victory in himself, believing that heaven bestowed success by reason of wisdom and valor, and turned his attention to Hannibal." His strategy was to weaken the Carthaginians by numerous skirmishes which hit at stragglers and scouts, while at the same time keeping clear of the main body of Hannibal's troops, and at all events to avoid pitched battles (whence his name Cunctator, "Delayer"). His strategy was criticized by his soldiers, by the Romans, and by the enemy as well, who scorned him for a coward. Only Hannibal realized how wise he

was, and determined to force him into an engagement. Among Fabius' own commanders was Minucius, his master of horse, who was seditious in his criticism of Fabius. When, having been trapped at Casilinum, on the Volturnus river, the Carthaginian not only escaped but spared the acres of Fabius when he burned the surrounding fields (to make it appear that Fabius was in collusion with him), the abuse of Fabius became violent. Fabius was summoned to Rome to assist in sacrifices and put his army in charge of Minucius, with orders not to give battle or engage the enemy. Minucius disobeyed and won a minor victory which was greatly exaggerated in Rome, whereupon he was, in a most unusual step, made co-dictator with Fabius. Rather than rotate the command, Fabius divided his forces with Minucius. Hannibal lured Minucius into battle. Fabius saw that his colleague was being destroyed. He exclaimed, "Hercules! How much sooner than I expected, but later than his own rash eagerness demanded, has Minucius destroyed himself!" Then he took the field and rescued Minucius, who publicly proclaimed his mistake, thanked Fabius, and put himself once more under his command. At the end of six months Fabius put down his office of dictator, as prescribed by law, and the war was again conducted by consuls—Paulus Aemilius and Terentius Varro succeeding him in command. At the outset they followed the policy of Fabius. But Varro boasted that he would conquer the enemy in a day, collected a force of 80,000 men, engaged Hannibal at Cannae (216 B.C.), and was defeated with frightful losses. Rome was almost defenseless, but Hannibal did not follow up his victory by marching on the city. In their terror and confusion the Romans again looked to Fabius, and he became consul for the third time (215 B.C., and again in 214). He limited the period of mourning and the offering of sacrifices in order to conceal to some degree the extent of the Roman losses, sent envoys to the oracle of Delphi, and when Varro returned saw that he was welcomed at Rome without recrimination. Two armies were sent out: one under Fabius, who now came to be called the "Shield of Rome," and the other under the daring and swift-moving Claudius Marcellus, Rome's sword. In spite of his victories and the Italian cities that had gone over to him after the victory of Cannae, Hannibal's army was exhausting itself on foreign soil. He almost lured Fabius into battle, but unfavorable auspices prevented Fabius from beginning operations, and he was saved. In 209 B.C. Fabius became consul for the fifth time and won Tarentum, thanks to the treachery of some Bruttians in the city. Rather than acknowledge that his victory was won by betrayal instead of arms, he put the Bruttians who had made it possible to the sword, killed many Tarentines, sold others into slavery, and plundered the city. Among the spoils was a statue of Hercules, which he sent to Rome and had set up near a statue of himself. The loss of Tarentum, which he had held for three years, was a great blow to Hannibal and won a great triumph for Fabius. Nevertheless, the Carthaginians were still in Italy. In 205 B.C. Scipio became consul and proposed to carry the war to Carthage. Whether from jealousy or from some other reason, Fabius did all he could to hinder and oppose him, but Scipio's view prevailed. The threat to Carthage forced Hannibal's recall from Italy and Fabius died (203 B.C.) before Hannibal's defeat in Africa by Scipio.

Fabius Pictor, Caius (pik'tor, -tôr). Early Roman painter, active c300 B.C. He was of the Fabian gens, and to judge by a passage in Cicero, the cognomen Pictor ("the Painter") was given him not in admiration, but in disapprobation of a man of such lineage engaging in such an occupation as painting. There is a record of only one of his works, the decoration (c304 B.C.) of the temple of Salus on the Quirinal, which probably depicted a Roman victory over the Samnites. There is no record of any Roman painting prior to this. These decorations perished when the temple of Salus was destroyed by fire in the time of the emperor Claudius.

Fabius Pictor, Quintus. Roman annalist. He served in the Gallic war in 225 B.C., as also in the Second Punic War, and was sent to Delphi, after the battle of Cannae in 216 B.C., to consult the oracle as to how the Roman state could propitiate the gods. He was the author of a history of Rome, written in Greek, including the period of the Second Punic War. This history, which is now lost, was highly esteemed by the ancients.

Fabricius Luscinus (fa-brish'us lu-sĭ'nus), **Caius.** Roman consul (282 B.C. and 278 B.C.), general, diplomat, and censor (275 B.C.); died c250 B.C. He was an envoy to King Pyrrhus in 280 B.C. to arrange for the ransom of Roman prisoners. Pyrrhus is said to have attempted to bribe him but Fabricius, poor as he was, refused the offers, much to the admiration of the king. He was noted for his incorruptibility, austerity and poverty. In the *Aeneid* Anchises pointed out the spirit of Fabricius, "princely in his poverty," waiting in the Underworld to be born, when Aeneas visited his father in the Underworld to learn about the future of his race and empire.

Faesulae (fē'sū-lē). [Modern name, **Fiesole**.] An ancient Etruscan town in C Italy, about three miles NE of Florence. It became an ally of Rome, to which it adhered during the campaigns of Hannibal. Stilicho defeated an army of Gothic invaders here in 406 A.D. Beautifully located on a hill above Florence, it is one of the oldest bishoprics in Tuscany, rich in monuments from ancient times, the Middle Ages, and the Renaissance period. It has Etruscan and Roman remains, among them baths and an amphitheater.

Falerian (fa-lir'i-an). See **Faliscan**.

Falerii (fa-lir'i-ī). [Also: **Falerium Vetus**; modern name, **Città Castellana**.] Town in Latium, about 27 miles N of Rome. According to some accounts it was founded by Halesus, either a bastard son or a companion of Agamemnon, who fled from Mycenae when Agamemnon was murdered, founded Falerii and taught its inhabitants the Mysteries of Hera. The town belonged to the Etruscan Confederation and was destroyed (241 B.C.) by the Romans.

Falerium Novum. Town in Latium, three miles NW of Falerium Vetus (Falerii), established by the Romans c240 B.C., where the inhabitants of Falerium Vetus were resettled after the destruction of their city by the Romans in 241 B.C. It has interesting and well-preserved fortifications in ashlar tufa, with arched gates ("Porta di Giove" and "Porta del Bove"), and remains of a theater and amphitheater. In mediaeval times, the inhabitants abandoned Falerium Novum and moved back to Falerium Vetus, now Città Castellana. (JJ)

Falernus Ager (fạ-lẽr'nus ã'jẽr). In ancient geography, a fertile territory in Campania, Italy, situated N of the Volturnus, from 20 to 25 miles N of Naples. It was celebrated for its wines.

Faliscan (fạ-lis'kạn). [Also: **Falerian**.] Ancient Italic language of the Falisci or Faliscans. It is a dialect related to Latin, and now known only from inscriptions, glosses, and proper names.

Falisci (fạ-lis'ī). [Also: **Faliscans**.] Italic people, inhabitants of Falerium Vetus or Falerii (modern, Città Castellana) in ancient Etruria. They spoke a dialect closely akin to Latin. Falerii was considered a member of the Etruscan League from the 5th century B.C. on; it was subjugated by the Romans in 241 B.C. Some older authorities have thought that the group might have been of Sabine origin.

Faliscus (fạ-lis'kus), **Gratius**. See **Gratius Faliscus**.

Famagusta (fä-mä-gös'tä). [Also: **Famagosta**; Latin, **Fama Augusta**.] See **Arsinoë**, city of Cyprus.

Fanum Fortunae (fã'num fôr-tū'nē). [Modern name, **Fano**.] In ancient geography, a town of C Italy, situated on the Adriatic Sea near the mouth of the Metaurus River. There was a temple of Fortune there, from which the town took its name. There was also a temple of Jupiter and one of Augustus. The town was held by Julius Caesar in 49 B.C.; Augustus later sent a colony there and built a wall around the town. The architect Vitruvius describes a basilica which he said was built at Fanum from his designs. Parts of the wall and a triumphal arch dedicated to Augustus remain.

Farnese Bacchus (fär-nā'zā bak'us). Greek torso of the 4th century B.C., in the Museo Nazionale at Naples. It is of the school of Praxiteles.

Farnese Bull. A copy of a large group of Greek sculpture of the Trallian school (1st century B.C.), in the Museo Nazionale at Naples. It represents the chastisement of Dirce by her stepsons for her treatment of their mother, Antiope, by binding her to the horns of a bull. It is much restored, but is considered very remarkable for its composition and execution. It was discovered in the Baths of Caracalla in 1546 in a mutilated condition and was initially restored under the supervision of Michelangelo and later by the Milanese sculptor Bianchi.

Farnese Flora (flō'rạ). Ancient statue in the Museo Nazionale at Naples. The goddess holds her Ionian tunic with her right hand as she steps forward, the motif being a familiar one in archaic statues of Venus. The figure is considered remarkable for its grace, despite its height of 11½ feet.

Farnese Heracles (her'ạ-klēz) or **Hercules** (her'-kū-lēz). Greek statue in the Museo Nazionale at Naples executed by Glycon of Athens. The demigod is represented undraped, leaning on his club. The bearded head is somewhat small, and the muscular development prodigious. The statue, which is a copy of a Heracles by Lysippus, dates from the early empire (1st century B.C.).

Farnese Homer (hō'mẽr). Ancient bust in the Museo Nazionale at Naples. Admirable in execution and remarkable for the profound intellectuality of its expression, it is perhaps the finest example of its familiar type, which is that universally associated with Homer.

Farnese Juno (jö'nō). Colossal antique bust of Juno (Hera), in the Museo Nazionale at Naples. The expression is one of calm repose, high and unbending. The hair is bound with a simple fillet. It has been demonstrated that this bust is probably a copy of a Hera made by Polyclitus (c423 B.C.) for the temple at Argos.

Farnese Minerva (mi-nẽr'vạ). Greek statue of Pallas (Athena Parthenos), found at Velletri, Italy, and now in the Museo Nazionale at Naples. The type is that of the great statue of the Parthenon. The goddess wears the Attic helmet with a sphinx and two figures of Pegasus, and the aegis on her breast. The arms are restored; the right is extended to hold the Victory, and the left raised to sustain the spear.

Fasces (fas'ēz). In Roman antiquity, bundles of rods, usually of elm or birch, with an ax bound in with them, the blade projecting. They were borne by lictors before the superior Roman magistrates as a badge of their power over life and limb. The magistrates lowered the fasces in the presence of the popular assembly to signify that it had the sovereign power. Officials of different rank were entitled to a varying number of fasces, and officials of a lower rank saluted those of a higher rank by lowering the fasces. When a magistrate died his fasces, along with his arms, were carried reversed behind his bier. The adoption of the fasces as the symbol of the authoritarian political movement organized in Italy by Mussolini led to the use of such terms as "fascism," "fascist," and "fascist party," and imitative developments in Spain, Germany, Argentina, and elsewhere.

Fasti (fas'tī). Roman calendars listing for each month those days which were feast days, market days, administrative days, and others. The list of the *dies fasti* was for a long time accessible only to the patricians. This put all others at a great disadvantage because the courts sat and certain proceedings of the state could be undertaken only on the *dies fasti*. Days when the courts were closed and certain business could not be done were called *dies nefasti*. In 304 B.C. the list was published and thereafter made available to all.

Fasti. Poetical Roman calendar, by Ovid, in six books. In it, Ovid describes, and attempts to explain, the origins and ceremonies connected with certain Roman festivals. It was Ovid's intention to compose 12 books, one for each month of the Roman year; at the time of his banishment to Tomis on the Euxine, in 8 A.D., he had completed the first six books, which have come down to us. Apparently his drafts and fragments from the other six books were destroyed. (JJ)

Fasti Capitolini (kap"i-tō̯-lī'ni). Marble tablets containing a register of the Roman consuls and other chief magistrates of certain years. They were excavated at Rome in 1546 or 1547, and preserved in the Capitol, whence their name.

Fates (fāts). In Roman mythology, the three goddesses of destiny who preordained the course and outcome of every human life. Their Latin name, Fata, is the plural of *fatum*, meaning an unalterable decree of the gods, hence, fate. Because they functioned at every human birth, they became identified with the Moerae, three goddesses of Greek religion who are also called Fates. This identification gave rise to the development of

the three Roman Parcae, or Fates, from the original Roman birth-goddess, Parca.

Faun (fôn). In Roman mythology, one of a class of demigods or rural deities, sometimes confounded with satyrs. The form of the fauns was originally human, but with a short goat's tail, pointed ears, and small horns; later they were represented with the hind legs of a goat, thus taking the type of the Greek Pan.

Faun of Praxiteles (prak-sit'e̯l-ēz). Ancient Greek statue by Praxiteles, the finest surviving copy of which is in the Capitoline Museum at Rome. The youth leans on a tree stump, nude except for a panther skin over the shoulder. The face betrays his animal kinship by little except the unusual hollow in the nose and the slightly pointed ears.

Faunus (fôn'us). Ancient Italian god of forests and wild life, an agricultural and pastoral fertility deity who later became identified with the Greek Pan. He had two annual festivals, in December and February, called Faunalia, accompanied by libations of milk and wine, sacrifice of goats, and the performance of games. In the Roman mythology, he figures as the brother, father, or consort of Bona Dea. In ancient legend, Faunus was a son of Picus, grandson of Saturn. He was a Latin king and the father of Latinus. There was an oracle of Faunus, in the city founded by Latinus, which instructed Latinus to wed his daughter Lavinia to a stranger. It was for this reason that Latinus refused the suit of Turnus for his daughter's hand, and accepted that of Aeneas. Faunus taught the Latin peoples their agriculture and religion.

Fausta (fôs'ta̯), **Cornelia.** Daughter of the Roman dictator L. Cornelius Sulla by his fourth wife, Caecilia Metella; born c88 B.C. She married at an early age C. Memmius, by whom she was divorced. In 55 B.C., she married T. Annius Milo. She was notorious for her conjugal infidelity. The historian Sallust is said to have been one of her paramours.

Faustulus (fôs'tu̯-lus). In Roman mythology, the shepherd who found the abandoned twin infants Romulus and Remus, took them home, and with his wife fostered them until they reached manhood.

Favonius (fa̯-vō'ni-us). In Roman mythology,

the gentle west wind, bringer of spring and the rebirth of vegetation, hence regarded as auspicious: identified with Zephyr.

Felix (fē'liks). Surname of **Sulla, Lucius Cornelius.**

Felix, Antonius. Roman procurator of Judea, 1st century A.D. He was a freedman of Antonia, mother of the emperor Claudius I, and was the brother of the latter's favorite, the freedman Pallas. He was appointed procurator of Judea c55 A.D., and governed his province from Caesarea, whither Saint Paul was sent to him for trial after his arrest at Jerusalem (Acts, xxiii. 23, 24). He married Drusilla, daughter of Agrippa I and wife of Azizus, king of Emesa, whom he induced her to desert, and procured the assassination of the high priest Jonathan, who had offended him by unpalatable advice. He was recalled c60 A.D., and was saved from the consequences of his tyranny and extortion by the intercession of his brother with the emperor Nero.

Ferentinum (fe-ren-tī'num). [Modern name, **Ferentino.**] In ancient geography, an important town of the Hernici, situated about 48 miles SE of Rome. It was captured by the Romans in 364 B.C., and its inhabitants were given the citizenship after 195 B.C. The town was located on a hill and was strongly fortified. The powerful walls, polygonal masonry repaired in ashlar, survive in almost their entire extent, as do several gates, including the famous Porta Sanguinaria, or Bloody Gate, an arched postern gate, and an interesting corbelled sally port.

Ferentum (fe-ren'tum). [Modern name, **Ferento.**] Ruined city in C Italy, about 5½ miles N of Viterbo. It contains extensive Etruscan, Roman, and medieval remains which have been excavated. The ancient theater is of particular interest. Ferentum was the birthplace of the emperor Otho.

Feronia (fē-rō'ni-a). An ancient Italian goddess, presiding over woods and orchards. In later Roman mythology she was regarded especially as the patroness of freedmen. Her most celebrated shrine was at the foot of Mount Soracte in Etruria. In the *Aeneid*, she is named as the mother of Erulus (q.v.), to whom she gave three sets of weapons and three separate lives.

Fescennia (fe-sen'i-a). A Tuscan city on the Tiber. Its people were allies of Turnus, the Rutulian, in the war against Aeneas in Latium.

Fescennine Verses or **Songs** (fes'e-nīn, -nin). Ancient Roman popular verses or songs: so named, according to Festus, from Fescennia in southern Etruria. They were recited or sung at rustic merrymakings, and especially at popular harvest festivals.

Festus (fes'tus), **Sextus Pompeius.** Latin scholar and lexicographer, active perhaps in the middle of the 2nd century A.D. He epitomized (in 20 books, of which half is extant) a glossary of Latin words and phrases entitled *De Verborum Significatu*, by Verrius Flaccus, which is now lost.

Ficoroni Cist (fē-kō-rō'nē). Cylindrical bronze box found near Palestrina, Italy, in 1745, and acquired by the Museo Kircheriano at Rome. It is important because its incised decoration, representing the victory of Polydeuces (Pollux) over Amycus, is one of the finest surviving examples of Greek line drawing. The box is over 1½ feet high, and rests on three feet; the handle of the cover is formed by a group consisting of Bacchus and two satyrs.

Fidenae (fi-dē'nē). In ancient geography, a town of the Sabines in Latium, situated on the Tiber River about five miles NE of Rome. Anchises predicted the founding of this town to Aeneas when the latter visited his father in the Underworld.

Fidentia (fī-den'shi-a, -sha). [Modern name, **Fidenza;** formerly **Borgo San Donnino.**] In ancient geography, a town on the Via Aemilia, in N Italy, about 14 miles NW of the city of Parma. It was the site of a victory of Metellus Pius over Carbo, the leader of the Marian faction, in 82 B.C.

Fides (fī'dēz). The Roman personification and goddess of faith or fidelity, commonly represented as a matron wearing a wreath of olive or laurel leaves, and having in her hand ears of corn or a basket of fruit. The temple of Fides on the Palatine Hill in Rome was a meeting place for the Senate and a depository of international documents. In connection with sacrifices to Fides, the right hand was bound in a white cloth to indicate that honor dwelt in the right hand.

Fields of Mourning. In the *Aeneid*, a region in the Underworld inhabited by the souls of unhappy lovers who had committed suicide. On his visit to the Underworld, Aeneas saw Dido in the Fields of Mourning and tried to speak to her, but she turned her head aside and ignored him.

Firmum (fêr'mum). [Modern name, **Fermo.**] In ancient geography, a town of C Italy, situated on a hill overlooking the Adriatic Sea. It was founded as a Roman colony, 264 B.C. Remains of a Roman amphitheater and of the ancient walls may be seen.

First Triumvirate. See **Triumvirate, First.**

Flaccus (fla'kus), **Caius Valerius.** See **Valerius Flaccus, Caius.**

Flaccus, Quintus Fulvius. Roman soldier and statesman; fl. 3rd century B.C. He was consul in 237, 224, 212, and 209 B.C., censor in 231, pontifex maximus in 216, and urban praetor in 215 B.C. During his third consulship he won an important victory at Beneventum over the Carthaginians under Hanno. He laid siege to Capua, occupied by the Carthaginians, and though compelled to go to Rome, where Hannibal had caused a diversion, he returned and freed Capua from the invaders.

Flaccus, Marcus Fulvius. Roman politician, grandnephew of Quintus Fulvius Flaccus; fl. 2nd century B.C. After the death of Tiberius Gracchus (133 B.C.), of whom he had been a strong supporter, Flaccus took his place in the commission appointed for the redistribution of the land. He was consul, 125 B.C., and proposed that the allies of Rome be granted the citizenship. His proposal was rejected by the Senate, by whom he was considered a dangerous "democrat." He was sent out of Rome on the excuse of protecting the Massilians, allies of Rome, against the Ligurians. Successful in this, he returned to Rome in triumph, but left again (122 B.C.) to go to Carthage with Caius Gracchus to found a colony. He was killed in Rome in 121 B.C., at the same time as Caius Gracchus was killed.

Flamen (flā'men). A Latin word, possibly meaning "he who burns the sacrifices." In Roman antiquity the *flamen* was a priest devoted to the service of one particular deity. Originally there were three priests thus named: the *flamen Dialis,* consecrated to Jupiter; the *flamen Martialis,* sacred to Mars; and the *flamen Quirinalis,* who superintended the rites of Quirinus (Romulus). The number was gradually increased to 15, but the original three retained priority in point of rank, being styled *majores,* and elected from among the patricians, while the other 12, called *minores,* were elected from the plebeians. They held their office for life and could only be removed under special conditions. They were freed of all the responsibilities of civic life and took no part in politics. Their characteristic dress included the white conical cap called the *apex.* This was made from the hide of a sacrificed animal and had an olive branch and a woolen thread at its peak. The *flamines* wore their caps at all times out of doors. The *flamen Dialis,* as the priest of Jupiter, was dedicated with his wife and children to the god. He had to be chosen from parents who followed the old patrician form of marriage, in which an offering of a cake was made to Jupiter in the presence of the priest and the *flamen Dialis,* with ten witnesses. He must be married himself, and if his wife died he resigned his office. Certain prohibitions were attached to the office. He was not allowed to leave his home at night; he was not permitted to view any one at work, therefore the lictor who preceded him called on all to stop their toil as he approached; he was forbidden to look upon armed men, or to touch any unclean thing, and if he did so he must resign. Because he was also forbidden to see or have about him anything in the shape of a chain, the fastenings of his robe, which must have been woven by his wife, were clasps. The *flamen Dialis* also had certain privileges, such as a seat in the Senate and the services of a lictor and heralds. The duties of the *flamines* were to offer daily sacrifices. For the *flamen Dialis* every day was a holy day, on which he must wear his ceremonial dress and carry the sacrificial knife. The wife of the *flamen Dialis* was a priestess of Juno and had certain insignia. She wore a purple fillet woven through her hair, covered her head with a veil, and wore a long woolen robe. She also carried a sacrificial knife. The *flamines majores* drove to the Capitol in two-horse chariots on the 1st of October and there offered sacrifice to Fides Publica, the Roman personification of the honor of the people.

---

actọr; up, lūte, pụll; oi, oil; ou, out; ŦH, then; ḍ as d or j, ṣ as s or sh, ṭ as t or ch, ẓ as z or zh.

Flaminian Way (fla̱-min'i-a̱n). [Latin, **Via Flaminia**.] One of the oldest and most famous highways of ancient Rome. It was 209 miles long, extended from Rome to Ariminum (Rimini), and was built by the censor Caius Flaminius in 220 B.C. Its superintendence was held to be so honorable an office that Augustus himself assumed it in 27 B.C., as Julius Caesar had been curator of the Appian Way. Augustus restored it through its entire extent, in commemoration of which triumphal arches were erected to him over the road at Ariminum and at Rome; the arch at the former place still exists. Much of the old pavement survives, together with many tombs by the roadside.

Flamininus (flam-i-nī'nus), **Titus Quintius** (or **Quinctius**). Roman general and statesman; born c230 B.C.; died c174 B.C. He was consul in 198 B.C., defeated Philip V of Macedon at Cynoscephalae in 197, and proclaimed, at the Isthmian Games at Corinth, the freedom of Greece from Macedonian rule in 196 B.C. In 195 B.C. he defeated Nabis, tyrant of Sparta, and returned (194) to Rome in triumph. He was sent (192 B.C.) on a diplomatic mission to Greece and succeeded in rallying the wavering Greek states to the Roman side against Antiochus III of Syria. He negotiated with Bithynia for the surrender of Hannibal who had sought asylum there, but Hannibal committed suicide (183 B.C.) before any conclusion was reached.

Flaminius (fla̱-min'i-us), **Caius**. Roman general and politician; killed in battle 217 B.C. He was tribune of the people in 232 B.C., in which year he procured the passage of a law distributing the *Ager Gallicus Picenus* (an area along the Adriatic coast) among the plebeians, for which he won great popularity. He defeated the Insubres (near modern Milan) while consul in 223 B.C., and while censor in 220 B.C. constructed two celebrated public works which bore his name: the Circus Flaminius for the plebeians, and the Flaminian Way. He was made consul for the second time in 217 B.C., after Hannibal had invaded Italy. He disapproved of the policy advocated by Fabius Maximus, which was to wear Hannibal out by harassment rather than by engaging him in pitched battles. Numerous unfavorable portents frightened the Romans on the advent of Hannibal, but Flaminius scorned them. He ordered the tribunes to call out the army for the purpose of attacking Hannibal. When he sprang to his horse the animal trembled with fear and threw him. But even that ominous portent did not deter Flaminius. He met Hannibal at Lake Trasimenus (217 B.C.) in Tuscany. The opposing forces engaged in such a furious struggle that the occurrence of an earthquake in the midst of the battle is said to have gone unnoticed. The forces of Flaminius were nearly annihilated: 15,000 were slain and another 15,000 were taken prisoner. Flaminius, responsible for the disaster, fell in the battle. Hannibal sought his body, to give honorable burial to a valiant opponent, but it had disappeared.

Flaminius, Caius. Roman general; fl. 2nd century B.C.; son of Caius Flaminius (d. 217 B.C.). He served as quaestor under Scipio Africanus the Elder in Spain. He was elected praetor in 193 B.C., and obtained Hispania Citerior as his province. In 187 he became consul with M. Aemilius Lepidus, and in 181 B.C. he founded the colony of Aquileia near the head of the Adriatic Sea.

Flavian (flā'vi-a̱n) **Amphitheater**. Amphitheater at Rome, just SE of the Forum. It was begun by Vespasian (T. Flavius Sabinus) in 72 A.D. and completed in 80. For 400 years it was the seat of gladiatorial shows. The axes of this chief of amphitheaters are about 617 and 512 feet; of the arena, about 282 and 177 feet. The exterior was ornamented with four tiers of engaged columns with their entablatures, the lowest three enclosing arches, and the highest walled up, with square windows in every second intercolumniation. The material of the interior is stone, of the inner passages and vaults largely brick and concrete. The marble seats accommodated between 40,000 and 50,000 people. Sailors from the imperial fleet were detailed to handle the great awnings which protected the spectators from the burning sun. The interior was faced with marble. In the substructions there is a most elaborate system of chambers, passages, dens, and drains. Despite the enormous mass of the existing ruin, it is estimated that a large part (perhaps as much as two-thirds) has been carried away in the Middle Ages and later, for building material. The name Colosseum, not encountered in the literature before the 8th century A.D. but probably in popular use long before that, was derived from a colossal gilded bronze statue of Nero which once stood nearby.

Flavius (flā′vi-us), **Cnaeus.** Early writer on Roman law who was active in the 4th century B.C. He was the son of a freedman, and became secretary to Appius Claudius Caecus. In his time in Rome information as to the days on which cases might properly be pleaded (known as *fasti*) remained exclusively in the possession of the patricians. Flavius obtained possession of the forms pertaining to the law of practice, and a calendar of the days (*fasti*) on which cases could be pleaded. This information was invaluable to the plebeians, as any infraction of the forms, or any error in the day would automatically cause the loss of a case. Flavius published this vital information in a collection known as the *Ius Civile Flavianum.* He was afterward made a senator by Appius Claudius, and was elected curule aedile in 304 B.C.

Flood. In Greek mythology, the means which Zeus employed to destroy the wicked men of the Age of Iron. According to most accounts, only Deucalion, the son of Prometheus, and his wife Pyrrha were spared to create a new race of men. Other accounts say that Megarus, a son of Zeus, was warned by cranes and fled to Mount Gerania, which was not covered by the flood; also Cerambus was saved. The latter was changed into a beetle by nymphs and flew off to Mount Parnassus.

Flora (flō′ra). Ancient Italian goddess of flowers and spring, and perhaps of love. Her cult in later Roman religion was influenced by foreign rites; her festival, the Floralia, was celebrated from April 28 to May 1 with mummery and games and the type of license associated with all fertility festivals.

Florence (flor′ents). [Latin, **Florentia;** Italian, **Fiorenza,** now **Firenze.**] Ancient town in Tuscany, on the banks of the river Arnus (Arno), probably established in the 1st century B.C. as a Roman colony, traces of whose checkerboard plan and a few streets have survived. In the Middle Ages and Renaissance it was a center of intense creative activity. Driven by Dante, Boccaccio, Petrarch, Macchiavelli, and Galileo, and the artists Cimabue, Giotto, the della Robbias, Donatello, Botticelli, da Vinci, Michelangelo, Raphael, Cellini, and their hardly less distinguished pupils, Florence became the intellectual capital of Italy and the artistic capital of Europe. The Galleria degli Uffizi contains, in addition to splendid Florentine paintings, a major collection of Greek and Roman sculptures, and the archaeological museum holds important Etruscan, Greek, and Roman ceramics, bronzes, and some sculptures. (JJ)

Florus (flō′rus), **Lucius Annaeus.** Roman historian who was active at the beginning of the 2nd century A.D. He was the author of an abridgment of Roman history to the time of Augustus (*Epitome de Gestis Romanorum*), founded chiefly on Livy. By some scholars he has been identified with the rhetorician and poet P. Annius Florus.

Fons (fōnz). In Roman mythology, the god of springs. He was the son of Janus and Juturna. There was an altar to Fons on the Janiculum in Rome, and at the time of his festival, in October, fountains and springs were decorated with wreaths and garlands were thrown into their waters as offerings to him.

Formiae (fôr′mi-ē). [Modern name, **Formia;** formerly **Mola di Gaeta.**] Town in Latium, C Italy, situated on the Gulf of Caieta, about 44 miles NW of Neapolis (Naples). An ancient town of the Volsci, on the Appian Way, it became a Roman city with limited rights of citizenship in 322 B.C., and with full rights in 188 B.C. It was a summer resort of rich Romans from the time of the late republic; Cicero had a villa here. Remains of ancient Roman structures are still standing.

Fornax (fôr′naks). In Roman mythology, the goddess of grain and specifically, the goddess of ovens. Her festival, the Fornacalia, was celebrated in February on different days, one day for the state, and one each for the *curiae* (tribal divisions) of Rome.

Fortuna (fôr-tū′na). In Roman religion, the goddess of fortune and good luck, corresponding to the Greek Tyche. She was worshiped in Rome in many aspects: as goddess of chance or luck she was called *Fors Fortuna;* as goddess of women, *Fortuna* *muliebris;* as patron of newly-wedded girls, *Fortuna virginensis;* as goddess of virility in men, *Fortuna virilis.* She was also famous as *Fortuna Redux* whose festival, the Augustalia, was celebrated Oct. 3–12. She had oracular shrines at Antium and Praeneste. At Praeneste she was called *Primigenia,* and regarded as the oldest daughter of Jupiter.

Forum Appii (fō′rum ap′i-ī). In ancient geography, a station on the Appian Way, about 40 miles SE of Rome.

Forum Boarium (fō′rum bō-ā′ri-um). Early cattle market of ancient Rome. It was bounded on the N by the area called the Velabrum, on the E by the Palatine Hill, on the S by the Aventine Hill at the extremity of the Circus Maximus, and on the W by the Tiber River. It is said that at an early date gladiatorial shows were given here, and that human sacrifices were made by burial alive.

Forum Holitorium (hō-li-tō′ri-um). Vegetable market of ancient Rome. It occupied the southern extremity of the Campus Martius, beneath the Capitoline Hill, stretching into the Velabrum, and separated from the Forum Boarium only by the Servian Wall. Of the 15 or more temples known to have stood in this district of Rome, three which stood side by side have been found incorporated into the later church of San Nicola in Carcere. It has been suggested that these temples were those dedicated to Spes (*Hope*), Juno Sospita, and Dis Pater or Janus; but no certain proof is available. (JJ)

Forum Julium (jō′li-um, jōl′yum). Earliest of the imperial forums of ancient Rome, designed to relieve the crowding of the Forum Romanum. It was begun by Julius Caesar (46 B.C.), and practically adjoined the northern side of the Forum Romanum at its eastern end. It was surrounded with porticoes, and its central area was occupied by a richly adorned peripteral temple of Venus Genetrix. Some finely arcaded and vaulted chambers of the enclosure exist near the southwest angle; they were probably offices for legal business.

Forum of Augustus (ô-gus′tus). Second of the imperial forums of ancient Rome; dedicated in 2 B.C. The existing remains include very impressive stretches of the enclosing wall, one of the entrance arches now called Arco de' Pantani, and some columns and walls of the temple of Mars Ultor.

Forum of Nerva (nėr′va̲). [Also: **Forum Palladium, Forum Transitorium.**] Fourth of the imperial forums of ancient Rome; built by Domitian and dedicated by Nerva in 97 A.D.

Forum of Trajan (trā′jạn). Largest and the northernmost of the imperial forums of ancient Rome, adjoining the NW side of the Forum of Augustus, and lying between the northeastern declivity of the Capitoline Hill and the Quirinal. It consisted of three parts: 1) the forum proper, 2) the huge Basilica Ulpia, and 3) the temple of Trajan, with its colonnaded enclosure. Between the temple of Trajan and the Basilica Ulpia rises the column of Trajan, beneath which was the emperor's mausoleum. To create an area for this lavish monumental display, Trajan cut away a large ridge of tufa which extended from the Capitoline to the Quirinal. The forum was completed for Trajan by the architect Apollodorus of Damascus in 114 A.D.

Forum Pacis (pā′sis) or **Forum of Vespasian** (ves-pā′zha̲n). Third of the imperial forums of ancient Rome. It was the southernmost of the imperial forums, and lay behind the Basilica Aemilia, which fronted on the Forum Romanum. It was built to enclose the temple of peace which was dedicated by Vespasian in 75 A.D. in honor of the taking of Jerusalem, and is described by Pliny as one of the four finest buildings of Rome. In it were dedicated the spoils of the Jewish temple, represented on the Arch of Titus; and here too Vespasian placed the works of art taken by Nero from Delphi and other Greek cities. A massive stretch of the exterior wall of this forum still stands, near the western end of the basilica of Constantine, with a fine flat-arched doorway of travertine.

Forum Palladium (pa̲-lā′di-um). See **Forum of Nerva.**

Forum Romanum (rō̲-mā′num). Famous Roman forum which from the time of the kings formed the political center of ancient Rome. Beginning in a hollow on the eastern slope of the Capitoline Hill, its long and comparatively narrow area stretched in a direction south of east beneath the northern declivity of the Palatine Hill. Its western end was occupied by the *tabularium,* or office of the archives, in front of which stood the temples of Concord and of Vespasian. On its southern side were the temple of Saturn, the Basilica Julia, the temples of Castor and Pollux and of Vesta, and on its northern side the arch of Septimius Severus, the Curia, the Basilica Aemilia, and the temples of Antoninus and Faustina and of Romulus. In the middle of the eastern part rose the temple and rostra of Julius Caesar. The more ancient and famous rostra from which Cicero spoke were at the western end. The area was neglected and abused during the Middle Ages and Renaissance and although it has been thoroughly excavated and painstakingly studied by generations of scholars, many difficult problems of topography remain unsolved.

Frentani (fren-tā′nī). Ancient Italian people related to the Samnites, dwelling along the Adriatic coast northwest of Apulia. They were subjugated by the Romans in 304 B.C.

Frigidus (frij′i-dus). [Also: **Frigidus Fluvius.**] In ancient geography, a small river in what is now NW Yugoslavia: noted for its coldness. In its valley Theodosius defeated the forces of Eugenius and Arbogast in 394 A.D.

Frogs, The. Comedy of Aristophanes, produced 405 B.C. and awarded the first prize. Aeschylus, Sophocles, and Euripides having died, Dionysus is dissatisfied with the new poets who have come to take their place at his festivals. He decides to go to Hades and fetch Euripides back to earth. Disguised as Heracles, with a lion's skin, he goes to Hades with his servant, but immediately shows how unworthy he is of Heracles' mantle by exhibiting the utmost cowardice before the creatures of Hades. Frightened, he hands the lion's skin to his servant and pushes him forward. Relieved of his fears, he seizes the lion's skin and makes boasts—the passages are hilarious. In Hades Dionysus finds not only Euripides but also Sophocles, who has no desire to return to earth, and Aeschylus as well. He is embarassed to have to choose between Euripides and Aeschylus. They each present their claims to be chosen. Dionysus seems about to choose Euripides, but at the last moment, on impulse, he selects Aeschylus. The play is named for the chorus, representing the frogs that lived in the marshes

near Eleusis, where Dionysus passed on his way to Hades.

Frontinus (fron-tī′nus), **Sextus Julius.** Roman writer. He was born c30 A.D. and died c103. He fought in Britain and held public office under the emperors Vespasian, Nerva, and Trajan. Nerva appointed him superintendent of aqueducts. From experience gained in this post he wrote *De Aquis Urbis Romae,* an interesting history and description of the water supply of Rome, and the laws governing its use and maintenance. This work, published in the time of Trajan, survives. Also in the time of Trajan he served as augur and as consul. Among other of Frontinus' works still extant are: *Strategemata,* which describes instances of military strategy taken from Greek and Roman campaigns, and excerpts from a work on land surveying.

Fronto (fron′tō), **Marcus Cornelius.** Roman rhetorician and orator. He was born at Cirta c100 A.D., in Numidia, and died c166. By his eloquent oratory he earned the admiration of the emperors Hadrian and Antoninus Pius, and was put in charge of the education of the young Marcus Aurelius and Lucius Verus. For a time (143) he served as consul, but ill health compelled him to give up this post. He corresponded with Marcus Aurelius and a collection of his letters, some in Greek, survives. Fronto was an advocate of a return to the more classic style of earlier Roman letters.

Frusino (frö′sē̦-nō). [Modern name, **Frosinone.**] In ancient geography, a town of the Hernici, in C Italy, about 53 miles SE of Rome. Conquered by the Romans in 304 B.C., it later became a colony of Rome.

Fucinus, Lacus (fū′si-nus lā′kus). [Modern name, **Fucino, Lago di Fucino** (or **di Celano**).] Former lake in C Italy, near the towns of Avezzano and Celano. Mentioned in the *Aeneid* as a limpid lake which wept for Umbro, a snake charmer who was killed by a Trojan in the war between Aeneas and the Rutulians under Turnus. It was drained by Prince Torlonia, who began the work in 1852. It had been partly drained in the reign of Claudius. It had no outlet, and measured about 37 miles in circumference.

Fulvia (ful′vi-a̦). Roman matron, wife of Publius Clodius, then of Curio, and later of Mark Antony. She fomented a rising (the

Perusine war) against Octavian in 41 B.C., in order to draw Antony away from Egypt and Cleopatra. By Clodius she was the mother of Claudia. When Fulvia was later married to Mark Antony, this daughter Claudia was given to Octavian (Augustus) in marriage in order to draw closer the two leading figures in Rome after the murder of Caesar. Augustus quarreled with Fulvia and divorced Claudia. Fulvia's son by Mark Antony, who fled to the image of the god Julius for sanctuary when Antony was defeated, was slain at Augustus' order. Fulvia died at Sicyon, Greece, in 40 B.C.

Fundi (fun'dī). [Modern name, **Fondi**.] In ancient geography, a town of the Volsci, situated on the Appian Way, near the Gulf of Tarracina between Rome and Naples, Italy. Because the inhabitants granted the Romans safe passage through their territory they were given limited citizenship by the Romans (c388 B.C.). In 188 B.C. they received full citizenship. Parts of the ancient walls and gates remain.

Furculae Caudinae (fėr'kū-lē kô-dī'nē). Latin name of the **Caudine Forks**.

Furiae (fū'ri-ē) or **Furies**. In Roman mythology, goddesses adopted from the Erinyes of Greek mythology.

—G—

Gabii (gā'bi-ī). In ancient geography, a city in Latium, Italy, situated about halfway between Rome and Praeneste at the foot of the Alban Hills; one of the oldest of the cities belonging to the Latin federation. It was a nameless site at the time when Aeneas visited his father in the Underworld. Anchises pointed out to him the shade of the man waiting to be born who would found the city. According to Roman legend it was conquered by Tarquinius Superbus in the following manner: His youngest son, Sextus, presented himself before Gabii in the guise of a fugitive from his father's tyranny, and was received by the Gabines as their leader, whereupon Sextus sent to Rome for further instructions. The messenger found Tarquin in his garden. Without saying a word, the king knocked off the heads of the tallest poppies. The messenger returned to Sextus, who saw the meaning of the parable, and cut off the heads of the chief men of Gabii, which was then surrendered to Tarquin. The most notable remains of antiquity is the barnlike shell of a temple cella in the local tufa, dating most plausibly from the 2nd century B.C., perhaps of the temple of Juno of Gabii. Gabine tufa, *lapis Gabinus,* was quarried in substantial quantities for new construction at Rome.

Gabinian Law (ga-bin'i-an). [Latin, **Lex Gabinia**.] In Roman history: 1) Law passed in 67 B.C., by which Pompey was invested for three years with unlimited command over the whole Mediterranean and its coasts for 50 miles inland, and received unconditional control of the public treasuries of the provinces, for the purpose of conducting the war against the pirates. 2) Law passed in 58 B.C., which forbade loans of money at Rome to legations from foreign countries, the object of which was to prevent such legations from borrowing money to bribe the senators.

Gabinius (ga-bin'i-us), **Aulus**. Roman tribune (67 B.C.); died at Salona, in Dalmatia, c47 B.C. He proposed a law giving Pompey command against the pirates, for which reason the law was called the Gabinian Law. (See article immediately preceding.)

Gabrias (gā'bri-as). See **Babrius**.

Gadara (gad'a-ra). In ancient geography, a city of the Decapolis in Syria, situated about seven miles SE of the Sea of Galilee, probably the capital of Peraea; the modern village of Umm Qeis (Um Keis). It was rebuilt by Pompey. There are remains of a large Roman theater, not excavated in a hill but entirely built up of masonry on vaulted substructions and in good preservation, and of a smaller theater on the same site. Orthography has led the place to be associated with the parable of the Gadarene swine (the herd of swine into which demons were cast from two men and which then perished. Matt. viii. 28; Mark, v. 1; Luke, viii. 26). The textual variants (Gadarenes, Gerasenes, Gergesenes) in the several books have led some to believe that the miracle occurred either at Gadara or at Gerasa (modern Jerash, in Jordan), but modern scholarship identifies the scene with Kersa, a town on the E shore of the Sea of Galilee on the Wadi Samak, where the physical setting is more in consonance with the Biblical description than it is at either Gadara or Gerasa.

Gadeira (ga-dī′ra) or **Gadira.** The Greek name for Gades (q.v.). It was here that Heracles was believed to have stopped on his way to fetch the cattle of Geryon, and erected the Pillars of Heracles, one on the continent of Africa and one on the continent of Europe.

Gades (gā′dēz). [Phoenician, **Gadir**; Greek, **Gadeira** or **Gadira**.] In ancient geography, the remotest colony of the Phoenicians in the west. It was founded c1100 B.C. beyond Gibraltar at the NW extremity of an island, about 12 miles long, which lies off the W coast of Spain, and occupied almost exactly the same site as the modern city of Cádiz. It was the headquarters of the western commerce of the Phoenicians, and contained various temples of the Phoenician gods. The Carthaginians used Gades as a base for their conquest of Spain. It fell to the Romans in 206 B.C.

Gaea (jē′a). [Also: **Gaia, Ge.**] In Greek mythology, the goddess of the earth. Some say she was the child of Air and Day. Others say she was sprung directly from Chaos. She was the mother of Uranus (the sky-god), Pontus (a sea-god), and the mountains. She bore Uranus in her sleep and by him became the mother of the Hecatonchires, the Cyclopes, the Titans, and the Titanesses. Because Uranus hid the Cyclopes in Tartarus, Gaea plotted against him. She gave Cronus, one of the Titans, the sickle with which he cut off Uranus' genitals when all the Titans except Oceanus attacked their father. Drops of blood from this mutilation fell on Gaea and she bore the Erinyes and the Melic nymphs. Gaea prophesied that Cronus, who had deposed his father, would be dethroned himself by one of his children. When Cronus was later attacked by his son Zeus, Gaea advised Zeus to release the Cy-

clopes, who had again been imprisoned in Tartarus by Cronus. By her son Pontus, Gaea was the mother of Nereus, Phorcys, Thaumas, Eurybia, and Ceto. After the defeat of the Giants by Zeus, Gaea, enraged, lay with Tartarus and brought forth the monster Typhon. She is also said by some to have been the mother of Ladon, the dragon that guarded the golden apples of the Hesperides; of Antaeus, a king in Libya who was killed by Heracles; of Charybdis, the sea monster; of the 24 Giants born at Phlegra in Attica; and of the earth-born serpent-kings Erechtheus and Cecrops. Gaea was invoked as a witness to oaths. She was worshiped with the sacrifice of a black lamb and her priestesses drank bull's blood, considered to be deadly poison to ordinary mortals. She was honored as the mother of all, who nourishes her children and gives them rich blessings. She was also regarded as an Underworld deity who reclaims her children in the end. Her cults were very numerous. The earliest oracle at Olympia was hers, as was also the first oracle at Delphi. Some say Apollo stole the latter from her, but others say she gave it to the Titaness Phoebe and it was from her that Apollo got it. The Romans identified Gaea with their Tellus.

Gaeeochus (ji-ē′ō-kus). Epithet of Poseidon, meaning "Earth-moving." See **Ennosigaeus**.

Gaeta (gä-ē′tä). See **Caieta**.

Gaeta, Gulf of. See **Caieta, Gulf of**.

Gaetulia (jē-tū′li-a). In ancient geography, the land of the Gaetuli, mentioned in the *Aeneid* as a warlike tribe that threatened Dido and Carthage. It was a region in N Africa, S of Mauretania and Numidia, extending from the land of the Garamantes W to the Atlantic. The Gaetulians were subjected to Roman rule about the time of Christ.

Gaia (gā′a). See **Gaea**.

Gaius (gā′us). See **Caius**.

Galata (ga′la-ta). According to legend, a princess of Gaul, said to have been the ancestress of the Gauls of Alesia, and hence of all the Gallic race, by her brief union with Heracles. He passed through that region, and founded Alesia, on his journey to fetch the cattle of Geryon.

Galatea (gal-a-tē′a). In mythology, a sea-nymph, the daughter of Nereus and Doris, who frolicked on the shores of Sicily near

Mount Aetna. She was loved by Polyphemus, the one-eyed Cyclops, who pursued her constantly, singing of his love for her and of the gifts he could offer her. But Galatea loved the handsome and youthful son of Faunus and a sea-nymph. He was Acis, and she gave him the love Polyphemus so ardently desired. One day as Polyphemus was playing love songs about Galatea on his shepherd's pipe, he chanced upon her, lying in the arms of Acis. In a rage he attacked them. Galatea plunged into the sea to escape, momentarily abandoning her lover, and Polyphemus hurled a huge stone at Acis and crushed him. Galatea, returning in search of Acis, caused the rock which covered him to crack open, and from the cleft the blood of Acis flowed out and was transformed into the river which bears his name.

Galatea. In mythology, a beautiful ivory statue, made by the sculptor Pygmalion, son of Belus, who lived on the island of Cyprus. He fell in love with his work of art and asked Aphrodite, at a festival in honor of the goddess, to give him a wife like the statue. Flames leaped up from the altar to show that the goddess had heard his plea, and when he returned home and kissed the statue it came to life. As the wife of Pygmalion, Galatea bore Paphus and Metharme.

Galatea. In Greek legend, Cretan mother of a daughter (called Leucippus) who brought the girl up disguised in boy's garments in order to deceive her husband who had ordered that the child be killed at birth if it were a girl. Eventually Galatea and Leucippus took refuge in the temple of Leto. Galatea prayed that her daughter might be changed into a boy, and the transformation took place. This same story is told by Ovid, in the *Metamorphoses,* of Telethusa, whose daughter Iphis was transformed by the help of Io to a young man.

Galatea. Character in Vergil's third eclogue. She hid herself among the willows in order to be followed. In literature, she is symbolic of coquetry.

Galatia (ga̱-lā′sha̱). In ancient geography, a division of Asia Minor, lying between Bithynia and Paphlagonia on the N, Pontus on the E, Cappadocia and Lycaonia on the S, and Phrygia on the W; originally a part of Phrygia and Cappadocia. It was conquered and settled by a Celtic people which crossed the Hellespont in 278 B.C. It was made a Roman province in 25 B.C. Theodosius subdivided it into Galatia Prima and Galatia Secunda. See also under **Gaul.**

Galba (gal′ba̱), **Servius Sulpicius.** Roman emperor (68–69). He was born c3 B.C. near Tarracina; died at Rome, Jan. 15, 69 A.D. The son of an aristocratic and ancient Roman house, he claimed descent from Jupiter on the one hand, and from Pasiphaë, wife of King Minos of Crete, on the other. Various omens foretold his future role as emperor. During the reign of Tiberius it was predicted that he would become emperor when he was an old man. Tiberius, who expected to be safely dead by that time, was unmoved by the prediction and did not interfere with Galba's career. He took part in public affairs and, though still under the legal age, was made praetor (20 A.D.). While holding that office he had charge of the Games, at which, it is said, he introduced the spectacle of tight-rope-walking elephants. He was next appointed governor of the province of Aquitania for a year, and in 33 served as consul for six months. Under Caligula he became governor of Greater Germany and acquitted himself well, raising the standard of discipline and repelling a barbarian raid into Gaul (39). When Caligula was murdered (41) Galba was urged to make himself emperor. He won the favor of Claudius by refusing, and served the emperor well. In 45 he was named proconsul of Africa for two years. He restored order there and won a great reputation for his justice. On his return to Rome he received great honors. Nevertheless, he went into virtual retirement, apparently in fear of his life for, according to Suetonius, he never went anywhere during this period without a second conveyance that carried 10,000 gold pieces—to tide him over in case sudden flight became necessary. In his retirement at Fundi he was offered the governorship of Hispania Tarraconensis (Tarragonian Spain) by the emperor Nero and accepted it (60). He at first set about administering his office with vigor. Then, lest he win the disfavor of Nero by winning too great renown as an administrator and thus appearing as a possible rival, he became less active and careless in his duties. Even so, Nero feared him and

gave a secret order for his assassination. By
chance Galba discovered it. Shortly afterward, revolt broke out in Gaul, and he joined
the insurrection of Caius Julius Vindex (68),
and declared himself governor of all Spain,
in the name of the Roman Senate and the
Roman people. He accepted the title of
commander-in-chief, began to raise an army,
and announced his rebellion against Nero.
His acts, according to Suetonius, were supported by propitious omens: a ring with a
stone, engraved with an image of Victory
raising a trophy, was found in the city where
he made his headquarters; a ship carrying
arms, but with no living person aboard,
drifted ashore at Tortosa. Just as it appeared
that his rebellion might fail through defec-
tions and the death of Vindex, news came
from Rome that Nero was dead and that the
praetorians had revolted and come out in
his favor. Galba at once assumed the title
of Caesar, and cruelly punished those who
had resisted his rebellion. Arrived at Rome
he soon lost the support of the Senate and
the moderates. He removed many traditional
privileges and immunities, savagely punished
innocent men and protected his infamous
friends. His unpopularity at once became apparent; the army violently opposed him because he refused to carry out a promise of
gifts to the soldiers. The people opposed
him for his miserliness. The soldiers in Germany refused to swear allegiance to him.
Thinking it was because he had no son (his
wife and two sons had died and he had long
refused to consider remarriage) he adopted
Calpurnius Piso Frugi Licinianus as his successor. But Marcus Salvius Otho, an early
supporter, had hoped to succeed him, and
now organized a revolt among the praetorians
and marched against Galba. On false news
that the rebels had surrendered, Galba went
out to meet them, and was attacked in the
Forum. Some say he realized his attackers
meant to kill him, and bared his throat to
their swords. No one came forward to defend him. His body was left where he was
slain. The remains of his mutilated body
were eventually buried in his own garden.

Galen (gā′lẹn). [Latin, **Claudius Galenus**.]
Greek physician and philosophical writer,
born at Pergamum, in Mysia, Asia Minor,
c130 A.D. He died c200, greatly esteemed
by his contemporaries. His father Nicon was
a mathematician and an architect, who saw
to it that his son was well-educated. He
completed his studies in philosophy in his
native city, and began studying medicine at
about the age of 16, traveling and furthering
his studies in Smyrna, Corinth, and Alexandria. He returned (157) to Pergamum and
took the post of surgeon to the gladiators
there for the purpose of increasing his knowledge by treating their many and varied
wounds. He went (162) to Rome, where
he lectured on anatomy and became a much-
sought-after physician. After a few years
he was compelled to leave Rome by the attacks of his rivals and traveled in Greece and
Asia, returning to Pergamum in 169. From
there he was summoned to Rome by the
emperor Marcus Aurelius. The emperor
wanted Galen to accompany him on his expedition against the Germans, but Galen did
not go, remaining in Rome as the attending
physician to the emperor's son Commodus.
He worked at Rome for some time, and apparently eventually returned to Pergamum.
Galen was a prolific writer and is credited
with some 500 works, on medicine, logic,
grammar, ethics, philosophy, and literature;
he wrote on comedy and prepared commentaries on Plato and Aristotle. His medical
writings included all branches of medicine:
anatomy, physiology, pathology, pharmacology, and treatment, and were translated
widely, into Arabic, Hebrew, and Syriac. So
extensive were his writings, and so widely
imitated, or rather so often were works falsely
attributed to him, that Galen himself wrote a
descriptive catalogue of his writings, *De
Propriis Libris*. Some 100 treatises known to
be, or considered, genuine are extant. Galen's
work in medicine and physiology remained
the standard for more than 1000 years until
it was upset, in the 16th century and after,
by the work of such men as Harvey. The
reason for its long life was Galen's method
of accurate observation; his facts, derived
from experimental data, were accurate, but
since his experiments were not performed on
human beings, some inaccuracies were present.

Galeus (gā′lẹ̄-us). In mythology, a lizard,
the son of Apollo. The Galeotae, soothsayers

of Sicily, declared that Galeus was their ancestor.

Galinthias (ga-lin'thi-as), or **Galanthis** (-this), or **Galen** (gā'len). In Greek mythology, a faithful handmaid of Heracles' mother Alcmene. Hera conspired with Ilithyia and the Moerae to delay the birth of Heracles for nine days and nights, the Moerae sitting outside the door with knees crossed and hands clasped in sympathetic magic. Galinthias, to help Alcmene end her long labor, mendaciously announced to the waiting goddesses that the birth had taken place. At this news they jumped up, uncrossing their legs and unclenching their hands, thus breaking the spell, and Heracles was born. Galinthias laughed at the goddesses she had tricked and Ilithyia seized her by the hair and changed her into a weasel and, according to some accounts, because she had lied about the birth of Heracles, she was condemned to bear her young through her mouth. Later Hecate pitied her and made her one of her handmaidens, and Heracles erected a shrine for her at Thebes.

Gallic Wars (gal'ik). Name usually applied to Julius Caesar's military campaigns while he was proconsul (58–51 B.C.) of Cisalpine and Transalpine Gaul. He repulsed the Helvetii as they came over the Alps, pursued them to Bibracte, where he defeated them, and then routed their king, Ariovistus. In 57 B.C. he subdued the Belgic tribes, and in 56 he defeated the Veneti. In 55 B.C. he threw back a German invasion and crossed the Rhine by erecting a bridge near Cologne. In 54 B.C. he invaded Britain for the second time, having previously landed in Kent, and in 53 B.C. he crushed a Belgian revolt, crossed the Alps in the dead of winter (regarded as one of his most brilliant exploits), and put down a dangerous revolt in Gaul, led by Vercingetorix. The campaigns are described fully in Caesar's *Commentaries* (*Commentarii de Bello Gallico*), one of the great classics of Latin literature, published in 51 B.C., in seven books (the eighth book being by Aulus Hirtius, one of Caesar's lieutenants).

Gallipoli (gal-ip'ō-lē). See **Callipolis**.

Gallipoli Peninsula. Modern name of the ancient Chersonesus Thracica, a long tongue of land between the Hellespont and the Gulf of Saros.

Gallus (gal'us). In mythology, a priest of Cybele who emasculated himself in the service of Cybele. From then on it was the usage that these priests should be eunuchs. Their worship consisted essentially of wild and boisterous rites and the name was associated with that of the river Gallus, in Phrygia, whose waters were fabled to make those who drank them mad.

Gallus (gal'us), **Caius Asinius.** Roman politician and writer, consul with C. Marcius Censorianus in 8 B.C. He married Vipsania, formerly wife of Tiberius. He was condemned to death by the Senate (30 A.D.), at the instigation of Tiberius, and died of starvation after an imprisonment of three years. He was a son of C. Asinius Pollio. His works, all of which are lost, included *De Comparatione Patris et Ciceronis,* to which the emperor Claudius replied in his defense of Cicero.

Gallus, Caius Cornelius. Roman poet, orator, general, and politician. He was born at Forum Julii (modern Fréjus), in Gaul, 69 or 66 B.C. He committed suicide in 26 B.C. He supported Octavian, commanded a part of his army at the battle of Actium in 31 B.C., pursued Antony to Egypt, and was made first prefect of Egypt in 30 B.C. He incurred the enmity of Augustus, was deprived of his post, and was exiled by the Senate. Virtually nothing of Gallus' poetry survives, but he was outstanding among the poets of his age for the development of the love elegy. Among others he is said to have influenced Vergil.

Gamelion (ga-mē'li-on). The seventh month of the Attic year. It consisted of 30 days, and corresponded to the latter half of January and the first part of February.

Ganges (gan'jēz). [Hindi, **Ganga;** also, in its upper course, **Bhagirathi.**] Sacred, and greatest, river of India. It rises (under the name of the Bhagirathi) in the Himalayas, near the Tibetan border, and is called the Ganges after its junction with the Alakanada. In its upper course it flows through gorges and mountain valleys, emerging onto its extensive plain at Hardwar. It flows SE across the largest and most densely peopled plain of India, finally emerging upon its great delta of 17,000 square miles where the main stream now enters the Meghna estuary of the Bay of Bengal. At various times it has followed numerous different courses in the delta region, which is traversed by many branching distributaries. Its chief tributaries are the Jumna, Ramganga, Gumti, Gogra, Gandak, Kosi, Atrai, Son, and Jamuna (the main stream of the Brahmaputra). The length of the main stream is 1557 miles. It was formerly navigable from Hardwar, and from Allahabad for larger vessels. It is no longer navigable because of the large amounts of water taken out for irrigation. On it are situated Calcutta, Patna, and many holy places, such as Benares, Allahabad, Hardwar, and Gangotri.

Ganymeda (gan-i-mē′da). Another name for Hebe, handmaiden of the gods. See **Hebe**.

Ganymede (gan′i-mēd) or **Ganymedes** (gan-i-mē′dēz). In Greek mythology, a beautiful Trojan youth, the son of Tros and Callirrhoë. He was transferred to Olympus (according to Homer, by the gods; according to others, by the eagle of Zeus, or by Zeus himself in the form of an eagle, or by Eos, goddess of the dawn, from whom he was taken by Zeus), to become the cup-bearer of the gods, and became immortal. To compensate his father for the loss of his son, Zeus gave Tros a golden vine and two immortal horses which could run like the wind over water or standing grain. Ganymede supplanted Hebe in her function as cup-bearer, his presence in Olympus thus annoying Hera and giving the goddess another reason for hating the Trojans. Ganymede was later regarded as the genius of water, especially of the Nile, and he is represented in the Zodiac by the constellation Aquarius. In Latin the name appears as Catamitus, whence the English term catamite.

Garamas (ga′ra-mas). Another name for Amphithemis, son of Apollo and Acacallis. Also, according to the Libyans, the name of the first man born to Mother Earth.

Garden of the Hesperides. A legendary garden owned by Atlas, on Mount Atlas, either in Mauretania, in the land of the Hyperboreans, or on an island beyond the stream of ocean. In this garden grew the tree with the golden apples, gift to Hera from Mother Earth. It was guarded by the Hesperides, daughters of Atlas, hence the name.

Garganus (gär-gā′nus). A mountain in Apulia. In this mountainous region, according to the

Aeneid, Diomedes built a city after he had been driven out of his home by his wife and her lover when he returned from the Trojan War. The region, a mountainous peninsula projecting into the Adriatic Sea, was later known as Monte Gargano; the highest point is Monte Calvo (3460 feet).

Gargaphia (gär-gā′fi-a), **Vale of.** In Greek mythology, the vale where Actaeon was torn to pieces by his own hounds, after being transformed into a stag in punishment for having seen Artemis bathing. It was used by Jonson as the scene of *Cynthia's Revels*.

Gargaron (gär′ga-ron), **Mount.** [Also: **Mount Gargarus.**] In ancient geography, the highest summit of Mount Ida, Mysia, in what is now NW Turkey.

Gasterocheires (gas″ter-ọ-kī′rēz). In Greek mythology, seven gigantic Cyclopes, who went with Proetus from Lycia, when Proetus and his brother Acrisius divided the kingdom between them, and built the massive walls of Tiryns.

Gate of Italy (it′a-li). Gorge in the Italian Tyrol, in the valley of the Adige River near Rovereto, N Italy.

Gates of Dreams. In Latin mythology, two sets of gates in the Underworld. Through the gates made of horn pass the dreams that are to come true. Through the gates of ivory pass the dreams that are sent to deceive mortals.

Gaugamela (gô-ga-mē′la). In ancient geography, a place in Assyria, near the modern Mosul, the scene of Alexander's victory (331 B.C.) over Darius III of Persia (called the battle of Arbela).

Gaul (gôl). [French, **Gaule**; German, **Gallien**; Italian, Latin, and Portuguese, **Gallia**; Spanish, **Galia**.] In ancient geography, the country of the Gauls; in an inexact use, France. It was divided into Cisalpine Gaul and Transalpine Gaul, and is often taken as equivalent to Transalpine Gaul. The name Galatia was also sometimes used, specifically Celtic or Roman Galatia. In the later Roman Empire Gaul comprised the dioceses of Spain, Gaul, and Britain, and corresponded to Spain, Portugal, a small strip of Morocco, France, Belgium, Switzerland, the Netherlands and Germany to the Rhine, England, Wales, and the S part of Scotland.

Gaul, Cisalpine. [Latin, **Gallia Cisalpina**,

Gallia Citerior.] In ancient history, that part of Gaul lying on the S side of the Alps. It extended from the Alps S and E. A Roman colony was founded (282 B.C.) at Sena Gallica. Part of the country was reduced between the First and Second Punic Wars, Mediolanum (Milan) and Comum (Como) being captured, and the conquest was completed in 201–191 B.C. It was made a Roman province, and was incorporated (42 B.C.) with Italy.

Gaul, Cispadane. [Latin, **Gallia Cispadana.**] In ancient geography, the part of Cisalpine Gaul S of the Padus (Po) River.

Gaul, Transalpine. [Latin, **Gallia Transalpina.**] In ancient geography, that part of Gaul which lay beyond the Alps (that is, N and NW of the Alps from Rome). It comprised in the Roman period Narbonensis, Aquitania, Lugdunensis, and Belgica. Its ancient inhabitants were Gauls, Iberians, and Germans. Many remains of early inhabitants have been discovered, especially in the center of Gaul (Auvergne, and elsewhere). The Gallic antiquities are especially numerous in the N (Brittany). Some Greek colonies were planted in early times in the S. The Roman settlements were made first in the SE in the end of the 2nd century B.C. Gaul was thoroughly conquered (58–51 B.C.) by Julius Caesar. Augustus divided it into four provinces.

Gaul, Transpadane. [Latin, **Gallia Transpadana.**] In ancient geography, the part of Cisalpine Gaul N of the Padus (Po) River.

Gauls (gôlz). The people of ancient Gaul, described as tall and blond, and classified as Continental Celts. They included not only the Celtic Belgae, but numerous named tribes inhabiting Gaul and extending even into Galatia, Asia Minor, which was settled by them in the 3rd century B.C.

Gaumata (gô-mä′ta̱) or **Gaumates** (-tēz). Median magus. See **Smerdis, False.**

Gaurus (gô′rus). [Modern name, **Monte Barbaro.**] In ancient geography, a mountain in Italy, about seven miles W of Neapolis (Naples). Here, c342 B.C., the Romans under Valerius Corvus defeated the Samnites.

Gaza (gä′za̱). [Also: **Ghazze, Ghazzeh.**] Seaport and important trading place in SW Palestine, near the Mediterranean coast, about 50 miles SW of Jerusalem: one of the five chief cities of the ancient Philistines. The town was taken by Alexander the Great in 332 B.C. after a two-months' siege.

Ge (jē). See **Gaea.**

Gedrosia (jē-drō′zha̱). In ancient geography, a country in Asia, corresponding nearly to the modern Baluchistan and SE Iran. It was bounded on the N by Drangiana and Arachosia, on the E by India, on the S by the Indian Ocean, and on the W by Carmania. It was a province of the Persian Empire, and voluntarily submitted to Alexander the Great when he passed the winter at nearby Seistan (330–329 B.C.). He made it a satrapy with its capital at Pura. On his return journey from India (325 B.C.), Alexander elected to march through the trackless deserts of coastal Gedrosia, to parallel the voyage of Nearchus along the coast. With little water and failing supplies, parched by the heat and exhausted by the shifting sands through which they marched, the army suffered great losses in the wastelands of Gedrosia. Some say the force was reduced to one-quarter its size; others say Alexander lost more men in the desert of Gedrosia to heat, thirst, and exhaustion, than he lost in all his campaigns.

Gegania gens (jē-gā′ni-a̱). In the history of ancient Rome, a patrician house or clan which traced its origin to the mythical Gyas, one of the companions of Aeneas. On the destruction of Alba by Tullus Hostilius it was transplanted to Rome, and rose to considerable distinction in the early period of the republic. Its only recorded cognomen was Macerinus.

Gela (je′lä). [Former name, **Terranova di Sicilia.**] City on the S coast of the island of Sicily. Ancient Gela, on whose site the modern town is built, was founded (689 B.C.) by colonists from Crete under the leadership of Entimus, and by colonists from Rhodes under the leadership of Antiphemus, the two groups having united to found the city. The city, on a hill between the sea and a plain, was named for the nearby Gelas River, called "its own wild river." The Rhodians called the fortified citadel of the new city Lindii, after their own city of Lindus in Rhodes. The colonists adopted Dorian institutions in their new home. About 100 years after the founding of Gela, colonists from the city founded Acragas (Agrigentum), which became the second most important city of ancient Sicily. Under the tryant Hippocrates (died 491 B.C.), Gela flourished and extended its power over Naxos, Zancle, Camarina, and other Greek cities of Sicily. Gelon, who succeeded Hippocrates as tyrant, won control over Syracuse. He moved his court and half the inhabitants of Gela to Syracuse, leaving his brother Hieron in charge of a greatly reduced Gela. Henceforth, Gela which had been the most powerful Greek city in Sicily, gave place to Syracuse. In 405 B.C. the Carthaginians attacked and laid siege to Gela. The inhabitants defended their walls courageously. They appealed to Dionysius the Elder, tyrant of Syracuse, for aid, and he did indeed march out with the apparent intention of helping them to drive off the Carthaginians. However, he seems to have betrayed them, and instead of helping them, he persuaded them to march out under cover of darkness and abandon their city. By the terms of a peace he afterward negotiated with Cathage, Gela fell to the Carthaginians, who destroyed it. Some of the inhabitants afterward moved back and rebuilt it, and it was fortified again by Timoleon in 338 B.C. In 312 B.C. Agathocles, tryant of Syracuse, massacred 4000 of the inhabitants in the course of a war with Carthage, and it was finally destroyed in 282 B.C. by the Mamertines, after which the few remaining inhabitants were transferred to a neighboring town. Remains of temples of the 6th and 5th centuries B.C. have been found at the site, and recent excavations have uncovered long stretches of the 4th century B.C. city walls, with superstructure of mud brick on a socle of carefully fitted ashlar stone masonry, a discovery of extraordinary importance for the history of military architecture. Smaller finds are tastefully displayed in the new museum.

Gelanor (jē-lā′nôr). In Greek legend, a king of Argos. Danaus landed in his kingdom and claimed his throne. Gelanor was persuaded to yield it peacefully to him by an omen: a wolf came boldly down from the hills and attacked a herd of cattle and killed the leading bull. The Argives interpreted this to mean that their leading bull, Gelanor, would be killed by the bold Danaus if he didn't give up his throne. Rather than suffer the fate of the bull, Gelanor gave up his throne.

Geleon (jel′e-on). According to Greek tradition, one of the four sons of Ion. One of the four ancient tribes of Athens was named for him. His brothers were Aegicores, Argades, and Hoples.

Gellius (jel′i-us), **Aulus**. Roman grammarian, born c123 A.D.; fl. in the 2nd century. After receiving an education in rhetoric at Rome he went to Athens to study philosophy. While there he became interested in the Greek writers and read widely in their works. On his return to Rome he wrote *Noctes Atticae*, based on the material he had read and studied in the long evenings in Athens. The work was in 20 books. Of the eighth book only chapter-headings and brief fragments survive. His work is valuable as a conscientious account of all that he could learn about archaic literature and language, laws, philosophy, and natural science.

Gelon (je′lon) or **Gelo** (je′lō). Tyrant of Gela (491 B.C.) and later of Syracuse (485 B.C.), in Sicily; died 478 B.C. He was the son of Deinomenes, a descendant of a noble and priestly family. In the wars against Naxos, Zancle, Leontini, and Syracuse carried on by Hippocrates, tyrant of Gela, Gelon distinguished himself as a general of cavalry. On the death of Hippocrates (491 B.C.), Gelon offered his support to the sons of Hippocrates, but on gaining power from an unwilling people, he swept aside the sons of Hippocrates and made himself tyrant. In 485 B.C. the nobles of Syracuse, who had been driven out by the people, appealed to Gelon for aid. He used their appeal as a pretext for marching against Syracuse, won control of it and made himself master, not only of the common people but of the nobles who had appealed for his aid as well. Gelon moved his court and half the inhabitants of Gela to Syracuse, which possessed great natural advantages for defense and for shipping. He enlarged Syracuse to include a high promontory on the mainland as well as the island of Ortygia, which was the site of the original city, and enclosed both within one great wall from the sea on one side to the inner harbor on the other. A new agora was laid out close to the harbor near the wall and installations for shipping were constructed to utilize the geographical advantages of the enlarged city. To secure inhabitants for his enlarged city he razed the city of Camarina to the ground and moved its inhabitants to Syracuse. New citizens were also drawn from the cities of Megara, a northern neighbor of Syracuse, and Euboea, farther up the coast. The nobles from these places became citizens of Syracuse. The common people were sold into slavery. Gelon was himself of the noble class and, though tolerant of the whims of the populace, he preferred his own class and looked upon the commons as "a thankless neighbor." At his own court he was supported by his brothers Polyzalus and Hieron. Envoys from Athens and Sparta went to seek Gelon's aid in the war that Xerxes was preparing to wage on Greece. According to Herodotus, Gelon offered his assistance on condition that he be made commander of all the Greek forces, or, failing that, if he were made commander either of the land forces or of the fleet. Otherwise he would neither go himself nor send aid. He made this offer, he said, in spite of the fact that the Greeks had refused to help him against the Carthaginians. The Greeks could not accept his conditions and sailed home. As it happened, Gelon was fully engaged in Sicily. He was closely linked by ties of marriage to Theron, tyrant of Acragas. Theron quarreled with Terillus, tyrant of Himera, and drove him out. Terillus sought aid from the Carthaginians, who brought a vast army into Sicily under the command of Hamilcar, to recover Himera for Terillus. Theron besieged in Himera by the Carthaginians, appealed to Gelon for aid. Gelon immediately hastened to his rescue with a large force. By a stratagem he got some of his horsemen into the city. There they found Hamilcar sacrificing at the great altar of Poseidon. They captured and killed him, and set fire to his ships. When Gelon received the signal that they had been successful Gelon marched his army against the land forces of Hamilcar and, after a long and desperate struggle, won a complete victory (480 B.C.). The forces of the Carthaginians were annihilated. Some say this great victory of Gelon's over the Carthaginians fell on the same day as the victory of the Greeks over the Persians at Salamis. By the victory

Gelon repulsed for some time to come the encroachments of the Carthaginians in Sicily. He died 478 B.C., leaving instructions to his brother Polyzalus to marry his widow, Damareta, daughter of Theron, and to share the rule of Syracuse with another brother Hieron.

Gelonus (je-lō′nus). According to Herodotus, a son of Heracles and a fabulous serpent-tailed woman of Scythia. His brothers were Scythes and Agathyrsus. Because he failed to draw Heracles' bow and put on his girdle in a certain way, complying with Heracles' instructions, his mother sent him out of the land.

GEMINI
Pictured according to ancient descriptions

Gemini (jem′i-nī). The third sign of the zodiac—the Twins—which the sun enters about May 21. Also, a zodiacal constellation. It represents the two youths Castor and Pollux, sitting side by side. In the heads of the twins respectively are situated the two bright stars which go by their names—Castor to the west, a greenish star intermediate between the first and second magnitudes; and Pollux to the east, a full yellow star of the first magnitude.

Genetrix (jen′e-triks). An epithet of Venus, meaning "Mother," and applied to her as the mother of the Julian family through her son Aeneas, and thus of all the Romans.

Genetyllis (jen-e̩-til′is). [Also: **Gennaides.**]

In Greek mythology, a goddess, protectress of births, a companion of Aphrodite. The name is also used as an epithet of Aphrodite and of Artemis. In the plural, Genetyllides, it is applied to a body of divinities presiding over childbirth, and attached to the train of Aphrodite.

Genius (jē′ni-us). In Roman mythology, the presiding divinity of a place, person, or thing; a deity attending the individual which determines his character, conduct, and destiny.

Gerania (jẽr-ā′ni-a̱). A mountain in Greece to which Megarus, a son of Zeus, fled when Zeus sent a flood to destroy wicked mankind. Deucalion and Pyrrha also survived the flood, but on Mount Parnassus.

Gerasa (jẽr′a̱-sa̱). [Modern name, **Jerash**.] In ancient geography, a city of the Decapolis, in Palestine, about 56 miles NE of Jerusalem. The site contains many antiquities. The forum, which is oval and 300 feet long, is surrounded by a range of Ionic columns, many of which still stand with their entablature. From it extends a great colonnaded street, intersecting the entire city, and crossed at right angles by another. More than 100 columns still stand along the street. They seem to have formed a series of porticoes with galleries above. Among the remains are those of a great temple, the cella of which (66 by 78 feet) is in great part standing, together with many columns of the peristyle. A theater has 28 tiers of seats still remaining above ground, with one precinction (landing), to which vaulted passages give access. In the back wall of the precinction there are small chambers, perhaps boxes. A gallery surrounds the top of the cavea. A smaller theater on the same site is equally perfect and interesting. Gerasa was important in the early Christian period, and the early churches, incorporated in pagan temples and other structures, are important for understanding the development of church architecture and the history of the early church.

Gerenia (jẽr-ē′ni-a̱). A Laconian town on the border of Messenia. It was formerly called Enope. Nestor lived here for a time, whence his epithet "Gerenian Nestor." He either was brought up here in his childhood, or fled to this place when Pylus was captured by Heracles. To Gerenia, Nestor brought the bones of Machaon, the physician, after the Trojan War, and at the tomb and sanctuary of Machaon in Gerenia, men were cured of diseases.

Gergovia (jẽr-gō′vi-a̱). In ancient geography, a Gallic town, situated in the region known today as the Plateau de Gergovie, S of what is now Clermont-Ferrand, France. Caesar besieged it (52 B.C.), and was defeated here by Vercingetorix. There are some relics on the site.

Germania (jẽr-mā′ni-a̱). In ancient geography, the region included between the Mare Germanicum (North Sea), Mare Suevicum (Baltic Sea), Vistula River, Ister (Danube) River, and Rhenus (Rhine) River (from near Mainz to near Emmerich); often extended to include certain territories W of the Rhenus. In the first sense it was never a part of the Roman Empire.

Germanicus (jẽr-man′i-kus). See **Claudius I.**

Germanicus. See **Drusus, Nero Claudius.**

Germanicus, Claudius Tiberius. Original name of **Britannicus.**

Germanicus Julius Caesar (sē′zar). Roman general, born 15 B.C.; died near Antioch, Oct. 9, 19 A.D. He was the son of Nero Claudius Drusus and Antonia the Younger, and was the nephew of the emperor Tiberius, by whom he was adopted. Germanicus was a noble example of the finest Roman traits: he was handsome, brave, kind, and possessed of a gift for winning the respect and devotion of his troops, his relatives, and the Roman people. He was skilled in Greek and Roman oratory and letters and translated Greek works into Latin. His modest manner of living endeared him to the common people. His care to make sacrifices at the tombs of famous men emphasized his own humility and piety. His personal qualities so endeared him to Augustus that the latter had considered, some say, making Germanicus his heir, but decided instead on Tiberius and ordered him to adopt Germanicus. Added to his other qualities was great military ability. While still under the legal age for such offices he served as quaestor and as consul. He was in Germany with his troops when news of the death of Augustus arrived (14 A.D.). His devoted troops would have proclaimed him emperor in place of Tiberius, but he was loyal and forbade them to do so. The Senate appointed him commander of the forces in Germany. He conducted three campaigns against the Germans (14–16 A.D.), and in the latter year defeated Arminius in a great battle on the Campus Idistavisus between what are now Minden and Hameln, Germany. His successes and his popularity roused the jealousy of Tiberius and he was recalled, but the wild acclamation of the crowd at the triumph he was awarded at Rome (17 A.D.) did nothing to dispel the fears and jealousy of Tiberius. In 18 A.D. he was placed in command of the forces in the East and went there to restore order. He defeated the king of Armenia and reduced Cappadocia to the status of a province. He was taken ill at Antioch and died there, 19 A.D. His body was found to be covered with dark splotches and poison was suspected. It was said that Cnaeus Piso, the governor of Syria, poisoned him at the request of Tiberius. When his body was cremated, some say, his heart was not consumed. This was considered confirmation that he had been poisoned, for a heart steeped in poison was thought to be proof against fire. When news of his death reached Rome the people were wild with grief: temples were stoned, altars were overturned, and heads of families threw the household gods into the streets. Even the barbarians, both those fighting among themselves and those fighting against Rome, ceased fighting to mourn him. Cnaeus Piso was condemned to death by the Senate when he returned to Rome. Germanicus was married to Agrippina, the daughter of Marcus Vipsanius Agrippa and Julia, the daughter of Augustus. She bore him nine children, two of whom died in infancy and a third in early childhood. Of the remaining children who survived him, Agrippina the Younger became the mother of the emperor Nero; two other daughters, Drusilla and Livilla, led

HERACLES AND TRIPLE-BODIED GERYON
Black-figured Attic amphora, Exekias, 550–525 B.C. Eurytion lies wounded, his name written backwards over his shoulder; Heracles' name appears off his forehead; Geryon's name is inscribed along his legs; Exekias has put his signature under Heracles' raised arm. *Louvre*

notoriously immoral lives; his two sons, Nero and Drusus, were executed as public enemies during the reign of Tiberius, and his third son, Caius, became the emperor Caligula.

Gerrha (jer′a). [Also: **Gerra.**] In ancient geography, a city of Arabia Felix, situated on the Persian Gulf. It was important in the 7th and 6th centuries B.C., under the Assyrians, Babylonians, and Persians.

Geryon (jē′ri-on, ger′i-on) or **Geryones** (jē-rī′ō-nēz). In Greek mythology, a monster with three heads or three bodies and powerful wings, dwelling in the island of Erythea in the far west; son of Chrysaor and Callirrhoë. He possessed a large herd of red cattle guarded by Eurytion (his shepherd) and the two-headed dog Orthus. To carry away these cattle was the tenth labor of Heracles, which he successfully performed, after killing the shepherd, the dog, and Geryon himself. According to a later account, Chrysaor was a renowned king in Iberia, the father of three brave sons who were symbolized in the three-headed Geryon. When Heracles went there to steal the cattle the three sons headed three forces against him. Heracles separated them and killed Chrysaor's three sons.

Getae (jē′tē). Ancient tribal people formerly inhabiting Dacia, which corresponds approximately to what is now Rumania. They were so called by the Greeks; the Romans called them Daci.

Giants, Gigantes (ji-gan′tēz). In Greek mythology, an earth-born race which sprang from the blood of Uranus when he was mutilated by his son Cronus. From the drops of blood which fell on Phlegra in Attica, 24 sons were born to Gaea (Earth). They had the bodies of serpents and the heads of men. Gaea, and their own rage because Zeus had banished the Titans to Tartarus, inspired them to wage war on the gods. Armed with tree trunks and rocks, they attacked Olympus. The war was frightful. Hera prophesied that only a mortal, wearing a lion's skin and protected by a magic herb, would be able to slay the Giants. Zeus sent Athena to Heracles. While Eos, Helius, and Selene, as commanded by Zeus, ceased to pour their light on the world, Athena helped Heracles find the herb and brought him to the battle. The gods succeeded in wounding many of the Giants but only Heracles could deliver the death blow. Those Giants who were not killed on Olympus fled to Arcadia, near Trapezus, and there, attacked and wounded by the gods, were finished off by Heracles. According to ancient accounts the ground in the region still smoldered from the thunderbolts Zeus hurled at the Giants, and plowmen often turned up huge bones in their fields. Other accounts say the final stand of the Giants took place on the Phlegraean Plain, which borders the Bay of Naples near Cumae in Italy, and that they are buried under mountains there, where they rumble and explode from time to time as volcanos.

Gitiadas (ji-tī′a-das). Greek sculptor and architect who was active in the beginning of the 6th century B.C. Some say he constructed the bronze temple in which the bronze image of Athena was housed in Sparta, and for which reason she was called Athena Chalkioikos, "Of the Bronze House."

Glauce (glô′sē). Another name for Creusa, daughter of Creon, king of Corinth. See **Creusa.**

Glauce. In Greek legend, a daughter of Cychreus, king of Salamis. Telamon, who fled to Salamis after the death of his brother, Phocus, married her and succeeded her father as king of Salamis. She died and he married Periboea.

Glaucia (glô′sha). In Greek legend, a daughter of the Trojan river-god Scamander. When Heracles attacked Troy and sacked it Deimachus, one of his companions who had been Glaucia's lover, was killed. She sought protection and Heracles took her back to Hellas with him. She bore Deimachus' son, whom she named Scamander. Heracles later made him a king in Boeotia, where he renamed the Inachus River Scamander, after himself.

Glaucus (glô′kus). In Greek legend, a son of Hippolochus and grandson of Bellerophon. He was a captain of the Lycians, allies of Troy in the Trojan War, a valiant hero, and the close friend and cousin of Sarpedon. He met Diomedes face to face in combat, and in response to Diomedes' challenge, said that as a grandson of Bellerophon he would fight anyone. On learning of his ancestry Diomedes planted his spear in the ground. He recalled that his own grandfather, Oeneus, was a close friend of Bellerophon, and declared that the grandsons should con-

actor; up, lūte, pull; oi, oil; ou, out; ҭн, then; ḏ as d or j, ş as s or sh, ṭ as t or ch, ẓ as z or zh.

tinue the friendship. As an expression of the ancient friendship he gave his bronze armor to Glaucus. Glaucus, whose wits were addled by Zeus, gave his pure gold armor to Diomedes in return—the classic example of getting the worst of a bargain—and they parted friends. Glaucus accompanied Sarpedon at the siege of the fortifications surrounding the Greek ships and was wounded by Teucer. Later, although wounded, he called on Apollo to help him rescue Sarpedon's body, as his friend had asked with his last breath. Apollo heard his prayer and cured his wound. Glaucus then rallied the Trojans and with them defended Sarpedon's body until it was borne away by Apollo. Later, when fighting for possession of Achilles' body, Glaucus was slain by Telamonian Ajax. His body was rescued by Aeneas and taken to Troy, from whence it was borne to Lycia by Apollo, for funeral rites.

Glaucus. A fabled fisherman of Boeotia, one of the Argonauts. According to some accounts, he was a son of Poseidon, or of Anthedon, who saw a dead fish that was laid on a certain grass come back to life again. Glaucus ate some of the grass and, leaping into the sea, was transformed into a sea-god and became an attendant of Poseidon. Among many others, he loved the sea-nymph Scylla. Circe, or perhaps it was Amphitrite, who also loved Glaucus, changed Scylla into a hideous sea-monster out of jealousy that she had won Glaucus' love. Glaucus had the gift of prophecy, and is represented in the *Aeneid* as the father of Deïphobe, a priestess of Apollo and Trivia at Cumae—the Cumaean Sibyl.

Glaucus. In Greek legend, a son of Minos, king of Crete, and Pasiphaë. While still a child he disappeared one day and could not be found. His parents at last consulted the oracle at Delphi and were told that whoever could give the best comparison concerning a heifer that changed its color three times a day would find that lost child. Polyidus, an Argive descendant of the seer Melampus, compared the changing colors of the heifer—from white to red to black—with a ripening mulberry, which follows the same color changes. Minos thereupon ordered him to find Glaucus and he at length did find

him, drowned in a vat of honey. Minos then told him that since he had found the child he must now restore him to life, and locked him in a tomb with the dead child. As Polyidus, in despair, sat in the tomb, he saw a snake crawl into the crypt and approach the body of Glaucus. Polyidus killed it with his sword. Presently the serpent's mate crawled up and deposited a magic herb on the dead snake, whereupon the dead snake slowly came to life. Polyidus seized the herb and laid it on the body of Glaucus, where it had the same miraculous results. He and the restored Glaucus were released from the tomb and Minos, in his joy at finding his son alive, gave Polyidus rich gifts and asked him to teach the art of divination to Glaucus. Polyidus did as he was commanded, but just before he sailed from Crete to return home to Argos, he asked Glaucus to spit into his open mouth. Glaucus did so and immediately forgot all Polyidus had told him about divination. Apparently spitting into the mouth of the teacher was the time-tested way to make the pupil forget what his master had taught him.

Glaucus. In Greek legend, a son of Sisyphus and Merope. He lived near Thebes and was the father of Bellerophon. Glaucus refused to let his mares breed, on the theory that they were better racing horses if they did not breed, and so offended Aphrodite. She punished him by feeding his mares on a magic herb, hippomanes, which drove them mad. When Glaucus harnessed them to his chariot for the race at the funeral games for Pelias, they became frenzied, overthrew the chariot, and plunged Glaucus to the ground. They then tore their master to pieces and devoured his flesh.

Glaucus. According to Herodotus, a Spartan known for his justice and integrity. His reputation for honesty was so widespread that a man of Miletus came to him and asked him to keep a sum of money which he had brought with him. He gave Glaucus certain tokens, with instructions that he should turn over the money left in his keeping to those who would bring him matching tokens. Glaucus agreed to take care of his money and to give it to the bearers of matching tokens. Many years later the sons of the Milesian came to Glaucus. They brought with them matching tokens, and asked for the money their father had deposited with him. Glaucus claimed he had no recollection at all of such a matter. However, he advised the Milesians to return after four months, in case his memory should be refreshed. The Milesians departed, convinced that they would never see their money. Glaucus went to the oracle at Delphi and asked whether he should swear he had never received the money and keep it. The priestess answered he might as well do as he wished, for those who keep their oaths die ultimately, even as do the false-swearers. But—the priestess warned Glaucus—the god of oaths has a son who would surely take vengeance on a perjuror by destroying all his offspring, whereas oath-keeping men leave flourishing offspring behind them. Glaucus, acknowledging the rebuke, instantly apologized to the priestess for asking such a question. However, the priestess replied that to entertain such a thought as perjury and to ask the oracle to confirm him in his plan was as bad as if he had actually done the deed, and the priestess sent him away. Glaucus recalled the Milesians and gave them their money. But the inevitable consequences foretold by the priestess because he had entertained the notion of perjury overtook him: not a single descendant of Glaucus survived in Sparta.

Glaucus. Greek sculptor in metals; fl. c6th century B.C. He lived at Chios but belonged to the Samian school of art. He is said to have been the inventor of the art of welding iron.

Glaucus of Rhegium (rē′ji-um). Greek writer of the late 5th century B.C. He wrote a book about poets in which he gave the names and dates of poets, described their styles, and what poets influenced them. He began his listing of poets with Orpheus who, he said, "admired nobody, because at that time there was nobody."

Glenus (glē′nus). According to Greek legend, a son of Heracles and Deianira.

Glessariae (gle-sā′ri-ē). In ancient geography, a chain of islands stretching from the Rhenus (Rhine) to the estuary of the Albis (Elbe), noted for the abundance of amber found there. They were sometimes called the Electrides after the islands in Greek legend, and also the Amber Islands.

Glycera (glis′e-ra). Name of several notorious Greek courtesans; in particular, a mistress of Menander, and a favorite of Horace.

Glycon of Athens (glī′kon, ath′enz). Greek sculptor; fl. about the 1st century B.C. He made the Farnese Hercules, which was found in the Baths of Caracalla in 1540 with an inscription by Glycon. It was probably executed in the 1st century B.C. and is a copy of a Heracles by Lysippus.

Gnomic Poets (nō-mik). Collective name applied to a group of Greek poets, active about the 6th century B.C., whose works are characterized by moral teachings and maxims on life. Although the list included in this title varies, the elegiac writers Solon, Theognis, Simonides of Ceos, and Phocylides are generally included.

Gnossus or **Gnosus** (nos′us). See **Cnossus.**

Gnosticism (nos′ti-sizm). A term applied to a religious philosophy of salvation, or rather a group of philosophies, widely spread throughout the Orient (Egypt, Syria, Persia) in the early centuries of the Christian era, growing out of the Hellenistic epistemologies but emphasizing the importance of divine revelation. Some Gnostics at first considered themselves members of the Christian community. They acknowledged the Godhead of Christ, but presently introduced elements of secrecy, mysticism, and superstition which proved incompatible with Christian theology; eventually they broke away to form a number of splinter sects. The most important were those established by Simon Magus, in Syria, and Manes (or Mani) in Persia. The latter founded the Manichaean sect which became indeed a distinct faith and in which Zoroastrian and Christian beliefs were fused. Voluminous Gnostic writings in Greek, Latin, Coptic, Syriac, and Armenian have survived, and a recent sensational find at Chenoboskion in Egypt yielded 13 bound codices containing some 40 new Gnostic texts. Gnosticism in its various manifestations lost ground before the spread of Christianity and Mohammedanism, but in Middle Asia Manichaeanism survived throughout most of the first millennium. (JJ)

Gobryas (gō′bri-as). Persian noble. He was one of the seven conspirators who, according to Herodotus, procured the death of Smerdis the Magian (the False Smerdis) in 521 B.C. and raised Darius I to the throne.

Golden Age, The. According to Hesiod's account of the Creation, this was the period of the first race of men, who lived during the reign of Cronus. There were no women in the Golden Age. Men lived like gods. They knew neither sorrow nor toil, old age nor sickness. It was a period of patriarchal simplicity, when the earth yielded its fruits spontaneously and spring was eternal. When it was time for men to leave the earth, Death came gently and led them off in a peaceful sleep.

Golden Apples of the Hesperides. In Greek mythology, Gaea presented Hera with the tree which bore the golden apples as a wedding gift. The tree was planted in a garden in the remote West, on Mount Atlas in Mauretania, or in the land of the Hyperboreans, or perhaps on an island beyond the stream of Ocean. It was guarded by the Hesperides, daughters of Atlas, or of Hesperus, the evening star or the personification of the West or of sunset, and by the 100-headed, sleepless dragon Ladon. As one of his labors, Heracles fetched the golden apples to Eurystheus, but as it was unlawful for a mortal to possess the apples they were restored to the garden through the good offices of Athena. In one version Heracles prevails upon the giant Atlas, who holds the sky on his shoulders, to wade out across Ocean and fetch the apples for him while Heracles holds the sky in his stead. This incident is an occasional subject of Greek art, as on one of the metopes of the temple of Zeus at Olympia.

Golden Ass, The. [Alternative and original title, **Metamorphoses**.] Romance of a fantastic and satirical character, by Apuleius, written in the 2nd century A.D.; probably his earliest work. It was said to have imitated a portion of the dialogue, *Lucius or the Ass*, of Lucian. The best-known episode in it is that of Cupid and Psyche, which was taken from a popular legend or myth. Some of the adventures of Don Quixote and of Gil Blas are drawn from this source, and Boccaccio used many of the comic episodes. The author relates the story in his own person. His dabbling in magic results in his transformation into an ass, a form in which, however, he retains his human intelligence.

Golden Bough, The. The mistletoe. The Cumaean Sibyl told Aeneas to find the Golden Bough if he wished to visit the Underworld, for only with it in his possession would Charon allow him to pass the Styx. The Golden Bough would serve him as a passport to the Underworld as it was sacred to Proserpina (Persephone).

Golden Fleece, The. The fleece of pure gold taken from the winged ram which Hermes sent to snatch Phrixus and Helle away from the altar as they were about to be sacrificed. The ram flew with them to Colchis but as they crossed the Hellespont Helle fell into the sea which has since borne her name. Phrixus arrived safely in Colchis and sacrificed the ram, as instructed, to Zeus. The Fleece was hung up in Colchis and guarded by a dragon. It was recovered from King Aeëtes by the Argonautic expedition under Jason, with the help of Medea, the daughter of King Aeëtes. Modern travelers have reported that in the Caucasus gold dust is obtained by staking fleeces in the river gravels, which after some weeks are lifted out, dried and burned, leaving as residue the gold which had clung to the wool, and suggesting a possible origin for the oriental phase of the legend.

Golden Horn. Inlet of the Bosporus, in European Turkey, forming the harbor of Istanbul, and separating Pera and Galata from the main part of Istanbul. Length, about five miles.

Golden House. Palace of Nero in Rome, which occupied the valley between the Palatine and Esquiline hills, and connected the palaces of the Caesars with the gardens of Maecenas. It was built after the great fire of 64 A.D., and was so large that it contained porticoes 2800 feet long and enclosed a lake where the Flavian Amphitheater ("Colosseum") now stands. The forecourt contained a colossus of Nero 120 feet high. The profuse splendor of this residence is described by Suetonius and Tacitus. It was further adorned by Otho, but the remains are scanty, as most of its site was restored to public use by the Flavian emperors, who built on it the Flavian Amphitheater and the baths of Titus.

Golden Mount, The. Name applied to the

fat, fāte, fär, fãre, errạnt; net, mē, hėr ardẹnt; pin, pīne; not, nōte, mŏve, nôr,

Janiculan Hill of Rome with reference to its yellow sand composition.

Golden Verses. Greek verses attributed to the school of Pythagoras, a condensation of the morals drawn by earlier epics.

Gongylus (gon'ji-lus). Corinthian captain who reached Syracuse (414 B.C.) before Gylippus, and urged the Syracusans not to give up their resistance to the Athenians, and encouraged them with the news that help from Corinth and a Spartan general, Gylippus, were on the way. The Syracusans persisted in their resistance to Athens as he advised.

Gonippus (go-ni'pus) and **Panormus** (pa-nôr'mus). According to Pausanias, two Messenian youths who impersonated the Dioscuri. During the Second Messenian War with Sparta they dressed themselves in white tunics, purple cloaks and egg-shaped caps and rode into the Spartan camp, where a feast of the Dioscuri was being celebrated. The Spartans thought the gods had come among them and fell down and worshiped them. Gonippus and Panormus rode into their midst, slew many with their, spears, and then galloped off to Andania. From that time forward the Dioscuri hated the Messenians and signally aided the Spartans in the war.

Good Fame or **Good Repute.** Goddess, usually identified with Artemis. There was an altar and an image of the goddess of Good Repute in the market-place of every town in Boeotia and Locris. An image of her was also in the market-place at Corinth.

Gordian Knot. A knot tied by Gordius in the cord that connected the pole and the yoke of the ox-cart in which he was riding when he or his son Midas was chosen king of Phrygia. It was so intricate as to defy all attempts to untie it; and the oracle of the temple in which the cart was preserved declared that whoever should succeed in undoing it would became master of Asia. Alexander the Great solved the difficulty by cutting the knot with his sword, and the oracle was fulfilled.

Gordium (gôr'di-um). In ancient geography, a town in N Galatia, Asia Minor, near the river Sangarius (Sakarya). It is noted as the capital of the Phrygian kingdom of the 8th and 7th centuries B.C. In the neighborhood are many large burial mounds, one of which, recently excavated by a University of Pennsylvania expedition, proved to contain an intact royal burial, one of the most important post-war archaeological discoveries. Also exhibited at Gordium was the intricate Gordian Knot, which Alexander solved by cutting through it with his sword. (JJ)

Gordius (gôr'di-us). According to tradition, a Phrygian peasant who became king. One day as he was driving his ox-cart a royal eagle settled on the pole and remained there as he drove along. He made for the city of Telmessus where there was a famous oracle, but as he came to the gate of the city he was met by a prophetic maiden who noted the eagle on the pole of the cart and told him to make sacrifices to Zeus at once. He consented to do so if she would marry him. She agreed to do this as soon as the sacrifices were made. In the meantime the king of Phrygia died, and the oracle told the Phrygians that their new king was approaching with his bride in an ox-cart. As the Phrygians debated in the market-place Gordius arrived in his ox-cart. The Phrygians, noting the eagle and the maiden, at once proclaimed him king. Gordius dedicated his cart, together with the yoke which was fixed to it with an intricate knot, to Zeus. It was afterward deposited in the temple at Gordium, a city founded by Gordius, and the oracle pronounced that he who could untie the knot joining the yoke and the ox-cart would become lord of all Asia. The cart and yoke were guarded in the temple for centuries. To this place came Alexander the Great. He looked at the knot, heard the oracular pronouncement concerning it, and with one stroke of his sword cut right through the knot.

Gorgias (gôr'ji-as). Greek rhetorician and sophist, born at Leontini, Sicily, c485 B.C. He lived to be about 100 years old and died at Larissa, in Thessaly, 376 B.C. In 427 B.C. he went to Athens to ask for aid for his native city against the Syracusans. His eloquence won him great esteem as well as success in the object of his journey, and he went home. Later he returned to Athens and traveled about Greece teaching the art of rhetoric. His object in his teaching was to train his disciples in the art of persuasion, so that they could speak effectively on any subject. He wrote a philosoph-

---

actọr; up, lūte, pu̇ll; oi, oil; ou, out; ᵺ, then; ḍ as d or j, ş as s or sh, ţ as t or ch, ẓ as z or zh.

ical treatise in which he denied that positive knowledge is attainable; hence he confined himself to teaching oratory. Although he doubted if he could teach anything, claiming only that he was a good speaker, he won many disciples. He made speeches at Athens, Delphi, and Olympia, among others, which were published and by which the art of rhetoric was spread throughout Greece. Two exercises in rhetoric are extant which are attributed to him on doubtful grounds. One of Plato's *Dialogues* is named for him.

Gorgo (gôr′gō). Daughter and only child of Cleomenes, king of Sparta (c519–c487 B.C.). As a child she advised her father to send away the Samian who was trying to bribe him to go to the aid of Samos lest the Samian, who kept increasing his offer, corrupt her father. Gorgo married Leonidas, the half-brother of Cleomenes. It is said that before the outbreak of the Persian War Demaratus, co-king of Sparta who had been deposed by Cleomenes and had fled to Susa, sent a message warning the Spartans that Xerxes was preparing to march against Greece. He dared not send a message openly, so wrote it on a tablet which he then covered with wax. The tablet which the messenger presented to the Spartans thus appeared to be blank. Gorgo suggested that they scrape the wax off the tablet and they would surely find writing underneath. Her suggestion was acted upon and the message of warning from Demaratus was found.

Gorgoneion (gôr-gō-nī′on). A mask of the Gorgon or the head of Medusa as an attribute of Athena, who bore it on her breast in the midst of her aegis, and also on her shield.

Gorgons (gôr′gonz). In Greek mythology, three daughters of Ceto and Phorcys (whence they are called Phorcides) dwelling in the Western Ocean near Night and the Hesperides (in later mythology, in Libya). They had originally been beautiful maidens but were transformed into such horrible winged monsters, with coiling serpents for hair, brazen claws, and staring eyes, that all who looked upon them were turned to stone. Their names were Stheno, Euryale, and Medusa. Medusa, the only one of the three who was mortal, was slain by Perseus.

Gorgophone (gôr-gof′ō-nē). In Greek legend, the daughter of Perseus and Andromeda.

She married Perieres, king of Messenia and son of Aeolus, and had two sons: Aphareus and Leucippus. When Perieres died she married Oebalus, king of Sparta, and bore him two sons: Tyndareus and Icarius. According to some accounts, she was the first widow to remarry, as it was the custom up to then for women to commit suicide on the death of their husbands.

Gorgythion (gôr-jith′i-on). In Homeric legend *(Iliad)*, a Trojan, a son of Priam. He was slain by one of Teucer's arrows when Teucer was attempting to kill Hector.

Gortyna (gôr-tī′na). [Also: **Gortyn.**] In ancient geography, an important Dorian city in S central Crete, near Mount Ida. According to legend, Zeus, in the form of a white bull, landed near here after swimming the sea with Europa on his back. Traditionally founded by Gortys, son of Rhadamanthys, Gortyna was an important center of Cretan civilization, second only to Cnossus. After the Roman conquest Gortyna replaced Cnossus as the leading city of Crete. It became the capital of the Roman province of Crete and Cyrenaica when the island was subdued by the Romans in 66 B.C. The famous Gortynian Code was discovered here in 1862 and 1884. Nearby are the remains of a temple of Pythian Apollo, the earliest parts of which

GORGON
From the west pediment of the Temple of Artemis, beginning of the 6th century B.C.
Corfu

fat, fāte, fär, fãre, errant; net, mē, hèr ardent; pin, pīne; not, nōte, möve, nôr,

date from the 7th century B.C., and a temple of Isis from the era of Greco-Roman civilization. Attached to the latter is a small crypt that seems to have played some part in the rites of initiation into the mysteries of Isis. Also at Gortyna are the remains of a basilica of St. Titus, companion of St. Paul, who brought Christianity to the island and became the first bishop of Gortyna. His grave is said to be nearby.

Gortynian Inscription (gôr-tin′i-an). An extensive and famous law code, found at Gortyna in Crete, a small part in 1862 and the rest in 1884. It dates from the 5th century B.C., although it contains references to laws of the 6th and 7th centuries B.C. It was inscribed, in the Cretan dialect of Greek, in ten great tables on a marble wall, in the "Boustrophedon" or "Ox-plough" script. In this script the first line is written from left to right, the succeeding line begins at the right and goes to the left, and so on, in the same manner as the ox draws the plow back and forth across a field. The Romans enclosed the wall on which the inscription appears in an arcade, where it may be seen today on the inner wall. The inscription is of great value as giving what is practically a code of early Greek civil law, prescribing in detail economic and social rules for the preservation of tribal estates and of the state, and, to a considerable extent, the procedures by which the laws were carried out.

Gortys (gôr′tis). According to some accounts, a son of Rhadamanthys of Crete. He inherited land in Crete from his father and the Cretan city of Gortyna is named for him. But some say Gortys was an Arcadian.

Gortys. In Greek legend, a son of Stymphalus. He was said to be the founder of the city of Gortys, in Arcadia, on the river of the same name. Also; a son of Tegeates of Arcadia. Some say this Gortys migrated voluntarily to Crete, and there founded the Cretan city of Gortyna; but the Cretans say Gortyna was founded by their own Gortys, son of Rhadamanthys.

Gournia (gôr′ni-a). In ancient geography, a town on the E end of the island of Crete. Remains uncovered on the site present the only extensive picture of a Minoan village, with private houses and a small palace, to be found on Crete.

Gracchus (grak′us). The distinctive *cognomen* of a branch of the Roman gens Sempronia: especially, the sons of Cornelia, the daughter of Scipio Africanus, and Tiberius Sempronius Gracchus (died 154 B.C.). They were: 1) Tiberius Sempronius Gracchus, born 168 or 163 B.C. He married Claudia, daughter of Appius Claudius, and was the brother-in-law of Scipio Africanus Minor whom he accompanied in his expedition against Carthage (146 B.C.). He was appointed quaestor in 137 B.C., and as such served under the consul Caius Hostilius Mancinus in the Numantine war in Spain. He was elected tribune of the people for 133 B.C. At this period the class of independent farmers of small holdings was rapidly disappearing from Italy. The land was being absorbed by the great estates of the rich and cultivated by slave labor; and the peasantry were forced to seek refuge in the cities, especially Rome, where they swelled the ranks of the unemployed. Gracchus sought to bring about a greater subdivision of the land and to restore the class of independent farmers by reviving, with some modification, the Licinian law, passed in 367 B.C. but allowed to fall into abeyance, which limited the amount of public land that each citizen might occupy. His proposals were carried in the *comitia tributa* in spite of the opposition of his colleague, who was deposed. At the end of his term he tried, contrary to precedent, to secure reelection, and a disturbance arose in consequence, in which he and 300 of his followers were killed. 2) Caius Sempronius Gracchus, younger brother of Tiberius. He served under his brother-in-law Scipio Africanus Minor in Spain, and was quaestor in Sardinia from 126 to 123 B.C., when he was elected tribune of the people. He renewed the agrarian law passed by his brother Tiberius, and brought forward a series of resolutions seeking to undermine the existing aristocratic republican form of government, securing the support of the poorer plebeians of the capital by the regular distribution of grain at the expense of the state. He was reëlected to the tribuneship in 122 B.C., but failed of election in 121 B.C., in consequence of the opposition among all classes to his project of extending the rights of citizenship to the Latins and Italians, and as the result of a campaign by the aristocratic party to discredit him by having one of their henchmen offer even more to the people than Gracchus did. He was killed in a disturbance which ensued in the city in 121 B.C. These two sons of Cornelia—the accomplished Roman woman who answered the boasts of a Roman matron about her jewels by pointing to her sons and saying, "These are my jewels"—were pointed out to Aeneas by Anchises when he visited the latter in the Underworld. Their spirits were awaiting to be born then and their illustrious future had already been decided, according to the *Aeneid*—which was, of course, written long after they had died.

Graces, The Three. In Roman mythology, the Gratiae, personifications of grace and beauty. In Greek mythology, they are the Charites, daughters of Zeus. The names generally given to the Charites are Euphrosyne, Aglaia, and Thalia. In Sparta and in Athens only two were recognized. They were worshiped at Athens, Messene, and elsewhere in Greece, but they had no cult in Rome. See **Charites.**

Graces, The Three. Antique undraped marble group preserved in the Opera del Duomo at Siena, Italy. It is the foundation of many of the Renaissance and modern representations of the subject.

Gradivus (grā-dī′vus). A Roman epithet of Mars, as the god of war.

Graeae (grē′ē). [Also: **Graiae.**] In Greek mythology, three daughters of Ceto and Phorcys. They were sea-goddesses, old from birth, having been born with gray hair. They had but one eye and one tooth between the three of them which they passed back and forth. They were the protectors of the Gorgons, and inhabited a plain in the farthest reaches of Libya, where the light of neither the sun nor the moon ever shone. Perseus visited them to learn where the Gorgon Medusa could be found, and compelled them to give him the information he sought by seizing their only eye and tooth. Their names were Dino, Enyo, and Pemphredo.

Graecia (grē′sha), **Magna.** See **Magna Graecia.**

Graiae (grā′e, grī′ē). See **Graeae.**

Granicus (gra-nī′kus). A small river in Mysia, Asia Minor, flowing into the Propontis (the modern Sea of Marmara or Marmora). It was named by Homer as one of the rivers of the Troad which, after the Trojan War had ended, was diverted from its course by Apollo and Poseidon and sent against the wall which the Greeks had erected to protect their ships, to wash the wall into the sea. On its banks Alexander the Great won (334 B.C.) his first victory over the Persians. See **Rhesus,** river.

Gratiae (grā′shi-ē). A Roman name for the Graces.

Gration (grā′shi-on). In Greek mythology, one of the Giants, son of Gaea and the blood of Uranus, who waged war on the gods. In the battle Artemis wounded him with an arrow and Heracles killed him.

Gratius Faliscus (grā′shus, -shi-us, fa-lis′kus). Roman poet; fl. in the late 1st century B.C. He was the author of a poem on the chase and the management of hunting dogs, entitled *Cynegetica*, parts of which survive. He was called Faliscus because he claimed descent from the ancient Falisci.

Great Eleusinia (el-ū-sin′i-a). The chief annual festival in honor of Demeter and Persephone, celebrated at Athens and Eleusis in September and October.

Great Mother. In ancient mythologies, the goddess of birth and fertility: an almost worldwide concept. Cybele is the Great Mother of ancient Anatolia whose cult spread throughout the whole Mediterranean region. Ishtar was the ancient Babylonian and Assyrian Great Mother; the Sumerian Great Mother was Nana; the Phoenician was Astarte; the Egyptian was Isis. Anahita was the Great Mother of ancient Iranian religion. The Greeks identified Cybele with their Rhea, and later her cult became fused with those of Artemis and Aphrodite. The Romans identified her with Ops and Bona Dea, and later with Venus. The North American Indians also have their mother goddesses, Earth Mothers, Corn Mothers, and others, who are all nature and fertility deities. The ancient Peruvians had the concept; Pachamama was their great Mother Earth. Various other South American Indians also conceive of a great chief deity whom they regard as the common mother of all things. The concept is widespread in primitive African Negro religions. Surinam Negroes worship a Gro Mama, or Great Mother.

fat, fāte, fär, fāre, errant; net, mē, hèr ardent; pin, pīne; not, nōte, möve, nôr,

Greece (grēs). [Modern Greek, **Ellas**; ancient Greek, **Hellas**; Latin, **Graecia**.] In the widest sense the ancient name includes the Greek Colonies in Asia Minor, Sicily, Africa, and elsewhere; in its restricted and more usual meaning it is the peninsula S of the Cambunian Mountains, with the neighboring islands. Peninsular Greece comprised Thessaly, Epirus, Central Greece (including Acarnania, Aetolia, Doris, Western Locris, Eastern Locris, Phocis, Boeotia, Attica, and Megaris), and the Peloponnesus (including Corinthia, Sicyonia, Phliasia, Achaea, Elis, Arcadia, Argolis, Laconia, and Messenia). The chief islands were Crete, Rhodes, Cos, Samos, Chios, Lesbos, Tenedos, Imbrus, Samothrace, Thasus, Lemnos, Scyrus, Euboea, Salamis, Aegina, the Cyclades, Thera, Cythera, and the Ionian Islands (including Zakynthos [Zante], Cephalonia, Ithaca, Leukas, Corcyra [Corfu], and others). Cyprus was sometimes included, and in later times Macedonia and Thrace. The following are some of the more important facts and incidents of ancient Greek history: Dorian invasion of the Peloponnesus (c1100 B.C.); commencement of the hegemony of Sparta (6th century B.C.); Persian wars (500 to c449 B.C.); hegemony transferred to Athens (c477 B.C.); Peloponnesian War (431–404 B.C.); hegemony of Sparta (404–371 B.C.); of Thebes (371–362 B.C.); hegemony of Macedon commenced 338 B.C.; rise of Aetolian League and renewal of Achaean League (c280 B.C.); independence of Greece proclaimed by Flamininus (196 B.C.); final subjection of Greece to Rome (146 B.C.); Greece made (in great part) into the Roman province of Achaea (27 B.C.). Later, Greece formed part of the Byzantine Empire.

Greek Religion. The religion of the Greeks is a composite of beliefs and practices of the original inhabitants (Pelasgians), the Achaeans and other northern invaders, and various people with whom contact was established at different times (Crete, Asia Minor, Egypt, etc.). A strong interplay of various elements is probably responsible for the failure of the Greek religion to become a unified logical system. In addition to gods worshiped throughout Greece, there were many deities and heroes whose shrines were the focal points for local cults. An outstanding feature of the religion is the fact that at the period of its greatest development in Classical Greece, we find innumerable aspects of earlier practices and aspects of ritual which suggest contradictory beliefs being followed at the same time. One explanation for the frequently immoral acts of the gods as related in mythology lies in syncretism, or the attempt to identify the Olympian gods with numerous local divinities of the earlier inhabitants with whom the invading Achaeans came into contact.

The Minoan civilization of Crete (c2500–1500 B.C.) and its counterpart or development at Mycenae (c1500–1100 B.C.) reveal practices and beliefs which influenced the later religion and which in some aspects persisted through the Classical period. Although it is impossible in all cases to separate with certainty those aspects which were brought to Greece before or during the earlier periods from those which had existed there previously, there is abundant evidence of extensive borrowing. Among these early aspects of the religion, we find evidences of animism, fetishism, totemism, tabus, human sacrifice, scapegoats, omens and oracles, local hero cults, and ghosts and spirits. Various myths have been explained, either partially or in full, on the basis of these early beliefs. An example may be found in the story of Theseus and the Minotaur. The *Labrys* (double-ax) is a prominent object in Cretan worship, and the Labyrinth, which is the home of the Minotaur, may be nothing more than "the place of the double-ax." Nilsson believes that the tabus relating to childbirth and death are the basis for the later ideas of purity and impurity found in the Classical and Post-Classical periods. Among the chief concerns of this earlier period of religion appear to be the promotion of fertility and the appeasement of ghosts and spirits. These aspects persist throughout the Classical period and are an essential part of the worship of the chthonian or subterranean divinities.

The Homeric or Olympian gods are the most prominent feature of the Classical period. Although the Homeric poems in no sense are basically a religious work, their great authority during this period resulted in the acceptance of their presentation of the gods, who are the deities of the invading Achaeans. They are anthropomorphic with personalities which are more sharply defined than their functions. Athena and Ares are both concerned with war, but there is no mistaking their individual personalities. Herodotus states that "(Homer and Hesiod) are they who taught the Greeks of the descent of the gods, and gave to all their several names, and honors, and arts, and declared their outward form." Although this statement indicates the high esteem in which Homer was held during this period, it cannot be accepted literally. The 12 gods of the Olympian Pantheon have been shown to be of various origins. Zeus is the chief god of the invaders. Hera may have come from Ionia; she was the chief deity of Argos taken over by the Achaeans. Artemis and Athena appear to be of Minoan or Mycenaean origin. Dionysus (of little importance in Homer) and possibly Ares are derived from Thrace. Cyprus was the original home of Aphrodite, whereas Hestia, Demeter, and possibly Hermes are deities of the Pelasgians or primitive Aegean people. Apollo and Hephaestus are probably from Anatolia in Asia Minor. The origin of Poseidon is uncertain, but if he was a god of the Achaeans, he could not have been at first a god of the sea.

The Homeric poems were largely instrumental in defining the relationship between gods and humans in this period. The gulf between them was unbridgeable, and any attempt of a human to trespass on divine prerogatives was an act of *hybris* (arrogance) to be punished severely. In the *Nekyia,* Odysseus sees that the worst torments are visited in Tartarus upon humans, such as Tantalus, Sisyphus, and Ixion, who have offended the gods. Since immortality is an attribute of the gods, it follows that man cannot be immortal, and it is this aspect of the Olympian worship which may have been a factor in the persistence of earlier beliefs which held out a promise of immortal life. Although men could not criticize the gods whose actions might have appeared unjustified on occasion, the gods were not completely lawless and fickle. Zeus, in the first book of the *Odyssey*, is a god of righteousness and not the author of evil. Both in the *Iliad* and the *Odyssey* the right of the

stranger to hospitable treatment is recognized as a law of the gods.

It was during the Classical period that the outward manifestations of the Greek religion assumed their most splendid form. Numerous temples were erected throughout Greece, and the efforts of the greatest architects and sculptors were devoted to them. In his Funeral Oration, Pericles gives an indication of the importance of the religious festivals to the Athenians. The maintenance of the temples and the furtherance of the Olympian religion was a function of the state, or *polis*. The religion did not require its adherents to subscribe to a set of beliefs or dogma. The individual fulfilled his function by participating in the public ceremony. There was little or no conception of the modern view of personal religion. As each cult had its own priests, there never was a unified priesthood to exert an undue influence. The festivals were joyous occasions, although it is possible to see in certain of them traces of earlier beliefs. Thus, in the *Anthesteria,* the appeasing of spirits took place, but it was cloaked and overlaid by ritual of a later date.

A prominent feature of the religion was the Mysteries, which held a promise of immortality for the initiates. Of particular importance in this respect were the Eleusinian Mysteries and the cult of Orphism, in which sacred symbols were revealed and symbolic rites were performed. Orphism, which was an adaptation of the Dionysiac worship, was the earliest "book religion" in Greece, and placed great emphasis on a rebirth cycle. Its stress on purity throughout life is an indication of the turning of Greek thought toward the more modern view.

The decline of the polis with its ensuing problems caused the Greek philosophers to seek other answers. Although the pre-Socratics during the Classical period had evolved systems which required no gods, or gods completely at variance with those of Homer, the changing political and economic conditions during the 5th and 4th centuries B.C. hastened the process. The Sophists proclaimed that there were no absolute standards of morality and rejected divine establishment of laws. The various philosophical schools established ethical doctrines which could not be reconciled with the traditional Olympian worship. In many ways the maxims of the philosophers found their way into early Christian thought. (AH)

Griffins (grif′inz). In Greek mythology, fabulous monsters, sometimes called "the Hounds of Zeus." They were said to have been generated between the lion and the eagle, and to combine the head, front, and wings of an eagle with the body and hindquarters of of a lion. Their duty was to guard the mines of gold and the river of gold which flowed in the region of the Hyperboreans from the one-eyed Arimaspi, who were always trying to steal it. The figure of the griffin is seen on ancient coins, and is borne in coat-armor. It is also a frequent motive in architectural decoration.

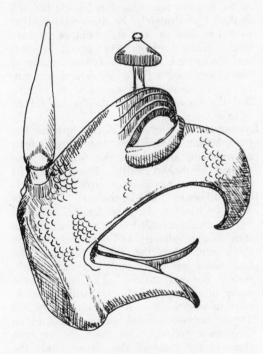

GRIFFIN
Bronze found at Olympia, mid-7th century
B.C. *Olympia*

Grumentum (grö-men′tum). In ancient geography, a town in Lucania, S Italy, situated on the Aciris (now Agri) River near the modern Grumento Nova.

Grynaeus (grī-nē′us). An epithet of Apollo from the famous shrine and oracle of Apollo in Gryneum in Mysia.

Gryneum (grī-nē′um) or **Grynea** (grī-nē′a̯). In ancient geography, a small Aeolian city in Mysia, on the shore of the Aegean Sea. It was noted for a sanctuary and ancient oracle of Apollo, as well as a white marble temple, and a grove sacred to Apollo.

Gyas (ji′as). In the *Aeneid,* a Trojan who accompanied Aeneas on the flight from Troy. He commanded one of the ships of Aeneas' fleet. In the funeral games held for Anchises in Sicily, Gyas captained one of the boats; becoming impatient with his helmsman he tossed him overboard and took the helm himself, but it was too late. His boat came in third. He fought valiantly in the war against the Latins.

Gygaea (jī-jē′a̯) or **Gyge** (jī′jē̯). In the *Iliad,* a nymph of the lake in Lydia of the same name. She was the mother of Iphition, by Otrynteus.

Gyges (jī′jēz) or **Gyes** (jī′ēz). In Greek mythology, one of the Hecatonchires, the 100-handed giants who were the children of Uranus and Gaea. His brothers were Cottus and Briareus.

Gyges (gī′jēz, jī′-). A king of Lydia (c685–c653 B.C.), and the founder of a new dynasty. Pressed by the Cimmerians, he invoked the help of Assurbanipal, and submitted to his supremacy. Afterward he allied himself with Psammetichus, king of Egypt, against Assyria, and seems to have fallen (c653 B.C.) in one of the repeated attacks of the Cimmerians, who were no longer checked by the Assyrian power. Plato's story is that Gyges, a shepherd of the king of Lydia, after a storm came upon a hollow, bronze horse in a chasm. Within the horse lay a corpse from which he took a magic ring which had the property of making the wearer invisible. Wearing the ring, Gyges killed the king, and thus became king himself. Herodotus tells still another story: Gyges was the trusted aide of Candaules who was king of Lydia and a descendant of Heracles. Candaules was madly in love with his wife and thought she was the most beautiful woman in the world. So carried away was he with the wonder of her beauty that he wished Gyges to see her naked, which was unlawful to do, so that his words might be confirmed by Gyges' eyes. He commanded Gyges to hide in the chamber where he and the queen slept and to behold her naked loveliness. Gyges was shocked at the idea but in the end obeyed his master as he valued his life above his honor. Candaules' wife entered the chamber, as Candaules had assured Gyges she would do, put off her clothes and went to bed, but out of the corner of her eye she saw Gyges hiding behind the door. She did not cry out or make any mention that she had seen him and Gyges slipped out of the room, as he thought, unobserved. The next day the queen sent for him. She informed him that she knew he had spied on her with her husband's aid, and had seen her naked which was unlawful. She now gave Gyges the choice of two alternatives: either he must kill Candaules and take her as his wife, that thus he would have looked on what was his own, or he must die himself, that only Candaules should have looked on what was his own. Gyges, who was truly loyal to his master, tried to appease her but the queen was immovable, and Gyges chose his own life rather than loyalty to the king. The queen gave him instructions for killing Candaules, in the very chamber where Gyges had spied on her. She gathered trusted friends to her support and Gyges slipped into Candaules' chamber at night and killed him as he slept. He then took the queen as his wife and declared himself king of Lydia. The Lydians were aroused to great wrath by the murder of their king and attacked Gyges, but as the attack was indecisive they agreed to consult the oracle at Delphi to learn whether Gyges should be allowed to reign. The priestess gave an answer favorable to Gyges and the Lydians accepted him as their king. Gyges sent rich offerings to Delphi, one of the earliest of the barbarians to do so, among them large amounts of silver and six golden goblets. In addition to confirming him as king, the priestess foretold that in the fifth generation the descendants of Gyges would suffer revenge at the hands of the descendants of Heracles. The king in the fifth generation was his descendant Croesus.

Gylippus (ji-lip′us). Spartan general; fl. 5th century B.C. He was a son of Cleandrides, who was expelled in 446 B.C. from Sparta after having been found guilty of taking bribes from the Athenians, exhibiting a weakness of character that his son apparently inherited. During the Peloponnesian War he was sent in 415 B.C. to help Syracuse against Athens. He defeated the Athenian forces in several engagements, compelling them to surrender (414–413 B.C.) with their generals, Nicias and Demosthenes. Later (404 B.C.), after the capture of Athens by Lysander, he was sent by that general to Sparta with the treasure taken in Athens, but he was unable to resist the temptation of unsewing the bags which contained large amounts of silver and of extracting from each bag a "considerable amount." He then sewed up the bags again and delivered them to the Spartan magistrates as he was ordered to do. Unfortunately, he did not know that each bag had in it a statement of its contents. When the bags were opened, his theft was discovered, and he was found guilty of having embezzled public funds and was sentenced to death. He managed to escape, fled the country, and died, like his father, in exile.

Gymnopaediae (jim-nō-pē′di-ē). Spartan festival, lasting several days. Spectacular feats of wrestling and choral dancing were performed by naked youths, accompanied by songs celebrating Spartan exploits.

Gynaecothoenas (jin″ē-kō-thē′nas). Epithet of Ares. Charillus, king of Sparta, deceived by an oracle invaded Tegea. The Tegean men fought valiantly and were just holding their own, when the Tegean women, who had taken up arms and lain in ambush, rushed out and drove back the Spartans, many of whom, including Charillus himself, were taken prisoner. After their victory, the Tegean women offered sacrifice to Ares on their own account, and gave the men no share in the meat of the victims; only the women ate of it. For this reason Ares was given the name "Gynaecothoenas" (*Feasted by the Women*).

Gythium (jith′i-um, ji-thī′um). [Modern name, **Gytheion.**] In ancient geography, a seaport in Laconia, Greece, situated on the Gulf of Laconia. According to tradition, when Heracles asked the priestess at Delphi how he could be cured of a sickness afflicting him she refused to answer. He seized the tripod from her and threatened to set up his own oracle. Apollo came to the rescue of his priestess and strove with Heracles. Zeus parted them and compelled them to compose their quarrel. After this Apollo and Heracles together founded the city of Gythium, where images of Apollo, Heracles, and Dionysus stood side by side in the market-place. Near Gythium is a stone on which Orestes is said to have sat to rest when he had been driven to madness by the Furies. As he sat on the stone his madness left him. Off the coast of Gythium is the island of Cranaë, where Helen first yielded in love to Paris after he had carried her off from Sparta. On the mainland opposite the island was a sanctuary of Aphrodite Migonitis (*Uniter*), but afterward Menelaus set up near the sanctuary an image of Thetis and the goddesses Praxidicae (*Extracters of Justice*).

—H——

Habrocomas and Anthia (hab-rō-kō′mas; an′-thi-a). See **Abrocomes and Atheia.**

Hades (hā′dēz). One of the 12 Olympian gods, he was the lord of the Underworld, feared alike by mortals and gods, as ruler of the dead and for his terrible justice. No soaring temples rose in the bright air of Greece in his honor, nor were festivals celebrated to glorify him. When mortals called on him they struck the earth with their hands and invoked him with oaths and curses. He reigned in a splendid palace, and, besides his function of governing the shades of the dead, he was the giver to mortals of all treasures derived from the earth and was given the name Pluto (*Wealth*). Hermes conducted the shades of the dead to his kingdom, and from there they never escaped. Hades took pride in the growth of his kingdom, and once complained to Zeus about Asclepius, who was raising the dead, that if he were allowed to continue this practice the population of the Underworld would not increase as it should.

Hades was the son of Cronus and Rhea. Like his sisters before him he was swallowed by Cronus as soon as he was born, and later was disgorged with them when Zeus, aided by Metis, tricked Cronus. In the war between Zeus and Cronus, Hades was given a cap of invisibility by the Cyclopes. (The cap symbolized the invisible world of which he was the ruler; the name Hades happens also to mean "the Unseen.") Wearing it, he crept into the presence of Cronus and stole his weapons. When Cronus was defeated, Hades, Zeus, and Poseidon drew lots from a helmet to see what regions of the universe each would control. By the lots Zeus was assigned to the heavens, Poseidon to the sea, and Hades to the Underworld. The earth was to remain open to all. Hades descended to his kingdom and seldom appeared thereafter on earth.

Some say that Aphrodite, queen of love, inspired love in the heart of Hades because she wished to show her power in the Underworld. He fell in love with Peresphone, daughter of Demeter and Zeus, and asked Zeus for her hand. Zeus did not like to deny his brother, nor did he want to cause suffering to Demeter, thus he took the position that he would not interfere in the matter. Hades took this as consent. In his golden chariot, drawn by four black horses, he arose through a cleft in the earth, swooped down on Persephone as she was gathering flowers in a meadow, and carried her back to the Underworld with him. Persephone was a most unwilling bride, and all the time she was in his kingdom she refused to eat. Demeter caused the earth to be barren until her daughter should be restored to her, and Zeus was compelled to send Hermes to Hades with a command to him to restore Persephone to her mother, otherwise the race of men would die and the gods would lose their rich sacrifices. Hades had no choice but to obey. However, before he sent Persephone off with Hermes, he reproached her and reminded her that it was no discreditable thing to be the wife of the lord of the Underworld, and he persuaded her to eat seven pomegranate seeds. For those who have eaten the food of the dead must return to the world of the dead. In this way he brought it about that Persephone was compelled to spend a portion of each year with him, as queen of the Underworld. Pedsephone bore him no children. She was a careful wife, and transformed the nymph Minthe, whom Hades would have seduced, into the fragrant mint plant. Again, when Hades was eyeing the nymph Leuce she was transformed into a white poplar tree, and thenceforward stood beside the Pool of Memory in the Underworld. Heracles, come here to seize the dog Cerberus, plucked the leaves of the poplar and made a wreath for his head. The leaves were black, the color of the Underworld, but the divine sweat of Heracles' brow as he labored with Cerberus bleached the leaves where they touched his skin, which is why one side of the leaves of the poplar gleams whitely, while the other side is dark. Heracles was one of few who succeeded in visiting the realm of Hades and escaping from it. As one of his labors for Eurystheus he was required to drag up the dog Cerberus from Tartarus. When he boldly demanded the dog, the god agreed to let him take it if he could do so without weapons. Heracles succeeded. While he was in Tartarus Heracles freed Theseus, who had gone there with Pirithous with the purpose of abducting Persephone. Hades had invited them to be seated when they made their arrogant demand for his wife, and as soon as they did so they found themselves bound fast to the Chairs of Forgetfulness. Heracles was able to wrench Theseus from his seat, but Pirithous had to be abandoned. Orpheus so charmed Queen Persephone and the shades of the dead that Hades agreed to allow him to take Eurydice, his dead wife, back to earth with him on condition that he not look back until he reached the upper air. Orpheus, in his anxiety, looked back too soon and Eurydice was lost forever. Some say that at the command of Zeus Hades came to earth to fetch Sisyphus, the greatest knave that ever lived, to Tartarus. Sisyphus persuaded Hades to try on a pair of golden handcuffs, once they were on Sisyphus locked them and kept Hades a prisoner. As long

as Hades was a prisoner no one could die, not even the most grievously wounded. Ares came to the rescue and freed Hades. On another occasion when Hades visited the earth he took part in the war between Heracles and the Pylians. The god fought against Heracles, was wounded by him and was compelled to withdraw.

As he had no temples, he had very few names. The Greeks preferred not to think of him. The cypress and the narcissus were sacred to him. In art he is represented in a form kindred to that of Zeus and that of Poseidon, and bearing the staff or scepter of authority, sometimes in company with Persephone or the dog Cerberus. The Romans also called him Pluto, and identified him with their Dis or Orcus.

Hades. [More properly, **The House of Hades.**] The lower or subterranean world in which dwelt the spirits of the dead. Sometimes it was said to be situated in the west. The souls in Hades were believed to carry on there a counterpart of their material existence: those of the righteous without discomfort, amid the pale sweet blooms of asphodel, or even in pleasure, in the Elysian Fields; and those of the wicked amid various torments in Tartarus. Hades was surrounded by five rivers, of which the Styx (across which Charon ferried the souls of the buried dead) and Lethe (the river of forgetfulness) are the best known. The gates were guarded by the monstrous three-headed (sometimes 50-headed) dog Cerberus to prevent the shades from escaping to the upper world.

Hadrian (hā′dri-an). [Also: **Adrian**; full Latin name, **Publius Aelius Hadrianus.**] Roman emperor (117–138 A.D.); nephew and ward of Trajan, whom he succeeded. He was born probably at Italica, in Hispania Baetica (near modern Seville, Spain), Jan. 24, 76 A.D.; died at Baiae, Italy, July 10, 138. He held several positions in various parts of the empire under Trajan, accompanying him in his campaigns. On the death of Trajan, it is said, he succeeded to the emperor's place through the slyness of Plotina, Trajan's wife, who announced Trajan's adoption of his nephew, then withheld news of Trajan's death until Hadrian could consolidate his position. Renouncing the policy of conquest, he abandoned the new provinces of Armenia, Mesopotamia, and Assyria, and established the Euphrates as the eastern boundary of the empire. In 119 he began a progress through the provinces, in the course of which he began the construction of the wall that bears his name, designed to keep the Picts and the Scots out of Britain. He returned finally about 131, having visited Gaul, Germany, Britain, Spain, Mauretania, Parthia, Asia Minor, Athens, Sicily, Rome (for a year), Syria, Palestine, Arabia, and Egypt. He promulgated the *Edictum perpetuum* (c130), a collection of the edicts of the praetors by Salvius Julianus. This formed the groundwork for the *Corpus juris* of Justinian. In 132 a revolt was occasioned among the Jews by the planting of the Roman colony of Aelia Capitolina on the site of Jerusalem, and the building of a temple to Jupiter Capitolinus on the site of the Temple; the revolt, led by Bar Kochba, was suppressed in 135. Hadrian devoted himself to building and strengthening the position of the emperor. Through the *Edictum*, lawmaking by the praetors was ended; thereafter laws became a màtter of senatorial confirmation of the suggestions of the emperor. He reduced taxes, provided for less arbitrary treatment of slaves, and fostered regulations to reduce immorality. His public works include the wall in Britain, similar structures in Germany, the Pantheons of Rome and Athens, and the temple of Olympian Zeus at Athens, as well as many other buildings in Rome and in the provinces. He was a patron of the arts and himself a poet; perhaps his most famous composition is the address to his soul, supposed to have been said on his deathbed, beginning: "*Animula, vagula, blandula,*" (Little soul, evanescent, pleasant . . .). Hadrian's first choice as his successor, Lucius Ceionius Commodus, died Jan. 1, 138, and Hadrian then chose Antoninus (Antoninus Pius) on condition that Antoninus would adopt Commodus' son (later the emperor Commodus) and Antoninus' own nephew (later the emperor Marcus Aurelius).

Hadrian's Villa. Assemblage of ancient ruins, near Tivoli, perhaps the most impressive in Italy. It included the Greek and Latin theaters, so-called; an odeum, *thermae* (baths), a stadium, a palace, several temples, spacious structures for guards and attendants, and many subsidiary buildings and devices.

Of most of these there are extensive remains; and here were found many of the fine statues now in Roman museums.

Hadrian's Wall. A wall of defense for the Roman province of Britain, constructed by Hadrian between the Solway Firth and the mouth of the Tyne. The work has been ascribed to Severus and others, but was probably constructed under Hadrian alone.

Haedui (hed′ū-ī, hē′dū-ī). See **Aedui.**

Haemon (hē′mọn). In Greek legend, the son of Creon, king of Thebes. He loved Antigone, daughter of Oedipus, but was ordered by his father to bury her alive because she had defied his order and built a pyre for the corpse of her brother Polynices. Haemon, according to some accounts, agreed to slay Antigone but secretly married her and hid her away. She later bore him a son which Creon recognized as her child because it bore the mark of a serpent, as did all the descendants of Cadmus. Creon again ordered her death, as well as that of the child, and when she was killed Haemon killed himself on her tomb. According to Sophocles, Antigone was killed immediately for her defiance of Creon and Haemon committed suicide on her tomb.

Haemonia (hẹ-mō′ni-ạ). An ancient name for Thessaly.

Haemus (hē′mus). In Greek mythology, a son of Boreas and Orithyia. He was a king in Thrace and the father, by Rhodope, of Hebrus. Haemus and Rhodope were so happy in their marriage that they assumed the names of Zeus and Hera. For their presumption, the gods transformed them into mountains, the peaks in the Balkans that bear their names. The whole range, now called the Balkan mountains, was once called the Haemus range.

Hageladas or **Hagelaides** (haj-ẹ-lā′dạs). See **Ageladas.**

Hagios Elias (ä′yôs ē-lē′äs). [Also: **Hagios Ilias, Mount Saint Elias.**] Mountain summit in Greece, in the Taÿgetus range about 11 miles S of Sparta. It is the highest point in the Peloponnesus. Elevation, about 7903 feet.

Hagno (hag′nọ). In Greek mythology, Arcadian nymph who, according to the Arcadians, was one of the nymphs who took care of the infant Zeus after he was born on Mount Lycaeus in Arcadia. A never-failing

actọr; up, lūte, pŭll; oi, oil; ou, out; ᴛн, then; ḍ as d or j, ṣ as s or sh, ṭ as t or ch, ẓ as z or zh.

spring on the mountain was given her name. This spring had the wonderful property of bringing rain to a parched land. When there was a prolonged drought the priest prayed to its waters and made sacrifices. Then he lowered an evergreen oak branch to the surface of the water. When the water was stirred, a mist rose. This mist formed a cloud, drew other clouds to it, and caused rain to fall on the Arcadians.

Hagnon (hag'non). According to tradition, the Athenian founder of Amphipolis, in Macedonia. He was honored as a hero by the Amphipolitans. When the Spartan general Brasidas won Amphipolis, 424 B.C., the Amphipolitans were so charmed by him that after his death the monuments and honors of Hagnon were transferred to his name.

Halcyon (hal'si-on). An old and poetical name of the kingfisher. This bird was fabled to lay its eggs in nests that floated on the sea about the time of the winter solstice, and to have the power of charming the winds and waves during the period of incubation, so that the weather was then calm. The name comes from Alcyone, the wife of Ceyx, who was transformed into a kingfisher because of grief over the death of her husband, who died at sea. A dried kingfisher was regarded as protection from the thunderbolt of Zeus.

Halcyon Days. In Greek fancy, days of fine and calm weather about the winter solstice, when the halcyon (kingfisher) was believed to brood, especially the seven days before and as many after the winter solstice. They are named for Alcyone when, as a kingfisher, she hatches her eggs on the sea. In this period Zeus stills the sea for her safety and that of her young.

Halesus (hal'e-sus). In the *Aeneid*, a bastard son, or a companion, of Agamemnon. He fled from Mycenae to Italy when Agamemnon was murdered. In Latium he founded the town of Falerii and taught its inhabitants the Mysteries of Hera. Since he hated everything Trojan he gathered the warlike tribes of the Campania and went to the aid of Turnus in his war against Aeneas.

Halia (hal'i-a). A sea-goddess of Rhodes. By Poseidon she was the mother of six sons and a daughter, Rhode. They were brought up on the island of Rhodes, which takes its name from Halia's daughter. Aphrodite, who had

been insulted by the six sons of Halia, inspired them with madness and they assaulted their mother. Poseidon hid them in the earth, where they became demons. Halia hurled herself into the sea and was deified as the sea-goddess Leucothea, according to some accounts, but this same story is told of Ino, the mother of Melicertes, and the same name is given to Ino after she became a sea-goddess. In the *Iliad* Halia is named as a Nereid.

Haliacmon (hal-i-ak'mon). [Modern name, **Vistritsa.**] In ancient geography, a river of Macedonia which empties into the Myrtoan Sea (Thermaic Gulf).

Haliartus (hal-i-ar'tus). In ancient geography, a city of Boeotia, Greece, situated on the S shore of Lake Copaïs, about 14 miles NW of Thebes, and under the shadow of Mount Tilphusius. Nearby it ran the Lophis River. According to some accounts, the stream once did not exist. The ruler of Haliartus went to the oracle at Delphi to inquire how he could get water for his city, and was told to kill the first man he met. The first man he met on his return was his son Lophis. He struck him with his sword, wounding but not killing him. The lad ran about wildly, and where drops of his blood fell water rose from the earth and became the stream afterwards called Lophis in his honor. At Haliartus there was also the spring of Tilphusa, where the seer Tiresias was buried, and there was a hero-shrine of Cecrops, the son of Pandion. Haliartus was important because of its location on the main route between N and S Greece. In the Persian War the inhabitants threw in their lot with the Greeks. The Persians overran the town and burned it (480 B.C.). In 395 B.C. the Spartan general Lysander was defeated and killed at Haliartus by the Thebans. The city was completely destroyed in 171 B.C. by the Romans, because it had favored the cause of Perseus, king of Macedonia.

Halicarnassus (hal''i-kär-nas'us). In ancient geography, a city in Caria, Asia Minor, situated on the island of Zephyria close to a promontory of the mainland. The island was eventually united to the mainland and the city extended to include both. It was colonized by Dorians from Troezen and perhaps Argos who came to the region, according to tradition, under the leadership of Anthes. The city was a member of the Dorian Hexapolis for a time, but was later excluded from the religious rites when the Halicarnassian Agasicles, in defiance of the laws, carried off to his own house the bronze tripod he had won at the games for Apollo. In the time of the Persian War it was ruled over by Artemisia, queen of Caria, who commanded her own ship in the Persian fleet that was defeated by the Greeks at Salamis (480 B.C.). Following the Persian War it was for a time a member of the Delian Confederacy. Later, by the Peace of Antalcidas (the "King's Peace"), it fell to Persia and was governed by satraps as part of Caria. Among these satraps was Mausolus, whose wife Artemisia built (352 B.C.) his tomb, the famous Mausoleum, celebrated as one of the seven wonders of the ancient world. Scopas and other renowned sculptors of the time cooperated in the building of the tomb. It consisted of a quadrangular peristyle of Ionic columns on a high basement, above which rose a pyramid of 24 steps, supporting a *quadriga* (a chariot drawn by four horses), in which stood a huge statue of Mausolus. Important remains of the sculptured decoration are in the British Museum. In 334 B.C. Alexander the Great besieged the city, took it, and sacked it, and it never recovered its former importance. The city is famous also as the birthplace of the historians Herodotus and Dionysius. The site is now occupied by the Turkish town of Budrum.

Halicyae (hal-is′i-ē). [Modern name, **Salemi**.] Town on the island of Sicily, about 40 miles SW of Panormus. It was a Greek town originally, then came under Carthaginian influence, and submitted to the Romans in 262 B.C.

Halirrhothius (hal-i-rō′thi-us). In Greek mythology, a son of Poseidon. Ares killed him at the spring of Asclepius, claiming that he had attempted to violate Alcippe, the daughter of Ares. For the murder Ares was tried on the hill in Athens that henceforth came to be known as the Areopagus, and was acquitted.

Halitherses (hal-i-thėr′sēz). In the *Odyssey*, an Ithacan seer who understood the flight of birds. When two eagles flew over the assembly gathered by Telemachus and suddenly began tearing at each other, Halitherses interpreted this to mean that Odysseus would return and tear the suitors of Penelope to pieces. For this reason he advised them to go home and leave the halls and fortunes of Odysseus in good state for their master's return.

Haloa (ha-lō′a). An ancient Greek festival, celebrated in the month Poseideon (December–January), in honor of Demeter and Kore and Dionysus. The festival was held at Athens when the vines were cut and the new wine was tasted. It was also connected with the time of threshing. During the festival first fruits were carried from Athens to Eleusis, games and sports were held on the threshing-floors, and a procession in honor of Poseidon was held. The festival was under the presidency of women; a priestess offered the first fruits; no animal victim was offered in sacrifice. Some say the festival commemorated the death of Icarius, who introduced the vine into Attica. Women celebrated the festival alone. Phallic symbols were handled and the women exchanged all manner of crude and bawdy jests. At the end of the festival there was a great banquet, at which wine was served and various foods, the "gentle foods" given by Demeter, were eaten. Prohibited foods at the banquet were the pomegranate, in this case considered as a food for the dead, since the eating of it had drawn Persephone back to Hades for certain parts of the year. Apples, cocks, eggs, the red sea-mullet and certain other fishes were also prohibited. Cakes in the shape of the phallus were set upon the tables.

Halys (hā′lis). A river of Paphlagonia, about 800 miles long (the modern Kizil Irmak), the longest river in Asia Minor. Phineus directed the course of the Argonauts past it. It is famous for the defeat of Croesus, king of Lydia, brought about by his misinterpretation of the ambiguous oracle given him by the priestess of Delphi: "If Croesus passes over the Halys he will destroy a great empire."

Hamadryad (ham-a-drī′ad). In Greek mythology, a wood-nymph supposed to live and die with the tree to which she was attached. The hamadryad is the presiding deity of the tree and shares in its joys and sorrows; whatever wounds the tree wounds the hamadryad.

actǫr; up, lūte, pull; oi, oil; ou, out; ᵺ, then; d̠ as d or j, ş as s or sh, t̠ as t or ch, z̠ as z or zh.

Hamilcar (ham'il-kär, ha̲-mil'kär). Carthaginian general of the 5th century B.C. During the Persian War envoys of Xerxes went to Hamilcar and arranged with him an attack on the Greek settlements of Sicily, so that the latter could not, as requested by the homeland, send aid against the Persians. The occasion for the Carthaginian attack against Sicily was a quarrel between two Greek states there, in which the Greek tyrant of Himera was driven out of his city by the tyrant of Acragas and appealed to Hamilcar for aid. Hamilcar seized the opportunity to reduce Greek power in Sicily. He sailed with a huge armament to recover Himera and besieged the city (480 B.C.). He proposed to enlist the aid of the Greek gods to help defeat the Greeks in Sicily, but as he was unfamiliar with the forms and ceremonies, he sent to Selinus, a Greek city under Carthaginian dominion, requesting the people to send priests who could properly perform the ceremonies for a great sacrifice to Poseidon. Hamilcar's messenger to Selinus was intercepted by the forces of the tyrant of Acragas. They rode to the camp of Hamilcar on the appointed day and asked admittance as the men Hamilcar had sent for. The Carthaginians, unaware of the deception since all Greeks looked alike to them, admitted them to the camp by the sea. As Hamilcar stood waiting by the great altar of Poseidon he was overpowered and slain, and his ships were fired. The waiting Greek army, under the command of Gelon, tyrant of Syracuse, who had come to aid the tyrant of Acragas, received the signal that the trick had been successful and marched around the other side of the city where Hamilcar's land army was encamped and attacked it. After a desperate battle Gelon's forces were successful; Hamilcar's great force was utterly destroyed. The Carthaginians, unwilling to admit that Hamilcar was slain by a trick at the altar of the Greek god Poseidon, said that he stood throughout the hard-fought battle beside an altar of the Phoenician god, Baal, and that all day victims were hurled into the fire that blazed mightily. But when he saw his army in full retreat he offered himself as the greatest victim to his god; he leaped into the fire on the altar and was consumed in the flames.

Hamilcar Barca (or **Barcas**) (bär'ka̲, bär'ka̲s). Carthaginian general, drowned in Spain, c229 B.C. He was the father of Hannibal; his surname Barca means "lightning." He held (247–244 B.C.) Mount Ercte (Monte Pellegrino), Sicily, against the Romans, transferred his troops and held (244–241 B.C.) Mount Eryx (Monte San Giuliano), and raided Roman positions as far as the mainland. At the end of the First Punic War in 241 B.C., he retired to Africa undefeated. There, his troops, their promised rewards being withheld by the Carthaginian government, revolted and Hamilcar was called to defeat them. He suppressed the rising of the mercenaries (241–238 B.C.), and became dictator of Carthage. He began (236 B.C.) the reduction of Spain to a Carthaginian province in order to have a base from which to strike at Rome, but was drowned while withdrawing from a siege.

Hannibal (han'i-ba̲l). Carthaginian general, 5th century B.C., grandson of Hamilcar. His life was dominated by a desire to avenge the death (480 B.C.) of his grandfather at Himera, in Sicily. At an advanced age he persuaded Carthage to send a force to Sicily in reply to a request for aid from Segesta, a Greek city at war with Selinus. A great force was prepared and sailed to Sicily under command of Hannibal. The fleet reached Sicily, and the armed force marched to Selinus. Selinus had never been attacked in the 250 years since its founding and was completely unprepared to withstand the Carthaginians. Its inhabitants resisted valiantly but after nine days the city fell to Hannibal (410 B.C.), and it became the first Greek city in Sicily to be taken by the Carthaginians. Such military installations as existed were destroyed, its people were slaughtered or carried off into slavery, but the city itself was allowed to stand. Hannibal now set out to fulfill his real purpose in the expedition to Sicily, which was the destruction of Himera, the scene of his grandfather's defeat and death. He besieged Himera and breached its walls by means of mines. The defenders drove his soldiers out. Just at that time appeared a fleet of 25 ships, sent from Syracuse to relieve Himera. Hannibal spread abroad a rumor that he was going to attack Syracuse, and the commander of the Greek fleet, having heard the rumor and believing it to be true, immediately decided to withdraw. He offered to take the inhabitants of Himera to safety in his ships. About half of the inhabitants, all he had room for, boarded the ships and the fleet sailed. The remaining inhabitants continued desperate resistance to the Carthaginians. They maintained their resistance until the Syracusan fleet returned to rescue them, but just as it appeared the forces of Hannibal again breached the walls, poured into the town, and by the time the Greek ships reached the harbor, Himera was already in Hannibal's hands. It is said that on the very spot where his grandfather had been slain Hannibal sacrificed 3000 human victims to appease his shade and avenge him. Afterward he completely destroyed the city and left the spot barren. Hannibal then returned in triumph to Carthage. In 406 B.C. he again invaded Sicily at the head of a great force and laid siege to Acragas. Because the ground about the city was low and made the siege difficult, he decided to build a great causeway, from which height his forces could attack the fortifications more effectively. He plundered the neighboring cemeteries of their grave stones and tombs to get material for the causeway. It is said that when the tomb of Theron, former tyrant of Acragas, was being broken into it was struck by a thunderbolt and seers advised that it be spared. Before the causeway was finished plague broke out in Hannibal's camp; he fell victim to it and died. The Carthaginians decided that the gods were angry because of the desecration of the cemeteries. They sacrificed a boy to their god Moloch and then completed the causeway, without further disturbing the tombs.

Hannibal. The great Carthaginian general, eldest son of Hamilcar Barca; born 247 B.C.; committed suicide at Libyssa, Bithynia, probably 183 B.C. He was with his father in Spain after c238 and, at his father's request swore, at the age of nine, his enmity to Rome, which had defeated Carthage in the First Punic War (261–241 B.C.). Following Hamilcar Barca's death in 228 B.C. Hannibal's brother-in-law Hasdrubal succeeded to the command of the Carthaginian forces in Spain; Hasdrubal was assassinated in 221 B.C. and Hannibal was chosen leader of the army. He

set about extending the Carthaginian domain in Spain and by 219 B.C. had reached the Ebro, controlling all of Spain south of that river except the city of Saguntum (modern Sagunto, near Valencia), an ally of Rome. Hannibal laid siege to the city, despite specific warnings from Rome that such action would lead to war, and in eight months took it. When the Carthaginian government would not repudiate his action by surrendering Hannibal to the Roman envoys, the Romans declared for war. Hannibal now conceived a daring plan and in the spring of 218 B.C. marched northward, crossed the Pyrenees, evaded a Roman force sent to intercept him, reached the Rhône, and in October, with snow already in the high passes, crossed the Alps into Italy. Only some 26,-000 men survived the crossing (which was probably by way of the Little St. Bernard Pass) of about 35,000–40,000 that had started, yet this crossing of the Alps in late autumn, with supplies and with the Carthaginian war-elephants, is still considered perhaps the greatest military achievement in history. At the Ticinus River and again at the Trebia in December, Hannibal scored victories over the Romans and secured control of the Padus (Po) Valley. Reinforced by Gaulish tribesmen, he marched south in the spring of 217 B.C., crossed the Apennines, and at Lake Trasimenus cut to pieces a Roman army under the command of the consul Caius Flaminius, who was killed in the battle. Rome now had no army capable of risking another defeat in the field and Fabius Maximus, who was appointed military dictator, dared not risk a general engagement. Hannibal decided against storming Rome itself and instead marched through Italy into Apulia, destroying as he went, but suffering the harrying attacks of Fabius, whose tactics won him the surname Cunctator ("Delayer"). Hannibal wintered on the Apulian plains and early the next summer (216 B.C.) faced the largest army Rome had ever put into the field, about 54,000 men at Cannae. Skillfully he encircled them, pushed one group in on another until the Roman position was confused, and then cut them to pieces with his cavalry; more than half the Roman force was killed. As a result of the victory, several Italian tribes came over to the Carthaginians,

actǫr; up, lūte, pu̇ll; oi, oil; ou, out; ᴛʜ, then; ḏ as d or j, ş as s or sh, ṭ as t or ch, ẓ as z or zh.

as did Capua, where Hannibal wintered in 216–215 B.C. Syracuse deserted the Roman cause and allied itself with Carthage; Philip V of Macedon became an ally, although he never did send material aid. Hannibal had now reached the peak of his power; Rome, in his eyes, was impregnable, and her nearer allies were not deserting her; his failure to attack Rome after Cannae, when she was probably helpless, has been criticized as his fatal mistake. He campaigned in southern Italy for several years, captured Tarentum in 213 B.C., and in 210 won a victory at Herdoniae, but the strain on his manpower was great. In 212 B.C. Syracuse, under siege for three years, fell to the Romans, and in 211 B.C. Capua, too, was captured and sacked, despite Hannibal's attacks on the surrounding Roman armies and a feint on Rome itself. Help was required from Carthage's armies elsewhere, and Hannibal's brother Hasdrubal, who had been fighting the Romans in Spain, crossed the Alps with a large force. But before Hannibal could reach him from the south Hasdrubal was defeated and killed at the Metaurus in 207 B.C. Hannibal took refuge in the mountains of Bruttii, where he maintained an unassailable position for some years. At last, with help not forthcoming, with Mago defeated in Liguria, and with Scipio advancing victoriously in Africa against Carthage itself, he was recalled to Carthage in 203 B.C. There he hastily put together an army of his veterans from Italy and a levy from the African tribes and met the Romans at Zama in 202 B.C.; the Carthaginian force was practically annihilated and Carthage had to make peace. To pay the resulting indemnity (Carthage also gave up all claims to the Mediterranean islands), Hannibal, appointed chief magistrate, reformed the financial structure of the Carthaginian state and thereby came into conflict with the oligarchy. But his methods succeeded and within a few years Carthage was not only paying the indemnity but was reëstablishing itself as a Mediterranean power. Alarmed, Rome thereupon demanded that Carthage surrender Hannibal and he was forced to flee (c195 B.C.). He stayed in Syria for some time as a general with Antiochus III, but when Syria was defeated by the Romans he once again fled, to the court of Prusias, king of Bithynia. There

the Romans again sought him and demanded his surrender by Prusias. Rather than give up to his sworn enemies, Hannibal committed suicide; the year 183 B.C. is given as the date of his death by Livy, the same year that Scipio Africanus and Philopoemon, general of the Achaean League in Greece, died, but the specific date is conjectural.

Hanno (han'ō). Carthaginian navigator; fl. probably in the early 5th century B.C. He led a colonizing expedition to the western coast of Africa. An account of his voyage (*Periplus*) is extant in a Greek translation taken from a Phoenician text. He probably reached the coast of what is now Sierra Leone or Liberia. Hanno's account, used by Ptolemy, remained the standard until after the Portuguese Gilianes' voyage past Cape Bojador (on the coast of what is now Spanish Sahara) in 1433.

Hanno. [Called **Hanno the Great.**] Carthaginian leader; fl. in the 3rd century B.C. He was the leader of the aristocratic party at Carthage and an opponent of Hamilcar Barca and Hannibal. He opposed the war with Rome and all other trans-Mediterranean adventures. His opposition to paying Hamilcar's troops led to their revolt, and his refusal to support Hannibal with sufficient aid was a principal contributory cause of Hannibal's failure.

Harma (här'ma). In ancient geography, a city of Boeotia, Greece. The name means *Chariot,* and was given to the city, some say, because here the chariot bearing Amphiaraus was swallowed up when the earth opened as he fled from Thebes.

Harmodius (här-mō'di-us) and **Aristogiton** (a-ris-tō-jī'ton, ar"is-tō-). Killed 514 B.C. Two Athenian youths who killed Hipparchus, tyrant of Athens, in 514 B.C. They are represented as entertaining a strong affection for each other, which remained unaltered despite the endeavors of Hipparchus to draw that of the young and beautiful Harmodius toward himself. Enraged at the indifference of Harmodius, Hipparchus put a public insult upon him by declaring his sister unworthy of carrying the sacred baskets at the religious procession of the Panathenaea, in revenge for which the youths organized a conspiracy to overthrow both Hipparchus and his brother Hippias. They chose the feast day of the Panathenaea for the execution of their plot because it was the only day when the citizens could meet together, armed, without arousing suspicion. They had only a few accomplices, but they hoped that the stir made by the death of Hipparchus would rouse the citizens to throw off the yoke of tyranny. However, revolution was incidental, and was hoped for only as a means of saving themselves. As the time for the festival arrived the conspirators saw Hippias standing in the Ceramicus talking with one of their accomplices. They immediately concluded, falsely, that their plot was exposed and resolved to act at once. They found Hipparchus by the Leocorium and struck him down. Harmodius was captured by the guards and slain on the spot. It is said that Hippias, to whom the news was brought as he still stood in the Ceramicus, kept his features composed as if nothing had happened, pointed to the armed men in the procession whom he thought were implicated in the plot, ordered them to withdraw and had them disarmed. Aristogiton escaped temporarily through the excited crowd, but was shortly captured. When put to torture to reveal his accomplices, he named the principal friends of Hippias, who were executed. When pressed for further revelations, he answered that there remained no one whose death he desired, except the tyrant. Aristogiton then died under torture. Following the death of Hipparchus, Hippias, who hitherto, according to Thucydides, had maintained the laws, beautified the city, and carried out the wars of the Athenians and the sacrifices as prescribed, now became fearful of further plots. From this time on his rule became more oppressive, so that, according to Thucydides, and Herodotus also, the death of Hipparchus deepened, rather than lessened, the tyranny of the Pisistratidae. At the time of the murder of Hipparchus not much attention was paid to Harmodius and Aristogiton by the citizens. But as the rule of Hippias became more oppressive the conspirators came to be regarded as heroes, and after the expulsion of Hippias (510 B.C.), they were honored as such. A statue of them was placed in the market-place, on the way to the Acropolis opposite the Metroum; a copy of this is in the Museo Nazionale at Naples. They were the first

men to have their statues set up in the market-place at Athens. The subject of Harmodius and Aristogiton became a favorite with painters and sculptors when popular fancy transformed them from murderers to tyrannicides.

Harmonia (här-mō′ni-a̱). In Greek mythology, a daughter of Ares and Aphrodite. Zeus gave her to Cadmus when he became king of Thebes, and all the gods attended their wedding. Among the gifts to Harmonia was a necklace fashioned by Hephaestus which was said to guarantee beauty to its possessor. Some say Hephaestus gave it to Cadmus, and he gave it to Harmonia. Others say this had been a gift of Zeus to Europa; and still others say it was given by Aphrodite to Harmonia. Harmonia was also given a *peplus*, or robe, by Athena, and some say Athena gave her both the necklace and robe. These two gifts, handed down to the descendants of Cadmus, brought great grief to their possessors, and played a part in the Expedition of the Seven against Thebes as well as in the war of the Epigoni. They were at last taken to the temple of Apollo at Delphi, where the god saw to it that they brought no further disasters. There they remained until the 4th century B.C., when they were carried off by a bandit. Harmonia bore Agave, Autonoë, Ino, Semele, and Polydorus to Cadmus. Although Harmonia and Cadmus were turned into serpents by Zeus, their tomb was to be found in the land of the Encheleans in Illyria. See **Cadmus**.

Harmonia. A naiad; according to some accounts, she was the mother of the Amazons by Ares.

Harmonides (här-mō′ni-dēz). Another name for Phereclus, meaning the son of Harmon, who built the ships in which Paris abducted Helen.

Harmost (här′most). In Greek antiquity, the title of the governors appointed by the Spartans, during their supremacy after the Peloponnesian War, over subjected or conquered cities. The *harmost* was, in effect, a military governor.

Harmothoë (här-mō′thō̱-ē̱). In Greek mythology, the wife of Pandareus and the mother of Aëdon, Cleothera, and Merope. When her husband was punished for his part in the theft of the golden dog that guarded the infant Zeus, Harmothoë fled to Sicily and there died in misery.

Harpagus (här'pa̤-gus). General of Cyrus; fl. 6th century B.C. According to Herodotus, he was descended from a noble Median house, and was the attendant of Astyages, who charged him with the duty of exposing the infant Cyrus, grandson of Astyages. Instead of performing that duty in person, he delegated it to the herdsman Mitradates, who substituted a still-born child of which his wife had just been delivered. When the identity of Cyrus, who had been brought up by Mitradates and his wife as their own child, was discovered, Astyages punished Harpagus by serving up to him at a banquet the flesh of his own son. Harpagus waited until Cyrus had grown to manhood, then incited him to rebel against Astyages, and effected the downfall of the latter by deserting with the army to Cyrus. He was afterward one of the most trusted generals in the service of Cyrus, and played a prominent part in the conquest of Asia Minor.

Harpalyce (här-pal'i-sē). In Greek mythology, a daughter of Clymenus of Arcadia. She bore a son as the result of an incestuous union with her father, and afterwards cut up the child and served it as food to Clymenus. Clymenus learned what she had done and slew her. She was turned into a bird of prey.

Harpalyce. A daughter of Harpalycus, legendary king of Thrace. Her father had trained her in the arts of hunting. After his death she became a huntress and pillaged the peasants and shepherds. They finally caught her in a net, killed her, and celebrated her death annually with a mock fight at her grave.

Harpalycus (här-pal'i-kus). In Greek mythology, a son of Hermes, noted for his fearsome appearance when fighting, who, according to some accounts, taught boxing to the youthful Heracles.

Harpies (här'piz). In Greek mythology, winged daughters of Thaumas and Electra, daughter of Oceanus. They were winged monsters, ravenous and filthy, having the face and body of a woman and the wings of a bird of prey, with the feet and fingers armed with sharp claws, and the face pale with hunger. They served as ministers of divine vengeance. Sometimes they punished criminals themselves, as they tormented Phineus for impiety; sometimes they caught criminals and handed them over to the Erinyes for punishment, as in the case of Merope, Cleothera (or Cameiro), and Clytië, who were punished by the Erinyes for the crimes of their father, Pandareus. The Harpies carried off the souls of the dead and defiled the food of their living victims. They were commonly regarded as two (Aello and Ocypete) or three in number (Celaeno), but occasionally several others were mentioned. Homer mentions only one, named Podarge. They were

HARPIES
Black-figured Greek vase.

originally personifications of storm-winds sent by the gods to carry off offenders, and were later personified as fair-haired, winged maidens, their features and characteristics being more or less repulsive at different times and places. The Harpies have been to some extent confounded with the Sirens because of their form, being represented as women in the upper parts of their bodies and as birds below.

Harpina (här-pī'na̤). According to Pausanias, a daughter of the river-god Asopus. According to the people of Elis, she was the mother of Oenomaus by Ares. Oenomaus founded a city in Elis and named it after her.

Harudes (ha̤-rö'dēz). [Also: **Charudes.**] German tribe first mentioned by Caesar as in the army of Ariovistus. In the campaigns of Tiberius the Harudes were situated on the lower Albis (Elbe), at the base of the Cimbrian peninsula (Jutland). Nothing is known of their ultimate fate.

Haruspex (ha̤-rus'peks). One of a class of

minor priests or soothsayers in ancient Rome, of Etrurian origin, whose function it was to inspect the entrails of victims killed in sacrifice, and by them, as well as by certain natural phenomena, to interpret the will of the gods. Their duties were thus similar to those of the augurs, who, however, occupied a much higher position in the state.

Hasdrubal (haz′drṳ-bal, haz-drö′bal). [Also: **Asdrubal**.] Carthaginian general and politician, who died in Spain, 221 B.C. He rose to prominence as a leader of the democratic party in Carthage in the interval between the First and Second Punic wars, and married a daughter of Hamilcar Barca, whom he accompanied to Spain in 238 B.C. He subsequently returned to Africa to assume command in a war against the Numidians, and reduced them to submission. In 229 B.C. he succeeded his father-in-law as commander in Spain, where he founded the city of Carthago Nova (New Carthage, modern Cartagena), and largely extended the Carthaginian power, fixing by treaty the boundary between the Carthaginian and Roman possessions in Spain at the Iberus (Ebro). He was assassinated by a Celtic slave whose master he had put to death.

Hasdrubal. [Also: **Asdrubal**.] Carthaginian officer of high rank in the army of Hannibal in Italy. He contributed greatly to the victory of Cannae in 216 B.C. by a cavalry charge on the rear of the Roman infantry after having put the Roman horse to rout.

Hasdrubal. [Also: **Asdrubal**.] Carthaginian general; son of Hamilcar Barca and younger brother of Hannibal (c247–c183 B.C.); died 207 B.C. He was left in charge of the Carthaginian forces in Spain when Hannibal set out on his expedition to Italy in 218 B.C. He maintained the war against the Romans under the brothers Cnaeus and Publius Scipio with varied success until 212 B.C. Then, having been reinforced by two armies under Mago and Hasdrubal (d. 200 B.C.), son of Gisco, he was enabled to inflict a decisive defeat upon Cnaeus, who fell in the battle, Publius having been killed a short time previously in a cavalry engagement. He was defeated by Scipio Africanus at Baecula (Bailén) in 209 B.C., and probably in the same year crossed the Pyrenees on his way to join his brother in Italy. He crossed the Alps in 207 B.C., but was attacked and defeated by the Romans under Caius Claudius Nero and Marcus Livius on the Metaurus (Metauro) River in the same year before he could effect a junction with Hanibal. He fell in the engagement, and, according to Livy, his severed head was thrown into the camp of Hannibal by the victorious Romans.

Hasdrubal. [Also: **Asdrubal**.] Carthaginian general, son of Gisco; died c200 B.C. He was sent to Spain with an army in 214 B.C., and on the departure (c209 B.C.) of Hasdrubal, son of Hamilcar, on his expedition to join Hannibal in Italy, was left with Mago in command of the Carthaginian forces in Spain. He was defeated with his colleague at Silpia by Scipio Africanus in 206 B.C., was in command of an army opposed to Scipio in Africa in 204 B.C., when his camp near Utica was fired by the Romans and nearly the whole of his army destroyed, and is said by some authorities to have taken poison to escape the fury of the Carthaginian populace.

Hasdrubal. [Also: **Asdrubal**.] Carthaginian general. He was commander-in-chief in the war against Masinissa in 150 B.C. Having sustained a decisive defeat, he was punished with exile. He was, however, recalled on the outbreak of the Third Punic War in 149 B.C., and was placed in command of the forces outside the walls of Carthage. He defeated the consul Manilius in two engagements (c148 B.C.). He subsequently became commander of the forces within the city, which he defended with great obstinacy against Scipio Aemilianus in 146 B.C. He finally surrendered, and, after gracing the triumph of Scipio, was allowed to spend the rest of his life in honorable captivity. It is said that at the time of his surrender his wife upbraided him for cowardice, and threw herself and her children into the flames of the temple in which she had taken refuge.

Hearth, Goddess of the. See **Hestia**.

Hebe (hē′bē). In Greek mythology, the goddess of youth and spring; the personification of eternal and exuberant youth, and, until supplanted in this office by Ganymede, the cupbearer of Olympus. She was a daughter of Zeus and Hera, who gave her as wife to Heracles after his death and deification, as a reward for his achievements. She bore him two sons. Hebe was worshiped as Dia in certain localities, and in this aspect she is associated with Aphrodite. Powers of rejuvenation were ascribed to her. The Romans called her Juventas.

MARRIAGE OF HERACLES AND HEBE
Greek vase, 4th century B.C.

Hebrus (hē′brus). [Modern name, **Maritsa.**] A river of Thrace, about 300 miles long, that flows into the NE Aegean Sea. The maenads who attacked and dismembered Orpheus flung his head and his lyre into this river. There they miraculously floated, the lyre playing a plaintive air and the head murmuring sadly, and crossed the sea to the island of Lemnos.

Hecaleius (hek-a-lī′us). Epithet of Zeus. When Theseus was on his way to capture the Marathonian bull he was entertained by an old woman named Hecale. She vowed to sacrifice a ram to Zeus if he returned safely. When he returned, having been successful, Hecale had died. Theseus established Hecalesian Rites to honor her and Zeus Hecaleius.

Hecamede (hek-a-mē′dē). In the *Iliad*, a daughter of Arsinous of Tenedos, who was captured when Achilles took Tenedos and was awarded to Nestor as part of the spoils of war. She became the handmaiden and servant of Nestor in the Trojan War.

Hecataeus of Abdera (hek-a-tē′us; ab-dir′a). Greek philosopher and historian, active in the 4th century B.C. He appears to have accompanied Alexander the Great on his Asiatic expedition. He wrote a work on the Hyperboreans, and another on Egypt. Some critics also attribute to him a work on the Jews. A small number of fragments of his work survive.

Hecataeus of Miletus (mī-lē′tus, mi-). Greek chronicler and geographer, born at Miletus, c550 B.C. and died c476 B.C. He was descended from an ancient and illustrious family at Miletus, in Asia Minor. He thought he was the 16th generation in direct descent from a god until the priests of Egyptian Thebes disabused him of this notion. In his search for knowledge he traveled throughout the Mediterranean, in the Persian Empire, Egypt, and possibly also in Pontus, Libya, and Iberia. Most of our knowledge of him comes from Herodotus, who frequently consulted his description of the earth, and who disagreed with him about the source of the Nile and the existence of the river Oceanus, but otherwise respected him as a man of greatness. At the time of the Ionian revolt against the Persians (500–494 B.C.), the people of Miletus consulted him as a wise man. He urged them not to rebel against Darius, but his advice was ignored. He then urged them to seize the treasury of Apollo before the Persians got it, and to build a fleet with it which would command the Aegean. Again his advice was ignored, and Miletus was defeated. Subsequently Hecataeus served as ambassador to Artaphernes, satrap of Sardis under Darius I, whom he prevailed upon to treat the conquered insurgents with mildness. Hecataeus wrote of history as he knew it; that is, of times that have since come to be regarded as mythical but were considered to be historical in his own time. Sometimes he abandoned the Greek tradition in favor of the Egyptian tradition. In the fields in which he operated: literature, geography, and history, he was a great figure and represented the spirit of his age in his search for knowledge, his rationalistic approach, and his literary performance. Fragments of his work remain.

Hecate (hek′a-tē). [Also: **Hekate.**] In Greek mythology, a triple goddess combining the concepts of moon-goddess, earth-goddess, and Underworld-goddess. She had powers over the sky, earth, and sea, and was also a giver of riches and good fortune. As moon-goddess, she was identified with Artemis. As Underworld-goddess, she was an attendant of Persephone; and as leader of souls of the dead she was associated with ghosts, magic, and witchcraft. She was invisible to mortals, but dogs could see her pass; and she was often conceived of as tearing through the night followed by a pack of spectral hounds. Hounds were sacred to her. Hecate was also a crossroads-goddess, and as such was represented with triple bodies back to back. In this aspect the Romans named her Trivia. She was also identified variously with Demeter, Rhea, and Persephone.

Hecatomb (hek′a̱-tom, -töm). In ancient Greece, a great public sacrifice of oxen or other beasts. Homer speaks of hecatombs being offered, as by Agamemnon and Hector, to propitiate the gods. Hecatomb means literally "100 oxen," but a sacrifice so costly must rarely have been performed, the word coming to mean no more than a sacrifice of unusual importance: (JJ)

Hecatombaeon (hek″a̱-tom-bē′on). The first month of the Attic year, containing 30 days, and corresponding to the last half of July (roughly) and the first half of August. It was a month in which sacrifices were offered to the gods, whence its name.

Hecatompedon (hek-a-tom′pe̱-do̱n). Popular name of an early temple of Athena on the Acropolis at Athens. Its foundations, buried beneath the Parthenon, cannot be seen, but its dimensions and plan can be deduced from its name (*hecatompedon* means "100-foot") and from elements of the entablature and pediment sculptures which have survived, and which indicate a date before 550 B.C., in the time of the Pisistratids. It was a modest Doric temple of the limestone known as *poros,* restored with tristyle-in-antis porches at front and rear. The Hecatompedon was demolished between 490 and 480 B.C. to make way for a new and larger marble temple of Athena, the "Older Parthenon," which in turn was destroyed in scaffolding by the Persians in 480 B.C.

The name *Hecatompedon* is also used to designate the cella of the third temple of Athena to rise on this spot, the Parthenon, construction of which was begun in 447 B.C.

Although the name implies that the Parthenon cella was 100 feet in length, it was actually somewhat less, 91½ Doric feet as measured by Dinsmoor; the name doubtless arose from association with the Pisistratid Hecatompedon. (JJ)

Hecatompylon (hek-a-tom′pi-lon). A name for Thebes in Egypt, meaning "100-gated," a city said to have been founded by Heracles as he passed through Egypt on his way to the west to fetch the cattle of Geryon.

Hecatonchires (hek-a-ton-kī′rēz). Greek name, used collectively, for the 100-handed monsters Briareus (also called Aegaeon), Cottus, and Gyges (or Gyes). The Roman name was *Centimani.*

Hector (hek′to̱r). The Trojan hero of the *Iliad.* He was the son of Priam and Hecuba (but some say he was a son of Apollo), the Crown Prince of Troy, and the leader of the Trojans and their allies in the defense of Troy against the Greeks. He did not approve of the war and unsuccessfully tried to stop it by negotiation and by individual combat, as when he suggested the duel between Menelaus and Paris. He scorned his brother, Paris, as a beautiful coward and seducer of women, and often wished him in Hades. Nevertheless, Hector fought valiantly and was the bravest of the Trojans, as his honor compelled him to fight for his family and for his country. His bravery was the greater because he knew he was doomed to die and that Troy would fall. For sheer love of glorious combat he challenged the Greeks to send a champion against him in single combat. Telamonian Ajax won, by lot, the honor of fighting him and they struggled all day, with neither able to achieve victory. At the end of their duel each expressed admiration for the courage and skill of the other. Hector gave Ajax his sword as a gift. Ajax gave Hector his girdle in exchange.

In what is probably the most touching and tender scene in the *Iliad,* Andromache, his wife, begs him to withdraw from the field and to seek safety inside the city walls, for her sake and that of their son, as well as for his own. With understanding and compassion, for he foresees her gloomy future, he convinces her that he must go, for he cannot evade his destiny. He expresses the hope that his baby son, who now shrinks in terror from his father's glittering war helmet, will be proud of his father and will be a better man. Gently he salutes her and leaves to rejoin the fighting. Aided by Apollo, he leads the Trojans against the ramparts protecting the Greek galleys, smashes open the gates, and fires the ships. He slays Patroclus, the intimate friend of Achilles, and puts on his armor. The death of Patroclus causes Achilles to renounce the wrath that has kept him inactive during the struggle, and he enters the battle to avenge Patroclus. Achilles drives the Trojans back into the city. Hector is left alone before the walls to face him. Seized by a moment of human fear Hector flees. Three times Achilles pursues him around the walls of Troy. Now Hector masters his fear and stops to face his enemy. And now the gods forsake him. Athena deludes him by appearing in the guise of his

recognizes the armor that Hector is wearing, knows that there is a chink in the armor at the throat. He plunges his spear through the chink, and Hector falls. Achilles slits the tendons of Hector's heels, and takes the girdle that had been given to Hector by Ajax and passes it through the slits. Then he fastens the girdle to his chariot and drags the body of his fallen enemy through the dust to the Greek camp. Daily thereafter Achilles maltreats Hector's body, but it is preserved from all signs of injury by the gods, who anoint it with nectar and ambrosia. Thus, when Priam comes at last to ransom it, the body is still fresh. Priam returns to Troy with the body of his son and, as all Troy mourns, gives it funeral honors. Even Helen mourns the death of Hector, for he had always been kind to her and protected her from the spite of some of the Trojan women.

RANSOM OF HECTOR'S BODY
Red-figured Attic skyphos, early 5th century B.C. Hector's body lies under the couch on which Achilles rests; aged Priam is at the left. *Vienna*

brother. Hector hurls his spear at Achilles then turns to his supposed brother for another weapon. He finds no one is there and realizes that the moment has come to meet his inevitable fate. His request to Achilles that his body be restored to Priam for burial is wrathfully scorned; and Achilles, who

Great "shimmering-helmeted" Hector was one of the noblest characters of Greek literature—valiant, honorable, compassionate, reasonable, skillful in arms, and handsome in body. He paid due respect and honor to the gods, especially to Zeus, who in turn protected him often, but could not save him

fat, fāte, fär, fãre, errant; net, mē, her ardent; pin, pīne; not, nōte, mȯve, nôr, from his appointed fate. Some say that the bones of Hector were later taken to Thebes in Boeotia, and buried beside the fountain of Oedipus there. This was done in obedience to a command of the oracle, which recommended that the Thebans gain possession of the bones of Hector if they desired prosperity for their land. Others say they were moved at the command of Apollo, who ordered the reburial of Hector's body in a city that had taken no part in the Trojan War, in order to lift a plague that struck Greece. Hector was still worshiped at Troy in the time of the Roman Empire; even, in fact, after the state had recognized Christianity. The Emperor Julian was taken to the sanctuary of Hector in the Troad by the bishop. There he saw a bronze statue of Hector in a little shrine, before which embers of sacrificial fire were still glowing on an altar. The Emperor asked in surprise if people still sacrificed to Hector. The bishop replied that Hector was one of their good townsmen, and if people paid their respects to him it was no more than Christians did to their martyrs.

Hecuba (hek′ū-ba̱) or **Hecabe** (hek′a̱-bē). In Greek legend, a daughter of Dymas of Phrygia, or, as some say, of Cisseus. She was the second wife of Priam, king of Troy, and bore him 19 of his 50 sons. Her oldest son, Hector, was sometimes said to be the son of Apollo, as was her son Troilus. Among Hecuba's other sons were Paris, Deïphobus, Helenus, Polites, Antiphus, and Polydorus. Her daughters included Cassandra, Creusa, Laodice, and Polyxena. Before Paris was born Hecuba dreamed that she had given birth to a bundle of faggots tied with fiery serpents. She woke screaming that Troy was in flames. This dream was interpreted to mean that the child she was about to bear would bring destruction to Troy if he and his mother were not killed to prevent it. A second pronouncement said that the child born to a royal Trojan that day must be destroyed with his mother or Troy would fall in ruins. Hecuba bore Paris on the day of the later prophecy and Priam spared them both. Later, on the urgent advice of seers, he gave the infant to his herdsman with instructions to kill him. Some say Hecuba bribed the herdsman to spare her child.

In any event, Paris was not destroyed and when he appeared in Troy as a young man he was welcomed delightedly by his parents. During the Trojan War Hecuba pled with Hector to keep himself apart from the struggle but to no avail. When he was pursued to the walls by Achilles, she begged him to save himself but he refused; he stood and faced Achilles and met his death before his mother's eyes. For reasons that have never been satisfactorily explained, Hecuba, with Helen, questioned Odysseus, when he crept into Troy to steal the Palladium, and let him go without denouncing him as the spy he was. In this case, Hecuba acted with Helen. Later she beseeched Menelaus to kill Helen as the cause of the disasters which had overcome Troy and the house of Priam. In the sack of Troy Hecuba saw her son Polites and her husband slain by Neoptolemus. Only her children Cassandra, Polyxena, and Polydorus now remained to her. In the division of the spoils Hecuba was awarded to Odysseus, perhaps in fulfillment of some promise he had made to her when he secretly entered Troy, or perhaps to prevent her from revealing that he had appeared in any but a heroic light on that occasion. As the woman who once had been the proud queen of a rich kingdom waited to be carried off as a slave, she was informed that Cassandra and her daughter-in-law Andromache were to be the captives of Agamemnon and Neoptolemus respectively; and that, on the advice of Odysseus, her grandson Astyanax must be destroyed lest at some future time he raise an army and march against the Greeks. The aged, broken queen left Troy in flames and sailed with her captors across the Hellespont to Thrace. Here the Greeks were held by unfavorable winds. To appease Achilles and secure favorable winds, Hecuba's last remaining daughter was sacrificed on the tomb of Achilles. Hecuba wished that she might have died with her city, and counted Priam lucky that he had not lived to see his city fall and his children destroyed. In the midst of these shattering griefs the body of her son Polydorus was brought to her. He had been sent with a rich treasure to Polymnestor of Thrace for safe-keeping. Polymnestor had betrayed his trust, some say in his greed for gold, slain the young prince, and cast his body into the sea. It was washed ashore at Hecuba's feet. In a sudden fury for revenge Hecuba, with Agamemnon's connivance, lured Polymnestor and his two young sons into her tent, with a story that she had concealed a great hoard of Trojan gold there. Once they were inside Hecuba and other Trojan women attacked him, put out his eyes, and killed his two sons. Cassandra's prophecy that Hecuba would never go to Greece was fulfilled. The Greeks would have stoned her to death for the blinding of Polymnestor and the murder of his two sons, but she was transformed into a bitch, Maera, and ran howling off into the wilderness. Others say that she was taken to Thrace by Odysseus, but that she so hideously condemned the Greeks for their barbarity and treachery and uttered such constant invectives that they put her to death. Her spirit was transformed into a black bitch that leaped into the sea and swam off to the Hellespont. Even the gods agreed that Hecuba had not deserved to meet such an end.

Hecuba. A tragedy by Euripides, exhibited in 425 B.C. Before the tent of Agamemnon, on the coast of Thracian Chersonese, the ghost of Polydorus appears. Because of his youth, this son of Priam and Hecuba had been sent to Polymnestor in Thrace, with much gold, for safety during the Trojan War. As long as Hector lived and Troy was victorious, Polymnestor took good care of him. But when Troy fell Polymnestor murdered Polydorus for the gold and threw his body into the sea. Now the Greeks, having vanquished Troy, are prevented from sailing for home because the shade of Achilles demands the sacrifice of Polyxena, Priam's daughter, to honor his deeds in the war. The ghost of Polydorus prophesies that she will be sacrificed, and that his mother will see two corpses.

Hecuba, dressed as a slave, appears with a chorus of captive Trojan women. She tells them she has dreamed of Polydorus and Polyxena, and they sadly warn her that Polyxena must be sacrificed to Achilles' shade before the Greeks can sail. They say that Agamemnon wanted to spare her but Odysseus convinced him that Achilles' spirit demanded this honor. Polyxena joins her mother and learns of her impending fate. She regrets the sorrow this will cause her mother but she will be glad to die, for death will be a happier fate than life as a slave. When Odysseus comes to take her away, Hecuba reminds him of the time he entered Troy in disguise. Helen recognized him and warned Hecuba of his presence, but in response to his pleas Hecuba spared him. Now she pleads with him to spare her child. He denies her pleas. Polyxena refuses to plead for her life. She longs to die. Hecuba begs Odysseus to take her instead of her daughter. It was she who bore that son Paris who killed Achilles with his arrows, so she should be sacrificed. Again Odysseus denies her. Achilles' ghost, he says, demands Polyxena. Hecuba swoons as he takes Polyxena off.

Talthybius, Agamemnon's herald, comes to the despairing Hecuba. He has compassion for the fallen queen. He would rather die than fall so low. He has come to inform Hecuba that she may claim her daughter's body for burial. All the Greeks, he says, watched Achilles' son lead Polyxena to be sacrificed. She did not flinch from the knife but died heroically, as the Greeks freely acknowledged, by the hand of Achilles' son. Later Agamemnon comes to Hecuba to command her to fetch Polyxena's body, since he has, at her wish, forbidden the Greeks to touch it. He finds Hecuba with the corpse of Polydorus in her arms. His body had been washed up on the beach and brought to Hecuba. She appeals to Agamemnon, in the name of her daughter Cassandra, who is his captive, and as a champion of the right, to help her to avenge herself on Polymnestor. Polymnestor has betrayed his old friend, murdered Polydorus and cast his body into the sea, for the sake of the gold Polydorus had brought with him from Troy. Agamemnon would like to help her if it can be done without the knowledge of the Greeks. All Hecuba requires is his permission to bury Polyxena and Polydorus together and his promise to send Polymnestor to her. To his doubts that feeble, unarmed women can do much, she replies that it was women who killed the sons of Aepytus, and women who depopulated Lemnos. He agrees to send Polymnestor to her.

When Polymnestor enters with his two young sons Hecuba inquires about Polydorus. He assures her all is well with him. She then speaks about a secret hoard of gold, and adds that she has a treasure of jewels in her tent, brought with her from Troy. All go into the tent. The chorus of women, remaining outside proclaims that the penalty for murder will soon be paid. At this Polymnestor screams from within the tent that he has been blinded and his children murdered. Hecuba comes out of the tent, Polymnestor groping after her and shouting for help. He tells Agamemnon, who has returned, that he killed Polydorus lest he reassemble the Trojans and start another war on the Greeks. In pain and anguish of heart he tells him that Hecuba and the captive women duped him, disarmed him, killed his children, and blinded him. Hecuba scoffs at Polymnestor's tale that he murdered Polydorus to help the Greeks. He did it for the gold, but if he really wants to help the Greeks he should give it to them. Agamemnon judges that Polymnestor, who is guilty of guest-murder, the foulest crime, has got what he deserved. Polymnestor prophesies that Hecuba will turn into a red-eyed bitch. He tells Agamemnon a bath of blood awaits him in Argos, and prophesies the death of Cassandra and Agamemnon at the hands of his wife Clytemnestra. Agamemnon orders the soldiers to take him away and leave him on a desert island. He then commands Hecuba to bury her children quickly for, following the sacrifice of Polyxena on Achilles' funeral pyre, a favorable breeze has sprung up, and they will sail for Greece at once.

Hegeleos (hē-jel′e-os). In Greek legend, a son of Tyrsenus, and a grandson of Heracles. He taught the Dorians how to play the trumpet and set up a sanctuary of Athena Salpinx (*Trumpet*) in Argos.

Hegemone (hē-je′mō-nē). In Athens only two Charites (Graces) were recognized. Hegemone (Queen) was one of them. See **Charites.**

Hegeso (hē-jē′sō), **Monument of.** Monument in Athens, Greece, on the Street of Tombs, remarkable for the beauty of its relief-stele of the 4th century B.C.

Helen (hel′en). [Also: **Helen of Troy.**] In Greek legend, the "all-glorious" woman whose divine beauty led to a disastrous war which ended in the complete destruction of Troy and the empire of King Priam. Various stories are related concerning her birth, but certain it is that Zeus was her father. Some say that Zeus pursued Nemesis; that she fled from him, transforming herself from one animal to another to escape. At last she took the form of a goose and flew off. Zeus assumed the form of a swan, overtook her and ravished her. Nemesis laid a blue and silver egg which was found by Leda, wife of Tyndareus. She took it home and hid it in a chest, and from this egg Helen was born. Others say that Hermes found the egg Nemesis had laid and tossed it between Leda's knees, and it was from this that Leda bore Helen. The most common account is that Zeus, in the form of a swan, made love to Leda, and she bore him Helen. Helen's brothers were the twins, Castor and Polydeuces, of whom Polydeuces, and sometimes both, are said to be the sons of Zeus. Her sister was Clytemnestra, the child of Tyndareus. From childhood Helen was famed for her beauty. As a child, some say at the age of 12, she was kidnaped by Theseus and Pirithous and taken to Athens. Theseus, having lost his wife, intended to make Helen his bride. However, the Athenians frowned on this exploit of Theseus and, to avoid their displeasure, he sent her to Aphidna with his mother for safe-keeping. Helen's loyal brothers swooped down on Aphidna and rescued her, and carried her back to Sparta. As she grew to marriageable age the richest and most powerful princes of Greece sought her hand. Tyndareus, her supposed father, turned none of the suitors away. On the other hand, he dared not choose any one among them lest the others turn on him in wrath. Odysseus, not one of Helen's suitors, suggested a scheme whereby Tyndareus might award his daughter's hand without incurring the anger of the disappointed suitors. He advised Tyndareus to require each of the suitors to take an oath, on the joints of a horse, by which each would swear to come to the aid of the man who became Helen's husband in the event that any ill should come to him because of his marriage. Diomedes,

Ajax, Teucer, Patroclus, Philoctetes, Idomeneus, and many others willingly took the oath. Tyndareus gave her to Menelaus, whom he also made the heir to the throne of Sparta. Whether Menelaus was also Helen's choice is not known. Helen bore Menelaus one daughter, Hermione, and, some say, three sons. However Helen and Menelaus may have felt about each other, the gods had decreed that their marriage was doomed. Some say Zeus wanted to make Helen famous for having embroiled Europe and Asia in a devastating war, or that he wanted to exalt the demigods. Some say Aphrodite was punishing Tyndareus, who had once overlooked her when he was sacrificing to the gods, by causing his daughters to become notorious adulteresses. Whatever the reason, the gods deliberately caused the war and took an active role in its progress. As Homer pictures Helen, she was the helpless tool of the gods, neither responsible for her beauty nor the disasters it caused.

Aphrodite had promised Paris, son of King Priam of Troy, the fairest woman in the world if he awarded her the golden apple which Eris had tossed among the wedding guests at the marriage of Peleus and Thetis. Paris did award Aphrodite the apple. Helen was the fairest woman in the world and already married. Yet Aphrodite set all in train to carry out her promise. Paris, with the blessing of his father, sailed to Sparta, telling no one the true object of his journey. In Sparta he was courteously welcomed and entertained by Menelaus. Apparently Menelaus felt perfectly secure in the affections of Helen, for though it was obvious to everyone that Paris was madly in love with Helen and making no effort to hide it, at the end of nine days Menelaus sailed off to Crete to attend his grandfather's funeral. He left his kingdom and the task of entertaining his distinguished and handsome Trojan guest in charge of Helen. The night of Menelaus' departure Helen eloped with Paris, taking a son and a great treasure with her. Paris' fleet was delayed by storms sent by Hera, and more time elapsed in side journeys to Cyprus, Phoenicia, and Egypt, before Paris arrived in Troy and formally married Helen. She bore him several children, all of whom perished in infancy. The entire city of Troy fell in love with Helen; old men stood at the walls to watch her pass; Priam vowed he would never let her go. Embassies from the Greeks demanding her return were summarily dismissed. The resolution of Paris and Priam to keep Helen did not weaken even when the Greeks gathered a great fleet of over 1000 ships and raided the coasts of the Troad. This resolution was concurred in by most of the Trojans. Men like Antenor, who advised from the very beginning that she be restored to her husband and reparations made, were regarded as traitors.

After nearly ten years of raids and attacks on the allies and cities of the Troad, the Greek fleet was beached off the plain of Troy and the city was besieged. Violent encounters followed between the Greeks under Agamemnon and the Trojans under Hector, then Paris and Menelaus, by agreement between the Greek and Trojan chieftains, fought in single combat to decide who should have Helen. This was a sensible solution to avoid further bloodshed by limiting the fighting to the two men most intimately concerned. If the gods had not intervened, the Trojan War would have ended here. Menelaus was about to strangle Paris in this duel when Aphrodite snatched him away in a mist and restored him to Helen. Helen was by no means grateful; she chided both the goddess and Paris. She would have preferred to go back to Menelaus and her homeland, but was compelled to accept the bidding of the goddess. In the *Iliad,* Helen's elopement is the dynamic force which sets off the great struggle between the Greeks and Trojans, but once the struggle is in progress Helen plays a minor role. Homer makes no criticism of Helen. His attitude is one worshipful of her beauty and sympathetic to her plight as a pawn of the gods. Following the interference of Aphrodite in the duel between Menelaus and Paris, full-scale war broke out again. As the Greeks massed on the plain Priam called Helen to him and asked her to identify various outstanding Greeks he could see from the towers of Troy. She named and characterized such heroes as Ajax, Odysseus, and others, and looked for her brothers among the throng, unaware that they had died and been deified. Watching the Greeks and remembering her happy life in Sparta, Helen regretted the trouble she, at Aphrodite's hands, had caused, and longed for her husband and her daughter. She was one of the chief mourners at the death of Hector. He had always been gentle and compassionate with her, and had ever turned aside the anger of others. As she grieved over Hector's death she lamented her years in Troy (20, according to Homer), and wished she had died rather than have caused so much anguish to so many. Following the death of Paris, Helen feared that she, now without a protector, would suffer the anger of the Trojans for the misery she had caused, but Deïphobus and Helenus, brothers of Paris, quarreled for her hand. She was awarded to Deïphobus, because of his brave deeds. The Trojans disapproved of this marriage by force.

When Odysseus crept into the city in disguise to steal the Palladium, which the Greeks had learned protected the city as long as it remained in the citadel, Helen recognized him. She took him, cringing and appealing for mercy, to Hecuba. Hecuba and Helen questioned him and let him go free, without telling anyone he had been there. Some say Helen did this to prepare for her return to Menelaus. Others say she succeeded, as she thought, in getting valuable information about the Greeks' plans from Odysseus. But Odysseus returned with Diomedes, and this time the Palladium was stolen from the citadel. Troy's days were numbered. The Greeks sailed away behind the island of Tenedos and left the Wooden Horse on the beach before Troy. The Trojans jubilantly hauled it inside the walls, deluded into the belief that it would please Athena and give them dominion over Europe. Helen, accompanied by Deïphobus, walked around the Wooden Horse. To test whether there were indeed, as Cassandra proclaimed, armed men hidden inside it, Helen imitated the voices of the wives of the Greek warriors and called out their names. So true was her imitation that Anticlus would have replied, and Menelaus and Diomedes wanted to leap out of the horse on hearing her voice, but Odysseus restrained them all. Some say Aphrodite, in disguise, appeared to Helen and told her Menelaus was in the Horse, and that she walked around it to help the Trojans, but Athena came to prevent her from helping the

Trojans and caused her to light a signal fire which burned from the roof of her house all night and advised the Greeks it was safe to return. Others say it was Sinon who, after releasing the Greeks from inside the Wooden Horse, lighted the beacon to summon the Greek fleet back. He opened the gates of Troy and the Greeks streamed silently inside the walls and sacked the city. Menelaus made straight for Helen's house. Though he had proclaimed that he would kill her, he was passionately in love with her and could hardly wait to get her back. Deïphobus, with whom Menelaus and Odysseus found Helen, was slain and horribly mangled. Menelaus instantly forgave Helen. He was more than willing to blame the elopement, as she did, on the gods. She feared the anger the Greeks would harbor against her, and went among them in shame, but she was so beautiful everyone "marveled to see the glory of loveliness of that all-flawless woman"; no one reproached her. She accompanied Menelaus to his ship and they passed the rest of the night in sweet converse.

Following the destruction of Troy, Menelaus quarreled with Agamemnon and sailed immediately, without offering due sacrifice to the gods. To punish him, Athena drove his fleet off course, and afterward he and Helen were delayed eight years on their journey home. Helen feared the welcome she would get in Greece, but as it turned out, she and Menelaus, who returned to Sparta with rich treasure, lived among their people in great prosperity and harmony. So deep was the affection and understanding between Helen and Menelaus, according to Homer, that she could refer ruefully to the aberration which had caused her to leave her husband and embroil Europe and Asia in a disastrous war. There is a story that the poet Stesichorus wrote a scurrilous account of Helen's elopement. Some time later he went blind and learned that Helen had taken away his sight to punish him for dishonoring her name. He wrote a new account, which he called the true one, and repudiated the former one as spurious. According to his revised version, Helen never went to Troy at all. Zeus sent Hermes to carry her off in a cloud. She was taken to Egypt and left under the protection of the king there. The Helen for whom

Menelaus and all the Greeks fought Hector and all the Trojans was a phantom, fashioned from a cloud by Hera. While they fought over this wraith the real Helen, blameless of any infidelity to Menelaus, remained in Egypt, bemoaning the awful fate which had caused her name to be dishonored. Seven years after the end of the Trojan War Menelaus, who had been completely taken in by the phantom Helen, touched at Egypt after a storm had wrecked his fleet. There he found his own true, beautiful, and virtuous wife. They were joyously reunited as the phantom Helen disappeared.

There are as many accounts of Helen's end as there are of her birth. Some say that Helen was threatened by Orestes when she and Menelaus at last landed in Sparta, because he considered her the cause of all his troubles. She was borne off in a cloud to Olympus, at Zeus' command, where she joined her brothers as a goddess who protects mariners. Others record that Menelaus died in Sparta and that Helen, friendless, fled to her former friend Polyxo in Rhodes. Polyxo, the wife of Tlepolemus who was killed in the Trojan War, avenged her husband's death by inciting her servants to hang Helen. But others say that Helen and Menelaus lived happily together; that Menelaus was made immortal as the son-in-law of Zeus, and that he and Helen went to the Elysian Fields together where they wander hand in hand. Still others say that Achilles had fallen in love with her when he saw her on the walls of Troy, and that at the end of her life with Menelaus in Sparta, she went to the island of Leuce which had been given to Achilles by Poseidon. There she married Achilles and lived happily with him and his companions, Antilochus, Patroclus, and the two Ajaxes. Mariners who sailed near the wooded shores of the island could hear their voices floating over the water as they recited the verses of Homer which recounted their exploits. A special shrine to Helen, as a goddess of beauty, was erected at Therapne, and an annual festival was held there in her honor.

Helen. A drama by Euripides, written about 412 B.C. In this drama Euripides presents the view that Helen, daughter of Zeus and Leda, and wife of Menelaus, king of Sparta, never went to Troy at all. Hera, angry with Paris for awarding the prize for beauty to Aphrodite, substituted a phantom Helen, shaped from a cloud, for the real Helen whom Aphrodite had given to Paris as a reward for giving the golden apple of beauty to her. Paris, unaware of the substitution, took the phantom back to Troy with him, while the real Helen was spirited away by Hermes and left under the protection of King Proteus of Egypt. There she remained, lamenting the evil fate that had made her name a byword of infamy, although she was innocent of dishonoring her husband. Because of the anger and wiles of Hera, Greeks and Trojans perished by the Scamander in Troy for a wraith; the whole war, for which Helen was held to be the cause, was fought for a cloud. After seven years, Menelaus, who had been continually prevented from reaching his homeland by violent storms, was shipwrecked on the Egyptian coast. He found Helen, and after learning that the Helen he had captured at Troy was nothing but a phantom, and that his wife had been noble and virtuous throughout the long years, he joyously claimed her. By trickery they were able to escape from Theoclymenus, the son and successor of Proteus, who had determined to marry Helen, and return to Sparta. Thus the will of the gods, absolutely incomprehensible to mortals, was fulfilled, while Euripides calls attention to the futility of war.

Helena (hel'e-na). Greek painter; daughter of the Egyptian Timon. She is said to have lived in the time of the battle of Issus (333 B.C.), and to have painted a picture of that subject. This picture was hung by Vespasian in the Temple of Peace at Rome. The great Pompeian mosaic of the battle of Issus must have been made about this time, and is perhaps a copy of the picture.

Helena. Island off the coast of Attica, between Cape Sunium and the island of Ceos. Helen is said to have landed there first on her return with Menelaus from Troy, and the island was named for her.

Helenor (he-lē'nôr). In the *Aeneid,* the son of a Lydian king and a slave-girl from Licymna. He had fought at Troy and accompanied Aeneas in his flight from that city to Italy. He was one of the principal defenders of the garrison in the war between the Trojans, under Aeneas, and the Latins, under

fat, fāte, fär, fāre, errant; net, mē, hėr ardent; pin, pīne; not, nōte, möve, nôr,

Turnus, when Turnus attacked it while Aeneas was away seeking help.

Helenus (hel'ẹ-nus). In Greek legend, a son of Priam and Hecuba, and the twin of Cassandra. When he was a child the twins were left outside while others celebrated in the temple of Apollo. Sacred serpents came and licked their ears and gave them prophetic powers. When later, Paris proposed to set out for Sparta with the secret intention of abducting Helen, Helenus agreed with Cassandra that Troy would go up in flames if he made the trip, but their prophecies were ignored. In the Trojan War he fought bravely, killing many and wounding Achilles and Menelaus. After the death of Paris, he contended with Deïphobus for Helen's hand. She was awarded to Deïphobus, who forcibly married her, and Helenus withdrew from the city and went to live on Mount Ida. The Greeks learned from Calchas that only Helenus could tell them what protected Troy and determined to seize him. Odysseus captured him in the temple of Apollo and took him to the Greek camp. Helenus agreed to give the required information on condition that he be sent to a land far from Troy at the close of the war. He said Troy could not be taken unless a bone of Pelops was brought to the Greek camp, that Neoptolemus, son of Achilles, must join the fighting, and that the Greeks must steal the Palladium that protected Troy as long as it remained in the city. After the war Helenus advised Neoptolemus to go to Molossia. He also told him to wait two more days before sailing, and prophesied that storms would overtake the others. In gratitude for his advice Neoptolemus took Helenus with him when he left Troy, and bequeathed him Andromache, captive and concubine of Neoptolemus, on his death. Helenus also told Neoptolemus to build a city where he found men living in houses whose foundations were of iron, walls of wood, and roofs of wool. It was because of this advice that Neoptolemus later settled in Epirus, where he came upon a group who were camped under blankets supported by spears. Some say that Neoptolemus also gave Helenus his mother, Deidamia, for a wife. Later, after the death of Neoptolemus, Helenus acquired Andromache (Hector's wife), and a part of Neoptolemus' kingdom in

Epirus, thus becoming a ruler over Greeks. He built a miniature Troy, with a copy of the Scaean Gate, near a river which he named Xanthus after the river of Troy. He entertained Aeneas when the latter stopped there on his way from Troy to Italy, and made certain prophecies regarding his fate. He told Aeneas that the voyage and dangers ahead were yet great, that a sow with 30 new-born piglets would mark the site of the city Aeneas was to build, that he should avoid the east coast of Italy because it was peopled by Greeks, that he should sail around Sicily to avoid Scylla and Charybdis, that he should pay particular homage to Hera, and that he should consult the Cumaean Sibyl. He then gave Aeneas a plumed helmet that had once belonged to Neoptolemus and many other presents and guides and sent him on his way.

Heliadae (hẹ-lī'a-dẹ). A name given to the seven sons of Helius and Rhode, daughter of Poseidon. They were thought to be especially gifted in knowledge of astrology. For the murder of one of the brothers, the other brothers were scattered through various lands.

Heliades (hẹ-lī'a-dẹz). A name for the daughters of Helius and the nymph Clymene. Their grief for the death of their brother, Phaëthon, was so great that the gods in pity transformed them into poplar trees. There they stand, eternally weeping tears of amber, on the banks of the Eridanus River into which Phaëthon fell when struck by a thunderbolt of Zeus.

Helicaon (hel-i-kā'on). In Greek legend, a son of Antenor and Theano, and the husband of Laodice, a daughter of Priam. He was horribly wounded in the fall of Troy and was rescued by Odysseus. His family was spared by the Greeks, because Antenor had advised the Trojans to return Helen, and later migrated to the northern coast of Italy.

Helice (hel'i-sẹ). In ancient geography, a city of Achaea, on the south coast of the Gulf of Corinth. According to some accounts, it was founded by Ion, son of Apollo and Creusa, and named for his wife Helice, daughter of King Selinus of Aegialus. Men of Helice went to the Trojan War under the command of Agamemnon. Poseidon had a temple there. In 373 B.C., according to Pausanias, some suppliants who had fled to his temple and taken refuge in his famous sanctuary were dragged away from the altars by the Achaeans. To punish them for this impiety Poseidon sent an earthquake against the Achaeans. Helice was shaken to the ground and was then swallowed up in the sea by a tidal wave; none of its inhabitants was left alive.

Helicon (hel′i-kon, -kọn). [Also: **Elikon, Helikon, Zagora**.] Mountain range in S central Greece, on the N shore of the Gulf of Corinth, about 50 miles NW of Athens. According to legend Helicon and Cithaeron were brothers. Cithaeron was fierce and brutal. He murdered his father and attempted to hurl gentle Helicon from a rock, whereupon the brothers were transformed by the gods into the mountains which bear their names. Helicon became the home of Apollo and the Muses. Wild Cithaeron became a mountain on which unwanted infants were often exposed to die. Helicon contained the fountains of Aganippe and Hippocrene. Peak elevation, about 5868 feet.

Heliconian (hel-i-kō′ni-an). Epithet of Poseidon, meaning "Of Helice," from the town in Achaea of that name. The Ionians founded the sanctuary of Heliconian Poseidon at Helice, and it was very holy to them. When they were driven out by the Achaeans they took the cult of Heliconian Poseidon to Athens with them. From Athens the Ionians went to the coasts of Asia, and their worship of Heliconian Poseidon went with them. They established altars there, as at Miletus, and also founded a precinct and altar of Heliconian Poseidon at Teos. At Helice, the Achaeans removed some suppliants from the altar of Heliconian Poseidon and killed them. As punishment Poseidon visited upon their city complete destruction. First an earthquake swallowed it up, then a flood inundated it.

Heliodorus (hē″li-ọ-dō′rus). Greek novelist, born at Emesa (modern Homs), Syria, and active toward the end of the 4th century A.D. One of the two best Greek novelists, according to some scholars (the other was Longus), he was the forerunner of a new and buoyant movement in the writing of romances. His strength lay in his control of plot, his skill in narrative, and in the lively power and quality of his writing. According to one account, given as typical of Heliodorus, he was a bishop of the Christian Church. His works aroused the criticism of his colleagues and he was asked either to give up writing romances or his bishopric. He resigned his bishopric. Some say, however, that this is an apochryphal tale, and that Heliodorus the bishop was another individual. An extant novel by Heliodorus is the *Ethiopica*, in ten books, which served as a model to later Greek novelists.

Heliopolis (hē-li-op′ọ-lis). [Ancient Egyptian, **An** or **On**; modern name, **Matarieh, Matariya**; known as the "**City of the Sun-God**."] In ancient geography, a city in Lower Egypt, on the Pelusiac branch of the Nile. According to legend, it was founded by Actis, a son of Helius and Rhode, who named it for his father. It was situated on the edge of the desert, about four miles E of the apex of the Nile delta. It was a seat of learning ("the university of Egypt") and of the worship of the sun-god Ra. Its site is about six miles N of Cairo.

Heliopolis. [Modern name, **Baalbek, Baalbec, or Ba'albek**.] Ancient city of Syria, situated on the slope of the Anti-Libanus mountains, about 34 miles NW of Damascus; now a small town in E Lebanon. Famous in modern times chiefly for its ruins, it was a center of the worship of Baal as sun-god, whence both the original and Greek names. The city was a Roman colony (Colonia Julia Augusta Felix) under Augustus, and was adorned, especially with the great temple of Jupiter which he began, by Antoninus Pius. There are also remains of temples to Bacchus and Venus. Its decline began with its capture by the Arabs, and it was totally destroyed by an earthquake in 1759. The site is famous for the ruins of the great temples on its acropolis. The older portions of the acropolis wall, made of huge stones, are of Phoenician or kindred origin, and date from the time when the worship of Baal was still supreme. Aside from these sections of the wall, all the structures now remaining are Roman or later in time, and are interesting for their grouping, their great size, and the beauty of the materials. The site has been known to Europeans since the 16th century, and its monuments have been studied and sketched by many explorers.

fat, fāte, fär, fāre, errạnt; net, mē, hėr ardẹnt; pin, pīne; not, nōte, mȯve, nôr,

Helius (hē'li-us). The sun-god (called Hyperion by Homer). He was the son of the Titan Hyperion and the Titaness Thia, and was the brother of Eos and Selene. By Clymene he was the father of Phaëthon. Aeëtes, Circe, and Pasiphaë were his children by Persa. Helius is also known as a god of herds and flocks, who keeps his own sacred flocks on Trinacria (Sicily), an island which was given to him by Zeus after it was formed in the battle between the gods and Giants, and on the island of Erythea. Helius is represented as a strong and beautiful youth, with heavy waving locks and a crown of rays, driving a four-horse chariot. He keeps his horses in a magnificent stable built for him by Hephaestus, and each morning rises from the ocean on the east and drives across the heavens in his glowing car, descending at evening into the western sea. At night, while asleep, he is borne along the northern edge of the earth in a golden boat or cup made by Hephaestus to his rising-place in the east. Because of his passage through the sky nothing escapes the notice of Helius. It was he who warned Hephaestus of the love affair between Ares and Aphrodite, who saw Hades abduct Persephone, who told Artemis that Oeneus of Calydon had forgotten to include her in his sacrifice of first fruits to the gods. Rhodes, the principal seat of his worship, came into Helius' hands in the following manner: when Zeus was parcelling out various cities and islands to the gods he forgot Helius. Helius offered to take as his portion an island which was just then rising out of the sea. This was Rhodes, and Helius made it his own. There he became the father of seven sons and a daughter by the nymph Rhode. His sons became rulers of the island and their descendants built his famous statue, the Colossus of Rhodes. In later times Helius was confused with Apollo because of his association with the sun. The Romans identified him with their Sol.

Helius. Roman court favorite; died 68 A.D. He was prefect of Rome and Italy during the absence (67–68) of Nero in Greece, being invested with full power of life and death even over the senatorial order. He was put to death, with Locusta, the poisoner,

and other of Nero's creatures by Nero's successor, the emperor Galba.

Helladians (he-lā'di-anz). In Byzantine geography, a name coined to describe the people of Hellas, the region in and near the Greek peninsula, to distinguish them from those speaking Greek, or the Hellenes.

Helladic (he-lad'ik). A term coined by prehistorians to denote the material culture of the bronze age (c3000–c1100 B.C.) of the mainland of Greece, and its three chronological divisions: Early Helladic c3000–c1950 B.C., Middle Helladic c1950–c1650 B.C., Late Helladic c1650–c1100 B.C., each in turn subdivided into two or more phases. The term Mycenaean is synonymous with Late Helladic in this context and is freely substituted for it. Parallel terms are Cycladic, denoting the bronze-age culture of the islands of the Aegean (Cyclades), and Minoan, denoting the bronze-age culture of Crete. (JJ)

Hellanicus (hel-a-nī'kus). Greek chronicler or logographer. He was born at Mytilene, in Lesbos, possibly c480 B.C. and lived until some time after 406 B.C. He is said by Suidas, probably erroneously, to have lived with Herodotus at the court of Amyntas of Macedonia. The same doubtful authority states that he died at Perperene, on the coast of Asia Minor, opposite Lesbos. He is known to have lived before Thucydides, who mentioned his now-lost work *Atthis* (a history of Attica), which in its turn mentioned the battle of Arginusae (406 B.C.), and is thought to have been younger than Herodotus. Using local written and oral records, he collected what he thought to be a mass of facts, but which in many cases were local or general myths, legends, and versions of events distorted for local purposes, and put these into chronological order according to a system of his own devising. He wrote a history of Persia, including in it many Greek stories, and preserved many Greek legends (which he thought of as historical events in danger of being lost) in his histories of the Aeolians in Asia Minor. He wrote about the descendants of Deucalion and histories of Media and Assyria from the time of Ninus to his own day. He went to Argos and wrote the legends of that region and also published a list of the priestesses of Hera at Argos, as well as a list of the victors of the games of

actor; up, lūte, pull; oi, oil; ou, out; ŦH, then; ḍ as d or j, ş as s or sh, ṭ as t or ch, ẓ as z or zh.

Apollo at Sparta. These lists, considered to be accurate, were important as providing a chronological basis for the history of the past, but to this chronology he fitted the myths and legends of which he wrote. Next he went to Athens and wrote his *Atthis,* in which he gave long lists of the names of kings of Attica in an attempt to account for a period beginning more than a thousand years before the first Olympiad. His artificial and invented lists, with his method of using local data uncritically, have at times put obstacles in the way of obtaining historical fact, and he was called a liar by Ephorus, careless by Apollodorus, and less reliable than Homer, Hesiod, and the tragic poets by Strabo. Nevertheless, he attempted to be systematic, and was conscientious in following a method of recording, even when he had to invent to complete the record, and even when what he recorded was in no sense history. Only fragments of his works survive.

Hellas (hel′as). In ancient geography, originally a town and small district in Phthiotis, Thessaly, later extended to denote the lands inhabited by the Hellenes, modern Greek Ellas. The terms Greek and Greece were never applied by the Greeks to themselves, being used by Italians first to designate the Hellenes of S Italy (Magna Graecia) and subsequently extended to include the Hellenes of the mainland. (JJ)

Helle (hel′ē). In Greek legend, the daughter of Athamas and Nephele, and a sister of Phrixus. The two children flew away on the winged ram with the golden fleece to escape the death plotted for them by their stepmother. Helle fell off and was drowned in the Hellespont, whence its name, meaning "Sea of Helle."

Hellen (hel′en). In Greek legend, a son of Deucalion and Pyrrha. He married Orseïs and settled in Thessaly. Through his sons, Aeolus, Xuthus, and Dorus, he was the eponymous ancestor of the entire Hellenic race. Aeolus was the founder of the Aeolian tribe; the sons of Xuthus, Achaeus and Ion, founded the Achaean and Ionian tribes; and Dorus was the founder of the Dorian tribe.

Hellenes (hel′ēnz). Ancient Greeks; properly, the Greeks traditionally so called from Hellen, son of Deucalion and Pyrrha, the legendary ancestors of the true Greeks, consisting of the Dorians, Aeolians, Ionians, and Achaeans.

Hellespont (hel′es-pont). [Modern name, **Dardanelles.**] Strait connecting the Propontis (Sea of Marmara) with the Aegean Sea, and separating the Chersonesus Thracica (Gallipoli peninsula) from Asia Minor. It was named for Helle, the sister of Phrixus. As she and her brother were escaping from Orchomenus on the back of a golden-fleeced ram, Helle lost her hold and fell into this strait, which ever after bore her name. It was celebrated in the legend of Hero and Leander. It was crossed by Xerxes in 480 B.C., and by Alexander the Great in 334 B.C. Length, about 45 miles; average width, 3 to 4 miles; narrowest point, about 1¼ miles.

Helos (hē′los). In ancient geography, a town in Laconia, situated near the sea, about 25 miles SE of Sparta. It was said to have been founded by Helius, the youngest son of Perseus. The Dorians reduced it by siege and reduced the inhabitants to slavery and carried them off to Sparta.

Helvetii (hel-vē′shi-ī). A Celtic people which in the time of Caesar occupied a district east of the Jura, north of the Lacus Lemannus (Lake of Geneva), and west and south of the Rhenus (Rhine), in what is now Switzerland. They were defeated by Caesar in 58 B.C., and thoroughly subjugated by Augustus in 15 B.C.

Hemera (hem′er-a). In Greek mythology, a daughter of Erebus and Nyx (Night). Later she came to be identified with Eos (Dawn) when, as she accompanied Helius, she changed from Dawn and became Day.

Hemerasia (hē-mer-ā′zha). An epithet of Artemis, meaning "She who Soothes." There was a sanctuary of Artemis Hemerasia in Arcadia on the spot where Melampus cured the daughters of Proetus of their madness.

Hemithea (hē-mith′e-a). In Greek legend, a daughter of Cycnus of Colonae and Proclea. She was the sister of Tenes and was banished with him by her father and accompanied him to Tenedos. Some say Achilles fell in love with her when the Greeks landed on Tenedos on their way to Troy, and that it was a quarrel over her that led Achilles to kill Tenes. Others say that after Achilles killed Tenes he pursued Hemithea. He would have caught her but the earth parted and swallowed her up.

Henioche (hē-nĭ′ō̯-kē). Epithet of Hera, meaning "Charioteer." Suppliants at the oracle of Trophonius, at Lebadia, sacrificed to Hera Henioche.

Hephaestion (hē-fes′ti-on). Macedonian of Pella; died at Ecbatana (now Hamadan, Iran), 324 B.C. He was the intimate friend and companion of Alexander the Great, whom he accompanied on the campaigns in Asia. Alexander called him "the friend of Alexander," whereas his other close companion he named "the friend of the king." When Alexander crossed the Hellespont (334 B.C.) and laid a garland on the tomb of his hero and supposed ancestor, Achilles, Hephaestion did homage at the grave of Patroclus, for he was linked to Alexander as Patroclus was to Achilles. When Alexander increasingly adopted barbarian (Oriental) customs as he continued his conquest of Asia, Hephaestion did the same, although other of Alexander's closest companions resented the influence the barbarians seemed to be wielding on their king. On the march into India, Hephaestion, with three regiments, went by the Khyber Pass to the Indus River, where he was to arrange transport for the crossing of the army. On the return from India Alexander rested at Ecbatana, the Median capital. Thousands of poets and actors came from Greece to entertain the king; great feasts and celebrations were held. Hephaestion fell ill of a fever. He disregarded his physician's orders to rest and abstain from feasting, and joined Alexander at a banquet. He suffered a relapse and died. Alexander was wild with grief. He ordered the manes and tails of the horses and mules to be cut, razed the fortifications of neighboring cities as a sign of mourning, crucified the physician who attended Hephaestion, and forbade the playing of music until an oracle of Ammon arrived instructing him to sacrifice to Hephaestion and worship him as a hero. He fell on the tribe of the Cossaeans and destroyed them, some say as a sacrifice to Hephaestion. When he arrived in Babylon, 323 B.C., he caused a funeral pyre 200 feet high to be raised, on which his friend's body was burned. For the funeral, of unsurpassed magnificence, he had set aside 10,000 talents. The last honor he paid his friend was the erection of shrines, in which Hephaestion would be worshiped as a hero, at Alexandria in Egypt and in other cities.

Hephaestus (hē-fes′tus). One of the 12 Olympian gods, he was the god of fire and the divine smith. With Athena, he was the patron of handicrafts, and through his skill as a craftsman he was one of the chief promoters of civilization and of city life. He was the creator of all that was beautiful and mechanically wonderful in Olympus, especially arms and armor for the gods. At the festival of the Apaturia, when children were enrolled as citizens, Hephaestus was honored as the god of fire. In general, he was a beneficent god, much loved by mortals and gods alike for his kindness and his skill in the peaceful arts.

Some say that Hephaestus was the son of Hera alone, that he had no father. They say Hera produced him alone after Athena was born from the head of Zeus to show that she too could have a child without anyone's help.

DIONYSUS CONDUCTING HEPHAESTUS TO OLYMPUS
Red-figured Attic crater, 5th century B.C.
Munich

But others say Zeus was his father. When he was born, he alone of the ideally beautiful gods was ugly, and Hera, in disgust, flung him out of heaven. He fell into the sea and was rescued by Thetis and Eurynome. The Nereids treated him kindly and kept him with them in a cavern beneath the sea for nine years. It was because of her kindness that Hephaestus, in the Trojan War, made new armor for Achilles, son of Thetis. While living under the sea Hephaestus, "equally skilled in both hands," made a golden throne to which he attached golden mesh fetters, so fine they were invisible. This he sent to Hera, to punish her for hurling him out of heaven. When she sat on the throne she was immediately held fast by the invisible fetters. The gods of heaven sought to persuade Hephaestus to return to Olympus and free her. He refused. Ares threatened him with force. Hephaestus compelled him to withdraw by menacing him with molten missiles. Dionysus came to try his persuasions. Hephaestus trusted Dionysus and received him. Dionysus got him drunk and led him to Olympus, where he at last agreed to free Hera. From then on he took his place among the gods and was greatly loved by them, and made them beautiful bronze palaces. But Zeus, angry with Hera because she had caused Heracles to be shipwrecked on the isle of Cos, punished her by hanging her out of heaven with anvils attached to each of her feet. Hephaestus remonstrated with him, and sought to help his mother. Enraged at his interference, Zeus flung him again from heaven. Through one whole day he fell, and landed at last on the island of Lemnos. Half-dead, he was rescued and cared for by the Lemnians, for which reason Lemnos became one of his favorite haunts. Some say both his legs were broken in this fall, and that he was ever after lame. But others say he was born lame. He made himself golden maidens that had the power to move by themselves, and these helped him to walk and assisted him in his forge. And in his forge he made golden tripods on wheels, that went of themselves to the gatherings of the gods. He never again interfered in the quarrels of Zeus and Hera. On the contrary, he tried to persuade his mother to yield to the will of her husband in the future.

Some say that before he freed Hera from the throne to which she was bound by invisible chains, he won from her a promise that Aphrodite would be given to him for a wife. He paid rich marriage gifts to Zeus for her and she was married to him. But she was an unwilling wife. She preferred the straight and handsome Ares, and frequently entertained him when Hephaestus was absent. Helius, who sees everything in his passage through the skies, saw Aphrodite and Ares together and reported it to Hephaestus. Hephaestus determined to expose the guilty pair. He fashioned a net so fine it was invisible and as strong as it was fine, and placed it over his marriage bed. Then he told his golden wife that he was going on a journey to Lemnos. As soon as he had gone, Ares came joyously to his house and embraced Aphrodite on the marriage bed. Instantly the lovers were caught in the golden mesh and could not escape. Hephaestus returned and called all the gods to witness his dishonor. The gods came and laughed mightily at the plight of Aphrodite and Ares, but the goddesses stayed at home, out of modesty. Hermes was frankly envious of Ares as he viewed the glorious body of Aphrodite, and confessed that he would gladly change places with him. Zeus refused to have anything to do with the matter and rebuked Hephaestus for exposing the dishonor to his name. But Poseidon, fired with love by the sight of Aphrodite, offered, if Ares should default, to make good the marriage gifts Hephaestus had given Zeus for Aphrodite's hand and which he now demanded be returned. Hephaestus accepted his offer and freed the lovers. Aphrodite went to her island of Cyprus and was there purified by her nymphs. Ares went to Thrace. But in a short time all was as before. Hephaestus loved Aphrodite so passionately that he gladly took her back on her terms. Aphrodite bore no childen to Hephaestus, but he was the father of Palaemonius the Argonaut, who was lame like his father. He was also the father of Erichthonius. Some say that Poseidon, for a joke, told Hephaestus that Athena would welcome his advances. When she came to his forge for new weapons he attempted to embrace her. She repulsed him, and his seed fell on her leg. The goddess brushed it off with a piece of wool, which she then cast from her. It fell on Mother Earth, and from this accidental union Erichthonius was born. This encounter did not seem to mar the friendly relations between Athena and Hephaestus,

fat, fāte, fär, fãre, errᶏnt; net, mē, hėr ardᶒnt; pin, pīne; not, nōte, mȯve, nôr, for they were often associated in various exploits. Some name Charis, one of the Graces, as a wife of Hephaestus; and some name Aglaia, the youngest of the Graces, as his wife.

In the Trojan War Hera called on him to come to the aid of Achilles. For Achilles had so choked the Scamander River in Troy with the bodies of those he had slain that the river rose up against him to drown him. Hephaestus sent his flames and dried up the river, and the river-god promised to take no further part in the war. Hephaestus used his skill for peaceful purposes usually, and it was greatly against his will and only because he was commanded to do so by Zeus, that he forged fetters and bound Prometheus to a crag in the Caucasus. At the time he mourned that his great art, so often employed for the good of mankind, should be used for such a cruel purpose, even though it was his own fire that Prometheus had stolen and given to man, for which Zeus punished him. Among the marvelous works said to have been created by Hephaestus were bronze palaces for the gods, the fire-breathing bronze-hoofed bulls that Aeëtes required Jason to yoke; Talos, the bronze man who guarded the island of Crete for King Minos; Ariadne's wonderful crown that was afterward set in the heavens; the armor of Achilles; the bronze castanets with which Heracles frightened the Stymphalian birds, and Heracles' golden breastplate; and the necklace of Harmonia that brought sorrow to all who possessed it. It was also Hephaestus who fashioned the figure of Pandora, into which the gods breathed life. But some say the only truly authentic work from the hand of Hephaestus that survived was the scepter he made for Zeus. Zeus sent it to Pelops by Hermes, and ultimately it passed into the hands of Agamemnon. This scepter came to be the most precious possession of the people of Chaeronea, who say they found it on the borders of their land. They worshiped it under the name *Spear,* and offered sacrifices to it daily. It was kept in a house selected by the priest and near it stood a table on which meats and all kinds of cakes were offered. The Lycians also claimed to have one of the works of Hephaestus, a bowl that was dedicated by Telephus in the temple of Apollo.

Lemnos, once a volcanic isle, was of course a favorite place of Hephaestus, and there he had a forge, manned by the Cyclopes. A volcanic island of the Lipari group was said to be the site of another of his forges, and Mount Aetna in Sicily was also said to lie over one of the forges of Hephaestus. In Athens Hephaestus was honored with a splendid marble temple, the Hephaesteum, and an altar. The *Chalkeia,* a feast of the metal workers, honored him and Athena; and at the *Hephaestia* a torch race was run in his honor. He was sometimes known as Mulciber (*Melter*), by the Romans, who identified him with Vulcan. In art he was represented as a bearded man, usually with the short sleeveless or one-sleeved tunic and the conical cap, and holding the smith's hammer and tongs.

Heptanesus (hep-ta-nē'sus). The seven principal inhabited islands of the Ionian Sea: Corcyra, Paxos, Leucas, Ithaca, Cephallenia, Zacynthus, and Cythera. (JJ)

Heptaporus (hep-tap'o-rus). Named by Homer (*Iliad*) as one of the rivers of the Troad which, after the Trojan War had ended, was diverted from its course by Apollo and Poseidon and sent against the wall which the Greeks had erected to protect their ships. The rivers so diverted from their courses, with the aid of Zeus, washed the wall into the sea. See **Rhesus,** river.

Hera (hēr'a). [Also: **Here.**] One of the 12 Olympian gods, the greatest feminine divinity of Olympus, queen of heaven; daughter of Cronus and Rhea; wife and sister of Zeus, and inferior in power to him only. She was the goddess of women and childbirth, the type of virtuous womanhood, and of the wife and mother. Honored by the Greeks in these capacities, she yet appears in their myths as an extremely unpleasant and rather spiteful goddess, driven to it perhaps by the turmoils of her own married life. She was a sky-goddess, as Zeus was a sky-god. The ancients attributed the storms in the heavens to the quarrels of Zeus and Hera. Aeolus, keeper of the winds, released them at her command.

Like her sisters before her, Hera was swallowed up by Cronus as soon as she was born, and was cast out with them when Zeus duped his father into drinking an emetic. Many places where she was worshiped claimed to be her birthplace. The Samians said she was born on their island. In antiquity they pointed out a tree near the Imbrasus River under which they claimed she was born. At Samos an image of Hera was annually hidden at the seashore, where it was annually discovered, as part of her worship. Argos also claimed to be her birthplace. She contended with Poseidon for control of it; the dispute was submitted to the river-gods Inachus, Cephissus, and Asterion, who decided in favor of the goddess. Samos and Argos were the chief seats of her worship, although the Arcadians claimed that they

HEAD OF HERA
From a coin of Cnossus, 4th century B.C.
Museum of Fine Arts, Boston

were the first to worship her. According to the *Iliad*, Argos, Mycenae, and Sparta were the three cities most loved by her. Near Mycenae was the national Argive shrine of the goddess, the Heraeum, where the great image of her by Polyclitus was housed. In Argos the years were named according to the priestesses of Hera who served in the Heraeum. Some say Hera was brought up by Temenus, son of Pelasgus, in Arcadia, where the Seasons were her nurses. Temenus erected three shrines of Hera: one of Hera the Child, in commemoration of her early years under his care; one of Hera the Bride, in honor of her marriage to Zeus; and a third of Hera the Widow, in memory of a time when she quarreled with Zeus and left him.

Homer says that Hera dwelt at some time in her youth with Oceanus and Tethys, for whom she always had a high regard. When she reached marriageable age her brother, Zeus, courted her, but she repulsed him. He assumed the form of a cuckoo and approached her, some say on Mount Thornax in Argolis, others say it took place in Crete. Deceived, she picked up the bird and nestled it in her bosom. Zeus at once resumed his own form and ravished her. Thus was she persuaded to marry him. Almost as many places as claimed to be her birthplace also claimed to be the scene of her marriage, which took place in the spring. The wedding was attended by all the gods, who brought gifts. Gaea presented her with a tree bearing golden apples, which was set out in the Garden of the Hesperides and guarded by the daughters of Atlas. The wedding night, which lasted 300 years, was spent on the island of Samos. Each year thereafter Hera was said to renew her virginity by bathing in the spring of Canathus in Argos. In all things except the capacity to bestow the power of prophecy, Hera's powers, though great, were inferior to those of Zeus. He often confided in her and sometimes even took her advice, but zealously guarded his right to do as he pleased in any given case. When the arrogance of Zeus became unbearable to the gods they plotted against him and bound him as he slept. Through the intervention of Thetis he was freed by Briareus. To punish Hera, the ringleader in the plot, Zeus fastened bracelets of gold on her wrists, anvils on her feet, and hung her out of heaven. Only when the gods pleaded with him and promised never again to revolt did he relent and restore her to Olympus. When the Giants waged war on the gods it was Hera who prophesied that they could never be slain by the gods, but only by a mortal who was protected by a magic herb. She took vigorous part in the battles against the Giants. Porphyrion sought to violate her, Zeus sprang to her aid and wounded him, and Heracles, the mortal of her prophecy, slew Porphyrion.

Hera bore Ares, Hephaestus, and Hebe to Zeus. Hephaestus was born lame, and in disgust Hera flung him out of heaven. To punish her, Hephaestus, a master-smith, built a magnificent chair and sent it to her. When she sat in it the arms closed about her and held her fast. The gods tried in vain to free her. At last Dionysus went to Hephaestus, got him drunk, and led him to Olympus where he freed his mother. When she saw what a gifted craftsman he was, Hera became reconciled with Hephaestus and set up a forge for him on Olympus. Hera was also said to be the mother of Ilithyia, the birth-goddess, and of Python, the serpent she sent to pursue Leto throughout the world before she bore Apollo and Artemis, the children of Zeus. And some say that, angry because Zeus bore Athena from his own head without any help from her, she bore the monster Typhon without the help of Zeus and gave him to the serpent at Delphi to rear.

The marriage of Zeus and Hera was the only proper marriage on Mount Olympus, but it was an exceedingly stormy one. Any subject was a cause for argument. Once they disputed as to which sex enjoyed the pleasures of love more. Hera contended the masculine sex did. Zeus assured her that the feminine sex did. The dispute was submitted to Tiresias, who had lived both as a woman and as a man, for decision. His answer was that if the pleasures of love were counted as ten, women enjoyed nine parts and men one. Hera was so infuriated by his judgment, some say, that she struck Tiresias with blindness. The unflagging interest of Zeus in other women, mortals or immortals, was a constant source of anger to Hera. Whenever possible she punished the objects of Zeus' readily bestowed love, even when, as was often the case, they had submitted reluctantly to his caresses, and she was as vindictive to the children of Zeus by other women as she was to their mothers. She sent a gadfly to pursue Io, whom Zeus had transformed into a heifer when Hera was about to discover him dallying with her. Echo, a nymph who tried to protect Zeus by chattering with Hera and so delaying her that she did not come upon Zeus and Io until he had changed the form of Io, was punished by Hera. She was permitted to go on talking, as she loved to do, but her conversation was limited to the repetition of the last words of whomever had spoken to her. Hera transformed Callisto, mother of Zeus' son Arcas,

into a bear. Zeus placed Callisto's image among the stars. Such an honor to one of her rivals so infuriated Hera that she induced Poseidon to forbid the image of the Bear ever to sink into his waters, which is why the constellation of the Bear never sets. By a trick she caused the destruction of Semele, and later drove Athamas mad, so that he killed his own son, because Athamas sheltered the infant Dionysus, son of Zeus and Semele; or, as some say, because Athamas put aside the wife Hera had given him and took another in her place. As for Dionysus, some say Hera commanded the Titans to tear him to pieces. He was restored through the agency of Athena, but when he was grown Hera recognized him and drove him mad.

The two most afflicted objects of Hera's enmity were Heracles and the Trojans. Basic to her hatred of Heracles was that he was the son of a rival. Even before he was born she hated him. Zeus boasted before his birth that the king of the Perseid line was about to be born. Hera tricked Zeus into giving the most solemn oath that the first child born that day to the house of Perseus would become master of the land. Having secured the oath, she hastened to the house of Sthenelus and caused Nicippe, his wife, to produce her child before its time. She then kept Ilithyia, the birth-goddess, from going to the aid of Alcmene, who was momentarily expecting her child, and delayed the birth of Heracles. Thus, in fulfillment of his oath, Zeus was forced to allow Eurystheus, son of Sthenelus and Nicippe, to be supreme over Heracles, his own son by Alcmene. But the name Heracles means "Glory of Hera," and was perhaps given because through Hera's enmity he was forced to accomplish mighty deeds. Some say that by a trick Hera was duped into nursing Heracles, but he nursed so vigorously she turned him over to his own mother, unaware whose child he was. When he was an infant in his cradle she sent huge serpents to attack him. He strangled them. Throughout his life she tormented him. She drove him mad, so that he killed his children by Megara. Some say she was responsible for the poisonous, many-headed Hydra, whose killing was one of the labors imposed on Heracles by Eurystheus. Hera sent an enormous crab to help the Hydra when Heracles attacked it, but to no avail; he killed the Hydra. Hera set the image of the crab in the heavens, as Cancer, one of the signs of the Zodiac, to reward it. As another of his labors, Heracles was sent to fetch the cattle of Geryon. Hera came to Geryon's aid and fought Heracles, but he wounded her in the right breast and she was forced to withdraw. Even so, as he was leading the cattle back to Eurystheus, she sent gadflies to sting them and they scattered in a frenzy, so that he was forced to roam widely in order to recover them. She set the dragon Ladon to guard the Apples of the Hesperides, and set his image among the stars after he was killed by Heracles. Once when he was returning from Troy, Hera bribed Sleep to lull Zeus, and when he had succumbed she ordered up a great storm and caused Heracles to be shipwrecked on the island of Cos. Some say it was on this occasion that Zeus was so angered by her that he hung her out of heaven. In his war against Pylus, Hera took the side of Pylus and engaged in the fighting. Again Heracles wounded her. On only one occasion did she fail to hamper him. This was when he fought against the sons of Hippocoön. He was so grateful for her indifference in this case that he sacrificed goats, the only victims available, to her and built a shrine of "Goat-eating Hera" in Sparta. The Spartans were the only ones to give her this name and to offer goats to her. When Heracles was suffering and begged for death, Philoctetes lighted his funeral pyre to bring his suffering to an end. Some say Hera punished Philoctetes for his compassion by sending the serpent that bit him when he accompanied the Greeks to the Trojan War. But when at last Heracles was burned and made immortal, Zeus persuaded her to go through a ceremony that imitated the birth process and to adopt him as a son, and she gave him her daughter Hebe in marriage.

The reason for her relentless hatred of the Trojans came from the Judgment of Paris. Hera, with Aphrodite and Athena, contended for the Apple of Discord, the golden apple that was thrown among the wedding guests at the marriage of Thetis and Peleus, and was inscribed "To the Fairest." Zeus refused to rule as to which of the three goddesses was the fairest and recommended them to consult Paris, son of Priam, who was reputed to be a fine judge of beauty. The goddesses sought Paris and put the problem to him. Each of them offered a handsome bribe if he would award the apple to her. Paris, as is well known, accepted Aphrodite's bribe— the most beautiful woman in the world for his wife—and gave the apple to her. This brought down the unending wrath of Hera on Paris and, by extension, on all Trojans. She took an active part in the Trojan War that resulted when Paris carried off his reward—Helen, wife of King Menelaus of Sparta—and lent her aid to the Greeks on every occasion. When the Trojans had hurled back the Greeks with ruinous losses, Hera again prevailed on Sleep to lull Zeus, and with the aid of Aphrodite's magic girdle, which she borrowed for the occasion, so aroused desire in Zeus that he forgot all about the war and gave himself up to love and sleep. While he was so occupied, the Greeks sallied out against the Trojans and inflicted heavy losses. Again Zeus raged when he learned how she had tricked him, and forbade the gods to take any part in the war for a time. At last, however, fearful that the Trojans would be utterly destroyed when Achilles rejoined the fighting, he gave his permission for the gods to interfere as they wished. Hera attacked Artemis and scattered her arrows. She encouraged Athena to attack Aphrodite, and when the Xanthus River rose up to engulf Achilles for glutting its waters with the bodies of slain Trojans, Hera prevailed on Hephaestus to set the river afire and forced its withdrawal from the strife.

Pelias felt the wrath of Hera because, in his youth, he dragged Sidero from Hera's altar where she had sought refuge, and because Pelias withheld honors that were due the goddess. She favored Jason against Pelias, partly for the above reason, and partly because, to test Jason, she disguised herself as a crone and asked him to carry her across the swollen Anaurus River. Jason courteously obliged, although he found his burden heavy, and won unceasing gratitude and help from the goddess in his later exploits.

Hera was worshiped throughout the Greek world, especially as a protectress of women. Among the festivals celebrated in her honor were the *Daedala,* celebrated at Plataea, the

fat, fāte, fär, fãre, errạnt; net, mē, hėr ardẹnt; pin, pīne; not, nōte, mŏve, nôr,

Heraea, celebrated in Argos, and the Heraean Games, celebrated at Olympia in Elis. There were temples and shrines of Hera in many places, the most famous of which were the Heraeum, near Mycenae in Argolis, the great temple in Samos, and her ancient temple at Olympia. The temple of Hera Prodromia (*Guide*) at Sicyon was said to have been founded by Phalaces, son of Temenus, because Hera guided him on the road to Sicyon. In a sanctuary of Hera Protectress, on the road from Sicyon to Phlius, the men celebrated a festival by themselves. The women's temple there was called the Nymphon. Before the temple of Hera Anthea (*Flowery*) at Argos, was a common grave of women who came to help Dionysus in a war against the Argives. Every spring, a flower festival was celebrated in honor of Hera Anthea by the women of the Peloponnesus. The Spartans had a sanctuary of Hera Hypercheiria (*Protectress*), because she saved the land when the Eurotas River was flooding it. This sanctuary was dedicated in obedience to an oracle. The Spartans also had a temple of Argive Hera, said to have been founded by Eurydice, a daughter of Lacedaemon and the wife of Acrisius. The Eleans poured libations and sang hymns to Hera Ammonia at Olympia once a month; this name for the goddess was given her as the wife of Zeus Ammon, the Libyan name for Zeus. The Argives, and many others, sacrificed cows to Hera. Sacred to her also were the cuckoo, the crow, and, in later times, the peacock. The pomegranate, symbol sometimes of fruitfulness and sometimes of death, was also sacred to her.

Homer describes Hera as "Ox-eyed," "White-armed," and in general as a majestic personage to whom the other gods and goddesses paid homage. He also shows her as passionately punishing the Trojans by whatever means she could contrive. In art the goddess is represented as a majestic woman, fully clad in flowing draperies, characteristically with a crown on her brow, and bearing a scepter. The renowned statue of Hera by Polyclitus in the Heraeum in Argolis remains only in description or, as some scholars think, in the copies, the Farnese and Ludovisi Junos. By the Romans Hera was early identified with their Juno, originally a distinct

divinity; and the Latin name is often incorrectly given to the Greek goddess.

Heraclea (her-a-klē′a). In ancient geography, a city of Magna Graecia, situated near the Gulf of Tarentum, in what is now Lucania, S Italy, near the modern village of Policoro. It was established as a colony of Tarentum, and was the scene of a victory of Pyrrhus, king of Epirus, over the Romans in 280 B.C. It was this victory and that of Asculum in the following year, in which Pyrrhus lost heavily, which gave rise to the saying "a Pyrrhic victory," meaning a gain made at great cost to the victor.

Heraclea Minoa (mi-nō′a). [Also: **Heraclea.**] In ancient geography, a city on the S coast of Sicily, about 18 miles NW of Acragas.

Heraclean Tables (her-a-klē′an). [Latin, **Tabulae Heracleenses.**] Two fragmentary bronze tablets discovered near Heraclea in Magna Graecia about the middle of the 18th century, and preserved at Naples. They contain a Latin inscription (a copy of the *Lex Julia municipalis*), and also a much earlier Greek inscription.

Heraclea Perinthus (her-a-klē′a pe-rin′thus). See **Perinthus.**

Heraclea Pontica (pon′ti-ka). [Also: **Heraclea;** modern Turkish name, **Ereğli.**] In ancient geography, a city in Bithynia, Asia Minor, situated on the Euxine Sea about 100 miles E of what is now Istanbul, Turkey. According to legend, it was founded by the Mariandyni and named for Heracles in gratitude to him for repelling the Bebryces and restoring the land to the Mariandyni. According to some accounts, it was near here that Heracles came up from the Underworld with Cerberus, and as the three-headed dog of Hades emerged into the light foam fell from his jaws. From this foam sprang the poisonous aconite plant, which flourished in this region thereafter. Colonists from Megara later settled at Heraclea (c560 B.C.) in obedience to the advice of an oracle to settle on land that had been dedicated to Heracles.

Heraclea Sintica (sin′ti-ka). In ancient geography, a town in Macedonia, situated about 40 miles NE of Therma (now Salonika); the modern Zeruokhori.

Heraclea Trachinia (tra-kin′i-a). [Called **Heraclea.**] In ancient geography, a town in Malis, C Greece, about six miles W of Thermopylae; a Spartan colony founded in 426 B.C.

Heracles (her'a̯-klēz). [Latin, **Hercules**.] The mightiest and most famous of Greek heroes. His deeds were fabulous for the courage and strength which he displayed in performing them and his name—Herculean, a Latinized form—has become synonymous for prodigious strength, courage, or size. His sufferings, largely as a result of Hera's antagonism, were equally heroic and were endured by him with immense fortitude. Beginning with the circumstances of his birth every characteristic and deed of his life was extraordinary. Zeus, having decided to father a hero to end all heroes, chose Alcmene, wife of Amphitryon of Tiryns, to be the hero's mother. She is said to have been the last mortal woman whom Zeus embraced. Since she was impeccably chaste Zeus appeared to her in the guise of her husband, and caused the sun and stars to halt in their courses so that the night the god spent with her was three times as long as usual. When the day arrived on which Heracles was to be born, Zeus exultantly vowed that the first male child born that day would reign over the descendants of Perseus. Hera, as usual inflamed by the infidelities of her husband, hurriedly arranged to delay the birth of Heracles and to hasten the birth of Eurystheus, son of Sthenelus, king of Mycenae. She summoned Ilithyia, the birth-goddess, to sit outside Alcmene's door at Thebes with crossed knees and clenched hands. By this magic Alcmene's labor was prolonged until Galinthias, a handmaiden of Alcmene's, falsely announced the birth of Heracles, whereupon Ilithyia was so startled that she jumped up, uncrossing her knees and relaxing her hands, and allowed Heracles to be born. In a rage at the deception, Ilithyia seized Galinthias and changed her into a weasel. But by this time Eurystheus had already been born and Zeus, although he was furious, was obliged to honor his vow. Nevertheless, he persuaded Hera to agree that Eurystheus should be king but that Heracles, after performing ten great labors for Eurystheus, should become immortal. Alcmene, now aware that she had been seduced by a god, abandoned her child out of fear of the jealousy of Hera. The babe was found by Athena, the friend and patron of Heracles throughout his life, who gave him to Hera to rear, pretending that she did not know what child it was. Hera took the child but the infant sucked so forcefully that Hera refused to nurse him and, unaware of his parentage, unwittingly gave him to his own mother to bring up. Alcmene had produced another son, a twin half-brother of Heracles, by Amphitryon. This was Iphicles, younger than Heracles by one night, and the two children were bedded down together. Hera was not long in ignorance of the true origin of Heracles, who at this time was called Alcaeus. She sent two serpents into the cradle where Heracles and Iphicles were sleeping. The infant Heracles grasped the serpents in his bare hands and strangled them.

In his youth Heracles was taught to drive a chariot by Amphitryon, to wrestle by Autolycus or by Harpalycus, son of Hermes, to shoot with the bow and arrow by Eurytus, to fence by Castor. His studies in literature were supervised by Linus, son of the river-god Ismenius, and he was given instruction on the lyre by Eumolpus. It happened that on one occasion Linus attempted to improve his performance on the lyre by boxing his ears. In a rage Heracles flung the lyre at him and killed him. He was acquitted of a murder charge on the ground that he had resisted an aggressor, but Amphitryon sent him to tend his flocks around Mount Cithaeron to keep him out of trouble. While there he went to Thespiae to hunt the Thespian Lion which roamed over Mount Helicon and Mount Cithaeron and was ravaging Amphitryon's flocks. According to some accounts, he killed the lion, skinned it, and wore its pelt as a cloak, using the massive head as a kind of helmet. Others say it was the Nemean Lion's skin he wore, and that Alcathous killed the Thespian Lion. In any event, Heracles so impressed Thespius, founder and king of Thespiae, that he wished to have descendants by Heracles and gave him his 50 daughters to bring about the desired end. All but one of the 50 maidens was delighted with the attentions of Heracles, and between them they produced 51 sons, including two sets of twins. The one who refused his advances was condemned to lifelong virginity as a priestess in his temple. Of these 51 sons, Heracles later sent 40 to colonize the island of Sardinia, as he had been commanded to do by an oracle.

Heracles next followed his foster father Amphitryon to Thebes. He found the city under bondage to Erginus, king of the Minyans, and compelled to pay annual tribute to Erginus. Heracles met the heralds who had come to collect the tribute, cut off their ears and noses, which he threaded on a string and hung around their necks, tied their hands behind their backs, and sent them back to Erginus. As was to be expected, Erginus raised a force to punish Thebes for this outrage. The Thebans, having been disarmed in previous wars with the Minyans, would have surrendered, but Heracles rallied them and armed them with the shields and spears which were hanging in the temples as offerings to the gods. Under his leadership the Minyans were defeated and Erginus was slain, and thenceforth the Minyans were compelled to pay a tribute to the Thebans twice as large as the one they had been exacting from Thebes. In gratitude to Heracles, Creon, king of Thebes, gave him his daughter Megara in marriage.

The fame of Heracles spread far and wide. Eurystheus now summoned him to perform the ten labors. Heracles deemed it unworthy of him to serve an inferior mortal like Eurystheus, and became so despondent at the idea that in a fit of madness, inspired by Hera, he killed his children. Restored to sanity, and purified by Thespius, he went to the Oracle at Delphi for instructions. The priestess now gave him the name Heracles (*Glory of Hera*) because he would obtain glory as a result of Hera's enmity, and ordered him to begin his labors for Eurystheus so that he could become immortal.

The first labor was to bring Eurystheus the hide of the Nemean Lion. This animal, which could not be killed by iron, bronze, or stone, had its lair in a cleft in Mount Tretus, between Mycenae and Nemea. Heracles blocked one entrance of the cleft, which ran through the mountain, so that the lion could not escape, followed the creature in and strangled it. He then skinned the lion and ever after used its shaggy pelt as a cloak. Eurystheus was so terrified at the sight of

Heracles clad in the lion's skin, with its fierce head serving as a cap, that, some accounts say, he ordered him to report his successes from outside the city walls in the future.

The second labor was to kill the many-headed Hydra that lurked in the Lernaean swamp and wasted the surrounding area with its noisome breath. According to some accounts the Hydra had nine heads, one of which was immortal. Others say there were as many as 100 heads. The difficulty in killing it was that as fast as one head was cut off, two fire-breathing heads grew in its place. As Heracles struggled with the monster Hera sent a huge crab to help the monster by biting Heracles' feet. Heracles crushed the crab, which Hera then translated to the heavens as the constellation Cancer. He now called upon Iolaus, companion of many of his exploits, and as fast as Heracles sliced off one of the Hydra's heads Iolaus seared the stump with hot pitch. In this way it was decapitated of all its heads. Heracles dipped his arrows in the Hydra's venom, and coated them with such a lethal poison that whoever was wounded by one of them, no matter how superficially, was doomed to die. Eurystheus refused to recognize this labor, on the ground that Heracles had not performed it alone: Iolaus helped him.

On his way to perform the next labor, the capture of the Erymanthian Boar, Heracles visited Pholus the centaur, in a cave on a mountain. Pholus entertained him by opening a cask of wine which had been given to him by Dionysus. The other centaurs smelled the wine and were maddened by the fumes. They attacked Heracles, and were aided in their onslaught by a torrential rain. This gave them a distinct advantage, for with their four feet they could maintain their footing in the slippery mud of the mountainside, whereas Heracles was constantly slipping to his knees. Even so, he killed many of them and drove the rest off. They fled to Chiron in Malea, whither he pursued them, and there by accident wounded his friend Chiron with one of his arrows. The wound could not be healed because of the Hydra's venom on the arrow which caused it. On the other hand, the centaur Chiron was immortal and could not die. Later, he was finally released from his suffering by a generous act of Prometheus, who offered to assume Chiron's immortality so that Chiron could die. Pholus also died as a result of this engagement. In withdrawing an arrow from one of the fallen centaurs he unfortunately dropped it. It pricked his foot and he died instantly. Heracles buried him on the mountain and named it Mount Pholoe in his honor. He now pursued the Erymanthian Boar, which he was ordered to take alive. He chased it to the north and finally caught it in a deep snow drift or, as some say, with a net, and returned to Eurystheus carrying the Boar on his shoulders. Eurystheus hid in a specially constructed bronze vessel, buried in the ground, when he learned that Heracles was approaching with the Boar. (Some say it was this deed that so terrified Eurystheus that he ordered Heracles to report his future successes from outside the city walls.)

The fourth labor was to catch the golden-horned Hind which dwelt near the Cerynean river in Arcadia. Since the Hind was sacred to Artemis it had to be taken alive. Heracles pursued it for a year and finally caught it as it drank at the river Ladon. With one perfect shot of his bow he transfixed the forefeet of the Hind and captured it. As he carried it off on his shoulders Artemis reproached him for harming one of her creatures. The goddess forgave him when he pleaded that he was carrying out the command of Zeus in performing the labors for Eurystheus.

The fifth labor was to drive off the bronze-beaked birds that were infesting the Stymphalian marsh. They were huge pestilential birds with iron feathers, and were sacred to Ares. As they flew over the countryside they dropped their feathers and killed many of the countrymen, and their filthy habits were destroying the crops. Athena gave Heracles a bronze rattle which he shook violently and so startled the birds that they rose in flight and he was able to pick off many of them with his arrows. The rest fled to the island of Ares where they were later encountered by the Argonauts.

For his sixth labor Heracles was commanded by Eurystheus to cleanse the stables of Augeas, king in Elis. Augeas was the possessor of large and magnificent herds but his stables had not been cleaned for years. Heracles approached him and offered, without telling him that he had been sent for this purpose, to cleanse the stables before nightfall in return for the payment of one-tenth of the cattle. Augeas agreed, and called his son Phyleus to witness the bargain. He did not expect to have to make the payment as he felt it would be impossible to accomplish the task in the time stipulated. However, Heracles diverted the Alpheus and Peneus Rivers from their courses, washed them through the stables and carried out his end of the bargain as proposed. Augeas refused to pay. He said that the river-gods had helped Heracles, and furthermore, he had learned that Heracles was commanded to carry out this task by Eurystheus. Heracles called on Phyleus to state whether Augeas had promised a payment of one-tenth of his cattle. Phyleus supported Heracles and urged his father to pay. In a rage, Augeas banished his son and expelled Heracles. Heracles swore he would get his revenge. He then proceeded to Olenus and killed Eurytion, a centaur who tried to ravish the daughter of the king there. But some say this centaur attacked the daughter of Eurystheus, and that Heracles generously aided his enemy by slaying the centaur.

The seventh labor was to bring back the Cretan Bull beloved by Pasiphaë from Crete. King Minos offered to help in this task but Heracles subdued the bull by himself, and rode on its back as it swam the sea from Crete to Greece. Eurystheus took one look at the bull and turned it loose. It roamed the countryside until it came to Marathon and thereafter became known as the Marathonian Bull.

When he had accomplished this labor Heracles established the Olympic Games, dedicated to Zeus, on the banks of the Alpheus River. He paced off the stadium and won all the contests himself in the first Games. The gods gave him valuable gifts: Athena gave him a robe, Hephaestus a war-club and coat of mail, Poseidon horses, Hermes a sword, Apollo bow and arrows; but on the whole Heracles preferred to fight with a club he cut himself from a wild olive tree, or with his bow and arrows.

fat, fāte, fär, fãre, errant; net, mē, hėr ardent; pin, pīne; not, nōte, möve, nôr,

For his eighth labor Heracles captured the man-eating mares of Diomedes of Thrace. Diomedes, a son of Ares and Cyrene, fed his animals on human flesh. Heracles tamed them by feeding them the flesh of their master. He founded the city of Abdera, in memory of his servant Abderus who had been killed as he tended the mares while Heracles captured Diomedes. He then returned with the mares to Eurystheus, who consecrated them to Hera.

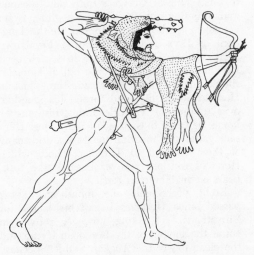

HERACLES
Red-figured Greek volute crater, Euphronius, end of the 6th century B.C. *Museo Pubblico, Arezzo*

The news of Jason's expedition to Colchis to recover the Golden Fleece now came to Heracles' ears and he interrupted his labors to join the Argonauts. They unanimously chose him as their leader but he would not take the honor from Jason, who had organized the expedition. It was Heracles who reminded the Argonauts that their goal was Colchis when he thought they lingered overlong enjoying the favors of the women of Lemnos. Heracles took his squire, Hylas, with him on the voyage, and when the Argonauts stopped in Mysia Hylas, who had gone to fetch water at a spring, disappeared. Heracles delayed so long in his search for Hylas that the Argonauts sailed without him.

Heracles wandered through Mysia, searching for Hylas and commanding the Mysians to do likewise. Ever after, once a year the Mysians sacrificed to Hylas, calling his name aloud and pretending to search for him.

Heracles returned to Eurystheus and learned that Admete, his daughter, had a fancy for Hippolyte's girdle, and that his ninth labor was to fetch it. Hippolyte was a queen of the Amazons, who dwelt near the Thermodon River that flows into the Euxine Sea (Black Sea), and her girdle was a belt given to her by her father Ares. On his way to the Amazon country Heracles landed on the island of Paros and carried off two hostages in revenge for the slaying of two of his crew who had gone to fetch water. In Mysia he was entertained by Lycus, and helped that king to defeat Mygdon, king of the Bebryces, and gave the land he seized from the Bebryces to Lycus, who named it Heraclea in his honor. Proceeding then to the port of the Amazons, he was graciously welcomed by Hippolyte, who freely consented to give him her girdle. But Hera stirred up the Amazon women with a rumor that Heracles was attacking their queen. They marched against him and he, thinking he had been tricked, killed Hippolyte, took the girdle, and set out for Hellas, taking Antiope, a sister of Hippolyte, with him as a captive. On his way home he passed Troy and saw a beautiful maiden chained to a rock. On inquiring the reason for this he learned that she was Hesione, the daughter of Laomedon, king of Troy, and that she was being offered as a sacrifice to a sea-monster sent by Poseidon to punish Laomedon. Heracles offered to slay the monster on condition that Laomedon give him the immortal horses of Tros which Zeus had given Tros in compensation for his abduction of Ganymede. Laomedon agreed to the conditions, whereupon Heracles leaped fully armed into the jaws of the monster, hacked about in its belly for three days, and then emerged, victorious but completely bald. Laomedon refused to honor his agreement, now that the danger was passed, and Heracles departed, vowing revenge. He sailed to the island of Thasus, where he subdued the Thracians, and finally arrived at Mycenae, where he presented the girdle to

Eurystheus. The captive Antiope was given to Theseus.

His tenth labor, to fetch the cattle of Geryon from the island of Erythea, took him over most of Europe. Heracles went to Crete, gathered a large force, and rid the island once and for all of wild beasts in gratitude to the Cretans for their hospitality. He sailed from Crete to Libya. There he wrestled with Antaeus, a giant whose strength increased as his body came in contact with the earth. Heracles overcame him by holding him aloft and crushing his ribs. He then subdued all Libya and put it under cultivation. Next he went to Egypt and killed Busiris, who was in the habit of sacrificing strangers. Heracles allowed himself to be bound and led to the altar, then he suddenly burst his bonds and killed Busiris. In Egypt he founded the 100-gated city of Hecatompylon, or Thebes. From Egypt he went to Gadira and set up the Pillars of Heracles, one on each continent. According to some accounts, this passage between Calpe (Gibraltar) and Abyla (Ceuta) was very wide and Heracles built each side out so that his Pillars make the passage narrower and thus keep ocean monsters out of the inner sea. Others say that the two continents were joined and that Heracles cut a passage between them so that the waters of the ocean could mingle with those of the inner sea. In any event, setting up the Pillars was hot work under the broiling sun. Heracles sent a threatening arrow at the Sun for sending such heat. But the Sun was amused at his presumption and indulgently gave him a golden goblet in which to cross the sea. Heracles apologized and set off in the goblet for Erythea. There he killed Orthus, the hound that guarded Geryon's cattle, and Eurytion, the herdsman. He then slew Geryon and took his cattle. Passing through Liguria on his way home he was attacked by two sons of Poseidon and their forces. When he had used up all his arrows he prayed to Zeus for help. Zeus sent a shower of stones which Heracles hurled at his attackers and so repelled them. The place where this event occurred, between Massilia (Marseilles) and the Rhodanus (Rhone) River is still noted for its many stones about as big as a man's fist, and is

called the Stony Plain (Plaine de la Crau.) He then crossed the Alps, marched to the Tiber and, pitching his tent where Rome now stands, was hospitably received by Evander, a Trojan immigrant who became a king in Latium. In Italy he slew the monstrous three-headed Cacus, who was terrorizing the countryside, and being weary from this effort went to rest at Paestum, but cicadas made such a noise he could not sleep. He prayed for relief and Zeus banished the cicadas from Paestum, where they have not been heard again from that day to this. One of Geryon's bulls now escaped and, stepping into the sea at Rhegium, swam across to Sicily. It wandered to the kingdom of Eryx and was put into Eryx' own herd. When Heracles came in search of it Eryx agreed to surrender the bull if Heracles should defeat him in a wrestling match. Heracles killed him and turned his kingdom over to the natives. Resuming his journey home, he came to the Ionian Sea. Here Hera sent gadflies to madden the cattle, and many of them escaped to Thrace. Those which Heracles did not recover became the forebears of the Thracian cattle.

Eight years and one month had now passed since Heracles began his labors for Eurystheus. That king, however, refused to count the slaying of the Lernaean Hydra and the cleansing of the Augean Stables, because in the one case Heracles had the help of Iolaus and in the other he did it for pay. Thus two more labors were laid on him. The eleventh was to fetch the Golden Apples of the Hesperides, the apples which had been given to Hera as a wedding gift and which were guarded by the Hesperides, daughters of Atlas, and by the 100-headed dragon, Ladon. Heracles did not know where the apples were to be found. He journeyed to the Eridanus River and there, at the prompting of the river-nymphs, seized the sea-god Nereus as he slept. Nereus went through many transformations in an effort to escape but Heracles held him fast and compelled him to give the information he wanted. On the advice of Nereus he went to Rhodes where, being hungry, he took a bullock from a cart, killed it, roasted it, and ate it. Meanwhile the owner of the bullock stood on a hill at a safe distance and cursed helplessly.

fat, fāte, fär, fāre, errạnt; net, mē, hèr ardẹnt; pin, pīne; not, nōte, mŏve, nôr,

For this reason it became the custom in that country to curse when sacrificing to Heracles. Next he passed through Arabia, where he slew Emathion, crossed Libya, and again received a golden goblet from the Sun in which he crossed the sea to the Caucasus. He found Prometheus chained to a crag there, while vultures daily gnawed at his liver. Heracles killed the vultures and freed Prometheus, who assumed Chiron's immortality and thus permitted the suffering centaur, accidentally wounded by one of Heracles' poisoned arrows, at last to die. In the land of the Hyperboreans Heracles found the olive tree, which he took home with him, and acting on instructions from Prometheus he approached the Titan Atlas, in whose garden the tree with the golden apples grew. Heracles offered to hold up the heavens while Atlas fetched the apples, as he had been advised not to pluck them himself. Atlas demurred, in fear of the dragon, whereupon Heracles sent an arrow over the garden wall and killed Ladon. He then shouldered the heavens while Atlas went for the apples. When Atlas returned he offered to take the apples to Eurystheus himself as long as Heracles was so obliging as to hold up the heavens. Heracles agreed but asked Atlas to relieve him a moment so that he could pad his shoulders and make his burden less uncomfortable. Atlas resumed the burden and Heracles, who had no intention of taking over Atlas' monotonous job, walked off. He gave the apples to Eurystheus, but as it was unlawful to possess them they were restored to the garden through the good offices of Athena.

For his twelfth and last labor Heracles was to fetch Cerberus from Hades. To prepare for the task he went to Eleusis and asked the priest to initiate him into the Eleusinian Mysteries. However, since it was a rule that only Athenians could properly be initiated and he was a foreigner, Demeter established the Lesser Mysteries in his honor, which were celebrated at Agrae on the Ilissus River. Duly purified, he descended to Hades through an opening at Taenarum in Laconia, or as some say, at Heraclea on the Euxine Sea, guided by Athena and Hermes. As he stepped from Charon's boat—he had persuaded the ferryman of the

Styx to take him across by assuming a terrifying expression—all the shades fled in fear except Meleager and Medusa, who boldly faced him. He would have run his sword through Meleager but was assured that he had nothing to fear from ghosts, and as they then engaged in friendly conversation, Heracles promised Meleager that he would marry Deianira, Meleager's sister, on his return to earth. In Hades Heracles found Theseus and Pirithous immobilized on Chairs of Forgetfulness. He freed Theseus and took him back to earth with him, but was unable to free Pirithous. He also rolled away the stone with which Demeter had flattened Ascalaphus for talebearing concerning Persephone's food in the Underworld, but Demeter immediately transformed Ascalaphus into a short-eared owl as an alternate punishment. Hades, persuaded by Persephone, allowed him to take Cerberus on condition that he capture him without weapons. This he did by grasping him firmly around the neck and choking him until the hound submitted. He returned to earth with Cerberus by an entrance near Troezen, or some say through a cave in the land of the Mariandyni on the Euxine Sea. When he had shown Cerberus to Eurystheus he returned the hound of Hades to the Underworld.

Now that he had finished his labors for Eurystheus Heracles gave his wife Megara to his faithful friend Iolaus, as he feared to have more children by her, remembering how he had slain her children in his madness. He sought Eurytus in Oechalia and asked for the hand of his daughter Iole. Eurytus, who had learned archery from Apollo and had in turn taught it to the youthful Heracles, had promised his daughter to whoever could defeat him in an archery contest. Heracles defeated him but Eurytus, claiming that Heracles used divine arrows, and fearful because of his former madness, refused to give up his daughter. Heracles departed, and shortly thereafter some of Eurytus' mares were missing. He was convinced that Heracles had stolen them. His son Iphitus, who had urged his father to carry out his bargain and give Iole to Heracles, claimed Heracles was innocent, and in truth it was the well-known thief Autolycus who had taken them. Iphitus set out to find

Heracles and prove his innocence. He met him as he was returning from Pherae, having brought Alcestis up from the Underworld, where he wrestled Hades himself, and restored her to Admetus, and gained Heracles' promise of assistance in a search for the cattle, but unfortunately, Hera sent another spell of madness, in which he hurled Iphitus from the walls of Tiryns and killed him.

Once again in possession of his senses, Heracles was overcome with remorse and asked Neleus of Pylus to purify him. Neleus, with the backing of his sons, refused. Deïphobus of Amyclae purified him for the murder. Even so, he was plagued by disease and went to consult the Oracle at Delphi to learn how he could be cured. The priestess refused to have anything to say to him, whereupon Heracles seized her tripod and threatened to set up his own oracle. Apollo rushed onto the scene to defend his priestess and the dauntless Heracles attacked the god. Zeus separated them by hurling a thunderbolt between them and the priestess hurriedly gave him instructions. She told him to sell himself as a slave and give the purchase price to the sons of Iphitus. Omphale, queen of Maeonia, bought him. For her he seized the Cercopes, deceitful men who had been turned into apes by Zeus, and, hanging them head down from a pole, carried them to Omphale. He killed Syleus for his unpleasant habit of forcing travelers to compete with him in tilling his vineyards. Omphale, impressed with his deeds, freed him and married him and bore him a son, Lamus. It is said that while in Omphale's services, Heracles and the queen sometimes exchanged garments. This is the foundation for the story that Heracles worked for Omphale dressed in women's clothes and that he was so effeminate as to engage in spinning and weaving.

Freed of his service, Heracles returned to the Peloponnesus to carry out his vows of revenge on Laomedon, Augeas, Eurytus, and Neleus. He sailed to Troy in six ships and attacked the city. Telamon of Salamis, who accompanied him, was the first to breach the wall. Angry that anyone had gotten ahead of him in valor, Heracles was about to kill Telamon but paused as he noticed Telamon hastily piling up stones. When he asked the reason for this Telamon said he was building an altar to Heracles the Victor. His ready answer mollified Heracles and saved Telamon from certain death. Heracles sacked Troy and killed Laomedon and all of his sons except Podarces, who had advised Laomedon to pay Heracles as he had promised for destroying the sea monster. He gave Hesione, Laomedon's daughter, to Telamon. She ransomed Podarces with her veil and thus he gained the name Priam, "Ransomed." Heracles turned over Laomedon's ruined kingdom to him. On his way home from Troy Hera sent violent storms that shipwrecked Heracles on the island of Cos. He was then urgently sought out by Athena, who asked his assistance in the war against the Giants which was now raging on the plain of Phlegra. The goddess helped him to find the magic herb that would protect him and they hurried off to the battle. Although the gods had wounded many of the Giants Heracles was required to dispatch them, as an oracle had foretold that only a mortal could kill them.

He next turned his attention to Augeas. He collected an Arcadian army but was repelled by the sons of Actor and Molione. Eurystheus banished him from Tiryns and he attacked and killed Eurytus, the son of Augeas, near Cleonae, where a temple to Heracles was erected, some say by himself. He made a second attack on Augeas in Elis in which he killed Augeas and gave the kingdom to Phyleus because the latter had supported Heracles in the matter of the payment Augeas had promised. He then marched against Neleus, who had refused to purify him for the murder of Iphitus, and slew Neleus and all of his sons except Nestor. According to some accounts, in this battle he also wounded Hades, Hera, and Ares, who fought on the side of Neleus. He fought against the Spartans, to avenge the death of a son of his friend and to punish them for aiding Neleus, and defeated Hippocoön, who had seized the throne from his brother Tyndareus, and restored Tyndareus.

On his way home he stopped in Tegea, where he was entertained by Aleus. He ravished Auge, daughter of Aleus, a priestess in the temple, and she later bore his son, Telephus. Returning then to Pheneüs, he stayed there five years. At the expiration of this time he left for Calydon and fulfilled the promise made to Meleager in the Underworld to marry Deianira, daughter of Oeneus. First however, he had to overcome the river-god Achelous, who was also one of Deianira's suitors. Achelous fought in the shape of a serpent and then in the form of a bull. Neither form helped him. Heracles seized him by a horn and hurled him to the ground with such force that the horn broke off. This horn eventually became the Cornucopia, the "Horn of Plenty."

Heracles marched with the Calydonians against the Thesprotian city of Ephyra, slew the king and ravished his daughter, who subsequently bore him Tlepolemus. At a banquet with Oeneus he impatiently cuffed the lad who poured water over his hands for the libation. The boy died as a result of what Heracles considered a light tap. It was clearly an accident but Heracles, overcome by remorse, insisted on taking the penalty, which was to go into exile. He set off with Deianira for the kingdom of Ceyx, in Trachis. On the way it was necessary to cross the Evenus River. Nessus, a centaur, offered to ferry Deianira across on his back while Heracles, swimming, went ahead. As they neared the shore Nessus attempted to violate Deianira. Her screams drew instant action from Heracles. He sent one of his poisoned arrows into the centaur. Before he died Nessus advised Deianira to preserve his blood as it would be a potent love charm in the event that Heracles' interest in her should waver, as it was constantly doing. She secretly gathered the blood and kept it in a vial.

At Trachis they were hospitably received, and Heracles fought as an ally of Aegimius, king of the Dorians, against the Lapiths. Among other deeds he performed at this time: he killed Cycnus, the son of Ares and Pelopia, who killed strangers and used their polished skulls to build a temple to his father; he slew Amyntor, who had refused to give Heracles his daughter, on the ground that he already had a wife, and took Astydamia, Amyntor's daughter, by force and became the father of Ctesippus by her; he gathered an army with which he attacked Eurytus, father of Iole, slew him and his

sons, and took Iole captive. On his way back from this war he went to Cenaeum, the extreme northwestern point of Euboea, and prepared to sacrifice to Zeus. He sent his herald Lichas to Trachis to get the robe he customarily wore when sacrificing. Deianira learned from Lichas that Iole was with Heracles and decided that the time had come to make use of Nessus' love charm. She rubbed the dried blood of Nessus on the robe and sent it off with Lichas. After the herald left she noticed that the ground on which a drop of the blood had fallen was smoldering, and in terror she tried to recall Lichas, but it was too late. Lichas gave the robe to Heracles, who put it on and prepared his sacrifice. As the heat of his body warmed the robe the blood of the centaur with which it was covered melted, and suddenly it seared Heracles' body as with a sheet of fire. He tried to pull off the robe and his skin came with it. He was in torment, and it was caused by his own arrow which had poisoned Nessus' blood. According to some accounts he leaped into the waters of a stream to cool his burning body, but the only effect of this was to cause the water to bubble and steam, which it has done from that day to this and accounts for its name, Thermopylae, "hot springs." In a frenzy he hurled the innocent Lichas into the sea, and swore to kill Deianira. However, she had learned the effects of Nessus' love charm and hanged herself. On the advice of Apollo, Heracles repaired to Mount Oeta and built a great pyre. He secured a promise from his son Hyllus to marry Iole, and mounted the pyre. No one had the courage to light it for him, in spite of his pleas to be released from his sufferings. Only Philoctetes, in compassion, found the heart to set it alight. In return for this he was given the bow and arrows of Heracles. As the pyre blazed up, a flash of lightning blinded all present; a cloud passed under Heracles' body and bore it away. The pyre was instantly consumed and as no bones were found all took it for granted that Heracles had been carried to Olympus. Zeus took him to Olympus in a four-horse chariot and persuaded Hera to adopt him as a son. This the goddess did, partly because she had no choice, but also partly in gratitude because Heracles had protected her in the war with the Giants when one of the Giants sought to violate her. She even permitted him to marry Hebe and acquiesced when he was made gate-keeper of Olympus.

The Locrians began to sacrifice to Heracles as a hero immediately after his death. They were followed in this by the Thebans, but it was the Athenians who first worshiped him as a god. The general opinion was that Heracles' immortal parts, reft from his blazing pyre, went to Olympus, but his mortal parts went as a shade to the Underworld, and Odysseus saw it when he visited the Underworld.

Heracles was worshiped throughout the Mediterranean world. Each town and city added some act or exploit to the hero's life which would identify him with their own people. The legion of sons he was supposed to have fathered gave many places a direct ancestor who was a son of Heracles. Only Euripides speaks of Heracles as being the father of one daughter, Macaria. The Romans took over Heracles, whom they called Hercules, lock, stock, and barrel, and added some incidents to his life which were exclusively connected with their own history and nation. Every town, village, and city, wished to be connected in some way, no matter how slightly, with the great hero. This perhaps accounts for the incredible number of exploits which were added to the list of his accomplishments.

Heracles, Labors of. According to some accounts, Heracles was obliged to perform only ten labors for Eurystheus, but because Eurystheus refused to count two of them, Heracles performed 12 great labors. The order of the 12 labors differs in the accounts given by different writers, and even the labors themselves differ. Following is a list that includes those labors generally regarded as the 12 great labors of Heracles: 1) the strangling of the Nemean Lion; 2) the killing of the Lernaean Hydra; 3) the capture of the Erymanthian Boar; 4) the capture of the Cerynean Hind; 5) the cleaning of the Augean Stables; 6) the slaughter of the Stymphalian Birds; 7) the capture of the Cretan Bull; 8) the capture of the man-eating mares of Diomedes of Thrace; 9) the securing of the girdle of Hippolyte, queen of the Amazons; 10) the fetching of the red oxen of Geryon; 11) the procuring of the Golden Apples of the Hesperides; 12) the bringing to the upper world the dog Cerberus, guardian of Hades. Labors that are sometimes substituted for some of those on the above list by other writers are: the strangling of the serpents; the battle with the centaurs on Mount Pholoe; the killing of the guest-slayer Cycnus; and the rearing of the Pillars of Heracles to hold up the heavens.

Heracles the Dactyl (dak'til). In Greek mythology, one of the five Dactyls of Crete who, according to some accounts, protected the infant Zeus on Mount Ida in Crete. Afterward he went, with his brothers, to Elis to propitiate Cronus. Some say he engaged in a race with his brothers at Olympia in Elis, and that this was the origin of the Olympic Games, and that they were held every fifth year because there were five brothers. And some say that Heracles the Dactyl had brought back the wild olive from the land of the Hyperboreans and crowned the winner in this first race with a wreath made from its branches, thus establishing the custom of crowning the victor with wreaths of the wild olive. Heracles the Dactyl is also said to have built the first altar to Zeus at Olympia, constructing it from the ashes of the bones of victims he had sacrificed. The image of Heracles found floating on a raft in the sea between Chios and Erythrae and won by the Erythraeans with a rope made of women's hair was said to be of Heracles the Dactyl, not Heracles son of Alcmene.

Heracleum (her-a-klē'um). [Also: **Candia, Heraklion, Herakleion, Iraklion, Megalokastron.**] City on the N coast of the island of Crete, near the site of ancient Cnossus.

Heraclidae (her-a-klī'dē). Descendants of Heracles; specifically, in Greek legend, certain Achaean chiefs claiming descent from Heracles, who in prehistoric times joined the Dorian migration to the Peloponnesus. The sons of Heracles were said to have been expelled from their heritage in the Peloponnesus by Eurystheus (to whom Hera had given the region) and to have settled in Attica. The most notable of their descendants who joined the Dorians were Temenus, who in the partition of the conquered territories obtained Argos; Procles and Eurysthenes, who obtained Lacedaemon; and Cresphontes, who obtained Messenia. The invasion of the Peloponnesus by the Heraclidae in alliance with the Dorians was commonly referred to as the return of the Heraclidae.

Heraclidae, The. Drama by Euripides. See **Children of Heracles, The.**

Heraclides (her-a-klī′dēz). Greek philosopher, born in Pontus, and active in the 4th century B.C. He went to Athens in his youth and became a disciple of Plato and Speusippus. He wrote on a number of subjects, including philosophy (uncritically following and exaggerating Plato's spirit of mysticism), geography, grammar, poetry, and mathematics, but only fragments of his work remain.

Heraclitus (her-a-klī′tus). Greek philosopher, born at Ephesus, Asia Minor, probably c535 B.C., and died there, probably c475 B.C. He was of a noble family and of distinctly aristocratic temper. When the democracy came into power after the defeat of the Persians he withdrew to the country and pursued his studies. He looked with scorn not only on his fellow Ephesians but on many of his fellow philosophers as well. He is one of the earliest of the metaphysical school, and was known as the "Dark" or "Weeping" philosopher (the latter in contrast to Democritus' epithet the "Laughing" philosopher) because of his depth of concept and his misanthropy. He held a theory of the relativity of things: nothing was absolute, all was subject to change and constantly changing; the individual is part of a general harmony in the world and virtue consists of becoming part of that harmony by denial of individuality. All things flow; the basic principle of life is fire, which changes to water, then to earth, and then back again. But it is the process of change itself that governs, and this operates according to certain laws, whether they be of Nature to restore a balance, or of Fate, or of Justice, which brings retribution. Only the gods have perfect wisdom, according to Heraclitus, and as they are also subject to change they will be destroyed also. The ideas of Heraclitus were expressed in the ardent terms of a prophet, but in such diffi

cult oracular language that he was called "the Obscure" by the ancients. The Ephesians nevertheless thought highly of him, and engraved his image on the coins of Ephesus for centuries. Fragments of his great work, *On Nature,* in three books, are extant.

Heraea (hē-rē′a). In ancient geography, a city in W Arcadia, on the Alpheus River; according to tradition, it was founded by Heraeus, son of Lycaon. Among the temples were those of Pan and of Hera, and of Dionysus Citizen and Dionysus Giver of Increase.

Heraea. An Argive festival, celebrated every five years in honor of Hera. The priestess of Hera rode in a car, drawn by white oxen, to the Heraeum, the national shrine of the Argives near Mycenae. A procession accompanied the priestess, the soldiers bearing their arms. As part of the festival, oxen were sacrificed to the goddess, a great feast was provided, and games were held. One of the contests peculiar to this festival was to hurl the javelin at a shield while running at full speed.

Heraean (hē-rē′an) **Games.** Games established by Hippodamia in honor of Hera, in gratitude to the goddess for her help in bringing about the marriage of Hippodamia to Pelops. The games consisted of a single race in which the contestants were virgins of different ages. The prize was an olive wreath and a part of a cow that was sacrificed to Hera.

Heraeum (hē-rē′um) or **Heraion** (-rī′on). National shrine of the Argives, and one of the most sacred sanctuaries of Hera, situated near Mycenae, in Argolis. It was to this shrine that Cleobis and Biton pulled their mother in a barrow so that, as a priestess, she could take part in the rites. In the temple they went peacefully to sleep, never to wake again. This was the answer the goddess gave to their mother's prayer for a fitting reward for her devoted sons. Some say it was at this temple, within two miles of Mycenae, that Agamemnon heard the vows of the Greek chiefs that they would take Troy or die in the attempt. The site of the temple is on a slight rise between the streams Eleutherios and Asterion. The waters of the Eleutherios were employed by the priestesses of the goddess in purification ceremonies. The Argives claimed Hera was nursed by three daughters of the river-god Asterion, whose names were Euboea, Acraea, and Prosymna. On the banks of the river grew a plant, also named asterion, which was offered to Hera, and of which garlands were woven for the image of the goddess. The ancient temple dated from the 6th century B.C. This temple burned when, it is said, a priestess tending the sacred fire fell asleep. A new temple was built in its place (c423 B.C.), of which the Argive Eupolemus was said to be the architect. The new temple contained the celebrated chryselephantine colossal statue of Hera by the sculptor Polyclitus. The ivory and gold seated image wore a crown on which were embossed figures of the Graces and the Horae. In one hand the goddess held a pomegranate, symbol of fertility; in the other hand she held a scepter on which a cuckoo perched. The cuckoo signifies that Zeus first won Hera when he assumed the form of a cuckoo. Next to the goddess was an ivory and gold image of her daughter Hebe. Also in the temple was an ancient image made of wild pearwood, brought to the Heraeum from Tiryns, which the Argives had conquered and destroyed. The silver altar in the precinct was decorated with a representation of the marriage of Hebe and Heracles. Before the temple were statues of former priestesses of the goddess, including one of the unfortunate priestess whose nap had brought destruction to the old temple. The shield Menelaus took from Euphorbus at Troy was dedicated in the ancient temple, and in Roman times the Emperor Hadrian dedicated a peacock, bird sacred to Hera, made of precious stones in the new temple. Cleomenes, the Spartan king (c519–c487 B.C.), thought he had received assurance from an oracle that he would take Argos. He attacked the Argives near Tiryns and they fled for refuge into a sacred grove. As all efforts to force them out failed, Cleomenes set fire to the grove and burned them to death. Afterwards he asked the name of the grove. On learning that it was a grove sacred to Argus he feared that the oracle had been fulfilled, that he had taken the grove Argus and would not take the city Argos. He visited the Heraeum and made sacrifices to the goddess to learn whether he should proceed in his attempt to take Argos.

When he made his offerings a flame flashed from the breast of the image of the goddess. This was a sign to Cleomenes that he should not attack Argos, for only if the fire flashed from the head of the image were the omens considered to be propitious. The Heraeum was excavated (1892–1895) by the American School at Athens, and more recently by the French School. A very valuable collection of archaic terra-cottas was recovered, as well as architectural and sculptural remains. The sculptures of the pediment depicted on one side the birth of Zeus and the war of the Giants, on the other the taking of Troy. Large fragments of these have been recovered.

Herceius (hėr-sē′us, -sī′us). Epithet of Zeus, meaning "Of the Courtyard." It came from the custom of placing an image of Zeus in the forecourt of temples and palaces. There was, for an example, an altar of Zeus Herceius before the house of Oenomaus at Pisa. In the sack of Troy, Priam was killed by Neoptolemus before the image of Zeus Herceius. Sthenelus later carried away this image as part of his share of the spoils of war. The image had three eyes, two in the usual place and a third in the forehead. The presence of the three eyes was to indicate that Zeus exerted his powers in heaven, the sea, and in the Underworld, some say. Sthenelus took the image to Argos and set it up at Larissa, the name of the citadel in Argos.

Herculaneum (hėr-kū-lā′nē-um). Ancient city in Campania, S Italy, near the coast, about six miles SE of Naples, directly at the W foot of Mount Vesuvius. Like Pompeii it was overwhelmed in the eruption of 79 A.D. The city was buried deep under heavy volcanic ash which solidified to a form of tufa. The ancient town was forgotten, and modern Resina grew up over its ruins. In 1709 an inhabitant of Resina sunk a well which reached the ancient theater, and brought to light sculptures and marble facings. Further search was made, solely for the marbles and works of art, and subsequent excavations were undertaken by the Italian government, but were very unscientifically and irregularly conducted, and the galleries pierced were in great part filled again. Under the French rule (1806–15) systematic explorations were instituted; a little was done between 1828 and 1837; then nothing until Victor Emmanuel caused (1869) the resumption of the work. The most important remains are the theater, basilica, prison, some interesting private dwellings, and portions of several streets paved with lava. In Herculaneum were found a number of carbonized manuscripts on papyrus, some of which have been deciphered, and some of the best-known statues in the Naples Museum, including the Agrippina, Sleeping Faun, Aristides, and busts of Plato and Demosthenes.

Hercules (hẽr′kū-lēz). The Roman name for Heracles (q.v.). (For the Labors of Hercules, see **Heracles, Labors of.**) The Romans adopted the Greek hero Heracles, lock, stock, and barrel, and added to the legends assembled about his name some purely Roman adventures. According to the Romans, Hercules stopped at Rhegium on his way back to Greece with the cattle of Geryon. Here one of the bulls from his herd swam across the strait from Rhegium to Sicily. Heracles followed to recover the bull, wrestled with King Eryx, son of Aphrodite, in whose herd his bull was hidden, killed him and won his kingdom, which he left until one of his descendants should come to claim it. The Romans also claimed that while in Italy Hercules freed King Evander from the domination of the Etruscans; that he killed King Faunus, who sacrificed strangers on the altar of his father Hermes, and that by Faunus' widow he was the father of Latinus, the ancestor of the Latins; that he founded Pompeii and Herculaneum; and that he went on in Sicily to the spot where the city of Syracuse was later founded and established the festival commemorating the rape of Proserpina (Persephone) near the sacred chasm of Cyane through which, according to the Romans, Pluto carried off Prosperina to the Underworld. With these and many more legends, the Romans linked the peoples of Italy and the rise of their own state with Hercules, whom they worshiped as a hero and a god of physical strength, courage, and related qualities.

Hercules. An ancient constellation, between Lyra and Corona Borealis, representing a man upon one knee, with his head toward the south, and with uplifted arms. The an-

cients did not identify the constellation with Hercules; the moderns place a club in one hand, and a branch of an apple tree, with the three heads of Cerberus, in the other.

Hercules Furens (fū′renz). Drama by Euripides. See **Madness of Heracles.**

Hercyna (hẽr-sī′na̤). In Greek mythology, a fountain-nymph of Lebadia in Boeotia, and a playmate of Persephone. Once as they were playing, a goose she was holding escaped and fled into a cave. Persephone pursued it and lifted the rock in the cave under which it was hiding. A spring immediately gushed forth from the place where the rock had lain, which became the source of the Hercyna River. Near the source of the river in the cave stone images were placed. On the bank of the river was a temple of Hercyna, with an image of the maiden holding a goose in her arms. The bones of Arcesilaus, brought back from Troy by Leïtus, were entombed beside the river. Across the river was a grove sacred to Trophonius, in which there was an image said to have been made by Praxiteles. Those who sought to consult the oracle of Trophonius had first to bathe in the waters of the river Hercyna.

Hercynian Forest (hẽr-sin′i-a̤n). [Latin, **Hercynia Silva**; Greek, **Herkynia Hule.**] In ancient geography, a mountain range forming the N boundary of what was then known as Europe, and seemingly identified by Aristotle with the Alpine mass. Caesar described it as a nine days' journey wide and a 60 days' journey long, apparently including all the mountains and forests in S and C Germany. It has been variously represented as in C Germany, and as identical with the Böhmerwald, the Thüringerwald, and others.

Hermae (hẽr′mē). Square stone pillars, symbolic of the god Hermes, that were set up in his honor in the doorways of houses and temples, and at cross-roads and streets. On the top of the square pillar an image of the head of Hermes rested. In the midst of the Peloponnesian War (415 B.C.), all the Hermae in Athens were found to have been mutilated. This was just at the time when an expedition was to be sent out against Sicily, and the Athenians were struck with terror by the mutilation of the Hermae, and felt it was an evil omen for the expedition. Alcibiades, one of the generals of the expedition, was ac-

cused of being ringleader in a plot to overthrow the democracy and the mutilation of
the Hermae was ascribed to him. However,
it was decided to put off his trial until he
returned from the expedition. But while he
was away in Sicily, before the Athenians had
had any success there, the Athenians became
frenzied over the mystery of the mutilation
of the Hermae and recalled him to stand his
trial. Numerous accusations were lodged
against many leading men of Athens. Alcibiades did not return but fled into exile.
Meanwhile, a young Athenian of good family
confessed that he had been one of those who
mutilated the pillars and named his companions. In later times it was thought that
this confession had been made only to calm
the populace, and the mystery of the mutilation of the Hermae was never solved, but it
had many repercussions, and years later was
brought up to haunt some of the oustanding
men in Athens.

Hermann (her′män). See **Arminius**.

Hermaphroditus (hèr-maf-rō̯-dī′tus). In Greek
mythology, a son of Hermes and Aphrodite,
born on Mount Ida. In his youth he journeyed to Caria, where he came to the fountain in which dwelt the nymph Salmacis.
Salmacis fell in love with his beauty, which
combined that of Hermes and Aphrodite, but
he rejected her advances and begged her to
go away. As he bathed in Salmacis' pool the
nymph dived into its clear water and clung
to him, praying they might be united in one
person. Her prayer was answered; the bodies
of Hermaphroditus and Salmacis were fused
into one being combining both male and female attributes.

Hermes (hèr′mēz). One of the 12 Olympian
gods. He was the messenger of the gods,
the bringer of dreams, the god of flocks and
herds, and of the market-place; he was god
of commerce and trade, of inventions, science,
and the arts, and of craft in oratory. As an
ancient fertility god, he became also a god
of wealth, hence of luck, hence of thieves.
He conducted the souls of the dead to Hades,
and thus was a link between the worlds of
the living and the dead, equally beloved in
both. The story of Hermes is that while Hera
slept Zeus went to a cave on Mount Cyllene,
in Arcadia, and there embraced Maia, the
daughter of Atlas. In this same cave his son

Hermes was born to Maia one day at dawn.
The infant was wrapped in swaddling clothes
and laid on a winnowing fan, but he refused
to stay in his cradle. On the very first day
of his life he crept to the entrance of the cave,
and there, on the threshold, he found a
tortoise. He greeted the tortoise with joy,
took it up, scooped out the flesh from its shell,
and bound it with ox hide. To the sounding
box he made in this manner he attached

HERMES
Black-figured Attic amphora, 6th century
B.C. *Museum of Fine Arts, Boston*

horns, which he connected at their free ends
with a bridge of reed. From the bridge he
strung seven sheep-gut strings to the sounding box. (Some say he strung only three
strings, others say it was four, and that it
was Apollo who added the strings that make
the seven-stringed lyre.) After he invented
a plectrum he tried out his new musical instrument; he plucked the strings and sang of
the love of Zeus and Maia and of his own
birth. Then, being hungry, he set off to the
meadows of Pieria, where the cattle of
Ápollo were grazing. Here he selected 50

head from the herd and prepared to make off with them. But to cover his tracks, he made huge sandals of oak bark, fastened together with woven grasses, and put them on the hoofs of the cattle. But some say he made the cattle walk backward, to disguise their path, and that he put the sandals on his own feet and camouflaged himself with branches as well. All agree that he was the inventor of sandals, and that he made them to help him carry out his theft of Apollo's cattle. As he started off with the cattle for Pylus, on the Alpheus River, he was spotted by an old man who was cultivating his crops in the nearby fields. Hermes promised the old man rich crops if he would say he had not seen him. According to some accounts the old man agreed; but others say he would make no promise. Hermes proceeded with the cattle to the Alpheus River, where he fed them, penned them in a cave, and built a fire by scraping sticks of wood together. He was the first to build a fire in this manner. He killed two of the steers, roasted their flesh, and nailed their hides to the rocks. The flesh of the roasted steers he cut into 12 portions but, though he was hungry, he ate none of it himself, as it was a sacrifice to the gods. Some say he did eat of the flesh, and that this was the first flesh sacrifice made to the gods. He then quenched the fire, threw his sandals into the river, and returned to Cyllene, where he slid through the keyhole into the cave, and was back in his cradle before his absence had been discovered, having, in the first 24 hours of his life, invented sandals, a method of making fire by rubbing sticks together, the first flesh sacrifices to the gods, and the lyre, to say nothing of having stolen his brother Apollo's cattle. Some say his mother saw him as he slid back into his cradle and pulled the covers around his neck; and she chided him, and predicted he would come to a bad end. He at first innocently answered that he was much too young to do anything that merited such a rebuke, then reproached her for talking to him as if he were a "wordless babe," assured her that he would get along all right, and would look after her too. As he had already made up his mind to be a god, he promised her that they would dwell among the immortals. For, he said, if his father Zeus would not make

him a god he would make himself one. At dawn the next day Apollo discovered that 50 of his cattle were missing. Some say Apollo searched fruitlessly for them, and finally offered a reward for their return. Silenus and his companions, eager for the reward, set out to track down the missing cattle. They came to the cave in Cyllene and heard strange music issuing from it. They questioned the nymph Cyllene about the music and learned from her that a marvelous child had been born the day before, who had invented a new instrument from ox hides and sheep gut. The Sileni were suspicious, especially when they heard of the ox hide, and charged that this marvelous child had stolen the cattle of Apollo. Cyllene was indignant at this ridiculous charge. Just then Apollo arrived, guided thither by a long-winged bird, some say, but others say he knew by divination that Hermes had stolen his cattle. They say that when Apollo noticed the loss of his cattle he asked the old man working in the fields if he knew what had become of them. The old man answered that many passed by as he worked and he could not know them all, but he did especially notice a child, a mere babe, driving cattle backward. Apollo found the tracks and the strange imprints made by the sandals Hermes had invented, and although he didn't understand the strange tracks, he knew where to look for his lost cattle.

Now he arrives, full of wrath, at the cave on Cyllene and charges Hermes with the theft. Hermes cowers in his cradle as Apollo sweeps through the cave looking for his cattle, in vain. He threatens Hermes. Hermes answers that he is a mere infant, who knows nothing of such things and is interested only in his mother's milk. After all, he says, he was born only yesterday, and scarcely understands the meaning of the word "cattle." Apollo is beguiled by the cheekiness of his infant brother. Nevertheless, as Hermes refuses to say where the cattle are and protests his innocence, Apollo hales him off to Zeus. Zeus, too, is amused by Hermes' lies, but orders him to restore the stolen cattle, and asks Apollo to forgive his baby brother. Hermes submits to the will of Zeus; he leads Apollo to Pylus and brings the cattle from the cave where he had hidden them.

actor; up, lūte, pu̇ll; oi, oil; ou, out; ᵺн, then; ḍ as d or j, ş as s or sh, ṭ as t or ch, ẓ as z or zh.

Now Apollo notes the two hides nailed to the rock, and resolves to punish Hermes. But the willow bonds he makes to bind him fall to the ground and sprout. Apollo asks what he did with the two steers he killed, and is told that they were sacrificed to the 12 gods. Surprised, Apollo says he knows of only 11 gods; who is the twelfth? Hermes modestly names himself. As Apollo prepares to set his cattle to graze Hermes plucks his lyre, which up to now he has kept hidden under his swaddling clothes, and sings of the creation of the world and of the gods. Apollo is enchanted with the music. He agrees to give Hermes the cattle in exchange for the lyre, and promises to honor him and his mother. Hermes hands the lyre over and in his turn promises never again to steal anything of Apollo's. They become fast friends. As the cattle graze Hermes invents a shepherd's pipe of reeds and pipes on it guilelessly. Apollo, hearing it, demands this instrument too, and offers in exchange the golden wand with which he herds his cattle. But Hermes bargains. He will exchange the pipe for the golden wand *and* instruction in the art of prophecy. Apollo gives him the golden wand, which will make him a warder of cattle and bring him wealth, but will not teach him the art of prophecy. However, he tells Hermes of the three sisters, the Thriae, who dwell on Mount Parnassus and who will teach him the art of divining by pebbles. In addition to learning this, Hermes also invented the art of divining by knucklebones. Apollo names him god of flocks, cattle, and all animals, and tells Zeus of the deeds young Hermes has already performed. Zeus appoints him herald of the gods, gives him a herald's staff wound with white ribbons, which must be respected by friend and foe, and a round hat and winged sandals, and Zeus appoints him protector of travelers, god of treaties and commerce. Thus Hermes is enrolled as one of the gods. Hades appoints him as the god who summons the dying by laying his golden staff gently on their eyes, and Hermes becomes Pterseus (*Destroyer*), because he is the herald of Death, and Psychopompus, because he conducts the dead souls to the Underworld. Sometimes Hermes uses his staff merely to bring sleep to mortals, and as such he is the bringer of dreams and to him libations are poured before bedtime. In time Hermes shared with Apollo the honors given to the god of the *palaestra* (athletic contests), and feasts called *Hermaia* were dedicated to him as the god of athletic skills that make men strong and handsome.

As herald of the gods Hermes performed many errands. After the flood that Zeus sent to destroy wicked men, Hermes was sent to ask Deucalion, who survived it, what he wished for. Deucalion wished for men to repopulate the earth. It was Hermes who sent the ram with the fleece of gold to rescue Phrixus and Helle when their father was about to sacrifice them. At the command of Zeus he killed 100-eyed Argus, set by Hera to guard Io after she had been transformed into a heifer. Because of this Hermes won the epithet Argeiphontes (*Slayer of Argus*). He guided Perseus to the Phorcides when he was on his mission to fetch the head of Medusa, gave him the adamantine sickle to cut off the Gorgon's head, and restored the cap, wallet, and sandals to the nymphs when Perseus was through with them. It was Hermes who led the goddesses—Athena, Aphrodite, and Hera—to Paris to be judged for the prize of beauty that Eris had thrown among the wedding guests at the marriage of Thetis and Peleus. Some say Hermes, at the command of the gods, carried Helen off to Egypt and delivered her into the charge of the king, and that the Helen Paris carried off to Troy, and for whom the Greeks and Trojans fought a disastrous war, was only a phantom, a wraith created by Hera to punish the Trojans. In the Trojan War he aided the Greeks, with the permission of Zeus, but when Hector was killed by Achilles, Hermes, in disguise, led Hector's aged father Priam to the camp of the Greeks and spirited him into Achilles' tent so that he could ransom his son's body. He then conducted the grieving old king, with Hector's corpse, safely back to Troy. By his cunning and his gift for crafty language Hermes often helped the gods. He retrieved the sinews of Zeus that had been cut out and hidden by the monster Typhon and restored them to Zeus, who then conquered Typhon. He helped to rescue Ares when he was imprisoned in a bronze vessel by Otus and Ephialtes. To him was entrusted the infant Dionysus to save him from the wrath of Hera. He took Dionysus to Ino and Athamas and persuaded them to rear him as a girl. When Hera drove Ino and Athamas mad, Zeus transformed Dionysus into a kid, and in that guise Hermes took him to the nymphs of Nysa. In the gods' war with the Giants Hermes wore the cap of invisibility, loaned to him by Hades, and overcame the giant Hippolytus. As a god who had connections with the Underworld he bore a message from Zeus to Hades, demanding the release of the abducted Persephone so that the earth might not become barren because of Demeter's sorrow, and he brought Persephone back to her mother Demeter in his chariot. On the other hand, he forcibly restored Sisyphus to the Underworld, from which he had escaped by a trick. But he fetched up Protesilaus, killed in the Trojan War, to spend a few hours with his wife on earth. It was Hermes who sold Heracles for three talents to Omphale, to purge him of his crime of murdering Iphitus. Hermes was sent by Zeus to help Atreus in his struggle for the throne of Mycenae; and again, he was sent to warn Aegisthus not to seduce Clytemnestra while her husband was off at the Trojan War. He gave the lyre to Amphion and gave the magic herb moly to Odysseus to protect him from the spells of the enchantress Circe. Altogether, Hermes was a most helpful god; a deity of great ingenuity, craft, and, on the whole, good will.

Like most of the gods, Hermes had many loves. Apemosyne, daughter of King Catreus of Crete, rebuffed him. However, as she was returning from a spring one day he spread fresh hides in her path, and when she attempted to run from him she slipped and fell; he seized her and ravished her. Some say Hermes was the father of Eros by Aphrodite, and some say he was the father of Pan by Penelope. He also loved Herse, daughter of Cecrops, and she bore him Cephalus who was carried off by Eos, and Ceryx, the first herald of the Eleusinian Mysteries. Other sons were: Autolycus, the notorious thief; Echion and Eurytus the Argonauts; Daphnis, who invented bucolic poetry; Myrtilus, the charioteer of Oenomaus, for whose murder Pelops erected the first temple of Hermes in the Peloponnesus; Abderus, who accompanied Heracles to Thrace to fetch the man-eating mares of Diomedes and perished there.

In recognition of his role as protector of travelers and wayfarers, square pillars were set up in his honor. They were called *Hermae,* and were to be seen at cross-roads, lanes, byways, and before houses. In addition, there were heaps of stones at the cross-roads to which passing travelers added their stones in tribute to Hermes. An image of Hermes of the Gateway stood at the entrance to the Acropolis. As god of the Market-place his image stood near the Painted Portico in Athens. Another image, bearded and made of stone, stood in the market-place at Pharae. Here there was an oracle of Hermes. In front of the image was a hearth to which bronze lamps were fastened. At nightfall, the inquirer at the oracle burned incense on the hearth, filled and lighted the lamps, put them on the altar to the right of an image of a coin called a "copper," then he whispered his question into the ear of the image of Hermes. Having asked his question, the inquirer stopped his ears and left the market-place, when he unstopped his ears. The first words he overheard thereafter constituted the oracular response. Hermes was called Cyllenian (*Of Cyllene*), for his birthplace; Epimelius (*Keeper of Flocks*), and the god who brought fertility to flocks and fields; Pronaos (*Of the Fore-temple*) and had an image said to have been made by Phidias at the entrance to the Acropolis at Thebes; he was Acacesius (*Of Acacesium*) after Acacus, founder of Acacesium, because, some say, as a child he lived in Acacesium and Acacus was his foster-father; he was Dolius (*Crafty*); Champion, especially at Tanagra where he led the youths of the city against invading Eretrians, and where there was a wild strawberry tree under which he was said to have been nourished; he was Spelaites (*Of the Cave*); and Promachos (*Defender*). He was the god of luck and of profit; whatever was found by chance was a gift of Hermes. He was born on the fourth of the month and that day and number were sacred to him. His worship, which was particularly strong in Arcadia, its ancient seat, extended throughout Greece. In art he was sometimes represented bearded, but after the archaic period usually as a graceful and vigorous youth, slightly draped, with *caduceus* (staff), *petasus* (round hat), and *talaria* (winged sandals) as attributes. The most noted artists of antiquity executed works in which Hermes was the subject. One of the most beautiful as well as one of the best-known statues of antiquity that have been preserved is the *Hermes Carrying the Infant Dionysus,* found in the ruins at Olympia. The Roman Mercury, their god of commerce, became identified with Hermes.

Hermes Carrying the Infant Dionysus (hėr'-mēz; dī-ọ-nī'sus). Subject of sculptured groups by several ancient artists, including one by Praxiteles which the Greek traveler Pausanias says he saw (c170 A.D.) in the Heraeum, or Temple of Hera, at Olympia. A superbly executed and well-preserved marble group found in the cella of the Heraeum by the German excavators was assumed at the time to be the group recorded by Pausanias and to be the original by Praxiteles. Since that day some experts have asserted that 1) the workmanship and finish are not referrable to the time of Praxiteles, and 2) there is reason to think Praxiteles' original was of bronze; therefore, these scholars argue, the group found was not the original, but a copy substituted in ancient times, conceivably after Pausanias' visit. In the group, Hermes carries the babe on his left forearm, which rests on a tree stump. His right hand, now missing, held something which caught the child's attention, probably a bunch of grapes. A greatly inferior adaptation of this group was found in the theater of Minturnae in 1933. (JJ)

Hermesianax (hėr-mē-sī'ạ-naks). Greek elegiac poet of the 4th century B.C. He was born at Colophon, in Ionia, was a contemporary of Alexander the Great and Demosthenes, and a friend of Philetas. He wrote love elegies. One long fragment of his work *Leontion,* in three books, remains. It consists mainly of a list of lovers of mythology and legend.

Hermione (hėr-mī'ọ-nē). In Greek legend, the daughter of Helen and Menelaus. She was nine years old when her mother eloped with Paris and left her in Sparta. Menelaus gave her into Clytemnestra's charge while he sought the return of Helen. She was betrothed to Orestes at the command of Apollo, but some say that toward the end of the Tro-

jan War when oracles foretold that Troy could not be taken without the presence of Neoptolemus, Menelaus promised her to Neoptolemus in return for his aid at Troy. Others say she was given to Neoptolemus because Orestes, pursued by the Furies for the murder of his mother, could not marry her. She married Neoptolemus long after he returned from the war accompanied by his captive and concubine Andromache. Hermione bore no children to Neoptolemus and accused Andromache, whom she constantly referred to as a barbarian, of putting a spell on her. Neoptolemus went to Delphi to consult the priestess concerning his wife's childlessness. While he was gone Hermione plotted to kill Andromache and her sons by Neoptolemus. She was prevented from doing so by the timely arrival of Peleus, grandfather of Neoptolemus. In fear of her husband's wrath for what she had tried to do, Hermione attempted to kill herself by hanging, but was saved by her handmaidens. She later married Orestes, who some say had a hand in Neoptolemus' death at Delphi, and bore him a son, Tisamenus.

Hermione. In ancient geography, a city on the E coast of the Peloponnesus, near Troezen. According to tradition, it was founded by Hermione, a grandson of Phoroneus, but some say the Hermionians were Dryopes who had been driven out of Doris by Heracles. The rock from beneath which Theseus took up his father's tokens was on the road between Troezen and Hermione. The most ancient city of Hermione contained temples of Apollo Platanistus (*Of the Plane Tree*), sanctuaries of Demeter Thermasia (*Warmth*), Poseidon, and Athena. The old city was moved back a short distance from the coast. In the newer city there was a temple of Aphrodite Pontia (*Of the Deep Sea*) and Limenia (*Of the Harbor*), in which maidens and widows about to marry sacrificed. Annually, the Hermionians held a festival to Dionysus of the Black Goatskin. A sanctuary of Demeter Chthonia was said to have been founded by Clymenus, son of Phoroneus. It was named in honor of an Argive maiden, Chthonia, who received Demeter when she was searching for Persephone. An annual festival was held in her honor, in the course of which a procession of wreath-decked maidens led cows, also adorned with wreaths, to the temple. One cow at a time was induced to enter the temple, where four elderly women waited and slaughtered the cow with an ax when it came inside. Four cows were dispatched in that manner. All Hermionians took part in the ceremony outside the temple, but the most sacred object within was never seen by any man. Hermione was noted for having its own private entrance to Hades. Consequently, the thrifty Hermionians considered it unnecessary to put a coin under the tongue of a corpse to pay Charon to ferry it across the Styx. By this entrance, the Hermionians claimed that Heracles dragged Cerberus, the Hound of Hell, up to the light, and Hades, they said, carried Persephone to his realm through this chasm. In the Trojan War men of Hermione joined the Greeks before Troy under the leadership of Diomedes. When the Dorians invaded the Peloponnesus, Dorians from Argos settled in Hermione. In the Persian War Hermione sent three ships to join the Greek fleet at Salamis (480 B.C.), and its name was inscribed on the trophy dedicated at Delphi as having taken part in the victory of Plataea (479 B.C.).

Hermippus (her-mi′pus). Greek satirical poet, active about the end of the 5th century B.C. He was an older contemporary of Aristophanes, and a writer of the Old Comedy. His first victory was in 435 B.C. An enemy of Pericles, he attacked Aspasia, his mistress, and charged her with impiety. Fragments of his satirical, abusive work survive.

Hermocrates (her-mok′ra-tēz). Syracusan general and politician; killed at Syracuse, c407 B.C. At a congress at Gela attended by delegates from all the Greek cities of Sicily and called (425 B.C.) for the purpose of considering whether the cities should ally themselves with Athens against Syracuse, Hermocrates formulated a policy of Sicily for the Sicilians. He advised the representatives not to invite outsiders in to settle the quarrels of the Greek cities with each other, and to unite to repulse any interference in their affairs by outsiders. His policy was not adopted, nor in the end was he able to follow it himself, but for the time being the intervention of Athens in Sicilian affairs was postponed. Ten years later an Athenian expedition arrived in Sicily at the request of Segesta, which was engaged in a quarrel with Selinus, and to restore Leontini, which had been taken by Syracuse. Hermocrates was appointed general to defend Syracuse. A fleet was assembled and walls were built. With the aid of the Spartan general Gylippus, who came in response to Syracusan appeals for help, the Athenians were completely defeated at sea (413 B.C.), and cut to pieces or enslaved as they attempted to retreat overland. After the defeat of the Athenians Hermocrates was appointed commander of a fleet that was sent to the aid of Sparta in the Aegean and took part in the battle of Cynossema (411 B.C.). While he was gone a resurgence of democratic feeling in Syracuse was used by his political opponent, Diocles, to secure his banishment and to deprive him of his command. He went to Persia and served the Spartans under the satrap Pharnabazus. In 408 B.C. he returned to Sicily, but was not allowed to return to Syracuse. He built a small fleet, hired mercenaries, and gathered a band of followers from Himera, the city just destroyed by the Carthaginians, and set about to drive back the Carthaginians. He had great success and hoped now to win back his own city, but Diocles prevented his recall. Hermocrates thereupon went to the ruins of Himera and gathered the bones of the soldiers of Diocles who had fallen there and whose bones Diocles had neglected to inter. Hermocrates loaded the bones on wagons and sent them into Syracuse, while he waited outside the city walls, hoping to be recalled. Diocles was banished for having failed to bury the dead, but Hermocrates was not recalled. All else failing, he now resolved to take the city by force. With a few followers he was secretly admitted to the city by his supporters inside it, but before the main body of his supporters could join him his presence in the city became known, and he was overpowered and slain (c407 B.C.).

Hermodorus of Ephesus (her-mō-dō′rus; ef′e-sus). Greek philosopher, of the 5th century B.C. He is said to have gone to Rome and to have assisted the decemvirs in drawing up the laws of the Twelve Tables at Rome in 451 B.C.

Hermogenes (her-moj′e-nēz). Greek rhetorician of the 2nd century A.D. He was born at Tarsus, in Cilicia, and in his youth went to

Rome. There he earned the admiration of the emperor Marcus Aurelius for his skill and power in oratory. He wrote a work on rhetoric, in five books, which became a standard text for the subject, and which still survives.

Hermonthis (hėr-mon′this). [Modern name, **Armant, Erment.**] In ancient geography, a town in the Thebaid, Egypt, situated on the Nile about eight miles SW of Thebes. It was a seat of ancient worship, and important ruins remain, notably those of a temple built in the time of Cleopatra.

Hermus (hėr′mus). [Modern name, **Gediz.**] In ancient geography, a river of Asia Minor, said to have gold-bearing sands in its channel. On it was located Sardis, the Lydian capital of King Croesus. The river was also called Sarabat.

Hernici (hėr′ni-sī). Ancient Italian people, allied to the Sabines, dwelling in the Apennines about 40 miles SE of Rome. Their capital was Anagnia (Anagni). They were subjugated by the Romans in 486 B.C., and revolted (unsuccessfully) in 387 and 362 B.C. and in 306 B.C.

Hero (hē′rō). In Greek legend, a priestess of Aphrodite at Sestos, on the Hellespont, beloved by Leander, who swam across the Hellespont every night from Abydos to see her. One night Leander was drowned and Hero, heartbroken, drowned herself also.

Hero or **Heron** (hē′ron). Alexandrian "mechanist" and mathematician, active probably c150 A.D. He was the inventor of *Hero's fountain*, in which a jet of water is maintained by compressed air, and of a machine acting on the principle of Barker's mill, in which the motion is produced by steam. One of his extant works describes a machine that manipulated mechanical actors through a four-act tragedy, including a shipwreck and a fire, without any further aid once the machine had been set in motion. In geometry he wrote the *Metrica*. Fragments of his *Commentary on Euclid's Elements* survive in Proclus and in the work of an Arabian writer. His *Mechanica* in three books exists in an Arabic version. Surviving also are his *Pneumatica*, in two books, *Barulcus* (a treatise on the raising of heavy weights), *Belopoeica* (a treatise on the making of darts), *On the Dioptra, On Mirrors, On Automaton-*

making, and a treatise on the making of a machine called the "Cheirobalistra."

Herodas (hē-rō′das) or **Herondas** (-ron′-). Greek satirical poet; fl. c3rd century B.C. He seems to have lived on the island of Cos, but little is known of him beyond a few lines quoted by other writers, and the eight poems of his literary mimes in iambic scazons, preserved in a papyrus manuscript in the British Museum. These poems show him to have been a realist who portrayed in vivid manner, and in a particular style and meter, the speech and incidents of everyday life.

Herodes Atticus (hē-rō′dēz at′i-kus), **Tiberius Claudius.** [Sometimes called **Atticus Herodes.**] Greek rhetorician, born at Marathon, c101 A.D., and died there, c177. He was the son of an old and rich family and was soundly educated in rhetoric and philosophy. His eloquence won the admiration of the emperor Hadrian, who appointed him to public office. In 129 he returned to Athens and became distinguished as a teacher. In 140 Antoninus Pius invited him to Rome to become the tutor of Marcus Aurelius and Lucius Verus, and rewarded him with public offices, including that of consul (143). He inherited great wealth from his father, which he used for the benefit of his fellow citizens. He is notable for his interest in public works during the period of government influence, building such structures as the Odeum at Athens, another odeum at Corinth, a stadium at Delphi, baths at Thermopylae, and an aqueduct at Canusium, as well as restoring many ruined buildings in Greece. Fragments of his writings survive.

Herodianus (hē-rō-di-ā′nus) or **Herodian** (hē-rō′di-an). Greek historian, born about 170 A.D., died about 240 A.D. He lived at Rome, where he held public office. His history of the Roman emperors, from the death of Marcus Aurelius (180) to the accession of Gordianus III (238), survives.

Herodianus Aelius. Greek grammarian, born at Alexandria, who was active in the 2nd century A.D. He went to Rome and became friendly with Marcus Aurelius. His chief interest was the study of grammar and in reducing it to a system. A work of his on the words and unusual forms in the *Iliad* was epitomized, with other studies of the *Iliad,* in the 3rd century A.D. His work on anomalous words and a short Atticist lexicon are extant. He is considered one of the greatest, and the last, of the original Greek grammarians.

Herodorus (hē-rō-dô′rus). Greek historian of Heraclea on the Euxine Sea. He was active at the end of the 6th century B.C. His work, critical history of the earliest records, was chiefly concerned with his native town and with Heracles, who had seized the land on which it stood from the Bebryces and given it to the Mariandyni; it also included mention of the Argonauts and the descendants of Pelops. His approach to the early records— that is, to the myths—was an attempt to give a rationalistic account of such stories as that of Prometheus and Laomedon, for example, and to fit them into some sort of chronological order. Of Laomedon, who, according to the myth, refused to pay Apollo and Poseidon as promised for building the walls of Troy, Herodorus explains that Laomedon took money from the treasuries of other temples to build the walls and never repaid it. Of Prometheus, chained to a rock and gnawed by an eagle in the myth, Herodorus says Prometheus was a Scythian prince, the Eagle was a river of that name which regularly overflowed its banks and flooded the country. The Scythians imprisoned Prometheus, punishing the prince for the evils that fell on them, and he was freed only when Heracles, with the aid of science, improved the channel of the river and it ceased to flood the country. Although he believed the common tradition that the Nemean Lion had fallen from the moon, he explained it on the ground that the moon was another earth, populated by some of the strange beasts and birds spoken of in the stories but never seen on earth in his day. In furtherance of his work of critically examining and recording the early records, Herodorus made extensive geographical studies. The questing mind that prompted Herodorus to search for rational explanations of the myths, the only explanations men had for the universe and the basis of their theology, must be admired as a step forward in man's search for knowledge.

Herodotus (he-rod′ō-tus). Greek historian, called "The Father of History." He was born at Halicarnassus in Asia Minor, probably c484 B.C.; died, c424 B.C. According to the commonly accepted account of his life, gleaned chiefly from his own works, he was the son of Lyxes and Dryo, persons of means and station at Halicarnassus. He fought against the Persians, who controlled Halicarnassus, and against Lygdamis, the tyrant of his native city. Before Lygdamis was overthrown Herodotus fled to Samos. On the fall of the tyrant he returned to Halicarnassus, but for some reason, perhaps a political one, he soon left and went to Athens. There he found a second home, and became a friend of Sophocles, and possibly of Pericles also. Ultimately, he went as a citizen to the model colony of Thurii which Athens founded (443 B.C.) on the site of the ruined city of Sybaris in south Italy. There he wrote his history, and there he died. The Greek word from which our word "history" comes means "a learning or knowing by inquiry." Herodotus was a seeker of knowledge and information. His search led him to travel widely. He visited Egypt; traveled in what was then known as Asia as far as Susa and Ecbatana; journeyed around the Euxine Sea to the mouths of the Ister (Danube); visited the Crimea and the land of the Colchians. He went to Tyre in Phoenicia and to Cyrene in Libya. He knew Greece well, having traveled, perhaps as a professional story-teller, to Dodona, Acarnania, Delphi,. Thebes, Athens, Tegea, Sparta, and Olympia, and he also traveled along the coast of Thrace. What he learned he set down in his history of the Persian Wars to 479 B.C. His *History* is a work in nine books, which men later named after the nine Muses. The first six books are occupied with what might be called the background of the wars, the last three books are concerned with the mighty forces which were in motion and the course of the war down to 479 B.C. In the opening sentence of his work he announces that he publishes the results of his researches in the hope of preserving the memory of the deeds of men, and of preventing the great and glorious actions of the Greeks and the barbarians (Persians) from losing their due meed of glory. In doing so he means to set down a record of the reasons for the struggle between the Greeks and the barbarians. Beginning with a rationalized account of the seizure of Io and her removal from Greece to Egypt, followed by the theft

actọr; up, lūte, pụll; oi, oil; ou, out; ᴛʜ, then; ḍ as d or j, ṣ as s or sh, ṭ as t or ch, ẓ as z or zh.

of Medea from Colchis (representing Asia) by Jason, and the abduction of Helen by Paris and the war which the Greeks waged on Troy (again, representing Asia), Herodotus details the ancient reasons for enmity between Asia and Greece. He then takes a long leap through time to the period of Croesus, the first Asiatic ruler to subdue the Ionian cities. He describes the power of Croesus and his fall to Cyrus, and gives a vivid, anecdotal, and broad-minded picture of the reigns of Cyrus, Darius, and Xerxes, describing the wars they fought, their reasons for fighting them, and the course of the engagements which took place. In the course of so doing, Herodotus finds occasion, by means of what modern writers call "flashbacks," to describe what he had learned of the origin and ancestry of the peoples and customs of the areas in which he had traveled. His history includes a fascinating collection of the myths, legends, and folk tales of the peoples whose lands he visited, with plentiful references as well to those of the Greeks. He has been criticized by some for discursiveness, for the inclusion of material not strictly relevant to his theme, and for what seems, to some, to have been a naïve acceptance of patently unacceptable stories and conclusions. However, we can hardy blame Herodotus for accepting as true what was regarded as truth in his time, and we must be grateful for the liveliness with which he paints the picture of the ancient world. And because of his discursiveness and inclusiveness much has been preserved which would otherwise have been lost. The anecdotes he relates—perhaps, it is true, with the idea of entertaining his audience—give an immediacy to the work which may account for its vitality even today. Whatever he quoted in the way of conversations (and he quoted some which could not have taken place), stories, oracles, or fantastic incidents, is revelatory of the ideas and attitudes of his own time. In many cases Herodotus cites the sources of his information. Often he repeats what "was told" to him by people he had reason to believe, under the circumstances of his age and the state of knowledge at the time. Sometimes he gives his information or descriptions without comment, and sometimes he repeats stories that he quite frankly says he does not

believe himself. But over all, there is a sympathy and understanding of peoples and their differences, an admiration for the worth even of enemies, which is a winning tribute to the compassion and curiosity of the author, and makes him lively and interesting reading even more than 2000 years after his death.

Heroic Age. One of the five Ages of Man described by Hesiod. It followed the Bronze Age and preceded the Iron Age. Men of the Heroic Age were descended from mortals and fought gloriously and for the joy of combat in the Trojan War. The siege of Thebes and the expedition of the Argonauts were among other glorious exploits of the Heroic Age. At the end of their days, the men of the Heroic Age were transported to the Elysian Fields.

Herophile (hē-rof'i-lē). A legendary prophetess of Delphi. She is said to have lived before the Trojan War, for she foretold that Helen would be reared in Sparta and would be the ruin of Europe and Asia, and that for her sake the Greeks would capture Troy. She claimed that her mother was immortal, a nymph of Trojan Mount Ida, and that her father was a mortal. She was an attendant at the temple of Apollo Smintheus but spent most of her life in Samos, with occasional visits to the sanctuaries of Apollo at Clarus, Colophon, and Delphi. At Delphi she stood on a high rock and chanted her oracles. She died in the Troad and was buried in the grove of Sminthian Apollo, whom at various times she claimed as a husband and a brother in her oracles.

Herophilus (hē-rof'i-lus). In Greek mythology, a son of Aphrodite and Poseidon.

Herophilus. Greek anatomist and physician at Alexandria; born at Chalcedon, in Bithynia; fl. c300 B.C. He was a pioneer in dissection and is credited with early descriptions of the brain, the liver, and the genitals, and with being the first to describe motor and sensory nerves as different in function. Among his writings were commentaries on Hippocrates, a manual for midwives, and notes on the causes of sudden death.

Herostratus (hē-ros'tra-tus). Ephesian who set fire to the temple of Artemis (Diana) at Ephesus, one of the seven wonders of the world (allegedly, on the night of the birth of Alexander the Great), in order to immortalize himself.

fat, fāte, fär, fāre, errant; net, mē, hėr ardent; pin, pīne; not, nōte, möve, nôr,

Herse (hėr′sē). In Greek mythology, one of
the three daughters of Cecrops, the half-
man, half-serpent king of Attica, and
Agraulos. Hermes, beholding her in a procession for Athena, fell in love with her and
bribed Agraulos the Younger to facilitate a
visit to her. Agraulos took the bribe but refused to do anything to help Hermes because she had been inspired by Athena with
gnawing envy of her sister's good fortune
in being loved by a god. In anger, Hermes
turned Agraulos to stone and sought Herse.
She bore him two sons, Cephalus and Ceryx.
Long before this happened, however, Athena
had given Agraulos and her daughters a
chest to guard. She cautioned them not to
open the chest. Some time after the dèath
of Agraulos the Younger, Herse and her
mother and sister could no longer control
their curiosity. They opened the chest and
were horrified to find therein an infant which
was half-child and half-serpent. Maddened
by this discovery, they leaped from the
Acropolis and were killed. Athena was so
grieved when she learned of their deaths
from her sacred crow that she dropped the
huge stone she was carrying to fortify the
Acropolis, and it became Mount Lycabettus.
She also changed the crow's feathers from
white to black for bringing her bad news,
and forbade all crows from ever again visiting the Acropolis.

Hersilia (hėr-si′li-a). In Roman legend, a
woman of the Sabines. When Romulus invited the Sabines to the celebration of ˙the
Consualia and, by arrangement with his followers, fell upon the Sabine women and
carried them off because of the lack of women
in his new city of Rome, Hersilia was taken
by Romulus and became his wife, according
to some accounts. The Sabines waged war
on the Romans to recover their women, who
had become quickly adjusted to their Roman husbands, and were driven off. Romulus prepared to carry the war against the
Sabines but, some say, Hersilia persuaded
him to forgive the parents of the stolen
women for trying to regain their children,
and instead, to receive the Sabines into the
new state of Rome. Some say that Tullus
Hostilius, the third king of Rome (672–640
B.C.), was a grandson or great-grandson of
Hersilia and Romulus.

Hesiod (hē′si-od, hes′i-). Greek didactic poet,
born at Ascra, on the slopes of Mount Helicon
in Boeotia, and, according to some scholars,
active in the 8th century B.C. His youth,
according to a poem attributed to him, was
spent in rural pursuits at his native village.
He left Ascra, it is thought, because of a
lawsuit brought against him by his brother
on the death of their father, and went to
Naupactus where he settled. As far as can
be learned, he spent all his life in these two
places, except for a short trip he once took
across the Euripos to Chalcis, where he participated in some funeral games and won a
tripod which he dedicated to the Muses.
He especially avoided southern Greece, it is
said, because an oracle had foretold his
death at Nemea. In the end he did die in
the sacred precinct of Nemean Zeus in Locris.
According to tradition he was murdered by
the brothers of a woman who bore him a
son in his old age. The murderers flung his
body into the sea, but dolphins bore it back
to land, and by order of the oracle at Delphi
a tomb was built for his bones in Orchomenus. The son born to him in his old age
was said by some to have been the lyric poet
Stesichorus. The obscurity of his life has
led some critics to adopt the opinion that
the name does not represent an actual person, but is a mere personification of the
Boeotian or Hesiodic school of poetry, as
opposed to the Homeric or Ionic. Among
the numerous works ascribed to him are
Works and Days, the *Theogony,* and *The
Shield of Heracles.* Hesiod says that he was
tending his flocks when the Muses visited
him. They announced to him, "We know
how to tell many false things true-seeming,
but we know how to speak the real truth
when we will." From then on Hesiod became a poet. *Works and Days* is in the form
of an address to his brother, and exhorts
him to live justly and gain wealth by honest
toil (instead of by suing him!); it contains
myths and fables, gives notes on agriculture
and navigation, tells what days are lucky
and unlucky for agricultural and nautical
undertakings, praises hard work, and lays
down precepts for moral guidance. It also
reveals that Hesiod shared the popular superstitions, that he was a woman-hater, and
that he felt he lived in an evil age. In this

poem appears the story of Pandora, descriptions of the Four Ages of Man (or five, including the Age of Heroes), and a noted description of Winter. According to the Boeotians, this poem is the only authentic work of Hesiod. The *Theogony* attempts to reduce to order the stories of the origin of the earth and the origin and relationships of the gods. According to Herodotus, it was Homer and Hesiod who first composed the genealogies of the gods, gave them their names and occupations, and described them. The *Theogony* contains the most ancient materials of mythology and is one of the principal sources of our knowledge of the mythology of the early Greeks. A third poem, *The Shield of Heracles,* is also attributed to Hesiod, but his authorship is now doubted by most scholars. It describes the shield made by Hephaestus for Heracles and used by him in his fight against Cycnus the robber. Fragments of other works attributed to Hesiod, particularly of the *Catalogues,* survive.

Hesione (hē-sī'ō-nē). In Greek legend, a daughter of Laomedon, king of Troy, and Leucippe. On the advice of an oracle she was chained to a rock on the shores of Troy as a sacrifice, to be killed by a sea-monster sent by Poseidon to devastate the land because Laomedon had refused to pay Poseidon and Apollo for their help in building the walls of Troy. Passing by Troy, Heracles saw her and when he learned the reason for her pitiful situation he offered to slay the monster and free her. Laomedon promised to pay him with the marvelous horses that Zeus had given to compensate for the abduction of Ganymede. Heracles slew the monster and freed Hesione but once the danger was removed Laomedon refused to honor his promise. Heracles vowed revenge. After some time he returned and attacked Troy. He killed Laomedon and all of his sons except Podarces (Priam), sacked the city, and took Hesione captive. He gave her to Telamon, who had aided him in his attack, and she bore him a son, Teucer, the half-brother of Telamonian Ajax. According to some accounts, when Priam, the new king of Troy, had reëstablished his kingdom he sought the return of his sister, and sent his son Paris with a fleet to bring her back.

Paris took the occasion to go to Sparta and seduce Helen and bring her back to Troy, thus causing the Trojan War. Others say that Hesione fled from Telamon to Miletus, where King Arion found her and married her. She bore a second son, Trambelus, whom Arion reared as his own son, although he was the child of Telamon, and who was afterward killed at Troy by Achilles.

Hespera (hes'pėr-a̱). In Greek mythology, the daughter of Erebus and Nyx (Night). The name for Eos when, as she accompanied Helius, she had passed through the heavens to the western shore and had become Evening.

Hespere (hes'pėr-ē). In Greek mythology, one of the Hesperides. She changed herself into a poplar tree at the approach of the Argonauts to the Tritonian Lake. See **Hesperides.**

Hesperia (hes-pir'i-a̱). According to the ancient Greeks, the region of the west, especially Italy, and sometimes, according to the poets, the Iberian peninsula. Aeneas, having stopped in Crete on his flight from Troy, was told in a dream to go to the land of his fathers, Hesperia, and found a new nation.

Hesperides (hes-pėr'i-dēz). In Greek mythology, three maidens, Hespere, Erytheïs, and Aegle, who guarded the tree with the golden apples which Gaea (Earth) caused to grow as a marriage gift for Hera. According to Hesiod they were daughters of Nyx and Erebus; in later accounts they are named as the daughters of Atlas and Hesperis. They dwelt in the gardens of the west, or among the Hyperboreans, or in Libya; the location of their garden is variously given. Ladon, a 100-headed dragon, helped them guard the apples, but to no avail, Heracles came and slew Ladon and obtained some of the golden apples to take to Eurystheus. The Hesperides were also visited by the Argonauts, who had been blown to the coasts of Libya by a storm and then lifted in the *Argo* by a mighty wave which washed them into the interior and left them stranded. They carried their ship over the desert to the Tritonian Lake and came to the Hesperides, who first transformed themselves into dust and earth before the Argonauts, and then into trees—Hespere into a poplar, Erytheïs into an elm, and Aegle into a willow. The reason for their fear at sight of the Argonauts was that only the day before Heracles had come and taken the golden apples. When they found the Argonauts were not hostile they told them how to find a spring which Heracles had caused to gush up from the earth in the desert and wished them good luck.

Hesperis (hes'pe̞-ris). According to some accounts, the mother by Atlas of the Hesperides. She was the daughter of Hesperus.

Hesperus (hes'pe̞-rus). Personification of the evening star, in Greek mythology; son of Astraeus and Eos (according to Hesiod): identified with the planet Venus. The Latin name for it was Vesper.

Hestia (hes'ti-a̞). One of the 12 Olympians. She was the eldest daughter of Rhea and Cronus and, like Artemis and Athena, was a virgin goddess. This came about because Apollo and Poseidon were rivals for her love. She settled their quarrel by vowing to remain a virgin forever. For thus preventing strife from breaking out on Olympus Zeus ordered that the first victim of every public sacrifice be dedicated to Hestia. As goddess of the hearth and the hearth fire, Hestia was intimately linked with every Greek family, for the hearth was the center of Greek life. She presided over individual well-being and the duties of hospitality. Hestia, who remained aloof from the wars and disputes in which the other gods and goddesses reveled, was worshiped as a beneficent and kindly goddess. Her shrine was a sanctuary for suppliants, and her fire, both in private and public hearths, was sacred. The Romans identified her with their Vesta.

Hetruria (he̞-trö'ri-a̞). See **Etruria**.

Hexapolis (hek-sap'o̞-lis), **Dorian**. In ancient Greek history, a name given to a league of six Dorian cities: Lindus, Ialysus, Camirus (all in Rhodes), Halicarnassus, Cnidus, and the island-city of Cos.

Hicetaon (hi-se-tā'o̞n). In the *Iliad*, a son of Laomedon, and a descendant of Dardanus, Ilus, and Tros. Like his brother Priam, he was too old to fight in the Trojan War, and served as a counselor. In this capacity he advised the Trojans to restore Helen to Menelaus, although he felt the Trojans could not be blamed for fighting for such as she, who

was like to a goddess immortal in face and figure.

Hiera (hī'e̞-ra̞). According to some accounts, the wife of Telephus, and a leader of the Mysian women, allies of the Trojans in the war against the Greeks. She was slain in battle by Nireus. Some say she was a daughter of King Priam of Troy, and that she surpassed Helen in beauty.

Hierapolis (hī-e̞r-ap'o̞-lis). [Eng. trans., "Sacred City."] Ancient city in Phrygia, Asia Minor, near Laodicea. It was held sacred on account of its hot springs and cave called "Plutonium," and was the birthplace of Epictetus.

Hierapolis. Ancient city in Syria, about 50 miles NE of Beroea (Aleppo); the Greek Bambyce, and the modern Membij.

Hiero I (hī'e̞-rō) or **Hieron I** (-ron). Tyrant of Syracuse, who died 467 B.C. He was the brother of Gelo, whom he succeeded as tyrant in 478 B.C. Cyme (Cumae), the northern outpost of the Greek settlements on the Italian coast, harried by its neighbors the Etruscans, appealed to Hiero for aid. He sailed at the head of a large Syracusan fleet and defeated the Etruscans at the Battle of Cyme (474 B.C.). Thenceforth Etruscan power in Italy declined. Hiero and Syracuse, like the other Greek settlements in Italy and Sicily, were strongly attached to their motherland, and honored and preserved Greek customs and Greek gods. From the spoils taken from the Etruscans at Cyme, Hiero dedicated a fine bronze helmet at Olympia. Hiero's court was wealthy and luxurious, and its ruler a generous patron of literature. The poet Pindar was an ardent admirer of Hiero and was a welcome guest at his court. He wrote the *First Pythian Ode* to celebrate the victory at Cyme. Hiero reverenced the sacred sanctuary at Delphi, to which the tyrants of Syracuse made rich gifts. He sent his horses and chariots to take part in the great games at Olympia. His entries won victories there in 476, 472, and 468 B.C., and at the Pythian Games, in which he also participated, in 482, 478, and 470 B.C. Pindar and Bacchylides, another poet who was welcomed at his court, commemorated his victories in their odes. To memorialize the founding of the city of Aetna, which Hiero accomplished by removing all

actǫr; up, lūte, pull; oi, oil; ou, out; ᴛʜ, then; d̦ as d or j, ș as s or sh, ț as t or ch, z̦ as z or zh.

the inhabitants of Catana and repeopling and renaming it, Aeschylus, visiting at Hiero's court, wrote a play, *Women of Aetna*. The play has been lost, and the city as Aetna did not long survive; it soon became Catana again. A quarrel between Hiero and Theron, tyrant of Acragas, was settled, so it is said, by the poet Simonides, who spent the last years of his life in Syracuse. Under his successor, the work of Hiero as a tyrant was undone. His defeat of the Etruscans at Cyme was a lasting benefit to the Greek settlements of Italy, and his generosity as a patron of literature bore fruit which survives to our own age.

Hiero II or **Hieron II.** King of Syracuse, born c307 B.C.; died 216 B.C. He became (275 B.C.) general of the Syracusans, and as a result of his victory over the Mamertines, who were spreading into Syracusan territory, was chosen king in 270 or in 265 B.C. The Carthaginians, looking for a chance to gain possession of a base in Sicily, came to the Mamertines' aid, but they in turn had called on Rome for help. Hiero therefore became an ally of Carthage in 264 B.C., but driven back by the Romans, he became a permanent ally of Rome in 263 B.C. and remained on their side during the First and Second Punic wars.

Hieronymus of Cardia (hī-e̱-ron′i-mus; kär′-di-a̱). Greek general and historian; fl. end of the 4th century B.C.; died c250 B.C. He was possibly one of Alexander the Great's generals. After Alexander's death he joined Eumenes, was taken prisoner by Antigonus, who pardoned him, and was later made military governor of Boeotia by Demetrius Poliorcetes. He wrote a carefully documented history of the Diadochi (successors of Alexander) from the death of Alexander to the Pyrrhic War. His work was an important source for Arrian's history of Alexander the Great. Hieronymus lived to an extremely advanced age and died at the court of Antigonus Gonatas.

Hilaira (hil-a̱-ī′ra̱) or **Hilara** (hi-lā′ra̱). In Greek mythology, daughter of Leucippus. She was a priestess of Artemis. She and her sister Phoebe were betrothed to their cousins, Idas and Lynceus, but Castor and Polydeuces carried them off and had sons by them. According to some accounts, the bitterness

which now arose between the two sets of twins, Idas and Lynceus, and Castor and Polydeuces, led to the death of Castor.

Himera (him′e̱-ra̱). In ancient geography, a town on the N coast of Sicily, about 30 miles E of Panormus (Palermo). Famous warm springs, sacred to the nymphs, were located here. The city was founded, 648 B.C., by Greek colonists from Euboea. Here (480 B.C.) Gelon of Syracuse defeated the Carthaginians under Hamilcar. By a trick, the forces of Gelon secured entrance to Hamilcar's camp and slaughtered him as he stood by a great altar of Poseidon. Hamilcar's grandson Hannibal (d. 406 B.C.) conquered Himera (408 B.C.), sacrificed 3000 men on the spot where his grandfather had been killed to appease his shade, and completely destroyed the city to avenge his grandfather's defeat and death. No city was ever again raised on the spot. Afterward Thermae Himerenses (the modern Termini Imerese) was the chief town in the vicinity. Himera is also known as the birthplace of Stesichorus.

Himera. Ancient name of two rivers in Sicily, one (the modern Salso) flowing S, and the other (the modern Grande) flowing N past the ancient town of Himera.

Himeros (hī′me̱r-os). The god of longing or desire closely associated with Eros.

Himerus (hī′me̱r-us). In Greek legend, a son of Lacedaemon and Taÿgete. Aphrodite caused him to ravish his sister Cleodice unwittingly. When he realized what he had done he leaped into the river which was sometimes known by his name, but was more generally called the Eurotas River.

Himilco (hi-mil′kō). Carthaginian navigator; fl. c500 B.C. According to Pliny he conducted a voyage of discovery from Gades (modern Cádiz) northward along the coast of Europe, perhaps as far as Britain. It is inferred from passages in the *Ora Maritima* (c400 A.D.) of Festus Avienus that the voyage of Himilco may have extended to the Sargasso Sea, though similar seaweed patches occur off Portugal.

Himilco. Carthaginian general (fl. c400 B.C.). He was a cousin of Hannibal (d. 406 B.C.), whom he accompanied at the siege of Acragas (406 B.C.). In order to attack the walls, Hannibal ordered a causeway to be built and plundered the tombs of cemeteries outside

Acragas for material. Plague broke out and Hannibal was one of its first victims. Himilco succeeded to the command. Feeling that the gods were angry at the plundering of the tombs, Himilco sacrificed a boy to the Carthaginian god Moloch, and finished building the causeway, but without taking any more material from the tombs. He besieged the city and at the end of eight months the defenders, in despair, decided to abandon their homes and their gods. Practically the entire population marched out at night, unhindered by the Carthaginians, and left their city to be plundered and occupied (406 B.C.) by Himilco's forces. The following year he marched against Gela, besieged the city, and took it when its inhabitants also fled. In 397 B.C. Himilco returned to Sicily to protect the Carthaginian cities from the attacks of Dionysius the Elder, tyrant of Syracuse. He retook the city of Motya, captured and almost completely destroyed by Dionysius the year before, and founded a new city, Lilybaeum, nearby, and the city of Tauromenium on the heights above the Sicilian city of Naxos. He defeated the Syracusan fleet at Catana and marched to besiege Syracuse. His army encamped in a marsh, but Himilco pitched his tent on higher ground, in a precinct of Olympian Zeus. This insult to Greek gods, and a more horrendous sacrilege—the plundering of a temple of Demeter—were thought by the Syracusans to have caused the plague that now broke out in the Carthaginian camp. The pestilence so weakened the besiegers that a well-planned assault by the besieged on the plague-stricken camp succeeded, and the forces of Himilco were defeated. But Himilco himself came to a secret arrangement with Dionysius, treacherous on both sides, whereby, in return for the payment of 300 talents, Dionysius allowed Himilco to escape with 40 triremes and his Carthaginian soldiers, leaving his allies and mercenaries to their fate at the hand of Dionysius. Upon returning home Himilco committed suicide.

Hipparchus (hi-pär′kus). Younger son of Pisistratus and brother of Hippias. The brothers succeeded their father (527 B.C.) and reigned as tyrants of Athens conjointly. The night before the Panathenaic Festival, according to Herodotus, Hipparchus dreamed that a tall and handsome man stood over him and made the following statement: "Bear thou unbearable woes with the all-bearing heart of a lion,/Never, be sure, shall wrongdoer escape the reward of wrong-doing." The next day Hipparchus offered sacrifices to ward off the evil portended by the dream and then led the Panathenaic procession. While leading it he was murdered (514 B.C.) by Harmodius and Aristogiton, Gephyraeans whose ancestors were said to have come to Boeotia from Phoenicia with Cadmus and who, being driven from Boeotia, fled to Athens for refuge. The murder of Hipparchus did not end the tyranny of the Pisistratidae but, according to Herodotus, merely exasperated them. Hipparchus was a great patron of the arts. It was his invitation which brought the poets Anacreon and Simonides to Athens. The great advances in vase-painting, sculpture and architecture of Pisistratid Athens are due in great part to this cultured ruler.

Hipparchus. Greek astronomer; considered the father of systematic astronomy; born at Nicaea, Bithynia, c190 B.C.; died c125 B.C. He catalogued 850 or more stars, invented the planisphere, and made a number of important discoveries including the eccentricity of the solar orbit, some of the inequalities of the moon's motion, and the precession of the equinoxes. Only one of his own writings survives, *In Eudoxi et Arati Phaenomena,* but Ptolemy acknowledged his indebtedness to Hipparchus for the Ptolemaic theory of the universe. He is credited also with development and extension of the use of trigonometry.

Hipparete (hi-pa̱-rē′tē). Daughter of Hipponicus and sister of Callias; fl. end of the 5th century B.C. Her father gave her in marriage to the Athenian general Alcibiades. He continued his public affairs with various courtesans after the marriage and she left him and went to live with her brother. Later, she sued him for divorce. When she appeared in court, in person rather than by proxy, he strode in, picked her up, and carried her through the agora to his house. This was according to the law. A wife suing for divorce must appear in court in person so that her husband might, if he so desired, reclaim her as his property. Hipparete then

actọr; up, lūte, pull; oi, oil; ou, out; ᴛʜ, then; ḍ as d or j, ş as s or sh, ṭ as t or ch, ẓ as z or zh.

continued to live with him until her death, which took place shortly thereafter.

Hippasus (hip′a-sus). In Greek mythology, son of Leucippe and a grandson of Minyas. When Dionysus came to Orchomenus and invited the daughters of Minyas to join his revels, they refused. They were driven mad and offered Hippasus as a sacrifice. They tore him to pieces and devoured him.

Hippia (hip′i-a). Epithet of Athena, meaning "Horse-goddess." She is credited with having invented the war-car and drove her own chariot in the war between the gods and the Giants. The people of Acharnae, a division of Attica, invoked Athena Hippia.

Hippias (hip′i-as). Tyrant of Athens, 527–510 B.C. He was the eldest son of Pisistratus and with his brother Hipparchus succeeded him as ruler of Athens, 527 B.C. After the murder of Hipparchus (514 B.C.), he became sole ruler and tyrant of Athens. As a result of the extremely harsh rule to which he subjected the Athenians the Alcmaeonidae, who had been banished by the Pisistratidae, joined other exiles and sought to free Athens. With the assistance of the Spartans under Cleomenes, the Athenians compelled Hippias to leave the country (510 B.C.). He went to Sigeum on the Scamander River in Asia Minor. Later the Spartans, fearing lest a free Athens become as strong as Sparta, sent to Hippias in Sigeum, invited him to Sparta, and proposed to restore him to power in Athens. However, the allies of Sparta, especially the Corinthian representative, rebuked the Spartans for seeking to restore a tyrant, and since they refused to participate in the undertaking it was abandoned. Hippias went again to Sigeum where he embarked on an intense program of interesting Artaphernes, nephew of the Persian king Darius, in making war against Athens. The Athenians learned of his activities and sent messengers to Artaphernes, to whom he replied that if they valued their safety they must take back Hippias. As the Athenians refused to do this henceforth they were open enemies of the Persians. Hippias accompanied Artaphernes when he invaded and took Eretria. A dream convinced him that he would be restored to Athens with all his former power and that he would live to old age in his native land. He now assumed the role of guide to the Persians and led them to the plain of Marathon, as he considered it a favorable ground for the Persian cavalry. When he had arrived at Marathon it happened that he sneezed violently and as he was then of advanced years, probably well over 60 at the time, one of his teeth was forced out by the violence of his sneeze and fell in the sand. Hippias searched for it but could not find it. To him this was the fulfillment of his dream and it now seemed to him that after all the land would never fall to the Persians, and that all his share of it would be the part occupied by his lost tooth. In the ensuing battle of Marathon (490 B.C.) the Persians were completely defeated, and Hippias died shortly thereafter, c490 B.C.

Hippias. Greek sophist and polymath, born about the middle of the 5th century B.C. He was a contemporary of Socrates. He came to Elis and taught and wrote in various parts of Greece, especially in Athens, and acquired great wealth and fame. In his teaching his main object seems to have been to teach his students how to be successful. He occupied himself in rhetorical, philosophical, and political studies. He was also well-versed in poetry, music, mathematics, painting, sculpture, and handicrafts. Out of his own richly furnished mind he could produce, at short notice, arguments to buttress any side of a question. Plato, in two dialogues, criticized him by characterizing him as vain of his memory and method and arrogant in his teaching. One of the great contributions of Hippias was to Greek chronology, and consisted in publishing a list of the Olympiads, with their successive victors. This provided a point of departure of inestimable value to history.

Hippocamp or **Hippocampus** (hip′ō-kamp, -kam′pus). In Greek and Roman mythology, a sea-horse with two forefeet and a body ending in the tail of a dolphin or other fish. The car of Poseidon and those of other deities were drawn by such sea-horses.

Hippocoön (hip-ō′kō-on). In Greek legend, a son of Oebalus of Sparta and the nymph Batia. He was the half-brother of Tyndareus and Icarius, and banished them both in order to make himself ruler of Sparta. He was attacked and slain by Heracles, because his sons had killed a friend of Heracles, and

Tyndareus was restored to the throne of Sparta.

Hippocoön. According to legend, a comrade and kinsman of Rhesus, king of Thrace and ally of the Trojans. Hippocoön was roused by Apollo when Diomedes and Odysseus, having entered the Trojan camp as spies, were slaying Rhesus and the Thracians. Hippocoön gave the alarm, but it was too late and the Greek pair escaped with the marvelous horses of Rhesus. Hippocoön later accompanied Aeneas on the flight from Troy to Italy.

Hippocrates (hi-pok′ra̱-tēz). Father of Pisistratus. Once when he went to the games at Olympia, as he was sacrificing, the water in the cauldrons for the victims began to boil, although there was not as yet any fire beneath them. A soothsayer interpreted this prodigy as a warning to Hippocrates: if he were unmarried he should remain so, that he might never have a son; if he already had a wife he should put her aside; and if he already had a son he should disown him. Hippocrates disregarded the advice of the soothsayer. Afterward he became the father of a son. Hippocrates was a descendant of Neleus (Nestor's father) and named his son Pisistratus, after Nestor's son of that name.

Hippocrates. [Called the **Father of Medicine.**] Greek physician, born on the island of Cos, c460 B.C.; died at Larissa, Thessaly, c377 B.C.. Nothing definite is known of his life: he is said to have been a descendant (17th or 19th in direct line) of Asclepius, to have traveled widely, and to have practiced in various places. Of the 72 (or 87) medical works attributed to him, it is not known which, if any, he wrote; there is, however, general recognition of a Hippocratic school of medicine and a corpus of Hippocratic treatises that were preserved in the Alexandrian library. The Hippocratic physician discarded the philosophic approach and also the ancient customs and beliefs in his insistence that the effect must have a cause; moreover, the effect was the result of ascertainable causes and was not of supernatural origin. Climate, food, even the kind of government under which the patient lived had to be considered. Observation was the keynote of the teaching of Hippocrates; of necessity

his knowledge of anatomy was weak, since current religious beliefs did not sanction vivisection, and his theories of essences or humors were incorrect. But his observation was sharp enough to make the *facies Hippocratica,* described in his *Prognostics,* a still recognizable symptom in the dying patient. His *Aphorisms* contains the famous "Life is short, but art is long." The Hippocratic Oath, taken by doctors today, is perfectly in harmony with Hippocrates' reported medical practice, even though it was not written by him.

Hippocrates. Tyrant of Gela, in Sicily; died 491 B.C. He extended the power of Gela over Naxos, Zancle, and other Greek cities of Sicily. He waged war on Syracuse and defeated the Syracusans at the Helorus River, but was prevented from taking Syracuse when aid arrived for that city from Corinth and Corcyra. He was killed while attacking the city of Hybla (491 B.C.).

Hippocrates of Chios (kī′os). Greek mathematician; fl. at Athens, 470–400 B.C. He wrote an *Elements of Geometry,* now lost. The third and fourth books of Euclid's *Elements* are to some extent based on the work of Hippocrates, who is said to have proved that the areas of circles are to each other as the squares of their diameters. His best-known work is on the "lunes of Hippocrates," certain figures bounded by two intersecting arcs of circles.

Hippocrene (hip′o̱-krēn, hip-o̱-krē′ne̱). Fountain on Mount Helicon, in Boeotia, sacred to the Muses. Traditionally it sprang up from a hoof mark of Pegasus, and is alluded to as a source of poetic inspiration.

Hippocurius (hip″o̱-kū′ri-us). Epithet of Poseidon, meaning "Horse-tending." He had a sanctuary at Sparta.

Hippodamas (hi-pod′a̱-mas). In Greek mythology, father of Perimele. He flung his daughter into the sea when he learned that she had been ravished by the river-god Achelous.

Hippodameia (hi-pod-a̱-mē′a̱, -mī′a̱). See **Briseis.**

Hippodamia (hi-pod-a̱-mī′a̱). In Greek legend, a daughter of Oenomaus, king of Pisa and Elis, and Sterope. Either because of incestuous love for her or because an oracle had declared that he would die at the hands of one of her offspring, her father refused to give her in marriage. He compelled her suitors to run a race with him, from Olympia to the Isthmus of Corinth. If Oenomaus, who gave the contestants a head start, overtook them he flung his spear into their backs and killed them. When Pelops came wooing Hippodamia, she fell in love with him and bribed Myrtilus, Oenomaus' charioteer, so that Pelops could win. Pelops also bribed Myrtilus; he won the race, and Oenomaus was killed. Hippodamia established games to Hera, the Heraean Games, in gratitude for her marriage to Pelops. She bore him many children, among them: Pittheus, Atreus, Thyestes, Copreus, and Sciron. She became jealous of Pelops' affection for his bastard son Chrysippus. Some say she murdered Chrysippus but was recognized and fled. Others say she and her sons Atreus and Thyestes were implicated in the murder. However it was, she fled to Argolis and killed herself. Later her bones were brought back and buried at Olympia. Annual sacrifices were made by women in her sanctuary.

the proper grouping of dwelling-places. The plans of three cities were specifically attributed to him: Piraeus, the port of Athens; Thurii, a colony established by Athenians and others in 443 B.C. on or near the deserted site of Sybaris in the toe of Italy; and Rhodes. At Piraeus and Rhodes, rectangular street plans have in fact been detected, although it is not certain that these go back to the 5th century B.C., and by 408 B.C., when Rhodes was laid out, Hippodamus would have been at least 70 years old; Thurii has not been excavated. The checkerboard plan of Olynthus in Macedonia, dates from c425 B.C., during Hippodamus' active period, and it has been suggested that this was designed either by Hippodamus himself or by engineers trained in his atelier. (JJ)

Hippolochus (hi-pol′ọ̄-kus). In Homeric legend (*Iliad*), a son of Bellerophon, and the brother of Isander and Laodamia. He resigned his claim to his father's kingdom in favor of his nephew Sarpedon. His son was Glaucus, Sarpedon's devoted comrade.

Hippolyte (hi-pol′i-tē) or **Hippolyta** (-tạ). In

PELOPS AND HIPPODAMIA
Red-figured Attic amphora, 5th century B.C. *Museo Pubblico, Arezzo*

Hippodamia. In Greek legend, a daughter of Butes, or, as some say, of Adrastus. She married Pirithous. Pirithous did not invite Ares and Eris to their wedding, and some say that out of spite they caused an outbreak of battle between the Lapiths and the centaurs at the wedding festivities. Hippodamia was married only a short time when she died.

Hippodamus of Miletus (hi-pod′ạ-mus; mī-lē′tus, mi-). Greek architect and engineer, born c480 B.C., considered by the Greeks to have been the father of city-planning. According to Aristotle, it was he who introduced the principle of straight, wide streets and

Greek legend, a queen of the Amazons; a daughter of Ares and Harmonia, or, according to other accounts, of Otrera or of Aphrodite and Ares. She dwelt near the Thermodon River on the Euxine Sea, and was the possessor of a famous girdle, a gift to her from Ares, which Heracles was told to fetch as one of his labors for Eurystheus. When Heracles came to her shores she received him graciously and voluntarily agreed to give him the girdle. However, Hera stirred up the Amazon women with a rumor that Heracles was about to abduct their queen. They armed themselves and prepared to attack.

fat, fāte, fär, fãre, errạnt; net, mē, hèr ardẹnt; pin, pīne; not, nōte, mŏve, nôr,

Heracles, suspecting treachery, killed Hippolyte and took her girdle. According to other accounts, Heracles got the girdle in exchange for one of Hippolyte's sisters whom he had captured; or by engaging in personal combat with Hippolyte and slaying her; or even from Theseus, who had secured the girdle and gave it to Heracles in exchange for Antiope, a captive Amazon princess.

Hippolyte. Name sometimes given to the Amazon queen who bore Hippolytus to Theseus. See **Antiope.**

Hippolytus (hi-pol′i-tus). In Greek mythology, one of the Giants, a son of Gaea and the blood of Uranus, who waged war on the gods. In the battle, Hermes, hidden in Hades' cap of invisibility, felled him and Heracles killed him.

Hippolytus. In Greek legend, a son of Theseus and the Amazon Antiope. When Theseus had sons by his lawful wife Phaedra, he sent Hippolytus from Athens to Troezen where his grandfather Pittheus made him his heir. Hippolytus was a handsome, athletic, and chaste youth. He built a temple to Artemis in Troezen and devoted himself to the worship of that goddess to the exclusion of others. By this devotion to Artemis he denied the power of Aphrodite, and she resolved to punish him. She caused Phaedra, his stepmother, to fall madly in love with him. Phaedra followed him to Troezen and covertly watched him every day as he exercised on the gymnasium ground, jabbing the pin of her jeweled brooch in the leaves of a nearby myrtle tree in her frustration. After some time, encouraged by her nurse, Phaedra sent Hippolytus a letter in which she confessed her love for him and invited him to share her couch. Hippolytus was horrified. He destroyed the letter, his only evidence that she had made the advances, and reproached Phaedra. She, fearing he might expose her, wrote a letter to Theseus accusing Hippolytus of committing the acts she wished he had committed, and then hanged herself from the lintel. When Theseus read the letter he accused Hippolytus and without listening to the protests of his son, who had come to Athens, banished him from the city. Theseus called on Poseidon to punish Hippolytus. As Hippolytus drove furiously along the coast road in his chariot, Poseidon sent a huge wave from the sea. Riding the crest of the wave was a great bull, or according to some accounts, a sea monster. The horses were terrified and shied and reared. Hippolytus prevented them from plunging over the cliffs but they had swerved from the road. Either the reins caught on a fig tree by the roadside or the axle of the chariot wheel struck the tree bole. The chariot overturned and Hippolytus, entangled in the reins, was dragged to his death. Too late Theseus learned that his son was innocent. Some say the body of Hippolytus was buried beside that of Phaedra in a tomb in Troezen near the myrtle tree, the leaves of which still bear the scars of being jabbed by Phaedra's brooch. The people of Troezen paid Hippolytus divine honors, brides cut off a lock of their hair and dedicated it to him. But some say the people of Troezen did not believe Hippolytus was killed by his horses, and that he was not buried in Troezen. They say his spirit went to Tartarus and there Artemis demanded that Ascelpius restore him to life. Asclepius, with the aid of an herb, did as she requested, but since it was against divine law for the dead to return to life Artemis wrapped him in a cloud, transformed his appearance and rapt him off to Italy. She changed his name to Virbius and sent him to live in her sacred grove in Aricia. There, with the permission of the goddess, he married the nymph Egeria. No horses were allowed in the sacred grove. Priests of the temple were drawn from runaway slaves. See **Aricia.**

Hippolytus. A tragedy by Euripides, exhibited 428 B.C. and won first prize. It treats the vengeance which Aphrodite brought on Hippolytus for denying the power of love. Seneca and Racine, among others, wrote tragedies based on this legend.

The scene is before the palace of Theseus in Troezen, whither Theseus has withdrawn in a self-imposed exile for slaying a kinsman. Aphrodite enters and vows to punish Hippolytus for scorning her and dedicating himself to the chaste goddess Artemis. It is not because he worships Artemis that Aphrodite punishes him; it is because he fails to honor her as well, for the chaste huntress and the goddess of love merit equal reverence. This day will see her vengeance on Hippolytus, and on Phaedra, the young wife of Theseus, as well. She sees Hippolytus approaching, and withdraws.

Hippolytus enters with his fellow huntsmen and sings praises to Artemis. A servant advises him to honor Aphrodite too, but Hippolytus answers that men may choose the gods they will worship, and he has chosen pure Artemis. He departs. His servant is troubled, and prays that Aphrodite will forgive Hippolytus, for this is the folly and extremism of youth. As the servant leaves a chorus of Troezenian ladies enters. They speak of the unhappy state of Phaedra, who seems ill and longing to die. They ask what curse has fallen on their young queen.

Phaedra approaches with her nurse and her handmaidens. The conversation between Phaedra and the nurse expresses the fevered longings of the one and the concern of the other. The nurse does not know why Phaedra is so unhappy, for her mistress will not tell the reason. She coaxes Phaedra, reminds her of her children, mentions Hippolytus. His name brings a cry from Phaedra. She loves her children, she says, but fate has conquered her. Her hands are pure but her soul is stained. She longs for death, for her death will be her honor. She recalls the unnatural love of her mother Pasiphaë, and her sister Ariadne's betrayal of her father and country out of love for Theseus. At length she reveals that she is passionately in love with Hippolytus, the young son of Theseus and the Amazon Hippolyte. The nurse is horrified, the chorus of women grieves. Phaedra tells of her sleepless nights. She has mused on the unhappiness of men's lives, and concludes that it is not inborn folly that causes suffering, but the failure of men to do what they know is right. When she was smitten with love for Hippolytus she tried to overcome it with self-control. Unsuccessful, she has resolved to die rather than shame Theseus. The nurse has been thinking the matter over. After all, she says, it is not so unusual; many have had the same experience, and it would be a poor thing if Phaedra could help those she loves only by dying. Everyone must yield to Aphrodite, she says, and cites numerous cases—Zeus and Semele, Eos and Cephalus. If even the gods capitulate Phaedra, too,

must bow; Phaedra has tried to be too perfect. Since a god has willed that she love Hippolytus, she must accept the god's will and yield, as it is presumptuous to try to be stronger than the gods. Phaedra instantly sees through the nurse's compromising and practical reasoning, and rejects it. Life is more than honor, the nurse insists. Phaedra is shocked, and begs her not to weaken her determination to die rather than yield to her love. The nurse persuades her that she has a charm to soothe love and goes off. The chorus sings of the awful power of love and the grief it can bring. Presently Phaedra and the Troezenian women hear the voice of Hippolytus from within the palace. The nurse has told him of Phaedra's love for him. He is shocked and angry, and curses the nurse. He comes from the palace, aghast at what he has heard, and makes a long speech denouncing women. He is defiled just to have heard the nurse's suggestion that he betray his father. If he hadn't been trapped into giving an oath that he would not reveal what the nurse subsequently told him, he would go straight to Theseus. As it is, he cannot break his oath. He leaves. Phaedra sends the nurse away; the latter justifies her action by telling how welcome it would have been if it had worked. Phaedra declares that she intends to die, but wants to leave no stain of dishonor on her sons or on Theseus. At the same time, she wants to punish Hippolytus; to teach him that all the gods must have their due. Phaedra withdraws. The chorus sings that Phaedra's marriage to Theseus was doomed from the start, because Aphrodite was offended. A cry is heard from within—Phaedra has hanged herself. Theseus enters and is stunned by the news. He orders the doors opened and Phaedra is revealed hanging from a lintel. He apostrophizes his dear, dead wife. Why did she do it, he mourns; what broke her heart? The chorus grieves with him, and shudders at the woe they know is still to come. Theseus sees a note. In it Phaedra accuses Hippolytus. Enraged, Theseus calls on Poseidon as his father, reminding the god that he had once promised Theseus three curses. He wishes to use one now, and asks Poseidon to destroy his son. The chorus, sworn to silence by Phaedra, cannot tell

Theseus his son is innocent. Hippolytus enters and sees Phaedra dead. Theseus assails him as a traitor who would have betrayed his father. Hippolytus veils his head in horror. Theseus bids him reveal himself, and reviles him for having pretended to be so chaste. Hippolytus is a vile hypocrite, convicted by Phaedra in her letter, to which her suicide is a witness. He banishes Hippolytus. Hippolytus swears that he is innocent, that he never betrayed his father, nor even thought or dreamed of such a thing. Phaedra guarded her honor with dishonor, he says, and he can say no more because of his oath. Theseus, ignoring the pleas of the chorus and the denials of Hippolytus, banishes his son on the spot. Hippolytus leaves. The chorus laments. A messenger enters and announces that Hippolytus is near death, that the curse Theseus invoked has already operated. Poseidon sent a monster from the sea that caused the horses of Hippolytus' chariot to rear as he drove along the shore. The chariot was overturned and Hippolytus, entangled in the reins, was dragged along and so mangled that he is now at the point of death. The messenger, though a servant of Theseus, believes Hippolytus was innocent—no matter how many women hanged themselves nor how many letters they had written before doing so. Theseus is not so glad to hear of his son's approaching death as he had expected to be. He orders bearers to bring his son to him. The chorus of women sings of the power of love to bring unbending hearts low. Artemis, veiled in a cloud, addresses Theseus: Hippolytus was innocent; Phaedra was nobly resolved not to reveal the love Aphrodite had inspired in her for Hippolytus; the misguided act of a doting nurse, who sealed the lips of Hippolytus with an oath, precipitated the disaster. Phaedra wrote a lying letter to protect her honor. Artemis accuses Theseus of condemning Hippolytus too hastily. Even Poseidon, she says, though he fulfilled the curse as he had promised, finds him wicked. But Theseus may yet be forgiven, for the whole disastrous chain was set off by Aphrodite to punish Hippolytus for denying her power.

Bearers bring in Hippolytus. He cries to Zeus to behold the injustice that has rewarded his upright life. He longs to die and be free from pain. Artemis addresses him. He pities his father and wishes men's curses could strike the gods as the gods' curses strike men. Artemis soothes him, promises that he will ever be remembered in Troezen by the offerings of hair from girls who are about to marry. She bids Theseus take his son in his arms, then, because she cannot look on death, she disappears. Hippolytus forgives his father and dies. As Theseus mourns the chorus sings of the great blow that has fallen on the city with the loss of one so mighty.

Commentators say Euripides changed the last few lines of this drama to commemorate the death of Pericles, which occurred just before the play was presented. The lines as they stand, translated by A. S. Way, are:

"On the city hath lighted a stroke without warning,
On all hearts desolation.
Rain down, O ye fast-dropping tears of our mourning!
When the mighty are fallen, their burial-oblation
Is the wail of a nation."

Hippomedon (hi-pom′e̞-don). In Greek legend, a son of Aristomachus. He was an Argive and was one of the seven chieftains who marched against Thebes to restore Polynices to the throne. He perished in the expedition. Some say he was slain by Ismarus, others say he was overcome by a cloud of Theban missiles after he had nearly drowned in the Ismenus River. His body was recovered by Theseus after the Thebans had refused honorable burial to those who fell at Thebes. He was the father of Polydorus, one of the Epigoni.

Hippomenes (hi-pom′e̞-nēz). In Greek legend, the son of Megareus and Merope, and the grandson of Poseidon. As a woman-hater, he went to sneer as he watched Atalanta race against her suitors, but remained to fall in love with her. With the help of Aphrodite he resolved to race Atalanta and to win her. Aphrodite gave him three golden apples which, during the course of the race, he cunningly threw in front of Atalanta. She, who had at one time vowed to remain a virgin, stooped to pick them up and lost ground. In this way Hippomenes won the race and won Atalanta for his wife. According to some accounts, Atalanta had already fallen in love with Hippomenes at sight, and thus was the more ready to take advantage of any delay which would permit him to win. In his joy at winning Atalanta Hippomenes forgot to give proper thanks to Aphrodite, and the goddess became his enemy. She induced him to commit a sacrilege in the temple of Cybele. Cybele, in her turn punishing, turned him and Atalanta into lions and yoked them to her car. According to other accounts it was Zeus who turned them into lions; Hippomenes is also known as Melanion.

Hipponax (hi-pō'naks). Greek iambic poet, born at Ephesus in the 6th century B.C.; fl. 540–537 B.C. According to tradition he was a lame, deformed beggar, who invented the "halting iambic" (choliambic meter), or "scazon" (limping), so-called because it has a spondee or trochee in the last foot rather than the expected iambic foot. In this meter he composed his satirical verses, or perhaps they should more properly be called abusive verses. They were directed against all who offended him, and especially against women. He was banished (540 B.C.) by the tyrants of his native city to Clazomenae, and lived the rest of his life there in poverty. In this place two sculptors, Bupalus and Athenis, caricatured him. He avenged himself on them in such bitter, abusive verse that, according to tradition, they were driven to suicide. He is reputed to have been the first to parody epic poems. Only fragments of his work survive.

Hipponicus (hi-pon'i-kus). Athenian of the 5th century B.C. He was the father of Callias and of Hipparete, wife of Alcibiades.

Hipponous (hi-pon'ō-us). In Greek legend, one of the last Trojans slain by Achilles. Achilles, wounded and dying, kept his fighting spirit to the end and slew Hipponous just before he died.

Hipponous. According to legend, the father of Periboea. He ordered his daughter to be slain because she claimed the child she was about to bear had been fathered on her by Ares.

Hippothoë (hi-pō'thō-ē). According to legend, a daughter of Mestor (son of Perseus and Andromeda) and Lysidice (daughter of Pelops). She was carried off to the Echinades

islands by Poseidon, to whom she bore Taphius, the colonizer of Taphos.

Hippothous (hi-pō'thō-us). In Greek legend, a son born secretly to Alope, daughter of Cercyon, a king in Arcadia. Poseidon was his father. Alope gave him to a nurse and ordered that he be exposed to die, but he was saved by shepherds and taken to Cercyon, who recognized the mantle in which the infant was wrapped as belonging to his father. He ordered the child exposed again, and again he was saved. Theseus later killed Cercyon and put Hippothous on the throne of Arcadia in his place.

Hippothous. Named in the *Iliad*, as a captain of Pelasgians, allies of Troy in the Trojan War. He was slain by the spear of Telamonian Ajax as he tried to drag the body of Patroclus to the Trojan camp.

Hippys (hip'is). Greek historian who lived at Rhegium, 5th century B.C. He was the earliest collector and writer of the myths, traditions, and legends of Sicily and Italy.

Hire (hī'rē) or **Hira** (hī'ra). See **Ire**.

Hirpini (hėr-pī'nī). Ancient Italian people, of Samnite stock, living in southern Samnium in the district near Beneventum, subjugated by the Romans in 290 B.C.

Hirtius (hėr'shi-us), **Aulus.** Roman politician; killed near Mutina (Modena), Italy, 43 B.C. He was a friend of Caesar and the reputed author of the eighth book of Caesar's *Commentaries on the Gallic War,* and of the history of the Alexandrian war. As consul with Pansa (43 B.C.) he defeated Antony at Mutina, but less than two weeks later was killed in another battle there.

Hissarlik (hi-sär-lik'). See **Troy**.

Histiaea (his-ti-ē'a) or **Hestiaea** (hes-). In ancient geography, a city on the NW coast of Euboea, Greece, opposite Thessaly, colonized by Thessalians. In the Trojan War Greeks from "vine-clad" Histiaea fought under the command of Elephenor, captain of the Abantes. In 447–446 B.C. it was conquered by Athens under Pericles and Tolmides. Its inhabitants were driven out and fled for refuge to Macedonia; the territory was annexed by Athens, and nearby the deserted city the Athenians sent colonists to found the city of Oreus. After the defeat of Athens in the Peloponnesian Wars, Oreus fell under the dominion of Sparta. The Athenian colonists

fat, fāte, fär, fãre, errant; net, mē, hėr ardent; pin, pīne; not, nōte, möve, nôr,

were expelled, the ancient name Histiaea was restored. In 207 B.C. Attalus II conquered the city, lost it to the Romans, and reconquered it, 200 B.C.

Histiaeus (his-ti-ē′us). Tyrant of Miletus, through the friendship of Darius the Persian, at the end of the 6th century B.C. He was executed at Sardis, Asia Minor, 494 B.C. When Darius attacked Scythia (c512 B.C.), the Ionian leaders who were allied to Darius and who had been left to guard the bridge by which Darius crossed the Ister (Danube), considered whether they would revolt against Darius and regain their freedom. Histiaeus urged them not to revolt and suggested a means by which they could preserve the bridge from the attacks of the Scythians. To reward him for this service Darius promised him whatever boon he asked. Histiaeus asked for Myrcinus on the Strymon River in Thrace, that he might build a city there. His request was granted. Histiaeus took the town and began to raise a wall about it. Darius now feared that he meant to make himself master of the area. He sent for Histiaeus, on the pretext that he needed his advice, compelled him to relinquish the throne of Miletus, and kept him in honorable confinement at the court of Susa, Miletus being left under the regency of Aristogoras, nephew and son-in-law of Histiaeus. Histiaeus longed to return to Miletus but could not go as Darius pretended he needed him, nor could he send out any messages to Aristagoras as he was closely watched. He finally hit on the following scheme: He chose his most trusted slave, shaved his head, and pricked a message on his scalp. When the hair had grown back he sent the slave to Aristagoras in Miletus with instructions to Aristagoras to shave the head of the messenger and look at it. Aristagoras did as commanded and found orders to revolt against Darius. Histiaeus incited the revolt because he thought if Miletus rebelled Darius would send him to quell the revolt. All Ionia revolted and, as he had planned, Histiaeus was sent to put it down. Being now freed of Darius' restraint, he warred against Persia. He was finally captured in Mysia and handed over to the Persian satrap Artaphernes. The latter, fearing that Darius might even now forgive Histiaeus because of his former service, impaled his body, cut off his head and sent it back to Darius at Susa.

Hittites (hit′īts). Ancient people in Asia Minor c2000–1200 B.C., traditionally descended from Heth, son of Canaan, the son of Ham. They settled in the region of Hebron on the hill, are mentioned as one of the seven principal Canaanite tribes, and sometimes as comprising the whole Canaanite population. Hittite kings are mentioned who seem to have dwelt N of Palestine. About the middle of the 9th century B.C. they disappear from Biblical history. Some scholars, however, distinguish the latter as Syrian Hittites, whom they consider a different group from the Canaanite Hittites. Historically it is assumed that the Hittites were a people of Indo-European stock who invaded the region known as Cappadocia c1800 B.C., conquered its people, and retained their power in Asia Minor until c1200 B.C., when they were overcome by Rameses II. Thothmes III of the XVIIIth Dynasty fought with them c1600 B.C. in Megiddo. Later Seti attacked them c1350 B.C., and Rameses II (the supposed Pharaoh of the oppression) defeated them at Kadesh, on the Orontes, c1200 B.C. and married a Hittite princess. Attacks by the so-called "sea-nations" followed by Thracian, Phrygian, and Assyrian invasions finally overthrew them late in the 12th century B.C. Monuments have been discovered since 1872 in Hama, Aleppo, Carchemish, Cappadocia, Lycaonia, and Lydia, which would show that the Hittite empire once spread over the greater part of Asia Minor; and it may be that from there they at one time pushed their way into N Syria. The question whether they formed one people with the Hittites of the Canaanite stock remains an open one. The inscriptions on these monuments are in hieroglyphic characters.

Homadus (hom′a-dus). In Greek legend, a centaur who attacked Heracles on Mount Pholoe. Heracles drove him off, and he fled. Later he tried to violate Alcyone, the sister of King Eurystheus, and Heracles killed him.

Homagyrius (hom-a-ji′ri-us). Epithet of Zeus. At Aegium, in Achaea, Agamemnon assembled the leading princes and heroes of Greece to consult with them about making war against Troy, when Paris carried off

Helen. Thereafter, the sanctuary at Aegium was named the sanctuary of Zeus Homagyrius (*Assembler*).

Homer (hō'mėr). Poet (fl. before 700 B.C.) to whom is assigned by very ancient tradition the authorship of the *Iliad* and the *Odyssey*, and of certain hymns to the gods (*Homeric Hymns*). Other poems also, as the *Batrachomyomachia* (Battle of the Frogs and Mice), were with less certainty attributed to him. Seven cities (Smyrna, Rhodes, Colophon, Salamis in Cyprus, Chios, Argos, and Athens) contended for the honor of being his birthplace; of these, the best evidence connects him with Smyrna. He was said to have died on the island of Ios. The tradition that he lived on the island of Chios, and in his old age was blind, is supported by the *Hymn to the Delian Apollo.* Modern criticism, especially that stemming from the great scholarly debate of the 19th century, when the Homeric works were the focus of classical study, has led to doubt whether such a person as Homer existed at all, the great epics which bear that name being supposed to be, in their existing form, of composite character, the product of various persons and ages. It is possible, however, that the nucleus of the *Iliad*, at least, was the work of a single poet of commanding genius; debate still continues, the only agreement being that in the *Iliad* and the *Odyssey* we have the prototype of epic poetry. According to Herodotus, Homer lived c850 B.C.; others give a later date, and some a date as early as 1200 B.C. His poems were sung by professional reciters (rhapsodists), who went from city to city. They were given substantially their present form under Pisistratus or his sons Hipparchus and Hippias, who ordered the rhapsodists to recite them at the Panathenaic festival in their order and completeness. The present text of the poems, with their division into books, is based upon the work of the Alexandrine critics.

Homeric Hymns (hō-mer'ik). Group of Greek hexameter poems, five of considerable length and 29 shorter, anciently ascribed to Homer. Each is inscribed to and relates a legend concerning a god or goddess. The most noted are the *Hymn to the Delian Apollo,* in which an account is given of the birth of Apollo and of the ancient festival at Delos (the author describing himself as the blind bard of rocky Chios), the *Hymn to the Pythian Apollo,* and the hymns to Hermes, Demeter, and Aphrodite.

Homeridae (hō-mer'i-dē). Ancient Greek clan at Chios claiming to be descended from Homer. They recited epics and poems purporting to be by him and it is thought by some scholars that they gave polished form to the *Iliad* and the *Odyssey* and may have written the *Homeric Hymns* and other poems attributed to him.

Homeromastix (hō″mer-ō-mas'tiks). See **Zoilus.**

Hoples (hop'lēz). According to tradition, one of the four sons of Ion. One of the four ancient tribes of Athens was named for him. His brothers were Aegicores, Argades, and Geleon.

Horace (hor'as). [Full Latin name, **Quintus Horatius Flaccus.**] Roman poet, born at Venusia (modern Venosa), in Apulia, Dec. 8, 65 B.C.; died at Rome, Nov. 27, 8 B.C. His father, a freedman, owned a small farm. He took his son to Rome to be educated as were the sons of knights and senators, and guided his son's education with great solicitude. Horace has left a picture of one of his masters, Orbilius, who pounded their lessons into his pupils by the aid of frequent floggings. To complete his education, Horace went to Athens to study philosophy. While he was there Caesar was murdered. Like many young men of his day he was fired with enthusiasm for republican ideas and joined the republican army of Brutus, in which he served as a *tribunus militum.* He took part in the battle of Philippi (42 B.C.), in which, as he tells us, he threw away his shield, a reference to the fact that his side was defeated and he fled. He says Mercury rescued him, trembling as he was, and spirited him away in a mist to safety. He then returned to Rome where for a time he was in want which, he says, gave him the courage to turn to poetry. At Rome he became acquainted with Vergil and Asinius Pollio. Through Vergil and Varius he met Maecenas who became his literary patron and lifelong friend. He became reconciled to the rule of Augustus and lauded his work in peace. Despite his connections in high places he did not fawn or flatter the emperor or his patron, and refused the post of private secretary that Augustus offered to him. Maecenas gave him a farm in the Sabine hills (33 B.C.) which became his favorite dwelling place. He retired to it frequently, delighted with the simple life of the country, soothed by the Falernian wine he celebrated in his writings, and free to meditate, write, and entertain. When in Rome he lived modestly and enjoyed being a spectator of the lively Roman scene. He died in his 57th year, only a few months after Maecenas, and was buried on the Esquiline Hill near the tomb of Maecenas. His works (all publication dates are approximate) are *Satires,* conversation pieces in hexameters (first book 35 B.C., second 30 B.C.); *Epodes* (30 B.C.), often in iambics, with a refrain; *Odes* (first three books 23 B.C., fourth 13 B.C.), lyrics in various meters of great originality, beauty, and melody, modelled on the Greek poets Sappho, Alcaeus, Anacreon, and Simonides; *Epistles* (first book 20 B.C., second 13–8 B.C.), personal letters in hexameters addressed to friends; *Carmen Saeculare* (17 B.C.), composed at the request of Augustus for the Secular Games in 17 B.C. and sung by a chorus of boys and girls; and *Ars Poetica* (23–15 B.C.), a treatise on the art of poetry, especially dramatic poetry. The work of Horace does not burn with passion. Rather it is illuminated by urbanity, irony, gentle self-deprecation, and passages of free lyricism in which he extols the virtues of the simple life, the beauties of nature, and the joys of friendship. A gentle shadow sometimes falls because of his consciousness that whether prince or pauper, the end for all men is dust and shade. Probably no other Roman poet has had so great an influence on modern poetry, both in English and in the Romance languages.

Horae (hō′rē). In Greek mythology, three nature-goddesses who preside over the changes of the seasons and the accompanying course of natural growth and decay. According to Homer, they are handmaidens of Zeus, who guard the gates of heaven and control the weather; according to Hesiod, they are daughters of Zeus and Themis, named Eunomia ("Good Order"), Dice ("Justice"), and Eirene ("Peace"), guardians of agriculture and also of social and political order. Their number varied from two, as at Athens (Thallo, goddess of spring flowers, and Carpo, goddess of summer fruits), to four.

The dance of the Horae was a symbolized representation of the course of the seasons.

Horatii (hō-rā′shi-ī), **The Three.** In Roman legend, three brothers celebrated in the reign of Tullus Hostilius (672–640 B.C.), for their combat with the three Curiatii of Alba Longa. Tullus, king of Rome, was preparing to war on Alba Longa because of some cattle raids. The ruler of Alba Longa said the two cities were foolish to fight each other and so become weak and an easy prey for their common enemy the Etruscans. Since a war would make one of the cities master of the other, he proposed that the issue be decided by single combat between representatives of the two armies. Tullus agreed. On the Roman side were three brothers—the Horatii; they volunteered to fight the three Curiatii of the Alban side, and the two armies drew up to watch the combat. The Curiatii succeeded in killing two of the Horatii and the Romans groaned, for they feared they would become subject to Alba. The lone Horatii brother who remained was untouched by any wound. The three Curiatii had all suffered wounds. Horatius could not defend himself if he were attacked by all three Curiatii at once. He resorted to guile. He pretended to flee, and as the wounded Curiatii pursued him at unequal distances because of their injuries, he turned and slew them one at a time as they came up. As a result of his victory Alba Longa fell under Roman dominion. Horatius was returned to Rome in triumph. As he entered the city his sister Horatia saw him and noted that the cloak he wore was one she had woven for one of the Curiatii to whom she was betrothed. She immediately began to lament and call on her dead lover's name. Horatius, enraged to see her tears in the hour of his triumph, unsheathed his sword and plunged it into her breast. "Go to your betrothed," he said, "with your ill-timed grief, since you have forgotten your brothers, both dead and living, and have forgotten your country. So perish every Roman woman who mourns a foe!" Because he had taken the law into his own hands, Horatius was brought to trial. His father pleaded with the Roman people not to deprive him of his last remaining child, one who had done so much for Rome. Horatius was acquitted, but that it should not appear that anyone could take the law into his own hands with impunity, he was ordered to endure a ritual punishment. A beam, symbolizing a yoke, was erected across the street and he was compelled to pass under it with his head covered, as a token that he submitted to the yoke of Roman law. The beam remained in place for centuries, restored from time to time by the state, and came to be known as "the Sister's Beam." Horatia was buried in a stone tomb on the spot where she had died by her brother's sword.

Horatius Cocles (hō-rā'shus, -shi-us; kok'lēz, kō'klēz). See **Cocles, Publius Horatius.**

Horcus (hôr'kus). See **Orcus.**

Horn of Plenty. In Greek mythology, a horn of the goat Amalthea, or of a goat belonging to the nymph Amalthea, which nursed the infant Zeus. The horn was said to be always full of whatever food and drink one desired. For the Romans, the Horn of Plenty—*Cornu Copiae* (Cornucopia, q.v.)— was the horn of Achelous, the river-god who had taken the form of a bull to fight Heracles and lost one of his horns in the struggle. This Horn of Plenty was always full of fruits and flowers.

Horoscope (hor'ō-skōp). The Greek term *horoskopos* "hour-watcher," Latin *horoscopus*, may mean 1) a diagram of the Zodiac as it appeared at a particular moment, e.g. at the birth of a child, showing the 12 constellations or Signs ("houses") of the Zodiac and the distribution among them of the seven visible planets or "wanderers" (Mercury, Venus, Mars, Jupiter, Saturn, Sun, Moon); or 2) a horizontal line, bisecting such a diagram, which represented the horizon and indicated the position of the sun in relation to the horizon. From the horoscope or "aspect" of the stars at a critical moment, as at birth, astrologers professed to foretell the fortune of the client. (JJ)

Hortensian Law (hôr-ten'shi-an, -shan). In the history of ancient Rome, a law, adopted probably in 286 B.C., which decided that the decrees (*plebiscita*) of the Comitia Tributa should be binding on all citizens, patricians as well as plebeians.

Hortensius Hortalus (hôr-ten'shi-us, -shus; hôr'ta-lus), **Quintus.** Roman orator, born 114 B.C.; died 50 B.C. He was a leader of the aristocratic party, a minor historian, collector of art, and a composer of love poems.

Catullus twice addresses him. As a pleader he defended the notorious Verres (70 B.C.), whose conviction by Cicero was a notable defeat for Hortensius. Many stories circulated concerning his luxurious habits. (JJ)

Hyacinthia (hī-a-sin'thi-a). A Spartan resurrection festival celebrated at Amyclae in Laconia, in honor of Hyacinthus and of Apollo. It was celebrated for three days in July, and commemorated sorrow for the death of vegetation, joy for the harvest, and trust in the annual renewal of nature. The first day of the festival was devoted to silent mourning for Hyacinthus at his grave in the sanctuary of Apollo. The following days of joy and hope were celebrated with processions of singing youths and maidens to the temple of Apollo, with games, sacrifices, and feasts.

Hyacinthides (hī-a-sin'thi-dēz). In Greek mythology, the daughters of Hyacinthus the Spartan. They were Aegleis, Antheis, Lyctaea, and Orthaea, and were sacrificed in Athens on the advice of the oracle to save the city when it was attacked by Minos, king of Crete, to avenge the murder of his son. The city was wracked by plague and earthquakes and it was thought that the sacrifice of the maidens would bring relief from these as well as protection from Minos. However, the sacrifice was unavailing, and the Athenians were compelled to yield to Minos and pay him tribute of their sons and daughters before the plague and earthquakes stopped.

Hyacinthus (hī-a-sin'thus). [Also: **Hyacinth.**] In Greek mythology, a beautiful youth, the son of Amyclas, king of Amyclae in Laconia. He was loved by Thamyris the poet, by Apollo, and by Zephyr (the West Wind). Thamyris was defeated in a musical contest by Apollo, and blinded, which removed him as a rival for the affections of Hyacinthus. But one day when Apollo was teaching young Hyacinthus to throw the discus, or a quoit, Zephyr seized the discus and blew it back against Hyacinthus with such force that it killed him. From his blood Apollo caused the hyacinth to spring, and upon the petals of the plant was thought to be marked the exclamation AI ("woe!"). Hyacinthus represents the death of young things just as they are approaching the full bloom of their beauty, as fruits and flowers that flourish in the spring but die under the heat of the summer sun. The tomb of Hyacinthus was at Amyclae, under the great image of Apollo. Sacrifices were offered to him as a hero and his festival, the *Hyacinthia,* was observed at Amyclae during three days in July. Modern scholarship sees in Hyacinthus an agricultural or vegetation deity, and in his annual festival a typical resurrection ritual.

Hyacinthus. A Spartan who moved to Athens with his four daughters. See **Hyacinthides.**

Hyades (hī'a-dēz). [Also: **Hyads.**] In Greek mythology, a group of nymphs, the daughters of Aethra and Atlas, and the sisters of Hyas. They grieved so over the death of their brother that they were translated to the heavens as the seven stars in the head of the constellation Taurus. Others say the Hyades were the nymphs of Nysa who nurtured the infant Dionysus, and that they were translated to the heavens by Zeus as a reward for their care of his son. The rainy season, which begins with their rising, is a mark of their continuing care, for the rain they send nurtures the vine sacred to Dionysus. The Romans, through a mistaken etymology, called the constellation Succulae (*Little Pigs*).

Hyas (hī'as). In Greek mythology, a son of Aethra, daughter of Oceanus and Tethys, and Atlas. He was a mighty hunter who sought a lioness and her cubs and was killed by a Libyan boar. His sisters grieved so for him they were placed among the stars as the Hyades.

Hybla (hī'bla). [Also: **Hybla Magna, Hybla Geleatis, Hybla Major.**] In ancient geography, a city in Sicily, on the S slope of Mount Aetna, about 11 miles NW of Catana (Catania); believed to have been at or near the modern Paternò.

Hybla Heraea (he-rē'a). In ancient geography, a town of S Sicily, W of Syracuse. It was an ancient Sicel town. Hippocrates, tyrant of Gela, besieged the town, 491 B.C., and was killed while attempting to breach its walls. The modern city of Ragusa lies on the slopes of the hill where ancient Hybla Heraea stood.

Hybla Minor (mī'nor). [Also: **Megara Hyblaea.**] In ancient geography, a city on the E coast of Sicily about 12 miles N of Syracuse. The celebrated Hyblaean honey, mentioned frequently by ancient poets, may have been produced in the vicinity. It is often confused with Hybla on Mount Aetna, sometimes called Hybla Major.

Hydaspes (hi-das'pēz). Ancient name of the Jhelum River, a river in the Punjab, West Pakistan, rising in Kashmir and joining the Chenab about 80 miles NE of Multan; in its upper valley is the Vale of Kashmir. On its banks Alexander the Great defeated Porus in 326 B.C.

HERACLES AND THE LERNAEAN HYDRA
Black-figured Greek amphora.

Hydra (hī'dra). In Greek mythology, a monstrous dragon of the Lernaean Spring, in Argolis, represented as having nine heads, each of which, being cut off, was immediately succeeded by two new ones unless the wound was cauterized. The destruction of this monster (by searing each neck as he cut off the head, with firebrands supplied by Iolaus) was one of the 12 labors of Heracles.

Hydra. An ancient southern constellation, representing a sea-serpent. It is of Babylonian origin, like most of the ancient constellations. It is bounded by the ancient constellations Canis Minor, Argo, Centaurus, Virgo, Corvus, Crater, Leo, and Cancer, and by the modern constellations Sextans and Monoceros (which separates it from Canis Major). It contains one star of the second magnitude, and about 400 stars visible to the naked eye.

Hydria (hī'dri-a). In ancient Greece, a large vase, used especially for carrying water. It has a capacious body with a narrow mouth and usually a broad rim, and three handles: one at the back extending above the rim, and a smaller one on each side.

Hydrus (hī'drus). [Modern name, **Otranto.**]

actor; up, lūte, pull; oi, oil; ou, out; ᴛʜ, then; d̪ as d or j, s̩ as s or sh, t̩ as t or ch, z̩ as z or zh.

In ancient geography, a seaport of Apulia, SE Italy, called by the Romans Hydruntum, situated about 45 miles SE of Brundisium. It was founded by colonists from the Dorian city of Tarentum and retained its Greek language and culture until the 11th century.

Hyettus (hī-et′us). In ancient geography, a village of Boeotia, Greece, near Lake Copaïs. It was founded, some say, by an Argive named Hyettus who killed his wife's lover and fled to the Boeotian king Orchomenus. The king gave him land and he founded this village. Hyettus is the first man recorded as having exacted the punishment of death from an adulterer. Later, in the time of Dracon, the concept was established that an adulterer caught and killed was himself, by his act, the cause of his own death. In the village of Hyettus was a temple of Heracles, with an image of unwrought stone. The sick went to this temple to be cured.

Hygea (hī-jē′a). [Also: **Hygieia**.] In Greek mythology the goddess of health. She was the daughter of Asclepius; in later myth, his wife. In later myth also, she became the goddess of mental health.

Hyksos (hik′sōs, -sos). ["Princes of the Desert"; wrongly called (from an incorrect etymology) the "Shepherd Kings."] Name given to the kings of Egypt, of a foreign (probably Semitic) race, whose rule (c1800–c1575 B.C.) fell between the XIIIth and the XVIIIth Dynasties. They introduced into Egypt the horse and chariot.

Hylaeus (hī-lē′us). In Greek mythology, a cloud-born, Arcadian centaur. According to some accounts, he pursued Atalanta during the Calydonian Hunt with the intention of violating her, but she repulsed and slew him. Others say he was slain by Heracles in the battle with the centaurs on Mount Pholoe. And still others say he was killed by Theseus in the battle between centaurs and Lapiths.

Hylas (hī′las). In Greek legend, a son of Thiodamas, king of the Dryopians, and the nymph Menodice. Heracles slew Thiodamas and carried off his young son, Hylas, who became his squire and beloved companion. He accompanied Heracles as an Argonaut. When the Argonauts landed in Mysia, Hylas went to the fountain of Pegae to fetch water while Heracles searched for a tree from which to make an oar. Dryope, the nymph of the fountain, fell in love with Hylas as he stopped to draw water, and pulled him into the spring to dwell thereafter with her and her sister nymphs. It was because he stayed to search for Hylas that Heracles was left behind by the Argonauts and did not take part in the recovery of the Golden Fleece.

Hyllus (hil′us). In Greek legend, a son of Deianira and Heracles. He took his dying father to Mount Oeta, built a funeral pyre at his request, and promised to marry Iole, daughter of Eurytus of Oechalia. He learned from Heracles that his death, as a result of Nessus' blood having been rubbed on his sacrificial robe by Deianira, fulfilled an old prophecy that no living mortal would destroy him, but that he would die because of a dead enemy. Hyllus could not bear to carry out his father's last request, which was to light the pyre on which Heracles was lying. This was done by Philoctetes. After the apotheosis of Heracles, Hyllus joined with the Athenians in a war against Eurystheus, captured him, and, according to some accounts, cut off his head. He then successfully invaded the Peloponnesus, but a plague broke out and he was warned by the oracle at Delphi to withdraw and to await the third crop before he returned. Hyllus took this to mean three years, and at the expiration of this time he returned. In order to avoid bloodshed he offered to engage in single combat with a representative of Mycenae, on the condition that if he was victorious the kingdom of Mycenae would be his, but if he lost the Heraclidae would withdraw for fifty years. Echemus, king of Tegea, accepted his challenge. In the duel Hyllus was slain and was buried in Megara. The Heraclidae honored his agreement and withdrew from the Peloponnesus. The oracle at Delphi explained that the third crop meant the third generation, not the third year, as Hyllus had interpreted it.

Hyllus. In Greek legend, a son of Heracles and the nymph Melite. Heracles had gone to the home of Nausithous, king of the Phaeacians, to purify himself after the murder of his children. There he violated Melite, who bore him Hyllus. Hyllus migrated from Phaeacia to the Cronian Sea, and was later slain.

---

fat, fāte, fär, fāre, errạnt; net, mē, hėr ardẹnt; pin, pīne; not, nōte, mŏve, nôr,

Hymen (hī′mẹn) or **Hymenaeus** (hī-mẹ-nē′us). Originally, the marriage song among the Greeks. The names were gradually personified, and Hymen, the marriage song personified, was invoked as the god of marriage. According to legend he was the son of Apollo and one of the Muses, or of Dionysus and Aphrodite, or, in some accounts, a mortal youth who was invoked in hymeneal songs. He is represented as a beautiful youth, more serious than Eros, carrying a bridal torch.

Hymettius (hī-met′i-us). Epithet of Zeus, from his image on Mount Hymettus at Athens.

Hymettus (hī-met′us). A mountain ridge in Attica, Greece, lying SE of Athens. For a few minutes just before dusk it sometimes glows with a soft violet color, and from this Athens has the epithet "violet-crowned." In ancient times the mountain was celebrated for its honey, and also for its bluish-gray marble. Elevation, about 3368 feet.

Hyperbolus (hī-pẻr′bọ-lus). Athenian politician and demagogue; killed at Samos, c411 B.C. He was a lamp-maker who rose in politics during the Peloponnesian War. His pretensions made him the butt of the comic poets and he endured all manner of abuse, but cared not at all what men said of him and continued to pursue his ambitions. Thucydides called him "a rascal and a disgrace to the city." He was allied with Alcibiades, leader of the radical party, against Nicias, leader of the aristocratic party. In 417 B.C. he engineered a vote of ostracism in an attempt to get rid of Nicias. He thought the radicals would vote against Nicias and that he would be ostracized; if not, the supporters of Nicias would surely vote against the radical Alcibiades. In either case one of them, so he reasoned, would be removed and he could compete on more equal terms against the one who remained. But Alcibiades deserted him and joined forces with Nicias. In the resulting vote Hyperbolus was himself ostracized and sent into exile. Candidates for ostracism had been the leaders of the state, prominent men whose very prominence and influence were considered to be a possible danger to the democracy. Ostracism was thus a backhanded honor. When the vote fell on Hyperbolus it was felt that the process of ostracism had been degraded. He was the last Athenian ever to be ostracized; afterward, the practice fell into disuse. He went to Samos and was murdered there (c411 B.C.) by the oligarchic party that supported the government of the Four Hundred at Athens.

Hyperboreans (hī-pẻr-bō′rē-anz). In early Greek legend, a people who were believed to live beyond the north wind, and were not exposed to its blasts, but enjoyed a land of perpetual sunshine and abundant fruits. They were free from disease, violence, and war. Their natural life span was said to be 1000 years, and was spent in the worship of Apollo, who was said to pass the winter among them. No one ever actually described their land, and its existence was doubted by some in ancient times, but Abaris, who in legend went around the world on an arrow, claimed to have visited it. According to Herodotus, those who were supposedly neighbors of the Hyperboreans—for example, the Scythians—never mentioned them, but they were named by Hesiod. Again according to Herodotus, those who had the most to say about the Hyperboreans were the people of Delos. The Delians claimed that two Hyperborean maidens, Hyperoche and Laodice, brought offerings of the first fruits wrapped in wheaten straw to Delos. They were accompanied by five men. When the Hyperboreans found that their envoys to Delos did not return they no longer sent their envoys direct to Delos. They sent their offerings to the Scythians, who passed them on to their neighbors, and eventually the offerings, given in honor of Apollo, reached Delos. Some say Apollo came from their land. It was also claimed that the Hyperboreans sent the birth-goddess Ilithyia to assist Leto on Delos when she was about to bear Apollo. Some said that the wild olive was brought from their land into Greece by Heracles. And some said that it was the Hyperboreans who first established the oracle of Apollo at Delphi where, later, they sent a temple made of bees' wax and feathers. The Hyperboreans Pagasus and Agyieus were said to have established the oracle. When the Gauls attacked Delphi (279 B.C.), Pagasus and Agyieus were said to have appeared in superhuman form and to have driven them away. In later times the Greeks gave the name Hyperboreans to inhabitants of northern countries generally.

Hypercheiria (hī-pèr-kī'ri-ạ). Epithet of Hera. The Spartans, in obedience to an oracle, raised a sanctuary of Hera Hypercheiria (*Protectress*) in their land, when the goddess saved them from the Eurotas River which was flooding its banks. At Sparta, mothers sacrificed to a wooden image of Hera Aphrodite when their daughters were about to be married.

Hyperenor (hī-pẹ-rē'nôr). In Homeric legend (*Iliad*), a Trojan, the son of Panthous and Phrontis. He was the brother of Polydamas and Euphorbus, and was slain by Menelaus when the Greeks drove the Trojans back from the Greek ships, as Zeus slept.

Hyperenor. One of the Sparti who sprang from the earth when Cadmus sowed the dragon's teeth. See **Sparti.**

Hyperesia (hī-pẹ-rē'shạ). Town of Achaea, on the coast. Men of Hyperesia went to the Trojan War under the command of Agamemnon. The name of the town was later changed 'to Aegira (q.v.).

Hyperides (hī-pẹ-rī'dēz or hī-per'i-dēz). One of the Ten Attic Orators, born c390 B.C.; died 322 B.C. He studied with Plato and Isocrates and achieved an important position in Athenian forensic circles. His gay private life and natural wit made him a favorite topic of comedy. In politics he was allied with Demosthenes against the Macedonian Party which favored peace with Philip of Macedon. After the destruction of Thebes (335 B.C.) by Alexander, he and Demosthenes, only with the greatest difficulty, escaped being handed over to the Macedonians. In 324 B.C. he was one of the prosecutors of Demosthenes, on charges of bribery. However, in seeming to prosecute Demothenes, Hyperides actually defended him, and his action in this case led to no breach in their friendly relations. After the death of Alexander, Hyperides and Demosthenes joined forces to rouse the Peloponnesus to war. The Lamian War broke out and was pursued to disaster for Greece. The Macedonian general demanded the surrender of Hyperides and Demosthenes. His death sentence was signed but he fled to a temple in Aegina for refuge. He was seized there, and by or-

der of the Macedonian commander Antipater was put to death in 322 B.C. Some consider the work of Hyperides to rank next to that of Demsothenes in forcefulness, and superior to it in charm. Large fragments of five speeches, found in Egyptian papyri in the 19th century, show that his work was marked by forthrightness, humor, and grace.

Hyperion (hī-pir'i-on). In Greek mythology, a Titan, one of the sons of Gaea and Uranus. By the Titaness Thia he was the father of Eos (*Dawn*), Helius (*Sun*), and Selene (*Moon*). In the *Odyssey* he is identified with Helius, and in late mythology with Apollo.

Hypermnestra (hī-pèrm-nes'trạ). In Greek mythology, one of the 50 daughters of Danaus. When she and her sisters were about to be married to the 50 sons of Aegyptus, Danaus gave each of them a sharp pin or dagger and ordered them to kill their husbands on the wedding night. Hypermnestra, divinely inspired, looked on her sleeping husband Lynceus and could not bear to kill him. She told him of her father's plot and begged him to flee. To inform her of his safety she asked him to light a beacon when he reached Lyncea, 60 furlongs away, and she promised to answer his signal. Lynceus escaped and made known his safety to her. Danaus was enraged by her disobedience. He imprisoned her and would have killed her but the Argives acquitted her and she dedicated an image to Aphrodite in gratitude. Later Danaus reluctantly reunited her with Lynceus. But some say Lynceus returned and won her back by force and killed Danaus. Hypermnestra bore Abas, the ancestor of Perseus, to Lynceus.

Hypnos (hip'nos). In Greek mythology, the god of sleep; son of Erebus and Nyx (Night), and brother and companion of Thanatos (Death). He is usually represented as a winged figure accompanying Thanatos. He had three sons named Morpheus, Icelus, and Phantasus, regarded as dream-bringers. Hypnos is identified with the Roman Somnus.

Hypseus (hip'sūs). In Greek mythology, a son of the nymph Creusa and the river-god Peneus. He was king of the Lapithae and the father, by the naiad Chlidanope, of Cyrene.

Hypsipyle (hip-sip'i-lẹ). In Greek legend, a

daughter of Thoas, king of Lemnos. When the women of Lemnos rose up and killed all the men because they had abandoned their true wives for captive women, Hypsipyle secretly spared her father and set him afloat on the sea in a chest. She then became queen. By the time the Argonauts landed in Lemnos on their way to find the Golden Fleece, Polyxo, aged nurse of Hypsipyle, was easily able to change the attitude of the Lemnian women toward men. They invited the Argonauts to stay and share their island. Hypsipyle entertained Jason and by him became the mother of twin sons. According to some accounts, when the Lemnian women later learned that Hypsipyle had spared her father they rose against her, killed her sons and sold her into slavery to Lycurgus, king of Nemea, under whom she became the nurse of Opheltes, his son. According to other accounts, her sons were not killed, but rescued her and returned her to Lemnos, after she had carelessly allowed Opheltes to be slain by the bite of a serpent. Her sons were Euneus and Thoas, and according to Homer, Euneus supplied the Greeks at Troy with wine from Lemnos during the Trojan War.

Hypsipyle was the subject of a play by Euripides, lost from the manuscript tradition but fortunately now represented by extended passages on papyrus recovered from the village dumps of Greco-Roman Egypt.

Hypsistus (hip-sis′tus). Epithet of Zeus. Cecrops, king of Athens, was the first to worship Zeus Hypsistus (*Most High*), and he established the rule that no living creature was to be sacrificed to Zeus Hypsistus. Instead, cakes were offered on his altars. Of the many images of Zeus Hypsistus, as at Corinth, on the Acropolis at Athens, at Olympia, the oldest was the one in Sparta. The Spartan image was of bronze, so made in separate pieces that the limbs were held to the torso by nails. This image was said to have been made by Clearchus of Rhegium.

Hyrcania (hėr-kā′ni-a). In ancient geography, a region in W Asia, around the S end of the Hyrcanum Mare (Caspian Sea); now part of N Iran.

Hyrie (hī′ri-ē). In Greek mythology, the mother by Apollo of that Cycnus who flung himself over a cliff in anger at his friend Phylius. She grieved so over her son's death

that, according to some accounts, she was transformed into a pool. Others say she was turned into a swan along with her son.

Hyrmina (hėr-mī′na) or **Hyrmine** (-nē). In Greek legend, a daughter of Epeus and granddaughter of Endymion. She married Phorbas the Lapith and bore him Actor, who founded the city in Elis, on the coast, which he named Hyrmine after her. Her grandsons, the Actoridae, or Moliones as they were sometimes called, shared in the government of Elis during the reign of Augeas.

Hyrnetho (hėr-nē′thō). In Greek legend, a daughter of Temenus, a son of Aristomachus who won Argos as his share of the Peloponnesus. He favored his daughter and her husband over his sons, and proposed to leave his kingdom to Hyrnetho and her husband Deiphontes. When they learned of this, his sons—Agelaus, Eurypylus, and Callias—hired assassins to murder their father. Hyrnetho accompanied her husband when he marched to Epidaurus and took over the land without a struggle. Her brothers tried to persuade her to abandon Deiphontes, and when she refused they carried her off in their chariot and then, pursued by Deiphontes, they killed her. Deiphontes and his sons buried her in a place that came to be known as the Hyrnethium, and established a hero-shrine in her honor. It was the custom to place in her shrine branches and twigs that fell from olive trees. See also, **Deiphontes**.

Hyrtius (hir′shi-us). Named by Homer (*Iliad*) as a leader of the Mysians, allies of Troy in the Trojan War. He was wounded by Telamonian Ajax at the battle for the Greek ships, when the Trojans had driven their forces onto the very ships. But Poseidon in disguise helped the Greeks, and it was with his aid that Hyrtius was driven back.

Hysiae (hī′si-ē). In ancient geography, a city in Argolis, Greece, situated in the mountains west of Lerna. Here Argos defeated the Spartans in battle (traditional date, 669 B.C.).

Hysiae. Village of Boeotia, Greece, situated on the lower slopes of Mount Cithaeron, on the border between Attica and Boeotia. There was a temple of Apollo here, and a sacred well, from which oracles could be obtained by drinking the waters at night. The village, once part of Boeotia, fell under

Athenian control following a war between Athens and Boeotia (509 B.C.), in which the Boeotians were defeated. In the Persian War, the Persians and Greeks faced each other across the Asopus River near here (479 B.C.). The Greeks, instructed by an oracle to fight on the plain of Eleusinian Demeter, found at Hysiae, thanks to the intervention of Zeus, a very ancient sanctuary of Eleusinian Demeter, and in the battle of Plataea nearby they thoroughly defeated the Persians. The Persian general Mardonius was slain, and some say his tomb was at Hysiae.

Hystaspes (his-tas′pēz). Persian general; fl. c517 B.C. He was an Achaemenid, related to and a contemporary of Cyrus the Great. Ordinarily, it would have been he who succeeded to the vacant throne when Cambyses III died without issue, but instead Hystaspes saw his son Darius I become king and served under him. He was satrap of Parthia and Hyrcania, and is thought by some to have been the patron of Zoroaster. Among his other sons were Artabanus, Artaphernes, and Artanes.

I

Iacchus (ĭ′a-kus). In Greek mythology, a divinity peculiar to Athens, and important for his intimate connection with the Eleusinian mysteries. His mother is variously given as Demeter, Persephone, or Semele; his father as Zeus or Dionysus. He is undoubtedly a personification of the ritual cry raised by the worshipers of Dionysus, and the resemblance of his name to Bacchus (Dionysus) easily led to his identification with the latter. His image, crowned with myrtle and bearing a torch, was carried in the famous procession from the Eleusinium at Athens to the *sekos* (sanctuary) at Eleusis, and he presided over the mysterious rites there. He was sometimes called the Phrygian Bacchus, who, as a son of Demeter, was distinct from the older Dionysus.

Iache (ĭ′a-kē). In Greek mythology, a nymph, one of the companions of Persephone.

Ialmenus (ī-al′me-nus). In Greek legend, a a son of Ares and Astyoche. He and his brother, Ascalaphus, accompanied Jason in the *Argo* on the expedition for the Golden Fleece. Like his brother, he was a suitor for the hand of Helen, daughter of Zeus and Leda. And like the other suitors, he took an oath that he would come to the aid of the man who became Helen's husband in the event that any ill befell him as a result of his marriage. When Helen was carried off to Troy by Paris, Ialmenus became a leader of the Boeotians and served as a chief of the Greek sentries in the Trojan War that followed.

Ialysus (ī-al′i-sus). Ancient city in N Rhodes, on the NW coast of the island about six miles SW of the modern city of Rhodes. According to Homer, it was founded by Tlepolemus, a son of Heracles. Other accounts say it was built by the Telchines and named for a Danaid, or the city took its name from the hero Ialysus, grandson of Helius. It was a Dorian city, and a member of the Hexapolis (League of Six Cities); it flourished c1000 B.C. About the 4th century B.C. it was surpassed by the city of Rhodes, and declined.

Iambe (ĭ′am-bē). In Greek mythology, a daughter of Celeus and Metanira, of Eleusis. When Demeter in her search for Persephone stopped at the house of Celeus, Iambe tried to cheer her up with somewhat bawdy stories. For this reason ribald songs came to be sung at a certain point in the Eleusinian mysteries.

Iamblichus (ī-am′bli-kus). Syrian Neoplatonic philosopher, born at Chalcis c250 A.D. in Coele-Syria (modern El Bika); he died c325 A.D. His main work was an encyclopedia of Pythagorean doctrine in nine books, of which four or five remain. In his mathematical books, Pythagorean mysticism is carried to the extreme. Iamblichus believed in divination and magic and was reputed to have worked miracles. He mentions the first pair of amicable numbers (220 and 284), but the interest of the Pythagoreans in the properties

fat, fāte, fär, fāre, errant; net, mē, hèr ardent; pin, pīne; not, nōte, mŏve, nôr,

of numbers makes it virtually certain that they were not his own discovery but were already known by the time he wrote. The philosophy of Iamblichus is a development of a reasoned system of paganism as opposed to Christianity.

Iamus (ī'a-mus). According to Greek tradition, a son of Evadne and Apollo. His mother abandoned him through shame, and he was nursed by two serpents who fed him honey. From them and from his father Apollo he received the gift of prophecy and founded a family of seers called, after him, Iamidae.

Ianthe (ī-an'thē). According to legend, a beautiful maiden of Phaestus, in Crete. She was the daughter of Telestes. She loved and was loved by Iphis, the daughter of Telethusa. Telethusa had brought Iphis up as a boy, because her husband intended to kill her child if it was a girl. Thus Ianthe supposed that she was in love with a young man. The two young people were betrothed, but Telethusa and Iphis, fearing the revelations marriage would bring, delayed the ceremony. At last, when it could be delayed no longer, Telethusa entered the temple and prayed to Io for aid. Her prayer was answered. As she left the temple Iphis was transformed into a man. The next day Ianthe and Iphis were married.

Iapetus (ī-ap'e-tus). In Greek mythology, a Titan; son of Uranus (the sky) and Gaea (the earth); father by the nymph Clymene of Prometheus (and therefore ancestor of the human race), Epimetheus, Atlas, and Menoetius. He was thrown by Zeus into Tartarus after the Titans were overthrown.

Iapygia (ī-a-pij'i-a). In ancient geography, a name used vaguely by the Greeks for a region approximating what is now the SE part of Italy.

Iapygians (ī-a-pij'i-anz). Under the general name of Iapygians there were commonly included five distinct tribes of Italy: the Messapians, the Peucetians, the Calabrians, the Salentinians, and the Daunians. The first-named are spoken of by Strabo as the inhabitants of the Iapygian peninsula, eastward of Tarentum and Brundisium.

Iapyx (ī-ā'piks). A son of Daedalus. He was the mythical ancestor of the Iapyges, a people of southeastern Italy.

Iarbas (ī-är'bas). In Roman legend (*Aeneid*), a son of Jupiter Ammon and a ravished African nymph. He was king of the Gaetulians in Numidia and sold Dido the land on which she built Carthage. He wished to make Dido his queen but she rejected his suit. When he learned from Fama (Rumor) that Dido had given her affections to Aeneas he prayed to Jupiter. He asked if it was in vain that he had brought the worship of Jupiter to Africa and built a hundred shrines in his honor, since Jupiter permitted Dido to pledge her love to Aeneas. Jupiter answered his prayer by sending Mercury (Hermes) to command Aeneas to leave Carthage and pursue his destiny in Italy.

Iardanus (ī-är'da-nus) or **Iardanes** (ī-är'da-nēz). In Greek legend, a king in Lydia, the father of Omphale, who succeeded him as ruler.

Iardanus. [Also: **Jardan, Jardanus;** modern name, **Iardhanos**.] In ancient geography, a river of Elis, Greece, that had the same name as the Phoenician river, the Jordan. Homer mentions it in the *Iliad* as the place where Nestor and the Pylians fought against the Arcadians in his youth and where he slew Ereuthalion.

Iasion (ī-ā'zi-on). In Greek mythology, a Titan, or according to other accounts, a son of Zeus and the Pleiad Electra; the twin of Dardanus and a founder of the Trojan race. Demeter fell in love with him at the marriage of Cadmus and Harmonia and he lay with her in a "thrice-plowed field" and begot Plutus (the wealth-giver, especially the giver of agricultural bounty). For this association with the goddess, Zeus struck Iasion dead with a thunderbolt. This myth is probably the rationalization of some very early Greek fertility rite associated with Demeter in her aspect as a grain-goddess.

Iaso (ī-ā'sō). In Greek mythology, a daughter of Asclepius, and the sister of Aigle, Hygea, and Panacea. She was a goddess of healing.

Iason (ē-ā'son). See **Jason.**

Iasus (ī'a-sus). According to some accounts, the father of Atalanta. He was so disappointed not to have a son that he exposed her on a mountain in Calydon to die. Through the intervention of Artemis she was saved and when, as a young woman, she won honors in the Calydonian Boar Hunt, Iasus was glad to own her as his daughter.

Iberia (ī-bir′i-ạ). [Latin, **Hispania.**] In ancient geography, the peninusla of SW Europe, now known as the Iberian Peninsula.

Iberia. In ancient geography, the region bounded by the Caucasus Mountains on the N, (ancient) Albania on the E, Armenia on the S, and Colchis on the W; now largely the E portion of Georgian Soviet Socialist Republic.

Iberians (ī-bir′i-ạnz). Prehistoric inhabitants of the Iberian Peninsula, thought to have entered the region perhaps from Africa, as far back as the New Stone Age. Various theories have been advanced in regard to them: 1) that they preceded the Celts in Spain and merged with them to the extent of interabsorption; 2) that they were identical with the Basques (a supposition now discredited). They were a short, dark people to whom are attributed various characteristic neolithic cairns and dolmens which survive in sections of North Africa, Spain, Portugal, and Great Britain. They were eventually conquered and absorbed by the Romans.

Ibycus (ib′i-kus, ī′bi-). Greek lyric poet who was born at Rhegium, Italy, and flourished in the second half of the 6th century B.C. He spent much time wandering around Greece before he settled at the court of Polycrates of Samos and later at that of Periander. Fragments of his poems indicate that they dealt with mythological themes (the Funeral Games of Pelias, the Sack of Troy, and the Calydonian Boar Hunt) written in the style of Stesichorus, and with personal love-songs. According to tradition, he was murdered by robbers near Corinth, and called on a flock of passing cranes to bear witness. Shortly afterward, during the performance of a play in a Corinth theater, one of the murderers, at sight of some cranes flying overhead, involuntarily exclaimed, "the avengers of Ibycus." Suspicion was aroused and the murderers identified. Hence the "cranes of Ibycus" became a proverb for the belief that "murder will out."

Icaria (ī-kār′i-ạ). [Also: **Ikaria, Nicaria, Nikaria, Kariot.**] Island in the Aegean Sea, situated about 13 miles W of Samos. According to legend, it was to this island that Daedalus brought the body of his son Icarus after the latter, flying so close to the sun as to melt the wax holding his wings together, fell into the sea and was drowned. Daedalus buried his son here and named the island after him. Area, about 99 square miles; length, about 25 miles.

Icaria. Site in the Rapedosa valley, Attica, Greece, N of Mount Pentelicus, excavated and identified (1888) by an expedition from the American School at Athens. Here, according to the legend, wine-making and the Dionysiac cult were introduced into Attica by Dionysus himself, and here was born Thespis, who, by the changes he introduced into the old dithyrambic songs, became the originator of tragic drama, with Icaria as the theater.

Icarian Sea (ī-kār′i-ạn). [Latin, **Mare Icarium.**] In ancient geography, part of the Aegean Sea surrounding Samos and the neighboring small island of Icaria, along the coast of Asia Minor. In Greek legend it is the scene of the drowning of Icarus, son of Daedalus, and was named for him.

Icarius (ī-kār′i-us). In Greek mythology, an Athenian who entertained Dionysus, not knowing he was a god. As a reward for his hospitality, Dionysus taught Icarius the cultivation of the vine and the art of winemaking. Icarius offered some wine to a band of peasants but as they did not mix it with water they got drunk from it. Thinking themselves poisoned, they killed Icarius and buried his body under a pine tree. See **Erigone.**

Icarius. In Greek legend, the son of Gorgophone, daughter of Perseus, and her second husband Oebalus. He was the brother of Tyndareus of Sparta and the father of Odysseus' wife Penelope.

Icarus (ik′ạ-rus, ī′kạ-). In Greek legend, the son of Daedalus and a Cretan slave, Naucrate. He was imprisoned with his father in the labyrinth that Daedalus had built for King Minos. Freed by Pasiphaë, Daedalus and Icarus escaped from Crete with the aid of wings that Daedalus made by threading feathers together and fastening them with wax. Before they flew off, Daedalus warned his son not to fly too low lest the sea wet his wings and make them heavy, and not to fly too high lest the sun scorch them. Above all he warned Icarus to follow his father

fat, fāte, fär, fãre, errạnt; net, mē, hėr ardẹnt; pin, pīne; not, nōte, mŏve, nôr,

closely and not to be diverted by the creatures he would see in the sky. They passed the islands of Delos, Paros, and Samos safely. Icarus then became over-confident as he soared through the air and forgot his father's warnings. In his pleasure at wheeling in flight he flew so near the sun that the wax bindings of his wings melted and he fell into the sea and was drowned. Daedalus rescued his corpse and buried it on an island now known as Icaria in the Icarian Sea. Some say that it was Heracles who buried his body on the island where his body was cast up.

Icelus (īs′e̯-lus). The dream-god who sent dreams of birds and beasts. He was the child of Nyx (*Night*) and the brother of Hypnos (*Sleep*) and Thanatos (*Death*). Men called him Phobetor, "the Terrifier," but the gods named him Icelus.

Ichnousa or **Ichnusa** (ik-nö′sa̯). Greek name for the island of Sardinia. The name means "footprint," and was given to the island because of its shape. It was also called Sandaliotis, from its resemblance to a sandal.

Ichor (ī′kôr, ī′kėr). An ethereal fluid believed to flow instead of blood in the veins of the gods.

Ichthyocentaur (ik″thi-ọ-sen′tôr). In Greek mythology, a fabulous creature of the sea with the body of a man, the legs of a horse, and the tail of a fish. The Ichthyocentaurs were attendants of Triton and other sea-gods.

Icos (ī′kos). An island in the Aegean Sea, near the coast of Thessaly and Euboea. Peleus, father of Achilles, on his way to Molossia to join his grandson Neoptolemus, was cast ashore there by storms, and died and was buried there.

Ictinus (ik-tī′nus). Greek architect; fl. in the middle of the 5th century B.C. With Callicrates, he was the chief designer of the Parthenon, begun 448 B.C., dedicated 438 B.C. He also designed the temple of Demeter and Persephone at Eleusis, and the temple of Apollo Epicurius at Bassae near Phigalia (the sculptured Ionic frieze of this temple is among the treasures of the British Museum). Ictinus and Phidias were identified with Pericles in the execution of his great scheme of public works.

Ida (ī′da̯). In Greek mythology, one of the nymphs who took care of the infant Zeus

when his mother hid him in a cave on the island of Crete to save him from being devoured by his father Cronus. Also, a nymph of Mount Ida who, according to some accounts, was the mother, by Zeus, of the Dactyls, the discoverers of iron and the art of iron-working, in Crete.

Ida, Mount. [Modern name, **Psiloriti**; Latin, **Ida Mons.**] Mountain in C Crete, the highest peak of the island. According to Greek mythology, the infant Zues was raised on Mount Ida by Amalthea. Elevation, about 8195 feet.

Ida, Mount. A mountain in the range of the same name in Phrygia and Mysia, Asia Minor. At the base of it was the Troad, whose capital was Troy. The mountain, described in the *Iliad* as "many-fountained," was a seat of Zeus and had a grove sacred to him and an altar to him. It was from here that Zeus directed the Trojan War on many occasions and watched the progress and weighed the fates of his favorites. Mount Ida was also known as the place from which Zeus carried off Ganymede, as the site of the Judgment of Paris, and as a seat of worship of Cybele. The highest peak of the mountain was also known as Gargarus or Gargaron (5749 feet).

Idaea (ī-dē′a̯). In Greek legend, the second wife of Phineus. She falsely accused of wicked acts his two sons by Cleopatra, his first wife. Phineus had them imprisoned and flogged daily. When the accusations were proven false by Calais and Zetes, brothers of Cleopatra, Phineus restored his sons and sent Idaea back to her father in Scythia.

Idaea. In Greek mythology, a nymph of Mount Ida in the Troad. She married Scamander when he came to Phrygia from Crete and bore him a son, Teucer.

Idaean Mother, The (ī-dē′an). Another name for Cybele, deriving from her sanctuary on Mount Ida. Other names are Mater Idaea, and the Great Mother of the gods.

Idalium (ī-dā′li-um). [Also: **Idalia**; modern village name, **Dali**.] In ancient geography, a town and promontory on the coast of Cyprus, with a temple to Aphrodite, who was sometimes called Idalia.

Idas (ī′da̯s). In Greek legend, the son of Arene by Poseidon, but brought up as the son of Aphareus, Arene's husband. He was a man of great valor, a skilled bowman, a

---

actọr; up, lūte, pu̇ll; oi, oil; ou, out; ᴛʜ, then; d̦ as d or j, ş as s or sh, ț as t or ch, z̦ as z or zh.

strong man with the spear, and the devoted brother of Lynceus. The brothers took part in the Calydonian Hunt, and accompanied Jason on the *Argo* in the quest for the Golden Fleece. As an Argonaut, Idas boasted that his own spear was of more help to him than was Zeus, and was chided for blasphemy by Idmon the seer. Orpheus stilled the ensuing quarrel between them by playing his lute. Later Idas slew the boar which had attacked and killed Idmon, and still later, when the Argonauts arrived in Colchis, he objected violently when Jason decided to seek the assistance of Medea. Idas considered it an insult to his manly valor and skill as a warrior to accept help from a woman.

Idas and Lynceus were betrothed to their cousins, the Leucippides, but Castor and Polydeuces carried the Leucippides off and had sons by them, thus earning the enmity of Idas and Lynceus. Idas fell in love with Marpessa, the daughter of Evenus. To win her he had to defeat her father in a chariot race, and did so with the help of a winged chariot given to him by Poseidon. Apollo also loved Marpessa. When he learned that Idas had won her he engaged in a duel with him—Idas was one of very few who dared challenge the gods—but Zeus intervened and said Marpessa could choose between Apollo and Idas. She chose Idas, because she feared the immortal would too soon tire of her. After the death of Aphareus Idas and Lynceus resolved their quarrel with Castor and Polydeuces and made a raid with them for some cattle in Arcadia. In the division of the spoils Idas and Lynceus won the cattle by a trick and drove them off. Later Castor and Polydeuces stole the cattle from them, and hid in a hollow tree to waylay Idas and Lynceus. Lynceus, whose sight was so keen he could see through a tree trunk, spotted them. He and Idas rushed up and in the fight that broke out Lynceus and Castor were killed, and Zeus, to protect his son Polydeuces, hurled a thunderbolt that killed Idas.

Idmon (id′mon). In Greek legend, an Argonaut, the son of Apollo and Cyrene, but reared as the son of Abas of Argos. He was a seer (his name means "the knowing one") who learned the augury of birds from Apollo. At the start of the expedition in the *Argo* he predicted that though there would be grievous trials, both coming and going, the Argonauts would bring back the Golden Fleece. He also predicted that he would not return with them. This prophecy was fulfilled in the land of the Mariandyni, where he was attacked and killed by a wild boar.

Idomeneus (ī-dom′e̯-nūs, ī″dō-me̯-nē′us). In Greek legend, the son of Deucalion. He was king of Crete, and was renowned for his courage, and for his good looks. As a former suitor of Helen he commanded a fleet and sailed to join the Greeks in their expedition against Troy to recapture Helen from Paris. Although he was no longer young, he fought with the courage of a wild boar and accounted for many Trojans with his spear. With others, he volunteered to meet Hector in single combat but was eliminated in the drawing of lots. He and the two Ajaxes were the chief defenders of the Greek fortifications against Hector's attack. On his way home after the war his ship was beset by storms. He prayed to Poseidon to abate them, promising to sacrifice the first thing he met upon landing. This, to his sorrow, was his son. True to his vow, he prepared the sacrifice, but was interrupted by a pestilence which swept Crete. On this occurrence Leucus, who had first become the paramour of Idomeneus' wife Meda and then murdered her and seized the throne, banished Idomeneus from Crete. He went to Bruttii, where he ended his days.

Idothea (ī-dō′thē̯-a). In the *Odyssey*, a nymph, the daughter of the sea-god Proteus. She told Menelaus, becalmed on the island of Pharos on his way home from the Trojan War, how to catch Proteus when he went to sleep with the seals and how to force him to tell what god was angry and kept Menelaus so long from home.

Idyia (ī-dī′ya̯). In Greek legend, a daughter of Tethys and Oceanus. She was the wife of King Aeëtes of Colchis and, according to some accounts, the mother of his son Apsyrtus.

Iliad (il′i-a̯d). Greek epic poem, composed, according to tradition, by Homer sometime during or before the 8th century B.C. With its companion poem, the *Odyssey*, it is one of the greatest epics of world literature and one of the earliest examples of literary invention. It describes, in 15,693 dactylic hexameters, events that took place early in the tenth year of the Trojan War. In the course of the long poem many references are made to mythological and legendary events which took place prior to the outbreak of the war. Remarkable for the surpassing majesty and beauty of its language, it also demonstrates intimate knowledge of human nature, explicitly illuminates human character, and powerfully extols the might and virtues of warriors. Homer attributes somewhat mortal motives to the immortals—the gods and goddesses, moved by jealousy, pride, love—who actively participated in the affairs of the heroes. They caused the war, interfered in its progress, and struggling among themselves decided its outcome.

The participants on each side who appear in the following summary are:

Greeks

Calchas	Patroclus ✓
Agamemnon ✓	Nestor ✓
Achilles ✓	Odysseus ✓
Menelaus ✓	Eurypylus
Diomedes	Machaon
Telamonian Ajax ✓	Teucer
Ajax the Lesser	Myrmidons

Trojans

Hector ✓	Dolon
Paris ✓	Rhesus
Aeneas	Priam ✓
Helenus	Polydamas
Antenor	Sarpedon

Gods and goddesses who aided the Greeks:

Thetis	Poseidon
Hera	Hermes
Athena	Hephaestus

Gods and goddesses who aided the Trojans:

Apollo	Artemis
Aphrodite	Xanthus, river-god
Ares	Leto

(See also under their separate entry names, and under **Trojan War** and **Aeneid**.)

Book I: In the tenth year of the Trojan War, Apollo sends a plague against the Achaeans (they were never spoken of as Greeks by Homer; he called them Achaeans, Argives, and Danaans interchangeably). Calchas, a seer, explains that Apollo is punishing them because Agamemnon, "king of men," refuses to restore the captive Chryseis to her father Chryses, Apollo's priest, who had approached Agamemnon with an offer of ransom. Aga-

memnon, after much debate, agrees to return her but insists on taking Briseis, a captive who had been awarded to Achilles as his "meed of honor," in her place. This is the cause of the quarrel between Achilles and Agamemnon and the reason for the famous "wrath of Achilles" which is the theme of the *Iliad*. Achilles withdraws from the fighting, foretelling the day when Agamemnon will desperately need him to save the Achaeans from the fury of "man-slaying" Hector. Achilles appeals to his mother, "silver-footed" Thetis, to intercede with Zeus. When she does so Zeus promises to give victory to the Trojans until the Achaeans acknowledge the honor due to Achilles and Agamemnon atones for his insult. With this promise, Zeus sets himself against Hera and Athena who favor the Achaeans.

Book II: Zeus causes the Achaeans to resume the warfare by sending a deceptive dream to Agamemnon, telling him to assemble his forces for the capture of Troy. Iris, the messenger of the gods, warns the Trojans that the Achaeans are massing and advises them to do the same. There follows a catalogue of the captains of the Greeks, Trojans, and their respective allies.

Book III: Chided by Hector for cowardice and for causing the war by stealing Menelaus' wife Helen, Paris agrees to a single combat with Menelaus to decide who shall have Helen and to avoid the carnage of further warfare. The Greeks and Trojans are delighted by the prospect of settling the war in this manner and oaths of friendship are exchanged by the two armies. In the duel, Menelaus is about to conquer when Aphrodite rescues Paris and spirits him away to Helen. She, the innocent cause of the long war, yearns for her homeland and Menelaus. When Paris is restored to her, she bitterly reproaches both him and the goddess.

Book IV: Following the rescue of Paris, Zeus in Olympus deliberately taunts Hera and Athena with being less careful of their favorites, the Achaeans, than Aphrodite is of Paris. Disguised as a Trojan, Athena then appears to Pandarus, a famed Trojan archer, and dares him to shoot at Menelaus and win fame for himself. Hera deflects the arrow and Menelaus is only slightly wounded. Agamemnon immediately calls the Greeks to arms for this violation of the oath·of friendship. At the same time the Trojans rally and battle is joined. Many heroes on both sides are slain as Athena aids the Greeks and Apollo upholds the Trojans.

Book V: As the battle rages, the gods take an ever more active part. Athena endows Diomedes with unconquerable courage and skill as he slashes through the Trojans, even spurring him to wound Aphrodite as she bears her son Aeneas, whom Diomedes had felled, from the field. Ares then goes to the aid of the Trojans at Aphrodite's behest and helps them stand off the Achaeans until he in his turn is wounded by Diomedes. Content that the furious struggle continues, Hera and Athena withdraw to Olympus.

Book VI: The tide of battle swings back and forth. Helenus, Hector's brother, tells him to return to the city and instruct their mother and other Trojan matrons to offer sacrifices to Athena. He does so, and visits his wife Andromache and his baby son. Andromache pleads with him not to make her a widow. Sadly and gently he tells her he must return to the battle, for although he knows Troy is destined to be destroyed it is his fate ever to be in the forefront of the struggle. Meanwhile, Diomedes and Glaucus, squaring off to fight each other, discover that their fathers had been friends and swear oaths of friendship instead. They exhange armor, and Glaucus, beguiled by Zeus, gives up his gold armor for Diomedes' bronze armor—the classic example of getting the worst of a bargain. It is at this encounter that Glaucus expresses the ruling ambition of the heroes on both sides: "Ever to be of the best."

Book VII: Hector, returning to the battle with Paris, wreaks havoc among the Achaeans. Watchful Athena hurries down from Olympus to sustain her favorites, but she is intercepted by Apollo, who is championing Hector. The two gods decide to withdraw from the battle for one day and to inspire Hector to challenge the Greeks to a single combat, not for any prize but for the love of combat itself. Ajax is chosen by lot to accept the challenge and they fight to a standstill until nightfall. Antenor, "prudent in counsel," advises the Trojans to restore Helen, but Paris refuses. A truce is declared for burial of the dead, and the Greeks improve their opportunity by building a wall and digging a moat to protect their ships.

Book VIII: Zeus now orders the gods and goddesses to refrain from helping the Greeks, while he goes to Mount Ida and from there tips the scales in favor of the Trojans. Under his protection Hector ravages the Achaeans. Hera and Athena think to defy Zeus and go to their aid, but Zeus, divining their intention, sends Iris to warn them not to interfere. He prophesies that Hector will fight unconquered until Achilles emerges from his tent and joins the battle to avenge the death of his friend Patroclus. Twice Hector drives the Greeks back, but the coming of darkness prevents him from surmounting the ramparts and putting the torch to their ships.

Book IX: Hector's onslaughts arouse fear and confusion among the Greeks. Agamemnon, admitting that he was wrong in angering Achilles, offers to make amends. Nestor, "wise counselor," advises that a delegation be sent to Achilles by which Agamemnon will offer to restore Briseis and give him many other great gifts if Achilles will come to their aid. Achilles' pride cannot be bought in this manner, however. Recalling that Thetis had foretold that if he fought at Troy he would gain undying fame but have a short life, he refuses the offer and threatens to sail for home the next day.

Book X: In despair, for his own rashness and for the life of his men, Agamemnon seeks further counsel. At a meeting of the chiefs it is decided to send a spy to the Trojan camp. Diomedes and Odysseus volunteer to go. On the way they meet Dolon, a Trojan who had been sent to spy on them. They capture him, and after learning that Rhesus, a king of Thrace and a Trojan ally, is located at some distance from the Trojan camp, they slay Dolon. Next they find Rhesus, slay him and twelve of his men, steal his horses and return to the Greek galleys.

Book XI: At dawn, Eris alone of the gods descends to the strife. The Achaeans fight savagely. Many Trojans are slain before Zeus again tips the scales in favor of Hector. Then Diomedes, Eurypylus, and the surgeon, Machaon, are wounded by shafts from Paris' bow. Agamemnon and Odysseus are also wounded. Ajax is betrayed by Panic. All withdraw to the ships. Achilles, watching

fat, fāte, fär, fãre, errȧnt; net, mē, hėr ardẹnt; pin, pīne; not, nōte, mȯve, nôr,

from his ship, sees Nestor race to the galleys in his chariot. He sends Patroclus to learn what wounded hero Nestor is driving. For Patroclus "this was the beginning of evil." He sees Machaon, wounded, and hears a long speech in which Nestor laments his advancing years, recalls the glorious exploits of his youth, and reminds Patroclus that his father had sent him off to the war with Achilles charging him "ever to be of the best." As a peroration, Nestor urges Patroclus to come clothed in Achilles' armor and leading his Myrmidons, if Achilles, unmoved by the travails of his countrymen, still refuses to fight.

Book XII: Meanwhile Hector, fighting like a whirlwind, drives the Greeks to their ships. An eagle flying over drops the serpent it holds in its talons just as the Trojans are about to assail the moat and wall protecting the ships. Polydamas interprets this as an evil omen, but Hector scorns him, saying that there is only one omen, "to fight for our country." Despite the Greeks' maniacal defense of the ramparts, Sarpedon, an offspring of Zeus, breaches the walls, while Hector smashes open the gates with a huge stone and leaps inside. The Trojans pour in after him.

Book XIII: Satisfied with the Trojan's progress, Zeus then turns his eyes to more peaceful scenes. But Poseidon, in anger at Zeus and with pity for the Achaeans, evades Zeus' order not to interfere by assuming mortal shape and circulating among the desperate Greeks. He rallies them to battle and inspires them with fresh valor and might. With his encouragement they resume their furious defense of the ships. Many heroes on both sides are slain but neither side gains the advantage.

Book XIV: Agamemnon wants to put to sea in the ships but Poseidon appears to him in mortal form and prophesies the rout of the Trojans. Hera, too, resolves to help them indirectly. By trickery she persuades Aphrodite to loan her the magic girdle of love, seduces Zeus with blind desire, and bribes Slumber to lull him to sleep. With Zeus thus occupied Hector is stunned by a stone and the Trojans are driven onto the plain as Poseidon turns back the tide of the battle.

Book XV: Zeus wakes from his trick-induced

sleep to see the Trojans fleeing. He reviles Hera and sends her to Olympus to have Poseidon recalled, and to despatch Apollo to heal Hector of his wound. He reminds Hera of his promise to Thetis and again foretells Hector's death by Achilles' hand. In the meantime he determines that Hector shall have the glory. Once more the Achaeans draw back as Hector, restored by Apollo, fights like a flame. Patroclus hears the rush of the Trojans on the ramparts and speeds off to Achilles, while Hector, protected by Apollo, approaches the ships. Zeus grants him the glory of firing the ships, though he knows that death and destruction are the ultimate fate of Hector and Troy.

Book XVI: Patroclus, weeping for the Achaeans, reproaches Achilles for his pitiless spirit. Achilles boasts that the Trojans would not now be threatening the ships if Agamemnon had not, by his insult, caused him to withdraw, and again refuses his help, but yields to Patroclus' ardent plea that he be allowed to go to their aid. He clothes Patroclus in his own armor, loans him his immortal horses—Balius and Xanthus—and puts him in command of the Myrmidons. Hector and the Trojans immediately perceive the change in the tide of battle and fall back. Sarpedon is slain as he tries in vain to stop Patroclus' murderous progress, whereupon a savage struggle takes place over possession of his corpse. As Pàtroclus pursues the Trojans to the walls of the city, Apollo comes to Hector's aid. The god stuns Patroclus and loosens his armor. Euphorbus wounds him and Hector slays him with his spear. Dying, Patroclus breathes that it was the gods and not Hector who had slain him.

Book XVII: The death of Patroclus brings on a prodigious struggle for his body. Hector dons the armor he had stripped from him and fights in the vanguard. Menelaus, fearing that Hector will conquer, sends Antilochus to tell Achilles that his comrade has been slain and to urge him to come and rescue his corpse.

Book XVIII: Achilles covers his head with ashes when he learns of the death of Patroclus. Thetis hears her son weeping and comes from the depths of the sea to comfort him. She reminds him of his prayer that the Achaeans should suffer because of Agamemnon's insult. He replies with bitter reproaches on himself for that anger which had caused him to withdraw to his tent, leading to the death of so many Achaeans and ultimately to that of his beloved comrade. He swears to kill Hector. Since he has lost his armor, Thetis urges him to wait until next morning when she will return with new armor forged by Hephaestus. Iris now comes, a messenger from Hera, to tell Achilles to show himself on the ramparts, that the mere sight of him, protected by Athena's flaming egis, will terrorize the Trojans. When they see him the Trojans are confounded and Patroclus' corpse is rescued. Polydamas, seeing that Achilles has now come out against them, advises the Trojans to withdraw to the city, but Hector scorns his advice.

Book XIX: When Thetis returns at dawn Achilles calls an assembly and renounces his wrath. Agamemnon admits his error and blames his rash act in taking Briseis on Ate, the goddess of blindness and mischief. He restores Briseis to Achilles and gives him great gifts in atonement. Achilles, refusing to eat until Patroclus is avenged, puts on his new armor, bridles his immortal horses, and calls on the Achaeans to follow him into battle.

Book XX: Zeus now tells the gods to intermingle in the fight as they choose, lest Achilles, returning to the battle, should defy fate and destroy Troy. Hera, Athena, Poseidon, Hermes, and Hephaestus take the Achaeans' part. Ares, Apollo, Artemis, Leto, Xanthus, and Aphrodite go to the side of the Trojans.

Book XXI: With a ferocious onslaught, Achilles drives the Trojans back to the banks of the Scamander, or Xanthus, as it was called by the gods. There Hera delays the Trojans with a thick cloud and Achilles slaughters them in droves. The river-god is horrified. He asks Achilles not to choke up his streams with Trojan corpses. When Achilles boastfully denies him, the river overflows its banks and pursues Achilles to the plain. To save him, Hera sends Hephaestus to set the river afire. Then the gods begin to quarrel among themselves. Athena sets upon Ares and then Aphrodite. Hera attacks Artemis and scatters her arrows. Apollo returns to the plain, and by assuming the shape of a Trojan, induces Achilles to chase him, thus drawing

him away from the city and preventing him from overtaking Hector and the Trojans.

Book XXII: When the Trojans are safely inside the walls Apollo reveals himself to Achilles, who acknowledges that he could not defeat a god and turns back to the city. Hector reproaches himself for disregarding Polydamas' advice when Achilles first appeared on the ramparts, and for causing the losses the Trojans have suffered. He resolves to meet Achilles and defend the city, and ignores his father's and mother's pleas to come into the city for safety. As Achilles draws near Panic invades Hector. Three times he flees around the walls with Achilles in ardent pursuit. Zeus pities Hector, but when he weighs Achilles and Hector in the scales, Hector is doomed. Apollo now appears to Hector to give him courage so that he will engage Achilles and meet his fate. Then Apollo forsakes him, and Athena deludes him by appearing to him in the shape of his brother. But when Hector, having hurled his spear at Achilles in vain, turns to his supposed brother for another one, there is no one there. Now Hector knows that the gods have deserted him. Making a futile charge at Achilles with his sword, Hector is mortally wounded when Achilles drives his spear through a chink in the armor at Hector's throat. Hector's dying request for a proper burial is rejected by Achilles. The Achaeans gather around and run their swords through the fallen hero. Insatiate Achilles lashes Hector's feet to his chariot and drags Hector's body to the Greek ships.

Book XXIII: Achilles now prepares to bury Patroclus as he had promised he would do as soon as Hector was killed. The funeral rites include a magnificent feast and a huge pyre surrounded by 12 slain Trojan princes and sacrifices of sheep, cattle, horses, and dogs. Following the burning of Patroclus' body the funeral games are held: chariot race, boxing and wrestling matches, foot race, sword duel, shotput, and archery contest.

Book XXIV: Each day as he mourns, Achilles drags Hector's body three times around the tomb of Patroclus. This treatment of an honorable enemy offends Zeus. He sends an order to Achilles to yield the body to Priam when he comes for it. At the same time, Iris bears a message to Priam to go alone to

Achilles, bearing rich gifts, and ransom his son's corpse. As a good omen for Priam, Zeus sends an eagle, and he commands Hermes to protect and guide Priam to the heart of the enemy's camp. On the way, Hermes, in disguise, tells Priam that Hector's body has been protected by the gods with nectar and ambrosia and is as fresh as a dewdrop. He smuggles Priam into Achilles' tent where the latter is astounded to see the old king and, his desire for vengeance sated, listens to him with compassion. He weeps for Patroclus as Priam mourns for Hector. Kissing the hands that had slain his son, Priam begs him to accept ransom and deliver the body. Achilles agrees, as he had been ordered to do by Zeus. He asks Priam how many days he wants to mourn Hector and promises to hold the war in abeyance during that time. Hermes spirits Priam and Hector's body away in the night so Agamemnon will not learn of Achilles' compassion and interfere. On the return to Troy the whole city, led by Andromache, Hecuba, and Helen, mourns for Hector for nine days. On the tenth day his body is burned. On the eleventh the flames of the pyre are extinguished with wine and Hector's funeral rites have been accomplished.

Ilias Latina (il′i-as la-ti′na). Condensation (1st century A.D.) of the *Iliad,* the "Latin Homer," in 1070 painstaking Latin hexameters, of uncertain authorship. (JJ)

Ilias Parva (pär′va). Title of a lost epic, treating of the events of the closing weeks of the Trojan War, from the fatal contest for the arms of Achilles to the admission into Troy of the Wooden Horse, usually attributed to the epic poet Lesches of Mytilene (7th century B.C.). (JJ)

Ilion, Ilios, Ilium (il′i-on, -os, -um). Names for Troy, meaning the city founded by Ilus. See **Troy.**

Ilione (il-ī′ō-nē, -ō′nē). [Also: **Iliona.**] In Greek legend, the oldest daughter of Priam and Hecuba. She was the wife of Polymnestor, king of Thrace, and the mother of his son Deïpylus. Entrusted with the care of her young brother, Polydorus, Ilione purposely confused the two children so that if one died the other would succeed to the throne. According to some accounts, Polymnestor, bribed by the Greeks to kill Polydorus,

by mistake killed his own son, whereupon Ilione first blinded and then killed him.

Ilioneus (il-ī-ō′nē-us, il-ī′ō-nūs). In the *Aeneid,* a Trojan who accompanied Aeneas on his flight from Troy. He commanded one of the ships of the fleet and was separated from the others when they were assailed by a great storm off Sicily. Aeneas thought he had perished but when Aeneas, wrapped in a mist by Venus to protect him in a strange land, approached Dido, he found Ilioneus standing before her and asking for asylum. Ilioneus told Dido that they were not pirates, but Trojans who were on their way to Hesperia. Later, when the Trojans landed in Italy, Ilioneus acted as an emissary from Aeneas to Latinus. He gave Latinus presents, relics from Troy, and asked for a plot of land on which the Trojans might settle.

Ilioneus. In Homeric legend (*Iliad*), a Trojan hero, the only son of Phorbas. Peneleus pierced him through the eye-socket with his lance, then cut off his head and waved it on the end of his lance as he taunted the Trojans. This is one of the few instances of brutality for its own sake in the *Iliad.*

Ilissus (i-lis′us). [Modern Greek name, **Ilissos** or **Eilissos.**] In ancient geography, a small river in Attica, Greece, flowing just S of Athens. It was on the banks of this river that Orithyia, the daughter of Erechtheus, was playing when Boreas swooped down in a great gust of wind and carried her away to Thrace to be his consort.

Ilithyia (il-i-thī′ya). [Also: **Eileithyia.**] The goddess who presides over childbirth, sometimes called the daughter of Hera. In her role as the goddess who helps women in childbirth she can either hasten or delay delivery. Hera enlisted her aid to delay the birth of Heracles until after Eurystheus, whose arrival was speeded up, was born. On the Hill of Cronus, near the site of the Olympic Games, an infant was transformed into a serpent, and so terrified the Arcadians, who were warring on the Eleans, that they fled with great losses. The spot where the serpent then disappeared into the hill was marked by a shrine to Ilithyia. In it priestesses fed a snake on cakes of honey in memory of this miracle. The Romans identified Ilithyia with Juno, whom they called Lucina in this aspect.

Ilium (il'i-um). See **Troy**.

Iliupersis (il″i-ū-pėr′sis). In classical mythology, archaeology, etc., the destruction of Troy or Ilium; hence, a poem or an account treating of the destruction of Troy, or a graphic or plastic representation of the destruction of Troy, or of some episode connected with its fall.

Illyria (i-lir′i-a̟). [Greek, **Illyris, Illyria.**] In ancient geography, a region in the W part of the Balkan peninsula, N of Greece. Its boundaries are vague. In the second millennium B.C. this region was occupied by tribes speaking an Indo-European language and collectively known as Illyrians. The S part of Illyria came early under Greek influence. According to some legendary accounts, Cadmus fled to this region with his wife after the death of his grandson Pentheus, who had denied the divinity of Dionysus. He settled among the Encheleans who defeated the Illyrians in war and made Cadmus their king. In his old age Cadmus had a son, Illyrius, for whom the Illyrians were named. Historically, the Greeks, apparently attracted by the mines in the interior, began colonizing the coast in the 6th century B.C. and continued for a number of centuries thereafter. The kingdom of Illyria, with Scodra as its capital, was important in the 3rd century B.C., and was overthrown (168 B.C.) by Rome. The region formerly known as Illyria is now occupied principally by Yugoslavia and Albania.

Illyrians (il-ir′i-a̟nz). People of ancient Illyria, including groups later known as Dalmatians and Pannonians; but the term is most commonly applied to the tribes who inhabited the coastal region of the Balkan peninsula north of what is now Albania. They were a warlike, piratical people, who threw off all Greek attempts to subjugate them. The Romans conquered them in the 3rd century B.C. and under Augustus the country, called Illyricum, was organized as a Roman province.

Illyrius (i-lir′i-us). According to legend, a son born to Cadmus in his old age. He became ruler of Buthoë, a city built in Illyria by Cadmus, after the death of Cadmus.

Ilus (ī′lus). In Greek legend, a son of Dardanus and the brother of Erichthonius. According to some, he was the grandnephew of Dardanus and son of Tros. Having been victorious in a wrestling match in Phrygia, he was awarded 50 youths and 50 maidens as a prize. He was also given a spotted cow and told to follow it until it should lie down. On that spot he was to erect a city. Ilus carried out his instructions and followed the cow until it came to rest on a hill in the Trojan plain. There he built Ilium, named for himself. He prayed to Zeus for a sign that he had chosen well, and was answered by finding a wooden image in the ground in front of his tent. This was the Palladium. Apollo told Ilus that as long as the Palladium remained within its walls the city would be safe. Ilus was the father of Laomedon, by Eurydice, daughter of Adrastus, and the grandfather of Priam.

Ilus. Another name for Ascanius, the son of Aeneas and a descendant of Ilus, founder of Troy.

Imbrasus (im′bra̟-sus). A river of the island of Samos. Near its waters Ancaeus the Argonaut, son of Poseidon and Astypalea, was born.

Imbrex (im′breks), **Licinius.** [Also known as **Publius Licinius Tegula.**] Latin poet; fl. c200 B.C.; known as a writer of comedies and of at least one hymn.

Imbrius (im′bri-us). In the *Iliad,* a son of Mentor. He came from Pedasus and married Medesicaste, a daughter of King Priam of Troy. Priam treated him as one of his own children. In the Trojan War he fought on the side of the Trojans and was slain by Teucer. Locrian Ajax cut off his head and hurled it among the Trojans.

Imbrus (im′brus). [Also: **Imbros.**] An island in the NE Aegean, situated just W of the Hellespont. Near here, according to the *Iliad,* was a deep chasm under the sea where Poseidon stabled his horses while he went to observe the Trojan War and to help the Achaeans. The island was won for Athens by Miltiades just before the outbreak of the Persian War. Like its neighbor Samothrace, it was a center for the worship of the Cabiri (q.v.).

Imhotep (im-hō′tep). Egyptian architect, physician, and adviser to King Zoser; probable designer of the oldest pyramid, the famous Step-Pyramid at Sakkara; fl. 3rd Dynasty (c3190–3100 B.C.). In later mythology, he

fat, fāte, fär, fâre, errant; net, mē, hėr ardent; pin, pīne; not, nōte, möve, nôr,

acquired divine status as the first-born son of Ptah and Sekhmet, with whom he formed the Memphic triad. In this concept, he was the god of knowledge, akin to Thoth, and was identified by the Greeks with Asclepius.

Inachus (in′a̱-kus). In Greek mythology, the god of the river Inachus, son of the Titan Oceanus and his sister Tethys, whose children were the Oceanids and the rivers of the world. He was the first king of Argos and was the father of Io and of Phoroneus by the nymph Melia. When Poseidon contended with Hera for control of Argolis, Zeus asked the river-gods Inachus, Cephissus, and Asterion to mediate the quarrel. The river-gods decided in favor of Hera. Poseidon was enraged that they had awarded Argolis to Hera and to punish them dried up their rivers so that they ceased to flow in the summer.

Inachus. [Modern Greek name, **Inakhos** or **Inachos.**] In ancient geography, a river in Argolis, flowing into the Gulf of Argolis SE of Argos.

Indiges (in′di-jēz) or **Indigites** (in-dij′i-tēz). A Roman term by which mortals, such as Aeneas and Romulus, were known when they were deified after death. The specific meaning of the term when applied to Roman gods is not clear.

Indus (in′dus). [Also: **Sind**; Sanskrit, **Sindhu.**] Chief river of Pakistan. It rises among the Himalayas of W Tibet, and flows NW through gorges in Tibet and Kashmir. Near the N part of Kashmir it turns S and flows SW through Pakistan (Punjab and Sind) into the Arabian Sea. It has formed an extensive delta. Its chief tributaries are the combined rivers of the Punjab (Jhelum, Beas, Chenab, Ravi, and Sutlej, entering through the Panjnad) and the Kabul. By means of the Sukkur Barrage, in Sind, the Indus irrigates several million acres of land. The volume of water in the Indus varies greatly, with floods in the spring and summer, and low water in winter; because of this extreme variability and silt deposition, it is not much used for navigation. Alexander the Great returned from India (325 B.C.) by the Indus valley, proceeding to Patala.

Inessa (in-es′a̱). [Modern name, **Biancavilla.**] Town on the island of Sicily, S of Mount Aetna and about nine miles NW of Catana. It was a Greek settlement.

Inferi (in′fer-ī). The Roman name for the inhabitants of the infernal regions, the dead. It is also the name of the gods of the lower world in contrast with the Superi, the gods of heaven. *Inferiae* were the sacrifices offered by the Romans to the souls of deceased members of their families.

Ino (ī′nō). In Greek mythology, a daughter of Cadmus and Harmonia, and the sister of Semele, Agave, Autonoë, and Polydorus. She married Athamas, king of Orchomenus, after he had abandoned his first wife, Nephele, by whom he had two children, Helle and Phrixus. Ino also had two children by Athamas, Learchus and Melicertes. She plotted to destroy Phrixus and Helle so that her own children would be the heirs. By some means she parched all the grain seed secretly, so that when it was planted no crops grew and there was a famine. Messengers were sent to consult the oracle and returned with the news, as they had been bribed to do by Ino, that the gods could be propitiated and starvation avoided if Phrixus were sacrificed to them. Athamas took Phrixus and Helle to a mountain top and prepared to sacrifice them. Just as he was about to put the knife to their throats, however, Hermes sent a miraculous winged ram with fleece of gold which rescued them and bore them off on his back. Hera punished Athamas for abandoning Nephele, whom she had arranged for him to marry in the first place, by driving him mad. In his frenzy he killed Learchus and would have killed Ino. She escaped, carrying her son Melicertes in her arms, and leaped into the sea. However, Zeus was grateful to her for sheltering his son Dionysus and transformed her into a sea-goddess who was known thereafter as Leucothea. Melicertes became the sea-god Palaemon. It was in her capacity as sea-goddess that Leucothea saved Odysseus from drowning when his raft was shattered in a storm. She gave him her veil and helped him to reach shore on the island of the Phaeacians.

Insubres (in′sū-brēz). Ancient Gallic people in Cisalpine Gaul, dwelling north of the Padus (Po), in the vicinity of Mediolanum (Milan). They were finally made subject to Rome in 194 B.C.

Insula Herculis (in′sū-la̱ her′kū-lis). [Modern

name, **Asinara.**] Island off the NW coast of Sardinia.

Intaphernes (in-tạ-fėr′nēz). A Persian noble who, with Darius, was one of seven conspirators who overthrew the False Smerdis and made Darius ruler of the Persians. Among the privileges which the six were to enjoy when Darius was made king was that they were free to enter the palace unannounced whenever they chose, except when the king was with a woman. This privilege led to the death of Intaphernes. Acting on it, he wished to enter the palace on a matter of business with the king. Guards sought to bar his way on the grounds that the king was with a woman. Intaphernes thought they were lying, and drawing his scimitar, he cut off their ears and noses and strung them on his bridle. The guards went to Darius and told him what had happened. Darius, fearing that this was part of a plot against him, secretly consulted the other conspirators. He learned from their answers that they knew nothing at all of Intaphernes' insolence. Relieved on this score, Darius seized Intaphernes, his children and his close relatives, put them in fetters and condemned them to death. Each day the wife of Intaphernes stood before the palace gate weeping. Darius took pity on her and offered to grant her as a boon the life of one of the condemned family. She answered that if she could save the life of one only she chose that of her brother. Darius was surprised at this choice and asked why she had not chosen her husband or one of her children. Her answer was that the gods might grant her another husband and more children, but as her father and mother were dead she would never have another brother. Darius saw the worth of such reasoning. He not only spared her brother's life but that of her oldest son as well. Intaphernes, with the rest of his children and relatives, was put to death.

Inuus (in′ū-us). A name for the Roman god Faunus in his role as fertility god of cattle and good spirit of the forests, fields, and pastures.

Io (ī′ō). In Greek mythology, a beautiful daughter of the river-god Inachus. She was a priestess of Hera at Argos. Zeus saw her as she wandered by the river and fell in love

with her. He appeared to her in dreams and told her she had inspired his heart with love. One day he overtook her as she returned from the river. She fled from his embrace. He called a dark cloud to cover the earth, seized her, and ravished her. From her seat on Olympus Hera saw the cloud which appeared from nowhere and, ever suspicious of her notoriously unfaithful husband, she hurried down to earth to investigate. Zeus, hearing her approach, transformed Io into a beautiful pure white heifer, so that Hera should not discover his love-affair and heap angry recriminations on his head. Hera was acutely suspicious on finding Zeus in the company of a heifer and inquired where it had come from. He had had no time to think what he would say and improvised a tale that the heifer had sprung from the earth. Hera admired it and asked Zeus to give it to her as a gift. He was most reluctant but dared not risk further questions by refusing this gift to his wife, and turned Io over to Hera. She set the 100-eyed Argus to guard the heifer and went off, if not satisfied with his explanation at least content that she had foiled whatever plan he had in mind for the heifer. Argus, whose 100 eyes were never all asleep at once, guarded Io vigilantly. By day he allowed her to graze; at night he tied her up. Inachus searched in vain for his daughter. At length he came upon Argus and his charge. Io ran up to her father and licked his hand, but he had no idea this was his daughter. In despair that she could not speak to him and tell him of her plight she at last traced her name in the dust with her hoof—the hoofprint of a cow still spells her name. Inachus was desolate when he realized what had happened to his daughter, but he was powerless and Argus soon drove her on to new pastures. At length Zeus, in pity for Io, sent Hermes to slay Argus and set Io free. Hermes lulled all his 100 eyes to sleep and cut off his head. But Io was still not delivered. The shade of Argus pursued her, and Hera sent a gadfly to torment her. Half-crazed by the continual stings of the gadfly, she wandered distractedly through Greece. The Ionian Sea is so-named because she swam across it to Thrace. There she found Prometheus, bound to a rock. She pleaded with him to tell her if the future held any

fat, fāte, fär, fãre, errạnt; net, mē, hėr ardẹnt; pin, pīne; not, nōte, möve, nôr,

hope. He could not be immediately encouraging. He told her that much weary wandering lay ahead of her. Hounded by the gadfly, she would cross over into Asia—the place where she crossed, he said, would be known as Bosporus, "Ox-ford"—then after many years of wandering and suffering she would arrive at the Nile. Here at last she would regain her true shape. Zeus would touch her and she would bear him a son, Epaphus. With a frenzied cry Io left Prometheus and fled, stung by the gadfly. All turned out as he had predicted. She came at last to the Nile, was retransformed into her own shape, and bore Epaphus after Zeus touched her. She married Telegonus, king of the Egyptians, and set up images to Demeter. The Egyptians called the goddess Isis, and they also gave Io the name Isis, which may be the reason why images of the goddess are shown with a cow's horns. The descendants of Epaphus were Aegyptus, Danaus, Cepheus, and Phineus, and ultimately, as Prometheus foretold, a male child was born, a mighty archer, who brought about the release of Prometheus; he was Heracles. According

mation into a horned heifer was represented by the crescent moon.

Iobates (i-ob′a̤-tēz). In Greek legend, a king in Lycia and the father of Antia, wife of Proetus. He received Bellerophon kindly when he came to him with a message from Proetus, and after entertaining him hospitably for nine days he read the message. In it Proetus asked him to kill Bellerophon, charging that he had insulted Antia. Iobates did not want to offend the gods by slaying Bellerophon himself. He sent him, in turn, to kill the Chimaera, to fight the Solymi, and then to fight the Amazon women. As Bellerophon was successful in each case Iobates set an ambush to kill him, but Bellerophon slew the Lycian heroes who sprang on him from ambush and returned to Iobates. He decided that Bellerophon must have divine aid and therefore must be innocent of the crimes charged against him by Proetus. Iobates then gave him his daughter in marriage and a wide domain to rule over in Lycia. The message from Proetus to Iobates is the earliest reference to writing in European literature.

HERMES ABOUT TO SLAY ARGUS, THE GUARD OF THE HEIFER IO
Red-figured Attic hydria, 5th century B.C. *Museum of Fine Arts, Boston*

to later rationalizations of the Io story, she was not seduced by Zeus at all. Rather, it was a group of Phoenician traders who landed in Argos and carried her off to Egypt. Later the Greeks identified Io with Isis, the Egyptian moon-goddess. The starry skies symbolized the 100-eyed Argus; her transfor-

Iocaste (i-ō-kas′tē). **Jocasta.**

Iodama (i-od′a̤-ma̤). According to Greek tradition, a daughter of Itonius. Some say she ʼvas a priestess in the temple of Athena Itonia in Boeotia, between Alalcomenae and Coronea. She went into the sacred precinct at night and Athena appeared to her. When

Iodama saw the Gorgon's head on Athena's aegis she was turned to stone. Fires were lighted daily on the altar, and chants were thrice intoned, saying Iodama lived and desired fire. Others say Athena was a daughter of Itonius and that Iodama was her sister, and that the goddess accidentally turned her to stone by allowing her to see Medusa's head on her aegis.

Iolaus (i-ō-lā′us). In Greek legend, the son of Iphicles. He was the nephew, faithful friend, and companion of Heracles, and accompanied him as he carried out his labors for Eurystheus, sometimes acting as Heracles' charioteer and sometimes as his armor-bearer, but in all cases giving whatever aid he could to his beloved uncle. Heracles loved him dearly, but when, in a spell of madness inspired by Hera, he killed his children, he also attacked Iolaus, but the latter escaped his attacks and comforted Heracles when his senses were restored to him. Later Heracles gave Megara, the mother of his murdered children, to Iolaus as his wife. Iolaus led 40 of Heracles' sons by the daughters of Thespius to Sardinia and founded a colony there. He established the city of Olbia and named the colonists Iolarians after himself. Hercules established a sanctuary of Iolaus in Sicily. Iolaus returned to Greece and became the protector of Heracles' children after the latter had become immortalized. When the son of Theseus gave the children of Heracles sanctuary in Marathon, causing a war with Eurystheus, Iolaus, by then an old man, armed himself with weapons which he took from the walls of the temple. Despite protests that he was too old and weak to fight, he jumped into a chariot and drove into the battle, first praying to the gods to be given youth and strength for one day. Two stars lit on the yoke of his chariot, and cast a shadow over him. When the shadow lifted Iolaus was revealed as a stalwart youth. He pursued and captured Eurystheus and took him back to Alcmene, mother of Heracles, to give her the privilege of deciding the fate of her son's enemy. But some say Iolaus cut off Eurystheus' head and Alcmene then gouged out his eyes with a spike.

Iolcus (i-ol′kus). [Modern name, **Volos**.] In ancient geography, a city of Thessaly, in NE Greece, situated on the Gulf of Pagasae. Its king, Aeson, was deprived of his throne by Pelias. Jason, son of Aeson, came to reclaim the throne and was sent to Colchis to recover the Golden Fleece by Pelias. Iolcus, or nearby Pagasae, is, according to tradition, the point from which the Argonauts set forth on their expedition to recover the Golden Fleece. The site of Iolcus was occupied from ancient times. Remains of the Mycenaean and Geometric periods have been found there. The ancient city occupied a height that rose abruptly above the shore.

Iole (ī′ō-lē). In Greek legend, a daughter of Eurytus, king of Oechalia. Heracles sought her for a wife and was promised her hand if he defeated Eurytus in an archery contest. When Heracles won, her father refused to keep to his bargain. Heracles vowed revenge, and in the meantime he married Deianira. He later slew Iphitus, son of Eurytus, and afterward gathered an army, attacked and killed Eurytus and his sons, and took Iole captive. Deianira, to whom Heracles sent Iole, had nothing but pity for the youthful captive, but she was determined to recapture Heracles' affections if possible. She sent him a robe anointed with what she thought was a love charm. But it turned out to be a poison that entered Heracles' blood and ended his mortal life. Hyllus, his son, married Iole, as he had promised his dying father he would do, and Deianira hanged herself.

Ion (ī′on, ī′on). According to Greek tradition, a son of Creusa, daughter of King Erechtheus of Athens, and Apollo; eponymous ancestor of the Ionians. His mother abandoned him as an infant in the cave where Apollo had ravished her, and when, overcome by remorse and anxiety, she returned to fetch him, no trace of the child was to be found, and she feared he had been carried off by eagles. But Apollo had sent Hermes to rescue his son, and Ion was taken to the temple of Apollo at Delphi, where he was reared by the priestess. By the time he was grown to young manhood he had become a priest in the service of Apollo at Delphi. Meanwhile, Creusa had married Xuthus, an alien from Thessaly who had come to Athens and saved the city in a war with the Eu-

fat, fāte, fär, fāre, errant; net, mē, her ardent; pin, pīne; not, nōte, mōve, nôr, boeans. Creusa and Xuthus ultimately went to Delphi to ask the oracle why they had no children. There Creusa met the young priest. By command of the oracle, he was given to Xuthus as a son. Creusa, driven nearly to madness by grief for her own lost son and jealousy over Xuthus' new son, sought to poison Ion. By the intervention of the gods the poisoned wine which she intended for him was poured on the ground, doves that sipped it died, and her plot was discovered. At this, Ion tried to kill Creusa, but again the gods intervened, and mother and child were made known to each other and reunited. Ion returned to Athens with Creusa and Xuthus, who was not informed that he was his wife's own son. Ion married Helice, daughter of King Selinus of Aegialus, and succeeded his father-in-law as king of the Aegialeans. The name of his people was changed to Ionians. They afterward colonized the coast of Asia Minor, which became known as Ionia. Ion gave his assistance to the Athenians in a war against the Eleusinians and, being successful in this, was made king of Athens. The four sons of Ion and Helice—Geleon, Hopletes, Argades, and Aegicores—became the ancestors of the four Ionic tribes.

Ion. A play by Euripides, exhibited between 413 and 408 B.C. It treats the legend of Ion, son of Creusa and Apollo, who was abandoned by his mother as an infant, was miraculously rescued, and ultimately became king of Athens and ancestor of the Ionian race.

The scene is at Delphi, in the court of the temple of Apollo. The great altar of sacrifice stands in the center. Hermes enters and relates the history of Creusa, daughter of Erechtheus, king of Athens. She has come to the temple to ask the oracle why she and her husband Xuthus have no children. Hermes tells what he thinks is going to happen, and withdraws behind some laurel bushes to see how it all works out.

A young priest enters, accompanied by worshipers. He praises Apollo and orders his followers to purify themselves at the Castalian Spring while he purifies the temple, which, since he has neither mother nor father, has been his home and which he proudly serves. A chorus of Creusa's handmaids enters and sings of the glories of the temple. Creusa enters. The young priest is moved by the sight of her tear-stained face and feels drawn to her. He asks the reason for her weeping, for people usually rejoice in Apollo's temple. She answers that she weeps for a memory and over the wrongs of women and the injustices of gods. By his questions to her and her answers he draws from her the history of the kings of Athens. Coming to her own time, he learns that she was given to Xuthus, an alien, to reward him for having saved Athens in a war with the Euboeans, and that they have now come to the temple to ask the oracle why they remain childless. He tells her his story—that he was abandoned as an infant and brought up in the temple—and they pity each other. Creusa says she has come alone to the shrine on behalf of a friend. Her friend was ravished in a cave by Apollo, bore a son as a result, and abandoned the child in the very cave where the god had violated her. Now her friend is tormented by grief and anguish over the fate of the child she abandoned, and hopes to learn from the oracle what became of him. In fact, this story ascribed to a friend is Creusa's own story. The priest warns her not to put questions to the oracle that indicate a god had acted the part of a villian, and that no one should seek to reveal what the gods wish to hide. Creusa cries out at the injustice of Apollo, and asks the priest to say nothing of all this to Xuthus, who is now approaching. Xuthus enters and announces that he has learned from the oracle of Trophonius that he will take a son home with him. He goes to the inner temple of Apollo to learn how he is to gain this son. Creusa leaves to place boughs on the altar. Alone, the ardent priest is disturbed by Creusa's story that Apollo ravishes maidens and forsakes infants; he refuses to believe that the gods have one law for mortals and another for themselves—if this be true, the temples of the gods will soon be abandoned. He departs. The chorus invokes Athena, praying for an heir of Erechtheus for the throne of Athens. As the priest returns Xuthus comes from the temple and embraces him with joy, for he has learned that the first man he meets on leaving the temple is his son. The

actor; up, lūte, pull; oi, oil; ou, out; ᴛʜ, then; ḍ as d or j, ş as s or sh, ṭ as t or ch, ẓ as z or zh.

young man is not so enthusiastic; he wants to know who his mother is. Xuthus can't tell him, but thinks she may have been a maenad with whom he dallied during the festival of Dionysus, before he married Creusa. The priest reluctantly acknowledges him as his father, but longs to know who his mother was. The chorus rejoices for Xuthus, and prays for good fortune for Creusa. Xuthus plans a feast for his son, after which they will return to Athens, but his new son is troubled: he fears he will not be welcomed in Athens for the Athenians have no love for aliens, and not only is Xuthus an alien but his son has the stain of bastardy. Moreover, Creusa will hate him as a son of Xuthus she cannot share, and will hate Xuthus who no longer shares her childlessness. He thinks of the blessings and peace of his present life and fears the future. Xuthus tells him he must accept his fate, and names his new son Ion ("coming"), because he met him at his "coming-forth" from the temple. Xuthus and Ion depart. The chorus sings of Creusa and her new woe. Their loyalty is to her, the Athenian, rather than to Xuthus, the alien, and they resolve to tell her, in defiance of Xuthus' command, of his new-found son. By the time the chorus finishes their feeling for Xuthus has developed from one of beneficent indifference to definite dislike because he has been lucky and Creusa hasn't. Creusa now approaches with an old servant and learns that she has no son but that Xuthus has. The old servant instantly jumps to the conclusion that Xuthus' son is a bastard, and is incensed at this additional insult to Creusa. He invents a tale to account for this son: he is the child of a slave to whom Xuthus turned when Creusa bore him no children. Creusa immediately accepts his tale and laments that she has been betrayed by both mortal and immortal lovers. Now for the first time she tells the story of her son by Apollo, and cries out against the god for adding to her suffering by giving Xuthus a son when she has lost hers. The servant, deeply troubled, questions her. She tells the whole story and repeats her accusations against Apollo. She abandoned her child in the hope that Apollo would save his own son. All are bitter at the god for forsaking her and her child. On the urging of the servant she decides to avenge herself by slaying the son Apollo has given to Xuthus. She will put a drop of the Gorgon Medusa's blood—given to Erechtheus by Athena and to her by Erechtheus—into the wine cup the servant will hand to Ion at the feast. The chorus agrees it is better for Ion to die than for Athens to be ruled by an alien. Creusa and her servant depart. The chorus prays for her success. Soon the servant rushes back, searching for Creusa. When he presented the wine cup, Ion poured the wine on the ground because of some sacrilege; doves flew down to sip it and instantly died, uncovering the plot. Now the Delphians seek Creusa, to stone her. When she rushes in the chorus tells her to fly to the altar as a suppliant. As she does so Ion enters. He reviles Creusa, and calls on his unknown mother. As he prepares to seize Creusa the priestess of the temple enters, carrying a casket which holds the clothes he was wearing when he was left at the temple. She gives the casket to Ion as a clue to his mother and tells him to search for her. Ion weeps. His mother must have suffered as much in losing him as he did in losing her. Yet he would rather not know who she is than learn that she is unworthy. Creusa glimpses the robes in the casket and cries out. She recognizes them as those in which she wrapped her new-born child, and proves that she knows them by describing the embroideries on them. Mother and child are made known to each other and embrace. Happy to have found his mother, Ion is still troubled, for he cannot understand why Apollo has caused them to suffer. The goddess Athena now appears, sent, she says, by Apollo to tell Ion that he is the god's son, and that he must go to Athens with Creusa; that he will become king, and that his four sons will father four Athenian tribes. The goddess warns Ion and Creusa not to let Xuthus know that Ion is really Creusa's son, and predicts that Creusa will have sons by Xuthus. Creusa and Ion join in praising Apollo, and rejoice that their sufferings are ended.

Ionia (ī-ō′ni-a̱). In ancient geography, a maritime region on the W coast of Asia Minor, including Chios, Samos, and the adjacent islands. It included the mainland cities of

Phocaea, Clazomenae, Erythrae, Teos, Lebedus, Colophon, Ephesus, Priene, Myus,
Miletus, and later Smyrna. According to
tradition, it was colonized about the 11th
century B.C. by Ionian refugees fleeing from
the Greek mainland before the invading
Dorians. Conquered by Croesus in the middle of the 6th century B.C., it passed later to
Persia, was the scene of an unsuccessful revolt, 500-494 B.C., became, on the close
of the Persian War, a dependent ally of
Athens, but passed again to Persia in 387,
and to Macedonia in 334 B.C. Later it fell
to Pergamum and Rome. Ionia was noted
for its wealth, and for the early development of art, music, philosophy, and literature.

Ionian Islands (ī-ō´ni-an). In ancient geography, the islands lying in the Ionian Sea
W of Greece, and including Corcyra or Kerkyra (Corfù), Paxos, Leucas (Levkas),
Ithaca (Ithaki or Thiaki), Cephallenia
(Kephalonia), Zacynthus (Zante) and many
smaller islands. Cythera, off the southern
coast of the Peloponnesus, is sometimes
counted among the Ionian Islands. The
seven principal islands may be referred to
as the Heptanesus. (JJ)

Ionians (ī-ō´ni-anz). People of ancient Ionia,
either refugees from the Greek mainland,
possibly organized by Athens, who colonized
the region, or, according to some scholars, a
mixed Hellenic group who became even more
mixed by intermarriage with the indigenous
groups of the region. It is supposed that
the Ionians received an alphabet of conso-
nants from Phoenician traders, to which they
made the enormous contribution of adding
vowels. According to tradition, the Ionians
were descendants of Ion, son of Apollo and
Creusa. They were driven out of their land
in the Peloponnesus by the Dorian invaders,
the Heraclidae. The Ionians fled to Attica
where they were received kindly and settled. Under the sons of Codrus, legendary
Athenian king, the Athenians say that the
Ionians embarked on colonizing expeditions
to Asia. But some say Codrus was really
a Messenian, and they say the Athenians
claimed him and his descendants to rein-
force their claim that Athens was the mother
of the Ionian cities. But the Athenians point
to the "tunic-trailing Ionians" mentioned by

Homer in the *Iliad* as being Athenians. The
Ionians attacked the coasts of Asia for the
purpose of establishing colonies, seized cities
already there, and in some cases founded
new ones. They had 12 cities in Asia and
would admit no more. They were: Miletus,
Myus, and Priene, in Caria; Ephesus, Colophon, Lebedus, Teos, Clazomenae, and
Phocaea, in Lydia; Erythrae and the island-
cities of Samos and Chios. These 12 cities
were the counterparts of the 12 cities they
had formerly had in Aegialus. According to
Herodotus, though they spoke different dialects of Attic Greek, they were all most
anxious to be considered pure Ionians as
distinct from the Dorian and other nations
of Asia. And as he points out, though their
cities were in fact colonized by Abantes,
Minyans, Cadmeans, Dryopians, Phocians,
and others who were not even Ionian in
name, since they set such store by it, he was
willing to let them call themselves Ionians.
The true test of the Ionian race was that they
came from Attica and celebrated the feast of
the *Apaturia,* Herodotus says. This feast
was held once a year, and at this time all
children born in the preceding year whose
birth entitled them to citizenship were registered. All the Ionian cities, except Ephesus
and Colophon, prohibited by reason of an
act of bloodshed, celebrated the Apaturia.
And all the Ionians gathered to celebrate
the feast of Panionia at the temple of Heliconian Poseidon, near Mycale. This united
them culturally and preserved their distinction from other Greek nations in Asia.

Ionian Sea. [Italian, **Mar Ionio**; Latin, **Mare
Ionium.**] Part of the Mediterranean between Greece on the E and S Italy and Sicily
on the W.

Ionic Order (ī-on´ik). In architecture, one of
the three Greek orders, so named from the
Ionic race, by whom it was held to have been
developed and perfected. The distinguishing
characteristic of this order is the volute of
its capital. In the true Ionic the volutes
have the same form on the front and rear,
and are connected on the flanks by an ornamented roll or scroll, except in the case of
the corner capitals, which have three volutes
on their two outer faces, that on the external
angle projecting diagonally. The spiral fillets of the volute are continued along the

face of the capital, beneath the abacus. The shaft, including the base and the capital to the bottom of the volute, is normally about nine diameters high, and is generally fluted in 24 flutes, separated by fillets. The bases used with this order are various. The Attic base often occurs, and is the most beautiful and appropriate. The architrave is normally formed in three bands, each projecting slightly beyond that below it, the whole crowned by a rich molding. The frieze frequently bears figures in relief. The cornices fall under three classes: the simple but richly molded and strongly projecting Greek cornice, and the less refined dentil and modil-

IONIC ORDER
A) volute; B) anthemion band; C) shaft; D) base

lion (Roman) cornices. Beautiful examples of the Ionic order are the Erechtheum and the Temple of Nike Apteros on the Acropolis at Athens. The details of the Erechtheum are notable for the delicate elaboration of their ornament; but the interior capitals of the Propylaea are, in their simple purity of line, perhaps the noblest remains of the Greek Ionic. The order was probably evolved by the Ionian Greeks from forms found in Assyrian architecture.

Ion of Chios (ī'on, ī'on; kī'os). Greek writer, born c490 B.C., and died before 421 B.C. He was an aristocrat and was the friend of Cimon and the Spartan king, Archidamus. He wrote lyric poems, tragedies, and a cosmological work in prose. The Alexandrian critics placed him on their list of outstanding tragic poets. Among his writings was a book of memoirs which included descriptions of noted persons who visited Chios. A long anecdote about Sophocles survives from this in the work of Athenaeus.

Iophon (ī'ō-fon). Distinguished Greek tragic poet, the son of Sophocles. According to a well-known but doubtful story, in Sophocles' later years Iophon tried to have the management of his estates transferred to his hands on the grounds that Sophocles was incompetent to manage them. In his defense, Sophocles read to the jury an ode from the *Oedipus at Colonus,* which he was then writing, proved that he was in full possession of his faculties, and kept charge of his own affairs.

Ios (ī'os). [Also: **Nio.**] Island in the Aegean Sea, one of the Cyclades, about 12 miles SW of Naxos. Length, about 11 miles; area, about 46 square miles.

Ioxus (ī-ok'sus). In Greek legend, a grandson of Theseus and Perigune. He led a colony to Caria where his descendants, the Ioxids, worshiped the wild asparagus and refused to burn or destroy it, because it had sheltered their ancestor Perigune.

Iphianassa (if″i-a-nas'a). Named by Homer (*Iliad*) as a daughter of Agamemnon. She was offered by her father to Achilles as a wife if he would forget his quarrel with Agamemnon and return to fight at the side of the Greeks, in the tenth year of the Trojan War.

Iphianassa. In Greek legend, a daughter of Proetus and Antia. With her two sisters, she was driven mad, for offending either Dionysus or Hera, and was cured by Melampus. She later married Bias, brother of Melampus.

Iphicles (if'i-klēz, ī'fi-klēz). In Greek legend, the twin brother of Heracles; son of Amphitryon (a mortal) and Alcmene, Heracles being the son of Zeus and Alcmene. According to some accounts, Amphitryon wanted to find out which of the two boys was his own son. He therefore put two harmless serpents in the cradle where the infants were sleeping. Heracles grasped the serpents firmly and strangled them, laughing as he did so, but Iphicles screamed and tried to hide. Thus Amphitryon knew that Iphicles was his son. But others say that Hera introduced the serpents, which were deadly, into the cradle to destroy Heracles but was frustrated by the fearless strength of Heracles. Iphicles was the father of Iolaus, the faithful companion of Heracles. Iphicles and Heracles were also companions in several adventures before Iphicles was killed in the war which Heracles waged against Augeas, king of Elis.

Iphiclus (if′i-klus, ī′fi-). In Greek legend, the only son of Phylacus, king of Phylace. He was a famous runner, who was reputed to be able to run over a field of standing grain without bending it, and to be able to speed over the sea. Nevertheless, he was beaten by Nestor in a footrace, according to Nestor. According to some accounts, he was one of those who joined Jason on the expedition of the Argonauts. His father was the possessor of famous flocks and herds and Melampus, the seer, tried to steal them for his brother Bias. Being caught, Melampus was imprisoned, but freed when he told Phylacus how Iphiclus could be cured of his childlessness. Melampus said that Iphiclus had been frightened when, as a child, he saw his father approaching him with a bloody knife with which he had been gelding rams. Phylacus stuck the knife into a tree and ran to comfort Iphiclus. Melampus instructed Phylacus to find the knife, scrape rust from it into wine, and give the wine to Iphiclus. After this had been done Iphiclus and his wife Clymene had two sons: Protesilaus, who was the first Greek killed at Troy, and Podarces, who then took command of the Phthians in his place.

Iphiclus. In Greek legend, a son of Thestius. He took part in the Calydonian Boar Hunt and in the expedition of the Argonauts to Colchis.

Iphicrates (ī-fik′ra-tēz). Athenian general, from Rhamnus; fl. first half of the 4th century B.C.; died c353 B.C. He was noted for his military reforms. He equipped his soldiers, called *peltasts,* with light shields and javelins,

which gave them much greater mobility for the raiding tactics he increasingly employed than the heavy armor worn by the hoplites. He emphasized drill and discipline; he lengthened the swords and javelins the soldiers carried, and introduced the wearing of leggings, called "Iphicratid boots." In the Corinthian War (c391 B.C.) he attacked a band of 600 Spartan hoplites and destroyed them. In 388 B.C. he was sent to the Hellespont with 1200 peltasts and defeated a Spartan force near Cremaste, and assured Athenian command of the Hellespont and the Bosporus, for the time being at least. With his band of mercenaries he served various princes of Thrace. About 378 B.C. he married a daughter of the Thracian king Cotys. He later served the king of Persia, and then returned to Athens. From there he was sent to the relief of Corcyra, besieged by the Spartans. On his way he encountered a fleet of ten Syracusan ships, sent to help Sparta. He attacked and captured all but one of them (372 B.C.). As a captain of mercenaries he served sometimes against his own country. He was adopted by Amyntas, king of Macedonia, and with the fleet he was operating off the Macedonian coast he helped to secure the throne for Perdiccas, son of Amyntas, on the latter's death (368 B.C.). He sided with the Thracian king Cotys against Athens in a war over the Chersonese, but the Athenians later pardoned him, and made him commander, with Timotheus and Chares, of a fleet to put down a revolt of Chios. Timotheus and Iphicrates, experienced soldiers, disagreed with Chares' plan to attack Chios and refused to take part in it. Chares was driven off with losses. He accused Iphicrates and Timotheus of treachery. They were tried, but Iphicrates was able to secure his acquittal.

Iphidamas (i-fid′a-mas). In Homeric legend *(Iliad),* a Trojan, the son of Antenor and Theano. He was brought up by his grandfather Cisseus in Thrace, and married there. When he learned of the Greek attack on Troy he left his bride, sailed to Percote where he left his 12 ships, and journeyed overland to Ilium to aid his kinsmen. He bravely attacked Agamemnon but his spear failed to penetrate Agamemnon's shield and Agamemnon killed him with a sword thrust.

Iphigenia (if″i-jē-nī′a). In Greek legend, a

daughter of Agamemnon and Clytemnestra, and a sister of Orestes and Electra. Her father sacrificed her to Artemis at Aulis, where the Greek fleet was prevented from sailing to Troy by violent storms, to appease the goddess for the death of one of her creatures and to obtain favorable winds. However, as the knife was put to her throat Artemis snatched her up and substituted a hind in her place. Agamemnon thought that she had been taken to live among the gods, but Artemis wafted her to Tauris. There she became a priestess in the temple which contained a sacred image of Artemis. Her duty was to prepare all strangers who inadvertently landed in Tauris as victims to be sacrificed in the temple. After some time, two Greeks were brought before her to be cleansed before they were sacrificed. She gloated over the opportunity thus presented to avenge herself on the people who had been willing to slay her at Aulis, but in the course of talking to the two strangers and of hearing of many whom she had known, her love for her country and her people revived and she resolved to help them escape. First she would give them a message to take to her brother. She handed a scroll to one of the Greeks and, reciting the message contained in it, directed him to give it to Orestes. At that he handed it to his companion. When suitable proof was forthcoming that this was indeed Orestes the three made plans to escape which, with the aid of Athena, they subsequently did, taking the sacred image with them. According to some accounts, Iphigenia ended her days as a priestess in a temple, set up at Brauron, which thereafter housed the sacred image brought from Tauris. Iphigenia is sometimes said to have been the daughter of Theseus and Helen, and to have been adopted and brought up by her aunt, Clytemnestra. See *Iphigenia in Aulis* and *Iphigenia in Tauris*.

Iphigenia in Aulis. A drama by Euripides, produced after his death by his son, 405 B.C. The play opens outside the tent of Agamemnon in the Greek camp, as Agamemnon, in distress, tells an old servant that glory is bound up with peril, and ambition with trouble. The servant, remarking that since he is a mere mortal, joy and sorrow will be his lot and the will of the gods will prevail,

asks why he is troubled. Agamemnon relates the oath which Tyndareus compelled the suitors of Helen to take: that they would defend and protect the man she took as a husband. Now they are gathered at Aulis in fulfillment of their oath, to help Menelaus recapture Helen, who has been carried off to Troy by Paris. Agamemnon wishes someone else had been chosen commander. He has learned from the seer Calchas that the winds which hold them in Aulis are caused by the wrath of Artemis and only the sacrifice of Iphigenia will appease the goddess and send favorable winds. On the advice of Odysseus he has written to Clytemnestra commanding her to send their daughter to Aulis on the pretext that she is to be married to Achilles. Now his feelings as a father choke him. He has written the truth to Clytemnestra and asks the old servant to take it to prevent Iphigenia from journeying to Aulis.

Menelaus, who snatched the letter from the servant's hand, now enters and accuses Agamemnon. He reminds him that he sought out the glory of being captain of the Greeks. Furthermore, for his own pride's sake he agreed to the sacrifice of Iphigenia to obtain favorable winds so that he could lead his thousand ships against Troy. By changing his mind he has shown that he isn't fit to wield the power he craved, and all Hellas will suffer if a wife can be stolen from her husband with impunity. Agamemnon answers that he can't restore a virtuous wife to Menelaus, and he will not harm his own child to regain a beautiful but faithless wife for Menelaus.

A messenger announces the arrival of Iphigenia, with Clytemnestra and Orestes, and that everyone is curious as to her reasons for coming. Agamemnon, heartbroken, feels that as leader of the expedition he must carry out the sacrifice of his daughter, and is tormented by the responsibilities that fall on the highborn. His grief moves Menelaus, and he apologizes for his angry words. He offers to give up Helen and advises Agamemnon to disband the fleet. Agamemnon fears it is too late: Calchas will have told the oracles and the opinion of the armies will compel him to carry them out. They cannot kill

Calchas, as Menelaus now suggests, for Odysseus will stir up the mob against them.

Clytemnestra, radiant at the thought of the approaching marriage, greets Agamemnon with delight. Iphigenia, of all his children the one who loves him most, thinks he is sad to give her to a husband when he tells her it breaks his heart to part with his child. He interrupts Clytemnestra's eager questions and commands her to return to Argos. She refuses: he can command the army, but she will do what is fitting for a bride. Sad and worried, Agamemnon goes.

Achilles enters and complains about the delay in sailing. His men are restive; they want to proceed to Troy or return home. Clytemnestra joins him and is humiliated when she understands from his talk that he knows nothing of a proposed marriage. They both now learn for the first time, from the servant, of the oracles and of Agamemnon's trick to get Iphigenia to Aulis, and of his determination to sacrifice her. Achilles, angry and insulted that his name has been dragged into the affair, offers to help Clytemnestra save Iphigenia.

Iphigenia comes before Agamemnon, weeping, and when he asks why, Clytemnestra bluntly asks him if he means to murder his child. Both women plead with him, but he says the sacrifice must be carried out so that the fleet can sail and so that Hellas will hereafter be safe from wife-snatchers and raiders. As he leaves, Achilles returns, and tells them that the whole fleet has now learned of the oracles and demands that the sacrifice take place. When he raised his voice against it he was stoned. Even his own Myrmidons clamor for it and Odysseus has been named leader of a group to seize Iphigenia. As he again offers to fight to save her, Iphigenia speaks: she is willing to die to save Hellas; she will do it gloriously and her name will be blessed. Achilles, though admiring her unselfishness, urges her to think again, and if she changes her mind he will fight at the very altar to save her. When they are alone, Iphigenia tries to comfort Clytemnestra by picturing the glory she will have as the benefactress of Greece, and tells her she will go to the sacrifice alone. They depart.

Soon a messenger comes and calls Clytemnestra. His message is that, just as Calchas put the gleaming knife to Iphigenia's throat Iphigenia vanished, and in her place was a hind with its throat cut. Agamemnon comes and confirms the story. He says they are blest because their daughter has been chosen by the gods. Clytemnestra must take Orestes and go home now. He is going to Troy.

Iphigenia in Tauris. A play by Euripides, produced sometime between 413 and 408 B.C. As the play opens, Iphigenia is discovered before a barbaric temple on a desolate sea-coast. She stands near a blood-stained altar, and speaks of her ancestors and relates that her father thought he had killed her at Aulis. But Artemis carried her away and substituted a hind in her place as a sacrifice. The goddess had wafted her to Tauris where, as a priestess, she now prepares mortal victims to be sacrificed. Lately she has been saddened by a dream that convinces her that her brother Orestes is dead.

She goes into the temple and Orestes and Pylades enter furtively. Orestes reminds Pylades of his wanderings as a result of the slaying of his mother. Now he has come to Tauris, at Apollo's command, to fetch a sacred image of Artemis that lies in the temple. As Pylades encourages him, they leave, to hide until nightfall when they will attempt to steal the image.

Iphigenia returns, accompanied by her serving women, exiles like herself. She tells them of her dream and of her intention to perform funeral rites for Orestes. As she finishes the ceremonial rites a herdsman enters and describes two strangers who have been caught and who will be sacrificed to Artemis. He says they are Greeks and that one of them is mad. Iphigenia vows to be pitiless to these Greeks, the first who have fallen into her hands, since it was the Greeks who would have sacrificed her at Aulis. The bound victims are brought before her. She questions them and learns that Troy has fallen; Helen is living happily in Sparta with Menelaus; Calchas and Achilles are dead; Odysseus has not yet reached his home; Agamemnon is dead by his wife's hand; Clytemnestra has been slain by her son Orestes, and Electra is alive and unwed. On hearing of her family and her country Iphigenia's love for her people revives. Impulsively she offers to save the two Greeks and asks them to take a message to Argos. She will tell them what is in the message in case the scroll on which it is written should come to harm. She hands the scroll to Pylades, recites her message, and tells him to deliver it to Orestes. Thereupon, Pylades hands it to Orestes and says her message has been delivered. Orestes proves to her that he is really her brother and they are joyous in reunion. He tells her why he has come to Tauris. Immediately the three plan their escape from Thoas, king of the Taurians. Orestes suggests that they kill Thoas, but Iphigenia refuses to do this: Thoas has been kind to her. Instead, she proposes to tell him that Orestes, a matricide, must be purified in salt water, and that the image, which he had touched, must be purified also. In that way they will make their way to the sea, where a ship is moored, and make their escape. Iphigenia carries out this plan when Thoas comes, and tells him he must go into the temple and that all should cover their eyes during the ceremony of purification. The scheme succeeds and the three escape to the ship. As Thoas waits the end of the purification ceremony a messenger comes to tell him that the priestess has gone off with the strangers in a ship, but strong winds have driven them back to shore. Thoas, determined to recapture and kill them, is halted by the appearance of Athena. She tells him it is the will of the gods for Iphigenia to return to Greece with Orestes. At the same time she bids Orestes take the image to Greece and construct a temple for it. At the high festival in the temple she instructs that a sword must be touched to a man's throat, enough to draw a single drop of blood, as a record that Orestes had been saved from being sacrificed. Thoas, seeing that nothing will be gained from struggling against the gods, allows Iphigenia, Orestes, and Pylades to depart, and frees as well the exiled women who had attended Iphigenia.

Iphimedia (if″i-me̯-dī′a̯). In Greek mythology, the wife of Aloeus and the mother, by Poseidon, of Otus and Ephialtes, who were called the Aloidae, after their mother's husband. Iphimedia and her daughters were taken to Naxos by pirates, but were rescued by her sons, who then made themselves masters of the island.

Iphinoë (i-fin′ō̯-ē̯). In Greek legend, a daughter of Antia and Proetus. With her sisters, Iphianassa and Lysippe, she was driven mad, for offending either Dionysus or Hera. When Melampus sought to cure them the sisters fled wildly to Arcadia. Iphinoë died on the way.

Iphinoë. In Greek legend, a woman of Lemnos, who acted as Queen Hypsipyle's messenger when she invited Jason and the Argonauts to land and make themselves comfortable in Lemnos.

Iphis (ī′fis). In Greek legend, an Argive, the son of Alector. Polynices sought his advice when he wished to persuade Amphiaraus to join him in the expedition against Thebes. Iphis said that Eriphyle, wife of Amphiaraus, feared she was losing her looks and suggested to Polynices that he bribe her with the necklace of Harmonia (said to make its wearer beautiful), on condition that she persuade her husband to join the expedition. Some accounts list Eteoclus, son of Iphis, as one of the Seven against Thebes.

Iphis. According to legend, a maiden of Crete who was brought up as a boy. Before she was born her father had ordered her mother, Telethusa, to put the expected child to death if it turned out to be a girl, because he could not afford to bring up a girl. Io appeared to Telethusa in a dream and advised her to deceive her husband if the child was a girl, and to bring it up as a boy, and promised to help Telethusa if necessary. When Iphis was born the deception was carried out and the father, unaware of it all, in due course betrothed his supposed son to a beautiful Cretan maiden, Ianthe. Iphis fell desperately in love with Ianthe, and the love was returned. Telethusa delayed the marriage as long as she could. When delay was no longer possible, Telethusa prayed to Io and reminded her of her promise of aid. As Telethusa and Iphis left the temple, Io answered her prayers and Iphis was transformed into a man.

Iphition (i-fish′i-on). In Homeric legend (*Iliad*), a Trojan. He was the son of Otrynteus and the nymph of Lake Gygaea, and was slain by Achilles in the Trojan War.

Iphitus (if′i-tus, ī′fi-). In Greek legend, a son

of Eurytus, king of Oechalia; he was the
brother of Iole. He and his brother, Clytius,
joined Jason on the expedition of the Argonauts to Colchis. Iphitus tried to persuade
his father to honor the agreement which he
had made with Heracles: to give him his
daughter Iole if Heracles defeated him in an
archery contest, but when Heracles won
Eurytus refused to carry out his agreement.
Later, Eurytus missed some of his cattle, and
thought Heracles had taken them for revenge.
He sent Iphitus to bring them back. Iphitus
thought Heracles was innocent. Nevertheless he followed him and told him about the
missing cattle, Heracles, inwardly seething
because he erroneously thought Iphitus
suspected him, took him in to a tower in Tiryns,
asked him if he could see the cattle, and
when Iphitus admitted that he could not,
Heracles hurled him to his death. Iphitus
was the possessor of a famous bow, said by
some to have been given to Eurytus by
Apollo. Iphitus gave the bow to Odysseus,
who had gone to Iphitus' land in search of
some missing cattle, and it was afterwards
used by Odysseus to slay the suitors of
Penelope.

Iphthime (if'thi-mē, if-thī'mē). In the *Odyssey*, a daughter of Icarius. She was a sister
of Penelope, whose shape Athena assumed in
order to appear to Penelope in a dream and
to assure her that Telemachus was safe, and
that he was protected by the gods.

Ipoctonus (i-pok'to-nus). Epithet of Heracles.
The people of Erythrae in Asia Minor worshiped Heracles under this name because he
killed the bugs that attack the vines. The
name means "Worm-" or "Grub-killer."

Ipsus (ip'sus). In ancient geography, a town
in W central Asia Minor, in Phrygia. Here,
in 301 B.C., Lysimachus and Seleucus defeated and slew Antigonus, and brought to
an end the wars carried on by the successors
of Alexander the Great.

Ire (ī'rē) or **Ira** (-ra). Ancient town in Messenia, on the eastern shore of the Gulf of
Messenia. It was one of the seven gift cities
offered by Agamemnon to Achilles if he
would give up his quarrel with Agamemnon
and return to the battle in the Trojan War.
Later Abia, nurse of a descendant of Heracles, built a temple of Heracles here. When
Cresphontes became master of Messenia he

changed the name of Ire to Abia in honor of
her.

Irene (ī-rē'nē). In Greek mythology, the goddess of peace; one of the three daughters of
Zeus and Themis known as the Horae (goddesses of order and the seasons). The Romans identified their Pax with Irene.

Iris (ī'ris). The "wind-footed" messenger of
the gods, and the goddess of the rainbow—
the arc that touches sky and earth. She was
the daughter of Thaumas and Electra and
was the sister of the Harpies. She could go
to the ends of the earth or even to the Un-

IRIS
Red-figured Attic vase, 5th century B.C.

derworld on her golden wings, and traveled
along the rainbow, carrying messages to gods
as well as to men. In the *Iliad* she is the
messenger from Zeus who warns the gods not

to help their favorites, or stir up the courage of the Trojans. Later she was considered more especially as the messenger of Hera. She was sent by Hera to tell Peleus to prepare for his marriage to Thetis; to warn the Boreadae not to kill the Harpies; to tell Menelaus that Paris had carried off Helen; to release Dido's soul from her body after she had committed suicide in despair over being abandoned by Aeneas. As a messenger, Iris had no will of her own, but must convey the commands, for good or ill, as she was instructed to do. Some say that as Hera's messenger she carried a jug of water which put perjurers to sleep.

Iron Age. In classical mythology, a name given to the last (and the worst) of the four ages of mankind or the world, as described by Hesiod and Ovid. It is an age of hard work and agricultural toil, of constant care and trouble, of shame and falsehood, of moral, mental, physical, and spiritual decay; a period in which the only thing that triumphs is Evil. In this age, the land, which was formerly common to all, is divided into private property and becomes a source of conflict. Iron and gold are discovered and find use as material for arms in the wars that continually erupt. The evils of men are so great that Justice leaves the earth and retires to Olympus. It is in marked contrast to the first, and best, age, the Golden Age, when Cronus (Saturn) ruled, and is inferior even to the Silver Age, when people were foolish and arrogant, and to the Bronze (or Brazen) Age, which was an age of war. Hesiod, who described the Ages of Man, and with particular bitterness his own Age of Iron, also wrote of the Age of Heroes, in which men descended from gods fought gloriously and at the end of their days were transported to the Elysian Fields. This Age preceded the Iron Age.

Irus (ī'rus). In the *Odyssey*, a nickname given to Arnaeus, a beggar of gigantic stature whose size deluded him into thinking he was as strong as he looked. He kept watch over the suitors of Penelope and was employed by them as a messenger, whence his nickname. When Odysseus, disguised as a beggar, returned to his own palace, Irus threatened him and told him to be off. He wanted no other beggars poaching on his territory.

Odysseus refused to leave and Irus, egged on by the amused suitors, challenged him to a fight, hoping that his challenge would not be accepted. Odysseus was glad to accept, however, and with one mighty blow knocked him out of the palace. He never begged in those halls again.

Isaeus (ī-sē'us, -zē'-). One of the Ten Attic orators, and a professional writer of speeches. He was born at Chalcis or Athens c420 B.C.; died 350 B.C. He was a pupil of Isocrates and, some say, a teacher of Demosthenes. His 11 extant orations, mainly on contested inheritances, provide considerable light on the private law of Athens.

Isander (ī-san'dėr). In Homeric legend (*Iliad*), a son of Bellerophon, and the brother of Hippolochus and Laodamia. He resigned his claim to his father's kingdom in favor of his nephew Sarpedon. While fighting against the Solymi he was slain by Ares.

Isauria (ī-sô'ri-a). In ancient geography, a district in Asia Minor on the northern side of the Taurus range, bounded by Phrygia on the N, Lycaonia on the E, Cilicia on the S, and Pisidia on the W. The surface was rugged. The inhabitants were famous in guerrilla warfare. They were defeated by Servilius in 76 B.C., and by Pompey, but continued unsubdued.

Ischepolis (is-kep'ọ-lis). In Greek legend, a son of Alcathous, king of Megara. He went to join Meleager in the hunt for the Calydonian Boar and was slain. His body was returned to Megara and buried near the law courts there.

Ischia (ēs'kyä). [Ancient names, **Aenaria, Pithecusa.**] Volcanic island in the Tyrrhenian Sea, situated about 16 miles W of Naples. It was early colonized by Greeks from Eretria and Chalcidice, but was abandoned by them because of the volcanic eruptions of Monte Epomeo. Hieron I, tyrant of Syracuse, sent a garrison there (c470 B.C.) but they refused to stay when the volcano erupted again. The island has many hot springs and was known as a spa from Roman times. In ancient times it was known as Pithecusa (q.v.).

Ischys (is'kis). In Greek mythology, a son of Elatus of Arcadia. Coronis, beloved by Apollo, was unfaithful to the god with Ischys. White crows reported her infidelity to Apollo and were turned black for bringing the bad

fat, fāte, fär, fãre, errant; net, mē, hėr ardent; pin, pīne; not, nōte, möve, nôr,

news (which the all-seeing god already knew), instead of remaining to peck out the eyes of Ischys. Ischys was slain, either by a thunderbolt of Zeus or by an arrow of Apollo.

Isernia (ī-sėr′ni-ạ). See **Aesernia.**

Ishtar (ish′tär). [Also: **Istar.**] Principal goddess of Assyrian and Babylonian mythology, great mother-goddess or earth-mother goddes of love, fertility, sex, and war. As mother-goddess she was identified with the Sumerian Nana or Inanna, Phoenician Astarte or Ashtoreth, Greek Aphrodite, Roman Venus. She was also associated with the planet Venus. In her warlike character she was conceived of by the Babylonians as ruling the morning star; as goddess of love she ruled the evening star. The Assyrians distinguished between the Ishtar whose shrine was at Arbela, who presided over battles, and Ishtar of Nineveh, in whom the voluptuous aspect predominated. Ishtar also occurs as an appellation, or generic name, for a goddess in general. The story of Ishtar and her lover Tammuz, his death, her mourning for him, and her descent to the Underworld to bring him back, the parching of the earth in her absence, and the return of vegetation with her return is the great vegetation myth of Asia Minor and the Mediterannean region.

Isis (ī′sis). In Egyptian mythology, the chief female deity; the sister, wife, and female counterpart of Osiris, and the mother of Horus. The most famous of all Egyptian goddesses, she was distinguished by the solar disk and cow's horns on her head, and in this aspect was often identified with Hathor. She was identified by the Greeks with Athena and Demeter. Her worship in a modified form, as a nature-goddess, was introduced subsequently to the Alexandrine epoch into Greece, and was very popular at Rome from the end of the Republic. The Greek and Roman priests and priestesses of Isis wore a special costume, and had as an attribute a form of dance rattle, the *sistrum*, which traveled with the cult of Isis through the Roman Empire as far as Gaul. On her statue was an inscription mentioned by Proclus: "I am that which is, has been, and shall be. My veil no one has lifted. The fruit I bore was the Sun"; hence the well-known allusion to a mystery as covered with "the veil of Isis." In Egypt she

was also identified with Sothis, the Dog Star, and in later days with the planet Venus. As Neith she was the divine originator and patroness of weaving and other womanly arts. Her cult persisted in Europe until the latter half of the 6th cenutry A.D.

Island of the Sun. An island where the magnificent oxen of the Sun (Helius) lived. Whoever ate of the oxen was doomed to death. It was here that Odysseus lost his entire company because, in spite of warnings given them by Circe and Odysseus, they slew and roasted some of the cattle. The island was Trinacria (Sicily).

Islands of the Blest. Another name for the Elysian Fields, or Elysium, the last home of heroes, sons of the gods, and those whose noble lives or participation in the Mysteries of Demeter earned them the happiness of dwelling there.

Ismarus (is′mạ-rus). In Greek legend, a Theban who killed Hippomedon in the war of the Seven against Thebes.

Ismarus. A city of the Cicones, on the northern shores of the Aegean Sea. It was sacked by Odysseus on his way home from Troy. It was from this city that Odysseus took the wine which he later used to such advantage on Polyphemus, the chief of the Cyclopes.

Ismene (is-mē′nẹ). In Greek legend, a daughter of Oedipus and Jocasta, and the sister of Antigone, Eteocles, and Polynices. She dared not join Antigone in her defiance of Creon when he forbade anyone to bury the body of Polynices, who had been slain attacking Thebes. Ismene wanted to share Antigone's punishment when the latter was led away to her death for her defiance, but Antigone scorned her. She told Ismene that since she had cautiously refused to act in defiance of Creon because she desired to live, now she must live.

Ismenium (is-mē′ni-um). Place in Boeotia where there was an oracle of Apollo. Oracles were given as a result of the inspection of entrails of victims.

Ismenus (is-mē′nus). According to Greek tradition, a son of the river-god Asopus and Metope. He went to Boeotia and settled on the banks of the small river that flows by Thebes and is called the Ismenus River in his honor.

Isocrates (ī-sok′rạ-tēz). One of the Ten Attic

Orators, a professional speech-writer and teacher of rhetoric. He was born (436 B.C.) at Athens, the son of a wealthy flute manufacturer, and received a good education. When his father lost his money in the Peloponnesian Wars Isocrates was compelled to earn his living. He studied with Gorgias, and then went to Chios, where he taught rhetoric. On his return to Athens he opened a school (c392 B.C.) of rhetoric and philosophy. This school, intended to further the study of history, dialectics, mathematics, literature, and the use of language, was highly successful. He numbered among his pupils statesmen, poets, historians, and the orators Isaeus, Hyperides, and Lycurgus. Isocrates' view of life, expounded in his *Speech on the Exchange of Property,* was to steer a middle course between the purely practical and the purely philosophic. He defended his course on the ground that the practical man lacks culture and imagination, while the philosopher becomes too detached from life. He found that his course was much criticized from both directions, but his school and the culture he imparted in it were extremely popular. It is said that through shyness and because of a weak voice he kept aloof from an active public life. He attempted to exercise political influence through his writings. His *Panegyricus,* written (380 B.C.) for the Hundredth Olympiad, extolled the contributions of Athens to Greece, urged the Spartans to share supremacy of Greece with Athens, and exhorted all the Greek states to abandon their rivalries and unite against the barbarians. He was a friend and admirer of Evagoras of Salamis who alone fought against the Persians for eight years. When Evagoras was assassinated Isocrates transferred his admiration to his son. In 356 B.C. Isocrates addressed himself to Archidamus, king of Sparta, urging him to unite the Greeks on the mainland and free the Greeks in Asia. Archidamus failed him. Isocrates recognized that Philip of Macedon was the rising power. With unimpaired patriotism after the first peace with Philip (346 B.C.), he addressed him and urged him to seize the magnificent opportunity he now had to unite Greece, make himself the champion of liberty, and become the benefactor of the world. His views on Philip and the

Macedonians made him extremely unpopular. He lived, in full vigor of mind and body, nearly 100 years, and saw all his hopes for Greek unity and democracy completely crushed. In 338 B.C., a few days after the Battle of Chaeronea in which Philip defeated the Athenians and the Boeotians, Isocrates died. Some say he starved himself to death in despair over the loss of Greek liberty. Isocrates was a master of style, whose influence extended to all subsequent Greek prose. According to Gilbert Murray, the essay-writing of Isocrates' school "forms in one sense the final perfection of ancient prose, in another the ruin of what was most characteristically Attic or indeed Hellenic. It is smooth, self-restrained, correct, euphonious, impersonal. . . . It has lasted on from that day to this, and is the basis of prose style in Latin and in modern languages." Of the *Orations of Isocrates,* which he did not speak himself but wrote for others, 21 are extant.

Issus (is'us). In ancient geography, a town in Cilicia, SE Asia Minor, situated near the head of the Gulf of Issus, about 45 miles E of what is now Adana, Turkey. Here Alexander the Great defeated (333 B.C.) the Persians under Darius III; Septimius Severus defeated (194 A.D.) his rival Pescennius Niger; and Heraclius defeated (622) a Persian army.

Ister (is'tėr). An ancient name for the Danube River.

Istria (is'tri-a). [Also: **Ister, Istropolis.**] In ancient geography, a colony of the Milesians, founded about the time of the Cimmerian invasion of Asia Minor (7th century B.C.), near the mouth of the Ister (the modern Danube). It was a trading center for the lower Danube basin for many centuries.

Istvaeones (ist-vē'ō-nēz). Group of ancient Germanic tribes inhabiting the Rhine region, mentioned by Tacitus, and including the Batavi, Bructeri, Chatti, Sicambri, Tencteri, Ubii, and Usipetes. The last four tribes are also mentioned by Julius Caesar: the Tencteri and Usipetes as having invaded Gaul in 55 B.C., the Sicambri whose villages he burned, and the Ubii whom he protected against the Suebi (Suevi).

Isus (ī'sus). In Homeric legend (*Iliad*), a bastard son of Priam. In the early days of

fat, fāte, fär, fãre, errạnt; net, mē, hėr ardẹnt; pin, pīne; not, nōte, mŏve, nôr,

the Trojan War he was captured, with his half-brother Antiphus, by Achilles but was released for ransom. Later, he joined the battle and in the tenth year of the war was slain by Agamemnon.

Italica (i-tal′i-ka̤). Ancient Roman town in Spain, near Seville; founded by Scipio Africanus in 206 B.C. It has ruins of an amphitheater, and is said to have been the birthplace of three emperors: Trajan, Hadrian, and Theodosius I.

Ithaca (ith′-a̤-ka̤). [Modern Greek, **Ithake, Thiaki.**] One of the Ionian Islands, about two miles NE of Cephallenia. According to tradition, it was the center of the island kingdom of Odysseus, which comprised in addition, the islands of Dulichium, Same, and Zacynthus, and was the site of his palace. As described in the *Odyssey,* it has no plains suitable for agriculture or the rearing of horses, but has a topography well adapted for goats. The location of Ithaca, commanding the routes to Corcyra, Elis and Triphylia, and the western entrance to the Gulf of Corinth, could have given it the maritime importance it had as Odysseus' kingdom. From this island he sailed with 12 ships to accompany the Greeks to Troy. Some say that the topographical descriptions given by Homer in the *Odyssey* fit the island Leukas more accurately than Ithaca. And other scholars, in consideration of the topographical details, point out that Homer was writing poetry, and his descriptions are not necessarily to be taken as a geographical guide, although in fact they have been so taken, successfully in some cases. Excavations by archaeologists have not been able to support either claim; the question remains an open one.

Ithomatas (i-thō′ma̤-ta̤s). Epithet of Zeus, meaning "Of Ithome." When Polycaon and Messene first came into the Peloponnesus they established a precinct of Zeus Ithomatas on the summit of Mount Ithome in Messenia. Subsequently the worship of Zeus Ithomatas was neglected, but it was reëstablished by Glaucus, the grandson of Cresphontes. The Messenians claimed that Zeus was born in their land, and was reared by two nymphs— Neda, for whom a river was named, and Ithome, for whom Mount Ithome was named. The Messenians carried water from the

spring, where the infant Zeus was said to have been bathed after he was born, to the sanctuary of Zeus Ithomatas. The image in the temple was made by Ageladas. The priest of Zeus Ithomatas, who was chosen annually, kept the image in his house; annually also a festival, the *Ithomaea,* was held. In the First Messenian War with Sparta, the oracle at Delphi told the Messenians that the side that first set up 100 tripods in the precinct of Zeus Ithomatas would win. The Messenians set about making tripods, but the Spartans learned of the oracle also, and one of their number fashioned 100 tripods of clay and secretly entered the precinct where he set them up. Again, when Aristodemus, the Messenian leader in the war, was about to sacrifice to Zeus Ithomatas, the victims rushed into the fire of their own accord; this too, was an omen of Messenian defeat and in fact the Messenians lost the war. In the Second Messenian War the besieged Messenians became suppliants at the altar of Zeus Ithomatas, and were allowed to depart under a truce, because the Spartans were warned by an oracle not to harm the suppliants of Zeus Ithomatas. In 371 B.C. when the new city of Messene was founded with the aid of Epaminondas, the Messenians sacrificed to Zeus Ithomatas when the foundations of their new city, of which Mount Ithome was one wall, were laid. The Messenians claimed that Leuctra, in Laconia, was once a part of Messenia, because once a fire destroyed a forest there, and when the ground was bared a statue of Zeus Ithomatas was found to have been dedicated there. The finding of the image confirmed the Messenians in their claim that Leuctra had once been Messenian.

Ithome (i-thō′mē). A strong, natural fortress west of the Pamisus River in the western mountains of Messenia. To it the Messenians withdrew in the First Messenian War with Sparta (8th century B.C.), and walled it. In the Second Messenian War (7th century B.C.), under the command of Aristomenes, they were again defeated after a long struggle, but were permitted to withdraw from their fortress on Mount Eira unharmed on condition that they never return to the Peloponnesus. Before he left, Aristomenes returned to Ithome and in a remote spot buried the mysteries that had been brought to Messenia by Caucon. Nearly 300 years later, the mysteries were recovered, owing to a dream had by Epaminondas, the Theban conqueror of the Spartans at Leuctra (371 B.C.). His dream instructed him to restore the Messenians to the land where the mysteries were found. He recalled them from their exile all over the Greek world, and to the music of flutes helped them to lay out a new city, which bore the name Messene. Ithome formed the citadel of the new city, and one side of its boundaries.

Itius Portus (ish'i-us pôr'tus). In ancient geography, the place from which Caesar sailed for Britain; generally identified with Boulogne or Ushant (Ile d'Ouessant).

Itonia (i-tō'ni-a). Epithet of Athena. Some say the goddess was the daughter of the Boeotian Itonius. There was a sanctuary of Athena Itonia in Boeotia, at which the annual assemblies of the Boeotians were held. At another sanctuary of Athena Itonia, between Pherae and Larisa in Thessaly, Pyrrhus dedicated thè shields he took from the Gallic mercenaries of Antigonus II (273 B.C.). Pyrrhus, king of Epirus, caused the following inscription to be put with the shields: "Pyrrhus the Molossian hung these shields taken from the bold Gauls as a gift to Itonian Athena, when he had destroyed all the host of Antigonus. It is no great marvel. The Aeacidae (descendants of Aeacus) are warriors now even as they were of old."

Itonius (i-tō'ni-us). In Greek mythology, a Boeotian, said by some to be the father of Athena and Iodama.

Itylus (it'i-lus, ī'ti-). In Greek mythology, the only child of Aëdon and Zethus. Aëdon, jealous of Niobe and her seven sons and seven daughters, plotted to slay Niobe's oldest son as he slept with Itylus. By mistake she killed Itylus and was transformed by Zeus into a nightingale, forever mourning for her son.

Itys (ī'tis, it'is). In Greek legend, the son of Tereus and Procne, killed and served as a meal to his father by Procne and her sister Philomela. Tereus had seduced Philomela and torn out her tongue. After the revenge of the sisters, they fled, with Tereus in pursuit. See **Procne**.

Iulus (ī-ū'lus). In Latin legend, a son of Ascanius (son of Aeneas) or, according to

DEATH OF ITYS
Red-figured Attic kylix, early 5th century
B.C. Procne holds her son Itys, as Philomela
gesticulates. *Louvre*

other accounts, a surname of Ascanius himself.

Ivory Gate. In classical mythology, the gate of sleep by which false dreams are sent from the lower world.

Ixion (ik-sī'on, ik'si-on). In Greek mythology, a son of Phlegyas, king of the Lapithae. In order to avoid paying the gifts he had promised so that he might marry Dia, daughter of Eioneus, he constructed a hidden pit in front of his palace, in which he placed a red-hot charcoal fire. When Eioneus came to the palace he fell into the pit and was consumed by the fire. Aeschylus names Ixion as the first murderer. Nevertheless, Zeus purified him and even invited him to dine with the gods. But Ixion had no gratitude. On the contrary, he planned to seduce Hera, sister and wife of Zeus. Zeus forestalled him in this by substituting a cloud in the form of Hera in Ixion's arms. The cloud-born woman, Nephele, eventually bore Centaurus, ancestor of the centaurs, to Ixion but in the meantime Ixion was punished for his presumption in daring even to think of embracing Hera. He was fixed to a fiery wheel and revolves eternally in the deepest reaches of Tartarus, in the section of Hades reserved for the desperate men who have sinned against the gods.

fat, fāte, fär, fāre, errant; net, mē, hèr ardent; pin, pīne; not, nōte, möve, nôr,

Iynx (ī'inks). In Greek mythology, a daughter of Pan and Echo. According to some accounts, it was she who caused Zeus to fall in love with Io, by putting a spell on him. She was transformed by Hera into a wryneck, a kind of woodpecker.

——J————

Janiculum (jạ-nik'ụ-lum). [Also: **Mons Janiculus, Mons Aureus**; Italian, **Monte Gianicolo**.] Long ridge or hill in Rome, on the W bank of the Tiber, extending S from the Vatican, and opposite the Capitoline and Aventine hills. It is the highest of the seven hills of Rome, attaining an elevation of about 276 feet. At its highest point, guarding the Via Aurelia which here crosses the Janiculum, was an early blockhouse. Where the 3rd-century wall of Aurelian (270–275 A.D.) crosses the Via Aurelia was the Porta Aurelia, dismantled in 1643 and replaced by the modern Porta San Pancrazio. Nearby are the buildings of the American Academy. (JJ)

Janus (jā'nus). In Roman mythology, the ancient god of doorways and the special patron of the beginning of all undertakings, explained as the spirit of the doorway, its *mana* or *numen*. As god of beginnings his blessing was sought for the beginning of each day, month, and year, and at births, the beginning of life. As a Roman deity, he was credited with having given man the knowledge of agriculture, civil law, and coinage. As the protector of doors and gateways, he was represented as holding a staff or scepter in the right hand and a key in the left; and as the god of the sun's rising and setting he had two faces, one looking to the east, and the other to the west. His temple at Rome was kept open in time of war, and was closed only in the rare event of universal peace. His festival, the *Agonia* or *Agonalia,* was celebrated on January 9.

Jason (jā'sọn). In Greek legend, a son of Aeson. His mother is variously named as Perimede, Amphinome, Alcimede, and Polymede. Pelias, the half-brother of Aeson, seized Aeson's throne in Iolcus and would have killed Jason but his mother pretended that he had been born dead and lamented over him. She then spirited him away to Chiron the centaur, who brought him up on Mount Pelion. When he reached manhood, Jason returned to Iolcus to claim the throne. On the way he came to the Anaurus River. It was in flood and an old hag waiting on the bank asked him to carry her across. Jason did so, although many others had refused her request. (The old hag was Hera in disguise, and from then on she aided and protected Jason.) As he was crossing the river he lost one of his sandals in the mud. He arrived therefore before Pelias, clad in a leopard skin, but wearing only one sandal. Now Pelias had been warned to beware of a man wearing one sandal, and when he saw Jason he was frightened. He asked Jason who he was. Jason told him his name and his errand, and the relationship between the two was revealed. Pelias assured Jason that he would be glad to give up the throne in his favor, but that he was troubled by the ghost of Phrixus, which haunted him with the demand that the Golden Fleece of the ram on which Phrixus had escaped from Orchomenus, and which now hung in a grove in Colchis, be restored to Hellas. Once the Fleece was brought back, Pelias assured him, he would be glad to give up the throne. Jason agreed to go to Colchis to secure the Golden Fleece. Other accounts say that when Pelias saw Jason shod with one sandal, he asked him what he would do if he knew someone threatened his life. Jason replied that he would send him to Colchis to fetch the Golden Fleece. Hera had put these words into his mouth, wishing to bring glory to Jason and to punish Pelias.

However it happened, Jason made ready to go to Colchis. Many heroes of Greece responded to his call to help him secure the Fleece, among them Heracles, Iphiclus, Admetus, Oileus, Telamon and Peleus, Idmon, Castor and Polydeuces, Mopsus, Augeas,

Idas and Lynceus, Meleager, the Boreadae, various sons of Hermes, Poseidon, Apollo, and many others. A ship was built at Pagasae and named the *Argo* after Argus, who built it with Athena's help. Those who sailed in her became known as the Argonauts. Jason was made commander of the expedition. The *Argo* sailed from Pagasae, and after a brief stop on the coast of Magnesia, went to Lemnos. There the Argonauts were beguiled for more than a year by the Lemnian women who, having killed all the males on the island, were delighted to welcome the Argonauts. Jason became the father of two sons, Euneus and Nebrophonus, by Hypsipyle, the Lemnian queen. After more than a year had passed, Heracles, according to some accounts, reminded the Argonauts of their mission and they continued their journey. In the course of the voyage the Argonauts landed among the Doliones, and by a tragic mistake killed their king Cyzicus. In Mysia they lost Heracles, who was separated from his companions while he searched for his squire Hylas. On the island of the Bebryces, Amycus, their king, challenged any member of the crew of the *Argo* to a boxing contest. He was defeated and killed by Polydeuces, and his followers were crushed by the Argonauts. Continuing, the Argonauts landed at Salmydessus in Thrace, where they found Phineus, a son of Agenor or Poseidon. He was living in misery, tormented by Harpies who defiled his food, and blinded by Zeus because of his power to predict the future accurately. The Boreadae banished the Harpies and Phineus gave the Argonauts much valuable advice on how to avoid the pitfalls that lay ahead of them. Leaving Phineus, they passed safely through the Symplegades, the "Clashing Rocks," sailed by the land of the Mariandyni after having been welcomed there by the king, and passed the country of the Amazons, and the island of Ares. There they found King Aeëtes' four grandsons who had been shipwrecked, and took them aboard the *Argo* to return them to Colchis.

After many adventures in which Jason was often discouraged, they arrived in Colchis, the kingdom of Aeëtes where hung the Golden Fleece. King Aeëtes was enraged when he learned the errand of the Argonauts, but he planned to avoid giving up the Fleece by making Jason submit to a test which he was sure would destroy him. He agreed to give Jason the Fleece if he could yoke two fire-breathing bulls, plow a field, and sow it with the dragon's teeth which Athena had given to Aeëtes. These dragon's teeth had come from Thebes where Cadmus had killed the dragon, sown some of the teeth, and given the rest to Athena. Hera and Athena, anxious for Jason, appealed to Aphrodite to aid him. The goddess of love and beauty bribed her son Eros with a golden ball, and he caused Medea, daughter of Aeëtes, to fall in love with Jason by piercing her with one of his arrows at the instant when Medea's eyes lighted on Jason. Torn between her filial duty and the great love which had come to her so suddenly, Medea decided to betray her father by telling Jason how he could succeed in the trial of courage which her father had set for him. She met Jason in a grove at night and offered her help. Jason promised to take her to Iolcus and to marry her in return for her aid. She gave him the Charm of Prometheus which made invulnerable for one day the person and weapons of whoever was anointed with it. This protected him from the fire-breathing bulls. She told him that when he sowed the dragon's teeth, armed men would spring up. He must cast a stone among them, whereupon they would fight each other to the death. Jason followed her instructions and successfully carried out the test that Aeëtes had set for him.

Aeëtes, however, was enraged. He knew that Jason had succeeded only with the help of Medea, and plotted to seize and kill him. Medea warned Jason of her father's intentions. She lulled the never-sleeping dragon and allowed Jason to steal the Golden Fleece; then they fled to the ship and sailed from Colchis, pursued by Aeëtes. Some say Apsyrtus, brother of Medea, went with them, and that Medea cut him to pieces and flung the parts of his body into the sea. This delayed Aeëtes in his pursuit, because he stopped to gather the pieces of his son's body for burial. Others say Apsyrtus pursued Jason with a large fleet, that he was lured into meeting Medea alone, and that Jason sprang out on him from ambush and killed him. The Argonauts then continued their flight. But they were harassed by many ills. At last the sacred oak of Dodona, which had been placed in the hull of the *Argo* by Athena, spoke to Jason and informed him his woes would not cease until he had been purified for the murder of Apsyrtus. He was to go to the island of Circe where the enchantress would sprinkle the blood of a pig on his hands and purify him.

After being purified, Jason and the Argonauts continued their journey. They passed the Sirens successfully, and with the help of Thetis navigated safely by the Wandering Rocks and Scylla and Charybdis. They landed at length on Drepana (also known as Corcyra) and were received by Alcinous, king of the Phaeacians. Here the Colchians caught up with them and would have taken Medea, but Arete, wife of Alcinous, persuaded her husband not to give up Medea if she were already married to Jason. But if they were not married he would hand Medea over to the Colchians. Arete immediately arranged a wedding. When the Argonauts at last returned to Iolcus (for more detailed information on the voyage of the *Argo*, see **Argonautica**), Jason learned that his father and mother were dead and that the king Pelias, having heard a false rumor that the Argonauts had all perished, had slain his young brother, Promachus. Jason planned to attack Pelias and seize the throne. However, Medea disposed of Pelias single-handed by means of her magic arts. Jason arranged good marriages for the three daughters of Pelias and out of fear of vengeance resigned the throne of Iolcus to Acastus, the son of Pelias. He then took the Golden Fleece to Orchomenus and hung it in the temple of Zeus. Next he dedicated the *Argo* to Poseidon on the Isthmus of Corinth. Then he and Medea went to Corinth where they lived happily together for ten years and became the parents of several children, some say seven boys and seven girls.

At the end of this time Jason proposed to leave Medea and to marry Glauce (or Creusa), daughter of Creon, the king of Corinth. Medea reminded him of all he owed to her. But Jason persisted in his plan to abandon Medea, although he offered to make suitable provision for her and her children. Medea, inflamed by his ingratitude, sent a robe to Glauce as a wedding gift. It was impregnated with magic and the instant Glauce put it on, it burned her to ashes. Her father also was consumed by the flames which sprang from it. Medea fled in a winged chariot drawn by dragons, after killing some of her children, and Jason too was forced into exile for being false to his oath to Medea. He wandered friendless about Greece and at last came to the Isthmus of Corinth where he had beached the *Argo*. As he sat in the shadow of its hull, remembering his past glorious exploits, the prow of the old ship broke off and fell on him, killing him instantly. To show that the *Argo* was innocent of his death, its image was set among the stars. The legend of Medea's betrayal and revenge spawned many variants. In Euripides' tragedy, for instance, Jason and Medea, with two sons, are living in exile at Corinth when the king offers Jason his daughter's hand in marriage, and with it the right of succession. It is Jason's eagerness to embrace this opportunity to repair his fortunes which triggers Medea's insane response.

Jaxartes (jak-sär′tēz). In ancient geography, a river (modern Syr Darya) of Scythia, in C Asia. Alexander the Great crossed the river (328 B.C.) and penetrated Scythia. Returning, he founded a city on the banks of the Jaxartes where it crossed the borders of Sogdiana. He named the new city Alexandria Eschata (*Furthest*), because it was intended to mark the northeastern limit of his empire. In succeeding centuries, the name of the city was changed to Khodjend. It is now Leninabad, in the Tadzhik Soviet Socialist Republic, U.S.S.R.

Jocasta (jō-kas′ta) or **Jocate** (-tē). [Called in Homer: **Epicaste**.] In Greek legend, a daughter of Menoeceus of Thebes and the sister of Creon. She was married to Laius, king of Thebes. When her son was born, Laius had his feet pierced and bound and ordered him exposed on Mount Cithaeron, because an oracle had foretold that his son would slay him and marry his mother. But his orders were not carried out. Oedipus, his infant son, fell into the hands of Polybus of Corinth and was brought up by him and his wife Merope as their own son. On reaching manhood, Oedipus fled from Corinth, because he regarded Polybus and Merope as his parents and he had been made aware of the oracle by visiting Delphi. On the road he met Laius and, unaware of his true identity, killed him. He then solved the riddle of the Theban Sphinx, thus causing her death, and went to Thebes where he was made king and given the newly widowed Jocasta for a wife. Jocasta bore him two sons, Eteocles and Polynices, and two daughters, Antigone and Ismene. When dark hints began to gather that Oedipus himself might be the murderer of Laius, for whom all Thebes—led by Oedipus—was seeking in order to lift a plague, Jocasta tried to persuade him to give up his investigations. She also pleaded with him to cease his inquiries into his origin. To his talk of oracles she cited many which, as she thought, had not come true. She said an oracle had told Laius that he would be slain by his son, but that his son had been exposed, and Laius was killed by robbers. But all the reassuring things she told him became hollow as the pieces of Oedipus' story fell into place. When Jocasta learned the horrifying truth that he was actually her son, his father's murderer, and the father of her children, she hanged herself.

Josephus (jō-sē'fus), **Flavius.** [Usually shortened to **Josephus.**] Jewish priest, soldier, statesman, and historian; born at Jerusalem, 37 A.D.; died at Rome, sometime between 95 and 100 A.D. The son of a priest and descendant of royalty, he studied Hebrew law and Greek and Hebrew literature. After spending three years in the desert with Banus, a hermit, he was chosen to serve as a delegate to Nero in 64. Upon his return from Rome, he was appointed governor of Galilee by the Sanhedrin, the great council of the Jews at Jerusalem. In 66 he was active in the Jewish revolt against Rome, and led in the defense of Jotapata for 47 days before he surrendered to Vespasian. He won the favor of the latter (as he had previously won that of Nero's mistress Poppaea Sabina) by making predictions calculated to please his hearers (he told Vespasian that he would become emperor). He went with Vespasian to Alexandria, was later

freed, adopted the family name of Vespasian (Flavius), became a Roman citizen, and was given a pension and a considerable estate in Judea. He continued to enjoy the protection of Vespasian, and later of Titus and Domitian (he was with Titus at the fall of Jerusalem in 70 A.D.). His works are a *History of the Jewish War*, in seven books, first written in Aramaic and then translated into Greek; *Antiquities of the Jews*, in 20 books, dealing with the history of the Jewish people from the beginning of time to the year 66; *Vita* (his autobiography), in which he denies the charges made by his enemy, Justus of Tiberias, that he was responsible for the Jewish rebellion; and *Contra Apionem*, two essays in which he defends the Jews against the attacks of Apion, an anti-Semitic Alexandrian.

Juba I (jö'ba). [Also: **Iuba.**] Committed suicide, 46 B.C. King of Numidia, an ally of Pompey. He defeated the Caesareans under Curio in 49 B.C., and in 47–46 B.C. supported Metellus Scipio, whose forces were defeated at Thapsus. Following this, Juba died by his own hand at Zama.

Juba II. [Also: **Iuba.**] King of Mauretania, son of Juba I of Numidia; died c19 A.D. He was taken to Rome (46 B.C.) as a young child to form part of Caesar's triumphal procession and eventually became a protegé of Octavian. He was made king of Numidia c30 B.C., married Cleopatra Selene, daughter of Antony and Cleopatra, in 29 B.C., and was transferred by Augustus to Mauretania in 25 B.C. He established his capital at an old Carthaginian depot, Iol, which he renamed Caesarea (modern Cherchel). He was noted as a man of broad culture, as an art collector and author, in Greek, of many works on history and natural history, now all lost. (JJ)

Jugurtha (jö-gér'tha). [Also: **Iugurtha.**] Executed at Rome, 104 B.C. King of Numidia; son of Mastanabal and grandson of Masinissa. On the death of his uncle Micipsa in 118 B.C., he and Micipsa's two sons inherited the kingdom. He usurped western Numidia in 117 B.C. and eastern Numidia in 112. A war with Rome commenced as a result in 111, and he contended against Metellus in 109 and 108 and against Marius in 107 B.C. He was captured by Sulla, was exhibited by

Marius in a triumphal procession at Rome in 104 B.C., and was then put to death by strangling.

Julia (jöl'ya̲). Daughter of Julius Caesar and his first wife Cornelia. She was born c83 B.C.; died 54 B.C. She was betrothed to Servilius Caepio, but instead became the wife of Pompey the Great in 59 B.C. At this point in his career Caesar needed Pompey's armies and his influence, and he used his daughter as a means of gaining Pompey's support. When she died in childbirth, Caesar gave a gladitorial show and a public banquet in her honor.

Julia. Daughter of Augustus Caesar and Scribonia, born 39 B.C.; died at Rhegium, 14 A.D. She was married in 25 B.C. to Marcus Claudius Marcellus, on whose death in 23 B.C. she became the wife of Marcus Vipsanius Agrippa, by whom she became the mother of Caius and Lucius Caesar, Agrippa Postumus, Julia, and Agrippina. After Agrippa's death in 12 B.C., she married Tiberius for reasons of state. Her private life was the scandal of Rome, and it was particularly galling to Augustus when he learned of it, as he regarded himself as the upholder of public morals. Tiberius divorced her, and Augustus banished her, first to the island of Pandataria, and afterward to Rhegium.

Julia. Daughter of Marcus Vipsanius Agrippa and Julia, daughter of Augustus Caesar; died 28 A.D. She seemed to have inherited the vices of her mother, and was banished by Augustus in 9 A.D. to the island of Trimerus.

Julian Calendar. A calendar instituted by Julius Caesar, radically reforming the lunar calendar previously in use at Rome, whose intercalations had invited political manipulation. Advised by Sosigenes, a Greek astronomer from Alexandria, Caesar added 80 days to the year 46 B.C., giving it 445 days in all, to bring the civil year into agreement with the solar. He made 45 B.C. the first year of a new calendar based on the ancient solar calendar of Egypt, with 12 months of 31 or 29 days, totaling 365 days; unlike the Egyptian calendar, provision was made for the intercalation of one extra day every four years. (This, the most accurate calendar devised up to that time, nevertheless incorporated an error of three days every 400

years. By the time of Pope Gregory XIII this amounted to ten days, necessitating the further correction contained in Gregory's Bull of February 24, 1582, giving us the Gregorian Calendar, now in general use.) Even Caesar's calendar suffered a mishap at the start; for some years the intercalary day was mistakenly added every *third* year instead of every fourth (the Romans counting both ends of a period, as usual), resulting in an error which was discovered and corrected during the principate of Augustus. The lengths of the months in days, however, have remained unchanged since the time of Augustus. (JJ)

Julian Emperors. Collective name for the Roman emperors Augustus, Tiberius, Caligula, Claudius, and Nero, as members by birth or adoption of the family of Julius Caesar.

Juno (jö'nō). In Roman mythology, the queen of heaven, the highest deity in the Roman pantheon next to Jupiter, of whom she was both the sister and the wife. As a daughter of Saturn she was identified with the Greek Hera. She was the special protectress of marriage. Under her auspices the bride was conducted to the bridegroom's house, the door posts were anointed to bring her favor, and the marriage girdle was untied. The month of June (named for her) is still the popular marriage month. She was also guardian of women from birth to death. The *Matronalia,* her most famous festival, was celebrated on March 1 by every matron and virgin. And ever woman had her own tutelary *juno,* conceived of as a kind of guardian spirit. As *Juno Lucina* (Light-bringer) she was invoked during childbirth as the goddess who brings from darkness into light. A table was spread for her in the house where a child was born, and a gold piece was deposited in the treasury of her ancient temple in the sacred grove at Rome on the birth of a boy. In Rome a temple was erected in 344 B.C. by Camillus to *Juno Moneta,* the epithet being explained by later Romans as derived from the warning of the goddess on the occasion of an earthquake. A mint was established in this temple in the 3rd century B.C. and thus the epithet *Moneta* in various forms became associated with matters of finance. As *Juno Regina* she headed the state cult along with Jupiter. Her chief temple on the Capitoline Hill close to that of Jupiter contained her sacred geese. As *Juno Curitis* she was regarded as a war-goddess, especially worshiped by the Sabines, and she was represented as clad in a goatskin mantle bearing a shield and an uplifted spear, and accompanied, like Athena, by a sacred serpent. As *Juno Lanuvina* she had a special cult and priesthood at Lanuvina, where her sacred serpents ate the cakes offered by virgins and refused all others. The raven was sacred to her as the protectress of citadels.

In the *Aeneid,* Juno was the implacable enemy of Aeneas because: 1) she feared that the Trojans would destroy her favored city of Carthage, 2) she still hated all Trojans for the Judgment of Paris, and 3) she resented the taking of Ganymede who was made a favorite of Jupiter. It was she who bribed Aeolus to unloose the winds that shipwrecked the Trojans on the shores of Carthage. When Dido fell hopelessly in love with Aeneas, Juno thought to unite them in marriage. First, however, she arranged a plot with Venus to unite them without marriage. She sent a storm which isolated them in a cave where Dido submitted to Aeneas. When, on orders from Jupiter, Aeneas later left Carthage without marrying Dido, Juno, in pity for her desperate plight, sent Iris to part Dido's agonized soul from her body. It was Juno who incited the Trojan women to burn the ships while Aeneas was celebrating funeral games in honor of Anchises in Sicily; who sent Alecto to arouse the Latin women under Amata against Aeneas; who goaded Turnus to war and opened the gates of war herself when Latinus refused to do so. Jupiter allowed her to delay the death of Turnus in the war with Aeneas, but nothing could change Aeneas' ultimate fate, which was to found a great race in Italy. Juno at last gave up her struggle to prevent the fulfillment of Aeneas' destiny, asking only that the Latins be allowed to keep their name and language, so that the line would be Roman and the very name of Troy erased. To this Jupiter consented.

Juno Inferna (in-fėr'na). A Roman name for Proserpina as a goddess of the lower world.

Junones (jö-nō'nēz). In Roman mythology, guardian deities of women.

Juno Stygia (sti'ji-a). In Roman mythology, a name for Proserpina, goddess of the Underworld.

Jupiter (jö'pi-tėr). [Also: **Jove.**] In Roman mythology, the supreme deity, predominantly a sky-god. The name *Jupiter* (*Iuppiter*), also found in Latin as *Diespiter*, reveals its original conception as a sky-god by its linguistic connection with *diēs* (Latin: "day"), and *dēus* (Latin: "god"). The second element of the name represents the Latin word for "father." It is related to Greek *Zeus.* Jupiter was both brother and husband of Juno. As a son of Saturn (Uranus) and Ops (Rhea), he was identified with the Greek Zeus, and was the embodiment of the might and national dignity of the Romans. The central seat of his cult was the Capitoline Hill at Rome, where as god of the state he had the title of Optimus Maximus (*Best and Greatest*). He was the bringer of light, of the dawn as well as of the full moon, and the days of the month when the moon was full were sacred to him. His priests sacrificed a white lamb on these days in his honor. He was the "Thunderer," whose weapon was the thunderbolt, and all places struck by lightning were sacred to him. As god of the sky, he was the originator of all atmospheric changes. Farmers honored him at the time of the spring sowing as well as at the time of the harvest, and a special festival was celebrated in his honor in his capacity as rain-god. He controlled and directed the future, and sacrifices were offered to secure his favor (with that of Janus) at the beginning of every undertaking. Except for Mars, he was the most honored as the god of victory in war. He was also the guardian of property, whether of the state or of individuals, and also guardian of honor, the keeping of oaths, treaties, vows, and the laws of hospitality. It was Jupiter who brought blessings and good fortune to the family as well as to the nation. White, the color of the light of day, was sacred to him: hence white animals were offered to him in sacrifice, his priests wore white caps, his chariot was drawn by four white horses, and the consuls were dressed in white when they sacrificed to him upon assuming office. The eagle was especially consecrated to him. As the most honored god of Rome, elaborate festivals were celebrated for him. Among them were the Roman Games, the oldest and greatest festival, originally celebrated in September by victorious generals in honor of Jupiter. Originally of one day's duration, the Roman Games finally came to cover a span of 15 days.

In the *Aeneid,* Jupiter consoles Venus for the ills besetting her son Aeneas by predicting the success of Aeneas in Latium; a 30-year reign for his son Ascanius; a 300-year rule by the Trojan dynasty; and after that the birth to a priestess and Mars of twin sons who would found the Roman nation. He also prophesied that the time would come when the children of Troy would enslave the children of Agamemnon, Diomedes, and Achilles, and rule in Argos, and foretold the birth of Julius Caesar, named after Iulus, who would rule from sea to sea. Jupiter sent Mercury to Aeneas in Carthage to command him to leave Dido and get on with his destiny; if he did not care about himself, he must consider the heritage of Ascanius. He sent torrential rains to quench the fires that the Trojan women had set to burn the fleet in Sicily. As did Zeus in the *Iliad,* Jupiter said he would not interfere in the fighting between Aeneas and Turnus for a time when Venus and Juno expressed their grievances about the fate of these two respectively. Although he allowed Juno to put off the death of Turnus for a time, he assured her that this would not change the outcome of the war, and ultimately he commanded her to give up her attempts to prevent Aeneas from fulfilling his destiny. Fate was on the side of Aeneas. However, he conceded to Juno that the new race which Aeneas would found should be known as a Latin race and keep its Latin tongue, in order to erase the name of Troy and Trojan, so hated by Juno. Thus it was that the line became established as Roman.

Justitia (jus-tish′i-a̱). In Roman mythology, the personification of Justice, similar to Greek Dikê (Dice).

Juturna (jö-tẻr′na̱). A Roman goddess of springs. She is named in the *Aeneid* as the sister of Turnus. She was loved by Jupiter and by him made goddess of lakes, rivers, and springs, and was also given immortality. In the war between the Trojans under Aeneas, and the Latins under Turnus, Juno sent Juturna to give Turnus whatever help she could. She inflamed the Latins by sending a false omen, and thus inspired Tolumnius to break the truce which had been declared. In the mêlée that followed she replaced Turnus' charioteer and drove his war car away from the fighting in order to protect him. At length he recognized that his charioteer was his sister in disguise, leaped out of the chariot and returned on foot to the battle. When Turnus later fought in single combat with Aeneas, she recognized the owl that plagued her brother during the fight as one of the Furies sent by Jupiter. Knowing herself defeated by Jupiter in her struggle to preserve Turnus, she lamented the immortality that caused her to outlive her brother, and abandoned him to his fate. There was a pool sacred to Juturna in the Forum at Rome.

Juvenal (jö′ve̱-nal). [Full Latin name, **Decimus Junius Juvenalis.**] Roman rhetorician and satirical poet of the age of Trajan; fl. c50–130 A.D. Little is known of his life. Sixteen of his satires (in five books) are extant; they display an epigrammatic style that is bitingly used to expose the flagrant vices of the Roman society of his day.

Juventas (jö-ven′ta̱s). In Roman mythology, the goddess who protected the *iuvenes,* men of military age. She had a shrine in the cella of Minerva in the great temple on the Capitoline, and a temple close to the Circus Maximus. Juventas has been erroneously identified as the Roman counterpart of Hebe (q.v.) and as a goddess of youth.

K

Kalamai (kä-lä′mē). An unimportant ancient village at the foot of Mount Taÿgetus in Messenia, S Greece, now known as Kalámi. The name has been transferred to the modern port city of Kalamai or Kalamata, near the mouth of the Nedon river, which stands on the site of Pherae (Pharae) of Homeric legend. (JJ)

Kalamai or **Kalamata** (kä-lä-mä′tä). The modern port city which stands on the site of the Homeric Pherae or Pharae in S Messenia. The name *Kalamai* is borrowed from an ancient village (now Kalami) which stood several miles further inland. See **Pherae.** (JJ)

Kalamata (kä-lä-mä′tä). See **Kalamai.**

KALPIS
Black-figured, warriors fighting, c510 B.C.
Metropolitan Museum of Art

Kalpis (kal′pis). A water-vase, usually of large size, resembling the hydria, and like it having three handles, but differing from the hydria in that the posterior handle does not extend above the rim.

Kamares or **Camares** (ka-mä′res). A cave on the S slope of Mount Ida in Crete. In it the British School of Archaeology found important remains of the Middle Minoan civilization; particularly the polychrome vases painted in white, red, and yellow on a black glazed ground that came to be known as "Kamares ware."

Kanish (kä′nish). [Modern name, **Kultepe.**]

In ancient geography, a town in C Asia Minor, in the Anatolian plateau, about 100 miles N of what is now Adana, Turkey. Silver was mined here for Assyria c1900 B.C.; it was a Hittite center.

Kea (ke′ä), or **Keos** (ke′ôs). See **Ceos.**

Kephallenia (ke″fä-le-ne′ä). See **Cephallenia.**

Kephisos (ke-fe-sôs′). See **Cephissus.**

Keres (ke′rez). In Greek mythology, malign or evil spirits associated with death, sometimes regarded as souls of the dead, or as goddesses dealing death through the medium of disease. In late mythology, they became identified with the Furies.

Khios (ke′ôs). See **Chios.**

Khubur (kö′bur). In Babylonian mythology, the river between the land of the living and the land of the dead, which souls had to cross to reach the Underworld. It is analogous to the Styx of later Greek cosmogony.

Kithairon (ke-the-rôn′). See **Cithaeron.**

Knights, The. Comedy of Aristophanes which was exhibited in 424 B.C. and won first prize. It was a comedy with a political target— Cleon, an Athenian demagogue and leader of the democratic party, who opposed efforts to make peace with Sparta during the Peloponnesian Wars. In the play an elderly gentleman, Demus, falls completely into the power of his scheming Paphlagonian slave, a leather-monger. (The slave represents Cleon, whose father was a tanner.) After a wild struggle, in which the participants fling the most uninhibited abuse at each other, the Paphlagonian loses his control over Demus to a vendor of black puddings, who has won by out-lying, out-cheating, and out-stealing the Paphlagonian. In the end, the black-pudding vendor is transformed into an honest man, Demus recovers control of his own destiny, and an eloquent appeal to patriotism closes the play.

Knossos (nos′os). See **Cnossus.**

Kolonos Hippios (ko-lō′nos hip′i-os). See **Colonus.**

Kore (kō′re). [Also: **Cora.**] In Greek mythology, one of the names of Persephone, daughter of Zeus and Demeter. She was called Kore or Cora especially in her fertility-cult aspects. The meaning of the name is "Maiden."

Korinthos (kô′ren-thôs). See **Corinth** and **Corinthia.**

Kos (kos). See **Cos.**

Kyklades (kē-klä′thes) or **Kykladon Nesoi** ka̧-klä′thôn nē′sē). See **Cyclades**.

Kylix (kī′liks). [Also: **Cylix**.] In ancient Greece, a vase or cup of elegant form, used for drinking. The kylix was usually broad and shallow, with or without a slender foot, and provided with two handles not extending above the rim. Those with the slender foot closely resemble modern champagne glasses.

Kythera (kē′thē-rä) or **Kytherion** (kē-thē′rē-ôn). See **Cythera**.

—L———————

Labdacus (lab′da̧-kus). In Greek legend, a son of Polydorus, king of Thebes, and Nycteis. He was king of Thebes himself, and was the father of Laius, and the grandfather of Oedipus. Labdacus gave his name, Labdacidae, to Oedipus and his children.

Labeo (lā′bē-ō), **Attius**. First-century A.D. Latin poet, reported to have made Latin hexameter translations, evidently of no great merit, of the *Iliad* and the *Odyssey*. (JJ)

Laberius (la̧-bir′i-us), **Decimus**. Roman knight, born c115 B.C.; died at Puteoli, Italy, in January, 43 B.C. He was the author of mimes or popular farces, comic and satirical poems, an epic poem on Caesar's Gallic War, a prose work containing anecdotes, and others. Titles, some lines, and a prologue (given when Caesar compelled him, though a knight, to act in a mime) are extant.

Labienus (lab-i-ē′nus), **Quintus**. Roman general; son of Titus Labienus. As a republican opposed to Antony and Octavian, and commander of Parthian mercenaries, he invaded (41–40 B.C.) Syria and Asia Minor where after some successes, he was defeated and killed in 39 B.C.

Labienus, Titus. Roman general; killed in battle, 45 B.C. He was early a partisan of Caesar and helped him to secure the office of Pontifex Maximus (63 B.C.). He was distinguished as Caesar's legate in the Gallic War, and acted for Caesar whenever the latter had to be away in Rome. As a general in Gaul, he defeated the Treviri (54 B.C.), made an expedition against Lutetia (Paris, 52), and defeated the Aedui (52 B.C.). When civil war broke out, he joined Pompey (49 B.C.). After the defeat at Pharsalus he fled to Africa. From there he went to Spain and joined the forces of the younger Pompey, and was killed at the battle of Munda, 45 B.C.

Labors of Heracles or **Hercules**. See **Heracles, Labors of**.

Labyrinth (lab′i-rinth). "Place of the double ax," from *labrys* "double-bladed ax." In Greek legend, a vast maze built at Cnossus by the Athenian artificer Daedalus at the command of Minos, ruler of Crete. It was built as a place in which to confine the Minotaur, the child with a bull's head and human body born of the union of Queen Pasiphaë with a handsome bull in the royal stables. On the walls and furnishings of Minos' great palace at Cnossus the double ax appears repeatedly, suggesting that it was a symbol of Minos' regal authority, so that "Hall of the Double Axes" would be an appropriate epithet for this extensive structure. The concept of a labyrinth as a maze would thus have arisen later, in consideration of the Labyrinth's hundreds of rooms and endless corridors, and the difficulty of a stranger in finding his way about it. (JJ)

Lacedaemon (las-e-dē′mon). In Greek mythology, a son of Zeus and the Pleiad Taÿgete. Some say he married the niece of Taÿgete, also named Taÿgete, who bore him a son, Himerus, and a daughter, Cleodice. But others say he married Sparta, the daughter of Eurotas, and inherited her father's kingdom. He named the people of his kingdom (formerly called Leleges) Lacedaemonians after himself, and named the Mountain Taÿgetus after his mother. He founded a city in Laconia, and named it Sparta after his wife, from which the name finally was applied to the entire kingdom. There was a hero-shrine of Lacedaemon at Alesiae in

Laconia, and the Spartans claimed that it was he who instituted the worship of the Graces, of whom there were only two, according to the Spartans, named Cleta and Phaenna.

Lacedaemon. See **Laconia** and **Sparta,** both in ancient Greece.

Laches (lā′kēz). Athenian general; fl. last half of the 5th century B.C. He commanded an expedition to Sicily, 427 B.C. The expedition accomplished little largely because Laches and his treasurer were more interested in enriching themselves than in pursuing the interests of Athens. He later (423 B.C.) presented to the Athenian assembly the proposals for a one-year truce with Sparta, drawn up by Nicias and Plistoanax. He appears in the dialogue of Plato which bears his name.

Laches. One of the dialogues of Plato; a conversation on courage between Lysimachus, the son of Aristides, and Melesias, the son of the elder Thucydides (who are considering the question of the education of their sons), the generals Nicias and Laches, and Socrates.

Lachesis (lak′e-sis). In Greek mythology, one of the three Moerae or Fates. As first explained by Hesiod, Lachesis assigns the lot of life to each person, Clotho spins the thread of it, and their sister Atropos cuts it. (JJ)

Laconia (la-kō′ni-a). [Also: **Lacedaemon, Laconica.**] In ancient geography, the SE division of the Peloponnesus, Greece, lying S of Argolis and Arcadia, and E of Messenia. It was traversed by the Eurotas River. Chief city, Sparta.

Laconia, Gulf of. [Modern Greek, **Lakonikos Kolpos;** Latin, **Laconicus Sinus.**] Arm of the Mediterranean S of Laconia, Greece.

Lade (lā′dē). In ancient geography, a small island in the Aegean Sea near Miletus. Near it, in 494 B.C., the Persian fleet defeated the Ionian Greeks.

Ladon (lā′don). In Greek mythology, a many-headed dragon or serpent that had the power of human speech and never slept. According to some accounts he was the son of Ceto and Phorcys. Others say he was the son of Typhon and Echidna, or that he was earth-born. He was set to guard the Apples of the Hesperides, either by Hera or by Atlas, and was slain by Heracles when he came to steal the apples. He was then translated to the heavens as the constellation Serpentarius.

Ladon. In ancient geography, a river in Arcadia, Greece. Rising in the mountains near Pheneüs, it is, according to Pausanias, the most lovely river in Greece. The river-god of the Ladon was, according to some accounts, the father of Daphne beloved by Leucippus and Apollo. The nymph Syrinx fled to the Ladon, pursued by Pan, and on its banks she was transformed into a reed. Pan, not knowing which reed was Syrinx, cut the reeds he found in the place where she was last seen and made them into a musical instrument called the syrinx, or Pan's pipes.

Laelaps (lē′laps). According to legend, a marvelous hound that was given to Procris, wife of Cephalus, by Artemis. The hound had the power of always catching whatever it pursued. Amphitryon borrowed the hound to catch a vixen that had been sent to plague Thebes. The vixen had the gift of always out-running its pursuers. As Laelaps, the dog that always caught its quarry, chased the vixen that could never be caught, Zeus settled the matter by turning them both into stone. According to some accounts it was Minos who had received Laelaps from Artemis, and gave him to Procris in return for her favors.

Laelius (lē′li-us), **Caius.** Roman general and consul; fl. c200 B.C. He was a friend of the elder Scipio Africanus, whom he accompanied on his campaign in Spain (210–206 B.C.). In 205 B.C. he led an expedition to Africa, and in the battle of Zama (202 B.C.) distinguished himself as commander of the cavalry. He served as aedile (197), praetor (196), and consul (190 B.C.).

Laelius (lē′li-us), **Caius.** [Surnamed **Sapiens,** meaning "the Wise."] Roman statesman and philosopher, praetor in 145 B.C., consul in 140 B.C., and closely associated with the younger Scipio Africanus. He is the chief character in the *De Amicitia* of Cicero, which is therefore often called *Laelius,* and appears as a speaker in Cicero's *De Senectute* and *De Republica.* He was one of the aristocratic party in opposition to the reforms of the Gracchi.

Laertes (lā-ėr′tēz). In Greek legend, a son of Acrisius the Argive. He was married to Anticlea, daughter of Autolycus. Some say he was one of the Argonauts who went on the expedition to secure the Golden Fleece. In Homer Laertes is represented as the father of Odysseus. Later writers said that Odysseus was the son of Sisyphus, but he passed as the son of Laertes. During the long absence of Odysseus at the Trojan War and after it, Laertes retired to his farm in the country and grieved for his son. He was still living when Odysseus returned, was joyously reunited with him, and helped him confront the fathers of the suitors of Penelope, whom Odysseus had slain on his return.

Laertiades (lā″er-tī′a-dēz). "Son of Laertes," e.g., Odysseus.

Laestrygones (les-trig′ō-nēz). [Also: **Laestrygonians**.] In the *Odyssey*, a race of cannibal giants visited by Odysseus in a remote country, where "the nights are so short that the shepherd driving his flock out meets the shepherd who is driving his flock in," clearly an echo of some traveler's tale of northern latitudes. Eleven of Odysseus' 12 ships moored in their nearly landlocked harbor and went to scout the countryside, while only Odysseus anchored outside. The ships in the harbor were attacked and destroyed by the man-eating Laestrygones, who devoured their crews, only Odysseus' ship escaping. Later writers placed the Laestrygones in Sicily, S of Mount Aetna, and Roman authors blandly transferred them to Formiae (Formia) in Latium. (JJ)

Laevinus (lē-vī′nus), **Publius Valerius**. Roman consul, 280 B.C. He advanced with an army to meet Pyrrhus at Heraclea, and when Pyrrhus sent word to him that he would act as mediator between the Romans and the Greeks in Italy, Laevinus replied that he "neither accepted Pyrrhus as a mediator nor feared him as an enemy." At the battle which took place, 280 B.C., he was defeated by Pyrrhus with heavy losses on both sides.

Lais (lā′is). [Also: **Laïs**.] Name of two Greek courtesans celebrated for their beauty. The elder, probably a native of Corinth, lived in the 5th century B.C., and was famous for her beauty and for her vices. She died at Corinth, where a monument (a lioness tearing a ram) was erected to her. The younger (born probably in Sicily, and brought to Corinth when a child) lived in the middle of the 4th century B.C. Apelles is said to have induced her to follow the life of a courtesan. She is said to have been slain in Thessaly by women whose jealousy she had aroused.

Laius (lā′us, lā′yus). In Greek legend, a son of Labdacus, king of Thebes. He succeeded to the throne of Thebes but was expelled by Amphion and Zethus. He went to the court of Pelops at Pisa and was hospitably received. There he fell in love with Chrysippus, the bastard son of Pelops, and carried him off to Thebes. Pelops pursued him to Thebes but when he arrived Chrysippus was dead, some say by his own hand and some say his death was engineered by Hippodamia, wife of Pelops. Pelops forgave Laius and he was restored to the throne. He married Jocasta, daughter of Menoeceus, but time passed and she bore him no children. Laius consulted the oracle and was told he should not mourn his childlessness, for the child Jocasta bore him would kill him. Even so, Jocasta did ultimately produce a son to Laius but he, remembering the oracle, had the infant's feet pierced and bound and ordered him exposed on Mount Cithaeron. His order, unknown to him, was not carried out and the child, who was named Oedipus, "Swollen-footed," was reared by Polybus of Corinth as his own child. Hera sent a monster to punish Thebes because Laius had abducted Chrysippus. This monster, a Sphinx, ravaged Thebes by killing all who could not answer a riddle she propounded. Laius set out for Delphi to ask the oracle how he could free Thebes of the Sphinx. On the way he met Oedipus, neither knowing who the other was, and ordered him out of the road. Oedipus refused to move and angrily struck Laius' charioteer when the latter treated him violently. When he saw a chance, Laius struck the young stranger full on the head with his goad. Oedipus, enraged, set upon him, and killed him and all his companions save one, who escaped. Thus the oracle was fulfilled.

Lamachus (lam′a-kus). Athenian general, killed in Sicily, 414 B.C. With Alcibiades and Nicias he was one of the three commanders in charge of the Athenian expedition to Sicily, 415 B.C. He was not a rich man and had to be reimbursed for all expenditures he made for himself on his campaigns. Perhaps for this reason he was mocked by the comic poets. However, he was a brave and able soldier. When the Athenian expedition arrived in Sicily to aid the Egestaeans against the Selinuntines, allies of Syracuse, the commanders learned to their dismay that the Egestaeans were unable to advance the gold they had promised. Lamachus, with a purely military view, advised the Athenians to attack Syracuse at once, although this had not been the announced target of the expedition. He argued that Syracuse was the real enemy, and that the Athenians should take advantage of the unprepared state of the Syracusans and the panic into which the sight of the Athenian flotilla would throw them; for after a time, he warned, the Syracusans would recover their composure and prepare themselves for battle, and the advantages of surprise would be lost. The advice of Lamachus was ignored. In a skirmish before the city of Syracuse Lamachus was killed, 414 B.C.

Lamia (lā′mi-a). In Greek mythology, a daughter of Belus. She was a beautiful Libyan queen who was loved by Zeus. Zeus gave her the power to take out and replace her eyes at will. Hera, out of jealousy, killed all Lamia's children except Scylla; thereafter, because she could not revenge herself on Hera, Lamia sought to destroy the children of men. She is usually depicted with a serpent's body and beautiful woman's head. In later belief she was regarded as a seducer of young men. Keats's poem *Lamia* treats of this story.

Lamia. Athenian courtesan; fl. in the early 3rd century B.C. She possessed great influence over Demetrius Poliorcetes (Demetrius I of Macedonia).

Lamia. Town in C Greece, near the head of the Gulf of Lamia (an arm of the Aegean Sea). It was an ancient city of Malis, where Antipater was besieged in 323 B.C.

Lamia, Gulf of. [Also: **Malian Gulf**; Latin, **Maliacus Sinus**.] Arm of the Aegean Sea, S of Thessaly, Greece.

Lamian War (lā′mi-an). War (323–322 B.C.) in which Athens and its allies were defeated by Macedonia under Antipater; so named from the siege of Lamia by the allies.

Lampadion (lam-pā′di-on). Conventional name for a lively provocative courtesan in later Greek comedy.

Lampetia (lam-pē′shi-a). In the *Odyssey*, a daughter of Helius and the nymph Neaera.

She and her sister Phaethusa tended Helius' cattle on Trinacria (Sicily), and it was she who informed Helius of the theft and slaughter of some of his cattle by the companions of Odysseus. In consequence, Zeus, at the request of Helius, sent a great storm which destroyed all of them except Odysseus, who had not eaten of the flesh of the divine cattle.

Lampsacus (lamp′sa-kus). [Modern village name, **Lapseki**.] In ancient geography, a city in Mysia, Asia Minor, on the E shore of the Hellespont. It was colonized by Ionian Greeks from Phocaea, fell to Persia following the Ionian revolt (499 B.C.), allied itself to Athens at the end of the Persian Wars (479 B.C.) and paid Athens a large tribute. Its location on the Hellespont made it important to Athens as one of the cities that controlled the grain route. When Lampsacus revolted against Athens (411 B.C.), the revolt was put down. The Spartan Lysander besieged and took the city (405), but with the signing of the King's Peace (387), it fell again to Persia. It was occupied for Alexander the Great by his general Parmenio (335), and ultimately, c196 B.C., became an ally of Rome. Ancient Lampsacus was a center of worship of the nature-god Priapus, a god of fertility.

Lamus (lā′mus). In Greek legend: 1) a son of Heracles and Omphale, queen of Libya to whom Heracles had been sold as a slave. Omphale freed Heracles, married him, and bore him Lamus. 2) The king of the Laestrygones in Italy. His people overwhelmed 11 of Odysseus' ships when they stopped there on the way home to Ithaca, and devoured their crews.

Lanuvina (lan-ū-vī′na). An epithet of Juno, deriving from Lanuvium, the site of her chief sanctuary.

Lanuvium (la-nū′vi-um). [Modern village name, **Lanuvio**, formerly **Città Lavinia**.] In ancient geography, a town in Latium, Italy, about 20 miles SE of Rome. It was a center of the worship of Juno Sospita, the succoring goddess.

Laocoön (lā-ok′ō-on). In Greek legend, a priest of Apollo at Troy who had offended the god by marrying and becoming the father of children, and who had profaned the image of the god. He was chosen by the Trojans to propitiate Poseidon in the last year of the

fat, fāte, fär, fāre, errant; net, mē, hėr ardent; pin, pīne; not, nōte, möve, nôr,

Trojan War, because the Trojans had slain their former priest of Poseidon. When the Wooden Horse was seen on the beach before Troy, Laocoön hurled his spear into its side and urged the Trojans not to take it inside the walls. It was a trap, he declared, as he utttered the words, "I fear the Greeks, especially when they bring gifts." While the Trojans hesitated, a great serpent sent by Apollo to punish Laocoön for his earlier offenses came slithering out of the sea, and grasped Laocoön and his two sons in its coils. The serpent crushed them to death and carried them off to the shrine of Athena. The Trojans erroneously concluded that Laocoön had been punished for doubting the holiness of Athena's gift—as they thought of the Wooden Horse—and for dishonoring it by thrusting his spear into its side. They thereupon resolved to take the Wooden Horse inside the walls to Athena's shrine, with disastrous results.

Laocoön. In Greek legend, a son of Oeneus of Calydon by a serving woman. He was the half-brother of Meleager, whom he accompanied on the expedition of the Argonauts to Colchis.

Laocoön. Sculpture in the Vatican Museum, Rome, showing the Trojan priest of Apollo and his two young sons attacked by two great serpents, as narrated by Aeneas to Dido in Vergil's *Aeneid,* Book II, and frequently elsewhere. It is an important work of Hellenistic sculpture—Pliny the Elder regarded it as the greatest of all sculptures. According to Pliny, the sculptors were three, Agesander, Athenodorus, and Polydorus, all of Rhodes. It was discovered at Rome in 1506. (JJ)

Laodamas (lā-od′a-mas). In Greek legend, a son of Eteocles and grandson of Oedipus. He became king of Thebes after the death of his father. In the defense of Thebes when it was attacked by the Epigoni, Laodamas killed Aegialeus, the only one of the Epigoni to be killed, but was in turn slain by Alcmaeon.

Laodamas. In the Odyssey, a Phaeacian, the son of Alcinous. Unaware of the identity of Odysseus, he challenged him to take part in the games and athletic contests which were held when Odysseus was cast ashore on Phaeacia.

Laodamia (lā-od-a-mī′a). In classical legend, a daughter of Acastus. She was the wife of Protesilaus, and missed him so when he went to Troy that she made a wax image of him to keep her company. When she learned that he had been slain at Troy by Hector she prayed to the gods to let him revisit her from Hades, if only for three hours. Zeus permitted Hermes to bring the shade of Protesilaus from the Underworld for three hours. While with his wife, Protesilaus exhorted her to follow him when it was time for him to return to the Underworld. At the end of the three hours Laodamia stabbed herself so that she could go with him.

Laodamia. In the *Iliad,* a daughter of Bellerophon, and the sister of Isander and Hippolochus. She was the mother of Sarpedon of Lycia by Zeus. Artemis slew her in anger.

Laodice (lā-od′i-sē). In the *Iliad,* a daughter of Priam and Hecuba. According to Homer, she was the fairest of Priam's daughters. She was the wife of Helicaon, son of Antenor. When Acamas journeyed to Troy with Diomedes to demand the return of Helen, Laodice fell in love with him and bore him a son, Munitus. When Troy fell, she prayed that she might be swallowed up by the earth rather than live a life of dishonor as a slave and concubine of the Greeks. The earth parted and she was swallowed up as she had prayed.

Laodice. The name Homer gives to Electra, daughter of Agamemnon and Clytemnestra.

Laodicea (lā-od-i-sē′a, lā″ọ-di-sē′a). [Full Latin name, **Laodicea ad Lycum.**] Ancient city in Phrygia, Asia Minor, in the valley of the Lycus, a tributary river of the Maeander (modern Menderes), about 50 miles N of Aradus. It was founded under the Seleucids, by Antiochus II (c250 B.C.) and named after his wife, Laodice. It was an important early Christian center, and in the Apocalypse is one of the congregations to which an epistle is addressed. Its great heap of ruins still attest to it former splendor.

Laodicea. [Full Latin name, **Laodicea ad Mare.**] Ancient city on the coast of Syria about 50 miles S of Antioch. It was known for its commerce in wine and fruit from the surrounding country, and in modern time has given its name to *Latakia* tobacco. (AH)

Laodocus (lā-od′ō-kus). In Greek legend, a son of Apollo and Phthia. He lived in the land of the Curetes. Aetolus, son of Endymion, forced to flee from his country, came to the land of the Curetes, slew Laodocus and his brothers, Dorus and Polypoetes, seized the land, and named it Aetolia for himself.

Laomedon (lā-om′e-don). In Greek legend, a son of Ilus and Eurydice, and a descendant of Dardanus. He was a king of Troy. To punish Apollo and Poseidon, Zeus sent them to work for Laomedon and they built the walls of Troy. But when their year of service was up, he refused to pay them. Instead, he threatened to cut off their ears, bind them, and ship them abroad to be sold as slaves. In revenge, Poseidon sent a sea-monster to ravage Troy. Heracles rescued Hesione, Laomedon's daughter, who had been chained to a rock to appease the monster, and offered to slay the beast in return for the famous horses of Tros, immortal horses which had been given to Tros by Zeus to atone for the loss of Ganymede, and which had been handed on to Laomedon. Laomedon agreed, but once again refused to honor his agreement. In a fury, Heracles attacked Troy and killed Laomedon and all his sons except Podarces (Priam).

Laothoë (lā-oth′ō-ē). In the *Iliad*, a daughter of Altes, king of the Leleges. She was Priam's concubine and the mother of his two youngest sons, Lycaon and Polydorus.

Laphria (laf′ri-a). An epithet of Artemis, possibly deriving from a word meaning "spoils taken in war." Pausanias mentions that this surname is a foreign one and that the image of Artemis in this shrine was brought in from another place. But some say the Calydonians called her Laphria because a man named Laphrius set up an image of the goddess in Calydon. Others say she was given this epithet because her wrath, originally strong, against Oeneus and the Calydonians rested more lightly (*elaphroteron*) as time passed. A festival called Laphria was held in her honor annually at Patrae. At this festival the Patraeans set up a circle of green logs around her altar, and on the fire that was lighted within the circle they hurled great numbers of live wild beasts.

Laphystius (la-fis′ti-us). Epithet of Zeus, from his sanctuary on Mount Laphystius in Boeotia. It was at the altar of Zeus Laphystius that Athamas was preparing to sacrifice his children, Phrixus and Helle, when a golden-fleeced ram came and carried them off. In obedience to an oracle, the people were about to sacrifice Athamas for his attempted murder of his children, when Cytissorus, the son of Phrixus, came to the land from Colchis and rescued him. This rescue brought the anger of the gods on the descendants of Athamas, and henceforth it was forbidden to the oldest son of his race to enter the temple of Zeus Laphystius; if one defied the prohibition, he was to be sacrificed. When Jason returned from Colchis with the Golden Fleece, he dedicated it in the temple of Zeus Laphystius.

Laphystius, Mount. A mountain near Orchomenus, in Boeotia. Athamas had his palace at the foot of this mountain. It was on its summit that he was preparing to sacrifice his son Phrixus when the latter was rescued and carried off on the back of a miraculous winged ram with fleece of pure gold.

LAPITH AND CENTAUR
Metope from the south face of the Parthenon,
438–432 B.C. *British Museum*

Lapithae (lap′i-thē) or Lapiths (lap′iths). A Thessalian people descended, according to some accounts, from Lapithes, a son of Apollo and Stilbe. Others say the Lapithae were descendants of Ixion. One of their kings was

Pirithous. On the occasion of his marriage to Hippodamia the centaurs, who as cousins of Pirithous had been invited to the wedding, got drunk from drinking wine unmixed with water and attacked the bride. A fierce struggle broke out between the Lapithae and the centaurs when the Lapithae resisted the attacks of the centaurs on their women. This episode resulted in the expulsion of the centaurs from Mount Pelion. Later the centaurs invaded the territory of the Lapithae and overwhelmed them. Those Lapithae who escaped fled to Mount Pholoe in Elis from which they were also subsequently driven by the centaurs. The remnants of the Lapithae finally settled in Malea.

Lapithes (lap′i-thēz). According to some accounts, a son of Apollo, and a descendant of Oceanus and Tethys. He ruled the region about the Peneus River, the land of his grandfather, the river-god Peneus. His sons, Phorbas and Periphas, became kings after him and named their subjects Lapiths, or Lapithae, after their father.

Lararium (lär-ār′i-um). A part of a Roman house in which the Lares were placed. In effect, it was a private shrine or chapel. The lararium was next to the family hearth, which was in early times located in the *atrium* (the entrance hall of a Roman house, in early times used as a ceremonial room and for such general domestic purposes as cooking and dining; later, except among the poor, reserved as a general reception room). The togaed image of the *Lar familiaris* stood, between the images of the two Penates, in the lararium. The images were greeted each morning by the family with a prayer; after the principal meal of the day was served, a reserved portion of it was placed on a ceremonial table in the lararium as a gift to the family household gods. To celebrate special family occasions, as birthdays or the safe return from a journey, garlands were hung about the images, and offerings, including wine and animals, were made to them. A lararium was found in the House of the Menander (Casa del Menandro) at Pompeii.

Larentalia (lar-en-tā′li-a). Ancient Roman festival celebrated Dec. 23, during which offerings were made to the dead, especially at the shrine of Acca Larentia, nurse of Romulus and Remus, field-goddess, and protestress of the city. The *flamen Quirinalis* offered sacrifices on the spot where Acca Larentia was said to have disappeared.

Lares (lār′ēz). In Roman religion, a class of benevolent spirits presiding over the house and family. They were looked upon also as protectors of the state and city, and as very powerful for evil if not duly respected and propitiated. The public Lares, originally two in number, were the guardians of the unity of the state, and were honored with temples and an elaborate ceremonial. After the time of Augustus, at least, each division of the city had also its own public Lares (*Lares compitales*). The private Lares differed for each family, and were worshiped daily in the house, being domiciled sometimes on the family hearth but usually in a special niche with the Penates. Food was offered to them at every meal. They received also special recognition upon every occasion of festivity, public or private, and on certain days devoted particularly to them, and claimed tribute alike from the bride upon entering the family and from the youth upon attaining his majority. The chief of the private Lares in each family, the domestic or household Lar (*Lar familiaris*) was the spirit of the founder of the family. To the family spirits were often added in later times, among the household Lares, the shades of heroes, or other personalities who were looked upon with admiration or awe. In their character as malignant divinities, the Lares were commonly classed as *lemures* or *larvae*. The division of Lares into *compitales* and *familiares* is the basis of two theories as to their origin: 1) they were originally farm-land deities; 2) they were the ghosts of the dead.

Larissa (la-ris′a). According to tradition, a daughter of Pelasgus the Argive. The citadel at Argos was named for her, as were also two cities in Thessaly: one on the Peneus River and one on the sea.

Larissa. [Also: **Larisa**.] A city in Thessaly, NE Greece, situated on the Peneus River. According to legend, it was here that Acrisius was killed by his grandson Perseus. The discus Perseus was hurling in an athletic contest went wild and struck and killed Acrisius, thus fulfilling the prophecy that a son of Danaë would slay her father. Larissa became the seat of the Aleuadae, a Thessalian family prominent in organizing the Thessalian Confederacy in the 6th century B.C. The Aleuadae welcomed artists and writers from southern Greece to their court. In the Persian War Larissa was allied to Xerxes. The Aleuadae Dynasty was overthrown toward the end of the 5th century B.C. Philip II of Macedon brought Larissa under his control, c344 B.C. In 196 B.C. it became the capital of the Thessalian Confederacy organized by the Romans.

Larissa Cremaste (krē-mas'tē). In ancient geography, a town in Phthia, SE Thessaly, Greece, situated near the coast opposite the northern tip of Euboea. According to some accounts, this was the site of Achilles' city. The ancient citadel was taken by Demetrius Poliorcetes, 302 B.C.

Larius, Lacus (lā'ri-us lā'kus). [Modern name, **Lake Como.**] Lake in N Italy, traversed by the Addua River and famous for its scenery.

Lars Porsena (lärz pôr'se̱-na̱). See **Porsena, Lars.**

Larvae (lär'vē). In Roman mythology, spirits of the dead who were forces for evil, as contrasted with the Lares. They haunted the living as ghosts or specters and had the power to drive the living mad. They were the spirits of the wicked. The name *Lemures* (q.v.) was also given these spirits.

Larymna (la̱-rim'na̱). In ancient geography, a city of Boeotia, Greece, situated on the coast. It was said to have been named for a daughter of Cycnus, son of Poseidon who was transformed into a swan. The city once belonged to Opus but voluntarily joined the Boeotians.

Las (läs). An ancient town in Laconia, on the Gulf of Laconia. Some say it takes its name from Las, who founded it, and who was slain by Patroclus. Others say it gets its name from the rocky hill on which it stands. It was said to have been captured by the Dioscuri. Men of Las went to the Trojan War under the command of Menelaus.

Lassithi (la̱-sē'thē). [Also: **Dhikti.**] Modern name of a mountain in Crete. The ancient name of the mountain was Dicte, where the cave in which some say Zeus was born is located.

Lasus (lā'sus). Greek dithyrambic poet of Hermione; fl. 6th century B.C. He went to the court of Hipparchus at Athens, where

he made some innovations in the dithyrambs sung at the festivals of Dionysus.

Latin League (lat'in). Confederation of the cities in Latium, existing in Italy in the earliest historic times and continuing until 338 B.C., when the Latin towns were finally incorporated in the dominion of Rome, following the Great Latin War (340–338 B.C.), which resulted from the towns' attempts to make themselves equals of Rome within the League or to secede if that were not possible. According to the earliest tradition, the League included 30 cities, among which Alba Longa held the preëminent place. After the fall of Alba, Aricia, Lanuvium, and Tusculum, with other important communities not originally included, were united with the League. The confederation held assemblies in the grove of Ferentinum, below Marino in the Alban Hills, and had a common religious sanctuary in the temple of Jupiter Latiaris on the summit of the Alban Mount (Monte Cavo), where annual sacrifices were celebrated.

Latini (la̱-tī'nī). [Also: **Latins.**] Italic-speaking farmers who settled in Latium soon after 1000 B.C., deriving their name from the region they occupied. Before the dawn of Italian history their dialect of Italic had become a distinct language, thenceforth known as Latin. To Latin- and Sabine-speaking colonists was attributed the founding of Rome (traditionally, in 753 B.C.; excavations near the Forum have revealed burials still older). (JJ)

Latinus (la̱-tī'nus). In legend, according to the Greeks, a son of Circe and Odysseus, The Romans say that his father was Heracles and his mother was the widow or the daughter of Faunus, or that he was a son of Faunus and the nymph Marica. He was a king of Latium, whose capital was Laurentum. He had established the city and named his colonists Laurentes, after a laurel tree which he found on the site and dedicated to Phoebus. He was the father of one daughter, Lavinia, by his wife Amata, and had no sons. A swarm of bees settled on the sacred laurel tree; this was considered an omen that indicated the arrival of a stranger. About the same time, Lavinia's hair caught fire at the sacred altar but did not burn. Latinus consulted the oracle and learned that he should give his daughter in marriage to a

fat, fāte, fär, fãre, errạnt; net, mē, hėr ardẹnt; pin, pīne; not, nōte, mŏve, nôr,

stranger rather than to Turnus, whom her mother was very anxious for her to marry. Latinus welcomed Ilioneus, the representative of Aeneas, when he came bearing gifts from Troy. He said he remembered that the Auruncan elders used to say that Dardanus was born in Latium. He decided that Aeneas was the stranger the oracle had recommended as a husband for his daughter, and sent him a present of horses that had been bred by Circe. However, Juno did not intend to let Aeneas settle in Italy so peacefully. She sent Alecto to stir up the Latin women, to goad Turnus, and to inflame the countrymen. Latinus could not subdue the desire for war, and so he gave up the reins of government. As the war went on and Mezentius, a Latin ally, was killed, Latinus called a council. On learning that Diomedes refused his aid, and in fact counseled the Latins not to wage war on the Trojans, he **proposed** to cede land to Aeneas, or to pro**vide** him with ships that he might seek a **home** elsewhere. But Turnus refused to take this advice. He urged continuance of the war and the Latins met with disaster. When Turnus offered to meet Aeneas in single combat at last, Latinus again offered to make peace, but as Turnus again refused, Latinus accepted the vow of Aeneas that if he should be victorious, peace and equality would be established between the Latins and the Trojans. Aeneas was victorious, and because of this vow the Latins and Trojans lived thereafter in peace.

Latium (lā'shi-um). In ancient geography, the part of C Italy lying along the Mediterranean SE of Etruria and NW of Campania. The name was originally restricted to the land of the Latini or Latins, chiefly comprised in the Roman Campagna. Its chief cities formed the Latin League, which was at war with Rome, 340–338 B.C., and was incorporated with Rome after 338 B.C. In an extended sense Latium (also Latium Adjectum or Novum) was the region from the Tiber to the Liris or to Mount Massicus, including the territories of the Latini, Hernicans, Volscians, and Auruncans, and (in part) of the Aequians. According to legend, Saturn fled to this region from Jove and gave it the name Latium to suggest the refuge he had found. Under Saturn's beneficent

rule a golden age flourished in Latium. It was the home of the Latins, and became the home of the Trojans when the latter, under the leadership of Aeneas, were guided there by destiny to found a second Troy.

Latmus (lat'mus). In ancient geography, a mountain range in Caria, Asia Minor, E of Miletus. There was a sanctuary to Endymion here because it was on this mountain, according to legend, that Endymion slept forever while Selene, the moon-goddess, came to gaze on his ever-youthful beauty.

Latona (la-tō'na). In mythology, the mother of Apollo and Diana. A Latin name of Leto.

Laughing Philosopher. An epithet of **Democritus.**

Laurentum (lô-ren'tum). In ancient geography, a city in Latium, Italy, situated near the coast between Ostia and Lavinium, about 16 miles S of Rome: the capital of ancient Latium. According to the *Aeneid*, it was founded by the Laurentes, men who colonized Latium under Latinus. They got their name from the sacred laurel tree which was found in the spot where the city was built.

Laurium (lô'ri-um). [Also: **Laurion;** modern name, **Lavrion.**] Low hills at the SE extremity of Attica, Greece. They were celebrated in ancient times as the site of silver mines that helped Athens to arrive at commercial greatness. Shafts of these mines, galleries of which remain, went down as much as 400 feet. From the silver **mined** here the Athenians minted coins that circulated throughout the world, and enjoyed such a high reputation that it was considered unwise to change the design. For this reason, lest a newer design be looked upon with suspicion in the remote parts to which Athenian traders ventured, the ancient coins, with the head of Athena on one side and her owl on the other, retained their original archaic design. In the time of the traveler Pausanias (2nd century A.D.), who described the shafts and galleries of the mines, the silver ore had been exhausted. Centuries later the mines were reopened, and produced lead and zinc. Near Laurium is the modern seaport of Lavrion.

Lausus (lô'sus). In the *Aeneid,* a son of the Etruscan king Mezentius. As commander of 1000 men he joined Turnus in his war against Aeneas. In a duel with Pallas, son

---

actor; up, lūte, púll; oi, oil; ou, out; ŦH, then; ḍ as d or j, ş as s or sh, ṭ as t or ch, ẓ as z or zh.

of Evander, with whom he was evenly matched as to age, skill, and weight, Turnus intervened and slew Pallas. Later Lausus went to the aid of his father when the latter was wounded by Aeneas. He saved his father's life but in so doing lost his own. Aeneas, in pity for his youth and filial devotion, honored the youth by sending his fully-armed body back to Mezentius on his shield.

Lavinia (la̱-vin'i-a̱). In Roman legend, the only daughter of Latinus, king of Latium, and Amata. Her mother wished her to marry Turnus, king of the Rutuli, but an oracle had advised Latinus to give her to a foreign leader. It was thus that Latinus welcomed Aeneas, believing he was the alien of whom the oracle had spoken. In the course of sacrifices at the altar Lavinia's hair caught fire and blazed up without being consumed. This was interpreted to mean that she would have a glorious fate but her people would suffer war. She married Aeneas and became the ancestress of the inhabitants of Lavinium, a city named for her.

Lavinium (la̱-vin'i-um). In ancient geography, a city in Latium, Italy, about 17 miles S of Rome. According to the *Aeneid*, it was built by Aeneas and named after his Latin wife, Lavinia.

Lay of Ethiopia (ē-thi-ō'pi-a̱). See **Aethiopis.**

Lay of Telegonus (tel-e̱-gō'nus). See **Telegonia.**

Leander (lē-an'de̱r). In Greek legend, a youth of Abydos, the lover of Hero. Each night he swam the Hellespont to visit her secretly. Marriage was forbidden them because Hero was a priestess of Aphrodite at Sestos. One stormy night the light in the tower, by which his course was guided, was extinguished, and he perished. His body was washed ashore, and on discovering it Hero threw herself into the sea and was drowned.

Learchus (lē-är'kus). In Greek mythology, a son of Athamas, king of Orchomenus in Boeotia, and Ino, daughter of Cadmus of Thebes. Driven mad by Hera, his father mistook him for a stag and pierced him with an arrow.

Lebadia (le-bä'di-a̱) or **Lebadea** (le-ba̱-dā'a̱). A town in Boeotia, Greece, famous for its oracle of Trophonius. The town was said to have been named for Lebadus, an Athe-

nian who settled there. The oracle was on the slope of a mountain across the Hercyna River and beyond a sacred grove in which there were many sanctuaries. According to tradition, for a long time the Boeotians were ignorant of the oracle of Trophonius within their borders. Once, during a drought, they sent to the oracle at Delphi to learn how the drought might be broken. The priestess instructed them to go to Trophonius. They were at a loss where he could be found, and Saon, a Boeotian, searched in vain. At last he saw a swarm of bees and decided to follow them. Where the bees disappeared into the ground, he found the oracle of Trophonius, and it was he, they say, who established the rites to be observed there. The procedure for appealing to the oracle was most involved. After elaborate purification ceremonies, the suppliant ate the flesh of a ram that had been sacrificed to the shade of Agamedes, brother of Trophonius. He was then led to the Hercyna River by two boys 13 years of age. They bathed and anointed him. He then drank from a spring, called the Water of Lethe, to make him forget the past. Then he drank from another spring called the Water of Memory, so that he would recall whatever he was told by the oracle. Dressed in a prescribed costume and wearing fillets on his head like a sacrificial victim, he was led to the cave where the oracle was housed. Holding barley and honey cakes in his hands he descended a ladder into a pit, until he reached a narrow opening. There unseen hands pulled him through and he received a stunning blow on the head. While he was still unconscious from the blow, a voice spoke and prophesied. As soon as the prophetic voice ceased the suppliant was returned, feet first, through the opening, hauled up the ladder, and seated on the chair of Memory, where he repeated all that the voice had said while he was unconscious. When he recovered consciousness, the suppliant found that he no longer had the barley and honey cakes: they were taken from him while he was in the second cavern, before the prophetic voice spoke. The ceremonies for consulting the oracle were so shattering that a long time passed before the suppliant recovered his ability to laugh; and especially solemn people were said to "have been to Trophonius." The oracle of Trophonius was one of many consulted by Croesus, King of Lydia, before he decided to make war on Cyrus, King of the Persians. Trophonius is one of the chthonian deities, the worship of whom is in sharp contrast to that of the Olympian gods.

Lebedos (leb'e-dos). In ancient geography, an Ionian seaport in Lydia, Asia Minor, about 25 miles NW of Ephesus. It was one of the 12 Ionian cities of Asia, and according to tradition, was colonized by Andraemon, son of Codrus, legendary king of Attica, as leader of an expedition of Ionians and Boeotians.

Lechaeum (le-kē'um). One of the harbors of Corinth. According to tradition, it was named for Leches, child of Poseidon and Pirene. There were a sanctuary and a bronze image of Poseidon there.

Lecheates (lek-ē-ā'tēz). Epithet of Zeus. Near Aliphera in W Arcadia was a stream called Tritonis. The people of Aliphera claimed that it was here that Athena was born from the head of Zeus, and they worshiped her above all other deities. Because of this, they set up an altar of Zeus Lecheates (*In Childbed*) at Aliphera.

Lecythus (les'i-thus) or **Lekythos** (lek'i-thos). A small oil- or perfume-vase of ancient Greece, of tall and graceful proportions and narrow neck. In Attica a particular class of lecythus was used, especially in funeral rites. The neck and the foot of these Attic lecythi are covered with black glaze, and the body has a clear white ground upon which are drawn with a brown outline figures and designs, often of remarkable delicacy and elegance. Unlike nearly all other examples of Greek vase-painting, these figures and designs are frequently filled out with bright and naturalistic colors.

Leda (lē'da). In Greek mythology, a daughter of Thestius, king in Aetolia. Her father gave her in marriage to Tyndareus of Sparta. Some say she found a blue and silver egg, dropped by Nemesis, lying in a marsh. She took it home and hid it. From it Helen was born, the daughter of Zeus. Others say that Hermes threw the egg between Leda's knees and that from this she bore Helen. But the most common account is that Zeus fell in love with Leda, transformed himself into a swan, and in this form embraced her. She subsequently bore an egg from which Helen and Polydeuces, her children by Zeus, were born. By her husband she was the mother of Castor, twin-born with Polydeuces, and Clytemnestra. But the paternity of her twins, Castor and Polydeuces, is disputed. Clytemnestra was the daughter of Leda and Tyndareus, Helen of Leda and Zeus. Homer says that Tyndareus fathered Castor and Polydeuces also, but others make one or both the sons of Zeus. According to some accounts, Leda hanged herself because of her shame over the notorious elopement of Helen with Paris. Odysseus saw her shade when he visited the Underworld on his way home after the Trojan War. Pausanias, traveling in Greece in the 2nd century A.D. says that in the sanctuary of the Leucippides in Sparta there was an egg suspended by a ribbon from the roof-tree, and that this was supposed to be the egg that Leda had brought forth.

Leges Regiae (lē'jēz rē'ji-ē). Ancient Roman traditional laws. Upon being subsequently written down, they were arbitrarily ascribed to various kings.

Leibethra (lī-bē'thra). See **Libethra**.

Leïtus (lē'i-tus). In Homeric legend (*Iliad*), a captain of Boeotians at the siege of Troy. He was wounded by Hector in the struggle for possession of the body of Patroclus. However, he recovered, and was the only one of the Boeotian chiefs to return home safe from Troy. He brought back with him the bones of Arcesilaus and buried them near the oracle of Trophonius at Lebadia. The tomb of Leïtus was at Plataea.

Leleges (lel'e-jēz). Ancient people who lived on the coasts of Greece, Asia Minor, and the islands of the Aegean. According to the Spartans, they were descendants of Lelex, the first king of the people later known as Lacedaemonians, but in his time called Leleges. They are sometimes associated with the Carians of SW Asia Minor. Homer (*Iliad*) speaks of them as a warlike and war-loving people of western Asia, who were allies of the Trojans in the Trojan War. Like "Pelasgi," the term is often used loosely by the Greeks to mean "aborigines," the older stratum of population found in the Aegean when the first Greek immigrants arrived c1950 B.C.

Lelex (lel'eks). According to Lacedaemonian tradition, he was the first king of the Lacedaemonians, and called his people Leleges after himself. Some say he was a son of Poseidon and Libya, the daughter of Epaphus, and that he came to Megara from Egypt and became king of Megara. This was a Megarian tradition. The son of Lelex was Myles, who succeeded him as king.

Lemnos (lem'nos). [Also: **Limni, Limno, Limnos.**] Island in the NE Aegean Sea. The surface is hilly and fertile, and in antiquity produced considerable grain crops. It has hot springs and a harbor on the S coast at modern Moudhros. It was sacred to Hephaestus in ancient times because, when he was hurled out of heaven by Zeus, he landed on the island, and the islanders who found him took care of him. According to legend, the Lemnian women, under their queen Hypsipyle, murdered all the men of the island for cohabiting with their Thracian female captives. Afterward, the island was purified every year of the guilt of this mass murder, which included the slaying of all male children as well as their fathers. Ceremonies of purification lasting nine days were held, during which time all fires on the island were put out. At the end of the nine days and after sacrifices had been offered to the dead, new fire was brought from Delos. The Argonauts stopped at Lemnos for supplies soon after they began their voyage to Colchis to secure the Golden Fleece. They found the island populated only by women. They were hospitably greeted and stayed for some time, Jason fathering the twin sons of Hypsipyle, their queen, and the other Argonauts leaving an island soon repopulated with a race called, for their fathers, the Minyans. Students see in the myth evidence of a former gynocracy (rule by women). Both Aeschylus and Sophocles wrote plays, now lost, on the story. When the Greeks sailed against Troy to recover Helen, they also stopped at Lemnos. It was here that Philoctetes was bitten by a serpent, according to some accounts, and because the wound would not heal and gave off a noisome smell, Philoctetes was abandoned in a lonely part of the island. However, the Greeks needed his arrows, given to him by Heracles, and in the tenth year of the war they returned to Lemnos and fetched Philoctetes, nearly dead from his wound and starvation, back with them to Troy.

Lemnos was conquered in the reign of Darius I by the Persians. It was gained for Athens by Miltiades c500 B.C. According to Herodotus, the history of this conquest was as follows. Some Pelasgians who had settled near Athens were banished and went to settle in Lemnos, where they drove off the descendants of the Argonauts. Later, the Pelasgians, wishing to avenge themselves on the Athenians, made a raid on Brauron while the Athenian women were celebrating the festival of Artemis there, and carried them off to Lemnos and made them their concubines. The sons born to these women were brought up by their mothers in the Attic manner, and they banded together against the legitimate sons of the Pelasgians and their wives. As boys the sons of the Athenian women banded together against the sons of the Pelasgians and sought to rule them, therefore the Pelasgians feared what they might do when they grew up. The Pelasgians resolved to slay all the sons of the Athenian concubines, and their mothers as well. For this slaughter, and for the extirpation of the males of Lemnos by the Lemnian women under Hypsipyle, evil and savage actions came to be known as "Lemnian deeds," a phrase which became proverbial in Greece for acts of atrocity. After the murder of the Athenian women and their sons the land of the Pelasgians in Lemnos ceased to be fertile; their women and cattle were less fruitful. The Pelasgians sent to the oracle at Delphi to learn how they could recover their former prosperity, and were told they must grant the Athenians whatever satisfaction they demanded for the abduction of the Athenian women from Brauron and their subsequent murders. The Pelasgians sent to the Athenians to learn what recompense would satisfy them. The Athenians told them to deliver up their land to them in a condition of flourishing prosperity. This was too high a price. The Pelasgians replied that they would do so when a north wind brought a ship from their land to Lemnos in one day. This they were sure would never happen, as Athens is far to the south of Lemnos. Nevertheless, according to Herodotus, they were compelled to fulfill their promise. Some years later Miltiades, the Athenian, while he was ruler of the Chersonese for the Athenians, sailed from the Hellespont during the time of the Etesian winds and reminded the Pelasgians of their oath. The people of Hephaestia in Lemnos yielded, and gave themselves up. Those of Myrina scorned Miltiades, but he besieged them, subdued their city, and brought Lemnos under Athenian dominion. Later, in the time of Pericles, when colonists went out to Lemnos from Athens, they took with them a bronze statue of the goddess Athena made by Phidias, and dedicated it on the Acropolis. The statue, which in ancient times was regarded as among the most beautiful of the works of Phidias, has been lost, but copies of it survive. The island remained a possession of Athens, except for a 10-year period of Spartan control, until Greece was conquered by the Macedonians. Lemnos was noted throughout antiquity, and into modern times, for a product called "Lemnian earth" which was supposed to have unusual medicinal properties. To modern times it has been used as a cure for certain wounds and infections, and in ancient times it was also highly regarded as a cure for snake bite. On a fixed day each year a priestess went to the bare hill where the earth was dug, performed certain rituals, and supervised the digging of a prescribed amount of the earth. The earth was prepared in blocks, each of which was stamped with a head of Artemis and with the word "Lemnos," whence the name. In modern times the ceremony of digging the Lemnian earth was carried out on Aug. 6th; the blocks were stamped, and then distributed for sale by apothecaries. The island of Lemnos is about 20 miles long, and has an area of about 180 square miles.

Lemovices (lem-ō̱-vī′sēz). Tribe in ancient Gaul, occupying territory near the Arvernian border. They are mentioned by Julius Caesar as supporting Vercingetorix in his revolt of 52 B.C. The French province of Limousin derived its name from them.

Lemures (lem′ū̱-rēz). [Also: **Larvae**.] Among the ancient Romans, the spirits of the dead considered as evil-disposed specters or ghosts, who were supposed to do mischief at night to the living, and were exorcised annually with a ceremonial ritual by the head of each household during the festival called *Lemuralia* or *Lemuria*. There were also games and other public observances of the festival.

Lemuria (lē̱-mū̱′ri-a̱). Ancient Roman festival celebrated annually on May 9, 11, and 13 for the *lemures*, or spirits of the dead. At midnight the head of the family rose and, standing in his bare feet, made a sign with his fingers and thumb to keep off any ghosts. He washed his hands three times, then turned around and put black beans into his mouth. Turning his head to one side, he spat out the beans and thus redeemed his own family. It was believed that the ghosts followed him as he spat out the beans and, if no one was watching, picked them up. The father afterward washed again, struck a brass gong, and begged the ghosts to leave with the words, "Shades of my fathers, depart!" Nine times he repeated this command, and having done all as required, considered that his house was purified of the ghosts of his ancestors. The third day of the Lemuria was celebrated especially by merchants to insure a year's good luck in business.

Lenaea (le-nē̱′a̱). In Greek religion, one of the four Attic festivals in honor of Dionysus. It was celebrated in the ancient sanctuary of that god, called the *Lenaeum*, believed to be to the west of the Acropolis. It was the second of the series of Dionysiac festivals, and took place at the end of January and the beginning of February (on the 12th, 13th, and 14th days of the month Gamelion). There was a great public feast, followed by a procession with jesting and mockery to the theater, where, on the occasion of this festival, dramatic contests in both tragedy and comedy were held. See **Dionysia**.

Lenaeus (le-nē̱′us). An epithet of Dionysus, derived from the Greek word *lene*, "maenad," or *lenos*, "vat."

Lentini (len-tē̱′nē). See **Leontini**.

Lentulus (len′tū̱-lus), **Publius Cornelius**. [Surnamed **Sura**.] Roman politician; executed at Rome, Dec. 5, 63 B.C. He was praetor (75 B.C.), and a conspirator with Catiline in 63 B.C. He planned to kill Cicero and burn Rome. He divulged the plot to the Allobroges in the hope of securing their assistance and they betrayed the plot. The conspirators in Rome were seized; they confessed and were executed. He received his surname, Sura, because when Sulla accused him of carelessness with public funds (81 B.C.), instead of defending himself he held out the calf of his leg (*sura*). This was in imitation of boys who did this to receive punishment when they committed a fault in their games.

Leo (lē'ō). The fifth sign of the zodiac—the Lion—which the sun enters about the 23rd of July. Also, a zodiacal constellation, supposed to represent a lion. It is easily found, for the pointers of the Great Bear point southerly to its brightest star, Regulus, distant about 45 degrees from the southernmost of them. Four stars in the body of Leo form a characteristic trapezium, and those about the neck and mane make a sickle.

LEO
Pictured according to ancient descriptions.

Leochares (lē-ok'a-rēz). Athenian sculptor, who was active about the middle of the 4th century B.C. He was a pupil of Scopas and associated with him on the mausoleum of Halicarnassus. He is probably represented by the Ganymede and eagle of the Vatican, supposed to be a copy of his celebrated work.

Leonidas (lē-on'i-das). King of Sparta, early in the 5th century B.C. He was reputed to be the 20th generation in direct descent from Heracles, and became king of Sparta, c490

B.C., on the death of his two elder brothers, who died childless. When Xerxes marched with his host against Greece and invaded the mainland as far as the borders of Locris, Leonidas went to defend the narrow pass at Thermopylae (480 B.C.), through the mountains south of the Sinus Maliacus. Through it ran the main road into Greece by which the Persian land forces meant to enter Locris and press on to the Peloponnesus. Under his command Leonidas had a force of 4000 soldiers, including 300 Spartans, 700 Thespians, and groups of varying numbers from Arcadia, Corinth, Mycenae, Thebes, and other cities. The plan was to send him more soldiers as soon as the Olympic Festival, which fell at this time, was over. However, before reinforcements arrived, Xerxes learned from his spies the small size of the force which opposed him. He questioned Demaratus, a former Spartan king who had fled to Xerxes before the Persian invasion and who now accompanied him. Did Demaratus think these Spartans, whom his spies had observed combing their hair and going through gymnastic exercises, would dare fight the host of the Persians? Demaratus assured him that the Spartans were the bravest of the Greeks, that it was their custom to dress their hair when they were about to risk their lives in battle, and that they were trained to give up their lives in glorious combat rather than retreat or surrender. Xerxes was incredulous. He thought it was ridiculous that such a small force would attempt to resist his vast army. He waited four days, thinking the Greeks would surely retire. Finding that they did not do so, he sent the Medes and Cissians against them The Greeks fought like gods in the narrow pass, caused immense slaughter among the barbarians, and compelled them to withdraw. Xerxes next sent his Persian Immortals against them. This was a band of 10,000, called Immortals because when one of their number fell he was replaced immediately, that the number might remain always at exactly 10,000. They too suffered enormous casualties and fell back. The next day the Persians attacked again, and were again driven back. Now as Xerxes pondered what should be done, a Malian, one Ephialtes, out of desire for gain betrayed the Greeks. He went to Xerxes and offered to lead the Per-

fat, fāte, fär, fãre, errant; net, mē, her ardent; pin, pīne; not, nōte, möve, nôr, sians across the mountains by a path he knew so that they could attack the Greeks from the rear. Xerxes gladly accepted his services. At nightfall he sent a band of Persians off under the guidance of Ephialtes. Leonidas was first warned of the destruction that was coming by the seer Megistias, who learned of it from his sacrificial victims. The seer's warning was confirmed by scouts. On learning of the destruction that was imminent, Leonidas decided that he and his Spartans could not honorably withdraw, but he allowed the soldiers from all the other cities to retire, except the Thebans, who had come unwillingly in the first place, and whom he kept as hostages. The Thespians remained of their own accord, refusing to desert Leonidas. According to Herodotus, who gives us a description of the heroic defense of the pass, Leonidas had earlier been told by an oracle that either Sparta or its king must fall before the barbarians. He chose to remain and perish at their hands, thus fulfilling the oracle, that Sparta might be spared. The next day, the Persians fell upon them again. Leonidas and his forces met the attack with unparalleled courage, knowing they were doomed to die. They boldly sallied out from the narrow pass and in a furious onslaught slew many of the barbarians before them and flung others into the sea. On this wild day the brave Leonidas perished in furious battle. Many valiant Spartans and brave Persians, among them kin of Xerxes, also died. After inflicting immense casualties and losing many of their own number, the Greeks, except the Thebans who surrendered, again withdrew to the pass. Here they were attacked on their other side by the Persians who had crossed the mountain. A smaller band now, they formed a tight group on a hillock near the entrance to the pass and continued to defend themselves. They fought with immortal valor until not one Greek survived. A stone lion in honor of Leonidas was set up to mark the spot where the Spartans perished, and the names of the 300 Spartans were engraved on a pillar, set up in Sparta, which existed at least until the 2nd century A.D. In honor of the 4000 of the original group, before Leonidas sent the allies away, an inscription marked the spot, which read:

Here did four thousand men from Pelops' land
Against three hundred myriads bravely stand.

The Spartans alone were immortalized in another inscription:

Go, stranger, and to Lacedaemon tell
That here, obeying her behests, we fell.

It is said that Xerxes, examining the field after the battle, came upon the body of Leonidas and knew him to be the Spartan king and commander. He ordered the head cut off and the body hung on a cross. This was a measure of his wrath against Leonidas, for ordinarily fallen enemies were honorably treated. It is also said that Xerxes tried to conceal the number of men he had lost, 20,000, in this engagement with first 4000 and then 1000 Greeks. He buried 19,000 of his dead in trenches which he camouflaged with branches. The bodies of 1000 he left scattered about the field. But this attempt at deception fooled no one. Many years after his death the bones of Leonidas were removed to Sparta by Pausanias, the victor at Plataea. In after times, speeches were annually delivered over the tombs of Leonidas and Pausanias, and contests were held in which none save Spartans could compete.

Leonidas of Tarentum. Greatly admired Greek epigrammatist of the 3rd century B.C. About 100 of his epigrams appear in the *Anthology.* (JJ)

Leonnatus (lē-ō̇-nā′tus). General of Alexander the Great; died 322 B.C. He was one of the ablest of Alexander's generals. On the return from India Alexander pursued the Malli and attacked them in their city, the modern Multan, 325 B.C. He recklessly mounted the wall of the city and leaped down among his enemies before his men had gained entrance into the city. Leonnatus was one of three who succeeded in scaling the wall to go to his aid. He guarded the king, who had been wounded as he faced his enemies, until rescue arrived. On Alexander's death (323 B.C.), Leonnatus received the satrapy of Hellespontine Phrygia. He fell in battle against the Athenians and their allies while seeking to relieve Antipater who was blockaded in Lamia.

Leonteus (lē-on′tūs). In the *Iliad,* a son of Coronus and a suitor of Helen before she married Menelaus. He was a leader of the Greeks at Troy and, with Polypoetes, held off Asius as he besieged the Greek fortifications. By slaying Orestes, Hippomachus, Antiphates, Menon, and Iamenus, he halted the Trojan attack.

Leontini (lē-on-tī'ni). [Modern name, **Lentini**.] In ancient geography, a city of Sicily, situated on a plain between two hills, about 21 miles NW of Syracuse. It was founded by Chalcidian Greeks from Sicilian Naxos, 729 B.C. Hippocrates of Gela took it, 498 B.C., and to it Hiero of Syracuse removed the inhabitants of Catana and Naxos. In 433 B.C. Leontini entered into an alliance with Athens to counteract the growing power of the Corinthian city of Syracuse, and in 427 B.C. an Athenian expedition was sent out to Sicily, largely owing to the urging of Gorgias of Leontini, but the expedition accomplished little. In 423 B.C. the city was taken by Syracuse. The restoration of Leontini was one of the objects of the second expedition undertaken by Athens against Sicily, 415 B.C. The expedition failed signally to accomplish its objects and brought disaster to Athens. After being devastated by the Carthaginians, 406 B.C., the independence of Leontini was restored briefly by a treaty of peace between Dionysius the Elder, tyrant of Syracuse, and the Carthaginians, but in 404 B.C. the city surrendered to Dionysius rather than risk annihilation at his hands. In the Second Punic War it was besieged and taken by the Romans under Marcellus, 214 B.C.

Leonymus (lē-on'i-mus). A legendary general of Croton. He was wounded in battle, and his wound did not heal. On the advice of the oracle at Delphi he sought out the spirit of Ajax on the island of Leuce, the "White Island," according to tradition, located at the mouth of the Ister. There he saw the two Ajaxes, Achilles, Antilochus, Patroclus, and Helen. He was cured of his wound and returned. It was Leonymus who brought back the message from Helen that Stesichorus, the poet, had been struck blind by her because of the infamous poems he wrote about her.

Leos (lē'os). According to legend, a herald, who informed Theseus that the sons of Pallas had divided their forces to attack Athens. One of these forces was hidden in ambush. Because of the information Leos gave him

Theseus surprised and killed them. Because he had informed on the sons of Pallas, their descendants in Pallene never intermarried with the people of Agnus from which Leos came. They would not permit their heralds to make the customary introduction to their proclamations, *"Akouete leoi!"* (Hearken, ye people!) because the word *leoi* reminded them of the treachery of Leos.

Leos. According to some accounts, a son of Orpheus. During his time Attica was afflicted by a crippling famine. The oracle of Delphi said the famine would be ended if there was a human sacrifice. Leos offered his three daughters—Praxithea, Theope, and Eubule—for the good of the state, and the famine was ended. Some say the three girls gave their lives of their own accord for the public good. In any event, the famine was over, and ever after the three maidens were worshiped at a shrine called the Leocorium in the district of the Ceramicus at Athens. It was beside this shrine that Hipparchus was slain by Harmodius and Aristogiton.

Leosthenes (lē-os'the-nēz). Athenian general; died 322 B.C. He was commander of the combined Greeks armies in the Lamian War, 323 B.C., defeating Antipater and forcing him to take refuge in Lamia, the siege of which city gave the war its name. Leosthenes was killed in the course of the siege.

Leotychides (lē-ō-tik'i-dēz). King of Sparta, c491–c476 B.C. He was the son of Menares and was reputed to be a direct descendant of Heracles. All his ancestors except the seven immediately preceding him had been kings of Sparta. Cleomenes, co-king of Sparta with Demaratus, sought to depose Demaratus, and agreed to make Leotychides king in his place if the latter would help him against the Aeginetans. Leotychides was the more willing to destroy Demaratus because Demaratus had stolen the bride to whom he was betrothed and married her himself. Leotychides brought charges against Demaratus, claiming he was not the true son of Ariston. The priestess of Delphi, bribed by Cleomenes, confirmed his charges, and Leotychides became king in his place. In fulfillment of his agreement he then assisted Cleomenes in a successful attack on the Aeginetans. Leotychides commanded the Spartan fleet that sailed against the Persians at Mycale in Asia

Minor, and defeated them there in 479 B.C., traditionally on the same day as the Greeks at Plataea defeated the Persian forces under Mardonius. Later he commanded the Spartans in a war against Thessaly and might have conquered the whole region but for his probable acceptance of a bribe. Discovered in his tent with a large sum of silver, he was brought to trial and fled, or was banished, from Sparta. His house was destroyed and he took refuge at Tegea where he subsequently died, c469 B.C.

Lepidus (lep'i-dus), **Marcus Aemilius.** [Surnamed **Porcina.**] Roman consul (137 B.C.) and orator. He was sent into Spain during his consulship, and conducted an unsuccessful war against the Vaccaei.

Lepidus, Marcus Aemilius. Roman politician; died c77 B.C. He was the father of Lepidus the triumvir (died 13 B.C.). He was praetor of Sicily, 81 B.C., took the side of Sulla in the civil war, but then abandoned him and with Pompey's help became consul, 78 B.C. He unsuccessfully attempted to alter Sulla's constitution and was then ordered to a provincial post by the Senate to remove him from Rome. On his way to his post, Transalpine Gaul, he began to raise an army in defiance of the Senate, which thereupon declared him an enemy of Rome. Pompey and Catulus led the resistance when he marched on Rome, 77 B.C., and defeated him in the Campus Martius. He went to Sardinia and died shortly thereafter.

Lepidus, Marcus Aemilius. Roman politician; died 13 B.C. He was consul, 46 B.C., and took the side of Caesar in the civil war. When Caesar was assassinated (44 B.C.), Lepidus was at the head of an army preparing to go to Gaul. In the disturbances that followed Caesar's death he allied himself with Mark Antony, and became a member of the Second Triumvirate with Octavian and Antony in 43 B.C. Octavian and Antony took away his provinces of Spain and Gaul and relegated him to a minor role in the affairs of government. He was later given command of 20 legions in Africa and became so convinced of his strength that he demanded an equal role in the Triumvirate, but without success. In 36 B.C. he sailed to Sicily to raise rebellion against Octavian but was betrayed by the soldiers, who went over to the latter. Lepidus was sent into permanent exile, which he passed at Circeii.

Lepini (lā-pē'nē), **Monti.** Italian name of the Volscian Mountains.

Lepontine Alps (lē-pon'tin, -tīn). [Italian, **Alpi Lepontine.**] That part of the Alps which extends from the Simplon Pass E to the Splügen Pass. It comprises the St. Gotthard, Ticino, and Adula Alps. Highest peak, Monte Leone (about 11,655 feet).

Lepreum (lep'rē-um). City of Elis on the coast of the Cyparissian Gulf. Some say that the city was founded by Minyans who had come from the island of Lemnos and settled there. They say the city was named for Lepreus, who challenged Heracles to a series of contests and was killed. Others say the city got its name from the disease that afflicted the inhabitants. The disease was called leprosy but was not the same as the modern disease of that name. It was a skin affection in which the skin became whitish in color, rough, and scaly. The people of Lepreum wished to be thought Arcadians, but they were in fact Eleans, and when they won in the Olympic Games, were announced as Eleans from Lepreum. Near Lepreum was the spring of Arene, said to have been so named for the wife of Aphareus.

Lepreus (lep'rē-us). According to tradition, a son of Caucon. He founded the city of Lepreum near the Messenian border of Elis. This city, named after him, or as some say because of the leprosy that attacked the earliest settlers of the district, became the chief seat of his father's worship. Lepreus incurred the enmity of Heracles because he advised Augeas to bind Heracles when the latter asked to be paid for cleaning the Augean stables. Later, on learning that Heracles was on his way to the city, Lepreus, at his mother's urging, agreed to receive Heracles and ask his forgiveness. Heracles agreed to do so, but challenged him to three contests: throwing the discus, drinking the greatest quantity of water, and eating an ox. Heracles won the first two, but Lepreus ate his ox the faster. Immediately he challenged Heracles to a duel, in which Lepreus was clubbed to death.

Leptis Magna (lep'tis mag'na). [Also: **Leptis, Neapolis;** modern name, **Lebda.**] In ancient geography, a seaport in N Africa, on the

Libyan coast just E of the present town of
Homs, said to have been founded by Sidonians. After the Second Punic War it was
conquered by the Numidians, but in the wars
waged by Jugurtha for control of Numidia,
it appealed to Rome for protection and became an ally. It was the birthplace of
Septimius Severus, Emperor of Rome 193–
211 A.D., who embellished it with handsome
buildings and extensive public works, including Septimius' great arch. Beginning in the
4th century it was repeatedly raided from
the desert and its population dwindled; its
ruins remain today, however, the most imposing of Roman Africa. The most recent
explorations have indicated the presence of
a Punic settlement underlying the imperial
city.

Lepus (lē′pus). ["The Hare."] An ancient
southern constellation, situated south of Orion
and east of Canis Major. Its brightest star
is in a line from the middle star of Orion's
Belt through the sword of Orion.

Lerna (lėr′na). In ancient geography, a
marshy region and town in Argolis, Greece,
S of Argos, and situated on the Gulf of
Argolis. It is said that out of love for Amymone, daughter of Danaus, Poseidon caused
a never-failing spring to gush forth here,
which became the source of the never-dry
river of Lerna. Some say the marsh of Lerna
was the home of the Nereids. On the banks
of the river the many-headed Lernaean Hydra
was born under a plane tree. It lived in the
marsh and was so devastating that the name
Lerna became synonymous with evil in the
saying, "A Lerna of evils." To the marsh
came Heracles, who sought out the monster,
and with the aid of Iolaus slew it. In the
marsh was the bottomless Alcyonean Lake
that once the Emperor Nero tried, and failed,
to sound. Some say this lake was an entrance
to Hades. Into it, they say, Dionysus
plunged when he went to Hades to seek his
mother. His descent to Hades was remembered annually with secret rites on the banks
of the lake at night. Vine-wreathed trumpets
pealed forth to summon the god up from the
depths. According to some accounts, the
heads of the sons of Aegyptus, murdered on
their wedding night by their brides, the
daughters of Danaus, were buried at Lerna.
The Danaids were afterward purified for the

murders in the waters of Lerna by Athena
and Hermes but this did not save them from
punishment in Hades. Danaus raised a shrine
to Athena on the bank of the river Pontinus
that flows through the marsh. In a sacred
grove on the slopes of Mount Pontinus, west
of the marsh, were images of Demeter,
Dionysus, and Prosymna, the latter said to
be one of the nurses of Hera. Lerna was a
place where murderers went for purification.
The river Lerna was also called Amymone,
after the daughter of Danaus loved by Poseidon.

Lernaea (lėr-nē′a). Epithet of Demeter.
Mysteries were celebrated in honor of Lernaean Demeter (*Of Lerna*) at Lerna. Here,
some say, Hades disappeared into the earth
with Persephone.

Lerus (lē′rus) or **Leros** (lē′ros). [Also: **Lero.**]
Small, rocky island in the Aegean Sea, about
32 miles S of Samos and lying N of Calymna.
In the course of the Ionian revolt against
Persia, which began 499 B.C., Aristagoras,
one of the chief instigators, was forced to
flee from Miletus to Myrcinus in Macedonia
by the successes of the Persians. Hecataeus
the historian proposed to the Ionians that
they retire to Lerus with its deep and well-
protected harbors, fortify it, and prepare to
resist the Persians from there, or make it a
base for a later return to Miletus. His advice was not taken. Area of the island, about
28 square miles.

Lesbia (lez′bi-a). Name by which Clodia, the
favorite of Catullus, is referred to in his
poems.

Lesbian Adventures (lez′bi-an), **The.** [Also:
Lesbiaca.] Greek romance, attributed to
Longus.

Lesbos (lez′bos). [Also: **Lesvos, Mytilene,
Mitylene, Mytilini;** Italian, **Metelino;** Turkish
Midillü.] Mountainous and fertile island in
the N Aegean Sea, lying just off the coast of
Asia Minor opposite ancient Mysia. It was
to this island, according to legend, that the
dismembered head of Orpheus floated after
it had been tossed into the Hebrus River by
the maenads. His lyre also landed here and
remained until, at the request of Apollo and
the Muses, it was translated to the heavens
as the constellation Lyra. In the Trojan
War, Lesbos belonged to Priam's realm and
was assaulted and taken by the forces of

Achilles. In later times the noble families of Lesbos claimed descent from Agamemnon. The island was colonized by Aeolians and was one of the strongest Aeolian centers. In the late 7th and early 6th centuries B.C. Pittacus, known as one of the Seven Sages of Greece, became tyrant and put an end to the internecine wars that divided the island. Later in the 6th century B.C. Polycrates, tyrant of Samos, defeated the Lesbians in a sea fight when they came out against him to aid Miletus. The Lesbians he captured in the battle were put in chains and compelled to build the moat around the castle at Samos. The island came under the dominion of the Persians and revolted, along with the Ionian cities, in 499 B.C. through hatred of the satrap Coes set over them by Darius. They furnished men and ships to Histiaeus, a leader of the revolt. However, in the battle of Lade (494 B.C.) for the relief of Miletus to which the Lesbians sent 70 ships, the Lesbians sailed away without joining the battle, and the following year Lesbos again fell to the Persians. After the Persian War Lesbos joined the Confederacy of Delos, under Athenian leadership, as an ally that contributed ships and was not required to pay tribute. In 428 B.C. Lesbos, a free ally, revolted against Athens. The Athenians sent a fleet, besieged Mytilene, which had now become the chief seat of resistance as well as the center of affairs of the island, and compelled its surrender. The Athenians voted in assembly to put the entire adult male population of Mytilene to death and to sell the women and children into slavery. A ship was sent to Mytilene bearing the order, but the day after the vote was taken in Athens reaction set in, the vote was rescinded, and a second ship, whose crew was promised large rewards if the first ship was overtaken, set out for Lesbos to countermand the first terrible order. The second ship arrived at Mytilene almost at the same time as the first ship, whose commander had not been in a hurry to deliver his fatal message. The ringleaders of the revolt were executed, the Lesbian fleet was taken over by Athens, and the walls of Mytilene were pulled down, but the population of Mytilene was spared. A second revolt, 412 B.C., was also put down. In the last years of the Peloponnesian War

the island was frequently attacked by the Spartans and their allies and parts of it were taken. Most of it was won back for Athens by Thrasybulus. It joined the second Athenian Confederacy in 377 B.C. and remained loyal. Later in the 4th century B.C. it fell to Macedonia. It was taken by Mithridates of Pontus (88 B.C.), and when he was defeated by the Romans, it became part of the Roman province of Asia. The five chief cities of ancient Lesbos were Mytilene, Methymna, Antissa, Eresus, and Pyrrha. The island was celebrated in ancient times as a seat of literature. In the 7th century B.C. it produced the musician Terpander, the Cyclic poet Lesches, and the poet Arion of Methymna who was credited with inventing the dithyramb, or cyclic chorus. The lyric poets Sappho and Alcaeus were contemporaries of Pittacus in the 6th century B.C. The philosophers Theophrastus (c372–c287 B.C.) and Cratippus (1st century B.C.) were also natives of Lesbos. Area of the island, about 630 square miles.

Lesches (les′kēz) or **Lescheus** (les′kūs). Greek cyclic poet, born at Pyrrha near Mytilene, and active in the 7th century B.C. He was the reputed author of a lost poem entitled *The Little Iliad,* in four books. It was designed to be a sequel to the *Iliad* of Homer, and related the events which followed the death of Hector, namely, the fate of Telamonian Ajax, the exploits of Odysseus, and the fall of Troy.

Lesser Eleusinia (el-ū-sin′i-a). An annual festival at Athens, held as a prelude to the Great Eleusinia in the last days of February and early days of March.

Lethe (lē′thē). In Greek mythology: 1) The personification of oblivion; a daughter of Eris. 2) The river of oblivion, one of the streams of Hades, the waters of which possessed the property of causing those who drank of them to forget their former existence. The dead drank upon their arrival in Hades; and souls destined for reincarnation had to drink of it to forget everything they had seen before returning to earth. Ariosto places Lethe in the moon; Dante places it in purgatory.

Leto (lē′tō). [Latin, **Latona**.] In Greek mythology, a daughter of the Titans Coeus and Phoebe. Some say she was the gentle wife of Zeus, before he married Hera, and bore him the twins Apollo and Artemis. But others say Zeus pursued her after he was married to Hera, and that he transformed himself and Leto into quails before he ravished her. Hera was wild with jealousy when she learned Leto was to bear the children of Zeus. She sent the serpent Python to pursue her. She ordered that no place on earth where the sun shone should receive Leto. As the time for the birth of her children approached, Leto was rejected by heaven, earth, and sea; she fled before Python hopelessly. Some say the South Wind bore her to Ortygia, a tiny island near Delos, and that there she bore Artemis without pain; but others say Poseidon sent a dolphin that carried her over the sea on its back. As soon as Artemis was born she helped her mother across the sea to Delos, another tiny island, which was the only spot on earth to offer her hospitality. There, leaning against a palm tree on the side of a mountain and shaded from the sun, or as some say, in a cave, Leto bore Apollo after nine days of labor. Up to this time Delos had been a floating island; it now became anchored or, as some say, four pillars sprang up from the bottom of the sea to hold it in place because of the kindness to Leto. As the birthplace of Apollo it became one of his favorite and most sacred shrines. In a later time no one was permitted to be born there: women near the time of their confinement were removed to a nearby island. And no one was permitted to die there: the very ill were also carried to a nearby island so that they might not pollute the sacred place. Some say both Artemis and Apollo were born on Delos. According to some accounts, Hera continued to harass Leto, and compelled her to flee from Delos shortly after her children were born. She arrived at last in Lycia. Exhausted, she came to a lake in a valley. She knelt to drink of its waters for she was faint from hunger and thirst. Peasants gathering rushes on the brim of the lake tried to prevent her from drinking, and ended by muddying the waters so that she could not drink. To punish them, Leto said they should live forever in this lake of theirs that was so precious to them: she transformed them into frogs. An altar was raised to Leto on that spot. Apollo at length killed the Python and Leto went to Delphi. On her way she stepped into a sacred grove to perform some rites. Tityus, the giant son of Elara and Zeus, attacked her and attempted to violate her. Apollo, hearing her cries, rushed to her defense and with his arrows slew Tityus. Apollo and Artemis were ever devoted protectors of their mother's honor. When Niobe boasted of her lineage, her beauty, her riches—and above all—of her children, and called on the people of Thebes to worship her instead of Leto who had only two children, Leto called on Apollo and Artemis to avenge the insult and the insolence of Niobe. Apollo and Artemis swept down and killed all the seven sons and seven daughters of Niobe. As the mother of the Olympians Apollo and Artemis, Leto went to dwell in Olympus and was worshiped in connection with her children.

Letrini (let-rī′ni). [Modern name, **Pirgos** or **Pyrgos.**] Town in Elis, said to have been founded by Letreus, son of Pelops. In the temple of Artemis the Letrinians worshiped the goddess as Alphaea, because it was at Letrini that she daubed her face and the faces of her nymphs with white clay to escape the embraces of the river-god Alpheus.

Leucaeus (lö-sē′us). Epithet of Zeus, meaning "Of the White Poplar." Some say Heracles brought the white poplar to Elis from Thesprotia, where he found it growing on the banks of the Acheron River, and that he burned the thigh bones of victims being sacrificed to Zeus at Elis on the wood of the white poplar. Thenceforth the Eleans used only the wood of the white poplar in sacrificing to Zeus. There was a temple of Zeus Leucaeus at Lepreum in Elis.

Leucas (lö′kas). [Also: **Leucadia, Leukados, Levkas**; Italian, **Santa Maura.**] One of the Ionian Islands, W of Aetolia and Acarnania in Greece. The island is separated from the mainland by only a narrow channel, and the ancients considered it as a peninsula which had been artificially made into an island by a man-made channel. Some say the island was named for Leucadius, a brother of Penelope, who was a king in Acarnania. And some say Leucas is the island described in the *Odyssey* as Ithaca, the center of the island kingdom of Odysseus. Those who hold this view claim that Homer's description fits

fat, fāte, fär, fãre, errant; net, mē, hèr ardent; pin, pīne; not, nōte, möve, nôr,

Leucas and profess to recognize the site of Odysseus' palace at Nidri on the east coast. The great bay of Ithaca described by Homer is identified with the bay of Vlikhon. Other spots specifically described in the *Odyssey* have been identified by those who hold the view that Leucas was the home of Odysseus. The surface of the island is hilly and mountainous. A rocky promontory (Cape Doukato) was the site of a temple of Apollo which, according to some accounts, was built by Cephalus. It was from this cliff that Cephalus, grieving for his wife Procris whom he had unwittingly slain, leaped into the sea. Aeneas and his companions stopped on their way from Troy to Italy and held Trojan Games on Leucas. Near the ancient temple of Apollo on the promontory in the SW part of the island is a steep cliff, known as Sappho's Leap, from which the poetess Sappho is said to have thrown herself into the sea. The ancient city of Leucas was founded by colonists from Corinth in the 7th century B.C. These colonists are said to have made Leucas into an island by cutting a canal across the isthmus. The canal later was silted up, for in 425 B.C. the Peloponnesian fleet was hauled across the Isthmus. In the time of Augustus the canal was cleared and the channel deepened. Bronze-age tombs and pottery found on the island indicate that it was occupied in Mycenaean times.

Leuce (lö′sē). In Greek mythology, a nymph who was pursued by Hades. To prevent him from violating her, she was transformed into a white poplar tree and stands beside the Pool of Memory in the Underworld.

Leuce. In ancient geography, a wooded island off the mouth of the Ister river (Danube) in the Euxine Sea. According to some accounts in Greek mythology, Poseidon, at the request of Thetis, gave this island to Achilles and to it he retired after he was slain at Troy. His shade was joined by his companions Patroclus, Antilochus, the two Ajaxes, and Helen. There was a temple of Achilles there that contained an image of him and one of Helen. According to tradition, seamen were permitted to land and make sacrifices, but had to leave the island before sunset. No one could live on the island and women were absolutely forbidden to set foot on it. Achilles and his companions made merry there, and mariners sailing nearby claimed they could hear the voices of Achilles and his friends singing the verses of Homer, and sometimes the clashing of shields and the sound of horses stamping their hoofs were said to be wafted over the waves.

Leucerae, Lacus (lö-sēr′ē lā′kus). [Modern name, **Lake Lecco.**] Southeastern arm of Lacus Larius (Lake Como), NW Italy. Length, about 13 miles.

Leucippe (lö-sip′ē). One of the daughters of Minyas, king in Orchomenus. See **Minyades.**

Leucippe. According to legend, the mother of Teuthras, king in Mysia. When her son was smitten with madness and a violent skin disease for killing a boar that had fled to the temple of Artemis, Leucippe, taking the seer Polyidus with her, appeased the goddess with rich sacrifices. When Teuthras was restored to sanity and his skin disorder was cured, Leucippe built an altar to Artemis. She caused a boar, with the head of a man, to be made of gold. This image, when threatened, sought refuge in the temple of Artemis and cried, "Spare me!", even as did the real boar which Teuthras had impiously slain.

Leucippe. Daughter of Thestor, sister of Theonoë and Calchas. See **Thestor.**

Leucippides (lö-sip′i-dēz). In Greek mythology, the daughters of Leucippus: Phoebe, a priestess of Athena, and Hilaira, a priestess of Artemis. They were betrothed to their cousins, Idas and Lynceus, but were carried off by Castor and Polydeuces and became the mothers of sons by them.

Leucippus (lö-sip′us). In Greek mythology, a son of Oenomaus. He loved the nymph Daphne, but she was a follower of Artemis and scorned men. Leucippus disguised himself as a maiden and was accepted as a companion of Daphne and her friends in their hunting expeditions. Apollo also loved Daphne, and he advised the maidens to bathe naked to be sure that all were maidens. When the disguise of Leucippus was thus revealed Daphne and her companions set upon him and tore him to pieces.

Leucippus. In Greek legend, the son of Gorgophone and Perieres, brother of Aphareus, and grandson of Perseus. He shared the rule of Messene with his brother when Perieres died. He was the father of the Leucippides: Phoebe and Hilaira.

Leucippus. Greek philosopher, active c450 B.C. He originated an Atomic theory, according to which the atom is the irreducible solid, the basic substance of which all matter, whatever its shape, size, or ability to move, is composed.

Leucon (lö′kon). In Greek mythology, a son of Athamas, king of Orchomenus in Boeotia, and Nephele, a cloud-born woman. He sickened and died because of his father's crimes.

Leucopetra (lö-kop′e̲-tra̲). [Modern Italian name, **Capo dell' Armi.**] In ancient geography, a promontory at the SW extremity of Italy.

Leucopetra. In ancient geography, a village on the Isthmus of Corinth. Here (146 B.C.) the Romans under Mummius defeated the Achaean League under Diaeus.

Leucophryne (lū″ko̲-frī′nē). An epithet of Artemis. She was worshiped as Leucophryne by the Magnesians of Asia. The sons of Themistocles dedicated a bronze statue of Artemis Leucophryne on the Acropolis because their father had been made governor of Magnesia in Asia by the Persian king. The epithet Leucophryne was taken from Leucophrys, a town in the valley of the Maeander River, where there was a very holy sanctuary of Artemis. At Magnesia on the Maeander was a magnificent Ionic temple of Artemis Leucophryne that was the third largest temple in Asia. The image in it wore a mural crown. The lower part of the body of the image resembled a pillar, and fillets hung from the outstreched arms of the upper part.

Leucophrys (lū-ko̲′fris). An ancient name for the island of Tenedos. It was renamed Tenedos for Tenes, son of Cycnus, who landed there safely with his sister Hemithea when they had been cast into the sea in a chest by his father because of a false accusation, made against Tenes by Phylonome, second wife of Cycnus.

Leucothea (lö-koth′e̲-a̲). A sea-goddess, formerly the mortal Ino who had been metamorphosed into a goddess when she leaped into the sea to escape from her husband Athamas whom Hera had driven mad. She gave Odysseus a veil to buoy him up when Poseidon in a great storm destroyed the raft on which he had left the island of Calypso. Leucothea advised Odysseus to abandon the fragments of the raft and with the help of the veil to swim to Phaeacia, after which his troubles would be over. See also, **Ino.**

Leucothoë (lö-koth′o̲-ē). In Greek mythology, a Babylonian princess who was transformed into a sweet-smelling plant by Apollo.

Leuctra (lök′tra̲) or **Leuctrum** (-trum). A city on the eastern coast of the Gulf of Messenia. It was claimed by the Lacedaemonians. The Messenians, who also claimed it as formerly a part of Messenia, said it was named for Leucippus, a descendant of Perseus.

Leuctra. In ancient geography, a locality in Boeotia, Greece, about seven miles SW of Thebes. It is celebrated for the victory (371 B.C.) gained here by the Thebans under Epaminondas over the Spartans under Cleombrotus. The battle is significant as the decisive end of Spartan military supremacy in Greece and as a tactical turning point in military history, Epaminondas's victory being the result of his concentration of overwhelming force at a single point in the enemy line. He did this by strengthening the left wing of his phalanx to a depth of 50 men and by having it advance ahead of the other wing.

Leucus (lö′kus). A legendary Cretan who became the paramour of Meda, wife of King Idomeneus, while the king was away at the Trojan War. He murdered Meda and her daughter, and took the throne of Crete. When Idomeneus returned to Crete after the war, Leucus banished him, using as a pretext the occurrence of a pestilence following his arrival.

Leucus. In the *Iliad,* a valiant companion of Odysseus. He was slain at the siege of Troy by Antiphus, a son of Priam.

Leukothea (lö-ko̲-thē′a̲). See **Leucothea.**

Levadia (le-vä′thyä), or **Levadhia, Levadeia, Livadia.** See **Lebadia.**

Levana (le-vä′na̲). In Roman religion, a goddess of childbirth and protectress of children.

Liber (lī′bėr). In Italian mythology, a god of the vine and wine, worshiped as a fertility god, who became identified with the Greek Dionysus. He was honored, with his female counterpart, Libera, at the festival *Liberalia,* celebrated on March 17.

Libera (lib′e̲-ra̲). In Italian mythology, a goddess of the vine and wine, partner of the wine-god Liber, worshiped as a fertility goddess. She became, in this capacity, identified with the Greek Persephone.

Liberalia (lib-ẹ-rā′li-ạ). An ancient Roman festival celebrated annually on March 17 in honor of Liber and Libera.

Liberalis (lib-ẹ-rā′lis), **Antoninus**. See **Antoninus Liberalis.**

Libertas (li-bėr′tas). The Roman personification of Liberty. She was represented wearing the Phrygian cap which symbolized liberty and sometimes with the dagger. There was a temple to Libertas on the Aventine Hill.

Libethra (lī-bē′thrạ). In ancient geography, a place at the foot of Mount Olympus where the remains of Orpheus, gathered by the Muses, were said to have been buried; the nightingales were said to sing more sweetly here than anywhere else in the world. According to legend, an oracle of Dionysus came to Libethra from Thrace, saying that when the bones of Orpheus were seen by the sun, their town would be destroyed by a boar. The people forgot the oracle. One day a shepherd leaned against the pillar on which the urn containing the bones of Orpheus was supported. The shepherd fell asleep, and presently began to sing sweetly in his sleep. Other shepherds heard him and crowded up to listen. They jostled each other in their eagerness, crowded about the pillar, and overturned it, so that the urn fell to the ground and broke open. The bones within it were exposed to the sun. The following night a torrential rain fell. The river Sys (*Boar*) flooded its banks, breached the walls of Libethra, overturned the sanctuaries of the gods and the houses of men, and drowned the inhabitants and their animals. At a later time, Macedonians from Dium came to the place, took the bones of Orpheus, and carried them to their own city.

Libitina (lib-i-tī′nạ). Ancient Italian goddess of gardens and vineyards. By confusion with the word "libido" she was mistakenly regarded as a goddess of passion. Later Venus became identified with her as Venus Libitina, especially in her aspect as goddess of death and of burials. In this aspect she was later identified with Proserpina. By tradition, a piece of money was deposited in her temple for every one who died in Rome.

Libra (lī′brạ). The seventh sign of the zodiac—the Balance—which the sun enters about September 23. Also, a zodiacal constellation, representing an ordinary pair of scales. This constellation was not commonly used among the Greeks, its place being occupied by the Chelae, or Scorpion's Claws. It is found, however, in all the Egyptian zodiacs, going back to 600 B.C.; but there is reason to believe that it is not as old as the rest of the zodiac (that is, 2000 years or more B.C.).

Library. Before the time of Aristotle, we hear of individuals who possessed private collections of books; and evidence of an industry of copying manuscripts and of a market in used books suggests a reading public; but it was Aristotle who first set out deliberately to collect copies of those works which interested him. The Greek kings of Egypt set the pattern for large state libraries. Either Ptolemy I Soter (ruled, first as satrap, later as king, 323–283 B.C.), or Ptolemy II Philadelphus (285–246 B.C.) established the Library at Alexandria which was said eventually to have possessed several hundred thousand volumes. (It should be noted that the unit usually translated "book," the *volumen,* literally, "roll," is the optimum size of a papyrus scroll convenient to handle, corresponding to a "book" of Herodotus, Thucydides, or Livy, or to 30–40 pages of modern print.) Under the direction of successive eminent scholars, the Library and the associated Museum at Alexandria became an institute for advanced research, and as a center of Hellenistic literary production and criticism was without rival in the ancient world, though the library founded by Eumenes II at Pergamum enjoyed wide fame and was reputed to contain 200,000 rolls. According to Strabo, Aristotle's disciple Theophrastus left the manuscripts of the master's works to one Neleus of Scepsis, whose descendants, to keep them out of the hands of the kings of Pergamum, stored them in a cellar. In one perhaps not fully reliable account, the Library of Alexandria was destroyed by fire while Caesar was besieged there, and subsequently, it is said, Antony presented the Pergamene books to Cleopatra as the nucleus of a new collection. In Rome, by the 1st century B.C., large private libraries had become commonplace (Lucullus, Cicero, Atticus, Varro, Caesar); Augustus established in Rome two libraries of Greek and Latin works; a special type of building suited to library practice was designed, and examples are known at Athens, Ephesus, Leptis Magna, and elsewhere. One of the most startling events of archaeology was the discovery at Herculaneum, in 1752, of a private library of 1800 or more rolls, complete with bookcases and a reading table; unfortunately, the papyrus had so deteriorated that the rolls have defied the most painstaking attempts to unroll them. (JJ)

Liburnia (lī-bėr′ni-a̯). 1) In ancient geography, a country in Illyria, along the Adriatic Sea, corresponding to the W part of modern Croatia, Yugoslavia. The inhabitants were celebrated as navigators and pirates. 2) A fast, light cutter developed by the inhabitants of Liburnia, originally for piracy, the *liburna* or *liburnica*. The Romans adopted it and it became an indispensable part of the imperial fleet.

Liburnum (lī-bėr′num) or **Liburni Portus** (lī-bėr′nī pōr′tus). [Modern name, **Livorno**; English, **Leghorn**.] Seaport of C Italy, on the Ligurian Sea.

Libya (lib′i-a̯). In ancient geography, a name of varying signification, denoting Africa, or Africa excluding Egypt, or Africa excluding Egypt and Ethiopia.

Libyan Desert (lib′i-an). [In Egypt, **Western Desert**.] In ancient times, the Sahara; now restricted to an extremely barren and partly sandy desert region extending from the W side of the Nile valley to E central Libya. Area, about 750,000 square miles.

Libyans (lib′i-anz). Inhabitants of ancient Libya, a Hamitic-speaking group. Their extinct languages and dialects, called Old Libyan, belonged to the Hamitic group of languages.

Libyan Sea. [Latin, **Libycum Mare**.] In ancient geography, that part of the Mediterranean which extends from what is now Tunisia E to Egypt.

Licata (lē-kä′tä). See **Phintias**.

Lichas (lī′kas). In Greek legend, a herald of Heracles. He escorted the captive Iole to Deianira, and tried to protect Deianira from the knowledge that Heracles had transferred his affections to Iole and intended his wife to share her house with his captive. Deianira gave the ceremonial robe which she had anointed with what she thought was a love charm to Lichas to take to Heracles. When Heracles put it on he was soon consumed as by a fire, for the love charm turned out to be a poison. Lichas, although he was innocent of any evil intent—as indeed, was Deianira—hid from his master's fury, but Heracles found him and, condemning him for being the bearer of the fatal robe, flung him into the Euboean Sea. Lichas turned to stone as he whistled through the air, and his stone body formed a small reef onto which sailors feared to step because they did not want to hurt Lichas.

Lichas. According to Greek tradition, a Spartan who was sent to the oracle at Delphi to learn how he could find the bones of Orestes, after the Spartans had learned from the oracle that they would not be victorious in their wars against the Tegeans until they secured the bones of Orestes from Tegea. The priestess told Lichas to go where two winds meet, where stroke meets stroke, and where evil rings upon evil. There he would find the bones he sought buried in the earth. The oracle instructed him to bring them to Sparta and make Sparta the master of Tegea. Lichas went to Tegea and came to a smithy. The smith was forging a sword of iron, instead of the usual bronze. When Lichas commented on this unusual sight, the smith told him stranger things had happened than the forging of an iron sword. He volunteered that he had found an enormous coffin containing an equally enormous skeleton when he was digging a well beneath the smithy floor. Lichas remembered the oracle and deduced that the winds referred to were those that came from the smith's bellows, the strokes were those of the hammer, and the evil upon evil was the iron sword beaten by the iron hammer, as iron was the symbol of the cruel days of the Iron Age. He returned to Sparta with the information he had gathered. The Spartans sent him back to Tegea, disguised as a fleeing slave, and he sought refuge with the smith. During the night he stole the bones from the coffin and escaped with them to Sparta. In this way the Spartans secured the bones of Orestes, and under their protection secured ascendancy over the Tegeans.

Licinian Laws or **Rogations** (lī-sin'i-an). Laws proposed by the Roman tribunes Caius Licinius Calvus Stolo and Lucius Sextius in 376 B.C. and passed in 367 B.C. They provided that one of the consuls must be a plebeian; that no person could occupy more than 500 *jugera* (somewhat more than 300 acres) of the public land; that interest on debts should be deducted from the principal and the balance paid in three years; and that plebeians should be admitted to the College of the Sibylline Books. There were provisions limiting the cattle on the public lands and limiting the slave labor on large estates.

Licinius (lī-sin'i-us). [Full name, **Caius Licinius Calvus Stolo**.] Roman tribune (377 B.C.) who proposed the Licinian Laws. The laws brought a peaceful end to the struggle between patricians and plebeians. Licinius, who was active 377–361 B.C., was consul in 364 and 361 B.C. He was afterward fined for possessing more of the public land than was allowed by his own laws.

Lictor (lik'tor). Among the ancient Romans, one of a number of officers required to be free-born (though freedmen were admitted to the office under the empire), whose functions were to attend a magistrate, bearing the fasces, in some cases with the ax and in others without it, in order to clear the way and enforce due respect, and also to arrest offenders and to scourge or behead condemned persons. According to tradition, Romulus established the custom of having the lictors precede the magistrate. Some say that the idea was taken from the Etruscans and that the number represented the 12 Etruscan cities. Magistrates were entitled to a number of lictors according to their rank, a dictator having 24, a consul 12, a praetor six (at first only two within the city walls), etc. The *flamen Dialis*, or priest of Jupiter, and the vestals also had lictors, but, it is believed, without fasces.

Licymnius (lī-sim'ni-us). In Greek legend, a son of Electryon and Midea. He was the uncle and companion of Heracles. In his old age he unfortunately stumbled between Tlepolemus, the son of Heracles, and a servant he was punishing. Tlepolemus acci-

dentally struck him with a club and killed him.

Ligarius (li-gãr'i-us), **Quintus.** Roman commander; fl. in the middle of the 1st century B.C. He was an adherent of Pompey, and was defended before Caesar by Cicero.

Liguria (li-gū'ri-a). In ancient geography, the country of the Ligurians, in NW Italy and SE France. At the time of Augustus it was included between the Mediterranean and the rivers Varus, Padus, Trebia, and Magra. Originally it extended beyond these limits. It was at war with Rome from c200 B.C. to c120 B.C., and was finally subjugated in 14 B.C.

Ligurians (li-gū'ri-anz). Ancient eponymous inhabitants of Liguria, occupying a region from the Mediterranean coast into SE Gaul. One group of Ligurii, of mixed Celtic and Germanic stock, was subjugated by Rome.

Ligurian Sea. [Italian, **Mar Ligure**; French, **Mer Ligurienne**; Latin, **Mare Ligusticum**.] That part of the Mediterranean Sea which lies between Liguria and Corsica.

Lilybaeum (lil-i-bē'um). [Modern name, **Marsala**.] In ancient geography, a city on the W coast of Sicily. According to Greek tradition, it was founded by Eryx, the son of Aphrodite and the Argonaut Butes. In actuality, it was founded in 396 B.C. by the Carthaginian general Himilco to take the place of the Carthaginian stronghold of Motya, which had been destroyed (398 B.C.) by Dionysius the Elder of Syracuse and recaptured by Himilco (397 B.C.). Lilybaeum became the chief stronghold of the Carthaginians in Sicily; it resisted Dionysius and Pyrrhus (368 B.C. and 276 B.C. respectively) and the Romans during the First Punic War (264–241 B.C.), who occupied it only at the end of the war. It was used as the place of Scipio's embarkation for Africa in the Second Punic War (218–201 B.C.).

Limenia (lim-e-nī'a). An epithet of Aphrodite in her aspect as goddess of the sea, meaning "Of the Harbor."

Limnae (lim'nē). In ancient geography, a section of Athens, Greece, important as the seat of the earliest cult of Dionysus and the first rudimentary dramatic performances at Athens.

Limnae or **Limnaeum** (-um). A place in Laconia sacred to Artemis Orthia (*Upright*), because the wooden image of Artemis was said to have been brought from Tauris by Orestes and Iphigenia to this spot.

Limnaea (lim-nē'a̤). An epithet, meaning "Of the Lake." It was applied to Artemis when she was identified with Britomartis of Crete.

Limnatis (lim-nā'tis). An epithet of Artemis, meaning "Of the Lake." There was a sanctuary of Artemis Limnatis on the road to Epidaurus. At another temple of Artemis Limnatis on the border between Messenia and Laconia, Spartan maidens who were visiting the shrine were attacked, some say, by Messenian youths, and this brought on a war between Messenia and Sparta.

Limni (lēm'nē) or **Limno** (lēm'nô) or **Limnos** (lēm'nôs). See **Lemnos.**

Limnoria (lim-nō'ri-a̤). In Greek mythology, a daughter of Nereus and Doris.

Limon (lī'mon). In Greek legend, a son of Tegeates of Tegea and Maera, and the brother of Scephrus. When Apollo was investigating the rulers who had refused to receive Leto before her children were born, he came to Tegea with his sister Artemis. Scephrus took him aside and talked privately with him. Limon thought Scephrus was accusing him to Apollo, rushed forth and murdered his brother. Artemis pursued Limon and shot him with her arrows. Afterward, at the festival of Apollo Agyieus (*God of the Streets*) the pursuit of Limon by Artemis was commemorated by having the priestess of Artemis pursue a man.

Lindus (lin'dus). In ancient geography, a city on the southeast coast of the island of Rhodes, situated on a commanding and readily defended height. Cadmus is said to have stopped there in his search for Europa and to have built a temple to Poseidon. According to some accounts, the city was founded by the Telchines and named after one of the Danaids who died there on the flight to Argos. Homer wrote that Tlepolemus, the son of Heracles, fled to the island of Rhodes after accidentally killing Licymnius, and that Lindus was one of the three cities his followers founded on the island. He also names it as a contributor to the nine Rhodian galleys that Tlepolemus brought to the side of the Greeks in the Trojan War. Prehistorically colonized by settlers from Crete, it was a Dorian city from about 1000 B.C., and

was a member of the Dorian Hexapolis—six Dorian cities on or near the coast of Asia Minor. In the centuries preceding the Persian Wars it was an important port of over 100,000 inhabitants, owing to its strategic location and wide commerce throughout the Mediterranean. It was also the mother city of many colonies on the neighboring islands and on the coast of Asia Minor. Cleobulus, one of the Seven Sages of Greece, was tyrant of Lindus in the 6th century B.C. A lofty promontory, rising abruptly from the sea, formed the acropolis of the city, and was crowned with a Doric temple of Athena Lindia. Remains of the temple, of majestic propylaea, and of a theater, may still be seen. Lindus was the capital of the island of Rhodes until 408 B.C., when the three principal cities of the island—Lindus, Camirus, and Ialysus—jointly founded the city of Rhodes and made it the capital. With the growth of the city of Rhodes as a religious, political, and commercial center, Lindus lost its commanding importance in the ancient world. Modern Lindos, a village of about 1000 inhabitants, occupies the site of the ancient city at the base of the acropolis.

Linus (lī'nus). In Greek mythology, a son of Apollo and Psamathe, daughter of Crotopus of Argos. Psamathe feared the wrath of her father and left her child on a mountain to die, but he was found and brought up by shepherds. Psamathe, learning of this, was relieved to know her son lived, but when he was a youth, he was torn to pieces by dogs that belonged to her father, and Psamathe was unable to disguise her grief. Crotopus realized that the slain youth was his daughter's son and condemned her to death. In grief and anger over the double loss, Apollo sent a monster, Poena, who stole young children from their mothers. This monster brought great sorrow to the land, and at last Coroebus slew it. Argos was then afflicted by a plague. The Argives sent to the oracle at Delphi to learn how they could free themselves from the plague, and were told they must sacrifice to Psamathe and Linus. They did this but the plague continued. At last Coroebus confessed that he had slain Poena. He was commanded by the priestess at Delphi to take a tripod and set forth from Delphi; where the tripod should fall to the ground, he was to raise a temple. Coroebus followed her instructions. The tripod fell to the ground on Mount Gerania; there he raised a temple of Apollo and founded the city of Tripodisci, named for the tripod. The plague now ceased, and thenceforth Linus was honored by a festival, called Arneis (*Feast of Lambs*) because he had been reared by shepherds among lambs, and by the singing of songs of lamentation called "Lini" in his memory.

Linus. According to some accounts, the son of the muse Calliope and Oeagrus, and thus a brother of Orpheus. Others give him different fathers, including Apollo, Hermes, and Amphimarus, a son of Poseidon, and different mothers, including the muses Urania and Clio. In any event, he was regarded as a great poet and as the musician who invented melody and rhythm; and it is said he was slain because of Apollo's jealousy of his talents. This Linus was the teacher of Thamyris and Orpheus. His portrait adorned the walls of a cave on Mount Helicon, and to it sacrifices were offered just before the annual sacrifices to the Muses. The body of Linus is supposed to have been buried at Thebes.

Linus. In Greek mythology, a son of the river-god Ismenius and one of the Muses. He was a skilled musician who had been taught by Apollo and who in turn taught Orpheus. He tried to instruct Heracles, but was slain when Heracles, in a fit of impatience, hurled the lyre at his head.

Linus. Song of lamentation for the death of vegetation or for the "killing" (i.e., cutting or reaping) of the vine and grain, anciently sung in Phoenicia and W Asia at the time of vintage and harvest. Sappho identified Linus with Adonis, and the Linus song with the Adonis songs, sung all over W Asia, Asia Minor, and into Greece and the Mediterranean region as the Adonis cult spread. Sir James G. Frazer suggested that the name Linus was a corruption of the words *ai lanu,* meaning "woe to us," expressing grief for the death of Adonis, symbolized in the cutting of the grain. Herodotus mentions a like song of mourning being sung by Egyptian reapers.

Lion of Chaeronea (ker-ọ-nē'ạ). Colossal marble figure of a seated lion, erected by the Thebans over the common tomb of their troops who fell in the Battle of Chaeronea in 338 B.C., when Philip II of Macedon crushed the united armies of the Greek states and ended Greek resistance. In the 19th century a brigand chief, hoping that the marble contained gold treasure, blew it up; in 1902 the fragments were reassembled, and the figure was eventually restored and replaced on its original pedestal. (JJ)

Lipari Islands (lip'ạ-ri; Italian, lē'pä-rē). Group of islands in the Tyrrhenian Sea, N of Sicily. The chief islands are Lipari (Lipara), Stromboli (Strongyle), Salina (Didyme), Vulcano (Thermessa or Vulcania), and the small islands of Alicuri (Ericussa), Filicuri (Phoenicussa), and Panarea (Euonymus or Hicesia). See **Aeoliae Insulae.**

Lipoxaïs (lī"pok-sā'is). Traditionally, the eldest son of Targitaus, the first inhabitant of Scythia. He was the founder of the Scythian race called the Auchatae. See **Colaxaïs.**

Litae (lī'tē). The daughters of Zeus, personifications of Prayer, especially prayers of repentance. In the *Iliad* they are described as halting of foot and with downcast eyes. They are appointed to follow in the footsteps of Sin, but Sin, being swift of foot, outruns them and causes many to falter and fall. The Litae come to heal the fallen, and if they are welcomed by the sinner, Zeus listens when the Litae intercede; but if they are repelled, they request that Zeus punish the offender.

Liternum (li-tėr'num). In ancient geography, a town in Campania, Italy, situated on the W coast about 14 miles NW of Naples, between Cumae and the mouth of the Volturnus River. It was noted principally as the place to which Scipio Africanus the Elder withdrew towards the end of his life. He died at Liternum and his tomb was there.

Lituus (lit'ū-us). In Roman antiquity, a staff with a recurved or crooked tip, used by the augurs in the ill-understood ritual of divination known as quartering the heavens. It was supposed to be of Etruscan origin.

Lityerses (lit-i-ėr'sēz). In Greek legend, a Phrygian farmer, bastard son of King Midas. He compelled his guests to engage in reaping contests with him in his fields. Whoever reaped less than he did had his head cut off and wrapped in a sheaf. Daphnis, who had come to Lityerses' home in search of Pimplea,

actọr; up, lūte, pu̇ll; oi, oil; ou, out; ŦH, then; ḍ as d or j, ṣ as s or sh, ṭ as t or ch, ẓ as z or zh.

was compelled to enter a reaping contest with him, but Heracles took his place, killed Lityerses and hurled his body into the Maeander River.

Livia Drusilla (liv′i-a̤ drö-sil′a̤). First Roman empress, born 56 B.C.; died 29 A.D. She was the daughter of Livius Drusus Claudianus and was married first to Tiberius Claudius Nero (the father of her sons Tiberius and Drusus), who was compelled to divorce her (38 B.C.) in order that she might become the wife of Octavian, the future emperor Augustus. She was accused of committing various crimes, even of hastening the death of her husband, in her endeavor to secure the succession to her son Tiberius. For a time after the accession of Tiberius she was all-powerful in the state, but was soon forced to retire from public affairs by her son.

Livius (liv′i-us), **Titus.** Latin name of **Livy.**

Livius Andronicus (an-dro-nī′kus, an-dron′i-kus), **Lucius.** Early Roman dramatic poet and actor, called by some the founder of Roman epic and dramatic poetry. He was a Greek, born (c284 B.C.) in the colony of Tarentum in southern Italy. When Tarentum was conquered, he was taken to Rome as a slave (242 B.C.). His master, from whom he took his name, freed him, and he entered upon the occupation of teaching Latin and Greek. He translated the *Odyssey* for his pupils' use and his translation became the Roman textbook used for centuries. In 240 B.C. he presented a drama in the Greek style in Rome with such success that it became the impetus for the development of dramatic poetry in Rome. His plays, also, were translated from the Greek.

Livius Drusus (drö′sus), **Marcus.** See **Drusus, Marcus Livius.**

Livy (liv′i). [Latin name, **Titus Livius.**] Roman historian, born at Patavium (Padua), 59 B.C.; died there 17 A.D. He went to Rome in his youth and soon became acquainted with the most important men of his time, including Augustus, although Livy was well-known for his republican principles. He has been called the most important prose writer of the Augustan Age. He wrote a comprehensive history of Rome from the founding of the city to the death (9 B.C.) of Drusus, in 142 books, of which only 35 are extant (1–10 and 21–45), although the content of

the lost books (except for two) is known through epitomes. His history has sometimes been criticized on the ground that he had a tendency to include a good story without adequate basis, and was rather too ready to accept statements and data without thorough critical evaluation. An object of his work was to revive the patriotism of his contemporaries by presenting to them, in brilliant and vivid style, a stirring account of their great heritage. His work abounds in descriptions of events and of the people who took part in them; the speeches he put into their mouths show that his own training in rhetoric had been thorough. His work, renowned in Roman days, has served as a constant source of information of early history ever since. Livy also wrote several philosophical dialogues and a work on rhetorical training, now lost. He spent the greater part of his life (over 40 years of which were given to his history) at Rome.

Lochia (lō-kī′a̤ or lō′ki-a̤). An epithet of the goddess Artemis as the protectress of women in childbirth.

Locri (lō′krī or lok′rī) or **Locri Epizephyrii** (ep″i-ze-fir′i-ī). [Modern name, **Gerace.**] In ancient geography, a city on the SE coast of what is now Calabria, founded before 680 B.C. by colonists from Opuntian and Ozolian Locri in Greece and probably also by Lacedaemonians. The severe law code prepared for the city by the famous lawgiver Zaleucus, about 650 B.C., appears to have been the first written legal code in Europe, widely copied in Magna Graecia. At one time closely allied with Syracuse, it survived the usual wars with its Greek neighbors, the Bruttians, Pyrrhus, Rome, and the Carthaginians without fatal injury, and was well-known to Polybius. Excavations have revealed a Doric temple of about 500 B.C. and traces also of an Ionic temple of the 5th century B.C., built over the foundations of a predecessor. (JJ)

Locri Epicnemidii (ep″ik-nē-mid′i-ī). Ancient Greek people dwelling along the Malian Gulf, north of Phocis; so named from Mount Cnemis.

Locri Epizephyrii (ep″i-ze-fir′i-ī). See **Locri.**

Locri Opuntii (ō-pun′shi-ī). Ancient Greek people living N of Boeotia and opposite Euboea; so named from Opus, their chief town. The name is sometimes taken to include also the country of the Locri Epicnemidii. According to Pindar, the Locrians were named for Locrus, a descendant of Deucalion, who named his people for himself. His foster son was Opus (or Opous), for whom the chief city was named. In the Trojan War Ajax the Less, an Opuntian Locrian, brought 40 ships to the Greek expedition against Troy. Because it was claimed (some say, falsely, by Odysseus), that he violated the sanctuary of Athena in seizing Cassandra who had taken refuge there during the sack of Troy, the wrath of Athena fell on the Opuntian Locrians. Ajax himself perished at sea on the way home, some say by a thunderbolt hurled at him by Athena, and his fellow countrymen reached their homeland only after great difficulty. They annually honored their former leader by launching a ship fitted with black sails and laden with gifts. Once the ship was launched, it was burned to the water's edge. The Locrians were afflicted with a terrible plague which they learned was caused by Athena. In order to free themselves of the plague they had to send two maidens to the temple of Athena at Troy each year for 1000 years, or as some say, two maidens who must be replaced when they died so that there were always two Locrian maidens in the temple. The maidens were chosen by lot from the 100 noblest families of Locris. They were sent at different times of the year so that the Trojans would not know when to expect them, and they arrived in the Troad in secrecy. If they were caught, they were slain; their bones were burned with the wood of wild trees that had never born fruit, and their ashes were scattered on the sea. If they escaped capture by the Trojans they entered Troy secretly, some say by the conduit or sewer which Odysseus is said to have used to enter Troy during the Trojan War. Once inside the temple they were safe. Wearing the single tunic of the slave, with their heads shorn and their feet bare, they served as priestesses, sweeping and sprinkling the sacred precinct. Once one of the Locrian priestesses was killed in the temple, and the Locrians stopped sending the girls to Troy. They were immediately smitten with plague again, and so they resumed their penance of sending the maidens to Troy. There is abundant historical evidence that this custom was well known to the Greeks of the Classical and Hellenistic periods, that it persisted for 1000 years, and that it ended not before the 1st century A.D., warranting our assumption that this was a real penance imposed for a real offense, e.g., Ajax the Lesser's violation of Cassandra at the altar of Athena, an example of continuity not matched elsewhere in ancient history.

Locri Ozolae (oz'ọ-lē). Ancient Greek people living along the N coast of the Corinthian Gulf, W of Phocis. Its chief towns were Amphissa and Naupactus.

Locris (lō'kris, lok'ris). In ancient geography, name applied to a division of C Greece, occupied by the Locri Epicnemidii, the Locri Opuntii, and by the Locri Ozolae. Locris was the home of Oileus, the Argonaut who was the father of Ajax the Lesser. The Locrians were allies of the Greeks in the Trojan War. As skilled bowmen, they wore no helmets and carried no shields, and were therefore valueless for close fighting.

Locrus (lō'krus). According to tradition, a descendant of Deucalion. He was king of the Locrians, whom he named after himself.

Locusta (lō-kus'tạ). [Also: **Lucusta**.] Professional poisoner living at Rome c54 A.D. Juvenal speaks of her as the agent for ridding many a wife of her husband, and Tacitus as "long reckoned as among the instruments of government." She was employed by Agrippina to prepare a poison for the emperor Claudius. She was executed in the reign of Galba (c68 A.D.).

Longinus (lon-jī'nus), **Dionysius Cassius.** Greek critic and philosopher, born c210 A.D.; executed 273 A.D. The great work entitled *On the Sublime*, an essay on literary style, has been traditionally credited to him, but modern criticism has demonstrated the improbability of his having written it. This essay is probably the work of a writer who lived in the 1st century A.D.

Longinus, Caius Cassius. See **Cassius Longinus, Caius.**

Longus (long'gus). Greek romancer and sophist, who was active probably in the 3rd or 4th century A.D. He is the reputed author of the pastoral romance *Daphnis and Chloë*, which is noted for its poetic quality, grace of

---

actọr; up, lūte, pùll; oi, oil; ou, out; ŦH, then; ḍ as d or j, ş as s or sh, ṭ as t or ch, ẓ as z or zh.

language, and loyalty to an older principle of beauty in literature for its own sake.

Lotis (lō′tis). In Greek mythology, a nymph who fled from a pursuer and was turned into a lotus tree. There are several variations on this story, in one of which it was a naiad who fled and was turned into a water lily.

Lotophagi (lō-tof′a-jī). "Lotus-Eaters"; in the *Odyssey*, the name of a people in whose country storm-driven Odysseus lands with his crews. There they are offered a plant called Lotus. Some of Odysseus' men eat of this and lose all desire to return to their friends and native land, so that Odysseus has to have them brought back by force and shackled to their rowing-benches. The Greeks applied the name *lotus* to a number of different plants, none reported to have narcotic effect; the ripe seed pod of the opium poppy, however, somewhat resembles the seed pod of the true lotus, suggesting that possibly back of Homer's allusion lay some traveler's encounter with opium. One reading the *Odyssey* passage uncritically would conclude that the land of the Lotus-Eaters was along the North African coast, Cyrenaica or Tripolitania; the geography of Odysseus' adventures defies systematic analysis, but later geographers agreed in locating the Lotophagi in Cyrenaica. (JJ)

Lotus (lō′tus). A name given by the Greeks to several distinct species of plants, shrubs, and small trees, whose flowers, leaves, fruit, seeds, or tubers were used as human or animal food. A people (of North Africa?) who use a kind of lotus for food, and offer it to Odysseus' men with unfortunate results, are called Lotophagi or "Lotus-Eaters." (JJ)

Loxias (lok′si-as). An epithet of Apollo, meaning "Crooked" or "Ambiguous." Apollo was the god who interpreted the will of Zeus to men, but they did not always interpret his prophecies correctly, whence this epithet. One of the most famous examples of misinterpretation was that of Croesus, king of Lydia, to whose question whether he should make war on the Persians, the priestess of Apollo replied that if he did so, he would destroy a great empire. Croesus, well-satisfied with this answer, waged war on Cyrus. A great empire was destroyed, but it was the empire of Croesus. Later Croesus reproached the priestess, and was told that he had not

asked which the empire would be. Croesus humbly accepted the blame for his own hasty and ill-informed act. Cassandra, to whom Apollo had given the gift of prophecy but turned it into a curse by decreeing that no one would believe her true prophecies, particularly used the epithet Loxias when invoking Apollo.

Luca (lö′ka). [Modern name, **Lucca**.] City in N Italy, NE of Pisae. Presumably established in Etruscan times, but its first certain appearance in history is in 56 B.C., when Caesar summoned Pompey and Crassus to Luca and there organized with them the First Triumvirate. Later, perhaps in Augustus' time, a veteran colony was sent there. Careful study has recovered the plan of the central city and traces of the forum and buildings: theater, amphitheater, temple, and aqueduct; and the churches of S. Giovanni, S. Frediano, and S. Alessandro incorporate shafts and capitals of ancient columns removed from other Roman structures. (JJ)

Lucan (lö′kan). [Full Latin name, **Marcus Annaeus Lucanus**.] Roman poet and prose writer, born at Corduba, Spain, 39 A.D. He was the grandson of Seneca the rhetorician, and the nephew of Seneca the philosopher. From an early age he gave evidence of his rhetorical and poetic talents. He was appointed to public office by Nero, but the latter's favor soon changed to jealousy. Nero had a high regard for his own poetic talents, and forbade Lucan to recite his poems in public, as he was becoming too popular. To avenge his treatment by the emperor Lucan took part in the conspiracy of Piso. He was betrayed, and by a promise of pardon was induced to turn informer, but, after denouncing his mother and his other accomplices, he was condemned to death. He anticipated his punishment by causing his veins to be opened (65 A.D.). Lucan was the author of the *Pharsalia*, in ten books, an epic poem on the civil war between Caesar and Pompey. The poem follows such rigid chronological order, beginning before the Battle of Pharsalus and ending with the capture of Alexandria, that some refuse to recognize it as a poem at all, but regard it rather as a history. In this work Lucan showed himself to long for the lost days of liberty and to be a follower of Pompey.

fat, fāte, fär, fāre, errant; net, mē, hėr ardent; pin, pīne; not, nōte, mŏve, nôr,

Lucania (lö-kā'ni-a). In ancient geography, a division of S Italy. It was bounded by Campania, Samnium, and Apulia on the N and NE, the Gulf of Tarentum on the E, Bruttii on the S, and the Tyrrhenian Sea on the SW. The surface is mountainous. The inhabitants were Lucanians (a branch of the Samnites) and, on the coast, Greeks. It was reduced by Rome in the 3rd century B.C.

Luceria (lö-sē'ri-a). [Modern name, **Lucera.**] In ancient geography, a town in Apulia, SE Italy. According to some accounts, the golden armor of the Trojan Diomedes was deposited in the temple of Athena here. Others say Diomedes erected the temple of Athena, and that the Palladium, brought from Troy, was preserved in it. In the wars between the Romans and the Samnites (321 B.C.) Luceria took the side of Rome. It was later colonized by the Latins.

Lucian (lö'shan). Greek satirist, born at Samosata, Syria, c120 A.D.; died c200 A.D. He was born of a poor family and gained an education and training for rhetoric by his own persistent efforts. He traveled in Greece, Italy, and southern Gaul, earning his living as an orator and advocate. In middle life he went to Athens. In his impoverished old age he was given a governmental post in Egypt, which he retained to his death. He wrote satirical dialogues in the style of Plato, but with the emphasis on the comic rather than the philosophic. For a time he studied and followed the ideas of the sophists, but became disenchanted by the aridity of their thought in his time, by their disputes, and by the wide gulf which seemed to him to separate sophist teaching and practice. He was a keen observer, learned, honest, and possessed of a highly developed sense of the ridiculous. Because he was an independent thinker, attacking with pungent satire the religious beliefs of his time, according to Suidas he was called "the Blasphemer," and was torn to pieces by dogs (doubtless a pious invention). He wrote rhetorical, critical, and biographical works, romances, dialogues, and poems. Outstanding among his works are *The True History*, a parodied travelogue, and the satirical *Dialogues of the Gods* and *Dialogues of the Dead.* In these he mocked the popular religious beliefs, aimed specially pointed barbs at Eastern superstitions that

had filtered into the west, and at the oracle-mongers who fattened on these superstitions, and attacked also the popular beliefs concerning life after death. *Auction of Philosophers* is his satiric evaluation of various schools of thought. He did not think much of them.

Lucifer (lö'si-fer). The morning star; the planet Venus when it appears in the morning before sunrise; when it appears in the evening, it is called Hesperus, or the evening star. In Greek mythology Lucifer was personified, as the father of Ceyx, for example. The name Lucifer means "light-bringer," and is a Latin translation of one of the Greek names for the planet Venus, Phosphorus. Later, Lucifer is a name of Satan before his fall.

Lucilius (lö-sī'li-us), **Caius.** Latin satirical poet, born at Suessa Aurunca, Campania, Italy, c180 B.C.; died at Naples, 103 B.C. He was born to a distinguished and wealthy family, and received a good education. When he went to Rome, he became acquainted with the most distinguished men of his time, partly, no doubt, on account of his relationship to Pompey, and he was on intimate terms with Scipio the Younger and Laelius. He was the author of *Saturae*, satirical poems that covered a wide range of topics, including the political, social, and intellectual life of his times, as well as material drawn from his own experiences and his studies. In his poems he attacked individuals, no matter how powerfully placed, if he felt they merited attention. On occasions when something worthy of praise came to his attention, he was sincerely laudatory. With his exaggerations and mockery of so many facets of life, he presents a lively picture of the time. Fragments of his work survive. Horace was among later writers who used the satires of Lucilius as a model.

Lucina (lö-sī'na). In Roman mythology, the goddess who presided over childbirth, an aspect of Juno, and as such called Juno Lucina. The name was also applied to Diana corresponding to the Greek goddess Ilithyia, and to Hecate.

Lucretia (lö-krē'sha). [Also: **Lucrece.**] In Roman legend, the wife of Tarquinius Collatinus. She was violated by Sextus, the son of Tarquinius Superbus; on her husband's return she told of the deed and killed herself. Subsequent agitation organized by Junius Brutus culminated in a popular uprising which brought about the expulsion of Rome's seventh and last king, and the establishment of the republic, in or about 510 B.C. (JJ)

Lucrinus, Lacus (lö-krī′nus lā′kus). [Modern name, **Lake Lucrine.**] In ancient geography, a small salt-water lake in Campania, Italy, about nine miles NW of Neapolis.

Lucretius (lö-krē′shus). [Full name, **Titus Lucretius Carus.**] Roman philosophical poet, born at Rome, probably c94 B.C.; died there Oct. 15, 55 B.C. For his friend Memmius, an orator and poet, he wrote *De Rerum Natura* (On the Nature of Things), the first Latin treatment of Greek philosophy. It is a didactic and philosophical poem in six books, treating of physics and cosmology, of psychology, and (briefly) of ethics from the Epicurean point of view. The point of it is to prove that all things come to be and disappear according to natural law and are unaffected by the supernatural. This being the case, the fears and terrors aroused by superstitions are unnecessary. According to his thesis, the basic substance is the atom, from which proceed not only material things, as the earth and the substances of it, but the soul and spirit as well, and with the dissolution of the atom these also perish. Death prevented Lucretius from polishing his work, yet it is marked by simplicity and power, and passages of great beauty, in spite of the scientific approach with which he attacked his subject. It is said that Lucretius committed suicide, probably in a fit of insanity. According to a popular but doubtless erroneous tradition, his madness was due to a love philter administered by his wife.

Lucullus (lö-kul′us), **Lucius Licinius.** [Surnamed **Ponticus.**] Roman general, born c117 B.C.; died 56 B.C. He served under Sulla in the East, and was curule aedile in 79 and consul in 74 B.C. He defeated Mithridates VI of Pontus in Asia Minor, 74–71 B.C., defeated Tigranes near Tigranocerta in 69, and was recalled to Rome in 66 B.C. He was afterward famous for his wealth and his luxury. His villas at Tusculum and near Neapolis (Naples) were famous for their splendor, and he is said to have spent fabulous sums on his table (a rich banquet is

still called a Lucullan feast). One anecdote tells that his dining-rooms were coded, so that a message to his chef naming only the room in which dinner was to be served indicated the degree of extravagance and ostentation with which he wished to celebrate the occasion. He is said to have been the first to introduce cherries into Italy. He was also a collector of books and a patron of learning.

Lucumo (lū′kū-mō). Among the ancient Etruscans, the head of a patrician or noble family, uniting in himself the characters of priest and prince; in general, one of the Etruscan nobility.

Lugdunensis (lug-dū-nen′sis). [Also: **Gallia Lugdunensis.**] In ancient geography, a province of the Roman Empire, situated in Gaul. It extended from Lugdunum (modern Lyons) N to the line of the lower Seine (including Paris), and NW through Brittany to the ocean, including the upper course of the Seine and nearly the entire course of the Loire. It was conquered (58–51 B.C.) by Julius Caesar.

Luna (lö′na). [Modern site name, **Luni.**] In ancient geography, a city in Italy, on the coast E of what is now La Spezia. It was founded by the Etruscans and became a Roman town in the 2nd century B.C.

Luna. In Roman mythology, the goddess of the moon. She had at Rome an ancient sanctuary on the Aventine Hill and a temple on the Palatine. The latter was illuminated at night. She figured in calendar computation especially, but had no strong cult. She was also identified with the goddess Diana.

Lunar Calendar. A system of time-reckoning formerly much in use among primitive peoples, in which the principal division was the lunar or synodic month, determined by visual observation of new moon or full moon. The average length of this period is 29.5306 days, so that the lunar month was sometimes 29, sometimes 30, days in length. A lunar year of 12 lunar months, c354.36 days, is incommensurate with the solar year of c365.2425 days, falling about 11 days short and causing a cumulative error which most early societies were at pains to correct. The Mohammedan calendar, however, consists of precisely this type of lunar year, of 12 lunar months, without intercalation, usually 354 days in length, so that the Mohammedan months revolve through the tropical year, and 100 western or Gregorian years are equal to about 103 Mohammedan years. (JJ)

Lunisolar Calendar. Any primitive system of time-reckoning in which the lunar or synodic month, which averages c29.5306 days in length, is required to serve as a division of the solar or tropical year of c365.2425 days. Since these figures are incommensurate (12 lunar months of 354.3672 days falling nearly 11 days short of the tropical year), frequent correction is required to hold the solar and lunar years in rough correspondence. This correction most often took the form of an extra "intercalary" or "embolic" month added every second or third year, preferably in some cycle so that the intercalations might be known in advance. A cycle much honored in theory, though nowhere demonstrated in certain use, was the *octaeteris* or eight-year cycle, in which five years had 12 lunar months and three intercalary years had 13 months. In the course of eight years an error of 1.5894 days was produced under this system. Far more accurate was the *enneadekateris* or 19-year cycle in which 12 years had 12 months and seven years had 13 months. In the course of the 19 years an error of about two hours accumulated. This latter calendar, first proposed in Babylonia in the 5th century B.C. or earlier, and certanly employed early in the 4th century B.C., was widely adopted in Asia, and adaptations of it are still in use. Hellenistic astronomers speak also of cycles of 38 and 76 years, but these are merely multiples of the 19-year cycle, of which they represent minor refinements. The 19-year cycle is sometimes called the Metonic Cycle, from Meton, an Athenian astronomer who was said to have introduced it in the 5th century B.C., but the evidence from the records of centuries of observations available there, indicates that the computation had been performed earlier in Babylonia. (JJ)

Lupercal (lö′pėr-kal). Cave or grotto near the W angle of the Palatine Hill, in ancient Rome, dedicated, according to tradition, by the original Arcadian settlers to Lupercus, a fertility deity, or to Inuus, or to Pan. It was said to be the den of the she-wolf that suckled Romulus and Remus. As time went on the Lupercal was adorned architecturally, and its decoration was renewed by Augustus. Near the Lupercal was the Ficus Ruminalis, the fig tree beneath which Romulus and Remus were left by the retiring waters of the Tiber, and above it was the primitive thatched hut preserved to imperial days as a relic of Romulus. According to the *Aeneid*, the Lupercal predated the founding of Rome. Evander pointed it out to Aeneas shortly after the latter landed in Latium.

Lupercalia (lö″pėr-kā′li-a). One of the most ancient of Roman festivals, celebrated every year on February 15. The origin of the festival is older than the legend of Romulus and Remus and the wolf, with which, as with the Greek cult of Lupercus (or Faunus, or Inuus, or Pan), it was associated. It was a festival of expiation and was regarded also as a purification ceremony of the Palatine city and the surrounding land, and its purpose was to bring fertility to fields, herds, and individuals. It is said that in earlier times human victims were sacrificed in the Lupercal cave near the Porta Romana, after having been conducted around the walls. In historic times the sacrificial victims were goats and a dog (both symbolizing fertility). The blood of the sacrificial victims was smeared on the foreheads of two youths and then wiped off with wool moistened in milk. After a feast, the celebrants of the festival, naked except for a goatskin apron, ran around the old line of the Palatine walls, striking all whom they met with thongs cut from the skins of the slaughtered animals. These blows were reputed to endow women with fertility. The month of February takes its name from this festival, from *februum*, pl. *februa*, a word of Sabine origin meaning "a means of purification" and used to describe the thongs, the blows of which purified, and *februare*, "to purify."

Lupercus (lö-pėr′kus). In Roman mythology, a fertility god, often identified with Faunus, or with Inuus, or with Pan, as the protecting deity of shepherds. The festival called Lupercalia was celebrated in his honor.

Lupus (lū′pus). An ancient southern constellation—the Wolf—representing a beast held by the hand of the Centaur.

Luscinus (lu-sī′nus), **Caius Fabricius.** See **Fabricius Luscinus, Caius.**

Lusia (lö-sī'a̠). Epithet of Demeter. The Thelpusians say that when Poseidon, in the form of a stallion, ravished Demeter, who had taken the form of a mare and sought refuge from him among the herds of Oncus in Arcadia, she was so infuriated by his outrage that they gave her the name Erinys (*Fury*). But afterwards, they say, her anger abated, and she cleansed herself by bathing in the Ladon River. For this reason they gave her the name Lusia (*Bather*). In her sanctuary in their land they placed two images: one of Demeter Erinys and one of Demeter Lusia.

Lusitania (lö-si-tā'ni-a̠). In ancient geography, the country of the Lusitanians, comprising the modern Portugal N to the river Durius (Douro), and adjoining parts of W Spain. In a later, more extended use, it was one of the Roman provinces into which Hispania was divided by Augustus.

Lusius (lö'si-us). In ancient geography, a river in Arcadia. The name means "Bathing-river," and was given to it because Zeus was bathed in its waters after his birth. The river flows through the city of Gortys. At some distance away from its source it is called the Gortynius River, and it is noted for the coldness of its waters.

Lyaeus (lī-ē'us). In Greek mythology, the "Loosener," the god of wine and song who loosens care; an epithet or surname of Dionysus.

Lycabettus (lik-a̠-bet'us, lī-ka̠-) or **Lykabettos** (-os). Rocky hill rising in the E part of Athens to a height of about 910 feet above the sea. According to legend, it was originally a huge stone. When Athena, who was carrying it to fortify the Acropolis, heard of the death of Agraulos and her daughters by leaping from the Acropolis, in grief at their deaths she dropped the stone and formed Mount Lycabettus. It is a very conspicuous object in the landscape, presenting from most points of the city the general form of an abrupt, slightly concave cone; there is, however, beyond a slight depression, a long ridge N of it. Upon the top stands today a small chapel of Saint George. On the S slope is the large reservoir built by Hadrian and Antoninus Pius which still supplies the city.

Lycaeus (lī-sē'us) or **Lycaeum** (-um). Moun-tain in S Arcadia. Some Arcadians called it Olympus and others called it Sacred Peak, because, they say, there is a place on the mountain called Cretea, and here, where no living creature cast a shadow, Zeus was born to Rhea and was reared by the nymphs Thisoa, Neda, and Hagno. Here was a course where the Lycaean Games were held. On the spot where Zeus was born was a precinct sacred to Lycaean Zeus forbidden to mortals. Whoever ignored the rule and entered was destined to die within a year. On the summit of the mountain, from which a view over the whole Peloponnesus was possible, was an altar of Lycaean Zeus, on which sacrifices to the god were made in secret. On the east side of the mountain was a sanctuary of Apollo, at which an annual festival was held in his honor. As part of the festival sacrifices that were made in the market-place were carried to this sanctuary to the music of flutes. The mountain was also a center of the worship of Pan, who had a sanctuary there.

Lycaeus. Epithet of Zeus, meaning "Wolfish." Some say it comes from Mount Lycaeus, in Arcadia, and that the name was given him by Lycaon, who also founded the Lycaean Games in his honor. Others say it was given to him because Lycaon and his impious sons were changed into wolves by Zeus. There was a sanctuary of Lycaean Zeus at Megalopolis in Arcadia, and altars in many places, especially in Arcadia. The cult of Zeus Lycaeus is thought to have been an ancient pre-Hellenic cult with cannibalistic ritual, later syncretized with Zeus worship. Some say that in rites performed to Lycaean Zeus on Mount Lycaeus a human victim was sacrificed. Parts of the human victim were mixed with parts of animal victims and were cooked together. The mixture was then eaten at a banquet of the worshipers. It was believed that whoever happened to eat of the human flesh at this banquet was changed into a wolf for a Great Year, that is, for eight years. If, at the end of that time, he had eaten no human flesh during his wolfish incarnation, he was metamorphosed back to mortal form again in the ninth year. Pausanias tells of one Demarchus who spent eight years with the wolves as the result of these rites, regained his mor-

fat, fāte, fär, fãre, errant; net, mē, hèr ardent; pin, pīne; not, nōte, mȯve, nôr, tal form and, in the tenth year after being transformed into a wolf, won the boxing prize at the Olympic Games. His name was inscribed on the list of winners and noted by Pausanias there, but Pausanias points out that on the slab at Olympia his transformation into a wolf was not mentioned in connection with his exploits. Therefore Pausanias doubts that it ever happened, for surely if it had, such a remarkable event would have been mentioned.

Lycaon (lī-kā'on). According to Greek tradition, a son of Pelasgus, the first king of Arcadia, who succeeded his father as king. Some say he founded the city of Lycosura on Mount Lycaeus, and that it was he who gave Zeus the name Lycaeus and established the Lycaean Games in his honor. The Lycaean Games were older than the Panathenaea but not so old as the Olympic Games. Lycaon had 50 sons who became the founders of many of the cities of Arcadia. The youngest of them, Oenotrus, was said to have sailed to Italy and to have colonized Oenotria, of which he became king. This, according to some accounts, was the first expedition from Greece to found a colony. Besides his 50 sons, Lycaon was the father of one daughter, Callisto, beloved of Zeus. Some say it was a deed of Lycaon, typical of the general wickedness of mankind, that caused Zeus to send a flood to punish the race of men. Zeus, visiting the world in the guise of a mortal, came to the house of Lycaon. He informed Lycaon of his divinity, but Lycaon doubted that he was really a god, and decided to test him. He cut up and cooked a child (his own son Nyctimus, according to some accounts) and served the flesh to Zeus. For this impiety Zeus destroyed his house and transformed Lycaon into a savage wolf. Some say he also struck all the sons of Lycaon, except Nyctimus whom he restored, with his thunderbolt. But others say the sons of Lycaon were also turned into wolves. And some say, that at the sacrifice to Lycaean Zeus a man was transformed into a wolf. If, after nine years, he had not tasted human flesh, he became a man again. But if he had eaten human flesh, he remained a beast.

Lycaon. In Homeric legend, a son of Priam and Laothoë, and half-brother of Hector and Paris. While cutting shoots from a fig-tree in his father's orchard, he was captured by Achilles. Achilles sold him to King Euneus of Lemnos for a mixing bowl. Next he was ransomed by Eëtion of Imbrus and sent to Arisbe, from which he escaped. He returned to Troy but 11 days later he was again captured by Achilles, who this time, in spite of Lycaon's pleas, slew him and hurled his body into the Scamander river. Apollo assumed the form of Lycaon to rally Aeneas against Achilles when the Trojans fled before him after the death of Patroclus.

Lycaonia (lik-ā-ō'ni-a, lī-kā-). In ancient geography, a province in S central Asia Minor. It was bounded by Galatia on the N, Cappadocia on the E, Cilicia on the S, Pisidia on the SW, and Phrygia on the W. Sometimes it included Isauria, and sometimes it was included in Cappadocia. Chief city, Iconium.

Lyceum (lī-sē'um). Gymnasium and exercise-ground of ancient Athens, lying on the right bank of the Ilissus, at the place now called Ilissia, a short distance E of the palace garden. It was a sanctuary of Apollo Lycius (*Wolfish*). The story is that once when Athens was infested by wolves, Apollo ordered the people to sacrifice. They did so, and the smell of the sacrifice drove the wolves off. On the spot where the sacrifice was offered they dedicated the sanctuary and placed an image of Apollo Lycius in it. By the time of Pisistratus the Lyceum had become the chief gymnasium of Athens. It was noted for its fine groves of plane trees. Aristotle and his disciples formed the habit of discussing their philosophy while following the shady walks of this gymnasium, and hence received the name of Peripatetics. The Lyceum was burned in 200 B.C. by Philip V of Macedonia. The trees of the peaceful groves were cut down by Sulla (87–86 B.C.) to make siege engines when he was besieging Athens.

Lychnidus (lik'ni-dus) or **Lychnitis** (lik-nī'tis). In ancient geography, a lake in Illyria. The modern name of the lake (on the border of Albania and Yugoslavia) is Ohrid.

Lycia (lish'a). In ancient geography, a division of SW Asia Minor, bordering on the Mediterranean and on Caria, Phrygia, Pisidia, and Pamphylia. The Lycians were one of the peoples of Asia Minor who invaded

Egypt in the time of Ramses II and Merneptah. Its 23 cities formed the Lycian League. According to legend, Apollo had his winter palace in Lycia. Leto, his mother, was forced to flee from Delos after giving birth to her children, on account of the wrath of Hera. She wandered to Lycia and, being thirsty and worn, stopped at a pond to drink. Peasants who were gathering reeds at the edge of the pond tried to prevent her from drinking or from giving water to her children. They would not yield to her pleas and when she tried to drink, they muddied the water so that it was unfit to drink. To punish them for their malice Leto prayed that they might live in the pond forever, and the gods answered her prayer by changing them into frogs.

Lycians (lish'anz). [Also: **Lukki.**] Inhabitants of ancient Lycia, in SW Asia Minor. These people are first met as the Lukki in the Tel el-Amarna tablets of 1400 B.C. and in the list of invaders of Egypt from the E Mediterranean. Their occupation of Lycia took place probably at a later date. The attempt by the Lydians to subdue them failed, but they later were conquered by Harpagus, a general of Cyrus. Although they had to acknowledge the suzerainty of Persia, they remained practically independent. They were incorporated into Alexander's empire, and in the 3rd century B.C. belonged to the Ptolemies. At the beginning of the 2nd century B.C. Lycia was annexed by the Seleucid king Antiochus III; after his defeats by Rome the Romans (189 B.C.) turned the administration of Lycia over to Rhodes, but after three revolts the Lycians achieved independence (169 B.C.) and established federal institutions which survived until suppressed by Rome in the 1st century A.D. According to Homeric legend (*Iliad*), in the Trojan War the Lycians, under the command of Sarpedon and Glaucus, were allies of Troy. After the fall of Troy, according to the *Aeneid*, some of the Lycian allies accompanied Aeneas on his flight to Italy. Classification of the language of the Lycians was long a matter of conjecture, but it is now classified as belonging to the extinct Anatolian subfamily of Indo-European languages.

Lycius, Lyceius or **Lyceus** (lī-sē'us). An epithet of Apollo, meaning "Wolfish" or "Wolf-god." It refers to his function (as god of shepherds and herdsmen) as wolf-slayer. At one time also when Athens was overrun with wolves, Apollo was said to have rid the city of them. Danaus made the original temple of Apollo Lycius, in which was a wooden image, at Argos. He did this in gratitude for Apollo's help in securing the throne. When Danaus came to the land and sought the throne, Gelanor was king. The people debated whether to make Danaus king in his place. During the night a wolf came down from the hills and destroyed a bull in a herd of cattle outside the town. The Argives took this as an omen, that Danaus would destroy their king, and to prevent this, Gelanor stepped aside and Danaus became king. Danaus thought that the wolf that helped him was Apollo in disguise, or that Apollo had sent the wolf. But some have said that Lycius means "God of Light."

Lycomedes (lī-kọ-mē'dēz). In Greek legend, a king of Scyrus. He welcomed Theseus when that hero was blown to his shores by a storm but when Theseus decided to stay in Scyrus, on land that belonged to him, Lycomedes, under the pretext of showing him the land, treacherously led Theseus to a cliff and pushed him over. Afterwards Lycomedes announced that Theseus had fallen off the cliff while under the influence of wine. In another legend, Thetis, who knew that if her son Achilles went to Troy he would never return, tried to prevent Achilles from going to fight against the Trojans by sending him to the court of Lycomedes disguised as a girl. Lycomedes sheltered him but was unable to prevent Odysseus from finding him and carrying him off to Troy. Achilles left behind a son, Neoptolemus, by Lycomedes' daughter, Deidamia, whom Lycomedes brought up. When the oracles declared that Troy could not be taken without the aid of Achilles' son Lycomedes allowed Neoptolemus to depart for Troy.

Lycon (lī'kon). In Homeric legend (*Iliad*), a Trojan, slain by Peneleus.

Lycon. Greek Peripatetic philosopher; fl. in the 3rd century B.C.

Lycophron (lī′kō̯-fron). In the *Iliad,* a Greek who, having committed a murder, fled from his home in Cythera to the home of Telamonian Ajax, and later accompanied Ajax to the Trojan War. He was slain by Hector when the Trojans attacked the Greek ships.

Lycophron. A son of Periander, tyrant of Corinth (c625–585 B.C.). He learned that his father had been responsible for the death of his mother, Melissa, and withdrew from his father's court and refused to have anything to do with him. Periander sought to compel his return by forbidding the Corinthians to help him in any way, and Lycophron, harried from house to house, was reduced to near beggary in the streets. He went at length to Corcyra, a Corinthian colony. Periander wished Lycophron, as the more capable of his two sons, to succeed him as ruler of Corinth and sent many messengers, including his daughter, to try to persuade Lycophron to return. He at last agreed to do so when Periander promised that he would withdraw from Corinth if Lycophron would come back and take over the government. However, before Lycophron could depart for Corinth the Corcyraeans slew him to punish Periander for carrying off 300 Corcyraean boys of the noblest families.

Lycophron. Greek poet and grammarian; born at Chalcis in Euboea; fl. in the 3rd century B.C. He worked at Alexandria in the time of Ptolemy Philadelphus (285–247 B.C.). At Ptolemy's request he arranged the works of the Greek comic poets for the Library, and afterwards wrote a work on Greek Comedy, which is now lost. His only extant poem is the *Alexandra* or *Cassandra,* comprising about 1400 iambic verses, in which Cassandra predicts the results of the voyage of Paris to Sparta, the fate of the heroes at Troy, and the ultimate fall of the city.

Lycosura (lī-kō̯-sū′ra̯). In ancient geography, a city in S Arcadia, near the border of Messenia. According to tradition, it was founded by Lycaon, son of Pelasgus. Pausanias says it was the oldest city in the world, that from it the rest of mankind learned how to build cities, and that a sacred deer, weakened by great age, lived in Lycosura, about whose neck was a collar, on which was written,

"I was a fawn when captured at the time when Agapenor went to Troy."

Lycotherses (lī-kō̯-thėr′sēz). In Greek legend, a king of Illyria. He married Agave, daughter of Cadmus, who had fled to his country after the murder of her son Pentheus. Agave killed Lycotherses and gave his kingdom to her father, who had also fled from Thebes and had become ruler of the Encheleans.

Lyctaea (lik-tē′a̯). In Greek legend, a daughter of Hyacinthus the Spartan. See **Hyacinthides**.

Lycurgus (lī-kėr′gus). In Greek mythology, a son of Dryas. He was king of the Edonians in Thrace, and an opponent of the worship of Dionysus. When Dionysus and his attendants landed in his kingdom on their return from Asia, Lycurgus attacked them with an ox goad and scattered the god's followers. Dionysus himself escaped by fleeing under the sea to Thetis for protection. Lycurgus' arrogance in attacking a god aroused the wrath of Zeus who, according to some accounts, struck him blind. According to other accounts, he was driven mad by the gods and killed his own son with an ax under the mistaken impression that he was cutting down a vine. Thrace became barren after this horrible crime and the Thracians learned that their land would become productive again only when Lycurgus was punished. His people then seized and bound him and left him on Mount Pangaeus where he was torn to pieces by wild horses.

Lycurgus. According to Homer's *Iliad,* a king in Arcadia. He trapped Areïthoüs, the "Maceman," in a narrow place where he could not swing his club, slew him, and took his armor and his mace.

Lycurgus. In Greek legend, a king of Nemea. He bought Hypsipyle, queen of Lemnos, from the Lemnian women as a slave and made her nurse to his son Opheltes.

Lycurgus. Spartan legislator, the traditional author of the laws and institutions of Sparta. Some say he lived in the 9th century B.C. Others say he lived in the 7th century B.C.; and still others say he was not a historical person at all, but a legendary figure to whom was ascribed the authorship of the Spartan way of life which was so consistent that it was thought to have been developed by one person. According to Plutarch, Lycurgus was descended from the Heraclid Aristodemus, and was a descendant of Soüs and of the Eurypontid line of Spartan kings. He lived at a time when Sparta was in a state of anarchy. King Polydectes, his half-brother, died and left a wife who was about to bear a child. Lycurgus declared that if the child was a boy, he would be the king. Polydectes' widow proposed to Lycurgus that she should destroy her unborn child and marry him, and that he should claim the throne. He was shocked, but pretended he would be delighted to marry her at some later time, and persuaded her not to interfere with the natural course of her pregnancy. In due course she bore a son. Lycurgus proclaimed him king, named him Charilaus, and acted as his regent. The widow of Polydectes made accusations against him, and for the sake of peace in Sparta he went into voluntary exile. He went to Crete where, impressed by the sober and temperate character of the Cretans, he studied their laws with the view to applying them to Sparta. Some say he went from Crete to Asia Minor, where he first came in contact with the poems of Homer and transcribed them for his own people. And some say he also visited Egypt and that it was there that he got the idea, later introduced into Sparta, of separating the military class from the rest of the people. At last he returned to Sparta, resolved to make certain reforms and to restore order to his country. He went to consult the oracle at Delphi, to learn whether his plans were wise. As he entered the shrine the priestess exclaimed,

"O thou great Lycurgus . . .
Whether to hail thee a god I know not,
    or only a mortal,
But my hope is strong that a god thou
    wilt prove, Lycurgus."

Because of this oracle some afterwards claimed that Lycurgus was indeed a god, and there was a temple of Lycurgus erected in Sparta. But at the time, the response of the priestess encouraged him and he introduced his reforms. Some say it was he who established a body of 30 overseers or administrators, which included the two kings. These *ephors*, as they were called, proposed measures to the citizens who assembled before them. The citizens could vote to adopt or reject their proposals, but could not modify them nor propose measures of their own, and the ephors might withdraw their own proposals if they wished. The effect of having 28 ephors to act with the kings was to weaken the absolute power of the kings, but Sparta did not become a democracy through this because the voice of the citizens was so limited in state affairs. Another change attributed to Lycurgus was of great importance to the future development of Sparta. He is said to have called in all the gold and silver and to have established a system of iron money. The purpose was to reduce all the citizens to the same level and to eradicate the evils of greed and robbery which gold and silver brought in their train. The iron from which money was made was first quenched in vinegar so that it could not be worked and therefore had no practical use; it was so cumbersome that large amounts could not be transported or hidden; it was worthless in trade with other Greek states and therefore weakening luxuries were not imported into Sparta from other areas. Conditioned to valueless iron money, the Spartans became impervious to bribery. It was not until the time of Agis (died 399 B.C.) that gold and silver again came into use in Sparta. The entire education and training of Spartan youth was designed to create a military state, not for the purposes of conquest, but to protect Sparta in the midst of her enemies. Children were considered to belong to the state. Those that were puny at birth were exposed on Mount Taÿgetus. Lycurgus established rules for the training and physical development of young women so that they would bear strongs sons, and of young men so that they would become excellent and obedient soldiers. The males were brought up together according to prescribed rules from the age of seven. Even as men they ate together in a common mess. Not all the citizens favored the changes brought about by Lycurgus. The wealthy especially opposed them. Lycurgus was attacked and chased into the market place, where his attacker put out one of his eyes with his spear. The Spartans were ashamed that their leading citizen had been injured, and turned his at-

Panathenaic prize amphora, c 530 B.C.

a

b

c

Red-figured kylix, Phintias, c 520 B.C. (A) Heracles and Apollo struggling for the tripod
(B) Heracles slaying the giant Alcyoneus, in the presence of Hermes (C) Side view.

Red-figured hydria,
Phintias, c 510 B.C.
The Music Lesson.

Attic black-figured (white ground)
lecythus, c 515 B.C. Poseidon fishing.

Red-figured amphora, Cleophrades Painter, c 500 B.C.
Lid: Chariot race; Amphora: Athletes.

tacker over to him. Lycurgus punished him mildly by compelling him to serve him at table, and ultimately converted him into one of his greatest admirers. Lycurgus raised a temple to Athena Ophthalmitis in gratitude that he still had one eye, and the Spartans made a law that no one should carry as much as a staff in the public assemblies. To provide a livelihood for the citizens whose lives were entirely devoted to military training, the land was redistributed in lots which would produce certain amounts of grain, oil, and wine. It is said that once when he returned to Sparta from a journey at harvest time and saw all the stacks of grain standing, equal and alike, Lycurgus remarked with pleasure that "all Laconia looks like one family estate just divided among a number of brothers." The land was worked by *helots,* a slave class that was continually threatening to revolt. As part of the training of a Spartan youth, he was permitted to seek out and slay any helot who he thought might become a leader of rebellion.

When Lycurgus had brought about these changes and thought that they were good, he won a promise from the Spartans that they would observe his laws until he returned. He went to Delphi to learn from the priestess whether his laws were good. The priestess of Apollo assured him that they were, and that Sparta would thrive as long as they were followed. Lycurgus sent on the words of the priestess to Sparta. He sacrificed again to Apollo and said farewell to his relatives and friends. Determined to compel the Spartans to observe his laws until he returned, he resolved not to return at all and, some say, starved himself to death. But others say he went to Crete, the place of origin of many of his laws, and died there. His ashes were scattered on the sea, they say, so that his bones could never be collected and returned to Sparta and release the Spartans from their oath. And, of course, some say that there never was any such person as Lycurgus at all, but all admit that he, or his legend, had great effect on the development of the Spartan character.

Lycurgus. One of the Ten Attic Orators, born at Athens, c396 B.C.; died 324 B.C. He was the son of Lycophron of the aristocratic family of the Eteobutadae. With Demosthenes and Hyperides he was a leader of the anti-Macedonian party. He was thrice appointed manager of the Athenian finances for terms of five years each. During his tenure he improved the revenues of the city and beautified Athens with magnificent buildings. He was also responsible for causing copies of the plays of Aeschylus, Sophocles, and Euripides to be deposited in the public archives. Only one of his speeches, *Against Leocrates,* is extant. A man of unblemished patriotism and integrity himself, he accused Leocrates of cowardice for leaving the city after the battle of Chaeronea, and demanded the death sentence as punishment; Leocrates, however, was spared.

Lycus (lī'kus). In Greek legend, a son of Pandion the Younger and Pylia. He was the brother of Aegeus, Pallas, and Nisus. Pandion, king of Athens, was expelled from his kingdom. After his death his four sons marched against Attica and defeated their enemies. They then divided Attica among them. Aegeus, being the eldest, became king of Athens. Lycus became ruler of Euboea. But the brothers were not satisfied. They claimed Aegeus was an adopted son of Pandion and therefore not a true descendant of Erechtheus with no claim to the throne. Lycus intrigued aganst Aegeus, and at length became so threatening that Aegeus banished him. He went to Cilicia in Asia Minor where Sarpedon, brother of Minos of Crete, had made himself king. Lycus succeeded Sarpedon on the throne and the country was renamed Lycia after him.

Lycus. According to legend, a king of the Mariandyni in Mysia. He entertained Heracles and won his support in a war against the Bebryces, in which the Bebrycian king Mygdon was slain. He named Heraclea, land in Paphlagonia which was regained in this war, in honor of Heracles. When Heracles left, the Bebryces under the new king Amycus, attacked again and retook the land. Later, Lycus welcomed the Argonauts when they visited his kingdom on their way to Colchis. He built a shrine to Polyeduces, one of their number, because he had killed Amycus in a boxing contest, and sent his son Dascylus to join the Argonauts in gratitude to them for having defeated his ancient enemies, the Bebryces, in war.

actọr; up, lūte, pụll; oi, oil; ou, out; ŦH, then; ḍ as d or j, ş as s or sh, ṭ as t or ch, ẓ as z or zh.

Lycus. A legendary ruler of Thebes. He was the husband of Dirce and uncle of Antiope. To carry out his promise to Antiope's father, he attacked Sicyon, whither Antiope had fled, killed the king and took Antiope captive. Much later, he was slain by Antiope's sons, Amphion and Zethus, because of his cruel treatment of their mother. See **Antiope.**

Lycus. In Greek legend, a son of Lycus and Dirce. During the absence of Heracles he killed Creon, the father of Heracles' wife Megara, made himself king of Thebes in Creon's place, and threatened to destroy Megara and the children. of Heracles. Lycus dared do this because Heracles was occupied on the labor for Eurystheus of bringing Cerberus from Hades, and he had been gone so long that it was thought he would never return. However, he did return, his task successfully completed. And when he learned of Lycus' deeds, he killed him.

Lydia (lid'i-a). [Early name, **Maeonia.**] Ancient country, later a Roman province, on the W coast of Asia Minor, bordering on the Aegean Sea and on Mysia, Phrygia, and Caria. The earliest known inhabitants were Phrygians. Later it was invaded by Semites, who gave it the name of Lydia (compare the Old Testament Lud, descendants of Shem, Gen. x. 22). The name Maeonia was afterward confined to the E part of the country near the upper Hermus River, and Lydia to the W. About 700 B.C. a revolution overthrew the Semitic reign, and brought the native dynasty of the Mermnadae to the throne, with Gyges as first king. Under them Lydia rose to the position of a mighty kingdom extending from the coast to the river Halys (modern Kizil Irmak), with Sardis as capital. The prosperous Greek cities were brought either to subjection or alliance. But under the fifth and best-known of the dynasties, Croesus, the Lydian empire was brought to a sudden end by the Persian conqueror Cyrus, who in 546 B.C. captured Sardis and the king himself. From the Persians Lydia passed over, through Alexander the Great, to Syria, and later to Eumenes of Pergamum. During the Roman period Lydia formed a separate province, with Sardis as capital.

Lydians (lid'i-anz). People of ancient Lydia, in W Asia Minor. They are noted for having had a high level of civilization, attaining great wealth, and perhaps for instituting the first coined money. Their language, Lydian, is classified as belonging to the extinct Anatolian sub-family of Indo-European languages.

Lygdamus (lig'da-mus). Pseudonym of a Roman poet (late 1st century B.C.) of no exceptional talent, a member of Messalla's literary circle. Six elegies by him have survived and now constitute Book III of the Tibullan collection. (JJ)

Lygodesma (lī''gō-des'ma). An epithet of Artemis, meaning "Willow-bound." This epithet was given to her because, some say, the Taurian wooden image of the goddess brought back by Orestes and Iphigenia was found in a clump of willows, and tendrils of the willows had twined themselves about the image and held it upright. Another epithet applying to this Taurian image was Artemis Orthia (*Upright*), because the willows held it erect.

Lykabettos (lik-a-bet'os). See **Lycabettus.**

Lyncestes (lin-ses'tēz), **Alexander.** See **Alexander** (fl. 4th century B.C.).

Lynceus (lin'sūs). In Greek mythology, the son of Aegyptus and the husband of Hypermnestra. On the advice of Artemis, Hypermnestra spared her husband on their wedding night. She was the only one of the 50 daughters of Danaus to spare her husband. Danaus had given each of his daughters a slender dagger and had ordered them to kill their bridegrooms. Hypermnestra helped Lynceus to escape to Lyncea, where he lighted a beacon to inform her that he had arrived safely. She also lighted one to show that his message had been received, and this act was commemorated annually by the lighting of signal fires. Lynceus and Hypermnestra were subsequently reunited.

Lynceus. In Greek legend, the son of Aphareus and Arene and the brother of Idas. His sight was so keen he could see through the bole of a tree. See **Idas.**

Lyra (lī'ra). [Also: the **Harp.**] An ancient northern constellation, representing the lyre of Hermes or of Orpheus. The brightest star in this constellation is Vega (Lyrae), the fourth brightest star in the sky.

Lyrcea (lir-sē'a). In ancient geography, a place in Argolis to which Lynceus, husband of Hypermnestra, escaped when all his brothers (the sons of Aegyptus) were slain by their brides, the daughters of Danaus. When he arrived at Lyrcea, once called by his name Lyncea, he raised a flaming beacon as a signal to Hypermnestra that he was safe. On her part, she raised a beacon at Larissa, the citadel of Argos, in reply. By the time of the Greek expedition to Troy, Lyrcea lay in ruins.

Lyre (līr). The national instrument of ancient Greece, belonging essentially to the harp family, but with a sounding box. It was said to have been invented by Hermes on the same day he was born. He met a tortoise as he was stealing out of the cave that was his birthplace, scooped out its shell, and covered it with ox-hide; this was the sounding box. To this he attached two horns separated by

MUSICIAN WITH LYRE
Red-figured Attic cup, Duris
(fl. c500–470 B.C.). *Berlin*

a cross-piece and strung seven strings from the cross-piece across the tortoise shell. He gave the lyre to Apollo—who made it his instrument—to atone for stealing Apollo's cattle, also on the day he was born.

Lyrnessus (lir-nes'us). Mentioned by Homer in the *Iliad* as a city in Mysia allied to Troy. Early in the Trojan War it was attacked and sacked by Achilles, who murdered King Mynes and carried off his wife Briseis as his captive.

Lyrus (lī'rus). According to some accounts, a son of Aphrodite and Anchises, and the brother of Aeneas. He died childless.

Lysander (lī-san'dėr). Spartan commander, killed near Haliartus in Boeotia, 395 B.C. He was the son of Aristoclitus of the line of the Heraclidae. Reared in poverty and in the strict Spartan discipline, he showed himself unusually subservient, according to Plutarch, to men of influence and power with the object of furthering his own ambitions. He was appointed *navarch* (admiral) of the Peloponnesian fleet in 408 B.C. He sailed to Ephesus where the Spartans were cordially received, and set up a base there. At this time he became friendly with Cyrus the Younger, the son of the Persian king, Darius II, and the satrap at Sardis with jurisdiction over Cappadocia, Phrygia, and Lydia. Lysander won his complete confidence and promises of help for the Spartan cause by his refusal to accept any gift from Cyrus for himself. In 407 B.C. he defeated an Athenian fleet at Notium. According to Spartan law, he now had to give up his post as navarch, having served the legal term of one year. Callicratidas was appointed the new navarch but (again according to Plutarch) Lysander wished to hamper Callicratidas and sowed disaffection among his men before turning over his command. In 406 B.C. Callicratidas was defeated at Arginusae by the Athenians and fell in the battle. The Spartan allies and Cyrus the Younger wanted Lysander reappointed as admiral, but because of the Spartan rule that no man could twice be navarch, it was impossible to give him the title. He was, however, given the power. He went to Sardis and obtained funds from Cyrus the Younger, over whom he continued to exercise his influence. Cyrus entrusted him with the administration of his satrapy and the collection of the tribute therein while he went off to see his dying father, Darius II. Thus restored in funds and power, Lysander sailed forth. The Athenians sought to engage him at Ephesus, but he refused to meet them in

actọr; up, lūte, pùll; oi, oil; ou, out; ᴛʜ, then; ḍ as d or j, ş as s or sh, ṭ as t or ch, ẓ as z or zh.

battle there. Instead, after sailing to Attica where he conferred with Agis II, the Spartan king, he recrossed the Aegean, laid siege to Lampsacus on the east shore of the Hellespont, took it, and gave it over to his men to plunder. The Athenians determined to engage him and met him at Aegospotami. In the battle that finally took place there (405 B.C.) it was said that twin stars appeared on each side of Lysander's ship as he sailed into battle. These stars represented the Dioscuri, ever-protecting deities of Sparta. Lysander was completely victorious in the battle at small cost to Sparta. Three or four thousand Athenians were taken prisoner and put to the sword; only 20 Athenian ships escaped. Lysander was prevented from pursuing those by the quick action of the Athenian admiral Conon. It was the custom of the Greeks to unship their sails in preparation for a naval battle, and the Peloponnesians had deposited theirs at Cape Abarnis near Lampsacus before the battle of Aegospotami. Conon swooped down on the Cape and seized the sails. However, the complete defeat of the Athenians at Aegospotami was the effective end of the Peloponnesian War. Lysander sailed to blockade Athens. He set up Spartan *harmosts* (governors) over the Athenian cities of Greece and Asia, established Spartan supremacy, and restored Melos which had been taken and depopulated by the Athenians (416–415 B.C.), and also restored Scione, which had suffered the same fate (421 B.C.). At this moment the power of Lysander was supreme. Athens, on the verge of starvation because of the blockade, was compelled to ask for peace. According to the terms of it the Long Walls and the fortifications of the Piraeus were demolished to the piping of flutes; Athens surrendered all but 12 of her ships; her possessions were taken away from her; she was compelled to readmit those who had gone into exile, and to become a subordinate ally of Sparta. To memorialize his victory, Lysander set up twin golden stars of the Dioscuri as a trophy at Delphi. (These were the stars which were said to have disappeared in 371 B.C., just before the Battle of Leuctra in which the Spartan supremacy won in the time of Lysander was destroyed by the Thebans under Epaminondas.) Lysander sailed off to reduce Samos, but inter-

vened in Athenian politics to establish the Tyranny of the Thirty (404 B.C.) and to write a new constitution. He placed Spartan harmosts over the cities which had been freed from Athens, choosing for these posts friends whom he wished to reward, regardless of their capacity or honesty. His arrogance increased as he was successful in his ambitions. At Samos he was awarded, and graciously received, divine honors, the first living man to be so honored. The Samians changed the name of their festival of Hera to *Lysandria* in a slavish desire to win his favor. To please his friends, he wantonly ordered the death of their enemies. To exiles whom he distrusted, he promised amnesty if they returned; once they did so, he had them executed. He pillaged the coasts of Asia to reward his friends and to send rich treasure back to Sparta, but took nothing for himself. Such actions roused strong resentment in the Persian satrap and he complained to Sparta. Lysander was recalled. With him he carried a letter from the Persian satrap Pharnabazus who had been a faithful ally of the Spartans in their war against Athens. Lysander thought the letter justified his actions, but at the last moment Pharnabazus had substituted a highly critical account, denouncing Lysander, and it was this letter that he handed to the Spartan ephors with his own hand. The accusations of the letter and the fact that he had been duped by Pharnabazus into delivering it himself made Lysander's position in Sparta equivocal. With some difficulty, he secured permission to depart on a visit to the temple of Zeus Ammon in Libya. He subsequently returned, and such was his fame for his victory over the Athenians that he was influential in securing the throne for Agesilaus II on the death of Agis II. He encouraged Agesilaus to wage war on the Persian king, and accompanied him on an expedition to Asia, fully expecting that he would be the actual commander of the expedition because of his supposed influence with Agesilaus and his experience in the area. Agesilaus soon disabused him of that notion. He refused to aid those who came to him recommended by Lysander; on the other hand, he ostentatiously helped those known to be unfriendly to Lysander; finally, while he gave others of his train positions of com-

fat, fāte, fär, fãre, errant; net, mē, hėr ardent; pin, pīne; not, nōte, möve, nôr,

mand, he appointed Lysander as his official Carver-of-Meats. Lysander understood the insult, asked leave to depart and was granted permission. Unhonored, he sailed back to Sparta plotting revolution. He planned to unseat Agesilaus by changing the Spartan rule from hereditary kingship to elective kingship. To justify his proposals he sought favoring oracles from Delphi. The priestess there, as at Dodona, was impervious to both persuasion and bribery. The priests of Ammon were so incensed by his attempts to corrupt them that they sent word to Sparta denouncing him, but the Spartans acquitted him. In lieu of valid responses he gathered a number of spurious oracles to place before the Spartans. His intrigue failed and was not discovered until after his death. Sparta became involved in a war against Thebes in support of Phocis, the Spartan ally. Lysander marched out from the revived Spartan colony of Heraclea near Thermopylae, against Thebes. The Spartan king Pausanias, coming with a second force from the south, was to join him at Haliartus, in Boeotia. Lysander arrived first and attacked the town. The soldiers within it rushed out in a surprise raid, repulsed the Peloponnesians, and killed Lysander (395 B.C.).

A skillful diplomat and an able general, Lysander was for a time supreme in Greece. His great capacity was betrayed by his personal ambition, his harshness when he had won supreme power, and his irresponsible choices of subordinates. Personally incorruptible and scornful of wealth, he undermined the ancient Spartan discipline, which depended on iron money that had no real value and hence presented no temptation, by sending into the state great treasure taken by plunder. He thus opened up Sparta to the corruption brought by wealth and completely changed the Spartan character. Honest men considered him unscrupulous and deceitful, treacherous to his friends as well as to his foes. He justified his deceit in war by saying, "Where the lion's skin will not reach, it must be patched out with the fox's." Some say the image of a long-haired, bearded man that was set up in the treasury of the Acanthians at Delphi was that of Lysander to honor him for his part in winning Acanthus from Athens (424 B.C.).

Lysias (lis'i-as, li'si-as). One of the Ten Attic Orators. He was born in the Greek colony of Syracuse, c450 B.C., and died in 380 B.C. His father Cephalus, whose portrait appears in Plato's *Republic,* was invited by Pericles to come to Athens. There, at the Piraeus, he had a shield factory, and was the owner of some property. When he was 15 years old, Lysias went to Thurii, in Italy, and studied rhetoric. In 413 B.C. he took part in the defeat of the Athenians in Sicily, after which he returned to Athens and went into his father's business with his brother Polemarchus. When the Thirty Tyrants took control of Athens (404 B.C.), they attacked the wealthy aliens. Polemarchus was killed, much of his property was confiscated, and Lysias escaped to Megara. Henceforth Lysias espoused the cause of democracy and gave money to support it. In 403 B.C. the Tyrants were expelled. Lysias was given Athenian citizenship, but it was withdrawn shortly thereafter. Unable to take a part in the politics of the city, he occupied himself with writing speeches for others to deliver. One of the speeches, still extant, which he himself made was *Against Eratosthenes.* Eratosthenes was one of the tyrants, who had been given amnesty on the restoration of the democracy. Lysias was noted for being able to make the speeches he wrote for others sound as if they had been prepared by the person who gave them. It was said of him that he was never more persuasive and convincing than when he had a shaky case. Of his more than 200 speeches, 34 which bear his name are extant, though of some the authenticity has been challenged. Titles or fragments of a hundred others remain. They show him to have been somewhat cynical, able, and possessed of tact and agility. In style he avoided bombast, used simple and lucid language, and achieved his effects by vivid narrative description, concise points, and a faithful or skillful presentation of the character of the person who gave the speech.

Lysicrates (lī-sik'ra-tēz), **Choragic Monument of.** The best-preserved example of a type of structure once familiar at Athens, the choragic or choregic monument, built to commemorate a victory in a dramatic contest and to display the bronze tripod awarded the choragus who sponsored the winning produc-

actor; up, lūte, pull; oi, oil; ou, out; ŦH, then; d̠ as d or j, g̠ as s or sh, t̠ as t or ch, z̠ as z or zh.

tion. The Monument of Lysicrates is circular in plan on a square stepped base. It has six Corinthian columns, the intercolumniations closed by curved slabs of marble so that the columns appear engaged, carrying an Ionic architrave, sculptured frieze, and cornice. Above this is a single conical roof block terminating in a rich ornamental anthemion which supported the tripod. The dedicatory inscription names the archon Evaenetus, in whose year the contest was held, corresponding to 330 B.C. (335 B.C., according to others). The monument stands beside what was then called the Street of Tripods, approaching the Theater of Dionysus from the east.

Of other choragic monuments near the theater, that of Thrasyllus, 320 B.C., survives in ruinous condition above the topmost seats of the theater, marked by a cave cut into the rock of the Acropolis. Another, erected by a choragus named Nicias, 320/319 B.C., was later dismantled, and many of its stones were used to build the lower gate (Beulé Gate), of Roman date, at the western entrance of the Acropolis, in whose structure they can still be seen. (JJ)

Lysimachus (lī-sim′a-kus). Macedonian general under Alexander the Great. He was born probably at Pella, in Macedonia, c360 B.C.; and was killed at the battle on the plain of Corus, Asia Minor, 281 B.C. He was buried at Lysimachia, a town he founded in the Thracian Chersonese between Cardia and Pactye. He was a member of Alexander's bodyguard and served with distinction in the campaigns in Asia. According to one implausible account, Alexander, angered at Lysimachus, shut him up in a chamber with a lion. Lysimachus overpowered the beast and emerged unscathed. Ever after, Alexander treated him with great respect. Following Alexander's death Lysimachus received the kingdom of Thrace. He joined Cassander, Ptolemy, and Seleucus in the league against Antigonus in 315 B.C., assumed the title of king in 306 B.C., and was one of the victors at Ipsus in 301 B.C., when Antigonus was killed. In the division of Antigonus' realm, Lysimachus received a large part of Asia Minor. He destroyed Lebedos and Colophon and refounded Ephesus with inhabitants he removed from the former

cities. Demetrius, son of Antigonus, took advantage of his absence in Greece (297 B.C.) to renew the war. By the peace which ended the war Demetrius became king of Macedonia, but in 288 B.C. Lysimachus, with Pyrrhus, invaded Macedonia, and drove Demetrius out. Pyrrhus, king of Epirus, held the throne for a time, but was soon driven out in his turn by Lysimachus, who thus obtained Macedonia for himself. Before the battle of Ipsus Lysimachus had married Amastris, the widowed queen of Heraclea in Pontus. She later divorced him and he married Arsinoë, daughter of Ptolemy, to strengthen himself against Seleucus, who now appeared to threaten him. Amastris was slain by her sons. Lysimachus had them put to death. Arsinoë asked him to give her Heraclea, and he did so. Then to secure the succession for her own children, Arsinoë plotted against Lysimachus' eldest son Agathocles. He was accused of conspiring to seize the throne. Lysimachus believed the accusations and had him put to death. The widow of Agathocles fled to Seleucus, who at once invaded the territory of Lysimachus in Asia. The towns the latter had taken in Asia Minor rose up in revolt. He crossed the Hellespont to engage Seleucus. A battle took place in the plain of Corus in Lydia, and Lysimachus was killed (281 B.C.). It is said that his body, left lying on the field of battle, was guarded for several days by his dog, until it was recovered and delivered to his son Alexander.

Lysippe (lī-sip′ē). In Greek legend, a daughter of Antia and Proetus. With her sisters, Iphianassa and Iphinoë, she was driven mad for offending either Dionysus or Hera. Melampus, who finally came to terms with their father, effected their cure after pursuing them to Sicyon. Later Lysippe married Melampus.

Lysippus (lī-sip′us). Greek sculptor, a native of Sicyon, who was active c372–316 B.C. According to Pliny he revised the canon of Polyclitus, making the head smaller and the legs longer, and adjusting details to a greater elongation. This new canon has been preserved in the *Apoxyomenus* of the Vatican, a young nude athlete scraping from his skin with a strigil the olive oil which took the place of soap in the bath, thought to be a copy of the bronze original placed by Agrippa before his baths in Rome. Lysippus also developed and fixed the extreme athletic type in Heracles, whom he repeatedly represented. A small table figure of Heracles in bronze was made for Alexander, who carried it about with him in his campaigns. It was afterward owned by Hannibal and Sulla. The *Torso Belvedere* is supposed to have been copied from this figure by Apollonius of Athens. Among the statues in bronze which Lysippus was said to have made was a colossal figure of Zeus at Tarentum. This was taken to the Capitol at Rome, removed from there to the Hippodrome in Constantinople, and melted down in the 11th century. There was also a colossal statue of the sun-god in a four-horse chariot, as well as a statue of Heracles, second in size only to the colossus of Rhodes. Through Chares of Lindus the characteristics of Lysippus were transmitted to the great Rhodian school which produced the *Laocoön*. Lysippus was the favorite sculptor of Alexander the Great, and author of most of his

portraits in sculpture. An anecdote purporting to prove that, in an admittedly long and busy career, Lysippus made 1500 sculptures challenges credence.

Lysis (li′sis). Dialogue of Plato; the narration by Socrates of a conversation on friendship which took place in a palestra outside the walls of Athens, between himself, the youthful friends Lysis and Menexenus, Hippothales, and Ctesippus.

Lysistrata (li-sis′tra̱-ta̱). Comedy of Aristophanes, exhibited in 411 B.C. It concerns a strike called by the women, in which they refuse to have anything to do with the men until the latter make peace with Sparta. (Lysistrata, a coinage of Aristophanes, means "She who disbands the army.") The broad humor, founded largely upon the ostensibly uncontrollable appetite of the human male for the female, reinforced by its practical immunity as a recognized classic from censorship, has obtained for the *Lysistrata* repeated revivals in the present century. (JJ)

M

Ma (mä). Mother goddess of ancient Cappadocia in Asia Minor, identified with Cybele. The focus of her cult was her sanctuary at Comana, where her festivals were celebrated and where she was attended by a great troop of priests, priestesses, and sacred prostitutes. Roman soldiers, after they occupied Cappadocia, identified her with their own Bellona, and called her Ma Bellona.

Macareus (mak′a̱-rös). In mythology, a son of Aeolus, keeper of the winds, and Enarete. He and his five brothers and six sisters lived happily on the island where the winds were confined. Unaware that incestuous unions were displeasing to the gods, the brothers and sisters considered themselves married to each other. When Aeolus discovered this, he threw the child of Macareus and his sister Canace to the dogs, sent Canace a sword, with which she killed herself, and forced four of his other sons to seek homes in other lands.

Macaria (ma̱-kar′i-a̱). In Greek legend, the

daughter of Heracles and Deianira, the only daughter he ever had. In the war between Theseus (or Demophon, his son) and Eurystheus that followed the persecution of Heracles' children by the latter, an oracle prophesied that the Athenians would win only if one of Heracles' children was offered as a sacrifice. Macaria volunteered to serve as the sacrifice, and when it was suggested that lots should be drawn she scorned the suggestion, saying she wished to offer her life of her own free will, and not to give it up as a result of chance. She was sacrificed and the Athenians, who had given sanctuary to the harassed children of Heracles, won. The Macarian Spring at Marathon, where Macaria died, is named for her.

Macedonia (mas-e̱-dō′ni-a̱). [Also: **Macedon.**] In ancient geography, a country in SE Europe, of varying limits. It lay N of the Aegean Sea and Thessaly, E of Illyria, and W of Thrace, separated from Illyria by the Scardus Mountains. The chief rivers were the Axius (Vardar) and Strymon; the chief cities, Edessa, Pella, and Thessalonica. Macedonia was not originally a part of Hellas. It first became powerful under Philip II, who united the country and made the Macedonian army the best-trained army of his time. Philip, who became the master of Greece, was succeeded by his son Alexander the Great, the conqueror of the entire geographical area that came to be known as the Near East, making Macedonia the motherland of one of the greatest empires of history. After his death, its possession was contested by Alexander's successors, and was finally won (c278 B.C.) by Antigonus II (Antigonus Gonatas). The Macedonians were defeated by Rome at Cynoscephalae in 197 B.C., and finally at Pydna in 168 B.C., and Macedonia was made a Roman province in 146 B.C. Parts of it are now in Yugoslavia, Bulgaria, and Greece.

Macedonian Empire (mas-e̯-dō′ni-an). Empire built up by Philip II (who reigned 359–336 B.C.) and his son Alexander the Great (336–323 B.C.). It included at its greatest extent Macedonia, Greece, Thrace, Asia Minor, Syria, Egypt, Mesopotamia, Babylonia, Assyria, part of Armenia, and the countries comprised in what are now Iran, Afghanistan, Baluchistan, W India, and a large part of C Asia. The empire was divided under Alexander's successors, the chief divisions being Macedonia, Egypt, Syria, Pergamum, Bithynia, Rhodes, and Greek states.

Macedonians. Natives or inhabitants of ancient Macedonia, in which Hellenic culture and the Greek language were influential.

Macedonian Wars. Wars between Rome and Macedonia: 1) 214–205 B.C., when Philip V fought in alliance with Carthage; 2) 200–197 B.C., when Philip V was defeated by Flamininus at Cynoscephalae (197 B.C.); 3) 171–168 B.C., when Perseus was defeated by Aemilius Paulus at Pydna (168 B.C.); 4) 149–148 B.C., soon after which Macedonia was made a Roman province.

Machaon (ma̯-kā′on). In Homeric legend (*Iliad*) a son of Asclepius and a brother of Podalirius. He was famed as a surgeon and his brother as a physician. Both went from Oechalia with the Greeks to Troy. Machaon, regarded as one of the most valuable of all the Greeks for his skill in healing, was wounded by a three-barbed arrow shot by Paris, and was taken off the field of battle by Nestor. According to some accounts he was finally slain by the Amazon queen Penthesilea; according to others it was Eurypylus, son of Telephus, who killed him. Nestor took his bones back to Pylus where they became the center of a healing sanctuary.

Machaerus (ma̯-kē′rus). According to some accounts, a Phocian who killed Neoptolemus, at the command of the priestess, at the shrine of Apollo at Delphi, because Neoptolemus had impiously attempted to steal the sacrificial offerings on the altar.

Macrae (mak′rē). A place in Attica where, according to some accounts, Poseidon slew Erechtheus with his trident for killing Eumolpus, Poseidon's son and a priest of Eleusis, in the war between the Athenians and the Eleusinians. Here the earth opened and swallowed up Erechtheus.

Macrians (mak′ri-a̯nz). A people who dwelt near the Propontis. They were neighbors and enemies of Cyzicus and the Doliones. On the fatal night when the Argonauts were blown back to the kingdom of Cyzicus, the Doliones attacked them in the belief that they were Macrian raiders.

Macris (mak′ris). In Greek mythology, a daughter of Aristaeus and Autonoë. She was one of the nymphs of Nysa to whom Hermes brought the infant Dionysus to be cared for. The nymphs cared for him in a cave, sometimes said to be on Mount Helicon (the precise location of Nysa has never been settled), and fed him on honey. She was driven out of Euboea by the wrath of Hera and fled to Drepana, the island which was later called Corcyra, where she was kindly received by the Phaeacian natives. There she dwelt in a cave with a double entrance and granted great wealth to the Phaeacians. A town on the coast was named for her and the island itself was sometimes also called by her name. When the Argonauts landed in the island on their way home from Colchis, Jason and Medea were married in the cave of Macris.

Macro (mā′krō), **Naevius Sertorius.** Prefect of the Roman praetorians under Tiberius and Caligula. He was forced to commit suicide, 38 A.D.

Macron (mā′kron). Attic vase painter in the

red-figure technique, active at the end of the 6th and the beginning of the 5th centuries B.C. He decorated all but three of 30 vessels signed by Hieron as potter. Two hundred and forty extant works have been attributed to him, among them a skyphos (Boston) showing Paris carrying off Helen, on one side, and Menelaus recovering her on the other. This vessel, signed by Macron as painter and Hieron as potter, is the only extant one on which the signature of Macron appears in its entirety.

Maddaloni (mäd-dä-lō′nē), **Monte di.** See **Tifata.**

Madness of Heracles, The or **Hercules Furens.** A drama by Euripides, presented c416 B.C. The scene is before an altar of Zeus in front of the royal palace of Thebes. Amphitryon, the foster father of Heracles, tells of the dangers with which he, Megara, the wife of Heracles, and the children of Heracles are threatened, now that Heracles has been gone so long in the Underworld to fetch Cerberus that men think he will never return. These dangers arise from the fact that evil-hearted and discontented men have brought Lycus, a Euboean, into Thebes. He conspired against Creon, slew him, and usurped his throne. Lycus has determined to slay all that remain of the house of Heracles lest in the future they attempt to avenge Creon's death. Megara adds that they must resign themselves to death, as they have no friends and nowhere to turn. Amphitryon cannot resign himself. In spite of old age and terrible misfortune, he rejoices in life and "loves its hopes." He clings to a belief that Heracles will yet return and save them.

Lycus enters. He mocks Amphitryon's hopes of rescue by Heracles. The family of Heracles must die. Amphitryon calls Lycus a coward who would murder innocent children in their father's absence. He asks that they be allowed to go into exile, and says the Thebans are disgraced because they will not help the family of the man who did so much for their city. Lycus ignores him and commands that funeral pyres be erected for Heracles' family and for the Theban Elders who sympathize with Amphitryon but are too old and weak to fight. Megara counsels Amphitryon to die nobly since she is sure there is now no hope for them. She leads

her children into the palace to dress them in burial clothes. Before following her, Amphitryon rails at Zeus: the god makes less of an effort to protect his children than does the mortal father.

The chorus of Theban Elders sings of Heracles' 12 great labors for Eurystheus. At the end of their song they lament that old age prevents them from defending his family against Lycus. Megara, Amphitryon, and the children come out of the palace dressed in burial shrouds. In desperation, Megara involuntarily calls on Heracles to help them. Miraculously, he appears. They tell him of their terrible plight. He asks if he has no friends who would help his family, and sadly concludes that misfortune has no friends. He vows to destroy Lycus and the Thebans who have permitted his excesses. Since no one saw him enter the city, he will hide until Lycus comes and then attack him. He tells his family that he remained so long in the Underworld in order to rescue Theseus; then they all go into the palace.

Lycus enters. He says the time has come and asks Amphitryon where Megara and the children are. He follows them into the palace while Amphitryon gloats as he imagines the fate that awaits Lycus at the hands of Heracles. Presently he hears Lycus cry out. His cries alternate with the song the chorus of Elders sings of the retribution for the tyrant.

Iris and Mania (*Madness*) now appear. Iris says that now that Heracles' labors for Eurystheus are finished, Hera wants to stain him with the blood of his own kin. She commands Mania (a daughter of Uranus and Nyx) to take possession of Heracles. Mania pleads with Iris not to devise evil against Heracles, who has done such great things for the gods, as well as for mortals. But Iris warns her that she must not interfere with Hera's desires, and orders her to do as she is bid. Mania calls Helius to witness that she is carrying out orders against her will, and enters the palace. The chorus laments over the misfortunes the gods send Heracles. An uproar breaks out in the palace. A servant runs out and announces that in a fit of madness Heracles has slain his children under the impression that they are the sons of Eurystheus. Megara is dead also, and he would have killed Amphitryon but Athena appeared and hurled a great rock at him which knocked him unconscious, whereupon Amphitryon and the servants bound him. Now Amphitryon, grieving, comes from the palace and warns the elders to flee; Heracles has regained consciousness, burst his bonds, and is coming out, calling for his friends. He asks Amphitryon why he is weeping, and is gradually made to understand the horror he has wrought in a spell of madness. In despair, Heracles decides to kill himself. He warns Theseus, who now approaches, to keep away, lest he be tainted by Heracles' bloodguilt. Theseus had heard of the crimes of Lycus and had come to help Heracles. He sees the bodies of Heracles' children and learns what has happened from Amphitryon, as Heracles crouches with his head covered. Theseus seeks to comfort Heracles. He tells him to unveil his head, that he is his friend and remains so in misfortune. He attempts to hearten Heracles by telling him that a "royal-souled man" bears the blows of heaven and does not flinch. He persuades Heracles not to set his mind on suicide, and in response to his statement that no land will accept him because of his crimes, he invites Heracles to Athens, promises to purify him and to give him half of his kingdom. Athens, he says, will be honored for having helped a hero. Heracles expresses bewilderment about the motives of the gods, who have brought him such sorrow, and even wonders if the gods exist. He accepts the generous offer of Theseus, because it is braver to live than to die. He commits his children to Amphitryon for burial and laments. Theseus offers his hand to Heracles as a helper and a friend.

Maeander (mē-an′dėr). [Modern Turkish, **Menderes**.] In ancient geography, a river of W Asia Minor, flowing, with many windings, generally SW and W through Phrygia and Ionia to the Aegean Sea. The name is the origin of the word "meander." According to legend, Maeander, son of Cercaphus and Anaxibia, was at war in Phrygia. He vowed to the goddess Cybele that if he was victorious, he would sacrifice the first person who congratulated him on his return. He was victorious, and on his return he was met and congratulated by his son, his mother, and his sister. In fulfillment of his vow he sacrificed them. He then hurled himself into the river which afterward bore his name.

Maecenas (mē-sē′nas), **Caius Cilnius.** Roman statesman and patron of literature, died 8 B.C. He was descended from an ancient Etruscan family and belonged to the equestrian order. He appears in 40 B.C. as the agent of Octavian (afterward emperor under the title of Augustus) in negotiating a marriage with Scribonia, daughter of Libo, the father-in-law of Sextus Pompeius. He was entrusted with the administration of Rome during the absence of Octavian on an expedition against Pompey in 36 B.C., and after the battle of Actium in 31 B.C., when Octavian made himself master of the Roman world, urged him to establish an empire instead of restoring the Republic. He remained, with Agrippa, the chief adviser of Augustus down to 16 B.C., when he became estranged from his master and retired to private life. He was the friend and patron of Horace and Vergil, and wrote a number of works of which only fragments are extant. His name has become a synonym for the generous patron of the arts.

Maenads (mē′nadz). [Known also as **Bacchae** or **Thyiades**.] The female followers of Dionysus; priestesses of Dionysus. Their tradition sprang from those who accompanied the god when he roamed all over the world in a frenzy of madness inspired by Hera. The maenads celebrated the festivals of Dionysus with mad songs and boisterous courses in gay companies amid the crags of Parnassus and Cithaeron, particularly on the occasion of the great triennial festival of Dionysus. During the celebration they donned the *nebris* (fawnskin), chewed laurel leaves, and carried the ivy-twined, pine-cone-tipped thyrsus. Their faces and arms were sometimes painted or tattooed as a disguise during their orgies on the mountain tops when they became the lovers of Pan. The maenads, inflamed by wine and Dionysiac ecstasy, helped Agave tear her son Pentheus to pieces under the impression he was a young lion, because he had doubted the divinity of Dionysus. At the instigation of Dionysus, they attacked Orpheus at Dium in Thrace. They first murdered their husbands, who were in a temple where Orpheus was a priest of Apollo, and then tore Orpheus limb from limb, and hurled his head into the Hebrus River. Dionysus saved their lives from the vengeance this provoked by transforming them into oak trees, and ever after the maenads in that region were tattooed by their husbands as a warning against the murder of priests.

MAENAD
Red-figured Greek amphora, Cleophrades
Painter, c500 B.C. *Munich*

Maenalus (men′a-lus, mē′na-). In Greek mythology, the eldest son of Lycaon. According to some accounts, it was he who suggested that Lycaon place human flesh before Zeus when the god came to test the piety of Lycaon and his sons, to determine whether the god would recognize human flesh. According to some accounts, Maenalus, his father, and all his brothers except one were changed into wolves for this horrible deed. Others say Zeus slew Maenalus with his thunderbolt.

Maenalus. A mountain in Arcadia, sacred to Pan.

Maeon (mē′on). Named by Homer as the "godlike" son of Haemon. He was a Theban, one of the 50 valiant Theban warriors who were set to ambush Tydeus when he left Thebes after having fruitlessly attempted to persuade the Thebans to restore Polynices to the throne. As Tydeus made his way back to the camp of the Seven against Thebes, these 50 leaped on him from ambush. He slew them all except Maeon, who was allowed to escape and return to Thebes to tell what had happened. In the subsequent battle of the Seven against Thebes it is said that Maeon, in gratitude for being spared by Tydeus, buried the fallen hero's body with full funeral honors.

Maeonia (mē-ō′ni-a̱). An ancient name of Lydia, the country on the W coast of Asia Minor. The Maeonians were allies of Troy in the Trojan War. It was to Omphale, queen of Maeonia, that Heracles went as a slave after the murder of Iphitus, son of Eurytus. According to Herodotus, Tyrrhenians from Maeonia, who left their country to escape a famine, became colonizers and the ancestors of the Etruscans in Italy.

Maeotis (mē-ō′tis), **Palus.** Ancient name of **Azov, Sea of,** the shallow gulf opening from the north shore of the Euxine Sea, in the Chersonesus Taurica (Crimea).

Maera (mē′ra̱). In Greek legend, Icarius' faithful hound. He led Erigone to the spot where peasants had buried her father after killing him. The hound was later translated to the heavens and became the Lesser Dog Star.

Maera. Legendary daughter, or descendant of a daughter, of Atlas. She was the wife of Tegeates, and was buried with him at Tegea, although the Mantineans claimed she was buried in their land.

Maera. According to some accounts, the bitch into which Hecuba was transformed after she had blinded the Thracian king, Polymnestor.

Maggiore (mäd-jō′rā), **Lago.** See **Verbanus, Lacus.**

Magi (mā′jī). Members of the learned and priestly caste of Medians in ancient Persia who had official charge of the sacred rites, practiced interpretation of dreams, professed supernatural arts, and were distinguished by peculiarities of dress and insignia. They are believed to have been originally pre-Zoroastrian; but their beliefs are embodied in Zoroastrianism, and Zoroastrian priests were Magi. The word "magic" is derived from Magi.

actọr; up, lūte, pŭll; oi, oil; ou, out; ᴛʜ, then; d̲ as d or j, s̲ as s or sh, t̲ as t or ch, z̲ as z or zh.

Magna Graecia (mag′na̤ grē′sha̤). [Eng. trans., "Great Greece."] In ancient geography, the name given to the part of S Italy colonized by Greeks. Among the leading cities were Cumae, Croton, Sybaris, Metapontum, Locri, Rhegium, Tarentum, Thurii, Heraclea, and Neapolis. Colonization began in the 8th century B.C. and the most flourishing period was the 7th and 6th centuries B.C.

Magna Mater (mā′tẻr). A Roman name for Rhea or Cybele, meaning "the Great Mother," the mother of the gods.

Magnes (mag′nēz). One of the earliest (c500 B.C.) writers and founders of Attic comedy.

Magnesia (mag-nē′zha̤, -sha̤.) In ancient geography, the easternmost district of Thessaly, Greece, bordering on the Aegean Sea and the Pagasean Gulf.

Magnesia. [Sometimes called **Magnesia ad Maeandrum.**] In ancient geography, a city in Ionia, W Asia Minor, about 14 miles SE of Ephesus. The temple of Artemis Leucophryne, the remains of which still exist, was one of the most magnificent of ancient monuments, rebuilt c300 B.C. The frieze, now in the Louvre, bears reliefs of combats between Greeks and Amazons. There are also remains of a theater of the 4th century B.C., with later modifications, and of a large stadium.

Magnesia or **Magnesia ad Sipylum** (ad sip′i-lum). [Modern name, **Manisa** or **Manissa.**] In ancient geography, a city of Lydia, situated on the Hermus River. Here in 190 B.C. the Romans under Lucius Scipio, who had his famous brother Scipio Africanus the Elder as one of his lieutenants, defeated a vastly superior force under Antiochus the Great, king of Syria. Antiochus fled, sued for peace, and by the terms of it was compelled to withdraw behind the Taurus Mountains.

Mago (mā′gō). Carthaginian general; fl. 6th century B.C. He was the reputed organizer of the military system of Carthage.

Mago. Carthaginian naval commander; fl. 4th century B.C. He commanded the Carthaginians in the wars against Syracuse (396–392 B.C.), and was compelled by Dionysius of Syracuse to make a peace which put all the Greek cities of Sicily under the dominion of Syracuse. By this peace the Carthaginians were forced to withdraw to the western corner of Sicily. In a later war with Dionysius, Mago was killed in Sicily, c378 B.C.

Mago. Carthaginian general; fl. 4th century B.C. He was the commander of the Carthaginian forces in Sicily, 343 B.C., and allied himself with Hicetas, tyrant of Leontini, in his struggle with Timoleon who sought to overthrow the tyrants. Mago's conduct of the campaign was marked by inexplicable cowardice. On his return to Carthage he committed suicide, and his body was nailed to a cross by his countrymen.

Mago. Carthaginian general; died c203 B.C. He was a younger brother of Hannibal, whom he accompanied to Italy in 218 B.C. and in whose victories he shared in the first years of the war. He returned to Carthage and then was ordered to Spain (215 B.C.) to support his brother Hasdrubal there. When Hasdrubal went to Italy to support Hannibal, Mago remained in Spain. He was defeated by Scipio Africanus at Silpia in 206 B.C. He later landed in Liguria and was defeated in Cisalpine Gaul by the Romans (203 B.C.). On his journey back to Carthage he died of his wounds.

Maia (mā′ya̤, mī′a̤). In Greek mythology, a daughter of Atlas and Pleione. She was the eldest of the Pleiades, mother by Zeus of Hermes, and the nurse of Arcas after the death of Callisto. In Roman mythology she became identified with a primitive Italian goddess who was associated with fertility and growth. As such the Romans called her Maia Maiesta, and because of the fertility association identified her with the Phrygian mother-goddess, Cybele, and their own Bona Dea.

Maimacterion (mī-mak-tē′ri-on). The fifth month of the Attic year, corresponding to the end of November and the beginning of December. A festival to Zeus of the Storms was held in this month.

Malea (ma̤-lē′a̤). Easternmost of the three southern promontories of the Peloponnesus. Here Chiron had one of his caves, according to legend, and it was here that he received the wound from Heracles' poisoned arrow which led to his death. Some say Malea was the home of Silenus. Ships rounding this cape often encountered wind squalls and rough seas. Prudent masters, who preferred the Corinth isthmus portage to the risk of disaster off Cape Malea, contributed to the profits which made the wealth of Corinth proverbial. (JJ)

Malea. In ancient geography, the southernmost point of the island of Lesbos.

Maliacus Sinus (ma-lī′a̧-kus sī′nus). Latin name of **Lamia, Gulf of.**

Malian Gulf (mā′li-a̧n). See **Lamia, Gulf of.**

Malis (mā′lis). In ancient geography, a district of Greece, S of Thessaly, N of Doris, and W of Locris. Lamia and Heraclea were the chief cities.

Malli (mal′i). An ancient tribe of Dravidian stock, of NW India. They were a free and warlike tribe, dwelling on the banks of the Hydraotis (Ravee) River, near the confluence of the Hydaspes and Acesines. On his way home from India Alexander the Great passed through their territory. They resisted his advance and withdrew to their city, which may have been on the site of modern Multan. The city was taken, but the Malli took refuge in their citadel, from the walls of which they hurled a shower of arrows on Alexander and his men attempting to scale the wall with ladders. Alexander, eager to enter the citadel, seized a ladder and climbed up under cover of his shield. So many of his men sought to follow him that the ladder gave way, and he found himself on the wall with only three companions. His men shouted to him to jump back. Instead, he leaped in among the hostile Malli and sought to hold them off single-handed. His three companions on the wall followed him. One was killed instantly. Alexander slew the leader of the enemy with his sword, but was overcome by a hail of missiles and by a wound in the breast, and at last fell to the ground, faint from loss of blood. His loyal companions protected him: Peucestas held a shield over him while Leonnatus held off the enemy until the army forced the gates and stormed in to the rescue. The soldiers, infuriated, massacred the population within the citadel in revenge for the wounds sustained by Alexander. The king was, in fact, terribly weakened, and rumor quickly spread that he was dead. News of his death reached the main body of the army, encamped lower down on the Ravee River, and caused despair. To reassure his men,

Alexander had himself placed in a barge and carried down the river to the camp. When the army saw his litter in the barge, they thought it held his corpse until he waved to them. Once ashore, he even walked a few steps and the army went wild with relief and delight. Some of his friends rebuked Alexander for the adventure at Malli. A general, they said, had no right to endanger his army by leaving it without a commander by taking such personal risks. Alexander agreed that they were right. After the taking of the citadel, the Malli made complete submission to Alexander and were added to his empire.

Mallia (mä′li-a̧). In ancient geography, a city on the N coast of Crete, E of Cnossus. Remains of a palace, built in the same period as the first palaces of Cnossus and Phaestus but on a smaller scale, have been found there.

Malophorus (mal-of′ō-rus). Epithet of Demeter. Some say it means "Apple-bearer," and some say it means "Sheep-bearer." According to those who say it means the latter, she was given this name by those who first sheared sheep at Nisaea.

Malta (mâl′ta̧). The modern name of **Melita.**

Mamers (mā′mèrz). Ancient Italian (Oscan) name of the god Mars. He was worshiped originally as a god of the fields, with fertility associations.

Mamertine Prison (mam′èr-tīn). Name given to the Carcer Tullianum, the oldest prison in Rome, situated on the E slope of the Capitoline Hill. Its erection was attributed to Ancus Marcius (fourth king of Rome, 640–616 B.C.), and it was originally built over a well. The Tullianum consists of a large oblong upper chamber and a small underground circular chamber, built at different periods. Jugurtha, Lentulus, and others met death in this prison, and according to tradition Saint Peter and Saint Paul were imprisoned here. The name Mamertinus was given to it in medieval times.

Mamertines (mam′èr-tīnz). In ancient history, a band of Campanian mercenaries who became rulers of Messina, 289 B.C. Their requests for aid from the Carthaginians and then from the Romans (caused by an attack by Hiero of Syracuse) brought about the First Punic War, 264 B.C.

Mamurius (ma̱-mur′i-us). In Roman legend, a smith who made shields which were exact reproductions of the *ancile* (sacred shield) that fell from heaven. He made 11 copies of this shield, so exact that they could not be told apart. The purpose was to prevent recognition of the original shield and its possible theft. Mamurius was sometimes considered as a god himself and was sometimes identified with Mars. A special festival was held in his honor in March, during which hides were beaten with clubs in imitation of a smith's hammering.

Mandane (man′da̱-nē). A daughter of Astyages, king of the Medes. Her father dreamed that such a stream of water flowed from her that it covered all Asia. The interpretation of the dream by the Magi caused Astyages to give his daughter in marriage, not to a Mede, but to the Persian Cambyses, a member of a people at that time subject to the Medes. After she was married, Astyages dreamed that from her womb grew a vine that overshadowed all Asia. The Magi interpreted this to mean that his daughter's son would be a king if he did not die too soon. Terrified lest his grandson rule in his place, Astyages sent at once for his daughter. When she arrived, he saw that she was about to bear a child. He set guards about her with instructions to destroy the child the instant it was born. In due course Mandane was delivered of a son. He was immediately taken from her, and it was many years before she knew that the child she bore was not dead, as she had been led to believe. Her son was Cyrus the Great. He led a revolt against Astyages and became master of the Medes, and thus the dream was fulfilled.

Manes (mā′nēz). In Roman antiquity, the spirits of the dead considered as tutelary divinities of their family; the deified shades of the dead, according to the belief that the soul continued to exist and to have relations with earth after the body had perished. Three times a year a pit called the *mundus* was officially opened in the *comitium* of the Roman Forum, to permit the Manes to come forth. The Manes were also honored at certain festivals, as the *Parentalia* and *Feralia;* offerings were made to them, and a flame was maintained on the altar of the household for them.

Manetho (man′e̱-thō). Egyptian priest, a native of Sebennytus and a priest of Serapis at Alexandria. At the bidding of Ptolemy II Philadelphus (308–246 B.C.), founder of the Museum of Alexandria, he compiled, in Greek, the *Aegyptiaca,* a history of Egypt from earliest times to the death of Alexander the Great (323 B.C.). His compilation, however, survives only in quotations in later writers. The dynastic chronology which we now use is derived from his reconstruction of the Egyptian king-lists in old, middle, and new kingdoms (31 dynasties), though in part his reconstruction is irreconcilable with contemporary inscriptions and other evidence. (JJ)

Mania (mā′ni-a̱, mān′ya̱). In Roman religion, the goddess of the dead, called Mother or Grandmother of Ghosts. Woolen effigies of men and women were offered to her at the Compitalia (crossroads festival) in the hope that she would accept them in place of living persons. These effigies themselves were called *maniae,* as were also certain loaves and cakes made in human form and eaten at a similar festival at Aricia, near Rome. Mania has been referred to by various Latin writers as the mother of the Lares.

Maniae (mā′ni-ē). In ancient geography, a place, near Megalopolis in Arcadia, where there was a sanctuary called Maniae (*Madnesses*). Here, they say, Orestes was overtaken by the Furies, who caused him to go mad for the slaying of his mother. Nearby is a small earthen mound, surmounted by a stone finger and called the "Tomb of the Finger." In his madness Orestes saw the Furies as black goddesses. He bit off a finger and appeased them and then they appeared to him as white as he recovered his senses. Another sanctuary nearby marks the spot where he cut off his hair and offered it as sacrifice when he recovered his sanity. Orestes offered a sin-offering to the black goddesses to avert their wrath, and a thank-offering to the white goddesses in gratitude for the return of his senses. From this it became the custom to sacrifice to the Graces before sacrificing to the Furies. The spot where he recovered his senses was called Ace (*Remedies*). All this took place before

Orestes was tried by the court of the Areopagus.

Manilian Law (mạ-nĭ′li-ạn). In Roman history: 1) a law carried by the tribune Caius Manilius in 67 B.C. The law, which extended the voting privileges of freedmen, was annulled by the Senate because of violation of constitutional provisions. 2) to win the support of Pompey, Manilius proposed the conferring on him of extraordinary powers in the East, including the command of the Mithridatic War. Cicero supported this proposal in his oration *Pro Lege Manilia* (For the Manilian Law). Manilius was later tried on a charge, the nature of which is uncertain but probably involved *maiestas* (lowering the dignity of the Senate). Although he was defended by Cicero, Manilius was found guilty.

Manilius (mạ-nĭ′li-us), **Caius.** Roman tribune (67 B.C.); fl. in the first half of the 1st century B.C. He proposed the Manilian Law in connection with the voting privileges of freedmen and the law conferring on Pompey the command of the Mithridatic War.

Manilius, Marcus. Roman poet, contemporary of Augustus and Tiberius, author of the *Astronomica,* a didactic poem on astrology in expert Latin hexameters, of which books 1–5, 4258 lines, survive. The critical edition of the *Astronomica,* in five volumes, the revised edition of which was completed in 1937, was a life work of the English poet and great Cambridge scholar A. E. Housman. (JJ)

Manlius Capitolinus (man′li-us kap″i-tō-lĭ′nus), **Marcus.** Roman patrician, consul 392 B.C.; died 384 B.C. When Brennus and the Gauls attacked Rome, 390 B.C., most of the inhabitants fled. Brennus found the gates open and unguarded. He pillaged and burned the city and put to the sword those whom he took captive. Manlius and some companions fled to the citadel on the Capitoline Hill and successfully resisted Brennus who laid siege to the Capitol. In the course of the siege, Pontius Cominius, an envoy from the exiled dictator Camillus, secretly penetrated the enemy ring about the Capitol, and by a way he knew ascended the lower slopes of the Capitol and was hauled to the top by the defenders. He left by the same route, and returned safely to Camillus. A few days later one of the Gallic soldiers noticed the broken branches and gouged places in the hill which marked the path taken by Cominius up the slope, and he pointed this out to Brennus. The leader of the Gauls realized that there was a way to the top, and sent a force of Gauls up to attack the Capitol at night. According to tradition, the Gauls made their way in safety to the top, but as they were about to attack the Romans, some sacred geese in the temple of Juno heard them, cackled, and woke the sleeping Romans, who leaped up to defend themselves and the Capitol. The Gallic party was slain, and next day their leader was hurled from the rock into the enemy camp. Because he was the commander and preserved the Capitol from the Gauls, Manlius was given the surname Capitolinus (but some say his father before him had that name, and it had nothing to do with the defense of the Capitol). After the Gauls had been driven out of Rome, Manlius began (385 B.C.) to champion the cause of the plebeians against the patricians with a view to making himself ruler of Rome. In the following year he was arrested by Camillus, who had been appointed dictator by the Romans, and cast into prison. But Manlius had so won the people that when they learned of his imprisonment they went about the streets clad in mourning, and Camillus was forced to release him. Manlius continued his seditious activities against the Republic and was brought to trial. The Campus Martius, where the trial was held, was in full view of the Capitol. Marcus Manlius stretched out his hands toward it and recalled how he had gloriously defended it against the Gauls. This aroused so much sympathy that the judges dared not convict him. On the other hand, he could not be acquitted because proof of his crimes against the state was plain. Camillus settled it by transferring the place of the trial. Manlius was convicted of treason and hurled to his death from the Tarpeian Rock on the Capitol, so that this place was the scene of his greatest glory and his deepest shame. The house of Manlius on the Capitoline Hill was razed, a temple of Moneta was erected in its place, and henceforth it became the rule that no patrician should have a house on the Capitoline Hill. The events of Manlius' life were pictured on the shield which Vulcan made for Aeneas to protect him in his wars against the Latins.

Manlius Imperiosus Torquatus (im-pir-i-ō′sus tôr-kwā′tus), **Titus**. Roman hero of the 4th century B.C. He was elected military tribune in 362 B.C., and in 361 served under the dictator Titus Quintius Pennus against the Gauls. During this campaign he slew a gigantic Gaul in single combat in the presence of the two armies, and despoiled him of a *torques* (chain) which he placed around his own neck (whence the surname *Torquatus*). He was appointed dictator in 353 and again in 349 B.C., and was consul in 347, 344, and 340 B.C. During his third consulship, while engaged with his colleague Publius Decius Mus in a campaign against the Latins, he put to death his own son, who, contrary to orders, had fought and killed in single combat an enemy from the opposing army.

Manlius Torquatus, Titus. Roman general, died 202 B.C. He was consul in 235 and 224 B.C., and dictator in 208 B.C. During his first consulship he conquered the Sardinians, after whose subjugation the Romans enjoyed a brief period of universal peace, the temple of Janus being closed for the first time since the reign of Numa Pompilius at the very beginning of Roman history. He opposed the ransoming of the prisoners taken by Hannibal at Cannae in 216, and gained a decisive victory over the Carthaginians in Sardinia in 215 B.C.

Manlius Vulso (vul′sō), **Cnaeus**. Roman consul (189 B.C.); fl. 2nd century B.C. He defeated the Galatians in Asia Minor.

Mannus (man′us). Mythological ancestor of the ancient Germanic peoples. He is mentioned by Tacitus as being the father of three sons from whom the various Germanic tribes sprang.

Mantinea (man-ti-nē′a). [Also: **Mantineia**.] In ancient geography, a city in Arcadia, Greece, SW of Corinth. The original city of this name, some say, was founded by Mantineus, son of Lycaon, on another spot. In obedience to an oracle Antinoë, daughter of Cepheus of Tegea, led the inhabitants to a new location. She was guided to the new site by a serpent, for which reason the river flowing beside the city was named Ophis (*Snake*). The burial mound of Antinoë became the Common Hearth of the Mantineans.

Near an altar of Hera in the city was the tomb of Arcas. The daughters of Pelias, who fled hither after their father's death at Medea's hands, died in Mantinea and were buried here. At Mount Alesium nearby, was a famous sanctuary of Poseidon, said to have been built by Agamedes and Trophonius, into which it was forbidden to mortals to enter. In their temple at Mantinea, which was divided into two equal parts, the Mantineans had an image of Asclepius by Alcamenes in one part, and images of Leto and her children by Praxiteles in the other part. There were also in Mantinea sanctuaries of Zeus Savior, Zeus Giver-of-Gifts, the Dioscuri, Demeter, Athena, and Hera. Men of Mantinea went to the Trojan War under the leadership of Agapenor, son of Ancaeus the Argonaut. In the Persian War they were among the allies of Leonidas at Thermopylae and at the battle of Salamis (480 B.C.). In the Peloponnesian Wars Mantinea joined Elis to fight against Sparta and was defeated (418 B.C.). In 385 B.C. the Mantineans were defeated again by Sparta and their city was taken. Pausanias says the Spartans took the city by diverting the waters of the Ophis River against the walls made of unbaked brick. The bricks crumbled, and the Spartans rushed in and razed the city to the ground. It was restored by the Thebans, under Epaminondas, after 371 B.C., but the Mantineans treacherously negotiated with the Spartans to make a separate peace and betrayed their benefactors. Later they fought with the Spartans against the Thebans at Mantinea (362 B.C.) and were defeated. In honor of Alexander the Great's general, Antigonus, the Mantineans changed the name of their city to Antigonea, but its ancient name was restored during the reign of the emperor Hadrian.

Mantius (man′shus). In legend, a son of Melampus the seer. He was the father of Clitus, carried off by Eos for his beauty, and of the seer Polyidus.

Manto (man′tō). In Greek mythology, a daughter of the seer Tiresias. She also had the gift of prophecy. When Thebes was taken by the Epigoni, Manto, who had not fled from the city as her father advised the Thebans to do, was taken captive by Alcmaeon, the leader of the Epigoni. By Alcmaeon she became the mother of Amphilochus and Tisiphone. Later Manto was sent as part of the booty of Thebes to the temple of Apollo at Delphi. Apollo sent her to Colophon in Ionia, where she married Rhacius, king of Caria, and became the mother of the seer Mopsus, either by Rhacius or Apollo.

Manto. In Roman mythology, a seeress, the mother of Ocnus by the river-god of the Tuscan river. Ocnus founded the city of Mantua and named it for his mother.

Mantua (man′tū̠-a̠). [Italian, **Mantova.**] An ancient Etruscan town situated on a lake formed by the river Mincius. According to the *Aeneid* it was founded by Ocnus, a son of the Tuscan river-god and the seeress Manto, for whom the city was named. The town was further developed by the Romans and has long been known as the birthplace of the poet Vergil.

Maracanda (mar-a̠-kan′da̠). Ancient name of Samarkand, city in ancient Sogdiana, C Asia. Alexander the Great stopped here (327 B.C.) for some time on his expedition into India, and destroyed the ancient city. It was at Maracanda that Clitus, a friend of Alexander's, during a long evening of drinking, expressed resentment of the influence of the Orientals over Alexander. Rash words and insults were flung out; Alexander seized a spear and ran Clitus through.

Marathon (mar′a̠-thon). According to Greek tradition, a son of Epopeus. He fled from the violence of his father in the Peloponnesus to Attica. After his father's death he returned to the Peloponnesus and succeeded him as ruler of Ephyraea. He was succeeded by his son Corinthus, for whom the city of Corinth was named.

Marathon. A plain in Attica, Greece, near the modern village of Vrana, about 18 miles NE of Athens, between Mount Pentelicus and the sea. Pisistratus landed there when he returned from exile in Eretria, prepared his assault on Athens there, and from there made his successful march on Athens when he became tyrant for the third time (c546 B.C.). The plain is celebrated as the site of the battle of September, 490 B.C., between the Greeks (10,000 Athenians and 1000 Plataeans) under Miltiades, and 30,000 or more Persians under Datis and Artaphernes.

Hippias, son of Pisistratus, who had been expelled from Athens, led the Persians to the plain because it was considered ideal terrain for the Persian cavalry. The Athenians, having learned of the approach of the Persians at Marathon, marched their forces thither under ten generals. The Athenians sent Phidippides (or Philippides) to Sparta with an urgent request for aid, but for religious reasons the Spartans could not march out of Sparta until the moon was full. In the meantime the Athenians drew up their battle lines in a precinct of Heracles, and were joined by the Plataeans. Five of the Athenian generals advised against risking a battle because they were so greatly outnumbered. The other five, including Miltiades, son of Cimon, wanted to engage the enemy at once. Miltiades feared that in case of an even division, those who favored withdrawal would prevail. For this reason he persuaded Callimachus, the *polemarch* (war-archon) to vote for the attack and break the tie. Under Miltiades as commander the battle array was set; sacrificial victims gave favorable omens. The Athenians made a running charge out onto the plain against the Persians. According to some accounts, a fully-armed image of Theseus led the Athenians in their rush against the Persians. The latter thought that the few Greeks running against them without horses or archers were mad, and prepared to receive them. The Greeks fought gloriously in close array, and it was some time before the Persians crashed through the center of their line, the weakest part, and were victorious in that sector. But the Athenians on the right wing and the Plataeans on the left wing were victorious. They permitted the Persians they had overcome to flee, while they reformed their line and fell upon the Persians who, thinking they had won, were pursuing the Greeks of the center of the line. With their reformed line the Athenians and Plataeans overcame the Persians. (Ever after this day, it was the custom of the Athenians, in the sacrifices and festivals they held every fifth year at Athens, for the heralds to call down the blessing of the gods on the Plataeans equally with the Athenians.) The Greeks pursued the Persians to the shore, cutting down many, and seized seven of their ships, but the remainder of their fleet escaped. The

Persian fleet made a feint at Athens at Phalerum, the harbor of the city, and then sailed away to Asia. Athens was safe. In the Battle of Marathon the Persians lost, according to Herodotus, 6400 men, and the Athenians lost 192. After the full of the moon 2000 Spartans hurried up, so eager to lend their aid that they had made the march from Sparta in three days. They found the battle was over. However, they were anxious to see what the Persians looked like and went to the plain of Marathon and examined the slain. They praised the skill and bravery of the Athenians, then turned around and went home again. This victory ended Darius' attempt against Greece and is classed among the decisive battles of the world. The *soros*, a conical mound 40 feet high and 200 in diameter, which covers the Athenian dead, marks the central point of the famous battle. All doubt as to its identification was set at rest by an excavation made by the Archaeological Society of Athens, which disclosed ashes, charred remnants of the funeral pyre, and fragments of pottery dating from the beginning of the 5th century B.C. The modern marathon race is run over a distance approximating that run by the messenger carrying news of the victory in battle to Athens, a distance of 26 miles, 385 yards.

Marathonian Bull. See **Cretan Bull.**

Marcellus (mär-sel′us). The name of an illustrious Roman family. In the *Aeneid*, Aeneas saw the spirits of three members of the family waiting to be born when he visited Anchises in the Underworld. They were: 1) **Marcus Claudius**, who was born before 268 B.C. In 222 B.C. he became consul for his first of five terms, and defeated the Gauls at Clastidium, slaying with his own hand their leader, Viridomarus or Britomartus. He defended Nola against Hannibal in 216 B.C. For his daring and swift action in the Second Punic War, he came to be known as the "Sword of Rome," as Fabius Cunctator, his great colleague, became the "Shield of Rome." He captured Syracuse in 212 and, taking command in Apulia, contended against Hannibal in southern Italy until his death (208 B.C.) in a skirmish near Venusia (Venosa). 2) **Marcus Claudius**, consul in 51 B.C., was an adherent of Pompey and an

opponent of Caesar. He exiled himself to Mytilene after the battle of Pharsalus (48 B.C.). An appeal by the Senate in his favor caused Caesar to pardon him. He was killed on his way back to Rome, 45 B.C. 3) **Marcus Claudius**, the son of Octavia, born 42 B.C. He was the nephew of Augustus, and the adopted son and favorite of the emperor, whose daughter Julia he married. His early death (23 B.C.) was noted by Vergil (*Aeneid*) and other writers; Augustus read the funeral oration.

Marcius (mär′shus), **Ancus.** See **Ancus Marcius.**

Marcius, Cnaeus or **Caius.** See **Coriolanus.**

Marcomanni (mär-kō-man′ī). Group of ancient Germanic tribes, a branch of the Suevi, first mentioned by Caesar as in the army of Ariovistus. They were in frequent conflict with the Romans down to the 4th century A.D., when the name disappeared.

Marcus Andronicus (an-drō-nī′kus). See **Andronicus, Marcus.**

Marcus Annaeus Lucanus (a-nē′us lö-kā′nus). Full Latin name of **Lucan.**

Marcus Cornelius Fronto (kôr-nēl′yus fron′tō). See **Fronto, Marcus Cornelius.**

Mardonius (mär-dō′ni-us). Persian general, son-in-law and nephew of Darius, and cousin of Xerxes. After Darius had put down the Ionian revolt (494 B.C.), he sent Mardonius to resubdue Thrace and Macedonia, and to punish Athens and Eretria for the aid they had lent the Ionians. Mardonius succeeded in subduing Thrace, and Macedonia submitted, but on the way to punish the two Greek cities a violent storm shattered the Persian fleet off the promontory of Athos, and Mardonius returned to Susa, having carried out the more important part of his task. Darius died before he could punish the Greeks, who in the meantime had added to the Persian desire for vengeance by defeating Datis and Artaphernes at Marathon (490 B.C.). The desire to punish the Greeks burned fiercely in Mardonius, who besides hoped to win glory in an expedition against Athens. It was he, according to Herodotus, who continually urged Darius' successor Xerxes to make a punitive expedition against Greece. In the war that Xerxes undertook, after enormous preparation, the Persians captured and burned Athens, but suffered a humiliating defeat by the combined Greek fleet at Salamis (480 B.C.). Xerxes decided to return to Persia, and left Mardonius, at his earnest request, with a large land force to prosecute the war. The Persian forces under Mardonius withdrew to Thessaly and spent the winter. The Greek states that had so valiantly resisted at Salamis fell into violent disagreement on the best way to resist further Persian attacks. Mardonius, aware of this, tried to separate Athens from her Peloponnesian allies. He sent a distinguished ambassador to offer to repair the damage Athens had suffered from the Persians, and proposed an alliance with Athens, as with an equal and independent state. The terms were generous. According to Herodotus, the Athenians answered him in this manner, "We know, as well as you do, that the power of the Persians is many times greater than our own: we did not need to have that cast in our teeth. Nevertheless, we cling so to freedom that we shall offer what resistance we may. Seek not to persuade us into making terms with the barbarian—say what you will, you will never gain our assent. Return rather at once, and tell Mardonius that our answer to him is this, 'So long as the sun keeps his present course, we will never join alliance with Xerxes. Nay, we shall oppose him unceasingly, trusting in the aid of those gods and heroes whom he has lightly esteemed, whose houses and images he has burnt with fire.' And come not again to us with words like these; nor, thinking to do us a service, persuade us to unholy actions." On learning of this answer Mardonius broke camp and marched to Thebes and thence to Athens, which he found abandoned as the Athenians had again withdrawn to Salamis. Again he offered terms, and again his terms were rejected, as the Spartans rallied to the Athenians. A Spartan force was sent out under Pausanias. Mardonius, seeing his overtures were fruitless, burned Athens and resolved to withdraw from Attica, since the ground was not suitable for his cavalry, and was not advantageous for a retreat in case he should suffer defeat. He decided to return to the friendly neighborhood of Thebes, but first he marched into the region of Megara, the farthest point in Europe to which the Persians penetrated, ravaged it, and

afterward withdrew to Thebes. The Greeks under Pausanias advanced to Plataea. Mardonius came out to meet them, but on both sides the victims of sacrifices gave unfavorable omens and the battle was delayed. At last Mardonius resolved to ignore the omens, to still the fears roused by various oracles, and to begin the battle. In the struggle that followed, after much maneuvering and many harassing attacks by the Persian horse, Mardonius fought like a lion, and as long as he lived, his men defended themselves and killed many Greeks. But Mardonius was slain (479 B.C.) by a Spartan, and after his death the Spartans drove the Persians back, pursued them, and hacked them to pieces. When the battle was over, it was proposed to Pausanias, the victorious Spartan general, that he behead the corpse of Mardonius and hang the body on a cross, as Xerxes had done to Leonidas after Thermopylae. Pausanias replied that such actions were more fitted to barbarians than to Greeks, and even in barbarians they were detestable. Moreover, the great victory more than avenged Leonidas. The next day the body of Mardonius disappeared, and none could say who had taken it, although Herodotus says he knew of many who were paid large sums by the son of Mardonius on this account.

Margites (mar-jī′tēz). [Eng. trans., "The Booby."] Greek comic poem of uncertain date, with a fool and dandy for hero. Aristotle considered it the beginning of true comedy.

Mariandyni (mar″i-an-dī′nī). A people of Bithynia, dwelling on the south shore of the Euxine Sea. They founded Heraclea in honor of Heracles, who had subdued their enemies, the Bebryces. Later they welcomed the Argonauts; and built a shrine in honor of Polydeuces because he had killed their enemy Amycus, the new king of the Bebryces.

Marica (ma-rē′ka) or **Dea Marica** (dē′a). A nameless divinity worshiped in a grove at the mouth of the Liris River (modern Garigliano), below Minturnae, in S Latium. Excavations during the 1920's in swampy soil on the right bank of the Liris exposed the foundations of an Italic temple, referred to the 4th century B.C., and numerous humble votive offerings of terra-cotta. In Roman mythology the Dea Marica was said to have been the mother by Faunus of Latinus, and hence an ancestress of the Latins. During the empire Venus, in her role of sea-born goddess, was associated or identified with the Dea Marica, as if Marica were the equivalent of Marina, "Of the Sea." Modern scholars, however, explain Dea Marica as "Goddess of the Marsh," the spirit of the teeming wild life of the Minturnese swamps. It was in these swamps that Caius Marius was captured in 88 B.C., and through the grove sacred to the Dea Marica that he was conducted to the ship which took him to safe refuge in Africa. (JJ)

Maris (mä′ris). Named by Homer (*Iliad*) as a companion of Sarpedon of Lycia, in the Trojan War. He was a Carian, and was slain by Thrasymedes while defending the body of his brother.

Maritime Alps (alps). [French, **Alpes Maritimes**; Italian, **Alpi Marittime**.] Division of the Alps which lies on the border of France and Italy, between the Ligurian Apennines and the Cottian Alps. Peak elevation, about 10,817 feet; length, about 120 miles.

Marius (mãr′i-us), Caius. Roman general, born near Arpinum, Italy, 157 B.C.; died Jan. 13, 86 B.C. He was the son of poor and obscure parents, which probably accounted for his lifelong opposition to the aristocratic conservative party at Rome. He served with distinction under Scipio Africanus the Younger in the Numantine War in Spain (134 B.C.), and won the affection and respect of his commander. It is said that one evening when Scipio was sitting around the campfire talking with his men, one of them asked where Rome would find another such general when Scipio was gone. Scipio put his hand on Marius' shoulder and said, "Here, perhaps." This incident was supposed to have been a great inspiration to Marius. He became tribune of the people in 119 B.C. During his term of office he proposed a law to improve the election procedure, but also opposed a proposal for free distribution of grain to the people. When his term as praetor (115 B.C.) expired he cleared Spain of robbers; then he returned to Rome, where he won popularity and married Julia, the aunt of Julius Caesar. He was legate under the consul Caecilius Metellus, and fought with him against Jugurtha in Africa (109–

108 B.C.), winning great distinction and the devotion of his soldiers, whom he had organized into a well-disciplined force. Metellus became alarmed at his growing power and found excuses to delay him from returning to Rome to seek the consulship. But Marius returned in time and promised, if given command of the war in Africa, that he would either kill Jugurtha or take him alive. He became consul, 107 B.C., and soon alarmed the conservatives by his bold and insolent speeches. His policy was one of attack on the patricians to win the support of the delighted commons. He returned to Africa to finish the war (107–105 B.C.), but did not have the honor of capturing Jugurtha. This distinction fell to Sulla, a general serving under Marius, and this event was the beginning of the rivalry between them that ended in civil war. In 102 B.C. Marius illegally became consul, while he was outside Rome, and went to subdue the Cimbri and Teutones. He defeated (102 B.C.) the Teutones at Aquae Sextiae (Aix), and the Cimbri at the Raudian Fields near Vercellae (101 B.C.). For these successes in protecting Rome from the invaders he was named "Third Founder of Rome." He returned to Rome and sought the consulship again with the most servile flattery of the people. With the aid of two lawless mob leaders he had Metellus, whom he feared, expelled from Rome, and won the consulship for the sixth time, 100 B.C. In his efforts to get the office he had become even more objectionable to the aristocrats. He lost the favor of the people when he was unable to save one of the leaders who had helped him to win it. In the Social War he defeated (90 B.C.) the Marsi, but Sulla had also won great successes in the Social War, and was more than ever a threat to Marius. When the war was over, Rufus Sulpicius demanded that Marius be named commander of the war against Mithridates, and he invaded the Senate with his personal armed guard to enforce his demand. Sulla escaped to the house of Marius, from which he departed in secret to rejoin his army, and Marius was named to command the Mithridatic War. However, when tribunes went to take over Sulla's army, they were stoned. In Rome, Marius attacked the friends of Sulla, put many of them to death, and seized their

property. Sulla now marched on Rome at the head of his loyal army, and Marius fled (88 B.C.). He took ship from Ostia and sailed along the coast, but when the provision for his party ran out, his companions deserted him. He was put ashore and was found by a search party hiding in the marshes of the Liris River. Marius did not give up hope. An ancient oracle, which he quoted many times, said he would serve as consul seven times. Up to this time he had held the office six times, in 107, 104, 103, 102, 101, and 100 B.C. Until the oracle was fulfilled, he believed he was safe. He was ordered executed, but the people of Minturnae, where he was imprisoned, freed him and put him aboard a boat for Carthage. There he was joined by his son Marius the Younger. He learned that Cinna had seized power in Rome after Sulla's departure for the East, and was engaged in destroying the friends of Sulla to increase his own power. Marius decided to join Cinna, and soon after landed in Tuscany, where he gathered a force and joined Cinna (87 B.C.). He seized the grain ships and the port of Ostia, marched to Rome and bathed the city in blood as he gave full rein to his desire for revenge on Sulla and the aristocrats. In 86 B.C. he became consul for the seventh time, and the oracle was fulfilled. His thirst for blood was unassuaged, and even Cinna was shocked by his crimes. He had been consul for only a few days when news of Sulla's victory over Mithridates and his approach to Rome came to him. Marius had no more heart to fight him. He retired to his home and soon after sickened and died. According to Plutarch, the Romans were delirious with joy when they learned of his death.

Marmara (mär′ma̱-ra̱). See **Proconnesus.**

Marmara, Sea of. See **Propontis.**

Marmax (mär′maks). Said to have been the first suitor for the hand of Hippodamia, daughter of Oenomaus. As demanded by Oenomaus, he engaged in a chariot race with Oenomaus and he was the first of the many suitors to be killed by Oenomaus. Oenomaus also butchered Marmax′ horses and buried them in a tomb with their master beside the river Parthenia in Pisa. The river took its name from one of the mares. The tomb of Marmax and his mares was still shown to visitors in the 2nd century A.D.

Marmolada (mär-mō-lä′dä). [German, **Marmolata.**] Highest summit of the Dolomites, in N Italy. Elevation, about 10,965 feet.

Marmore (mär′mō-rā), **Cascate delle.** [English, **Falls of Terni.**] Series of cascades in Umbria, C Italy, SE of Interamna Nahars (Terni), in the Velinus River near its mouth. The spot has been celebrated for its beauty. Height of the falls, about 65 feet, 330 feet, and 190 feet, respectively.

Maro (mā′rō) or **Maron** (mā′rōn). In the *Odyssey*, a priest of Apollo at Ismarus in the land of the Cicones. When Odysseus and his companions were returning from Troy, they sacked the city of Ismarus but spared Maro and his family. In return Maro gave Odysseus some casks of wine of extraordinary strength. Odysseus later freed himself from Polyphemus by furnishing the latter with a plentiful supply of the undiluted wine.

Maro. Cognomen of the Roman poet Vergil (Publius Vergilius Maro). The name is thought to be an Umbrian word meaning "magistrate."

Marpessa (mär-pes′a̱). In the *Iliad*, known as the "beautiful-ankled" daughter of Evenus. Her father sought to prevent her marriage by challenging her suitors to a chariot race with him. He was invariably the winner and the unlucky suitors were slain. Idas, with the help of winged horses, succeeded in defeating Evenus and carried Marpessa off. Apollo, who also loved her, fought Idas, but Zeus intervened in the unequal struggle between a mortal and a god. He gave Marpessa the privilege of choosing between them, and she chose Idas. She feared Apollo would tire of her and preferred to risk her life and love with another mortal like herself. She was the mother of Meleager's wife, Cleopatra.

Marrucini (mar-ọ̈-sī′nī). Ancient Italian people dwelling near the Adriatic, north of Samnium, allied to the Marsi, an Italic people east of Rome. Their principal cities were Aternum (today Pescara) and Teate (today Chieti). They were subjugated by the Romans in 305 B.C. Their language is classified as a Sabellian dialect of the ancient Italic languages.

Mars (märz). In Roman mythology, the god of war. Aeneas learned from Anchises in the Underworld that Mars would father twin sons, Romulus and Remus, and thus be an ancestor of the Roman nation. Jupiter, Mars, and Quirinus (who was identified with Romulus) comprised an early triad. Mars was probably an ancient Italian god of fertility and vegetation before he was a Roman god, and in the primitive ten-month calendar the first month of the year, March, was named for him and was sacred to him. His transition from god of agriculture to war-god has not been satisfactorily explained, but it has been observed that wars usually started in the spring. It has also been claimed that 1) as a war-god, he guarded the fields of the people; 2) as a god whose function had not been clearly established, an agricultural people, frequently at war, identified him with both of these activities. His attributes are the sword, spear, and shield, and the wolf and the woodpecker are sacred to him. Sacrifices were offered to Mars before and during campaigns and generals solemnly invoked him before proceeding into battle. His priests (the Salii) danced dressed in armor in the great March festival. Bellona (Roman war goddess) was his charioteer, and wife, sister, or daughter. In later mythology, Mars became completely identified with the Greek Ares.

Marsala (mär-sä′lä). See **Lilybaeum**.

Marsi (mär′si). Ancient Italian people, inhabiting the area east of Rome. Their language is classified as a Sabellian dialect of the ancient Italic languages. Dwelling in the Apennines, they were among the most warlike of the Italian tribes and, according to Roman legend, were allies of Turnus in his war against Aeneas. Their friendship with Rome was of long standing and in 340 B.C. Roman soldiers were permitted to pass through their territory. Their demand for Roman citizenship in the Social War was granted.

Marsi. Ancient Germanic tribe first mentioned by Strabo, and also listed by Tacitus in his *Germania* as among the tribes descended from Mannus. The Marsi took part in the uprising under Arminius (9 A.D.), but disappeared after the campaigns of Germanicus. They were probably a part of the Sugambri, whom they adjoined on the southeast, west of the Cherusci and Chatti.

Marsian Hills. A name for the Apennines.

Marsic War. See **Social War.**

Marsus (mär′sus), **Domitius.** Roman poet of the Augustan Age, born c54 B.C.; died c4 B.C. He was the author of a collection of epigrams (*Cicuta*) and comic tales, a work on oratory, an epic (*Amazonis*), and erotic elegies.

Marsyas (mär′si-as). In Greek mythology, a satyr (or in some accounts a Phrygian or a peasant) follower of Cybele who was defeated by Apollo in a musical contest in the following manner: Athena had made a flute which she played at a banquet of the gods. Although the music was beautiful, Hera and Aphrodite could not stop laughing. Athena then played beside a stream. She saw from the reflection of her face in the water how playing the flute distorted her features, and threw away the flute with a curse on the person who picked it up. Marsyas found it and when he put it to his lips the flute played by itself, remembering the sweet strains Athena had drawn from it. Marsyas was delighted and went about the land entertaining the natives. He became so proud of his music-making that he declared Apollo himself could not do better. This boast came to the ears of Apollo, and the god challenged Marsyas to a contest, with the Muses acting as judges. As the Muses could not choose a victor, Apollo turned his lyre upside down and continued to play sweet hymns to the gods. Marsyas could not draw any sounds at all from his flute in an upside down position and the Muses awarded Apollo the victory. For his presumption in vying with a god Apollo flayed Marsyas alive and fastened his skin to a tree near the river in Phrygia which bears his name. Some even say the river was formed from the tears which the nymphs and satyrs shed over his death.

Martial (mär′shal). [Full Latin name, **Marcus Valerius Martialis.**] Latin poet, born at Bilbilis, Spain, c40 A.D.; died in Spain, c104. In the reign of Nero he went to Rome to study law, but instead took up writing poetry. He was a friend of Juvenal and Quintilian and worked under the patronage of Titus, Domitian, and other influential persons. Even so, when he returned to Spain (98) he was impoverished, but won wealthy patrons in his own land. With mordant wit he described the low moral tone of his times, but

fat, fāte, fär, fãre, errant; net, mē, hėr ardent; pin, pīne; not, nōte, möve, nôr,

he was abjectly sycophantic when he dealt with his patrons in high places. His 14 books of epigrams (86–98 A.D.) contain sharp pictures of the degenerate life of his time and formed the model for later epigrammatists.

Masinissa or **Massinissa** (mas-i-nis′ạ). King of Numidia, born c240 B.C.; died 149 B.C. He fought as ally of the Carthaginians in Spain, but later went over to the Romans. As an ally of Rome he served (204–203 B.C.) with Scipio against Syphax. Syphax was defeated and his capital fell, one of the prisoners being his queen Sophonisba, who had once been betrothed to Masinissa. Scipio refused to sanction their marriage and, rather than see Sophonisba paraded in triumph through Rome, Masinissa sent her a bowl of poison which she drank. He later served (202 B.C.) at Zama, the decisive battle of the Second Punic War. He became (201 B.C.) ruler of all Numidia and ruled in peace for 50 years.

Massagetae (mas-aj′ẹ-tī). In ancient times, a large tribe, thought by some to be a branch of the Scythians, dwelling beyond the Caspian and Aral Seas. Their dress was similar to the Scythians, according to the description of Herodotus, and like the Scythians they fought on horseback as well as afoot, with bows, spears, and battle-axes. Their land abounded in gold, which they used to adorn their heads, girdles, and breastbands, and with which they adorned the bridles and bits of their horses. They used bronze for their spears and arrow-heads, and made bronze breastplates for their horses. Among the Massagetae each man took a wife, but wives were shared in common by a simple device; when a man desired another woman, he hung his quiver above her wagon and this gave him license to embrace her as he pleased. The Massagetae considered it a great calamity to die of sickness or infirmity. Their custom was, if a man survived battle and lived to a great age, for the relatives of an aged man to come together and slay him, and a number of his cattle as well. The flesh of man and cattle was cooked together and eaten by his survivors. The Massagetae worshiped the sun above all gods and sacrificed horses to the sun, on the principle that the swiftest of gods must be honored with the swiftest of creatures. A warlike, nomadic tribe, they sowed no crops but lived on meat, milk, and fish. They drove the Scythians across the Rha River (Volga) into the land of the Cimmerians, who in their turn were pushed out by the Scythians. Cyrus the Great attacked the Massagetae, who were led by their queen Tomyris, and according to the general account met his death fighting them.

Massicus (mas′i-kus), **Mons**. [Modern Italian name, **Monte Massico**.] In ancient geography, a range of hills on the border of Campania and Latium, Italy. It was famous for its wines.

Massilia (mạ-sil′i-ạ). [Greek, **Massalia**; now, **Marseilles**.] An ancient Greek colony in southern France. It was founded by Phocaeans c600 B.C., and, according to legend, was visited by Heracles when he went to fetch the cattle of Geryon.

Massinissa (mas-i-nis′ạ). See **Masinissa**.

Massylians (mạ-sil′i-ạnz), or **Massyli** (mạ-sil′ī). A people of the northern part of Numidia. In the *Aeneid*, they are mentioned as noted horsemen who lived near Dido's Carthage.

Matera (mä-te′rä). Town in S Italy, situated above a steep ravine about 37 miles W of Tarentum. It was of strategic importance because of its location, and was occupied by Hannibal and then by the Romans. In the vicinity are found numerous prehistoric remains and caves.

Mater Matuta (mā′tėr mạ-tū′tạ). See **Matuta**.

Mater Turrita (tū-rī′tạ). A Roman name for Cybele. It comes from the mural or turreted crown in the form of a miniature city wall, which Cybele was often represented as wearing.

Matralia (mạ-trā′li-ạ). In ancient Rome, an annual festival celebrated on June 11 only by the citizen matrons in honor of the goddess Mater Matuta. The goddess was associated with the Greek goddess Leucothea, and the rites commemorated incidents of the Leucothea myths. In the performance of the sacred rites the women led a female servant into the sanctuary, flogged her, and drove her out again. This commemorated the persecution of Ino (who was later transformed into Leucothea by Zeus), by her husband's second wife. During the celebration of the Matralia the women embraced their nephews and nieces rather than their own children, in

actọr; up, lūte, půll; oi, oil; ou, out; ŦH, then; ḍ as d or j, ṣ as s or sh, ṭ as t or ch, ẕ as z or zh.

honor of Ino's kindness in rearing Dionysus, the son of her sister Semele and Zeus.

Matronalia (mat-rō̩-nā'li-a̩). In Roman antiquity, a festival celebrated by matrons on the first of March in honor of Juno.

Mattiaci (ma̩-tī'a̩-sī). Ancient Germanic tribe, a branch of the Chatti (first mentioned by Pliny), in the Taunus region, southward to the Moenus (Main) River, near Aquae Mattiacae (Wiesbaden). The Mattiaci are mentioned by Tacitus as being a people of keen spirit, but "dutiful to Rome."

Matuta (ma̩-tū'ta̩). [Also: **Mater Matuta**.] In Roman mythology, a goddess of birth, associated with Janus. She has been interpreted also as an old goddess of dawn, but no mythology supports this. Her festival, the *Matralia*, (q.v.) was celebrated on June 11 by Roman matrons.

Mauretania (mô-re̩-tā'ni-a̩). [Also: **Mauritania**.] In ancient geography, the NW part of Africa, corresponding to the N parts of Morocco and of W and C Algeria. Juba II of Numidia was confirmed (25 B.C.) king of Mauretania by Augustus. It was annexed (42 A.D.) to the Roman Empire by Claudius, and was divided into the provinces Mauretania Tingitana in the W and Mauretania Caesariensis in the E.

Mausoleum (mô-sō̩-lē'um). A magnificent tomb at Halicarnassus (Budrum) in SW Asia Minor, built for Mausolus, king of Caria, and his sister, wife, and queen, Artemisia, begun before Mausolus' death in 353 B.C. The names of the architects, Pythius and Satyrus, have been recorded, along with those of four famous sculptors, Bryaxis, Leochares, Scopas, and Timotheus. Vitruvius and Pliny have left summary descriptions from which it appears that the Mausoleum consisted of a colonnade, square in plan, surmounted by a pyramid, the latter crowned by a platform on which rested a marble four-horse chariot with statues of Mausolus and Artemisia by Pythius. Ancient critics acclaimed the whole as a great masterpiece and classed it among the seven wonders of the ancient world, so that thereafter any conspicuous monumental tomb might be called a mausoleum. The British Museum contains remains of three friezes and abundant other sculptures. (JJ)

Mausolus (mô-sō̩'lus). King or *dynast* of Caria, who died 353 B.C. He first appears in history in the revolt of the satraps against Artaxerxes II (Artaxerxes Mnemon) in 362 B.C. He married his sister Artemisia, who after his death completed at Halicarnassus the celebrated monument named after him, the Mausoleum. A Greek statue of Mausolus from the Mausoleum (352 B.C.) is in the British Museum.

Mavors (mā'vôrs). An old Latin name of Mars.

Maximus (mak'si-mus). A title, "greatest," given to Fabius, surnamed Rullianus, and to his descendants, the most illustrious of whom was Fabius Cunctator. Fabius Rullianus, who died about 290 B.C., was a consul and general, who distinguished himself in the Third War against the Samnites, over whom he gained the decisive victory of Sentinum in 295 B.C.

Maximus, Quintus Fabius. See **Fabius Maximus, Quintus.**

Maxyes (mak'si-ēz). Libyan tribe mentioned in ancient geography, situated in the eastern part of what is now Tunisia. As depicted on the Egyptian monuments and as described by Herodotus, its members let their hair grow long on the right side of their heads, shaved it close on the left, and painted their bodies red.

Mechaneus (me̩-kā'nūs). Epithet of Zeus, meaning "Contriver." An image of Zeus Mechaneus at Argos was the spot, some say, where the Argives who set out against Troy took an oath that they would continue to prosecute war until they either took Troy or died in the attempt. This image, with images of Artemis and Athena, was set on a bronze vessel in which, some say, the bones of Tantalus were held. According to Pausanias, these must have been the bones of that Tantalus who was married to Clytemnestra and was slain by Agamemnon. The bones of the Tantalus who was the friend of the gods and who was slain for abusing their friendship, rested in a tomb on Mount Sipylus.

Mecisteus (me-sis'tūs). In Greek legend, a brother of Adrastus, king of Argos. He is sometimes named as one of the Seven against Thebes. His son Euryalus the Argonaut was among the Epigoni who successfully attacked Thebes and avenged their fathers.

Meda (mē'da̩). In Greek legend, the wife of Idomeneus, king of Crete. While Idomeneus was away at the Trojan War, Meda was falsely informed that he had taken a concubine whom he was planning to bring back to Crete as his new queen. In a rage of jealousy Meda thereupon took Leucus as her lover. This led to her disaster, for shortly thereafter Leucus murdered her and her daughter, and seized the throne of Crete.

Medea (mē-dē′a̞). In mythology, a daughter of Aeëtes, king of Aea in Colchis, and Idyia. She was the granddaughter of Helius, and was noted as a sorceress, skilled in the use of drugs and poisons. To aid Jason, who had come to Colchis to secure the Golden Fleece and restore it to Hellas, Hera and Athena appealed to Aphrodite. Aphrodite bribed her son, Eros, to pierce Medea's′ heart with one of his arrows at the instant when her eyes fell on Jason as he entered her father's courtyard. Out of loyalty to her father and her country Medea tried to resist the surge of love for Jason which overwhelmed her, but she was powerless, as Hera and Athena had meant her to be; she yielded to her love and betrayed her father. She met Jason at night in the grove of Hecate. On coming face to face with the object of her love she was nearly speechless. But in return for his oath in the name of Hecate to take her away with him and to marry her, she told him how he could fulfill the task her father had set for him. She gave him the charm of Prometheus, an ointment which would render him and his weapons invulnerable for one day. This would protect him from the fire-breathing bulls that Aeëtes had commanded him to yoke. Once the bulls were yoked he must plow the field and sow the dragon's teeth in the furrows. Armed men would spring up from the dragon's teeth, she said, and he must hurl a stone among them, whereupon they would set to fighting among themselves until all were dead. The next day Jason followed her instructions to the letter, and all turned out as she had predicted. He performed the task Aeëtes had set for him, on the successful completion of which Aeëtes had promised to give him the Golden Fleece. Aeëtes, however, was in a furious rage. He knew well that Jason could not have accomplished this trial of his courage without Medea's help. He planned to seize and destroy Jason, burn the *Argo,* and attack the Argonauts. Medea

learned of her father's intention. She hurriedly sent for Jason, went with him to the orchard of Ares where the Golden Fleece was hanging, lulled the dragon that guarded it while Jason snatched the Fleece, and together they fled to the *Argo* and hurriedly put to sea. According to some accounts, Apsyrtus, the young brother of Medea, accompanied them; Medea slew him and cast the pieces of his dismembered body into the sea. Aeëtes, pursuing the Argonauts with a fleet, stopped to gather up the fragments of his son's body, and was soon outdistanced by the *Argo.* Other accounts say that Apsyrtus did not accompany Medea, but that he commanded a ship in pursuit of her. Jason would have surrendered Medea in violation of his oath to her. She persuaded him to adopt a different course. She sent word to her brother that she wished to return to Colchis with him, and arranged to meet him at a temple in a lonely grove. Apsyrtus met her at the appointed spot and as they talked, Jason leaped out from ambush and killed Apsyrtus. In either case, Medea's passion for Jason led to her brother's death. After suffering many hardships in their voyage, the Dodonian oak which Athena had placed in the hull of the *Argo* spoke and informed them that their woes would not cease until Jason and Medea had been purified by Circe for the murder of Apsyrtus. Accordingly, they proceeded to Circe's isle and were purified. They next successfully passed the isle of the Sirens as well as Scylla and Charybdis, and came to the island of the Phaeacians. Here they were received by Alcinous, king of the Phaeacians, and here the Colchians, still pursuing Medea, caught up with the Argonauts. Again, Jason would have surrendered Medea. She appealed to Arete, wife of King Alcinous. That worthy queen persuaded her husband to make a decision: if Medea was still a chaste maiden, he would restore her to her father; he would not separate husband and wife. A marriage was hastily arranged. To marriage music supplied by Orpheus, Jason and Medea were married in a cave, which became known as the sacred cave of Medea. The Golden Fleece and flowers decorated the marriage couch. The frustrated Colchians abandoned their pursuit. When the *Argo* at last came in

actǫr; up, lūte, pu̇ll; oi, oil; ou, out; ŦH, then; ḏ as d or j, ṣ as s or sh, ṭ as t or ch, ẓ as z or zh.

sight of the mainland of Greece a disastrous storm overtook it and lashed the ship for days. It was swept onto the shoals of Syrtis, and then borne on a great wave into the desert near the Tritonian Lake, where it was left high and dry. The Argonauts, encouraged by nymphs, placed their ship on rollers and propelled it over the desert to the Tritonian Lake. From there Triton guided them back to the sea. In the last stage of the journey the *Argo* sailed by Crete where, according to some accounts, Medea slew Talos, the bronze man who guarded the island, by pulling out the pin in his ankle which stoppered the life-giving ichor in his body.

suicide. No one knew of the successful return of the *Argo,* and Jason resolved to take advantage of surprise to kill Pelias and seize the throne, which was rightfully his anyway. Medea offered to get rid of Pelias by her own arts and, as had happened so many times, Jason was more than willing to let Medea do it. Medea appeared to the daughters of Pelias and informed them that she would make their father young again. To prove her powers she transformed an old ram into a skipping lamb by cutting up its body and boiling it in a cauldron with magic herbs. The daughters of Pelias were convinced by this demonstration and followed Medea's in-

MEDEA AND PELIAS

Black-figured Attic vase, 6th century B.C. Pelias sits at the left while Medea, next to him, works her magic on the ram; the daughters of Pelias are on the right. *British Museum*

By the time the *Argo* landed at Pagasae, the port from which it had originally sailed, King Pelias, who had sent Jason for the Golden Fleece, thought that he and his companions had all perished on the voyage, as he had hoped they would do. He had forced Aeson, father of Jason, to die by drinking bull's blood, and had killed Jason's young brother. Jason's mother had committed

structions. They approached their father as he slept under the influence of one of Medea's drugs, and cut his throat. They then cut him into pieces which they boiled in the cauldron. But Medea had put no magic herbs in this cauldron, and Pelias was irretrievably dead. His daughters, with the most loving intentions, had become his murderers. According to another story, when Jason and

fat, fāte, fär, fāre, errạnt; net, mē, hér ardẹnt; pin, pīne; not, nōte, möve, nôr,

Medea returned to Iolcus, they found Aeson alive, but weak and old. Jason asked Medea to take some of the years he might expect to live from him, and give them to his father. Medea assured him she could do better than this. She swept off in a winged chariot drawn by dragons and disappeared for nine days. In this time she had no contact with mortals, but spent her time collecting drugs and herbs known only to her and Hecate. At the end of the period she returned, sacrificed to Hecate, and cast Aeson into a deep sleep. She cut his throat, letting all the aged blood drain out, dismembered his body, and boiled the pieces in a cauldron in a liquid prepared from the magic herbs she had gathered. Aeson emerged from the cauldron restored to the physical condition he had enjoyed 40 years before. On seeing the magic restoration of Aeson, the daughters of Pelias begged Medea to do the same for their father. Medea agreed. But as noted before, Medea put no magic herbs into the cauldron with Pelias' body. After the death of Pelias, Jason seized the throne, but fearing vengeance he resigned it to Acastus, son of Pelias, and went with Medea to Corinth, where they lived happily for ten years, and Medea was highly thought of by the Corinthians. At the end of that time Jason decided to abandon Medea and their children, seven boys and seven girls, according to some accounts, and marry Glauce (or Creusa), daughter of King Creon of Corinth. Medea was in a frenzy when she learned of this proposal. She pleaded with Jason not to make a mockery of her love, and not to violate his sacred oath. She reminded him of all she had done for his sake—betrayed her father, killed her brother and Pelias, helped him to win the respect of the Corinthians, to say nothing of having borne him many children. Jason was obdurate. He offered to make some provision for Medea and their children but persisted in his plan to marry Glauce. Medea plotted a horrible revenge that would cause Jason great suffering and discredit him with the Corinthians. Pretending that she finally saw the wisdom of his plan, she sent Glauce a magnificent robe and chaplet as a wedding gift. The instant Glauce donned them, she was consumed to ashes. Creon, attempting to rescue his daughter, was destroyed by the flames which shot out from her body. The people of Corinth, in a raging desire for vengeance, seized the children of Medea from the altar in Hera's temple where they had gone as suppliants, and stoned them to death. For this reason, in expiation, each year thereafter seven boys and girls, with shaven heads and clad in black garments, were sent to spend a year in Hera's temple. Jason was scorned for having broken his oath to Medea, and reviled for the consequences of his broken oath. He wandered forlornly about Greece until his death. Euripides, some say bribed by the Corinthians to hide their own dishonor, wrote that Medea herself killed her children, as the worst possible revenge on Jason. Aegeus, king of Athens, had passed through Corinth, and had promised Medea sanctuary should she ever need it. In return she had promised to give him a son by her magic arts. She now fled from Corinth in a winged chariot drawn by dragons, which was sent to her rescue by Helius. Some say she went first to Thebes, where she cured Heracles of his madness. She then went to Athens, where Aegeus received her kindly, as he had promised, and married her. All went well until Theseus, the son of Aegeus, came to his father's court. Aegeus did not know his son, who had been born and brought up in Troezen. But Medea instantly recognized him, and feared him as a rival of her own son, Medeus. She prepared a wine-cup, poisoned it with aconite and prevailed on Aegeus to give it to the unknown youth. At the last instant Aegeus recognized the sword the young man was carrying as his own, and realized that this young stranger was his son. Medea fled; some say that Aegeus even provided an escort for her in gratitude for giving him the son as she had promised. With her she took Medeus, who some say was her son by Aegeus and others say was the only one of her children by Jason to escape the wrath of the Corinthians after the murders of Glauce and Creon. According to some accounts, she went to Italy after leaving Athens, and taught the tribes the art of snake-charming. At last she learned that her uncle Perses had seized her father's kingdom. She went to Colchis, taking Medeus with her, brought about the death of Perses, and restored Aeëtes to his throne. Medeus conquered additional ter-

actor; up, lūte, pull; oi, oil; ou, out; ŦH, then; ḏ as d or j, ş as s or sh, ṯ as t or ch, ẓ as z or zh.

ritory for the kingdom and gave his name to the Medes. Some say that Medea was made immortal by Hera, because she had repulsed the advances of Zeus, and that she went to the Elysian Fields. There she married Achilles and lived as a queen.

Medea. Tragedy of Euripides, produced 431 B.C. It deals with Medea's passionate reaction to Jason's decision to abandon her and her children and marry Glauce, the daughter of King Creon of Corinth.

The scene is before Medea's house in Corinth near the palace of the king. A nurse mourns the day when Jason sailed to Colchis, won the love of Medea, and caused her to use her supernatural powers against her own father in order to help him. Now all the love is turned to hate, for Jason has betrayed Medea and taken a royal bride, Glauce, the daughter of King Creon. In vain Medea reminded him of his promises and of all she had done for him. Now she has given herself up to grief and is like a stone, except when she thinks of her father and her native land. Even her children have become hateful to her. The nurse knows her well and is fearful of what she may do in her ungovernable wrath. The man who incurs it cannot think he will escape lightly.

Medea's children come in with a tutor, who tells the nurse he has heard Jason is preparing to yield to his new father-in-law's demand that he send Medea and her children out of Corinth. The nurse cannot believe he would be so treacherous, but asks the tutor to keep the children out of their mother's sight. She has seen Medea eyeing them savagely. From inside Medea is heard cursing her children and their father Jason, and calling down ruin on his house. The nurse shudders. She cannot understand why the children must share in their father's crime. She grieves for them, and notes that the highborn cannot easily change their moods. As for her, she would rather live to old age in security and with moderation than share the splendors and agonies of high birth.

A chorus of Corinthian women enters. They have heard Medea's cries and grieve for the sorrows of a house they have come to love. As they hear Medea long for death and revenge and call on Themis, goddess of justice, to bring Jason and his bride to de-

struction, they cluck among themselves at her lack of restraint. They advise the nurse to bring her out that they may give her the benefit of their advice. Medea comes out and justifies her grief to the Corinthian ladies. All she asks of them is their silence if she can devise a way to avenge herself on Jason, and on the king who gave him his daughter. The ladies agree to keep silent, for they think justice is on her side.

King Creon comes and orders Medea and her children into exile. He banishes the already homeless one because he fears her, and the evil she may do his daughter with her sorceries. She answers that she has been given a bad reputation, and begs him not to fear her. It is her husband she hates, but as for Creon, she wishes him prosperity and asks to be allowed to remain. He agrees, against his better judgment, to let her stay one more day to arrange her affairs, but then she must go.

When the chorus commiserates with her after Creon's departure, she answers that all is not yet lost, she will find a way to avenge herself on Jason and his bride. She swears by Hecate to destroy them both, and the king too. She, the daughter of a king and a granddaughter of Helius, will not be made an object of scorn by those of a lesser race.

Jason comes and berates her for the wild words that, he says, have caused Creon to exile her. He doesn't care what she says about him, but it was a mistake to include the king in her angry denunciation. She might have stayed in comfort if she had kept her temper. Now he has come to help her to prepare for her journey into exile, for though she hates him, he has no hard feelings toward her.

Medea reviles him. She recites the whole story: how she helped him to yoke the fiery bulls, slew the dragon, betrayed her father, killed her own brother, and slew his old enemy Pelias when they returned with the Golden Fleece to Iolcus. All these terrible deeds she committed for love of him. He has broken his oaths of faithfulness to her and has rewarded her by abandoning her and her children. And where can she go now, having betrayed her native land for his sake? Jason is irritated by her claim that it was to her he owed his safety and success. But

fat, fāte, fär, fāre, errant; net, mē, hėr ardent; pin, pīne; not, nōte, mŏve, nôr,

whether or no, Medea has had many advantages: she lives in Hellas, a civilized land of law instead of in barbarian Colchis. His marriage to the king's daughter will bring a powerful friend to her and to her children. It was a great step for him, an exile from Iolcus, to marry the daughter of the king of Corinth. He tries to convince her it was policy, not lack of love for her, that brought about his marriage. It was all done with the well-being of Medea and her children in mind. Medea scorns his arguments, and refuses his offers of help. Jason calls all to witness that he has done his best and departs.

Seeing the rage to which her former love for Jason has brought Medea, the chorus asks to be spared the shafts that cause such jealousy and wrath. As Medea sits before the house in despair, Aegeus, king of Athens, enters with his retinue. He is on his way from the oracle, where he sought to learn if he would ever have a son. Medea tells him the reason for her sad state. She asks him to receive her in his country, and promises that she will work her spells so that he will have a son. Aegeus says he will not take her away by force, for Corinth is his ally, but if she can reach his country by herself, he will receive her and be her champion.

Now that she is assured of asylum, Medea plots her revenge. She will destroy Creon, Glauce, and her own children. The chorus implores her not to slay her children. Medea sends for Jason. When he comes, she asks to be forgiven for the harsh words she had spoken. She has thought it over, she says, and decided he was right. She repents of her rage, and calls the children out to say goodby to their father. Jason is gratified that she has apparently come to her senses. He promises to have the welfare of the children always in mind. She gives the children a robe and a golden chaplet and instructs them to present these gifts to the princess. She asks Jason and the children to plead with Creon and his daughter to allow them, at least, to remain in Corinth.

When the children return with their tutor to say they have presented the gifts to Glauce and that their prayer to remain in Corinth has been granted, Medea is gloomier than ever. She knows now, since the gifts have been delivered, that she must slay her children. As she talks to them, her love for them almost sways her from her dark purpose but she hardens her heart. If she doesn't kill them, the Corinthians will when they learn how she has slain Glauce and Creon. With a cry that she fully understands the fearful deed to which she is being driven by rage, she takes the children into the house. Almost immediately she returns. A messenger comes from the palace and tells her to fly, for the princess had put on the robe and chaplet and has been consumed by the poison Medea's sorcery had embedded in them. Medea asks to hear the details, and learns that Creon, trying to help his daughter, was also destroyed by the poison. Now she will take the final step. She enters the house and murders her children. The chorus, mourning for them, yet cannot decide to go to their assistance. Jason comes rushing up. He has learned of the death of Creon and Glauce and wants to save his children from the wrath of the Corinthians. He cannot believe the chorus when they tell him Medea has killed them. He longs to kill her. She appears above the house, riding in a chariot drawn by winged dragons, sent by Helius to save her. She has the bodies of her children with her, and refuses to deliver them to Jason for burial. She will bury them herself, where their tombs cannot be defiled. As for Jason, she predicts a long, unhappy life for him and an inglorious end. Though the death of her children brings great grief to her, she is satisfied that Jason's is more grievous. He has earned suffering, for he is a breaker of oaths and of the laws of hospitality. She leaves in her chariot to go to the asylum King Aegeus had promised her.

Medes (mēdz). Inhabitants of Media, ancient country in what is now NW Iran. They first appear in history as Amadai in 836 B.C., when Shalmaneser, the Assyrian conqueror, received tribute from them. In 715 and 713 B.C. Sargon subjected them. In the second half of the 7th century they won their independence and were united under a single dynasty. The Medes were eventually defeated by the Persians under Cyrus, and absorbed into the Persian Empire. According to legend, the Medes were the descendants of Medeus, the son of Medea, who added the territory which they occupied to his grand-

actor; up, lūte, pŭll; oi, oil; ou, out; ŦH, then; ḑ as d or j, ş as s or sh, ṭ as t or ch, ẕ as z or zh.

father's kingdom of Colchis, after Medea fled with Medeus from Athens and returned to Asia.

Medeus (mē'dē-us). In Greek mythology, a son of Medea by Aegeus, king of Athens, to whom Medea fled after Jason abandoned her. Medea's plot to poison Theseus, the heir of Aegeus, was thwarted and she fled to Asia, taking Medeus with her. Together they killed Perses and restored Aeëtes, Medea's father, to the throne of Colchis. Medeus enlarged the kingdom and gave his own name to his new subjects, the Medes. According to other accounts, Medeus was Medea's oldest son and his father was Jason. He was educated by Chiron. Still others say he was the son of an Asiatic king whom Medea married after she fled from Aegeus and Athens.

Media (mē'di-a̯). Ancient country comprising the NW part of the Iranian highland, extending from the Caspian Sea to the Araxes (modern Aras). It was bounded on the NE by Hyrcania, on the E by Parthia, on the S by Susiana and Persis, and on the W by Assyria. It nearly corresponded to the modern Iranian regions of Azerbaijan, Ardilan, and Iraq Ajemi. Later the SE part of the country was called Great Media, and the NW, or Atropatene, Little Media. The Medes (Hebrew and Assyrian, *Madai*; Old Persian, *Mada*) are enumerated in Gen. x. 2 as among the descendants of Japheth; and they, together with the Persians, constituted the most important and powerful Indo-European population in W Asia. It is assumed that the country was originally settled by another (perhaps Turanian) tribe, and that the Medes gradually advanced from the NE to the W and SW. Media came into contact with Assyria at least as early as the end of the 9th century B.C., when it is mentioned as a conquered and tributary land. Tiglath-pileser III was the first Assyrian king who annexed Median territory; and Sargon II transplanted Israelitish war captives to Median cities, and claims in his annals of 713 B.C. to have received tribute from 45 Median chiefs. Sennacherib also received tribute from the Medes. Under Esarhaddon the Medes entered into alliance with the Mineans and the Cimmerians against Assyria, apparently without success. But from that time the Medes grew more united and more

powerful against tyrannical Assyria. The Assyrians had held Upper Asia from 1229–709 B.C. when the Medes successfully revolted, shook off Assyrian rule, and became self-governing. But their land was torn by robbery and lawlessness. According to Herodotus, Deïoces (c709–656 B.C.) made himself king of the Medes by following such a course of scrupulous justice in settling disputes and punishing the lawless that his name spread from his own village throughout the area, and he was requested by the Medes to become their king and restore law and order. Deïoces accepted the throne, demanded a palace for himself and a personal bodyguard, and caused the strongly fortified city of Ecbatana (or Agbatana) to be built. To widen the distance between himself and ordinary men and to increase the respect in which he was held, he made himself inaccessible to those who sought his favor or counsel, organized an elaborate ceremony for his audiences, and, having secured his power, ruled justly and consolidated the Medes into a nation. At his death he was succeeded by his son Phraortes (reigned 647–625 B.C. or, as some think, 678–625 B.C.). Phraortes attacked the Persians and brought them under his sway. He extended his conquests over lesser neighboring tribes, and at last attacked Assyria, but died in the expedition after a reign of 22 years (or, as some think, 53 years). He was succeeded by his son Cyaxares (625–584 B.C.), who was even more warlike than his predecessors and organized his confused forces into systematic companies. Cyaxares marched against Nineveh to complete the attack his father had begun, but was diverted from the expedition when Media was attacked and overrun by the Scythians. For 28 years thereafter the Scythians dominated Asia. At the end of that time Cyaxares regained control, expelled the Scythians, and recovered his empire. After the Scythians had been driven out, the Medes, in alliance with the Babylonian Nabopolassar, advanced once more against Nineveh, and brought about its downfall (612 B.C.). In the division of the Assyrian Empire, Assyria proper and Mesopotamia as far as Haran fell to Media, which, however, could not develop into a dominant power on account of the rise of the new Babylonian Empire under Nabopolassar and

Nebuchadnezzar. Under Cyaxares the Medes made war on Alyattes, king of the Lydians, because the Lydians refused to give up some Scythians who had fled as suppliants to the Lydians from the Medes. The war went on for five years, with neither side gaining an overall victory, although each side had won individual battles. One day (May 28, 585 B.C.) in the midst of the fighting, the sun was suddenly darkened; day became night. Alarmed by this omen (an eclipse of the sun, which had been foretold by Thales of Miletus), both sides sought peace. The matter was handed over to outside mediators and peace was arranged. To seal the peace, the daughter of Alyattes was given in marriage to Astyages, the son of Cyaxares. After a reign of 40 years Cyaxares died and was succeeded by this son. Astyages became the grandfather of Cyrus and was overthrown by him (550 B.C.), after which the fate of Media was bound up in that of Persia. Still it seemed to have preserved a kind of independence or particularism while united to Persia. Thus, the Old Testament writings speak of an empire of "the Persians and Medes." Only the Book of Daniel seems to assume the existence of a Median empire between the last Babylonian king, Nabonidus (Belshazzar), and Cyrus. After the destruction of the Persian Empire and in the division of Alexander's conquered territories Media fell to Seleucus, the founder of the Syrian monarchy, and later to the Parthian Empire. The old Medes were, according to the classical writers, a warlike people; in Isa. xiii. they are described as hard and cruel. The religion of the Medes was, according to Strabo, the same as that of the Persians, i.e., dualism. They worshiped, besides the sun-god Mithras, the moon, a goddess corresponding to Aphrodite, fire, the earth, winds, and water. The oldest capital of Media was Rhagae, on the site of modern Tehran. Deïoces moved the capital to his new city of Ecbatana (modern Hamadan), in the W part of the country, which remained the summer residence of the Persian and Parthian kings. To Media belonged also Behistun (ancient Baghistan), famous from the trilingual cuneiform inscription discovered there.

Median Wall (mē′di-an). In ancient history, a wall N of Babylon, extending from the Tigris to the Euphrates, built as a defense of Babylonia.

Mediolanum (mē-di-ō-lā′num). [Modern name, **Milano**; English, **Milan.**] In ancient geography, a town of the Insubres, in Cisalpine Gaul, situated in the plain between the Addua and Ticinus rivers. It was taken (222 B.C.) by the Romans under Scipio, and fell under Roman dominion permanently in 194 B.C.

Mediterranean Sea (med″i-te-rā′nē-an). [Latin, **Mare Internum, Mare Mediterraneum.**] Sea, the most important extension of the Atlantic, separating Europe on the N from Africa on the S, and communicating with the Atlantic Ocean by the Strait of Gibraltar, and with the Black Sea by the Dardanelles, Sea of Marmara, and Bosporus. It is divided into two major basins, the western reaching from Gibraltar to Sicily and Tunisia, and the eastern from there to Syria. Its chief branches are the Tyrrhenian Sea, Ionian Sea, Adriatic Sea, and Aegean Sea. The chief islands are the Balearic Islands, Corsica, Sardinia, Sicily, Malta, the Ionian Islands, Crete, Cyprus, and the Dodecanese Islands. The chief tributary rivers are the Ebro, Rhône, Po, and Nile. The Mediterranean has an important influence on the climate of the surrounding islands; it has given its name to a type of climate which characterizes these lands, with hot, sunny, dry summers and mild winters. Most of the rainfall occurs in autumn, winter, and early spring. The lands surrounding the Mediterranean basin are generally mountainous, and this enhances the scenery, already famous because of the brilliant blue of the skies and the water. The water of the Mediterranean is about ten percent more saline than that of the oceans. Tides are small; the connection with the Atlantic at the Strait of Gibraltar is only about nine miles wide. Each of the two major basins has a deep zone; the greatest known depth of the E Mediterranean, W of Crete, is about 14,450 feet; of the W Mediterranean (Tyrrhenian Sea), about 12,240 feet. Length, about 2200 miles; greatest width of sea proper, about 700 miles; area, about 963,600 square miles; average depth, about 4890 feet.

Medon (mē′don). In Homeric legend (*Iliad*), a bastard son of Oileus and Rhene, and half-brother of Ajax the Less. He had fled for asylum to Phylace, after he murdered his

actor; up, lūte, pŭll; oi, oil; ou, out; ᴛʜ, then; ḍ as d or j, ş as s or sh, ṭ as t or ch, ẓ as z or zh.

stepmother's brother, and from there joined the Greeks in the war against Troy. When Philoctetes had to be left behind because of a snake bite which could not be cured, Medon took his place as captain of the Phthians. He was slain by Aeneas.

Medon. In the *Odyssey*, a herald of Penelope's suitors and a supporter of Odysseus. He warned Penelope that the suitors were lying in wait for Telemachus with the intention of capturing and slaying him as he returned from his voyage to Pylus. Because of this friendly deed Odysseus spared Medon, when he returned and slew the suitors and their servants.

Meduacus Minor (med-ū-ā′kus mī′nôr). [Modern name, **Bacchiglione**.] River in NE Italy which flows past Vicentia (Vicenza) and Patavium (Padua) and empties into the Gulf of Venice.

her head, he attacked her with averted face, seeing only her reflection in the shield of Athena, who also guided his hand. From the decapitated body of Medusa, Pegasus and Chrysaor, the children of Poseidon, sprang full-grown. Perseus later gave the head to Athena, who used it on her aegis. According to some accounts, Athena also flayed Medusa's body and used the skin for her aegis; and drained the blood from the body and divided it with Asclepius. Athena used the blood to bring about war and death. Asclepius used his half to heal, and even to restore life. When Heracles went to the Underworld to fetch Cerberus, all the spirits fled in terror from him except fierce Medusa and valiant Meleager. In Roman mythology Medusa was said to have been, by Vulcan, the mother of the half-human giant Cacus.

Mefitis, Mephitis (mē-fī′tis). In Roman my-

PERSEUS AND THE GORGONS
Black-figured Attic vase, 6th century B.C. Perseus, between Athena and Hermes, has the head of Medusa in the wallet over his arm; Medusa's sisters pursue him. *Bibliothèque Nationale, Paris*

Medusa (mē-dū′sa, -za). In Greek mythology, one of the three Gorgons, daughters of Ceto and Phorcys, who dwelt in Libya. Medusa, the only one of the three who was mortal, was originally a beautiful maiden who was transformed into a hideous winged monster by Athena because with Poseidon she had violated one of the temples of that goddess. Her hair was changed into writhing serpents and her face was so fearful to look upon that whoever saw it was changed into stone. Accordingly, when Perseus sought her to cut off

thology, a goddess who averts pestilential exhalations.

Megacles (meg′a-klēz). An Athenian noble of the Alcmaeonid family. He was archon at the time of the uprising of Cylon (c632 B.C.) and was responsible for the death of the followers of Cylon in violation of a pledge to spare their lives if they surrendered. For violating the oath and insulting the gods, Megacles and the Alcmaeonids were tried for sacrilege, their property was confiscated, and they were driven into perpetual exile. The

fat, fāte, fär, fãre, errant; net, mē, hėr ardent; pin, pīne; not, nōte, mŏve, nôr,

bodies of those Alcmaeonids who had died between the time of the murders and the sentencing for sacrilege were dug up and reburied outside the city. Although the curse on the Alcmaeonids was not allowed to be forgotten for over 200 years, members of the family returned to Athens under an amnesty enacted by Solon.

Megacles. An Athenian noble, son of Alcmaeon. He lived in the 6th century B.C. He married Agariste, daughter of Clisthenes of Sicyon, who bore him Clisthenes, future ruler of Athens, and Hippocrates, later grandfather of Pericles. He was the leader of the party of the Coast in Athens, in opposition to Lycurgus, leader of the Plain. While they contended, Pisistratus at the head of a third party, the Hill, gained control. After a period of struggle in which Pisistratus was driven into exile, Megacles agreed to aid Pisistratus to return on condition that the latter marry his daughter. Pisistratus agreed and gained control of Athens a second time. However, as he already had two sons, and as the Alcmaeonids were under a curse for having slain the followers of Cylon, he refused to have children by the daughter of Megacles. Megacles was furious when he learned of this insult. He allied himself to the enemies of Pisistratus and drove him into exile a second time. But when Pisistratus was again restored (c544 B.C.), the Alcmaeonids fled and their property was seized.

Megaera (me-jē′ra). In late Greek mythology, one of the three Erinyes, or Eumenides, born of the blood of Uranus which fell on Gaea when Cronus mutilated him. Megaera was called "the Jealous One."

Megalesian Games (meg-a-lē′shan). In Roman antiquity, a magnificent festival with a stately procession, feasting, and scenic performances in the theaters, celebrated at Rome in the month of April in honor of Cybele and lasting for six days. The image of this goddess was brought to Rome from Pessinus in Galatia, about 203 B.C., and the games were instituted then or shortly afterward, in consequence of a sibylline oracle promising continual victory to the Romans if due honors were paid to her.

Megalopolis (meg-a-lop′ō-lis). In ancient geography, a city of Arcadia, Greece, situated on the Helisson River, not far from Mount Lycaon. The city was founded by Epaminondas after the battle of Leuctra (371 B.C.), in which he had defeated the Spartans. The new city was intended to form a link (with Messene, also a new city founded by Epaminondas, and with Mantinea) in a chain of strong cities to blockade Sparta. It was built on both banks of the river and was encircled by a double wall. The encircling mountains gave it added protection. The villages and towns of Arcadia were joined in a league, and populations of whole villages and levies from the chief cities (Tegea, Clitor, Mantinea, Orchomenus) were moved to the great new city, whose name means "Great City." The new inhabitants brought their local cults and images with them; altars were set up, temples were raised, a stadium was laid out, and public buildings were erected. The Arcadian cities and villages of the league were to be governed by an assembly in a federal system. The sessions of the assembly were held in the Thersilion. But the great plan of Epaminondas and the Arcadian League for a federal system and a strong city was a failure in practice. The peasants who had moved from their old homes became discontented and returned to their villages. The city was subjected to siege many times and was at last destroyed. When the traveler Pausanias passed that way in the 2nd century A.D. the city lay in ruins. Remains of a large theater, capable of accommodating 20,000 spectators, and of a great sanctuary of Zeus Soter (*Savior*) have been uncovered. The extraordinary design of the Thersilion, a vast roofed assembly hall whose supporting columns were artfully arranged in lines radiating from the *bema* (speaker's platform), has evoked the admiration of historians of architecture.

Megamede (meg-a-mē′dē). In Greek legend, the wife of Thespius, king of Thespiae in Boeotia, and the mother of his 50 daughters.

Megapenthes (meg-a-pen′thēz). In Greek legend, a son and successor of Proetus, king of Tiryns. He exchanged kingdoms with Perseus when the latter, in grief over the accidental slaying of his grandfather Acrisius, left Argos. Megapenthes took Argos and Perseus took Tiryns.

Megapenthes. In Greek legend, a bastard son of Menelaus and a slave girl. He was barred from succeeding to the throne of Sparta on account of his birth. After the death of Menelaus, Megapenthes and his twin brother, Nicostratus, according to some accounts, forced Helen to flee to Rhodes.

Megara (meg′a-ra). In Greek mythology, a daughter of Creon, king of Thebes. She was given in marriage to Heracles by her father, as a reward to him for conquering Erginus and the Minyans, who had been exacting tribute from the Thebans. Hera, ever jealous because Heracles was the son of Zeus, drove him mad, and in his frenzy he killed his children by Megara. Later, he gave Megara to his beloved nephew, Iolaus, for a wife, because he feared to have more children by her himself after his terrible experience. According to some accounts, Heracles killed Megara also during the spell of madness in which he killed his children.

Megara. Town on the Isthmus of Corinth in central Greece, situated between the Halcyon Sea, the Corinthian Bay, and the Saronic Gulf. The town, whose name is the plural of the Greek word *megaron* (the great central hall of the bronze-age palaces), is about 21 miles west of Athens. The ancient city, whose early inhabitants were Carians, was situated on the route leading from central Greece to the Peloponnesus. According to ancient tradition, Megara once belonged to Athens, for its king, Pylas, left it to Pandion, king of Athens. Nisus subsequently became king, founded the port of Nisaea, and named the area Nisa after himself. During his reign his land was attacked by Minos, king of Crete, who harried the Greek states that would not join him in a war against Athens to avenge the death of his son, Androgeus. The Boeotians said that Megareus, a son of Poseidon, went to help Nisus in the war, that he was killed and buried on the citadel, and that the place was named Megara for him. But the Megarians themselves, according to tradition, told a different story. They said their land was first ruled by Lelex, who came there from Egypt, and that Sciron, a descendant of Lelex, married a daughter of the Athenian king Pandion. Sciron (later slain by Theseus) struggled with Nisus for the throne of Nisa (Megara). Their dispute was arbitrated by Aeacus, who awarded the throne to Nisus but gave command of the

army to Sciron. The Megarians said that Megareus, the son of Poseidon mentioned above, was connected to their history by marriage with Iphinoë, daughter of Nisus, and that he succeeded his father-in-law on the throne and named the kingdom for himself. For the Megarians preferred to forget that their land was ever attacked and destroyed by Minos, as indeed it was. They said that Megareus succeeded Nisus, and that he was in turn succeeded by Alcathous, son of Pelops, who had slain the Cithaeronian lion and married the daughter of Megareus. But their story was intended to cover their shame at their defeat by Minos, for when Alcathous came to Megara from Elis after the Megarians had lost everything in the war with Minos, it was necessary for him to rebuild the walls of the city that had been razed by the Cretans. He raised an altar to the gods called Prodomeis (*Previous Builders*), and with the help of Apollo built new walls. Near the wall was the stone where Apollo rested his lyre while he helped Alcathous. This stone, when struck by a pebble, gave out the musical note of the lyre. Megara had two citadels, one called Caria, after Car, the son of Phoroneus. Some say Alcmene, on the advice of an oracle, was buried in Megara and that her tomb was here. Hyllus, son of Heracles, slain in a duel with Echemus, was also buried here, as was Hippolyte the Amazon. She fled to Megara after the defeat of her Amazon forces by Theseus and died of a broken heart and was buried in a shield-shaped tomb. Near her tomb was the grave of Tereus. Pandion, who was buried on the Rock of Athena Aethyia (*Gannet*), had a shrine in Megara, and there were also shrines of Ino, whom the Megarians say was washed ashore in their land and buried after being found by two maidens, and of Iphigenia, who they say died in Megara. Some say Calchas the seer was a Megarian, and that Agamemnon raised a sanctuary of Artemis when he succeeded in persuading Calchas to accompany the Greeks to Troy. Among the many sacred places in Megara was a rock called Anaclethris (*Recall*) where Demeter called to Persephone when she was searching for her after she had been abducted by Hades. The Megarian women regularly performed a ritual that commemorated this incident of Demeter

fat, fāte, fär, fāre, errant; net, mē, hèr ardent; pin, pīne; not, nōte, möve, nôr,

calling for Persephone. Among the temples of Megara was a temple of Artemis Agrotera and Apollo Agraeus raised by Alcathous in gratitude for his success in killing the Cithaeronian lion, and a temple of Artemis Savior in gratitude for her help in resisting a group of Persians from the forces of Mardonius in the Persian War (480 B.C.). They say that when Codrus was king of Attica the Dorians invaded his kingdom on their way back to the Peloponnesus. They captured Megara and gave it to their Corinthian allies, and thus made it Dorian.

The Megarians were among the first to send out colonies to the Euxine (Black) Sea region. They founded Chalcedon on the Thracian Bosporus first; then, scolded by the oracle for their blindness, founded Byzantium (667 B.C.) on the opposite and more advantageous shore. The founding of this city that controlled the entrance to the Euxine Sea, assured the penetration of Greek colonists in the region. They also founded Selymbria on the north coast of the Propontis, and Heraclea on the coast of Bithynia. This last, according to legend, had been named Heraclea by Lycus, king of the Mysians, because Heracles had helped him in a war against the Bebryces. The Megarians colonized it in obedience to instructions from the priestess at Delphi. She told them to found a colony on the Pontus (another name for the Black Sea) in a land dedicated to Heracles. In the west the Megarians established the colonies of Hybla Minor (Megara Hyblaea) and Selinus in Sicily. Theagenes, tyrant of Megara (640–600 B.C.), beautified the city and brought water to it by an aqueduct, parts of which remain. His daughter married Cylon, a noble who attempted to seize the citadel at Athens (c632 B.C.). He failed, and in the ensuing wars with Athens Megara was weakened and lost much of its power and influence. Under the inspiration of Solon, the Athenians wrested Salamis from Megara and further weakened it, for this island, in the possession of one, was a threat to the other city. Following a dispute with Corinth, Megara accepted an Athenian garrison and constructed (459 B.C.) the Long Walls that linked the city with her port Nisaea. Shortly afterward, Megara quarreled with the Athenians again and drove out the garrison. In

retaliation, Pericles promulgated (432 B.C.) a decree that excluded Megara from Athenian markets. This was a disastrous economic blow. In addition, the Athenians annually ravaged the land and blockaded their coasts. Megara appealed to Sparta, and this was one of the causes of the Peloponnesian Wars, in which Megara served as a battleground for Sparta and Athens. Ultimately, the city fell into the hands of the Macedonians and afterward the Romans controlled it. Megara was the birthplace of Euclid, the founder of the Megarics, or Megarian school of philosophers, and of Theognis, the poet. The Megarians were noted for their gay temperament, and Megara was said to be the birthplace of comedy. The area surrounding Megara is called the **Megaris** (q.v.) or **Megarid**.

Megara Hyblaea (meg′a-ra hī-blē′a). See **Hybla Minor**.

Megareus (me-gar′ē-us). In Greek mythology, a son of Oenope and Hippomenes. He was an ally of Nisus, father of Scylla and ruler of Nisa (afterwards Megara), and married Iphinoë, another daughter of Nisus. Megareus had two sons, one of whom, Euippus, was killed by a lion that was ravaging Mount Cithaeron. Megareus promised his throne and his daughter, Euaechme, to whomever should kill the lion, and gave both to Alcathous who accomplished this deed. Nisa then became known as Megara, after Megareus. He was buried near the acropolis of the city.

Megarics (me-gar′iks). School of Greek philosophy, founded by Euclid of Megara, which combined the ethical doctrines of Socrates and the metaphysics of the Eleatics.

Megaris (meg′a-ris). In ancient geography, a district in Greece which formed part of the isthmus connecting the Peloponnesus with C Greece and lay SW of Attica and NE of Corinthia. The surface is largely mountainous. Chief town, Megara.

Megaron (meg′a-ron). The great central hall of the Homeric house or palace. In large houses of this early time there was a *megaron* for the men and the entertainment of guests, and another, more secluded, for the women of the household. The plan and disposition of such megara, with the ceremonial family hearth in the middle, was clearly exposed in the excavations of Schliemann and Dörpfeld at Tiryns in the Peloponnesus.

Megarus (meg'a-rus). In Greek mythology, a son of Zeus who, according to some accounts, was saved from the flood with which Zeus engulfed the world to punish mankind. He was awakened by screaming cranes and fled to Mount Gerania which was not covered by the flood waters.

Megasthenes (mē-gas'the-nēz). Greek historian, active c300 B.C. He spent considerable time (315–291 B.C.), as the ambassador of his friend and companion the Syrian ruler Seleucus (Seleucus Nicator), to Sandrocottus (Chandragupta), king of the Prasii in India, whose capital was probably near the modern Patna. Based on information he got about the people and the country while he was there, he wrote a geographical and historical work on India which was the chief source of the later Greek information on the subject, especially Arrian's *Indica*.

Meges (mē'jēz). In the *Iliad*, a son of Phyleus "the Horseman." He was a nephew of Odysseus and commanded the Epeans against the Trojans. He slew many but was himself saved by wearing his father's mail-plated corselet. As a son of Phyleus he was also spoken of as "Phylides."

Megistias (mē-jis'ti-as). An Acarnanian seer, said to be a descendant of Melampus. He was in the train of Leonidas at the defense of the pass of Thermopylae (480 B.C.). From observing his sacrificial victims he foresaw the imminent doom of the Greeks. Scouts soon confirmed his deduction with news that the Persians were coming by a path over the mountain to attack the Greeks in the rear. Leonidas gave Megistias permission to retire with the allies when they left him alone with the Spartans and Thespians to resist the Persians. Megistias scorned to desert Leonidas himself, but sent his only son back with the allies. He died along with the Spartans and Thespians in their heroic defence of the pass, and was memorialized by the poet Simonides as follows:

> The great Megistias' tomb you here may view,
> Whom slew the Medes, fresh from Spercheus' fords.
> Well the wise seer the coming death foreknew,
> Yet scorned he to forsake his Spartan lords.

Meilichius or **Milichius** (mī-lik'i-us). Epithet of Zeus. At the altar of Zeus Meilichius (*Gracious*), near the Cephissus River in Attica, Theseus was purified by the descendants of Phytalus for the slaying of his kinsman Sinis. There was an altar of Zeus Meilichius at Sicyon. The white marble image of Zeus Meilichius at Argos was made by Polyclitus. This image was dedicated as part of the purification for a mass murder. One thousand picked men had been chosen to protect Argos against the continual attacks of Sparta. This elite corps was unbounded in its arrogance toward their fellow countrymen. The leader of the group seized a maiden as she was being conveyed to her bridegroom, carried her off to his camp, and ravished her. While he slept the young woman put out both his eyes and then fled to the people of Argos as a suppliant. The people refused to give her up to the followers of the blinded chief, and a battle between the 1000 men and the people took place, in which the people won and put to death all the 1000 soldiers. The image of Zeus Meilichius by Polyclitus was dedicated as an offering and as part of their purification, for having shed the blood of their kinsmen.

Mela (mē'la), **Pomponius**. Roman geographer, born at Tingentera, Spain, and active about the middle of the 1st century A.D. He was the author of *De Situ Orbis,* or *De Chorographia* (in three books), a compendium of geography and of manners and customs, based mostly on ancient Greek sources. His geography is in the form of a voyage, starting from North Africa and describing the countries of the then known world as the supposed voyage continued until it ended at West Africa. His is the earliest extant account of the ancient world written in Latin.

Melaenis (me-lē'nis). An epithet of Aphrodite in her aspect as a goddess of death-in-life, meaning "Black." But some say she was called Melaenis because men invoke her for their love-making at night.

Melampus (me-lam'pus). In Greek mythology, a son of Amythaon of Pylus and Idomene, and the brother of Bias. The brothers went with Neleus when the latter invaded Messene and captured the city of Pylus. According to some accounts Melampus was the first mortal who enjoyed the power of foretelling the future. In his youth he rescued some young serpents whose parents had been killed by servants who wanted to kill the off-spring also. Melampus buried the parent serpents. In return the young serpents licked his ears as he slept; and when he awoke he had the power to understand the language of birds and beasts and thus learned many secret things. Furthermore, Apollo taught him the art of augury by means of the entrails of sacrificial victims. Melampus was also said to have been the first to mix wine with water, to build temples to Dionysus and to establish certain mysteries in his honor, and the first to act as a physician. He was strongly attached to his brother Bias. Bias fell in love with Pero, a daughter of Neleus and the sister of Nestor. Neleus, compelled to choose among the many suitors for Pero's hand, agreed to award her to that one who could steal the prize cattle of Phylacus of Phylace, in Thessaly. Melampus agreed to help his brother obtain the cattle and win Pero. By his prophetic powers he learned that whoever tried to steal the cattle would win them as a gift, but only after having served a year in prison. Melampus went to the building where the cattle were housed, prepared to spend a year in prison before he would gain them. The ferocious dog that guarded them gave the alarm and Melampus was captured by the minions of Phylacus and imprisoned. He had been confined exactly a year when he overheard some woodworms talking in the beams of his prison. One of them asked another how much longer they must gnaw at the beams. The other answered that they would have gnawed through the beam by the following morning. Melampus instantly set up a clamor to be removed to another cell, saying the building would collapse before morning. Although his guards scoffed at his story, Phylacus permitted him to be moved. Next day his former prison collapsed as the woodworms finished gnawing through the beams. Phylacus was much impressed by this evidence of Melampus' gift of prophecy. He agreed to free Melampus and give him the cattle if he could cure his son Iphiclus of his childlessness. Melampus undertook to do so. He sacrificed two bulls to Apollo and invited the birds to feast on their carcasses which he left lying on the altars. Two vultures flew down to eat the sacrificial victims. Melampus listened to their speech and learned from it that Iphiclus had been frightened as a child when he watched his father gelding rams and saw him with the bloody knife. Phylacus plunged the knife into the trunk of a tree and ran to comfort his child. Since then Iphiclus had been impotent. The vultures agreed that the only cure for his condition would be to scrape some of the rust from the knife, which remained buried in the tree trunk where Phylacus had thrust it, mix the rust with wine, and give it as a potion to Iphiclus for ten successive days. But the vultures concluded that probably there was no one other than themselves wise enough to employ such a cure. However, Melampus, having overheard them, at once prepared the potion as they had suggested and gave it to Iphiclus. In the course of time he was cured and had a son. Phylacus now willingly gave Melampus his cattle. Melampus gave them to Bias and his grateful brother was able to present them to Neleus and win Pero. Melampus now went to Argos. There the daughters of Proetus, co-king of Argos, were afflicted by madness because they had denied the divinity of Dionysus, and went raging about the countryside. Melampus, at the request of Proetus, offered to cure his daughters in return for one-third of his kingdom. Proetus scorned to accept such a high price. The result was that increasing numbers of the women of Argos were seized with madness and roamed wildly through the mountains. Proetus had no alternative. He went to Melampus and offered to accept his terms. Melampus, seeing Proetus' need had increased, increased his price. He now demanded another third of the kingdom for his brother Bias as the price of curing the Argive women. Proetus had no choice but to agree. Melampus pursued the Argive women and drove them to a well where he purified them. He then pursued the three daughters of Proetus—Lysippe, Iphianassa, and Iphinoë—across Arcadia and overtook the first two near the river Styx. The third, Iphinoë, had died in flight. Melampus married Lysippe, and Bias, whose wife Pero had died, married Iphianassa. Proetus partitioned his kingdom as he had agreed. Melampus was the father of Antiphates, who was the father of Heracles' com-

panion Oïcles, and he was the father of Mantius, who in his turn fathered Clitus, carried
off by Eos. The family of seers founded by
Melampus was known as the Melampodidae.

Melanion (mē-lā′ni-on). In Greek legend, a
son of Amphidamas of Arcadia. He is sometimes named as the youth to whom Aphrodite
gave the golden apples so that he could win
a race with Atalanta and win her as his bride.
See **Atalanta.**

Melanippe (mel-a-nip′ē). In Greek mythology,
the name given to the foal which Thea, transformed as the mare Euippe, bore. After it
was born Poseidon transformed the foal into
an infant girl who was given the name Arne.
See **Arne.**

Melanippe. In Greek legend, an Amazon
queen, a daughter of Ares. She ruled a city
near the Thermodon River. According to
some accounts, when Heracles came to the
land of the Amazons in quest of Hippolyte's
girdle, he captured Melanippe, sister of Hippolyte, and held her until Hippolyte ransomed her by giving him the girdle.

Melanippus (mel-a-nip′us). In Greek legend,
a Theban who was one of the defenders of
the city when it was attacked by the Seven
against Thebes. He wounded Tydeus but
Amphiaraus cut off Melanippus' head and
gave it to Tydeus and told him to gulp Melanippus' brains. Tydeus did this and thus
Melanippus, although dead, caused the death
of Tydeus.

Melanippus. A legendary son of Theseus
and Perigune. He was the father of Ioxus,
who took out a colony to Caria.

Melanippus. In the *Iliad,* named as a son
of Hicetaon. He went from Percote and
lived in Priam's palace in Troy, where he was
treated as one of the king's own children. In
the Trojan War he was slain by Nestor's son,
Antilochus.

Melanippus. Beloved of Comaetho, with
whom he profaned the temple of Artemis in
Patrae. See **Comaetho.**

Melanthius (mē-lan′thi-us). In the *Odyssey,*
a goatherd of Odysseus. He was not faithful
to his master in the 20 years while Odysseus
was away, but instead toadied to the suitors
of Penelope. When Odysseus returned disguised as a beggar, Melanthius met him on
his way to the palace, and reviled and attacked him. In the fight between Odysseus

and the suitors, Melanthius was captured as
he tried to slip away and fetch weapons for
the suitors. He was strung up to a beam
where he could watch the combat. When it
was over and all the suitors were dead Melanthius was taken down, his nose, hands,
and feet were cut off, he was disemboweled
and the severed members were thrown to
the dogs.

Melantho (mē-lan′thō). In the *Odyssey,* a beloved handmaid of Penelope, who was treated
almost as a daughter. She proved faithless
while Odysseus was away at the Trojan War
and in the years of wandering after it, and
became the mistress of one of Penelope's
suitors, Eurymachus. When Odysseus returned disguised as a beggar, she mocked
him. After Odysseus had slain the suitors, he
killed those of his servants who had been
faithless during his absence, among them
Melantho.

Melanthus (mē-lan′thus). Another name for
Thymbraeus, a son of the priest Laocoön.
See **Antiphas.**

Melanthus. In Greek legend, a king of Messenia, who was descended from the royal
Messenian family of Neleus. He was driven
out of his kingdom by the Dorians, and went
to Athens. There he became king, as the
successor of Thymoetes, the great-grandson
of Theseus. Melanthus was succeeded on the
throne of Athens by his son Codrus, the last
king of Athens.

Melanthus of Sicyon (sish′i-on). [Also: **Melanthius.**] Greek painter (4th century B.C.),
especially noted as a colorist, one of the great
Sicyonian school founded by Eupompus. He
was a pupil of Pamphilus. Like his teacher,
he based his work on the scientific training
which characterized the artistic activity of
the Peloponnesian cities. He wrote a work
much used by Pliny in the compilation of his
thirty-fifth book.

Melas (mel′as). In Greek legend, a son of
Phrixus and Chalciope, and a grandson of
Aeëtes, king of Colchis. See **Phrontis.**

Melas. See **Clitus.**

Melas (mē′las), **Sinus.** [Modern name, **Gulf
of Saros.**] In ancient geography, the name
of a gulf in the extreme NE part of the
Aegean Sea, formed by the Thracian Chersonese.

Meleager (mel-ē-ā′jèr). In Greek legend, the

son of Oeneus, king of Calydon, and Althaea. When he was seven days old, the Fates told his mother that he would live until a log of wood then on the fire was completely consumed by the flames. Althaea immediately snatched the burning brand from the fire, quenched it, and hid the charred remains. As a youth, Meleager accompanied Jason on the quest for the Golden Fleece, and was wounded by the Colchians as the Argonauts fled with Medea and the Fleece. He married Cleopatra, daughter of Idas and Marpessa. However, when the hunt for the Calydonian Boar was organized, Atalanta joined it and Meleager fell in love with her. According to some accounts, he had a son, Parthenopaeus, by her. Some of the greatest warriors of Greece joined in the chase for the boar. Atalanta, who hunted at Meleager's side, was the first to wound it; others also drew its blood, and Meleager dealt the death blow. He awarded the boar's hide and tusks to Atalanta as a prize for drawing first blood. Two of his uncles objected to giving Atalanta the prize, and in a rage, Meleager slew them. A war with the Curetes for possession of the boar's hide followed. Meleager refused to defend Calydon because his mother had put a curse on him for the death of his uncles, her brothers. He scorned the rich gifts the Calydonians offered him, withdrew from the battle, and amused himself with his wife. At last, the Curetes being about to scale the walls of Calydon, Meleager yielded to the entreaties of his wife, his mother and his friends. He joined in the battle and repulsed the Curetes, at the same time killing two more of his uncles. Althaea, maddened by the death of all her brothers, took the half-burned brand which she had snatched from the fire so many years ago and hurled it into the flames. As it was consumed, Meleager felt a fiery breath scorch him and he died. He was a celebrated warrior, and when, in after years, Heracles visited Hades and frightened the spirits of the dead into fleeing before his sword, Meleager held his ground. Medusa was the only other spirit who dared face the mighty Heracles in the Underworld.

Meleager. Macedonian general, distinguished under Alexander the Great. He was killed c323 B.C.

Meleager. Greek epigrammatist of Gadara in Palestine, who was active about the 1st century B.C. He was a scholar, teacher, and poet, who wrote love poems of great sweetness, and elegies of great tenderness. His collected epigrams, entitled *Stephanos* (Wreath), form the nucleus of the earliest anthology known in world literature.

Meleagrides (mel-ē-ag′rī-dēz). The sisters of Meleager of Calydon. They grieved so at his death that Artemis took pity on them and changed all, save Deianira and Gorge, into guinea hens.

Melete (mel′e-tē). In older Greek mythology, one of the Muses: the muse of Practice.

Meletus (me-lē′tus). Athenian tragic poet; fl. 5th century B.C.

Melia (mē′li-a). In Greek mythology, a nymph who was the mother of Phoroneus and Aegialeus by Inachus, the god of the river of that name in Argos. Aegialeus died childless and Phoroneus founded the city in Argos which afterward bore that name.

Melia. In Greek mythology, a nymph, the daughter of Oceanus. Apollo carried her off and she bore the god two sons: Tenerus, to whom his father gave the art of divination, and Ismenus, for whom the river at Thebes was named.

Meliad (mē′li-ad). In Greek mythology, a nymph of fruit trees or of flocks.

Meliboea (mel-i-bē′a). In Greek legend, a maiden of Ephesus who flung herself from the roof on her wedding day, because her parents would not let her marry Alexis, the man of her choice. She was miraculously saved in her fall and lived to escape and marry Alexis.

Meliboea. In Greek mythology, a daughter of Niobe and Amphion. According to some accounts, she was spared when the other daughters of Niobe were slain by Artemis, because she offered up a propitiatory prayer to Leto. According to these accounts she was given the name Chloris which means "pale," and under this name became the wife of Neleus.

Melicertes (mel-i-sėr′tēz). In classical mythology, a son of Athamas, king of Orchomenus, and Ino, daughter of Cadmus of Thebes. His father, inspired with madness by Hera, sought to kill him, but his mother snatched him up in her arms and leaped into the sea with him. The gods transformed him into a sea-god and he was henceforth known as Palaemon. As a sea-god he rode on the back of a dolphin to Corinth. His identification with the Phoenician Melkarth is uncertain. He was worshiped on the coast, especially at Megara and the Isthmus of Corinth, where his mortal body was cast ashore. His uncle Sisyphus founded in his honor the Isthmian Games, held every four years; whenever they were neglected, famine struck the locality. By the Romans he was identified with Portunus, god of harbors.

Melic (mel'ik) **Nymphs.** In Greek mythology, nymphs who sprang from the blood of Uranus when he was mutilated by Cronus. They were distinguished by the spears of ash they carried, and were also said to be the nymphs of ash trees. With many others, they are sometimes said to have taken care of the infant Zeus in a cave on the island of Crete.

Melië (mel'i-ē). In Greek mythology, a nymph of Bithynia, the mother, by Poseidon, of Amycus, king of the Bebryces.

Melissa (me̯-lis'a̯). In Greek mythology, a Cretan nymph who helped her sister Amalthea care for the infant Zeus by feeding him on honey, while her sister supplied goat's milk. Her name, which means "bee," was also applied to other nymphs and sometimes to priestesses.

Melissa. In Greek legend, the wife of Periander, tyrant of Corinth, who murdered her in a fit of jealousy. Herodotus recounts that she sent Periander word from the land of the dead that she was unclad and cold because her clothes had not been burnt for her at the time of burial; whereupon Periander gathered together many costly garments and burned them in a pit for her.

Melisseus (me̯-lis'ös). According to some accounts, a king in Crete, and the father of Adrastea and Ida, the nymphs who nursed the infant Zeus.

Melissus (me̯-lis'us). Greek philosopher and admiral, who was active in the middle of the 5th century B.C. As an admiral of the Samian fleet he once defeated Pericles. He was a disciple of Parmenides and a representative of the Eleatic school. Fragments of his writings have been preserved.

Melita (mel'i-ta̯). [Modern name, **Malta.**] Island in the Mediterranean Sea, about 60 miles S of Sicily. It was colonized by the Phoenicians c1000 B.C. Greek colonies were established in the 8th century B.C. but the Greeks were driven out by the Carthaginians and the island remained a Carthaginian stronghold until taken by Rome in 218 B.C., during the Second Punic War. The *Acts of the Apostles,* Chs. 27, 28, tell how Saint Paul was shipwrecked on the island (c60 A.D.) and converted many of the inhabitants to Christianity. It was occupied successively by Vandals, Goths, Byzantines, Arabs, and Normans, and when the Turks expelled the Knights of St. John from Rhodes, the Emperor Charles V, in 1530, presented Malta to them; they have since been known as the Knights of Malta. Among the ancient remains are substantial stone ("megalithic") structures of the second millennium B.C., and some have proposed to identify Melita with Ogygia, the island on which the nymph Calypso detained Odysseus. (JJ)

Melite (mel'i-tē). In Greek mythology, a water nymph of the Phaeacians, the daughter of the river-god Aegaeus. When Heracles went to the land of the Phaeacians to be purified, he fell in love with Melite and she became the mother of his son Hyllus, who emigrated across the Cronian Sea and was ultimately killed by the Mentores of Illyria.

Melitene (mel-i-tē'nē). In ancient geography, a district in E Cappadocia, Asia Minor.

Melkarth (mel'kärth). [Also: **Melcarth, Melkart.**] Tutelary god of the Phoenician city of Tyre, an aspect of the Canaanite Baal. He was annually burned in effigy on a great pyre by the people of the city and in the Tyrian colonies. The Greeks identified Melkarth with their own Heracles, who cast himself upon a burning pyre. In Cyprus Melkarth was worshiped side by side with Adonis. He is represented riding on a sea-horse, on the ancient coin of Tyre. His temple at Tyre was celebrated for its magnificence. Women were not allowed to enter the temples of Melkarth (nor those of Heracles).

Melos (mē'los). [Italian, **Milo.**] Volcanic island of the Cyclades, SE Greece. The great harbor which the island partially encircles was caused by volcanic action. Remains of three prehistoric cities have been found at Phylakopi on the island. The two oldest date from the early Minoan period (3400–2100 B.C.) and the Middle Minoan period (2100–1580 B.C.) and indicate a Minoan civilization that developed independently of Crete. The latest of the three cities dates from the Mycenaean period. Obsidian produced on Melos was early used in the manufacture of knives and spear-points, and was an important item of export. Melos was a Dorian colony from ancient times, and was never under the control of Athens as the other islands were following the Persian War. In the Peloponnesian Wars it remained neutral until an Athenian armament came to attack it. Thucydides presents a discussion between Athenian and Melian envoys, which clearly indicates the desire of Melos to remain at peace and in liberty and the undisguised intention of Athens to force the island into submission. The crux of the Athenian argument was that "the strong do what they can and the weak suffer what they must." The Melians, relying on the justice of their cause and the gods, decided to resist (416 B.C.). After a siege of some months they surrendered. All the adult males were put to death by the Athenians, and the women and children were enslaved. Later the Athenians sent out colonists and took the island for themselves. Melos is noted for the Venus of Melos (Venus de Milo) found in the ruins of the ancient city of Melos in 1820, now in the Louvre at Paris. Area of the island, about 57 square miles.

Melpomene (mel-pom′ẹ-nē). In Greek mythology, one of the daughters of Zeus and Mnemosyne. Originally the muse of song and musical harmony, she was looked upon later as the especial patroness of tragedy. She is generally represented as a young woman, bearing the tragic mask and often the club of Heracles, and with her head wreathed with vine leaves in token of her relation with the dramatic deity, Dionysus. According to some accounts, Melpomene was the mother of the Sirens by Achelous. See **Muses.**

Melus (mel′us). In Greek mythology, a companion of Adonis, son of Cinyras of Cyprus. He married Pelia, a kinswoman of Cinyras, but he and his wife grieved so when Adonis was killed in his youth by a boar, that Aphrodite transformed Melus into an apple tree and Pelia into a dove.

Memnon (mem′non). A mythical Aethiopian king, the son of Eos and Tithonus, who came to the aid of the Trojans. The Trojans, shattered by the loss of Hector and then of their ally Penthesilea, the Amazon queen, were considering flight or the surrender of Helen. The arrival of Memnon with his Aethiopians inspired them with new courage. In the furious battle Memnon killed Antilochus, son of Nestor, but ordered Nestor to withdraw as he did not wish to fight an old man. For a time Memnon was irresistible, and as he forced the Greeks back to their ships, Nestor called on Achilles to avenge Antilochus. When Achilles and Memnon, both descendants of gods and endowed with great prowess, met face to face, their fates had already been sealed. Memnon's black fate came to his side. Achilles plunged his sword through Memnon's breast and "snapped the chord of life." Myrmidons stripped him of his armor, while the Trojans fled in terror. Grief-stricken Eos veiled her face and the earth was in shadow as her other children slipped down and rescued Memnon's body. Drops of blood which fell from his corpse became a river, the Paphlagonia, whose waters, so it was said, annually flowed with blood on the anniversary of Memnon's death. His Aethiopian soldiers, whom the gods did not desert, were transformed into birds that flew off mourning their lord. The Greeks and Trojans watched in awe as the whole Aethiopian horde vanished. The body of their fallen leader was carried to the banks of the Aesepus River, where his transformed soldiers darted and wheeled with wailing cries about his tomb. From the ashes of his funeral pyre a great flock, the Memnonides, rose in the air and circled the pyre three times. The fourth time the flock divided. The birds of the two groups made fierce attacks on each other until they fell into the ashes of the funeral pyre as offerings to the dead hero. Annually the Memnonides are said to rise, fight, and fall on Memnon's tomb. On the death of her son, Eos vowed she would withdraw her light from the world. The Horae, however, conducted her to Zeus, who commanded her to resume her daily course. This she did, but each morning she weeps tears of dew in memory of her son. The ancients depicted Memnon as a youth of marvelous strength and beauty. His original home was said to be at Susa in Elam, where his temple or monument, the Memnoneum, was situated. The Greeks gave his name to one of the colossi of Amenophis III at Thebes in Egypt, a great stone statue called "the vocal Memnon" because the stone, when reached by the rays of the rising sun, was said to give forth a sound resembling that of a breaking chord.

Memnonides (mem-non′i-dēz). According to legend, the ashes that rose from the funeral pyre of Memnon were transformed into birds that annually rise, fight, and fall on his tomb. See **Memnon.** Other accounts say the Memnonides are maidens, companions of Memnon, who mourned so over his death that the gods in pity transformed them into birds, and that they also annually visit the tomb and drop water from the Aesepus River on it.

Menaechmi (mē-nēk′mī). Comedy of Plautus, the plot of which turns upon the comical mistakes arising from the resemblance of twin brothers. It was translated into English in 1594 by "W.W." (William Warner) and frequently since. Shakespeare used its plot as the basis of his *The Comedy of Errors.*

Menaechmus (mē-nēk′mus). Greek mathematician; fl. at Athens, c365–350 B.C. A pupil of Eudoxus, friend of Plato, and tutor of Alexander the Great, he is best known as the probable discoverer of the conic sections. None of his works has survived.

Menander (mē-nan′dēr). Athenian comic poet, born at Athens, 342 B.C.; said to have been drowned c291 B.C. He was the son of a wealthy and distinguished family and received a good education. He lived so comfortably in Athens, enjoying his friends, especially Epicurus, that when Ptolemy I of Egypt invited him for a visit, he refused to go. Menander, who made his first appearance in 322 B.C., was the chief of the writers of the New Comedy. He was highly regarded by the ancients for his wit, his skill in plot devising, his inventiveness, and his vivid characterization. His works abound in maxims, which were separately collected in anthologies in a later day. He wrote more than 100 plays, each with its love story. The titles of some 80 are known, with numerous fragments available to modern scholars. Earlier papyrus finds in Egypt brought to light whole scenes and enabled scholars to reconstruct a few plots, notably *Epitrepontes*

(The Arbitration) and *Perikeiromene* (She Is Shorn of Her Locks). In the former a foundling infant, aided by slaves, recovers his rights and finds his parents who had been estranged because of him. In the latter, a soldier-lover maltreats and loses his mistress but regains her as wife after he repents. The appearance in 1959 of the first edition of the *Dyscolus* (The Grouch), edited from a papyrus now in a private collection in Switzerland, caused an international sensation among classical scholars. Lacking only a few lines, it is the only complete play of Menander published up to this time (1961); opinions of its literary and dramatic merits are divided. According to rumor, the manuscript which yielded the *Dyscolus* contains two, or three, additional unpublished plays. Through Plautus and Terence, Menander's influence passed to modern writers of comedy of manners. He won first prize only eight times, but was later extolled as supreme in depicting lively, natural characters in domestic difficulties. He took from Homer's *Odyssey* and from tragedy the theme of family reunion and recognition of lost relatives, but is original in his treatment of good women sinned against, and men reformed by love for them.

Menapii (mē-nā′pi-ī). Ancient Gallic people in Gallia Belgica, formerly living in what is now Belgium and S Netherlands. They are mentioned by Julius Caesar as being the only Gallic people never to sue for peace during the whole Roman conquest of Gaul.

Mende (men′dē). In ancient geography, a city on the Pallene peninsula, in Chalcidice. It revolted from Athens, 423 B.C., and gave allegiance to the Spartan general Brasidas.

Menderes (men-de-res′). Modern Turkish name of the **Maeander,** and also of the **Scamander.**

Menderes, Little. See **Caÿster.**

Menelaeum (men-e-lā′i-um). A hill on the banks of the Eurotas River in Laconia, on which the hero-shrine of Helen and Menelaus has been found. The cult of Helen and Menelaus was observed there until the Dorian invasion, c1100 B.C. On the site, remains of a small temple of the 5th century B.C. have been found. Other remains indicate that this temple replaced a much earlier one, in which Helen and Menelaus were honored.

Nearby, traces of houses of the Mycenaean period have also been found.

Menelaus (men-ẹ-lā′us). In Greek legend a son of Atreus and Aërope. He was the brother of Agamemnon and Anaxibia. Following the murder of their father by Aegisthus, Menelaus and Agamemnon were sent, some say as children, to Polyphides, lord of Sicyon. Next they went to the court of Oeneus in Calydon. Ultimately they were brought back to Argos by Tyndareus and expelled Aegisthus, Agamemnon becoming king of Mycenae and Menelaus becoming king of Sparta. Menelaus was a suitor of Helen, supposedly the daughter of Tyndareus and Leda, but said to have been a daughter of Zeus, who embraced Leda in the shape of a swan. So many noble and valiant princes of Greece sued for the hand of Helen that Tyndareus feared to award her to anyone lest the disappointed suitors turn on him in wrath. Odysseus advised him to require all the suitors to take an oath that they would aid the one who succeeded in case any ill should come to him as a result of his marriage to Helen. The suitors readily took the oath, and Tyndareus then gave Helen to Menelaus. Whether he was also Helen's choice has never been definitely ascertained. She bore Menelaus a daughter, Hermione, and according to some accounts, three sons. Menelaus cordially welcomed Paris when he came to Sparta with the secret intention of carrying off Helen. After entertaining Paris royally for nine days Menelaus, with appalling obtuseness, for it was obvious that Paris was madly in love with Helen, sailed blandly off to Crete to attend the funeral of his maternal grandfather. The night after he sailed, Helen eloped with Paris, taking with her a great treasure and a son. On learning of the abduction, Menelaus appealed to Agamemnon at Mycenae to raise an army and sail against Troy. Agamemnon sent messages to the kings and princes of Greece, reminding them of the oath they had taken as suitors of Helen and declaring that the abduction was an insult to all Greece; that if it was not avenged, they risked losing their own wives. The heroes answered his call. An army and fleet were mustered which assembled at Aulis. For the first nine years the Greeks raided the coasts of Asia Minor

at intervals, and for considerable lengths of time were at home in Greece. Then the fleet reassembled at Aulis, and after the sacrifice of Iphigenia to appease Artemis, they put to sea and arrived at the island of Tenedos. Menelaus and Odysseus were sent as envoys to Troy to demand the return of Helen. Their mission was unsuccessful. They would, in fact, have been murdered by the angry Trojans except for the intervention of Antenor, who sheltered the envoys and secured safe passage for their return in the name of the laws of hospitality and of war. The Greek fleet now sailed to Troy and the city was attacked. A truce was then arranged and, with the approval of both armies, Menelaus met Paris in single combat: the winner to have Helen and thus conclude the war. Menelaus had by far the best of the battle, and would have slain Paris but for the intervention of Aphrodite, who spirited him away in a mist and restored him to Helen. The truce was broken when Athena caused Pandarus to shoot at Menelaus an arrow which merely grazed him, and the war was resumed. Menelaus fought bravely, killing many Trojans. He accepted Hector's challenge to single combat but was dissuaded by Agamemnon from submitting his name for the drawing of lots, and Telamonian Ajax fought Hector. He boldly rescued Odysseus when he was wounded and cut off by the Trojans. He wounded Helenus, the Trojan seer and brother of Paris, and, aided by Athena, killed Euphorbus, who had just wounded Patroclus, and protected the body of Patroclus when he was slain by Hector and helped to carry it back to the Greek ships. After the deaths of Achilles and Telamonian Ajax, Menelaus proposed that the Greeks give up the war and return home. He cared more for his Greeks, he said, than for Helen. But this suggestion was put forth purely for psychological reasons. As he expected, the Greeks protested that this would be cowardly and vowed to fight harder than ever. Calchas the seer encouraged them by recalling that Troy was fated to fall in the tenth year of the war, which was now passing. When the Greeks decided to abandon direct siege of the city and to penetrate it by stratagem, Menelaus was one of those who entered it in the

Wooden Horse. Remembering the kindness of Antenor when he had gone as an envoy to Troy, Menelaus hung a leopard's skin in front of Antenor's house, when the Greeks stole out of the Wooden Horse, as a sign that the house and family of Antenor should be spared in the destruction of the city. During the sack of Troy he searched for Helen, vowing he would kill her. He found her with Deïphobus, to whom she had been forcibly married after the death of Paris. According to some, it was Menelaus who slew Deïphobus and horribly mangled his body. He raised his sword against Helen in the presence of Agamemnon, but was prevented, as he had expected to be, from plunging it into her breast. For Menelaus, whatever he might have said, still passionately loved Helen and could hardly wait to get her back. This was possibly owing to the interference of Aphrodite. They withdrew to his ship and he completely forgave her. He was willing to blame her infidelity, as did she, on the will of the gods. When the city was destroyed, Menelaus wanted to sail immediately. Agamemnon insisted they first sacrifice to the gods. The brothers quarreled and parted; Menelaus never saw his brother again. He put to sea but was caught in a great storm and lost all but five of his ships. Except for Odysseus, he was the last of the Greeks to return home. For eight years he was buffeted about the Mediterranean, sailing to Libya, Phoenicia, Cyprus and Egypt, and collecting a vast treasure. On the island of Pharos, in the mouth of the Nile, he was becalmed for many days. Idothea, a sea-goddess, told him he must catch the sea-god Proteus and force him to tell why Menelaus was prevented from returning home. Idothea helped him to disguise himself and some of his companions as seals and hid them among the seals of Proteus' herd, among which the sea-god took his midday nap. To prevent them from suffocating from the stench of the seal skins in which they were wrapped, Idothea filled their nostrils with ambrosia. Proteus, unaware that masqueraders had joined his herd, came to take his usual nap among them. As he slept, Menelaus seized him, and held him firmly as the sea-god rapidly transformed himself into a lion, then to a serpent, to a panther, and even to run-

ning water. Proteus was thus compelled to prophesy. He said the gods were preventing Menelaus from getting home because he had not made proper sacrifices. He must return to Egypt and sacrifice to Zeus, and then favorable winds would permit his return. He also told him that Agamemnon had been murdered by Aegisthus and Clytemnestra, that Ajax the Lesser had perished at sea, and that Odysseus was held on an isle by Calypso. Menelaus returned to Egypt as instructed, offered sacrifices, and then sailed easily to Sparta with Helen. He arrived to find that Orestes had avenged the murder of Agamemnon by slaying Aegisthus and Clytemnestra. He then raised a temple to Zeus in Sparta in honor of Agamemnon. Telemachus, son of Odysseus, later visited Menelaus in search of news of his father, and found him and his beautiful Helen living in perfect harmony in the midst of splendid prosperity. So complete was their understanding that Helen could ruefully refer to the aberration which had caused her to run off with Paris and win an affectionate smile from Menelaus. Hera made Menelaus immortal, because he was a son-in-law of Zeus, and he and Helen ultimately departed this world and went to dwell in the Isles of the Blest.

Menestheus (me-nes'thūs). Named by Homer as a son of Peteus of Athens. While Theseus was absent in the Underworld Menestheus became regent of Athens. He welcomed the Dioscuri, who had been ravaging Attica as they searched for their sister Helen, and made them honorary citizens of Athens. He was a bold fighter and strategist and as a former suitor of Helen he was bound by his oath to aid and defend her husband. It was thus that he led 50 ships against Troy when Paris stole Helen and took her there. At the end of the war he helped persuade Agamemnon that Aethra, mother of Theseus, who had been taken to Sparta when Helen was rescued by her brothers from Attica, and who had later been carried to Troy, should be restored to Athens. According to some accounts, Menestheus did not return to Athens after the war, but went to Melos where he became king. Others say he died at Troy.

Menesthius (me-nes'thi-us). In the *Iliad,* a son of Areïthoüs, the "Maceman," and Phylomedusa. He was a lord of Arne who joined the Greeks in the Trojan War and was slain by Paris.

Menippe (me̯-nip′ē). In Greek mythology, a daughter of Orion. She and her sister Metioche offered themselves up as two virgins for sacrifice in order to dispel a plague which had fallen on Boeotia.

Menippus (me̯-nip′us). Cynic philosopher, born at Gadara, Palestine, active in the middle of the 3rd century B.C. He was originally a slave. He was noted for his satirical jests upon the follies of mankind, especially of philosophers. His writings, which combined prose and verse, are lost. Varro and Lucian later used Menippus as a model in their satirical writings.

Meno (mē′nō). [Also: **Menon.**] Dialogue of Plato; a conversation between Socrates, Meno (Menon), a slave of Meno, and Anytus upon the teachability of virtue.

Menodice (men-od′i-sē). In Greek mythology, a nymph, the mother of Hylas, Heracles' squire, by Thiodamas, king of the Dryopians.

Menoeceus (me̯-nē′sūs). In Greek legend, a descendant of one of the Sparti, the men who sprang from the dragon's teeth sown by Cadmus. He was the father of Jocasta and Creon. When a plague broke out in Thebes, some time after the marriage of Oedipus and Jocasta, the seer Tiresias said the plague would be dispelled if one of the descendants of the Sparti would give his life for the city. Menoeceus thereupon leaped to his death from the walls to save the city.

Menoeceus. In Greek legend, the son of Creon, king of Thebes, and a grandson of the Menoeceus named above. In the war of the Seven against Thebes, Tiresias, the seer, again prophesied that Thebes would remain safe only if a descendant of the Sown Men freely gave his life for the city and appeased Ares, who was still angry over the death of the Sown Men brought about by Cadmus. Creon refused to sacrifice his son but Menoeceus, knowing of the prophecy, disobeyed his father's command to flee, and killed himself before the gates of the city. Others say he took part in the fighting, being young and inexperienced and knowing that he would be killed, and was slain in that way.

Menoetes (men-ē′tēz). In Greek mythology, a cowherd who tended Hades' cattle on Ery-

thea. It was he who warned Geryon that Heracles was stealing his cattle, although Heracles had not touched any of the cattle of Hades. Later, when Heracles went to the Underworld to fetch Cerberus, he slaughtered one of Hades' cows to give blood to the spirits of the dead. Menoetes challenged him for stealing Hades' cattle as he had Geryon's, and in the wrestling match which followed Menoetes would have been crushed to death by Heracles' strong arms had it not been for the intervention of Persephone who rescued him.

Menoetius (me̯-nē′shi-us). In Greek mythology, a Titan, the son of Iapetus and Clymene, and the brother of Atlas, Epimetheus, and Prometheus. He was killed by a thunderbolt of Zeus and hurled down to Tartarus when the Titans warred against the gods.

Menoetius. In Greek legend, a son of Actor and Aegina. He was an Argonaut and the father of Patroclus, whom he took from Opus in Locris to the court of Peleus after Patroclus had killed a young friend in a childish argument. When Patroclus left with Achilles to join the Greeks in the war against Troy, Menoetius charged him ever to do his best, and if he was not so skillful in arms as Achilles, at least he could fight at his side and aid him with wise counsel and gentle suggestions.

Menon (mē′non). Thessalian mercenary; killed c400 B.C. He was one of the leading generals in the expedition of Cyrus the Younger against Artaxerxes. After the death of Cyrus at Cunaxa (401 B.C.) the Greek mercenaries, who had been victorious in the battle against Artaxerxes in which Cyrus was killed, refused to surrender when Cyrus' oriental troops fled, and forced the Persians to supply them with provisions and a guide back to Sardis. The satrap Tissaphernes became their guide. After crossing the Tigris and proceeding into Media, hostility between the Greeks and their Persian escort broke out. Tissaphernes invited all the Greek generals (five of them), including Menon, as well as the leading Greek captains to a conference in his tent. When they were gathered there, he treacherously caused the captains to be taken and slain. The generals were sent off to the Persian court in chains. Menon was put to torture and finally killed.

actor; up, lūte, pull; oi, oil; ou, out; ᴛʜ, then; ḏ as d or j, ṣ as s or sh, ṭ as t or ch, ẓ as z or zh.

Mentes (men'tēz). In the *Odyssey*, a captain of the Taphians, whose form Athena took when she went to the house of Odysseus to encourage Telemachus to journey in search of news of his father. In the *Iliad*, Mentes was a leader of the Cicones, whose form Apollo assumed to spur Hector to obtain possession of Patroclus' body.

Mentor (men'tor). In the *Odyssey*, an Ithacan to whom Odysseus, when about to depart for the Trojan War, entrusted the care of his house and the education of his son Telemachus. His name has become a synonym for a faithful adviser.

Mentores (men'tôr-ēz). A people of Illyria. According to legend, when Hyllus, son of Heracles and the Phaeacian nymph Melite, went to settle in their country, they killed him.

Mercedonius (mêr-se̱-dō'ni-us) or **Mercedinus** (mêr-se̱-dī'nus). Among primitive peoples, the most widely-used system of time-reckoning was the "lunisolar" calendar, in which some form of intercalation was employed to keep two incommensurate periods, the solar year of 365+ days and the lunar year of 354+ days (12 lunar months averaging 29.5306 days), in rough correspondence. In a calendar ascribed to Numa Pompilius, traditional second king of Rome (c700 B.C.), an attempt was made to correct the cumulative discrepancy of the lunisolar year by intercalating, between February 23 and 24, in every second year, a short, non-lunar, month of 22 or 23 days, called *Mercedonius* or *Mercedinus*. Such a calendar would present a relatively sophisticated type of intercalation, and modern scholars consider that this calendar was probably developed much later than the period of Numa Pompilius. (JJ)

Mercury (mêr'kū-ri). In Roman mythology, the god of commerce, who became identified with the Greek Hermes and took on various other attributes of Hermes, such as being messenger of the gods. His cult came from S Italy into Rome c495 B.C. Mercury was the tutelary deity of thieves and tricksters; he became also the god of science, eloquence, and of the arts, and the patron of travelers and athletes. It was he who guided the shades of the dead to the Underworld. He is represented in art as a young man, usually wearing a winged hat and the talaria or winged sandals, and bearing the caduceus, and often a purse.

Meriones (mer-ī'ō̱-nēz). In Homeric legend (*Iliad*), a son of Molus. He went from Crete as an aide to Idomeneus, a former suitor of Helen, when the latter joined the Greek fleet waiting at Aulis to sail to Troy. Noted as an archer, he slew many Trojans, and was one of several who accepted Hector's challenge to single combat but was eliminated in the drawing of lots. When Odysseus went to spy on the Trojan camp, Meriones loaned him his bow and quiver and his famous helmet studded with boar's tusks. After the death of Patroclus he helped Menelaus to carry off his body, while the two Ajaxes held off the Trojans; and in the funeral games for Patroclus he won the archery contest from Teucer by shooting a pigeon in midair.

Mermerus (mêr'me̱-rus). A son of Jason and Medea. See **Alcimedes**.

Mermnadae (mêrm'na̱-dē). Last dynasty of the Lydian kings, beginning with Gyges (c685 B.C.) and ending with Croesus (560–546 B.C.). Besides these kings it included Ardys, Sadyattes, and Alyattes.

Merope (mer'ō̱-pē). In Greek mythology, a daughter of Atlas and Pleione, one of the seven Pleiades. She was the wife of Sisyphus, king of Corinth. When Sisyphus was taken to the Underworld for betraying secrets of Zeus he told Merope not to dress him in burial clothes. Thus he was able to convince Persephone that he had not had proper burial, and won her permission to return to earth to see that the proper rites were carried out. However, Sisyphus did not escape for long, and when he returned to the Underworld for good, Merope, ashamed because she was the only one of the Pleiades to have a husband who was a prisoner in the Underworld, left her six sisters in the heavens and is now no longer visible. According to another account, her shame is due to the fact that she, alone of the sisters, married a mortal.

Merope. In Greek mythology, a daughter of Oenopion, king of Chios. She was loved by Orion who, for her sake, cleared the island of Chios of wild animals. Oenopion agreed to give Merope to Orion in marriage in return for this service, but kept delaying the fulfillment of his promise. At last Orion, in a drunken state, insulted the maiden. Oenopion called on Dionysus to punish him. While he was in a deep sleep, Oenopion blinded him. Merope is also sometimes called Aero.

Merope. In Greek mythology, a daughter of Pandareus and Harmothoë, and a sister of Cleothera and Aëdon. When their father was punished by the gods for his part in a theft, the goddesses took charge of his daughters. Aphrodite, Hera, Artemis, and Athena endowed them with beauty, wisdom, strength, and skill. But they were snatched away by the Harpies one day when the goddesses were not attending them, and handed over to the Erinyes, who hounded them for their father's crimes.

Merope. In Greek legend, an Arcadian; she was the wife of Cresphontes, a king in Messenia and a descendant of Heracles. Two of her sons and her husband were killed in a rebellion, and Polyphontes, who succeeded Cresphontes, married her. Her third son, Aepytus, had been hidden in Arcadia to save him, during the rebellion. When he grew up he returned to Messenia and with the help of his mother, who at first did not recognize him, he murdered Polyphontes and assumed the throne.

Merope. The name sometimes given to the wife of Polybus, king of Corinth, who brought up Oedipus and led him to believe that she was his mother. See **Periboea.**

Merops (mē′rops). In Homeric legend (*Iliad*), a Percosian who excelled in the art of divining. He tried to prevent his two sons, Adrestus and Amphius, from joining the Trojans, as he knew they would never return from the war, but was unsuccessful in his attempts to help them escape their fate, which was to die at Troy.

Merops. A legendary king of Aethiopia. He was the husband of Clymene and the foster father of Phaëthon.

Mesopotamia (mes″o-pō-tā′mi-a). [From Greek, meaning "Between Rivers"; Hebrew, **Aram Naharaïm.**] Country between the Euphrates and Tigris. It is usually divided into Upper Mesopotamia (ancient Chaldea) and Babylonia. It is a great lowland plain, and was formerly very extensively irrigated and cultivated; in recent decades there has been a considerable extension of the irrigated area. It was invaded and conquered several times

by the Egyptians and has belonged at different times to the Median, Persian, Macedonian, Syrian, Parthian and Roman empires.

Messa (mes′a). Harbor town in Laconia, on the W coast of the Taenarum promontory. It was described by Homer as "abounding in pigeons," and men from this port accompanied Menelaus to the Trojan War.

Messala (or **Messalla**) **Corvinus** (me-sā′la, me-sal′a, kôr-vī′nus), **Marcus Valerius.** Roman general, official, orator, historian, and patron of literature (64 B.C.–8 A.D.) He fought for Antony at Philippi (42 B.C.) but later was on Octavian's side at Actium (31 B.C.). He was consul in 31 B.C.

Messalina or **Messallina** (mes-a-lī′na), **Valeria.** Roman empress. Before 41 A.D., she became the third wife of Claudius who afterward ascended the imperial throne. Their children were Octavia, later married to Nero, and Britannicus (Claudius Tiberius Caesar). She was a woman of infamous vices, and during a temporary absence of her husband publicly married her favorite, Caius Silius. Her partner in influence over Claudius, the freedman Narcissus, informed the emperor, and she was put to death (48 A.D.) by order of Claudius.

Messana (me-sā′na) and **Messene** (me-sē′nē). [Modern name, **Messina.**] Messene was the name given (c664 B.C.) to the ancient city of Zancle in Sicily, situated on the extreme NE corner of the island, on the strait that separates it from the mainland of Italy. After the Messenians were defeated in the Second Messenian War with Sparta, many of them went to Sicily, according to tradition, on the invitation of the tyrant of Rhegium, a city diagonally S across the strait from Zancle. They defeated the Zancleans, made a treaty of friendship with them, and changed the name of Zancle to Messene, after their own country. Early in the 5th century B.C. the city came under the control of the tyrant of Rhegium, and henceforward it was known as Messana. In the struggle for control of Sicily between Carthage and the powerful Greek city of Syracuse, Messana changed sides many times. In 405 B.C. it was declared independent at the insistence of the Carthaginian general Himilco. When Dionysius, tyrant of Syracuse, renewed the war, 398 B.C., Himilco attacked Messana. Most of the inhabitants had fled, and Himilco took an abandoned city (396 B.C.). He pulled it to the ground, and destroyed its walls and buildings so completely that it was said no one would have known a city ever existed on the site. In the following year Dionysius rebuilt it and settled colonists from Italy and some exiles from Greek Messenia there. It fell again into the hands of the Carthaginians and was freed by Timoleon, 343 B.C. When the wars between Carthage and Syracuse broke out again, it sided with Carthage. It was seized by the Mamertines (288 B.C.), allies of Rome, who sought the aid of Rome and thus initiated the First Punic War. At the end of the war (241 B.C.) it became a free city allied to Rome. In the Roman civil wars following the assassination of Caesar, Messana was on the side of the enemies of Octavian, and was taken and sacked by the forces of Octavian (35 B.C.). Owing to its location the city sprang up many times after destruction, and it soon revived and again became a flourishing port.

Messapia (me̦-sā′pi-a̦). In ancient geography, the peninsula at the SE extremity of Italy, often used as synonymous with Calabria or Iapygia. The name derives from its prehistoric Illyrian inhabitants.

Messene (me̦-sē′nē). According to tradition, the daughter of Triopas, son of the Argive Phorbas. She married Polycaon, son of Lelex, and accompanied him, with a band of Argives and Spartans, to the country which came to be named Messenia after her.

Messene. A city in Messenia, Greece, on the slope of Mount Ithome, about 19 miles SW of Megalopolis. According to tradition, after the defeat of the Spartans at Leuctra (371 B.C.), their Theban conqueror Epaminondas dreamed that he was instructed to restore the Messenians to their land, from which they had been driven by the Spartans. In his dream he was told to recover a secret thing which the dream directed him where to find, and on that spot to found a city for the Messenians. Epaminondas sent an envoy to find the secret thing of his dream. It turned out to be the Messenian mysteries, buried by Aristomenes before he fled from Messenia after the Second Messenian War. On this spot, which was at Mount Ithome, Epaminondas helped the Messenians, whom he had

recalled from their exile, to lay out the foundations of their city (369 B.C.), and to the piping of flutes the heavy walls were raised. The walled city had the practical advantage of serving as a fortress against Sparta. In the city the Messenians dedicated a statue of Zeus the Savior in the market-place, and raised temples of Poseidon, Aphrodite, and Demeter, as well as a temple of Messene, daughter of Triopas, who had given her name to the Messenians and to their new city. The bones of Aristomenes were recovered from Rhodes at the command of an oracle, and interred in a tomb in the city. Annually certain rites were held at his tomb. A bull was bound to the pillar that stood on the grave of Aristomenes. If the bull, struggling to free himself, rocked the pillar, it was an omen of good fortune for the Messenians. If the pillar was not moved by the struggling bull, misfortune was portended. The ancient city of Messene is noted now for its extensive ruins at the modern village of Mavromati.

Messene. City in Sicily, see **Messana.**

Messenia (me̦-sē′ni-a̦). In ancient geography, a division of the Peloponnesus, Greece. It was bounded by Elis and Arcadia on the N, Laconia (separated by Mount Taÿgetus) on the E, and the sea on the S and W. It contained the fertile valley of the Pamisus and enjoyed a milder climate than its neighbor across Mount Taÿgetus. For these reasons it was enviously eyed by the Lacedaemonians whose land was rocky and infertile. According to tradition, Polycaon, son of the Lacedaemonian king, Lelex, married Messene, the daughter of Triopas, an Argive. With a band of Spartans and Argives Polycaon marched into the land west of Mount Taÿgetus and took it, and named it Messenia after his wife. When Polycaon's line died out, the Messenians summoned Perieres, the husband of Gorgophone, daughter of Perseus, to be their king. His throne passed to his two sons, Aphareus and Leucippus, who were supposed to reign as co-kings, but in fact Aphareus was the master. When his twin sons Idas and Lynceus died without heirs, the kingdom passed to Nestor, son of Neleus. The descendants of Nestor held the kingdom until the Dorian invasion and the return of the Heraclidae to the Peloponnesus. In the Dorian invasion, the sons of Aristomachus—

Aristodemus, Temenus, and Cresphontes—drew lots to decide which of the three regions of the Peloponnesus each would receive. Cresphontes, by a trick, got Messenia, which was regarded as the choicest portion of the Peloponnesus. In later times the Messenians and Lacedaemonians quarreled. The Lacedaemonians claimed that Messenians attacked a group of Lacedaemonian maidens who were on their way to a festival of Artemis at a sanctuary shared by both Messenians and Lacedaemonians and ravished the maidens, and killed the Spartan king, Teleclus, who tried to protect them. The Messenians claimed this was not the case at all. They said a band of Spartan youths, disguised as maidens, set upon them and that the Messenians killed them in self-defense. This incident was a cause of much friction, and in the next generation war broke out between the two kingdoms. The real cause of the war was the desire of the Spartans to control the rich areas of Messenia. The war, which some say began in 743 B.C., and certainly took place in the 8th century B.C., was carried on sporadically for 20 years. The Messenians protected themselves as best they could but were weakened by their losses and by disease. They withdrew to Ithome and carried on the war from there. All the omens predicted Spartan victory. The oracles told the Messenians that since they had won the land by guile (Cresphontes' trickery with the drawing of the lots), they would lose it by guile. Unfavorable omens appeared: the shield on the armed statue of Artemis fell to the ground; when the king was about to sacrifice victims to Zeus at Ithome, the citadel of the Messenians, the rams rushed into the flames of their own accord; dogs howled every night and at last fled to the Spartan camp. Aristodemus, the king of Messenia, was informed by an oracle that the willing sacrifice by her father of a Messenian virgin would save Messenia. He proposed to sacrifice his daughter, but her affianced husband, in an effort to save his beloved, said she was not a virgin but was about to become the mother of his child. Aristodemus was enraged at this slur on his honor. He slew his daughter and opened up her body to prove that she was not about to bear a child. But his impious act, carried out in a rage on the

daughter he loved, did not satisfy the demands of the oracle for a voluntary sacrifice, and the death of his daughter was in vain. He was visited by evil dreams and, despairing for the fate of Messenia, he committed suicide on his daughter's tomb. About 724 B.C., according to some accounts, the war came to an end in Spartan victory. The Messenians fled from Ithome. The Spartans razed it to the ground and captured other towns. The victors compelled the Messenians to take an oath that they would never rebel and that they would give one-half of the produce of their fields to Sparta. In addition, the Messenians were compelled to attend the funerals of Spartan officials in the future, a particularly humiliating illustration of their defeat.

In the years that followed, the Messenians chafed under the Spartan yoke so that they welcomed the fiery speeches of Aristomenes, an ardent patriot who grew up in their midst at the beginning of the 7th century B.C. He urged them to revolt and free themselves from Sparta. Under his leadership the Second Messenian War broke out in the first half of the 7th century B.C. Some give the dates of it as 685–668 B.C. In this war Aristomenes performed prodigious feats, on at least one occasion driving the Spartans back in confusion, and several times escaping when he was taken prisoner. The Arcadians were allies of the Messenians, but through bribery their king betrayed the Messenians, without letting his own people, who cherished a warm friendship for the Messenians, know that he was doing so. He ordered the Arcadians to withdraw in the midst of a battle, and led them to the rear through the Messenian lines, thus throwing the Messenians into such confusion as the Arcadians fled through their midst that they were surrounded by the Spartans and suffered heavy losses. The survivors were led to Mount Eira by Aristomenes, and from there carried on their defense. The Messenians were besieged for 11 years, when they were again betrayed, this time by an adulterous woman. They fled to Arcadia, where they were warmly received and where the Arcadians, on learning that their king had betrayed their allies, stoned him to death. Aristomenes went to Rhodes, where he died, and many of the Messenians went to Sicily,

actor; up, lūte, pu̇ll; oi, oil; ou, out; ᴛʜ, then; ḍ as d or j, ş as s or sh, ṭ as t or ch, ẓ as z or zh.

where they captured the town of Zancle and changed its name to Messene (664 B.C.). The Spartans now had Messenia and divided it among themselves, except for Asine, which remained separate. Those Messenians who were left were reduced to slavery and became helots. But before Aristomenes fled from Messenia, he took a casket and buried it on a remote spot of Ithome, for an oracle had foretold that if this casket with its secret contents was kept by the Messenians, they would one day recover their country. The hatred of the Messenians for the Spartans never faltered; in 464 B.C. the Messenian helots revolted. This was at a time when Sparta was stricken by earthquakes to punish her for seizing suppliants at the sanctuary of Poseidon at Taenarus and putting them to death. The Messenian helots took refuge in their old fortress of Ithome, and held out against the Spartans for five years. At the end of that time they surrendered, and were allowed to withdraw from the fortress unharmed on condition that they never return to the Peloponnesus. The Athenians offered them a new home at Naupactus on the Corinthian Gulf (455 B.C.). The Messenians aided the Athenians in the Peloponnesian War. It was a Messenian plan that helped the Athenians capture a force of Spartans in Pylus (425 B.C.). With part of the spoil they took from the hated Spartans on this occasion, the Messenians commissioned the sculptor Paeonius to make an image of Victory, hovering in the air over a soaring eagle, which they dedicated in the Altis of Zeus at Olympia. After the Battle of Aegospotami (405 B.C.) in which the Spartans defeated the Athenians, the Messenians were driven from Naupactus. Some went to Rhegium and Sicily, but many went to Libya. At the Battle of Leuctra (371 B.C.), the image of Aristomenes appeared to aid the Thebans against the Spartans. Epaminondas, the Theban general who defeated the Spartans at Leuctra, dreamed that he was instructed to restore the Messenians to the Peloponnesus, and was told in his dream how to find the land he should give them. He sent a servant to the spot indicated to him in his dream; the servant dug there and found the casket hidden nearly three centuries earlier by Aristomenes. The secret contents

which Aristomenes had hidden were the mysteries that had originally been brought to Messenia by Caucon in the misty past. Epaminondas recalled the Messenians and restored them to Ithome, where the casket was found. He helped them to lay out (369 B.C.) a new city, Messene, one side of which was formed by the old fortress of Ithome. The Messenians, who had been wandering for generations all over the Greek world, now returned home.

Messenia, Gulf of. [Also: **Gulf of Korone.**] Inlet of the Mediterranean, S and E of Messenia, Greece.

Messina, Strait of. [Italian, **Stretto** (or **Faro**) **di Messina**; Latin, **Fretum Siculum.**] Strait in the Mediterranean, separating Sicily from the mainland of Italy. Width in narrowest part, about two miles.

Mesta (mes'tä). See **Nestus.**

Mesthles (mes'thlēz). In Homeric legend (*Iliad*), a son of Talaemenes and the nymph of the lake of Gygaea. He was a leader of the Maeonians, allies of Troy.

Mestor (mes'tôr). In mythology, a son of Perseus and Andromeda. By Lysidice he was the father of Hippothoë.

Mestra (mes'tra). In classical mythology, a daughter of Erysichthon of Thessaly. Poseidon, who loved her, gave her the power to change her form at will. She was the wife of Autolycus. See **Erysichthon.**

Meta (mē'ta). In Roman antiquity, a conical column or post, or usually a group of three such posts, at each end of the race course of a circus, marking the place where the chariot racers turned.

Metabus (met'a-bus). In Roman legend, the father of Camilla, who became the ally of Turnus in the war against Aeneas. He was a ruler in Privernum, but was expelled by his people for his tyrannical rule. He fled with his infant daughter Camilla, and on coming to the Amasenus River, hotly pursued by his former subjects, he fastened his daughter to his spear, vowed to dedicate her to Diana if he was successful, and hurled her across the flood. She reached the other side safely, Metabus swam across and retrieved her, and both escaped. He lived the rest of his life in the forests, gave Camilla to be nursed by a brood mare, and as she grew up taught her the arts and skill of hunting and horsemanship.

Metageitnion (met-a-gīt'ni-on). The second month of the Attic year, having 29 days, and corresponding to the last part of July and the first part of August.

Metamorphoses (met″a-môr-fō'sēz). Poetical work by Ovid, in 15 books. The work is a collection of some 250 stories taken from Greek mythology, Roman and Latin folk tales, legends and myths, and including also some tales from the East. The unifying element in the collection is that all of the stories have to do with transformations: for an infinite variety of causes, gods, men, and animals are transformed in an infinite variety of ways. Written in hexameters, each story leads smoothly to the next one to make the work a whole rather than a collection of separate, unconnected tales. Besides being a literary production of interest, charm, and artistry the *Metamorphoses* is a treasury of myth and legend, gleaned by Ovid from the works of ancient poets and other writers and transformed by him into a literary masterpiece of immortal interest. His work has been an undiminished source of inspiration and influence for western European literature.

Metamorphoses. See **Golden Ass, The.**

Metanira (met-a-nī'ra). In Greek legend, the wife of Celeus, king of Eleusis, and the mother of Abas, Demophoön, and Triptolemus. She and her family sheltered Demeter when she was searching for Persephone. See **Demophoön** and **Triptolemus.**

Metaphysics (met-a-fiz'iks). Celebrated work by Aristotle. It consists of 13 books, more or less disconnected and imperfect, dealing with the doctrines of his predecessors and with various metaphysical topics.

Metapontum (met-a-pon'tum). [Also: **Metapontium.**] In ancient geography, a city in S Italy, situated on the Gulf of Tarentum, about 25 miles SW of Tarentum. It was founded by Achaeans from the mainland of Greece at an early date. The city became an important manufacturing and shipping center, and enjoyed great prosperity. Two archaic peripteral Doric temples are known at Metapontum: one, of about 520 B.C., attributed to Apollo and now known as the Chiesa di Sansone; the other, of about 500 B.C., of which 15 columns still stand, is now called the Tavole Paladine. In addition, Pliny mentions a temple of Hera notable for having wooden columns. Archaeologists have reported a theater, tombs, and traces of fortification walls. The religious philosopher Pythagoras, forced out of Croton where he had founded his famous brotherhood, took refuge at Metapontum, where he died. The order was later revived at Metapontum, but in the late 4th century B.C. it became finally extinct. (JJ)

Metaurus (me-tôr'us). [Modern name, **Metauro.**] Small river in Italy, which flows into the Adriatic about 28 miles NW of Ancona. The battle of the Metaurus was a victory gained at the river, S of Ariminum (Rimini), in 207 B.C., by the Romans under the consuls Marcus Livius Salinator and Claudius Nero over the Carthaginians under Hasdrubal. Nero had eluded Hannibal in S Italy, and made a forced march of 250 miles with 7000 men. Hasdrubal was slain, and his army nearly annihilated. Hannibal was thus left in a hopeless position, unable to get reserves, in S Italy. This victory is ranked as one of the decisive battles of the world.

Metellus (mē-tel'us), **Lucius Caecilius.** Roman general; died c221 B.C. As proconsul he defeated the Carthaginians at Panormus in 250 B.C.

Metellus, Quintus Caecilius. [Surnamed **Macedonicus,** meaning "the Macedonian."] Roman general; died 115 B.C. As praetor he was distinguished for his victories in Macedonia and Greece (148–146 B.C.). He was consul in 143, and censor in 131 B.C.

Metellus, Quintus Caecilius. [Surnamed **Numidicus,** meaning "the Numidian."] Roman general; died c91 B.C. He was a nephew of Metellus Macedonicus. As consul and proconsul he defeated Jugurtha in Numidia in 109 and 108 B.C. He was exiled (c100 B.C.) by his political opponents.

Metellus, Quintus Caecilius. [Surnamed **Pius.**] Roman general; died c64 B.C. He was a son of Metellus Numidicus. He was commander under Sulla in the civil wars, was consul in 80 B.C., and commanded later in Spain against Sertorius.

Metellus, Quintus Caecilius. [Surnamed **Creticus,** meaning "the Cretan."] Roman general; died probably c56 B.C. He was consul in 69 B.C., and subdued Crete (68–66 B.C.).

Metellus Celer (sē'lẽr), **Quintus Caecilius.** Roman statesman; died 59 B.C. He was praetor in 63 B.C., opposed the conspiracy of Catiline, and was consul in 60 B.C.

Metellus Nepos (nē'pos), **Quintus Caecilius.** Roman stateman; died c55 B.C. He was a partisan of Pompey. He was tribune in 62 and consul in 57 B.C.

Metellus Pius Scipio (pī'us sip'i-ō), **Quintus Caecilius.** Roman statesman; committed suicide 46 B.C. He was the son of Scipio Nasica, and the adopted son of Metellus Pius. He was consul with Pompey in 52 B.C., and Pompeian commander in Syria and Egypt.

Meter (mē'tẽr). An epithet of Athena, meaning "Mother," given to the goddess by the women of Elis. After Heracles had sacked Elis and killed the men, he decided to repopulate the city, and ordered the widows of the Eleans to lie with his own soldiers. The Elean women prayed to Athena that they might conceive sons at their first embrace with the soldiers of Heracles. Athena answered their prayer and gave them sons, and in gratitude the Eleans raised a sanctuary of Athena the Mother.

Methone (meth-ō'nē). In ancient geography, a town in Messenia on the coast of the Ionian Sea. Some say it was named Methone for a daughter of Oeneus, son of Porthaon, who took refuge with Diomedes after the fall of Troy. Others say the name comes from the underwater rock reef which protects the harbor of the town. Diomedes dedicated an image to the winds in the temple at Methone, because his prayer for the cessation of harassing winds that were harming the city was answered. This was the same town that was formerly known as Pedasus, and was one of the seven gift cities offered by Agamemnon to Achilles during the Trojan War, if he would give up his quarrel with Agamemnon and return to battle to help his fellow Greeks against the Trojans. In the Peloponnesian Wars the city was besieged by the Athenians (431 B.C.), but it was saved by the arrival of a Spartan force under Brasidas. When Epaminondas restored Messenia after 371 B.C., the city was given to Nauplians.

Methone or **Methana** (mē-thā'na). In ancient geography, a peninsula of the Peloponnesus, between Troezen and Epidaurus. It was captured and garrisoned by the Athenian general Nicias, 425 B.C., and served as a base from which the Athenians raided Spartan territory.

Methone. In ancient geography, a city of Macedonia, situated near the mouth of the Haliacmon River, on the W side of the Thermaic Gulf. It was called Pierian Methone, from the Pierian forest where the Muses were said to dwell. Some say it was founded by Methon, a son of Orpheus. It was colonized by Euboeans. In the Peloponnesian Wars it was loyal to Athens, and later served, at various times, as a base of operations against the Macedonians.

Methone. In ancient geography, a town of Thessaly, near the Gulf of Pagasae. It was said that men of Methone went to the Trojan War under the leadership of Philoctetes. The ruins of an ancient acropolis are to be found here.

Methydrium (mẹ-thid'ri-um). In ancient geography, a city in E Arcadia, Greece. According to tradition, it was founded by Orchomenus, the son of Lycaon. Its name, which means "Between the Waters," was given it because it is on a high knoll between two rivers. The people of Methydrium claimed that it was on a mountain nearby, Mount Thaumasius (*Wonderful*), that Rhea deceived Cronus by giving him a stone to swallow after the birth of Zeus. On the summit of the mountain was Rhea's cave, into which only women sacred to the goddess could enter. Methydrium was also noted for its temple of Poseidon Hippius. Methydrium was abandoned some time after 371 B.C. when its inhabitants went to dwell in the new city of Megalopolis.

Methymna (mẹ-thim'na). In ancient geography, a city in Lesbos.

Metioche (mẹ-tī'ō-kē). In Greek legend, a daughter of Orion. She was the sister of Menippe, and with her sister offered herself as a sacrifice to dispel a plague from Boeotia.

Metion (mē'ti-on). In Greek mythology, a son of Erechtheus, king of Athens, and Praxithea. After the death of Erechtheus his sons quarreled over the succession. Metion threatened to kill his brother Cecrops, who had been awarded the throne. Metion died, but his sons expelled Pandion, son of Cecrops, from Athens.

Metis (mē′tis). In Greek mythology, a Titaness, the daughter of Oceanus and Tethys. She was the first wife of Zeus. It was she who advised Zeus to mix mustard and salt into the honeyed drink of Cronus in order to make the latter regurgitate the brothers and sisters of Zeus whom Cronus had swallowed as soon as they were born. When Metis became pregnant, Zeus learned from an oracle that her first child would be a girl, and that if she bore a second child, it would be a boy who would dethrone his father. Zeus thereupon swallowed Metis. Some time later he was passing near Lake Triton and was assailed by a frightful headache. Prometheus, or possibly Hephaestus, split his skull with an ax and out leaped fully-armed Athena, the daughter of Zeus and Metis. Metis is also known as the personification of Prudence and Insight, and Zeus claimed that she often gave him advice from within him.

Metiscus (me̱-tis′kus). In Roman legend, the charioteer of the Rutulian chief, Turnus. Juturna, the sister of Turnus, assumed the guise of Metiscus and took his place in the chariot in order to drive Turnus away from the fighting and save his life.

Meton (mē′ton). Athenian astronomer of the 5th century B.C. He attacked the problem of devising a calendar which would reconcile the incommensurate periods of the sun (year) and moon (month), and announced the discovery of the *enneadecateris*. This was a lunisolar calendar of 235 months or 19 years, of which 12 years had 12 lunar months each and seven years had 13 lunar months each. At the end of each 19-year cycle sun and moon returned to their apparent starting-points with a variation of about two hours. For this he was acclaimed; but there is no evidence that the enneadecateris was adopted at Athens before 338 B.C. Students of the astronomical achievement of Babylonia, where records of continuous observations at least from the 8th century B.C. were available for study, have shown that the 19-year correlation was known there early in the 5th century B.C., suggesting that instead of making an independent discovery, Meton may have constructed his cycle on data already well known to Babylonian astronomers. The

enneadecateris was officially adopted by the Hellenistic dynasty of the Seleucids in western Asia, who dated their era from 312–311 B.C., and it became the model for the Persian, Chinese, and Jewish calendars, and the method by which the date of Easter is calculated in advance. In recognition of his association with it, the enneadecateris is sometimes called the Metonic Cycle. (JJ)

Metope (met′ō̱-pē). In Greek mythology, a Stymphalian nymph, a daughter of the river-god Ladon. She was the wife of the river-god Asopus, and bore him two sons and a number of daughters, among them Aegina and Thebe.

Metope. In architecture, a slab inserted between two triglyphs of the Doric frieze, sometimes, especially in late work, cut in the same block with one or more triglyphs. It was so called (*metope*, "opening," "window") because in the primitive Doric architecture in wood, of which the later triglyphs represent the ends of the ceiling-beams, the metopes were left open as windows, and were thus literally apertures between the beams. The metopes were often ornamented with paintings or with sculptures in high relief, but they were more usually left plain.

Metroum (me̱-trō′um). A sanctuary of the Mother of the Gods (Rhea). The most celebrated was that of Athens, which stood at the foot of the hill known as Colonus Agoraeus, on the west side of the market-place or Agora. The story is that one of the begging priests of Rhea came to Athens and initiated the women into the rites of the Mother of the Gods. The Athenians did not understand the rites, and killed the priest by casting him into a pit. At once plague broke out in Athens. The oracle told the Athenians to propitiate the murdered priest. To do so they built a shrine on the site of the murder and dedicated it to the Mother of the Gods. In the shrine they dedicated a statue of the begging priest. It was a rule of this sacred precinct that no one could enter it after eating garlic. Festivals called *Galaxia,* at which a mixture of barley and milk was eaten, were held here in honor of the Mother of the Gods. In the Metroum was the large jar in which Diogenes was supposed to have lived. The Metroum was the official depository of the state archives, including such documents as a copy of the accusation against Socrates, the plays of Aeschylus, Sophocles, and Euripides, and the will of the philosopher Epicurus. The excavations in the Agora by the American School of Classical Studies at Athens have revealed the foundations of an early temple, which was destroyed by the Persians in 480 B.C. and not rebuilt, and an altar. On this site was later built a group of buildings known as the Metroum-Bouleuterium complex, a combination of cult-place for the worship of the Mother of the Gods, the state archives, and the *Bouleuterium,* or council-house of the Five Hundred. Somewhere in this complex stood a famous cult statue, attributed variously to Phidias or Agoracritus. (JJ)

Mettus (met′us) or **Metius** (mē′shus), **Fuffetius.** An Alban general who was put to death for treachery by Tullus Hostilius (legendary third king of Rome, 672–640 B.C.). The scene of his death was prophetically depicted on the shield that Vulcan made for Aeneas when he fought against the Latins in Italy. According to the *Aeneid,* he was torn to pieces by horses.

Mezentius (me̯-zen′shus). In Roman legend, a king of Caere or Agylla in Etruria. He was noted for his cruelty, one of his practices being to bind live men to corpses, face to face, so that they died a lingering death. His people revolted against his oppressive rule and he fled with his son Lausus to Turnus, the Rutulian, and joined him in the war against Aeneas. The Etrurian subjects of Mezentius, angered with Turnus for receiving him, joined the war on the side of Aeneas. Mezentius fought bravely and killed many of the enemy. He came face to face with Aeneas and was wounded by him, but was saved by the intervention of Lausus who took the death blow intended for his father and perished. In a frenzy of grief over the loss of his son Mezentius mounted a horse and again sought Aeneas. Finding Aeneas, Mezentius told him that he had indeed destroyed him by slaying his son. Aeneas wounded his horse and Mezentius, already wounded, fell. He refused to ask for mercy, since, he said, he had never thought it a crime to kill when he made war. Aeneas put him to the sword.

Micipsa (mi-sip′sa̯). Son of Masinissa; died

118 B.C. He was the chief ruler of Numidia after Masinissa's death in 149 B.C.

Micon of Athens (mī′kon; ath′enz). Greek painter and sculptor, active in the first half of the 5th century B.C. He was a contemporary of Polygnotus, with whom he worked in the Painted Portico (*Stoa Poikile*) at Athens. In the Painted Portico he painted the *Battle of Theseus and the Amazons.* In the picture of *The Battle of Marathon* in the Painted Portico, on which he also worked, were portraits of Callimachus, Miltiades, and possibly Aeschylus. On the walls of the Theseum he painted the story of Theseus proving to Minos that he was a son of Poseidon. When Theseus arrived in Crete with the tribute of young maidens and young men from Athens, Minos was attracted by one of the young girls and sought to seize her. Theseus rebuked him, claiming the right to do so as a son of Poseidon. Minos mocked him. He himself was a son of Zeus, he said, and called aloud to Zeus to give him a sign. There was an instant clap of thunder. Then Minos drew a ring from his finger and hurled it into the sea, telling Theseus that if he was indeed a son of Poseidon, he should leap into the sea and retrieve the ring. Theseus dived below the waters. Dolphins came to guide him and Nereids restored the ring. While under the sea he met Thetis, or as some say, Amphitrite, wife of Poseidon, who gave him a jeweled crown. With the ring and the crown he returned to Minos. He restored the ring to Minos and gave the crown to Ariadne as a bridal gift. Among other works by Micon was an incident from the voyage of Jason for the Golden Fleece that he painted in the temple of the Dioscuri at Athens, and a statue of the Athenian Callias, victor in Olympiad 77 (or 468 B.C.).

Micythus (mis′i-thus). Son of Choerus. He was a slave of Anaxilas, tyrant of Rhegium. When Anaxilas died (476 B.C.) he left Micythus the tyranny in trust for his children. Micythus managed it well, except for a war in which thousands of the citizens of Rhegium lost their lives, and when the children of Anaxilas grew up and demanded an accounting of his trust, the report he gave them was so satisfactory, according to some accounts, that they begged him to stay on as tyrant. But he refused and sailed off, accompanied by the good wishes of the common people. He went to Tegea in Arcadia, where he ultimately died. Micythus made many offerings at Olympia in fulfillment of a vow he had made for the recovery of his son, who was ill of a wasting disease. His son recovered and Micythus carried out his vow. On one of the offerings set up was inscribed his gratitude and his vow.

Midas (mī'dạs). In Greek mythology, a Phrygian king, the son of Cybele and a satyr. Some say he was the son of Gordius, who became king of Phrygia, but others say he was adopted by Gordius who was childless, and succeeded him as king. Midas had famous rose gardens in which, it was said, the sweetest roses in the world grew of themselves. When Dionysus passed through his lands, Silenus, who was in his train, fell behind and was captured by peasants. They took him to King Midas. Silenus amused the king by telling him fantastic tales of the strange lands he had visited with Dionysus. Midas treated him kindly and after some days restored him to Dionysus. The god was grateful to Midas and offered to grant him the 'fulfillment of any wish he might make. Midas asked that whatever he touched might be turned to gold. Dionysus granted his wish, although he thought it an unworthy one, and Midas at once tested it. He touched the pillars of his palace, the grain in his fields, the very earth itself: all were instantly turned to gold. Midas was delighted. However, when he was hungry and would eat, or thirsty and would drink, whatever he put into his mouth was also turned to gold. Deeply regretting his greedy wish, he prayed to Dionysus, acknowledging that he had done wrong to ask such a gift and praying that it might be taken from him. Dionysus pitied him. He told Midas to go and bathe in the headwaters of the Pactolus River to free himself of his ruinous gift. Midas obeyed his instructions. His miraculous powers were washed off in the river, whose waters and sands ever after bore grains of gold. Midas promoted the worship of Dionysus and founded the city of Ancyra. He also sent gifts to the shrine of Delphi, the first foreigner to do so, and dedicated his throne there, where it remained a thing worthy to see for a long time. But now Midas made another stupid mistake.

Apollo and Pan engaged in a musical contest with Tmolus as judge. Tmolus awarded the prize to Apollo, but Midas disagreed with the award and maintained that Pan was the winner. For having ears so unfitted to judge the god's music, Apollo caused long ass-ears to grow from the head of Midas. In deep humiliation he concealed them under a cap, but he was unable to conceal them from his barber. Midas warned the barber, on pain of death, not to reveal his secret. The barber was tormented because he could not tell his strange news to a soul. Unable to keep it to himself any longer, he went to the bank of the driver, dug a deep hole there, and whispered into it, "King Midas has ass's ears." Then he filled in the hole and went away relieved. But reeds growing on the spot whispered the secret and soon it was known throughout the land. When Midas realized that his disgrace was common knowledge, he ordered the barber to be killed and then drank bull's blood, and so died himself.

Midea (mid'e-ạ). In Greek legend, a woman of Phrygia. She was the mother of Licymnius by Electryon. Licymnius was married to Perimede, sister of Creon, king of Thebes.

Midea. In ancient geography, a city in C Argolis. This area of Argolis was ruled by Proetus, brother of Acrisius, and passed to his son, Megapenthes. When Perseus, cousin of Megapenthes, accidentally killed his grandfather Acrisius, he did not want to return to Argos. He exchanged his kingdom with Megapenthes and so became ruler of Midea, Tiryns, and Mycenae, which he founded. Electryon, son of Perseus, succeeded him as ruler, and when he in his turn was accidentally slain by Amphitryon, Sthenelus, father of Eurystheus, seized the kingdom. He kept Mycenae and Tiryns for himself, but gave the rest of the country, with Midea as its capital, to Atreus and Thyestes, the sons of Pelops. By the time Pausanias passed this way in the 2nd century A.D., Midea lay in ruins.

Migonitis (mī-gō-nī'tis). An epithet of Aphrodite in her aspect as goddess of love, meaning "Uniter." Paris raised a sanctuary to Aphrodite Migonitis on the Greek mainland opposite the island of Cranaë, because on the island he first embraced Helen after he had carried her away from Menelaus in Sparta.

Mikonos (mik′ō-nos, mī′kọ-nos; Greek, mē′kô-nôs). See **Myconus**.

Milan (mi-lan′). See **Mediolanum**.

Milazzo (mē-lät′tsō). See **Mylae**.

Milesians (mī-lē′zhạnz). Inhabitants of Miletus (q.v.).

Milesian Tales (mī-lē′zhạn). Short stories, usually witty and frequently erotic if not obscene, greatly in vogue among the Greeks and Romans. Aristides of Miletus (fl. c100 B.C.) wrote or more likely compiled, in Greek, a work now lost, the *Milesiaca*, a collection of such short stories. In the 1st century B.C. the Roman historian Cornelius Sisenna published a Latin translation, which as the *Milesiae Fabulae* had wide popularity. They are mostly lost, but specimens survive in Petronius' *Satyricon* and Apuleius' *Metamorphoses* ("The Golden Ass."). The best is the merry tale of the Widow of Ephesus, in the *Satyricon*. They are the antecedents of Boccaccio's *Decameron* and a never-ending stream of such compositions. (JJ)

Miletus (mī-lē′tus). According to Greek tradition, a son of Apollo and Aria (Deione, according to Ovid), born in Crete. Minos, Rhadamanthys, and Sarpedon, the sons of Europa, quarreled for the love of Miletus. The beautiful youth preferred Sarpedon. Minos went to war against them and Miletus fled with many followers to Caria in Asia Minor. There he killed thè giant, Asterius, who had been ruling the land, and whose bones, when they were disinterred, measured ten cubits in length. Miletus founded the city and kingdom of Miletus and married Cyaneë, daughter of the river-god of the Maeander. She bore him the twins Byblis and Caunus.

Miletus. In ancient geography, a city in Caria, SW Asia Minor, situated on the coast opposite the mouth of the Maeander River. It was the principal settlement of the 12 Ionian cities in Asia. According to tradition, it was taken by Miletus, son of Apollo and Aria, who fled to Caria from Crete with a large fleet. There he found a city ruled by Asterius, son of the giant Anax, and inhabited by a people called Anactorians. Miletus overcame the natives, killed Asterius and buried him on the island of Lade. He seized the city and named it after himself. In later times, Neleus, son of Codrus the legendary king of Athens, is said to have led a colonizing expedition of Ionians from Attica and, having landed at Miletus, his companions mixed with the inhabitants and brought their own culture to the region. Some say Neleus and his followers destroyed the old city and built a new one.

Historically, Miletus is thought to have been founded about the 12th century B.C. by Ionian Greeks. The city was attacked by the Lydian kings from the time of Gyges (c685–c653 B.C.) to the time of his great-grandson Alyattes (c617–560 B.C.). Alyattes attacked Milesia (the walled city and its surrounding territory) year after year at the time of the harvest. He marched his forces to the piping of flutes and the strumming of harps through the countryside and burned the standing grain, but did not destroy the houses as he wanted the owners to return and plant new crops that he could again plunder. He harried Miletus in this way because he could not take the city by direct attack, since it was strongly walled and commanded the sea, and he thought by this means to force it into submission. In all this time, only Chios of the Ionian cities sent any aid to Miletus. In the sixth year of Alyattes' war (Lydians had been carrying on the war more or less regularly for 12 consecutive years), when the Lydians set fire to the grain, a violent wind carried the flames to the temple of Athena Assesia and burned it to the ground. Afterward, Alyattes fell into a lingering sickness, and on inquiry at Delphi was told that no answer would be forthcoming until he rebuilt the temple of Athena Assesia. Alyattes sent a herald to Miletus to ask for a truce, that he might have time to build the temple. At this time Thrasybulus, the most famous of the Ionian tyrants, was tyrant of Miletus. Under his rule Miletus flourished brilliantly and planted Milesian colonies on the Euxine Sea. Thrasybulus had been informed of the oracle and was expecting that Alyattes would ask for a truce. He arranged for all the meager supply of grain in the area to be brought to the market-place, and when the herald of Alyattes arrived, he found the Milesians feasting and making merry. The herald was astonished, and reported what he had seen to Alyattes. He too was astonished at the apparent prosperity of the Milesians after so many years of war and destruction of their crops, and decided it was not worthwhile to pursue his war against a people who flourished so in adversity. He ended the war and made an alliance of friendship with Miletus. He then built two temples of Athena at Assesus to make up for the one that had been burned, and recovered from his sickness. Thus, according to Herodotus, the ruse of Thrasybulus with the food was successful in ending the war.

During the reign of Croesus, son and successor of Alyattes, Miletus seems to have submitted to Lydian rule on favorable terms. When Croesus was conquered by Cyrus, Miletus alone of the Ionian cities was not subject to attack, because the Milesians, well aware of the weakness and divisions of Ionia, made an alliance with Persia on the same terms as the one they had with Lydia, rather than joining the weak league of Ionian cities in an attempt to resist. Miletus had reached a great peak of prosperity by the time Darius became king of Persia. Her goods were sent throughout the Greek world; Milesian coins bearing the figure of a lion turned up wherever trade was carried on; over 60 Milesian colonies had been founded, among them were Istria on the Adriatic, Sinope, Trapezus, Cyzicus, and many others on the Euxine Sea, and Abydos on the Hellespont. Milesian traders settled in Naucratis in Egypt, and built a temple of Apollo there. The oracle of Apollo at Branchidae in Milesian territory was famous. But Miletus had suffered much from internal disorders, and asked the Parians to compose the differences between the different factions in their country. The Parians, according to Herodotus, went through the land outside the city walls, noting down the names of the owners of any farms that were prosperous in the midst of the desolation caused by civil strife. When they had completed their survey, they proposed that those who had shown they could maintain their own property in the midst of disorder should be made the governors over the others.

In the time of Darius, Histiaeus was tyrant of Miletus. He had accompanied Darius to the Hellespont when the latter invaded Thrace, and he supported Darius because Darius maintained the tyrants. But later Darius called Histiaeus to his court at Susa and kept him there as his friend and counselor, so he said, and Histiaeus, anxious to return to Miletus but constrained to remain in Susa, became one of the inciters of the Ionian revolt against Persia. Under the guidance of his nephew and son-in-law, Aristagoras, who had succeeded him as tyrant of Miletus, the city played a leading part in the revolt (499 B.C.). The revolt was determined upon for the wrong reasons; it was badly planned and ineffectually carried out. The Persians gave it their full attention and put it down with determination. The Ionians were defeated in a sea battle at Lade by a Phoenician fleet sent against them by Persia. Then the attack was concentrated on Miletus. The city was besieged by sea and land, mines were driven under the walls, and the city was taken in 494 B.C., nearly six years after the revolt broke out. The fall of the city fulfilled an oracle that had been given by the priestess at Delphi:

Then shalt thou, Miletus, so oft the contriver of evil,
Be to many, thyself, a feast and an excellent booty.

For now the Persians killed most of the men, put the women and children into slavery, and plundered and burned the oracle and temple at Didyma (Branchidae). Herodotus, who tells of these things, fairly adds that the Milesians who were carried off to the court of Darius at Susa received no injury at his hands, but were settled by him in another part of his empire. Nor had Darius ordered the burning of Apollo's temple, and he rebuked the officer responsible because, he said, "Apollo had always told the truth to the Persians." The Athenians were grief-stricken over the capture of their daughter city Miletus, and showed their grief in their treatment of the poet Phrynichus. When his drama, *The Capture of Miletus*, was presented, it is said that the entire audience burst into tears. A law was passed that the drama should never be presented again to remind the Athenians of their loss, and Phrynichus was fined.

After the Persian defeat at Mycale in 479 B.C., the Persians withdrew from the coast and Miletus joined the Delian League, from which it revolted in 412 B.C. In 334 B.C. the city was captured by Alexander the

Great. Miletus was a flourishing trading city, a great colonizer, and a center of literature and philosophy. It was the birthplace of the philosophers Thales and Anaximander, and of the traveler Hecataeus, and the courtesan Aspasia.

Milo (mī′lō) or **Milon** (mī′lon). Greek athlete, famous for his strength, born at Croton, Magna Graecia, Italy, and active in the last part of the 6th century B.C. He was six times victor in wrestling at the Olympic Games and six times at the Pythian, and many stories were told of his extraordinary feats of strength, of which the best-known is his carrying a heifer, four years old, on his shoulders through the stadium at Olympia, then slaying it with his fist and eating the whole of it in a day. He is said to have been devoured by wolves which attacked him while his hands were caught in a cleft tree which he had endeavored to rend.

Milo, Titus Annius Papianus. Roman partisan leader, a rival of Clodius; killed in Lucania, Italy, 48 B.C. The gangs of toughs hired by the two rivals kept Rome in constant uproar during the struggle between Pompey and the conservative group on the one hand, and the democratic party on the other. Milo, an adherent of Pompey, was tribune of the plebs in 57 B.C. and had Cicero recalled from exile. The struggle came to a climax in 52 B.C., when Milo and Clodius met by chance at Bovillae; Milo's band, at his orders, set upon Clodius' and Clodius was killed. Feeling ran high and Milo, after a trial, was exiled to Massilia. Cicero's speech in his behalf was not delivered for fear of violence; the oration (*Pro Milone*) which we possess is an expanded version published after the trial. Milo joined with Marcus Caelius Rufus in a revolt (48 B.C.) against Caesar and was killed. He was married to Sulla's daughter Fausta.

Milo (mē′lō). Italian name of **Melos**.

Miltiades (mil-tī′a̤-dēz). Son of Cypselus, lived 6th century B.C. He governed the cities of the Chersonese (Gallipoli Peninsula), which came into his possession, according to Herodotus, in the following manner: The Dolonci, a Thracian tribe of the Chersonese, sent envoys to Delphi to inquire of the oracle how they could settle a war they were waging against their northern neighbors. The priestess told them to take back to the Chersonese with them the first man to offer them hospitality after they left the temple. The envoys journeyed all the way from Delphi to Athens without being offered hospitality, but when they passed the house of Miltiades, he noticed their strange dress and the lances they carried and called them into his house for refreshment and lodging. After they had eaten, the Dolonci told Miltiades of the oracle and urged him to accompany them to the Chersonese. This was during the reign of the tyrant Pisistratus in Athens, and Miltiades, his political enemy, chafed under his government. He agreed to accompany the Dolonci and took with him many Athenians as colonists. Arrived in the Chersonese, Miltiades became as autocratic a ruler, over the Dolonci and the Athenians who had come with him, as Pisistratus was over the Athenians in Athens. He built a wall across the narrow neck of the Chersonese to safeguard it from attacks. Next he crossed the Hellespont (Dardanelles) and attacked Lampsacus. In the engagement he was taken prisoner, but when Croesus, king of Lydia, an admirer of Miltiades, heard of this he threatened to cut down the Lampsacenes "like a fir" unless they released Miltiades. The Lampsacenes learned from one of their wise men that the particular reference to the "fir" was made because the fir of all trees is the only one that does not put forth new shoots when it is cut down, but dies completely. They immediately freed Miltiades. After his death the people of the Chersonese made sacrifices to Miltiades as the founder of their country, and established games in his honor, in which Lampsacenes were forbidden to take part.

Miltiades. Athenian general, c550–489 B.C. He was the son of Cimon and the nephew of Miltiades, son of Cypselus, whom he ultimately succeeded as ruler of the Chersonese (c524 B.C.). When he arrived in the Chersonese to take up the government, he confined himself in his house on the pretext of mourning his brother, his immediate predecessor. According to Herodotus, the leading men of the area came to his house to offer him comfort. Miltiades had them all cast into prison, although they had shown no enmity to him, and made himself tyrant. He married

Hegesipyle, daughter of Olorus, king of Thrace. When Darius I, king of Persia, subdued Thrace and then marched into Scythia (c516–513 B.C.), Miltiades commanded the Chersonesites at the Ister (Danube) against the Scythians. Darius crossed into Scythia by means of a bridge he caused to be built over the Ister. He left Ionians to guard the bridge against his return. The Scythians circled around the forces of Darius and reached the bridge before him as he retreated from their country. The Scythians urged the Ionians to destroy the bridge and prevent Darius from using it on his return. According to Herodotus, Miltiades also advised the destruction of the bridge but was outvoted by Ionian tyrants loyal to Darius. Thus he became an enemy of the Persian king. That this story is of doubtful validity is shown by the fact that Miltiades was not disturbed subsequently by Darius. He went back to the Chersonese at the request of the Dolonci. During the Ionian revolt against Persia that broke out in 499 B.C., Miltiades seized the islands of Lemnos and Imbrus. As the forces of Darius drew nearer to the island of Tenedos, Miltiades fled to Athens (493 B.C.). On his arrival there he was accused of tyranny, but was acquitted by his fellow citizens because his conquest of Lemnos and Imbrus brought them under Athenian dominion. Darius resolved to punish Athens and Eretria for their part in the Ionian revolt and sent Artaphernes and Datis at the head of an expedition to attack them. The Persians took Eretria, enslaved the population, and burned the temples. They then pushed on toward Athens. Led by Hippias, exiled tyrant of Athens, they landed at Marathon. Before the threat of the Persian attack Miltiades was made one of the ten generals to direct the defense. He was a bitter enemy of Hippias; he was the best acquainted of all the Athenians with Persian methods of warfare, and he became the guiding spirit of the resistance at Marathon. According to the traditional account, the ten generals were equally divided on the question of resisting the Persians at Marathon. Miltiades, hot for the attack, persuaded the polemarch Callimachus who had the power (at this time in Athenian history) to supervise military matters and to cast a vote with the generals. According

to Herodotus, Miltiades told Callimachus that by his vote he could make his country free or could enslave it. Callimachus voted to attack. The Persians, planning an amphibious invasion of Athens, embarked part of their army on ships and the remainder began to march on Athens. On the plain of Marathon they were met by the Greeks, led into a trap by the apparent collapse of the Greek center, and slaughtered by the more heavily-armed though outnumbered Greeks. Miltiades then turned quickly and marched back to Athens to face the threatened landing from the Persian ships, but the Persians, rather than land, drew off and gave up their expedition. After this great and decisive victory Miltiades was held in the highest esteem by the Athenians. He was given command of a fleet of 70 Athenian ships, with which he attacked, for reasons now uncertain, the island of Paros. The Parians withdrew into their city and submitted to siege. According to their account as given by Herodotus, Miltiades, unable to overcome them, received a Parian priestess, Timo, who suggested to him if he wished to take the city he must do certain things in the sacred precinct of Demeter which lay outside the walls of the city. He acted on her advice, went to the precinct, leaped over the wall, and proceeded to the sanctuary. There, according to Herodotus, he was overcome with horror at what he was about to do (Herodotus does not know what it was), and turned back, but on leaping again from the wall he injured his leg. Because of his injury and the stubbornness with which the Parians resisted, he was forced to withdraw from Paros after a siege of 26 days without adding anything to the wealth or power of Athens. On his return to Athens he was charged with having deceived the Athenians concerning the use of the 70 ships they had granted him. His life was spared because of his former contributions to Athens, but he was fined 50 talents. His wound had turned gangrenous so that he could not defend himself, and he died of it before the fine could be paid, but this was ultimately done by his son Cimon. The Parians, when they learned of Timo's treachery, asked the oracle if she should not be put to death. They were told by the oracle to spare her, as it had been decreed that Miltiades would come to an unhappy end and Timo had been merely the instrument that lured him to his destruction.

Milvian Bridge (mil′vi-an). [Also: **Mulvian Bridge**; Italian, **Ponte Milvio**; Latin, **Pons Milvius** or **Mulvius**.] Ancient bridge across the Tiber River N of Rome, built, to replace an earlier wooden structure, by Aemilius Scaurus in 109 B.C., at the crossing of the river by the Via Flaminia. It was the site of the victory of Constantine over Maxentius (312 A.D.) and of the vision of Constantine of a cross in the sky, which led him to embrace Christianity. The bridge was reconstructed in the 13th century, and was again repaired in the 19th century. Of the four original main arches, two survive, and the bridge continues in use for heavy traffic.

Milyas (mil′i-as). In ancient geography, a region in SW Asia Minor, of uncertain extent, usually including parts of Lycia and Pisidia.

Mimas (mī′mas). In Greek mythology, one of the Giants, a son of Gaea and the blood of Uranus, who waged war on the gods. In the battle he was burned by a ladle of molten metal flung at him by Hephaestus and was killed by Heracles.

Mimas. In Roman legend, a son of the Trojan Theano, born on the same night as Paris. He was a follower of Aeneas and fled with him from Troy. In the war that the Latins waged on Aeneas and his Trojans when they arrived in Italy, Mimas was slain by Mezentius.

Mimnermus (mim-nėr′mus). Greek elegiac poet, of Colophon. He was an older contemporary of Solon and was active c630–600 B.C. He was a master and creator of the romantic or erotic elegy, and was chiefly celebrated for his work *Nanno,* of which fragments only remain. In this collection of poems, named for a beautiful flute-player who did not return his love because he was so old, he evokes past lovers, urges youth to enjoy love while they can, and laments the passing of time that brings a chill to love. Fragments of rich and spirited war poems also remain. Because of the great romantic beauty of his language the ancients called him "the sweet singer," and his influence on later erotic elegists was great.

Mincius (min′shi-us). [Italian, **Mincio**.] River in N Italy, a tributary of the Padus (Po),

which it joins about 11 miles SE of Mantua.

Minerva (mi-nėr′va). In Roman mythology, one of the three chief divinities, the other two being Jupiter and Juno. The chief seat of the cult of all three was the great temple on the Capitoline Hill. Minerva also had a sanctuary on the Aventine Hill, especially popular with artists and poets, and one on the Caelian Hill. Minerva was originally an ancient Italian goddess adopted from the Etruscans by the Romans. She was the goddess of wisdom and inventiveness, the patroness of the arts of women, especially spinning and weaving, and a goddess of artisans, a more important patronage in Etruria than in Rome. She was also the goddess of artists, sculptors, actors, poets, physicians, teachers, and students. Her chief festival was the *Quinquatrus,* celebrated on March 19, the date of the founding of her temple, and lasting for five days. Sacrifices were offered, gladiatorial contests were held, and social gatherings were enjoyed by those under her patronage. In Roman myth, Minerva was the virgin daughter of Jupiter, the supreme god, and hence was identified, as the Romans came more and more under the influence of Hellenic culture, with the Greek Athena. Like Athena, Minerva was represented in art with a grave and majestic countenance, armed with helmet, shield, and spear, and wearing long full drapery, and on her breast the aegis.

Minos (mī′nos, -nos). In Greek mythology, a son of Europa and Zeus, born on the island of Crete. He was the brother of Rhadamanthys and Sarpedon. Asterius, king of Crete, married Europa and adopted her three sons as his heirs. When they grew up the brothers quarreled over the affections of Miletus, a son of Apollo and Aria and, when Miletus showed a preference for Sarpedon, Minos drove him out of the country and banished Sarpedon. Minos married Pasiphaë, daughter of Helius and Persa. She bore him Acacallis (Acalle), Ariadne, Androgeus, Catreus, Glaucus, and Phaedra, and, some say, Deucalion, the father of Idomeneus. Minos was also the father of sons by the nymph Paria and was, according to some accounts, the lover of Procris, wife of Cephalus. He pursued Britomartis and others. Upon the death of Asterius, Minos wished to become king of Crete. He declared that he had received the kingdom from the gods, and in proof of his special favor in their sight he claimed that whatever he prayed for would be accomplished. As he was sacrificing to Poseidon, he prayed that a bull might emerge from the sea, which he promised he would then sacrifice to Poseidon. Poseidon answered his prayer by sending a magnificent white bull from the sea. Minos was so enchanted with the handsome specimen that he put the bull among his own herds and sacrificed another in its place. He became king of Crete and established laws which it is said he received from Zeus, who met Minos in a cave and gave him the laws. But Poseidon punished Minos for his failure to fulfill his vow by sacrificing the bull which he had sent him from the sea. He caused Pasiphaë to conceive an unnatural passion for the bull. With the help of Daedalus, the marvelous smith who had fled to Crete and had been welcomed by Minos, she was able to gratify her passion, and ultimately bore Asterius, or Asterion, called the Minotaur, a monster with the head of a bull and the body of a man. Minos, to conceal this evidence of disgrace to himself and Pasiphaë, commanded Daedalus, on the advice of an oracle, to build the Labyrinth in which to hide the Minotaur. The bull escaped from the herds of Minos and ravaged the island until Heracles came and, as one of his labors, subdued the bull and rode on its back across the sea to Hellas. The bull was turned loose in Hellas. It ravaged the plains about Marathon and became known as the Marathonian Bull. Some say Androgeus, son of Minos, journeyed to Athens and took part in the Panathenea. He was victorious in all his contests and, out of jealousy, King Aegeus of Athens sent him to slay the bull. Androgeus was himself slain in the attempt. But others say that it was Theseus who slew the bull and that Aegeus caused Androgeus to be ambushed while he was on his way to Thebes, because Aegeus feared that Androgeus was conspiring in a revolt that was brewing against the rule of Aegeus. Androgeus bravely fought those who attacked him from ambush but was slain. Minos had by this time made himself master of the sea, the first ruler to do so, and when he learned of the death of Androgeus, he vowed vengeance on Athens. He won

the support of some of the island princes to his projected war against Athens. He bribed with gold the princess Arne of Siphnus to become his ally, and sought the help of Aeacus of Aegina, but Aeacus refused to aid him and allied himself to the Athenians. Minos attacked Nisa on the Isthmus of Corinth. Scylla, the daughter of King Nisus, saw Minos as she watched the battle from a tower, and fell in love with him. She resolved to betray her father and to help Minos. In fulfillment of this resolve she crept into her father's bed chamber at night and cut off a magic golden, or some say purple, lock of his hair. This lock of hair protected the life and kingdom of Nisus. Scylla gave it to Minos who willingly accepted it, and the city fell into his hands. But he scorned Scylla for betraying her father and refused to take her with him to Crete. He could not subdue Athens, and prayed to Zeus to avenge his son's death. His prayer was answered: all Hellas was shaken by earthquakes and afflicted by famine. An oracle instructed the leaders of the Greek states to request Aeacus, king of Aegina, to pray to their gods on their behalf. When this was done, the earthquakes ceased everywhere except in Attica. The Athenians now sought advice from the oracle at Delphi. They were informed that they must submit to whatever demands Minos might make if they wished to be spared further earthquakes. Minos demanded that they send a tribute of seven youths and seven maidens to Crete every nine years. The Athenians were compelled to submit; the youths and maidens were sent to Crete and there were devoured by the Minotaur. The third time the Athenian youths and maidens came to Crete, Theseus, son of King Aegeus, was one of their number. With the help of Ariadne, daughter of King Minos, he slew the Minotaur and escaped with Ariadne and his fellow Athenians. Minos, who had welcomed Daedalus the smith when he first came to Crete, and later employed him to build the Labyrinth, now discovered that Daedalus had helped Pasiphaë to indulge her passion for the bull. He imprisoned Daedalus and his son in the Labyrinth. Some say Pasiphaë freed them but they could find no ship to take them from the island, and others say Minos had simply forbidden Daedalus to leave Crete. He escaped with his son by means of wax wings which he constructed. He flew to Italy, having lost his son in the sea on the way, and went to the court of King Cocalus in Sicily. Minos resolved to secure his return. As he did not know where Daedalus had gone he resorted to a stratagem to find him. He procured a many-chambered shell and, taking it with him as he sailed about the Mediterranean, he offered a rich reward to the man who could pass a thread through it. When he landed in Sicily, he showed the shell to King Cocalus, who undertook to have the shell threaded as Minos desired. Cocalus gave the shell to Daedalus, who succeeded in threading the shell with the aid of an ant and some honey. When the threaded shell was returned to Minos, he knew he had found Daedalus, as no one else could have found such an ingenious solution. He demanded the surrender of Daedalus.

lowers and they buried him in a fine tomb in Camicus in Sicily. Later his bones were restored to Crete. Minos was the greatest ruler of his time, and was regarded as a friend of Zeus, who made him a judge in the Underworld. He divided the good from the bad and assigned the spirits to their final home in Tartarus. Cases that were too difficult for Rhadamanthys and Aeacus, the other judges of Tartarus, were turned over to Minos. Ruins of a palace at Cnossus (q.v.) in Crete, said to have been the palace of Minos and occupied in the first half of the second millennium B.C., were excavated by Sir Arthur Evans early in the 20th century, and a maze, distinct from the palace, has been found which may have been the Labyrinth of Daedalus. Archaeologists generally agree, however, that the Labyrinth was the Palace of Minos itself (*labyr-inthos*, "Place of the Double Ax," from *labrys*, "double-ax").

THESEUS SLAYING THE MINOTAUR
Black-figured Attic hydria, 6th century B.C. *Museum of Fine Arts, Boston*

Cocalus did not at once refuse. Instead he invited Minos to remain as a guest in his palace, and as Minos was resting in his bath the daughters of Cocalus, who did not want to lose Daedalus, poured boiling water or hot pitch on Minos and scalded him to death. Cocalus returned his body to his Cretan fol-

Minotaur (min'ō-tôr). Literally, "Minos-bull." The monstrous offspring of Queen Pasiphaë and the Cretan Bull. He had a human body and the head of a bull. He was confined in the Labyrinth at Cnossus and fed with human flesh; he devoured the seven youths and seven maidens whom Minos compelled the Atheni-

fat, fāte, fär, fâre, errạnt; net, mē, hėr ardẹnt; pin, pīne; not, nōte, möve, nôr, ans to send him periodically as a tribute. The Minotaur was killed by the son of Aegeus, the hero Theseus, with the assistance of Minos' daughter, the princess Ariadne, who thereupon eloped with Theseus. The Cretans claimed that there was no such animal, and that Pasiphaë had an intrigue with one Taurus, a general under Minos, and that one of her children rather too closely resembled Taurus. Another, and anthropologically very attractive, explanation is that for certain rituals, as in many other primitive contexts, the priest, or priest-king of Cnossus wore an animal-head mask, in this case a mask representing a bull, and that the story of the figure with a human body and bull's head may have reached the Greek mainland with a bronze-age traveler who had happened to observe such a ritual without fully understanding it. (JJ)

Minthe (min′thē) or **Menthe** (men′-). In Greek mythology, a nymph who was transformed into a mint plant by Persephone to prevent her from being seduced by Hades. Or, as others say, she was a nymph transformed by Hades into a mint plant to protect her from the jealousy of Persephone. In either case, she became a mint plant because she had aroused the interest of Hades. Mint was used in funeral rites, and the barley water which Demeter drank at Eleusis when she was searching for Persephone was flavored with mint.

Minturnae (min-tèr′nē). The Roman historian Livy mentions three *oppida* (cities) of the Aurunci or Ausones, an Italic people of Ausonia, on the border between Latium and Campania, which were captured by the Romans on the same day, he says, and by the same stratagem, in 314 B.C. These three *oppida* were Ausona, Vescia, and Minturnae or Menturnae. A Roman citizen colony was founded at Minturnae in 295 B.C. The site of Minturnae has never been lost; it lies in the Vescian Plain, on the right bank of the river Liris (the modern Garigliano) a mile from its mouth. Before excavation enough classical remains survived above ground (three temples, a theater, an amphitheater, an aqueduct, and, if anyone had looked for them, sections of the fortification wall) to suggest the size and importance of the ancient city. On the right bank of the Liris, near

its mouth, excavations by Mingazzini in the 1920's revealed the primitive temple of the obscure local Dea Marica (q.v.), now explained as the Goddess of the Marsh, with extensive deposits of votive offerings.

Excavations sponsored by the University of Pennsylvania Museum in 1931–1934 identified at the river's edge the colony of 295 B.C., in a *castrum* or fortified camp plan strikingly similar to the famous 4th century B.C. *castrum* of Ostia, but walled in polygonal limestone, much enlarged later in the 3rd century B.C. by an extension of the fortifications in ashlar tufa. The *decumanus*, the principal street and east-west axis of the colony, was the Via Appia, surveyed in 312 B.C. and thus anterior to the Roman settlement. In the enlarged city, a block fronting on the Via Appia became the forum, with a small temple of Jupiter and *tabernae* (shops or booths), which burned about 200 B.C. Following this fire the temple of Jupiter was replaced by a larger Capitolium, dedicated to the "Capitoline Triad," Jupiter, Juno, and Minerva, and to replace the *tabernae* a large three-winged porticus, or colonnade, was erected. In the time of the Gracchi Minturnae was the scene of a slave insurrection, ruthlessly crushed by the crucifixion of the leaders. The city is famous as the locale of one of the adventures of the dictator Caius Marius, who, fleeing from Sulla in 88 B.C., was trapped in the Minturnese marshes and imprisoned in the city, where he so awed his guards and the town fathers that they released him and provided safe transportation to Africa.

Destroyed in another fire, which according to the excavators occurred about 45 B.C., the forum buildings were rebuilt in the fashion of the Augustan period. In the block east of the forum, straddling the foundations of the by then dismantled colony wall, was built a temple of Julius Caesar, enclosed, like the Capitolium, within the wings of a three-winged porticus. In a trapezoidal area north of the forum, between the porticus and the city wall, a theater was erected, the back of whose scene was the wall of the porticus. At about the same time an aqueduct in reticulate masonry, still one of the striking sights of the countryside, was built to bring water from copious springs on the slopes of the

Montes Aurunci, about nine miles away to the north. A little later a new temple, dedicated probably to Augustus, or to Augustus and Livia, was squeezed into the forum, between the Capitolium and the east wing of the forum porticus; in the foundations of this temple were reused 29 altars from the *compitalia,* street-corner shrines which had been damaged in the fire of c45 B.C. These altars, inscribed with the names of more than 300 slaves and freedmen and the names of their patrons, are at once a directory of prominent families and a mine of information about the ethnography of Minturnae in the early 1st century B.C.

During the empire additional temples, baths, and an amphitheater were built, the forum expanded into the area south of the Via Appia, the city gates were embellished, water from the aqueduct was conducted in underground lead conduits to fountains throughout the city, and the familiar forests of statues and other dedications crowded the public areas. The country outside the walls was dotted with villas of the well-to-do, and a few hundred yards upstream the Liris was bridged with a single great masonry arch. Minturnae became Christian and had its own bishop, but before 590 A.D. the site was abandoned and the see was merged with that of Formia. The Liris bridge having fallen, ferry service was reëstablished and from this the deserted site received the name of Traetto, which passed also to the medieval town growing, thanks to stones removed from the ruined city, on a hilltop three miles inland. In the 19th century the name was changed to Minturno.

As for the other *oppida* of the Aurunci, Ausona and Vescia, they disappeared long ago. The modern hamlet of Ausonia, on the Via Ausonia, which crosses along the base of the Montes Aurunci from the Via Appia to the Via Latina, has no connection with ancient Ausona. Suessa, or Sessa Aurunca, a Latin colony on the slopes of the extinct volcano known as Roccamonfina, may stand on the approximate site of ancient Vescia, and perhaps reflects an alternate pronunciation of the ancient name. (JJ)

Minucius Rufus (mi-nū′shus rö′fus), **Marcus.** Roman commander; fl. last half of the 3rd century B.C. He was named *magister equi-* *tum* (master of the horse, or cavalry commander) under the dictatorship of Fabius Maximus Cunctator (217 B.C.). As did the Roman soldiers, citizens, and the Carthaginian enemy, he scorned the harrying tactics of Fabius against Hannibal, and urged an attack on him. In the absence of Fabius he engaged in a skirmish with a part of Hannibal's forces in disobedience of an order from Fabius, and won a victory which was greatly exaggerated in Rome. Fabius threatened to punish him but such was the joy in Rome over the success of Minucius that, in an unusual step, Minucius was named co-dictator with Fabius. The Roman army was divided between the two commanders. Minucius moved the troops in his command to a separate camp beyond a hill that separated him from Fabius. Hannibal, occupying the hill, lured Minucius into a battle, surrounded him and would have destroyed him if Fabius had not rushed to his rescue and driven off the Carthaginians. According to the accounts, Fabius uttered no word of recrimination against Minucius, but the latter publicly acknowledged his mistake, presented himself in Fabius' camp to thank him, and put himself once more under the command of Fabius. Minucius fell at the battle of Cannae (216 B.C.).

Minyades (min-ī′a-dēz) or **Minyae** (min′i-ē). In Greek legend, the daughters of Minyas, king of Orchomenus. They were Alcithoë, Leucippe, and Arsinoë (or Arsippe, or Aristippe). They scorned to take part in the wild revels of Dionysus, and sat quietly at home, spinning and performing their other household tasks. Dionysus appeared to them as a girl, and invited them to take part in the revels but they refused. He then appeared to them as a bull, a lion, and finally as a panther. He caused wine and milk to flow from their spindles, and followed this by causing their spindles to sprout and put forth ivy leaves. At length he drove them mad to punish them for their sacrilege, and they were overcome by an insatiable desire for human flesh. By lot, they chose Hippasus, the child of Leucippe, tore him to pieces and ate him. This is the basis for the assumption that in Orchomenus the human sacrifice was always chosen from the royal family. The murder of Hippasus was annually commem-

fat, fāte, fär, fãre, errant; net, mē, hėr ardent; pin, pīne; not, nōte, möve, nôr,

orated at Orchomenus by a feast of atonement and a ritual of seeking Dionysus. The
Minyadae, according to some accounts, were
transformed by Dionysus into bats. Others
say that Hermes changed them into birds.

Minyans (min'yanz) or **Minyae** (min'yē,
min'i-ē). In Greek tradition, a prehistoric
people, descendants of Minyas, who founded
Orchomenus in Boeotia, and there established his family. Another branch is found
at Iolcus in Thessaly and the Argonauts were
often called Minyans because they sought
to satisfy the ghost of Phrixus, grandson of
Minyas, by restoring the Golden Fleece to
Hellas. Furthermore, Jason was a descendant of Minyas through his mother, who was
the granddaughter of Minyas. One of the
early exploits of Heracles was the defeat of
the Minyans under their king Erginus.

Minyan Ware (min'yan). In the classification
of ceramics which, in the absence of written
records, is the principal basis of relative
chronology in the Greek bronze age, two
wheel-made wares widely associated with
the Middle Bronze (Middle Helladic) Period are spoken of, perhaps inaccurately, as
Minyan Ware. "Gray Minyan," the older of
the two, dates from Middle Helladic 1,
c1950–c1800 B.C. "Yellow Minyan" is associated with Middle Helladic 2, c1800–
c1600 B.C. When heated sufficiently, Gray
Minyan ware becomes yellow, suggesting
that the change in fashion resulted simply
from a technical improvement in the kiln
which made possible a higher firing, tem-
perature. The cultural break which was
once considered to close the Middle Helladic
Period is no longer accepted. Archaeologists
now consider that Middle Helladic 2 developed into the following period, Late Helladic
1 (Mycenaean 1), without a break, the
earliest phases of the so-called Mycenaean
pottery ware being essentially Yellow Minyan
ware to which decoration in color has been
added. The name Minyan was applied to
the gray ware by Heinrich Schliemann, who
first identified it in his excavations at
Boeotian Orchomenus, legendary seat of
King Minyas. (JJ)

Minyas (min'i-as). In Greek legend, a king
of Orchomenus in Boeotia. He had migrated
from Thessaly to Orchomenus and founded
the kingdom. He was famous for his great
wealth and was the first king ever to build
a treasury. His daughters were transformed
into bats for refusing to take part in the
worship and revels of Dionysus. See **Minyades.**

Minyeius (min-i-ē'i-us). In ancient geography,
a name given by Homer to the Anigrus River
in Elis. Its waters were said to cure certain skin diseases and other maladies. Fish
living in its evil-smelling waters were in-
edible. See **Anigrus.**

Misenum (mī-sē'num). [Modern name,
Miseno.] A promontory at the NW entrance
to the Bay of Naples, sheltering a small harbor also known as Misenum. In the period
of Greek activity it served as a port of
Cumae, but was presently eclipsed by
Puteoli, whose greater harbor area enabled
it to serve a vast and growing commercial
enterprise. Misenum became a fashionable
resort for well-to-do Romans, whose custom
it shared with Baiae, Puteoli, and Pausily-
pus Mons (modern Posilipo). In 31 B.C.
Agrippa established the headquarters of the
imperial fleet at Misenum, and it was from
here in 79 A.D. that Pliny the Elder, as
fleet admiral, sailed to his death in the
eruption of Vesuvius. (JJ)

Misenus (mī-sē'nus). In Roman legend, a son
of Aeolus. He was a herald and trumpeter
and had been a comrade of Hector in Troy.
With Aeneas, he fled from Troy when the
city was sacked by the Greeks at the end of
the Trojan War. At Cumae in Italy while
Aeneas was visiting the Sibyl, Misenus challenged the gods to a musical contest. To
punish him for his arrogance, Triton seized
him and drowned him. Meanwhile, Aeneas
was told by the Sibyl to find the body of a
comrade and bury it. He did not know at
the time that Sibyl referred to Misenus, but
learned of his death soon thereafter, found
his body and buried it. The fame of Misenus
is preserved in the headland of Campania
that is named for him, Cape Misenum.

Mistretta (mēs-trät'tä). See **Amestratus.**

Mithra (mith'ra) or **Mithras** (mith'ras). In ancient Persian belief, a god of light and truth,
and an ally of Ahura-Mazda in his struggle
against evil and darkness. The worship of
Mithra had a secret ritual which is imperfectly known at present. The sacrifice of a
bull and the application of bull's blood to

---

actọr; up, lūte, pu̇ll; oi, oil; ou, out; ᴛʜ, then; d̩ as d or j, ṣ as s or sh, ṭ as t or ch, ẓ as z or zh.

a candidate for initiation appear to be part of the ritual which was performed in artificial caves. The candidate underwent a number of ordeals, after which his forehead was marked. There were seven grades, each of which may have had its own initiation ceremony. The identification of Mithra with the sun is shown in various dedications. In Vedic mythology, he is Mitra, a sun-god and ruler of the day. The popularity of his cult in Asia may be shown by the frequent occurrence of the name *Mithridates*. His worship was introduced into Rome, chiefly by soldiers and Asiatic merchants. After Pompey had wrested Pontus in Asia Minor from the Persians, the worship of Mithra superseded the Dionysia, and was prevalent throughout the Roman Empire. In the 2nd century A.D. Mithraism was stronger than Christianity in the Roman Empire.

Mithridates or **Mithradates VI** (mith-ri-dā′tēz or mith-ra̩-dā′tēz). [Also: **Mithridates VI Eupator;** called **Mithridates the Great.**] King of Pontus (120–63 B.C.), born 132 B.C.; died 63 B.C. He succeeded his father at about the age of 11, but his mother made so many attempts to have him slain that he fled to the mountains and lived as a hunter until he felt strong enough to overcome his enemies. He became noted in antiquity for his courage, his strength, his skill in military arts, and for his swiftness of foot. He was a daring rider, skilled hunter, and tremendous eater, and had an enormous capacity for drinking. With these physical qualities was united a keen intelligence. He surrounded himself with Greek men of letters and awarded prizes to the greatest poets, as he did also to the best eaters. But it was an uneasy state to be among his friends, for he distrusted everyone and was ruthless to any who threatened or seemed to threaten him. In 111 B.C. he returned to Sinope and regained his throne by casting his mother into prison and putting his younger brother to death. Ultimately, he murdered his mother, his own sons, and the sister Laodice whom he had married, and once killed all the concubines in his harem to prevent their falling into the hands of his enemies. Having secured his power, he at once undertook a program of conquest. He subjugated the peoples on the eastern shore of the Euxine Sea, and conquered what is now the Crimea and southern Russia. He next attacked Paphlagonia, Cappadocia, and Bithynia, client states of Rome, which caused the interference of that power. He had seized the thrones of Bithynia and Cappadocia. Sulla, as propraetor of Cilicia, restored Ariobarzanes to the throne of Cappadocia . (92 B.C.) and Nicomedes III was restored to his throne in Bithynia. Mithridates prepared for war on Rome in consequence, and the First Mithridatic War broke out in 88 B.C. Mithridates rapidly made himself master of all the Roman possessions in Asia Minor, except Magnesia on the Maeander, and caused a general massacre of the Roman inhabitants, said to have numbered 80,000, or according to others, 150,000. He also instigated a rising of the European Greeks, to whose aid he sent a formidable land and naval force under his general Archelaus. Mithridates was now at the height of his power. His general controlled the sea, his sons were in Thrace and on the Bosporus, he himself had won large areas of Roman interest in Asia, and he sat in Pergamum, handing out provinces and principalities to his friends. There an omen of evil came to him. As he sat in the theater a Victory, bearing a crown in her hands, was being lowered over him so that the crown would be deposited on his head. As it was about to touch his head, the mechanism failed; the Victory fell and was smashed to pieces. The portent was followed by the defeat of Archelaus by Sulla at Chaeronea in 86 and at Orchomenus in 85 B.C. Sulla crossed the Hellespont to Asia. Mithridates was forced to sue for peace. He met Sulla at Dardanus in the Troad in 84 and was compelled to accept the peace the Roman general dictated. Mithridates surrendered his fleet, paid a heavy war indemnity, and restored all his conquests, retaining Pontus only. He did not honor all the terms of the peace, failing to evacuate Cappadocia completely, and the Second Mithridatic War broke out in 83. The propraetor Murena invaded Pontus, but was defeated and forced to withdraw. Peace was restored in 81 on the basis of the treaty of Dardanus. In 74 the Third Mithridatic War broke out, occasioned by an attempt on the part of Mithridates to take possession of Bithynia,

fat, fāte, fär, fãre, errạnt; net, mē, hér ardẹnt; pin, pīne; not, nōte, mȯve, nôr, which had been bequeathed to the Romans by his son-in-law Nicomedes III, late king of Bithynia. Mithridates defeated Marcus Aurelius Cotta at Chalcedon in 74 but was expelled from his own kingdom by Lucullus, and took refuge with his son-in-law Tigranes, king of Armenia. Lucullus defeated the latter at Tigranocerta in 69, but was unable to prevent Mithridates from reconquering Pontus and ravaging Bithynia and Cappadocia because his troops mutinied. Lucullus was superseded by Cnaeus Pompeius Magnus (Pompey the Great), who defeated Mithridates in 66 B.C. and compelled the surrender of Tigranes at Artaxata. Mithridates fled to Panticapaeum (modern Kerch in the Crimea), and was planning a new campaign when his troops revolted. He tried to commit suicide by poison. He had taken small doses of poison for years, however, and his body was immune to its action. He was compelled to order a mercenary soldier to kill him. His body was sent to Pompey, who caused it to be buried in the royal tomb at Sinope.

Mithridatic Wars (mith-ri-dat'ik). Three wars between Rome and Mithridates, king of Pontus. The Romans were commanded in the First (88–84 B.C.) by Sulla and his lieutenant Fimbria; in the Second (83–81 B.C.) by Murena; and in the Third (74–63 B.C.) by Lucullus, later by Pompey the Great. In the last Mithridates and his ally Tigranes were defeated, and Pontus was annexed to Rome in 63 B.C.

Mitra (mī'trạ). A long band of stuff, leather, or metal, used variously as a girdle or headband by the women of ancient Greece. It is mentioned in the *Iliad* and has been found on archaic statuettes discovered in excavations at Delphi, Olympia, and elsewhere.

Mitrephorus (mit-rē'fôr-us). An epithet of Dionysus, because he wore a band around his head.

Mnemon (nē'mon). In Greek epic, a companion of Achilles, given to him by his mother Thetis, to warn Achilles that he should not kill a child of Apollo, or Apollo would bring about his death. Achilles killed Tenes, a son of Apollo, on the island of Tenedos, and then, realizing what he had done, killed Mnemon for not reminding him.

Mnemosyne (nẹ-mos'i-nē, -moz'-). In Greek mythology, a Titaness, the daughter of Uranus and Gaea. She was the goddess of memory. Zeus visited her nine nights and she bore him the nine Muses.

Mnemonides (nẹ-mon'i-dēz). A name for the Muses, from their mother Mnemosyne.

Mnesicles (nes'i-klēz). A brilliant Athenian architect of the Periclean period, known from literary sources to have been the designer of the magnificent *Propylaea*, or entrance-gates, of the Acropolis of Athens. The construction of the Propylaea was begun in 437 B.C. and left unfinished in 432 B.C., before the outbreak of the Peloponnesian War. From his skill and versatility in adjusting the design of the Propylaea to sloping ground, it has been suggested that Mnesicles was also the architect of the split-level *Erechtheum*, whose builder is otherwise unknown. (JJ)

Modena (mô'dā-nä). See **Mutina.**

Moerae (mē'rē). [Also: **Moirai.**] In Greek mythology, the three birth goddesses, identified with the Fates. Homer uses the name in the singular, as of a single divinity, and also in the plural. He also calls them the "spinners of the thread of life." They are spoken of as daughters of Night and Darkness, and also as daughters of Zeus and Themis. Hesiod represented them as three: Clotho (the spinner), Lachesis (disposer of lots), and Atropos (the inevitable). The first spins the thread of life, the second fixes its length, and the third severs it. Their attributes were, respectively, a spindle, a scroll, and for Atropos, a scale or scissors. Their duty was to see to it that the fate allotted at birth was duly carried out. They were more powerful than the gods themselves, as Homer frequently states, and whoever attempted to defy the Moerae was certain to be visited by Nemesis.

Moeragetes (mē-raj'ẹ-tēz). An epithet of Apollo, meaning "Leader" or "Guide of the Fates." This name was also applied to Zeus, and there was an altar of Zeus Moeragetes at Olympia. Images of Apollo Moeragetes and Zeus Moeragetes were set up at Delphi.

Moesia (mē'shi-ạ). In ancient geography, a northeastern province of the Roman Empire, lying N of the Balkans, S of the Danube, and W of the Black Sea, corresponding to the N and C parts of modern Bulgaria and Serbia. It was made a Roman province c16 B.C., was divided under Domitian into Moesia Superior (in the W) and Moesia Inferior (in the E), and was overrun by Goths in the 3rd and 4th centuries A.D.

Moirai (moi′rī). See **Moerae**.

Molione (mō̰-lǐ′ō̰-nē). In Greek mythology, the mother of Cteatus and Eurytus, twins who were sometimes said to be joined together at the waist, by Actor. When she learned that Heracles had killed her sons in Elis, she asked the Eleans to avenge their death. The Eleans declined to take on this task, whereupon Molione put a curse on any Elean who entered the Isthmian Games. The Eleans respected the curse by refusing thereafter to take part in the Isthmian Games.

Moliones (mō̰-lǐ′ō̰-nēz). In Greek mythology, the twin brothers Eurytus and Cteatus. They were the sons of Molione and Poseidon, but as they were brought up by Actor, the husband of Molione, they are also called the Actoridae. According to some accounts they were joined together at the waist. Nestor, relating the heroic exploits of his youth to spur Patroclus into battle during the Trojan War, tells how he was about to conquer the Moliones when they were spirited away in a mist by Poseidon. Later they defeated Nestor in a chariot race. They repelled Heracles when he attacked their uncle, Augeas, in Elis, but were later ambushed and slain by Heracles at Cleonae. The sons of Cteatus and Eurytus sailed to Troy to take part in the Trojan War. As descendants of Molione they were also known as Moliones.

Molorchus (mol-ôr′kus). In Greek legend, a peasant who dwelt near Mount Tretus, the home of the Nemean Lion. His son was killed by the lion, and as he was preparing to sacrifice to Hera to propitiate the goddess, Heracles, on his way to hunt the lion, stopped at his hut. He told Molorchus to wait 30 days. If at the end of that time Heracles had not returned, Molorchus should sacrifice to Heracles the Hero; but if Heracles returned safely, they would sacrifice to Zeus together. Heracles returned on the thirtieth day, having successfully slain the lion, and they sacrificed to Zeus as planned. Some say Heracles made changes in the Nemean Games on this occasion, and that Molorchus planted the grove in which the games were subsequently held. It is also said that Molorchus founded a city in Nemea, which he named for himself.

Molossians (mō̰-los′i-anz). Ancient tribe of Epirus, in N Greece. They occupied at first a district in the center but ultimately their kings ruled over all Epirus. Their breed of huge hounds was famous.

Molossus (mō̰-los′us). In Greek legend, the son of Neoptolemus and Andromache, eponymous ancestor of the Molossians.

Molurian (mol-ö′ri-an) **Rock.** A cliff over the sea near Megara on the Saronic Gulf. It was from this rocky crag that Ino is said to have leaped into the sea with her son Melicertes when she fled from her maddened husband Athamas of Orchomenus. The Molurian Rock was also famous as the spot from which Sciron hurled travelers into the sea, until he himself was thrown from it by Theseus.

Molus (mō′lus). In Greek mythology, a son of Ares and Demonice. He was the brother of Evenus and the father of Molione.

Moly (mō′li). A fabulous herb of magic power, represented as having a black root and a milk-white flower; it is said by Homer to have been given by Hermes to Odysseus to counteract the spells of Circe.

Momus (mō′mus). [Also: **Momos** (-mos).] According to Hesiod, the son of Nyx (Night). He is the personification of mockery, ridicule, and censure. He criticized Hephaestus for not putting a door in the breast of the man he had made, so that the inmost secrets of his heart could be revealed. He found fault with Aphrodite because her sandals made too much noise, and criticized Zeus for putting the bull's horns where the bull could not see them.

Moneta (mō̰-nē′ta). A Roman epithet of Juno, meaning "Adviser" or "Warner." In gratitude for timely warnings, it was said, a temple of Juno Moneta was built on the northern summit of the Capitoline Hill. Connected with this temple were a state office and workshop for the manufacture of coins. This came to be known colloquially as the Moneta, and eventually passed into western languages, e.g., Italian, *moneta*, French, *monnaie*, and English, *money, mint*. (JJ)

Monopteron (mō̰-nop′te-ron) or **Monopteros** (-ros). A type of Greek or Roman temple, usually circular and without an enclosed cella, composed of columns arranged in a ring and supporting a cupola or a conical roof. The temple of Rome and Augustus on

---

fat, fāte, fär, fāre, errant; net, mē, her ardent; pin, pīne; not, nōte, möve, nôr,

the Acropolis of Athens, east of the Parthenon, was an example of a monopteron.

Monumentum Ancyranum (mon-ū-men′tum an-si-rā′num). A long inscription in parallel Latin and Greek versions, containing the text of the *Res Gestae Divi Augusti,* the official biography of the emperor Augustus, which was inscribed on the walls of the temple of Rome and Augustus at Ancyra (Ankara) in Galatia, Asia Minor, and discovered there in 1855. Fragmentary copies have also been found at Apollonia and Antioch in Pisidia. (JJ)

Mopsuestia (mop-sǭ-es′chi-a). [Later Latin name, **Hadriana Mopsuhestia;** modern village name, **Misis.**] In ancient geography, a city of Cilicia, S Asia Minor, on the Pyramus River E of Tarsus. The city was favored by the emperor Hadrian and received special privileges from him; it was renamed in his honor.

Mopsus (mop′sus). In Greek mythology, a Lapith. He was the son of Ampycus and a nymph, and was taught the augury of birds by Apollo himself. He took part in the battle between the Lapiths and the Centaurs, and it was he who recognized as the soul of the Lapith Caeneus the bird which flew out of the pile of trees and logs under which Caeneus was buried. Mopsus also took part in the Calydonian Hunt, and later went from Thessaly to Iolcus to join Jason on the voyage of the *Argo* to Colchis for the Golden Fleece. On the way back from Colchis the Argonauts were driven into the shoal waters of Syrtis in Libya, and were carried by a great gale into the desert. Mopsus wandered about in search of water and was bitten by a serpent. This serpent was one of those which sprang up from the drops of blood that fell from the severed head of Medusa when Perseus was carrying it back to Seriphus, and the bite was therefore fatal to Mopsus. Afterward he was worshiped as a hero in Libya, and there was an oracle of Mopsus there.

Mopsus. In Greek legend, a son of Rhacius, king of Caria, and Manto, daughter of the famous seer, Tiresias. He was a noted seer also. In a contest with the seer Calchas, at Colophon, after the Trojan War, Mopsus gave the correct number of figs growing on a fig tree, and accurately predicted the time of birth and the number of pigs in the litter that

a sow was about to produce. Calchas, who had been mistaken in both cases, died, as it had been foretold he would do when he met a seer wiser than himself. Mopsus was the founder, with Amphilochus, of the city of Mallus in Cilicia. When Amphilochus returned to Argos, Mopsus ruled alone. But Amphilochus later returned to Mallus, and wished to share in the rule of the city which he had helped to found. Mopsus and Amphilochus quarreled so violently for control of the throne that it was finally suggested they should engage in a combat to see which should rule. In the duel that followed they killed each other. Afterward a common oracle was set up of Mopsus and Amphilochus, which became as celebrated for accuracy as the oracle at Delphi. Questions were put to it on wax tablets, and the answers were revealed in dreams.

Morgantina (môr-gan-tē′na). City in Sicily, in the district known as Serra Orlando, near Aidone, under excavation by an expedition from Princeton University, which has revealed the market-place, public buildings, houses, fortifications, and a cemetery. The culture is native Sicilian under Greek influence; after the Roman annexation of Sicily, Morgantina rapidly declined. The identification of the site as Morgantina, not known previously, emerged from study of the coins found in the excavations. (JJ)

Morpheus (môr′fūs or môr′fę-us). In Greek mythology, one of the sons of Hypnos, or Sleep. Morpheus was the god of dreams who imitated human forms and voices, and was therefore summoned when a dream of human beings was required, as distinct from the bringer of dreams of animals or phantoms. It was Morpheus, for example, who appeared to Alcyone as her husband Ceyx, to inform her that Ceyx had been drowned. He is more prominent in literary allusion than in mythology itself, and hence, by extension, is very commonly referred to as the god of sleep.

Morpho (môr′fō). An epithet of Aphrodite, meaning "Shapely." An image of Aphrodite Morpho, representing the goddess veiled and with fetters about her feet, was dedicated by Tyndareus. It was said that it represented the modesty and loyalty demanded by the marriage tie.

Moschion (mos-kī′on). Greek tragic poet; fl. 4th century B.C. Fragments of his work survive.

Moschus (mos′kus). Greek bucolic poet of Syracuse, active in the 2nd century B.C. He claimed to have been a pupil of Bion, but this seems to be a dubious claim. He modeled his poems after those of Theocritus. The work of Moschus was more ornate and less simply based on an unaffected love and understanding of nature than that of his model. Among the eight extant poems of Moschus, one treats the story of Europa; one, which has been widely imitated, is supposedly a description by Aphrodite of the deceptive qualities of her runaway son Eros; a third is a pastoral lament for Bion. The last is doubtfully ascribed to him. His work is usually printed with that of Bion and Theocritus.

Mossynoeci (mos-ī-nē′sī). A people of Pontus. They were said to perform private and intimate acts in public and public acts in private, and starved their king to death if he made a mistake in handing down his judgments. The Argonauts on their way to Colchis passed by their country but did not stop.

Motya (mot′ya̱). [Modern name, **S. Pantaleo.**] In ancient geography, a Carthaginian city of western Sicily. It was situated on an island in a small bay on the extreme western coast of Sicily. The island is almost completely enclosed in the bay: an arm of the mainland stretches across the north and ends in a long spit of land and protects the bay to the W, or sea side. The city on the island was completely walled, and was connected to the mainland by a causeway. In 398 B.C. Dionysius the Elder, tyrant of Syracuse, marched at the head of a large force and besieged it. To protect themselves from his siege engines, the inhabitants destroyed the causeway. Dionysius drew his ships ashore on the bay and set to work to build a new causeway, a much larger one than that destroyed, in order to attack the city, not with his fleet, but with his siege engines. The Carthaginians sent a fleet to the relief of Motya and blockaded the fleet of Dionysius in the bay. Instead of launching his galleys against the Carthaginian fleet Dionysius marched his army around the bay and attacked them from the shore with catapults

that hurled great stones against the ships. This was a new weapon with which the Carthaginians were not prepared to cope. They sailed out of the bay and lurked out of reach of the catapults. Dionysius then put his own ships on great rollers and hauled them across the arm of land to the north, and launched them in the sea on the other side. The Carthaginians decided not to engage him. Leaving the Motyans to their fate, they sailed back to Carthage. Dionysius was now free to besiege the city, his mole having been completed. Because the space in the city was limited, the inhabitants built up into the air. Stone towers as high as six stories studded the city. The towers were out of reach of ordinary siege engines. Dionysius redesigned his engines, putting the operating force atop siege towers of a height to be effective against the towered city. The siege he thus mounted against Motya became a kind of aerial warfare with the besieged and besiegers struggling from the tops of the towers. Those on the siege towers rained stones on the city with catapults, while below the rams of Dionysius battered at the walls. Those defending the city retaliated with flaming pitch hurled at the wooden siege towers, but to no avail. The forces of Dionysius breached the wall and entered the city. This by no means was the end. From their towers the defenders rained missiles and fire on the invaders. The attackers brought in their siege engines and flung bridges across to the towers of the defenders, so that much of the fighting was carried on on these bridges high in the air. Many were flung to their death. Every tower had to be taken individually as the Motyans had no thought of surrender. Day after day the struggle was renewed and each night it ceased as both forces rested. The Motyans could not hope to drive off the Greeks, but they were determined to make a Greek victory costly. Many of Dionysius' men were slain, and he decided on a night attack. He entered a part of the town that was still being defended and completely surprised the Motyans. His forces poured in and massacred the inhabitants, who continued their heroic resistance to the end. At last Dionysius stopped the slaughter. Those who survived were sold into slavery, and the city was given over to

fat, fāte, fär, fãre, errạnt; net, mē, hėr ardẹnt; pin, pīne; not, nōte, mŏve, nôr,

his soldiers to plunder. It was a great victory for Dionysius and his new methods of siege warfare, but the next year the Carthaginians returned and recaptured Motya. They, however, did not restore it. Instead they founded a new city, Lilybaeum, on the south side of the bay.

Motyca (mō′ti-ka̱) or **Mutyca** (mū′ti-ka̱). [Modern name, **Modica**.] In ancient geography, a town of Sicily, situated on a hill between two valleys, near the Mauro River, in the SE corner of Sicily. It was a town of the ancient Sicels.

Mulciber (mul′si-bėr). In Roman mythology, an epithet of Vulcan, meaning "the Melter."

Mulius (mū′li-us). In Homeric legend (*Iliad*), a spearman of Augeas, and the husband of Agamede, daughter of Augeas. Nestor killed him in the war between the Eleans and the Pylians. Nestor recounted this exploit of his youth to Patroclus in order to goad him into joining in the battle against the Trojans when the Trojans were about to set fire to the Greek ships. Nestor lamented that he no longer had the vigor he had possessed when he killed Mulius.

Mummius (mum′i-us), **Lucius**. [Surnamed **Achaicus**.] Roman consul, active in the middle of the 2nd century B.C. During his consulship (146 B.C.) he defeated the Achaean League and captured Corinth, completing the Roman conquest of Greece. Mummius is noted for the barbarity with which he treated Corinth; according to contemporary sources, all its inhabitants were killed, its art treasures were sent to Rome, and the city was burned to the ground. The material brought to light in the extensive excavations by the American School of Classical Studies at Athens, however, indicates that the city was not completely depopulated, that some inhabitants survived or, having fled, returned to maintain life in the ruins until the city was officially refounded in 44 B.C.

Munda (mun′da). In ancient geography, a town in S Spain, of undetermined location. It is noted for the victory gained (45 B.C.) there by Julius Caesar over the sons of Pompey.

Munippus (mū-nip′us). In Greek legend, the son of Cilla, sister of King Priam, and Thymoetes. He was born earlier on the same day as Paris was born to Priam and Hecuba.

Because of a prophecy that a son born to a woman of the royal house would cause the destruction of Troy, Priam had Cilla and her infant put to death. Actually, the prophecy referred to Hecuba and Paris.

Munitus (mū′ni-tus). In Greek legend, a bastard son of Laodice, daughter of Priam and Hecuba, and Acamas, son of Theseus and Phaedra. He was brought up by his great-grandmother Aethra, a captive in Troy. At the fall of Troy Acamas rescued him, but after he had landed in Thrace with his father, he was bitten by a snake and died.

Munychia (mū-nik′i-a̱). One of the three harbors serving Athens in the vicinity of Piraeus. The name *Munychia* is also given to the citadel (height, 284 feet) of Piraeus. On the hill at Munychia was a temple of Artemis. According to legend, once a bear sought refuge in the temple; the people rushed in after it and killed it. At once plague struck the populace, and they learned it would be lifted only if one of the citizens volunteered to sacrifice his daughter. One of the inhabitants agreed to sacrifice his daughter to Artemis. He dressed her and prepared her for the sacrifice, but at the last minute substituted a goat, clad in his daughter's clothes, and sacrificed it in her place. After the death of Hipparchus Hippias fortified the hill of Munychia, in 510 B.C. The democratic opponents of the Thirty Tyrants seized the hill of Munychia, occupied the temple of Artemis, and in the following conflict (403 B.C.) inflicted such damage on the Thirty that they were thrown from power and sought refuge at Eleusis.

Munychion (mū-nik′i-on). The tenth month of the Attic year. It included the latter part of April and the early part of May. A festival of Artemis Munychia was especially celebrated at Munychia, the port of Athens, where her shrine stood, in this month. It commemorated the battle of Salamis.

Musaeus (mū-zē′us). Legendary Greek poet and seer of Attica, associated with Orpheus (as a pupil or, in some accounts, as a son). To him were attributed various poems connected with the mysteries of Demeter at Eleusis, over which he was said to have presided. According to some accounts, he initiated Heracles into the mysteries at Eleusis before he went to the Underworld to fetch

Cerberus. He was buried at Athens and his tomb was on the Museum, SW of the Acropolis.

Musaeus. [Surnamed **Grammaticus.**] Greek grammarian who flourished about the 5th century A.D. He was the author of the celebrated love epic *Hero and Leander,* of which the 340 verses that have been preserved show intense feeling.

Musagetes (mū-sạ-jē′tēz). An epithet of Apollo as patron of the Muses.

Muses (mū′zez). Originally there were three Muses: Melete (*Meditation*), Mneme (*Memory*) and Aoede (*Song*). According to the earliest writers, the Muses were goddesses of memory, then inspiring goddesses of song, and later, divinities presiding over poetry, the sciences, and the arts, while at the same time having springs and streams as their special province. According to later tradition, Mnemosyne (*Memory*) bore nine daughters, the Muses, to Zeus, who lay with her nine nights. They were born in Pieria (and hence called Pierides), and there they frolicked around the sacred Pierian springs; or disported in their sacred grove on Mount Helicon in Boeotia, where the winged horse Pegasus had made the Hippocrene Spring for them by stamping his hoof on the earth; or visited the inspirational Castalian Spring on Mount Parnassus; or went to Olympus where they entertained the gods. As companions of Apollo they learned singing, dancing, and poetry, and shared the mastery of the lyre with him. Because they presided over the musical arts, they were sometimes called on to judge musical contests, as that between Apollo and Marsyas, or challenged to enter them themselves, as by the Sirens, who were defeated and lost their wings, or by the daughters of Pierus, who were also defeated, and changed into magpies. The Muses attended the marriages of Peleus and Thetis and Cadmus and Harmonia, where they entertained the guests at the weddings with music and song. The Muses were the mistresses of healing and prophecy, which they sometimes taught to others, as to Aristaeus, and they had many sanctuaries, sacred groves, and springs throughout the Greek world. Anyone inspired by the "violet-crowned" Muses was blessed and highly venerated, for "Happy is he whom the Muses love, and

sweet flows his voice from his lips." The nine Muses and their attributes were: Clio, the muse of history, who wears a wreath and carries a scroll; Euterpe, of music, who carries a double flute; Thalia, of comedy, who has an ivy wreath, a comic mask, and a shepherd's staff; Melpomene, of tragedy, with a tragic mask, an ivy wreath, and sometimes a club or a sword; Terpsichore, of choral dance and song, with a lyre; Erato, of lyric and amorous poetry, with the lyre; Polymnia or Polyhymnia, of the inspired and stately hymn and religious dance, who is usually shown veiled and thoughtful; Urania, of astronomy, who holds a globe; and last of all, Calliope, the chief of the Muses, of heroic or epic poetry, who carries a tablet and stylus. The Muses were intimately associated in legend and in art with Apollo, who as the chief guardian and leader of their company was called Musagetes. The Romans identified their Camenae with the Greek Muses.

Museum (mū-zē′um). The name means "Sanctuary of the Muses," and so was applied not only to established shrines of the Muses but also loosely to schools dedicated to the pursuit of poetry, literature, rhetoric, philosophy, science, and music. In Athens, the Museum was a hill almost directly south of the Acropolis, the farthest E of the group of hills on the SW side of the city; named from an old shrine of the Muses located on it. On the summit stands a conspicuous monument, ornamented with niches, Corinthian columns, statues, and a relief-frieze, to Philopappus, grandson of the last king of Commagene, who became an Athenian citizen. The slopes of the hill, particularly on its southern extension, abound with curious rock-cuttings, for the most part vestiges of prehistoric Athens. These include house foundations, stairs, meeting places with seats, and the so-called prison of Socrates and tomb of Cimon. Between this hill and the Pnyx passed the road to the Piraeus between the Long Walls. The rock is deeply cut by the ruts of chariot wheels and an artificial water channel.

Museum. The most famous Museum was that of Alexandria in Egypt, founded about 280 B.C. by Ptolemy II Philadelphus as an institute for advanced research, populated by scholars attracted from the whole Greek East and

fat, fāte, fär, fãre, errạnt; net, mē, hėr ardẹnt; pin, pīne; not, nōte, möve, nôr,

supported by the revenues of the state and afterward by the Roman emperors. At its head was a presiding scholar or high-priest (*hiereus*) of the Muses. Associated with it, but apparently administratively distinct, was the Library, an earnest attempt to gather under one roof the world's store of written learning. It is said that as an incident of the siege of Julius Caesar in Alexandria, 47 B.C., the Library was fired; but a new collection of books was constituted, and the Museum and Library continued in existence through the 4th century A.D. (JJ)

Mutina (mū'ti-na). [Modern name, **Modena**.] City of Italy, situated on the Via Aemilia, NW of Bononia (Bologna). Near here, 44–43 B.C., Decimus Junius Brutus was blockaded by Mark Antony, and was relieved by Hirtius, Pansa, and Octavian (the future Augustus), who defeated Antony.

Mutinus (mū-tī'nus) or **Mutunus** (mū-tō'nus). Ancient Italian god, personifying the sexual function of marriage. Later, in Roman mythology, he became identified with Priapus.

Mutyca (mū'ti-ka). See **Motyca**.

Mycale (mik'a-lē). In ancient geography, a mountain in Lydia, Asia Minor, N of Miletus. Here were gathered about 60,000 of the forces of Xerxes, left behind to guard Ionia after the defeat of the Persians at Salamis (480 B.C.). Part of the Persian fleet, not wishing to risk another naval fight with the Greeks, also withdrew to Mycale. There the ships were dragged ashore and a rampart was built around them to protect them and to form a defense for the soldiers. The Greek fleet under Leotychides pursued the Persians to Mycale. Seeing that the Persians did not venture out to meet them, the Greeks disembarked. As the Greeks prepared for battle, a rumor spread through the camp that the Greeks had defeated the Persians at Plataea on that very day. A herald's wand was found lying on the beach, according to Herodotus, which was an indication of the miraculous means by which the news had come from Plataea to Mycale so swiftly. Heartened by the rumor and the sign, the Greeks rushed eagerly into the battle. The struggle was grim and hard-fought on both sides, with neither giving ground at first. When the Athenians on their wing succeeded in breaking through the line of Persian wicker shields, the Persians withdrew into the entrenchment they had created with the ships and the surrounding rampart. The Athenians were so hot in pursuit they swarmed into the entrenchment after them and took the fortress. The Persians fled, and the Greeks fired their ships and took great booty. Thus on the same September day in 479 B.C., or so the story goes, the Persians in Greece under Mardonius were defeated at Plataea, and the Persians in Ionia were defeated at Mycale.

Mycalessia (mī-ka-lē'shi-a). Epithet of Demeter, from her sanctuary at Mycalessus in Boeotia. This sanctuary was said to be opened up each morning and closed each night by Heracles the Dactyl. A marvelous property of this sanctuary was that offerings of fruit placed before the image in the sanctuary in the autumn remained fresh throughout the following year.

Mycalessus (mī-ka-lē'sus). In ancient geography, a city in Boeotia. It is said to have been so-named from the Greek word for "low," because the cow guiding Cadmus in Boeotia lowed at this place. Diïtrephes, the Thracian, came to Mycalessus as he led his Thracians back to their country (c413 B.C.). He took the town and put the entire population to the sword. It is for this reason that the statue of Diïtrephes set up on the acropolis at Mycalessus showed him pierced by many arrows. At Mycalessus was a remarkable sanctuary of Demeter Mycalessia.

Mycenae (mī-sē'nē). In ancient geography, a city in Argolis, Greece, about 14 miles SW of Corinth. It was a very ancient settlement, dating from perhaps the 20th century B.C., and was conspicuous in Greek legend and history. According to tradition, Argolis was inhabited by Pelasgians, who fell under the domination of Danaus when he arrived from Egypt with his 50 daughters. The kingdom of Danaus in Argolis was subsequently divided among his descendants. Acrisius became ruler of Argos. His brother Proetus ruled the neighboring region of Tiryns. When Perseus, grandson of Acrisius, unwittingly killed Acrisius, he did not wish to remain in Argos. He exchanged his inheritance with his cousin Megapenthes and became ruler of Tiryns. As Perseus proceeded toward Tiryns, he was overcome by thirst. He stooped to pluck a mushroom and drank the water from its cap. Pleased that he thus quenched his thirst, he founded a city on the spot and named it Mycenae for the mushroom (*mykos*). Nearby the spot where this occurred is a spring, called by the ancients *Persea,* which still gives sparkling water to the inhabitants. Some say, however, that Perseus named his city from the cap of his sword, which happened to fall off at this spot, and which has a Greek name very similar to the word for mushroom. At all events, he fortified the city, which was on an eminence rising from the fertile plain, easily defendable and in a position to command routes to and from the sea. He secured the aid of the Cyclopes to build the wall of the city, which is sometimes called "the Cyclopean City," from the huge irregular stones that form its wall. Sthenelus, son and successor of Perseus, received Atreus and Thyestes, sons of Pelops, into his realm when they fled from their father. On the death of Eurystheus, son of Sthenelus, Atreus became king, ended the Perseid dynasty and established that of the Pelopidae, which became the equal of any kingdom in the Peloponnesus. Signs of fire found in the excavations at Mycenae are attributed to the struggles that took place when Atreus assumed mastery. Atreus was followed by his brother Thyestes, who in turn was succeeded by Agamemnon, son of Atreus and brother of Menelaus. The rulers between Perseus and Agamemnon cover the period of time between about the middle of the 14th century, when the city was founded by Perseus, and the fall of Troy, the traditional date of which is 1183 B.C. In the time of Agamemnon, Mycenae was at its apogee. Tiryns, Argos, and Midea were subject to him, as was most of the Peloponnesus and the neighboring islands. As master of a strong maritime empire he exercised influence over most of the Greek mainland and the islands, and drew supporters from the entire area when he led the expedition to Troy to recover Helen. The murder of Agamemnon on his return from his successes at Troy by his wife Clytemnestra and her lover Aegisthus, provides the material for some of the most dramatic pages of Greek tragedy. After an interval in which Mycenae was ruled by Clytemnestra and Aegisthus, Agamemnon was succeeded by his son Orestes and his grand-

son Tisamenus. During the reign of Tisamenus the Dorians invaded the Peloponnesus, took Mycenae, and destroyed its citadel. Thereafter, the influence and power of Mycenae was in eclipse.

MYCENAEAN WARRIOR
Mycenaean crater, c1200 B.C.
National Museum, Athens

As in many cases, history and legend are closely intertwined at Mycenae. Archaeologists consider that the earliest city to occupy the site dated from about the 20th century B.C. In succeeding centuries close relations were established between Mycenae and

Crete, and remains of a distinctly Cretan character, dating from 1600–1400 B.C., have been found in tombs on the site along with other evidences of Cretan domination in this period. Following the establishment of the city of Perseus, c1350 B.C., a distinctively Mycenaean culture developed throughout the area and spread to Asia Minor in the east and to Sicily in the west. In the period of its greatness the kings of Mycenae were the peers of the kings of Egypt and Babylon. From the end of the 12th century B.C. the importance of Mycenae declined so completely that nothing more is heard of it until the Persian Wars, when 80 Mycenaeans went to the aid of Leonidas at Thermopylae and later 200 shared in the victory at Plataea (479 B.C.). The Argives, roused to jealousy by the pride which the Mycenaeans took at having their names inscribed on the tripods at Delphi after the Battle of Plataea, attacked Mycenae and destroyed it c470 B.C. The city never recovered from this attack. Only a village remained on the site. The traveler and writer Pausanias visited there in the 2nd century A.D., and saw parts of the old walls and the Lion Gate (which was never completely obscured). He also claimed to have seen the graves of Atreus and Agamemnon in the citadel, as well as the graves of Clytemnestra and Aegisthus outside the walls (for they, as murderers, could not be buried in the citadel). Modern scholars doubt that Pausanias actually saw the graves, for they must have been covered over; rather, it is thought that they were described to him by local inhabitants who knew of them by tradition. From the time of Pausanias until the 19th century Mycenae was a forgotten village. In that century the site was rediscovered by travelers, and various objects that were uncovered were carried off. It was not until the end of the century that the city as a famous and immensely valuable historical and archaeological site again came to the attention of the world. The original excavations were made by Heinrich Schliemann in 1876–77. Following the account of Pausanias, Schliemann discovered the Grave Circle of Mycenae with its royal shaft graves. Five graves were rapidly cleared and yielded a rich treasure. Later work was done on the site by the Archaeological Society of Athens.

The Mycenae of the *Iliad*, "that well-built city and fortress," the "golden," "wide-wayed" city especially loved by Hera, as well as the city of much earlier times, has been steadily emerging through archaeological expeditions ever since, notably those undertaken by the British Archaeological Society under Prof. A. J. B. Wace, which were interrupted in 1939 by the outbreak of World War II, and those of the Greek Archaeological Society in the 1950's. In the latest excavations (1952 and following years), a new grave circle has been disclosed, which includes the graves of the ruling families of the 17th and 16th centuries B.C. The shaft graves found by Schliemann and those in the new grave circle uncovered in 1952 were cut into the rock, sealed off, and covered over. They contained many skeletons and objects of value that decorated the bodies of the dead when they were interred. This is of interest as it shows that at the time of these burials the Mycenaeans did not burn their dead, as they did according to the Homeric poems of a later age. Rather, they buried them with all the accoutrements of the living—ornaments, utensils, and weapons. However, once the flesh had disappeared from their bones, no more concern was expressed for their souls or for their journey to the other world, and it appears that the skeletons were somewhat unceremoniously moved to one side to make room for new arrivals in the tombs. Excavations at the site of Mycenae have supplied some of the oldest materials for the study of Greek architecture and art. The site consisted of an acropolis, occupying the apex of a hill, and the lower town, the confused ruins of which are spread over its slopes. The acropolis is triangular, and is surrounded by a massive wall of huge stones (Cyclopean stones), partly shaped. It is entered by the Gate of the Lions, which dates from the 14th century B.C. This gate is at the end of a walled passage so placed that the right, or unshielded, side of an enemy would be exposed to the defenders within the citadel. The opening of the gate is about ten feet wide and high, tapering toward the top, with monolithic jambs and a huge lintel. Above the lintel a large triangular opening is formed by corbeling, and the great slab, two feet thick, which fills this, bears the remarkable relief of two facing rampant lions separated by a column. Close inside of this gate, in a double circle of upright stones 80 feet in diameter, were found shaft graves containing golden ornaments and masks, inlaid sword-blades, and other objects whose discovery astonished the scientific world. According to legend, these were the tombs of Atreus, Electra, Agamemnon, Cassandra, and others of the period. Modern scholars place the date of the tombs earlier than the time of Agamemnon, between the 19th and 16th centuries B.C. Excavations have disclosed on the acropolis a prehistoric palace resembling that at Tiryns, and remains of palaces and temples of later periods that were super-imposed on it. Remains still exist of the ramp on which, perhaps, Clytemnestra placed the royal purple for the feet of Agamemnon on his triumphant return from Troy. The bath in which she almost immediately there-after slew him disappeared when part of the acropolis was destroyed in a landslide. This is the acropolis that the tutor points out to Orestes, in Sophocles' *Electra*, as "a treasure-house of gold . . . the ancestral home of the family of Pelops, a house of death if ever there was one." The most important monu-ments of the lower town are the great "bee-hive" tombs, commonly called treasuries. Of these, one sometimes called "the treasury of Atreus" and sometimes "the tomb of Agamem-non," is a typical example. The interior is a circle about 50 feet in diameter and slightly less in height, covered with a pseudodome formed by corbeling in the horizontal courses of the wall. Indications are that the inner surface of the tomb was decorated with medallions in metal and painted designs. The discoveries at Mycenae threw a flood of light upon the earliest Greek art, particularly in pottery. They were the first important finds of their class, which has since been recognized in a large proportion of Greek settlements of sufficient age, and is every-where distinguished as Mycenaean. My-cenaean ornament includes geometric decora-tion, foliage, marine and animal forms, and the human figure. Mycenaean art was prac-ticed and developed through several cen-turies, and existed contemporaneously with the succeeding dipylon style of decoration, which began c1000 B.C. Among the objects

found in the second grave circle, excavated 1952 and following years, are: bronze dag-gers, spears, swords, and the remains of a leather scabbard; pottery, including painted vases, amphorae, and jars; engraved gems; gold ornaments, including bands, buttons, and ear clips; beads of semi-precious stones; rock crystal bowls and pins with rock crystal heads; and gold cups. The chief objects found at Mycenae are in the National Mu-seum at Athens.

Myconus or **Mykonos** (mik'ō̆-nos, mī'kō̆-nos). [Also: **Mikonos**.] Island in the Aegean Sea, one of the Cyclades. Area, about 33 square miles. It lies E of Delos, and according to legend was one of the moorings which an-chored Delos, hitherto a floating island, to the sea floor when Leto went to Delos to bear her twin children, Apollo and Artemis. The body of Ajax the Less, which had been recovered from the sea, was buried here by the sea-goddess Thetis.

Mygdon (mig'don). In Greek legend, a king of the Bebryces. While waging war against the Mariandyni, he was slain by Heracles, their ally. He was succeeded by his brother Amycus.

Mylae (mī'lē). [Modern name, **Milazzo** or **Melazzo**.] Seaport on the N coast of the island of Sicily, about 18 miles W of Mes-sana. Near here the Roman fleet under Duilius gained its first naval victory over the Carthaginians in 260 B.C., and Agrippa de-feated Sextus Pompey's fleet in 36 B.C.

Mylasa (mī-lā'sa). [Also: **Mylassa**; modern town name, **Milâs**.] In ancient geography, an inland town in SW Asia Minor, in Caria. It was the capital of the later Carian kingdom.

Myles (mī'lēz). In Greek tradition, a son of Lelex, who succeeded his father as king in Laconia. Myles was credited by the Spartans as being the inventor of the water-mill as a means of grinding grain. He was succeeded by his son Eurotas.

Mylitta (mī-lit'a). In Babylonian mythology, a fertility and birth goddess, identified by Herodotus with the Greek Aphrodite, and by other writers with Ishtar. Her cult demanded that every woman serve in her temple as a sacred prostitute, until released by a fee from a stranger. The money for the service was given in the name of the goddess.

Mynes (mī'nēz). In Homeric legend (*Iliad*),

a son of King Evenus. He was king of Lyrnessus and the husband of Briseis. Because he had sheltered Aeneas, Achilles raided his land during the Trojan War, killed him and his brother Epistrophus, and carried off his wife as a captive.

Myonnesus (mī-ō̧-nē′sus). In ancient geography, a promontory on the coast of Ionia, W Asia Minor, about 27 miles NW of Ephesus. Near it the Romans gained (190 B.C.) a naval victory over the Syrians under Antiochus III.

Myra (mī′ra̧). In ancient geography, a city in Lycia, SW Asia Minor, situated near the S coast. An ancient theater here is among the finest in Asia Minor.

Myrina (mi-rī′na̧). According to Homer (*Iliad*), the wife of Dardanus. A hill near Troy, "Thorn-hill," was named by the gods as her funeral mound.

Myrina. Very extensive Greek necropolis, near Izmir (Smyrna), Asia Minor, discovered c1870, and systematically excavated by the French School at Athens between 1880 and 1882, known for terra-cotta figurines.

Myrina. In ancient geography, a city of the island of Lemnos. The site is now occupied by the town of Kastron.

Myrmidon (mėr′mi-do̧n, -don). In Greek mythology, according to some accounts, a king whose daughter was visited by Zeus in the form of an ant. Her children were therefore called Myrmidons.

Myrmidons. A warlike tribe of Phthiotis, Thessaly, that originated on the island of Aegina. According to Greek mythology, Hera sent a pestilence on Aegina, which was named for one of her rivals for the affections of Zeus. The streams were polluted and a plague of serpents appeared. Men and animals died by the thousand and the island was almost depopulated. Sacrifices to the gods had no effect. At last Aeacus, the king of the island and a son of Zeus, prayed to his father to restore his people by sending him as many men as the ants that were crawling up an oak tree in the sacred grove. Zeus answered with a flash of lightning and the next day the ants had been transformed into magnificent warriors, and the plague had lifted. Aeacus named his new subjects Myrmidons in memory of their origin. Emigrants from Aegina to Thessaly continued to hold the ant sacred in their new land. According to Homer, the Myrmidons were led by Achilles in the Trojan War, and performed their warlike duties as faithfully and tirelessly as the ants for which they were named.

Myron (mī′ro̧n). Greek sculptor; fl. c450 B.C. He was a native of Eleutherae on the frontier between Attica and Boeotia, and a pupil of Ageladas of Argos. Polyclitus and Phidias were reputedly his fellow pupils. Myron worked, exclusively or primarily, in bronze, a medium which released the artist from the static poses of sculpture in marble and made possible the athlete statues for which he became famous. He considered the subject more from the standpoint of action than of proportion, and represents the attitudes of the active rather than the beauty of the passive athlete. In this he was considered supreme. His most representative work was probably the *Discobulus* or discus-thrower, described by Quintilian and Lucian, of which inadequate copies can be seen in the British Museum, the Vatican, and the National Museum (Museo delle Terme) in Rome. His group of Athena and Marsyas is represented by the Athena in Frankfurt and the Marsyas of the Lateran, as well as on coins and on a marble vase in Athens. Myron's bronze cow on the Pnyx at Athens was a popular Greek and Roman favorite. (JJ)

Myrrha (mir′a̧). In Greek mythology, the daughter of Cinyras, king of Paphos. Afflicted by an unnatural love for her father because her mother had boasted that Myrrha was more beautiful than Aphrodite, she tried to hang herself. Her devoted nurse saved her and took her to her father, disguised as a young girl who was in love with him. Ultimately Cinyras discovered that she was his own daughter and in horror sought to kill her. She fled and was transformed by the gods into a twisted tree that ever weeps tears of bitter resin, the myrrh tree. The trunk of the tree split open and delivered Adonis, the child of her incestuous union. Myrrha is also sometimes called Smyrna.

Myrtilus (mėr′ti-lus). In Greek legend, a son of Hermes. Accompanied by Oenomaus, king of Elis, he drove the chariot in the races which Oenomaus demanded of the suitors of his daughter, Hippodamia. As Oenomaus had horses born of the wind, he always won the races and killed the defeated suitor. When Pelops sought Hippodamia's hand, he bribed Myrtilus to let him win the race. Hippodamia, having seen Pelops and fallen in love with him, also bribed Myrtilus. Myrtilus substituted wax pins in the axles of the chariot, and as the race was nearing its end, the wheels spun off, it overturned, and Oenomaus, tangled in the horses' reins, was killed, but before he died he laid a curse on Myrtilus. Pelops then set off with Hippodamia and Myrtilus. Myrtilus now demanded his reward—half of the kingdom of Oenomaus—and Pelops answered by hurling him into the sea at Geraestus, the southernmost tip of Euboea. This part of the Aegean Sea was thereafter known as the Myrtoan Sea. While drowning, Myrtilus cursed the house of Pelops, a curse which brought many woes on his descendants. Hermes set Myrtilus' image among the stars as the constellation Auriga (the Charioteer). His body was washed ashore and buried behind a temple of Hermes in Arcadia. The ghost of Myrtilus haunted the stadium at Olympia, and charioteers made sacrifices to it so that it would not frighten their horses and bring disaster to them in their races.

Myrtle (mẻr'tl). A tree sacred to Aphrodite. Myrtle nymphs cared for Aristaeus in Cyrene, and taught him to make cheese, to raise bees, and to cultivate the olive.

Myrtoan Sea (mẻr-tō'an). [Latin, **Mare Myrtoum.**] In ancient geography, that part of the Aegean Sea S of Argolis, Attica, and Euboea.

Mys (mis). Greek artist who was active in the latter part of the 5th century B.C. He was famous for chasing designs on or working reliefs on metal. From a design of Parrhasius he engraved the battle between the Lapiths and Centaurs on the inside of the shield of the great bronze statue of Athena Promachus on the Acropolis. From another design of Parrhasius he made the Sack of Troy in relief on a cup.

Mysia (mish'i-a). In ancient geography, a district in NW Asia Minor. It was bounded by the Propontis on the N, Bithynia on the NE, Phrygia on the E, Lydia on the S, the Aegean Sea on the W, and the Hellespont on the NW. The region is traversed by mountain ranges. There were many Greek cities on the coasts. It belonged successively to Lydia, Persia, Macedon, Syria, Pergamum, and Rome. The Mysians were probably allied to the Lydians. They assisted the Khita (Hittites) against Rameses II.

Mysia. Epithet of Demeter, said to have been from Mysius, an Argive who entertained Demeter when she came to Argos in her search for her daughter. Inside the sanctuary of Demeter Mysia on the road from Mycenae to Argos was another sanctuary, of burnt brick, and in this were images of Demeter Mysia, the Maid, and Hades. The sanctuary of Demeter Mysia near Pellene in Achaea was surrounded by a grove, in which there were many springs. At this place there was a festival lasting seven days in honor of Demeter. On the third day of the festival all the men withdrew, even male dogs being excluded. The next day the men returned and the two sexes mocked and jeered at one another.

Myson (mī'son). Attic potter and painter, active early 5th century B.C. Forty-seven extant vessels are attributed to him. One of the finest of these is an amphora (Louvre) showing Croesus on his pyre. It is in the red-figure technique.

Mytilene (mit-i-lē'nẹ). [Also: **Mitylene, Mytilini;** former name, **Kastro.**] Town on the E coast of the island of Lesbos. In ancient times it was the chief city of Lesbos, the home of Sappho, and an important maritime power of the Aeolian Greeks. It revolted from Athens in 428 B.C., and was subjected in 427 B.C.

Myus (mī'us). In ancient geography, one of the 12 Ionian cities of Asia Minor. It was in Caria, situated on the Maeander River, about 11 miles NE of Miletus. According to tradition, it was colonized by Ionians from Attica, under the leadership of Cyaretus, son of Codrus, the legendary king of Athens. The city took part in the Ionian revolt against the Persians, and was subdued. In later centuries, the arm of the sea on which Myus was located was silted over, and turned the inlet into a lake. The lake became a breeding ground for gnats, and they became such a pest that the people of Myus abandoned their city, taking their gods with them, and withdrew to Miletus.

N

Nabis (nā'bis). A son of Demaratus and tyrant of Sparta from 207 to 192 B.C. when he was killed. He was conquered by the Romans under Flamininus in 193 B.C.

Nabonidus (nab-ō-nī'dus). [Babylonian, **Nabu-na'id.**] Last king of Babylonia (556–c538 B.C.). He was the father of Belshazzar. He seems to have belonged to the priestly class, and was zealous in the repairing of sanctuaries, but neglected the gods Merodach (or Marduk) and Nabu (or Nebo), on account of which he estranged himself from the priesthood; this to some extent facilitated the easy conquest of the Babylonian Empire by Cyrus of Persia in 538 B.C. According to Eusebius, Nabonidus after the fall of Babylon fortified himself in Borsippa, and when this was taken by Cyrus, the conqueror generously gave him a region in Carmania as his residence. But from a cylinder (cuneiform record) of Cyrus it seems that Nabonidus was treacherously delivered into the hands of Gobryas, the general of Cyrus, and died in a mysterious manner. It appears, from inscriptions of his which have been recovered, that he had a strong historical interest, and several historical statements of great importance for the chronology of the Babylonian Empire are recorded by him.

Nabopolassar (nab"ō-pō-las'ar). [Babylonian, **Nabu-bal-uçar.**] Founder of the new Babylonian Empire, active c625–604 B.C. He ruled, it seems, first over Babylonia as viceroy of Assyria. He then entered into an alliance with the Median king Cyaxares, who gave his daughter in marriage to Nabopolassar's son Nebuchadnezzar, and by their united efforts the destruction of the Assyrian Empire was brought about in 606 B.C.

Naevius (nē'vi-us), **Cnaeus.** Roman dramatic and epic poet, born c270 B.C. He served in the army in the First Punic War, and afterward wrote an account of it in verse. Like earlier Roman writers, his account began with the flight of Aeneas from Troy, and brought the history of Rome through the First Punic

War. He also wrote tragedies modeled after those of the Greeks, and attempted to dramatize events of his own country's history, as with his drama of the youth of Romulus and Remus. He was most successful as a writer of comedy, in which he did not merely translate the Greeks but freely adapted them to his own ideas. In his comedies he treated his own times, and attacked the Roman nobles so bitterly that he was thrown into prison. He was later freed, but was banished and died in exile at Utica, in Africa, c201 B.C.

Naiads (nā'adz, nī'-). In Greek and Roman mythology, female spirits presiding over springs, rivers, streams, and fountains. The Naiads were represented as beautiful nymphs with their heads crowned with flowers, lighthearted, musical, and beneficent. Their beneficence extends to the life-giving properties of water.

Name, See **Nomen.**

Naos (nā'os). "Dwelling-place"; the Greek word for temple (Latin *aedes*), the stately residence reserved for a god on his visits to the community. The term is also applied to the principal chamber of a temple, in which stood the image of the god and where the valuable properties of the cult were stored (Latin *cella*). Except for a few circular temples (*tholoi*), Greek temples were generally rectangular, with the long axis running east to west (but north to south at Bassae) and the entrance at the east. Rarely we hear of altars within the cella. The main altar, at which important sacrifices were performed, regularly stood in the open air facing the entrance; a temple sanctuary (*temenos*) might, however, contain several subsidiary altars and occasionally small buildings of temple form called treasuries. The simplest form of Greek temple is a single room with an open (prostyle) or partly enclosed (in-antis) columned porch. Embellishments may take the form of porches at both front and rear (amphiprostlye), or colonnades completely surrounding the cella (peristyle). (JJ).

Napaeae (nạ-pē′ẹ). In Roman mythology, nymphs of a dell.

Naples (nā′plz). See **Neapolis.**

Nar (när). [Modern name, **Nera.**] A shallow, sulphurous river in Umbria.

Narbo (när′bō). [Modern name, **Narbonne.**] A city in Gaul near the Mediterranean coast, known in pre-Roman times as a Celtic market-town and in 118 B.C. refounded by the Romans as Colonia Narbo Martius. After Caesar's Tenth Legion had been settled there, the province of Gallia Narbonensis was established, with Narbo as its capital, a distinction later lost to Nemausus. (JJ).

Narbonensis (när-bọ-nen′sis). [Also: **Gallia Narbonensis.**] Province of the Roman Empire, occupying the S and SE parts of Gaul, named for its first capital Narbo. It extended from the Alps SW along the Mediterranean to the Pyrenees. The N border was near the line of the Cebenna (Cevennes), the Rhodanus (Rhône), and the Lacus Lemanus (Lake of Geneva). The area of the province corresponds approximately to French Provence. Among its leading cities were Massilia (Marseilles) and Narbo (Narbonne), on the coast; Arelate (Arles), Nemausus (Nîmes), Arausio (Orange), and Vienna (Vienne), in the valley of the Rhodanus (Rhône); and Tolosa (Toulouse), inland to the west. The Roman ruins of Provence are famous: at Arles, a theater, an amphitheater, the forum, and town walls; at Nîmes, a fine temple, the so-called Maison Carrée, erected by Agrippa in 16 B.C., an amphitheater, and a gate, and nearby the splendid aqueduct known as the Pont du Gard; at Orange, a theater, a municipal arch, and fortifications; at Vienne, a well-preserved temple and a circus. Narbo became a Roman colony in 118 B.C.; colonies were later established at Arelate, Arausio, and Nemausus, and probably also at Vienna and Tolosa. (JJ)

Narcaeus (när-sē′us). In Greek tradition, a son of Physcoa and Dionysus. He founded a temple of Athena Narcaea at Elis and introduced the worship of Dionysus in Elis.

Narcissus (när-sis′us). In mythology, a son of the river-nymph Liriope and the river-god Cephissus. When he was born, the seer Tiresias told his mother that he would live to old age only if he never came to know himself. By the time he was a youth he was so beautiful that he was loved by many young men as well as maidens, but he scorned them all out of pride in his own beauty. The wood-nymph Echo fell in love with him and followed him. Narcissus heard her rustling in the forest and called to learn who was there. She could only repeat his last words, since she had been deprived of the power to speak any but the last few words another had spoken. When, therefore, Narcissus called out to his unseen admirer to come to him, she approached him with delight. But Narcissus scorned her love, as he had that of all others and Echo, yearning for love of him, wasted away until nothing was left of her but her voice, ever repeating the last words spoken by others. At length Aminius, whose love for Narcissus had also been scorned, prayed to the gods that one day Narcissus' love would be cruelly denied him, as he had denied others. Nemesis, or as some say, Artemis, heard the prayer and caused Narcissus, who was weary and hot from hunting, to go to a pool deep in the forest to refresh himself. As he bent to drink, he glimpsed his own image in the still surface of the pool and instantly fell in love with it. Each time he stretched his arms into the spring to clasp the image it disappeared. Nothing could tear him away from the spring and he cried to the gods in despair at the cruelty of the fate which denied him from embracing his love. As he lay day after day by the pool pining, he wasted away, adoring his own image. Dying, he prayed that the object of his love which was so beautiful, would outlive him, and when he breathed his last, his body disappeared. In its place was a lovely flower, with a golden center surrounded by white petals: the narcissus, whose bulb came to be useful as a narcotic. Another flower sometimes called narcissus, but more commonly called the iris, was created by Zeus to help Hades seize Persephone. It was a purple and silver blossom, and when Persephone saw it she wandered off from her attendant maidens in delight to pluck it. When she was alone the earth parted, Hades leaped out in his chariot and carried her off.

Narcissus. Freedman of the Roman emperor Claudius; died 54 A.D. He acquired a complete ascendancy over the emperor. He assisted the empress Messalina in procuring the deaths of C. Appius Silanus and others. Afterward he was the chief instrument in bringing about the execution of Messalina herself. He was put to death on the accession of Nero.

Narcissus. Roman athlete; fl. latter part of the 2nd century. He strangled the emperor Commodus in 192 A.D.

Narni (när′nē) or **Narnia** (när′ni-a). See **Nequinum.**

Naucratis (nô′kra̱-tis). In ancient geography, a city in Egypt, situated on the Canopic mouth of the Nile, not far from Saïs and about midway between modern Cairo and Alexandria. It is believed to have been founded by Milesian colonists not later than the 7th century B.C., and was described by Athenaeus and Herodotus as celebrated for its potters and florists. According to Herodotus, Amasis II (fl. c569–525 B.C.) encouraged the Greeks to settle in Naucratis, the only city where the Greeks were allowed to trade, and gave them land for their temples and altars. The site remained unknown till it was discovered by W. M. Flinders Petrie in 1884. The very extensive and important remains that have been excavated include ruins of the famous Hellenium, a temple built jointly by the Ionians, Dorians, and Aeolians, who owned the temple and appointed the governors of the port; temples of Zeus, Hera, Apollo, and Aphrodite, built by the Aeginetans, Samians, and Milesians; and pieces of pottery in great variety and profusion.

Naupactus (nô-pak′tus). [Also: **Naupaktos, Navpaktos, Lepanto.**] City in Locris, Greece, situated on the Gulf of Corinth, opposite Patrae. According to some accounts, the Dorian invasion of the Peloponnesus was launched from here. The name of the city means "city of ship-building," and some say it was Cresphontes, others say it was Aristomachus, and still others say it was Temenus, who here built the vessels for the Dorian invasion. Just west of the city was a sanctuary of Asclepius, and a rock covered with inscriptions expressive of gratitude to the god of healing may still be seen there. In the 5th century B.C. the Athenians established a naval base here, having taken the city from the Ozolian Locrians, and thus won a stra-

tegic base for the control of the Gulf of Corinth. About 464 B.C. the Messenians had revolted against Sparta. Athens went to help the Spartans put down the revolt, but as the Spartans feared growing Athenian power more than the revolting Messenians, the Athenians were requested to withdraw. The Athenians got their revenge for this snub by giving Naupactus to the Messenians who were defeated and compelled to leave Ithome, where they had resisted Sparta. In the Peloponnesian Wars (431–404 B.C.), the Messenians offered Naupactus to Athens as a naval base against Sparta. It was a band of Messenian scouts who led the Athenians around to the Spartan rear when the latter were besieged on the island of Sphacteria, and brought about their surrender (425 B.C.). In gratitude for thus humiliating their age-long enemies the Messenians of Naupactus dedicated the famous statue of Victory, by Paeonius, at Olympia. After the defeat of the Athenians at Aegospotami (405 B.C.), the Spartans drove the Messenians out of Naupactus.

Nauplia (nô′pli-a). [Also: **Nafplion, Nauplion, Navplion.**] Town in S Greece, situated at the head of the Gulf of Nauplia (also called Gulf of Argolis), about 25 miles SW of Corinth. It was the port of ancient Argos. According to tradition, the city was founded by Nauplius, the son of Poseidon and Amymone. It was the place where Agamemnon landed when he returned from Troy and, so some say, knelt to kiss the soil of his native land. South of the city a rocky cliff rises to a height of about 700 feet above the gulf. This was the ancient citadel of the city. Its name, Palamidi, recalls Palamedes, that son of Nauplius who was treacherously killed by his fellow Greeks in the Trojan War.

Nauplia, Gulf of. [Also: **Gulf of Argolis** (or **Argos**); Greek, **Argolikos Kolpos;** Latin, **Argolicus Sinus.**] Arm of the Aegean Sea, indenting the E coast of the Peloponnesus, Greece. Length, about 30 miles.

Nauplius (nô′pli-us). In Greek legend, a son of the Danaid Amymone and Poseidon. He was a celebrated navigator who discovered the art of steering by the constellation of the Great Bear. He was also the founder of Nauplia, the port of Argos.

Nauplius. In Greek legend, a son of Clytonaeus, and a descendant of Nauplius the navigator. He was a king of Nauplia, and he too was a famous navigator. He was one of the Argonauts who accompanied Jason on the expedition for the Golden Fleece. Aleus, king of Tegea, on discovering that his daughter Auge was about to bear a child whose father she claimed was Heracles, gave Auge to Nauplius with instructions to drown her, but he prudently took her to Nauplia and sold her to traders from Caria. Catreus, king in Crete, believing that he would meet his death at the hands of one of his own children, gave his daughter Clymene to Nauplius with instructions to sell her as a slave. Instead, Nauplius married her, and by her became the father of Oeax and Palamedes. The latter joined the Greeks in the Trojan War but was betrayed and killed by the Greeks at the instigation of Odysseus. Nauplius demanded satisfaction for his son's murder but was refused it. To avenge himself on the Greeks for the murder of his son, he visited the wives of the Greek heroes who were fighting at Troy. He told them that their husbands had taken concubines whom they intended to bring home as wives. Some unhappy women committed suicide as a result of his talk. Others were encouraged to commit adultery. Thus, Nauplius was partly responsible when Clytemnestra, wife of Agamemnon, became the mistress of Aegisthus, when Aegialea, wife of Diomedes, took Cometes as a lover, and when Meda, wife of Idomeneus, abandoned her husband for Leucus. In further revenge for the death of Palamedes, Nauplius decoyed the Greeks, returning home from the war in their ships, by lighting huge beacon fires on the coast of Euboea and causing them to dash their ships against the Capharean Rocks, thinking they were heading for safe harbors. Bold sailor as he was, Nauplius at length met his death by drowning after he himself followed a false beacon and was shipwrecked.

Nausicaä (nô-sik'a̱-a̱). In the *Odyssey*, the daughter of Alcinous, king of the Phaeacians. Inspired by a dream, she went with her maidens to wash on the shore near where Odysseus, who had just escaped from the sea, was sleeping. She gave him food and clothes when he appeared before her, naked and bleeding, and directed him to the palace. She discreetly advised him to go to the palace alone, rather than in her company, and told him to address himself to her mother first, rather than to her father, the king. Nausicaä has given her name as a model of discretion and tact.

Nausithous (nô-sith'ọ̄-us). In Greek legend, a son of Poseidon and Periboea. He was the king of the Phaeacians and led them to their island home of Scheria, also known as Phaeacia and Corcyra. He aided Heracles' son Hyllus (the younger of the two sons of Heracles by this name) to emigrate. Nausithous was the father of Alcinous.

Nausithous. In Greek tradition, a native of Salamis who was employed by Theseus as his helmsman on the voyage to Crete. The Pilots' Festival, held at Phalerum, where Theseus set up monuments to Nausithous and Phaeax, the pilot, was celebrated in their honor.

Nautes (nō'tēz). Named in the *Aeneid* as an aged Trojan who accompanied Aeneas on the flight from Troy. He was famed for his wisdom, having been taught by Pallas Athena herself. When the women of Aeneas' company, discouraged with continual voyaging, burned the ships in Sicily, Aeneas toyed with the idea of settling down in Sicily instead of going on to Italy. Nautes advised him instead to leave those who were discontented in Sicily, to repair the ships, and to proceed to his destined home with those who still had a thirst for glory.

Navarino (nä-vä-rē'nō). See **Pylus.**

Naxos (nak'sos). [Also: **Naxia.**] Island in the Aegean Sea, about 170 square miles in area. It is the largest and most fertile of the Cyclades, and is celebrated for its wine, olives, fruit, and vegetables. According to some accounts, it was anciently known as Strongyle, and was seized by Butes, a son of Thracian Boreas. He used it as a base from which to make piratical raids on passing ships. As there were no women on the island, he sailed to Drius in Thessaly with his followers. There he found the women celebrating the festival of Dionysus and attacked them. Butes was driven mad by Dionysus, who was invoked by one of the women Butes sought to ravish, and drowned himself in a well. His Thracian followers seized the women, among them Iphimedia, wife of Aloeus, and her daughter Pancratis, and returned with them to Strongyle. The sons of Iphimedia, Otus and Ephialtes, pursued the abductors, and captured the island, which they renamed Dia. Thracians dwelt on Naxos for 200 years, when they were driven out by a prolonged drought. It was afterward settled by Carians, whose king was Naxos, and for whom they in their turn renamed the island. The grandson of this king is said to have been the king who hospitably received Theseus and Ariadne when they stopped there on their way from Crete to Athens. While they rested at Naxos, Dionysus appeared to Theseus in a dream and commanded him to leave Ariadne on the island and depart for his homeland. Theseus did as he was bid, and Dionysus carried Ariadne away. The Naxians claimed that Dionysus was reared on their island by the nymphs Coronis, Philia, and Clide. For this reason Dionysus especially loved Naxos and caused its wine to be noted for its excellence, as the island became noted as a center of the worship of Dionysus. The Naxians were celebrated warriors and distinguished themselves at the battles of Salamis (480 B.C.) and Plataea (479 B.C.). Naxos was a member of the Confederacy of Delos, and revolted but was subdued by Athens c467 B.C. Near it Athens won a naval victory over Sparta in 376 B.C.

Naxos. [Also: **Naxia.**] Chief town of the island of Naxos, in the Cyclades, situated on its NW coast.

Naxos. [Also: **Naxus.**] In ancient geography, a seaport on the east coast of Sicily, just north of Mount Aetna. It was founded by Chalcidians who were accompanied by Ionians from the island of Naxos. The traditional date of its founding is 735 B.C. It was always especially highly regarded by the Greeks because it was their first settlement in Sicily. According to legend, the founders of Naxos were driven to Sicily by winds sent by Apollo. They erected an altar of Apollo Archegetes (*Founder*) on the spot where they landed, and it became the custom for envoys from Greece always to go first to this altar and offer sacrifice when they landed in Sicily. Colonists from Naxos founded the Sicilian cities of Catana and Leontini. Naxos sided with the Ionian cities of Sicily against

Syracuse and the Dorian cities, and was one of the few allies of Athens in the Sicilian expedition of 415 B.C. In 403 B.C. traitors inside the city accepted gold to open the gates to Dionysius the Elder, tyrant of Syracuse. Dionysius destroyed its walls and its dwellings, sold most of the inhabitants as slaves in Syracuse, and gave the land to the Sicels to win their support. The few Naxians who managed to escape at length found a home in the new town of Tauromenium.

Neaera (nē-ē′ra). In Greek mythology, the mother, by Strymon, of Evadne, who married Argus, the son of Niobe and Zeus.

Neaera. Said to have been a daughter of Pereus. She married her cousin Aleus, king of Tegea, and bore him a daughter, Auge, and three sons, Cepheus, Lycurgus, and Aphidamas.

Neaera. In the *Odyssey*, a nymph, the mother of Lampetia and Phaethusa, children of Helius. Her two daughters tended the wondrous herds of Helius on the island of Trinacria (Sicily).

Neapolis (nē-ap′ō-lis). [Also: **Parthenope;** modern **Naples.**] In ancient geography, a city of S Italy, situated on a magnificent bay, S of Rome. It was founded by colonists from the Greek settlement of Cumae, c600 B.C., and was first called Parthenope. When new colonists came from Chalcis and Athens and built themselves a settlement, Parthenope came to be known as Palaeopolis, the "old city," and the new settlement was called Neapolis, the "new city." In 327 B.C. Palaeopolis was besieged and taken by the Romans, and its name disappeared from history. Neapolis became a dependency of Rome, to whom she was a faithful ally. It was a strongly fortified town and resisted the efforts of Pyrrhus to take it, 280 B.C. In the civil wars it was betrayed to the partisans of Sulla (82 B.C.). They entered it and slaughtered the inhabitants. However, the city soon revived and became once more a prosperous port. Because of its climate and the beauty of its surroundings ("See Naples and die," Italian proverb) the city was a favorite resort of wealthy Romans and of the emperors. Vergil, who wrote most of the *Georgics* here, wished to be buried on a hill overlooking the city. The glorious beauty of the Bay of Naples, with Mount Vesuvius rising dramatically in the background, has for centuries been celebrated by poets and writers.

Nearchus (nē-är′kus). Attic painter and potter in the black-figure style, active c570 B.C. Over 40 cups with his signature are extant. He was one of the foremost makers and painters of the Little Master cups, so-called because of the exquisite miniature paintings that decorated them. A fragment of a cantharus (Athens) signed by him, shows Achilles and parts of three horses and represents the moment when Achilles was preparing to rejoin the battle against the Trojans to avenge Patroclus.

Nearchus. Macedonian officer, born in Crete, active in the second half of the 4th century B.C. He was an intimate friend and trusted officer of Alexander the Great, and was admiral of the fleet which Alexander sent out (325–324 B.C.), and voyaged from the mouth of the Indus to that of the Euphrates. An account of his voyage is given by Arrian in his *Indica*.

Nebris (neb′ris). A fawn skin worn as a special attribute by Dionysus and his attendant train (Pan, the satyrs, the maenads, etc.), and assumed on festival occasions by priests and priestesses of Dionysus, and by his worshipers generally.

Nectar (nek′tar). In classical mythology, the drink or wine of the Olympian gods, poured out for them by Hebe and Ganymede, the cup-bearers of Zeus. It was reputed to possess wondrous life-giving properties, to impart a divine bloom, beauty, and vigor to him so fortunate as to obtain it, and to preserve all that it touched from decay and corruption. In the *Iliad*, Thetis preserved the body of Patroclus by dripping nectar through his nostrils. Although nectar and ambrosia are usually considered the drink and food respectively, of the gods, in ancient literature nectar is occasionally defined as the food and ambrosia as the drink of the gods.

Neda (nē′da). When Zeus was born to Rhea on a mountain top in Arcadia, she prayed to Gaea for water in which to bathe him. In answer to her prayer the river Neda gushed forth. According to the legend, Neda, a river-nymph, was one of the nymphs who cared for the infant Zeus.

Neith (nē′ith). [Also: **Net.**] In early Egyptian mythology, a personification of the female principle, called mother of the gods. She was the mother of the sun-god, Ra, but herself unbegotten. She was the chief divinity of the city of Saïs, single, supreme, self-existent and self-producing. In some interpretations of her function she was thought to personify parthenogenesis. Identified by the Greeks with Athena, she was represented as a woman wearing the crown of lower Egypt.

Nekyia (nek′wi-a). The "Book of the Dead," a name given to the eleventh book of the *Odyssey*. (JJ)

Neleus (nē′lūs). In Greek mythology, a son of Tyro and Poseidon, and the twin of Pelias. His mother exposed the twins on a mountain but they were rescued by shepherds and Neleus was nursed by a bitch. When the twins grew up, they avenged the cruel treatment their mother had suffered at the hands of her stepmother, but later they quarreled. Pelias seized Iolcus and Neleus went into exile in Messenia. There he captured the city of Pylus. It throve so under his management that it is sometimes said to have been founded by him. He married Chloris, the only daughter of Niobe who survived when her other daughters were slain by Artemis because of Niobe's arrogance. Chloris bore him 12 sons. Heracles asked Neleus to purify him for the murder of Iphitus, but Neleus refused, and all his sons, except Nestor, supported their father's refusal and refused to receive Heracles. In revenge, Heracles later attacked Pylus, captured it and burned it, and killed all the sons of Neleus except Nestor. Neleus himself escaped and lived to dwell again in the rebuilt city.

Nelides (nē-lī′dēz). An epithet of Nestor, meaning "Son of Neleus."

Nemausus (nē-mô′sus). [Modern name, **Nîmes.**] An important Roman town in the valley of the Rhodanus (Rhône) River, in the Roman province known as Provincia (modern Provence). Established as a colony in 16 B.C., Nemausus prospered greatly, as the impressive remains of Roman buildings indicate: The "Maison Carrée," a handsome and well-preserved hexastyle Corinthian temple built by Agrippa, an amphitheater, a gate, and a great aqueduct, one imposing section of which survives as the Pont du Gard.

fat, fāte, fär, fāre, errant; net, mē, hėr ardent; pin, pīne; not, nōte, mŏve, nôr,

Eventually Nemausus replaced Narbo as capital of the province of Gallia Narbonensis. (JJ)

Nemea (nḗ'mḗ-ạ, nḗ-mḗ'ạ). In ancient geography, a valley in Argolis, Greece, about 11 miles SW of Corinth. Some say Nemea was named for a daughter of the river-god Asopus. Nearby was Tretus, the cave with the double entrance which, according to legend, was the haunt of the Nemean Lion. As the first of his 12 labors for Eurystheus, Heracles blocked one of the entrances, entered the cave, and choked the lion to death. To Nemea came the Seven on their way to wage war against Thebes. They asked Hypsipyle, nurse of Opheltes, son of Lycurgus, king of Nemea, where they might find water. She put down her young charge in the grove of Nemean Zeus and led them to a spring, later called Adrastea. While she was gone, a snake bit Opheltes and caused his death. In his honor the Nemean Games were founded. Of the 4th century B.C. Doric temple of Zeus three columns still stand. Excavations by French and American archaeologists have revealed the plan of the temple, notable for its sunken *adytum* or crypt at the rear of the cella, and a great altar, a palestra, a gymnasium, and an athletes' bath. The stadium lies in a recess in the neighboring hills.

Nemean (nḗ-mḗ'ạn). Epithet of Zeus, from his temple at Nemea in Argolis. A grove of cypress trees surrounded the temple, and it was in this grove that Opheltes was left by his nurse while she showed the Seven against Thebes where they could find water. Here Opheltes was bitten by a serpent, and died of its poison. His grave was on the spot, in an enclosure that also contained altars. Nearby was the grave of Lycurgus, his father. Near the temple was a spring, called Adrastea, perhaps because it was to this spring that the nurse of Opheltes led Adrastus and his Argive followers. Another sanctuary of Nemean Zeus was at Argos.

Nemean Games (nḗ-mḗ'ạn or nḗ'mḗ-ạn). One of the four great national festivals of the ancient Greeks (the others being the Olympian, Pythian, and Isthmian games). The Nemean Games were celebrated in the valley of Nemea near Cleonae, in the second and fourth years of each Olympiad, near the temple of the Nemean Zeus, some Doric columns of which are still standing. They are said to have been instituted originally in memory of Opheltes, the young son of Lycurgus, king of Nemea. The games consisted of athletic contests, equestrian exercises, and musical contests. The victor's garland at the Nemean Games was made of parsley (parsley being sacred to the dead in ancient Greece).

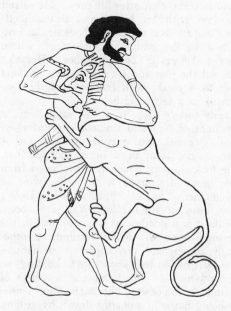

HERACLES STRANGLING THE NEMEAN LION
Black-figured Attic amphora, 6th century
B.C. *Museum of Fine Arts, Boston*

Nemean Lion. In Greek mythology, a huge lion that could not be killed with any weapon of iron, bronze, or stone. Some say it was the offspring of Typhon and Echidna; others say the two-headed dog Orthrus fathered it. It dwelt in a cleft in Mount Tretus, between Mycenae and Nemea. The first labor of Heracles was to slay the Nemean Lion, which had been ravaging the countryside. He arrived at Cleonae, near Mount Tretus, and stopped at a peasant's hut. The peasant, one Molorchus whose son had been killed by the lion, was just on the point of offering a sacrifice to Hera. Heracles told him he intended to kill the lion, and instructed

Molorchus to wait 30 days. If at the end of that time Heracles had not returned, then Molorchus must offer sacrifices to Heracles the hero, but if Heracles did return, then the sacrifice should be offered to Zeus. Heracles left Molorchus and proceeded to Mount Tretus. He encountered the lion but could make no impression on it with either his arrows, sword, or club. The lion withdrew to its lair unharmed. Heracles blocked up one end of the double-entranced lair and went into the cleft after his prey. He seized the lion with his hands and strangled it. He slung the lion across his shoulders and returned to the house of Molorchus, where they sacrificed to Zeus together. Heracles skinned the lion and ever afterward used its hide as a cloak, with the head of the lion serving as a terrifying helmet.

Nemesis (nem'e̦-sis). In Greek mythology, a daughter of Nyx and Erebus. According to some accounts, Zeus pursued Nemesis and at last, in the form of a swan, violated her. She took the egg which was produced from this union and gave it to Leda, wife of Tyndareus of Sparta. From this egg Helen, the cause of the Trojan War, was born. Nemesis is a goddess of law and justice, the personification of divine retribution, especially for human presumption. Sometimes she is represented as winged, holding an apple bough in one hand and a wheel of fortune in the other. She is also represented as being borne in a chariot drawn by griffins. By extension she is popularly regarded as a goddess of the inevitable. In the shrine of Nemesis at Rhamnus in Attica were two temples, the earlier, dating perhaps from the morrow of the first Persian invasion of 490 B.C., a modest distyle-in-antis structure, the other, a hexastyle peripteral temple by the nameless Periclean architect who built the temples of Hephaestus and Ares in Athens and of Poseidon at Sunium, begun about 436 B.C. and, probably in consequence of the Peloponnesian War (431–404 B.C.), never finished. It contained a cult statue of Parian marble by Agoracritus, fragments of which are said still to lie in the vicinity. Marble reliefs from its pedestal have survived, and are in the National Museum, Athens. In Augustus' time the temple was rededicated to the empress Livia. (JJ)

Nemetes (nē̦-mē'tēz). Ancient Germanic tribe, first mentioned by Caesar as being in the army of Ariovistus, king of the Suevi. The Nemetes were situated at the left side of the middle Rhenus, east of the Vosegus (Vosges), in the region about present-day Speyer, where they still remained after the defeat (58 B.C.) of Ariovistus.

Nemorensis, Lacus (nem-ō̦-ren'sis, lā'kus). [Italian, **Lago di Nemi**; English, **Lake Nemi.**] A small lake about 17 miles SE of Rome, noted for its beauty. It occupies the crater of an extinct volcano in the Alban Mountains. Nearby is a lonely wood in which there was a temple to Diana where all the Latins joined in her worship. Among the many legends connected with this shrine was one that in the wood there was a tree which bore a golden bough. Whoever plucked the bough and slew the priest of the shrine succeeded him as the new priest and retained the honor until he in his turn was slain. It was in the hope of finding analogies which might provide an explanation of this cult that Sir J. G. Frazer embarked upon the extended research in primitive religion and magic which culminated in the publication of his monumental *Golden Bough*. The "golden bough" itself has, with some plausibility, been explained as mistletoe.

Neocastro (ne"ô-kas'trô). See **Pylus.**

Neocorus (nē̦-ok'ō̦-rus). In Greek antiquity, the guardian of a temple, in some cases, merely a janitor or temple-sweeper, in others, a priestly officer of much dignity, having charge of the treasures dedicated in the temple. Under the Roman imperial dominion the title was accorded by the Senate to certain cities regarded as custodians of the ceremonial worship of Rome and of the emperor.

Neoptolemus (nē̦-op-tol'e̦-mus). [Also: **Pyrrhus.**] In Greek legend, the son of Achilles and Deidamia, the daughter of Lycomedes, king of Scyrus. After the death of Achilles in the Trojan War, Helenus, a Trojan seer who was captured by the Greeks, told them that Troy could not be taken without the aid of Neoptolemus. Odysseus and Diomedes were accordingly sent to Scyrus to fetch him. He eagerly consented to accompany them in spite of the tears and entreaties of his mother to remain safe in Scyrus. Some say he was only 12 years old at the time, and his name which was originally Pyrrhus means roughly, "he went to war young." On his arrival at Troy he went immediately into battle. Odysseus gave him Achilles' armor, Athena sent him glory, and he drove back Eurypylus, grandson of Heracles, who would surely have fired the Greek ships but for Neoptolemus. Night put an end to the battle. Next day it was resumed with increased ferocity. Neoptolemus led the Myrmidons against the Greeks and after a fierce struggle, he killed Eurypylus. Troy would have fallen before the Greek onslaught, but Zeus capriciously decided to save it by veiling it in a cloud, while Apollo saved Deïphobus from Neoptolemus by hiding him in a mist, and Thetis prevented her grandson Neoptolemus from coming face to face with Aeneas out of respect for Aphrodite, mother of Aeneas. Though Paris had been killed, the Greeks decided, with the assistance of the gods, not to try to take Troy by direct attack. Instead they proposed to build a great Wooden Horse and enter the city secretly and attack from within. Neoptolemus scorned the plan as cowardly. He preferred to win by valor. However, he was the first to volunteer to go in the Wooden Horse once the plan was adopted. Inside the city he fought ferociously. He found Priam and Hecuba before the altar of Zeus in the courtyard of Priam's palace, killed their son Polites and then slashed off Priam's head with one stroke of his sword when the aged king feebly attacked him. He then dragged the headless body to Achilles' tomb and left it there to rot. According to some accounts, it was Neoptolemus who hurled Astyanax, still a "wordless babe," the son of Hector and Andromache, from the towers of Troy. After the fall of the city, in which he took Andromache as his captive and concubine, the shade of Achilles appeared to him in a dream. Achilles announced that Priam's daughter Polyxena must be sacrificed on his tomb, or else Achilles' wrath would be even greater than when Briseis was taken from him, and he would send disastrous storms to prevent the Greeks from sailing. Neoptolemus related his dream and, over the protests of Agamemnon who thought there had been enough bloodshed, the sacrifice was carried out; Neoptolemus

wielded the knife as priest. Odysseus recounted the glorious exploits of Neoptolemus to Achilles when he saw him in the Underworld on his way home from Troy.

Neoptolemus now set sail for Molossia, whither Helenus had advised him to go. According to some accounts, in a shipwreck on the way he lost the arms of Achilles, which had been awarded to Odysseus over the claims of Telamonian Ajax, and which Odysseus had given to Neoptolemus. Thetis washed the arms ashore at the tomb of Ajax on Cape Rhoeteum. Arrived in Molossia with his captive Andromache, whom, some say, he treated kindly and who bore him sons, he learned that his grandfather Peleus had been banished from his kingdom of Iolcus. He went to Iolcus, drove out the usurpers and regained the throne. Next he went to Epirus and built a city near the Oracle of Dodona. But his father's death still troubled him, and he went to the shrine of Apollo at Delphi and upbraided the god for, as he thought, causing Achilles' death. He plundered and burned the shrine and departed for Sparta, where he claimed Hermione, daughter of Menelaus. Although she had been promised to Orestes, son of Agamemnon, the Spartans gave her to Neoptolemus. But she bore him no children, and was intensely jealous of Andromache. Neoptolemus set off again to Delphi to inquire why Hermione was barren. He was told he must appease Apollo for his earlier action of destroying the shrine. Accounts of his death vary. Some say he was slain at Delphi by Apollo's priests. Others say he took the sacrifices he had offered to appease the god from the altar and was slain by Machaereus. Still others say Orestes was the instigator of his murder. In any case, his body was buried in the precincts of the temple and the Delphians made annual offerings to him as a hero. His shade was borne off to the Elysian Fields by the immortal horses, Balius and Xanthus, which had wept at the death of Patroclus and Achilles and now were united with their master in the Underworld.

Neoptolemus. King of Epirus; fl. 4th century B.C. He was the father of Olympias and the grandfather of Alexander the Great.

Nepenthes (nē-pen'thēz). A plant that, mingled with wine, had an exhilarating effect, removing sorrow. In the *Odyssey*, it was an Egyptian drug which lulled sorrow for the day, and was given to Telemachus by Helen when he visited the court of Menelaus seeking information about Odysseus.

Nephele (nef′e̯-lē). In Greek mythology, a cloud, shaped by Zeus into the form of Hera to protect Hera from the amorous advances of Ixion. By this cloud Ixion became the father of Centaurus, the sire of the centaurs. At Hera's command, Athamas later married this phantom and became the father by her of two sons, Phrixus and Leucon, and one daughter, Helle. But Athamas tired of his phantom wife and fell in love with Ino, the daughter of Cadmus. Nephele, learning of his attachment, and being abandoned by Athamas, complained to Hera. The goddess vowed vengeance on Athamas and carried out her vow by causing Athamas to lose Ino and all his children.

Nepos (nē′pos, nep′os), **Cornelius.** Roman historian, born probably in Cisalpine Gaul; active in the 1st century B.C. He was a friend of Cicero and Catullus, and wrote love poetry, a three-book *Chronica,* anecdotes, and lives of Cicero and Cato, all lost. His only extant work, *De Excellentibus Ducibus Exterarum Gentium,* is a section from the *De Viris Illustribus,* biographies of celebrated men, a larger work of his now lost. In this work he treated Roman and Greek lives of famous generals and historians in separate sections.

Nepos, Quintus Caecilius Metellus. See **Metellus Nepos, Quintus Caecilius.**

Neptune (nep′tūn). In Roman mythology, the god of the sea. He was originally a water god and rain giver, and thus associated with the growth of vegetation; but he came to be identified by the Romans with the Greek Poseidon. There was a temple to Neptune at Rome in the Circus Flaminius where he was worshiped as patron of horses and horsemen, and a temple on the Campus Martius erected by Agrippa to commemorate a naval victory. Neptune, in the *Aeneid,* calmed the storm aroused by Aeolus at Juno's request, lifted up the sunken ships, dispersed the clouds and restored the sun for Aeneas and his fleet. He promised Venus he would give Aeneas calm seas until he arrived at the harbor of Cumae, but in return for the lives

he saved he demanded the life of one. The one he took was Palinurus, the steersman. In art Neptune is usually represented as a bearded man of stately presence, with the trident as his chief attribute, and the horse and the dolphin as symbols.

Nequinum (nē-kwī′num). [Also: **Narnia**; modern name, **Narni.**] In ancient geography, a town of Umbria in C Italy, on the Via Flaminia. It was situated on the Nar River about 43 miles N of Rome. The Umbrian town was captured by the Romans, 299 B.C., and colonized by them. The Roman name of the town was Narnia.

Nera (nā′rä). [Ancient name, **Nar.**] Small river in C Italy, a tributary of the Tiber. Terni is situated on it.

Nereid Friezes (ner′e̯-id). Four friezes from the Nereid monument at Xanthus in Lycia, now in the British Museum. The widest frieze represents a battle between Greeks and Asiatics; the others represent episodes of war, the chase, banquet, and sacrifice.

Nereids. In Greek mythology, sea nymphs, the 50 daughters of Nereus (whence the name) and Doris. The most famous among them were Amphitrite, Thetis, and Galatea. The Nereids were beautiful maidens helpful to voyagers, and constituted the main body of the female, as the Tritons did of the male, followers of Poseidon. They were imagined as dancing, singing, playing musical instruments, wooed by the Tritons, and passing in long processions over the sea seated on hippocamps and other sea creatures. They were also held to assist mariners in distress and were therefore especially worshiped on the islands, along the coasts, and at the mouths of rivers. Works of ancient art represent them lightly draped or nude, in poses characterized by undulating lines harmonizing with those of the ocean, and often riding on sea monsters of fantastic forms.

Nereus (ner′ūs). In Greek mythology, a seagod; the son of Pontus and Gaea. He was the husband of Doris, and the father of the 50 Nereids. On the whole he was a gentle and kindly god, but he had the power of changing his shape at will, and like Proteus, only by holding on to him firmly through all his transformations could one force him to answer the questions one asked of him. Heracles caught him and forced him to tell him how he could obtain the golden apples of the Hesperides.

Nerites (ner'i-tēz). In Greek mythology, a son of Nereus and Doris, and a brother of the Nereids. Aphrodite loved him as long as she lived in the sea. Because he would not follow her when she left the sea, she turned him into a mussel.

Neritos (ner'i-tos). In ancient geography, a small island near Ithaca, whose sheer cliffs rise abruptly from the sea. According to Greek legend, it belonged to Laertes in his young days.

Nero (nē'rō, nir'ō). [Full name, **Nero Claudius Caesar Drusus Germanicus**; original name, **Lucius Domitius Ahenobarbus**.] Roman emperor (54–68A.D.); born at Antium, Italy, Dec. 15, 37 A.D.; committed suicide near Rome, June 9, 68. He was the son of the consul Cn. Domitius Ahenobarbus and Agrippina (daughter of Germanicus Caesar). His father died when he was three years old and, since his mother had been banished the year before by the emperor Caligula, Nero was taken into the house of his aunt Domitia Lepida. The emperor Claudius recalled Agrippina, who at once began an unrelenting campaign to have Nero succeed Claudius in place of his son Britannicus. Agrippina married Claudius in 49 and persuaded him to adopt Nero as his son the following year. Seneca was recalled from exile and became his tutor. In 55 Nero married Octavia, the daughter of Claudius by Messalina. In 54 Claudius was poisoned by Agrippina, probably with the knowledge of Nero. She caused Nero to be proclaimed emperor to the exclusion of Britannicus, the son of Claudius, who was Nero's ward. The partisans of Britannicus made no great resistance; Nero was well received by the public, and the opening of his reign was propitious. His former tutors, the philosopher Seneca and Burrus, commander of the pretorian guards, were placed at the head of the government. The early years of his reign were marked, on the whole, by clemency and justice. To be sure, he caused his rival, Britannicus, to be removed by poison (55) but such removals of threats to the imperial power had become so common as to be taken for granted, and did not particularly arouse resentment against him. The Senate recovered some of its power, taxes were lowered, many abuses were corrected, and the provinces were left in peace. In this time a great struggle for domination over the young emperor was being waged by Agrippina and Seneca. Agrippina's influence had been supreme, for she had made him emperor. But when Nero fell in love with Acte, a beautiful freedwoman, and was encouraged in the affair by Seneca, Agrippina rebuked, harried, and ultimately threatened her son. Nero deprived her of her Roman and German bodyguards, took away her power, and sent her away from his palace. Her continued threats and violent behavior so frightened him that he decided to put her out of his way. It is said he tried three times to poison her, but that each time she had taken an antidote in advance. He had a mechanical contrivance rigged up in her bedroom that would hurl the ceiling down and crush her as she slept, but someone revealed the presence of the device. Later, he pretended reconciliation and invited her to visit him at Baiae. He arranged to have the galley in which she arrived collide with another so that it was no longer seaworthy. After a seemingly affectionate reunion, he kissed her and put her aboard a vessel for her return home. This vessel was so constructed that it would collapse and fall apart on signal. On the way home the vessel collapsed as planned, but Agrippina saved herself by swimming to shore. In the end, Nero sent a group of soldiers to surround her house and murder her in her bedroom (59). Then at once he became fearful of the consequences of his crime, and claimed to be haunted by her ghost. He said the Furies hounded him with whips and flaming brands, and he asked magicians to intercede with her ghost and compel it to cease haunting him. The report was circulated that Agrippina had died as a result of her own plots against him, and congratulations came to him from all quarters that he had been spared. He was tumultuously welcomed when he returned to Rome. In 61 a savage revolt erupted in Britain. One Roman legion was destroyed before it was put down. Burrus died in 62, whereupon Seneca retired from public life. Freed from the restraint of his former advisers, Nero gave free rein to a naturally tyrannical and cruel disposition. He divorced Octavia in order to marry Poppaea, who had been his mistress for several years. He had several times tried to strangle Octavia, and when he divorced her, his act was so unpopular that he banished her to the island of Pandataria and shortly afterward had her put to death (62). Poppaea ultimately died (65) from the effects of a kick administered by her brutal husband. He also married Statilia Messalina, whose husband he murdered. In 63 the Romans lost the province of Armenia. Having been accused of kindling the fire which in 64 destroyed a large part of Rome, he sought to divert attention from himself by ordering a persecution of the Christians, whom he accused of having caused the conflagration. Traditionally, Peter and Paul both died in this persecution, but this is unlikely. Legend states that Nero, having set the fire, watched it spread while playing music on his lyre. The fire raged for six days, subsided, and then broke out anew. Nero made what provision was possible to shelter the many who were made homeless, brought in food from Ostia, and lowered the price of grain. In the rebuilding of the city an attempt was made to prevent future conflagrations by leaving open spaces about the new houses which were to be at least partly of stone, and by replacing the narrow winding alleys with broad streets. Nero took the opportunity offered by the fire to erect the "Golden House" between the Palatine and Esquiline Hills. It was built with no consideration for cost, decorated with gold and precious stones, and surrounded by magnificent grounds. The provinces were taxed heavily to pay for it. From the time of the fire Nero's popularity waned rapidly. The fire was thought to be a sign of the wrath of the gods, and was followed by a plague. In addition, his personal and public excesses, his wild extravagance, his cruelty and licentiousness, disgusted and terrified the people. A group of enemies conspired to murder him and put Caius Calpurnius Piso, a young noble who was one of his closest companions, in his place. The conspiracy was discovered (65) and the leaders were put to death. Nero was terrified by the plot and the extent of the enmity against him it revealed. He seized many citizens and had them put to death, among them Seneca. From this time on he killed Roman citizens more or less at will. From his youth Nero had been interested in the lyre and singing; he had studied and worked at this interest, and had arrived at a point where he considered himself a serious and accomplished musician. In 67 he went to Greece and entered as a contestant in the chariot races and musical competition. To accommodate him, all the great festivals were held in one year. He won the prizes in every contest, whether he actually competed or not, but he usually went through the motions of competing on the same terms as the other entrants. He was pleased with his reception in Greece and made lavish presents. While there he planned to cut a canal across the Isthmus at Corinth, and even went so far as to remove the first spadeful of earth himself. When he returned to Italy (68) he had great sections of the walls of the towns he visited torn down to permit his entry, as was fitting to a victor in the Greek games, and gave many musical entertainments, from which no one was permitted to depart while he was still performing. In his absence in Greece unrest at Rome had increased. More dangerous to him was the unrest and outright spirit of rebellion that had arisen in the provinces. Revolt broke out in Gaul. It was put down, and the troops who quelled it offered the throne to their commander. He refused it. This revolt was followed by one in Spain where Galba, the leader, proclaimed himself emperor. When Nero at last decided to take action to save his tottering power he found himself deserted even by his palace guards. He fled from Rome to the house of a freedman and there, with the aid of his secretary, stabbed himself and expired just as the troops who had been sent to take him alive arrived. Acte, the beautiful freedwoman he had earlier loved, had his body buried in the family tomb on the Pincian Hill. Many people refused to believe he was dead, and in ensuing years several appeared who pretended, with success in certain quarters, to be Nero. With the death of Nero the line of the Julian emperors came to an end. Suetonius tells that when Livia was returning to Rome after marrying Augustus, an eagle swooped down and deposited a white pullet in her lap. The pullet held a laurel twig in its beak. She kept the pullet and planted the twig. The pullet produced a great flock of poultry and the twig grew into a luxuriant tree. The Caesars henceforth were crowned with laurel from this tree in their triumphs. The deaths of the Julian emperors were foretold by the tree, whose leaves unfailingly wilted just before one of them died. In the last year of Nero's reign the original laurel tree, and those that had been raised from it as slips, died at the root, and the whole flock of chickens, descended from the original pullet, also died, thus faithfully prophesying the death of Nero and the end of the Julian line.

Nero, Caesar Tiberius Claudius. See **Tiberius.**

Nero, Caius Claudius. Roman consul in 207 B.C. He marched against Hasdrubal, and (with Marcus Livius Salinator) defeated him in the decisive battle of the Metaurus in 207 B.C.

Nero Claudius Drusus (klod'i-us drö'sus). See **Drusus, Nero Claudius.**

Nerva (nėr'va̞), **Marcus Cocceius.** Roman emperor (96–98 A.D.); born c30 A.D.; died Jan. 27, 98. He was consul with Vespasian in 71 and with Domitian in 90, and was raised to the throne (96) after the latter was murdered. He was a mild and just ruler and accomplished reforms in laws, taxation, and expenditures. He was unable, however, to control the Praetorian Guard and therefore adopted (97) Trajan as his successor.

Nervii (nėr'vi-ī). Ancient warlike people of the Belgic Gauls, dwelling in the neighborhood of the Sabis (Sambre) River. They opposed the Romans but were defeated (57 B.C.) by Julius Caesar.

Nesiotes (nes-i-ō'tēz, nē-shē-). See **Critius and Nesiotes.**

Nessus (nes'us). In Greek legend, a centaur slain by Heracles. He carried Deianira, Heracles' wife, across the river Evenus; but when he attempted to ravish her, Heracles shot him with a poisoned arrow. Dying, Nessus secretly declared to Deianira that his blood would preserve her husband's love, and she put it in a vial and took it with her. Later she rubbed the dried blood on a sacrificial robe and sent it to Heracles, hoping thereby to regain his love which he had transferred to his captive, Iole, and to speed his return home. Heracles donned the robe to offer sacrifice; the garment clung to his flesh, which was torn off with it. The herald, Lichas, who brought the robe, was cast by the raging hero into the sea, and Deianira hanged herself when she learned what had happened. Heracles built and ascended a pyre, had it set on fire, and was carried off from it to Olympus, thus fulfilling a prophecy that no living man would kill him but that he would die as the result of action by a dead enemy.

Nestor (nes'tọr). In Greek legend, one of the 12 children of Neleus, king of Pylus, and Chloris, only surviving daughter of Amphion and Niobe. In his youth he took part in the Calydonian Hunt. Nestor was the only one of Neleus' sons to receive Heracles when the latter came to Pylus to ask Neleus to purify him for the murder of Iphitus. Although Nestor urged his father to do it, Neleus refused. Because of his good intentions in this case, when Heracles later attacked Pylus and killed the rest of Neleus' sons, he spared Nestor and gave him the city of Messene. He was the first to swear an oath by Heracles and came to be much loved by him. But some say Nestor was away in Gerenia at the time of Heracles' attack. In Homer he is spoken of as the "Gerenian Horseman." At his father's order Nestor made war on the people of Elis, because they had stolen a chariot that Neleus had sent to compete in the games. He acquitted himself gloriously, taking rich booty, although this was his first experience of war. The Eleans retaliated, and Nestor, on foot because his father thought he was too young to control warhorses, furiously counter-attacked and cut a wide swath through their ranks. He slew an Elean and continued the battle from his dead enemy's chariot. He would have killed the Moliones but Poseidon spirited them away in a mist. The Eleans fled, and Nestor was given the honors for this victory. A truce was arranged and funeral games were held. Nestor won all the contests except the chariot race, and he lost that only because the Moliones committed a foul. He also fought against the Arcadians and took a valiant part in the battle between the Lapiths and the centaurs. Nestor recalled the glorious deeds of his youth when he rallied the Greeks during the dark days of the Trojan War. He succeeded to the throne of Messenia and lived in Pylus, where remains of his palace have recently been found. He had already governed two generations of men, and was ruling a third, when the Trojan War started. Nevertheless he immediately joined Agamemnon's forces, to which he contributed 90 ships. He accompanied Menelaus on his journey to recruit the Greek princes, former suitors of Helen, for the war against Troy. He also went on the mission to Scyrus to fetch Achilles. He became Agamemnon's most trusted and skillful adviser in the war, his "utterance flowed from his smooth tongue sweeter than honey." His name has become a synonym for a wise old man, an elder statesman. He was a bold fighter in spite of his advanced age, and was a master of cavalry and infantry tactics. Agamemnon cherished him and said if he had but ten Nestors, the war would soon be over. Nestor and Odysseus always agreed on the course which should be followed in the conduct of the war. It was Nestor who advised the Greeks to take advantage of a truce in the fighting for burial of the dead, to dig a moat and to raise a wall as protection for the Greek ships drawn up on the beach before Troy. His sound judgment, firm and kindly character made him respected by all. In rallying or advising the Greeks he made many long speeches—the privilege of an old man—citing the magnificent exploits of his own career as a spur to the Greeks. He tried to prevent the quarrel between Agamemnon and Achilles over the captive Briseis. He told them Priam and the Trojans would rejoice if they knew how the Greek chiefs were quarreling among themselves. In this he was unsuccessful. Later he advised Agamemnon to try to resolve the quarrel by restoring Briseis to Achilles and sending him rich gifts. But Achilles refused to accept this peace offer. Nestor, however, did persuade Patroclus, the great friend of Achilles who had withdrawn from the war with him, to don Achilles' armor and lead his Myrmidons against the Trojans. Nestor took full part in the fighting. At one point when his chariot horses were wounded and became unmanageable, Nestor was in danger of his life. Antilochus, his youngest son, came to his rescue. He saved Nestor but lost his own life when Memnon attacked and killed

him. Nestor rushed to attack Memnon, but the Aethiopian told him to withdraw; he did not wish, he said, to wage war on an old man. Nestor grieved for his lost youth, and lamented that his brave heart had been "tamed by time." When, following the death of Achilles, Thetis offered his armor to the bravest of the Argives who had rescued his body, Telamonian Ajax and Odysseus both claimed Achilles' arms. Ajax suggested that Idomeneus, Nestor, and Agamemnon should decide between them. Nestor was filled with foreboding. The careless gods, he said, had laid a great woe on them, because whoever lost in the choice would be lost to the Greeks. He suggested that they should let the Trojan captives decide which one, Ajax or Odysseus, had done them the most harm. In that way the loser's wrath would be turned against the Trojans, and not against his fellow Greeks. This was done, but Nestor proved right in predicting that whoever lost would be lost to the Greeks, for Ajax committed suicide. Nestor was one of the few who had a prosperous voyage home after the war. He took the bones of the physician Machaon back to Pylus with him, and placed them in a sanctuary; many came to be healed there. Odysseus' son Telemachus, in search of news of his father, visited Pylus ten years after the Trojan War had ended. He found Nestor, now at a very advanced age, governing a prosperous kingdom, surrounded by bold, intelligent sons, and blessed by the gods; for he had always been just, courteous, valiant, and one who paid due honor to the gods. By his wife Anaxibia (or Eurydice, as Homer names her), he had two daughters and seven sons. He lived out his days peacefully and died at a very old age. Some say he lived 300 years, because Apollo added to his life span all the years that were denied his uncles, the sons of Niobe and Amphion slain by Apollo. The substantial bronze-age palace, discovered and excavated by a University of Cincinnati expedition directed by Carl W. Blegen, several miles inland from Pylus in Messenia, is plausibly believed to be Nestor's palace. The large numbers of clay tablets found there, inscribed in the syllabic script known as Linear B, essential to Ventris' decipherment of the language as an early form

fat, fāte, fär, fāre, errạnt; net, mē, hėr ardẹnt; pin, pīne; not, nōte, mŏve, nôr,

of Greek, are no doubt from the archives of one of Nestor's successors.

Nestus (nes'tus). [Also: **Mesta.**] River in SE Europe, rising in SW Bulgaria and flowing generally SE through NE Greece to the Aegean Sea opposite the island of Thasus.

Nicaea (ni-sē'a̧). [Anglicized, **Nice;** Greek, **Nikaia;** modern Turkish name, **Iznik.**] In ancient geography, a town in Bithynia, Asia Minor, situated on Lake Ascania, about 58 miles SE of Constantinople. It was founded in the 4th century B.C., and was one of the chief cities of Bithynia. It was the seat of the two Councils of Nicaea, at the first of which (325 A.D.) the Nicene Creed was formulated and decreed.

Nicaea. [Modern name, **Nice.**] In ancient geography, a town on the coast of Liguria, founded by colonists from Massilia (present Marseilles) in the 1st century A.D.

Nicander (ni-kan'dėr, nī-). Greek poet, grammarian, and physician, born at Colophon in Asia Minor, probably about the middle of the 2nd century B.C. He was a priest of Apollo and a physician, and lived in Pergamum and Alexandria. He wrote widely on agriculture and on mythological transformations, only fragments of which survive. Two poems, on treatment of wounds inflicted by poisonous animals and on poisons and their antidotes, are extant.

Nicaria (nī-kär'i-a̧). See **Icaria,** island.

Nicator (nī-kā'tôr, -tor). See **Seleucus I.**

Nicator, Demetrius. See **Demetrius II** (of *Syria*).

Nicias (nish'i-as). Athenian general and politician; killed 413 B.C., in Sicily. He was the son of Niceratus and, although he was wealthy, he was the leader of a moderate party at Athens. He favored peace with Sparta and was continually opposed by Cleon and others who had lately won influence in the assembly and who pursued a policy of empire and war with Sparta. Nicias maintained his popularity with the people by his deserved reputation for incorruptibility, his undeserved reputation as a general, and his conspicuous piety. In the latter connection, he played a leading part in the "cleansing" of Delos. This was done (426 B.C.) to propitiate Apollo that he might never again send plague to Athens. The bodies of the dead were removed from

their tombs on Delos and transferred to another island. It was ordered that henceforth those on the island who were near death, or women who were about to bear children, should be removed to neighboring Rhenia to keep Delos pure. Under his leadership the Athenians reëstablished the ancient games of Apollo and held them every four years at Delos. A few years later all the inhabitants were moved from the island to complete the purification. Such manifestations of piety were intensely gratifying to the Athenians. Nicias ever held their respect and support. He was *strategus* (general) when the Spartans were besieged in Sphacteria (425 B.C.), and replied to the taunts of Cleon, who claimed he would capture the Spartan garrison himself if he were commander, by resigning his command to Cleon in order to permit the latter to carry out his boast. To the surprise of all, Cleon did so. To counteract the growing influence of Cleon that ensued from this success, Nicias went to the Peloponnesus and established a garrison at Methone (425 B.C.), and captured the island of Cythera (424 B.C.) from which the Athenians could raid Sparta. In 423 B.C. he negotiated a one-year truce with Sparta. The truce was violated in Thrace, whither Nicias now sailed at the head of a fleet of 50 ships and recovered Mende which had revolted. In 421 B.C. he was the chief Athenian negotiator of a peace, with Plistoanax the Spartan king, that was to last for 50 years. In 420 B.C. Alcibiades was elected strategus and Nicias was not. An expedition was made against Epidaurus; Sparta came to her assistance; Athens claimed Sparta had broken the peace. Nicias was returned as strategus (418 B.C.), continued to advocate peace, but found himself, through the vagaries of political fortunes, now in alliance with the warlike and far from pious Alcibiades.

In 416 B.C. Segesta, a city of Sicily, asked Athens for aid in a war with her neighbor Selinus. Alcibiades was all eagerness for a war in Sicily. He painted a glowing picture of the aggrandizement of Athens as the result of such a war. The younger generation of Athens responded to his clamor for war as if in a hypnotic trance. Nicias opposed sending aid to Segesta. In the first place, he doubted—correctly as it turned out—that the Segestaeans had the money they promised for the war. He pointed out that the Athenians had enough enemies near at hand without going abroad for more. Even if an expedition to Sicily should succeed, it would be impossible to keep an enemy subdued at such a distance. It would be more to the purpose to concentrate on the enemies at hand. But the Athenians were so in love with the idea of conquering Sicily, about which they had only the vaguest ideas, that they paid no attention at all to his good advice, nor were they deterred in the least when he presented a formidable estimate of the cost of such an expedition. They voted all he asked for and made him, against his wish and judgment, one of the three commanders of the expedition with full power to help Segesta against Selinus, restore the Leontini to their city that had been taken by Syracuse, and promote Athenian interests in all matters. The other two commanders were Alcibiades and Lamachus. The most splendid and costly armament ever prepared by one city for the longest passage away from home ever attempted, sailed in a carnival atmosphere from the Piraeus (415 B.C.), libations having been poured and prayers uttered by a herald. At Corcyra the fleet, 134 galleys, was divided into three squadrons, each under one of the three commanders. Arrived at Rhegium, Nicias wanted to sail directly against Selinus to settle the affair of the Segestaeans. Alcibiades prevailed on him to prepare for an attack on Syracuse, but before it could be mounted, Alcibiades was recalled to Athens to answer a charge of impiety. Nicias and Lamachus divided the command between them. Lamachus now urged immediate attack on Syracuse, while the Syracusans were still unprepared and overawed by the size of the armament the Athenians had brought against them. Nicias rejected his advice. Instead the summer was spent sailing about, engaging in ineffectual skirmishes, while Nicias tried to make up his mind. In the meantime, the Syracusans recovered from their first shock and began energetic preparations to defend themselves. The Athenians frittered away their time, their money, and their striking power sailing up and down the coast, and then returned to Syracuse. In the first engagements there they were successful, but in one of them Lamachus was slain (414 B.C.), leaving the sole command to Nicias. He was not only incapable of making decisive moves but was ill. The Syracusans sent to Sparta and Corinth for aid and the Spartan general Gylippus arrived to aid them. A furious contest of building walls about Syracuse took place between the Athenians, to protect access to their ships and cut off the city, and the Syracusans, to protect their city and cut off the Athenians. As the strength of Syracuse under Gylippus grew, Nicias sent to Athens for help. Demosthenes and Eurymedon were sent out with a fleet. Demosthenes, driven back in an attempt to take one of the heights of Syracuse, advised Nicias to withdraw while he could still save his fleet, as he was convinced that Syracuse, made strong by her own preparations and by her allies, could not be taken by siege, and as he realized the danger in which the Athenian fleet was placed in the harbor. Nicias was fearful of his reception in Athens if he should retreat from Syracuse, and would not leave unless he was ordered to do so from Athens. To receive such an order would take a long time. He would not even withdraw to Catana, from which his army would have room to maneuver in open territory as Demosthenes advised, for at Syracuse the Athenians were cramped by the physical limitations of the location. When Gylippus returned to Syracuse with reinforcements, Nicias saw that his position was hopeless and decided to withdraw under cover of darkness. All was in readiness and the Syracusans were unaware of his intention. But that night there was an eclipse of the moon. One might have said the gods were aiding the Athenians with total darkness for their withdrawal. But many regarded the eclipse as an evil omen. Nicias consulted the soothsayers and decided to wait the 27 days they had prescribed. In that time the Syracusans learned that he meant to retreat. Emboldened by this obvious sign of weakness, they resolved to prevent the withdrawal they would earlier have welcomed. They defeated the Athenians in a sea fight and bottled their remaining ships in the harbor. The crews refused to board the ships for another attempt to get through the enemy fleet. Nicias was now compelled to retreat overland. Even in this extremity he let time help the Syracusans. They were celebrating their sea victory and would have been in no condition to march out and stop the Athenians, but Nicias delayed, duped by a stratagem of the Syracusan Hermocrates. When he led his forces overland in retreat, the Syracusans were ready and attacked them as they fled. The forces were divided between Demosthenes and Nicias, Eurymedon having been slain. Those under Demosthenes fell behind and were forced to surrender. Nicias, unaware of the surrender, pushed on to the Asinarus River. His men were harried by Syracusan attacks and many were lost; they were exhausted by lack of provisions and by thirst. When they came to the Asinarus River, they tumbled into it like madmen to allay their thirst. The Syracusans and their Peloponnesian allies, lined atop the steep opposite bank, butchered them with arrows and javelins as they drank. Nicias, who had now learned of the surrender of Demosthenes, offered to surrender. The Syracusans might do as they liked to him if they would stop the slaughter of his men. Gylippus accepted his surrender. According to Thucydides, Gylippus would have preferred to lead Nicias back as a captive, but the exultant Syracusans butchered him, and Demosthenes as well. The men were enslaved and imprisoned in a quarry. A few escaped and brought back the terrible news to Athens—news that the entire armament was destroyed and that those who were not killed were enslaved. This was the greatest disaster Athens had ever suffered and she did not recover. According to Thucydides' account of it in his *History of the Peloponnesian Wars,* if any one man was responsible for it that man was Nicias, whose incapacity and indecision along with his obstinacy were not only incredible but tragic for Athens. In his defense it must be said that he was personally brave, scrupulously honest, pious to the point of blind superstition, and commander of the expedition by popular demand and against his own will.

Nicias of Athens (ath′enz). Greek painter of the 4th century B.C., a younger contemporary of Praxiteles. When Praxiteles was asked which of his works in marble he valued most, he is said to have answered, "Those on which Nicias has set his mark." Pliny explains this expression by the comment, "So much importance did Praxiteles attach to the *circumlitio* (tinting of color) applied by Nicias." This passage was for a long time the principal foundation for the theory that the Greeks painted their statues, which is now confirmed by the works themselves. Nicias was noted for his skill in giving a third dimension to his pictures by the proper use of light and shade, and was celebrated for his painting of female figures and other subjects which gave scope for dramatic treatment. Among the latter was a *Rescue of Andromeda* and one of *Odysseus Questioning the Dead in the Underworld.* Ptolemy of Egypt offered a large sum for this latter picture, but Nicias preferred to make a present of it to Athens.

Nicias, Peace of. Peace arranged by the Athenian general Nicias with Sparta (421 B.C.), by the terms of which there was to be a 50-year truce between Athens and Sparta. The peace was broken almost immediately.

Nicippe (nī-sip′ē). In Greek legend, a daughter of Pelops and Hippodamia. She was the wife of Sthenelus, the Argive king. When she was about to bear a child, Hera hastened her labor so that her child, Eurystheus, would be born before Alcmene's child and would, in accordance with an oath given by Zeus, become high king of the Perseid people. Thus it was that Nicippe's son Eurystheus was able to exact the 12 labors from Alcmene's son Heracles.

Nicolaus of Damascus (nik-ō-lā′us; da-mas′kus). Greek historian; born at Damascus; fl. in the 1st century B.C. The Jewish king Herod the Great was his patron, and he became friendly with Augustus when he accompanied Herod on a visit to Rome. He wrote a universal history from the time of the Assyrian empire to his own day in 144 books; a life of Augustus, and an autobiography. Fragments of his work survive.

Nicomachean Ethics (nī′′kō-ma-kē′an). Ethical treatise by Aristotle, believed to be a series of his lectures edited by his son.

Nicomachus (nī-kom′a-kus). Greek painter, active about the middle of the 4th century B.C. He was noted for the speed and excellence with which he painted. One of his paintings famous in antiquity was *The Rape of Persephone.*

Nicopolis (ni-kop′ō̇-lis, nī-). Ancient city in Cappadocia, Asia Minor, founded by Pompey to commemorate his victory there over Mithridates VI in 66 B.C.

Nicopolis. In ancient geography, a city in Epirus, Greece, situated on the Gulf of Arta. It was founded by Octavian (later the emperor Augustus) in commemoration of his victory at Actium in 31 B.C. The site contains many Roman antiquities.

Nicopolis. Ancient city near Alexandria, Egypt, founded (24 B.C.) by Augustus to commemorate his defeat of Antony.

Nicosthenes (ni-kos′thi-nēz). Attic potter of the 6th century B.C. His work is known from about 100 extant vessels bearing his signature. The decorator of his vessels worked in the black-figure style and is called the Nicosthenes Painter.

Nicostrata (nī-kos′tra̤-ta̤). In Greek legend, a daughter of the river-god Ladon. She was the wife of Echenus but by Hermes was the mother of Evander. She persuaded Evander to murder Echenus, and when they were banished from Arcadia for this crime, she accompanied him to Italy, whither he emigrated. It was she who chose the site of the city he founded, Pallantium, near the Tiber River. It is the present site of the Palatine Hill. According to some accounts, it was she also who brought the alphabet to Italy and adapted it for use by the Latins. Others say the alphabet was a contribution which Heracles made to the Latins. In Italy Nicostrata's name was changed to Carmenta in recognition of her gift of prophecy.

Nicostratus (nī-kos′tra̤-tus). According to some accounts in Greek legend, a son of Menelaus and Helen. Some say that with his bastard brother Megapenthes he drove Helen out of Sparta after the death of Menelaus. Nicostratus was worshiped as a hero by the Lacedaemonians.

Nicostratus. Name of two Greek comic poets; the first, a writer of Middle Comedy, was said to be a son of Aristophanes. The second, a writer of New Comedy, was active at the end of the 4th and the beginning of the 3rd century B.C.

Night. In Greek mythology, the "Subduer of Gods and Men;" the child of Chaos. See **Nyx.**

Nike (nī′kē, nē′kā). [Latin, **Victoria.**] In Greek mythology, the goddess of victory, especially victory in war. According to Hesiod she was a daughter of Styx, whom she accompanied to aid Zeus in his war against the Titans. After the victory of Zeus

NIKE LOOSING HER SANDAL
Relief from the south face of the Temple of Nike Apteros on the Acropolis at Athens, c409, B.C. *Acropolis Museum, Athens*

in this struggle Nike remained on Olympus. She was identified often with Athena, and by the Romans with their Victoria. She was regularly represented as a winged maiden, usually as alighting from flight, her most frequent attributes being a palm branch in one hand and a garland in the other, or a fillet outstretched in both hands; sometimes she holds a herald's staff.

Nike Apteros (ap′te̤-ros) or **Wingless Victory, Temple of.** See **Athena Nike, Temple of.**

Nilus (nī′lus). The river-god of the Nile River.

Nineveh (nin′e̤-ve). [Latin, **Ninus.**] In ancient geography, an important city, for a long time the capital of the Assyrian Empire, situated on the E bank of the upper Tigris opposite what is now Mosul, and surrounded in ancient times by a shallow river (Khosr). The site, now marked by the two mounds of Kuyunjik and Nebi Unus, was first identified in 1820 by J. C. Rich, political resident of the East India Company at Baghdad. The first attempts at excavation were made in 1842 by Paul Emile Botta, who, however, met with slight success; these were followed on a more extended scale by Sir Austen Henry Layard (1845–47, 1849–51), by Hormuzd Rassam (1854), by George Smith (1873–76), the work being again taken up by Rassam on the death of Smith, and by King and Thompson (1903–05). As a result of these excavations, the general outline of a city about three miles long, the remains of four palaces and numerous sculptures, and thousands of tablets (principally from the so-called library of Assurbanipal) were discovered. The greater part of these are now in the British Museum. The city had a perimeter of from seven to eight miles, the ruins of the walls showing a height in some parts of 50 feet. It was in existence as early as the time of Hammurabi (c1950 B.C.). Shalmaneser I (1330 B.C.) built a palace at Nineveh and made it the city of his residence. Shamshi-Adad V (824–811) decorated and restored the temple of Ishtar, famous for a special phase of the cult of the goddess. Adadnirari III (811–782 B.C.) built a new palace on the site of the mound Nebi Yunus. For a time Nineveh was neglected, Sargon II (722–705 B.C.) the founder of the new dynasty, abandoning it as the capital for a new town Dur Sharrukin (Khorsabad) which he built and made his residence. His son, Sennacherib (705–681 B.C.), was, however, a special patron of Nineveh. He surrounded it with a wall, replaced (695 B.C.) the small palace at the NE wall by a large one, built another palace which he filled with cedar wood and adorned with colossal bulls and lions, and beautified the city with a park. The Old Testament (2 Kings, xix. 36, Isa. xxxvii, 37) mentions Nineveh as the residence of Sennacherib. Esarhaddon (680–668 B.C.) finished a temple, widened the streets, and beautified the city, forcing the kings whom he conquered to furnish materials for adorning the city and palaces.

Nineveh succumbed (c608 B.C.) to the combined attack of the Medes under Cyaxares and the Babylonians under Nabopolassar.

Nine Worthies. Nine heroes of ancient legend and medieval chivalric romance. In one of the latter, the *Triumphes des neufs Preux,* the author feigns that there appeared to him in a vision nine heroes, and in a second vision a tenth hero, i.e., Joshua, David, Judas Maccabaeus, Hector, Alexander the Great, Julius Caesar, and then Arthur, Charlemagne, Godfrey of Bouillon, and finally Bertrand du Guesclin. They charge him to undertake the description of their lives and feats, in order that Lady Triumphe, who appears with them, may decide which of them has deserved her crown. The nine heroes of this romance are not infrequently mentioned in English literature. Shakespeare alludes (in *Love's Labour's Lost*) to the Nine Worthies. They also appear in the verses which precede the Low German history of Alexander the Great. They figure in tapestry and paintings. This selection of thrice three heroes may have originated in the Welsh *Triads,* where the three pagan, Jewish, and Christian trinities are enumerated as follows: Hector, Alexander, and Julius Caesar; Joshua, David, and Judas Maccabaeus; Arthur, Charlemagne, and Godfrey de Bouillon. Guy of Warwick is sometimes substituted for Godfrey.

Ninus (nī'nus). In Greek legend, the eponymous founder of Nineveh and of the Assyrian Empire; husband of Semiramis, the famous Assyrian queen. She is said to have coaxed Ninus into giving her full power for five days; he did so, and on the second she had him put to death.

Ninus, Tomb of. In Roman legend, the spot outside the city of Babylon where Pyramus was to meet Thisbe under a mulberry tree, and where he, thinking Thisbe had been slain by a lion, killed himself. Thisbe, returning to the spot and finding him dying, killed herself too, and ever after the berries of the mulberry tree were dyed red from their blood.

Niobe (nī'ō-bē). In Greek legend, the first mortal woman loved by Zeus. She bore him Argus and Pelasgus. Some say she was the mother of Phoroneus and the wife of Inachus. Others say she was the daughter of Phoroneus.

Niobe. In Greek mythology, the daughter of Tantalus, and thus a sister of Pelops. She was the wife of Amphion, king of Thebes, and the mother of seven sons and seven daughters, and extremely proud of this fact. (Other accounts give various numbers for her children, ranging from four to 20.) The Theban women, inspired by a seeress, were making offerings to Leto when Niobe appeared among them. In her arrogance she mentioned her ancestors, Tantalus, Atlas, even Zeus, who was her father-in-law as well as her ancestor. She spoke of the wealth and power of her husband, her own beauty, and above all, of her sons and daughters. She reminded the worshipers of Leto that Leto had only two children, and that both earth and sea had refused her a place to bear them until the tiny island of Delos sheltered her. For these reasons she considered that the Thebans should worship her instead of Leto, and finally prevailed on them to do so. Apollo and Artemis, Leto's children, took instant revenge for their mother. Apollo slew Niobe's sons, and Artemis killed her daughters. (Some say one son and one daughter were spared.) Zeus prevented the burial of the children by turning the Thebans into stone. After nine days, the gods themselves performed the burial rites. Niobe, distracted by grief, wandered to Mount Sipylus, where she was changed by Zeus into a marble statue whose face is continually wet with tears.

Niobids (nī′ō-bidz). The term means "Children of Niobe." The *Slaughter of the Niobids,* when Apollo and Artemis avenged Niobe's affront to their mother Leto by slaying Niobe's seven sons and seven daughters with their arrows, attracted at least two able sculptors. Copies of individual figures by them, separated by considerations of style into a 5th-century B.C. group and a 4th-century B.C. group, survive in European museums. Assigned to the 5th-century group is the superb Niobid in the National Museum (Museo delle Terme) in Rome, and a boy and a girl in Copenhagen. A collection of 18 statues in the Uffizi in Florence, the Chiaramonti Niobid in the Vatican, and others are assigned to the 4th-century group. The theme, offering a variety of postures, standing, running, crouching, kneeling, and pros-

trate, with perhaps 18 figures (Apollo, Artemis, Niobe, 14 children, and the *paedagogus* or tutor), would have lent itself admirably to the triangular composition of a temple pediment, and it is likely that one or both groups were originally so designed and erected, to be eventually shipped to Rome. It has been suggested that the 5th-century group represents the missing S pediment of the temple of Apollo at Bassae. The identification of the sculptors is in dispute. (JJ)

Nireus (nī′rös). Named in the *Iliad* as a son of Aglaia and Charopus. He was the fairest of the Greeks who went to Troy except Achilles, but his good looks were linked with a weakling's prowess. He was slain by Eurypylus, grandson of Heracles.

Nisa (nī′sa). Ancient name of **Megara.**

Nisaea (nī-sē′a). In ancient geography, a region in Media (perhaps near the Caspian Gates), famous for its breed of horses.

Nisaea. The port of the ancient city of Nisa (later **Megara**), founded by Nisus, according to Greek tradition, and named for him.

Nisibis (nis′i-bis). [Modern names, **Nisibin, Nusaybin.**] In ancient geography, a town in Mesopotamia. At various times an Armenian, Parthian, and Persian stronghold, it was taken by Lucullus in 68 B.C., and afterward (from the Persians) by Trajan.

Nisus (nī′sus). According to Greek tradition, a son of Pandion. He and his three brothers conquered Attica and divided it between them by lot. Nisus drew Nisa, afterwards called Megara, and his claim to it was confirmed by Aeacus. He founded and gave his name to the port of Nisaea. Nisus had one purple (or golden) lock of hair, on which his life depended. The prophecy was that if it was cut off he would die. When Nisus was attacked by King Minos of Crete, his daughter Scylla fell in love with Minos, and cut the lock. Nisus died and Minos was successful, but Minos refused to take Scylla to Crete with him, as she had expected him to do, and sailed without her. She leaped into the sea and swam after his ship, pursued by her father who had been transformed into an osprey or sparrow-hawk. The body of Nisus was buried in Athens, in a tomb behind the Lyceum.

Nisus. In Greek and Roman legend, a son of Hyrtacus and the nymph Ida. He came from

Arisbe and fought at Troy. He was a companion of Aeneas on the flight from Troy and was famed for his devotion to his young friend Euryalus. At the funeral games for Anchises in Sicily Nisus was winning in the foot race when he slipped in a pool of blood and fell. To help his friend win, he rolled into the path of the next contestant and enabled Euryalus to win. In the war with the Rutulians, while Aeneas was away from the camp seeking help from Tarchon, the garrison was surrounded by the enemy. Nisus and Euryalus slipped away from the besieged camp to go for help but were discovered by the enemy when light glittered on the shining helmet Euryalus had placed on his own head after stripping it from one of the sleeping foes he had killed. In the fight which then broke out Nisus and Euryalus were separated and Euryalus was slain. Nisus, who might have escaped, turned on Volscens, the slayer of Euryalus, and killed him, but was then felled himself by enemy wounds. The Rutulians cut off his head and mounted it on a spear and exhibited it before the walls of the besieged garrison.

Nisyrus (ni-sī'rus). An island near Cos in the Dodecanese. According to tradition, it was formed during the war between the Giants and the gods when Poseidon broke off a piece of Cos with his trident and hurled it at the Giant Polybutes, burying Polybutes under it. Men of Nisyrus sailed against Troy in the Trojan War under the leadership of descendants of Heracles.

Nocera Inferiore (nō-che'rä ēn-fä-rē-ō'rä). See **Nuceria Alfaterna.**

Noëmon (nō-ē'mon). In the *Odyssey*, an Ithacan who, inspired by Athena, gave Telemachus a ship in which to make his voyage to Pylus in search of news of Odysseus. Later, by asking Antinous when Telemachus would return, he gave away the secret that Telemachus had departed.

Nola (nō'la̤). Town in Campania, S Italy, about 15 miles NE of Neapolis. Possibly founded by Etruscans, it became subject to Rome in 313 B.C. It was the scene of battles (216, 215 B.C.) between Marcellus and Hannibal in the First Punic War, and was also the site of the death of Augustus in 14 A.D.

Nomen (nō'men). "Name." In Classical Athens, and in Greece generally, a person was known by his given name: Sophocles, Pericles, Aristophanes, Andromache, Aspasia. Such names were freely coined: Aristarchus "excellent ruler," Evangelus "of good tidings," Philippus "fond of horses," Zenodotus "gift of Zeus," Berenice "bearing victory," Dorothea "gift of heaven," Eurydice "wide-judging," etc. Many are patronyms, e.g. in *-ides*: Callicratides "descendant of Callicrates," Euripides "descendant of Euripus," Atreides "son of Atreus," etc. To distinguish between two men of the same given name the father's name, in the genitive ("son of"), was added: Thoukydides Olorou (Thucydides son of Olorus, the historian), Thoukydides Melesiou (Thucydides son of Melesias, the statesman and general). In formal records the name of the *deme* or parish in which the family was registered was also added: Sokrates Sophroniskou Alopekeus, Socrates son of Sophroniscus, of the deme Alopece. Sons rarely took the given name of their father, but frequently took that of a grandfather.

In early Rome an adult male had two names, a *praenomen* (Aulus, Caius, Lucius, Marcus, Quintus, Tiberius, etc., usually abbreviated to one or two letters, of which the number was fixed at about forty) and a clan or gentile name (*nomen gentile* or *gentilicium*, e.g. Aurelius, Julius, Lucretius, Ovidius, Terentius, Valerius, Vergilius, of which the number was fixed at about 1000): Servius Tullius, Appius Claudius, Caius Marius, Aulus Hirtius. Several emperors were commonly known by their *praenomina*: Tiberius, Caius ("Caligula"), Titus. To distinguish between individuals of the same name, a nickname (*cognomen*) was used, usually inspired by a distinguishing feature, desirable quality, or fancied resemblance, not invariably flattering: Ahenobarbus "red-beard," Albinus "white-haired," Balbus "stammering," Caecus "blind," Calvus "bald," Celsus "tall," Crassus "fat," Dentatus "toothy," Florus "shining," Glabrio "hairless," Laevinus "lefty," Lentulus "slow," Lepidus "elegant," Longus "tall," Macer "lean, skinny," Naso "big-nose," Niger "dark," Paulus or Paullus "shorty," Plautus "flat-foot," Pulcher "handsome," Rufus "red-haired," Strabo "squint-eyed" (Greek *strabon*), etc.; Carus "dear," dim. Carolus "little dear," Felix "happy, lucky," Frugi "honest, thrifty," Tacitus "silent," Valens "powerful," dim. Valentinus, etc.; Aquila "eagle," Catulus "puppy," Corvus "raven," Falco "hawk," Gallus "cock," Lupus "wolf," Mus "mouse." Toponyms (place names) also appear: Coriolanus, Norbanus, Sabinus, Soranus, Tusculanus. In the course of time these *cognomina* or nicknames came to be officially recognized, and thereafter most Romans had at least three names, *praenomen, nomen,* and *cognomen,* in that order: Publius Ovidius Naso, Quintus Horatius Flaccus, Publius Vergilius Maro. Most Romans appear in history under their gentile names: Ovid, Horace, Vergil; Cnaeus Pompeius Magnus is Pompey the Great, Tiberius Claudius Nero Germanicus is the emperor Claudius. But many Romans are better known by their *cognomina*: Caius Julius Caesar, Marcus Tullius Cicero, Cnaeus Domitius Ahenobarbus, Marcus Terentius Varro, etc. An adopted child took the name of his adoptive father, adding a second *cognomen* (ending in *-anus*) to indicate the *gens* or clan to which he had been born: The emperor Augustus was first Caius Octavius; on his adoption by his great-uncle Caius Julius Caesar (by the latter's will) he became Caius Julius Caesar Octavianus, and between 44 B.C. and 27 B.C. he is properly known as Octavian. In 27 B.C. the Senate conferred on him the title Augustus, by which he is thereafter known. Military commanders often took a second *cognomen* recalling a victorious campaign: Africanus, Asiaticus, Macedonicus, Numantinus. A slave on emancipation received the *praenomen* and *nomen* of his master, keeping his own given name as a *cognomen*: Heliodorus, slave of P. Claudius, as a freedman became P. Claudius Heliodorus. In theory, members of families bearing the same gentile name were presumed to be descended from an ultimate common ancestor; but widespread adoption, and the assumption of their patrons' names by freedmen, accelerated the dilution of blood-lines which had presumably far advanced before the beginning of written history. Families sharing the same gentile name might identify themselves by coupling a distinctive *cognomen* permanently to the gentile name, e.g. the Cornelii Scipiones and the Cornelii Lentuli, individuals adding a second cognomen (if necessary, a third) for personal identification: L.

Cornelius Scipio, L. Cornelius Scipio Barbatus, Cn. Cornelius Scipio Calvus, P. Cornelius Scipio Africanus Major and his son P. Cornelius Scipio Africanus Minor, P. Cornelius Scipio Nasica, L. Cornelius Scipio Asiaticus, etc. P. Cornelius Scipio Aemilianus Africanus Numantinus was the adopted son of P. Cornelius Scipio Africanus Minor, the *cognomen* Aemilianus showing that he was born to the *gens* Aemilia; he earned the further *cognomina* Africanus and Numantinus by his successes in Africa and Numantia (Spain). Brothers having the same *cognomen* could be distinguished by second *cognomina* or by distinct *praenomina*: Tiberius Sempronius Gracchus and Caius Sempronius Gracchus, the famous liberal tribunes; Marcus Tullius Cicero, Quintus Tullius Cicero. Father and son might have identical names, Marcus Tullius Cicero the orator being the third in line to bear the name and his son the fourth. In identifying the sponsors of legislation or public works the gentile name was regularly used: *Lex Junia de Peregrinis,* a law ordering non-citizens expelled from Rome, sponsored by the tribune M. Junius Pennus; Aqua Marcia, the aqueduct built by the praetor Q. Marcius Rex in 144 B.C.; Via Flaminia, the highway north from Rome to Ariminum, built by the censor C. Flaminius in 220 B.C. (but Via Appia, built by Appius Claudius; Appius is a *praenomen*). Among non-Romans the term "gentiles" referred to Roman citizens, those officially enrolled in a Roman *gens* and bearing one of the thousand recognized gentile names, as distinguished from non-citizens.

A Roman woman took as her name the feminine form of her father's gentile name; Junia, Valeria. Cicero's first wife was Terentia, daughter of one Terentius; their daughter was Tullia, the Tulliola "Little Tullia" of his letters. This is the origin of many given names of women in English-speaking lands: Celia (Latin Caelia), Cicely (Caecilia), Cornelia, Emily (Aemilia), Hortense (Hortensia), Julia, Lucy (Lucia), Marcia, Virginia, etc. Sisters were distinguished by ordinal *cognomina*: Secunda, Tertia, etc. (JJ)

Nomentum (nō-men'tum). In ancient geography, a town of Latium, about 13 miles NE of Rome. It was a nameless site when Aeneas visited his father in the Underworld. Anchises pointed out to him the shade of the man waiting to be born who would found the city. The village of Mentana later occupied this site.

Nomia (nō'mi-a̱). In Greek mythology, a nymph to whom Daphnis had sworn to be faithful. When he was seduced while drunk, Nomia punished him for breaking his vow by blinding him.

Nonacris (nō-nak'ris). In ancient geography, a city in N Arcadia, Greece. It was named for the wife of Lycaon. Nearby was the famous river Styx, by which the Arcadians swore their most binding oaths. In the Aroanian Mountains above Nonacris was the cave where the daughters of Proetus fled in their madness. On the spot where Melampus cured them of their madness was a sanctuary of Artemis called Hemerasia (*She who Soothes*) by the people of Clitor.

Nonnus (non'us). An Egyptian Greek from Panopolis, who lived in the early part of the 5th century A.D. His epic, *Dionysiaca*, in 48 books, which he wrote as a pagan, is a collection of the legends of the Dionysiac cycle, and is an important source of those legends. Later, Nonnus became a Christian, and wrote a paraphrase of the Gospel of St. John in Greek hexameters. As a poet, he evolved a system of stress accents which he added to the hexameter.

Nora (nō'ra̱, nôr'a̱). In ancient geography, a fortress in Cappadocia, Asia Minor, situated at the foot of Mount Taurus, near Lycaonia. Eumenes was besieged (320–319 B.C.) here by the forces of Antigonus.

Norax (nō'raks). In Greek mythology, a son of Hermes and Erythea, the daughter of Geryon. He went to Sardinia and founded the city of Nora, the oldest city in the island.

Norba (nôr'ba̱). In ancient geography, a city in Latium, Italy, on a spur of the Lepini Mountains, overlooking the Pontine Marshes, about 35 miles SE of Rome. Norba is noted for its well-preserved fortification walls of massive polygonal ("Cyclopean") masonry in local limestone, with an imposing main gate and sally ports, which were formerly held to be of very early date, the 6th or 7th century B.C., but are now assigned to the late 4th or early 3rd century B.C. Within the outer circuit are many retaining walls and foundations in polygonal limestone, including the sub-

structures of at least two temples. Norba was destroyed by Sulla during the civil wars; on the next eminence to the E lies its successor, the medieval town of Norma. (JJ)

Norcia (nôr'chä). See **Nursia.**

Noricum (nor'i-kum). In ancient geography, a country in Europe, bounded by Germany (separated by the Danube) on the N, Pannonia on the E, Pannonia and the land of the Carni on the S, and Vindelicia and Rhaetia (separated partly by the Inn) on the W. It corresponded mainly to the later Lower and Upper Austria S of the Danube, Salzburg, Styria, Carinthia, and parts of Tirol and Bavaria. It was conquered by the Romans c15 B.C., and made a Roman province.

Notium (nō'shi-um). In ancient geography, the port of Colophon, near Ephesus. Near it the Spartan fleet under Lysander defeated (407 B.C.) the Athenians.

Notus (nō'tus). In Greek mythology, the south or southwest wind. Notus was the son of Astraeus or Aeolus and Eos, and the brother of Zephyrus, Boreas, and Eurus. He was the wind of fog and mists, dangerous to shepherds on the mountain tops or to mariners at sea, but a friend of thieves.

Nuceria Alfaterna (nū-sir'i-a̱ al-fa̱-tér'na̱). [Modern name, **Nocera Inferiore.**] In ancient geography, a town in S Italy, situated about 20 miles SE of Neapolis. An ancient Oscan town, it was occupied by the Romans in 307 B.C., destroyed by Hannibal in 216 B.C., sacked by the revolting slaves under Spartacus in 73 B.C., and recolonized by Augustus and Nero.

Numa Pompilius (nū'ma̱ pom-pil'i-us). According to Roman legend, the second king of Rome (715–673 B.C.). He was a Sabine from Cures, born, so it is said, on April 21, the day Rome was founded. He married Tatia, daughter of Tatius, king of the Sabines. She died, and henceforth he was said to have turned to the nymph Egeria, who advised him on matters of state and religion. Numa was 40 years old when an embassy came from Rome to invite him to become king. His first reaction was to decline the honor with vigor. He enjoyed his quiet life and informed the embassy that a man must be mad to exchange a peaceful life of contemplation for the uncertainty and upheaval that being king of the warlike Romans would entail. He was at length persuaded that "the work of a true king is a service rendered to the gods," and accepted the throne. Many favorable omens accompanied him to Rome, and he was accepted as king with great joy. As king he tried to soften the warlike character of the Romans, and to turn their interest to matters of religion and ritual. For Romulus, recently deified, he appointed a priest called the *flamen quirinales*. He established the institution of the high priests, called the *pontifices*. The chief of these, the Pontifex Maximus, was charged with the duty of interpreting the will of heaven, was overseer of public ceremonies and private sacrifices, and overseer of the vestal virgins, consecrated by Numa. Numa is said also to have laid down rules concerning burial and mourning, established the priesthoods of the Salii and the Fetiales, reformed the calendar, and divided the people into tribes according to their work. In all he did Numa claimed he was guided by the Muses, among whom one in particular, Tacita (*the Silent one*), was honored, and by his nymph Egeria. Above all, Numa maintained peace, sometimes by playing on the superstitious fears of the people to compel them to follow his course. The doors of the temple of Janus, open in time of war, were closed for 43 years in the reign of Numa. When he died, his laws were buried in one stone coffin and his body in another. Some say the laws were found 400 years later, but were reburied as it was thought unlawful to publish them. Some say Numa had a daughter, Pompilia, who was the mother of Ancus Marcius, king of Rome (640–616 B.C.); and some say he had four sons, Pompon, Pinus, Calpus, and Mamercus, each of whom was the founder of a noble Roman family.

Numantia (nū-man′sha). In ancient geography, the capital of a Celtiberian people, the Arevaci, situated on the Durius (Douro) River near what is now Soria, Spain. It was famous on account of its siege by the Romans under Scipio Aemilianus, beginning in 134 B.C. It was taken and destroyed in 133 B.C.

Numantine War (nū′man-tin). War between the Romans and the Celtiberians of N central Spain, 143–133 B.C., ending in the destruction of Numantia in 133 B.C.

Numanus (nū-mā′nus). In Roman legend, the brother-in-law of Turnus, lord of the Rutulians. In the war between Turnus and Aeneas he taunted the Trojans and boasted of how he would annihilate them. He was slain by an arrow from the bow of Ascanius.

Numidia (nū-mid′i-a). In ancient geography, a country of N Africa, corresponding nearly to the modern Algeria. It was bounded by the Mediterranean on the N, the territory of Carthage on the E, the desert on the S, and Mauretania on the W. In Roman legend (*Aeneid*) it was occupied by tribes hostile to Dido and Carthage. The peoples in the E and W were united in a kingdom under Masinissa. This was dismembered after the defeat of Jugurtha in 106 B.C., and the E part became a Roman province shortly after the death of its king Juba in 46 B.C.

Numina (nū′mi-na). In ancient Roman mythology, protective spirits—of the home, the fields, the crafts, individuals, and the like. The Numina of orchards and gardens were later identified with Pomona and Vertumnus, those of the home became the Lares and Penates. Gradually the Numina were differentiated and acquired names for their specific roles. *Numen* (singular form of *numina*) is a supernatural power or influence, corresponding in significance to the term *mana*, the extraphysical power prominent in Melanesian and Polynesian belief.

Numitor (nū′mi-tôr). In Roman legend, the father of Rhea Silvia, and the grandfather of Romulus and Remus. Numitor was a king of Alba Longa. He was deposed by a younger brother and was restored to his throne by the famous twins, who killed the uncle. Anchises pointed out the spirit of Numitor, waiting to be born, when Aeneas visited the Underworld.

Nursia (nėr′sha). [Modern name, **Norcia**.] An ancient Sabine city, about 42 miles SE of Perusia (Perugia). According to the *Aeneid*, its people were allies of Turnus in the war against Aeneas.

Nycteus (nik′tūs). In Greek legend, the brother of Lycus and the father of Antiope. When he learned that Antiope was about to produce Amphion and Zethus, her children by Zeus, his wrath caused her to flee, and he asked Lycus to capture and punish her. He died, either in the battle to capture Antiope from the king of Sicyon to whom she had fled, or by suicide.

Nyctimene (nik-tim'e-nē). In Greek legend, the daughter of Epopeus, king in Lesbos. After being ravished by her father, she hid in a forest. Athena transformed her into an owl.

Nyctimus (nik'ti-mus). The youngest, according to Greek legend, of the 50 sons of Lycaon of Arcadia. Some say that Lycaon was a pious king, who warned his sons that the gods were ever visiting the earth in disguise to observe mortals. His proud and arrogant sons decided to test whether a visitor who claimed to be Zeus was indeed that god. They cut up their young brother Nyctimus, boiled his flesh and served it to Zeus. Zeus, instantly aware of the nature of the meat set before him, in anger turned the sons of Lycaon into wolves; or as some say, struck them dead with his thunderbolt. He restored Nyctimus to life. Others say Lycaon was as impious as his sons and took part in this means of testing Zeus and was turned into a wolf. It was because of the lawlessness and impiety of Lycaon and his sons, according to some, that Zeus determined to punish mankind by sending a great flood.

Nymphaea (nim-fē'a). An epithet of Aphrodite in her aspect as goddess of love, meaning "Bridal." Theseus dedicated an image of Aphrodite Nymphaea when he made the youthful Helen, whom he had abducted with the help of Pirithous, his bride.

Nymphaea. Name sometimes given to the island of Calypso.

Nymphs. Inferior divinities, imagined as beautiful maidens, eternally young, who were considered as guardian spirits of certain localities and objects, or of certain races and families, and whose existence depended upon that of the things with which they were identified. They were generally in the train or company of some other divinity of higher rank, especially with Apollo, Artemis, Dionysus, Hermes, and Pan, and were believed to be possessed of the gift of prophecy and of poetical inspiration. Nymphs of rivers, brooks, and springs were called naiads; those of mountains, oreads; those of woods and trees, dryads and hamadryads; those of the sea, Nereids. The nymphs aided humans upon occasion, and guarded the places, tree, spring, mountain, etc., they themselves inhabited. The nymphs were wooed and won by gods and mortals alike and from them sprang many heroes. They also played a part in many of the activities of the gods and in general were a protective influence. Groves and grottoes sacred to the nymphs throughout Greece received offerings of lambs, milk, oil, and wine.

Nysa (nī'sa). The spot to which the infant Dionysus was sent by Zeus to protect him from the wrath of Hera. According to Greek mythology, the young god was nurtured in a cave in Nysa by nymphs who fed him on honey. The sacred place has never been definitely located and is probably mythical, but it was claimed by many areas where the vine is cultivated. It has been variously named as a mountain in Thrace, a city on a mountain in India, a city in Caria about 45 miles E of Ephesus, Mount Helicon in Greece, and a remote place in Aethiopia. Nysa was also the name of one of the nymphs who cared for Dionysus.

Nysaean Nymphs or **Nyseides** (nī-sē'an, nī-sē'i-dēz). The nymphs who cared for the infant Dionysus on Mount Nysa, after Ino, his mother's sister who had first cared for him, died. To hide him from Hera, who was jealous because he was the child of Zeus by Semele, the nymphs covered him with ivy leaves. This plant was ever afterward associated with Dionysus. The Nysaean nymphs, Bromie, Cisseis, Erato, Eriphia, Macris, Nysa, and Polyhymno, were rewarded by being placed among the stars by Zeus, after which they became known as the Hyades.

Nyx (niks). In Greek mythology, the daughter of Chaos. She was the goddess of night, a very ancient cosmological personification. By Erebus, her brother, she was the mother of Hypnos (Sleep), Thanatos (Death), Moros (Doom), Cer (Fate), Dreams, Momus (Blame or Mockery), Oïzys (Misery), the Hesperides who guarded the Golden Apples, the three Fates (Lachesis, Atropos, and Clotho), Nemesis, Deceit, Friendship, Old Age, and Strife. Nyx, riding in a chariot and accompanied by stars, led forth the brothers Sleep and Death at the close of day, and was a force for both good and evil for man, as she brought sleep and rest or darkness and

actor; up, lūte, pull; oi, oil; ou, out; ᴛʜ, then; d̪ as d or j, ş as s or sh, t̪ as t or ch, ẓ as z or zh.

death. Nyx was even reverenced and feared by Zeus, whom she instructed. When Sleep, bribed by Hera, lulled Zeus so that Hera could rouse a great storm and shipwreck Heracles on the isle of Cos, Zeus on awaking threatened to hurl Sleep down to Erebus. But Nyx intervened, and Zeus bowed to her will and spared Sleep. Nyx had little or no cult worship, but was revered for her oracular powers, which were made known from a cave.

O

Oak. Tree sacred to Zeus. The rustling of the leaves in the grove at Dodona was interpreted by priests to reveal the will of Zeus.

Oaxes (ō-ak′ses). A river of Crete. According to some accounts, the nymph Anchiale bore the Dactyls in a cave near this river.

Oceanids (ō-sē′a-nidz). In Greek mythology, 3000 ocean-nymphs, daughters of the sea-god Oceanus, and his consort Tethys.

Oceanus (ō-sē′a-nus). In the belief of ancient geographers, a swift and unbounded stream that encircled all the world, from which all earthly rivers were believed to rise. Oceanus was later taken to be the outer sea, which we know as the Atlantic Ocean.

Oceanus. In Greek mythology, a Titan, the son of Gaea and Uranus. He lived with his wife Tethys in the farthest west, and never attended the meetings of the gods on Olympus, or took part in their quarrels. He and Tethys were the parents of 3000 sons, who were the river-gods of all the rivers of the world, and of 3000 daughters, the sea- and river-nymphs. Oceanus was the oldest of the Titans, and on the fall of Cronus submitted to the sovereignty of Zeus. Oceanus and Tethys brought up Hera, and to them she fled during the war between the Titans and the gods, in which Oceanus took no part. In art Oceanus was represented as an aged, bearded man, sometimes with bull's horns on his head or with a garland of crab's claws, and surrounded by creatures of the deep.

Ocellus Lucanus (ō-sel′us lū-kā′nus). Greek philosopher; born in Lucania; fl. 5th century B.C. He was a follower and possibly a pupil of Pythagoras. Writings attributed to him are of doubtful authenticity.

Ochimus (ok′i-mus). In Greek mythology, one of the seven sons of Helius. In a quarrel among the brothers one of the brothers was slain. All the brothers except Ochimus and Cercaphus fled from Rhodes, and Ochimus became king. He married a nymph, Hegetoria, who bore him Cydippe.

Ochus (ō′kus). Original name of **Darius II** (of *Persia*).

Ocnus (ok′nus). In Greek mythology, the droll of the Underworld and personification of delay or futile effort. He is described as forever plaiting a straw rope, which his ass devours as fast as he makes it: or sometimes he is shown loading the ass with sticks which keep falling off.

Ocnus. In Roman legend, an Etruscan, the son of the Tuscan River and the seeress Manto. He founded Mantua and gave it his mother's name. He commanded a group who went to the aid of Aeneas in his war against Turnus and Mezentius.

Ocrisia (ok-rī′shi-a). In Roman legend, a slave in the house of Tarquin and Tanaquil. A phantom appeared to her as she was making an offering of food on the hearth. On Tanaquil's advice she clothed herself as a bride and waited alone in the room for the phantom. In this guise a god, either Vulcan or Lar, visited her and she became by him the mother of Servius Tullius.

Octavia (ok-tā′vi-a). Sister of Caius Octavius (Octavian; after 27 B.C. known as Augustus). She died 11 B.C. She was the wife first of Caius Marcellus, and afterward of Mark Antony. Her son by Caius Marcellus was the first husband of her brother Octavian's (Augustus) daughter Julia. Octavia was married to Mark Antony to cement the alliance between Augustus and Mark Antony. When Antony went to the East and carried on his affair with Cleopatra with flagrant disregard for Roman morality and the feelings of his wife, Augustus used this as one of his reasons for making war on Antony and eliminating him as a rival for power in Rome. Octavia was divorced from Antony in 32 B.C.

Octavia. Daughter of Claudius I and Messalina; born c40 A.D.; killed 62 A.D. She was the wife of Nero. He divorced her in order to marry Poppaea and soon afterward contrived to have her killed, after banishing her to the island of Pandataria.

Octavian (ok-tā'vi-an). Name by which Caius Octavius, who afterward became Augustus, was known after he became the heir of Julius Caesar and, under the terms of his will, took the name Caius Julius Caesar Octavianus. After 27 B.C. he is properly known as Augustus.

Octavian Library. Library at Rome, founded by the emperor Augustus in honor of his sister Octavia. It was destroyed in the fire which raged at Rome in the reign of Titus (79–81 A.D.).

Octavius (ok-tā'vi-us), **Caius.** Original name of Augustus.

Octavius, Cnaeus. Roman consul in 87 B.C. and killed at Rome in that year. He was an adherent of Sulla, while his colleague, Lucius Cornelius Cinna, was an adherent of Marius. He was killed by the followers of Cinna while Sulla was absent fighting against Mithridates VI in the East.

Ocypete (ō-sip'ē-tē). In Greek mythology, one of the Harpies, a daughter of Thaumus and the Oceanid Electra. See **Harpies.**

Ocyrrhoë (ō-sir'ō-ē). In Greek mythology, a daughter of Chiron and the nymph Chariclo. She was named for the river on whose banks she was born. She had learned the healing and hunting arts of her father, and was also endowed with the gift of prophecy. When Asclepius, the infant son of Apollo, was brought to be reared by Chiron, Ocyrrhoë prophesied that he would bring healing and health to all the world; that he would even be able to restore the dead to life; that by so doing he would rouse the envy of the gods, who would cause Zeus to strike him dead with his thunderbolt; and that after being a lifeless corpse he would be immortalized and thus twice fulfill his destiny. She also foretold the sufferings that would befall Chiron as a result of an accidental wound from one of Heracles' arrows.

Ocyrrhoë bewailed her ability to know the future, for by her own gift she knew that she incurred the wrath of heaven and would be punished by the gods. Her foreknowledge was correct. The gods, angered because she correctly predicted the future, transformed her into a mare and gave her the name Hippo.

Odeum (ō-dē'um). "Singing-place." The odeum was a form of roofed theater, generally smaller than the great open-air theaters of Greece and Rome. It was developed primarily for musical performances, because the volume of sound produced by early stringed and reed instruments was insufficiently audible in open-air theaters. The earliest recorded example is the Odeum of Pericles at Athens, built in the 5th century B.C., burned in the 1st century B.C., and reconstructed by Ariobarzanes II, king of Cappadocia. Agrippa built an odeum in the Athenian Agora, and in the 2nd century A.D. Herodes Atticus built odea at Athens and Corinth. In the absence of special buildings for the purpose, an odeum could conveniently serve as a meeting-place for a *bouleuterium* (town council) or *ecclesiasterium* (public assembly), and with this versatility odea were widely built throughout the Roman provinces. (JJ)

Odeum of Herodes Atticus (hē-rō'dēz at'i-kus). A roofed theater at Athens, at the SW foot of the Acropolis. It was built in the middle of the 2nd century A.D. at the expense of the wealthy statesman, litterateur, and art patron Herodes Atticus, in memory of his wife Regilla, for whom it is sometimes called the Odeum of Regilla. It is of Roman plan, semicircular, about 260 feet in diameter, with about 33 rows of seats and well-preserved stage and scene. As elsewhere, the revetment of the seats and scene-building, pavement, etc., were removed before the liberation of Greece from the Turks, but are currently being restored, and the odeum is again used for dramatic presentations, concerts, etc. Herodes Atticus also built an odeum at Corinth. (JJ)

Odysseus (ō-dis'ūs, ō-dis'ē-us). [Latin: **Ulixes, Ulysses.**] One of the leading Greek heroes in the Trojan War. He not only survived the war but eventually, after ten years of wandering, returned safely to his home in

actor; up, lūte, pull; oi, oil; ou, out; ŦH, then; ḏ as d or j, ṣ as s or sh, ṭ as t or ch, ẓ as z or zh.

Ithaca. He has many epithets; "wily," "crafty," "Odysseus of many devices," are a few of them. In Homer he is represented as a brave man of great wisdom and ingenuity, always ready with a stratagem to save the day and never wanting in sage counsel or valor. But Pindar thinks that Odysseus owes his reputation to Homer, and that he was, in fact, merely "a supple liar." In later literature Odysseus often appears as unscrupulous, shrewd, and deceitful. Ordinarily in Homer the heroes are described as "glorious," "man-slayer," "flawless," or in other abstract terms, but Odysseus receives some physical description. He had red hair and, though he had broad shoulders so that when he was seated he looked as mighty as any man, he had short legs and showed when he stood up that he was somewhat under the expected height. Odysseus passed as the son of Laertes and Anticlea, but some say that Sisyphus was his father. His name, which means "the angry one," was given to him by his grandfather Autolycus, father of Anticlea. Autolycus so named his grandson because he himself had made many enemies in his lifetime and expected Odysseus to be a target for some of them. In his boyhood Odysseus visited Autolycus on Mount Parnassus and received rich gifts from him. During a boar hunt on this visit he was wounded in the leg and bore the scar the rest of his life. Odysseus went, as did many of the heroes and princes of Greece, to the court of Tyndareus at Sparta. Unlike the others, he was not a candidate for the hand of Tyndareus' daughter Helen. He wanted to marry Penelope, the daughter of Icarius. Tyndareus feared to choose from among the many suitors for Helen's hand, lest in selecting one he offend the others and make powerful enemies. Odysseus proposed a way for him to choose one suitor without antagonizing the others. It was to make them all swear, on the joints of a dismembered horse, that they would come to the aid of the man who became Helen's husband in the event that any ill should come to him as a result of his marriage to her. Tyndareus adopted his suggestion, the suitors took the oath, and Helen was given to Menelaus. In return for this good advice Tyndareus agreed to help Odysseus win Penelope. Some say

he won her as the result of a foot race that Tyndareus arranged for him to win. In any event, he married Penelope and took her with him to his home in Ithaca. There he ruled wisely and won the devotion of his subjects. Penelope bore him a son, Telemachus. While his son was still an infant Paris abducted Helen, her former suitors were called upon to honor their oath, and all was set in motion for a great expedition to Troy to recover her. Agamemnon, brother of Menelaus and the commander of the expedition, learned that it could not succeed without Odysseus. He and Menelaus, accompanied by Palamedes, went to Ithaca to secure his services. Odysseus had been warned by an oracle that if he went to Troy, he would be gone 20 years and would return alone and destitute. When the envoys arrived, they found Odysseus plowing with an ox and an ass yoked together, and flinging salt over his shoulders into the furrows. On his head was a Phrygian peasant cap. He pretended not to recognize his visitors and gave every sign that he had taken leave of his senses. But Palamedes suspected him of trickery. He seized the infant Telemachus and flung him in front of Odysseus' advancing plow. Odysseus immediately turned out to avoid injuring his son, and confessed that he had feigned madness to escape going to Troy. He was now compelled to join the Greeks in their expedition, but he never forgave Palamedes for unmasking him, and when the Greeks were later gathered before Troy, he succeeded in having Palamedes accused of treachery and brought about his death.

Calchas the seer foretold that Troy could not be taken without Achilles. Odysseus was one of the ambassadors who went to Scyrus to fetch him. Some say Achilles had been hidden away among the women of Lycomedes' court by his mother Thetis to prevent him from going to the war. Odysseus appeared at the court and asked for him. Lycomedes let him search the palace but Achilles was not to be found. Odysseus now asked if he might make presents to the women of the court. He displayed girdles, jewels, and such ornaments as would appeal to women. As the women crowded around to look at his gifts Odysseus caused a trumpet

fat, fāte, fär, fāre, errant; net, mē, her ardent; pin, pīne; not, nōte, möve, nôr, blast and a clatter of arms to be heard from the courtyard. Instantly one of the young women seized the sword and shield which Odysseus had cunningly included in the gifts he was displaying, and made ready to fight. Thus was Achilles unmasked and brought to join the Greeks. But others say Odysseus and Nestor found Achilles not at Lycomedes' court, but at his father's court, that Peleus readily consented to let his son join the Greek expedition and sent Achilles off with good advice and the company of his tutor Phoenix and his dear friend Patroclus. When the Greek fleet was wind-bound at Aulis and Agamemnon learned that only the sacrifice of his daughter Iphigenia could appease Artemis and cause favorable winds, it was Odysseus, according to some, who devised the scheme of sending for Iphigenia on the pretext that she was to be married to Achilles, and so persuaded Clytemnestra to let her come to the Greek camp, where she was sacrificed. The Greeks then had favorable winds and put to sea. They stopped at the island of Lesbos where Odysseus wrestled the king, Philomelides, and overcame him. Then they went to Tenedos. At some point before the actual siege of Troy Odysseus accompanied Menelaus to Troy as an envoy to seek the voluntary return of Helen. This mission failed. In the conduct of the war before the walls of Troy Odysseus and Nestor were Agamemnon's most trusted advisers. No matter how hopeless the Greek situation appeared, Odysseus would not hear of giving up and returning home. On his advice a rampart was built to protect the Greek ships on the beach. He was a member of the embassy which tried to patch up the disastrous quarrel between Agamemnon and Achilles, as a result of which Achilles had withdrawn from the fighting. This embassy was unsuccessful, and the Greeks suffered catastrophic losses without the aid of Achilles. With Diomedes, Odysseus made a scouting raid on the Trojan camp. He killed the Thracian Rhesus, who had just come up to the aid of the Trojans, and seized his marvelous horses, because there was a prophecy that if the horses of Rhesus grazed on Trojan pastures and drank the waters of the Scamander River, Troy could not be taken. In furious fighting the next day

Odysseus was wounded and cut off by the Trojans, but was rescued by Menelaus. In this engagement many of the leading Greek heroes were wounded and the Trojans breached the wall protecting the ships. Agamemnon proposed that the Greeks give up the struggle, put to sea in their galleys, and return to Greece. Odysseus scorned this proposal and successfully urged the continuance of the war. After the death of Achilles, Thetis decreed that her son's armor, made by Hephaestus, be awarded to the bravest of the Greeks. Only Odysseus and Telamonian Ajax dared claim them. Ajax was always the enemy of Odysseus. He said Odysseus fought with words, but when swords were flying Odysseus disappeared. He reminded Odysseus that he had sought to avoid coming to Troy in the first place. For his part, Ajax wished that he had not come, for it was on the advice of Odysseus that wounded Philoctetes, possessor of the bows and arrows of Heracles, had been abandoned alone on the island of Lemnos, and it was due to the machinations of Odysseus that Palamedes had been destroyed. He accused Odysseus of cowardice for keeping his ships in the center of the line, where there was less danger, while Ajax had his ships on the exposed flank. But Ajax despaired of winning by speech, for in that field Odysseus clearly dominated; therefore, he challenged Odysseus to duel with him for the armor of Achilles. Odysseus replied that wisdom increases strength. He listed his contributions to the war and declined to duel with Ajax on the ground that he was still suffering from his wound. Agamemnon did not know how to choose between these two valiant and valuable warriors. Nestor mourned that the careless gods had sent them a great evil by making them choose between two such great men, as whoever lost in the choice would be lost to the Greeks. According to some accounts, Nestor suggested that the Greeks allow the captured Trojans to decide which of the two had done them the most injury, for perhaps thus the wrath of the loser would be turned against the Trojans rather than against his fellow Greeks. The decision of the captive Trojans caused the arms of Achilles to be awarded to Odysseus. Others say the arms were awarded as a result of a secret vote of the Greek leaders. Ajax was infuriated with the decision, and sought to kill Odysseus, but Athena inspired him with madness and he captured a ram under the impression that it was Odysseus, and flogged it unmercifully. Restored to his senses, Ajax was so appalled and humiliated by what he had done that he committed suicide. According to some accounts, Agamemnon refused burial to the body of Ajax, and ordered it exposed as prey for the birds, but he was persuaded by Odysseus to allow the burial on the ground that Ajax had made valiant contributions to the Greeks, and with the warning on the part of Odysseus that yesterday's enemy might become tomorrow's friend. He offered to help in the burial rites for Ajax, and said he would never have claimed the armor of Achilles if he had realized how much it meant to Ajax. Later Odysseus gave the armor to Neoptolemus, the son of Achilles.

When it was learned that Troy could not be taken without the bows and arrows of Heracles, Odysseus went with Diomedes to Lemnos to fetch Philoctetes, the possessor of the bow and arrows. Philoctetes had been abandoned on Lemnos at the suggestion of Odysseus when the Greeks were on their way to Troy, because he had suffered a noisome wound. Now when Odysseus appeared to ask him to go to Troy, Philoctetes' first impulse was to shoot him. But such were the persuasive powers of Odysseus, and the influence of the gods, that Philoctetes agreed to accompany him to Troy. Again with Diomedes, Odysseus went to Scyrus to fetch Neoptolemus, son of Achilles, to Troy, because an oracle said Troy could not be taken without him. On learning that only Helenus knew the oracles that protected Troy, Odysseus captured him and brought him to the Greek camp. Some say Odysseus secretly entered Troy with Diomedes to steal the Palladium, a sacred image which Helenus said protected the city as long as it remained in the citadel. Some say Diomedes climbed on Odysseus' shoulders to scale the wall of the city and got the Palladium himself, and that as the two were returning to the Greek camp Odysseus thought to kill Diomedes and gain the credit for securing the Palladium

for himself. He stepped behind Diomedes, but Diomedes saw the glint of his naked sword in the moonlight as he lifted it to strike him, whirled around and disarmed Odysseus, and drove him with the flat of his sword back to the Greek camp. And some say Odysseus, disguised in rags and matted with blood, entered Troy secretly and alone on another occasion, was recognized by Helen and Hecuba, questioned by them, and allowed to return unharmed to the Greek camp. Again, some say that the idea for the stratagem of the Wooden Horse by which Troy was finally taken came from Odysseus, but others say he merely took the credit for it, as usual. All agree that he was one of those who entered Troy in the Wooden Horse. In the sack of Troy he accompanied Menelaus to the house of Deïphobus, where Helen was, and had a part in the slaying of Deïphobus. According to some accounts, it was Odysseus who persuaded Agamemnon, against his will, to sacrifice Polyxena on the tomb of Achilles, and to dash Astyanax, the young son of Hector, to his death from the walls of Troy. Odysseus took Hecuba as his share in the spoils of the city, some say to prevent her from revealing his craven attitude when he secretly entered Troy and was discovered by her and Helen.

After the sack of Troy Odysseus departed with his ships for his home in Ithaca. At the outset of his voyage he was driven by a storm to the coast of Thrace, north of the island of Lemnos. He plundered the town of Ismarus, belonging to the Cicones, where he lost a number of his followers. Next he was driven to the country of the Lotophagi (the Lotus-Eaters) on the coast of Libya; then to the goat island, which lay a day's voyage to the north of the Lotophagi. Leaving behind all his ships except one, he sailed to the neighboring island of the Cyclopes (which some locate on the W coast of Sicily), where with 12 companions he entered the cave of the one-eyed Cyclops, Polyphemus, a son of Poseidon. Polyphemus devoured six of the intruders, and kept Odysseus and the others prisoners. Odysseus made Polyphemus drunk with wine, put out his one eye with a burning pole, and escaped with the remnant of his companions by concealing himself and them under the bellies of the sheep which the

fat, fāte, fär, fãre, errᶐnt; net, mē, hėr ardᶒnt; pin, pīne; not, nōte, möve, nôr, blinded Cyclops let out of his cave (he ran his hands over their backs, but forgot that his enemies might be clinging to their bellies). Thenceforth, however, Odysseus was pursued by the anger of Poseidon, who sought to avenge the injury inflicted on his son. After further adventures, in which he lost all his ships except one, he arrived at the island of Aeaea, inhabited by the sorceress Circe.

ODYSSEUS AND THE SIRENS
Red-figured Greek stamnos, c490 B.C.
British Museum

He remained with her a year and she bore him, according to some accounts, three sons —Agrius, Latinus, and Telegonus. At her insistence he made a journey to Hades, where he consulted the shade of the seer Tiresias. He then sailed by the island of the Sirens (which some locate near the W coast of Italy), passed between Scylla and Charybdis, and arrived at Trinacria, the island of Apollo, or of the Sun. Here his companions killed some of the sacred oxen belonging to the god with the result that they were all drowned in a shipwreck after leaving the island. Odysseus escaped with his life to the island of Ogygia, inhabited by the nymph Calypso, with whom he lived eight years. She bore him twin sons, Nausithous and Nausinous. Leaving Ogygia on a raft built with the assistance of the nymph, he was again shipwrecked, but reached the island of the Phaeacians, where he was discovered naked by Nausicaä, the daughter of their king Alcinous. Clothed, and presented at court, he told his story. He was carried to Ithaca by the hospitable Phaeacians, and after slaying the suitors of his wife Penelope who had been wasting his property during his long absence,

was welcomed by his wife and subjects. (For a fuller description of the return of Odysseus, see **Odyssey.**) He now sacrificed to Hades, Persephone, and Tiresias, and on the advice which Tiresias had given him when he visited him in Hades, he set out to appease Poseidon. He went on foot, carrying an oar, until he came to a people who had never seen the sea. They asked him why he was carrying a winnowing fan. Here he set up the oar and sacrificed to Poseidon. Some say he married Callidice, the queen of this land, which was Thesprotia, and became its king and had a son by his new wife. When she died he gave the kingdom to this son, Polypoetes, and returned to Ithaca, which Penelope had been ruling in his second absence in the name of their young son, Poliporthis. An oracle had foretold that Odysseus would meet his death at the hands of his son. For this reason he banished Telemachus. Tiresias had added to this prophecy that Odysseus' death would come from the sea. Now Telegonus, his son by Circe, came searching for his father. He landed on Ithaca, unaware that it was his father's island home. Odysseus, equally unaware that the apparent raider was his son, rushed to the shore to repel him. Telegonus killed him with his spear, which was tipped with the spine of a sting ray, and thus the prophecies were fulfilled.

Odyssey (od'i-si). Epic poem, in 24 books, attributed to Homer, and generally thought of as a companion to the *Iliad*. Some critics, both ancient and modern, who have acknowledged the Homeric origin of the *Iliad*, attribute the *Odyssey* to a different author. These critics believe that the *Odyssey* is a later poem. It celebrates the ten years of wandering and trials endured by Odysseus as he struggled to reach his home in Ithaca after the close of the Trojan War.

Book I: In a council, while Poseidon is absent, Athena secures the consent of the gods to the return of Odysseus to his homeland. He has been prevented from returning after the Trojan War by the anger of Poseidon and is languishing on the isle of Ogygia with the nymph Calypso. Athena, disguised, advises Telemachus, son of Odysseus to rebuke the suitors of Penelope, his mother, who are wasting the substance of the absent Odysseus, and then to go to Pylus, home of Nestor, and Sparta, where Menelaus lives, to see what he can learn of Odysseus.

Book II: Telemachus rebukes the assembled suitors for eating up his inheritance. Antinous, most insolent of them, reminds him that Penelope has tricked them. Pretending she would make her choice when she finished a shroud she was weaving, each night she raveled out what she had woven during the day. Until she chooses a husband from among them, Antinous says the suitors will continue to make merry in the halls of Odysseus. That night Telemachus boards a ship, provided and manned by Athena's aid, telling only his old nurse, Euryclea, what he intends to do and swearing her to secrecy.

Book III: In Pylus, Nestor can tell him only that the gods had scattered the Achaeans on their way home from Troy. He gives him a chariot to go to Menelaus, and sends his son with him.

Book IV: In Sparta, Menelaus tells him that he has learned from Proteus, a sea-god, that Odysseus is held on the island of Ogygia by Calypso. Meanwhile in Ithaca, Antinous and the other suitors plan to waylay and kill Telemachus on his return.

Book V: Spurred on by Athena, Zeus sends Hermes to command Calypso to send Odysseus home. The nymph agrees and informs Odysseus of his imminent departure. After a brief and understandable doubt concerning Calypso's motives, Odysseus welcomes the approaching end of his eight-year stay on her island. He builds a raft, Calypso gives him provisions, and he sails. But Poseidon is enraged when he sees Odysseus skimming over the sea, and determines that if he cannot defy Zeus and prevent Odysseus from reaching Ithaca, at least he will make it difficult. He raises a mighty storm that shatters the raft. A sea-nymph, Leucothea, comes to Odysseus' aid; she gives him a veil which bears him up until he reaches a rocky island, the home of the Phaeacians. There he drags himself into a wood, covers himself with leaves and falls into a deep sleep.

Book VI: Athena now inspires Nausicaä, daughter of Alcinous, king of the Phaeacians, to go to the beach with her maidens to wash her garments. Their happy cries awaken Odysseus. Naked and bruised as he is,

he approaches them and asks their aid. Nausicaä directs him to her father's palace and advises him to approach her mother, Arete.

Book VII: Hidden in a mist by Athena he arrives at the palace. As he nears Arete, the mist lifts and, falling on his knees, he appeals for help. Alcinous offers the stranger hospitality.

Book VIII: The next day there is a great feast and athletic contests in which Odysseus shows his skill, and dancing. Twice when the blind minstrel, Demodocus, sings of the Trojan Wars, Alcinous notes that the stranger weeps. He tells the minstrel to cease his song and, addressing Odysseus, asks him to tell who he is and why he weeps.

Book IX: He says he is Odysseus, son of Laertes, from Ithaca, and begins his story. After leaving Troy he sacked Ismarus, city of the Cicones, and took great treasure, but his men refused to leave and were set upon by neighbors of the Cicones. Many were killed. A violent storm then drove his fleet to the land of the Lotophagi, the Lotus-Eaters, but they did not linger there for fear of the lotus, fruit of forgetfulness. Stopping next at an island near the land of the Cyclopes, he took a skin of wine and 12 comrades and went to that land. On finding a vast cave, well stocked with wine and cheese, his men urged him to steal the stores and leave, but he decided to await the return of the cave-dweller. Polyphemus, a huge, one-eyed giant, returned at dusk, drove in his flocks and barred the entrance to the cave with a great boulder. On discovering his guests he seized and ate two of them. Odysseus dared not kill him for if he was successful he and his companions would be trapped in the cave. In the morning Polyphemus devoured two more men before driving his flocks out and again barring the entrance to the cave. For his evening meal he took two more of Odysseus' unfortunate companions, and asked Odysseus his name. Odysseus replied that he was "Noman." He offered Polyphemus the wine he had so wisely brought with him, and when the Cyclops fell into a drunken sleep, Odysseus and his men poked out his one eye with a stake they had sharpened in the fire for this purpose. In a frenzy of pain the giant sought his tormen-

fat, fāte, fär, fãre, errạnt; net, mē, hẽr ardẹnt; pin, pīne; not, nōte, mõve, nôr, tors. His howls were heard by neighboring Cyclopes but when they questioned him from outside the cave, he answered that "Noman" had wounded him and they went away, saying he was mad. Next morning when Polyphemus rolled the stone away to let his flocks out, Odysseus and his comrades clung to the thick fleece of the ram's bellies and rode out safely. Polyphemus passed his hands over the back of his flock as they went out but it did not occur to him to feel underneath. Running to his ship, Odysseus flung back a taunting shout at Polyphemus. The giant hurled a great crag after them, and sorrowfully recalled that an oracle had foretold his blinding by Odysseus, but he hadn't expected Odysseus to be so puny as "Noman." He prayed to his father, Poseidon, to avenge him. This was the reason for Poseidon's unrelenting anger at Odysseus.

Book X: From the land of the Cyclopes Odysseus went to the cliff-edged isle of Aeolus, the king of the winds. He entertained them and gave Odysseus a bag in which all the winds were tied up. As they came within sight of Ithaca his men, thinking the bag contained gifts which Odysseus was keeping for himself, opened the bag; the winds flew out and drove them back to Aeolus. That king refused to help again such men who were hateful to the gods, and they departed, compelled to use their oars until they came to the land of the Laestrygoni (Man-eaters). Odysseus alone anchored his ship outside their harbor and thus escaped when the Laestrygoni attacked his other 11 ships and devoured their crews. He fled in the last ship of his fleet to Aeaea, home of the enchantress Circe. There he sent half his forces, led by Eurylochus, to explore. Eurylochus, who had not entered Circe's palace with the others, returned and told Odysseus that his men had been turned into swine by the sorceress and begged Odysseus to fly. However the latter was determined to rescue them, and with the aid of a magic herb given him by Hermes, proved himself invulnerable to Circe's charms and compelled her to change his men back to men from the swine into which she had transformed them. After this Circe was very agreeable, entertained them nobly, and they remained with her a year. She then told Odysseus he must go to Hades and visit the shade of Tiresias, the seer, before he could get home.

Book XI: Circe sent a favorable wind and the ship arrived at the fog-shrouded land of the Cimmerians at the edge of the world, and followed the stream of Oceanus. Odysseus performed the sacrifices as Circe had directed and the souls of the dead appeared. Tiresias came, and Odysseus allowed him to drink the blood of animals he had sacrificed. The seer told him of the journey he must make and of Penelope's suitors, and said Odysseus would vanquish them. The shade of Odysseus' mother appeared and told him she had died grieving for him.

Book XII: From Hades Odysseus returned to Aeaea to bury Elpenor, one of his companions who had died there. Circe warned him of the Sirens, of Scylla, a monster with 12 legs and six hideous heads bearing three rows of teeth each, who inhabited a rocky cave and seized passing mariners, and of Charybdis, a violent whirlpool he must pass. She told him how to pass these threats with the minimum loss and also warned him, as Tiresias had done, not to harm the cattle of the Sun if they touched the island where they were pastured. When they drew near the Sirens' isle, Odysseus filled the ears of his crew with wax, but he had himself lashed to a mast and listened to the Siren's song. He begged his men to release him when he heard it but they ignored his pleas and the danger was safely passed. With great skill the whirlpool of Charybdis was navigated, but six men were seized by Scylla and devoured. Wearied and discouraged, they arrived at Trinacria, the island of Helius. Odysseus, mindful of the warnings of Tiresias and Circe, wanted to sail on. His exhausted men insisted on landing, and promised not to harm the cattle of Helius. Storms kept them on the island and when their food gave out they decided, on a day when Odysseus was off praying to the gods, that they might as well die from eating Helius' cattle as from starvation. Odysseus was in despair when he learned of the feast they had eaten, and rightly so, for shortly after they again set sail Zeus sent a fierce storm and shattered the ship with a thunderbolt to punish them. Only Odysseus survived the wreck. He was swept back to Charybdis but saved himself by grasping a timber of the broken ship and paddling with his hands. Nine days later he landed at Ogygia, the isle of Calypso. She treated him kindly through his eight years' stay there, but he longed for his homeland and Penelope his wife. With this episode Odysseus brings the tale of his wanderings to a close.

Book XIII: The Phaeacians promise him a ship for the voyage to Ithaca, and at nightfall they take him aboard and sail. As he sleeps, they put him ashore on Ithaca and leave him, surrounded by many gifts. When he wakes alone, he does not recognize his surroundings and thinks that the Phaeacians have deceived him. However, Athena appears and reassures him. She helps him hide his treasure in a cave and then transforms him into an old beggar, advising him to seek Eumaeus, a swineherd who has been faithful to him during his absence, for help, and cautioning him not to betray his real identity to Eumaeus.

Book XIV: Eumaeus does not recognize him but treats him kindly and gives him meat and wine, meanwhile bemoaning the continued absence of his master Odysseus. Odysseus assures him that his master will return but Eumaeus is not convinced. In answer to questions about himself Odysseus invents a tale, including an episode in which he says that he has seen Odysseus. The words and deeds of Eumaeus confirm his loyalty to Odysseus but the time has not yet come for Odysseus to reveal himself.

Book XV: Athena visits Telemachus in Sparta and inspires him with a burning desire to go home. He leaves Menelaus, who gives him rich gifts, and returns to Pylus with Nestor's son. There he goes directly to his ship and sails. He lands on Ithaca near the hut of Eumaeus, as advised by Athena, and tells his crew to take the ship into port, thus frustrating the plans of Antinous and the suitors to waylay his ship and kill him.

Book XVI: Eumaeus is delighted to see Telemachus safely returned and goes at once to the palace to give Penelope the good news. As soon as he leaves, Athena transforms Odysseus into his own shape again and he reveals himself to his son, telling him that it is with Athena's help that he has come home,

the suitors. He says he will go to the and that with her help he will overcome palace as a beggar to learn what is going on and to decide what he must do, before anyone realizes he is home.

Book XVII: When Eumaeus returns, Telemachus leaves to go home. Shortly thereafter Odysseus, again in the guise of a beggar, with Eumaeus sets out for the palace. Odysseus finds his home filled with Penelope's suitors, who are eating and drinking at his expense. They mock him as they give him the food he begs, and Antinous throws a footstool at him, but he holds his peace. Penelope sends for him to ask whether he knows anything of Odysseus and he sends word that he will talk to her after the suitors have gone, as this course of action will be more discreet.

Book XVIII: Irus, a common beggar, fearing Odysseus as a rival, is encouraged by the suitors to engage in a fist fight with Odysseus. The suitors think it is great sport and are delighted when Odysseus nearly kills him. Odysseus tries to warn Amphinomous, the best of the suitors, of the imminent arrival of Odysseus and the ruin of the suitors, but Amphinomous, though troubled, ignores him. Now Penelope appears and reminds her uninvited guests that it is customary for wooers to present gifts. Odysseus is delighted with her guile and the rich gifts it draws. When she withdraws from the hall, the merrymaking continues. The suitors entertain themselves by mocking Odysseus and he enrages them with his bold answers. A brawl over the audacity of the beggar is avoided only because Telemachus accuses the suitors of being too far gone in wine and and suggests that they go home.

Book XIX: As advised by Odysseus, Telemachus then takes the suitors' weapons from the hall and hides them. Penelope comes to question the beggar. He begs her not to ask his name, and invents a story of his wanderings. He says he has seen Odysseus and predicts his early return. In spite of her tears he does not reveal his true identity. She thanks him and orders Euryclea, an old nurse, to wash the stranger's feet. In the act of doing so Euryclea recognizes him by an old scar on his leg, and would cry out but Odysseus grasps her throat and warns

fat, fāte, fär, fãre, errant; net, mē, hėr ardent; pin, pīne; not, nōte, möve, nôr,

her to keep silence. Then Penelope describes a dream of 20 geese in the dooryard who were destroyed by an eagle and he tells her it means that Odysseus will return and slay the suitors. She says it must be soon, for she has decided to make a trial of her suitors and choose the one who can string Odysseus' great bow and shoot an arrow through the eyes of 12 ax heads set up in a row, as Odysseus himself used to do. He advises her to do this at once, and assures her that Odysseus will be among the contestants.

Book XX: The following day the banquet hall is prepared for a great feast. Odysseus meets Philoetius, one of his cattle drovers, and learns that he has been as loyal as Eumaeus. He tells Philoetius that Odysseus will soon be home.

Book XXI: Penelope joins the feast, bringing Odysseus' great bow with her, and announces the contest and her intention of marrying the winner. Odysseus withdraws to the courtyard with Eumaeus and Philoetius, proves that he is their master by showing his scarred leg, and enlists their aid to kill the suitors. When Penelope leaves the banquet hall one of the suitors tries to string the bow but is unsuccessful. Eumaeus, over the violent protest of the suitors, then hands it to Odysseus, as he has been instructed to do. Meantime, Euryclea has sent the servants away and Philoetius has taken his post guarding the entrance to the hall. Odysseus takes up the bow, strings it easily, and shoots an arrow through the ax heads which Telemachus has set up.

Book XXII: He then strips off his rags, takes an arrow and shoots Antinous in the throat. The suitors spring up, thinking it is an accident. Now Odysseus tells them who he is and vows to kill them all. As their shields and spears have been hidden by Telemachus, they seize their swords and rush on Odysseus, but to no avail. With his mighty bow and with the aid of Telemachus, Eumaeus, Philoetius, and above all, of Athena, all the suitors are slain. Next he rounds up the servants who have been faithless, orders them to clean up the bloody hall, and then Telemachus hangs them.

Book XXIII: Penelope cannot believe that it is really Odysseus. She lays a trap for

him by telling the servants to move his bed. He proves his identity when he says they cannot move his bed, as he had made it himself from a living olive tree that was enclosed by the walls of the palace. At this Penelope falls into his arms. He tells her briefly of his adventures, and of the journey Tiresias has commanded him to make to a people who have never heard of the sea in order to appease the anger of Poseidon.

Book XXIV: Next day Odysseus visits his father, Laertes. In the meantime the Ithacans have discovered the slaying of the suitors. They bury their dead and resolve to avenge them. As Odysseus and his party are returning from Laertes' home, they are met by the Ithacans, fathers of the suitors. A fight breaks out and Odysseus and his group are about to conquer when Athena intervenes and advises Odysseus to make peace with them forevermore.

Oeagrus (ē'a̯-grus). In Greek legend, a king of Thrace. By the muse Calliope he was the father of Orpheus and, some say, of Linus the musician.

Oeax (ē'aks). In Greek legend, a son of Nauplius and Clymene, and the brother of Palamedes, the inventor. The brothers joined the Greek army which attacked Troy. When Palamedes was killed, through the machinations of Odysseus, Oeax informed his father of the murder by writing the message on oars, which he dropped into the sea. He and his father became the implacable enemies of Agamemnon, because he had refused satisfaction for the death of Palamedes. In his scheme for revenge, Oeax told Clytemnestra that Agamemnon was bringing home Cassandra, and provoked her to murder Agamemnon. His enmity extended to Agamemnon's children, Orestes and Electra.

Oebalus (ē'ba̯-lus). In Greek legend, a king of Sparta. He was the second husband of Gorgophone, daughter of Perseus. His sons by Gorgophone were Tyndareus and Icarius. His son Hippocoön was said to have been born to him by the nymph Batia.

Oedipus (ed'i-pus, ē'di-). In Greek legend, the son of Laius, king of Thebes, and Jocasta, and a descendant of Cadmus. Because of an unfavorable oracle, Laius caused his son's feet to be pierced with a spike and bound when he was born (this accounts for his name, which means "swollen-footed"), and ordered him to be exposed on Mount Cithaeron. However, the shepherd into whose hands he gave the infant was too tenderhearted to leave him to die on the mountain side. Instead, he gave him to a shepherd from another district. The second shepherd gave him to Polybus, king of Corinth. Polybus and his wife Merope (or Periboea), being childless, brought Oedipus up as their own son. When he was grown to manhood, Oedipus was taunted about his origin. Hints were thrown out that he was not the true son of his father. Oedipus questioned Polybus. The king protested and sought to punish those who had made the accusations but, still uneasy in his mind, Oedipus secretly set out to consult the oracle at Delphi. To his horror the priestess told him that he would slay his father and sire children on his mother. Determined to prevent the fulfillment of this awful prophecy Oedipus did not return to Corinth but made his way to a new land. On his way from Delphi where three roads crossed, Oedipus met an older man in a chariot, who ordered him out of the road. Oedipus refused to move and a quarrel arose. Oedipus was struck and defended himself. The stranger, angry in his turn, lashed out at Oedipus with his goad. Enraged, Oedipus set on him and killed him and all his train, save one who escaped. He

OEDIPUS AND THE SPHINX
Red-figured Attic amphora, late 5th century
B.C. *Museum of Fine Arts, Boston*

then proceeded on his way. On the outskirts of the city of Thebes he was stopped by a Sphinx. This monster had been terrorizing Thebes by stopping passers-by and compelling them to answer a riddle: What goes on four legs in the morning, two legs at noon, and three legs in the evening? Whoever failed to give the correct answer, and all had failed, was slain by the Sphinx. Oedipus, when the riddle was put to him, answered that it was man: In infancy he crawls on all fours, in youth he walks upright on his two legs, and in the evening of his life he needs the aid of a staff. On hearing the correct answer the Sphinx killed herself and Thebes was freed of her ravages. When Oedipus arrived in the city, he learned that the king had recently been murdered, and that his successor, his brother-in-law Creon, had proclaimed that whoever vanquished the Sphinx should become king of Thebes and marry the former king's widow, Jocasta. Oedipus was accordingly made king and married Jocasta. By her he became the father of two sons, Eteocles and Polynices, and of two daughters, Antigone and Ismene. Oedipus and Jocasta dwelt in perfect harmony and Thebes prospered. Then a plague struck the city. Cattle and men died, no young were born, the sound of weeping filled the streets. Oedipus sent Creon to the oracle at Delphi to learn the cause of the plague. On his return Creon reported that the plague would be lifted when the murderer of Laius was found and punished. Oedipus now issued a proclamation decreeing that whoever had knowledge of the murderer and sheltered him would be shunned by all Thebans and subject to banishment. He called down all sorts of terrible punishments on the murderer and on those who knew of him and concealed their knowledge. After some time the seer Tiresias was brought to the city on the advice of Creon. Tiresias at first refused to do more than hint at the identity of the murderer but, goaded by the anger of Oedipus, at last revealed that it was Oedipus himself who had murdered Laius. The tragic story gradually unfolded. The shepherd who supposedly had exposed Oedipus as an infant was found and confessed that he had given the child to a shepherd of Corinth. News came from Corinth of the death of

Polybus, and at the same time, the fact that he was not the real father of Oedipus was revealed. All of the pieces of the story fell into place and it became horrifyingly clear that the prophecy the priestess at Delphi had made to Oedipus had come true: He had slain his father and become the father of his own sisters and brothers by his mother. Jocasta hanged herself when she learned the truth. Oedipus despairingly blinded himself and as a consequence of his own order, was shunned by all the people of Thebes. With his daughter Antigone to guide him, he left Thebes and wandered about Greece, endlessly pursued by the Furies. He came at last to Colonus in Attica. There he was befriended by Theseus and at last found peace in death. He was buried and mourned by Theseus and the faithful Antigone. Some say that Oedipus continued to rule Thebes after he learned of the crimes he had unwittingly committed, that he married again, that it was this second wife who bore his four children, and that he finally fell in battle and was honored with funeral games. Others say that once, after his misfortunes, his sons gave him the slave's portion of a sacrificial victim—the haunch, rather than the shoulder. To punish them for their scorn, he laid on them a curse that they should divide their inheritance by the sword. Oedipus was worshiped as a hero after his death. According to some accounts, his bones were treasured as the guardians of the country's safety. Some say the resting-place of his bones was a secret. Others say his grave was in the sanctuary of Demeter at Eteonus, and still others say his bones were taken to Athens.

Oedipus at Colonus (kō-lō′nus). Drama by Sophocles, produced c401 B.C., concerning the fate of Oedipus. The first scene is near a grove of trees in the countryside. Oedipus, self-blinded, banished from Thebes, clothed in rags, and with only his daughter, Antigone, for guide and protector, has wandered here in search of refuge. Antigone leads him to a rock and helps him to be seated. She describes the scene to him, telling him it must be a sacred place. As they wonder where they are, a stranger enters. He urges them to leave the spot where they are resting because, he says, it is sacred to the Eumen-

ides and no human being has ever set foot in it before. In reply to questions put to him by Oedipus, who refuses to move, the stranger says they are near Athens, whose king is Theseus. However, the grove is in land belonging to Colonus and he departs to consult with its people as to whether Oedipus may remain or not. Oedipus prays to the Eumenides to grant him refuge, for Apollo has promised it. Some Elders of Colonus arrive. Their first horror at the idea of a stranger's violating their sacred grove turns to pity when they see the wretched old man, and they are impressed with his noble bearing despite his rags. When they learn he is Oedipus, whose story they know, they urge him to leave lest he pollute their city. Antigone pleads with them. Her plea moves them, but fear of the gods is stronger than pity. They ask Oedipus to respect the laws of their land and leave the sacred grove. Oedipus reminds them of the reputation of Athens for sheltering the weak. He chides them for fearing his name and for betraying their reputation by forcing him, an afflicted old man, away. The crimes he committed he tells them, were committed in innocence. He commands them not to darken the bright name of Athens, and assures them that they will offend the gods if they drive him out, for now he is under the protection of the gods. His presence will bring a blessing to Athens. His arguments sway the elders. They will lay the matter before King Theseus for decision. While they await the arrival of Theseus, Ismene, a second daughter of Oedipus, approaches. She has been searching for them. She greets her father and her sister with joy, then grieves that she brings a message of evil concerning her brothers, Polynices and Eteocles. When Oedipus first left Thebes, she says, the brothers allowed their uncle, Creon, to rule. Now they are grown and are contending for the throne. Polynices, driven out of Thebes by Eteocles, has raised an army in Argos and intends to march against Thebes. An oracle of Apollo has predicted that the army that has possession of Oedipus will win. Creon, wishing to keep mastery, is on his way to seize Oedipus, dead or alive. He will never take him into the city, for he killed his father and cannot be buried there, but he will take him

---

actor; up, lūte, pull; oi, oil; ou, out; ᴛʜ, then; ḍ as d or j, ş as s or sh, ṭ as t or ch, z̧ as z or zh.

to the borders of the city. Eteocles and Polynices also know of the oracle. Oedipus is incensed. After neglect, abuse, and banishment at their hands, his sons will now seek him for their own advantage. He vows that none of them shall ever benefit from him.

The elders of Colonus advise Oedipus to make amends to the Eumenides, whose sacred grove he has violated. Ismene offers to perform the rites for him and departs. The elders have heard the story of Oedipus. They ask to hear from his own lips whether what they have heard is true, namely that he married his mother and had children by her, that he killed his own father. Oedipus replies that it is all true, but that he did it in innocence, for the Thebans gave him a bride but he did not know she was his mother. He killed a man in self-defense, but he did not know it was his father. Now, he says, the oracle has promised that he will bring a blessing to the land that offers him refuge.

Theseus enters and expresses compassion for the miserable state of Oedipus and his daughters. He promises Oedipus asylum and departs. Antigone warns that Creon is approaching. He comes and with smooth words invites Oedipus to return to Thebes, so that the shame of his exile and the unhappy condition of his daughters may be erased. Oedipus is wrathful to hear Creon's hypocrisy. He knows, he says, that Creon will not take him back into Thebes at all, and that Creon is seeking his own advantage because of the oracle. Rather than return with him Oedipus curses him and his own sons. Creon threatens him. If he cannot take Oedipus, he will seize his daughters. Ismene has already been taken. He orders his guards to seize Antigone. They carry her off. Creon prepares to seize Oedipus but Theseus returns and forbids him, and also sends his men to rescue the daughters of Oedipus. As for Creon, Theseus says he will be dealt with according to the laws of Athens. In the meantime, he accuses Creon of disgracing and dishonoring the name of Thebes. Creon tries to justify himself. He flatters Theseus and Athens for the rule of law and respect for the gods. Then he recites the crimes of Oedipus, mentions the pollution his presence brings, and says he would spare Athens from it. Oedipus cries out that he knows the

story better than anyone. He lashes out against Creon for telling his disastrous history again, and shames him. Again he declares his innocence. The oracle that he would slay his father was given before he was even born. And as for marrying his mother, Creon should be ashamed to drag out the story of his own sister again. The Athenians, Oedipus says, know not only how to rule themselves but how to protect the weak. Theseus orders his men to recover Ismene and Antigone. He assures Oedipus he can stay in Athens in peace and, taking Creon with him, he leaves. He returns shortly with Antigone and Ismene. Overjoyed, Oedipus thanks and blesses Theseus. Theseus tells him a man has rushed up to Poseidon's altar as a suppliant, and that he wishes to see Oedipus and asks for assurance that he will be allowed to depart in safety after he has done so. Theseus adds that this suppliant has come from Argos. When Oedipus hears this he realizes it is his son Polynices, and at first refuses to see him, but yields to Antigone's pleas that he hear his son, whom, he says, he hates. Polynices enters. He berates himself for his neglect of his father. His errand is to ask his father's friendship in the war against Eteocles for the throne. Oedipus answers him with wrath. He reminds him that he was no kinder to his father than Eteocles has been. He knows why they all seek him now, after abandoning him for so long. It is because they need him. As he refused Creon, he now refuses Polynices, and predicts that the brothers will both die if Polynices marches against Thebes. The inheritance he leaves for his sons is a place to die in. In sending Polynices away, he prays that the brothers will kill each other. Polynices prepares to leave. He begs his sisters to give him honorable burial if he falls at Thebes. Antigone reminds him that the oracle and the curse will both fail if he does not attack Thebes and pleads with him to spare his own city. Polynices answers that he will not inform his allies of the oracle, and that having raised an army he must fight or he will be branded a coward. He goes. A clap of thunder is heard. Oedipus calls on his children to send for Theseus, for the thunder is a sign from Zeus that his death is near. Thunder peals again, and yet a

fat, fāte, fär, fãre, errạnt; net, mē, hėr ardẹnt; pin, pīne; not, nōte, mȯve, nôr,

third time. Theseus appears and Oedipus welcomes him. He wants to keep his promise that his body will bless Athens before he dies. Theseus alone is to know the spot where he dies. Theseus must reveal it to none save his successor, for the body of Oedipus in Athenian soil will protect Athens from Thebes. Now Oedipus, the blind one, helped by the gods, leads his daughters and Theseus away. As the elders wait, a messenger comes. Oedipus first purified himself, then said farewell to his daughters and commended them to the care of Theseus. He sent them away, keeping only Theseus with him. When the messenger looked back, Oedipus had disappeared, and Theseus was holding his hand before his eyes as if blinded by a great light. The death of Oedipus was quiet; only Theseus knows how it came. Antigone returns, grieving, followed by Theseus. He cannot yield to her plea to know where her father's grave is for he gave his oath in return for the promise of Oedipus to protect his country from harm.

Oedipus Rex (**Tyrannus**), or **Oedipus the King.** Tragedy by Sophocles on the story of Oedipus of the cursed house of Labdacus. The date of its first production is not known. With dramatic power and logical motivation, it perfectly illustrates the conception of the tragic hero, defined by Aristotle as "a man who is highly renowned and prosperous, but one who is not preëminently virtuous and just, whose misfortune, however, is brought upon him not by vice and depravity but by some error of judgment or frailty."

The scene is before the palace of Oedipus at Thebes. Seated on the steps of the altars are a number of suppliants, their hair bound with white fillets of wool. Oedipus comes from the palace to learn their prayer. An aged priest of Zeus says that the city is beset by a plague—vines and cattle are dying, women are producing stillborn infants. As Oedipus once before saved them by killing the dread Sphinx, before he was king, they turn to him again, now that they have made him their king. Oedipus knows of the plague; he suffers for the city, for its people, and for himself. He has sent Creon, son of Menoeceus, to the oracle at Delphi to learn how the plague can be lifted. As he wonders why his emissary has not returned, Creon

enters with a message from the oracle. The word is that the plague will be lifted when the man who killed Laius has been found and driven from the city. Laius, the last king before Oedipus, was murdered by a band of robbers as he was returning from Delphi. Because Thebes was so troubled by the Sphinx at that time, the search for his murderers was not pursued. Oedipus resolves that he will find the murderers and purge Thebes. The suppliants are comforted by his promise and leave. A chorus of Theban Elders enters and sings an ode, mourning the plague and praying to the gods to save the city from the pestilence that is smiting down her children. Oedipus speaks to them. If the man who killed Laius is in Thebes, let him declare himself, and his only punishment will be exile from the city. If any one knows who the murderer is, he must declare it. But if any one knows and does not declare it, that man shall be banished from the life and shelter of Thebes and hounded by the gods. If it were a member of his own household, Oedipus would carry out this punishment, and he charges all of them to do the same. Apollo has spoken to them from Delphi; they must obey the god. Since he, Oedipus, now rules in the place of the slain man, is married to his former wife, and since his children will be heirs to the kingdom, Oedipus has more obligation than any of them to find the murderer of Laius. He will, he says, champion the cause of Laius as if he were his own father. If any disobeys his command to reveal the murderer, he prays that the gods will smite that man.

Tiresias, the blind seer whom Oedipus has called to the palace for help, is led in by a boy. He refuses to answer the questions of Oedipus, saying that it will be better for all if he keeps his peace, yet he knows the man they are seeking. This infuriates Oedipus. Tiresias assures him that the future will come of itself; Oedipus may rage all he likes, but he will remain silent. However, he cannot carry out his intention. Under the lash of Oedipus' tongue he is goaded into saying that Oedipus himself was the slayer of Laius. When Oedipus realizes that Tiresias means what he says, he hotly concludes that this is a plot, planned with Creon, the queen's brother, to ruin him. Tiresias tells him Creon is not a plague to him and that he is his own plague, but Oedipus concentrates on the thought of a plot. The chorus tries to calm them. Tiresias speaks again and tells Oedipus that though he has eyes, he cannot see the misery he is in, nor understand where he is living, nor with whom. He predicts that the curse of Oedipus' mother and father will drive him from Thebes. Oedipus, in a rage, tells him to be gone, but calls him back when Tiresias mentions his parents, and asks who they were. Tiresias predicts that this day will reveal all to him.

The chorus, alone, sings an ode of foreboding, but refuses to believe Oedipus guilty. Creon enters. He has heard the charges of a plot laid against him and has come to face the king. Oedipus berates him. Creon tries to assure him, and asks not to be convicted without some proof. The chorus approves his defense, but Oedipus is not appeased and vows to kill him.

Jocasta, who has heard their angry voices, joins them and begs them to cease their quarrel when the city is already so afflicted. She urges Oedipus to believe Creon's oath that he is his friend. No one wants to tell her the cause of their quarrel, but Oedipus says he will, for he honors her above all others. He tells her he has been accused of murdering Laius. Jocasta seeks to relieve his mind. An oracle said Laius would die by the hand of his own son. But Laius was killed at a place where three roads cross by a band of robbers. His own son, and hers, had been abandoned on a mountain side with his ankles pinned together, when he was only three days old. Therefore the oracle was not fulfilled; the gods can change the future as they will.

Oedipus is not calmed by this story. He questions Jocasta. Where was the place where the three roads cross? She answers that it was on the way from Delphi, and the slaying happened just before Oedipus came to Thebes. As Oedipus questions her and hears her answers, he becomes more agitated. He tells that when he was a youth, son of King Polybus and Queen Merope of Corinth, he overheard some drunken youths say he was not the true son of his father. Vexed and troubled, he went to Delphi to question the oracle. There he was told he

would kill his father, and then marry his mother and have children by her. After that, to prevent the fulfillment of the oracle, he refused to return to Corinth. Instead he came to Thebes. On the way he met a chariot at a place where three roads crossed, disputed the passage, and in anger slew the old man riding in it. Thus, he must be the man to suffer his own proclaimed punishment for the murder of Laius, unless the one man who escaped from the retinue of Laius and for whom he has sent, swears by his story that Laius was set upon by a band of robbers. If he does, Oedipus is innocent, for he was alone when he killed the old man in the chariot. No matter what the man says, Jocasta insists that he cannot change the story now for the whole city has heard it, but besides, the oracle had said Laius would die by the hand of his son, and his son had perished when he was an infant.

They go into the palace, but Jocasta soon comes out and makes offerings on the altar of Apollo. She prays for an end to Oedipus' terrors and to the uncleanness that befouls them all. A messenger comes seeking Oedipus to tell him that his father Polybus is dead and that the people of Corinth want him for their king. Jocasta is delighted, for now it is impossible for the oracle that Oedipus will kill his own father to come true. Oedipus is relieved too, but still fears the second part of the oracle, namely that he will marry his mother. The messenger, overhearing, tells him to be easy about that, for Merope after all, is not his mother, and Polybus was not his father. The messenger is perfectly sure of this because he himself gave Oedipus into the hands of Merope. He had received Oedipus as an infant, with his ankles pinned together, from a shepherd on Mount Cithaeron, and had given him to Polybus and Merope. This tale gives a new direction to Oedipus' thoughts. He wants to find the shepherd and unravel the mystery of his birth. Jocasta begs him not to continue his researches. She implores him to take her advice and give it up. But he is so determined to discover whether he is of noble or base birth that the details the messenger has given him mean nothing to him. They do to Jocasta who hopes he will never know who he is. When he persists

fat, fāte, fär, fãre, errạnt; net, mē, hèr ardẹnt; pin, pīne; not, nōte, möve, nôr, in questioning the shepherd, who has now been brought in, she rushes into the palace. The shepherd, with the greatest reluctance, is forced to reveal what Jocasta has realized is true: Oedipus is the son of Laius and Jocasta. The shepherd had been given the infant to expose on the mountain, so that the oracle concerning the death of Laius would not be fulfilled. But his heart was touched by the child, and instead he gave him to the messenger now standing before them. Now Oedipus realizes that the oracle he had received at Delphi and which he tried so desperately to circumvent, has been fulfilled. He rushes into the palace in a frenzy. A second messenger comes out and announces that Jocasta, in horror at what she has learned, has hanged herself. As he finishes speaking Oedipus staggers forth, his face streaming with blood from his empty eye sockets. Feeling he was no longer worthy to look on the sun he had plucked out his own eyes. He calls down ruin on the man who preserved him as an infant so that he could grow up and commit these horrors. As he swore to do to the murderer of Laius, he commands, Creon, who now becomes king, to banish him from the city. He leaves Thebes to free it from the pestilence of his presence.

Oeneus (ē′nūs). In Greek legend, a son of Portheus. He was king of Calydon in Aetolia. He married Althaea and was the father of Toxeus, Meleager, Tydeus, Deianira, and Gorge, although some accounts say Ares was the father of Meleager and Dionysus the father of Deianira. Dionysus gave him a vine plant and he is said to have been the first to cultivate grapes. Bellerophon visited Oeneus at his court and they exchanged guest gifts of lasting friendship, a fact that assumed great significance for their respective grandsons, Glaucus and Diomedes, in the Trojan War. Agamemnon and Menelaus were sheltered by Oeneus for a time after their father's death. Because he neglected to offer first fruits to Artemis when he made offerings to the other gods and goddesses, the goddess sent a savage boar to lay waste his land. The boar was slain by Meleager in a hunt in which many great heroes took part. Afterward Artemis inspired a war over possession of the boar's hide to harass the Calydonians.

In his later days Oeneus was driven from his throne by rebels and restored to it by his grandson Diomedes.

Oeno (ē′nō). In Greek mythology, one of the three daughters of Anius, king of Delos. She was given the power by Dionysus to turn whatever she wished into wine. See **Elaïs**.

Oenochoë (ē-nok′ō-ē). In Greek antiquity, a small vase of graceful shape, with a three-lobed rim, the central lobe forming a mouth adapted for pouring, and a single handle reaching above the rim: used for dipping wine from the crater and filling drinking cups.

Oenoë (ē-nō′ē). An island of the Cyclades in the Aegean Sea. Here Thoas, king of Lemnos, is said to have landed when he was cast adrift in a chest by his daughter Hypsipyle to save him from the Lemnian women. The name of the island was later changed to Sicinus, after the child that Oenoë, the water-nymph, bore to him.

Oenoë. In ancient geography, a place in C Argolis. Oeneus, king of Calydon, was driven out of his kingdom and took refuge with Diomedes at Argos. Diomedes treated him as a father. When Oeneus died, Diomedes buried him in Argolis and the Argives named the place Oenoë after him.

Oenomancy (ē′nō-man-si). A mode of divination among the ancient Greeks, from the color, sound, and other peculiarities of wine when poured out in libations.

Oenomaus (ē-nō-mā′us). In Greek legend, a son of Ares and a nymph, or of Ares and the Pleiad, Sterope. He was a king of Pisa and Elis. His wife Sterope, a daughter of Acrisius, bore him three sons, Leucippus, Hippodamus, and Dysponteus, and one daughter, Hippodamia. Either because he was in love with her himself or because he feared one of her offspring would cause his death, he determined not to let her marry. However, he did not say this was the case. He said he would wed Hippodamia to the suitor who could beat him in a chariot race from Olympia to the Isthmus of Corinth. If Oenomaus, who gave each suitor a head start while he sacrificed at Olympia, overtook the suitor in the race, he flung his spear into the suitor's back. But if a suitor won, Oenomaus would have to die and Hippodamia would be given to the victor. However, since Oenomaus' horses were given to him by Ares and were the swiftest in Greece, Oenomaus always won. He had already defeated 12 or 13 suitors and nailed their heads to the door of his palace when Pelops, son of Tantalus, came to race for Hippodamia's hand. Pelops' horses and winged chariot had been given him by Poseidon, but to make absolutely sure of winning, he bribed Oenomaus' charioteer Myrtilus, a son of Hermes. Myrtilus substituted wax pins in the axles of Oenomaus' chariot. As the racers neared the goal on the Isthmus, Pelops, with Hippodamia in the chariot beside him, was in the lead. Oenomaus in a furious attempt to overtake him was suddenly cast out of his chariot. The wheels had flown off. He was dragged along, tangled in the reins, to his death. But some say Pelops won and Oenomaus killed himself, or that Pelops, on winning, killed him. But before Oenomaus died, he put a curse on Myrtilus for betraying him and prayed that Myrtilus would die at the hands of Pelops.

Oenone (ē-nō′nē). In Greek legend, a nymph of Mount Ida. A daughter of the river-god Oeneus, she was versed in the arts of healing, which had been taught her by Apollo, and in the arts of divination, which she learned from Rhea. She was loved by Paris when he lived as a simple shepherd on Mount Ida, and bore him a son, Corythus. When Paris returned to his father's palace and later decided to sail to Sparta, Oenone begged him not to leave her, but her pleas were unavailing. As she said goodby to him, she told him to return to her if he was ever wounded, as she alone could heal him. Toward the end of the Trojan War he did return, grievously wounded. Oenone, jealous of Helen and maddened by Paris' desertion, scornfully told him to get Helen to heal him. She knew Helen could not do this, and in the night Oenone ran through the forest to find Paris. Some say her love for him compelled her to seek him out to cure him. But she arrived too late. Paris was already dead and lying on his funeral pyre. Muffling her face in grief, Oenone flung herself on the lighted pyre, clasped Paris in her arms, and died in the flames with him. Their ashes were mixed in one urn and buried beneath a huge mound. Two pillars were erected on it, facing in opposite directions, for the ancient jealousy persisted in the marble.

Oenophyta (ē-nof′i-ta). In ancient geography, a place in Boeotia, Greece, about 23 miles N of Athens. Here the Athenians under Myronides defeated (456 B.C.) the Boeotians.

Oenopion (ē-nō′pi-on). In Greek mythology, a son of Dionysus and Ariadne, and a king of Chios, which he had inherited from Rhadamanthys of Crete. He was the father, by the nymph Helice, of Merope. He promised his daughter to Orion in return for killing the wild beasts of Chios, but kept delaying the marriage. Orion assaulted Merope, while under the spell of too much wine, and Oenopion punished him by blinding him as he slept. When Orion returned from the East with his sight restored Oenopion hid from him in a palace under the earth built for him by Hephaestus. Oenopion had been taught how to make wine by his father Dionysus, and it was he who first realized that it was wise to mix the wine with water for drinking purposes.

Oenotria (ē-nō′tri-a). In ancient geography, a name given by the Greeks to the S part of Italy, which was colonized by Oenotrians. The name was ultimately changed to Italy. It was to this region that Aeneas and his Trojan followers went to fulfill their destiny.

Oeonus (ē-ō′nus). In Greek legend, a young relative of Heracles who accompanied him to Sparta. As he was walking about the streets one day, a dog rushed out and attacked him. Oeonus threw a stone at the dog in self-defense and killed it. The sons of Hippocoön surged forth and beat Oeonus with cudgels. Heracles rushed up to protect him, but he was too late; Oeonus had been beaten to death. On this occasion Heracles was injured in the thigh and was compelled to withdraw. Later he resolved to wage war on Hippocoön and this time he killed him and his sons. In gratitude for having avenged the death of Oeonus Heracles raised a sanctuary of Athena Axiopoenus (*Just Requital*) in Laconia and dedicated a shrine of Asclepius Cotyleus (*Of the Hip-joint*) on the road to Therapne for the healing of his wound.

Oeta (ē-ta), **Mount.** A mountain in S Thessaly. Here Heracles built his own funeral pyre when he was suffering from the agonies caused by the poisoned garment sent to him by his wife. Since he was too strong to die,

fat, fāte, fär, fāre, errant; net, mē, hėr ardent; pin, pīne; not, nōte, möve, nôr,

he cast himself on a pyre of his own building and prevailed on Philoctetes to set it alight. A cloud descended on the pyre and when it had lifted, all trace of Heracles had vanished. Nearby is the pass of Thermopylae, into the stream of which Heracles had flung himself to get relief from his burning pain. Its waters brought no relief to Heracles. On the contrary, he caused the waters to bubble and steam, hence the name, which means "burning" or "hot passage."

Oetylus (ē'ti-lus). An ancient town in Laconia, on the Taenarum promontory. It was named for a hero of Argive descent, and sent many heroes to the Trojan War under the command of Menelaus.

Ogmios (og'mē-ọs). Ancient Gallic god of eloquence, equated with the Old Irish Ogma. The Romans, when they invaded Gaul, identified Ogmios with their own Mercury.

Ogygia (ō-jij'i-ạ). In classical geography, the island of Calypso, referred to in the *Odyssey*. Plutarch says it lies due west, beneath the setting sun.

Ogygus (oj'i-gus). A legendary Boeotian king, said to have sprung from the soil or, as some say, the son of Poseidon. During his reign Lake Copaïs overflowed its banks and inundated the region with a great flood that came to be known as the Ogygian Flood.

Oicles (ō-ik'lēz). In Greek legend, an Argive, the son of Antiphates. He was the father of Amphiaraus the seer. He accompanied Heracles on his expedition against Troy to punish Laomedon. Oicles was left to guard the ships while Heracles attacked Troy. The Trojans, hurriedly armed, set upon the ships to burn them but Oicles, fighting heroically, held them off until his companions could launch the ships and escape. Some say Oicles was killed in this action. Others say he survived it and was still alive when his grandson Alcmaeon was driven mad by the Furies, and that he gave asylum to Alcmaeon.

Oileus (ō-i'lūs). A legendary king in Locris. He had gone as an Argonaut with Jason on the quest for the Golden Fleece, and was wounded near the island of Ares, when an iron feather dropped from one of the birds of Ares on him. He was known as a "sacker of cities." By his wife Eriopis he was the father of Ajax the Less, and by Rhene, his concubine, he was the father of Medon.

Olbia (ol'bi-ạ). In ancient geography, a city in Scythia, a Greek colony from Miletus, near the confluence of the Borysthenes (the modern Dnieper) River and the Hypanis (modern Bug).

Olbia. An ancient settlement on the northeast coast of the island of Sardinia. It had the best harbor on the coast and its traditional founding is attributed to an expedition from Thespiae and Attica led by Iolaus. (AH)

Old Man of the Sea. In Greek mythology, a name for Nereus, the god who came to be thought of as the god of the Mediterranean, as distinct from Oceanus, the personification of the outer sea. This title or name is also given to Phorcys.

Olen (ō'len). A mythical poet of Lycia. He was reputed to be the first to sing hymns to the gods in connection with the worship of Apollo at Delphi. To him was attributed the legend of Apollo's visit to the Hyperboreans.

Olenus (ō'lē-nus). In ancient geography, a town on the coast of Achaea. It was one of the 12 towns occupied by the Achaeans after the Ionians had left the region. In the time when Dexamenus was king of Olenus, Heracles is said to have visited his kingdom, having just finished the labor of cleansing the Augean Stables; there he saved the daughter of Dexamenus from marriage with the centaur Eurytion. Olenus did not grow in size and was finally abandoned by its inhabitants because it was so small as to be defenseless.

Oliarus (ō-li-ăr'us) or **Olearus** (ō-lē-ăr'us). [Modern name, **Antiparos.**] Island in the Cyclades, SW of Paros, celebrated for a stalactite grotto. Length, about eight miles.

Olive. Tree sacred to Athena. In a legendary contest between Poseidon and Athena for possession of the city of Athens, Poseidon struck the rock of the Acropolis with his trident and a well of salt water gushed forth. Athena planted the olive tree beside the well, and as this was considered the more useful and valuable gift, Athena was awarded the city. The well and the olive tree were in the temple of Erechtheus. When the Persians under Xerxes captured and sacked Athens (480 B.C.), they killed the Athenians who had rushed to the Acropolis for safety and burned the temple with the olive tree in it. But when the Athenians returned to the citadel to offer sacrifices, they found a fresh shoot growing out of the old trunk. The olive tree could still be seen on the Acropolis as late as the 2nd century A.D. Some say Heracles, having reëstablished the Olympic Games, went back to the land of the Hyperboreans and asked Apollo's priests to give him some of the wild olive trees growing there. He wanted the trees to provide shade for the precinct of Zeus at Olympia. The priests gave him a tree which he planted in the precinct of Zeus. From that time on, he decreed that the victors in the contests should be crowned with olive leaves. This was to be their sole reward, because he had not received payment for his labors for Eurystheus. His decree was honored. Branches for the victors' crowns were cut from the tree in the sacred grove of Zeus with a golden sickle, by a boy of noble birth, both of whose parents were still living.

Cultivation of the olive was an important feature of agricultural life in the ancient world. In Greece the expansion in olive culture came after the Persian Wars when expanded maritime activity made it possible both to import grain and to export olive oil. Cultivation in Italy increased after the Punic Wars. Methods of cultivation described by ancient authors are still followed.

Olonos (ọ-lọ′nos). See **Erymanthus.**

RED-FIGURED EYE-CUP, OLTOS, c530–520 B.C.
Munich

Oltos (ol′tos) or **Oltus** (-tus). Attic vase-painter, active c530–510 B.C. Two kylixes (cups) signed by him as the painter are extant, and over 100 other cups have been attributed to him. Among his works is a large kylix (Tarquinia) on which the gods on Olympus are shown. An eye cup (Munich) decorated on the inside in black-figure style shows Dionysus with a drinking cup; on the outside the decoration is in red-figure and consists of two large eyes separated by a flute case on one side and two large eyes separated by a nose on the other. Another cup (Munich) in red-figure has Priam with a train of gift bearers before Achilles to ransom the body of Hector. Oltos also worked, to a less degree but with great success, on the larger vessels, as the amphora and stamnos.

Olympia (ọ-lim′pi-ạ). In ancient geography, the site of a celebrated sanctuary of Zeus and of the Olympic Games, the most important of the great public games of classical antiquity. Situated in Elis in the valley of the Alpheus River at its confluence with the Cladeus River, its location and importance caused it to be spared the incessant warfare that harassed most of the rest of Greece. The area was originally a part of Pisatis, whose capital was Pisa, but came, after many engagements between Eleans, Pisans, Spartans, and Argives, under the control of Elis early in the 6th century B.C. Through centuries of warfare and change in Greece, Olympia remained a relatively peaceful spot, remote from political upheavals and protected by its geographical location. It was primarily a religious center, where the athletic contests in honor of the gods gradually took on more importance than the religious ceremonies that brought them into being. The site is a peaceful valley, cooled by numerous pine trees, once washed by two rivers, and protected at the north by the low wooded Hill of Cronus. The origins of the sanctuary and of the games are anterior to history; according to tradition the games were reorganized, in obedience to the Delphic oracle, in the 9th century B.C. The list of Olympic victors goes back to 776 B.C., which is the first of the four years of the first Olympiad, but the Olympiad system of chronology did not come into accepted use until much later. South of the Hill of Cronus at Olympia was the Altis, a sacred enclosure that was the religious center. It was surrounded by a low wall, the location of which was changed from time to time through the centuries to enlarge the enclosure. Inside the Altis was the 6th century B.C. Doric temple of Zeus, built from the spoils that were taken from the Pisans by the Eleans. Libo, the architect who designed the temple shortly after the Elean victory, did not live to see its completion, which was not accomplished until the middle of the 5th century B.C. The greatest treasure of the temple, which was richly decorated within and without, was the statue of *Olympian Zeus* by Phidias. In front of the temple, facing the east, were many statues given as votive offerings at various times. Among them was the *Nike* of Paeonius, given by the Messenians to celebrate a victory over the Spartans. Inside the north wall of the Altis was the ancient temple of Hera, in the cella of which stood the famous *Hermes and the Infant Dionysus,* by Praxiteles. Between the temples of Zeus and Hera, on a slight rise, was a sanctuary of Pelops, enclosed by a pentagonal stone wall. Black rams were here sacrificed to Pelops, who was honored at Olympia only slightly less than Zeus, and in memory of whom, some say, the first games

HEAD OF APOLLO
From the west pediment of the Temple of
Zeus at Olympia, 470–456 B.C. *Olympia*

were instituted. East of the temple of Hera stood the *Metroum,* a temple dedicated to the Mother of the Gods, and south of the Metroum, roughly in the middle of the Altis, was a very ancient altar of Zeus made of ashes of victims mixed with the waters of the Alpheus River. In addition, there was a profusion of statues of gods, heroes, and victors scattered within the Altis, as well as numer-

ous other buildings that were erected in later times. Outside the Altis, to the west, was the *Bouleterium,* dating from the 6th and 5th centuries B.C. Here sat the Upper Council, or Boule, that managed affairs at Olympia. Also to the west were a gymnasium and palestra where the athletes trained for the contests. At the northwest corner of the Altis stood the *Prytaneum,* the chief administrative building at Olympia, where the priests and other officials took their meals and where visitors of importance and victors were entertained. In half the building was the sacred hearth of Hestia, on which a fire was kept burning at all times. To the east of the Altis was the stadium, capable of seating 20,000 spectators, where the foot races were held. German archaeologists have uncovered the marble starting line, marked off in equal spaces for the contestants, and the finish line, 192.27 meters away. South of the stadium was the hippodrome, where the chariot races were run. In addition, the site at Olympia was occupied by a number of *thermae,* chiefly of Roman date, the treasuries of various Greek cities and states, numberless statues and works of art, and steles with commemorative inscriptions. The Olympic Games were formally abolished (394 A.D.) by the emperor Theodosius as a relic of paganism. The monuments were much shattered by earthquakes in the 6th century, and as time went on were progressively buried by landslides from Cronus and inundations of the Cladeus (now dry), and the Alpheus, in one of which the hippodrome was entirely washed away. Sand and earth were deposited to a depth of from ten to 20 feet over the ruins. Nor was man free from responsibility in the destruction of the monuments. The heads of many statues were lopped off to destroy the pagan idols, and much material from the temples and other buildings was carried away for use in humbler structures. The French *Expédition de Morée* made· (1829) some superficial excavations, and recovered some sculptures (now in the Louvre) from the temple of Zeus. In six seasons of work after 1874, the German government laid bare down to the ancient level the greater part of what survives of the sanctuary. The sculptural finds include the *Hermes* of Praxiteles and the *Nike* of Paeonius, which are now in the Museum at Olympia, along with large fragments from the pediments of the temple of Zeus as well as fragments of metopes from the same temple. In the departments of architecture and epigraphy the German excavations, resumed after World War II, rank as the most important that have been made. The antiquities discovered are preserved on the site. Olympia as a religious and athletic center did not seek to exercise influence on political affairs, and it was perhaps for this reason that it was respected as a peaceful island in the midst of the constantly warring Greek city-states, that armed soldiers were not permitted to pass through its territory, and that guarantees of safe conduct through hostile areas could be given to contestants and spectators going to the games. For centuries, the festival at Olympia gave one point of unity to the Greeks perpetually at odds with each other. In its Golden Age, Olympia developed a high standard of personal excellence in the games, and served as a widely-attended showplace for the presentation of Greek ideas and for the exhibition of some of the finest achievements in Greek art, poetry, literature, and philosophy.

Olympians (ō-lim′pi-ạnz). The 12 high gods of Greek mythology, so named because they dwelt on Mount Olympus. They are usually counted as follows: Zeus, the supreme god who ruled over all; Hera, his consort and sister; Hestia, another sister; Poseidon, his brother; the four daughters of Zeus, Athena, Hebe, Artemis, and Aphrodite; his four sons, Hermes, Ares, Apollo, and Hephaestus. Demeter and Dionysus are sometimes added to the original 12, and sometimes also Heracles.

Olympian Zeus. Great statue of Zeus in the sanctuary at Olympia. It was one of the Seven Wonders of the Ancient World, and in ancient times it was considered a misfortune to have died without beholding it. The statue, of ivory and gold, with painted draperies, was made by Phidias, whose workshop near the sanctuary at Olympia existed into the Christian era and later became a Byzantine church. Phidias was assisted in executing the statue, which was considered, with the statue of Athena in the Parthenon, his masterwork. According to tradition, when Phidias was commissioned to make the statue

he was asked what model he would use, and was said to have replied that he would use Homer's description:

"Thus spoke the son of Cronus, and with
    darkling eybrows he nodded.
Then the ambrosial locks of the King
    flowed waving about him,
Down from his head immortal; . . ."

When the statue was finished, Phidias prayed for a sign from Zeus that the god found it acceptable. Immediately a bolt of lightning struck the floor of the temple in front of the image, signifying the pleasure of Zeus in the work. Many eminent travelers of the ancient world testified to the extraordinary beauty and majesty of the statue, but only Pausanias attempted to describe it in detail. He tells of the god on his throne, his head wreathed with the wild olive. In his right hand was an image of Victory; in his left hand was an ornamented scepter on which perched an eagle. On his feet were golden sandals, and his robe was decorated with figures of animals and flowers. The throne was of gold, jewels, ebony, and ivory, and was decorated with many figures from mythology. According to some accounts, the Emperor Caligula wished to transport the image to Rome, and replace the head of Zeus with an image of his own, but the ship he sent for the purpose was struck by lightning and lost. Whenever, later, any of his men attempted to lay hands on the statue, they were driven back by a loud peal of laughter from the image. The image has been completely lost. Some say it was lost in a fire about 408 A.D., or that it was destroyed in Constantinople, whither it had been taken, about 475 A.D. Only representations of it on coins remain. The descendants of Phidias held the office of Burnishers of the Image for generations; they anointed the ivory with oil to keep it from cracking.

Olympias (ō-lim′pi-ạs). Wife of Philip II of Macedon, and mother of Alexander the Great; put to death 316 B.C. The daughter of Neoptolemus, king of Epirus, she met Philip at Samothrace, where he had gone to be initiated into the mysteries, and married him in 357 B.C. According to tradition, before Alexander was born, she dreamed a thunderbolt fell on her body and that from it flames spread out in all directions and then were extinguished. This was taken as an omen that her son would have brilliant successes. Of a strongly mystical temperament, it is said that at the religious orgies she twined tame serpents about her body, a sight men could not bear to see. Once also, it is said, Philip found a serpent lying beside her as she slept. From that time on he found her distasteful and turned his attention to other women. Her proud and tumultuous spirit was roused to fury and desire for revenge by his flagrant infidelities. She found some satisfaction in turning her son against his father. In 337 B.C. Philip inflicted the supreme insult by casting her aside altogether and marrying Cleopatra, the niece of his general, Attalus. At the wedding feast Attalus asked the assembled company to pray for a legitimate heir, thus bringing into the open rumors that Olympias was, though more discreet, no less unfaithful than Philip, and that Alexander was not his son. Alexander hurled a cup into Attalus' face for his insult to his mother. Philip rose to run his son through with his sword but tripped over a couch as he lunged. After this Alexander took his mother to her old home in Epirus. She continued to intrigue against Philip for revenge and for power. At the marriage of Philip's daughter to her brother, the king of Epirus, Philip was murdered as he walked in the wedding procession. Olympias did not wield the dagger that killed him, but it has been said on the basis of evidence of doubtful validity that she was the architect of the plot. Still thirsting for revenge, she caused the infant son of Philip and Cleopatra to be slain in his mother's arms and compelled Cleopatra to hang herself. This not only avenged her honor but also cleared a possible rival from Alexander's path. After Alexander's accession (336 B.C.) she maintained her influence at court, especially during Alexander's absences in his campaigns. She constantly wrote to him, advising him not to enrich his companions, lest they seek his throne, and pouring out accusations against Antipater, left behind as regent of Macedonia. Alexander sent her many gifts from the spoils he took in Asia but did not allow her advice to influence his conduct of affairs. Antipater in his turn sent letters of accusation against Olympias. Alexander read them

and remarked that Antipater did not realize how easily all his words could be washed out by the tears of a mother. Having made an enemy of Antipater, when Alexander died (323 B.C.), she prudently retired to Epirus once more. From there she opposed the growth of the power of Cassander, Antipater's son, but he besieged her at Pydna, and, after her capitulation, had her slain.

Olympias. Spring, near Trapezus in Arcadia. Every other year, according to the Arcadians, the spring ceased to flow; instead, fire rose up. The Arcadians said that here the battle between the gods and the giants took place, and here the Arcadians offered sacrifices to the lightning, thunder, and hurricanes.

Olympic Games (ō-lim′pik). [Also: **Olympian Games.**] The greatest of the four Panhellenic festivals of the ancient Greeks. The others were the Nemean, the Pythian, and the Isthmian games. They were celebrated at intervals of four years in honor of Zeus at Olympia on the Alpheus River in Elis. The contests were held outside a sacred enclosure called the Altis, at the foot of the Hill of Cronus. The Altis contained many temples and other religious structures, was dotted with a profusion of statues of gods, heroes, and victors, and was the site of a very ancient altar of Zeus. Outside the Altis were civic buildings, treasuries, gymnasia, baths, and the stadium and hippodrome where the contests were held. Various accounts are given of the origin of the games. Some say that Heracles, the eldest of the five Curetes of Mount Ida in Crete, who guarded the infant Zeus, came to Olympia and matched his brothers in a running race, and crowned the winner with a wreath of wild olive. He established the custom of holding the games every fifth year because there were five brothers, they say. But some say Zeus wrestled at Olympia with Cronus for control of the universe, and that he established games to celebrate his victory over Cronus, and that Apollo was an early Olympic victor, having beaten Hermes in the foot race and Ares in the boxing contest. Others say the games were established by Pisus, founder of the city of Pisa in Elis that was destroyed in the time of Nestor by the Eleans. And still others say that the games commemorated the chariot race between Pelops and Oenomaus for the hand of Hippodamia, daughter of Oenomaus, won by Pelops. At all events, there was a sanctuary of Pelops at Olympia of great antiquity, and he was honored there only slightly less than Zeus. Some say Olympia was the site of an ancient oracle of Gaea and of Zeus, and that the first games date from the second millennium B.C. In the earliest times the games were purely local, and membership in them was limited. Later, it is said, they were refounded and reorganized by Heracles, who paced off the stadium himself. The local games, originally celebrated in honor of local gods and heroes, gradually resolved into a festival honoring the greatest of the gods, Zeus, and became a Panhellenic festival in which membership was open to all free Greeks. At intervals in the early centuries the celebration of the games lapsed. They were revived, allegedly in the 9th century B.C., by Iphitus, descendant of that Aetolian Oxylus who assumed the throne of Elis on the return of the Heraclidae to the Peloponnesus. He is said to have appealed to the oracle at Delphi for a means of stopping the constant wars, and was told by the priestess to reëstablish the games. It was Iphitus too, some say, who in obedience to a command of the oracle first crowned the victors in the contests with wreaths of wild olive. From about this period dates the *Sacred Truce*, under which contestants going to the games were guaranteed safe conduct. The Sacred Truce was later extended to cover the full month in which the games were held, so that spectators as well as contestants could proceed to Olympia in safety. Records of the victors at the games were kept from 776 B.C., and the period of four years intervening between one celebration and the next, called an Olympiad, is notable as the measure by which the Greeks computed time. The name given to each Olympiad was that of the victor in the foot race. At the beginning of the 6th century B.C. the Eleans wrested control of Olympia from the Pisans, and henceforward Olympia was relatively inviolate, and was gradually enriched with the magnificent temples and many works of art that made it a center of pilgrimage throughout the Greek world. Until 472 B.C. the games all took place on the same day, on the day of the first full moon after the summer solstice. After

this, the festival lasted for a week, and in this period of the summer solstice the contests were held in the cool of the morning. In the evening, by the light of the full moon and pine torches, banquets and feasts were held at which hymns of victory and paeans to the gods were sung. The festival was in two parts: the first consisted of offerings to Zeus, and to the other gods and to heroes; the second, in which men, and later boys also, took part, consisted of the athletic contests. After the 5th century B.C. all the contestants, except those in the chariot race, competed in the nude. The earliest contest was the foot race, run in the stadium that Heracles was said to have paced off. In 708 B.C. the pentathlon was added. This consisted in a combination of five separate contests—wrestling, spear-throwing, discus-hurling, leaping, and a foot race—in each of which some contestants were eliminated, and in which the victor in the last contest was the winner of the pentathlon. The pancratium, consisting of boxing and wrestling matches, was a later addition. Gradually, more contests were added, including chariot racing, competitions between trumpeters and heralds, oratorical contests, literary, poetic, and painting competitions and the like, until there were 24 separate contests, held over the course of several festivals, in which any free Greek could participate. Later, the Romans also were allowed to take part. The emperor Nero added a musical contest, in which he was, of course, the victor. No Greek who had any personal stain on his honor could enter; slaves were not admitted to competition, although they could observe; and women were forbidden even to observe except on certain days. A law was passed that any married woman caught observing on the prohibited days must be tossed to her death from nearby Mount Typaeum. Only one woman was ever caught, and she escaped the penalty because of the glorious record of her family in the games. The story was that one Pherenice or Callipatira, a widow, disguised herself as a trainer and took her son to compete in the games. He won his match and she, in jumping over the enclosure in which the trainers were kept during the competition, exposed her person and unmasked herself. Although she escaped the penalty, a law was passed that in future trainers must strip before entering the arena. In the Council Chamber at Olympia was an image of Zeus, holding a thunderbolt in each hand, called the "Oath-god." Here the contestants, their families, and their trainers took an oath on slices of boar's flesh that in nothing would they sin against the Olympic Games. The athletes swore that they had spent at least ten months in preparation for the games and that they would observe only fair means in attempting to win their contests. The games were supervised by priests and the rules were rigidly enforced, any infractions being punished by fines or forfeiture of the prize. The fines were used to erect images of Zeus called *Zanes*. These images were set up along the way leading to the stadium, to remind the athletes on their way to their contests of the penalties of breaking their oath. The victors in the contests were crowned with wreaths of wild olive that had been cut with a golden knife by a boy whose mother and father were still living. The victors were also permitted to set up suitably inscribed statues of themselves in the Altis. The festival ended with sacrifices at the six double altars of the gods. These altars were reputedly set up by Heracles, one altar for each pair of the twelve Olympians. When a victor returned home, he was received with extraordinary distinction and enjoyed numerous honors and privileges. He rode in a chariot drawn by four white horses to the temple of the most important god of his home area and deposited his victor's wreath on the altar as an offering to the god. After this there was a banquet for the victor at which a hymn was sung in his honor. Such hymns were sometimes composed by the most celebrated poets, as those of Pindar. Often valuable perquisites were given to the victor, for in winning he was thought to be in divine favor and honored his home city as well as himself. After the Peloponnesian Wars the games deteriorated somewhat. The principle, carefully maintained up to this time, that the contestants at the festival must be amateurs of good character and superb fitness was abandoned, and Olympia became an arena for professional athletes. The emperor Hadrian sought to restore the former splendor of the games and for a time they regained

some of their former glory and attracted many spectators and gifts. The games were held regularly, regardless of war or disaster, from 776 B.C. to 393 A.D. In 393 A.D. the emperor Theodosius abolished them as a symbol of pagan idolatry.

Olympus (ō-lim′pus). In Greek legend, a Phrygian flute-player who was taught the art of flute-playing by Marsyas and improved upon it. His Phrygian descendants were said to have inherited the art and the 7th century B.C. Olympus who introduced the art among the Asiatic Greeks was regarded as his descendant. In the contest between Apollo and Marsyas Olympus was associated with Apollo. Olympus was taught how to play the syrinx by Pan.

Olympus. In ancient geography, the name of various mountains, but especially of one (elevation, about 9794 feet) on the borders of Macedonia and Thessaly, regarded as the especial home of the chief gods of Greek mythology. Hence the word is often used to mean heaven. The Mysian Olympus was on the borders of Mysia, Bithynia, and Phrygia in Asia Minor. Others were in Lydia, Lycia, Cyprus, Laconia, and Elis. There are believed to have been 14 in all.

Olynthiac Orations (ō-lin′thi-ak). Series of three orations delivered (349–348 B.C.) at Athens by Demosthenes for the purpose of inducing the Athenians to assist Olynthus against Philip II of Macedon.

Olynthus (ō-lin′thus). In ancient geography, a city in Chalcidice, Macedonia, situated near the head of the Toronaic Gulf near the neck of the Pallene peninsula. It was a city of the Bottiaeans, a Thracian tribe, until 479 B.C. At that time Artabazus, the Persian general who had escorted the defeated Persian king to the Hellespont, returned to Chalcidice and, suspicious that Olynthus was about to revolt against Xerxes, captured the city and sacked it. The inhabitants were led to a nearby marsh and slaughtered. Artabazus then handed the city over to the Chalcidians, who had been loyal to Persia, and from this time Olynthus became a Greek city. The city revived under the Macedonian king, Perdiccas. He instigated a revolt of the cities of Chalcidice against Athens and persuaded the inhabitants of the neighboring cities to unite within the walls of Olynthus against Athens (c433 B.C.). Perdiccas later appealed to Sparta for aid against Athens, and Olynthus became the base for the operations of the Spartan general Brasidas in the area. With his successes Perdiccas turned against Sparta and renewed his alliance with Athens. Olynthus became independent and the center of a powerful Chalcidian League. The league, at first an association of equals, soon came to be dominated by Olynthus, which sought to compel neighboring cities to join. They appealed to Sparta and a force was sent against the city, 382 B.C., and Olynthus was compelled to surrender, 379 B.C., but only after having inflicted heavy losses on the Spartans. The city soon recovered its power and its place as the head of a confederacy even more powerful than the earlier one. It was allied with Philip II of Macedon, who had sought its favor by giving it the city of Potidaea. However, as Philip's power grew, Olynthus became alarmed and abandoned her alliance with him. When he demanded the surrender of his half-brother, who had found refuge in the city, the Olynthians refused his demand and he marched against the city. Olynthus appealed to Athens for aid. In the Olynthiac Orations Demosthenes urged the Athenians to send aid to Olynthus. His main argument was that Philip must be crushed before he became so powerful as to threaten Athens, and that the place to crush him was Olynthus, far from the borders of Attica. Athens sent soldiers to the north, but had delayed their departure too long. The city was captured by Philip (348 B.C.) before the Athenians arrived. He so completely destroyed the city that a few years later it would have been hard to realize a city had ever existed on the spot. The inhabitants that were not slain were sold as slaves or scattered in neighboring cities.

Omphale (om'fạ-lē). In Greek legend, a daughter of Iardanus. She was the wife of Tmolus, king in Lydia, and some say she was the mother of Tantalus by Tmolus. On the death of her husband, Omphale became ruler of Lydia. It was she who bought Heracles as a slave when he was ordered to sell himself to expiate the murder of Iphitus. He performed many services for her, in the course of which he captured the Cercopes, and killed Syleus, Lityerses, and a serpent that was ravaging the countryside. In gratitude, Omphale, who had now learned his real identity, freed him and became his mistress. She bore him several sons, among them Lamus. When Heracles had completed his service, some say at the end of a year, others say at the end of three years, Omphale gave him rich gifts and he returned to Tiryns. Some say that Omphale forced Heracles to dress in women's clothes and to perform women's work. This was a story spread by Pan. Heracles and Omphale did sometimes exchange their clothes, as it amused the queen to behold the brawny Heracles in her delicate garments. On one occasion when they were dressed in each other's clothes, Pan sought to ravish Omphale as she slept in a cave with Heracles. Feeling the silken garments in the dark, he mistakenly attacked Heracles and was kicked across the cave for his pains.

APOLLO SEATED ON THE OMPHALOS
Red-figured Greek vase

Omphalos (om'fạ-los). A sacred stone in the temple of Apollo at Delphi, believed by the Greeks to mark the "navel" or exact centerpoint of the earth. This point was located by Zeus. He released two eagles in opposite directions. They flew until they met, at Delphi, and thus determined the center of the earth. The stone set up to mark the spot was the one Rhea gave to Cronus to swallow in the place of her new-born son, Zeus; for it was the custom of Cronus to swallow his children as soon as they were born. When Zeus grew up, he forced Cronus to disgorge his sisters and brothers and the stone. It was then set up at Delphi and daily anointed with oil. Extant representations show it as a stone of a conical shape, often covered with a kind of network called *agrenon,* similar in character to the sacred garment so called, or wreathed with votive fillets. The Delphic or Pythian Apollo is often represented as seated on the omphalos, in his chief sanctuary, and statues have been found, the feet of which rest on a truncated omphalos.

Onatas (ō-nā′tas). Aeginetan sculptor and painter, a contemporary of Ageladas, the teacher of Phidias. He was active c500–460 B.C. He was especially famous for his statues of athletes. Pausanias has described many of his works, as the *Apollo* of Pergamum, the *Ten Greek Heroes* casting lots to see which would take up the challenge of Hector to single combat, and a group representing Hiero of Syracuse in the chariot in which he won the victory at the Olympic Games.

Onchestus (on-kes′tus). In ancient geography, a city of Boeotia, Greece, near Thebes. It was named for a son of Poseidon, was sacred to that god, and contained a temple and image of Onchestian Poseidon.

Oncium (on-sī′um). Place in Arcadia, ruled by Apollo's son Oncus. Here, according to legend, Demeter, wearied from her search for Persephone, and being pursued by Poseidon, transformed herself into a mare and grazed in the fields. But Poseidon was not fooled. He transformed himself into a stallion and attacked her. From this union the nymph Despoena and the fabulous horse Arion were born.

Oneiros or **Oniros** (ō-nī′ros). The personification of dreams. He was a winged god who dwelt in the land of the sunset.

Onesimus (ō-nē′si-mus). See **Euphronius,** painter and potter.

Onomacritus (on-ō-mak′ri-tus). Greek prophet and mystic poet at the court of the Pisistratidae at Athens, about 530–485 B.C. He is said to have edited the poems of Musaeus for the Orphics. He was for a time a great friend of the Pisistratidae but was banished from Athens by Hipparchus when it was discovered that he was inserting one of his own oracles among the supposed oracles of Musaeus, namely, that the island of Lemnos would one day disappear into the sea. Later he was reconciled to the sons of Pisistratus, who had been banished themselves from Athens, when they went to Susa to persuade Xerxes to make war on the Athenians. To help the Pisistratidae to sway Xerxes, who was at first cool to the idea of the war, Onomacritus recited oracles which seemed to promise success in a war against Athens. At the same time, he carefully omitted to mention a great number of oracles that prophesied disaster for the Persians. According to Herodotus, the favorable oracles he mentioned to Xerxes had great weight in swaying that monarch to the idea of war.

Opheltes (ō-fel′tēz). In Greek mythology, a son of Lycurgus, king of Nemea. He was left alone by his nurse Hypsipyle, former queen of Lemnos, while she went to get water for the Seven against Thebes, who had stopped in Nemea on their way to Thebes. While she was gone, Opheltes was bitten by a serpent and died. The Nemean Games were celebrated in his honor.

Ophion (ō-fī′on). In Greek mythology, a great serpent who was created, some say, by Eurynome, and with her was the first lord of creation. They created the Titans, according to some accounts, and ruled them from Olympus until they were forced to yield to Cronus and Rhea; after this they disappeared into the sea.

Ophiuchus (of-i-ū′kus). An ancient northern constellation, representing a man holding a serpent, whence its name, Serpent-bearer. The serpent is now treated as a separate constellation. Also called **Serpentarius.**

Ophthalmitis (of-thal-mī′tis). An epithet of Athena, meaning "Of the Eye." Lycurgus, the Spartan lawgiver, incurred the enmity of some of the Spartans with his laws. One of his enemies struck out one of his eyes. Lycurgus fled to a spot near the Bronze House in Sparta, and was saved by the Spartans from losing his remaining eye. In gratitude he set up an image of Athena Ophthalmitis, because it was near her temple, the Bronze House, that he was rescued.

Opimius (ō-pim′i-us), **Lucius.** Roman consul in 121 B.C. He was put forward by the Senate to oppose the reforms of Caius Gracchus and, as the leader of the optimates, killed Gracchus and 3000 of his followers in 121 B.C. He was afterward exiled for accepting bribes from Jugurtha, king of Numidia.

Opis (ō′pis). In Greek mythology, a Hyperborean maiden who was a companion of Artemis. Some say Orion pursued her, and that it was because of this that Artemis killed him. Opis and Arge, a Hyperborean companion, were said to have come to Delos at the same time as Artemis. The Delian maidens dedicated locks of their hair to them, and they were invoked by the Delians, as well as by the other islanders and the Ionians, in a hymn that Olen made for them. The Delians scattered the ashes from the sacrifices burnt on the altar of Artemis over the tomb of Opis and Arge, which was behind the temple of Artemis, facing the east.

Opisthodomus (op-is-thod′ō-mus). In Greek architecture, an open vestibule within the portico at the end behind the cella in most ancient temples, corresponding to the pronaos at the principal end, into which opens the main entrance. It was sometimes used as a place for preserving the temple treasure.

Oppian (op′i-an). Greek poet of Cilicia, who was active in the latter part of the 2nd century A.D. He was the author of a poem on hunting, *Cynegetica,* for which he was rewarded by the emperor Caracalla. To Oppian, although possibly to another Oppian, of Syria, of the first half of the 3rd century A.D., is attributed a poem in five books on the subject of fishing, *Halieutica.* (AH)

Oppius (op′i-us), **Caius.** Friend and contemporary of Julius Caesar, reputed in antiquity to be author of the history of the African war. This work, however, is usually ascribed to Aulus Hirtius.

Ops (ops). In Roman mythology, a very old harvest and fertility goddess, hence also construed as a goddess of plenty. She was the wife of Saturn, with whom she shared a temple on the Capitoline, and the mother of Jupiter. Ops dwelt in the earth, and for this reason she was invoked by worshipers who were seated and in contact with the ground. At her festival honoring her as the goddess of sowing and reaping, only the vestal virgins and one of the priests could be present. Later the Romans identified Ops with the Greek goddess Rhea.

Optimus Maximus (op′ti-mus mak′si-mus). A Roman epithet of Jupiter, "Best and Greatest."

Opus (ō′pus). In ancient geography, a town on the Gulf of Euboea. It was the capital of Opuntian Locris, and was said to have been named for Opus, the foster son of Locrus, an early king of the Locrians. Opus was the home of Patroclus, Ajax the Less, and, some say, of Theano, the wife of the Trojan Antenor.

Oracle. In classical antiquity: 1) an utterance given by a priest or priestess of a god, in the name of the god and, as was believed, by his inspiration, in answer to a human inquiry, usually respecting some future event, as the success of an enterprise or battle, or some proposed line of conduct. Such oracles exerted for centuries a strong influence upon the course of human affairs, the belief of both the medium and the questioner in their divine inspiration being in most cases genuine. The oracles themselves, however, were often ambiguous or at least obscure. The prestige of the chief oracular seats of Greece was powerful in the promotion of good government and justice. 2) the deity who was supposed to give such answers to inquiries. 3) the place where oracular answers were given; the sanctuary, temple, or adytum whence the supposed supernatural responses proceeded. The Greeks surpassed every other nation in both the number and the celebrity of their oracles. Those of Zeus at Dodona in Epirus, of Apollo at Delphi, and of Trophonius near Lebadia in Boeotia enjoyed the highest reputation.

Orbilius Pupillus (ôr-bil′i-us pū-pil′us). Roman grammarian and schoolmaster, the teacher of Horace. The epithet "plagosus" was given to him by Horace on account of the floggings which his pupils received from him, and the name Orbilius has often since been used in literature for a teacher of this type.

Orchomenus (ôr-kom′e-nus). In ancient geography, a city in Arcadia, Greece, about 33 miles W of Corinth. According to tradition, it was founded by Orchomenus, son of Lycaon, who gave it his own name, and it became one of the leading Arcadian cities. Nearby the city was a wooden image of Artemis set in a cedar tree, from which the people called the goddess "Lady of the Cedar." Arcadians from Orchomenus took part in the Battle of Plataea (479 B.C.) and had their names inscribed, with others, on the pedestal of an image of Zeus that was dedicated at Olympia.

Orchomenus. In ancient geography, a city in Boeotia, Greece, situated on the Cephissus River, about 55 miles NW of Athens. According to tradition, it was first named Andres, for Andreus, son of the river-god Peneus. Athamas, having lost his wife and his children, joined Andreus here, and was given land about Mount Laphystium. In later times, Eteocles became king in the land. He was, the Orchomenians claimed, the first to sacrifice to the Graces, of whom he numbered three. Eteocles died childless and Phlegyas ascended the throne. He named the people Phlegyans. He was a warlike king, and in their folly the Phlegyans attacked Delphi. They drove back the picked force that was sent against them but were themselves driven back by the god. Chryses, son of Poseidon, succeeded Phlegyas, and was in turn succeeded by his son Minyas, from whom the people took the name Minyans. In the time of Minyas Orchomenus was very rich; Minyas was the first to build a treasury for his wealth. The son of Minyas was Orchomenus, and from him the land came to be called thereafter Orchomenus. When Erginus, son of Clymenus, became king of Orchomenus, he exacted tribute from Thebes because a Theban had accidentally slain his father. Heracles waged war on Erginus and defeated him, and thereafter Thebes ceased to pay tribute. The sons of Erginus, Agamedes and Trophonius, were famous builders, and from their time Orchomenus reached a high degree of civilization. It is thought that in this period the earliest attempts were made to drain Lake Copaïs on the borders of Orchomenus. After the death of Agamedes and Trophonius, Ascalaphus and Ialmenus, sons of Ares, led the Minyans who accompanied the Greeks to Troy. The city was noted for its wealth and its many sanctuaries. The people worshiped the Graces, in whose honor they held a festival. They sacrificed annually to Actaeon as a hero, and they had sanctuaries of Dionysus and the Graces, and a cult of Asclepius. The

tomb of Minyas was in the city. In obedience to an oracle given them by the priestess of Delphi during a pestilence, the Orchomenians recovered the bones of Hesiod from Naupactus and buried them in their city. In the time of its greatness Orchomenus sent colonists to Asia Minor.

Orchomenus became a member of the Boeotian Confederacy at the beginning of the 7th century B.C. In the Persian War it was on the side of the Persians. Up to the time of the Peloponnesian Wars, Orchomenus was the equal of Thebes, but following that long struggle Thebes became a democracy, and the aristocracy that ruled Orchomenus took the side of Sparta and became an enemy of Thebes, fighting against that city at Coronea and Haliartus. When the Thebans defeated Sparta at Leuctra (371 B.C.) they would have destroyed Orchomenus, but Epaminondas persuaded them to spare it. However, in 364 B.C. they destroyed it without mercy. It was rebuilt in 353 B.C. by the Phocians, but was destroyed again by the Thebans in 349 B.C. Philip of Macedon rebuilt it anew, but the city never recovered its former power and wealth. In 87 B.C., Sulla defeated Archelaus, the general of Mithridates VI, king of Pontus, before the walls of Orchomenus. The site contains important remains of antiquity, going back to the Neolithic Age. Modern excavations have uncovered one city built atop another, as at Troy, the oldest of which dates from before 3500 B.C. Fragments of vases and frescoes, on which are depicted buildings and scenes of bull-leaping, and designs similar in style to those of Cnossus and Tiryns, have been recovered at the site. The so-called treasury of Minyas is a very ancient tomb of the Mycenaean beehive type. The plan is circular, 45 feet in diameter, covered by a pseudo-dome formed by corbeling in the stones of the wall.

Orcus (ôr′kus). In Roman mythology, a god of the Underworld, identified with the Greek Horcus, god of oaths, who punished perjurers. Orcus was later identified with the Greek Underworld god, Hades, and still later with Pluto. The word eventually became synonymous with Hades as a place.

Oreads (ō′rē-ạdz). Nymphs of the mountains. They were especially associated with Artemis because they dwelt on the mountains where she hunted, and were her companions in hunting, dancing and frolicking. Because of their association with Artemis they were particularly honored by hunters. They were also connected with the worship of Pan and as such were honored by shepherds.

Orestea (ō-res-tē′a̩). A dramatic trilogy by Aeschylus, for which he won first prize in 458 B.C. It is founded on the history of the family of Agamemnon, and treats the theme of the curse on the house of Atreus, which caused much suffering, and the reconciliation

of the tragedies *Agamemnon,* which takes place in Argos following the fall of Troy and ends with the murder of Agamemnon by his wife Clytemnestra; *The Choëphoroe,* in which Orestes, son of Agamemnon, who has grown up in exile, returns at Apollo's command and avenges his father by murdering Clytemnestra and her paramour Aegisthus; and *The Eumenides,* in which Orestes, relentlessly pursued by the Furies, is at last tried before the Areopagus and acquitted by the vote of Athena, whose vote cast in Orestes' favor breaks a tie. See separate entries.

ORESTES SLAYING AEGISTHUS
Red-figured Attic pelike, early 5th century B.C. *Vienna*

and the end of the curse by the application of moral laws. The two laws chiefly operative are that the doer must suffer and that man learns by suffering. Though it may take several generations, as it is shown to do here, man eventually learns the folly of wrongdoing, and learns not only how to avoid suffering but how to do right. The *Orestea* consists

Orestes (ō-res′tēz). In Greek legend, a son of Agamemnon and Clytemnestra, and the brother of Electra and Iphigenia. Before Agamemnon returned victorious from Troy and was slain by Clytemnestra and her lover Aegisthus, Orestes had been spirited away to Strophius, king of Phocis. In the eighth year following the murder of Agamemnon he returned in secret to Mycenae, accompanied by his friend Pylades, to avenge his father's death. He went to his father's grave, left offerings on it of locks of his hair, and prayed to his father's spirit for his sanction in the deed he was about to commit. Electra, who had been kept in a state of misery by Clytemnestra and Aegisthus, and who constantly accused her mother of adultery and murder, publicly longed for the return of Orestes to avenge their father's death. Orestes revealed himself to his sister and told her he had come at the command of Apollo to kill Clytemnestra and Aegisthus. He was greatly troubled by the deed he was planning, as to slay one's own kin was the most heinous crime in the sight of gods and men. He found that Electra had no such doubts about it, as the gods also laid an obligation on sons to avenge their fathers. Caught in the dilemma of angering the gods if he failed to avenge his father's death, and of incurring the wrath of the Furies if he killed his mother, Orestes wavered. Electra and Pylades stiffened his will to carry out the command of Apollo and to shed blood for the blood that had been shed. By a ruse he secured entrance to the palace and came face to face with his mother. She did not recognize him at first but when he made himself known to her, she understood what was about to happen. Despite her pleas to spare the mother who had given him life and despite his own doubts, he killed her, calling the gods to witness that he was obeying a command of Apollo and reminding them of the horrible crimes she had committed. He also killed her paramour, as Hermes had told Aegisthus he would do many years before, if Aegisthus persisted in his plan to seduce Clytemnestra and destroy Agamemnon. The murder of Aegisthus could readily be justified as a proper fate for an adulterer. But there was no escape from the avenging Furies who immediately began hounding Orestes for the murder of his mother. After great pain and suffering, and spells of madness, in one of which he bit off his own finger to appease the Furies, he felt that he had been purified of his guilt by his sufferings. He had been purified many times in this period but to no avail, for the Furies still pursued him. He now made his way to Athens to stand trial before the Areopagus. Apollo was his advocate. The chief of the Furies was his prosecutor. Athena was present as an impartial judge to see that justice was done. The jury was evenly divided as to the verdict, whereupon Athena cast a vote to break the tie. She decided on the side of Orestes, on the ground that he had suffered for his guilt and been purified. She persuaded the avenging Furies to accept her verdict on the side of mercy, and from then on they took up their residence in a grotto on the side of the Acropolis and became known as the Eumenides, the "kindly ones," who protected suppliants. The acquittal of Orestes lifted the curse which had tormented three generations of the House of Atreus. Some say that this verdict did not render Orestes immune to suffering because not all of the Furies accepted it; those that did not continued to harass him. He went to the shrine of Delphi and asked Apollo's aid. The priestess told him he must go to Tauris and secure a wooden image of Artemis from a temple there and restore it to Attica. Orestes and the faithful Pylades set out for Tauris, although it was well known that the Taurians sacrificed strangers who landed on their shores. The two friends landed, were captured, and brought before the priestess to be prepared for sacrifice. At first the priestess gloated over the two Greeks who had fallen into her hands. She was Iphigenia, daughter of Agamemnon, and she was glad to sacrifice Greeks, as the Greeks so many years before would have sacrificed her when they were windbound at Aulis. Only the intervention of Artemis had saved her. As she talked to the two men, one of whom seemed mad, she felt drawn to them and decided to help them escape. In the course of her conversation with them she told her own history. Orestes then declared that he was her brother. After joyous reunion they made plans to escape and, aided by Athena, succeeded in leaving Tauris and returning to Greece with the image. Some say that they went to Sminthe where they were overtaken by the king of the Taurians, but escaped again. Others say they were driven to Rhodes by a storm and set up the image there. Still others say the image was taken back to Attica, as commanded by the priestess of Delphi, and set up in a temple at Brauron, where Iphigenia became a priestess. But many places claimed the image: it was said to have been taken to Italy, Susa, Cappadocia, and Sparta, and all claimed they had the original sacred image. Finally cured of his madness and freed from the persecutions of the Furies, Orestes went to Delphi and there was reunited with his sister Electra. He then returned to Mycenae and slew Aletes, descendant of Thyestes who had siezed the throne, and became ruler of Mycenae. His next project was to bring about the murder of Neoptolemus, son of Achilles, at the shrine of Delphi, and to marry Hermione, daughter of Menelaus. He had been betrothed to Hermione but Menelaus had given her to Neoptolemus, some say in return for the latter's help at Troy, but others claim that Orestes' madness had caused Menelaus to give her to Neoptolemus. When Menelaus died, Orestes was invited by the Spartans to become their king. By conquest he added a large part of Arcadia to his kingdom, and he would have taken Achaea also, but the oracle at Delphi warned him against it. In the end he left Mycenae and went to Arcadia, where he founded the city of Orestia. There, in his old age, he was bitten by a serpent and died. He was buried at Tegea. Later the Spartans, informed by an oracle that they would continue to lose their battles with the Tegeans as long as the bones of Orestes remained in Tegea, sent Lichas to Tegea to locate the whereabouts of Orestes' grave. He learned that Orestes' bones had been discovered under the forge of a Tegean smith; he stole them and returned with them to Sparta, where they were reïnterred. After that the Spartans were victorious over the Tegeans. Orestes' son Tisamenus succeeded him as king. The tragedy of Orestes, caught between the necessity to avenge his father and the crime of killing his mother if he did so, is treated in *The Choëphoroe* of Aeschylus, the *Electra* of Sophocles, and the *Electra* and *Orestes* of Euripides. The expiation of his crime and his release from suffering are treated in *The Eumenides* of Aeschylus, and *Iphigenia in Tauris* by Euripides. See these entries.

Orestes. Drama by Euripides, produced 408 B.C. It concerns the wild events that followed the murder by Orestes of his mother

Clytemnestra to avenge her murder of his father Agamemnon. The scene is at the palace in Argos. Orestes sleeps while his sister Electra watches over him. She recounts the evils that have befallen the race of Tantalus. He suffers in Hades because he offended the gods. His descendants—Pelops, the brothers Atreus and Thyestes, and Agamemnon, son of Atreus—have all been under a curse. Now Electra sits with her brother who has been driven mad by the Furies because, at Apollo's command, he slew his mother to avenge his father's murder. For six days he has taken no food. During most of his waking hours he has been raving with madness. On this day the Argives will decide whether to stone him, and her too for the part she played, for their mother's murder, or whether they will force them to kill themselves. Their only hope lies in Menelaus who has just landed at Nauplia. In fear of the Argives, who lost their sons at Troy for her sake, Menelaus has sent Helen to the palace in secret. There she now mourns for her sister Clytemnestra. Helen comes from the palace and asks Electra to make offerings at the tomb of Clytemnestra in her name, as she is ashamed to be seen by the Argives. Electra mocks her belated virtue, and suggests that Helen send her daughter Hermione to make the offerings. Helen adopts the suggestion. She gives Hermione locks of her hair to lay on Clytemnestra's tomb, and instructs her to make drink-offerings of milk and honey, and to pray to Clytemnestra for a kindlier mood towards Helen. When they leave, Electra notes that Helen cut off only the tips of her hair, so as not to mar her beauty. She is still the Helen of old, and Electra hates her for the ruin she has brought—to the Greeks, to the house of Agamemnon, and particularly, to Orestes and Electra.

A chorus of Argive women, friendly to Electra, enters softly so as not to disturb sleeping Orestes. Electra asks them to go away quietly, but they remain. She says he will die, so faint has he become, and she is fated to die too. They are both victims of Apollo's command to kill their mother. Orestes wakes. His madness has left him temporarily. Electra informs him of the arrival in Argos of Menelaus and Helen, and adds that the daughters of Tyndareus (Helen and Clytemnestra) are beacons of reproach and infamy. At the mention of his mother Orestes becomes terribly agitated. He cries out that the Furies are leaping upon him. He raves, but calms somewhat when he sees how this makes Electra suffer. He blames Apollo, who commanded him to commit a heinous crime and then deserted him. He begs Electra to go and rest, for she is his only support and must take care of herself for his sake. Assuring him that she will never forsake him, that she will live or die with him, she agrees to go into the palace.

The chorus of Argive women prays to the Eumenides to spare Orestes. Menelaus enters and greets them. His homecoming after so many years of wandering is darkened by the fearful news of his brother's death, Clytemnestra's crime, and her murder by Orestes. Orestes clasps the knees of Menelaus as a suppliant. He has come at the hour of greatest need. Menelaus is appalled at the sight of wild-appearing Orestes, and asks what sickness is killing him. Orestes replies that it is conscience, grief, and madness; yet he killed his mother in obedience to Apollo. Now the god has abandoned him. The Argives hate him. None will purify him. This is the day they will decide on his death. He cannot escape, for the Argives have surrounded him. His only hope is in Menelaus, who has appeared in his prosperity to Orestes in his misery. Tyndareus is seen approaching. This deepens the suffering of Orestes, for Tyndareus was good to him as a child and he has made a foul return for his kindness. Tyndareus welcomes Menelaus, reviles Orestes, and chides Menelaus for speaking to the criminal. Menelaus answers pacifically that Orestes is the son of one he loved, and that the Greek way is to honor those of kindred blood. Tyndareus argues that Orestes should have had his mother brought to trial for her crimes, which he does not condone, instead of taking the law into his own hands. He has made himself as vile as his mother by killing her. If this principle of blood for blood is carried on, he asks, where will the killing end? Tyndareus holds no brief for either of his daughters, but he upholds the rule of law rather than that of blood vengeance. He warns Menelaus not to try to

help Orestes, who is loathed by the gods for his crime, and ends by saying that but for his daughters, he would have had a happy life. Orestes seeks to defend himself. He recites his mother's crimes—she took a lover while Agamemnon was away at war, and slew Agamemnon with her lover's help when he returned victorious. If Orestes had remained silent, he would have been guilty of condoning her crimes and would have been hounded by the shade of his unavenged father. Over and above all this, Apollo commanded him to commit the murder, and so it is Apollo's sin, not his. Tyndareus scorns his defense. Before he leaves to encourage the Argives to sentence Orestes to death by stoning, he warns Menelaus that if he aids Orestes he will never set foot in Sparta again. Menelaus is shaken by this parting threat. Orestes, seeing that he hesitates, addresses him again, saying that Menelaus owes it to him to help him, even if he has to commit a wrong to do so, for Agamemnon went to Troy to "heal the sin and the wrong-doing of thy wife," and was murdered on his return. He pleads with Menelaus to save him, so that the line of Agamemnon will not die.

Menelaus wavers. He alone cannot fight the Argives. Instead, he will try to persuade them by words to spare Orestes and Electra. When he leaves, Orestes cries out against the ingrate who has forgotten the deeds of Agamemnon in his behalf. He has been betrayed by Menelaus, the one man from whom he might have expected help. Pylades, his true friend, comes to him in his despair. Pylades is not surprised that Menelaus has betrayed Orestes, "by the traitor wife the traitor husband made!" He encourages Orestes to try to escape and promises his help. They leave to visit Agamemnon's tomb. The Argive women chant about the curse on the house of Tantalus that has brought about the terrible murder of a mother by her son. Electra enters, followed by a messenger who informs her that the Argives have voted death to her and Orestes, and that they have scorned Orestes' defense of his act. Electra despairs. The curse on the house of Tantalus, felt by all his descendants, is now about to destroy the last of his line in Orestes and herself. Orestes and Pylades return. Electra cannot submit quietly to her fate; she longs to live. Pylades says if they all have to die, he would first like to bring some suffering to Menelaus. He proposes that they go to Helen, pretending to bemoan their fate, and that they seize and kill her. It will be only right to kill one who has caused such grief to Hellas, and they will also be avenged on Menelaus, who in his cowardice and greed for the throne has abandoned his kinsmen. If they do not succeed in killing Helen, they will set fire to the palace and perish with it. Electra suggests that they seize Hermione as a hostage and force Menelaus to let them go, on the threat of killing his daughter. Thus they will escape death and at the same time punish Menelaus by killing Helen. All agree on the plan, and pray to Agamemnon for help. Orestes and Pylades enter the palace. Electra gives the signal, and Helen is heard to cry out from within. Electra savagely exhorts her brother to slay her. The Argive women tell her that Hermione is nearing. Electra greets her in subdued fashion and tells her she and Orestes are to die. The cry Hermione heard, she says, was from Orestes pleading with Helen. She begs Hermione to join her prayers to those of Orestes. Hermione hurries into the palace. Soon her cry that she has been seized is heard. A Phrygian slave rushes out and describes the attack on Helen. When she was about to be slain she vanished, perhaps carried off by the gods. Menelaus now rushes in. As he stands outside the palace Orestes and Pylades, with Hermione, look down on him from above. Orestes threatens to murder Hermione and set fire to the palace if Menelaus does not persuade the Argives to spare him and make him their king. Menelaus is trapped. He calls on the Argives to rescue Hermione, as flames leap up from the palace. Now Apollo appears in the clouds above with Helen. The god calls for peace between Menelaus and Orestes. He says he has rescued Helen at the command of Zeus, and that henceforth she will dwell on Olympus. Orestes must go into exile for a year, then stand trial at Athens for his mother's murder. Ultimately he will marry Hermione. He commands Orestes to give Electra in marriage to Pylades. Menelaus must return to Sparta. Orestes will finally be restored to sanity and to the throne of Argos.

Oreus (ō′rē-us). In ancient geography, a city on the NW coast of Euboea, Greece, situated opposite Thessaly. See **Histiaea.**

Orgetorix (ôr-jet′ō-riks). Helvetian conspirator shortly before the time of Caesar's war with the Helvetians in .58 B.C. According to Caesar's account, he planned to conquer Gaul with the Helvetians, but was detected by them plotting with other chiefs to seize control of the tribe. He escaped immediate trial, but committed suicide afterward.

Orion (ō-rī′on). In Greek mythology, a giant hunter, the son of Poseidon and Euryale. He visited Chios and fell in love with Merope, daughter of King Oenopion. For her sake he cleared the island of wild beasts. But Oenopion, who had promised her in marriage to Orion, kept postponing the wedding day. Frenzied by wine, Orion attacked Merope and was punished by Oenopion with the aid of Dionysus, by having his eyes put out while he lay in a drunken sleep. Orion learned from an oracle that if he went to the East and turned his eyes to Helius as he rises from the ocean stream, his sight would be restored. He kidnaped a young worker from Hephaestus' workshop on Lemnos and with him for a guide set off for the East, and had his sight restored. Eos fell in love with him and accompanied him on his return journey. He was dissuaded from pursuing Oenopion for revenge by Artemis, whom he met on his way to Crete and whose passion for hunting he shared. Together they pursued the pleasures of the hunt and caused Apollo to become uneasy, for he feared that his virgin sister might become enamored of Orion as Eos had been. Apollo sent a giant scorpion to attack Orion, and when he found he could not overcome the scorpion, Orion leaped into the sea to escape. When his head was but a distant speck on the sea, Apollo tricked Artemis, who was unaware that it was Orion, into transfixing it with an arrow. She was stricken with grief when she learned that she had killed her hunting companion, and sought Asclepius to restore him to life, but Asclepius had been killed by a thunderbolt of Zeus. Artemis then placed the image of Orion in the heavens as the constellation Orion, the mighty hunter, eternally pursued by the scorpion. His spirit went to the Asphodel Fields and Odysseus saw him hunting there when he visited the Underworld. According to another account, Artemis slew Orion because he pursued her chaste companions, the Pleiades, but as the Pleiades were far from chaste, this version seems unreasonable. Still others say Orion was killed by the scorpion, whose image was also translated to the stars.

Orion. A constellation situated in the southern hemisphere with respect to the ecliptic, but the equinoctial crosses it nearly in the middle. This constellation is represented by the figure of a giant with a sword by his side. It contains seven stars which are very conspicuous to the naked eye; four of these form a quadrangle, and the other three are situated in the middle of it in a straight line, forming what is called the *Belt* or *Girdle of Orion.* They are also popularly called *Jacob's staff, Our Lady's wand,* the *Yard-wand,* etc.

Orithyia (ôr-i-thī′ya). In Greek legend, a daughter of Erechtheus, king of Athens, and his wife Praxithea. Boreas fell in love with her and wished to marry her but her father, fearing the wild wind of Thrace, delayed the marriage. Boreas became impatient and one day as Orithyia was playing on the bank of the Ilissus River, he swooped down and carried her off in a gust of wind to his home in Thrace. The children of Orithyia were Cleopatra, Chione, and the winged twins, Calais and Zetes.

Orneae (ôr′nē-ē). In ancient geography, a city in Argolis, traditionally named for Orneus, son of Erechtheus. Men of Orneae went to the Trojan War under the command of Agamemnon, and Menestheus, grandson of the founder of their city, led a body of Athenians to help Agamemnon destroy Troy. At some later time, the inhabitants of Orneae were removed to Argos by the Argives and their city was abandoned.

Orneus (ôr′nūs). In Greek legend, a son of Erechtheus, king of Athens, and Praxithea. With his brother Metion he caused Cecrops, another brother who had been chosen to succeed Erechtheus, to flee from Athens.

Ornytus (ôr′ni-tus). In Greek legend, a leader of the Arcadians. He quarreled with Agamemnon as the Greeks were assembled at Aulis and waiting for favorable winds to sail to Troy. As a result of this quarrel he refused to accompany the Greeks. Athena appeared to him in disguise and tried to persuade him not to take his followers and go home, but to go with the Greeks to Troy. Ornytus angrily wounded the goddess, whom he did not recognize, with his spear. As punishment for this Athena appeared to him in a dream when he returned home. She caused him to fall sick and sent a pestilence on his fields. On appealing to an oracle he learned that he could appease the goddess by erecting a statue to her.

Oroetes (ô-rē′tēz). A Persian noble who was appointed a governor of Sardis by Cyrus the Great. He retained this post under Cambyses. He resolved to destroy Polycrates, ruler of Samos (c540–522 B.C.). Some say his hatred of Polycrates was inspired by one of his fellow Persians who reproached Oroetes because he had not conquered Samos and brought it under the dominion of Persia. Others say Polycrates had deeply offended Oroetes by his contemptuous treatment of a herald of Oroetes. Oroetes sent the herald to Polycrates on some mission and Poylcrates received him as he was lying on his couch with his back to the herald. At no time during the interview did he deign to turn over and face the messenger from Oroetes, nor did he address one word to him. Whatever the reason, Oroetes, having learned that Polycrates had the mighty ambition to make himself master of the sea, sent a messenger to him. The message he bore was that Oroetes had been warned that Cambyses meant to destroy him. At the same time Oroetes said he was aware of Polycrates' great ambition, and also that Polycrates lacked the means of attaining it. If Polycrates would, therefore, come to the aid of Oroetes and save him from Cambyses, for his part Oroetes would supply Polycrates with the wealth to make himself master of the sea. However, lest Polycrates should doubt that Oroetes possessed enough wealth to make it worthwhile, he invited Polycrates to send a trusted messenger to whom he would show his treasure as a proof. Polycrates was delighted, as he was in great need of gold to build up his fleet. He sent a messenger as Oroetes had invited him to do. Oroetes filled eight great chests with stones. Over the stones he spread a layer of gold. These chests he showed to the messenger from Polycrates, who in due course reported on the vast wealth of Oroetes to his master. Polycrates decided to go to Sardis and rescue Oroetes from Cambyses and gain the promised treasure. Against the advice and warnings of his friends, soothsayers, and his own daughter, he went to Sardis with some of his followers. As soon as Polycrates came into his hands, Oroetes seized him and put him to death and hung him on a cross. Oroetes let the Samians in the train of Polycrates return to their homes but the foreigners who had come with him, including Democedes, he kept among his own slaves. Not long after this Oroetes killed the Persian who had reproached him about Samos, and during the time of the False Smerdis he did nothing to help the Persians regain the throne. When Darius became king, Oroetes showed great insolence toward him, even going so far as to kill one of his messengers. Darius longed to take vengeance on him, but since he had only recently ascended the throne and since Oroetes was very powerful in Sardis and was surrounded by a guard of 1000 men, Darius had to attack him by indirect means. He sent a volunteer to Sardis who contrived that Oroetes was murdered by his own bodyguard, whose loyalty to the king of Persia proved to be greater than that to Oroetes. After his death the treasures and slaves of Oroetes were taken to Susa.

Oropus (ō-rō′pus). In ancient geography, a seaport in Attica, Greece, bordering on Boeotia, situated on the Euripus, about 23 miles N of Athens. It belonged originally to Boeotia, but in the struggles for it between Attica and Boeotia, the former won control of it. Near Oropus was a sanctuary of Amphiaraus, whose divinity was first established by the Oropians, who gave the cult to the rest of Greece. In the sanctuary was a temple and a white marble image of Amphiaraus, and the oracle of Amphiaraus, the Amphareum, was very famous. Sometimes the oracle gave responses in verse, but generally responses were given in dreams. The questioner at the oracle purified himself, sacrificed to Amphiaraus and to all those whose names were on the altar. He next sacrificed a ram, flayed it, and spread its skin on the ground. At night the questioner stretched out to sleep on the ram's skin and the answer to his question came to him in his dreams. Near the sanctuary was a spring into which those who had been cured of diseases as the result of responses from the oracle threw gold and silver coins.

Orpheus (ôr′fūs, ôr′fē̇-us). In Greek legend, a son of Oeagrus, king of Thrace, and the muse Calliope and, some say, the brother of that Linus who was slain by Heracles. But according to some accounts, Orpheus was the son of Apollo. Whoever his father was, Orpheus was the most famous poet and musician in Greek legend. Apollo gave him the lyre and the Muses taught him to play it so beautifully that trees and stones danced to his music and wild beasts were tamed by it. He was taught the Mysteries of Rhea by the female Dactyls in Samothrace and on a visit to Egypt he saw the Mysteries of Osiris. In imitation of these latter he invented the Mysteries of Dionysus and instituted them in Thrace. He taught the Mysteries of Dionysus to Midas, the Phrygian king, among others. Orpheus accompanied Jason and the Argonauts on the expedition to Colchis for the Golden Fleece. With his music he soothed quarrels that sprang up among the Argonauts, made the arduous labor of rowing seem lighter, and drowned out the songs of the Sirens, thus enabling the Argonauts to pass their island in safety on the return voyage. Only Butes succumbed to the charms of the Sirens and leaped overboard. According to some accounts, the Sirens were so chagrined at being out-charmed by Orpheus that they committed suicide, but in Homeric legend they were still on their island when Odysseus passed by a generation later. On the island of the Phaeacians Orpheus sang the marriage song at the wedding of Jason and Medea. When he returned from the voyage of the *Argo* Orpheus married Eurydice and went to dwell among the Cicones of Thrace. One day as Eurydice was walking in the meadows, Aristaeus saw her and tried to ravish her. As she fled from him she stepped on a viper which bit her ankle, and she died of the poisoned sting. Orpheus was inconsolable and resolved to bring her back from the Underword. He descended to Tartarus, some say through an entrance in Thesprotia, and so charmed Charon that the ferryman freely carried him over the Styx. Cerberus, the watch-dog of Tartarus was also charmed by his music, and the judges of the Underworld interrupted their task to listen, and the tortures of the wicked were temporarily suspended. Even Hades' heart was softened, and he agreed to let Eurydice return to earth on condition that Orpheus was not to look back as she followed him until she reached the light of the sun. Orpheus gladly accepted this condition and led the way, playing upon his lyre. Eurydice followed, guided by the music. When he reached the light of the sun, he could wait no longer; he looked back eagerly to see Eurydice. But she had not yet stepped into the sunlight and so he lost her forever. After

had neglected the worship of the god and now honored the sun above all. Orpheus protested against human sacrifice and objected to the orgies of the maenads. Others say the women set upon him in revenge for his scorn. While their husbands were worshiping in the temple the women rushed at Orpheus. One hurled a stone at him, but the stone, charmed by his music, dropped harmlessly at his feet. Then the clamor of the women was so great the music was drowned out. The women fell upon him and tore him limb from limb. They flung his head and lyre into the Hebrus River. From there they floated, still singing, across the sea to the island of Lesbos. As the head lay on the shore of Lesbos a serpent approached to bite it, but Apollo appeared and turned the

DEATH OF ORPHEUS
Red-figured Greek vase, 5th century B.C.

this second loss he retired to Thrace and kept apart from all women. Many maidens sought to win his love but he scorned them and gave his attention to lads in the first bloom and beauty of youth. When he played his lyre, the trees and rocks gathered to listen. One day as he was thus playing, he was set upon by the Ciconian women. Some say Dionysus inspired them with madness because Orpheus

serpent to stone. The head was placed in a cave at Antissa, where it prophesied continually until Apollo, fearful lest it become more famous than his oracle at Delphi, commanded it to cease prophesying. The lyre was first placed in the temple of Apollo at Lesbos and its image was placed in the heavens as a constellation. The Muses, grieving over the loss of the poet, gathered

actor; up, lūte, pull; oi, oil; ou, out; ᴛʜ, then; ḍ as d or j, ṣ as s or sh, ṭ as t or ch, ẓ as z or zh.

his limbs and buried them at the foot of Mount Olympus, and ever since, the nightingales of this region sing more sweetly than anywhere else in the world. The Ciconian women sought to wash the blood of Orpheus from their hands in the Helicon River, but the river-god, not willing to be an accessory in any way in the murder of Orpheus, dived underground and did not reappear for several miles. The women were transformed where they stood into oak trees as a punishment for the murder of Orpheus, and there they stood throughout time. In Zone in Thrace was another ring of oak trees left standing in the midst of a dance they had been performing as Orpheus played for them. A religious sect arose, perhaps in the 5th century B.C., called the Orphics. They claimed Orpheus as their founder and adopted some Oriental and Egyptian ideas of purification and expiation. According to the Orphics, Orpheus was a more ancient poet than Homer and they attributed many poems, hymns, and prayers to him, some of which survive.

Orpheus, Eurydice, and Hermes (ū-rid′i-sē; hẻr′mēz). Replica of an Attic high relief of the school of Phidias, in the Museo Nazionale, Naples. The group is shown just at the moment when Orpheus, having looked back, must lose his wife forever.

Orseïs (ôr-sē′is). In Greek mythology, a nymph who married Hellen and bore him Aeolus, Zuthus, and Dorus. Xuthus was the father of Ion and Achaeus. Thus Orseïs was the ancestress of the four great Hellenic nations: Dorians, Aeolians, Ionians, and Achaeans.

Orsippus (ôr-sip′us). An athlete of Megara, Greece. He is said to have won the foot race at Olympia (720 B.C.) by running naked while his competitors wore loin cloths as was the custom, and thus was the first to compete in the nude. Afterward, this became the custom. He was buried at Megara.

Orthaea (ôr-thē′a). A daughter of Hyacinthus the Spartan. See **Hyacinthides.**

Orthia (ôr′thi-a). An epithet of Artemis, meaning "Upright," because the image of Taurian Artemis, brought back to Greece by Orestes and Iphigenia, was found among willows at Limnaeum, in Laconia, according to some accounts, and willow tendrils growing about it held it upright. It is likely that Orthia represents a goddess of the Dorians with whom Artemis was identified. See also, **Lygodesma.**

Orthrus (ôrth′rus). In Greek mythology, the son of Echidna and Typhon, and the brother of Cerberus. He was a two-headed monster who guarded the cattle of Geryon. By Echidna, his mother, he was the father of the Sphinx, the bane of the Thebans until it was slain by Oedipus. Some say that he was the father by the Chimaera of the Nemean Lion that ravaged the vale of Nemea until it was slain by Heracles. When Heracles came to fetch the cattle of Geryon, Orthrus rushed against him barking furiously. Heracles attacked him with his club and killed him.

Ortygia (ôr-tij′i-a). In ancient geography, a small island at the entrance to the great harbor of Syracuse, Sicily. It was famous in the sieges of that city. It is the site of the fountain of Arethusa, a sacred spring. Arethusa was transformed by Artemis into a spring as she fled from the river-god Alpheus. The spring flowed under the sea from Greece and arose in Ortygia. Alpheus pursued her under the sea and the waters of the Alpheus of Elis at last mingled with those of Arethusa in Ortygia. It was said that a flower thrown into the Alpheus River in Greece would float under the sea and rise in Arethusa's spring in Ortygia.

Ortygia. An ancient name of Delos. It means "Quail," and was so named because Asteria, daughter of Coeus the Titan, leaped into the sea to escape the embraces of Zeus and was transformed into a quail. The island where she came safely ashore was named for her.

Orvieto (ôr-vye′tō). See **Urbibentum.**

Orythaon (ôr-i-thā′on). In Greek legend, a Trojan comrade of Hector. He was one of the last Trojans slain by Achilles. Achilles, dying from the wound inflicted by Paris or by Apollo had not lost his fury for fighting; he hurled his spear with his last breath and killed Orythaon.

Oschophoria (os-kō-fō′ri-a). A festival of Dionysus celebrated at Athens in the Fall, when the grapes ripen. It was believed to have been established by Theseus, when he returned safely from Crete, in gratitude to

fat, fāte, fär, fāre, errạnt; net, mē, hẻr ardẹnt; pin, pīne; not, nōte, mŏve, nôr,

Athena and Dionysus, who had come to him while he was at Naxos on his way home, or in honor of Dionysus and Ariadne. For the festival two youths whose parents were living were chosen from each of the ten Athenian tribes. Carrying clusters of grapes on shoots of vine, the 20 youths raced from the sanctuary of Dionysus at Limnae in Athens to the sanctuary of Athena Sciras at Phalerum. The name of the festival comes from the vines they bore, and means "Fruit-bearing." The winner of the race received a goblet with a drink of wine, cheese, meal, and honey, and was given an honored place in the procession that followed the race. This procession was led by two youths disguised as maidens. They represented two of the youths who went to Crete with Theseus as part of the Athenian tribute to Minos, and who, some say, disguised themselves as girls and killed the guards while Theseus was in the Labyrinth. Fourteen women took part in the sacrifice that followed the procession. They commemorated the mothers of the seven youths and seven maidens who made up the tribute to Minos and who were saved by Theseus.

Osiris (ō-sī'ris). In Egyptian mythology, the god and judge of the dead, and lord of the Underworld. He was also believed by the ancient Egyptians to have given them their religious rites, their knowledge of agriculture, and the other arts of civilization. Probably the most widely known myth about Osiris is that he was the son of Geb (earth) and Nut (sky), consort of his sister Isis, that he was killed by his envious brother, Set, cut up into 14 pieces and scattered over Egypt, and avenged by his posthumous son, Horus, who killed Set. Isis recovered the scattered fragments of his body and buried them here and there in Egypt; and each of these places became a center of the Osiris cult. The gods then gave Osiris immortality and made him judge and guardian of the dead. Osiris was originally an ancient fertility god who became associated with the fertility-giving Nile, and because of his death, resurrection, and immortality story, became associated with the setting and forever-rising sun, and thus with Ra, the sun-god. His chief center of worship was at Abydos. In art he was portrayed as a bearded human figure in mummy swathing,

wearing the crown of Upper Egypt, and bearing in his hands, which protruded from the swathing, the shepherd's crook and flail (both agricultural symbols). The Greeks identified Osiris with Dionysus, Isis with Demeter, and Set with Typhon.

Osroene or **Osrhoene** (oz-rō-ē'nē). [Also: **Orrhoene.**] In ancient geography, a region in the NW part of Mesopotamia. Its chief city was Edessa (modern Urfa).

Ossa (os'a). Mountain in the E part of Thessaly, Greece, situated NW of Pelion and separated from Olympus on the N by the Vale of Tempe. According to myth, Pelion was piled atop Ossa by the giants when they stormed Olympus. Elevation, about 6400 feet.

Ostia (os'ti-a). In ancient geography, a city in Latium, Italy, situated on alluvial soil on the left bank of the river Tiber near its ancient mouth, about 15 miles SW of Rome. According to Roman tradition it was the oldest colony of Rome, founded by Ancus Marcius, fourth king of Rome (640–616 B.C.), but extensive excavations have revealed nothing earlier than the 4th century B.C. To the period of about 340 B.C. is assigned the plan of the earliest Roman settlement, in the form of a Roman camp (*castrum*), consisting of a rectangular fortification bisected by a north-south street, the *cardo*, and by a west-east street, the *decumanus*. The walls, and the four gates where these streets enter the castrum, are of the ashlar tufa masonry which is so typical of Republican construction in and near Rome that it is of little use as a criterion of dating, the most that can be said of it being that it would not be out of place any time between 500 and 50 B.C. Parallel to the walls, both inside and outside the castrum, are strips of land about 40 feet wide, reserved for military purposes and forbidden to private construction, clearly defined by streets, the external and internal pomerial streets, so called because they mark the defense zone known as the *pomerium*. Of the four areas corresponding to city blocks within the walls, part was taken up by temples and a forum or market, the rest being available for residential purposes; but the population quickly outgrew the fortified space and expanded outside the walls. During the Punic Wars, especially the Second Punic War, Ostia became a naval base of crucial importance to Rome. In the disturbances of the time of Sulla, during which Ostia was sacked by Marius, a new and greatly enlarged fortification wall was built in ashlar tufa masonry strikingly similar to that of the 4th century castrum, enclosing an area now calculated at c170 acres, in spite of which Ostia was sacked again in 68 B.C., this time by pirates, an act of unprecedented boldness which led to Pompey's *imperium* in 67 B.C.

Rome's increasing need for grain, other foodstuffs, and building materials imported from Spain, North Africa, Sicily, and Egypt, caused the rapid growth of Ostia as the commercial port of Rome. Ostia built a theater and behind it a vast colonnade where the corporations which organized the import and export trade and the barge services on the Tiber had their offices. Vulcan remained the chief god of Ostia, but the cosmopolitan and polyglot population introduced the oriental cults of Magna Mater, Isis, Mithras; and, soon after, if not before 200 A.D., Christ. To overcome continual silting by the Tiber, Claudius and later Trajan constructed artificial harbors, connected to the sea and to the Tiber by canals. In the 2nd century A.D. Ostia reached its peak as one of the greatest cities of the Empire; the population then exceeding 200,000 and perhaps approached 300,000. The growing population caused crowding that was only partly relieved by the development of great five-story *insulae* (apartment houses), with central courts, interior staircases, windows, and balconies, directly anticipating those of modern cities. Before 300 A.D., however, there is evidence of depression; taxes and liturgies became increasingly onerous, and the population began to decline.

On an island in the Tiber, the Isola Sacra, was the cemetery of the prosperous freedmen who made up the bulk of the commercial class. It has been meticulously excavated, like much of Ostia itself, by the distinguished Italian archaeologist Guido Calza. There is a small museum of sculpture, and important collections of Latin and Greek inscriptions. Outside the walls stands the small modern village of Ostia, but the area within the walls is unoccupied and the shore has advanced two miles from its ancient line. The Tiber has eroded a small sector along the northern boundary of Ostia, and for centuries Ostia was quarried by Roman princes for building materials and objets d'art, but it remains one of the most impressive archaeological sites of ancient Italy. (JJ)

Ostracism (os'tra-sizm). A political measure employed under restrictions of law among the Athenians, by which citizens whose presence seemed embarrassing to the state were banished by public vote for a term of ten years, with leave to return to the enjoyment of their estates at the end of the period. It has its name from the tablet of earthenware (*ostrakon*) on which every voter wrote the name of the person he desired to ostracize. Ostracism was practised in some other democratic states of Greece, as Argos and Megara, but the method of its administration, except in Athens, remains obscure. Aristides, Themistocles, and Cimon were among those who were banished by ostracism. Hyperbolus was ostracized in 417 B.C. He was a demagogue, called "a rascal and a disgrace to the city" by Thucydides. Hitherto, ostracism had been employed against statesmen whose very qualities of leadership might pose a threat to the democracy. When it was employed against Hyperbolus the practice was considered to have been degraded, and thereafter fell into disuse.

Otanes (ō-tā'nēz). A Persian nobleman of the 6th century B.C. According to Herodotus, when the False Smerdis ascended the throne of Persia, following the death of Cambyses, Otanes began to suspect that this Smerdis was not the true son of Cyrus because he never left the palace and never received any of the Persian noblemen. Otanes suspected that he was really a Median magus who had usurped the throne with the help of his brother, a magus who had been left in charge of Cambyses' household when the latter departed on his expedition to Egypt. Otanes sought to prove his suspicions. His daughter, Phaedima, had been one of the wives of Cambyses and was taken as a wife by Smerdis after the death of Cambyses. Otanes sent a message to her, asking if the man who shared her couch was truly Smerdis, the son of Cyrus, or some other man. Phaedima answered that she did not know because she had never seen Smerdis the son of Cyrus.

Otanes then instructed her to ask Atossa if the man they both knew as their husband was truly Smerdis, for surely Atossa, the sister and wife of Cambyses and the sister of Smerdis, would know whether the man she called her husband was her own brother. Phaedima replied that she was never permitted to see the other wives of Smerdis. Otanes was now more than ever convinced that the man was not truly Smerdis. He instructed his daughter to perform the following test: When the king came to her, she was to feel his ears as he slept. If he had ears he was truly Smerdis, but if he had no ears he was the magus, for his ears had been cut off as punishment for a crime. Phaedima did as her father commanded, and reported that the man who came to her as king had no ears. Now Otanes was certain that this was an impostor. He confided his information to two other Persian nobles, who, as it happened, had already entertained the same suspicions, and the three decided to take three more loyal Persians into their confidence. At this time Darius, the son of Hystaspes, came to Susa and he was made a seventh member to plan how they should remove the false king. The names of the seven conspirators were Otanes, Aspathines, Gobryas, Intaphernes, Megabyzus, Hydarnes, and Darius. Darius urged instant action, for if so many already knew what he thought he alone knew, more would find out soon and warn Smerdis. In fact, he threatened that unless they acted at once, he himself would betray them to Smerdis rather than take the risk of being betrayed himself. Otanes would have preferred more men to aid them, and he counseled delay but was overruled. The seven set out at once for the palace, succeeded in entering it, and themselves cut down the False Smerdis and his brother. Following his death and exposure, the capital was in a ferment. The conspirators now met to decide on a government to succeed Smerdis. Otanes favored a government by the people. He pointed out the excesses of Cambyses and the insolence of Smerdis as evils attendant on a monarchy, in which the monarch can do as he likes and is answerable to no one. Otanes thought it was inevitable that the power which is customarily vested in a monarch leads to excessive pride and arrogance and promotes great envy in those who aspire to such power; thus the kingdom is continually in turmoil. He thought the excesses and unlimited power of monarchs could be avoided by a democracy, but Otanes was overruled. The conspirators decided to choose one of themselves as king. Hereupon Otanes said that as he neither wanted to rule or to be ruled, he would withdraw his name from consideration for the role on one condition: that none of them or their descendants should ever claim the right to rule over him or his descendants. The others agreed, and thenceforward the family of Otanes was the only free family in Persia. Its members submitted to the rule of the king or not, as they chose, although they were compelled to obey the laws of the land like all other Persians. Later Otanes successfully commanded an expedition for the conquest of Samos.

Otho (ō′thō), **Marcus Salvius.** Emperor of Rome (January–April, 69); born 32 A.D.; committed suicide, in April, 69. He was governor of Lusitania under Nero, whose mistress was Poppaea Sabina, Otho's wife. He overthrew Galba by a conspiracy after helping him gain the purple, and was in turn overthrown by Vitellius.

Othrys (oth′ris). Mountain range in the S part of Thessaly, Greece, due S of Ossa and SW of Pelion. Peak elevation, about 5665 feet. According to Greek mythology, it was a part of the domain of Aristaeus, and was the headquarters of the Titans when they waged war against the gods.

Otionia (ō-shi-ō′ni-a). In ancient mythology, a daughter of Erechtheus, king of Athens, and his wife Praxithea. She gladly submitted to being sacrificed when an oracle told her father that Athens would secure victory in a war between the Athenians and the Eleusinians, if he would sacrifice his youngest daughter. On her death two of her sisters, Pandora and Protogonia, killed themselves, as they had taken an oath that if one of them must die by violence, they would also die.

Otranto (ô′trän-tō). See **Hydrus**.

Otus (ō′tus). In Greek mythology, a son of Poseidon and the brother of Ephialtes. See **Aloidae**.

Otus. In the *Iliad*, a leader of Epeans and a comrade of Meges in the siege of Troy. He was slain by Hector's comrade and counselor Polydamas.

Ovid (ov′id). [Full Latin name, **Publius Ovidius Naso.**] Roman poet of the Augustan Age, who was born at Sulmo, in the mountains of the Abruzzi in Italy, March, 43 B.C.; died at Tomi, near the Euxine Sea, 17 or 18 A.D. He was the son of a wealthy and prominent landowner who wanted him to enter the legal profession, and for this purpose sent him to Rome to be educated. There he had a splendid training under two of the most noted rhetoricians of his day, Porcius Latro and Arellius Fuscus. He completed his education by traveling for more than a year to Athens, Troy, Asia Minor, and Sicily, with Aemilius Macer, the poet and contemporary of Vergil. He held a number of minor posts in the government, but his drive for poetic expression exerted itself to the disappointment of his father, and he gave up all pretensions to a career in the government service to devote himself to his poetry which, he said, flowed from his lips of its own accord, and to living a life of unfettered pleasure. He had some connection with the younger members of the palace circle, had powerful allies in government posts, and was the friend of the poets Tibullus, Propertius, and Horace. He was married three times, first to a wife who was given to him by his father when he was yet very young. This marriage ended in divorce, as did his second marriage. For his third wife, who was of the prominent and powerful Fabian family, he seems to have had warm affection and respect, and after his marriage to her he produced his more serious work, or perhaps "less frivolous" would be a better description, as Ovid was not noted for the seriousness of his work but for the elegance of his writing, his gracefully evocative descriptions of the beauties of nature, the vividness of his imagination, and his skill as a story-teller. For reasons now unknown, he was banished by Augustus in 9 A.D. to Tomi on the Euxine (Black) Sea. Some think he may have had knowledge of one of the affairs of the notorious Julia, granddaughter of the emperor, which he failed to report, and that this was the reason for his exile. From his own writing we learn that he admitted to an error, but not to a crime. Another reason for his banish-

ment may have been his publication of *Ars Amatoria* (Art of Love) which was in conflict with the moral reforms of the emperor. In any event, Augustus never recalled him from his banishment, and Tiberius, successor of Augustus, paid no attention to his constant and anguished appeals to be allowed to return. In spite of the mild form of his banishment, which permitted him to retain his civic rights and his property, to be exiled among semi-barbarians was most dire punishment for the sophisticated and cultivated Ovid, who by his own account would rather have lived in his own age and in Rome than any age of which history has a record or any other place. It was to no avail, he died an exile, in 17 or 18 A.D.

Among his works was a tragedy, *Medea,* which has been lost, but which enjoyed a high reputation among his contemporaries. Apparently he never again tried his hand in this form. Of his *Amores* (Love Poems), a collection published in 2 B.C. (following an earlier publication) is extant, and contains 49 elegies on the poet's life and his love for his mistress, Corinna. But some think that this lady was not much more than a fictional love. The *Heroïdes* is a collection in the form of letters written by the heroines of various myths or legends to their lovers. Published in 2 B.C. was his immoral *Ars Amatoria* (Art of Love), in three books, a handbook on the arts of love which described in sensual and light-minded detail the means and methods of engaging in and carrying on love affairs. The first two of these books was for the instruction of men, the third was directed to women. In the course of the work he illustrated various points by retelling the stories of famous lovers of mythology, as Cephalus and Procris, and Theseus and Ariadne. This work shocked the official court of Augustus, while it titillated those permitted to have private opinions, for the emperor was trying at that time, with little success, to improve and elevate the lowered moral tone of the higher echelons of Roman society. Ten years after its publication, when Ovid was banished, an edict against the *Ars Amatoria* was also published. *Ars Amatoria* was followed by *Remedia Amoris* (Cures of Love), thought by some to have been written as a kind of apology for the

fat, fāte, fär, fāre, errant; net, mē, hèr ardent; pin, pīne; not, nōte, mŏve, nôr, earlier work, but with no diminution of its sensual quality. From his exile in Tomi, Ovid wrote a number of poems, *Tristia,* of lamentation concerning his exile, and letters, *Epistulae ex Pontus,* in which he expressed his sorrow in his exile and his ardent desire, never fulfilled, to be recalled to the life and the city he loved. The *Fasti* is a poem in six books (out of 12 contemplated, one for each month), on the Roman calendar, and describes the ceremonies and rites of Roman religion in his age. He had begun this work before he finished the *Metamorphoses,* and stopped work on it at the time of his exile. In addition, he wrote a treatise on the use of cosmetics, *Medicamina Faciei Femineae,* fragments of which remain, and a poem in imitation of Callimachus' poem of the same name, *Ibis,* which was an attack on an enemy held in some part responsible for his exile.

Perhaps the most influential and most widely read of Ovid's works has been the *Metamorphoses,* a collection of myths drawn from Greek, Latin, and Eastern sources, all of which had one element in common: that they dealt, no matter how tenuous the connection, with a miraculous transformation. In the 15 books of the *Metamorphoses* Ovid treated a sure knowledge of mythology with untrammeled imagination and graceful language. He dextrously maneuvered through intricate plots and relationships so that one story led almost imperceptibly to another. To his quick sense of what a story is, he added compassion for his human protagonists and a lightly irreverent treatment of the immortal gods. The work is a treasure of myth and legend which has provided a source of information and inspiration to succeeding western literature and art, and which is still read in modern times, if perhaps without the same sense of charm and delight that it held for the readers of his own time. Written entirely in the hexameter, rather than the elegiac couplet which he used in other works, the work covers the field of mythology from the transformation of Chaos to the ordered universe of earth, sea, and sky, down through the myths of Greek and Latin cultures to the transformation of Julius Caesar into a star. This last was included as a tribute to the divinity of Augustus, the adopted son of Caesar, but it did not benefit Ovid, for just

as he had finished the long poem and begun revising it, Augustus banished him. In his despair it is said that Ovid gave his work to the flames. Obviously, and fortunately, there were copies of it in existence at the time, and though he never finished the revision he had intended, his work was preserved in spite of his dramatic gesture, and was published by friends after he had gone into exile. And although he felt it stood in need of revision and lamented from exile that he had not done it, Ovid was in no doubt as to its worth as it stood, for the closing lines of the *Metamorphoses* read, "My work is complete: a work which neither Jove's anger, nor fire nor sword shall destroy, nor yet the gnawing tooth of time. That day which has power over nothing but my body may, when it pleases, put an end to my uncertain span of years. Yet with my better part I shall soar, undying, far above the stars, and my name will be imperishable. Wherever Roman power extends over the lands Rome has subdued, people will read my verse. If there be any truth in poets' prophecies, I shall live to all eternity, immortalized by fame."

Oxyderces (ok-si-dėr′sēz). Epithet of Athena, meaning "Bright-eyed." Diomedes, whom the goddess so inspired with valor in the Trojan War that he attacked even the gods themselves, was wounded by an arrow of Pandarus during the struggle. Mist darkened his eyes and he faltered, but Athena came to him, healed his wound, and cleared the mist from his eyes. After the Trojan War Diomedes dedicated a sanctuary of Athena Oxyderces at Corinth.

Oxylus (ok′si-lus). In Greek tradition, an Aetolian who was exiled for a year to Elis for an accidental homicide. As he was returning to Aetolia he was met by the Heraclidae—Cresphontes, Temenus, and their nephews Procles and Eurysthenes. The Heraclidae, preparing for their invasion of the Peloponnesus, had been told by an oracle to choose the man "with three eyes" for a leader. Oxylus was driving a one-eyed mule and the Heraclidae took him as the leader indicated by the oracle. Oxylus asked that they give him Elis as his reward for leading them into the Peloponnesus, and they promised to do so. But he feared that when they saw what a pleasant land it was they would break their promise, and so he led them through Arcadia. When he came to Elis, he hoped to get the kingdom without a battle, but the Eleans would not give up so easily. However, they agreed to a duel in which the winner would get the kingdom. The champion who fought for Oxylus was an Aetolian slinger. He won and Oxylus be-

came king. He allowed the Eleans to keep their land and did not disturb their worship of their heroes. He brought in Aetolian colonists and enlarged the city, and the land prospered. In obedience to an oracle, he sought Agorius from Helice in Achaia, as he had been commanded to take a descendant of Pelops as co-founder.

— P —

Paches (pa′kēz). Athenian commander; fl. at the end of the 5th century B.C. He was sent to capture Lesbos, which had revolted from Athens in 428 B.C. After a winter siege the city of Mytilene, the chief Lesbian city, surrendered to him, 427 B.C., on condition that the Mytileneans would be allowed to send a delegation to Athens to plead their cause, and that Paches would not imprison, enslave, or put to death any of the inhabitants of the surrendered city. He accepted the terms and invested the city. On learning that a Peloponnesian fleet had been seen coming to the relief of Mytilene, Paches set out after it and the Peloponnesians fled. Paches went on to Ionia, seized Notium, and gave it to a faction in Colophon. Afterward, Paches was called to account for his activities by his enemies. As he was giving his account of his generalship in court he drew his sword and killed himself.

Pachynus (pa-kī′nus). Rock-strewn cape at the southeastern extremity of Sicily, now called Cape Passero.

Pactolus (pak-tō′lus). In ancient geography, a small river of Lydia, Asia Minor, a tributary of the Hermus. It was long celebrated for its gold, but its sands had ceased to produce by the time of Augustus. In Greek legend, it was the river in which Dionysus told Midas to bathe in order to free himself of the gift, which had become a curse, of having everything he touched turn to gold. This was the reason why the sands of the river afterwards bore grains of gold.

Pacuvius (pa-kū′vi-us), **Marcus.** Roman tragic poet, born c220 B.C., at Brundisium, Italy, and died at Tarentum, c130 B.C. He went

to Rome, where he was a pupil of his uncle, the poet Quintus Ennius, and spent most of his life there, returning to Brundisium only at an advanced age. Fragments or titles totaling about 400 lines of 13 of his tragedies, in imitation of the Greek, survive. Cicero accused him of faulty use of Latin, which suggests that his native tongue may have been Greek, or at least that he was brought up in a Greek-speaking community.

Padua (pa′dū-a). English form of Italian Padova, Latin Patavium (q.v.).

Padus (pā′dus). A Latin name of the Po; equated with the mythical Eridanus River by Greek and Roman writers.

Paean, Paeon (pē′an, -on). An epithet of the gods of healing applied to Apollo and then to his son Asclepius. Originally a hymn to a help-giving god, especially Apollo, asking for aid in war or other trouble, or giving thanks for aid received; hence, a war-song sung before battle in honor of Ares, or after battle as a thanksgiving to Apollo; in later times, a hymn in praise of other gods, or even of mortals.

Paean, Paeeon, or **Paeon.** According to Homer, the physician of the gods. He healed Hades when the latter was wounded by Heracles, and cured Ares when he was wounded by Diomedes during the Trojan War.

Paedotrophus (pē-dọ-trō′fus). An epithet of Artemis, meaning "Nurse of Children." At Sparta a festival was held in her honor and little boys were brought to her temple by their nurses. The Ionian Greeks presented her with clippings of boys' hair at their annual festival of the Apaturia. She was worshiped by girls as the guardian of their

fat, fāte, fär, fāre, errạnt; net, mē, hėr ardẹnt; pin, pīne; not, nōte, mŏve, nôr,

maiden years, and when the time came for them to marry they offered her a lock of their hair and their girdles.

Paeligni (pē-lig′nī). [Also: **Peligni.**] Ancient Italic people who were neighbors of the Marsi and Sabines, and whose chief towns were Corfinium and Sulmo. In the 3rd century B.C. they unsuccessfully resisted Roman ascendancy in the region. Their language, called Paelignian, was one of the ancient Oscan dialects.

Paeon (pē′on). According to tradition, a son of Endymion. His father organized a running race at Olympia, the winner of which was to succeed him on the throne of the region later known as Elis. Paeon raced against his brothers Epeus and Aetolus and lost. Angry at his defeat, Paeon went into exile in the region beyond the Axius River and founded the race that bore his name, the Paeonians.

Paeonia (pē-ō′ni-a). Epithet of Athena, meaning "Healer." Altars and images of Athena Paeonia were raised at Athens and Oropus, among other places.

Paeonia. In ancient geography, the land between the Strymon and Axius (modern Vardar) rivers, lying on the north border of Macedonia and the western border of Thrace. The Paeonians claimed descent from colonists from Troy, and fought as allies of the Trojans in the Trojan War. According to Herodotus, they practised polygamy, and, among other deities, they worshiped Dionysus and Artemis. Also according to Herodotus, several tribal chieftains struggled for control of Paeonia. Two brothers sought the aid of the Persian king, Darius, to win power. In a typically devious manner, they dressed their sister, a tall and beautiful woman, in rich clothing and sent her to draw water for them by a way which passed the spot near Sardis where Darius was sitting in state. On her head she bore a pitcher, with one arm she led a horse, and all the while as she walked she spun flax. Darius was struck by her beauty and her industry. He sent men to follow her and observe what she did. When she came to the river she watered the horse, filled the pitcher and set it on her head, and returned by the way she had come, spinning all the while. Darius commanded that she be brought to him. She arrived with her brothers. Darius

asked of what nation the woman was. Her brothers said she was their sister and that they were all Paeonians. Darius had never heard of Paeonia. He asked where it was and what had brought them to Sardis. They told him Paeonia was a land not far beyond the Hellespont, and that they had come to put themselves under his protection. They added, in answer to his questions, that all the women of Paeonia were as beautiful and industrious as their sister. Thereupon Darius resolved to have the hard-working Paeonians moved from Europe into Asia, and sent word to his general Megabazus in Thrace to bring the Paeonians to him. Megabazus did, in fact, make war on Paeonia, and conquered the lower part of it. He could not conquer the Paeonian tribes on Mount Pangaeus or the Paeonian lake-dwellers. Herodotus says the lake-dwellers had their houses built on platforms resting on piles in the middle of the lake. The platforms were connected to the land by a single narrow bridge. The independent Paeonians in later times raided Macedonia and united with the Illyrians to harass Macedonia until they were finally subdued (358 B.C.) by Philip II of Macedon. Paeonia became a district of Macedonia after the Roman conquest.

Paeonius (pē-ō′ni-us). Greek sculptor of Mende in Thrace, active in the latter part of the 5th century B.C. Some say he was one of the sculptors who worked on the decorations of the temple of Zeus at Olympia, and among the figures by him there was a group representing the chariot race between Pelops and Oenomaus. Paeonius made the statue of Victory which the Messenians dedicated at Olympia in honor of the defeat of their ancient enemies the Spartans at Sphacteria and Cythera (425 B.C.), and in celebration of their part in the defeat. The statue, a contemporary marble copy of a bronze original, was discovered in 1875 with its inscription, and gives a perfect idea of this master's style.

Paestum (pes′tum). City in Lucania, in southern Italy, situated near the sea. Founded as Posidonia, a colony of Sybaris, c600 B.C., it quickly achieved prosperity, as its great Doric temples indicate. These temples include: a temple of Hera, c530 B.C., known in later times as the Basilica; a temple of

Athena, c510 B.C., known later as a temple of Ceres; a temple dedicated to Hera, c450 B.C., but later called the temple of Poseidon. Each of these temples preserves its peristyles, or outer colonnades, intact, and the temple of Poseidon (Hera) further preserves its interior supports, small Doric columns in two stories. Excavations of two more temples of Hera at the mouth of the river Silarus (Sele), five miles to the north, have produced delightful sculptured metopes in the archaic style that are now displayed in the Paestum museum. Together, these temples form an outstanding gallery of Doric architecture, surpassed in impressiveness and wealth of information only by the Periclean buildings of Athens. Yet no ancient writer ever happened to mention them. Beginning about 400 B.C. native Italian tribes, the Lucani, attacked Posidonia and soon gained control of the city, whose inhabitants they are said to have oppressed. The greater part of the city fortifications, two and a half miles in circuit and still preserved throughout their entire length, appears to be of Greek construction, with extensive repairs attributed to the Lucanians. Four main gates survive, as well as a number of posterns and sally ports, some blocked up, and many towers. Of these towers, those later adapted for use as farm buildings have survived almost intact. From this period date also a number of painted Lucanian tombs. After the collapse (275 B.C.) of Pyrrhus' invasion of Italy, Posidonia fell under the domination of the Romans, who established there (273 B.C.) a Latin colony under the name of Paestum, the name by which it is now usually known (Italian, Pesto). To the period of Roman domination belong new temples, an amphitheater, houses, and paved streets. Under the Empire, however, malaria increased and the population declined. To this circumstance we must credit the partial survival of the three great temples and the superb fortifications, which a more vigorous population would surely have dismantled to obtain their stones for building material. The temple of Athena (known as the temple of Ceres) became a church, and still contains traces of Christian tombs, but after a destructive Saracen raid in the 9th century the site was deserted. Paestum's temples remained un-

known to western scholarship until 1745, when the Italian traveler Antonini described them. Recent excavations by Claudio Pellegrino Sestieri have revealed streets, Roman houses, fresh data on the history of the fortifications, painted tombs, and an extraordinary underground ritual chamber containing a bed and jars of offerings. (JJ)

Pagae (pa′jē). In ancient geography, a seaport on the Gulf of Corinth, surrounded by the hills of the Megaris. There was an ancient oracle of Hera here, and here too, Aegialeus, son of Adrastus, reputedly had his tomb, having fallen in the siege of the Epigoni at Thebes. In the Persian War a force from the army of Mardonius was lost in the hills nearby at night. In fear of hostile forces, they fired off a volley of arrows. The arrows struck a rock at Pagae which, according to tradition, Artemis caused to groan. The Persians, thinking they were hitting their enemies, shot off all their arrows, and when day broke they were easily overcome, having exhausted their ammunition, and were slain by the Greeks. The rock at Pagae, bristling with the Persian arrows, was shown for centuries as one of the sights of the region. In gratitude for her help, the inhabitants of Pagae raised a bronze image of Artemis Savior at Pagae.

Pagasae (pag′a-sē). A principal seaport in Thessaly, in NE Greece. Here the *Argo* was said to have been built and from here it sailed. To this port the *Argo* returned after the journey to Colchis. Many ancient ruins of the city remain. Near it is the modern city of Volos.

Pagasus (pag′a-sus). Named by some as a Hyperborean priest who established the worship of Apollo at Delphi.

Painted Portico or Colonnade. [Also: **Stoa Poikile.**] A portico in the market-place, at Athens, founded by Pisianax. The walls of the portico were covered with paintings. One of the pictures showed the Athenians arrayed against the Spartans at Oenoë in Argolis, the date of which incident is unknown. Another, by Micon of Athens, was of Theseus fighting the Amazons. A third, by Polygnotus, showed the Greeks victorious at Troy gathered in an assembly to consider the outraging of Cassandra by Ajax the Lesser; and a fourth, by Micon and Panaenus, portrayed the fighting at the Battle of Marathon, in which were portraits of Callimachus the polemarch and Miltiades. Pausanias the traveler saw the paintings in the 2nd century A.D., but by the end of the 4th century they had disappeared. The Athenians dedicated the shields they had taken from the Spartans on the island of Sphacteria in 425 B.C. in the Painted Portico, and covered them with pitch so that they would not rust. Zeno, the philosopher, walked with his disciples in the Painted Portico, and discussed philosophy with them, whence came their name Stoics, from the *stoa* (colonnade, or portico), in which they developed their principles.

Palaces of the Caesars (sē-zᶐrz). Vast congeries of constructions in Rome, begun by Augustus and added to by successive emperors, occupying the Palatine Hill. Though the buildings are in ruinous condition, the plans have been in large part recovered by excavation, with fragments sufficient for a far-reaching restoration; and many imposing walls and vaults, with interesting wall paintings and graffiti, remain in position.

Palaemon (pᶐ-lē'mon). In classical mythology, a sea-divinity into which Melicertes was metamorphosed when Ino, his mother, fleeing from her frenzied husband Athamas, leaped into the sea bearing him in her arms. See **Melicertes.**

Palaemonius (pᶐ-lē-mō'ni-us), or **Palaemon.** In Greek legend, an Argonaut from Aetolia. He was said to be the son of Lernus of Olenus, but to have been actually the son of Hephaestus. Like his father, he had crippled feet. His lameness did not interfere with his heroic actions, for he was of great might and valor.

Palaephatus (pᶐ-lē'fᶐ-tus). Greek historical writer of the late 4th century B.C. In his writings he attempted to rationalize the myths and religion by asserting that the gods were originally mortals who, because of their great deeds, came to be looked upon after their deaths as gods through the awe and superstition of lesser mortals. A later extract of his work, called *Of Incredible Things,* survives.

Palamedes (pal-ᶐ-mē'dēz). In Greek legend, a son of Nauplius and Clymene, and the brother of Oeax. He was one of Agamemnon's chief lieutenants and went with Agamemnon and Menelaus to Ithaca to secure the services of Odysseus in the war against Troy for the recapture of Helen. Now Odysseus had been warned by an oracle that if he went to Troy he would be gone 20 years and would return alone and destitute. When, therefore, Palamedes, Agamemnon, and Menelaus arrived in Ithaca he pretended to be mad. Palamedes realized that this madness was feigned. According to some accounts, he snatched up Telemachus, the infant son of Odysseus, and made as if to put him to the sword. Other accounts say the envoys found Odysseus plowing with an ox and an ass and sowing salt, and that Palamedes flung Telemachus in front of the plow. In either case, Odysseus showed by his instant reaction to protect his son that he was not mad at all. Thus Palamedes won the valuable services of Odysseus for the Greeks. But Odysseus never forgave him for unmasking his feigned madness and plotted to destroy him. When the Greeks were encamped before Troy he contrived to make Palamedes appear as a traitor. He compelled a Trojan prisoner to write a letter, supposedly sent by Priam to Palamedes, in which a sum of gold sent as a reward for Palamedes' treachery was mentioned. Odysseus then killed the prisoner and buried gold near Palamedes' tent. He caused the letter to be found and read by Agamemnon and gave sufficiently broad hints so that the gold was also found. This was evidence for the Greeks, and they stoned Palamedes to death as a traitor. Some say Agamemnon was privy to this plot and encouraged it because he feared Palamedes. Others say Odysseus and Diomedes induced Palamedes to descend into a well, with the claim of a great treasure there, and then buried him under a shower of stones. For the murder of Palamedes, Nauplius became a burning enemy of Agamemnon and other Greek heroes, and avenged himself on them in his own way. Palamedes, noted as an inventor, was said to have added letters to the alphabet, to have invented weights and measures, dice, the discus, and the lighthouse. He was worshiped as a hero on the island of Lemnos.

Palatine (pal'ᶐ-tīn) **Hill.** See **Palatium.**

Palatium (pᶐ-lā'shi-um). [Also: **Mons Palatinus.**] One of the seven hills of Rome, SE of the Capitoline and dominating the Forum from the S; traditionally, the hill at whose foot Romulus and Remus were washed ashore, where Romulus took the auspices, where he plowed the magic furrow that marked the *pomerium,* and the site of the first settlement at Rome. Archaeological confirmation for this is lacking, and the suggestion that the Palatium had still earlier been a pasture is commended by no more than a dubious etymology—*pascere,* "drive to pasture." Much built over in later times, the Palatium preserves of primitive structures a few courses of fortification walls in tufa and little else. Since householders on the hill could reach the Forum in a few moments, it became the fashionable residence of the wealthy and the politically ambitious, and we hear of many prominent citizens of the late Republic who had houses there: M. Fulvius Flaccus, Q. Lutatius Catulus, M. Livius Drusus whose house was bought by Crassus and then by Cicero, Cicero's brother Quintus Cicero, Q. Hortensius, M. Aemilius Scaurus, Mark Antony, and many others. When Octavian established the principate he acquired the house of Hortensius and added to it to form a suitable imperial residence; later emperors extended these quarters until they occupied almost the whole of the Palatium. Romans who had business at the offices of the emperor spoke of going *ad Palatium* (to the Palatium); from this came the secondary meaning of palatium as the residence of any head of state or church, English "palace." The Palatium also had temples of Jupiter, Victoria, Magna Mater (Cybele), Apollo, and other divinities, and relics of Romulus, whose locations are still in controversy. (JJ)

Palermo (pä-ler′mō). See **Panormus.**

Pales (pā′lēz). In old Italian and Roman mythology, a deity, protector of shepherds and flocks, sometimes regarded as a god and equated by the Romans with Pan or Faunus; also sometimes regarded as a goddess and identified with Vesta. The festival of Pales was the Palilia or Parilia, celebrated April 21 (the reputed anniversary of the founding of Rome) for the increase of flocks.

Palestra, Palaestra (pa̤-les′tra̤). In Greek antiquity, a public place appropriated to exercises under official direction, in wrestling and athletics, and intended especially for the benefit of athletes training to contend in the public games. Also, wrestling and athletics themselves.

Palestrina (pal-e̤s-trē′na̤; Italian, pä-läs-trē′nä). See **Praeneste.**

Palici (pa-lī′sī). In mythology, twin sons of either Zeus and Thalia or Hephaestus and Aetna. They were born in Sicily. Their mother feared the jealousy of Hera and asked to be concealed in the earth. Twin boys arose from her hiding place near Mount Aetna in Sicily, and this became the seat of their worship. They were regarded as the personifications of two warm sulphur springs nearby and oaths were taken by these springs, death being the penalty for a false oath. Their shrine came to be famed as a seat of justice, as an oracle, and as a sanctuary or place of refuge, especially for runaway slaves.

Palilicium (pal-i-lish′i-um). Name given by the Romans to the Hyades, and especially to Aldebaran, the brightest of them, because this group of stars set on the day of the Palilia (April 21), originally a festival for the increase of herds, dedicated to Pales, later celebrated as the anniversary of the founding of Rome.

Palinurus (pal-i-nur′us). In Roman legend, a son of Iasus. He was Aeneas' steersman on the voyage from Troy to Italy after the Trojan War. When the Trojans left Carthage, Palinurus advised them to put into Eryx to avoid a storm. But Neptune, who at Venus' request had calmed the storms, required one life in return for the many he had spared. Thus it was that after the Trojans left Eryx, Somnus (Sleep), taking the form of Phorbas, lulled Palinurus, causing him to fall asleep, and pushed him overboard. Palinurus woke, swam for four days, and finally reached shore. There, having reached Italy as Apollo had promised, he was murdered by barbarous natives. Aeneas met his shade when he visited the Underworld. The shade of Palinurus, wandering in the marshes surrounding the Styx, unable to cross the river because he had not been properly buried, asked Aeneas to bury him and let the shade rest. On his return to the upper world, the Sibyl promised Aeneas that the natives who had killed Palinurus would bury him and atone for his death, and that the place where he had come ashore in Italy would keep his name forever. For this rea-

fat, fāte, fär, fãre, erra̤nt; net, mē, hėr arde̤nt; pin, pīne; not, nōte, mȯve, nôr,

son Cape Palinurus on the west coast of Italy received his name.

Palinurus or **Palinurum** (-um). [Modern names, **Cape Palinuro, Cape Spartimento.**] Promontory on the W coast of Italy, situated in Lucania. It was the scene of shipwrecks of Roman fleets in 253 and in 36 B.C., and of the legendary drowning of Palinurus.

Palladium (pạ-lā′di-um). A wooden image of a maiden supposed to have been sent from heaven as a gift to the Trojans as a pledge of the safety of Troy so long as it should be preserved within the city. According to one account, when Ilus had marked out the limits of Troy, he prayed to Zeus for a sign that he had chosen an auspicious site for his city and that his efforts would be successful. The next morning he found a legless image of a maiden half buried in the ground in front of his tent. She was three cubits high (about five feet), and in her right hand she held a spear, in her left a distaff and spindle (or a shield), and she was wearing the aegis. Athena had made the image in memory of her dead playmate, Pallas, and set it up on Olympus, but when Electra, the Pleiad who had been violated by Zeus, accidentally touched it, Athena hurled it out of Olympus. On discovering the image Ilus was told by Apollo to guard it, as the city in which it was kept could not be taken. Another account says that the image came from heaven while Ilus was building a temple, and that it fell through an opening in the still uncompleted roof and landed on the spot where it afterward remained. However it came to Troy, it brought marvelous protective powers with it. It was for this reason that Diomedes and Odysseus entered Troy secretly toward the end of the Trojan War and carried it off, after which Troy fell to the Greeks. In Roman legend, Aeneas rescued the sacred image from the burning city of Troy, took it to Italy, and it became established at Rome. It is said to have saved Rome from the sack of the Gauls in 390 B.C. Many cities in both Greece and Italy claimed and disputed the possession of the original.

Pallanteum (pạ-lan-tē′um). A town in Italy, founded by Arcadians from Greece, descendants of Pallas. According to legend, Evander, to whom Aeneas came when he reached Latium after his flight from Troy, was king in the town. The site of the town was later known as the Palatine Hill in Rome.

Pallantium (pạ-lan′shi-um). In ancient geography, a city in Arcadia, founded by Pallas, a son of Lycaon. According to legend, from here Evander, son of Hermes and a nymph, daughter of the river-god Ladon, was sent out to found a colony. He went to Italy, and there on the banks of the Tiber River founded a town, Pallanteum, which he named for his native town in Arcadia. This name was later shortened, and the Palatine in Rome is supposed to be the site of Evander's town.

Pallas (pal′as). In Greek mythology, one of the Giants, a son of Gaea and the blood of Uranus, who waged war against the gods. In the battle Athena crushed him with a stone and Heracles killed him. Athena then stripped him of his skin and afterward wore it as a garment.

Pallas. In Greek mythology, a Titan, the son of Crius and Eurybia, and the brother of Astraeus and Perses. By Styx he was the father of Zelus, Nike, Cratus, and Bia. According to some accounts, he was also the father of Chryse, wife of Dardanus, who gave her husband the sacred images of the gods as a wedding gift.

Pallas. In Greek legend, one of the four sons of Pandion and Pylia, born at Megara. He and his brothers, Aegeus, Lycus, and Nisus, divided Attica between them, and Pallas received the southern part as his portion. He was the father of 50 giant sons. He and his sons attacked Aegeus, king of Athens, claiming that he was not a true descendant of Erechtheus, but a bastard. They were, however, betrayed by the herald Leos and defeated by Theseus, son of Aegeus. When Theseus later became king of Athens, he killed Pallas and those of his sons who had survived previous battles.

Pallas. In Greek mythology, a daughter of Triton, in Libya. She was a youthful playmate of Athena who was accidentally killed by the goddess. In grief, Athena put the name of Pallas before her own name. The goddess also made a wooden image of Pallas which later was flung out of heaven and landed before the tent of Ilus, founder of Troy. This image was placed in the temple, and as the Palladium, became the guardian of the safety of Troy as long as it remained

actọr; up, lūte, půll; oi, oil; ou, out; ᴛʜ, then; d̦ as d or j, ş as s or sh, ț as t or ch, z̧ as z or zh.

within the city. Scholars agree that the name Pallas was originally a title of the goddess Athena who is often called Pallas Athena.

Pallas. In Roman legend, a son of Evander, king of Pallanteum on the Tiber River in Italy. Evander sent Pallas to fight at the side of Aeneas in his war against Turnus. Pallas was slain by Turnus, who stripped him of his armor. Aeneas returned the body of Pallas to his father on his shield, with great pomp. Later, in a final struggle with Turnus, Aeneas recognized the belt which Turnus was wearing as belonging to Pallas. This so enraged Aeneas that instead of sparing Turnus' life, as he had intended to do, he killed him.

Pallas. A favorite freedman and financial secretary of the emperor Claudius. He persuaded Claudius to marry Agrippina and to adopt her son, Nero. When Nero succeeded Claudius, he deprived Pallas of his offices (56 A.D.) and finally put him to death (62), ostensibly because of his wealth. Many stories circulated concerning his intimacies with Nero's mother and his immense wealth. (PM)

Pallene (pa-lē'nē). See **Cassandra.**

Pamisus (pa-mī'sus). Chief river of Messenia, Greece. Its waters made the Messenian fields fertile, and in honor of it the kings of ancient Messenia made annual sacrifices to it. It flows into the Gulf of Messenia.

Pamphilus (pam'fi-lus). Greek painter of the first half of the 4th century B.C. He came from Macedonia and worked chiefly at Sicyon, as a teacher in the school founded there by Eupompus. Among his pupils was Apelles. He was the first to base the teaching of art on scientific principles, maintaining that painters had to have a knowledge of arithmetic and geometry in order to perfect their art. He is also said to have been responsible for introducing drawing as a school subject in Sicyon.

Pamphylia (pam-fil'i-a). In ancient geography, a mountainous region in Asia Minor, bounded by Pisidia on the N, Cilicia on the E, the Mediterranean Sea on the S, and Lycia on the W. It was successively under the rule of Lydia, Persia, Macedon, Syria, Pergamum, and Rome.

Pamphylian Gulf (pam-fil'i-an). [Also: **Pam-**

phylian Sea.] Ancient name of **Antalya, Gulf of.**

Pamphylicus Sinus (pam-fil'i-kus sī'nus). Latin name of **Antalya, Gulf of.**

APHRODITE AND PAN PLAYING FIVE-STONES
Engraved Greek bronze mirror, 4th century
B.C. *British Museum*

Pan (pan). A woodland god and god of pastures and of flocks. According to most accounts, he was a son of Hermes. It has even been claimed that he was a son of Penelope, wife of Odysseus, by her suitors, or of Amalthea, the goat who nursed Zeus, but others say he was a very ancient god, and was the son of Cronus and Rhea, or of Zeus. He was born with horns, a beard, tail, and goat legs. Pan never lived in Olympus, but dwelt in Arcadia where he guarded his flocks and herds, played with the mountain-nymphs, and aided hunters. Although he did not dwell with the gods he was associated with Cybele, Dionysus, and Aphrodite. Early in the 5th century B.C. his worship, which was native to Arcadia, spread over the rest of Greece and was strongest in country areas. He passed his days in comparative idleness, playing on his pipes and resting. It was his custom to frighten any who disturbed his noonday rest with a sudden shout, and this was the reason shepherds did not play on their pipes at midday. Sudden terror (panic) without reasonable or visible cause was attributed to his influence. It was Pan's sudden shout, in the long war between the gods and

Titans, which finally caused the precipitous retreat of the Titans. Another shout so frightened the monster Delphyne, who was guarding Zeus, disabled by Typhon, that Hermes was able to free Zeus. Some say Pan stopped Phidippides, the messenger whom the Athenians sent to ask Sparta for aid on the eve of the Battle of Marathon, as he ran to Sparta. The god asked him why the Athenians neglected him, when he was so friendly to them and would aid them in the future as he had in the past. The Athenians believed that Pan caused the panic which helped them to rout the Persians later at Marathon (490 B.C.). Afterward, the Athenians erected a cave-shrine to Pan on the Acropolis and established annual sacrifices and torch-races in his honor. Pan taught Apollo the art of prophecy and taught Daphnis to play the pipes. He considered himself a fine musician and, on boasting of his skill, was challenged to a contest by Apollo. Midas and Tmolus, the god of the mountain, were the judges. Tmolus decided in favor of Apollo; Midas obstinately favored Pan, but as everyone else agreed with Tmolus Apollo was the victor. By the nymph Echo, Pan was the father of Iynx; by Eupheme, the father of Crotus; and he boasted that he was the lover of all of Dionysus' maenads at the time of their wild orgies on the mountain tops. Pitys escaped his amorous advances by becoming transformed into a fir tree, and ever afterward Pan wore a wreath of pine about his head. Syrinx escaped him by turning into reeds along the Ladon River. Pan cut the reeds and, as they made a gentle singing sound, bound them together and invented the Pan-pipes. Of all the gods, Pan was the only one whose death was announced. A sailor, Thamus, on a ship voyaging to Italy, heard a voice shout across the waves telling him to proclaim that "the great god Pan is dead." When he reached Italy Thamus did as he was bid and the land mourned. The story of Pan's death was described by Plutarch in the 1st century A.D. but shrines, altars, mountains, old oaks, pine trees, and caves sacred to Pan were still honored and much frequented over a century later. The tortoise was sacred to Pan. The Romans identified Pan with their god Inuus, and sometimes also with Faunus.

Panacea (pan-a-sē′a). ["All Healer.] A goddess of healing. She was a daughter of Asclepius, and was the sister of Hygea, Iaso, and Aegle.

Panachaea (pan-a-kē′a). Epithet of Demeter, from her sanctuary at Aegium, in Achaea.

Panaenus (pa-nē′nus). Greek painter, active about the middle of the 5th century B.C. He was a brother or a nephew of Phidias, and worked with him on the great statue of Zeus at Olympia, of which, some say, Panaenus painted the drapery. He also worked with Micon on the painting of the *Battle of Marathon* in the Painted Portico at Athens.

Panaetius (pa-nē′shi-us), **Painter.** See **Euphronius**, painter and potter.

Panaetius. Greek Stoic philosopher of Rhodes, born c185 B.C.; died c109 B.C. He was the friend (at Rome) of Laelius and Scipio the Younger. In 129 B.C. he became head of the Stoa at Athens. Of his work, on which Cicero based some of his writing, only fragments have survived.

ATHENA
Black-figured Panathenaic amphora.
British Museum

Panathenaea (pan-ath-e-nē′a). In ancient Greek religion, the great festival celebrated annually in July/August (and every fourth year with greater pomp) at Athens in honor of Athena. Traditionally, it was founded by Erechtheus, as a festival of Athena. Theseus changed it to the Panathenaea, a festival of all the Athenians. The manner of its celebration was elaborated and fixed in the time of Pisistratus. There were athletic and musical contests, races, and various games. A chief feature of the celebration was a procession of women to the Acropolis bearing a mast to which was fastened a magnificent peplus which they had embroidered for the goddess. In the procession were also youths and maidens bearing various symbolic implements and leading sacrificial animals, and also chariots and cavalry. It is this procession which was commemorated in the splendid Ionic frieze which encircles the cella of the Parthenon. The prize given to winners of the various contests was olive oil in amphorae bearing a depiction of the goddess, the olive having been the specific gift of Athena to the people.

Pancratis (pan′kra̱-tis). In Greek mythology, a daughter of Aloeus and Iphimedia, and a sister of the Aloidae. She and her mother were carried off to Naxos by Thracians, but were rescued by the Aloidae.

Pancratium (pan-krā′shi-um). In Greek antiquity, a gymnastic contest or game combining wrestling and boxing. The combatants fought naked, with bare fists or with the soft cestus, and the contests were, at Olympia as almost everywhere, regulated by strict rules to guard against unfairness. The contest was, however, very severe, as the fight was continued until one of the adversaries either was killed—which often happened—or acknowledged his defeat.

Pandareus (pan-dăr′ē̱-us). In Greek mythology, a son of Merops. He was a native of Miletus in Crete, and was the father, by Harmothoë, of Aëdon, Cleothera, and Merope. He stole the golden dog which Hephaestus had made to guard the infant Zeus from the temple of Zeus at Dicte, and gave it to Tantalus to keep for him. When he later asked Tantalus to return it to him Tantalus denied that it had ever been in his possession. Hermes discovered the whereabouts of the dog, on Mount Sipylus, and restored it to the temple. Tantalus was buried under Mount Sipylus for his lies and Pandareus fled to Sicily. There he was slain by Zeus. His daughters were brought up by Aphrodite, with the assistance of Artemis, Athena, and Hera. According to other accounts, it was Tantalus who stole the dog, and Pandareus

who received it for safe-keeping, and for his part in the theft Pandareus was slain by Zeus or turned into stone.

Pandarus (pan′da̱-rus). In Homeric legend (*Iliad*), a Trojan, the son of Lycaon. A renowned archer, being the possessor of a bow given to him by Apollo, he came from Zeleia, at the foot of Mount Ida, to aid the Trojans in the war against the Greeks. The Greeks and Trojans, both tired of the war, exchanged oaths of friendship and agreed that the winner of a duel between Paris and Menelaus should have Helen and all her possessions. This duel was inconclusive because when it appeared that Paris might lose Aphrodite snatched him away in a cloud. Following this, Athena, in the guise of Laodocus, appeared to Pandarus and urged him to shoot at Menelaus and win fame for himself. Beguiled by the goddess, Pandarus treacherously aimed an arrow at Menelaus. Athena deflected it so that Menelaus was only wounded, but the truce had been broken by the Trojans, and the war was resumed. Pandarus, "peer of immortals," wounded Diomedes and, encouraged by Aeneas, sought to kill him, although by that time he was convinced that the gods were protecting Diomedes, as indeed they were. In their second encounter, Pandarus wounded Diomedes with his spear and then was slain by Diomedes.

Pandarus. In the *Aeneid,* a son of Alcanor of Mount Ida in Troy, reared by the woodnymph Iaera. He was one of the companions of Aeneas on the flight from Troy. In Italy Aeneas left him to guard the gate of the Trojan garrison when he himself went to seek help from Tarchon for his beleaguered forces. Pandarus and his brother Bitias opened the gate and slew the followers of Rutulian Turnus as they poured into the garrison. In the mêlée Bitias was killed. When Pandarus saw that his brother was dead he shut the gate, leaving many of his comrades outside and locking in some of the Rutulians, notably Turnus. He hurled his spear at Turnus but Juno deflected it. Turnus took advantage of the divine intervention and split the head of Pandarus in two with his sword.

Pandataria (pan-da̱-tār′i-a̱). [Modern name, **Ventotene.**] In ancient geography, an island in the Tyrrhenian Sea, W of Naples. It was the place of banishment of Julia, the licentious daughter of Augustus; Agrippina, Julia's daughter and wife of Germanicus; and Octavia, daughter of Claudius and Messalina.

Pandemos (pan-dē′mos). Epithet of Aphrodite, originally alluding to her function as a civic or social goddess, but later referring to her as goddess of earthly or physical love.

Pandion (pan′di-on). In Greek legend, a king of Athens, father of the twins Butes and Erechtheus, and of Procne and Philomela. He died of grief following the transformation of his daughters into a nightingale and a sparrow, respectively. See **Procne**.

Pandion. In Greek legend, one of the two sons of Phineus and Cleopatra. His brother was Plexippus. The brothers were blinded by Phineus, who had abandoned their mother and married Idaea, as a result of false accusations made against them by their stepmother. According to some accounts, their sight was later restored and they were given Phineus' kingdom by their uncles, Calais and Zetes.

Pandion. Named by Homer as a companion and squire of Teucer, and bow-carrier for Teucer.

Pandion the Younger. In Greek legend, a son of Cecrops. He was a king of Athens, and by Pylia was the father of Aegeus, Lycus, Nisus, and Pallas. When he and his sons were driven out of Athens by his nephews the Metionidae, he fled to Megara, his wife's home, and succeeded her father Pylas to the throne. Pandion never returned to Athens. He was given a hero's honors in Megara.

Pandora (pan-dō′ra). According to Greek mythology, Prometheus defied Zeus, stole fire from heaven and gave it to men. Zeus punished Prometheus for loving mankind too well, and took his revenge on men by sending an evil which counterbalanced the benefits of the gift of fire. He commanded Hephaestus, the master smith, to create a maiden. She was a most beautiful creation. Athena taught her woman's work, Aphrodite endowed her with beauty, Hermes gave her a deceitful nature, the Charites and the Horae adorned her with delicate raiment, flowers, and a crown of gold. She was called Pandora because all the gods of Olympus gave her gifts. Zeus ordered Hermes to take her to Epimetheus as a gift. Prometheus, still loving

mankind, shut up in a casket all the evils which might plague the world. This was given to Pandora as a dowry. Prometheus warned Epimetheus not to accept any gift from Zeus but Epimetheus forgot the warning, and only remembered it when it was too late. He married Pandora, and forbade her to open her box, as Prometheus had instructed him to do. But as Pandora had been created as a scourge to mankind, she one day yielded to her curiosity and opened the box. All the evils which Prometheus had imprisoned therein flew out and from that time on brought misfortune to men. Only hope remained. Some say this was at the order of Zeus. Others say it was Prometheus who gave wild hope to men. At all events, until the arrival of woman, in the shape of Pandora, men lived without evil and hardship, but with her coming, the world became a dangerous and unhappy place.

Pandora. In Greek legend, a daughter of Erechtheus, king of Athens, and his wife Praxithea. When her sister, Otionia, was sacrificed to bring victory to Athens, in the war with the Eleusinians, Pandora fulfilled a vow and killed herself.

Pandorus (pan-dō′rus). In Greek legend, a son of Erechtheus, king of Athens, and Praxithea. After the death of Erechtheus his sons quarreled over the succession. Cecrops was appointed king by Xuthus, who had been asked to settle the dispute. But Metion and Orneus were not satisfied. They threatened to kill Cecrops. He fled, and Pandorus joined him and founded a colony in Euboea.

Pandosia (pan-dō′sha). In ancient geography, a town in Bruttii, Italy, situated on the Acheron River, near what is now Cosenza. Here Alexander I, king of Epirus, was defeated and slain (326 B.C.) by the Bruttians.

Pandrosos (pan′drō-sos). In Greek mythology, a daughter of Cecrops, king of Athens, and Agraulos. She was a priestess of Athena, in whose temple on the Acropolis grew the sacred olive tree, given to Athens by Athena. She leaped to her death from the Acropolis. See **Herse**.

Paneas (pan′ē-as). [Roman name, **Caesarea Philippi**; modern name, **Baniyas**.] Village in SW Syria, at the foot of Mount Hermon, about 40 miles SW of Damascus: said to have been named by the Greeks for the god Pan.

actor; up, lūte, pull; oi, oil; ou, out; ᴛʜ, then; d̩ as d or j, s̩ as s or sh, t̩ as t or ch, z̩ as z or zh.

Pangaeus (pan-jē'us) or **Pangaeum** (-um), **Mount.** A mountain in Thrace, near the mouth of the Strymon River on the shore of the Aegean Sea. Here, according to legend, Lycurgus was pulled apart by wild horses in punishment for his crime (induced by madness which Dionysus had inspired) of killing his son, Dryas. It was also the place where Orpheus rose to greet the dawn and proclaim Apollo, in defiance of the ritual of Dionysus. The mountain was rich in gold and silver. Philip II of Macedon in 358–357 B.C. seized it and from its mines secured the funds to build his military organization.

Panhaema (pan-hē'ma). A field on the island of Samos where, according to tradition, Dionysus killed the Amazon women who opposed him on his return from India. He killed so many of them that the place was named Panhaema (All-bloody) to commemorate them.

Panhellenius (pan-he-lē'ni-us). Epithet of Zeus as "God of all the Greeks." It was to Zeus Panhellenius that Aeacus sacrificed on the mountain top in Aegina, to beseech him to end the drought that afflicted all Greece. Zeus answered his prayers and sent rain. Afterward, Aeacus established a sanctuary of Zeus Panhellenius on the mountain top in Aegina. The Roman emperor, Hadrian, dedicated a temple of Zeus Panhellenius in Athens in the 2nd century A.D.

Panhellenius. A mountain on the island of Aegina. Aeacus made sacrifices on it, at the request of the Athenians, to end a drought in Greece. His rites were followed by a thunderclap and a deluge of rain. He built a sanctuary to Zeus there, and ever afterward it was a sure sign of rain when a cloud veiled the mountain top.

Panionia (pan-i-ō'ni-a). In ancient Greece, a festival convening all Ionians for the worship of Poseidon. By the end of the 5th century B.C. it had been superseded in importance by the festival of Ephesus. See **Panionium.**

Panionium (pan-i-ō'ni-um). A temple of Poseidon at Mycale in Asia Minor, where the Ionians of the 12 Ionic cities of Caria (Miletus, Myus, and Priene), of Lydia (Ephesus, Colophon, Lebedus, Teos, Clazomenae, and Phocaea), of the islands of Samos and Chios, and of Erythrae on the mainland opposite Chios, gathered to celebrate the Panionia, in honor of Poseidon. These Ionians decreed that this temple should be closed to the other states of Ionia. The Ionians met at the Panionium to discuss matters of public business and policy. At one time Thales of Miletus suggested in a meeting at the Panionium that the Ionian cities unite and establish a central government, and suggested. Teos, as the center of Ionia, as the logical place for the central government. His advice was disregarded. The Ionian cities maintained their separate laws and policies and were easily picked off by Croesus, Cyrus, and Darius.

Pannonia (pa-nō'ni-a). In ancient geography, a Roman province, bounded by the Ister (Danube) on the N and E, Moesia and Illyricum on the S, and Noricum on the W. It was made a Roman province by Tiberius (c9 A.D.), and divided by Trajan into Upper Pannonia in the W and Lower Pannonia in the E (c106 A.D.).

Panomphaeus (pan-om-fē'us). An epithet of Zeus as the sender of ominous and prophetic voices.

Panopeus (pan'ō-pūs). In Greek legend, a son of Phocus (son of Ornytion) and Asteria. He was the twin of Crisus, with whom he struggled in his mother's womb. The hatred thus begun persisted throughout their lives. Panopeus took the part of Aegisthus and Clytemnestra, while Crisus and his family sided with Orestes. He took part in the Calydonian Boar Hunt and also allied himself with Amphitryon, foster father of Heracles, in the war against the Taphians and Teleboans. Before going into battle he swore in the name of Athena, as did the other allies, that he would not hide any of the spoils which might be taken in the war. He was the only one to break his oath and was punished for so doing by becoming the father of a cowardly son, Epeus, who, nevertheless, accompanied the Greeks to Troy and built the Wooden Horse. Panopeus was also the father of Aegle, for whom, some say, Theseus abandoned Ariadne on the island of Naxos.

Panopeus. In ancient geography, a city of Phocis. It was named for Panopeus, father of that Epeus who built the Trojan Horse, and was peopled by Phlegyans. Homer mentions it as one of the cities that sent men against Troy in the Trojan War. Among the wonders of Panopeus described by Pausanias, who visited it when the city was in ruins, were two very large, clay-colored stones that gave off an odor like the smell from the skin of a man. The people of Panopeus claimed these stones were all that remained of the clay from which Prometheus fashioned the human race. Near Panopeus was the reputed tomb of Tityus. Panopeus was destroyed by the Persians (480 B.C.), rebuilt, destroyed by Philip of Macedon following the Sacred War (346 B.C.), and never recovered from the destruction of Sulla (86 B.C.).

Panoptes (pan-op′tēz). In Greek legend, an epithet, meaning "All Eyes," of the 100-eyed giant, Argus. He was slain by Hermes.

Panormus (pa̱-nôr′mus). See **Gonippus.**

Panormus. In ancient geography, a city on the N coast of Sicily, lying at the foot of a mountain. Harbors on both sides of the ancient city accounted for its name, which means "All-haven." The city was founded in very ancient times by the Phoenicians, came under the power of Carthage, and was one of the most important Punic centers in Sicily. It remained a Punic city until 254 B.C., when it was taken by the Romans. The modern city on the site is Palermo, noted for its mild climate and the beauty of its location.

Pansa (pan′sa̱), **Caius Vibius.** Roman consul in 43 B.C. He was the colleague of Hirtius with whom he defeated Antony at Mutina, 43 B.C. He died the same year.

Pantelleria (pän″tel-le-rē′ä). [Also: **Pantalaria, Pantellaria.**] Island in the Mediterranean Sea, off the W tip of Sicily. It was highly favored as a place to which members of the imperial family and other prominent persons were banished in the time of the Roman empire. See **Cossura.**

Pantheon (pan′thē-on). In 27 B.C., M. Vipsanius Agrippa, son-in-law of the emperor Augustus, ordered the construction of the Pantheon, a temple dedicated to the "All-Holy Ones" (not to "All the Gods," as is sometimes asserted), in the Campus Martius, Rome. The Pantheon of Agrippa was burned in 80 A.D., restored by Domitian, and destroyed about 110 A.D. The structure which now stands on the site was built between 120 and 124 A.D. at the orders of the emperor Hadrian, who repeated Agrippa's dedicatory inscription on the entablature of the façade.

As it stands, it is a rotunda of concrete faced with brick, c142 feet high and c142 feet in internal diameter, and c182 feet in external diameter, the walls being more than 20 feet thick. It is roofed with a coffered dome in which is a circular open skylight about 29 feet in diameter, and entered through a handsome vestibule with 16 Corinthian columns of granite with marble capitals. The great bronze doors are variously reported to be ancient, or to have been removed for reuse and replaced in the 16th century. The interior walls are decorated with rectangular and semicircular niches, once elegantly revetted in marble, which was later removed for reuse elsewhere. The dome was originally covered with gilded bronze tiles which at the orders of the emperor Constans II were removed in 662 A.D. and carried off to Constantinople. In 609 A.D. the Pantheon became a church, dedicated to Sancta Maria ad Martyres, later Santa Maria Rotonda. As a church, it contains tombs of members of the Italian royal family, including two kings, Victor Emmanuel II and Humbert I, and of Raphael and other artists. In spite of many changes, it is the best preserved Roman temple, and illustrates as very few Roman buildings do the Roman sense of scale and proportion, and the integrity of their construction. (JJ)

Panthous (pan′thō̱-us). In Greek legend, a priest of Apollo at Delphi. Priam sent an envoy to consult the oracle at Delphi concerning the site of Troy, when he was about to rebuild it after its destruction by Heracles, but the envoy fell in love with Panthous and brought him back to Troy, without consulting the oracle. Priam made him a priest of Apollo in Troy and he became one of his trusted advisers. By the time of the Trojan War he was too old to fight but acted as one of Priam's counselors. He was the father of Euphorbus, Hyperenor, and Polydamas.

Panyasis (pa-nī′a̱-sis, pan-i-ā′sis). Greek poet of Halicarnassus, an uncle or cousin of Herodotus. He was active in the first half of the 5th century B.C., and was put to death by the tyrant Lygdamis, c454 B.C., as leader of the party which opposed the tyrant. He was the author of the epic *Heraclea*, in 14 books, that dealt with the deeds of Heracles. Only fragments of the work survive. By some, he is ranked next after Homer among the epic poets. Others place him fourth, after Homer, Hesiod, and Antimachus. Besides his epic, he wrote elegies.

Paphian Goddess (pā′fi-an). In ancient Greek religion, Aphrodite, as goddess of sexual love. The term arose from the worship paid her at her cult center at the city of Paphos, in Cyprus.

Paphlagonia (paf-la-gō′ni-a). In ancient geography, a country in Asia Minor, bounded by the Euxine Sea on the N, Pontus (separated by the Halys) on the E, Galatia on the S, and Bithynia on the W. According to Homer, the inhabitants were specially noted as breeders of mules. In the Trojan War the Paphlagonians were allies of Troy and were led by Palaemenes. The country was semi-independent under Persian and Macedonian rule. It passed later to Pontus, and to Rome in 65 B.C.

Paphos or **Paphus** (pā′fos, -fus). In Greek legend, a son of Pygmalion and Galatea. He succeeded his father as king of Cyprus. The city on Cyprus, which bears his name and was one of Aphrodite's favorite cities, was founded by his son and successor Cinyras, according to Greek tradition.

Paphos. In ancient geography, the name of two cities in Cyprus. Old Paphos was situated near the SW coast. According to legend, it was founded by Cinyras, the grandson of Pygmalion, and it was he who built the celebrated temple of Astarte, or Aphrodite, of unburned brick and wood on a stone foundation measuring 164 by 220 feet. The famous image of the goddess was a *baetylus* (a conical meteoric stone). The temple stood in a large enclosure whose walls were likewise of sun-dried brick on a massive stone foundation. Cinyras named the city for his father Paphos, who was the son of Pygmalion and Galatea. The city was sacred to Aphrodite and was one of her favorite haunts. New Paphos was situated on the W coast eight or ten miles NW of Old Paphos. It was a commercial center. Aphrodite is said to have risen from the sea near Paphos.

Papirius Cursor (pa-pir′i-us kėr′sôr, -sor), **Lucius.** Roman consul five times and dictator twice, hero of the Second Samnite War. As dictator he won a victory over the Sam-

nites in 309 B.C. His name became a byword for great strictness and severity.

Papirius Cursor, Lucius. Roman consul and general in the Third Samnite War (298–290 B.C.); son of the hero of the Second Samnite War. According to Pliny, he erected the first sun-dial at Rome.

Paraebius (pa-rē′bi-us). In Greek legend, a friend of Phineus, in Salmydessus in Thrace. His father had cut down a hamadryad's tree, despite the pleas of the nymph to be spared. As a result he and his children were cursed. Phineus told Paraebius how he could lift the curse on himself by proper sacrifices to a nymph. Ever after, Paraebius loyally tended to the needs of the blinded and Harpy-harried Phineus. When the Argonauts visited Phineus on their way to Colchis, it was Paraebius who prepared the altar and sacrifices which they required.

Parallel Lives. Formal title of the chief work of Plutarch, consisting of biographies of 23 Romans and 23 Greeks, arranged in pairs (one Greek and one Roman), and four separate biographies. The arrangement as we have it is probably not as in the original; some biographies have been lost. The comparisons at the end of each pair (some of these are missing) are perhaps not by Plutarch. Various writers, including Shakespeare, have drawn upon Plutarch's work. See **Plutarch.**

Parcae (pär′sē). Three Fates of Roman mythology. Originally there was one (named Parca), a birth goddess who decided the destiny of the newborn. She was early equated with the Greek Moerae, and thus the concept became triplicate.

Parchment. A favorite writing material in antiquity. The Latin term was *membrana Pergamena* (Pergamene skins), the Hellenistic kingdom of Pergamum in Asia Minor having been a center of preparation of sheepskins for international commerce. The phrase, shortened to *Pergamena*, became *parchemin* in French and *parchment* in English. With its great durability, and its excellent writing surface and light color, against which black and colored inks contrast agreeably, it was the finest writing material known to the ancients, and many of the oldest surviving manuscripts are on parchment. Its substantially higher production cost, compared with the

fat, fāte, fär, fāre, errant; net, mē, hėr ardent; pin, pīne; not, nōte, mōve, nôr,

abundant papyrus of Egypt, tended to limit its use to compositions of permanent importance, except during those periods when artificially high prices set on papyrus by the Ptolemies made parchment and vellum commercially competitive. (JJ)

Paria (pãr'i-a). In Greek mythology, a nymph. She was loved by Minos, king of Crete, and bore him four sons: Eurymedon, Nephalion, Chryses, and Philolaus. Her sons colonized the island of Paros in the Cyclades and named it for their mother. Heracles, on his way to fetch the Apples of the Hesperides, stopped at Paros for water. Two of his men were killed. In retaliation he killed the sons of Minos and Paria.

Parian (pãr'i-an) **Chronicle.** [Also **Marmor Parium.**] A marble tablet, found at Paros (1627), on which were engraved a number of dates relating to Greek history, especially literary and religious history, from the time of Cecrops, king of Athens, to the time of the Athenian archon Diognetus, 264 B.C. The times of the founding of various festivals, victories of poets in contests, and dates of their births and deaths, are among the data inscribed in the 93 lines which remain of the Chronicle. Among others, the time of the arrival of Demeter in Eleusis is given, as well as the first sowing of corn by Triptolemus in the plain of Eleusis; and the first celebration of the Mysteries of Demeter by Eumolpus is placed in the reign of Erechtheus. According to the Chronicle, iron was discovered on Mount Ida in Crete in the time of Pandion I of Athens. The dates given are according to the kings and archons of Attica, progressing backward in time from the period of Diognetus. The Parian Chronicle was part of a group of ancient sculptures and antiquities collected by Thomas Howard, 14th Earl of Arundel, and presented to the University of Oxford in 1667. A smaller fragment of the Parian Chronicle was found at Paros in 1897 and is preserved in the local museum.

Parilia (pa-ril'i-a). See **Pales.**

Paris (par'is). [Also: **Alexander.**] In Greek legend, a son of Priam and Hecuba. Before he was born his mother dreamed that she had given birth to fiery serpents and awoke screaming that Troy was in flames. Her dream was interpreted to mean that the child she would bear would bring disaster to Troy. On the day Paris was born another prophecy was made: that the child born to a royal Trojan that day would cause the ruin of Troy and that therefore he and his mother should be destroyed. Priam, despite the pleas of priests and seers to kill Paris, who was born late that day, could not destroy his wife and child, and gave the child to a herdsman with instructions to kill him. The herdsman exposed Paris on Mount Ida, but when he returned after a few days he found the infant alive and well, having been suckled by a she-bear. He carried him home and brought him up with his own son. Paris became a shepherd on Mount Ida and lived happily with Oenone, a nymph, the daughter of the river-god Oeneus. He was disporting with Oenone and innocently tending his flocks on Mount Ida when Hermes approached and told him he had been selected to judge a contest between goddesses: Eris had thrown a golden apple, marked "To the Fairest," among the wedding guests at the marriage of Peleus and Thetis. Athena, Aphrodite, and Hera each claimed the prize. Zeus had refused to settle the dispute and had advised the goddesses to consult Paris. They agreed to accept his decision. Hera promised to make him ruler of all Asia if he awarded the apple to her; Athena promised him victory in all his battles, as well as wisdom and beauty; Aphrodite promised him the fairest woman in the world as his wife. Paris awarded the apple to Aphrodite, and thus won the eternal hatred of Athena and Hera for himself and for all Trojans. The fairest woman in the world was Helen, wife of Menelaus, king of Sparta. Before she married Menelaus, her foster father made all her suitors swear an oath that they would take up arms for the man she married if any evil ever came to him because of his wife. By chance, Paris shortly after the contest returned to Troy and was discovered to be the supposedly lost son of Priam and Hecuba. (Some say Hecuba had bribed the herdsman not to destroy her infant.) The priests immediately urged that he be put to death before he could cause the destruction of Troy, as the oracles had foretold, but Priam would not consent and welcomed his handsome son warmly. Without divulging his true purpose,

actor; up, lūte, pull; oi, oil; ou, out; ᴛʜ, then; ḑ as d or j, ş as s or sh, ṭ as t or ch, ẓ as z or zh.

which was to go after Helen, Paris asked Phereclus to build him a fleet in which he could sail to Sparta, and when it was ready he sailed off, in spite of the burning admonitions and prophecies of Cassandra, his pro-

to attend his grandfather's funeral. That same night Helen, swept on by the fate which Aphrodite had spun for her, eloped with Paris, taking one of her sons and a great treasure with her. On the way to Troy they were

HELEN, PARIS, ANDROMACHE, HECTOR
Black-figured Attic vase, 6th century B.C. *Wurzburg*

phetic sister, that his voyage would bring ruin to Troy. Helenus, a seer and a brother, added his warnings, but Priam ignored them and permitted Paris to sail. Oenone, his nymph, also tried to dissuade him from his journey, but her tears were unavailing. As she bade him farewell she told him to return to her if he was ever wounded, because only she could heal him. Arrived in Sparta, Menelaus welcomed him courteously, entertained him for some days, and then, oblivious of the apparent fact that Paris was headlong in love with Helen, Menelaus left for Crete

driven to Cyprus by storms, and later spent some months in Egypt, fearing pursuit by Menelaus. When they finally arrived at Troy they were married, and all Troy fell in love with Helen's glorious beauty. No one blamed Paris. According to some accounts, Helen bore Paris several children, all of whom died as a result of an accident in their childhood. In spite of envoys and threats Paris refused, with the full consent and approval of the Trojans, to give up Helen. The Trojan War, in which all the Greek suitors of Helen who had taken the oath took part, followed. After

fat, fāte, fär, fāre, errạnt; net, mē, hėr ardẹnt; pin, pīne; not, nōte, möve, nôr,

nearly ten years of war Menelaus and Paris arranged, with the approval of both the Greek and Trojan armies, to fight in single combat, the winner to have Helen and end the war. In the duel, Paris was about to be overcome by Menelaus when Aphrodite spirited him away and restored him to Helen. Hector, brother of Paris, frequently accused him of being a coward and a wife-stealer, but in truth Paris fought bravely. He wounded Diomedes, Machaon, and Eurypylus, and led a group at the attack on the Greek fortifications. But each time that it was proposed that he restore Helen to Menelaus, as after the death of Hector and later the deaths of Penthesilea and Memnon who had come to aid the Trojans, he refused and accused those who made the proposals of cowardice, or what was worse, treachery. According to most accounts Paris, with the help of Apollo, mortally wounded Achilles by shooting an arrow into his vulnerable heel. He attacked Telamonian Ajax, who was defending the body of Achilles, and was flattened by a huge stone flung by Ajax. Again, he fearlessly attacked Philoctetes, who had been brought from Lemnos with the arrows he had inherited from Heracles. This attack was Paris' downfall. His arrow missed Philoctetes, but he was wounded by one of the poisoned arrows Philoctetes aimed at him. He withdrew from the battle in great pain, as the poison invaded his body. No one could cure his wound. In his desperate need he sought out Oenone, his deserted nymph, who alone could heal him. He implored her to free him of his pain, declared that it was fate which had made him desert her, and asked her forgiveness. But Oenone had also been wounded, by desertion and jealousy. She scornfully advised Paris to go to Helen to be cured. Deserted in his turn by Oenone, Paris died of his wound. The Trojans did not mourn him, for he was the cause of all their woes. His death frightened Helen, for she did not know what the Trojans would do with her now that Paris was dead. But Oenone's deep love for Paris reasserted itself. Her heart was pierced with grief. She left her home in the night and ran through the woods to the pyre on which Paris was lying. Muffling her face, she leaped into the flames and died in the fire, with Paris clasped in her

arms. Their ashes were mingled in one urn and a common burial mound heaped over it. Two pillars were erected at the burial mound, facing in opposite directions because the jealousy which Oenone harbored for Helen still lived in the marble pillars.

Parisii (pa̱-ris′i-ī). Ancient Gallic tribe occupying a small town called Lutetia on an island in the Sequana (Seine), at the time of Caesar's conquest of Gaul. They gave their name to the city of Paris.

Parma (pär′ma̱). [Latin: **Parma, Colonia Julia Augusta.**] City in N Italy, situated between Bononia (Bologna) and Placentia (Piacenza). It became a Roman military colony in 183 B.C. and was of great strategic importance because of its location on the Via Aemilia. It was destroyed by Mark Antony in the civil wars, and was rebuilt by Augustus under the name of Colonia Julia Augusta.

Parmenides (pär-men′i-dēz). Greek philosopher, born at Elea (Velia), in Italy, and active about the middle of the 5th century B.C., in the Eleatic school of philosophy. In his native town he was noted for his wise laws and blameless life; in respect to the latter, his fame was such that the expression "a Parmenidean life" became proverbial among the Greeks. He is believed to have arrived (c450 B.C.) at Athens at the age of 65, which suggests a birthdate of c514 B.C. According to some accounts, in Athens he became acquainted with his younger contemporary Socrates. He was a follower of Xenophanes, and the teacher of Zeno, and he embodied his ideas in a didactic poem in hexameters, *On Nature,* in two books. In a proem to the poem, he tells how he rode to the daughters of the Sun, who took him through the stone gates of Night and Day, to the goddess Wisdom. She told him he must seek the truth and how to go about it. In the first book, *On the Way of Truth,* he outlines his belief in one unchangeable state of being. It is not something in the process of being created or of having been created. It is there—perfect, whole, unchangeable; "that that is, is; that that is not, is not." In the second book, *The Way of Falsehood or Illusion,* he puts forth the view that the idea of non-existence, of phenomena in nature, of changing states, of becoming, is false and illusory; the idea of substantive change, of existence being created from non-existence, is opinion, and not truth. Fragments of his work survive.

Parmenio (pär-mē′ni-ō) or **Parmenion** (pär-mē′ni-on). Macedonian general, born c400 B.C.; executed without trial, on the orders of Alexander the Great, 330 B.C. He was the leading councilor and ablest general of Philip II of Macedon, who sometimes called him his only general. He defeated the Illyrians (356 B.C.); acted as envoy of Philip at the signing of a peace treaty with Athens, 346 B.C.; and when Philip was preparing war to liberate the Greek cities of Asia Minor from Persian control, he crossed the Hellespont with an advance force. Philip was murdered before he could carry out his plan to drive back the Persians. Parmenio won control of the Hellespont and kept it. When Philip's successor, Alexander the Great, arrived (334 B.C.), he had a base from which to launch his invasion of an expedition into Asia. Parmenio served Alexander as loyally and well as he had served Philip. He commanded the left wing at the battles of Granicus, Issus, and Arbela. Perhaps because of his experience and because he was old enough to be Alexander's father, he sometimes gave him advice, which was seldom taken. When the Macedonians came to the Granicus River, where the Persians were arrayed to meet them, Parmenio advised Alexander to wait until morning to cross the river and make his attack, before the Persians had time to draw up their line. Alexander's characteristic reply was that he would disgrace the Hellespont, which he had already crossed, if he allowed himself to be detained by a miserable stream such as the Granicus, even for a night. The Macedonians crossed and defeated the Persians (334 B.C.). Again, some time after the battle of Issus (333 B.C.) the defeated Darius sent to Alexander asking to ransom his family and proposing to cede to Alexander all of his kingdom west of the Euphrates River. Parmenio said he would accept the offer if he were Alexander. Alexander remarked, "So would I, if I were Parmenio," and proceeded to draft an imperious letter to Darius in which he refused his terms and demanded his surrender in person. On the eve of the battle of Gaugamela (331 B.C.), Parmenio advised a night attack against the vastly superior forces assembled under Darius. In this case, Alexander said, "I will not steal a victory," and ordered the attack for the morning. The Persians facing Alexander were completely routed and he would have pursued Darius who fled on horseback, but Parmenio was in difficulties in his sector and sent to Alexander for aid. Before Alexander came up the enemy was routed, thanks to the Thessalian cavalry. Some say that from this time Alexander had less confidence in Parmenio. However, he was left in charge (330 B.C.) of the enormous treasure the Macedonians had assembled at Ecbatana, the capital of Media, when Alexander at last found an opportunity to pursue Darius. Philotas, son of Parmenio, was also a general in Alexander's army. With the rich spoils taken and distributed to the Macedonians, Philotas began to lead a wildly extravagant life, and to rival Alexander himself in the rich gifts he gave his friends. Parmenio wrote to his son to be "less great," for he knew Alexander had received accusations against Philotas. Alexander became convinced that Philotas was conspiring against him, had him accused, tried, and put to death. He then sent messengers to Media with orders to kill Parmenio, against whom there was no charge; but the fact that he was the father of Philotas made him an object of danger to Alexander. The murder of Parmenio (330 B.C.), a loyal general who had rendered great service to two generations, marked a departure from Alexander's ordinarily generous and mild conduct toward his friends.

Parmensis (pär-men′sis), **Caius Cassius.** See **Cassius Parmensis, Caius.**

Parnassus (pär-nas′us). [Also: **Liakoura.**] Mountain ridge in Greece, about 83 miles NW of Athens, and situated mainly in ancient Phocis. Some say the mountain was named for Parnassus, a son of Poseidon and the nymph Cleodora. Others say this Parnassus was a mortal. In any case, he is said to have founded the oldest city at Delphi and to have discovered how to tell the future by observing the flight of birds. The ancient city founded by Parnassus was destroyed in the great flood Zeus sent to punish wicked mankind. Some of the inhabitants of Parnassus' city were warned by wolves of the coming of the flood and escaped up the

fat, fāte, fär, fāre, errant; net, mē, hėr ardent; pin, pīne; not, nōte, mŏve, nôr,

mountain. There they founded a new city called Lycoria (*Mountain-wolf-city*). Deucalion and Pyrrha, who some say were the only ones to survive the flood, landed on Mount Parnassus as the waters ebbed, and there in obedience to a command of the gods recreated the human race. Mount Parnassus suffered again when Phaëthon lost control of the horses that draw the chariot of the sun. The flaming chariot came too near the earth and set the mountain afire. It was on Parnassus that Odysseus, visiting the home of his grandfather Autolycus, received a gash from a wild boar's tusk and carried the scar the rest of his life. The mountain was sacred to Apollo, the Muses, Dionysus, and the nymphs, and hence was regarded as the seat of music and poetry. On its slopes was located the most famous of all Greek oracles, that of Apollo at Delphi. The mountain was a favorite place for the orgies that were celebrated in honor of Dionysus. On its slopes was the Corycian cave, sacred to Pan. In the Persian Wars, the Delphians took refuge in the mountain peak when Xerxes sent an army against Delphi, but the mountain itself, according to Herodotus, protected the sacred oracle: two enormous crags broke off from it, rolled down, and crushed the Persian forces (480 B.C.). Guerrilla bands hid out in the mountain and used it as a base from which to make damaging raids on the armies of Mardonius before the battle of Plataea (479 B.C.). Highest summit, Lycoria (8068) feet).

Parnethius (pär-nē'thi-us). Epithet of Zeus, from his bronze image on Mount Parnes, near Athens.

Parnopius (pär-nō'pi-us). An epithet of Apollo, meaning "Locust-god," because he dispelled a plague of locusts from Attica.

Paros (pār'os). Second largest island of the Cyclades; in the Aegean Sea W of Naxos. It is composed of a single mountain, famous in ancient times for its white marble. According to tradition, the island was first colonized by Arcadians. These were later joined by Ionians from Athens. Colonists from Paros, including the poet Archilochus, went to the island of Thasus early in the 7th century B.C. Because Paros had been an ally of the Persians at Marathon (490 B.C.), the victorious Athenian general Miltiades attacked it after the defeat of the Persians, but was unable to take the island. In 480 B.C. Paros again sided with the Persians. After the expulsion of the Persians from Greece (479 B.C.) Paros was forced by the Athenians to pay a heavy fine, to join the Confederacy of Delos, and to pay the highest tribute to the Confederacy treasury of any of the islands. Remains of many ancient structures have been found on the island, among them sanctuaries of Asclepius, Aphrodite, and of Delian Apollo, and a grotto of Ilithyia. Parian marble was exported from the 6th century B.C., and was used by the most famous of the Greek sculptors. Some of the tunnels in the mountain by which the marble was quarried can still be seen. One of the most interesting finds made on the island was that of the Parian Chronicle. Area of the island, about 81 square miles; length, about 15 miles.

Parrhasius (pạ-rā'shi-us). Greek painter, considered one of the greatest of antiquity. He was born at Ephesus and was active in Athens, c400 B.C., as one of the chief representatives of the Ionic school. He was said to have had a painting contest with Zeuxis, another leading painter of the Ionic school. Zeuxis painted a bunch of grapes, which so deceived the birds that they swooped down and pecked at them. But Parrhasius painted a curtain which deceived Zeuxis himself, and won the contest. The anecdotes of Pliny about all the painters of this time indicate extraordinary realism carried to the point of actual illusion, as in the above case. There were many pen-and-ink sketches by Parrhasius still in existence in the time of Pliny. Among his principal works were *The Personification of the Demos of Athens,* probably suggested by Aristophanes, in which he portrayed great variety of psychological expressions in depicting the many types that made up the Athenian people; a *Prometheus;* the *Heracles* at Lindus; the *Theseus* at Athens, afterward on the Capital at Rome; a *Contest of Ajax and Odysseus for the Arms of Achilles;* and a *Madness of Odysseus.* He was one of the first to observe and utilize the proportions in human anatomy, and was skilled in the use of delicate coloring, as well as interested in catching rather violent activity in facial expressions.

actọr; up, lūte, pu̇ll; oi, oil; ou, out; ŦH, then; ḍ as d or j, ş as s or sh, ţ as t or ch, ẓ as z or zh.

Parthenia (par-then'i-a̱). Another name for the island of Samos.

Parthenia (pär-thē'ni-a̱). An epithet of Athena as the chief of the three virgin goddesses: Athena, Artemis, and Hestia.

Parthenius (pär-then'i-us). In Greek legend, a son of Phineus and Cleopatra. He and his brother, Pandion, were blinded by Phineus when their stepmother, Idaea, made false accusations against them. Parthenius is also known as Plexippus. See **Pandion.**

Parthenius. Greek poet of Nicaea, brought to Rome as a slave and then freed; active in the 1st century B.C. Only a few fragments of his elegiac poetry remain. A collection of his prose stories of unhappy lovers survives, culled from ancient writers and dedicated to Cornelius Gallus. The stories are illustrative of romantic Alexandrian literature. (PM)

Parthenius. A river of Paphlagonia; a gentle river, where Artemis bathed to refresh herself after hunting.

Parthenius, Mount. In ancient geography, a mountain in Arcadia. Some say Telephus, son of Heracles and Auge, was born on the mountain, and abandoned there. A sacred enclosure marked the spot where the infant was found and suckled by a deer. Near the sanctuary of Pan on Mount Parthenius, Phidippides, the Athenian runner, met the god when he was on his way to Sparta to seek aid for Athens just before the battle of Marathon (490 B.C.), and Pan assured him of his interest in the Athenians. The mountain was noted for its many tortoises, the shells of which would make good lyres, but the people of the mountain would not permit the tortoises to be taken because they were considered sacred to Pan.

Parthenon (pär'thē-non). The popular name for the splendid marble Doric temple of Athena Polias (Athena of the City), built on the Acropolis of Athens, between 447 and 438 B.C. It represents the peak achievement of Greek architecture. It was the third of three temples of Àthena on this site. The first was a modest Doric temple of the limestone known as poros, restored with tristyle-in-antis porches at front and rear, the so-called Hecatompedon or "100-foot" temple. The foundations of this temple, buried beneath the later Parthenons, cannot be seen, but its dimensions and plan can be deduced

from elements of the entablature and pediments which have survived, and which indicate a date somewhat earlier than 550 B.C., in the time of the Pisistratids.

In the wave of enthusiasm which followed the repulse of the Persians at Marathon in 490 B.C., the Hecatompedon was deliberately demolished to make place for the second temple, a more pretentious structure. This was the "Older Parthenon," designed as a hexastyle Doric temple, of marble from the quarries then recently opened on Mount Pentelicus, and was the first large construction in Pentelic marble. When the Persians, return-

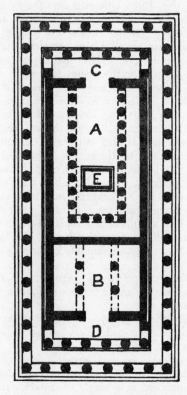

PLAN OF THE PARTHENON
A) cella; B) opisthodomus (or Parthenon);
C) pronaos; D) epinaos (or opisthodomus);
E) site of the statue of Athena

ing in 480 B.C., captured and burned Athens, the Older Parthenon was in scaffolding; construction had proceeded only as far as the limestone platform, the steps, and, to a height

fat, fāte, fär, fāre, errant; net, mē, hėr ardent; pin, pīne; not, nōte, mȯve, nôr,

of from two to four drums each, the columns of the peristyle. In the fire these were badly damaged. Before the battle of Plataea (479 B.C.), the Greek allies had sworn not to rebuild the sanctuaries which had been burned and thrown down by the Persians, but to leave them in perpetuity as memorials of barbarian impiety. In accordance with this, the older Parthenon stood in ruin for 30 years; but in 449 B.C. Pericles annulled the oath, and ordered plans drawn up for the most magnificent temple yet seen. The architects were Ictinus and Callicrates, the sculptor in charge was Phidias. They designed an octastyle Doric temple, of Pentelic marble, with 17 columns on the flanks, measuring 101 by 228 feet on the top of the stylobate. Within the peristyle, two steps up from the stylobate, was the cella, itself divided into two chambers, the cella proper, called the *Hecatompedon,* in which was the cult statue, and a rear room called the *Parthenon,* the chamber of the Virgin (*parthenos,* "virgin"), each approached through a hexastyle portico. The cella had interior supports in the form of small Doric columns in two stories, the Parthenon in the form of four tall, slender, Ionic columns. The sculptured decorations, designed by Phidias and executed under his supervision, the finest architectural sculpture created in the Greek world, consisted of the east and west pediments, a Doric frieze of 92 metopes, and an Ionic frieze in low relief which ran completely around the naos within the peristyle, at the top of the cella wall and above the columns of the vestibules. The east pediment represented the birth of Athena, when Hephaestus split Zeus' aching head open with an ax. The west pediment represented the contest between Athena and Poseidon for chief place in the worship of the Athenians. The 92 metopes of the Doric frieze carried scenes in high relief of the battles of gods and giants on the east front, centaurs and Lapiths on the south, Amazons and Athenians on the west, and the fall of Troy on the north. The superb Ionic frieze, 523 feet in length, represented the Panathenaic procession of officials, youths and maidens, and sacrificial animals, that was the high point of the great festival of Athena held every four years. Phidias himself executed the gold and ivory (chryselephantine) cult

statue of Athena, tinted ivory for the face and throat, arms, and feet, and gold for the clothing, armor, and attributes, 42 feet in height. The staggering expenditure on the Parthenon and its brilliant decorations was severely criticized by those who opposed governmental extravagance in any form, by those who were a little sensitive about the source of the funds, which Athens had blandly diverted to its own purposes from the reserves of the Delian Confederacy, and by those who hoped to profit by discrediting or embarrassing Pericles. Even after the dedication some residue of bitterness found expression in the litigation traditionally so dear to Athenian hearts. Phidias, for instance, was accused of having converted to his personal advantage some of the gold for the cult statue with which he had been entrusted, but refuted the charge by revealing that he had cast the gold in artfully fitted plates which could be dismantled, verified by weighing, and reassembled. Again, he was accused of impiety in that among the figures in the scene of the battle of Marathon, on Athena's shield, he had included recognizable portraits of himself and Pericles. Whatever the validity of the charge, it is known that Phidias left Athens and lived in exile for some years.

When its service to the pagan goddess was completed, the Parthenon was converted into a church of the Theotokos, the Mother of God. In 1204 (or 1208 A.D.) the Frankish Dukes of Athens turned it over to Rome. About 1460, after the Turkish conquest, it became a mosque. In 1687, during a siege of Athens by the Venetians under Morosini, a Venetian cannon ball exploded gunpowder stored in the mosque by the Turks, destroying the cella, the pronaos, 14 columns of the peristyle, and the mosque; afterward the Turks built a smaller mosque amid the wreckage. In 1801–3 Lord Elgin removed a great number of "architectural marbles," and as the Elgin Marbles they are among the chief treasures of the British Museum. These include 18 figures from the pediments, almost half of the frieze, and 15 metopes. Those sculptures which remain in place on the Parthenon have suffered grievously from weathering. Dominating the whole city from its position on the highest eminence of the

Acropolis, of the golden rust color characteristic of weathered Pentelic marble, the Parthenon has survived age, wars, and changing times as a memorial to that surge of intellectual and artistic grandeur which we known as the Golden Age of Pericles. (JJ)

him defeat the enemies of the king of Mysia. Later, against the advice of Atalanta, he was one of the Seven who marched against Thebes under the command of Adrastus. In the attack he was slain by Periclymenus. Before he died, he asked that his head be shorn

PARTHENON
View from the southwest

Parthenopaeus (pär″thē-nō-pē′us). In Greek legend, a son of Atalanta. According to some accounts, he was the son of Melanion (or, as some say, Hippomenes), who had won the race with Atalanta by means of the golden apples provided by Aphrodite. Some say he was a son of Ares. Still others say he was the son of Meleager, who had fallen in love with Atalanta when she joined the Calydonian Boar Hunt, and that she exposed the child when he was born, on Mount Parthenius. A she-bear found him and suckled him until he was found by shepherds and taken to Corythus, their master. At the same time, Telephus, son of Heracles, who had been abandoned by his mother Auge, was found and the two children were brought up together. According to some accounts, Parthenopaeus accompanied Telephus to Mysia when the latter went in search of his mother, and acted as his spokesman, and also helped

and his hair sent back to his mother. His body was one of those reclaimed by Theseus and the Athenians, after the Thebans had refused burial to those who were slain, and was returned to Athens for burial.

Parthenope (pär-then′ō-pē). In Greek mythology, a siren who threw herself into the sea because her singing could not beguile the hero Odysseus. She drowned, and her body was cast up on the shore of Naples, for which reason her name is sometimes given for Naples.

Parthenos (pär′the-nos). Epithet meaning "Virgin," given to several Greek goddesses, as for instance Artemis and Athena. It was also given to Hera in her aspect as a maiden.

Parthia (pär′thi-a). In ancient geography, a country in W Asia, situated E of Media and S of Hyrcania. It was the nucleus of the Parthian Empire.

Parthian Empire (pär′thi-an). Ancient Iranian

fat, fāte, fär, fãre, errant; net, mē, hėr ardent; pin, pīne; not, nōte, möve, nôr,

monarchy, comprising a great part of the territories of the first Persian Empire. It extended at its height to the Euphrates River, Caspian Sea, Indus River, and Indian Ocean. It was established by Arsaces, the first king, who overthrew the rule of the Seleucidae and reckoned 248/7 B.C. as the Year 1 of the Arsacid or Parthian Era, and rose to great power under Mithridates I and II. The Parthians were often at war with Rome. Their empire was overthrown by the new Persian dynasty of the Sassanidae c224 A.D.

Parthians (pär'thi-anz). People of ancient Parthia in Asia. They were skilled horsemen and excelled in fighting on horseback with bows and arrows. The expression "a Parthian shot" means a parting shot or, in modern usage, the last word in an argument. This is in allusion to the custom of the ancient Parthians of shooting at an enemy from horseback with the horse turned away as if in flight.

Parysatis (pa-ris'a-tis). Daughter of Artaxerxes I (Artaxerxes Longimanus), wife of Darius II, and mother of Artaxerxes II (Artaxerxes Mnemon) and Cyrus the Younger. She was active c400 B.C. She was notorious for her crimes, especially those committed in revenge for the failure and death of her son Cyrus, whom she had attempted to aid in usurping the throne.

Pasargadae (pa-sär'ga-dē). One of the tribes that made up the Persian nation. Herodotus says they were the noblest of the tribes and the one from which the royal line of Achaemenidae sprang. According to some accounts, in the last violent battle Cyrus fought against his Median grandfather Astyages, the Pasargadae fought with outstanding valor. Cyrus named the new city he built, the capital of ancient Persia, Pasargadae in their honor. It has been identified in the ancient site conspicuous in the little valley now called Meshhed-Murghab, NE of the ancient Persepolis. Cyrus built here two palaces and founded temples; here he was buried; and his city became a place of pilgrimage and religious instruction for the Persians. Darius afterward moved the capital to Persepolis, but a great treasury remained in Pasargadae which fell into the hands of Alexander the Great when he conquered the Persians in 336 B.C. When Alexander returned from India

he found that the tomb of Cyrus in Pasargadae had been looted. He ordered the perpetrators of this crime found and punished, and ordered the tomb to be restored. The architectural remains of the city, though in ruins, are important.

Pasiphaë (pa-sif'a-ē). In Greek legend, a daughter of Helius and Persa, and the sister of Aeëtes and Circe; like her sister she was a mistress of the black arts. She married Minos, king of Crete, and was the mother of Acacallis, Ariadne, Androgeus, Glaucus, Catreus, and Phaedra, among others. Poseidon had sent a magnificent white bull to Minos, which the latter had promised to sacrifice to the god. But Minos hated to slay the handsome creature and sacrificed another bull in its place. Poseidon punished Minos for this breach of his oath by causing Pasiphaë to fall in love with the bull. Pasiphaë confessed her bizarre passion to Daedalus, the marvelous smith and builder who was living in Crete at that time. He built her a wooden image in the shape of a cow and made it possible for her to enter the structure and consort with the white bull. As a result of this union she produced the monstrous Minotaur, half-man and half-bull. To hide the disgraceful story of his wife's passion Minos asked Daedalus to construct a labyrinth, and in it the Minotaur and, some say, Pasiphaë as well, were hidden. When Minos later learned that Daedalus had helped Pasiphaë to gratify her unnatural lust he locked Daedalus up in the labyrinth also, but Pasiphaë freed him and, some say, helped him to escape from Crete. There was an oracle of Pasiphaë at Thalamae in Laconia, where answers were given in dreams.

Pasiphaë. An epithet of Aphrodite in her aspect as a goddess of the heavens, meaning "Shining on all."

Pasiteles (pa-sit'e-lēz). Greek sculptor, a native of Magna Graecia, of the 1st century B.C. He acquired Roman citizenship (c87 B.C.) when the southern cities were admitted to that privilege. He followed the modern method of elaborating his work in clay, and wrote five books on artistic matters much quoted by Pliny. Pasiteles and his school affected a kind of pre-Phidian style. Many pseudo-archaic works are ascribed to them.

Pasithea (pa-sith'e-a). One of the Graces, children of Zeus and Eurynome. Hera promised her to Hypnos (*Sleep*) if the latter would aid her by putting Zeus to sleep, as part of her plot to prevent Zeus from aiding the Trojans in the Trojan War.

Patara (pat'a̱-ra̱). In ancient geography, a city in Lycia, Asia Minor, situated on the coast. There are remains of a theater dating from the time of Hadrian.

Patavium (pa̱-tā'vi-um). [Modern name, **Padova**; English, **Padua**.] City in NE Italy, situated on the Meduacus Minor River, about 20 miles W of Venetia (Venice). According to legend, it was founded by Antenor, who came to this place when he was spared by the Greeks in the sack of Troy. It became a capital of the Veneti, and by 174 B.C. it was subject to Rome. It was the birthplace of the Roman historian Titus Livius (Livy), 59 B.C.–17 A.D., whose literary style the rival historian Asinius Pollio ridiculed as *Patavinitas* (Patavinity), and of Asconius Pedianus. (JJ)

Paterculus (pa̱-tėr'kū-lus), **Caius Velleius**. Roman soldier and historian, born c19 B.C.; died after 30 A.D. He is the author of an extant epitome of Roman history distinguished by lavish praise for Tiberius.

Paternò (pä-ter-nô'). Town on the island of Sicily, situated on the S slope of Mount Aetna. Nearby is the site of the ancient Hybla or Hybla Major.

Patizeithes (pa-ti-zī'thēz). Median magus who was left in charge of Cambyses' household when the latter went on his campaign against Egypt. Patizeithes plotted a revolt against Cambyses and carried it out by setting his brother Gaumata on the throne under the name of Smerdis. See **Smerdis, False.**

Patmos (pat'mos; Greek pät'môs). [Also: **Patino**; Italian, **Patmo**.] Island of the Dodecanese, situated in the Aegean Sea, about 20 miles SW of Samos. It was colonized first by Dorians, who were later joined by Ionian colonists. In the Roman period the barren volcanic island was frequently used as a place of banishment for political exiles. There is a monastery bearing the name of Saint John the Divine, and a cave pointed out where, according to legend, the apostle saw the visions of the Apocalypse. Area of the island, about 22 square miles.

Patrae (pā'trē). [Modern name, **Patras**.] A city on the N coast of Achaea in the Peloponnesus, at the western end of the Gulf of Corinth. According to tradition, Eumelus first settled in the land and became king over a few subjects in a town called Aroë. Triptolemus visited him and taught him how to cultivate corn. Together, Eumelus and Triptolemus founded a second city, and named it Antheia after the son of Eumelus, who had been killed when he rashly tried to yoke the dragons of Triptolemus' chariot. A third city, Mesatis, was built between the two. Later Patreus, a descendant of Amyclas and Lacedaemon, came with Lacedaemonian followers. He drove out the inhabitants of the cities, built a wall which enclosed Aroë, and named his new city Patrae after himself. Many years before, after the Trojan War, Eurypylus, son of Euaemon, received a chest as his part of the spoils of victory. He was driven mad by the image of Dionysus inside the chest and went to Delphi to inquire concerning his malady. The priestess told him to find a people making a strange sacrifice and to settle there. Ultimately he came to Aroë, where he found the people sacrificing a youth and a maiden to Artemis, to propitiate her for the crime of Comaetho and Melanippus, who had polluted her shrine. Eurypylus understood that this was the strange sacrifice indicated by the priestess and settled in Aroë. The people recognized him as the leader foretold by an oracle and made him their king. Thereafter Eurypylus recovered his sanity and the Patraeans ceased to make human sacrifices to Artemis. The tomb of Eurypylus was in Patrae, and ever after the people of the city sacrificed to him as a hero at the festival of Dionysus. In Patrae there was an oracle of Demeter, where the priestesses gave answers to cure the sick by reading from a mirror lowered into Demeter's well. In the Peloponnesian War Patrae supported Athens. After occupation by Rome Augustus established a Roman colony at Patrae, which had been abandoned for some time. The city was, and still is, an important port for travelers from Italy.

Patrai (pä'trē) or **Patras** (pa̱-tras', pat'ra̱s). See **Patrae.**

Patroclus (pa̱-trō'klus). In Greek legend, a native of Opus in Locris. His father was Menoetius. His mother is variously named as Sthenele, daughter of Acastus; Polymele, daughter of Peleus; Periapis, daughter of Pheres; or Philomele, daughter of Actor. As a youth he had accidentally slain a friend in a childish argument over jackstones, and had fled to the court of his uncle Peleus. There he became the intimate friend and inseparable companion of Achilles. He was a suitor of Helen and had sworn to defend and assist whomever she chose as her husband in the event that any ill came to him as a result of his marriage. Thus, he accompanied Achilles and his Myrmidons to Troy when the Greeks sailed to recapture Helen from Paris. On the way to Troy their ships landed in Mysia and the Myrmidons ravaged the country, under the impression that it was a part of the Troad. The king, Telephus, drove them back to their ships but was in his turn repelled and wounded by Achilles, with the staunch assistance of Patroclus. In the years of the war before

Agamemnon. Patroclus withdrew from the fighting with him. However, they both kept close watch of the battle, and after a furious struggle in which Hector drove the Greeks back to their ships, they saw a chariot racing toward the ships bearing a wounded man. Patroclus was sent to find out who it was. "This for Patroclus was the beginning of evil." He learned that it was Machaon, the surgeon, and that the Greeks had just barely prevented Hector from setting fire to their ships. Nestor pleaded with Patroclus to urge Achilles to come to the aid of his beleaguered friends or, if he refused that, at least to send his Myrmidons under Patroclus' command to their aid. Patroclus started back to Achilles with the message. On the way he met Eurypylus, who had been wounded by Paris, and learned that Ajax, Diomedes, and Odysseus had also been wounded, and that Eurypylus thought nothing could now stop Hector

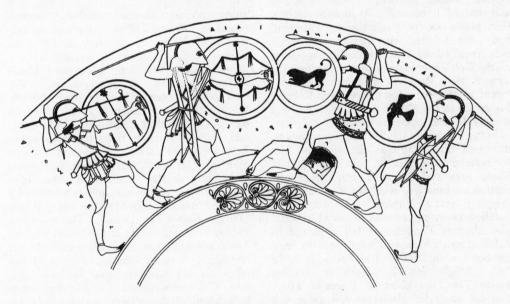

STRUGGLE FOR THE BODY OF PATROCLUS
Red-figured Attic kylix, Oltos, c520–510 B.C. The figures over the fallen Patroclus are, from the left: Diomedes, Ajax, Aeneas, and Hippasus. *Berlin*

the actual siege of Troy Patroclus took part with Achilles in raids and captures of many cities that were allied to Troy. In the tenth year of the war Achilles withdrew his ships and men from the Greek camp and threatened to sail home, because of his anger at

from destroying the Greek host. Patroclus attended to his wound and sped back to Achilles with the news. In spite of his pleas to give up his anger Achilles refused to join the battle, but he did yield to Patroclus' request to borrow his armor and his Myrmidons so that Patroclus could lead them into battle. Achilles helped him into the armor and cautioned him to drive the Greeks away from the ships but not to go onto the plain, lest a victory by Patroclus tarnish the glory of Achilles. Patroclus entered the fray with a furious onslaught. Aided by Zeus, he drove the Trojans back to the plain and, in defiance of Achilles' command, pursued them to the walls of the city. There Apollo came to the Trojans' rescue. Patroclus slew Cebriones, Hector's brother and charioteer, and struggled with Hector over his body. Three times he attacked the walls, each time killing nine Trojans. The fourth time he attacked, Apollo smote him and stunned him, his helmet fell off and his armor was loosened. Euphorbus wounded him with his spear and Hector dealt him the death blow. With his dying breath Patroclus defied Hector, saying it was the gods who had slain him, not Hector. Hector stripped off Achilles' armor and donned it himself. A furious struggle then broke out for possession of Patroclus' body, but Achilles, who had learned of his dear friend's death from Antilochus, appeared on the Greek fortifications and so terrified the Trojans that Menelaus and Meriones, protected by the two Ajaxes, were able to carry his corpse to the Greek camp. Achilles was wild with grief over the death of his comrade, and Briseis, Achilles' captive princess, expressed his epitaph as she mourned him by remembering that he was ever gentle. Thetis preserved Patroclus' body from corruption, and made it whole of its wounds by dripping nectar through his nostrils, as Achilles, mourning, refused to bury the body. The ghost of Patroclus at last appeared to Achilles in a dream and asked him to bury the body so that the soul of Patroclus could rest. Prophesying the death of Achilles before Troy, the ghost of Patroclus asked that his ashes be placed in the same urn with those of Achilles. And so, when Achilles died, it was done.

Patroclus. Uninhabited island off the Cape of Sunium. It was named for Patroclus, an admiral in command of an Egyptian fleet that came to help the Athenians c267–263 B.C. There was an ancient fortification on the island.

Patrous (pa̯-trō′us). An epithet of Zeus, mean-

ing "Paternal." This name was also applied to Apollo. In the Dorian invasion of the Peloponnesus, the sons of Aristomachus (Temenus, Cresphontes, and the twin heirs of their brother Aristodemus), successfully won the region and divided it between them by lot. They set up three altars to Zeus Patrous and cast lots for the division of it between them. After they had cast lots they found signs lying on the altars where they had sacrificed. Temenus drew Argos, and the sign on his altar was a toad. The seer interpreted this to indicate that the followers of Temenus should remain in the city, for the toad loses its strength when it walks. The sons of Aristodemus drew Lacedaemon. On their altar was found a serpent, and the seer told them their people would be terrible in attack. On the altar of Cresphontes, who had won Messenia by a trick, a fox was found, and the seer said his people would be wily.

Paulus (pô′lus), **Lucius Aemilius.** Roman consul in 219 and 216 B.C. He was the colleague of Varro in the Roman defeat at Cannae, 216 B.C., where he was killed.

Paulus, Lucius Aemilius. [Surnamed **Macedonicus**, meaning "the Macedonian."] Roman general, born c229 B.C.; died 160 B.C. He was the son of Lucius Paulus, who took part in the defeat at Cannae (died 216 B.C.), and claimed descent from the philosopher Pythagoras. His sister Aemilia was the wife of Scipio Africanus. His wife Papiria was a daughter of the consul Maso. She bore him two sons, one of whom was adopted by Scipio Africanus and took the name Scipio (Publius Scipio Aemilianus). The other was Fabius Maximus. Aemilius divorced Papiria. There seemed to be no good reason for the divorce, and in explanation a story of another Roman who divorced his wife was told: This man's friends were surprised when they heard of the divorce; was his wife not discreet, was she not beautiful, did she not give him sons? In reply he held out his shoe and asked, "Is this not handsome? Is it not new? But no one of you can tell me where it pinches my foot." Afterward, Aemilius married again and had two more sons.

Aemilius was noted in Rome for his integrity and his courage. In 193 B.C. he was elected aedile over 12 competitors. He was made augur in 192 B.C. and devoted himself to the study of the ancient rituals, which he performed with the most precise regard for the forms. In military matters he was equally exact in observing the established customs and practices. He was sent to Spain (191 B.C.) as praetor and defeated the revolting barbarians, slaying about 30,000 of them and subduing 250 cities. He restored order and left the province (189 B.C.) having refused to enrich himself by as much as a penny through plunder of the province. In 182 B.C. he was elected consul and undertook an expedition against the Ligurians, whom he defeated, though their forces outnumbered his by five to one. Because the Ligurians formed a buffer between the Gauls and the Romans he did not treat them harshly. He seized their ships in which they had been making piratical raids, but restored the captives he had taken. When he returned to Rome he was not made consul again, as he expected to be, and gave himself up to his duties as augur and to the education of his sons, the elder of whom he introduced to the men of affairs in Rome.

The Romans had been successful in their wars on all fronts save that with Perseus, king of Macedonia. He defeated them in several engagements, though he was not considered an especially skillful general. The Romans felt disgraced by the defeats and sought a new commander for the war. Aemilius was urged to run as consul, but declined at first on the grounds of his age, and perhaps out of pique at not being chosen consul again when he returned from his successful Ligurian campaign. But he was at length persuaded to stand for the office and was chosen consul in 168 B.C. for the second time. Now in his sixties, he became commander of the Roman forces in the war against Perseus. It is said that when he went home after being made consul he found his little daughter in tears, and learned she wept for the death of her "little Perseus," a pet dog. Aemilius knew this for a favorable omen. Before he set out to join the army he made a speech to the Romans, in which he announced that the first time he became consul he had sought the office. This time he had become consul because

the Roman people needed a general. Therefore he cherished no feelings of gratitude for the office. On the contrary, if the people had confidence in him they must not attempt to tell him what to do. All he required of them was that they vote the necessary supplies and money to carry on the war, for if they sought to command their commander his campaigns would be as ridiculous and as unsuccessful as those of his predecessors. Such frank speaking greatly impressed the Romans. They voted what he asked for. He joined the Roman army near Mount Olympus in Greece, about which Perseus had set up his camp, and by an encircling movement prepared to attack Perseus at Pydna (168 B.C.). That night the moon changed color many times and finally disappeared. Some say the Romans, according to their custom, tried to call her light back by clashing bronze utensils and by holding up many torches toward the heavens. Others say Aemilius, a well-educated man, knew an eclipse of the moon would take place, and had forewarned his men so that they would not take it as an evil omen. But the Macedonians were terrified, and rumor spread rapidly through their ranks that it portended the eclipse of a king. Aemilius sacrificed 11 heifers to the moon. At daybreak he sacrificed 20 oxen to Hercules without getting favorable omens for the coming battle. When the twenty-first victim was sacrificed the omens were favorable, on condition that the Romans did not initiate the attack. Aemilius vowed hecatombs and games to Hercules if he should be successful. During the day he occupied himself about his camp, waiting until afternoon, when the sun would be in the eyes of the enemy and not blinding his own men. Careful not to defy the omens produced by the sacrificial victims, he did not take the offensive, but tricked the Macedonians into beginning the attack. His strategy was spectacularly successful: 25,000 Macedonians were slain, while he lost only between 80 and 100 of his own men. Perseus was routed, thus ending the Third Macedonian War. Perseus fled to Pella, later sailing to Samothrace where he took refuge in the temple of the Dioscuri with his wife and children. But his enraged Macedonians seized him and themselves gave him into the hands of Aemilius. After the victory at Pydna, Aemilius rested his army, while he traveled about Greece. One of his journeys was to Delphi, where he set up a statue of himself on the pillar Perseus had raised for a statue of himself. He visited Olympia and held games, offered sacrifices, gave feasts, and won the admiration of the Greeks. Of the plunder taken from Perseus, he kept none himself, but sent it all to Rome except for some books he allowed his sons to take from the library of Perseus. After freeing the Macedonian cities and exacting tribute from them for Rome (less than they had paid to their own king), Aemilius marched into Epirus and, on orders from the Roman Senate, allowed his soldiers to plunder it. The sack of Epirus did not satisfy them, for it yielded but little. They thought with envy of the rich treasure that had gone to Rome, and were ready to join in a vote to deny Aemilius a triumph when he returned. However, a veteran, covered with wounds, made a speech in honor of Aemilius, the soldiers changed their minds, and he was voted a triumph. It was celebrated in November, 167 B.C. Three days were required for the procession carrying the captured armor and spoils from the victory of Pydna to pass. Perseus, who had begged to be spared the humiliation of marching in the procession, was scorned by Aemilius for his cowardice. Aemilius pointed out one way in which he could avoid being exhibited as a captive, but Perseus could not bring himself to take his own life at that time. He marched in the procession with his two sons and his daughter, following his own chariot and captured armor and accompanied by many captive Macedonian nobles. At the end of the procession came Aemilius, clad in a purple robe, carrying a spray of laurel, and riding in his war chariot. His triumph was held in the midst of personal disaster. Five days before it was celebrated the elder of the two sons by his second wife died. Three days after the triumph the second son died. Aemilius took this as an evil sent by the gods to balance the good fortune he had met with in war. The Romans continued to reward him. In 164 B.C. he was made censor, a post of great honor because of its power over the

senators and life of the Romans. Four years later, after a brief illness, he died, having enjoyed many honors from the Republic, and leaving to it two sons, one of whom, Scipio the Younger, destroyed Carthage (146 B.C.) and became the most influential Roman of his day.

Pausanias (pô-sā′ni-as). Son of the Spartan king Cleombrotus and nephew of Leonidas. He was a Spartan general. When Leonidas I, the Spartan king, died at Thermopylae, Cleombrotus, his brother, became regent for Pleistarchus, the son of Leonidas; Cleombrotus died in 480 B.C. and Pausanias became regent. At the earnest request of the Athenians, when Mardonius occupied Attica for a second time (479 B.C.), the Spartans sent out Pausanias, in command of a force of Spartans, to the aid of the Athenians. At Plataea he commanded the Spartans and Tegeans, the other Greek forces having withdrawn according to plan, in a battle against vastly superior numbers of Persians under the command of Mardonius. Pausanias and his Spartans and Tegeans won a glorious victory (479 B.C.) Mardonius was killed in the battle and it was suggested to Pausanias that he behead and crucify the body of Mardonius to avenge Leonidas, whose body had been mutilated in this manner by the Persians after the Battle of Thermopylae. Pausanias replied to this suggestion that such acts were more suited to barbarians than to Greeks, and even in barbarians were detestable. Moreover, he considered Leonidas to have been amply avenged by the Persian lives that were taken, not only at Plataea, but in his own battle at Thermopylae. Pausanias ordered the booty of the Persian camp to be gathered. A tenth part of it was dedicated to Apollo at Delphi. Other portions were offered to the gods at Olympia and on the Isthmus. The rest was divided among the soldiers according to their merits. Pausanias himself received ten of every kind of thing found in the Persian camp—women, horses, camels, money, vessels, etc. Herodotus says that when Pausanias came upon the rich war-tent of Mardonius, he commanded the Persian captive cooks and bakers to prepare a banquet in the Persian manner. When he saw the rich couches, covered with gold and silver, tables inlaid with the same

fat, fāte, fär, fãre, errant; net, mē, hėr ardent; pin, pīne; not, nōte, mōve, nôr, precious metals, and the feast that was spread on them, he ordered his own men to prepare a Spartan meal. Then he called the Greek generals to see both meals. He told them he wanted them to see the folly of the barbarians who, when they had such fare as this, had come to rob the Greeks of their poverty. After Plataea Pausanias led his forces against Thebes, because the Thebans had made common cause with the Persians, and demanded the surrender of the Theban chiefs whom he held responsible for the alliance of Thebes with the Persians. The Thebans refused to give these men up and the city was attacked. Thereupon two Theban chiefs, Timagenidas and Attaginus, volunteered to surrender to Pausanias to spare the city further siege. But when agreement was made with Pausanias, Attaginus fled and escaped, and sent his children to Pausanias in his place. Pausanias, however, refused to hold them guilty, for he did not consider the children responsible for their father's offense. But the other men surrendered by the Thebans he took to Corinth and slew. In 478 B.C. he continued the war against Persia, took Cyprus and, when he was besieging Byzantium (which he subsequently took, 477 B.C.), he set up a great bowl as an offering at the entrance to the Euxine Sea. Later, Pausanias seems to have nourished an ambition to become tyrant of Greece, and to this end he seems to have conducted a treasonable correspondence with Xerxes. He was recalled to Sparta for trial but was acquitted of the charges. He then returned to Byzantium and seized the Straits, but was driven out (c475 B.C.) by the Athenians under Cimon. Returning to Sparta, he plotted a revolt of the helots. This was exposed at the last moment and he was forced to flee. He took refuge in the sanctuary of Athena on the Acropolis of Sparta, and was starved to death there by order of the ephors as a punishment for his treason (c466 B.C.).

Pausanias. Spartan king, colleague of Agis I; reigned 445–426 and 408–394 B.C. He brought an end to the civil war in Attica that followed the defeat of Athens in the Peloponnesian War, and helped the Athenians to restore their democracy (403 B.C.). He was known to be an opponent of the Spartan general Lysander. In a Spartan attack on Thebes (395 B.C.) Pausanias marching from the south, was to meet Lysander marching from the north, at Haliartus. Lysander arrived first and was forced into battle by the Haliartians and was killed. By the time Pausanias arrived an Athenian force had come to the aid of the Thebans, and Pausanias felt his position was hopeless. He recovered the body of Lysander and then asked for a burial truce, thereby admitting defeat. Afterward, the Spartans accused him of betraying Lysander and of refusing to fight, and condemned him to death. However, since he did not return to Sparta, the sentence could not be carried out, and he died an exile in Tegea.

Pausanias. Greek geographer and traveler, active in the middle of the 2nd century A.D. He was a native of Lydia, and traveled widely in Greece, Macedonia, Asia, Palestine and Egypt. Ultimately he settled in Rome and wrote his *Periegesis,* or *Description of Greece,* in ten books. The ground covered includes Attica, Megara, Corinth, Philius, Argolis, Aegina and the neighboring islands, Laconia, Messenia, Elis, Olympia, Achaea, Arcadia, Boeotia, Phocis, and Locris. Some of what he describes he actually saw himself, some he read about in books that may have been as much as 300 years old at the time he wrote, and some of his information he gleaned from talking to the natives of the regions he visited. Some critics have rather scorned the work of Pausanias because it is unsystematic, diffuse and even—in a few cases—inaccurate. However, the material he preserved in his work from the ancient writings and his own observations, and the information he picked up, make his work a rich source of information about religious cults and mythology; it provides the most complete clue existing to the monuments of art and architecture of ancient Greece; it contains historical data that might otherwise have been lost; and its topographical notices are a primary source for scholars and archaeologists. Heinrich Schliemann, the great German archaeologist and discoverer of the rich Circle Graves of Mycenae, was led to the site from reading Pausanias.

Pausias (pô′si-as, -shi-). Greek painter of Sicyon, active in the middle of the 4th century B.C. He was a pupil of Pamphilus and a contemporary of Apelles. He made a special study of forseshortening, and was the first to paint ceiling-panels. A famous picture was the *Stephanoplocus* or *Stephanopolis,* painted from Glycera, a flower girl of Sicyon. He painted *Love,* without his bow and arrows and carrying a lyre, in the Tholos (*Round House*) at Epidaurus, and also a picture of *Drunkenness* staring at himself from the bottom of his cup. He was especially attracted by the possibilities of encaustic (the technique of using heated wax to apply colors on stone or wood), and developed it to a high degree of perfection.

Pax (paks). In Roman mythology, the goddess of peace. She was the personification of both civil peace and peace among nations. She was a fairly late addition to the pantheon, almost unknown before Augustus; but her cult is credited with fostering the popularity of the empire.

Paxos (pak'sos, päk-sôs'). [Also: **Paxoi.**] Small island of the Ionian Islands, about eight miles SE of Corfu. It is noted for the production of olive oil. According to a famous story found in Plutarch and mentioned by Rabelais and Milton among others, it was from Paxos that mariners heard the great voice announcing "Pan is dead."

Peace, The. Comedy of Aristophanes, exhibited in 421 B.C. and awarded the second prize. Its aim was to commend the anticipated peace of Nicias.

Peacock. This bird was sacred to Hera. She set the 100 eyes of Argus, the "All-seeing," in the peacock's tail as a reminder of the murder of Argus by Hermes.

Pedaeus (pe-dē'us). Named by Homer (*Iliad*) as an illegitimate son of Antenor, who was raised by Antenor's wife Theano as tenderly as her own sons. He was slain in the Trojan War by Meges.

Pedasians (pē-dā'shanz). A people of Caria, dwelling above Halicarnassus. According to Herodotus, when any evil was about to befall them, the priestess of Athena grew a long beard. The Pedasians alone, of all Caria, resisted subjugation by Persia but were overcome in the end.

Pedasus (pēd'a-sus). A Trojan, named in the *Iliad* as the twin of Aesepus. See **Aesepus.**

Pedasus. A town in Messenia, which Homer described as "vine-clad." It was one of the cities Agamemnon promised to Achilles if he would give up his quarrel and join the Greeks in the battle to defend their ships.

Pedasus. A town in the Troad, near the Satniois River, that was sacked by Achilles.

Pedasus. In Homeric legend (*Iliad*), a horse captured by Achilles in the sack of Thebes in Cilicia, and yoked to his immortal horses. Patroclus borrowed him, along with Achilles' armor, when he led the Myrmidons against Hector. Pedasus, being mortal, was slain by Sarpedon.

Pegae (pē'jē). A spring in Mysia. The nymph of the spring fell in love with Hylas, when he stooped to draw water, and drew him into the spring to dwell with her.

Pegasus (peg'a-sus). In Greek mythology, the winged horse that sprang from the blood of Medusa when she was slain by Perseus. His father was Poseidon. Athena gave him to the Muses and with a stroke of his hoof he caused the poetically inspiring fountain Hippocrene to well forth, on Mount Helicon in Boeotia. Bellerophon, on the advice of a seer, sought Pegasus when he undertook to slay the Chimaera for Iobates, king of Lycia. Some say the seer told Bellerophon to go and sleep in the temple of Athena, if he would find the winged horse. Bellerophon followed his advice, and dreamed that the goddess appeared and spoke to him. When he woke he found a golden bridle at his feet. Carrying this, he found Pegasus drinking at the Pirene spring in Corinth. He threw the bridle over the horse's neck. Thus Pegasus was tamed and willingly carried Bellerophon to hunt the Chimaera. Because he could fly above it on the back of Pegasus, Bellerophon was able to kill the Chimaera. Later Bellerophon sought to fly to the heavens. Zeus sent a gadfly that stung Pegasus. He reared in pain and Bellerophon was hurled to earth. Pegasus went to Olympus and was stabled with the steeds of Zeus. Ultimately his image was placed among the stars as a constellation.

Pegasus. An ancient northern constellation. The figure represents the forward half of a winged horse. The center of the constellation is about 20 degrees north of the equator, and four bright stars in it form a large square.

fat, fāte, fär, fāre, errant; net, mē, hèr ardent; pin, pīne; not, nōte, möve, nôr,

Peiraeus (pē-rē′us) or **Peiraieus.** [Greek, Peiraievs.] See **Piraeus.**

Peirene (pī-rē′nē). See **Pirene.**

Peirithous (pī-rith′ō-us). See **Pirithous.**

Peisenor (pī-sē′nôr). A herald of Ithaca, noted in the *Odyssey* as "skilled in sage counsels."

Peisistratus (pī-sis′tra-tus). See **Pisistratus.**

Peitho (pī′thō). In Greek mythology, a cult title of Aphrodite, and also a separate, lesser deity, attendant on Aphrodite, interpreted as a personification of persuasion, especially to love.

Pelagon (pel′a-gon). Named in the *Iliad* as one of Sarpedon's Lycian comrades in the Trojan War. He helped Sarpedon away from the battle when he was wounded by Tlepolemus, son of Heracles, and it was he who drew out the spear that had been driven into Sarpedon's thigh.

Pelasgi (pe-laz′jī). [Also: **Pelasgians.**] Ancient people believed by the Greeks to have been widely spread over Greece and the coasts and islands of the Aegean Sea and the Mediterranean generally. All accounts of the Pelasgi now available are legendary, and their ethnological position is uncertain. According to mythology, they were sprung from Pelasgus and were the original inhabitants of Argos. The Athenians claimed that Pelasgians were ancient dwellers in Attica, and that they built the earliest fortification wall of the Acropolis, which was called the "Pelasgian wall." Pelasgians were also supposed to have lived in the Troad, south of Mount Ida, and are mentioned in the *Iliad* as allies of Troy in the Trojan War. Archaeological research has indicated that three or four, or more, groups of pre-Hellenic migrants in the Aegean area preceded the first Greeks in Greece, but it is not now possible to identify the Pelasgians with any one of these groups rather than another, nor is there any way of inferring their linguistic affinities. Perhaps the historical Greeks lumped together under this term a number of non-Greek-speaking, "aboriginal" populations in the lands bordering the Aegean. (JJ)

Pelasgia (pe-laz′ji-a). Ancient name of Arcadia, said to have been called this after Pelasgus, the first king of the area.

Pelasgiotis (pe-laz-ji-ō′tis). In ancient geography, a division of C Thessaly, Greece.

Pelasgis (pe-laz′jis). Epithet of Demeter, from her sanctuary at Argos, named for Pelasgus, who is said to have founded the sanctuary.

Pelasgus (pe-laz′gus). In Greek mythology, according to some accounts, the first man, a son of Earth who sprang from the soil of Arcadia and taught those who followed him to build huts and sew tunics of pigskin. He was the father of that Lycaon whose impieties caused Zeus to send the flood. Others say Pelasgus was the son of Zeus and Niobe, and the founder of the Pelasgian race. Still others, that he was the son of Phoroneus, and thus the grandson of the river-god Inachus, and that he was the founder of the Pelasgian division of the Greeks.

Pelegon (pē′le-gon). Named by Homer (*Iliad*) as a son of Periboea and the river-god of the Axius River in Paeonia. He was famed for his powerful spear, and as the father of Asteropaeus.

Peleus (pē′lūs, pē′lē-us). In Greek legend, a king of the Myrmidons in Thessaly. He was a son of Aeacus and Endeïs, and the brother of Telamon and the half-brother of Phocus. He was born on the island of Aegina. Peleus and Telamon were jealous of Phocus because he was their father's favorite and excelled at athletic games. Acting on the advice and encouragement of their mother, they challenged Phocus to an athletic contest in the course of which Phocus was killed. Some say he was struck by a discus and then beheaded with an ax. The brothers were accused of the murder and fled. Peleus went to Phthia, where he was purified by Eurytion, the adopted son of King Actor. He married Polymela, Actor's daughter, and received one-third of the kingdom. But he was again forced to flee for having accidentally killed Eurytion in the Calydonian Hunt, of which they were both participants. He went to Iolcus and was again purified; this time it was Acastus, a son of Pelias, who performed the rite. In Iolcus, Cretheïs, wife of Acastus, falsely accused Peleus of making improper advances to her, and when Polymela learned of the charges she hanged herself. Acastus, who believed his wife's accusations against Peleus, challenged him to a hunting contest. Peleus had a magic sword made by Daedalus, and with it he soon killed many beasts. Acastus claimed that they were his victims but Peleus proved that he had slain the animals by producing their tongues, which he had had the forethought to cut out and keep to one side. During the night Acastus stole and hid Peleus' sword, and left with his followers, but the sword was restored to Peleus by Chiron, the centaur, who also protected him from other centaurs

PELEUS WRESTLING THETIS
Red-figured Attic stamnos, c470 B.C.
Metropolitan Museum of Art

who were minded to murder Peleus. Peleus then departed to Chiron's cave. Here a messenger from Hera came to him to tell him that he was to marry Thetis, the sea-goddess who had scorned the amorous advances of Zeus. Zeus had given up his pursuit of Thetis when he learned that she would bear a son who would be greater than his father, but to punish her for rejecting him he vowed that she would not marry a god but would be yoked to a mortal. Chiron warned Peleus that Thetis would be a reluctant bride, and advised Peleus to seize her as she took her midday nap in a cave on the shores of a small island off Thessaly. Peleus hid behind a myrtle bush near the cave, and watched as the naked goddess rode on the back of a dolphin to the island. When she had entered the cave and fallen asleep he followed Chiron's advice, seized the sleeping goddess and held on to her manfully as she

changed herself into fire, water, a lion, and a serpent in her attempt to escape. At last she yielded. Peleus and Thetis were married near Chiron's cave on Mount Pelion as the gods, seated on their twelve thrones, looked on approvingly, the Muses sang, and the 50 Nereids who accompanied Thetis danced. The gods gave wedding gifts: an ashen spear, golden armor, and a pair of immortal horses, Balius and Xanthus. The only one of the immortals who was not invited to the wedding was Eris, goddess of discord, and this deliberate slight led to the interminable struggle and disaster of the Trojan War, for Eris hurled the Apple of Discord among the wedding guests which led to the Judgment of Paris and the Trojan War. Peleus and Thetis passed through Trachis, where Peleus' herds were attacked by a wolf sent by the mother of Phocus to avenge her son's murder, but Thetis turned the wolf to stone with a glance. They next proceeded to Iolcus, which Peleus captured, and where he killed Acastus and his lying wife, Cretheïs, and hacked her body to pieces. He then led an army of his Myrmidons into the city. Some say the Myrmidons had fled with him from Aegina, others say they sprang from an army of ants supplied by Zeus. Thetis bore seven sons to Peleus. Each of the first six she held in the flames to burn away their mortal parts and sent the immortal remainder to Olympus. Peleus happened to see her as she was performing this rite on their seventh son, Achilles. He screamed in fright. Thetis dropped the child, left Peleus and returned to her home in the sea. (The best known tale is that Thetis plunged the infant Achilles into the Styx and made every part of him invulnerable except his heel.) Peleus never saw her again, although she permitted him to hear her voice from time to time. Peleus accompanied Heracles on his voyage to fetch the girdle of the Amazon queen, and again when Heracles attacked and sacked Troy to punish Laomedon. He also accompanied Jason on the voyage of the *Argo* to Colchis. He was too old to fight at Troy, but he gave his ashen spear, golden armor, and immortal horses to his son Achilles when the latter set off for the war. Peleus outlived his famous son, who was mightier than his father as had been prophesied, and he outlived his grandson, Neoptolemus. According to some accounts, although old and weak he protected and preserved the life of Neoptolemus' bastard son by Andromache, after the Trojan War, when Menelaus and his daughter Hermione would have killed Andromache and her child out of jealousy. In his old age, and after he had been expelled from Iolcus by the sons of Acastus, Thetis spoke to Peleus, advised him to return to the cave where he had first mastered her, and await her there. She promised that she would come and confer immortality on him, and carry him away to live with her under the sea. But, according to some accounts, Peleus, although he went to the island as instructed, became impatient. In quest of news of Neoptolemus, he set out across the sea, was caught and shipwrecked in a great storm, died and was buried on an island near Euboea before Thetis had a chance to make him immortal.

Pelias (pē′li-as). In Greek legend, a son of Tyro and Poseidon, twin-born with Neleus. The twins were exposed on a mountain to die but were rescued. A horse belonging to the rescuer kicked Pelias and bruised his face, whence his name, which means "livid" or "black and blue." When the twins grew up they learned that Tyro was their real mother, and proceeded to avenge her for the mistreatment she had received at the hands of Sidero, her stepmother. They found her before the altar of Hera, where she had gone for sanctuary, and Pelias slew her. For this act in the temple of Hera, Pelias incurred the anger of Hera and later suffered from the goddess' displeasure. It is also said that Pelias withheld sacrifices to Hera, which made her the more resolved to punish him. Tyro married Cretheus, founder and king of Iolcus, and he adopted Pelias and Neleus. After the death of Cretheus, Pelias and Neleus quarreled. Pelias forced Neleus into exile. But when he was warned by an oracle that a descendant of Aeolus would cause his death, Pelias killed all the descendants of Aeolus he could find except his half-brother Aeson, a son of Cretheus and Tyro and the rightful heir to the throne. He kept Aeson as a prisoner. Pelias married Anaxibia, a daughter of Bias, or Phylomache, a daughter of Amphion, and became the father of

Acastus and several daughters. Among the latter was Alcestis, who had many suitors. According to some accounts, Pelias gave her to Admetus of Pherae, because he alone of the suitors met the conditions set up by Pelias: to yoke a lion and a wild boar to his chariot and drive them around a race-course. But others say Jason arranged the marriage of Alcestis and Admetus. A second oracle warned Pelias to beware of a man wearing one sandal. When, therefore, a youth clad in a leopard's skin and wearing but one sandal appeared before him Pelias resolved to destroy him. On learning that the youth was Jason, his nephew, he agreed to resign the throne to him, but said he was troubled by the ghost of Phrixus, which demanded proper burial and the return of the Golden Fleece, now in Colchis, to Hellas. He assured Jason he would give up the throne once these things were accomplished. He did this in the expectation that Jason would never return from the dangerous errand. Jason accepted his proposal and departed with a band of heroes and demigods to fetch the Fleece. After some time had passed Pelias was sure that Jason had perished. He was about to kill Aeson, father of Jason, but allowed him to commit suicide by drinking bull's blood. Aeson's wife thereupon uttered a curse on Pelias and hanged herself. (According to other accounts, aged Aeson was still living when Jason and Medea returned, and was restored to youthful vigor by Medea's magic.) Pelias murdered the young son of Aeson. Jason, however, returned to Iolcus with Medea and the Fleece. Medea tricked the daughters of Pelias into murdering their father. She appeared to Pelias and told him Hecate had empowered her to rejuvenate him. She transformed an old ram into a skipping lamb to demonstrate her powers. Pelias was convinced and allowed himself to be drugged into a deep sleep. His daughters, instructed by Medea, cut his throat, dismembered his body, and cast the pieces into a cauldron. But Medea added no magic herbs to the brew as she had done with the ram, and the daughters of Pelias unwittingly brought about his miserable end.

Pelides (pe̱-lī′de̱z). An epithet meaning "Son of Peleus," applied especially to Achilles, and sometimes to his son Neoptolemus.

---

actọr; up, lūte, pửll; oi, oil; ou, out; ꜰʜ, then; ḑ as d or j, ş as s or sh, ṯ as t or ch, ẓ as z or zh.

Pelike (pel′i-kē). In ancient Greece, a large vase resembling the hydria, but with the curve between the neck and the body less marked, and having only two handles, attached to the neck at or near the rim and extending to the body.

Pelion (pē′li-on). Mountain in Thessaly, N Greece, near the coast, SE of Ossa. It was the legendary home of the centaurs, and known especially as the dwelling place of Chiron, the wise centaur who was tutor to Achilles. It was near his cave on Mount Pelion, that Peleus and the sea-nymph Thetis were married. The two mythical giants known as the Aloidae piled Mount Ossa on Olympus and then Pelion on Ossa in their attempt to reach heaven.

Pella (pel′a). In ancient geography, the capital of Macedonia (c400–167 B.C.). It was the birthplace of Alexander the Great.

Pellegrino (pel-lā-grē′nō), **Monte.** See **Ercta.**

Pellene (pe-lē′nē). In ancient geography, a town in E Achaea, on the borders of Sicyon. The people of the town said it was named for the Titan Pallas, but the Argives claimed it was named for Pellen, a son of Argive Phorbus. The town was one of the 12 towns occupied by the Achaeans after the Ionians left the region. Pellene was on the lower slopes of a hill, and boasted an ivory-and-gold image of Athena in the temple, that was said to have been made by Phidias before he made the famous statue of Athena in the Parthenon. The Pellenians claimed that a deep shrine beneath the pedestal of this statue was filled with damp air, and this dampness preserved the ivory of the image. Behind the temple was a grove of Artemis Savior, and nearby was a sanctuary of Dionysus Lampteros (*Torch-bearer*). The Pellenians held a festival in his honor, during which they took blazing brands to the sanctuary at night, and set bowls of wine throughout the city. The Pellenians also held games in honor of Apollo Theoxenius (*God of Strangers*), whose shrine was in their city. In addition, there were sanctuaries of Artemis and Ilithyia. Pellene fell under the dominion of Alexander the Great, who appointed one of their own sons despot over them. Thereafter the Pellenians would not even mention his name, though he had won two prizes at the Isthmian games and four at the Olym-

pian, because he had permitted the conqueror to set him up as a tyrant over his own countrymen.

Pelopia (pe-lō-pī′a) or **Pelopea** (-pē′a). In Greek legend, a daughter of Thyestes, and the niece of Atreus. She was separated from her father in the quarrels between Thyestes and Atreus, and went to Sicyon where she became a priestess. Thyestes had been advised by the oracle at Delphi to father a son by his own daughter, in order to get revenge on Atreus (who had killed three of Thyestes' sons and served them to Thyestes at a banquet). He found Pelopia sacrificing to Athena, at night, attacked and ravished her. She did not know who her attacker was in the darkness, but she managed to steal his sword, and hid it in the temple of Athena. Thyestes fled. Shortly afterward, Atreus came to Sicyon in search of Thyestes, because the oracle had ordered him to bring Thyestes back from exile. Atreus saw Pelopia, fell in love with her, and asked the king, thinking she was the king's daughter, for her hand in marriage. The king, Thesprotus, was anxious to have Atreus for an ally, and did not tell him that Pelopia was not his own daughter, but gladly gave his consent to the marriage. Pelopia later bore a son, the child of Thyestes, and exposed him on the mountain to die, but he was found by shepherds and brought to Atreus. Atreus thought Pelopia had temporarily taken leave of her senses after giving birth to her son, and brought up the child, Aegisthus, under the impression that it was his own son. A few years later, Aegisthus was ordered by Atreus to kill Thyestes, who had fallen into his hands again. Thyestes escaped the young boy's attack (some say Aegisthus was only seven years old at this time), but recognized the sword in his hand as the one which had been taken from him the night he attacked Pelopia. When he learned from Aegisthus that the sword had been given him by his mother he asked Aegisthus to bring Pelopia to him. She came, and recognized her father joyfully, but on learning that the sword she had stolen from her ravisher was her own father's, and that he was the father of her son, she plunged the infamous sword into her breast and died.

Pelopia. In Greek mythology, the mother by

Ares of that Cycnus who was slain by Heracles at Pagasae.

Pelopidae (pe-lop′i-dē). A name for the descendants of Pelops, applied especially to Atreus, Thyestes, Agamemnon, Menelaus, and Orestes.

Pelopidas (pe-lop′i-das). Theban general, killed at Cynoscephalae, Thessaly, 364 B.C. He was the great and good friend of the Theban patriot Epaminondas, and like him hated the Spartan overlords of the city, but unlike Epaminondas, Pelopidas went to Athens as an exile. Aware that Thebes could not be freed by force, he resolved to free it by guile. With six friends, all disguised as hunters, he crossed Mount Cithaeron and mingled with the Theban peasants who returned within the city walls at nightfall. In this manner the conspirators entered the city safely. Another conspirator hid them in his house. Still another conspirator invited the Spartan polemarchs to his house for a great banquet, at which, as a special lure, he promised the presence of some beautiful women in whom the Spartans were interested. In the course of the banquet, it is said, a letter was delivered to one of the Spartan polemarchs, but he, enjoying himself, said he would tend to business the next day, and put it away unread. The letter advised him that a conspiracy was afoot. The Spartans called for the women who had been promised them. When all the attendants had left the room the women, heavily veiled, were brought in and seated themselves beside the Spartans. They were invited to lift their veils by the amorous Spartans. As they did so the "women" buried daggers in the bodies of their hated Spartan masters, for the women were Pelopidas and his six companions. Following the deaths of the polemarchs, Pelopidas and his friends went to the houses of other Spartan leaders and killed them, and freed the political prisoners. Those Theban patriots who hated the Spartans but had felt the time was not ripe for action, now joined Pelopidas and the revolution was successfully proclaimed. Athenian volunteers who had helped in securing the overthrow of Sparta were afterwards repudiated by Athens. But in this manner Thebes was liberated (379 B.C.). Later, Pelopidas was one of the Theban generals in the army of Epaminondas.

The night before the battle of Leuctra, some say, a vision came to Pelopidas as he slept. Nearby his tent were the tombs of the Leuctrides, daughters of a local hero, Scedasus. Pelopidas dreamed that he saw the Leuctrides crying at their tombs and cursing the Spartans. Scedasus appeared to him and commanded him to sacrifice a maiden with auburn hair to the Leuctrides if he wished to defeat the Spartans in battle. The vision disturbed Pelopidas. Next day he related it to the generals and seers of the army. Some said such a maiden should be sacrificed at once, and cited the sacrifice of Macaria, daughter of Heracles, to bring victory against Eurystheus, and that of Menoeceus, son of Creon, for the defense of Thebes. Others held that such sacrifices would never be demanded by gods. While they were discussing the matter, a filly with a shining red coat broke away from the herd and ran through the camp. One of the soothsayers who was discussing the vision of Pelopidas cried out to him that here was the sacred victim, a maiden sent by the gods to be sacrificed. All agreed to accept the gift of the gods. They wreathed the head of the colt with flowers, led her to the tombs of the Leuctrides, prayed, and sacrificed her. On that same day, the Thebans overcame the Spartans at Leuctra (371 B.C.). Pelopidas brought Thessaly under Theban protection and arranged an alliance with Macedonia, and took hostages, including young Philip, who was to become the ruler of Macedonia. In 368 B.C., when he was on his way home, he stopped at the camp of Alexander of Pherae who, without his knowledge, had become an ally of Athens. Alexander detained him, but he was released through the intervention of Epaminondas in command of a Theban army. In 364 B.C. he started for Thessaly again at the head of an expedition. Before he left there was an eclipse of the sun, an evil omen. At Cynoscephalae (364 B.C.) he defeated the forces of Alexander of Pherae. However, in the moment of victory he happened to spy Alexander himself, and rashly rushed against him. Alexander escaped to his guards and Pelopidas, pursuing recklessly, was killed.

Peloponnesian War (pel″ō-pō-nē′zhan, -shan). War between Athens and its allies on one side and the Peloponnesian confederacy under the lead of Sparta and its allies (Boeotia, Phocis, Megara, and others) on the other. Argos, bound by treaty with Sparta, remained neutral. The war was carried on from 431 to 404 B.C. The Peloponnesian War actually consisted of two wars, the Archidamean War (431–421 B.C.) and the Decelean War (414–404 B.C.) and the uneasy Peace of Nicias between them; the first war is named for Archidamus, then king of Sparta, the second for Decelea, a town in Attica whose seizure by the Spartans signaled the beginning of open warfare once more. Thucydides, in tracing the causes and history of the Peloponnesian War, relates that the Corcyraean colony of Epidamnus, weakened by civil war, appealed to Corcyra for help. Corcyra refused aid. The Epidamnians went to the oracle at Delphi and were instructed to deliver their city to Corinth. The Corinthians agreed to accept and protect Epidamnus, partly because of the oracle, but mostly because they hated the insolent (as they considered them) Corcyraeans. This led to a war between Corinth and Corcyra, in which Corinth suffered defeat. Later Corcyra arranged an alliance with Athens, and when Corinth attacked Corcyra, Athens sent a fleet to the assistance of the Corcyraeans. At about the same time (432 B.C.) revolt broke out in Potidaea, a Corinthian colony, but an Athenian city by forced alliance. The Potidaeans were aided by the Corinthians, while Sparta refused to arbitrate the disputes with Athens as Pericles offered to do. These two outbreaks emphasized the friction between Sparta, of whom Corinth was the chief naval ally, and Athens, and added to the fear of Sparta, a land power, of the growing power of Athens, a sea power. Embassies went back and forth between the two powers. The Spartans demanded that the Athenians drive out the curse of the goddess. This was a reference to the curse laid on the Alcmaeonidae, whose ancestors had impiously slain the followers of Cylon (c632 B.C.) who had been promised safe conduct if they withdrew from the altar in the Acropolis of Athens. The curse was that the Alcmaeonidae were to be exiled from Athens. For a time they were exiles, but they had gradually returned. The Spartans pretended that they were upholding the honor of the gods in their demand but in actuality it was a device to get rid of Pericles, the most powerful man in Athens and a member of the Alcmaeonidae. By submitting this demand on religious grounds they hoped to win allies. The Athenians answered their demand by ordering the Spartans to drive out the curse of Taenarus. This referred to the Spartan slaying of the Spartan regent Pausanias (c466 B.C.). He had taken refuge in the Bronze House (sanctuary of Athena) on the Acropolis at Sparta when he realized that the Spartans were about to seize him for his intrigues against Sparta with the Persian king. The Spartans barricaded him in the temple and starved him to death. It was called the curse of Taenarus because it was there that Pausanias was betrayed by his messenger. In this instance it was the Spartans who had dishonored the gods. All these incidents and demands were pretexts. Basically the Peloponnesian War resulted from the reaching of the saturation point in the alliances of both of the chief Greek powers, Athens and Sparta. Athens had built up, following the Persian Wars at the beginning of the 5th century B.C., a great league of city-states around the Aegean Sea, while Sparta had developed a confederacy of land powers covering the Peloponnesus and part of northern Greece. With her fleet, Athens could shut off the food supply of the Spartans. It was thus the clash of a sea power with a land power; Athenian strategy, determined initially by Pericles, was to avoid land battles and to wait for Sparta's military efforts and Athenian raids to exhaust her; Sparta would try to starve Athens out, besieging her, laying the countryside to waste, and alienating her allies. To say that the struggle was between oligarchic Sparta and her allies on one side and democratic Athens and her allies on the other has more ideological than actual significance; in truth, both ruled absolutely and solely for their own benefit, and both were subject to dissension caused by enemies within who were opposed to their ruling system.

The war began over economic measures taken by Athens against Megara. The Megarians appealed to Sparta, and in the winter of 432–431 B.C. Sparta declared war.

Attica was invaded in the spring of 431, but the inhabitants of the countryside were removed to within the walls of the Athens-Piraeus area (the "long walls" from Athens to the sea), and all that Sparta accomplished was to destroy some crops and farms. In 430–429 plague struck crowded Athens and many died, Pericles among them. Lesbos revolted, 428, but by 427 the revolt had been suppressed by the Athenians. An Athenian fleet on its way to Sicily was driven by a storm into Pylus harbor (Navarino, as it is known in later history); the general Demosthenes seized the city as a base for operations against Sparta. Sparta in turn sent troops to Sphacteria, an island in Pylus bay, and they besieged the Athenians. Cleon, who had replaced Pericles as the popular leader in Athens, was sent to assist Demosthenes, and with the help of Messenian allies, bitter enemies of Sparta, the Spartan force on Sphacteria was captured. This was an almost unbelievable event, since the Spartans had won the reputation throughout Greece of never surrendering, but of fighting on to victory or death. In 422, after indecisive military operations by both sides throughout Greece, both Cleon and Brasidas, the Spartan military leader, were killed. The Peace of Nicias was negotiated in 421, but it was soon broken by both sides. In 418 the Spartans defeated the Athenians and their allies at the battle of Mantinea and restored their control over the Peloponnesus. Except for local fighting, however, the war had practically died out. A war had, meanwhile, been going on in Sicily among the city-states of that island and when Segesta appealed (416) for aid to Athens, a huge expedition was sent out by which the Athenians hoped to establish their hegemony over the island and provide a great outlet for their trade. But, just before the fleet sailed the sacred statues of Hermes throughout Athens were discovered to be mutilated; suspicion fell on Alcibiades, the principal promoter and one of the leaders of the expedition, and he was recalled. He fled to Sparta and the expedition continued under Nicias, whose temporizing led in 413 to the complete defeat of the Athenians, the fleet being wiped out and few of the men returning home. Fighting in Greece broke out once more in 414 and the

Spartans began to make headway, not only in Attica but also in Ionia in Asia Minor, where Abcibiades had made a military agreement with Tissaphernes, the Persian satrap. Alcibiades' purpose apparently was to make it apparent to both sides that the war was pointless. In 411 he convinced a number of Athenians that the alliance between Sparta and Persia could be broken if an oligarchic government, one less repugnant to Persia than the Athenian democracy, could be set up. As a result, in that same year a small group of citizens seized power at Athens. Alcibiades, who had been recalled, now led the Athenians to victories at Cynoscema (411), Abydos (411), and Cyzicus (410), but when the Spartans asked for peace the war party at Athens refused, and once again the government reverted to a more democratic form. During an absence of Alcibiades (407), the Athenian fleet was defeated at Notium by Lysander, who had built a fleet with money received from the Persians; again Alcibiades fled, this time for good. Conon became chief of the Athenian military forces, and was defeated at Lesbos (406). The Athenians rebuilt their fleet and in the same year defeated the Spartans at Arginusae in a great naval battle. The Athenians at home, however, were shocked to learn that the commanders of the fleet had refused to stop their pursuit of the Spartan ships to pick up from the water their own shipwrecked sailors; eight of the commanders were tried and executed, thus removing most of the efficient leaders. What ensued was almost inevitable; at Aegospotami on the Hellespont, the Athenian fleet drawn up to shore was caught by the Spartans and annihilated (405). The supply route from the Euxine Sea was now in Spartan hands; Athenian communication with her allies was cut off. Sparta set up governments in the various cities of the Athenian allies and began a siege of Athens by sea and land. After eight months of negotiation, and the execution of Cleophon, who had persisted in his demands that Athens continue to resist, the Athenians surrendered in 404 B.C. The war resulted in the end of Athenian leadership in Greece. For a time Sparta replaced her, but by 370 B.C. the weakness of Spartan leadership in government brought about the loss of Spartan power and Thebes became the principal city of Greece. Thucydides' history of the Peloponnesian War, down to 411 B.C., is the principal and most accurate source. For the period from 411 B.C., when Thucydides' history breaks off, to the end of the war in 404 B.C., the only connected narrative history is the *Hellenica* of Xenophon, composed in imitation of Thucydides' style but without the latter's awesome authority.

Peloponnesus (pel″ō-po-nē′sus). [Also: **Morea, Peloponnesos, Peloponnese.**] Leaf-shaped peninsula forming the S part of continental Greece. It is practically an island, attached to the mainland only by the narrow rocky Isthmus of Corinth, and separated from it by the Gulf of Corinth and the Saronic Gulf on the north. To the east is the Aegean Sea; to the west the Ionian Sea. It has an area of 8356 square miles, and measures about 160 miles in its greatest length. Sharp high mountains divide the parts of the peninsula one from the other and in ancient times communication was easier by sea than by land. The chief rivers are the Eurotas (or Iri) and the Alpheus. According to legend, when Pelops, son of Tantalus, was driven out of his land in Paphlagonia by barbarians he settled on Mount Sipylus in Lydia. But the Trojan king would not permit him to remain, and he came to the country of Oenomaus, ruler of Pisa and Elis in the Peloponnesus. He won Hippodamia, daughter of Oenomaus, in a chariot race and succeeded to Oenomaus' throne. His kingdom became rich and powerful, and he subjugated the surrounding country which he then renamed *Peloponnesus* (Pelops' island). In ancient times the principal divisions of the Peloponnesus were, in clockwise order, Argolis, Laconia, Messenia, Elis, and Achaea, all of which bordered on the sea. Arcadia, occupying the mountainous center of the peninsula, alone was without an exit to the sea. Of the ancient Pelasgian population of the peninsula, only that of Arcadia, which boasted of its pure race, remained relatively unmixed by successive invasions. The Achaeans and Aeolians moved into Argolis, Laconia, Messenia, and Elis. Danaus and Pelops represented invaders from Egypt and Asia Minor. The so-called Mycenaean civilization that developed in the Pelopon-

nesus, centered about Mycenae, was equalled only by the earlier Minoan civilization of Crete. Under the rule of Agamemnon, grandson of Pelops, Mycenae dominated all of Argolis, most of the Peloponnesus and the islands, and extended its influence to continental Greece. Such was the influence of Agamemnon that when he sailed against Troy to recover Helen, princes from all over Greece rallied to his cause and joined his expedition. In succeeding generations, the Peloponnesus was invaded by the Epeans who came from Aetolia and of whom Augeas was a king, by the Caucones who spread out from Arcadia into Elis, and by Ionians, said to have come from Attica. About 1100 B.C. the Dorian invasion of the Peloponnesus took place. This invasion by people from the north is also called the "return" of the Heraclidae. The basis of the claim of the Heraclidae to the Peloponnesus was that their ancestor Heracles had conquered large parts of it and left it in trust for his descendants. All of the Peloponnesus except Arcadia, which made an agreement with the Heraclidae, fell under Dorian domination. By the 7th century B.C. the Peloponnesus was divided into the city-states of Corinth, Sicyon, Argos, Sparta, Elis, and the 12 Ionian cities of Achaea. Arcadia, divided into independent cities, retained its homogeneity as a race. In the 7th century B.C. Argos was the dominant power. By the next century its power had been eclipsed by that of Sparta. For the next 300 years affairs in the Peloponnesus revolved around the activities of Sparta. After the downfall of Sparta at Leuctra (371 B.C.) the cities and states of the Peloponnesus united in various leagues, against Sparta, against Macedonia, and against the Romans. The Peloponnesus was conquered by the Romans, 146 B.C., and became the Roman province of Achaea.

Pelops (pē′lops). In Greek legend, a son of Tantalus and a grandson of Zeus. His sister was Niobe. Tantalus was on terms of great intimacy with the gods and dined at their table, but he betrayed their friendship by stealing the nectar and ambrosia upon which they fed, and gave it to his mortal friends so that they could enjoy the immortality it conferred. He also, in his pride, invited the gods to dine, and served them his son

Pelops, whom he had cut up and cooked to test whether the gods would recognize human flesh. All the gods except Demeter refused to touch the repast, being quite well aware what had been set before them. But Demeter, mourning for her lost daughter, inadvertently ate a piece of Pelops' left shoulder. Tantalus was horribly punished by the gods for his crimes. They then ordered Hermes to restore Pelops by cooking his flesh in the same cauldron, after which Rhea breathed life into the reformed body, and an ivory shoulder was substituted for the one Demeter had eaten. (Pindar was aghast at this revolting story. He claimed that Poseidon had fallen in love with the beauty of Pelops and had stolen him away. Pindar said the other story was a lie, and a reflection on gods and mortals alike.) Restored, Pelops was so beautiful that Poseidon carried him away to Olympus and fed him on ambrosia. He returned to his father's kingdom in Paphlagonia, but was driven out and went to Elis, where he sued for the hand of Hippodamia, daughter of Oenomaus. He won her, with the aid of winged horses and a golden chariot that could skim across the waves given to him by Poseidon, by defeating her father in a chariot race. Myrtilus, a son of Hermes and a charioteer of Oenomaus, accepted a bribe from Pelops to help Pelops win the race, and he removed a pin from the axle of Oenomaus' chariot and caused the death of Oenomaus. Afterward, Pelops hurled Myrtilus into the sea when he tried to collect his payment. As he fell, Myrtilus laid a curse on the House of Pelops which brought disaster to many of his descendants. The murder of Myrtilus also aroused the wrath of Hermes. Hephaestus purified Pelops for the murder and he built a temple to Hermes to appease that god. He then succeeded to the throne of Oenomaus and, "smiter of horses" as he was termed by Homer, made himself master of the whole region which he renamed Peloponnesus after himself. He was rich and powerful, and envied by all the princes of Greece. A sanctuary of Pelops, containing his bones, was dedicated to him at Olympia by his descendant, Heracles, and annually a black ram, roasted on a fire of white poplar-wood, was offered to him. His chariot, his golden

sword, and the spear-shaped scepter made by Hephaestus, were preserved long after his death in various sanctuaries in Greece, and he was regarded by the Achaeans as their ancestor. The spear-shaped scepter was awarded to the people of Chaeronea who worshiped it as their most important deity, offering victims and a rich variety of food to it daily. Towards the end of the Trojan War, Helenus told the Greeks they must fetch the shoulder of Pelops, among other things, if they expected to defeat the Trojans. Agamemnon accordingly sent envoys to Pisa to secure the ivory shoulder. This ivory shoulder was first revealed to Pelops himself when he mourned the death of his sister Niobe by baring his breast. Incidentally, he was the only one to mourn that arrogant woman. According to Pausanias, the ship carrying the shoulder back to Greece, after the Trojan War, was sunk in a storm. Years later, when a plague was ravaging Elis, a fisherman pulled up the huge bone in his net, and according to instructions from the oracle at Delphi, gave it to envoys from Elis. The envoys returned with it to Elis and the plague was lifted. The fisherman was honored by being made custodian of the sacred bone. Among the many children of Pelops were Atreus, Thyestes, Alcathous, Pittheus, the bastard Chrysippus, who was his favorite and aroused the jealousy of Hippodamia, Copreus the herald, Sciron the bandit, and Astydamia, said to have been the mother of Amphitryon.

Pelops. According to some accounts, one of the twin sons Cassandra bore to Agamemnon. See **Teledamas.**

Pelorus (pe̱-lō′rus). In Greek mythology, one of the armed men who sprang from the earth when Cadmus sowed the dragon's teeth. His name means "Serpent" or "Dragon." See **Sparti.**

Pelusium (pe̱-lō′shi-um). In ancient geography, a city at the NE extremity of the Nile delta, Egypt, SE of modern Port Said, at what was called the Pelusiac mouth of the Nile. It was a frontier fortress of Egypt toward Syria. Herodotus tells of an Egyptian king, Sestos, who was a priest of Hephaestus, who scorned and neglected the warrior class in Egypt, and took from them the rich land that had been granted to them. When, therefore, Sennacherib led a force of Arabians and Assyrians against Egypt, the warriors refused to respond to the call of Sestos for their aid. The king, in despair, entered the temple of Hephaestus and lamented. He fell asleep in the temple and dreamed that the god came to him and told him not to despair, to march against the Assyrians with whatever forces he could muster, and that the god would come to his aid. Sestos called together the traders and artisans and marched with them to Pelusium, relying on the god's help. The two armies encamped opposite each other. During the night an army of field mice attacked the camp of the Assyrians; they devoured the strings of their bows and ate the straps of their shields. Next day great numbers of Assyrians were slain as they had no weapons with which to defend themselves, and the rest fled. According to Herodotus, there was in his time a statue of Sestos holding a mouse in his hand, in the temple of Hephaestus, and bearing an inscription admonishing the beholder to look on him and "learn to reverence the gods." It was at Pelusium that Assurbanipal defeated Tirhaka of Egypt; and it was here that Cambyses, son of Cyrus, defeated the Egyptians under King Psammetichus, the last Egyptian king (525 B.C.), and reduced Egypt to a Persian province.

Pemphredo (pem-frē'dō). One of the Graeae, a daughter of Ceto and Phorcys. See **Graeae.**

Penates (pē-nā'tēz). In ancient Roman religion, the two gods of the store-room, protectors of the food supply and guardians of the general welfare of the household. They were said to have been brought from Samothrace to Troy and from Troy to Italy by Aeneas. They were household gods who presided over families and were worshiped in the interior of every dwelling. They had their own place on every hearth where a fire was kept burning for them. Every household had its Penates, and there were also public Penates of the state, whose seat, originally at Lavinium, was in the temple of Vesta at Rome where they were served by vestal virgins. The Penates were associated with the Lares as household gods, and their names were sometimes used interchangeably. They were also associated with Vesta. Roman priests and other officers made annual offerings to the state Penates.

Peneius (pē-nē'us). See **Peneus.**

Peneleus (pē-nel'e-us). In Homeric legend (*Iliad*), a leader of the Boeotians in the Trojan War. He thrust his spear through the eye-socket of Ilioneus, then cut off his head and raised it aloft on the javelin for all the Trojans to see. This is one of the few instances of brutality for its own sake in the *Iliad*. Later Peneleus slew Lycon, and was then himself wounded by Polydamas.

Penelope (pē-nel'ō-pē). In Greek legend, the daughter of Icarius of Sparta and the naiad Periboea. According to some accounts, at her father's command she was hurled into the sea, but purple ducks bore her up and conveyed her to shore, hence her name, which means "duck." Odysseus was one of her many suitors. He advised Tyndareus, foster father of Helen, how to choose a husband for his daughter without making enemies of Helen's disappointed suitors. In return for his advice, Tyndareus helped Odysseus to win a suitor's foot-race for Penelope in Sparta. Icarius protested when Odysseus set out with his bride for Ithaca, but Penelope signified her desire to go with her husband by drawing her veil over her face, and they proceeded to Ithaca. Telemachus, the son of Penelope and Odysseus, was only an infant when Odysseus left for the Trojan War. The war lasted ten years. Many more years elapsed after it was over and Odysseus did not return. Consequently, he was presumed dead by many in his kingdom and Penelope was besieged by suitors. She was described by Homer as a beautiful woman, with great charm and intelligence, and enormous character. Besides, she was the mistress of rich estates. Over 100 suitors, princes of the kingdom, sought to win her. They plotted to murder Telemachus, just coming to manhood, and seize the throne. Penelope, hoping Odysseus would return, refused to choose a husband from among her suitors. She said she must first finish a shroud she was weaving for her father-in-law, Laertes. Each day she worked at her loom; and each night she secretly unraveled what she had done. This went on for three years before her ruse was discovered. In the meantime, the suitors daily made themselves at home in the palace of Odysseus, eating up his flocks and herds, drinking his wine, seducing his servants, and wasting his substance. At the end of nearly 20 years, Penelope was hard-pressed by the wooers. Telemachus was not strong enough to expel them, and she did not know which way to turn, although Athena visited her frequently in one guise or another to encourage her. When she learned that Telemachus had secretly left for Sparta to seek news of his father and that the suitors planned to ambush and kill him on his return, she hid her fears and boldly chided the wooers for their evil designs. She reminded Antinous, the most insolent of them, that Odysseus had protected his father when he was harassed by enemies. The suitors replied with soothing words and increased their clamor for her decision as to which of them she would take as her husband. Telemachus, aided by Athena, escaped their ambush and returned safely. At the same time Odysseus at last came home. He appeared disguised as a beggar, and so complete was the disguise Athena had given him that no one recognized him. (He did reveal his true identity to Telemachus, and later, to two faithful servants.) Penelope heard that a stranger had come to the palace. She sent for the beggar, who had already observed her demanding bridal gifts from the suitors in the great hall and secretly applauded her prudence in getting what she could from them. She was immediately drawn to the beggar, and questioned him closely. He assured her that Odysseus lived, that he had seen him, and promised his immediate return. Penelope, hopeful but not convinced, ordered a servant to bathe and refresh the beggar. She told him a dream she had had, in which 20 geese, feeding in the yard, were attacked and destroyed by an eagle. The beggar said the geese represented the suitors, and the eagle represented Odysseus, who would come home and destroy them. In a state of sorrow and great uneasiness, Penelope told him she was being compelled to choose from among the suitors, and that she had decided to accept the one who could string her husband's great bow and shoot an arrow through the eye holes of 12 axes set up in a row, as her husband could do. The beggar urged her to carry out her plan at once, and the

next day Penelope announced the contest. None of the suitors could even bend the bow to string it. Odysseus seized it and, as the suitors reviled him for his arrogance, Penelope left the hall. He strung the bow easily and turning on the suitors killed every one of them, aided by Athena, Telemachus, and his two faithful servants, Eumaeus and Philoetius. Euryclea brought the news that Odysseus had returned and destroyed the suitors, but Penelope was dubious. Odysseus had been gone so long, and she had grieved so much and had so many troubles, that her hope of good fortune was nearly killed. But Odysseus was not worried, and calmed his son, who was rebuking Penelope for her coldness. He told Telemachus there were certain signs, known only to the two of them, by which they would know each other. To test him, Penelope gave an order to have his bed moved. Odysseus was exasperated. No one could move his bed, he said, because he himself had carved it from a living olive tree that grew through the palace. Thus he proved that he was not an impostor and Penelope welcomed him warmly, apologizing for her previous coolness and doubts. Penelope is regarded as the model of the chaste and faithful wife, who bore her sufferings during the absence of her husband with great nobility and fortitude. She is pictured as a tender mother and a paragon of the domestic virtues. According to later accounts, Odysseus left her again to appease Poseidon, and Penelope ruled Ithaca in his place. Odysseus was mistakenly killed by his son Telegonus, the child of Circe, and Penelope then married Telegonus. Other accounts say that Penelope was not faithful to Odysseus, that she became the mother of Pan by Hermes, or as the result of consorting with all her suitors; as Pan was a very ancient god, long before the time of Penelope, these stories are obviously later embroideries.

Peneus (pē-nē′us). In Greek mythology, the river-god of the Peneus, a great river of Thessaly. He was the son of Tethys and Oceanus. By Creusa, a naiad, he was the father of Hypseus, king of the Lapiths. He was also the father of Daphne, whose plea for help as she fled from the embraces of Apollo he answered by transforming her into a laurel tree. He was the grandfather (some say, the father) of Cyrene, mother of Aristaeus.

Peneus. [Also: **Peneius.**] River in the Peloponnesus, Greece, sometimes also called the Gastuni. It drains into the Ionian Sèa.

Peneus. [Also: **Peneius.**] Principal river in Thessaly, Greece, sometimes also called the Salembria. It traverses the Vale of Tempe and flows into the Gulf of Salonika about 26 miles NE of Larissa.

Pentapolis (pen-tap′ō-lis). State consisting of five cities, or a group of five cities; the term was used in ancient geography in speaking of a variety of groups: 1) In Cyrenaica, Africa, a district comprising Cyrene, Apollonia, Barca, Arsinoë (near what is now Bengasi), and Berenice (or Hesperides; modern Bengasi), with their neighboring territories. 2) In Palestine, five cities including Sodom, Gomorrah, Admah, Zeboim, and one other. 3) Five cities of the Philistines: Ashkelon, Gaza, Gath, Ekron, and Ashdod. 4) Five Dorian cities in Asia Minor: Cnidus, Cos, Lindus, Camirus (on the island of Rhodes), and Ialysus. 5) Five cities in Italy: Rimini, Ancona, Fano, Pesaro, and Sinigaglia, with part of the exarchate of Ravenna; this, also called Pentapolis Maritima, was later included in the States of the Church (Papal States).

Pentelicus (pen-tel′i-kus). [Also: **Brilessus, Mendeli.**] Mountain in Attica, Greece, about 12 miles NE of Athens; noted especially for a variety of white marble resembling Parian, but denser and finer-grained, apparently inexhaustible quarries of which have from antiquity been worked in this mountain. The Parthenon, the Propylaea, and other Athenian monuments are built of it, and from it are carved the famous sculptures known as the Elgin Marbles. Elevation, about 3638 feet.

Penthesilea (pen″the-si-lē′a̱). In Greek legend, an Amazon queen. She left her home in Thermodon, fleeing the reproaches which followed the accidental killing of her sister Hippolyte, and came to the aid of the Trojans in the last year of the war, after Hector had been killed. Her arrival put new hope into the Trojans, and the flashing beauty which glowed in her face as she vowed to slay Achilles convinced them that she would do even as she said. Only Andromache, who had lost her husband to Achilles' spear, questioned the wisdom of such a boast. Clad in armor given her by Ares, Penthesilea led her

12 Amazon princesses into battle, but as Priam prayed for her success, an eagle clutching a dove in its talons flew screaming over his head; it was a gloomy omen. Penthesilea slashed about her mightily and the Greeks fled in panic. Achilles, mourning for Patroclus, at last heard the din of the fray and hurriedly joined the struggle. Penthesilea, whose path to death was strewn with the glory of killing many Greeks, leaped like a leopard to meet him. But her hour of glory was over. Her lance splintered on Achilles' magic armor. He wounded her in the breast with his sword, and as she debated whether to ask for mercy he impaled her and her horse with his spear. When she fell he gloated over her but when he removed her helmet and saw the wonder of her beauty, "like a child of Zeus sleeping," he fell wildly in love with her and was filled with remorse. Ares was so enraged by the death of his daughter that he would have killed Achilles, but was prevented from doing so by Zeus. Thersites mocked Achilles, who remained sorrowfully at Penthesilea's side, and roused the hero's wrath. Achilles dashed him to the ground. He permitted Agamemnon and Menelaus to restore Penthesilea's body to Priam and she was given funeral honors as a beloved daughter by the Trojans. She, and the Amazon princesses, were buried beside the bones of Laomedon.

Pentheus (pen′thūs). In Greek legend, a son of Agave and Echion and a grandson of Cadmus. He succeeded his grandfather as king of Thebes. When Dionysus arrived in Thebes and invited the Thebans to join in his revels Pentheus, who disapproved the extravagances of the new religion, forbade his people to take part. He seized and imprisoned the maenads who had come with Dionysus from Asia. However, the fetters which bound them dropped from their limbs, the doors of prisons opened of their own accord, and the prisoners were freed. Pentheus resolved to capture and imprison Dionysus himself, against the advice of Cadmus. The latter warned him not to despise the gods or resist their will. But Pentheus scorned the claim that Dionysus was a god. And he mocked the prophecy of the seer Tiresias that he would be torn limb from limb if he denied the divinity of the god. Dionysus al-

fat, fāte, fär, fãre, erra̱nt; net, mē, hėr arde̱nt; pin, pīne; not, nōte, möve, nôr, lowed himself to be taken before Pentheus, and tried to persuade him to accept the new god. As Pentheus refused, and added his doubting comments on the divinity of Dionysus, the god resolved to punish him. He inspired Pentheus with madness, and under the pretext of sending him to spy on the revels of the women on Mount Cithaeron, he induced him to disguise himself as a woman. Pentheus then went to the mountain and climbed a tree from which he could view the revels. The women, among them his mother Agave, spied him in the tree. Frenzied with religious ecstasy, they mistook him for a wild beast. They shook the tree and finally tore it up by the roots. They then set upon Pentheus and, with Agave as leader, tore him limb from limb. Agave, still under a spell of madness, bore his head proudly back to the palace and exhibited it as the head of a young lion which she had overcome. The fate of Pentheus is often cited as an example, in ancient writing, of the swift fate which overtakes those who question, defy, or resist the gods.

Peparethos (pep-a-rē′thos). [Modern name, **Skopelos.**] Island in the Aegean Sea, about 16 miles from Euboea, and SE of Thessaly. It was famous in ancient times for its wines. According to legend, the island was part of the realm of Rhadamanthys of Crete, brother of King Minos, and was bequeathed by him to Staphylus, son of Ariadne and Dionysus, god of wine.

Peplus or **Peplum** (pep′lus, -um). A richly ornamented, shaw-like upper garment worn by women. It was thrown over one arm and then wrapped around the body in various ways. It was frequently ascribed to female divinities, particularly to Athena, for whose statue in the temple of Athena a ceremonial peplus was woven every year by the highborn maidens attached to the person of the priestess of Athena, and presented at the Panathenaic festival.

Peraea (pē-rē′a). In ancient geography, a maritime district on the coast of Caria, Asia Minor, opposite Rhodes.

Perdiccas I (pėr-dik′as). King of Macedonia, the legendary founder of the Macedonian kingdom, active c650 B.C. Herodotus tells the following story concerning him: Perdiccas, a descendant of Temenus, the Heraclid who won Argos as his share of the Peloponnesus, fled from Argos with his brothers, Gauanes and Aeropus. They went first to Illyria, and then to Macedonia. Arrived in Macedonia, the three brothers hired themselves out as laborers to the king; one tended the horses, another the cows, and Perdiccas, the youngest, looked after the young stock. At this time even the kings were poor, and the king's wife prepared the meals. She noticed that each time she baked bread the loaf for Perdiccas swelled to twice its normal size. She pointed this phenomenon out to the king, who recognized it as an omen but did not understand what it meant. In fear he ordered the three brothers before him and commanded them to leave his kingdom. They agreed to go but first demanded to be paid their wages. At this the king was infuriated. The sun, shining down the chimney of the room in which they were standing, made a patch of sunshine on the floor. Pointing to this the king said, "There are the wages you deserve; take them." The two older brothers were stunned at this injustice, but Perdiccas took a knife and made a mark around the patch of sunlight and said he accepted the payment. Then he took the light of the sun on his breast three times, and the brothers departed. When the king learned of this last gesture, and was warned that it must have some meaning, he sent horsemen after the brothers, to slay them. But they had crossed a river, one revered in Argos, and when the horsemen came to the river its waters rose and swelled so that the horsemen dared not cross over and thus the brothers escaped. They went to Mount Bermius, which is so cold that no one can ascend it. Some say this mountain is near the wonderful rose gardens of Midas. From this mountain Perdiccas and his brothers gradually conquered all of Macedonia, and Perdiccas became king.

Perdiccas II. King of Macedon, c450–413 B.C. He was at one time an ally of Athens, but became an adversary and stirred up a revolt of the cities of Chalcidice against Athens (433–432 B.C.). He persuaded the inhabitants of the Chalcidian cities on the coast to abandon them and retire to the strong city of Olynthus to oppose Athens. It was largely owing to the maneuvering of Perdiccas that the Chalcidians invíted the Spartan general Brasidas into the region. Perdiccas helped to defray the expenses of the Spartan army, and Mende, Acanthus, and Scione were won over to Sparta. Shortly afterward Perdiccas again changed sides. He abandoned Brasidas in a perilous position and helped Athens to prevent reinforcements from coming to his aid.

Perdiccas III. King of Macedon (364–359 B.C.). He was a son of Amyntas and a brother of Philip II of Macedon. With the aid of an Athenian fleet under Iphicrates, various pretenders to the Macedonian throne were crushed and Perdiccas secured it under the regency of Ptolemy Alorus. He assassinated Ptolemy, who had killed his brother Alexander and had married Eurydice, the mother of Alexander, Perdiccas, and Philip. He then threw off the influence of Thebes and allied himself to Athens. Perdiccas was killed, 359 B.C., in battle against the Illyrians.

Perdiccas. One of the generals of Alexander the Great; assassinated in Egypt, 321 B.C. He was the son of Orontes, an independent prince of Macedonia. Before setting out to conquer Asia Alexander impoverished himself by giving away his estates, farms, and revenues to his friends so that they would have enough money and provisions to follow him in comfort. Perdiccas asked him what he had kept for himself. "My hopes," Alexander is said to have replied. Perdiccas then announced that Alexander's soldiers would be the partners in his hopes, and refused to accept the estate Alexander offered to him. After the death of Alexander (323 B.C.) Perdiccas became regent for Alexander's son who was subsequently born to Roxana. He wished to keep Alexander's empire intact, although he allied himself to Ptolemy, who wished to break it up, against Antipater and Antigonus. He set out to subdue Asia Minor and conquered Cappadocia, 322 B.C. Antigonus had refused to help him in the conquest of Asia Minor, and when Perdiccas set out against him he fled to Antipater and Craterus and asked their aid on the ground that Perdiccas intended to seize the throne. Ptolemy abandoned Perdiccas and joined them. Perdiccas moved to attack the allies but was unsuccessful in an attempt to cross the Nile at Pelusium and was defeated. His soldiers mutinied and murdered him.

Perdix (pėr'diks). In Greek mythology, the sister of Daedalus and the mother of Talos, who was also sometimes called Perdix. When Daedalus killed Talos, jealous because he rivaled him as a smith, Perdix hanged herself and was changed into a partridge. The name "Perdix" means partridge. She was also known as Polycaste (q.v.).

Pereus (pėr'ūs). In Greek legend, a son of Elatus and Laodice, daughter of Cinyras. His daughter Neaera married her cousin Aleus and became the mother of Auge and several sons.

Perga (pėr'ga). [Also: **Perge**.] In ancient geography, a city in Pamphylia, Asia Minor, long noted for the worship of Artemis. A Roman theater here is one of the finest surviving.

Pergamos (pėr'ga-mos). [Also: **Pergamum**.] Name given in the *Iliad* to the citadel or walls of Troy. Also, the Trojan citadel of Helenus in Epirus, which was made to resemble that of Troy.

Pergamum (pėr'ga-mum). [Also: **Pergamus**; modern name, **Bergama**.] The word appears to mean "citadel" or "stronghold." In ancient geography, a city in Mysia, Asia Minor, about 50 miles N of Smyrna. The city was raised to importance by the famous victory of Attalus I over the Gauls in the latter half of the 3rd century B.C. Attalus I celebrated this victory by dedicating a series of bronze statues on the acropolis of Pergamum, and later a second series at Athens. Of some of these statues marble copies survive: *The Dying Gaul* in the Capitoline Museum, Rome; the *Ludovisi Gaul*, and the head of a *Dying Asiatic*, in the National Museum (Museo delle Terme), Rome; another *Dying Gaul* and *Dying Asiatic*, and a *Dead Amazon*, in the National Museum, Naples; and others elsewhere. To the son of Attalus, Eumenes II, are due the great extension of the city as well as its architectural adornment, and during his reign occurred the remarkable development of Pergamene sculpture, on lines much more modern in spirit than the older Greek art. The same king founded a famous library here. His chief buildings were placed on a succession of terraces on the summit of the acropolis, which rises 900 feet above the plain, and on the other lower terraces immediately outside the powerful acropolis walls. The city remained prosperous under the Romans, and under the empire many fine buildings were erected on the acropolis, and beside the river below. In 1878 the Prussian government sent to the site an exploring expedition under Alexander Conze and Karl Humann. Their investigations were continued for several years, and to them are due the rediscovery of Pergamene art and the mass of information regarding later Greek architecture which together form one of the most remarkable archaeological acquisitions of that century. There are also a Greek theater, a Roman amphitheater, and remains of several temples. An Ionic temple of the finest Greek design is on the slope of the acropolis; the cella with its ornamented doorway remains unusually perfect. The temple of Athena Polias, a Doric peripteros of six by ten columns, of late Greek date, measuring 42½ by 72 feet, occupied a terrace surrounded on two or three sides by a handsome stoa of two stories, Doric below and Ionic above, with a balustrade sculptured with warlike trophies in the second story. The Great Altar of Zeus, with its high-relief sculptures of the *Battle of Gods and Giants,* is one of the landmarks of Hellenistic art. The continuous frieze is seven feet high and 400 feet long. The temple of Trajan, occupying a large terrace toward the summit of the acropolis, was a Corinthian peripteros of white marble.

Pergamum, Kingdom of. Ancient Greek kingdom in Asia Minor. It rose to prominence under Attalus I in the 3rd century B.C. Attalus III died in 133 B.C., and bequeathed the kingdom to Rome. It was made a Roman province under the name of Asia. See **Attalus I, II, III; Eumenes II; Pergamum.**

Pergamus (pèr′ga-mus). According to Greek tradition, a son of Neoptolemus and Andromache. After the death of Neoptolemus Andromache married Helenus and went with him to the new city he founded. When he died she went to Asia, according to some accounts, and took Pergamus with her. There he conquered the king of Teuthrania, in Asia Minor, and won the city, which he renamed Pergamum, after himself.

Perialla (per-i-al′a). A priestess of Delphi who was bribed by Cleomenes, king of Sparta, to say that Demaratus was not the true son of Ariston and was therefore not rightfully a king of Sparta. The fact that she had taken a bribe was later discovered and she was forced out of her office.

Periander (per-i-an′dèr). Tyrant of Corinth (c625–585 B.C.). He was a son of Cypselus, whom he succeeded on the throne of Corinth. At first he ruled mildly, but became ever more harsh as time passed. According to Herodotus, he sent a messenger to Thrasybulus, tyrant of Miletus, to inquire how best to secure his government. Thrasybulus took the messenger to a field of wheat. Without saying a word Thrasybulus walked through the field, knocking off and throwing away the ears of wheat that grew the highest. He then, still without replying to the question Periander's messenger had asked him, sent the messenger back to Corinth. Periander, on hearing of this performance from his messenger, understood that Thrasybulus was advising him to destroy all the leading citizens. He immediately set about to follow this advice, and went at it with great energy, slaying the leading citizens. One day he stripped the clothes off all the women of Corinth whom he had ordered to go to the temple of Hera, because a message from the Thesprotian oracle said that his wife Melissa, whom he had slain, was cold. She sent word that the clothes buried with her did not keep her warm because they had not been burned. He caused the clothes he now stripped from the Corinthian women to be burned in a pit. It was during Periander's reign, according to Herodotus, that Arion, the musician, was set upon by the crew of the ship in which he was returning to Corinth, and was compelled to cast himself into the sea. A dolphin took him on its back and bore him to Corinth. Periander disbelieved the story Arion had to tell him when he arrived in Corinth. When the ship on which Arion had set sail from Italy arrived Periander questioned the crew concerning Arion. They assured him that Arion was safe in Italy, enjoying great prosperity. Periander thereupon produced Arion, gave them the lie, and put them to death. By his wife Melissa Periander had two sons. When they were 17 and 18 years old respectively they were entertained by Procles, their mother's father. He treated them with great kindness and interest, and one day asked them if they now knew who had caused the death of their mother. The older boy, a dull youth, paid no attention to the question and later forgot that it had even been asked. Lycophron, the younger son, realized that it was his father who had slain his mother. When he returned to Corinth he refused to have anything to do with his father, and was cast out by him. Ultimately he found refuge in Corcyra. As Periander advanced in years he wished for the return of Lycophron. He realized that his older son was doltish and wished Lycophron to succeed him on the throne. Lycophron was at last persuaded to return when Periander agreed that he would withdraw from Corinth if Lycophron would return, but before Lycophron could depart the Corcyreans, angry at Periander because he had abducted 300 boys from the best families and sent them to Lydia to become eunuchs, seized Lycophron and put him to death. Thus an oracle, pronounced before the birth of Cypselus, father of Periander, was fulfilled. It was to the effect that Cypselus and his sons—but not his grandsons—would rule Corinth. Despite almost universal agreement on the despotism of Periander, he appears to have acted for the good of Corinth, establishing colonies to the north, promoting trade, extending Corinthian influence, and developing a program of public works. He is usually counted among the Seven Wise Men of Greece.

Periapis (per-i-ā′pis) or **Periopis** (-ō′pis). A daughter of Pheres. According to some accounts, she was the mother of Patroclus.

Periboea (per-i-bē′a). In Greek legend, a daughter of Alcathous, king of Megara, and granddaughter of Pelops. She was Telamon's second wife, and the mother of Telamonian (or Great) Ajax.

Periboea. In Greek legend, the wife of Polybus, king of Corinth. Oedipus, exposed as an infant, was found by shepherds and brought to Polybus. He and Periboea, being childless, took him and brought him up, allowing him to think he was their own son. According to another account, Periboea found Oedipus in a chest that floated ashore and pretended to all, except her husband, that she had borne the child herself.

Periboea. In Greek mythology, a daughter of Hipponous of Olenus, who claimed she was with child by Ares and was sent by her father to Oeneus in Calydon to be destroyed. Instead Oeneus, having lost his wife and his son Meleager, married her and by her became the father of Tydeus.

Periboea. Named by Homer (*Iliad*) as a daughter of Acessamenus, a king in Thrace. She was the mother, by the river-god of the Axius River, of Pelegon.

Peribolus (pe-rib′ō-lus). In Greek antiquity, a consecrated court or inclosure, generally surrounded by a wall, and often containing a temple, statues, etc.

Periclean (per-i-klē′an) **Architecture.** A classification under which are listed a number of marble temples and other buildings erected in Attica during the intellectual and aesthetic hegemony of Pericles. The period of Periclean architecture began with the eclipse of Cimon and Ephialtes in 461 B.C. and survived the death of Pericles (429 B.C.). At Pericles' instigation and under his close supervision, Athens embarked on a broad program of civic embellishment. A partial list of Periclean buildings, with their locations, style, architects, and approximate dates, follows: Temple of Hephaestus, formerly called the Theseum (Athens; Doric; the Theseum architect (q.v.); c449–c444B.C.); Temple on the Ilissus (Athens; Ionic; Callicrates; c449 B.C.); Hall of the Mysteries (Eleusis; Doric; Ictinus and others; c450 B.C.); Parthenon (Athens; Doric; Ictinus and Callicrates; begun 447 B.C., dedicated 438 B.C.); Odeum of Pericles (Athens; architect unknown; after 450 B.C.?); Temple of Poseidon (Sunium; Doric; the Theseum architect; c444–c440 B.C.); Temple of Ares (Athens; Doric; the Theseum architect; c440–c436 B.C.); Propylaea (Athens; Doric; Mnesicles; c437–c432 B.C.); Temple of Nemesis (Rhamnus; Doric; the Theseum architect; c436–c432 B.C.). Buildings begun after Pericles' death continued the traditions he established: Temple of Athena Nike (Athens; Ionic; architect unknown, possibly Mnesicles; begun 421, finished 405 B.C.); Stoa of Zeus (Athens; Doric; architect unknown; last quarter of the 5th century B.C.). To this list may properly be added temples outside of Attica, by architects in the Periclean tradition: Temple of Apollo (Bassae; Doric; Ictinus; c450–c425 B.C.); Temple of

Apollo (Delos; Doric; architect unknown; c425 B.C.). (JJ)

Pericles (per'i-klēz). Athenian statesman, general, and orator, born probably c495 B.C.; died 429 B.C., of the plague, at Athens. He was a member of a powerful and influential family of Athens, of the tribe of Acamanthis. His father Xanthippus fought at the battle of Mycale (479 B.C.) and was prominent politically. His mother Agariste, a member of the Alcmaeonidae, and a niece of Clisthenes, dreamed a few days before he was born that she had given birth to a lion. He received an excellent education. He studied music and politics with Damon, heard the lectures of the Eleatic philosopher Zeno, and was chiefly instructed and strongly influenced by Anaxagoras of Clazomenae, whose rationalistic philosophy and scientific approach freed his pupil and friend to a large extent from the superstitions of his age. As an example of the methods of Anaxagoras, it was said that a ram's head, from which a single horn grew, was brought to Pericles. Soothsayers said this meant that the two factions of Athens would unite under Pericles. Anaxagoras took the specimen, dissected it, and showed that the single horn was developed owing to physical causes. In the event, both Anaxagoras and the soothsayers were honored: Anaxagoras for his science; the soothsayers because Pericles did in fact become the head of a united Athens.

As a member of a powerful family and as a leader, Pericles was not immune to personal attacks. His head was long and pointed and the comic poets gleefully spoke of him as "Onion Head." To cover up the malformation of his head, statues and pictures of Pericles always portrayed him helmeted. His critics said he was vain, proud, and supercilious. However, he was a man of great self-control and patience, and pursued his course. This was, at first, to stay out of public life, for he feared that his many advantages—good looks, wealth, oratorical gifts, and powerful connections, might draw too much envy and lead to his ostracism. (Ostracism was a means to secure the exile of any man who might be a potential source of unrest, disorder, or danger to the state; it was not necessary for a man to have committed a crime, civic or otherwise, to be ostracized.)

After the disappearance of Aristides, Themistocles, and Cimon from public life, Pericles became prominent. His policy was to win the support and respect of the masses. This he did with money and by weakening the authority of the Areopagus, whose members came from the richest classes of the state. At the same time, he instituted democratic reforms. He reorganized state office-holding so that henceforth the office-holders were paid, thus making it possible for all citizens to accept office, and even to seek it. His personal life was simple, with limited social connections, and he made it a point not to make many public appearances or speeches. He was a speaker of such eloquence that he was called "Olympian," but he wisely realized that his eloquence would lose its golden lustre if people heard it too frequently. His chief rival at first was Cimon, whom he caused to be ostracized (c459 B.C.), but who was recalled later. After the death of Cimon, Thucydides emerged as a rival. Pericles wooed the masses with diversions, and sent out colonies—to the Chersonese, Naxos, and Sybaris, which had been destroyed three times and was now rebuilt as Thurii. Through these colonies he siphoned off some of the excess population of Athens, and at the same time strengthened the outposts of the empire. He sent envoys throughout the Greek world, calling for the fulfillment of the sacrifices that had been promised during the Persian War and for the rebuilding of the temples that the barbarians had destroyed. However, owing to Spartan resistance to it, this Pan-Hellenic project, of which Athens would have been the leader, failed. He declared that the rebuilding of the temples was a sacred duty, in gratitude for the help the gods gave the Greeks in the Persian War. To fulfill it, Pericles set about beautifying the city. His critics claimed he used the money of the Delian League for this purpose. The funds, contributed by the allies, had been kept in the Treasury at Delos. Pericles transferred the funds to Athens (454 B.C.) and justified the transfer on the grounds that Athens must fulfill her sacred duty to the gods, that Athens had earned it by keeping the Persians at bay during and after the Persian Wars as she had undertaken to do, and on the ground that it provided employment at home. He made Phidias superintendent of all public building. Under his charge Periclean architecture was created; the Parthenon was built, a temple of Initiation at Eleusis was erected, the long walls between Athens and Piraeus were finished, a temple of Athena Nike was built on the southwestern side of the Acropolis, a temple of Hephaestus rose on the Hill of Colonus, and one of Poseidon was built at Sunium. The temples were adorned within and without by magnificent sculptured groups, as the pediments of the Parthenon, and images of the gods, notably the statue of Athena in the Parthenon, by Phidias. During the construction of the Odeum a workman was injured. Pericles cured him, thanks to the instructions the goddess Athena gave him in a dream it is said, and in honor of this cure he caused a golden statue of the goddess, made by Phidias, to be placed near the altar on the Acropolis.

With the ostracism of his opponent Thucydides (441 B.C.), Pericles became sole master of Athens. From then on, according to Plutarch, he was a changed man. He became much sterner with the people, and controlled them through the two-edged sword of hope and fear. At the same time, he was careful of the public good, and although he had great power and opportunity, he did not add a single drachma to the estate his father had left him. He maintained himself as undisputed master of Athens through his wisdom and his eloquence, and never lost sight of the fact that his acts were subject to review by the people at the end of each year. As it was, he was chosen one of the ten generals of Athens year after year and, in fact, he was the general among generals.

His policy of increasing Athenian power and influence on the Greek mainland met with little success. Aegina remained an unwilling ally, Megara and Boeotia were lost, a revolt in Euboea was quelled, and the Thirty Years' Peace was arranged with Sparta (446–445 B.C.). In the Sacred War (448 B.C.) he had seized the temple of Delphi, which had been handed over to the Delphians by the Spartans, and restored it to the Phocians. The Spartans had engraved on the left side of the bronze wolf, by the great altar, their privilege of consulting the oracle first. Pericles caused a claim for the same privilege for

the Athenians to be engraved on the wolf's right side. However, the friendship with the Phocians was short-lived. As a result of these setbacks, he turned his attention to strengthening Athens as a sea power. In 448 B.C. peace was concluded with the Persians. He pacified the Chersonese and secured the Greek cities of the Pontus.

Pericles' wife bore him two sons, Xanthippus and Paralus, but the couple was so unhappy that they separated by mutual consent. She married another and he took as his mistress Aspasia, a beautiful, intelligent Milesian, who excelled at political discussion and was a friend of some of the leading thinkers of the day. She was attacked by the comic poets as the "new Omphale," Cratinus plainly called her a prostitute, others spoke of her as Deianira and Hera. Some said she wrote Pericles' speeches. It was said that she urged Pericles to wage war on Samos, to avenge her native city of Miletus. He conquered Samos (440 B.C.), and established a democracy, then sailed off, leaving a few ships behind. The Samians revolted, seized the Greek ships and branded their Athenian prisoners on their foreheads with an owl, symbol of Athens. Pericles returned to Samos, besieged it for nine months and forced its surrender. He razed the walls and levied a fine on the Samians. On his return to Athens he celebrated a magnificent funeral for the fallen and was chosen to make the funeral oration, a speech which won him much applause.

In 433 B.C. he sent a small fleet to observe in the war between Corcyra and Corinth. The fleet was to assist the Corcyraeans defensively. This was one of the incidents that marked the prelude to the Peloponnesian War, and was an excuse for the Spartans to claim that Athens had broken the Thirty Years' Peace. Pericles offered to submit all questions in dispute between Athens and Sparta to arbitration, but Sparta refused. Embassies went back and forth. The Spartans demanded that the Athenians drive out the curse of the goddess. This was a reference to the followers of Cylon, who (c632 B.C.) were slain after having been promised safe conduct if they would come out of the temple on the Acropolis where they had fled as suppliants after an abortive attempt to

Red-figured stamnos, Berlin Painter,
c 490 B.C. Athena with warriors.

Red-figured psykter, Pan Painter, c 490
B.C. Artemis between Apollo and Evenus.

Attic red-figured kylix, 490–480 B.C.
Departing warrior.

Attic red-figured crater, mid-5th century
B.C. Heracles and warriors.

Enlarged
Impressions
of Sealstones:

Cretan sealstone and
impression, 2200–
1350 B.C.

Cretan, 1500–1100
B.C.

Greek, green steatite;
Man and Woman;
8th century B.C.

Greek, steatite; Lion
attacking a man;
8th–7th century B.C.

Greek, carnelian
scarab; Lion attack-
ing a bull; late 6th
century B.C.

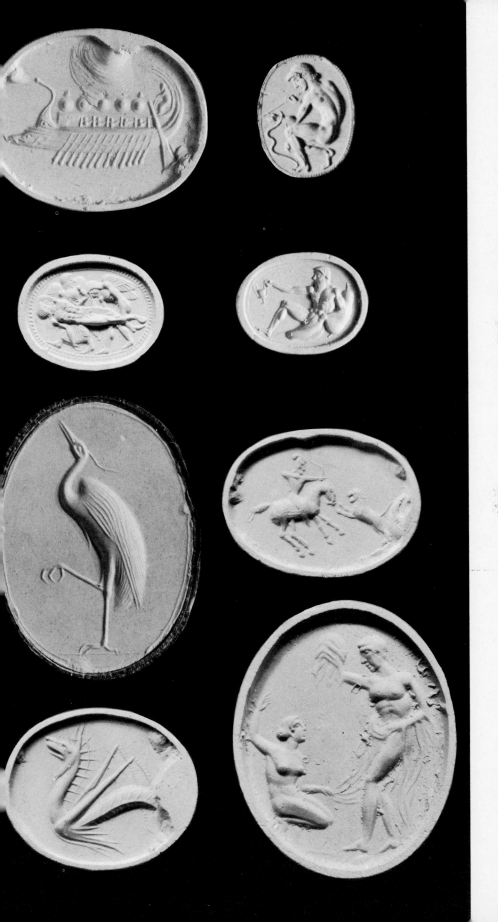

Enlarged
Impressions of
Sealstones:

Greek, burnt chalcedony; Warship;
c 500 B.C.

Greek, chalcedony;
Archer; 500–490 B.C.

Etruscan, carnelian;
Sleep and Death with
the body of Memnon; early 5th century B.C.

Greek, black jasper;
Satyr with wineskin
and cantharus; c 460
B.C.

Greek, chalcedony;
Heron; 5th century
B.C.

Graeco-Roman chalcedony; Lion hunt;
5th–4th century B.C.

Greek, chalcedony;
Winged monster;
450–400 B.C.

Greek, carnelian or
chalcedony; Man
and Woman; third
quarter, 5th century
B.C.

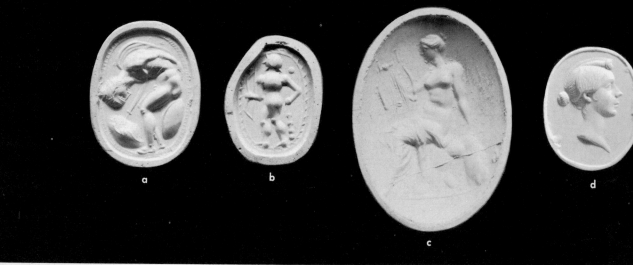

Courtesy of The Metropolitan Museum of Art

Enlarged impressions of sealstones: a) Etruscan, carnelian; Suicide of Ajax; 4th century B.C. b) Etruscan, carnelian; Heracles with bow and club; 4th–3rd century B.C. c) Hellenistic; Woman with lyre; 3rd–2nd century B.C. d) Roman, sard from a ring; Bust of a girl; Augustan Age.

From left to right: Gold earring, 4th century B.C. Gold fibula, S. Italy, 4th century B.C. Gold buckle, S. Italy, 4th century B.C.

win control of the city. The curse was that the family of the Alcmaeonidae should be exiled from Athens forever. The Alcmaeonidae had returned to Athens and Pericles was the most prominent member, as well as the most powerful man in Athens. The Athenians replied with a demand that the Spartans drive out the curse of Taenarus, referring to the slaying of Pausanias, and the death of some suppliants at the temple of Poseidon at Taenarus. These were pretexts. The Spartans had decided on war as the only means of arresting the growing power of Athens.

After listening to their allies and ambassadors from Athens who sought peace, the Spartans declared that the Thirty Years' Peace had been broken and decided for war (431 B.C.). Pericles' strategy was to allow the Spartans to exhaust themselves by attacks on Athens, while Athens remained inside its walls. He remained unmoved by the pleas of many to attack the Spartans. He sent out a fleet to harass the Peloponnesus and the Spartans withdrew, but returned the next year. In that year (430 B.C.), plague broke out in crowded Athens. His enemies blamed it on Pericles. He manned a fleet, and was on board, ready to sail, when there was an eclipse of the sun. In spite of the unfavorable omen he sailed, but his expedition was not very successful, and when he returned he was deprived of his command and fined. He was now attacked by many, including his son Xanthippus. But the latter died of the plague, and Pericles withdrew with dignity, only losing his composure when his younger son also succumbed to the plague. A year later he was recalled to power in Athens by the people, but soon he too fell a victim to the plague and died, in 429 B.C.

The empire of which Pericles was the leader was composed of many unwilling states; they were ruled with an autocratic hand, were deprived of all control over their policies and destinies, and were compelled to contribute to the treasury at Athens. At home, his law (451–450 B.C.) that only those whose parents were legally wedded Athenians could be citizens was most undemocratic and limiting; the law rose to plague him in his connection with Aspasia the Milesian.

At the summit of power he had, naturally, many enemies. He was attacked indirectly through Phidias, who was accused of stealing the gold he was supposed to have used on his statue of Athena. This accusation was disproved, since Phidias had provided that the gold could be removed for weighing. Phidias was next accused of impiety, because he showed his own and Pericles' likenesses on the shield of the goddess. He was cast into prison and died, or as some say, he died an exile. Coming closer, the critics of Pericles attacked Aspasia as an alien, but he was able to protect her. In addition, his old friend and teacher, Anaxagoras, was accused of impiety and fled. Plutarch claims that because of these troubles Pericles was anxious for war. Other witnesses do not bear out this conclusion. Rather, war between the two most powerful states of Greece was inevitable since they could not agree, as Cimon had so devoutly hoped, on a course by which their powers would be united.

The contributions of Pericles to Athens and to the western world were great. He ended the Persian Wars, confirmed Athens as the leading sea power of Greece, and established democratic reforms that tended to strengthen Athenian democracy. He brought commercial prosperity to the city, which he so beautified that the period of his ascendancy came to be known as the Golden Age of Athens, and he encouraged art and literature. The funeral oration which he gave for the dead who first fell in the Peloponnesian War contrasts Sparta and Athens and is a testament of his ideas of and ideals for Athens. In it he describes the Athenian democracy as he sees it: an administration that favors the many rather than the few, whose laws provide equal justice for all, and whose offices are open to any one with capacity; an administration that is made possible and strengthened by public and private respect for magistrates and the law. To this is added: diversion for the spirit in the form of public games and sacrifices, beautiful buildings, and a flourishing commerce that brings the products of the world to Athens. In military affairs and foreign policy, Athens is a city open to the world, welcoming all, even at the risk of being observed by an enemy, because the native spirit of the Athenians is its greatest strength and protection. In developing these points he names Athens the school of Hellas, and proudly declares to the Athenians that we "have left imperishable monuments behind us."

Pericles the Younger. Athenian commander; executed 406 B.C. He was the son of Pericles and his mistress Aspasia. By a Decree of the People he was declared legitimate in 429 B.C. He was one of the Athenian commanders who defeated the Peloponnesians under Callicratidas in the sea fight at Arginusae (406 B.C.). In this battle, which was an Athenian victory, 25 Athenian ships and their crews were lost. For some reason, unknown, the other ships did not stop to pick up the men in the water. The Athenians felt that many of these men might have been saved, and anger over their loss raged against the commanders who had not ordered their rescue. Eight of the commanders were tried by the Athenian Assembly, rather than by constituted courts, for criminal negligence. The commanders were found guilty, their property was confiscated, and they were condemned to death. Pericles was one of six who were actually executed (406 B.C.).

Periclymenus (per-i-klĭ′me̱-nus). In Greek mythology, the oldest son of Neleus and Chloris (or Meliboea, daughter of Amphion and Niobe). Poseidon gave him boundless strength and the power to assume whatever shape he wanted. Some time after the journey in the *Argo*, in which he took part, he attempted to defend Pylus, his father's kingdom, against Heracles. In combat with Heracles he changed himself into a lion, a serpent and a bee. Lastly he transformed himself into an eagle and tried to peck out Heracles' eyes, but as he flew away to dodge Heracles' club, the hero seized a bow and shot him.

Periclymenus. In Greek legend, a Theban, the son of Poseidon and Chloris, who was a daughter of Tiresias, the seer. He was a defender of Thebes in the war of the Seven against Thebes, and slew Parthenopaeus. He attacked Amphiaraus, and would have killed him, but Zeus caused the earth to split open and Amphiaraus, alive and in his chariot, was swallowed up.

Perieres (per-i-ē′rēz). In Greek legend, a son of Aeolus of Thessaly and Enarete. He be-

came king of the Messenians, at their request, and married Gorgophone, daughter of Perseus. She bore him Aphareus, who succeeded him, and Leucippus.

Perigune (per-i-gū′ne̱). In Greek legend, a daughter of Sinis the "Pine-bender." When Theseus encountered Sinis and struggled, successfully, to overpower him, Perigune, in terror of Theseus, ran and hid from him. He found her cowering among wild asparagus and rushes, appealing to the shrubs to hide her, and promising them that she would never burn or destroy them if they would protect her from Theseus. Theseus assured her that he meant her no harm, and so convinced her that she fell in love with him. He embraced her and in due time she bore him Melanippus. Theseus later gave her to Deioneus of Oechalia. The descendants of Perigune in Caria, who were called Ioxids because Ioxus, grandson of Perigune, led a colony to Caria, made it a practice not to burn the wild asparagus and rushes. Instead they revered these plants for their service to Perigune.

Perilaus (per-i-lā′us). In Greek legend, a son of Icarius. He was a cousin of Clytemnestra and some say it was he who accused Orestes and demanded vengeance for the murder of Clytemnestra from the Furies.

Perimedes (per-i-mē′dēz). In Greek legend, a son of Eurystheus. He was slain by the Athenians in the war which they waged against the forces of Eurystheus in defense of the children of Heracles, and also in defense of the right of the Athenians to give sanctuary to whomever they pleased.

Perimedes. In the *Odyssey*, one of the companions of Odysseus in his wanderings on the return to Ithaca after the Trojan War. He accompanied Odysseus on his visit to the Underworld.

Perimele (per-i-mē′le̱). In mythology, a daughter of Hippodamas. The river-god Achelous fell in love with her and ravished her. Hippodamas was enraged with his daughter and hurled her into the sea, but as she was falling Achelous caught her and held her up. He prayed to Poseidon that she might be given a resting place or become a place, herself. His prayer was answered: Perimele was transformed into an island off the mouth of

fat, fāte, fär, fāre, errant; net, mē, hėr ardent; pin, pīne; not, nōte, mȯve, nôr,

the Achelous River. She became one of the Echinades Islands.

Perinthus (pe-rin′thus). [Also: **Heraclea Perinthus.**] In ancient geography, a city in Thrace, strongly situated on a cliff on a peninsula on the Propontis about 55 miles W of Byzantium. It was part of the realm of Darius the Great, and revolted against him when he was on his expedition in Scythia. After the Persian Wars (479 B.C.) it became a member of the Confederacy of Delos, to which it paid tribute. The city made a successful defense against Philip II of Macedon in 340 B.C. Eski Ereğli is the name of the town now occupying the site.

Peripatetics (per″i-pa-tet′iks). Followers of Aristotle (384–322 B.C.). They were so called from his teaching while walking up and down or from "Peripatos," a covered walking-place in a school. Theophrastus and Straton succeeded Aristotle as leaders of the school and transformed Aristotelian philosophy into scientific research. After the 1st century, B.C., the Peripatetics wrote commentaries and expositions of Aristotle, thus preserving Aristotle's philosophical speculations in metaphysics and logic for later generations. The school became eclectic and eventually turned to Neoplatonism. In the Middle Ages the word was often used to signify "logicians."

Periphas (per′i-fas). According to some accounts, an ancient king of Attica, before the time of Cecrops. He was renowned for his justice and piety, and was called "Zeus" by men. For this presumption Zeus wanted to destroy him, but was persuaded by Apollo to change him into an eagle instead, and he became king of the birds.

Periphas. In Homeric legend (*Iliad*), a son of Ochesius. He was called a giant by Homer, and named as the bravest by far of the Aetolians in the Trojan War. Ares slew him, when the god entered the battle at Aphrodite's request to help the Trojans, and stripped him of his armor.

Periphas. In Homeric legend (*Iliad*), a son of Epytus. He was a Trojan herald, whose shape Apollo assumed in order to spur Aeneas on in the struggle for possession of Patroclus' body.

Periphetes (per-i-fē′tēz). In Homeric legend (*Iliad*), the only son of Copreus of Mycenae. His father had once served as messenger between Eurystheus and Heracles. While defending the Greek ships in a phalanx of shields against Hector, Periphetes tripped on his buckler and fell on his back. Hector thereupon ran up to him and thrust his javelin into his breast.

Periphetes. In Greek legend, a Giant. Some say he was a son of Poseidon, but others say he was a son of Hephaestus and Anticlea, and like Hephaestus, he was lame. He lived at Epidaurus, and was in the habit of attacking travelers with a huge iron club (he was sometimes called Corynetes, "Cudgel-bearer"). When he attacked Theseus, who was passing that way, Theseus seized the club from his hands and battered Periphetes to death with his own club. Ever after, Theseus carried the huge club and used it to good effect.

Periphetes. In Homeric legend (*Iliad*), a Mysian ally of the Trojans. He was slain and stripped of his armor by Teucer.

Periplus (per′i-plus). Title of ancient reports of navigations of explorers, and manuals for the use of navigators. The oldest extant is by the younger Scylax of Caryanda in Caria, assigned to the time of Alexander the Great. There were also similar works by Nearchus, Agatharchides, Hanno, Timagenes, and others.

Peripteros (pe-rip′te-ros). A temple of which the cella is surrounded by a single range of columns.

Peristyle (per′i-stīl). In architecture, a range or ranges of columns surrounding any part, as the cella of a Greek temple, or any place, as a court or cloister, or the atrium of a classical house.

Pero (pē′rō). In Greek legend, a daughter of Neleus, king of Pylus, and Chloris, daughter of Amphion and Niobe. She was the sister of Nestor. She had many suitors and her father promised her to the one who could bring him the cattle of Phylacus (or his son, Iphiclus). She was finally won by Bias, who with the help of his brother Melampus, a seer, got possession of the cattle. She was said by some to be the mother of the river-god Asopus, by Poseidon. She died young and Odysseus saw her shade when he visited the Underworld on his way home from the Trojan War.

Perpenna (pėr-pen′a) or **Perperna** (-pėr′na), **Marcus.** Roman general in Spain, lieutenant of Sertorius, whom he put to death. He was defeated and put to death by Pompey, c72 B.C.

Persa (pėr'sa). In Greek mythology, a daughter of Oceanus and Tethys. She was the mother of Aeëtes, Circe, Pasiphaë, and Perses, by Helius.

Persae (pėr'sē). Tragedy of Aeschylus. See **Persians, The.**

Persephone (pėr-sef'ọ-nē). [Also: **Core, Kore,** meaning "the Maiden."] In Greek mythology, the daughter of Zeus and Demeter. Hades fell in love with her and sought permission from Zeus to make her his wife. Zeus neither gave his consent, for he knew Demeter would not want to lose her daughter in the Underworld, nor withheld it, for fear of offending Hades. One day as Persephone was gathering flowers in a meadow with her companions, Hades suddenly appeared in his chariot drawn by four black horses and seized her. As she struggled to escape, the earth opened and the chariot disappeared into the chasm bearing Hades and the unhappy maiden in it. Demeter was wild with grief over the loss of her daughter. She wandered tirelessly over the world searching for her. Some say Enna, in Sicily, was the place where Hades carried off Persephone; others say Colonus in Attica, Hermione or Lerna in Argolis, Pheneus in Arcadia, Nysa in Boeotia, a place in Crete, and various other places visited by Demeter in her search for her daughter were the scene of the abduction. But the priests of Demeter said she was carried off from Eleusis in Attica. Demeter learned from Hecate that Hades had abducted her daughter with the tacit consent of Zeus and carried her off to his realm to be his wife. In her wrath, Demeter withdrew her gifts of fertility from the earth; fields and vineyards ceased to bear. Zeus, fearing the destruction of mankind, sent Hermes to Hades with a command to restore Persephone to her mother, on condition that she had eaten nothing while in his kingdom. Persephone had eaten some seeds of a pomegranate—one, three, six, or seven—and for that reason was compelled to spend part of each year as Hades' wife in his kingdom, where she lived with him in a palace, had a grove of black poplars sacred to her, and exercised great powers. She allowed Heracles to re-store Alcestis to earth when she had given her life that her husband might live; deceived by Sisyphus, she gave him permission to return to earth to make arrangements for his own burial, which he said had not been properly performed; and she accepted a myrtle bough from Dionysus in return for permitting him to take his mother Semele from Hades' kingdom to Olympus. Occasionally she was compelled to deal with a rival. She transformed the nymph Minthe into a mint plant when she observed Hades dallying with her. For the same reason, the nymph Leuce was transformed into a white poplar that stood beside the Pool of Memory in Hades. Variations on the story of Persephone were that she was the daughter of Zeus and the nymph of the river Styx in Hades; that she was the mother of Zagreus and Dionysus by Zeus. The annual disappearance from the earth of Persephone brought death to vegetation. When she appeared to spend the rest of the year with her mother the earth flowered in rebirth. Persephone and Demeter were worshiped as the Great Goddesses, the central figures of the Eleusinian Mysteries, from which a concept of immortality evolved. Persephone was also worshiped as "the Maid," whose name it was unwise to utter. Symbolically, Demeter and Persephone were interpreted as two aspects of the grain goddess, Persephone representing the new young grain, Demeter the ripened harvest. Persephone is also associated with the mother-goddess Aphrodite in the fertility myth regarding the vegetation-god Adonis. Adonis dwelt with Persephone under the earth for one-third of the year, and spent the other eight months with Aphrodite in the world. Persephone's cult name was Core, or Kore, "the Maiden," and in this aspect she figured in the Eleusinian mysteries. She was associated with Dionysus in the Eleusinian mysteries when, under the name Iacchus, he represented her brother, her son, or her bridegroom. In the Peloponnesus she was honored with a festival of flowers, the Anthesphoria. In later times Persephone came to be identified with Hecate, a dread goddess of darkness and of spirits. As a virgin who dwelt with her mother, Persephone was represented as a beautiful maiden, and had a flowing cornuco-

fat, fāte, fär, fãre, errạnt; net, mē, hėr ardẹnt; pin, pīne; not, nōte, möve, nôr,

pia, a sheaf of wheat, and the cock as her attributes. As the stern queen of the Underworld, she held a torch or a pomegranate, symbolizing death and rebirth. The Romans called her Proserpina and made little or no change in the myth or its interpretation. She was especially worshiped in Sicily, which was sacred to Demeter and Persephone and where many festivals were held in their honor.

Persepolis (pẽr-sep'ọ̄-lis). In ancient geography, one of the capitals of the Persian Empire, about 35 miles NE of what is now Shiraz. It became the capital under Darius I, was captured by Alexander the Great c330 B.C. and subsequently burned, and is still noted for the ruins of its palaces. The most remarkable monuments are grouped on a terrace of smoothed rock and masonry, approximately rectangular in plan, though with irregular projections, measuring 940 by 1550 feet, and attaining in front the height of 43 feet, of fine polygonal masonry, while at the back it is dominated by the rock of the foothills behind. The chief buildings on the terrace were the Propylaea and the great hypostyle hall of Xerxes, the Hall of 100 Columns, attributed to Darius, and the residence palaces of Darius and his successors. In the palace of Darius carved reliefs of men fighting animals occur, based on Assyrian originals; in that of Xerxes the sculptures represent subjects pertaining to royal luxury. Great figures of bulls, often set up before the portals, recall the Assyrian practice. The chief explorations are due to Eugène Napoléon Flandin and P. Coste in 1840–41, and to F. Stolze and Andreas prior to 1882. In 1891 some excavations were made by Herbert Weld Blundell, and casts of the sculptures and inscriptions taken by a private expedition sent out from England. The site was carefully investigated in the 1930's by an expedition representing the University of Chicago and the University of Pennsylvania, under Ernst Herzfeld and Erich F. Schmidt.

Perses (pẽr'sēz). In Greek mythology, a son of the Titan Crius and Eurybia, and the father of Hecate by Asteria. This Perses, or another of the same name, was said by some to be the son of Persa and Helius, and the brother of Aeëtes, Circe, and Pasiphaë. He seized Colchis from his brother, Aeëtes, and was afterward slain either by Medea or by her son Medeus, when Medea returned to Colchis from Greece.

Perseus (pẽr'sūs, -sē-us). In Greek mythology, a son of Zeus and Danaë. He was born in a bronze underground chamber in which Acrisius had imprisoned Danaë to prevent her from having any traffic with men. He did this because he had been warned by an oracle that his grandson would kill him. But Zeus visited Danaë in a shower of gold and she bore him Perseus. Acrisius was reluctant to kill his own grandson, for fear of the wrath of the gods. He therefore placed mother and child in a chest and cast it into the sea. The chest floated to the island of Seriphus. There it was recovered by Dictys, a fisherman. He took Danaë and her son to his house and sheltered them; Perseus grew up under his care to be a fisherman. Polydectes, brother of Dictys and king of the island, saw Danaë and fell in love with her. By this time Perseus had grown to be a strong and handsome youth. Some say Perseus objected to the marriage which Polydectes tried to force on his mother. Others say Polydectes simply wanted to get rid of Perseus. At any rate, Polydectes summoned his friends to his palace and asked them to make contributions to him for a wedding present to Hippodamia, daughter of Pelops, whom he pretended he was going to marry. He asked his friends to give him horses. Perseus, a poor fisherman, could give no such gift. Instead he agreed to fetch the head of the Gorgon Medusa as his contribution. Some say he idly promised he would even fetch the head of Medusa to prevent Polydectes from marrying Danaë, and that Polydectes immediately accepted his offer. Others say Perseus, humiliated by his inability to give a horse as the others were promising to do, proudly offered to fetch the head of Medusa instead. This then was his mission, and Polydectes thought he had seen the last of him, for he expected him to be killed on this dangerous errand. Perseus sailed to Greece, without telling his mother of his daring plan, to consult the oracle at Delphi and learn where the Gorgons might be found. The oracle directed him to a land where the people eat only acorns. Perseus took this to mean Dodona, the site of the oracle of the talking oak trees. The priests of Dodona, however, could not tell him where to find the Gorgons. They did tell him that Athena and Hermes would help him. As he wandered about searching for information Perseus met Hermes and learned from him that only the nymphs of the North could tell

PERSEUS FLEEING FROM A GORGON
Red-figured Greek amphora, c490 B.C.
Munich

him where the Gorgons dwelt, and that only the Graeae, who lived at the foot of Mount Atlas in Libya, could direct him to the nymphs. Hermes accompanied him on his journey to the Graeae. These shadowy old women shared one eye and one tooth between them and lived in a land that knew no sunlight. They were sisters of the Gorgons. As they came to the sisters, Hermes advised Perseus to steal their eye and their tooth as these were passing from hand to hand, and to keep them until the Graeae revealed the home of the nymphs. Perseus followed his instructions. The Graeae, compelled by their need for the eye which Perseus had snatched from them, told him how to find the nymphs of the North. He then set off with Hermes to find the nymphs, who lived in the far northern land of the Hyperboreans. The nymphs treated him kindly and gave him a wallet, winged sandals, and a cap of darkness. They also told him where to find the

Gorgons. Hermes gave him an unbreakable sickle. Athena gave him a polished shield. She told him not to look directly at the Gorgons, for they were so revolting and frightening with their snaky locks that whoever looked on them was instantly turned to stone. She showed him how to use the shield as a mirror so that he need not look directly at the Gorgons, and told him how he would recognize Medusa, the only one of the Gorgons who was not immortal. Perseus flew over the ocean on his winged sandals until beneath him he saw the Gorgons reflected in the polished shield. He swooped down and, using the shield as Athena had directed, cut off Medusa's head with one sweep of Hermes' sickle and put it into the wallet the nymphs had given him for this purpose. From the blood of Medusa sprang Pegasus, the winged horse, and Chrysaor. Her sisters woke up and pursued Perseus, but as he was wearing the cap of darkness he was invisible and they soon gave up the chase. Hermes and Athena now left him and he flew off, carrying the head in the wallet. Drops of Medusa's blood that fell on the land as he flew over it turned into serpents, and thenceforth this land was infested with poisonous snakes. Some say that Perseus, on his way to find the Gorgons, visited Atlas and asked his hospitality. Atlas, remembering a prophecy given him by Themis that the golden apples would one day be stripped by a son of Zeus, from the trees which he guarded, refused to entertain him. As Perseus returned with the head of Medusa, he again stopped at the house of Atlas, exhibited the head of Medusa and turned Atlas to stone to punish him for his inhospitality. There Atlas stands to this day, a mighty mountain called by his name. Continuing his journey, Perseus flew to Chemmis, the home of his ancestor Danaus in Egypt. He stopped there briefly to refresh himself. The Egyptians honored him with an image in the sacred precinct of the temple of Chemmis; they said that a huge sandal belonging to Perseus frequently is found, and that on the occasions when the sandal comes to light all Egypt prospers. The Egyptians worshiped Perseus with games in the Greek manner. Perseus next flew over the coasts of Aethiopia and saw a beautiful maiden chained to a rock on the shore. He fell in love with her at sight, and flew down to inquire the reason for her unhappy state. She told him she was Andromeda, daughter of Cepheus, king of Aethiopia. She was chained to the rock as a sacrifice to a sea-monster that Poseidon had sent to ravage the land. Perseus offered to slay the monster if in return Cepheus would give him Andromeda in marriage. Cepheus was delighted to agree. Perseus took the head of Medusa from the wallet and laid it on some seaweed, which instantly turned to coral, in case he should need it to kill the monster. But it was not necessary. As the beast emerged from the sea Perseus flew above it, swooped down and cut off its head with a single blow. He then raised altars and sacrificed to Hermes, Athena, and Zeus, and claimed his bride. At the wedding festivities Phineus, who some say was the brother of Cepheus and some say was a son of Agenor, burst into the hall and claimed the bride. Andromeda had been betrothed to him before the monster was sent by Poseidon, but when she was chained to the rock as a sacrifice Phineus had given up his interest in her. Now that all was safe, he reasserted his claim to her. Perseus refused to give up Andromeda. He fought off Phineus and his companions, killing many, but he was seriously outnumbered and must surely have perished if he had not exposed the head of Medusa and turned Phineus and his followers to stone. After this he departed with Andromeda for Seriphus. Arrived there, he learned that his mother and the kindly Dictys, whose wife had long since died, had been forced to flee because of the violent importunities of Polydectes. They had taken refuge in a temple. Perseus set off for the palace, where Polydectes and his friends were gathered at a great banquet. As he entered the banquet hall all eyes turned to him. He held up the head of Medusa and Polydectes and all his companions who had been unfriendly to Danaë were instantly turned to stone. A circle of lifeless boulders on Seriphus marks the site of this event. Now Perseus sought his mother and Dictys. He made Dictys king of the island, and with his mother and his wife he set out for Argos to find his grandfather. Acrisius, who had heard all about his glorious exploits, remembered the oracle that warned he would be killed by his grandson and fled to Larissa. Thither Perseus followed him. Some say he took part in funeral games at Larissa unaware that Acrisius was among the spectators. However that may be, in the discus throwing contest Perseus' discus was caught by the wind, struck Acrisius and killed him. Thus the oracle was fulfilled, as oracles invariably are. Perseus was reluctant to return to Argos after he had killed his grandfather, even though it was an accident. He exchanged his kingdom of Argos with his cousin Megapenthes for the kingdom of Tiryns. In his new kingdom he fortified Midea and Mycenae. Some say indeed, that Perseus founded Mycenae; that one day when he was thirsty a mushroom sprang up and provided water. He founded the city on this spot and named it Mycenae in honor of the mushroom (*mykos*). Perseus gave the sandals, wallet, and cap of darkness to Hermes, who restored them to the nymphs. He gave the head of Medusa to Athena. The goddess placed the head in the center of her shield, or aegis. Andromeda bore Perseus six sons: Perses, from whom the kings of Persia were said to have sprung, Alcaeus, Sthenelus, Heleus (or Aelius), Mestor, and Electryon, and one daughter, Gorgophone. As far as is known, Andromeda rejoiced in the undiluted affection of her lord, a rare occurrence for the wives of Greek heroes. Perseus was worshiped as a hero in Athens and Seriphus, and had a shrine on the road between Argos and Mycenae.

Perseus. Last king of Macedon, son of Philip V, whom he succeeded in 179 B.C. He began war with the Romans in 172 B.C. and defeated them in several engagements. The Romans elected Aemilius Paulus as consul and sent him to Greece to command the Roman forces against Perseus, whose army was encamped near Mount Olympus. Aemilius brought his forces up by an encircling movement and prepared to attack Perseus at Pydna (168 B.C.). On the eve of the battle an eclipse of the moon brought terror to the Macedonians, who took it as an omen of the eclipse of Perseus. Perseus had great treasure, but was so miserly he refused to pay his mercenaries and duped his allies. He kept his treasure but was soundly defeated by Aemilius Paulus at Pydna and fled to Pella.

From there he sailed to Samothrace and took refuge, with his wife and children, in the temple of the Dioscuri. His gold was stolen by Cretan sailors and the Macedonians, enraged by his flight, his oppressive rule, and by their defeat which they attributed to him, seized him and turned him over to Aemilius Paulus. Perseus begged to be spared the humiliation of being exhibited as a captive in a triumphal procession. Aemilius scorned him for his cowardice, and suggested that he could avoid the humiliation by committing suicide. Perseus could not bring himself to this step. With his children, his captured chariot and armor, he was paraded as a captive before the throngs of Rome (167 B.C.). In the end, some say, Perseus starved himself to death in prison. Others say the soldiers who guarded him prevented him from sleeping so that at length, worn out, he died.

Persians (pėr'zhạnz, -shạnz). Native inhabitants of ancient Persia. Their name is derived from the district which in antiquity was known as Persis, the modern Fars. They were originally nomadic immigrants who entered the region through Caucasia, mingling with and dominating the people already there. They were well established in the Persis region by the 6th century B.C., and under Cyrus and his successors continued to build a great empire. According to Greek legend, the Persian kings were descended from Perses, son of Perseus and Andromeda, from whom they took their name.

Persians, The. A drama by Aeschylus, produced 472 B.C. It concerns the disasters which overcame the might of Persia under Xerxes. The play can be read as a great patriotic eulogy of the outnumbered Greek forces which defeated the Persians at Salamis (480 B.C.). (Aeschylus himself fought at Marathon and probably at Salamis.) At the same time, it treats the punishment which the gods meted out to Xerxes for his presumption in defying divine law; a punishment which was delivered by human and natural forces.

The scene is in Susa, the home of the Persian kings. A chorus of Persian Elders enters. They speak of themselves as having been left in charge while Xerxes has gone off at the head of a mighty host to invade Greece. They are uneasy because they have had no news of the Persian forces. They name the leaders and allies who accompanied Xerxes on his march across the Hellespont by a bridge of boats, and seek to reassure themselves that the great Persian power is irresistible. Nevertheless, they are aware that the gods can, if they wish, make a mockery of the greatest power, and they are uneasy lest the gods have deluded Xerxes.

Atossa, mother of Xerxes, enters. She adds to their feeling of impending catastrophe by confessing to anxiety about her son's fate, and asks the Elders to interpret a dream she had that seemed to prophesy disaster for Xerxes. She dreamed two beautiful women appeared, one clad in Persian and the other in Greek dress. A feud broke out between the two; Xerxes resolved to settle it and yoked both women to his car. One of the women bore her situation proudly; the other struggled, broke the harness, and dragged the chariot violently, snapping the yoke. Xerxes was hurled to the ground. Darius, his father, came to commiserate with him and Xerxes rent his garments in grief. When she woke Atossa was disquieted. She prepared to propitiate the gods and pray them to avert evil from her son but hesitated to do so because of another omen: an eagle, pursued by a falcon, fled to the altar of Apollo for safety, but was overtaken and slain by the falcon. The Elders do not attempt to interpret her dream. They advise her to make sacrifices to the gods, offer libations to Earth, and pray to the spirit of her dead husband Darius to send blessings on Xerxes and Persia. Atossa accepts their advice, but first she would like to know something about these Athenians Xerxes has marched against. The Elders tell her where Athens is, that if Athens is subdued all Hellas will submit, that their wealth is in silver, and that they own no man to be their master. But here comes a messenger, the Elders say, and he will tell them how matters stand with Xerxes and his forces. The messenger rushes in. He cries out that disaster has overtaken the Persians at Salamis. To the questions of the Elders and Atossa he gives a list of the Persian leaders lost at Salamis, tells of the destruction of the Persian fleet in the narrow straits. To Atossa's question about the size of the Greek fleet that dared attack the Persians he replies that if numbers had counted the Persians must surely have won, for they greatly outnumbered the Greeks, but the gods sided with the Greeks. Not only was the fleet cut to pieces, he adds, but a picked body of troops who had been sent to a neighboring island to harry whatever Greeks fled there for safety had instead been destroyed by the victorious Greeks. Xerxes, watching the battle, tore his garments in despair and ordered a retreat. The Persian ships that were not destroyed put out to sea in disorder. The army, retreating overland, was harried by hunger and thirst, many perished, but the army suffered the greatest loss when they came to the Strymon River. It unseasonably froze over, and as the Persians crossed, the gods caused the rays of the sun to melt the ice and a great number were drowned.

Atossa and the Elders lament over these terrible tidings. Atossa fears for her son. The Elders fear for the nation; some now under the Persian yoke will rebel, so they think, when they hear how the might of Xerxes has been destroyed. Atossa and the Elders invoke the divinities of the nether world to send forth the spirit of Darius. The Elders, calling on the deities of Earth, eulogize Darius; they recall his wisdom and the benefits he brought Persia. The ghost of Darius is now seen to rise from his tomb. He asks why the earth groans, what is the unexpected evil that weighs down the Persians? As the Elders are reluctant to speak he addresses himself to Atossa. She tells him of the disasters the messenger has described and of the ruin of Xerxes' forces. Darius grieves that it was his son on whom these evils have fallen. He laments that Xerxes in his presumption thought he could triumph over the gods who had separated Europe and Asia by building a bridge across the Hellespont. Atossa defends her son: he had been taunted into making the expedition by constant reminders of how much his father had added to the empire. Darius lists the various rulers of Persia down through his own time and adds that none has brought such disaster to the empire as Xerxes has now done. He advises the Persians not to fight the Greeks, for though they have no such hosts of allies as the Persians, the land itself is their ally, inflicting famine and thirst on an invading

army. Furthermore, Darius predicts that the picked body of troops still remaining in Hellas will be destroyed at Plataea. The Persians will now suffer their crowning disaster as punishment for their presumptuous pride and impious thoughts, for they ravaged the images of the gods in Greece and burned their temples. Because they wrought evil they will suffer an equal measure of evil. Zeus, he says, chastises overweening pride and corrects with a heavy hand. He advises Atossa to prepare to receive Xerxes, and the chorus to enjoy the day, even in the midst of troubles, for wealth is of no use to the dead. As the ghost of Darius departs, Atossa and the chorus of Elders lament. Atossa leaves for the palace to prepare for the return of her son. The Elders sing of the blessings Persia enjoyed under Darius.

Xerxes, in tattered robes, now approaches with a few of his followers. He laments the savage mood of Fortune that has brought him low, and wishes he had died with his men. The Elders question him, and learn that all the leaders for whom they inquire are dead. The most desolate picture of complete destruction of Persia's mighty army and fleet is painted by Xerxes. He advises the Elders to lift their voices in lamentation, beat their breasts, tear their hair, rend their garments, and give themselves up to mourning. The Elders respond with cries of woe for their fallen nation.

Persian Wars. In ancient Greek history, the wars between the Persians and the Greeks, commencing in 500 B.C. and ending c449 B.C. According to Herodotus, the enmity between Asia (that is, the non-Greek world beyond the Hellespont) and Greece stretched back into the mists of mythical antiquity. The Phoenicians, he says, went to Argos to trade and carried off Io along with other Argive women. Later the Greeks landed at Tyre on the Phoenician coast and stole Europa, more or less in retaliation. They then exacerbated the ill feeling between Asia and Greece by going to Colchis and carrying off Medea. In the next generation, Paris the son of Priam went to Sparta, eloped with Helen, and set off the long war that brought disaster to Troy. These were ancient causes. In 499 B.C. the Ionian Greeks revolted against their Persian overlords. The revolt was put down in 494

actọr; up, lūte, pŭll; oi, oil; ou, out; ᴛʜ, then; ḍ as d or j, ş as s or sh, ṭ as t or ch, ẓ as z or zh.

B.C., but not before Athenians and Eretrians had come to the aid of the Ionians and had burned the Lydian city of Sardis. Darius was so inflamed by this daring and insolent interference by the Greeks in Persian affairs that he had one servant whose sole duty was to remind him three times each day to "Remember the Athenians," and take vengeance on them. To punish them the Persians were provoked to attempt the conquest of European Greece. With this object in view, three grand expeditions were undertaken, each of which was repelled. In 492 B.C. Darius put Mardonius, his son-in-law, over all other generals and sent him out. Mardonius embarked at Cilicia, sailed along the coast, stopping along the way to remove the Ionian tyrants and establish democracies, and joined his land army at the Hellespont. From there he crossed into Europe with the intention of punishing Athens and Eretria. On the way he reconquered Thrace and Macedonia by land, and took the island of Thasus without a struggle. When his fleet was off Mount Athos a violent storm arose and destroyed many of his ships. Meantime, on land the army was attacked by Thracians, and though they were repelled and conquered, Mardonius was forced to return to Persia without fulfilling his mission of punishing Eretria and Athens. Darius was more than ever resolved on vengeance, but first he sent heralds throughout Greece demanding earth and water as token of submission to his rule. Many states and the neighboring islands submitted and gave up the tokens, but not the Athenians. Darius sent out a second expedition (490 B.C.) under Artaphernes (his young nephew), assisted by the experienced general Datis. The Persian fleet sailed from Samos. Naxos was taken on the way. Delos, from which the Delians had fled, was not only spared as a religious center, but gifts were made there by the Persians. Other islands were subdued and compelled to furnish men to the Persian army. The fleet advanced to Eretrian territory, besieged the fortress and took it through the betrayal of some prominent Eretrians. The Persians burned the temples, even as Sardis had been burned, and enslaved the populace. From Eretria the Persians proceeded to the plain of Marathon, guided thither by Hippias, ex-

iled son of Pisistratus, who hoped to return to power in Athens by means of a Persian victory. At Marathon the Athenians, aided by the Plataeans, met them and, although vastly outnumbered, administered a resounding defeat (Sept. 12, 490 B.C.). The Persian fleet, which was relatively intact, sailed to the waters off Athens, then, without making an attempt on the city which was now defended by soldiers who had returned from Marathon, the Persians sailed away. Greece was safe for the moment. The valor and ability the Athenians had shown ennobled them among the Greeks and gave them the confidence to resist the Persians at a later date.

On hearing of the defeat of his army, Darius was more resolved than ever on the conquest of the Greeks, and set about preparing for a new expedition with great energy, but died before he could embark on it. Xerxes, his heir, was at first cool to the idea of war against the Greeks. He was persuaded by his cousin Mardonius that the Greeks must be punished and the prestige of Persian arms restored. Artabanus, his uncle, advised him against war, but yielded before the force of a dream which, according to Herodotus, both he and Xerxes had, and which commanded him to make war on Greece. In addition, exiles from Athens urged war, and the seer Onomacritus, who had come to Susa with the Pisistratidae, produced many oracles in favor of war, prudently neglecting to mention any which foretold disaster. Herodotus relates that after Xerxes had decided for war he had another dream: that he was crowned with olive branches, the boughs of which stretched to the ends of the earth, and suddenly the wreath upon his brow vanished. Soothsayers interpreted this to mean that his power would cover the earth and all men would become his subjects. For the next four years he continued his preparations for the war, so that in all, since the defeat of Marathon, nearly ten years elapsed before the third expedition was undertaken in 481–480 B.C. under Xerxes. This expedition is said to have consisted of an army of about 100,000 men, exclusive of European allies, and a fleet of 1000 ships. At the moment of departure of the expedition, the sun, in a clear and cloudless sky, was suddenly obscured; day became night. Xerxes was full of alarm at this omen, but the soothsayers assured him that the gods were simply foretelling to the Greeks the destruction of their cities, for it was the sun who spoke to the Greeks, whereas it was the moon who spoke to the Persians. Before the army crossed the Hellespont into Europe, spices were burned on the bridges they had constructed, and they were strewn with myrtle boughs. At sunrise Xerxes poured a libation into the sea from a golden goblet, prayed to the sun that evil would not overtake him in his conquest, and cast the golden goblet along with a golden bowl and a sword into the sea. After the whole army had crossed a prodigy occurred, says Herodotus. A mare gave birth to a hare. This signified that Xerxes would lead his great host against Greece with splendor and power but would have to run for his life to regain the spot from which he set out. But Xerxes ignored the prodigy and marched forward. His army forced the pass of Thermopylae, after a heroic defense by the Greeks under the Spartan Leonidas, for Leonidas chose to lead the fight and die himself that the oracle might be fulfilled, to wit:

Oh! ye men who dwell in the streets of broad Lacedaemon,
Either your glorious town shall be sacked by the children of Perseus,
Or, in exchange, must all through the whole Laconian country
Mourn for the loss of a king, descendant of great Heracles. . . .

Xerxes marveled at the courage of the Spartans, and at the valor which impelled them to fight to victory or to death. He pushed on with his army and destroyed Athens (480 B.C.). But the Athenians had their own oracles and their own valor. They retired to Salamis. In the same year, 480 B.C., the Persian fleet fought the indecisive battle of Artemisium, and then tested the valor of the Athenians and their allies at Salamis. There they were completely defeated in a great sea fight (Sept. 20, 480 B.C.). Xerxes left Mardonius to prosecute the war and retreated to Persia. Mardonius fell at the battle of Plataea in 479 B.C., on the same day, according to some, that the Persian fleet under Mardontes was defeated at the battle of Mycale. Hitherto the Greeks had acted on the defensive; they now assumed the offensive, gaining the victories of the Eurymedon in 466 or 465 B.C. and of Salamis in Cyprus in 449 B.C. After the battle of Salamis negotiations for peace were opened, and, although no formal treaty was adopted, peaceable intercourse was gradually restored on the basis of existing political relations; this is known as the Peace of Callias, named for the Athenian ambassador to Artaxerxes who negotiated it. By some the name Persian Wars is restricted to the period between 500 and 479 B.C., inclusive, during which the Greeks acted on the defensive.

Persis (pér'sis). In ancient geography, a country in Asia, lying SE of Susiana, S of Media, and W of Carmania. It was the nucleus of the Persian Empire, and corresponded nearly to the modern Fars.

Persius (pér'shi-us, -shus). [Full name, **Aulus Persius Flaccus**.] Roman satirist; born at Volaterrae, in Etruria, 34 A.D.; died 62 A.D. He went to Rome when he was 12 years old and was educated there by eminent teachers of the day. His most revered teacher was Lucius Annaeus Cornutus, under whom he studied Stoic philosophy. He gave up early attempts at writing poetry and, influenced by the work of Lucilius and Horace, turned to the writing of satiric verse. His six satires, written in hexameters, are actually homilies advocating stoic ethical values; their language is obscure and strained.

Perugia (pa-rö'jạ). Italian name of **Perusia** (q.v.).

Perusia (pē-rö'shạ). City in C Italy, situated on hills above the Tiber River, N of Rome. The ancient city was one of the 12 principal cities of the Etruscan federation. The city submitted to Roman rule in 309 B.C. In 41 B.C. Octavian, the future Augustus, besieged and captured it; this is the Perusine War of the historians. Eventually becoming a colony, its name thereafter was Colonia Vibia Augusta Perusia.

Pervigilium Veneris (pér-vi-ji'li-um ven'ér-is). A bright and charming poem of love and springtime, the *Vigil of Venus,* written in trochaic meter by an anonymous but cultured pagan, perhaps in the 4th century A.D. (JJ)

Pescara River (pās-kä'rä). [Also, in its upper

course, **Aterno.**] River in C Italy which flows into the Adriatic near the town of Pescara.

Pessinus (pes′i-nus) or **Pesinus** (pe-sī′nus). In ancient geography, a city in Galatia, Asia Minor, situated near the Sangarius (Sakarya) River about 80 miles SW of what is now Ankara. It was long noted for the worship of Cybele.

Petalism (pet′al-izm). In ancient Syracuse, a mode of banishing citizens whose influence seemed dangerous, modeled on the ostracism at Athens, from which it differed in little except that the voter wrote the name of the person he recommended for banishment on an olive leaf and not on a tablet of earthenware, and that the stated period of banishment was five years, and not ten as at Athens. The law, which in any case was not in effect for long, was repealed 452 B.C., because it deterred the best citizens from taking part in public affairs.

Petra (pē′tra). In ancient geography, a city in Arabia Petraea. The site was early occupied on account of its proximity to the caravan route between Arabia and Egypt. From the 3rd century B.C. or earlier it was a stronghold of the Nabataeans. The site consists of a precipice-enclosed valley on the NE side of Mount Hor, approached only through narrow gorges. The sandstone rocks are brilliantly colored in many different hues, and are greatly worn by the action of water. Petra is famous for its rock-cut architectural remains, dating from after the establishment of Roman rule in 105 A.D. These remains have been looked upon by many as those of temples and palaces, but are merely the façades, many of them considerable in scale and elaborate in ornament, of rock tombs, with motifs borrowed from Assyrian, Egyptian, and Greek architecture. They gain in effectiveness by their situation and by the marvelous coloring of the rock. The buildings of the town are in an extreme state of ruin, except for the rock-cut theater.

Petronius Arbiter (pē-trō′ni-us är′bi-tėr), **Caius** (also **Titus**). Companion of the emperor Nero, mentioned by Tacitus, Pliny the Elder, and Plutarch. An aristocrat who proved his talent and energy as governor of Bithynia, he was regarded at the emperor's court as the *arbiter elegantiae* or authority in matters of entertainment and good taste (hence his name). His influence, we are told by Tacitus, aroused the jealousy of Tigellinus, commander of Nero's body-guard, who falsely accused him of treason. When Petronius was placed under house arrest at his estate near Cumae he anticipated the death sentence by opening his veins. Surrounded by feasting friends, he died slowly and without the customary heroics (66 A.D.). The overwhelming majority of scholars identify Petronius with the author of the *Satyricon*, a novel that in its amused, somewhat cynical detachment from and satire of the contemporary scene chimes perfectly with Petronius' character. It deals with numerous topics, institutions and literary questions of the Neronian age, and in language and style shows very many parallels with Seneca. Preserved in fortunately extensive fragments, the *Satyricon*, while partly indecent by today's standards, is nevertheless an immensely entertaining work full of wit, satire, parody. A large part is formed by the *Cena Trimalchionis* (Trimalchio's Dinner), the satirical description of a banquet given by a rich and vulgar freedman. This episode comprises short stories about lycanthropy and witchcraft; other portions contain a brief epic, many poetic passages, a critique of rhetoric and art, the story of the Matron of Ephesus, and many other good things. Petronius is also the reputed author of a number of poems preserved outside the *Satyricon* that show genuine poetic talent and felicity of expression. (HS)

Phaea (fē′a). In Greek legend, sometimes said to be the woman who reared the Crommyonian Sow (q.v.). This name was also applied to the sow itself.

Phaeacians (fē-ā′shanz). A legendary seafaring people who inhabited the island of Corcyra, or as some say, Scheria. According to some accounts they considered themselves to be of the blood of Uranus, because the sickle with which Cronus mutilated his father was flung into the sea by Cronus, either near their island or to form it, and its people were sprung from the drops of Uranus' blood on the sickle. Others say they were descendants of Phaeax, a son of Poseidon. And some say they emigrated to their island to get away from their noisy neighbors, the Cyclopes. As descendants of Poseidon, the Phaeacians

fat, fāte, fär, fāre, errant; net, mē, hėr ardent; pin, pīne; not, nōte, mŏve, nôr,

were extraordinary navigators and mariners. Their ships traveled the seas without the aid of steersman or helm, knowing of themselves the course they must take. Muffled in misty clouds and darkness, they flew over the waters like birds. On their island the Phaeacians lived in the midst of splendid prosperity and happiness, remote from wars and often enjoying visits from the gods themselves. Traditionally they were extremely hospitable to other seafarers and never refused their aid in danger and shipwreck. The women, thanks to Athena, were as skilled in weaving as the men were in seamanship. Jason and Medea stopped among the Phaeacians, during the reign of Alcinous, and were hospitably received. Odysseus was cast ashore on their island when the raft on which he sailed from Calypso's shores was broken up in a great storm. Nausicaä, the daughter of Alcinous, encountered him on the beach and directed him to her father's magnificent palace of bronze, gold, and silver. There the Phaeacians clothed and fed him and after hearing his story promised to convey him to Ithaca in one of their ships. They gave him rich gifts and put him aboard a ship at night. While he slept the ship skimmed over the sea to Ithaca, and the sleeping Odysseus was gently put ashore. On the return to Phaeacia, Poseidon, enraged that the Phaeacians who were of his own blood had given aid, comfort, and rich treasure to his enemy, sought permission from Zeus to punish the Phaeacians. Zeus advised him to turn the ship into stone and to raise a mountain which would overshadow their island. Just as the ship was in sight of the harbor, on its way back from Ithaca, Poseidon turned it to stone, and there it can be seen to this day. On seeing this disaster Alcinous remembered that an oracle had foretold Poseidon's anger because they convoyed mortals. The Phaeacians therefore sacrificed to Poseidon, to appease him and to plead with him not to raise up a mountain over their city. Withdrawing into their battlemented island they resolved that henceforth they would no longer give safe escort to mortals who came to them from the sea.

Phaeax (fē'aks). In Greek mythology, a son of Corcyra and Poseidon. He was born on the island named for Corcyra and became the ancestor of the Phaeacians. Some say he piloted the Athenian fleet which carried Theseus and the other Athenian youths and maidens who were going to Crete as tribute to King Minos, because the Phaeacians were skilled pilots. And it was Phaeax who steered them away to safety after Theseus killed the Minotaur and the Athenians escaped to the ships. Theseus afterward established the Pilots' Festival in his honor.

Phaedima (fē'di-ma). A daughter of the Persian nobleman Otanes. She was one of the wives of Cambyses. After the death of Cambyses she was given as wife, as was the custom, to his successor. At her father's command she risked her life to discover that the man who was posing as Smerdis, son of Cyrus, was an impostor. She discovered this by feeling for his ears as he slept. But he had no ears, thus confirming the suspicion of her father that the man who was posing as Smerdis was really a Median magus who had had his ears lopped off as a punishment for a crime. Following the death of the impostor, Phaedima became one of the wives of Darius, who succeeded him. See **Smerdis, False.**

Phaedo (fē'dō) or **Phaedon** (fē'don). Greek philosopher, born at Elis, Greece, and active in the first part of the 4th century B.C. He was a disciple of Socrates. His name is given to a celebrated dialogue of Plato, which purports to be the last conversation of Socrates, with an account of his death.

Phaedra (fē'dra). In Greek legend, a daughter of Minos, king of Crete, and Pasiphaë. She was the sister of Ariadne. After the death of Minos, her brother Deucalion became king of Crete, and made an alliance with Theseus of Athens. To bind the alliance he gave Theseus Phaedra for wife. She bore him two sons, Acamas and Demophon. By Antiope the Amazon Theseus was the father of Hippolytus. He was a chaste and handsome youth. Theseus sent him to Troezen where he raised a temple to Artemis. Phaedra fell in love with him and followed him to Troezen. She built a temple to Aphrodite which overlooked the gymnasium where Hippolytus daily exercised. It is said that in her frustration at watching the unobtainable youth, Phaedra pierced the leaves of a nearby myrtle tree with the pin of her jeweled brooch, and that the leaves still bear the marks of her jabbings. Although she confided her feelings for Hippolytus to no one, her nurse, seeing that she ate little and slept less, soon guessed the truth. She encouraged Phaedra to send a letter to Hippolytus, confessing her love. Hippolytus, shocked to read such a letter, destroyed it and went to Phaedra to reproach her. She, fearing he might expose her, wrote a letter to Theseus in which she accused Hippolytus of actually committing the deeds she only wished he had done, and then hanged herself. Some say it was Aphrodite who caused Phaedra to fall in love with Hippolytus, because he had dedicated himself to Artemis, thus denying the power of Aphrodite, and Phaedra was the innocent victim implicated in the punishment of Hippolytus by Aphrodite.

Phaedrus (fē′drus). Athenian philosopher; born c450 B.C.; died c400 B.C. He was a friend of Socrates and is immortalized in the name of one of Plato's dialogues, the *Phaedrus*. In this, thought to be one of Plato's early works and noted as one of the most poetic, certain types of Greek rhetoric are attacked; the preëxistence and immortailty of the soul are asserted; and the doctrine of the transmigration of souls is expounded.

Phaedrus. Roman fabulist; born c15 B.C.; died c50 A.D. Originally a Macedonian slave who was brought to Rome as a boy, he became a freedman of Augustus. His five books of fables in verse are apparently renderings of Aesopian fables current in his day. Phaedrus was the principal medieval source for the fables of Aesop (q.v.).

Phaenias (fē′ni-as) or **Phanias** (fan′i-as). Greek philosopher and historian; born in Lesbos; fl. last half of the 4th century B.C. He went to Athens where he was pupil and follower of Aristotle. Only fragments of his works on history and philosophy are extant.

Phaestus (fes′tus). [Also: **Phaistos**.] In ancient geography, a city of Crete, situated in the middle of the south side of the island, on a hill 300 feet above the plain of Mesara. To the N and W, Cretan Mount Ida, where some say Zeus was born, rises above the plain. The city is mentioned by Homer in the *Iliad* as one which sent men against Troy under the leadership of Idomeneus. It was one of the most ancient cities of Crete. According to legend it was founded by Minos, whose nephew Gortys, son of Rhadamanthys, later destroyed the citadel and added the area to his realm. Remains at the site show that there were three distinct periods of occupation. The first structures date from the neolithic age. In the second period, c2000 B.C., a palace was built on the site, remains of which indicate a highly developed and prosperous civilization. This palace was destroyed, or partly destroyed, c1700 B.C., by some catastrophe, either by earthquake, or by enemy raids. However, the interruption in the prosperity of Phaestus was temporary, and a second and larger palace was constructed on the ruins of the first. This too was destroyed by means unknown, c1400 B.C.; after this the site was relatively unoccupied and was ultimately crowned by a temple of the classical period. Among present remains are traces of the structures of all three periods. Work on the excavation of the site, begun in 1900 by the Italians under Federigo Halbherr and continued in subsequent years, is still proceeding. The palace, which lies on terraces of differing levels connected by large and small staircases, follows the general plan of that at Cnossus but on a smaller scale and with more refinement. The general plan of the installations on the site includes a large paved court where dances and games were held, a theater, rooms for the performance of sacrifices, with channels to collect the blood of victims, gypsum shelves for the exhibition of statues and cult objects, an ingenious system for supplying the area with water and an intricate drainage system. The palace itself, approached through a propylaeum, had a large central court with porticoes, at least on the east and west sides, a great colonnaded reception hall that was approached by a majestic stairway, *megaron* (central hall), guest rooms, baths, storage areas, and other chambers for the use of the royal family and those occupied in serving it. The women's quarters were separate from the men's. Only the king, by a private stairway, could pass the sentry who guarded the women's quarters. Remains of a bathroom and bath have been found. The bath was a sunken chamber, with steps lead-

fat, fāte, fär, fāre, errant; net, mē, hėr ardent; pin, pīne; not, nōte, mŏve, nôr,

ing down to it, surrounded by a balcony on which a maid might stand to pour water over her mistress. Some say, however, that such a sunken chamber had ceremonial significance, and was used for purification rites. As at Cnossus, careful and brilliant provision was made for insulating the palace against the hot sun of summer and the bitter winds that swept down from the north in winter. The plaster of the walls was mixed with straw to provide air spaces, even as is done today in the houses of the Cretan farmers. Two sets of doors, with an air space between them, protected the main chambers from drafts or heat. For light and ventilation the palace had light wells, covered at the top and with openings cut in the walls below the roof. Of the many finds at Phaestus, a clay disc that had been hardened and preserved in the fire that destroyed the palace was unique. On the two faces of the Phaestus Disc appear pictographic inscriptions in spiral form, which, according to a recent effort at decipherment, can be read as Greek, and list Cretan shrines to be visited by the pious traveler.

Phaëthon (fā′e-thon). In Greek mythology, a son of Helius and Clymene. When his boasts that he was a son of Helius were jeered by his companions, he asked his mother to give him some proof of his paternity. Clymene advised him to go to his father's palace and question him in person. Phaëthon joyfully set out for the palace, which some say was in Colchis. On appearing before Helius he was assured that he was indeed his son, Helius even offering to grant him any boon he demanded as proof. Phaëthon immediately asked permission to drive his father's chariot (the sun) across the heavens. Helius, regretting his promise, tried to persuade Phaëthon to choose some other boon. He knew that Phaëthon would not be able to control the fiery horses that drew the chariot, and that such an expedition would end in disaster. But Phaëthon insisted and as Helius had given his oath he now sorrowfully fulfilled it. As Helius had foreseen, Phaëthon had not the strength to control the horses, nor was he familiar with the path the chariot must take across the heavens. Moreover he was frightened by the monsters—the Scorpion,

Crab, Serpent, and others—that menaced the path. The horses, missing the firm hand that usually reined them in, charged about the heavens in a frenzy of freedom. They soared so high that the heat of the chariot did not reach the earth and earth shivered, but the North Star became warm. Then they swooped down, setting fire to the clouds and coming so close to earth that it burst into flames. Some say the brown people of Ethiopia got their color when the chariot came too close and scorched them. The heat of the chariot, skimming so close to the earth, dried up rivers and set the land afire. Zeus, to preserve the earth and to protect Olympus from burning, hurled a thunderbolt and struck Phaëthon. He fell, blazing, into the Eridanus River. The horses broke from the yoke and scattered across the heavens. Helius kept the earth dark for a day in his grief for his son, after which he corralled his horses and resumed his daily course through the heavens. Nymphs of the Eridanus buried Phaëthon and erected his tomb. His mother and sisters came weeping to the river bank. The sisters lamented so grievously that the gods in pity turned them into poplar trees which stand on the river bank, weeping tears of amber.

Phaëthon. In Greek mythology, a son of Eos. His father was Cephalus, whom Eos had loved at sight and carried away from his rightful wife, Procris. Aphrodite stole Phaëthon and carried him off to be an attendant in one of her most sacred temples. He was called Adymnus by the Cretans; the name meant the morning and the evening star to them.

Phaëthon. Named by Homer as one of the ever-young steeds that draw the chariot of the Sun.

Phalanthus (fa-lan′thus). According to tradition, a Spartan hero who founded Tarentum in Italy (traditional date, 707 B.C.). Before he set out he was told by the oracle at Delphi that when he felt rain under a cloudless sky (*aethra*) he would win both a territory and a city. He didn't give much thought to the oracle and set out for Italy in his ships. On the way he was shipwrecked, but rescued and borne to shore by a dolphin. As he won many victories over the barbarians of Italy but took no cities,

actor; up, lūte, pull; oi, oil; ou, out; ᴛн, then; d as d or j, s as s or sh, t as t or ch, z as z or zh.

he remembered the oracle. He thought it was impossible for rain ever to fall from a cloudless sky and that therefore the oracle meant he would never take a city. He thus despaired. His wife sought to comfort him. She took his head between her knees and began to pick lice out of his hair. Seeing him so unhappy she wept for him, and covered his head with her tears. Then Phalanthus realized the meaning of the oracle, for his wife's name was Aethra. On that very night he seized the city on the Taras river from the barbarians. This city was named Tarentum, after Taras, a son of Poseidon. Coins of Tarentum showed Phalanthus riding on the dolphin's back in memory of the divine protection that brought him to Italy.

Phalaris (fal′a-ris). Tyrant of Acragas in Sicily from c570 to c554 B.C., notorious for his cruelty (notably his human sacrifices in a heated brazen bull). The inventor of the bull was the first victim to be roasted alive. The spuriousness of some 148 epistles which passed under his name was shown by the classical scholar Richard Bentley in his *Epistles of Phalaris* (1697).

Phalereus (fa-lē′rös, fa-lir′ē-us), **Demetrius.** See **Demetrius Phalereus.**

Phalerum (fa-lir′um). [Also: **Phaleron.**] In ancient geography, a seaport in Attica, Greece, on a small bay S of Athens and E of Piraeus. According to legend, Theseus sailed from here on his way to Crete with the tribute of youth and maidens demanded by King Minos. Shrines of Nausithous and Phaeax, pilots of Theseus on this voyage, were erected in Phalerum, and the Cybernesia (*Steering Festival*) was held in their honor. It was from this port also that Menestheus set sail with his fleet for the Trojan War. In ancient times Phalerum was the port of Athens, but after the time of Themistocles it was abandoned as the port of Athens because he built up and fortified the Piraeus, a more advantageous and better protected location.

Phalerus (fa-lē′rus). In Greek legend, a son of Alcon, the skilled archer and companion of Heracles. Phalerus was also skillful in the art of archery. He joined Jason on the expedition for the Golden Fleece, and was the representative of Athens in the *Argo*.

Phanagoria (fan-a-gō′ri-a). In ancient geography, a Greek colony situated on the penin-

sula now called Taman, opposite the Crimea.

Phanes (fā′nēz). An Orphic deity. According to some accounts, Phanes was born from a silver egg laid by Nyx, and afterward created the earth, sky, sun, and moon. Other accounts have him born from an egg fashioned by Cronus in the Aether. He is also called Eros, Ericapaeus, Metis, and Protogonus (First-born).

Phantasus (fan′ta-sus). According to some accounts, a child of Nyx (*Night*), and the brother of Hypnos (*Sleep*) and Thanatos (*Death*). Others say he was a son of Hypnos (Latin, Somnus). Phantasus is the god of dreams who causes dreams of inanimate objects. His brothers are Morpheus, Icelus, and Phobetor.

Phaon (fā′on). Legendary boatman of Mytilene, loved by the poetess Sappho. According to the legend, when old and ugly he carried the goddess Aphrodite across the sea and would accept no payment. For this she rewarded him with youth and beauty. Sappho is said to have leaped into the sea because her love for him was not returned.

Pharae (fā′rē, fär′ē). See **Pherae.**

Pharnabazus (fär-na-bā′zus). Persian satrap of Phrygia; fl. c400 B.C. After the complete failure of the Athenian expedition to Sicily (415–413 B.C.) Pharnabazus, with the idea of recovering the Athenian cities of Asia Minor for Persia, made an alliance with Sparta. He was a loyal and energetic ally, aiding the Spartans with men and above all, with money, and providing vigorous support to them to the end of the Peloponnesian War. Though he continued as a friend of Sparta he did not approve of the high-handed methods of the Spartan leader Lysander in Asia Minor and secured his recall. When the Spartans waged war against the Persian king Artaxerxes they treacherously turned on Pharnabazus (399 B.C.). King Agesilaus led an army against his satrapy and plundered it up to the walls of the city where Pharnabazus lived (395 B.C.). Pharnabazus asked for a meeting with Agesilaus. Agesilaus arrived first and sat down on the grass. Members of Pharnabazus' train came and began to spread rich rugs for their master, but when he saw that Agesilaus sat simply on the ground he took his seat beside him and waved away his minions with their luxurious carpets. He addressed the Spartan king. He reminded him that he had ever been a loyal and generous friend of Sparta, that he had never betrayed his trust as other satraps had done, but had throughout helped Sparta in the war against Athens. Now the Spartans rewarded him by ravaging his province so that he could hardly get his dinner except by picking up the scraps the Spartans left. Was this, he asked with dignity, a fitting reward for the services he had rendered to Sparta? Agesilaus answered that since Sparta was at war with the Persian king she must harass and fight against all the parts of his empire, including the province of Pharnabazus. Agesilaus invited him to revolt against the king and to join the Spartans as an ally. Pharnabazus displayed the same loyalty to his king as he had shown as an ally of Sparta. If Artaxerxes, he replied, replaced him and put another in command over him as satrap, he would be glad to become the friend and ally of Sparta. But as long as he held a post of command under the king he would support him with all his strength and would fight against his enemies with all his might. Agesilaus was so impressed with his loyalty that he agreed to withdraw from the territory of Pharnabazus at once, and to respect it in the future. Afterward, Pharnabazus joined the Athenian admiral Conon to his fleet, and with him defeated the Spartans at Cnidus, 394 B.C. The following year he accompanied Conon with a fleet and attacked the shores of Laconia. On his return to his satrapy he left the fleet with Conon, and gave the Athenians money to rebuild the Long Walls and to fortify the Piraeus. He opposed the King's Peace (387 B.C.), brought about by Spartan diplomacy, but accepted it on being given a daughter of King Artaxerxes in marriage. He attempted (385 and 373 B.C.) unsuccessfully to invade Egypt.

Pharnaces I (fär'na-sēz). King of Pontus (c185–169 B.C.). He conquered Sinope in 183 B.C., and unsuccessfully made war on Eumenes II of Pergamum.

Pharnaces II. King of Pontus (c63–47 B.C.); son of Mithridates VI (Mithridates the Great) of Pontus. On the suicide of Mithridates in 63 B.C., he revolted and made himself master of that part of his father's dominions lying along the Cimmerian Bosporus. He afterward invaded Pontus, but was defeated by Caesar at Zela in 47 B.C. In the triumph celebrated at Rome for this victory, one of the chariots carried the inscription: "Veni, vidi, vici" (I came, I saw, I conquered).

Pharos (fā'ros, fär'os). An island in the mouth of the Nile, opposite ancient Alexandria. It was one of the legendary homes of the sea-god Proteus, and there he kept one of his herds of seals. Menelaus was becalmed on Pharos for 20 days on his way home from the Trojan War, and succeeded in leaving the island only after catching and consulting Proteus. Ptolemy I and Ptolemy II, Greek kings of Egypt, erected a celebrated lighthouse on Pharos, which was one of the seven wonders of the ancient world.

Pharsala (fär'sä-lä). See **Pharsalus**.

Pharsalia (fär-sā'li-a). Epic poem in ten books, by Lucan (Marcus Annaeus Lucanus), on the civil war between Pompey and Caesar.

Pharsalus (fär-sā'lus). In ancient geography, a city in Thessaly, Greece, about 23 miles S of Larissa; the modern Pharsala. It is celebrated for the great battle fought near it, June 29 or Aug. 9, 48 B.C., in which Caesar with 22,000 legionaries and 1000 cavalry totally defeated Pompey and his army of 45,000 legionaries and 7000 cavalry.

Phaselis (fa-sē'lis). In ancient geography, a seaport in Lycia, Asia Minor, situated on the W shore of the Pamphylian Gulf (the modern Gulf of Antalya). According to tradition, the spear of Achilles was dedicated in the sanctuary of Athena here.

Phasis (fā'sis). [Modern name, **Rion**.] In ancient geography, a river of Colchis emptying into the Euxine Sea. Here the Argonauts anchored before approaching King Aeëtes with a demand for the return of the Golden Fleece.

Phegeus (fē'jūs). In Greek legend, a son of Alpheus. He was a king of Psophis. He purified Alcmaeon for the murder of his mother, Eriphyle, and gave his daughter Arsinoë to Alcmaeon for a wife. Alcmaeon betrayed Arsinoë and married Callirrhoë, without letting either Phegeus or Arsinoë know of his new attachment. When Phegeus learned of it he ordered his sons to kill Alcmaeon, and they did so before Arsinoë's eyes. She was still unaware of Alcmaeon's treachery, and would not listen to her father's explanation of it. She prayed that her father and her brothers would die before the new moon, to avenge the death of Alcmaeon. Phegeus gave her away as a slave. Meantime, Callirrhoë learned of the murder of Alcmaeon and prayed that her infant sons by him would grow up overnight and avenge their father's death. Her prayer was answered; her sons found the sons of Phegeus, killed them and Phegeus too, before the appearance of the new moon in the heavens. Thus the prayers of both betrayed wives of Alcmaeon were answered.

Pheidon (fī'don). King of Argos; fl. probably in the middle of the 7th century B.C. He reunited the practically independent Argive cities under his strong and able rule and Argos again played a prominent part in the affairs of the Peloponnesus. He marched at the head of an army across Arcadia to Olympia, seized the management of the Olympic Games from the Eleans, and presided over the festival himself. Afterward he restored control of the games to Pisa, in whose territory the sanctuary of Zeus at Olympia was, and who had presided over the games until Elis wrested control away from them. Pheidon also introduced a system of weights and measures into Argos which was adopted also in the Peloponnesus and in Athens. He is also said to have struck the first Greek coins in Aegina.

Phemius (fē'mi-us). In the *Odyssey*, a minstrel and bard, who entertained the suitors of Penelope during the absence of Odysseus. Odysseus spared him when he returned and destroyed the suitors, because Phemius had sung for them against his will, and because the person of a poet and singer was sacred.

Phemonoë (fē-mō'nō-ē). According to some accounts, the first priestess of Apollo at Delphi, and the first to sing in hexameter verse. She predicted the death of the dragon that guarded the sacred spring at Delphi at Apollo's hands, and his purification by the Cretans, in the following verses:

At close quarters a grievous arrow shall
Apollo shoot
At the spoiler of Parnassus; and of his
blood-guilt
The Cretans shall cleanse his hands, but
the renown shall never die.

Pheneüs (fe'nē-us). In ancient geography, a city in N Arcadia, Greece, on a river of the same name. The river once flooded its banks, and marks on the surrounding hills showed how high the water had risen. Some say that before Heracles went to Thebes he dug two chasms at the base of the hills to draw off the river, and dug a ditch through the plain to drain the rivers flowing into the Pheneüs and to prevent flooding. The city was said to have been founded by Pheneüs, an Arcadian aboriginal for whom it was named. On the acropolis was a temple of Athena Tritonia. There was also an image of Poseidon Hippios and a sanctuary of Artemis Hippias (*Horse-finder*), both founded by Odysseus, who found in Pheneüs the mares he had lost and for which he had been searching all over Greece. Thereafter Odysseus pastured his mares in Pheneüs and left instructions for their care. The sanctuary of Apollo at Pheneüs was said to have been founded by Heracles in gratitude for his victory over Augeas and the Eleans. Iphicles, brother of Heracles, was wounded in the fighting. In a fainting condition he was brought to Pheneüs, where he died. His tomb is in Pheneüs, where he was worshiped as a hero. There was a sanctuary of Eleusinian Demeter at Pheneüs, wherein the ritual was the same as at Eleusis. The people of Pheneüs claimed that Demeter visited their city in her wanderings, that Damithales and Trisaules welcomed her, and that she gave to them all manner of pulse except the bean, which the Pheneatians considered to be impure. Above all, the Pheneatians worshiped Hermes, and celebrated the Hermaea in his honor. Behind the temple of Hermes in Pheneüs was the grave of his son Myrtilus. Myrtilus, the charioteer of Oenomaus, was flung into the sea by Pelops. The Pheneatians said his body was washed ashore, that they recovered it, and brought it to Pheneüs, where he was thereafter worshiped as a hero in rites performed at night.

Pherae (fē'rē). In ancient geography, a city in Thessaly, Greece, about 25 miles SE of Larissa. According to legend, it was the home of Admetus and Alcestis. In the 4th century B.C. it became an important power under the tyrant Jason, who united Thessaly under his command. The later revolt of

fat, fāte, fär, fāre, errant; net, mē, hėr ardent; pin, pīne; not, nōte, mōve, nôr,

Thessaly against the tyrants of Pherae presented Philip II of Macedon with an opportunity to extend his power into Greece.

Pherae or **Pharae** (fa'rē). [Modern name, **Kalamai** or **Kalamata**.] City in Messenia, on the Gulf of Messenia, said to have been founded by Pharis, a son of Hermes and Phylodameia, one of the daughters of Danaus. Pherae was one of the seven gift cities offered by Agamemnon to Achilles if he would compose his quarrel with Agamemnon and return to battle in the Trojan war. Diocles, prince of Pherae, sent his twin sons Orsilochus and Crethon to accompany the Greeks in the war against Troy. They were slain in battle by Aeneas. Diocles entertained Telemachus on his journey to Sparta to seek news of his father after the Trojan War. Following the death of Diocles, Nichomachus and Gorgasus, sons of Machaon and grandsons of Asclepius, succeeded to the kingdom. The Pheraeans raised a sanctuary to them, for they naturally had healing powers, and a temple of Tyche (*Fortune*). At Pherae there was also an oracle of Hermes, which was much consulted by the sick. The first chance words that were heard on leaving the oracle constituted the oracular answers to questions that had been asked of it.

Phereclus (fer'e-klus). In Homeric legend (*Iliad*), a son of Tecton. He was especially loved by Athena, who gave him great skill and cunning in all kinds of handwork. Phereclus was the builder of the ships which Paris used when he carried off Helen. In the war that was caused by this abduction, Phereclus was slain by Meriones.

Pherecrates (fer-ek'ra-tēz). Greek writer of Attic comedy, an older contemporary of Aristophanes, who won his first victory in 437 B.C. He wrote on topical matters, such as the impudence of slaves and an attack on a new style of music; and he was also intrigued by the idea of a possible utopia. In his play *Miners,* now lost, he described a golden age that is taking place somewhere under the earth. His one political drama was an attack on Alcibiades. Fragments of his work survive.

Pherecydes (fer-e-sī'dēz). Greek chronicler, a native of the island of Lerus; fl. 5th century B.C. He lived at Athens, where he was a contemporary of Herodotus and Thucydides,

and compiled a chronicle, in ten books, of myths connected with the early history of Attica. It was he who related how the infant Dionysus was nursed by the Hyades, and he, also, who told how Zeus hid Elara from Hera in a cave under the earth, where she bore him Tityus.

Pherecydes of Syros (sī'ros). Greek mythologist and cosmologist, born on the island of Syros and active in the middle of the 6th century B.C. He is sometimes reckoned among the Seven Wise Men of ancient Greece. Fragments of his work on the origin of the world and of the gods survive. He was an Orphic and is said to have originated the doctrine of the transmigration of souls. He was one of the earliest writers of Greek prose.

Pheres (fer'ēz). In Greek legend, a son of Cretheus and his niece Tyro. He was the brother of Aeson and Amythaon, and the uncle of Jason, whom he supported in his claim to the throne of Iolcus. Pheres was the founder and king of Pherae, in Thessaly. He was the father of Admetus, who succeeded him, and of Idomene and Periapis, who was sometimes said to be the mother of Patroclus.

Pheres. A son of Jason and Medea. See **Alcimedes.**

Pheretima (fer-e-tī'ma). Mother of Arcesilaus, king of Cyrene and descendant of that Battus who founded the kingdom. Arcesilaus was driven out of his kingdom by a revolt and fled to Samos. Pheretima went to Salamis in Cyprus for refuge, and asked King Evelthon who controlled Salamis to give her an army that she might restore her son. The king gave her many rich gifts which she accepted, saying each time that she did so that the gift was a good thing, but what she really wanted was an army. At last the king gave her a golden spindle and wool for spinning, and told her this, not armies, was the kind of gift he gave to women. Arcesilaus, however, managed to recover his throne and Pheretima returned to Cyrene with him. Then he flouted an oracle, was forced to flee, and was slain in the market-place of Barca whither he had gone. Pheretima this time fled to Egypt and demanded that the Persian governor there avenge her son's death. The governor turned over an army and a fleet to her. Herodotus, who tells this story, says the troubles of Pheretima were but a pretext for the expedition; the real reason was the desire of the Persians to conquer Libya. In any case, the forces of the Persians besieged Barca, and after nine months took it by a fraud. The leading citizens were handed over to Pheretima who crucified them and maimed their wives. But, ends Herodotus, Pheretima did not escape the anger which the gods hold for those who mete out over-harsh punishment. On her return to Egypt her body was infested with worms that ate her living flesh and so caused her death.

Phiale (fī′a̱-lē). In ancient Greece, a flat, saucer-shaped vase used for pouring religious libations.

Phidias (fid′i-a̱s). Greek sculptor; the son of Charmides. He was born probably at Athens, c490 B.C.; died c430 B.C. He studied with Hegias of Athens, and later with Ageladas of Argos, who may have come to Athens in the time of Cimon. He became later, under Pericles, a counselor in political affairs at Athens as well as chief sculptor, and was a sort of supervisor of public works. Among his first works were 13 figures at Delphi ordered by Cimon, son of Miltiades, to commemorate the victory at Marathon, in which Miltiades was represented among gods and heroes. To this early period are ascribed also the *Athena Area* at Plataea, and the *Athena Promachus*, or bronze colossus, on the Acropolis at Athens. This figure was probably more than 30 feet high, and could be seen for a great distance. The statue, made in 460–450 B.C., was the largest ever made in Athens. The pedestal was discovered in 1845. The statue of *Olympian Zeus* at Elis, his greatest work and described by Pausanias, is supposed to have been about 42 feet high, seated and holding a Nike (Victory) in his hand. The flesh was of ivory and the drapery of gold, with inlaid or inscribed decoration. The throne itself, which rose above the head of the statue, was elaborately carved and decorated. Both throne and statue were surrounded with statues and paintings. Ancient writers also selected for special distinction his *Lemnian Athena*, dedicated c450 B.C. By 444 B.C. Phidias must have been at Athens, and intimately associated with Pericles in his transformation of the city. All the great monuments of Athens, including the

Parthenon, were erected at this time, within a period not longer than 20 years. The work of Phidias culminated in the *Athena Parthenos*, a chryselephantine (gold and ivory) statue of Athena in the cella of the Parthenon. It was finished and consecrated in 438 B.C. The figure was about 38 feet high, standing, and held a Nike in her right hand. The *Varvakeion Athena* at Athens (discovered in 1881) represents the statue, but inadequately. The enormous expense of these works, which was paid with money exacted from the allies of Athens, brought both Pericles and Phidias into difficulties. According to Plutarch, Phidias was accused of appropriating the gold devoted to the statue to his own use. The gold was removed, weighed, and found to be intact. He was then accused of sacrilege in representing Pericles and himself on the shield of the goddess. In one version he was condemned, thrown into prison, and died there, possibly of poison. The actual style of Phidias is best represented in the well-known fragments of the frieze of the Parthenon. Among the independent statues by Phidias was an *Amazon* at Ephesus which took second prize in competition with Polyclitus. This is supposed to be represented by the *Amazon Mattei* of the Vatican.

Phidippides (fī-dip′i-dēz). Athenian herald and athlete. When the Persians landed at Marathon (490 B.C.), he was sent as a courier from Athens to Sparta, asking the latter city's help against the invader. On the way he was met by Pan, near Mount Parthenius. The god asked him why the Athenians, to whom he had always shown himself friendly, neglected him, and promised to aid them in the coming struggle with the Persians. Phidippides continued his journey to Sparta, covering the 150-mile distance in two days, according to Herodotus. In Sparta he delivered the Athenian call for aid. The Spartans, highly sympathetic, promised to go to the assistance of the Athenians, but regretted that for religious reasons they could not set out until the full of the moon. When they did arrive the battle was over; the Athenians, with Plataean aid, had soundly beaten the Persians at Marathon. On his return to Athens Phidippides reported his conversation with Pan, and after the battle of Marathon the Athenians raised a sanctuary to the god under the Acropolis, for they considered that he had helped them as he promised, and caused the Persians to withdraw in panic before the Athenian onslaught.

Phigalia (fi-gā′li-a). In ancient geography, a town in the SW corner of Arcadia, Greece. According to tradition, the town was founded by Phigalus, a son of Lycaon. Nearby, on Mount Elaius, was a cave, sacred to Black Demeter. The Phigalians said that after Poseidon in the form of a stallion ravished Demeter, who had taken the form of a mare to escape his attention while she was searching for her lost daughter in Arcadia, Demeter gave birth to a girl child, whom they called "The Mistress." She then clothed herself in black and shut herself up in this cave on Mount Elaius. Following this the crops throughout the land died, and none could find the goddess to restore fertility to the land. At last Pan, roaming through Arcadia, discovered her whereabouts and reported to Zeus. The Phigalians said Zeus sent the Fates to appeal to her and thus appeased her wrath. The Phigalians set up an image of the goddess in the cave where she had hidden. It was a figure of a woman seated on a rock, but instead of a woman's head it had a horse's head ("Mare-headed Demeter"), out of which grew serpents and strange beasts. In one of her hands the image bore a dolphin; in the other was a dove. In succeeding years the image was burned, which was a sign that the king himself would soon die. Thereafter the Phigalians did not replace the image, and they neglected the festivals of Deo, another name for Demeter. Barrenness then fell on their land and they consulted the oracle at Delphi. The priestess advised them to honor Deo.

After this the Phigalians resumed their care of Demeter's shrine and honored her more than ever. They caused the sculptor Onatas to make a new image. On the altar built before the cave, worshipers offered grapes, other cultivated fruits, honeycombs, and raw wool. Near Phigalia was a temple of Apollo designed by Ictinus. See **Bassae**.

Phigalian Marbles (fi-gā′li-an). See **Bassae**.

Philadelphus (fil-a-del′fus), **Attalus**. See **Attalus II**.

Philadelphus, Ptolemy. See **Ptolemy II**.

Philammon (fi-lā′mon). In mythology, a son of Chione and Apollo, twin-born with Autolycus, whose father was Hermes. Philammon was noted for his singing and his playing on the lyre. See **Chione**, daughter of Daedalion.

Philemon (fi-lē′mon, fī-). See **Baucis and Philemon**.

Philemon. Greek poet of the New Comedy, born c360 B.C. either at Soli in Cilicia, or at Syracuse in Sicily. He died at an extremely advanced age at Athens, c262 B.C. He came to Athens early in life and appeared as an author in 330 B.C. The grant of Athenian citizenship to Philemon is known through inscriptions. His chief rival was the poet Menander, whom he eclipsed many times in the contests, as in his own age the sharp comedy of Philemon on subjects taken from ordinary life was more appealing than the delicate wit of Menander. It is said that he passed some time at the court of the king of Egypt. Of the 97 plays he wrote only fragments survive. He wrote the plays on which the *Mercator*, the *Mostellaria*, and the *Trinummus* of Plautus were based.

Philetaerus (fil′′e-tē′rus). Greek poet, son of Aristophanes; writer of Middle Comedy. Titles of 13 of his works survive.

Philetas (fi-lē′tas). Greek poet and prose writer; born on the island of Cos. He was a younger contemporary of Demosthenes and was active in the second half of the 4th century B.C. As a young student he was so thin that the comic poets said of him that he would have blown away if he hadn't carried lead in his shoes. He acted as tutor to Ptolemy II in Alexandria and to the poet Theocritus. Philetas was one of the first to write Alexandrian elegy. The love elegies he wrote for his mistress Battis, or Bittis, were much admired at Alexandria and Rome. Only fragments of them survive. He also wrote on Homer and wrote an epyllion (miniature epic) about the intrigue of Odysseus and Polymela.

Philia (fi-lī′a). In mythology, a nymph of the island of Naxos. According to some accounts, she helped care for the infant Dionysus when he was sent to Naxos by Zeus for safe-keeping.

Philip I (fil′ip). Legendary third king of Macedonia. According to Herodotus, he was the son of Argaeus and the grandson of Perdiccas.

This Perdiccas was a descendant of the Heraclid Temenus, who fled from Argos to Illyria and thence to Macedonia which, with his two brothers, he brought under his control. Perdiccas was succeeded by Argaeus, who was in turn succeeded by Philip I.

Philip II. King of Macedon (359–336 B.C.), born 382 B.C.; assassinated at Aegae, the old capital of Macedonia, in 336 B.C. He was the son of Amyntas II and Eurydice, and the father of Alexander the Great. Philip lived some years as a youth at Thebes, whither he had been taken as a hostage (367 B.C.), and it was from the Boeotians, under the guidance of Epaminondas whom he knew and admired, that he received his military training. For some reason he was permitted to return to Macedonia (364 B.C.). The Macedonian kings, from their ancient fortress capital at Aegae, had power over all the area on the north and northwest coasts of the Thermaic Gulf (ancient Myrtoan Sea, modern Gulf of Salonika). Beyond this area of relatively complete control, their power extended to the borders of the Illyrians in the west and to those of the Paeonians in the north, but the tribes within the region, with the active assistance of the Illyrians and Paeonians, continually contested Macedonian rule. King Perdiccas, older brother of Philip, was slain (359 B.C.), in one of the frequent wars with the Illyrians. His son Amyntas, the legitimate heir, was a child. Philip became guardian of Amyntas and immediately undertook to overcome the domestic and foreign enemies of Macedonia. His first problem was to beat back the pretenders to the throne. He defeated an Athenian fleet that came to the aid of one of them. Out of respect and admiration for the Athenians, he released without ransom those whom he had taken prisoner. His other rivals were also repulsed. The Macedonian kings were of Greek stock and Philip's lifelong policy was to identify himself with Greece and Greek culture. Having secured his power at home he next subdued the Paeonians and the Illyrians (358 B.C.), thus clearly establishing his control over his troublesome neighbors. In the same year he made a secret agreement with the Athenians by which he undertook to recapture their colony of Amphipolis on the coast of western Thrace in return for the free city of Pydna, on the west coast of the Thermaic Gulf. He took Amphipolis (358) which commanded the gold mines of Mount Pangaeus in Thrace, deceived the Athenians and kept it. As they had been perfectly willing to betray Pydna they had no just grounds to cry treachery against Philip. This did not prevent them from doing so, however. He fortified Crenides, a gold-mining settlement on the coast of Thrace opposite the island of Thasus, and renamed it Philippi for himself. The capture of Amphipolis and the fortified settlement of Philippi gave him control of a gold-mining area which made Macedonia the richest state in Greece. About this time he abandoned the old inland capital at Aegae and moved his court to Pella, somewhat nearer the sea. He took Pydna and Potidaea and handed them over to the Olynthian Confederacy. Wielding supreme authority, he now set aside his nephew and took the title of king. The next year was devoted to consolidating his power and improving his army. Men of all tribes were put under arms and had constant practice in actual warfare. The Macedonian phalanx, so skillfully and successfully used by Philip and later by his son, was organized and drilled into a mobile, effective weapon. In 357 he married Olympias, daughter of a prince of Epirus, a stormy and mystic princess who ultimately caused his death. In 356 she bore his famous son Alexander. He captured Methone (c353), the last city of Athens on the Thermaic Gulf, and on the invitation of the Thessalians, he marched into Thessaly to take part in the Sacred War against Phocis. He was forced to withdraw by the Phocians, but the following year he returned and made himself master of Thessaly, having decisively beaten the Phocians who were in temporary control there. At Thermopylae (352) he was momentarily checked by a force sent by Athens, Sparta, and Achaea to oppose his descent into Greece. In the same year he carried on successful campaigns in Thrace.

By 352 B.C. Philip had organized a formidable army and secured his treasury by control of the gold mines on the coasts of Thrace. He had subdued the rebellious tribes on his borders and won control of the lands along the north Aegean from Thermopylae to the Propontis. His ambition was to unite all

Greece under the overlordship of Macedonia and to bring the Greek culture which he admired, and of which he considered himself an heir, to Macedonia. He admired Athens above all Greek states and would have preferred to win her friendship. But Athens rejected his friendly overtures. The city that had once been the leader of the Greek world hoped to recover her power in the Aegean and to bring down Macedonia. At about this period Demosthenes in Athens began delivering the speeches known as the *Philippics,* warning the Greeks that Philip would eventually conquer all Greece unless he were opposed. On the other hand, there were some who saw in Philip a potential uniter of the quarreling Greek states. Their view did not prevail. Athens took every opportunity, no matter how flimsy and dangerous to herself and her interests, to oppose Philip. In 349 Philip marched against Chalcidice to punish Olynthus, which had betrayed him in collusion with Athens. Most of the cities of Chalcidice submitted without a contest. Those that did not were taken by force and destroyed, as was Stagira, a city which he later restored and repopulated in honor of the philosopher Aristotle, whom he had invited to become tutor to his son Alexander. In 348 Philip took Olynthus and destroyed it completely. The orations of Demosthenes known as the *Olynthiacs,* whose purpose was to stir the Athenians to aid Olynthus, resulted in the sending of an Athenian force to the rescue of Olynthus. But the Athenians arrived too late. Olynthus had fallen; the city was razed and its citizens sold into slavery. Philip maintained his tolerant spirit toward Athens; envoys sent from there to Pella were courteously received. A peace was made but, thanks to the intransigence of Demosthenes, the terms were not so broad as to include the alliance between Athens and Macedonia, which Philip wanted. When, as a result of the Sacred War, Phocis was expelled from the Amphictyonic Council (346 B.C.), Macedonia took her place, and Philip presided over the Pythian Games held in the same year. In 342, by campaigns in Thrace, he made the Thracian kingdom a dependency of Macedonia and built the city of Philippopolis there as a center of Macedonian influence. In 340–339 he besieged

Perinthus and Byzantium. Athens supported his enemies in the region, and without a fleet his sieges were unsuccessful. In 339 the Amphictyonic Council called on him for aid against the Locrians of Amphissa in a new Sacred War. Philip at once answered the summons. He captured Amphissa, and then went into Boeotia where Athens and Thebes, alarmed at his growing influence in Greece, had united to oppose him. He completely defeated their combined forces at Chaeronea (338 B.C.). He placed a Macedonian garrison over Thebes, but true to his policy of respect and friendship for Athens (which was very shabbily rewarded on the whole), he treated Athens leniently. He released the Athenian prisoners without ransom and gave Oropus to Athens, but compelled her to surrender the Chersonesus to Macedonia. He returned the Athenians who fell in the battle of Chaeronea to Athens for burial, under a guard of honor that included his son. The Athenians set up a statue of Philip in the agora in gratitude for his generosity. After this, Philip marched into the Peloponnesus which submitted without a struggle, except for Sparta, which suffered devastation at his hands for its obstinacy.

Philip was now master of all Greece. He summoned all the Greek states to a congress at Corinth. All except Sparta sent representatives. In the following year (337 B.C.) he was elected commander of the Greek forces to liberate the Greek cities of Asia Minor from the Persians, and to avenge the barbarous acts against the Greeks and their gods committed by the Persians in the days of Xerxes. An advance expedition was sent to the Hellespont under Parmenio, but Philip was assassinated before he could take the field. Despite his genius as a conqueror and administrator he could not keep order in his own household. His wife Olympias, whose reputation was not stainless (to such a degree that it was whispered that Philip was not the father of her great son Alexander), became inflamed at the infidelities of Philip. He had conceived a profound distaste for her when he found a serpent lying beside her as she slept. He had attachments with many women, some of whom were temporarily acknowledged as wives in the polygamous Macedonian court. He fell in love with

Cleopatra, niece of his general Attalus, and added to the fury of Olympias by definitely casting her aside to marry Cleopatra. At the wedding feast, Attalus proposed a toast and publicly hoped for a *legitimate* heir. Alexander dashed a cup of wine in the face of Attalus for the insult to his mother. Philip rose to slay his son with his sword, but tripped over a couch as he lunged at him. With scorn, Alexander pointed to his father as a "man who would pass from Europe to Asia but trips in passing from couch to couch." After this Alexander fled the court of Philip and went with his mother to Epirus. When a son was born to Philip and Cleopatra, Alexander feared lest his place in the succession be disturbed. The fire kindled in Olympias by her supposed wrongs had not in the least cooled. She found, with Alexander's knowledge, a tool for her longed-for vengeance. At the marriage of Philip's daughter to the king of Epirus, a pawn of Olympias named Pausanias rushed at Philip as he marched in the wedding procession and stabbed him with a Celtic dagger. Pausanias was caught and killed; Olympias, sister of the bridegroom, was avenged, as she thought, and Alexander's succession was assured. Philip's death fulfilled an oracular pronouncement. The oracle of Trophonius had warned him to beware of a chariot, and because of this Philip never entered one. But it was to no avail: on the ivory hilt of the dagger Pausanias plunged into his side was engraved the figure of a chariot. Philip had done what no Greek state was strong enough to do: he united Greece. His reign marks the end of the old city-state system in Greece and the growth of a Greek nation. By his organization of the army and his selection of generals, he prepared the way for Alexander's conquests.

Philip III (of *Macedon*). [Also: **Philip III Arrhidaeus.**] King of Macedon 323–317 B.C.; murdered 317 B.C. He was an illegitimate son of Philip II. He was proclaimed king by the troops after Alexander's death in 323 B.C. His own death was caused by Olympias, widow of Philip II and mother of Alexander.

Philip IV (of *Macedon*). King of Macedon; son of Cassander. He reigned for a few months c297 B.C.

Philip V (of *Macedon*). King of Macedon (220–179 B.C.); born 238 B.C.; died 179 B.C. He was a son of Demetrius II. His father died while he was still a child, and the kingdom was governed by a regent, a cousin of Philip's. Philip assumed complete power when the regent died, 220 B.C. He was at war with the Aetolian League (220–217), was allied with Carthage and at war with Rome (later also with the Aetolian League) 214–205 B.C., and began the second war against Rome in 200. He was defeated by Flaminius at Cynoscephalae in 197 B.C., and was thereafter at peace with the Romans, recognizing them as his masters and concentrating on his own Macedonian kingdom. Philip's reign marks the disappearance of Greece as a world power.

Philippi (fi-lip′ī). In ancient geography, a city in Macedonia, about 73 miles NE of Thessalonica. It was founded by Philip II of Macedon in 358 B.C., and is famous as the site of the two battles in 42 B.C., in which Octavian and Mark Antony defeated the republicans under Brutus and Cassius. A Christian church was founded here by Paul, who addressed to the congregation the Epistle to the Philippians.

Philippics (fi-lip′iks), **The.** Group of orations of Demosthenes, directed against Philip II of Macedon. In these orations Demosthenes urges his fellow Athenians to resist conquest by Philip. They comprise the First Philippic, urging the sending of a military force to Thrace, delivered in 351 B.C.; three orations (also called the *Olynthiacs*) in behalf of the city of Olynthus (destroyed by Philip), delivered in 349–348; the oration *On the Peace* (346); the Second Philippic (344); the oration *On the Embassy* (343); the speech *On the Chersonese* (341); and the Third Philippic (341 B.C.). A Fourth Philippic has also survived. The name is also given to a series of 14 orations of Cicero against Mark Antony, delivered in 44–43 B.C. The word "philippic" has come, therefore, to mean any speech of caustic denunciation.

Philippides (fi-lip′i-dēz). See **Phidippides.**

Philistus (fi-lis′tus). Greek historian of Syracuse, born c432 B.C.; died 356 B.C. He held high office under the tyrant Dionysius the Elder, but then fell from favor for some reason and was banished by the tyrant. He went to Adria on the Adriatic coast and there occupied himself by writing a history of Sicily which was an important source of the history of Syracuse, especially of his own time. His work, in 13 books, covered the history of Sicily from the earliest times through the capture of Acragas (Agrigentum) by the Carthaginians (406 B.C.), the reign of Dionysius the Elder, and part of the reign of Dionysius the Younger, by whom he was recalled. In the reign of Dionysius the Younger he returned to Syracuse, but he was against the philosophical ideas of an ideal state with which Plato was seeking to inculcate Dionysius the Younger, and worked for the restoration of the tyranny. For a time he was successful, and Plato returned to Athens. When Dionysius the Younger was deposed by Dion (357 B.C.) and took refuge in the island citadel of Syracuse, Philistus brought a fleet to the relief of Dionysius. Philistus was defeated in a sea-fight and he was captured. According to Plutarch, the Syracusans subjected him to great cruelty as a defender of tyrants. He was dragged through the streets by one leg by boys while the Syracusans mocked and jeered him, recalling that he had once told Dionysius that "he must not run away from his tyranny on a swift horse, but wait until he was dragged from it by the leg." His head was cut off and his body was thrown into the quarries. Other accounts relate that he committed suicide when Dion defeated him in a naval encounter.

Philius (fil′i-us). Epithet of Zeus, meaning "Friendly." In the sacred enclosure of the Great Goddesses (Demeter and her daughter), at Megalopolis in Arcadia, was a temple of Zeus Philius. The image in the temple was made by Polyclitus, and showed the god holding a thyrsus on which an eagle perched.

Philo (fī′lō). Greek sculptor of the time of Alexander the Great. Among his works was a statue of Alexander's friend Hephaestion and an image of Zeus that was set up at the entrance to the Bosporus.

Philo. Athenian architect; fl. latter part of the 4th century B.C. He built the portico to the great temple at Eleusis for Demetrius Phalereus (c318 B.C.), and ship installations at the Piraeus. The latter were destroyed by Sulla (86 B.C.).

Philo or **Philo Judaeus** (jö-dē′us). [Also: **Philo of Alexandria.**] Hellenistic Jewish philosopher of Alexandria; born probably at Alexandria, c30 B.C.; died c45 A.D. He went to Rome (c40 A.D.) at the head of an embassy of five Jews, to plead with Caligula for the uninterrupted exercise of their religion, a privilege that had been suspended because the Jews refused to give the emperor divine homage. His philosophy sought to reconcile Hellenistic doctrines, such as Neoplatonism, with the teachings of the Pentateuch. His work had a great influence upon early Christian literature.

Philo of Larissa. Greek philosopher; fl. in the first half of the 1st century B.C. He left Athens during the Mithridatic Wars and went to Rome, where he became a teacher of rhetoric and philosophy. Cicero was one of his pupils.

Philochorus (fil-ō-kôr′us). Greek historian; fl. at Athens in the first half of the 3rd century B.C. He opposed Demetrius Poliorcetes and his son Antigonus Gonatas, who put him to death after Athens was taken. Of his *Atthis,* a history of Attica in 17 books, fragments survive.

Philocles (fil′ō-klēz). Greek tragedian, nephew of Aeschylus. Of the many tragedies he wrote in the manner of Aeschylus, only fragments remain. He is notable for having won the first prize over Sophocles' *Oedipus Rex,* but the play with which he won it is lost.

Philoctetes (fil-ok-tē′tēz). In Greek legend, a son of Poeas, king of Meliboea in Thessaly. He was the only one who had the compassion and courage to set the funeral pyre of Heracles alight when that hero laid himself down and begged to be released from his suffering. As a reward, Heracles gave him his bow and arrows. Some say Heracles also made Philoctetes promise not to reveal his grave. When the Greeks assembled to sail against Troy to recover Helen, Philoctetes, as one of her former suitors, commanded seven ships. After the second mustering at Aulis the Greeks sailed to Tenedos. There, as they were sacrificing to Apollo, Philoctetes was bitten by a water-snake; some say Hera punished him in this manner for helping her enemy, Heracles. His wound did not heal, and became so repulsive that the Greeks put him ashore on the island of Lemnos and abandoned him. Some say however, that he was bitten on the small island of Chryse, near Lemnos, where for centuries an altar of Philoctetes, a bronze serpent, bow, and breastplate could be seen. The island had disappeared beneath the sea by the 2nd cen-

PHILOCTETES
Red-figured Greek lecythus, c430 B.C.
Metropolitan Museum of Art

tury A.D. Still others say Philoctetes was not bitten by a snake at all, but accidentally stepped on one of Heracles' poisoned arrows, and that this was a punishment for revealing Heracles' grave, by stamping on it meaningfully when he was questioned. In any event, on the advice of Odysseus he was abandoned on Lemnos and lived there in misery, clothing himself with the feathers of birds, eating what he could catch, and suffering horribly from his festering wound. After the death of Achilles the Greeks learned that Troy could not be taken without the arrows of Heracles and hurriedly sent Odysseus and Diomedes to fetch Philoctetes from Lemnos. He would have slain them in his anger at their heartless desertion but, aided by Athena and the shade

of Heracles, Odysseus persuaded him to accompany them to Troy. There he was healed by Podalirius (or as some say, by Machaon), and seemed like one reborn. He went immediately into battle, and one of his arrows killed Paris. He disapproved of the proposal to take Troy by the stratagem of the Wooden Horse, as he preferred to fight bravely in the open, but yielded and was one of those who entered the city by this means. At the end of the war Philoctetes returned to his home but was forced to flee from it by rebels. He went to the Campanians in Italy, and founded the cities of Petelia and Crimissa. Nearby he founded a sanctuary of Apollo the Wanderer, in which he dedicated the bow and arrows of Heracles. When he died he was buried beside the Sybaris River.

Philoctetes. Drama by Sophocles, produced in 409 B.C. It concerns Philoctetes, abandoned on the desolate island of Lemnos by the Greeks on their way to Troy because of a malodorous wound, and Neoptolemus, son of Achilles, who comes with Odysseus ten years later to fetch him to Troy.

Odysseus and Neoptolemus, accompanied by a chorus of sailors, land on the desolate coast of Lemnos. Neoptolemus, having found the cave where Philoctetes lives, is moved to pity by the bed of leaves, the crude cup, and tattered garments drying in the sun. Philoctetes is nowhere in sight. Now Odysseus reveals that Philoctetes hates him because he holds him responsible for his desertion on Lemnos. He must be tricked into accompanying them to Troy, since he cannot be taken by force. Neoptolemus, whom Philoctetes has never seen, must tell him that he has deserted the Greeks and is returning to Scyrus, because when he joined the Greeks at their urgent request, they refused to give him his dead father's armor, but gave it instead to Odysseus. The idea of lying and trickery, second nature to Odysseus, is repugnant to the straightforward son of Achilles, who prefers to trust in his strength and courage and would "rather lose by fair means than win by foul." Odysseus commends this sentiment, but says age and experience have shown him the necessity for cunning. Not only is Philoctetes invincible with his arrows, but Troy cannot be taken without him. As a good soldier, Neoptolemus must obey the commands of his leaders to return with Philoctetes. Odysseus hides, and the sailors comment on the desolate country and express sympathy for the sufferer compelled to live there. Philoctetes hobbles in, his foot raggedly bandaged. In his hand he holds the bow of Heracles. Joyfully he sees the strangers and longs to hear if they are Greeks. Neoptolemus says he is a Greek on his way home from Troy, and pretends he has never heard of Philoctetes. Commenting bitterly on the loyalty of the Greeks, Philoctetes tells how he was stung by a serpent and abandoned by his comrades as he slept, because they could not bear his noxious, incurable wound. Suffering from loneliness and pain, he could barely keep alive with the aid of his bow. Above all, he expresses his hatred of Odysseus and the Atreidae who forsook him. Neoptolemus truly sympathizes with him, yet he tells the story Odysseus prepared. Philoctetes believes him at once and eagerly asks for news of his comrades, but when Neoptolemus prepares to leave he begs to be taken with him. The sailors add their pleas, and Neoptolemus consents, even promising to take Philoctetes to his home in Oeta. At this moment two sailors, disguised as merchants, approach, and tell Neoptolemus they have just come from Troy, and that the Greeks are pursuing him. They say Odysseus and Diomedes have sailed to fetch Philoctetes, because they have learned from Trojan Helenus, captured by Odysseus, that Troy cannot be taken without these two. When the men depart Philoctetes begs Neoptolemus to put to sea at once, to escape pursuit, but Neoptolemus lingers. He asks about the bow, and if he may hold it. Philoctetes willingly gives it to him, because of his goodness, he says, and adds that no one else has ever handled it. In a moment he asks Neoptolemus to return it, and he does so, almost involuntarily, and thanks Philoctetes and calls him his friend. They go into the cave. Alone, the chorus sings of the misery of Philoctetes: even wicked Ixion did not suffer as does this good and innocent man. As they come from the cave, Philoctetes is overcome by a spasm of pain. The young man wants to help him, and Philoctetes hands him the bow. Neoptolemus

promises that it will not fall into other hands. As the pain becomes more cruel, Philoctetes begs to be burned on a pyre, as he had ended the suffering of Heracles and been given the bow as a reward. Neoptolemus, deeply moved, promises not to leave him, as Philoctetes drops to the ground in an exhausted sleep. The chorus advises Neoptolemus to be off with the bow. He hesitates, and Philoctetes wakes, overjoyed to find his noble friend still there. Now as Neoptolemus prepares to help him to the ship he pauses. The complete trust Philoctetes has shown makes it even harder to carry out the trick Odysseus planned. He can betray neither a weak and wounded man who trusts him, nor his own instincts. He tells him the truth. Philoctetes is stunned. He refuses to go to Troy. He demands the bow he so trustingly handed over. Neoptolemus starts to return it, but Odysseus rushes up and forbids it. Philoctetes is beside himself as he understands that Odysseus has made Neoptolemus a stalking horse for this plot. Odysseus tries to calm him; his wound will be cured, he says, and he will have the glory of helping to conquer Troy; but nothing can persuade Philoctetes. He would rather die, and even attempts to leap from the rocks but the sailors hold him back. Seeing it is hopeless, Odysseus persuades Neoptolemus, who still has the bow, to leave. The sailors sympathize with Philoctetes, but they cannot help him in defiance of their leader and they hold him responsible if he chooses to die alone on Lemnos. Determined and hopeless, Philoctetes crawls back into his cave as the sailors leave. Neoptolemus returns. Despite the arguments of Odysseus he has decided to right the wrong he committed and restore the bow to Philoctetes. He calls Philoctetes from the cave, assures him that he is his friend, and gives him back his bow. Now he tries to persuade Philoctetes to go to Troy. He says his wound is a punishment from heaven because he invaded the sanctuary of Chryse, that it will never be cured unless he goes to Troy, where the sons of Asclepius will heal him and where, with his bow, he will bring about the destruction of Troy. All this the Greeks have learned from Helenus. But Philoctetes' hatred of Odysseus and the Atreidae is implacable; he will not rejoin them, instead, he reminds Neoptolemus of his promise to take him home. Neoptolemus pauses, makes up his mind, and says he will carry out his promise. As they turn to leave, the shade of Heracles appears. It is the will of heaven, he says, for Philoctetes to take the bow and go to Troy. He will be cured; he must kill Paris, and take part in the sack of Troy. To Neoptolemus, he says that Troy cannot be conquered unless he and Philoctetes are there. Philoctetes yields to the will of Heracles, bids farewell to Lemnos, and departs for Troy with Neoptolemus.

Philodemus (fil-ọ-dē′mus). Greek Epicurean philosopher; born in Gadara, Palestine; fl. in the 1st century B.C. He was a contemporary of Cicero, who admired his poetic style but decried his manner of living. Thirty-four love epigrams by Philodemus have been preserved in the *Palatine Anthology,* and fragments of his prose works on various subjects were recovered in the excavation of Piso's villa at Herculaneum.

Philoetius (fi-lē′shus). In the *Odyssey,* a cowherd who remained faithful to his master, Odysseus, during his long absence at the Trojan War and the ten years following it. He was one of the few to treat Odysseus hospitably when he returned to his homeland disguised as a beggar, and showed by his conversation with his disguised master that he had taken faithful care of his cattle and was longing for his return. When Odysseus finally revealed himself to his faithful servant, Philoetius promised to help him destroy Penelope's suitors, and was one of the few who fought beside him in the great hall of the palace at the battle in which all the wooers were slain.

Philolaus (fil-ọ-lā′us). Greek philosopher of the 5th century B.C., one of the chiefs of the Pythagoreans. Fragments of his works are extant.

Philomela (fil-ọ-mē′la). In Greek legend, a daughter of Pandion, king of Athens. She was the sister of Procne, and was transformed into a swallow by the gods. See **Procne.**

Philomele (fil-ọ-mē′lē). In Greek legend, a daughter of Actor. According to some accounts, she was the mother of Patroclus.

Philomelides (fil″ọ-mẹ-lī′dēz). In Greek legend, a king of Lesbos. It was his custom to compel travelers or guests to wrestle with him. He always won, and killed his opponents until Odysseus wrestled with him and defeated him when the Greeks stopped at Lesbos on their way to Troy, after the sacrifice of Iphigenia.

Philomelus (fil-ọ-mē′lus). Phocian general of the 4th century B.C., who rallied his countrymen to resist the heavy fines that had been levied on them by the Amphictyonic League that charged them with impiety. He cited the Homeric verses from the *Iliad,* "Phocian warriors . . . . Those who possessed Cyparissus and likewise Pytho the rocky." These verses he made the basis of a claim that Phocis rightfully owned Delphi (Pytho), and proposed to seize it. With the rich treasures of the sanctuary in their possession the Phocians could raise levies to resist the Amphictyonic League. The Phocians took Delphi and fortified the treasury with a wall. Philomelus wished the oracle to continue its prophecies, for he did not want to alienate the rest of the Greek world, but the priestess refused. He threatened the priestess and in alarm she told him to do as he liked. Taking this as permission, he availed himself of the treasures of the sanctuary. One of those said to have been taken by him was the great golden shield given to Delphi by the Lydian king, Croesus. Philomelus and the soldiers he hired with the proceeds of the treasures held off their enemies for years but at last suffered defeat at Neon, on the slopes of Mount Parnassus. Philomelus fought bravely but, covered with wounds, was driven to the edge of a cliff. There, rather than submit to capture, he hurled himself over it to his death.

Philon (phī′lon). See **Philo.**

Philonis (fil-ọ′nis). A name sometimes given for the mother of Philammon and Autolycus. See **Chione.**

Philopoemen (fil-ọ-pē′men). General of the Achaean League, called "the Last of the Greeks" because, so it is said, Greece produced no more illustrious men after him. He was born at Megalopolis, Arcadia, Greece, c252 B.C.; drank poison at Messene, Greece, 183 B.C. His father Craugis, an aristocrat, died in Philopoemen's infancy, and he was brought up by a Mantinean exile who lived at Megalopolis. He was well educated, and from childhood showed an interest in and aptitude for the military arts. In young manhood he occupied himself with hunting, tilling his lands, studying the philosophers, reading military histories, and studying the more warlike parts of Homer. He is described as of splendid physique, powerful, modest in dress and manner, frugal at table, and homely. Concerning his plain features, Plutarch tells that once, after he had become general of the Achaean League, he arrived as a guest at a house in Megara. His hostess who had never seen him before noted his simple dress and homeliness and thought he was a servant. She set him to work chopping wood, which he did without protest or explanation. When his host came home and found his distinguished guest performing the work of a servant he asked the meaning of it. Philopoemen gravely told him he was "paying the fine of my deformity."

In 223 B.C. Cleomenes III of Sparta made a surprise attack on Megalopolis at night and seized t h e market-place. Philopoemen escaped with a group of young men. He persuaded them not to treat with Cleomenes, as they were willing to do, but to go back and win Megalopolis by force of arms. He and his group joined with the Achaeans and Arcadians, and the Macedonians under Antigonus, and met and defeated the Spartans at Sellasia, 222 B.C. In the battle Philopoemen, a cavalryman, saw that the infantry would decide the battle. He voluntarily gave up his horse and joined the foot-soldiers. He fought with great bravery and skill. It is said that an enemy spear pierced both his thighs and pinned his legs together. In his determination to keep fighting, he sank to his knees and by a violent movement of his legs broke the enemy spear. Antigonus was filled with admiration for him and invited him to serve under him in Macedonia. Philopoemen declined. Instead he sailed to Crete as a leader of mercenaries and took part in a civil war there. When he returned to Megalopolis, after 11 years, he was named commander of the Achaean League. With authority and discipline he shaped his forces into a splendid fighting machine. The mettle of the forces was tested at the Larisus River (210 B.C.) when, with his allies, he defeated the Eleans and the Aetolians and killed their commander. He was now greatly admired and was given the opportunity to reorganize the infantry. He replaced their short spears and oblong wicker shields with long spears and round shields, and gave the foot-soldiers breastplates and greaves to protect their bodies. He was insistent that the soldiers keep their armor bright, that the glitter of shining armor might terrify the enemy. Following the defeat of the Eleans and Aetolians, he engaged the Spartan tyrant Machanidas at Mantinea (207 B.C.). The Achaeans seemed to have lost the battle, but Philopoemen regrouped his forces, chose new ground for his attack, and drew victory from defeat; Machanidas was slain and his severed head was exhibited to the Achaeans. Following the victory he went on and took Tegea, and marched into Laconia and pillaged it at will. After this he was so idolized that when the harpist at the Olympic Games began the ode:

Who to Greece gives the great and glorious
   jewel of freedom,

all eyes turned to Philopoemen, and the whole company burst into applause. His name alone inspired fear in his enemies: the Thebans withdrew from Megara when it was rumored that Philopoemen was coming to the aid of the city; Nabis, the new tyrant of Sparta, evacuated Messene (201 B.C.) on news that Philopoemen, no longer a general but a private citizen, had arrived before the city with the army; Philip V of Macedon so feared him he tried to have him assassinated. When his term as general was up Philopoemen went back to Crete. For this he was much criticized, as he left Megalopolis hard-pressed by its enemies. By request, he returned to his country some years later and again became commander of the Achaeans (altogether he was commander eight times). Philip V had been defeated by the Romans. Nabis of Sparta was at war with Rome and the Achaeans. Philopoemen defeated the Spartans, burned their camp at Gythium, compelled the Spartans to join the Achaean League (191 B.C.), and prevented the Romans from entering the city of Sparta. For this last the Spartans, having got rid of Nabis, offered him rich gifts, which he refused. In 184 B.C. the city of Messene revolted. Philopoemen sent Lycortas to quell the revolt, which was the second that had broken out in Messene, then, with a small band, he decided to go to Messene himself, unaware that Lycortas was already on his way back. In a skirmish Philopoemen was wounded in the head, taken captive, and carried off as a prisoner. According to Pausanias, the aristocrats clamored for his death, while the people, who called him the "Father of the Greeks" wanted to save him. Someone sent him poison, and rather than endure the shame of having been taken alive, he drank the poison. His bones were later returned to Megalopolis; many statues were set up to honor him for his successes against tyrants. One at Tegea described him as the "author of blameless freedom." Thirty-seven years after his death (146 B.C.) certain of the Romans wanted to destroy the statues. The Greek general and historian Polybius defended Philopoemen, and the Roman consul Mummius, noted for the barbarity with which he had ravaged Greece, refused to dishonor Philopoemen; the statues of the man who had reorganized the forces of the Achaean League and used them so effectively were allowed to stand.

Philotas (fil-ō'tas). Macedonian general, killed 330 B.C., in Drangiana, C Asia. He was the son of Parmenio, general who served Philip as well as Alexander. Under Alexander, Philotas commanded the heavy cavalry of the Macedonian forces. On the successful expedition into Asia great treasures were taken as spoils and distributed among the Macedonians. Philotas made an ostentatious display in gift-giving and indulged himself in the most arrogant extravagance and luxury. He is said to have boasted to his concubine, Antigone, who had been given to him as part of his share in the spoils, that the victories for which Alexander took credit were won by his father and himself. Antigone repeated his indiscreet and boastful words to his enemies, and they came at last to the ears of Alexander. While in Drangiana, a plot to kill Alexander was uncovered; Philotas was accused. Though boastful and arrogant, no proof that he was connected with the plot was brought forward. However, he is said to have admitted that he knew of the existence of a plot but had done nothing about it. The Macedonians, before whom his case was laid by Alexander, found

him guilty, pierced him with their javelins, and killed him.

Philoxenus (fi-lok'se-nus). Greek dithyrambic poet, born in the island of Cythera, c435 B.C., died at Ephesus, 380 B.C. When Cythera was conquered by the Athenians he was taken as a prisoner of war to Athens and sold as a slave to Melanippides, the dithyrambic poet. Melanippides educated him and set him free. Philoxenus went to Syracuse to the court of Dionysius the Elder. Dionysius fancied himself as a poet, and when Philoxenus criticized his work, he sent him to work in the stone quarries. Philoxenus escaped from Sicily and traveled in Greece and Asia Minor, giving performances of his work. He avenged himself on Dionysius by writing a dithyramb which was his masterpiece. It was entitled *Cyclops* and parodied the unsuccessful love of the clumsy, one-eyed Cyclops for the nymph Galatea. Dionysius was blind, or partially blind, in one eye. The 24 dithyrambs of Philoxenus, fragments of which remain, were very popular with the ancients for their wit and variety of melody.

Philyra (fil'i-ra). In Greek mythology, a daughter of Oceanus. She lived on an island named for her. Cronus, in the infancy of Zeus, lay with Philyra, deceiving Rhea. When he was discovered by Rhea Cronus changed himself into a stallion. Philyra gave birth to Chiron, half-horse and half-god (or man), as the result of Cronus' transformation. She prayed to be relieved of her burden of nursing her unnatural child and was metamorphosed into a linden tree, the flowers of which came to be frequently used in medicine, and the bark of which was used in foretelling the future.

Phineus (fī'nūs, fin'e-us). In Greek mythology, a son of Agenor and Telephassa and the brother of Cadmus and Europa. After searching vainly for his sister Europa when she was abducted by Zeus, he settled down and became king of Salmydessus in Thrace. He married Cleopatra, daughter of Boreas, and had two sons. Then he abandoned Cleopatra and married Idaea, daughter of Dardanus. According to one account, he was blinded by Zeus because of his unerring prophecies—Zeus wanted the gods alone to know the secrets of the future—and was tormented by the Harpies who defiled his food so that he was perpetually on the verge of starvation. When the Argonauts, accompanied by Cleopatra's brothers Calais and Zetes, landed on Phineus' shores they promised to help him. As winged sons of Boreas (the North Wind), Calais and Zetes swiftly overtook the horrible creatures and would have slain them, but Iris was sent to forbid them to kill "the hounds of Zeus" and to promise that they would no longer torment Phineus. In return, Phineus gave them valuable advice for their journey. He told them how they could safely pass the Symplegades, or Clashing Rocks, how to drive away the birds of Ares so that they could land on the island of Ares, and predicted that Aphrodite would assist them when they arrived in Colchis. According to some accounts, Phineus was blinded by Zeus because he had blinded his own sons on receipt of false accusations against them from Idaea. As a punishment, he could choose between death or blindness. When he chose blindness, Helius sent the Harpies to torment him because of his impiety in choosing never to look upon the sun again. In this version, Phineus was killed by his sons, whose sight had been restored, and they became rulers of his kingdom.

Phineus. In classical mythology, a brother of Cepheus, king of Ethiopia, and the uncle of Andromeda, to whom he was betrothed. When Andromeda was chained to a rock as a sacrifice to a sea monster, to punish her mother for boastfulness, Phineus lacked the courage or ability to slay the monster and rescue the maiden. Perseus, on his way home from killing Medusa, slew the monster and won Andromeda for his bride. But Phineus, since the monster was safely dead, invaded the palace during the wedding feast with a mob and claimed Andromeda, saying she had been promised to him. With his followers he attacked Perseus. A fierce struggle broke out, in which many were killed, but Perseus won the battle and retained his bride by exhibiting the head of Medusa and so turning Phineus and his remaining companions to stone. In other accounts the man who claimed Andromeda and was turned to stone by Perseus was named as Agenor of Tyre.

Phintias (fin'ti-as). Attic potter and painter,

active at the end of the 6th and the beginning of the 5th centuries B.C. His signature as painter appears on four extant vessels, as potter on three. A cup (Munich), c520 B.C., is inscribed "Deiniades made, Phintias painted." The inside of the cup has a Silen with a drinking cup. One side of the outside shows Heracles and Apollo struggling for the Olympic tripod; the other side shows Heracles slaying the giant Alcyoneus, as Hermes watches. The decoration is executed in the red-figure style. A hydria (Munich) c510 B.C., also in red-figure style, shows a music lesson, and on the shoulder, two hetairai playing the game of cottabus.

Phintias. See **Damon and Pythias.**

Phintias. Tyrant of Acragas in Sicily; fl. 280 B.C.; founder of the coastal city of Phintias, modern Licata. (JJ)

Phintias. [Modern name, **Licata.**] Greek city on the S coast of Sicily, at the mouth of the river Himera (modern Salso), between Gela and Acragas. It was founded c284 B.C. by Phintias, tyrant of Acragas, who in 282 B.C. settled there the refugees from the destruction of Gela by the Mamertines. (JJ)

Phlegethon (fleg'e-thon). In Greek mythology, one of the five rivers surrounding Hades. It was a river of fire which flowed into the Acheron.

Phlegraean Fields or **Plain** (flē-grē'an). [Italian, **Campi Flegrei.**] Volcanic district lying W of Naples, Italy, bordering on the Bay of Naples, where according to some accounts, the Battle of the Giants and the Gods was brought to a conclusion with the defeat of the Giants. According to other accounts, the battle was finished on the Phlegraean Plain of Chalcidice, in northeastern Greece, under the generalship of Athena.

Phlegyas (flej'yas). In mythology, a son of Ares and Chryse. He was king of the Lapithae and lived near Orchomenus in Boeotia. He was the father of Ixion and Coronis. When he learned that his daughter had born Asclepius to the god Apollo he violated Apollo's shrine at Delphi and was slain by the god. As further punishment he was condemned to Tartarus, the region of Hades reserved for the worst criminals— those who had sinned against the gods. There he stood beneath a rock which was forever on the verge of falling and was continually hungry because his food was contaminated by one of the Furies.

Phlias (flī′as). In Greek legend, a son of Dionysus. He dwelt near the springs of Asopus in Araethyrea and joined Jason on the expedition of the *Argo* to Colchis.

Phliasia (flī-ā′shi-a). In ancient geography, a small district in the Peloponnesus, Greece, NW of Argolis, NE of Arcadia, and S of Sicyonia. According to legend, the first king of the land was the earth-born Aras, who named the country Arantia after himself and founded a city on the Arantine Hill. His son changed the name to Araethyraea in honor of his dead sister, and by this name it was known to Homer and mentioned in the *Iliad* as having sent men to the Trojan War under the command of Agamemnon. Finally, Phlias gave the land its third name of Phliasia and named the city Phlius. Some say this Phlias was a son of Dionysus and that he was an Argonaut. Others say he was a grandson of Temenus, one of the Heraclidae who successfully invaded the Peloponnesus. The Phliasians were Argives originally, but when the Dorians conquered the Peloponnesus they came to terms with them and became Dorian.

Phlius (flī′ūs). In ancient geography, a city in Phliasia, Peloponnesus, Greece, about 14 miles SW of Corinth, situated on the upper reaches of the Asopus River. It was founded by Dorians from Argos. The people of ancient Phlius had a very holy sanctuary of Hebe, or Ganymeda as they called her. One of the honors accorded to the goddess was that she could pardon suppliants. All who sought her in her temple situated in a cypress grove on the citadel won full forgiveness, and prisoners set free by her dedicated their fetters in her temple. There were also temples of Hera, Demeter, and Asclepius at Phlius. The rising of the constellation they called the Goat was accompanied by violent storms that did great damage to the vines. The people of Phlius had a bronze image of a she-goat in the market-place that they honored and adorned with gold to appease the constellation Goat and save their vines. Behind the market-place was a House of Divination. Here, they say, Amphiaraus, at that time an ordinary man with no special powers, entered and slept a night. Thenceforward he was endowed with the power of prophecy. Not far from Phlius was the Omphalos (*Navel*), the center of the Peloponnesus, they say. Heracles visited Phlius on his way back from the Garden of the Hesperides, and here Oeneus came from Aetolia to entertain him. It was on this occasion, they say, that Heracles in a fit of impatience accidentally killed the cup-bearer Cyathus. A shrine near the sanctuary of Apollo at Phlius commemorated this accident; in it was a stone image of Cyathus holding out a cup to Heracles. At nearby Celeae the Phliasians celebrated the mysteries of Demeter in Eleusinian fashion every fourth year. The Phliasians claimed that these mysteries were established in Phliasia by Dysaules, who, they say, was a brother of Celeus, driven out of Eleusis by Ion. Phlius, usually an ally of Sparta, drove out its oligarchs after the Peloponnesian Wars. The Spartan king Agesilaus reduced it by siege and forced it to receive a Spartan garrison (381–379 B.C.). Henceforth it was either allied to Sparta or remained neutral.

Phobetor (fō-bē′tôr). The name men gave to Icelus, the god who brought dreams of animals and birds. The name means "the Terrifier."

Phobus (fō′bus). In late Greek mythology, a son of Aphrodite and Ares, and an attendant of Ares, the god of war. He personifies the fear which terrifies whole armies and causes rout.

Phocaea (fō-sē′a). In ancient geography, the most northerly of the 12 Ionian cities of Asia, situated on the Aegean Sea about 28 miles NW of Smyrna. The inhabitants were Phocians by descent. To commemorate Psamathe the Nereid, they put the figure of a seal on their earliest coins, because Psamathe had transformed herself into a seal to escape the embraces of Aeacus. Her efforts were unsuccessful; she bore Phocus, the ancestor of the Phocians in Greece. When the Phocians emigrated to Asia and colonized Phocaea they won their land by agreement with the natives and settled among them without warfare. Phocaea was admitted to the league of Ionian cities when the inhabitants accepted a descendant of Codrus, legendary king of Athens, as their ruler. The Phocaeans were great sailors and according to Herodotus were the first of the Greeks to explore the coasts of the Adriatic and Tyrrhenian Seas, and to set out colonies in that area. Phocaea was the mother-city of Massilia, later Marseilles, France. The Phocaeans even sailed to the shores of Spain. According to Herodotus, when they arrived at Tartessus, a colony founded by the Phoenicians in Spain, the ruler was so impressed by them that he invited them to leave Phocaea and settle in his country. When they declined his invitation he gave them money to wall their city in Asia. When Phocaea was attacked by Harpagus, general of Cyrus, in 540 B.C., their wall momentarily protected them, and they asked for a day in which to consider whether they would submit to Persian domination. This was granted them, and the Phocaeans, rather than submit to slavery, used their day of grace to load their families, and as much of their goods as possible, aboard their vessels and sailed away. Harpagus, on entering the city next day, found it empty. After a brief stop at Chios the Phocaeans decided to go to Cyrnus (Corsica), where years before they had established a colony, Alalia, and settle there. Before they left, however, they sailed back to their own city, surprised the Persian garrison and put them to the sword. Then they dropped a huge mass of iron in the sea and swore they would not return to Phocaea until the iron floated to the surface. But some of the Phocaeans were so saddened at the thought of leaving their homes that they immediately broke their oath and deserted their comrades and returned. The remainder went to Cyrnus and settled there for a time, but found it expedient to withdraw, following a sea-battle with the Carthaginians and Etruscans, to Rhegium. It is said that the Carthaginians landed the Phocaean captives they took in the sea-battle on the shore and stoned them to death. Afterward, men and animals passing the spot where the stoning took place were afflicted: their bodies became palsied or their limbs paralyzed. The people sent to Delphi to inquire about this matter and were told to honor the dead Phocaeans with funeral rites and games, a practice which was followed annually for many years. The Phocaeans finally established themselves at Elea in Italy.

Phocion (fō′shi-on). Athenian statesman and general; born c402 B.C.; put to death 318 B.C. He was of a good Athenian family, and in his youth was a pupil of Plato and Xenocrates. As a young man he attached himself to the Athenian general Chabrias, whose admiration he won. Chabrias advanced him, and he commanded the left wing of the Athenian fleet in the sea-fight with the Spartans off Naxos in 376 B.C. that resulted in an Athenian victory. Even after the death of Chabrias, Phocion continued to honor him and showed his loyalty by his care for Chabrias′ son, Ctesippus, an intractable and capricious youth. Once on an expedition Ctesippus harried him with criticism and advice. Phocion exclaimed, "Chabrias, Chabrias, surely I make you a large return for your friendship in enduring your son." Phocion early established a reputation for unimpeachable honesty, and won the admiration of the Athenians because no amount of money could tempt him. He was devoted to the interests of the state and impervious to public criticism. Of a kind and gentle nature, he was forbidding in appearance, and never hesitated to tell the Athenians wherein lay their errors. He was a forceful speaker, capable of putting great good sense into very few words. He never sought the favor of the people. On the contrary, he invariably publicly disapproved of their actions. Once, it is said, when he delivered an opinion and it was approved by all, he turned to a friend and asked, "Can it be that I am making a bad argument without knowing it?" The great object of his civil policy was peace with Macedonia, because Athens was not in a position to oppose her. He frequently exposed those who spoke in favor of war as being either unwilling or unable to fight. Demosthenes, the most fiery advocate of war, once said to him, "The Athenians will kill you, Phocion, should they go crazy." To which he replied, "But they will kill you, should they come to their senses." Although he was an outspoken advocate of peace, and although he never sought the office, he was appointed general by the Athenians 45 times. Because of his reputation for justice and honesty, he alone of the generals sent out by Athens to the allies was welcomed by them. In 348 B.C. he was sent to put down a revolt in Eretria, in the island of Euboea. The victory he won there consisted mainly in avoiding defeat. In 339 B.C. he was sent to the Hellespont to the relief of Byzantium, which was undergoing siege by Philip II. Chares, the Athenian who had preceded him, had accomplished little since the Byzantians so distrusted him they refused to allow him in their city, but for Phocion they threw open their gates. Philip was forced to withdraw and Phocion recovered some cities he had taken. Then, having sustained a wound, he returned to Athens. In 344–343 B.C. he answered an appeal from Megara for aid, and helped to build the long walls from Megara to her port. His immutable policy was peace, and he tried to persuade Athens to accept Philip's terms. Demosthenes urged war, but recommended that it be waged as far from Attica as possible. "My good sir," said Phocion, "let us not ask where we can fight, but how we shall be victorious. For in that case the war will be far away; but wherever men are defeated every terror is close at hand." The Athenians followed Demosthenes, and were disastrously defeated by Philip at Chaeronea (338 B.C.). Phocion recommended that the kindly overtures of Philip after the defeat be accepted. Philip trusted and admired him; Athens was granted peace on moderate terms and Philip returned the Athenian dead with a guard of honor. Phocion disapproved of the sacrifices of rejoicing that were proclaimed by the Athenians when Philip was murdered (336 B.C.), for, said he, the force that had defeated them at Chaeronea was diminished now by only one man. He opposed Demosthenes' speeches against Alexander, and after the destruction of Thebes (335 B.C.) strongly advised the Athenians to surrender the leaders of the war party, including Demosthenes, demanded by Alexander, because in Phocion's view they were responsible for bringing Athens low by their fiery speeches and their violent policies. Phocion was one of the envoys sent to Alexander. He advised him to end the war in Greece and, if he sought glory, to fight the barbarians. Alexander made him his guest and friend, and when he

returned to Athens Alexander sent him a gift of 100 talents because, "Alexander judges that you alone are a man of honor and worth." Phocion refused to accept the gift. Alexander was angered because he would not accept anything from him. Thereupon Phocion asked for the release of four men who had been taken. Alexander released them. Later (324 B.C.), Alexander offered him the revenues of any one of four cities. Phocion again refused the gift. When the Athenians murmured against Alexander he told them, "Either be superior in arms or be friends with those who are superior." After the death of Alexander and the defeat of the Athenians at Crannon (322 B.C.) by Antipater, Phocion went to Antipater at Thebes as an envoy of Athens. The terms imposed by Antipater were harsh, but Athens had no choice but to accept them. Phocion won the confidence of Antipater as he had of Philip and Alexander, and became virtual ruler of Athens under him. Antipater said he had two friends at Athens: Phocion, whom he could not persuade to take anything, and Demades, to whom he could never give enough. On the death of Antipater, Philip Arrhidaeus, the imbecile half-brother of Alexander, was king under the control of Polysperchon. Polysperchon was an opponent of Cassander, son of Antipater. He persuaded the Athenians to try Phocion, now a very old man, on a false charge of treason. In a frenzy of madness, as Demosthenes had predicted, the Athenians refused to hear his defense and condemned him. He drank the hemlock in May, 318 B.C. As an added indignity, he was at first denied burial, but a friend took his body and burned it. His wife gathered his bones and buried them under his own hearth. Very soon the Athenians regretted their madness. They gave his bones public burial and raised a statue to him in the market-place.

Phocis (fō'sis). In ancient geography, a region in S central Greece. It was bounded by Locris on the N, Boeotia on the E, the Corinthian Gulf on the S, and Doris and Locris on the W. It was colonized by Phocus of Corinth, the son of Ornytion, and was named either for him or for Phocus, the son of Aeacus, who went there with his followers from the island of Aegina. Phocians played their part in the Trojan War under the command of Schedius, son of Iphitus. Orestes was sent to King Strophius in Phocis after the death of Agamemnon, according to some accounts, to protect him from Clytemnestra and Aegisthus. Before the Persian invasion of Greece the Phocians fought against the Thessalians. They buried empty water jars just beneath the surface of the ground, and when the Thessalian cavalry charged, their horses, falling into the jars, were lamed or crippled and the cavalry was thrown into complete confusion. Enraged, the Thessalians gathered a large army to hurl against the Phocians. The latter consulted the oracle at Delphi and were told:

"I will match in fight mortal and immortal,
And to both will I give victory, but more
   to the mortal."

Puzzled by this equivocal response, the Phocians sent 300 picked men against the Thessalians. All perished. Terrified, the Phocians gathered their women, children, and valuables and made a huge pyre. They left 30 men to guard it and gave them orders to set it alight and cause all to burn if the Phocians should lose in the battle they were about to engage in with the Thessalians. This gave rise to the expression "Phocian despair," for a forlorn hope. With the picture of their women and children before their eyes, the Phocians attacked desperately, and won. Thus the oracle was fulfilled, for the watchword of the Thessalians was "Itonian Athena," and the watchword of the Phocians was "Phocus," a mortal's name. In gratitude, the Phocians sent offerings to Delphi. In a later attack, the Phocians smeared themselves with chalk and put on white armor. When they appeared at night the Thessalians thought they were spirits, not their enemies from Phocis, and the Phocians slaughtered them wholesale. When the Persians made their successful way into Greece the Phocians were compelled to join them, but they deserted as soon as possible and afterward took part in the Greek victory at Plataea (479 B.C.). The Phocians had periodically controlled and lost Delphi. In 357 B.C. they seized it again. The Thebans fought against them for ten years until at last Philip of Macedon intervened on the pretext of restoring order to Greece and put

an end to the war, 348 B.C. This war was called the Phocian War and also, the Sacred War. The cities of Phocis—Lilaea, Hyampolis, Anticyra, Parapotamii, Panopeus, and Daulis —were captured and destroyed. Only Abae, whose citizens were free from impiety, was spared as it had not shared in the seizure of the sanctuary. The Phocians now lost their share in the sanctuary and in the assembly. Their votes in the Amphictyonic League were given to the Macedonians. In the following years some of the cities of Phocis were rebuilt. The Phocians allied themselves with Athens and took part in the disastrous battle of Chaeronea where the allies were defeated by Philip. In the 3rd century B.C., when the Gauls attacked, the Phocians fought savagely in order, some say, to defend Delphi and atone for their earlier crimes against the sanctuary. The region is mountainous and contains Mount Parnassus. As a region it was especially important because of its chief place, Delphi.

Phocus (fō′kus). In Greek mythology, a son of Aeacus and the Nereid Psamathe. He was a great favorite of his father and his skill in athletic contests aroused the jealousy of his half-brothers, Telamon and Peleus. To avoid a conflict with them he left Aegina, the island home of his father, and settled in Phocis with his followers. According to some accounts, Phocis was named for him. On a visit to Aeacus he was challenged to a contest by his brothers in the course of which they killed him. He was the father of the twins Crisius and Panopeus.

Phocus. In Greek tradition, a son of Ornytion of Corinth. He colonized the region around Delphi in Phocis and according to some accounts this area is named Phocis after him. He purified Antiope, who had wandered to his land maddened by Dionysus for the death of Dirce, and later married her.

Phocylides (fō-sil′i-dēz). Greek poet of Miletus, in Ionia, who lived in the latter part of the 6th century B.C. He wrote witty gnomes (maxims or epigrams), a few fragments of which remain. Nothing is known of his life.

Phoebe (fē′bē). In Greek mythology, a Titaness, the daughter of Uranus and Gaea. According to some accounts, Eurynome gave her dominion over the Moon. By Coeus she was the mother of Leto, and thus the grandmother of Artemis and Apollo. Some say she at one time controlled the oracle at Delphi but gave up her powers to her grandson Apollo. The name Phoebe became synonymous with the moon in later writings, and hence synonymous both with Artemis and the Roman Diana, as identified with the moon.

Phoebe. In Greek mythology, a daughter of Leucippus. She was a priestess of Athena. With her sister she was carried off by Castor and Polydeuces. See **Leucippides.**

Phoebe. According to some accounts, a daughter of Tyndareus and Leda, and the sister of Clytemnestra, Helen, Castor, and Polydeuces. This extra, little-heard-of sister, is sometimes also known as Timandra.

Phoebus (fē′bus). In late Greek mythology, Apollo in his aspect of sun god and dispenser of light. As Phoebus, Apollo took on many of the attributes of the older sun god, Helius, but never the chariot.

Phoenicia (fē-nish′a). In ancient geography, the strip of land on the coast of S Syria, between Mount Lebanon and the Mediterranean Sea. It was about 200 miles in length, and its width did not exceed 35 miles at the maximum; area, about 4000 square miles. But the rivers (fed by the snows of Lebanon) which irrigated it, and the energy and enterprise of its inhabitants, made this narrow tract of land one of the most varied in its products, and gave it a place in history out of proportion to its size. The principal rivers were the Leontes (Litani), N of Tyre, and the Orontes (Nahr el Asy) in the N. The cedars of the mountains furnished building material; the coast furnished sand for glass and the purple snail for dyeing; and the inland plains were covered with orchards, gardens, and grain fields. Though the coastline was not deeply indented, the skill of the inhabitants secured them harbors. The ancient inhabitants of Phoenicia, the Phoenices of the classical writers (*Poeni* or *Puni* designating the Carthaginians), are now considered by many scholars to have been Semites of the Canaanites, and their country Canaan. In Greek legend, the Phoenicians are counted as the descendants of Phoenix, the son of Agenor and Telephassa, and the brother of Cadmus and Europa. When Europa was carried off he went, at his father's command, in search of her. He traveled westward from his native Canaan, to what later became known as Carthage, whose people took the name Punic from him. But since he did not find Europa he returned to Canaan, after his father's death, and the land was named Phoenicia in his honor, and its people Phoenicians. According to classical writers, the Phoenicians emigrated from the Erythrean Sea. This would favor the assumption that the Phoenicians were identical with the Punti of the Egyptian monuments. The language of the Phoenicians was closely akin to Hebrew. They worshiped as principal divinities Baal and Astarte, besides the seven planets under the name of Cabiri. Phoenicia never formed a single state under one head, but rather a confederacy of cities. In the earliest period (1600–1100 B.C.) Sidon stood at the head of Phoenician cities; c1000 Sidon lost the hegemony to Tyre; in 761 B.C. Aradus was founded in the N extreme of the country; and from these three cities Tripolis (the modern Tripoli in Lebanon) was settled. South of Tripolis old Byblos was situated, while Berytus (Beirut) in the N did not become prominent before the Roman period. To the territory of Tyre belonged Akko or Acco (Acre), later called Ptolemaïs. Separated from the rest of Phoenicia lay Joppa (Jaffa), on the coast of Palestine, which the Maccabees united with Palestine. The constitution of these Phoenician townships was aristocratic, headed by a king. The earliest king of Tyre mentioned in the Old Testament was Hiram, a contemporary and friend of David and Solomon. After Hiram six kings are supposed to have ruled until Ethbaal or Ithobal, the father of Jezebel, wife of Ahab. Under Ethbaal's grandson, Pygmalion, contentions about the throne led to the emigration of his sister Elissa (Dido in Vergil) and the foundation of Carthage, the mighty rival of Rome. In the middle of the 9th century B.C., Phoenicia shared the fate of Syria at large. After the battle of Karkar (853 B.C.) it became tributary to Assyria. It made a struggle for independence under Shalmaneser IV, but was brought to submission by his successor, Sargon. In 609 B.C. Phoenicia came for a short time into the hands of Necho II, king of Egypt.

Tyre was besieged for 13 years (585–572 B.C.) by Nebuchadnezzar. Cyrus brought Phoenicia with the rest of the Babylonian possessions under Persian supremacy. But, owing to their skill in navigation, the Phoenicians retained an independence of sorts. In 351 B.C. Sidon was destroyed by Artaxerxes III. The same fate befell Tyre at the hands of Alexander the Great in 332 B.C. In 64 B.C. Phoenicia was annexed by Pompey to the Syrian province of the Roman Empire. Less original and productive in the domain of thought and higher culture, the Phoenicians excel other members of the Semitic family in contributions to material civilization. They were the merchants and manufacturers of antiquity. They were the most skillful shipbuilders and boldest navigators. All along the Mediterranean, even beyond Gibraltar, they established colonies. They sent colonies to Cyprus, Crete, and England, and it is not improbable that they worked the tin mines of Cornwall. They even ventured to circumnavigate Africa. The principal articles of their commerce were precious stones, metals, glassware, costly textiles, and especially purple robes. Their skill in architecture was exhibited in the temple of Solomon. Their alphabetic writing became the parent of all the European alphabetic systems now in use. According to the Greek legends, the alphabet was brought to Crete by Cadmus, when he was searching for Europa, and from there to Greece. The Phoenicians also transmitted a knowledge of mathematics and of weights and measures to other nations. Of the Phoenician literature only a few fragments in Greek translation have come down to us. Among the numerous Phoenician inscriptions, the most important is that of the sarcophagus of the Sidonian king Eshmunazar (who reigned in the 4th century B.C.), found in 1855, and now at Paris.

Phoenician Maidens, The. A play by Euripides, c409 B.C. It treats the myths and legends attached to the city of Thebes. The play is named for its chorus, a band of Phoenician maidens dedicated to the service of Apollo at Delphi. They stopped at Thebes on their way to Delphi and were detained there by the siege of the Seven against Thebes. The Phoenician maidens,

from the land of Cadmus, founder of Thebes, observe and comment throughout the play, and describe, in vivid choral odes, the history of Thebes and of the descendants of its founder.

Oedipus blinded himself in horror when it was revealed to him that the oracles from which he had sought to flee had been fulfilled: unaware of his own parentage he had killed his father, married his mother, and fathered two sons and two daughters by her. In Euripides' version of the Oedipus story, Jocasta does not kill herself when she learns that the man who became king of Thebes after killing the Sphinx, and to whom she was given in marriage by the grateful Thebans (her husband Laius having been killed by an unknown murderer), is her own son. She and Oedipus remain in the palace at Thebes, where their sons, Eteocles and Polynices, seek to conceal their father's disgrace by keeping him hidden, and neither honor nor love him. In anger, Oedipus curses them: ". . . that they should divide their inheritance by the sword." Eteocles and Polynices think to avert the curse by alternately ruling Thebes. Eteocles, the elder, rules first. At the end of a year he refuses to give up the throne as he had agreed to do, and banishes Polynices. Polynices goes to the court of Adrastus, king of Argos, marries the daughter of Adrastus, and returns with an army of Argives, led by seven chieftains, to win his inheritance by force of arms. Jocasta seeks to reconcile her sons, and thereby avoid a war that would ruin them and the city. She arranges a parley between them, while the Argive army is gathered before the walls of Thebes. But her efforts are fruitless. To the demand of Polynices that the kingdom be turned over to him in accordance with their agreement, Eteocles replies that he will not give up his power, that having been king he will not now submit to being subject to Polynices. Polynices returns to the Argive camp. Eteocles arranges the defense of Thebes with his uncle Creon, Jocasta's brother. Before he leaves to appoint the Theban champions to defend the seven gates of Thebes against the seven Argive leaders, he consents to the marriage of his sister Antigone to Creon's son Haemon; bequeaths Thebes, in the event of his death, to Creon; and commands Creon not to allow the burial of Polynices on Theban soil if he too should fall in battle. Creon consults the blind Theban seer Tiresias concerning the fate of Thebes and learns that only the death of Creon's son, Menoeceus, can save the city from the Argives. According to Tiresias, it is Ares' will to avenge the earth-born dragon that was killed by Cadmus when the city was founded with the death of a descendant of one of the Sown Men (Sparti). Creon refuses to sacrifice his son to save the city, and orders him to fly before Tiresias' oracle becomes known and the people demand his death. Menoeceus agrees to do as his father commands. But instead, he goes to the ramparts and nobly takes his own life to save Thebes. The Argives attack and are driven back. As Jocasta, informed by a messenger, rejoices that her sons still live and that Thebes is safe, she is told that Eteocles and Polynices, to avoid further bloodshed, have agreed to settle their conflict by a duel. She rushes off to prevent the duel but arrives too late: the brothers have slain each other. In despair, Jocasta kills herself on her sons' bodies. Creon, seeking the comfort of his sister in his grief for his dead son, learns that she is dead, and Eteocles and Polynices as well. He announces that he is now king and forbids anyone, on pain of death, to bury Polynices. Antigone, who hears this command, vows she will defy Creon and bury her brother. She calls her father from the palace. Blind Oedipus is led forth, hears that his curse on his sons has been carried out, and is banished by Creon, who says Thebes can never prosper as long as Oedipus remains. Antigone promises to bury Polynices and to accompany her father into exile. She and her father leave together to go to Athens, where Oedipus has learned from an oracle that he will die.

Phoenix (fē'niks). According to some accounts, a son of Agenor of Canaan (afterwards Phoenicia) and Telephassa. He was the brother of Cadmus, Cilix, Thasus, Phineus, and Europa. When Europa was carried off by Zeus in the form of a bull, Phoenix, with his brothers, was sent by Agenor to find her. He journeyed beyond Libya to what afterwards became Carthage in his search for her. After his father died he returned to his own country and became king there. It was renamed Phoenicia in his honor, and he came to be regarded as the ancestor of the Phoenicians.

Phoenix. In Greek legend, a son of Amyntor and Cleobule. At his mother's request he seduced his father's mistress, and was denounced by her to Amyntor. To punish him, Amyntor blinded him and put a curse on him: that he should never have a son of his own. Phoenix fled to the court of Peleus, where he was kindly received. Peleus persuaded Chiron to restore his sight, and then made him ruler of the Dolopians. He became the preceptor and foster father of Achilles, son of Peleus, and thus the curse of childlessness was to some extent overcome. He accompanied Achilles to the Trojan War. Phoenix tried, unsuccessfully, to persuade Achilles to give up his wrath at Agamemnon over the captive Briseis. Later he, as one whom Achilles loved and respected, was one of the ambassadors to offer him rich gifts and the restoration of Briseis if he would give up his quarrel and come to the aid of the Greeks. When Achilles rejected this attempt to settle the quarrel, Phoenix elected to remain with him. He commanded a group of the Myrmidons under Patroclus when that hero prevailed on Achilles to loan him his armor and his men so that he, at least, could go to the aid of his countrymen. After the death of Achilles he was one of the envoys to Scyrus to fetch Neoptolemus, son of Achilles, to the war. At the end of the war he left Troy with Neoptolemus but died on the way home to Greece.

Phoenix. [Also: **Phenix.**] Greek name for the ancient Egyptian mythological bird, the *bennu,* a bird of great beauty which, after living 500 or 600 years in the Arabian wilderness, the only one of its kind, built for itself a funeral pyre of spices and aromatic gums, lighted the pile with the fanning of its wings, was burned upon it, but from its ashes rose new and young. The Phoenix was the Egyptian symbol for the rising sun and the hieroglyph for the sun. In Christian symbolism the Phoenix represents resurrection and immortality. The story exists in Arabia, Persia, and India. It is mentioned in the Old Testament (Job, xxix. 18). In heraldic symbolism the Phoenix is always represented in the midst of flames.

Pholus (fō′lus). In Greek legend, a centaur who lived in a cave on Mount Pholoë and guarded the wine given to the centaurs by Dionysus. Heracles visited him and, in accordance with the oracles, Pholus opened the wine of Dionysus to serve to him. The other centaurs were attracted by the aroma of the wine and maddened by its fumes. They attacked Heracles. Their mother sent a torrential rain to help them—as they were four-footed they could fight in the mud whereas Heracles, with only two feet, was continually slipping and falling. Nevertheless, Heracles killed many of the centaurs and drove the rest away. Pholus, his friend, in extracting an arrow from a fallen centaur marveled that such a slender weapon could be so deadly. It fell from his hand and pierced his foot slightly. Heracles tried to save him from succumbing to the poisoned arrow, but since it had been dipped in the venom of the Lernaean Hydra its effect, even in the slightest wound, was deadly and Pholus died. Heracles buried him on the mountain and named it after him, Mount Pholoë.

Phorbas (fôr′bas). In Greek legend, a son of Lapithes. He freed the Rhodians from a plague of serpents, and was honored by them as a hero. He was placed in the heavens as the constellation Ophiuchus (the Serpent-holder). Another Phorbas was a famous boxer, who challenged pilgrims en route to Delphi to contend with him, killed them, and eventually was slain by Apollo.

Phorbas. Named in the *Iliad* as a wealthy cattle owner, beloved of Hermes. His only son Ilioneus was slain by the Boeotian, Peneleus, in the Trojan War.

Phorbas. Named by Homer in the *Iliad* as a leader of the Phrygians, allies of Troy. He was slain by Telamonian Ajax in the struggle over possession of the body of Patroclus.

Phorcids (fôr′sidz). [Also: **Phorcides, Phorcyads, Phorkyads.**] In Greek mythology, the children of Phorcys and Ceto: Ladon, Echidna, the Gorgons, the Graeae, and according to some accounts, the Hesperides.

Phorcys (fôr′sis). [Also: **Phorcus, Phorkys.**] In Greek mythology, a son of Gaea and Pontus (Outsea) or Nereus. He was a sea-

deity, a leader of the Tritons, and was the brother and consort of Ceto (a sea-goddess) and father of the Phorcids (especially the Graeae) and the Gorgons, and in some accounts of the Sirens and Scylla also.

Phorcys. A harbor on the island of Ithaca on the shore of which the Phaeacians left the sleeping Odysseus when, after an absence of 20 years, he was at last restored to his homeland.

Phormio (fôr′mi-ō). Athenian admiral; fl. last half of the 5th century B.C.; died probably c428 B.C. He went with reinforcements to the blockade of Potidaea (432) and helped to surround the city. In 430 B.C. he commanded a fleet of 30 ships that captured Amphilochian Argos on the Ambracian Gulf, sold the Ambraciots, who had taken the city, into slavery, and restored the Amphilochian inhabitants. He then went to Naupactus and guarded the western entrance to the Gulf of Corinth. The following year he twice defeated superior Spartan fleets sent against him in the Gulf of Corinth.

Phormion (fôr′mi-on). According to Greek tradition, a Spartan who acquired the house once lived in by the Dioscuri. When they came to him as strangers he regretfully denied their request to sleep in their old room, because his daughter was occupying it. Next day the maiden and everything belonging to her had vanished. Only images of the Dioscuri and a table on which was some silphion (a medicinal herb) remained in the room.

Phormis (fôr′mis). Greek comic poet in Syracuse; fl. early in the 5th century B.C. Titles of seven of his works survive.

Phoroneus (fôr-ō′nē-us). In Greek mythology, a son of Inachus and the ash nymph Melia, and the brother of Io. He was the first to found a market town; its original name, Phoronicum, was later changed to Argos, and he is regarded as the founder of Argos. In the contest between Hera and Poseidon over Argos, Phoroneus was a judge. According to some accounts, he was the first man, and the one who discovered the use of fire, after Prometheus had stolen it. He established the worship of Hera, who had won in the contest for Argos, and is generally credited with being the originator of civilization in the Peloponnesus. According to some accounts, he married the nymph Cerdo and was the father of Iasus, Agenor, and Pelasgus, who divided the Peloponnesus between them. Others say his wife was Teledice, and his children were Apis and Niobe.

Phoronicum (fôr-ō′ni-kum). A city in the Peloponnesus, founded by Phoroneus, brother of Io. Its name was later changed to Argos. It was said to have been the first market town, and the first in the Peloponnesus to establish the worship of Hera.

Phosphorus (fos′fō-rus). In Greek mythology, the morning star; a son of Astraeus and Eos. It is also the name of the planet Venus when seen in the early dawn. Phosphorus is sometimes depicted as a youth carrying a blazing torch.

Phreattys (frē′at-is). In ancient geography, a place near the sea at Piraeus. Here exiled men, against whom some new charge had been brought, stood on a ship at sea and defended themselves while the judges listened from the shore. In the same manner, Teucer defended himself before Telamon, when he returned from the Trojan War without his half-brother Ajax, and before him, Telamon had defended himself to his father Aeacus on the charge of murdering his brother Phocus.

Phrixus (frik′sus). In Greek legend, a son of Athamas, king of Orchomenus in Boeotia, and Nephele, a cloud-born woman whom Athamas married at Hera's command. Phrixus was falsely accused by his aunt of making amorous advances to her. Actually, he had honorably scorned her approaches to him. In addition, Athamas' new wife, Ino, wished to remove him as an heir of Athamas so that her own children could inherit the kingdom. She therefore arranged a famine in the land and bribed messengers to bring word from the oracle at Delphi that only the sacrifice of Phrixus to the gods would lift the famine. As Athamas was about to put the knife to his throat a winged, golden-fleeced ram, sent by Hermes, arrived at the altar. Phrixus and his sister Helle leaped on the ram's back and were borne away through the skies. Helle fell off over the strait which now bears her name, Hellespont. Phrixus was carried safely to Colchis. There he was kindly received by the king, despite the Colchians' reputation for unfriendliness, and sacrificed the ram as he had been instructed to do. Its golden fleece, guarded by a dragon, was fastened to an oak tree in a grove sacred to Ares. In Colchis, Phrixus married Chalciope, daughter of King Aeëtes. On his death he was denied proper burial. His ghost haunted Pelias, who had seized the throne of Iolcus, demanding proper burial rites and the return of the Golden Fleece to Hellas. This provided a ready pretext when Pelias sought to get rid of his unwelcome nephew Jason. See **Argonauts, Jason, Medea.**

Phronima (fron′i-ma). According to Herodotus, a daughter of Etearchus, a king in Crete. Her stepmother made false accusations of improper behavior against her and convinced Etearchus that her charges were true. Etearchus asked a guest in his house, one Themison, to swear that he would perform whatever service Etearchus required of him. Themison, having sworn that he would do so, was requested by Etearchus to take Phronima and hurl her into the sea. Themison was indignant at the trickery which compelled him to do such a deed. He took Phronima and sailed from Crete. When the ship was at sea he lowered her over the side by a rope and, when she had been thoroughly immersed, hauled her aboard again, little the worse for her ducking. On arriving at the island of Thera Themison gave Phronima to Polymnestus, to whom she subsequently bore a son, Battus. This Battus later, at the bidding of the oracle at Delphi, founded Cyrene in Libya.

Phrontis (fron′tis). In Greek legend, a son of Phrixus and Chalciope, and the grandson of Aeëtes, king of Colchis, and Athamas, king of Orchomenus. With his brothers he sailed from Colchis with the intention of going to Orchomenus to claim their inheritance from Athamas. On the way they were shipwrecked and rescued off the island of Ares by Jason and the Argonauts. Phrontis and his brothers, Argus, Cytissorus, and Melas, returned to Colchis with the Argonauts.

Phrontis. Named by Homer as the wife of the Trojan Panthous. She was the mother of Euphorbus, Hyperenor, and Polydamas.

Phrygia (frij′i-a). In ancient geography, a country in Asia Minor, of varying boundaries. In the Persian period it comprised Lesser Phrygia, on the Hellespont, and Great

Phrygia in the interior, bounded by Bithynia and Paphlagonia on the N, the Halys River on the E, the Taurus Mountains on the S, and Mysia, Lydia, and Caria on the W. Later the Galatians settled in the NE part. The inhabitants (Phrygians) were of undetermined origin, but are believed to have come from Europe. The country was overrun by the Cimmerians in the 7th century B.C., and was ruled later by Lydia, Persia, Macedon, and Rome. Gordius, who tied the Gordian knot, and Midas, his son, who possessed the golden touch, were legendary kings of Phrygia. Named by Homer as the "land of the vineyard," it was the home of the pious and devoted couple, Baucis and Philemon; the oak and linden tree growing from one trunk, into which they were changed as a reward for their hospitality to Zeus, could be seen there. Phrygia was invaded by the Amazons in the years preceding the Trojan War, and in the war the Phrygians allied themselves to Troy.

Phryne (frī'nē). [Original name, **Mnesarete**.] Boeotia-born, 4th century B.C. Athenian courtesan. She is supposed to have been the model of the picture *Aphrodite Anadyomene* by Apelles, and of the statue of the Cnidian Aphrodite by Praxiteles. According to legend, she was defended on a capital charge by her lover Hyperides; and when he failed to move the judges by his oratory, he bade her uncover her bosom, after which they voted her acquittal.

Phrynichus (frin'i-kus). Attic poet, son of Polyphradmon. An older contemporary of Aeschylus, he was active early in the 5th century B.C. He is credited with several innovations, such as using an actor in addition to the leader of the chorus, and placing female characters on the stage. Titles of nine of his works on mythological and contemporary subjects survive. One of these latter, *Capture of Miletus,* caused the audience to burst into tears, because it reminded the Athenians of what they considered their own misfortune, the fall of Miletus (494 B.C.) to the Persians. Phrynichus was fined and a law was passed that this drama should never be produced again (the first case of censorship on record). Another of his plays, *Phoenissae* (Phoenician Women) won first prize for him. It took its name from the

wives of the Phoenician sailors who formed part of the navy of King Xerxes in the Persian War. The scene was at the Persian court where the elders were awaiting news of the war. Themistocles, Athenian hero of the war, was patron of the chorus. The drama is said to have been the model for the great Aeschylean tragedy, *Persians.* Only fragments of the work of Phrynichus survive, but the songs he wrote were popular long after his death.

Phrynichus. Greek poet of the Old Comedy, contemporary and rival of Aristophanes. In 405 B.C. his comedy, *Muses,* took second prize when Aristophanes won with *The Frogs,* but in general he was not a very formidable rival. Fragments of some of his plays survive.

Phthia (thī'a). In Greek mythology, mother by Apollo of Dorus, Laodocus, and Polypoetes.

Phthia. In Homeric legend (*Iliad*), the concubine of Amyntor. Phoenix, son of Amyntor, seduced Phthia to please his mother. Phthia accused him to Amyntor, and in a rage the latter blinded Phoenix and laid a curse on him that he should never have children of his own. It was because of his father's hatred that Phoenix fled to the court of Peleus and became the beloved tutor and companion of Achilles.

Phthia. In ancient geography, a district and town in Thessaly. According to Greek legend, Peleus was the king of the region, to which he fled from Aegina after the murder of his brother Phocus. It was also the home of Aristaeus before he went to Ceos, and was the native town of Achilles.

Phthiotis (thī-ō'tis). In ancient geography, a region of Thessaly, bordered on the E by the Maliacus Sinus (Gulf of Lamia). It was in ancient times a home of the Achaeans.

Phylacus (fī'la-kus). In Greek mythology, a descendant of Ares. He was a son of Deion and Diomede, and was the king of Phylace. He owned a fine herd of cattle which he prized above all things except his son, Iphiclus. Melampus tried to steal the cattle for his brother Bias, who needed them to win a bride, but he was caught by Phylacus and imprisoned. After a year Melampus convinced Phylacus of his prophetic powers

actor; up, lūte, pull; oi, oil; ou, out; ᵺH, then; d̦ as d or j, ș as s or sh, ț as t or ch, z̦ as z or zh.

and was freely given the cattle in return for curing Iphiclus of sterility.

Phyle (fī'lē). In ancient geography, a fortified place in Attica, on Mount Parnes, commanding the shortest route between Athens and Thebes. It was one of a series of fortresses that guarded the mountainous border of Attica. When (404 B.C.) the Thirty Tyrants ruled Athens Thrasybulus, who had sought refuge in Thebes, resolved to overthrow the tyrants. With 70 partisans he left Thebes and seized the fortress of Phyle. The tyrants sent a force against him and prepared to force his surrender by a blockade of the fortress. However, a snowstorm compelled the attackers to withdraw. Some months later another expedition was sent against Phyle but they were ambushed by Thrasybulus and suffered heavy losses. From Phyle Thrasybulus marched to Piraeus, seized Munychia, and succeeded in overthrowing the Thirty (403 B.C.).

Phyleus (fī'lē-us, -lūs). In Greek legend, a son of Augeas, king of Elis. He witnessed Heracles' oath to cleanse the Augean stables in one day and his father's oath to pay Heracles one-tenth of his cattle if the task was performed on time. When Augeas refused to fulfill his part of the bargain, claiming he had never made it, Phyleus reminded him that he had been a witness to his oath. Augeas angrily banished his son and he went to Dulichium. Phyleus, father of Meges, was a famous horseman beloved of Zeus.

Phyleus. In Greek legend, a king of Ephyra in Thesprotia. He was the father of Astyocheia, who was carried off by Heracles when he attacked Ephyra and slew Phyleus.

Phylius (fī'li-us) or **Phyllius** (fil'i-us). In mythology, the beloved friend of Cycnus who faithfully carried out the tasks of taming wild birds and a lion to prove his love, but refused to give Cycnus a bull which he won as a prize. Cycnus flung himself over a cliff and was transformed into a swan.

Phyllidas (fil'i-das). Theban patriot; fl. in the first half of the 4th century B.C. He plotted with the Theban exile Pelopidas to overthrow the pro-Spartan polemarchs of Thebes who were sustained by a garrison of 1500 Spartans in the Theban citadel. Phyllidas was the secretary of the polemarchs. He arranged a great banquet, supposedly in honor of the polemarchs, for the day following the secret entry into the city of Pelopidas and his six fellow conspirators. Phyllidas lured the polemarchs to his banquet by promising them the company of some beautiful noblewomen whom they desired. In the course of the feast the polemarchs asked for the promised women. Phyllidas said they would come only when the polemarchs were alone. The attendants were dismissed and the women entered, heavily veiled. When the polemarchs requested them to raise their veils and expose their beauty the "ladies" plunged daggers into the bodies of the polemarchs and the few friends who had remained with them, for according to plan, the "beautiful women" were Pelopidas and his six colleagues in the plot to free Thebes. As a result of the deaths of the polemarchs and other political murders which immediately followed, the Spartan garrison withdrew from the citadel (378 B.C.) and the Thebans regained control of their city.

Phyllis (fil'is). In Greek mythology, a princess of Bisaltia in Thrace. On his return from the Trojan War, Demophon, son of Theseus, landed at Thrace. Phyllis fell in love with him and married him, and he became king. After a time Demophon wished to return to Athens and, after promising Phyllis that he would return within a year, he made ready to leave. Phyllis gave him a casket which she said contained a charm, and told him not to open it until he had decided he would never return to her. At the end of the year Demophon had not returned. Phyllis invoked Rhea to curse his name, took poison, and died. At the same time, Demophon decided to open the casket. The sight of its contents (which remained forever unknown) is said to have driven him mad and caused his death. Another Thracian Phyllis fell in love with Demophon's brother Acamas, who had stopped in Thrace on his way to the Trojan War. When she learned of the fall of Troy she made eager visits to the shore to welcome him on his return, but as days passed and he did not come (storms had delayed him), she died of grief and was transformed into an almond tree by Athena. The next day Acamas arrived. He embraced the trunk of the almond tree, whereupon it instantly burst into flower. The Athenians

fat, fāte, fär, fāre, errant; net, mē, hėr ardent; pin, pīne; not, nōte, möve, nôr,

performed dances annually in honor of Phyllis and Acamas.

Phyllis. In ancient geography, a river of Bithynia, passed by the Argonauts on their way to Colchis.

Phyllis. In ancient geography, a mountain of Thessaly, the source of the Apidanus and the Enipeus Rivers.

Phylo (fī′lō). An attendant and handmaiden of Helen at the court of Menelaus.

Phylomache (fil-om′a̰-kē). According to some accounts, a daughter of Amphion, and the wife of Pelias, by whom she was the mother of Acastus and Alcestis.

Phylonome or **Philonome** (phil-on′ō-mē). In Greek legend, the second wife of Cycnus of Colonae. She falsely accused Tenes, her stepson, of making advances to her and produced witnesses to attest to her lies. Cycnus banished his son. When Cycnus later learned that she had lied about Tenes he buried Phylonome alive.

Phytalus (fit′a̰-lus). In Greek mythology, one of the inhabitants of Eleusis who received Demeter when she was searching for Persephone. As a reward for his kindness to her Demeter gave him the fig tree and taught him how to cultivate it. His sons later purified Theseus for the murders he had committed on his way to Athens.

Phyteus (fit′ē-us). In Greek mythology, Apollo as the Pythian god, i.e., as killer of the dragon, Python, and specifically as god of the Delphic oracle.

Phyxius (fik′si-us). Epithet of Zeus, naming Zeus as a protector of fugitives. Deucalion sacrificed to Zeus Phyxius (*God of Escape*), when he landed safely after the great flood sent by Zeus to destroy impious men. Phrixus sacrificed to Zeus Phyxius, when he arrived safely at Colchis, the golden-fleeced ram on which he had escaped from Boeotia.

Piacenza (pyä-chen′tsä). See **Placentia**.

Piazza del Campidoglio (pyät′tsä del käm-pē-dō′lyō). Open square on the Capitoline Hill at Rome, the Area Capitolina of the ancient city. Until 1477 it was the general market of the city and remained the center of civic life after the market was removed to another location. The Senatorial Palace or city hall is mentioned as early as 1150. In 1538 the equestrian statue of Marcus Aurelius was placed here, and in 1559 a plan was made,

under the direction of Michelangelo, according to which the present arrangement of the buildings has been carried out: the Senatorial Palace in the center, the Palace of the Conservatori on the right, and the Capitoline Museum on the left.

Picenes (pī-sē′nēz). Specifically, the people of Picenum in ancient Italy, ethnologically and linguistically related to the Illyrians. The term is also a generic regional and cultural term, however, for all the people E of the Apennines from Rimini to Vasto. The Picenes were a warlike merchant people, practiced earth burial, and had many amber and ivory ornaments and carvings, and bronze figures and bowls.

Picenum (pī-sē′num). In ancient geography, a territory in Italy, lying between the Adriatic Sea and the Apennines. It was bounded by Umbria on the NW and W, the Sabines on the SW, and the Vestini on the S. It was reduced by Rome in 268 B.C., and took part in the Social War against Rome in 90 B.C. Capital, Asculum Picenum.

Pictones (pik-tō′nēz). Ancient Gallic people, mentioned by Julius Caesar as living on the coast of what is now France, along the S bank of the Loire River. Their ancient town of Limonum is the modern Poitiers, to which they gave their name.

Picumnus (pi-kum′nus) and **Pilumnus** (pi-lum′nus). In Roman religion, two fertility gods associated with marriage and especially with childbirth. When a birth was about to take place they prevented the forest-god Silvanus from entering the house by beating the threshold with ax and pestle. Offerings were made to them after a delivery.

Picus (pī′kus). In ancient Italian mythology, a god of agriculture. According to Ovid, he was a son of Saturn and was a king in Italy. He was also said to have been the father of Faunus. He was a handsome and athletic youth, a trainer of horses, a mighty hunter, and a seer. Nymphs pursued him, but he scorned them all except Canens, reputed to be a daughter of Janus. He married Canens and they were devoted to each other. One day while he was hunting boars Circe saw him from afar and fell in love with him. She sent a phantom boar across his path, which he instantly pursued and so was separated from his companions.

As he searched alone in the forest, Circe approached him and declared her love. But Picus announced his unshakable love for Canens and spurned Circe. To punish him, she invoked her magic and transformed him into a handsome bird, a woodpecker. His companions, who came upon her and accused her of foul play toward their young leader, were changed into wild beasts. Some think, however, that the story of Picus is a rationalization of the sacred bird of Mars, the woodpecker.

Pielus (pī′ẹ-lus). According to Greek tradition, a son of Andromache and Neoptolemus, son of Achilles. Alexander the Great traced his descent from Neoptolemus and Andromache through this Pielus, one of whose descendants, they say, was Olympias, mother of Alexander and sister of King Neoptolemus of Epirus.

Pieria (pī-ir′i-ạ). In ancient geography, a district in N Thessaly, Greece. Apollo pastured his herd of cows here, and it was from here that they were stolen by the child Hermes. It was the legendary birthplace of Orpheus and of the Muses. Mount Olympus was in the district.

Pierides (pī-ir′i-dēz). In Greek mythology, the Muses. They were so named from Pieria in Thessaly, their reputed birthplace.

Pierides. In Greek legend, nine maidens of Pieria, in N Thessaly. They were so proud of their numbers and of their voices that they challenged the Muses to a contest on Mount Helicon. River-nymphs were selected to be the judges. When, not unexpectedly, the Muses were adjudged the winners, the Pierides hurled abuse on them. It was for this reason, not because of their arrogance in challenging the Muses, that they were turned into magpies with endless power to chatter and scold. The Pierides were so named and the incident thus reported by Nicander of Colophon, a poet of the 3rd century B.C. They are also said to be the daughters of Pierus, a king of Macedonia.

Pietas (pī′ẹ-tas). In Roman mythology, the personification of piety, dutiful respect, and family affection. Her symbol is the stork. A temple was built in her honor in Rome, in 191 B.C., by Acilius Glabrio. The occasion for the building of the temple was said to have been in honor of a daughter who had saved her father, condemned to starvation, by feeding him from her own breast.

Pillars of Heracles, or **Hercules** (her′kụ-lēz). In ancient geography, the two opposite promontories Calpe (Gibraltar) in Europe and Abyla in Africa, situated at the E extremity of the Strait of Gibraltar, at the outlet from the Mediterranean into the Atlantic. According to some accounts, a land bridge once joined the two continents and Heracles carved it apart to let the waters of Ocean mingle with those of the inner sea. Others say the waterway between the two continents was once much wider and Heracles narrowed it to keep ocean monsters out of the inner sea. Still others say that he set up the stone pillars to commemorate his successful voyage to the island of Erythea to fetch the cattle of Geryon. Whatever his reason, all agree that it was during his journey on this errand that he erected the Pillars.

Pilumnus (pi-lum′nus). A Roman fertility god, sometimes thought to have been the inventor of the idea of crushing grain with a pestle. See **Picumnus**.

Pimplea (pim′plẹ-ạ). In ancient geography, a city and fountain in Pieria sacred to the Muses.

Pimpleides (pim-plē′i-dēz). A name of the Muses, from Pimplea in Pieria.

Pincian Hill (pin′shi-ạn). [Latin, **Mons Pincius**.] Hill in the N part of Rome, extending in a long ridge E from the Tiber River. It was not one of the traditional Seven Hills, though separated by but a narrow interval from the Quirinal. In antiquity, as at the present day, it was noted for its beautiful gardens. The view from it toward Saint Peter's is famous.

Pindar (pin′dar). Greatest of the Greek lyric poets (518–438 B.C.). He was born in Cynoscephalae, near Thebes in Boeotia, to an aristocratic family, the Aegidae, who traced their ancestry to Aegeus and before him to Cadmus of Thebes. From childhood he showed great aptitude for and interest in music. He learned to play the lyre and flute at home, then went to Athens to learn music and how to train choruses from Agathocles (or Apollodorus of Athens). By the time he was 20 he had achieved a reputation as a poet. According to tradition, he was once beaten in a contest by the poetess Corinna,

fat, fāte, fär, fāre, errạnt; net, mē, hėr ardẹnt; pin, pīne; not, nōte, mŏve, nôr,

who also advised him to lay on the mythological adornments to his poems with a lighter hand. While still in his twenties he wrote for the princes of Thessaly and the nobles of Aegina. He wrote for and visited the leading families of Rhodes, Tenedos, Athens, which he especially loved, as well as King Alexander of Macedon, and the tyrants Theron of Acragas in Sicily, and Hiero of Syracuse, at whose court he lived for a time (476–472 B.C.). He was known and honored on every hand for his genius and for his piety. He was an ardent supporter of traditional religion, had special privileges at Delphi, and after his death his ghost was supposed to feast annually with Apollo. A Dorian aristocrat, he was as proud of his ancestry as he was of his genius, and considered himself the equal of any man with whom he might associate. The myths with which he embellished his work were often what he considered to be part of his family history. His morality was indissolubly linked to the Dorian aristocratic tradition—the heroic tradition of Heracles and the Aeacids. Best of all he loved to write, for their descendants, of the glorious exploits of Heracles and the Aeacids. Although he lived during the Persian War he did not offer his gifts to further the cause of the Greeks against the Persians, for he was purely a poet, inspired to commemorate an earlier age. He wrote widely, in many modes, including *Hymns* (to Persephone, to Fortune, and the like), *Paeans* (to Apollo of Delphi and Zeus of Dodona), *Choral dithyrambs* to Dionysus, *Processional songs, Choral songs for maidens, Choral dance-songs, Encomia* (laudatory odes), *Scolia* (festive songs to be sung at banquets by a *comus* or festive troop), and *Dirges* (to be sung to the flute, with choral dance). Of all these only fragments survive. His 44 *Epinicia* (Victory Odes) to the winners of the Olympian, Pythian, Nemean, and Isthmian games have come down to us almost in their entirety. In the victory odes for the winners of the games Pindar mentions the victor himself only in passing, as it were. The burden of the poems concerns the locale from which the victor came and such mythological adornments concerning it as Pindar could work in, with occasional sharp philosophic comments. The myths of which

he wrote he believed in implicitly, as Stesichorus before him had believed that the myths were actual history, but like Stesichorus, Pindar corrected the stories when he felt that was in order. For example, it was incredible to him on religious grounds that Tantalus would have served up his son Pelops as a feast for the gods, and that Demeter would have absent-mindedly eaten the shoulder of Pelops at the feast before she realized on what flesh she was feeding. Pindar would not admit that the immortal gods would permit such shocking barbarity, or that Tantalus would have committed it. In his account therefore, he said that Pelops was carried off by Poseidon, and that in his absence the horror story that he had been served up to the gods was invented. With his strong affection for and pride in the Aeacids, Pindar bore a resentment against Odysseus who brought such torment to Ajax, and said that it was to Homer that Odysseus owed his great reputation, that actually Odysseus was nothing but "a supple liar." But Pindar did give Homer full credit for telling the whole story of the glorious prowess of Ajax. Pindar wrote in the Ionic dialect, in a style that was almost archaic, rich in imagery, and difficult. So truly a poet of the dialect was he that he comes through only imperfectly in translation. The music he composed, and to which his poems were sung, has been lost. He lived to a great age and died in the theater in Argos. So reverenced was his name that Alexander the Great, more than a hundred years later, spared his house and his descendants when he captured and sacked Thebes.

Pindus (pin′dus). Range of mountains in Greece, between Thessaly on the E and Epirus on the W. Greatest elevation, about 7665 feet.

Pirae (pī′rē). The name of a village between Formia and Minturnae on the Via Appia, mentioned once by the Latin author Pliny the Elder, who describes it as deserted in his time (1st century A.D.). It has been identified with a substantial fortification of polygonal limestone at the modern seaside village of Scauri, five miles W of Minturnae. The existence of a town of this name in the 1st century B.C. has been confirmed by the Minturnae excavations, in whose inscriptions the name of a slave owner Pirana or Peirana, "woman from Pirae," appears four times. (JJ)

Piraeus (pī-rē′us). [Also: **Peiraeus, Peiraieus, Peiraievs, Piraieus.**] Seaport of Athens and the chief port of Greece, situated on the Saronic Gulf about 5 miles SW of Athens, on the west side of the Munychian peninsula. The ancients believed the Piraeus was once an island, and its name is taken to mean "land across the water." In ancient times Phalerum, which could be seen from the Acropolis, was the port of Athens, but Themistocles recognized the advantages of the Piraeus with its three harbors, even though it was farther away from Athens than Phalerum, and built it into a formidable port. The three harbors of the Piraeus were the great harbor on the west side of the peninsula, and the smaller, circular harbors of Munychia and Zea on the east side. Because of these harbors Themistocles thought the Piraeus even more important than Athens himself, and perhaps if he had been a tyrant would have compelled the Athenians to give up their city and move to the port. He advised them if they were ever hard-pressed to withdraw to the Piraeus, but they never did. During his archonship (493–492 B.C.) he fortified the harbor and built it up as a port. In c450 B.C. Hippodamus of Miletus remodeled the city, laying out the streets in squares or rectangles, the so-called gridiron system. The great ship sheds there were one of the glories of Athens. Among the artifacts found on the site of the ship sheds are marble plates, with a great eye painted on them. These plates were fastened to the bow of the ships, providing an eye so that the ship could see where it was going. The port was connected to Athens by long walls, and ultimately the whole area, Athens, Piraeus, Munychia and Zea, was enclosed in a single fortification. At the end of the Peloponnesian Wars (404 B.C.), the Spartans destroyed the fortifications. They were rebuilt in 394 B.C. by Conon, who also founded a sanctuary of Aphrodite near the SE rim of the great harbor. Sulla destroyed the fortifications (c86 B.C.) and they were never rebuilt. At the Piraeus there was a sacred precinct of Athena Savior with a bronze image of the goddess holding a spear; and there was a precinct of Zeus Savior with a bronze image of the god holding a staff and Victory. Annually a public sacrifice was offered to Zeus Savior with a public festival, boat races, and a procession. Those who had been saved during storms at sea made offerings at the sanctuary of Zeus Savior. Themistocles founded a sanctuary of Aphrodite at the NE extremity of the Piraeus. There were, among other religious sites, at least two theaters of Dionysus there. The bones of Themistocles, who died in Magnesia in Asia, were brought back to Greece by his sons and buried at Piraeus.

Piren or **Peiren** (pī′rēn). In Greek mythology, a son of Glaucus, and the brother of Bellerophon. According to some accounts, Bellerophon was compelled to flee from Corinth because he had accidentally killed Piren. Others say he killed Bellerus, the tyrant of Corinth.

Pirene (pī-rē′nē). A daughter of the river-god Achelous, or of the river-god Asopus and Metope. Her son by Poseidon, Cenchrias, was accidentally slain by Artemis. Pirene wept so copiously that she was metamorphosed into a fountain, which was located at Corinth.

Pirene Spring. A spring behind Aphrodite's temple on the Acrocorinth, the citadel of Corinth, or one just outside the city gate. Some say it was caused to flow to supply Corinth with water forever by the river-god Asopus. He did this in return for information supplied him by Sisyphus about the fate of Aegina, a daughter of Asopus, who had been carried off by Zeus. Others say the spring gushed forth when Pegasus, the winged horse, struck the ground with his hoof. It was while Pegasus was drinking at this spring that Bellerophon slipped the golden bridle over his neck and captured him. American archaeologists have found what is undoubtedly the Pirene Spring of the classical period within the city, just off the agora.

Pirithous (pī-rith′ō-us). [Also: **Peirithous.**] In Greek legend, a Lapith prince, the son of Ixion and Dia, daughter of Eioneus, or, as some say, a son of Zeus and Dia. He heard of the great exploits of Theseus and resolved to find out whether he could live up to his reputation for strength and courage. To carry out his resolve he invaded Attica and made a raid on a herd of cattle near

fat, fāte, fär, fāre, errant; net, mē, hėr ardent; pin, pīne; not, nōte, mōve, nôr,

Marathon. Theseus pursued him, whereupon Pirithous turned in his tracks to confront him and test his mettle. But when he saw Theseus, who showed every sign of his reputed valor, he had a change of heart. Instead of fighting him he admitted his wrong and put himself in Theseus' hands, to ask of him whatever recompense he desired. Theseus answered that the only recompense he wanted was the friendship of Pirithous. They then swore an oath of friendship which both kept until death. Pirithous married Hippodamia, daughter of Butes. He invited Theseus and many noted guests to the wedding, at which the centaurs were also present, but he did not invite Eris and Ares, and they determined to punish him for the slight. The centaurs became unruly as the result of taking too much wine, which in their ignorance they had failed to dilute with water, and attacked the bride. Pirithous, with the ready assistance of Theseus, fought them off and drove them from the wedding festivities. Pirithous was a member of the hunt for the Calydonian Boar and some say he accompanied Theseus on his expedition to the land of the Amazons. He had a son, Polypoetes, by Hippodamia, who later fought in the Trojan War. When Hippodamia subsequently died, Pirithous determined to seek a daughter of Zeus for a wife. He made a compact with Theseus by which they agreed to abduct Helen, the supposed daughter of Tyndareus, and draw lots to see which would win her. They bound themselves by oath that the winner would assist the loser to gain the bride he might seek. On the successful abduction of Helen, Pirithous lost in the drawing of the lots. He chose Persephone as the wife he would seek, and in spite of the efforts of Theseus to dissuade him he insisted that no other woman would suit him. Theseus, bound by his oath, descended to Tartarus with him and demanded Persephone from Hades. Hades, who received them courteously, invited them to be seated. Unwittingly, they took seats on Chairs of Forgetfulness, and instantly the chairs grew about them. They were unable to move. They sat there for years. Heracles, on a mission to fetch Cerberus from Tartarus, found them and answered their pleas for help. He wrenched Theseus from his chair but Pirithous, whose impious idea it was to invade the world of the dead and steal Persephone, remained fast to his chair, and there he sits through eternity.

Pirous (pī'rō-us). In Homeric legend (*Iliad*), a son of Imbrasus. In the Trojan War he was a captain of the Thracians, allies of Troy. They were described by Homer as top-knot wearers. He felled Diores with a huge stone and then stabbed him. In his turn he was slain by the javelin of Thoas.

Pisa (pī'sa). The name of Oenomaus' realm in Elis. It was said to have been founded by Pisus, a son of Perieres and a grandson of Aeolus. The mound of the murdered suitors of Hippodamia, daughter of Oenomaus, was here, and after he married Hippodamia and became king of Pisa in place of Oenomaus, Pelops sacrificed to them annually. When Pelops died his bones, according to some accounts, were placed in a chest and kept in a small building near the sanctuary of Artemis Cordax in Pisa. The Pisans were hostile to the Eleans. In 748 B.C. they brought in a tyrant of Argos and held the Olympic Games with him. In 668 B.C. they again took control of the games from the Eleans with an army. The Eleans did not recognize these games held under the auspices of the Pisans, and called them Non-Olympiads. In the 6th century B.C. the Pisans made war on the Eleans and were destroyed with their allies. Henceforth, the name of Pisa was Olympia.

Pisa (pē'sä). [Ancient name, **Pisae**.] City in C Italy, situated on the Arno River. Ancient Pisae, on the same site, was only two miles from the sea, but deposits in the delta of the Arno have so built out the land that the city is now six miles from the Mediterranean Sea. The ancient city was one of the 12 federated towns of Etruria. It became a Roman colony in 180 B.C., and was important for its location on the Aemilian Way and as an outpost against the Ligurians.

Pisae (pī'sē). Ancient name of **Pisa**, city in C Italy.

Pisander (pī-san'dėr). In Homeric legend (*Iliad*), a son of Maemalus. He was a captain of the Myrmidons sent out by Achilles with Patroclus, and was a man who excelled at fighting with the spear.

Pisander. [Also: **Peisandros**.] Early epic poet

actor; up, lūte, pull; oi, oil; ou, out; ᴛн, then; d̦ as d or j, ş as s or sh, ț as t or ch, z̦ as z or zh.

of the 7th or 6th century B.C. He was a native of Camirus in Rhodes, and wrote an epic, *Heraclea*, in two books, only fragments of which survive. It is thought that he was the first in literature to describe the labors of Heracles and fix their number as 12, and that it was he who gave to Heracles the attributes of the lion skin and the club.

Pisatis (pī′sa̤-tis). In ancient geography, a region in the NW of the Peloponnesus. It became a part of Elis.

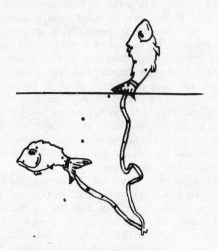

PISCES
Pictured according to ancient descriptions

Pisces (pis′ēz). The twelfth sign of the zodiac —the Fishes—which the sun enters about February 19. Also, a zodiacal constellation, supposed to represent two fishes united by a ribbon attached to their tails. One of the fishes is E, the other S, of the square of Pegasus.

Piscis Australis (pis′is âs-trā′lis). An ancient southern constellation—the Southern Fish. The figure represents a fish which swallows the water poured out of the vase by Aquarius.

Pisidia (pi-sid′i-a̤). In ancient geography, a territory in Asia Minor. It was bounded by Phrygia on the N, Isauria and Cilicia on the E, Pamphylia on the S, and Lycia on the SW, and was traversed by the Taurus Mountains. It was conquered by Rome.

Pisistratidae (pī-sis-trat′i-dē). Hippias and Hipparchus, the two sons and successors of Pisistratus.

Pisistratus (pī-sis′tra̤-tus). [Also: **Peisistratus.**] Tyrant of Athens, 561–527 B.C. (with intervals). He was born c605 B.C., the son of Hippocrates, a descendant of Neleus, and was named for Nestor's son Pisistratus. He was a relative of Solon with whom, in spite of political differences, he remained on friendly terms to the end of Solon's life. At a time of civil strife between two factions in Athens Pisistratus seized the opportunity, at the head of a third party of agricultural followers whose support he won by the promise of liberal land laws, to gain power for himself (c561 B.C.). According to Herodotus, he achieved power in the following manner: He gashed himself and his mules, then drove his chariot into the market place of Athens. Displaying his wounds, he asked for a guard to protect him, reminding the Athenians of his brave exploits when he led an army against the Megareans (c570 B.C.) and recovered Salamis for the Athenians and captured the Megarean port of Nisaea as well. The Athenians granted him a guard armed with clubs. With this, Pisistratus revolted, captured the citadel, and secured power in Athens. Having established himself in power, however, he made no upsetting changes in the laws or offices but administered the government according to the established usages and was a wise ruler. Only a short time passed before the leaders of the other two factions, the aristocratic parties, Megacles and Lycurgus, composed their differences and drove Pisistratus out (c560 B.C.). He went into exile. The harmony between Megacles and Lycurgus was short-lived. Megacles sent a herald to Pisistratus and offered to restore him to power on condition that Pisistratus marry his daughter. He agreed. But the problem of how his restoration was to be accomplished had to be overcome. The device used was, according to Herodotus, extremely silly in view of the fact that the Athenians were reputed to be the cleverest of the Greeks, but it worked. Pisistratus found an unusually tall and beautiful woman, dressed her in armor, and drove her in a cart to the city. Heralds preceding the procession proclaimed that this was the goddess Athena, and that it was her wish that the Athenians restore Pisistratus. The Athenians accepted the hoax and he regained power

fat, fāte, fär, fāre, errant; net, mē, hẽr ardẹnt; pin, pīne; not, nōte, möve, nôr,

(c559 B.C.), and then married the daughter of Megacles. Pisistratus already had grown sons, and as the Alcmaeonidae, of which family Megacles was a member, were under a curse for breaking their oath in regard to the followers of Cylon, Pisistratus resolved not to have any children by his new wife. Megacles learned that the childlessness of his daughter was deliberate and was roused to anger against Pisistratus. He again composed his differences with the party of Lycurgus and plotted to expel Pisistratus, but he, learning of the plot, fled to Eretria (c556 B.C.). He spent the next ten years scheming how to regain power in Athens. He and his sons Hippias and Hipparchus collected money, armed mercenaries and allies who were in their debt, and set out to return to Athens. They landed near Marathon and were joined by many who, as Herodotus says, "loved tyranny better than freedom." But others says the rule of Pisistratus was not unpopular, and that it was on the whole beneficial. At first the Athenians ignored the movements of Pisistratus, but when they realized he had left Marathon and was approaching the city with an army they gathered forces to resist him. The two forces encamped opposite each other. An Acarnanian soothsayer announced to Pisistratus:

> Now has the cast been made, the net is out-spread in the water,
> Through the moonshiny night the tunnies will enter the meshes.

Pisistratus understood the saying and instantly acted on it. He fell upon the Athenian army just after they had finished their midday meal and were relaxing in their camp, and put them to rout. He now became ruler of Athens for the third time (c544 or 541 B.C.), and this time he took vigorous measures to secure his power. The Alcmaeonidae fled the country. Pisistratus took land from his enemies and gave it to his agricultural followers. He made peace with the neighboring states. He oriented Athenian diplomacy towards Ionia in an effort to make the Aegean Sea the area of Athenian hegemony. He took the city of Sigeum from the Mytilenaeans by force of arms and established his bastard son Hegesistratus as tyrant there. He beautified the city of Athens, gave his support to the art of poetry, encouraged the dramatic representations that were given at the festivals of Dionysus, and changed the character of the Panathenean festival to give it a national rather than a local flavor. In the latter years of his rule he commissioned a learned body to establish a definitive text of the *Iliad* and the *Odyssey*. This version, which collated and set in order the many bits and sections recited by the rhapsodists, is the one from which all subsequent texts of Homer are derived. Under his just and beneficent rule Athens was strong, prosperous, and at peace. At his death (527 B.C.), Pisistratus left his sons Hippias and Hipparchus in control of the city.

Pisistratus. In the *Odyssey*, one of the sons of Nestor. He welcomed Telemachus when he arrived in Pylus in search of news of his father, and accompanied Telemachus on his journey to Sparta to see what news Menelaus could give him.

Piso (pī'sō), **Calpurnius.** Name of a family of the Gens Calpurnia distinguished in Roman history. Among the members were the following: Lucius, a censor, consul (133 B.C.), and author; Lucius, a politician, father-in-law of Julius Caesar, consul in 58 B.C., and later a member of the party of Mark Antony; Cnaeus, governor of Syria under Tiberius—according to some accounts he poisoned Germanicus at the request of Tiberius, but when he returned to Rome and showed documents as evidence of Tiberius' complicity, Tiberius destroyed the documents and disavowed him, and he was sentenced to death by the Senate; Caius, the leader of an unsuccessful conspiracy against Nero in 65 A.D. who committed suicide when the plan fell through; and Lucius, the successor of Galba for four days, put to death by Otho (69 A.D.).

Pistor (pis'tôr). In Roman mythology, an epithet of Jupiter, meaning "the Baker." When the Gauls were besieging Rome Jupiter advised the Romans to bake bread and throw it to the enemy, thus deluding them into thinking that the Romans had plenty of provisions.

Pistoria (pis-tôr'i-a). [Modern name, **Pistoia**.] City in C Italy, situated near the Umbro River, about 20 miles NW of Florence. It was colonized by the Romans in ancient times. Nearby the conspiracy of Catiline was crushed (62 B.C.) when his forces were destroyed and he was killed.

Pistoxenus (pis-toks′e̯-nus) **Painter.** See **Euphronius,** painter and potter.

Pitana (pi-tā′na̯) or **Pitane** (-nē̯). In Greek mythology, a nymph, mother by Poseidon of Evadne. She concealed the fact that she was to bear a child, and when it was born gave it to Aepytus, son of Elatus, to bring up.

Pithecusa (pith-e̯-kū′sa̯) or **Pithecusae** (-sē̯). [Also: **Aenaria.**] In ancient geography, a volcanic island in the Tyrrhenian Sea, situated about 16 miles W of Naples. The name, given it by the Greeks, means "Apes' island." According to legend, Zeus became disgusted with the Cercopes, a people notorious for their lying and cheating habits. He changed them into apelike animals covered with long yellow hair, deprived them of speech so that they could no longer plague humanity with their lies, and exiled them to this island which bears their name. Modern name of the island is **Ischia.**

Pittacus (pit′a̯-kus). Greek politician and poet, born c650 B.C., in Lesbos; died c569 B.C. He was chiefly responsible for the overthrow of the tyrant of Mytilene (c611 B.C.). He won the confidence of the people and was elected by them to be their ruler for a term of ten years. He restored order in Mytilene by banishing the nobles who resisted his power, among them the poets Alcaeus and Sappho, and he secured domestic peace by the enactment of wise laws and a firm rule. At the end of the ten years for which he had been chosen he voluntarily relinquished his power. After his death he was enrolled as one of the Seven Wise Men of ancient Greece.

Pittheus (pit′thūs). In Greek legend, a son of Pelops and Hippodamia. He was king in Troezen, a city which he named after his brother and which he dedicated to Athena and Poseidon, and was said to have been the wisest man of his time. He founded an oracle of Apollo in Troezen, dedicated an altar to Themis, and was a teacher of oratory and rhetoric. He gave his daughter Aethra to King Aegeus, who was paying him a visit, and reared and instructed their son Theseus, in Troezen. Later he adopted Hippolytus, son of Theseus and Antiope, and made him heir to the throne of Troezen.

Pityocamptes (pit-i-ō̯-kamp′tēz). The name given to Sinis, meaning "Pine-bender." See **Sinis.**

Pitys (pi′tis). In Greek mythology, a nymph who fled from Pan and was changed into a fir tree. Pan used the branches of the tree for a garland for his head.

Pityusa (pit-i-ū′sa̯). [Modern names, **Spetsai, Petza, Spetzia.**] Island in S Greece, at the entrance to the Gulf of Nauplia, about 28 miles SE of Nauplia. Length, about 5 miles.

Pius (pī′us), **Metellus.** See **Metellus, Quintus Caecilius** (died c64 B.C.).

Placentia (pla̯-sen′sha̯). [Modern name, **Piacenza.**] City in N Italy, situated on the Padus (Po) River E of its junction with the Trebia (Trebbia) River, about 40 miles SE of Mediolanum (Milan). Founded by the Romans in 218 B.C. as a fortress against the Gallic tribes, it served as a place of retreat for the remnants of the Roman army after the defeat at the Trebia (218 B.C.) by Hannibal. In 205 B.C. Hasdrubal unsuccessfully besieged it; in 200 it was burned by the Gauls; and in 190 B.C. it was recolonized, and a few years later was made a terminus of the Aemilian Way. In the time of Augustus part of the ancient city was named Julia Augusta.

Planctae (plang′tē). "Wandering Rocks," perhaps referring to the shifting channel between Sicily and Italy. When the Argonauts on their roundabout way home from Colchis reached the Planctae, Thetis and her Nereids lifted the *Argo* in the air, carried it past the Planctae, and set it in the water safely on the far side of the dangerous shifting rocks.

Plancus (plang′kus), **Lucius Munatius.** Roman soldier, orator, and consul (42 B.C.). He served under Julius Caesar in the Gallic and civil wars, and attached himself successively to Brutus, Anthony, and Octavian (it was he who proposed in the Senate that the title of Augustus should be bestowed on the last-named). Horace addressed to him Ode vii, Book I.

Planet. The word means "wanderer." The ancients observed that, in addition to the fixed stars in the sky, there were seven light-giving bodies which wandered among them, and which they accordingly called "planets." These were the sun and the moon, and the five which we now speak of as the visible planets, named after Roman gods, Mercury, Venus, Mars, Jupiter, and Saturn. To these were ascribed magic or even divine powers, and from the belief that their positions relative to each other, or to the signs of the zodiac, had favorable or disastrous influence upon human fortunes arose the pseudo-science of astrology, whose practitioners pretend to interpret these aspects as prophetic of outcomes and as guidance in future undertakings.

From the seven planets came the seven days of the week, each with a god in charge. The days of the seven-day week, with their Latin names and the French, Italian, and English derivatives, are

Latin	Italian	French	English
Dies Solis			(Sun-day)
Dies Lunae	lunedì	lundi	(Mon-day)
Dies Martis	martedì	mardi	
Dies Mercurii	mercoledì	mercredi	
Dies Iovis	giovedì	jeudi	
Dies Veneris	venerdì	vendredi	
Dies Saturni			Satur(n's)-day

(In the English week, Tuesday, Wednesday, Thursday, and Friday are named after Norse gods.) (JJ)

Plataea (pla̱-tē′a). [Also: **Plataeae**.] In ancient geography, a city in Boeotia, Greece, situated at the foot of Mount Cithaeron, about 30 miles NW of Athens. Some say that the original inhabitants were sprung from the earth, and that the city was named for the nymph Plataea, a daughter of the river-god Asopus; there was a hero-shrine of Plataea in the city. The Plataeans knew of only two kings in their history: Cithaeron for whom the mountain was named, and Asopus for whom the river separating Plataea from Thebes was named. Plataeans were among many Boeotians who accompanied the Greeks in the Trojan War. The Plataeans played a valiant part in the Persian War. They helped the Athenians defeat the Persians at Marathon (490 B.C.). The part they played in the battle of Plataea (479 B.C.) was so glorious they were awarded the meed of valor after the defeat of the Persians. With their share of the booty from the victory they raised a temple of Athena Area (*Warlike*), and in it placed a wooden image of the goddess, with head, hands, and feet of marble, said by some to have been made by Phidias. On the walls of the temple was a painting by Polygnotus, showing Odysseus after he had slain the suitors, and a painting by Onasias which depicted the expedition of the Seven against Thebes. Because of their valor at the battle of Plataea the Plataeans were excused from all further contributions to the war against the Persians, and undertook to celebrate the anniversary each year. Annually deputies came from all parts of Greece to sacrifice to Zeus Savior. No slaves were allowed to take part in this ceremony that was sacred to the memory of men who died for liberty. On the day of the celebration a trumpet call to battle was sounded at dawn. Immediately, a procession was formed, in which chariots laden with myrtle boughs were followed by a black bull and young men carrying wine and milk for libations. The procession marched to the entrance of the city where the graves of those who fell in the battle were located near an altar of Zeus, God of Freedom. There the archon washed the little pillars on the monuments of the dead with water and rubbed them with oil and perfumes. Then the black bull was slain and the archon called on the shades of the dead to come and feast on its blood. Next he poured wine from a bowl and presented it to the men who had died for the liberty of Greece. This ceremony was performed annually at least until the 1st century A.D. Every fifth year games, called Eleutheria, were celebrated in honor of Zeus Eleutherios (*God of Freedom*), in which races by men in armor were the most important contest. The Plataeans also celebrated the festivals known as the Great and Little Daedala. Plataea was unsuccessfully attacked by the Thebans in 431 B.C., besieged by the Spartans and their allies in 429 B.C., taken and destroyed by them in 427, and restored in 387 B.C. In 373 B.C. the Plataeans, wary of the Thebans, went out of their city to the fields only when they knew the Thebans were meeting in assembly and would not attack. The Thebans, learning of this policy, went to their assembly armed, marched out of it, and attacked Plataea while the inhabitants were at work in the fields. They took the city, destroyed all but its sanctuaries, and barred the gates against the Plataeans, so that though they lost their city they at least kept their lives, and many of them went to Athens. They were restored to their own city and rebuilt it after Philip of Macedon conquered Thebes and her allies at Chaeronea (338 B.C.).

Plataea, Battle of. When Mardonius occupied

actọr; up, lūte, pŭll; oi, oil; ou, out; ᴛʜ, then; ḏ as d or j, ş as s or sh, ṭ as t or ch, ẓ as z or zh.

Attica for a second time, the Spartans sent out Pausanias, in command of a force of Spartans, to aid the Athenians (479 B.C.). On learning that the Spartans were on the march Mardonius withdrew from Attica, which was unfavorable terrain for the operation of his cavalry, and went to Thebes whose people were allied to the Persians. Pausanias arrayed the Spartans, Tegeans, Athenians, and all the other allies (according to Herodotus, a force of over 100,000) near Plataea. The Persians who faced him under Mardonius numbered, again according to Herodotus, 300,000. (Most modern historians consider these figures much too high.) Both armies offered sacrifices and the victims in each case foretold victory if they stood on the defensive, but not if they began the attack or if they crossed the Asopus River which separated them. Owing to these circumstances neither side wished to begin the attack, and for ten days the battle was delayed, although the Persian cavalry made harassing raids from time to time. In the meantime the Greek forces were daily augmented by soldiers flocking in. In the interval Aristides, who commanded 8000 foot-soldiers under Pausanias, sent to Delphi for an oracle. The response from the priestess was: "The Athenians shall be victorious if they address their prayers to Zeus, Hera of Cithaeron, Pan, and the nymphs Sphragitides; if they sacrifice to the heroes Androcrates, Leucon, Pisander, Damocrates, Hypsion, Actaeon, and Polyidus; and if they fight only in their own country, on the plain of the Eleusinian Demeter and of Persephone." All the conditions of the oracle were satisfied except the last ones, since the Athenians under Aristides were not fighting on their own soil nor in the plain of Eleusinian Demeter. Because of this, Aristides thought the Greeks should withdraw to Attica and meet the Persians there. However, while the matter was debated, the Plataean general Arimnestus was visited by Zeus in a dream, and was told by the god that the Greeks had misinterpreted the oracle, that there was a plain of Eleusinian Demeter nearby if they would look for it. On learning of the dream Aristides searched the area, and found a very ancient sanctuary of Demeter, which was well situated for battle. The Plataeans removed the boundary of their

territory and gave the land to the Athenians, so that, in accordance with the oracle, the Athenians would fight on their own soil, in the plain of Eleusinian Demeter. On the eleventh day that the Greeks and Persians faced each other across the Asopus River, the Persians had a consultation. Some Persian chiefs were in favor of withdrawing to the fortified city of Thebes, where provisions were available, and by means of bribes buying up the Greek chiefs one at a time, and so ending the war without a battle. But Mardonius, proud of his army, sure that his superior numbers would overcome the Greeks, and worried by diminishing provisions, decided to ignore the advice of his generals and the warnings of the victims, and attack on the next day. That night Alexander of Macedon, who was of Greek descent, rode to the Greek camp and warned of the impending attack, because, he said, he did not want to see Greece exchange freedom for slavery. He asked the Greeks, if they should be victorious, to secure his freedom, then rode back and took his place in the Persian line. The following day the Persian cavalry attacked and grievously harried the Greeks. During the night the Greeks withdrew according to plan, but the Spartans and Tegeans, their faithful allies, were delayed in their withdrawal by the intransigence of a Spartan general who misunderstood the reason for the withdrawal and considered it a disgrace. He proposed to remain with his forces and fight. While Pausanias reasoned with him the Athenians and the other allies withdrew, and the Spartans and Tegeans were left alone to face the Persians. The Athenians to whom they sent for help were unable to come up immediately as they had been set upon by the Greek allies of Persia. Pausanias ordered his forces to hold their line but not to fight until he had obtained favorable omens from sacrificial victims. The omens were unfavorable and he ordered new victims. Meanwhile the Persians were nearing the immobilized forces and hurling weapons against them, so that some were killed without making any resistance, in accordance with the command of Pausanias. As the omens were still unfavorable and the Persians were rushing on, Pausanias lifted his eyes, streaming with tears, to heaven and implored Hera to grant that if they must be unsuccessful in the coming fight they might at least acquit themselves with valor. According to Herodotus, who tells us this story, at that moment the sacrificial victims gave favorable omens, and he ordered his line into action. The Tegeans rushed against the Persians; Pausanias attacked the Persian line of wicker shields. When the line was pierced a furious struggle took place near a temple of Demeter. Both sides fought with the utmost courage. As long as Mardonius was alive and led a body of picked men, the Persians attacked tirelessly. But when Mardonius was slain the Persians took flight and Pausanias with his Spartans and Tegeans won a glorious victory against enormous odds. Herodotus says that though the battle was fought close to a sacred grove of Demeter, as the oracle of Delphi had commanded, not a single Persian died on the sacred soil, while around it, in unconsecrated ground, great numbers were slain. He concluded that the goddess herself kept the Persians out of her sacred grove. The Spartans and Tegeans pursued 'the fleeing Persians to the rampart they had built in Theban territory and besieged it. With the aid of the Athenians, who had shaken off their attackers and now came up, they breached the wall of the rampart and slaughtered the Persians inside. Herodotus gives the number of Persians and their allies who were lost as over 250,000. Others say that though the slaughter was undoubtedly great, Herodotus exaggerated the number here as he did the number on both sides in this battle. According to Plutarch, the Greeks lost 1360 men. Legend says the successful battle of Plataea (479 B.C.) took place in the morning of the same day that saw, in the afternoon, the defeat of the Persians at Mycale in Asia Minor.

Platanistius (plạ-tạ-nis'ti-us). An epithet of Apollo, meaning "God of the Plane-tree Grove."

Plato (plā'tō). [Original name, **Aristocles**.] Greek philosopher, who was born, some say, on Apollo's birthday, 428 or 427 B.C., at Athens. He died at Athens, 348 or 347 B.C. He was an associate of Socrates ("my elderly friend") until the latter's death, and was the founder of the Academic school, of which Theaetetus, Eudoxus, and Aristotle were members. Plato's father, Ariston, traced his descent from Codrus, the legendary king of Athens. His mother, Perictione, also of aristocratic birth, was a descendant of Solon. But from association with other members of his family he became familiar with the background and outlook of democracy in its Periclean form. As a young man, he had had a thorough training in music, mathematics, and letters; he was also an accomplished athlete and a witty writer. With his ability, family background, and political connections, he would naturally have proceeded to take part in public life, but for the tragic death, in 399 B.C., of Socrates. For a time thereafter he withdrew to Megara, to the home of Eucleides, and there is a tradition that he spent some years in travel, visiting Egypt, Cyrene, Sicily, and parts of Italy, before returning to Athens in 387 B.C. There he founded his school in the garden of a gymnasium that had been named Academy for the hero Academus, who told the Dioscuri where they could find their sister Helen after she had been abducted by Theseus and Pirithous. In later life (367 and 361 B.C.) Plato was invited to Syracuse with the idea of initiating its ruler, Dionysius II, into the philosophy suitable for a "philosopher-king." It is said that Plato sought to teach Dionysius philosophy from the ground up, and started him out with geometry, for which Dionysius soon lost his enthusiasm. Jealousies and misunderstandings made the situation impossible, and Plato's freedom of movement was for a time curtailed. On the return voyage, it is said that his vessel was intercepted, and that Plato, as a captured enemy alien, was exposed for sale in the slave market at Aegina. He was purchased by a former pupil, who restored him to the Academy, which he never again left. The Academy, over which he presided for forty years altogether, was attended by large numbers of educated men, and even by women. Plato's teaching was carried on in the manner of informal conversations with his followers. He never married. To the end of his long life he pursued his activities of teaching and writing and, it is said, he was engaged in composing one of his works when a gentle death overtook him. Plato himself regarded academic teaching as his main activity, but shortly after the death of Socrates he commenced the series of *Dialogues* upon which, for the modern reader, his influence as a great philosopher chiefly depends. In the earlier *Dialogues* we see depicted a "Socrates made young and handsome," the embodiment of courage, temperance, justice, and wisdom: moving freely in society, among young men, among intellectuals, sometimes in happy, sometimes in trying circumstances. Always we feel his challenge to "tend our souls," i.e., to become "friends of ideas," members of the new spiritual Academy. The *Dialogues* are dramatic, not doctrinal, presentations. Nevertheless, the modern reader finds himself impelled to participate in the discussions, and to construct from somewhere within himself what he takes to be implied in the Socratic ideal of reflective citizenship. This is always something beyond the "tendance of the soul," which was all that Socrates himself claimed as the content of his mission in life. In the series of *Dialogues* culminating in the *Republic,* the modern reader senses the pull of a consistent philosophy: uncompromising idealism applied to the construction of a perfect human community. Such a community exists only in idea; but the neophyte is urged to walk in its ways, whatever his local citizenship. Actually, what emerges in the mind of the modern reader is usually a mirror-image of what idealism that reader's mind possesses within itself. Accordingly, what is acclaimed as "the philosophy of Plato" varies with the background and outlook of the acclaimer. Neverthless, it is upon the subjective interaction of modern minds with the *Dialogues* representing "middle Platonism," especially the *Republic,* that Plato's great influence still depends. It is thought to go beyond the teaching of Socrates, but not beyond the spirit of his teaching.

The later *Dialogues* are more technical. They throw light upon the studies pursued in the Academy and provide a somewhat abstract and arid intellectual training. They also present views of three rival philosophic schools: 1) an abstract idealism, 2) a concrete and rather naïve realism, and 3) a form of humanism which is regarded as a precursor of modern pragmatism. The earlier idealism is apparently refuted (in the *Parmeni-*

des), the highest good is sought in "the mixed life" (*Philebus*), and in the latest *Dialogue* (*The Laws*), the transcendentalism of the *Republic* is withdrawn in favor of a "second-best" or "model" city, in which full justice is done to the teachings of experience. At the same time, the *Laws* end with an expression of faith in the Academy as the most vital of social institutions.

Plato. Athenian comic poet, active 428–389 B.C. He is ranked among the very best of the poets of the Old Comedy. He carried on a poetic contest with Aristophanes, and attacked the demagogues Cleon, Hyperbolus, Agyrrhius, and Cleophon. Fragments only of his works are extant.

Plato. Greek bust in bronze, of the first half of the 4th century B.C., in the Museo Nazionale, Naples, once supposed to represent the great philosopher. Many consider it a bearded type of Dionysius; some, the famous Poseidon of Tarentum.

Plautus (plô'tus). [Full name, **Titus Maccius Plautus.**] Roman comic dramatist, born at Sarsina, Umbria, Italy, c251 B.C.; died 184 B.C. Although he was unquestionably the most famous and most popular of ancient Roman writers of comedy, the details of his life are virtually unknown. Some say he came to Rome and worked for a miller, and that it was while thus employed that he first began to write comedies in verse. It seems reasonably certain that he was intimately connected with the stage from a comparativly early age, if only because of the remarkable knowledge of stage technique manifested in his plays (indeed, his works remain today among the most widely read and enjoyed of the Latin classics). He drew much from Menander and the other dramatists of the Greek New Comedy (including stock characters, such as the clever, unscrupulous slave, and stock situations, involving mistaken identity and carefully contrived misunderstandings between two lovers), but he wrote in the popular idiom of his day. As a result his plays do not merely ape those of the Greeks, but are vigorous, often coarse, always amusing examples of practical stagecraft. His works were extremely popular in his own day, and were read and often adapted by such later writers as Molière who modeled his *Avare* (*Miser*) on a play of Plautus, and by Jonson, and Shakespeare. Of his comedies, 21 (nearly all complete) are extant. Among them are *Amphitruo*, notable for being a comic treatment of a mythical subject (but the subject of Amphitryon has been a favorite with writers of all ages, comic and otherwise), *Captivi, Aulularia, Trinummus, Rudens, Miles Gloriosus, Mostellaria, Pseudolus,* and *Menaechmi.*

Plavis (plä'vis). [Modern name, **Piave.**] River in Italy, which flows into the Adriatic Sea about 20 miles NE of Venetia (Venice).

Pleiades (plē'a̧-dēz, plī-). [Also: **Pleiads.**] In Greek mythology, the daughters of Atlas and Pleione. They were born on Mount Cyllene in Arcadia, and their names are: Alcyone, Celaeno, Electra, Maia, Merope, Sterope (or Asterope), and Taÿgete. According to some accounts they were transformed into doves by the gods to protect them from Orion who had been pursuing them for five years, and their images were set among the stars. Others say they killed themselves in grief for their sisters, the Hyades, and were placed among the stars by the gods. Only six of them are visible in the cluster because Merope, ashamed that she was the only one of the sisters to have married a mortal, withdrew. Other accounts say it is Electra who is missing, and that she withdrew so that she would not be compelled to witness the fall of Troy, founded by her son. Literally, Pleiades means "The Weepers;" they are also called the Seven Sisters. Their rising is the signal that the time for the spring sowing is at hand, and their setting marks the time of harvest. See individual entries.

Pleione (plē-ī'ō̧-nē). In Greek mythology, a daughter of Oceanus and Tethys. She was the wife of Atlas and the mother of the seven Pleiades. See **Pleiades.**

Plexippus (plek-si'pus). In Greek legend, a brother of Althaea, the mother of Meleager. He took part in the Calydonian Hunt and was later killed by Meleager for trying to take the boar's hide from Atalanta, to whom Meleager had awarded it. It was because of the murder of her brother that Althaea cast into the fire the charred block of wood which, according to a prophecy at his birth, would bring the end of Meleager's life when it had burned to ashes.

Plexippus. In Greek mythology, a son of Phineus and Cleopatra. He was also known as Parthenius. See **Pandion,** son of Phineus.

Pliny (plin'i). [Called **Pliny the Elder;** full Latin name, **Caius Plinius Secundus.**] Roman naturalist, born at Novum Comum (now Como), Italy, 23 A.D.; perished in the eruption of Vesuvius, Aug., 79 A.D. He went to Rome in his early youth, served in Africa, and was, at the age of 23, commander of a troop of cavalry in Germany. While there, it is said, the ghost of Drusus Nero (Roman general who died in Germany, 9 A.D.), appeared to him as he slept and asked Pliny to rescue his memory from oblivion. Inspired by this dream, Pliny undertook to write a complete history of the German Wars. He produced the *Bellorum Germaniae Libri,* in 20 books, which no longer is extant. He returned to Rome and studied law, was procurator in Spain under Nero (c70–72), and was charged with other official duties in various parts of the empire. His literary work, which was conducted with extraordinary industry in the intervals of his official labors (scarcely a waking moment of day or night being left unoccupied), extended into the departments of tactics, history, grammar, rhetoric, and natural science. His reading was enormous; it is said that he made notes on all the books he read on the ground that no book was so bad that there wasn't some good in it; and he was called the most learned man of his day. Of his writings, only his *Natural History (Historia Naturalis)* is extant. An elaborate and valuable scientific encyclopedia in 37 books, it covers anthropology, zoology, pharmacology, and mineralogy. He drew his material from nearly 500 authors of antiquity to which he applied his own standards of criticism. For example, he rejected some material from the Greeks as being manifestly impossible and unscientific, but on the other hand, in the books on the anthropology of man and the animals, he included descriptions of fabulous creatures and marvelously made men as part of his array of "facts." He describes the "Umbrella-foots," who turned on their backs and used their big feet to protect them from the sun; and he tells of winged horses, unicorns, Tritons, and Nereids. Yet, at the same time, he records many sound scientific observations. In the last books of the work he treats the use of minerals in medicine and in art and in connection with the latter describes many art works—paintings and sculpture—of antiquity. The death of Pliny, vividly described by his nephew Pliny the Younger in a letter to the historian Tacitus, was the result of his efforts to observe more closely the eruption of Vesuvius, and to aid those who were in danger.

Pliny. [Called **Pliny the Younger;** full Latin name, **Caius Plinius Caecilius Secundus.**] Roman author; born at Novum Comum (now Como), Italy, 62 A.D.; died 113. He was a nephew of the elder Pliny, under whose will he was adopted as a son. He was a consul in 100, and later (111 or 112) governor of Bithynia and Pontica. He was a friend of Trajan and Tacitus. His *Epistles* and a eulogy of Trajan have been preserved. The most celebrated of his letters is one to Trajan concerning the treatment of the Christians in his province and describing their practices.

Plisthenes (plĭs'thḗ-nēz). [Also: **Pleisthenes.**] In Greek legend, a son of Atreus and his first wife Cleola. He was brought up in Thyestes' court. According to some accounts, Thyestes sent Plisthenes to kill Atreus, but Atreus killed him instead, unaware that he was his own son. Others say Atreus sent messengers to murder Thyestes' son, and that Thyestes, learning of the plot, arranged it so that Plisthenes was slain instead. Some say it was to avenge the death of Plisthenes that Atreus later cut up, cooked, and served Thyestes' sons to him at a banquet. Another Plisthenes was the son of Pelops and Hippodamia, and some say he was the father by Aërope of Agamemnon and Menelaus.

Plotae (plō'tē). According to some accounts, floating islands in the Ionian Sea. To these islands the Boreadae pursued the Harpies who had been tormenting Phineus. Here they were commanded by Iris not to slay the "Hounds of Zeus" and received a promise from Iris that the Harpies would torment Phineus no more. Therefore, the Boreadae turned back, and the islands then became known as the "Islands of Turning," the Strophades.

Plutarch (plö'tärk). Greek essayist, author, and priest of Pythian Apollo, born c46 A.D. at Chaeronea, Boeotia, Greece; died there, c120. He was educated at Athens, traveled in Egypt, and spent some time in Rome, where he became acquainted with the emperor Hadrian who made him procurator of Greece. Among his many works are the *Opera Moralia,* essays on ethical principles. One such is a dialogue to show the moral superiority of many animals over man in which the speakers are Circe, Odysseus, and a pig; in this discussion the pig is the winner. Others, the titles of which indicate Plutarch's interests, are *On Virtue and Vice, On the Late Vengeance of the Deity, On Superstition,* to name a few of the 60 essays attributed to him in this group. These essays, aside from their own interest, are valuable for the numerous and frequently long citations in them from Greek poems that have since been lost. He wrote on religion, as *On the Oracles of the Pythian Priestess, On Isis and Osiris, Why the Oracles Are Silent,* extremely valuable and interesting for the archaeological material and religious history preserved in them; on natural history, as *On Rivers,* which also included mythological references; on history and literature, as in *Greek* and *Roman Questions.* Among many other extant works is a letter, *Consolation to His Wife,* on the loss of their young daughter, which indicates that he had been initiated into the mysteries of Dionysus and his acceptance of the comfort of the belief that the soul is immortal. He is most celebrated as the author of 46 "Parallel Lives." These *Lives* are paired, for the most part, so as to consider one famous Greek and the famous Roman who most closely parallels him, as Theseus and Romulus, for example, the legendary founders of Athens and Rome. To his sympathetic, humane, and hero-worshiping (especially of the Greeks) *Lives* he brings quotations and material from many sources: solid historical fact, glorious legend, and his own ethical and religious reflections. According to K. O. Müller (*History of the Literature of Ancient Greece*), "In spite of all exceptions on the score of inaccuracy, want of information, or prejudice, Plutarch's lives must remain one of the most valuable relics of Greek literature, not only because they stand in the place of many volumes of lost history, but also because they are written with a graphic and dramatic vivacity, such as we find in few biographies, ancient or modern."

fat, fāte, fär, fāre, errant; net, mē, hėr ardent; pin, pīne; not, nōte, mŏve, nôr,

Pluto (plö'tō). In Greek mythology, a cult name of Hades, god of the infernal regions. The word means "rich one" or "wealth-giver," and thus he is associated with Plutus. Pluto is commonly the name used for him in the Persephone abduction myth. The Romans called him Dis.

Plutus (plö'tus). In Greek mythology, a personification of wealth; a son of Iasion and Demeter, and intimately associated with Irene, goddess of peace, who is often represented in art holding the infant Plutus. Zeus is said to have blinded him in order that he might not bestow his favors exclusively on good men, but should distribute his gifts without regard to merit (however, by some accounts he was later cured and gave wealth only to those whom he could see were honest).

Plutus, The. Comedy of Aristophanes, produced 388 B.C. It concerns Plutus, the god of wealth, who, being blind, distributes his favors indiscriminately. The play takes up various schemes by which Plutus' eyesight may be restored, so that his wealth will be distributed with a more just hand. The comedy ridicules rising theories concerning a more equitable distribution of wealth among the classes.

Pluvius (plö'vi-us). In Roman mythology, an epithet of Jupiter in reference to his function as rain-giver.

Plynteria (plin-tē'ri-a). One of the two principal days of a festival held at Athens in honor of Athena from the nineteenth to the twenty-fifth of the month Thargelion (last of May and beginning of June). This was a "washing" festival. The image of the goddess was removed from the Erechtheum on the Acropolis and the garments enfolding it were taken off. Veiled, so that the eyes of the populace could not behold it, the image was carried in a solemn procession to the sea. Those who marched in the procession carried cakes of dried figs in their hands. At the seaside the image was washed in sea water. The garments were also washed. The immersion in sea water was a purifying rite, as Iphigenia pretended she would purify the image of Artemis in Tauris, polluted by being seen by a matricide, by washing it in the sea. The rites of washing the image were performed by priestesses called Plyntrides. The day on which this ceremony fell was considered an unlucky one, because the goddess was not in her temple, and therefore no public business was transacted on this day. The companion day of the Plynteria was the Callynteria, which fell earlier in the month Thargelion, and involved the cleansing of Athena's temple. Both were in preparation for the offering of first fruits to the goddess.

Pnyx (niks). Hill between the Museum Hill and the Hill of the Nymphs, above the Agora, in the group SW of the Acropolis, at Athens, Greece; also, a famous ancient place of public assembly established on the N slope of this hill, beneath the summit. The place of assembly consists of a terrace, bounded at the back by a vertical cutting 13 feet high in the rock at the summit of the hill, and supported by a curved retaining wall, built of well-jointed polygonal masonry in huge blocks. Some of the courses of this retaining wall have disappeared, so that the terrace now slopes downward, while originally it was level or ascended slightly toward the back. The length of the terrace is 395 feet and its width 212 feet. The back wall is not straight, but forms an open obtuse angle, at the apex of which projects a huge cube of rock, rising from three steps and ascended by a small flight of steps in the angle at each side. This is the *bema,* or orators' platform, from which Demosthenes and other great Athenian political orators delivered their harangues.

Po (pō). [Latin, **Padus, Eridanus.**] Largest river in Italy. It rises in Monte Viso (*Mons Vesulus*) in the Alps on the French border, flows NE and then generally E, traversing a wide, fertile, and nearly level plain, and empties by several mouths into the Adriatic Sea (*Mare Adriaticum*). Its chief tributaries are the Tanaro (*Tanarus*) and Trebbia (*Trebia*) on the right, and the Dora Baltea (*Duria Major*), Sesia (*Sessites*), Ticino (*Ticinus*) (draining Lake Maggiore, *Lacus Verbanus*), Adda (*Addua*) (draining Lake Como, *Lacus Larius*), Oglio (*Ollius*) (draining Lake Iseo, *Lacus Sebinus*), and Mincio (*Mincius*) (draining Lake Garda, *Lacus Benacus*) on the left. The chief places on its banks are Turin (*Taurosia*), Piacenza (*Placentia*), and Cremona.

Podalirius (pod-a-lī'ri-us). In Greek legend, a son of Asclepius. He and his brother

Machaon, both "excellent leeches," accompanied the Greeks to the Trojan War as physicians. According to some accounts, Podalirius healed Philoctetes of his noisome wound when he was brought from Lemnos to Troy in the last year of the war. Others say it was Machaon who cured him. Podalirius tended the wounds the Greeks received at the hands of the Trojans as well as the wounds they gave each other, as at the funeral games for Achilles. When Machaon was killed Podalirius was wild with grief and was only prevented from taking his own life on his brother's grave by the persuasion of Nestor. Later he was among those who entered Troy in the Wooden Horse. He did not sail for Greece at the close of the war, but went overland to Colophon in Caria and then, searching for a place to settle, he chose Syrnos, in Caria, a spot ringed by mountains. He selected this site to fulfill instructions given by the oracle to go where he would be safe, even if the skies should fall. He shrewdly considered that the mountains surrounding his new home would hold up the skies if they should temporarily slip from their moorings.

Podarces (pō-där′sēz). The original name of Priam. When Heracles attacked Troy to punish Laomedon for reneging on his promise, he killed Laomedon and all of his sons except Podarces. He took Hesione captive and awarded her to Telamon. Hesione was given the chance to ransom any of the prisoners she chose and she chose her brother Podarces, after which he took the name Priam.

Podarces. In Homeric legend (*Iliad*), a son of Iphiclus, a grandson of Phylacus, and a descendant of Ares. He was the younger brother of Protesilaus. When Protesilaus was slain, in fulfillment of the prophecy that the first Greek to land at Troy would die, Podarces assumed command of the Phthians who had followed the brothers to Troy.

Podarge (pō-där′jē). In Greek mythology, a Harpy. She was the mother, by Zephyr (the West Wind) of the immortal horses Balius and Xanthus, which Poseidon gave to Peleus at his marriage to Thetis. The horses afterward went to the Trojan War with Achilles.

Podes (pō′dēz). In Homeric legend (*Iliad*), a Trojan. Though not of noble blood, he was a comrade and table companion of Hector. He was slain by Menelaus in the struggle for possession of the body of Patroclus.

Poeas (pē′as). In Greek legend, a king of Meliboea, in Thessaly. He was an Argonaut and, according to some accounts, as the Argonauts passed Crete on their way home Poeas killed Talos, the bronze man of Crete, by shooting him in his vulnerable heel with a poisoned arrow. When Heracles, in agony as the result of the burns of a poisoned robe, begged that someone would light the funeral pyre on which he was lying, only Poeas had the courage and sympathy to cast the brand which set the pyre afire. In return Heracles gave him his bow and arrows, which Poeas later gave to his own son Philoctetes to take to Troy. Others say it was Philoctetes, at the command of Poeas, who set fire to the pyre and received the bow and arrows.

Poena (pē′na). [Also: **Poine**.] A goddess of punishment and a companion of Nemesis. Poena is also pictured as a monster who robbed mothers of their children. She was sent by Apollo to ravage Argos to punish Argos for the deaths of Linus and Psamathe. The depredations of Poena ceased when the Argives raised a temple to Apollo and established a festival in honor of Linus and Psamathe.

Polemarch (pol′e-märk). A title of several officials in ancient Greek states. At Athens the polemarch was the third archon, who was, as late as Marathon (490 B.C.), the titular military commander-in-chief, and was later a civil magistrate having under his especial care all strangers and temporary sojourners in the city, and all children of parents who had lost their lives in the service of their country.

Polemon (pō′le-mon). Platonic philosopher of Athens, the successor (314 B.C.) of Xenocrates as head of the Academy. He died 270 B.C.

Polias (pol′i-as). An epithet of Athena in her role as protectress of cities. There was a temple of Athena Polias (*Of the City*) on the Acropolis at Athens. In it was a wooden image of Hermes said to have been dedicated by Cecrops. Other temples of Athena Polias were at Troezen, Erythrae in Asia Minor, and Arcadia.

Poliatas (po-li-ā′tas). An epithet of Athena,

meaning "Keeper of the City." At the sanctuary of Athena Poliatas at Tegea the priest entered but once a year.

Polieus (pol′i-ūs). Epithet of Zeus, meaning "Urban." There were altars and images of Zeus Polieus in many cities in Greece and on the Acropolis at Athens. In the time when Erechtheus was king of Athens, the following ritual was observed: An ox was killed before the altar of Zeus Polieus. The unknown slayer left the ox where it was and went into exile. When the slain ox and the ax were discovered the ax was tried for murder and was acquitted. From this arose the custom of placing barley and water upon the altar of Zeus Polieus before sacrificing to him. The ox intended for the sacrifice, left to itself, would go to the altar and eat the barley. The priest would run out, slay the ox, and then cast aside the ax and run away. The other priests of Zeus Polieus then tried the ax for murder, as if they did not know who had killed the ox, and acquitted it.

Poliorcetes (pol″i-ôr-sē′tēz), **Demetrius.** See **Demetrius I** (of *Macedonia*).

Polites (po-lī′tēz). In Greek legend, one of the 50 sons of Priam. His mother was Hecuba. Because of his great speed, he served as a sentinel on a barrow outside the walls of Troy when the city was attacked by the Greeks. He fought bravely when the Greeks, with the aid of the Wooden Horse, overran the city. He was the last of Priam's sons to survive, and was killed before his father's eyes by Neoptolemus, who cut him down before the altar of Zeus in the courtyard of Priam's palace.

Polites. In the *Odyssey,* one of the companions of Odysseus on his long wanderings after the Trojan War. He was one of those turned into swine by Circe, and rescued by Odysseus.

Poliuchus (pol-i-ū′kus). Epithet of Athena, meaning "City-protecting." There was a sanctuary of Athena Poliuchus on the citadel in Sparta.

Pollio (pol′i-ō), **Caius Asinius.** Roman politician, military commander, orator, author, critic and patron of literature. He was born c76 B.C.; died at Tusculum, Italy, 5 A.D. He was an adherent of Julius Caesar, took part in the battle of Pharsalus (48 B.C.), and later commanded against Pompey's son in Spain.

After the assassination of Caesar he became a partisan of Mark Antony, and was named governor of Transpadane Gaul. In 40 B.C. he was consul and helped to reconcile Octavian and Antony. He defeated the Parthians in Illyria in 39 B.C. For this victory he was honored with a triumph at Rome, and with the booty taken from the Parthians he caused a public library, the first such, to be erected in Rome. Henceforth he retired from public life and devoted himself to literature. He was a patron of Vergil and Horace. When he was governor of Transpadane Gaul he withdrew Vergil's estate from the lands being distributed to the veterans and thus saved it for the poet. Vergil addressed one of his eclogues to him. Of his own works—tragedies, a history of the civil wars of his own day, and speeches—only a few fragments of the speeches are extant.

Pollux (pol′uks). Latin name of Polydeuces. See **Dioscuri.**

Polybius (pō̄-lib′i-us). Greek historian; born at Megalopolis, Arcadia, Greece, c204 B.C. He is said to have died as the result of a fall from his horse, c120 B.C. He was a son of Lycortas, who was a general and statesman of the Achaean League and a friend of Philopoemon. For the first half of his life Polybius was occupied with the military and diplomatic work of the League, which he hoped to keep independent. He went to Egypt with his father and Aratus as an ambassador of the League (181 B.C.), and became the commander of the League's cavalry. In the war between the Romans and Perseus of Macedonia his desire was to keep the League neutral, but he was sent as commander of a cavalry troop to the aid of the Romans (169 B.C.). However, the Romans did not avail themselves of the assistance thus offered, and afterward Polybius and the Achaeans were charged with lack of zeal in the Roman cause. With 1000 prominent Achaeans he was taken to Rome as a hostage (166 B.C.) and kept there for 17 years. As a cultivated hostage, as distinct from a captive, he became acquainted with some of the leading men of Rome. Aemilius Paulus, who defeated Perseus (168 B.C.), made him the tutor of his sons Fabius and Scipio Africanus the Younger. He became the friend and adviser of Scipio who (151 B.C.) secured permission for Polybius,

actor; up, lūte, pull; oi, oil; ou, out; ᵷH, then; ḍ as d or j, ş as s or sh, ṭ as t or ch, ẓ as z or zh.

and those of his fellow Achaeans who had survived, to return to their homes. After a short stay at home he accompanied Scipio on his campaigns and was with him when Carthage was captured (146 B.C.). In the meantime the Achaean League had risen against Rome and been disastrously defeated; Corinth was destroyed (146 B.C.); the League was prostrate. Polybius returned to his home and used his good reputation with the Romans to win what concessions he could for his defeated countrymen from their conquerors. When Greece became a Roman province he was given the task of organizing it. This he did so honorably from the standpoint of the conquering Romans, and so skillfully as the representative of a conquered people, that both honored him. Statues in his honor, inscribed with laudatory phrases, were raised at Mantinea, Pallantium, Tegea, and Acacesium. The statue at Acacesium bore the words, "Hellas would never have come to grief if she had obeyed Polybius in all things, and, having come to grief, she found succor through him alone." Later Polybius spent much time in Rome and in long journeys to gather material for the completion of his *History*. This *History*, which covered in detail the period from 220 to 145 B.C., was in 40 books, of which five survive intact. Parts of the remaining books have been preserved in the works of other Greek and Roman historians, and there are also some fragments extant. Polybius took a philosophical view of history as a means of teaching men, by an investigation of causes and an honest record of facts, how to avoid disaster and improve themselves. To the story of wars that made up a large part of his *History* he could bring his own wide experience as a general and tactician and as an observer of other generals, notably Scipio. In detailing causes he had his own first-hand knowledge of Roman politics and institutions and of the affairs of Hellas. In furtherance of his desire to present facts he traveled widely, to see for himself the terrain of important battles, and to inspect sites and records; for example, he crossed the Alps himself before he wrote of Hannibal's crossing of them. In addition, he made careful use of official documents. Succeeding generations have honored and read Polybius for his accuracy, his under-

standing, and his willingness to recognize the skill, organization, and superior political and military institutions of the enemies of his own country.

Polybus (pol'i-bus). In Greek legend, the king of Corinth, husband of Periboea, or Merope, to whom Oedipus was brought as an infant after shepherds had found him on the mountain with his ankles pierced. Polybus brought Oedipus up to believe he was his own son, and it was to avoid fulfillment of the prophecy that he would kill his father that Oedipus left Corinth and went to Thebes. Polybus died peacefully of old age.

Polybus. In Homeric legend (*Iliad*), a Trojan; named by Homer as a son of Antenor and Theano, and a leader of a group of Trojans who assaulted the Greek fortifications in the tenth year of the Trojan War.

POSEIDON SLAYING POLYBOTES
Red-figured Greek vase, 4th century B.C.

Polybotes (pol-i-bō'tēz). In Greek mythology, one of the Giants, a son of Gaea and the blood of Uranus, who waged war on the gods. In the battle he fled to Cos. Poseidon pursued him there and broke off a chunk of the island, hurled it at Polybotes and buried him under it. The new island thus formed became known as Nisyrus.

Polycaste (pol-i-kas'tē). In Greek mythology, the sister of Daedalus. She was the mother of Talos, a gifted smith. Daedalus, jealous of the boy's skill, hurled him from the top of the Acropolis. Polycaste was so grief-stricken over her son's death that she hanged herself and was metamorphosed into a bird. Some say the bird that chattered and laughed while the sorrowing Daedalus later buried the body of his own son Icarus, was Polycaste, delighted to see Daedalus suffer as she had suffered. The Athenians built a sanctuary in honor of Polycaste beside the Acropolis. Polycaste is also sometimes called Perdix.

Polyclitus (pol-i-klī′tus) or **Polycletus** (-klē′tus). [Sometimes called **Polyclitus of Sicyon**; also known as **Polyclitus the Elder**.] Greek sculptor and architect in the last half of the 5th century B.C., an older contemporary of Phidias. He is associated with the high development of abstract proportion which characterizes Greek sculpture. He seems to have realized the athletic type of ideal to the entire satisfaction of the Greek world, and made a figure embodying the accepted proportions, which was called "the canon." This canon is supposed to have been a simple figure carrying a spear (*doryphorus*), described by Pliny and now represented by several copies. The best of these was found at Pompeii, and is in the museum at Naples. Another statue of almost equal importance is mentioned by Pliny, and called *diadumenus* (i.e., an athlete binding a fillet about his head). The best copy is in the British Museum. The most important monumental work of Polyclitus was the chryselephantine Hera at Argos, which has completely disappeared; representations of it are found on coins. An Amazon Polyclitus made for Ephesus, also lost, was considered by the ancients to be the equal, if not the superior, of the Amazon of Phidias. In general, Polyclitus worked in bronze, and confined himself to statues of athletic victors.

Polyclitus the Younger. Greek sculptor of Argos; fl. c400 B.C.

Polycrates (pō-lik′ra-tēz). He was a son of Aeaces. By an insurrection he made himself master of Samos (q.v.) and was tyrant of the island from c540 to 522 B.C. In the beginning he shared control with his two brothers, but then killed one, banished the other, and made himself sole ruler. He had an alliance of friendship with Amasis, king of Egypt. He built a fleet and waged war throughout the eastern Mediterranean, plundering friend and foe alike on the theory that friends are much more pleased if what has been taken from them is restored than they are to be spared in the first place. Polycrates overcame the Lesbians at sea when they came to the aid of Miletus, and forced his Lesbian captives to dig a vast moat around his palace at Samos. Good fortune attended all his endeavors. He lived in a magnificent style and was a patron of literature and the arts. He enjoyed such great prosperity and good luck that his friend and ally, Amasis of Egypt, became uneasy. He wrote to Polycrates to this effect: The uninterrupted good fortune of Polycrates disturbs him, because he knows that the gods are envious and will bring him down. Amasis is more pleased when the good fortune of his friends is mingled with an occasional setback, for in that way the gods are appeased. He has never known a man whose extreme good luck did not end in calamity. He therefore suggests to Polycrates that, to distract the gods from too close a scrutiny of his prosperity, he take the thing that is dearest to him and cast it away where it can never be found. In this way he will suffer a grievous loss and, in the eyes of the gods, his good fortune will have been tempered. Polycrates read the message from Amasis and found his advice good. He considered which of his treasures it would grieve him most to lose and decided on a signet ring, an emerald set in gold. He put to sea in a 50-oared ship and when he was well out, he hurled the ring into the sea. Then he returned home and grieved for his loss. Shortly thereafter a fisherman caught a splendid fish. It was such a superb specimen that he decided to give it to Polycrates. He took it to the palace and presented it to him. Polycrates was pleased with the gift and asked the fisherman to dine with him. In preparing the fish servants cut it open; within it they found Polycrates' ring. With joy they restored it to their master. Polycrates immediately sent word to Amasis and told him the whole story. Whereupon Amasis concluded that it was not given to man to divert fate from its destined path on his fellow men. He was so certain that Polycrates would end in disaster that he straightway dissolved his alliance of friendship with him, that he might be spared having to grieve over a friend when disaster inevitably overcame Polycrates. This, at any rate, is the reason that Herodotus gives for the end of the alliance between Polycrates and Amasis. When Cambyses was preparing war against Egypt (c525 B.C.), Polycrates offered him assistance and sent him a number of ships manned with those whom Polycrates thought were the most likely to rebel against his rule. These ships he gave to Cambyses with instructions never to allow the men to return home. However, some of this crew escaped, or deserted, or never got to Egypt at all. They returned to Samos and defeated Polycrates in a sea-fight, but were defeated by him when they attacked him on land. They then appealed to the Spartans for aid against Polycrates. In the meantime Polycrates imprisoned the wives and children of his loyal subjects so that they would not go over to the rebels. He threatened to burn the prisoners if his subjects joined the exiles. The Samian rebels succeeded in gaining the assistance of Sparta. Some say the Spartans agreed to help the Samian exiles out of gratitude. Others say it was to punish Samos for stealing a bowl Croesus had sent them, and an embroidered linen corselet sent them by Amasis. The Corinthians also joined the Samian exiles in their war against Polycrates, to avenge an old insult. The Spartans brought a strong force and attacked Samos. For 40 days they besieged the island. Then, finding they were making no headway, they lifted the siege and sailed away. Polycrates now conceived the ambition to become master of the sea. Oroetes, a Persian who had been made governor of Sardis by Cyrus, aware of Polycrates' ambition and determined to destroy him, sent him a message in which he avowed that Cambyses, Cyrus' successor, was seeking Oroetes' life. He offered Polycrates all his wealth to enable him to become lord of the sea if Polycrates would come to his rescue and carry him away from Sardis. In the meantime, he invited Polycrates to send a trusted messenger to whom he would show all the wealth which he would give to Polycrates. Polycrates sent his messenger. The wily Oroetes filled eight chests with stones, and covered these with a layer of gold. These he showed to the messenger from Polycrates, who in his turn reported to his master. Hearing of this great store of gold, Polycrates, de-

spite many warnings from seers and from his friends, decided to go to Oroetes in person. His daughter dreamed that she saw Polycrates hanging in the air, washed by Zeus and anointed by the sun. Even this dream did not deter him. On the contrary, he threatened to keep his daughter unwed if she did not cease her entreaties to him to remain at home. Accompanied by many friends he sailed off to Oroetes. In Sardis Oroetes set upon him and killed him in a manner which (according to Herodotus who tells these events) was too horrible to describe. Oroetes crucified the dead body of Polycrates, rains sent by Zeus washed it, and the sun's rays anointed it. Thus the dream of Polycrates' daughter was fulfilled. His end also confirmed the gloomy predictions which his friend Amasis of Egypt had entertained concerning the disasters which were certain to befall any man whose good fortune was uninterrupted.

Polydamas (pō-lid'a̱-ma̱s). In Greek legend, a son of Panthous and Phrontis. He was the brother of Euphorbus and Hyperenor, and was a close friend of Hector. In the Trojan War he showed himself as a daring and courageous fighter, but as an even more courageous and skillful strategist who dared argue with Hector about the conduct of the war. In the attack on the Greek fortifications he advised Hector not to take his horses and chariots through the Greek moat lest the Greeks, in a counterattack, force them back into the narrow moat where there would be no room to maneuver and they would become easy targets for the Greeks. Instead, he advised that they attack on foot. Hector was pleased to follow this advice and the attack was successful. But as they prepared to breach the wall an eagle, clutching a serpent in its talons, flew over. The serpent, still alive and writhing, bit the eagle and the eagle screamed and dropped it to the ground. Polydamas interpreted this to mean that the Trojans, if they attacked the wall now, would miss the prize and many would fail to return, even as the eagle had failed to return with its prey to its nest. He therefore urged Hector to withdraw and regroup his forces. Hector scorned his advice, and accused him of being frightened by the confusion of battle. Polydamas smarted under this rebuke but continued to advise what he thought was sensible and possible. When Achilles had driven the Trojans back simply by appearing unarmed at the ships, Polydamas again advised withdrawal. He said they should withdraw into the city and fight from there, but again his advice was scorned. Later, as Hector stood alone outside the walls he remembered what Polydamas had advised and regretted that he had not followed his counsel. He felt that the approaching defeat was his fault for ignoring Polydamas. After the death of Hector, and later that of Penthesilea, the Trojans withdrew to the city in terror. Polydamas now counseled that they neither flee, as some urged, nor wait the arrival of other help, as others suggested. Rather he advised they should restore Helen with rich gifts to Menelaus. To the accusation of Paris that this was cowardice, Polydamas replied that he preferred wise discretion to foolish valor. His interest was in protecting the city, whereas Paris was bringing ruin to Troy. But the proposal to restore Helen which he had made many times was never carried out. Nor was his final plea to retire and fight from the walls and towers of the city heeded, for each time aid came to the Trojans they sallied out of the city and fought on the plain. Polydamas was probably right in all his advice, but the end result had already been determined by the gods.

Polydamas. A native of Scotussa in Thessaly; active in the latter part of the 5th century B.C. He was said to be the tallest man of his age, and a great athlete who won victories in the pancratium at the games and had his statue at Olympia. Among his legendary feats of strength, it is said: that he slew a lion on Mount Olympus with his bare hands; that he seized a huge and fierce bull by its hind feet and hung on to it despite the creature's leapings and lurchings, until at last the bull escaped, but only by leaving its hind hoofs in the hands of Polydamas; that he stopped a chariot going at full speed by grasping it with one hand. The Persian king heard of his exploits and sent for him. He journeyed to Susa, where he challenged three of the Persian Immortals to fight him at once, and he killed all three. His exploits were inscribed on the pedestal of his statue at Olympia. But at last he perished through his own

strength. He went into a cave under a mountain with some companions. When the roof of the cave began to crack his companions fled, but Polydamas, arrogant in his strength, thought he could hold up the roof with his hands. The mountain fell in on him and killed him.

Polydectes (pol-i-dek'tēz). In Greek legend, a son of Magnes and a nymph. He was the brother of that Dictys who rescued Perseus and Danaë when they were washed ashore on Seriphus. Polydectes was king of Seriphus. He wanted to marry Danaë, but was prevented from doing so by Perseus. In order to get rid of Perseus, Polydectes sent him to get the head of Medusa, on the pretext that this would be a suitable gift for him to give for his supposed plan to marry Hippodamia, daughter of Oenomaus. Polydectes was convinced that Perseus would be killed on this errand. While Perseus was away, Polydectes sought Danaë but she fled with Dictys and hid in a temple. When Perseus returned he searched for and found his mother and learned of the treachery of Polydectes. He went to the court and turned Polydectes and his followers to stone by revealing to them the head of Medusa.

Polydeuces (pol-i-dū'sēz). The twin brother of Castor. See **Dioscuri.**

Polydora (pol-i-dō'ra). Named by Homer (*Iliad*) as a daughter of Peleus and the half-sister of Achilles. By Spercheus, the river-god, she was the mother of Menesthius. Later she married Borus, who reared Menesthius as his own son.

Polydorus (pol-i-dō'rus). In Greek legend, the youngest son of Priam and Hecuba. During the Trojan War he was sent to Polymnestor, a king in Thrace, for safe-keeping, along with a great store of treasure. Polymnestor betrayed the Trojan allies and went over to Agamemnon. He murdered Polydorus and stole the treasure he had brought with him. After the war, when Aeneas landed in Thrace and attempted to found a city, the blood of Polydorus gushed black from the ground and the voice of Polydorus warned Aeneas not to settle there. The voice further told of Polydorus' murder by Polymnestor and of his anguish because he had not been given honorable burial. Aeneas performed funeral honors for Polydorus, and then, in accordance with his advice, sailed away.

Polydorus. A fleet runner; named in the *Iliad* as the youngest son of Priam and Laothoë. Priam had forbidden him to take part in the Trojan War, but he defied his father, charged into the battle to show off his great speed, and was slain by Achilles.

Polydorus. In Greek legend, a son of Cadmus and Harmonia. He became king of Thebes when Cadmus left the city to go into exile in Illyria. Polydorus was the father of Labdacus and the ancestor of Oedipus.

Polydorus. In Greek legend, a son of Hippomedon. He was one of the Epigoni who successfully marched against Thebes.

Polydorus. Rhodian sculptor, associate of Agesander in carving the Laocoön group.

Polygnotus (pol-ig-nō′tus). Greek painter, born on the island of Thasus. He was active in Athens c475–447 B.C. He was identified with Cimon in the reconstruction of Athens, and seems to have had about him a large school or force of assistants. In recognition of his merit as an artist he was given Athenian citizenship. He worked on the Painted Portico in Athens, where a picture of *The Capture of Troy* was attributed to him. In this picture Elpinice, sister of Cimon, appeared as Laodice, daughter of King Priam. Among his other known works was the *Marriage of the Dioscuri to the Leucippides* in the sanctuary of the Dioscuri at Athens, and very celebrated paintings of the *Capture of Troy* and the *Descent of Odysseus into Hades* at Delphi. Polygnotus introduced transparent draperies and many realistic effects; for example, Pausanias tells that a hare in the picture of the marriage of the Dioscuri was greatly admired for its lifelike effect.

Polyhymnia (pol-i-him′ni-a), or **Polymnia** (po-lim′ni-a). One of the nine daughters of Zeus and Mnemosyne. She is the muse of the sublime hymn and also of pantomime and the religious dance. In art she is usually represented in a meditative attitude, heavily draped, and without any attribute. See **Muses.**

Polyidus (pol-i-ī′dus). In Greek mythology, a seer of Corinth, and a descendant of Melampus. He advised Bellerophon to capture the winged horse Pegasus in order to kill the Chimaera. He was visiting in Crete when Glaucus, young son of King Minos, disappeared and could not be found. On likening a heifer—which changed color from white to red to black—to a mulberry which changes color in the same order as it ripens, Polyidus was informed that, in accordance with instructions from an oracle, he must find Glaucus. He found Glaucus drowned in a vat of honey, and was then told he must restore the drowned child to life. Polyidus, watching by the dead child, saw a serpent glide near the body. He killed it. Presently another serpent approached, and finding its mate dead it slid off and returned with an herb which it laid on the dead serpent's body, whereupon the dead serpent was slowly revived and glided away. Polyidus took the herb and applied it to the corpse of Glaucus. The child too, was restored to life. Polyidus was given rich gifts by Minos, who commanded him to teach the arts of divination to Glaucus. Polyidus did so, but before he left Crete he commanded Glaucus to spit into his open mouth. As soon as Glaucus did so he forgot all Polyidus had taught him. Polyidus prophesied that his own son Euchenor, who was longing to join the Greeks in the Trojan War, would either die in his home, worn out by affliction, or fall at Troy if he accompanied the Greeks. Knowing the alternatives, his son went to Troy, where he perished from one of Paris' arrows.

Polymastus (pol-i-mas′tus). An epithet of Artemis, meaning "Many-breasted." The name came from the image of the goddess ("Diana of the Ephesians") in her magnificent temple at Ephesus. The image had many breasts and bore a mural crown on its head; the figure had no legs but ended in a point, and was decorated with a number of mystical animals. Artemis Polymastus was a fertility goddess, as shown by the many breasts. She was originally an Asiatic divinity, who was adopted by the Greeks as they colonized the region, and to whom they gave the attributes of their own Artemis in Greece.

Polymela (pol-i-mē′la) or **Polymele** (-lē). Named by Homer as a daughter of Phylas. She was loved by Hermes and by him had a son, Eudorus, who commanded a battalion of Myrmidons under Patroclus at Troy. After Eudorus was born Polymela was wooed and won by Echecles, a son of Actor, and Eudorus was brought up as his own son by Echecles.

Polymela. In Greek legend, a daughter of Actor. Her father gave her in marriage to Peleus. Informed, falsely, that Peleus intended to desert her for Sterope, daughter of Acastus and Cretheïs, she hanged herself.

Polymelus (pol-i-mē′lus). Named by Homer (*Iliad*) as a Lycian ally of the Trojans. He was slain by Patroclus.

Polymnestor (pol-im-nes′tor). In Greek legend, a king in Thrace and the husband of Ilione, oldest daughter of Priam. Polydorus, the youngest son of Priam and Hecuba, was sent to Polymnestor with great treasure for safe-keeping during the Trojan War. Polymnestor changed sides and went over to Agamemnon. He murdered Polydorus and stole the treasure. When Hecuba, brought as a captive to Thrace after the war, learned of Polydorus' death—according to some accounts, his body was washed ashore at her feet—she, with other captive Trojan women, blinded Polymnestor and killed his children.

Polynices or **Polyneices** (pol-i-nī′sēz). In Greek legend, a son of Oedipus and Jocasta. After the withdrawal of Oedipus from Thebes, Polynices and his brother Eteocles agreed to share the throne of Thebes by ruling alternately. Eteocles, the elder, ruled first, but when his term came to an end he refused to relinquish the throne on the grounds of Polynices' violent character, and banished Polynices. He fled to Argos, to the court of King Adrastus. There he fell into a quarrel with Tydeus of Calydon, who had also fled to Argos. Adrastus separated them and, remembering an oracle which told him to yoke his daughters in marriage to a boar and a lion, he gave his daughter Aegia (or Argia) to Polynices, who bore the device of a lion on his shield, and promised to restore him to his lands. Aegia bore Polynices a son, Thersander. Adrastus now proposed to march on Thebes and began to assemble the leaders of the expedition of the Seven against Thebes. Polynices bribed Eriphyle, wife of the seer Amphiaraus, to persuade her husband to accompany the expedition by giving her the necklace of Harmonia which he had brought with him from Thebes. This necklace had been given to Harmonia as a wedding gift by Aphrodite, and had a history of bringing disaster to its possessor. In the war on Thebes, Polynices met Eteocles face to face and in single combat to decide who should have the throne, the brothers killed each other. All the other Argive leaders were slain except Adrastus, who fled on his winged horse Arion. Creon, uncle of Polynices and Eteocles, succeeded to the throne of Thebes. He gave orders that the bodies of the Argive dead should remain unburied. Polynices' body was cast out of the city to become the prey of scavenger birds because he had treacherously attacked his own city. But Antigone, the sister of Polynices, defied Creon's order and gave her brother's body a ritual burial. Creon sentenced her to death for disobeying his order.

Polypemon (pol-i-pē′mon). Another name for Procrustes. He acquired the name Procrustes from his habit of cutting up travelers to make them fit the bed he provided for their night's lodging. He was the father of Sinis, the "Pine-bender." Father and son were slain by Theseus.

Polyphemus (pol-i-fē′mus). In Greek mythology, a one-eyed giant, the chief of the Cyclopes. He was a son of Poseidon and the owner of great flocks and bountiful gardens. He loved Galatea, the daughter of Nereus and Doris, and for love of her tried to tame his wild appearance and gave up his savage ways. But Galatea loved Acis and paid no attention to the songs of love that Polyphemus played to her on his shepherd's pipe, nor to his promises of gifts and honors. When Polyphemus, sighing of love for Galatea, came upon her lying in the arms of Acis, he was enraged. Galatea escaped his wrath, but Acis was crushed under a huge rock hurled at him by Polyphemus.

Telemus, a seer, had warned Polyphemus that one day Odysseus would come and put out his single eye, but Polyphemus scorned the prophecy. When Odysseus, with some of his companions, appeared in his cave, Polyphemus rolled a great stone before the entrance and imprisoned them. Each day thereafter he devoured some of them when he returned from the fields with his sheep, until the wily Odysseus made him drunk and put out his eye with a wooden stake especially sharpened for that purpose. Polyphemus screamed in pain and rage, but when his brothers gathered outside the cave and asked who was wounding him he replied, "Noman," for that was the name Odysseus had given him, and his brothers went away. The Greeks escaped the next day by clinging to the bellies of the sheep which Polyphemus let out of the cave to graze. As they fled to the shore and their ship Odysseus could not resist shouting back to Polyphemus and telling him who he really was. Polyphemus recalled the prophecy of Telemus and was chagrined, because he had expected Odysseus, if he ever came, to be a bigger man. As the mocking Greeks sailed off Polyphemus called on his father Poseidon to avenge him; and this was the reason that Poseidon prevented Odysseus from returning to his homeland for such a long time.

Polyphemus. In Greek legend, a son of Elatus of Arcadia. He fought the Lapithae in his youth and in his later years, though his limbs were enfeebled, he kept his martial spirit and joined Jason in the quest for the Golden Fleece. In Mysia, Hylas, Heracles' squire, disappeared. While Polyphemus and Heracles searched for him the Argonauts, after waiting some time, sailed away and left them. Polyphemus founded the city of Crius in Mysia and died in the land of the Chalybes.

Polyphides (pol-i-fī'dēz). In Greek legend, a son of Mantius and a grandson of Melampus the seer. Apollo made Polyphides the best of all seers after Amphiaraus, also a descendant of Melampus, was swallowed up by the earth in the war of the Seven against Thebes. The son of Polyphides was Theoclymenus.

Polyphides. In Greek legend, a king of Sicyon. He sheltered Agamemnon and Menelaus in their youth, when they were brought to his court by faithful servants after the murder of Atreus. Later he sent them on to Oeneus of Calydon.

Polyphontes (po-li-fon'tēz). According to tradition, a brother of Cresphontes, king of Messenia. He murdered Cresphontes and two of his sons in a rebellion, and married Merope, Cresphontes' widow. A third son of Cresphontes and Merope had been sent away for safety during the rebellion, and survived, unknown to Polyphontes. He secretly returned to Messenia and announced to Polyphontes that he was the murderer of Cresphontes' third son, Aepytus. When Merope heard of his coming, and learned that Aepytus was no longer in the place where she had sent him for safe-keeping, she resolved to kill this self-confessed murderer. But when she went to do so he was revealed to her as her own son Aepytus, come in disguise to kill Polyphontes. Thereupon Merope and Aepytus resolved to kill Polyphontes and did so. Others say that Polyphontes was not the brother but the uncle of Cresphontes, and that it was Cresphontes who slew him.

Polyphrasmon (pol''i-fras'mon) or **Polyphradmon** (-frad'mon). Greek tragic poet, son of Phrynichus; fl. 5th century B.C.; defeated by Aeschylus' Theban tetralogy, 467 B.C.

Polypoetes (pol''i-pō-ē'tēz). In Greek legend, a son of Pirithous and Hippodamia. He became king of the Lapiths when Pirithous failed to return from his expedition to the Underworld. In the Trojan War he was a leader of the Greeks and, with Leonteus, he held off Asius of Arisbe when the latter invaded the Greek fortifications with his chariots. Polypoetes slew Astyalus, Damasus, Pylon, and Ormenus. At the funeral games in honor of Patroclus he was the winner in the shotput.

Polypoetes. According to Greek tradition, a son of Apollo and Phthia. He dwelt in the land of the Curetes. Aetolus, son of Endymion, forced to flee from his country, came to the land of the Curetes. There he slew Polypoetes and his brothers Dorus and Laodocus, seized the land, and named it Aetolia for himself.

Polypoetes. According to some accounts, a son of Odysseus and Callidice, queen of Thesprotia. He was born after Odysseus returned from his wanderings following the Trojan War. Odysseus had come to Thesprotia to appease Poseidon, and married Callidice. On the death of Callidice Odysseus turned the kingdom over to Polypoetes and returned to Ithaca.

Polyporthis (po-li-pôr'this). According to some accounts, a son of Odysseus and Penelope, born after Odysseus returned from his long wanderings following the Trojan War.

Polysperchon (pol-i-spėr'kon) or **Polyperchon** (pol-i-pėr'kon). Macedonian general in the

service of Alexander the Great; born c380
B.C.; died after 303 B.C. He succeeded
Antipater as regent in 319 B.C. He was
superseded by Cassander, son of Antipater.

Polytechnus (pol-i-tek′nus). In Greek mythology, the father by Aëdon of Itys. Much
the same story is told of Polytechnus and
Aëdon as that concerning Tereus and Procne,
with some variations. According to this
story, Polytechnus and Aëdon were punished
for boasting that their love was greater than
that of Zeus and Hera. They were forced
to compete with each other on the understanding that the loser would present the
winner with a slave. Polytechnus, who lost,
went to bring Aëdon's sister, Chelidon, back
with him. On the way he violated her and
threatened her with death if she revealed
his act. To punish him the sisters killed
Itys and served him to his father at a feast.
When Polytechnus, horrified at this deed,
pursued them, he was captured by his wife's
servants, bound, smeared with honey, and
left to be eaten alive by ants. Aëdon would
have released him but her brothers forbade
it, and Zeus changed him into a woodpecker,
Aëdon into a nightingale, and Chelidon into
a swallow. In a quite different story, Aëdon
is given as the wife of Zethus, and her child
is called Itylus. See **Aëdon.**

Polyxena (pō-lik′sē-na). In Greek legend, a
daughter of Priam and Hecuba. Achilles
saw her, either in the temple of Apollo or
on the walls of Troy at the time of the ransoming of Hector's body, and fell in love
with her. He tried by secret negotiations to
persuade either Hector or Priam to give her
to him, but the price demanded was too high
and involved either treachery (Hector), or
abandoning Helen to the Trojans (Priam).
As he was dying from Paris' wound Achilles
is said to have requested that Polyxena be
sacrificed on his barrow, and after the fall of
Troy the shade of Achilles appeared to
Neoptolemus, his son, in a dream, and
warned that he would send high winds to
prevent the Greeks from sailing for home if
Polyxena was not sacrificed to appease his
shade. Calchas, the seer, confirmed that only
the death of Polyxena would bring favorable
winds. Agamemnon was unwilling to shed
more blood but he was ultimately persuaded
by Odysseus to agree to the sacrifice, and a
herald was sent to fetch Polyxena from her
mother's side. She accompanied the herald
willingly as she had, she said, nothing to live
for except dishonor and slavery. She bared
her throat to the sacrificial knife with such
courage that even the Greeks were overawed
and gave her honorable burial. After her
death, the storm winds were stilled and a
favorable breeze permitted the Greeks to sail.
Some say the sacrifice of Polyxena occurred
at Troy. Others say it took place after the
Greeks and their captives had already left
Troy and landed in Thrace. Other accounts
say that Polyxena had fallen in love with
Achilles, and had run away from Troy to
join him in the Greek camp, and killed herself at his death. She was the subject of a
lost tragedy by Sophocles, and of the tragedies *Hecuba* by Euripides and *Troades* by
Seneca, but she is not mentioned by Homer.

Polyxenus (pō-lik′se-nus). In Greek legend, a
son of Agasthenes and grandson of Augeas,
king in Elis. In command of ten Elean
ships he accompanied the Greeks to the Trojan War from which he returned safely. He
had a son Amphimachus, named for his friend
who was slain at Troy. Amphimachus was
the father of Eleus, during whose reign the
Dorians gathered under the sons of Aristomachus for the return to the Peloponnesus.

Polyxo (pō-lik′sō). In Greek legend, an aged
nurse of Hypsipyle, queen of Lemnos. The
Lemnian women had killed all the men of
the island and Polyxo urged Hypsipyle to
welcome the Argonauts when they asked to
land at Lemnos on their way to Colchis.
She advised Hypsipyle to invite them to stay
so that they should become protectors of
the island and father sons by the Lemnian
women to prevent the race from dying out.

Polyxo. In Greek legend, a native of Argos
who married Tlepolemus, son of Heracles.
According to some accounts, Helen fled to
her home in Rhodes after the death of
Menelaus, but Polyxo, a former friend, caused
her to be hanged to avenge the death of
Tlepolemus in the Trojan War.

Polyzelus (pol-i-zē′lus). Brother of Gelon,
tyrant of Gela and Syracuse; fl. in the early
part of the 5th century B.C. He succeeded
Gelon as general of the Syracusan army and
tyrant of Syracuse. He sent his race horses
and chariots to compete in the Olympic and

actor; up, lūte, pull; oi, oil; ou, out; ŦH, then; ḍ as d or j, ş as s or sh, ţ as t or ch, ẓ as z or zh.

Pythian games, as did other tyrants of Sicily. A fragmentary inscription found at Delphi, in association with fragments of the monumental four-horse chariot group of which the famous bronze *Charioteer* is the principal surviving piece, suggests that Polyzelus may have been the dedicant.

Pometia (pō-mē'shi-ạ) or **Pometii** (-ī). A city of the Volsci in S Latium. It was a nameless site when Aeneas visited his father in the Underworld. Anchises pointed out to him the shade of the man waiting to be born who would found the city. The Volscian town became a Roman colony in 382 B.C. In ancient times the city was also called Suessa Pometia, perhaps the modern Torre Petrara, or Mesa.

Pomoerium or **Pomerium** (pō-mē'ri-um). Explained as *pro-moerium,* the term appears originally to have signified a sacred zone outside, or outside and inside, the walls of a fortified Italic town. In such a zone the erection of buildings was prohibited, in order to keep the space clear for the movement of troops in defense, and to deny an attacker possible access to the battlements via the roofs. Roman writers tell of an obviously very old ritual in which the limit of the pomerium was marked by a furrow made by a bronze plow to which were yoked a bull and a cow. The sod turned over by the plow symbolized the earthen mound of the *agger,* while the trench cut by the plow represented the *fossa* or ditch at the foot of the agger. This is one form of magic circle; the Romans believed they had inherited the ritual from the Etruscans. Magic or apotropaic circles are, however, widely familiar in ancient Italy, Greece, and Indo-European contexts generally; they are no monopoly of the Etruscans, and the practice may well have been Italic. In the legendary founding of Rome, Romulus cut a furrow in this manner. When Remus leaped over it in mockery, his act constituted a desecration for which Romulus killed him. At some colonies, the limit of the pomerial zone was apparently fixed by streets. The excavators of Ostia and Minturnae believe that they have identified such streets, parallel to the city walls at a distance of some 40–60 feet from them. In classical Rome, the pomerium marked the official boundary of the ritually consecrated

city, purified by regular lustrations, within which certain activities were prohibited. Since the growing populace repeatedly built out beyond this boundary, there were successive proposals to extend the pomerium so as to bring new residential areas within its protection. In this connection, we hear of such enlargements of the boundaries by Sulla, Caesar, Augustus, Claudius, Vespasian, Hadrian, and Aurelian; the details concerning these enlargements are, however, clouded in scholarly controversies not yet resolved. (JJ)

Pomona (pō-mō'nạ). In Roman mythology, the protecting goddess of fruit trees; a wood-nymph devoted to their cultivation. Her delight was in pruning and grafting them, and so great was her devotion to her orchards that she refused to have anything to do with the many suitors who wooed her. Silenus, Priapus, the followers of Pan, and the satyrs tried to win her, but she fenced herself in in her orchards and refused their suits. Vertumnus, god of gardens and orchards, fell in love with her. He attempted to win her by adopting various disguises. At last he appeared to her in his own glowing beauty and received her happy consent to share her orchards with him.

Pompeia (pom-pē'ạ). Second wife of Julius Caesar, and a granddaughter of Sulla. Her marriage to Caesar, which took place in 67 B.C., was terminated in 61 B.C. She was charged with misconduct during the ceremonies of the Bona Dea. These rites were extremely sacred, and men were rigorously excluded from them. During one performance of the rites, a male intruder dressed in woman's clothing was detected in the house. He was found to be Publius Clodius, a notorious scoundrel reputed to be the lover of Pompeia. This was a colossal scandal and it was charged that Pompeia had arranged or connived at his presence there. Neither the charge of impiety nor of infidelity with Clodius was ever proved. This being so, it was asked of Caesar why he divorced her. The future master of Rome answered that "Caesar's wife must be above suspicion."

Pompeii (pom-pā'ē). Ancient city in Italy, situated on the Bay of Naples 13 miles SE of Naples, nearly at the foot of Mount Vesuvius. It was a flourishing provincial town,

fat, fāte, fär, fãre, errạnt; net, mē, hẻr ardẹnt; pin, pīne; not, nōte, mõve, nôr,

containing many villas. It was severely injured (63 A.D.) by an earthquake, and was totally destroyed (79) by an eruption of Vesuvius. Owing to the preservation of the ruins practically intact to the present day by the layer of ashes and pumice that buried them, the remains of Pompeii afford in many ways the most complete information we possess of Roman material civilization. Some excavations were made on the site in antiquity, in the effort to recover buried treasure, but Pompeii and its tragic end were soon forgotten. In 1748 some peasants came accidentally upon a few ancient works of art in a ruined house, and the Bourbon sovereigns of Naples thereupon caused searches to be made for similar objects. Between 1808 and 1815 Joachim Murat instituted the first scientifically conducted excavations. After his fall the work went on more or less irregularly until the Bourbon kingdom ended in 1860. It thereafter progressed with system and regularity under Giuseppe Fiorelli. Most of the oval area included within the walls has now been thoroughly explored. Excavators have now uncovered about two-fifths of the city which in 79 had an area of about 160 acres. The great theater, of the time of Augustus, is one of the most perfect of Roman antiquity, semicircular in plan, with a diameter of 322 feet. The temple of Isis is a small Corinthian tetrastyle prostyle structure raised on a basement in a peristyle court upon which open the lodgings of the priests. Many interesting objects connected with the cult were found here, and skeletons of the priests amid surroundings indicating that they had sought, too late, to flee. The so-called House of Castor and Pollux is curious as being a double house with a large peristyle court common to the two parts. Each part has its atrium and all its subdivisions complete. The exterior contrasts with the usual plainness by its stucco decoration in panels and arabesques. The so-called House of Marcus Lucretius is a double house, remarkable also for having had three stories, and for its beautiful reception room (*tablinum*) and dining room. The so-called House of Meleager is notable for its paintings and other decorations. In the atrium there is a marble table supported by winged griffins. The peristyle court, with 24 Ionic columns, is the finest in Pompeii. The so-called House of Pansa is one of the largest and most elaborate dwellings of Pompeii, measuring 120 by 300 feet. The so-called House of the Faun is perhaps the best in style of the ancient city. The usual wall paintings are here replaced by mosaics. The famous *Dancing Faun* and the mosaic of the *Battle of Issus* came from this house.

Pompeius Magnus (pom-pā′us mag′nus), **Cnaeus**. Roman general, elder son of Pompey the triumvir; put to death, 45 B.C. After the defeat of his father at Pharsalus (48 B.C.) by Caesar, Cnaeus Pompeius joined his brother Sextus in Spain. The brothers were defeated by Caesar at Munda, in Spain, 45 B.C. Cnaeus escaped but was captured shortly afterward and put to death.

Pompeius Magnus, Sextus. [English, **Pompey**; called **Pompey the Younger.**] Roman soldier; younger son of Pompey (Cnaeus Pompeius) the Great; born 75′ B.C.; killed at Miletus, 35 B.C. His forces were defeated by Julius Caesar at Munda in 45 B.C. He became powerful as commander of a fleet on the coasts of Sicily and Italy, and by cutting off Rome's grain supply from Africa, hoped to starve the Romans into receiving him again. He was defeated in a naval battle by Agrippa in 36 B.C., and fled to Asia Minor, where he was captured and executed.

Pompey (pom′pi). [Called **Pompey the Great**; full Latin name, **Cnaeus Pompeius Magnus.**] Roman general, born 106 B.C.; murdered in Egypt, Sept. 28, 48 B.C. He was the son of Cnaeus Pompeius Strabo, a Roman general, under whom he served (89 B.C.) in the Social War. As a youth Pompey was noted for his temperate manner of living, for his skill in war, his honorable character, and his availability to those who sought his favors. Strabo was hated for his avarice, and his soldiers mutinied against him, but such was the respect and affection they had for Pompey that he was able to persuade them to return to their general. After his father Strabo died he was accused of misappropriation of the public funds. Pompey defended him so brilliantly that the praetor in charge of the case offered him his daughter Antistia in marriage. Lucius Cornelius Cinna, a leader of the popular party, supporter of Marius and opponent of Sulla, seized control of

Rome during Sulla's absence. He was slain in 84 B.C. and was succeeded by Carbo, another leader of the popular party. Pompey resolved to join the conservative party of Sulla, but not before he had collected an army. In a short time he had gathered three legions with all their equipment in Picenum, forced the followers of Carbo to give way, and defeated a combined force of three generals sent against him (83 B.C.). When he at last met Sulla he arrived as a young general of proven abilities. Sulla greeted him as *Imperator* and, wishing to reward him, persuaded him to divorce Antistia and to marry a connection of his, one Aemilia, who was at the time married and about to bear a child. Pompey divorced Antistia and married Aemilia, who subsequently died in childbirth. Pompey now went to Sicily and successfully cleared the island of Sulla's Marian enemies. Carbo was seized on the island of Pantelleria, dragged before a tribunal in chains, and condemned to death. From Sicily Pompey crossed over to Africa where, within 40 days, he had conquered the followers of Marius, subdued Numidia, and once more made the name of Rome respected in Africa. When he returned to Rome (81 B.C.), Sulla came to greet him and gave him the title *Magnus* (Great), which Pompey kept and handed down to his sons. However, Sulla opposed Pompey's demand for a triumph because, he said, the laws did not permit a triumph to one who had been neither praetor nor consul, and moreover, Pompey was too young—24—to be a senator and was still a knight. Pompey pointedly remarked that "more [people] worship the rising than the setting sun," and when Sulla saw how popular he was he allowed him his triumph, regardless of the laws. Pompey's obvious popularity and power soon made Sulla uneasy, and relations between them became less warm. After Sulla's death (78 B.C.), Marcus Aemilius Lepidus (father of the triumvir) sought to change Sulla's constitution, gathered an army, and made himself master of Cisalpine Gaul and part of Italy. Pompey was named general, and with the consul Caius Lutatius Catulus he marched against Lepidus. He went to Mutina, where Marcus Junius Brutus (father of Caesar's chief assassin) commanded the

forces of Lepidus and compelled his surrender. Brutus was permitted to retire, but after he had withdrawn Pompey treacherously sent men after him to slay him (c77 B.C.). Lepidus was driven out of Italy. Pompey next had himself named proconsul and went to Spain to help Metellus Pius in the war against Sertorius. He was in Spain from 76 to 71 B.C. and, after the death of Sertorius, defeated his successor Perpenna and ended the war. He returned to Rome at the time of the revolt of Spartacus, the so-called Servile War, and went to assist Crassus. Crassus defeated the main body of the forces of Spartacus (71 B.C.), but Pompey, marching up, came upon those fleeing after the defeat by Crassus and wiped them out and received much of the credit for ending the Servile War. He demanded a triumph for his victories in Spain and asked permission to stand for the consulship. The Senate opposed him because he had not held the required offices, but he joined with Crassus, and since each had an army poised at the gates of Rome the Senate withdrew its opposition. He had his triumph, his second, and became consul with Crassus (70 B.C.). During their term, in which they publicly disagreed, the tribunes and censors were restored, and the Senate was compelled to share the administration of justice with the knights.

While Rome had been preoccupied with wars and civil wars, the pirates who ever infested the Mediterranean had become increasingly powerful and bold. They had 1000 ships, had taken 400 cities, plundered temples, and so interfered with the grain supply on which Rome depended that the city was in great distress. Gabinius, a friend of Pompey, proposed a decree by which Pompey was to be given enormous power for the purpose of clearing the seas of the pirates. When the decree was read there were many who saw the dangers in the great power it would give to one man and they opposed it. But the Gabinian Law was passed (67 B.C.), and Pompey was granted power to take what money he needed, to equip a large fleet, and to enroll crews and fighters at his discretion. In three months he drove the pirates from the sea. He took 20,000 prisoners, most of whom were humanely allowed to settle in small towns in Cilicia and Greece. To reward him, Manilius proposed that the provinces of Lucullus, other territory, and command of the Mithridatic War be given to him. This law was also opposed by some senators. Catulus, renowned for honor and virtue, spoke against it as he had against the Gabinian Law. Cicero supported it, for reasons of personal policy. The law was passed (66 B.C.), and its effect, in conjunction with the Gabinian Law, was to give Pompey unlimited power on land and sea. Opponents of the law were well aware of its effect. "We have at last then, a sovereign," they said, "The Republic is changed into a monarchy." Having received command of the war against Mithridates, thus publicly humiliating Lucullus and denying the services he had already rendered, Pompey set out for the East. He defeated Mithridates at the Euphrates, but Mithridates escaped. Tigranes, king of Armenia, surrendered to Pompey, who fined him 6000 talents and restored certain of his lands. Pompey surged through the East with his army, defeated the Iberians, went into Colchis, marched back to quell a revolt of the Albanians, converted Syria into a Roman province (64 B.C.), reduced Judaea (63 B.C.), founded cities, administered justice, settled disputes between cities, and with imperial power restored order. As he was returning to Rome after his splendid victories he learned what all Rome knew: that his third wife, Mucia, had betrayed him with Caesar. He called Caesar "my Aegisthus," and sent Mucia a divorce. When he later married Caesar's daughter Julia (59 B.C.) he was heavily criticized. On his arrival in Rome he voluntarily disbanded his army. The triumph he was awarded (61 B.C.) for the conquest of Asia was the most magnificent Rome had ever seen. This was the apex of his career. From this time, as Plutarch says, "he was insensibly ruined by the weight of his own power." He had as little talent for politics as he had greatness as a general and soon frittered away the great popularity he had won. He turned away from the conservative party and allied himself with Publius Clodius, a renegade patrician, at whose demand he abandoned his old friend Cicero. He allowed Caesar

to reconcile him with Crassus, formed with them the First Triumvirate (60 B.C.), and filled the city with his loyal soldiers to secure the command of Gaul for Caesar for five years. But he could not control the street mobs of Clodius, who openly scorned him, and he had lost the respect of the Senate when he abandoned Cicero. He secured the restoration of Cicero, who reconciled him with the Senate, and then was given the task of supplying Rome with grain. In this position he was again master at Rome, and he carried out his task with great success. Meantime, Caesar was tremendously successful in Gaul, and was intriguing against Pompey. He crossed the Alps and wintered at Luca. Pompey and Crassus met him there (56 B.C.), renewed the triumvirate, agreed to seek the consulship again, and to procure another five-year term for Caesar in Gaul. By means of bribery and street mobs, Crassus and Pompey won the consulate (55 B.C.) and Caesar got his command in Gaul. In the division of the provinces between the consuls, Pompey took Africa and Spain; Crassus got Syria and command of a war against the Parthians. Pompey did not set out for his provinces. He was severely criticized for jaunting about Italy with his young wife, Julia, and leaving the administration of his territories to his lieutenants. Crassus was killed in his war with the Parthians (53 B.C.), and the year before that Julia had died. The links, always fragile, between Caesar and Pompey were now broken, and their rivalry for control of Rome came out in the open. The city was in a ferment. It was proposed that Pompey be made dictator, but Cato successfully opposed this. However, the disorder was so great that Cato later endorsed the proposal that he be named sole consul, and this was done (52 B.C.). In the midst of the political confusion Pompey married Cornelia, the widow of Crassus' son, and allied himself to the conservative party. He served as sole consul for five years, and in this time restored order and embarked on a policy of legislation designed to curb Caesar. He felt so secure in his power that he scorned Caesar and refused to gather an army against him. Caesar's agents circulated freely in Rome, armed with booty that they liberally distributed in bribes to win opponents of Pompey. When at last Caesar crossed the Alps with an army Pompey had no force with which to oppose him. Before he could collect one he learned that Caesar had crossed the Rubicon. Pompey hesitated, bewildered by the sudden collapse of his influence, and unable to decide on any of the conflicting plans offered him. Italy was in a ferment; Rome was in a state of wildest confusion. Those outside the city flocked in, while those in it were making all haste to leave. As the uncertainty and confusion reached a climax, Pompey declared that he would consider all who stayed in Rome as enemies. With many prominent men he left the city to Caesar, and when the latter pursued him he took ship at Brundisium and sailed to Macedonia. Caesar was now master of Italy, but Pompey still controlled the sea. Many eminent men, looking to him to save the Republic, joined him; among them was the consul Labienus, who had been greatly honored by Caesar, and Marcus Junius Brutus, whose father Pompey had caused to be murdered, as well as Cicero. Caesar did not follow him immediately. First he went to Spain, conquered Pompey's troops there, and added them to his own army. Then he went to Macedonia and asked Pompey for a conference. Pompey refused to meet him, seized all the ports, and cut off Caesar's supplies, forcing him to withdraw to Thessaly. Pompey's plan, a sound one, was to exhaust Caesar, but his followers were eager to give battle. They claimed Caesar's withdrawal to Thessaly was a sign of weakness, and urged Pompey to return to Rome. He did not want to appear to flee before Caesar a second time (as he had at Brundisium), and hoped to defeat him in Thessaly. He yielded to the demands of his subordinates, for nothing that had happened in his life had prepared him to accept the abuse and criticism they now heaped on him for refusing to fight. A council of war was held at Pharsalus, in Thessaly, at which it was decided to engage Caesar. Caesar was relieved, "At last," he said, "we shall fight men and not famine." In the battle that followed on Aug. 9, 48 B.C., Pompey, with a force of 45,000 legionaries and 7000 cavalry, was utterly routed by Caesar, with 22,000 legionaries and 1000 cavalry.

For the first time in his life Pompey knew what it was to be defeated and to flee. In a small boat he went to Mytilene to fetch his wife Cornelia and his son. He sailed to Egypt and sent to the young king, Ptolemy XIII, to ask for asylum. Ptolemy's advisers persuaded him to kill Pompey, some say, for "dead men don't bite." Pompey was waiting in his boat off shore for the king's decision. A few men came to him in a small and humble boat. He suspected from their lack of ceremony and the insignificance of their equipage that Ptolemy did not mean to welcome him with honor. Nevertheless, he got into their boat. When they neared the beach his freedman Philip leaped out to help him ashore. He stretched out his hand to Philip, and as he did so was stabbed in the back. Some say it was one of his former centurions who killed him for Ptolemy. Others in the boat set on him and killed him with many blows. They cut off his head, stripped his body, and left it naked on the shore. Philip washed it in sea water, wrapped it in one of his own garments and, using an abandoned fishing boat as a pyre, burned it. When Caesar reached Egypt and learned of his murder he ordered the assassins executed; the ashes of his fallen rival were restored to Cornelia, who buried them on his estate near Alba.

Pompilius (pom-pil′i-us), **Numa.** See **Numa Pompilius.**

Pomponius (pom-pō′ni-us), **Lucius.** [Surnamed **Bononiensis,** meaning "of Bononia" (Bologna).] Roman writer of plays; fl. at the beginning of the 1st century B.C. About 70 titles of his short, lively plays remain.

Pomponius, Publius. [Called **Secundus.**] Roman tragedian of the 1st century A.D. After the death of Sejanus (31 A.D.), whose partisan he had been, Pomponius was restricted in his movements by Tiberius. He was later freed by Caligula. He became consul in 44, fought against the Chatti in 50, and received triumphal honors from Claudius for his victories. Of his tragedies, much admired in his own day, only fragments remain.

Pomptinae Paludes (pomp-tī′nē pa-lö′dēz). [English, **Pontine Marshes.**] Marshy district in the region of Latium, C Italy, between the Tyrrhenian Sea and the Volscian Mountains, and extending about 31 miles from Tarracina to near Velitrae. From ancient times it had been a notoriously malarial swampland, due to a lack of natural drainage, and from 160 B.C. many attempts were made to drain it, notably those by Cethegus and Trajan. The area, finally drained and improved in the 1920's and 1930's is traversed by the Appian Way.

Pontia (pon′sha̱). An epithet of Aphrodite in her aspect as goddess of the sea, meaning "Of the Deep Sea."

Pontiae (pon′shi-ē) or **Pontia** (-sha̱). [Modern name, **Ponza.**] Chief island of the Pontine group, situated in the Tyrrhenian Sea about 67 miles W of Naples: a place of exile for state prisoners under the early Roman emperors.

Ponticus (pon′ti-kus). See **Lucullus, Lucius Licinius.**

Pontine Islands (pon′tin, -tīn). [Modern name, **Ponza Islands.**] Group of small volcanic islands W of Naples.

Pontine Marshes. See **Pomptinae Paludes.**

Pontus (pon′tus). In Greek religion, a personification of the sea. He is variously mentioned as both son and consort of Gaea, the earth goddess, and as the father of Nereus, Ceto, Phorcys, and others.

Pontus. In ancient geography, a country in Asia Minor. It was bounded by the Pontus Euxinus (Black Sea) on the N, Colchis on the E, Armenia on the SE and S, Cappadocia on the S, Galatia on the SW, and Paphlagonia on the W. It became independent of Persia in the 4th century B.C., and rose to · great power with extended boundaries under Mithridates VI. After the victories of Pompey (66 B.C.) it was reduced to its former limits, and was eventually made a Roman province.

Pontus Euxinus (ūk-sī′nus). [Latin form of the Greek name of the **Euxine Sea,** or **Black Sea.**] The Greek word *euxeinos* may be translated "friendly to strangers." The Black Sea having been notably treacherous to Greek mariners with their keelless ships, the legend arose that it had once been called the *Axeinos,* "hostile to strangers." It was said that its name had been changed in the hope of placating its spirit, as the Greeks were said to have changed the name of the Erinyes (Furies) to Eumenides "the Kindly-Disposed." (JJ)

Popilian Way (pō-pil′i-a̱n). See **Via Popilia.**

Poppaea Sabina (po-pē′a̱ sa̱-bī′na̱). Wife of Otho, and mistress, and subsequently wife, of Nero. She was divorced from the former and married the latter in 62 A.D. She is usually blamed as the person who chiefly influenced Nero in his murder of his wife Octavia, her sister Antonia, his mother Agrippina, the philosopher Seneca, and others. He is said to have kicked her so severely, in a fit of rage, that she died (65 A.D.).

Populonia (po-pū-lō′ni-a̱). In ancient geography, a town of the Etruscans, situated on the coast of Etruria on the N end of a promontory projecting into the Mediterranean Sea and opposite the island of Elba. According to the *Aeneid* it was one of the Etruscan towns that lent assistance to Aeneas in his war with the Latins. Sulla took the town by siege about the beginning of the 1st century B.C., and thereafter it declined. Tombs dating from the 9th century B.C. have been found near the site of the ancient town.

Porcia (pôr′sha̱). See **Portia.**

Porcina (pôr′si-na̱). Surname of **Lepidus, Marcus Aemilius** (consul 137 B.C.).

Porinus (pō-rī′nus). Sixth century B.C. Greek architect, associated with Antistates, Antimachides, and Callaeschrus in preparing the original plans for the Olympieum, the colossal temple of Zeus Olympius at Athens projected by the Pisistratids. (JJ)

Poros (pô′ros). See **Calauria.**

Porphyrion (pôr-fī′ri-on). In Greek mythology, one of the Giants, a son of Gaea and the blood of Uranus, who waged war on the gods. During the battle Eros pierced him with an arrow, Zeus felled him with a thunderbolt for attempting to violate Hera, and Heracles killed him with one of his arrows. With other Giants, he was buried under volcanic mountains when the gods, aided by Heracles, won the battle.

Porsena (pôr′se̱-na̱), **Lars.** [Also: **Porsenna.**] In Roman legend, a king of Clusium in Etruria, who gained power over Rome in the 6th century B.C. He was allied with the banished Tarquins against Rome, and the scene in which he besieged Rome to compel the Romans to take back the banished Tarquin was depicted on the shield which Vulcan, at the request of Venus, made for Aeneas, long before any of these events could have taken place. He was celebrated in the legends of Tarquin, Horatius Cocles, and others.

Porta Romana (pôr′tä rō-mä′nä). See **Arch of Augustus.**

Portia (pôr′sha). [Also: **Porcia.**] Wife of Bibulus (consul, 59 B.C.) and later of Marcus Junius Brutus, leader of the conspiracy that resulted in the assassination of Caesar. When she learned of her husband's death at Philippi she is said to have killed herself by swallowing live coals (42 B.C.). Most scholars believe, however, that she died before Brutus in 43 B.C.

Portici (pôr′tē-chē). Town and commune in S Italy, in the Campania, situated on the Bay of Naples about 5 miles SE of Naples; a seaside resort. Near here is the site of ancient Herculaneum, covered in 79 A.D. by ashes from the eruption of Vesuvius, which, wet with rain and flowing as warm mud, filled the streets and houses and there hardened into stone.

Portoferraio (pôr-tō-fer-rä′yō). See **Argoön.**

Porto Torres (pôr′tō tôr′räs). See **Turris Libisonis.**

Portunus (pôr-tū′nus). [Also: **Portumnus.**] In Roman mythology, a god, protector of ports and harbors. It is thought he may originally have been associated with Janus as protector of doors, gates, and entrances. Like Janus, he is represented with a key. There was a temple to Portunus at the mouth of the Tiber, and there an annual festival was held in his honor in August. Portunus was identified with the Greek Palaemon or Melicertes.

Portus Trajani (pôr′tus trạ-jā′nī). See **Centumcellae.**

Porus (pō′rus). Indian king who governed the land between the Hydaspes and Acesines rivers (in what is now the northern Punjab); killed c318 B.C. When Alexander the Great advanced to the Hydaspes River (326 B.C.), some of the reigning princes of the lands through which he passed voluntarily submitted to him and kept much of their powers. Porus, a powerful prince, prepared to resist and gathered an army on the farther bank of the Hydaspes to prevent Alexander from crossing it. His most formidable weapon was a large corps of elephants, the sight and smell of which drove Alexander's horses into a frenzy. The river was swollen by seasonal rains and for a time the two armies faced each other from opposite banks. Alexander made many feints, as if to put his army in motion, but in the end he marched 16 miles up the river with part of his army, crossed, and attacked Porus from his own side. Porus, mounted on a magnificent elephant, was in the thick of the fighting, and was wounded. His elephants, so formidable when met head on, were maddened by attacks from all sides, threw their riders in many cases, and raged about trampling friend and foe alike. According to Plutarch, Porus' own elephant maneuvered him tenderly through the strife, and when it felt Porus weakened by arrow wounds, the elephant knelt down for Porus to dismount and plucked the arrow from his body with its trunk. When Porus saw his army routed he did not flee, but turned his elephant and rode off. Messengers from Alexander persuaded him to return. Alexander asked him how he expected to be treated. Porus replied, "Like a king." He was. Alexander treated him royally and gave him back his kingdom, somewhat enlarged in area, which he was to govern as a dependent of Macedonia. After the death of Alexander, Porus was treacherously slain (c318 B.C.) by the Macedonian general Eudemus.

Poseideon (pō-sī′dē-on). The sixth month of the Attic year, corresponding to the latter half of December and the first half of January.

Poseidon (pō-sī′don). One of the 12 Olympian gods, son of Cronus and Rhea, brother of Zeus and Hades. He was lord of the sea and navigation. The Arcadians say that when Rhea bore Poseidon she laid him in a flock of lambs in Arcadia to save him from Cronus, and gave Cronus a foal to swallow in his stead. A spring near Mantinea called "the Lamb" was named by the Arcadians as the place near which Poseidon was hidden. Some say he was brought up by the Telchines of Rhodes, who forged the trident with which he cleft rocks, caused fountains and springs to gush forth, and raked the sea into mighty storms. But the general account is that Poseidon, like his brothers and sisters before him, was swallowed up by his father Cronus as soon as he was born. Zeus tricked Cronus into disgorging the children he had swallowed, and the brothers immediately plotted to dethrone their father. The Cyclopes provided them with weapons, giving the trident to Poseidon, and they waged war on the Titans, of whom Atlas was the leader since Cronus had become too feeble for the role. The Titans were defeated; Cronus was overthrown and fled. Zeus, Hades, and Poseidon cast lots in a helmet to divide up the universe among them. Poseidon drew the sea as his realm. Zeus drew the heavens, and Hades

POSEIDON
Red-figured Greek amphora, Nikoxenus Painter

drew the underworld; earth and Olympus were shared by all. Poseidon built an underwater palace for himself near Aegae, in Euboea. In its stables he kept his white chariot horses with bronze hoofs and golden manes, and a golden chariot. Clad in a robe of gold he rode the sea in this equipage, accompanied by sporting dolphins, tritons, and other sea creatures. At his approach storms were dispelled, the waves flattened, and the sea smiled. At first Zeus, Hades, and Poseidon were equal in power, but gradually Zeus came to be the acknowledged master of them all. He was so overbearing that the gods and goddesses on Olympus revolted and bound him as he slept. Through the inter-

vention of the Nereid Thetis, Zeus was freed by Briareus. Enraged at their rebellion, Zeus punished the gods. He sent Poseidon and Apollo as servants to King Laomedon of Troy, who commanded them to build a wall about his city. Some say Poseidon and Apollo were assisted in their task by Aeacus, a son of Zeus, because if the wall was built by the gods alone it would have been invulnerable. When the wall was finished, Laomedon refused to pay Poseidon and Apollo as he had promised. On the contrary, he threatened to cut off their ears and send them off in chains. Poseidon sent a sea-monster to scourge Laomedon's country, and would not recall it until Laomedon agreed to sacrifice his daughter Hesione to it. Laomedon exposed Hesione on a rock for the monster, but Heracles came along and slew it, and gave Hesione to his friend Telamon.

Poseidon was ever seeking to increase his realm, trying as he could to encroach on the land and add it to his sea kingdom. He contended with Athena for control of Athens. He struck the rock of the Acropolis with his trident and caused a fountain of sea water to gush forth. Athena planted an olive tree as her gift to the city and claimed the city for herself. Poseidon challenged her to single combat, and she accepted. However, Zeus forbade them to fight, and ordered their dispute submitted to the gods and goddesses for settlement. All the gods voted in favor of Poseidon and the goddesses voted in favor of Athena, and since Zeus had refused to take part, Athena won by one vote and claimed the city. Poseidon was so enraged he sent a flood over the Thriasian plain. In the end he was reconciled to Athena, and shared her temple, the Erechtheum, on the Acropolis. In his part of the temple the well of sea water he had caused to spring forth was housed, and whenever the south wind blew a sound of the sea could be heard coming from it. He contended with Hera for control of Argolis. Their dispute was submitted to the river-gods Cephissus, Inachus, and Asterion. The river-gods awarded the land to Hera. This time Poseidon, since, some say, he had promised to send no more floods, dried up the rivers, so that ever after their beds were dry in summer. Danaus came into the land with his 50 daughters and urged them to find some way to propitiate Poseidon. Amymone, one of his daughters, was seized by a satyr one day while hunting. Poseidon, hearing her cries, came to her rescue and hurled his trident at the satyr. The satyr dodged and the trident pierced a rock from which a spring immediately gushed forth. Poseidon fell in love with Amymone and embraced her. She bore him a son, Nauplius, and Poseidon promised that the spring his trident had brought forth would never fail. As the fountain of Amymone, it is the source of the Lerna River, which does not dry up in the summer. But some say Poseidon, in this contest with Hera for Argolis, inundated Argos, and was finally persuaded by Hera to withdraw the waters, and that because of the flooding he was called Prosclystius (*Flooder*). The Argives raised a sanctuary to Poseidon Prosclystius at the point in Argos where the flood ebbed. And some say he sent brine to kill the roots and seeds in the land about Hermione, but when he was propitiated by sacrifices and prayers he stopped sending the brine and the plants grew and the land prospered. For this reason he was called Phytalmios (*Nourishing*). Poseidon vied with Helius for control of Corinthia, and was awarded the isthmus by Briareus. The land became sacred to him and altars of Isthmian Poseidon were raised. In a second contest with Athena, he claimed Troezen. Zeus ordered them to share control, and the Troezenians worshiped him as "King." He even claimed Aegina, an island belonging to Zeus, and Naxos, the island of Dionysus, but his claim in each case was useless.

Poseidon and Zeus were rivals for the love of the Nereid Thetis, but when they learned from an oracle that she would bear a son greater than his father, they both lost interest in her. Poseidon then courted Amphitrite, another Nereid. She fled, and he sent Delphinus as ambassador to plead his cause. Delphinus was successful and Amphitrite agreed to marry Poseidon. As a reward, Poseidon set the image of Delphinus among the stars as the constellation of the Dolphin. Amphitrite bore Triton, Rhode, and Benthesicyme to Poseidon. He was a very inconstant husband and had nearly as many love affairs as Zeus. When Amphitrite learned of his love for the sea-nymph Scylla, she trans-

formed the unfortunate nymph into a monster with six hideous dogs' heads, and 12 long arms. Poseidon also wooed Medusa, once a beautiful maiden, but because he made love to her in one of Athena's temples the goddess transformed her into a hideous snaky-haired Gorgon. When Perseus cut off Medusa's head, the monster Chrysaor and the winged horse Pegasus sprang from her spilled blood; these were her children by Poseidon. He carried off Tyro, daughter of Salmoneus, and, hidden by a huge violet sea wave, ravished her. She bore him Pelias and Neleus. By Libya, a daughter of Epaphus and a granddaughter of Zeus, he was the father of the Phoenician kings Agenor and Belus. He seduced Alope, daughter of King Cercyon of Arcadia. She bore him a son, Hippothous. When Alope died he transformed her into a spring. The nymph Caenis was seized and embraced by him, and he promised to fulfill whatever wish she might ask. She asked to be transformed into an invulnerable man. He carried out his promise, and as a man she was named Caeneus. Aethra, daughter of King Pittheus of Troezen, having been embraced by Aegeus, king of Athens, was ordered in a dream to wade across to the island of Sphaeria and make an offering in the temple there. While she was there Poseidon came upon her and ravished her. For this reason, some say that he was the father of Theseus. Most say Aegeus was his father, but Poseidon many times came to his aid, and promised to fulfill any three wishes Theseus might ask of him. Theseus used one of his wishes to request the destruction of his own son Hippolytus, who he thought had betrayed him with his wife Phaedra. Poseidon sent a great sea-monster, riding the crest of a huge wave, to frighten the horses drawing the chariot of Hippolytus. The horses bolted, overturned the chariot, and dragged Hippolytus to his death. By Gaea Poseidon was the father of Antaeus, king in Libya, whose strength increased as his body had contact with the earth. Antaeus forced strangers to wrestle with him, and when he had slain them he used their skulls to build a temple to his father Poseidon. Antaeus was slain by Heracles. Amycus, king of the Bebryces; Cycnus who was transformed into a swan; Busiris, king of Egypt; Orion whose image

fat, fāte, fär, fãre, errạnt; net, mē, hėr ardẹnt; pin, pīne; not, nōte, möve, nôr,

was placed among the stars; the Argonauts Ancaeus and Euphemus; Halirrhothius, slain by Ares, and Eumolpus, priest of Eleusis slain by Erechtheus, were among his many sons. He won Aphrodite's gratitude by offering to pay off her marriage gifts to Hephaestus when she had been discovered with Ares. She bore him Rhodus and Herophilus. He pursued Demeter who was desperately searching for her lost daughter Persephone. Demeter sought to escape by transforming herself into a mare. Poseidon changed himself to a stallion and ravished her. She bore him the marvelous horse Arion and Despoena, a nymph. Some say it was because he transformed himself into a stallion on this occasion that he had the epithet Hippios (*Horse*). At the foot of Mount Alesium in Arcadia, Agamedes and Trophonius built a sanctuary of Poseidon Hippios from oak logs. Some say that a sea wave rose up in the sanctuary. Odysseus dedicated an image of Poseidon Hippios at Pheneüs in Arcadia, and there was an altar of Poseidon Hippios at Olympia. He was especially worshiped by this name in Attica, perhaps because, as some say, he created the horse by striking the rock of the Acropolis with his trident. Some say Poseidon was the father of Athena, and a blue-eyed statue of the goddess in Athens was taken as evidence of his paternity.

In the Trojan War, Poseidon aided the Greeks whenever possible. At one time he disguised himself as the seer Calchas in order to talk to the Greeks and inspire them with renewed courage for the fight, but he was recognized as a god by his well-formed legs. He aided the Greeks because he had never forgotten that Laomedon cheated him when he built the walls of Troy. But when the Greeks took advantage of a truce for burial of the dead to build a great wall about their ships, Poseidon complained to Zeus that the Greek wall might rival the wall he himself had built about Troy with the aid of Apollo. Zeus soothed him by assuring him that as lord of the sea he could break down the Greek wall whenever he wished, and after the war was over Poseidon diverted the courses of several rivers, washed them against the Greek wall and destroyed it. Though he favored the Greeks in the war, he once rescued Aeneas when he was wounded, out

of pity for the Trojan hero. After the war, he joined with Athena to harass the Greeks on their return from Troy by sending great storms at sea. The change of heart of the gods toward the Greeks was occasioned in part by the supposed arrogance of Ajax the Lesser. Poseidon's greatest anger was reserved for Odysseus. On the way home Odysseus stopped at the island of Polyphemus the Cyclops, a son of Poseidon. To escape from him Odysseus blinded Polyphemus. The latter called on Poseidon for vengeance. To avenge his son, Poseidon harried Odysseus unmercifully, and prevented him from returning home for ten years.

In earliest times Poseidon was a god of the depths of the earth. In this aspect he was thought to cause earthquakes, whence his title "Earth-shaker," and was especially worshiped in regions subject to earthquake, as Sparta and Thessaly. It was Poseidon, for example, who cleft the earth with one of his earthquakes and created the Vale of Tempe in Thessaly. In most ancient times he shared the oracle at Delphi with Gaea. When Apollo slew the Python that guarded the oracle and seized it for himself, he gave the island of Calauria, off the coast of Troezen, to Poseidon in exchange for his half of the oracle. Poseidon came increasingly to be worshiped solely as a god of the sea, who had sovereignty over all its waters, everything in them, and navigation on them. He raised storms and caused shipwreck or calmed the waters at his pleasure; he also gave victory at sea, and because he could send favorable winds or victory he was called Soter (*Giver of Safety*). His temples were usually to be found on promontories and headlands jutting into the sea; typical were those at Taenarum and Sunium, where in the latter place ruins of his temple may still be seen. As god of the sea he was the "Earth-girdler," for the sea was thought to be a vast band surrounding the earth. He was particularly worshiped by seafaring peoples, who claimed descent from him. The island of Chios, for example, was named for a son of Poseidon; Nauplia, the port on the Gulf of Argolis, was founded by his son, Nauplius; the Phaeacians, greatest sailors of legend, were said to be his descendants. Away from the sea, Poseidon was worshiped as the donor of the life-giving waters of springs and fountains. He was also worshiped as a god of horses. His worship was very ancient and extended throughout the Greek world. The Ionians of Helice in Achaea had a very holy sanctuary of Heliconian Poseidon. When they were expelled from Helice they went to Athens, where they continued to worship Heliconian Poseidon. Afterward, the descendants of these Ionians emigrated to the coasts of Asia Minor and colonized the region that came to be known as Ionia. They carried Heliconian Poseidon with them and spread his cult in the expanding Greek world. They raised altars to him near Miletus and in Teos, and in their chief sanctuary on the promontory of Mycale, the Ionians celebrated their great festival in honor of Heliconian Poseidon called the Panionia. As for the original site of the cult of Heliconian Poseidon, Helice in Achaea, Poseidon caused it to be swallowed up by an earthquake and drowned in a flood, because the Achaeans dragged some suppliants from his altar in the shrine there.

The horse, dolphin, and pine tree were sacred to Poseidon. Bulls, especially black ones, were sacrificed to him, and sometimes flung alive into rivers to propitiate him. In Ionia and Thessaly bull-fights were held in his honor. His chief festival was the Isthmian Games, which were held every other year on the Isthmus of Corinth. In these games, of which he was the patron, the victors were crowned with wreaths of his sacred pine. After the victory of the Greeks over the Persians at Plataea (479 B.C.) the Greeks used part of the Persian booty to erect a bronze statue of Isthmian Poseidon ten feet high. Other great statues of Poseidon stood at harbors and on promontories. In art Poseidon is represented as a majestic figure; his most common attributes are the trident, the dolphin, and the horse. The original Roman or Italic Neptune became assimilated to him.

Poseidonius (pos-ī-dō'ni-us). See **Posidonius.**

Posidippus or **Poseidippus** (pō-sī-dip'us). Greek poet, one of the most distinguished of the writers of the New Comedy. He was born in Cassandrea, Macedonia, and was active in the first half of the 3rd century B.C. His first work appeared in 289 B.C. Only fragments of his work survive.

Posidonia (pos-i-dō'ni-a). Original name of **Paestum.**

Posidonius (pos-ī-dō'ni-us). [Also: **Poseidonius.**] Greek Stoic philosopher; born at Apamea, Syria; fl. at the beginning of the 1st century B.C. He was educated at Athens under the philosopher Panaetius and became known as the most learned man of his time. He traveled widely in western Europe and North Africa in furtherance of his scientific researches, and then went to Rhodes, where he became head of the school of Stoic philosophy. Cicero was one of his pupils. He was active in the affairs of Rhodes and was sent as an envoy to Rome (86 B.C.). Among his Roman friends were such eminent men as Marius and Pompey. He was greatly interested in astronomy, mathematics, natural history, geography, and mythology, and wrote widely on these subjects as well as on philosophy. He also wrote a history of the period 146–88 B.C., continuing the *History* of Polybius. None of his work, except some meager fragments, survives.

Postvorta (post-vôr'ta). In Roman mythology, a goddess to whom was attributed a knowledge of the past. See **Antevorta.**

Pothos (pō'thos). The personification of desire and longing. A companion of Aphrodite, along with Eros, Himeros, and the Graces.

Potidaea (pot-i-dē'a). [Also: **Cassandrea.**] In ancient geography, a city in Macedonia, situated on the Pallene peninsula, the most westerly of the peninsulas of Chalcidice. The city was founded by colonists from Corinth (c600 B.C.). The Persians, on their way back to the Hellespont after their defeat at Salamis (480 B.C.) attempted to take Potidaea and besieged it, but after three months gave up the siege and withdrew. As a result of a quarrel between Athens and Corinth over Corcyra, Potidaea revolted against Athens (433 B.C.), of whom she had become a tributary ally after the Persian War. Athens sent a force to subdue the city. Corinth sought the aid of Sparta to defend it. The revolt of Potidaea was one of the precipitating causes of the Peloponnesian Wars. The Athenians besieged the city for a year and reduced its inhabitants to starvation. According to Thucydides, they were so driven by their hunger that in certain instances they ate human flesh. The city surrendered (430

B.C.). By the terms of the surrender the inhabitants and their auxiliary soldiers were allowed a free passage out of the city, the men with one garment apiece, the women with two, and a fixed sum of money was allotted them for the journey. Later the Athenians sent colonists to repopulate the city. The city joined the Chalcidian League early in the 4th century. In 364–362 B.C. it fell again under Athenian dominion. Philip II of Macedon captured it (c356 B.C.) and handed it over to Olynthus. The city was largely destroyed, probably during the Olynthian War (348 B.C.), but was rebuilt by Cassander, son of Antipater, who renamed it Cassandrea for himself. For a time it was very powerful, but it was finally destroyed by the Huns. Ruins of the ancient wall are to be found on the site.

Potniae (pot′ni-ẹ). In ancient geography, a city of Boeotia, Greece. The city had a grove of Demeter and the Maid. Once when the people were sacrificing to Dionysus they became so inflamed with wine that they killed the priest. The city was afterwards smitten by a plague and envoys were sent to Delphi to seek relief. The priestess told them they must sacrifice a boy, but later a goat was substituted by the god himself, who shot a goat and put him in the place of the boy victim. For this reason the inhabitants raised a temple of Dionysus the Goat-shooter. A well in Potniae had the property of driving mares that drank its waters to madness. Between Potniae and Thebes was the place where, some say, the earth opened and swallowed up Amphiaraus and his chariot as he fled from Thebes. A small enclosure marked with pillars was erected about the spot. It was said that birds would not perch on the pillars nor beasts crop the grass of the sacred enclosure.

Pozzuoli (pōt-tswô′lẹ). See **Puteoli.**

Pozzuoli, Bay of. Northwestern arm of the Bay of Naples.

Praeneste (prẹ-nes′tẹ). [Modern name, **Palestrina.**] In ancient geography, a city in Latium, Italy, situated on a lofty hill about 23 miles ESE of Rome. According to legend, it was founded by Caeculus, a son of Vulcan. It was built probably as early as the 8th century B.C., and was often opposed to Rome, especially in 380 B.C. when it was captured

by Camillus, and in the Latin War (340–338 B.C.), and was later allied with Rome until the time of the Social War (90–88 B.C.), when it received the Roman franchise. It was taken by the partisans of Sulla from the Marians under the younger Marius in 82 B.C. With its clear air and refreshing breezes, it became a favorite summer resort of the Roman nobility (the residence of Augustus, Horace, Tiberius, and Hadrian), and was celebrated for the temple of the goddess Fortuna Primigenia. Connected with the temple was an oracle, the *sortes Praenestinae* (Praenestine lots), which was consulted in the following manner: Contained in a receptacle were a number of small oak tablets, on which were inscribed enigmatic sentences. When a petitioner wished to consult the oracle, a child drew one of these and handed it to him. He was at liberty to interpret it as he saw fit. Ruins of ancient Praeneste are still visible. These include long sections of fortification wall in polygonal limestone masonry, assignable to the 4th or 3rd century B.C., the vast sanctuary of Fortune, majestically constructed in ascending terraces on the hill slope and still the subject of endless study and discussion, and a large Nile landscape in mosaic. From the cemetery have come the famous Praenestine cists (decorated caskets, as the Ficoroni Cist, q.v.) and the Praenestine fibula (ornamental clasp), with the earliest inscription in Latin. (JJ)

Praenestine Way (prẹ-nes′tīn, -tin). See **Via Praenestina.**

Praetor (prē′tọr). In Roman history, a title which originally designated the consuls as the leaders of the armies of the state. Later (from about 367 B.C.) one praetor, and from about 242 B.C. two praetors were appointed as colleagues to the consuls, and specifically as judicial officers, one of whom (*praetor urbanus*) tried causes between Roman citizens, and the other (*praetor peregrinus*) causes between foreigners, or between foreigners and citizens. After the discharge of his judicial functions a praetor had often the administration of a province, with the title of propraetor, or sometimes proconsul. When the dominions of Rome were extended beyond Italy, the number of praetorships was increased, and finally, under the empire, became 18 or even more. The *praetor urbanus* was the first in rank, and was specifically *the Praetor.*

Praetorian Camp (prē-tō′ri-an). [Also: **Pretorian.**] Camp of the Praetorian Guard at ancient Rome, first permanently established by Tiberius, outside the city walls. It formed a square of about 1500 feet to a side, and was enclosed by a brick-faced wall ten feet high, strengthened with towers at its gates. The camp was included by Aurelian (c212–275 A.D.) in his new line of fortifications, and still forms an abrupt projection in the wall on the NE. The fortifications of Aurelian are three times as high as those of Tiberius, but not so well built. The latter, embedded as they are in the newer work, can still be followed for a considerable distance. Within the camp there were monumental buildings with mosaics and marble incrustation. Constantine the Great (274–337 A.D.) abolished the Praetorian Guard, and pulled down the wall of their camp on the side toward the city.

Praetorian Guard. A body of troops originally formed by the emperor Augustus to protect his person and his power, and maintained by successive Roman emperors down to Constantine: so called as practically continuing the organization and functions of the *praetoria cohors,* or select troops which attended the person of the praetor or the general of the Republic. These troops were under a special organization, and had special privileges of rank and pay, raising them above the ordinary soldiery. They soon acquired a dangerous power, and for a considerable time raised and deposed emperors at their pleasure.

Prasiae (prā′si-ē) or **Prasia** (-a). A coast town of Laconia. The inhabitants claimed that after Dionysus was born, Cadmus placed Semele and her infant in a chest and cast it into the sea. The chest came ashore at Prasiae, and when it was opened Semele was dead. The Prasiaeans gave her a splendid funeral and took care of the infant. After some time Ino came wandering to Prasiae and agreed to take care of the infant Dionysus. The cave where she nursed him was still shown in the 2nd century A.D.

Prasiae. In ancient geography, a place in Attica where there was a temple of Apollo especially connected with Hyperborean Apollo. First fruits of the Hyperboreans, wrapped in wheaten straw, were sent here. From here, the Athenians took them to Delos. There was a monument to Erysichthon at Prasiae, for he died on the return voyage from Delos after having delivered the Hyperborean first fruits there.

Pratinas (pra′ti-nas). Greek dramatist of Phlius, in the Peloponnesus, who performed at Athens. He was a contemporary and rival of Aeschylus, with whom he first competed c500 B.C. He wrote satyr plays, which he is believed to have invented, as well as tragedies, dithyrambs, and choral odes. Fragments of his work survive.

Praxidicae (prak-sid′i-sē). In Greek religion, three goddesses of justice, especially of retribution. They were often solemnly sworn by, but always in the open air (even their temple had no roof). The singular form of the name was an epithet of Persephone.

Praxis (prak′sis). Epithet of Aphrodite, meaning "Action." In the temple of Aphrodite at Megara was an ivory image of Aphrodite Praxis.

Praxiteles (prak-sit′e-lēz). Greek sculptor, born at Athens about the end of the 5th century B.C. He was the son of the sculptor Cephisiodotus, and was a younger contemporary of Scopas. His activity lasted until about the time of Alexander the Great, or 336 B.C. Nearly threescore of his works are mentioned in old writers. The characteristics of his work—relaxed and graceful strength, extraordinary modeling and delicate contours—are shown in the statue of *Hermes Carrying the Infant Dionysus,* identified by Pausanias' description, and found at Olympia in 1877. Of the many works described with admiration and enthusiasm by the ancient writers, the *Hermes* and three heads are the only surviving originals of Praxiteles. Various works in modern museums are copies of his work. Among them is the *Satyr* of the Capitol in Rome (the *Marble Faun* of Hawthorne's novel). Of this there is a story that Phryne, a courtesan who sometimes served as the model for Praxiteles, once asked him to give her the most beautiful of his works. Loverlike, as Pausanias says, he agreed to do so, but couldn't say which he thought was most beautiful. She sent a slave to give him the alarm that fire had broken out in his studio. Praxiteles rushed to the studio, crying that his work was all wasted if fire had destroyed his *Satyr* and his *Eros.* Having found out what he most valued, Phryne chose to take the statue of *Eros.* The original *Satyr* was in a temple of Dionysus at Athens. Other copies of his work are a beautiful torso discovered in the Palatine, and now in the Louvre; the *Apollino* of the tribune in Florence; and the *Apollo Sauroctonus* (Lizard-slayer) of the Vatican. His most celebrated work was the *Aphrodite of Cnidus,* which, next to the *Zeus* of Phidias, was the most admired of the statues of antiquity. Of the *Aphrodite,* it is said that Praxiteles was commissioned to execute a statue of Aphrodite for the Athenians. He made two, one of which was a nude, the first time the female figure had been sculptured without drapery. The Athenians considered the two statues and chose the more conventional draped one. The Cnidians eagerly purchased the nude. This is the statue that came to be known as the *Aphrodite of Cnidus.*

Praxithea (prak-si'thē-a̱). In Greek legend, the wife of Erechtheus, king of Athens. She had four sons, among them, Cecrops who succeeded his father, and seven daughters. She permitted her youngest daughter Otionia (or Chthonia) to be sacrificed when Athens was attacked by the Eleusinians under Eumolpus, grandson of Praxithea. An oracle had foretold that such a sacrifice would save Athens. Protogonia and Pandora, two other daughters killed themselves at the same time, as they had vowed that if one of them must die by violence they would die, too.

Prexaspes (prek-sas'pēz). A faithful Persian attendant of Cambyses II (King of Persia, 529–c521 B.C.) Cambyses ordered him to slay his brother Smerdis (Bardiya), because while Cambyses was in Egypt he dreamed Smerdis sat on the royal throne and his head touched the heavens. Prexaspes returned to Susa and killed Smerdis, either by drowning him or during a hunting expedition. He then returned to Cambyses and reported that he had carried out his orders. On one occasion Cambyses asked Prexaspes what the Persians were saying about him. Prexaspes answered that they praised him greatly but said that he was overfond of wine. Cambyses was furious. He said he would shoot an arrow at the son of Prexaspes; if he hit the child in the heart the Persians who said he was overfond of wine and mad were liars; if he failed to hit the child in the heart, they were speaking the truth. Straightway he carried out his threat. He shot the son of Prexaspes with an arrow, had the body cut open and showed Prexaspes that his arrow had pierced his son's heart. Prexaspes, seeing that he was mad, agreed that the Persians who said Cambyses was mad were liars. Some time later two brothers, Median magi, planned a revolt against Cambyses. One of them looked very much like Cambyses' murdered brother Smerdis, and assumed the same name. While Cambyses was still in Egypt he set himself on the throne, stated that he was Smerdis, son of Cyrus, and declared himself king. Cambyses, hearing of this, thought Prexaspes had betrayed him, and had not slain Smerdis after all. He charged him with betrayal, but Prexaspes assured him his brother was dead. He helped him to learn that it was another Smerdis, a magus, who had rebelled and seized the throne. Thus it was that Cambyses' dream that Smerdis sat upon the royal throne and his head touched the heavens was fulfilled, but it was not his brother Smerdis, but another, and he had caused his brother's murder for nothing. In a rage Cambyses sought to mount his horse, wounded himself on his sword, and shortly thereafter died. Smerdis the rebel magus being still on the throne, Prexaspes now swore that he was the real Smerdis, brother of Cambyses, and also swore that he had not killed him, since it was unsafe to acknowledge the truth after the death of Cambyses. Later Smerdis the magus enlisted the aid of Prexaspes. To quiet rumors that were springing up he asked Prexaspes to go to the top of a tower and announce that the Persians were ruled by Smerdis the son of Cyrus, and no other. He knew that Prexaspes was the man most likely to be believed in this matter. Prexaspes agreed. He went to the tower, recited the genealogy of the Persian kings from the time of Achaemenes, said that he himself, at the command of Cambyses, had killed Smerdis the son of Cyrus, and that the present Smerdis was a magus and an impostor. Then Prexaspes hurled himself head first from the tower and perished.

Priam (pri'am). In Greek legend, a son of Laomedon, king of Troy, and Strymo; and a descendant of Dardanus and Tros. He was originally named Podarces, "swift-footed." When Heracles sacked Troy to punish Laomedon for reneging on his agreement to pay Heracles for the destruction of a sea-monster, Podarces and his sister, Hesione, were taken captive. Laomedon and his other sons were slain. Hesione was awarded to Telamon and was allowed to ransom any one of the captives. She ransomed Podarces with her veil. Henceforth he was called Priam, meaning, according to popular etymology, "redeemed." Heracles gave Laomedon's ruined kingdom to Priam, because he had urged Laomedon to pay Heracles as promised. Priam rebuilt the city on the old site and restored the kingdom to a state of great wealth and prosperity. He first married Arisbe, the daughter of Merops, the seer. By her he had one son, Aesacus. After the birth of this son Priam gave Arisbe to Hyrtacus for a wife, and he married Hecuba. Priam was said to have fathered 50 sons, 19 of them by Hecuba, and 12 daughters. They all lived about the palace court-yard with their wives and husbands. Among Priam's children were Hector, Paris, the twins —Helenus and Cassandra—Deïphobus, Polites, Polydorus, Antiphus, and Troilus; and among his daughters there were Creusa, Laodice, and Polyxena. According to some, Hector and Troilus were Hecuba's sons by Apollo. Ominous portents before the birth of Paris caused Priam to order him to be exposed at birth, but he was saved, and restored as a young man, although seers and prophets urged that he be destroyed or he would bring ruin to Troy. Priam gave his approval when Paris asked for a fleet to sail to Sparta, possibly under the impression that Paris would demand satisfaction for the abduction of Hesione. And when Paris returned, after many months, with Helen of the flawless beauty, Priam, like all Troy, fell in love with her, vowed he would never let her go, and did not chide Paris at all for his flagrant breach of hospitality. He refused all requests by Greek envoys for the return of Helen, and as he was too old to fight himself he entrusted the command of the Trojans to

his son Hector. One after another he saw his sons fall before the ferocious onslaughts of the Greeks. When Achilles rejoined the Greeks in their siege against Troy, Priam watched from the towers as Achilles drove Hector to the walls of the city. He pleaded with his son to come inside the walls, but Hector remained to face Achilles and death. The Trojans saw Achilles' barbarous treatment of Hector's body before he dragged it away to the Greek camp behind his chariot. Iris appeared to Priam with a message from Zeus which advised Priam to go to Achilles alone and ransom Hector's body. With one frail companion the aged king set out, carrying great treasure. Hermes came to guide him and spirited him into the tent of Achilles. Some say Achilles was sleeping and that Priam might easily have murdered him and avenged the death of his son. But Priam is always pictured as a man of honor, grave, courteous, and humane, with an abiding interest and love for his children. He appealed to Achilles on his knees for the return of Hector's body. The old king pointed out that few had done what he was doing, kissing the hands that had killed his son. Achilles and Priam wept together—the one for his dead friend, the other for his son. Achilles was touched by the dignity and frailty of the bereaved king who reminded him of his father. He promised to give him Hector's body and to allow the Trojans a truce of as many days as they required to perform funeral honors for Hector. In pride and grief Priam then conveyed his son's body back to Troy and the whole city mourned. In succeeding days Priam was encouraged by the arrival of Penthesilea, Memnon, and Eurypylus, only to see them all fall before the enemy. He also lost Paris, the cause of all the disaster. Now the Greeks resorted to stratagem; they left the Wooden Horse before the walls of Troy. Over the flaming protests of his prophetic daughter Cassandra, and in spite of numerous portents of doom, Priam agreed that the Horse should be drawn inside the city. The sack of Troy followed. The king prepared to join the fighting in defense of his city but was dissuaded, on the grounds of his age and weakness, by Hecuba. He mourned the loss of his sons and wished he had died rather than see the destruction of Troy. With Hecuba he was seated before the altar of Zeus in the court-yard of his palace when his young son Polites rushed in. He was followed by Neoptolemus, and was slain before his father's eyes. In a last glow of wrath Priam attacked the slayer of his son, but Neoptolemus swung on him and slashed off his head with one sweep of his sword. He then dragged the decapitated body to Achilles' tomb and left it there to rot.

Priam. In the *Aeneid*, a son of Polites, the son of Priam. He was a youthful companion of Ascanius on the flight of the Trojans, under Aeneas, to Italy.

Priamid (prī'a̯-mid). A name applied to any one of the 50 sons of Priam, king of Troy.

Priapus (prī-ā'pus). In Greek mythology, a god, a son of Dionysus and Aphrodite, the promoter of fertility in crops, cattle, and women. A statue of him was set up in vineyards and gardens to promote fertility, and he was honored in the city as well as in the country. Sometimes also known as Ithyphallus, he is depicted as a faunlike deity with penis always erect. In Rome he was identified with Mutinuus (or Mutunus), another fertility god. The first fruits of garden and field were sacrificed to him. Poems composed in his honor were called Priapea. In the Middle Ages he became the protector of cattle, herds, shepherds, farmers, and fishermen, and of women in childbirth.

Priene (prī-ē'nē). In ancient geography, one of the 12 Ionian cities of Asia. It was in Caria, N of Miletus. According to tradition, it was colonized by Ionians and Thebans, who went there under the leadership of a grandson of Codrus, the legendary king of Athens. In the 4th century B.C. the city was rebuilt on the rectangular "gridiron" plan. The site contains many ruins and is a fine example of ancient town planning. The temple of Athena Polias, dedicated 340 B.C., was an Ionic peripteros of six by 11 columns, of marble, graceful in proportion and with delicate decorative sculpture.

Priscus (pris'kus), **Helvidius.** Roman patriot; son-in-law of Thrasea Paetus. He was exiled by Nero, and again by Vespasian, who put him to death for his fanatic republicanism. He was quaestor in Achaea under Nero, trib-

une of the people in 56 A.D., and later praetor (70).

Privernum (prī-vėr'num). In ancient geography, a town of C Italy, about 47 miles SE of Rome. It was an ancient Volscian town. About the time when Aeneas landed in Italy, Metabus, the tyrant of the town, was expelled from it because of his tyranny. His daughter Camilla was forced to flee with him. The modern town near the ancient site is Priverno.

Probus (prō'bus), **Marcus Valerius.** Roman scholar and critic, born at Berytus in Syria; fl. in the late 1st century A.D. His work was devoted to study of republican Roman authors and to critical commentary on the Roman poets.

Prochoös (prō'kọ-os). In Greek antiquity, a small vase of elegant form, resembling the oinochoë, but in general more slender, and with a handle rising higher above the rim: used especially to pour water on the hands before meals were served (and also to pour from for libations).

Prochyta (prok'i-ta̯). Ancient name for Procida, an island at the entrance of the Bay of Naples.

Procida (prô'chē-dä). [Ancient name, **Prochyta.**] Island at the entrance of the Bay of Naples, about 13 miles SW of Naples, belonging to the province of Napoli, Italy. The surface is rocky and volcanic.

Proclea (prō-klē'a̯). In Greek legend, the first wife of Cycnus of Colonae. She was the mother of Tenes and Hemithea.

Procles (prō'klēz). According to Spartan tradition, a son of Aristodemus. He was the twin of Eurysthenes. Because their father died while they were still infants, the Spartans wished to make one of them king but did not know which was the older. On the advice of the oracle of Delphi they made the twins co-kings, and ever after Sparta had two kings. But because they observed their mother as she tended her children, they decided that Eurysthenes was the first-born, because his mother always bathed and nursed him first, so they honored him more than Procles. Procles' line was thus the junior line of the two royal Spartan houses. His son, Soüs, had a son Eurypon, who was so renowned for his deeds that the descendants of Procles were called after him "Euryponti-dae."

---

actǫr; up, lūte, pu̇ll; oi, oil; ou, out; ᴛʜ, then; ḍ as d or j, ş as s or sh, ţ as t or ch, ᶎ as z or zh.

Procne (prok'nē). In Greek legend, a daughter of Pandion, king of Athens. She was the sister of the twins Butes and Erechtheus, and of Philomela. Her father gave her to Tereus, king in Thrace, in marriage, as a reward to Tereus for his aid in defeating the enemies of Pandion. Their wedding was not blessed by the Graces nor by Hera, but the people of Thrace rejoiced at the marriage of their king, and were delighted when a son, Itys, was born to the royal couple. After five years, Procne longed to see her sister and Tereus went to Athens to fetch Philomela for a visit. Pandion yielded to the pleas of Philomela and to the even more ardent ones of Tereus, who had fallen in love with his wife's sister on sight but did not betray himself, and consented to let Philomela go to Thrace with her brother-in-law. The voyage went well, but when they landed Tereus, true to the violence for which the Thracians were noted, could no longer restrain his feelings. He ravished Philomela. She begged him to slay her, as she could not bear to face her sister after such a double betrayal, and when Tereus refused, she vowed vengeance. To silence her, Tereus cut out her tongue and imprisoned her. He returned to Procne and told her that Philomela had died on the voyage. In her prison Philomela wove a tapestry on which was pictured the whole story of her ravishment, maiming, and imprisonment by Tereus. She sent the tapestry by a servant as a gift to the queen, her sister. Procne examined the tapestry and read in it the story of the wrongs that had been done her sister and herself. In secret she went to the house where Philomela was imprisoned and was reunited to her. The sisters returned to the palace secretly and planned their revenge on Tereus. Equally maddened by the faithlessness and crimes of Tereus, the two sisters murdered the child Itys, Procne's son, cut up his flesh, cooked it and served it to Tereus. After he had eaten Procne told him of what his banquet had consisted, and at the same moment confronted him with Philomela. The grief and horror which Tereus knew at the fearsome death of his son temporarily stunned him and the sisters fled. Tereus was then consumed by a bloodthirsty rage. He pursued Procne and Philomela, and was about to kill them near Daulis, when suddenly the gods transformed Procne into a nightingale, whose song is eternally of grief for her son. Philomela was changed into a swallow, and Tereus became a hoopoe, forever pursuing her. In some Latin versions of the myth, the roles of the sisters, or of the birds into which they were transformed, were reversed.

Proconnesus (prō-kon̯-nē'sus). [Modern name, **Marmara.**] Island in the W part of the Propontis. It has marble quarries, for which it has been noted since ancient times. Area, about 50 square miles.

Proconsul (prō-kon'sul). In ancient Rome, an officer who discharged the duties and had, outside of Rome itself, most of the authority of a consul, without holding the office of consul. The proconsuls were almost invariably persons who had been consuls, so that the proconsulship was a continuation, in a modified form, of the consulship. They were appointed to conduct a war in or to administer the affairs of some province. The duration of the office was one year.

Procris (prō'kris). In Greek legend, a daughter of Erechtheus, king of Athens, and the sister of Orithyia. She was married to Cephalus and loved him deeply. He was carried off by Eos, the goddess of Dawn, and returned to Procris in disguise to test her fidelity. After many protestations of love and the offerings of rich gifts, Procris, who had been grieving for her husband, yielded. Cephalus immediately denounced her, revealed himself, and deserted her. According to some accounts, she fled from Athens and forswore the company of men, devoted herself to hunting as a companion of Artemis. Artemis gave her a marvelous hound, Laelaps, that could not fail to catch his quarry, and a spear that always hit its target. Others say Procris fled to Crete after Cephalus deserted her, and there she was seduced by King Minos, and that it was he who gave her the hound and the spear, which he had received from Artemis. She later joined Cephalus on a hunting expedition, disguised as a beautiful youth, Pterelas, and agreed to give him the hound and the spear, but only for love. Cephalus accepted this proposal and she then revealed herself as his wife. The couple was happily reunited and spent some years in devotion to each other. But

Artemis was displeased by the manner in which her gifts were being handed around. She caused Procris to suspect that Cephalus was still meeting a lover in secret. She had overheard him calling on a breeze to cool him, and thinking it was a lover he summoned, she jealously followed him on one of his hunting trips. As she spied on him from a thicket the bushes which hid her moved; Cephalus, thinking the movement was caused by a wild beast, hurled his spear and transfixed her. Her spirit fled to the Underworld, where Odysseus saw her when he visited there on his way home from the Trojan War.

Procris. In Greek legend, the eldest daughter of Thespius, king of Thespiae, and Megamede. By Heracles, who had come to Thespiae to hunt a lion, she was the mother of twin sons.

Procrustes (prō-krus′tēz). In Greek legend, an outlaw who lived near the road to Athens, in Attica. It was his custom to offer hospitality to travelers. He had a bed (named for him the Procrustean bed) which he insisted his guests use. Those who were too short he stretched on a rack to fit it, and those who were too long had their legs sawed off to the proper length. Some say he had two beds; one short which he offered to tall travelers, then cut off their legs to fit it; and one long on which he stretched short travelers. Theseus, who passed his house on his way to Athens, killed him. He was also known under the names of Damastes, Polypemon, and Procoptas. He was the father of Sinis, the "Pine-bender."

Proculus Julius (prō′kū-lus jū′li-us). In Roman legend, a citizen to whom Romulus appeared in a vision shortly after he had been carried off to heaven by the lightning. He told Proculus, "My Rome shall be the capital of the world; so let the Romans cherish the art of war, and let them know and teach their children that no human strength can resist Roman arms." After saying this, Romulus departed on high. Proculus reported the vision to the Roman people and thus assured them that Romulus had become immortal.

Prodicus (prod′i-kus). Greek sophist and rhetorician. He was a native of the island of Ceos, and was active in the second half of the 5th century B.C. He spent much time at Athens, as an ambassador from Ceos, and was a friend of Euripides and a contemporary of Socrates. In his lectures he laid great emphasis on the proper discrimination of synonyms. It was Prodicus who told the story of Heracles at the crossroads, faced with a choice between two women, one of whom represented Pleasure, the other Virtue. Heracles, according to the fable, chose Virtue. The fable is preserved in Xenophon's *Memorabilia*.

Prodromia (prō-drō′mi-a). Epithet of Hera, meaning "Pioneer." The name was given to the goddess by Phalaces, son of Temenus, because he said Hera guided him on the road to Sicyon, where he later raised a temple of Hera Prodromia.

Proetus (prō-ē′tus). In Greek legend, a son of Abas, king of Tiryns in Argolis. He and his twin Acrisius fought in their mother's womb and continued the struggle ever afterwards. Proetus violated Acrisius' daughter, Danaë, lost control of the throne to his brother, and fled to Iobates, king of Lycia. Iobates gave him his daughter Antia in marriage and helped him to win back Tiryns from Acrisius, which Proetus then turned into a fortress with the aid of the Gasterocheires. Proetus and Antia had three daughters: Iphianassa, Iphinoë, and Lysippe, who were driven mad for offending either Dionysus or Hera. Melampus offered to cure them but Proetus thought the price—a part of his kingdom—too high. Then all the women of Tiryns went mad and Proetus was forced to use, and pay for, Melampus' services to cure them. Bellerophon fled to the court of Proetus and was hospitably received by him. However, Antia fell in love with Bellerophon and when he spurned her advances she accused him falsely of making love to her against her will and demanded his death. Proetus feared to offend the gods by killing one to whom he had offered hospitality so he sent Bellerophon to Antia's father, Iobates, with a secret message instructing Iobates to kill Bellerophon. Proetus had a son, Megapenthes, who succeeded him as ruler of Tiryns.

Promachorma (prō-ma-kôr′ma). Epithet of Athena, meaning "Protectress of the Anchorage." There was a sanctuary of Athena Promachorma at Buporthmus (*Ox-ford*), on the promontory of Argolis, near Hermione.

Promachus (prom'a̱-kus) or **Promachos** (prom'-a̱-kos). A diety, as Athena or Apollo, who fights before some person, army, or state, as a protector or guardian. In art and archaeology the type is distinguished by the attitude of combat, often with upraised shield and the spear or other weapon extended threateningly. Also, an epithet of Athena, meaning, "the Defender."

Promachus. Named by Homer in the *Iliad* as a Boeotian leader. He was slain by Acamas, son of Antenor, as he stooped to strip the armor from Archelochus, brother of Acamas, whom he had just killed.

Promachus. In Greek legend, a son of Parthenopaeus the Arcadian. He was one of the Epigoni who successfully marched against Thebes to avenge their fathers.

Prometheus (prō̲-mē'thē̲-us). In Greek mythology, a Titan, the son of Iapetus and the nymph Clymene, or as some say, the son of Themis, who revealed the secrets of the future to him. His brothers were Epimetheus, Atlas, and Menoetius, all of whom suffered at the hands of Zeus. He was the father of Deucalion, king of Phthia, and warned him that Zeus was going to send a flood to destroy mankind; he advised Deucalion to build an ark to save himself and his wife. When the Titans waged war on the Olympian gods, Prometheus, who knew what the outcome would be, took the side of Zeus, after the Titans had scorned his advice, and helped him to defeat the Titans and make himself king. According to some accounts it was Prometheus who split the skull of Zeus so that Athena, fully armed, could spring from his head. She taught Prometheus many arts and these he passed on to man. Some say Prometheus created man by forming an image from the clay and water of Phocis, into which Athena then breathed life. He caused man, alone of the animals, to walk erect and lift his head to the sun and the stars. He taught men the use of numbers and letters, how to build ships and sail the seas, how to cultivate the fields and tame beasts to work for them; all human arts come from Prometheus. When Zeus was firmly in power he took no thought for mankind and would have blotted out the race of men altogether. Only Prome-

theus interceded for man and Zeus relented. Prometheus was once called upon to judge which parts of a sacrificial animal should be reserved to the gods and which to men. He cut up a bull and placed all the flesh into one bag, made of the bull's hide. But on top of the good flesh he laid the stomach of the bull, the least appetizing part of the animal. In a second bag he placed all the picked bones of the animal, but disguised the fact that there were only bones in the bag by covering them with a layer of rich

PROMETHEUS
Black-figured Cyrenaic vase, 6th century
B.C. *Vatican*

fat. He asked Zeus to choose one of the two bags. The one chosen would contain the parts reserved for the gods in a sacrifice. Zeus, either because he was duped, or because he wished an excuse to punish men, chose the bag containing the bare bones, and henceforth bones wrapped in fat were offered the gods in sacrifices. But Zeus was angered by this successful deception and decreed that though men would have the flesh of the animals they would have to eat it raw, as he would now withhold the gift of fire from mankind. Prometheus, ever pitying mankind's vulnerable state, stole fire from heaven and, carrying it in a fennel reed, gave it to

fat, fāte, fär, fãre, errạnt; net, mē, hẽr ardẹnt; pin, pīne; not, nōte, mŏve, nôr,

man. Zeus counterbalanced this great bene-fit by sending Pandora, the first mortal woman, to Prometheus' brother, Epimetheus, for a wife. Prometheus warned his brother not to accept any gift from Zeus, but Epimetheus married her anyway. Zeus punished Prometheus for stealing the divine fire by ordering Hephaestus to bind him in fetters to a rock in the Caucasus forever. Prometheus, bound to his lonely rock, proclaimed that Destiny had declared his ultimate deliverance and that Zeus would one day be dethroned because of a foolish marriage, even as he himself had dethroned his father Cronus. Prometheus said he knew all these things from his mother. (His name means "forethought".) Zeus sent Hermes to learn from Prometheus what marriage would cause his downfall, so that he could avoid it, but Prometheus, defiant even in chains, refused to reveal his secret. To add to his torment Zeus hurled the rock to which he was chained into Tartarus and sent an eagle which daily tore at Prometheus' liver (which was nightly restored). For 1000 years, or as some say, 30, Prometheus hung on his rock in torment. Heracles came to the Caucasus, where the rock had now emerged, after one of his labors, and begged Zeus to free Prometheus. Zeus was willing to do so because Prometheus had warned Zeus in time not to marry the Nereid Thetis, as she would bear a son greater than his father. But Prometheus could not be freed until some other immortal would go to Tartarus in his place. Chiron, doomed to eternal suffering because he had been accidentally wounded by one of Heracles' poisoned arrows, gladly gave up his immortality to end his own and Prometheus' sufferings. Zeus consented to this exchange but decreed that Prometheus must eternally wear a ring, containing a stone of the rock to which he had been chained, to show that he had been a prisoner. This was the first instance of a ring being worn. Heracles shot the eagle which had tormented Prometheus, and he was set free. To honor Prometheus, men began to wear rings, as he was compelled to do, and wreaths, because he was ordered to crown himself with a willow wreath when he was freed. Zeus set the arrow with which Heracles killed the eagle among the stars as the constellation Sagitta.

Prometheus went back to Olympus and resumed his role as adviser to the gods. He was honored with an altar, shared by Hephaestus, and an annual torch race in Athens.

Prometheus Bound. A tragedy by Aeschylus, of uncertain date. It is the first of a trilogy, the other two parts of which, *Prometheus Unbound* and *Prometheus the Fire-bearer,* have been lost. In this trilogy Aeschylus treats the legend of the Titan Prometheus who pitied frail and vulnerable man and gave him the precious gift of fire to improve his pitiable state. In stealing fire and giving it to man Prometheus defied a law of heaven and incurred the wrath of Zeus. *Prometheus Bound* tells of the awful punishment which Zeus visited on Prometheus for his defiance and of the manner in which Prometheus, continuing to defy Zeus, met his punishment.

The scene is a rocky gorge in Scythia. Cratus (Power) and Bia (Force) enter, carrying Prometheus as a captive. They are accompanied by Hephaestus. Cratus turns Prometheus over to Hephaestus to bind in chains. Hephaestus is reluctant to fetter one of his fellow gods but dares not defy Zeus, yet he regrets the cruelty of Zeus that demands such a punishment. Cratus and Bia urge Hephaestus, whose own fire Prometheus has stolen, to use his craft and not delay any more; he must carry out his orders, for only Zeus is free. Hephaestus forges the fetters and binds Prometheus to the lonely rock, lamenting that his art is, for the first time, used to bring harm rather than good; he groans for Prometheus' sufferings, but does as he is commanded to do by Zeus, and leaves. Cratus taunts the now immobilized Prometheus, asking him if the mortals for whom he stole divine fire will now help him, and then departs. Throughout this prologue Prometheus scorns to speak to the minions of Zeus. Now alone in the silence of the gorge he calls all nature to witness what he suffers at the hands of another god. He recalls how he stole fire and hid it in a reed to give it to men, and charges that Zeus has become his enemy because he loved mankind too well. A chorus of Oceanids enters, drawn in a winged car. They say they heard the sound of iron being forged and have come from their cavern in

actor; up, lūte, pull; oi, oil; ou, out; ᴛʜ, then; ḍ as d or j, ṣ as s or sh, ṭ as t or ch, ẓ as z or zh.

the ocean to learn the reason. They speak of Zeus as the new ruler who has brought new laws. Prometheus reveals that he knows of one who will try to unseat Zeus, and that Zeus will call upon him in vain to reveal the secret. The Oceanids observe that the calamity which has befallen Prometheus has not broken his spirit. He repeats that the pride of Zeus will be humbled, and that one day Zeus will ardently seek the friendship of Prometheus. The Oceanids ask why he is bound. He relates how he advised the Titans to accept Zeus but they scorned his advice. He took the side of Zeus and helped him to dethrone Cronus and become the ruler of the gods. But Zeus, once in power, took no thought for man and would have blotted out mankind altogether. Only Prometheus opposed the plan. He had mercy for mortals but could find none for himself. He gave mankind hope and fire and this is the reason for his punishment. The Oceanids conclude that Prometheus erred to defy the ruler of the gods, and advise him to seek release for his sufferings. He answers that he has acted with his eyes wide open: he knew in advance what the consequences would be. Oceanus enters and asks what he can do to help Prometheus. Prometheus bitterly asks if he has come to look upon his ruin, to see the friend who helped Zeus to a throne now suffering torments. Oceanus advises him to be more prudent in his language, lest Zeus overhear, and to use his cunning to seek some respite from his sufferings. He offers to intercede with Zeus. Prometheus reminds him of the fate of Atlas and Typhon, and speaks of the implacable anger of Zeus. He advises Oceanus to look after himself, and adds that he will only incur the wrath of Zeus if he interferes to help Prometheus. Oceanus, saying the calamity of Prometheus will be a lesson to him, departs. The chorus sings that the whole world laments for Prometheus. He answers by recalling his pity for mankind—all human arts, he says, come from Prometheus. He could be endlessly inventive for man but was not able to escape disaster for himself. To the chorus' statement that he should not care more for mortals than for himself he replies that Destiny, before whom even Zeus must bow, has

decreed his deliverance. He will not divulge his secret as the time has not yet come, but he knows that one day he will be freed from his present bondage. The chorus sings, offering a prayer that they may never offend Zeus. They chide Prometheus for not fearing Zeus enough and for honoring mortals too much, especially since feeble men can do nothing to help him in his present straits. Io, transformed into a heifer, enters, bewailing her miserable state. What has she done, she asks, that Zeus causes her to suffer so? She asks Prometheus who he is and why he is in chains. He tells her, and agrees to tell her what he knows of her future, though "loth to bruise her heart." But first the Oceanids want to hear Io's story. She tells of the sufferings she has endured at the will of heaven: how she confessed to her father Inachus the dreams she had of being wooed by Zeus, and how her father, after consulting the oracle at Delphi, drove her into exile lest he incur the anger of Zeus. Then she was transformed into her present shape of a heifer and was driven by a gadfly to wander over the earth, ever pursued by the shade of Argus. Now she wants to know what is to come, no matter how terrible it is. Prometheus tells her that Hera has more evils in store for her: she will be driven into Asia. She longs to die. They cannot die, Prometheus says, and he will know no relief until Zeus loses his supremacy. He assures Io that this will happen, and it will come about through Zeus' own folly. He will take a bride whose son will be mightier than the god, and unless Prometheus is freed this son will dethrone Zeus. He tells Io she will wearily journey until she arrives at the Nile delta. There she will establish her home and her family. Zeus will gently touch her and she will bear Epaphus, who will become lord of the region. He prophesies the flight of the 50 Danaids, descendants of Epaphus, to Argos, and tells that one of the 50 will spare her husband on the wedding night, when her sisters kill their bridegrooms, and that from this one a royal race will rise in Argos that will produce Prometheus' deliverer. All this, he says, he has learned from his mother Themis. Io, driven by the gadfly, departs in despair. The chorus sings a prayer that they will never be loved by any one outside their station, after seeing the misery it has brought to Io. Prometheus again declares that Zeus will be humbled, and only he knows how to prevent the disaster to Zeus. When the irresistible champion comes, Zeus will find out what a difference there is between ruling and being a slave. The leader of the chorus advises Prometheus to be more discreet in his words, lest Zeus contrive even worse torments for him. Prometheus answers that he is fated not to die, and is prepared for anything. Hermes, the "lackey of Zeus," now enters. He has come to find out what marriage it is that will bring about the dethronement of Zeus. Prometheus tells him to trudge back the road he came; he is not going to reveal his secret and he would not exchange his hard lot for Hermes' menial one. Prometheus continues to mock Hermes, and refuses to reveal the knowledge that will prevent Zeus from being overthrown. Prometheus' pride is undiminished by his sufferings. Hermes warns him of further tortures, of the lightning and of the eagle that will gnaw at his vitals. The leader of the chorus cautions Prometheus to abandon his pride and accept wise counsel. Prometheus answers that he knows all that is to come, and Zeus, no matter what he does, cannot destroy Prometheus. Hermes thinks his mind is unhinged. He warns the chorus to leave before Zeus looses the lightning, and departs. Lightning flashes, thunderbolts split the rock on which Prometheus is chained. The chorus scatters. As an additional punishment for refusing to disclose his secret Prometheus sinks slowly down to Tartarus through the chasm opened by the lightning, crying out to Mother Earth to witness the wrongs he endures at the hands of Zeus.

Prometheus, Charm of. According to Greek legend, a plant or flower that rose from the ground where the drops of ichor fell from Prometheus as the eagle gnawed at his liver. This herb conferred invulnerability on the person and weapons that were anointed with it. The invulnerability lasted for one day. Medea gave an ointment of it to Jason to protect him from the fire-breathing bulls which her father required him to yoke.

Pronaos (prō-nā'os). An open vestibule or portico in front of the naos or cella of a Greek temple.

Pronaus (prō-nā'us). Epithet of Athena, meaning "Of the Fore-temple." The image of Athena Pronaus on the Hill of Apollo, near the Ismenus River at Thebes, was made by Scopas.

Pronoea (prō-nē'a) or **Pronoia** (-noi'a). Epithet of Athena, meaning "Forethought." Croesus, king of Lydia, sent rich gifts to the temple of Athena Pronoea at Delphi.

Pronuba (prō'nö-ba). An epithet of Juno applied to her in her role as the goddess who presides over marriage.

Propertius (prō-pèr'shus), **Sextus.** Roman elegiac poet, born at Assisi, in Umbria, Italy, between 54 and 48 B.C.; died after 16 B.C. He lost his father at an early age, and lost his estates, 42 B.C., when the land was given to the Roman veterans. Nevertheless, enough remained of his patrimony to educate him. He went to Rome, c34 B.C., and later spent some time at Athens in furtherance of his studies. He began to write at an early age. Many of his love poems concern his passion for his mistress Hostia, who appears as Cynthia in the poems, and who shared his interest in literature and encouraged him to develop his poetic powers. The intimate relationship between Propertius and Hostia began in 28 B.C. and lasted, with various eruptions of jealousy on both sides, storms and reconciliations, until 23 B.C. During this time Propertius published the first of his four books of poetry and dedicated it to his mistress. His work was immediately recognized and he came to the attention of Maecenas, who became his patron. This association brought him into contact with other writers, notably Vergil and Ovid, who became his friends. The affair with Hostia, which suffered a definite break in 23 B.C., may have been resumed. Even after her death he wrote of her. Propertius is presumed to have died young, as the last of his work dates from 16 B.C. His poems, many of which deal with his love for Cynthia and his own melancholy thoughts, and a few of which deal with the events of his day, are noted for their richness of imagination, the ardor of his passion, his awareness and love of beauty, and by his unusual use of his wide vocabulary. He has been ranked next to

Catullus as the poet of the transports and torments of the passion of love.

Propoetides (prọ-pọ-ē'ti-dẹz). In mythology, maidens of Amathus, in Cyprus. They flagrantly denied the divinity of Aphrodite. To punish them Aphrodite caused them to become wantons, and later they were turned into stone. Some say it was the sight of these women and their immoral lives that made Pygmalion decide to remain a bachelor, and to carve a statue of a woman who would be free from their faults.

Propontis (prọ-pon'tis). [Modern name, **Sea of Marmara** or **Marmora**.] Sea communicating with the Euxine Sea on the NE by the Thracian Bosporus, and with the Aegean Sea on the SW by the Hellespont. Length, about 170 miles; greatest width, about 50 miles.

Propylaea (prop-i-lē'ạ). Monumental gateway to the Acropolis at Athens, begun 437 B.C. by Mnesicles. It consists of a central ornamented passage and two projecting wings, that on the N with a chamber (the Pinacotheca) behind its small portico. The central passage has on both W and E faces a magnificent hexastyle Doric portico. At about two thirds of its length it is crossed by a wall pierced with five doorways, the widest and highest in the middle. An inclined way passes through the wider middle intercolumniations of both great porches and the large central door; this way was flanked between the W portico and the door by six tall Ionic columns, whose capitals supply the most beautiful type of the order.

Propylaeum (prop-i-lē'um). An important architectural vestibule or entrance to a sacred inclosure or other precinct, as that of the Acropolis of Athens, or that of the sanctuary of Eleusis; usually in the plural: *propylaea.* In its origin it was a strongly fortified gateway, but it became developed into an ornamental structure, often elaborate and magnificent, with which were combined gates of more or less defensive strength.

Prosclystius (pros-klis'ti-us). Name given to Poseidon, meaning "Flooder," because he flooded a large part of Argolis when the river-gods awarded the land to Hera instead of to him. Hera persuaded him to send the sea back, and the Argives erected a sanctuary to him at the spot where the tide ebbed.

Proserpina (prọ-sėr'pi-nạ). Latin form of **Persephone.**

Prostaterius (pros-tạ-tē'ri-us). An epithet of Apollo, meaning "Protecting." In the sanctuary of Apollo Prostaterius at Megara there were images of Apollo, Artemis, and Leto by Praxiteles.

Protagoras (prọ-tag'ọ-rạs). Dialogue of Plato; the narration by Socrates of a conversation which took place in the house of Callias, a wealthy Athenian, between himself, the Sophists Protagoras, Hippias, and Prodicus, Hippocrates, Alcibiades, and Critias. The theme of this celebrated dialogue is virtue, its nature, unity, and teachableness; it is also a study of the sophistic teachers in the person of one of their best representatives, the famous Protagoras of Abdera. It closes with the well-known conclusion of Socrates that virtue is knowledge.

Protagoras of Abdera (ab-dir'ạ). Greek Sophist, born c485 B.C. at Abdera, in Thrace; died c411 B.C. He was the earliest of the class of teachers called Sophists who accepted payment for his teachings. He traveled throughout Greece teaching, but spent a great deal of time at Athens, where he was acquainted with the leading men of his day, among them the poet Euripides who was his good friend. He was highly esteemed for his learning. At the request of Pericles, with whom he is said to have spent an entire day arguing various theories of punishment, he drew up the laws for the new colony of Thurii (444 B.C.). In his teaching Protagoras took as his point of departure a belief that man has an inherent sense of justice, that the soul (or psyche or character) can be shaped by education, and that social and political virtue can be taught. His tools were grammar (which he systematized by distinguishing the parts of speech), rhetoric, music, and poetry. The last two were to bring the soul into the harmony and rhythm essential for the attainment of virtue. The education of the soul, as distinct from education in certain techniques that might be learned once and for all, was considered by Protagoras to be a lifelong process. In the last years of his life he wrote a treatise *On the Gods,* that began as follows, "In regard to the gods I cannot know that they exist, nor yet that they do not exist; for many things hinder such knowledge—the obscurity of the matter, and the shortness of human life." He was charged with impiety because of this work, although in it he did not deny the existence of the gods, and fled from Athens. On his way to Sicily he was lost at sea. Protagoras is best known from his famous dictum on the relativity of all knowledge, "Man is the measure of all things; of those which are, that they are; of those which are not, that they are not."

Protesilaus (prō-tes-i-lā′us). In Greek legend, a son of Iphiclus (whose impotence was cured by Melampus), and an uncle of Philoctetes He and his brother Podarces came from Phylace to join the Greeks in the war against Troy. According to a prophecy, the first man to set foot on Trojan ground was destined to be killed. Protesilaus, who some say knew of the prophecy, was the first to leap ashore and was killed, either by Hector or by Euphorbus. He was buried in Thracian Chersonese and was awarded divine honors. Nymphs planted a grove about his barrow, and it is said that the leaves of the trees which faced Troy withered rapidly and fell to the ground, whereas the leaves on the trees away from Troy stayed green all winter. Protesilaus was married to Laodamia, daughter of Acastus (others say his wife was Polydora, daughter of Meleager), and when she learned of his death she grieved so that the gods permitted him to return from the Underworld for three hours to visit her. He used this time to urge her to follow him to the Underworld, and when the time came for his departure she committed suicide.

Proteus (prō′tē-us, prō′tūs). In classical mythology, an oracular sea-god, the son of Oceanus and Tethys, who had the power of assuming different shapes. If caught, however, and held fast through all his many changes until he reassumed his own shape, he was compelled to answer questions. With the help of Idothea, daughter of Proteus, Menelaus disguised himself in a seal skin and caught Proteus when he took his daily nap among his seals on the island of Pharos in the Nile Delta. He forced Proteus to tell him how he could escape from Pharos, where he was becalmed on his way home from Troy, and to tell him what had happened to the Ajaxes, Agamemnon, and Odysseus. Aristaeus also overcame Proteus on his island home,

and forced him to tell him why his bees sickened and died.

Proteus. According to Euripides, a king of Egypt who lived on the island of Pharos. He married Psamathe, widow of Aeacus, and by her was the father of Theoclymenus and the prophetess Theonoë. In one version of his story, he kept and protected Helen when she was wafted to Egypt from Sparta, while a phantom Helen went with Paris to Troy.

Prothoënor (prō-thō-ē′nôr). Named by Homer (*Iliad*) as a son of Areïlycus. He was a leader of the Boeotians at the siege of Troy, and was felled by Polydamas when the Trojans attacked the fortifications protecting the Greek ships.

Protogenes (prō-toj′e-nēz). Greek painter; born at Caunus, in Caria, Asia Minor (or at Xanthus in Lycia); fl. in the second half of the 4th century B.C. He spent most of his life at Rhodes. He was noted for the care and time he spent on each of his paintings, and is said to have put four layers of paint on some of his works so that if the first layer wore off the next would replace it. Among his most famous works was the *Ialysus,* of which the subject was the hero who founded the town that bore his name on Rhodes. Protogenes is said to have spent seven years in completing the picture. It was at Rhodes for at least 200 years, then was carried off to Rome and placed in the Temple of Peace, where it perished when the temple was destroyed by fire. Another of his famous works was the *Resting Satyr* on which he worked at Rhodes all during the siege of the city by Demetrius Poliorcetes (305–304 B.C.), regardless that the garden in which he worked was in the midst of the enemy camp. It is said that Demetrius, on learning of the artist's presence, took measures to protect him and his work. He also had paintings in the Propylaea and the Bouleterium at Athens. It is said that Protogenes was a poor and self-taught man, whose great skill and art went unrecognized until Apelles, his great contemporary, publicly and generously expressed his admiration for them.

Protogenia (prō″tō-je-nī′a) or **Protogenea** (-ē′a). According to some accounts, the daughter of Deucalion and Pyrrha. She was the first woman to be born after the great flood that Zeus sent on the world and from which only

---

actor; up, lūte, pull; oi, oil; ou, out; ᵺ, then; d̦ as d or j, ş as s or sh, ț as t or ch, z̧ as z or zh.

Deucalion and Pyrrha survived. Her name means "First-born." Some say she was the mother, by Zeus, of Aëthlius, the first king of the land that came to be known as Elis.

Protogonia (prō″tō-gō-nī′a̞). In Greek legend, a daughter of Erechtheus, king of Athens, and his wife Praxithea. When her sister, Otionia (or Chthonia), was sacrificed to bring victory to Athens, in the war with the Eleusinians, Protogonia fulfilled a vow and killed herself.

Provincia (prō-vin′shi-a̞, -sha̞). [Also: **Gallia Provincia, Provincia Gallica**.] In ancient geography, the part of Gaul conquered by the Romans at the end of the 2nd century B.C. It corresponded originally to the later Provence, Dauphiné, and Languedoc.

Prylis (prī′lis). In Greek legend, a seer. He was the son of Hermes and a nymph, and accompanied the Greeks to Troy. According to some accounts, it was he, inspired by Athena, who suggested the ruse of the Wooden Horse as a means of overcoming Troy.

Prytaneum (prit-a̞-nē′um). A public hall in ancient Greek states and cities, housing and typifying the common ritual or official hearth of the community. That of Athens is especially famous. In it the city extended hospitality both to her honored citizens and to strangers. The prytanes, or chief magistrates, were entertained in it at the public charge, together with those who, on account of personal or ancestral services, were entitled to this honor.

Prytanis (prit′a̞-nis). Named by Homer (*Iliad*), as one of the Lycian companions of Sarpedon. He was slain by Odysseus as he tried to protect Sarpedon, who had been taken off the field, wounded.

Psamathe (sam′a̞-thē). In Greek mythology, a daughter of Crotopus of Argos. Fearing her father's wrath, she exposed the infant Linus whom she had born to Apollo, but he was found and reared by shepherds. In his youth he was torn to pieces by dogs and Psamathe's intense grief over his death revealed that she was his mother. When Crotopus perceived this he condemned her to death. Apollo sent a monster to destroy the children of Argos in revenge, and withdrew his punishment only when a shrine had been erected between Argos and Delphi. The songs of mourning for Linus and Psamathe,

sung by the Argive women at Apollo's command, were sung annually at this shrine and became known as Linus songs.

Psamathe. In Greek mythology, a Nereid. She attempted to escape the attentions of Aeacus, who wished to marry her, by changing herself into a seal, but in vain. By Aeacus she was the mother of Phocus. She sent a fierce wolf against Telamon and Peleus, half-brothers of Phocus, to avenge their murder of her son. Thetis, sister of Psamathe, turned the wolf to stone. After the death of Aeacus Psamathe married Proteus, king of Egypt, and bore him Theoclymenus and Theonoë.

Pseudo-Smerdis (sö′dō-smėr′dis). See **Smerdis, False**.

Psiax (sī′aks). Attic vase-painter, active c520 B.C. Formerly called the Menon Painter, from an amphora (Philadelphia) made by the potter Menon, he was later identified by two vases signed by him as painter and by Hilinus as potter. Twenty-eight other vessels have been attributed to him. With the Andocides Painter, he was one of the earliest to use the red-figure style. Active when this style was beginning to replace black-figure, he worked in both, and sometimes used both on the same vessel.

Psophis (sō′fis). In ancient geography, a town in NW Arcadia. Some say it was founded by Psophis, a descendant of Lycaon. Others say Psophis was a daughter of Eryx, the despot of Sicania (Sicily). They say Heracles violated her, but refused to take her to his land. He left her with a friend (Lycortes), who lived at Phegia in Arcadia. The sons born to Psophis and Heracles—Echephron and Promachus—were brought up in Phegia, and when they grew up they changed the name of the place to Psophis after their mother. They also established a sanctuary of Erycine Aphrodite in Psophis. Alcmaeon, son of Amphiaraus, fled here after killing his mother. He married the daughter of King Phegeus, but was forced to flee again by order of the oracle of Delphi. Later he returned and was murdered by the sons of Phegeus. His tomb was in Psophis; surrounding it were great cypresses called "Maidens." Since they were sacred to him they were never cut down and reached gigantic height. Because of their enmity toward the Argives on account of Alcmaeon, the people of Psophis took no part in the Trojan War. The river Erymanthus, near which Heracles slew the Erymanthian Boar, runs through Psophis. Nearby was a temple of Erymanthus containing an image of the river-god.

Psyche (sī'kē). In Greek mythology, a mortal maiden, beloved by Eros, the god of love, who after long tribulation and suffering was accorded her place among the gods as the equal of her god consort. Psyche as personification of the soul came into Greek mythology in the 4th–5th centuries B.C. Psyche as soul symbolized by a butterfly first appeared in the 5th century B.C. Before this the soul was conceived of and depicted either as a bird or as the spirit-double of the individual. For the myth, see **Cupid and Psyche.**

Psychopompus (sī″kō-pom'pus). An epithet of Hermes as the conductor or guide of souls or spirits to the Underworld.

PSYKTER
Red-figured, 5th century B.C.

Psykter (sik'tėr). A type of Greek vase used for cooling wine. The body is of conoid form, with short cylindrical neck and a somewhat tall cylindrical foot, adapted in form for insertion in the crater, and for standing on the table. It was sometimes supported on a tripod.

Psyttalia or **Psyttaleia** (sit-a-lī'a). An islet lying between Salamis and the mainland of Greece. With the Greek fleet anchored in the harbor at Salamis the Persians, planning a sea fight, sent a body of troops to Psyttalia, partly for the purpose of enclosing the Greeks and partly in the hope of destroying them as the wrecks of their fleet drifted to the island after the battle. In the event, the Persian fleet was beaten, and the Persian troops on Psyttalia were attacked and cut to pieces by the Greeks under the command of Aristides and totally destroyed (480 B.C.).

Pteleon (tel'e-on). Name which Cephalus assumed when he returned, in disguise, to his wife Procris after he had been carried off by Eos, the goddess of Dawn. In his guise as Pteleon, Cephalus tested his wife's fidelity.

Pterelas (ter'e-las). Name that Procris assumed when she appeared to Cephalus, disguised as a beautiful youth, to try and regain his love. It is said that when Cephalus leaped into the sea, he called the name "Pterelas," because it was under that name that his wife won back his love.

Pterelaus (ter-e-lā'us). In Greek legend, a son or grandson of Poseidon, who had provided him with one gold lock of hair which conferred immortality on Pterelaus. He was king of the Teleboans. With the Taphians he attacked Electryon's kingdom, killed his eight sons, and stole his cattle. Electryon's daughter Alcmene had been promised to Amphitryon, but she would not allow the marriage to be consummated until her brothers were avenged. Amphitryon therefore made war on Pterelaus. Comaetho, daughter of Pterelaus, saw Amphitryon and fell in love with him. To help him she plucked the golden lock from her father's head. Pterelaus died and Amphitryon achieved a crushing victory over the Taphians and Teleboans.

Pteria (tir'i-a). In ancient geography, a place in Cappadocia, Asia Minor: the modern Boğazkale, Turkey. It was the scene of a battle between Cyrus the Great and Croesus c554 B.C.

Ptolemaïs (tol-e-mā'is). In ancient geography, a city in Cyrenaica, W of Cyrene.

Ptolemaïs. [Also: **Ptolemaïs Theron.**] In ancient geography, a town on the W coast of the Red Sea.

actọr; up, lūte, pùll; oi, oil; ou, out; ᴛʜ, then; ḍ as d or j, ṣ as s or sh, ṭ as t or ch, ẓ as z or zh.

Ptolemy I (tol'e̯-mi) (of *Egypt*). [Surnamed **Soter,** meaning "Savior" or "Preserver," and **Lagi,** "Son of Lagus;" Latin, **Ptolemaeus.**] King of Egypt (306–285 B.C.), founder of the Greek dynasty in that country. He was born c367 B.C.; died 283 B.C. He was the alleged son of Lagus, a Macedonian of ignoble birth, and Arsinoë; but as Arsinoë had been the concubine of Philip II of Macedon, he was commonly supposed by his contemporaries to be the son of that monarch. He was one of Alexander the Great's most trusted generals, serving as one of those who guarded the king's person, and holding a place of high command. He accompanied Alexander throughout the Asiatic campaigns, of which he wrote a history. On the journey of Alexander to the oracle of Zeus Ammon in Libya, Ptolemy records as evidence of divine interest in Alexander that two snakes slithered along in front of the Macedonians to guide them through the trackless desert to the shrine, where the priest addressed Alexander as a son of Zeus. Ptolemy was one of those given a Persian princess, Artacama, for a bride at the great marriage festival celebrated by Alexander at Susa (324 B.C.), but after the event the princess seems to have disappeared from Ptolemy's history. In the distribution of the provinces on the death of Alexander in 323 B.C. Ptolemy obtained the government of Egypt. He managed to gain possession of Alexander's body and carried it off to Memphis until a suitably magnificent burial could be arranged. In so doing he incurred the enmity of Perdiccas, who had become regent of Asia. Ptolemy formed an alliance with Antipater against Perdiccas. He married Eurydice, daughter of Antipater, to strengthen the alliance but later put her aside in favor of his own half-sister Berenice. Perdiccas invaded Egypt in 321 B.C. but was murdered by his own troops. In the involved struggles of the Diadochi (the "successors" of Alexander) Ptolemy periodically invaded, won, and lost part of Syria; won, lost, and won Cyprus; subdued Cyrene; took Corinth, Megara, and Sicyon in Greece, but did not retain them. He afterward concluded an alliance with Cassander, Seleucus, and Lysimachus against Antigonus, who fell in the battle of Ipsus in 301 B.C. He assumed the title of king in

306 or 304. In 304 B.C. his efficient support of the Rhodians against Demetrius enabled them to repel his formidable attack, whence he received the surname Soter or Preserver from the Rhodians, who thereafter awarded him divine honors. During his reign Alexandria became the Egyptian capital; the library was founded by him and he made the city a place where scholars could work. He abdicated in 285 B.C., in favor of Ptolemy II, his son by Berenice.

Ptolemy II (of *Egypt*). [Surnamed **Philadelphus;** Latin, **Ptolemaeus.**] King of Egypt (285–246 B.C.); son of Ptolemy I. He was born in the island of Cos, 309 B.C., and died 246 B.C. He annexed Phoenicia and Coele-Syria, encouraged commerce, literature, science, and art, and raised the Alexandrian Museum and Library, founded by his father, to importance. He completed the Pharos, and is credited by ancient writers with authorizing the Bible translation known as the Septuagint, and the Egyptian history of Manetho.

Ptolemy III (of *Egypt*). [Surnamed **Euergetes,** meaning "Benefactor"; Latin, **Ptolemaeus.**] King of Egypt (246–221 B.C.); son of Ptolemy II, whom he succeeded in 246 B.C. He was born c282 B.C., and died 221 B.C. To avenge the murder of his sister Berenice in a dynastic intrigue, he invaded (c245) Syria and captured Babylon, but was recalled in 243 B.C. by a revolt in Egypt. He expanded the Egyptian fleet and gained control of the eastern Mediterranean, and further extended his domain by his marriage to Berenice of Cyrene.

Ptolemy IV (of *Egypt*). [Surnamed **Philopator,** meaning "Father-loving"; Latin, **Ptolemaeus.**] King of Egypt (221–203 B.C.); son of Ptolemy III. He was born c244 B.C., and died 203 B.C. He defeated Antiochus the Great at Raphia in 217 B.C., but in general he was an ineffective ruler; he held his throne by murdering several near relatives.

Ptolemy V (of *Egypt*). [Surnamed **Epiphanes,** meaning "Illustrious"; Latin, **Ptolemaeus.**] King of Egypt (203–181 B.C.); son of Ptolemy IV. He was born c210 B.C., and died 181 B.C. His dominions were overrun by Antiochus III, who had agreed to divide the Egyptian possessions with Philip V of Macedon, and saved only by the interference of Rome. He married Cleopatra, daughter of Antiochus, in the winter of 193–192 B.C., in accordance with a treaty of peace concluded with Antiochus some years previously. The Rosetta Stone commemorates his assumption of his majority in 196 B.C.

Ptolemy VI (of *Egypt*). [Surnamed **Philometor**, meaning "Mother-loving"; Latin, **Ptolemaeus**.] King of Egypt (181–145 B.C.); son of Ptolemy V. He was born c186 B.C., and died 145 B.C. The early years of his reign were a regency under his mother. He was captured during an invasion of Egypt by Antiochus IV, King of Syria, in 170 B.C., whereupon his younger brother Ptolemy VIII proclaimed himself king. He was presently released by Antiochus, and for a time reigned conjointly with his brother. Expelled by his brother, he sought relief in person at Rome in 164 B.C., and was reinstated at Alexandria, his brother being forced to retire to Cyrene, which he was allowed to hold as a separate kingdom. He supported Demetrius II in the struggle in Syria against Alexander Balas and was killed in the battle near Antioch that saw Demetrius' final triumph.

Ptolemy VIII (of *Egypt*). [Surnamed **Euergetes** (and called **Ptolemy Euergetes II**) or **Physcon**, meaning "Potbelly"; Latin, **Ptolemaeus**.] King of Egypt (170–116 B.C.). He was born c184 B.C.; and died 116 B.C. He was a younger brother of Ptolemy VI, on whose death in 145 B.C. he usurped the throne, putting to death the legitimate heir Ptolemy VII (surnamed Neos Philopator), and marrying the widowed queen, his sister. (For history previous to this event, see Ptolemy VI). He was expelled from Alexandria by the populace, who supported his wife, in 130 B.C. but recovered his capital in 127. His very evil reputation is probably due to his usurpation of the throne, the murder of the prince, and his later murder of his son by his sister, who would have succeeded him, and thus is well-founded. He married (c130 B.C.) his wife's daughter by her first husband, Ptolemy VI.

Ptolemy IX (of *Egypt*). [Surnamed **Lathyrus** or **Soter**, meaning "Savior," "Preserver"; called also **Ptolemy Soter II**; Latin **Ptolemaeus**.] King of Egypt (116–81 B.C.); son of Ptolemy VIII. He died in 81 B.C. On the death of his father he ascended the throne conjointly with his mother, Cleopatra. He was, in 108 B.C., expelled from Egypt by Cleopatra. He succeeded, however, in maintaining himself in Cyprus, which he held as an independent kingdom until the death of his mother in 88 B.C., when he was recalled by the Alexandrians. They had in the meantime expelled his brother, who had reigned as Ptolemy X.

Ptolemy X (of *Egypt*). [Called **Ptolemy Alexander I**; Latin, **Ptolemaeus**.] King of Egypt (108–88 B.C.); brother of Ptolemy IX; died 88 B.C. He was made joint ruler with his brother, and after his expulsion (108 B.C.) ruled alone. After his mother's death, he was attacked and deposed by Ptolemy IX, and was killed fighting against his brother in Cyprus.

Ptolemy XI (of *Egypt*). [Called **Ptolemy Alexander II**; Latin, **Ptolemaeus**.] King of Egypt (80 B.C.); son of Ptolemy X. He ruled after the death of his uncle, Ptolemy IX, having married the widow of his predecessor through the offices of the Roman Sulla. Ptolemy very shortly thereafter killed her and was murdered himself by an outraged mob (80 B.C.).

Ptolemy XII (of *Egypt*). [Surnamed **Neos Dionysus** or **Auletes**, meaning "Flute-player"; Latin, **Ptolemaeus**.] King of Egypt (80–51 B.C.); illegitimate son of Ptolemy IX. He died 51 B.C. He succeeded to the throne on the extinction of the legitimate line of the Ptolemies in 80 B.C. He was expelled by the populace in 58, but was restored by the Romans in 55 B.C.

Ptolemy XIII (of *Egypt*). [Latin, **Ptolemaeus**.] King of Egypt (51–47 B.C.); son of Ptolemy XII; died 47 B.C. He ascended the throne conjointly with his sister Cleopatra, whom he expelled in 49 B.C. The reinstatement of Cleopatra by Caesar in 48 B.C. gave rise to war. Ptolemy was defeated on the Nile, and was drowned in the flight.

Ptolemy XIV (of *Egypt*). King of Egypt (47–44 B.C.); brother of Cleopatra; died 44 B.C. For political reasons Julius Caesar had Cleopatra marry her adolescent younger brother, but she had him killed in order that her son by Caesar, Caesarion, might reign as Ptolemy XV.

Ptolemy (of *Mauretania*). King of Mauretania and last of the Ptolemaic line; son of Juba II

---

actor; up, lūte, pŭll; oi, oil; ou, out; ᴛʜ, then; ḏ as d or j, ş as s or sh, ṭ as t or ch, ẕ as z or zh.

and grandson of Antony and Cleopatra. He was summoned to Rome and put to death by Caligula (40 A.D.), whose cupidity had been excited by his great wealth.

Ptolemy. [Full Latin name, **Claudius Ptolemaeus.**] Alexandrian astronomer, geographer, and mathematician; born at Alexandria; fl. in the first half of the 2nd century A.D. His influence extended to the 17th century and was second only to that of Aristotle. His astronomic system is strictly geocentric: the sun, planets, stars, and heavens revolving about the earth; though it requires an intricate system to support his theory, the theory explains the phenomena Ptolemy knew. The Copernican system superseded it (16th and 17th centuries) because it was simpler, not because the Ptolemaic system was proved false. His greatest work, the *Mathematike Syntaxis* or *Megale Syntaxis* (Great Collection), summed up the achievement of Greek astronomy to his day; translated into Arabic (the *Almagest*), it greatly influenced Arab astronomical thought. He elaborated trigonometry to accommodate astronomy as a mathematical discipline, and catalogued 1028 stars. In his *Geographical Treatise* he first technically used the terms "parallel" and "meridian." He adopted Posidonius' incorrect estimate of the circumference of the earth; his overestimate in the extent in longitude of Eurasia was one of the factors of Columbus' discovery. Other works of which the Greek originals have not been recovered have survived in Arabic or in Latin translation. His recorded observations (at Canopus) extended from 127 to 151 A.D.

Ptoüs (tō'us). In Greek legend, a son of Athamas and Themisto, who gave his name to Mount Ptoüs in Boeotia. Near the mountain was a sanctuary of Ptoan Apollo. The oracle of the sanctuary never lied, and had the capability of answering in whatever tongue a question was put to it. During the Persian War Mardonius sent an envoy to consult the oracle and the answer was given, to the surprise of the Thebans who accompanied the Persian envoy, in Carian, the language of the envoy.

Publicola (pub-lik'ō-la). Name given to Publius Valerius, legendary Roman statesman and general of the 6th century B.C., who was renowned for his eloquence and his generosity. He was one of several prominent citizens who

sought to throw off the harsh rule of the Tarquins, and helped Lucius Junius Brutus to drive them out following the rape of Lucretia, wife of Tarquinius Collatinus, by the son of Tarquin the Proud. Following their expulsion, the Romans decided not to entrust their affairs to one leader but to divide the rule between two consuls. Valerius fully expected to be chosen as one of the consuls for his aid in driving out the Tarquins, and withdrew from public affairs in disappointment when Collatinus was chosen instead as the colleague of Brutus. However, he was one of the first of the senators to take the oath against the Tarquins, and swore to defend Roman liberty with his sword.

Tarquin sent envoys from Gabii, whither he had gone for refuge, to treat with the Romans, but Valerius barred their admission to the city. Next, Tarquin sent to say he resigned all claim to the throne, and asked only that his treasure be sent to him, that he and his dependents might not be in want. The Romans decided to cast out the treasure with the tyrant and admitted envoys to collect and dispose of his effects. The envoys used their time in Rome to conspire against the Republic. They met with members of the Aquilii and Vitelii families and wrote letters to Tarquin outlining a plot to kill the consuls and restore him as ruler of Rome. Some say they bound themselves to secrecy by drinking the blood of a human sacrifice. By chance, Vindicius, a slave in the house of the Aquilii, overheard their plot. Fearing that the consuls, both of whom were related to members of these two houses, would not believe him, he chose to go to Valerius, who was noted for his availability and for his justice. When Valerius heard of the plot he rushed to the house of the Aquilii with trusted aides and found the letters of which Vindicius had informed him. While he was still in the house the Aquilii returned and set upon him, but he successfully fought them, twisted their gowns around their necks, and dragged them to the Forum. Valerius produced Vindicius, an accusation was lodged, and the letters of the plotters were read. Among the conspirators were two sons of Brutus. Brutus handed them over to the lictors who put them to death for their crime against Rome; then Brutus withdrew from the Forum. Collatinus, the other consul, would have restored Vindicius to his masters and allowed the conspirators to depart from Rome. Valerius opposed him. He sent for Brutus, who returned to the Forum and called on the Roman people to pass judgment on the other conspirators; for, he said, he had already passed judgment on his own sons. The people put the matter to a vote and condemned the conspirators, and they were executed on the spot. Collatinus resigned the consulship and withdrew from the city. Valerius was elected consul in his place (509 B.C.). Vindicius was freed and made a citizen, the palace of Tarquin was razed and the Campus Martius, on which it stood, was rededicated to the god Mars.

However, Tarquin had not given up his intention of regaining power in Rome. He received aid from the Tuscans and approached Rome with a great force. The consuls led the Roman troops against them. Brutus and Aruns, son of Tarquin, killed each other in the battle; both sides sustained such losses that each thought itself defeated. The Romans were thoroughly disheartened. Valerius was uncertain what to do. In the night a divine voice issued from a nearby grove and proclaimed, "The Tuscans have lost one more man than the Romans." This inspirited the Romans and discouraged the Tuscans, most of whom thereupon withdrew; those who remained were taken prisoner by the Romans. When the dead were counted, it was found that there was one more Tuscan corpse than Roman. Valerius returned to Rome in a chariot drawn by four horses, pronounced the funeral oration of Brutus and buried him with honor, and was himself honored with a triumph. With the death of Brutus Valerius was the sole ruler, and soon the Romans complained that he exercised kingly power and lived royally in a palace on the hill. Informed of these criticisms, he hired workmen and ordered them to demolish his palace during the night. The Romans were pleased that he heeded their criticisms, but were saddened by the loss of so fine a palace; and they were ashamed that Valerius had no place to live but was compelled to go about from house to house among his friends. They gave him a piece of ground and built him a new, less magnificent, house. Sensible

of their fear of tyrants, he gave up many of the trappings of power, but such was the force and charm of his personality that the people obeyed him without question and he actually increased his personal power. To strengthen the Republic he brought the Senate, reduced in numbers by the Tarquins, up to strength. He promulgated liberal laws and revised the tax laws to make them more equitable and less onerous. To guarantee the public funds, he made the temple of Saturn the treasury and gave the people the right to elect two treasurers, or quaestors. And lastly, he ceased to rule alone: Marcus Horatius became his fellow consul. For his justice, his service to the Republic and to the Roman people, he was named Publicola, "The People's Respectful Friend."

Before Tarquin's second war against Rome, a prodigy occurred that greatly heartened the Romans. While still king he had begun the temple of Capitoline Jupiter, and had ordered artists of Veii to make a terra-cotta chariot to be placed atop it. Although he was driven out of Rome before the temple was completed, the artists went ahead and molded the chariot and set it in the fire to harden, whereupon it swelled to such a size that they could hardly withdraw it from the kiln. Soothsayers said this meant success for the people who possessed the chariot, and the Tuscans refused to give it to the Romans. Shortly afterward, in the course of games at Veii, the winner of the chariot-race was driving out of the arena. Suddenly his horses bolted, and in spite of his efforts to control them, they carried him off to Rome. The people of Veii were alarmed at this, and ordered the Tuscan artists to give up their earthen chariot to the Romans. Meanwhile, Tarquin had found assistance with Lars Porsena of Clusium, the most eminent and the most powerful ruler of Italy. He declared war on Rome and marched toward the city. Publicola, who was consul again, marched out to meet him. In the following battle Publicola received so many wounds he had to be carried from the field. The Romans retreated in dismay within their walls, leaving Horatius Cocles, with Titus Herminius and Spurius Lartius, to resist the Etruscans at the bridgehead. Horatius valiantly held back the Etruscans until the bridge behind him was destroyed, then leaped into the Tiber and swam to the city. The Etruscans laid siege to Rome. Publicola was eager to treat with the Etruscans but Tarquin arrogantly refused to have anything to do with him. This angered Lars Porsena. The Etruscan leader, it is said, was impressed by Mucius Scaevola, who secretly entered the Etruscan camp and, when caught, held his hand in the fire to demonstrate the valor of the Romans. Lars Porsena agreed to a parley with the Romans and peace was made. The Romans gave ten young men and ten virgins to the Etruscans as hostages; among the latter was Valeria, daughter of Publicola. One day the maidens were bathing in the river. Cloelia, one of them, swam across to freedom and urged the others to do the same. When his daughter appeared to him, Publicola was angry at the violation of the Roman pledge, and immediately returned her and the other maidens to the Etruscan camp. In the peace treaty, Lars Porsena showed great magnanimity to the Romans, who sent him a throne decorated with ivory as a token of their gratitude.

At a later time, many women of Rome were afflicted by a strange disorder; their children were either still-born or born deformed. Publicola consulted the Sibylline Books, sacrificed to Pluto, restored certain games, and, the gods being thus appeased, the unusual births no longer occurred.

Altogether, Publicola was consul four times. He won Appius Claudius, a powerful Sabine ruler, to the side of Rome. He gave him, and the 5000 men he brought with him, land in Rome, made them citizens, and gave Appius a seat in the Senate. The other Sabines considered Appius a traitor. They marched to Fidenae and prepared an ambush against the Romans. Publicola learned of it and put the Sabines to rout, and was honored with a triumph. He died soon afterward, full of years, greatly honored and loved, and having seen his work for the establishment of the Republic prosper. He was buried at the public expense in the city, an honor awarded only to those who had performed great services for their country, and was mourned by the women of Rome for a year.

Publilian Laws (pub-lil′i-an). In Roman history: 1) A law passed c471 B.C., through the efforts of the tribune Publilius Volero. It 'transferred the election of tribunes from the centuries to the *comitia tributa* (q.v. under **Comitia**), and its passage marked the concession of the right of initiating legislation to the plebeians. 2) Laws proposed by Publilius Philo c339 B.C. They provided that one censor must be a plebeian; that the *plebiscita* (laws passed by the comitia tributa) should apply to all citizens; and that laws presented to the centuries should be previously approved by the *curiae* (q.v. under **Comitia**).

Publilius (pub-lil′i-us). [Surnamed **Syrus**, meaning "the Syrian."] Latin writer of mimes; fl. in the 1st century B.C. He was born in Syria and was brought to Rome in his youth as a slave. He so charmed his Roman master by his intelligence and wit that he freed him and gave him a careful education. Publilius wrote mimes, short farcical presentations, and acted in them, winning great applause by the pieces themselves, his acting, and his clever improvisation. His works contained many pithy sayings that were later incorporated in the works of other writers and are the only examples of his work that survive. "Beneficium accipere, libertatem est vendere." (To accept a favor is to sell one's liberty.) "Necesse est multos timeat, quem multi timent." (He must fear many, whom many fear.) These are among the sayings of Publilius that have been preserved in a collection called *Sententiae* (Aphorisms).

Publius Aelius Hadrianus (pub′li-us ē′li-us hā-dri-ā′nus). Full Latin name of **Hadrian.**

Publius Cornelius Dolabella (kôr-nēl′yus dol-a-bel′a). See **Dolabella, Publius Cornelius.**

Publius Ovidius Naso (ō-vid′i-us nā′sō). Full Latin name of **Ovid.**

Pudicitia (pū-di-si′shi-a). In Roman mythology, the personification of Modesty or Chastity.

Punic Wars (pū′nik). [Also: **Carthaginian Wars.**] Three wars waged (264–241 B.C.; 218–201 B.C.; 149–146 B.C.) between Rome and Carthage, resulting finally in the total destruction not only of Carthaginian power, but also of Carthage itself. The First Punic War began in 264 B.C. Its nominal cause was the interference of the Romans in behalf of the Mamertines who were under siege at Messana (now Messina), Sicily, by Hiero of Syracuse.

Its actual cause was the inevitable, and irreconcilable, friction between the growing commercial ambitions of Rome, and the established position of Carthage as the chief trading community of the Mediterranean. The leading events were the following: naval battles of Mylae and Ecnomus; unsuccessful invasion of Africa by Regulus; battles of Panormus and Drepanum; campaigns of Hamilcar Barca (father of Hannibal) in Sicily; Roman naval victory (ending the war) at the Aegates (Aegadian Isles, now the Egadi Islands) in 241 B.C. By the peace, Carthage ceded western Sicily and paid a large indemnity. The seat of war was Sicily, Africa, and the Mediterranean. The Second Punic War began in 218 B.C. Its immediate cause was Hannibal's conquest of Saguntum (an ally of Rome) in 219 B.C. It was carried on in Spain, Italy, Sicily, and Africa. The following were the leading events: Hannibal's invasion of Italy after crossing the Alps in 218 B.C.; battles of Ticinus, Trebia, Lake Trasimenus, and Cannae; campaigns in Spain; conquest of Syracuse by Marcellus; invasion of Italy by Hasdrubal, defeated at the Metaurus; final defeat of Hannibal at Zama in 202 B.C. By the peace, 201 B.C., Carthage ceded possessions in Spain and the Mediterranean and paid a heavy tribute, Numidia became an ally of Rome, and the Carthaginian fleet was reduced. The chief commanders were Hannibal for Carthage and the elder Scipio Africanus and Fabius Maximus for Rome. The Third Punic War began in 149 B.C. Its nominal cause was the attack by Carthage on Massinissa. Carthage was besieged by land and sea by the younger Scipio Africanus, and was taken and destroyed in 146 B.C. The city of Carthage was destroyed with a thoroughness which was to have few, if any, parallels until the 20th century, when improved weapons made wholesale destruction somewhat easier than it was for the Romans. The site of the city was plowed, some say, and salt was sown in the furrows, that nothing might ever grow there again. Carthaginian territory was divided between Rome and Numidia.

Pupillus (pū-pil′us), **Orbilius.** See **Orbilius Pupillus.**

Puteoli (pū-tē′ọ̇-lī). [Modern name, **Pozzuoli.**] Ancient town in S Italy, situated on the Bay of Pozzuoli about seven miles W of Naples; commercial center for Rome's eastern trade and a fashionable villa resort. Founded by political refugees from the Greek island of Samos, c521 B.C., Puteoli became a Roman colony in 194 B.C. and developed into one of the greatest ports of Italy (it was the port of the town of Cumae), and a winter and seaside resort for wealthy Romans; it declined later in competition with the Roman port of Ostia. The site is noted for its Roman ruins, including harbor installations, amphitheater, houses, and temples (the so-called Temple of Serapis is really an ancient market-place).

Pyanepsia (pī-a-nep′si-a̱). In ancient Athens, an annual festival of Apollo, celebrated in the Attic month Pyanepsion (October-November). It had the character of a harvest feast, and was said to be called Pyanepsia from a dish of beans which was cooked and eaten at that time. As part of the celebration, an offering called the *Eiresione* was carried by a boy, both of whose parents were living, to the temple of Apollo. It consisted of a branch of olive or laurel bound with white and purple wool and hung with offerings of fruit, cakes, and pots of olive oil, wine, and honey. The boy was accompanied by a procession, and a song, also called Eiresione, was sung. At the temple the branch was deposited as an offering to the god. Similar branches were hung before the doors of houses, where they remained until they were replaced the following year at the time of the festival. The Pyanepsia later came to be associated with vows made by Theseus. He was supposed to have returned from Crete to Attica on the eighth day of Pyanepsion and to have cooked the few remaining provisions in one pot to feed his hungry crew. Therefore, on this day the Athenians went to the shore and cooked beans in pots to honor his memory. The Pyanepsia also honored the Horae.

Pyanepsion (pī-a-nep′si-on). The fourth month of the Attic year, corresponding to the last of October and the first of November. The feast of the Pyanepsia was held in this month.

Pydna (pid′na̱). In ancient geography, a town in Macedonia, situated near the Thermaic Gulf, about 30 miles SW of Thessalonica. It is notable for the victory gained near it in 168 B.C. by the Romans under Aemilius Paulus over the Macedonians under Perseus, causing the overthrow of the Macedonian monarchy.

Pygmalion (pig-mā′li-on). In Greek legend, a son of Belus, a marvelous sculptor, and a king of Cyprus. According to some, he was disgusted by the evil lives he saw some women leading, and withdrew from the society of women, resolved to remain a bachelor. He made an exquisite ivory statue of an ideal maiden, more beautiful than any he had ever known, and as he gazed upon its loveliness he fell in love with the statue. At a festival in honor of Aphrodite he prayed the goddess to send him a maiden like the statue. As he prayed the flames of the altar leaped up to show that the goddess had heard him. When Pygmalion returned to his house he kissed and caressed the statue and was overjoyed to find that Aphrodite had indeed endowed it with life. The maiden, Galatea, and Pygmalion were married in the presence of Aphrodite and afterward had a son, Paphus, who name was sometimes given to the island of Cyprus. Other accounts say Pygmalion fell in love with Aphrodite herself, and made his wonderful statue when his love was rejected. But the goddess was pleased with his homage, and breathed life into the statue.

Pygmalion. Legendary king of Tyre. He was the brother of Queen Dido, and murdered her husband for his riches. He kept the deed a secret but Sychaeus, Dido's husband, appeared to her in a dream and told her what had happened, and warned her to flee. It was for this reason that Dido and her companions went to North Africa where they founded the city of Carthage.

Pygmies (pig′mēz). In Greek legend, a race of men whose height equalled one *pygme*, that is, the distance from the elbow to the knuckles, or about 13½ inches. Homer represents the Pygmies as dwelling on the southern shores of Ocean, and as being warred upon by the cranes in their annual migrations. The battle with the cranes started because once a beautiful Pygmy, Gerana, considered herself more beautiful than Hera and Artemis. As a punishment for her pride Hera changed her into a crane and caused her to be hated by her people. Heracles, as he was sleeping, was once attacked by Pygmies, but he laughed at them, gathered a few up in his lion's skin and took them to Eurystheus (or

to Omphale). The African Pygmies described by Herodotus, and once supposed to be equally fabulous, were apparently the same as the remarkable race or races of dwarfs found by explorers in various parts of equatorial Africa.

Pylades (pil′a-dēz). In Greek legend, a son of Strophius, king in Phocis, and of Agamemnon's sister. When Orestes was brought to Strophius' court to protect him from the evil designs of Aegisthus, Pylades became his intimate and faithful friend. He accompanied Orestes when he returned in secret to Mycenae, and reminded him of the command of Apollo when Orestes wavered in his decision to kill his mother to avenge his father's murder. After the murder of Clytemnestra by Orestes the Furies pursued him. Pylades, disowned by his father for his part in the murder, refused to desert Orestes and accompanied him in his wanderings. He also went with him to Tauris to secure the sacred image of Artemis, although it was well-known that the Taurians sacrificed any strangers they caught landing on their shores. On his return from Tauris, Pylades married Electra, sister of Orestes. She bore him two sons, Medon and Strophius.

Pylae Ciliciae (pī′lē si-lish′i-ē). Latin name of the **Cilician Gates.**

Pylaemenes (pil-ē′me-nēz). Named by Homer (*Iliad*) as a king of the Paphlagonians. He led his men to Troy as an ally of the Trojans in the Trojan War. He was slain by Menelaus.

Pylaeus (pil-ē′us). Named by Homer (*Iliad*) as a son of Lethus and the brother of Hippothous. He was a captain of Pelasgians, allies of Troy in the Trojan War.

Pylas (pī′las). In Greek legend, a king of Megara. Pandion the Younger fled to his court when he was driven out of Athens by his enemies. Later, Pylas left Megara because of a murder, and gave his throne to Pandion. Pylas went to Messenia, where he founded the city of Pylus. Neleus drove him out and took over the city, which thereafter became known as the home of the Neleids and of Nestor. Pylas went into Elis and founded another city, "sandy Pylus."

Pylia (pil′i-a). In Greek legend, a daughter of Pylas, king of Megara. When Pandion the Younger fled to his court Pylas gave him

Pylia for wife. She bore Aegeus, Lycus, Nisus, and Pallas to Pandion.

Pylus (pī′lus). In ancient geography, a town in N Messenia, Greece, situated N and E of the Gulf of Navarino. The "sandy Pylus" of the *Iliad* and the *Odyssey,* it was about two and a half miles from the Bay of Pylus. (The bay has since been converted into a lagoon by a sandbar that blocks its mouth.) According to some accounts, this Pylus was founded by Pylas, who came into the region from Megara and whose companions were Leleges. It later fell into the hands of Neleus, who raised the city to such renown that Homer called it "the city of Neleus." Heracles captured Pylus from Neleus because the latter had refused to purify him for a murder. He gave it in trust to Nestor, the son of Neleus, because he was the only one of the sons of Neleus to receive him. This act by Heracles was the basis of the later claim of Cresphontes, one of the Heraclidae, to Pylus as part of the inheritance of the descendants of Heracles. In ancient times Pylus was a place of considerable importance. Nestor's palace was the peer, in size and wealth, of the palace of Agamemnon at Mycenae. Until 1939 the location of the palace of Nestor had been a matter of dispute; some placed it farther north, in Elis, and some placed it on the western promontory of the Gulf of Navarino that was known in ancient times as Coryphasium. In 1939 Prof. Carl W. Blegen, of the University of Cincinnati, located the palace of Nestor at Epano Englianos, a plateau about two and one-half miles from the modern village of Chora, when he and a Greek team uncovered the foundations and floor of the palace there. In 1952 and succeeding years, excavations under Prof. Blegen's direction have revealed the existence of a large palace dating from about 1300 B.C. Remains uncovered give a clear outline of the size and ground plan of the palace. Lying in a NW-SE direction on the plateau, the palace is roughly a huge rectangle that is divided lengthwise into three unequal parts. The central and largest portion is occupied, beginning at the SE end, by a portico, vestibule, great hall, and storage magazines. A narrow aisle on the southerly side has many small chambers. On the northerly side a wider aisle holds, from the

southeast to the northeast, the queen's apartments, a bathroom, stairways to the upper floors, and more storage spaces. It is thought the palace had at least two stories, the walls of the first story being of soft limestone blocks, and those of the upper story being of crude brick. Fragments of pottery of all sizes and descriptions have been dug up. In one pantry alone, over 2800 drinking cups were found; these were shaped like champagne glasses, and the number of them was ascertained by counting the stems. The work of the excavators has revealed that the floors and walls of the palace were covered with plaster and decorated with paintings of dolphins, octopuses and other marine creatures, linear designs, floral patterns, winged griffins, and human figures in armor. The great hall, or throne room, was surrounded by an inside balcony from which the ladies, whose apartments were on the second floor, could observe the men. There was an intricate drainage system by which water from the roofs and terraces of the palace was collected and carried off by underground limestone conduits. A large, circular, decorated hearth was found in the throne room where, presumably, slices of bulls' thighs wrapped in fat were roasted when Nestor entertained. A smaller circular hearth was found in the queen's apartments. Fragments of terracotta chimney pots to carry off the smoke from the hearth fires have also been discovered. The remains of a bathroom, in which there was an unbroken tub, have also been found. In a wing connected to the palace by a kind of ramp, another tub has been located. A huge altar unearthed in a portico before this wing indicates that this area may have been the household shrine. One of the most important finds in the excavation of the palace was the discovery of what was apparently an archive room. In this were hundreds of clay tablets and fragments inscribed with the Linear Script B. These tablets were the first to be found on the mainland of Greece and prove that the Greeks had a written language at least as early as 1300 B.C. At the time the tablets were found the Linear Script B, so-named by Sir Arthur Evans who found it in Crete, had not been deciphered. It was at last deciphered in 1952. The inscriptions on the tablets list inventories of olive oil, wheat, figs, and other stores of the royal household, as well as accounts of work to be done and goods to be supplied to the palace. The palace was destroyed by fire, as indicated by the fused condition of the rocks, and the site was never again occupied, so that the outline of the original structure has not been confused by the remains of later buildings, as at Mycenae and Tiryns. In the neighborhood of the palace many tombs have been discovered, some of which have been excavated. In them were found swords with ivory handles, bits of gold leaf, small art objects, and other funerary offerings. Skulls have been found that may even be those of the heroes of Homer. The modern seaport of Pylos, on a promontory at the SE end of the Gulf of Navarino, is a town founded early in the 19th century. In the neighborhood is a vast cave, with oddly shaped rock formations. This is said to be the cave where the cattle of Neleus and Nestor were kept. Because the sandy soil, whence its name "sandy Pylus," was unfit for growing grass, the cattle were driven to this area for grazing and were sheltered in this grotto. The modern Pylos has also been called **Navarino** and **Neocastro.**

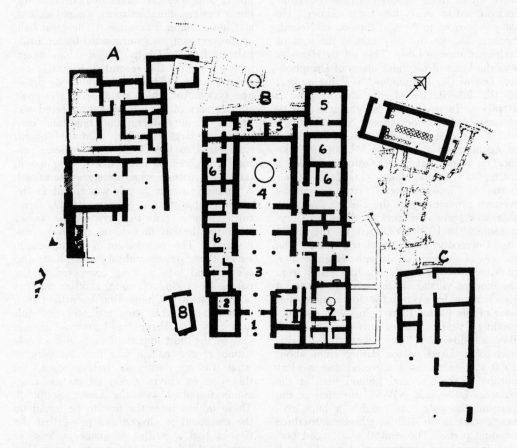

PLAN OF NESTOR'S PALACE AT PYLUS
A) older palace; B) main palace with: 1) propylaeum, 2) anteroom, 3) series of porticoes and vestibules, 4) great hall with throne, central hearth, four columns, 5) magazines for the storage of oil, wine, etc., 6) storage magazines and pantries, 7) queen's apartments, 8) archive room where Linear Script B tablets were found; C) wing thought to have contained the palace shrine. *American Journal of Archaeology*

Pyraechmes (pir-ek′mēz). Named by Homer (*Iliad*) as a captain of the Paeonians, allies of the Trojans in the Trojan War. He was slain by Patroclus.

Pyramus and Thisbe (pir′a-mus, thiz′bē). In classical legend, two Babylonian lovers. They were forbidden to see each other by their parents, and talked together through a crack in the garden wall. They finally planned to defy their parents and to meet under a mulberry tree that grew beside the tomb of Ninus, outside the city walls. Their rendezvous was set for the hours of darkness. Thisbe was the first to arrive at the trysting place. As she waited for her lover she was frightened away when a lion, whose jaws were dripping with blood from a recent kill, came to drink at the spring nearby. She fled into a cave, dropping her veil as she ran off. The lion seized the veil and mauled it about so that it was daubed with blood and then loped off. Pyramus, who now arrived, saw the blood-stained veil and instantly concluded that Thisbe had been killed. In despair, because he had asked Thisbe to undertake the secret meeting and now felt himself responsible for the death of his love, he killed himself under the mulberry tree that was to have been the meeting place. After a time Thisbe dared return. She found Pyramus dying, and resolved that death should not separate them. She seized the sword with which Pyramus had slain himself and plunged it into her own breast. Ever after, the berries of the mulberry tree, which were originally white, ripened to a dark purple, in memory of the blood of Pyramus and Thisbe which was shed because of their love for each other, under its boughs.

Pyrene (pī-rē′nē). In Greek legend, a daughter of Bebrys, a king in the Pyrenees. Heracles ravished her when he visited her father's kingdom on his labor to fetch the cattle of Geryon. According to some accounts, she gave birth to a serpent. She fled from her father's anger and was killed by wild beasts. Heracles found her body and buried it. Some say that this princess gave her name to the range of mountains in which her father's kingdom was located: the Pyrenees.

Pyrene. In Greek mythology, mother by Ares of that Cycnus who fought with Heracles at the Echedorus River in Macedonia.

Pyreneus or **Pyrenaeus** (pī-rē-nē′us). According to legend, a Thracian warrior who seized the lands of Daulis and Phocis and made himself king. He saw the Muses on their way to their temple on Mount Parnassus and invited them to take shelter in his palace from a sudden storm. When the weather cleared and the Muses prepared to depart, Pyreneus barred their way and attempted to assault them. The Muses escaped from him by flying off. Pyreneus, maddened for his arrogance, sought to pursue them. In his madness he leaped from a tower and fell to his death.

Pyrgi (pir′jī). In ancient geography, a town of Etruria, situated on the coast W and N of Caere. It was celebrated for its rich temple of Leucothea which was plundered by Dionysius the Elder (384 B.C.).

Pyrgos (pir′gôs). [Also: **Pirgos.**] See **Letrini**.

Pyrigenes (pir-ij′e-nēz). An epithet of Dionysus, meaning "Born of" or "Amid Fire," because he was snatched from his mother's womb when she was destroyed by the blazing majesty of Zeus and his thunderbolts.

Pyriphlegethon (pir-i-fleg′e-thon). Another name for Phlegethon, the river of fire in the Underworld.

Pyris (pir′is). Named by Homer (*Iliad*) as a Lycian companion of Sarpedon. When Patroclus entered the battle to drive the Trojans back from the Greek ships, he slew Pyris.

Pyronia (pir-ō′ni-a). Epithet of Artemis, meaning "Fire-goddess." From the sanctuary of Artemis Pyronia on Mount Crathis, the Argives took fire for their ceremonies at Lerna.

Pyrrha (pir′a). In Greek mythology, a daughter of Epimetheus. With her husband Deucalion she survived the flood which Zeus sent to destroy the wicked race of man. In fulfillment of the instructions of an oracle, after the flood she helped to found a new race to repeople the earth. See **Deucalion**.

Pyrrha. The name assumed by Achilles when, disguised as a girl, he was hidden in the court of Lycomedes on the island of Scyrus by his mother Thetis. She sent him there in the hope that he would not go to Troy, for she knew that he was fated to die if he joined the Greeks in the fighting at Troy. Achilles was sometimes also known as Cer-

actor; up, lūte, pull; oi, oil; ou, out; ᵺH, then; ḏ as d or j, ṣ as s or sh, ṭ as t or ch, ẕ as z or zh.

cysera during the period when he was hiding in Lycomedes' court.

Pyrrhic (pir′ik). An ancient Grecian warlike dance, in quick and light measure, accompanied by the flute. It consisted chiefly in adroit and nimble steps and motions of the body, intended to represent the attempt to avoid strokes of an enemy in battle and to inflict injury upon him. It was performed under arms, and the movements and practice necessary were looked upon as training for service in the field.

Pyrrho (pir′ō). Greek philosopher; born in Elis c360 B.C.; died c270 B.C. He accompanied Alexander the Great on his eastern expedition then returned to Elis, where he lived in poverty, although highly honored by his fellow countrymen. The Athenians also honored him and gave him citizenship. He was the founder of the Skeptical school of philosophy.

Pyrrhus (pir′us). Another name for Neoptolemus, son of Achilles.

Pyrrhus. King of Epirus, and one of the greatest generals of antiquity; born c318 B.C.; killed at Argos, Greece, 272 B.C. He was the son of Aeacides, king of Epirus, and Phthia. His father claimed descent from Neoptolemus (also called Pyrrhus), son of Achilles. While Pyrrhus was still an infant the Molossians revolted, overthrew Aeacides, and killed his family and his friends. Pyrrhus was saved and carried off by loyal friends of his family. According to Plutarch, as the party fled before the Molossians they came to a raging river and had no means of crossing it. The people they saw on the other side could not understand their shouts over the roar of the flood. In desperation one of the party inscribed the name of the royal fugitive on a piece of bark, weighted it with a stone, and hurled it across the river. The men on the other side read it, understood the urgent need of the party to cross, hastily constructed a raft, and came over to fetch them. The first man who touched the bank happened to be named Achilles. He took young Pyrrhus in his arms and conveyed him to safety across the river. Pyrrhus was taken to the court of Glaucias, king of Illyria. King Glaucias hesitated to give him asylum, out of fear of Cassander, an enemy of Aeacides. As he pondered, so the story goes,

the child crept to him and pulled himself to his knees by grasping the king's robe. Glaucias was moved to compassion and took the child into his own household and brought him up with his own sons until he was 12 years old. At that time Glaucias sent him back to Epirus at the head of an army and restored him to his throne. Some say, however, that Glaucias did not restore him with an army, but that he was recalled by the Epirotes. At the age of 17 he went to Illyria to attend the marriage of one of the sons of Glaucias. While he was gone the Molossians revolted again and set his cousin Neoptolemus on the throne. Pyrrhus went to Demetrius Poliorcetes, son of Alexander's general Antigonus, who was related to him by marriage. The successors of Alexander the Great were still struggling for control of his empire. Pyrrhus joined Demetrius and Antigonus against Lysimachus, Seleucus, Ptolemy, and Cassander, and fought bravely at the battle of Ipsus, 301 B.C. Demetrius and Antigonus were defeated, and Pyrrhus went as a hostage to Ptolemy in Egypt. There he noted that Berenice, wife of Ptolemy, exercised great influence. He courted her and won her good will, and made such a splendid impression on Ptolemy that he was given his stepdaughter Antigone in marriage. Out of gratitude, he later named his first son Ptolemy, and named a city he founded in Epirus Bereniceïs. Antigone secured men and money for him, and helped him to win back his kingdom (295 B.C.), the government of which he at first shared with the usurper, his cousin Neoptolemus. However, the divided rule was highly unsatisfactory to both parties. Partisans of Neoptolemus plotted to kill Pyrrhus. He was informed of the plot and forestalled the conspirators by killing Neoptolemus and making himself sole ruler. He was now in position to pursue his own ambitious plans. He first interfered in the affairs of Macedon, still at the mercy of those struggling to win control, and then seized the coast of Macedon and the regions of Ambracia, Acarnania, and Amphilochia. He was persuaded to meet his opponents to discuss peace. When sacrifices were to be made preparatory to swearing to the peace, a boar, a bull, and a ram were brought forth as victims. The ram dropped dead. Soothsayers predicted that one of the three kings negotiating the peace would die, whereupon Pyrrhus refused to swear to the articles. Shortly after this Alexander, king of Macedon at the peace negotiations, was murdered by Demetrius, thus fulfilling the prediction. Demetrius made himself king of Macedon, and thus a rival of Pyrrhus who had resolved to win control of the unhappy country. Pyrrhus won victories, great renown for himself by his bravery, skill, and daring, and the admiration of the Macedonians he defeated, who compared him to Alexander the Great. In the meantime, Demetrius had gone into Epirus and was ravaging it. Pyrrhus returned, and under a truce kept much of the Macedonian territory he had won.

Pyrrhus devoted himself exclusively to military affairs. After the death of Antigone he took several wives, for political reasons, and did all he could to foster the warlike natures of their various sons. It is said that when one of the latter asked him to which of them he would leave his kingdom, he replied, "To the one who has the sharpest sword." He won great fame and devotion from the Epirotes, who called him "the Eagle." "If I am an eagle," he said, "you have made me one; for it is on your arms, as upon wings, that I have risen so high." He was noted as a beneficent prince, who was quick to forgive an injury and even quicker to repay a kindness. In 286 B.C. he embarked on a plundering raid into Macedon. Meeting no resistance, he advanced as far as Edessa (Aegae). Then Demetrius raised a force and he withdrew, losing a considerable number of his men to the harassing attacks of Demetrius on the way. Demetrius planned to win back Asia, but was unwilling to leave so dangerous an enemy as Pyrrhus behind him. For this reason he made peace with him. Seleucus, Ptolemy, Lysimachus, kings respectively of Asia, Egypt, and Thrace, became alarmed at the preparations of Demetrius for war. They took up arms against him and urged Pyrrhus to do the same. Encouraged by a vision of Alexander the Great that came to him in a dream, Pyrrhus marched against Demetrius. He took Beroea on the Haliacmon River. Demetrius returned to drive him out, but

the Macedonians went over to Pyrrhus; Demetrius, deserted by his army, disguised himself and fled. Pyrrhus won his camp without striking a blow. Lysimachus now arrived and demanded half the kingdom. Pyrrhus did not feel strong enough to defeat him and yielded to his demand. When Demetrius had been driven from Athens by Pyrrhus, Lysimachus felt strong enough to attack Pyrrhus. He attacked his camp at Edessa, cut off his supplies, and compelled him, through hunger, to retire to Epirus, thus ending his influence and power in Macedonia in the same year in which he had won it (286 B.C.) Now, says Plutarch, Pyrrhus might have enjoyed the peaceful possession of his own kingdom, but he had no talent for peace. The people of Tarentum, engaged in a war with the Romans, asked him to come and command them. He immediately envisioned a conquest of the western world and gathered his host. Plutarch quotes a supposed conversation between Pyrrhus and one of his most trusted lieutenants, Cineas. "Suppose," said Cineas, "that you conquer the Romans, what then?" He would go and conquer Sicily. "And supposing a successful conquest of Sicily." Next he would win Africa. "And after that?" He would settle back and enjoy peace and prosperity. "But," persisted Cineas, "you have that now. Why risk men, treasure, and the horrors of war for what you already have?" Pyrrhus could give no answer, which made him somewhat discontented with Cineas but in no way changed his mind. He set out for Italy with 3000 horse, 20,000 foot, 20 elephants, 2000 archers, and 500 slingers. On the way his fleet was scattered by a great storm. He reached Italy with a small number of horse, 2000 foot, and two elephants. At Tarentum he found the people frivolously dissipating their time and strength; he immediately and sternly organized them for the war they had asked him to command. He learned that the Roman consul, Laevinus, was approaching with a large army, and sent word to him that he would act as mediator between the Romans and the Greeks in Italy. Laevinus replied that he "neither accepted Pyrrhus as a mediator nor feared him as an enemy," and continued his march. Although all his forces had not yet arrived, Pyrrhus resolved to act. He rode out to observe the Roman camp, and remarked with admiration that "the disposition of these barbarians has nothing of the barbarian in it." In the battle that followed at Heraclea (280 B.C.) Pyrrhus defeated the Romans, but lost many of his best men. He took the Roman camp and won many cities that had been allied to Rome. He advanced toward Rome itself and sent an embassy to the Senate, offering generous terms of peace. As the Senate considered whether to accept, Appius Claudius, who had built the Appian Way and had brought water from the Anio to Rome, had himself led into the Senate. He was blind, and now, he said, he wished he were deaf as well, so that he would not hear the Romans, who boasted that they could have defeated Alexander the Great, trembling before Pyrrhus who could not even hold Macedon. When he finished speaking the Senate voted for war, and sent word to Pyrrhus that when he had left Italy they would be glad to make a treaty of friendship with him; otherwise they would continue to fight him. The Roman Fabricius came to discuss ransom for the Roman prisoners and made a deep impression on Pyrrhus by his absolute refusal to accept any of the gifts offered him. Fabricius learned of a plot to poison Pyrrhus, and warned him of it. In gratitude, Pyrrhus freed the prisoners without ransom. When the Romans again rejected his peace offers he attacked at Asculum in Apulia, on the slopes of the Apennines. A fierce battle raged, which was ended by the coming of night. The next day on ground suitable for effective operation by his elephants, Pyrrhus drove the Romans back and defeated them (279 B.C.). In the two days Pyrrhus lost all his best officers and many men whom he could not replace. When he was congratulated on his victory he said, "Another such victory and we are done!" (Whence the expression "Pyrrhic victory.")

Following his victories in Italy, Pyrrhus was invited by the Greeks of Sicily to drive out the Carthaginians. He went to Sicily, drove back the Carthaginians, took the strongly fortified city of Eryx (Lilybaeum), and offered splendid sacrifices to Heracles and held games in his honor. The Car-

thaginians offered to make peace, but he sent the reply he had received from Rome: that he would make peace with them when they had withdrawn from the island. His ambition was to conquer Africa, and in a very high-handed way he began to levy men and ships, and lost the good will of the Sicilians. His plans misfired; Rome and Carthage joined to oppose him; he decided to go back to Italy (276 B.C.). On the way he lost part of his fleet to Carthaginian attacks, and when he landed in Italy he was harassed by the Mamertines. In an engagement he was wounded in the head. One of the Mamertines tauntingly called for Pyrrhus to come forth. He strode through his army, his head streaming with blood, faced the man who had taunted him, and clove his skull with his sword. The Mamertines were dazzled with admiration, and henceforward left him alone. Returning to Tarentum, he attacked the Romans at Beneventum and was defeated (275 B.C.). He now returned to Epirus, marched into Macedon and took all before him, winning Aegae, and the admiration of the Macedonians, many of whom flocked to his standard. At the request of a Spartan dissident he marched into the Peloponnesus, plundered Laconia, and prepared to take the city of Sparta, but failed and withdrew. However, his "hopes grew as fast as they were cut off" and he marched to Argos, harassed as he went by the Spartans. By treachery he entered Argos at night. In the darkness and confusion his soldiers scattered and fought to little purpose. At daybreak Pyrrhus was greatly disturbed to see an image of a bronze bull and a wolf fighting, for an oracle had said he would die when he saw a wolf encountering a bull. As he observed the turmoil in the city, and the fact that his elephants could not operate in the confined space, he decided to withdraw, and sent orders to his son Helenus to break down a part of the wall of the city to facilitate his exit. His order was misunderstood. Helenus drove into the city with his forces. The streets were jammed, those trying to get out were blocked by those forcing their way in. The elephants went mad and added terror to the confusion. One elephant, searching for his fallen master, trod frantically on all

fat, fāte, fär, fãre, errant; net, mē, hėr ardent; pin, pīne; not, nōte, mõve, nôr,

before him until he found his master's body.
This he took up in his trunk and placed on
his tusks, then bellowing furiously he trampled on all around him. Pyrrhus saw his
position was hopeless. He removed his
plumed helmet and gave it to a friend, then
wheeled his horse and charged in among the
enemy. He received a slight wound in the
breast and turned to engage the man who
had accidentally made the thrust. This man's
mother was watching the battle from a nearby roof. Seeing her son in great peril she
seized a tile from the roof, threw it with all
her might, and struck Pyrrhus on the head.
He fell from his horse unconscious. Argives
who did not recognize him dragged him to
a nearby porch. There one who had served
under Antigonus recognized him and drew
his sword to cut off his head, but as he
raised his arm Pyrrhus opened his eyes and
gave him such a fierce look that he wavered,
and succeeded in only wounding the fallen
general on the face. After many blows, he
hacked off his head. Alcyoneus, son of
Antigonus, rode up and asked for Pyrrhus'
head. He took it to his father and flung it
at his feet. Antigonus struck him for an impious barbarian and then, grieving for the
changes Fortune brings to men, wept for his
grandfather Antigonus, killed at Ipsus, 301
B.C., and for his father Demetrius, who had
died in prison. He clothed the body of
Pyrrhus in rich garments and put it, with
the head, on a funeral pyre and burned it
with due honor. The life of Pyrrhus was
studded with possibilities. He might have
made Epirus a formidable kingdom. He
might have arrested the expansion of Rome
and won Sicily from the Carthaginians. Instead, when he left Italy he remarked
prophetically, "What a battleground I am
leaving to Rome and Carthage." Hannibal
is said to have ranked Alexander the Great
as the world's greatest general, and Pyrrhus
next to him.

Pythagoras (pi-thag′ō-ras, pī-). Greek philosopher and mathematician; born in the island
of Samos; died at Metapontum in Magna
Graecia, c497 B.C. Some say he was a follower of Pherecydes of Syros, and that he
made extensive journeys in the earlier part
of his life to study the civilizations of the
East, especially that of Egypt. As an ex

ponent of oligarchy he left Samos, c530 B.C.,
to escape the tyrant Polycrates, and went to
Italy where he settled at Croton. Here he
founded an ascetic brotherhood, governed
by strict rules, which had as its aim a moral
and religious reformation of mankind, as
well as the political purpose of supporting
aristocracies against democracies and tyrannies. Basic to their system was the Pythagoreans' belief in the transmigration and
purification of the soul. Pythagoras himself,
it is said, claimed that his body was inhabited
by the soul of Euphorbus, a Trojan who
wounded Patroclus at the siege of Troy.
Because they believed that the soul migrates,
not only from man to man but from man to
animal, the Pythagoreans did not eat meat.
Around the religious and moral facet of the
Pythagorean system there soon grew up a
suffocating tangle of superstition. Another
basic principle of the Pythagoreans was a
belief that the explanation of the physical
and spiritual world depends on number.
Pythagoras wrote nothing, but many works
were attributed to him, and it is almost impossible to distinguish between his own
theories and those formulated by his followers. However, it was due to Pythagoras
that mathematics was raised to the rank of a
science, and many early geometrical discoveries have been ascribed to the Pythagorean
thinkers. They are considered to have founded
the theory of numbers, and the mathematical
study of acoustics and music. They have
appeared to have been among the first (if
not, in each instance, demonstrably the very
first) thinkers to conceive of incommensurable
quantities, and of the earth as a globe. Their
emphasis on the study of numbers led on the
one hand to number mysticism (which is
what many modern readers now chiefly associate with Pythagoras and his school), and
on the other hand to a quantitative study
of nature. The brotherhood of the Pythagoreans in Croton rapidly increased, and for
a time had great influence, which was wielded
in political as well as spiritual affairs. In a
war between Croton and Sybaris, a neighboring city ruled by a tyrant, the Pythagoreans
won a decisive victory over the Sybarites
(510 B.C.), and so completely destroyed
their city, which had become proverbial for
its wealth and luxury, that the exact site

of the ancient city remained unknown until recently. Shortly afterward there was a reaction against the Pythagoreans. A number of them who had assembled in the house of Milo in Croton were destroyed when the house was set afire by their enemies. A wave of persecution broke out, and Pythagoras retired to Metapontum, where he ended his days.

Pythagoras. Greek sculptor, born in the island of Samos. He went to Rhegium, in Italy, where he was active in the first half of the 5th century B.C. He worked exclusively in bronze and rivaled his contemporaries, Polyclitus and Myron, in his statues of heroes and victors in the games. His statues, only one copy of which survives, were notable for lifelike play of the sinews and positions of the body.

Pytheas (pith'ē-as). Greek navigator and astronomer; fl. second half of the 4th century B.C. He was a native of Massilia (Marseilles), and visited the coasts of Spain, Gaul, and Great Britain. His works, only fragments of which remain, contain our earliest first-hand information concerning northwestern Europe.

PYTHIA ON THE ORACULAR TRIPOD
Red-figured Greek vase

Pythia (pith'i-a). The priestess who was said to hold communion with Apollo and receive his oracles in the inner sanctuary of the great temple at Delphi, throughout historic antiquity.

Pythiad (pith'i-ad). A period of four years between two consecutive celebrations of the Pythian games.

Pythian Games (pith'i-an). One of the four great national festivals of ancient Greece. They ranked next in importance to the Olympic Games and were celebrated in August, every four years. They were held at Delphi until 586 B.C., when they were transferred to the plain below Delphi; ultimately, a stadium was built on a ledge of the mountain above the sanctuary of Apollo. Before 586 B.C. the games were held every eight years, and consisted of a great festival in honor of Apollo (whence their name, from "Apollo Pythius," slayer of Python), in which the contests were of a musical nature. The contestants played hymns of praise to Apollo, accompanying themselves on the cithara (a stringed instrument of the lyre class), under the supervision of the priests of Delphi. After 586 B.C., athletic contests similar to those of the Olympic Games were added, but the principal interest of the Pythian Games continued to be the musical competition. In this cithara players and flute players, accompanied by singers, performed songs and hymns on the theme of Apollo's battle with the Python at Delphi, and his victory over the monster. The winners in the various divisions of the competition were awarded a wreath of bay leaves from the Vale of Tempe and a palm branch. Like the Olympic Games, the Pythian Games probably lasted until 394 A.D., when they were abolished by Theodosius.

Pythias (pith'i-as). See **Damon and Pythias.**

Pythius (pith'i-us). In Greek religion, an epithet or surname of Apollo in reference to him as the slayer of Python. Apollo Pythius was worshiped especially at Delphi.

Pythius. According to Herodotus, a Lydian who lived in Celaenae. He is said to have given Darius the Great a golden plane tree and a golden vine. When Xerxes came to Celaenae in his preparation for invading Greece, Pythius entertained him lavishly and offered him money for the prosecution of the war. Xerxes was amazed, and asked the extent of his wealth. Pythius replied that he had 2000 talents of silver, and just 7000 short of 4,000,000 gold darics, all of which he would gladly give to Xerxes, as he would still be rich from the produce of his great land holdings. Xerxes was greatly charmed by the offer of Pythius, and by the reception, so different from others he had received, given him and his army by Pythius. Not to be outdone in generosity, he not only declined to accept Pythius' money but gave him 7000 gold darics, so that he would round out his 4,000,000, and declared himself a friend of Pythius. At the time when the army of Xerxes prepared to leave Sardis for Abydos, the sun was suddenly darkened in midday, says Herodotus. Pythius was frightened by this evil omen. He went to Xerxes and asked a boon. Xerxes promised to grant whatever he asked. At this Pythius reminded the king that he had five sons who had been called into service in the army of Xerxes, and asked that Xerxes allow the eldest son to remain behind with his father. Xerxes was angered by his request as much as he had earlier been charmed by his generosity. He declared that his own relatives and friends were being called on to risk their lives and now, as he had earlier matched the generosity of Pythius with greater generosity, so he would match his insolence in making such a request with greater insolence. He would spare Pythius and four of his sons because of the entertainment Pythius and offered his army, but he ordered his minions to find the eldest son of Pythius and cut him in two. The two halves of his body were to be placed at either side of the road, that the army of the king might march between them as it left Sardis.

Pytho (pī′thō). Another name for Delphi. It is derived from "Python," the monster that guarded the shrine until it was killed by Apollo.

Python (pī′thon). In Greek mythology, a huge female dragon or serpent born from the mud of the Flood. She guarded the cave and chasm at Delphi and there was killed by Apollo, who thus became henceforth the possessor and motivating deity of the oracle at Delphi. A ritual drama representing the killing of the dragon by the god was annually reënacted there. Also, in classical antiquities and in the New Testament, a soothsaying spirit or demon; hence, also, a person possessed by such a spirit; especially a ventriloquist. Some ancient writers speak of the serpent Python as having delivered oracles at Delphi before the coming of Apollo, and during the Roman imperial period we find the name often given to soothsayers. The spirit was supposed to speak from the belly of the soothsayer, who was accordingly called a ventriloquist.

Pyxis (pik′sis). In ancient Greece, a type of cylindrical vase or box with a cover, used especially by women, as for the toilet.

—Q————

Quadi (kwā′dī). Ancient Germanic tribe, a part of the Suevi, the eastern neighbors of the Marcomanni in Bohemia. The Quadi were originally allies of the Marcomanni, but later (in the 4th century A.D.) appear in incursions into Roman territory. They were ultimately included under the common name Suevi.

Quadrantaria (kwad-ran-tā′ri-a). A disparaging nickname of Clodia, the profligate aristocrat, sister of Clodius and contemporary of Catullus and Cicero. The insinuation contained in the name is that she sold her favors for a trifle, the *quadrans* being a small coin, a farthing. In one version, a lover, taking leave of her embraces, presented her with a bag of coins, which on examination turned out to be *quadrantes*. (JJ)

Quadriga (kwad-rī′ga). A two-wheeled chariot drawn by four horses, which were harnessed all abreast. It was used in racing in the Greek Olympic Games and in the Circensian Games of the Romans.

Quadrigarius (kwad-ri-gā′ri-us), **Claudius.** Roman annalist; fl. at the beginning of the 1st century B.C. He wrote a history of Rome from the destruction of the city by the Gauls (c390 B.C.) to his own time c80 B.C. Fragments of his work survive.

Quaestor (kwēs'tor). In ancient Rome, a member of one of two distinct classes of magistrates: 1) One of two public accusers (*quaestores parricidii*) whose duty it was to lay accusations against those guilty of murder or other capital offense, and to see to the execution of the sentence. This magistracy was in existence at an early period and is mentioned in the Twelve Tables but became obsolete about 366 B.C., its functions being transferred to other officers. 2) One of the officers (*quaestores classici*) having the care administration of the public funds; a public treasurer. It was his duty to receive, pay out, and record the public finances, including the collection of taxes, tribute, etc. Quaestors accompanied the provincial governors, proconsuls, or praetors, and received everywhere the public dues and imports, paid the troops, etc. After Julius Caesar, some of their functions were given to the praetors and some to the aediles. The number of quaestors was originally two, but was gradually increased to 20. Under Constantine the *quaestor sacri palatii* was an imperial minister of much power and importance.

Quintilian (kwin-til'yan). [Full Latin name, **Marcus Fabius Quintilianus.**] Roman rhetorician; born at Calagurris (Calahorra), Spain, c35 A.D.; died c95 A.D. He was educated at Rome, returned to his birthplace as a teacher of oratory, and went back to Rome with Galba in 68, and taught oratory there for 20 years in a school which he opened in the reign of Vespasian. He was patronized by Vespasian and Domitian, and was given the rank of consul by the latter for his services in educating his grandnephews. His most celebrated work is his *Institutio Oratoria,* which exerted a powerful influence in its day. It is the most elaborate ancient treatise on education, as well as one of the most important ancient documents of literary criticism.

Quintius (kwin'shi-us, -shus) or **Quinctius** (kwingk'shi-us, -shus), **Flamininus.** See **Flamininus, Titus Quintius (or Quinctius).**

Quintus Horatius Flaccus (kwin'tus hō-rā'shus flak'us). Full Latin name of **Horace.**

Quintus Fabius Maximus (fā'bi-us mak'si-mus). See **Fabius Maximus, Quintus.**

Quintus Ennius (en'i-us). See **Ennius, Quintus.**

Quirinal (kwir'i-nal). [Latin, **Mons Quirinalis.**] Farthest north and the highest of the seven hills of ancient Rome, lying NE of the Capitoline and NW of the Viminal. It takes its name from an old Sabine sanctuary of Quirinus.

Quirinalia (kwir-i-nā'li-a). In ancient Rome, a festival in honor of Quirinus, celebrated on Feb. 17, on which day Romulus was said to have disappeared in a thunderstorm.

Quirinus (kwi-rī'nus). The name given to the deified Romulus. It was also sometimes applied to Augustus, and sometimes to the Roman nation.

Quirites (kwi-rī'tēz). An ancient division of the Sabines, especially of those who lived near and around the city of Cures. Numa Pompilius, the second king of Rome (715–673 B.C.), came from Cures. His people were amalgamated with the Romans, and all came to be called Quirites in their civil capacity. The name *Quirites* pertained to them in addition to that of *Romani,* the latter designation having application in their political and military capacity.

R

Rabirius (ra-bē'ri-us), **Caius.** Roman poet of the age of Augustus. Fragments of an epic on the wars between Mark Antony and Octavian (Augustus) are attributed to him.

Rabirius, Caius. Roman senator, fl. 1st century B.C. In 63 B.C., at the instigation of Julius Caesar, he was accused by the tribune Titus Labienus of the murder of Lucius

Appulieus Saturninus, which had taken place in 100 B.C. Caesar revived an obsolete procedure and acted, with Lucius Caesar, as judge in the trial of Rabirius, who was defended by Cicero. Rabirius was condemned, but before the decision could be ratified by the people, Quintus Metellus Celer, the praetor, dissolved the assembly.

Rabirius, Caius Postumus. Nephew and adopted son of Caius Rabirius. He was defended successfully by Cicero (54 B.C.) when Gabinius brought charges of extortion against him. Cicero's speech (*Pro Rabirio Postumo*), used for his defense, survives.

Ragusa (rä-gö′zä). See **Hybla Heraea.**

Ramnes (ram′nēz) or **Ramnenses** (ram-nen′sēz). One of the three tribes into which the ancient Roman people were said to have been divided. Traditionally, this group represented the Latin element in the composition of the nation.

Raphia (ra-fī′a). [Modern name, **Rafa.**] In ancient geography, a city on the coast of Palestine, SW of Gaza. Near it Ptolemy IV defeated (217 B.C.) Antiochus III.

Raudian Fields (rô′di-an). [Latin, **Campi Raudii.**] In ancient geography, a noted plain in N Italy, probably near Vercelli, but by some located near Verona. It was the scene of a battle in 101 B.C., in which the Cimbri were annihilated by the Romans.

Raurici (rô′ri-sī). [Also: **Rauraci.**] Ancient Germanic tribe, first mentioned by Caesar. They were situated in the neighborhood of Basel, on the upper Rhine in the territory north of the Helvetii, whom they had joined in their attempted migration, 58 B.C.

Raven. In Greek mythology, a bird sacred to Apollo. Originally its plumage was pure white, but in anger with the raven for bringing him the message that Coronis, one of Apollo's loves, had been unfaithful to him, Apollo changed the raven's feathers to black.

Ravenna (rä-ven′nä). City in N Italy, about six miles from the Adriatic Sea. It was probably founded by the Etruscans, and came later (c191 B.C.) into the hands of the Umbrians and the Romans, who developed it into the chief naval station on the upper Adriatic coast. The historical importance of Ravenna really begins in 404 A.D., when because of its defensibility and the protection of the fleet, the emperor Honorius (395–

425 A.D.) moved the imperial residence there.

Rea Silvia (rē′a sil′vi-a). See **Rhea Silvia.**

Reate (rē-ā′tē). [Modern name, **Rieti.**] In ancient geography, a town of C Italy, situated on the Velino River, about 42 miles NE of Rome, in a region celebrated by Vergil and Cicero for its fertility. The town was the chief town of the Sabines.

Reggio di Calabria (räd′jō dē kä-lä′brē-ä). See **Rhegium.**

Reggio nell'Emilia (nel-lä-mē′lyä). See **Regium Lepidum.**

Regillus (rē-jil′us), **Lake.** In ancient geography, a small lake near Rome (perhaps near Frascati). It is traditionally the scene of a victory of the Romans over the Latins c496 B.C. that gave Rome preëminence in Latium.

Regium (rē′ji-um). See **Rhegium.**

Regium Lepidum (lep′i-dum). [Modern names, **Reggio nell'Emilia, Reggio, Reggio Emilia.**] City in N Italy, supposed to have been founded by Marcus Aemilius Lepidus, c187 B.C., in the course of the construction of the Aemilian Way, on which it lies.

Regulus (reg′ū-lus), **Marcus Atilius.** Roman general; died c250 B.C. He was consul in 267 B.C., and as consul again in 256 during the First Punic War, he defeated the Carthaginian fleet at Ecnomus, invaded Africa, and defeated the Carthaginian army. The Carthaginians asked for peace, but Regulus laid down such harsh terms that they could not accept them and resolved to continue the war. In 255 B.C. the Carthaginians under the Spartan general Xanthippus defeated Regulus and took him prisoner. According to Roman tradition, after the Carthaginian defeat at Panormus by the Roman proconsul Metellus (250 B.C.), the Carthaginians sent Regulus, who had been held in captivity for five years, with an embassy to Rome to ask for peace or an exchange of prisoners. Regulus is said to have given his word that he would return to Carthage. When his embassy produced no results because he himself strongly advised the Senate not to accept the Carthaginian terms, he refused to follow the advice of friends who urged him to stay in Rome. Instead, he went back to Africa and was tortured to death. Later, Carthaginian prisoners who were handed over to his family were put to death with most cruel tortures. Some say the story of

Regulus was afterward invented to justify the torture which his family had inflicted on the Carthaginian prisoners. In any case, the story of the honor and bravery of Regulus became a favorite with the Romans.

Remi (rē′mī). Tribe of the ancient Belgae in Gaul, dwelling in the vicinity of what is now Reims (their capital). They aided Julius Caesar in his Gallic wars.

Remus (rē′mus). In Roman legend, the twin brother of Romulus. It is said that when Romulus had plowed the magic furrow symbolizing the fortification of the future city of Rome, Remus contemptuously leaped over it, an act of desecration for which Romulus or his lieutenant killed him. See **Pomoerium, Romulus**. (JJ)

Res Gestae (rēz jes′tē). "Things accomplished, achievements," a term applied to official or unofficial biographies of kings and emperors, of which the Res Gestae of Augustus (the *Monumentum Ancyranum*) and of Charlemagne are the best-preserved examples. (JJ)

Resheph (rē′shef). In Syrian mythology, the god of war, disease, plague, and fire. The Phoenicians identified him with Apollo in his function of sender and dispeller of plagues. In Egypt Resheph was depicted as a bearded war-god bearing various weapons.

Rhadamanthys (rad-a-man′this). In Greek mythology, a son of Europa and Zeus, and the brother of Minos and Sarpedon. When Europa married Asterius, king of Crete, he adopted her sons and made them his heirs. The brothers quarreled over the youth Miletus. Minos drove the youth from Crete, Sarpedon fled, and Rhadamanthys made his peace with Minos, and on the death of Asterius received one-third of his kingdom. He was renowned for his wise and just rule, and established laws which were followed in Crete and in the Ionian islands. He obtained the laws from Zeus, who received him in a cave every ninth year. Rhadamanthys divided his kingdom among his sons and nephews. He fled from Crete to Boeotia, some say because he had killed a kinsman. There, according to some accounts, he married Alcmene, the mother of Heracles, after the death of Amphitryon. They lived in Ocalea and their tomb was shown in Haliartus. But some say he married Alcmene in the Elysian Fields. Zeus was devoted to Rhadamanthys and would have liked to spare him the burdens of old age. However, if he gave this blessing to one of his sons, the other gods might justifiably claim the same boon for their children, so he wisely gave up the idea. But he appointed Rhadamanthys as one of the three judges in the Underworld, where one of his special duties is to bring to justice those whose crimes have gone undetected on earth.

Rhadine (rad′i-nē). According to legend, a maiden of Samos who was compelled to marry a tyrant of Corinth, although she loved another. Her lover, Leontichus, followed her to Corinth in a cart; the tyrant seized him and killed him and Rhadine, and threw their bodies into the cart. Later he took pity on them and buried their bodies, so that their souls would not have to wander homeless for 100 years, as they would have done if they had not received proper burial.

Rhaetia (rē′sha). [Also: **Raetia**.] In ancient geography, a province of the Roman Empire. It was bounded by Vindelicia (at first included in it, but afterward made a separate province as Rhaetia Secunda) on the N, Noricum on the E, Italy on the S, and Helvetia on the W, corresponding to the modern canton of Graubünden, Switzerland, the N part of Tirol province, Austria, and part of the Bavarian and Lombard Alps. It was conquered by Tiberius and Drusus in 15 B.C., and was made a Roman province soon after.

Rhaetian Alps (rē′shan alps). [Latin, **Alpes Raeticae**.] Term of varied signification, applied in ancient times to the mountainous regions of Rhaetia, but in modern times generally to the chain of the Alps extending from the neighborhood of the Splügen Pass to the valley of the Adda, divided by the Engadine and Bergell into the Northern and Southern Rhaetian Alps. Peak elevation, Piz Bernina (about 13,295 feet), in the Bernina group.

Rhaetia Secunda (sē-kun′da). See **Vindelicia**.

Rhamnes (ram′nes). In Roman legend, a haughty Rutulian chief and prophet, favored by Turnus. He was slain by Nisus in the war between the Latins and Trojans.

Rhamnus (ram′nös). In ancient geography, a place in Attica, at the head of a wooded glen overlooking the Euripus, and not far from Marathon. There were two temples here:

fat, fāte, fär, fāre, errant; net, mē, hėr ardent; pin, pīne; not, nōte, mŏve, nôr,

one was a temple of Nemesis and the other, smaller one, was perhaps a temple of Themis. Nemesis was a goddess implacable to men of violence. Some say her wrath fell on the Persians who landed at Marathon (490 B.C.), and that she helped the Athenians defeat them because the Persians were so sure of defeating the Athenians that they brought marble with them to make a trophy. In her anger at their pride, Nemesis caused their defeat. Phidias used the marble they had brought with them to celebrate their victory to make a statue of Nemesis. On her head was a crown with deer and small images of Victory. In her left hand she held an apple branch; in her right, a cup engraved with figures of Aethiopians. On the pedestal of the image Helen was shown being led by Nemesis, said by some to be her mother, to Leda. The temple of Nemesis here was a Doric hexastyle peripteros, with 12 columns on the flanks, measuring 37 by 98 feet. The cella had pronaos and opisthodomos.

Rhea (rē′a). The great mother goddess; she was a Titaness, the daughter of Gaea and Uranus. She was the sister and wife of Cronus, and bore him Hestia, Demeter, Hera, Hades, and Poseidon, for which reason she is often called the mother of the gods. Cronus seized each of his new-born children and swallowed them, because it had been prophesied that he would be dethroned by one of his sons. When it was time for Zeus to be born, Rhea fled to Mount Lycaeus, according to some accounts, and there in a spot where no shadow is cast gave birth to Zeus. She entrusted her infant to Gaea, who gave him to the nymphs of Crete. But some say Rhea bore Zeus in Crete, either in a cave on Mount Ida or on Mount Dirce. And some say that when she was bearing Zeus she pressed her fingers into the earth of the Cretan cave and that the Dactyls were generated by her fingers, five females from her left hand and five males from her right hand. Rhea wrapped a stone in swaddling clothes and presented it to Cronus, who swallowed it. According to some accounts, Rhea was also the mother of the Curetes, who guarded the infant Zeus in Crete. She assisted Zeus, when he was grown, to compel Cronus to disgorge his other children. Rhea purified Dionysus of the murders he had committed during his madness, and initiated him into her mysteries. As an emissary from Zeus she persuaded Demeter to make the earth fruitful again when that goddess, in despair over the loss of her daughter Persephone, had withdrawn her life-giving blessings and caused the earth to become barren. She also used her influence to persuade her son Hades to allow Persephone, whom he had carried off to the Underworld, to spend part of her time on earth. The cult of Rhea was associated with fertility rites. One of the oldest places of her worship was in Crete, where she hid the infant Zeus from Cronus. She was often associated with the great Asian mother goddess Cybele. The Romans identified her with their Magna Mater, or with Ops.

Rhea Silvia (rē′a sil′vi-a). [Also: **Ilia, Rea Silvia.**] In Roman legend, daughter of Numitor, king of Alba Longa, and a descendant of Aeneas. Her uncle deposed Numitor, killed her brother, and had Rhea Silvia consecrated as a vestal virgin so that she could not beget any heirs who would restore their grandfather. But Mars fell in love with her and visited her, and she bore him the twins Romulus and Remus.

Rhegium (rē′ji-um) or **Regium.** [Modern name, **Reggio di Calabria.**] In ancient geography, a city in Bruttii, S Italy, situated on the Straits of Messina, on the tip of the toe of the Italian boot. According to legend, Heracles came to Rhegium on his way back to Hellas with the cattle of Geryon. He lay down to sleep but was prevented from so doing by the noise of cicadas. He prayed to the gods to stop their noise. They heard his prayer, and from that day forward cicadas were never again heard in Rhegium. The city was founded by Greek colonists in the 8th century B.C. as a sister city to Zancle, and became an important port and prosperous city. It was allied to Athens by treaty (433 B.C.) and took part with Athens in action against Syracuse (427 B.C.) which was waging war on the Athenian ally Leontini, but in the later Athenian expedition against Syracuse (415 B.C.) Rhegium remained neutral. In 391 B.C. the city was besieged by Dionysius the Elder, tyrant of Syracuse, who not only wanted it for its dominating position on the straits, but also desired to punish Rhegium for an insulting refusal to give him a

actor; up, lūte, pull; oi, oil; ou, out; ᴛʜ, then; d̯ as d or j, s̯ as s or sh, t̯ as t or ch, z̯ as z or zh.

maiden of their city in marriage. At the time, the Italian cities came to the aid of Rhegium, and the siege was raised. Two years later (389 B.C.), in the continuing struggle with Dionysius, Rhegium was compelled to surrender her fleet, and in 387 B.C. he besieged the city. The inhabitants held out for ten months, when they were compelled by starvation to surrender. Those who could not raise the money to ransom themselves were sold into slavery. The city was soon rebuilt and its activity as a port revived. In 280 B.C. the city was seized and its male inhabitants massacred following the revolt of a Roman mercenary garrison that had been admitted within the walls during the invasion of Italy by Pyrrhus. In 270 B.C. the Romans successfully besieged it and freed it from the mercenaries. Rhegium remained a loyal ally of Rome throughout the Punic Wars. It kept its Greek character into the time of the Roman Empire.

Rhene (rē'nē). Named by Homer *(Iliad)* as the mother of Medon by Oileus, whose concubine she was. Medon was half-brother of Ajax the Less.

Rhenia (rē'ni-a). In ancient geography, an uninhabited island near Delos, thought by some to be the island once known as Ortygia, where Artemis was born. The island served as a graveyard for the Delians, since no one was allowed to die or to be buried in the sacred island of Delos. When Polycrates, tyrant of Samos, captured Rhenia he dedicated it to Apollo and bound it to Delos with a chain.

Rhesus (rē'sus). According to some accounts, the son of Strymon, the river-god, and the Muse Calliope. Homer names him as the son of Eioneus. He was a Thracian king who came as an ally of Troy in the tenth year of the Trojan War. He arrived at a time when Hector had driven the Greeks back to their ships and Hector received him somewhat bitterly, accusing him of coming only when the Trojans were successful. Rhesus defended his delayed arrival on the ground that he had been fighting off his own enemies in Thrace. He promised to beat the Greeks once and for all the next day. On the night of his arrival he and his followers, who were encamped at some distance from the Trojans, were attacked by Diomedes and Odysseus. Those two Greeks had come as spies from the Greek camp. On the way they encountered Dolon, a Trojan spy, learned from him of Rhesus' arrival with his wonderful horses, and where he had pitched his tents. Diomedes and Odysseus then killed Dolon and proceeded to find Rhesus. They killed him and 12 of his followers as they slept, and captured his horses. It was important to the Greeks to capture the horses, as it had been prophesied that if they fed on Trojan fodder or drank the waters of the Scamander before Troy—which they had not yet done—the city could not be overthrown.

Rhesus. A Greek drama, attributed to Euripides. As the play opens, Hector, before his tent in the Trojan camp, bewails the setting of the sun that prevented him from burning the Greeks' ships. The fires he sees burning in the Greek camp convince him that the Greeks are about to flee as a result of the murderous attack he has made on them during the day. Aeneas does not agree that the fires are in preparation for departure. He persuades Hector not to attack, but instead, to send a spy to the Greek camp to learn their plans. Dolon, who volunteers to go as a spy on condition that he be awarded Achilles' immortal horses, dons a wolfskin for a disguise and, bragging that he will return with the head of Odysseus, departs. A messenger now announces the arrival of Rhesus, king of Thrace. Hector, who says he is a blunt man, tells Rhesus he should have come sooner. He owed his throne to Hector and should have come to his aid. Now, in their moment when victory is imminent, the Trojans don't need Rhesus. Rhesus justifies himself by saying that he had to fight off his own enemies, the Scythians, before he could come to Troy, but now that he has arrived he will make an end of the ten-year war in one day. He asks for the honor of fighting Achilles but on learning that he has withdrawn in anger from the war, he vows to capture Odysseus. Hector accepts his help and takes him off to his camp site.

Diomedes and Odysseus now enter, in search of Hector. They have already met and killed Dolon, as they themselves set out to spy on the Trojan camp. On finding that Hector is nowhere about, Odysseus suggests

fat, fāte, fär, fāre, errạnt; net, mē, hėr ardẹnt; pin, pīne; not, nōte, mŏve, nôr,

that they return to the ships, but Diomedes is unwilling to return without killing someone of their enemies. Athena now appears and tells them to slay Rhesus, never mind the others, as their fate is to die by other hands. They go in search of Rhesus. As they leave, Paris enters; Athena, pretending to be Aphrodite, assures him that she will protect him and Troy. Next Odysseus, pursued by sentinels, runs in, but he gives the watchword which he learned from Dolon, lulls the guard, and slips away.

The departure of Odysseus is swiftly followed by the entrance of a charioteer, wailing that Rhesus has been slain, and lamenting that he died as a fool might have done, without even the glory of fighting, but in his sleep. The charioteer, warned by a dream, woke up to find Rhesus and his followers dead. He thinks that Hector either committed the murder, or ordered it done to gain possession of Rhesus' horses. Hector, infuriated that two unarmed men had been allowed to escape, recognizes the raid as the work of Odysseus, and worries about Dolon who has not yet returned. As he waits, the muse, mother of Rhesus, appears in the heavens, bearing her son in her arms. He was slain by Odysseus, she says, and she curses Odysseus, Diomedes, and Helen, who caused the war. The muse tells how she was ravished by Strymon, the river-god, and in her shame left her son to be reared by nymphs. She had begged him not to go to Troy but he had disregarded her pleas and Athena had brought about his disaster. After predicting the death of Achilles, the muse, still with her slain son in her arms, disappears. Hector resolves to carry the fight to the Greek ships.

Rhesus. In Homeric legend *(Iliad)*, a river near Troy which Poseidon and Apollo diverted from its course, after the Trojan War, and caused to turn against the wall which the Greeks had built to protect their ships. It raged nine days against the wall, with other rivers diverted for the same purpose, and washed the wall into the sea. Poseidon had complained to Zeus about the wall, saying that the Greeks had offered no hecatombs to the gods when they built it, and fearing that the great wall which he and Apollo had built for Laomedon would suffer by com-

parison with this man-made wall. It was then that Zeus promised him that the Greek wall would be destroyed. Zeus helped to destroy it by sending torrential rains during the nine days that the rivers were raging out of their courses against it. The other rivers that helped to destroy the Greek wall were the Aesepus, Caresus, Granicus, Heptaporus, Rhodius, Scamander, and Simois.

Rhianus (ri-ā'nus). Greek poet and Homeric scholar; born in Crete; fl. in the second half of the 3rd century B.C.; contemporary of Eratosthenes. He had been a slave and had served as an overseer of a palestra (a public exercise ground). He obtained an education, and at Alexandria studied and worked on various recensions of Homer. He wrote epigrams in the Alexandrine manner, and epics. The most celebrated of his epics was the *Messeniaca*, in six books, about the Second Messenian War and the great deeds the hero Aristomenes performed during it. A few of the epigrams of Rhianus survive.

Rhigmus (rig'mus). In the *Iliad*, a son of Pires. He was a Thracian who allied himself with the Trojans and was slain by Achilles.

Rhinthon (rin'thon). Greek poet of Tarentum; fl. c300 B.C. He was the son of a potter and is noted as the inventor of burlesque tragedy, called *hilarotragoedia*, or cheerful tragedy. Into the tales of tragic myths he wove comic scenes. Fragments of his work survive.

Rhinthonic Comedy (rin-thon'ik). Variety of ancient Roman comedy, named after Rhinthon of Tarentum, a writer of travesties of tragic subjects. No specimens have survived.

Rhipaei Montes (ri-pē'ī mon'tēz). Range of snowy mountains supposed by the ancient Greeks to be at the extreme north of the world. Their exact location was never agreed upon. As the area of the known world increased, they were pushed farther and farther north. They did not finally disappear from maps until the Renaissance.

Rhode (rō'dē). In Greek mythology, a nymph, the daughter of Poseidon and the nymph Halia. She was born on the island of Rhodes and was the mother by Helius of seven sons and one daughter. She is sometimes said also to have been the mother of Phaëthon.

Rhodes (rōdz). [Greek: **Rhodos, Rodos**; Italian, **Rodi**; Latin, **Rhodus.**] Island in the Aegean Sea, SW of Asia Minor and separated from the coast by a channel about seven miles wide. One of the Dodecanese Islands, it is about 45 miles long and about 545 square miles in area. The surface is mountainous and hilly. It is noted for its fertility and has an active commerce. The inhabitants are largely Greek. According to traditional accounts, Rhodes was first inhabited by the Telchines, who nursed the infant Poseidon there. When he grew up he fell in love with Halia, a sister of the Telchines, and by her had six sons and one daughter, Rhode or Rhodos. These six sons outraged the goddess Aphrodite and committed other evil deeds. To punish them, Aphrodite drove them mad, and Poseidon sank them under the ground. Some say that when Zeus was parceling out the lands to the gods he absentmindedly forgot to award any to Helius, and when he thought of it, he was distressed. Helius offered to take an island that was just then rising from the great flood Zeus had sent over the world. Helius went there and found Poseidon's daughter Rhode, with whom he fell in love and for whom he named the island Rhodes. Thus, the island came to be known as "the Bride of the Sun." Rhodes is the scene of many myths and legends. Danaus, fleeing with his daughters from Egypt, stopped there and founded a temple of Athena at Lindus. Cadmus, searching for Europa, also touched at the island. He founded a temple to Poseidon in fulfillment of a vow he had made during a storm at sea, and also dedicated a bronze cauldron inscribed with Phoenician letters. According to some accounts, this was how the Phoenician alphabet was brought to the Greek world. Althaemenes, the son of Catreus of Crete, fled to Rhodes to escape an oracle that predicted he would kill his father. He built a temple to Zeus on Mount Atybrus, the highest point on the island, from which it was claimed he could see his beloved homeland. The flight of Althaemenes to Rhodes and his settlement there provide a legendary explanation for prehistoric colonization of the island by Cretans. Tlepolemus, the son of Heracles, also sought refuge on Rhodes, and became its king before he sailed to join Agamemnon in the war against Troy. His followers founded the three cities of Lindus, Camirus, and Ialysus

and laid the legendary basis for the Dorian invasion of Rhodes about 1000 B.C. Some say that Helen, after the death of Menelaus, fled from Sparta because of the enmity with which she was regarded, and sought asylum in Rhodes with her former friend Polyxo, wife of Tlepolemus. But Polyxo now hated her because of the death of Tlepolemus in the Trojan War, and inspired her maids to hang Helen. At one time Rhodes was so infested by serpents that it was called "Ophidea." The inhabitants sent to the oracle of Apollo at Delphi for relief, and were told to admit Phorbas, son of Lapithes, to colonize the island. The Rhodians sent for Phorbas, who came with his companions and destroyed the serpents. After his death he was accorded a hero's honors by the grateful people. Some say the three chief cities of the island—Ialysus, Lindus, and Camirus—were named for three daughters of Danaus who died there. Others say they were named for three grandsons of Helius, and that they founded the cities after a great flood and divided the island into three parts, each of the cities being the center of the area which each of the brothers ruled.

In prehistoric times Rhodes was colonized by Phoenicians and Cretans, and later by Dorians, and its three cities formed, with Halicarnassus, Cnidus, and Cos, the "Dorian Hexapolis." At the beginning of the 6th century B.C. the island fell under the domination of the Persians. After the Persian War it joined the first Athenian Confederacy, 478 B.C., from which it withdrew by revolt at the end of the 5th century. In 408 B.C. Lindus, Ialysus, and Camirus founded the city of Rhodes on the NE tip of the island. The new city became the capital, replacing Lindus, and rapidly grew into a flourishing commercial, religious, and political center, thanks to its location and its wide commerce throughout the Mediterranean. The city later came under the influence of Sparta, from which it freed itself in 394 B.C. In 378 it entered the second Athenian Confederacy, from which it withdrew in 356 B.C. After the death of Alexander the Great, who had imposed a garrison on Rhodes as an ally of Persia against the Macedonians, the Rhodians allied themselves to Egypt and successfully withstood a year's siege by the

Macedonians. Following this success, Rhodes entered into relations with Rome, and it was in this period that it reached the height of its importance and influence. Its commerce was carried on throughout the Mediterranean world. The code of maritime law developed by Rhodes was so good that 300 years later the Emperor Augustus adopted it for his entire empire. The city became an outstanding artistic and literary center. Lysippus the sculptor made his famous *Chariot of the Sun* there, and a distinctive Rhodian school of sculpture developed that numbered among its members Chares of Lindus, who made the famous *Colossus of Rhodes*; Philiscus, author of a group of the Muses; Apollonius and Tauriscus of Tralles, who executed the famous statue of the Dirce group, the so-called *Farnese Bull;* and Athenodorus, Polydorus, and Agesander, creators of the massive *Laocoön* group. Aeschines, the Athenian exile, founded a school of rhetoric at Rhodes that was later attended by Cato, Cicero, Caesar, Brutus, and other Romans. Splendid examples of Mycenaean pottery, dating from the 10th century B.C. and earlier have been found at Rhodes, and a distinctive style of glazed vases decorated with deer, the lotus flower, palm trees, and geometric designs, was in full flower by the 7th and 6th centuries B.C. The island was wholly sacred to Helius. Chariot-races, athletic and musical contests were held annually in the summer at the festival celebrated in his honor. Four horses were hurled into the sea each year at the festival as a sacrifice to him. About 278 B.C. the colossal bronze statue by Chares of Lindus was erected to Helius. This *Colossus,* one of the Seven Wonders of the ancient world, stood on the breakwater which protected the harbor of the city of Rhodes. It stood until 224 B.C., when it was hurled down by an earthquake; its fragments were melted down in 656 A.D. Augustus recognized Rhodes as a city allied to Rome. The emperor Vespasian incorporated it into the Roman Empire.

Rhodius (rō′di-us). Named by Homer as one of the rivers of the Troad. The Rhodius, after the Trojan War had ended, was diverted from its course by Apollo and Poseidon and sent against the wall the Greeks had erected to protect their ships. The rivers so diverted from their courses, with the aid of Zeus, washed the wall into the sea. See **Rhesus,** river.

Rhodius, Apollonius. See **Apollonius Rhodius.**

Rhodope (rod′ō-pē). In Greek legend, a beautiful maiden skilled in hunting; she was a companion of Artemis. She incurred the wrath of Aphrodite by taking an oath to Artemis that she would eschew the society of men. To punish her for denying her power, Aphrodite caused her to fall in love with a hunter she met in a cave. Artemis, enraged in her turn at this violation of an oath, changed Rhodope into a spring in the cave. This spring came to be used as a test for virginity. A maiden whose virtue was in question was required to write that she was a virgin on a tablet and then, holding the tablet in her arms, to step into the spring. If her tablet expressed a lie the spring rose up to her neck and covered the tablet. If her tablet expressed the truth the water did not touch it.

Rhodope Mountains. Mountains of NE Greece, sacred to Dionysus. According to legend, Rhodope was the wife of Haemus, king of Thrace, who was changed into a mountain because she considered herself more beautiful than Hera.

Rhodopis (ro-dō′pis) or **Rhodope.** According to some accounts, a beautiful maiden whose sandal was carried off by an eagle while she was bathing. The eagle flew to Memphis and deposited the sandal with Psammetichus, the king. He regarded this as an omen, was enchanted with the beautiful sandal, and determined to find the owner. When he found Rhodopis he made her his queen. But others say that Rhodopis was a beautiful courtesan, a Thracian by birth, who was taken as a slave to Samos and thence to Naucratis in Egypt. She was ransomed for a vast sum by Charaxus, the brother of Sappho the poetess. She remained in Naucratis, became wealthy, and left as a memorial of herself a number of iron spits for roasting whole oxen. These she gave as a present to the shrine of Delphi.

Rhodus (rō′dus). In mythology, a son of Aphrodite and Poseidon.

Rhoecus (rē′kus). In mythology, a Greek youth who noticed that an oak tree was about to fall and propped it up. In so doing he saved the life of the dryad that inhabited the tree and won her gratitude. She promised to give Rhoecus whatever he asked as a reward. He asked for her love and she consented to give him this gift, telling him that she would send him a bee as a messenger with instructions. When Rhoecus departed he fell in with some companions and forgot all about the bee, so that when it came he impatiently brushed it away and injured it. In anger at Rhoecus for so quickly forgetting her and for injuring her messenger, the dryad blinded Rhoecus.

Rhoecus. Greek sculptor and architect; fl. c500 B.C. He was a native of Samos, where he built the famous temple of Hera, called by Herodotus one of the three greatest works of all Greece. Rhoecus was also supposed to have been the inventor of casting statues in bronze.

Rhoeo (rē'ō). In Greek mythology, a daughter of Staphylus and Chrysothemis. Apollo seduced her, and when her father discovered that she was with child he locked her in a chest and set her adrift on the sea. The chest was wafted to the island of Delos, or as some say, to the shores of Euboea. There Rhoeo's son was born. She named him Anius, because of the "trouble" he had caused her. He became Apollo's priest and king of Delos.

Rhoeteum (rē-tē'um), **Cape.** A promontory on the Hellespont where Telamonian Ajax was buried, and to which Thetis washed the arms of Achilles after Neoptolemus lost them in a shipwreck.

Rhoetus (rē'tus). According to some accounts, one of the giants who battled against the gods. He was hurled into Tartarus by Zeus.

Rhoxolani (roks-ō-lā'nī). See **Roxolani.**

Rhyton (rī'ton). In ancient Greece, a type of drinking-vase, usually with one handle. In its usually curved form, pointed below, it corresponds to the primitive cup of horn. The lower part of the rhyton is generally molded into the form of a head of a man or, more often, of an animal, and is often pierced with a small hole through which the beverage was allowed to flow into the mouth.

Rieti (rye'tē). Modern name of **Reate.**

Rimini (rē'mē-nē). Modern name of **Ariminum.**

Rion (rē-ôn'). See **Phasis,** river.

Robigalia (rō-bi-gā'li-a). An annual festival in honor of Robigus and Robigo, supposedly instituted by Numa. The festival included a procession along the Via Claudia to the sacred grove of these two gods, about five miles outside Rome. The festival was held in April; prayers and incense were offered, a young dog and a sheep were sacrificed, and races were held.

Robigus (rō-bī'gus). In Roman mythology, an agricultural deity who protected growing grain from blight, or who was the personification of the blight. The female deity with the same function was Robigo.

Rodope or **Rodopi** (rod-ō'pē). See **Rhodope Mountains.**

Roma (rō'ma). In Roman legend, a daughter of Evander. According to some accounts, Evander founded Rome and named the city after his daughter. Roma came to be the personification of the city of Rome, and was worshiped as a goddess. During the reign of the Emperor Augustus, a circular shrine was raised on the Acropolis at Athens to the goddess Roma, where she was worshiped jointly with Augustus. The worship of Roma had begun as early as 195 B.C. In the 2nd century A.D. the Emperor Hadrian raised a temple to Roma and Venus. The figure of Roma appeared on the coins of the Roman Empire, where she was shown as a seated, robed figure, with a statue of Victory in her hand.

Roman Religion. The religious beliefs of the Italic tribes, of which Rome was a part, had a common origin with other Indo-European-speaking peoples who in prehistoric times began a series of migrations into Europe. However, from the 5th to the 1st century B.C., the only period for which reliable documentary evidence is available, the religion of the Italian people was already a composite of influences coming from the pre-Italic inhabitants—Etruscans (probably of Anatolian origin), Illyrians on the east coast, Greek colonists (and through them influences from the Near East), and trans-Alpine immigrants. In spite of these influences, a number of beliefs persisted which were genuinely native to the Romans and other Italians. The kernel of old Roman religion rested in the belief in impersonal spirits (*numina*) dwelling in some particular place or object. These numina, mostly concerned with the innumerable aspects of natural order, were thought to be present everywhere—in trees, stones, springs, groves—and to be able, if not properly placated, to inflict harm. This belief in impersonal spirits (that is, spirits which never attained the full personality of anthropomorphic gods) is reflected in the writings of such sophisticated poets as Ovid and Vergil. Ovid's description of the Aventine grove reveals this early stratum of Italic belief in nameless, awe-inspiring spirits: "There was a grove below the Aventine dark with the shade of holm-oaks, you might say, 'there is a spirit there (*numen inest*).'" We also hear of Ovid saying to his reader that Vesta, the hearth-spirit, should be considered "nothing more than the living flame." The same feeling of religious mystery, and fear, is found in Vergil's *Aeneid* (Book VIII) when Evander shows the site of the future city of Rome to Aeneas: "Hence he leads him to the abode of Tarpeia and the Capitol, gleaming now-a-days with gold, but once bristling with forest undergrowth. Even then the spot's dread awfulness brought fear to the timid countrymen; already they quaked before wood and rock." Evander continued: "This grove, this hill with its wooded top, some god, what god we know not, has for his dwelling." Hence, to the Roman, certain objects and places inspired in him a feeling of awe (*religio*) which compelled him to offer up prayers and sacrifices to these vague forces of nature in order to win their favor.

Greek contact with the Romans as far back as the 5th century B.C., and even earlier, resulted in the Italian deities' taking on certain attributes of their Hellenic parallels. Even among the early Italians certain greater personalized powers, such as Jupiter, Juno, and Diana, were sufficiently similar to some of the Olympian deities to be identified with them. In the course of time a number of Greek and Asiatic gods were introduced into Roman cult, some as new deities (as, Apollo, Cybele, Aesculapius), some under the names of nature gods with whom they were often identified in a superficial way (as, Demeter with Ceres, Aphrodite with Venus, Persephone with Libera). In this way the following major deities were established by analogy to the Greek form of religion:

Roman	Greek
Jupiter	Zeus
Juno	Hera
Neptune	Poseidon
Minerva	Athena
Mars	Ares
Venus	Aphrodite
Diana	Artemis
Vulcan	Hephaestus
Vesta	Hestia
Mercury	Hermes
Ceres	Demeter

After the Second Punic War, Greek ideas irresistibly made their way to Rome and it became more and more common to identify the gods of Rome with those of Greece. Thus the original significance of many Roman deities was either obscured or lost entirely. Under the influence of Hellenism, Roman gods became highly anthropomorphic. Statues of the gods in the forms of men and women were raised in the temples, and Roman writers, borrowing from the vast store of Greek myths, depicted their gods with all the moral weaknesses of men.

When the Romans prayed to the gods, they usually asked for material blessings rather than spiritual guidance. If examples of moral virtue were sought, they could be found in the lives of Roman soldiers and patriots, or in philosophy, which, like so many other things, was borrowed from the Greeks and adapted to Roman interests. Failure to receive help from the gods was taken to mean that the gods were angry with the petitioner. To regain favor, prayers and sacrifices were offered according to an exact ritual. If the favor was not granted the god had simply failed to fulfill his part of the agreement. The head of the family, the *paterfamilias*, could conduct his own religious services without the aid of an intermediary between himself and the deity to whom he addressed his prayers. However, prayers offered for the welfare of the state had to be offered in the most precise manner; they could not be left to any casual arrangement. Prayers and sacrifices on behalf of the state were placed in the hands of priests who were specially trained in the complicated rituals. A chief pontiff (*Pontifex Maximus*) and a kind of advisory board (*collegium pontificum*) assisted the chief magistrate in his sacral functions. Prayers and sacrifices for the good of the state were offered according to a ritual which, if not performed flawlessly, might result in being denied the favor of the gods. It was the function of the *pontifices* to know the proper religious course of action and the proper prayer-formula for regular festivals and for any religious crisis that might arise. They also had the duty of formulating the religious character of every day of the year, of keeping the knowledge of festival days throughout the year, and of seeing to it that they were duly announced to the people each month. There was no division between church and state, between civil officials and priests, for religious and political powers were one in the state. Civil officials were often members of particular priesthoods. In imperial times, the emperor himself took over the office of the chief pontiff. The Romans, believing that the gods were willing to express their approval or disapproval by signs, sought to know the will of the gods before undertaking any public action. Hence official diviners, called augurs, attempted to discover by the observation of signs, usually the flight or action of birds, whether the gods did or did not approve a proposed action. Predictions were also based on the observation of the entrails, especially the liver, of sacrificial animals by soothsayers (*haruspices*) who had inherited their skill from the Etruscans.

Rome was tolerant of religions other than her own, and even permitted the worship of foreign deities within the capital itself, though cults involving sensual or secret rites were at times forbidden. Adherents to Judaism and Christianity were excluded from this tolerance since the Romans regarded them as hostile to the gods of the state because of their obstinate refusal to offer incense on their altars. Fearing divine retribution for allowing such insults to the gods to go unpunished, and generally disliking anything resembling a secret society, the Romans persecuted Jews and Christians as subversives and enemies of the state. (PM)

Roma Quadrata (rō′ma kwod-rā′ta). Earliest fortified Rome, occupying the Palatine Hill and a quadrangular enclosure surrounding its base. This oldest fixed area or *pomerium* was looked upon with reverence, and was marked by boundary stones as late as the empire.

Rome (rōm). City in C Italy, the capital and center of the Roman republic and empire of ancient times. It is situated on both banks of the Tiber River, about 15 miles from its mouth. Evidence exists of settlements on the site dating from c1000 B.C. The legendary date of the foundation of the city is April 21, 753 B.C., when Romulus, the first king of Rome, built his settlement on the Palatine Hill known as *Roma Quadrata* (Square Rome) because the fortifications of his settlement enclosed it in a square. To gain wives for his followers Romulus invited the Sabines to a celebration of sacred games and, in the midst of it, captured the women and drove off the men. The women brought about a reconciliation between the Romans and Sabines; the latter were united in one race with the Romans and took up settlements on the Capitoline and Quirinal Hills, the former of which was added to the city. The area between the Palatine and Capitoline served as a common Forum. Traditionally, the seven kings of Rome were: Romulus (753–715 B.C.); Numa Pompilius (715–672 B.C.); Tullus Hostilius (672–640 B.C.), who destroyed Alba Longa, joined the Albans to the Romans, and added the Caelian Hill to the city; Ancus Marcius (640–616 B.C.), who added the Aventine Hill, the Janiculum, and the port of Ostia; Tarquinius Priscus (616–578 B.C.), who laid out the Circus Maximus; Servius Tullius (578–534 B.C.), who added the Quirinal and Viminal Hills and, so some say, the Esquiline Hill also, and built the Servian Wall that enclosed all the seven hills of Rome; and Tarquinius Superbus (534–510 B.C.), who laid the foundations of the temple of Capitoline Jupiter, and who was expelled by Lucius Junius Brutus, the founder of the Roman Republic (509 B.C.). The early history of the Republic is one of almost continuous warfare with the various tribes of Italy and with the Gauls of the north. About 390 B.C. the Gauls, under Brennus, captured and burned the city. It was hastily rebuilt as soon as the Gauls were driven out. By 265 B.C., having defeated the Etruscan and Latin federations, the Samnite tribes, and the Greek cities in S Italy, Rome had become the ruler of Italy, which was ultimately linked to the city by a network of magnificent roads. Among the many splendid roads were the Appian Way (Via Appia), which ran south and terminated at Brundisium, the Flaminian Way (Via Flaminia), running northeast to Ariminum on the Adriatic Sea, the Aurelian Way (Via Aurelia), running northwest to Pisa and continued by Augustus into Gaul, and the Latin Way (Via Latina), which was an inland road that ran south and joined the Appian Way at Capua. Rome clashed with Carthage, the leading maritime power of the Mediterranean, in the three Punic Wars (264–241 B.C., 218–201 B.C., and 149–146 B.C.), and with the final defeat of Carthage became not only the dominant sea power in the Mediterranean, but also the most powerful state in the ancient world.

By 61 B.C., when Julius Caesar became propraetor in Spain, Rome held sway over all Italy, Narbonensis, all of Spain and Portugal except the north coast of the Iberian peninsula, North Africa from Carthage east to the Nile, Phoenicia, large areas of the Parthian empire, Media, Armenia, Pontus, Bithynia, much of Asia Minor, all of Greece, and the eastern shore of the Adriatic Sea. Under Caesar and, after the replacement of the Republic by the Empire, under Augustus, Trajan, and Hadrian, Rome became the capital of a dominion which encompassed at its height virtually all of the world as it was then known to most people: the entire Mediterranean basin; to the N, Gaul, Britain, and what was later to be W Germany and the Netherlands along the banks of the Rhine River; the Alpine countries; to the E the Danube basin down to the Black Sea, the Balkans, Greece, Asia Minor, Syria, and Palestine; the North African shore from Egypt to Morocco; and all of Spain and Portugal. The Roman legions were unquestionably the best disciplined and most effective major military force known in the world to that time. The fact that they did not penetrate to India, as did the army of Alexander the Great, is probably chiefly attributable to what was long a basic Roman strategic attitude toward its military efforts, namely that the legions should take, fortify, and hold territory, which would then be developed and colonized as integral por-

tions of a single economic and (eventually) cultural unit. Compared to those of the early Roman emperors, Alexander's conquests were a brilliant military tour de force, but comprised an empire which it was far beyond actual Macedonian power to hold together. The Romans, who understood far better than anyone before them the logistic perils of too extended lines of communication, were not interested, for most of their history, in conquests which could not be consolidated and brought within the defensible empire. The existence of India and China was certainly known to the scholars and geographers of Rome under the emperors, but the thought of bringing them into the Empire was hardly one which would occur to leaders as shrewd and thrifty, in a military sense, as the early Roman emperors. It was during the period of early and middle Empire that the wealth of all these countries poured into Rome, and that the buildings which became the admiration of the centuries were erected.

Among the many existing remains of the Roman city are the Forum Romanum, with the arches of Titus, Septimius Severus, and Constantine, the Flavian Amphitheater or "Colosseum," Forum of Trajan, the temples of Concord, Fortune, Saturn, and Neptune, the Basilica of Constantine, the palace of Caligula, Christian and Jewish catacombs, and others; the Thermae (Baths) of Diocletian are near the Central Station; outside the old Servian Wall are the Theater of Marcellus, the well-preserved Pantheon, the Mausoleum of Augustus, and the Thermae (Baths) of Caracalla; the monument of Hadrian is on the right bank of the Tiber River.

Romulus (rom′ụ̄-lus). In Roman legend, the founder of Rome (753 B.C.) and its first king (753–716 B.C.). Venus complained to Jupiter about the misfortunes that were overwhelming her son Aeneas on his flight from Troy. Jupiter assured her that he had not changed his mind about the destiny of the Trojans. He told her that after a 300-year reign by the descendants of Aeneas, twins would be born to a princess of Trojan blood and one of these twins would become the founder of an unlimited empire. Aeneas, too, was given a glimpse into the future when he visited his father Anchises in the Underworld. The twins foretold by Jupiter were Romulus and Remus, the sons of Mars and the vestal Rhea Silvia, and thus grandsons of Numitor and descendants of Aeneas. Amulius, the brother of Numitor, had seized the throne. He now ordered the infant sons of his niece to be drowned, lest they grow up and avenge their grandfather. The babes were put into a chest and cast into the Tiber. But, under the protection of the gods, the chest floated down the river and was washed by a great tide up onto the banks near the Palatine Hill. There they lay under a fig tree. A she-wolf heard their cries and came and suckled them. Some say too, that a wood-pecker sent by Mars brought them food in its beak. The twins were found by a shepherd and brought up as his foster sons. Ultimately, Remus was brought before Numitor in some dispute and was recognized as his grandson. Romulus and Remus killed Amulius, restored Numitor to the throne, and went off to found a new city on the hills. Remus wanted to build the new city on the Aventine Hill. Romulus preferred the Palatine, the site of an ancient city of Trojan origin. A flight of birds favored the choice of Romulus and he immediately set to work to build the walls of his city. Remus, disappointed that his choice of a site had not prevailed, mocked the fortifications Romulus was building, and leaped scornfully over the walls. Romulus was infuriated and killed his brother. Romulus' settlement prospered but there were no women in the new town. Under the pretense of celebrating games, Romulus invited the Sabines to come with their wives and daughters for a festival. When the celebration was in full swing the young Romans seized the Sabine women and drove off the men. A war broke out which was settled at length by making the Sabines and the Romans equal in the new settlement. The new city, Rome, expanded and prospered under the wise rule of Romulus. At the end of his successful life Mars was permitted by Jupiter to descend from the heavens, in the midst of a fearful storm of thunder and lightning, and carry Romulus off in his chariot to the heavens. Thereafter he was worshiped as a god by the Romans, who gave him the name Quirinus and erected

temples in his honor. His wife was spared the grief of losing her husband: she was carried off to the heavens on a star and became known as Hora.

Romus (rō′mus). In Roman legend, a son of Aeneas or of his son Ascanius. According to some accounts, Aeneas died in Phrygia and did not reach Italy at all. These accounts say that it was this Romus who went to Italy and founded Rome. Such accounts are, of course, completely at variance with the *Aeneid.*

Roscius (rosh′us), **Quintus.** Greatest of Roman comic actors; died c62 B.C. He was a native of Solonium, near Lanuvium, in Latium. He was presented by Sulla with a gold ring, the symbol of equestrian rank, and was the instructor and friend of Cicero, who defended him in a lawsuit.

Rosetta Stone (rō-zet′a). An inscribed stone found in 1799 by soldiers of Napoleon near the Rosetta Mouth of the Nile (whence its name). A decree of the priests of Memphis, of 196 B.C., honoring Ptolemy V Epiphanes (210–181 B.C.) for his benefactions was recorded on it in three scripts—Egyptian hieroglyphs, Egyptian demotic or cursive, and Greek. The hieroglyphic text is broken at top and sides, but the demotic and Greek texts are almost complete. In the hands of Champollion and other scholars the Rosetta Stone became the key to the decipherment of the hieroglyphic script and the eventual analysis of the Egyptian language, which had survived as Coptic. Ceded to the British in 1801, the Rosetta Stone is in the British Museum. (JJ)

Roxana (rok-san′a, -sā′na). [Also: **Roxane.**] Wife of Alexander the Great; murdered at Amphipolis, Macedonia, 311 B.C. She was a Bactrian princess, the daughter of King Oxyartes, and was married to Alexander in 327 B.C. Alexander took other wives, according to the Oriental custom he increasingly followed, perhaps with the view to linking the Barbarians more closely with their Macedonian conquerors. In 324 B.C. he married Statira, daughter of Darius III, at Susa. After his death Roxana, then carrying his child, sent for Statira, who did not know Alexander had died. With the help of Perdiccas Roxana killed Statira and her sister, threw their bodies into a well, and filled it up with earth. At Babylon she bore Alexander's posthumous son, who was accepted by the Diadochi (Alexander's generals and successors) as co-king with Alexander's half-brother Arrhidaeus. Roxana went to Macedonia, where she sided with Olympias, Alexander's mother, against Cassander, and was put to death with her son by order of Cassander, 311 B.C.

Roxolani (roks-ọ-lā′nī). [Also: **Rhoxolani**.] One of the main divisions of the ancient Sarmatian people, situated in the region of the Tanais (Don) River about the beginning of the Christian era. They made frequent attacks on the Roman provinces, but later, with other Sarmatian tribes, allied themselves with Rome.

Rubi (rō′bē). [Modern name, **Ruvo di Puglia**.] In ancient geography, a town of Apulia, SE Italy. Many ancient Apulian vases of the 5th–2nd centuries B.C. have been discovered here.

Rubicon (rō′bi-kọn). In ancient geography, a small river in Italy, near Rimini. In the later Roman Republic it was the boundary between Italy proper and Cisalpine Gaul. The crossing of it by Julius Caesar, in 49 B.C., took place despite contrary orders to Caesar from the Senate, and signalized Caesar's irrevocable decision to proceed against Pompey, which meant civil war. From this event, the phrase "cross the Rubicon" has since come to describe any act or decision of irrevocable import. It has been identified with the Rugone, Uso, and Fiumicino rivers.

Rufia (rō-fyä′). See **Alpheus River**.

Rufus (rō′fus), **Marcus Caelius**. See **Caelius**.

Rufus, Publius Sulpicius. See **Sulpicius Rufus, Publius**.

Rugii (rō′ji-ī). Ancient Germanic tribe first mentioned by Tacitus. They were originally situated on the Baltic Sea, west of the mouth of the Vistula River. In the 5th century A.D. they appeared south of the Carpathians, where they are mentioned among the people in the army of Attila. They founded a kingdom on the Danube, including parts of Roman Noricum, which was overthrown late in the same century. They then joined the Ostrogoths (East Goths), with whom they subsequently disappear from history. With Jutes, Angles, Saxons, and possibly Frisians,

they seem to have taken part in the conquest of Britain, where their name is preserved in Surrey (old English, *Súthryge*) and in Eastry in Kent (Old English, *Eást-ryge*).

Ruinous Dream. In the *Iliad*, a dream sent by Zeus to Agamemnon which led the latter to believe that the opportunity had come to seize Troy at last, after nearly ten years of besieging it. The dream was sent by Zeus in fulfillment of his promise to Thetis to punish Agamemnon for his arrogant seizure of Achilles' captive Briseis. For in the struggle that followed as Agamemnon led his forces against Troy, Achilles refused to take part.

Rullianus (rul-i-ā′nus). See **Fabius Maximus, Quintus**.

Rullus (rul′us), **Publius Servilius**. Roman tribune of the people (63 B.C.). He sponsored a law for redistribution of lands to the advantage of the poorer citizens. Cicero made four speeches (three extant) against the measure, which was withdrawn, being obviously an attempt on the part of the party of Caesar to lay the onus of oppression on the aristocratic party.

Rumina (rō′mi-nạ). In Roman mythology, a minor goddess associated with the suckling of infants, both human and animal. There was a shrine of Rumina at the foot of the Palatine Hill near the Lupercal, where milk, not wine, was offered. Here, under a fig tree, Romulus and Remus were said to have been suckled by the she-wolf.

Rumor. According to Homer, "Zeus' own messenger." Vergil says she was the last child of Earth, and was a sister of Enceladus and Coeus. She is a swift-footed, feathered monster with a sleepless eye under each feather; and for every eye she has a tongue, a voice, and an ear. Rumor terrorizes whole cities with mixtures of truth and falsehood. Rumor brought the story of Dido and Aeneas to the ears of Iarbas, her rejected suitor. He appealed to Zeus, with the result that a message was sent from Zeus ordering Aeneas to depart for Italy. It was Rumor again, who brought to Dido the dread word that Aeneas was preparing to depart in secret. When Aeneas had landed in Italy, Rumor spread the news that Latinus had been advised by an oracle to give Lavinia to a stranger.

Rupilius (rō-pil′i-us), **Publius**. Roman politician, consul in 132 B.C. He is noted for the severity with which he prosecuted the followers of Tiberius Gracchus. He was subsequently brought to trial and condemned for persecuting them. In the meantime, he had suppressed a slave war on the island of Sicily in 131 B.C., and had organized the island as a Roman province.

Rusellae (rö-sel′ē). In ancient geography, a city of the Etruscan League, situated near the Umbro (Ombrone) River about six miles NE of what is now Grosseto. It was conquered (c300 B.C.) by the Romans. There are various remains of antiquity on the site.

Ruteni (rö-tē′nī). Ancient tribe in S Gaul, occupying what later was Rouergue. Defeated by the Romans in 121 B.C., they nevertheless retained a degree of autonomy and were allies of Caesar in 52 B.C.

Rutuli (rö-tū′lī) or **Rutulians** (-li-anz). In Roman legend, an ancient tribe of Latium, dwelling south of the Tiber, whose capital was Ardea. Their king Turnus was famous in connection with the legends of Aeneas, especially as a rival for the hand of Lavinia, and led the Rutuli to war against Aeneas and his Trojans when they landed in Italy.

Ruvo di Puglia (rö′vō dē pö′lyä). See **Rubi.**

Sabazius (sa-bā′zhus). In Thracian and Phrygian mythology, a god partially identified by the Greeks with Zeus and with Dionysus. His worship, which was orgiastic, was closely connected with that of Cybele and Attis, and was introduced into Athens in the 5th century B.C. It was introduced into Rome, and flourished throughout Italy after the 2nd century A.D. Sabazius was primarily a god of agriculture and of the regrowth of vegetation. His symbol was the snake, and a golden snake was used in the celebration of his mysteries. When he was identified with Zeus or Jupiter his symbol was the thunderbolt.

Sabellians (sa-bel′i-anz). Ancient Italic people which included the Sabines, Samnites, Lucanians, Piceni, Vestini, Marrucini, Frentani, Marsi, Paeligni, and others. Their language was Oscan.

Sabine Mountains (sā′bīn). Range of mountains E of Rome, near the E border of Latium. It is a branch of the Apennines. The highest point in the range is about 4200 feet.

Sabines (sā′bīnz). [Latin, **Sabini.**] Ancient people of C Italy, who lived chiefly in the mountains N and NE of Rome. They were allied to the Sabellians, Umbrians, and Oscans, and the Samnites were probably descended from them. They were defeated by Rome in 290 B.C. and formed subsequently

an important ethnic element in the composition of the Romans. The so-called rape of the Sabine women is a notable incident in the legendary history of early Rome. (According to one account of it, Romulus invited the Sabines to a celebration of games, and the Roman youths utilized the occasion to carry off several of the Sabine women for wives.) The chief town of the Sabines was Reate (now Rieti).

Sabinum (sa-bī′num). Country villa of Horace, his "Sabine Farm," the gift of Maecenas, situated not far from Tivoli. It is celebrated in his poetry.

Sabinus (sa-bī′nus). In the *Aeneid,* a planter of vines. He was said to be the forefather of the Laurentes (Latins) and the founder of the Sabine race.

Sacae (sā′sē). [Also: **Sakas.**] Ancient nomadic people dwelling in C Asia near the sources of the Oxus (modern Amu Darya) and the Jaxartes (Syr Darya). They invaded India in the 2nd century B.C. and are regarded as probably having been one of a number of Scythian peoples.

Sacer (sā′sėr), **Mons.** Latin name of the Sacred Mount.

Sacred Band. Band of 300 Thebans formed to take part in the wars of the 4th century B.C. against Sparta. The band was made of 150 pairs of devoted friends, sworn to

protect each other and their country. The
Sacred Band was especially distinguished at
Leuctra in 371 B.C., and was destroyed by
Philip of Macedon at Chaeronea in 338 B.C.
Under Epaminondas the Sacred Band was
organized into a flying wedge that spear-
headed all attacks.

Sacred Mount. [Latin, **Mons Sacer.**] Hill
about three miles NE of Rome, beyond the
Anio (Aniene) River. It is noted in Roman
history as the place of temporary emigrations
of the plebeians, undertaken in order to
extort civil privileges. The first (c494 B.C.)
led to the establishment of the tribunate;
the second (449 B.C.) resulted in the abolition of the decemvirate.

Sacred Nine. Poetic epithet of the Muses.

Sacred Wars. In Greek history, wars undertaken by members of the Amphictyonic
League in defense of the shrine of Delphi.
There were four of these wars: 1) In c600–
590 B.C. (or 596–586), the Amphictyons
overthrew Crisa and Cirrha. 2) Athens aided
the Phocians in recovering Delphi, c448 B.C.
3) In 357–346 B.C., the Phocians, at first
successful against the Thebans, Locrians, and
others, were overthrown by the aid of Philip
of Macedon, who joined the allies in 352 B.C.
Phocis was replaced by Philip in the League.
4) In 339–338 B.C., the Amphictyons appointed Philip to punish the Locrians of
Amphissa for sacrilege; his successes led to
the union of Athens and Thebes against him
and their defeat at Chaeronea in 338 B.C.

Sacred Way. See Via Sacra.

Sacred Way. Ancient road in Greece from
Athens to Eleusis, starting at the Dipylon
Gate and traversing the Pass of Daphne.
Over it passed every autumn from Athens
the solemn procession for the celebration in
the shrine of the great Eleusinian sanctuary
of the mysteries in honor of Demeter, Persephone, and Iacchus. For almost its whole
length it was bordered with tombs and
chapels. At the beginning of the road, in
the area known as Ceramicus, a number of
the tombs remain in place, practically uninjured. Further along the modern road to
Eleusis, whose line is almost identical with
that of the Sacred Way, many architectural
fragments are still visible, and some can be
identified from the descriptions of Pausanias.
At one point on the road is the monastery

at Daphne which exhibits, in contrast with its
Byzantine architecture, some remnants of
French Gothic work. It was founded by the
French dukes of Athens, and contains their
tombs, but occupies the site of a temple to
Apollo. Further on, toward the Bay of
Salamis, there are considerable remains of a
sanctuary to Aphrodite.

Sacriportus (sak-ri-pōr′tus). In ancient geography, a locality in Latium, Italy, near
Praeneste. Here Sulla decisively defeated
(82 B.C.) the forces of the younger Marius.

Saepinum (sē-pī′num). [Modern name, **Altilia.**] Small place in C Italy about 20 miles
N of Beneventum. The Roman walls of the
ancient town remain practically perfect.

Sagitta (sạ-jit′ạ). An insignificant but very
ancient northern constellation—the Arrow—
placed between Aquila and the bill of
Cygnus. It is, roughly speaking, in a line
with the most prominent stars of Sagittarius
and Centaurus, with which it may originally
have been conceived to be connected.

SAGITTARIUS
Pictured according to ancient descriptions

Sagittarius (saj-i-tā′ri-us). The ninth sign of
the zodiac—the Archer—which the sun enters
about November 22. Also, a zodiacal constellation representing a centaur (originally
doubtless some Babylonian divinity) drawing
a bow. The constellation is situated east of
Scorpio, and is, especially in the latitudes

of the southern United States, a prominent object on summer evenings.

Saguntum (sạ-gun′tum). [Modern name, **Sagunto.**] In ancient geography, a town in E Spain, situated near the Mediterranean Sea, about 15 miles N of what is now Valencia. A Roman theater and the ruins of an ancient citadel are preserved; there are scattered remains also from the Iberian, Carthaginian, and Moorish periods. The ancient town, according to legend founded by Greeks, actually is more likely to have been an Iberian town. Around 228 B.C. the town, disturbed by the growth of Carthaginian power, concluded an alliance with Rome. The Carthaginian leader Hannibal attacked the town in 219 B.C. and conquered it after a siege of eight months. The Romans rebuilt the town after 214 B.C., but it failed to regain its former importance.

Saitis (sạ-ī′tis). Epithet of Athena, from Sais, the Egyptian goddess with whom Athena was identified. Danaus is said to have raised a sanctuary of Athena Saitis on Mount Pontinus near Lerna, where the heads of the husbands his daughters had murdered were buried.

Salacia (sạ-lā′shạ). In Roman mythology, the consort and cult partner of Neptune. She was an ancient Italian goddess and is thought to have been the spirit of springing water. She later became identified with the Greek Amphitrite.

Salamis (sal′ạ-mis). In mythology, a daughter of the river-god Asopus and Metope. Poseidon fell in love with her and carried her off to an island in the Saronic Gulf. She bore Poseidon a son, Cychreus, who became king of the island, which was subsequently named Salamis in honor of his mother.

Salamis. [Also: **Koulouri.**] Island of Greece, in the Saronic Gulf, S of Attica and opposite the harbor of Athens. It is about ten miles long. The island was said to have been named for Salamis, daughter of the river-god Asopus. Her son by Poseidon, Cychreus, had been made king of the island for his service in slaying a serpent that was ravaging the land, at that time known as "the Serpent Isle." During the reign of Cychreus Telamon fled here when he was banished from Aegina for the murder of Phocus. Cychreus welcomed him and gave him his daughter in marriage. Later, some say, Cychreus became so cruel that he was expelled and went to Eleusis to become an attendant of Demeter, but the Salaminians founded a sanctuary of Cychreus and worshiped him as a hero. Telamon succeeded him on the throne. His son, Great Ajax, was born on the island, and from here he sailed in command of 12 ships to join the Greeks in the war against Troy. Near the harbor is the stone on which Telamon sat and watched his two sons, Ajax and Teucer, put out for Aulis to join the Greek fleet. The people of Salamis honored Ajax and his son Eurysaces, and in the temple of Ajax was an ebony image of him. In early times, Salamis was independent, and was contended for by the Megarians and Athenians; for whichever of the two cities controlled Salamis menaced the other city. Solon aroused the Athenians to "recover" Salamis. A force was organized, of which Pisistratus was one of the generals. Under his command, Nisaea, the Megarian port opposite Salamis, was taken. This was followed by the occupation of the island itself. The Megarians and Athenians made peace and agreed to submit their dispute to arbitration. The Spartans, called on to judge the merit of their claims, awarded the island to Athens (c596 B.C.) because of the connection of Cychreus with Eleusis, and also because of the lines in the *Iliad* that connect Salamis and Athens, they read:

Ajax from Salamis led his warships; twelve was number

Led them and stationed them where the Athenians stood in battalions.

After the destruction of Athens in the Persian War the Persian fleet of Xerxes assembled off Salamis, with the intention of engaging the Greek fleet. The Athenians had withdrawn to the island with their families before the Persian advance on Athens, and wanted to make a stand against them there. The Greeks of the Peloponnesus were reluctant to fight, as they thought, for the benefit of the Athenians, and preferred to protect the Peloponnesus by constructing a great wall across the isthmus. Themistocles, the great Athenian commander, feared that the vote in the assembly would go against his plan to fight at Salamis, and that the allies would elect instead to withdraw and defend the

Peloponnesus. He first threatened to withdraw the Athenian fleet and when that failed to change the plans of his allies, he resorted to stratagem. He sent a confidential messenger to the Persians to tell them that the Greeks were disorganized and in panic, as indeed they were, and to advise them that this would be the time to attack. The Persians promptly accepted the advice. They sent a force to occupy the island of Psyttalia, which lies between the jutting promontory of Salamis and the mainland, ordered their Egyptian allies to sail around Salamis and cut off a Greek retreat through the Bay of Eleusis, and moved their own ships in to block the Greeks behind the island of Psyttalia. While the Greeks, unaware of these maneuvers, were still disputing in council, Aristides arrived from Aegina and announced that it was now too late to argue, as they were surrounded. Themistocles had chosen the narrow waters of Salamis for the engagement with the Persians because it was best suited to the Greek ships, and in the narrow space the Persian ships would be at a disadvantage. In addition to his determination to protect Megara, Aegina, and Salamis, which would be abandoned if the Greeks withdrew to the Peloponnesus, he considered the strait of Salamis the ideal spot and opportunity for a decisive battle with the Persians. Demaratus, the Spartan king who had been exiled and who had fled to the court of Xerxes, accompanied him on his expedition into Greece. Some say that before the battle of Salamis he was walking with an Athenian exile in the plain near Athens. They observed a huge dust storm, raised as if by the feet of thousands of marching men, rising in the direction of Eleusis, and out of it they heard a great cry, like the cry given at the festival of Eleusis. Demaratus asked his Athenian companion what the dust and the cry could mean. The Athenian answered that it was a token of disaster for the forces of Xerxes, for as there were no men where the dust rose it must have come by divine means, and the cry was certainly a divine one; and since both came from Eleusis it was a message of good fortune for Athens. If the dust moved off in the direction of the Peloponnesus it indicated defeat for the land forces of Xerxes;

if it went toward the ships it indicated disaster for the fleet. As the two watched the dust formed a great cloud, rose in the air, and moved toward the ships. Now Demaratus and his companion knew that the fleet of Xerxes would suffer defeat, but they decided not to tell Xerxes of the omen, lest in his anger he cut off their heads. When the Greeks saw that they no longer had a choice they prepared for battle. At dawn, Sept. 20, 480 B.C., the Greeks put to sea in their fleet. The Persians attacked, and at once the Greeks started to back water as Themistocles had told them to do to lure the Persians through the narrow strait. Then one ship, either Athenian or Aeginetan, darted out from the line and attacked the enemy. As it was engaged the other Greek ships came to its aid and battle was joined. Some say that at this time a phantom in the shape of a woman appeared to the Greeks and cheered them on in a voice that was heard from one end of the line to the other, but first she rebuked them, saying, "Strange men, how long are you going to back water?" And some say that Cychreus appeared in serpent form during the battle and aided the Greek fleet. The Persians fought bravely, for Xerxes was watching the battle from the mainland, but their heavy ships were unable to maneuver in the narrow space, and those in the van who tried to withdraw were soon entangled with those that were eagerly forcing their way forward from the rear. By the end of the day a large part of the fleet was either destroyed or disabled. The Persians were compelled to withdraw to Phalerum, having suffered an overwhelming and decisive defeat. After the Persian War Salamis remained under Athenian control until it passed to Macedon in 318 B.C.; it was restored to Athens c230 B.C.

Salamis. In ancient geography, a city on the E coast of Cyprus, near what is now Famagusta. Teucer, the half-brother of Telamonian Ajax, was banished by his father on his return to Salamis from the Trojan War, because he had not brought back the bones of Ajax for burial. He sailed to Cyprus and was given permission to found a city, which he named Salamis after his homeland. In the Roman period the city was rebuilt as Constantia. Near it, a naval victory was gained (306 B.C.) by Demetrius Poliorcetes over Ptolemy I and his allies.

Salarian Way (sạ-lãr′i-ạn). See **Via Salaria**.

Salassi (sạ-las′ī). Ancient Ligurian (or perhaps Celtic) tribe which occupied the valley of the Duria Major, in NW Italy. They were in conflict with the Romans (143 B.C. and later), and were finally subdued in 25 B.C.

Salembria (sạ-lem′bri-ạ). See **Peneus**.

Salentinum Promontorium (sal-ẹn-tī′num promọn-tō′ri-um). A Latin name of **Santa Maria di Leuca, Cape**.

Salerno (sạ-lér′nō), **Gulf of**. [Also: **Gulf of Paestum**; Italian, **Golfo di Salerno**.] Arm of the Mediterranean Sea, on the W coast of Italy, SE of the Bay of Naples.

Salernum (sạ-lér′num). [Modern name, **Salerno**.] Town in S Italy, situated on the Gulf of Salerno SE of Naples. It became a Roman colony in 194 B.C.

Salii (sal′i-ī). Roman priests of Mars. They guarded the shield that fell from heaven, and according to tradition their order was established in the reign of Numa. They had charge of the sacred shields called ancilia, which they bore once a year in solemn procession through the city with hymns and dances.

Salina (sä-lē′nä). [Ancient name, **Didyme**.] One of the Lipari Islands, in the Mediterranean Sea about four miles NW of Lipari. Length, about six miles.

Sallust (sal′ust). [Full Latin name, **Caius Sallustius Crispus**.] Roman historian; born at Amiternum, in the country of the Sabines, Italy, c86 B.C.; died c34 B.C. He was elected tribune of the people in 52. In 50 B.C. he was expelled from the Senate by the censors on the ground, according to some, of adultery with Fausta, the daughter of the dictator Sulla and wife of Titus Annius Milo, but more probably for political reasons, inasmuch as he was an active partisan of Caesar. He accompanied Caesar in 46 B.C. on his African campaign, at the conclusion of which he is said to have amassed a fortune by injustice and extortion. This fortune enabled him to retire from public life, as he was compelled to do on the death of Caesar, and to devote himself to the literary life. He also used it to lay out the magnificent pleasure ground, situated in the N part of Rome, E of the Pincian Hill, known as the Gardens of Sallust. He wrote *Catilina* or *Bellum Catilinae,* on the conspiracy of Catiline, and *Jugurtha* or *Bellum Jugurthinum,* on the war with Jugurtha, both of which are extant and show him to have been biased. His most important work was his *Historiae,* in five books, of which only fragments are extant. It contained a survey of ancient times, a brief description of the civil war between Marius and Sulla, and a detailed history from 78 to 67 B.C. Sallust modeled himself on Thucydides, in his attempt to present the truth and the causes of events, and in the use of speeches by the various men who shaped events, or were shaped by them, to reveal their characters and the general attitudes of the times.

Salmacis (sal′mạ-sis). In mythology, a nymph of a fountain of the same name in Caria. She fell in love with Hermaphroditus, who had come to drink at the spring. He, a mere youth, rejected her advances, and begged her to go away and leave him alone. Salmacis withdrew into the forest but kept watch on Hermaphroditus. When he, tempted by the clear water, dived into the pool Salmacis dived in after him and clung to him. As he struggled to escape she prayed that he might never be separated from her. Her prayer was answered as their bodies were fused into one, neither completely male nor completely female. Hermaphroditus, realizing that he no longer existed as a man, prayed that whatever man bathed in that pool should emerge from it only half a man. This accounts for the tradition concerning the fountain in Caria of this name: that whoever drinks of it or bathes in its waters becomes effeminate.

Salmoneus (sal-mō′nẹ-us). In Greek mythology, one of the sons of Aeolus and Enarete. He left Thessaly and went to Elis, where he founded the city of Salmonia on the Enipeus River. His wife Alcidice died in giving birth to Tyro, a maiden of surpassing beauty. He next married Sidero, who ill-treated his daughter Tyro. Salmoneus was an arrogant and violent ruler, who considered himself godlike. In his insolence he imitated Zeus to such an extent that he confused himself with the god. He had a chariot so constructed, with bronze drums covered with hides, that there was a clangor as of thunder

fat, fāte, fär, fãre, errạnt; net, mē, hėr ardẹnt; pin, pīne; not, nōte, möve, nôr,

when he drove through the streets. On the festival day of Zeus he dashed through the streets in his thundering chariot hurling firebrands in imitation of the lightning, and calling on the people to worship him as Zeus the Thunderer. The vengeance of Zeus was swift. Real thunder roared and a bolt of lightning struck him dead and put the city in flames. He was hurled down into Tartarus, where Aeneas saw him when he visited Anchises in the Underworld on his way to Italy.

Salonika (sal-ō-nē′ka͟, sa͟-lon′i-ka͟). [Also: **Salonica, Saloniki, Thessalonike, Thessaloniki.**] See **Thessalonica.**

Salonika, Gulf of. See **Thermaic Gulf.**

Salpinx (sal′pingks). Epithet of Athena, meaning "Trumpet." Athena was credited with having invented the trumpet. Hegeleos, grandson of Heracles, founded a temple of Athena Salpinx at Argos and taught the Dorians how to play the trumpet.

Salus (sā′lus). In Roman mythology, a goddess personifying health and prosperity, identified with Valetudo, with whom the Greek Hygea was identified. From 302 B.C. there was a temple to Salus, as the goddess who protected the welfare of the Roman people, on the Quirinal. The ancient attributes of Salus were ears of grain, pointing to an original agricultural function, which became lost in her aspect of health-giver. She was supplicated in times of epidemic and on the emperor's birthday.

Samarkand or **Samarcand** (sam-a͟r-kand′). See **Maracanda.**

Same (sā′mē). Another name for Cephallenia, an island in the Ionian Sea west of the Gulf of Corinth. Under this name it is mentioned in the Odyssey as the home of some of Penelope's suitors.

Samicon (sam′i-ko͟n) of **Samicum** (-kum). In ancient geography, a city of Triphylia in Elis, Greece, situated on a high plateau of Mount Makistos. It was the meeting place of the six Minyan cities of Triphylia, and was noted for its temple of Samian Poseidon. Still visible are parts of the fortifications, built by the Eleans as a defense against the Spartans and Arcadians, probably in the 4th century B.C.

Samnites (sam′nīts). Ancient Italic people of Samnium, in C Italy. Their language was Oscan and hence they were culturally and linguistically close to the Sabellians. It is thought that the Samnites may have been descended from the ancient Sabines.

Samnite Wars (sam′nīt). In Roman history, the wars between Rome and the Samnites. The First Samnite War (343–341 B.C.), broke out when Rome answered an appeal from Capua and other towns of Campania for aid against the Samnite hill tribes who were invading the lowlands of Campania. The war was concluded (341 B.C.) by a treaty with the Samnites, under which they withdrew from Campania and the towns of that lowland area put themselves under Rome's protection. The Second Samnite War (328–304 B.C.), erupted when the Samnites went to the defense of Palaepolis, which had been sending raiders into Campania and had drawn a declaration of war from Rome as a result. In the course of the war the Romans suffered a disastrous defeat at the Caudine Forks (321 B.C.) and were forced to agree to a humiliating peace. But as Rome continued to strengthen herself with allies the Samnites renewed the war, 316 B.C., to put an end to the increasing power of their enemy. The Samnites were joined in the last years of the war by the Etruscans, Umbrians, Marsi, Paeligni, and others. However, when the Romans invaded Samnite territory, and took their town of Arpinum, the Samnites concluded peace (304 B.C.) by renewing the former treaty with Rome. The Third Samnite War (298–290 B.C.) was caused by an attack of the Samnites on the Lucanians, Roman allies. Rome took the offensive and captured one Samnite stronghold after another. The Samnites found allies in the northern tribes, the Umbrians, Etruscans, and Cisalpine Gauls. The Roman consuls, Quintus Fabius Maximus Rullianus and Publius Decius Mus, marched at the head of four legions and defeated the Samnites and their allies at Sentinum after a desperate struggle in which Decius and 8000 Romans were lost. After this defeat the allies abandoned the Samnites, and although they continued the war alone for five more years their power was broken, and they were at last compelled, 290 B.C., to conclude a peace, by the terms of which they became allies of Rome.

Samnium (sam'ni-um). In ancient geography, a mountainous district in C Italy. It was bounded by the country of the Marsi, Paeligni, and Frentani on the N, Apulia on the E, Lucania on the S, Campania on the SW, and Latium on the W, and was originally inhabited by the Samnites.

Samos (sā'mos). Island in the Aegean Sea, off the W coast of Asia Minor, from which it is separated by a narow strait; colonized by Ionians, c1100–1000 B.C. The island, with an area of 181 square miles, is mountainous (highest point, 4725 feet), but has land of notable fertility. According to one tradition, Samia, daughter of the river-god Maeander, married Ancaeus the Less who accompanied Jason on the quest for the Golden Fleece, and who as king of the Leleges named his island kingdom for his wife. The Samians said that Hera was born on their island, near the Imbrasus River; and the willow tree under which she was born still stood in the sacred precinct and was shown to the traveler Pausanias in the 2nd century A.D. On the island, Zeus and Hera spent their wedding night, which lasted, some say, for 300 years. Samos was one of the chief seats of the worship of Hera, and one of her most ancient temples was here. It was raised, some say, by the Argonauts, and the ancient image within it was brought by them from Colchis. In the time of Herodotus the temple of Hera on Samos was the largest then known. Among the offerings in the temple was an embossed bronze bowl, sent by the Spartans as a gift to Croesus, king of Lydia. The Spartans claimed the Samians stole the bowl when the ship carrying it to Croesus touched at their port. The Samians said it arrived in their island after Croesus had been defeated by Cyrus, and that it was sold by the Spartans to some Samians, who then offered it to the temple. Amasis, king of Egypt, sent two wooden statues of himself to the temple, because of his friendship with Polycrates, tyrant of Samos. A linen corselet, in which were woven the figures of many animals and which was embroidered in gold and silver thread, was also dedicated in the temple. This was also a gift of the Spartans, but it had been intended for Amasis, and the Spartans said the Samians stole it. Mandrocles, a Samian engineer, built a bridge across the Bosporus for Darius when he was preparing to march against Thrace. Darius honored him with great gifts, part of which Mandrocles used to have a picture painted in the temple of Hera. The picture showed the bridge, with Darius sitting on a seat of honor and watching his army cross over into Thrace. Under the picture was the following inscription:

> The fish-fraught Bosporus bridged, to Hera's fane
> Did Mandrocles this proud memorial bring;
> When for himself a crown he'd skill to gain,
> For Samos praise, contenting the Great King.

The Samians were great sailors, and ventured as far west as Tartessus. With part of the proceeds of such a voyage they caused to be made a bronze vessel, with griffins embossed on it, and resting on three ten-foot kneeling figures wrought of bronze; this they dedicated in the temple. Ionians and Epidaurians colonized Samos in very early times, and it became a flourishing commercial and shipping center. Polycrates made himself master of the island c540 B.C., built up a great fleet, captured many of the neighboring islands, and overcame the Lesbians in a sea fight. He compelled his Lesbian prisoners, weighted down with chains, to dig a moat around his castle. In making himself master of Samos he caused many prominent men to go into exile. They sought help from Sparta to secure their return and overthrow Polycrates. The Spartans, to punish the Samians for the theft of the bronze vessel intended for Croesus and the theft of the linen corselet intended for Amasis, agreed to help the exiled Samians. The Corinthians, because of an old grievance, joined the Spartans. They assembled a fleet and besieged Samos. When the place had not fallen after a siege of 40 days the Spartans and their allies withdrew and sailed back to the Peloponnesus. Polycrates, who had slain one of his brothers and banished another, Syloson, in winning control of Samos, had an alliance of friendship with Amasis, king of Egypt. According to legend, this friendship was broken off by Amasis because he feared lest the unfailing good fortune of Polycrates bring down on him the wrath of the gods, who are ever jealous of and seek to humble the pride of men. Legend aside, the friendship between Samos and Egypt ended during the reign of the successor of Amasis, when Polycrates offered his aid to Cambyses, the enemy of Egypt.

The Samians were great and daring sailors, versatile traders, and under Polycrates maintained a luxurious court of which the poet Anacreon was an ornament. During his rule some remarkable feats of engineering were executed. An underground aqueduct over 1000 feet long beneath a hill 900 feet high was constructed to bring water into the city. He completed the magnificent temple of Hera, the largest of its time. Another engineering triumph carried out by the Samians was the construction of a great mole to protect their harbor. The fears of Amasis that the gods would bring evil to his too fortunate friend Polycrates were fulfilled. Oroetes, the Persian satrap at Magnesia, lured him there with the promise of great treasure for his fleet, seized him upon his arrival, and caused him to be slain. Maeandrius, successor of Polycrates, raised an altar to Zeus the Protector of Freedom and prepared to grant Samos a democratic government, but when he saw that if he gave up the tyranny someone else would seize it, he kept his despotic power. Samos was the first city, Greek or barbarian, to fall under the sway of Darius I. Some say Darius attacked Samos as a favor to Syloson, banished brother of Polycrates. This Syloson had performed a friendly act for Darius while the latter was still unknown and powerless. When Darius became king of the Persians Syloson reminded him of the incident and asked the return of Samos as a reward. Henceforth Samos was subject to the Persians. During the Ionian Revolt the Samians rose, and engaged their fleet with other Ionian units in defense of Miletus, but in consequence of an agreement made by the Samian captains with the Persians, when the battle was joined all but 11 of the Samian ships deserted their Ionian allies and sailed away (494 B.C.). This treachery was humiliating to many Samians. Furthermore, they did not enjoy living under Persian dominion. They honored the captains who had remained to fight with their allies, and then many of them left Samos and went

to settle in Zancle in Sicily. Samos remained under Persian control, and fought, at the battle of Salamis (480 B.C.), under Persian command. The following spring the Persian fleet mustered at Samos, but by this time the Samians had had enough of Persian rule. They sent envoys to the Spartan admiral Leotychides, urging him to free the Ionian cities, promising that the Ionians would rise up, and assuring him of the friendship and help of Samos. Leotychides agreed; some say he was convinced by the good omen that appeared in the name of the Samian envoy: he was Hegesistratus, "Leader of Armies." The Greek fleet sailed and when it appeared off Samos the Persians, rather than risk battle, withdrew to join their land army at Mycale opposite Samos. As the Greeks pursued them and prepared to engage them on land, the Persians disarmed the Samians who were in their army. They suspected them of complicity, because they could not help but note that the Samians had ransomed many Athenian prisoners taken by the Persians and returned them to Greece. Even though disarmed, the Samians did all in their power to help the Greeks at Mycale, and the Persians suffered a disastrous defeat (479 B.C.). After the Persian War Samos was one of the leading maritime members of the Confederacy of Delos, from which it revolted, 440 B.C. Pericles besieged it, 439 B.C., put down the revolt and established a democratic government there. In the last years of the Peloponnesian Wars it was one of the most faithful friends of Athenian democracy, but afterward it was besieged by the Spartan Lysander, who restored the oligarchy (404 B.C.), and fell under Spartan influence. It was retaken by Athens, 366 B.C., and colonized by Athenians. After the death of Alexander the Great it fell to the sway of his general, Ptolemy, later bowed to Philip V of Macedon, was given by the Romans (189 B.C.) to the kings of Pergamum, and became part of the Roman province of Asia, 133 B.C. Mark Antony captured and sacked it, 39 B.C., and Augustus restored its freedom. Among the famous sons of Samos were the philosopher Pythagoras, the astronomer Conon, and the sculptor and architect Rhoecus, who is said to have invented casting in bronze and who was the architect of the famous temple of Hera.

Samos. [Also: **Same.**] Ancient city in Cephallenia.

Samosata (sạ-mos'ạ-tạ). In ancient geography, a fortified town in Commagene, Syria, situated on the right bank of the Euphrates; residence of the kings of Commagene and important commercial center. It was the birthplace of Lucian.

Samothrace (sam'ọ-thrās). [Also: **Khora, Samothrake, Samothraki.**] Wild, rocky island in the N part of the Aegean Sea, belonging to Greece, opposite the mouth of the Hebrus River and NW of the island of Imbrus. According to legend, it was the isle of Electra, daughter of Atlas, who bore Dardanus to Zeus in Arcadia. Dardanus, some say, went to Samothrace after the great Deucalian flood and established the mysteries there and the cult of the Great Goddesses, whose images he brought with him to the island. Afterward, Dardanus left Samothrace on a raft borne up by inflated skins and sailed to the coast of Asia Minor, where he founded Troy. According to Homer, Poseidon ascended the highest mountain of Samothrace to observe the progress of the Greeks during the Trojan War. Some say Cadmus stopped in Samothrace when he was searching for his lost sister Europa. The island was famed in ancient times as the center of highly revered mysteries, those of the Cabiri, concerning which little is known. The rocky and difficult coast of the island, and the lack of anchorages, protected it from invasion, rendered it politically unimportant, and conserved the ancient mysteries intact. These mysteries assumed great importance under the Hellenistic rulers, and came to rival those of Eleusis in importance. It was when he went to Samothrace to be initiated into the mysteries that Philip II met Olympias, who became his wife and the mother of Alexander the Great. Arsinoë Philadelphus, the daughter of Ptolemy I who married her brother Ptolemy II, was banished to Samothrace and became patroness of the sanctuary. She subsequently escaped and married Ptolemy II, but continued her benefactions to Samothrace. She and Ptolemy dedicated the most important buildings on the island. Perseus, last king of Macedonia, fled to Samothrace after his defeat by Aemilius Paulus (168 B.C.)

and sought refuge in the sanctuary; he was captured there and taken prisoner. At Samothrace a French expedition found (1863) the famous statue called the *Victory of Samothrace,* now in the Louvre. Among the remains discovered on the island are the ruins of a temple dating from the 6th century B.C., ruins of a later temple, probably that dedicated by Ptolemy II, and a few rows of seats of an ancient theater. A New York University expedition directed by Karl Lehmann has, in a number of excavation campaigns since 1939, exposed the central area of the sanctuary. The area of the island is about 71 square miles; its highest point, 5248 feet.

Sanchuniathon (san-kū-nī'ạ-thon). [Also: **Sanchoniathon.**] Legendary chronicler of ancient Phoenicia, said to have lived before the Trojan War, whose works (allegedly founded upon records preserved in the temples) Philo Byblius pretended to have translated.

Sancus (sang'kus). In Roman mythology, a primitive god sometimes identified with Dius Fidius, and also called Semo Sancus. He was probably a god of the lightning, and was worshiped as a god of oaths, of the public laws of hospitality and of nations, and he was also worshiped as the protector and preserver of safety on the roads. Oaths taken in his name must be made under the open sky; for this reason his temples, one on the Quirinal and another on the island in the Tiber, had holes in the roof. Sancus was sometimes identified with Hercules.

Sandrocottus (san-drọ-kot'us) or **Sandrokottos** (-os). [Also: **Chandragupta.**] The founder of the Maurya or Magadha kingdom in India (capital, Patna). He died c286 B.C. He reigned c322–c298 B.C. According to the Greek tradition he was an Indian king who in the time of Seleucus I (Seleucus Nicator) ruled over the Gangaridae and Prasii on the banks of the Ganges. He was of humble origin, and was the leader of a band of robbers before obtaining the supreme power. In the troubles following the death of Alexander, he extended his sway over the greater part of N India, conquering the Macedonians left by Alexander in the Punjab. Seleucus invaded his dominions, but did not succeed, and, concluding a peace, ceded to Sandrocottus his conquests in the Punjab and the country of the Paropamisus, receiving in return 500 war elephants. For many years afterward Seleucus had as his ambassador at the court of Sandrocottus, Megasthenes, to whose work entitled *Indica* later Greek writers were chiefly indebted for their accounts of India. The king is supposed to have abdicated and later to have committed suicide. The identification of Chandragupta with Sandrocottus admits of no reasonable doubt. This identification is of the utmost importance to Indian chronology, in which everything depends upon the date of Chandragupta as ascertained from that of Sandrocottus as given by the classical writers. Hindu and Buddhist writers are entirely silent as to Alexander, but show that Chandragupta overthrew the dynasty of the Nandas and "established freedom in India by the help of robbers." His capital was Pataliputra (in Greek, Palibothra), the modern Patna. The dynasty of the Nandas is often spoken of as the "nine Nandas," meaning "nine descents," or according to some, "the last king Mahapadma and eight sons." Mahapadma Nanda was the son of a Sudra (the lowest of the four castes of India), and so by law a Sudra himself. He was a tyrant. The Brahman Chanakya is represented as having brought about his fall. Chandragupta was then raised to the throne and founded the Mauryan dynasty, of which the great Asoka was the third king. The commentator on the Vishnupurana says that he was a son of Nanda by a low-caste woman named Mura (whence he and his descendants were called Mauryas). The Buddhists claim that the Mauryas were of the same family with Buddha, the Sakyas.

Sangarius (sang-gār'i-us) or **Sagaris** (sag'a̯-ris). A river of Bithynia. The river-god, a son of Oceanus and Tethys, imprisoned his daughter Nana and left her to die, because he discovered that she was about to bear a child. Nana had eaten an almond from a tree that had grown up from the blood of a mutilated son of Cybele, and this almond had impregnated her. She was cared for by her mother and bore a son, Atys, who was exposed to die but was rescued and brought up by shepherds. According to some accounts, Sangarius was the father of King Priam's wife, Hecuba.

Santa Maria del Sole (sän'tä mä-rē'ä del sō'lä).

Circular temple at Rome, on the left bank of the Tiber opposite the Tiber island. The cella is circular, 33 feet in diameter, with a peristyle of 20 graceful Corinthian columns 32 feet high. The entablature and the ancient roof are gone. The probable date of the temple (later a church) is the 2nd or 3rd century A.D.

Santa Maria di Leuca (dē le'ö-ka̯), **Cape**. [Also: **Cape Leuca**; Latin, **Salentinum Promontorium**.] Cape at the SE extremity of Italy.

Santa Maria in Cosmedin (ēn kôz-mä-dēn'). Very early church at Rome, with ancient columns, raised choir, crypt, medieval ambos and tabernacle, fine mosaic pavement, and medieval campanile. The church is important as having replaced the ancient Temple of Ceres, Liber, and Libera, a large peripteral structure, with Composite columns, which served as the treasury and record-office of the aediles. Ten peristyle columns and parts of the cella wall remain *in situ*. In the vestibule is preserved a large ancient mask with pierced mouth and eyes popularly called the *Bocca della Verità*. It was originally set in a pavement to permit water to drain into a sewer, or perhaps an outlet for steam in a bath; but the lively imagination of the Romans, not content with so prosaic an explanation, holds that it was used in administering oaths, the person swearing being required to hold his hand in the mouth, which closed on perjurers and liars.

Santa Maria sopra Minerva (sō'prä mē-ner'vä). Church at Rome, so named, like the similarly named temple at Assisi, from being built over a temple of Minerva: the only medieval church in Rome which retains Gothic forms and decoration. The church contains beautiful tombs, notable paintings by Filippino Lippi and others, and important sculptures, among them Michelangelo's *Christ with the Cross*.

Santa Maura (mou'ra̯). See **Leucas**.

Santorin (san-tō-rēn'). See **Thera**.

Saon (sā'ọn). In Greek legend, a Boeotian who went to Apollo's shrine at Delphi to seek advice in a time of drought. He was advised by the priestess to go to Lebadia. There a swarm of bees led him to a cave which had opened up to swallow Trophonius after he had slain his brother Agamedes. At the cave, which had become an oracle of Trophonius,

Saon got instructions from the oracle for ending the drought, and afterward established the worship of Trophonius.

Sappho (saf´ō). Greek lyric poet; fl. c600 B.C. She appears to have been a native of Mytilene, in Lesbos, where she probably spent her life. According to Suidas, her father's name was Scamandronymus, her mother's Cleïs. She had a brother, Larichus, who in his youth acted as cup-bearer in the prytaneum of Mytilene, an office assigned only to beautiful youths of noble birth. Another brother, Charaxus, a merchant, became enamored of the courtesan and slave Doricha, surnamed Rhodopis, at Naucratis in Egypt, and purchased her freedom at an immense price. So much is known of the brothers from Sappho's poems. She also mentions a daughter, named Cleïs. Her husband's name is said to have been Cercolas or Cercylas of Andros. She was a contemporary of Alcaeus, with whom she maintained friendly relations, and with whom she shared the supremacy of the Aeolian school of lyric poetry. She appears to have given instruction in the art of versification, and to have been the center of a literary coterie of women who were attached to her by ties of warmest affection and intimacy. According to some accounts, she was banished with others of noble family, including her fellow poet Alcaeus, by Pittacus, who overthrew the tyrant Myrsilus and took the reins of government for ten years. Some say she went to Sicily, but seems later to have returned to Mytilene. There is no foundation for the story that she threw herself from the Leucadian promontory (Leucas) into the sea, out of love for a beautiful youth, Phaon, who disdained her advances. Two odes, preserved in the works of others, and a number of fragments remain of the nine books of lyric poems she wrote. A number of additional fragments were found in the papyri discovered at Oxyrhynchus in Egypt in 1900. She wrote in a wide variety of styles and meters, in the language commonly spoken by her compatriots rather than in the literary language of the day. Her work— lyrics, elegies, *epithalamia,* or wedding songs —was notable in her own day and ever after for its intensely personal quality and the melodious grace of her language. Her love poetry, says Gilbert Murray, has "unrivaled splendor of expression for the longing that is too intense to have any joy in it, too serious to allow room for metaphor and imaginative ornament." Simplicity of language and immediacy of emotion are indelibly characteristic of her poems, as the following fragments eloquently testify. "Some say the fairest thing on the black earth is a troop of horsemen, others a band of foot-soldiers, others a squadron of ships. But I say the fairest thing is the beloved." "Like the sweet apple which reddens upon the topmost bough,/A-top on the topmost twig—which the pluckers forgot somehow,—/Forgot it not, nay, but got it not, for none could get it till now." (Rossetti). She was known and admired all over the Greek world soon after her death. The Greeks named her "the Tenth Muse," and called her "the Poetess" as Homer was called "the Poet."

Sarcophagus (sär-kof´a-gus). Typically, a coffin consisting of a rectangular box of stone with a heavy stone cover, often decorated. The word means "flesh-eating," and is also applied to a kind of limestone so active that it consumed the products of decomposition, which suggests that this limestone was once the material of choice for coffins of this type. The term has since come to be applied to coffins of marble, porphyry, and other stones, terra-cotta, lead, wood, and other materials; it is properly used only for coffins in which the whole corpse was buried, not for smaller chests in which the ashes of cremated bodies were deposited. The most famous with classical connotations are the Haghia Triadha sarcophagus, of terra-cotta, with scenes of ritual painted in polychrome, dating from the Cretan bronze age, and the famous collection found at Sidon in Phoenicia, which includes the splendid Alexander Sarcophagus and the Sarcophagus of the Mourning Women. In Hellenistic and Roman times sarcophagi sculptured with scenes from mythology, some executed with exquisite taste and skill, became popular among the well-to-do, and led to important developments in Early Christian art. Stone sarcophagi are readily adapted for re-use as baths, baptismal fonts, wateringtroughs, dye vats, etc., and have been widely perverted to such purposes wherever found. (JJ)

Sardinia (sär-din´i-a). [Italian, **Sardegna;**

fat, fāte, fär, fãre, errant; net, mē, hèr ardent; pin, pīne; not, nōte, möve, nôr,

Greek: **Ichnousa** or **Ichnusa, Sardo;** Latin, **Sardinia.**] Island in the Mediterranean Sea, situated between Corsica and Tunisia, about 150 miles W of the Italian mainland. The surface is largely mountainous, particularly in the E part of the island. It has an area of 9302 square miles. It was called Ichnusa by the Greeks who traded there in ancient times, because it is shaped like a man's footprint (*ichnos*). According to some accounts, it was first settled by Libyans, whose leader was Sardus and for whom the island was named. Some say Aristaeus, grieving over the death of his son Actaeon, went to Sardinia to live. Norax, said to have been a son of Hermes, sailed to Sardinia from Iberia and founded the city of Nora. Iolaus, companion of Heracles, also went to Sardinia, with a group of Athenians. He founded Olbia. He was worshiped as a hero by the Sardinians as late as the 2nd century A.D. Other legendary colonists in Sardinia were some Trojans who escaped from Troy with Aeneas. They were blown off their course on the way and landed in Sardinia, where they settled down with the Greeks who were already there. In later years, when Libyans came and attacked, they destroyed the Greeks, but the Trojans took to the hills and escaped, and kept their name of Ilians. Ultimately, Sardinia was conquered by the Carthaginians (c500 B.C.) and the Romans (238 B.C.). According to legend, there were no snakes and no wolves on the island, and only one poisonous plant. This plant was something like celery, and those who ate of it were said to die laughing, hence the expression, "sardonic laughter."

Sardis (sär′dis). [Also: **Sardes.**] In ancient geography, the capital of Lydia, Asia Minor, situated at the foot of Mount Tmolus, on the Pactolus near the Hermus. It was a flourishing city under Croesus. Cyrus the Great defeated the forces of Croesus before the walls of Sardis (546 B.C.), and after a short siege took the city. According to Herodotus, Croesus, who had been rescued from a blazing funeral pyre, watched the Persians plundering Sardis. He turned to Cyrus and asked, "What is it, Cyrus, which those men yonder are doing so busily?" "Plundering your city," Cyrus replied, "and carrying off your riches." "Not my city," answered Croesus, "nor my riches. They are not mine

any more. It is your wealth which they are pillaging." Cyrus was so struck by this view he halted the plundering. In the revolt of the Ionian cities against Darius (499 B.C.) the Athenians and Eretrians marched with a revolting Ionian force to Sardis and burned the city (c498 B.C.). The Athenians and Eretrians then returned home, but the burning of Sardis brought the wrath of Darius on the Greeks of Europe and was an important cause of the Persian Wars against Greece. The city was rebuilt and became the residence of the Persian satraps of W Asia. It submitted to Alexander the Great without a struggle in 334 B.C. The tomb of Alyattes at Sardis is a conical tumulus 1180 feet in diameter and 142 feet high, with a sloping base-revetment of massive masonry. The Temple of Cybele, a famous sanctuary, in its existing remains of Hellenistic date, was an Ionic dipteros of eight by 17 columns, with three ranges of columns on the front, and measured 144 by 261 feet. The columns are 6½ feet in diameter and about 58½ feet high.

Sarmatia (sär-mā′sha). In ancient geography, according to Ptolemy, a territory extending from the Vistula River on the W to the Rha (Volga) River on the E, and N to the Mare Suevicum (Baltic Sea). It comprised a large part of what is now S Russia and E Poland, and was occupied by the Sauromatae and Scythians.

Sarmatians (sär-mā′shanz). See **Sauromatae.**

Sarnus (sär′nus). In ancient geography, a small river in Italy, which flows into the Bay of Naples near Pompeii; the modern Sarno. Near it the Goths were totally defeated (553 or 552 A.D.) by the Romans.

Saron (sä′ron). A legendary king of Troezen. According to the story, he was a great hunter. Once when he was pursuing a doe the animal fled before him into the sea. Saron followed the doe into the water and swam after it until he came to the open sea. Then his strength failed him and he drowned. The Saronic Gulf was named after him.

Saronic Gulf (sa-ron′ik). Arm of the Aegean Sea, lying SW of Attica and NE of Argolis, Greece. It contains the islands of Salamis and Aegina. Also called Gulf of Aegina.

Sarpedon (sär-pē′don). In Greek legend, a son of Zeus and Laodamia. He became ruler of the Lycians when his uncles withdrew their claim to the kingdom, and with his close friend and cousin, Glaucus, led the Lycians to the defense of Troy in the Trojan War. In the last year of the war, when the city was directly attacked by the Greeks, Sarpedon chided Hector, claiming that he was leaving the hardest fighting to the allies. He, he said, had no reason to fight, no quarrel with the Greeks, yet as a faithful ally he would do his best. When the Trojans and their allies attacked the fortifications around the Greek ships Sarpedon was in the forefront of the battle. Addressing his friend Glaucus, he said that as they had been honored the most as kings now they must fight the most to repay their loyal subjects for that honor, and prove themselves worthy of being honored. Charging into the battle, he exhorted Glaucus: together they would go on to glory; if successful it would be their own; if not, it would add to the glory of whoever stopped them. He breached the Greek wall and was the first into the Greek encampment. Although he was assailed by Telamonian Ajax and Teucer, Zeus protected him. Zeus grieved that his son was fated to die at the hands of Patroclus, who entered the struggle after the Greek ships had been set afire, and for a time considered saving him from his fate. However, Hera reminded him that the sons of other gods were fighting before Troy. If Zeus saved his son from his fate as a mortal, another god might wish to do the same. With sorrow Zeus accepted her point. As Patroclus and Sarpedon struggled, Zeus sent a shower of bloody raindrops on the Trojan plain to express his grief at his son's approaching death. Sarpedon fell, mortally wounded. Dying, he called on Glaucus to rescue his body and his arms. Glaucus, wild with grief, withdrew the spear which Patroclus had imbedded in his friend's body, and as it left Sarpedon's side his spirit fled with it. A violent struggle then broke out for possession of his body. The Greeks succeeded in gaining his armor—later it was given as a prize in the funeral games for Patroclus—but Zeus sent Apollo to rescue the corpse and bear it away from the range of weapons. Apollo wafted it away, cleansed it in a stream of pure water, and anointed it with ambrosia to erase the marks of battle. He then delivered it into the hands of Slum-

ber and Death and it was borne back to Lycia for funeral honors.

But some say Sarpedon was the son of Zeus and Europa, and the brother of Minos and Rhadamanthys, and that he fled from Crete following a quarrel with Minos. He went to Cilicia, which was named Lycia after his successor, made himself king there, and it was because Zeus gave him the boon of living for three generations that he was among those who went to Troy.

Sarsina (sär′si-na̱). In ancient geography, a town of C Italy, in Umbria. The Roman poet Plautus was born there, c251 B.C.

Satrae (sā′trē). Ancient tribal people of Thrace, of whom little is known except that they worshiped Dionysus. Herodotus mentions them as never having been subject to any city-state or empire. They are sometimes interpreted as a mythical people, eponymously identified with the satyrs, who are also traditionally of Thracian origin.

Saturn (sat′ẽrn). [Latin, **Saturnus**.] In Roman mythology, a god of agriculture, believed to have been a king in the reign of Janus, who instructed the people in agriculture, gardening, and the like. The Romans identified him with the Greek Cronus who, driven out by Zeus, fled to Italy bringing with him the arts of agriculture and establishing the Golden Age. His wife was Ops, identified with the Greek Rhea, and he was the father of Picus. An ancient temple at the foot of the Capitoline was dedicated to him and Ops; in chambers in the substructure were the offices of the Roman treasury. The festival of the Saturnalia, on Dec. 17, was celebrated in his honor; it was a time of merriment and exchange of gifts, which facilitated the transition to the Christmas-New Year festival of the Christians. Saturn was also the name given to one of the seven planets for which the days of the week were named; *Saturni dies* survives as our Saturday.

Saturnalia (sat-ẽr-nā′li-a̱). In Roman religion, the festival of Saturn, celebrated Dec. 17–23. During his festival sacrifices were offered in the open before his temple, banquets were given, schools and the courts were closed, war was interrupted, and no punishment of criminals took place during the days of his festival. The period of the festival was one of joy and merrymaking, gifts were exchanged, slaves were served by their masters, games were played. It was a week of feasting and mirthful enjoyment for all, one week in which the joys of the Golden Age were recaptured.

Saturninus (sa-tėr-nǐ′nus), **Lucius Appuleius.** Roman demagogue. He was quaestor in 104 B.C. and tribune of the people in 103 and 100 B.C. Politically he was a supporter of Marius and ardently sought the favor of the popular party. With the aid of his personal bodyguard, bribery, and murder, he helped Marius to be elected consul for the sixth time, 100 B.C., and was himself made tribune of the plebs for the second time. As tribune he proposed that land north of the Po, won from the Cimbri by Marius, be distributed to Marius' veterans, and that colonies be founded in Sicily, Greece, and Macedonia. Furthermore, he demanded that the Senate should swear to approve the laws proposed by the tribunes. Only Metellus Numidicus refused to be intimidated by Saturninus and his unruly band. He refused to swear the required oath and was banished. Saturninus secured the passage of his agrarian laws following a period of great disorder. At the end of the year (100 B.C.) he was elected tribune again for the following year. At the same time his lawless ally, Glaucia, sought to become consul. The senatorial candidate for the consulship was Memmius. Partisans of Saturninus and Glaucia murdered Memmius. The tide of public feeling turned against Saturninus and Glaucia, and though Marius was greatly indebted to them he was ordered by the Senate to take up arms against Saturninus. Saturninus was defeated in the Forum, and was slain by a mob who removed tiles from the building where he had been imprisoned and pelted him to death with them.

Satyr (sā′tėr). A sylvan deity, representing the luxuriant forces of Nature, and closely connected with the worship of Bacchus. Satyrs are represented with a somewhat bestial cast of countenance, often with small horns upon the forehead, and a tail like that of a horse or a goat, and they frequently hold a thyrsus or wine-cup. Late Roman writers confused the satyrs with their own fauns, and gave them the lower half of the body of a goat. Satyrs were common attendants on Bacchus, and were distinguished for lasciviousness and riot.

Satyricon (sa-tir′i-kon). Traditional title of one of the two Latin novels we possess (the *Golden Ass,* by Apuleius, being the other). Ascribed by the overwhelming majority of scholars to Petronius Arbiter (d. 66 A.D.), it is believed to have been composed before 61 A.D. The work is preserved only in fragments, the largest of which, containing the *Cena Trimalchionis* (Dinner of Trimalchio), was discovered c1650. Formally, the work is a Menippean satire (mixture of prose and poetry); its literary genre is the picaresque novel. The narrator, one of a trio of thoroughly immoral but amusing scoundrels, recounts their disreputable adventures as wandering scholars in Campania. Love affairs (normal and abnormal) alternate with literary criticism, folk-tales about werewolves and witches, and satire on the ostentatious bad taste of the newly rich freedman class personified in Trimalchio and his guests. Other parts of the work are the story of the *Widow of Ephesus* (possibly of Oriental origin and of considerable influence on later European literature); a short epic, as a counterblast to Lucan's treatment of epic; and many poetic passages. Apart from its merits as a work of genuine wit, the novel is of great interest to students of Latin and Romance linguistics: here, almost for the first time after Plautus, the Latin spoken by the lower classes (which had been overshadowed by the literary language) emerges; it was from this "vulgar," i.e., popular, Latin, and not from the polished, high-class Latin of most classical authors, that the Romance languages evolved. (HS)

Sauromatae (sou-rō-mā′tē) or **Sarmatae** (särmā′tē), later called **Sarmatians** (sä-mā′shanz). Ancient nomadic Indo-Iranian people, related to the Scythians, who inhabited what came to be known as the S Russian and N Caucasian steppes. According to Herodotus, the Sauromatae were descendants of Amazon women who had come to the shores of Lake Maeotis after their defeat at Athens by Theseus. These Amazons became the wives of young Scythians and with them migrated north beyond the Tanais River and took up their homes there. In imitation of the warlike character of their ancestresses, the Sauromatae women, says Herodotus, in his day dressed like men, hunted on horseback, either alone or with their husbands, and even took

actor; up, lūte, pull; oi, oil; ou, out; ᴛʜ, then; ḏ as d or j, ş as s or sh, ṭ as t or ch, ẕ as z or zh.

the field in time of war. They had no iron and instead used bone for their spear tips and arrowheads. The Sauromatae also, according to Herodotus, lassoed their quarry in hunting, and cut thin sheets from horses' hoofs and bound them together into scaly shields for use in warfare. According to the legend of the Argonauts the Sauromatae were enemies of King Aeëtes of Colchis. Jason offered to conquer them if Aeëtes would then give him the Golden Fleece. His offer was refused. Historically, the Sauromatae dominated the S Russian and N Caucasian steppes from the 4th century B.C. to the 3rd century A.D. During the reign of Marcus Aurelius (161–180 A.D.), they moved westward and invaded Dacia (Rumania). They were heavily influenced by the Greek colonies in the Black Sea region; their art is a mixture of the old Siberian "animal style" and Hellenistic elements. They became allied with Rome against the German tribes, but by the 3rd century A.D. they had become either completely dispersed or absorbed in the German migrations.

Savior. An epithet of Artemis, under which she was worshiped at many places. There was an ancient sanctuary of Artemis Savior in Megara because the goddess saved Megara during the Persian War. A force of Persians from the army of Mardonius lost their way in the hills at night. They shot their arrows into the darkness to find out if there was a hostile force nearby. The arrows struck rocks, which the goddess caused to groan. The Persians, hearing the groans, thought they were striking their enemies and shot off all their arrows. At dawn the Megarians attacked them, and since they had used up all their arrows, the Persians were unable to defend themselves and were killed. The rock, at Pagae, with arrows still stuck in it, was one of the sights shown to the traveler Pausanias centuries later. In gratitude, the Megarians raised an image of Artemis Savior at Megara, and another like it was raised at Pagae. Theseus also erected a temple of Artemis Savior, at Troezen, in gratitude for her help in overcoming the Minotaur. The people of Boeae, in Laconia, also worshiped Artemis Savior, because when they did not know where to settle, she sent a hare to guide them. They followed the hare until it went to earth

under a myrtle tree. There they founded their city, Boeae, and worshiped Artemis Savior, and the myrtle tree. Zeus was also given the epithet Savior.

Scaean Gate (sē'an). The northwest gate of the city of Troy. When the Scaean Gate was opened it signified war. It was by this gate that the Trojans departed from the city when they fought the Greeks and by which they entered it when fleeing before Achilles. As had been prophesied, Achilles was slain by an arrow, some say of Apollo, before the Scaean Gate.

Scaevola (sē'vō-la, sev'ō-), **Caius Mucius.** Roman hero. According to legend, when Lars Porsena was besieging Rome in 509 B.C., Scaevola, concealing a dagger about his person, went to the king's camp with the intention of putting him to death, but killed instead a royal secretary whom he mistook for Porsena. He was threatened with death by fire unless he revealed the details of a conspiracy which he said had been formed at Rome for the purpose of assassinating Porsena, whereupon he thrust his right hand into a sacrificial fire burning on an altar hard by, and permitted the flames utterly to consume the flesh and bones. This extraordinary demonstration of disregard for physical pain so excited the admiration of Porsena that he ordered Scaevola to be released. The story, which is perhaps as widely known as the one about the Spartan boy who remained impassive while a fox devoured his entrails, probably stems from an etiological legend hinging upon the name Scaevola, which means "left-handed."

Scaevola, Publius Mucius. Roman orator and jurist. He was tribune of the plebs, 141 B.C., praetor, 136 B.C., and consul in 133 B.C., at the time when the disturbances caused by the Gracchi were at their height. Although he opposed the extremism of the Gracchi he did not favor the policies of the conservative aristocratic party, and was an opponent of Scipio Africanus the Younger. He was Pontifex Maximum in 130 B.C. He is noted for the publication, in 80 books, of a digest of the official annals of Rome. Cicero speaks of his high reputation as a lawyer.

Scaevola, Quintus Mucius. Roman jurist, known as "the Augur," to distinguish him from Quintus Mucius Scaevola, the Pontifex

Maximus. He was born c159 B.C., and died c88 B.C., and was, in fact, an augur. He was tribune of the plebs, 128 B.C., aedile, 125, and consul, 117 B.C. He was celebrated for his knowledge of the law, civil as well as religious. In his old age he gave legal instruction to Cicero, who mentions him in several of his treatises.

Scaevola, Quintus Mucius. Roman jurist; killed 82 B.C. He was the son of Publius Mucius Scaevola. He was a tribune of the people in 106 B.C., curule aedile in 104, and consul in 95 B.C. He was subsequently proconsul of the province of Asia, and ultimately became Pontifex Maximus. He was prominent during the Social War (91–88 B.C.), which one of his laws, intended to limit Roman citizenship, did much to bring on, was proscribed by the Marian party in the civil war that followed, and was killed in sanctuary. Excerpts from his writings are preserved in the *Digest.* His honorable character is lauded by Cicero, who studied under him when he was Pontifex Maximus.

Scamander (ska-man′dėr). In the *Iliad,* a plain where the Greeks assembled for the assault on Troy. It was the plain of a river of the same name which rose near Mount Ida and emptied into the Hellespont near Troy. It was believed that the waters of the river made the hair a beautiful color, and for this reason Aphrodite, Athena, and Hera bathed in it in preparation for the contest before Paris for the golden apple. The river was honored as a god by the Trojans and had its own priests. It was one of the rivers in the Troad which Poseidon, with the aid of Apollo, diverted from its course for nine days in order to wash down the wall which the Greeks had built to defend their ships. The destruction of the wall, because Poseidon feared that this man-made structure would overshadow the wall he and Apollo had built for Laomedon, took place after the Trojan War was over. The gods called the river and the river-god Xanthus, but men called it the Scamander. As a river-god, Xanthus was the son of Oceanus and Tethys, and the father of Teucer, the first king of the Trojans. See **Xanthus**, river-god.

Scamandrius (ska-man′dri-us). Another name for Astyanax, son of Andromache and Hector.

Scamandrius. In the *Iliad,* the son of Strophius.

He had been taught skill in archery by Artemis herself, but it availed him nothing when Menelaus attacked him at close range and slew him with his spear.

Scephrus (skef′rus). In Greek mythology, a son of Tegeates. When Apollo and Artemis roamed about Greece, seeking out for punishment all those who had refused aid to Leto when she was looking for a place to bear her children, they came at last to Tegea. In Tegea Scephrus met Apollo and went aside to have a private conversation with him. Limon, brother of Scephrus, observed their private parley, and feared that Scephrus was accusing him to the god. He rushed forth and murdered his brother. Artemis immediately pursued Limon and shot him. After this famine fell on the land and when the priestess at Delphi was consulted concerning this she ordered the Tegeans to mourn for Scephrus. Ever after, at the feast of Apollo Agyieus (*God of the Streets*) rites were performed in honor of Scephrus and, to commemorate the pursuit of Limon by Artemis, the priestess of Artemis pursued a man.

Schedius (skē′di-us). In Homeric legend (*Iliad*), a son of Iphitus and Hippolyte. He was one of the suitors of Helen and as such had given his oath to help her husband if any evil befell him as a result of his marriage. When Paris carried off Helen, Schedius and his brother Epistropus went from Panopeus in Phocis at the head of the Phocians to assist Menelaus to recover Helen from Troy. Schedius was slain by Hector in the struggle for possession of the body of Patroclus.

Scheria (skir′i-a). In the *Odyssey,* the island of the Phaeacians where Odysseus landed after shipwreck and was welcomed by Nausicaä and her father, the king. The people of the island were wonderful navigators, and conducted Odysseus to Ithaca overnight. The actual place most commonly suggested as identical with Scheria is Corfu, but this identification is highly questionable.

Schoenius (skē′ni-us). A Boeotian who is named by some as the father of Atalanta.

Scione (ski-ō′nē or si-ō′nē). In ancient geography, a city on the Pallene peninsula, in Chalcidice. It revolted from Athens, 423 B.C., and gave allegiance to the Spartan general Brasidas. He was received as a hero there, covered with garlands, and crowned with a golden crown.

Scipio (sip′i-ō). [Called **Scipio the Elder**; full name, **Publius Cornelius Scipio Africanus**.] Roman general; son of Publius Cornelius Scipio; born c236 B.C.; died probably 183 B.C. He served at the battle of the Ticinus (Ticino) River (218 B.C.), where he is said to have saved his father's life, and also at Cannae (216 B.C.) where he was one of the few Roman officers to survive. He became aedile in 212, and was appointed to the chief command in Spain as proconsul in 210 B.C. He landed at the mouth of the Iberus (Ebro) River and captured Carthago Nova (Cartagena), the Carthaginian port and headquarters in Spain, and with it took a rich store of war supplies. In 209 B.C. he defeated Hasdrubal, Hannibal's brother, but could not prevent him from marching to Italy to aid Hannibal. Scipio won over many of the Spanish chiefs to his side, and in 206 B.C. decisively defeated the Carthaginians at Ilipa and completed the conquest of Spain. The following year he was elected consul and was given Sicily as his province. Hannibal was at this time operating in southern Italy. Scipio was an ardent advocate of carrying the war to Africa. Over the objections of the Roman nobles he invaded Africa, 204 B.C., and the following year defeated Scyphax, the Numidian ally of Carthage, and a Carthaginian army under Hasdrubal (son of Gisco). The Carthaginians refused to accept his peace terms, although they were moderate, the war was continued, and in 202 B.C. he defeated Hannibal, who had been recalled from Italy to defend Carthage, at the battle of Zama. Carthage was compelled to submit, accepted the reasonable terms that Scipio offered for peace, and the Second Punic War was brought to a conclusion (201 B.C.). When Scipio returned to Rome he was welcomed with the greatest enthusiasm. He accepted the surname Africanus but disclaimed the other honors the grateful Romans would have given him. In 199 B.C. he was censor, but otherwise for the next few years after the end of the war he lived quietly, withdrawn from the political scene. In 194 B.C. he was consul for the second time, and in 193 he went to Africa to mediate a dispute between the Numidian king, Massinissa, and Carthage. In 190 B.C. his brother Lucius was given chief command in the war against Antiochus III of Syria. Scipio accompanied him as legate and between them they decisively defeated Antiochus. On their return to Rome, however, Lucius, who had taken the name Asiaticus, was accused of diverting to his own use some of the money paid by Antiochus to Rome, was tried, condemned, and fined. In 187 B.C. enemies of Scipio brought a charge against him of having accepted a bribe from Antiochus. On the day of the trial he completely reversed the popular mood and won their enthusiastic acclaim by reminding them that it was the anniversary of his victory of Zama. In the end the crowd marched to the Capitol with him to give thanks to the gods for such a noble citizen and to pray for more like him. After this Scipio retired to his country estate at Liternum, on the coast of Campania, where he remained until his death. Scipio was the father of Cornelia, who became the mother of the Gracchi.

Scipio. [Called **Scipio the Younger**; full name, **Publius Cornelius Scipio Aemilianus Africanus Numantinus**.] Roman general; born c185 B.C.; died 129 B.C. He was the second son of Aemilius Paulus Macedonicus (c229–160 B.C.) and Papiria, daughter of the consul Maso. His father's sister was Aemilia, wife of Scipio Africanus the Elder. When he was a young man he was adopted by Scipio Africanus, the elder son of Scipio Africanus the Elder, whence his name. He accompanied his father on the campaign against Perseus, king of Macedonia, and took part in the battle of Pydna (168 B.C.). When the battle ended in Roman victory, young Scipio was missing. His father grieved, and the men in the army, who admired the young soldier's bravery, set out to look for him. However, he soon returned to the camp with several companions, covered with blood but glowing with enthusiasm, and announced that he had been pursuing the enemy. On his return to Rome he pursued his studies, with special attention to literature. Lucilius and Terence the poets, and Panaetius the philosopher were among his friends. Polybius, the Greek general and historian who had been brought to Rome as a hostage,

fat, fāte, fär, fāre, errạnt; net, mē, hėr ardẹnt; pin, pīne; not, nōte, mŏve, nôr,

with 1000 other prominent Achaeans, became his intimate friend and adviser. Scipio secured (151 B.C.) the release of the Achaean hostages and they returned home. In the same year he went as military tribune to Spain where he served with distinction and won the respect of the Spanish tribes. In 149 B.C., on the outbreak of the Third Punic War, he went as military tribune to Africa, and by his personal bravery and skill saved the army of the consul Manilius from destruction. In 147 B.C., although he was under the legal age, he was appointed consul with Africa as his province. He besieged Carthage with great vigor, skill, and bravery, and despite the heroic resistance of the defenders of the citadel took it, 146 B.C. Polybius, who accompanied him, describes the war in his *History*. In accordance with instructions from Rome he leveled Carthage to the ground. Some say the land on which it stood was plowed and sowed with salt so that no city could ever rise on it again. When he returned to Rome he was given a splendid triumph. He acted as censor, 142 B.C., and in his term attempted to raise the moral level of the age by removing some of the more notorious men from the ranks of the senators. One who had been degraded brought charges of high treason against him (139 B.C.), but he defended himself brilliantly in speeches which were greatly admired in his time but are now lost; he was acquitted. In 134 B.C. he was again elected consul, with Spain as his province. He reorganized the Roman army that had been vainly trying to take Numantia there, and in 133 B.C. captured the city and established Roman power in Hither Spain. For his success in the capture of Numantia he was given the surname Numantinus. On his return to Rome, 132 B.C., he allied himself with the aristocratic party against the popular party, although the latter was led by his brothers-in-law the Gracchi. He appears to have been a moderate, not so much attracted by the conservatism of the aristocratic party as he was repelled by the extremism of the popular party. He was found dead in his room one morning after a tempestuous day in the forum, and was commonly supposed to have been assassinated. Scipio the Younger was one of the outstanding examples of all that was best in the Roman character in the waning days of the Republic. He was a brave and brilliant soldier, and a cultivated man of public honor and private virtue.

Scipio, Cnaeus Cornelius. Roman general; killed 212 or 211 B.C. He was the brother of Publius Cornelius Scipio. He was consul in 222 B.C., when with his colleague M. Claudius Marcellus he completed the subjugation of Cisalpine Gaul. He was appointed legate in Spain in 218 B.C., and was associated with his brother in the Spanish campaigns against the Carthaginians.

Scipio, Publius Cornelius. Roman general; killed 212 or 211 B.C. He was consul in 218 B.C., when he attempted unsuccessfully to prevent Hannibal's passage of the Rhodanus (Rhône), and was defeated at the Ticinus (Ticino) River and (with Sempronius, his co-consul, who insisted on fighting against his advice) at the Trebia (Trebbia) River. In 217 B.C. he defeated the Carthaginian fleet at the mouth of the Iberus (Ebro), whereby he gained for the Romans the supremacy of the sea. With his brother, Cnaeus Cornelius Scipio, he gained several victories over the Carthaginians in Spain, but was defeated and slain with his brother, possibly due to the desertion of native tribes who had been wooed away by Carthaginian gold. He was the father of Scipio Africanus the Elder.

Scipio, Quintus Caecilius Metellus Pius. See **Metellus Pius Scipio, Quintus Caecilius.**

Scira (skī′ra). See **Scirophoria.**

Sciras (skī′ras). Epithet of Athena. A sanctuary of Athena Sciras was set up at Phalerum by Scirus, a seer who came from Dodona to help the Eleusinians in their war against Athens, and it is from his name that the epithet comes. He fell in battle in the war, near the river which henceforth bore his name. Another sanctuary of Athena Sciras was raised at Salamis, and another was erected on the road between Athens and Eleusis.

Sciron (sī′ron). In Greek legend, a son of Pylas, and as such the uncle of Theseus; but some say he was a son of Poseidon or of Pelops. He was a robber who frequented the Molurian Rocks overlooking the sea near Megara, and forced strangers passing by to wash his feet. While they were doing so he would kick them off the rocks into the sea, where they were devoured by a turtle. When Theseus passed by on his journey from Troezen to Athens, he hurled Sciron himself into the sea, and his bones are said to form the high cliffs which still exist in the region. But some say that Sciron quarreled with Nisus over control of Megara and, in accordance with a judgment of Aeacus, was given command of the armies while Nisus retained the throne. And they say that he was an upright man, whose daughter Endeïs married Aeacus and was the mother of Peleus and Telamon. And that Theseus killed him when he captured Eleusis many years after he had become king or ruler of Athens. Later Theseus instituted the daytime Isthmian Games, formerly mysterious nocturnal rites in honor of Melicertes, in honor of Sciron.

Scirophoria (skir-ọ-fō′ri-ạ). [Also: **Scira, Skirophoria.**] Ancient Greek festival celebated at Athens on the twelfth of the month Scirophorion (June–July) in honor of Athena (or more anciently in honor of Demeter and Persephone). The feature of the celebration was a procession from the Acropolis to the village of Sciron, where pigs were sacrificed and Athena was importuned to prevent too great summer heat. The festival is said to be named for the huge white umbrella (*skiron*) which was carried over the head of the priestess of Athena and the priest of Poseidon during the march.

Scirophorion (skir-ọ-fō′ri-on). The twelfth and last month of the Attic year, containing 29 days. It corresponded to the last part of June and the first part of July. A festival in honor of Athene, the *Scirophoria*, was celebrated in this month.

Scopas (skō′pạs). Greek sculptor and architect; born in the island of Paros; fl. 4th century B.C. His first important work was the temple of Athena Alea at Tegea, built on the site of an older temple. The sculptures of it included scenes of the Calydonian Boar Hunt and the battle between Achilles and Telephus. Battered fragments of these sculptures remain. Scopas probably went to Athens c377 B.C., and remained there 25 years, when he went to Halicarnassus to superintend the sculpture of the Mausoleum. The fragments from this monument in the British Museum probably give us our most reliable information as to Scopas' style; but he is generally conceded to have led, or to have typified, a departure from the earlier serene, reposeful treatment of sculpture to the expression of strong emotion in facial expressions and in the movements of the figures. A doubtful passage of Pausanias suggests that he is represented in the sculpture recovered from the Artemisium at Ephesus. The *Apollo Citharoedus* of the Vatican has been associated with Scopas as a copy of his statue. The original of one Niobe group was by either Scopas or Praxiteles, probably Scopas.

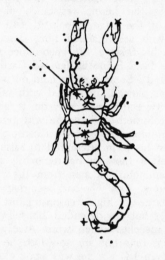

SCORPIO
Pictured according to ancient descriptions

Scorpio (skôr′pi-ō). The eighth sign of the zodiac—the Scorpion—which the sun enters about October 24. Also, a zodiacal constellation which is prominent in early summer in the skies of the southern United States (where the whole of the magnificent tail clears the horizon). It contains the first magnitude red star Antares and several of the second magnitude. With the Chaldeans and Greeks it extended over one-sixth of the planetary circle, the scorpion being represented with exaggerated claws embracing a circular space where Libra is now placed. From this irregularity it may be inferred that the constellation is older than the zodiac, which was formed before 2000 B.C. Libra, though later, is of no small antiquity, since it appears in the Egyptian zodiacs. Its adoption by Julius Caesar in his calendar made it familiar. Ptolemy, however, though living in Egypt nearly two centuries later, follows Babylonian and Greek astronomers in covering the place of Libra with the scorpion's claws.

Scotia (skō′shi-ạ). An epithet of Aphrodite in her aspect as a goddess of death-in-life, meaning "The Dark One."

Scribonia (skri-bō′ni-ạ). Wife of Octavian, the future Augustus, whom he married in 40 B.C. and divorced in 39 B.C., some said because he couldn't stand her nagging. She was the mother of his only child, Julia, and ultimately accompanied Julia into exile.

Scylaceus (sil-ạ-sē′us). In Greek legend, a Lycian companion of Glaucus and Sarpedon, allies of the Trojans. In the closing days of the war he was wounded by Ajax the Lesser but escaped death, as it was his fate to die beside the wall of his own city. He fled alone to his home city and was met at the walls by the Lycian women. They questioned him about their husbands and sons who had gone to fight at Troy, and when he told them they had all been slain, in grief and rage the women stoned Scylaceus to death as the bearer of the evil news. His tomb was built of the stones, which killed him, and stood beside Bellerophon's tomb. Afterward, at Apollo's command, Scylaceus was worshiped as a god.

Scylacium (si-lā′shum) or **Scylaceum** ˙(sil-ạ-sē′um). [Modern name, **Squillace**.] In ancient geography, a town on the coast of Bruttii, in the toe of the Italian boot, near the Gulf of Tarentum. It is mentioned in the *Aeneid* as "ship-wrecking," from its rocky coast. It was founded by Ionian colonists and became part of the dominions of Dionysius the Elder of Syracuse.

Scylla (sil′ạ). In classical mythology, a sea-nymph. Some say she was a daughter of Phorcys and Crataeis. Others say Zeus and Lamia were her parents. Echidna, Typhon and Triton are also mentioned as the parents of Scylla. Glaucus, the sea-god, fell in love with her and wooed her with promises and prayers, but she scorned him. He asked Circe's aid to win the love of Scylla. Circe, however, notoriously susceptible, fell in love

with Glaucus herself, and when she realized that his love for Scylla was unswerving she resolved to avenge herself on Scylla, whom Glaucus preferred to her. She concocted a mixture of magic herbs and sprinkled them on the pool in an arm of the sea where Scylla was wont to bathe, uttering a magic

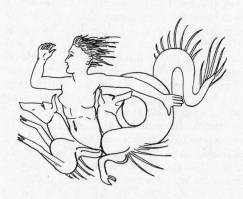

SCYLLA
Coin of Acragas (Agrigentum), late 5th century B.C. *Museum of Fine Arts, Boston*

spell at the same time. When Scylla went into the pool she was transformed. The upper part of her trunk and her head, which had not been immersed in the pool, remained that of a beautiful maiden. But her waist was girdled with the necks and heads of six hideous dogs. Her lower limbs were changed into a dolphin's tail. There she stands, rooted in the sea, and whenever a ship passes near the dogs' heads reach out and grasp six seamen and devour them. Some say Scylla was transformed by Amphitrite, who was jealous because Poseidon was enamored of her, and that she had 12 arms and six terrible heads with three rows of teeth in each head. She barks like a young dog and no longer bears any resemblance to the lovely maiden she was. The lower part of her body rests in a cave in the middle of a smooth, mountainous rock in the sea which none can ascend. She eats marine animals and any seamen who are unfortunate enough to come within her reach. Odysseus lost six of his best men when he sailed too near Scylla in order to avoid Charybdis on his way home from the Trojan War. Some say Scylla seized one of Geryon's cattle from Heracles when he passed her way, and that Heracles wrathfully slew her, but Phorcys burned her corpse and she rose anew from the ashes.

Scylla. In Greek legend, a daughter of Nisus, king of Nisa (later Megara). When Nisa was attacked by Minos, king of Crete, Scylla, watching the siege from the walls of the city, saw Minos and fell in love with him. Her father had one purple (or golden) lock of hair on which his life and the safety of the city depended. For love of Minos, Scylla cut off this lock as her father slept and took it to Minos. Her father died and the city fell to his enemy, but Minos refused to take Scylla with him to Crete because he was revolted by her crime, although he willingly took advantage of it to gain the city. He sailed off without her. Scylla, hated by her own countrymen and distracted at being abandoned by her former enemy, leaped into the sea and swam after Minos' ship and clung to its stern. There her father, who had been transformed into an osprey, saw her and attacked her with his beak. Scylla loosed her hold on the ship and just as she started to drown she was transformed into a ciris, a kind of lark whose name means "shearer."

Scylla. [Modern names, **Scilla** or **Sciglio**.] Promontory in S Italy, projecting into the Strait of Messina.

Scyllaeum (si-lē′um). In ancient geography, a promontory in Argolis, Greece, projecting into the Aegean: the easternmost point of the Peloponnesus. According to tradition, it was named for Scylla, who betrayed her father Nisus for love of Minos, king of Crete. When, thanks to Scylla's betrayal, Minos had defeated the forces of Nisus, he refused to take Scylla back with him to Crete, on the grounds that she was a parricide. Scylla swam out to his ship, but he ordered his men to drive her off. Some say she drowned, and that her body was washed up on this promontory, and that it was not buried but torn to pieces by sea birds. Others say she was transformed into a sea bird.

Scyllias (sil′i-as). A Greek of Scione. According to a story told by Herodotus, when the Persian fleet took up its position at Aphetae

(480 B.C.) off Thermopylae, and secretly sent a large squadron around Euboea to cut off the Greek fleet that was stationed at Artemisium, Scyllias dived into the sea at Aphetae and did not come up until he reached the Greeks at Artemisium, a distance of ten miles. There he warned the Greeks, who were contemplating retreat, of the Persian maneuver. But Herodotus adds that it was his opinion that Scyllias actually went in a boat. At all events, the warning brought by Scyllias, plus a great storm that wrecked many of the Persian ships, decided the Greeks against retreat, and prepared them for the inconclusive sea fight at Artemisium.

Scyllis (sil′is). Greek sculptor of the archaic period, active c580 B.C., and said to have invented the art of carving in marble. See entry under **Dipoenus** and **Scyllis.**

Scyphius (sif′i-us). According to some accounts, the name of the first horse, which Poseidon claimed to have created out of the earth.

Scyrus (sī′rus) or **Scyros** (-ros). Island in the Aegean Sea about 25 miles E of Euboea. Theseus, returned from the Underworld to find himself no longer wanted in Athens, went to Scyrus where he had estates. There he met his death at the hands of Lycomedes, who pushed him over a cliff. Later, according to legend, Achilles was hidden at the court of Lycomedes to prevent him from going to the Trojan War. His son Neoptolemus was born on Scyrus, and left from there to go to the Trojan War after the death of Achilles. The island was conquered (469 B.C.) by the Athenians under Cimon, who also found there bones proclaimed as the bones of Theseus and restored them to Athens. Length of the island, about 19 miles.

Scythes (sith′ēs). According to Herodotus, Heracles, returning with the cattle he had stolen from Geryon, came to the land later known as Scythia. There, overcome with cold and weariness, he drew his lion's skin around him and went to sleep. When he woke up his mares, that he had loosed for grazing, had disappeared. He looked for them and came upon a curious serpent-tailed maiden. She admitted she had his mares but would not release them until he became her lover, and she kept him with her, although he was longing to be on his way.

fat, fāte, fär, fãre, errant; net, mē, hér ardent; pin, pīne; not, nōte, möve, nôr,

When she finally permitted him to depart she told him she would bear him three sons, and asked him what she should do with them. Heracles instructed her to watch them, if she saw any one of them bend the bow as he now bent it, or girdle himself as he now demonstrated, she should make this one stay in the land with her where she was ruler. Any who failed to perform these acts as Heracles performed them she should send away out of the land. In due time the woman bore triplets, Agathyrsus, Gelonus, and Scythes. When they were grown their mother tested them as Heracles had ordered. Only Scythes performed the tasks as Heracles had done. His mother sent his brothers out of the land, but Scythes she kept with her. He became the ruler of the people who took their name, Scyths, and the name of their country, Scythia, from him.

Scythia (sith′i-a̱). In ancient geography, a name of varying meaning. It designated at first a region in what is now S European Russia and Rumania, inhabited by the Scythians. They resisted the invasion of Darius I of Persia. Since they had neither forts nor cities, carried their tents with them wherever they went, and were accustomed to fight from horseback, their method of avoiding destruction from invaders was to refuse to stand and make a fight. When Darius invaded their country they decided, according to Herodotus, not to meet the Persians in open conflict but to retreat by a distance of one day's march before the enemy, destroying the wells and driving off their cattle as they withdrew. In this way they led the Persians all over their land, never engaging them. Darius, at his wits' end at this strange manner of warfare, sent heralds to the Scythians. They sent back presents to him: a bird, a mouse, a frog, and five arrows. Asked the meaning of these presents, the Scythian herald refused to give it. They were at last interpreted in this way: unless the Persians could turn into birds and fly away, or into mice and burrow in the ground, or into frogs and retreat to the marshes, they would never escape from Scythia but would be killed by the Scythian arrows. Ultimately Darius came to the conclusion that this was indeed the case, and retreated from Scythia, without having subdued the country. After the time of Alexander the Great Scythia was subjugated by the Sarmatians and others. Later Scythia denoted N Asia and much of C Asia, divided by the Imaus Mountains into Scythia Intra Imaum and Scythia Extra Imaum. As a Roman province it comprised the lands immediately S of the mouths of the Danube.

Scythica (sith′i-ka̱), **Chersonesus.** An ancient name of the Crimea.

Scyths (siths) or **Scythians** (sith′i-anz). Indo-European people, described by Herodotus, who penetrated into what is now S Russia in the 7th century B.C. According to their own account, as given in Herodotus, their nation was founded by Targitaus, a son, he claimed, of Zeus and a daughter of the river-god Borysthenes. Targitaus had three sons: Lipoxaïs, Arpoxaïs, and Colaxaïs. During their rule a golden plow, yoke, battle-ax, and drinking-cup fell from the heavens. When the eldest son approached to pick them up, flames burst from them and forced him back. The same thing happened when the second son approached. But when Colaxaïs made the attempt the flames subsided and he grasped the implements, whereupon his brothers turned over the kingdom to him. From him sprang the tribe known as the Royal Scythians, in whose charge the golden implements remained. The Greeks told a different story of the origin of the Scythians. According to their account, the Scythians were descended from Scythes (q.v.), who was a son of Heracles and a serpent-tailed maiden. Because Heracles had worn a golden goblet attached to the clasp of his girdle when he was in their land, the Scythians wore goblets attached to their girdles. According to Herodotus' account, the Scythians built no temples or altars, but worshiped gods whose Greek names were Hestia, Zeus, Apollo, Aphrodite, Heracles, and Ares. Of all peoples they were most hostile to foreign customs, and particularly hated those of the Greeks and ruthlessly prevented their adoption. In battle the Scythian soldier drank the blood of the first man he killed, and cut off the heads of all others and took them to the king, for he was rewarded by the number of heads he presented. The Scythians scalped their fallen enemies, treated the skin, and used it for various purposes. Although the principal Scythic kingdom developed between the Borysthenes (Dnieper) and Tanais (Don) rivers, Scythian invaders crossed Asia Minor and reached Syria (c650–620 B.C.). Archaeological remains of Scythic culture have

SCYTHIAN ARCHER
From the west pediment of the so-called
Temple of Aphaea at Aegina, c510 B.C.
Munich

been found as far west and southwest as Hungary and Bulgaria. Although the Scythian rulers were nomads, other groups within their kingdoms were agricultural. Metallurgy and pottery were highly developed among them; their "animal style," with vivid representations of men, horses, reindeer, and other subjects is famous. Also noted are Scythian burial mounds, in which concubines, slaves, horses, and a great wealth of gold and furnishings were buried with the remains of a ruler. The Scythians reached the apex of their power in the 6th century B.C.; it de-

clined after prolonged wars with the Greek colonies on the Euxine (Black) Sea, the Celts in the areas now known as the Balkans and central Europe, and the Sauromatae in what is now S Russia. Politically, they succumbed in the 2nd century B.C.

Seduni (sē-dū′nī). Ancient Gallic tribe in the upper valley of the Rhodanus (Rhône), in what is now SW Switzerland. They opposed Julius Caesar in the Alps, but were defeated in 57 B.C.

Segesta (sē-jes′ta). In ancient geography, a city in Sicily, situated near the coast, about 27 miles W of Panormus. According to some accounts, it was founded by Acestes, son of the Trojan woman Egesta and the river-god Crimisus, and was therefore Trojan, and not Greek, in origin. Segesta was often at war with Selinus, and was an ally of Athens in the Peloponnesian War, the disastrous Sicilian expedition of 415 B.C. of the Athenians being allegedly to aid Segesta. It became a dependent of Carthage c400 B.C., was sacked (307 B.C.) by Agathocles, and had its name changed to Dicaeopolis, and passed under Roman supremacy in the time of the First Punic War. There are ruins near the modern Alcamo and Calatafimi. The Greek temple, though never finished, is one of the most complete examples surviving. It is Doric, hexastyle, with 14 columns on the flanks, on a stylobate of four steps. The architectural details are of the best period. All the 36 peristyle columns are still standing, and the entablature and pediments are almost whole. There is also a Greek theater, of the 4th century B.C., with Roman modifications. In plan it is more than a semicircle; the diameter is 209 feet, that of the orchestra 54 feet; the length of the stage is 91 feet. The cavea is in great part rock-hewn.

Segusiani (sē-gū-si-ā′nī). In the time of Julius Caesar, a Gallic people living in the valley of the Rhodanus (Rhône), in the vicinity of what is now Lyons.

Segni (sā′nyē). See **Signia.**

Seistan (sā-stän′). [Also: **Sistan.**] See **Drangiana.**

Sejanus (sē-jā′nus), **Lucius Aelius.** Roman courtier; died 31 A.D. He was the son of Seius Strabo, a Roman knight, commander of the Praetorian Guard, and was a native of Vulsinii in Etruria. He became the favorite of the emperor Tiberius, who raised him to the command of the Praetorians, and, following the withdrawal of Tiberius to Capri, he became for a time the virtual ruler of Rome. With a view to usurping the imperial power, he poisoned (23 A.D.) Drusus, son of the emperor, with the assistance of Livia the wife of Drusus, whom he had seduced, and induced the emperor to banish Agrippina the widow of Germanicus. His design was ultimately discovered, and he was put to death.

Selemnus (se-lem′nus). A river in Achaea. According to legend, it was named for a local youth, a shepherd who kept his flocks on its banks. Selemnus, the youth, was loved by the sea nymph Argyra who came from the sea each night and slept by his side. But as Selemnus grew older he began to lose his beauty and Argyra ceased to visit him. Selemnus died of love for her, and Aphrodite turned him into a river. But even as a river Selemnus remained faithful to Argyra, continued to love her and mourn her. To relieve him, Aphrodite caused him to forget Argyra. For this reason, it was said that those in love could forget their passion by washing in the waters of the Selemnus.

Selene (se-lē′nē). In Greek mythology, a daughter of the Titans Hyperion and Thia, and the sister of Eos and Helius. Some say Pan, in disguise, persuaded her to ride off on his back and then seduced her. She is also said to have borne a daughter to Zeus who was worshiped in Athens with her father. One night she came upon Endymion sleeping in a cave on Mount Latmus in Caria. She instantly fell in love with him and kissed his closed eyelids. By Endymion she became the mother of 50 daughters. Some say that when he later returned to the same cave he fell into a deep sleep from which he has never awakened, and that nightly Selene gently kisses him as she adores his unchanging youth and beauty. Some say Endymion himself asked Zeus to put him into an eternal sleep because he did not want to grow old. But others say it was Selene who caused him to sleep forever, so that his beauty would not fade and so that she alone could embrace him. Selene was the goddess of the moon, a beautiful winged maiden whose golden diadem casts a soft light on the earth. Her chariot was drawn by white cows, whose horns symbolized the crescent moon. She was worshiped at the time of the new and the full moon. Later Selene was identified with Artemis and with the Roman Diana.

Seleucia (se-lō′sha). [Also: **Seleuceia**.] In ancient geography, a city in Cilicia, Asia Minor, situated near the coast, about 70 miles SW of Tarsus. There are remains of a Roman hippodrome.

Seleucia. [Also: **Seleuceia**.] In ancient geography, a city in N Pisidia, Asia Minor, near the frontier of Phrygia.

Seleucia. [Also: **Seleuceia**; sometimes called **Seleucia Pieria**.] In ancient geography, a city in Syria, situated on the coast N of the mouth of the Orontes: the port of Antioch. It was built by Seleucus I. There are many antiquities on the site.

Seleucia. [Also: **Seleuceia**.] In ancient geography, a city near the Tigris, about 17 miles below Baghdad. It was built largely from the ruins of Babylon by Seleucus I, 312 B.C., and was one of the largest cities of the East. It was plundered by Trajan, and was destroyed by Avidius Cassius in 164 A.D.

Seleucids (se-lō′sidz). [Also: **Seleucidae**.] Royal dynasty in Syria which reigned from 312 B.C. to c64 B.C.; descended from Seleucus I (Seleucus Nicator).

Seleucus I (se-lō′kus). [Surnamed **Nicator**, meaning "Conqueror."] King of Syria; born 358 B.C.; died 280 B.C. He was the father of Antiochus I. Following the sudden death of Alexander the Great in 323 B.C. his chief generals, including Perdiccas, Seleucus, Antipater, Antigonus, Ptolemy, Eumenes, Craterus, and Lysimachus, being men equally of ambition and of violence, began without delay to contend among themselves for power and dominion. Perdiccas became regent for the dead conqueror's posthumous son but Antipater also claimed the regency and was supported by Ptolemy, Antigonus, and Craterus. Thus began the intermittent struggles known as the Wars of the Diadochi (Successors), which continued until 281 B.C. Seleucus was Perdiccas' chief supporter, but following the latter's defeat by Ptolemy, he engaged in the conspiracy which led to the assassination of Perdiccas in 321 B.C. In 312

B.C. he secured control of Babylonia. The city of Seleucia was built as the capital of this realm, superseding Babylon. Ambitious more than any of the others of the Diadochi to reëstablish Alexander's empire in its fullness, he invaded India, but after a defeat at Pataliputra (now Patna) in 305 B.C. he made peace with the Indian monarch Chandragupta on terms including a gift by the latter of 500 elephants. In 306 or 305 B.C., following the example of Antigonus, he assumed the title of king. In 301 B.C. he joined with Lysimachus, Ptolemy, and Cassander, son of Antipater (who died in 319 B.C.), to defeat and kill Antigonus, whose ambition threatened all the other surviving Diadochi, at the battle of Ipsus. In the division of spoils following this victory, Seleucus received Syria. Thereafter he extended his rule over a large part of Asia Minor, and his power reached its height with the defeat and death of Lysimachus in 281 B.C. Following this his ambition overreached itself, as the sequel showed. Aspiring to dominate the original seat of Alexander's power, he invaded Macedonia, where in 280 B.C. he was assassinated at the instigation of Ptolemy II. Seleucus I instituted the tight, efficient system of administration, modeled on Persian absolutism, which characterized the rule of the Seleucids.

Seleucus II. [Surnamed **Callinicus**, meaning "Gloriously Victorious."] King of Syria; died 226 B.C. He was the eldest son of Antiochus II and the father of Antiochus III. This monarch of the Seleucid dynasty hardly deserved his surname; his story is more interesting for what was done with, for, and to him, than for any achievement of his own. His mother was Laodice, whom his father, in the course of diplomacy, put aside to marry Berenice, daughter of Ptolemy II and sister of Ptolemy III of Egypt. These formalities completed, Antiochus returned to live with Laodice, but presently she poisoned him and proclaimed their son Seleucus king (247 B.C.). Berenice summoned Ptolemy III to support the claim of her infant son to the throne, but before Egyptian aid could arrive, Seleucus procured the murder of Berenice and his rival. Ptolemy wrested parts of Syria and Asia Minor from Seleucus, who later recovered some of the lost territory. His redoubtable mother, however, backed a revolt by his younger brother Antiochus Hierax, to whom Seleucus was constrained to yield a portion of his kingdom in Asia Minor, after a battle at Ancyra (modern Ankara) in 235 B.C. His death a few years later was due to accidental causes.

Seleucus III. [Surnamed **Soter**, meaning "Savior."] King of Syria (226–223 B.C.); eldest son of Seleucus II. He tried to retake Asia Minor from Attalus of Pergamum but failed. He was killed in a conspiracy.

Seleucus IV. [Surnamed **Philopator**, meaning "Father-loving."] King of Syria (187–175 B.C.). He inherited a diminished empire from his father, Antiochus III. He was assassinated in a plot led by Heliodorus and was succeeded by his brother Antiochus IV.

Seleucus V. King of Syria (125 B.C.). He was killed in a plot directed by his mother, Cleopatra Thea.

Seleucus VI. King of Syria (96–95 B.C.).

Selinus (sē-lī′nus). In ancient geography, a city in SW Sicily, situated near the coast about 48 miles SW of Panormus (Palermo), near what is now Castelvetrano. The city, named for the wild celery that abounds in the region, was the westernmost settlement of the Greeks in Sicily. It was built (c628 B.C.) by colonists from Megara and Hybla Minor and soon became rich and powerful. A quarrel between it and Segesta brought about the Athenian expedition (415 B.C.) to Sicily in the Peloponnesian War. In 410–409 B.C. the city was besieged by a huge Carthaginian force under Hannibal (grandson of Hamilcar), and after stubborn resistance was stormed and sacked. Most of the inhabitants were slaughtered, a few were sold into slavery, and a few escaped to Acragas. Selinus was the first of the Greek cities of Sicily to fall to Carthage. The following year it was rebuilt and fortified by Hermocrates, but under a treaty of 405 B.C. it became a subject city to Carthage. It never recovered its prosperity, and was utterly abandoned in the First Punic War when its few inhabitants were moved to Lilybaeum. Besides remains of the walls built by Hermocrates, the site retains the ruins of seven important Doric temples, several of them among the most archaic examples of the style known, and metopes, also in the archaic style, from an eighth temple have also been found. These temples were thrown down by earthquakes and lie in complete ruin, except that part of the peristyle of Temple "C" was restored some years ago, and since 1958 the complete peristyle and entablature of Temple "ER" have been spectacularly reërected from its fallen stones. The metopes are now in the museum at Palermo.

Sellasia (se̜-lā′zha̜). In ancient geography, a place in Laconia, Greece, a few miles NE of Sparta. Here the Lacedaemonians under Cleomenes III were totally defeated (222 B.C.) by the Macedonians and their allies under Antigonus III.

Selli (sel′ī). Priests of Zeus in his sacred grove at Dodona. They slept on bare earth, did not bathe their feet, and made their bread of acorns instead of grain. Perseus sought their advice when he wanted to secure the head of Medusa.

Selymbria (se-lim′bri-a̜). In ancient geography, a city on the north coast of the Propontis, founded in the 7th century B.C. by colonists from Megara.

Semaleus (se̜-mā′le̜-us). Epithet of Zeus, meaning "Sign-giving." There was an altar of Zeus Semaleus on Mount Parnes near Athens. Among the signs Zeus gave to indicate to mortals that he had heard their prayers were the thunderclap and the lightning flash. Sometimes he sent an eagle as an omen. If the eagle flew to the right the omen was propitious; if it flew to the left it was an omen of misfortune.

Semele (sem′e̜-lē). In Greek mythology, a beautiful daughter of Cadmus and Harmonia, and the sister of Ino, Autonoë, Agave, and Polydorus. She was loved by Zeus. Hera learned that she was about to bear Zeus' child and, jealous as always of her rivals for the affections of Zeus, appeared to Semele in the guise of her old nurse. She hinted to Semele that her lover was not really divine, and suggested to Semele that she ask him to prove his divinity by appearing to her in the same majesty as he appeared to Hera. When next he visited her Semele asked that he grant her a request. Zeus swore by the Styx that he would grant her whatever she asked. However, when he learned her request he urged her to change it, but she persisted and Zeus, bound by his oath, appeared to her with his thunderbolts and the lightning. His blazing majesty burned Semele to ashes. Zeus seized her unborn child and sewed it up in his thigh until the time for its birth should arrive. This child was the god Dionysus. When Dionysus was grown he descended to Tartarus at Lerna and bribed Persephone with a gift of myrtle to release his mother. He ascended with her at Troezen, changed her name to Thyone, in order to delude the other shades who might be jealous of her good fortune, and took her to Olympus. Semele was worshiped at Athens during the Lenaea with singing, dancing, and the sacrifice of a young bull.

Semiramis (sē-mir′a̜-mis). In Assyrian legend, the wife of Ninus, the founder of Nineveh. She was the daughter of the Syrian goddess Derceto, and was endowed with surpassing beauty and wisdom. She beguiled Ninus into making her queen for five days, had him killed, assumed the government of Assyria, and built the city of Babylon with its hanging gardens. If we are to believe the legends, she conquered Persia, Egypt, Ethiopia, and Libya, and organized a campaign against India. Some of the exploits of Semiramis are identical with those attributed to the goddess Ishtar, and she was identified with Ishtar in a fertility aspect. The historical original of these legends was possibly Sammu-ramat, the only Assyrian queen whose name is recorded on the monuments.

Semnones (sem-nō′nēz). Ancient Germanic tribe, a principal branch of the Suevi, first mentioned by Strabo, who describes them as subject to Maroboduus. They were situated in an area from about the middle course of the Albis (Elbe) River E to the Viadua (Oder) River. They are mentioned for the last time at the end of the 2nd century A.D., in the so-called Marcomannic War.

Semo Sancus Dius Fidius (sē′mō sang′kus dī′us fid′i us). See **Sancus**.

Sempronius (sem prō′ni-us). [Full name, **Tiberius Sempronius Longus**.] Roman consul in 218 B.C.; died c210 B.C. He was a colleague of Publius Cornelius Scipio, with whom he was defeated by Hannibal on the Trebia (218 B.C.).

Senate. In ancient Rome, a body of citizens appointed or elected from among the patricians, and later from among rich plebians also, or taking seats by virtue of holding or of having held certain high offices of state. Originally the Senate had supreme authority in religious matters, much legislative and judicial power, the management of foreign affairs, and similar activities. At the close of the Republic, however, and under the Empire, the authority of the Senate was little more than nominal. The original Senate of the patricians numbered 100; after the adjunction of the Sabines and Luceres, the number became 300, and so remained with little change until the supremacy of Sulla. Julius Caesar made the number 900, and after his death, it became over 1000, but was reduced to 600 by Augustus, and varied under subsequent emperors. The struggle between the senatorial party and the popular party, beginning late in the 2nd century B.C. under the Gracchi, culminated in the fall of the Senate from real power after the assassination of Julius Caesar in 44 B.C. Apparently, administration of the large and varied Roman possessions had become too great a burden for the Senate to accomplish successfully, and graft and corruption were widespread before the Senate's powers were curtailed.

Seneca (sen′e̱-ka̱), **Lucius Annaeus** (or **Marcus Annaeus**). [Called **Seneca the Elder** or **Seneca the Rhetorician**.] Roman writer; born at Corduba (now Córdoba), Spain, c54 B.C.; died c39 A.D. He was the father of Lucius Annaeus Seneca (c4 B.C.–65 A.D.) the philosopher, and the grandfather of Lucan. He studied at Rome in the time of Augustus, was a friend of the leading orators and rhetoricians of his day, and was a great admirer of the style of Cicero. His writing consisted of imaginary legal cases (*Controversiae*) demonstrating the uses of rhetoric, exercises in oratory (*Suasoriae*), and a history of Rome from the civil wars to his own time. Of his work only five books of the *Controversiae* and one of the *Suasoriae* survive.

Seneca, Lucius Annaeus. [Called **Seneca the Younger**.] Roman Stoic philosopher; born at Corduba (now Córdoba), Spain, c4 B.C.; died at his villa near Rome, 65 A.D. While still a child, he was brought by his parents to Rome, where he presently studied rhetoric and philosophy and rose to prominence in early manhood as a pleader of causes. He

was a senator under Caligula. In the first year (41 A.D.) of the reign of Caligula's successor Claudius, he was banished to Corsica at the instigation of the empress Messalina, who accused him of improper intimacy with Julia, the daughter of Germanicus. He was recalled in 49 through the influence of Agrippina, the new wife of Claudius, and was entrusted with the education of her son Nero. On the accession of his pupil in 54 he obtained virtual control of the government, which he exercised in concert with Sextus Afranius Burrus, prefect of the Praetorian Guard. The restraint which his counsel imposed on the emperor made his tenure of power precarious, and on the death of Burrus in 62 he petitioned for permission to retire. The permission was withheld; nevertheless, he largely withdrew from the management of affairs. He was ultimately charged with complicity in the conspiracy of Caius Calpurnius Piso, and was ordered by Nero to commit suicide. When the centurion who delivered the order refused him a tablet on which to write a will he turned to his sorrowing friends and family and said that since he could not leave them anything else he would leave them the highest gift of all—the pattern of his own life. He exhorted his friends to accept his death with the consolations of philosophy, embraced his wife tenderly, and with the utmost composure opened his veins. Seneca was highly popular as a philosophical writer in his own day. Theoretically he was a Stoic, but his interest leaned more to a practical and wise conduct of life than to abstract speculations. His pursuit of philosophy never interfered with his acquisition of great wealth. His many writings, in the style of his time, reveal his wide knowledge, and abound in aphorisms. His writings consist of the prose works *De Ira, De Consolatione ad Helviam Matrem, De Consolatione ad Polybium, De Consolatione ad Marciam, De Providentia, De Animi Tranquilitate, De Constantia Sapientis, De Clementia* (addressed to the emperor Nero), *De Vita Beata ad Gallionem, De Otio aut Secessu Sapientis, De Beneficiis, Epistolae ad Lucilium, Apocolocyntosis*, and *Naturales Questiones;* and the tragedies, on the Greek model, *Hercules, Troades, Phoenissae* or *Thebais, Medea, Phaedra* or *Hippolytus*,

Oedipus, Agamemnon, Thyestes, and *Hercules Oetaeus.*

Senones (sen-ō′nēz or sen′ō-nēz). Ancient people of Gaul, dwelling between the Adriatic and the Apennines. They were conquered by the Romans c283 B.C. and expelled from their lands. Another group of Senones was known to Caesar in C Gaul, whose territory bordered on that of the Belgae. They opposed Caesar in the revolt (52 B.C.) of Vercingetorix.

Sentinum (sen-tī′num). In ancient geography, a city in Italy, near the Apennines, about 37 miles SW of Ancona, near what is now Sassoferrato. It is noted for the decisive victory gained (295 B.C.) there by the Romans under Quintus Fabius Maximus Rullianus and Publius Decius Mus over the allied Samnites and Gauls.

Sepeia (sē-pī′a̤). In ancient geography, a place in Argolis, Greece, situated on the Gulf of Argolis, W of Nauplia. Cleomenes I, king of Sparta, believing he had received assurance from an oracle that he would take Argos, marched his forces to this place and prepared to attack (c494 B.C.). Such was the reputation of the Spartans that the Argives were terror-stricken. They could think of no plan to counter-attack or defend themselves and at length resolved that each time they heard the Spartan herald shout a command to the Spartan troops they would give the same command and execute the same maneuver. When Cleomenes observed their tactics he was at first perplexed but soon thought of a way to trick the Argives. He ordered his herald to shout the command to the Spartans to disarm and take their midday meal. The Argives thankfully gave the same command and fell to eating. Whereupon Cleomenes, who had secretly given another order, set upon the Argives and drove them headlong before him. They took refuge in a sacred grove. Cleomenes attempted to lure them out by calling out the names of the leading warriors and announcing that they had been ransomed. When they came out he seized them. The Argives within the grove learned from their scouts what was happening to those who responded to Cleomenes' call and thereafter refused to answer when they heard their names. Cleomenes did not wish to invade the sacred grove. Instead he set fire to it and burned the Argives who had sought sanctuary in it. Six thousand Argives perished. Afterward Cleomenes thought to inquire to whom the grove was sacred. When he learned it was sacred to Argus he concluded that the oracle was fulfilled, some say. He had taken Argus but would not take Argos. He withdrew his forces. From this disaster Argos never fully recovered its former power and equality with Sparta.

Sepias (sep′i-a̤s). A cape or promontory in Thessaly. Here, according to legend, Peleus caught Thetis as she slept in a cave and, although she transformed herself to many shapes, he clung to her. The name comes from the sepia fluid of a cuttlefish into which she last changed herself. The cape was sacred to the Nereids.

Sequani (sek′wa̤-nī). Ancient people of E Gaul who dwelt E of the Aedui, from whom they were separated by the Arar (Saône) River, and W of the Jura Mountains. They were allied with the Arverni against the Aedui. They invited Ariovistus and the Germans across the Rhenus (Rhine), allowed the Helvetii passage through their country in 58 B.C., and joined the league revolting against Caesar in 52 B.C.

Serapis (sē-rā′pis). Ancient deity of Egyptian origin, whose worship was officially promoted under the Ptolemies and was introduced into Greece and later to Rome. Serapis was the dead Apis bull, honored under the attributes of Osiris; he was lord of the Underworld and identified with the Greek Hades. His worship was a combination of Egyptian and Greek cults, and was favored by the Ptolemies for political reasons.

Serbonis, Lacus (sér-bō′nis, lā′kus). [**Serbonian Lake.**] In ancient geography, a bog or morass between the Isthmus of Suez, the Mediterranean, and the Nile delta. According to legend the monster Typhon lies under it.

Sergestus (sér-jes′tus). In the *Aeneid,* a Trojan who accompanied Aeneas on his flight from Troy. His ship was separated from the others in a great storm after the Trojans left Sicily and Aeneas, driven on the shores of Carthage, thought he had been lost, but he turned up safely at Dido's court. Later, Aeneas ordered him to prepare the ships in secret for a speedy departure after Aeneas

actǫr; up, lūte, pull; oi, oil; ou, out; ᴛн, then; d̲ as d or j, s̲ as s or sh, t̲ as t or ch, z̲ as z or zh.

had received a message from Jupiter, via Mercury, that he must leave Dido and proceed with his destiny, which was to found an empire in Italy. Sergestus took part in the boat race in the funeral games that were held for Anchises in Sicily, but he drove his boat on a reef and came in last. He was the supposed founder of the Sergian family in Rome.

Seriphus (se̯-rī′fus) or **Seriphos** (-fos). Island of the Cyclades, in the Aegean Sea about 26 miles N of Melos. Here, according to legend, the chest containing Danaë and the infant Perseus was cast ashore. The island was a place of banishment during the Roman Empire. Area, 25 square miles; length, nine miles.

Serpens (sėr′penz). An ancient northern constellation intimately connected with, but not treated as a part of, Ophiuchus.

Serpent Column. Bronze column at Constantinople; the base of the golden tripod set up in the sanctuary at Delphi from the spoils of the Persians at Plataea in 479 B.C. It was placed in the spina of the hippodrome by Constantine. It consists of three intertwined serpents, whose diverging heads are now broken, and is 18 feet high.

Serrai (se′rē̯). See **Serres.**

Serres (ser′ē̯s). [Also: **Seres, Serrai.**] Town in N Greece, situated in Macedonia near the N end of the lake Cercinitis. The town is of great antiquity, the site on which it lies having been occupied since pre-Hellenic times. The ancient names of the town, in the territory of the Paeonians, were Siris, or Sirrhae. Xerxes stopped here on his march into Greece, 480 B.C., and left the sacred car and horses of the Sun here for safe-keeping. When he returned after his defeat at Salamis and demanded the return of the chariot and the mares, he learned that they had somehow fallen into the hands of the Thracians.

Sertorius (sėr-tō′ri-us), **Quintus.** Roman general; assassinated 72 B.C. He served under Marius in the wars against the Cimbri and the Teutones, served in Spain in 97 B.C., and was quaestor in 91 B.C. When civil war broke out (88 B.C.) in Rome, he opposed the aristocratic party that was headed by Sulla and became commander of one of the armies that besieged Rome under Marius and Cinna. He was not, however, in favor of the blood-shed that followed Marius' success in gaining control of Rome. He was praetor in 83 and went to Spain as Marian commander either in the same or the following year. When Sulla gained control of Rome, Sertorius was proscribed and fled to Mauretania, where he captured Tingis (Tangier), and waged war, generally with success, against the Sullan commanders. At the request of the Lusitanians, he returned to Spain and became their leader against the Romans. He was opposed by Quintus Caecilius Metellus Pius after 79, and also by Pompey after 77 B.C. Following the death of Sulla, he was joined by Marcus Perpenna (or Perperna) and other Romans (77 B.C.). Neither Pius nor Pompey could defeat him. However, Perpenna grew jealous of his power, and intrigued with other Roman officers against him, and assassinated him, 72 B.C.

Servian Wall (sėr′vi-an̯). Name popularly given to a fortification wall in Rome, of local tufa in headers and stretchers revetting an earth embankment, of which substantial sections are preserved, e.g. in the entrance plaza of the railroad station and on the Aventine. These sections indicate an original thickness of 14 to 15 feet and an original height, where required by the terrain, of 30 feet or more, eventually increased to 50 feet. In Rome, masonry of this type is notoriously difficult to date, and earlier scholars identified this wall with fortifications traditionally ascribed by Roman writers to Servius Tullius, sixth king of Rome (578–534 B.C.). Historical considerations, however, indicate that at the time of its capture by the Gauls, c390 B.C., Rome was protected by no such wall, and it is now generally assigned to the generation following 390 B.C. A date of 377 B.C. has been suggested. Any major systemization by Servius Tullius of the defenses of Rome presumably took the form of an earth *agger*. (JJ)

Servile Wars (sėr′vil). Three wars conducted by the Romans against insurgent slaves: 1) The first war (134–132 B.C.) was occasioned by an insurrection in Sicily. The slaves were led by the Syrian Eunus who styled himself King Antiochus, defeated several Roman armies, and maintained himself at Henna (modern Enna), but was ultimately captured and executed. 2) The second war (102–99

fat, fāte, fär, fāre, errạnt; net, mē, hėr ardẹnt; pin, pīne; not, nōte, möve, nôr,

B.C.) was occasioned by an insurrection, also in Sicily, under Tryphon and Athenion, which was put down by the consul Manius Aquillius. 3) The third war (73–71 B.C.), also called the War of the Gladiators, was occasioned by bands of gladiators who had escaped from a gladiatorial school at Capua and occupied Vesuvius, whence, under the command of two Gauls and the Thracian Spartacus, they plundered the neighborhood. They were joined by runaway slaves, defeated four Roman armies in succession, and wandered about Italy, even threatening the capital, but were finally put down by Marcus Licinius Crassus and Cnaeus Pompeius (Pompey the Great). Spartacus fell in the fighting.

Servilia (sẽr-vil′i-ạ). Daughter of the Roman consul Quintus Servilius Caepio; fl. 1st century B.C. By her first husband, Marcus Junius Brutus, she was the mother of that Marcus Junius Brutus who was one of the chief assassins of Caesar. Her second husband was Decimus Junius Silanus. According to some accounts, she was the mistress of Caesar and the woman most loved by him.

Servilius Caepio (sẽr-vil′i-us sē′pi-ō), **Quintus**. See **Caepio, Quintus Servilius**.

Servius Sulpicius Galba (sẽr′vi-us sul-pish′us gal′bạ). See **Galba, Servius Sulpicius**.

Servius Tullius (sẽr′vi-us tul′i-us). According to Roman legend, the sixth king of Rome. He succeeded Tarquinius Priscus, and is said to have reigned 578–534 B.C. According to some accounts, he was the son of a slave woman who had been brought to Rome from the captured city of Corniculum. Others said his mother was a noblewoman of Corniculum who came to live in the palace of Tarquinius Priscus as a friend of Tanaquil, wife of Tarquinius. When Servius was an infant, a prodigy occurred. As he was sleeping in his cradle flames burst from his head. Attendants at the palace were alarmed and called Tanaquil. She said they must not wake the child and then, because she was expert at augury, she told Tarquinius the prodigy foretold that one day Servius would be a protector of the royal house. From that time on Servius was reared as a son of the royal family. He grew up to be greatly honored by the Roman Senate and the Roman people. The sons of Ancus Marcius, fourth king of Rome, considered that Tarquinius Priscus had unjustly won the throne, which should have fallen to one of them. They plotted against Tarquinius, and sent two shepherds to him on the pretense of asking him to settle a dispute. In the course of their argument before Tarquinius one of the shepherds smote him on the head with an ax. The shepherds fled. Tanaquil had the dying king removed to an inner chamber. She persuaded Servius to give out that the king was wounded only, and she prevailed on him to act in the king's place until he should recover. Servius did as she advised; he dealt with the Senate and pretended from time to time to consult the king, who was, in fact, dead. At last when Rome was restored to order and the sons of Ancus had fled, tricked into a belief that their plot had failed, a sound of great mourning rose from the palace and the news was announced to the Romans that Tarquinius Priscus was dead. Servius assumed the throne without being appointed king by the Comitia. He was a wise and capable king. He defeated the people of Veii in war, and when he returned to Rome in triumph he found the Romans no longer questioned his right to be king. He was noted for his reform of the constitution through the institution of the tribes, classes, centuries, and Comitia Centuriata. The people were so divided that the rich had to bear a larger share of the burden of supporting the state; in return, they were extended certain privileges. In drawing up the lists of the tribes Servius took a census of Rome. He expanded Rome by adding the Quirinal and Viminal Hills and, according to tradition, surrounded it with a wall known as the Servian Wall. He also persuaded the nations of Latium to raise a shrine of Diana in Rome, and thus they tacitly acknowledged Rome as the chief city of Latium. Servius had two daughters, both named Tullia, who were married to the sons, or as some say, the grandsons, of Tarquinius Priscus. Their names were Lucius and Aruns. The daughter who was married to Aruns was ambitious, restless, and unscrupulous. Her husband was mild and lacking in ambition. She contrived the death of her husband and of her sister and married Lucius, who shared her ambition and her temperament. She spurred him on to seize the throne from Servius, her own father. He went to the Senate and seated himself on the throne. Servius, now an old man, hurried to the Senate and challenged him. Lucius Tarquinius seized his father-in-law, carried him out and flung him into the street. In the disorder and confusion Servius was separated from his attendants. He made his way alone along the street, suffering from his injuries. As he did so a band of men sent by Tarquinius, some say at the suggestion of Tullia, overtook him and slew him. Presently Tullia came by and, so it is said, drove her chariot over her slain father's body. Tarquinius seized the throne and, as an instance of his wanton cruelty, forbade burial of his dead father-in-law. The reign of Servius marked the end of legitimate kings of Rome. Before him they had been named to the throne by the Comitia. He took the throne without being so named, but his reign was subsequently legalized. Tarquinius, his son-in-law, seized the throne by force.

Sesia (se′zyä). See **Sessites.**

Sesostris (sē-sos′tris). In Greek legend, a king of Egypt, said to have conquered vast areas in Asia and Africa. His legendary exploits are said to be founded on the deeds of Ramses II and others.

Sessites (ses′i-tēz). [Modern name, **Sesia.**] River in NW Italy, which rises in the Alps and joins the Padus (Po) about six miles E of Bodincomagus (Casale Monferrato).

Sestos (ses′tos) or **Sestus** (-tus). In ancient geography, a town in the Chersonesus Thracica, situated on the European shore of the Hellespont, opposite Abydos. It is noted as the residence of Hero in the legend of Hero and Leander, and as the place of debarkation of the army of Xerxes in his invasion of Europe. In Homeric legend (*Iliad*), men of Sestos went to the aid of Troy during the Trojan War.

Set (set). [Also: **Seth;** Greek, **Typhon.**] In Egyptian mythology, the brother, opponent, and slayer of Osiris. He was the god of darkness, night, and evil. Originally, he was a war god who insured victories for Egypt, only much later did he become the personification of evil. With the division of Egypt among the gods, Upper Egypt was assigned to Set, Lower Egypt to Horus. He was called Typhon by the Greeks. In Egyptian

art he is shown with a strange animal's head, having a pointed muzzle and high, square ears.

Setia (sē′shạ). [Modern name, **Sezze.**] In ancient geography, a town in C Italy, situated in the foothills of the Volscian Mountains, SE of Rome. It was a Volscian town, and became a Latin colony in 382 .B.C. Sulla captured it in 82 B.C. Among the Roman architectural remains on the site are fortification walls and a theater.

Seven against Thebes (thēbz), **Expedition of, the.** Polynices and Eteocles, the sons of Oedipus, agreed to rule Thebes alternately, each to rule a year and then give way to the other. Eteocles, the elder, ruled first, but when his term was ended he refused to give up the throne and banished Polynices. Polynices went to Argos. There King Adrastus gave him his daughter Aegia (or Argia) in marriage and promised to restore him to the throne of Thebes. Adrastus sought the help of six chieftains for his expedition against Thebes. He first called on his brother-in-law Amphiaraus. Now Amphiaraus was a seer and he knew that if the expedition were undertaken it would end in disaster and that Adrastus alone would survive it. He was therefore reluctant to go and tried to discourage others. But in an earlier time Adrastus and Amphiaraus had quarreled and would have attacked each other. They were prevented from so doing by Eriphyle, the wife of Amphiaraus and the sister of Adrastus. She composed their quarrel and extracted a promise from them that in future she should have the deciding word in any dispute which arose between them. Polynices learned of this agreement and acted on a suggestion that he bribe Eriphyle to persuade Amphiaraus to join Adrastus in the expedition. He gave her the necklace of Harmonia which he had brought with him from Thebes and begged her to compel Amphiaraus to join the expedition. Eriphyle succumbed to the bribe although she had been forbidden by Amphiaraus to accept any gifts from Polynices. She reminded him of his promise to let her settle any disputes between him and Adrastus and thus forced Amphiaraus agreed to go but left instructions him to take part in the war on Thebes. for his sons to kill their mother and march on Thebes when they grew up. The other leaders of the Seven against Thebes were Capaneus and Hippomedon, both Argives, and Parthenopaeus, the Arcadian son of Atalanta, Tydeus of Calydon, and Polynices of Thebes. Some writers don't count Tydeus and Polynices as leaders but name Eteoclus and Mecisteus, brother of Adrastus, in their places. The leaders set out at the head of their forces and proceeded to Nemea. There they sought water. They approached Hypsipyle, a former Lemnian queen who had been sold as a slave to Lycurgus, king of Nemea, and who was now acting as nurse to his son Opheltes. Hysipyle temporarily abandoned her young charge to lead the Argives to a spring. While Opheltes was alone a serpent attacked him. The Argives returned and slew the serpent but the child was already dead. They buried his body and founded the Nemean games in his honor. Ever after this the judges at the games wore dark robes in mourning for Opheltes, and the victors were crowned with parsley, a symbol of mourning. Opheltes' grave was in a sacred enclosure in Nemea, in which altars were set up. Amphiaraus said the death of Opheltes was a bad omen for the expedition, and renamed the child Archemorus, which means "Bringer" or "Beginner of Doom." The Seven then went on to Cithaeron. Here they paused and sent Tydeus ahead to Thebes as an envoy to demand the restoration of Polynices. The Thebans refused. Now the Argives approached the walls of Thebes. One champion was assigned to each of the seven gates of the city. Within the walls Eteocles assembled his forces. He assigned one Theban chieftain to each gate to match those of his enemies. Eteocles then consulted the seer Tiresias and was told that Thebes would be victorious if a son of Creon voluntarily sacrificed himself to Ares. In spite of his father's protests, Menoeceus, son of Creon, slew himself before the gates. The Argives attacked. Capaneus, boasting that not even Zeus could stop him, set about to scale the wall on a ladder and was struck dead by a thunderbolt of Zeus. Hippomedon was slain by Ismarus, or as some say, he was overcome by a cloud of missiles hurled by the Thebans after he had nearly drowned in the Ismenus River. Par-

thenopaeus was slain by Poseidon's son Periclymenus. Tydeus was wounded by Melanippus and died of his wound. Amphiaraus fled in his chariot. He was pursued by Periclymenus but Zeus made this virtuous man immortal. Before Periclymenus could hurl his spear into Amphiaraus' back Zeus cleft the ground with his thunderbolt and Amphiaraus, his chariot and his charioteer vanished into the chasm. Polynices and Eteocles met in single combat to decide who should have the throne and killed each other. Only Adrastus of the attacking force survived the disaster. He fled on the winged horse Arion which, some say, was the offspring of Demeter and Poseidon. Following the death of Eteocles, his uncle, Creon, succeeded to the throne of Thebes. He cast out the Argive dead and gave orders that their bodies were to remain unburied and at the mercy of scavenger birds. Antigone defied his order, recovered the body of her brother Polynices, and buried it. Adrastus fled to Athens, or as some say, to Eleusis, and laid an olive branch on the altar of the god as a sign that he was seeking divine protection. He appealed to Theseus and the Athenians to compel Creon to return the dead for burial. Theseus recovered the bodies and they were given funeral honors. But some say it was the wives of the fallen heroes who came as suppliants praying for the return of their husbands' corpses, and some say that Theseus made a successful war on Thebes to recover the bodies.

Seven Against Thebes, The, or **Septem** (sep'-tem). A tragedy by Aeschylus, produced 467 B.C. In it the curse on the sons of Oedipus—Eteocles and Polynices—that they shall divide their inheritance by the sword, is fulfilled as the Argives, at the instigation of Polynices and under the leadership of Adrastus, attack Thebes.

The scene is the Acropolis at Thebes. Eteocles, king of Thebes, addresses the citizens. He tells them that if Thebes is victorious it will be owing to the gods, but if it is overthrown he, as king, will bear the responsibility. Therefore he intends to instruct them on their duties. Their principal duty is to come to the aid of their city and their country's gods. Since the Argives are preparing to assault the city he orders the

Thebans to man the walls. A scout enters. He informs Eteocles that the Argives have chosen seven great warriors to lead the attack on the seven gates of Thebes. These warriors are even now casting lots to decide how they will be assigned to the seven gates. The scout urges Eteocles to act with speed, to send the city's best warriors to defend the gates. As for him, he will go to see what more he can learn of the Argive's plans. Eteocles appeals to the gods not to let Thebes be ruined because of a father's curse and leaves to make arrangements for the defense of the city.

At once a chorus of Theban maidens comes rushing forward. They clasp the sacred images, pour out their fears of the enemy, and make wild appeals to all the gods in turn to protect the city and save them from slavery. Eteocles returns and berates them for their expressions of terror. To fling themselves before the altars in this fashion disheartens the soldiers, spreads a poison of cowardice among the townsfolk, and helps the enemy. The women admit they were terrified and ran to the gods they could trust for protection. Eteocles does not object to their honoring the gods, but fear is contagious, he says, and he does not want it to spread through the city. The sound of battle is heard from without. Again the women stir with alarm. Eteocles orders them to return to their homes and pray that the gods will be on the side of Thebes. He assures them that he is now going to post warriors at the gates and adds that he too will take part by defending one of the seven gates. When he leaves the terror of the Theban women revives. They pray that the gods will protect the city and keep its maidens from captivity, for they know and now describe the horrors of war.

Eteocles and the scout approach from opposite directions. The scout describes the positions of the enemy. He names and describes the character, motto and shield device, appearance, and the impious boasts of the champions the Argives are sending against each of the seven gates. As he names and describes each one Eteocles chooses the Theban champion whom he considers appropriate to oppose him. Against the boastful and rash Tydeus he sends the son of Astacus,

who was sprung from the Sparti and whose modesty, discretion, and valor will counterbalance the wild boastfulness of Tydeus. As the scout proceeds to name the Argive chieftains, Eteocles announces the Theban who will best oppose him. The sixth Argive named by the scout is Amphiaraus, the wise seer who, according to the scout's information, upbraided Polynices for waging war against his own city. Against him Eteocles sends one who is wise, brave, and reveres the gods, although Eteocles is convinced that Amphiaraus will not attack the gates as, being a seer, he knows he is doomed. The scout now names the seventh Argive champion, Polynices, Eteocles' own brother. He is violently clamoring to meet Eteocles face to face and vows to kill him or drive him into exile. Eteocles, realizing that his father's curse is operating, names himself as the Theban to oppose Polynices, whose name means "much strife." The chorus burst out in fresh alarm. They urge Eteocles not to risk the impiety of killing his own brother. But he feels he cannot with honor refuse to take his part in the battle, nor can he escape the curse his father laid on him and his brother. He departs to defend the seventh gate.

The Theban maidens lament the woe brought on by a father's prayer. They sing the story of Laius, how he defied Apollo's command not to produce a son and thus brought doom on himself, his son Oedipus, and his grandsons, Eteocles and Polynices. The Theban maidens express their fear that the overthrow of the ruling house of Thebes will result in the destruction of the city. As they finish their ode a messenger enters. He tells them to be of good cheer, for the city is safe; six gates were successfully defended. At the seventh, Eteocles met Polynices and the brothers killed each other. His news is followed by the arrival of a procession bearing the bodies of Eteocles and Polynices. Antigone and Ismene, sisters of Eteocles and Polynices, accompany the procession. In a long hymn the chorus laments the evil fate of the house of Laius, a fate which its members brought on and fulfilled themselves. Antigone and Ismene sing an antiphonal dirge. The inheritance which the brothers divided by the sword is to be a space in their father's tomb.

In an additional episode at the end of the drama, which is thought to be spurious, a herald enters and announces that Eteocles, brave defender of the city, is to be buried with full honors. The body of Polynices, who would have destroyed his own city, is to be cast out as prey for the dogs. Antigone declares that she will give burial to her brother Polynices alone, if necessary. The Theban maidens announce that they will accompany her in a funeral procession for Polynices. For the state, they say, changes its idea of what is just with the changing times; and they will also honor the funeral rites for Eteocles.

Seven Hills of Rome (rōm). The seven hills on which Rome was originally built, included within the circuit of the Servian Wall. They are the Palatine, the Capitoline, the Quirinal, the Aventine, the Caelian, the Esquiline, and the Viminal. The elevations are inconsiderable, the highest, the Quirinal, rising 226 feet above the sea, and the lowest, the Aventine, 151. The Capitoline and the Aventine rise above the left bank of the Tiber, the former to the N. The Palatine lies between them, a little back from the river. N of the Palatine, the furthest N of the seven, is the Quirinal, and on the E are the Viminal, the Esquiline, and the Caelian, respectively NE, E, and SE of the Palatine.

Seven Sages. Seven men of ancient Greece, famous for their practical wisdom. A list commonly given is made up of Thales of Miletus, Solon of Athens, Bias of Priene, Chilo of Sparta, Cleobulus of Rhodes, Periander of Corinth, and Pittacus of Mytilene. Of the Seven Sages the story was told that once the Coans (inhabitants of the island of Cos) hauled up a great catch in their nets. Some strangers bought their catch, sight unseen. When they investigated it they found in it a golden tripod, said to have been dropped by Helen on her return voyage from Troy. When the Coans learned of the find they wanted their catch and its precious relic returned to them. The strangers refused to return it and war broke out. When this dragged on without reaching a decision it was decided to appeal to the priestess of Apollo at Delphi. She decreed that the tripod should be given to the wisest man.

With the willing consent of the Coans the tripod was sent to Thales of Miletus. He, however, modestly disclaimed the honor, saying that Bias of Priene was the wisest man. Accordingly it was sent on to him. He also refused to accept the honor of being named the wisest man, and suggested one of the other sages, and so the tripod went to each of them, and each of them was wise enough to know that he was not the wisest man. In the end, the tripod was dedicated to Apollo, some say to Ismenian Apollo at Thebes, and others say to Apollo at Delphi.

Seven Wonders of the World. The seven most remarkable structures of ancient times. These were the Egyptian pyramids, the Mausoleum erected by Artemisia at Halicarnassus, the Temple of Artemis at Ephesus, the walls and hanging gardens at Babylon, the Colossus at Rhodes, the statue of Zeus by Phidias in the great temple at Olympia, and the Pharos or lighthouse at Alexandria. The walls of Babylon sometimes replace the last.

Sextus (seks'tus). In Roman legend, the son of Tarquinius Superbus. He was said to have raped Lucretia (wife of Tarquinius Collatinus) and thus to have caused her to take her own life. See **Tarquinius Sextus**.

Sextus Julius Frontinus (jöl'yus fron-tī'nus). See **Frontinus, Sextus Julius**.

Sextus Pompeius Festus (pom-pē'us fes'tus). See **Festus, Sextus Pompeius**.

Sezze (sāt'tsā). See **Setia**.

Sibyls (sib'ilz). In ancient mythology, certain old women or young maidens reputed to possess special powers of prophecy or divination and intercession with the gods in behalf of those who resorted to them. They dwelt in caves or by springs, and under the influence of a frenzy supposedly inspired by a god, they uttered prophecies, often in equivocal language. Heraclitus, in the 6th century B.C., mentioned one prophetess named Sibyl, whose legend spread to various localities; by c350 B.C. she was mentioned as many. Different writers mention from one to ten Sibyls, enumerated as the Persian, Libyan, Delphian, Cimmerian, Erythraean, Samian, Cumaean, Hellespontine or Trojan, Phrygian, and Tiburtine. Of these the most celebrated was the Cumaean Sibyl (of Cumae in Italy) whose story is that she appeared before Tarquin the Proud and offered him nine books for sale. He refused to buy them, whereupon she burned three, and offered the remaining six at the original price. He again refused them; she destroyed three more, and offered the remaining three at the price she had asked for the nine. Tarquin, astonished, bought the books, which were found to contain directions as to the worship of the gods and the policy of the Romans. As the earliest Sibyl was thought to have dwelt on Mount Ida in the Troad this accounts for the introduction of foreign gods into Rome. These Sibylline Books, or books professing to have this origin, written in Greek hexameters, were kept with great care at Rome, and consulted only by the direction of the Senate. They were destroyed at the burning of the Temple of Jupiter in 83 B.C. Fresh collections were made, which were finally destroyed soon after 400 A.D. The 14 or 15 Sibylline Oracles referred to by the Christian fathers, and still extant, have no connection with the Sibyls of mythology. They belong to early ecclesiastical literature, and are a mixture of Jewish, Hellenistic, and later Christian material. In composition they seem to date from the 2nd century B.C. to the 3rd century A.D.

Sicanian (si-kā′ni-an). A name arbitrarily given to the neolithic phase of the pre-classical, non-Italic population of Sicily (perhaps ultimately of North African origin) which was in occupation when the exploring Phoenicians and Greeks arrived in the island. In Greek and Roman writers the Sicani or Siculi are the earliest inhabitants of Sicily; Sicania and Sikelia, or Sicilia, are used side by side. In Ovid, Sicania is a poetic alternative for Sicilia. In the chronological table based on ceramic classifications, the Sicanian (neolithic) phase is followed by First Siculan and Second Siculan (bronze-age) phases, and the Third Siculan (iron-age) phase. (JJ)

Siceli (si-sel′ī) or **Siculi** (sik′ū-lī). A people of ancient Italy, to which they had come from N Africa. They crossed the Straits of Messina to Sicily and occupied the eastern portion of the island, which takes its name from them. These were the people whom the Greeks first found in Sicily, and their culture was displaced, in large part, by that of the Greeks.

Sicharbas (si-kär′bas). See **Acerbas**.

Sicilian Bull (si-sil′yan). Bronze bull made as an instrument of torture by Perillus for the use of the Sicilian tyrant Phalaris. Persons selected for torture were placed in the bull's hollow body, which was then heated, the muffled screams of the victims evidently contributing to the mirth of the onlookers. As with other such devices, legend has it that Perillus was its first victim. (JJ)

Sicily (sis′i-li). [Latin, **Sicilia**; Greek, **Sikelia**; ancient names, also: **Trinacria** and **Sicania**.] Island in the Mediterranean Sea, SW of the mainland of S Italy, from which it is separated by the Strait of Messina. The surface is largely hilly or mountainous, with the volcanic structure of Mount Etna in the E and several ranges in the N. The largest plain is around Catania. The climate is subtropical, with hot, dry summers and mild, humid winters. In ancient times the island was called Trinacria, "Three Capes," from the three promontories of its roughly triangular shape—Pelorum, Pachynum, and Lilybaeum. It is thought to be the island mentioned in the *Odyssey* as the place where Helius pastured his sacred cattle. The land is very fertile and produced an abundance of grain. According to Sicilian tradition the island was the favorite home of Demeter, who gave the gift of grain to its people before any others, and taught them how to make use of the gift. The Sicilians claimed that the rape of Persephone took place in the meadows about the town of Henna (Enna), which lie in the center of the island. The spot, one of extraordinary beauty and noted for its abundance of violets, was called "the navel of Sicily." Near it were sacred groves, a grotto, and the chasm through which Hades bore Persephone to the Underworld.

The location of Sicily, midway between the eastern and western ends of the Mediterranean and stepping-stone between Italy and Africa, gave it great strategic importance, and made it a battleground for successive waves of colonists and invaders. The earliest inhabitants of which anything is known were the Sicanians, for whom the island was once called Sicania. They were pushed back by the Siceli who moved over from Africa and occupied the eastern half

fat, fāte, fär, fãre, errant; net, mē, hėr ardent; pin, pīne; not, nōte, möve, nôr,

of the island, which henceforth was called for them, Sicily. In the northwest corner were the Elymi, a people who had come perhaps from Asia Minor and occupied the area in very ancient times. At an early date the Phoenicians established settlements on the coasts of Sicily. But the most important of the early immigrants were the Greeks, whose influence endured for centuries. The earliest Greek colonizers were Chalcidians from Euboea who, c735 B.C., founded the town of Naxos, near what later became the Corinthian colony of Syracuse (c734 B.C.). The Greeks pushed the Phoenicians out of their settlements, mostly trading posts, and the latter withdrew to strong areas in the north and west, near the Elymian towns of Eryx and Segesta. Other early Greek settlements on the rugged eastern coast were the Chalcidian cities of Leontini and Catana (729 B.C.), Dorian Megara Hyblaea (726 B.C.), Zancle (715 B.C.), Gela (689 B.C.), Himera, the only Greek settlement on the northern coast (648 B.C.), Selinus (628 B.C.), Camarina (599 B.C.), and Acragas (582 B.C.). The Greek cities flourished; close ties were maintained with the homeland, and the intellectual and cultural vigor of the Greek mainland took firm root and proliferated in Sicily. Behind the Greek cities of the eastern coast were the Sicel and Sicanian settlements. West of them were the strong Phoenician towns of Panormus, Solus, and Motya. These last looked to the Punic city of Carthage to protect them from the encroachments of the Greeks. In the first half of the 6th century B.C. a large force was sent from Carthage which won some Greek territory for the Punic cities of the island. This century saw also the consolidation of certain areas of Greek Sicily, and by the beginning of the 5th century B.C. large areas were under the sway of tyrants, as those of Acragas, Syracuse, Zancle, and Himera. With Greece engaged in a desperate struggle against the might of Persia, Carthage seized the opportunity presented by a quarrel between Sicilian tyrants to interfere in Sicily and to win additional influence there. Hamilcar invaded Sicily at the head of a great armament. He was resoundingly defeated at Himera (480 B.C.), where he lost his life. For the next 70 years the Car-

thaginians remained on the sidelines in the struggles between the rival cities of Sicily. In that time Athens engaged in an expedition (415–413 B.C.) to the island designed to curb the growing power of the Corinthian colony of Syracuse and to establish Athenian domination of the island. The Athenian expedition was not only a failure; it was a disaster for Athens. Possibly the greatest effect of it for Sicily was to show the Sicilian cities that they had attained a status of political independence and equality with the city-states of Greece. Political independence was cherished, but not more than the Greek cultural heritage. In 409 B.C. the Carthaginians returned and won firm control of the western part of the island. The history of the next century is of wars with Carthage, in which the leading Sicilian participant was the great city of Syracuse. In the course of the wars mercenaries from Campania settled in Sicily, and later gave the Romans their pretext for interference in the island. In the First Punic War (264–241 B.C.) between Rome and Carthage, Sicily was a battle-ground. When the war ended, Carthage withdrew from the island and the western half became a Roman province (241 B.C.). The eastern half remained free as an ally of Rome. In the Second Punic War (218–201 B.C.), Syracuse revolted against Rome. The revolt was put down after a two-year siege by Marcellus (211 B.C.), and the entire island became a Roman province and the prey of a series of plundering Roman officials.

Sicinus (sik'i-nus). [Modern name, **Sikinos.**] An island of the Cyclades, about 19 miles S of Paros. According to legend Thoas, king of Lemnos, was pulled ashore here after he had been cast adrift in a chest by his daughter Hypsipyle to save him from the wrath of the Lemnian women. The island, which had been known as Oenoë, was named Sicinus after a son born to Thoas by the water-nymph Oenoë. Length, nine miles.

Sicinnus (sik-in'us). A household slave and tutor to the sons of Themistocles. When the Greeks, assembled at Salamis, began to dispute whether they should retire to the Isthmus for the coming battle with the Persians (480 B.C.), Themistocles sent Sicinnus with a message to the Persian fleet. The purpose of this stratagem was to compel the Greeks to fight at Salamis, which Themistocles thought was the most advantageous location for them. Sicinnus was secretly put aboard a merchant ship and sent to the Persian fleet. He pretended Themistocles was friendly to the Persians and gave as a message from him that if the Persians attacked at once they would find the Greeks arguing among themselves, terrified, and an easy conquest. The Persians acted on this advice at once. Sicinnus disappeared. After some time Themistocles freed him and made him a Thespian citizen.

Siculi (sik′ū-lī). See **Siceli.**

Siculum (sik′ū-lum), **Fretum.** Latin name of **Messina, Strait of.**

Siculus (sik′ū-lus). See **Diodorus.**

Siculus, Titus Calpurnius. See **Calpurnius Siculus, Titus.**

Sicyon (sish′i-on, sis-). In ancient geography, a city in the N part of the Peloponnesus, Greece, situated near the Gulf of Corinth, about ten miles NW of Corinth. According to legend, the city was founded by Aegialeus, son of the river-god Inachus, and was first called Aegialea after him. In later times, Sicyon, son of Metion and grandson of Erechtheus, according to some accounts came to Aegialea from Attica as an ally. He became king and changed the name of the city and region to Sicyon and Sicyonia respectively. Once wolves prayed on the flocks of the Sicyonians and they sought relief through an oracle. The oracle directed them to a certain spot where they would find a dry log. They were instructed to mix the bark of the log with meat and set it out for the wolves. They did so, and when the wolves ate the meat they fled and never returned. A sanctuary of Apollo Lycius (*Wolf-god*) was raised and the log was dedicated in it, but none could say from what kind of tree it had come. Near the sanctuary of Apollo Lycius was a sanctuary of Asclepius. The Sicyonians claimed the healing god came to them from Epidaurus, in the shape of a serpent and riding in a chariot drawn by two mules.

After the Dorian invasion Sicyon was part of Argive territory. Early in the 7th century B.C. Orthagoras became tyrant. He exercised a benevolent despotism and Sicyon flourished. His dynasty reached a peak of power and influence under Clisthenes, who contended against Argos, put an end to the recital of the Homeric poems because they exalted the Argives, suppressed the cult of the Argive hero Adrastus who had ruled Sicyon for a time, and changed the names of the Sicyonian tribes so that they should not share the names of the Argive tribes. He gave his daughter in marriage to Megacles, son of Alcmaeon the Athenian. With the Amphictyonic League, he went to the aid of Delphi (c590 B.C.), against Crisa, because Crisa claimed control over the oracle and exacted tolls from visitors to it. He helped to crush Crisa and assured the independence of the oracle. In the time of its greatest prosperity Sicyon had rich treasuries at Delphi and Olympia and was renowned for its painters, of whom Eupompus, Pamphilus, and Pausias were the most famous. After the reign of Clisthenes, Sicyon was so weakened by internal struggles between the aristocratic and democratic factions that it was able to play only a minor role in the Persian War. Afterward, Athens sought to control it. Pericles led an expedition against it but failed to subdue it. In 368 B.C. the city fell under the domination of Epaminondas. The city was destroyed by Demetrius Poliorcetes, 303 B.C. He moved the inhabitants away from the harbor to the citadel, which he considered to be healthier and safer, and built a new city there. Sicyon joined the Achaean League, 251 B.C., was taken with the rest of the Peloponnesus, by the Romans, and was destroyed, 23 A.D., by an earthquake. An ancient theater at the foot of the Acropolis where the new city of Demetrius Poliorcetes stood, was excavated by the American School at Athens. It is a large and important monument. At the bottom of the cavea there is a row of seats of honor, in the form of benches with backs and arms. Access to the cavea from without is facilitated by two vaulted passages. There is a covered underground passage from the middle of the orchestra to the interior of the stage structure. Other excavators have found remains of a council chamber and of a Doric temple of Artemis.

Sicyonia (sish-i-ō′ni-a̧, sis-). In ancient geography, the territory surrounding Sicyon,

a) Gold stater of Croesus, 561–546 B.C. b) Silver stater, Aegina, early 6th century B.C. c) Silver stater, Corinth, early 6th century B.C. d) Silver stater, Poseidonia, second half of 6th century B.C. e) Silver stater, Croton, second half of 6th century B.C. f) Silver stater, Sybaris, second half of 6th century B.C. g) Silver tetradrachm, Syracuse, c 530–510 B.C. h) Silver tetradrachm, Athens, late 6th century B.C. i) Silver tetradrachm, Gela, early 5th century B.C. j) Silver tetradrachm, Syracuse, c 485–479 B.C. k) Silver tetradrachm, Athens, 5th century B.C.

l) Silver tetradrachm, Aenus, c 450 B.C. m) Silver tetradrachm, Mende, c 450–423 B.C. n) Silver tetradrachm, Naxos (Sicily), second half of 5th century B.C. o) Silver decadrachm, Syracuse, late 5th or early 4th century B.C. p) Silver stater, Tarentum, c 420–380 B.C. q) Silver tetradrachm of Alexander the Great, c 336–334 B.C. r) Silver stater, Cnossus, 4th century B.C. s) Silver tetradrachm of Demetrius Poliorcetes, 292–291 B.C. t) Silver tetradrachm of Lysimachus, early 3rd century B.C. u) Silver tetradrachm of Mithridates VI of Pontus, 76/5 B.C.

Courtesy of The American Numismatic Society

a) Roman as, 3rd century B.C. b) Silver didrachm of S. Italy, 222–205 B.C. c) Silver denarius of S. Italy, 182–172 B.C. d) Silver denarius, 78–77 B.C. e) Silver denarius, Rome, c 44 B.C. f) Silver denarius of Augustus, 15–12 B.C. g) Gold coin of Tiberius, 14–37 A.D. h) Bronze sestertius of Caligula, 37–38 A.D. i) Bronze sestertius of Claudius, 41 A.D. j) Bronze sestertius of Nero, 64–66 A.D. k) Bronze sestertius of Titus, 80–81 A.D.

Roman aqueduct, c 19 B.C., Nemausus. (Pont du Gard, Nîmes)

Mary E. Dolbeare

Left: Roman bridge, 1st century B.C., Córdoba.

Spanish National Tourist Office

Spanish National Tourist Office

Roman aqueduct, 53–117 A.D., Segovia.

Left: Roman wall, 3rd century B.C., Lugo.

Spanish National Tourist Office

Greece, and bounded by the Gulf of Corinth on the NE, Corinthia on the E, Argolis and Phliasia on the S, Arcadia on the W, and Achaea on the NW. According to some accounts, Aegialeus, son of the river-god Inachus and the nymph Melia, was the first inhabitant of the land. He founded the city of Aegialea and named the region about it Aegialus for himself. After Apollo and Artemis had killed Python at Delphi they set out for Aegialea to be purified, but turned aside at a place called Fear and went to Crete instead. Plague fell on Aegialea. Seers told the people to appease Apollo and Artemis. Seven youths and seven maidens were sent as suppliants to the river and the gods, persuaded by the suppliants, came to the citadel and lifted the plague. In gratitude, the Sicyonians raised a sanctuary to Persuasion on the citadel. In the ceremonies regularly celebrated in memory of this event the images of the deities were first taken to the sanctuary of Persuasion. Then they were carried to the temple of Apollo. This temple was raised to Apollo by Proetus when his daughters recovered from their madness. Here Meleager dedicated the spear with which he had slain the Calydonian boar. The flutes of Marsyas, flung into the Maeander River in Phrygia, were brought by the river to the banks of the Asopus River in Sicyonia. Here they were found by a shepherd, who took them to the temple and dedicated them to Apollo. During the reign of Apis, who ruled before Pelops came into the Peloponnesus, Aegialea became very powerful. He extended his control to all the territory south of the Isthmus and named it Apia after himself. In a later age Sicyon, son of Marathon according to some accounts, but others say he was a son of Metion and a grandson of Erechtheus, came from Attica as an ally during a war. He became king and changed the name of the region to Sicyonia. His descendants, whose blood, they claimed, was mixed with that of various gods, ruled after him. Adrastus, king of Argos, inherited Sicyonia and became its king for a time, but afterward he returned to Argos and the throne of Sicyonia was occupied by a series of demigods. With the rise to power of the Pelopidae the power of Sicyonia declined. Agamemnon led an army against it and took

it. Henceforth Sicyonia was under the domination of Mycenae. In the Trojan War men of Sicyonia sailed against Troy under the command of Agamemnon. The Dorians entered Sicyonia c1100 B.C. but did not devastate it because its ruler at that time was, as the invaders claimed to be, a descendant of Heracles. Under the Dorians it was made part of Argive territory.

Side (sī'dē). In ancient geography, a town in Pamphylia, Asia Minor, situated on the Gulf of Pamphylia, near what is now Antalya, Turkey. The site contains a Roman theater, in part excavated from a hillside and in part built up of masonry. The cavea, greater than a semicircle, has 26 tiers of marble seats below the precinction and 23 above it. A number of vaulted passages lead from the precinction to the exterior. The diameter is 409 feet; that of the orchestra, 125 feet.

Sidero (sī-dē'rō). In Greek mythology, the second wife of Salmoneus. For her cruel treatment of her stepdaughter Tyro, the sons of Tyro avenged their mother when they grew up. They pursued Sidero to the temple of Hera, dragged her away from the altar where she had sought refuge, and killed her.

Sidon (sī'don). [Modern name, **Saida**.] Oldest city of ancient Phoenicia. From the 17th century B.C. to c1100 B.C. it held supremacy in Phoenicia, and established most of the Phoenician colonies. Later it was surpassed by Tyre, but long continued to hold an important position among the mercantile cities of the ancient world. In 351 B.C. it was destroyed in consequence of a revolt against the Persian king Artaxerxes III, but was rebuilt and was still a wealthy city about the beginning of the Christian era. During the Crusades it was several times destroyed. The ancient necropolis, long known and exploited, has yielded numerous monuments of the most diverse ages and civilizations, from the oldest Phoenicians still under Egyptian influence, through the various stages of Greek art. In 1887 an important discovery was made, consisting of an intact subterranean mausoleum of several chambers, containing 22 sarcophagi, several of them bearing polychrome sculptures in relief of the best Greek art, and almost uninjured. The sarcophagi were transported to the museum at Constantinople, where they form one of the most important existing collections of ancient art. The Greek sarcophagi were not executed at Sidon, but were imported from different places and at different times. Their usual form is that of a temple. Four only are completely covered with sculpture; but these four rank with the finest existing productions of Greek art, and are the only sarcophagi known which belong to the best period of sculpture. The oldest is of Lycian form, with centaurs and Lapiths, and hunting scenes. The second, dating from the beginning of the 4th century B.C., is called "the Sarcophagus of the Weeping Women," from the graceful figures in the intercolumniations of its Ionic colonnade. The third bears varied scenes from the life of an Oriental ruler. The fourth is so splendid that its discoverers may be pardoned for proclaiming it the sarcophagus of Alexander. Four of its six sculptured panels represent hunting or battle scenes in which the portrait of Alexander, almost contemporaneous, actually figures. It is no doubt the tomb of an Oriental prince who had enjoyed the companionship of the Macedonian conquerer.

Siena (sye′nä). [Ancient names: **Sena Julia, Colonia Julia Senensis**.] City in C Italy. It was founded by the Etruscans, and became a Roman town in the time of Augustus.

Sigeum (sī-jē′um). In ancient geography, a promontory and town in the Troad, at the mouth of the Hellespont about five miles NW of Troy. It was the legendary station of the Greek fleet during the Trojan War and, according to tradition, the tomb of Achilles was here. Sigeum was colonized by settlers from the island of Lesbos. With the encouragement of Miletus, Athens seized Sigeum, but lost it early in the 6th century B.C. when Pittacus, tyrant of Mytilene, won it back for Lesbos. Athens regained control (c535 B.C.), during the rule of Pisistratus.

Signia (sig′ni-a̱). [Modern name, **Segni**.] In ancient geography, a town in C Italy, situated near the Volscian Mountains, about 30 miles SE of Rome. It is notable for important Italic remains, which include massive fortifications in polygonal limestone masonry, with a picturesque corbelled gate—the Porta Saracinesca—a postern gate, and several sally ports, other fortifications in ashlar tufa, and an Italic triple-cella temple of the late 3rd or early 2nd century B.C. The cella walls of the temple, of ashlar tufa, incorporated in the ancient church of San Pietro, survive to nearly their original height. The temple stands on a double terrace of rough polygonal limestone (Cyclopean) construction, once thought to indicate an earlier building period but now considered contemporary with the existing temple. Signia was said to have received a Latin colony in 495 B.C., and the polygonal fortifications were formerly assigned to this period, though some scholars, deceived by their primitive appearance, considered them earlier still. It now appears safer to refer them to the period of the Punic Wars in the 3rd century B.C., when Signia was an important defensive outpost of Rome. (JJ)

Silarus (sil′a̱-rus). [Modern names, **Sele, Silaro**.] River in S Italy which flows into the Mediterranean about 17 miles SW of Salernum. Near it, in 71 B.C., Spartacus was defeated and slain by the Romans under Crassus.

Silenus (sī-lē′nus). In Greek mythology, a forest-god, depicted as a shaggy, full-bearded old man, with horse ears, and sometimes horse legs, usually drunk, and often riding on an ass or on a wine-vessel. He was reported to be extraordinarily wise, and if caught could be made to reveal his wisdom and give answers to questions. The Phrygian king Midas is said to have plied Silenus with wine and questions and received astounding answers; but nobody learned what Silenus told Midas, except that it would be better never to be born. In the 6th century B.C. Silenus became associated with Dionysus and thereafter appeared in the Dionysian frolics and processions attended by troops of satyrs. He became credited with being the foster father and boon companion of Dionysus. The term *sileni* (plural) is applied to a group of woodland spirits or semideities, who were much confused with the satyrs, whom they resembled, except that the sileni were old and were differentiated from the goatlike satyrs by their horselike characteristics. They, too, were characterized as wise, drunk, and prophetic. They were credited with being wonderful musicians, and with having taught Dionysus the secrets of the vine and wine-making. Socrates was compared to Silenus in wisdom, irony, and appearance.

Silures (si-lö′rēz). Ancient people of Britain, formerly dwelling in the hills of what is now SE Wales, at the period of the Roman conquest. The geological term Silurian is derived from this tribal name.

Silvanus, Sylvanus (sil-vā′nus). Ancient Roman god of untilled land, i.e., land outside of recognized boundaries. He was therefore somewhat feared, and was propitiated every time new ground was broken or new land cleared of trees. Every farmhouse had three Silvani: one to protect the boundaries, one to protect the farmhouse, and one to protect the herds. He was later rather freely identified with the Greek satyrs and sileni.

Silver Age. This was the second age of man created by the gods. It followed the Golden Age and was less glorious. The time of childhood and helplessness was long. The duration of manly strength was short, owing to the tendency of men to war against each other. Man in the Silver Age was less devout, and failed to make sacrifices to the gods. It was not an entirely bad age, however; there were men of honor, and after mortal life was over men were thought to live on as spirits.

Silvia (sil′vi-a). In Roman legend, a daughter of Tyrrheus, a herdsman of Latinus. She had taught a pet stag to obey her, and to return each night to its stall. The Trojans, who had landed in Latium with Ascanius, egged on by the goddess of mischief Alecto, and unaware of the tame nature of the stag, killed it. This deed aroused the Latins against the Trojans, and was one of the precipitating causes of the war between the Trojans under Aeneas and the Latins under the leadership of Turnus.

Silvius (sil′vi-us). In the *Aeneid,* when Aeneas visited his father in the Underworld to learn his destiny, Anchises pointed to the shade of Silvius, among others, as one waiting to be born. He told Aeneas that Silvius would be his last child, born in his old age, and that Lavinia would bear him in sylvan surroundings. Anchises predicted the rule of his line in Alba Longa. This name was borne by several of the descendants of Aeneas who were kings of Alba Longa.

Silvius Aeneas (sil′vi-us ē-nē′as). See **Aeneas Silvius.**

Simois (sim′ō-is). In Homeric legend (*Iliad*), the god of the river of the same name near Troy. It was at the mouth of this river that Protesilaus leaped ashore from the Greek ships and became the first Greek to be slain in the Trojan War. Toward the end of the war Xanthus, also a river-god, called on Simois to help stop Achilles when he was murderously attacking the Trojans. Simois flooded his banks and washed stones and tree trunks against Achilles in a raging torrent, but all to no avail. Hephaestus, at Hera's request, came to the aid of Achilles and set the rivers afire. After the war was over Simois was one of the rivers which Poseidon, with the aid of Apollo, diverted from its course for nine days in order to wash down the wall which the Greeks had built to defend their ships. The wall was destroyed because Poseidon feared that this man-made structure would overshadow the wall he and Apollo had built for Laomedon, if it were left standing. Simois the river-god was one of the many sons of Oceanus and Tethys.

Simois. A small stream near Buthrotum in Epirus. Helenus, who went to this region after the Trojan War, named the stream after the river of the same name in the Troad.

Simoisius (sim-ō-is′i-us). In the *Iliad,* a Trojan youth who was named after the Simois River because he was born on its banks. He was slain by Telamonian Ajax in the Trojan War.

Simonides of Amorgos (sī-mon′i-dēz a-môr′gos). [Also: **Semonides.**] Greek iambic poet; born in Samos; fl. c660 B.C. He led a colony from Samos to the island of Amorgos, whence his surname. He was a younger contemporary of Archilochus, less personal and intense in expression. Among his works was an elegy on the history of Samos, now lost, and a satiric poem in which he ascribed the least pleasing qualities in women to the animals that were distinguished for those qualities or characteristics, as, a fat lazy woman is compared to a pig, an obstinate woman to a donkey, an ugly one to a monkey, and so on. He quoted Homer, calling him "the man of Chios," in the line "Like generations of leaves, even so are men's generation," in an elegy in which he exhorted men to enjoy life while they are still young enough to do so, for "mortal men have only a short space to be young." Fragments of his work have been preserved.

Simonides of Ceos (sē'os). Greek lyric and elegiac poet; born at Iulis, island of Ceos, 556 B.C.; died at Syracuse, c469 or 467 B.C. While still a young man he became famous for his culture and his poetic gift. He was a contemporary of Pindar and Bacchylides (his nephew), and was a friend of many of the great men of his day. The tyrant Hipparchus was his friend and patron at Athens. After the murder of Hipparchus, Simonides left Athens and went to Thessaly where he was welcomed at the court of Scopas. He returned to Athens after the battle of Marathon (490 B.C.), and wrote some of his most celebrated elegies on the heroes of Marathon and Thermopylae. His elegy on the men who had fallen at Marathon was preferred to that of Aeschylus. His epitaph for the Spartans who fell at Thermopylae (480 B.C.) is moving, simple, and justly famed:

Go, stranger, and to Lacedaemon tell
That here, obeying her behests, we fell.

Toward the end of his life (c476 B.C.) he was summoned to Sicily to mediate a dispute between the tyrants Theron and Hiero I, and spent the remainder of his life at the court of Hiero at Syracuse. His poetry, among the best of ancient Greece, was in many forms, including epigrams, lyrics, epitaphs, threnodies, and, especially, hymns for the victors in athletic contests. Grace of language, sincerity of sentiment, and the simplicity with which he employed his vast learning are notable characteristics of his work. A poem on Danaë, cast on the sea in a chest with her infant Perseus, was acclaimed by the ancients for its "unsurpassed pathos."

Sinis (sī'nis). In Greek legend, a son of Polypemon and Sylea. He was a thug who lived on the Isthmus of Corinth. He was given the name of Pityocamptes (*Pine-bender*) because it was his custom to require travelers who came his way to help him bend down tall pine trees until their tops touched the ground. Sinis would then let go his hold and the tree, freed from his restraining hold, would spring upright, hurling the unlucky traveler into the air as from a catapult; when he fell to the ground he was dashed to pieces. Or as some say, Sinis bent two pines to the ground and tied his victim between them. When he released the arched trees thy sprang upright, tearing the victim in two. Theseus, on his way to Athens, encountered Sinis. He overpowered him and treated Sinis as Sinis had treated others.

Sinoeis (sin-ọ-ē'is). Epithet of Pan, given to him because, some say, he was nursed by the nymph Sinoë. In the temple at Megalopolis in Arcadia was an image of Pan Sinoeis.

Sinon (sī'nọn). In Greek legend, a cousin of Odysseus. He accompanied the Greeks to Troy and volunteered to remain behind and allow himself to be captured when the Greeks resorted to the stratagem of the Wooden Horse in the tenth year of the Trojan War. The Greeks built the Horse and left it on the beach before Troy. They then put out their camp-fires and sailed away behind the island of Tenedos. As the Trojans swarmed out of the city to inspect the huge image, Sinon arranged for himself to be captured. He was brought before Priam in chains and cast himself on the mercy of his former enemy. He said he had been a squire of that Palamedes whose death was brought about by Odysseus, and because he knew the secret of Palamedes' death Odysseus wanted to destroy him. The Greeks, he said, resolved to secure favorable winds so that they could return to their homeland, proposed to propitiate Athena with a blood sacrifice as they had formerly sacrificed Iphigenia at Aulis. Calchas, inspired by Odysseus, had chosen Sinon for the victim, but at that moment a breeze sprang up and the rush to sail permitted Sinon to make his escape. Priam listened courteously to his tale, and as he finished it ordered the fetters removed from his limbs and promised him asylum. The king then inquired the meaning of the Wooden Horse. Sinon, well coached by Odysseus, explained that it was an offering to propitiate Athena for the theft of the Palladium from Troy; that it had purposely been made huge so that the Trojans could not take it into their city, for if they

fat, fāte, fär, fãre, errạnt; net, mē, hėr ardẹnt; pin, pīne; not, nōte, mȯve, nôr,

succeeded in doing that Troy would become the master of Europe. In spite of the warnings of Cassandra and Laocoön, all worked as Odysseus had foreseen: the Trojans feverishly breached their walls and took the Wooden Horse inside the city. During the night Sinon gave the signal to the warriors concealed in the Horse to come out and signaled to the fleet to return from Tenedos. He opened the gates to the city and Troy, which for years had resisted frontal assaults, at last fell through the treacherous stratagem of the Wooden Horse.

Sinope (si-nō′pē). In Greek mythology, a daughter of the river-god Asopus and Metope. According to some accounts, Apollo fell in love with her and carried her off to a peninsula in the Euxine Sea to a city which later bore her name. Some say she bore Apollo a son, Syrus, who became king of the Syrians and named his people after himself. Zeus also fell in love with Sinope, and sought to gain her affections by promising to give her whatever she asked for. She craftily demanded that he assure her of lifelong virginity. He was compelled

cinnabar, which takes its name from Sinope. In 183 B.C. it was conquered and became the capital of Pontus. It was later (70 B.C.) subdued by Lucullus and became a Roman city. According to myth, Sinope was named for the daughter of the river-god Asopus.

Sintians (sin′shanz). A name for the people of Lemnos. The Sintians took care of Hephaestus when he was flung out of heaven.

Siphnus (sif′nus). [Also: **Siphnos**.] Island of the Cyclades, in the Aegean Sea about 24 miles NE of Melos. In ancient times there were rich mines of gold and silver in the island, the yield of which, according to Herodotus, was annually divided among the citizens and made them the richest of the islanders. The Siphnians furnished a treasury at Delphi which was equal to the grandest there, and at the time asked the oracle how long their wealth and good things would last. The answer of the priestess was as follows:

When the Prytanies' seat shines white in
    the island of Siphnos,
White-browed all the market—need then
    of a true seer's wisdom—

BATTLE OF GODS AND GIANTS
From the north frieze of the Treasury of Siphnus at Delphi, before 525 B.C. The figures are, from the left: two helmeted Giants, Dionysus, Cybele in her lion-drawn car, two Giants, Apollo, Artemis, a fleeing Giant, a fallen warrior, three Giants coming to the attack. *Delphi*

by his oath to grant her wish and Sinope thenceforth enjoyed a solitary couch. It is said that she frustrated the intentions of the river-god Halys in the same fashion.

Sinope. [Modern name, **Sinop.**] An ancient city and seaport located on a peninsula in the Pontus Euxinus (Black Sea). It has an excellent harbor. It was colonized by Milesians in the 8th century B.C. and became an important Greek commercial and colonizing center. One of its chief exports was

Danger will threat from a wooden host,
    and a herald in scarlet.

The Prytanies' seat referred to the prytaneum, or town-hall. About this time the building was covered with Parian marble. In the war of the Samian exiles to overthrow Polycrates, tyrant of Samos, the exiles, seeing they were temporarily at a stand, sailed to Siphnus in their scarlet-painted wooden ships. They asked the Siphnians to lend them money out of their great store. The Siphnians refused. The Samian exiles made war on them and defeated them; thus was the oracle fulfilled. The Siphnians, Ionians of Athenian stock, were among the few Ionian islanders who refused to give earth and water to the Persians as tokens of submission. In the Persian War they contributed a 50-oared ship to the Athenian fleet at Salamis. According to legend, King Minos of Crete, in his war on Athens to avenge the death of his son Androgeus, won the support of Siphnus by bribing the Princess Arne with gold. The area of the island is 29 square miles; its length is ten miles.

Sipylus (sip′i-lus). In ancient geography, a mountain in Lydia, Asia Minor, near Smyrna. A female image, believed by the Greeks to represent Niobe, was here carved out of the mountain rock. The limestone rock out of which it was carved dripped with moisture after rain, and as the water flowed over the face of the figure, disintegrating and disfiguring the stone as it ran, the Greeks considered that they beheld in it Niobe weeping for her children. The figure was, in fact, originally that of the great goddess of Asia Minor, known usually as Cybele.

Sirbonis (sėr-bō′nis), **Lacus.** See **Serbonis, Lacus.**

Sirens (sī′renz). In Greek mythology, a group of sea-nymphs who by their singing fascinated those who sailed past their island, and lured them to their deaths. According to some accounts they were the daughters of Terpsichore and the river-god Achelous. Half birds and half maidens, they had once been sweet-singing maidens, companions of Persephone. When the latter was snatched away by Hades the Sirens searched in vain for her, and at last prayed that they might be given wings so that they could search the seas. The gods gave them wings, but to preserve their sweet songs the upper half of their bodies remained those of maidens. Later, the Sirens lost their wing feathers and their power to fly after being defeated by the Muses in a singing contest. In art they are often represented as hideous, malevolent, and monstrous, with the head, arms, and breasts of young women, and the wings and lower body, or only the feet, of birds. Homer mentions two Sirens; three are often depicted; but they are usually thought of as a large group. Odysseus passed them safely by sealing the ears of his companions with wax and lashing himself to the mast. Orpheus saved the Argonauts from their enchantment by singing even more enchantingly. The Sirens were doomed to die when mortals could resist them (they leaped into the sea and became rocks). In early belief they were thought of as accompanying the souls of the dead from earth to Hades.

SIRENS
Greek funeral marble of Chios

Siris (sī′ris). In ancient geography, a city of Magna Graecia, Italy, situated at or near the mouth of the Siris River.

Siris River. [Modern Italian name, **Sinno.**] In ancient geography, a small river in Italy, flowing into the Gulf of Tarentum in what is now the province of Potenza. Near it Pyrrhus defeated (280 B.C.) the Romans in the battle of Heraclea.

Sirius (sir′i-us). [Also: **Dog Star.**] According to legend, Orion's dog, who accompanied him wherever he went, and was placed with him in the heavens forever following at his master's heels, as the constellation Canis Major. As a star, Sirius is a brilliant one, the brightest in the heavens.

Siros (sē′rôs). See **Syrus.**

Sisamnes (sis-am′nēz). A Persian, active in the 6th century B.C. He was one of the Royal judges. Cambyses, discovering that he had accepted a bribe to give an unrighteous sentence, had him slain and flayed. He had the skin of Sisamnes tanned as leather, cut into strips, and stretched across the seat of the throne on which the royal judge sat when dispensing justice. Cambyses then appointed Otanes, son of Sisamnes, as judge in his father's place, and recommended him never to forget that the throne on which he sat was webbed with his father's skin.

Sisenna (si-sen′ạ), **Lucius Cornelius.** Roman historian; born c119 B.C.; died 67 B.C. He was the author of a work on Roman history, the *Historiae,* of which a number of fragments survive. It dealt particularly with events of the early 1st century B.C., the Social War and the civil war of Sulla. (JJ)

Sistan (sē-stän′). See **Seistan.**

Sisyphus (sis′i-fus). In Greek mythology, a son of Aeolus, and a brother of Salmoneus and Athamas. He lived on the Isthmus of Corinth and was married to Merope, one of the Pleiades, who bore him Glaucus (father of Bellerophon), Ornytion, and Sinon. According to some accounts, he was the founder of Ephyra (later Corinth), where he promoted the trade and navigation of the city and founded the Isthmian Games in honor of Melicertes. Others say Medea bequeathed him the kingdom of Corinth when she fled from there. Homer names Sisyphus as the craftiest of mortals. At one time Sisyphus noticed that his fine cattle were disappearing, and suspected his neighbor Autolycus, a noted thief. But he could not prove anything because Autolycus had the ability to change the color of the cattle or add to or subtract horns from them at will. Sisyphus put a secret mark on the hoofs of his animals, and next day traced them to Autolycus. When he went to reclaim them he took the opportunity to ravish Anticlea, daughter of Autolycus, who subsequently bore him Odysseus (as Anticlea was the wife of Laertes, Odysseus was brought up as Laertes' son). Later Sisyphus seduced Tyro, daughter of his brother Salmoneus, in the execution of an oracular pronouncement that he should have sons by his niece if he wished to regain Thessaly, which Salmoneus had seized from him. However, Tyro killed the children she bore him. In exchange for a permanent spring, with which Asopus the river-god supplied Corinth, Sisyphus informed Asopus that Zeus had abducted his daughter Aegina. Zeus punished him for talebearing by commanding Hades to take him away to the Underworld, but when Hades came for him Sisyphus tricked him so that he was powerless. As long as Hades was compelled by Sisyphus to remain on earth no one could die. After a few days of this horrible state Ares rescued Hades and Sisyphus was led off to the Underworld. Before he went, however, Sisyphus instructed his wife not to perform burial rites for him. Arrived in the Underworld, he appealed to Persephone, saying he had not been properly buried, and requesting the privilege of returning to earth to arrange for his burial, after which he promised to return. Persephone granted his request, and of course Sisyphus broke his promise as soon as he saw the light of day. Hermes was commanded to pursue him and to carry him back to the Underworld. For his various crimes and deceptions Sisyphus was given the punishment of being compelled to push a huge stone up a slope. As fast as he got it to the top the stone slipped away from him and rolled down again. Thus he is eternally pushing a stone which eternally escapes just when he is on the point of completing his labor. Odysseus saw him toiling away at this task when he visited the Underworld. As one of the great sinners, Sisyphus is confined to Tartarus.

Skopelos (skop′ẹ-lọs). See **Peparethos.**

Skyphos (skī′fos). In ancient Greece, a large drinking-cup shaped like the kylix, and, like it, with two handles not extending above the rim, but without a foot.

Skyros (skē′ros). See **Scyrus.**

Sleep. [Greek, **Hypnos**; Latin, **Somnus.**] In classical mythology, the brother of Death (Thanatos) and the child of Night (Nyx). Sleep dwelt in the Underworld, in a cave near the misty land of Cimmeria where the rays of the sun never reached. No birds or beasts lived in the land, and the only sound came from the murmuring of the river Lethe as it washed over the pebbles in its bed. Poppies and other drugs grew in profusion before the cave of Sleep. Inside the cave, he rested on a sable-draped couch, surrounded by empty dreams. Sleep was often called on by the gods to deliver dreams to mortals or for other reasons. In the *Iliad,* Sleep was bribed by Hera to lull Zeus so that he would neglect the Trojans and give the Greeks a chance to win. Sleep was not anxious to do Hera's bidding in this case, because he remembered the anger of Zeus when he had lulled him to sleep before so that Hera could shipwreck Heracles on the isle of Cos. Sleep escaped that time only with the help of Night and by changing himself into a bird. Hera overcame his reluctance and he once again lulled Zeus to sleep.

Smerdis (smėr′dis). [Also: **Bardiya.**] A son of Cyrus the Great, and the younger brother of Cambyses. Cyrus made him governor of the provinces in the east before he died. He accompanied Cambyses on his campaign against Egypt, but was sent back to Persia by his jealous brother because, according to Herodotus, Smerdis was the only one of all the Persians able to bend a bow that the Aethiopians had sent to Cambyses. Cambyses then dreamed that Smerdis sat on the royal throne and that his head touched the heavens. He interpreted this to mean that Smerdis would seize his throne. To prevent this, Cambyses ordered his trusted aide Prexaspes to return to Persia and secretly to slay Smerdis. Prexaspes successfully carried out this command (c523 B.C.), but the death of Smerdis was not generally known, and a false Smerdis arose and assumed his place and name.

Smerdis, False. [Original name, **Gaumata.**] A Median *magus* (priest). His brother Patizeithes was left in charge of the king's household when Cambyses, son of Cyrus the Great, left Susa to attack Egypt. Patizeithes conceived a bold plan to rebel against Cambyses and seize the throne. He knew that Smerdis, son of Cyrus, had been secretly slain at Cambyses' order. His brother Gaumata bore a strong resemblance to Smerdis. Patizeithes engineered a revolt, which consisted in setting Guamata on the throne, announcing that he was Smerdis, son of Cyrus, and sending heralds throughout the land and beyond its borders to proclaim that Smerdis, not Cambyses was the true king. When this news reached Cambyses he concluded that Prexaspes, the trusted aide whom he had ordered to slay

Smerdis, had betrayed him and had not carried out his orders. He charged Prexaspes with treachery. Prexaspes assured Cambyses that he had carried out his orders and had buried Smerdis with his own hands, and that the man who had sent out the heralds proclaiming Smerdis was king could not be Smerdis, son of Cyrus, unless the dead could return to life. Prexaspes called the herald who had brought the news before him and questioned him; he learned that the herald had never seen Smerdis but had received his orders from Patizeithes, the magus left in charge by Cambyses. Prexaspes immediately divined what had happened: that Gaumata, the brother of Patizeithes, had set himself up as Smerdis and seized the throne. Cambyses determined to return to Susa and expose the impostor, but as he leaped to his horse he was wounded by his own sword. The wound did not heal. When he realized that his end was near he called the chief Persians to him and related to them that because of a false dream he had caused his brother Smerdis to be slain. He assured them that the Smerdis now occupying the throne was an impostor. He charged his chiefs not to allow the throne of Persia to remain in the hands of the Medes, but to recover it, taking whatever means were necessary. After the death of Cambyses Prexaspes swore that he had not killed Smerdis, as it was unsafe for him to admit it now that a Smerdis was on the throne. The chiefs who had heard the words of dying Cambyses thought he had invented his tale out of hatred of his brother and in the hope of causing his downfall, so Smerdis the magus was undisturbed in his reign. He ruled for seven months, and in this time freed all the nations under his sway from war service. But in the eighth month there were some who began to suspect he was not truly Smerdis, for he never left the palace and no one was allowed to see him. One of those whose suspicions were aroused was Otanes, a Persian nobleman. His daughter Phaedima had been among the wives of Cambyses, and on his death she was taken over, with the other wives, by Smerdis. Otanes sent word asking his daughter if the man who shared her couch was actually Smerdis, the son of Cyrus, or some other man. She replied that she did not know, as she had never seen Smerdis, and furthermore, she could not ask because all the wives had been separated by the new king and were forbidden to communicate with each other. Otanes was now sure that this king was an impostor. He instructed his daughter, when the king came to her bed, to feel his ears while he slept. If he had ears it was truly Smerdis, the son of Cyrus, but if he had no ears it was Gaumata the magus, because during the lifetime of Cyrus, Gaumata the magus had had his ears cut off as a punishment for a crime. Phaedima, in spite of the risk, agreed to do as her father commanded. She subsequently reported that the man who came to her as the king had no ears. Otanes knew now that this man was Gaumata, an impostor. He shared his information with five others whose suspicions had been aroused, and when Darius the son of Hystaspes came to Susa on official business, they took him also into their confidence. Darius urged instant action lest, since so many already knew the king was an impostor, others take action instead. He threatened to reveal their conspiracy to Smerdis himself if they did not act at once. The six others agreed to make an immediate attack on the king in his palace and set out. Meantime the false Smerdis had decided to make a friend of Prexaspes, since he alone knew for certain of the death of Smerdis. Prexaspes was won by his bribes and agreed to go to the top of a tower and proclaim to the people that the Persians were ruled by Smerdis, son of Cyrus, and none other. When he had mounted the tower, however, Prexaspes, a loyal Persian, recited the genealogy of the Persian kings and ended by saying that he had, at the command of Cambyses, killed Smerdis son of Cyrus; that the present ruler was an impostor, a Median magus. Then calling down curses on the Persians if they did not regain the throne from the Medes, he leaped from the tower to his death. Darius, Otanes, and the other conspirators learned of these events as they were on their way to attack Smerdis. All except Darius favored postponing the attack because of the turmoil into which Prexaspes' statements and death had thrown the capitol. As they argued with Darius two pairs of

vultures, pursued by seven hawks, flew over. The hawks overtook the vultures and clawed them with their talons and goaded them with their beaks. This omen convinced them that they should immediately carry out their plan. They proceeded to the palace. As prominent Persian nobles they were admitted without question, but being accosted by eunuchs in the courtyard, they forced their way past and entered the palace. They found the two brother magi within, discussing the revelations of Prexaspes, set upon them and killed them (521 B.C.). Darius and the others decapitated them, mounted their heads on pikes, and went out of the palace, exhibiting the heads and shouting that the impostor was dead. When the Persians realized how they had been hoodwinked they turned on all the other magi and killed every one they could lay their hands on. Ever after, the anniversary of the day was celebrated by a great festival called the Slaughter of the Magi, and no magus dared to show his face abroad on that day.

Smilis (smĭ′lis). Aeginetan sculptor, c580–540 B.C. Some say he was a contemporary of Daedalus. Among his works were the images of the Horae (Seasons) in the temple of Hera at Olympia, and an image of Hera in her temple at Samos.

Smintheus (smin′thē-us, -thūs). An epithet of Apollo, referring to his function as mouse god. Mice were associated with disease and its cure, and white mice were kept in Apollo's temples to protect against pestilence and to prevent plagues of mice.

Smyrna (smėr′na). A daughter of Cinyras. See **Myrrha.**

Smyrna. [Modern name, **Izmir.**] In ancient geography, a city on an arm of the Aegean Sea, in Lydia, Asia Minor. It had been one of the 12 Aeolian cities, but was seized by Ionians from Colophon (shortly before 688 B.C.) and compelled to join the Ionian League. Thanks to its location it became a flourishing and rich commercial city, and hence a target for the Lydian kings who were extending their power over the Ionian cities. The Lydian king Alyattes (c617–560 B.C.) conquered and destroyed it. Almost 300 years later a vision came to Alexander the Great commanding him to rebuild the city and to bring back the people of Smyrna. The vision having been verified by the oracle at Clarus, Alexander sent his generals Lysimachus and Antigonus to rebuild and enlarge the city, and it became one of the chief cities of Asia Minor. It was destroyed by earthquakes in 178 and 180 A.D. and again restored by Marcus Aurelius. Smyrna was one of the cities that claimed to be the birthplace of Homer. It was also the first Ionian city to send to the Olympic Games a contestant who won the victor's crown (688 B.C.).

Social Wars. In Greek history: 1) A war (357 or 358–355 B.C.) in which Athens was defeated by her former allies Byzantium, Chios, Cos, and Rhodes. 2) A war between the Achaean and Aetolian leagues (219–217) B.C.) in which Philip V of Macedon defeated Sparta and her allies.

Social War. [Also: **Marsic War.**] War (90–88 B.C.) between Rome and most of her erstwhile Italian allies (*socii*) in C and S Italy, including the Marsi, Paeligni, Samnites, and Lucanians. It was caused by the refusal on the part of the Romans to extend the privileges of Roman citizenship to the allied peoples. The Italians formed a new republic with its capital at Corfinium. The chief Roman commanders were Marius and Sulla. Rome made concessions, granting citizenship to those who would stop fighting, and thus split the allies and suppressed the rebellion.

Socrates (sok'ra̲-tēz). Greek philosopher, born at Alopece in Attica, c470 B.C.; died at Athens, 399 B.C. He was the son of Sophroniscus, a sculptor, and of Phaenarete, a midwife. He was not a prepossessing figure, having been compared in looks to a Silenus or satyr. His indifference to his outward appearance was well known throughout Athens. Equally well known were his indifference to bodily comforts, his splendid health, and his remarkable physical endurance. His marriage late in life to the shrewish Xanthippe, who bore him three sons, resulted in many apocryphal tales concerning her bad temper. He at first adopted his father's art; in the time of Pausanias a group of draped Graces by him was said still to have stood on the approach to the Acropolis. He soon, however, devoted himself entirely to the pursuit of philosophy, and became famous through the persistence and skill with which, in conversation with the Sophists and with everyone

who would take part in the discussion, he conducted the analysis of philosophical and educational ideas ("the Socratic method"). This analysis consisted of a directed sequence of questions; the answers ideally would indicate that the knowledge of the subject belonged to all and that a good teacher could evoke the best from his disciples. However, he did not call himself a teacher and took no pay from his followers, as the Sophists did. Indeed, he claimed no special wisdom, and when he learned that the oracle of Delphi had named him as the wisest man in the world, he set out to find a wiser and prove the oracle wrong. In the end he concluded that the oracle was perhaps right, for he was wisest in that he knew the extent of his ignorance. He was above all a searcher after a knowledge of virtue (which indeed he identified with knowledge), and was in himself the noblest exponent of the ethical life of the Greeks. In the Peloponnesian War, he served at Potidaea (431 B.C.), where he saved the life of his brilliant pupil Alcibiades. He served also at Delium (424 B.C.), where Alcibiades saved his life, and at Amphipolis (422 B.C.). He was a member of the Council of 500 and of the Prytanies (406 B.C.), at which time he refused to call for a vote on the condemnation of the six generals who had won the battle of Arginusae but had failed to stop and rescue the men in the water from their own wrecked ships. Socrates refused because it was against the law to try the generals collectively in the first place. He did not flee from Athens when the government was taken over by the Thirty Tyrants, but in 404 B.C., at the risk of his life, he defied their orders to arrest Leon the Salaminian. He is the chief character in the dialogues of Plato, in which his teachings are set forth (greatly modified by Plato's own views), and is the subject of the *Memorabilia* of Xenophon. Socrates left no writings of his own. His most famous pupils were Plato, Xenophon, and Alcibiades. He was bitterly attacked by Aristophanes as a Sophist and innovator, and drew upon himself by his mode of life and the character of his opinions the enmity of many others. In 399 B.C. he was accused of impiety (the introduction of new gods) and of corrupting the youth. His chief accuser was an obscure man, one Meletus, but behind him was Anytus. It was true Socrates questioned accepted religious practice, as he questioned everything. It was also true that he had a profound effect on the young men of his day who were his followers. Anytus had a son who was an ardent admirer of Socrates. Anytus forbade him to take part with others in the discussions presided over by Socrates, and the young man neither pursued his philosophical interests nor any profession suggested by his father. He took to drink. Anytus was a prominent democrat, a patriot who had helped to overthrow the tyrants. When his voice was added to others who accused Socrates he was brought to trial. Socrates could have avoided the trial by leaving Attica when the charges were brought against him, as many confidently expected him to do. Failing that, he might have won acquittal if he had used his skill in argument or the influence of his friends to deny the charges. He did neither. He was now an old man of 70. He had spent his life, except for periods of military service, in the Athens he loved. The defense he spread before his 501 judges, artistically recreated by Plato in his *Apology*, was no defense. He easily refuted some of the wilder charges, but on the main accusations he refused to make a defense. An inner voice, a personal daemon or divine inspiration, he said, spoke to him, exhorting him to seek the truth, and warning him against any evil or improper act. He would be compelled by his inner voice to continue his questioning, his search for truth, and his efforts to induce others to tend their souls. This was his life, his mission, and this he must carry out. His justification of his life and his expressed intention of continuing his practices alienated his judges and he was found guilty by a majority of 60. The penalty was death, but according to Athenian practice a defendant could propose a lighter penalty than that proposed by his judges. Socrates stated what all knew: that he was a poor man, and that for his services the state should really feed him at the public table in the Prytaneum. He proposed as an alternate penalty that he be fined 60 minae— a sum so ridiculously low that it was an insult to the judges, who now, by a much larger

majority, imposed the death penalty. He was imprisoned in Athens, but execution of the sentence was delayed because of a law that no one should be put to death while the sacred ship of Athens was on its annual mission to Delos. It was a month before the ship returned. In that time Socrates' devoted friends visited him in his prison. Plato gives accounts of those visits and the conversations held in some of the dialogues, and in them expresses Socrates' teachings and ideas. One of the most moving documents of compassion, humanity, and greatness is the *Crito*. In it the aged Crito tries to persuade his old friend to flee and escape his sentence. Socrates leads him gently through all the old arguments he has maintained through a lifetime, and convinces him that such flight as Crito urges would be a denial of the principles he has been living by all his life, one of which is obedience to the law. He had been duly condemned under the laws of Athens, by which he had always lived. He would not deny them now. Crito sadly admits the justice of the argument and the triumph of the spirit which poses it, but his affections are not comforted. The *Phaedo* of Plato shows Socrates talking with his followers on the last day of his life. The subject of discussion is Socrates' unshakable belief in the immortality of the soul. When all points have been resolved the closing lines of the dialogue describe in homely detail the taking of the hemlock and, finally, the simplicity and serenity with which the aged philosopher brought his life to a close.

Socrates, Apology of. See **Apology of Socrates.**

Sogdiana (sog-di-ā′na). [Also: **Sogdiane.**] In ancient geography, a large region in C Asia, lying N of Bactriana, between the Oxus (modern Amu Darya) and Jaxartes (modern Syr Darya), in the vicinity of Bukhara and Samarkand. It was invaded by Alexander the Great.

Sol (sol). In Roman mythology, the name of the sun god, given to two separate deities. One, called Sol Indiges, was native, and became associated with Helius and Phoebus Apollo. The other was Sol Invictus, an epithet of the Indo-Iranian Mithra. His cult, a transplant from the East, by the 3rd century A.D. had become, if not the chief cult of Rome, at least equal in importance to the cult of Jupiter.

Soli (sō'lī). In ancient geography, a city on the coast of Cilicia, Asia Minor, about 26 miles SW of Tarsus. It was destroyed by Tigranes of Armenia, and was rebuilt by Pompey and called Pompeiopolis. The corruptness of the Greek spoken there was proverbial, whence the word "solecism."

Solon (sō'lon). Athenian law-giver (born c638 B.C.; died, c559 B.C.). He was the son of Execestides, who claimed descent from the last Athenian king, Codrus. The family had been a wealthy as well as a noble one, but because his father had dissipated his fortune Solon was obliged to engage in trade. His business activity caused him to travel widely, especially in Ionia, and gave him contacts with and knowledge of foreign lands and rulers, as well as a wide experience of affairs. He built up his own fortune, not that he was an admirer of wealth, but he thought there was no odium attached to it if it were gained justly. His own comment on wealth was:

"For often evil men are rich, and good men poor;
But we will not exchange with them
Our virtue for their wealth, since one abides alway,
While riches change their owners every day."

He was a cultivated man, and by his own account, a persistent seeker of wisdom, who grew old "ever learning new things." He wrote poetry, in the Ionic dialect, at first for his own amusement, but later and principally as a means of teaching and exhorting his fellow Athenians to pursue the course he thought they should follow, a course determined by Justice. Fragments of his poetry, the earliest surviving Athenian writings, are extant, and Athenian school-boys for generations after him learned his poems by heart. He early turned his attention to political ethics and to a consideration of improvement in the laws governing the Athenians. Plutarch mentions a conversation between Solon and one Anacharsis. The latter scoffed at Solon for his belief that injustice could be eliminated by law, for the laws, he said, are like spiders' webs: they entangle the weak but are torn to pieces by the strong. Solon replied that men would keep their agreements when they were convinced that it was to their advantage to do so.

As a statesman Solon realized that control of the island of Salamis, lying opposite the port of Athens, was essential for the safety of the city. Because previous attempts to win it from Megara had ended in failure and the Athenians were tired of the war, a law was passed in Athens forbidding the mention of the name Salamis. Solon considered this disgraceful. He composed a poem inciting the Athenians to "recover" Salamis and, pretending madness to evade the law, recited the poem in the agora and so aroused the ardor of the populace that an expedition was undertaken under his leadership. Some say that in obedience to a command of the oracle at Delphi he rowed across to the island at night and made sacrifices to propitiate the heroes of Salamis—Cychreus and Periphemus. He returned to Attica, gathered a force of 500 men and sailed against Salamis and captured the city (c600 B.C.), and erected a temple to Euryalius (Ares) on the promontory where he had landed. This, however, did not end the dispute between the people of Megara and Athens over control of Salamis, and the matter was submitted to a board of Spartan judges for arbitration. The Spartans awarded it to Athens, some say on the basis of these verses from the *Iliad:*

Ajax from Salamis led his warships; twelve was the number
(Led them and stationed them where the Athenians stood in battalions).

And some say they awarded Salamis to Athens because Solon proved to them that Eurysaces, son of Ajax, had become a citizen of Athens and had brought the island with him. In any case, Solon now became prominent in public affairs. In later times his defense of the temple of Apollo at Delphi against the people of Cirrha (c590? B.C.), added to his prestige. Many urged him to make himself tyrant but he refused, saying, "a tyranny is a lovely place but there is no way down from it."

In his time there was great social and political unrest in Athens. The three main parties were the Hill, that favored a democracy, the Plain, that favored an oligarchy, and the Shore, that fell somewhere in between.

Solon was well aware of the strife in the city and the reasons for it. Driven by greed, he exclaimed, the leaders enrich themselves unjustly, sparing neither the wealth of the state nor the temple treasures, and undermining the ancient foundations of justice. But, he declared, Justice, though silent, knows all the past and present, and never fails to come in time to punish. In 594 B.C. he became archon and was given broad powers to correct the abuses existing between the very rich and the very poor, and which were causing such unrest that civil war was threatened. These abuses, and the conflicts between classes, arose out of the impoverishment of the small landowners and the miserable condition of the free laborers. The small landowners were forced to pay such ruinous rates on money they borrowed that they were crushed, and, as Solon said, the black earth itself was enslaved. The free laborers received only one-sixth of what they produced as wages, and fell into debt in order to live. At this time a debtor who could not pay could be taken as a slave by his creditor. When Solon assumed office he immediately declared that debts which entailed slavery were annulled, and declared free those who had been enslaved according to previous contracts. This act, which freed many, was celebrated by a public feast. He made other reforms. He limited the area of land that could be owned by one person in order to curtail the growth of large estates; he forbade the exportation of Attic products, save for olive oil, because so much grain was exported by large proprietors for high prices that not enough remained to feed the population; and he made laws for the encouragement of trade and manufactures. In this time there were four tribes in Athens, named for the four sons of Ion: Geleon, Aegicores, Argades, and Hoples. Solon divided the people of the four tribes into four classes according to wealth, and assigned taxes and civic responsibility to each class in accordance with its ability to pay or participate. He reformed the constitution, the so-called constitution of Draco, retaining those features he considered good and changing others. By his reforms some political rights were granted to the peasants, who prior to this had been citizens with no rights; and he

reconstituted the courts to give all four classes of citizens, chosen by lot, a share in the administration of justice. For this last alone he may be called the founder of Athenian democracy, for by it he gave the citizens some control over the administration which governed them, as public officials were answerable to the courts. He established the Council of 400, consisting of representatives from the three upper classes of the four tribes of Athens, to prepare the business of the Assembly; and he changed the function of the Council of the Areopagus, henceforth to be composed of former archons, to lessen its power. Public officers were to be chosen by lot and by election. Choosing by lot left the decision to the gods; it also insured that no class would have a monopoly. In some cases, a certain number of names were drawn and those so chosen in turn elected one of their number to office. In addition, a law was adopted that would disfranchise a citizen who refused to take sides in times of disagreement. The purpose of it was to compel the citizens to accept their civic responsibilities. Laws concerning the marriages of heiresses, wills, the dress of women, burial and mourning, were also adopted; all were designed to remove inequities or to eradicate excesses that had arisen, as in dress and mourning customs. Solon's laws were inscribed on wooden panels. Every citizen was required to swear to obey them, and they were to remain in force for 100 years.

Solon's reforms, based on his ideas of justice, satisfied no one. They antagonized the rich, who lost some of their property and power, and failed to satisfy the poor, who had hoped for the redistribution of the large estates and for the cancellation of their debts. Solon seems to have decided that there would be less pressure to tamper with his new laws if he were not there to be pressured. He therefore asked permission to leave Athens for ten years. In this time he traveled widely, visiting Egypt, Cyprus and probably Asia Minor. At Cyprus he helped the king to lay out a new city, which was called Soli in his honor. According to a story of Herodotus, in the course of his travels he visited Croesus, king of Lydia, who was at that time one of the richest and most powerful monarchs of the known world. Croesus thought the traveling Athenian, whose reputation for wisdom had preceded him, would surely be impressed by the wealth and power of the Lydian king. He therefore asked Solon to name the happiest man in the world, certain that his own name would be given in answer. Solon named an obscure Athenian, Tellus. To the shocked question of Croesus as to why this man was happiest, Solon replied it was because he had lived an honorable life, had children whom he lived to see grow up and have children of their own, and died a glorious death fighting for his country, for which he was given a public funeral and paid the highest honors by the Athenians. Croesus recovered his poise and asked Solon to name the second happiest man, thinking this time he would surely be named. Solon named Cleobis and Biton, because they had honored their mother and were rewarded with a peaceful death by the goddess Hera. Croesus now became angry; did Solon put so little value on his wealth and power that he rated Croesus even below ordinary men? Solon's reply was that no man can be called happy until his life has ended happily, for the gods are jealous of their power and will seek to bring misfortune to him who enjoys too great prosperity. Riches above the needs of man do not necessarily bring happiness, but a healthy man who has no misfortunes, who sees his children grow up, and who ends his life well, can be called happy. For, added Solon, "in every matter we must mark well the end; for oftentimes God gives men a gleam of happiness, and then plunges them into ruin." This story of Herodotus is undoubtedly apochryphal, for Solon left Athens shortly after he had been archon and was away only ten years. Croesus did not succeed to the throne of Lydia until 560 B.C. However, true or not, it illustrates an ethical and religious principle of the Greeks of the time and for some generations thereafter.

All of Solon's reforms had been made with the object of forestalling a tyranny and of restoring peace to Athens. In his last days he saw the city he had set on the road to democracy fall into the power of a tyrant in spite of his efforts. Pisistratus, a friend of Solon, seized control and established a tyranny (561 B.C.). The aged Solon, so it is said, went into the agora and urged the citizens to throw off the tyranny. The city, he cried, would not perish by the will of the gods but by the folly of her citizens. His words were not heeded. He went to his house and placed his arms before the door, saying he had done all he could for his country and its citizens must now do likewise. His friends feared for his life because of his open opposition to Pisistratus. They urged him to leave Athens and when he refused asked him on what he relied to protect him from the tyrant. "On my old age," he is said to have answered. He was in no danger however. Although their political views were opposed, Pisistratus retained his friendship and respect for Solon. He lived a full and enjoyable life in Athens, and ultimately was inscribed as one of the Seven Sages of Greece. When he died, c559 B.C., his body was burned and the ashes were scattered over the island of Salamis. His name has passed into the English language as a synonym for a legislator or a wise official.

Solus (sō′lus). [Also: **Soluntum.**] In ancient geography, a city on the N coast of Sicily, about 12 miles SE of Panormus. It was an ancient Phoenician colony.

Solymi (sol′i-mī). In Greek legend, famed warriors of Asia Minor. Proetus, desiring to get rid of Bellerophon but not willing to slay him because he had come as a guest, sent Bellerophon to fight the Solymi with the idea that he would surely be killed. Contrary to his expectations, Bellerophon conquered them.

Somnus (som′nus). In Roman mythology, the personification and god of sleep. He became identified with the Greek Hypnos. He was a twin brother of Death (Mors or Thanatos) and a son of Nyx. In art the two are represented alike as youths, often sleeping or holding inverted torches. See **Sleep.**

Sophilus (sof′i-lus). Athenian potter and vase-painter in the black-figure style, active at the end of the 7th and the beginning of the 6th century B.C. His signature has been preserved on the fragments of three vases. A fragment from a large mixing bowl (Athens), signed "Sophilus made me," shows a chariot race on the shoulder, and is inscribed "Patroclus' funeral games," a rare instance of a vase-painter giving a title to his painting. Spectators watching the race sit in a grandstand. Beside one of the spectators the name Achilles is inscribed.

Sophocles (sof'ō̲-klēz). One of the three great tragic poets of Greece, ranked with Aeschylus, his older contemporary, and Euripides, his younger contemporary. He was born, 496 B.C., at Colonus, in Attica; died 406 B.C. Sophillus (or Sophilus), his father, was a wealthy Athenian citizen and gave him a sound education in music, gymnastics, and dancing. He appears to have been noted for his youthful beauty, and was chosen to lead the chorus in the paean of thanksgiving for the victory at Salamis (480 B.C.). According to some accounts, he took the part of Thamyris the blind musician in one of his plays, and in another he played the part of the young princess Nausicaä. In his long life he several times held public office, perhaps partly as an acknowledgment of his fame as a dramatist and his genial qualities as a man. In 440 B.C. he was appointed one of the generals in the war which Pericles led against Samos, and in 413 B.C. he was one of the Ten Commissioners appointed, after the failure of the expedition to Sicily, to govern Athens. He seems to have made singularly few enemies, to have lived serenely, enjoying the respect and affection of his fellow citizens to the end of his long life. In his last years, so it is said, his older son, Iophon, became jealous of the affection Sophocles had for his grandson Sophocles, son of Iophon's half-brother. Iophon sought to have the administration of his father's thriving financial affairs turned over to him, on the ground that his father was mentally incompetent. Sophocles is said to have convinced the judges of the soundness of his mind by reading to them an ode from his *Oedipus at Colonus,* which he was then writing. Some say, however, that this tale is a fiction invented by the comic poets, and maintain that the poet lived in rare tranquillity to the end of his days.

Sophocles first won first prize, in competition with Aeschylus, in 468 B.C. He won first prize 20 times, second prize many more times, and was never awarded anything lower than that. Of the more than 120 tragedies he wrote, known by title or from fragments,

only seven have survived intact. They are: *Ajax,* perhaps the earliest of the extant plays, about the humiliation and suicide of the valiant warrior; *Antigone,* c440 B.C., from the saga of the Labdacids, which presents the conflict between the claims of the state and those of a higher, spiritual realm; *Oedipus Rex* (or *Oedipus the King, Oedipus Tyrannus*), which seems to be a later play than the *Antigone* (but the events of which precede it in the Theban saga) and which was considered by Aristotle as a perfect tragedy; *Electra,* on a subject with which both Aeschylus and Euripides concerned themselves; *Women of Trachis,* about Deianira's love for Heracles, the sorrow it caused her, and the hero's death; *Philoctetes,* produced 409 B.C., which presents young Neoptolemus, directed by crafty Odysseus, in an attempt to persuade Philoctetes to join the Greeks before Troy; and *Oedipus at Colonus,* produced by Sophocles' son in 401 B.C., concerning the mystic end of Oedipus. A long fragment of a satyr play, *Ichneutae* (The Trackers), is also extant. This tells about the search for Apollo's cattle, stolen from him by the new-born infant Hermes.

To the form of tragedy Sophocles added scene painting and a third actor. He increased the number of the chorus from 12 to 15 and reduced the proportion of the play given to the chorus, thereby accelerating the progress of the action. He did not write trilogies, as Aeschylus had done; each play is complete in itself. Sophocles was greatly admired by the ancients, and ever since, as a master of form, for the drive and directness with which his tragedies march to a conclusion, for his character drawing and for dramatic irony. He presented the sagas around which all tragedies were required to be written without comment, molding them by technical skill and transmuting them by genius. The ancients respected him for his calm and steady adherence to the traditional religion. His works, stunning in their effectiveness, glowing in their poetry, did not lacerate, as did those of Euripides, the quivering and vulnerable sensibilities of the audience. All his tragic figures were noble in their suffering. Of Euripides, Sophocles is reputed to have said, "He paints men as they are," implying that they are presented with all their doubts and waverings, all the conflicting impulses of human weakness and strength. Of himself, Sophocles said, "I paint men as they ought to be." His characters are the possessors of a few strongly etched qualities which, given a particular set of circumstances, make the end inevitable. Oedipus is brave, rash, persistent. He determines to learn the truth about the murderer of Laius. He is not hampered in his search for the truth by an imagination that would hint to him how unfortunate that truth might be. With the utmost concentration and power, with no vitiating philosophical digressions, the play marches inexorably to the overwhelming moment when Oedipus learns the truth. Having learned it, he suffers as intensely as he had pursued it. The work of Sophocles was considered the very perfection of tragedy. After his death it became the criterion and ideal of classic tragedy. He died in 406 B.C., before the final defeat of Athens by Sparta in the Peloponnesian Wars. After his death the Spartans under Lysander invaded Athens. According to legend, Dionysus appeared to Lysander in a dream and commanded him to honor with all the usual honors of the dead the new siren. As a result of the vision Lysander granted a truce, and the poet was buried on the road to Decelea, where an image of a siren marked his tomb. The Athenians worshiped him as a hero and offered annual sacrifice to him.

Sophonisba (sof-ọ-niz'bạ) Carthaginian woman; died c204 B.C. She was a daughter of Hasdrubal, son of Gisco. She was betrothed to the Numidian prince Masinissa, but was afterward married in 206 B.C., for political reasons, to Syphax, the rival Numidian ruler. Her husband was defeated by Masinissa, who acted as an ally of the Romans while Syphax was an ally of the Carthaginians, in the Second Punic War. Sophonisba fell into the hands of the conqueror, who married her, but was compelled by Scipio to reject her. She committed suicide by poison sent by Masinissa to prevent her from falling into the hands of the Romans. She has been the subject of many tragedies.

Sophron (sō'fron). Syracusan writer of comedy; fl. c440 B.C. He was noted for his mimes—usually humorous studies of little

scenes from daily life. He wrote in some kind of rhythmical prose which the ancients considered poetry. Only fragments of his works have survived.

Sora (sō'rä). Town of C Italy, situated on the upper Liris river, about 62 miles SE of Rome. It was an ancient Volscian town. The Romans captured it three times, in 345, 314, and 305 B.C. In 303 B.C. they finally secured its annexation to Rome by sending a strong colony there. In the time of Augustus, soldiers from the Fourth Legion colonized it.

Soracte (sō-rak'tẹ). [Italian, **Monte Soratto, Monte Sant'Oreste.**] Mountain in Italy, near the Tiber river, about 25 miles NE of Rome. There is an extensive view from its summit, and it was known in ancient times for its temple of Apollo. Elevation, 2260 feet.

Sorrento (sôr-ren'tō). See **Surrentum.**

Sosias (sō'si-ạs). Attic potter, active at the beginning of the 5th century B.C. The painter who decorated his work, in the red-figure style, is known as the Sosias Painter. Of two works definitely attributed to him, a kylix (Berlin) shows Achilles binding up the wounds of Patroclus and is admired for the subject and the concentrated rendering thereof.

Sosigenes (sō-sij'ẹ-nēz). Alexandrian astronomer; fl. in the 1st century B.C. At the bidding of Julius Caesar, he devised (47 B.C.) a solar calendar. His calendar was based on the fixed 365-day solar calendar of the Egyptians, but unlike the Egyptian calendar, provided an intercalary day every fourth year, the antecedent of our Leap Year, to absorb the fractional day (assumed to be 0.2500 day; the correct figure is c0.2425 day) of the solar cycle. As the Julian Calendar, this was adopted as the official calendar of the Roman state and passed into western Europe generally, and continued in use unchanged until the 16th century, when the slowly accumulating error amounted to 11 days. In 1582 A.D. Pope Gregory XIII ordered that the calendar be adjusted by omitting 11 days, and provided a corrected intercalation which will hold the calendar in agreement with the tropical year for several thousand years to come. As the Gregorian Calendar, this is the calendar by which we reckon time today. Sosigenes was also the author of various astronomical works, including one on *Revolving Spheres,* but of these only isolated fragments remain. (JJ)

Sosipolis (sō-sip'ō-lis). Native deity of Elis, worshiped in the sanctuary of Ilithyia at the foot of Mount Cronus at Olympia. The deity was tended by an old woman, who brought water for his bath and fed him barley cakes kneaded with honey. The story of Sosipolis is that the Arcadians invaded Elis. A woman holding an infant to her breast came to the Elean generals, in obedience to a command given her in a dream, and offered her child to fight for the Eleans. The Elean generals placed the naked child in front of their army. When the Arcadians advanced, the infant was transformed into a writhing serpent before their eyes. The Arcadians were thrown into confusion by this miracle and were defeated by the Eleans. On the spot where the serpent went into the ground the Eleans raised a sanctuary and named the god Sosipolis (*Savior of the State*), and decided to worship Ilithyia the birth-goddess with him because she brings sons to help men.

Sospita (sos'pi-ta). In Roman mythology, an epithet of Juno as a goddess of healing.

Soter (sō'tėr). Epithet of Zeus, meaning "Savior." When Heracles went to Nemea to slay the lion, he stopped at the house of one Molorchus, whose son had been killed by the lion. Molorchus was about to sacrifice a ram to Hera. Heracles asked him to wait, and if he did not return at the end of 30 days to sacrifice to him as a hero, but if he did return, he promised Molorchus that together they would sacrifice to Zeus Soter. When he had killed the lion, he returned to the house of Molorchus on the thirtieth day and found him preparing to sacrifice to Heracles as a hero. Instead, they sacrificed together to Zeus Soter. Of the bronze image of Zeus Soter in Thespiae the story is told that there was a dragon that used to ravage the countryside. In obedience to a command of a god, a youth was sacrificed to the dragon each year to appease it and prevent it from attacking the city. At last a youth volunteered to be sacrificed in order to save his beloved friend, whose name had been drawn by lot. The youth who volunteered made himself a breastplate, the outside of which was covered

with fishhooks with the barbs turned out. The idea was that when the dragon swallowed him he would be killed by the fishhooks, and though the youth himself would be killed, in future his countrymen would be safe. There were many sanctuaries of Zeus Soter, as at Troezen, Epidaurus, Aegium in Achaea, Mantinea and Megalopolis in Arcadia, and in Messenia.

Soter. Epithet of various Greek gods referring to their power to save from peril. In Hellenistic times it was also applied to various rulers in Egypt, Syria, and in other areas where Greek culture had made itself felt. Ptolemy I of Egypt was perhaps the most famous mortal recipient of the title.

Sounion (sön'yôn). See **Sunium.**

Sown Men. See **Sparti.**

Sparrow. . Bird sometimes considered to be sacred to Aphrodite.

Sparta (spär'ta). Ancient city in Laconia, Greece, situated on the Eurotas River. From the city the entire kingdom (which was called Lacedaemon as well as Laconia and Laconica) came to be known as Sparta. According to some accounts, Sparta was a daughter of Eurotas, for whom the river was named. She married Lacedaemon, son of Zeus and Taÿgete, and he inherited his father-in-law's kingdom. Lacedaemon founded a city which he named Sparta for his wife, and ultimately the whole kingdom took her name. According to Homer, this city of Sparta was one of those most loved by Hera. Sparta was famous in myth and legend. Among the many monuments of the ancient city were the grave of Orestes near a sanctuary of the Fates; a sanctuary of Athena Celeuthea (*Lady of the Road*) founded by Odysseus in gratitude for having won the race in Sparta by which he also won Penelope for his bride; the Hellenium, in which, some say, the Greeks deliberated before sailing to Troy to secure the return of Helen (and others say the Greeks deliberated here when they were preparing to repel Xerxes in 480 B.C.). Near the Hellenium was the tomb of Agamemnon's herald Talthybius. And there were many other sites and monuments connected with mythological and legendary figures, as well as many religious sites. The famous temple of Athena of the Bronze House, said to have been begun by Tyndareus, was on the acropolis at Sparta. Legend says that Heracles attacked Sparta, to punish Hippocoön and his sons, and that, being successful, he restored Tyndareus, foster father of Helen, to the throne and left the kingdom in trust for his sons and descendants. Menelaus succeeded his father-in-law as king of Sparta. To avenge the wrong to their king when Helen was carried off by Paris, many men from Sparta took part in the Trojan War. On the earlier conquest of Heracles the Heraclidae (Dorians) based their claim to Sparta when, under the sons of Aristomachus (a descendant of Heracles), they invaded the Peloponnesus. The Spartans claimed it was Aristodemus himself, the son of Aristomachus, who marched into the Peloponnesus and claimed Sparta; but others say he had died on the eve of the invasion, and that it was his twin sons, Procles and Eurysthenes, who won Sparta as their territory in the drawing of the lots with their uncles Cresphontes and Temenus. It was for this reason (that Procles and Eurysthenes shared the throne), that Sparta alone of the Greek states had two kings and two royal houses.

By the legislation of the semi-legendary Lycurgus, Sparta became a powerful state. A conservative, aristocratic governmental system was developed, in which every moment of the lives of its citizens was strictly regulated. The purpose of the regulation was to develop a nation continually poised for war. In this Sparta was eminently successful. In the first place, the citizen was freed from the necessity of gaining his livelihood. The land was divided into lots. Each Spartan obtained a lot, which then belonged irrevocably to him and his descendants. It could not be sold or divided. The land was cultivated by the helots, virtual slaves, who belonged to the Spartan master and could not be either sold or freed by him; but under certain circumstances the state might emancipate a helot. Of the produce which the helots drew from the land certain amounts of grain, wine, and fruit went to the Spartan lot-holder. Any over these specified amounts was left to the helots who cultivated the land. Trade and commerce were carried on by the Perioeci (*Dwellers-around*) who, though free, enjoyed none of the rights of citizenship. Thus the Spartan citizen was free to devote himself to the service of the state. When a child was born it was examined by representatives of the state, and if it was found to be weak or imperfect it was exposed on Mount Taÿgetus to die. At the age of seven years boys were given into the care of the state, and their training was entirely directed to the ends of complete obedience and the cultivation of devotion to the state. This training was supported by exposing the children to all sorts of hardships to strengthen them and make them invulnerable to hardships. A well-known story of Spartan self-control and self-discipline is of the Spartan boy who stole a fox, hid it under his cloak, and stood motionless and silent while the fox gnawed at his vitals. At the age of 20, Spartan youths were permitted to marry, but since at the same time they entered military service and were compelled to live in barracks, they could not enjoy a home or family life. At 30 the Spartan was considered a man and won the full rights of citizenship. Thenceforward however, they continued to eat with their army comrades at public messes. Spartan women were also subjected to a discipline by the state. They were encouraged to develop their bodies in gymnastic exercises, so that they might bear strong sons. Their devotion to their country surpassed their maternal instinct. In the development of Sparta as an armed camp there was no place for luxury or soft living, and Spartan simplicity became proverbial. As a further effect, the concentration on developing superb soldiers left no room for the encouragement of original thinkers—poets, dramatists, artists. The valor of the Spartan fighting man also became proverbial. The Greeks in general, for centuries, could not imagine a Spartan surrender or a Spartan captive. The death of the 300 Spartans under Leonidas at Thermopylae (480 B.C.) was considered typical of the Spartan way in war, and illustrated on a large scale the command of the Spartan matron to her son about to go to war, to come back with his shield or on it. Yet contrary to expectation, though always in a state of preparedness, Sparta was reluctant to initiate war and, on the whole, rather slow to engage in it even when her own interest

fat, fāte, fär, fãre, errạnt; net, mē, hėr ardẹnt; pin, pīne; not, nōte, mŏve, nôr,

was manifestly affected. In the 8th and 7th centuries B.C. Messenia was conquered. Arcadia, Messenian ally, later acknowledged Spartan supremacy. In the 6th century B.C. Sparta succeeded in conquering Tegea, the most powerful of the Arcadian cities. According to legend, Tegea had previously been invulnerable to Spartan attacks. An oracle told the Spartans they must bring back the bones of Orestes to Sparta if they would conquer Tegea. When this was accomplished, through the agency of the Spartan Lichas, Tegea was overwhelmed.

By the middle of the 6th century B.C. Sparta had established its supremacy over Argos, and was the leading Greek state and acknowledged as such by the other states. The Spartans had an alliance with Croesus. When the Ionian cities revolted they sought, in vain, the aid of Sparta. When the Persian invasion threatened (490 B.C.), the Spartans were prevented by a religious holiday from assisting the Athenians at Marathon. By the time the holiday was over and the Spartans came hurrying up, the Athenians had utterly routed the Persian forces. The Spartans were filled with admiration, and closely examined the battlefield where the great victory had taken place. With the approach of the second Persian invasion (480 B.C.), Sparta was the acknowledged leader of the Greeks and played a leading part in the Persian War and the Greek victory therein. After the Persian War Sparta retained its place as the leading land power, but the sea power of Athens had developed and now seemed to threaten Spartan supremacy. With various allies, Sparta fought against Athens in the Peloponnesian Wars (431–404 B.C.) and emerged victorious. The years 404–371 B.C. followed as the period of Spartan hegemony in Greece. At the height of its power the city of Sparta remained unwalled. It is said that when someone asked Agesilaus, the Spartan king (398 B.C.) why Sparta was unwalled, he pointed to the citizens in arms and replied, "These are the walls of Lacedaemon." But the period of Spartan ascendancy was short. Sparta had many enemies, and the arid military policy prevented the natural growth of the state. In 371 B.C. the Spartans were defeated at the battle of Leuctra by the Thebans under Epaminondas. At this time the two stars symbolizing the Dioscuri, patrons of Sparta, fell from their place in the temple and disappeared forever. This was the end of Spartan power. Sparta passed under Roman rule in 146 B.C.

Spartacus (spär′ta̯-kus). Thracian who became a Roman slave and gladiator at Capua. He headed an insurrection of slaves (Servile War) in Italy in 73 B.C., and routed several Roman armies, but was ultimately defeated by Crassus on the Silarus River and slain (71 B.C.).

Sparti (spär′tī). In Greek mythology, a race of fully-armed men that sprang from the soil when Cadmus sowed the dragon's teeth. The name means "the Sown Men." Cadmus hurled stones into their midst when they sprang from the earth and they fell upon each other and fought until only five survived. These five: Chthonius, Echion, Hyperenor, Pelorus, and Udaeus, became the ancestors of the noble families of Thebes.

Spelaites (spē-lā′i-tēz). An epithet of Hermes, meaning "Of the Cave." The people of Themisonium gave him this epithet because when they were being attacked, Hermes appeared to their generals in a dream and told them where to find a cave in which they should hide their women and children for safety. As Apollo and Heracles also appeared in the same dream, they too had this epithet.

Sperchius (sper-kī′us). [Also: **Hellada, Spercheius, Sperkhios**.] River that rises in Mount Othrys and flows through Thessaly into the Gulf of Lamia near Thermopylae. In Homeric legend (*Iliad*), the river-god Sperchius was the father of Menesthius by Polydora. Peleus, the father of Achilles, swore he would sacrifice Achilles' hair to the river if Achilles returned safely from the Trojan War. Knowing he would not return, Achilles cut off his hair and burned it on the pyre of Patroclus.

Spermo (sper′mō). In Greek mythology, one of the three daughters of Anius, king of Delos. She was given the power by Dionysus to turn whatever she wished into grain. See **Elaïs**.

Sperthias (sper′thi-as) and **Bulis** (bū′lis). Two Spartans. According to Herodotus, Darius the Great sent heralds to Sparta demanding earth and water from the Spartans as a token that they submitted to him. The Spartans cast the heralds into a well and told them to fetch their own earth and water. This was a violation of the immemorial sanctity, recognized by all nations, of the persons of heralds. The descendants of Talthybius, Agamemnon's herald, who held the hereditary right to the office of herald in Sparta, went to the temple of Talthybius there and called down his wrath on the Spartans. Thenceforth victims at sacrifices failed to give good omens. After this had gone on a long time the Spartans were extremely troubled. They called for two Spartans willing to give their lives for their country. Sperthias and Bulis, Spartan noblemen, offered themselves. They volunteered to go to Xerxes, son of Darius and present ruler of Persia, and submit to death at his hands to atone for the deaths of the Persian heralds at the hands of the Spartans. On their way to Susa they were received by the satrap Hydarnes. He pointed out to them many evidences of the advantages accruing to the friends of the Persian ruler, and asked them why they would not consent to become friends with Xerxes. They replied that he knew only half the story. Having always been a slave he was pleased to live in comfort, but if he had ever tasted liberty, such as they knew, he would urge them to fight to the death to retain it. Leaving Hydarnes, they went to Susa. There they refused to bow their heads before Xerxes, claiming that they worshiped no man, that this was not why they had come to Susa, and repelling with force those who sought to compel them to make obeisance to Xerxes. They addressed him, telling him they had come to give their lives to atone for the Persian heralds slain by the Spartans. Xerxes, "with true greatness of soul," according to Herodotus, answered that he would not do as the Spartans had done. He would not break the laws honored by men of all nations regarding the persons of heralds. He allowed Sperthias and Bulis to return home, and because of their noble willingness to die the anger of Talthybius was temporarily appeased, only to rise up again and visit itself on the sons of Sperthias and Bulis 60 years later.

Speusippus (spū-sip′us). Athenian **philosopher**; born c407 B.C.; died 339 B.C. He was a nephew and disciple of Plato, and became head of the Academy after Plato's death (347 B.C.). Only stray fragments of his work survive which testify to his interest in mathematical theory, ethics, and biological investigation.

Sphacteria (sfak-tir′i-a̱). [Also: **Sphakteria, Sphagia.**] Small island off the promontory of Messenian Pylus. Here the Spartans were cut off by the Athenians. They took refuge on what was thought to be an impregnable height at one end of the island. Their ancient enemies the Messenians, who were aiding the Athenians, discovered a perilous path up the cliffs in the rear of the Spartan position. They led the Athenians up the cliffs so that they now commanded the rear as well as the van of the Spartans and the Spartans surrendered (425 B.C.). Though the force of Spartans that surrendered was comparatively small, the victory was enormous, for up to this time the Spartans had such a reputation for fighting to the death that it was thought they were never taken alive. A bronze shield, found in a cistern near the temple of Hephaestus in Athens, bears an inscription recording its dedication by the Athenians, "from the Lacedaemonians at Pylus."

Sphinx (sfingks). In Greek mythology, the monstrous daughter of Echidna and Orthrus, or as some say, of Echidna and Typhon. She had the head of a woman, the body of a lion, the tail of a serpent, and eagle's wings. The Sphinx was sent by Hera or Apollo to punish Thebes for the crimes of Laius, king of Thebes. She frequented a high rock near the gate of Thebes and waylaid passers-by, asking them: "What creature with one voice walks on four legs in the morning, on two at noon, and on three in the evening?" She hurled those who could not answer the riddle to their deaths from her rock, or as some say, she devoured them. When Oedipus came to Thebes, he answered correctly: "Man, who crawls on all fours as a babe, walks upright in his prime, and needs a staff in old age." The Sphinx thereupon perished (or killed herself), and Oedipus entered Thebes as deliverer of the people from the monster.

Spodius (spō′di-us). An epithet of Apollo,

meaning "God of Ashes," for the ashes of sacrificial victims.

Spoletium (spō-lē′shum). [Modern name, **Spoleto**.] Town of C Italy, situated on a branch of the Via Flaminia, about 60 miles NE of Rome. It was attacked (217 B.C.) by Hannibal after the battle of Trasimenus, but he was driven off. The town was a battleground during the civil wars and its territory was annexed by Sulla, 82 B.C. Under the empire it again became a prosperous town. There are many Roman remains in Spoletium, including a theater, amphitheater, bridge, a triumphal arch of Drusus and Germanicus (21 A.D.), houses, and parts of walls.

Spoleto (spō-lä′tō). See **Spoletium.**

Sporades (spor′a-dēz). Group of Greek islands in the Aegean and neighboring seas. The name is variously applied. It includes Melos, Thera, Cos, and others, and sometimes Samos, Chios, Lesbos, and others.

Sporus (spō′rus). Favorite of the emperor Nero. He was a beautiful youth of slave parentage, and is said to have possessed a striking resemblance to Nero's wife Poppaea Sabina. After her death in 65 A.D., Nero had him castrated and dressed as a woman, and gave him the name of Sabina, publicly going through the ceremony of marriage with him in Greece in 67. Sporus fled with Nero from Rome on the insurrection of Galba in the following year, and was reputedly present at his suicide. He was afterward intimate with the emperor Otho, a former companion in debauchery of Nero, and ultimately, under Vitellius, committed suicide to avoid the indignity of appearing as a girl on the stage.

Squillace (skwēl-lä′chā). See **Scylacium.**

Stagira (sta-jī′ra). [Also: **Stagirus**.] In ancient geography, a city on the coast of Chalcidice, Macedonia, about 43 miles E of Thessalonika: the birthplace of Aristotle. It was colonized from Andros.

Stagirite (sta-jī′rīt). See **Aristotle.**

Stamnos (stam′nos). In ancient Greece, a large water- or wine-vase closely resembling the hydria, but generally with a shorter neck, and provided merely with the two small handles on the sides of the paunch, the larger handle behind being absent.

Stamphane (stäm′fä-ne) or **Stamphanes** (stäm′fä-nes). See **Strophades.**

Staphylus (staf′i-lus). In Greek mythology, a son of Dionysus and Ariadne. He inherited the island of Peparethos from Minos of Crete. Staphylus married Chrysothemis, who bore him three daughters, Molpadia, Rhoeo, and Parthenos.

Statira (sta-tī′ra). Wife of Artaxerxes II Mnemon (c436–358 B.C.), king of Persia. She was put to death by Parysatis.

Statira. Wife of Darius III (Codomannus), the Great King of Peria; died c333 B.C. At the battle of Issus (333 B.C.), Alexander completely defeated the forces of Darius. He fled, abandoning his mother, wife, and children in his pavilion near the battlefield. Alexander pursued him and retrieved the cloak and armor that Darius discarded in his flight. When Alexander returned with them to his camp he heard the wailing of women and learned that the wife and family of Darius had become his captives, and that they grieved, thinking Alexander had slain Darius because he returned to the camp with the accoutrements of Darius. Alexander sent word to comfort them, saying that Darius had escaped and still lived. He also assured the women that he would accord them every honor and service due to their royal state. Statira was reputed to be the most beautiful princess then living but Alexander did not molest her in any way. On the contrary, he did not seek her out but gave orders for her comfort. She died in childbirth while still Alexander's captive.

Statira. Daughter of Darius III (Codomannus); slain 323 B.C. On his return journey from India Alexander the Great married her at Susa (324 B.C.). When Alexander died (323 B.C.), Roxana, another of his wives, sent for Statira, who did not know he was dead. Roxana murdered Statira and her sister and flung their bodies into a well and covered them with earth.

Statius (stā′shus), **Publius Papinius.** Roman poet; born c45 A.D., at Naples; died c96. His father, who was also a poet, gave him his training. Statius became court poet to Domitian, on whose favor he depended, and whose good will he kept by means of the most sycophantic flattery. He wrote the epic *Thebais*, in 12 books, on the struggles of the sons of Oedipus to win control of Thebes,

actor; up, lūte, pull; oi, oil; ou, out; ᵺ, then; ḏ as d or j, ş as s or sh, ṭ as t or ch, ẕ as z or zh.

and an unfinished epic called *Achilleis*. His miscellaneous poems appeared in the collection called *Silvae*.

Statius Caecilius (sē-sil′i-us). See **Caecilius Statius.**

Stator (stā′tôr). Epithet of the Roman god Jupiter as the stayer of flight, especially the flight of armies.

Stentor (sten′tôr). In Greek legend, a Greek herald before Troy, who, in Homer's *Iliad,* had a voice as loud as those of 50 men together. The adjective "stentorian" is derived from his name.

Stenyclaros (sten-i-klā′ros). [Also: **Stenyclerus, Stenyclarus.**] In ancient geography, a city in Messenia. Cresphontes, who won Messenia as his share of the Peloponnesus in the return of the Heraclidae (Dorian invasion), built his palace there and made it his capital. In Stenyclaros was the Boar's Tomb where, some say, Heracles took an oath on slices of boar's flesh. A great battle between the Spartans and Messenians was fought at the Boar's Tomb in the Second Messenian War, in which the Spartans were put to rout, but Aristomenes, the Messenian commander, was prevented by the Dioscuri from pursuing them. The Dioscuri sat in a wild pear tree and caused Aristomenes to lose his shield. While he hunted for it the Spartans escaped.

Stepteria (step-tē′ri-a). A ritualistic festival commemorating the slaying by Apollo of the Pytho that guarded the oracular chasm at Delphi. The ceremony was reënacted every eighth year. According to the ritual, a hut of boughs was set up on the threshing-floor at Delphi. A boy, both of whose parents were living, was selected to enact the chief role. He went to the hut with his companions, upset the table for offerings within, destroyed the hut by fire and, presumably, destroyed the serpent whose house the hut was as well. The youth then fled to Tempe, where he underwent purification rites, and then, crowned with a laurel wreath, was led back to Delphi in a sacred procession.

Stereobate (stėr′e-ọ-bāt). In architecture, the substructure, foundation, or solid platform upon which a building is erected. In columnar buildings it includes the stylobate, which is the uppermost step or platform of the foundation upon which the columns stand.

Sterope (stėr′ọ-pē). In Greek mythology, a daughter of Pleione and Atlas; one of the Pleiades. She was the mother of Oenomaus by Ares. With her sisters, her image was placed among the stars. She is also known as Asterope. See **Pleiades.**

Steropes (stėr′ọ-pēz). In Greek mythology, one of the Cyclopes, a son of Gaea and Uranus. His brothers were Arges and Brontes. See **Cyclopes.**

Stesichorus (stē-sik′ọ-rus). Great lyric poet who was active in the middle of the 6th century B.C. His name was originally Tisias but he was given the name Stesichorus (marshal of choruses) in recognition of his office as director of choruses. He was a Locrian who went to Himera in Sicily and ultimately retired to Catana when the tyrant Phalaris triumphed. The eight-sided grave of Stesichorus, outside the gate named for him, was pointed out as one of the sights of Sicily in Roman times. Among the great contributions of Stesichorus were his invention of the simple narrative style of lyric and his transporting of the epic to the west. But his greatest contribution was in his lyrical recording and remodelling of the myths, especially those of Thebes and Troy. In a critical spirit, but with perfect faith, he set down the great stories, altering the details as it seemed good to him but never doubting that what he wrote about had really happened. Later poets took the versions of the stories, and the incidents and episodes he added, as their point of departure. An outstanding example of his willingness to alter the epics, as well as an example of his faith, is in his story of Helen of Troy. An early poem of Helen, now lost, apparently took the usual view that Helen had too easily succumbed to the temptations presented by Paris, had betrayed her husband and her country, and had wantonly provoked a long and disastrous war. Later in his life Stesichorus went blind. He thought this was a punishment on him from Helen for the scandalous things he had written about her. Besides, by this time it had begun to seem incredible that the Trojans would allow their kingdom to be destroyed just to indulge Paris. Like others after him, Stesichorus began to think that the Trojans did not give up Helen to the Greeks because she was not in their midst, that she had never gone to Troy at all. According to some accounts, a citizen of Croton who had gone to the island of Leuce to be cured of a wound by the shade of Ajax the Lesser, had there seen Helen, now married to Achilles. She commanded the Crotoniat to take a message to Stesichorus, saying that the loss of his sight was due to her displeasure because he had libelled her. Stesichorus, on receiving the message, recanted. He wrote a Palinode (a poetic recantation) which commenced, "That tale was never true! Thou didst not go aboard the well-benched ships, nor reach the towers of Troy." A public declamation by Stesichorus of these verses appeased the anger of Helen and his sight was restored. He was the first to advance the theory, for the above reasons, that Helen did nòt go to Troy at all, that the war was fought for a phantom, a wraith carried off by Paris, while the true Helen was living virtuously in Egypt. Stesichorus was tremendously admired by the ancients, who called him "the lyric Homer." Only fragments of his work survive.

Stesimbrotus (stes-im′brŏ-tus). Greek biographer; born on the island of Thasus; fl. at the end of the 5th century B.C. He was a contemporary of Cimon and Pericles. He went to Athens in the time of Pericles and wrote biographies on political figures in Athens: Themistocles, Pericles, and Thucydides. He was, not unnaturally since the Athenians had compelled Thasus to remain in the confederacy, violently opposed to the Athenian empire and much of his work was devoted to attacks against it.

Stheneboea (sthen-e-bē′a). The name sometimes given to the daughter of Iobates, king of Lycia, who married Proetus of Corinth and falsely accused Bellerophon. See **Antia**.

Sthenelaus (sthen-e-lā′us). In the *Iliad*, a Trojan who was slain by Patroclus.

Sthenele (sthen′e-lē). A daughter of Acastus. According to some accounts, she was the mother of Patroclus by Menoetius.

Sthenelus (sthen′e-lus). In Greek legend, a son of Actor. He was a comrade of Heracles in the war against the Amazons, and was struck by an arrow and wounded. On his return to Paphlagonia he died of his wound and passed to the Underworld. When the Argonauts passed his burial mound on their way to Colchis, Persephone yielded to his request to go from the world of the dead to the world of the living so that he could see once more heroes such as he used to be. The Argonauts stopped when they saw his spirit looking at their ship, and at the urging of Mopsus sacrificed to his spirit, after which his spirit returned to the world of the dead.

Sthenelus. In Greek legend, a son of Capaneus. He was one of the Epigoni, sons of the Seven against Thebes, and one who returned safely. As a close friend of Diomedes, "to his heart, the dearest of mortals," he went with Diomedes from Argos to fight with the Greeks in the Trojan War. When Diomedes was wounded by Pandarus, Sthenelus pulled out the arrow that had lodged in his shoulder. With Diomedes, he swore that he would stay and fight at Troy until the city was destroyed, even if Agamemnon should, as he proposed doing, induce the Greeks to withdraw and go home. Sthenelus was one of those who later entered Troy in the Wooden Horse.

Sthenelus. In Greek legend, a son of Perseus and Andromeda. He seized the throne of Mycenae, after banishing Amphitryon. When Atreus and Thyestes fled from the Peloponnesus he invited them to Mycenae, thus paving the way for the rule of the Pelopids, or the House of Atreus, over Mycenae. His wife Nicippe was about to bear a child when Zeus, awaiting the birth of his son Heracles, vowed that the first child born that day to a descendant of Perseus would reign over the Argives. Hera hastened Nicippe's birth pangs and she was delivered of Eurystheus, a seven-months child, hours before Heracles was born. This was why Heracles was a servant of Eurystheus, and why the latter succeeded his father as ruler of Mycenae.

Sthenias (sthen′i-as). Epithet of Athena, meaning "Strong." The Troezenians worshiped Athena Sthenias, and raised a temple to her on the citadel at Troezen.

Sthenius (sthen′i-us). Epithet of Zeus. The rock near Troezen under which Aegeus hid the tokens by which Theseus would be identified was known as the altar of Zeus Sthenius (*Strong*). When Theseus succeeded in moving it and recovering the tokens, the name was changed to the Rock of Theseus.

Stheno (sthē′nō, sthen′ō). A Gorgon, one of the daughters of Ceto and Phorcys. See **Gorgons**.

Stichius (stik′i-us). In the *Iliad*, a captain of

the Athenians in the Trojan War. He was a comrade of Menestheus, and was slain by Hector in the struggle at the Greek fortifications.

Stiria (stī-rī′a) or **Stiritis** (stī-rī′tis). Epithet of Demeter, from her sanctuary at Stiris in Phocis. The image in the sanctuary showed the goddess bound in ribbons.

Stoa (stō′a). A *porticus* or colonnade, a very important type of public building in ancient Greece and Italy. The term means "row of columns." In its simplest form the stoa was a long, narrow, one-story structure, its roof supported on the side facing the street, market-place, or temple enclosure by columns, on the other side by a blank wall, with ends open or closed. The plan was elaborated in various ways: with a second row of columns, with a second story, with projecting bays at each end, with two wings (forming an L), with three wings (forming three sides of a square or rectangle, the open side regularly toward the south to take the fullest advantage of winter sun and summer shade), with four wings, with a row of shops behind the columns, and so on. In the Athenian Agora one stoa has a wall on the longitudinal axis and columns on either long side, in effect, two stoas back-to-back. In Rome one porticus has no solid wall, the roof being supported solely by columns. At Delos the term stoa is applied to a large enclosed rectangular building, the Hypostyle Hall. Less sturdy in construction than temples, stoas were particularly vulnerable to earthquake, fire and the crowbars of vandals, and no stoa or porticus has survived intact; the Stoa of Attalus, at Athens, restored as the Agora Museum by the American excavators of the Agora, demonstrates better than any other the usefulness and adaptability of this popular and widespread building type. Stoas in Greece, and porticus in Rome, were places where lawyers and business men met their clients, magistrates conferred, teachers lectured, idlers lounged, and citizens generally took refuge from rain and sun. In the lexicon of philosophy, *The Stoa* refers to the Stoa Poikile or Painted Colonnade, bordering the Athenian Agora, where Zeno the Stoic and his successors lectured. (JJ)

Stoics (stō′iks). Disciples of the philosopher Zeno, who founded the sect c308 B.C. He taught that men should be free from passion, unmoved by joy or grief, and submit without complaint to the unavoidable necessity by which all things are governed. The Stoics are proverbially known for the sternness and austerity of their doctrines, and for the influence which their tenets exercised over some of the noblest spirits of antiquity, especially among the Romans. Their system appears to have been an attempt to reconcile a theological pantheism and a materialist psychology with a logic which seeks the foundations of knowledge in the representations or perceptions of the senses, and a morality which claims as its first principle the absolute freedom of the human will. The Stoics teach that whatever is real is material; that matter and force are the two ultimate principles; and that matter is of itself motionless and unformed, though capable of receiving all motions and all forms. Force is the active, moving, and molding principle, and is inseparably joined with matter; the working force in the universe is God, whose existence as a wise, thinking being is proved by the beauty and adaptation of the world. The supreme end of life, or the highest good, is virtue, that is, a life conformed to nature, the agreement of human conduct with the all-controlling law of nature, or of the human with the divine will; not contemplation, but action, is the supreme problem for man; virtue is sufficient for happiness, but happiness or pleasure should never be made the end of human endeavor. The wise man alone attains to the complete performance of his duty; he is without passion, although not without feeling; he is not indulgent but just toward himself and others; he alone is free; he is king and lord, and is inferior in inner worth to no other rational being. The sect takes its name from the Stoa Poikile, or Painted Colonnade, a building bordering the Agora of Athens, in which Zeno and his successors lectured.

Stolo (stō′lō), **Caius Licinius Calvus.** See **Licinius** (fl. 377–361 B.C.).

Stone People. In Greek mythology, the race of men that sprang up after the flood which only Deucalion and Pyrrha survived. To repopulate the earth, Deucalion and Pyrrha hurled the stones of earth, their mother, behind them. The stones thrown by Deucalion became men; those hurled by Pyrrha became women.

Strabo (strā′bō), **Cnaeus Pompeius.** Roman statesman; killed by lightning, 87 B.C. He served Rome as quaestor in Sardinia (103 B.C.), praetor (94), propraetor in Sicily (93), and consul (89 B.C.). He took part in the Social War and was sponsor of the law that granted to the inhabitants of Transpadane Gaul the same privileges as were enjoyed by the Latin colonies. He was the father of Pompey the triumvir.

Strabo. Greek geographer, born at Amasia, Pontus, 63 B.C.; died c24 A.D. He was educated at Nysa and at Rome. On the conclusion of his education in philosophy he devoted himself to the study of history and geography. He traveled extensively, making visits to Asia Minor, Egypt, Greece, and Italy. His historical work was a history, in 47 books, the last 42 books of which were a continuation of Polybius to his own time. Only fragments of this work survive. His great *Geographica*, in 17 books, has survived almost intact, and has been the most important geographical work to come down to us from ancient times. It is written as scientific geography, after the system of Eratosthenes, and is an invaluable source for descriptions of countries and peoples, their customs and manners, and historical and geographical material. The first two books contain certain introductory material, including criticism of earlier geographers. Books III–X are devoted to Europe, XI–XVI to Asia, XVII to Egypt and North Africa.

Strato (strā′tō) or **Straton** (strā′ton). Greek peripatetic philosopher of Lampsacus, the successor of Theophrastus in the presidency of the Lyceum in 288 B.C.; died c268 B.C. He was called "the Naturalist" because he declared the intervention of a deity in nature unnecessary.

Stratonice (strat-ō-nī′sē). Daughter of Demetrius I of Macedonia, and wife of Seleucus I, and later of his son Antiochus I; fl. c300 B.C. Seleucus, discovering his son's passion for her, gave her to him, and at the same time made him king of the provinces of upper Asia.

Strongyle (stron′ji-lē). [Modern name, **Stromboli**.] Northernmost of the Aeoliae Insulae (Lipari islands), N of Sicily: famous for its constantly active volcano (elevation, about 3038 feet).

Strongyle. An ancient name of the island of **Naxos.**

Strophades (strof′a-dēz; Greek, strô-fä′thes). [Also: **Stamphane, Stamphanes, Strofadhes;** Italian, **Strivali.**] Group of small islands W of the Peloponnesus, Greece. Hither the sons of Boreas were said, in Greek legend, to have pursued the Harpies, and here they turned back from their pursuit. The Harpies remained on the islands, which took the name, meaning the islands of turning, from the fact that the Boreadae, Calais and Zetes, turned back here. Later, Aeneas stopped here and the Harpies harried his exhausted men, and predicted that the Trojans would one day be so hungry they would be compelled to eat their tables. They also prophesied a long and difficult journey for Aeneas and his men.

Strophius (strō′fi-us). In Greek legend, a king in Phocis. His realm was at the foot of Mount Parnassus. He married a sister of Agamemnon, who bore him a son Pylades. Orestes was sent to him after the murder of Agamemnon for protection from the wicked designs of Aegisthus, and was brought up in his court. Strophius disowned his son, Pylades, the faithful friend of Orestes, for his part in Orestes' murder of Clytemnestra.

Strymon (strī′mon). [Modern name, **Struma**.] A river of Thrace which empties into the Aegean Sea. It was reputed to be the nesting ground of the cranes which fought the Pygmies. The river-god, according to some accounts, ravished the muse Calliope, or Euterpe, and fathered Rhesus, the Thracian king who went to the aid of Hector and was killed by Diomedes and Odysseus.

Strymonic Gulf (strī-mon′ik). [Also: **Gulf of Orfani;** Latin, **Strymonicus Sinus**.] Arm of the Aegean Sea, indenting the coast of Macedonia, Greece, E of the peninsula of Chalcidice, at the mouth of the Strymon River.

Stylobate (stī′lō-bāt). In architecture, a continuous basement upon which columns are placed to raise them above the level of the ground or a floor; particularly, the uppermost step of the stereobate of a columnar building, upon which rests an entire range of columns. It is distinguished from a pedestal, which, when it occurs in this use, supports only a single column.

Stymphalides (stim-fā′li-dēz). In Greek legend, a flock of fierce man-eating birds near Lake Stymphalus. They had bronze claws, beaks, and wings, and could discharge their own feathers like arrows. To kill them was the sixth labor of Heracles.

Stymphalus (stim-fā′lus). In Greek legend, a son of Elatus and Laodice, daughter of Cinyras. He was a king in Arcadia. When Pelops came into the Peloponnesus he waged war on Stymphalus, but could not defeat him by force of arms. He invited Stymphalus to meet with him for discussion under truce, and when Stymphalus came to his camp, he murdered him, dismembered his body, and cast his limbs to the four winds. This treacherous murder by Pelops brought a terrible drought on all Greece, which was lifted only when, on the advice of the oracle at Delphi, Aeacus prayed to Zeus for relief. Stymphalus in Arcadia is named for him.

Stymphalus. In ancient geography, a district and lake in the NE part of Arcadia, Greece. According to tradition, it was named for Stymphalus, the grandson of Arcas. In the ancient city, which was later moved to a new site, lived Temenus, son of Pelasgus. Temenus, some say, reared Hera and founded three sanctuaries for her. About the spring and lake of Stymphalus dwelt the savage, man-eating Stymphalian birds that were shot down as one of the Labors of Heracles. The birds were carved on the sanctuary of Stymphalian Artemis, and behind the sanctuary stood figures of maidens, in white marble, with the legs of birds. The Stymphalus River, the source of which is a spring, disappears, says Pausanias, into the earth through a chasm, and reappears in Argolis as the Erasinus River. Once, when the festival of Stymphalian Artemis was carelessly observed, a log of wood fell into the chasm and blocked it up. The river backed up and flooded the plain. Shortly thereafter, a hunter pursuing a deer followed it as it fled into the marshy plain. The chasm opened and swallowed up deer and hunter, and the river followed them into the chasm and dried up the plain. After this warning the inhabitants of Stymphalus celebrated the festival of Stymphalian Artemis with due care. The people of Stymphalus joined with the Argives of their own accord but they were, in fact, as Homer says, Arcadians.

Styx (stiks). In Greek mythology, a nymph, the daughter of Oceanus and Tethys. Because she was the first of the deities to go to the aid of Zeus when the Titans attacked him, Zeus took her children, among them Nike, to Olympus. He also made her the goddess by whom the most inviolable oaths were sworn. Styx dwelt on the western shore of the river Styx, near the edge of night, in a house with silver pillars. She guarded the Aloidae, who were tied to pillars with living serpents as a punishment for having attacked Olympus. Some say Styx was the mother of Persephone by Zeus.

Styx. In Greek mythology, one of the five rivers surrounding Hades, over which the ghosts of the dead who have been properly buried must pass. The river is so sacred that the gods swear by it. When one of the gods takes an oath by the Styx, Iris brings water from the river in a golden cup. Punishment for breaking an oath taken by the Styx consists in banishment from the councils of the gods for nine years. In ancient geography Styx was also the name of a river that flowed by the city of Nonacris in Arcadia. The water trickles down from a high cliff and flows into the Crathis River, or, as some say, it flows to Tartarus. The waters of the Styx were believed to bring death to all who drank them. Among the wonderful properties of the water it was claimed that it broke all things of glass, crystal, stone, and pottery, and corroded all metals. The only material that could withstand it was a horse's hoof. The Arcadians swore their most binding oaths by their river Styx. Hither the daughters of Proetus fled when they were struck by madness, and near here Melampus overtook them and cured them.

Subura (sö-bū′ra). Valley in ancient Rome, on the N side of the Fora, and extending between the Viminal and Esquiline hills. It was drained by the Cloaca Maxima.

Suessa Aurunca (swes′a a-rung′ka). A town on the SW slopes of the extinct volcano now known as Roccamonfina, commanding the pass between Roccamonfina and the Mons Massicus of wine-growing fame. On this site was established in 313 B.C. the Latin colony of Suessa Aurunca, which survives today as Sessa or Sessa Aurunca. It was the birthplace of the Latin satirist Caius Lucilius. To the imperial period belong an amphitheater and numerous architectural fragments from temples and other buildings, while in the neighborhood is a celebrated Roman bridge, the Ponte Ronaco (= Aurunco), still in daily use. It has been suggested that Suessa preserves an alternate pronunciation or dialectal form of Vescia, a lost city of the Ausones, and if so Suessa may stand over or near the site of ancient Vescia; but no traces of a pre-Roman Suessa have been identified. If, as a single late reference indicates, Roccamonfina last erupted in 269 B.C., Vescia may have been buried by ash, like Pompeii, and may still be awaiting the discoverer's spade. (JJ)

Suessiones (swes-i-ō′nēz). Ancient people of Gallia Belgica, allied to and situated near the Remi, in the vicinity of what is now Soissons, which was named after them. They were subjugated (57 B.C.) by Julius Caesar.

Suessula (swes′ū-la). In ancient geography, a place in Campania, Italy, about 13 miles NE of Naples. It is the traditional scene of a Roman victory over the Samnites in the First Samnite War (343–341 B.C.).

Suetonius (swē-tō′ni-us). [Full name, **Caius Suetonius Tranquillus**.] Roman biographer and historian; fl. in the first part of the 2nd century A.D. He was a teacher of rhetoric in Rome, and a great friend of the younger Pliny who was influential in securing many favors for him and with whom he traveled to Bithynia in 112. He was private secretary to Hadrian (c119–121) and then devoted himself to his literary pursuits. He collected information and notes on all sorts of matters and wrote about them. His chief work is *Lives of the Caesars*, which contains biographies (of an anecdotal character) of the first 12 Caesars, including Julius. The work is important for its revelations concerning the private life of the emperors. Fragments of his *De grammaticis* and of other works are extant.

Suevi (swē′vī). Ancient Germanic people mentioned by Caesar, who describes them as the largest and most warlike of the German tribes. At the time of Tacitus the name Suevi had become a generic term for all

the Germans to the north and east. They occupied all C Germany W of the Oder River, from the boundaries of the Harudes, who alone intervened between them and the Baltic, to the Danube River. In the first half of the 5th century A.D. the Suevi appeared as neighbors and allies of the Alamanni, with whom they acted as one folk. Either name has been used for the whole people, but they were probably two closely related groups. Together they were crushingly defeated by the Franks under Clovis. Subsequently the Suevi were settled about the headwaters of the Danube River, where their name was preserved in Swabia (Schwaben).

Suiones (sö-yō′nēz). [Also: **Suyones**.] Ancient Germanic people of Scandinavia, mentioned by Tacitus in *Germania* as living on the Baltic and having readily maneuverable ships with a prow at each end. They appear later to have occupied what is now the S part of Sweden.

Sulla (sul′a), **Lucius Cornelius**. [Surnamed **Felix**.] Roman general and dictator; born c138 B.C.; died 78 B.C. He was the son of an obscure and impoverished patrician family, and as a young man was compelled to live in lodgings for lack of his own estate. This fact was remembered by his enemies when he subsequently became wealthy in the service of the state. Towards the end of his life he took the surname Felix (*Fortunate*) in grateful acknowledgment to the gods, who always smiled on his undertakings as will presently appear. According to Plutarch, he loved a wealthy woman of plebeian birth and so charmed her that when she presently died she left him all her fortune. His stepmother also left him her property. He thus arrived at a fairly comfortable financial state and prepared to enter public life. In 107 B.C. he was appointed as quaestor to the consul Marius, and went to Libya to serve in the war against Jugurtha (107–106 B.C.). Sulla made friends with the Numidian king, Bocchus, who was also the father-in-law of Jugurtha. Bocchus plotted with Sulla to surrender Jugurtha to him. At some risk to himself Sulla put himself in Bocchus' power for the purpose of executing the plot. Bocchus secured the presence of Jugurtha by trickery and, though he wavered as to whether it would be more to his advantage to seize Sulla, decided Jugurtha was more of a danger to him and surrendered him to Sulla and ended the war. Marius, as consul, was honored with a triumph for the war, but Sulla was publicly credited with the seizure of Jugurtha. For his pride's sake he had a seal ring made, on which was engraved a figure of Bocchus surrendering Jugurtha to him. The prominence Sulla won in the Numidian war was not pleasing to Marius. Nevertheless, he concealed his jealousy and used Sulla to good advantage in subsequent campaigns. Sulla served under him during his second and third consulships (104 and 103 B.C.), and won the friendship of the Marsi for Rome. Becoming aware that Marius was acting to halt his advancement, he attached himself to Catulus, co-consul with Marius. Catulus, less ambitious or more indolent than Marius, gave Sulla free rein. He subdued the Cimbri and Teutones (104–101 B.C.) in the Alps and returned to Rome. In 93 B.C. he became praetor as the result of lavish expenditures, and in 92 B.C. as propraetor of Cilicia he defeated the general of Mithridates VI and restored Ariobarzanes to the throne of Cappadocia. In this war, carried on with the help of Roman allies, he slew many Cappadocians and Armenians, and received an envoy of the Parthian king Arsaces, who asked for friendship and alliance with Rome. He then returned to Rome, where the breach with Marius became open rivalry when Bocchus dedicated some images at Rome that portrayed Sulla accepting the surrender of Jugurtha. The rivalry between Marius and Sulla to control Rome was submerged by the outbreak of the Social War, 90 B.C. The war was so-called because it was a war between Rome and her Italian allies (*socii* meaning allies). Sulla achieved great fame by his exploits in the war, which included the defeat of the Samnites and the capture of Bovianum (89 B.C.). In 88 B.C. he became consul with Pompey. He brought the Social War to an end by the capture of Nola, and then by lot was chosen commander of the war against Mithridates, which had been renewed by the latter in attacking Rome's allies. Marius wanted the command of this war and his attempts to get it brought on civil war in Rome. Many omens are said to have foretold the civil conflict. Mice gnawed at the sacred gold in the temple; keepers caught one of them in a trap. It produced five young and immediately ate three of them. A trumpet rang out in a shrill and dismal tone and amazed and terrified the people. Seers said this foretold a change in conditions at Rome and a new age of man. While the Senate sat to consider these prodigies a sparrow flew into their chamber with a grasshopper in its mouth. The bird threw part of the insect on the Senate floor and flew off with the rest of its body. Seers interpreted this gloomily as a sign of trouble among the Romans. Marius allied himself to Sulpicius Rufus, an unscrupulous and dangerous popular leader who was tribune of the plebs. He proposed that Marius be made general in command of the Mithridatic War, and when the Senate refused to act he roused a mob against them. In the mêlée Pompey's son was killed. Sulla fled to the house of Marius, who might have killed him, but allowed him to escape. He fled to his army at Nola. In the meantime Sulpicius had deposed Pompey as consul and secured command of the Mithridatic War for Marius. But when the tribunes arrived at Nola to take over the army for Marius they were stoned by Sulla's troops, whose loyalty he had won by his flattery, his military successes, and the plunder he helped them to secure. When Marius learned of his defiance of the tribunes he attacked Sulla's partisans in Rome, slew many of them, and seized their property. Thus the civil war began.

It is said that a vision came to Sulla at this time. He dreamed a goddess stood beside him and gave him a thunderbolt. She named his enemies and invited him to strike them with the thunderbolt. He did so and they at once vanished. Encouraged by this omen, he marched on Rome; the first Roman ever to lead a Roman army against Rome. When he entered the gates of the city some of the people showered his army with rocks and tiles hurled from the roof tops. He ordered the houses fired, friend and foe alike. Marius could not stop him from entering the city. He fled to a temple for refuge, and then left the city. Sulla was now master.

fat, fāte, fär, fāre, errạnt; net, mē, hėr ardẹnt; pin, pīne; not, nōte, möve, nôr,

He called the Senate together and had Marius and Sulpicius condemned to death in absentia. He had won a political and military but not a popular victory. The people distrusted him as an arrogant aristocrat and feared him because he had shown his scorn of their tribunes. Nevertheless, he was the master. In 87 B.C. he set out to command the war against Mithridates. He went to Athens, which sided with Mithridates and was the center of his activity in the west, and laid siege to the city. When he needed timber for his siege engines he ruthlessly cut down the sacred groves of the Academy and the Lyceum. When he needed money for his operations he sent to Epidaurus, Olympia, and Delphi and removed the treasures from their temples. At Delphi the priests thought to frighten away his envoys by causing a musician to play the flute in an inner chamber and informing them that the music came from the god, who forbade them to harm his shrine. The envoys were fearful and relayed the message to Sulla. He sent back word that the music had been misinterpreted: the god was playing to welcome a friend; the envoys were ordered to proceed with the pillaging of the shrine. Among the treasures taken from Delphi was the great silver bowl dedicated there by the Lydian king Croesus. Sulla promised that he would replace the treasures necessity compelled him to seize from the temples. He took Athens (86 B.C.) by treachery, marched into the city at night and gave it over to his men to plunder. The streets ran with blood. But thanks to the pleas of some Roman senators in his train he did not destroy the city. He went on to take the Piraeus and burned it. From here he took his forces into Boeotia, met the forces of Mithridates' general Archelaus at Chaeronea and defeated them (86 B.C.). In the following year reinforcements came to Archelaus. An enemy charge inflicted damage on Sulla's troops and they fell back. As they retreated Sulla jumped from his horse and pushed toward the enemy on foot, crying, "For me, O Romans, an honorable death here; but you, when men ask you where you betrayed your commander, remember to tell them, at Orchomenus." His men rallied and next day defeated Archelaus

at Orchomenus (85 B.C.). In 84 B.C. he went into Asia and defeated Fimbria, a Marian leader who sought to take his command, and compelled Mithridates to come to terms with him. Mithridates and Sulla met at Dardanus in the Troad. Mithridates agreed to give up Asia (Asia Minor) and Paphlagonia; to restore the kings of Bithynia and Cappadocia, whose thrones he had seized; to pay an indemnity to Rome; and to contribute 70 ships to the Roman fleet. Sulla for his part guaranteed Mithridates in the territory that was left him and made him an ally of Rome.

In the meantime, terrible news had reached him from Rome. Marius had returned (87 B.C.) and captured the control of the city. Sulla's wife had come to him in Athens and told him of the destruction of his property in Rome and of the wholesale slaughter of his friends. Having concluded peace with Mithridates he now prepared to return to Rome. His soldiers, who had taken enormous booty while in his service, voluntarily swore allegiance to him. He sailed across to Italy (83 B.C.) and landed at Brundisium. By this time Marius had died (86 B.C.) and the opposition to Sulla was led by Cinna, Carbo, and the Younger Marius. Sulla defeated the forces sent against him by Marius the Younger and the consul Norbanus, then defeated Marius at Signia, near Praeneste. Marius escaped to Praeneste, but arrived after the gate had been closed. He was hauled up over the walls by a rope to safety. Sulla's generals, Pompey, Crassus, Metellus, and Servilius, were equally victorious in their areas. At last Carbo, the remaining leader of the opposition, fled to Libya (82 B.C.). The Samnites had taken advantage of the civil war to march on Rome. Sulla defeated them at the Colline Gate (82 B.C.) and was again master of Rome. He issued a sweeping proscription against his enemies. By the proscription any one who wished could kill with impunity anyone whose name appeared on the proscribed list. Many on the list were Sulla's enemies. Others were the owners of fine properties Sulla wished to take, for himself or for his friends. The sons and grandsons of those who were proscribed lost their civil rights. This was the first time in

Roman history, but not the last, that a reign of terror was inaugurated by means of a proscription. Marius the Younger committed suicide. Sulla caused to be slain all those in the city of Praeneste who had helped Marius —to the number of 12,000.

Sulla now made himself dictator, thus reviving an office that had lapsed 120 years earlier, celebrated a magnificent triumph for the Mithridatic War, and took the surname Felix (*Fortunate*) to acknowledge his debt to the gods. In 80 B.C. he became consul. His activities had resulted in the crushing of all opposition and the expropriation of the property of Marius' followers to the advantage of Sulla's. As master of Rome he made various constitutional reforms. He reorganized and restored the power of the Senate and weakened the power of the tribunes. He established a system of courts of justice. To support the political system he established military colonies on large grants of land throughout Italy. One of Sulla's enemies was Julius Caesar. He pursued the latter to such an extent that he was forced to change his lodging nightly. Finally, Sulla yielded to the pleas of the aristocratic party (*optimates*) to forgive Caesar. As he did so he warned those who pleaded in Caesar's behalf that the man they pleaded for would one day destroy their party. In this he was an excellent prophet. The personal life of Sulla was as vigorous and ruthless as his military life. In his hours of relaxation he enjoyed the company of actors and jesters, drank deep, and gave himself to every form of voluptuousness. He could show the most benign patience with his friends, or the most brutal anger. Of himself he said he never failed to reward his friends' kindnesses or to punish his enemies' wrongs, and this was inscribed on his monument. However, frequently the kindnesses of friends were transformed in his eyes into the wrongs of enemies. He was married at least four times. One of his wives was Caecilia, daughter of the pontifex maximus Metellus. He married her when he was 50 years old, having put aside previous wives, and always showed her the greatest deference. Yet when at last she was dying he divorced her and had her removed to another place so as not to pollute

his house with her death. This however, was in accordance with the custom, and did not at all hinder him from giving her a magnificent funeral. He resigned the dictatorship in 79 B.C. and retired to Puteoli, where he amused himself with his actor friends and finished his *Memoirs*. He died quietly in 78 B.C., was given a splendid public funeral, and was buried in the Campus Martius.

Sulmo (sul'mō). [Modern names; **Sulmona, Solmona**.] Town of C Italy. It was a Roman town, in the region of the Sabines, from ancient times. The town was taken and sacked by Hannibal, 211 B.C. It is the birthplace of the poet Ovid, its most famous son.

Sulpicia (sul-pish'a̱). Roman poetess of the Augustan age, daughter of Servius Sulpicius Rufus. Six charming short elegies by her, in which she speaks of her love for Cerinthus, have survived in the collected works of the elegist Tibullus (Book IV, nos. 7–12). (JJ)

Sulpicius Galba (sul-pish'us gal'ba̱), **Servius.** See **Galba, Servius Sulpicius.**

Sulpicius Rufus (rö'fus), **Publius.** Roman politician and orator; born c121 B.C.; killed 88 B.C. Prior to his tribunate in 88 B.C. he had been a member of the aristocratic party (*optimates*) but upon becoming a tribune of the plebs he switched his allegiance to the popular party (*populares*). It is said that he had a personal bodyguard of 3000 young men who kept Rome in a turmoil and Sulpicius powerful, and that he bought popularity by selling the Roman citizenship for a price. He was a partisan of Marius, the leader of the popular party, and proposed that he be made general in command of the war against Mithridates (88 B.C.). The consuls, Sulla and Pompey, refused to let the matter come to a vote. Sulpicius used his bodyguard to stir up a riot against them. Both fled. Sulpicius deposed Pompey from his consulship and took the command of the Mithridatic War away from Sulla, who had won it by lot, and gave it to Marius. However, the tribunes who went to Nola to take over Sulla's army were stoned by his loyal troops. Sulla led them against Rome, made himself master of the city, and condemned Sulpicius and Marius, who had fled, to death in absentia. Sulpicius was killed by a slave Sulla had freed for the express purpose of killing him. Afterward, Sulla caused the slave to be hurled to his death from the Tarpeian Rock.

Summanus (su-mā'nus). In Roman mythology, a god of thunderstorms, specifically the sender of thunderstorms at night. Summanus may originally have been an epithet of Jupiter as "Dweller in the most high places"; but the separate identity of this god as a nocturnal thunder deity has now been long accepted.

Sunium (sō'ni-um) or **Sunium Promontorium** (prom-on-tō'ri-um). [Also: **Sounion, Cape Colonna.**] In ancient geography, a lofty headland running into the sea at the SE extremity of Attica. At the summit, enclosed by a fortification wall and approached through propylaea or formal entrance gates, are the striking ruins of a splendid Periclean Doric hexastyle temple of the sea-god Poseidon, designed by the *Theseum Architect,* constructed c444 B.C. to replace an earlier temple, and conspicuous far out to sea. It is built of a local marble which unlike Pentelic marble has not weathered to a russet patina, but retains its dazzling whiteness. The view of the Aegean and its islands from the temple terrace is superb. Outside the sanctuary, at a little distance, are the foundations of an Ionic temple of Athena, unusual in that it had exterior columns on the front (E) and one flank (S) only. According to Homer, Phrontis, pilot of Menelaus, was struck down by the arrows of Apollo as his ship rounded Sunium on the return from Troy. (JJ)

Superi (sū'pē-rī). A Roman name for the gods. It was sometimes used also of mortals, to distinguish them from the Inferi: that is, the dead in the Underworld.

Suppliant Maidens, The. A drama by Aeschylus, of uncertain date. It is concerned with the Danaids, daughters of Danaus and descendants of Zeus and Io, and their flight from hated marriage with their cousins, the sons of Aegyptus. They have fled over the sea from Egypt to Argos, where they appeal to Pelasgus, king of Argos, for asylum. The scene is a sacred precinct with images of the gods, on the shore near Argos.

A chorus of maidens, daughters of Danaus, enters the sacred precinct. In a choral song

that rises in dramatic intensity the maidens tell why they have come to Argos, which they regard as their ancestral home, as it was the home of Io, the mother of their race. They pray the land to receive them, and to repel the hated, pursuing sons of Aegyptus, marriage with whom would, they insist, be impious. They appeal to the justice of the gods to uphold them in their cause, and especially invoke Zeus the all-powerful to protect them. It is Hera's hatred of Io, they say, that has caused their troubles. Zeus would risk the charge of injustice, they contend, if he denied their prayers.

Danaus enters. He advises his daughters to be prudent, and to accept his counsel, which is that they cast themselves before the altars as suppliants; for an altar, he tells them, is stronger than a castle. He observes men approaching the precinct. His daughters must explain their plight and ask asylum. Moreover, they must make their plea with due modesty, as they are aliens, fugitives, and in need. Pelasgus enters. From their garments he observes that they are not Greeks. He asks who they are. Before replying, the maidens would like to know who he is. They learn that he is the king of a large and prosperous realm—Argos. For their part, the chorus asks him a series of questions about Zeus, Io, and Hera. By his answers: that Io of Argos was transformed into a heifer by Zeus, wandered through many lands before she arrived at the Nile and at the "touch" of Zeus bore Epaphus, Pelasgus himself relates their ancestry, for they are descendants of Epaphus. It is thus made clear that they are connected with Argos and have a claim on that land. He now learns that they are the daughters of Danaus, and that they have fled to the land of their ancient origin to escape marriage with the sons of Aegyptus. Pelasgus, hearing their pleas, is caught: if he refuses sanctuary to the maidens he offends the gods; if he grants sanctuary he risks war with the sons of Aegyptus. He proposes to submit the question to his citizens. The maidens contend that it is his responsibility alone. He tries a reasonable approach. It is a good thing, he suggests, for cousins to marry, as it strengthens the family. They brush this aside. Perhaps the laws of the land sanction such mar-

actor; up, lūte, pull; oi, oil; ou, out; ᴛʜ, then; d̪ as d or j, s̪ as s or sh, t̪ as t or ch, z̪ as z or zh.

riages, he asks. The maidens cry for Justice. It is not an easy question for Pelasgus to decide and he refuses to decide it. He will consult with his people; thus if the event turns out unfortunately they will not be able to throw the blame on him. Now the maidens, with savage determination, threaten to hang themselves by their own girdles before the sacred images if he refuses their plea for asylum. Pelasgus repeats that the two courses open to him are equally fraught with danger: the unknown terrors which would result from offending the gods, or the known and dreaded evils of war with the sons of Aegyptus. He sends Danaus to lay the boughs of suppliants at other altars throughout Argos and so arouse the compassion of his people for the Danaids. Pelasgus also departs to persuade his people to vote to protect the suppliants, regardless of the ills such a course may bring to the state. Left alone, the maidens pray to Zeus. They relate the story of Io and ask Zeus to protect them, Io's descendants, as it is within his power to do, and express their trust in him. Danaus returns and informs them that the Argives, by an overwhelming vote, have decided to give them sanctuary. Pelasgus made a persuasive speech but Zeus brought about the favorable result. The maidens respond with a fervent hymn of gratitude. They pray for rich blessings on the people of Argos. Danaus now announces that he sees an Egyptian fleet approaching. He urges his daughters to be calm and departs to give the alarm. The maidens, recalling the lewdness and savagery of the Egyptians, resolve to die rather than submit. A herald from the sons of Aegyptus enters and roughly orders them to the ships. His command is followed by threats. He has no use for these gods before whom the maidens pray; they are not his gods. As the maidens continue to defy him he attempts to lay hands on them and compel them. At this point Pelasgus enters. He accuses the herald of barbarism and declares that he will protect the maidens. To the herald's demand to know who he is Pelasgus replies it is not important: if the maidens decide to go of their own free will the herald may conduct them, but the people have voted never to surrender them against their will. The herald blusters and threatens war, but leaves.

Pelasgus again assures the maidens and goes to make ready for war. Danaus returns. He commands his daughters to offer sacrifices to the gods for their saviors, the Pelasgians (Argives), and tells them to protect their chastity, for which they have made such a long flight. The chorus of Danaids and a group of their attendant maidens, who have hitherto been silent, alternate in singing the praises of Argos. The Danaids repeat their vows to Artemis to remain virgins, thus denying the power of Aphrodite, and declare that under no circumstances will they marry any of the race of Aegyptus. Their handmaidens advise them to moderate their prayer, as it is not good to ask too much of heaven. The balance of Zeus requires both Artemis and Aphrodite, but the Danaids are obstinately determined to follow Artemis in this matter.

Suppliant Women, The. Tragedy by Euripides, produced c420 B.C. Following the disastrous defeat of the Seven against Thebes, of whom only Adrastus survived, the Argives sent to Thebes and asked permission to recover the bodies of their dead for burial. The Thebans defied all the laws of warfare and religion by denying their request. (The play on this subject was produced during the Peloponnesian Wars between Athens and Sparta, and contains many Euripidean warnings against the folly of war, as well as eulogizing Athens as a humane nation that upholds the sanctity of law.)

The scene is in a court of the temple of Demeter at Eleusis. Aethra, mother of Theseus, is seated on the steps of the great altar in the middle of the court. About her are the mothers of the slain Argive chiefs and their handmaids, and nearby Adrastus is lying prostrate. Aethra is attached to the Argive women by woolen fillets that stretch to them and to her from the olive boughs the suppliants have placed on the altar. No one but the ruler can remove these fillets without committing sacrilege. Aethra prays for prosperity for Athens as she recounts the sad lot of these mothers. The women implore her, as one still blessed with a son, to help them recover their dead, for without proper burial their sons will be homeless and accursed in Hades (want of proper burial was deemed a worse calamity than death itself by the Greeks). Theseus, summoned by a herald, enters, and is troubled to see mourners in the temple, for this is an evil omen. He learns from Aethra who they are and why they have come, and addresses himself to Adrastus. Adrastus relates how he gave his daughters to two aliens, Tydeus and Polynices, at the command of an oracle, and waged war on Thebes to reclaim the inheritance of his son-in-law Polynices. In making war he admits that he flouted other oracles. Worse still, he refused to accept a compromise offered by Eteocles that would have prevented the war, and in self-blame he exclaims,

"Oh foolish states, which might by parley end Feuds, yet decide them in the field of blood!"

Now he humbly kneels to young Theseus and begs him to "save my dead." He appeals as a poor man to a rich one, and has come to Athens rather than to another state because the Spartans are heartless and the other states are neither strong enough nor compassionate enough to help him. Theseus chides him for greediness in attacking Thebes, and for foolishness in flouting the will of the gods. If he were to yield to the wishes of Adrastus he could not defend himself to his Athenians. He therefore bids Adrastus depart and not seek to pull down Athens in his own downfall. Adrastus replies that he has already been punished for his folly and his crimes. He wants help, not judgment, from Theseus; since Theseus denies him, he and his suppliants will withdraw. Aethra breaks in; she weeps for the Argive women. Theseus is surprised; their woes are no concern to her since they are not of her blood. But she insists she must speak for his and Athens' honor; he must not err by denying their appeal as suppliants. He is bound to champion the oppressed, for on that rests his fame. Moreover, he must honor the law of burial. His former brave deeds will be as nothing if in this case he refuses to take up the sword in behalf of the suppliants. Theseus is swayed by her words. He agrees to help the Argives, but first he will gain the approval of the Athenians for his undertaking. As he leaves the chorus praises Athens.

Theseus shortly returns with a herald, whom he instructs to go to Creon of Thebes and ask, as a neighbor and as a right, the return of the slain. If Creon refuses, the herald is instructed to tell him that Athens will fight to uphold the laws of burial. Before he has finished his instructions a Theban herald enters and demands the despot of the city. Theseus corrects him; there is no despot in Athens: its people are free. The herald expresses his scorn for a city that is ruled by an unreasoning mob, and lists all the disadvantages of a democracy. Theseus retorts by citing the advantages of a democracy—where the law is written down, known to all, and applied to all, and the disadvantages of tyranny—where the tyrant kills off possible rivals, seizes the produce of the worker, and ravishes the maidens. Recollecting himself, he tells the herald to get on with his message, and suggests that in future Creon send a less talkative herald. The message is a command to Athens to refuse to receive Adrastus, or if he is already there, to drive him out; it reminds Athens that she has nothing to do with the Argives, advises the Athenians to savor the joys of peace and avoid matters which are of no concern to them. To be discreet, the herald adds, is also to be brave, for ". . . were death in view when votes are cast, Never warfrenzied Greece would rush on ruin." Adrastus and the chorus break in, but Theseus stops them; the message is addressed to him and he will reply. Creon is not master of Athens, he tells the herald, and in seeking to recover the bodies for burial Athens is simply upholding the most sacred laws. This is a common cause of all Greece, not only of Argos;

Never to Greeks shall it be said, that when It fell to me and Athens to uphold Heaven's ancient law, that law was set at naught.

If war results it will be a war forced by Creon, not by Athens. The Theban herald warns that meddling Athens will never prevail and departs. Theseus goes to call his men to arms. He declines the company of Adrastus in his army, lest the pollution of which Adrastus was guilty in his war become associated with and sully the noble purpose of Theseus in his war. The Argive women, left alone, fear that new reproaches will be heaped on them if the Athenians lose in the war. They tremble at the unpredictability of the gods, and pray to Zeus to champion the

Athenians. A messenger now enters and informs them that Theseus, in full scale battle, has defeated Creon, but he refused to sack Thebes, for he had fought only for a pure purpose and not for gain or vengeance. He is bringing back the slain Argive chiefs, but the other dead he prepared for burial himself and entombed them. The Argive women rejoice that their sons will now be buried but mourn anew their deaths. They wish they had never married, rather than look upon their sons' corpses. Theseus enters with a procession carrying the biers of the Argives. He respects the mourning of the Argives, then asks that the gallant deeds of the slain chiefs be recounted for his young Athenians. Adrastus points out and characterizes each of the heroes—Capaneus, "true friend;" Eteoclus, "rich with honor;" Hippomedon "eager to yield his land his body's best;" Parthenopaeus, "unmatched in purity;" Tydeus, "dread reasoner in the logic of the shield." Capaneus, felled by a thunderbolt of Zeus, is to be buried separately (to the Greeks one struck by lightning became sacred), funeral pyres are erected for the others. Adrastus cries out to the mothers to look upon their dead sons, and is rebuked by Theseus for adding to their anguish. Adrastus admits his fault, for:

Short is life's span: behoves to pass through this
Softly as may be, not with travail worn.

The procession moves off, as the chorus mourns. Suddenly Evadne, wife of Capaneus, is seen mounting the cliff above his pyre. She cries out that she will end her life in the same fire that destroys her beloved husband's body. Her father Iphis, come to search for her, is just in time to see her leap into the flames. He is heartbroken. He has lost his son Eteoclus, and now sees his daughter die. If he had known what suffering comes from having children he would never have had any. He laments that man cannot live twice in one life, to profit by what he learns. Broken and alone, he wanders off to die. A procession enters bearing urns with the ashes of the dead chiefs. The chorus of mothers and children of the dead mourn; the sons of the slain chiefs pray that they may grow up to avenge their fathers. Theseus admonishes the Argives

to honor Athens for recovering their dead. Athena appears in her chariot above the temple and instructs Theseus to extract an oath of eternal friendship from Argos in return for the ashes of the dead Argives he has given them. (The goddess is less generous than the mortal Theseus.) She then addresses the sons of the Argive chiefs and predicts that they will avenge their fathers. Theseus promises to obey her will, and prays for her continued guidance so that Athens may prosper.

Surrentum (su-ren'tum). [Modern name, **Sorrento.**] Town in S Italy, situated on cliffs high above the Bay of Naples, about 16 miles SE of Naples. It has been famous since ancient times for its location and its wine, and has always been a popular resort. In ancient times its most celebrated temples were those of Athena and of the Sirens. It has numerous Roman remains, including villas and temples.

Susa (sö'za̤, sö'sa̤). [Biblical name, **Shushan.**] In ancient geography, the capital of Susiana or Elam, "the City of Lilies," situated near the Choaspes (Karkheh) River, S of modern Dizful in Iran. It was destroyed in 645 B.C. by Assurbanipal. The Achaemenid kings of Persia made it their winter residence, and provided it with a citadel. It was still flourishing in the 12th century A.D. It is frequently mentioned in the books of Daniel and Esther. The site at present exhibits a group of high and large mounds, forming together a diamond-shaped figure about 3½ miles in circuit. Excavations were made in 1851 by Loftus in one of the mounds, disclosing the palace of Artaxerxes II, the chief feature being a fine colonnade of 340 feet front. The excavations of M. A. Dieulafoy, between 1884 and 1886, laid bare beneath these ruins those of the palace of Darius the Great, and showed that the upper strata of the mound are formed by superposed layers of ruins.

Susiana (sö-zi-ā'na̤, -an'a̤). Province of the Persian Empire, corresponding to the Biblical Elam and to the region of modern Iran known as Khuzistan. It was an independent state after the first destruction of Nineveh, and was subdued by Sargon II. Its capital was Susa.

Swan. One of the birds sacred to Aphrodite.

Sybaris (sib'a̤-ris). In ancient geography, a city of Magna Graecia, S Italy, situated near the Gulf of Tarentum. It was founded (720 B.C.) by Achaean and Troezenian colonists. It was celebrated for its wealth, and its inhabitants were proverbial for their luxury (whence the epithet "Sybarite"). It was destroyed (510 B.C.) by the Pythagorean inhabitants of Croton. A second Sybaris rose upon the ruins of the first, but it never flourished, and was finally absorbed in the Athenian colony of Thurii (443 B.C.). Herodotus is said to have been one of the colonists. The site has been covered so deeply by earth eroded from the nearby hills that no sign of occupation appeared above ground, and archaeologists had searched in vain for its precise location, until in 1953 Donald F. Brown explored the plain with a coring tool and brought up specimens of datable pottery which established its position and approximate limits beyond reasonable doubt. The modern village near the site is Terranova di Sibari. (JJ)

Sybota (sib′o̯-ta̯). In ancient geography, a small town on the coast of Epirus, Greece, opposite the S end of Corcyra (Corfu). Near it was fought (432 B.C.) a naval battle between Corcyra (aided by Athens) and Corinth. The Corinthians won the sea fight, but withdrew the next day.

Sychaeus (si-kē′us). In Roman legend, a priest of Hercules in Tyre. He was Dido's husband, and was murdered by her brother Pygmalion for his wealth. After the murder he appeared to Dido in a dream and informed her of her brother's treachery. He warned her to flee the country and told her where his treasure was hidden so that she could take it with her. He was reunited with Dido in the Underworld. Sychaeus was sometimes also known as Acerbas.

Syennesis (si-en′e̯-sis). Name common to all the kings of Cilicia mentioned in history, especially that of a vassal of Persia, at the time of the expedition of Cyrus the Younger (401 B.C.).

Syleus (sil′e̯-us, -ūs). According to some accounts, a king in Aulis, but others say he lived in Lydia. He compelled passing strangers to work in his vineyard. Heracles, when he was in the service of Omphale, ravaged his vineyard and killed Syleus.

Syloson (sil′o̯-so̯n). A son of Aeaces, and the brother of Polycrates of Samos. Polycrates

seized the power in Samos and sent Syloson into exile. He went to Memphis in Egypt. It was while he was there that Cambyses made his successful expedition against Egypt and came to Memphis. According to Herodotus, one day Syloson, wearing a scarlet cloak, happened to go to the market-place. Darius, at that time a mere member of Cambyses' body-guard and with no particular prospects, chanced to see Syloson, admired his cloak, and asked if Syloson would sell it to him. Syloson, on impulse, said there was no price he would take for his cloak, but that he would freely give it to Darius and did so. After Darius had gained the throne of Persia, Syloson, still an exile, went to Susa and presented himself as a benefactor of the king. Darius could not think what Greek he was indebted to, and asked that the man who so described himself be brought to him. Syloson came before him and reminded him of the incident of the cloak. Darius remembered, and was the more grateful to Syloson because at the time when he made his gift he could not know that Darius would ever be in a position to do anything for him. He offered to give Syloson great gifts of gold and silver. But Syloson replied that he did not want gold and silver; he asked instead that Darius restore Samos to him, as his brother Polycrates was dead and the island was under the rule of a slave. Darius agreed to make him this gift. He sent forces to besiege Samos. They took it and it was restored to Syloson.

Sylvanus (sil-vā′nus). See **Silvanus**.

Symaethis (sim-ē′this). A sea-nymph, the mother by Faunus of Acis.

Syme (sī′mē). [Also: **Simi, Symi**.] Small island off the SW coast of Asia Minor, about 15 miles N of Rhodes.

Symplegades (sim-pleg′a̯-dēz). In Greek legend, two rocky cliffs at the entrance to the Euxine Sea. The ancients believed that they clashed together in order to crush any vessel that tried to pass between them. Legend has it that Jason's ship, the *Argo*, got safely through by sending a dove first, and slipping through quickly while the rocks were opening for the bird.

Symposium (sim-pō′zi-um), **The**. Philosophical dialogue by Plato, consisting of an account given by Aristodemus of a banquet at the house of the tragic poet Agathon after one of his victories. At the banquet, together with other less famous persons, Socrates, the physician Eryximachus, Aristophanes, and (in the latter part of the work) Alcibiades, discuss the nature and praise of Eros (love).

Symposium, The. Work by Xenophon, describing the character of Socrates.

Synnada (sin'a̱-da̱). [Modern name, **Eskikarahisar**.] Ancient city in Phrygia, famous for its ruins of old palaces. The city was known for its marble quarries, and from the time of Constantine was the capital of Phrygia Salutaris.

Syphax (sī'faks). King of the Massaesylians in W Numidia; died c201 B.C. He vacillated between Roman and Carthaginian alliances, and was often at war with Masinissa, but was finally allied with Carthage and married Sophonisba, daughter of Hasdrubal. He overran all of Numidia, but was defeated by Scipio in 203 B.C. and taken prisoner to Rome.

Syracuse (sir'a̱-kūs, -kūz). [Italian, **Siracusa**; Latin, **Syracusae**.] City of Sicily, situated on the island of Ortygia off the E coast of Sicily. In ancient times the largest and wealthiest city of Sicily, it was a Dorian city, founded (c734 B.C.) by Corinthian colonists under the leadership of Archias, on a site that was seized from earlier settlers. In the next century Syracuse began founding her own colonies in Sicily, and laid the foundations for the dominating position she attained among the Greek cities of the island. The government of the city was oligarchic and democratic by turns. Gelo (died c478 B.C.), tyrant of Gela, in answer to an appeal by Syracusan nobles who had been expelled by the people, made himself master and tyrant of Syracuse in 485 B.C. The splendid location of Syracuse made it a center of commerce and shipping. The island on which it stood was in the northeast part of a bay about five miles in circumference. Gelo connected the island by a causeway to Achradina, a mainland height on a promontory that commands the island. The island now became a peninsula that dropped down and enclosed the bay on the northeast. He built a wall that ran down to the bay across the promontory behind the fortified height of Achradina and enclosed it, the causeway, and

the island of Ortygia in one unit. The Great Harbor of Syracuse, as the bay became, was thus protected on the north by the citadel of the city on the island and by fortified Achradina, and on its southern side by the promontory called Plemmyrion. Safe inside the Great Harbor was anchorage for a vast number of ships. On the sea side of the causeway was another, smaller harbor. Gelo shifted at will populations from cities he had conquered to populate his enlarged city, giving the nobles he imported the citizenship and making slaves of the common people who were compelled to settle in Syracuse. He joined with Theron, tyrant of Acragas, to drive the Carthaginians out of Greek Sicily, and defeated them at Himera, 480 B.C. After his victory he brought Syracuse to a peak of power and prosperity and extended its dominion. Under his successor, his brother Hiero I (ruled 478–467 B.C.), who defeated the Etruscans and destroyed their influence in southern Italy, the magnificent court of

HEAD OF ARETHUSA, OR OF DEMARETA, WIFE OF GELON OF SYRACUSE
Silver decadrachm of Syracuse, struck to commemorate the victory of Gelon over Hamilcar at Himera, 479 B.C. *Museum of Fine Arts, Boston*

Syracuse attracted and welcomed such poets from the mainland of Greece as Aeschylus, Pindar, Simonides, and Bacchylides. Spiritual and cultural ties to the great shrines of Greece were jealously preserved by the thriving city in the west. Hiero I was followed

by his brother Thrasybulus, whose lack of capacity coupled with a harsh and cruel rule
precipitated a revolution. He was overthrown, a democratic government was established, and to celebrate freedom regained the
Syracusans set up a huge statue of Zeus
Eleutherius (*Deliverer*) and instituted annual
games in his honor. Syracuse flourished and
continued to expand, by colonizing and by extending its influence over neighboring areas,
until the great expedition (under Nicias,
Alcibiades, and Lamachus) was sent (415–
413 B.C.) from Athens to check the Syracusan
advance, to gain influence in Sicily, and as
an attack on Athens' enemy Corinth. The
Athenian expedition was a disaster for
Athens. The vast armament that set out
from Athens with such splendor and such
hope was completely destroyed. The prisoners taken by the Syracusans were set to work
in the huge quarries that are still a feature
of Syracuse.

Syracuse took its place now, not as the
equal of the cities of Greece, but as a strong
power to which they could turn, as did
Sparta, for assistance. Syracuse was triumphant, but greatly weakened by the long
struggle with Athens, and almost immediately
had to defend herself against attack from
Carthage. The democracy which had been
joyfully restored after the defeat of the
Athenians seemed unable to cope with the
Carthaginians. Dionysius I was named sole
general to counter the Carthaginian menace
(405 B.C.). The fortunes of Syracuse vis-à-vis
Carthage rose and fell. Dionysius made himself absolute ruler. In the course of his
reign he defended Syracuse from a siege by
the Carthaginians (397 B.C.), defeated them,
and drove them out of all but the western
corner of Sicily. Under Dionysius (c430–
367 B.C.), Syracuse became the most powerful
city in the Greek world, which is to say, the
most powerful state in Europe at the time.
At its greatest extent, the empire of Syracuse
included most of Sicily and the southern
part of the peninsula of Italy, into which
Dionysius had successfully penetrated. The
various parts of the empire were attached to
Syracuse in varying degrees of dependence,
alliance, and association. Dionysius enlarged and beautified the city, and improved
its defenses to make it the best fortified, as

well as the most magnificent, city in Sicily.
He also improved the docks and increased
the fleet to give Syracuse the strongest naval
force in the Mediterranean. In succeeding
years Syracuse suffered under the tyranny of
Dionysius the Younger (c395–after 343 B.C.),
son of Dionysius I, expelled him, and was
governed for a time by Dion (c408–353 B.C.),
a follower of Plato and a theoretical democrat
who had tried to make of Dionysius the
Younger a constitutional monarch. Syracuse
fell again to Dionysius the Younger, but was
then freed by Timoleon, a Corinthian general sent out by the mother city to free
Syracuse from tyranny and from an invading
Carthaginian force (343 B.C.). About 317
B.C. Agathocles (361–289 B.C.), with an
army of Campanian mercenaries and Greek
exiles, and with the encouragement of Carthage, made himself tyrant. He restored order to the city, which had been rocked by
revolution. Under Hiero II (c307–216 B.C.),
Syracuse enjoyed more than 50 years of
peace, and flourished greatly under his beneficent rule. In the First Punic War between
Rome and Carthage (264–241 B.C.; Syracuse
had suffered her own Punic Wars), Syracuse
was on the side of Rome, but Hieronymus
(grandson of Hiero II), finding Rome a
greater threat than Carthage ever was,
changed sides in the Second Punic War
(218–201 B.C.). He was dethroned in 215
B.C., and his family was murdered. Marcellus, the Roman consul and general, made
such demands that the Syracusans, abetted
by Carthage, determined to resist. Marcellus
laid siege to the city in 214 B.C. The city
was heroically defended; the inventions of
the great Archimedes played havoc with the
Roman ships in the Great Harbor. The city
held out until the defenders, weakened by
plague and lack of supplies, were compelled
to submit (211 B.C.). Marcellus allowed his
army to plunder the city, and many of its
treasures were carried off to Rome. Though
Marcellus had given strict orders to spare
and protect Archimedes, in the confusion he
was slain as, oblivious of the turmoil about
him, he worked out a problem in the sand.
Syracuse now became a Roman city in what
was ultimately the Roman province of Sicily.
Syracuse is famous for its Greek antiquities,
including, on the island of Ortygia, remains

of Doric temples of Apollo (6th century B.C.) and Athena (5th century B.C., the modern cathedral) that rest on foundations of even older temples. There are also a Greek theater, a Roman amphitheater, parts of walls and aqueducts, remains of a great fortress on the slope inland from Achradina, Roman houses, and numerous other remains. On the west side of the island of Ortygia is the celebrated fountain of Arethusa, which according to legend represents the nymph Arethusa. She fled the embraces of the river-god Alpheus and was transported to Syracuse by Artemis, where she was changed to a fountain. The river-god dove under the sea and came up in Ortygia to mingle his waters with those of the fountain of Arethusa. Through the marshes about Syracuse runs the stream Cyane. According to legend, the nymph Cyane saw Pluto (Hades) carrying off Proserpina (Persephone). She tried to persuade him to release Proserpina but he ignored her and plunged into the earth with his captive. Cyane wept so that she was changed into a fountain, the source of the stream.

Syria (sir′i-a). The region of this name described by the ancients lay probably between the Euphrates and the Mediterranean and between the N part of Arabia and the Taurus Mountains, and thus included Lebanon, Palestine, and Jordan. The inhabitants were Hittites, Arameans, Canaanites, Hebrews, and Phoenicians. (Sometimes lower Mesopotamia was included, and the names Assyria and Syria were used interchangeably by some ancient writers; this larger region is also called Aram in the Bible.) Syria became subject to Assyria c733 B.C. and was later under Babylon, Persia, and Macedon. Part of it was conquered by Seleucus Nicator and the name Syria was given to the whole realm of his descendants, the Seleucids, which had Antioch as its capital and embraced a great part of the Macedonian conquests in Asia. It was conquered by Pompey c65 B.C. and annexed to the Roman Empire.

Syrinx (sir′ingks). In Greek mythology, a mountain-nymph of Arcadia. She was a huntress, like the goddess Artemis, and like her wished to remain chaste. Pan caught sight of her one day on Mount Lycaeus and pursued her. The nymph fled through the forests until she came to the river Ladon. There she prayed to the nymphs of the stream to rescue her. Just as Pan grasped her she was transformed into reeds, and as the wind blew through them they gave off a gentle singing sound. Pan cut the reeds into unequal lengths and fastened them together into a Pan's pipe, or Syrinx.

Syrus (sī′rus) or **Syros** (sī′ros). [Also: **Siros, Syra.**] The most populous and richest island of the Cyclades. The philosopher Pherecydes, the teacher of Pythagoras, was born on the island, and a cave on the north of the island called the Grotto of Pherecydes, is said to have been his home. The chief town of the island is Hermoupolis, "Hermes' city." Area of the island, about 31 square miles; length, 11 miles.

Syrtis (sèr′tis). In ancient geography, a large embayment of the Mediterranean Sea, in Libya, the N coast of Africa. According to legend, it was a vast quicksand, where the *Argo* was driven by a great storm when the Argonauts were on their roundabout way home to Iolcus from Colchis.

T

Tabulae Heracleenses (tab′ū-lē her″a-klē-en′ sēz). Latin name of **Heraclean Tables.**

Tacitus (tas′i-tus), **Cornelius.** Roman historian, noted also as an orator; born c55 A.D.; died probably after 117. He was praetor in 88 and consul in 97. He was a friend of the younger Pliny. His extant works include *Dialogus de Oratoribus*, an "attempt to demonstrate and explain the decay of oratory in the imperial period, in the form of a dialogue between literary celebrities of the time of Vespasian"; a biography of his father-in-law Julius Agricola (*De Vita et Moribus Julii Agricolae*); the *Germania*, a celebrated ethnographical work on the Germans; the *Historiae,* a narrative of events in the reigns of Galba, Otho, Vitellius, Vespasian, Titus, and Domitian, of which only the first four books and the first half of the fifth book survive; and the *Annales,* a history of the Julian dynasty from the death of Augustus. Of the last work only by chance have parts survived. Originally in 16 or more books, books 1–6 depend upon a single manuscript, books 11–16 upon another single manuscript, and books 7–10 are lost. His style is compact, condensed to the utmost brevity, so that he has come to be regarded by students as a paragon of difficulty. He is devoted to objective truth, and takes rank as one of the world's most able writers on history.

Tacticus (tak'ti-kus), **Aeneas.** See **Aeneas Tacticus.**

Taenarus (tē'na̤-rus) or **Taenarum** (-rum). Locality, city, cape, and river, at the extremity of Laconia, Greece. Near the river in this locality, according to ancient legend, there was a back entrance to Tartarus which was used by those who evaded Hermes, the conductor of the dead to Tartarus, and by those who had no coin under their tongues to pay Charon to ferry them across the Styx. It was a cave-like temple. Some say Heracles brought up Cerberus from Hades through it. Theseus too was said to have used this entrance when he descended to Hades in quest of Persephone. Near here there was a spring. Formerly those who looked into it could see ships and harbors, but a woman washed dirty clothes in it, and after that nothing could be seen in its waters. There was also an oracle of the dead at Taenarus. To those who summoned them, the dead appeared while they were asleep and answered their questions. Some Spartan suppliants once fled to the sanctuary of Poseidon here, but were seized by the Spartans and put to death. For this impiety Sparta was shaken by earthquakes (464 B.C.).

Tages (tā'jēz). An Etruscan divinity, commonly represented as a beautiful youth.

Tainaron (te'nä-rôn). See **Taenarus.**

Talaemenes (tal-ē'me̤-nēz). Named by Homer *(Iliad),* as a Maeonian, the father of Mesthles and Antiphus, allies of Troy.

Talaria (ta̤-lā'ri-a̤). In classical mythology and archaeology, the sandals, bearing small wings, worn characteristically by Hermes or Mercury and often by Iris and Eos, and by other divinities, as Eros and the Furies and Harpies. In late or summary representations of the deity the sandals are sometimes omitted, so that the wings appear as if growing from the ankles, one on each side of the foot. Sometimes, especially in archaic examples, the talaria have the form of a sort of greaves bearing the wings much higher on the leg. They symbolize the faculty of swift and unimpeded passage through space.

Talaus (tā'lā̤-us). In Greek legend, a son of Bias and Pero and a great-grandson of Cretheus. He went from Argos to join Jason as one of the Argonauts, and was wounded in the battle with the Bebryces in the course of the journey. Talaus was the father of Adrastus, Mecisteus, and Eriphyle. He was killed by Amphiaraus in a war between the descendants of Bias and those of Melampus over control of the kingdom.

Talos (tā'los). [Also: **Perdix, Talus.**] In Greek mythology, a son of Polycaste, or Perdix, sister of Daedalus. He was an even more marvelous smith than Daedalus, to whom he had been apprenticed when he was ten years old. It is said that he invented the saw: using the spine of a fish as a model he cut teeth in an iron blade. He was also said to have invented the potter's wheel and the compass for describing circles. Daedalus was intensely jealous of his nephew's skill. His desire to destroy Talos was spurred, some say, by a rumor that Talos had incestuous relations with his mother. He lured Talos to the top of a tower and pushed him over. He then gathered up the corpse but was discovered before he could bury it. The soul of Talos was transformed into a partridge, a bird which does not soar on the heights, as Talos remembered his fall, but flutters near the earth and lays its eggs on or near the ground. His body was buried in Athens.

Talos. In Greek mythology, a man of bronze. Some say he was created by Hephaestus. Others say he was sprung from ash trees and that he was the last one left of the sons of the gods. He was entirely of bronze. In his ankle was a pin which stoppered the ichor that ran through his body in a single vein and sustained his life. Zeus gave him to

Europa to be the guardian of Crete. Three times a day he marched around the shore of Crete, inspecting for invaders. These he repelled by hurling great rocks at them or, if they came too close, he heated himself red-hot and burned them by clasping them in his arms. When Jason and Medea, returning to Iolcus from Colchis, sailed near the shores of Crete in the *Argo,* Talos prevented them from landing by hurling stones at them. Medea called to him and induced him to let them land by promising him a magic potion. Instead she gave him a sleeping draught, and while he slept she pulled out the pin in his ankle. All the life-giving ichor in Talos' single vein flowed out and he died. But others say Talos scraped his ankle against a rock and, the pin being loosened, he bled to death. Still others say he met his death when he was shot in the ankle by an arrow.

Talthybius (tal-thib'i-us). In Greek legend, Agamemnon's herald. He accompanied Menelaus and Odysseus to Cyprus to seek the aid of King Cinyras in the Trojan War. As Agamemnon's herald throughout the Trojan War he had many unpleasant missions to perform. It was he who went to bring Iphigenia to be sacrificed at Aulis. He fetched Briseis when she was taken from Achilles and given to Agamemnon to make up for the loss of Chryseis. He had to tell Hecuba, after the fall of Troy, that she was to be Odysseus' captive, that Cassandra would be taken by Agamemnon, and that Andromache would go to Neoptolemus. Talthybius, for all his gruesome message-bearing, seems to have been a compassionate man. He pitied the fallen queen, Hecuba. When it was his sad duty to tell her that Astyanax, her young grandson, must die, and that her daughter Polyxena must be sacrificed on Achilles' tomb, he shuddered for her sorrows and hoped he would die rather than fall so low as the once great queen had done. When Agamemnon was slain by Clytemnestra after the war, Talthybius, according to some accounts, took care of his young son Orestes and hid him from Aegisthus. According to some accounts, he emigrated to Crete and founded Tegea there. He died either at Mycenae or in Sparta. There was a shrine to him in Sparta and a family, said to have

been descended from him, had the hereditary function of state heraldry there.

Tammuz (tam'uz). [Also: **Thammuz**.] Ancient Babylonian god of agriculture, flocks, herds, and vegetation. He was beloved by Ishtar, who traveled into the Underworld to bring him back to earth. He personifies the life-giving powers of spring, and his annual death and resurrection symbolize the annual death and regrowth of vegetation. In his honor a feast was held every year, beginning with the new moon of the summer month Tammuz. This was a period of mourning for the death of Tammuz and a period of rejoicing for his rebirth. His story and his cult parallel those of the Phrygian Attis, the Egyptian Osiris, the Phoenician and Greek Adonis, the Old Norse Balder, and others.

TANAGRA FIGURINE
Berlin

Tanagra (tan'a-gra, ta-nag'ra). In ancient geography, a town of Boeotia, Greece, situated near the Asopus River, about 24 miles NW of Athens. The inhabitants in ancient times claimed descent from Apollo and Poseidon, and said their town was named for Tanagra, a daughter of Aeolus or, as some say, of the river-god Asopus. Among the temples of Tanagra in antiquity were those of Themis, Apollo, Aphrodite, Hermes, and Dionysus. In the last was a marble image of the god by the sculptor Calamis. There was also an image of a headless Triton. According to legend, a Triton attacked the women of Tanagra when they went to bathe in the sea to purify themselves before celebrating the rites of Dionysus. The women called on the god to protect them; he came and killed the Triton after a great struggle. But others say the Triton used to come from the sea and attack the cattle of the Tanagraeans. To catch him, a bowl of wine was set on the beach. The Triton drank of it and fell into a drunken slumber on the sand, whereupon a man of Tanagra cut off his head. Some say the tomb of Orion was at Tanagra. The tomb of the lyric poetess Corinna was also there, with a painting depicting her binding her hair with the victor's crown after a contest with Pindar. A victory was gained here in 457 B.C. by the Spartans over the Athenians and their allies. Its extensive necropolis has made this obscure town famous, for from it came (c1874) the first of the charming Tanagra figurines of terra-cotta which drew attention to the antiquities of this type. Such figurines, previously ignored, have since been eagerly sought and found in great quantities not only at Tanagra but upon a great number of sites in all parts of the Greek world.

Tanais (tan'a̱-is). Ancient Greek (Milesian) colony near the head of the Palus Maeotis. The colony dates from c500 B.C. and was probably founded by settlers from Panticapaeum.

Tanais. [Modern name, **Don.**] In ancient geography, a river of Scythia, flowing generally south to empty into the Palus Maeotis. A trade route to Central Asia was said to follow the valley of this river.

Tanaquil (tan'a̱-kwil). In Roman legend, the wife of Tarquinius Priscus (q.v.), fifth king of Rome.

Tanarus (tan'a̱-rus). [Modern name, **Tanaro.**] River in NW Italy. It rises in the Ligurian Alps and empties into the Po.

Tanit (tä'nit). [Also: **Tanith.**] Carthaginian goddess, identified with the Phoenician mother goddess, Astarte. The Greeks identified her with their own goddess Aphrodite.

The Romans confused her with Juno, the reason being that as goddess of women and childbirth she resembled Juno in her Lucina aspect. Tanit possessed also the same moon-goddess aspect as her counterpart Astarte.

Tantalus (tan'ta̱-lus). In Greek mythology, some say Tantalus was a son of Zeus, or of Tmolus, the god of Mount Tmolus in Libya. Others say he was a king of Argos or of Corinth, or of Sipylus in Libya. He was the father of Pelops, Niobe, and Broteas. Tantalus was most fortunate in being on intimate terms with the gods and dined often at their table. But he abused the confidence of the gods. He stole the nectar and ambrosia on which they fed, and which confers immortality on those who partake of it, and gave it to his mortal friends. He also, according to some accounts, committed a horrible crime. When the gods were invited to dine with him, he cut up his son Pelops and boiled the pieces in a cauldron. Some say he served the gods this gruesome meal to test their omniscience. The gods were instantly aware of the contents of the dish set before them and all, except Demeter, refused to eat of it. She was so preoccupied with her grief over the disappearance of her daughter Persephone that she distractedly ate part of the left shoulder. Pindar, on the other hand, says that Poseidon had fallen in love with Pelops and stolen him away. Zeus punished Tantalus for his ingratitude for the favors bestowed on him by the gods by destroying his kingdom. Tantalus then committed a third crime. Zeus had been guarded in his infancy by a golden dog made by Hephaestus. It was stolen by Pandareus and given into Tantalus' hands for safe-keeping. When Pandareus came to claim the dog, Tantalus swore by Zeus that he knew nothing about it. Zeus heard that Tantalus had taken an oath in his name and sent Hermes to investigate. On learning that the oath was false, he crushed Tantalus under a huge stone on Mount Sipylus. Some say, however, that Tantalus stole the golden dog himself, and that Pandareus was the receiver. But the fact remains that Tantalus swore falsely in the name of Zeus that he knew nothing of the matter. Zeus continues to torment Tantalus in Tartarus, the Underworld. For his first two crimes he is condemned to stand forever in water up to his neck, but whenever he stoops to drink of it, the water recedes. Around him grow trees bearing luscious fruits, but when he stretches a hand to eat one of them, they sway beyond his reach. For his third crime, a huge stone perches constantly over his head, ever on the verge of falling and crushing him. It is from Tantalus, and his fate of ever having food and drink just beyond his grasp, that the word "tantalize" is derived.

Tantalus. In Greek legend, a son of Broteas. He was a king of Pisa. He was married to Clytemnestra, daughter of Tyndareus of Sparta, and had one son by her. Agamemnon attacked Pisa, killed Tantalus and his infant son, and forced Clytemnestra to marry him. The bones of Tantalus were buried in a large bronze vessel at Argos.

Taormina (tä-ôr-mē′nä). See **Tauromenium**.

Taphiae (tā′fi-ē). [Also: **Teleboides**.] In ancient geography, a group of the Ionian Islands W of Acarnania, Greece. Homer called the people of the islands "Lovers of the oar." The Taphians raided the cattle of Electryon, father of Alcmene, and killed eight of his sons. Amphitryon, husband of Alcmene, raised an army, marched against the Taphians, defeated them, and gave their lands to his allies.

Taphius (tā′fi-us). In Greek legend, a son of Hippothoë (granddaughter of Perseus) and Poseidon. He was born in the Echinades islands. He went to the island of Taphos, colonized it, and called the people Teleboans, because he had gone "far from his native land." His son was Pterelaus, who was made immortal by Poseidon with a gift of one golden, or purple, lock of hair which rendered him invulnerable.

Taranis (tar′a-nis). Ancient thunder god of Gaul, identified by the Romans with their own Jupiter. He is said to have been worshiped with human sacrifices.

Taranto (tä-rän′tō). See **Tarentum**.

Taraxippus (ta-rak-sip′us). In Greek antiquity, a pillar shaped like a round altar at the turning-point of the course in the hippodrome at Olympia, which was believed mysteriously to terrify the competing horses, and thus cause the frequent accidents at this point of the course. Some say Taraxippus, "Horse-scarer," was Olenius, an Elean skilled in

horsemanship; others say he was Dameon, who accompanied Heracles against Augeas and was killed with his horse by Cteatus, son of Actor, who buried man and horse together. And some say that on this spot Pelops sacrificed to Myrtilus, whom he had murdered and cast into the sea, and named the empty mound he raised "Taraxippus" because of the trick by which Myrtilus frightened the horses of Oenomaus and allowed Pelops to win the race for his daughter Hippodamia's hand. Others say Taraxippus is Oenomaus himself; and still others say it is Alcathous, one of the suitors of Hippodamia, who met his death here in the race with Oenomaus for her hand, and who out of spite frightens the horses of all other racers. Whoever Taraxippus was, he was thought to frighten the horses in chariot races unless propitiated by the sacrifices which charioteers carefully offered him before their races.

Taraxippus. Said by some to be the ghost of Glaucus, the owner of mares that he refused to allow to breed and by which he was torn to pieces. It was said to haunt the Isthmus of Corinth and frighten horses at the Isthmian Games, causing the death of many charioteers. Others said Taraxippus was a dwarflike spirit that rode behind men on horseback and frightened their horses. It was thought to be the spirit of a rider or driver who had been killed, and sacrifices were offered to propitiate it.

Tarchetius (tär-kē′ti-us). In Roman legend, a king of Alba Longa. He was haunted by a phantom that emerged from his hearth, and was told that if his daughter married the phantom, the child of their union would become famous. When his daughter refused and sent a maid in her place, Tarchetius, enraged, was on the point of killing both but was warned by Vesta in a dream to spare them. Twins were born to the maid, who gave them to Teratius to protect them from Tarchetius. Teratius left them near a stream and they were nursed by a wolf and fed by birds until they were found and cared for by a shepherd. When they grew up, they overthrew Tarchetius. This story, told by Plutarch, is one of several variants of the story of Romulus and Remus and the subsequent founding of Rome.

Tarchon (tär′kon). In Roman legend, a Lydian

who went to Italy with Tyrrhenus and founded the Etruscan race. He gave his name to the city of Tarquinii and later, as leader of the Etruscans, he agreed to help Aeneas in his war against Turnus and the Latins.

Tarentinus Sinus (ta-ren-tī'nus sī'nus). [Modern name, **Gulf of Taranto**.] Arm of the Mediterranean, on the S coast of Italy. It separates the "heel" of the peninsula from the "toe," projecting into the "foot" about 85 miles.

Tarentum (ta-ren'tum). [Also: **Taras**; modern name, **Taranto**.] In ancient geography, a city of SE Italy, situated on a sheltered harbor on the N coast of the Gulf of Tarentum. The ancient name of Taras was given to it, according to some accounts, in honor of a son of Poseidon of that name. According to tradition, this ancient Dorian city was founded by Phalanthus, c707 B.C., who led a colony across the sea from Laconia and raised the city. It prospered, owing to its fertile soil, its protected harbor, and its manufacture of fabrics, dyed wools, and pottery, which were known throughout the Mediterranean area. Tarentum established colonies of her own on the east coast of Italy, and became the most powerful city of Magna Graecia. In the 4th century B.C. the city was threatened by the Lucanians, appealed to Sparta for aid, and received a force from there under the command of King Archidamus. The Spartan expedition was ineffectual. King Archidamus fell in battle (338 B.C.). Tarentum next appealed to Alexander of Epirus, uncle of Alexander the Great. He beat back the Italian tribes with great energy. The speed and vigor with which he established his control came to seem a greater threat to Tarentum than the Italian tribes had been. However, having greatly weakened the enemies of Tarentum, Alexander was treacherously slain and Tarentum was freed from both native and foreign threats for a time. At the beginning of the 3rd century B.C. the growing power of Rome became a menace. The Tarentines invited Pyrrhus, king of Epirus, to come and command them in a war against Rome. He arrived to find the city luxuriating in its wealth and making no great effort to arm itself for the coming war. After great but costly successes against Rome,

Pyrrhus went to Sicily. Tarentum was defeated by the Romans, 272 B.C., and became a Roman ally. In the Second Punic War the city was captured by Hannibal. It was taken (209 B.C.) and plundered by Fabius Cunctator, thanks to betrayal by some Bruttians in the city. Fabius slew many of the Tarentines and sold 30,000 others into slavery. Among the spoils which he removed from the city was a statue of Heracles. This he sent to Rome and caused it to be set up near a statue of himself. In 123 B.C. the city was colonized by Rome with the new name Colonia Neptunia, and an attempt was made to revive its industry. Architectural remains of antiquity include a Doric temple on an island in the harbor, and a Roman aqueduct.

Targitaus (tär-gi-tā'us). Said by some to have been a son of Zeus and a daughter of the river-god Borysthenes. He was said to have been the first inhabitant of Scythia. His sons were Arpoxaïs, Lipoxaïs, and Colaxaïs, the legendary founders of several Scythian tribes.

Tarne (tär'nē). In the *Iliad*, another name for Sardis, the capital of Lydia.

Tarpeia (tär-pē'a). In Roman legend, daughter of Spurius Tarpeius, governor of the citadel of Rome on the Capitoline Hill. Following the rape of the Sabine women by Romulus, Titus Tatius, king of the Sabines, waged war on Rome. Tarpeia, a vestal virgin, was accustomed to go outside the citadel to fetch water from the sacred spring of the Camenae. She was approached by Titus Tatius who bribed her with gold to admit armed men into the fortress. Some say she betrayed the fortress to the Sabines in return for "what they wore on their left arms." She meant their gold bracelets, but as they entered, the Sabines cast their shields upon her (which they also bore on their left arms) and she was crushed to death. The Tarpeian Rock was named for her.

Tarpeian Rock (tär-pē'an). [Latin, **Mons Tarpeius**.] Originally, the name of the entire Capitoline Hill in Rome, or at least of the peak occupied by the citadel, in memory of the treason of Tarpeia in connection with the Sabine siege; later, that part (*Rupes Tarpeia*) of the cliff of the Capitoline over whose precipice, according to tradition, con-

actor; up, lūte, pull; oi, oil; ou, out; ᴛʜ, then; ḍ as d or j, ş as s or sh, ṭ as t or ch, ẓ as z or zh.

demned criminals were hurled; now unrecognizable owing to artificial and natural
changes in the rocks.

Tarquinii (tär-kwin′i-ī). [Former name, **Cor-
neto Tarquinia**; modern name, **Tarquinia**.]
City in Latium, in C Italy, about 44 miles
NW of Rome. Its name derives from Tarchon, the Etruscan ally of Aeneas. The
town, surrounded by walls and fortifications,
has numerous Etruscan and Roman antiquities, and a necropolis of great interest, containing notable murals. One of the 12 chief
Etruscan cities, it submitted to Roman rule
in the 3rd century B.C. In Roman legend
it was the original residence of Tarquinius
Priscus.

Tarquinius Collatinus (tär-kwin′i-us kol-a-tī′-
nus). In Roman legend, the husband of
Lucretia, and a kinsman of Tarquinius Superbus. His wife was ravished by Tarquinius
Sextus, son of Tarquinius Superbus. The
outrage precipitated revolt against the Tarquins and they were driven out of Rome
(509 B.C.). The kings of Rome were succeeded by two consuls. Lucius Junius Brutus who led the revolt was one, and Tarquinius Collatinus as the man who had most
reason to hate Tarquinius Superbus and his
family was the other. Some say that Tarquinius resigned his consulship and withdrew
from Rome because he had appeared too mild
in punishing the conspirators who sought to
restore Tarquinius Superbus, and thus he
earned the distrust of the Romans. Others
say the Romans hated the very name Tarquinius and had no confidence in Collatinus
because of his family connections. Their
uneasiness reached such proportions that Brutus sought to quiet them by asking Collatinus
to leave Rome. "Depart, our friend . . ."
he is said to have urged, "the people are
persuaded that with the family of Tarquinius
the kingship will vanish from among us."
Collatinus was astonished at the evidence of
distrust. However, since Brutus promised
that he could take his possessions with him
and would even add to them if they were insufficient, Collatinus decided it was better
to go before the temper of the people became
dangerous and forced him to flee empty-
handed. He resigned his consulship and
retired to Lavinium.

Tarquinius Priscus (pris′kus), **Lucius.** In Ro-

man tradition, the fifth king of Rome. He
succeeded Ancus Marcius and was said to
have reigned 616–578 B.C. Mistakenly
called, in Roman accounts, Lucumo, which
was a title given to Etruscan princes and
priests, he was the son of Demaratus, a Greek
from Corinth who had gone as a colonist to
the Etruscan city of Tarquinii. A man of
great wealth, his wife was Tanaquil, a woman
of exalted birth, intelligence and ambition.
She persuaded him to leave Tarquinii, where
the Etruscans denied him the honor due him
because they regarded him as an alien up-
start, and remove to Rome, a new and growing city where he could achieve a position
of power and influence. When they reached
the Janiculum at Rome, an eagle flew down,
plucked off his cap, and flew up to heaven
with it. The eagle circled, dived, and gently
placed the cap back on his head. Tanaquil,
expert at augury, was delighted with the
omen of greatness brought by the eagle from
Jupiter. They continued into the city and
took a house there. In Rome he adopted
the new name of Lucius Tarquinius Priscus.
He quickly made many friends with his generosity and courtesy, and soon became an intimate friend of the king, who consulted
him on many matters and named him as
guardian of his children. When the king
died, Tarquinius sent his sons, now young
men, off on a hunting expedition and urged
the Comitia to choose a king without delay.
He was unanimously chosen by the Comitia.
One of his first acts was to double the size
of the Senate in order to be sure of senators
favorable to himself. Tarquinius Priscus
marked out the Circus Maximus; defeated
the Latins again and took much booty and
many cities from them; defeated the Sabines
and added their city of Collatia to Rome;
drained the marshes about Rome and built
the original *cloacae* (sewers); undertook the
work of raising a wall about Rome; and laid
the foundations for a temple of Jupiter on
the Capitol, as he had vowed to do during
the Sabine war. The sons of Ancus had
never been reconciled to the fact that Tarquinius succeeded their father. They plotted
against him, and sent two desperate shepherds to see him on the pretense that the
shepherds wished him to settle a dispute.
According to plan, the shepherds quarreled

violently before Tarquinius. Having listened to one of them, he turned his head to hear the other; the first shepherd took that opportunity to cleave his head with an ax, and Tarquinius died shortly thereafter.

Tarquinius, Sextus. Youngest son of Tarquinius Superbus. He was sent to Gabii by his father, who had failed to take that city by storm. According to some accounts, he told the Gabini he was fleeing the harshness of his father, and so won their confidence that they awarded him a position of great power in their councils. He continually urged the Gabini to make forays against Rome, and in these he was the leader. According to plan, the Gabini were successful in these raids and the reputation of Sextus became so great that his was the most influential voice in the city. He sent an envoy to his father, so the story goes, telling him he was now in control of Gabii and asking his father for instructions. In a procedure reminiscent of that of Thrasybulus, tyrant of Miletus, replying to Periander (c625–585 B.C.), tyrant of Corinth, Tarquinius is said to have refused to utter a word to the envoy of Sextus. Instead he walked about his garden with him, knocking off the heads of the tallest poppies that grew there. When the envoy returned and described his actions, Sextus knew he was to get rid of the leading men in Gabii. This he did by means of false charges, murders, and exile. Thereupon he delivered an unresisting city to Tarquinius. Later, when the Romans were besieging the Rutulian city of Ardea, Sextus and other young nobles fell to discussing the virtues of their wives. On the suggestion of Tarquinius Collatinus they agreed to ride to Rome and surprise their wives. Lucretia, wife of Collatinus, was found to be industriously engaged with her maids in household tasks. The other wives were feasting and amusing themselves. Lucretia easily won the palm for being the most virtuous of the wives. Sextus was aroused not only by her beauty but also by her reputation for chastity. He returned to her house in Collatia some nights later by himself. Lucretia received him graciously as a colleague and kinsman of her husband. During the night he entered her chamber and ravished her, after threatening that if she did not submit, he would kill

her and lay the naked body of a slave beside her so that she would appear convicted of adultery in its vilest form. When Sextus left her, she sent for her husband and her father, revealed what had happened and, adjuring them to avenge her, committed suicide. This deed of Sextus precipitated the revolt against the Tarquins and resulted in their expulsion from Rome (509 B.C.). Sextus fled to Gabii, but there, because of his former cruelties and betrayals, he was put to death by the outraged Gabini.

Tarquinius Superbus (sö-pėr′bus), **Lucius.** In Roman tradition, the seventh and last king of Rome (534–510 B.C.); son of Tarquinius Priscus, and son-in-law of Servius Tullius. In the traditional account he was married to Tullia, daughter of Servius Tullius. His brother Aruns was also married to a daughter of Servius Tullius, who was also named Tullia. According to some accounts, Tullia, wife of Aruns, was ruthless and ambitious; her husband was neither. Tullia, wife of Lucius Tarquinius, was of the same mild disposition as Aruns. Tullia, wife of Aruns, contrived the murder of her husband and of her sister, and married her brother-in-law, Lucius Tarquinius. Some say she continually urged him to seek the throne which, she claimed, her own father occupied unjustly. Lucius Tarquinius was of the same mind. He won many young Romans to his side by extravagant promises and with this backing went to the Senate House and seated himself on the throne. When Servius, now an old man, hurried to the Senate and challenged him, he seized the aged king, carried him out of the chamber, and flung him into the street. In the confusion, the aides of Servius were scattered or fled. At Tullia's suggestion, some say, Tarquinius sent agents to pursue Servius as he made his way alone through the streets and slay him. Later Tullia, on her way home, drove her chariot over her dead father's body. With the supporters he won to his side, Tarquinius made himself master of Rome. He immediately showed his cruelty by refusing to permit the burial of his father-in-law's body. One of his first acts was to demand a bodyguard, lest another attempt to seize power, as he had successfully done. To consolidate his power he tried capital offenses himself without the assistance of advisers. Thus he assumed the power of life and death over his enemies. He reduced the Senate by bringing charges against many of its members, sentencing some to death and others to exile, and seizing their property in either case. He broke with the tradition that the king consult the Senate, and he made war, signed treaties, and concluded peace without referring to that body. In order to strengthen himself outside Rome he made friends with the cities of the Latin peoples. By bribery and fraud he secured the death of the one Latin leader who dared speak against him, Turnus Herdonius. For his arrogant flaunting of traditional Roman forms and his tyrannical acts, Tarquinius was given the name Superbus, "the Proud." Tarquinius began the wars against the Volsci, which continued intermittently for the next 200 years. He seized Pometia from them. He waged war on Gabii, but when he could not storm the city, according to Livy, he resorted to guile. He sent his youngest son, Sextus, as his agent. Sextus went to Gabii as a suppliant, claiming that his father was as harsh to his children as he was to his subjects, and asked asylum of the Gabini. The Gabini were completely taken in by his words, admitted him to their city, and gradually gave him such power that he was able to deliver the city to Tarquinius without a struggle. Tarquinius also made peace with the Aequi, made an alliance with the Etruscans, and sent out colonists from Rome to Signia and Circeii. In Rome he engaged on a vast program of public works, among which was a temple of Jupiter which he proposed to raise with the plunder from the Volscian city of Pometia. All the ancient shrines, except that of Terminus, on the Capitol were moved, so that the place would clearly belong to Jupiter. The Romans became restless under the harsh rule of Tarquinius. In the palace a prodigy occurred when a snake glided out of a wooden pillar. Tarquinius dared not entrust the interpretation of such a prodigy to the Etruscan soothsayers who usually performed this service, and sent his sons Titus and Aruns to Delphi. According to legend, the priestess told them he who first kissed his mother would become king of Rome. Lucius Junius Brutus, their cousin who accompanied them,

on hearing this pretended to stumble, fell, and kissed the earth, the Great Mother. During a siege of Ardea, a city of the Rutulians, Sextus, the youngest son of Tarquinius Superbus, rode to Collatia and there ravished Lucretia, wife of Tarquinius Collatinus. She called her husband and her father to her, revealed what had happened, asked them to punish the criminal, and then plunged a dagger into her breast. Lucius Junius Brutus, who was present, lifted the dagger, dripping with Lucretia's blood, and swore to pursue and drive out of Rome Tarquinus Superbus, his wife, and his evil children. A similar oath was sworn by the others present. They carried the corpse of Lucretia to the market-place in Collatia. A great crowd gathered, and all who saw Lucretia's body remembered some evil Tarquinius Superbus had brought to him. Brutus urged them to take up arms and march on Rome. They did so, and a crowd gathered in the Forum. Brutus, who had always appeared slow-witted, amazed the assemblage with an impassioned speech calling for the expulsion of the Tarquins. Meanwhile, Tarquinius Superbus, at Ardea, learned what was going forward. He hurriedly set out for Rome but found the gates barred against him on arrival. He went into exile at Caere but by no means gave up his hopes of returning to Rome as king. A plot to kill the consuls who succeeded him as rulers of Rome failed. He appealed for aid to the people of Tarquinii and Veii. They sent forces to help him but they were defeated by the Romans under the consul Publius Valerius (Publicola), in a battle in which Brutus, the first consul, was killed. Tarquinius next sought aid from Lars Porsena of Clusium, the most powerful of the Etruscan kings. The forces of Lars Porsena besieged Rome. This action ended after some months in a peace treaty between Rome and Lars Porsena. Tarquinius again appealed to Lars Porsena, but this time, after parley with eminent Romans, Lars Porsena refused him aid, and said he would no longer give him asylum. Tarquinius Superbus went to the Latin city of Tusculum to live with his son-in-law. About 500 B.C., in a war between the Romans and Latins, he took part and was wounded at Lake Regillus. He never regained power in Rome, and died, some say, at Cumae, 495 B.C.

Tarracina (tar-a-sī′na). [Also: **Anxur**; modern name, **Terracina**.] In ancient geography, a town of C Italy, situated on the Mediterranean Sea about 58 miles SE of Rome. It was an ancient Volscian town and was taken by the Romans in 406 B.C. Roman remains include the ancient forum, whose original paving survives as the paving of the piazza in front of the cathedral (the dedicatory inscription, A. AEMILIVS.A.F., can be clearly read in the channels cut for the inlay of bronze letters, though the letters themselves were long ago pried up as scrap metal); a temple on whose foundations stands the cathedral; another temple, of the Augustan or post-Augustan period, with three cellas, exposed by World War II bombing; extensive city walls of polygonal limestone masonry of various periods, the earliest probably to be referred to the founding of a Roman citizen colony in 329 B.C.; paved stretches of the Via Appia; tombs; on the hill above the city, further fortification walls of concrete and rubble ("opus incertum") of c100 B.C., and the imposing substructure of a large temple of Jupiter Anxur, of about the same date; on the shore road just east of the city is a famous piece of Roman engineering—the scarp or vertical cut in the rock face made to permit the Via Appia to pass at sea level. (JJ).

Tarsus (tär′sus). In ancient geography, the capital of Cilicia, Asia Minor, situated on the Cydnus River. It was an important city in the Persian period, became partly Hellenized and the seat of a school of philosophy, and received important concessions from the Romans. It was the birthplace of the apostle Paul.

Tartarus (tär′ta-rus). In Greek mythology, an earth-god; some say he came into being after Gaea, but others say he was the child of Gaea and Aether (Air). By Gaea he was the father of the monster Typhon.

Tartarus. Deep and sunless abyss, according to Homer and also to earlier Greek mythology, situated in the lowest region of the Underworld. Here Zeus imprisoned the rebel Titans. Later poets described Tartarus as the place in which the wicked were punished.

Sometimes the name is synonymous with the lower world in general.

Tartessus (tär-tes′us). In ancient geography, a city and region in the SW part of the Iberian Peninsula, near the Pillars of Hercules. It was noted for its commerce. It is associated with Gades (modern Cádiz) and also with the Biblical Tarshish.

Tatius (tā′shus), **Titus.** In Roman legend, a king of the Sabines who attacked Rome after the rape of the Sabine women. The women, however, brought about a reconciliation, and Tatius is said to have ruled thereafter conjointly with Romulus.

Taura (tôr′a). In Roman mythology, a sterile cow, such an animal being sacred to the infernal gods.

Tauri (tô′rī) or **Taurians** (tô′ri-anz). An ancient warlike and barbarous people dwelling in the Chersonesus Taurica (Crimea), thought by some to have been the same as the Cimmerians. According to some accounts, when Iphigenia was about to be sacrificed at Aulis in order to appease Artemis and bring favorable winds for the Greek fleet on its way to Troy, she was miraculously spirited away and a hind was left in her place. She was transported to the Taurians by Artemis and became a priestess in her temple there. As described by Herodotus, the Taurians worshiped Artemis in the following manner. They offered as sacrifice to the virgin goddess all strangers who were shipwrecked on their coasts, and all Greeks who were forced by the weather to put into their harbors. After the victim was made ready, he was struck on the head with a club. His head was severed from his body and nailed to a cross, while the body was hurled from the cliff on which the temple stood into the sea, or as some said, the body was buried. In the time of Herodotus, the Taurians claimed that the goddess to whom they sacrificed these victims was Iphigenia, the daughter of Agamemnon. When a Taurian took a captive in war, he cut off his head, carried it to his house and nailed it to a tall pole above the house, so that thereafter the whole house was under the protection of the captive's head.

Taurian Games (tô′ri-an). [Also: **Tarentine** or **Terentine Games**.] Name under the Roman republic for the games called secular (*ludi* *saeculares*) under the empire.

Taurica (tô-ri-ka̤), **Chersonesus**. An ancient name of the Crimea (peninsula).

Taurini (tô-rī′nī). Ancient Ligurian people which dwelt in the valley of the upper Po, Italy.

Taurisci (tô-ris′ī). Celtic people which dwelt in the ancient Roman province of Noricum in the Alps. The Taurisci were the chief tribe of the region and became tributary to Rome c35 B.C.

Tauromenium (tô-rō-mē′ni-um). [Modern name, **Taormina**.] In ancient geography, a city on the NE coast of Sicily, just N of Mount Aetna. It was founded by the Carthaginian general, Himilco, 397 B.C., on the hills above the old Greek city of Naxos which had been destroyed by Dionysius the Elder of Syracuse. Himilco intended it as a stronghold for the Sicels and as a bastion against the Greeks. A few years later it was unsuccessfully besieged by Dionysius, to whom it was ultimately awarded, 392 B.C., in the conclusion of a peace treaty with Carthage. Dionysius settled his mercenaries there. After the death of Dionysius it became independent and received (358 B.C.) the former inhabitants of Naxos within its walls to revive ancient Naxos in Tauromenium. In the Punic Wars between Rome and Carthage it was allied with Rome. It was a place of refuge for the rebellious slaves in the Roman civil war, and in the reign of Augustus it became a Roman colony. There are architectural remains of antiquity, especially two Roman theaters, one of which rests on Greek foundations, remains of a 3rd-century B.C. Greek temple, known as the temple of Serapis, into which the church of S. Pancrazio has been built, and walls, houses, and tombs of the Roman period. The modern city of Taormina, on the ancient site, is famous for the magnificent views it commands of Mount Aetna to the south and the mountains of Calabria across the sea in the Italian peninsula.

Taurus (tô′rus). According to a Cretan story, Taurus was a general under King Minos. At funeral games held for Androgeus, Taurus won all the contests he entered. The prizes which he won were Athenian youths and maidens sent every nine years as tribute to Minos to atone for the death of his son

Androgeus. Thus, according to the Cretans, there was no Minotaur, part man and part bull, who devoured the young Athenians, but a powerful and arrogant general, whose name means "bull," who won the Athenians as prizes and employed them as slaves. When Theseus came as part of the tribute, he asked permission to take part in the contests. Minos was annoyed with the arrogance of Taurus and in addition suspected him of an intrigue with Queen Pasiphaë (this accounts for the story that Pasiphaë loved a bull). He gladly gave Theseus his permission to compete in the games, and was delighted when Theseus three times hurled Taurus to the ground in a wrestling match. He rewarded Theseus by giving him the young Athenians who had been sent to Crete as tribute, and allowed them to depart with him.

TAURUS
Pictured according to ancient descriptions.

Taurus. The second sign of the zodiac—the Bull—which the sun enters about the 20th of April. Also, a zodiacal constellation representing the forward part of a bull. It contains the star Aldebaran of the first magnitude, and the striking group of the Pleiades.

Taurus Mountains. Great mountain range in Asia Minor, along the S coast. It extends from the SW extremity of the peninsula to near the NE angle of the Mediterranean Sea.

fat, fāte, fär, fãre, errạnt; net, mē, hér ardẹnt; pin, pīne; not, nōte, mȯve, nôr,

The Anti-Taurus is an offshoot to the NE. The chief pass is known as the Cilician Gates. Highest point, about 12,250 feet.

Taxila (tak'si-lạ). In ancient geography, a city in the Punjab, India, in the vicinity of the modern Rawalpindi. Alexander the Great reached it, 326 B.C., in his march into India, and was obsequiously received.

Taxiles (tak'si-lēz). Indian king in the Punjab who received Alexander the Great, 326 B.C., on his march into India. His real name was Omphis, but he was called Taxiles after his city, Taxila.

Taxiles. Leading general of Mithridates VI; fl. in the 1st century B.C.

Taÿgete (tā-ij'ẹ-tē). In Greek mythology, a daughter of Pleione and Atlas; one of the Pleiades. She was transformed into a hind by Artemis so that she could escape the pursuit of Zeus. In gratitude, she dedicated a hind to Artemis, which some say was the Cerynean Hind captured by Heracles. Zeus discovered Taÿgete's disguise and ravished her. She became the mother of Lacedaemon and then hanged herself on the mountain which thereafter bore her name, Mount Taÿgetus. With her sisters', her image was placed among the stars. See **Pleiades.**

Taÿgetus (tā-ij'ẹ-tus). Highest mountain range in the Peloponnesus, Greece. It is situated in the W part of Laconia, on the border between Laconia and Messenia, extending into Arcadia. Length, 70 miles; highest point, Hagios Elias (about 7903 feet). The mountain was named for the Pleiad Taÿgete who bore Lacedaemon to Zeus. On one of the peaks, sacred to Helius, horses were sacrificed by the Spartans. On the wild slopes, haunt of deer, bears, wild goats, and other animals, weak and sickly Spartan infants were exposed to die, so that the state would not have the burden of rearing any children that would not be fit soldiers.

Tearless Battle. Battle (367 B.C.) between the allied Arcadians and Argives on one side and the Spartans on the other: so called because the Spartans did not lose a man as they inflicted great loss on the Arcadians and drove them back.

Tecmessa (tek-mes'ạ). In Greek legend, a daughter of Teuthras, a king in Thrace. Telamonian Ajax attacked her father's city, killed him, and carried off Tecmessa as his concubine along with rich treasure. She was treated with all the honor due a wife and loved him dearly. She bore him one son, Eurysaces.

Tectamus (tek'tạ-mus). In Greek legend, a son of Dorus; he is said to have taken a colony to Crete, where he became the father of that Asterius who ultimately married Europa.

Tegea (tē'jẹ-ạ). In ancient geography, a city in E Arcadia, Greece. The Tegeans said that it was originally the land around their city that was named for Tegeates, son of Lycaon, and that the city itself, also named for him, was founded by Aleus. Tegea was the site of a famous temple of Athena Alea, founded by Aleus. The ancient temple was burned, c394 B.C., and as restored by Scopas it was a Doric peripteros of six by 13 columns, measuring 72 by 154 feet. There were many sanctuaries, as of Aphrodite, Artemis, Demeter and the Maid, and many images. In the sanctuary of Ilithyia was an image of "Auge on her Knees," because, some say, when Aleus gave her to Nauplius to take her off and drown her because she had profaned the temple of Athena Alea with Heracles, she fell on her knees before the temple of Ilithyia and gave birth to a son. But others tell a different tale. Most of the altars of the Tegeans stood on a lofty site in their city, and here the Tegeans feasted annually.

Men of Tegea went to join the Greeks in the war against Troy under the command of Agapenor, son of Ancaeus the Argonaut. The Tegeans were the first of the Arcadians to defeat the Lacedaemonians. Charillus, king of Sparta, deceived by an oracle into thinking he could conquer Tegea, took fetters with which to bind his Tegean prisoners and attacked Tegea. His attack was unsuccesful. Aided by the Tegean women, who took up arms, the Tegeans defeated the Lacedaemonians and took many captives. In honor of their capture of the Spartans the Tegeans thereafter held a festival, the *Halotia* (Capture Festival). The fetters the Spartans had brought were placed on themselves, and they were forced to till the fields of the Tegeans as slaves. Many times the Spartans sought to conquer the Tegeans, but each time they were repulsed. According to legend, there were two reasons why Tegea was invulnerable to Sparta. First, some say that Athena gave Cepheus, king of Tegea and the son of Aleus, a lock of the hair of Medusa and that this protected the city. The sanctuary of Athena Poliatas (*Keeper of the City*) was also called Eryma (*Defense*) for this reason. Second, some say that the bones of Orestes were buried in Tegea and that as long as they rested there the Spartans could not defeat the Tegeans. At last the Spartans learned from the priestess of Delphi that they must secure the bones of Orestes and restore them to Sparta if they would conquer Tegea. Lichas, a Spartan, by trickery discovered that the bones of Orestes were buried beneath a forge in Tegea, secured their removal, and restored them to Sparta. After this, whenever the Spartans contended with the Tegeans, they were always victorious.

In the Persian War, 500 Tegeans served under Leonidas at the Pass of Thermopylae but did not take part in the final struggle and defeat there, as they were sent away with the other allies when Leonidas learned that the Persians had been led around the mountain and were about to cut off the Greeks in the pass. At the Battle of Plataea (479 B.C.) the Tegeans claimed the right to command one wing of the army facing the Persians. They based their claim to this distinction on the feat of their ancestor Echemus, who had slain Hyllus when the Heraclidae first invaded the Peloponnesus. Their claim did not prevail; the Athenians put forth more cogent reasons why they should have the honor. However, the Spartans, whose right to command one wing no one questioned, placed the Tegeans next to themselves in recognition of their courage. They did well in doing so, for in the great struggle at Plataea that decided the fate of Greece, through a confusion in commands the Spartans alone were left to face the army of Mardonius, and their Tegean allies remained firmly at their side and rushed into the fray with them. The Tegeans were the first to enter the wooden fortress to which the Persians had been driven by the onrush of the Spartans and the Tegeans, and they were the first to reach and plunder the tent of Mardonius. Among the booty given to the

Tegeans for their part in the battle was a bronze manger from which the Persian horses fed. The Tegeans placed it in the temple of Athena Alea at Tegea. According to Herodotus, of the 1500 Tegeans who took part in the engagement, 16 fell and were buried with full honors in a common grave on the field at Plataea. Tegea sided with Sparta in the Peloponnesian and Corinthian wars, was later a member of the Arcadian Confederacy against Sparta, fought against Sparta at Mantinea in 362 B.C., and was a member of the Aetolian and Achaean leagues.

Tegeates (te-jē′a̯-tēz). In Greek tradition, the son of Lycaon, for whom the region around the city of Tegea, founded later by Aleus, was named. Some say it was in the time of Tegeates that Apollo and Artemis visited Tegea to punish the persecutors of Leto. Tegeates sacrificed to them and appeased them. The tomb of Tegeates and his wife Maera was in Tegea. The sons of Tegeates were Cydon, Gortys, and Archedius. Some say they migrated to Crete and founded the cities of Cydonia, Gortyna, and Catreus there. But the Cretans denied this. They said Cydon, a son of Hermes and Acacallis, founded Cydonia; Catreus, son of Minos, founded Catreus; and Gortys, son of Rhadamanthys, founded Gortyna.

Tegyrius (te-jī′ri-us). In Greek legend, a king of Thrace. Eumolpus fled to his kingdom with his son Ismarus when he was forced out of Libya, and Tegyrius received him kindly. But Tegyrius, on discovering that Eumolpus was plotting against him, later drove him out of the kingdom. Still later, he was reconciled with Eumolpus and made him heir to his throne.

Teiresias (tī-rē′si-a̯s). See **Tiresias**.

Telamon (tel′a̯-mon). In Greek legend, a son of Aeacus, king of Aegina, and Endeïs. He was the brother of Peleus and the halfbrother of Phocus. Telamon and Peleus were jealous of Phocus because of his skill as an athlete and because he was their father's favorite. Encouraged by their mother, they schemed to kill him. In the course of an athletic contest to which they had challenged him, Phocus was struck by a discus, as if accidentally, and then slain with an ax. Which one of the brothers administered the fatal blow is not certain, but together they buried Phocus' body and fled. Telamon went to Salamis and sent back messengers to his father claiming he had no part in the murder. Aeacus forbade him to set foot on Aegina. In order to discuss the matter with Aeacus, Telamon secretly caused a mole to be built out into the sea from Aegina. He then stood on the end of the mole and shouted his plea of innocence to Aeacus. But Aeacus refused to believe him and Telamon returned to Salamis. There he married Glauce, daughter of King Cychreus, and succeeded Cychreus to the throne. When Glauce died, Telamon married Periboea. She was about to bear a child when Heracles visited at their court on his way to attack Troy. He prayed that Telamon's wife would bear a son as tough and brave as a lion. An eagle at once swooped down and Heracles declared this to be a sign that his prayer had been heard. Almost immediately thereafter Periboea was delivered of Telamonian Ajax. Telamon accompanied Heracles on his voyage against Troy and was the first to break through the wall and enter the city. Heracles was instantly enraged that Telamon had exceeded him in bravery and prepared to strike Telamon dead. But Telamon realized that he had aroused Heracles' wrath by his impetuous valor. With great presence of mind he began to collect stones. Heracles paused in the act of hurling his spear at Telamon to ask what he was doing. The quick-witted Telamon answered that he was building an altar to Heracles the Victor. Heracles was mollified and the attack proceeded. In the capture of Troy by Heracles, Telamon was awarded Hesione, a daughter of Laomedon and the sister of Priam. He took her back to Greece and she bore him Teucer, a noted archer. Priam sought repeatedly for the restoration of his sister but was denied satisfaction each time. Partly on this account Priam later felt completely justified in refusing to restore Helen to Menelaus after she had been abducted by Paris. Both of Telamon's sons took a valiant part in the second war against Troy, for the recapture of Helen. Thus the oracle which prophesied that the descendants of Aeacus would twice take Troy was fulfilled. Apollo had pro-

claimed this oracle at the time when the walls of Troy were built by him and Poseidon, with the help of the mortal Aeacus. At the end of the Trojan War Teucer returned to Salamis with the news that Ajax had committed suicide. Telamon banished him, even as he had been banished in his youth, claiming that he had not protected his brother's interests and blaming Teucer because he had not prevented his brother's death. Telamon took part in the Calydonian Hunt. He accompanied Jason and the Argonauts on the expedition to Colchis in quest of the Golden Fleece. He was a friend of Heracles and went with him to Thermodon when Heracles went there to fetch the girdle of the Amazon queen.

Telamon. In ancient geography, a place on the coast of Etruria, Italy, about 76 miles NW of Rome. Near here the Romans nearly annihilated (225 B.C.) an army of Gauls.

Telchines (tel-kī′nēz). In Greek mythology, nine children of the Sea (Thalassa). According to some accounts they had dogs' heads and flippers for hands. They were the first inhabitants of Rhodes and founded the cities of Lindus, Camirus, and Ialysus, which they named for three of the Danaids. With Caphira, a daughter of Oceanus, they nurtured the infant Poseidon who had been entrusted to them by Rhea, and made his trident. Later he fell in love with one of their number, Halia, and by her became the father of six sons and one daughter. The Telchines were renowned as smiths, and made the sickle with which Cronus castrated his father Uranus. They possessed the evil eye, could change their shape at will, could summon rain, clouds, snow, and hail, and were the first to make images of the gods. Zeus wanted to destroy them because of their magic powers and because of the unhealthy mists they caused, but Artemis warned them and they fled. Those who settled in Boeotia were destroyed in a flood. Those who went to Lycia were destroyed by Apollo.

Teledamas (tē-led′a-mas). According to some accounts, one of the twin sons Cassandra bore to Agamemnon. He and his brother Pelops were murdered in their infancy by Aegisthus and his followers at Mycenae. His tomb was near his mother's at Mycenae.

Telegonia (tel-ẹ-gō'ni-ạ). [Also: **Lay of Telegonus.**] Cyclic poem by Eugammon of Cyrene (c566 B.C.). It was a continuation of the *Odyssey,* and was named from its hero Telegonus, son of Odysseus and Circe, who slew his father and married Penelope. The poem completed the Trojan Cycle.

Telegonus (tẹ-leg'ọ-nus). In Greek legend, a son of Circe and Odysseus, born when Odysseus, on his way home from the Trojan War, stopped and lingered some time with Circe. Years later Circe sent Telegonus to find his father. He landed on the shores of Ithaca, under the impression that it was Corcyra, and set about to raid the island. Odysseus came to repel the invader. Each was ignorant of the other's identity and in the struggle Telegonus came face to face with Odysseus and killed him with his spear, which was tipped with the spine of a sting ray. Thus the prophecy which Tiresias had made to Odysseus in the Underworld—that his death would come from the sea—was fulfilled. Telegonus returned to Circe's isle with Telemachus and Penelope, and married Penelope. He was said to have been the founder of Tusculum and Praeneste in Latium, according to some accounts. Circe made Telegonus and Penelope immortal and they eventually went to dwell in the Isles of the Blest.

Telegonus. In Greek mythology, a son of Proteus. He married Io when she at last reached the Nile after her long wanderings and had been restored to her own form by Zeus. He was killed by Heracles, whom he had challenged to a wrestling match as the latter returned from his expedition to fetch Hippolyte's girdle.

Telemachus (tẹ-lem'ạ-kus). In Greek legend, a son of Odysseus and Penelope. While he was still an infant, his father left Ithaca to go to the Trojan War. In the long absence of Odysseus` Telemachus grew up. Although he was manly, straightforward, and intelligent, he was not able to exercise authority over the numerous suitors who came to woo his mother and who wasted the property of his father in eating and drinking at his expense. In the twentieth year of Odysseus' absence Athena appeared to Telemachus in the form of Mentes, a captain of the Taphians, and encouraged him to call a council of the Ithacans to ask the wooers to go home. The suitors refused to leave and mocked the youthful Telemachus. Athena advised him to seek information about Odysseus. She provided a ship for him in which he sailed to Pylus to question Nestor. Nestor sent him on to Menelaus in Sparta. In neither place did he hear any recent news of his father and Athena again appeared to him and told him to go home. She warned him that his mother's suitors were lying in wait to kill him, told him how to avoid them, and instructed him to go to the house of the faithful swineherd Eumaeus. Telemachus followed her instructions. At the house of Eumaeus he was reunited with his father, who had at last landed in his own country and had gone to Eumaeus, to whom he appeared in the guise of a beggar. Together, Odysseus and Telemachus planned to expel the suitors. They went to the palace of Odysseus and in due course attacked and killed the arrogant suitors. After Odysseus was reunited with Penelope and resumed control of his estates, he learned from an oracle that he would meet his death at the hands of his son. Thinking that this meant Telemachus, he banished him to the island of Cephallenia. But it was another son, Telegonus, who caused the death of Odysseus. Unaware of his father's identity, Telegonus, the son of Circe and Odysseus, landed on the shores of Ithaca and killed Odysseus. When he realized he had killed his father, he took the body of Odysseus back to the land of Circe. Telemachus and Peneople went with him. Circe made them all immortal and married Telemachus.

Telemus (tē'lẹ-mus). In Greek mythology, a noted seer who journeyed to Sicily and there encountered Polyphemus the Cyclops. He warned Polyphemus that his single eye in the middle of his forehead would one day be gouged out by Odysseus. Polyphemus laughed at the prophecy. He remembered it only after Odysseus, having blinded him, was sailing safely away.

Telephassa (tel-ẹ-fas'ạ). In Greek mythology, the wife of Agenor and the mother of Cadmus, Cilix, Phineus, Phoenix, Thasus, and Europa. She went with her son

Cadmus to Rhodes and from there to Thrace, where she died. She is sometimes also called Argiope.

Telephus (tel′e̯-fus). In Greek legend, a son of Heracles and Auge, a priestess of Athena. He was abandoned on Mount Parthenius by his mother but was nursed by a doe and found by herdsmen who took him to King Corythus. On reaching manhood he was told by the oracle of Delphi to sail to Mysia for news of his parents. There he learned from King Teuthras, now married to his mother, of his parentage. He married Teuthras' daughter, Argiope, and later became king of Mysia. According to other accounts, Telephus, speechless, went to Mysia accompanied by Parthenopaeus, son of Atalanta, who acted as his spokesman. In Mysia he defeated the enemies of Teuthras and was rewarded by being given Auge, the king's adopted daughter, as his wife. On the wedding night Auge attempted to kill him, as she was faithful to Heracles, but a serpent slithered into the room and prevented it. Thereupon Auge cried out to the spirit of Heracles, and Telephus was miraculously informed that she was his mother and Heracles was his father. In the early years of the Trojan War the Greeks landed in Mysia and ravaged it under the impression that it was part of the Troad. Telephus had driven them back to their ships when Achilles and Patroclus appeared. He turned to run from them but tripped on a vine and was wounded by Achilles' spear. The Greeks then sailed away. Telephus' wound did not heal. He was told by Apollo that only he who caused it could cure it. Having gone in disguise to Mycenae, at Clytemnestra's suggestion he snatched up the infant Orestes and told Agamemnon he would kill the child unless he healed his wound. Because there was a prophecy that the Greeks could not take Troy without the aid of Telephus, Agamemnon sent for Achilles, who cured the wound by scraping rust from his spear onto it. Telephus had agreed to pilot the Greeks to Troy but afterward refused to carry out his promise, claiming that his wife was Priam's daughter. However, he charted the course that the Greeks successfully followed to get to Troy.

Telesilla (tel-e̯-sil′a̯). Lyric poetess of Argos at the end of the 6th century B.C. It was said that she became a poetess because, when she consulted the oracle about her health, she was told she would find health with the Muses. She was renowned for her poetry—hymns to Artemis and Apollo—only small fragments of which remain. Cleomenes, the Spartan king (c519–c487 B.C.), attacked the Argives and they fled for refuge to a grove sacred to Argus. Cleomenes set fire to the grove and burned them to death. Argos now being undefended, Cleomenes marched against the city. Telesilla rallied the women; they armed themselves and defended the walls with great valor. The Spartans were dismayed, for if they defeated the women it would be a victory without honor. If, on the other hand, the women defeated them, it would be a devastating disgrace. Faced with the dilemma, the Spartans withdrew. Some say this was a fulfillment of the oracle that:

> Time shall be when the female shall conquer the male, and shall chase him Far away, gaining so great praise and honor in Argos

The statue of Telesilla before the sanctuary of Aphrodite at Argos represented her with her books lying at her feet, and in her hands was a helmet she was in the act of placing on her head.

Telesphorus (te̯-les′fôr-us). A deity attendant on Asclepius, who appeared in dreams and healed the sick or wounded. In ancient art he is represented as a child, often with Asclepius.

Telesterion (te-les-ter′i-on). A hall of initiation (*telesthenai* "to be initiated"), where the rites and ceremonies of admission to membership in the mystery religions were performed; especially, that at Eleusis near Athens. The Telesterion at Eleusis, at first a shrine of modest dimensions, was several times rebuilt on a larger scale. In its final 5th-century B.C. form it was a large building, square in plan, enclosing an area of about 29,000 square feet, with a Doric portico of 12 columns, and six entrances. The roof was supported by seven rows of six columns, like the hypostyle halls of Egypt, and along the four walls were eight rows of narrow stone seats. A religious drama or pageant

based on the myth of Demeter was performed in this hall for the candidates for
initiation. The initiates were forbidden to
reveal the details of the ceremony, and the
secret was kept so well that modern scholarship has not penetrated it. However, there
are hints that the ceremony told of the rape
by Hades of Demeter's daughter Persephone,
Demeter's search, her kindly reception at
Eleusis, and her gift of agriculture. (JJ)

Teleus (te-lē'us). Epithet of Zeus. The altar
of Zeus Teleus (*Full-grown*) at Tegea had
an image that was square, like the Hermae.

Tellus (tel'us). The Roman equivalent of
the Greek earth-goddess Gaea. When her
temple was dedicated in Rome in 286 B.C.
an earthquake occurred. Because of this
she was especially invoked during earthquakes. She was also a goddess by whom
oaths were sworn. Tellus was worshiped as
a goddess of marriage, and especially as a
goddess of the fruitfulness of fields and
cattle. Festivals were held in her honor
to ensure fruitful harvests from the sowing
of seeds and fertility among the cattle. Her
worship included fertility sacrifices, such as
a cow with an unborn calf. The ashes of
the calf were kept by the vestal virgins and
afterward used in rites of purification. Like
many other earth deities, she was also associated with rites for the dead.

Telmessus (tel-mes'us). In ancient geography,
a town on the coast of Lycia, Asia Minor.
The town was noted for its oracle of Apollo.
Croesus, withdrawing to Sardis after an
indecisive engagement with Cyrus, found
that the outskirts of Sardis were swarming
with snakes. The horses left the pastures
and went to feed on the snakes. Croesus
sent to the soothsayers of Telmessus to learn
the meaning of this strange portent. The
Telmessians sent word that the prodigy
meant that foreign invaders would come and
subdue his people, for the serpent, they
said, is a child of earth, and the horse is a
warrior and an alien. But by the time the
message from the Telmessian soothsayers
arrived, Croesus had already been captured
by Cyrus and the Persians were plundering
his capital. Among the important antiquities
on the site of the ancient town is an
ancient theater, well preserved and of good
style.

Telphusa (tel-fū'sa). In Greek mythology, a
nymph of a spring in Boeotia. According
to some accounts, she persuaded Apollo
not to erect a temple and oracle at her
spring but advised him to go to Delphi
where, since she was a prophetess, she
knew he would have to overcome the Python. Apollo punished her by hiding her
spring under rocks near which he built an
altar.

Temenos (tem'e-nos). In Greek antiquity, a
sacred enclosure or precinct; a piece of
land marked off from common uses and
dedicated to a god; a precinct, usually surrounded by a barrier, allotted to a temple
or sanctuary, or consecrated for any reason.

Temenus (tem'e-nus). In Greek legend, a son
of Aristomachus, a descendant of Heracles,
and brother of Cresphontes and Aristodemus.
With his brothers, he proposed to invade the
Peloponnesus and win the land that they
said had been left in trust for them by their
ancestor Heracles. When a fleet and army
were assembled at Naupactus, an Acarnanian
seer came to them, chanting prophetic verses.
The Heraclidae (descendants of Heracles)
feared he was a magician sent by the Peloponnesians to destroy them and so they
slew him. After this Aristodemus, some
say, was killed by a bolt of lightning, the
fleet was destroyed, and the army had to be
disbanded because of famine. Temenus
consulted the oracle and learned that these
calamities had come to punish them for the
death of the seer. Temenus and his relatives were instructed to banish the slayer
for ten years and to take "the Three-eyed
One" for a guide. Obeying the oracle, the
slayer was banished. Temenus, with Cresphontes, Eurysthenes and Procles (twin
sons of the dead Aristodemus), looked about
for "the Three-eyed One." They met
Oxylus, an exile from Aetolia, driving a
one-eyed mule, decided he was "the Three-
eyed One," and took him as their guide.
He led them to Elis and they conquered
the Peloponnesus. Oxylus received Elis as
his reward. The brothers and their nephews
decided to divide the rest of the Peloponnesus between them by lot. They were to
cast their lots into an urn and he whose
lot came up first was to receive Argos,
second Laconia, and third Messenia. The

fat, fāte, fär, fāre, errant; net, mē, hèr ardent; pin, pīne; not, nōte, möve, nôr,

lot of Temenus came up first and he was assigned Argos. The sons of Aristodemus won dominion over Laconia. Cresphontes, who greatly desired the rich land of Messenia, won it by a trick. He put a clod of earth into the urn and poured water on it. As it was melted by the water, his lot came up last. After the lot-drawing, the Heraclidae set up three altars to Zeus Patrous (*Paternal*) and on the altar of each a sign appeared. On the altar of Temenus there was a toad. The seer interpreted this to mean that his people must stay in the city, for the toad loses its strength when it walks. Temenus was the father of three sons, Agelaus, Eurypylus, and Callias, and one daughter, Hyrnetho. He favored his daughter and her husband, Deïphontes, and proposed to leave his kingdom to them. When his sons learned of this they hired assassins to kill him as he bathed in the river. Nevertheless, though mortally wounded, he managed to pass on his kingdom to his daughter before he expired. It was to this Temenus that the Temenidae, who later colonized Macedonia, traced their ancestry.

Temenus. According to Greek tradition, a son of Pelasgus who, according to some accounts, brought up Hera in Arcadia. At Stymphalus he raised three shrines in honor of Hera. In the first she was worshiped as a child because he had brought her up; in the second she was worshiped as a bride to commemorate her marriage to Zeus; and in the third as a widow because she had left Zeus and had come to live at Stymphalus.

Tempe (tem′pē), **Vale of.** Valley in E. Thessaly, Greece, deeply cleft between Olympus on the N and Ossa on the S, and traversed by the Peneus (or Salambria) River. It has been celebrated from ancient times for its beauty and savage grandeur. Tempe was one of the chief seats of the cult of Apollo. Some say the god went there after slaying the Python at Delphi and purified himself by bathing in the waters of the Peneus. Daphne, daughter of the river-god Peneus, was one of Apollo's earliest loves. She fled his embraces and was transformed into a laurel tree. Henceforth a delegation from Delphi went every eight years to Tempe to fetch laurel for the Pythian Games at Delphi. Length, about five miles.

Tempestates (tem-pes-tā′tēz). In Roman mythology, goddesses of the winds and storms. Sacrifices of black female lambs were offered to them, and shrines were erected for them, in order to gain safety in sea voyages.

Tencteri (tengk′te̯-rī). Ancient Germanic tribe first mentioned by Caesar, who describes them as having been driven by the Suevi (59 B.C.), together with the Usipetes, out of their original home. The Tencteri were defeated by Caesar in 55 B.C. in Gallic territory near the confluence of the Mosa (Maas) with the Rhenus (Rhine). They afterward joined other tribes in wars against Rome, and were probably merged ultimately with the Alamanni. According to Tacitus in *Germania,* they excelled in horsemanship.

Tenea (ten′e̯-a̯). In ancient geography, a town in the region of Corinth. The inhabitants claimed to be Trojans who were taken prisoner by Agamemnon on the island of Tenedos and afterward allowed to settle in Greece. They worshiped Apollo, said by some to be the father of Tenes, above all other gods.

Tenedos (ten′e̯-dos). A small island in the Aegean Sea situated off the Troad, on the NW coast of Asia Minor. It was known in the legends of the Trojans as an island sacred to Apollo, and was named for Tenes, a son of Apollo. The Greeks landed in Tenedos on their way to Troy, killed Tenes, and ravaged the island. It was to this island that the Greeks withdrew when they left the Wooden Horse on the beach at Troy to delude the Trojans into the belief that they had sailed for home. Historically, the island was settled by Aeolians, was subjugated by the Persians, and was in alliance with Athens in the 5th century B.C. Length, about seven miles.

Tenes (ten′es). In Greek legend, a son of Apollo, or as some say, of Cycnus, and Proclea. His stepmother Phylonome fell in love with him but he honorably rejected her amorous advances. She then denounced him to Cycnus, accused him of seeking to ravish her, and called Eumolpus, a flute-player, as her witness. Cycnus believed her, and to punish Tenes, he put him and his sister Hemithea in a chest and set them adrift on the sea. The chest went aground on an island near the coast of Asia Minor. Tenes became king of the island and named it Tenedos after himself. Cycnus later learned that Tenes had been blameless in the affair with Phylonome. He had the flute-player who had born false witness stoned to death, and buried Phylonome alive. Cycnus then sailed to Tenedos to ask forgiveness of his son. Tenes at first refused to allow him to moor his ship in the waters of Tenedos. Afterward, however, he forgave his father and Cycnus settled near him on Tenedos. When the Greeks sailed from Aulis the second time on their way to Troy, they coasted by Tenedos and sought to land. Tenes tried to prevent them from landing by hurling rocks at them from a cliff. Achilles swam ashore and killed Tenes. The Greeks landed and ravaged the island. But some say the Greeks were allowed to land peaceably but that Achilles seduced Hemithea, sister of Tenes, and in the resulting quarrel killed Tenes. In killing Tenes Achilles had carelessly forgotten his mother's warning that if he killed a son of Apollo, he would die by Apollo's hand. Thetis, mother of Achilles, had even sent a servant, Mnemon, whose sole duty was to remind Achilles not to slay a son of Apollo. When Achilles realized that he had forgotten his mother's warning, he killed Mnemon for failing in his duty. Tenes was buried on Tenedos and a shrine was erected to him. He was worshiped as a god after his death. No flute-player could enter the sacred precincts of his shrine because a flute-player had borne false witness against him, and it was forbidden to utter the name Achilles in these precincts.

Tenos (tē'nos). [Also: **Tino, Tinos**.] An island of the Cyclades, SE of Greece. Here, according to legend, Heracles slew the Boreadae as they were returning from funeral games for Pelias. He killed them because they, on the voyage of the *Argo*, had persuaded the Argonauts not to wait while Heracles searched for his lost squire Hylas in Mysia. Thus Heracles was left behind. Over their burial mound in Tenos Heracles erected two columns, one of which sways at the breath of the North Wind (Boreas). In modern times the island is one of the most prosperous of the Greek islands, and exports marble and wine. Length, about 17 miles; area, 79 square miles.

Tenth Muse. See **Sappho.**

Tentyra (ten'ti-ra). [Also: **Tentyris**; modern names, **Dendera, Denderah**.] Town in Upper Egypt, situated on the Nile. It is celebrated for its temple of the cow-goddess Hathor, which notwithstanding its late date, begun by Ptolemy XII (Ptolemy Auletes), and the great *pronaos* (columned hall outside the temple proper) added as late as the time of Tiberius, is one of the most interesting buildings in Egypt, owing to its almost perfect preservation, even to the roof. The imposing hexastyle pronaos has four ranges of Hathoric columns; on its ceiling is a noted sculptured zodiac, combining Egyptian and classical elements. Next to the pronaos is a hypostyle hall (ceiling supported on columns) of six columns, from which three chambers open on each side, and beyond this is a vestibule before a large hall in which stands an isolated cella. This hall is surrounded by a series of chambers, one of which in the middle of the back wall contained the emblematic *sistrum* (an instrument in the form of a metal rattle) of the goddess. The whole interior surface is sculptured, the art, however, being inferior. On the roof there is a small six-chambered temple to the local divinity Osiris-An.

Teos (tē'os). In ancient geography, one of the 12 Ionian cities of Asia Minor, situated on the W coast, about 25 miles SW of Smyrna. According to tradition, it was first inhabited by Minyans from Orchomenus who went there with Athamas, descendant of that Athamas who was the son of Aeolus. They were later joined by Ionians, Athenians, and Boeotians. The Teians fell under the dominion of the kings of Lydia. When Croesus was attacked by Cyrus, the Ionian cities rejected the overtures of Cyrus, thinking he could not defeat Croesus, and when Cyrus conquered Croesus he set out to bring the Ionian cities under his sway. All, except Miletus, resisted. Harpagus, general of Cyrus, approached Teos and prepared to take the walled city by building a mound of earth up around the wall. The Teians, rather than submit to slavery under the

Persians, abandoned their city. They embarked all the inhabitants in their ships and sailed off to Thrace, where they founded Abdera. Among the ruins at Teos is a noted temple of Dionysus, a beautiful Ionic hexastyle peripteros on a stylobate of three steps.

Terence (ter′ens). [Full Latin name, **Publius Terentius Afer.**] Roman comic poet; born at Carthage, c195 B.C.; died c159 B.C. He went early to Rome as a slave of Publius Terentius Lucanus, and was soon liberated, thereupon taking his patron's name. He became a friend of the younger Scipio and of Laelius, and went to Greece after bringing out his plays. The material of his works was rather freely adapted from the Greek playwrights Menander and Apollodorus. He left six comedies: *Andria, Hecyra, Heautontimorumenos, Eunuchus, Phormio,* and *Adelphi.*

Terentia (te̩-ren′shi-a̩). First wife of Cicero, to whom she bore a son and a daughter. He divorced her in 46 B.C.

Tereus (tē′rös). In mythology, a king of Thrace, who went to the aid of Pandion, king of Athens, when the latter was beset by enemies. Pandion showed his appreciation by giving Tereus his daughter Procne in marriage. Tereus was transformed into a hoopoe for the outrage he committed on Philomela, the sister of Procne. See **Procne.**

Terminalia (ter-mi-nā′li-a̩). Ancient Roman festival celebrated annually in honor of Terminus, the god of boundaries. It was held on the 23rd of February, its essential feature being a survey of boundaries.

Termini Imerese (ter′mē-nē ē-mā-rā′sā). See **Thermae Himeraeae.**

Terminus (ter′mi-nus). In Roman mythology, the god who presided over boundaries and landmarks. He was represented with a human head, but without feet or arms, to intimate that he never moved from whatever place he occupied. He was given a place in the temple of Jupiter, and for this reason is sometimes interpreted as an aspect of Jupiter.

Terpander (ter-pan′der). Greek musician and poet; born at Antissa, Lesbos, Greece; fl. mid-7th century B.C. He was undoubtedly a historical person, but very little is known about him, and some of what is told is probably legend rather than fact. He is said to have won the prize in musical con-

tests at Delphi four times and to have won the laurel for music at the Carnean Games in 676 B.C. According to some accounts, he was summoned to Sparta c650 B.C., in conformity with a revelation by the oracle at Delphi, to bring about peace between contending groups in that city-state, to lead the Spartan choruses in the religious festivals, and to teach the Spartans his new musical system. Henceforward the Spartans followed Terpander's style and did not look with favor on any deviation from it. He has been called the father both of Greek classical music and of lyric poetry, and it seems certain that he was in fact a poet, a composer, and a player of stringed instruments. Strabo wrote that to the four strings which the lyre formerly had Terpander added three more; but others understand that his innovation was in the form of the *nome,* or ode recited to music, which he divided into seven parts, where previously there were four. Terpander has in fact been credited with the origination of musical notation, but this is considered very doubtful. He was, in any case, the earliest Greek musician of whom we have even fragmentary historical knowledge.

Terpsichore (terp-sik′o̩-rē). One of the nine daughters of Zeus and Mnemosyne. She is the muse of the dance, the patroness of lyric poetry, the choral dance, and the dramatic chorus developed from it. In the last days of the Greek religion her province was restricted to lyric poetry. In art she is usually represented as bearing a lyre. According to some accounts, Terpsichore was the mother of the Sirens. See **Muses.**

Terracina (ter-rä-chē′nä). See **Tarracina.**

Terra Mater (ter′a̩ mā′ter). [Also: **Terra.**] In Roman mythology, a goddess, the personification of the earth. She is the same as Tellus. Latin writers also referred to the Germanic earth goddess, Nerthus, as Terra Mater.

Terra Sigillata (ter′a̩ sij-i-lā′ta̩). Term used to denote a type of Hellenistic pottery, decorated in molded reliefs in imitation of embossed metal ware, used principally for bowls and plates for table service. The peak of the art was achieved at Arretium in Etruria, whose potters in the 1st century B.C. perfected a ware with a biscuit of high quality, delicate designs, and a distinctive bright red glaze, thanks to which Arretine Ware became widely popular and was imitated in S Gaul and eventually in N Gaul, Germany, Pannonia, and even Britain, where it was formerly known as Samian Ware. Vessels of Arretine origin are often stamped with the name of the maker, study of which has enabled scholars to reconstruct the organization of the workshops. (JJ)

Testaceus (tes-tạ-sē′us), **Mons.** [Modern name, **Monte Testaccio.**] Hill in the S part of Rome, SW of the Aventine Hill, on the left bank of the Tiber. It is about 115 feet in height above the surrounding area, and 2500 feet in circumference, and is formed entirely of the fragments of pottery vases, chiefly amphorae, from the extensive warehouses which once lined the neighboring quay. The potters' stamps on the fragments show that this rubbish heap was still used in the 4th century A.D., and it is believed to have been begun about the inception of the empire.

Tethys (tē′this). In Greek mythology, a Titaness, the daughter of Gaea and Uranus. She was "the lovely queen of the sea," the wife of Oceanus, and the mother of all the rivers and 3000 Oceanids.

Teucer (tū′sėr). In Greek legend, a son of the Cretan prince Scamander and the nymph Idaea. He was born in Phrygia, whither Scamander had come to escape a famine in Crete. Teucer succeeded his father and became the first king of Troy, for which reason the Trojans are sometimes called Teucrians. According to some accounts, Aeneas and his companions were told to seek the home of their ancestors after they fled from Troy. Thinking the oracle referred to Scamander, or Teucer, they mistakenly went to Crete. Teucer's daughter Batia married Dardanus, a Thracian prince, who succeeded to the throne on Teucer's death. But some say it was Teucer who emigrated to Phrygia from Crete, and that he found Dardanus there and was welcomed by him. Still others say Teucer emigrated from Attica, founded Troy, and received Dardanus when he landed in Phrygia.

Teucer. In Greek legend, a bastard son of Telamon and Hesione, and adoring half-brother of Telamonian Ajax. He was a master of archery. He had been one of Helen's suitors before she married Menelaus, and as such was compelled to live up to his oath to aid Menelaus in any difficulty arising from his marriage. Therefore he joined the Greeks who went to Troy to recapture Helen. In the war he fought bravely at Ajax' side, at times using his brother's shield as a protection. He darted out from behind the enormous shield carried by Ajax, shot his lethal arrow, and then retired behind the shield. With his arrows he killed many, and tried several times to kill Hector. The first time, he struck Gorgythion instead; the second time, Apollo deflected his arrow and he killed Archeptolemus, Hector's charioteer. On his third try, Hector wounded him by hurling a great stone that struck him in the shoulder just as he was about to shoot. When he fell, Ajax again protected him with his shield. He wounded Glaucus, Sarpedon's comrade, when the Trojans breached the Greek wall, and assailed Sarpedon himself, but Zeus protected the latter. Again, Zeus caused his bowstring to snap as he once more aimed at Hector. The death of Ajax by suicide caused him bitter grief. As he stood over his fallen body, he recognized the sword Ajax had used to kill himself as the one Hector had given him, and recalled that Hector had been tied to the back of Achilles' chariot by the girdle Ajax had given him. He defied Menelaus' order not to bury Ajax, and with the wife and young son of Ajax as witnesses, buried him in the sands of Troy. When he returned to Salamis, Telamon forbade him to land and banished him because he had not brought back Ajax' bones, nor his wife, nor his son. He then went to Sidon, where he was hospitably received by Belus, father of Dido, and got help from him to conquer Cyprus. He married the daughter of the king who had given the island his name, built a city there which he named Salamis after his home in Greece, became king of Cyprus, and founded a dynasty of kings which traced their descent from him.

Teucrians (tū′kri-ạnz). Another name for the Trojans, from their ancestor Teucer.

Teumessus (tū-mes′us). In ancient geography, a place near Thebes in Boeotia, which was the home of the Teumessian vixen, a fox that, by an edict of the gods, could not be caught.

The vixen ravaged the countryside and at last Amphitryon set Laelaps, a dog fated to catch whatever it pursued, to chase the vixen. Under these circumstances, Zeus turned both animals to stone. Teumessus was also named as a place where Europa was hidden by Zeus. A sanctuary of Telchinian Athena at Teumessus was said by some to have been raised by Telchines from Cyprus.

Teuthis (tū'this). [Also, known as **Ornytus**.] In Greek legend, a leader of Arcadians from the village of Teuthis. When the Greeks were windbound at Aulis, Teuthis quarreled with Agamemnon and threatened to withdraw with his Arcadians. Athena came to persuade him not to withdraw, but he was so angry he struck the goddess with his spear and wounded her in the thigh. Teuthis then led his army back to Arcadia. Once at home, he was struck by a wasting disease and famine fell on his village, alone of the Arcadian villages. The oracle of Dodona told the inhabitants how they might appease the goddess. In addition, they made an image of Athena, showing the wound in her thigh, and dedicated it in the temple. The image, with its thigh wrapped in a purple bandage, was seen by the traveler Pausanias in the 2nd century A.D.

Teuthrania (tū-thrā'ni-a̯). In ancient geography, a region of Mysia, Asia Minor.

Teuthras (tū'thras̯). In Greek legend, a king in Mysia. Once while hunting, he raised a great boar and pursued it. The boar fled to the temple of Artemis and as Teuthras overtook it there, it cried out in a human voice to be spared as one of Artemis' creatures. Teuthras ignored the plea for mercy and ruthlessly killed it. This so enraged Artemis that she restored the boar to life and punished Teuthras with madness and disease. His mother at length appeased Artemis with rich sacrifices and Teuthras was cleansed of his disease and purified of his madness. This Teuthras gave refuge to Auge when she fled to his kingdom. According to some accounts, he married Auge. When her son Telephus later arrived in Mysia in search of news of his parents, Teuthras welcomed him. Telephus helped Teuthras to rout his enemies, and as a reward was given the daughter of Teuthras for a wife and made heir to his kingdom. Others say Teuthras adopted Auge

as his daughter when she fled to him, and that when Telephus appeared, Teuthras offered him Auge in return for his aid in driving off his enemies. But on the wedding night the relationship between Auge and Telephus was revealed and Teuthras, learning of it, sent them both back to their homeland with his blessing.

Teuthras. A legendary king of Phrygia and the father of Tecmessa. He was slain by Telamonian Ajax, and his daughter was taken captive by Ajax.

Teuthras. In the *Iliad*, a Magnesian ally of the Greeks. He was slain by Hector when Ares took part in the fight to help the Trojans.

Teutobod (tū'tō̯-bod). King of the Teutones, defeated by Marius at the battle of Aquae Sextiae (modern Aix), 102 B.C.

Teutoberg (tū'tō̯-bėrg) **Forest.** [German, **Teutoburger Wald** or **Teutoburgerwald**.] Low, wooded mountain range in NW Germany, extending from the vicinity of Osnabruck in Hanover SE through North Rhine-Westphalia. It is known in different parts as the Lippischer Wald, Osning, and by other names. A victory was gained in this area (exact locality undetermined) in 9 A.D. by the Germans under Arminius (Hermann) over the Romans under Varus, the Roman army being nearly annihilated. Peak elevation, about 1535 feet.

Teutones (tū'tō̯-nēz). [Also: **Teutoni**.] Ancient Germanic people which, with the Cimbri, defeated three Roman armies in the years 109–105 B.C., and were nearly destroyed by Caius Marius at Aquae Sextiae (Aix), 102 B.C. The Teutones are mentioned later as dwelling near the lower Albis (Elbe) River and eastward.

Thais (thā'is). Athenian courtesan; fl. in the last part of the 4th century B.C. She was the mistress of Alexander the Great, whom she accompanied on his expedition into Asia. She is alleged (undoubtedly erroneously) to have incited him to set fire to Persepolis. After the death of Alexander she became the mistress of Ptolemy, king of Egypt, and bore him two sons.

Thalamae (thal'a̯-mē). In ancient geography, a place on the promontory of Taenarum in Laconia, where there was an oracle of Pasiphaë, which, in this case, was a title of the moon. This oracle was consulted during sleep and responses were given in dreams. Nearby, at Pephnus, there was a large rock in the sea which was said to have been the birthplace of the Dioscuri and from which Hermes carried them off to be reared at Pellana. The Laconians placed on the rock small bronze images of the Dioscuri, which were so fashioned as not to be moved even though the sea washed over them.

Thalassa (tha̱-las'a̱) or **Thalatta** (-lat'a̱). In later Greek mythology, the personification of the sea. She was a goddess of the sea who was sometimes thought of as the mother of Aphrodite by Zeus, but this was not the traditional version of the origin of Aphrodite. In other accounts she was the wife of Pontus and the mother by him of fish children. Again, she was said to be the mother of the Telchines.

Thales (thā'lēz) or **Thaletas** (tha̱-lē'ta̱s). Lyric poet and musician of Sparta; born in Crete; fl. about the 7th century B.C.

Thales. Greek philosopher, astronomer, and geometer; born at Miletus, Asia Minor, c640 B.C.; died c546 B.C. He was one of the seven wise men of ancient Greece, the earliest of the Ionian natural philosophers, and has been called the father of European science and philosophy. He stands at the historical point where myths and cosmogonies no longer satisfied man's curiosity concerning the origin of the world. Thales sought an original substance from which all things arise, and believed that substance to be water. His interest in the nature of the universe led him to various studies, and to him are attributed various discoveries in geometry and astronomy. He is said to have learned, for example, that a circle is bisected by its diameter, and to have found that the height of a pyramid could be determined by measuring its shadow at an hour of the day when a man's shadow was the same length as a man. On May 28, 585 B.C., the Medes and the Lydians were engaged in a battle, in the course of a war that had beeen going on intermittently for six years. In the midst of the battle the sun was darkened and day became night. The combatants, terrified by this sign from heaven, laid down their arms and concluded a peace. "This event," says Herodotus, "had been foretold by Thales, the Milesian, who forewarned the Ionians of it, fixing for it the very year in which it actually took place." His correct prediction of the eclipse of the sun spread Thales' fame among the ancients. When Cyrus was engaged in the conquest of the Ionian cities, according to Herodotus, Thales advised them to unite in one political unit, with a capital on the island of Teos, to defend themselves. His advice, based on the weakness their disunity caused and the evident intention of Cyrus to pick them off one by one, was not taken. His reputation as an abstract philosopher, it is said, brought the criticism that he was impractical; according to the story, he then went into the olive-oil business and made a fortune. He is memorable, not only for his actual discoveries, but for being the first to base a philosophy on natural phenomena alone without recourse to the supernatural.

Thalia (tha̱-lī'a̱). One of the nine daughters of Zeus and Mnemosyne, she is the muse of comedy. By Apollo, according to some accounts, Thalia was the mother of the Corybantes. In later art she is generally represented with a comic mask, a shepherd's crook, and a wreath of ivy. See **Muses.**

Thalia. In Greek mythology, a daughter of Zeus and Eurynome, one of the Charites (Graces).

Thallo (thal'ō). In Greek mythology, the Attic name of one of the Horae, whose names as fertility spirits vary locally. Thallo presided over the growth of vegetation.

Thamus (thā'mus). An Egyptian sailor who, according to tradition, was in a ship bound for Italy when he heard a shout across the water. A voice called his name and told him when he reached Italy to proclaim that "the great god Pan is dead." Thamus did as he was bid and all the people mourned.

Thamyris (tham'i-ris). A legendary Thracian poet and musician who fell in love with the handsome youth Hyacinthus. Apollo was his rival for the affections of Hyacinthus, and when he overhead Thamyris boast that he could vie with the Muses in singing, he reported this boast to the Muses. They pursued Thamyris and overtook him at Dorium. To punish him for his boasting they blinded him, took away his voice, and caused him to forget his skill on the lyre.

Thanatos (than'a̱-tos). Ancient Greek personification of death. He was not worshiped as a god. In ancient Greece as elsewhere in the world, death personified was a folk concept. Later he became prominent in literary allusion. He was regarded as a healer and remover of pain; he was inexorable in his purpose, and unbribable. Hesiod said he was even hated by the gods. In the *Iliad* he is the son of Nyx (Night) and the brother of Hypnos (Sleep).

Thapsacus (thap′sạ-kus). [In the Bible, **Tiphsah;** modern village, **Dibse.**] In ancient geography, a town in Syria on the W bank of the Euphrates. It was an important crossing place in ancient times. Here Xenophon crossed when he accompanied the expedition of Cyrus the Younger; and here also Alexander the Great crossed the Euphrates.

Thapsus (thap′sus). In ancient geography, a town in N Africa, situated on the coast about 30 miles SE of what is now Sousse. Here Julius Caesar totally defeated (46 B.C.) the remnants of the army of Pompey that had been reorganized under Cato, Scipio, and Juba, and ended the African phase of the civil war. It is said that Caesar's forces were in a near panic when they learned of the size of the army Juba was leading against them. Caesar's psychology for encouraging his men was to exaggerate the size of the enemy's forces, giving exact figures, as he claimed, to keep them from spreading rumors, and also to spur them to fight for their lives before an overwhelming force. Any who doubted their ability to win or the facts he had given them were invited to embark on a leaking ship and put to sea where they would be the plaything of the winds. As noted above, this psychological approach was effective.

Thargelia (thär-jē′li-ạ). Ancient Greek festival celebrated in honor of Apollo at Athens, on the 6th and 7th of the month Thargelion, the month in which Apollo was born and which was sacred to him. (Thargelion was equivalent to the last of May and the beginning of June.). In the festival certain purification ceremonies were enacted and offerings of the first fruits of the harvest, raw fruits and bread from the first grain, were made to the god. On the first day of the festival the city was cleansed of any pollution that might be in it. Two men, usually

condemned criminals, were led out of the city. One of them, wearing black figs about his neck, represented the men of the city; the other, who wore white figs, represented the women. These men were called *pharmacoi,* and in them was embodied any evil that might have resided in the city. To them all such evil was transferred; they were the magical means by which the city was cleansed; they were scapegoats. The pharmacoi were driven forth to the piping of flutes and beaten with branches of fig trees and with leeks. The fig branches were strong and would thoroughly scourge the evil clinging to the pharmacoi. The leek was a powerful purgative. According to some accounts, the pharmacoi were in early times stoned to death, and burned in fires made of the wood of wild trees, and their ashes were scattered on the seashore. Thus the evil attached to them was also scattered and could never return to plague the city. In later times it is thought that the pharmacoi were hurled from a height, as a symbol of their destruction, but were caught as they fell and then were banished from the city. These purification rites were to propitiate Apollo and expiate evil, so that he would not, in his wrath at the presence of pollution in the city, send the burning sun to dry up the harvest or cause pestilence to fall on the people. Pharmacoi were employed on other occasions and at other places besides Athens when pestilence, plague, or famine struck, to remove whatever impurity had brought down the wrath of a god and caused affliction to a city. The remaining day of the Thargelia was devoted to the offering of first fruits of the harvest to Apollo, now that the city was cleansed. Boys, both of whose parents were living, carried branches twined with wool and with offerings of the fruit of the earth hanging from them, to the sanctuary of Apollo and placed them before the doors there. Similar wool-twined branches were placed before the door of every Athenian house. A musical contest was held, the winners of which dedicated in the sanctuary of Pythian Apollo the tripods they won.

Thargelion (thär-jē′li-on). The eleventh month of the Attic year, containing 30 days, and corresponding to the last part of May and the first part of June. The great festival in

actor; up, lūte, pùll; oi, oil; ou, out; ᴛʜ, then; d̦ as d or j, ş as s or sh, ț as t or ch, z̦ as z or zh.

honor of Apollo and Artemis, the *Thargelia*, was held in this month.

Thasus (thā'sus). In Greek legend, a son of Agenor of Canaan (afterward Phoenicia) and Telephassa. He was the brother of Cadmus, Cilix, Phineus, Phoenix, and Europa. When Europa was carried off by Zeus in the form of a bull, Agenor sent his sons to search for her. Thasus ended his search on the island of Thasus, which he colonized, and which took his name.

Thasus. An island in the N part of the Aegean Sea, S of E Macedonia, lying about four miles from the mainland. The surface is mountainous. It was colonized by Ionians from Paros about the end of the 8th century B.C., who either subdued or expelled the Thracian aborigines. Herodotus mentions having seen the rich gold mines that provided such a source of wealth to the inhabitants. Thasus carried on a prosperous trade with the Thracians, the Egyptians, and the Phoenicians, and by the 6th century B.C. had developed a flourishing civilization of its own. Histiaeus the Milesian fortified (c494 B.C.) the chief city (which had the same name as the island) with marble walls to protect it from attack. Darius the Great compelled the Thasians to dismantle the fortifications (491 B.C.); they were reconstructed, but again partly destroyed (464 B.C.) at the command of the Athenians. However, large parts remain to this day. During the Persian Wars Thasus was under the dominion of the Persians. The island later belonged to the Delian League, revolted c465 B.C. but was besieged and subjugated by Cimon. During the Peloponnesian Wars it changed hands between Athens and Sparta several times. It was subject to Philip V of Macedon, and later became a free city under the Romans, who accorded it a favorable position because, unlike the rest of Greece, it had favored Rome in the Mithridatic Wars. Polygnotus the painter (beginning of the 5th century B.C.) and Stesimbrotus the writer (end of the 5th century B.C.) were natives of the island. The French School of Athens engaged in excavations at Thasus from 1910. Among the notable remains are the ruins of the walls about the ancient citadel, with a block engraved with the name of the builder, a Hellenistic theater, the foundations of a

temple of Pythian Apollo (5th century B.C.), and remains of two altars on the terrace of a sanctuary of Poseidon and a huge altar of Hera as protectress of ports. On the latter it was forbidden to sacrifice goats. There are also remains of sanctuaries of Dionysus and Heracles, and a museum houses numerous statues and fragments. According to legend, the island was colonized by Thasus, for whom it was named. He was a son of Agenor of Phoenicia. Wearied of searching for his sister Europa he settled on the island in accordance with instructions he received from the oracle of Apollo at Delphi. The chief protecting deities of the island in ancient times were Dionysus and Heracles.

Thasus. Chief town and ancient capital of the island of Thasus, situated on the N coast.

Thaumas (thou'mas). In Greek mythology, a son of Pontus and Gaea. He was the husband of Electra, daughter of Oceanus. Their children were the Harpies, Aello and Ocypete, and Iris of the "fast-flying feet" who became the messenger of the gods.

Thaumasium (thou-mā'si-um). In ancient geography, a mountain in Arcadia, Greece. Here, according to some accounts, Rhea gave Cronus a stone wrapped in swaddling clothes. Under the impression that it was his newborn son Zeus, Cronus swallowed the stone.

Thea (thē'a). In Greek mythology, a daughter of Chiron the centaur. She was a chaste companion of Artemis but was ravished by Aeolus, king of Magnesia in Thessaly. She feared her father's wrath if he should learn that she was about to bear a child. To protect her, Poseidon transformed her into a mare, Euippe, until after her child was born. When her foal Melanippe was born, Poseidon set the image of the mare among the stars as the constellation of the Horse, and transformed the foal into a baby girl.

Theaetetus (thē-ē-tē'tus). Athenian mathematician (died 369 B.C.); a disciple of Socrates. He is the principal character in one of the most famous of Plato's dialogues, named for him.

Theagenes (thē-aj'e-nēz). According to Pausanias, a son of Timosthenes, of Thasus. But some say that a phantom was his father, that Timosthenes was a priest of Heracles and that it was the phantom of the god himself who was the father of Theagenes, and that thus he was the last of the Heraclidae. He was a great athlete and was said to have won 1400 times in the games. When he died, one of his enemies went every night to the bronze statue of Theagenes at Thasus and flogged it. The statue avenged itself by falling on the man and killing him. The sons of the dead man prosecuted the statue for murder. It was convicted and hurled into the sea. After this the land of Thasus became barren. The Thasians went to Delphi to consult the priestess on this matter and were told to take back their exiles. They obeyed, but the land remained barren. Again they went to Delphi. This time they were told, "But you have forgotten your great Theagenes." They were at a loss how to recover the statue of Theagenes which was at the bottom of the sea, but some fishermen were sent out and caught it up in a net. The Thasians set it up and ever after sacrificed to it as to a god. Many other places had statues of Theagenes, to which they offered sacrifices as to one who cures diseases.

Theagenes. Tyrant of Megara; fl. 7th century B.C. He obtained 'a bodyguard, ·overthrew the wealthy nobles of Megara, and made himself tyrant (c640 B.C.). His daughter was married to the Athenian Cylon, whom Theagenes encouraged to attempt to win control of Athens. The attempt ended in failure. Theagenes constructed an aqueduct for Megara during his rule. He was at length overthrown and banished from Megara.

Theano (thē-ā′nō). In Greek mythology, the wife of Metapontus, king of Icaria in Attica. She had no children and feared that her husband would abandon her if she remained childless. She tricked him by adopting twin boys who had been exposed to die and presenting them to Metapontus as her own children. The twins were the sons of Poseidon and Arne: Boeotus, founder of the Boeotians, and Aeolus, who became guardian of the winds. They had been ordered exposed by Desmontes, foster father of Arne, who had blinded and imprisoned their mother. Later Theano produced twin sons of her own. When they grew up, she became jealous because Metapontus, thinking that all four were his children, preferred Aeolus and Boeotus. She engineered a plot against them, advising her own sons to take advantage of a hunting expedition to kill Boeotus and Aeolus. They attempted to do so but, with the aid of Poseidon, Aeolus and Boeotus killed the sons of Theano and carried their dead bodies back to the palace. When Theano learned how her plot had miscarried, she committed suicide.

Theano. In Greek legend, a daughter of Cisseus, king of Thrace, and Teleclia. She was the wife of the Trojan Antenor, and among her sons were Acamas, Agenor, Archelochus, Helicaon, Iphidamas, and Polybus. She also tenderly reared Antenor's bastard son Pedaeus. Antenor and Theano believed that Helen and her possessions should be returned to Menelaus, and according to some accounts, they entertained Odysseus and Menelaus when they came on a mission to Troy to secure Helen's return. Theano was a priestess of Athena and, according to some accounts, it was she who gave the sacred Palladium to Odysseus and Diomedes when they entered the city in secret some time after the death of Hector. For these reasons the Greeks spared Antenor and Theano after the fall of Troy, and they crossed to Thrace and from there went to the northern part of Italy where, according to tradition, they eventually founded the city of Patavium (Padua).

Thebae (thē′bē). Latin form of **Thebes**.

Thebaid (thē′bā-id), **The.** An epic poem in 12 books by the Roman poet Publius Papinius Statius (c45–96 A.D.), based on the quarrel between Polynices and Eteocles for possession of Thebes which culminated in the expedition of the Seven against Thebes. It was published about 91 A.D. In the Middle Ages the *Thebaid* was widely admired, but modern scholarship does not accord it the status of a great work. (JJ)

Thebais (thē′bā-is). Greek epic poem of the Theban Cycle, of unknown authorship, relating to a legendary war between Argos and Thebes.

Theban Cycle (thē′ban). Group of legends or epics relating to the war between Argos and Thebes.

Thebe (thē′bē). In Greek mythology, a daughter of the river-god Asopus and Metope. She was the twin sister of Aegina, and like her was carried off by Zeus. She was known as the nymph of Thebes and, according to some accounts, married Zethus, one of the brothers who built the lower city. The name of the city, formerly Cadmea, was changed to Thebes in her honor.

Thebes (thēbz). [Modern Greek, **Thevai**: Latin, **Thebae**.] In ancient geography, the chief city of Boeotia in Greece. According to tradition, Cadmus the Phoenician came to Thebes following, in obedience to the command of the oracle of Delphi, a cow that had white moons on its flanks. Where the cow sank to rest, he was instructed to build his city. This it did at Thebes and there Cadmus slew the dragon that guarded the fountain of Ares and sowed its teeth to raise a race of warriors. But some say that before Cadmus came into the land it was occupied by the Ectenes, whose king Ogygus, or Ogyges, was an aborigine who reigned before the great flood that Zeus sent to engulf Hellas. The Ectenes perished by pestilence. The land was occupied by the Hyantes and Aones, and it was in this time that Cadmus came and built the upper citadel, called the Cadmea, where he had his own house. The room in the house where his daughter Semele gave birth to Dionysus was barred to men as late as the 2nd century A.D., when the traveler Pausanias visited Thebes. (Excavations at Thebes have uncovered the remains of what is called the "palace of Cadmus.") The city was first called Cadmea and its inhabitants were known as Cadmeans. Later Amphion and Zethus came and conquered it and built the lower city and the walls. The name was changed to Thebes in honor, some say, of the nymph Thebe, daughter of the river-god Asopus. She was the wife of Zethus. Thebes was celebrated as the birthplace of Dionysus, Heracles, the seer Tiresias, Amphion and Zethus, and many others. It was the scene of the exploits and tragedies of the Labdacids, descendants of Cadmus, the family of which Laius, Oedipus, and his descendants were members. It was the target of the Expedition of the Seven against Thebes, caused by the rivalry between Polynices and Eteocles, sons of Oedipus; and of the war of the Epigoni, undertaken by the sons of the original Seven, in which the Thebans were overcome and the city was taken. King Thersander, grandson of Oedi-

pus, was slain in Mysia in the early years of the Trojan War. His grandson, Autesion, became king of Thebes, but on the advice of the oracle left the city and brought to an end the long line of Labdacid kings of Thebes. Within 60 years of the end of the Trojan War Thebes had become the capital of the cities of Boeotia. The wall of the ancient city was pierced by seven gates—the Electran, Proetidian, Neïstan, Crenaean, Hypsistan, Ogygian, and Homoloid Gates. Outside the Electran Gate, on a slight eminence, was the temple of Ismenian Apollo. The priest in the temple was a boy of noble family who served for one year. He was called a "laurel-bearer," from the wreath of laurel he wore. Heracles was one of these laurel-bearers, according to some accounts, and his foster father Amphitryon dedicated in the temple a bronze tripod in his name which was inscribed with the "Cadmean" letters said to have been introduced into Greece by Cadmus. Before the temple was a stone called "Manto's chair." She was the prophetic daughter of Tiresias; and within the temple was an image of Apollo of cedar wood, made by Canachus. Among the treasures of the temple were a shield, spear, and tripod, all of solid gold, dedicated by King Croesus of Lydia. The site of the temple was discovered in 1910. Among the sights of Thebes were a sanctuary of Heracles decorated with marble sculptures representing most of his great labors; a temple of Artemis Euclia (*Of Good Repute*) with an image by Scopas, before which was a stone lion dedicated by Heracles after he defeated Erginus; the spring where Oedipus washed off the blood that had splattered on him when he slew his father; the spring where Cadmus slew the dragon of Ares and brought down the wrath of that god on his descendants; a shrine and tomb of Amphion outside the Ogygian Gate, and, farther off, a shrine of Iolaus, the companion of Heracles; the tomb, near the Neïstan Gate, of Menoeceus, son of Creon, who voluntarily leaped from the walls of Thebes to his death in order to propitiate Ares and save the city when the Seven attacked it; a sanctuary of Athena near the Hypsistan Gate, where Cadmus, having killed the dragon, sacrificed a cow to the goddess; a temple containing ancient wooden images of Aphrodite, said to

have been made from the figureheads of the
ships that brought Cadmus to Greece and
dedicated by his wife Harmonia; the grave
of Trojan Hector near the fountain where
Oedipus cleansed his hands, for Hector's
bones were brought to Thebes in obedience
to an oracle; a temple of Ammon containing
an image dedicated by Pindar; and Pindar's
tomb.

Modern scholars say Thebes was early
settled by Boeotians from Thessaly, and that
by the 7th century B.C. it was the capital of a
loose confederation of Boeotian cities, from
which, however, the wealthy Boeotian city
of Orchomenus held aloof. In 509 B.C. the
Boeotian city of Plataea sought the protection
of Athens and became a staunch ally of that
city and the implacable enemy of Thebes.
The protection that Athens rendered Plataea
caused a quarrel between Athens and Thebes
and they became enemies. When Xerxes invaded Greece, Theban troops under Leonidas
at Thermopylae (480 B.C.) served unwillingly,
according to Herodotus, and after the defeat
of the Greek forces there, the Thebans allied
themselves openly with Persia, fought on the
Persian side, and shared in the Persian defeat at Plataea (479 B.C.). Some say the
Thebans fought on the side of the Persians
against their will, compelled by their aristocratic rulers who hated Athenian democracy.
After the Persian War the rivalry with Athens,
now stronger than ever, flared anew. In a
battle at Tanagra (457 B.C.) the Thebans,
with the aid of the Spartans, defeated the
Athenians but could not press their advantage, and were defeated by the Athenians
at Oenophyta in 456 B.C. During the
Peloponnesian Wars Thebes was the bitter
enemy of Athens and rendered aid to Sparta.
The partnership with Sparta was an unequal
one, however, and there were many Theban
voices raised against Sparta in the years immediately following the long wars. Following a defeat at Coronea (394 B.C.) Thebes
was forced to yield to Sparta (392 B.C.). In
382 B.C. the Spartans, by a conspiracy with
malcontents within the city, gained control
of the citadel of Thebes. They arranged to
seize it on the day when the Thesmophoria
was being celebrated, for on that day only
women, celebrating the feast, occupied it.
The Spartans thus took it without resistance

and established a government friendly to
Sparta. This government, and the Spartan
officials in Thebes, were overthrown (379
B.C.) by a most daring coup of Pelopidas, the
Theban general and good friend of Epaminondas. Under command of Epaminondas,
the Thebans defeated Sparta at the battle
of Leuctra (371 B.C.) and again at Mantinea
(362 B.C.), and established Theban hegemony of Greece. Epaminondas was killed at
Mantinea and those who assumed power in
Thebes exercised power over the Boeotian
cities so tyrannously that they earned for
Thebes a hatred that ultimately led to the
destruction of the city. Thebes took part in
the Sacred War (354 B.C.) that was carried
on intermittently about Delphi for ten years.
She was allied with Athens in the attempt to
hold back Philip of Macedon and was defeated with her at Chaeronea (338 B.C.), and
was severely treated by Philip, who stationed
a Macedonian garrison in the city. On the
death of Philip the Thebans rebelled. Philip's
son, Alexander the Great, marched against it
and subdued it. At his side fought the
Boeotian enemies of Thebes. Alexander gave
the beleaguered city every opportunity to
surrender without bloodshed, but the defenders refused, the citadel was taken, and
6000 Thebans were massacred before Alexander put a stop to the slaughter. He entrusted the fate of the city to the hands of
his Greek allies; they decreed that the people
be sold into slavery and the city razed to the
ground. At the command of Alexander, one
house was spared, that of Pindar the poet,
which stood alone among the ruins. Before
Alexander took the city, the Thebans were
warned of their black fate by a prodigy: a
spider spun a black web over the entrance
to the sanctuary of Demeter, the temple in
which, in happier times, the shields of the
Spartans who fell at Leuctra had been dedicated by the victorious Thebans. The city
was rebuilt by Cassander, who restored the
ancient walls, but it lapsed into insignificance
under the Roman Empire. Remains of the
walls of the ancient city are still to be seen
but much of the ancient city now lies buried
under 15 to 20 feet of earth.

Thelpusa (thel-pū′sạ). In ancient geography,
a town in Arcadia, Greece, on a hill near the
Ladon River. It was said to have been

named for a daughter of the river-god Ladon. The Thelpusians named Demeter Erinys (*Fury*) because of her great rage when Poseidon, transformed into a stallion, attacked her when she was disguised as a mare and was grazing with the mares of Oncus. Afterward, Demeter's wrath abated, and she bathed herself in the river and they gave her the name Lusia (*Bather*). The Thelpusians had images of the goddess of both names. Their image of Fury held a torch in one hand and a chest in the other. The Thelpusians also said they were the first to give the name Hippios (*Horse*) to Poseidon, because of the horse Arion that Demeter bore to him. Some say the infant Asclepius, son of Apollo and Coronis, was exposed at birth in Thelpusa, and was found by Autolaus, an illegitimate son of Arcas. For this reason the Thelpusians had a sanctuary of Asclepius Pais (*Boy*). They also had a sanctuary of the 12 gods.

Themis (thē′mis). In Greek mythology, a Titaness, the daughter of Gaea and Uranus. She was the mother by Zeus of the Moerae (Fates)—Atropos, Clotho, and Lachesis; of the Horae (Seasons); and of Prometheus. Early mythology says that she received the oracle of Delphi from Gaea, and the prophetic gift remained one of her attributes, for she warned her son Prometheus of what was in store for him. Later Themis, no longer the wife of Zeus, is the "fair-faced divinity," the handmaiden of the gods who presides with Zeus over justice and order, and sits on the throne beside him as his trusted counselor. She is the patron goddess of the rights of hospitality and a protector of the oppressed. It was Themis who told Deucalion and Pyrrha how to repopulate the earth after the disastrous flood which had swept away all mankind save these two. Themis, with the power of foretelling the future, told Poseidon, and after him Zeus, that Thetis the Nereid whom both were pursuing, would bear a son greater than his father. Because of this Zeus abandoned his designs on Thetis and wed her to Peleus. Themis, who became the personification of law, custom, and justice, was worshiped especially in Athens, Delphi, Olympia, Thebes, and Troezen.

Themiste (thē-mis′tē), or **Themis**. According

to legend, a daughter of Laomedon and Eurydice. She married Capys, the son of Assaracus, and was the mother of Anchises.

Themisto (thē-mis′tō). In Greek legend, a wife of Athamas. According to some accounts, Athamas married her after he had settled in Thessaly, having been banished from Boeotia after the death of Ino and his sons, and raised a new family. But others say that Ino, the wife of Athamas and the mother of his sons Learchus and Melicertes, went out hunting one day and did not return. A blood-stained robe that was found convinced Athamas that Ino had been killed by wild beasts. After a brief period of mourning he married Themisto. But Ino had only gone to Mount Parnassus for a prolonged revel with the maenads and by the time Athamas learned that she was still alive Themisto had borne him twin sons. Athamas tried to conceal Ino as a nurse for his young children but Themisto learned her true identity, although she pretended not to know who Ino was. She went to the nursery and told the new nurse to prepare mourning garments for the two sons of the former wife of Athamas, and told the new nurse (Ino) that the garments were to be used on the next day. The next day Themisto ordered her servants to break into the nursery and kill the two children who were dressed in mourning garments. The servants obeyed her orders but Ino, suspecting foul play by Themisto, had dressed the children of Themisto in mourning garments rather than her own children. Thus it was the children of Themisto that were killed. When Athamas learned of their deaths he went mad, killed his son Learchus and would have killed Ino and Melicertes, but she took her son in her arms and leaped into the sea. Themisto, learning of the death of her children by her own orders, killed herself.

Themistocles (thē-mis′tō-klēz). Athenian statesman and commander, born c528 B.C.; died, in Asia, c462 B.C. He became a political leader in opposition to Aristides, who was ostracized in 483 B.C., and, recognizing the continued Persian threat, was instrumental in increasing the naval resources of Athens. He persuaded the Athenians to use the money in their treasury to build up the fleet to 200 ships. When Xerxes made ready to invade Greece, the Athenians consulted the oracle at Delphi. The priestess predicted utter destruction for the Athenians and urged them to fly. The Athenians again sought the priestess as suppliants, and said they would not leave the precinct until they received a more favorable response. The priestess answered them thus:

When the foe shall have taken whatever
  the limit of Cecrops
Holds within it, . . .
Then far-seeing Zeus grants this to the
  prayers of Athena:
Safe shall the wooden wall continue for
  thee and thy children.

. . . .

Yet shall a day arrive when ye shall meet
  him in battle.
Holy Salamis, thou shalt destroy the offspring of women,
When men scatter the seed, or when they
  gather the harvest.

Though this seemed somewhat more hopeful, it was open to various interpretations. Some thought "the wooden wall" referred to the Citadel of Athens, which had originally been of wood. Others thought "the wooden wall" meant the ships, but those who took this view were disturbed by the reference to Salamis and thought it meant that the fleet would be defeated there. Themistocles now came forward. According to his interpretation, "the wooden wall" meant the ships, and the inclusion of "Holy Salamis" indicated a victory there. The Athenians, determined to preserve their liberty at any cost, adopted his view and prepared to defend themselves with their fleet. Themistocles went as one of the commanders of a Greek expedition to Thessaly while Xerxes was preparing to pass into Europe from Asia, but the expedition withdrew on the advice of messengers from Macedonia. Later, at Artemisium, he is said to have accepted a bribe from the Euboeans to make a stand at Artemisium and protect the Euboeans. He used part of the money to bribe other commanders, who wished to withdraw, and the remainder he kept for himself, unknown to anyone. The battle fought at Artemisium, at the same time as the land battle at Thermopylae, was inconclusive, but the Persians suffered great losses through storms at sea. When Athens was at length overrun by the Persians, the Athenian fleet withdrew to Salamis. Themistocles wanted to engage the Persian fleet there, but had great difficulty persuading the other captains to do so, particularly the most important of the allies, the Spartans, who wished to retire to the Isthmus, build a wall across it, and defend the Peloponnesus. Themistocles understood that the Greek fleet, because of its superior maneuverability, could do great damage to the Persian fleet in the enclosed area of Salamis, whereas in the open sea the Persians would have the advantage. To force the hand of his unwilling allies, Themistocles sent a messenger to the Persian fleet. The burden of his message, which was true, was that the Greeks, in fear of the Persians, were on the point of flight; that they were at odds with each other; and that now was the time for the Persians to strike. The Persians took cognizance of the message and redeployed their land and sea forces to surround the Greeks at Salamis. While the Greek captains argued, Aristides, the old enemy of Themistocles, but one with him in his desire to preserve Greek liberty, came to them and told them their arguments were now academic, as they were surrounded. Thus, thanks to Themistocles, the matter was taken out of their hands; they had no option but to fight on the site Themistocles had chosen, and won a magnificent victory at Salamis (480 B.C.). After the victory and the flight of the Persians, Themistocles was out-voted in his desire to pursue the Persians to the Hellespont and destroy the bridges which they must use to return their land forces to Asia. Seeing that the allies would not go, he prevailed on the Athenians to give up the pursuit. At the end of the war all Greece rang with the fame of Themistocles, but through the jealousy and rivalry of the commanders, the Athenians withheld the honor that was his due to him—the crown of victory. He went to Sparta and was received and honored as no other stranger had ever been honored by the Spartans. When the Persians had withdrawn, the Athenians returned to rebuild their ruined city. Themistocles urged them to drop everything and rebuild the walls of the city, and also to build a walled way between Athens and her port, Piraeus, so that they would always have access to their fleet. The Athenians did as he advised,

actor; up, lūte, pull; oi, oil; ou, out; ŦH, then; d̦ as d or j, ş as s or sh, ț as t or ch, z̧ as z or zh.

but after the dangers of the war had passed, there were many in Athens who were bitterly jealous of Themistocles. The story of his bribe to remain and fight at Artemisium came out, and he was ostracized (c471 B.C.). He lived in exile in Argos and elsewhere. He was charged with complicity in the treason of the Spartan Pausanias, who planned to rule Greece with Persian aid; learning that the Athenians planned to seize him, as the Spartans had seized Pausanias, he fled. He went to Corcyra, and ultimately to Asia, where he sent a message to King Artaxerxes. He made a claim on the friendship of Artaxerxes, son of Xerxes, because, he said, he had prevented the Athenians from sailing to the Hellespont and destroying the bridges by which the Persian army of his father returned to Asia. He asked to be allowed to stay in Asia one year, at the end of which time he promised to present himself to the king. Artaxerxes granted his request. Themistocles spent his year of grace learning the Persian language and customs of the country.' At the end of the year he arrived at the court of Artaxerxes and was received with every evidence of respect and honor. He put his genius at the service of Artaxerxes and was rewarded by being named governor of the district of Asiatic Magnesia. Thucydides speaks of Themistocles as a man who exhibited "the most indubitable signs of genius," one who had an extraordinary and unparalleled claim on Greek admiration because of his native capacity, his ability to meet any emergency, and his wisdom as to present courses and future prospects. Though there was a story that he committed suicide, because he failed in his promises to the Persian king, Thucydides says he died of disease. A monument to him was set up in Magnesia. Because he was charged with treason, he could not lawfully be buried in Athens, but relatives secretly took up his bones and buried them in his native soil.

Theoclymenus (thē″ō-klī′mē̲-nus). In the *Odyssey*, a son of the seer Polyphides and a descendant of Melampus. He was also a seer. He was compelled to flee from his home in Argos for committing a murder, and met Telemachus when the latter was at the court of Nestor in Pylus in search of news of his father Odysseus. Telemachus gave Theoclymenus his protection and took him back to Ithaca. There Theoclymenus told Penelope that Odysseus still lived and would soon return, as he was actually then in his homeland. Theoclymenus also prophesied their end to Penelope's suitors, but they mocked his words.

Theoclymenus. According to Euripides, a son of Psamathe and Proteus, king of Egypt. He succeeded his father. Having determined to marry Helen, who had been transported to Egypt while a phantom Helen went to Troy, he became a fierce enemy of the Greeks and killed any who chanced to land in his country. He was about to kill his sister Theonoë because she had not told him that Menelaus had landed in Egypt, and as a result Menelaus succeeded in escaping with Helen, but the Dioscuri (Helen's brothers) appeared in the heavens and told him to spare her; that all had been done at the will of the gods.

Theocritus (thē̲-ok′ri-tus). Greek idyllic poet; born at Syracuse; fl. in the 3rd century B.C. He lived at Cos, at Alexandria, where Ptolemy Philadelphus was his patron, and at Syracuse, where Hiero II was his patron. Two of his 32 surviving *Idylls* are appeals to his patrons. Theocritus is credited with being the inventor of pastoral poetry. Ten of the *Idylls* describe, with gently nostalgic sweetness, the life of herdsmen, shepherds, and fishermen. The life so described is on the one hand idealized and on the other marked with touching and realistic detail. The *Adoniazusae* is in mimetic style and tells of the adventures of two Syracusan women at the great feast of Adonis at Alexandria. His *Dirge on Daphnis* has been widely imitated, both by the ancients and later poets. Other surviving *Idylls* are love poems, studies of the ordinary life of the people, and two occasional poems which "are not only gems in themselves, but leave the fragrance of a lovable character behind them." (Gilbert Murray). The Roman poet Vergil was strongly influenced by Theocritus, and eight of Vergil's ten *Eclogues* are modelled after or inspired by Theocritus' *Idylls*.

Theognis (thē̲-og′nis). Greek elegiac and gnomic poet; born in Megara; fl. in the middle or last part of the 6th century B.C.

He was an aristocrat, who lived at a time when the noble class was being tumbled from power and its position as the cultural leader of the state by uprisings of the people. Theognis saw his friends slain, lost his fortune, and was driven into exile, from which he returned only after many years. His work is then, not unnaturally, everywhere marked by a violent hatred of the "demos," "who knows no standard to tell them what is noble and ignoble, because they have no tradition," and by his exhortations to preserve the ideals of culture of his own class, which has standards and tradition. The works of Theognis are largely directed to the young nobleman Cyrnus, squire and intimate of the poet. They are maxims, precepts by which Cyrnus will attain the noble manhood expected of one of his class. He is exhorted by Theognis to tell the truth, to avoid the company of base men, to fight bravely, and to be loyal to his friend. The work of Theognis that survives was preserved in an anthology that was used in the 3rd century B.C. as a book of precepts for the young. The collection includes interpolated selections from Solon, Mimnermus, Tyrtaeus, and others.

Theogony (thē-og′ō-ni), **The**. Ancient Greek poem of 1022 lines, attributed to Hesiod, treating of the origin of the order of nature from chaos and the origin of the gods.

Theonoë (thē-on′ō-ē). In Greek legend, a daughter of Thestor, and the sister of Calchas who accompanied the Greeks to Troy, and of Leucippe. While at play on the seashore near Troy she was captured by pirates and sold to King Icarus of Caria, whose mistress she became. Some time later a handsome young priest of Apollo arrived in Caria. Theonoë fell in love with him but he scorned her advances. Theonoë, enraged, resolved to have the priest slain, but did not want to ask her slaves to commit the sacrilege of killing a priest, so she ordered that one of the foreign slaves must slay him. The foreign slave went to the room where the priest was confined and announced that he had been ordered to kill him but that he refused to do so; rather, he would kill himself, but first he wanted to tell how he came to be in such a sad plight. The priest announced that

he was Thestor, the father of Theonoë and Leucippe, and that he had fallen into the hands of the king's concubine while searching for his lost daughter Theonoë; then, as he made ready to kill himself, the priest of Apollo revealed that he was really Leucippe, Thestor's own daughter, disguised as a priest at the command of the oracle of Delphi and engaged on the same errand as Thestor, namely, a search for Theonoë. Father and daughter wept in each other's arms and then resolved to kill the king's wicked mistress. They entered Theonoë's apartments and Leucippe announced to her that for lusting after the young priest, she must prepare to die at the hands of Thestor, son of Idmon. Hereupon Theonoë revealed that she was the daughter of Thestor who had been carried away by pirates years before and had not recognized her father and sister. Now all three rejoiced and gave thanks to Apollo. King Icarus, being informed of their history, gave Theonoë her freedom and sent them all home together.

Theonoë. According to Euripides, a daughter of Psamathe and Proteus, king of Egypt. She was a prophetess and knew that Menelaus had landed in Egypt, seven years after the Trojan War ended. She decided not to tell her brother, who was wooing Helen, because Helen had been brought to Egypt to be protected by Proteus until Menelaus could claim her. By her silence she allowed Menelaus and Helen to escape.

Theophane (thē-of′a-nē). In Greek mythology, a beautiful maiden, the cousin of Phrixus and Helle. She had many suitors, among them Poseidon. To get her away from the other suitors he carried her off to the island of Crumissa. When her other suitors followed, he transformed her into a ewe and himself into a ram and the inhabitants of the island into cattle. The suitors, arriving and finding no people, slew the cattle and began to eat them. Poseidon changed them into wolves. In his form of a ram he married Theophane and she bore him the ram with the golden fleece that bore Phrixus to safety in Colchis and whose fleece was the object of the expedition of the Argonauts.

Theophrastus (thē-ō-fras′tus). Greek philosopher and naturalist; born at Eresus, Lesbos, c372 B.C.; died c287 B.C. After studying philosophy at Lesbos he went to Athens, where he became first a pupil of Plato and then a disciple of Aristotle. His name was originally Tyrtamus. Aristotle gave him the name Theophrastus (*Divine Speaker*) in acknowledgment of his power of language. Aristotle made him the guardian of his son, bequeathed him his library, and named him as his successor at the Lyceum. His *History of Plants* and other botanical works were the most important contributions to botanical science of antiquity. His other scientific-philosophical work is also important in the development of scientific thought. Theophrastus is also remembered for his 30 short *Characters*, vivid vignettes of such types as The Flatterer, The Grumbler, and The Boastful Man.

Theopompus (thē-ō-pom′pus). King of Sparta who took Messenia for Sparta in the First Messenian War. His tomb was near the sanctuary of Lycurgus in Sparta.

Theopompus. Greek historian and rhetorician; born in Chios, c378 B.C.; died about the end of the 4th century B.C. In his youth he went to Athens with his father, who had been forced to leave Chios because of his pro-Spartan leanings. In Athens Theopompus became a pupil of Isocrates the orator. He mastered the techniques of oratory so thoroughly that he not only spoke with success throughout Greece, but even won (351 B.C.) in a rhetorical contest sponsored by Queen Artemisia of Pergamum in honor of her husband Mausolus. He returned to Chios under the patronage of Alexander the Great, but on the death of the latter was again obliged to leave, as his aristocratic views and Macedonian leanings made him extremely unpopular. He went to Alexandria and there disappears from history. The *Hellenica* of Theopompus, in 12 books, was a continuation of the History of Thucydides to 394 B.C. His *Philippica*, in 58 books, was a history of his own times, in which Philip II of Macedon was the central figure. He included so many disgressions in the latter work that, so it is said, when Philip extracted the digressions the work was reduced to 16 books. The *Philippica* is thought to be the only Greek work concerning Philip which made an honest attempt to portray the man and his deeds and which recognized his greatness as well as his weaknesses. Only fragments of these works survive.

Theoricon (thē-or′i-kon) In ancient Athens, a public appropriation, including, besides the moneys for the conduct of public festivals and sacrifices, supplementary to the impositions (liturgies) on individuals for some of these purposes, a fund which was distributed at the rate of two obols per person per day to poor citizens, ostensibly to pay for their seats in the theater or for other individual expenses at festivals. The funds of the Theoricon were deposited in the Theoric Fund which ultimately became so important that a special minister was required to manage it. The use to which the Theoric Fund was put was influential in gaining the good will of the people and came to be a political weapon of some importance. In the time of Demosthenes the money of the fund, thanks to his influence, was used for military purposes.

Theoxenius (thē-ok-sē′nus). An epithet of Apollo, meaning "Strangers' God."

Thera (thir′a, thē′ra). [Also: **Thira, Santorin.**] Volcanic island in the S part of the Cyclades. According to legend, it rose from the sea when Euphemus the Argonaut flung into the sea at this spot a clod of earth given to him as a gift by Triton. It became the home of the descendants of Euphemus, and was known by the name Calliste. According to Herodotus, Cadmus stopped at Calliste when he sailed in search of Europa, and left a colony there. His descendants were on the island eight generations later when Theras, a Spartan, brought emigrants from Sparta to the island and founded a colony. In his honor the island was renamed Thera. It was from Thera that Battus later, at the command of the oracle of Delphi, colonized Libya. This was the colony that was sent forth to Cyrene in 631 B.C. The island rises steeply from the sea, and has long been celebrated for its volcanic activity. The sea forced a way into the volcanic cone and provided a deep anchorage for ships, almost at the center of the island. At times the water at certain spots can be seen to bubble from the subterranean pressures of the volcano. An eruption of the volcano occurred in 1956. Area of the island, 30 square miles; length, 10 miles.

Theramenes (thę-ram′ę-nēz). Athenian politician and military commander; executed 404 B.C. He was one of the leaders in the establishment (411 B.C.) of the oligarchic rule of the Four Hundred, which he later opposed for its extremity. He served at Cyzicus, Arginusae, and elsewhere, and was instrumental in procuring the condemnation of the Athenian generals after Arginusae. He was one of the negotiators (405–404 B.C.) for peace with Sparta, became one of the Thirty Tyrants, and through the influence of Critias was forced to drink poison.

Therapne (thę-rap′nē). In Greek legend, a daughter of Lelex, who gave her name to a town in Laconia between Amyclae and Sparta, near the Eurotas River. Some say Helen and Menelaus were buried here, and sacrifices were offered to both as to a goddess and a god, and festivals were held for them. There was a sanctuary there which some thought was a sanctuary of Helen but others say it was a temple of Menelaus. At Therapne, according to some accounts, there was a burial place of the Dioscuri.

Therimachus (thę-rim′ą-kus). According to some accounts, the eldest son of Heracles and Megara. He was intended to succeed Eurystheus but was slain by Heracles in a fit of madness.

Theritas (thę-rī′tas). Epithet of Ares, under which he was worshiped in Laconia. Young dogs were sacrificed at the sanctuary of Ares Theritas on the road from Amyclae to Therapne in Laconia, the oldest sanctuary of Ares. The image in the temple was said to have been brought from the temple of Ares in Colchis by the Dioscuri. Some say the name Theritas was given Ares because he had a Colchian nurse named Thero. Others say this name comes from a word meaning "wild beast," and was given to him because he is a war and battle god, and when one engages in battle one must cast aside all qualities of gentleness and humanity.

Therma (thėr′mą). In ancient geography, a city of Macedonia, situated at the head of the Thermaic Gulf (Gulf of Salonika), which was named for the city. Xerxes stopped here in his invasion of Greece, 480

B.C. It was held briefly by the Athenians just before the Peloponnesian Wars. About 316 B.C. Cassander founded the city of Thessalonica nearby and Therma was absorbed in it.

Thermae Himeraeae (thėr′mē him-ėr-ē′ē) or **Himerenses** (him-ėr-en′sēz). [Modern name, **Termini Imerese**.] In ancient geography, a town on the N coast of Sicily. It was founded (407 B.C.) by the Carthaginians, near the site of Himera, which they had destroyed. The town was on the hill above "the hot baths of the Nymphs" mentioned by Pindar. Its name, Thermae, refers to the hot springs, and the name Himeraeae signalizes the old Greek city that was destroyed. Greek settlers soon came to live in the Carthaginian town of Thermae Himeraeae and made of it a Greek town. Much contested between Syracusans and Carthaginians, it finally became a Roman town. Among scanty remains of antiquity are those of a Roman theater.

Thermaic Gulf (thėr-mā′ik) or **Thermaicus Sinus** (thėr-mā′i-kus sī′nus). Northwesternmost arm of the Aegean Sea, situated W of the Chalcidice peninsula. Length, about 70 miles.

Thermasia (thėr-mā′si-ą). Epithet of Demeter. Demeter Thermasia (*Warmth*) was worshiped at Hermion and Troezen.

Thermodon (thėr′mō-don). In ancient geography, a river of Pontus. The area about its mouth was traditionally the home of the Amazons.

Thermopylae (thėr-mop′i-lē). Hot salt springs on the border of Locris; the name means "hot gates." According to some accounts, Heracles, preparing to sacrifice to Zeus after his conquest of Eurytus, donned a ceremonial robe his wife sent to him here. The robe had been secretly anointed by his wife with the dried blood of his fallen enemy, the centaur Nessus. When the heat of the sacrificial fires melted the blood poisoned by one of Heracles' own arrows, the robe clung to Heracles and seared and stung his flesh. Maddened by the burning pain, he leaped into the waters to cool his body, but the heat of his flesh was so intense it caused the waters to bubble and steam. Ever since, these springs have been hot. The springs are at the narrow pass of the same name which runs from Thessaly to Locris, between Mount Oeta and a marsh bordering the Maliacus Sinus (Gulf of Lamia). (The configuration of the land has been somewhat changed in modern times.) Through it passed the only road from N to S Greece. Here occurred (480 B.C.) one of the most famous conflicts of the Persian Wars. A small band of Greeks under the Spartan Leonidas defended the pass against a vast army under Xerxes. Their position was betrayed, and Leonidas sent away his troops, except for 300 Spartans and 700 Thespians. These remained and with unmatched courage resisted the Persians until all were slain. According to Herodotus, two Spartans had been sent to the rear before the final battle, because they were afflicted by diseases of the eye. When they heard of the assault being made against Leonidas, one of them ordered his slave to bring him his armor and lead him to the battle. The slave did so and fled; his master plunged into the fight and perished with his friends. The other Spartan afflicted with a disease of the eyes used his sickness as an excuse to stay away from the battle and later returned to Sparta. There he was greeted with disgrace. No Spartan would give him a light to kindle his fire, nor would any Spartan speak with him. But this man, Aristodemus, redeemed himself later at the battle of Plataea (479 B.C.). Another Spartan who survived because he had been sent as an envoy to Thessaly by Leonidas was in such disgrace when he returned to Sparta that he hanged himself. In 279 or 278 B.C., the allied Greeks attempted unsuccessfully to prevent the passage of the Gauls under Brennus through the pass; and here, in 191 B.C., the Romans under Glabrio defeated Antiochus III of Syria.

Thero (thē'rō). According to some accounts, a nurse of Ares, thought to be from Colchis.

Theron (thē'ron). Tyrant of Acragas in Sicily (488–472 B.C.). His daughter Damareta was married to Gelon, tyrant of Syracuse, with whom Theron had close political ties. Under Theron, whose rule is said to have been mild and just, Acragas prospered and became second only to Syracuse in wealth. A quarrel between Theron and Terillus, tyrant of Himera, gave the Carthaginians an opportunity to interfere in Sicily. Theron united with Gelon to drive them out (480 B.C.), and as a result he won control of Himera. After the war he devoted himself to the enlargement and beautification of Acragas. In his time the foundations were laid for the row of temples along the south wall of the city that were brought to magnificent completion only long after his death.

Thersander (thėr-san'dėr). In Greek legend, a son of Polynices and Argia. He was one of the Epigoni who marched against Thebes to avenge their fathers for their disastrous defeat in the expedition of the Seven against Thebes. Thersander, like his father before him, bribed Eriphyle, mother of Alcmaeon. He gave her the robe of Harmonia to influence her son to command the expedition of the Epigoni. His boast, after the successful completion of the war, that the success was due to him because of his bribe, was overheard by Alcmaeon and led to Eriphyle's death at the hands of her son. Thersander became king of Thebes after the city was captured. By his wife Demonassa he was the father of Tisamenus. Thersander, in company with Diomedes, brought forty ships to the Trojan War. According to some accounts, he was killed when the Greeks raided the kingdom of Telephus in Mysia. Telephus drove the Greeks back, all except Thersander, who bravely withstood him and was killed. Diomedes performed the funeral rites for his burial in Mysia and a shrine was erected to him. But others say Thersander survived the battle in Mysia, went on with the Greeks to Troy, and ultimately was one of those who entered Troy in the Wooden Horse.

Thersilion (thėr-sil'i-on). The convention hall of the federal assembly of the Arcadian League at Megalopolis, named for its founder, built in the 4th century B.C., and notable for its size (over 35,000 square feet), and the ingenious arrangement of the interior columns supporting the roof, which, in order to reduce to the minimum their obstruction of the view from any part of the hall, are ranged in lines radiating from the speaker's platform. The Thersilion is connected to the theater of Megalopolis,

with which it forms an architectural whole;
its Doric entrance portico of 14 columns
faced the auditorium and served as a permanent scene. Megalopolis was destroyed
in 222 B.C. and the Thersilion apparently
was not rebuilt. (JJ)

Thersilochus (thėr-sil'ọ̄-kus). In the *Iliad*, a
Paeonian ally of the Trojans. He was slain
by Achilles on the banks of the Xanthus
as he sped in full flight before the raging
Achilles after the death of Patroclus.
Aeneas met his shade in the Underworld
when he visited Anchises there.

Thersites (thėr-sī'tēz). In the *Iliad*, a son of
Agrius of Aetolia. He was bowlegged, lame,
and deformed in the shoulders. Homer
says that he was the ugliest Greek at Troy.
He roused the wrath of Odysseus by accusing Agamemnon of greed and Achilles of
cowardice. Odysseus beat him and threatened to drive him off in dishonor if he
again heard him assail the name of
Agamemnon. His impudent, quarrelsome,
abusive nature made him disliked by his
fellow Greeks. No one mourned when
Achilles, enraged because Thersites had
mocked him for his grief over the death of
Penthesilea, smote him so hard that his teeth
fell out, accompanied by his gushing blood,
and he fell to earth dead.

Theseum (thȩ̄-sē'um). A hieron or sanctuary
near the Agora of Athens, dedicated to the
hero-king Theseus, but not yet identified by
the Agora excavators. Here were reburied,
as those of Theseus, the bones brought by
Cimon from Scyrus; on its walls were famous
paintings, and it was a familiar place of
refuge. The well-preserved Periclean marble
temple which stands on the terrace dominating the Agora on the west was formerly
considered to be a temple of Theseus, and
is pictured under the name of Theseum in
many older works on the antiquities of
Athens. It has now been shown beyond
reasonable doubt that this temple was dedicated to Hephaestus, or to Hephaestus and
Athena, and it is probable that the real
sanctuary of Theseus did not contain a
temple. In the meantime, however, the
erroneous identification had suggested a
name, the "Theseum Architect," for the
otherwise nameless architect who designed
the temple of Hephaestus and other struc-

tures, and this designation continues in use.
(JJ)

Theseum Architect. A name, inspired by the
erroneous identification of the Theseum at
Athens with the temple of Hephaestus, retained as a convenient designation for the
otherwise nameless master architect who
designed the Periclean marble temples of
Hephaestus and Ares at Athens, of Poseidon
at Sunium, and of Nemesis at Rhamnus. (JJ)

Theseus (thē'sös, thē'sȩ̄-us). In Greek legend,
an Athenian hero, the Athenian counterpart
of Heracles, who traced his descent from
Erechtheus and Pelops. Aegeus, king of
Athens, being childless, consulted the oracle
at Delphi. He could not interpret the answer the priestess gave him and later, when
visiting Pittheus, son of Pelops, in Troezen,
he told Pittheus the oracular pronouncement
and asked what it meant. Pittheus, renowned for his wisdom, did not interpret
the response. He entertained Aegeus lavishly and when he was flushed with wine,
he sent his own daughter Aethra in to him.
Aegeus embraced her. The same night
Aethra, in obedience to a dream, waded
across the sea to a nearby island and was
ravished by Poseidon. For this reason Poseidon is sometimes called the father of
Theseus, and indeed many times he came
to the hero's aid, but generally Theseus is
called the son of Aegeus. Before Aegeus
left Troezen, he placed a sword and a pair
of sandals under a huge stone. He told
Aethra if she should bear a son, to rear him
in secret in Troezen, lest the 50 sons of
Pallas should seek to destroy him. When
she thought he was strong enough, she
was to take him to the rock. If he could
lift it and recover the sword and sandals,
Aegeus said, she was to send him to Athens.
Aegeus then departed. In due course
Aethra bore a son and named him Theseus,
because of the tokens Aegeus had "deposited" under the rock, but some say he
took this name later. He was reared in
Troezen by his grandfather Pittheus. When
he grew to young manhood, Theseus journeyed to Delphi to offer the first clippings
of his hair to Apollo, as was the custom. He
was a strong, spirited, intelligent youth.
On his return, Aethra told him the story of
his birth and led him to the rock under

which the tokens lay. Theseus easily lifted it and recovered the sword and sandals. Then, following the instructions of Aegeus, he set out for Athens. Aethra and Pittheus urged him to go by sea, as the land route was made dangerous by brigands, monsters, and terrorists. But Theseus, in the hope of emulating his greatly admired relative Heracles, determined to follow the more hazardous overland route. He wished, he said, to present his father with a sword that had been blessed by use. He promised to wrong no man but to punish any who attacked him.

Near Epidaurus he met Periphetes, the "Club-bearer," who attacked travelers with his bronze club and beat them to death. Theseus seized the club and used it against Periphetes, slaying him. He was then so pleased with the huge club that he kept it as his own and carried it with him ever after, as Heracles had done with his club of olive wood. At the Isthmus of Corinth he came upon Sinis, the "Pine-bender," who compelled travelers to help him bend down pine trees. When, by main strength, Sinis and the traveler were holding the top of the arched tree to the ground, Sinis would let go. Without his strength the tree snapped upright, flinging the traveler into the air and then dashing him to his death on the ground. But some say Sinis bent two trees to the ground, tied his victim to the two trees, then released them. As the trees sprang upright, the victim was torn apart. Theseus slew Sinis by the same means. He found Perigune, daughter of Sinis, hiding in the rushes in terror of him. He persuaded her that he would do her no harm and won her love. She bore him Melanippus. Theseus later gave her to Deioneus of Oechalia. Theseus next slew the Crommyonian Sow, a savage beast said by some to be the offspring of Echidna and Typhon. The animal had been roaming the countryside, terrorizing the inhabitants. This sow, also called Phaea, was said by some not to have been an animal at all, but an evil female robber, whose greed and habits won her the name of sow. Theseus dispatched her and proceeded on his way. At the Megarian cliffs he came upon Sciron, whose custom it was to compel travelers to wash his feet as he sat near the edge of the cliff. As they squatted to carry out his bidding, he kicked them into the sea. Theseus refused to obey him. Instead he hurled Sciron into the sea. But some say it was not on the journey to Athens that he killed Sciron, whom they call an upright man, but later, when he captured Eleusis from the Megarians. Proceeding to Eleusis, he met Cercyon the wrestler and overcame him, not by strength but by skill, as Theseus was the first to understand the principles of wrestling. Next he encountered Damastes, called Procrustes, "Stretcher." He had two beds in his lodging, one short and one long. It was his evil practice to lure travelers to spend the night in his house. Short travelers he place on the long bed, and stretched them out until they fitted the bed. Tall travelers were given the short bed, and had as much of their limbs lopped off as was necessary to fit them to the bed. But some say Procrustes had only one bed which he used in both manners. Theseus killed him. At the Cephissus River Theseus came to the home of the Phytalidae, the sons of Phytalus. They purified him of the murders he had committed and treated him with courtesy. These were the first on his journey to receive him in a friendly manner. He later rewarded them by making them priests of a temple of Artemis which he raised in Troezen. Proceeding to Athens, Theseus passed an uncompleted temple of Apollo on the outskirts of the city. Masons working on the roof of the temple spied him and jeered his youthful appearance. They pretended they thought he was a girl and coarsely wondered that he should be walking about alone. Theseus made no reply to their taunts. Instead he unyoked an ox from the masons' cart and hurled the animal high into the air above the roof of the temple. Without more ado he went on to find his father's house.

In the years since he had visited Pittheus in Troezen and embraced Aethra, Aegeus had married Medea, the sorceress whom Jason brought back with him from Colchis. She bore him a son, Medeus, and feared that Theseus, whom by her arts she recognized the instant he came to Athens, would displace her son in the affections of Aegeus and as heir to his throne. She plotted to

fat, fāte, fär, fāre, errant; net, mē, hėr ardent; pin, pīne; not, nōte, möve, nôr,

kill Theseus. Aegeus did not know that the youth who appeared before him, and whom he had never seen before, was his own son. Some say that at Medea's suggestion he sent Theseus to capture the Marathonian Bull. This bull had been brought over the sea from Crete by Heracles and was ravaging the countryside. Theseus subdued the bull and dragged it by its horns through Athens and sacrificed it to Apollo. But some say he did this later, after he had been recognized as the son of Aegeus. Medea persuaded Aegeus, who still had not learned that this was his son, that the young stranger was a threat to him. She induced Aegeus to offer him a cup of wine that she had poisoned with aconite. This occurred at a banquet held in the temple on the Acropolis where Aegeus lived. As Theseus lifted the cup to his lips, Aegeus caught sight of the hilt of the sword the young man was wearing. By the serpents twined about the hilt he recognized it as his own sword and realized that this must be his son. He dashed the cup from Theseus' hand. The spot where it fell was afterward barred off in the temple. Aegeus was overcome with joy at this meeting with his valiant son, and all Athens celebrated. Medea, for her plots, was expelled from Athens, and her child with her. The sons of Pallas, brother of Aegeus, claimed that Aegeus was not a true descendant of Erechtheus, and they had been plotting to seize the throne. The arrival of Theseus put their plans out of joint and they resolved to divide their forces and attack the city from two sides. But Theseus was warned of their intentions by the herald Leos. He fell upon one of the forces of the Pallantids and slew them. Those in the other force scattered.

When he had been in Athens but a little while, the time came for the Athenians to send the tribute which King Minos of Crete exacted every nine years with the sanction of the gods, because the Athenians had caused the death of his son Androgeus. This tribute consisted of seven youths and seven maidens who were selected by lot and sent to Crete, there to be devoured by the Minotaur, the monstrous son of Pasiphaë, who was kept concealed in a winding labyrinth. The most common account is that Theseus won the hearts of the Athenians by volunteering to be one of the seven youths. Some say, however, that his lot was drawn; and others say that Minos came from Crete to select the young Athenians himself, and that he instantly chose Theseus. The custom was to send the youths and maidens to Crete in a ship fitted with a black sail as a sign of mourning for the loss Athens suffered. Theseus assured Aegeus that he meant to slay the Minotaur and return. Aegeus gave him a white sail, or as some say, a scarlet one, and instructed him to replace the black sail with it if he was successful in escaping from Crete. Before his departure Theseus made vows and prayers to Apollo at Delphi, and was told by the priestess to take Aphrodite as his guide. When the youths and maidens of the tribute were gathered at the shore, he sacrificed to Aphrodite, and his victim, a she-goat, was transformed into a he-goat as it died. With this favorable omen the Athenians departed. At that time the Athenians were not so skilled at navigation as they were to become later. Theseus took as his pilots for the voyage to Crete Nausithous of Salamis and Phaeax, who some say was the ancestor of the Phaeacians. The *Cyberneria,* or Pilots' Festival, was afterward celebrated at Phalerum in their honor. When the Athenians arrived in Crete, Minos came down to the shore to look them over. He was favorably impressed by one of the maidens in the group and would have seized her. Theseus sprang forward in anger and forbade him to touch any of the maidens who had been sent as tribute. He said that as a son of Poseidon he would protect the virgins who had come with him to Crete. Minos mocked his claim to be a son of Poseidon. He took a ring from his finger and, hurling it into the sea, commanded Theseus to prove he was a son of Poseidon by retrieving the ring. "First," said Theseus, "prove that you are, as you claim, a son of Zeus." Minos prayed to Zeus for a sign and immediately there was a loud clap of thunder and a flash of lightning. Theseus acknowledged this proof. He leaped into the sea to prove his own claim. A school of dolphins escorted him to the underwater palace of Thetis the Nereid.

actor; up, lūte, pull; oi, oil; ou, out; ᴛʜ, then; đ as d or j, ş as s or sh, ṭ as t or ch, ẕ as z or zh.

She, or as some say, Amphitrite, gave him a jeweled crown and sent out the Nereids to find the ring. When they recovered it, they gave it to Theseus, who then emerged from the sea carrying the ring, which he restored to Minos, and the jeweled crown, which he later gave to Ariadne as a wedding gift. For among those who had witnessed his defiance of Minos over the maiden, and had seen him subsequently leap into the sea and recover the ring, was Ariadne, the daughter of Minos. She fell in love with Theseus on the spot. This was the work of Aphrodite, whom Theseus, as advised, had taken as his guide. Ariadne resolved to save him from death in the labyrinth. She had a ball of magic thread from Daedalus, the builder of the labyrinth, which had the property, as it was unwound, of leading whoever held it to the heart of the labyrinth. By rewinding it one could follow it out of the labyrinth. Ariadne offered to help Theseus in exchange for his promise to take her away from Crete with him as his wife. She gave him the ball of thread, told him to fasten one end of it to the lintel of the labyrinth as he entered and unwind the ball until he came to the Minotaur. To escape from the labyrinth he had only to rewind the thread. He followed her instructions, found and slew the Minotaur, which he offered as a sacrifice to Poseidon, and returned to the entrance where Ariadne awaited him. Together with the Athenians who had accompanied him to Crete, they fled to their ship and escaped. Theseus took the precaution of knocking holes in the hulls of the Cretan ships before he left, and thus the Cretans were not immediately able to pursue them.

The Cretans did not accept this story of the Minotaur, offspring of Pasiphaë and a bull. They claimed there was no such animal, and said that the labyrinth was simply a dungeon where the Athenians were kept until they were either offered as sacrifices at the funeral games for Androgeus, or given as prizes. They said that the most powerful general under Minos was one Taurus (bull). He was a great athlete and bully. According to the Cretans, they held funeral games for Androgeus, at which the prizes were Athenian youths and maidens given to the winners as slaves. Taurus always won. The Cretans resented his prowess and his arrogance. Theseus, coming as part of the tribute, asked permission to take part in the games. Minos, in the hope that he might defeat Taurus and also because he suspected Taurus of carrying on an intrigue with Pasiphaë, gave his consent. Theseus wrestled Taurus and, to the delight of Minos and the watching Ariadne, three times hurled him flat and pinned his shoulders to the ground. Minos was so pleased by the humiliation of Taurus that he released the Athenians, sent them back to Athens with Theseus, and gave him his daughter Ariadne for wife. So much for the Cretan story.

After leaving Crete, carrying Ariadne with him, Theseus put in at the island of Naxos. There, as she slept, he abandoned her. Some say Dionysus appeared to him in a dream and demanded her; others that Athena appeared to him in a dream and warned him to leave her; others that his ship, with him in it, was driven to sea by a storm, and when he returned Ariadne had disappeared. Still others say he abandoned her out of love for a daughter of Panopeus. In any event, he did not take Ariadne to Athens with him. He sailed from Naxos to the island of Delos and dedicated an image of Aphrodite in the temple of Apollo there. Around an altar made of horns taken entirely from the left side of the head he danced the so-called Crane Dance, which in its weavings and circlings imitated the winding passages of the labyrinth. (The Delians continued to perform this dance at least as late as the first century of the Christian era.) In Delos he also instituted athletic contests and established the custom, the first to do so, of awarding the palm to the victor. He then sailed for Attica. Some say it was grief over the loss of Ariadne that caused him to forget to change the black sail. Others say it was jubilation at escaping from Crete and joy at beholding the shores of Attica that made him forget. In any event, Aegeus, anxiously looking out to sea, scanning the horizon for a glimpse of a sail, saw a black sail and read in it a message that his son was dead. In his despair he hurled himself from the Acropolis and was killed,

fat, fāte, fär, fãre, errant; net, mē, hẻr ardẹnt; pin, pīne; not, nōte, mȯve, nôr, or, as some say, he flung himself into the sea which thereafter was called Aegean in his honor. Theseus landed and sent heralds with the good news to the city. The ship in which he voyaged to Crete, a 30-oared galley, was preserved by the Athenians to the end of the 4th century B.C.

Aegeus being dead, Theseus now became king. He destroyed his enemies and the sons of Pallas, and strengthened the kingdom by incorporating the 12 independent demes into which Attica had formerly been divided into one municipal unit, to which some say he gave the name Athens. He established an orderly democracy in which he was the leader, and divided the citizens into classes, each of which had its own duties and privileges. He was said, incorrectly as it happens, to have coined money, stamped with the image of an ox, to have established the Panathenaic Festival, which was open to all of Attica, and to have added Megara to the control of Athens. When he had done these things he gave up the throne and gave Athens a constitution, for the Delphic oracle now prophesied that Athens could sail the stormy seas with the security of an inflated pig's bladder. Some say the Isthmian Games, previously mysterious rites held at night in honor of Melicertes, came to be held as athletic and other contests in the daytime and in honor of Sciron at the instigation of Theseus. He secured a promise from the Corinthians, where the games were held, that the Athenians should occupy a place of honor equal in area to the space which could be covered by the sail of the ship in which they sailed to the games.

According to some accounts, Theseus accompanied Heracles on his mission to the Euxine Sea to fetch the Amazon's girdle. Heracles gave him the Amazon Antiope as a reward and he returned with her to Athens. But some say Theseus went to the Amazon country after the expedition of Heracles, and captured Antiope himself. At all events, the Amazons marched from the Euxine Sea against Athens to avenge the attack Theseus made on them. The war lasted three months and ended in a treaty. Some say Antiope, who bore Hippolytus to Theseus, was killed in this war, fighting at his side. Others say she was killed later, when Theseus made an alliance with Deucalion, who had succeeded his father Minos as king of Crete. He gave Theseus his sister Phaedra for wife. Antiope, infuriated at being cast aside, burst into the hall where the wedding ceremonies were in progress and threatened to kill Theseus. The doors were hastily closed and Antiope, with her attendant maidens, was killed. Phaedra bore Acamas and Demophon, who took part in the Trojan War, to Theseus. She later fell in love with her stepson Hippolytus and when he repulsed her advances she hanged herself.

Theseus was said to have ravished the daughters of Sinis and Cercyon—his love adventures paralleled those of Heracles; to have married Periboea, who later married Telamon and bore Ajax; to have sailed with Jason in the *Argo;* to have taken part in the Calydonian Hunt; to have aided the Lapiths in their war with the centaurs; to have recovered the corpses of those who fell at Thebes in the Expedition of the Seven against Thebes; and to have settled a boundary dispute between the Peloponnesians and the Ionians. Indeed, so many were the deeds of Theseus that the expression "Not without Theseus" came into use.

Pirithous, king of the Lapiths, heard such tales of the valor and spirit of Theseus he resolved to test whether he could live up to his reputation. He made a raid on Attica and drove off some of the cattle. Theseus pursued him. Pirithous stopped in his tracks and turned to confront Theseus. He was so impressed by him that he confessed he had done wrong and offered to do whatever Theseus commanded of him. Theseus, equally impressed, asked of him only that he be his friend. At the wedding of Pirithous Theseus helped to subdue the unruly centaurs who attacked the bride. The wife of Pirithous subsequently died. As Theseus was also a widower, he and Pirithous resolved to seek daughters of Zeus as wives. They decided first to abduct Helen, the beautiful ward of Tyndareus of Sparta, although she was but a child (some say ten years old) at the time. They carried out their plan, seizing the youthful Helen as she was sacrificing in a temple, and drew lots to see which would win her for his wife, on the understanding that the winner

actọr; up, lūte, pu̇ll; oi, oil; ou, out; ᴛʜ, then; d̦ as d or j, ș as s or sh, ț as t or ch, z̦ as z or zh.

should then help the loser to find a bride. Theseus won, but as he feared the disapproval of the Athenians, for his act might cause a war with Sparta, he sent Helen away to Aphidna in the care of his mother. Pirithous later reminded Theseus of his bargain, and informed him that he meant to take Persephone from Hades for his bride. Theseus tried to dissuade him from the perilous enterprise of descending to Tartarus to steal Persephone, but Pirithous insisted and Theseus was bound by his oath to help him in the undertaking. They descended to Tartarus through an entrance at Taenarus and demanded Persephone from Hades. He asked them to be seated. The chairs on which they sat were the Chairs of Forgetfulness and at once became part of their bodies. They could not move, and stayed where they were for four years. Then Heracles, in Tartarus to fetch Cerberus, found them and answered their appeal for help. He succeeded in wrenching Theseus off his chair, but he left a good deal of his flesh stuck to the chair, for which reason the descendants of Theseus were noted for their thinly covered buttocks. Heracles, however, could not free Pirithous, and he and Theseus returned to earth without him. Some say this Persephone sought by Pirithous was the wife of one Aidoneus, a king in Thesprotia, and he captured Pirithous and Theseus when they came to steal his wife. He threw Pirithous to the dogs and locked Theseus up in a dungeon, from which Heracles ultimately freed him.

When he returned to Athens after his long stay in Tartarus, Theseus found that the Dioscuri had recovered their sister Helen, and carried her and Theseus' mother off to Sparta, and that Menestheus had seized the throne of Athens. In his absence the people had become corrupt and they did not welcome him on his return. In sadness he went to the island of Scyrus, where he owned estates. Lycomedes, the king, welcomed him and pretended friendship. Under the pretext of pointing out to Theseus where his estates were located, he led him to a cliff, and while his back was turned, he pushed Theseus off the cliff to his death. According to tradition, at the Battle of Marathon (490 B.C.) an image of Theseus in full armor rose up and rushed at the head of the Athenians against the Persians. Afterward the oracle of Delphi ordered the bones of Theseus restored to Athens; Cimon, the Athenian general, went to Scyrus to find them, but the islanders refused to tell him where Theseus was buried. He was led to his grave by an eagle which he saw tearing the earth with its talons. On that spot Cimon dug and found a coffin containing huge bones which he took to be the bones of Theseus. He restored them to Athens, where they were buried in a tomb in the heart of the city. This tomb became a sanctuary for runaway slaves and the oppressed, whom Theseus had always championed. The Athenians worshiped Theseus as the founder of their city and as a hero, but they never succeeded in having him declared a god.

Thesmia (thes′mi-a). Epithet of Demeter. Trisaules and Damithales, who welcomed Demeter when she came to Arcadia, established her rites and built a temple of Demeter Thesmia (*Law-goddess*) under Mount Cyllene in Arcadia.

Thesmophoria (thes-mō-fō′ri-a). Ancient Greek festival in honor of Demeter Thesmophorus (*Law-giver*), who taught the arts of agriculture, fostered marriage, presided over family life and the birth of children, and initiated civil law. Some say the Thesmophoria had no connection with Demeter as a lawgiver, since the festival had nothing to do with laws, but rather was a fertility ceremony, in which certain sacred objects were "carried and laid down." In this connection, the *thes* of Thesmophoria is thought to have the same meaning as the *thes* of Theseus, "tokens deposited," and these tokens were in the main symbols of fertility, of the earth and of man. The festival, which was widespread throughout Greece, was especially important in Athens. It was celebrated by women only (no men were admitted to the rites) from time immemorial, from the 11th through the 13th day of Pyanepsion (October-November). The rites were said to have been introduced to the Pelasgian women by the daughters of Danaus, who brought them from Egypt when they fled to Argos. After the Dorian invasion (c1100 B.C.), the Thesmophoria was not celebrated in Dorian cities. The rites, which were carried on at night by the light of torches, came to be associated with certain incidents concerning the rape by Hades of Persephone and Demeter's search for her daughter. During the Thesmophoria the women celebrants lived in booths and strewed the plant *agnus castus* on their couches, as this plant was thought to be a specific against snakes. The women who took part in the Thesmophoria had to be free citizens, and it is thought that they had to be married women. Women in whose houses a death had occurred during the year could not take part in the festival as they had been polluted by death. On the first day of the festival, variously called Cathodos (*Downgoing*) and Anodos (*Uprising*), women who had purified themselves for a certain number of days carried pinecones and phallic cakes, both symbols of fertility, and went out to certain chasms or megara (*chambers*) in the ground. These were considered to be underworld dwellings of Demeter and Persephone. Into them the women cast suckling pigs. The women, on the same day, descended into the chasms, striking bronze gongs or shaking bronze rattles to dispel the snakes that had gathered to feed on the flesh of the pigs, and brought up the rotted remains; presumably, remains of those piglets that had been cast into the chasms the year before. This part of the ritual came to be considered a reënactment of the rape of Persephone, for when Persephone was gathering flowers in a meadow, a swineherd named Eubuleus was tending his swine nearby. The earth parted, Hades emerged and seized Persephone, and descended into the earth again with her through the chasm. The swine of Eubuleus were swallowed up at the same time. The procedure followed by the women was a fertility rite in that the pig was highly regarded as a symbol of fertility and the serpents that ate the remains thereof were sacred spirits of the earth. The second day of the festival was the Nestia, a day of fasting. On this day the rotted remains of the swine rested on the altars. The fast was strictly observed, prisoners were freed, the law courts were closed, and the Boule did not sit. The women fasted sitting on

the ground. Contact with the earth was a fertility ritual. The sitting on the ground came to be associated with an incident in Demeter's search for Persephone. When she neared Eleusis, the goddess sat down on the "Laughless" stone, near the "Well of Fair Dances," and grieved for her lost daughter. Thus the Nestia was a day of fasting and grief. The third day of the festival was the Calligenia (*Fair-born*), when the rotted flesh of the swine was scattered over the fields, for it was believed that if this flesh was mixed with seed, a good crop would follow. The Calligenia was a day of merrymaking and feasting. At Athens the feast was held on the Pnyx. Women refrained from intercourse preceding the festival, ate no pomegranate seeds during it, as the pomegranate was food for the dead, and wore no ornamentation.

Thesmophoriazusae (thes-mō-fō″ri-a̯-zō′sē), **The.** Comedy of Aristophanes, presented in 411 B.C. The women of Athens rise up against Euripides because in his tragedies he depicts women as such unpleasant characters. They decide to work out a suitable punishment for him at the Thesmophoria, a festival to which women alone are admitted. Euripides learns of their plot and ardently wishes to have a representative at the Thesmophoria to present his side of the case. His father-in-law Mnesilochus agrees to attend the festival disguised as a woman in order to speak for him. He does so but his disguise is discovered by the women, who turn him over to the authorities for trial on a charge of profaning the festival. Euripides devises a number of schemes, each more ridiculous than the last. From off-stage he hums fragments of his own plays, to which Mnesilochus, under guard on-stage, hums the answers, and thus a plot which results in the escape of Mnesilochus is arranged, and all ends well.

Thesmophorus (thes-mof′o̯-rus). Epithet of Demeter. There were sanctuaries of Demeter Thesmophorus (*Law-giver*) throughout Greece, as in Attica, Megara, Hermione, and Phocis. The sanctuary of Demeter Thesmophorus at Thebes was said to have been the house of Cadmus. The Thebans say that when Alexander the Great was approaching their city, they were warned by a spider which spun a black web across the doorway of the sanctuary. As Thesmophorus, Demeter presided over and protected the social order, marriage, the family, and childbirth.

Thespiae (thes'pi-ē). A city in Boeotia at the foot of Mount Helicon. It was founded by Thespius, who became its king. Heracles visited the city when he hunted the Thespian Lion. With Plataea it refused to give earth and water to the heralds of Xerxes, and it sent to Thermopylae 700 men who remained and perished with the Spartans. The Thespians fought against the Persians at Plataea in 479 B.C. and against Athens at Delium in 424 B.C. The walls of the city were later destroyed by Thebes. Thespiae was noted for the worship of Eros and the Muses and in it was Eros' most famous shrine.

Thespian Lion. In Greek legend, a lion that roamed the forests of Cithaeron and the glades of Mount Helicon, and preyed on the flocks of Amphitryon, foster father of Heracles. Heracles, as a young man, sought and found the lion. He killed it and wore its skin as a cloak. According to other accounts, it was the skin of the Nemean Lion that Heracles wore, and Alcathous was the man who slew the Thespian Lion.

Thespian Maids (thes'pi-an). The Greek Muses. They were so called because their games were performed at Thespiae, at the foot of Mount Helicon.

Thespis (thes'pis). Attic poet; fl. in the middle of the 6th century B.C. He is the reputed founder of tragic drama. It is said that "to rest his dancers and vary the entertainment" he introduced monologues and perhaps dialogues in the dithyrambic choruses, which until then had responded as a unit to the leader. He won his first victory in 534 B.C.

Thespius (thes'pi-us). In Greek legend, a son or descendant of Erechtheus, king of Athens. He was the founder and king of Thespiae in Boeotia, and the father of 50 daughters by his wife Megamede. Being anxious to have descendants by Heracles, he welcomed the hero when he came to Thespiae to hunt the Thespian Lion, and gave him all his 50 daughters. All except one were delighted with Heracles' attentions, and among them produced 51 male children, including two sets of twins. The one daughter who re-

fused Heracles' favors was forced to become a priestess in his temple and was thus condemned to lifelong virginity. Thespius' admiration and friendly relations with Heracles endured. He purified Heracles after the latter, in a fit of madness, had murdered his own sons. Later, at Heracles' order, he sent 40 of his 51 grandsons to colonize the island of Sardinia.

Thesprotia (thes-prō'sha). [Also: **Thesprotis**.] In ancient geography, a region in SW Epirus, Greece, lying near the sea.

Thesprotus (thes-prō'tus). In Greek legend, a son of Lycaon and king of Sicyon, to whose court Thyestes fled. There Thyestes ravished his own daughter Pelopia who was serving as a priestess. Thyestes then departed. Atreus came to the kingdom and asked for Pelopia in marriage in the belief that she was the daughter of Thesprotus. Thesprotus did not enlighten him as to her origin and, wishing to win the friendship of Atreus, gave her to him in marriage.

Thessalonica (thes″a-lō-nī′ka, -lon′i-ka). [Modern names, **Salonika, Salonica, Thessalonika**.] In ancient geography, a city and seaport of Macedonia, situated at the head of the Thermaic Gulf (Gulf of Salonika). It was founded, c316 B.C., by Cassander near the ancient city of Therma, which was absorbed by the new city. Cassander named his city after his wife, a sister of Alexander the Great. It became a Roman province in 146 B.C. Owing to its location on the Gulf and also on the Via Egnatia (large sections of which remain in the city), the Roman military road that ran from the coast of the Adriatic to the East, it became a flourishing commercial and intellectual center. Cicero went into exile at Thessalonica, 58 B.C., and Pompey took refuge there briefly after his defeat by Caesar, 49 B.C.

Thessalus (thes'a-lus). In Greek legend, a son of Heracles and Chalciope, daughter of Eurypylus of Cos. When Heracles was shipwrecked on Cos at the command of Hera, he was attacked by the natives and had to flee. He disguised himself in women's clothes and successfully evaded his attackers. Later, when he had rested, he fought them and was victorious. He married Chalciope, who later bore him Thessalus, subsequently a king in Thessaly. His sons, Antiphus and Phidippus, captained 30 ships against Troy in the Trojan War.

Thessalus. In Greek legend, a son of Jason and Medea. Some say he was stoned to death, along with his sisters and brothers, by the Corinthians to avenge the death of Glauce and Creon, and that he was buried in the sacred precinct of Hera in Corinth. Others say he escaped and went to Iolcus, where he found that Acastus, son of Pelias, had died. Thessalus took over the throne of Iolcus and named the people of the land Thessalians after himself.

Thessaly (thes′a̱-li). [Also: **Thessalia.**] District which in ancient times formed the NE division of Greece. It was bounded by Macedonia on the N (separated by a range of mountains including Mount Olympus), the Thracian Sea and Magnesia (or including Magnesia) on the E, Doris and Aetolia on the S, and Epirus on the W (separated by Mount Pindus). Thessaly contained the mountains Ossa, Pelion, and Othrys, and was traversed by the Peneus River that flowed through the Vale of Tempe. According to tradition, it was the original home of the Achaeans who migrated from there to Crete and to other parts of Greece, and laid the foundations for a highly developed civilization which did not, however, take root in Thessaly. The fertile land and location of Thessaly as the entrance to the Greek peninsula from the north attracted frequent invasions. Pelasgians invaded it in the 2nd millenium B.C. They were followed by the Minyans, whose story is told in the legends of Iolcus, Pagasae, and the expedition of the Argonauts. Various other tribes came into the region, including Achaeans from Phthia (part of Achilles' realm), and Boeotians. The men of Thessaly took part in the great united Greek expedition against Troy, Thessalus, a son of Heracles and a king in Thessaly, being one of the leaders of the Thessalians. After the Trojan War the land was invaded by a Dorian people of Epirus, who also claimed descent from Heracles. They were called Thessali, and gave their name to the whole region. The newcomers subjugated and enslaved the people of Thessaly, and established themselves as the military and ruling class. "Horse-breeding" Thessaly made cavalry the backbone of its military establishment. Sev-

eral powerful families were founded, as the Aleuadae at Larisa and the Scopadae at Crannon. They established oligarchic and aristocratic rule, and democracy was much delayed in the region. Pagasae and Pherae became the seats of powerful lords. In the 6th century B.C. these powerful families united in a loose confederation, which in times of emergency united under a common military commander, called a *tagus*. The area was divided into four regions: Thessaliotis, centering about Pharsalus; Pelasgiotis, around Larisa; Hestiaeotis, about Triccala; and Phthiotis, about Othrys. In the Persian Wars Thessaly, the gateway to Greece, was pro-Persian, as much from necessity, owing to its exposed position, as from choice. At times the united Thessalian Confederation presented a threat to Phocis and southern Greece, but more often the confederation was weakened by the ambitions of local leaders. Jason, tyrant of Pherae in the 4th century B.C., won domination of the confederation and for a time threatened southern Greece. Whatever his dreams of conquest may have been, they were cut short by his assassination. The Thessalian cities invoked the aid of Macedonia to resist Jason's successor, Alexander of Pherae. They found it no happier to be under foreign rule, and turned to Thebes. For a time Thessaly existed as a Theban protectorate, divided into tetrads, four political divisions based on geographical divisions. In 353 B.C. Philip II of Macedon entered Thessaly, at the invitation of the Thessalians, and subsequently made himself master of it. It remained more or less a vassal of Macedonia until 197 B.C., when it became a protectorate of Rome. Many of the cities of Thessaly, its mountains and valleys, are celebrated in Greek legend.

Theste (thes′tē). Sister of Dionysius the Elder (c430–367 B.C.) of Syracuse. Her husband Polyxenus became an enemy of Dionysius and fled from Sicily. According to Plutarch, Dionysius called his sister to him and chided her because she had not warned him that Polyxenus meant to flee. She retorted that she had not known of it, for if she had she would surely have gone with him and shared his fortunes, as she would far rather be known as the wife of Polyxenus the exile than as the sister of Dionysius the tyrant. Dionysius admired her courage in speaking thus to him, and the Syracusans honored her and continued to give her the services due to royalty even after the dissolution of the tyranny. When she died, all the citizens, so it is said, attended her funeral.

Thestius (thes'ti-us). In Greek mythology, a son of Ares. He was a king in Aetolia and the father of Althaea, who became the wife of Oeneus, and of Leda, who became the wife of Tyndareus. According to some accounts, he also had a son Calydon, whom he killed because he had been charged with incestuous relations with his mother. Thestius later drowned himself in grief and remorse over the death of his son.

Thestor (thes'tor). In mythology, a son of Apollo, according to some accounts; or a son of Apollo's son, Idmon the Argonaut. He was the father of Calchas, to whom he taught the art of prophecy. In later versions of his story he was said to have been the father also of two daughters: Leucippe and Theonoë. Theonoë was kidnapped by pirates, who took her to Caria where she became the mistress of King Icarus. Thestor set out to search for his daughter but was overtaken by a storm and shipwrecked on the coast of Caria. He fell into the hands of King Icarus, who did not know of his relationship to Theonoë, and he was made a slave. Leucippe later sought for news of her father and sister, whom she had not seen since she had been a child. The oracle at Delphi told her to go to Caria, disguised as a priest of Apollo, to search for them. In Caria Theonoë fell in love with the beautiful young priest, but her advances were rejected. Enraged, Theonoë then ordered that one of the slaves should put the young priest to death. Thestor was the slave chosen for the purpose. Thestor confronted the young priest, but instead of killing him, he recited his own name and history and prepared to plunge the sword into his own breast in his misery. Leucippe recognized that this was her father and revealed her true identity to him. Together they then planned to kill the king's mistress. They found her alone in her room and told her to prepare to die. However, before they killed her, they wanted her to know what noble persons she had persecuted. On hearing their names, it was Theonoë's turn to recognize her father, and the family was happily reunited. King Icarus nobly shared their joy. He gave them rich gifts and sent them all home to Greece.

Thetis (thē'tis). In Greek mythology, a sea-goddess, attended by fifty Nereids, the daughters of Nereus and Doris. Zeus fell in love with her and pursued her, but Thetis eluded him, thus earning the gratitude of Hera. Zeus gave up his pursuit, as Poseidon had also done, when he learned from Prometheus that Thetis would bear a son more powerful than his father. He promised her to Peleus, son of Aeacus. Thetis had no de-

THETIS RECEIVING THE ARMOR OF ACHILLES
FROM HEPHAESTUS
Red-figured Attic cup. *Berlin*

sire to marry Peleus, and since she had the power to transform herself at will she endeavored to escape him when he had caught her as she slept in a cave by the sea, by turning herself successively into fire, water, a lion, a serpent, and a fish. Peleus, as he had been warned to do by Chiron, maintained his grasp through these changes and she consented to marry him. All the gods and goddesses were present at their wedding except Eris, who had not been invited because of her disruptive influence, and who threw the Apple of Discord among the wedding guests in revenge. Thetis bore several sons to Peleus. One after the other she immersed them in flames to burn away their mortal parts and sent them to Olympus. Peleus happened in one night while she was performing this rite on Achilles. He screamed at the sight. Thetis dropped Achilles and fled to the sea. Peleus never saw her again, although she sometimes spoke to him and told him what to do while keeping herself invisible. According to some accounts, Thetis dipped Achilles into the River Styx and thus made him invulnerable except for the one place on his ankle where she held him.

On the whole, Thetis was a kindly goddess and rendered service to many of the gods. When Hera, Poseidon, and Athena bound Zeus in 100 fetters, Thetis summoned Briareus, who used his 100 hands to free him instantly. She gave Dionysus asylum beneath the sea when Lycurgus pursued him. She sheltered Hephaestus for nine years when Hera hurled him from heaven because of his lameness. At Hera's request, she lifted the *Argo* over the dangerous Clashing Rocks and then, with her Nereids, propelled it safely past Scylla and Charybdis. Because of her previous aid, Zeus granted her request to favor the Trojans to punish the Greeks for Agamemnon's insult to her son Achilles in the tenth year of the Trojan War, and Hephaestus willingly made armor for Achilles to replace that which he had loaned to Patroclus and which had been captured by Hector. After the death of Achilles it was Thetis who decreed that this magic armor should be awarded to the bravest of the Greeks. She prophesied accurately that if Achilles went to Troy he would die young; that if Achilles killed a son of Apollo he would die by Apollo's hand; that the first man to go ashore at Troy would be the first to die there.

Thia (thī′a). In Greek mythology, a Titaness, one of the daughters of Gaea and Uranus. By her brother Hyperion she was the mother of Eos (Dawn), Helius (Sun), and Selene (Moon).

Thiasus, Thiasos (thī′a-sus, -sos). A band or company assembled in honor of a divinity; especially, a Dionysiac band or procession in which men and women took part in character, with boisterous mirth and music, and bear-

ing attributes of the god. This term was specifically applied to the mythological band of nymphs, maenads, satyrs, etc., forming the personal followers of Dionysus, and often represented in sculpture and painting.

Thiodamas (thī-od′a-mas). A legendary king of the Dryopians. Heracles, passing through his land, found the king plowing with a yoke of oxen. Since he was hungry Heracles asked for one of the oxen. Thiodamas refused him, whereupon Heracles slew him and took his son Hylas as his squire. He killed and roasted the ox and ate it. Then he drove the Dryopians out of their city on Mount Parnassus and sent the leading citizens as slaves to Delphi. But some say this Thiodamas was a native of Rhodes, and that it was when Heracles was in Rhodes that he seized one of his oxen. Thiodamas fled to a nearby hilltop and from this safe position hurled curses on Heracles. Heracles was unimpressed and ate of the ox, which he had meantime roasted, to his satisfaction. But some say it was from this incident that the custom arose in Rhodes of uttering curses when sacrifices were made to Heracles.

Thirty Tyrants. Aristocratic body which usurped the government of Athens (404–403 B.C.). The most notable was Critias. They were expelled by the democratic party under the lead of Thrasybulus.

Thisbe (thiz′bē). In ancient geography, a city of Boeotia, Greece, named for a local nymph. There was a sanctuary of Heracles here, and the inhabitants celebrated a festival called the *Heraclia*.

Thisbe. See under **Pyramus and Thisbe.**

Thisoa (thī-sō′a). In Greek mythology, an Arcadian nymph who, according to some accounts, took care of the infant Zeus after he was born on Mount Lycaeus in Arcadia. A city in Arcadia was named for her.

Thoas (thō′as). In Homeric legend (*Iliad*), a son of Andraemon and Gorge. He was a king in Aetolia after Oeneus and his children had perished. As a former suitor of Helen, he had sworn to give aid to whatever man became her husband in case any difficulty came to him as a result of his marriage, and therefore he led the Aetolians against the Trojans in the Trojan War to restore Helen to her husband. During the war he accepted Hector's challenge to single combat but was eliminated in the drawing of the lots and the honor of fighting Hector fell to Ajax. After the death of Hector he was one of the Greeks who entered Troy in the Wooden Horse.

Thoas or **Thoön** (thō′on). In Greek mythology, one of the Giants, a son of Gaea and the blood of Uranus, who waged war on the gods. In the battle the Fates crushed his head with a bronze pestle and Heracles killed him.

Thoas. In Greek legend, a son of Hypsipyle and Jason, and the twin of Euneus. Other names sometimes given to him are Nebrophonus and Deïphilus.

Thoas. In classical mythology, a son of Ariadne and Dionysus, or according to some accounts, of Theseus. Rhadamanthys of Crete gave him the island of Lemnos for his kingdom. However, the Lemnian women rose against the men of the island and killed all the males. Thoas was saved by his daughter Hypsipyle, who concealed him in a chest and set him adrift on the sea. The chest landed safely on the island of Oenoë and there Thoas became the father of Sicinus by the nymph of the island. Thoas was the king of the Taurians when Iphigenia was brought to Tauris, having been saved by the gods from being sacrificed at Aulis. He made her priestess of Artemis in Tauris. When her brother came to steal the statue of the goddess and discovered that the priestess was his own sister, he suggested that they should kill Thoas and escape with the statue. Iphigenia would not agree to the slaying of Thoas because he had been kind to her. They did escape by a trick and Thoas, in anger, would have pursued and killed them but Athena appeared to him and told him it was the will of the gods that they should go free.

Thoön (thō′on). In the *Iliad*, a Trojan who, with Asius, ignored the advice of Polydamas not to drive the chariots against the Greek wall but to attack on foot. The chariots were successful in getting across the moat but in the press and commotion were unable to maneuver, as Polydamas had foretold, and Thoön was slain by Antilochus.

Thornax (thôr′naks), **Mount.** Mountain in Argolis. Here, some say, Zeus, in the form of a cuckoo, wooed Hera. She had rejected his advances when he courted her in his own

shape, but took the cuckoo and nestled it in her bosom. Zeus thereupon resumed his own shape and ravished her. Afterward, the name of the mountain was changed to Cuckoo.

Thoth (thoth, tōt). [Also: **Tat, Tehuti, Thot.**] In Egyptian mythology, originally a moon-god, later the god and inventor of speech and hieroglyphics or letters, of the reckoning of time and measurements, and the god of wisdom. He was the scribe of the gods, and kept the records of the dead in a book, which he read at the time of judgment. The cynocephalous ape and the ibis were sacred to him. He is represented as a human figure, usually with the head of an ibis, and frequently with the moon disk and crescent. In Hellenistic times the Greeks identified him with their Hermes.

Thrace (thrās). [Latin, **Thracia**; Greek, **Thraki.**] In ancient geography, a region NE of Macedonia, extending to the Ister (Danube) River on the N and the Euxine (Black) Sea on the E. As a Roman province it was bounded by the Haemus or Balkan Mountains (separating it from Moesia) on the N, the Euxine Sea and Bosporus on the E, the Propontis, Hellespont, and Aegean Sea on the S, and the Nestus or Mesta (separating it from Macedonia) on the W. The principal mountain range is the Rhodope; the principal river, the Hebrus (Maritsa). The climate was known for its severity, and the inhabitants for their ferocity and barbarity. Because of the severe climate and the fierce people Thrace was known as the home of Boreas, the North Wind, and the war-god Ares. The aborigines were scattered by invaders, who were in turn replaced by the various tribes called Thracians between 1600–1400 B.C. The affinities of the ancient inhabitants are unknown; they may have been ancestors of the Wallachs. The wide stretch of country between the lower course of the Ister and the shores of the Aegean and the Propontis was occupied in ancient times by the tribe of the Thracians, which Herodotus regards as the greatest of all peoples next to the Indi. The scanty remains of the Thracian language are enough to establish traces of its Indo-Germanic character, but not enough to define its position in the Indo-European family more closely. Certain it is, however, that from hence a large part of Asia Minor received its Indo-European-speaking population. In the first place, it is known that the Thracians themselves spread eastwards over the strait a considerable distance towards Asia. According to the unanimous opinion of antiquity, again, the Phrygians emigrated from Europe, and were originally connected with the Thracians. According to Greek legend, Orpheus, Linus, and Musaeus came from Thrace. In the Trojan War the Thracians, under their prince Rhesus, were allies of King Priam. From the 8th century B.C. the Greeks visited Thrace, and planted colonies at Byzantium, on the Chersonesus Thracica (Gallipoli Peninsula), and at Abdera, Perinthus, and elsewhere. Darius the Great invaded Thrace and when he withdrew he left his general Megabazus there and the latter subdued the region. The Thracian Greeks furnished 120 ships and many foot soldiers to the armament Xerxes led into Europe in 480 B.C. And it was in Thrace, at the mouth of the Hebrus River, that Xerxes reviewed his vast army, as enumerated by Herodotus. After the defeat of the Persians the Athenians dispersed the Persian garrisons Xerxes had left in Thrace. In the middle of the 5th century B.C. Teres, king of the Odrysae, the most powerful of the Thracian tribes, brought most of Thrace under his rule. During the Peloponnesian War, Sitalces, son of Teres, supplied Athens with troops and invaded Macedonia to little effect. The Spartan general Brasidas made an unsuccessful attempt to win the Athenian cities on the coast of Thrace. In the 4th century B.C. an alliance between Athens and Thrace proved ineffective. Philip II of Macedon won control of the area c340 B.C. Following the death of Alexander the Great, Thrace became for a time part of the dominion of Lysimachus, and then fell to Macedonia. With the defeat of the Macedonian king Perseus (168 B.C.), Thrace became independent under the protection of Rome, and subsequently, a Roman province.

Thracian Bosporus (thrā′shạn bos′pō̍-rus). Ancient name of the **Bosporus.**

Thracica (thrā′si-kạ), **Chersonesus.** Ancient name of the **Gallipoli Peninsula.**

Thrasybulus (thras-i-bū′lus, thrạ-sib′ū̍-lus). A 6th century B.C. tyrant of Miletus under whose rule the city prospered greatly, and who planted colonies of Miletus on the Euxine Sea. He successfully resisted the threats of the kings of Lydia. According to Herodotus, in the 12th year of a war with Alyattes, king of Lydia who had inherited the war from his father, Alyattes invaded Milesia and set the grain afire, as he had been doing annually. A gale of wind swept the fire to the temple of Athena at Assesus and burned it to the ground. Afterward, Alyattes fell sick and sent to inquire of the oracle at Delphi how he might be cured. His messengers were told by the priestess that she would not answer his inquiries until the temple of Athena at Assesus was rebuilt. Periander of Corinth, a friend of Thrasybulus, heard of the oracle and sent word of it to Thrasybulus, that he might be prepared. Therefore, when Alyattes sent heralds to Thrasybulus to arrange a truce during which the temple could be rebuilt, the heralds were met by a startling sight. Thrasybulus, foreseeing that Alyattes would send to him as a consequence of the oracle, had caused all the grain that was in the city to be brought into the market-place, and had ordered the people to set to feasting and revelry when he gave the signal. When the heralds arrived, they found the Milesians enjoying themselves as if there had never been any war at all, and amusing themselves in the market-place, surrounded by an abundance of grain. The heralds immediately reported this to Alyattes and he, who had thought that by this time the Milesians would have exhausted their supplies and be glad of a truce, on learning of the plenty they still enjoyed, instead of offering a truce made peace with Thrasybulus and ended the long war. After this Alyattes rebuilt the temple of Athena and recovered from his sickness. One of the reasons for the friendship of Thrasybulus and Periander was advice he had given Periander when the latter became ruler of Corinth. Periander sent a messenger to him, to ask what sort of government he should establish. Thrasybulus took the messenger into a wheat field, and as he talked, kept breaking off the heads of the tallest stalks and throwing the ears on the ground, but he never answered the question the messenger had brought from Periander. On his return to Corinth the messenger reported that he had no answer from Thrasybulus, and described his strange conduct in the wheat field. But Periander understood the meaning of his actions, and immediately sought out the leading men of his realm and destroyed them.

Thrasybulus. Athenian commander and statesman; killed 388 B.C. In 411 B.C. he was at Samos with the Athenian navy, and persuaded the sailors there to rise against the oligarchy of the Four Hundred that was governing at Athens, and to proclaim their allegiance to the democracy. Under his direction the Assembly that had been abolished at Athens was revived at Samos. He secured the return to Samos of Alcibiades and had him elected general. In 410 B.C. he commanded one division of the fleet that defeated the Spartans at Cyzicus. Following this, and other Spartan defeats, the Four Hundred at Athens were overthrown. Athens enjoyed some successes in its war with Sparta, but was ultimately defeated at Aegospotami (405 B.C.). Under the protection of the Spartan general Lysander, an interim body of 30, later known as the Thirty Tyrants, was chosen to govern Athens. Thrasybulus was driven into exile with other democrats. The exiles took refuge at the fortress of Phyle in Attica and resisted an army sent against them by Athens. In 403 B.C. Thrasybulus burst out of Phyle with the exiles and seized Munychia at the Piraeus. This led to the overthrow of the Thirty Tyrants and the reëstablishment of Athenian democracy. Thrasybulus aided Thebes against Sparta in 395 B.C., and commanded with great success in the Aegean Sea in 390 B.C. He was killed in his tent at Aspendus in Pamphylia by natives who were outraged by the violence of his soldiers.

Thrasydemus (thras-i-dē′mus). In the *Iliad*, a Lycian, also called Thrasymelus, the squire of Sarpedon. He was slain by Patroclus. Sarpedon received a mortal wound from Patroclus in avenging his death.

Thrasyllus (thra-sil′us). Athenian commander in the Peloponnesian War; put to death 406 B.C. He opposed the oligarchs in 411 B.C., and helped to overthrow them. He was one of the commanders at Cynossema in 411 B.C., and was a general at Arginusae in 406 B.C. and one of those who was executed for permitting the crews of sunken ships to drown

rather than breaking off the pursuit of the enemy to rescue them.

Thrasymedes (thras-i-mē′dēz). In Greek legend, a son of Nestor who accompanied his father to Troy and was a chief of the Greek sentries. He furnished his sword, shield, and bull–hide helmet to Diomedes when the latter went as a spy against the Trojan camp. With his father he battled against Memnon for possession of the body of Antilochus, his brother, but both were forced to withdraw. He fought bravely throughout the war and at its close returned safely to Pylus with his father. Telemachus met him there when he visited Nestor in search of news of his father.

Three Graces, The. See **Graces, The Three.**

Three Horatii (họ-rā′shi-ī), **The.** See **Horatii, The Three.**

Thriae (thrī′ī). In Greek mythology, three nymphs of Parnassus who nursed Apollo. They were seeresses who foretold the future by casting pebbles in water. At the request of Apollo they taught Hermes how to foretell the future by this method.

Thriambus (thrī-am′bus). An epithet of Dionysus, applied to him because he was the first to celebrate a triumph.

Thronium (thrō′ni-um). In ancient geography, a city in the Ceraunian Mountains, settled, according to tradition, by Locrians from Thronium on the river Boagrius and by Abantes from Euboea, who, in eight ships, were driven to this place by a storm on their way home from the Trojan War. They named the land about their new city Abantis. Later, they were expelled from their city by their neighbors of Apollonia, a colony of Corcyra.

Thucydides (thū-sid′i-dēz). Greek historian; born c460 B.C.; died c401 B.C. He was a native of Athens, belonged to a family which claimed blood relationship with Miltiades and Cimon, is said to have been a pupil of Antiphon of Rhamnus and of Anaxagoras, and possessed an ample fortune, part of which was invested in gold mines in Thrace, where he held a hereditary chieftainship. In 424 B.C. he was appointed general and was sent to Chalcidice. Brasidas, the Spartan general, was operating in Thrace and threatening Amphipolis. Thucydides had removed the squadron under his command to Thasus, where, some said, he owned gold mines. Brasidas made a forced march through the snow and won Amphipolis before Thucydides, to whom word had been sent, could arrive and protect the city. Thucydides withdrew to Eion on the Strymon River, which he defended from attack by Brasidas, but because he had failed to prevent the capture of Amphipolis, he went into exile; whether this exile was forced or voluntary is unknown. He returned to Athens 20 years later in 403 B.C. He was commonly supposed by the ancients to have died a violent death soon after, probably at Athens. Thucydides was a soldier and a typical Athenian, with the most vibrant interest in the political life of his city. He was an ardent admirer of Pericles. The abrupt end of his military career in no way lessened his interest in the course of the war; it did permit him to take a broader view of its overall course, and to study it with the most intense interest. In the first book of his *History of the Peloponnesian War* he austerely warns, perhaps as a thrust at Herodotus, that "The absence of romance in my history will, I fear, detract somewhat from its interest; but if it be judged useful by those inquirers who desire an exact knowledge of the past as an aid to the interpretation of the future, which in the course of human things must resemble if it does not reflect it, I shall be content." He clearly states his intention of applying the most rigid critical tests to his material to ensure that the truth will be uncovered, and he rather grandly pronounces that, "I have written my work, not as an essay which is to win the applause of the moment, but as a possession for all time." As to the real cause of the war, "the one which was formally most kept out of sight," it was, he says, "the growth of the power of Athens, and the alarm which this inspired in Lacedaemon." He proposed to recount the history of the war in sequence, by summers and winters, and he adhered to his plan. By the device of speeches put into the mouths of various participants in the war he characterized men and nations as he presented in this manner the conflicting claims of allies and adversaries. Of these speeches he says, "some were delivered before the war began, others while it was going on; some I heard myself, others I got from various quarters; it was in all cases difficult to carry them word for word in one's memory, so my habit has been to make the speakers say what was in my opinion demanded of them by the various occasions, of course adhering as closely as possible to the general sense of what they really said." Having announced his method and stated his aim, he set to work and with admirable lack of passion carried out his purpose. The *History* which he produced is analytical and political, as distinct from the earlier histories which evolved in consequence of the original meaning of the word history, "a learning or knowing by inquiry." The *History* breaks off in the twenty-first year of the war, 411 B.C. The last book, the eighth, contains none of the famous speeches and lacks the literary finish of earlier books, indicating that Thucydides did not have a chance to revise it.

Thurii (thū'ri-ī). [Also: **Thurium**.] In ancient geography, a city in Magna Graecia, Italy, situated near the ancient Sybaris and near what is now Terranova di Sibari. It was founded (452 B.C.) by fugitives from Sybaris who were soon expelled by Croton, and was refounded (c443 B.C.) by colonists from Athens and other cities. Hippodamus of Miletus was said to have drawn the plans for the Athenian colony, and the historian Herodotus was one of the colonists. It was defeated (390 B.C.) by the Lucanians, called Rome to its aid against Tarentum in 282 B.C., and later was subject to Rome. It was plundered (204 B.C.) by Hannibal, and was later the site of a Roman colony.

Thyestes (thī-es'tēz). In Greek legend, a son of Pelops and Hippodamia, and the brother and arch-rival of Atreus. Thyestes and Atreus fled from their home in the Peloponnesus because they were implicated in the murder of their half-brother Chrysippus. They were invited to Mycenae by Sthenelus, who had seized the throne there. When Sthenelus and his son Eurystheus were dead, an oracle proclaimed that Mycenae should be governed by a Pelopid. The question was whether it should be Atreus or Thyestes. In the rivalry between the brothers Zeus took the part of Atreus; Artemis favored Thyestes. Thyestes, who had become the lover of Aërope, wife of Atreus, now induced her to steal a golden-fleeced, horned lamb that Atreus possessed. It had been sent to him by Hermes, to increase the enmity between the brothers and thus to punish the Pelopids for the murder of Myrtilus by their father Pelops. Atreus had sacrificed the flesh of the lamb to Artemis in accordance with a vow, but had kept the fleece, stuffed it, and kept it hidden away in a chest. Once Thyestes had it in his possession, he claimed that the throne of Mycenae should go to whoever held the golden-fleeced lamb. Atreus, under the impression that the lamb was safely in his possession, was agreeable. It then developed that Thyestes, thanks to Aërope's treachery, had acquired the lamb. He would immediately have been made king but for the intervention of Zeus. The god sent Hermes to ask if Thyestes would withdraw in favor of Atreus if the sun reversed its course through the heavens. Thyestes agreed, and Zeus for one day caused the sun to go backwards across the sky. Atreus became king and Thyestes was banished. According to some accounts, Thyestes avenged himself by causing Atreus to kill Plisthenes, his own son by his first wife, under the impression that Plisthenes, who had been brought up by Thyestes, was the latter's son. When Atreus learned of Aërope's adultery with Thyestes, he sent for Thyestes on the pretext that he was willing to share his kingdom with him. When he arrived, Atreus seized his three sons —Aglaus, Orchomenus, and Callileon—from the altar of Zeus where they had fled for refuge. He cut off their limbs and boiled their bodies in a cauldron. He then invited Thyestes to a feast. Only when the banquet was over did Atreus order the bloody limbs of Thyestes' sons brought in to reveal to their father that he had eaten of his own sons' flesh. Sickened with horror, Thyestes pronounced a fearful curse on the house of Atreus, which brought disaster to his sons, and fled to Sicyon. There, in accordance with instructions from an oracle, he ravished his daughter Pelopia. She did not know his true identity, and in her struggle to escape seized his sword. Atreus came to Sicyon looking for Thyestes. He saw Pelopia and fell in love with her. Since he had killed

Aërope for her infidelity, he asked the king of Sicyon, who he thought was Pelopia's father, for permission to marry her. The king did not enlighten him as to her parentage, but gladly gave his permission. Later Pelopia bore Thyestes' son, Aegisthus. Atreus thought this was his own child, and rescued him when Pelopia left him on a mountain to die. Some years later, famine afflicted Mycenae. Atreus sent his sons, Agamemnon and Menelaus, to fetch Thyestes. They found him and brought him to Mycenae. Atreus imprisoned him and ordered young Aegisthus to kill him as he slept. But Thyestes awoke, recognized the sword which Aegisthus held unsteadily over him, and asked where he had found it. Aegisthus said his mother had given it to him, and Thyestes realized that this was his own son. He sent for Pelopia, who plunged the sword into her breast on learning that the father of her child was her own father. Aegisthus took the bloody sword to Atreus as proof that Thyestes was dead and, as Atreus thankfully sacrificed near the sea, Aegisthus and Thyestes set upon him and killed him. Thyestes at last became king of Mycenae. When he died, he was buried near the shrine of Perseus outside Mycenae, and a ram was placed over his tomb. None of this complicated horror story for control of Mycenae appears in Homer. In the *Iliad,* the scepter, made by Hephaestus, was given by Zeus to Pelops; Pelops bequeathed it to Atreus, who in turn passed it to Thyestes, and he handed it over to Agamemnon.

Thyia (thī′a̱). In Greek mythology, a daughter of the river-god Cephissus according to some accounts. Others say Castalius, a mortal, was her father. She was the mother by Apollo of Delphus, who gave his name to Delphi. Since she first sacrificed to Dionysus at Delphi and celebrated revels in his honor, her name was given to the followers of Dionysus, who were called Thyiades. The Delphians raised an altar in the sacred precinct of Thyia in gratitude to the winds that helped them in the Persian Wars by causing great storms that scattered the Persian fleet at Artemisium.

Thyiades (thī′ya̱-dēz). A name for the maenads or bacchantes. See **Thyia.**

Thymbraeus (thim-brē′us). In Greek legend,

one of the twin sons of the priest Laocoön. He was sometimes known as Melanthus. See **Antiphas.**

Thymbrius (thim'bri-us). In ancient geography, a small river near Ilium (Troy).

Thymele (thim'ẹ-lē). In Greek antiquity, an altar; particularly, the small altar of Dionysus which occupied the central point of the orchestra of the Greek theater, and was a visible token of the religious character of the dramatic representations. Literally, "a place for sacrifice."

Thymoetes (thī-mē'tēz). In Greek legend, an elder of Troy and a counselor of Priam. His son Munippus, by Cilla, sister of Priam, was born earlier on the same day that Hecuba bore Paris to Priam. According to a prophecy, the royal Trojan who bore a son that day must be destroyed, along with her child; otherwise the child would bring ruin to Troy. Priam took the prophecy to apply to Cilla and her son, and had them both killed. Many years later, after the death of Hector and Penthesilea at the hands of Achilles, Thymoetes advised the Trojans to flee their doomed city, as Achilles was irresistible. His advice in this instance was disregarded. However, when the Wooden Horse was discovered before the gates of Troy, Thymoetes advised, either from treachery in revenge for the death of Munippus, or because Troy's fate was already sealed, that the Trojans bring it inside the walls. This time his advice was heeded and brought disaster to Troy.

Thymoetes. In Greek legend, a son of Oxyntes; he was the great-grandson and last descendant of Theseus. He became king of Athens by murdering his brother. During a war he was challenged by the leader of the enemy to fight a duel to decide the contest. Thymoetes refused to accept the challenge. Melanthus, a Messenian exile, accepted the challenge and killed his opponent, and after this he replaced Thymoetes as ruler of Athens.

Thynias (thī'ni-as). A small desert island near the Bosporus in the southern part of the Euxine Sea. According to legend, here the Argonauts stopped on their way to Colchis and here Apollo appeared to them at dawn in a blaze of glory. On the advice of Orpheus they sacrificed a wild goat to Apollo

on an altar which they erected, and took an oath never to desert one another in time of danger. This oath was commemorated by a temple to the goddess Harmonia or Concord which was later raised on the island.

Thyone (thī'ọ-nē). The name that was given to Semele when she was translated to Olympus from Tartarus. Dionysus gave his mother this name so that the ghosts who were left in Tartarus would not be jealous that she had escaped.

Thyoneus (thī-ọ-nē'us). An epithet of Dionysus, meaning "Son of Thyone," which was the name given to his mother Semele when she ascended to Olympus and became immortal.

Thyrsus (thėr'sus). One of the most common emblems of Dionysus and his thiasus and votaries. It was a staff tipped with an ornament like a pine-cone and sometimes wrapped round with ivy and vine branches, and appears in various modifications in ancient representations. The bacchantes carried thyrsi in their hands when they celebrated their orgies.

Tiber (tī'bėr). [Also: **Tiberis, Tiberinus, Tibris, Tybris;** modern name, **Tevere.**] Second longest river in Italy. It rises in the Apennines about 20 miles NE of Arretium (Arezzo), flows generally S, and empties into the Mediterranean about 16 miles SW of Rome, which is on its banks. Its chief tributaries are the Clanis (Chiana), Nar (Nera), and Anio (Aniene).

Tiberinus (tī-bėr-ī'nus) or **Tiberius** (tī-bir'i-us). In Roman legend, a king of Alba Longa. He was drowned in the Albula River which was then renamed Tiber for him. In Roman mythology the god of the Tiber River, worshiped at Rome, was also called Tiberinus. The river-god appeared to Aeneas as he was worrying, on the eve of the war with Turnus, and told him not to give up. He advised Aeneas to locate his city on a spot where he would find a white sow with 30 piglets, and told him he would find the sow on the banks of the Tiber under some oak trees. He also advised Aeneas to go to Evander for help in his war. The 30 piglets of which Tiberinus spoke indicated that after 30 years Ascanius, son of Aeneas, would found the white town of Alba.

Tiberius. [Full name, **Tiberius Claudius Nero**

Caesar.] Second Roman emperor, born Nov. 16, 42 B.C.; died March 16, 37 A.D. He was a member of the ancient patrician Claudian family whose ancestors, according to some accounts, had come from the Sabine country to Rome in the time of Romulus. Others say the Claudians came to Rome in the 6th century B.C. His father was Tiberius Nero, who had been a quaestor and had been a commander of Caesar's fleet. His mother was Livia Drusilla, a woman of great force and ambition, and the intelligence to pursue it. Some say Tiberius was born at Fundi, but most say he was born on the Palatine Hill. His birth took place during the disorders that followed the assassination of Caesar, when Octavian, the future Augustus, had not yet consolidated his power. According to a tale told by Suetonius, Livia sought to foretell the sex of her unborn child by warming an egg in her hands. She and her handmaids kept the egg warm until it hatched; a strong cock with a spectacular comb emerged from the shell and foretold the greatness of her as yet unborn son. In his youth an astrologer was similarly encouraging, saying he would be a king without a crown. The childhood of Tiberius was extremely unsettled, as his parents were continually fleeing before the displeasure of Octavian. Tiberius Nero had turned against Caesar, even proposing that his assassins should be rewarded, and he sided with Mark Antony in his early bid for power. When Antony was reconciled with Octavian, Tiberius Nero returned to Rome (39 B.C.) with his family, and his mistaken enthusiasm for republican government was forgiven by Octavian. This forgiveness may have been prompted by the fact that Octavian saw Livia and fell in love with her. Though she had borne one child, Tiberius, and was about to produce another, Octavian compelled Tiberius Nero to divorce her and immediately made her his own wife (38 B.C.).

The young Tiberius began to appear before the public at an early age. He delivered his father's funeral oration at the age of nine. He was quaestor, praetor, and consul, each time before he was old enough legally to occupy the offices. He appeared as an advocate and as prosecutor before the Senate, fought against the Cantabrians in Spain, led an army to Armenia (20 B.C.), where he restored the king as a vassal of Rome, and served as governor of Transalpine Gaul (19 B.C.). In 15 B.C. he went with his brother Drusus to subjugate the Germans at the source of the Rhenus (Rhine) and the Ister (Danube). In 11 B.C. he carried on a successful campaign against the Pannonians. This was followed by other successes in Germany. Augustus appointed him tribune for five years in 6 B.C. Suddenly he decided to retire from public life. He gave as his reason his unwillingness to appear to compete for popular favor with Caius and Lucius, the grandsons of Augustus, who had now come of age. Livia, to whom no children had been born of her union with Augustus, tried to persuade him not to retire. Augustus refused to consent to his retirement, for following the death of Drusus, Tiberius was the most capable commander of the Roman armies. Tiberius went on a hunger strike in order to gain his wish, and at the end of four days Augustus reluctantly gave him leave to depart. He went to Rhodes, which he remembered from a previous visit as an idyllic spot. Some say his ardent wish for self-imposed exile came from his bitterly unpleasant marriage. He had first married Vipsania Agrippina, the daughter of Augustus' good friend and military commander, Marcus Vipsanius Agrippa. With her he was happy; she bore him a son, Drusus. When she was about to bear their second child, Augustus ordered Tiberius to divorce his beloved wife and marry his daughter Julia (12 B.C.). It was said that when afterward Tiberius happened to see Vipsania in the street, tears came into his eyes and he followed her with such a look of unhappiness on his face that Augustus arranged it so that he would never lay eyes on her again. After his forced marriage to Julia her licentiousness became increasingly flagrant, and since he could not divorce her, Tiberius at last got off to Rhodes leaving Julia and his son Drusus behind. In Rhodes he lived quietly. When he learned that Julia had been banished by her father for her adulteries, he asked permission to return to Rome. Augustus now refused it, and as his influence waned alarmingly, Tiberius came to be known as "the Exile." He continued to make application to Augustus for his return. Livia added her pleas, and Augustus was persuaded to change his mind. The message that he could return having been received, Tiberius set out for Rome (c2 A.D.), after an absence of seven years. Within three years of his return Caius and Lucius, natural heirs of Augustus, had died. Augustus adopted him and Agrippa Postumus (his last remaining grandson) as his sons (4 A.D.). Agrippa Postumus was accused of plotting against Augustus and was banished. Tiberius became the heir apparent.

For the next years he led the armies. He pacified Germany. Next he went to Illyria to suppress a revolt. The war was hard-fought and long. After three years he was victorious. This success was particularly important to Tiberius and to Rome, for it came at the time (9 A.D.) when the loss of Varus with three legions in Germany had plunged all Rome into mourning. From Illyria he went to Germany to salvage what he could from the defeat of Varus. On his return from Germany he celebrated a belated triumph for his Illyrian victory. He gave a great banquet with 1000 tables laid for his guests, and gave each man present three pieces of gold. Under customary procedure, Bato, the defeated Illyrian leader, would have been strangled. In a rare instance of magnanimity, Tiberius made him rich presents and gave him a house in Ravenna, because once during the war Bato had had the Romans trapped in a gorge and allowed them to escape rather than defeat them in an unequal fight. Tiberius used the spoils of the Illyrian war to restore the Temples of Concord and of the Heavenly Twins (Castor and Pollux). When Augustus was in his last brief illness, he summoned Tiberius to his side. Some said Augustus made Tiberius his heir partly at the insistence of Livia, but mostly because all his natural heirs, save Agrippa Postumus, were dead. And some say among Augustus' last words were these, "Alas, poor Rome, doomed to be chewed by those slow-moving jaws." Tiberius' enemies said Augustus never liked him. On the other hand, it appears that Augustus admired his military skill, and felt that he would be able to protect Rome from her enemies.

Tiberius did not immediately reveal the death of Augustus. First, Agrippa Postumus must be disposed of. Whether Livia or Tiberius gave the order for his death is not known, but when it was announced to him, Tiberius had the man who had carried out the order executed. He then went to the Senate to announce the death of Augustus. He asked for the protection of a Praetorian Guard for his person and assumed imperial powers, although he did not take the title of emperor. His assumption of power did not take place with unanimous approval. The soldiers in Germany clamored for Germanicus, their general, to take power, but he rebuked them and honorably refused to take advantage of their enthusiasm and affection. Other abortive plots against Tiberius were easily crushed. Tiberius conducted himself modestly as supreme ruler, although there was never any doubt as to who held the power. He refused to allow his followers to dedicate temples and priests to him as a divine being. He restored the authority and dignity of the consuls, and preserved the forms of republican government. He made some attempt to elevate the moral tone of life among the upper classes of Rome, which had become increasingly dissolute. He tried to control high prices with price ceilings, and limited to some extent the expense of public shows. An ardent student of Greek and Roman literature himself, he encouraged literature. He undertook tax reforms that greatly strengthened the financial condition of Rome. He abolished the ancient right of sanctuary and temples and also abolished foreign cults, especially those of the Egyptians and the Jews; it was in his reign that Christ was crucified. Remaining in Rome, he yet kept his generals and governors in the outposts on the alert by his frequent announcements that he was about to visit them, even going so far as to order transportation and food for his train. Then he would cancel the journey. He did this so many times he was given the nickname "Callipedes," from an actor whose specialty it was to give an imitation of a runner while never moving from one spot.

In 26 A.D. Tiberius left Rome to dedicate a Temple to Capitoline Jupiter at Capua and one to Augustus at Nola. From there

actor; up, lūte, pull; oi, oil; ou, out; ᴛʜ, then; d̦ as d or j, ș as s or sh, ț as t or ch, z̦ as z or zh.

he went to the island of Capreae (Capri), and remained there almost uninterruptedly until his death. Tiberius had never been popular at Rome. He was harsh and often cruel, as were his immediate predecessors, but unlike them, he apparently had no avenue to the affections of the people. In his days at Capreae he acquired a hideous reputation for the most grossly immoral practices and for savage cruelty, according to the Roman biographers who exaggerated and preserved his reputation for evil. He seemed to become indifferent to affairs of state, and carried them out by correspondence. He had always been considered stingy. He now became rapacious, confiscating estates at will and with almost no excuse. He was relentless toward his ex-wife Julia, and refused to ameliorate the harsh conditions of her exile. He quarreled with his mother, did not attend her funeral, refused to allow her to be deified, and annulled her will. He cared so little when his son Drusus died, so it is said, that when a delegation from Troy came, a month or so later, and offered him condolences, he replied by offering them condolences for the loss of their own eminent citizen, Hector. Some say he arranged to have Germanicus, his nephew and adopted son, and a very popular general, poisoned. He exiled Agrippina, wife of Germanicus, and had her flogged so severely she lost an eye, but he could not prevent her from starving herself to death. He accused the sons of Germanicus, his adoptive grandsons, of plotting against him and ordered them starved to death. The youngest son of Germanicus, Caius, called "Caligula," he spared. When apprised of the hatred and contempt in which he was held by the Romans, he said, "Let them hate me, so long as they fear me." He made his favorite, Sejanus, commander of the Praetorian Guard, and gave him unlimited power to punish his enemies, but when Sejanus began to acquire a following in his own right, Tiberius had him killed (31 A.D.). He rewarded informers and inflicted punishments indiscriminately. His reign, according to unfriendly Roman writers, was one of terror, and he was as much terrified as anyone, fully aware of his many enemies. He kept himself barricaded on Capreae. Suetonius tells that once he left the island and started for Rome. On the journey a pet serpent that he fed with his own hand was found nearly devoured by ants. Soothsayers told him it was a sign he must "beware the power of the mob." He started back to Capreae at once. He dreamed (still according to Suetonius), that a statue of Apollo he was planning to dedicate in the library of a temple of Augustus appeared to him and said, "Tiberius will never dedicate me." A few days before he died, the lighthouse at Capreae was struck by lightning. These signs of imminent death were fulfilled on March 16, 37 A.D., when he died at Misenum. News of his death, which some said was caused by poison administered on the order of Caius Caligula, provoked an outburst of joy. He was succeeded by Caius.

Tiberius Claudius Drusus Nero (klô′di-us drö′sus nir′ō). Full name of **Claudius**, emperor of Rome 41–54 A.D.

Tibris or **Tybris** (tī′bris). An ancient name of the **Tiber.**

Tibullus (ti-bul′us), **Albius.** Roman elegiac poet; born c54 B.C.; died 19 B.C. Although his family had lost considerable property in the civil wars, Tibullus was left with enough to live in comfort on his estate between Tibur and Praeneste. He was patronized by Messalla, who invited him to accompany him on a campaign in Aquitania, 31 B.C. Out of love for "Delia," he refused a later invitation by Messalla to go on a campaign in Asia. The works ascribed to Tibullus consist of four books, of which Books I and II, indubitably by Tibullus, include poems to his fickle mistresses "Delia" (Plania?) and "Nemesis." The six elegies which constitute Book III are by "Lygdamus," pseudonym of a fashionable poet of lesser talents, and Book IV contains six elegant short poems by the poetess Sulpicia, seven poems probably by Tibullus, and the anonymous and tasteless *Panegyricus Messallae.* Tibullus was much admired for his skill in verse and the graceful style in which he depicted the themes of love and the pleasures of country life. (JJ)

Tibur (tī′ber). [Modern name, **Tivoli.**] In ancient geography, a town in C Italy, situated on a height above the falls of the Anio River, about 15 miles E of Rome. It was

fat, fāte, fär, fāre, errant; net, mē, hėr ardent; pin, pīne; not, nōte, mŏve, nôr,

an ancient town of the Latins. Under the Romans it continued to flourish, and was especially known as a resort and celebrated for the picturesque Falls of the Anio. Tibur is also notable for two interesting temples of the republican period, a round temple of Vesta and a rectangular temple, sometimes attributed to Hercules, or to the Sibyl, for many centuries used as a church. At the foot of the hill are extensive deposits of the fine water-laid limestone known by the Romans as *lapis Tiburtinus*, in English as travertine, and at a little distance are sulphurous warm springs, the Aquae Albulae of the Romans, and the extensive remains of the villa of the emperor Hadrian. (JJ)

Tichomachia (tī″kō-ma-kē′a). Literally, "battle at the walls, assault," a name given to the 12th book of the *Iliad*. (JJ)

Ticinus (ti-sī′nus). [Modern name, **Ticino**.] River in Switzerland and Italy, formed by the junction of two headstreams flowing from the Alps. It traverses Verbanus Lacus (Lago Maggiore) and the Lombard plain, and joins the Po near Pavia.

Ticinus, Battle of the. Victory gained near the Ticinus (modern, Ticino River) and probably near Pavia, 218 B.C., by Hannibal over the Romans under Publius Scipio; chiefly a cavalry engagement.

Tifata (tī-fā′ta). [Modern name, **Monte di Maddaloni**.] Low mountain range near Capua, Italy, about 17 miles NE of Naples. Near it, in 83 B.C., Sulla defeated the Marian general Norbanus.

Tifernum Tiberinum (ti-fėr′num tib-ẹ-rī′num). In ancient geography, a city in Italy, on or near the site of the modern Città di Castello, about 20 miles from Arezzo.

Tigranes (tī-grā′nēz). King of Armenia; died after 56 B.C. He was a son-in-law of Mithridates the Great. He conquered Syria and part of Asia Minor, but was defeated by Lucullus in 69 B.C., surrendered to Pompey, and was deprived of his conquest.

Tigris (tī′gris). [Biblical name, **Hiddekel**.] River in Mesopotamia (modern Asiatic Turkey and Iraq) which is formed by headstreams that rise in the mountains of Armenia and Assyria, and flows S and SE to the Persian Gulf. The ancient cities of Nineveh, Calah, and Ctesiphon, among

others, were on it. According to Greek legend to account for the name of the river, Dionysus crossed it on a tiger's back.

Tigurini (tig-ū-rī′nī). One of the branches of the ancient Helvetii. They took an active part in the defeat of the Romans in 107 B.C., but were overwhelmingly defeated by Caesar in 58 B.C. Their capital may have been on the site of modern Zurich.

Timaeus (tī-mē′us). Greek Pythagorean philosopher of Locri in Italy; fl. c400 B.C. He was long reputed to be the author of a philosophical work entitled *On the Soul of the World*, but scholars now generally agree in assigning the work to a later period. He appears in Plato's dialogue named for him.

Timaeus. Greek historian; fl. c356–260 B.C. He was a native of Tauromenium in Sicily, a member of a noble and wealthy family. He was banished by the tyrant Agathocles in 317 or 312 B.C., and went to Athens where he remained until the last years of his life, before returning to his native country. He wrote a history of Italy and Sicily, in 38 books, from the earliest times to 264 B.C. His work was highly regarded for the care with which he used existing authorities, including Carthaginian and Phoenician archives. Fragments of the work are extant.

Timandra (tī-man′dra). According to some accounts, a daughter of Tyndareus and Leda, and the sister of Helen and Clytemnestra. Because Tyndareus once forgot to make proper sacrifices to Aphrodite, the goddess resolved to punish him by making all his daughters notorious adulteresses. She was first married to Echemus but deserted him to go off to Dulichium with Phyleus.

Timanthes (ti-man′thēz). According to Pausanias, an Olympic victor in the pancratium. He tried to maintain his strength by bending a great bow each day. When he found he could no longer bend the bow, he lighted a fire and cast himself into it.

Timanthes. Greek painter of Sicyon; born in the island of Cythnus in the Cyclades; fl. c400 B.C. He is known mainly as the painter of one of the great pictures of antiquity, the *Sacrifice of Iphigenia*, in which Agamemnon conceals his uncontrollable grief by covering his head with his mantle. This picture was a favorite of Cicero. Pliny's remark that there is "always something more implied than expressed in his work" is suggestive of bold and generalized execution.

Timocreon (ti-mok′rē-on). Greek poet of Rhodes; fl. first half of the 5th century B.C.; a contemporary of Simonides of Ceos. He is known for his bitter attacks on Themistocles and Simonides. Simonides wrote his epitaph, as follows: "Here lies Timocreon of Rhodes, who drank much, ate much, and said many evil things."

Timoleon (ti-mō′lē-on, tī-). Greek general and statesman, born at Corinth; died 337 or 336 B.C., at Syracuse. He was the son of Timodemus, of an illustrious Corinthian family. Timoleon was noted as a great patriot, for his mild and gentle disposition, for his hatred of tyrants, and for his personal courage. To illustrate his various characteristics—once in battle his brother, pierced by many wounds, fell and was in imminent danger of death. Timoleon rushed to his side, held his shield over his brother to protect him, and warded off the enemy until help arrived. This same brother afterwards got command of a body of mercenaries and threatened to make himself tyrant. Timoleon tried to reason with him and to persuade him not to attempt despotic power but failed to deter him and was mocked for his pains. Timoleon went with two companions to his brother's house, withdrew to a corner of the room, covered his head and wept while his companions, according to plan, assassinated his brother. Those who admired Timoleon credited him with putting his country before his family. His mother, however, did not take this view. Her anger at Timoleon so depressed him that he was only with difficulty persuaded not to starve himself to death, and he withdrew from public life. For the next 20 years he lived in obscurity.

When Dionysius the Younger, exiled tyrant of Syracuse, returned after ten years and reestablished himself as tyrant, the Carthaginians threatened Syracuse. The Syracusans sent to Corinth, their mother-city, for help. As the Corinthians, having decided to send help to their colony, debated who should be put in command of the expeditionary force, someone proposed that Timoleon be named. He was given the appointment and had begun collecting his forces when a letter from Hicetas, tyrant of Leontini, arrived,

saying there was no need to send forces to aid Syracuse as he had been appointed general by the Syracusans. His letter angered the Corinthians, who suspected a design to make himself tyrant of Syracuse, and made them more than ever eager to send Timoleon. A force was outfitted. When they were ready to sail, the priestess of Persephone dreamed that the goddess and her mother were preparing for a journey and said they were going to sail with Timoleon. Because of this favorable omen the Corinthians equipped a sacred trireme and named it for the goddesses. Timoleon went to sacrifice at Delphi before his departure. As he did so a crown that had been presented as a votive offering slipped from its place and fell on his head, indicating that he had been crowned by the god himself. These were the first of many omens noted by Plutarch, that showed Timoleon to be under divine protection. He set sail (344 B.C.) with ten ships to relieve Syracuse. Before Timoleon reached his destination, he learned that Hicetas had besieged Dionysius in the citadel of Syracuse and had made a treacherous agreement with the Carthaginians to prevent Timoleon from coming to the aid of Syracuse. Envoys of Hicetas met him at Rhegium, which, having thrown off its tyrant, welcomed him warmly. But 20 Carthaginian ships, sent thither by Hicetas, lay at anchor in the harbor. Timoleon understood that this was a threat, and realized that Hicetas and the Carthaginians meant to divide Sicily between them. As he could not pass by the Carthaginian fleet, he asked the envoys from Hicetas, who carried orders to him to return to Corinth, to present their proposals to him in a public meeting within the gates of Rhegium. The envoys agreed; the Carthaginians, the envoys, and the people of Rhegium went into the market-place. The gates were closed and speeches were begun. Timoleon, with the help of the Rhegines, delayed the proceedings with many speeches and counter-proposals. While he did so, nine of his ships quietly sailed past the unattended Carthaginian fleet. When word was brought to him of their escape, Timoleon slipped through the crowd, boarded the last of his ships, and sailed away. The Carthaginians, noted for their duplicity, were deeply chagrined at the trick Timoleon had played on them, and the people of Rhegium were delighted that the Carthaginians had been beaten at their own game.

Timoleon and his fleet put in at Tauromenium, whose ruler, Andromachus, hated tyranny and allowed him to use the city as a base. Hicetas sent the Carthaginian ships to Syracuse. Timoleon set out for Adranum where he met the forces of Hicetas that had come to meet him. While the ranks of Hicetas were still coming up, Timoleon attacked and routed them, though they were vastly superior in numbers. The people of Adranum came streaming out of the city to welcome Timoleon, of whose success they had had divine warning: the doors of the temple of Adranus, the Sicilian fire-god, had flown open of themselves, the spear of the god trembled, and sweat poured off the face of the image, all of which portended wonderful victories. After this victory the other Greek cities of Sicily, which had hitherto distrusted him and feared he wanted to make himself tyrant, flocked to Timoleon's side, and his forces were greatly increased. Dionysius, still shut up in the citadel at Syracuse, sent a message offering to surrender to him. Timoleon secretly sent 400 of his soldiers, all he could safely get through the enemy lines, to accept his surrender and take him off the island citadel. Timoleon shipped him to Corinth and his men took posesssion of all the stores, horses, and men that Dionysius had left in the citadel. Now the situation at Syracuse was this: Timoleon's men occupied the citadel; the forces of Hicetas occupied the mainland city and territory of Syracuse; and the Carthaginian fleet was in the harbor. Timoleon himself was at Adranum. Hicetas sent two men to assassinate him as he made a sacrifice at the altar. As they were about to attack him, a man in the crowd leaped at one of the would-be assassins and killed him, crying out that he had just recognized him as the man who had slain his father. The other assassin confessed the plot and all marveled at the manner in which the gods protected Timoleon. After the failure of the plot, Hicetas invited Mago, the Carthaginian commander, with 60,000 troops into the city of Syracuse, which had never fallen to Carthaginian

attack but was now handed over to them. Hicetas continued to besiege Timoleon's men in the citadel. In an attempt to prevent the besieged from receiving supplies, he went with Mago to take Catana, which was sending food to the citadel by small boat. Timoleon's commander in the citadel sallied out in their absence and seized the strongest part of the city as well as stores of supplies and arms. On the accomplishment of this, and perhaps because he feared that the Greeks might unite against him, Mago decided to leave Sicily and abandoned Hicetas. Timoleon jeered at the cowardice of the Carthaginians, attacked Hicetas, and took the city by storm without losing a man. He destroyed the island citadel that had been the refuge of tyrants, and on its site raised courts of justice. Italy and Greece rang with his fame and the glory of his success. After the wars and sieges, Syracuse was sadly depopulated. Timoleon sent to Corinth to ask for colonists. Many came, and the city began to revive.

The Carthaginians, smarting under the cowardice of Mago, now sent a force of 70,000 under Hasdrubal and Hamilcar to attack Timoleon. With his force of 5000 foot-soldiers and 1000 horse, he marched to meet the enemy. Some of his mercenaries deserted on the way because they had not been paid and because they thought it was folly to attack such an overwhelmingly superior force, but others joined him. On the march his army met some mules loaded with parsley. His soldiers were made uneasy by this because of the association of parsley with the dead. Timoleon heartened them by saying the material of victory crowns had come to them of its own accord, for victors at the Isthmian Games at that time were crowned with parsley. He took some of it and made a wreath for his own head, and his men followed his example. Coming up to the Crimisus River, he saw that the Carthaginians were crossing it. A torrential rain and hail storm, with flashes of lightning and peals of thunder, greatly impeded the Carthaginians with their heavy armor. As they crossed the river Timoleon fell on them and slaughtered them by the hundreds (341 B.C.). Some say 10,000 were killed. The spoils were so great it took his men three days to collect them all and raise their victory trophy. The most beautiful of the captured armor was sent to Corinth to be dedicated in the temple of Poseidon. The defeated Carthaginians sailed away under command of Gisco. Timoleon pursued Hicetas and captured him alive in the land of Leontini. Hicetas and his sons were put to death. The wives and daughters of Hicetas and his friends were brought to trial in Syracuse and, with no opposition from Timoleon, they also were put to death. The Carthaginians sued for peace, and now for a time the sieges and wars ended. Timoleon freed the other Greek cities from their tyrants; Greek Sicily was restored to order, its lands were repeopled, and its cities revived. Timoleon, having accomplished what he had set out to do, voluntarily laid aside the great powers that he had exercised. He remained in Syracuse, where he was honored as a common father by the Syracusans. In his old age he went blind, but the Syracusans did not falter in their gratitude to him and their affection and honor for him. Occasionally he was brought into their assembly to hear a debate. After listening carefully he would pronounce his opinion on the proper course to follow and the Syracusans took his advice. After a brief illness, he died (337 or 336 B.C.), was given a great public funeral, and his ashes were buried in the market-place. Timoleon, of excellent character, unusual capacity, and incorruptible patriotism, was one of very few whose ventures were so unfailingly rewarded with success that it was commonly believed that the gods had a special love for him and protected him.

Timomachus (ti-mom′a-kus). Painter, of Byzantium, fl. in the 1st century B.C. According to Pliny, Julius Caesar paid a large sum for two of his pictures, an *Ajax* and a *Medea*. The *Medea* of Timomachus was not less praised in song and epigram than the *Aphrodite* of Apelles (an echo of the original may perhaps be seen in some of the Pompeian wall paintings). His *Iphigenia in Tauris* and a *Gorgon* were also celebrated.

Timon (ti′mon). A semi-legendary Athenian misanthrope; fl. in the last part of the 5th century B.C. Disillusioned by the disappointments he received, he won a place in history by withdrawing from the society of men. He is the subject of the tragedy *Timon of Athens* by Shakespeare.

Timon of Phlius (fli′us). Greek Skeptic philosopher; fl. c280 B.C. He wrote satiric poems called *Silloi* (hence he was called "the Sillographer"), in hexameter verse, ridiculing all the dogmatic schools of philosophy. Fragments of his poems survive.

Timotheus (ti-mō′thē̦-us, -moth′e̦-us; tī-). Athenian naval commander; son of Conon; died, 354 B.C. He was an able commander who did much to restore the power of Athens after the Peloponnesian War. He made an expedition around the Peloponnesus in 376 B.C., and achieved some successes, the most important of which was to win Corcyra for Athens. He was ordered back to Athens on the conclusion of a peace with Sparta, 374 B.C. In his next command he was hampered by lack of money. The Athenians had voted certain measures to relieve Corcyra, which had been attacked by Sparta after Timotheus left, but had not voted the money to carry them out. Timotheus was compelled to lose valuable time collecting money and ships. When he returned from a cruise about the Aegean for this purpose he was accused of fraud, was relieved of his command and subjected to trial. Thanks to the intervention of Alcetas, king of Epirus, and Jason of Pherae, whom he had persuaded to join the second Athenian Confederacy, he was acquitted. But he was discredited in Athens and left to enter the service of the king of Persia. He later returned to Athens and was sent as leader of an expedition against Samos, which he captured, 365 B.C. He next was given command of the fleet that was operating off Macedonia and won great success in the area; he compelled Methone and Pydna to join the Athenian Confederacy, and won Potidaea, Torone, and other cities, but was unsuccessful in two attempts to take Amphipolis. In 356 B.C. he was one of three commanders sent to subdue rebellious Chios. He and Iphicrates, a co-commander, decided not to press the attack because of a violent storm. Chares, the third commander, attacked against their advice and without their support and was driven off with great loss. He accused Timotheus and Iphicrates of treachery. They were brought to trial on a charge of having accepted bribes from the Chians. Iphicrates was acquitted but Timotheus, who had made enemies by his arrogant manner, was fined 100 talents. Unable to pay such a large sum, he withdrew to Chalcis and died soon after. Afterward the Athenians regretted their harsh treatment of Timotheus and allowed his son to settle the fine for 10 talents. Timotheus was buried in the Ceramicus; statues in his honor were set up in the market-place and on the Acropolis.

Timotheus. Dithyrambic poet of Miletus; died c360 B.C. He made some innovations in the theater, in which he was encouraged by Euripides, and in music. Among other things, he increased the number of strings of the cithara to eleven.

Timotheus. Greek sculptor, probably from Epidaurus; fl. 4th century B.C. He is best known as the oldest of the four sculptors (the others being Scopas, Leochares, and Bryaxis) who created the Mausoleum, the tomb of Mausolus, satrap of Caria, at Halicarnassus, which was completed c333 B.C. The relief panel of the Amazon frieze from the southern face is attributed to Timotheus. It is thought that he also contributed sculptural ornamentation to the Temple of Asclepius at Epidaurus.

Tinia (tin′i-a̯). Chief god of the ancient Etruscan pantheon. He is equated with the Greek Zeus in that he was both supreme deity and thunder-god. His attribute was the triple thunderbolt, and any spot struck by him became sacred.

Tiphys (tī′fis). In Greek legend, a son of Hagnias of Boeotia. He was a skillful navigator. At the urging of Athena he joined the Argonauts and became their steersman by common consent. He steered the *Argo* through many perilous seas but did not reach Colchis. In the land of the Mariandyni he died after a short sickness.

Tiresias or **Teiresias** (tī-rē′si-a̯s). In Greek mythology, a son of Everes and the nymph Chariclo. He was a blind Theban seer, whose very long life was three times as long as that of an ordinary man's, or, as some say, lasted for seven generations. His mother was the intimate companion of Athena. According to some accounts, when Tiresias was a child he was roaming the

forests one day and chanced to go to the Hippocrene Spring on Mount Helicon to drink. At the moment when he arrived there, Athena and Chariclo were bathing in the pool. Athena laid her hand across his eyes, or some say splashed water into them, and blinded him because he had seen her in her bath. Chariclo chided the goddess for blinding her son. Athena answered that it was not by her will but by the law of the gods that whoever saw them without their permission would be blinded. To atone somewhat for the loss of his sight Athena gave him the gift of prophecy and divination, a long life, and the power to retain his mental accomplishments in the Underworld. Or as some say, she caused serpents to cleanse his ears so that he could understand the talk of prophetic birds. Quite another account of how Tiresias became blind has to do with the anger of Hera. According to this account, Tiresias once saw two snakes coupling on Mount Cyllene in Arcadia. He wounded them or, as some say, killed the female, and instantly he was transformed from a man to a woman. For seven years he lived as a woman and was notorious for his love affairs. At the end of that time he again saw two snakes coupling and, as some say, killed the male and was transformed once more into a man. Hera and Zeus, being engaged in an argument about which sex enjoys the physical aspects of love more, decided to consult Tiresias, who had experienced these aspects as both a man and a woman. Hera maintained that the male derived the most pleasure from love-making, and contended that this was why Zeus was so often unfaithful to her. Zeus mocked her and claimed that it was the female who enjoyed it most. On being appealed to, Tiresias agreed with Zeus. If the parts of the pleasure of love were counted as ten, he said, women got nine parts and men only one. This infuriated Hera and she struck Tiresias blind. Zeus, to make up for this, gave him long life and the art of soothsaying. But some say he was blinded because he revealed things to men that only the gods should know. In the reign of Oedipus and Jocasta a plague struck Thebes. Tiresias said it would cease only when the murderer of Laius, Jocasta's former husband, was found and punished. As no one knew who that murderer was Tiresias was at length compelled to inform them that it was Oedipus himself, who had unwittingly murdered his father and sired children on his mother. In the war of the Seven against Thebes, Tiresias predicted to Eteocles, a son of Oedipus who now ruled in his father's place, that Thebes would be victorious if a son of the royal house voluntarily sacrificed himself to Ares. Menoeceus, son of Creon, killed himself and the Seven were routed. Of the seven attacking leaders only Adrastus survived. Ten years later the Epigoni (sons of the Seven against Thebes) attacked the city to avenge their fathers. This time Tiresias advised the Thebans to negotiate with the Argives and to flee the city, for, he said, Thebes would fall when the last of the original seven died, and Adrastus was even now dying of grief over the death of his son Aegialeus who had fallen before Thebes. The Thebans fled and the city fell, as Tiresias had predicted. But Tiresias did not escape with the Thebans. He knew he was fated to die when Thebes fell into the hands of the Argives. As he drew water to drink from a spring, he suddenly died. Tiresias was the father of Manto, a prophetic daughter who was taken by Alcmaeon in the war of the Epigoni and later was sent to Delphi. Some say he had another daughter, Daphne, who became a Sibyl. Tiresias predicted that Narcissus would have a long life, if he never knew himself. According to some, he foretold the heroic exploits of Heracles to Alcmene when Heracles, as an infant, strangled the serpents Hera had sent to kill him. Odysseus, long prevented from returning home after the Trojan War, was instructed by Circe to go to Hades and consult Tiresias to learn the fate that awaited him when he reached his homeland of Ithaca. Tiresias told him Poseidon was angry over the blinding of Polyphemus and would cause him much trouble. He warned Odysseus not to eat the cattle of the sun on Trinacria, told him of the wooers who were besieging Penelope in Ithaca, and said he would avenge their insolence. He also instructed him to seek a land where the men knew not the sea, and told him how he would recognize this land. There he must make sacrifices to Poseidon, after which he could dwell in Ithaca in peace. He also told Odysseus that death would come to him from the sea. All that he predicted came to pass.

Tiro (tī′rō), **Marcus Tullius**. Roman freedman and amanuensis of Cicero; fl. in the 1st century B.C. He is said to have contributed to the development of the art of stenography.

Tiryns (tī′rinz). In ancient geography, a city in Argolis, Greece, situated near the coast SE of Argos, and about three miles N of Nauplia. According to tradition, the region was first occupied by Pelasgians, who fell under the domination of Danaus when he came to Argolis from Egypt with his 50 daughters. Following internecine wars, the kingdom of Danaus was divided among his descendants. Acrisius became ruler of the region of Argos and his brother Proetus became king of the area about Tiryns and founded the city. According to legend, he imported Cyclopes from Lycia to build its "Cyclopean" walls of enormous, irregular stones. Perseus, having accidentally slain his grandfather Acrisius, thus fulfilling an oracle, did not care to remain in Argos. He exchanged his kingdom with his cousin Megapenthes for Tiryns and removed to Tiryns with Andromeda, the wife he brought home from his adventures in Asia and Africa. Some even say Perseus was born in Tiryns, and point to an underground chamber there as the place where his mother Danaë was confined and was visited by Zeus in a shower of gold. Heracles was compelled to carry out his 12 labors for its king, Eurystheus. Some say the chamber was one Eurystheus caused to be dug and that he used it as a place in which to hide rather than face the terrifying Heracles when he returned to Tiryns to report on the successful conclusion of his various labors. After the death of Eurystheus, Tiryns, like the rest of Argolis, fell under the domination of Atreus, son of Pelops, who had made himself master at Mycenae. With the Dorian invasion of the Peloponnesus Tiryns recovered its independence from Mycenae. In the Persian Wars Tiryns sent 200 men to the Battle of Plataea (479 B.C.). Their names were inscribed on the tripods dedicated at Delphi in celebration of the Greek victory. In 468 B.C. Argos, jealous of the honor paid Tiryns for its part in the Persian Wars, in which

Argos had played no heroic part, conquered Tiryns and destroyed the city.

The city was built on a low rocky hill that rose above the plain of Argos. The ancient city, occupying the hill and the area of the plain at its base, was older than Mycenae, and dates from the 3rd millennium B.C. After 2000 B.C. the citadel on the summit of the low rock was enclosed by walls, within which remains of a pre-Mycenaean palace have been found. Tiryns is celebrated for its antiquities, including Cyclopean walls, gates, and the palace (excavated by Heinrich Schliemann and Wilhelm Dörpfeld, 1884–85). The citadel is a famous memorial of early Greek civilization. The massive walls, built of great blocks, some of which weigh as much as 13 tons, with the interstices filled with small stones, surround the summit of an oblong hill. In the *Iliad* Homer speaks of Tiryns as "mighty of ramparts." Pausanias, who visited it in the 2nd century A.D., said it was unnecesary to go to Egypt to see the pyramids when there were such wonders as Tiryns at home. The acropolis at Tiryns is divided into three terraces, of which the highest was occupied by the palace and royal quarters, and included the well-known galleries of arcades resembling pointed arches. These galleries gave on to chambers constructed in the thickness of the walls and were unique in Greek architecture. They were used as storage areas in time of peace and as armories and places of shelter in time of war. The middle terrace, north and west of the royal quarters, reinforced the acropolis and was occupied by those connected with the royal household. To the north, and separated by a wall, was the lower terrace where the garrison was quartered, and to which the population of the city at the base of the hill withdrew in times of invasion. As at Mycenae, the principal approach to the acropolis was by a passageway made of enormous blocks of stone, more carefully dressed and fitted than the surrounding walls, and was so placed that the right, or unshielded, side of an approaching enemy was exposed to the defenders in the citadel. Within the walls of the acropolis there are remains of an extensive prehistoric palace, with outer and inner courts, men's apartments, bathroom, and secluded women's quarters, the whole corresponding with the spirit of the Homeric picture. The floor plan of the palace is still plainly visible. A cistern and remains of a drainage system have been found at Tiryns, as well as a royal altar surrounded by a ditch into which the blood of sacrificial victims flowed. Wall paintings and other details of high interest were found by Schliemann.

Tisamenus (ti-sam′e-nus). In Greek legend, a son of Orestes and Hermione, daughter of Helen. He was ruler of Sparta and was slain by the descendants of Heracles when they attacked his country. According to other accounts, he was not killed by the Heraclidae but lost his life when he was driven out of Sparta and sought to conquer regions in the northern part of the Peloponnesus.

Tisamenus. In Greek legend, a son of Thersander (one of the Epigoni). He accompanied his father to Troy and assumed command of the Boeotians when he came of age.

Tisamenus. According to Greek tradition, an Elean, a seer of the family of the Iamidae. He consulted the oracle at Delphi to learn why he had fathered no children. The priestess told him he would win five glorious victories. Tisamenus thought she meant he would win five victories in the games, and set to work to perfect himself in the Pentathlon. At the Olympic Games he won four of his contests but lost the fifth, the wrestling match. The Spartans concluded that the priestess had meant that Tisamenus would win five victories in battle; they therefore sought to hire his services in their wars. Tisamenus, seeing how much they desired him, agreed to help them if they would admit him on equal terms as a Spartan citizen. The Spartans considered this too high a price to pay and refused. But when they were threatened with the danger of the Persians in the Persian War they approached him again and agreed to make him a citizen. Now Tisamenus raised his price: the Spartans must also give the citizenship to his brother. Because of their great need the Spartans agreed; Tisamenus and his brother became the only men, according to Herodotus, whom the Spartans ever admitted to citizenship. With his prophetic powers Tisamenus helped the Spartans to win five victories: at Plataea (479 B.C.); near Tegea

(473 B.C.) against the Tegeans and Argives; at Dipaea (c471 B.C.) against the Arcadians; against the Messenians (464 B.C.); and at Tanagra (457 B.C.) against the Athenians and the Argives.

Tisander (ti-san′dėr) or **Tisandrus** (-drus). In Greek legend, a son of Jason and Medea. Some say he was murdered by his mother for revenge on Jason when the latter proposed to abandon her and marry a Corinthian princess. Others say Tisander, with his brothers and sisters, was seized and stoned to death by the people of Corinth in revenge on Medea for the death of the Theban princess Glauce and her father Creon. The body of Tisander was buried in Hera's sacred precinct in Corinth by order of the priestess of Delphi.

Tisiphone (ti-sif′ọ̄-nē). In Greek mythology, one of the three Erinyes (Furies) or Eumenides, born of the blood of Uranus which fell on Gaea when Cronus mutilated him. She is the "Avenger" who scourges the guilty in the Underworld who have escaped punishment for their crimes while on earth. Tisiphone also responds to the requests of the gods to implant envy and jealousy in the hearts of mortals. Aeneas saw Tisiphone, dressed in a blood-stained robe and sitting on a crag, when he journeyed to the Underworld to visit his father.

Tisiphone. According to Euripides, a daughter of Alcmaeon and Manto the daughter of the seer Tiresias, who had been taken captive by Alcmaeon in the capture of Thebes by the Epigoni. Alcmaeon gave Tisiphone to Creon, king of Corinth, to bring up, after he had sent Manto to Delphi as part of the booty taken at Thebes. Tisiphone grew up to be a beautiful girl. The wife of Creon, fearful lest her husband become enamored of the girl's beauty, sold Tisiphone as a slave. The purchaser, unaware of her identity, was her father Alcmaeon.

Tissaphernes (tis-ạ-fėr′nēz). Persian satrap; executed c395 B.C. He became satrap in Asia Minor (413 B.C.). As an enemy of Athens, he stirred up revolt (412 B.C.) of the Athenian cities of Asia Minor and made an alliance with Sparta. He was hostile to Cyrus the Younger, and discovered and disclosed the latter's plans to Artaxerxes II. He took part in the battle of Cunaxa (401 B.C.),

in which Cyrus was killed, and acted as guide to the Ten Thousand Greeks during the early part of their return journey from Cunaxa. In the course of the march Tissaphernes gathered the Greek generals and captains of the Ten Thousand in his tent, treacherously had the captains slain and sent the generals in chains to the Persian court, where they were put to death. He was appointed chief ruler in W Asia by Artaxerxes, was defeated by Agesilaus of Sparta in 395 B.C., and was put to death through the influence of Parysatis, who blamed Tissaphernes for the death of her son Cyrus.

Titan (tī′tạn). In classical literature, the sun personified. The name Titan was often substituted by the Latin poets for Helius as god of the sun.

Titane (ti-tā′nē). In ancient geography, a town between Sicyon and Phlius in the region of Corinth, Greece. The inhabitants claimed that it was the place where Titan, brother of Helius, first lived and that it was named for him. At Titane there was a sanctuary of Asclepius, built by a son of Machaon after the Trojan War. In the temple were images of Asclepius, Hygea, Coronis, and others. During sacrifices to Asclepius, in which a bull, a lamb, and a pig were offered, the image of Coronis was removed to another part of the temple. Sacred serpents lived in the temple and were fed by the worshipers. There was a temple of Athena on the hill at Titane. At the bottom of the hill was an altar of the Winds. One night a year the priest offered sacrifices to the winds. He performed secret rites, including, some say, the charms of Medea, at four pits near the altar to quell the blast of the winds in the coming year.

Titania (ti-tā′ni-ạ). A poetical epithet applied to Diana, Latona, Pyrrha, and Circe.

Titans (tī′tạnz). In Greek mythology, the sons of Gaea and Uranus. They were Oceanus, Coeus, Hyperion, Crius, Iapetus, and Cronus. Their sisters, the Titanesses, where Tethys, Rhea, Themis, Mnemosyne, Phoebe, and Thia. Their descendants were also called Titans. Gaea incited them to make war on Uranus. They dethroned him and made Cronus ruler in his place. When Zeus succeeded Cronus, the sons of Iapetus, led by Atlas, made war on Zeus. After a long struggle, during which the Titans fought from Mount Othrys and the gods fought from Mount Olympus, Zeus secured the aid of the Cyclopes and put the Titans to rout. He hurled them all except Atlas into Tartarus and set the Hecatonchires to guard them. But some say they were banished and at length joined Cronus in the Isles of the Blest.

Titaresius (ti-tä-rē'si-us). In ancient geography, a river of Thessaly, called by Homer a branch of the dread river of oaths, the Styx. The seer Mopsus lived near its banks.

Tithonus (ti-thō'nus). In Greek mythology, a son of Laomedon, and a brother of Priam, king of Troy. Eos fell in love with his youthful beauty and carried him off. He became the father of two of her sons, Memnon and Emathion, and settled in the east. Toward the end of the Trojan War Priam bribed Tithonus with a golden vine to send his son Memnon to the aid of the Trojans. This led to Memnon's death. Eos beseeched Zeus to grant immortality to Tithonus. Zeus granted her request, but as she had forgotten to ask for perpetual youth for him, Tithonus grew older and older, and finally shriveled up so that there was not much more left of him but a chirping voice. Eos shut him up in a chamber and he was transformed into a grasshopper.

Tithorea (ti-thôr'ē-a). In ancient geography, a city of Phocis, on the slopes of Mount Parnassus. When the sun was passing through the constellation Taurus, the Tithoreans went to Thebes with the aim of stealing earth from the tomb of Amphion and Zethus there. They did this in accordance with an oracle of Bacis, which said that if they took earth from the tomb of Amphion and Zethus and placed it on the tomb of Antiope, Tithorea would have a good harvest and Thebes would not. Naturally, the Thebans wished to prevent such an outcome, and set a guard about the tomb of Amphion and Zethus at this time.

Titias (tish'i-as). In Greek legend, a champion boxer of the Mariandyni. On his return from the expedition to the Amazons Heracles came among the Mariandyni and took part in the funeral games for the king's brother. He sparred with Titias and accidentally killed him.

Titinius (ti-tin'i-us). Latin writer of comedies, an older contemporary of Terence; fl. first half of the 2nd century B.C. Fragments of 14 plays indicate his interest in the everyday life of his time.

Titthium (tit'thi-um). Mountain near Epidaurus where, according to some accounts, Asclepius was exposed by his mother Coronis, and where the herbs are still noted for their medicinal powers. According to a story told by the Epidaurians, a goatherd on the mountain, noticing that his bitch and a she-goat were missing, went in search of them and found them taking turns nursing an infant. He thought to approach the child, but as he did so a bright light shone all about it. This was a sign to the goatherd of the presence of a divinity and he left the child to the protection of the god who had made the sign.

Titus (tī'tus). [Full name, **Titus Flavius Sabinus Vespasianus**.] Roman emperor; born 39 A.D.; died September, 81 A.D. He was the son of Vespasian. He was called "the delight of mankind" because of his free distribution of gifts to his people. He was educated with Britannicus, served in the army, conducted the Jewish war after the departure of his father, and in 70 A.D. captured Jerusalem, for which he was given a triumph at Rome and in honor of which his brother Domitian erected the Arch of Titus. He was associated with Vespasian in the government, and succeeded to the throne on Vespasian's death, June, 79 A.D. Though dissipated in his habits before he became emperor, he devoted himself thereafter to bettering the lot of the Romans. He finished the Flavian Amphitheater ("Colosseum") and built the Baths of Titus. The eruption of Vesuvius that buried Pompeii, and a fire at Rome, occurred in his reign. On his death he was succeeded by his brother, the cruel and tyrannous Domitian.

Titus Livius (liv'i-us). Latin name of the Roman historian **Livy**.

Titus Lucretius Carus (lö-krē'shus kār'us). Full name of the poet **Lucretius**.

Titus Quintius (or **Quinctius**) **Flamininus** (kwin'shus, kwingk'shus, fla-mi-nī'nus). See **Flamininus, Titus Quintius** (or **Quinctius**).

Titus Tatius (tā'shus). See **Tatius, Titus**.

Tityus (tit'i-us). In Greek mythology, the giant

son of Zeus and Elara. Zeus hid Elara in a cave to protect her from the wrath of Hera, and there her son was born. A cave in Euboea was named the Elarium in her honor. When Tityus grew up Hera incited him to attack Leto. As she was on her way to Delphi, she withdrew to perform some private rite and Tityus assaulted her. As he seized her veil she cried out, and her children, Artemis and Apollo, instantly came to her aid and killed Tityus with their arrows. Because he had had the presumption to attack one of the immortals Tityus was sent to the farthest reaches of Tartarus. There he was stretched out (his body covered nine acres) and pegged down, and vultures were send to peck at his heart continually. Aeneas saw the awful punishment of Tityus when he visited the Underworld, and the distinguished painter Polygnotus depicted it in his painting of *Odysseus in the Underworld*, in the hall of the Cnidians at Delphi. The tomb of Tityus, a rounded barrow, was shown in Phocis, and in Euboea he was worshiped as a hero and had a shrine.

Tivoli (tē'vō-lē). See **Tibur**.

Tlepolemus (tle-pol'e̞-mus). In Greek legend, a son of Heracles and Astyocheia, and a grandson of Zeus. As a youth he accidentally killed his father's maternal uncle Licymnius, whom he loved dearly, and was forced by the other sons and grandsons of Heracles to flee. He built a fleet and, after many hardships, landed with his followers in Rhodes, where he founded cities and married Polyxo. As an ally of the Greeks he captained nine ships in the Trojan War. In the war he encountered Sarpedon, son of Zeus, and taunted him with a lack of courage, saying he could not really be the son of Zeus. He then attacked him and although he succeeded in wounding Sarpedon he was slain by the latter.

Tleson (tlē'son). Attic, potter of the 6th century B.C., who specialized in small cups. A group of these cups is known as the Little Master cups from the exquisite miniature paintings on them. The decorator of Tleson's cups worked in the black-figure style and is known as the Tleson Painter. A cup (British Museum) from the third quarter of the 6th century B.C. shows an almost prancing hunter, accompanied by his dog, carrying small animals on a pole slung over his shoulder. It is signed, "Tleson, son of Nearchus, made." Another cup (Metropolitan Museum, N.Y.), c540 B.C., has the same inscription.

Tmolus (tmō'lus). In Greek mythology, a son of Ares. He was a king in Lydia, the husband of Omphale, and, according to some accounts, the father of Tantalus. While out hunting on a mountain Tmolus saw and fell in love with one of the chaste companions of Artemis. He pursued her to the temple of Artemis where she sought refuge before the altar. There Tmolus found her and violated the sanctity of the temple by ravishing her. The maiden hanged herself, but before she died she called on Artemis to avenge her. Artemis sent a wild bull that attacked Tmolus, tossed him in the air with his horns, and caused him to fall on sharp stakes and stones. Tmolus perished as the result of his injuries. His son Theoclymenus buried him on the mountain where he died and named it Tmolus after him. As the deity of the forest-covered mountain, Tmolus wore a wreath of oak leaves on his head. He acted as judge in the musical contest between Pan and Apollo and proclaimed Apollo the victor.

Todi (tō'dē). See **Tuder**.

Tolumnius (tō-löm'ni-us). In Roman legend, a Latin chief and soothsayer, allied to Turnus in the war against Aeneas. As an augur he was called on to interpret a sign: a swan was seized by an eagle, which was then attacked by other swans and compelled to let the first swan go. Tolumnius said this meant that the Latins should not allow Turnus to engage in single combat with Aeneas, but should help him. A truce had been proclaimed to let Aeneas and Turnus fight it out. Tolumnius, as a result of the omen, threw his spear and broke the truce. In the general battle that followed he was slain.

Tomi (tō'mī). [Also: **Tomis**.] In ancient geography, a town on the coast of the Euxine (Black) Sea, near what is now Constanta (Constanza), Rumania. It was the place to which the outspoken Roman poet Ovid was banished.

Tomyris (tom'i-ris). Queen of the Massagetae, a large tribe dwelling in the plain beyond the Aral and Caspian Seas. Cyrus the Great, wishing to become lord of the tribe, sent an embassy to Tomyris inviting her to become his wife. Tomyris recognized, according to Herodotus, that his true purpose was to gain control of her kingdom and rejected his suit. Cyrus then prepared to conquer her kingdom by force, as guile had failed. He built boats to ferry his army across the river into her country. Tomyris sent an ambassador to him, and advised him to cease from making war, for he could not be sure that he would profit by the outcome. She counseled Cyrus to be content to rule over his own and allow her to rule her own. However, if Cyrus was unwilling to take her advice, she proposed that she would withdraw her forces three days' march within her frontier, or, if Cyrus preferred, he could withdraw his forces three days' march into his country; the withdrawing army would then wait until the other army caught up with it, whereupon they would engage in battle. Cyrus took council with the chief Persians. They advised him to let Tomyris invade his country. But Croesus, Lydian king who had been captured by Cyrus, objected; he said that if Cyrus let the Massagetae in and they defeated the Persians, the Massagetae would not withdraw and Cyrus would lose his country. On the other hand, if Cyrus defeated them, he would gain nothing but his own country. Moreover, it would be shameful to withdraw before a woman. ·Cyrus took his advice and sent word to Tomyris to withdraw, which she did. Cyrus now advanced against Tomyris. After three days' march he left one-third of his army, as Croesus had advised him to. This portion was the weakest third and he instructed them to make camp, to serve up a rich banquet, to drink wine and make merry. Meanwhile Cyrus withdrew with the rest of his army. The Massagetae attacked the forces in camp with one-third of their forces, and although the Persians resisted, they were overcome by the Massagetae. Then, as Croesus had foretold, the Massagetae fell on the feast which the Persians had been enjoying, and being unused to wine, drank of it until they were sated and fell into a stupor. Cyrus now returned and slew

many of them and took Spargapises, son of Tomyris, captive. Tomyris sent Cyrus a message, chiding him for overcoming the Massagetae with wine and not with arms. She warned him to restore her son and retire, or she would glut him with blood. Spargapises, restored to sobriety and finding himself a captive, begged to be freed from his bonds. Cyrus released him, and instantly he took his own life. Tomyris, learning his fate, regrouped her forces and attacked. In fierce, desperate hand-to-hand fighting, the Massagetae prevailed, hacked the Persian army to pieces and killed Cyrus himself. Tomyris filled a skin with human blood, found the corpse of Cyrus, decapitated it, and flung the head into the skinful of blood. She maltreated the body and apostrophized it, saying that even though she had conquered Cyrus in battle, he had conquered her through the death of her son, but, as she had sworn, she had glutted him with blood. This, according to Herodotus, is how Cyrus met his death at the hands of a woman.

Toronaicus, Sinus (tôr-ō-nā′i-kus sī′nus). [Also: **Gulf of Cassandra (Kassandra), Toronaic Gulf**.] Arm of the Aegean Sea, between the peninsulas of Cassandra and Sithonia.

Torone (tō-rō′nē). In ancient geography, a city on the Sithonian peninsula, in Chalcidice. It was captured by the Spartan general Brasidas, 423 B.C., with the aid of conspirators inside the city.

Torquatus (tôr-kwā′tus), **Titus Manlius**. See **Manlius Torquatus, Titus**.

Torrhebus (tō-rē′bus). According to legend, a son of Atys who was a king of Lydia. He is sometimes confused with Tyrrhenus, the founder of the Tyrrhenian or Etruscan people. In some accounts he is reputed to be the son of Zeus and Torrhebia. His chief claim to fame was that, inspired by the nymphs, he invented the Lydian mode in music.

Torso Belvedere (tôr′sō bel-ve-dir′). Ancient figure of Heracles signed by the Athenian sculptor Apollonius, now in the Vatican, Rome. It is ascribed to the middle of the 1st century B.C., and is remarkable for the anatomical knowledge evidenced by the sitting position of the figure.

Tower of the Winds. Horologium or water

clock erected by the Syrian Andronicus Cyrrhestes at Athens in the 1st century B.C. It is octagonal in plan, 26 feet in diameter, and 42 feet high. Toward the top of each face is sculptured a figure representing one of the eight principal winds, with appropriate attributes. The structure was surmounted by a bronze Triton which served as a weathervane.

Toxeus (tok′sūs). In Greek legend, a son of Oeneus of Calydon and Althaea. He was killed by his father's hand when he impudently leapt over a ditch that had been dug in defense of the city.

Trabea (trā′bē̱-a̱), **Quintus**. Latin writer of comedies; fl. first half of the 2nd century B.C. A very few fragments of his work survive.

Trabzon (träb-zôn′). [Also: **Trebizond**; ancient name, **Trapezus**.] A seaport in N Turkey, on the Black Sea. See **Trapezus**.

Trachiniae (tra̱-kin′i-ē). Tragedy by Sophocles, based on the legend of the death of Heracles at Trachis. See **Women of Trachis**.

Trachis (trā′kis). In ancient geography, a city of Greece, situated at the foot of Mount Oeta near Thermopylae. It was an important strategic point, and the legendary scene of the death of Heracles. The Spartan colony of Heraclea was established there in 426 B.C.

Trajan (trā′ja̱n). [Full Latin name, **Marcus Ulpius Trajanus**; surnamed **Dacicus** and **Parthicus**.] Roman emperor (98–117 A.D.); born in Italica, Spain, 53 A.D.; died at Selinus, Cilicia, July or August, 117. He entered the army at an early age, served as military tribune in various provinces, marched from Spain to Germany (c88), was made consul (91) and by Nerva consular legate in Germany, and was adopted by Nerva, and succeeded him on the latter's death in January, 98. He developed the defenses of the empire on the northeastern frontier, built many roads and other improvements, founded the institution of *alimenta* (for rearing poor children in Italy), and encouraged various reforms. He conducted (c101–106) a successful war against the Dacians under Decebalus, and annexed Dacia to the empire; the Column of Trajan at Rome commemorates this conquest. He incorporated (114) Damascus, and part of Arabia, into the empire, and carried on an indecisive war with the Parthians (114–116). There were revolts in the eastern part of the empire and among the Jews in the last part of his reign, but he died before he could organize a campaign to put down the rebels.

Trajanopolis (trā′′ja̱-nop′ō̱-lis). In ancient geography, a city in Thrace founded by Trajan.

Trajan's Wall. Name given to: 1) Remnants of a Roman fortification in Bessarabia, in the U.S.S.R., between the Prut River and the Black Sea. 2) Remnants of a Roman fortification in Dobruja, Rumania, between the Danube and the Black Sea.

Tralles (tral′ēz). In ancient geography, a city of Lydia or Caria, in Asia Minor, situated on a tributary of the Maeander River. According to tradition, it was founded by colonists from Argos and Thrace. A school of sculpture, known as the Trallian school, grew up there, and is best represented by the Farnese Bull, now in the National Museum at Naples.

Tranquillus (tran-kwil′us, trang-), **Caius Suetonius**. See **Suetonius**.

Transalpine Gaul (trans-al′pin, -pīn, gôl). See **Gaul, Transalpine**.

Transpadane Gaul (trans′pa̱-dān, trans-pā′dān). See **Gaul, Transpadane**.

Trapani (trä′pä-nē). See **Drepanum**.

Trapezus (tra̱-pē′zus). In ancient geography, a place in W Arcadia. Some say it was founded and named for Trapezus, a son of Lycaon. But some say its name means "table," and that here Zeus, disguised as a traveler, appeared to Lycaon. Lycaon did not believe him when Zeus said he was a god, and to test him served him a dish consisting of the flesh of his own son Nyctimus. Zeus thrust the table aside and changed Lycaon and his other sons into wolves, but restored Nyctimus to life. The people of Trapezus refused to abandon their city to join the new Arcadian city of Megalopolis (after 371 B.C.), but when the Arcadians would have compelled them, they left the Peloponnesus entirely and went to the Pontus, and were there welcomed by the city of Trapezus on the Euxine Sea (Pontus) that had the same name as their own Arcadian city.

Trapezus. [Also: **Trebizond**; modern name, **Trabzon**.] A seaport on the Pontus. It is

fat, fāte, fär, fāre, errant; net, mē, hėr ardent; pin, pīne; not, nōte, mŏve, nôr,

picturesquely situated on a tableland between two deep ravines. Next to Smyrna
(now Izmir) it was long the chief commercial city in Asia Minor, and a center
of transit trade between Europe and Armenia, Persia, and C Asia. It was a
dependency of the Greek colony of Sinope,
a resting place on the retreat of the Ten
Thousand Greeks, and an important city
about the time of Hadrian. (JJ)

Trasimenus, Lacus (tras-i-mē′nus, lā′kus).
[Modern names, **Lago Trasimeno, Lago di
Perugia**; English, **Lake Trasimeno, Lake
Perugia**.] Lake in Etruria, about ten miles W
of Perusia (Perugia). It has no natural
outlet. Elevation, about 850 feet; length,
about ten miles; depth, about 25 feet; area,
about 50 square miles.

Trasimenus, Battle of Lake. Victory gained by
Hannibal over the Romans under the consul
Flaminius, on the N shore of Lake Trasimenus (modern Trasimeno) in Etruria, in
the summer of 217 B.C. The Roman army
was nearly annihilated, and the consul was
slain.

Trebia (trē′bi-a̤). [Modern name, **Trebbia**.]
River in N Italy which joins the Po near
Placentia (Piacenza). Near it Hannibal
defeated the Romans under Sempronius
Longus and Publius Cornelius Scipio in
December, 218 B.C.

Trent (trent). See **Tridentum**.

Treveri (trev′e̤-rī) or **Treviri** (-i-rī). Ancient
Celtic people in E Gaul, who dwelt W of the
Rhine in what is now SE Belgium, Luxembourg, and W Germany. Their chief town
was Trier (Latin, Augusta Trevirorum).

Triangulum Boreale (trī-ang′gṳ̄-lum bō-rē̤-al′e).
An ancient northern constellation in the form
of the letter delta (Δ).

Triballi (tri-bal′ī). Ancient Thracian people
who lived between the Haemus and the
Ister (Danube). They were subdued by
Philip II of Macedon in 339 B.C., and again
in 335 B.C. by Alexander the Great. They
are last mentioned in historical records
during the reign of Diocletian.

Tribocci (trī-bō′sī). Ancient Germanic tribe,
first mentioned by Caesar as part of the
army of Ariovistus. The Tribocci were
situated on the middle Rhenus (Rhine), E
of the Vosegus (Vosges) Mountains, in the
region SW of what is now Strasbourg, where

they still remained after the defeat of
Ariovistus (58 B.C.). They were probably
merged ultimately in the Alamanni.

Tribune (trib′ūn). In Roman history, originally,
a magistrate presiding over a tribe, or representing a tribe for certain purposes; specifically, a tribune of the people (*tribunus
plebis*), an officer or magistrate chosen by
the people, from the time of the secession
(probably in 494 B.C.), to protect them from
the oppression of the patricians or nobles,
and to defend their liberties against any
attempts upon them by the Senate and
consuls. Their persons were inviolable, and
any one who transgressed in regard to the
respect due them was outlawed. These
magistrates were at first two, but their number was increased to five and ultimately to
ten, which last number appears to have remained unaltered down to the end of the
empire. The tribunes figured especially in
the assembly of the tribes (*comitia tributa*);
they could inflict no direct punishment, but
could propose the imposition of fines, and
from their personal inviolability could afford
protection to any person. With the advance
of time, they could bring an offending
patrician before the comitia, could sit in the
Senate, could stop summarily proceedings
instituted before any magistrate, could propose measures of state to the comitia or the
Senate, and finally could even issue peremp-
tory edicts and suspend decrees of the
Senate. Their powers were greatly curtailed
by the emperors. The name *tribune* was
also given to any one of general officers of
the legions (*tribunus militaris*), and to
certain other officers, as the *tribunus volup-
tatum*, or superintendent of public amusements, of Diocletian and later.

Tricca (trik′a̤). [Modern name, **Trikkala**.] In
ancient geography, a town of Thessaly, situated N of the Peneus River. It is mentioned
by Homer as the home of Machaon and
Podalirius, sons of Asclepius who accompanied the Greeks to Troy as physicians, for
like their father they possessed the art of
healing. Homer names Tricca as the "pasture of horses," and in antiquity it was
especially celebrated for the magnificent
horses raised there. There was in Tricca
a temple of Asclepius to which pilgrims
repaired for healing.

Tricrena (trī-krē′na). In ancient geography, mountains near Pheneüs, in Arcadia, where there are three springs (thus accounting for the name). Hermes was thought to have been bathed in these after he was born, and for this reason they were sacred to him.

Tridentum (trī-den′tum). [Modern name, **Trent.**] In ancient geography, a city in NE Italy, situated on the Athesis (Adige) River. It was a Celtic colony, was fortified by the Roman emperor Augustus, and served as a base for the campaign of Drusus (15 B.C.) which incorporated the Alpine countries into the Roman domain.

Trifanum (trī-fā′num), **Battle of.** Decisive victory in the Latin War, gained by the Romans at Trifanum (between Minturnae and Suessa Aurunca, in Italy), over the Latins and Campanians, c338 B.C.

Triglyph (trī′glif). In architecture, a structural member in the frieze of the Doric order, repeated at equal intervals, usually over every column and over the middle of every intercolumniation. The typical Greek triglyph is a massive block incised with two entire vertical grooves cut to a right angle, called *glyphs,* framed between three fillets, and with a semi-groove at each side. The block is grooved on both sides to receive the adjoining metopes, which are thin slabs slid into their places from above. The triglyphs represent the ends of the ceiling-beams of the primitive wooden construction.

Trikkala (trik′a-la). See **Tricca.**

Trimalchio (tri-mal′ki-ō). A rich freedman, the central figure in the *Cena Trimalchionis,* a long episode in the *Satyricon,* the novel ascribed to Petronius Arbiter (d. 66 A.D.). Trimalchio, vulgar and ostentatious but good-natured, embodies the newly-risen class of very rich freedmen that achieved economic and even political power during the first half of the 1st century A.D., especially under the emperor Claudius, and is satirized by Petronius. Trimalchio (a fictional character, of course) is a former slave of oriental origin who as a boy served the lusts of both his master and his mistress, was freed and has achieved fabulous wealth. The exquisite bad taste he displays at his feast, together with his ludicrous pretensions to culture, is satirized most wittily; the solecisms committed by him and his fellow-freedmen contrast amusingly with the choice language of his educated guests. The slangy, earthy speech of the lower classes, interspersed with Greek turns of phrase, with proverbs and riddles, is also of great interest to the student of Latin and Romance linguistics. (HS)

Trinacria (tri-nā′kri-a). Old name of Sicily, meaning "Three Points," referring to the three promontories Pachynus, Peloris, and Lilybaeum.

Trinovantes (trī-nọ-van′tēz). [Also: **Trinobantes** (-ban′-).] Ancient non-Belgic people of SE Britain, formerly living in what is now Essex. They sided with Julius Caesar against the Belgic settlers already in Britain. Their chief town was on the site of modern Colchester.

Trinummus (trī-num′us). Comedy by Plautus.

Triopium (trī-ō′pi-um). A temple of the five Doric cities of Asia Minor (Lindus, Ialysus, Camirus, Cos, and Cnidus), located on a promontory in Cnidus, which was itself at the end of a long peninsula. At one time there were six Doric cities that worshiped at this temple, but once at the Triopian games for Apollo the winner, a man of Halicarnassus, in defiance of the law took the tripods he had won home to his own house instead of dedicating them to Apollo in the temple. Thenceforth the people of Halicarnassus were forbidden to enter the temple.

Triphylia (trī-fil′i-a). In ancient geography, a region in the S part of Elis, disputed for centuries by Elis and Arcadia. There was a celebrated temple of Samian Poseidon at Triphylia, and it was the seat of a league of six Minyan cities. In the time of Herodotus most of its cities were in ruins. The warrior and historian Xenophon, exiled from Athens, lived for a time at Scillus in Triphylia, and there set down the *Anabasis,* the celebrated history of the march of the Ten Thousand.

Tripod (trī′pod). In pre-classical and classical antiquity, a seat, table, or other article resting on three feet. Specifically 1) A three-legged seat or table. 2) A pot or caldron used for heating water or boiling meat, and either raised upon a three-legged frame or stand, or made with three feet in the same piece with itself. 3) A bronze altar, originally identical in form with the caldron described above. It had three rings at the top to serve as handles, and in many representations shows a central support or upright in addition to the three legs. It was when seated upon a tripod of this nature, over a cleft in the

PROPHETIC TRIPOD OF DELPHI
Red-figured Greek hydria. *Vatican*

ground in the innermost sanctuary, that the Pythian priestesses at Delphi gave their oracular responses. The celebrity of this tripod, which was especially sacred to the Pythian Apollo and was a usual attribute of him, led to innumerable imitations of it, which were made to be used in sacrifice, and ornamented tripods of similar form, sometimes made of the precious metals, were given as prizes at The Pythian Games and elsewhere, and were frequently placed as votive gifts in temples, especially in those of Apollo.

Triptolemus (trip-tol′ē-mus). In Greek mythology, a favorite of Demeter. His symbol was an ear of wheat. He was everywhere honored as the one who taught the arts of agriculture to mankind. The Eleusinians said he was a son of Celeus and Metanira of Eleusis, or a brother or fellow townsman of Celeus. The Argives said he was a son of Trochilus, a priest of the mysteries in Argos, who fled to Attica and married a woman of Eleusis who bore him Triptolemus and another son Eubuleus. The Athenians claimed

he was the son of Celeus but others said Oceanus was his father and Gaea his mother, or that Dysaules was his father, or even Poseidon. The truth is that many were anxious to claim him because of his great gifts to mankind. Some say he was the only one to recognize the goddess Demeter when she sought shelter in the house of Celeus during her search for Persephone. Triptolemus was able to tell her that the earth had parted and a chariot drawn by black horses and bearing Persephone had disappeared into the chasm. He became a favorite of Demeter and she taught him her sacred rites and mysteries. She also gave him seed wheat, instructed him in the use of the plow, and sent him a chariot drawn by winged serpents in which to travel throughout the world instructing mankind in the arts of agriculture. He went through Europe and Asia spreading the knowledge of agriculture and, some say, he came at last to the land of Scythia. There he revealed his name and his mission to the king, Lyncus. Lyncus pretended to welcome him but, out of jealousy, resolved to kill him. As Triptolemus slept he attacked him with a sword. His effort was in vain; before he could harm Triptolemus, Demeter transformed Lyncus into a lynx. Triptolemus continued his journeying. According to some accounts, he was the founder of Eleusis and established the worship of Demeter there, as well as the festival called the Thesmophoria.

TRIPTOLEMUS ALOFT
Red-figured Greek hydria, c490 B.C.
Metropolitan Museum of Art

actor; up, lūte, pull; oi, oil; ou, out; ᴛʜ, then; ḍ as d or j, ş as s or sh, ṭ as t or ch, ẓ as z or zh.

He was honored in Eleusis with a temple dedicated to him, and was honored throughout as the patron of agriculture. Some say that when Demeter came to the house of Celeus in Eleusis, she acted as nurse for his son Demophoön, and would have made him immortal had she not been interrupted by the child's mother. In her anger at the interruption she dropped the child in the fire in which she had been burning away his mortal parts, and he perished. The goddess promised to bring great honor to his brother Triptolemus to atone for his loss.

Tritantaechmes (trī″tan-tēk′mēz). A son of Artabanus and nephew of Darius the Great of Persia. He was a Persian captain under Xerxes in the invasion of Greece, 480 B.C. According to Herodotus, when he heard that the prize for which men contested at the Olympic Games was not money but a crown of olive leaves he said, "Alas, Mardonius, what manner of men hast thou brought us to fight against, who contend not for money, but for honor."

Tritogeneia (trī″tō̱-jē̱-nī′a). Epithet of Athena. Some say it means "Trito-born" and derives from the fact that the goddess was born from the head of Zeus near the lake Tritonis in Libya. Depending on the meaning assigned to the first element, the name may mean "head-born," "born on the third day," "the third child," or "thrice-born."

Triton (trī′ton). In Greek mythology, a gigantic son of Poseidon and the Nereid Amphitrite. He was the brother of Rhode and Benthesicyme and dwelt at the bottom of the sea; he was also thought to frequent the Lake Tritonis in Libya. When the Argonauts voyaging home from Colchis were driven into the desert of Libya by a great storm, Jason propitiated the deities of the land by offering two bronze tripods that had been given to him by the priestess of Delphi before he set out for Colchis. Triton appeared and seized the tripods. In response to requests of the Argonauts he towed the *Argo* back to the sea. He gave Euphemus a clod of Libyan earth that made Euphemus and his descendants masters of Libya. In the later mythology Tritons appear as a class of minor sea-deities, figuring with Nereids in the train of the greater sea-gods. They were conceived as having human figures from the waist up

combined with those of fish from the waist down. A common attribute of the Tritons is a shell-trumpet, which they blow to raise or calm storms.

Triton. A river in Boeotia. According to some accounts, Athena lived in the nearby city of Athenae when she first came to Greece from Libya, via Crete. Also, the Nile River was sometimes called Triton.

Triton. [Modern name, **Garavos.**] In ancient geography, a river of Crete, rising E of Mount Ida and flowing N into the sea. Some say that it was while walking on the banks of this river that Zeus was smitten with a violent headache, following which Athena sprang fully-armed from his brow.

Tritonis (trī-tō′nis), or **Triton, Lake.** A vast lake that once covered a large part of the lowlands of Libya. Athena was sometimes said to have been born on the edge of this lake, hence her epithet "Tritogeneia." The Argonauts, swept onto the desert by a great wave, came at last to this lake and were shown a route to the sea by Triton. The lake was thought to have been formed by a tidal wave that engulfed the shores of Libya, and to have disappeared ultimately as a consequence of earthquakes. In classical times the lake covered 900 square miles, having shrunk considerably since mythological times. It has now shrunk to a salt lake about 120 miles long in SW central Tunisia, known as Shatt el Jerid, if indeed this body of water is to be identified with Lake Tritonis. Possibly the lake also once included the Shatt el Melghir, another salt lake about 100 miles long in NE Algeria.

Tritonis. In ancient geography, a stream near Aliphera in Arcadia, where, according to the Arcadians, Athena was born from the head of Zeus.

Triumvirate, First. In Roman history, an agreement or alliance formed in 60 B.C. by Julius Caesar, Pompey, and Crassus, for the purpose of dividing the power among them. Caesar obtained the consulship for the next year (59 B.C.) and a command in Cisalpine Gaul (extended to Transalpine Gaul) and Illyricum for five years (extended for five years more). Pompey received for his veterans assignment of lands, and for himself later the administration of the grain supply. By a renewal of the Triumvirate at Luca in

56 B.C., Pompey received the consulship and command in Spain, and Crassus the consulship and command in the East (where he was killed in 53 B.C.). The union between Caesar and Pompey was formally broken by the civil war in 49 B.C.

Triumvirate, Second. In Roman history, an alliance formed in 43 B.C. by Octavian (the future Augustus), Mark Antony, and Lepidus. The triumvirs were to have consular powers for three years; they appointed magistrates, and their decrees were valid as laws. Octavian received Africa and the islands; Mark Antony, Gaul; Lepidus, Spain and Narbonensis. The alliance was followed by a wholesale proscription, and by the overthrow of the republicans under Brutus and Cassius in 42 B.C. Lepidus was soon reduced to a minor position, and was eventually banished. By a treaty at Brundisium, Octavian received the West and Mark Antony the East. The union was broken in 31 B.C., and Mark Antony was overthrown in the battle of Actium.

Trivia (triv′i-a̱). In Roman mythology, an epithet, corresponding to the Greek *Trioditis,* of Hecate, meaning "the Goddess of Crossroads." The epithet also applied to Diana when she was identified with Hecate.

Troad (trō′a̱d). In ancient geography, the region in NW Asia Minor about the city of Troy, which was its capital. It included a number of allied and dependent cities, and extended to the Hellespont and the Aegean Sea. In the Trojan War the Greeks harried the cities of the Troad for nine years before they attacked the capital city itself.

Trochilus (trok′i-lus). According to some accounts, a priest of the mysteries at Argos. He fled from Argos and went to Eleusis. There he married and became the father of Triptolemus and Eubuleus.

Troezen (trē′ze̱n). In ancient geography, a city in the Peloponnesus, Greece, situated near the coast, about 39 miles SW of Athens. It was originally an Ionian settlement, but later became Doric. According to Pausanias, the Troezenians were "unrivalled glorifiers of their own country." They claimed that one Orus, a son of the soil, was the first king of their land, and that in his time it was called Oraea after him. His daughter had a son by Poseidon, whose name was Althepus, and he

renamed the land Althepia. During the reign of Althepus, the Troezenians said, Athena and Poseidon struggled for control of their country. Their contest was decided by Zeus, who ruled that Athena and Poseidon should share control of the territory. Thus the Troezenians worshiped, above all Athena Polias (*Of the City*) and Athena Sthenias (*Strong*), and Poseidon, whom they called King. The temple of Athena Sthenias was on the citadel. The dual worship was memorialized in ancient coins which had a trident on one side and a head of Athena on the other. Following Althepus, Saron, for whom the Saronic Gulf was named, was king. There was then a long break in the line of kings whose names were known by the Troezenians, until they came to Hyperes and Anthas, sons of Poseidon. These founded the cities of Hyperea and Anthea. Troezen and Pittheus, sons of Pelops, came into the land and allied themselves with the king, so that there were now three rulers. The three rulers were commemorated in the tomb of Pittheus, which had three white seats surrounding it where the three kings used to sit in judgment. When Troezen died, Pittheus united the cities of Hyperea and Anthea into one city, which he named Troezen after his dead brother, and by this name it continued to be known. Pittheus was noted for his wisdom, and was said to have taught the art of rhetoric in an ancient temple of the Muses raised by Ardalus, a son of Hephaestus. Pittheus had a daughter, Aethra, who became the mother of Theseus, either by Poseidon or by King Aegeus of Athens. Thus did Troezen, through the exploits of Theseus, become closely allied to Athens in the future history of the two states. The area about Troezen was dotted with sites connected with the youth of Theseus. He dedicated the temple of Artemis Savior in the agora in thanks for his safe return from Crete. Hippolytus, son of Theseus and the Amazon Antiope, was sent to live in Troezen when Theseus married Phaedra, so that he would not appear as a rival in Athens to his younger half-brothers. He raised the temple of Artemis Lycea (*Wolfish*) there, either because he drove the wolves out of Troezen, or because Lycea was a name of Artemis among the Amazons, his mother's people. In Troezen Phaedra fell in love with her stepson, with tragic consequences. She used to watch him practice in the exercise ground, and as she did so, she pierced the leaves of the nearby myrtle tree with the pin of her brooch as a relief to her frustration, for Hippolytus not only did not return her love; he was totally unaware of it and was horrified when he learned of it. On the spot where Phaedra spied on him, the temple of Aphrodite Catascopico (*Spy*) was raised, and the leaves of the myrtle trees of Troezen ever afterward bore a strange marking, as if they had been pierced. The tombs of Phaedra and Hippolytus were, in ancient times, pointed out to travelers in Troezen. They had been buried near each other.

The Troezenians claimed that Dionysus brought up his mother from Hades, and that Heracles dragged Cerberus to the light, in their territory. They also said they were visited by Orestes, and showed what was called "the Booth of Orestes." Since none could receive him until he had been purified of his mother's blood, Orestes lived in this booth. He was at last cleansed by water from the Hippocrene Spring at Troezen, for the Troezenians said that Bellerophon came to their city seeking the hand of Pittheus' daughter Aethra in marriage. His horse Pegasus caused the spring to gush forth by stamping his hoof on the ground, just as he had done in Boeotia. Before a marriage with Aethra could be arranged, Bellerophon was banished from Corinth. The descendants of those who purified Orestes commemorated the event by dining at this booth on certain days. The stone on which nine Troezenians purified him was still shown centuries later. Near an image of Hermes in the city was an ancient olive tree. It was said that Heracles, passing this way, leaned his club against the image. From his olive wood club sprang a shoot that grew into the tree. The sanctuary of Pan Lyterius (*Releasing*) was dedicated in gratitude to that god for sending a dream to the Troezenian magistrates in which was revealed the cure for an epidemic that was ravaging the populace. Among other sanctuaries were those of Zeus, Aphrodite of the Height, and Apollo.

The Troezenians took part in the Trojan War under the leadership of Diomedes.

When he returned he raised a temple of Seafaring Apollo because he survived the great storms that battered the Greeks on their voyage home from Troy. It was Diomedes, they say, who dedicated the famous ancient precinct of Hippolytus, raised a temple to him, and was the first to sacrifice to him as a hero. Priests of Hippolytus held their office for life. Among the honors accorded to him as a hero, maidens dedicated a lock of their hair in his temple before marriage. The Troezenians held strong views about their hero; they did not admit that he was dragged to his death by his horses. They said he was translated to the heavens as the constellation Charioteer.

Troezen early sent out colonists. In Caria they founded the cities of Halicarnassus and Myndus. In the Persian War the Troezenians received the women and children who were sent to them for safety as the Persians approached Athens (480 B.C.). Stone images set up in the agora afterward represented these fugitives and commemorated Troezenian hospitality. The Troezenians played a valiant part in the war. They sent five ships to join the Greek fleet, a thousand men to Plataea, and at the battle of Mycale (479 B.C.), Herodotus says that, after the Athenians, "the most valiant were the men of Corinth, of Troezen, and of Sicyon." In the middle of the 5th century B.C. Troezen came under the dominion of Athens. It was an unwilling partnership, and later the Troezenians took the side of Sparta in the disastrous Peloponnesian Wars.

Trogus (trō′gus), **Cnaeus Pompeius.** Roman historian; fl. c10 A.D. He was the author of a general history, *Historiae Philippicae*, in 44 books, partly preserved in an epitome by Justinus. Written in an elaborate narrative style, the work may have been based on Timagenes of Alexandria.

Troia (trō′ya). A Latin name of ancient **Troy.**

Troilus (trō′i-lus, troi′lus). In Greek legend, a younger son of Hecuba. He was acknowledged as a son of Priam but some say Apollo was his father. According to a prophecy, Troy would not fall to the Greeks in the Trojan War if Troilus reached the age of twenty. Some say Achilles saw Troilus and pursued him to the sanctuary of the temple of Thymbraean Apollo and killed him there, where, according to some accounts, Achilles himself was fated to die. Others say Achilles came upon him while he was exercising his horses near the sea and killed him, or that Troilus dared meet Achilles in face-to-face combat and, having fallen wounded, was dragged to his death by his own horses. In

ACHILLES SLAYING TROILUS
Red-figured Attic kylix, Euphronius, end
of 6th—beginning of 5th century B.C.
Perugia

any case, it was certainly Achilles who killed or caused the death of Troilus. The story of Troilus' tragic love for Cressida (or Cris-eyede or Criseida) comes not from ancient sources but from a poem by a 12th century troubadour. It relates that Troilus was in love with Cressida, a daughter of Calchas, who remained in Troy and was loyal to the Trojans. On the demand of Agamemnon she was restored to her father by Priam, and went to the Greek camp. She betrayed the undying love which she had sworn for Troilus by falling in love and yielding to the caresses of Diomedes.

Trojan Horse (trō'jan). In Greek legend, the huge wooden horse which the Greeks constructed and left on the beach before Troy in the last days of the Trojan War. The Trojans, believing it to be a sacrifice to Athena,

hauled it into the city. But inside the horse were armed warriors. They descended from it in the night, opened the city gates to their comrades, and brought about the fall of Troy. Thus the Greeks, who could not overcome the Trojans by direct assault, penetrated their city by stratagem and brought about its ruin from within. The phrase has come to mean a stratagem or method that appears innocent, or that is carried out in secret, which is used by a foe to penetrate his opponent's camp, literally or figuratively, and weaken it from within. See also, **Wooden Horse.**

Trojan War (trō'jan). A war between the Greeks and the Trojans, celebrated by ancient writers, notably by Homer in the *Iliad,* which is now thought to have taken place about 1200 B.C. The actual causes of the war have been obscured under layers of myth and legend in which brilliantly imaginative writers recorded the actual event. Trade routes sought by the vigorous and expanding Greek cities may have occasioned the struggle. An unfriendly or uncoöperative power in Troy, which commanded the entrance to the Hellespont, had to be subdued or, as it happened, to be utterly destroyed, to permit the expansion of the peoples of Hellas into the area about the Euxine (Black) Sea. Some of the figures named in the epics had historical prototypes; as Agamemnon and Nestor. Others were added as the creative invention of ancient writers demanded.

As developed in myth and legend, the cause of the Trojan War goes back to the marriage of Peleus and Thetis and was the result of a deliberate plan on the part of Zeus and Themis, for reasons never satisfactorily explained. All the gods and goddesses except Eris were invited to the wedding of Peleus and Thetis. Eris, goddess of discord, took her revenge for being left out by hurling a golden apple inscribed "To the Fairest" at the feet of the goddesses Athena, Hera, and Aphrodite as they stood talking together among the guests. Each of the three goddesses claimed that the apple was intended for her. They appealed to Zeus to settle the dispute, but he wisely refused to make a choice and referred them to a young shepherd on Mount Ida in the Troad who was reputed to be a great and fair judge of beauty. The young shepherd was Paris, son of Priam, king

actor; up, lūte, pull; oi, oil; ou, out; ŦH, then; ḍ as d or j, ṣ as s or sh, ṭ as t or ch, ẓ as z or zh.

of Troy, and to him the goddesses repaired. Athena offered him wisdom and victory in all his wars if he awarded the apple to her. Hera promised to make him rich and the lord of all Asia. Aphrodite offered him the most beautiful woman in the world for a bride. Paris awarded (the "Judgment of Paris") the apple to Aphrodite. From that time the Trojans, as the race of Paris, suffered the implacable hatred of Hera and Athena. Most of the Olympian deities freely took sides, playing active and decisive roles in the war that resulted from this judgment of Paris.

The fairest woman in the world was Helen, wife of Menelaus, king of Sparta. Paris, although married to the nymph Oenone, went to his father's palace in Troy, and was recognized as that son of Priam and Hecuba who had been left on the mountain to die in his infancy because of prophecies that he would cause the destruction of Troy. He had been saved and brought up by a shepherd. Delighted with his beauty and courage, Priam and Hecuba welcomed their new-found son despite the urgent warnings of Cassandra, Helenus, and other seers that he would bring ruin to Troy. Secretly thinking of Helen, the bride promised him by Aphrodite, Paris offered to go on a mission to Greece to discuss the return of Hesione, sister of King Priam, who had been carried off by Telamon some years before and whom the Greeks had refused to return. If he was unsuccessful in this mission, he volunteered that he might bring back some Greek princess as a hostage. Priam, again disregarding the warnings of his prophetic daughter Cassandra, provided a fleet and Paris set out. Menelaus received him kindly in Sparta and entertained him royally for nine days. At the end of that time, ignoring a fact obvious to all—that Paris was madly in love with Helen—Menelaus blandly sailed off to Crete to his grandfather's funeral, leaving his kingdom and the entertainment of his guest in Helen's charge. Helen eloped with Paris that same night, taking with her her young son and a great treasure, but leaving her only daughter Hermione behind in Sparta. Hera sent great storms that drove Paris' fleet off its course. Furthermore, to avoid pursuit by Menelaus, Paris sailed to Cyprus, Sidon, Phoenicia, and

Egypt, so that it was some time before he returned to Troy with Helen.

In the meantime Menelaus had learned of the abduction of Helen. He immediately went to Agamemnon in Mycenae and demanded that an expedition be assembled to sail against Troy and recover her. Agamemnon agreed to do this if peaceful means failed. He sent envoys to Troy to demand the restoration of Helen, but the Trojans refused. According to some accounts, they knew nothing of the matter because Paris had not yet landed in Troy with Helen. But once he did bring her to Troy, all Troy fell in love with her and Priam vowed he would never let her go. As a result, each of several embassies that demanded her return was rejected, and those Trojan advisers who on divers occasions throughout the war counseled that she be restored to her husband were scorned. As peaceful means of regaining Helen failed, Agamemnon called on the Greek princes to fulfill their oath. This oath had been taken under the following circumstances. Helen was so beautiful and had so many suitors that Tyndareus, her supposed father, feared to give her hand to any one of them lest the disappointed suitors turn against him. Odysseus suggested to Tyndareus that he require all the suitors to swear on the joints of a dismembered horse that they would go to the aid of whichever suitor won Helen's hand, in the event that any ill should come to him as a result of his marriage to Helen. Tyndareus adopted this course and all the suitors took the oath. The mightiest and richest princes of Greece had been suitors of Helen; all were now commanded to fulfill their oath and come to the aid of Menelaus. Moreover, Agamemnon added, if the Trojans were not punished for the theft of Helen, no Greek husband could be sure of his wife's safety. Odysseus, although not one of the suitors, was needed for his wisdom and skill. Reluctantly he came from Ithaca. Achilles, accompanied by his intimate friend Patroclus and leading his Myrmidons, came from Scyrus. Diomedes, fresh from his victory at Thebes, came with his friends Sthenelus and Euryalus. Idomeneus, king of Crete, brought his squire Meriones and 80 ships. Aged Nestor, noted for his wisdom, arrived from Pylus with his sons

Thrasymedes and Antilochus. Telamonian Ajax and his half-brother Teucer commanded a fleet from Salamis. Oïlean, or Lesser Ajax, and his half-brother Medon commanded the men of Locris. King Cinyras of Cyprus promised to send 50 ships but defaulted. Tlepolemus, son of Heracles, brought nine ships from Rhodes. Many other heroes and demigods joined Agamemnon's expedition. The Greek fleet, over 1000 ships strong, assembled at Aulis. There, while Agamemnon was sacrificing, a blue serpent with crimson markings on its back darted out, coiled its way up a plane tree and devoured eight nestlings and a mother sparrow in their nest. The serpent was then turned to stone. Calchas, the seer who advised Agamemnon throughout the war, said this was an omen that nine years would be swallowed up and that in the tenth year Troy would fall. Others made the same prophecy about the duration of the war. But some say the war lasted twenty years. Homer has Helen say it is now the twentieth year since she left Sparta.

The Greeks sailed from Aulis and raided the coasts of Asia Minor. Some say they did not know the course to Troy, and that they landed in Mysia and ravaged it under the impression that they were in the Troad. For some time they cruised along the coast, attacking and sacking cities. At length the fleet was scattered by violent storms and the ships returned to their homeland. After nine years, according to some accounts, the fleet again assembled at Aulis. This time unfavorable winds delayed their sailing. In accordance with a prophecy by Calchas, Agamemnon sacrificed his daughter Iphigenia and thus secured favorable winds. Telephus, a king of Mysia who had been wounded in the raids on his shores, had come to Greece to be cured of his wound. He marked out the course the Greeks should take to Troy, and the correctness of his course was confirmed by divination. The fleet sailed once more. They touched at Lesbos and then at the island of Tenedos, within sight of Troy. There Achilles attacked and killed Tenes, who tried to prevent the Greeks from landing on his shores. This Tenes was reputed to be a son of Apollo, and Thetis, among other warnings to her son Achilles, had told

him if he killed a son of Apollo, he would die by Apollo's hand. The death of Tenes by Achilles was only one of many signs and portents that foretold to Achilles that he would not survive the Trojan War. On Tenedos also, according to some accounts, Philoctetes, possessor of the bow and arrows of Heracles, was bitten by a snake with such disastrous results that the Greeks were at length compelled to abandon him on Lemnos. According to some accounts, Agamemnon sent Menelaus, Odysseus, and Palamedes to Troy from Tenedos to make a final demand for the return of Helen. They were unsuccessful, and would have been killed by the indignant Trojans if Antenor had not prevented such an outrage against the laws of war and of hospitality. The Greeks now sailed past Sigeum, the headland of Troy, and beached their ships within sight of the city. Protesilaus was the first to leap ashore and, in accordance with a prophecy that the first ashore at Troy would die, was killed; some say, by Hector. The siege of Troy itself which now began, the disastrous quarrel between Agamemnon and Achilles, the death of Patroclus, and the death and burial of Hector, noblest of the Trojans, comprise the *Iliad*, q.v. The Trojans were not without allies. Heroes and demigods, such as Aeneas, Sarpedon, and Glaucus had joined them, and after the death of Hector, Penthesilea the Amazon, and Memnon the Ethiopian son of Eos, came to the aid of Troy. After inflicting great damage on the Greeks and so discouraging them that Agamemnon considered withdrawal, each was in turn killed by Achilles, who drove the Trojans back into the city each time. But Achilles had run his course. Apollo, some say, directed an arrow from Paris' bow that pierced Achilles' ankle or heel, his one vulnerable spot. Achilles pulled out the arrow and flung it away; it was wafted back to Apollo. Enraged with his wound and blaming Apollo, Achilles with his last strength hurled his spear and killed a Trojan; then he expired. Telamonian Ajax bore his body back to the Greek ships through a raging press of Trojans who were trying to gain possession of their fallen enemy's corpse. The death of Achilles brought about the death of Telamonian Ajax. At the command of Thetis, the armor of Achilles was to be awarded to the bravest of the Greeks. Odysseus was given the honor and the armor. Ajax, who had great ground for thinking he deserved it, was inspired with madness by Athena. In his frenzy he slaughtered innocent cattle under the impression that they were Greeks who had been unfriendly to him. When Athena decided to restore him to sanity, he was appalled at what he had done. In despair at the humiliation he had brought on himself he committed suicide.

The loss of Achilles and Ajax discouraged the Greeks and, as had happened before, they talked of giving up the struggle and sailing for home. Calchas reminded them of the omen of the serpent and the sparrows, and that this was now the tenth year when victory was prophesied. He informed them that Troy could not be taken without the bow and arrows of Heracles. Their possessor Philoctetes was accordingly fetched from Lemnos and was healed of his wound by Machaon the physician; then with the arrows of Heracles he shot Paris. After the death of Paris, Deïphobus and Helenus, his brothers, struggled for Helen's hand. She was awarded to Deïphobus, who forcibly married her, and Helenus left the city. He was captured by the Greeks and told them that Troy could not be taken without the presence of a bone of Pelops, nor without Neoptolemus, son of Achilles, nor could it be taken as long as the Palladium remained in the citadel. Agamemnon immediately sent for the bone of Pelops, and to Scyrus for Neoptolemus. Eurypylus, descendant of Heracles, now came to the aid of the Trojans. He fought valiantly and again drove the Greeks back to their ships. But the gods intervened, as they had done from the beginning, and caused Neoptolemus to slay Eurypylus. Odysseus and Diomedes disguised themselves and entered Troy. Some say Odysseus was recognized by Helen and brought before Hecuba, that he told them the Greeks' plans and was allowed to go free. Another account is that this mission of Odysseus was a different one from the raid made with Diomedes, and was in the nature of a scouting sortie. When Odysseus and Diomedes made their raid Diomedes scaled the wall of Troy from the shoulders of Odysseus, gained the Palladium, and returned with it to the Greek camp. In any

event, it seems agreed that Odysseus at some time entered Troy secretly, was recognized by Helen and Hecuba, and was allowed to return to the Greek ships.

In all the years of the war there had been some in Troy who advised that Helen be restored to Menelaus, with all the treasure she had brought with her. This advice had always been scorned, and those who gave it were regarded almost as traitors. Now, after the disasters following the deaths of Hector, Penthesilea, Memnon, Eurypylus, and Paris, there were some in Troy who advised flight from the city, rather than be caught like rats in a trap. Others said the war should be carried on from the walls and towers of Troy rather than on the plain where the great battles had cost so many lives. But this advice, as militarily sound as the other was politically sound, was rejected.

The Greeks too had their hours of doubt and despair. It was now proposed to take the city by stratagem rather than by direct assault. The idea of the Wooden Horse was put forth, some say by Odysseus, who in any case took credit for the idea. This proposal was enthusiastically adopted, except by Neoptolemus and Philoctetes who protested that it was cowardly. Epeus, aided by Athena, built the Wooden Horse in three days. Odysseus now proposed that the Greeks leave it on the beach before Troy with the most valiant warriors concealed inside it. The fleet would sail away behind the island of Tenedos, the camp fires would be doused, and the Trojans would happily conclude that the Greeks had sailed for home. In addition, Odysseus proposed that some one be left behind with a tale to account for his presence, who would persuade the Trojans to draw the Wooden Horse with its deadly freight inside the walls of Troy. Sinon volunteered to carry out this part of the plan. When the Trojans saw that the Greeks had apparently departed, they swarmed out onto the beach to examine the great horse. As they wondered about it and heard Laocoön and Cassandra plead with them to destroy it or it would destroy Troy, Sinon, who had arranged to be captured, was dragged forward. He said he had just escaped being sacrificed by the Greeks, who

fat, fāte, fär, fâre, errạnt; net, mē, hėr ardẹnt; pin, pīne; not, nōte, mȯve, nôr,

had sailed for home in despair, and that the Wooden Horse was an offering to Athena, to propitiate the goddess for the theft of the Palladium. The offering had purposely been made huge so that it could not be taken inside the walls of Troy, for the city that possessed it would conquer Europe. On hearing this the Trojans, deaf to the warnings of Cassandra and Laocoön, resolved to take the enormous offering into the city. The fact that a serpent slithered from the sea and crushed Laocoön and his two sons in its coils, indicated to them that the gods had punished Laocoön for his doubts and confirmed them in their resolve to take the offering into the city. They breached the walls to make way for the horse and rolled it inside the walls, decorated it with flowers and performed ritual dances about it. Then the Trojans went wearily to bed. In the night Sinon gave the signal to the men in the Wooden Horse, lighted a beacon to advise the Greek fleet to return from Tenedos, and opened the gates of Troy. The Greeks streamed in and sacked the city. Priam was slain by Neoptolemus before the altar of Zeus in his courtyard. Deïphobus, Helen's new husband, was killed and horribly mangled. The Greeks protected the family of Antenor by hanging a leopard's skin over the door of his house, because he had protected early envoys from the Greeks and had consistently advised the restoration of Helen. Aeneas escaped with his father and son from the burning city, carrying the gods of Troy with him. Astyanax, young son of Hector, was hurled to his death from the towers of Troy. Polyxena, daughter of Priam, was sacrificed on Achilles' tomb. In the division of the captives, Odysseus took Hecuba, Agamemnon claimed Cassandra, and Neoptolemus took Andromache. When the Greeks departed with their captives, Troy was in flames. The city, which had been an important bastion guarding the Hellespont and thus the entry into the Euxine Sea, never regained its important role. In fact, for centuries, even the site was lost. See **Troy.**

Trojan Women, The. A tragedy by Euripides, written about 415 B.C. It is concerned with a day after the end of the Trojan War, and powerfully depicts the utter emptiness of war, for victor as well as vanquished.

Poseidon laments the destruction of Troy, a city for which he had affection because he, with Apollo, had built its walls. He recalls the infamous Wooden Horse and the disaster it brought Troy, and the death of Priam. He speaks of Hecuba weeping before the gates, unaware that her youngest daughter, Polyxena, lies dead on Achilles' grave, and that another daughter, Cassandra, is to be Agamemnon's concubine. He blames Hera and Athena, who combined to give the Greeks victory and to destroy the Trojan city and race. Athena enters and asks Poseidon's aid to punish the Greeks (whom she had helped for ten years) because Ajax had dragged Cassandra from Athena's shrine and the other Greeks had not rebuked him. Poseidon agrees, and promises to send great storms to harry and delay the Greeks when they sail for home. The immortals depart.

Hecuba enters. She weeps for Priam's 50 sons, perished in the war, and expresses her fear of being carried off as a captive by the Greeks. Talthybius, Agamemnon's herald, comes to tell her the Greeks have chosen their captives: Cassandra will go to Agamemnon, Andromache to Achilles' son, and Hecuba herself to Odysseus. He evades her questions about Polyxena by saying that her fate has been settled. Cassandra enters, apparently maddened by her suffering. Actually she is in a prophetic trance. Of Agamemnon she says that he has lost what most he loved—his wife and children—to his brother. Of the Greeks, she says they fought and fell on foreign soil, away from their loved ones, for nothing, whereas the Trojans died gloriously in defense of their own land. She predicts Hecuba's death in Troy, ten years of peril and wandering for Odysseus, and her own death and the destruction of Agamemnon, and departs with Talthybius. Andromache now enters with her son Astyanax. She tells Hecuba of the death of Polyxena as a sacrifice to Achilles, and wishes that she too had died. Talthybius, returning, with compassion informs Andromache that on the advice of Odysseus not to rear a hero's son, Astyanax must die. He urges Andromache to give up her child without a struggle so that the Greeks will not deny him proper burial. Crying out against Helen, the cause of all her suffering, Andromache kisses Astyanax and hands him over to be dashed to death from the towers of Troy. After Andromache's departure Menelaus enters. He says he fought to avenge himself on Paris, not to recapture Helen. Hecuba begs him to kill Helen, who was the cause of death and suffering to so many, but asks him first to allow Helen to speak in her own defense so that she, Hecuba, can list her crimes in answering that defense. Helen speaks. She blames Hecuba for bearing Paris and for refusing to destroy him as she had been warned to do; she speaks of the Judgment of Paris and says that she was the helpless prize he chose when bribed by the goddesses; she accuses Menelaus of callously going off to Crete and leaving her alone when Paris came to Sparta to visit them; and lastly, for her own part in the tragedy, she says she was ruled by Aphrodite, the goddess of love who could overcome even Zeus himself. Hecuba scorns the defense of Helen and again urges Menelaus to kill her, but he is shaken, and says he will punish her when they return to Argos. He and Helen leave. Talthybius now comes to Hecuba, bearing the lifeless body of Astyanax on his shield. He gives it to her for burial. Mourning, Hecuba sorrowfully asks why the Greeks, who have utterly destroyed the Trojan warriors, should have feared this child. Talthybius orders the Greek captains to set Troy afire and commands Hecuba to go to Odysseus' ship. Hecuba, a broken, lamenting old woman, leaves the dead child and departs as Troy crashes in flames.

Tropaean (trō-pē'an). Epithet of Zeus. The Dorians set up a sanctuary of Tropaean Zeus (*He Who Puts to Flight*) in Sparta after they had conquered the Achaeans of Amyclae.

Trophonius (trō-fō'ni-us). In Greek mythology, a son of Erginus the Argonaut, of Orchomenus, or, according to some accounts, a son of Apollo. He was the brother of Agamedes. He and his brother, born in their father's old age, were famous builders. According to legend, they built the temple at Delphi on foundations laid by Apollo, the temple of Poseidon at Mantinea, the cham-

ber of Alcmene in Thebes, and the treasuries of Augeas in Elis and of Hyrieus in Boeotia. To reward them for their labors on his temple Apollo told them to feast and be merry for six days, and on the seventh day they would receive the greatest gift in his power. They feasted and enjoyed themselves for six days. On the seventh they went to bed and died peacefully in their sleep. An easy death was Apollo's best gift. According to another account, when the brothers built the treasury for Hyrieus, king of Boeotia, they so constructed it that one stone could be removed allowing them to rob the treasury at will. Agamedes was caught in the act by a trap set by Hyrieus, and Trophonius cut off his brother's head and removed it so that no one would know who the thief was and he would not be implicated. Trophonius was at once swallowed up by the earth. He had an oracle in a cavern at Lebadia in Phocis, which enjoyed great repute for centuries. Croesus and many leading Greeks and Romans consulted it down to historical times. The ritual for consulting the oracle was most intricate, and of such solemnity that suppliants lost their ability to laugh for some time after consulting it; and it came to be said of unusually sober persons that they must have visited Trophonius. Suppliants at the oracle were addressed, once they had penetrated to an inner cavern, by the ghost of Trophonius in the form of a serpent. The payment to the oracle was made in the form of honey cakes. See **Lebadia.**

Trophonius. In Greek mythology, an ancient earth-god, whose worship was typical of the rites associated with the Chthonian divinities. These rites are in sharp contrast with those of the Olympian gods. (AH)

Tros (trōs). Named by Homer as a son of Erichthonius and a grandson of Dardanus. He gave his name to the Trojans, and the region about Troy, the Troad, is named in honor of him. By his wife Callirrhoë, daughter of the river-god Scamander, he had three sons, Assaracus, Ganymede, and Ilus, and one daughter, Cleopatra. Ganymede, most beautiful of mortals, was taken up into heaven by Zeus to become his cup-bearer. To atone for the loss of his son, Zeus gave Tros his immortal horses. Boreas fell in love with these mares and they bore swift fillies that bounded over the sea. The horses were ultimately inherited by Laomedon, grandson of Tros, who promised them to Heracles but failed to deliver them.

Troy (troi). [Also: **Ilium**; Latin, **Troia, Troja.**] Ancient city in Asia Minor, famous in Greek legend as the capital of Priam and the object of the siege by the allied Greeks under Agamemnon. According to legend, the city was founded by Teucer, an immigrant from Crete who was the son of the Cretan river Scamander and the nymph Idaea. From him the people were called Teucrians. In the reign of Teucer, Dardanus came to his kingdom from Samothrace. Teucer gave him land in the region and his daughter Batia in marriage. Dardanus built a city at the foot of Mount Ida which he called Dardania. Tros, the grandson of Dardanus, called his people Trojans and named the city Troy. One son of Tros was Ilus, the father of Laomedon and the grandfather of Priam. Another was Assaracus, the ancestor of Aeneas. And a third son was Ganymede, carried off to Olympus by Zeus. Ilion, the city that Ilus founded in obedience to an oracle, was joined with Dardania and Troy and the whole came to be called Troy or Ilium. The location of Troy near the Hellespont and the entrance to the Propontis and the Euxine Sea, gave it command of trade from the Aegean islands and Greece to the region about the Euxine Sea. It was the strongest power on the coast of Asia Minor. The Trojan War, celebrated in the *Iliad* of Homer, is now thought to have been waged to destroy this control and to secure access to the lands about the Euxine Sea. According to Homer, the war lasted ten years. The first nine were occupied in raids on the cities of the Troad which supplied and supported Troy, for Priam's rule extended from the island of Lesbos to the Hellespont to Phrygia. In the tenth year the city itself was attacked and finally fell. The date for its fall is c1200 B.C.

The site of this Homeric city was generally believed in antiquity to be identical with that of the Greek Ilium (the modern Hissarlik); and this view has been supported in later times, most notably by Heinrich Schliemann, who followed the descriptions in the *Iliad* literally and whose explorations (1871 *et seq.*) at Hissarlik laid bare remains of a series of ancient towns, one above the other. The third and later the second from the bottom he identified with the Homeric town, those levels showing the effects of a conflagration and massive ruins. On the other hand, some scholars regarded the situation of Ilium as irreconcilable with Homer's description of Troy, and preferred a site in the neighborhood of the later Bunarbashi, holding Schliemann's results to be inconclusive. More recent investigations indicate, however, that Schliemann was correct about the site, but that the sixth, or more probably, the seventh level was ancient Ilium. Schliemann's and subsequent excavations on the site have revealed that a city existed there as early as the 3rd millennium B.C. Priam's city, erected on the ruins of earlier cities, was on a mound commanding the plains of the Scamander River and its tributary the Simois. It was larger than the earlier cities and was surrounded by a massive wall, built in the reign of Laomedon, according to legend, by Apollo and Poseidon with the aid of Aeacus. The wall was pierced by gates, of which the Scaean Gate is mentioned in the *Iliad*. On the highest point within the walls rose the palace-fortress. On the lower slopes were the houses of the inhabitants of the city, remains of which have been found. Gold ornaments and pottery indicate that the city was of the level of the Mycenaean civilization. The city of Troy remained a center of interest throughout antiquity for its historic and legendary significance. Xerxes stopped there on his way to invade Greece (481 B.C.) and offered sacrifices at the shrine of Ilian Athena to the shades of the ancient heroes of the Trojan War. Alexander the Great stopped there, 334 B.C., and saw the arms the heroes of the Trojan War had carried, including the shield of Achilles. The Romans, claiming descent from Trojan Aeneas, honored it. Lucius Scipio offered sacrifice to Ilian Athena. Sulla rebuilt the city after it had been destroyed by his opponent, the Roman general Fimbria. Augustus honored the city and enlarged its territory. After the 4th century A.D. the city fell into ruins, its site was abandoned, and even the location of the historic city was forgotten and lost until Schliemann's discovery of it.

Trygon (trī'gon). Some say the infant Asclepius, son of Apollo and Coronis, was exposed to die near Thelpusa, in Arcadia. He was found by Autolaus, an illegitimate son of Arcas, and was given to Trygon who nursed him.

Tubantes (tū-ban'tēz). Ancient Germanic tribe located on the right bank of the Rhenus (Rhine) in territory afterward occupied by the Usipetes. Ptolemy, however, places the tribe further to the south, near the Chatti.

Tuder (tū'dėr). [Modern name, **Todi**.] In ancient geography, an Umbrian town of C Italy, situated on a height above the Tiber River, about 23 miles S of Perusia (Perugia). It has Etruscan and Roman antiquities, including walls, a temple, and a theater. Objects found here are in the museum at Florence and in the Vatican at Rome.

Tullia (tul'i-a̱). In Roman legend, one of two daughters of Servius Tullius. She was the wife of Aruns, brother of Tarquin (Lucius Tarquinius). She murdered her husband, and Tarquin, having killed his wife, married her, slew Servius Tullius, and proclaimed himself king. Tullia rode to the Senate house to greet her husband as king, and on her return drove over the dead body of her father, which lay in the way. The street through which she passed thereafter bore the name Vicus Sceleratus ("Abominable Street").

Tullia. Daughter of Cicero and Terentia; born c76 B.C.; died at Tusculum, 45 B.C. The beloved Tulliola of Cicero's *Letters,* she was the wife first of Calpurnius Piso, later of Furius Crassipes, and finally of Publius Cornelius Dolabella.

Tullus Hostilius (tul'us hos-til'i-us). According to tradition, the third king of Rome (672–640 B.C.). His grandfather Hostilius fought against the Sabines in the war that followed the rape of the Sabine women by Romulus and his followers. Tullus, who succeeded the pious and peace-loving Numa, was even more warlike than Romulus. The relations between Rome and the city of Alba were strained because of a series of cattle raids. Tullus prepared to make war on Alba. However, Mettius Fufetius, leader of the Alban forces, convinced him that they would be

foolish to fight; they would only weaken each other and become prey for the Etruscans. Since one or the other city must sometime be the ruler of both, Mettius proposed that the issue be decided by single combat. A set of male triplets, the Curiatii, from the Alban side, engaged a set of male triplets, the Horatii, from the Roman side. The Horatii won and Rome thus won dominion over Alba. In a later war that Tullus waged against Fidenae and Veii, Mettius, his supposed ally, endeavored to betray Tullus for it galled him that Alba was subordinate to Rome. Tullus discovered his strategy and outwitted him, but when the war was over Tullus exposed the treachery of Mettius and had him torn to pieces by horses. Tullus did not accuse the Alban soldiers of treachery, for they were only obeying orders. He removed the Albans to Rome, gave them the citizenship, and even named some of them as senators. As for the city of Alba, which according to legend had been founded 400 years before this time, he destroyed it utterly except for its temples. He added the Caelian Hill to the city of Rome to make room for the expanded population, and built his own house there, so that from his time it was the custom for the kings of Rome to live on the Caelian Hill. He built a Senate chamber, named for him the Curia Hostilia, which was used until its destruction by fire in 52 B.C. Tullus declared war on the Sabines and defeated them. With all his wars, Tullus had neglected the rites owed to the gods. A rain of stones fell on Alba and a voice commanded the people to make sacrifices for nine days. Plague broke out in Rome. Tullus was one of those afflicted. He hurriedly revived the religious rites of Numa but it was too late. His house was struck by a thunderbolt and he was consumed in the flames.

Turnus (tėr'nus). In Roman legend, the king of the Rutulians in Italy at the period of the arrival of the Trojans under Aeneas. His family origin was Mycenaean and he was a descendant of Inachus and Acrisius, as well as of Pilumnus. He was the handsome suitor of Lavinia, daughter of Latinus. His suit was favored by Lavinia's mother. Alecto the Fury visited him in his palace in

Ardea in the guise of an aged priestess and told him of rumors that Lavinia was to be married to Aeneas. As this did not rouse him sufficiently, Alecto revealed herself and planted a firebrand in his heart which enraged him and led him to call for war on Aeneas. He was informed by Iris, sent by Juno, that Aeneas was temporarily absent from his company of Trojans and that this would be a good time to attack. He attacked, although Latinus disapproved the war. To encourage his men he compared his cause to that of Menelaus, and said that once again the Trojans had started a war by stealing a bride. But he, he declared, would not resort to stratagems as the Greeks had done. He would fight in the open and win by arms, not by wiles. He wrought havoc among the Trojans whom he attacked in their garrison. By mistake he was cut off inside the Trojan fort. He slashed about murderously, killing many before he was forced to give ground. He retreated slowly and at last jumped into the Tiber to save himself. In later struggles Juno and his sister Juturna tried to save him by luring him away from the battle field, but he was a valiant, fearless fighter, and as soon as he discovered that they had duped him, he returned to the thick of the struggle. He refused all suggestions and pleas by Latinus to make peace with the Trojans, and insisted that he would repel the Trojan invaders. He slew Pallas, the son of Evander who had come to aid Aeneas, and tore off Pallas' sword belt on which scenes from the story of the Danaids were depicted. This sword belt, which he now girt on himself, led to his death. After great bloodshed Turnus met Aeneas in single combat to decide the issue. Jove sent an owl to plague him and it was a sign that Turnus' hours were numbered. He fought savagely but was wounded and fell. Aeneas would have spared him, but he caught sight of the sword belt of Pallas, which Turnus was wearing, and to avenge Pallas he thrust his sword through Turnus' throat.

Turpilius (tẽr-pil′i-us), **Sextus.** Latin comic poet; died c104 B.C. Titles of 13 works and some fragments survive.

Turris Libisonis (tur′is li-bis-ō′nis). [Modern name, **Porto Torres.**] Town on the island of Sardinia, situated on the Gulf of Asinara NE of modern Sassari. A Carthaginian and then a Roman settlement, the town still has remains of ancient times.

Tuscan Archipelago (tus′kan). Group of islands W of Tuscany, including Elba and some smaller islands.

Tuscan Sea. Name sometimes given to the part of the Mediterranean W of Tuscany, Italy.

Tuscany (tus′ka-ni). Region in C Italy, bounded on the N and E by the main range of the Apennines, on the W by the Ligurian and Tyrrhenian seas, and on the S by the regions of Umbria and Latium. It was the home of the Etruscans, and one of the earliest objects of Roman expansion.

Tusculum (tus′kū-lum). In ancient geography, a city in Latium, Italy, situated in the Alban Hills about 13 miles SE of Rome, near the modern Frascati. According to tradition its chief, Mamilius, joined Tarquinius Superbus against the Romans. Later it was allied with Rome. Under the Republic and Empire it contained villas of many Romans (Lucullus, Pompey, Brutus, and Cicero). It was destroyed near the end of the 12th century. Its ruins contain a Roman amphitheater and a theater.

Tutula (tö-tö′la). [Also: called by some, **Philotis.**] In Roman legend, a serving-maid of the first half of the 4th century B.C. The Latins threatened war against Rome, and demanded Roman free-born virgins as wives. The magistrates were in a quandary as to how to deal with the demand. Tutula proposed that she and other pretty serving-maids, dressed as free-born brides, should be sent to the Latins, and she would contrive that the Latins would be defeated. The Roman magistrates took her advice and sent her and a number of others dressed as brides to the enemy. During the night, the Roman maidens went about the enemy camp and stole the swords of the sleeping warriors. Tutula climbed a fig tree and, holding her cloak behind her to hide its light, signalled with a torch to the Romans that it was safe to attack. Roman soldiers poured into the camp and slew the sleeping, weaponless Latins.

Tyana (tī′a-na). In ancient geography, a city in Cappadocia, Asia Minor. Its ruins are about 75 miles NW of the modern Adana. It was the birthplace of Apollonius of Tyana, a 1st-century A.D. wandering teacher and sage.

Tyanaeus (tī-a̱-nē′us), **Apollonius.** See **Apollonius of Tyana.**

Tyche (tī′kē). In Greek mythology, the goddess of fortune. Some say she was the daughter of Zeus, by whom she was given the power to decide the lot of individual mortals. She could assure prosperity, wealth, and good luck, but she might capriciously deprive one of all good fortune for no reason at all, or because the beneficiary of her gifts failed to make proper sacrifices to her. The overwhelming aspect of Tyche was her uncertainty. She became identified with the Roman Fortuna and, like her, is depicted with the cornucopia of plenty and the wheel of fortune.

Tychius (tī′ki-us). In Homeric legend (*Iliad*), a Boeotian leather-worker who made the sevenfold spear-proof bull's-hide shield of Telamonian Ajax.

Tydeus (tī′dūs, tid′ē-us). In Greek legend, a son of Oeneus of Calydon. Some say he killed his brother, others say he killed his cousins, and still others say any deaths that he caused were accidental. In any case, he was banished from Calydon and went to the court of Adrastus, king of Argos. There he quarreled with Polynices, son of Oedipus, who had been banished from Thebes. Adrastus separated them and was reminded of an oracle which advised him to yoke his daughters in marriage to a boar and a lion. He gave his daughter Deïpyle to Tydeus, who had the device of a boar painted on his shield, and promised to restore Tydeus to his lands. Deïpyle bore Diomedes to Tydeus. Adrastus first proposed to restore Polynices, who bore the device of a lion on his shield and to whom he gave his daughter Aegia (or Argia), to the throne of Thebes. Tydeus, in the expectation that he would be restored on the successful completion of the expedition, was eager to march against Thebes and was one of the Seven who made up the leaders of the expedition. He was sent as an envoy to Thebes to demand the restoration of Polynices. The Thebans refused. Tydeus then challenged the leading Theban warriors to single com-

bat, and overcame each of his opponents until no more dared to meet him. On his way to rejoin the Argives where they had stopped at Cithaeron, he was set upon by 50 Theban warriors who attacked him from ambush. He killed them all except Maeon, whom he allowed to escape. In the attack on Thebes Tydeus was wounded by Melanippus. But as Tydeus was a favorite of Athena, the goddess came hurrying up with a drug she had procured from Zeus that would cure him and make him immortal. But Amphiaraus, who hated Tydeus because he was one of the causes of the war against Thebes, cut off Melanippus' head (some say Tydeus, though wounded, had killed Melanippus, others say it was Amphiaraus), and gave it to Tydeus, pretending it would cure him. Tydeus split the skull and gulped down the brains of Melanippus. Athena, arriving on the scene at that moment, was so revolted by this sight that she refrained from giving Tydeus the magic drug that would have immortalized him, and he died of his wound. Some say Maeon, in gratitude for being spared by Tydeus, buried his body.

Tydides (tī-dī′dēz). An epithet of Diomedes, meaning "Son of Tydeus."

Tylissus (tī-lis′us). In ancient geography, a town on the E slope of Mount Ida on the island of Crete. It was the site of a Minoan palace built about 1600 B.C. Many valuable objects of the Minoan civilization have been recovered from the site.

Tyndareus (tin-dār′i-us). In Greek legend, a son of Gorgophone, daughter of Perseus, and Oebalus, king of Sparta. His brothers were Icarius and Hippocoön. He succeeded his father to the throne but was driven out by Hippocoön and his sons, and fled to Thestius, king of Aetolia. There he married Leda, daughter of Thestius, who bore Helen, Castor and Polydeuces, and Clytemnestra. Some say Castor and Clytemnestra were the children of Tyndareus, the others having been fathered by Zeus. Others say only Clytemnestra was his child. But he passed as the father of them all. Once when sacrificing to the gods, Tyndareus carelessly forgot Aphrodite. To punish him, Aphrodite caused his daughters to become notorious adulteresses. Tyndareus was restored to the

fat, fāte, fär, fãre, errant; net, mē, hèr ardent; pin, pīne; not, nōte, mōve, nôr, throne of Sparta by Heracles. Helen had so many powerful suitors that he feared to give her to any one of them lest the others turn on him in wrath. In return for his promise to help Odysseus win Penelope, daughter of Icarius, Odysseus advised him to require the suitors to take an oath that they would come to the aid of the man who

daughter of Tyndareus, either Helen or Clytemnestra.

Typaeum (tī-pē'um), **Mount.** Mountain on the road to Olympia, in Elis. According to a law of Elis, any married woman caught observing the Olympic contests on prohibited days was cast to her death from this mountain.

ZEUS AND TYPHON
Black-figured Greek hydria, 6th century B.C. *Munich*

married Helen if any ill should come to him as a result of his marriage. Tyndareus followed this advice and, all the suitors having taken the oath, awarded his beautiful daughter to Menelaus, who also became his heir on the death of Castor and Polydeuces. Tyndareus also compelled Thyestes to relinquish the throne of Mycenae to Agamemnon, and forgave Agamemnon for slaying Clytemnestra's husband and making her his wife by force. Some say that Tyndareus and Leda reared their grandson Orestes following the death of Agamemnon, but when Orestes later killed Clytemnestra and her lover, Tyndareus caused him to be brought to trial for matricide. Tyndareus, whose tomb was at Sparta, was one of those said to have been raised from the dead by Asclepius.

Tyndaridae (tin-dăr'i-dē). A name applied to Castor and Polydeuces as the children of Tyndareus, their supposed father.

Tyndaris (tin'da̱-ris). A name applied to a

Typhon (tī'fon). [Also: **Typhoeus**.] In Greek mythology, the son of Gaea, who in anger over the defeat of her sons the Titans, by Zeus, lay with Tartarus and produced Typhon in a cave in Cilicia. He was a tremendous monster, whose body consisted of snakes from the hips down. On his long arms he had serpents heads in place of hands. By Echidna, Typhon was the father of many monsters: Cerberus, the Hydra, the Chimaera, Orthrus, the Sphinx of Thebes, the dragon that guarded the Golden Fleece, and some say he was also the father of the Nemean Lion and of the eagle that daily gnawed at the liver of Prometheus. Incited thereto by Gaea, Typhon attacked Zeus and the Olympian gods. They fled, taking the form of various animals to escape him. Zeus hurled a thunderbolt and a sickle at him and burned and wounded him. Typhon fled, but when Zeus overtook him he overcame Zeus and cut the sinews of his hands and feet. He took Zeus to the

actọr; up, lūte, pull; oi, oil; ou, out; ᴛʜ, then; d̦ as d or j, ș as s or sh, ț as t or ch, z̦ as z or zh.

cave in Cilicia, set a dragon to guard him, and hid the sinews. Hermes and Pan came to the cave and succeeded in stealing the sinews and restoring them to the god. Now that he could move again Zeus pursued Typhon with his thunderbolts. Typhon fled to Thrace and hurled mountains at Zeus, but Zeus struck him over and over again, and Typhon, wounded, made off. Some say he wandered to Egypt and lies beneath a lake there. Others say he went to Sicily and that there Zeus buried him under Mount Aetna. As Typhoeus, Typhon was the personification of violent, hot windstorms.

Tyre (tīr). [Arabic, **Es Sur**; French, **Sour, Tyr**; Latin, **Tyrus**; Hebrew, **Zor**; called "**Queen of the Sea.**"] Most important and, next to Sidon, the oldest city of Phoenicia; now a town in Lebanon. It consisted of a town on the mainland, which was the oldest part, and two rocky islands directly opposite. These islands originally contained only the temple of Melkarth and warehouses. In the 13th century B.C. they were more settled, and were later united by Hiram, the contemporary of Solomon, by an embankment. In the 11th century B.C. Tyre began, under its first king, father of Hiram, to rival its mother city Sidon, and soon supplanted it as queen of the Phoenician cities. Of its magnificence and luxury the prophet Ezekiel gives a detailed description. It established colonies in Sicily, Sardinia, Spain, Africa (Carthage), and sent out mercantile fleets as far as India and Brittany. Under Hiram Tyre reached the height of its prosperity and splendor. It then came into close friendly relations with Israel. Later, Ahab, king of Israel, married Jezebel, daughter of Ethbaal, whose great-granddaughter Elissa (Dido) is said to have founded Carthage. Tyre was often the aim of attacks by Eastern rulers. It became tributary to Assyria under Tiglath-pileser III (745–727 B.C.). Shalmaneser IV (727–722 B.C.) besieged it for five years, apparently without success. Under Nebuchadnezzar it stood a siege of 13 years (585–572 B.C.). Later it came under Persian supremacy. Alexander the Great reduced the city after a siege of nine months (332 B.C.), though he did not completely destroy it. From this blow Tyre never fully recovered, but it continued to have a degree of prosperity through its manufactures of metalwork, fine textiles, and purple dye. In the Roman period Tyre was still a prosperous city, and it retained some importance down to the Middle Ages. During the Crusades it often changed hands between the Christians and the Mohammedans, and was repeatedly destroyed.

Tyro (tī′rō). In Greek mythology, the beautiful daughter of Salmoneus and Alcidice. She was seduced by Sisyphus, her uncle, and bore him two sons, whom she destroyed. Her stepmother Sidero treated her cruelly. In Elis, to which Salmoneus had gone from Thessaly, Tyro fell in love with the river-god Enipeus, and spent many lonely hours on the banks of his river wooing him. But Enipeus did not respond to her overtures. Instead Poseidon took advantage of the situation. He disguised himself as Enipeus and invited Tyro to join him at the river. After casting her into a deep sleep he raised up a great wave to hide him and ravished Tyro. She bore him twin sons, Pelias and Neleus, but exposed them on the mountain rather than subject herself to the anger of her stepmother by acknowledging her children. Some say she put the children in a chest and set them afloat on the Enipeus River, but in either case, they were saved, and when they grew up they avenged their mother for the cruel treatment she had suffered at Sidero's hands by killing the latter. Tyro married Cretheus, who founded Iolcus and was another of her uncles, and by him was the mother of Aeson, Amythaon, and Pheres.

Tyrrhenians (ti-rē′ni-anz). An ancient people, said to be Lydians who emigrated to Italy under the leadership of Tyrrhenus of Lydia, from whom they took their name. It is thought that these Tyrrhenians were the ancestors of the Etruscans.

Tyrrhenian Sea (ti-rē′ni-an). [Latin, **Inferum Mare, Mare Tyrrhenum**.] That part of the Mediterranean Sea which lies W of Italy and is partly enclosed by the islands of Corsica, Sardina, and Sicily.

Tyrrhenus (ti-rē′nus). According to Greek tradition, a son of Atys of Lydia. In his time a great famine afflicted the land. According to Herodotus, the Lydians sought to alleviate their distress by the invention of all manner of games, and lived according to

fat, fāte, fär, fāre, errant; net, mē, hėr ardent; pin, pīne; not, nōte, möve, nôr,

the following schedule: one day they so occupied themselves with the games that they had no desire to eat, the next day they ate and played no games. In this way they went on for 18 years. The famine persisted, however, and the king decided to divide his nation and, as the result of the drawing of lots, to send one-half over the sea to a new land under the leadership of his son Tyrrhenus. In this way the Lydians under Tyrrhenus went to Umbria in Italy, and colonized that land. Afterward they took the name Tyrrhenians from their leader.

Tyrrheus (tĭ′rūs) or **Tyrrhus** (-rus). In Roman legend, a shepherd of King Latinus. He had a pet stag that tamely followed wherever he went or, if it wandered off, returned to its stall on the farm of Tyrrheus at night. Alecto, commanded by Juno to stir up the Rutulian peasants against Aeneas and the Trojans, caused Ascanius to kill the stag, unaware that it was a pet. The Rutuli were aroused to a great pitch of anger against the Trojans for this incident, and it was one of the precipitating causes of the war between the Trojans and the people of Latium. Lavinia, fearing her stepson Ascanius, afterward fled to the hut of Tyrrheus in the forest to bear her son, whom she named Silvius.

Tyrtaeus (tẽr-tē′us). Greek elegiac poet of Sparta, active in the middle of the 7th century B.C. He was so successful in encouraging the Spartans in the Second Messenian War that the Athenians claimed he was originaly from Attica. According to their tradition, the Spartans, during this war, were commanded by the oracle to take a leader from among the Athenians. The latter, not wishing to offend the oracle by denying a man to the Spartans, and at the same time not wishing to lend any aid or comfort to the Spartans, sent Tyrtaeus, a lame schoolmaster of no reputation. After their defeat by the Messenians at the battle of the Boar's Tomb, the Spartans were discouraged and afraid, but Tyrtaeus so inspired them with his poems, which they sang as they marched into battle, that they renewed the fight and beat the Messenians. Fragments of his poems are extant.

—U—

Ubii (ū′bi-ī). Ancient Germanic people first mentioned by Caesar, in whose time they were situated on the E bank of the Rhine, N of the Taunus region to the Sieg River. Made tributary to the Suevi, they sought Roman aid and protection in 55 B.C. Later (38 B.C.) Agrippa brought them across the Rhine. Their principal place, named Colonia Agrippina (modern Cologne), became the chief seat of Roman power on the lower Rhine. Tacitus mentions that the Ubii later called themselves Agrippinenses. They were merged ultimately with the Franks.

Ucalegon (ū-kal′e̦-gon). Named by Homer (*Iliad*) as a Trojan elder and counselor of Priam. In the *Aeneid* he is further described as a friend of Anchises. Aeneas speaks of the burning of his house on the night the Greeks descended from the Wooden Horse and destroyed Troy.

Udaeus (ū-dē′us). One of the armed men who sprang from the earth when Cadmus sowed the dragon's teeth. See **Sparti**.

Ufens (ū′fe̦nz). In the *Aeneid*, a chief of the Aequi who came from the mountainous district of Nursae to join Turnus in the war against Aeneas. He was slain by Gyas.

Ufens. [Modern name, **Ufente** or **Uffente**.] In ancient geography, a river of Latium flowing into the sea west of Tarracina.

Ulpian (ul′pi-a̦n). [Full Latin name, **Domitius Ulpianus**.] Roman jurist, born at Tyre; murdered c228 A.D. He held office from the time of Septimius Severus, was banished by Heliogabalus, and was a praetorian prefect under Alexander Severus; his reduction of the privileges of the Praetorian Guard eventually caused them to kill him. He wrote many commentaries and other legal works (*Ad Edictum, Ad Sabinum,* and others),

---

actȯr; up, lūte, pu̇ll; oi, oil; ou, out; ᴛʜ, then; d̦ as d or j, ş as s or sh, ț as t or ch, z̧ as z or zh.

largely used in the *Digest,* forming about one-third of that work.

Ultor (ul′tôr). A name given by the Romans to Jupiter and often to Mars, meaning "the Avenger."

Ulysses (ū-lis′ēz). Latin name of **Odysseus.**

Umbria (um′bri-a̱). In ancient geography, a region in Italy, E of Etruria and W of Picenum. The Umbrians took part in the Second Samnite War, but were defeated (308 B.C.) by Rome. After the Third Samnite War they were gradually Romanized.

Umbro (um′brō). A soothsayer and priest of the Marruvian tribe of the Marsi. Among other accomplishments, he was a snake charmer and could cure snakebite. His chief, Archippus, sent him to join Turnus in the war against Aeneas, where he fell to a Trojan spear.

Upis (ö′pis). Ancient pre-Hellenic goddess of childbirth, whose name was later given to Artemis in reference to her function as birth goddess.

Urania (ū-rā′ni-a̱). One of the nine daughters of Zeus and Mnemosyne. She is the muse of astronomy and celestial forces, and the arbitress of fate, second only to Calliope in the company of the Muses. Her usual attributes are a globe, which she often holds in her hand, and a little staff or a compass for indicating the course of the stars. According to some accounts, Urania was the mother of the poet Linus by Apollo. See **Muses.**

Urania. An epithet of Aphrodite in her aspect as a goddess of the heavens, meaning "Heavenly." This epithet was also applied to Aphrodite in her role as the goddess of pure and spiritual love.

Uranus (ū′ra̱-nus, ū-rā′nus). In Greek mythology, the god and personification of the sky. Some say he was the first ruler of the world, and that he received his scepter from Nyx (Night). According to others he was the first child of Gaea, born while she slept. The gentle, fertile rains he sent on her caused trees and verdure to grow, and brought forth the mountains as well. His children by Gaea were: the Hecatonchires, Briareus, Cottus, and Gyges, who each had 100 hands and were the most terrible of the sons of Uranus and Gaea; the Cyclopes, Arges, Steropes, and Brontes, tyrannous-souled giants who had one eye in the middle of their foreheads, and who gave the thunderbolts to Zeus; the Titans, Oceanus, Coeus, Hyperion, Crius, Iapetus, and Cronus who hated his father; the Titanesses, Tethys, Rhea, Themis, Mnemosyne, Phoebe, and Thia. Uranus hated the Cyclopes and hid them in Tartarus. This so aroused the fury of Gaea that she plotted with the Titans to destroy Uranus. While he slept, all the Titans except Oceanus attacked him. Cronus used a sickle that had been forged by the Telchines and given to him by Gaea to cut off his father's genitals. He flung them and the sickle into the sea. Drops of blood falling on Gaea (Earth) from the dismembered parts of Uranus caused Gaea to produce the Erinyes (Furies), the Melic nymphs, and some say Aphrodite was born from the foam which was caused when Uranus' genitals fell into the sea. Some say the sickle that Cronus hurled from him fell into the sea near Drepanum in Sicily. After the mutilation of Uranus the Titans released their brothers, the Cyclopes, and made Cronus their ruler, but as Uranus was dying he prophesied that Cronus would also be dethroned by one of his own children.

Urbibentum (ėr-bi-ben′tum). [Called in the Middle Ages, **Urbs Vetus,** whence the modern name **Orvieto.**] A walled town in Umbria, about 60 miles N of Rome, on a volcanic hill thought by some to be the site of the once wealthy Etruscan city of Volsinii, which the Romans destroyed in 280 B.C. In the neighborhood have been found prehistoric antiquities and an Etruscan cemetery. Bronzes and Greek vases from the cemetery are exhibited in the local museum. Fragments of architectural decoration in terracotta, discovered with the walls, indicate the presence of an Italic (or Etruscan) temple. (JJ)

Ursa Major (ėr′sa̱ mā′jor). The most prominent constellation of the northern heavens, representing a bear with an enormous tail. There is a rival figure for the same constellation—a wagon. Both figures are mentioned by Homer. The name of the bear is translated from some original Aryan language, since the constellation in Sanskrit is called *riksha*—a word which means in different genders a "bear" and a "star." As the seven stars of the Great Bear are in many languages called the Septentrions, it is probable the figure of the bear, which by its tail would seem to have originated among some people not familiar with bears, may have been the result of a confusion of sound. Draco appears to have had formerly a longer tail, twisting down in front of Ursa Major.

Ursa Minor (mī'nor). A constellation near the north pole, the figure of which imitates that of Ursa Major, which its configuration resembles. It also has a rival figure of a wagon, and is sometimes called the Cynosure, which seems to mean "dog's tail." During the greater part of history sailors have steered by Ursa Minor as a whole.

Usipetes (ū-sip'e-tēz). [Also: **Usipes, Usipii.**] Ancient Germanic tribe, first mentioned by Caesar, who describes them as having been driven by the Suevi (59 B.C.), together with the Tencteri, from their original homes. With the Tencteri they were defeated by Caesar on the W bank of the Rhine, whence they withdrew to the opposite side, to the north of the Sugambri. Ptolemy, who names them for the last time, places them further to the south, in the Main region. They were probably merged ultimately in the Alamanni.

Utica (ū'ti-ka). In ancient geography, a city in Africa, situated near the Bagradas (modern Medjerda) River, about 25 miles NW of Carthage. It was founded by the Phoenicians (c1100 B.C.), sided in the Third Punic War with Rome, and succeeded Carthage as the leading city in Africa. It was held by Cato for the Pompeians in 46 B.C. Following the victory of Caesar at Thapsus Cato committed suicide there.

—V—

Vacuna (va-kū'na). Ancient Sabine goddess, She was probably originally a goddess of agriculture, but the Romans later identified her variously with Victoria, Bellona, and Venus.

Vadimonis, Lacus (vad-i-mō'nis, lā'kus). In ancient geography, a small lake in Italy, near the Tiber River; the modern Laghetto di Bassano. Here the Romans under Fabius Maximus Rullianus defeated (310 or 309 B.C.) the Etruscans; in 283 B.C. the Romans defeated the combined north Italians and Gauls here.

Valens (vā'lenz), **Fabius.** One of the principal generals of Vitellius; fl. 69 A.D. He defeated Otho at Bedriacum.

Vale of Tempe (tem'pē). See **Tempe, Vale of.**

Valerius (va-lir'i-us), **Marcus.** [Surnamed **Corvus.**] Roman general; born c371 B.C.; died c270 B.C. He distinguished himself in the First Samnite War. He is said to have won his surname when, having accepted single combat with a giant Gaul, he was aided by a raven that flew in the face of his opponent and enabled Valerius to win.

Valerius, Publius. Real name of **Publicola;** (q.v.).

Valerius Antias (an'ti-as, -shi-as). Roman annalist; fl. in the first part of the 1st century B.C. He wrote a history of Rome in 75 books from the origins to his own time.

Valerius Flaccus (flak'us), **Caius.** Roman poet of the time of Vespasian, author of an armchair epic, the *Argonautica*, a Latin version, in eight books of limited merit, of the adventures of Jason and his companions in the *Argo*, which in Greek is represented by the *Argonautica* of Apollonius Rhodius. The Roman poet Publius Terentius Varro Atacinus, in the 1st century B.C., also wrote an epic *Argonautica* of which fragments survive. (JJ)

Valerius Maximus (mak'si-mus). Roman rhetorician and historian; fl. in the first part of the 1st century A.D. Of his life nothing is known except that he accompanied Sextus Pompeius to Asia in 27 A.D. He dedicated to Tiberius a collection of anecdotes collected for rhetorical purposes.

Vangiones (van-jī'ō-nēz). Ancient Germanic

actor; up, lūte, pull; oi, oil; ou, out; ŦH, then; ḏ as d or j, ş as s or sh, ṯ as t or ch, ẕ as z or zh.

tribe first mentioned by Caesar as in the army of Ariovistus. The Vangiones were situated on the left side of the middle Rhenus (Rhine), in the region about Borbetomagus (later, Augusta Vangionum, modern Worms). They were probably merged ultimately with the Alamanni.

Varini (va-rī′nī). Ancient Germanic people who dwelt near the Mare Suevicum (Baltic Sea) between the Albis (Elbe) and Viadua (Oder) rivers.

Varius Rufus (vãr′i-us rö′fus), **Lucius.** Roman elegiac, epic, and tragic poet; fl. in the last part of the 1st century B.C. He was an older contemporary and friend of Vergil, who left him and Plotius Tucca his literary remains on his death in 19 B.C. Varius Rufus and Plotius Tucca were ordered by Augustus to disregard Vergil's request that the manuscript of the *Aeneid* be burned if anything should happen to him, and as Vergil's literary executors to edit and publish the *Aeneid*. Varius' great tragic poem, *Thyestes*, was presented at the Actian Games and he was rewarded by Augustus with a large sum of money. Of this work, as of his other epic poems, only fragments survive.

Varro (var′ō), **Caius Terentius.** Roman politician; died after 200 B.C. He became consul, with Lucius Aemilius Paulus, in 216 B.C., and loudly criticized the harrying tactics of Fabius in the war against Hannibal. He boasted that he would defeat the enemy in a day, collected a force of 80,000–90,000 men and, in defiance of all advice, sought the enemy. He engaged Hannibal at Cannae in Apulia, and suffered a catastrophic defeat. According to some accounts, 50,000 Romans fell and 10,000–20,000 were taken captive. It was the most terrible defeat the Romans had ever sustained.

Varro, Marcus Terentius. Roman scholar and author, the most learned of the Romans of his time. He was born at Reate, Italy, 116 B.C.; died c27 B.C. He did not confine himself to scholarly pursuits, but held various public offices, and rose to the praetorship. He joined the party of Pompey, but was reconciled with Caesar (47 B.C.) and was made by him director of the great public library. Henceforth he took no part in politics. Nevertheless, he was proscribed by Antony (43 B.C.), in the Second Trium-

virate, but was saved by his friends. The total number of his works is about 74, comprising 620 books. Of these only two, *De Lingua Latina,* dedicated to Caesar, and *De Re Rustica,* survive (the former only in part). Among his lost books are a work on geometry, one on mensuration, and a nine-book encyclopedia, covering grammar, dialectics, rhetoric, geometry, arithmetic, astrology, music, medicine, and architecture. His historical and archaeological studies, quoted by later writers, are the indirect source of much of our modern knowledge concerning ancient Rome.

Varro, Publius Terentius. [Surnamed **Atacinus.**] Roman poet; born at Atax, in Narbonensis, 82 B.C.; died c37 B.C. Following the Alexandrian school, he was the author of the epic *Argonautica,* a work fashioned after that of Apollonius of Rhodes. Only fragments of his works survive.

Varus (vãr′us), **Publius Quintilius.** Roman general. He was consul (13 B.C.), governor in Syria (6–4 B.C.), and commander in Germany (6–9 A.D.). His rigorous measures led to a German alliance against him, and he was totally defeated by Arminius in the famous battle in the Teutoburger Wald (9 A.D.). When he saw that the battle was lost, he fell upon his sword. The three legions under his command were massacred to a man. This defeat profoundly affected the Romans; henceforth they abandoned the idea of a frontier on the Albis (Elbe). Augustus bitterly mourned the loss of the three legions, and the anniversary of the loss was observed in Rome as a day of mourning.

Vascones (vas-kō′nēz). People which dwelt in the N part of ancient Spain, the predecessors of the present Basques. They were subjugated by Augustus. When the Roman Empire disintegrated, they became subject to the Visigoths, but freed themselves at the end of the 6th century A.D., at which time they migrated northward and settled Vasconia, now Gascony.

Vase-painting. From the variety and domesticity of the subjects treated, Greek vase-painting is of the greatest importance for the light shed by it upon every phase of ancient life; and from the art side it is equally valuable, not only from the fine decorative and creative quality which it frequently shows, but from the information that it supplies regarding the great art of Greek wall and easel painting, which has almost entirely perished. Painted ware in Crete in the Early Minoan Period (2800–2000 B.C.; a date for the beginning of the period somewhat later than that suggested by Sir Arthur Evans) consisted of simple designs—bands, wavy lines, plumes, curvilinear patterns—in dark paint on light and light paint on dark backgrounds, using black, varying shades of red, and white. Middle Minoan (2000–1550 B.C.) ware adds naturalistic lily and other plant patterns. In the Late Minoan Period (1550–1100 B.C.), designs inspired by marine life, as befitted a sea power, are widely employed. Octopuses, dolphins, fish, shells, and marine growths, first naturalistic and later stylized, with the occasional admission of the human figure, are skillfully accommodated to the shapes and surfaces that they decorate. On the Greek mainland a parallel development occurred in the Mycenaean Age (c1600–1100 B.C.), so called from its center about Mycenae. Following the Dorian invasion (c1100 B.C.), a geometric style of decoration replaces the patterns of the Minoan-Mycenaean Period. Formal arrangements, in bands or zones, of parallel lines, zigzags, swastikas, maeanders or variations of the key design, and checkerboards completely cover the vase, and give to this period the name Geometric. Later in the period (9th and 8th centuries B.C.) the Attic potters, particularly, produced huge amphorae, some as much as five feet high, which in addition to the geometric zones sometimes carry a scenic frieze. Slim, angular human figures, drawn schematically in silhouette, appear in the friezes, the designs becoming freer with the advance of time. Called Dipylon vases, because many of them were found in the cemeteries outside the Dipylon Gate of Athens, and often used as monuments on graves, many of these show some part of the funeral ritual or procession in the frieze inserted between zones of geometric patterns. In the 8th and 7th centuries, increased trade activity with the cities of Ionia and beyond led to the introduction of Oriental motifs in vase decoration—palmettes, lotuses, rosettes, friezes of fabulous monsters, spirals. Geometric patterns gradually disap-

pear as the space reserved for a pictorial panel increases. On the mainland of Greece, Corinth was the most important center for the production of vases in the Ionic style. The characteristic feature of the Corinthian style is the superposition of bands of animals and monsters, with rosettes and elaborate flowered and fringed borders, the whole following very closely the Assyrian and Phrygian metalwork and embroideries, which were abundantly imported into Greece at this time. Proto-Corinthian vases (725–640 B.C.) progressed from a highly developed geometric style on small vessels, through a stage where friezes of monsters and animals predominated, to a late phase in which the decoration consists of finely executed miniature paintings, generally of mythological subjects. The class of vessels, larger on the whole, called Corinthian (c640–550 B.C.), continue the use of friezes of animals and then developed, in the 7th century, the technique known as the black-figure style. This style, perfected at Corinth and adopted by Athenian potters, shows little Oriental influence; it is thoroughly Hellenic. In black-figure the decoration is painted in black silhouette directly on the clay. Details within the silhouette are incised with a graver. Occasionally red, purple, or white are sparingly used for decorative accent. The subjects of the masters of the black-figure style are most often from mythology; Heracles, for example, with the great variety of his adventures, is a favorite subject; Theseus and Perseus are also popular. Scenes from daily life begin to appear. The drawing is strong and archaic; the effect is decorative. The heads of the human figures are in profile, but the eye is full face. Men's eyes are round, women's are almond-shaped. The flesh of women is white. Bodies are in profile or with the shoulders and chest front view, the hips and legs in profile. Among the masters of the black-figure technique are Timonidas of Corinth (early 6th century B.C.); his contemporary, Sophilus of Athens (q.v.); Nearchus (q.v.), painter and potter; Exekias (q.v.), painter and potter; Cleitias (q.v.), painter who worked with the potter Ergotimus; the Amasis Painter (q.v.); and the Tleson Painter (q.v.).

By the middle of the 6th century B.C.,

Athens eclipsed Corinth as the center of the production of painted vases. A new technique developed there, the red-figure style, in which the background is painted black and the reddish color of the vessel itself is reserved for the figures. Details of the figures are drawn in black or a diluted black. The advantage of this technique is that it liberates the artist from the engraver, the brush giving greater fluidity than the graving tool. The black ground also heightens and sets off the red figures. At the same time, it intensifies the design effect. The black-figure and red-figure style existed side by side for many years. Indeed some masters, as Epictetus (q.v.) and the Andocides Painter (q.v.), worked in both, and on occasion used both on the same vessel, black-figure on one side and red-figure on the other. Toward the end of the first quarter of the 5th century B.C., however, the red-figure superseded the black-figure, except in the decoration of Panathenaic amphorae, which, by tradition, continued to be painted in black-figure and in a traditional archaic manner. Subjects of the red-figure artists are at first from mythology, then increasingly from daily life, as, the potter's shop, the shoemaker's shop, the music lesson, feasting and dancing, etc. Over 500 artists of the red-figure style have been identified, not, however, by their own names. Their identities are variously indicated, sometimes from the potter who is known to have thrown their vessels, as the Cleophrades Painter (q.v.), the Brygos Painter (q.v.), Pistoxenus Painter, Sosias Painter (q.v.), Sotades Painter; sometimes from a distinctive subject of their paintings, as the Penthesilea Painter, Pan Painter, Niobid Painter, Achilles Painter; sometimes from the location of an example of their work, as the Berlin Painter, Chicago Painter, Providence Painter. Among those whose names are known are: Euthymides (q.v.), Euphronius (q.v.), Onesimus (q.v.), Duris (q.v.), Phintias (q.v.), Oltos (q.v.), Myson (q.v.), and Macron (q.v.).

Another technique, employed generally only for the interiors of kylixes and for the decoration of lecythi, covered the natural clay with a white or creamy slip, and used this as a surface for painting outline figures in various colors. Greek vase-painting reached its height in the 5th century B.C. Attic ware was distributed throughout the Mediterranean region. Many of the surviving examples were found outside the borders of the Greek mainland. After the 5th century the quality of painted vases declined, but the art survived until the 3rd century, when painted pottery was no longer produced.

Vediovis (vēd′yọ̄-vis). [Also: **Vedius, Vejovis.**] See **Veiovis.**

Veii (vē′ī). In ancient geography, a city in Italy, the most important of the Etruscan League, about 11 miles NW of Rome. It was frequently at war with Rome, especially in behalf of the restoration of Tarquinius Superbus. It was besieged and taken by the Romans under the leadership of Camillus in 396 B.C. Roman references to Veii as a center of fine sculpture in terra-cotta have been borne out by excavations both clandestine and official, which have produced striking figures of gods, Apollo, Artemis, and others, in the Villa Giulia Museum in Rome. According to Pliny the Elder, a Veientine sculptor named Vulca made terra-cotta statues for the Capitolium in Rome. Under the Empire the city sank into obscurity. In Rome, on the W side of the Piazza Colonna, is a portico of ancient Ionic columns, removed from Veii in 1838 and reërected here. (JJ)

Veiovis (vē′yọ̄-vis). A Roman deity, possibly of Etruscan origin, regarded by some scholars as a sort of anti-Jupiter, a god of the dead. He was represented as a youth, armed with arrows and accompanied by a goat.

Velabrum (vẹ-lā′brum). Area in ancient Rome, between the Capitoline and Palatine hills and the Tiber River, extending NE to the Forum Romanum. It was a marsh before the construction of the Cloaca Maxima.

Velia (vē′li-ạ). Locality in ancient Rome, identified as the ridge which extends from the Palatine Hill to the Esquiline Hill, and on which stand the Temple of Venus and Roma and the Arch of Titus. As it now exists, it has been much cut down from its original height.

Velia. The Italic name of Elea, a Greek colony on the coast of Lucania in Magna Graecia. It was said to have been founded (540 B.C.) by Phocaeans who emigrated from Asia Minor rather than submit to Persia. It was the center of the Eleatic School of philosophy. (JJ)

Velinus (ve̯-lī′nus). [Modern name, **Velino.**] River in C Italy which joins the Nar (Nera) above Interamna (Terni). Near its mouth is the noted waterfall Cascate delle Marmore, consisting of a series of three cascades.

Vellum. Leather, or perhaps more correctly calfskin, especially when used as a writing material. Of the oldest manuscripts which have survived to our time, a great number are on vellum, whose durability has enabled them to withstand centuries of handling and haphazard storage. (JJ)

Venedi (ve̯-ned′ī). [Also: **Vends, Veneds.**] Name applied by Tacitus and Pliny to an ancient people living along the right bank of the Vistula. Tacitus classified them as Germans; they are, however, considered to have been the ancestors of the Wends.

Venelia (ve̯-nē′li-a̯). In the *Aeneid,* a nymph, the mother of Aeneas' Rutulian enemy Turnus.

Veneti (ven′e̯-tī). Ancient Celtic people of NW Gaul, who carried on a considerable trade with Britain. They were defeated by Caesar in 56 B.C., in a naval engagement. The name survives in the town of Vannes.

Veneti. [Also: **Heneti.**] Ancient people of Italy, dwelling near the head of the Adriatic, beyond the Padus (Po) and Athesis (Adige) rivers. During the Second Punic War the Veneti passed under Roman rule. Their principal towns were Patavium (Padua) and Ateste (Este). Inscriptions from the 5th to 1st centuries B.C. indicate that they spoke an Illyrian language.

Venulus (ven′ū-lus). In the *Aeneid,* an Italian who joined Turnus in the war against Aeneas. He was sent by Turnus to Diomedes' city to ask his aid. On his return he reported that Diomedes advised Turnus and the Latins to come to terms with Aeneas. He refused to lend Turnus any aid, for he had had enough of fighting Trojans.

Venus (vē′nus). In Roman mythology, the goddess of grace and love. Originally she was an Italic goddess of gardens and growth, and only at a comparatively late period became identified with the Greek goddess of love, Aphrodite. In medieval times her name

became synonymous with earthly love as contrasted with spiritual love.

Venus de Milo (mī′lō). [Also: **Venus of Melos.**] Greek statue in the Louvre, Paris, perhaps the most admired single existing work of antiquity. It was found in 1829 on the island of Melos, and in date appears to fall between the time of Phidias and that of Praxiteles, or c400 B.C. The statue represents a majestic woman, undraped to the hips, standing with the weight on the right foot and with the head turned slightly toward the left. The arms are broken off, and there is a dispute as to their original position.

Venusia (ve̯-nū′shi-a̯). [Modern name, **Venosa.**] Town in S Italy. It was a station on the Appian Way, and the birthplace of the Roman poet Horace (65 B.C.).

Verbanus, Lacus (vėr-bā′nus, lā′kus). [Modern names, **Lago Maggiore, Lago di Verbano.**] Second largest lake of N Italy. It is traversed by the Ticinus River. It contains the Borromean Islands, and is famous for picturesque scenery. Elevation, about 633 feet; length, about 37 miles; area, about 82 square miles; greatest known depth, about 1220 feet.

Vercingetorix (vėr-sin-jet′ō-riks). Chief of the Arverni in Gaul, the leader of the great rebellion against the Romans in 52 B.C. He gained various successes against Caesar, but was besieged by him at Alesia and surrendered in 52 B.C. He was exhibited in Caesar's triumph at Rome in 46 B.C., and then by Caesar's order beheaded (c45 B.C.).

Vergil (vėr′jil). [Full Latin name, **Publius Vergilius Maro.**] Roman epic, didactic, and idyllic poet; born in Andes, near Mantua, Cisalpine Gaul, Oct. 15, 70 B.C.; died at Brundisium, Italy, Sept. 21, 19 B.C. He studied at Cremona, Mediolanum (Milan), and Rome, perhaps with the idea of becoming an advocate, but a career before the public did not appeal to his retiring nature, and he soon devoted himself to philosophy and poetry. His knowledge of Latin and Greek poets and of Roman history was extensive. Among earlier writers who influenced him was the Latin poet of Epicureanism, Lucretius. There are also many indications in his work of his particular interest in the works of the Greeks Theocritus and Apollonius of Rhodes. His great learning is a very evident ornament of his finest work. In 41 B.C. his

actor; up, lūte, pu̇ll; oi, oil; ou, out; ͭH, then; d̩ as d or j, s̩ as s or sh, t̩ as t or ch, z̩ as z or zh.

paternal estate near Mantua, where he had grown up, was confiscated for the benefit of the soldiery which had assisted Octavian in the civil war against Brutus and Cassius; but he was later indemnified through the intercession of Maecenas. Some think these events were celebrated in the first and ninth of his *Eclogues:* in the first, the chief figure of the poem is happy to be confirmed in the holding of his land while others about him are losing theirs, and in the ninth the chief figure, a farmer, seeks to prevent the loss of his farm. Whether these two poems are definitely associated with events in Vergil's own life is open to question. However, with the *Eclogues* Vergil came to the attention of Maecenas (c40 B.C.), who became his patron and benefactor. He also enjoyed the friendship and patronage of Asinius Pollio and Octavian (later Augustus). He was an intimate friend of Horace, whom he introduced to Maecenas. About 37 B.C. he settled at Rome; his later years were spent chiefly in or near Neapolis (Naples), where at his wish he was ultimately buried.

The *Eclogues* or *Bucolics* of Vergil, written 42–37 B.C., consist of ten poems generally on pastoral themes. The four books of the great didactic poem, the *Georgics* (written 37–30 B.C., at the request of Maecenas), celebrate pastoral life, and are considered by some to be Vergil's finest poetry. Crops and the weather are the subjects of the first book, the cultivation of the vine and the olive of the second, farm animals of the third, and beekeeping of the fourth. Lyricism, pathos, and a profound humanity, all expressed with the highest art, pervade these lines in celebration of the rural life. The last years of Vergil's life (c30–19 B.C.) were devoted to the creation of a national epic, the *Aeneid* (q.v.), that would do for Augustus and Rome what Homer had done for the Greeks, and by a celebration of its past history unite the Romans, not yet recovered from the civil wars, in a loyal nation dedicated to pursuing its destiny under the egis of Augustus. At the time of his death the work had not been completely revised, and he was planning to spend three years in this task. On his deathbed he asked that it be destroyed, but Augustus ordered his literary executors, Varius and Tucca, to publish it as it stood. It has lived as the great Roman epic, second only in classical literature, according to some opinions, to the epics of Homer.

Vergil the Magician. Legendary form which the historical Vergil assumed in the Middle Ages. The *Sortes Vergilianae,* divination by the use of Vergil's *Aeneid,* used as early as the 1st century A.D., seems to be the nucleus of his reputation for magic. To this were added certain widespread legends, locally attributed to him but elsewhere to other prominent figures, and around and through this disconnected series of anecdotes was built a fictional biography that made him a great magician and virtually ignored his literary achievements.

Veroia (ve'ryä). [Also: **Veria, Verria.**] See **Beroea.**

Veromandui (ver-ọ-man'dū-ī). [Also: **Viromandui.**] Ancient people of Belgic Gaul who lived on the upper Samara (Somme) River in the vicinity of what is now St.–Quentin.

Verona (vẹ-rō'nạ). City in NE Italy, in Cisalpine Gaul, situated on the Athesis (Adige) River. It was a Celtic settlement in ancient times, and became a Roman colony in 89 B.C. It was the birthplace of the poet Catullus. Verona has one of the best-preserved Roman amphitheaters of Italy, and other Roman antiquities, including a theater, gates, and large archaeological collections.

Verres (ver'ēz), **Caius.** Roman official; put to death under a proscription of Mark Antony, 43 B.C. He was praetor in 74 B.C., and later, as governor of Sicily (73–70 B.C.), plundered the island of property, art treasures, and the like. The Sicilians brought him to trial (70 B.C.) for his extortions. Cicero, who had offered his services to the Sicilians, undertook his prosecution. Verres was defended by Hortensius, who tried unsuccessfully to delay the trial to the following year when he would be consul. Cicero presented his evidence and Hortensius, unprepared, abandoned his client. Verres went into exile at Massilia (Marseilles) taking much of the loot from Sicily with him. Of the six orations against Verres composed by Cicero, only the first was actually delivered.

Verrucosus (ver-ū-kō'sus), **Quintus Fabius Maximus.** See **Fabius Maximus Verrucosus, Quintus.**

Vertumnus (ver-tum'nus). [Also: **Virtumnus.**]

Ancient Etruscan or Italic deity taken over by the Romans. Little is known of him except that he came to be regarded as presiding over gardens and orchards, and was worshiped as the god of the changing seasons. In later Roman mythology, Vertumnus fell in love with Pomona, a wood-nymph whose love of her orchards and gardens was greater than any love a man could inspire. To be near her, Vertumnus disguised himself as a laborer and worked in her gardens, orchards, and vineyards. At length he disguised himself as an old crone and visited her. In this disguise he caressed her and told her a parable. Pointing to an elm tree which supported an abundantly loaded grape vine, he said that the tree by itself would be of no use or of any interest, except for its leaves, and that the vine without the tree would lie unremarked upon the ground and unable to bear fruit; each brought usefulness and beauty to the other, and she would do the same if she took a husband. But, as one who loved her, the old crone advised her to take no one but Vertumnus, and proceeded to extol the virtues of that young god and to describe his love for orchards and gardens, so similar to hers. Moreover, Pomona was warned of the vengeance of Venus if she continued to deny the power of that goddess. The words had no effect on Pomona, however, and suddenly Vertumnus resumed his own shining form. Pomona, on viewing the beauty of the youthful god, instantly fell in love with him and gladly agreed to share her gardens with him.

Vescia (ve'sha). One of three *oppida* (an *oppidum* was a subject, provincial town), Ausona, Vescia, and Minturnae, of an Italic people known as the Ausones or Aurunci, who occupied the Vescian plain and the valley of the river Liris, on the border between Latium and Campania. According to Livy, these three oppida were captured by the Romans in 314 B.C., after which their independent history ceased, and the site of Vescia was lost. It has been suggested that Suessa (now Sessa) Aurunca, a Latin colony on the southwestern slopes of an extinct volcano now known as Roccamonfina, may reflect an alternate pronunciation or dialectal form of Vescia, in which case Suessa may lie over or near the site of Vescia; but no traces older than the Latin colony have been identi-

fied. The name survived in Ager Vescinus and Montes Vescini (JJ)

Vespasian (ves-pā'zhạn). [Full Latin name, **Titus Flavius Sabinus Vespasianus.**] Roman emperor (69–79 A.D.); born near Reate, Italy, Nov. 17, 9 A.D.; died June 24, 79 A.D. He was of humble origin, but rose to distinction in the army, and became consul in 51. He was afterward governor of Africa, and in 67 was appointed commander-in-chief against the insurgent Jews. He was proclaimed emperor in 69. His general Antonius Primus overthrew Vitellius in the same year, and Vespasian arrived at Rome in 70, leaving his son Titus to continue the Jewish war. The chief events of his reign were the destruction of Jerusalem by Titus (70), the victories of Agricola in Britain, and the suppression (70) of the revolting Batavians under Civilis. He restored discipline in the army and order in the finances, and expended large sums on public works, including the Flavian Amphitheater ("Colosseum"), which, however, he did not live to finish. He was said to have installed the first public comfort stations in Rome, which in some parts of Europe are still called "Vespasians." On his death he was succeeded by his sons Titus (79–81 A.D.) and the unspeakable Domitian (81–96 A.D.).

Vesta (ves'tạ). Hearth-goddess of the ancient Romans, equivalent to the Greek Hestia. She presided over both the private family hearth or altar, and the central altar of the city, the tribe, or the state. She was worshiped along with the Penates at every meal, when the family assembled round the altar or hearth, which was in the center of the house. Aeneas was said to have carried the sacred fire (her symbol) from Troy, and to have brought it to Italy, and it was preserved at Rome by the state in the sanctuary of the goddess which stood in the Forum. There was no image of Vesta; she was represented entirely by the fire. This fire was watched by six virgins, called "vestals," who prevented it from going out. If it did, it was rekindled by friction. Her festival, the *Vestalia*, was observed June 9–15, during which time her sanctuary was cleaned.

Vestal Virgin. Among the ancient Romans, a virgin consecrated to Vesta and to the service of watching the sacred fire, which was kept perpetually burning upon her altar. According to tradition, the vestal virgins, warned of the approach of the Gauls (c389 B.C.), took the sacred fire from the altars and fled from the city. As they were hurrying along the road with the sacred fire and sacred vessels from the temple, Lucius Albinus, also fleeing the barbarians with his family and household goods in a cart, came upon them. He piously removed his family and goods from his cart, took up the vestal virgins, and carried them to Caere. There they remained until the Gauls, who had taken the sacked Rome, were driven out. Some say that because the vestal virgins performed their sacred rites at Caere these rites afterwards came to be known as ceremonies, for the place of refuge of the vestal virgins. The institution of the vestal virgins was one of the oldest features of Roman religion, and was the last to perish with the rise of Christianity. The vestals were at first two, then four in number, afterward six. They entered the service of the goddess from six to ten years of age, their term of service lasting 30 years. They were then permitted to retire and to marry, but few did so, as it was supposedly unlucky. Their persons were inviolable, any offense against them being punished with death, and they were treated in all their relations with the highest distinction and reverence. A vestal who broke her vow of chastity was immured alive in an underground vault amid public mourning. There were very few such instances; in one of them, under Domitian (51–96 A.D.), the chief of the vestals was put to death under a false charge trumped up by the emperor.

Vestini (ves-tī'nī). Ancient people of C Italy, living E of the Sabines, and probably of Sabine affinities. The Vestini became allied with the Romans c300 B.C., and joined the Marsi in the Social War. They were subjugated by the Romans in 295 B.C.

Vesuvius (vē-sö'vi-us), **Battle of.** Victory gained near Mount Vesuvius, c340 B.C., by the Romans under Manlius Torquatus and Decius Mus over the Latin League.

Vesuvius, Mount. [Italian, **Monte Vesuvio.**] The only active volcano on the mainland of Europe, and unquestionably the best-known one in the world, situated on the Bay of Naples, Italy, about nine miles SE of Naples. It has two summits, the volcano proper (about

4200 feet high), and Monte Somma to the N (3730 feet). It was regarded in ancient times as extinct. Severe earthquake shocks occurred in 63 A.D., and the first recorded eruption took place in 79 A.D., destroying Pompeii, Herculaneum, and Stabiae. The popular belief that Pompeii, Herculaneum, and Stabiae were overwhelmed by streams of molten lava is mistaken; in the eruption of 79 A.D., Vesuvius sprayed into the atmosphere vast quantities of molten rock in the form of droplets charged with gases, which expanded as in the cooler air the drops solidified, forming *lapilli*, "pellets" of light, dry, warm "ash" (pumice). It was this ash which covered Pompeii to a depth of 16 to 20 feet, and Stabiae, in some places, to an even greater depth. On the SW slopes of the volcano, however, it rained, and the wet ash, falling to the ground as warm mud, flowed downhill and covered the lower slopes, including the entire resort of Herculaneum, where it hardened into the rock known as tufa, effectively sealing it off from discovery and clandestine excavation until the 18th century. Other more or less notable eruptions have taken place since 79 A.D., the most destructive being those of Dec. 16, 1631, and 1906. (JJ)

Via Aemilia (vī'ạ ē-mil'i-ạ). [English, **Aemilian Way.**] Important ancient Roman highway, the earliest in N Italy, connecting Placentia (Piacenza) and Ariminum (Rimini), where it met the Flaminian Way. Later branches extended from Ariminum to Bononia (Bologna), and thence to Aquileia, and from Placentia to Ticinum (Pavia), and the main road was extended from Placentia to Mediolanum (Milan) and Augusta Praetoria (Aosta). The original highway was built by Marcus Aemilius Lepidus in 187 B.C., and is still in use.

Via Appia (ap'i-ạ). Latin name of the **Appian Way.**

Via Aurelia (ô-rē'li-ạ). [English, **Aurelian Way.**] One of the chief ancient Roman highways. It was built toward the close of the republic, and extended from Rome, for the most part along the coast, to Pisae (Pisa), whence it was continued along the Ligurian shore to the Maritime Alps, and by Augustus was carried into Gaul. There are considerable remains of the road, notably along the Italian and French Riviera.

Via Cassia (kash'i-ạ, kas'-). [English, **Cassian Way**.] Ancient Roman highway which extended from Rome through Etruria to Arretium (modern Arezzo), and thence to Florentia (Florence) and Luca (Lucca). It was in existence before the end of the republic, but the time of its construction is unknown.

Via Clodia (klō'di-ạ). [English, **Clodian Way**.] Ancient Roman highway of the time of the republic, extending through Etruria on a line about parallel with the Via Cassia. It was a branch of the Via Cassia, which it left about ten miles from Rome, where its pavement still exists.

Via Egnatia (eg-nā'shi-ạ). Important ancient Roman military road, running from the coast of the Adriatic at Dyrrhachium (modern Durrës) through Illyria and Macedonia to Thessalonica (Salonika), and thence by Philippi through Thrace to Cypsela (Ipsala), near what is now Edirne. The road, built c130 B.C., takes its name from Egnatia on the Apulian coast. Its length was 534 Roman miles. There are abundant remains of the road, especially near Salonika.

Via Flaminia (flạ-min'i-ạ). Latin name of the **Flaminian Way**.

Via Latina (lạ-tī'nạ). [English, **Latin Way**.] One of the great and earliest highways leaving ancient Rome. It ran to Casilinum (near Capua), where it united with the Appian Way. A branch was later carried from Teanum to Beneventum. The Via Latina undoubtedly existed as a road for a long period before it was regularly constructed and paved. The invading forces of both Pyrrhus and Hannibal followed its course.

Via Ostiensis (os-ti-en'sis). [English, **Ostian Way**.] Ancient highway from Rome to Ostia. It followed the left bank of the Tiber, cutting across the larger bends of the river.

Via Popilia (pō-pil'i-ạ). Two ancient highways: 1) A highway from Capua to Rhegium that ran, inland, from the Appian Way at Capua for over 300 miles to Rhegium. 2) A 178-mile highway that ran along the Adriatic coast from Ariminum (Rimini) to Aquileia.

Via Portuensis (pôr-tū-en'sis). Ancient highway from Rome to the new imperial seaport Portus Trajani (Civitavecchia). Its course,

which can still be followed, is along the right bank of the Tiber.

Via Praenestina (pren-es-tī'nạ). [English, **Praenestine Way**.] Very ancient highway from Rome to Praeneste (Palestrina), whence it was continued to join the Via Latina at Anagnia (Anagni).

Via Sacra (sā'krạ). [English, **Sacred Way**.] First street of ancient Rome to be established on the low ground beneath the hills. It had its name either because on its line, according to tradition, Romulus made his treaty with the Sabine chief Tatius, or because on it lay several of the oldest and most revered sanctuaries of Rome. It began at the E end of the Forum Romanum, and ran along the S side of the Forum, past the Basilica Julia and the Temple of Castor and Pollux; then it turned at right angles and crossed the Forum, and turned again to skirt the N side of the Temple of Julius Caesar. It continued in front of the Temple of Antonius and Faustina and the Basilica of Constantine to the Arch of Titus. Under the empire it was extended hence past the Flavian Amphitheater to a point on the Esquiline Hill. The lava pavement of the Via Sacra, as it now exists, is almost all late in date; and it is probable that the course of the street was slightly altered from time to time to meet architectural exigencies.

Via Salaria (sạ-lār'i-ạ). [English, **Salarian Way**.] One of the most celebrated of ancient Roman highways. It ran from Rome up the Tiber valley to Reate (Rieti), then crossed the Apennines and went past Asculum Picenum (Ascoli Piceno) to the Adriatic. Here it branched, one road running N to Ancona and the other S to Hadria (Adria). The name means "Salt Road," and indicates that it originated in the track by which crude salt had been transported from drying-pans near the Tiber mouth to the interior of Italy since before the time of recorded history. Eventually the track was engineered and paved to Roman standards.

Via Valeria (vạ-lir'i-ạ). [English, **Valerian Way**.] One of the principal highways of ancient Rome. It continued a road which led from Rome to Tibur (Tivoli) to Lake Fucinus (Fucino) and the Marsic territory, and was afterward extended to the Adriatic at the mouth of the Aternus (Aterno). The time of its construction as far as Lake Fucinus (Fucino) is unknown; its continuation through the Apennines and in the Aternus valley was built by Claudius. Many portions of the roadway survive.

Victor. A Roman epithet often applied to Jupiter, Mars, and Hercules, and sometimes to other gods.

Victoria (vik-tō'ri-a̲). In Roman mythology, the personification of victory, equated to the Greek Nike. She was specifically a goddess of the Roman legions, and also of the emperors. Her temple at Rome dates back to 294 B.C.

Victory of Samothrace (sam'ō-thrās). [Also: **Winged Victory.**] One of the greatest art monuments of antiquity, found in Samothrace in 1863, and now in the Louvre, Paris. The colossal winged figure (of which the head has been lost) stands, with full drapery blown by the wind, on the prow of a trireme. The work is of Hellenistic date.

Victrix (vik'triks). A Roman epithet applied to Venus, Diana, Fortuna, and sometimes to other goddesses.

Vigiles (vij'i-lēz). Corps of police and firemen, organized under military discipline, in ancient Rome. Under Augustus they numbered 7000, were under the command of a prefect, and were divided into seven regiments, each of which had the guard of two of the 14 *regiones* of the city, and was subdivided into seven companies. The Vigiles were quartered in seven main barracks, or *stationes,* and 14 subordinate posts, or *excubitoria.* The remains of several of these barracks and posts have been discovered, and are remarkable for the magnificence of their decoration with marble incrustation and columns, mosaic pavements, statues, and mural paintings.

Villanovans (vil-a̲-nō'vanz). Pre-Etruscan people of N Italy, named from a cemetery excavated in 1853 at Villanova near Bologna. Their culture is believed to have been brought (c1000 B.C.) into the region by migrants from north of the Alps, who spread into Etruria, Latium, and through the Bologna area. It is characterized by cremation of the dead and urn-burial of the ashes.

Viminal Hill (vim'i-na̲l). [Latin, **Mons Viminalis.**] Northeasternmost of the group of seven hills of ancient Rome, E of the Quirinal and N of the Esquiline. The baths of Diocletian lie below it to the N.

Vindelicia (vin-de̲-lish'i-a̲, -lish'a̲). [Also: **Rhaetia Secunda.**] In ancient geography, a Roman province; sometimes united with Rhaetia. It was bounded by the Ister (Danube), the Aenus (Inn) (separating it from Noricum), and Rhaetia. Its chief town was Augusta Vincelicorum (Augsburg). The early inhabitants were probably of Celtic origin. Vindelicia occupied in general what is now the S part of Baden, Wurttemberg, and Bavaria, and the N part of the Tyrol.

Vindicius (vin-di'shus, -shi-us). In Roman legend, a Roman slave who belonged to the family of the Aquilii. By chance (c509 B.C.) he overheard envoys of the deposed Tarquin plotting with members of the Aquilii and Vitelii families to slay the consuls Brutus and Collatinus and restore Tarquin as king of Rome. He revealed the plot to Publius Valerius (Publicola) who, terrified that the conspirators might act at once if they realized their plot had been exposed, shut Vindicius up in his house and set his wife to guard him. Valerius immediately investigated, found that what Vindicius had said was true, and rounded up the conspirators, who by vote of the Roman people were thereupon slain. To reward Vindicius, Valerius procured a decree from the people granting him the freedom of the city with the right to join whatever tribe of the Roman citizens he chose, and giving him the franchise. Vindicius was the first slave ever to be enfranchised in this manner.

Violet-Crowned City. Name sometimes given to Athens. As seen from Athens, the deforested limestone flanks of Mount Hymettus, when lit by the late afternoon sun, reflect an extraordinary violet light observed nowhere else in nature. The epithet "violet-crowned" was first applied to Athens by the Theban poet Pindar. (JJ)

Virbius (vir'bi-us). In Roman mythology, a minor deity attendant on Diana (Artemis) of Aricia. According to some accounts, Hippolytus, restored to life by Asclepius, was carried in a cloud by Artemis (Diana) to Italy. He married Egeria and became ruler in Aricia under the name Virbius. His appearance and name were changed because it was against divine law for the dead to be restored to life, and the changes were for the purpose of disguising him, even as Dionysus changed the name of his mother to sneak her out of Tartarus and take her to the home of the gods. Virbius built a famous shrine to Diana (Artemis) in her grove at Aricia near Lacus Nemorensis (Lake Nemi). Some say he was the father of a second Virbius by the nymph Aricia. For restoring Hippolytus to life, a deed permitted only to the gods themselves, Asclepius was struck by a thunderbolt of Zeus.

Virgil (vẽr′jil). See **Vergil**.

Virginia. In Roman legend, the daughter of Virginius, a centurion, who was slain by her father to keep her from the power of the decemvir Appius Claudius (449 B.C.). This act led to the overthrow of the decemvirate.

Virginius (vẽr-jin′yus). In Roman legend, the father of Virginia.

VIRGO
Pictured according to ancient descriptions.

Virgo (vẽr′gō). The sixth sign of the zodiac— the Virgin—which the sun enters about Au-

gust 23. Also, a zodiacal constellation representing a winged woman in a robe holding a spike of grain in her left hand.

Viriathus (vi-rī′a-thus, vir-i-ā′thus) or **Viriatus** (vi-rī′a-tus, vir-i-ā′tus). Lusitanian shepherd who led a revolt against Rome following the proscriptions of the proconsul Galba (150 B.C.). By means of guerrilla tactics, he conducted a long and generally successful war (149–141 B.C.) against the Romans in the western part of the Iberian Peninsula. Having defeated the generals sent against him, his independence and that of the Lusitanians was recognized by a treaty with Rome. The Roman consul Cnaeus Servilius Caepio broke the treaty (140 B.C.), renewed the war, and bribed three friends of Viriathus to slay him (139 B.C.).

Virtus (vẽr′tus). In Roman mythology, the personification of courage, or the manly virtues.

Vitellius (vi-tel′i-us), **Aulus.** Roman emperor (69 A.D.); born 15 A.D.; killed at Rome, in December, 69 A.D. To say that he was a favorite of Tiberius, Caligula, Claudius, and Nero is to give eloquent testimony of his adaptability, servility, and profound knowledge of all forms of debauchery. He was appointed governor in lower Germany by Galba in 68, and was proclaimed emperor by the army at the beginning of 69. His generals Caecina and Valens defeated Otho, and he entered Rome in the middle of 69. His brief reign was marked by a rise in debauchery and license, but when the forces of Vespasian marched on Rome his followers dwindled. The Romans are said to have insisted that he keep the purple. His forces were defeated by those of Vespasian under Antonius Primus, and he was taken from hiding and murdered.

Vitruvius Pollio (vi-trö′vi-us pol′i-ō), **Marcus.** [Called **Vitruvius**.] Roman architect and engineer; born at Verona, Italy; fl. 1st century B.C. He was a military engineer under Caesar and Augustus. His treatise on architecture, in ten books (*De Architectura*), dedicated to Augustus, is the only surviving Roman treatise on the subject. His taste was strongly conservative. The work continually stresses the merits and charms of the unpretentious Roman architecture of earlier generations, which was rapidly disappearing from the Roman scene as at Augustus' bidding outmoded buildings were remodeled and sheathed with marble revetment or replaced entirely. It has been suggested that Vitruvius wrote in the vain hope of persuading Augustus to return to traditional decoration in stucco and terracotta. His description of a triple-cella temple in the Tuscan style, for example, which has been a source of controversy among historians of architecture for generations, is now regarded as a proposal for a temple he would have liked to build, rather than a description of an existing temple. Nevertheless, the book contains much useful material not elsewhere recorded. It was well known to Pliny the Elder, and on it was based much of the theory and practice of Renaissance and Neo-Classical architecture. (JJ)

Volaterrae (vol-a-ter′ē). [Modern name, **Volterra.**] Town in C Italy. It was one of the 12 leading Etruscan towns. Tombs of the Villanovan period have been found nearby. The town fell to Rome in 298 B.C. Ancient walls still surround the town.

Volcae (vol′sē). Celtic people of ancient Gaul, who, emerging from the Ister (Danube) Valley, pushed west and reached the Rhenus (Rhine) during the 4th century B.C., and settled in the region later called Languedoc. Split up in their earlier migrations, one group of the Volcae moved through Greece in the 3rd century B.C., creating great havoc. By the time of the Roman conquest of Gaul, the Volcae tribes had already largely lost their tribal identities.

Volos (vô′lôs). [Also: **Bolos.**] Town in NE Greece, on the coast about 32 miles E of Larissa: main harbor of Thessaly. In the vicinity are many ancient ruins; nearby were the sites of Iolcus and Pagasae, ancient seaports, both of which have been identified as the starting point of the Argonauts, and also of ancient Demetrias.

Volscens (vol′skenz). Named in the *Aeneid* as a Latin chief, a captain of cavalry who discovered Nisus and Euryalus as they crept through the Rutulian lines at night during the war between Aeneas and the Latins. Firelight reflected from the helmet Euryalus had taken from Messapus, a Rutulian he had slain, and put on his own head. Volscens saw the light flash, ambushed the two friends,

killed Euryalus, and was in turn slain by Nisus.

Volscian Mountains (vol′shan). [Italian, **Monti Lepini.**] Group of mountains in Italy, SE of Rome. They are W of the main chain of the Apennines, and S of the Alban Hills. Elevation, about 4420 feet.

Volscians (vol′shanz). [Also: **Volsci.**] Ancient Italian people who dwelt in S Latium. They were noted for their long wars against Rome. They were subdued by Rome in the last part of the 4th century B.C. In the *Aeneid* the Volscians are named as ardent supporters of Turnus in his wars against Aeneas.

Volsiniensis, Lacus (vol-sin-i-en′sis, lā′kus). Latin name of **Bolsena, Lake of.**

Volsinii (vol-sin′i-ī). One of the twelve capitals of the Etruscan Confederacy, destroyed by the Romans in 280 B.C., thought by some scholars to have stood on the site of **Urbibentum,** modern Orvieto. The Romans later refounded it some miles to the SW as Volsinii Novi, modern Bolsena, on the shores of the Lacus Volsiniensis or Lake of Bolsena. (JJ)

Volterra (vōl-ter′rä). See **Volaterrae.**

Volturnus (vol-tér′nus). [Modern name, **Volturno.**] River in Italy which traverses Campania and flows into the Mediterranean Sea about 21 miles NW of Neapolis (Naples).

Volumen (vō-lū′men). Latin, meaning literally "something rolled up, a roll, scroll." From this comes our word volume, but the ancient meaning was different. Prose works were composed in columns on sheets of papyrus eight to twelve inches high and usually not over nine inches wide. These could be glued together to form a roll as long as desired, but for convenient handling they were usually not over 30–35 feet long. For storage they were rolled up, the reader unrolling to expose one or two columns at a time. Before the development of the *codex,* formed of folded sheets arranged in quires like a modern magazine, written on both sides and bound flat, the necessary preliminary to publishing an extended prose work was to divide it into sections corresponding in length to such rolls. These are the *volumina* of ancient prose writers. Latin writers often refer to these as *libri* (books), which is why we have come to speak of the "books" of Herodotus, Thucydides, Livy, Tacitus, etc. Shorter in length than modern books, they are equivalent to longish chapters of 30–40 pages of print. The volumen was uneconomical, being written on one side only; it was bulky, and therefore wasteful of storage space; and it was difficult to consult for reference. When the codex appeared its superiority ultimately led to its adoption as standard, and the volumen was gradually superseded (JJ)

Voluptas (vō-lup′tas). Sometimes known in Roman mythology as the goddess of pleasure.

Vortumnus (vōr-tum′nus). See **Vertumnus.**

Vulca (vul′ka). Name of an Etruscan sculptor in terra-cotta of Veii, who, according to Pliny the Elder, made terra-cotta statues for the Capitolium in Rome. (JJ)

Vulcan (vul′kan). In Roman mythology, the god of fire, especially volcanic fire. Originally an independent, and not benevolent, deity, he became completely identified with the Greek Hephaestus, and as such patron of metallurgy and handicrafts. See **Hephaestus.**

Vulcanalia (vul-ka-nā′li-a). Ancient Roman festival in honor of Vulcan, celebrated on Aug. 23 with games in the Flaminian circus, near the temple of the god, and with sacrifices of burnt fishes. It was a festival of appeasement, for the prevention of forest fires and of the burning of granaries.

Vulcania (vul-kā′ni-a). [Modern name, **Vulcano.**] In ancient geography, an island between the Sicilian coast and Aeolian Lipara. According to legend, it was Vulcan's workshop. It was an island of volcanic origin and was supposed by Vergil to be connected by subterranean channels with Mount Aetna. The island was also called, in ancient times, Hiera.

Vulso (vul′sō), **Cnaeus Manlius.** See **Manlius Vulso, Cnaeus.**

Vulture. Bird sacred to Ares.

Vuvos (vö′vôs). See **Cocytus.**

W

Wall of Aurelian (ô-rē′li-an, ô-rēl′yan). Fortified enclosure of ancient Rome, of irregular outline, extending beyond the Servian Wall, particularly on the N (where it includes the Pincian Hill) and on the E and S (where it takes in the Monte Testaccio), and on the right bank of the Tiber enclosing the Vatican and Janiculum hills. The wall was constructed by Aurelian 271–275 A.D., and was repaired by Honorius, Theodoric, Belisarius, and later rulers; its circuit remains almost unaltered, and measures about 13 miles. The masonry of the wall is for the most part of brick, interrupted occasionally by stonework. Some older pieces in *opus reticulatum* are incorporated. The exterior height is about 55 feet, and there are 381 rectangular towers.

Wasps, The. Comedy of Aristophanes, produced in 422 B.C. and awarded the second prize. It satirizes the Athenian love of litigation and mocks Athenian judicial processes by presenting a dog prosecuting another dog for stealing a cheese. Of the two judges sitting on the case, one, Philocleon ("Love-Cleon"), is mad. The other, Bdelycleon ("Hate-Cleon"), is wise. Aristophanes is attacking Cleon in this play as he did in others, for the cheese represents Sicily, which an Athenian general was sent to take. Cleon prosecuted the general for shady financial transactions which led to the failure of his expedition to take Sicily.

Weeping Philosopher. Name given to **Heraclitus.**

Widow of Ephesus. The best surviving specimen of a literary genre once widely popular in Greece and Rome, witty short stories, usually erotic and frequently obscene, known as the *Milesiae Fabulae* or Milesian Tales. In "The Widow of Ephesus," preserved as a fragment of Petronius' *Satyricon,* a soldier posted at a crucifixion to prevent the relatives of the criminal from removing the cadaver for burial, hears the sound of mourning in a tomb in a nearby cemetery. He investigates, and finds a distraught young widow weeping over the body of her husband, attended only by her maid. He offers consolation, but while his attention is focused on the widow the relatives take the body down from the cross and escape with it, making the soldier himself liable to the death penalty. The soldier and his new friend are equal to this emergency; they mount the corpse of the husband on the cross and go off happily. (JJ)

Winged Victory. See **Victory of Samothrace.**

Wingless Victory, Temple of. See **Athena Nike, Temple of.**

Women of Trachis (trā′kis). [Also: **Trachiniae.**] A tragedy by Sophocles, of uncertain date, which treats the great Heracles —a law unto himself. Side by side with his heroic exploits, his undisciplined passions function, bringing suffering to his intimates and ending in death to his wife, his herald, and himself.

The scene is before the house of Heracles at Trachis. Deianira quotes to her old nurse the proverb: that no one should be called happy or unhappy until he is dead. She recalls her fear of marriage when the river-god Achelous wooed her, and her joy when Heracles overcame him and became her husband. This soon turned to sorrow as Heracles left her for long periods while he engaged in dangerous adventures, and she has known no peace of mind since she married him. They are exiles in Trachis because he killed Iphitus, but where her brave husband is now she does not know. It is 15 months since he left home and she is frantic with worry. The nurse advises her to send her son Hyllus to search for his father. But Hyllus knows where Heracles is. He tells his mother that after serving Queen Omphale as a slave to atone for the murder of Iphitus, he is now free and is waging war against Eurytus in Euboea. This news frightens Deianira, for Heracles had told her that this war would be his last exploit; after 15 months he would either meet his death or spend the rest of his days in peace. Hyllus departs in search of Heracles. A chorus of women of Trachis enters and sings an ode commemorating the suffering and worry of Deianira in her husband's absence. They advise her not to give up hope. Deianira answers that any woman who has been a wife and mother will understand her fears. A messenger enters and announces that Lichas, herald of Heracles, has come. As he talks, Lichas enters accompanied by a group of young female captives. Deianira eagerly demands his

news. Heracles has been victorious, he says, and indicates that the young girls are captives he has sent home. In answer to questions, he assures Deianira he does not know the history of one beautiful young captive who has aroused Deianira's pity. He must return to Heracles, who is preparing to sacrifice to Zeus on Cenaeum. After Lichas departs the messenger tells Deianira that he lied: the young captive was the cause of the war. Heracles fell in love with her and when her father Eurytus refused to give her up Heracles made war on him and ruined his kingdom. When Lichas returns to see what messages Deianira has for Heracles she questions him again about the young captive. He persists in his first story. She begs for the truth. She knows, she says, that the heart of man can change in its affections, and that no man, much less Heracles, can deny the god of love. This is certainly not the first time his affections have strayed, and she would not blame either Heracles or Iole, the innocent victim, but she cannot forgive a liar. Lichas now admits that the captive is Iole, daughter of Eurytus, who so aroused Heracles' desire that he destroyed her father's kingdom to capture her. He had lied to spare her pain. Deianira says she is resigned to this state of affairs and prepares to send gifts to Heracles by Lichas. The Trachinian women sing an ode on the power of Aphrodite, in which they describe the thundering battle between Heracles and the river-god Achelous for the hand of Deianira. Deianira returns from the house and confides that she will not share her house with Heracles' concubine. She refuses to bear the title of wife to Heracles when all the world knows he is Iole's man. She tells the women of her plan to recapture his love. Nessus the centaur once carried Deianira on his back across the Evenus River. He attempted to ravish her but her screams brought quick action from Heracles. He shot Nessus. As Nessus was dying, he advised Deianira to collect the blood that clotted around the arrow, to preserve it in a casket, out of the sunlight, and to use it for a love charm if the affections of Heracles should ever be transferred to another woman. Deianira has resolved to use this love charm at last. She has rubbed it on a tunic which

fat, fāte, fär, fāre, errạnt; net, mē, hėr ardẹnt; pin, pīne; not, nōte, mŏve, nôr,

she will send to Heracles by Lichas, and which he will wear when he sacrifices to Zeus. Even as she tells the women of her scheme she wonders if it is an evil thing that she is doing. The women think it is worth a try, and she gives the garment, impregnated with the dried blood of the centaur, to Lichas, with instructions that it must not be exposed to the sun until Heracles is ready to wear it. Lichas departs and Deianira enters the house. She immediately hurries back and tells the women that a bit of wool she had used to rub the centaur's blood onto the tunic fell to the ground and was instantly consumed; purplish bubbles oozed up from the earth on which it had fallen. Greatly disturbed by this portent, Deianira blames herself for believing that the centaur, dying of Heracles' arrow, would have wanted to help her. She now remembers that the arrows of Heracles had been poisoned by the blood of the hydra and desperately fears the effects the tunic, smeared with blood poisoned by these arrows, will have on Heracles. If he dies, she vows to kill herself. The women try to comfort her. Hyllus returns. He accuses her of killing Heracles. He describes the sacrifice Heracles was about to offer when Lichas came with the tunic, and the terrible suffering Heracles endured when he donned the garment and it was warmed by the heat of the sacrificial fire. It seemed to cling to him and sting and burn his flesh. In his agony and rage he hurled Lichas, who had brought it, onto a rock in the sea. But Deianira shall see for herself, for Hyllus has brought his dying father to Trachis. Hyllus calls on the Furies to punish Deianira for killing the greatest man in the world. She silently enters the house, as Hyllus departs to bring in Heracles. As the women of the chorus pity Deianira, who had sought only to regain her husband's love, they hear the sound of weeping. The nurse runs out. Deianira is dead, she cries. After going all through the house saying goodby to the memories it held for her, she stabbed herself with a sword before the nurse could stop her. As the women mourn, Heracles is carried in on a litter. He cries out in agony and begs for the end of his sufferings. This is the worst torment he has had to endure, he cries.

What monsters, gods, and men could not do to him the perfidious daughter of Oeneus has accomplished. Now he weeps like a girl, he says, felled by a woman. He commands Hyllus to bring his mother out of the house that he may make her suffer with him. Hyllus defends Deianira; she was only trying to win back his love by a charm of Nessus; when she learned of its evil result she killed herself. On learning that his tunic was anointed with the blood of Nessus, Heracles knows he is doomed. With no more thought of Deianira, whose innocence he ignores, he tells Hyllus of certain oracles. It was foretold that no living creature could kill him; only one who had passed the border between life and death could slay him; it is Nessus, his dead enemy, whom he had killed, who is now killing him. He asks Hyllus to swear to carry him to Mount Oeta, build a pyre there, lay his suffering body on it, and set the pyre alight. Hyllus recoils in horror at the command to burn his father's living flesh, but agrees to carry Heracles to Mount Oeta and to build the pyre. Heracles then commands him to marry the captive Iole, for he does not want any man other than his son to possess the women he has possessed. Hyllus protests that he cannot marry the woman who has caused the death of his mother and father, and calls it an act of impiety which he cannot perform, but yields at last and agrees to do it; though it is repugnant to him he will carry out his father's wish. Attendants lift the litter and prepare to carry Heracles to Mount Oeta. Hyllus asks the forgiveness of men for what he is about to do and cries out that the gods look down unmoved on the tragedies of men; all the strange and awful things they have seen, he tells the women of Trachis, come from Zeus.

Wooden Horse, The or Trojan Horse. An immense figure of a horse, built by Epeus, with which the Greeks tricked the Trojans and so took Troy, according to Greek legend. As described by the epic poet Tryphiodorus (5th century A.D.), it was built of wood from the plain of Ida, which had also provided wood for the fleet in which Paris sailed when he abducted Helen. It was white, had a purple mane fringed with gold, eyes of sea-green beryl and red amethyst,

actǫr; up, lūte, pŭll; oi, oil; ou, out; ᴛн, then; ḍ as d or j, ş as s or sh, ṭ as t or ch, ẓ as z or zh.

and had rows of ivory teeth in its jaws. The harness was purple, inlaid with ivory and bronze. Under the hoofs were wheels for propelling it. It was left on the beach before the walls of Troy. Inside many Greeks were hidden. Included among them was Epeus, although he was quaking with fear, because he was the only one who knew how to operate the lock on the trapdoor by which the Greeks had entered the horse. Sinon, a Greek left behind for the purpose, persuaded the Trojans that the horse was an offering to Athena, and they hauled it inside the walls in spite of the warnings of Cassandra and Laocoön. Cassandra, prophesying the evil it would bring, foretold the deaths of Priam, Polyxena, and Agamemnon, but no one believed her. Laocoön hurled his spear into its side and uttered the warning (as recorded in the *Aeneid*), "Timeo Danaos et dona ferentes." (I fear the Greeks even when they bring gifts.) Laocoön was destroyed by a sea monster and the Trojans mistakenly interpreted this as a punishment for his doubts. Once inside the walls, the Trojans decked it with flowers and performed the Crane dance around it. This was a dance which Theseus did before the altars of Delos, and its winding movements imitated his path as he escaped from the labyrinth of the Minotaur. With joy and relief the Trojans offered sacrifices to the gods, but the fires on the altars fizzled out, the victims didn't burn, the smoke rose blood red from the fires, and statues of the gods wept. Nevertheless the Trojans refused to be warned and went wearily to bed. During the night the Greeks let themselves out of the horse, opened the gates of Troy to their comrades who had returned from behind the island of Tenedos at their signal, and from within the city the Greeks laid waste the Trojan citadel.

Works and Days. Chief work of the ancient Greek poet Hesiod; so named because it deals with the labors of the farmer, and the lucky and unlucky days for performing them.

X

Xanthippe (zan-thip′ē, -tip′-) or **Xantippe** (zan-tip′ē). Wife of the Greek philosopher Socrates, proverbial for her shrewish disposition.

Xanthippus (zan-thip′us, -tip′-). Father of Pericles. He was of democratic tendencies, though of aristocratic family, and was partly responsible for the ostracism of Hipparchus (not Hipparchus the son of Pisistratus, but a kinsman) and Megacles. A few years later (484 B.C.) he was himself ostracized at the instigation of his opponents. However, when Athens was threatened by the Persian invasion under Xerxes he was recalled (480 B.C.), and named as one of the Athenian commanders in the war. Following the victory of the Greeks over the Persians at Mycale (479 B.C.), in which he commanded the Athenian fleet, he sailed to the Hellespont (478 B.C.) and captured the fortress of Sestos. After the Persian War he shared the direction of the affairs of Athens with Aristides and Themistocles. About 472 B.C. he joined with Aristides and others to bring about the ostracism of Themistocles.

Xanthippus. Spartan mercenary commander. He organized the Carthaginian army in the First Punic War, and won a victory over Regulus in 255 B.C.

Xanthus (zan′thus). In Homeric legend (*Iliad*), one of a pair of immortal horses. His mate was Balius. They were the children of Podarge the Harpy, and Zephyrus the West Wind. Poseidon gave them to Peleus the father of Achilles. Achilles loaned them to Patroclus and they wept when he was slain by Hector. Temporarily endowed with speech by Hera when Achilles in his turn yoked them for war, Xanthus promised him a safe return from this battle but foretold that soon thereafter he would be slain by a god and a hero.

Xanthus. In Homeric legend *(Iliad),* a Trojan, the son of Phaenops. He was slain by Diomedes.

Xanthus. In Homeric legend, the name given by the gods to the river-god of the Scamander River in the Troad. When Zeus at last gave permission to the gods to interfere in the Trojan War as they chose, Xanthus at first took no part. Then, horrified by the slaughter Achilles was wreaking, Xanthus asked him to kill on the plain and not to clog up his waters with Trojan corpses. Achilles scornfully rejected his plea. Then Xanthus rose up in anger, flooded his banks and pursued Achilles with tree trunks and boulders tumbling in his swollen waters and sought to drown Achilles. As the river raged after Achilles, Hera, alarmed for him, called on her son Hephaestus to set the river afire. He did so, and Xanthus surrendered before the holocaust, promised to withdraw from the battle and never to reënter it, no matter what happened. Xanthus had only entered the fray in the first place to protect his clear flowing streams from the pollution of Achilles' victims, which in their great numbers were strangling the river.

Xanthus. In ancient geography, a city in Lycia, Asia Minor, situated on the Scamander (or Xanthus) River near its mouth. It was besieged and destroyed by the Persian general Harpagus c545 B.C., and again by the Romans under Brutus, in 43 or 42 B.C. Important antiquities were discovered (c1838) there by Fellows. Among them is the so-called Nereid monument, a cella with a beautiful Ionic peristyle, dating from the middle of the 4th century B.C. The chief frieze, on the basement, represents a battle of cavalry and foot soldiers; the second frieze illustrates a siege; the third frieze, on the cella, is sculptured with sacrificial and feasting scenes; the fourth frieze, on the entablature, shows hunting episodes and homage to an offical personage. The principal parts of the monument have been transported to the British Museum.

Xanthus. [Modern name, **Koca.**] In ancient geography, a river of Lycia, Asia Minor, rising in the Taurus Mountains and flowing S to empty into the Mediterranean Sea.

Xenia (zē'ni-a̱). Epithet of Athena, meaning "Hospitable." There was a sanctuary of Athena Xenia at Sparta.

Xenoclea (zē-nō̱-klē'a̱). In Greek legend, a priestess of Apollo at Delphi. Heracles applied to her for an oracle to cure his disease, after the slaying of Iphitus. Because he had not been purified she refused to prophesy for him. Enraged, Heracles seized the tripod on which she sat and declared he would carry it off and establish his own oracle. Apollo arrived to protect his oracle and struggled with Heracles. Zeus intervened with his thunderbolt to part the contestants, commanded the oracle to give Heracles answers, and persuaded him and Apollo to become friends.

Xenocrates (zē-nok'ra̱-tēz). Platonic philosopher; born at Chalcedon 393 B.C.; died 314 B.C. He went to Athens in his youth where he became successively the pupil of Aeschines and Plato. He accompanied Plato on his visit to Syracuse, 361 B.C. He was a friend of Aristotle and when the latter was in Macedon succeeded Speusippus as head of the Academy, over which he presided for 25 years (339–314 B.C.). He served as a member of embassies to Philip II of Macedon and to Antipater. He refused to accept Athenian citizenship when it was later offered him because he disapproved the Macedonian influence in Athens. In his philosophy he closely followed Platonic ideas.

Xenophanes (zē-nof'a̱-nēz). Greek philosopher; born at Colophon, Asia Minor, c570 B.C.; died c480 B.C. He was a disciple of Anaximander. Driven from his homeland by the Persian invasion of 546 B.C., he traveled widely about the world as a rhapsode. He went to Italy, where he settled at Elea, 540 B.C., and founded the Eleatic school of philosophy. He is among the earliest critics of Greek religious tradition, especially those traditions which clothed the gods in the weaknesses of men. If horses and lions, he said, could make images of gods they would fashion them in their own likenesses. He cried out against the "lies" of Homer and Hesiod, who made the gods thieves and adulterers; rejected mysticism; and proclaimed his concept of a single supreme god who was not made in the image of man and who controlled the universe through thought. He was as scornful of the adulation accorded athletic victors as he was of the unworthy gods of the poets, likening the accomplishments of the athletes to the unthinking animals who perform labors of great magnitude. Fragments of his elegies and his *Satires* have been preserved.

Xenophon (zen′ō-fon). Greek soldier, historian, and essayist; born at Athens, c430 B.C.; died after 357 B.C. He was a son of Gryllus, of aristocratic background and sympathies. He was a disciple of Socrates. This came about, according to a popular story, in the following manner. In his youth Xenophon was walking in the streets of Athens and was stopped by the philosopher. Socrates asked him where various goods might be secured. The youth answered politely. Then Socrates asked, "And where can you get high-minded men?" Xenophon was unable to answer. "Then follow me," said Socrates. Xenophon did as he was bid, and remained ever after an admirer and defender of Socrates. However, his contact with him must have been of short duration. Proxenus, a Boeotian friend of Xenophon, invited him to join him in an expedition with Cyrus the Younger, brother of Artaxerxes II, the Great King of Persia. Socrates advised him to consult the oracle of Delphi, because he disapproved of the plan. Xenophon did so, but since he had made up his mind to secure the wealth and honor the expedition seemed to promise, he agreed to go on the expedition as a mercenary. At the outset the 10,000 Greeks in Cyrus' army did not know the true destination of their march, and when they learned that they were to fight the Great King it was too late to turn back. The battle was fought at Cunaxa, in Babylonia, 401 B.C. Cyrus was killed, and his oriental troops were defeated, but the Greeks were victorious in their sector. Artaxerxes wished only to rid himself of the 10,000 well-trained, menacing mercenaries. He offered them a guide for the journey to the sea. On the way the generals of the Greeks, as well as their captains, were treacherously slain on the order of their Persian guide Tissaphernes. The Greeks found themselves alone and leaderless in the heart of hostile country, over a thousand miles from Greece. With great presence of mind Xenophon, who had been serving without rank, rallied their spirits, scorned surrender,

and proposed the election of new officers to lead them to the sea. He was elected one of the generals and thereafter guided their march, through unknown and dangerous lands, in the face of barbarous enemies, until the glorious day early in 400 B.C. when those in the vanguard raised the joyous cry, "Thalassa!" (The sea!). From the heights above Trapezus they looked down on the Euxine Sea. Here Xenophon gave up his command of the 10,000. He thought of establishing a colony on the Phasis River but abandoned the idea when his life was threatened by those who opposed it. The whole heroic and incredible journey of the 10,000 was described by Xenophon in the *Anabasis* (the Up-going, i.e., The expedition up from the coast). Simple and direct, in parts almost a day-to-day record of events, the work has great immediacy as a description of stirring events by one of the chief participants. It was written much later, after he had served various Spartan harmosts and the Spartan king Agesilaus, who became his great friend. In 394 B.C. Athens declared war on Sparta. Xenophon was accused of "Laconism" and condemned. Thereafter he accompanied Agesilaus at Coronea in the same year. Afterward he retired to an estate at Scillus near Olympia, given to him by the Spartans, and spent the next 20 years in retirement.

In this period he wrote the *Anabasis;* the *Cyropaedia,* an idealized biography of Cyrus the Great in which Xenophon, sacrificing the truth, expressed his ideas on the education of a ruler; the *Memorabilia,* a defense and description of the life of Socrates as he remembered it, which evolves as a portrait of a man rather than a study of a philosopher. Other works were a *Symposium,* in which he sought perhaps to correct certain details and atmospheres of Plato's work of the same name; *Ways and Means,* concerning means of raising money for Athens without resorting to tribute; *Hiero,* a dialogue on government between Hiero of Syracuse and the poet Simonides; *Agesilaus,* a eulogy of his friend; *Hellenica,* a history in which he continues the history of Thucydides, though without that writer's lack of bias and without his accuracy, from 411 B.C. to the end of the Peloponnesian Wars, and on to the battle of Mantinea (362 B.C.). In this work Xenophon criticizes Sparta, which he had always admired greatly, for arrogance, and noted that punishment follows injustice. He also wrote *The Oeconomicus* which gives advice on household management and outlines the duties of husband and wife; essays on hunting and horsemanship, and other works. After Sparta's defeat by Thebes at Leuctra, 371 B.C., he was forced to leave Scillus and went to Corinth, where he spent his last years. In the meantime he had educated his sons, Gryllus and Diodorus, in the finest tradition. An alliance between Sparta and Athens against Thebes removed the old stigma of "Laconism"; the sons joined the Athenian army, and Gryllus fell at Mantinea, lauded for his courage. The image of Xenophon that comes to us across the centuries is of a noble, honest, heroic, and somehow endearing man, who did what he thought just without ambition, and who left in the *Anabasis* a stirring record of one of the most thrilling Greek exploits outside the proper history of Greece.

Xerxes I (zėrk'sēz). [Old Persian, **Khsayarsha**; in the Bible, **Ahasuerus.**] Son of Darius the Great and Atossa, born c519 B.C.; assassinated 465 B.C. Before Darius became king of Persia he had a wife and several sons. On his accession to the throne, following the death of Cambyses and the murder of the False Smerdis, Darius also took as part of his kingly possessions the wives of Cambyses who had fallen to Smerdis. Atossa was one of these, and came to be one of the most influential of the wives of Darius. To her and Darius, Xerxes was born as their first son and, according to Herodotus, Atossa was determined that he should be the heir rather than his older half-brothers, born before Darius was king and to another wife. It was finally decided, on the advice of the Greek exile Demaratus, that the sons born before the father was king or heir apparent, had no claim to the throne as they were the children of a private person; only the sons born to the king and the wife he had after he became king were legitimate heirs. Demaratus cited a similar instance in Spartan history in support of his point, which he had every wish of making in order to please the queen. Thus it was, that when Darius

was preparing a punitive expedition against Greece after the battle of Marathon, he appointed Xerxes as his heir. But Herodotus, who tells this story, adds the comment that with or without the suggestion of Demaratus Xerxes would have been named heir, because of the great influence of Atossa. On the death of Darius, Xerxes duly succeeded him (485 B.C.). At this time revolt had broken out in Egypt, and it seemed to Xerxes more important to put it down than to make an expedition into Greece. In the year following therefore, he marched against Egypt, subdued the country, and crushed it under a more tyrannical rule than that under which it had existed in the time of Darius. In the meantime, Mardonius, cousin of Xerxes, was aflame to win glory for himself, and to this end continually pressed on Xerxes the necessity to punish the Greeks, and at the same time he pointed out the advantages to Persia of extending her sway over Greece. To add to these persuasions, the Pisistratidae came as exiles from Athens to the Persian court and urged Xerxes to march against Greece, in the hope that they would be restored to power in Athens; and envoys from Thessaly also came and invited him into Greece and promised him all assistance should he do so. Xerxes consulted with his generals, and all save his uncle Artabanus agreed that a punitive expedition should be undertaken. They did so out of fear, according to Herodotus. Artabanus advised caution; he pointed out the difficulties; he reminded Xerxes that the lightning strikes the tallest tree, that the gods smite the most powerful men. Moreover, he advised him not to underestimate the Greeks. Xerxes scornfully rejected his advice as cowardly, and in his turn reminded Artabanus of the great deeds his forbears had accomplished with boldness. The decision to make war was made. But on thinking it over Xerxes decided that the advice of Artabanus was good, and he changed his plans. Next day he announced the cancellation of the expedition. All the generals were delighted, save Mardonius. However, according to Herodotus, a vision appeared to Xerxes in a dream and seemed to threaten him with destruction if he did not proceed against the Greeks. He discussed his dream with Artabanus, who tried to ex-

actor; up, lūte, pull; oi, oil; ou, out; ᴛH, then; ḏ as d or j, ş as s or sh, ṭ as t or ch, ẓ as z or zh.

plain it away, but when the figure of the dream appeared to Artabanus himself, and threatened him for persuading Xerxes to abandon the expedition, Xerxes and Artabanus concluded that the war on Greece was demanded by the gods.

Preparation now went forward with vigor in the following years. Four years were spent in gathering the host, the largest that had ever been assembled. In addition to a huge land army a fleet was gathered. At last all was in readiness, provisions were stored at strategic points on the route, beasts of burden were collected, cables for bridges were prepared, and the armies were gathered at Sardis. Xerxes sent heralds throughout Greece, except to Athens and Sparta, demanding earth and water as tokens of submission to his rule, for he thought surely they would send the tokens through fear of his overwhelming force. He then (Spring, 480 B.C.) proceeded toward Abydos on the Hellespont, where he had caused a bridge of boats to be constructed so that his vast army could the more easily cross into Europe. Some say that when he set out from Sardis for Abydos there was an eclipse of the sun, a token of ill omen for the Persians. Others say this omen occurred on his departure from Susa for Sardis. In either case, his priests, when called on to interpret the omen, said it foretold destruction for the Greeks, for the sun was the oracle of the Greeks, but the moon was the oracle of the Persians. Xerxes rode forth with his baggage bearers, beasts of burden, polyglot army and their camp followers, spearmen, sacred horses, and an empty chariot of the Persian god Ormazd drawn by eight milk-white steeds. The chariot was empty because it would have been impious for a mortal to ride in the god's car. On the way to Abydos the army passed through Troy, where Xerxes sacrificed 1000 oxen to Trojan Athena and poured libations to the heroes who fell in the Trojan War. At Abydos he reviewed his army from a white marble throne that he caused to be set on a hill outside the city. As he saw the whole plain and the strait filled with his army and his ships, he first congratulated himself and then wept. To the question of Artabanus as to why he wept he replied that it was out of pity for the shortness of man's

life, for he suddenly realized (so says Herodotus) that of all his tremendous host not one would be alive in a hundred years. Artabanus was still full of fears as to the outcome of the venture, and warned Xerxes of two great dangers: the land, that would not support the needs of the great army; and the sea, which had no harbors big enough to protect such a fleet in case of storms. Herodotus, who gives these conversations, could invent them after the fact, for it did indeed turn out that Xerxes' army, as other armies in later times that pushed too far from their base of supplies, suffered from lack of food and water; and parts of the great fleet were destroyed by storms. But that was in the future, and Xerxes was unmoved by his fears. After offering a libation from a golden goblet to the Hellespontine waters, or perhaps to the sun, he ordered his host to cross at Abydos. The crossing lasted seven uninterrupted days and nights. When the whole army was across a prodigy occurred: a mare gave birth to a hare. This could only mean, says Herodotus, that Xerxes would lead a great host against Greece but would have to run for his life to regain the point from which he had set out. But this omen as well as others was disregarded.

According to Herodotus, the number in the Persian train, including non-combatants and camp-followers, was 1,700,000. Later scholars estimate the number of fighting men at 180,000. Soldiers from all parts of the Persian empire and their allies made up the army. In the fleet, it was said, were 1207 ships furnished by the Phoenicians, Egyptians, Cyprians, Ionians, Lycians, and many others. Of these, those of the Phoenicians were superior in quality and numbers. Demaratus the exiled Spartan king accompanied Xerxes on the expedition, and was questioned concerning the valor of the Greeks, and whether they would resist the Persians. Xerxes thought they would not. Demaratus assured him on more than one occasion that the Spartans, at least, would never submit, and that if there were only 1000 Spartans they would nevertheless take the field. Xerxes laughed at what he considered to be wild words, and continued his march along the coast of Thrace, crossing the Strymon River and forcing the nations along the way to join his march. Near the promontory of Athos, across which a ditch had been cut for the passage of his ships, Xerxes separated from the fleet, and the army continued to Pieria, where the heralds he had sent out to demand earth and water from the Greek cities returned. They brought back tokens of submission from many, among them the Thessalians, Locrians, Achaeans of Phthiotis, Thebans, and all the Boeotians except the Plataeans and Thespians. According to Herodotus, the Greeks who did not give tokens of submission took the following oath: "From all those of Greek blood who delivered themselves up to the Persians without necessity, when their affairs were in good condition, we will take a tithe of their goods, and give it to the god at Delphi." Xerxes had sent no heralds to Athens and Sparta, for when his father Darius had done so his heralds to those cities were slain in defiance of the sacred laws protecting the persons of heralds. Although the Persian force was directed in name against the Athenians, the Greeks understood that it was in truth directed against them all, and it was for this reason that many determined to resist the Persian advance. But now that the Persian force was near, the hearts of many failed. Oracles predicted doom and allies deserted, but some of the Greeks maintained their courage. The Persian army reached Thermopylae and the fleet reached Cape Sepias off Euboea without suffering any battle losses. At Cape Sepias a violent storm, caused, the Athenians said, by their prayers to their kinsman Boreas, rose and destroyed 400 of the Persian ships, unnumbered men, and rich treasure. At Thermopylae Xerxes learned the truth of Demaratus' statements concerning the valor of the Spartans, for although the forces of Xerxes won the pass, it was only after the loss of thousands of Persians in the face of the resistance offered by Leonidas and his 300 Spartans and 700 Thespians. After the battle at Thermopylae and an inconclusive sea fight at Artemisium, the Persian army marched down the valley of the Cephissus River and on to Athens. At the approach of the Persians most of the Athenians withdrew with their families to the island of Salamis. A few took refuge on the citadel (Acropolis) and prepared to resist the Persians. They attacked the citadel, took it, massacred the defenders, and set fire to the temples on the Acropolis and burned Athens. Thus Xerxes had made himself master of Athens and carried out the vengeance his father had intended. But the war was not over. Themistocles the Athenian general, by a stratagem compelled the Greek allies who still had the will to resist to meet the Persian fleet at Salamis. As Xerxes watched from a hill overlooking the bay, he saw his fleet suffer disastrous defeat (480 B.C.). He now feared his restless Ionian subjects would break down his bridges and prevent his return into Asia if he did not fly at once, but to cover up his plans he continued warlike preparations against Salamis. However, he consulted his generals as to whether he should stay and conquer Greece or return to Persia. Only Artemisia the female admiral, of all his advisers, advised him to return to Persia and allay the fears of his people that would arise when they learned of the defeat at Salamis. On her advice and at the urging of Mardonius, he left the latter in charge of a large land force and hurriedly set out for the Hellespont. Arrived there, he found that storms had destroyed his bridge of boats, but his force was now so small that he was able to embark in ships and so return to Asia. On his return to Susa, weakened by the losses his arms had suffered and later by the defeat of the forces he left behind, at Plataea and Mycale (479 B.C.), he became involved with court intrigues. The power of Persia had been so severely weakened that it never fully recovered. Xerxes was assassinated in 465 B.C. in a palace conspiracy. Ahasuerus, the king of Persia who appears in the Book of Esther in the Old Testament, is identified with Xerxes I.

Xuthus (zö′thus). According to Greek tradition, a son of Hellen and the nymph Orseïs, and the brother of Dorus and Aeolus. He fled to Athens from Thessaly and there married Creusa, daughter of King Erechtheus, unaware that she had born a son to Apollo. At the shrine of Apollo in Delphi, whither he and Creusa had gone to seek the god's help because they had no children, Xuthus was told that the first person he met would be his son. As he left the sanctuary he met Ion, a young priest of Apollo, and claimed him as his son. Creusa learned, with the assistance of Apollo's priestess, that this was the son she had borne to the god and abandoned, but it was commanded that Xuthus should never know this. Xuthus was to consider Ion as a gift from the oracle at Delphi. Later, Xuthus and Creusa had two sons, Achaeus and Dorus. After the death of Erechtheus, Xuthus, with the consent of the chief claimants to the throne, appointed Cecrops to succeed Erechtheus. His decision was unpopular and he was banished from Athens and died in exile. Through his sons, Xuthus was the ancestor of the Achaeans and the Ionians.

Xypete (zī'pe̦-tē). One of the demes or villages of Attica, on the highway from Phalerum to Athens, in which was a temple of Hera in Xypete, sacked and burned by the Persians in 480 B.C., and thereafter left in ruin as a reminder of the impiety of the Persians; still lacking doors and roof, it was seen in the second century A.D. by the traveler Pausanias. The cult continued active in its ruined sanctuary; it appears in 5th-century B.C. financial audits, and possessed a statue of Hera by the sculptor Alcmaenes. (JJ)

—Z—

Zacynthus (za̦-sin'thus). Island of the Ionian group, Greece, about eight miles S of Cephallenia. It has often been visited by earthquakes. According to legend, Zacynthus was a companion of Heracles. He was entrusted with the care of the cattle taken from Geryon, and on his way to take them to Thebes was bitten by a serpent and died on this island in the Ionian Sea which afterward bore his name. The island was a part of the kingdom of Odysseus. It was originally colonized by Achaeans, who roamed the seas and, some say, founded Saguntum in Spain long before the Trojan War. Its position between the Peloponnesus and routes to the west made it an important station. It became a member of the Athenian Confederacy.

Zagreus (zā'grē̦-us). Divine child of Orphic mythology, later identified with Dionysus. The story is that Zeus, in serpent form, begat Zagreus on Persephone, and intended to bestow on him unlimited power. He set the Curetes to guard his cradle in a cave on Crete, and they clashed their weapons about him even as they had done for Zeus in his infancy. Hera, out of jealousy, induced the Titans to do away with the boy. They daubed their faces with gypsum to disguise themselves and came to Zagreus in the night. First they beguiled him to them with such toys as golden apples, a bull-roarer, dice, and tufts of wool, then they set upon him to kill him. Zagreus attempted to save himself by a series of rapid transformations. He changed himself into a lion, serpent, tiger, and bull, but the Titans grasped him firmly in this last transformation, tore him apart, and devoured him. Athena managed to save the child's heart. Some say she put it into a gypsum figure and breathed life into it, thus making Zagreus immortal; others say Zeus swallowed the heart of Zagreus and thus was enabled to rebeget Zagreus in the new Dionysus, son of Semele.

Zakynthos (zä'kēn-thôs). See **Zacynthus**.

Zaleucus (za̦-lö'kus). Traditional lawgiver of the Epizephyrian Locrians in Italy; fl. about the 7th century B.C. His laws were adopted by the city of Thurii, founded by the Athenians, 443 B.C.

Zama (zā'ma̦). In ancient geography, a town in N Africa, about 85 miles SW of Carthage. A decisive victory was gained near it in 202 B.C. by the Romans under Scipio Africanus over Hannibal. It ended the Second Punic War.

Zancle (zang'klē). In ancient geography, a town in the NE corner of Sicily, situated on a sickle-shaped harbor that gave the city its name (from the Greek word for sickle). The ancient coins of the city (later named

Messene) were engraved with a sickle, representing the harbor, within which a dolphin floated. The town commanded the narrow strait between Italy and Sicily. Originally occupied by pirates, it was colonized by Chalcidian Greeks in the 8th century B.C. According to tradition, when the Messenians were defeated by the Spartans in the Second Messenian War those who could escape fled the country. Many of them went to Sicily at the invitation of the tyrant of Rhegium. They defeated the Zancleans in battle, but refused to kill them when they fled to their altars as suppliants. Instead, they exchanged pledges with them to dwell together in peace, raised a temple of Heracles, and changed the name of the city to Messene (c664 B.C.), after their own country.

Zante (zan′tē). Another name for **Zacynthus** (q.v.).

Zariaspa (za-ri-as′pa). Another name for **Bactra,** capital of the ancient country of Bactria.

Zea (tse′ä). See **Ceos.**

Zela (zē′la). In ancient geography, a town in Pontus, Asia Minor, at or near what is now Zile, a farm-market town in Turkey. It was the scene of a victory of Mithridates VI over the Romans c67 B.C., and was famous for the victory by Caesar over Pharnaces II in 47 B.C. It was with reference to this battle that Caesar wrote the famous *"Veni, vidi, vici"* (I came, I saw, I conquered).

Zeleia (ze-lī′a). Named in the *Iliad* as a city at the foot of Mount Ida in the Troad. It was the home of the Trojan archer Pandarus.

Zeno (zē′nō). [Also: **Zeno of Elea.**] Greek philosopher of the Eleatic school, 5th century B.C. He was the favorite pupil of Parmenides. He went to Athens in his fortieth year, during the early youth of Socrates, and resided there many years. He is especially celebrated for his arguments designed to prove the inconsistency in the concepts of divisibility. Zeno's paradoxes were notable advances in the theory of infinity. The best known is the paradox of Achilles and the turtle: If the turtle be given a start, Achilles can never catch him since by the time Achilles reaches the point where the tortoise was the tortoise will have moved, and so on. Another has to do with an arrow in flight; at any moment the arrow occupies a given position and is therefore at rest; it is thus at rest during the whole flight. His doctrines are referred to in the *Parmenides* of Plato.

Zeno. Greek philosopher; born at Citium, in Cyprus, 335 B.C.; died 263 B.C. He was the founder of the Stoic school of philosophy. He studied philosophy under the Cynics at Athens, and founded his school, eclectic in its efforts to reach a consistent system, there at the Stoa Poikile ("Painted Porch"), whence its name. See **Stoics.**

Zeno. Epicurean philosopher at Athens; born at Sidon, in Phoenicia, c150 B.C.; died c78 B.C. He was an instructor of Cicero.

Zenodotus (ze̱-nod′o̱-tus). Alexandrian grammarian and critic; born at Ephesus; fl. in the 3rd century B.C. He was the first head of the Library at Alexandria. He was one of the early scholars to whom we owe our traditional explanation of the works of Homer. He studied the manuscripts of Homer in the Library, omitting lines which he considered spurious or later additions, and giving new interpretations to others. He was responsible for dividing the *Iliad* and the *Odyssey* into 24 books.

Zephyrus (zef′i-rus). [Also: **Zephyr.**] In Greek mythology, a personification of the west wind, poetically regarded as the mildest and gentlest of all the winds. He was the son of Eos and Astraeus, or of Aeolus. By the Harpy Podarge he was the father of the two marvelous horses, Balius and Xanthus, that Achilles took with him to the Trojan War. Zephyrus married the nymph Chloris, who bore him a son, Carpus. The Romans identified Favonius, their west wind, with Zephyrus.

Zetes (zē′tēs). An Argonaut, the winged son of Boreas and Orithyia, and the twin of Calais. See **Boreadae.**

Zethus (zē′thus). In Greek legend, a son of Antiope and Zeus and twin brother of Amphion. When the twins built the walls of Thebes Zethus boasted of his great strength in placing the huge stones, but Amphion, with his lyre, played so beautifully that the stones slid into place by themselves. According to some accounts, Zethus married Aëdon and was the father of Itylus. According to others, he married Thebe, from

actọr; up, lūte, pu̇ll; oi, oil; ou, out; ᵺн, then; ḏ as d or j, ș as s or sh, ṭ as t or ch, z̧ as z or zh.

whom the city of Thebes took its name. See
Amphion.

Zeus (zōs). The chief of the Olympian gods,
whose power is greater than that of all the
other gods together. The dual attitude of the
Greeks toward their gods is brilliantly illuminated by their contradictory concepts of
Zeus. He is "The Father of gods and men,"

ZEUS
Red-figured Greek psykter, Pan Painter,
c490 B.C. *Munich*

the supreme ruler who grasped kingly power
and from whom the power of mortal kings
is derived, as he gave the golden scepter
fashioned by Hephaestus to Pelops as a sign
of kingship. He is Cosmetas (*Orderer*),
who presides over the state as well as over
the family unit. He punishes crime, avenges
wrongs, protects suppliants. All the good
or evil that falls to the lot of man is distributed by the impartial hand of Zeus, who
draws the lot of man from two urns placed
at his side and weighs out man's fate on
golden scales. He is a god of the sky (his
name is derived from a word meaning
"bright sky"), who is considered to dwell
on all mountain tops, but whose special home
is Olympus. Thus he is "Olympian Zeus,"
the lord of heaven, in whose honor the Olym-

pic Games were celebrated at Olympia in
Elis. He wields the thunderbolt and the
lightning, he sends the sudden storm. He
is "The Cloud-gatherer" who drops the
beneficent rain, brightens the skies, or
breathes favorable winds as needed. He
is the founder and patron of all the institutions of civilization and religion, and the
maintainer of justice, law, and order. He is
the giver of oracles, with an ancient and
revered shrine at Dodona, at Olympia, and
other places. Because his will is not always
properly understood by mortals he is called
"Lord of the crooked counsel." In contrast to the great civilizing and ethical force
exerted by the worship of Zeus that pervaded
every phase of life, is the Zeus of the Greek
myths, abundantly endowed with the frail-
ties and appetites of mortals, and immor-
tally capable of indulging them. It is probable that the legends grew up locally to
connect specific local gods or heroes or
families with the great god Zeus. As the
stories were accepted throughout Greece
they were woven into the bewilderingly complex series of relationships, with incidents to
explain them, that present Zeus in two violently contrasting aspects—the god to whom
all honor and devotion was owed and given
as the supreme ruler of gods and men, and
the supermortal who could perform, on a
lavish scale, all that imperfect mortal men
would like to do.

Zeus was the son of Cronus and Rhea,
hence his surname Cronides (*Son of Cronus*).
An oracle of Gaea had foretold that Cronus
would be overthrown by one of his children,
even as he had overthrown his father
Uranus. To prevent the fulfillment of the
oracle, Cronus swallowed his children as
soon as they were born, first Hestia, then
Demeter, Hera, Hades, and Poseidon in
succession. When the time neared for Zeus
to be born Rhea resolved to forestall Cronus.
The Arcadians say Rhea went to Mount
Lycaeus, in Arcadia, and there at a place
called Cretea, where no living creature casts
a shadow, she gave birth to Zeus. The infant god was washed in the Neda River and
then conveyed by Gaea to the nymphs of
Crete. The Messenians claim his birthplace
was on Mount Ithome in their land. Thebes,
Aegium in Achaea, Olenus in Aetolia, Mount

fat, fāte, fär, fāre, errạnt; net, mē, hėr ardẹnt; pin, pīne; not, nōte, mŏve, nôr,

Ida in the Troad, and so many others that, as Pausanias justly says, it would be impossible to name them all, also claimed to be the birthplace of the god. The generally accepted account is that he was born in a cave on Mount Ida, in Crete, or in the cave of Dicte there. When Cronus demanded his last child, Rhea gave him a stone wrapped in swaddling clothes, which he promptly swallowed. The infant Zeus was handed over to the nymphs Adrastea and Ida, daughters of Melisseus. They fed him on honey and the milk of the goat Amalthea, and the Curetes crashed their shields to drown out the infant's cries so that Cronus would not discover how he had been tricked. When Zeus grew up he sought the Titaness Metis who, according to some accounts, was his first wife. She advised him of a potion by which he could compel Cronus to disgorge his brothers and sisters. Zeus disguised himself as the cup-bearer of Cronus and gave him the potion. Hestia, Demeter, Hera, Hades, and Poseidon were cast up, as was the stone Rhea had given Cronus in place of Zeus. The stone was set up at Delphi, and was called Omphalos (*Navel*), as being the center of the earth. Zeus, with his brothers as allies, made war on Cronus and the Titans. After the war had dragged on for ten years without a decision, Gaea told Zeus he would defeat Cronus and the Titans if he released the Cyclopes and the Hecatonchires (Briareus, Cottus, Gyges) whom Cronus had locked up in Tartarus. Zeus went to Tartarus and killed Campe the jaileress. He took her keys and freed the Cyclopes and the Hecatonchires. The Cyclopes forged the thunderbolt for him, gave a cap of invisibility to Hades, and a trident to Poseidon. With their help Cronus and the Titans were overcome, and all save Atlas were hurled into Tartarus, where the Hecatonchires were set to guard them. Having made themselves masters, Zeus, Hades, and Poseidon cast lots into a helmet to divide the rule of the universe. In the lot-drawing Zeus drew dominion over the heavens, Poseidon over the sea, and Hades over the Underworld. The earth and Olympus were to remain common to all. Because of superior divine endowment, Zeus became chief of the three rulers. He decreed that the oaths of the gods must be sworn by the waters of the Styx, because Styx and her children had voluntarily come to his aid in the war with the Titans. Some say Zeus was harsh in establishing himself as supreme ruler, and that his harshness extended to mankind. He denied them the gift of fire lest they make themselves the equal of the gods, and punished Prometheus, who in his pity for vulnerable and weak man stole fire from heaven and gave it to him. Zeus commanded Hephaestus to bind Prometheus to a crag in the Caucasus, where an eagle daily gnawed at his liver, which was renewed each night. Hera, Poseidon, Apollo, and the other gods, except peaceful Hestia, conspired against Zeus. They overcame him as he slept and bound him with thongs tied with a hundred knots. Thetis the Nereid called the hundred-handed Briareus to untie the knots and secured his release. As leader in the conspiracy, Zeus scourged Hera, and he punished Apollo and Poseidon by sending them to serve Laomedon, king of Troy. The other gods were forgiven on their promise never again to rebel against Zeus.

Some say Gaea, who had helped Zeus overthrow Cronus and the Titans with her advice, was enraged at the punishment Zeus meted out to them and brought forth a race of Giants to war against him. Others say the Giants waged war on Zeus because they were angered at his harsh treatment of their brothers the Titans. Because of an oracle that none of the Giants would perish at the hands of the gods, Zeus sent Athena to find Heracles and bring him to the aid of the gods. He ordered Helius, Selene, and Eos to dim their light, and so stop the battle, while Athena and Heracles searched for a magic herb that would render Heracles invulnerable. When they found it, Athena led Heracles to the Phlegraean Plain, which some say was in Chalcidice and some say was in Italy, where he did valiant service in routing the Giants. Gaea was more enraged than ever, and brought forth Typhon in the Corycian Cave in Cilicia. Typhon attacked the gods in heaven and they fled in terror to Egypt, transforming themselves into various animals to escape his fiery breath; Zeus took the form of a ram, but when Athena accused him of cowardice he assumed his own shape,

actọr; up, lūte, pŭll; oi, oil; ou, out; ŦH, then; ḏ as d or j, ş as s or sh, ṭ as t or ch, ẓ as z or zh.

hurled his thunderbolts at Typhon and struck him with an adamantine sickle. He struggled with Typhon on Mount Casius in Syria and was overcome. Typhon wrested the sickle from him and cut the sinews of the hands and feet of Zeus. In a helpless condition, Zeus was carried off to the cave in Cilicia by Typhon, who gave him to the dragon Delphyne to guard, and who hid the sinews of Zeus in a bearskin. Hermes and Pan stole into the cave, found the sinews of Zeus, and replaced them on his limbs. With renewed strength he sought out and attacked Typhon. He pursued him to Mount Nysa, where the Fates aided Zeus by deceiving Typhon into stopping to eat some fruits, under the pretense that they would restore his strength. Zeus came up, hurling thunderbolts. Typhon fled to Thrace and made a stand there. He flung whole mountains at Zeus, who parried them with his thunderbolts. They fell on Typhon and so crushed him that the stream ran red with his blood and was henceforth called Haemus (*Bloody*). As with failing strength Typhon fled through the sea, Zeus hurled Mount Aetna on him and crushed him beneath it forever. There was now no power, god or demigod, to question the authority of Zeus.

Zeus desired the Titaness Metis, and sought to ravish her. She transformed herself into various shapes to escape him, but he seized and violated her. An oracle of Gaea foretold that the child she would bear him would be a girl, and that if she bore him another child it would be a son who would overcome his father. On learning of this oracle, Zeus took a leaf from his father's book and straightway swallowed Metis and her unborn child. He maintained that Metis continued to give him good counsel from inside his belly. After some time had passed, Zeus was afflicted with a violent headache as he walked on the shores of the Lake Tritonis. Prometheus, or as some say, Hephaestus, took up a double-edged ax and smote his brow. Athena, child of Zeus and Metis, sprang fully-armed from his cloven skull. The Titaness Themis bore him the Horae, making him the father of the seasons, and the Moerae. Themis continued to sit by the side of Zeus and give him good counsel, and some call her his wife, but do not

explain why she retired from this position. The acknowledged wife of Zeus was his sister Hera. When Zeus first wooed her she rejected his advances. He transformed himself into a cuckoo and approached her in this guise. Hera took up the bird and nestled it in her bosom, whereupon Zeus resumed his own shape and ravished her. The incident was supposed by some to have taken place on Mount Thornax in Argolis, and because of it Zeus was given the surname Coccygius (*Cuckoo*), and the mountain was renamed Cuckoo. The marriage of Zeus and Hera was celebrated, some say, at Cnossus in Crete. In the temple that was raised on the spot sacrifices were annually offered, and a ceremony was held that reënacted the marriage. Zeus and Hera spent their wedding night, said to have lasted 300 years, on the island of Samos. Hera bore Ares, Ilithyia, and Hebe to Zeus. Their marriage, the only proper marriage on Olympus, was stormy, and marked by continual quarrels. With her spying and her constant recriminations Hera often brought humiliation on Zeus. There was always material at hand for a dispute. On one occasion they argued about which sex enjoyed love-making more. Zeus maintained that the female gets the most pleasure from making love. Hera insisted that women were mere instruments of masculine pleasure. They submitted their dispute to the Theban Tiresias for judgment. He was an authority because he had spent part of his life as a woman. Tiresias declared that if the parts of the pleasures of love-making counted as ten, the female enjoyed nine and the male one. Some say Hera was so vexed by his opinion that she blinded Tiresias. Zeus awarded him long life and prophetic powers. As the wife of Zeus, Hera had great powers and shared his confidence in many respects, but she could not control his interest in and intrigues with other women—goddesses and mortal maidens—despite the jealous watch she kept over his activities. He was the master, and made it plain that he would brook no interference. When Hera incurred his displeasure, as when she caused Heracles to be shipwrecked on the island of Cos, Zeus attached golden bracelets to her wrists and hung her out of heaven, with anvils attached to each of her feet. He had always the thunderbolt at his command to punish any impertinence or rebelliousness, and he had the power to cast out of heaven any who roused his anger, as he hurled Hephaestus to earth for interfering in one of his quarrels with Hera, and as he cast Ate, goddess of folly, out of heaven because she betrayed him into making a rash oath before the birth of Heracles.

Zeus was the father of many famous children—gods, demigods, and heroes. Some say Aphrodite was his daughter by the Oceanid Dione. Leto, daughter of the Titans Coeus and Phoebe, bore him the twin gods Apollo and Artemis. Maia, daughter of Atlas, was the mother of his son Hermes, whom he made the patron of travelers, commerce, and of treaty-making, as well as messenger of the gods. The god Dionysus, whose nurses he transferred to the heavens as the Hyades, was his son by Semele. Eurynome, a daughter of Oceanus, bore him the Charites (Aglaia, Euphrosyne, Thalia). Mnemosyne, with whom he lay for nine nights, bore him the Muses. He was the father of Demeter's daughter Persephone, and looked the other way when Hades carried her off, but later ordered Hades to restore her to her mother. He transferred the Pleiades to the heavens to save them, some say, from the unwelcome attentions of Orion. Of the Pleiades, Taÿgete was the mother of his son Lacedaemon, and Electra of his sons Iasion and Dardanus, the former of whom Zeus slew with a thunderbolt for lying with Demeter in a "thrice-plowed field." Some say he was the father of Pan by Hybris. Elara bore him Tityus. The first mortal woman Zeus embraced was Niobe, daughter (or wife) of Phoroneus; she bore him Argus and, some say, Pelasgus. In a celebrated incident, he pursued Io, daughter of the river-god Inachus, and when about to be discovered by Hera, he transformed Io into a white heifer. After long, tortured wanderings in this form, Io reached the Nile. There she assumed her own shape, Zeus "touched" her, and she bore him Epaphus. Among his other famous children (see separate entries) were Helen and Polydeuces, the children of Leda; Minos, Rhadamanthys, and Sarpedon

(allowed by Zeus to live for three generations), sons of Europa; Perseus, son of Danaë, whom he visited in a shower of gold; Amphion and Zethus, sons of Antiope; Arcas, son of Callisto whom he transformed into a bear to save her from the wrath of Hera and whose image he placed among the stars as the Great Bear; Aeacus, for whom he transformed ants into men, son of Aegina; and Heracles whom he made immortal, the son of Alcmene, the last mortal woman Zeus embraced. And some say he was the father of Endymion, who chose to remain ageless in eternal sleep; of Hellen, the ancestor of the Hellenes; and of many others. He vied with Poseidon for the favors of the Nereid Thetis, but when informed by an oracle of Gaea that her son would be greater than his father he gave her to a mortal, Peleus, in marriage.

As a god who punished wickedness and avenged wrongs, Zeus sent a great flood to destroy the men of the Bronze Age for their evil ways. From the flood Deucalion and Pyrrha were spared because of their piety, and in answer to their prayers Zeus instructed them how to repeople the earth. Some say he sent the flood because of the wickedness of Lycaon and his sons. For from time to time Zeus visited the earth in disguise to test the hearts of men. When he came to Lycaon's house he was served with human flesh. In disgust at such wickedness Zeus overturned the banquet table and resolved to wipe out mankind with a flood. Others say he first turned Lycaon and his sons into wolves and then sent the flood. But when he visited the humble house of Baucis and Philemon, and was hospitably welcomed and entertained by the poor and devoted couple, he rewarded them by granting them their wish that they might die together. Salmoneus, who in his arrogance imitated the lightning and thunder of Zeus, who took away the sacrifices of the god and ordered them made to himself, was struck down by a thunderbolt. Alcyone and Ceyx in their pride likened themselves unto Hera and Zeus. Zeus transformed them into a kingfisher and a gannet respectively. In anger at the murder of Apsyrtus by Jason and the Argonauts, Zeus sent great storms to blow the Argonauts off their course as they sailed for home. Some say that in the war of the Seven against Thebes, Zeus struck the Argive Capaneus with the thunderbolt for his boast, as he scaled the walls of Thebes, that not even the gods could stop him. He caused Tantalus to suffer fearful torments in Tartarus for abusing the friendship of the gods, and he fixed Ixion to a fiery wheel that whirls in the wind for boasting that he had lain with Hera. In fact, Ixion had embraced a cloud, made by Zeus in the shape of Hera to trick him and test him.

Many times Zeus acted as mediator in quarrels. When Apollo and Idas were fighting for Marpessa, he parted them and granted Marpessa the right to choose between the god and the mortal. On another occasion he came upon Apollo and Heracles fighting over the tripod at Delphi. He parted them with a thunderbolt and made them agree to become friends. When Laelaps, the hound fated to catch whatever he pursued, hunted the Teumessian vixen, fated never to be caught, Zeus solved the dilemma by turning both to stone. In the dispute between Athena and Poseidon for control of Athens, he appointed the gods and goddesses as judges. When they vied for Troezen he decreed that they must share it. Some say that he arbitrated the dispute between Aphrodite and Persephone for the love of Adonis, but others say he was disgusted by their sordid quarrel over the handsome youth and appointed Calliope to settle it. And he wisely refused to say for whom the golden apple was intended. It was inscribed "For the Fairest," and was flung among the wedding guests, at the marriage of Thetis and Peleus, by Eris, goddess of Discord. He referred Athena, Hera, and Aphrodite, the chief contenders for the apple, to Paris for a decision.

Mount Ida in the Troad was especially sacred to Zeus. In the *Iliad,* Homer represents that Zeus observed the Trojan War from his place on this mountain. The connection of Zeus with Troy was particularly close. Dardanus, the ancestor of the Trojans, was his son. Ganymede, son of Tros, king of Troy, was carried off by an eagle of Zeus to be his cup-bearer on Olympus. This was an insult to Hera, whose daughter Hebe

had hitherto filled this function, and was an additional reason for Hera's hatred of Troy and an extra cause of dissension with Zeus. When Ilus had built Troy, he asked Zeus for a sign that his city found favor in the sight of Zeus. In answer to his prayer the Palladium fell from heaven. Some say it landed before the tent of Ilus. Others say it fell into the temple of the Citadel, which was still unroofed, and landed on the place where it ever after stood. Apollo and Poseidon with, some say, the help of Aeacus, built the walls of Troy when they were compelled by Zeus to serve Laomedon. Some say that Zeus and Themis planned the Trojan War to glorify his daughter, Helen, by embroiling Europe and Asia for her sake, or to exalt the race of the demigods. In the war, Zeus promised Thetis that he would allow Hector and the Trojans to harass the Greeks until Agamemnon had atoned for the dishonor he had brought her son Achilles. He did this knowing that it would be a cause of bitterness to Hera, who favored the Greeks, and because he owed something to Thetis for having brought Briareus to his aid when he was bound by Hera, Apollo, and Poseidon. During the last year of the Trojan War he warned the gods and goddesses not to interfere on either side, and went off to Mount Ida to weigh the scales in favor of Hector, in fulfillment of his promise to Thetis. He sent Iris to forbid Athena and Hera to aid the Greeks against Hector, and foretold that Hector would not cease from battle until Achilles rejoined the war to avenge the death of Patroclus. In this, Zeus said that so Fate had ordained and that he was powerless to interfere with Fate. As the Trojans drove the Greeks back with heavy losses, Hera borrowed Aphrodite's magic girdle and so charmed Zeus that he forgot the battle for a while, and then was lulled by Sleep, who had been bribed by Hera. When he awoke and realized what had happened he threatened Hera, and ordered her to secure the withdrawal of Poseidon from the battle. After the death of Patroclus, Achilles reentered the war to avenge him, and Zeus now gave permission to the gods to take sides as they liked, for he feared lest the fury of Achilles bring immediate destruction on the Trojans if the gods did not take part. And, according to Homer, Zeus laughed in Olympus when he saw the tumult stirred up by Achilles against the Trojans and by the gods as they struggled among themselves. Zeus pitied Hector and would have saved him, but when he weighed his fate in the scales against the fate of Achilles, "down sank the doomful day of great Hector," and Zeus knew that the time had come for Hector to meet his black fate. But when Achilles killed Hector and abused his body, Zeus was angry. He sent Priam to ransom Hector's body and commanded Achilles to treat the old man kindly and to restore to him the body of his son. In the end, as Fate decreed, Troy was destroyed.

The countless epithets of Zeus, describing his special powers, incidents connected with his worship, protection, divine intervention, places of worship, etc., are too numerous to describe individually. See separate entries for descriptions of those in the following incomplete list: Aegiochus (*Aegis-bearing*); Anchesmius (*Of Anchesmus*); Apesantius (*Of Apesas*); Aphesius (*Releaser*); Atabyrian; Cappotas (*Reliever*); Catharsius (*Purifier*); Cenaean; Chthonius (*Of the Lower World*); Cithaeronian; Clarius (*Of Lots*); Croceatas (*Of Croceae*); Ctesius (*God of Gain*); Dodonian; Eleutherius (*God of Freedom*); Herceius (*Of the Courtyard*); Homagyrius (*Assembler*); Ithomatas (*Of Ithome*); Laphystius; Lecheates (*In Childbed*); Leucaeus (*Of the White Poplar*); Lycaeus (*Wolfish*); Mechaneus (*Contriver*); Megistus (*Almighty*); Meilichius (*Gracious*); Moeragetes (*Guide of Fate*); Hypsistus (*Most High*); Nemean; Panhellenius (*God of all the Greeks*); Patrous (*Paternal*); Philius (*Friendly*); Phyxius (*God of Flight*); Polieus (*Urban*); Semaleus (*Sign-giving*); Soter (*Savior*); Sthenius (*Strong*); Teleius (*Full-grown*); and Tropaean (*He who turns to flight*).

The eagle and the oak were sacred to Zeus. His worship was universal throughout Greece by the time of Homer, who describes him with due honor as "the father of gods and men," the god of grace and mercy, the protector of oaths, and of the rights and privileges of hosts and guests. He is the mightiest of the gods, "the Thunderer," "the Cloud-gatherer," the "Olympian lord of the lightnings," and the counselor who by a nod of his immortal head grants the prayer of the suppliant. He is the avenger of wrongs and the giver of victory. All the institutions of civilization and religion derive from Zeus, as do the powers of the other gods. The Romans identified their Jupiter with Zeus, and added the Zeus myths to the ancient Jupiter mythology. In art, the most famous statue of Zeus was the huge ivory and gold image made by Phidias for the temple at Olympia. See **Olympian Zeus.**

Zeuxis (zök'sis). Greek painter; born at Heraclea, in Lucania; fl. at the close of the 5th century B.C. He formed his style at Athens under the influence of Apollodorus, worked at various other cities, and finally settled at Ephesus. He is said to have introduced light and shadow into his paintings to give mass. He was also especially successful in achieving illusion. The story is told of a contest between him and Parrhasius. Zeuxis painted grapes so lifelike that birds came and pecked at them. Parrhasius painted a filmy drapery that deceived Zeuxis. Among his principal works were *Zeus on His Throne Surrounded by Gods, Eros Crowned with Roses* (in the temple of Aphrodite at Athens), the *Marsyas* (in the temple of Concord at Rome), the *Centaur Family* (described by Lucian), the *Alcmene of the Argentines, Heracles as a Child,* the *Helena* (in the temple of Lucanian Hera), and the *Boy with Grapes.*

Zodiac. An imaginary band in the sky, 16° wide, within which lie the paths of the sun, moon, and major planets, and having as its center the plane inclined to the earth's equator which defines the yearly path of the sun, called the ecliptic. The ancients, with their preference for duodecimal reckoning (12 is divisible by 2, 3, 4, and 6, 10 only by 2 and 5), thought to see a divine order in a 360-day year of twelve 30-day months (the fact that the actual figures are 365.2425 days, c12⁷⁄₁₉ months, and 29 *or* 30 days was not permitted to interfere with this idealization of the universe). They accordingly divided the ecliptic into 360 degrees, one degree supposedly marking one day's motion of the sun, and looked for, and found, 12 constellations which could be considered as marking each one 30° segment of the ecliptic, one month's movement of the sun. These are the constellations or "Signs" of the zodiac, among which move the seven planets. The Greek names of the constellations of the zodiac, with their Latin and English equivalents, are

Greek	Latin	English
Ichthyes	Pisces	Fishes
Krios	Aries	Ram
Tauros	Taurus	Bull
Didymoi	Gemini	Twins
Karkinos	Cancer	Crab
Leon	Leo	Lion
Parthenos	Virgo	Virgin
Zygos	Libra	Scales
Skorpios	Scorpio	Scorpion
Toxotes	Sagittarius	Archer
Aigokeros	Capricornus	Goat
Hydrochoos	Aquarius	Water-Carrier

(JJ)

Zoïlus (zō′i-lus). Greek rhetorician and cynic philosopher; fl. in the 4th century B.C. He was called Homeromastix (*Scourge of Homer*)

from his severe criticisms of Homer, whose works had too much of the fabulous for Zoïlus' taste. His name came to be applied to any carping critic.

Zone (zō′nē). In ancient geography, a place in Thrace where, according to tradition, wild oaks stand in ranks just as they were left, after having been led to this place from Pieria by the music of Orpheus.

Zoster (zos′tėr). In ancient geography, a place on the coast near Athens. The name, which means "Girdle," was given to it because here Leto, preparatory to bringing forth her children, loosened her girdle. The site was marked by altars to Apollo, Artemis, Leto, and Athena.

Zosteria (zos-tē′ri-a). Epithet of Athena, meaning "Girder." Amphitryon dedicated an image of Athena Zosteria at Thebes, because here he put on his armor when he went to fight against Chalcedon and the Euboeans. Some say Heracles raised two stone images to Athena Zosteria at Thebes after his successful defence of the city in the war with Erginus.

XX-1